The
Encyclopedia of
Nineteenth-Century
Land Warfare

OTHER BOOKS BY BYRON FARWELL

The Man Who Presumed: A Biography of Henry Morton Stanley
Burton: A Biography of Sir Richard Francis Burton
Prisoners of the Mahdi
Queen Victoria's Little Wars
The Great Anglo-Boer War
Mr. Kipling's Army
The Gurkhas
Eminent Victorian Soldiers
The Great War in Africa, 1914–1918
Armies of the Raj
Ball's Bluff: A Small Battle and Its Long Shadow
Stonewall: A Biography of General Thomas J. Jackson
Over There: The United States in the Great War, 1917–18

The
ENCYCLOPEDIA OF NINETEENTH-CENTURY LAND WARFARE

An Illustrated World View

BYRON FARWELL

W. W. Norton & Company

New York • London

For information about permission to reproduce selections from this book, write to Permissions,
W. W. Norton & Company, Inc., 500 Fifth Avenue, New York, NY 10110

This book is composed in Garamond
Composition by Techbooks
Manufacturing by Courier Westford

Book design by Charlotte Staub

Library of Congress Cataloging-in-Publication Data

Farwell, Byron.
The encyclopedia of nineteenth-century land warfare : an illustrated world view / Byron Farwell.

p.   cm.

Contents: v. 1. A–Z
Includes bibliographical references (p.   ).

ISBN 0–393-04770–9

    1. Military history, Modern—19th century Encyclopedias.
    2. Military art and science—History—19th century Encyclopedias.
    I. Title.

D361.F34   2001
355' .009'034—dc21   99-39854
                                                      CIP

W. W. Norton & Company, Inc., 500 Fifth Avenue, New York, NY 10110
www.wwnorton.com

W. W. Norton & Company Ltd., Castle House, 75/76 Wells Street, London W1T 3QT

For Ruth

Contents

Acknowledgments

❧

I AM INDEBTED in ways too numerous to mention to Leonard Thill, who added a new dimension to the concept of friendship by donating countless hours for more than five years, programming, indexing, checking conventions, and in general helping bring order to this work.

For all medical entries I have been much assisted by my good friend Dr. Robert J. T. Joy, a retired army colonel and emeritus chairman of the Medical History Department of the Uniformed Services University of the Health Sciences. There is not a more knowledgeable person in the field of military medical history or one more generous in sharing his vast knowledge. William Carey, Esq., an attorney in Berkeley Springs, West Virginia, has also been of assistance. I also wish to thank Dr. John Prados for many helpful suggestions and emendations. No university or foundation provided assistance for this work.

Foreword

Arma virumque cano. —Virgil

This is a work designed for both the scholar and the general reader of military history. Its entries include information on wars, revolutions, battles, sieges, spies, soldiers—and some marines and sailors who fought on land—technical military terms, weapons, armies, military awards, camp followers, and other aspects of nineteenth-century wars and military life. As diseases in all armies and in all wars except the Maori Wars and the short-lived Franco-Prussian War accounted for more deaths by far than from all weapons combined, attention has been paid to the most prevalent diseases affecting soldiers, available medicines, and medical arrangements of armies, including the political and military consequences of attempting to reduce the impact of that great filler of military hospitals, venereal disease.

In the nineteenth century at least five major developments shaped the nature of armies and the wars they fought: (1) The increased size of the world population permitted larger and larger armies. The population of Europe, in spite of large emigrations to the United States, doubled. (2) Advances in technology, particularly in the last quarter of the century, added greatly to the destructive power of weapons. (3) Largely the result of improved weapons, defensive tactics and strategies more often prevailed over the offensive, although the importance of this change was seldom realized at the time. It took many years for senior soldiers to realize that the breech-loading rifle and rifled cannon put an end to cavalry as an attack weapon and that the introduction of the machine gun at the end of the century put period both to the horse in battle and to massed infantry attacks. (4) War became more of a science in the last half of the century. At the beginning of the nineteenth century few officers received formal military education.

Armies throughout the world were largely officered by aristocrats and the gentry. The nineteenth century saw the introduction in Europe and the United States of schools designed to give young men training in the profession of arms and staff colleges that made officers more professional. (5) Finally, there was a dramatic change in the quality of the rank and file. The peasants, serfs, farm boys, slum dwellers, unemployed, and unemployable who served in the armies of the Napoleonic Wars were gradually replaced by better-educated and more competent men. Improved reward systems were developed, somewhat more palatable food was provided, and marginally healthier living conditions.

In the encyclopedia the length of an entry is not necessarily a measure of the magnitude of a conflict or the consequence of a person. Some lesser conflicts and some minor personalities are given at length because of their human interest or because more detailed information is not readily available elsewhere for readers of English. Thus, neither the Battle of Gettysburg nor the Battle of Waterloo is described in great detail, nor is there a full biography of Wellington, Napoleon, Lee, or Grant. However, the bloodiest war of the century, the Taiping Rebellion, is given a lengthy entry because it is probably little known to American or British readers, with the possible exception of the bit role played by "Chinese" Gordon.

Many may be surprised by entries such as Korean War, the Capture of Hanoi, and the Battle of Château-Thierry, names we usually associate with twentieth-century conflicts although they were the locations of earlier battles. "Concentration camp" and "commando" had different connotations in the nineteenth century. Words change their meaning. "Shrapnel" did not mean simply a metal fragment, as newspapers have now taught readers to believe, but a particular kind of shell invented by Major Henry Shrapnel, a British soldier. Other entries describe events not widely known: the American invasion of Canada, the military expedition against the Mormons, the bloody War of the Triple Alliance, and the British award to Mohandas Gandhi of two medals and a mention in dispatches for his support of the empire in two wars.

In an effort to reduce somewhat the use of "q.v." it has been omitted for technical military terms, names of well-known generals, major wars and battles, and well-known institutions, such as West Point; the reader can assume that all such are explained in an entry. Not every definition of a word is always given, only those applicable to armies and their operations.

While all the great captains have been included, it was not possible to include every general. In the American Civil War alone there were 425 Confederate generals and 583 Union generals. However, a number of interesting lives of men of lesser rank have been included.

It has also been impossible to list the thousands of battles in the century or the hundreds of South and Central American émeutes. In Panama alone in just the last half of the century there were five revolutions, some fifty major riots, and thirteen interventions by American forces. However, to avoid the impression that all battles were large-scale or politically significant, a smattering of smaller engagements has been included.

Much effort has been spent in trying to locate exactly where each battle occurred. This is often difficult because many engagements took place near villages that have since changed their names or are no longer extant. Physical features have also suffered name changes or have vanished. The Battle of Beecher's Island, for example, was fought on the western frontier where no such island now exists. Many battles are known by several names in several languages and sometimes in the same language. During the American Civil War Confederates tended to name battles after the nearest town; Federals named battles after physical features. Thus the Confederate battle named after the town of Sharpsburg is the Union Battle of Antietam Creek and the Confederate Manassas is Federal Bull Run. Often battles have received multiple names, even within the same command. During the American Civil War the Battle of White Oak Swamp, one of the Seven Days' battles of the Peninsular Campaign, for example, was also sometimes known as the Battle of Glendale, Nelson's Farm, Frayser's Farm, Charles City Crossroads, New Market Crossroads, or Turkey Bend.

Although cities in Western Europe and the United States have not changed their names or their spellings and all major non-English cities are known to English speakers by commonly accepted English equivalents, such is not the case elsewhere. I have throughout used nineteenth-century names; where cities and countries have changed their names or spellings, I have attempted to include the present name in brackets. Not everyone would recognize present-day Myanmar as the former Burma or Guangzhou as Canton.

All numbers in military histories must be regarded skeptically. In many accounts the round number of 5,000 may simply mean "a lot" or the number 50,000 may simply mean "beyond counting." Numbers are suspect in almost all accounts. The numbers of troops engaged, the number of guns, even the dates of battles, and casualty figures can usually be regarded, at best, as estimates. When, as frequently occurs, several sets of figures are available, they may vary by thousands, even tens of thousands. Three normally reliable sources list three different figures for the size of Napoleon's army at Austerlitz: 65,000, 70,000, and 73,000, the difference between the highest and the lowest being 8,000 men, an army in itself. The number of Allied soldiers at the Battle of the Alma in the Crimean War ranges from 51,000 to 63,000. I have in each case chosen the numbers that to me seem most plausible, but I could not defend any one.

Casualty figures in particular require a reader to keep a vigilant hold on his or her credulity. Even in small battles, where it ought to have been easy to count, there are major discrepancies. After the Battle of Hanover Court House Confederate General Lawrence Branch reported total losses of 243 killed and wounded; the wounded would be the larger number. But Union General Fitz-John Porter claimed to have buried 200 and to have captured 730. Three scholars have assiduously studied the casualties in battles of the American Civil War and have arrived at three sets of figures.

Scant attention has been given to the causes of wars. Any number of excuses exist for any country to declare war. As the poet Margaret Atwood has said, "Wars happen because the ones who start them think they can win" (*The Loneliness of a Military Historian*). It has been said that in Europe there always exist at least thirty causes for war. In wars of any length, the original causes tend to be forgotten, and the aims for which they are fought often change in the course of the war.

Having found errors in every reference book consulted, I cannot imagine that this one is without mistakes, although I hope none is grievous. I will be grateful to knowledgeable readers who point out my sins of omission or commission.

BYRON FARWELL
Hillsboro, Virginia

*The
Encyclopedia of
Nineteenth-Century
Land Warfare*

A

Abatis. Pl. abatis or abatises. An obstacle of trees felled so that their intertwined branches faced the enemy. Smaller branches were occasionally lopped, and the remainder was sharpened; trunks were sometimes buried or secured by crochet pickets, making their disengagement difficult. Abatis were found most useful in the defense of an isolated post or in blocking roads and mountain passes.

Abatis *Abatis at Petersburg, Virginia, for Confederate defense against Grant's attack*

Abbas II / Abbas Hilmi Pasha (1874–1944). A khedive of Egypt, the eldest son of Muhammad Taufiq Pasha (1852–1892), whom he succeeded to the khediviate in 1892. He was anti-British, and his attempt to appoint a prime minister without consulting the British agent resulted in a humiliating scolding. Shortly after, while touring Upper Egypt and Nubia with General Horatio Kitchener [q.v.], he created a sensation, referred to as a "frontier incident," when he openly criticized the efficiency of the British officers who were training the Egyptian army, an indiscretion that caused the downfall of his ministry. He was deposed by the British in July 1914 and died thirty years later in exile in Geneva, Switzerland.

Abbas Mirza (1783–1833). A Persian prince, the son and heir of Shah Fath Ali [q.v.], who conducted campaigns against Russia in 1800–13, and who in 1826–28, with help from his sons, tried unsuccessfully to prevent Russia from capturing Persian provinces in the Caucasus [see Russo-Persian Wars]. In 1821 he drove the Turks from the western mountains of Turkish Armenia (although Persia later lost Armenia in the Russo-Persian War of 1826–28), defeated the Turks in the Battle of Erzerum, and signed a peace treaty in 1823 [see Turko-Persian War]. In 1825 a border dispute with Russia erupted into war, and Abbas invaded the Lake Van area. He reached Tiflis (Tbilis) in Georgia but was defeated by Russians under General Ivan Paskievich [q.v.] in the Battle of Gandzha [q.v.]—also called Ganja, Elisavetpol, or Kirovagad—on 26 September 1826. He did not live to assume the throne. [See Russo-Persian Wars.]

Abd al-Kader. Algerian ruler. [See Abd el-Kader.]

Abd Allahi Muhammad Turshain, Khalifat al-Madhi. See Abdullahi, Kalifa.

Abd al-Qadir / Kader Pasha Hilmi (1837–1908). An Egyptian soldier and governor-general of the Sudan. The son of an Egyptian officer and a Syrian mother, he acquired a medical degree in Vienna but preferred the life of a soldier. He was promoted liwa and pasha [qq.v.] in 1874 and took part in the Abyssinian-Egyptian War [q.v.] in 1875–76. In February 1882 he was appointed governor-general and commander-in-chief of the Sudan. Unsuccessful in opposing the disastrous Hicks Pasha [q.v.] expedition to Kordofan, he was recalled exactly a year later.

Abd al Rahman wad al-Nujumi (d.1889). A Dervish emir who in 1881 became one of the earliest followers of El Mahdi [see Muhammad Ahmed]. In 1885, during the Mahdist conquest of the Sudan, he took a leading part in the siege and capture of Khartoum [q.v.]. Later that year, while he was in temporary command at Berber and Dongola, his army was defeated by an Anglo-British force at Ginnis [q.v.]. He was appointed to command a Dervish force designed to invade Egypt, but his army was defeated, and he himself killed at the Battle of Toski [q.v.].

Abd ar Rahman (1778–1859). A Moroccan prince who in 1822 succeeded his uncle to become sultan of Fez and Morocco. He allied himself with Abd el-Kader, the amir of Mascara [q.v.] in his war against the French [see Ab el-Kader Wars].

Abd el-Kader / Abd el-Kadir (1808–1883). Algerian leader of the Hashim tribe and marabout (holy man) of the Sufi Qadiriyya, a fundamentalist Islamic sect. In 1832, on the death of his father, he became amir of Mascara, whose capital was built on the slope of a mountain, 1,800 feet above sea level, 60 miles southeast of Oran. Soon afterward he succeeded in uniting many of the tribes in western Algeria in a war against the French [see Abd el-Kader Wars].

A charismatic leader, he possessed exceptional military and organizational abilities and became the most formidable adversary the French faced in North Africa. On 30 May 1837 he signed the Treaty of Tafna, by which France yielded to him most of the Algerian interior. On 23 December 1847 he surrendered to Colonel Charles Cousin-Montauban, later Count Palikao [q.v.], serving under General Louis Christophe Lamoricière [q.v.]. Although promised permission to emigrate to Alexandria or Syria, he was detained in France until 1852, when on 16 October he was freed by Napoleon III. He settled first in Turkey and then in Damascus, where in 1860 he saved 1,200 Christians from a fanatical Muslim mob during Druse-Maronite disturbances. For this he was awarded the Legion of Honor. In the Algerian Revolt of 1870–71 he recommended submission to France. He died in Damascus on 26 May 1883.

Abd el-Kader *Abd el-Kader, leader in a jihad against the French in Algeria, surrenders his sword.*

Abd el-Kader Wars (1832–34, 1835–37, and 1840–47). Abd el-Kader [q.v.] led Algerians in harassing attacks on the French until 1834, when by treaty France appointed him dey (or amir) of Mascara. The following year he renewed his attacks, generally defeating the French in numerous small battles. In 1837, in a second treaty (Treaty of Tafna), France ceded to him nearly all of the Algerian interior, confining itself to holding the ports of Oran, Algiers, Bougie, and Bône and their surrounding districts.

In December 1840 Marshal Thomas R. Bugeaud de la Piconnerie [q.v.] took command of French forces in Algeria and began a long, bitterly fought campaign to conquer the country. He abandoned the prevailing system of sprinkling small forces in blockhouses and instead sent out flying columns to harass recalcitrant Arab tribes, burning their crops and carrying off their cattle. At the same time he established an Arab Bureau [q.v.] composed of officers who spoke Arabic and were familiar with Arab customs and institutions and acted as an intelligence bureau.

After the capture of his stronghold at Takdempt in 1841 and defeats at Tlemcen in 1842 and at Smala [q.v.] in 1843 Abd el-Kader retreated into Morocco, where he raised an army of 45,000 and mounted a third revolt in which he was again defeated by Bugeaud de la Piconnerie on 14 August 1844 at the Isly River [q.v.]. A rebellion in the Dahra area

north of the Chelif River gave him the opportunity to lead still another revolt, in which he won several fights, including the Battle of Sidi Brahim in September 1845. Driven back into Morocco, he settled in the Riff. On 23 December 1847 he surrendered to Colonel Charles Cousin-Montauban, later Count Palikao [q.v.], serving under General Louis Christophe Lamoricière [q.v.].

Abdication of Napoleon (6 April 1814). At the urging of his marshals, Napoleon I abdicated in favor of his son, a provision the Allies refused to accept. Five days later on 11 April, yielding to Allied demands, he abdicated unconditionally and was exiled to the 86-square-mile island of Elba in the Mediterranean Sea between the northeast coast of Corsica and the Italian mainland, a miniature kingdom of which he was made the ruler. On 1 March 1815 he made good his escape and landed with a small force of about 1,000 men near Cannes. By 20 March he was back in Paris.

Abdul Ghafur. See Akhund of Swat.

Abdul Kerim Pasha (1811–1883). A Turkish general who took part in the Crimean War [q.v.] and in campaigns against Serbia in 1876 [see Turko-Serbian War]. He commanded a Turkish army in the Russo-Turkish War of 1877–78 [q.v.]. When defeated, he was banished.

Abdullahi, Khalifa (1846–1899), full name: Abd Allahi Muhammad Turshain, Kalifat al-Mahdi. One of the four sons of a holy man of the Taaisha Baggara of Darfur in the western Sudan, he was an early Dervish convert and the first to proclaim Muhammad Ahmed [q.v.] El Mahdi (the messiah). In 1881 El Mahdi appointed him one of four caliphs. A successful general in the Mahdist revolt against Egypt, he was in charge of the siege of Khartoum [q.v.], which fell on 26 January 1885 [see Mahdist Revolt; Gordon, Charles George]. Upon the death of El Mahdi on 22 June 1885, he seized power and retained it until he was routed by an Anglo-Egyptian army under General Kitchener [q.v.] in the Battle of Omdurman [q.v.] on 2 September 1898 [see Sudan, Reconquest of]. Fleeing south after the battle with a handful of followers, he was defeated and killed in the Battle of Umm Dibaikarat [q.v.] on 23 November 1899 by an Anglo-Egyptian force under Francis Reginald Wingate [q.v.].

Abdur Rhaman / Abd-er-Rahman Khan (1830?–1901). An Afghan chieftain and nephew of Dost Muhammad and of Shere Ali Khan [qq.v.]. [See Afghan Civil Wars.] After the death of Dost Muhammad he supported an unsuccessful rebellion against his younger uncle. He fled to Turkistan in 1870 but returned at the end of the Second Afghan War [q.v.], when, supported by the British, he was proclaimed amir of Afghanistan on 22 July 1880. Ruling until his death in 1901, he pacified the country and negotiated frontiers with the British and Russians.

Abensberg, Battle of (20 April 1809), Napoleonic Wars. Archduke Louis John Charles [q.v.] with 161,000 Austrians created considerable confusion among the French when seeking to trap French Marshal Louis Nicolas Davout [q.v.] at Ratisbon (Regensburg) [q.v.], Bavaria, he launched a surprise attack on 19 April 1809. Napoleon quickly arrived on the scene and the following day with 113,000 men launched a counterattack at Abensberg, 18 miles southwest of

Regensburg, upon the archduke's overextended center, splitting the Austrian forces and regaining the initiative. The Battle of Eggmühl or Eckmüth [q.v.] followed the next day.

Abeokuta, Battle of (16 March 1864), West Africa tribal war. The town of Abeokuta or Abbeokuta, 60 miles north of Lagos in what is today Nigeria, was originally a robbers' haunt. By about 1830 it had evolved into a refuge from slave hunters, and a strong surrounding wall had been constructed. In 1864 it was unsuccessfully attacked by forces under the fon of Dahomey (Benin), who suffered heavy losses, particularly among his amazon warriors [q.v.]. The town became the chief city of the Egbas, who made a treaty with the British in 1893.

Abercromby, John (1772–1817). A British soldier who, commissioned at age fourteen in the 75th Foot, was a lieutenant colonel by age twenty-two. He saw service in Flanders, the West Indies, Ireland, and Egypt and became a colonel in 1800. While traveling in France, he was seized and imprisoned when the Treaty of Amiens [q.v.] was revoked on 16 May 1803. He was released, however, and, having been promoted major general while a prisoner was in 1809 appointed commander-in-chief, Bombay. In this capacity he commanded the troops that captured Mauritius [q.v.]. In 1812 he was promoted lieutenant general.

Abercromby, Ralph (1734–1801). A British soldier credited with restoring British army morale after the defeats in the American Revolution. He took part in the Flanders Campaign of 1794, led a military expedition to the West Indies, participated in the abortive Helder Campaign, and in June 1800 took command of British forces in the Mediterranean. After failing to capture Cádiz, he was ordered to attack the French in Egypt. He landed on 8 March 1801 and on 22 March was mortally wounded in the final hours of the Battle of Aboukir [q.v.].

Abergoin / Abrogans / Aberginian. Words frequently used in the nineteenth century to denote American Indians. It is perhaps a misspelling of "aborigine."

Abkhazia, Insurrection in (1866). This province on the Black Sea at the west end of the Caucasus Mountains was annexed by Russia in 1864. Two years later on 8 August 1866 the Abkhazians, a Caucasian race akin to the Circassians, revolted. They were expeditiously quelled, but not until much blood had spilled.

Abo, Battle of (1808), Russo-Swedish War. Russians under General Karl Federovich Bagavut (1761–1812) defeated the Swedes under Count Karl Adlercreutz [q.v.] at this town (Turku in Finnish) in southwest Finland on the Gulf of Bothnia, 100 miles west-northwest of Helsinki.

Abomey, Occupation of (17 November 1892). In the Franco-Dahomey War [q.v.] a French force under Colonel (later General) Alfred Dodds [q.v.] occupied this capital of the kingdom of Dahomey (Benin), 60 miles north of Ouidah after Dahomean forces fired the town and then abandoned it. Dodds then proclaimed King Behanzin of Dahomey (d. 1906) deposed and acquired the submission of the majority of his chiefs.

Abor Raids. The Abors, an independent people living on the northeastern frontier of India, north of Lakhimpur, between the Miri and Mishmi hills in a mountainous area covered with thick rain forest, were in the habit of making frequent raids on their neighbors in the plains of Assam. First encountered by the British in 1826, in 1848 they extended their range and began to make raids and commit outrages upon Indians who were under British protection. Several expeditions sent against them failed to deter their depredations. From 1894 to 1900 the British attempted to blockade their territory but achieved only partial success. The Abors remained troublesome throughout the nineteenth century.

Abort, to. To cancel an operation before it is completed.

Aboukir / Abukir, Battles of (1799 and 1801), Napoleonic Wars. In the First Battle of Aboukir (25 July 1799) Napoleon's Armée d'Orient defeated a Turkish army of 15,000 under Mustapha Pasha (1779–1808) at this small village on a promontory at the western end of the Bay of Aboukir in northern Egypt.

The Second Battle of Aboukir, sometimes called the Battle of Alexandria, took place on 21 March 1801. In early March British General Ralph Abercromby [q.v.], ordered to destroy the French army left in Egypt after Napoleon's defeat at Acre in May 1799, successfully landed 14,000 to 18,000 men under fire at Aboukir Bay. After fighting a small action on 13 March, he advanced west along a narrow isthmus in the direction of Alexandria.

Meeting fierce resistance from Alexandria's French garrison under General Louis Friant (1758–1829), the British drew

Aboukir *In early March 1801 the British successfully land 14,000 to 18,000 men at Aboukir Bay. They go on to defeat the French at Cairo (June) and Alexandria (September).*

back into a fortified camp about four miles east of Alexandria and posted strong batteries of artillery on a ridge about two miles from the city. When French General Jacques François Menou [q.v.] arrived from Cairo with 10,000 reinforcements, the French launched a gallant but unsuccessful attack upon the British positions just before daybreak.

The battle was fought on a narrow spit of land between the sea and Lake Aboukir near the ruins of Nicopolis. The brunt of the attack was borne by Major General Sir John Moore [q.v.], who commanded 8,000 men of the Reserve Division. In the chaotic fighting on the right flank the soldiers of the 28th Foot (later the North Gloucestershire Regiment) earned a nickname and everlasting fame. Attacked front and rear, their colonel coolly ordered the rear rank "right about face," and they held fast until Moore led the 42nd Highlanders (Black Watch) in a fierce bayonet charge against the French flank. Permitted ever after to wear their cap badges in both the front and back of their headgear, the 28th Foot became known as the Fore and Aft. The regiment then celebrated Back Badge Day yearly on 21 March.

The French lost 1,160 killed and at least 3,000 in wounded and missing; the British lost 1,468. Both Abercromby and Moore were wounded, Abercromby mortally.

The British, now under General John Hely-Hutchinson (1757–1832), advanced upon Cairo, where the French garrison surrendered on honorable terms on 22 June; on 2 September Menou surrendered Alexandria.

(A naval battle fought in Aboukir Bay on 1 August 1798 between Rear Admiral Horatio Nelson [1758–1805] and Vice Admiral François Paul Brueys d'Aigalliers (1753–1798) is generally referred to as the Battle of the Nile.)

Abra. A word used in the American Southwest for a narrow pass or a narrow valley.

Abri. 1. A shelter, cover, or concealment. Sheds for arms in a camp to shelter them from rain, dust, etc.
2. A place of security for troops during bombardments.

Absent without Official Leave. A phrase used in the American and British armies referring to a soldier who is not where he is supposed to be. Commonly referred to as AWOL. In the nineteenth century punishment for such unauthorized absence varied from no disciplinary action to severe corporal punishment, usually depending upon the length of absence and the intent. In 1867 Lieutenant Colonel George Armstrong Custer [q.v.] was court-martialed and sentenced to suspension of rank and pay for a year for being absent without leave when he left his post to visit his wife.

The difference between "AWOL" and "desertion" is intent. To be considered: intent to return, intent simply to leave the army and go home, or intent to desert to the enemy. Intent is often difficult to determine.

Absterdam Projectile. A shell cast in a single piece with an expanding brass

ring projecting three-eighths inch beyond the base. It could be fitted with a percussion fuze.

Abtao, Battle of (7 February 1866), War of the Pacific. Near this small village in central Chile on the Pacific coast near Antofagasta (then part of Bolivia), Allied forces of Peru, Bolivia, and Chile defeated a Spanish force.

Abteilung. A German battalion.

Abu Anja. See Hamdam Abu Anja.

Abu Hamed, Battle of (7 August 1897), British reconquest of the Sudan. An Anglo-Egyptian flying column of 2,700 men with 1,300 camels, six Krupp 12-pounders, and four Maxim machine guns under Colonel Archibald Hunter (1856–1936) attacked at dawn and defeated Dervishes [q.v.] under Muhammad Zain Hasan (1873?–1903) near this Sudanese town on the north bank of the Nile (19°34′N) below the fourth cataract. Muhammad Zain Hasan was captured. Anglo-Egyptian losses were 80 killed and wounded, including 4 British officers.

Abu Hamed *Sudanese infantry of the Egyptian army charge at the Battle of Abu Hamed*

Abukir, Battle of. See Aboukir, Battles of.

Abu Klea, Battle of (17 January 1885), Gordon Relief Expedition. A large force of Dervishes [q.v.], perhaps 10,000, many armed with Remington rifles acquired from Egyptian soldiers who fell in the Battle of Kashgil [q.v.] in the ill-fated expedition of William Hicks Pasha [q.v.], attacked a 1,800-man British camel corps with three guns and a Gardner machine gun [q.v.] under General Sir Herbert Stewart (1843–1885) near a caravan station on the west bank of the Nile in the northern Sudan, 63 miles southwest of Ed Damer and 120 miles north of Khartoum. The British force was a flying column that had cut across the base of the Great Bend in the Nile in the hopes of relieving Charles ("Chinese") Gordon [q.v.], besieged at Khartoum. Although the Dervishes broke the British square, they were repulsed with more than 1,000 killed; British casualties were 10 officers, among them the celebrated Colonel Frederick Gustavus Burnaby [q.v.], said to have been the

Absterdam Projectile

An absterdam percussion fuze

Abu Klea *Members of the Mounted Infantry Camel Regiment at the Battle of Abu Klea*

strongest man in the army; 65 other ranks were killed and 82 wounded.

Abu Kru, Battle of. See Gubat, Battle of.

Abutment. The block at the rear of a rifle barrel (especially a breechloader) or a breech-loading cannon. Its function was the same as a breech plug [q.v.] or breech pin in a muzzle-loading firearm. There were many variations of this block.

Abyssinian Campaign, British (1868). In 1864 Theodore (Tewodros) II of Abyssinia (see Theodore of Abyssinia), enraged because Queen Victoria had failed to answer a letter he had sent her, relieved his feelings by imprisoning the British consul Charles Duncan Cameron (1826?–1870), along with other Europeans. The British responded by launching a punitive expedition under Major General Robert Cornelis Napier [q.v.] of the Bombay army. Napier's army consisted of 16,000 troops plus a number of civilians, mostly coolies, herdsmen, and drivers, for a total complement of 32,000 men.

For a British campaign of this era, Napier's was exceptionally well organized. Among its equipment were a portable railroad, telegraph lines, two water condensers, tools and materials to create a port facility, and a hospital ship. Among its numerous animals was a collection of elephants. The expedition landed at Zula (Mulkutto) on Annesley Bay on 2 January 1868. The march on Magdala [q.v.], then the Abyssinian capital in the north-central part of the country, began on 25 January. Some 420 miles were covered, including a climb to more than 9,000 feet. The first battle was fought at Arogee [q.v.], 3 miles north of Magdala, on 10 April, when an attack by the Abyssinians was repulsed for a loss of 30 wounded; the Abyssinians lost an estimated 500 killed and more wounded.

Magdala was stormed on 13 April 1868. Theodore had killed himself the day before. The British destroyed the place before leaving.

Prime Minister Benjamin Disraeli (1804–1881), addressing the House of Commons, declaimed: "They brought the elephant of Asia to convey the artillery of Europe to dethrone one of the kings of Africa, and to hoist the standard of St. George upon the mountains of Rasselas."

By 2 June the expedition had reembarked, and one month later Napier arrived at Dover with Theodore's seven-year-old son, Alamayou, who was subsequently presented to Queen Victoria and then sent to India to be educated. He returned to England at the end of 1871 and died at Leeds on 14 November 1879.

Abyssinian Civil Wars. Lij Kassa, an Abyssinian prince, became, on the death of his uncle, chief of the Abyssinian province of Kwara. A rival chief, Ras Ali, led a revolt, and the province was the seat of intermittent warfare between 1841 and 1847. During a tenuous peace Lij Kassa married the daughter of Ras Ali. Hostilities were resumed when Lij Kassa accused Ras Ali's mother of insulting him. In 1853 he completely routed the forces of Ras Ali at Gorgora on the southern shores of Lake Tana. After subduing a sufficient number of neighboring chiefs, Lij Kassa proclaimed himself Emperor Theodore of Abyssinia [see Theodore of Abyssinia]. His cruelties as emperor provoked numerous revolts, all of which he crushed. Quarrels with the British proved his undoing. When he imprisoned the British consul and other Europeans, the British sent an army under Robert Napier [q.v.] against him [see Abyssinian Campaign, British]. On the death of Theodore, Prince Menelik [q.v.], who, although named by his father ruler of the province of Shoa in central Abyssinia, had been in Theodore's power in Tigré, escaped to Shoa, where he built up an army.

In 1872 King Johannes, who had succeeded Theodore [q.v.], was about to advance upon Menelik when he was diverted by the Egyptian seizure of Massawa on the coast [see Abyssinian-Egyptian Wars]. It was not until March 1876 that Johannes was able to turn his attention to Menelik, who had taken advantage of the conflict with Egypt to make raids on Gondor.

Menelik had had to quell several rebellions against his rule, but with the advance of Johannes's army the Shoans presented a united front. Nevertheless, they were defeated, and in March 1878 Menelik was forced to make a humiliating obeisance to Johannes.

Abyssinian-Egyptian Wars (1872–76 and 1884–85). In 1872 Egypt seized and occupied Massawa (or Massaura), an Eritrean seaport on the Bay of Massawa, an inlet of the Red Sea, in the northern Abyssinian province of Bogos. King Johannes [q.v.], the Abyssinian negus negusti (king of kings), collected an army and with the help of Ras Walad Michael, the hereditary ruler of Bogos, defeated and almost annihilated an Egyptian force of 2,500 under Søren Adolph Arendup Bey [q.v.] in the Battle of Gundet [q.v.] on 17 November 1875.

The Egyptians launched an avenging expedition under Muhammad Ratib Pasha. Among its officers was a one-armed American soldier, William Loring [q.v.], a former Confederate general. Egyptian troops marched to Gura, sited on a plateau in central Eritrea five miles south of Decamere. Here they fortified the town and were reinforced by an Abyssinian force under Ras Walad Michael, who had quarreled with Johannes. On 7 March 1876 in the Battle of Gura the forces of Johannes defeated them a second time, and they retired after heavy losses of men and matériel.

In 1884, at the request of the British, Johannes consented to go to the relief of the Egyptian garrisons besieged by Mahdist forces under Osman Digna [q.v.], the Dervish emir, near the Abyssinian-Egyptian frontier [see Abyssinian-Sudanese Conflict]. In 1885 Ras Alula [q.v.], Abyssinian governor of Tigré, effectively relieved several garrisons, but before he could reach the garrison at Kassala [q.v.], famine had forced the town to capitulate. Advancing with a large force, ostensibly to retake Kassala, he soundly defeated Osman Digna at Kufit [q.v.], near Agordat, on 23 September 1885. Offended by Egypt's transfer of Massawa to the Italians, he then refused to make any further effort. In 1894 the Italians captured Kassala and held it for three years.

Abyssinian-Italian Wars. See Italo-Abyssinian Wars.

Abyssinian-Sudanese Conflict (1885–87). In September 1885 Abyssinian forces under Ras Alula [q.v.], Abyssinian governor of Tigré, defeated Dervish "Fuzzy-Wuzzies" [q.v.] under Osman Digna [q.v.] at Kufit [q.v.] on the east bank of the Nile 13 miles south-southeast of Qena (Qina).

In August 1887 the Dervishes under Hamdam Abu Anja [q.v.] attacked Takla Haymanot Adal and defeated him on the plain of Debra Sin, 30 miles west of Gondar and 21 miles north of Lake Tana [see Gondar, Battle of]. In 1889 Abyssinian King Johannes [q.v.] led an army of 150,000 into the Sudan and on 9 March attacked and defeated the Dervishes at Gallabat [see Gallabat, Battles of]. Thousands of prisoners were taken, the town was stormed and burned, but Johannes was mortally wounded by a stray bullet, and the dispirited Abyssianians retired. As they did so, the Dervishes turned and pursued, routing the Abyssinian rear guard and capturing King Johannes's corpse, which was sent to Omdurman, the Sudanese capital under the Mahdists, as proof that the Dervishes had won the battle. This ended the war.

Academic Board. The board of the United States Military Academy at West Point, consisting of the superintendent and heads of the departments of instruction, which recommends textbooks, annually examines cadets, ranks them, and proposes improvements. In the nineteenth century it was so influential that it sometimes challenged the authority of the superintendent.

Acanzi. Turkish light cavalry that formed the vanguard of the sultan's army.

Acapulco de Juárez, Insurrection of (11 January 1811), Mexican War of Independence [q.v.]. On the outskirts of the town of Acapulco a night attack by 1,000 insurgents led by Father José María Morelos y Pavón (1765–1815) and José Antonio Galeana (1780–1812) defeated a force of 3,000 Spaniards and Mexican loyalists commanded by Francisco Paris, governor of Acapulco Province. The insurgents captured 800 muskets, 5 guns, a large quantity of ammunition, and Paris's money chest at a cost of 200 killed and wounded.

Paris's forces suffered 400 killed and wounded; 700 were taken prisoner.

Acceptable Casualties. The number of killed and wounded a unit, an army, or a nation is willing to suffer or is capable of enduring before halting a battle by breaking or ending a war by surrendering.

Accessory Means of Defense. Artificial obstacles arranged to detain an enemy within a field of fire. Such obstacles include abatis, chevaux-de-frise, caltrops, entanglements, inundations, mines, palisades, small pickets, stockades, and trou-de-loup.

Accidental Line of Operations. This is not, as one might suppose, a line of operations [q.v.] arrived at by accident, but a line of operations different from that proposed in the original plan for a campaign.

Accidental Objective. When the mission is the destruction or dismemberment of an enemy, an accidental objective (position, place, line, or part of a country) is one determined by the enemy's location. If the enemy is greatly extended, a central point that would divide his forces might be the accidental objective. If the enemy is strongly concentrated, a point on the flank might be targeted.

Accidental Strategical Point. A position whose possession gives an advantage and causes an enemy to fight at a disadvantage or to retreat.

Accles Magazine. A patent ammunition magazine manufactured by the Colt Company for use with the ten-barreled Gatling [q.v.] gun Model 1883.

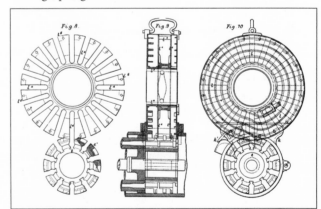

Accles Magazine *Details of the Accles positive feed, which allows cartridges to move in a circular path through the tracks of a propeller into the machine gun*

Accolade. In Britain, a ceremony conferring knighthood in which the sovereign or a representative touches with the flat of a sword the shoulders of the postulant.

Accord. The conditions under which a fort or a body of troops surrendered.

Accordion Effect. The bunching up followed by the stringing out of a marching column, mounted or on foot. Even such minor obstacles as a narrow bridge, a small stream, or a steep hill alter the pace and create an accordion effect that is the bane of marching troops and their commanders.

Accountant General of the Army. An officer in the British army who controlled military finances. One of the 1870 army reforms was the inclusion of the chief auditor in the office of the accountant general.

Accoutrements / Accouterments. Items other than clothing and weapons carried by soldiers, such as canteens, cartridge boxes, haversacks, bayonet slings, cap pouch [qq.v.], etc.

Accoutrements

À-Cheval Position. Troops placed so that a river or a highway passed through their center and formed a perpendicular to the front. Wellington's army at Waterloo [q.v.] was à-cheval on the Charleroi–Brussels road and the corps of Stonewall Jackson [q.v.] at Antietam [q.v.] was à-cheval on the Hagerstown Turnpike.

Achilles' Heel. The vulnerable or weakest part of a person, position, army, etc.

Achinese War (1873–1907). Achin or Acheh (today Atjeh) was a powerful Muslim sultanate in northern Sumatra that rebelled against Dutch rule. The rebellion was put down, and the capital and port city of Kutaradja (Koetaradja) captured in 1873 after two Dutch expeditions. Sporadic fighting followed, and the area was not completely pacified until the end of 1907.

Achselbander. German for aiguillettes [q.v.].

Achselklappen. German for shoulder straps.

Achseln. German for the cloth additions or "wings" added to the shoulders of uniforms. In British usage, often called swallows' nests.

Acknowledgment. A notice to the sender of a message that it has been received. The envelope in which the message was sent was often signed or initialed and given to the courier to return to the sender as proof that he had delivered the message.

Acoustical Shadow. A rare atmospheric phenomenon, sometimes called acoustic opacity, in which sounds are inaudible when close by but can be heard dozens of miles away. It is caused by changes of wind speed at different altitudes, wind direction, or changes in air temperatures at different altitudes. Woods, folds in the ground, wind direction, or air densities all are capable of blunting nearby sounds. The phenomenon was noted during several American Civil War battles: at Fair Oaks on 31 May 1862; Gaines's Mill on 27 June 1862; Iura on 20 September 1862; Perryville on 8 October 1862; Chancellorsville on 2 May 1863; and Gettysburg on 1 July 1863 [qq.v.].

Acquittance Roll. In the British army the list of the names of the men in each company and troop, recording their debts and credits and certified by the unit commander.

Acre, Battle of (27 May 1832), Turkish-Egyptian War of 1832–33. An Egyptian force under Ibrahim Pasha [q.v.] captured the seaport town of Acre, Syria (now Israel), from the Turks after a short siege.

Acropolis, Sieges of (1821, 1822, and 1827), Greek War of Independence. The Acropolis of Athens was besieged by the Greeks in 1821 and 1822 and by the Turks in 1827.

1. In May 1821 Muslim inhabitants of Athens who had survived a massacre by Greek insurgents took refuge in the Acropolis, where they were besieged until 30 June, when they were rescued by a Turkish force.

2. The following year the citadel was captured by the Greeks, who massacred the Turkish garrison.

3. Five years later the Turks returned and besieged a Greek force in the Acropolis. On 25 April 1827 the Greeks, with help from British officers, notably Sir George Church [q.v.], and the Royal Navy, attacked a Turkish camp near the St. Spiridion Monastery, cutting off the Turkish army under Reshid Pasha (1802–1858). Albanian troops (members of the Turkish army) at the monastery surrendered two days later and were massacred. On 4 May the Greek leader Georgios Karaïskakes (1782–1827) was killed in a skirmish. The following day the Greeks made a general assault on the main Turkish camp but were caught in the open by Turkish cavalry and routed. On 27 May the Greek garrison of the Acropolis capitulated and was allowed to march out with the honors of war [q.v.]. Mainland Greece was then again under Turkish rule, and Athens and its Acropolis remained in Turkish hands until 1833, when the kingdom of Greece was established.

Acs, Battle of (2 July 1849), Hungarian Revolution. At this small town in northern Hungary, 17 miles east of Györ, 25,000 Hungarians under Arthur van Görgey [q.v.] fought an indecisive battle with a vastly superior Russo-Austrian army under Prince Alfred Windisch-Graetz [q.v.].

Acting Assistant Surgeon. A private physician under contract to the American army who drew the pay and allowances of a first lieutenant, with an extra ration when serving west of the Mississippi River. [See Contract Surgeon.]

Action. 1. An engagement or battle between opposing forces.
2. A memorable act by a soldier or a unit.
3. A maneuver in which guns are brought into position or change position to open fire.

Active Defense. Defense of a place or position by active patrolling, raids, threats of offensive action, ruses, sallies, and other means of keeping an attacker off-balance. Karl von

Clausewitz [q.v.] wrote that "the defense form of warfare is intrinsically stronger than the offensive," and while Henri Jomini [q.v.] did not completely agree, both of these noted strategists concurred that an active defense was more effective than a passive defense [q.v.].

Active Duty. On the active list with full pay as opposed to being in the reserve or on half pay.

Active List. A list of all serving officers in an army.

Active Service. Being on a military campaign or in the theater of war; operations against or in the presence of an enemy.

Active Service and Peace Manoeuvres Forage Cap. In the British army a soft, brimless, foldable cap first described in the 1883 Dress Regulations, although similar caps with side flaps that could be folded down were in use at least as early as the Crimean War [q.v.]. British soldiers called the cap a tea cozy. Similar caps worn in the Austrian army were sometimes called Austrian caps.

Act of Grace. In Britain an act of Parliament that granted a general and free pardon to deserters or other offenders.

Act of Hostility. An unfriendly military, commercial, or diplomatic action causing or threatening to cause a state of war between two or more nations. The invasion of a friendly territory or the firing on the warship of a friendly nation is a military act of hostility. The embargo laid on British shipping in 1803 by Napoleon after the Peace of Amiens [q.v.] was a commercial act of hostility [see Continental System]. The verbal altercation in a social setting at the Kursaal of Ems on 13 July 1870 in which Count Vincent Benedeti (1817–1900), French ambassador to the court of Berlin, assailed the king of Prussia with French demands and the slap in the face administered to the French consul by the dey of Algiers on 30 April 1827 are instances of diplomatic acts of hostility.

Act of War. See Act of Hostility.

Aculco, Peasant Revolt of (1810–11). On 7 November 1810 at this small town in central Mexico (officially, San Jerónimo Aculco), 22 miles southeast of San Juan del Río, some 60,000 Mexican peasants led by Father Miguel Hidalgo y Costilla [q.v.], who had raised a revolt on 16 September of that year against the Spanish government, were routed by 15,000 Spanish and Creole troops under Félix María Calleja del Rey [q.v.], later Conde de Calderón. Dividing his forces into five columns, Calleja del Rey broke the insurgent front. Insurgent casualties were about 12,000 killed and wounded; Spanish losses were about 1,000.

Father Hidalgo regrouped his forces and retreated to Valladolid.

Acultzingo, Battle of (28 April 1862), French invasion and occupation of Mexico. Near this town in Sierra Madre Oriental, 17 miles southwest of Orizaba in eastern Mexico, an army of 7,500 French troops under General Charles Ferdinand Latrille de Lorencez [q.v.], commander of the French forces in Mexico, attacked a Mexican army of 10,000 under General Ignacio Zaragoza [q.v.], which held a strong position in the Cumbres Pass. Forced to retreat, the Mexicans fell back upon La Puebla, where they were attacked [see La Puebla, Battles of].

Adal, Takla Haymanot (d.1899). An Abyssinian (Ethiopian) ras (chief) charged with guarding the Sudanese frontier at Gallabat. In 1885, after Sudanese Mahdist Dervishes looted an Abyssinian church, Adal invaded the Sudan and defeated the Dervishes at the Battle of Gallabat [q.v.]. In August 1887 the Mahdist amir Hamdam Abu Anja retaliated by invading Abyssinia and decisively defeating Adal on the plain of Debra Sin, 30 miles west of Gondar [see Gondar, Battle of]. Adal himself escaped, but his son was captured; after the Mahdist sack of Gondar, Adal's wife and daughter were also taken prisoner. He himself died under mysterious circumstances, perhaps by poison.

Adama. A Fula amir who in the early years of the nineteenth century conquered an area in West Africa lying between the Bight of Biafra and Lake Chad. The region was called, after him, Adamawa.

Adams, Daniel Weisiger (1821–1872). An American lawyer and son of a federal judge. A fiery young man, he once killed in a duel a newspaper editor who had criticized his father. At the beginning of the American Civil War he became a Confederate lieutenant colonel and later colonel of the 1st Louisiana. On 23 May 1862 he was promoted brigadier general. He led the Louisiana Brigade at Perryville, Murfreesboro, where he was wounded, and Chickamauga [qq.v.], where he was again wounded and captured. Upon being exchanged, he commanded a cavalry brigade in Alabama. After the war he returned to the law.

Adams, John Wittington (1763–1837). A British soldier who became known as the father of the Bengal army. He entered the Honourable East India Company's service in 1780 and fought at Rohillas, Hyderabad, Malavelly, and Seringapatam. He became a field officer in 1809, and in 1813 he commanded the field force in the invasion of the Bewah and opened the campaign by a siege and capture by storm of the fort at Entarrie. During the Nepalese War [q.v.] he commanded at Kumaon (Kumaun). In 1817–18 he fought in the Third Maratha War [q.v.], and in January 1826 he took part in the storming of Bhurtpore [q.v.]. In 1830 he was promoted major general.

Adams, Robert (fl. 1850–1865). A British designer and manufacturer of pistols. In 1855 the British army adopted the Deane and Adams revolver pistol, which was largely Adams's design. He later converted the pistol to a breechloader, and this was adopted by the British service in 1868. He also developed a solid-frame metallic cartridge that was widely adopted by European armies. [See Adams Pocket Revolver; Adams Dragoon Revolver.]

Adams Dragoon Revolver. A percussion revolver caliber

.493 with a solid-frame construction developed about 1859 by Robert Adams [q.v.]. It had a 7-inch barrel, held five rounds, and weighed 44 ounces.

Adams-Onís Treaty (22 February 1819). A treaty signed by American Secretary of State John Quincy Adams (1767–1848) and Luis de Onís, the Spanish minister, in which Spain surrendered all claims to the Pacific Northwest and to West Florida. East Florida was ceded to the United States. The northern boundary of Spanish Mexico was drawn from the mouth of the Sabine River on the Gulf of Mexico northwest to the Pacific Ocean. Later, when Texas joined the United States, the Americans disputed the boundary.

Adams Pocket Revolver. Also known as the Beaumont-Adams pocket pistol. This five-round revolver was developed from a design of Robert Adams [q.v.] and Lieutenant Francis Edward Blackett Beaumont (1838–1899) of the Royal Engineers. It was manufactured by the London Armoury Company about 1860. A caliber .32, it weighed 24 ounces and had a barrel only 4½ inches long.

Addis Ababa, Treaty of (26 October 1896). A treaty signed after the defeat of the Italians in the Battle of Adowa [q.v.] on 1 March 1896 in which Italy recognized Abyssinian independence.

Addiscombe Seminary. A 58-acre estate at Croyden, Surrey, formerly the residence of the Earl of Liverpool. On 7 April 1809, by a resolution of the Honourable East India Company's court of directors, it was purchased by the company for the education of cadets destined to be commissioned in the military service of the company. Originally it only trained cadets to be artillerymen or engineers, but seven years after its founding it initiated training for the infantry as well. To be admitted, boys had to be older than fourteen and younger than eighteen. The entrance fee was £30. The company supplied all the needs of the cadets, including 2s.6d. per week pocket money.

The name was changed from Seminary to College a year or two before its closing in 1861, when the Honourable East India Company disappeared.

Additional Aide-de-Camp. Immediately before the American Civil War the 14 general officers then in the American regular army were allowed among them a total of 33 aides-de-camp and 46 additional aides. On 5 August 1861 an act of Congress authorized an unlimited number. [See Aide-de-Camp.]

Aden, Attacks on (1839). In 1835, when the port of Aden (now in Yemen) became an important coaling station, the British purchased rights there, including permission to station troops to protect their coaling. Three years later, when the British sent a small force to garrison the place, the local Arab authorities, who had fortified Aden, refused to allow the landing and declined to supply them with water. British ships retaliated by shelling their fortifications. Upon the port's surrender, troops were landed and installed in garrison. An Arab attack launched later in the year was repulsed.

Adjutant. An aide to a commanding officer of a military unit or garrison who assists in much of the detail of his work. In a battalion this is usually a lieutenant or captain. He is often the chief administrative officer of a unit, who keeps the books and records of the command, receives and promulgates orders, and, in the British and some other armies, is responsible for discipline. In the French army the adjutant is called the *aide-major*.

"Unexceptionable deportment is especially becoming to the adjutant" (Thomas Wilhelm, *A Military Dictionary and Gazetteer*).

Adjutant General. A high military functionary in the American and British services. In Britain the second member of the Army Council is styled adjutant general to the forces. A general officer at the head of a department at the Horse Guards [q.v.], he is responsible for keeping an account of each regiment and for overseeing all communications concerning leave, discharges, recruiting, and other personnel matters.

The American regular army for most of the nineteenth century had only one adjutant general, whose duties were to publish orders and to handle correspondence and other administrative details for the head of the army. In war he was responsible for establishing camps and hospitals and for the mustering of troops. Those performing these or similar functions in lesser units were styled assistant adjutant generals and served as executive officers or chiefs of staff. The same system prevailed in the Confederate army during the American Civil War [see Confederate Army].

In the United States each state has its own adjutant general, who performs cognate functions for state militia. In Germany, Russia, and other countries during the nineteenth century the adjutant general was an officer on the personal staff of the sovereign.

Adjutant's Call. A bugle call signifying that the adjutant [q.v.] is about to form a regiment or portion of it for a military ceremony.

Adlercreutz, Count Karl Johan (1757–1815). A Swedish general born in Finland who in 1808 was defeated by the Russians in Finland during the brief Russo-Swedish War [q.v.]. In 1809 he led the party of officers who deposed Swedish King Gustavus Adolphus (Gustavus IV) in a coup d'état [see Swedish Military Coup d'État]. In 1813 he served in Germany against Napoleon, and the following year in Norway.

Administration, Military. See Army Administration.

Administrative Commandant. In the British service, lines of communication were divided into bases, sections, and posts, the boundaries of which were usually the same as those organized for defense. An administrative commandant, appointed for each base, section, or post, was responsible to the inspector general for discipline, sanitation, interior economy, and the policing of his jurisdiction as well as for transport animals and personnel, including prisoners of war, passing through his area.

Adobe Walls, Battles of (24 November 1864 and 27 June 1874), American Indian Wars. Two battles took place at this hunter's fort on the South Canadian River in the Texas Panhandle in present-day Hutchinson County.

1. On 25 November 1864 Colonel "Kit" Carson [q.v.], leading New Mexico volunteers, fought a battle with Kiowa and Comanche Indians in which he was saved from disaster by his artillery. The Indians suffered the loss of 60 warriors and the destruction of many of their lodges as well as their food supplies laid in for the winter. Carson lost 2 killed and 10 wounded.

2. On 27 June 1874 between 700 Kiowas and Comanches under Lone Wolf [q.v.] and Quanah (1845?–1911) attacked the fort, but its 28 white defenders, including famed scout Billy Dixon (1850–1913), successfully repulsed the attack. About 15 Indians and 4 whites were killed.

Adowa / Aduwa / Adua, Battle of (1 March 1896), Italo-Abyssinian War. At this place in mountainous country in Tigré Province, 145 miles northeast of Gondar and 80 miles south of Asmara, Italian General Oreste Baratieri [q.v.] with an army of 20,000 men (Italians and Africans) foolishly launched an attack upon the 90,000-man army of Emperor Menelek II [q.v.], negus negusti, or king of kings, of Abyssinia (Ethiopia). Baratieri's leading brigade became separated from the main body and was surrounded and destroyed. His remaining three brigades soon met the same fate. The losses in killed and wounded were 4,600 Italians and more than 2,000 African allies; 1,600 Italians and 900 Africans were taken prisoner. The Abyssinians owned to a loss of 3,000, although the figure may have been higher. It was the worst defeat ever administered to a European colonial army by an indigenous force. When news of the disaster reached Italy, there was rioting in many cities; nearly 100 were killed in Milan alone.

Despite accounts in the European press of Abyssinian atrocities, the Italian prisoners of war were in fact treated humanely. On 9 April Italy sued for peace, and on 26 October it signed the Treaty of Addis Ababa [q.v.], which recognized the independence of Abyssinia. Baratieri was superseded by Antonio Baldissera [q.v.], and the defeat brought down the government of Premier Francesco Crispi (1819–1901).

Adrianople, Capture of (20 August 1829), Russo-Turkish Wars. This Turkish city (Edirne), on the banks of the Tundzka River at its confluence with the Maritsa (Meriç) River in European Turkey, was captured by German-born Russian General Ivan [Ivanovich] Dibich-Zabalkansky [q.v.], who outmaneuvered and outmarched the Turkish forces under Grand Vizier Mustafa Reshid Pasha (1802–1858), whom he had defeated in the Battle of Kulevcha [q.v.] on 11 June. The fall of Adrianople threatened Constantinople (Istanbul), and the Turks sued for peace. The city was again captured by the Russians in 1879 following the capture of the Turkish army at the Shipka Pass [q.v.].

Military historian John Keegan, who has described Adrianople as the "most fought over city on earth," has counted fifteen battles or sieges fought here.

Adrianople, Treaty of (16 September 1829). A treaty between Russia and Turkey following the Russo-Turkish War of 1828–29 in which the Russians gained the mouth of the Danube River and the eastern coast of the Black Sea.

Advance by Bounds, to. To move forward by fits and starts, often from cover to cover.

Advance by Echelon. Units adjacent to one another moving one at a time.

Advanced Covered Way. A terreplein on the exterior of the advanced ditch similar to the first covered way.

Advanced Ditch. A trench beyond the glacis of the enceinte.

Advanced Glacis. A secondary glacis outside the primary. It was usually used in conjunction with an abatis and trous-de-loup.

Advanced Guard. Any body of troops on the march or stationary that are positioned between the main body and the enemy to prevent surprise, remove obstacles, or clear away skirmishers. [See Van.]

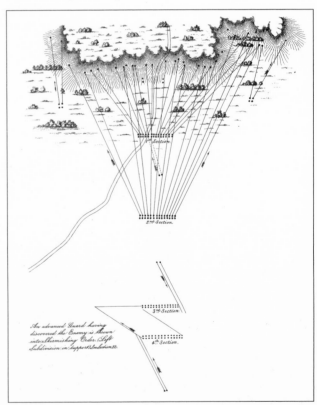

Advanced Guard *Diagrams of an advanced guard on the line of march and an advanced guard moving into skirmishing formation*

Advanced Lunette. A work resembling a bastion or ravelin having flanks formed upon or beyond a glacis. [See Lunette.]

Advanced Works. Defenses placed beyond the covered ways

of the enceinte and its outworks but still so connected as to be protected by covering fire from the general defenses.

Advising to Desert. Any soldier who advised another to desert in wartime committed an offense punishable by death. In peacetime in the American army the offender could receive any punishment except death that a court-martial might direct.

Adye, Sir John Miller (1819–1900). A British soldier, the author of *Recollections of a Military Life* (1895) and other books on military subjects, who served in the Crimean War, in the Indian Mutiny, and on the Northwest Frontier [qq.v.]. In 1875 he was promoted major general and appointed governor of the Royal Military Academy, Woolwich [q.v.]. In 1882 he was chief of staff to General Sir Garnet Wolseley [q.v.] during Arabi's Revolt [q.v.], and in 1884 he was made a colonel commandant of artillery.

Aeen. A tree found in India and Burma (Myanmar) that supplied the hard, heavy wood used to make handspikes, shafts, and yokes.

Aerial Photography. The first aerial photograph was taken from a balloon in 1858 by Félix Tournachon, pseudonym, Nadsar (1820–1910) over the outskirts of Paris, but officers were slow to see the military advantages until World War I.

Affair. A skirmish or small battle of no strategic significance.

Affamer. To lay such a close siege that the garrison and inhabitants face starvation.

Afghan Civil Wars. In 1793 Amir Timur died, leaving twenty-three sons to quarrel over the throne of Afghanistan. In the following twelve years three of the brothers occupied themselves in wresting the throne from one another. In 1803 Shuja-ul-Mulk (1780–1842), still another son of Timur, seized power and, although unpopular, reigned until 1815 when, while suppressing a revolt in the southern provinces, he was dethroned by his brother Shah Mahmud, who raised the standard of revolt in the north. Shuja-ul-Mulk, defeated in battle, fled to India.

Mahmud ruled for three years before being deposed in 1818 through the agency of the powerful Barakzai family. While the Barakzais waged fratricidal wars, the kingdom fell into anarchy and into the control of warlords. In 1835 Shuja-ul-Mulk made an unsuccessful attempt to regain his throne.

In that same year a powerful warrior, Dost Muhammad Khan [q.v.], proclaimed himself amir. He annoyed the British by renewing relations with Russia and disturbed them by refusing to accept a British Resident in Kabul, his capital. Consequently, in March 1839 an expedition under Sir John (later Lord) Keane (1781–1844) advanced through the Bolan Pass and entered Kandahar on 26 April. On 23 July Ghazni was taken, and on 7 August the army entered Kabul. [See Afghan War, First; Indus, Army of.] On 4 November 1840 Dost Muhammad surrendered, and the British reinstalled Shuja-ul-Mulk on the throne; Dost Muhammad was exiled to India. In November 1841, in a successful revolt led by Akbar Khan [q.v.], a son of Dost Muhammad, Shuja-ul-

Afghan Civil Wars *The British Army of the Indus files through the Bolan Pass on its way to Kandahar during the 1839 invasion of Afghanistan.*

Mulk (who was assassinated the following April) was toppled. Akbar humiliated and murdered both British envoys and drove the British army out of Afghanistan [see First Afghan War]. In December 1842 the British permitted Dost Muhammad to return. He quickly displaced Akbar and ruled for two decades.

Before his death on 9 June 1863, Dost Muhammad named as his successor Shere Ali [q.v.], his third son, passing over two elder sons, Afzul Khan and Azim Khan. A short time after Shere Ali assumed the throne, Afzul Khan led a revolt against him in the northern part of the country between the Hindu Kush and the Oxus. The fighting lasted for five years before the two came to terms.

Afzul Khan had a son, Abdur Rahman Khan [q.v.], an able and brave soldier who Shere Ali feared would attempt to replace his father on the throne. To frustrate any such designs, he threw Afzul Khan in prison, whereupon Abdur Rahman Khan wisely fled to Bokhara. While Shere Ali was suppressing a serious revolt in the south, Abdur Rahman reentered the country from the north with an armed force. Many of Shere Ali's troops mutinied and joined him. In March 1866, with the help of his uncle Azim Khan (d.1869), Abdur Rahman entered Kabul. Shere Ali led an army north from Kandahar, and the two forces clashed on 10 May at Sheikhabad. Abdur Rahman Khan, the victor, released his father and placed him on the throne while he himself assumed the governorship of the northern province. Shere Ali was routed after a second attempt to regain the throne. At the end of that year

Afzul Khan died, and his brother Azim Khan assumed the amirship.

In 1868 Shere Ali reentered the country and was met by a popular rising in his favor. On 3 January 1869 in the Battle of Tinah Khan [q.v.] he defeated Abdur Rahman Khan and Azim Khan, both of whom fled to Persia (Iran). Later Abdur Rahman Khan placed himself under Russian protection at Samarkand; Azim died in Persia in October 1869.

Shere Ali failed to maintain good relations with the British, who in 1878 for a second time invaded Afghanistan [see Afghan War, Second]. Shere Ali was deposed and his son Yakub Khan [q.v.] was installed on the throne. He was in turn deposed by the British when he permitted a rebellious mob and mutineers to kill the British Resident Pierre Louis Napoleon Cavagnari [q.v.] in 1880.

Afghan War, First (1839–42). In 1839 the British sent an army of 15,000, with 30,000 followers and a large herd of cattle, under General Sir John Keane (1781–1844) over the Bolan Pass and into Afghanistan. Its purpose was to replace the Afghan amir, Dost Muhammad [q.v.], with a more docile puppet, Shuja-ul-Mulk (1780–1842), a deposed amir whom the British had kept on the dole in India. Kandahar fell without a fight; Ghazni, after a stiff resistance. In August Kabul was occupied. Although the Afghans maintained control of the countryside, Shah Shuja-ul-Mulk was replaced on the throne, his authority propped up by British bayonets.

Because no major fighting ensued, the British reduced their garrison and, behaving as if they were in a friendly country, failed to fortify their positions. In 1841 the aged general William George Keith Elphinstone (1782–1842) took command. On 1 November of the same year the British camp at Kabul was shelled. A brigade sent out against the attackers was routed. A large army, outnumbering the British seven to one, had been raised by Akbar Khan, a son of Dost Muhammad [qq.v.]. The British tried to negotiate, but their envoys, Sir William Hay Macnaughton (1793–1841) and Sir Alexander Burns (1805–1841), were murdered. By November the Anglo-Indian garrison at Kabul was surrounded, and Afghans had seized a number of officers and their wives as hostages. Only Jalalabad, ably defended by General Robert Sale [q.v.], held fast. On 1 January 1842 the British in Kabul agreed to return to India and foolishly consented to give up almost all their artillery. In return the Afghans promised to provide for them and protect them on their retreat. They did neither.

On 6 January 1842, the Anglo-Indian army of 4,500 men with about 12,000 followers began its retreat to India. Struggling through snow in bitter weather, it was repeatedly attacked by Akbar Khan's Pathans in the passes. More soldiers, women, and children were given up as hostages until Akbar held 22 officers, 37 other ranks, 12 women, and 22 children. These, in the event, proved to be fortunate. Of the entire mass struggling toward India, only one European, Dr. William Brydon [q.v.], survived. Wounded and exhausted, he reached the frontier fortress town of Jalalabad, 80 miles from Kabul, on 13 January.

The retreat from Kabul was the most humiliating military disaster for the British in the nineteenth century. In response, the British ordered Major General Sir William Nott and Major General George Pollock [qq.v.] to move on Kandahar and Kabul. On 31 March General Pollock forced the Khyber

Pass with a loss of only 14 killed and then moved to capture Kabul. General Nott sallied forth from Kandahar and defeated the Afghans in a series of battles before joining Pollock at Kabul, where, as an act of retribution, Pollock destroyed the great covered bazaar. On 11 October he and Nott started back to India. In 1843 Dost Muhammad was restored to the amirship and reigned for twenty years.

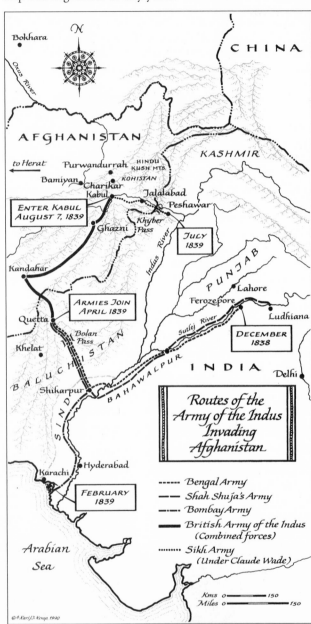

Afghan War, First *Map of the routes of the Army of the Indus invasion of Afghanistan*

Afghan War, Second (1878–80). In 1863, when Shere Ali succeeded his father, Dost Muhammad [qq.v.], as amir of Afghanistan, he alarmed the British by his warm response to Russian blandishments and his refusal to receive a British agent. In November 1878 the British invaded Afghanistan with three columns. Shere Ali died in February 1879 and was succeeded by his son, Yakub Khan [q.v.], who signed a treaty at Gandamak that ceded to the British the Khyber Pass and other strategic areas. Yakub Khan also agreed to receive a British agent in Kabul. Pierre Louis Napoleon Cavagnari [q.v.], the British-educated son of one of Napoleon's generals, was selected for the post and arrived on 24 July 1879 with an escort of 75 soldiers from the Corps of Guides. On 3 September, while Yakub Khan stood by, Cavagnari and his escort were massacred by an Afghan mob mostly composed of mutinous Afghan soldiers.

Again the British dispatched an army of retribution, this time under General Frederick Roberts, VC [q.v.], who marched into Kabul on 7 October. To avenge the murder of Cavagnari, he hanged nearly 100 Afghans believed to have taken part in the killing.

Roberts established a fortified camp outside the city at a place called Sherpur, where on 23 December 1879 he beat back an attack by an estimated 60,000 Afghans [see Sherpur, Battle of]. Afghan losses were believed to be 3,000. The British lost 5.

In February 1880 Abdur Rahman [q.v.], a grandson of Dost Muhammad, led an Afghan force equipped with modern Russian rifles across the Oxus into northern Afghanistan. Instead of opposing him, the British offered him the throne. Terms were agreed to at a durbar north of Kabul on 22 July 1880, and the British began their withdrawal.

At this same time Ayub Khan [q.v.], the ruler of Herat, a cousin of Abdur Rahman's and a claimant to the throne, marched on Kandahar with a force of about 20,000. A British force under Brigadier General George Burrows (1826?–1913) marched out of Kandahar to intercept him, and the two armies met near the village of Maiwand, about 40 miles west of Kandahar, on 27 July [see Maiwand, Battle of]. Burrows was soundly defeated and retreated into Kandahar, where he was soon besieged.

Learning of the disaster, Roberts, still in Kabul, made his famous march with 10,000 men from Kabul to Kandahar [see Kabul to Kandahar March]—313 miles in twenty-two days— and on 1 September defeated Ayub Khan in the Battle of Kandahar [q.v.], capturing his camp and routing his army for a loss of only 35 British killed; Afghan losses were estimated to be 600 killed.

The British then withdrew to India. Ayub Khan seized Kandahar, but was defeated by Abdur Rahman, who remained on the throne until 1901. A Third Afghan War was fought in 1919, when Amanullah Khan (1892–1960) became amir.

Afrancesados. The name given to those Spaniards, mostly from the upper social classes, who supported or collaborated with the French during the Peninsular War [q.v.]. They were also sometimes called Josefinos, supporters of King Joseph.

African Corps, Royal. A force of Africans, originally called Fraser's Corps, raised by the British in 1800, to defend the island of Gorée in Senegal. In 1804 it became the Royal African Corps. In 1805, 34 volunteers accompanied the expedition of Mungo Park (1771–1806) to the Niger River; only 6 returned.

Afridi Tribes, Military Expeditions against.   The Afridis, although less numerous than the Wazirs [q.v.], were the most powerful and incendiary of the tribes living on India's Northwest Frontier [q.v.]. They occupied, as they still do, the eastern spurs of the Safed Koh, and through their territory snakes the Khyber Pass, between what was in the last half of the nineteenth-century British India (today Pakistan) and Afghanistan. The Afridis were reputed to be cruel, brave, hardy, and untrustworthy. They were organized into many septs and subsepts, and their untrammeled ways bordered on anarchy; no single ruler could control them. Late in the century a number were enrolled into units of the Frontier Scouts [q.v.], such as the Khyber Rifles [q.v.], but the majority remained so bellicose that the British felt forced to launch numerous expeditions against them.

In 1850 General Colin Campbell [q.v.] led 3,200 troops against the Adam Khel Afridis after 1,000 attacked an Anglo-Indian body of sappers building a road, killing 12 and wounding 6. In that same year Charles Napier [q.v.] led another expedition against the Jowaki Afridis, a sept of the Adam Khel living in the area between the Kohat Pass and the Indus River. Three years later a punitive expedition of 1,700 troops swept through Afridi territory, destroying crops and villages, including the stronghold at Bori.

With some success the British tried bribing the Afridis, giving them an allowance for "guarding the passes," but in 1877, when the government of India proposed to reduce the allowance to the Jowaki Afridis, they cut telegraph wires and reverted to raiding British territory. In August of that year a punitive expedition of 1,500 men in three columns was organized under the command of Colonel Frederic David Mocatta (1828–1905), a veteran of the Second Sikh War of 1848–49, the Indian Mutiny in 1857–58 [qq.v.], the Usafazai Expedition of 1863, and the Hazara Field Force on Black Mountain in 1868 [see Black Mountain Expedition].

Although Mocatta's expedition did great damage, destroying crops and burning villages, the Jowaki Afridis persevered in their depredations. In a few months a stronger force of 7,400, organized into three columns led by Brigadier General Charles Patton Keyes (1825?–1896?), the commandant of the Frontier Field Force [q.v.], who had seen much action on the Northwest Frontier, was sent against them. After destroying their principal villages, Keyes occupied their territory for several months in 1877–78.

During the Second Afghan War [q.v.], from September 1878 to November 1880, the Zakka Khel Afridis opposed the British advance into Afghanistan and attacked their outposts.

Afghan War, Second *Major Pierre L. N. Cavagnari, British leader of the peace mission, and his aides breakfast as guests of the khan of Gandamak. His hosts murder him four months later and war begins again.*

After the war a British force of 2,500 under a redoubtable warrior, Brigadier General John Adam Tytler, VC [q.v.], descended upon their territory and forced their submission. The Afridis in the Khyber Pass who had persistently hectored the British throughout the war were subdued by an expedition under Lieutenant General Frederick Maude, VC [q.v.], which inflicted such damage that they gave no more trouble until the great uprising on the frontier in 1897. [See Tirah Campaign; Malakand Field Force.]

Afridi Tribes *A cartoon from* Punch, *12 February 1898, notes that "Someone has blundered" in the British expeditions against the Afridis.*

Afrikanders / Africanders. Afrikaans-speaking white South Africans, descendants of seventeenth-century Dutch with considerable admixtures of French, German, British, and other European nationalities. In the nineteenth century they were usually called Boers, an Afrikaans word for farmer. They fought two wars with the British (1881 and 1899–1902) as well as numerous wars with African tribesmen. [See Kaffir Wars; Anglo-Boer Wars.]

Afrikanders *Boers defend against the Ndebeles at the Battle of Vechtkop, October 1836.*

After-Action Report. The official report made after a battle, skirmish, or other engagement by the commanders of all units engaged. During the American Civil War these were often known as field returns.

Agent, Army. In the British army a person in the civil department under the paymaster general and over the regimental paymaster through whom every regimental concern involving money was transacted.

Agent Provocateur. A person employed to feign sympathy for a cause and to infiltrate a group in order to persuade its members to commit illegal acts, such as mutiny or rebellion.

Aggregate Strength. See Strength, Unit.

Agha. An honorary title for Turkish and Egyptian officers in general and in particular for officers below the rank of bey [q.v.]. Its use declined in Egypt after the creation of a regularly drilled and disciplined army by Muhammad Ali Pasha Husain (d.1884) in 1821–24.

Agiades. Pioneers or field engineers in the Turkish army who were employed in constructing field fortifications [q.v.].

Agnew. The name given to the uniform worn by female nurses of the Sanitary Commission [q.v.] in the American Civil War. It was said to be the first uniform worn by female army nurses, at least in the United States. It consisted of an issue army shirt worn with shirttail out over a full skirt without hoops. The collar was worn open, and the sleeves were rolled up. The name derives from Dr. David Hayes Agnew (d.1892), a Pennsylvania volunteer surgeon, who lent one of his shirts to a female nurse during the Peninsular Campaign [q.v.] of 1862.

Agordat, Battle of (21 December 1893), Italo-Abyssinian Wars. In northwest Eritrea, then an Italian colony, about 75 miles west of Asmara some 2,200 Italian troops and local tribesmen under Major General Giuseppe Arimondi (1845–1896) routed 11,500 Mahdist Dervishes [q.v.] under Ahmed wad Ali wad Ahmad [q.v.]. Mahdist losses were about 3,000, including the Dervish commander; Italian losses were 13 Italians and 225 allied tribesmen killed or wounded.

Agra, Sieges of (1803), Second Maratha War. The fortress at Agra, on the right bank of the Jumna River, 110 miles southeast of Delhi in central India, was twice besieged in the nineteenth century.

The first siege was begun on 4 October 1803, during the Second Maratha War [q.v.]. The fort and town, garrisoned by 7,700 troops of Doulet Rao Sindhia (d.1827), was besieged by a British force of 10,500 cavalry and infantry under General Sir Gerard Lake [q.v.]. On the 10th of the month Lake successfully attacked the forces in the town and captured 26 guns. On the 17th British batteries opened fire on the citadel, which surrendered the next day. The British captured an enormous quantity of stores, and a rich treasury was seized for prize money [q.v.].

The second siege began on 2 August 1857, during the Indian Mutiny [q.v.]. The British garrison of Agra sallied out to attack an army of 10,000 mutineers camped just four miles from the city. A significant portion of the garrison's sepoys deserted to the mutineers, and the British, hard pressed and short of ammunition, retreated into the Agra fort. In early October a flying column of four infantry battalions and two cavalry regiments under Colonel Edward Greathed

(1815?–1880?) of the 8th Foot put to flight 7,000 mutineers near the city. On 11 October Greathed entered Agra and relieved it.

Aguinaldo Insurrection against Spain. See Philippine Insurrection against Spain.

Aguinaldo Insurrection against the United States. See Philippine Insurrection against the United States.

Aguinaldo y Famy, Emilio (1869–1964). A Philippine revolutionary of mixed Chinese and Tagalog ancestry. He had little formal education but had studied law and was well acquainted with the histories of the French and American revolutions. American Admiral George Dewey (1837–1917), the "Hero of Manila Bay," found him "a soft-spoken, unimpressive little man" whose command of English was "quaint." Nevertheless, he was a

General Emilio Aguinaldo, August 1898

gifted guerrilla leader. In 1896 he led a revolution against Spain in which he managed to defeat a large Spanish force under the command of the islands' governor-general, Ramón Blanco y Erenas (1831–1906) [see Philippine Insurrection against Spain]. After agreeing to a truce in which the Spanish promised numerous social and political changes, he went into exile at Hong Kong, but when few of the promised reforms were initiated, he returned to rekindle the revolution. In 1898, when the Spanish-American War [q.v.] broke out, assured that America had no designs on the Philippines, he assisted American forces in defeating the Spaniards, particularly in the capture of Manila on 13 August 1898. Soon afterward, aware that he had been deceived, he mounted an open rebellion against American rule. He announced a "provisional dictatorship" and soon was instrumental in establishing an independent Visayan Republic with its capital at Malolos, northeast of Manila in south-west Luzon. There in September–November 1898 a constitution was framed in the Barasoain Church, and on 23 January 1899 a republic was proclaimed with Aguinaldo as president. The Americans were astonished. Admiral George Dewey later wrote: "I never dreamed that they wanted independence."

The revolt was quelled by American troops after a protracted war in which about 1,000 Americans were killed and some 3,000 wounded. Aguinaldo was captured in March 1901. [See Funston, Frederick; Philippine Insurrection against the United States]. The insurrection officially ended on 4 July 1902.

After a time spent in prison, Aguinaldo took the oath of allegiance to the United States. In 1935 he was defeated in a presidential election, and in 1945, during World War II, he was imprisoned for aiding the Japanese. He was released at the end of the war.

Ahmad Khel, Battle of (19 April 1880), Second Afghan War. British General Sir Donald Stewart [q.v.] with a force of 6,000 was attacked by some 15,000 Afghans while on a march from Kandahar to Ghazni. After an assault by 3,000 fanatical

Ghazis [q.v.] was repulsed, the Afghans retired, leaving 1,000 dead on the field. British losses were 17.

Ahmadnagar, Capture of (12 August 1803), Second Mahratta War. Major General Sir Arthur Wellesley (later Duke of Wellington), having captured Poona [q.v.], India, on 20 March 1803, moved 30 miles south with a portion of his force, 4,500 regulars, about half of whom were cavalry. After defeating an army of 30,000 cavalry and 10,000 infantry under Rughuji Bhonsla, the raja of Berar, and Sindhia [q.v.] at the junction of the Jua and Kelna rivers, he took 11,000 men and captured the hill fortress of Ahmadnagar, 64 miles east of Poona, considered the greatest fort in India. One Indian is said to have marveled: "These English are a strange people, and their general is a wonderful man. They came here in the morning, surveyed the wall, walked over it, killed all the garrison, and returned to breakfast!" It was not that simple, however. British losses were 79 Europeans and 62 sepoys killed or wounded; Maratha losses are unknown.

Ahmadu (d. 1902). A Tukulor sultan in West Africa from 1864, following the death of his father, Umar ibn Said Tal [q.v.]. Although he had assisted the French in overthrowing Mahmadu Lamine [q.v.], he suffered increasing aggression from them. On 3 January 1891, when the French decisively defeated the Tukulor army near the village of Tori, he fled with a small group of retainers east across the desert to Masina, which was ruled by one of his brothers, whom he deposed. When the French attacked him there, he was forced to take refuge in the Sokoto empire.

Ahmed Arabi Pasha. See Arabi Pasha.

Ahmed wad Ali wad Ahmad (d. 1885). A Mahdist (Dervish) amir and the cousin of the Khalifa Abdullahi [q.v.], who became governor of Kassala, 250 miles east of Khartoum, by alleging that the incumbent, Zaki Tamal [q.v.], planned to betray the town to the Italians. He was killed fighting the Italians in a battle near Agordat on 23 September 1885.

Aide-de-Camp. Often called an ADC in the British service and aide in the American. A staff officer of no fixed duty or of various duties who often helps with correspondence or assists in dispensing the hospitality and courtesies of a general's quarters. In nineteenth-century battles he carried orders from commanding officers.

In the British army it was common for titled officers to be attached to the commanding general's staff. Francis Grose (1731–1791) in his satirical *Advice to the Officers of the British Army* (1782) wrote: "An aide-de-camp is to his general what Mercury was to Jupiter, and what the jackal is to the lion." British army officers assigned as aide-de-camps were not removed from the lists of their regiments. Toward the end of the century, to avoid abuses, every aide-de-camp had to have served at least two years with his regiment and to have passed an examination.

Aide-de-camps often wear special insignia or aiguillettes [q.v.]. Early in the nineteenth century an ADC's coat bore distinctive "saw-edged" buttonhole loops of fine gold or silver wire.

Aide-de-Camp to the King / Queen. In Britain a largely honorary post for regular and militia officers involving no particular duties and carrying the rank of colonel in the army. On state occasions 6 were required to attend the sovereign. The number who could occupy the post was not fixed. In 1876 there were 33, of whom 8 were peers.

Aide-Major. An adjutant, later surgeon, in the French army.

Aid to the Sick and Wounded, National Society of. A British society formed on 4 August 1870. It collected and distributed money and stores and gave aid to the sick and wounded in the Franco-Prussian War, Serbo-Bulgarian War of 1876, Russo-Turkish War of 1877–78, and Second Anglo-Boer War [qq.v.] in 1899–1901.

Aiguillette. An ornamental plaited cord often ending with metal points, aiglets, or needles, worn over the shoulder and under the arm in one or more loops. It was worn by those performing special functions, such as aides-de-camp [q.v.], or, later, as a unit decoration, such as the French Croix de Guerre.

In Britain the aiguillette was worn by officers of the Life Guards and Horse Guards. In the American army it was for a time worn on the right shoulder of general officers, and at one time aiguillettes in some form were worn by adjutants of regiments, officers of the adjutant general's department, and others.

Aigun, Treaty of (May 1858). A treaty following the Second Opium War [q.v.] by which China ceded the left bank of the Amur River to Russia.

Aikuchi / Haikuchi. A Japanese dagger having a wooden hilt and horn fittings without a guard between the hilt and the single-edged, slightly curved blade. This was a favorite weapon for ritual suicide (seppuku or hara-kiri [q.v.]).

Aile. The wing or flank of an army or a fortification.

Air Bed. Although air beds of leather were known in the early eighteenth century, it was not until the invention of the airtight or macintosh cloth that they became practical and relatively inexpensive.

Air bed

A bed popular with officers on campaign consisted of a number of airtight compartments, each with a valve so that it could be inflated with a bellows. At one end a compartment larger than the others formed a bolster.

Airey Committee. A British committee formed in 1879 and chaired by General Richard Lord Airey (1803–1881) for the purpose of examining the advantages and disadvantages of short service enlistments and the linkage of battalions that would assign each regiment at least two. Its report proposed a short service of eight years with the colors and the establishment of large training depots. It counseled against battalion linkage. Not one of these proposals was adopted.

Air Gun. See Gas Guns.

Aizu, Battle of (6 November 1868), Boshin Civil War. The final battle in the Japanese war to restore power to the Meiji emperor in Japan. The samurai of the Tokugawa shogunate were defeated.

Aka Hills Expedition (1883). The inhabitants of the rugged Aka hills on India's Northeast Frontier [q.v.] known as brave and bold raiders saw no reason to change their ways when the area came under British protection, about 1829. In 1883 they went too far when they raided the British district of Darrang and carried off as hostages several Indian forest officers. In retaliation, an expedition 800 strong under General Rowley Sale Hill (1837?–1905?), commander of the Eastern Frontier District, was sent against them. The Aka Hills Expedition, as it was known, successfully curbed their raiding propensities.

Akbar Khan (d. 1849). An Afghan leader and a son of Dost Muhammad [q.v.]. After the British captured his father in 1839, Akbar Khan gathered an Afghan army, and in November 1841 he led an attack upon the British in Kabul. British envoys—Sir William Hay Mcnaghten (1793–1841) and Sir Alexander Burnes (1805–1841)—were murdered while attempting to negotiate, and the British garrison of 4,500 British and Indian troops under Major General William George Keith Elphinstone (1782–1842) was surrounded. On 6 January 1842 the troops and nearly 10,000 noncombatants were permitted to depart for India under a safe conduct, which proved to be worthless. The British were so harassed by Akbar Khan's troops and hostile Pathans that only one European, Dr. William Brydon [q.v.], and a few sepoys survived the march [see Afghan War, First]. The sixty-year-old Elphinstone, suffering from gout and generally poor health, was captured and died of dysentery. A few months later Akbar Khan was defeated by an Anglo-Indian army under Sir George Pollock [q.v.] that forced the Khyber Pass.

Akhalzic / Akhaltzikke / Akhaltskhe, Siege and Storming of (22 July–27 August 1828), Russo-Turkish War of 1828–29. Russian General Ivan Feodorovich Paskevich [q.v.] with 11,000 men and 50 guns, after advancing from Tiflis and capturing Kars [q.v.], laid siege to 40,000 Turks, mostly ill-disciplined irregulars, in the fortress at Akhalzic, a Georgian town on the left bank of the Kura River 65 miles east of Batum. When Paskevich sent a colonel under a white flag to demand the surrender of the place, he was fired upon and killed. On 27 August 1828 the fortress was taken by storm. Russian losses were 618 killed and wounded; Turkish losses were 5,000 killed or severely wounded; 600 Turks who had surrendered were murdered. Further Russian advances were halted temporarily by fierce Kurdish resistance on the upper Euphrates.

Akhulgo, Siege of (19 June–29 August 1839), Murid Wars. Akhulgo, the headquarters of the Murid rebel leader Shamyl [q.v.], was a rocky fortress aerie in Daghestan perched on an isolated peak rising 600 feet above the Köisu River; it was besieged by the Russians for seventy-one days. Although Shamyl had stocked his fortress with arms, ammunition, and supplies, the quantities were insufficient for so long a siege. When the Russians finally attacked, the Murids [q.v.], out of ammunition, fought with stones and, as a last resort, flung themselves onto the Russian bayonets. The women too fought, dashing their children and themselves onto the advancing enemy. Although the fortress was taken, Shamyl himself escaped to fight another day [see Murid Wars].

The fall of Akhulgo was a turning point in the Murid Wars. It hardened the resolve of Shamyl and his followers, intensified their hatred of the Russians, and sustained through adversity their desire for revenge.

Akhund of Swat, (1794–1874). Real name: Abdul Ghafur. A Muslim holy man living in the Swat Valley on the Northwest Frontier of India (Pakistan) who wielded considerable influence over tribesmen in the area and over Muslims throughout Central Asia. He was generally friendly with the British, but after his death later akhunds were less so, and in 1896–97 the British sent an expedition to the Swat Valley to put down violence resulting from civil war in Chitral [see Chitral Campaign].

Akindschi / Akindjis. Volunteer Turkish cavalry whose only tactic was a headlong dash at the enemy.

Alabama Red Rovers. An American volunteer company of about 60 men formed in 1835 in Courtland, Alabama, to help Texans win freedom from Mexico. Their bright red hunting shirts of linsey-woolsey made by women in the community gave the company its name. In December 1835 they marched out of Courtland. On 27 March 1836 near Presidio La Bahía (Goliad, Texas) almost all were killed in action or massacred after being taken prisoner, along with nearly 300 other Americans and Texans, on orders from Mexican General Santa Anna [q.v.]. [See Goliad Massacre.]

Aladja Dagh / Alaca-Dag, Battle of (14–15 October 1877), Russo-Turkish War of 1877–78. At this site in eastern Turkey Russian forces advancing through the Caucasus under Count Mikhail Tarielovich Loris-Melikov [q.v.] engaged a Turkish army under Ahmed Mukhtar Pasha. The Turkish force was broken up, and its heavily fortified camp captured. Turkish casualties were 6,000 killed and wounded, and 12,000 were taken prisoner, including 7 pashas; 22 guns were lost. Russian losses were 1,500 killed and wounded.

Pursued by the Russians, the survivors were forced to fall back upon their two main fortresses at Kars and Erzerum.

Alaibeg. A Turkish commander of a regiment of conscripted troops.

Alamo, Siege of (23 February–6 March 1836), War of Texan Independence. Mission San Antonio de Valero, a thick-walled Spanish Franciscan mission first established in 1718 near San Antonio de Bexar was secularized in 1793 and converted into a fort renamed Alamo (Spanish for cottonwood tree). For two weeks in 1836, 188 Texans and American adventurers commanded by William Barret Travis [q.v.] defended it against a besieging force of 3,000 Mexican regulars under General Antonio López de Santa Anna [q.v.]. With the defenders were several frontier heroes, among them James Bowie (1799–1836), reputed inventor of the bowie knife [q.v.], and David ("Davy") Crockett [q.v.]. When the fort was finally taken by assault, only 5 of its 188 defenders survived,

and these were shot. Only 30 noncombatants were spared. The Mexicans lost more than 1,500 men. On a wall of the fort was found written: "Thermopylae had its messenger of defeat; the Alamo had none."

It was while the siege was in progress that Texas was proclaimed a republic (2 March 1836) with Sam Houston as its army commander and later its president. After the battle Santa Anna marched east, toward Galveston, destroying all American settlements in his path. The Alamo was the first of eight battles Santa Anna was to fight against the Texans and Americans.

Not much of the original structure exists. Much was destroyed by the Mexican army, and much of the surviving structure has been altered. The American army occupied the place as a quartermaster depot during the Mexican War [q.v.] and about 1848 added two upstairs windows and a humped parapet to what had been the barracks. When the army moved out in 1873, it was largely neglected for twenty years. For a time it was a saloon and once a house of ill repute. In 1890 there were "improvements," including the demolition of the upper floors of the barracks. In 1905 the remaining structure was taken over by the Daughters of the Republic of Texas. It is still preserved as a public monument and administered by them, although on 21 April 1936 it was bought by the state of Texas.

Alarm Post. The place appointed for troops to assemble in case of alarm. In French, *place d'alarme*.

Alava, Miguel de (1771–1843). A Spanish general who, beginning in 1811, served on Wellington's [q.v.] staff as a liaison officer. He was with the fleet at Trafalgar and was present at Salamanca [q.v.]. At Orthez [q.v.] in 1814 he was wounded in the buttocks, a wound Wellington found amusing until soon after he himself suffered the same wound. Alava was present at Waterloo and Quatre Bras [qq.v.]. Shortly after, he was named a brigadier general in the service of Ferdinand VII (1784–1833). In 1834 he became president of the Cortes. He was ambassador to the Court of St. James's and later to France.

Alba de Tormes, Battles of. During the Peninsular War [q.v.] two battles were fought near this village on the Tormes River, 13 miles southeast of Salamanca.

First Battle (28 November 1809). A Spanish army of 30,000 infantry and 1,500 cavalry commanded by Don Lorenzo del Parque [q.v.] was defeated by 13,000 French infantry and 3,000 cavalry under French General François Étienne Kellermann (1770–1835). French casualties were fewer than 300; the Spanish lost 3,000 in killed, wounded, and captured, as well as nine guns and five standards.

Second Battle (10–11 November 1812). Wellington, holding the important bridge over the Tormes River with a mixed British and Portuguese force, was attacked by French forces under Jean Baptiste Jourdan [q.v.], Napoleon's elder brother King Joseph Bonaparte (1768–1844), and Nicolas Jean de Dieu Soult [q.v.], who deployed 18 guns and 12 voltigeur companies. On 10 November Wellington commenced a lengthy bombardment that was resumed for a few hours the next day before the French withdrew. Casualties among the Allies were 79 British and 44 Portuguese; the French lost 158.

Albanian Revolts. 1. In the late eighteenth century Muhammad Bushati, pasha of Scutari, threw off the Turkish yoke in northern Albania. In the early nineteenth century his son, Muhammad called Muhammad the Black, routed three Turkish armies that tried to retake the country. Not until the defeat of his grandson Mustapha by the Turks in 1831 was the power of the Bushati family broken.

2. In central Albania, Ali Pasha [see Ali Pasha of Jannina], known as the Lion of Jannina (Ioannina), established a virtually independent state. Ruthless, completely amoral, and untrustworthy, he managed for a time to deceive the sultan of Turkey, as well as Napoleon and the British government. By 1803 he controlled Epirus, most of Albania, Thessaly, and all the former Venetian towns except Parga; his sons held the pashaliks of Morea (Peloponnesus) and Mukhtar. Parga remained in French hands until the Pargiots rose in revolt and handed the town over to the British to save it from the clutches of Ali, who had bribed the commandant to surrender to him. Ali and his two sons were assassinated by order of Sultan Mahmud II of Turkey (1785–1839).

3. An Albanian revolt against Turkey in 1840 and another in 1880 were both suppressed by Dervish Pasha [q.v.].

Albeck, Battle of. See Haslach, Battle of.

Albert (Albrecht), Archduke Friedrich Rudolf, Duke of Teschen, (1817–1895), usually called Archduke Albert. An Austrian soldier and military writer, the son of Archduke Charles (Karl Friedrich), he entered the Austrian army at age twenty as a colonel of infantry. In 1848–49 he served in Italy and Sardinia as a volunteer under Count Radetzky [q.v.], and he commanded the Austrian force at Venetia in 1860–63. He became a field marshal in 1863, leading the Austrian army to victory at Custoza [q.v.] on 23 June 1866. That same year he was made commander-in-chief, succeeding Radetzky.

Freiherr (Baron) Franz Kuhn von Kuhnenfeld [q.v.], when war minister, took an extreme dislike to Albert and in his diary described him as an absolute incarnation of "Spanish absolutism, bigotry, ultramontanism, falseness and jesuitness." Kuhn was responsible for the dissolution of Albert's staff and his demotion from army commander to inspector general, a position in which he served from 1866 to 1895. He did much to modernize the army, instituting conscription, improving the general staff, and upgrading the railroad system. He died on 18 February 1895.

Albert, Friedrich Augustus (1828–1902). A German soldier and crown prince who in 1873 became king of Saxony. In 1849 he served as a captain in the Schleswig-Holstein War [q.v.] against the Danes. During the Seven Weeks' War [q.v.] of 1866 he commanded the Saxon forces opposing the Prussians under Prince Frederick Charles [q.v.]. He wisely did not defend Saxony, but fell back into Bohemia to join forces with the Austrians. He played a leading part in the battles in which the Prussians forced the line of the Iser. In the Battle of Gitschin [q.v.] he made a retreat in good order, and in the decisive battle of Königgrätz (or Sadowa) [q.v.], in which he commanded the extreme left flank of the Austrian position, he displayed great tenacity. [See Seven Weeks' War.]

When Saxony entered the Confederation of the Rhine, Prince Albert was given command of the Saxon army, which became XII Corps of the North German army. In the Franco-Prussian War [q.v.] he commanded the extreme left of the German army at Gravelotte–St. Privat [q.v.] and with his Saxons and the Prussian Guards made the attack at St. Privat that was the decisive action of the battle.

He played a leading role in the battles that preceded the Battle of Sedan [q.v.]. In the march on Paris he commanded the Fourth Army, known as the Army of the Meuse [q.v.], and during the siege of Paris [q.v.] his troops formed the northeast section of the investing force. After the armistice he commanded the army of occupation until the fall of the Paris Commune [q.v.]. Later he became a field marshal and an inspector general. On 29 October 1873, on the death of his father, he succeeded to the throne. He died on 10 June 1902.

Alberta Field Force (1885). When Cree Indians under Big Bear massacred settlers at Frog Lake in Saskatchewan, Canada, an Alberta rancher, Thomas Bland Strange, a former British soldier who had seen extensive service in India, organized a punitive expedition of militia and mounted police that he called the Alberta Field Force. He led them through rugged, heavily wooded terrain for 500 miles before he finally encountered the Indians at Frenchman's Butte, where he fought and won a pitched battle, compelling the surviving warriors to surrender and effecting the release of the white captives they had taken.

Albert Helmet. A metal helmet designed for heavy cavalry by Prince Albert of Britain (1819–1861), who was keenly interested in uniforms. The helmet was adopted by the Household Cavalry [q.v.] in 1842 and by line cavalry in 1847. It is still worn with little change by the Household Cavalry.

Albert Medal. A British decoration instituted in 1866 as a reward for bravery in saving life at sea. In 1877 it was extended to include as well heroic acts on land not performed in battle.

Albert Shako. A stiff tubular hat with peaks in front and back worn by British infantry, artillery, and engineers from 1844 to 1855.

Albini-Braendlin Rifle. A number of rifles by this name were manufactured, but the most successful was a .60 caliber rimfire rifle (sometimes spelled Albini-Brändlin) designed in 1865 by Admiral Augusto Albini (1830–1909) of the Italian navy. Its breechblock was similar to the American Springfield rifle, and it featured a hinged breech that was lifted when loading. Using this system, old muzzleloaders could be converted to breechloaders. Albini had his rifle manufactured by the Braendlin Armoury Company in Birmingham, England. In 1865 the British army tested it but rejected it in favor of the Snider [q.v.], which had a similar design. It was adopted by the armies of Bavaria and Württemburg and issued to Belgian regulars in 1867.

Albuera, La, Battle of (16 May 1811), Peninsular War. British General William Carr Beresford [q.v.] with 10,000 Spanish, 9,000 Portuguese, and fewer than 8,000 British troops took up a position blocking the fords and bridges across the Albuera River near the village of La Albuera, 13 miles southeast of Badajoz, Spain, in order to stop the advance of French Marshal Nicolas Jean de Dieu Soult [q.v.], who, with 24,260 men and 48 guns, was marching to relieve besieged Badajoz [q.v.]. In a pouring rain Soult sent a strong infantry force to attack the besiegers and take the town's bridge; at the same time he dispatched 4,000 cavalry and 19 battalions of infantry under André Masséna [q.v.] to force crossings defended by Beresford's weaker Spanish forces, one of which was two miles and one three miles south of La Albuera. The French scattered the Spanish at the fords, a British brigade hurrying to their aid was annihilated by French cavalry, and Soult swept down on Beresford's flank.

Two Spanish battalions on a small rise managed to hold off two French divisions until the British could bring up a division and launch a counterattack. The counterattack was not an unqualified success. Polish lancers (1st Vistula Lancers) and the French 2nd Hussars charged the flank of one British brigade and inflicted 60 percent casualties.

It was only with difficulty and after heavy losses that just as the rain ceased, Beresford was able to establish a stable defensive line of not more than 1,800 British infantry. The British position was precarious. A Spanish general refused to cooperate; two Portuguese brigades were held up by confused orders. The day was saved by the initiative of General Galbraith Lowry Cole (1772–1842) and Sir Henry Hardinge [q.v.], who brought up 4,000 men and launched an oblique attack that included a splendid charge by the Fusilier Brigade. The French retreated, and the battle ended, four hours after its start.

This battle has been called "the most murderous and sanguinary conflict" of the Peninsular War [q.v.]. Some formations stood as close as 40 yards from each other and fired until one side broke. A British private who was captured later described the scene after the battle "Men dead where the column had stood, heaped on each other; the wounded crying for assistance, and human blood flowing down the hill!" The French lost about 7,000 to 8,000; the Allies about 6,000. Of the 7,640 British engaged, 3,930 were killed or wounded. In his after-action report Beresford wrote: "Every individual nobly did his duty; and it is observed that our dead . . . were lying, as they fought, in ranks, and every wound was in the front." Wellington told Beresford: "You could not be successful in such an action without a large loss. We must make up our minds to affairs of this kind sometimes, or give up the game."

It was during this battle that Colonel William Inglis, wounded commander of the 57th Foot, called out to his men: "Die hard! Fifty-seventh!" They did. Of 579 engaged, 23 officers and 414 other ranks were killed or wounded. Ever after, the 57th and its successor, the Middlesex Regiment, were known as the Die Hards. In 1896 Lady Butler [q.v.], famous for her canvases of British battle scenes, was commissioned by the Middlesex Regiment to commemorate the regiment in this battle. Her *Steady the Drums and Fifes* vividly portrays the ordeal of standing steadfast under withering fire.

Albufera, Battle of (4 January 1812), Peninsular War. The battle took its name from a lagoon in east-central Spain near which French Marshal Louis Gabriel Suchet [q.v.] defeated a combined British and Spanish force under General Joachim Blake [q.v.].

Albuquerque, Mousinho d' (1855–1898). A Portuguese officer who joined the army in 1871 and served first in Portuguese India, where he became secretary general. He then served in East Africa, where he explored the hinterland of Mozambique and waged war against recalcitrant local tribes. In September 1894 he led an arduous expedition of 50 men from the Limpopo River to Gazaland, where he captured the troublesome Gungunhana [q.v.], paramount chief of Gazaland. He was appointed governor of Lourenço Marques (Maputo), and in 1896 he commanded the Portuguese forces in Mozambique. In 1897 he returned to Portugal. There for unknown reasons he soon after committed suicide.

Alcaide / Alcayde. A Moorish title used by the Spanish and French to denote a military officer in charge of a fort, prison, or town. The military equivalent of the civilian title of alcalde (mayor or magistrate).

Alcañiz, Battle of (23 May 1809), Peninsular War. Elements of the French III Army Corps—7,200 infantry, 550 cavalry, and 320 artillery with 18 guns—under General Louis Gabriel Suchet [q.v.], seeking to restore French power in Aragón, attacked a Spanish army of 8,000 infantry, 450 cavalry, and 19 guns under Captain General Joachim Blake [q.v.] entrenched in a line of hills east of Alcañiz. The French were repulsed, and Suchet was wounded in the foot. That night a panic broke out among the French troops, and they fled in disorder. Suchet ordered the initiator of the panic shot.

Alcolea, Battle of (28 September 1868), Carlist Wars. Marshal Juan Prim y Prats [q.v.], leading revolutionary forces against the tempestuous and authoritarian Queen Isabella II of Spain (1830–1904), defeated a royalist army at Alcolea, a village in southern Spain, 7 miles northeast of Córdova on the Guadalquivir River. Isabella was forced to flee to France, and a provisional government under Francisco Serrano y Domínguez [q.v.] wielded power until Amadeo Ferdinando María di Savoia (1845–1890) ascended the throne in 1871 as Amadeo (or Amadeus) I.

Alcolea Bridge, Battle of (12 June 1808), Peninsular War. In the first major battle to be fought on the Iberian Peninsula in this war French General Pierre Antoine Dupont de l'Étang [q.v.] with 13,000 troops defeated a Spanish force of 1,400 regulars and 12,000 volunteers under Manuel Novaliches [q.v.] at the Alcolea Bridge over the Guadalquivir River, near Córdova. Undefended, Córdova was subjected to frenzied plundering by French soldiers, who killed, robbed, and raped unchecked.

Aldershot / Aldershott. A British camp of instruction opened in April 1854 built on 7,063 acres of dreary waste on the confines of Hampshire, Surrey, and Berkshire. Subsequently, additional parcels of land, including forestland, were acquired. Initially troops were housed in wooden huts, each holding about 25 men; these were gradually replaced by brick barracks, completed in 1898, which could accommodate up to 15,000.

The new barracks were built on the border of the government land, the planners lacking the foresight to see that a civilian community would spring up nearby to provide beer halls, houses of prostitution, and other "haunts of dissipation" likely to debauch young soldiers. Aldershot did not become the principal training center of the British army until 1904. [See Knollys, William.]

Aldie, Affairs at (17 June 1863), American Civil War. During the Gettysburg Campaign in the neighborhood of Aldie, Virginia, 60 miles west-northwest of Alexandria near present-day Dulles International Airport, Federal cavalry launched inconclusive mounted and dismounted attacks against Confederate troops shielding the right flank of James Longstreet. Union casualties were 305; Confederate losses were probably just over 100. On the same day at Middleburg, Virginia, only 5 miles west of Aldie, Confederates annihilated the 1st Rhode Island Cavalry.

Aleppo, Capture of (16 July 1832), Turko-Egyptian War of 1832–33. Egyptian General Ibrahim Pasha [q.v.] defeated the Turks and captured Aleppo, Syria (today in Lebanon).

Alessandria, Convention of (15 June 1800). Austrian General Michael Friedrich Benoît Melas [q.v.], following his defeat by Napoleon at Marengo [q.v.], sued for peace, agreeing to surrender all remaining posts in the Milanese, the Piedmont, and Lombardy and to retreat east of the Ticino River.

Alexander, Edward Porter (1835–1910). A Confederate general in the American Civil War and the author of *Military Memoirs of a Confederate* (1907). He was born in Georgia and was graduated from West Point third of thirty-eight in the class of 1857. After teaching at West Point, he took part in the Utah Expedition [q.v.]. In 1859 he returned to the academy as an instructor. Working with Albert James Myer [q.v.], he developed a wigwag system of signal communication [q.v.]. After brief service in the West, he resigned his commission at the outbreak of the Civil War and joined the Confederate army.

As a captain he was General Pierre Beauregard's engineer and chief of signals in the First Battle of Bull Run, in which he sent the famous wigwag signal to Colonel Nathan Evans [q.v.] warning that the Confederate left flank was in grave danger, the first use of the system in battle. He later saw much service during the Peninsular Campaign, and fought at Second Bull Run and Antietam [qq.v.]. As a colonel he commanded James Longstreet's [q.v.] artillery on Marye's Heights in the Battle of Fredericksburg [q.v.] and was with Thomas ("Stonewall") Jackson at Chancellorsville. He also fought at Gettysburg, Knoxville, Cold Harbor, and Petersburg.

He ended the war as a brigadier general. After the war he taught at South Carolina University, was involved in business and in planting, and held several public offices. In 1891 he acted as engineer/arbitrator in the Nicaragua–Costa Rica boundary dispute.

Alexander I, Alexander Joseph of Battenberg, king of Bulgaria (1857–1893). A nephew of Tsar Alexander II of Russia who served in the Hessian army and in 1877–78 saw action in the Russo-Turkish War [q.v.]. In 1879 he was elected prince of the new autonomous principality of Bulgaria, and after a successful military coup in eastern Rumelia he became governor of that district as well. In 1885 he led his army against Serbia and won several battles. Overthrown and kidnapped through a Russian conspiracy, he was later restored, but he abdicated in 1886 and retired to Austria.

Alexander I, or Aleksandr Pavlovich, tsar of Russia

(1775–1825). On 24 March 1801 Alexander was placed on the throne through a conspiracy against his mad father, Tsar Paul I (1754–1801). He began his reign with sweeping reforms, establishing ministries and encouraging education and advances in science. In 1805 he formed a coalition with Prussia against Napoleon and was present at the Battle of Austerlitz [q.v.]. After further defeats at Eylau and Friedland [qq.v.], he held his famous meeting with Napoleon on a raft at Tilsit [q.v.] and joined the Continental System [q.v.]. However, after 1809 his relations with Napoleon deteriorated. In 1812, when Napoleon invaded Russia, Alexander refused to treat with the French even after the capture of Moscow and in a relentless campaign virtually destroyed the French army. [See Russian Campaign, Napoleon's; Russian Army.]

He further hastened the collapse of Napoleon by sending Russian armies into Central and Eastern Europe. After Napoleon's fall he played a leading part in the Congress of Vienna.

In later years he became a mystic and took scant interest in the governing of Russia.

Alexander II, Aleksandr Nikolaevich (1818–1881). A Russian tsar who was given a military education. He signed the Treaty of Paris, which ended the Crimean War [q.v.], in 1856. He reorganized the Russian army and in 1863–64 suppressed a Polish revolt. In the Franco-Prussian War of 1870–71 [q.v.] he was friendly to Germany. He was victorious in the Russo-Turkish War of 1877–78 [q.v.]. By his orders the Russian boundaries in Central Asia were extended (1868–81). He was killed by the explosion of a bomb thrown by a revolutionary in St. Petersburg. [See Russian Army.]

Alexandria, Battle of. See Aboukir / Abukir, Battles of.

Alexandria, Louisiana, Affairs at (30 April–8 May 1864), American Civil War. A number of small affairs occurred near this town in central Louisiana, about 100 miles northwest of Baton Rouge, during the withdrawal of Nathaniel Banks's Federal troops from the Red River Campaign [q.v.]. On 30 April 1864 at Hudnut's Plantation a Federal cavalry brigade of XIX Corps was surprised and defeated, losing 30 troopers; the following day Federals on the Rapides Road were attacked and driven to within 3 miles of Alexandria; on the evening of 3 May Confederates on the Bayou Road drove the Federals to within 3 miles of Governor Thomas Overton's plantation.

Alexinatz (Aleksinac), Battle of (1 September 1876), Turko-Serbian War. Serb forces with Russian volunteers, all under Russian leaders, were defeated by Turks under Suleiman Pasha (1840–1892) at this town in east-central Serbia on the southern Morava River, 17 miles north-northwest of Nis.

Alfaro, Eloy (1864–1912). An Ecuadorian general and political leader who led a revolt against President Luis Cordero in 1893–95 and in 1895 became dictator. He was president of Ecuador from 1897 to 1901 and again in 1907 until he was murdered in the uprising of 1911.

Alforja. Sometimes spelled alforche, alforge, alforka, and alforki. A Mexican word for saddlebags or the bags hung on either side of a pack animal. It was adopted by American soldiers serving in the Southwest.

Alger, Russell Alexander (1836–1907). An American soldier and politician. During the American Civil War he served in the Federal army and rose from the ranks to become a colonel. In 1884 he was elected governor of Michigan, and in 1897 he became secretary of war. In 1899, because of the inefficiencies and inadequacies of his department revealed during the Spanish-American War, President William McKinley (1843–1901) asked him to resign. He served as a U.S. senator from 1902 to 1907.

Algeria, French Conquest and Occupation of (1830 into twentieth century). In the early nineteenth century the Ottoman Empire claimed but could not rule North Africa. When the French attempted to conquer these lands, Algeria became the scene of frequent fighting between French forces and its indigenous peoples [see Algerian Revolts; Abd el-Kader Wars].

In June 1830 France sent an army of 37,000 men with 83 guns under General Louis de Bourmont [q.v.] to invade the country, which had been in turmoil for two decades. On 5 July the French captured the city of Algiers and expelled the dey [see Algiers, Capture of]. The subjugation of the interior proved more difficult, and not every Frenchman approved of the rush to acquire African territory, a passion that persisted throughout the century but was strongest between 1830 and 1847. Prime Minister Jules Ferry (1832–1893) later described it as a "steeplechase to the unknown."

French expansionist military operations were the responsibility of the Navy Ministry, but from 1830 to 1857 and from 1860 to 1870 Algeria became the responsibility of the War Ministry. From 1870 it was deemed an integral part of metropolitan France and came under the Ministry of the Interior

Algeria *Algiers falls to the French, 1830.*

with the War Ministry still responsible for the defense and administration of the southern Sahara. [See Algerian Revolts.]

Algerian-French Wars. See Abd el-Kader Wars; Algerian Revolts.

Algerian Revolts. With the surrender of Abd el-Kader [q.v.] in 1847 [see Algiers; Abd el-Kader Wars], the French conquest of Algeria north of the Sahara was largely complete, but the Saharan tribes were still largely unconquered and unrest persisted in many places, particularly the Constantine-Biskra area, where in 1848 some 4,000 French troops were involved in the siege of the desert oasis of Zaatcha [q.v.]. To protect northern Saharan caravan routes in Algeria, three French columns were sent south, and in December 1852 the oasis of Laghouat was occupied after heavy fighting. The desert towns of Touggourt and Ouargla were also occupied at this time.

Kabylia in the mountainous Djurdjura region in northeastern Algeria long remained unconquered. In 1853 General (later Marshal) Jacques César Randon (governor-general, 1851–57) directed three columns sent into the area, but Kabylia remained obdurate. In 1855 General Marie MacMahon [q.v.] led an unsuccessful expedition against them. Only in 1857, after the Crimean War, was Randon able to obtain three divisions and launch a successful invasion. Some tribes submitted without struggle, but 4,000 Kabylians held out at Icheriden [q.v.] until defeated by MacMahon in May. Randon then ordered Fort Napoléon built in the region as a "thorn in the flesh" of Kabylia, and by July the entire Djurdjura region of the Little Atlas Mountains, had been subjugated. This completed the French conquest north of the Sahara. In 1859 there was a revolt in the Aurès Mountains in the Saharan Atlas and the following year in the Hodna Mountains, a range in the Little Atlas Mountains in northeast Algeria.

In 1861 the Ouled-Sidi-Cheik people, who inhabited an area in the southern Oran district, revolted. Because the area abutted Morocco, where the insurgents were able to find refuge and rally support, they were not completely suppressed until 1883.

The French defeat in the Franco-Prussian War and the political turmoil in France considerably lowered France's prestige among native Algerians, and in March 1871 in the province of Constantine a chieftain named Muhammad al Mokhrani, aided by a son of Abd el-Kader [q.v.] proclaimed a war of liberation that became a jihad [q.v.] when the revolutionaries were joined by Chick al Haddad, a venerated religious leader. The insurrection spread to the Hodna Mountains and Kabylia and involved an estimated 800,000 people, including perhaps 100,000 warriors. Mokhrani was killed in one of the many engagements with French troops fought between April and June 1871. French suppression of the revolt was carried out with brutal severity and with heavy communal punishments and fines. French casualties, mostly from diseases, totaled 2,700 men.

In 1876 there was an uprising in the Al Amri oasis in the Biskra area, and in 1879 a marabout (Islamic holy man) in the Aurès Mountains led a revolt. In 1881 a marabout, Bou Amama, began harassing the French. In April 1882 he ambushed a small exploring expedition guarded by two Foreign Legion companies, killing 65. Bou Amama proved an elusive foe; he fled to Morocco and from there in 1904 organized yet another revolt.

Algiers, Capture of (5 July 1830). On 14 June 1830 a French force of 37,000 men under General Louis de Bourmont [q.v.] landed in Algeria, and on 5 July it captured Algiers. Other ports as well as some inland towns were also captured; the dey was expelled and France began its long conquest of North Africa [see Algeria, French Conquest and Occupation of].

Ali Bey. 1. A Turkish colonel of cavalry.
2. A Turkish commander of a district.

Alicante, Battle of (16 January 1812), Peninsular War. A French force of 4,000 infantry, 1,500 cavalry, and 6 guns under General Louis Pierre Montbrun [q.v.] attempted to take Alicante, a seaport city in southeastern Spain 77 miles south of Valencia, by a coup de main but was repulsed by the Spanish garrison of 6,000 under General Nicholas Mahy.

Ali Dinar Zakariya Mohammed al-Fadl (1865?–1916). A Sudanese prince and tribal leader. He assisted the Dervishes in one military expedition against a recalcitrant tribe but in 1898, after the Battle of Omdurman [q.v.], deserted the Mahdist cause. Collecting followers and weapons, he attacked the Dervish forces in Darfur. He captured its capital, Al Fasher, and seized the throne. In 1900 he was officially recognized by the Anglo-Egyptian Condominium (Sudanese government) as the sultan of Darfur. His undoing came in 1916, when he sided with Turkey and the Senusis and was defeated by Anglo-Egyptian forces. He was killed by a stray bullet.

Aligarh / Allyghur, Battle of (4 September 1803), First Maratha War. The 76th (Hindoostan) Regiment of Foot, part of British General Gerald Lake's [q.v.] army of 13,000 with 65 guns, attacked the walled city of Aligarh, the arsenal of Sindhia [q.v.], 43 miles north of Agra and 70 miles southeast of Delhi, defended by a Maratha force under Pierre Perron (1755–1834), a French adventurer. Although the city was strongly fortified and surrounded by a moat 100 feet wide and 10 feet deep, the main gate was blown in and the place stormed by a forlorn hope led by William Monson (1760–1807), who was severely wounded. At the end of the battle Perron and some of his French officers rode into the British lines and surrendered. The Maratha losses were estimated at 2,000; 281 guns were captured. The British lost 55 killed and 205 wounded.

Lake captured Delhi in September and Agra the following month.

Ali Musjid, Battle of (21 November 1878), Second Afghan War. At this fort in the center of the Khyber Pass [q.v.] British General Samuel James Browne [q.v.], employing a skillful turning movement, defeated a numerically superior Afghan force and captured 32 guns. Anglo-Indian losses were small.

Ali Pasha of Jannina (1741–1822). An Albanian who gained power in central Albania through murder, brigandage, and other unscrupulous methods. In 1787 he became pasha of Trikala and the following year he was made pasha of Jannina (or Jenina; today Ioannina, in Greece). He allied himself several times to Napoleon and several times to Britain, switching sides as it seemed advantageous. He plotted against the sultan of Turkey, his nominal ruler, and became involved in the Greek War of Independence [q.v.]. The barbarous culture he established in his court in Jannina was described by Lord Byron [q.v.] in *Childe Harold's Pilgrimage*. He was finally assassinated on orders from Mahmud II (1735–1839), the sultan of Turkey.

Alison, Archibald (1826–1907). A British officer who served as second-in-command during Wolseley's Ashanti Campaign [see Ashanti War, Second]. He led the Highland Brigade in the Battle of Tel el-Kebir [q.v.] in the Egyptian Campaign of 1882 [see Arabi's Revolt]. He became a full general in 1887. [See Alison Committee.]

Alison Committee. A British committee formed in 1881 chaired by General Sir Archibald Alison [q.v.] to determine the battle honors to which each regiment was entitled. It was decided that honors would be awarded only for those battles that had left a mark on British history, that only British victories would be included, and that a regiment would be entitled to the honors only if its headquarters and at least half its complement had been present. None of these edicts was strictly adhered to, but they provided some guidelines.

Aliwal, Battle of (28 January 1846), First Sikh War. Sir Harry Smith [q.v.] with 12,000 British and Indians decisively defeated a Sikh force of 20,000 under Runjar Singh at Aliwal, a village on the south bank of the Sutlej River in the Punjab, India, 6 miles west of Ludhiana and 90 miles east southeast of Lahore. The British took 67 guns at a cost of 151 killed, 422 wounded, and 25 missing; Sikh losses were estimated at 3,000.

Alkalak / Alkhalak. A long coat worn by cavalrymen in the Indian army.

All Arms. Infantry, cavalry, and artillery together.

Allahabad, Siege of (4–11 June 1857), Indian Mutiny. On 4 June 1857 in this holy Islamic city in northwest Hindustan mutinous sepoys of the 6th Bengal Native Infantry murdered their officers, including seven newly arrived young cadets, and every European civilian they could find. Colonel (later Brigadier General) James George Smith Neil [q.v.] of the 1st Madras Fusiliers marched promptly from Benares (Varanasi), reaching Allahabad on 11 June in time to save a small band of Europeans and loyal Sikhs sheltering in the fort. He suppressed the mutiny there with great severity, hanging hundreds.

Allard, Jean François (1785?–1839). A French soldier who enlisted in the 23d Dragoons in 1803. In 1806 he was a noncommissioned officer in Napoleon's bodyguard. During the Peninsular War he served in Spain and was twice wounded. Having earned a battlefield commission, he rose to the rank of captain. He rejoined Napoleon during the Hundred Days and was a captain of cuirassiers in the Battle of Waterloo. After the fall of Napoleon, he served the shah of Persia (Iran) until persuaded by Baptiste Ventura to join the Khalsa, the Sikh army of Ranjit Singh, who employed many foreigners, mostly French, to modernize his forces. Allard arrived at Lahore on 23 March 1822 and was given a commission. By 1829 he commanded a brigade of 3,000 cavalry with 200 guns. In 1834 he took eighteen months' leave and traveled to Europe with his wife and children. He returned with a consignment of arms and died soon after.

Allatoona Pass, Battle of (4–5 October 1864), American Civil War. During the Franklin and Nashville Campaign a vital Federal supply depot at Allatoona, Georgia, 12 miles southwest of Marietta, guarded by only 860 men under a lieutenant colonel, was threatened by Confederate troops. Anticipating an attack, Federal General William T. Sherman [q.v.] ordered a brigade from Rome, Georgia, under Brigadier General John Murray Corse [q.v.], to reinforce the garrison.

On the morning of 5 October Confederate General Samuel Gibbs French [q.v.] arrived before Allatoona, cut all the roads by which it could be reinforced, and, unaware of Corse's arrival, demanded the surrender of the garrison "to avoid a needless effusion of blood."

"We are prepared for the 'needless effusion of blood' whenever it is agreeable to you," Corse replied.

In the hard fighting that followed, Corse was wounded in the head by a Minié ball. The following day, when French broke off the action and withdrew, Corse sent a celebrated message to Sherman: "I am short a cheek bone and an ear, but am able to whip all hell yet."

Of 1,944 Federals engaged, 707 were killed or wounded. French reported a loss of 799 out of an assaulting force of "a little over 2,000."

Allen's Farm, Battle of. See Savage's Station.

All Sir Garnet. An expression signifying that a task or mission had been accomplished efficiently. It was inspired by General Sir Garnet (later Viscount and Field Marshal) Wolseley's well-earned reputation as an efficient officer, particularly his handling of troops in the Second Ashanti War [q.v.] of 1873–74.

Allowances. Money, rations, forage, goods, or services given to soldiers, usually officers, in addition to their pay for some particular purpose or to regiments for certain expenses. In the Indian army this was known as batta [q.v.]. No regulations in any army were as closely pondered yet as complicated as those relating to allowances, and perhaps no others were more likely to generate dissatisfaction and discontent. [See Pay.] Perhaps no army had as complex a system of allowances as did the British army.

Colonel's Allowance. Money allowed general officers of the British army who were given the honor of being appointed colonel of a regiment [q.v.]. In the Indian Staff Corps [q.v.] a colonel's allowance was given to lieutenant colonels who had served thirty-eight years, including twelve years in grade.

Lodging Allowance. An allowance given to officers, warrant officers, and sometimes privates who could not be provided for in barracks or in the field. These often included a food and light allowance to officers and sometimes noncommissioned officers even if quarters were provided. An officer in the field or otherwise away from home or one whose "on the strength" [q.v.] wife was in a hospital, continued to receive his lodging fuel and light allowances [see Wives of Soldiers]. Allowances were provided if an officer could not mess with his regiment, if he was on court-martial duty, if he was detained at embarkation points, and in a maze of other situations. Certain staff officers, such as adjutants, received extra pay and allowances, depending upon their duty. In the French army of Napoleon an allowance was given to officers before a campaign so that they could purchase needed clothing and supplies.

Horse Allowance. Money given to mounted officers when forage could not be supplied by the commissariat [q.v.].

Contingency Allowance. Money given to cover the cost of particular authorized items of expenditure, such as an allowance to commanders to cover the cost of burials, repair of weapons, and the bad debts of those who died.

Allyghur, Battle of. See Aligarh / Allyghur, Battle of.

Alma, Battle of (20 September 1845), Crimean War. In September 1854 the Allied expeditionary force landed at Yevpatoria (Evpatoria or Eupatoria) in Kalamita Bay, in the Crimea. It consisted of British infantry commanded by Lord Raglan [q.v.] and French forces commanded by Marshal Armand Jacques Le Roy St. Arnaud [q.v.] supported by 1,000 British cavalry and 128 guns, about 62,000 men in all.

In its advance on the Russian naval base at Sevastopol [q.v.], it encountered 36,400 Russians under General Prince Aleksandr Sergevich Menshikov and General Pëtr Dmitrievich Gorchakov [qq.v] in a strong defensive position on the south (left) bank of the Alma River, a small stream that empties into the Black Sea. The Russian right was anchored on a hill ridge, and its left flank, which was out of range of the guns of the Allied fleet in the Black Sea, was refused [see Refused Flank].

On 20 September, in the first land battle of the war for the French and British, the Allied force crossed the river. Before the British attack Sir Colin Campbell [q.v.] told his Guards regiments: "It is better that every man of Her Majesty's Guards should lie dead upon the field than that they should turn their backs upon the enemy." Because of poor liaison between the British and French commanders, the French attack was delayed, but the British stormed the heights and the Russians retreated. British losses were 362 killed and 1,621 wounded; French losses were 63 killed and 560 wounded. Russian losses numbered 1,800 killed and 3,700 taken prisoner, many of whom were wounded.

The road to Sevastopol [q.v.] was now open, but the Allies dithered and advanced in a leisurely fashion, enabling Count Frants Eduard Ivanovich Totleben [q.v.], the great Russian military engineer, to fortify the city strongly.

Marshal St. Arnaud died of cholera shortly after the battle; he was succeeded by General François Certain Canrobert [q.v.].

Alma *The 1st Division at the Alma during the Crimean War*

Almaraz, Capture of the Pontoon Bridge at (19 May 1812), Peninsular War. French Marshal Auguste de Marmont [q.v.] planned to cross the Tagus River at Almaraz, a town 27 miles southeast of Plasencia. Its fine sixteenth-century bridge had been so badly damaged in the Talavera Campaign of 1809 that the French were forced to build a pontoon bridge [see Talavera de la Reina, Battle of]. Wellington dispatched General Sir Rowland Hill [q.v.] with 7,000 men and 12 howitzers to attack the bridge and its defenses, which included Fort Ragusa with 6 guns and, on the opposite bank of the Tagus, Fort Napoleon, mounting 9 guns. In all, the French had only about 1,000 troops in the area.

Fort Napoleon was taken by storm by 900 men on the morning of the 19th, and the defenders of Fort Ragusa fled. The British lost 189 men; the French about 400 plus 18 guns and 12 pontoons.

The forts were blown up, and the pontoon bridge was dismantled. The old bridge, eventually repaired, became a major crossing over the Tagus.

Almeida, Sieges of (1810 and 1811), Peninsular War. This fortified commune in northeast Portugal, 25 miles northeast of Guarda, fell to French Marshal Michal Ney [q.v.] on 28 August 1810 after a ten-day siege. At seven o'clock on the previous evening a French shell had exploded the store of black powder in the fort's magazine, destroying all the ammunition and reducing most of the walls to piles of debris. Some 700 people, mostly soldiers, were killed.

The French occupied the town, and it was held by General Antoine François Brennier (1767–1832) when on 4 April 1811 it was invested by British and Portuguese forces under Wellington. An attempt by French Marshal André Masséna [q.v.] to relieve the town resulted in the Battle of Fuentes de

Oñoro [q.v.], eight miles south. On 10 May Brennier led the garrison on a successful sortie and broke out, a feat Wellington described in a dispatch two days later as "the most disgraceful military event that has yet occurred to us." Almeida remained in Allied hands for the duration of the war.

Almonacid, Battle of (11 August 1809), Peninsular War. At Almonacid de Toledo, 11 miles southeast of Toledo, French General Horace Sébastiani [q.v.] with about 14,000 effectives defeated a Spanish army of 16,000 under Francisco Venegas (d.1838), who lost half of his guns, all of his baggage, 3,500 dead, and 2,000 taken prisoner. The French lost 2,400.

Almorah, Battle of (25 April 1815), Nepalese War. Colonel (later Lieutenant General Sir) Jasper Nicolls (1778–1849) of the Honourable East India Company with 2,200 sepoys, 1,000 irregulars, and 10 guns assaulted and captured the fortified town of Almorah, garrisoned by 4,000 Nepalese Gurkhas. Almorah was in the western Himalayas, 160 miles northeast of Delhi, and its capture resulted in the Nepalese surrender on 26 April of the Kumaon (Kumaun) provinces and all of its forts.

Alpha. In the 1890s Alfred Krupp [q.v.] developed and began to manufacture large-caliber coastal defense guns. The first of these, a 24 cm gun, named Alpha, was followed in 1900 by Beta, a 30.5 cm gun.

Alpine Campaign of Garibaldi (July 1886), Wars for Italian Independence. Leading a small army of volunteers, Giuseppe Garibaldi [q.v.] won several small victories over Austrian forces at Lodrone (3 July), Monte Asello (10 July), Condino (16 July), Ampola (19 July), and Bezzecca (21 July).

Alsen, Battle of (29–30 June 1864), Schleswig-Holstein War. On the night of 29 June 1864 Prussians crossed to the island of Alsen, off the east coast of South Jutland, where the Danish garrison of Düppel (Dybböl) had taken refuge, and stormed the Danish entrenchments under heavy fire [see Düppel, Siege of]. With the fall of Alsen, the Danes surrendered, ending the war. This much-admired amphibious operation was planned by Chief of Staff Helmuth von Moltke [q.v.] the Elder, who later was the architect of the successful German strategy in the Franco-Prussian War of 1871–72.

Altafulla, Battle of (24 January 1812), Peninsular War. In Catalonia a French force of 8,000 from the garrison at Barcelona under General Maurice Mathieu, attempting to relieve the Spanish blockade of Tarragona [q.v.], advanced under cover of fog and routed a Spanish force of 4,000 under Joaquín Ibáñez, Baron Eroles (1785–1825). The Spanish suffered 600 casualties and lost two guns. Tarragona was relieved.

Alten, Sir Charles (Karl) (1764–1840). A British soldier of Hanoverian birth who served in the Hanoverian army from 1783 to 1803, when he joined the British army. He commanded the light infantry in the Hanoverian Expedition of 1805 and in Copenhagen in 1807. During the Peninsular War [q.v.] he served in Spain with the King's German Legion [q.v.] under Sir Thomas Moore [q.v.], and in 1809 he took part in the disastrous Walcheren expedition [q.v.], after which he returned to Spain and commanded a brigade at Albuera [q.v.]. On the death of General Robert Craufurd [q.v.], mortally wounded in the storming of Ciudad Rodrigo [q.v.] on 19 January 1812, Alten was given command of the Light Division, which he led through the remainder of the war in the peninsula.

In 1815 he led a division in the battles of Quatre Bras and Waterloo [qq.v.], where he was seriously wounded. He later served as Hanoverian minister of war and inspector general of the Hanoverian army. He became a field marshal in the Hanoverian army while retaining his major general's rank on the British half pay list.

Altiscope. A nineteenth-century name for a periscope.

Alula, Ras (1847–1897). The Abyssinian governor of Tigré. In 1884–85 he assisted in evacuating the Egyptian garrisons along the Sudanese-Abyssinian frontier to save them from the Dervishes [q.v.]. In 1885 he failed in an attempt to relieve the Egyptian troops besieged at Kassala in northeast Sudan. In 1886 he soundly defeated a force of "Fuzzy-Wuzzies" [q.v.] under Osman Digna [q.v.] at Kufit [q.v.], near Agordat. In 1887, when in the vanguard of the Abyssinian army marching on the Eritrean seaport of Massawa (Massaua), he destroyed an Italian column at Dogali [q.v.]. He died at Adowa.

Álvares de Arenales, Juan Antonio (1774–1831). An Argentine soldier who fought in the Argentine War of Independence (q.v.). He served under José de San Martín [q.v.] in the invasion of Chile and Peru and led expeditions into the interior of Peru in December 1820 and May 1821. In the first of these, on 6 December he defeated and captured the Spanish general, Diego O'Reilly. In 1822 he commanded the garrison of Lima.

Álvarez, Juan (1780–1867). A Mexican general who took part in the revolt against Spain in 1821 and joined Antonio López de Santa Anna [q.v.] in the overthrow of Agustín de Iturbi [q.v.] in 1822–23. In 1847 he served in the Mexican army in the war with the United States [see Mexican War]. In 1849 he became the first governor of the state of Guerrero in southwest Mexico. In 1854–55 he led a revolt against Santa Anna, and in 1861–62 he resolutely opposed the rule of Emperor Maximilian [q.v.]. [See Mexico, French Invasion and Occupation of.]

Alvear, Carlos María de (1789–1853). An Argentine general, educated in England, who was for a time a rival of José de San Martín [q.v.]. He forced the surrender of Montevideo in 1814 but was later defeated by José Artigas [q.v.]. He became governor of Buenos Aires but was forced to flee to Brazil in 1820. He commanded the Argentine army against Brazil in Uruguay in 1826 and won the Battle of Ituzaingó [q.v.] on 20 February 1827. Banished by the Argentine dictator Juan Rosas [q.v.] about 1830, he spent the remainder of his life in the United States, where in 1823 he had been for a brief time Argentine minister.

Alvensleben, Konstantin von (1809–1892). A Prussian soldier who entered the Prussian Guards from the cadet corps in 1827. In 1870, at the beginning of the Franco-Prussian War [q.v.], he succeeded Prince Frederick Charles [q.v.] in command of III Corps in the First Army of General Karl Steinmetz [q.v.] and won a victory at Spicheren [q.v.] on 6 August 1871. Later that month he took a leading part in the battles before Metz [q.v.], particularly at Mars-la-Tour. He became a general of infantry in 1873 and retired immediately after.

His brother Gustav von Alvensleben (1803–1881) was also a Prussian general of infantry and a corps commander in the Franco-Prussian War, playing an important role at Beaumont [q.v.].

Amalgamated Field Forage. A compound developed by the commissary department of the American army just before the American Civil War that reduced the bulk of animal forage. Chopped hay, bran, oats, and other grain were mixed in the proportions usually issued to cavalry horses, chemicals were added and the mixture was compressed by hydraulic power into solid cakes, each weighing 22 pounds. Four such cakes were packed in a canvas cover that converted to a nose bag. The blocks were restored to their original bulk by "friction and a few minutes' exposure to the air."

Amalinda, Battle of (1818), Fifth Kaffir War. The main battle in this South African war between Gaika [q.v.] and the forces of Ndhlambi (d.1829), who was his uncle and a rival Xhosa chief. Gaika was utterly routed. The battle was fought in an area of basinlike depressions called Kommetje Flats in Dutch and Amalinda in Xhosa that is now a suburb of East London.

Amatola Mountain, Battle of (1846), Axe War. The main battle of the Axe War [q.v.] in South Africa was fought near this mountain north of King William's Town in eastern Cape Colony between Xhosas under Sandilli [q.v.] and British and Cape Colony troops. Although Sandilli was defeated, he rallied his forces and successfully attacked the baggage train of an advancing British expedition, forcing its retirement.

Amazons. Corps of women warriors. In the West African kingdom of Dahomey (roughly today's Benin) an all-female unit was formed in the late eighteenth or early nineteenth century. In 1818 it was strengthened and organized into regiments by King Gezo (d.1858) when he assumed the throne. One-third of the female population was enrolled, and these were said to be "married to the fetish." Female captives were also sometimes enlisted. Members of the corps wore distinctive apparel that included a kilted blue skirt, a cartridge belt, and a distinctive red fez; their feet and torsos were bare. Richard Francis Burton (1821–1890), who saw them in 1862, estimated their number at 2,500; a later writer estimated 1,000. Foreigners were sometimes invited to "autumn maneuvers" in which the barefoot amazons customarily impressed all when they charged a wall of thorny acacia. The corps fought well against the French in 1892 [see Franco-Dahomey War].

During the War of the Triple Alliance [q.v.] Eliza Lynch [q.v.], the mistress of the Paraguayan dictator Francisco López [q.v.], formed a Paraguayan corps of women and is said to have led them in the Battle of Corumbá [q.v.].

In China the Taipings organized all women into military-type units, some of which, notably composed of women from the hardy Miao tribes, were formed into actual fighting units [see Taiping Rebellion].

The sultan of Djokjokarta (Jogjakarta or Jokayakarta) in what was the Dutch East Indies (Indonesia) maintained an armed bodyguard of women, some of whom were mounted.

European countries eschewed organizing women's units, although women often played parts in the émeutes of 1848. In Germany a small revolutionary unit of women formed in Baden included the daughter of executed revolutionary leader Robert Blum (1804–1848), who to muster support regularly rode about the town in a black velvet riding habit flourishing a red flag. [See Soldiers' Wives; Women Soldiers.]

Amba Alagai, Battle of (7 December 1895), Italo-Abyssinian War. Italian forces under Colonel Oreste Baratieri [q.v.] pushed too far inland from Eritrea and were defeated by an Abyssinian force led by Menelek II [q.v.] near this village in eastern Abyssinia.

Ambit. The compass or circuit of a fort, camp, or similar installation.

Amboina / Ambon, Occupation of (1810), Napoleonic Wars. In February 1796 this chief island of the Moluccas in the East Indies was captured from the Dutch by the British; it was returned to the Dutch following the Peace of Amiens [q.v.] on 25 March 1802. However, in 1810, after the Dutch had allied themselves with Napoleon, the British landed 130 troops of the 1st Madras European Infantry, some sepoys, and artillery and recaptured it with a loss of 4 killed and 9 wounded. The British remained in occupation until the Treaty of Paris on 30 May 1814, when the island was again restored to the Dutch.

Ambulance. Derived from the French *Hôpital ambulant* (mobile hospital). In American usage the word was used exclusively to mean a vehicle, but in the British and French armies it more often denoted a small field hospital. In the early nineteenth century it could also mean a medical dressing station.

Baron Dominique Jean Larrey [q.v.], a French military surgeon, is credited with the invention of the *ambulance volante* (moving hospital). In the French army at mid-century such an ambulance for infantry consisted of five wagons containing surgical instruments for amputating and trepanning, bandages, medicines, and 8,900 dressings. One such unit was assigned to each division and two to each corps headquarters. Ambulances for cavalry were similar but contained only three wagons and 4,900 dressings. French regimental surgeons in the Grande Armée often used a sturdy, four-horse *caisson d'ambulance* and sometimes a Wurst [q.v.] fitted with a hood.

For most of the century ambulance wagons had few, if any, springs. In the course of the American Civil War a Rucker pattern ambulance, a four-wheeled wagon with springs, was introduced. Because it was so comfortable, it was often used by general officers as their headquarters or personal wagons. After the war many officers serving in the West bought them and used them to transport their families and household goods from one post to another.

Amazons *Detail from* Armed Women with the King at Their Head, *a late eighteenth-century engraving from* History of Dahomey.

Just before the Crimean War George James Gutherie (1785–1856), who became a British surgeon at age fifteen and was three times president of the Royal College of Surgeons, designed the Gutherie ambulance cart, in which the badly wounded were laid at full length on the floor and on a stretcher slung from the roof, while those less seriously injured sat along the front, back, and sides; the backboard, let down, provided space for amputations. Medical chests could be slung underneath.

After the Battle of the Alma [q.v.] in the Crimean War the British had almost no means for bringing their wounded down from the heights, but the French were well supplied with *cacolets,* two chairs slung like panniers over the backs of

Ambulance *Top, an ambulance of American design used by the French in 1870; center, a French cacolet; bottom, a Gutherie ambulance.*

mules, devised during their wars in North Africa. Similar devices were soon adopted by the British army. In India the doolie [q.v.], or dhooly, was adopted.

The earliest use of pack animals for the transport of sick and wounded soldiers in the United States was the Thickle ambulance developed by Captain H. L. Thickle of the Louisiana Volunteers. A litter employing a single mule on which a man could be transported almost supine, it was patented in 1837 and used in the Second Seminole War [q.v.]. An improved single-mule litter was submitted to the surgeon general on 17 January 1877 by Dr. Henry McEldery (1845?–1898). The French developed a similar ambulance that was used in Mexico [see Mexico, French Invasion and Occupation of].

Late in the century armies finally equipped railroad cars to carry their wounded. In the American army an ambulance corps was not officially established until an act of Congress in 1864, near the end of the American Civil War.

Ambuscade. See Ambush.

Ambush. A trap in which individuals or units lie in wait for their enemies and attack by surprise.

Amelia Island Affair (23 December 1817). American marines, sailors, and soldiers removed the forces of Gregor McGregor [q.v.], a Scottish-born freebooter who had collected a band of adventurers and in June 1817 attempted to establish a revolutionary government on Amelia island, a sea island five miles long and four miles wide, separated from the mainland of northern Florida by salt marshes and extending south from the St. Mary's River. Using this base, he hoped to create a revolt against Spanish rule in Florida.

In 1862 Union forces captured the island from Confederates.

Amelia Springs, Battle of (5 April 1865), American Civil War, also called Battle of Jetersville. In the Appomattox Campaign [q.v.] Philip Sheridan sent a brigade of cavalry under Union Brigadier General Henry Eugene Davies (1836–1894) northwest from Jetersville, Virginia, in an effort to discover in which direction Lee was retreating. About five miles distant, near Amelia Springs, Davies encountered and attacked a large wagon train, routing the cavalry guard of about 400 men and capturing 5 guns, 400 animals, 11 flags, 320 white soldiers, and about 300 blacks; some 200 wagons were fired. Davies lost 20 killed and 96 wounded.

It is believed that the records of General R. E. Lee's headquarters were destroyed in this battle.

American Army. See United States Army.

American Association of the Red Cross. In 1865 Clara Barton [q.v.], a clerk in the U.S. Patent Office who had done some nursing on Civil War battlefields and had organized an agency that provided medical supplies and other aid to Union soldiers, was appointed by President Abraham Lincoln [q.v.] to handle correspondence with relatives of the missing. Through this work she became active in the International Red Cross [q.v.], and in 1877 she organized the American National Committee, which in 1881 became the American

Association of the Red Cross, a humanitarian society with the president of the United States as its president [see Red Cross, International]. In 1905 the name was changed to the American Red Cross.

It first functioned in wartime during the Spanish-American War [q.v.], when it offered nursing and medical assistance to the forces.

American Civil Disorders. Marines were used on 12 March 1824 to quell a riot in the Massachusetts State Prison. They were also used to restore order in Washington, D.C, during the Pug Ugly election riot of 1 January 1857, and on 17 October 1859 they were called out to capture John Brown [q.v.] and his gang at Harper's Ferry. Troops were called out in New York, Baltimore, and Washington, D.C., in April 1861 to quell rioting over conscription during the Civil War. After the war until late 1879 army troops were used as an occupation force in the former Confederacy and were dispatched to quell racially inspired riots in Memphis, New Orleans, Norfolk, Virginia, and elsewhere. In 1870 U.S. Marines were employed on 28 March to seize and destroy illicit distilleries in "Irishtown" (Brooklyn), New York. Troops were used as well to maintain order in strikes in Michigan in 1872, in the great railroad strike of July and August 1877, in the anti-Chinese rioting in Wyoming and Washington in 1885–86, and in miners' strikes in Coeur d'Alene, Idaho, in 1892 and 1894.

American Civil War (1861–65). Officially called the War of the Rebellion, a name that has been rarely used. After the war southerners often called it the War between the States or the War against Northern Aggression, appellations that were never used during the hostilities.

The causes of the war were a tangled tissue of political, economic, and social issues that estranged the primarily agricultural southern portion of the United States and the urban and industrial northern portion. James Murray Mason (1798–1871), a senator from Virginia, called the conflict a "war of sentiment and opinion by one form of society against another."

In 1861 the southern states with a population of about 5.5 million whites and 3.5 million blacks, mostly slaves, seceded from the Union and formed a separate Confederate States of America with its capital first in Montgomery, Alabama, and later in Richmond, Virginia, which was also the capital of the most populous southern state. The population of the northern states was about 22 million.

The U.S. army before the war consisted of only 1,098 officers, about a third of whom resigned to join the Confederacy, and 15,304 enlisted men, of whom fewer than 100 deserted. In the Confederacy each state formed its own army until a "provisional" Confederate army, which was intended eventually to become the standing army of the new republic, was formed [see Confederate Army].

The South had an inadequate railroad system, few good harbors, and not enough factories to supply its needs. The North possessed the world's best railroad network, factories of all sorts, and clear naval and military superiority.

Both sides evinced an equal determination to prevail, but because the South's basic aim was to defend itself and because Confederate geography determined the theaters of action, the military task of the North was the more difficult, requiring that it take the offensive. In the beginning there was scant recognition on either side that the technology of the Industrial Revolution could be mobilized for war and no notion that it would change the face of land warfare forever.

General Winfield Scott [q.v.], head of the Federal army, advised President Abraham Lincoln that it would take 300,000 men two years to quell the rebellion, but his assessment was optimistically ignored, and he himself was replaced in November 1861 by Major General George McClellan. The war that ensued was unmatched in scope by any previous war in the Western world in the nineteenth century, although it was not the bloodiest measured by the number engaged. [See War of the Triple Alliance.] The Union put in the field an army of more than a million men who were the best-equipped, best-fed, most powerful military force ever seen in the Western world. American armies fought some 2,400 known major battles and sieges, plus thousands of smaller actions, over a vast landscape of thousands of square miles with a fury that amazed the world and left hundreds of thousands killed or maimed.

The fighting began on 12 April 1861 with the southern bombardment of Fort Sumter, South Carolina. On 21 July the first major battle, the Battle of Bull Run [q.v.], or Manassas, Virginia, was won by the South.

In April 1862 General George McClellan began his Peninsular Campaign [q.v.], an attempt to reach Richmond from the east, but General Robert E. Lee, who replaced Joseph Eggleston Johnston [q.v.] as commander of the Army of Northern Virginia [q.v.], forced his withdrawal, later defeating the Union Army of the Potomac [q.v.] in a Second Battle of Bull Run [q.v.] on 29–30 August 1862. This was followed by a Confederate invasion of Maryland by forces under General Lee and a Union victory in the Battle of Antietam [q.v.], or Sharpsburg.

McClellan failed to pursue Lee when he retreated across the Potomac after the battle. He was replaced by General Ambrose Everett Burnside [q.v.], who was defeated by Lee at Fredericksburg [q.v.] on 13 December 1862 and was himself replaced by Joseph Hooker [q.v.].

The first major victory for the North was achieved by General Ulysses Simpson Grant, who in February 1862 forced the surrender of Fort Henry and Fort Donelson [q.v.] in Tennessee. After the Battle of Shiloh [q.v.], Tennessee, in April, the Union had command of the Mississippi River south as far as Vicksburg, Mississippi.

In the East the two greatest battles of 1863 were fought at Chancellorsville, Virginia, in May, and Gettysburg, Pennsylvania [qq.v.], in July. At Chancellorsville Lee defeated General Joseph Hooker [q.v.], and after a brilliant move that turned the Federal flank, Thomas ("Stonewall") Jackson was accidentally shot by his own men. At Gettysburg, Union General George Gordon Meade [q.v.] defeated Lee in a three-day battle. That same month Grant took Vicksburg [q.v.].

Many southerners hoped for the intervention of European powers on their side and although Britain, France, and Russia considered taking some such action, Lincoln's Emancipation Proclamation collapsed any budding venture on their part. In the summer of 1864 Grant embarked upon the bloody Wilderness [q.v.] Campaign, and the struggle became a war of attrition impossible for the Confederacy to win.

Union General William Tecumseh Sherman [q.v.] launched his successful Atlanta [q.v.] Campaign in May 1864, and this was followed by his "March to the Sea" [q.v.], in which he cut a wide swath of destruction through the Confederacy to the Atlantic Ocean. Lee's Army of Northern Virginia and Johnston's Army of Tennessee [qq.v.] could no longer withstand the pressures upon them. The war effectively ended when on 1 April 1865 Union General Philip Henry Sheridan [q.v.] fought and won a major battle at Five Forks [q.v.], Virginia; Petersburg and Richmond fell, and on 9 April 1865 Lee surrendered to Grant at Appomattox Court House [q.v.]. The last Confederate army surrendered at Shreveport, Louisiana, on 26 May 1865.

In the course of the war the North mobilized 2,128,948 men. Of these, 75,215 were regulars, 1,933,779 were volunteers, 46,347 were conscripts, and 73,607 were substitutes. The South mustered about 1,082,000. Of the 359,528 Federal dead, 110,070 were killed or mortally wounded in battle. Of the approximately 258,000 Confederate dead, about 94,000 died or were mortally wounded in battle. Both sides were woefully unprepared for such casualties. At the beginning of the war the Confederates had only 24 medical officers; the Union had only 98, and they could boast of only twenty thermometers and six stethoscopes among them.

It has been estimated that in the course of the war there were 10,455 military engagements of all kinds and sizes, including twenty-nine campaigns. The six leading theaters of war were Virginia (2,154 military engagements), Tennessee (1,462), Missouri (1,162), Mississippi (772), Arkansas (771), and West Virginia (632), while it was still part of Virginia before being admitted to the Union in 1863.

Although the war was watched with great interest in Europe, particularly in Britain and France, European generals and most other professional soldiers scorned the tactics of the American armies of amateurs and failed to absorb their military lessons.

American Long Rifle. See Kentucky Rifle.

American Peace Society. An organization with headquarters in Washington, D.C., founded in 1828 by William Ladd (1778–1881), a wealthy merchant and shipowner. Although it condemned all wars, it supported the Union Side in the American Civil War. It was dissolved in 1945. [See Washington Peace Conference.]

American War of 1812. See War of 1812.

Ames Gun. A rifled cannon manufactured by Horatio Ames of Falls Village, Connecticut, in which wrought-iron bars were formed into rings that were then lathed and fitted one inside the other to form disks that were welded in succession to the concave breech of a gun. The shape was that of a Dahlgren gun [q.v.].

Amherst, William Pitt, Earl Amherst of Arakan (1773–1857). A British diplomat and soldier who was Britain's envoy to Peking (Beijing) in 1816–17. He became governor-general of India in 1823 and in 1824–26 successfully waged war against Burma (Myanmar). [See First Burma War].

Amiens, Battle of. See Hallue, Battle of.

Amiens, Treaty of (27 March 1802), Napoleonic Wars. A peace treaty between France and Britain negotiated by Lord Cornwallis (1738–1805) that brought a general peace to Europe for the first time in a decade. Napoleon regarded it as merely a breathing space, and it lasted only until 17 May 1803, when Britain declared war on France, a shorter time than it had taken to negotiate the treaty.

Amin. An Arabic title for one entrusted with a particular duty or office.

Amin / Amir al-Raiya. The commander of a raiya [q.v.], about 2,000 men, in the army of El Mahdi [q.v.] in the Sudan.

Amin / Amir al-Ruba. The commander of ruba [q.v.], a unit of about 500 men in the Dervish army of El Mahdi [q.v.] in the Sudan.

Amir. An Islamic ruler of a tribe, province, or nation [see Amin].

Ammunition. 1. All projectiles, with their fuzes, propellants, and primers, fired from muskets, rifles, cannon, or other projectile launchers. Also all grenades, rockets, bombs, and mines.

A round of artillery ammunition consisted of (a) the projectile and its filling, (b) the cartridge, (c) the igniting element, and (d) the fuze, which was usually screwed into the head of the projectile, although sometimes into its base. Percussion fuzes were introduced about 1842, and reliable time fuzes in 1864.

A round of small arm ammunition for a rifle or pistol consisted of (a) a cartridge case, (b) a percussion cap, (c) a propellant charge, and (d) a bullet.

2. In British usage, the word "ammunition" preceding a noun indicated that the item was government issue—e.g., ammunition bread and ammunition boots.

Ammunition *The manufacture of ammunition for the American Civil War, Watertown Arsenal, Watertown, Massachusetts. Engraving by Winslow Homer*

Ammunition Allowance for Battle. In the last quarter of the nineteenth century the number of rounds of ammunition carried by an infantryman into action varied by country: Russia, 120; Austria, 119; Germany, 117; France, 92; and Britain and the United States, 100.

Ammunition Boxes. Stout wooden boxes of well-seasoned white pine in which ammunition was packed. Their lids were fastened with six two-inch screws and had rope handles on the ends. Such boxes were not quickly opened, and there was sometimes

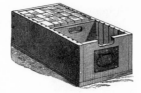

Ammunition box

danger of running out of ammunition because tools for opening them were scarce or could not be found, as was the case of the British in the Battle of Isandhlwana [q.v.] during the Zulu War of 1879 [q.v.].

Boxes containing artillery ammunition were painted in colors indicating their contents. In the American army shot boxes were olive; shell boxes, black, spherical case shot (shrapnel), red; and canister, a light drab.

Ammunition Chests. Four ammunition chests accompanied each field gun: one on the limber [q.v.] and three on the caisson [q.v.]. Their interior design varied according to the type of ammunition carried. Cannoneers could ride seated on the chests.

Ammunition Shoes. Protective soft shoes free of metal worn by soldiers and sailors using powder magazines.

Ammunition Train. The wagons, animals, and personnel organized to transport ammunition, often the reserve ammunition of an army or smaller unit.

Ammunition Train *Destruction of an ammunition train by Federal troops at Chickahominy Swamp. Drawing by Alfred Waud*

Amnesty. The pardon of a large group of people, as in 1869, when the American government pardoned all those who had waged war against the Union in the American Civil War, and in 1859, when the French pardoned those who had participated in the uprising in 1848.

Amoaful, Battle of (31 January 1874), Second Ashanti War. A British expeditionary force of 5,000 men and 12 guns under General Sir Garnet Wolseley [q.v.] dispatched to the Gold Coast (Ghana) of West Africa defeated an Ashanti force of about 12,000 after a fierce conflict at the village

of Amoaful, near Bekwai, 20 miles south of Kumasi. The British attack was led by the 42nd Highlanders (Black Watch). Total British casualties were 1 officer and 3 other ranks killed and 21 officers and 173 other ranks wounded. Ashanti losses are unknown, but the British buried 150 of their dead.

Amoy, British Capture of (26 August 1841), First Opium War. A British expeditionary force bombarded and captured Amoy (Szeming), a seaport town on an island in southeast China, the first port through which the Dutch and British had traded with China. The land forces, consisting of British regulars and Indian army contingents, were commanded by Sir Hugh Gough [q.v.]. The Lovell percussion musket [q.v.] was used here in action for the first time.

At the end of the war Amoy was opened as a treaty port under the terms of the Treaty of Nanking (Nanxiang or Nanjing).

Amoy, Taiping Capture of (20 March 1853), Taiping Rebellion. This seaport town in southeast China was captured by Taiping forces and held until recaptured by imperialist forces on 19 July 1864.

Amplitude. The range of an artillery piece.

Ampola, Italy, Battle of (19 July 1866). A successful battle fought by Giuseppe Garibaldi [q.v.] during his Alpine Campaign [q.v.].

Ampudia, Pedro de (fl.1840). A general who commanded the Mexican army on the Rio Grande in 1846 at the beginning of the Mexican War [q.v.]. On 24 September he surrendered to General Zachary Taylor [q.v.] at Monterrey [q.v.].

Amputations. In the nineteenth century nearly all wounded men seen by military surgeons had been hit in the extremities. Those hit in the head or torso usually died. On the Union side of the American Civil War, 75 percent of all operations involved amputation, and this or a higher percentage would be a valid statistic in wars throughout the century. At Gettysburg [q.v.] it was said that some surgeons worked from dawn to dusk for a week cutting off limbs. Surgeons became very skilled and could amputate an arm or leg within a few minutes. Amputations performed on men within 48 hours of their wound were twice as likely to survive as those amputated later.

The following statistics were compiled for the Union army:

	CASES	DEATHS	% FATAL
Fingers	7,902	198	2.5
Thighs	6,369	3,411	53.6
Upper Arms	5,540	1,273	23.0
Shins	5,523	1,790	32.4
Forearms	1,761	245	13.9
Toes	1,519	81	5.3
Knee Joints	195	111	54.9
Ankle Joints	161	119	73.9
Hip Joints	66	55	83.3

Amritsar, Treaty of (15 April 1809). An agreement signed by Charles Metcalfe (1785–1846) on behalf of the Honourable East India Company and Ranjit Singh [qq.v.], ruler of the Sikhs in the Punjab, which established the Sutlej River as the boundary between Sikh and British territories.

Amstetten, Battle of (5 November 1805), Napoleonic Wars. Near this village between Ems and Vienna, in Lower Austria, 21 miles east northeast of Steyr, Austrians and Russians, falling back on Vienna, fought a rearguard action against French cavalry under Marshal Joachim Murat [q.v.] and a contingent of Marshal Jean Lanne [q.v.]. The Austrians and Russians were defeated with a loss in killed, wounded, and prisoners of about 1,000.

Anabasis / Anabases. Any long, difficult, and dangerous military trek resembling the retreat in the fourth century B.C. of the 10,000 Greek mercenaries through Persian territory in Asia Minor to the Black Sea as described by Xenophon (434?–355? B.C.) in his *Anabasis.*

Anaconda Plan. The strategy recommended in 1861 by Lieutenant General Winfield Scott [q.v.], general-in-chief of the U.S. army, for defeating the rebellious southern states. Although seventy-four years old, obese, and infirm, Scott remained a brilliant general. Foreseeing at the beginning of the war the difficulty of fighting on exterior lines [q.v.], he advocated that the southern ports be blocked, that an army of 300,000 be raised at once, and that the South be invaded down the Mississippi Valley, thus crushing it as an anaconda does its prey. Politicians, optimistically envisioning a short war, ridiculed this sensible long-range plan.

Anarchy. An absence of an operable government, resulting in lawlessness and political disorders. It is sometimes occasioned by mutinous troops, and government and order are often restored by disciplined troops. [See Punjab, Anarchy in.]

Anatolia, Invasion of (December 1832), Egyptian-Turkish War. During Egypt's revolt against Turkey, Egyptian General Ibrahim Pasha [q.v.] invaded Anatolia, and on 21 December he defeated the main Turkish army under Turkish General Reshid Pasha (1802–1858) in the Battle of Konya [q.v.] in southwest-central Turkey. A desperate Turkey then called upon Russia for assistance.

Ancient and Honorable Artillery Company. The first regularly organized military company in America. It was formed in Boston in 1637 and modeled after the Honourable Artillery Company [q.v.] of London. In the nineteenth century the company was renowned for the eminent citizens among its members and for the splendor of its annual parade, which was followed by a sermon and a formal dinner.

Ancón, Treaty of (20 October 1883), War of the Pacific. A treaty signed by Chile and Peru, by which Peru formally ceded Tarapac Province to Chile and agreed to Chilean occupation of Tacna and Arica for ten years. (Tacna was not returned to Peru until 1929.)

Ancona. A much fought-over Italian port town on the Adriatic Sea, 117 miles southeast of Florence. It was a municipal republic under papal protection until captured by the French in 1797 and then by the Russians in 1799. In 1814 it was restored to the pope, but in 1832 it was occupied by the French. On 18 June 1849 the town was bombarded and captured by the Austrians, who proved to be unpopular rulers. In September 1860 the citizens rose in rebellion, and the Austrians were forced out. On 18 September, ten days after the fall of Castelfidardo [q.v.], an Piedmontese fleet carried the army of General Enrico Cialdini, Duca di Gaeta (1811–1892), to Ancona, which was besieged. The town was defended by a papal garrison commanded by French General Louis Christophe Léon Juchault de Lamoricière [q.v.]. After a resistance of more than a week, the boom guarding the harbor was broken, and on 29 September Ancona was surrendered and was in the power of Piedmont.

Andaman Islands. These two groups of islands at the eastern end of the Bay of Bengal were annexed by the Indian government in 1858 and, until seized by the Japanese in 1942, were used as an Indian penal settlement. The nearby Nicobar Islands were annexed in 1869. Many convicted Indian army soldiers when sentenced to "transportation" were sent to these islands for life or for long periods. A small infantry unit and a battalion of Indian military police garrisoned them. After a period of graduated labor marked by good behavior, a soldier convict could earn a ticket-of-leave, allowing him to send for his family and to work at a craft or on a farm to become self-supporting. The total convict population hovered around 12,000 for most of the century. A viceroy of India, Richard Southwell Bourke, sixth Earl of Mayo (1822–1872), was assassinated by a Muslim convict at Fort Blair, the capital, while on an official visit to the islands on 8 February 1872.

Anderson, Charles DeWitt (1827–1901). An American soldier who served in the Third Seminole War [q.v.] as a lieutenant and during the American Civil War rose to be a colonel in the Confederate service. When he was eleven years old, his family decided to emigrate to Texas from South Carolina. Both parents died on the voyage, and he and his brother were taken in by an Episcopal minister who raised them.

In 1846, on the recommendation of Sam Houston [q.v.], he was appointed the first Texan to attend West Point. He failed French and mathematics his first year and was dismissed in November 1848. However, on 27 June 1856 he was appointed second lieutenant in the 4th Artillery. In April 1861 he resigned from the U.S. army and was appointed a captain in the Confederate army. On 8 May 1862 he was elected colonel of the 21st Alabama. On 8 August 1864 he was forced to surrender Fort Gaines on the eastern point of Dauphin's Island at the entrance of Mobile Bay, and he spent the remainder of the war in prison.

After the war he engaged in railroad construction and built the Galveston, Texas, lighthouse. He spent the last six years of his life as a lighthouse keeper.

Anderson, George Thomas (1824–1901). An American soldier, called Tige, who left Emory College in Georgia to become a lieutenant in a volunteer Georgia cavalry regiment in the Mexican War [q.v.] and in 1855 entered the regular service, from which he resigned three years later as a captain of the 1st Cavalry. In 1861, at the beginning of the American Civil War, he entered the Confederate forces and was elected colonel of the 11th Georgia. He quickly rose to be a brigade commander fighting in the Seven Days' Battles, Second Bull Run, and Antietam [qq.v.]. He was promoted brigadier general on 1 November 1862. Severely wounded at Gettysburg [q.v.], he recovered to fight at Chickamauga [q.v.] and in the 1864–65 campaigns in Virginia, culminating at Appomattox.

After the war he became successively a freight agent, the chief of police of Anniston, Alabama, and a county tax collector.

Anderson, James Patton (1822–1872). An American soldier who, after practicing medicine in Mississippi, raised and commanded as a lieutenant colonel the 1st Battalion Mississippi Rifles in the Mexican War [q.v.]. After the war he served as U.S. marshal for Washington Territory and then as a congressman. A Confederate, he was appointed colonel of the 1st Florida Infantry at the beginning of the American Civil War. He fought at Shiloh, Murfreesboro, Chickamauga, Chattanooga, Ezra Church, and Jonesboro [qq.v.], where he was severely wounded. On 17 February 1864 he was promoted major general.

After the war he became a tax collector.

Anderson, Joseph Reid (1813–1892). An American soldier who was graduated from West Point in 1836. He resigned from the army the following year to become an engineer and manufacturer. After serving as chief engineer for the Shenandoah Valley Turnpike Company, he became an agent for the Tredegar Iron Works [q.v.] in Richmond, Virginia. Seven years later he owned the company. On 3 September 1861, at the beginning of the American Civil War, he was given a brigadier general's commission in the Confederate army. He commanded a brigade at Seven Days', where he was wounded, but he resigned on 19 July 1862, convinced that his most valuable contribution to the Confederacy was the manufacture of ordnance. He returned to the presidency of the Tredegar Iron Works, turning out guns and ammunition for Confederate armies and earning the sobriquet of the Krupp of the Confederacy.

After the war the Tredegar Iron Works was confiscated by the federal government. It was returned in 1867 and reorganized with Anderson again as president.

Anderson, Richard Heron (1821–1879). An American soldier, a West Point graduate of the class of 1842, whose 37 members surviving in 1861 supplied the Union and Confederate armies with 22 general officers. Anderson was a veteran of the Mexican War [q.v.], in which he won a brevet to first lieutenant. He was a captain of dragoons when he resigned on 3 March 1861 to become an infantry major in the Confederate army. On 18 July he was promoted brigadier general, and he served under James Longstreet [q.v.] through all the battles of the Army of Northern Virginia [q.v.]. He was promoted major general on 14 July 1862, and when Longstreet was wounded in the Battle of the Wilderness [q.v.], he was promoted a lieutenant general. In the Battle of Sayler's Creek [q.v.] he was defeated and his troops were routed. Because there was no command appro-

priate for his rank, he was sent home the day before Lee's surrender at Appomattox.

After the war he struggled against poverty as a minor South Carolina bureaucrat.

Anderson, Robert (1805–1861). An American soldier who, as a major, commanded Fort Sumter [q.v.], on the south side of the entrance to Charleston Harbor in South Carolina, when it was attacked by Confederates on 12 April 1861; he capitulated two days later. The attack on the fort marked the beginning of the American Civil War.

Anderson was graduated from West Point in 1825 and served in the Black Hawk War and the First Seminole War [qq.v.], in operations against Cherokees in Florida, and in the Mexican War [q.v.], in which he was severely wounded at Molina del Rey [q.v.] on 8 September 1847.

He finished the Civil War as a brigadier general and brevet major general. On 14 April 1865, the day Abraham Lincoln was shot, he reraised the American flag over Fort Sumter.

Anderson's Raid (27 September 1864), American Civil War. Led by William Anderson (1840–1864), a band of Confederate irregulars that included Jesse James (1846–1882) and his brother Frank (1843–1915) captured a stagecoach and a train at Centralia, Missouri, killing 24 unarmed Union soldiers who were on furlough as well as those civilians who tried to hide their valuables. Three companies of the 39th Missouri and a detachment from the 1st Iowa Cavalry, sent in pursuit, were ambushed and almost wiped out. Of the 147 Federal soldiers, 116 were killed, 2 were wounded, and others were unaccounted for.

Andersonville Prison. In the American Civil War a hastily constructed prison camp for captured Federal enlisted men that was in use from February 1864 to April 1865. Its proper name was Camp Sumter (for Sumter County, Georgia). Simply a log stockade with a stream running through it, located 55 miles southwest of Macon, Georgia, just northeast of Americus, it initially enclosed 16½ acres, finally expanded to enclose 26. Daily rations of cornmeal, beans, and (rarely) meat were the same as those issued to the always hungry Confederate soldiers, but the overcrowding of thousands of prisoners, the want of shelter, the lack of doctors and medicines, and the execrable sanitation facilities created a death rate that became horrendous.

In all, 49,485 Union prisoners were held in Andersonville in the fourteen months of its existence. The numbers there at any one time varied widely, but the death rate was always high. In September 1864, when the mean number of prisoners was 17,000, there were 2,700 deaths; the following month, when only 6,700 were confined, 1,560 died.

The exact number of deaths is unknown, but there are today 12,912 graves in the National Cemetery at Andersonville, more than 1,000 marked "unknown." The Confederate commandant of the camp, Captain Henry Wirz [q.v.], charged with "impairing the health and destroying the lives of prisoners," was hanged on 10 November 1865.

Andersonville was donated to the federal government in 1910 and was given to the National Park Service in 1971.

Andersonville Prison *Issuing rations at Andersonville Prison, Sumter County, Georgia*

Andes, Army of the. José de San Martín [q.v.] spent three years (1814–16) training an army of Chileans and Argentines in Cuyo Province, Argentina. In January–February 1817, with Bernardo O'Higgins [q.v.] in command of the Chilean contingent, he marched his Army of the Andes—3,000 infantry, 700 cavalry, and 21 guns—westward over the mountains through the snow-filled passes of the Gran Cordillera, a feat never before attempted, to attack and defeat the Spanish forces in the battles of Chacabuco and Maipo [qq.v.], thus securing the independence of Chile from Spain and providing San Martín with a base for moving north into Peru, the heart of the Spanish viceregal authority. In 1817 O'Higgins assumed the dictatorship of Chile; he was deposed by a revolution in 1823.

Andizhan / Andijan Uprising (1898). On 1 June 1898 a Russian force of 300 was surprised by Khohand rebels near this city in eastern Uzbek, 155 miles east-southeast of Tashkent on the upper Syr Darya River. Before the rebels were repulsed, 22 Russians were killed. Rebel losses were 11 killed, and their leader was captured. In October the government announced that 24 surrendered Khohand rebels had been hanged and 362 banished to Siberia.

Andréossy / Andréossi, Comte Antoine François (1761–1828). A French soldier and diplomat who served in the Revolutionary Army and under Napoleon. He became Napoleon's ambassador in London, Vienna, and Constantinople.

Andrews Hat. A soft felt hat with a wide brim that could be worn up or down and could be folded flat. It was designed by Irish-born Colonel Timothy Patrick Andrews (d. 1868) in February 1847, when he raised a regiment of voltigeurs and foot rifles to serve with the American army in Mexico. The hat, sometimes called the voltigeur hat, was the forerunner of the campaign hat adopted by the American army in 1872.

Andrews's Raid (April 1862), American Civil War. An incident sometimes called the Great Locomotive Chase. On the night of 12 April 1862 a group of 21 Ohio soldiers and 1 civilian, led by an adventurer named James J. Andrews (d. 1862), penetrated deep into Confederate territory to cut the railroad line between Marietta, Georgia, and Chattanooga, Tennessee. Dressed in civilian clothes, they boarded a north-bound train of the Western & Atlantic Railroad at Marietta. When the train stopped for breakfast at Big Shanty (Kenesaw, Georgia), they dismounted on the side opposite the station, disconnected the passenger cars, boarded the locomotive, named *General,* and steamed off, stopping periodically to cut telegraph wires and lay ties across the tracks to delay the Confederates, who were in hot pursuit in the locomotive *Texas.* After an 87-mile run the *General* ran out of fuel near the small town of Graysville in northwest Georgia, about 17 miles northwest of Dalton. The Federals fled on foot; all were soon captured.

Andrews was hanged on 7 June 1862 in Atlanta, and 7 others were hanged eleven days later; the survivors remained in prison until October, when 8 overwhelmed their guards and escaped; about a year later those remaining were paroled. They were among the first recipients of the Medal of Honor [q.v.], presented to them personally by Secretary of War Edwin M. Stanton [q.v.] on 26 March 1863.

Anesthesia. Anesthesia was first used in war in late March or early April 1847 at Veracruz, Mexico, during the Mexican War. When a German teamster had both legs injured by the accidental discharge of a musket, Dr. Edward H. Barton (1790?–1859), surgeon of the 3rd Dragoons, using "letheon" (sulfuric ether), amputated the most severely damaged leg.

One of those who witnessed the operation was Dr. John B. Porter (1804–1869), who also experimented with the use of ether but later reported: "In gunshot wounds, anesthetic agents are almost universally unnecessary, and are almost universally injurious. It was for this reason that they were entirely given up in the hospital at Vera Cruz."

Angareb. The common bed in the Sudan and Upper Egypt made from strips of rawhide lashed from side to side and end to end, across a frame. It was adapted by some British soldiers as a comfortable and portable field expedient.

Ang Chan (1791–1835). A king of Cambodia who sought to appease his warlike neighbors, Siam and Vietnam, by paying tribute to both. When his brother, Ang Snguon, with help from Rama II (1809–1924), king of Siam, raised a revolt in 1812, Ang Chan fled to Vietnam, where Gialong (or Gia Long; originally Nguyen-Anh, d. 1820), the Vietnamese emperor, assisted him in regaining his throne by dispatching an army. The Siamese withdrew without fighting.

Angle of Defense. In fortifications, the angle formed between a line of defense and a flank. The rule was that it should never be less than 90 degrees or more than 120 degrees.

Angle of Repose. The steepest angle possible for a pile of earth or other material to be heaped without sliding.

Angle of the Epaule. The angle formed by one face and one flank of a bastion.

Anglesey, First Marques. See Paget, Henry William.

Anglo-Bhutanese War (1864–65). In 1826 the British Honourable East India Company occupied the province of Assam in northeast India and annexed it to its Indian possessions, a move that began a long-lasting frontier dispute with neighboring Bhutan. About 1863 the Bhutanese occupied key mountain passes and rejected British demands that they give them up. In January 1865 the British sent a small expeditionary force to take the passes. It was thrown back, and the British were forced to evacuate their garrison at Dewangiri in southeast Bhutan, abandoning two mountain guns.

A second and successful expedition, led by Sir Henry Tombs [q.v.], was immediately formed. By the Treaty of Sinchula on 11 November 1865 Bhutan ceded to Britain the southern passes and the tract of land known as the Dwars. Dewangiri and the region around it were annexed to Assam. (The republic of India returned the area to Bhutan in 1949.)

Anglo-Boer Wars (1880–81 and 1899–1902). Often called South African or Boer Wars. Wars fought between Britain and the Boer inhabitants of southern Africa.

First Anglo-Boer War. Sometimes called the Transvaal War. In 1877 Disraeli's government annexed the ramshackle Boer republic in the Transvaal (officially, Republic of South Africa), but when the Gladstone government came into power, the Boers hoped that it would give them back their independence. When it failed to do so, they rose in revolt on 16 December, 1880, Dingaan's Day [see Blood River, Battle of] and besieged British garrisons throughout the Transvaal, including those at Pretoria, Potchefstroom, and Lydenburg [see Paardekraal]. British General Sir George Pomeroy Colley [q.v.] organized a force to relieve the garrisons and suppress the uprising, but he was soundly defeated at Laing's Nek on 28 January 1881 and decisively at Majuba Hill [qq.v.], where he was killed, on 27 February. The British sued for peace, and the Treaty of Pretoria on 5 April gave the Boers a large measure of self-government [see Bronkhorstspruit, Battle of].

Second Anglo-Boer War. The Jameson Raid [q.v.] created an understandable and justifiable distrust of the British on the part of the Boers. For protection the Transvaal (officially, the Republic of South Africa) formed a military alliance on 17

Anglo-Boer Wars *A Boer outpost in the Transvaal*

March 1897, with a neighboring Boer republic, the Orange Free State, and each began to acquire military supplies from Europe, including Britain. Sir Alfred Milner (1854–1925), the British high commissioner to South Africa, with the backing of Joseph Chamberlain (1836–1914), the colonial secretary, clearly provoked the Boers into declaring war.

War was officially declared on 12 October 1899, and a Boer army under Piet Joubert [q.v.] invaded Natal. The Boers enjoyed initial success, besieging Robert Baden-Powell [q.v.] in Mafeking on 13 October and Kimberley [qq.v.] on 15 October. After winning battles at Talana Hill on 20 October and at Elandslaagte [qq.v.] the following day, Joubert besieged a large British force under General Sir George White [q.v.] in Ladysmith [q.v.], northern Natal, on 2 November.

A large expeditionary force was assembled in Britain and sent to South Africa under the command of General Sir Redvers Buller, VC [q.v.]. On arrival, a part of this army was sent under the command of General Lord Methuen [q.v.] to attempt the relief of Kimberley and Mafeking [q.v.]; another part, under General William Gatacre [q.v.], was sent to attack the Boers who had crossed the Orange River and occupied Colesburg in northern Cape Colony; the remainder, under Buller's personal command, landed in Natal and attempted the relief of Ladysmith [q.v.]. All quickly came to grief.

During Black Week [q.v.] Gatacre was defeated at Stormberg on 10 December, Methuen at Magersfontein on 11 December, and Buller at Colenso [qq.v.] on 15 December. Buller suffered still further defeats at Spion Kop on 24 January 1900 and at Vaal Krantz [qq.v.] on 5 February, before he was superseded as commander-in-chief in South Africa by Lord Roberts [q.v.]. Methuen had failed to relieve besieged Kimberley and Mafeking.

When Roberts arrived with Lord Kitchener [q.v.] as his second-in-command, he dispatched his cavalry under General John French [q.v.] to relieve Kimberley; it was effected on 15 February 1900. Piet Cronjé [q.v.], fearing to be enveloped, attempted to flee but was trapped with 4,000 men and many women and children on the banks of the Moder River at a place called Paardeberg [q.v.], 23 miles southeast of Kimberley. Soon after, Mafeking, ably defended by Colonel Robert Baden-Powell, was also relieved.

At long last Buller relieved besieged Ladysmith on 28 February. Roberts entered Bloomfontein, capital of the Orange Free State, on 13 March and annexed the country as Orange River Province. After a delay caused by widespread illness among his troops, he marched into the Transvaal and occupied Johannesburg on 31 May. Pretoria, capital of the Transvaal, was entered on 5 June, and by August all the major

Anglo-Boer Wars *British troops fight from behind a redoubt at Honey Vest Kloot during the Second Anglo-Boer War.*

towns, railways, mines, and factories were in British hands. On 1 September 1900 the Transvaal was annexed, and in November Lord Roberts, considering his work completed, returned to Britain and a hero's welcome.

Lord Kitchener was left to mop up, as he assumed, but the Boer commandos in the field refused to surrender. Although all of the major set piece battles had been fought, able Boer leaders such as Martinus Theunis Steyn (1857–1916), Christiaan de Wet, Louis Botha, Jan Smuts, and Jacobus Hercules Delarey [qq.v.] carried on a guerrilla war that lasted until the Treaty of Vereeniging on 31 May 1902. Only by organizing a blockhouse system, placing women and children in concentration camps [q.v.], and carrying out a scorched-earth policy of slaughtering farm animals and burning crops was Kitchener finally able to bring the stubborn Boers to heel. David Lloyd George (1863–1945), the future prime minister, railed in the House of Commons: "You entered into these two republics [Orange Free State and the Transvaal] for philanthropic purposes and remained to commit burglary." Nevertheless, within five years the Boer leaders, notably the generals, again had their hands on the levers of government in South Africa.

Anglo-Burmese Wars. The British fought three wars in Burma (Myanmar) in the nineteenth century, in each of which it acquired more territory.

First Anglo-Burmese War (1824–26). In January 1824 a border dispute [see Assam, Attacks on] led the Burmese forces of King Bagyidaw (1819–37) to invade Cachar (Kachar), a district in south-central Assam just west of Manipur, then under British protection. On 5 March the governor-general of India declared war. On 10 May an Anglo-Indian force of 11,500 men, including four British regiments, under Archibald Campbell [q.v.] landed in Upper Burma and captured Rangoon (Yangon). On 28 May other fortified places nearby were successfully attacked. [See entries for Kamarut, Kemendine, and Kokein battles.] A British attack on the Shwe Dagon Pagoda at Kimendine (Kemendine) on 3 June failed to

dislodge the Burmese, but the temple complex was successfully assaulted on 10 June.

In July Campbell dispatched a force to Pegu, 47 miles northeast of Rangoon (Yangon). On 4 August it stormed the pagoda at Syriam. Heavy rains began in October, and sickness among the British troops delayed further operations. In November the British were besieged in Rangoon by Maha Bundoola, or Bandula (d. 1825), an able Burmese chief. Campbell, who had only some 5,000 effectives, requested reinforcements and the 47th Foot and two brigades of sepoys were sent to him. The siege was lifted, and on 16 December 1824 the Burmese stockade at Kokein was stormed.

Campbell led his army toward Prome, 150 miles up the Irrawaddy River, half marching by land and half carried in a flotilla of 40 gunboats. On 7 March 1825 his advance brigades attacked the stockades of Danubyu (Donabew) but were repulsed. When the attack was renewed on 1 April, the Burmese were defeated, and Maha Bundoola was killed. On 15 April, after three days of bitter fighting, Campbell entered Prome, on the left bank of the river, and on 5 May he established his headquarters there for the rainy season. During the next four months he lost 15 percent of his force to disease.

In September the Burmese sued for peace but refused to accept Campbell's terms. After repulsing a Burmese attempt to recapture Rangoon, British forces took control of the Tenasserim coast and moved on Burmese forces up the Irrawaddy to Wattee-Goung. The initial assault upon the stockades there on 16 November failed, but they were taken

Anglo-Burmese Wars *British infantry storm the Shwe Dagon Pagoda in the Second Anglo-Burmese War, 1852.*

ten days later. The British then advanced in two columns supported by the flotilla up the river. After three days of heavy fighting on 30 November–2 December, the Burmese army collapsed and the British moved upriver to Yandaboo, about 70 miles from Ava.

The Burmese again sued for peace, and on 26 December a truce was agreed upon. However, fearing that the Burmese were merely stalling, Campbell broke the truce and continued his advance. On 2 January 1826 Melloon, the last fortified place on the way to Ava, was stormed. The Burmese surrendered, and Burmese hegemony in Southeast Asia was shattered. By the Treaty of Yandaboo (Yandabu), signed on 24 February 1826, Burma was forced to cede Assam, Manipur, Arakan, and the Tenasserim coast to the British.

Second Anglo-Burmese War (1852). A precipitate action by a British naval officer was upheld by the governor-general. War was declared on 1 April 1852, and a force of 8,100, called the Army of Ava, under General Henry Thomas Godwin (1784–1853), was dispatched. The war began with a bombardment of Martaban, at the mouth of the Salween River opposite Moulmein, which was captured on 5 April 1852. Rangoon was occupied on 12 April, and the Shwe Dagon Pagoda complex was captured two days later after heavy fighting. Bassein was taken on 19 May, and Pegu [q.v.] on 3 June. On 9 October Prome was taken, Godwin encountering little resistance. On 21 November Pegu, which had been abandoned, was recaptured. On 20 January 1853 Pegu Province was annexed to British India.

In the course of the war a revolution took place in the Burmese capital. After a six-year reign King Pagan Min (d. 1880) was dethroned and replaced by his half brother Mindon Min (1814–1876), who accepted the British occupation of Pegu. In 1862 the Burmese provinces under British rule were amalgamated under a chief commissioner.

Third Anglo-Burmese War (1885). British-Burmese relations did not improve. Exasperated by "various incidents of Burmese truculence against British subjects," barbarous practices against the populace, and the intrigues of King Thibaw Min (1858–1916), son of Mindon Min, who, ignoring British interests, ousted a British teak company in favor of a French company, signed a contract with the French to build a railroad from Mandalay to the Indian frontier, and refused to accept a British envoy while he levied fines against British commercial interests, the Honourable East India Company issued a peremptory ultimatum on 22 October 1885. It was rejected, and in response 9,034 fighting men, 2,810 native followers, and 67 guns under General Sir Harry North Dalrymple Prendergast (1834–1913) were dispatched from India to Burma together with a flotilla of fifty-five steamers that carried the force up the Irrawaddy. The war was over in twenty days. King Thibaw surrendered on 28 November 1885, and Mandalay was occupied the next day. In 1886 Upper and Lower Burma were combined into a single Indian province, and the kingdom of Burma ceased to exist.

In addition to these three wars, more or less continual guerrilla warfare was waged throughout the century as the British battled dacoits and tribesmen in the interior, such as the Chins, Shans, Kachins, Karennis, and others, but Burma remained British until the Japanese invaded the country in 1942.

Anglo-Chinese Wars. See Opium Wars.

Anglo-Dutch War in Java. See Java War.

Anglo-Persian War (November 1856–April 1857). When an attempt to persuade Persian (Iranian) forces to lift their siege of Herat, on the Hari Rud River in northwestern Afghanistan, failed, the British, who supported the Afghans, declared war. On 1 November 1856 a British force of 5,670 men, of whom 2,270 were European, left India for Bushire, (Bushehr). With them were 3,750 camp followers, 1,150 horses, and 430 bullocks. It was commanded by Major General Foster Stalker of the Bombay army. On 7 December 1856 the British defeated the Persians in the Battle of Reshid [q.v.], and on 10 December 1856 they seized the port of Bushire on the Persian Gulf and repulsed an attack by a 6,000-strong Persian force. On 27 January 1857 Stalker was superseded by General Sir James Outram [q.v.]. Outram then moved 46 miles inland, where he defeated Persian General Shuja-ul-Mulk in the Battle of Khushab [q.v.]. On 26 March 1857 they captured Mohammerah (Khorramshahr) on the Karun River at its junction with the Shatt-al-Arab, after its guns had been silenced by the guns of Indian naval warships. Three river gunboats and 300 men ascended the Karun and routed 10,000 Persians at Ahwaz, 70 miles upstream.

The Persians sued for peace, and the former frontier between Afghanistan and Persia was restored. The shah ordered the seizure of the officers who ran away at the Battle of Mohammerah and had them publicly humiliated and dragged about by rings through their noses. Their general, however, who had had the wisdom to present the shah's chief minister with a small fortune, was given a sword and a robe of honor.

This war has been called the War for a Persian Lady, for the British envoy to the court of Persia had so embroiled himself in a quarrel with the Persian government over his intrigue with one of the shah's female relatives that in a fit of pique he had broken off diplomatic relations without consulting his government. The war was unpopular in Britain, and a lead article in *The Times* of London began: "Where Herat is, we neither know or care."

Angostura, Paraguay, Fighting near (August–December 1867), War of the Triple Alliance. The war saw much scattered fighting particularly in the area just north of Angostura at Ypacarai in south-central Paraguay. In a major battle lasting from 22 December to 30 December 1867, Paraguayans under Francisco López [q.v.] held off the combined armies of Brazil, Argentina, and Uruguay until forced by overwhelming numbers to retire, leaving behind 1,000 prisoners and six guns. López fled with a small detachment of cavalry, and Angostura surrendered on 30 December. The following day Asunción was occupied and sacked by Brazilians.

Angustura, Mexico, Battle of (21 February 1847), Mexican War. General Winfield Scott [q.v.] defeated a Mexican army under General Santa Anna [q.v.] at this village in northwest Mexico on the Mocorito River.

Animus Belligerent. The intent to go to war. Deliberate warlike acts with animus belligerent constitute a declaration of war. Nations have been known to declare that their bellicose acts had been committed without this intent and had been misunderstood. [See Act of Hostility.]

Anking, Fall of (10 August–5 September 1861), Taiping Rebellion. Chinese imperial and provincial forces under the redoubtable General Tsêng Kuo-Fan [q.v.] with a force of 160,000 moved on Anking (Hwaining or Nganking) in eastern China on the north bank of the Yangtze River between Nanking (Nanxiang or Nanjing) and Hankow, which had been held by 130,000 Taipings [see Taiping Rebellion] for nine years. It was captured on 5 September 1861.

Anonymat. Name given to Article 7 of the French ordinance of 10 March 1831, which provided anonymity to those enlisting in the French Foreign Legion [q.v.] and allowed recruits to embellish or reinvent their pasts.

Anquera. A piece of leather fastened to the back of a saddle that could be used as a pad for a second rider, protecting his clothing from the horse's sweat. Used in Mexico, California, and the American Southwest.

Anse des Pièces. The handles of cannon that serve to pass ropes, handspikes, or levers the more easily to move them. They were often made in the shape of dolphins, serpents, etc. [see Dauphins].

Ansei Purge (1858). A purge conducted in Japan by Ii Naosuke (1815–1860), who held the position of *tairo* (great elder) in the Tokugawa government, against those who threatened the power of the shogunate. He secured the election of twelve-year-old Iyemochi (1846–1866) as shogun with himself as premier, and in control of affairs, he signed treaties of friendship with the United States, Britain, Russia, and other Western powers without the emperor's approval.

Antelope Hills, Battle of (11 May 1858). Captain John ("Rip") Ford [q.v.] with 100 Texas Rangers and about an equal number of Indian auxiliaries from the Brazos Agency attacked a Comanche village north of Red River near the Antelope Hills. Some 300 Indians were routed, and 76 were killed.

Antietam, Battle of (17 September 1862), American Civil War. Called Battle of Sharpsburg by Confederates. A twelve-hour battle fought along Antietam Creek, just east of Sharpsburg, Maryland, between the Confederate Army of Northern Virginia [q.v.] under General Robert E. Lee, which totaled fewer than 50,000 effectives, and the Federal Army of the Potomac [q.v.] under General George B. McClellan [q.v.], numbering some 113,000, of whom only about 50,000 were actually engaged. Federals moved across Antietam Creek and attacked the Confederate positions on a low ridge where Thomas ("Stonewall") Jackson held the north end of the line, and James Longstreet [q.v.] the south end. A breakthrough on the Confederate right by Union General Ambrose Everett Burnside [q.v.] threatened to roll up the Confederate right flank, but Burnside's corps was itself struck on its left flank by Confederates under A. P. Hill [q.v.], who had just arrived on the field after taking the surrender of

Antietam *The charge across the Burnside Bridge during the Battle of Antietam, near Sharpsburg, Maryland*

12,000 Union troops at Harpers Ferry [q.v.]. Burnside's men were routed, and Lee's right flank was saved.

The best estimates for casualties have been given by Stephen W. Sears in *A Landscape Turned Red* (1994): Union losses were 2,108 dead, 9,540 wounded, and 753 missing for a total of 12,401; Confederate losses, more difficult to calcu-

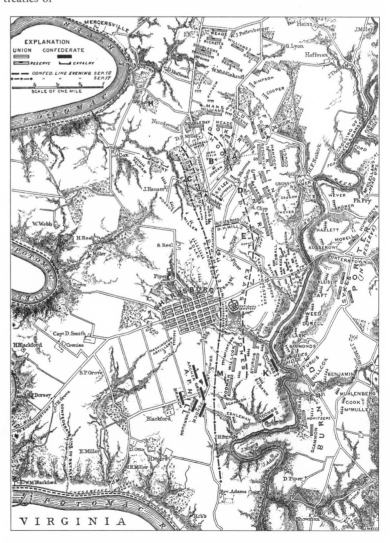

Antietam *The field of Antietam*

late accurately, were 1,546 dead, 7,752 wounded, and 1,018 missing, for a total of 10,316. The combined total for the twelve hours of fighting on 7 September 1862 was 22,717. No single day in any other American war before or since has been so bloody. It ended with both sides exhausted, occupying roughly the same positions with which they had started.

The armies rested the next day, and during the night of 18–19 September Lee retreated into Virginia. McClellan belatedly discovered the Confederates' departure and sent troops in pursuit, but they were repulsed on the banks of the Potomac.

The battle was one that Lee, with his back to the Potomac, ought not to have fought, but that he managed with great skill, shifting his units to the most threatened portions of his line as needed. McClellan, who had the power to crush the Confederates, failed to do so; he committed his forces piecemeal, did not push forward on 18 September, and allowed Lee's army to cross the Potomac to safety in Virginia.

Antiwar Movements. In the nineteenth century there were protests against conscription in a number of countries, and such religious groups as the Quakers, Dunkards, and Doukhobors refused to serve in armies, but no true antiwar movement existed until the Second Anglo-Boer War [q.v.], when a number of small antiwar groups such as the South African Conciliation Committee, the Stop the War Committee, and the Transvaal Committee were formed in England. Labeled "pro-Boer," they bickered among themselves and were unable to mount a coordinated campaign.

Anton, Karl, also called Charles Anthony (1811–1885). A Prussian soldier and prince of Hohenzollern-Sigmaringen who became a general and played a prominent part in the disputes over the reorganization of the Prussian army in 1853–62. From 1863 to 1871 he was governor of the Rhineland region of Westphalia.

Antwerp, Sieges of (November–December 1832), liberation of Belgium. In October 1830 a rebellion erupted, and an insurgent Belgian army was welcomed by the populace of the city. The Dutch garrison, led by Lieutenant General Baron David Hendryk Chassé [q.v.], retreated into the citadel and from there bombarded the city.

On 18 November 1832 a French army under Marshal Comte Maurice Étienne Gérard [q.v.] besieged the citadel, and on 23 December Chassé surrendered.

In 1839 Britain, France, Prussia, Russia, and Austria signed a treaty guaranteeing Belgium as an "independent and perpetually neutral state." Leopold of Saxe-Coburg (1865–1909), the maternal uncle of Queen Victoria, was named king.

Anything to Preserve the Union. A catch phrase much used in the American Civil War by Union soldiers when ordered to do something disagreeable.

Aong, Battle of (15 July 1857), Indian Mutiny. At this village near Cawnpore, India, about 240 miles southwest of Delhi, British and Sikh forces, 1,130 strong with eight guns under Sir Henry Havelock [q.v.], on the march to Cawnpore, routed 3,000 mutineers with two 9-pounders under Nana Sahib [q.v.]. A shortage of cavalry prevented British pursuit. The following day Havelock entered Cawnpore.

Aoungan. The war chief of a Dahomean village.

Apache and Navajo Wars. From 1860 and throughout the American Civil War, 1861–65, and until 1886 the federal army was forced to fight various Indian tribes, notably the Apaches in Arizona, formidable warriors of Athapascan stock, related linguistically to the Navajo (Navaho).

In 1860, alarmed by the growing incursion of white settlers, the Apaches and Navajos in the Southwest went on the warpath, killing, burning, and plundering over a wide area. In 1861 Cochise [q.v.], a Chiricahua Apache chief, along with other Indian leaders, was accused of cattle rustling and kidnapping. When he appeared at an army post to deny the charges, he was seized and imprisoned. He escaped with white hostages, whom he then offered to exchange for imprisoned Apaches. When negotiations failed, the Indians killed their white hostages, and in retaliation the soldiers killed a number of Apache prisoners. Enraged, Cochise joined forces with his father-in-law, Mangas Colorado [q.v.], of the Mimbres Apaches, and within sixty days some 150 whites in Arizona and New Mexico were slaughtered. In 1862 a "California Column," 3,000 California volunteers, recruited, organized, and led by General James Carleton (1814–1873), was ambushed in Apache Pass by 500 Chiricahua and Mimbres Apaches led by Cochise. Although the Indians occupied strong positions, they were finally driven out by artillery. Two soldiers and 10 Apaches were killed. The aged Mangas Colorado was captured and imprisoned at Fort McLane, New Mexico, where he was killed while "trying to escape." Cochise, unsubdued, led his warriors deeper into the Dragoon Mountains, from which they frequently swept out to raid, repeatedly attacking stagecoaches and murdering their passengers.

In 1864–65 Colonel Christopher ("Kit") Carson [q.v.], leading the 1st New Mexico Volunteers, waged a campaign in which more than 650 Apaches were killed and 9,000 taken prisoner. In 1869 Brigadier General Edward Otho Cresap Ord [q.v.] ordered his troops to hunt down Apaches "as they would wild animals."

When Carson and his men discovered the main Navajo base in Chelly Canyon and burned their crops and cut down their fruit trees, the Navajos surrendered and were settled on reservations on the Pecos River in New Mexico; Cochise and the Apaches retreated into the hills and mountains, descending periodically to make raids.

Apache War of 1871–73 *The 5th Cavalry, with Indian scouts, surprise an Apache camp in a cave on Salt River Canyon, Arizona, 1872.*

Apache War of 1871–73. Provoked by Apache raids on white settlements, a company of white men and Papago Indians on the night of 30 April 1871 fell upon peaceful Arivaipi Apaches at Camp Grant in southern Arizona. Some 108 of those in the camp were killed, and 29 children were taken to Mexico and sold as slaves. Because most of the men were out hunting, only 8 of those slain were warriors. The leaders of this assault were tried and acquitted.

The Camp Grant massacre provoked a massive Indian uprising. In 1872–73 Lieutenant Colonel (later Major General) George Crook [q.v.] launched a successful campaign against the Apaches in Arizona and New Mexico. In April 1873 most of the Indians, including Cochise, capitulated and were sent to live on the San Carlo Reservation in Arizona. Three years later, unhappy with their lot, they again rebelled. Some Kickapoos and Lipan Apaches fled to Mexico, where in May 1873 they were pursued by an expedition under Colonel Ranald Slidell Mackenzie [q.v.].

Apache War of 1876–86. The war began after drunken Apaches killed a white stationmaster and American troops responded by attempting to force all Indians in the Southwest to move to more remote areas. Marauding Apache bands under Victorio and Geronimo [qq.v.], later joined by Comanches and renegades, terrorized prospectors and ranchers in Arizona, in New Mexico, and across the border in Mexico. American troops under Generals Crook and Nelson A. Miles [q.v.] battled the Indians for years. In 1883 Crook induced a number to surrender, but Geronimo and his followers were not brought to heel until a year later after a campaign that lasted from 1 May until 9 June 1885. It was Crook's last fight with the Apaches.

Apache Pass, Affair at. See Bascom Affair.

Apache Scouts. Apaches were enlisted to fight Apaches. American General George Crook [q.v.] employed them for the first time in 1872. No expedition against Indians in the Southwest could be successful without their help in tracking down hostile Indians.

Aparejo. A simple form of packsaddle of padded leather, canvas, or quilted cloth used by American Indians and soldiers in the American West.

Apology. Among officers, an apology offered and accepted debarred the accepting officer from bringing forward the matter as a substantive accusation that might lead to a duel [see Dueling].

Apple River Fort, Battle of (24 June 1832), Black Hawk War. An indecisive battle between Black Hawk Indians and militia near present-day Galena, Illinois.

Appointment of Officers. In the British army, all appointments to the officer corps were made by the crown—i.e., the sovereign—and such was the case in most European armies.

In the American service army promotion to the rank of general officer required appointment by the president with the consent of the Senate, and in the early years of the century candidates were scrutinized for their political beliefs.

Second lieutenants [q.v.] were appointed from graduates of the United States Military Academy at West Point as long as there were brevet second lieutenants unassigned [see Brevet; West Point]. In filling remaining vacancies, consideration was sometimes given to deserving noncommissioned officers [q.v.] of good character who were unmarried, were over twenty-one and under thirty years of age, had at least two years' service, and had been recommended by their commanders and passed by a board of officers annually assembled. Noncommissioned officers so selected received a certificate, had the title Candidate prefixed to their rank, and wore a single gilt stripe on both sleeves, except those ineligible to become second lieutenants by reason of overage who wore a single stripe on the left sleeve only. The number of men commissioned from the ranks was small.

If vacancies still existed, civilian candidates under the age of thirty and over twenty-one were considered.

Promotions to the rank of captain [q.v.] were made regimentally, to the rank of colonel [q.v.] by arm (cavalry, infantry, or artillery) or by corps for staff departments, engineers, and ordnance. All vacancies to the rank of colonel in established regiments and corps were filled by seniority in peacetime. These rules, however, changed from time to time.

In the British service in the early years of the nineteenth century there was no limitation on age, and since promotion was by seniority as well as by purchase [q.v.], the sooner a young man was commissioned, the better. Many were commissioned before their teens and occasionally at birth.

Appointments, Officer's. The accoutrements of an officer.

Appomattox Campaign (25 March–9 April 1865), American Civil War. This was the final campaign of the war in Virginia. It may be said to have begun with the unsuccessful Confederate assault on Fort Stedman [q.v.], near Petersburg, on 25 March, which, followed by Grant's successful assault on 2 April, marked the end of the Petersburg Campaign [q.v.], and to have ended with the surrender of General Robert E. Lee at Appomattox Courthouse on 9 April 1865.

Lee with 50,000 men intended to retreat south to join forces with Joseph E. Johnston [q.v.]. To do so, he had to hold the line of the Southside Railroad, but Grant with 113,000 effectives moved with great vigor to prevent the linkage of the two Confederate armies. On 29 March he ordered Philip Sheridan [q.v.] to advance and cut the tracks of the South-side Railroad. Sheridan did so, winning a decisive victory at Five Forks [q.v.], just southwest of Petersburg, on 1 April. The next day Grant ordered two corps to attack the right of the Confederate defenses at Petersburg [q.v.]. The Confederate line crumbled, and the Confederates evacuated Richmond.

There were subsidiary engagements in the campaign at Quaker Road [q.v.] on 29 March, at White Oak Road and Dinwiddie Court House on 31 March, and in rearguard actions in Richmond.

Lee moved troops south toward Amelia Courthouse, a small village in south-central Virginia, where he expected to find supplies and to use the Danville & Richmond Railroad to shift his army toward Johnston. The Federal pursuit, led by Sheridan, was energetic. Rearguard cavalry affairs occurred at Namozine Church on 3 April and two days later at Amelia Springs [qq.v.]. Sheridan's arrival at Jetersville, seven miles southwest of Amelia Courthouse, cut the Confederate line of retreat by railroad, forcing Lee to move east, and a running fight occurred at Sayler's Creek [q.v.] on 6 April.

There were a number of other rearguard actions. The rear guard of Richard Ewell [q.v.] was cut off and destroyed. Other engagements were fought on 7 April at High Bridge and at Farmville [q.v.]. The final convulsions of the Army of Northern Virginia [q.v.] took place at Appomattox Station on 8 April and at Appomattox Courthouse, where Lee surrendered the following day.

Federal casualties in this campaign were 1,316 killed, 7,750 wounded, and 1,714 missing. Confederate losses were 6,266 killed and wounded; some 3,800 deserted. About 1,000 cavalry simply "left the ranks" and went home. Some 2,400 cavalry made their escape.

Appomattox Courthouse. Surrender at (9 April 1865), American Civil War. Early on the morning of 9 April 1865 some 1,600 Confederate infantry and 2,400 cavalry under General James Longstreet [q.v.] attacked Federal earthworks at Bent Creek Road near Appomattox Courthouse, Virginia, a village 25 miles east of Lynchburg. Within an hour superior numbers of Federal infantry had begun an envelopment of the Confederate right and Federal cavalry attacked the Confederate left. At the same time, the Federals launched vigorous attacks upon the Confederate rear guard. With his last supplies destroyed at Appomattox Station and unable to cut his way south, Lee realized that he must surrender. "There is nothing left for me but to go and see General Grant, and I would rather die a thousand deaths," he said to a staff officer.

At 3:45 P.M. on 9 April 1865 at the home of Wilmer McLean (who had moved from Manassas to avoid the war) General Lee surrendered the Army of Northern Virginia, now reduced to only 28,000 men, to General U.S. Grant, virtually ending the Civil War.

The terms of the surrender were generous: "The officers to give their individual paroles not to take up arms against the government of the United States until properly exchanged, and each company or regimental commander to sign a like parole for the men of their commands." Neither "side arms of the officers nor their private horses or baggage" had to be given up. Horses and mules claimed by Confederate enlisted men were left in their possession. (Grant's generosity was unwittingly a disaster for many southern farmers, for numerous Confederate cavalry horses carried communicable diseases, which were thus spread throughout the South, particularly in Virginia.)

On 18 April Joseph E. Johnston [q.v.] surrendered the last Confederate field army west of the Mississippi. The war conclusively ended on 26 May, when General Edmund Kirby Smith, finding himself isolated in a hopeless position, surrendered.

Approach. 1. The area in front of an enemy's line.

2. A besieger's fortified positions.

3. The route or method for an attacking force to advance upon a fortified place.

Approaches in Siege Operations. Zigzag saps, known as boyaux, were directed by the besiegers toward the enemy's fortifications. Protecting the boyaux were trenches dug perpendicular to them known as parallels and shorter demiparallels.

The great French military engineer Marquis Sébastien le Prestre de Vauban [q.v.] developed this methodical approach for attacking a besieged place. Later military engineers, such as Frants Eduard Ivanovich Todleben [q.v.], or Totleben, added refinements.

Approach March. That phase of a military operation in which troops move forward from assembly or concentration areas toward the enemy and contact is imminent. The approach march ends when the troops deploy and form line of battle. The term can be used for any movement in which there is no direct contact with the enemy. Thus a movement to the rear designed to lure an enemy to a more favorable battle site could also be termed an approach.

King Archidamus II, who reigned from 476 to 427 B.C., is said to have warned his Spartans about approach marches as they prepared to invade Athenian territory: "When invading an enemy's territory, men should always be confident in spirit, but they should fear, too, and take measures of precaution; and thus they will be at once most valorous in attack and impregnable in defense."

Appui. See Point d'Appui.

Apron. 1. A piece of sheet lead tied in place by ropes that covered the touchhole [q.v.] of a gun.

2. A garment covering the front of a person's body to protect clothing or as an adornment. Pioneers in infantry regiments and farriers in cavalry regiments wore aprons of leather even on parade. In the nineteenth century the hides of wild animals were sometimes used as aprons for certain band members.

Aquidabán River, Battle of (1 May 1870), War of the Triple Alliance. In the last battle of this bloody five-year war Francisco Solano López [q.v.], the Paraguayan dictator, with a force of 400 Europeans-Paraguayans and 5,000 Indians was attacked and cut to pieces by the combined forces of Argentina, Brazil (the largest contingent), and Uruguay. López was killed. His Irish mistress, Eliza Lynch [q.v.], escaped to Europe with her jewels.

The Paraguayan population, which had numbered about a million people before the war, was reduced to a quarter of that. Only 28,000 males over the age of fifteen survived.

Appomattox Courthouse *McLean's house, at Appomattox Courthouse, Virginia, where Generals Grant and Lee met for the surrender, 9 April 1865. Photograph by Alexander Gardner*

Arab Bureau. An organization created by General Thomas Bugeaud [q.v.] in 1840, when he was governor of Algeria, to administer the indigenous population and to gather information useful in controlling it. The bureau was manned by Arabic-speaking French officers, who in many remote areas actually made the laws, for until 1871 Algeria was administered as a military colony.

Arabian Wars (1801–42). Sometimes called the Egyptian-Wahhabi Wars. In March 1802 the Wahhabis in Arabia (followers of Muhammad Ibn Abdul Wahhabi, 1691–1787, an Islamic puritan), captured and sacked the Shiite holy city of Karabala, the site of the tomb of Husain (629?–680), one of the Prophet's grandsons, in present-day Iraq 55 miles south-southwest of Baghdad. Most of Karabala's inhabitants were massacred. The following year the Wahhabis captured Mecca (Makkah). In both instances, believing that all knowledge came from the Koran or the summa (a compilation of the Prophet's teachings and beliefs) and all else was suspect, they destroyed tombs and carried away religious objects and treasure.

In 1804 when the Wahhabis captured Medina (Medinah) from the Turks, the sultan of Turkey ordered Mehmet (or Mehemet or Muhammad) Ali [q.v.], viceroy of Egypt, to crush them. Mehmet Ali took his time obeying. Not until 1811 did he send an army of 15,000 to 20,000 men with 800 Turkish cavalry, all commanded by his seventeen-year-old son Tusun (1792–1816) into the Hejaz. Tusun's army was ambushed in a defile at a place called Jadeed Boghaz, and some 4,000 were slain for a Wahhabi loss of 600. In the following year Mehmet Ali himself took the field against the Wahhabis and enjoyed some initial success.

Tusun was then sent to Taraba, in the mountains east of Tayif, to attack the Buqum Arabs, led by a woman named Ghaliya, whom many believed to be a sorceress. He was once more repulsed.

Early in 1814 Mehmet Ali sent an expeditionary force under Zaim Oglou, an Albanian known for his ruthlessness and cruelty, to capture Qunfidha, a port on the Red Sea northeast of Asir in Arabia. The attack was successful, and all captured Wahhabis were slain. Undeterred, a month later a Wahhabi force retook the city, and Oglou was forced to flee in his ships, abandoning many of his men and much matériel.

Mehmet Ali himself led an expedition of 4,000 men into the Hejaz. Although he managed to slaughter many Wahhabis and to take 300 prisoner, only 1,500 of his own men returned, and only 300 of his 4,000 camels survived. Even though he had promised his captives quarter, he impaled 50 at Mecca, and the remainder were impaled at coffeehouses on the road to Jiddah, their bodies left to be eaten by vultures and dogs.

After a lull in the fighting in 1815 the struggle was renewed more successfully by a force under Ibrahim Pasha [q.v.], Mehmet Ali's son (or perhaps son-in-law), who landed at Yembo, the port of Medina, on 30 September 1816. In March 1817 he defeated the Wahhabis at Mawiya (Mawiyah) on a 4,000-foot-high central plateau in southwest Yemen east of Taiz. After a siege, ending in January 1818, he captured Shaqra in the central Nejd, about 100 miles west-northwest of present-day Riyadh, Saudi Arabia. He then sacked Huraimala, and on 14 April he began the siege of Deraiyeh (Deraya, Derayeh, Derayah, Dariyah, or Dariya), the capital of Wahhabism, which surrendered on 9 September. Abdullah, the Wahhabi commander, was taken to Constantinople (Istanbul) and beheaded; Deraiyeh was razed to the ground. On 11 December 1819 Ibrahim Pasha made a triumphal entry into Cairo.

In 1824 Abdullah's son, Turki (d.1834), headed an uprising and established a new Wahhabi capital at Riyadh, 10 miles west-northwest of the former site of Deraiyeh. Turki consolidated his power steadily until in 1834 he was murdered by his cousin Mishari. Turki's son, Faisul (d.1867), took the reins of power, but because he refused to pay the customary tribute to Egypt, he was captured and imprisoned in Cairo. In 1842 he managed to escape and reestablished Wahhabi power in central Arabia, where he ejected the Egyptian forces, fended off threats to his power by jealous tribal leaders, and, with difficulty, kept the peace between his two sons, Saud and Abdullah, until his death.

After Faisul's death the history of Arabia for the remainder of the century was a series of revolts, murders, bloody family feuds, and the efforts of Egypt and Turkey to gain control. For a time it seemed that Wahhabi power had dissipated, but in 1901 it again emerged virtually intact, led by the house of Abdul Agiz Ibn Saud (1880–1953).

Arabi Pasha (1839–1911), more correctly, Ahmed Arabi or Ahmad Urabi. An Egyptian officer who served twelve years as a conscript before he was commissioned in 1862. In 1875 he served in the Egyptian Campaign against Abyssinia. As a colonel he conspired with other officers against the government, protesting European influence, privileges, and control over Egyptian finances. On 1 February 1881 he and two other officers were court-martialed for disobedience. Their soldiers rescued them from prison, and Khedive Tewfik (1852–1892) was forced by his rebellious military to dismiss his minister of war.

A demonstration led by Arabi on 8 September 1881 forced the khedive to increase the size of the army and the pay of its officers. By the beginning of 1882 Arabi had acquired such ascendancy over the khedive that he first was named undersecretary for war and soon after was created a pasha and appointed minister of war. In that same year he led a nationalist revolt against the foreigners, mainly British and French, who virtually ruled Egypt [see Arabi's Revolt]. He was dismissed from his post after a British army under Sir Garnet Wolseley [q.v.] invaded Egypt and defeated the Egyptian forces in the Battle of Tell el-Kebir [q.v.] on 13 September 1882. He was captured, tried on 3 December, convicted, and sentenced to death, a sentence commuted to life imprisonment in Ceylon (Sri Lanka). In 1901 he was pardoned and returned to Egypt. He died in Cairo on 21 September 1911.

Arabi's Revolt (1882). A revolt against the khedive Muhammad Tewfik Pasha (1852–1892) led by Egyptian Colonel Ahmed Arabi Pasha [q.v.] to protest French and British control of the Suez Canal and of Egypt's finances. In response, a British fleet under Admiral Sir Beauchamp Seymour (1821–1895) shelled Alexandria, and although France refused to cooperate, an expeditionary force of 25,000 British troops led by General Sir Garnet Wolseley [q.v.] landed near Suez and in the battles of Tell el-Kebir and Kassassin [qq.v.] routed Arabi's forces and established virtual suzerainty over Egypt. British officers and noncommissioned officers were seconded to the Egyptian army, officers serving two ranks above their substantive British army rank. A British major general became the sirdar (commander-in-chief) of the Egyptian army.

Arab Uprising in East Africa. See Bushiri's Revolt.

Aragón, Army of. A Spanish army in the Peninsular War, formed in the autumn of 1808 with 23,758 men and six guns under Spanish General José Palafox [q.v.]. A second Spanish army of this name was formed in May–June 1809 with 14,200 men under General Joachim Blake [q.v.].

At the same time a French Army of Aragón with 11,000 men was formed in May 1809 under General Louis Suchet [q.v.].

Arakan Uprising (1811–15). Rebellious Arakanese attempted to drive the Burmese out of their territory. The Burmese protested to the British because the rebels were operating from bases in British territory, but the British were unable or unwilling to interfere.

Arakchiev, Aleksei Andrievich (1769–1834). A Russian soldier and administrator who became a cadet in the artillery at the age of thirteen. Before his twenty-ninth birthday he was a major general. From 1803 to 1807, as inspector general of artillery, he was influential in obtaining the number and quality of guns required to fight Napoleon. From 1808 to December 1809 he was war minister and responsible for the planning of the invasion of Finland [q.v.]. After the failure of Napoleon's Russian Campaign [q.v.] in 1812 he worked on rebuilding destroyed cities, notably the speedy reconstruction of Smolensk, and was responsible for the establishment of military colonies, in which soldiers lived with their families under military discipline on neglected lands to restore cultivation.

Araure, Battle of (5 December 1813), Venezuelan Revolution. Simón Bolívar [q.v.] won a decisive victory over 3,500 Spanish royalists at this village in western Venezuela, thirty-five miles south-southeast of Barquisimeto.

Arbuthnot and Ambrister Affair (1818), First Seminole War. In the course of a punitive expedition against the Seminole Indians in Florida, American General Andrew Jackson [q.v.] captured and court-martialed Alexander Arbuthnot (d. 1818), a Scots trader accused of instigating Indian raids into Georgia, and an English trader named Robert Chrystie Ambrister (1798?–1818) who was charged with inciting the hostile Seminoles against the United States. [See Mcgregor, Gregor.] Arbuthnot was hanged from the yardarm of his own trading vessel. Ambrister was shot. The executions were followed by a brouhaha in the British press, which denounced Jackson as a "ruffian" who had murdered two British subjects, but the British government chose to ignore the incident, as did President James Monroe (1758–1831).

Arc de Triomphe de l'Étoile. On 18 February 1806 Napoleon selected the Place de l'Étoile, then the western limit of Paris, as the site for his memorial arch. The arch was inaugurated on 29 July 1806 but was not completed until July 1836 in the reign of Louis Philippe. Built after the design by Jean Chalgrin (1739–1811) and adorned with hauts-reliefs, it stands nearly 164 feet high. On its sides are inscribed 158 military engagements of the Revolutionary and Napoleonic eras, beginning with the Battle of Valmy on 20 September 1792 and ending with the Battle of Ligny [q.v.], Napoleon's last victory, on 16 June 1815, as well as the names of 662 marshals, admirals, and generals who served with distinction from Valmy to Ligny.

Arc de Triomphe du Carrousel. Smaller than the great Arc de Triomphe de l'Étoile [q.v.] this arch was erected in Paris to celebrate the victories of 1805 and 1806. Much admired by Napoleon, it was designed by Charles Percier (1768–1838) and Pierre Fontaine (1762–1853). The sum of one million francs was allocated for the project, and this was to be collected from war reparations from the Netherlands. The site, between the Louvre and the Tuileries, was so named because Louis XVI (1754–1793) on the birth of his first child in 1781 had erected a giant carrousel here as part of a great celebration.

The cornerstone of the arch was laid on 7 July 1807. At the end of the year the Garde Impériale [q.v.], returning from its victories in the battles of Eylau and Friedland [qq.v.], was the first unit to pass beneath it.

Archduke Charles. See Charles Louis, archduke of Austria.

Archer, Branch Tanner (1790–1831). A Texas patriot who was born in Virginia but emigrated to Texas, where he took an active part in securing Texas independence. He served as secretary of war under President Mirabeau Buonaparte Lamar (1798–1859), the second president of Texas.

Archer, James Jay (1817–1864). An American lawyer and soldier, educated at Princeton, who fought with distinction in the Mexican War, winning a brevet. He was mustered out in 1848 and for a time practiced the law but returned to the army in 1855 as a captain of infantry. In 1861 he resigned his commission to become colonel of the 5th Texas in the American Civil War. On 3 June he was promoted a Confederate brigadier general. As a regimental or brigade commander he fought in every battle of the Army of Northern Virginia [q.v.] from Seven Days' through Gettysburg [qq.v.]. He was captured on 1 July 1863 and held prisoner for more than a year on Johnson's Island [q.v.], where his health failed. After being exchanged, he commanded again for a brief period before he died in Richmond on 24 October 1864.

Archers, Royal Company of. The sovereign's bodyguard for Scotland was formed in 1676 by an act of the Privy Council of Scotland. It is the Scottish counterpart to the English Gentlemen-at-Arms [q.v.].

Archibald Wheel. An iron-hubbed wheel used on the wagons and gun carriages of the American army.

Arcis-sur-Aube, Battle of (20–21 March 1814), Napoleonic Wars. At this town in Champagne Prince Karl Philip von Schwarzenberg [q.v.] of Austria with 60,000 men successfully, but with great difficulty, repulsed an attempt by Napoleon, leading 23,000 men, to sever his line of communication [q.v.]. The Austrians suffered 2,500 casualties; the French lost 1,700. Napoleon called

Archibald wheel

upon Marshals Auguste de Marmont and Édouard Adolphe Casimir Joseph Mortier, Duc de Trévise [qq.v.] to come to his aid with their 17,000 men, but en route, on 25 March, they encountered Schwarzenberg and in the Battle of Fère-Champenoise [q.v.] were beaten and driven back toward Paris, 75 miles west. The French suffered 3,000 casualties; the Allies about 4,000.

Ardant du Picq, Charles Jean Jacques Joseph (1831–1870). A French soldier educated at St. Cyr [q.v.] and in 1844 commissioned in the infantry. He fought in the Crimean War and in September 1855 was captured at Sevastopol [q.v.]. When released in December, after the war, he returned to duty. He served in Syria from August 1860 to June 1861 and took part in the attempt to restore order during the Druse-Maronite [q.v.] sectarian violence there. From 1864 to 1866 he served in Algeria, and he was promoted colonel in February 1869. During the Franco-Prussian War [q.v.] he was killed at the head of his regiment in the Battle of Colombey-Borny [q.v.] on 15 August 1870.

Noted as a military theorist, he made major contributions to the development of combat theory, particularly in discipline, unit cohesion, and the behavior of men in battle. Before his death he had published *Combat antique;* this was expanded, based on his manuscript for *Études sur les combat: Combat antique et moderne,* usually referred to as *Battle Studies,* which was published in part in 1880 and in its entirety in 1902.

He was one of the first to stress the psychological and behavioral aspects of the combat experience. He believed that battles were basically contests of wills, that it was more important to persuade the enemy that he was beaten than to inflict material losses, that everything should be sacrificed to the ferocity and momentum of the attack.

A French man of letters, Jules Barbey d'Aurevilly (1808–1889), said of him: "Never has a man of action, and in the eyes of universal prejudice, more splendidly glorified the spirituality of war." He greatly influenced many of the generals who fought in World War I, notably Marshal Ferdinand Foch (1851–1929).

Areizaga, Juan Carlos (d. 1816). A Spanish soldier who in 1809, during the Peninsular War [q.v.], served as a division commander under Joachim Blake [q.v.]. He was given command of the Army of La Mancha, but was defeated in the Battle of Ocaña [q.v.] on 19 November 1809, and he proved unable to prevent the French from overrunning Andalusia. His forces were dispersed in January 1810, and his command passed to General Manuel Freire (1765–1834).

Arendrup, Søren Adolph (1834–1875). A Dane who was commissioned in the Danish army in 1859 and was a first lieutenant of artillery in 1863 and retired as a captain. When he contracted tuberculosis, he removed to Egypt, where in 1874 he joined the Egyptian army as a lieutenant colonel, serving under General (Fariq) Charles Stone [q.v.], chief of the general staff. His specialty was ordnance; he had previously worked at the Finspong gun factory in Sweden. In 1875 he commanded the Egyptian forces in the Abyssinia-Egyptian War [q.v.]. He was killed in the Battle of Gundet [q.v.] in the Abyssinian highlands, a disaster to Egyptian arms.

Arentschildt, Alexander Carl Friedrich von (1806–1881). A Hanoverian general who fought in the Schleswig-Holstein War [q.v.] as a colonel and was promoted brigadier general in 1861. At the beginning of the Seven Weeks' War [q.v.] in 1866 he was promoted against his will to the rank of lieutenant general and given command of the Hanoverian army. He attempted to march on Bavaria, but his army was defeated in the Battle of Lagensalza [q.v.]. After the annexation of Hanover to Prussia, he refused an appointment in the Prussian army.

Argaon / Argaum / Argun, Battle of (29 November 1803), Second Maratha War. In this last battle of the war the Maratha chief Doulut Rao Sindhia (d. 1827), commanding the forces of the raja of Berar—10,000 infantry and 25,000 cavalry—made a last stand. His demoralized troops were defeated by a force of 11,000 British regulars and sepoys under Major General Sir Arthur Wellesley (later Duke of Wellington). Wellesley's victory was not an easy one. Two British sepoy battalions broke and fled, and for a time the situation was serious. British losses were 46 killed and 315 wounded. The Marathas lost an estimated 3,000 and all their elephants, baggage, and guns.

Argentine-Brazilian War (1825–28). In 1825, supported by Argentina, Juan Antonio Lavalleja (1784–1853), a Uruguayan patriot leading a small group called the Thirty-Three Immortals, declared Banda Oriental (Uruguay) independent of Brazil. In response, Brazil declared war on Argentina and blockaded the port of Buenos Aires. On 20 February 1827 an Argentine-Uruguayan army defeated the Brazilians in the Battle of Ituzaingó [q.v.] on the cisplatine pampas. Pressure from Britain, France, and the United States forced Brazil to abandon its blockade, and the British mediated a treaty that resulted in the independence of Uruguay.

Argentine-Brazilian War (1851). Argentine dictator Juan Manuel de Rosas [q.v.] attempted to annex Paraguay and Uruguay, but land and naval forces of Uruguay, Corrientes, and Brazil commanded by General Justo José de Urquiza [q.v.] defeated Rosas and thwarted his designs.

Argentine Civil Wars. In Argentina the revolution against Spain began on 25 May 1810, when a provisional junta was formed. Six years later the United Provinces of the Río de la Plata was proclaimed [see Argentine War of Independence]. In 1825 these became the Argentine Republic or Confederation.

The Spaniards and Creoles in Argentina frequently fought each other, and both waged frequent wars against Indian tribes. In October–December 1836 they united to campaign against the Borogas Indians, and the following year an uprising was brutally suppressed by troops under Colonel Antonio Ramírez.

On 3 February 1852 in the Battle of Caseros [q.v.] the seventeen-year rule of Argentine dictator Juan Manuel de Rosas [q.v.] was ended by a rebel force under Justo José de Urquiza [q.v.]. Buenos Aires had refused to recognize the authority of the Argentine Confederation in 1853, but when an Argentine army led by Urquiza, its new president, defeated an army of Buenos Aires dissidents under Bartolomé Mitre [q.v.] in the Battle of Cepeda [q.v.] on 23 October 1859, Buenos Aires again became part of Argentina.

In 1860 Buenos Aires, unhappy with its new condition, revolted. An army under Mitre, its governor, defeated the army of Urquiza in the Battle of Pavón [q.v.] in the province of Santa Fe on 17 September 1861. In 1862, in a rigged election, Mitre was elected president of a united Argentina.

On 12 October 1868 Colonel Domingo Faustino Sarmiento (1811–1888), an Argentine political leader, defeated Mitre and was elected president; he served until 1874. In November 1868 he suppressed an insurrection in Corrientes. In December 1873 he defeated the rebel leader Ricard López Jordán (d. 1888). In September 1874 Mitre led another revolution but was defeated by Sarmiento at Buenos Aires on 6 November. In 1878–79 General Julio Argentino Roca (1843–1914) fought a successful campaign against the Indians of Patagonia, pushing them south of the Río Negro, and in 1880 he was elected president, succeeding Nicolás Avellaneda (1836–1885), who had held office since 1874. In 1889 a group of "better-class citizens" of Buenos Aires formed the Unión Civica and in July 1890, aided by some regiments of the regular army, revolted. There was heavy fighting in the streets of Buenos Aires, and the town was bombarded. President Miguel Juárez Celmán (1847–1909), who had become president on 12 October 1886, was ousted and replaced by Carlos Pellegrini (1848?–1906), the vice-president. After a brief armistice, fighting resumed. An estimated 1,000 people lost their lives and much property was destroyed before the insurgents surrendered. There was a general amnesty, but army officers implicated in the rebellion were cashiered and exiled.

February 1891 saw conspiracies and rioting in Córdoba and Buenos Aires; in January 1892 there were disturbances and assassinations at Mendoza. In April there was an aborted revolution. In September some 30 officers who had joined the latest rebels were court-martialed. On 19 October in a revolt in the province of Santiago del Estrado the governor and his ministers were made prisoners. Peace was restored in November.

In October, and again in November 1892, insurrections flared in Corrientes Province but were suppressed by the army the following January. In March 1893 an insurrection in Catamarca was followed by others in various provinces. By the end of August the country was in a state of siege. Rebel forces ousted the government of Corrientes, and in September there was a revolt in Tucumán. Rosario was taken by the rebels on 25 September but retaken by the government on 1 October. By the end of February 1894 all the insurrections had been put down. The country spent the remainder of the century fighting locusts and floods, coping with a destructive earthquake and financial chaos until riots broke out in July 1901, followed by a frontier dispute with Chile in December.

Argentine Intervention in Uruguay (1842–52). Juan Manuel de Rosas [q.v.], dictator of Argentina, supported Uruguay's former president in a long civil war (1842–51) that involved an eight-year siege (1843–51) of Montevideo [q.v.], where Giuseppe Garibaldi [q.v.] was one of the defenders. In an effort to check the ambitions of Rosas in Argentina, France and Britain blockaded the Río de la Plata and landed forces in Uruguay. On 3 February 1852 Justo José de Urquiza [q.v.], with the help of troops from Uruguay and Brazil, defeated Rosas in the Battle of Monte Caseros [q.v.]. Rosas fled to England. Two years later Urquiza became the first constitutional president of Argentina (1854–60).

Argentine War of Independence (1806–16). In 1806 the British blockaded the Río de la Plata and landed troops in Argentina. They were defeated by a colonial force under Santiago Liniers [q.v.]—a Frenchman in the Spanish service—and forced to withdraw from Buenos Aires.

In 1807 the British returned with an 8,000-man army and seized both Buenos Aires and Montevideo, which they held until forced out by Liniers.

In 1810, when news that King Ferdinand VII (1784–1833) had been deposed and that Napoleon was invading Spain reached Buenos Aires, the Spanish viceroy was deposed and replaced by a junta that included Cornelio Savedra (1760–1828), Mariano Moreno (1778–1811), Manuel Belgrano (1770–1820), and Bernardino Rivadavia (1780–1845). The junta was in turn replaced by a triumvirate. Under its rule a congress met at Tucumán and declared Argentina independent. On 9 July 1816 Juan Martín de Pueyrredón (1776–1850) was inaugurated as supreme dictator.

Argentine War of Independence *An Argentinean gaucho, early nineteenth century*

Arínez, Hill of. See Vitoria, Battle of.

Arisaka. A Japanese service rifle, popularly called the Meiji rifle, introduced in 1897. It had a bolt action with a magazine that held five semi-rimmed 6.5 cartridges and was largely a copy of the Mauser [q.v.], although the cocking action differed. There were variants in future years, identified by the symbol and name of the current emperor's reign, e.g., the Meiji 30th Year 6.5 infantry rifle adopted in 1897, and the Meiji carbine of the same year.

Arista, Mariano (1802–1855). A Mexican general who took part in an unsuccessful attempt to suppress the Texas

Revolution [q.v.] in 1836. In the Mexican War [q.v.] he commanded the army that was defeated by American General Zachary Taylor [q.v.] at Palo Alto on 8 May 1846 and at Resaca de la Palma [qq.v.] on the following day. He became minister of war (1845–51) under José Joaquín Herrera (1792–1854) and in 1851 was elected president of Mexico, serving until 1853.

Arkansas Campaign of 1864 (23 March–3 May 1864), American Civil War, also known as the Expedition to Camden. This was part of the Red River Campaign [q.v.]. To prevent Confederate forces in southwest Arkansas from opposing the advance of Union General Nathaniel Banks [q.v.] on Shreveport, Louisiana, Union General Frederick Steele (1819–1868) was to have concentrated his forces and on 1 March 1864 was to advance on the Confederates. Instead, he lingered at Little Rock, Arkansas, until 23 March.

When he finally advanced, he fought numerous skirmishes: At Mount Elba on 30 March; at Spoonville (Terre Noire Creek) and Antoine on 2 April; at Elkin's Ford (Little Missouri River) on 4–6 April; and at Prairie d'Ann (between Arkadelphia and Spring Hill) on 11–13 April. He did not learn that Banks had abandoned his advance on Shreveport until 15 April, when he arrived at Camden, Arkansas.

Meanwhile Confederate General Edmund Kirby-Smith [q.v.] sent a column to cut off his retreat. Although the column captured 211 of his wagons at Mark's Mills on 25 April, Steele managed to carry on his retreat. On 29–30 April he was attacked while astride the Saline River at Jenkin's Ferry and lost his pontoon train. On 3 May, with the remnants of his force, he limped into Little Rock.

Arkansas Post, Capture of (11 January 1863), American Civil War. This Arkansas community, once the capital of Arkansas Territory, was the oldest white settlement in the lower Mississippi Valley. Located on the north bank of the Arkansas River about fifty miles from its confluence with the Mississippi, the town was captured on 11 January 1863 by a Federal force of about 30,000 men under General John A. McClernand [q.v.], after part of it had been lost for a time in a swamp. The expedition, although suggested by General W. T. Sherman, was not authorized by U. S. Grant [qq.v.]. It served no useful purpose, and Grant, who dubbed it a "wild goose chase," ordered McClernand to return to the vicinity of Vicksburg.

Union losses were about 1,100 out of 29,000 engaged; Confederate losses were some 4,900, of which all but about 200 were captured.

Arkansas Toothpick. In the American West, the name given to any large sheath knife, such as a bowie knife [q.v.].

Arlington National Cemetery. The largest (originally 200 acres; extended to 440 acres) and best-known national cemetery in the United States. It was established in 1864, during the American Civil War, at Fort Meyer across the Potomac from Washington, D.C., on land once owned by George Washington and later by Robert E. Lee. The title of the land was in dispute until 1883, when the U.S. government paid $150,000 to the son of General Robert E. Lee. The cemetery was administered by the War Department in the nineteenth century; at present it is administered by the Department of the Army.

The first soldier buried in the cemetery was a Confederate who had died in the hospital established there. The first Union soldier to be interred was William Christman of Pennsylvania, buried in Grave No. 19. Some 2,000 unknown soldiers of the Civil War, having been gathered from the Bull Run [q.v.] battlefield and on the route to the Rappahannock, were buried on the grounds, but the first ceremonial reburying of the American Unknown Soldier was not until November 1921. [See National Cemeteries, American.]

Arm. 1. As a noun, a weapon used for offense or defense.
 2. As a noun, a portion of an army [see Arms of the Service].
 3. As a verb, to furnish with weapons.
 4. As a verb, to adjust the firing mechanism of an explosive device to explode when triggered.

Armament. The process of preparing for war. The arrangements made for defense of a nation, a military unit, a fort, or other fixed fortification.

Arme Blanche. The romantic name given to the sword or to cavalry generally. Occasionally, particularly in French usage, used for other edged weapons, such as the bayonet and lance.

Armed to the Teeth. Fully prepared to do battle. First used by English statesman Richard Cobden (1804–1865) in a speech when he asked rhetorically: "Is there any reason we should not be armed to the teeth?"

Armée Coloniale. Often called simply La Coloniale, this was a French force composed of both European and native units that served in French colonies [see Armée d'Afrique]. It was established in 1900 from the Infanterie de Marine [q.v.]. French General Charles Mangin (1866–1925) said of the black Africans in this force that they represented "African civilization reborn and constitute our crowning achievement."

Armée Coloniale *An African instructor and an infantryman of the French colonial army*

Armée d'Afrique. The force used by the French to conquer and garrison Algeria, Tunisia, and Morocco. It consisted of four major entities: Chasseurs d'Afrique, Zouaves, Légion Étrangère (French Foreign Legion), and Infanterie Légère d'Afrique [qq.v.]. Originally these were recruited only from Europeans. Later some indigenous or mixed units, such as the Spahis, Tirailleurs, and Compagnies Sahariennes [qq.v.], were added.

Except for those of the Foreign Legion, the Armée d'Afrique had no training depots. Units formed training platoons with cadres and sent them into the desert for hands-on instruction. In the nineteenth century it did not have its own artillery.

Although its strength grew steadily in the nineteenth century, its composition varied little. In 1875 its infantry consisted of four regiments of Zouaves [q.v.], each with four battalions of four fighting companies; three regiments of Algerian Turcos [q.v.], organized like the Zouaves; one regiment of the Foreign Legion [q.v.], with four battalions of four companies; and five disciplinary companies. Its cavalry consisted of three regiments of Spahis [q.v.] and four regiments of Chasseurs d'Afrique, each with six squadrons; in all, 59 officers and 978 other ranks in each regiment.

Armée de Métier. An army of long-term professional soldiers.

Armée des Côtes de l'Océan. Sometimes called Armée de l'Angleterre. An army of 160,000 activated by Napoleon in May 1803 to protect French shores facing west. Six camps (later designated numbered army corps [q.v.]) were centered on Brest, Montreuil, Boulogne, St. Omar, Bruges, and Utrecht. In August 1805 they became part of the Grande Armée [q.v.].

Armée Métropolitaine. That part of the French armed forces that served in metropolitan France.

Armée Savants. Informal name for French artillerymen and army engineers.

Armenian Massacres of 1894–98. In the early nineteenth century the Ottoman sultans referred to their Armenian subjects as the "loyal community" because in contrast with the Greeks, Bulgarians, and Serbs, they were not rebellious.

Armenian Massacres of 1894–98 *An Armenian is arrested by Turkish soldiers in Constantinople, 1896.*

Nevertheless, beginning about 1878, a spirit of nationalism began to stir the Turkish Armenians, and in 1894 revolutionary bands attacked Turkish authorities and an attempt was made to form an Armenian state. The revolt was crushed with great brutality. In a four-year period Kurdish cavalry and Turkish infantry, on orders from Sultan Abdul-Hamid II (1842–1918), massacred an estimated 150,000. Further massacres occurred in 1909 and 1915.

Armistead, George (1780–1818). An American officer, born in Virginia. He became an ensign in the 7th Infantry on 14 January 1799. In 1814 he was a major and in charge of Fort McHenry [q.v.] in Baltimore's harbor when, during the War of 1812, it was attacked by the British. He was brevetted lieutenant colonel for his gallant defense of the fort.

Armistead, Lewis Addison (1817–1863). An American soldier who attended West Point from 1834 to 1836 but was dismissed, it was said, for breaking a plate over the head of Cadet Jubal Anderson Early [q.v.]. Nevertheless, in 1839 he was appointed a second lieutenant in the 6th Infantry. During the Mexican War [q.v.] he was twice brevetted. On 26 May 1861, at the outbreak of the American Civil War, he resigned to join the Confederate forces and was appointed a colonel of the 37th Virginia. On 1 April 1862 he was promoted brigadier general and assigned to command a brigade in the division of George Pickett [q.v.]. He led the brigade with distinction from the Peninsular Campaign through the Battle of Gettysburg [qq.v.]. On the third day of the latter battle his brigade formed the second rank of the division in Pickett's charge [q.v.]. Leading a handful of men, he scaled a stone wall and drove Union gunners from their guns but fell mortally wounded with his hand on a captured cannon. The Confederate attack ebbed, and he was left behind. He was carried to a Federal hospital, where he died on 5 July.

Armistice. An agreed-upon suspension of hostilities between belligerents either for a definite interval or for an indefinite period during which hostilities could resume upon notice being given by either side. An armistice is always temporary and does not mean peace. A general armistice, usually of a combined military and diplomatic nature, is valid at all points and lines of the belligerents and often is a prelude to a formal peace treaty. A limited or a local armistice applies to certain troops or certain times; it suspends hostilities over a wider area than a suspension of arms [q.v.] but includes less than the total of the belligerent forces.

Armor, Medieval. Suits of such armor were still worn late in the nineteenth century by warriors in Darfur Province in the Sudan and by those in Bornu in northern Nigeria.

Armored Cars. Automobiles mounting a small cannon or machine guns and protected by metal plates. In 1900 the Simms war car, capable of traveling 9 mph and mounting a 1½-pounder gun, was successfully demonstrated to the War Office in Britain, but it was not adopted, and no attempts were made to improve it.

Armored Trains. Railroad batteries, guns mounted on trains, were used in the American Civil War, the Franco-Prussian War, and the Second Anglo-Boer War [qq.v.].

Lieutenant Winston Churchill was captured during a Boer attack upon a British armored train in Natal, South Africa.

Armory or Armoury. See Arsenal or Armory.

Arms Chest. A portable locker for small arms [q.v.].

Arms of Honor. Muskets, rifles, swords, or other weapons presented to soldiers as a mark of honor, often suitably inscribed. In Napoleon's Grande Armée a pioneer's ax, a drummer's sticks, or a bugler's horn could be so presented.

Arms of the Service. In the nineteenth century there were only three basic arms—infantry, artillery, and cavalry—although engineers were also sometimes so classified. They were known as the line of the army or troops of the line. Each was sometimes associated with a different color, which was used for facings and trouser stripes. In the United States these were infantry blue, artillery red, and cavalry gold.

Arms Ornamentation. The decoration of edged weapons, a common practice in earlier centuries, continued into the nineteenth century in all parts of the world. The practice was often extended to the ornamentation of muskets, rifles, and cannon. Only the practice of ornamenting cannon died out with the century, although not completely; many guns manufactured in Asia continued to display ornamentation.

The incongruity of making weapons of destruction into works of art has puzzled some, and a few have seen a moral inconsonance in the practice. Robert Browning pondered the seeming inappositeness of embellishing weapons in his poem "A Forgiveness," published in 1876:

> I think there never was such—how express?
> Horror coquetting with voluptuousness,
> As in those arms of Eastern workmanship—
> Yataghan, kanjar, things that rend and rip,
> Gash rough, slash smooth, help hate so many ways,
> Yet ever keep a beauty that betrays
> Love still at work with the artificer
> Throughout his quaint devising. Why prefer,
> Except for love's sake, that a blade should writhe
> And flicker like a flame? . . .

[See Yataghan; Khanjar.]

Arms Rack. A frame or fitting capable of being locked for the temporary storage of small arms [q.v.]; usually found in barracks or on troopships. [See Bell of Arms.]

Armstrong, John (1758–1843). An American general and politician who in 1777 served in the Continental army during the American Revolution. He was elected a U.S. senator and on 6 July 1812 was appointed a brigadier general in the regular army. He resigned his commission on 6 January 1813 to become secretary of war and served until 27 September 1814. His ineptness was widely credited as the cause for most of the American failures in the War of 1812 [q.v.].

Armstrong, William George, Baron Armstrong of Cragside (1810–1900). The son of a prosperous English yeoman, he was privately educated. Although he became a

barrister, he was always interested in machinery, and his inventions ranged from "Armstrong's water-pressure wheel" to a hydraulic crane. He won prizes for his work, and both Oxford and Cambridge awarded him honorary degrees.

At the outbreak of the Crimean War [q.v.], he invented mines for blowing up Russian ships, and this turned his mind to ordnance. A newspaper account of the Battle of Inkerman [q.v.] on 5 November 1854, which dramatically described the struggle to manhandle into position an 18-pounder gun weighing 3 tons, caused him to wonder why it required a 5-inch–caliber gun of 3 tons to throw a shell weighing only 18 pounds. This led him to ponder how the weight of guns might be reduced.

At that time the barrel of a cannon was made by forging metal into the desired form and then boring a hole in it. Armstrong enclosed a steel cylinder with a twisted wrought-iron bar, welding the turns into a cylinder of internal diameter somewhat smaller than the steel lining. This jacket was expanded by heat, slipped over the core, and then contracted by cooling. Other rings, as desired, could be shrunk upon it. He persuaded the War Office to authorize him to make six such guns.

He conceived the notion of loading guns from the rear and invented both a wedge and a screw method for closing the breech. He also designed an elongated lead projectile capable of acting as shot, shell, or case shot, as well as a special percussion fuze.

As his first guns, completed in July 1855, were small 3-pounders, they were derided by artillery officers as "popguns." In response, Armstrong built a 6-pounder on the same principle while continuing experiments to improve his weapon, taking out eleven patents in all. On 16 November a committee on rifled cannon appointed by the secretary for war issued

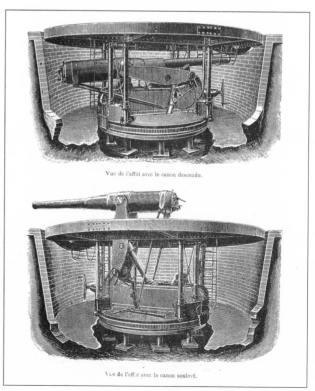

Armstrong Gun *An Armstrong gun with the cannon lowered (top) and the cannon raised (bottom)*

a most favorable report on his gun, and Armstrong patriotically presented all his patents to the government without charge and put his services and talents at its disposal. The following year he was knighted and appointed engineer of rifled ordnance at Woolwich [q.v.].

By 1863 British artillery was probably the finest in the world, but although Armstrong's guns had proved themselves in action in China in 1859–60, where 18-pounders were first used on 12 August 1860 to bombard Sinho (Hsin-ho) [see Opium Wars], there were still strong objections to breechloaders among conservative British gunners, who argued that it was more difficult to train cannoneers, that breechloaders were more expensive, that they did not work well in sandstorms, and that they did not weather well. In short, the British army returned to muzzleloaders.

Undaunted, Armstrong continued to improve his ordnance. Foreign governments proved more appreciative than his own, and through sales abroad he made a fortune. By 1880 he had developed a construction using small wired cylinders instead of jackets or hoops so efficacious that even the British army, whose artillery was now quite obsolete, returned to Armstrong's breechloaders on a substantial scale in 1882.

To the end of his life Sir William continued to experiment and invent. His interest in armor plate led him to produce steel of high-tensile strength by tempering it in an oil bath. Later in life he experimented with electricity. He was raised to the peerage in 1887.

Although Armstrong guns, in various calibers up to 600-pounders (13.3-inch), were used in the American Civil War by both sides, they predominated in northern armies. Fieldpieces had ranges up to 2,200 yards. The 3-inch breechloader fired a 10-pound projectile with lead driving bands around its middle. Not all of the Armstrong guns were breechloaders; those of larger caliber were sometimes muzzle-loaders.

In all, about 5,000 Armstrong guns in various calibers were produced for armies and navies.

Armstrong Gun. See William George Armstrong.

Armstrong's Mill, Battle of. See Dabney's Mills.

Army. The word has both general and specific meanings. It can mean a great multitude or the entire armed forces of a country or a cause. General Helmuth von Moltke [q.v.] wrote: "The Army is the most outstanding institution in every country, for it alone makes possible the existence of all civic institutions."

More specifically, an army consists of the land forces of a nation, exclusive of its marines. Even more specifically, in a military sense it is a unit of a national army consisting of two or more corps with supporting troops. When these are field armies, they are usually named after some geographical or political feature—e.g., the Army of Northern Virginia, Army of the Marne, Army of the Andes, Army of the Sutlej [qq.v.]. Armies were also sometimes numbered, and when they were numbered (rare in the nineteenth century), the number was written and capitalized: Second Army. During the American Civil War there were at least sixteen Union and twenty-three Confederate units that were called, officially or unofficially,

armies. Some of these, such as the so-called Army of the Allegheny with fewer than 3,000 men under Confederate Brigadier General Edward Johnson (1816–1873), were actually of only brigade size.

Army Administration. All the activities necessary to manage a military unit not encompassed by tactics or strategy. Supplying the needs of an army, including clothing, fuel, shelter, transport, medical care, pay, records, accoutrements, arms, ammunition, etc., has been complex in all armies, but perhaps nowhere has it ever been more bewildering than in the British army in mid-nineteenth century. Administration was then separate and distinct from command and discipline. The army belonged to the British sovereign. His or her representative for administration was the secretary of state for war, who was responsible for reconciling any differences between the sovereign's wishes and the desires of Parliament; the sovereign's representative for command and discipline of the army was the commander-in-chief, who for forty years of the nineteenth century was the Duke of Cambridge [q.v.].

The commander-in-chief had no control over troops outside Britain. Even in Britain he had no control over food and transport, which were the responsibilities of the Commissariat [q.v.], a branch of the Treasury. The Medical Department reported directly to the secretary of state for war, who was also responsible for army finances, except those of the "technical services"—i.e., the Royal Artillery and the Royal Engineers. The technical services were paid for by the master general of the ordnance [q.v.], who was also responsible for barracks and fortifications, as well as certain items of equipment, and was accountable to no one. Neither the secretary for war nor the commander-in-chief nor the chancellor of the exchequer had any responsibility for the size of the army or its cost. This was managed by the secretary of state for colonies. As a result of this administrative tangle, the army landed to fight in the Crimea [q.v.] with exactly twenty-one wagons to carry all its supplies, ammunition, gear, and impedimenta, and no fuel whatsoever.

Army and Navy Pensioners Employment Society. An organization founded in Britain in 1885 to provide suitable jobs for wounded and disabled servicemen. [See Corps of Commissionaires.]

Army Certificate of Education. Certificates awarded to British soldiers who learned to read, write, and figure. Introduced in 1860, the certificate came in three classes. The lowest (third class) required an ability to read and write short passages and do simple arithmetic. A third-class certificate was necessary before a private could be promoted to corporal; a second-class was required for promotion to sergeant; and a first-class was required for warrant officers (senior noncommissioned officers). By 1874, 32 percent of the rank and file held at least third-class certificates.

Army Corps. Large armies were usually divided into army corps, which consisted of two or more divisions and often special troops, artillery, and equipment. They were generally commanded by a senior major general or a lieutenant general [see General Officer]. It was Napoleon who conceived the idea for a *corps d'armée,* and all large armies in Europe followed his example. In the United States army corps were not formed until the American Civil War, when they were formed first by the Union army and then by the Confederate. [See Army Organization.]

Army Estimates. The British army's budget, known as estimates, was put forward each year for the approval of the House of Commons. When they were approved, the accountant general at the War Office from time to time made the requisite drafts, and the Treasury authorized the paymaster general of the forces to honor the drafts on the Bank of England, which provided the money.

The estimates followed a set format usually with the same headings. Those for 1879–80, for example—covering the period from 1 April 1879 to 31 March 1880, a period that included part of the Zulu War of 1879—were approved by the House of Commons and provided for 62,653 British troops to serve in India and to be charged against the Indian Treasury, plus 135,625 regulars to serve elsewhere. Also authorized were 26,218 horses, of which 10,830 were to serve in India.

The pounds sterling were broken down under six major headings:

1. Regular forces: pay and allowances   £4,944,200
2. Auxiliary and reserve forces   £1,258,500
3. Ordnance services (provisions, clothing, arms, stores)   £5,531,000
4. Works and buildings   £853,300
5. Various services (education, administration, etc.)   £432,900
6. Noneffective services   £2,625,800
   Total: £15,645,700

Army Hospital Corps. A unit of the British army formed in mid-century to care for the sick and wounded under the instruction of medical officers. The enlisted men, recruited from the army, acted as orderlies, cooks, and bakers or performed any other duty required of them. Because many of those recruited were too old or physically unfit, the corps was not a success.

Army in India. The British name for the forces of the Crown serving in India, including British regular army units and the Indian army [q.v.]. British troops serving elsewhere were responsible to the War Office, but those in India were the responsibility of the government of India, which paid, rationed, and equipped them. The commander-in-chief, India, was also the defense member of the viceroy's council from the term of Lord Kitchener [q.v.] onward.

Army List. A monthly publication of the British War Office which listed by regiment or corps the names and honors of all commissioned officers in the army and the Royal Marines. A larger, unofficial annual list, *Hart's Army List,* first published in 1840 for the year 1839, gave war services and additional information. The American equivalent of the official Army List was the Army Register [q.v.].

Army Medical Corps, Royal. See Medicine and Surgery, Military.

Army Mutual Aid Society. A mutual benefit society formed on 13 January 1879 by and for officers of the American army.

Army of Northern Virginia. See Northern Virginia, Army of.

Army of Observation. A military force designed to detect and intercept an approaching enemy force. If an army besieging a fort was large enough, it detached such a force to prevent a relieving force from approaching by surprise. If a neighboring country was a belligerent, an army of observation was usually posted to threatened points on the frontier to contain the belligerent's armies.

Army of Occupation. An army that remains in the territory of a defeated enemy to ensure that the terms of an armistice or peace treaty are complied with or reparations paid.

Army Organization. In the American, the British, and most European armies the smallest unit in an army was the squad (*escouade* in French, *escudra* in Spanish, *Korporalschaft* in German), or sometimes the section: from about five to a dozen men commanded by a noncommissioned officer. The next largest unit was the half company or platoon (*peloton* in French, *peletón* in Spanish, and *Zug* in German): two or more squads. But in the nineteenth century "platoon" was usually only a vague term for a small group of soldiers. An 1853 British military dictionary (Stocqueler) stated: "The word is obsolete except in the term 'manual and platoon exercise.'" The company, usually commanded by a captain, was the next largest unit and generally consisted of from 50 to 250 men; in the Union army during the American Civil War a full-strength company numbered 100 men. [See Fire Unit.]

Late in the century, in some armies, companies of artillery were called batteries, and companies of cavalry were called troops. The company was the smallest administrative unit. Two or more companies formed a battalion, but this was not always a unit within a regiment. In the Confederate army during the Civil War, for example, a battalion was always a separate unit, larger than a company but smaller than a regiment, commanded by a major or a lieutenant colonel. In the cavalry, units of battalion size were called squadrons or wings. [See Tactical Unit.]

A regiment (in the French army sometimes called a demibrigade) consisted of one or more battalions or several companies. In peacetime for most of the nineteenth century the British army contained a number of one-battalion regiments, all of which could be expanded by any number of battalions in time of war. The regiment was an administrative rather than a combat unit in the British service. A Union regiment of infantry at full strength in the American Civil War consisted of ten companies, each commanded by a captain, and one major, one lieutenant colonel, and one colonel commanding. A chaplain [q.v.] and one or more doctors were part of the colonel's staff. In peacetime the American army had no larger organizational unit than a regiment.

A brigade consisted of two or more regiments of infantry or two or more batteries of artillery, or it could include a mixed unit of all arms. A brigade might have artillery or cavalry attached and was commanded by a brigadier or a brigadier general (a major general in the German army). In the British army brigades were always ad hoc units commanded by a brigadier or a brigadier general [q.v.], whose rank was not always substantive. When a battalion of infantry was brigaded with (augmented by), even temporarily, a battery of artillery or any other additional unit, it became a brigade and the senior officer in the army (not necessarily in the regiment) assumed command. In Napoleon's army a brigade was commanded by a *maréchal de camp* or a *général de brigade*.

Two or more brigades of infantry plus cavalry, artillery, engineers, and other elements formed a division, which was usually commanded by a major general [q.v.] in the American and British armies but by a lieutenant general [q.v.] in German armies and a *général de division* in the French army. The division was usually the smallest unit containing all arms and services.

Two or more divisions formed an army corps [q.v.], and two or more corps made up an army, [q.v.] usually commanded by a full general [q.v.] or a field marshal [q.v.].

Army Register. A list of U.S. army officers on active duty and their services. In the British army this is called the Army List [q.v.].

Army Regulations. In the American army a printed work embodying all the acts of Congress and directives from the commander-in-chief for the management of the army in peace and in war.

Army Schools. In the U.S. many officers for the army were trained at the United States Military Academy at West Point, New York; in France, at St. Cyr or the Ecole Polytechnique [q.v.]; in Britain, infantry and cavalry were trained at the Royal Military College at Sandhurst [q.v.] in Berkshire, and artillery and engineers at the Royal Military Academy at Woolwich [q.v.], a metropolitan borough of London. For many years the Honourable East India Company maintained its own school, called a seminary, at Addiscombe [q.v.], near Croydon.

In the United States a number of individual states maintained military academies, among the most notable the Virginia Military Institute [q.v.] at Lexington, Virginia, and The Citadel [q.v.] in Charleston, South Carolina, both of which are still in existence.

The United States and many European countries maintained postgraduate schools for special training. In Britain the School of Musketry at Hythe, the School of Artillery at Shoebury, and the School of Instruction at Chatham for engineers were founded in the nineteenth century. The United States established an Artillery School in 1824. It was allowed to lapse briefly but was revived in 1867 as the Artillery School of Practice [q.v.]. The United States school of application for infantry and cavalry at Fort Leavenworth was begun in May 1881; in the 1860s the Corps of Engineers and the Signal Corps established schools of application; the schools for cavalry and light artillery were established at Fort Riley in 1893. The French established their cavalry school at Saumur [q.v.] and one for engineers and artillery at Metz [q.v.].

In Britain schools such as the Royal Hiberian Military School in Dublin and the Military Asylum [q.v.], which opened in 1803 at Chelsea, prepared boys for army commissions. The latter, known today as the Duke of York's School, is in Dover. Schools at posts, camps, and stations were established for soldiers' children toward the end of the century. Some British regiments hired their own schoolmasters.

Army Service Corps. In Britain, a branch of the Control Department, which supplied the army with clerks, mechanics, drivers, skilled workmen, etc. It was officered by the Supply and Transport subdepartment, whose ranks were commissary major, deputy commissary captain, and assistant commissary lieutenant. [See Intendance.]

Army Work Corps. In the Crimea during the Crimean War [q.v.] the British found they lacked the laborers needed to build roads, erect buildings, dig wells, and perform other manual labor. In response Sir Joseph Paxton (1801–1865), the designer of the Crystal Palace at the London Exhibition of 1851, raised a corps of workers for the government and sent them out in detachments until 3,500 men were engaged in all.

Arnaut. Albanian mercenary soldiers in the early-nineteenth-century Egyptian army of Mehmet Ali [q.v.]. They were noted for their greed and cruelty.

Arnaut *Two Arnauts, Albanian mercenary soldiers in the army of Mehmet Ali*

Arogee, Battle of (10 April 1868), Abyssinian Campaign. An Abyssinian army under King Theodore [q.v.] attacked a British force under Sir Robert Napier [q.v.] and was repulsed with heavy losses near this inland village in Abyssinia. The British suffered 30 wounded; the Abyssinians lost an estimated 700 killed and wounded.

Arrah Incident (July–August 1857), Indian Mutiny. Six British officials, who had sent their wives away to safety at the onset of the Indian Mutiny [q.v.], remained at their posts in Arrah (Shahabad), 35 miles west of Patna in Bihar Province. When the troops at Dinapur, 25 miles away, mutinied, the 6 retreated to a detached two-storied house, 50 feet square, which had been fortified and stocked with food, sherry, and brandy by Mr. Richard Vicar Boyle (1822–1908), a district engineer on the East Indian Railway. Here they were joined by a handful of other Europeans and several loyal Indians, including 50 Sikhs.

From Sunday, 26 July, to sunset on 2 August 1857, 16 Europeans and about 60 Indians successfully repelled all attacks from some 3,000 mutinous sepoys and armed insurgents led by a zemindar named Kur Singh (d.1858). A British relief force from Dinapur was disastrously repulsed. Rescue was finally effected after eight days' fighting by a small force, mostly 5th Fusiliers under an artillery officer, Major (later Sir) Vincent Eyre (1811–1881), who was recommended for, but did not receive, the Victoria Cross [q.v.].

The foresighted Mr. Boyle received no reward. Shortly after the siege he was seriously injured by a kick from a horse. He had scarcely recovered when he survived the shipwreck of a steamer on the Ganges. From 1872 to 1877 he was chief engineer for the Imperial Japanese Railways.

Array. The orderly arrangement or drawing up of an army in position of battle.

Arrears of Pay. A grievance voiced by soldiers in many, if not most, armies in the nineteenth century and earlier was the failure of the governments they served to pay their wages promptly. In the United States, acts of Congress of 16 March 1802 and 3 March 1813 clearly stated that American troops should never be more than two months in arrear of their pay unless circumstances made it unavoidable. Nevertheless, until the American Civil War it was the usual practice to pay troops only every two months, and frequently soldiers went without their pay for longer periods.

Arrest. In the British and American armies, privates in arrest were placed in confinement or under guard; noncommissioned officers [q.v.] were usually confined in their quarters; officers were confined to certain restricted areas, usually the limits of the garrison. In both armies an officer in arrest was not permitted to wear his sword. In an American (including Confederate) army on the march, field officers [q.v.] and staff officers [q.v.] in arrest marched in rear of their regiments; arrested company officers [q.v.] and noncommissioned officers marched in rear of their companies. It was considered indecorous for an officer in arrest to appear in public places.

Arrest *Arrest of a Blackfoot Indian on the western plains. Engraving by Frederic Remington*

Arriero. A term in use during and after the Mexican War [q.v.] of 1846–48 for a Mexican muleteer hired to handle army packtrains.

Arrowhead Bastion. A bastion with the orillons sharply cut back or recessed into the flanks, making the gorge narrow and giving the work an arrowhead appearance when viewed from overhead.

Arrows. 1. An arrow of a fortification was a defensive earthwork consisting of trench and parapet placed at a salient angle of a glacis and connected by a short passage to the covered way. [See Arrowhead Bastion.]

2. A missle, usually with a pointed tip of metal or stone fitted to a slender wooden shaft with a feathered end, dispatched by means of a bow. American troops in the American West and European troops fighting in Africa and Asia frequently contended with enemies fighting with bows and arrows. The arrows of American Indians in the West were usually 24 to 29 inches long, and their arrowheads (barbed if they were war arrows) were sometimes poisoned with rattlesnake venom or mixtures of crushed bees or crushed ants. Some Apaches mixed rattlesnake venom with the decomposed liver of a deer or antelope. The Pitt River Indians were said to mix the juice of wild parsnips with the decomposed liver of a dog.

Arrows *An Apache bow and quiver with arrows*

Arrow War. See Opium War, Second.

Arroyo dos Molinos, Battle of (28 October 1811), Peninsular War. Wellington sent General Rowland Hill [q.v.] with 10,000 Allied troops to attack French General Jean Baptiste Girard (1775–1815) with about 4,000 men at Arroyo dos Molinos in Estremadura, about 40 miles from the Spanish border. Thanks to a torrential storm, Hill was able to advance to within a half mile of the French before an alarm was raised. Girard tried desperately to break out on one road after another, but Hill had blocked all routes.

The British lost only 7 killed and 64 wounded; their Spanish allies, about 30. The French lost three guns and some 300 killed and wounded; 1,300 more were captured, including Prince Auguste Marie Raymond d'Arenberg, known as the Comte de la Marck (1753–1834) and General Guillaume Marie Anne Brune (1763–1815).

Arroyo Grande, Battle of (1842), Uruguayan Revolution. Uruguayans under the leader of the Colorado (Red) Party were totally defeated by Argentine troops under Uruguayan General Manuel Oribe (1796?–1857), who then laid siege to Montevideo [q.v.].

Arsenal or Armory. Strictly speaking, an arsenal is a place in which ordnance is manufactured or repaired and an armory (British: armoury) is a place in which ordnance is stored, but these two words have so often been used interchangeably that it is impossible to be sure which sense is intended. The word "depot" is also sometimes used to indicate a place in which arms are manufactured, repaired, or stored.

The principal arsenal and armory for the British army was located at Woolwich [q.v.]. In 1859 it employed 10,000 men and was stocked with 12,000 pieces of ordnance, of which some 700 were modern and of large caliber.

The first arsenals in the United States were established at Carlisle, Pennsylvania, and Springfield, Massachusetts [see Springfield Armory]. By 1847 there were seventeen arsenals and two armories; in 1860 the number was enlarged to twenty-three arsenals and armories, most in the North, and nine of the arsenals were quickly enlarged at the beginning of the Civil War.

In 1841 Henry Wadsworth Longfellow (1807–1872) wrote "The Arsenal at Springfield," probably the only poem ever written on such a subject. It begins:

> This is the Arsenal. From floor to ceiling
> Like a huge organ, rise the burnished arms;
> But from their pipes no anthem pealing
> Startles the village with strange alarms.

Arsenal *Photograph of the Chinese arsenal in Nanking*

Articles of War. On 3 April 1689 the British Parliament passed the first Mutiny Act [q.v.], which placed checks upon the powers of the sovereign over the army and provided for its management and regulation. The act listed military offenses and provided for courts-martial. The first Mutiny Act was effective only for six months, but it was renewed and, except for one three-year period (10 April 1698 to 20 February 1701) has been renewed, with alterations and amendments, every year.

The United States adopted a similar plan under a code of 1775, and later, under the Constitution, the Congress was made responsible for establishing rules and regulations for the army. In framing the original American Articles of War, published on 10 April 1806 and enlarged on 20 September of the following year, Congress used the Mutiny Act as a model. The 101 articles in the Articles of War established the legal code and trial procedures of the army and were, with little change, in force throughout most of the nineteenth century. One provision gave the president sole authority to institute courts of inquiry or to commute a sentence of death awarded by a court-martial; others reduced the maximum number of lashes that could be given as punishment from 100 to 50 and extended the previous prohibition against "traitorous or disrespectful words against the President" to a wide range of government officials.

Artificers. 1. Skilled workmen, soldiers, or civilians, including armorers, carpenters, blacksmiths, wheelwrights, harness makers.

2. Artillery artificers prepared ammunition, fuzes, and pyrotechnics and built and repaired gun carriages. Regimental and company artificers were handymen who maintained and sometimes built quarters, equipment, and vehicles.

Artificers seem never to have enjoyed a good name. Shakespeare (in 1596) spoke of "Another lean unwash'd artificer" (*King John*, iv, 2), and in 1797 Admiral Lord St. Vincent (1735–1823) in a letter to the first lord of the admiralty wrote: "All the artificers are thieves."

Artigas, José Gervasio (1774–1850). A Uruguayan soldier who was a captain in a Spanish national police force charged with protecting the western marches of Uruguay (then called Banda Oriental). In 1811 he led gauchos in an unsuccessful revolt against Spanish rule. He captured Montevideo from the Argentines in 1815 and lost it to the Portuguese at Tacuarembó in northern Uruguay in 1820. He then fled to Paraguay.

Artillery. 1. Crew-served mounted firearms of large caliber—i.e., too large to be hand-held.

2. That branch of a nineteenth-century army in which artillery was the primary weapon. One of the arms of the service [q.v.]. St. Barbara was its patron. On 22 May 1809 Napoleon said: "It is with artillery that war is made."

There were four main areas of improvement in artillery in the nineteenth century: breech loading, rifling, interior ballistics, and, in the last years of the century, recoil mechanisms. All these, except rifling, were perfected after the American Civil War, which ended in 1865. By the end of the century the old smoothbore muzzle-loading guns, howitzers, or mortars had given way to rifled breechloaders; artillery had increased in caliber and dramatically in range and rapidity of fire. The first rifled breechloader was manufactured in Italy in 1846. However, not until the general introduction of breechloaders could spiral rifling be used to best advantage and projectiles not be thrown off by the effect of windage.

Most improvements of fuzes and projectiles also occurred in the last half of the century although its early years were marked by such major steps as the invention of case shot or shrapnel [q.v.] by Lieutenant (later General) Henry Shrapnel [q.v.] and the development of the friction tube.

Smokeless powder, developed for both small arms and artillery at the end of the century, entirely changed the appearance of the battlefield and made locating the enemy's batteries more difficult.

All muzzleloaders were fired in the same way. First a bag of powder and then the projectile were inserted from the muzzle to the breech; a steel pick was then thrust through the vent (touchhole) to pierce the powder bag in the barrel; a priming tube of fine-grain powder and strands of "quick match" was inserted; the crew stood clear while a lighted portfire, lit by a slow match of a linstock in the rear of the gun, was applied to the primer, firing the gun.

Until almost the end of the century artillery tubes had to be relaid after each shot because the recoil threw the gun carriage back and out of line. The problem was largely solved, first by a series of springs and then by hydropneumatic devices. Quick-firing (QF) rifled guns, often called simply, but sometimes confusingly, rifles, were in use by all major armies by the end of the century. [See French 75.]

About 1810 Friedrich Krupp (1787–1826), a Prussian ironmaster, founded the Krupp Works [q.v.] at Essen. He was succeeded by his son Alfred (1812–1887), who about 1847 began to manufacture ordnance and developed a process for making cast steel [see Krupp Gustahlfabrik]. In 1861 his design for a breech-loading rifle was accepted by the Prussian army. At his death, control of his steel and munitions empire passed to his daughter, Bertha, for whom the Big Bertha of the First World War was named.

In France Henri Joseph Paixhans (1783–1854), a French artillery officer, invented one of the earliest guns for throwing explosive shells, and Napoleon III (1803–1873), who was deeply interested in artillery, helped develop the 12-pounder Napoleon howitzer [q.v.], which became the gun most widely used in the American Civil War.

In the United States Robert Parker Parrott [q.v.], a West Point graduate (1824) who resigned after twelve years in the army to establish a foundry, invented and patented in 1861 a rifled cannon using a expanding projectile, and he developed a method of strengthening cast-iron guns by shrinking wrought-iron hoops on the breech. Parrott guns [q.v.] were used by both Union and Confederate armies in the American Civil War. Thomas Jackson Rodman (1815–1871), another West Pointer, class of 1841, invented the Rodman gun [q.v.], made by casting successive layers of metal around a hollow core. John Adolphus Bernard Dahlgren (1809–1870), an American naval officer, developed the Dahlgren gun [q.v.] and a percussion lock.

In Britain Sir George Armstrong [q.v.] made numerous advances in the design of guns, fuzes, and projectiles. Sir Joseph Whitworth [q.v.], a mechanical engineer and inventor, discovered a new way to make ductile steel for guns and secured the standardization of screw threads (Whitworth threads).

In 1812 a British officer, William Congreve [q.v.], invented

Artillery *Gatling on full field carriage*

the Congreve rocket. It was adopted by the British army although its maximum range was only about 1,500 yards and it never achieved a high degree of accuracy. Its erratic behavior, noise, and glare generated panic when it was first used against the French in the Battle of Leipzig [q.v.] in October 1813. Employed in the British attack upon Baltimore in the War of 1812, it provided the "rocket's red glare" commemorated in the American national anthem. It was most effective when used against primitive peoples in Asia and Africa, but it also proved effective against American militia at the Battle of Bladensburg [q.v.]. It remained in use in the British service at least as late as 1860.

Hiram Stevens Maxim [q.v.], an American who emigrated to England, where he became a naturalized subject, was the inventor of a machine gun [q.v.] and in 1884 organized the Maxim Gun Company, which subsequently merged with the Nordenfeldt Company (1888) and was then absorbed into Vickers' Sons and Maxim (1893). A perceived problem was whether machine guns should be treated as infantry weapons or as artillery. Because their weight required a carriage and their efficient operation required a crew, they were usually considered, until the twentieth century, artillery pieces rather than infantry support weapons. However, in the nineteenth century indirect fire was almost unknown,

Artillery *An 18-pounder gun of the Royal Artillery*

and field artillery was usually pushed ahead of the infantry or cavalry.

At the end of the eighteenth century a French artillerist, Jean Baptiste Vacate Gribeauval (1715–1789), reformed French artillery. Building on his system, Napoleon developed French artillery into the best in the world. The length and weight of both the gun tube and the carriage were reduced for easier transport, and great strides were made in producing better ammunition: balls more truly spherical and more precisely sized and prefabricated cartridges, which eliminated loose powder and separate shot.

More efficient gun drill produced a more rapid rate of fire. In 1791 Napoleon formed batteries of horse artillery capable of accompanying cavalry, and in 1800 he established a driver corps of soldiers, ending the system of contracting with civilians for horses to move the artillery. (Britain formed horse artillery in 1793 and a driver corps in 1794.) There were improvements too in the harnesses, wagons, limbers, and caissons [qq.v.] used to bring ammunition, guns, and their gear into action.

For forts and coastal defenses the innovation of the century was the disappearing gun [q.v.], which could fire over a parapet [q.v.] and then disappear behind it, a weapon developed and most deployed in the United States.

The proper use and organization of artillery were subjects much discussed. In nearly all major armies most batteries were organized into "companies" of six to eight guns each, some of the reserve companies containing four guns and two howitzers. A battery of field or horse artillery usually consisted of four to six guns. When on a war footing, it included a battery wagon, a traveling forge, 112 horses, and for each gun a caisson and limber with 400 rounds of ammunition. Siege batteries usually had two or four guns and carried about 250 rounds per gun.

Experts could not agree on the proportion of guns to infantry. During the Peninsular War [q.v.] Wellington seldom had more than 1 gun per 1,000 infantry, but by the time he entered France he had 3 per 1,000. Napoleon preferred 2 guns per 1,000 infantry, each gun provided with more ammunition than was previously thought desirable. Many European powers followed his example. The British army believed that an army of 60,000 (50,000 infantry, 7,500 cavalry, and 2,500 artillerymen) ought to have 16 guns in reserve.

Napoleon, who began his military career as an artilleryman, always took a keen interest in this arm. His guns came to be affectionately known as the "Emperor's beautiful daughters." Increasingly he favored firing by massed batteries. The artillery of his Grande Armée provides a fair sample of the kinds of guns used by most armies in the field in the first half of the nineteenth century. A favorite was the 12-pounder, a 122 mm gun that could be fired at the rate of a round a minute with an effective range of 550 meters when firing canister, 900 meters when firing ball, and a maximum range with ball of about 1,800 meters. Each had a full crew of 15, of whom 8 were specialists.

Guns were usually classified by the weight of their projectile; howitzers, by the width of their barrel's bore. Muzzle-loaders fired round shot, merely a solid metal ball; canister, metal containers packed with musket balls, or grapeshot with musket balls in bags. Both the latter were antipersonnel devices in which nails, glass, stones, etc. could be substituted for musket balls. Good gunners could use fuzed shells

timed to explode in the air, but these required more art than science.

An 8-pounder with a caliber of 100 mm and a crew of 13 could fire twice as rapidly as the 12-pounders. Its maximum range was 1,500 meters, but its effective range, firing ball, was about 800 meters; firing canister, 450 meters.

For a brief five-year period (1804–09) a 6-pounder was popular. Firing canister, it had an effective range of about 450 meters and about 800 meters firing ball with a maximum range of 1,300 meters.

An 84 mm 4-pounder with a barrel 5 meters long could fire two or three rounds per minute. Although it had a maximum range of 1,200 meters, its effective range was 700 meters with ball and 400 meters with canister. It was for a time an integral part of a French infantry regiment.

A 6-inch howitzer with a caliber of 166 mm had a short barrel (2 feet, 4 inches) and a maximum range from 700 to 1,200 meters, depending upon the charge and fuze setting. Firing canister, it was effective only for 250 meters, but it could be devastating. Its rate of fire was about one round per minute.

Using ricochet fire, a gun (but not a howitzer) could increase its range by as much as 75 percent.

During the Napoleonic Wars [q.v.] the British army relied heavily on 6- and 9-pounder guns and a 5.5-inch howitzer. The Russian army relied upon its numerous 6- and 12-pounder guns and its 20-pounder, 10-pounder, and 3-pounder long-barreled howitzers known as unicorns.

[See Cannon; Howitzer; Mortars; Siege Guns; Gatling; Shot; Grapeshot; Canister; Columbiad; Shrapnel; Corps of Artillerists and Engineers.]

Artillery, Foot. Artillery pulled by horses or mules with the cannoneers on foot.

Artillery, Horse. Artillery units in which all the artillerymen rode, either on horseback or on the caissons and limbers. Horse artillery was intended to keep up with and operate in conjunction with cavalry.

Artillery, Foot *Mountain artillery carriage*

Artillery, Royal Regiment of. All the artillery in the British army was (and still is) considered part of a single regiment.

Artillery, Siege. Heavy guns, usually mortars or howitzers [qq.v.] of large caliber, used for destroying walls and thick defenses as required for sieges.

Artillery Boat. A boat carrying artillery; a gunboat.

Artillery Company. A military unit consisting of a battery of artillery.

Artillery Horses. The most desired artillery horses were between five and eight years of age, weighed between 900 and 1,200 pounds, and were well broken to harness. The load allotted to them was normally lighter than those used for commerce because allowance had to be made for bad roads, forage that was not always satisfactory, and the forced marches to which they were sometimes subjected. An average march for artillery horses on good roads was 15 to 20 miles per day, usually at a walk. The care of horses on the march was one of the most important duties of an artillery officer.

Artilleryman. 1. A cannoneer [q.v.].
2. A member of an artillery unit, or one whose assigned branch is artillery.

Artillery Park. 1. The totals of the guns, ammunition, wagons, etc. needed for siege or field artillery.
2. A place where artillery was camped or, during a siege, collected.
3. The reserve artillery.

Artillery School of Practice. A gunnery school, the first American service school of its kind, was established by the army in 1824 at Fort Monroe on Old Point Comfort, Virginia, as the United States Artillery School. Its purpose, according to Major General Jacob Brown [q.v.], was "to guard against the approaches of sloth and imbecility." It was allowed to lapse for a time during the American Civil War, but in 1867 it was revived as the Artillery School of Practice by William Farquhar Barry [q.v.], who had been chief of artillery for William Tecumseh Sherman [q.v.]. Barry was the school's commandant for ten years.

Artillery Supports. Troops, usually infantry, deployed to provide close protection for artillery from the fire of sharpshooters, infiltrators, cavalry raids, etc.

Artillery Train. A number of guns or other pieces of ordnance of an army or military expedition mounted on carriages and ready or capable of marching.

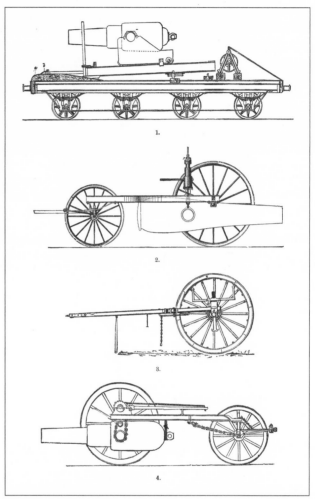

Artillery Train *Carriages: (1) iron-clad train; (2) American sling wagon; (3) improvised sling cart; (4) English iron sling cart*

Artillery, Siege *Germans pictured in Paris with heavy artillery during the siege of Paris*

Arya Samaj. A militant Hindu organization founded by Swami Dayananda (1824–1883) in 1874 to defend Hinduism against Western influences and create a Hindu state. The organization was the source of much conflict between Muslims and Hindus in the 1890s.

Asapes. Turkish peasant soldiers used as pioneers. In the Crimean War [q.v.] they were used for digging entrenchments.

Ashanti Army. During the second half of the seventeenth century various Akan-speaking peoples in West Africa organized themselves under a single sovereign, Osei Tutu (d. 1712), into the Ashanti (Asante) kingdom, whose economy was supported by the slave trade. The kingdom was basically a military union. All males were liable for service in its army, and attempts to avoid service were punishable by death. In the field the army was a well-orga-

Ashanti Army *An Ashanti warrior with a Danish musket called Long Dane*

nized force composed of scouts, advanced guards, a main body, two wings, the king's bodyguard, a rear guard, and a medical corps responsible for removing the dead and caring for the wounded. [See other Ashanti entries.] So successful were the Ashantis that by the end of the eighteenth century they occupied a territory larger than present-day Ghana.

Ashanti / Asante Civil War. Followed the Second Ashanti War [q.v.] of 1873–74. After King Kofi Karikari (called King Coffee by British soldiers) was deposed by the British, a devastating civil war broke out among the factions contending for the throne. It ended on 26 March 1888, when Agyeman Prempeh (1871?–1931) proclaimed himself ruler and took the name of Kwaka Dua III.

Ashanti-Fanti Wars (1807–20). The Fanti, or Fantes, a people occupying the coastal area of the Gold Coast (roughly present-day Ghana) refused the inland Ashantis, a militant nation, access to the coast and a direct market for their slave trade. At the same time they harbored fugitives from Ashantiland, refused to sell the Ashantis guns, powder, or lead, and otherwise provoked them. In 1807 the Ashantis launched an invasion. Under King Osei (or Osai) Tutu Kwadwo, who ruled from 1801 to 1824, they forcefully brought the Fanti and other more peaceful coastal tribes on the Gold Coast under their suzerainty. The Danish governor of the Gold Coast at the time wrote: "[T]he Assiabthees [*sic*], with sword and fire murder and destroy everything they meet with . . . many thousands of people not shot in battle, were murdered in cold blood." The Ashantis, having plundered the Fanti, withdrew.

There were further successful incursions in 1811, 1816, and 1820, and the Ashantis became indisputably the greatest power in West Africa.

Ashanti War, First (1824–31). In December 1823 the Ashantis, incensed by the British protection extended to

peaceful coastal tribes, particularly the Fantis, launched a series of attacks upon their territories. On 10 January 1824 Sir Charles M'Carthy (1770?–1824), the governor of Sierra Leone and a soldier dedicated to "the cause of Christianity and civilization in Africa," moved out against them with a small force of Africans, colonial militia, and volunteers. Eleven days later at Essamako [q.v.], near the village of Bonsaso, he encountered about 10,000 Ashantis. M'Carthy ordered the band of the Royal African Corps to strike up "God Save the King" [q.v.]. The Ashantis replied with music of their own and fell upon the British force, quickly routing it. Severely wounded, M'Carthy was seized by the Ashantis as he tried to order a retreat. He was later beheaded. His skull, appropriated, was used as a royal drinking cup.

Not until July 1824, after a battle on the open plain at Akatamanso, were the British able to drive the Ashantis back to Coomassie (Kumasi), their capital. Two years later they again invaded the coastal area, but on 7 August 1826 they were crushed by the British at Dodowah [q.v.], near Accra (Akkra). In 1831 the Ashantis gave up their suzerainty over the coastal tribes and agreed on the Prah River as the boundary between Ashantiland and British territory.

Ashanti War, Second (1873–74). After a decade of Ashanti raids upon the Gold Coast coastal tribes under British protection, the British mounted a major expedition and invaded Ashantiland with a force of 2,500 British regulars assisted by some African auxiliaries led by Major General Sir Garnet (later Field Marshal Lord) Wolseley, who issued advice to his troops before they set off: "It must never be forgotten by our soldiers that Providence has planted in the heart of every native of Africa a superstitious dread and awe of the white man, that prevents the negro from daring to meet us face to face in combat."

Both armies suffered from diseases. Smallpox weakened the Ashantis, and the British suffered greatly from a number of tropical disorders. However, the campaign went forward. In a general order Wolseley adjured his regulars: "Soldiers and

Ashanti War, Second *Ashantis wait in ambush for approaching British troops during the 1873–74 Ashanti War on the Gold Coast.*

sailors, remember that the black man holds you in superstitious awe; fire low; fire slow, and charge home; the more numerous your enemy, the greater will be the loss inflicted on him, and the greater your honour in defeating him." In the short, brisk campaign Wolseley defeated the Ashantis, razed Coomassie (Kumasi), their capital, and deposed their king (asantehene), Kofi Karikari. So efficiently had he conducted the campaign that the expression "All Sir Garnet," meaning anything perfectly arranged, came into common use. He had waged the war brilliantly, but near the end of his life he described it as "the most horrible war I ever took part in."

Ashanti War, Third (1895–96). Under a new ruler, Agyeman Prempeh (1871?–1931), the Ashantis renewed their depredations. [See Ashanti Civil Wars; Ashanti-Fanti Wars; Ashanti wars, First, Second.] On 27 December 1895 a British punitive expedition of about 2,500 men left Cape Coast Castle under the command of Colonel Sir Francis Scott. Major Robert Baden-Powell [q.v.], later to gain fame at the siege of Mafeking [q.v.] and to found the Boy Scout movement, was a member of the expedition.

Without opposition, the British entered Coomassie (Kumasi), the Ashanti capital, on 17 or 18 January 1896, and on the 20th Prempeh was forced to make a humiliating public submission. He was then exiled with other tribal chiefs. Although many of the European troops succumbed to malaria and other tropical diseases in the campaign, only one shot was fired in anger: An enraged British private shot his sergeant in the shoulder, a deed for which he was sent to prison for seven years.

This expedition was said to be the last time British troops campaigned in red tunics.

Ashanti War, Fourth (1900). On 13 March 1900 Sir Frederick Hodgson (1851–1925?), governor of the Gold Coast, set out from Accra (Akkra) with his wife and a large entourage to pay a state visit to Coomassie (Kumasi), capital of the Ashantis. On his arrival several days later he assembled the Ashanti tribal leaders and demanded that they give up their golden stool, adding, that he wished to use it as his ceremonial seat. The spirit of the Ashanti nation was embedded in, or symbolized by, this stool, a wooden one partly covered in gold, which the British erroneously assumed to be the king's throne. Under the terms of submission following the Third Ashanti War [q.v.] the "Golden Stool of the Ashantis" was to have been surrendered to the British. Instead, it had been hidden. Following Hodgson's demands, a search, conducted by British-led Hausa soldiers, was made without success. The demand and the search so inflamed Ashanti passions that Hodgson, a handful of Europeans, including 4 women, and the small British force at Coomassie were besieged in an improvised fort by an estimated 40,000 enraged Africans. In May the garrison was reinforced to number about 700 men, 16 of whom were Europeans, but their position remained perilous.

On 23 June Hodgson sallied out with a force of some 600 Hausas, carrying the noncombatants with him. Three Englishmen and 100 Hausas with rations for three weeks remained behind to man the fort. Maxim machine guns kept the Ashantis at bay. Although he suffered 100 casualties, Hodgson succeeded in reaching the coast on 10 July.

The plight of Hodgson and his people in Coomassie had been known to those on the coast, but because it was the height of the rainy season, local carriers were scarce and no local food was available. It was not until 2 July that a relief force had set out. Made up of Hausas and Yoruba troops, it was commanded by Colonel (later General Sir) James Willcocks (1857–1926), a veteran of the Second Afghan War [q.v.] and of campaigns on the Northwest Frontier [q.v.] who was now colonel-commandant of the West African Frontier Force. After surmounting appalling difficulties and fighting two sharp battles on the fourteenth and fifteenth the expedition reached Coomassie and, on the evening of the fifteenth, relieved the beleaguered little garrison.

The Gold Coast Constabulary and the West African Frontier Force, all armed with machine guns, came to the rescue, and the Ashantis and their allies were decisively defeated by Willcocks at Aboasu (Obassa) [q.v.] on 30 September.

Ashanti War, Fourth *The British evacuate their garrison at Coomassie (Kumasi), taking their wounded and war dead with them.*

Ashby, Turner (1828–1862). An American soldier born into a wealthy Fauquier County, Virginia, family who was a planter and businessman before the American Civil War. A superb horseman, he raised a volunteer cavalry troop for the Confederacy at the outbreak of the war and rose quickly from captain to colonel of the 7th Virginia Cavalry. Although General "Stonewall" Jackson maintained that he gave too little thought to discipline and drill, Ashby performed brilliantly for him during the Valley Campaign [q.v.] and was, over Jackson's objections, promoted brigadier general on 23 May 1862. Less than two weeks later, on 6 June, he was killed in a skirmish near Harrisonburg.

Ash Hollow or Blue Water, Battle of (3 September 1855), American Indian Wars. General William Selby Harney [q.v.] left Fort Leavenworth on 5 August 1855 with two companies of dragoons, six companies of infantry and a company of artillery, about 1,200 men, to retaliate for the massacre of a detachment of Company G, 6th Infantry on 19 August 1854 near Fort Laramie. On 3 September the expedition encountered about 200 Brulé Sioux under Little Thunder (d. 1879) at Ash Hollow, Nebraska, west of Fort Kearny, and killed 85; 70 women and children were taken captive. Little Thunder escaped.

Ashti / Ashtee / Ashta, Battle of (18 February 1818), Third Maratha War. An engagement fought on the banks of the upper Parbati River, 45 miles west-southwest of Bhopal, in which a British force under General Lionel Smith (1778–1842) defeated a force of 10,000 Maratha cavalry. Their commander, Baji Rao II (d. 1852), the seventh and last peshwa (ruler), who reigned from 1795 to 1818, fled the field before the action began. General Smith was severely wounded.

Asirghar / Asseerghur, Captures of (1803 and 1819), Maratha Wars. This strategic hill fortress at Burhanpur, on the Tapi River, 185 miles west of Nagpur, was twice captured by the British: first during the Second Maratha War in 1803 and again in the Third Maratha War in 1819 [qq.v.].

On 18 March 1819 Jaswunt Rao Holkar, ruler of Indore from 1797 to 1811, held the fort when he was besieged by the British under General Sir John Malcolm (1769–1833). Three days later the garrison was forced back into the upper fort, where it was bombarded until 7 April, when Jaswunt Rao Holkar surrendered. British losses were 313 killed and wounded; the Maratha garrison suffered somewhat less.

Askari. An African soldier, particularly in East Africa.

Askultsik, Battle of (August 1828), Russo-Turkish War of 1828. Near this town some 17,000 Russians under General Ivan Paskievich [q.v.] defeated 30,000 Turks, capturing all their baggage and artillery. Paskievich then laid siege to the town, defended by a garrison of 50,000, and after three weeks carried it by storm.

Aspern-Essling, Battle of (21–22 May 1809), Napoleonic Wars. In response to Napoleon's occupation of Vienna on 13 May 1809, 95,000 Austrians with 264 guns under Archduke Charles Louis [q.v.] of Austria concentrated near Vienna, on the north bank of the Danube. Napoleon threw up a bridge from Kaiser-Ebersdorf, a village six miles east of Vienna, and, in spite of difficulties from rising water, crossed with 23,000 troops and 60 guns to the island of Löbau (Löbo), six miles long and four and a half miles wide. From there he attempted to establish footholds on the north bank of the Danube at Aspern and Essling, two villages about five miles east-northeast of Vienna. He encountered fierce resistance. The villages were taken and retaken ten times. On the night of 22–23 May, despite reinforcement to a strength of 48,000 infantry, 7,000 cavalry, and 144 guns, he ordered a withdrawal to Löbau Island.

This was Napoleon's first defeat. His reconnaissance had been poor, he had not realized the nature of the Danube in flood, and he had seriously underestimated the ferocity of his opponents. Austrian losses were 23,300 out of perhaps 80,000; French losses were more than 21,000. Marshal Jean Lannes [q.v.] was killed.

The withdrawal completed, Napoleon ordered the construction of defensive works on the island (some of which are still extant) and for seven weeks did not again try to cross the Danube.

Aspromonte, Battle of (29 August 1862), Italian Wars of Independence. When the unification of Italy under King Victor Emmanuel II (1820–1878) was proclaimed on 17 March 1861, Pope Pius IX (Giovanni Maria Mastai-Ferretti, 1792–1878), who ruled Rome, refused to allow the city to be annexed. France backed his refusal and supported him with troops. This spurred Giuseppe Garibaldi [q.v.] to emerge from retirement and with 1,000 Red Shirts [q.v.], mostly Sicilians, he marched on Rome. Fearful of French intervention, King Victor Emmanuel II sent a force to stop him. On 29 August 1862, at this mountain ridge of the southern Apennines in Reggio Calabria, east of the Strait of Messina and Reggio, Italian regulars under Giorgio Guido Pallavicino-Trivulzio (1798–1878) defeated Garibaldi's Red Shirts in a small battle, scarcely more than a skirmish. Garibaldi himself was wounded, captured, and imprisoned in the Fortress of Varignano. He was released five weeks later.

Assail, to. 1. To attempt to break down a defended position or an enemy force by repeated onslaughts or bombardments.
2. To attack violently.

Assake, Battle of (30 January 1876), Russian conquest of Central Asia. Russian forces under Konstantin Kaufmann [q.v.] defeated rebellious Turkic inhabitants of Khokand [q.v.], a khanate in central Asia, located about 10 miles southwest of Andizhan [q.v.]. Assake was later called Zelensk and still later Leninsk. [See Khokand, Russian Conquest of.]

Assam, Attacks on (1824), Burmese-Assamese conflict. When the Burmese captured Assam, Assamese refugees fled to Manipur, then a British protectorate, and some established bases, which they used to attack the Burmese, as had the Arakanese in 1811–15 [see Arakan Uprising]. Burmese protests to the British were ignored [see First Anglo-Burmese War].

Assault. 1. A short, fast attack against a defended position such as a fort or gun emplacement.
2. The culminating phase of an attack, sometimes leading to hand-to-hand combat [q.v.].

In 1812 Karl von Clausewitz [q.v.] wrote: "On no account should we overlook the moral effect of a rapid, running assault. It hardens the advancing soldier against danger, while the stationary soldier loses his presence of mind" (*On War*).

Assault Bridge. See Pontoon Bridge.

Assault Position. The area occupied by troops between the line of departure [q.v.] and their objective. This is usually the last position offering concealment or protective cover.

Assaye, Battle of (23 September 1803), Second Maratha War. An engagement in the Deccan Campaign of Sir Arthur Wellesley (later Duke of Wellington) and one of the most remarkable victories of the nineteenth century. Moving against Doulet Rao Sindhia (d. 1827) of Gwalior, and Rughuji, ruler of Berar, the British found an unprotected ford over the swollen Kelna (or Kaitna) River, between the villages of Assaye and Bokerdum in northwest Hyderabad, south-central India, 45 miles northwest of Aurangabad. Crossing the river with about 13,500 British and Indian troops and 22 guns, mostly of small caliber, Wellesley attacked the combined Maratha forces, estimated at 50,000, including 20,000 renowned cavalry, and 98 guns. Repulsing strong cavalry attacks on both flanks, he launched an oblique attack upon the

Maratha's left flank and after fierce fighting routed the Maratha infantry, which left 1,200 dead, 4,800 wounded, and all its guns on the field. Wellesley's 5,000 native cavalry did not arrive on the field in time to take part in the action, but the British 19th Light Dragoons performed good service.

Wellesley's losses were heavy, 1,584 killed and wounded, of whom 650 were Europeans. At the end of his long military career he still considered this his bloodiest engagement for the numbers engaged.

Assaye Regiment. The name given to the 74th Highlanders (later Highland Light Infantry), which in the Battle of Assaye [q.v.] on 23 September 1803 lost all its 17 officers killed or wounded but continued to fight. The regiment was brought out of action by a sergeant major. Of the 550 other ranks, 384 were killed or wounded.

Assegai / Assagai. Originally any South African native spear, usually thrown. It was Shaka [q.v.], the great Zulu king who developed it into a short stabbing spear about three and one-half feet long with a broad leaf blade, turning it into a close combat weapon.

Assembly. A bugle call or drumbeat calling troops to assemble.

Assembly Area. The area in which a unit comes together for further action or to receive orders.

Assessment of Damages. In the British army a committee of officers met once a month to determine the damage soldiers had done to their barracks and the amounts to be deducted from the pay of those responsible.

Assistant. In the British army, assistant was the third grade of staff officer, after deputy quartermaster or deputy adjutant general. In the American army, assistant was the second grade in a staff position.

Association of Graduates of the Military Academy. An American association of West Point graduates organized in 1869 to "cherish the members of our Alma Mater and to promote the social intercourse and fraternal fellowship of its Graduates." Its president is always the oldest graduate; the association's other officers are appointed by him. In April 1884 it had 531 members and its president was a graduate of the class of 1818. Still extant, it annually publishes a *Register of Graduates*.

Asylum, Royal Military. An institution in Chelsea, Middlesex, England, for the education of sons of soldiers of the British regular army. The first stone was laid by the Duke of York [q.v.] on 19 June 1800. Preference was given first to orphans, next to those whose fathers had been killed or died in foreign service, and then to those who had lost their mothers and whose fathers were serving abroad. A similar institution for the maintenance and education of daughters was established at Southampton.

Ataman. A Cossack leader, sometimes called a hetman.

Atbara, Battle of (8 April 1898), reconquest of the Sudan.

An Anglo-Egyptian army of 15,000 men under General Horatio Herbert (later first Earl) Kitchener [q.v.] invaded the Sudan. Moving cautiously up the Nile, Kitchener captured Dongola [q.v.] on 21 September 1896 and Abu Hamed [q.v.] on 7 August 1897. On 8 April 1898 he attacked and defeated a Dervish [q.v.] force of 12,000 infantry, 4,000 cavalry, and 10 guns under Muhammad Ahmed, a Dervish amir, encamped behind a zeriba near the confluence of the Atbara River and the Nile. The Battle of the Atbara was the bloodiest fight in what Winston Churchill [q.v.] called the River War. The Anglo-Egyptian army lost 560 killed and wounded; the Mahdist forces suffered an estimated 6,000 killed, wounded, or captured; the remainder fled. Muhammad Ahmed himself was captured. About 4,000, including Osman Digna [q.v.] and most of the cavalry, escaped.

Atbara *Muhammad Ahmed, a Mahdist amir, under Sudanese guard after the Battle of Atbara*

Atchoupa, Battle of (20 April 1890), French-Dahomey War. French forces routed those of the fon of Dahomey (Benin) near this village in the hinterland of Porto Novo in the last battle of the war.

Atholl Grey. The shade of gray of the greatcoats and capes worn by British officers in the Foot Guards.

Atiradores. Marksmen in the Portuguese army.

À Titre Étranger. A foreigner in the French army. If an officer, he ranked below officers of equal grade who were *à titre français*. [See *Français de Fraîche Date*.]

Atlanta, Battle of (22 July 1864), American Civil War. Also known as Hood's Second Sortie. After his failure at Peach Tree Creek [q.v.] on 20 July 1864, General John Bell Hood [q.v.], commanding the Confederate Army of Tennessee [q.v.], fell back upon the defenses of Atlanta, Georgia, one of the few remaining Confederate manufacturing centers, containing mills, machine shops, and foundries. From here Hood directed General William Joseph Hardee [q.v.], commanding a corps in the Army of Tennessee, to attack the Federals under William Tecumseh Sherman [q.v.] who were attempting to invest the city. Hardee's attack was delayed. He was unable, as Hood had hoped, to get behind the Union forces, but he struck the left flank of Federal General James Birdseye McPherson [q.v.]. Although the surprise was complete and McPherson himself was killed, the Confederates were repulsed with a loss of some 8,500 men out of about 32,000 engaged. Federal casualties were 3,722 out of 30,477 engaged. Hardee accurately considered this battle "one of the most desperate and bloody of the war."

Sherman lacked the men necessary to invest Atlanta completely, so on 27 July he swung his forces westward to attack the railroads and sent much of his cavalry south to raid Confederate lines of communication. On 28 July at Ezra Church [q.v.], Georgia, Hood again atacked and was again repulsed with a loss of 4,300; Union casualties were 632. Hood then abandoned Atlanta after destroying supplies [see Atlanta Campaign].

Atlanta Campaign (1 May–8 September 1864), American Civil War. Union General William T. Sherman [q.v.] with approximately 110,000 men organized into seven infantry and one cavalry corps, was ordered by General U. S. Grant "to move against [Joseph E.] Johnston's army, to break it up, and to get into the interior of the enemy's country as far as you can, inflicting all the damage you can against their war resources. . . ." Sherman began his advance on 7 May 1864, moving toward Atlanta, Georgia, a vital commercial, industrial, and communications center of the Confederacy that was of both strategic and emotional importance. To forestall him, Johnston [q.v.] interposed his Confederate Army of Tennessee [q.v.], 60,000 infantry and 2,000 cavalry, but in three battles—at Dalton on 9 May, Resaca on 15 May [qq.v.], and Cassville on 19 May—Sherman outmaneuvered him, each time by holding the center and making a wide flanking movement around his own right.

When Sherman bypassed Johnston's position at Allatoona Pass on 24 May, Johnston positioned his army directly in his path. After small, indecisive battles at Dallas and New Hope Church [qq.v.], Sherman launched an assault upon Johnston's key position on Kenesaw Mountain [q.v.]. It was a Union disaster in which the Federals lost more than 3,000 men to the Confederates' 552, but on 2 July Sherman again turned the Confederate left. Two days later Johnston dug in at a line north of the Chattahoochee River. When Sherman again turned his position, Johnston fell back to Peach Tree Creek [q.v.], just north of Atlanta, and made plans for a counterattack.

Although Johnston with his inferior numbers had executed a masterful series of delaying actions with relatively small losses—Sherman had been able to average only one mile per day for two and one-half months—on 17 July he was summarily relieved of his command and was succeeded by John Bell Hood [q.v.]. Sherman later wrote that the Confederate government, by relieving Johnston, "rendered us most valuable service."

"Hood's first sortie," as it was sometimes called, was the Battle of Peach Tree Creek [q.v.], a Confederate disaster fought on 20 July. Federal losses were 1,600; Confederate losses 2,500. Hood then withdrew into the defenses of Atlanta and two days later executed "Hood's second sortie," another

disaster [see Battle of Atlanta]. At the end of August, abandoning all hope of defending Atlanta, he blew up ammunition and stores and abandoned the town. After evacuating its inhabitants, Sherman destroyed all its mills, factories, and public buildings, leaving the city a smoking ruin. The loss of Atlanta was a severe, irreplaceable loss to the South. Sherman now prepared to make his famous "March to the Sea" [q.v.].

Atrocities. Inexcusable, horrible, often barbaric crimes are committed in most wars, even those fought by civilized nations. Some of the most vicious in Europe occurred during the Napoleonic Wars [q.v.]. The Spanish responded to French indiscriminate looting by brutal and ferocious guerrilla activity, almost never taking prisoners.

In Portugal, after the Battle of Bussaco [q.v.], on 27 September 1810, the French occupied and sacked Coimbra, a town on the Mondego River, 108 miles north-northeast of Lisbon. When Marshal André Masséna marched out of the town on 5 October, he left behind 5,000 of his wounded. Soon after, General Nicholas Trant [q.v.] with his Portuguese irregulars raided the town and slaughtered most of them.

At Badajoz [q.v.] in April 1812, drunken British soldiery terrorized the Spanish population for three days. On 17 June 1809 Sir Arthur Wellesley, the future Duke of Wellington, wrote to Viscount Castlereagh (1769–1822) from Portugal: "It is impossible to describe to you the irregularities and outrages committed by the troops. . . . There is not an outrage of any description which has not been committed on a people who have received us as friends by soldiers who have never yet for one moment suffered the slightest want or the smallest privation. . . . We are an excellent army on parade, an excellent one to fight, but we are worse than an enemy in a country."

Both French and Italians employed torture and murder in the Calabrian War. In at least one instance prisoners were forced to eat the flesh of their tortured and slain comrades.

Atrocities were committed by both whites and Indians during the American Indian Wars. Those committed or said to have been committed by whites, such as those perpetrated at Wounded Knee [q.v.], have been the better known, but the most atrocius was the Fort Mims massacre [q.v.] of men, women, and children by Creek Indians.

The "Bulgarian atrocities" [q.v.] aroused the horror of

Atrocities *The atrocities of guerrilla warfare during the Spanish War of Independence, pictured by Goya in his famous* Disasters of War

Europe in 1876, when Turkish bashi-bazouks [q.v.] massacred some 12,000 Bulgarian Christians.

Attaché, Military. A military officer on the staff of a foreign embassy or attached in an official capacity to a foreign army for the purpose of reporting on military affairs to his own army. Not until 22 September 1888 did the American army send military attachés to embassies in the capitals of the five major European powers: Berlin, London, Paris, St. Petersburg, and Vienna. The following year, however, attachés were sent to sixteen foreign capitals, including Tokyo and Mexico City.

Attack, to. To assail forcefully with men and weapons. Winston Churchill in *The River War* (1899) wrote: "For what is more thrilling than the sudden and swift development of an attack at dawn?"

Attack Column. A formation developed by French General Lazare Nicolas Marguerite Carnot [q.v.] and perfected by Napoleon that enabled commanders to bring men onto the field rapidly and deploy them easily.

The *levée en masse* [q.v.] in 1793, which conscripted the entire male population of France and created fourteen new armies, brought into the service a mass of raw recruits who could not quickly be trained to face the fire of professional soldiers in conventional field formations. Well suited to inexperienced soldiers, the attack column, usually of battalion strength, brought men in close order onto a field and gave them cohesiveness and esprit. It also provided considerable flexibility, for it could easily be converted into other formations.

Attention. The position of a soldier when standing formally in ranks, of privates and noncommissioned officers when addressed by an officer, and of junior officers when reporting to senior officers. Also, the word of command to assume such a position. The position varied only slightly between armies. In the American army a soldier stood with his feet as close together as the conformity of the man permitted, heels together, and toes apart, forming an angle of approximately 45 degrees. His legs were straight without stiffness. Initially his arms hung naturally at his side. Only after the First World War were his thumbs pulled back to the seams of his trousers. His head and eyes were straight to the front with his chin in and the axis of the head and neck vertical.

Attestation. The Mutiny Act [q.v.] required that a British recruit be brought before a magistrate within four days of his enlistment to declare his assent to his enlistment, to swear that the pertinent parts of the Mutiny Act had been read to him, and that an oath had been administered by a magistrate.

Attila. A short-skirted tunic or jacket bearing cord or braid loops across the chest. Worn by hussars [q.v.] from the middle of the nineteenth century. It was sometimes called a husarka.

Attrition. The wearing down or wearing away of an army or smaller unit through steady losses of men and matériel. Such was General U. S. Grant's strategy in the spring and summer of 1864 during the American Civil War, when he calculated that he could lose 3 men to General R. E. Lee's 2 and still maintain numerical superiority. His bloody calculus proved to be correct.

Aubry de la Boucharderie, Comte Claude Charles (1773–1813). A French general who commanded the artillery under Napoleon until he was killed at the Battle of Leipzig [q.v.].

Auchmuty, Samuel (1756–1822). A British soldier who was born in New York City, where his father, Samuel (1722–1777), was rector of Trinity Church. When a young man, he served in the American Revolution in three cam-

Attack, to *Attack and great victory at the Battle of Song-hwan during the Sino-Japanese War, 1894*

paigns as a British volunteer with the 45th Foot. In 1777 he was rewarded with an ensigncy in that regiment and the following year a lieutenancy without purchase. In 1783 he exchanged into the 52d Foot and accompanied that regiment to India, where he saw action in the final war against Hyder (or Haidar) Ali (1722–1782) and took part in the campaigns against Tippoo Sultan (1751–1799) in 1790 and 1791 and against the Rohillas. He was promoted captain and earned a brevet of lieutenant colonel. In 1797 he returned to England and in 1800 was colonel of the 10th Foot. He fought against the French in Egypt and was knighted in 1803. In 1806 he was ordered to take reinforcements to South America. There he failed to capture Buenos Aires but succeeded in capturing Montevideo at a loss of 600 out of 4,800 men [see Buenos Aires, British Expedition to].

In 1808 he was promoted major general and in 1810 was appointed commander-in-chief, Madras. In 1811 he was in command of the expedition that attacked Java [see Java War]. He occupied Batavia on 8 August and on 8 September overcame the last Dutch resistance at Samarang. In 1813 he returned to England and was promoted lieutenant general, but he saw no further active sevice. In 1821 he was appointed commander-in-chief in Ireland. A few months later while riding in Phoenix Park he fell dead from his horse.

Audacity. The quality of being bold, almost reckless, was much admired by Napoleon and other successful generals as well as by both Henri Jomini and Karl von Clausewitz [qq.v.]. In 1838 Jomini wrote in *Précis de l'art de la guerre:* "My critics . . . want war too methodical, too measured; I would make it brisk, bold, impetuous, perhaps sometimes even audacious."

Auerstädt, Battle of (14 October 1806), Napoleonic Wars. Some 27,000 French troops with 44 guns under Marshal Louis Nicolas Davout [q.v.] engaged a Prussian-Saxon army of 62,000 with 230 guns under General Karl Wilhelm Ferdinand, Duke of Brunswick [q.v.], at this village (now called Auerstedt or Auerstädt) in the former Prussian province of Saxony. For more than six hours the French, standing across the Prussian-Saxon line of communication, withstood repeated assaults. Prussian-Saxon morale was sapped by word of the French victory over the main Prussian army at Jena [q.v.] that same day and by the mortal wounding of the Duke of Brunswick. When Prussian-Saxon ardor sagged, Davout counterattacked. French Marshal Jean Baptiste Jules Bernadotte [q.v.], belatedly marching to the sound of the guns with 20,000 men, came in behind the retreating Prussians and Saxons and routed them. Nevertheless, Bernadotte was severely censored by Napoleon for arriving late on the field. Davout was created Duke of Auerstädt for his achievement.

The Prussians and Saxons lost 115 guns, 10,000 killed and wounded, and 3,000 taken prisoner; the French lost 258 officers and 6,793 other ranks.

The battle is sometimes called the Battle of Jena-Auerstädt, for the two battles were fought on the same day. They destroyed Prussia as a military power for the time being.

Augereau, Pierre François Charles (1757–1816). A French soldier, the son of a fruit seller, who rose from private to a marshal of France and the title Duc de Castiglione. His mother was a German domestic. He joined the army in 1774, first serving in the Régiment de Clare Irlandais and subsequently changing regiments several times. In Naples he eloped with the daughter of a Greek merchant. In 1792 he was adjutant of light cuirassiers in the German Legion, and on 26 June 1793 he was promoted a captain of Hussars. He fought exceptionally well at Lodi and Castiglione.

On 19 May 1804 Augereau was one of the first to be created a marshal by Napoleon, and the following February he was awarded the Legion of Honor [q.v.]. In 1805 he served in Austria, and in 1806 he commanded Napoleon's left wing in the Battle of Jena [q.v.]. On 18 February 1807 he led his corps to near destruction in the Battle of Eylau [q.v.], where he was wounded in the arm. In 1809 he replaced Laurent St. Cyr [q.v.] as VII Corps commander and on 10 December captured Gerona [q.v.], a fortified Spanish commune 52 miles northeast of Barcelona. He was military governor of Catalonia until April 1810. In 1813 he won the Battle of Naumburg and subsequently was present in the Battle of Leipzig [q.v.]. After being defeated in the Battle of St. Georges on 18 March 1814 and losing Lyons on 23 March, he deserted Napoleon and refused to rally to him during the Hundred Days [q.v.].

Proud to be called "a child of the people," he retained his lower-class mannerisms all of his life. Louis Desaix [q.v.] described him succinctly as a "fine big man—handsome—large nose— has served in all countries, few equals as a soldier, is always bragging." He had a coarse sense of humor and a lust for money.

Augur, Christopher Colon (1821–1898). An American soldier who was graduated sixteenth in the West Point class of 1843. U. S. Grant was a classmate. He fought in the Mexican War [q.v.], and then served on the western frontier. In the Civil War he became a brigadier general of volunteers in the Union army. He was severely wounded at Cedar Mountain [q.v.] but recovered and rose to become a major general.

Aul. A fortified Caucasian hilltop village.

Aulic Council. The popular name for the unpopular Hofkriegsrath, a committee of the Austrian War Department composed of senior commanders. Designed to control strategy, it hampered field commanders with suggestions, requests for reports, and cumbersome paperwork until the Austrian defeat in the Battle of Austerlitz [q.v.], after which its powers were greatly reduced by Archduke Charles [q.v.].

Aumalé, Henri Eugène Philippe Louis d'Orléans, Duke of (1822–1897). The fourth son of King Louis Philippe, he entered the French army at age seventeen and served in Algeria, where in 1847 and 1848 he was governor-general. [See Smala, Battles of.] During the Revolution of 1848 he retired to England, where he wrote articles and pamphlets against Louis Napoleon. In 1867 he published *Les Institutions militaire de la France.* In 1873 he became a general of division, and in 1879 inspector general of the army. In 1886 he donated his Château de Chantilly to the nation.

Aurellé de Paladiner, Louis Jean Baptiste d' (1804–1877). A French soldier who served in the Crimean War and in the Franco-Prussian War, where, on 9 November 1870, he defeated a force of Bavarians at Coulmiers [q.v.], giving the

French their sole victory in the war. In 1875 he was elected senator for life.

Ausgleich. The creation through political compromise in 1867 of Austria-Hungary and the formation of three governments and three armies within the Hapsburg Empire: the Hungarian [see Honvéd], Austrian, and common or joint armies.

Auspicious Incident / Event (14 June 1826). Turkish: *Vakayt Hayriye.* On this date the janissaries [q.v.] in Constantinople (Istanbul) revolted after Sultan Mahmud II (1785–1839) issued an edict incorporating 150 men from each janissary battalion into his *eshkenji* [q.v.], or European-trained army. The janissaries marched on the palace, expecting to overthrow the sultan as they had overthrown other sultans, but Mahmud had anticipated them, and his *eshkenji* met them with grapeshot. Their barracks were bombarded, and their power was crushed. Some 6,000 were killed, and their corpses thrown into the Bosporus.

Austerlitz, Battle of (2 December 1805), Napoleonic Wars. This battle, fought two or three miles from the Moravian village of Austerlitz (Slavkov in Czech), 12 miles east-southeast of Brno (Brünn), is sometimes called the Battle of the Three Emperors, for the rulers of France, Austria, and Russia all were present on the field.

In late November 1805 Napoleon, with 73,200 troops and 139 guns, appeared to be in an uncomfortable position. To his northwest, at Prague, was Archduke Ferdinand of Austria (1769–1824) with 18,000 men; to his northeast lay Tsar Alexander I of Russia [q.v.] and Emperor Francis II of Austria (1768–1835) with 25,000 Austrians, 60,000 Russians, and 278 guns, the entire force commanded by Prince Mikhail Ilarionovich Kutuzov [q.v.]; to the south, beyond the Alps were 80,000 Austrians under the archdukes Charles Louis and John (Johann Baptist Joseph Fabian Sebastian) [qq.v.], who were prevented from crossing the mountains by a mere 20,000 French under Marshal Michel Ney and Auguste de Marmont [qq.v.]. Napoleon's task was to prevent these forces from uniting and to preserve his line of communication to Vienna, where he had left a garrison of 20,000. After Napoleon's great victory in the Battle of Ulm [q.v.] in Württemberg on 27 October 1805, Kutuzov had wished to retire to the Russian border and await reinforcements before again attacking the French. He was overruled by Tsar Alexander, who believed that Napoleon was in a vulnerable position. For his part, Napoleon assumed every appearance of irresolution. He feigned weakness, suggested an armistice, and talked of peace negotiations.

On 28 November the Allied army began to move south, intending to cut the French line of communication with Vienna. In response, Napoleon moved his army off the Pratzen Heights, a commanding plateau nine miles west of the city, near Austerlitz, and placed it on the low ground facing east. He deliberately overextended his right for two miles, putting it in plain view of enemy scouts. The bulk of his army was concentrated and concealed behind the Zurlan Heights, east of Brno, near Olmütz.

When the Allied army reached Austerlitz on 1 December and occupied the Pratzen Heights, its commanders saw Napoleon's overextended right flank and determined to crush it. At dawn the following day Russian General Count Friedrich Wilhelm von Buxhöwden (1750–1811) threw 40,000 men, more than one-third of the Allied army, on Napoleon's weak right. Although reinforced by 10,500 men

Austerlitz *Napoleon rests on the field after the Battle of Austerlitz, 1805.*

under Marshal Louis Davout [q.v.], the French line was forced to give ground. Napoleon then ordered a corps under Marshal Nicolas J. Soult [q.v.], previously hidden, to assault the Pratzen Heights.

The French stormed the heights and split the Allied center. Davout encircled the Allied left, rolled it up, and sent it flying in confusion. In the path of the Russian retreat lay a frozen lake, which the demoralized soldiers attempted to cross. French artillery fire, brought to bear on them, tore through the ice, and many drowned in the freezing water. Napoleon claimed that 20,000 were lost, but the lake was shallow and probably fewer than 2,000 were killed. The Allies did lose 38 guns and 130 horses in the lake.

The Allied right under Russian Prince Pëtr Bagration [q.v.] was successfully attacked by the marshals Jean Lannes and Jean Baptiste Jules Bernadotte with the help of the cavalry of the commander-in-chief, Marshal Joachim Murat [qq.v.], and Napoleon's victory was complete. In the early afternoon, snow began to fall, adding to the misery and confusion of the Allied soldiers.

The Russian Imperial Guard, led by Grand Duke Constantine (1779–1831), launched a reckless counterattack that was costly in lives and added to the chaos, for he tried to cross the line of the Austrian retreat. Two of Russia's finest regiments were almost annihilated. This Russian debacle led Napoleon to comment that "many fine ladies of St. Petersburg would lament this day." Only Prince Bagration, commanding the Russian cavalry, managed to parry Murat's repeated attacks and conduct an orderly retreat along the Danube Valley.

In the pursuit Marshal Davout ordered, "No prisoners! Let not one escape!" As a result, as one French officer said, "Until the last hour of the battle . . . not a single living enemy remained in our rear." The last shots were fired at four-thirty in the afternoon.

The Allies suffered 16,000 killed and wounded, plus more than 11,000 taken prisoner, and lost 180 guns and 45 standards; French casualties were 1,800 killed and 6,800 wounded. Napoleon's victory bulletin began: *Soldat! Je suis content de vous.* That night he wrote to his wife, Josephine: "The Russian army is not only beaten but destroyed."

Graduates of the newly created military school at St. Cyr [q.v.] participated in this battle, and 3 were killed.

Austerlitz is generally regarded as one of Napoleon's tactical masterpieces and has been ranked as the equal of Arbela, Cannae, and Leuthen. It wrecked the Third Coalition [see Napoleonic Wars], and it firmly established Napoleon's military reputation. Napoleon and Francis II agreed to meet, and the result was the Peace of Pressburg, signed on 26 December 1805, by which Venice was added to the kingdom of Italy, while Croatia, Istria, and Dalmatia were ceded to France; Swabia was added to Württemberg and the Tyrol, Vorarlberg, and other Alpine areas were given to Bavaria, a French satellite state.

Austrian Army. The four great Continental armies of the nineteenth century were those of France, Prussia, Russia, and Austria. Austria, or the Hapsburg Empire, before it became the Austro-Hungarian Empire after 1867, consisted of the Austrian hereditary lands (Austria and Slovenia), the Bohemian crown lands (Bohemia, Moravia, and Austrian Silesia), Galicia (southern Poland), Hungary (including Transylvania in present-day Rumania), Slovakia, Croatia, Slovenia, and Bukovina (now in Ukraine). During the course of the nineteenth century Austria lost lands in northern Italy but gained Bosnia-Herzegovina. The country contained about 25 million people.

Although the Austrian (particularly Hungarian) hussars [q.v.] were considered among the best cavalry in Europe, the remainder of the army was not generally of high quality before the reorganization of 1813, which established it on more modern lines and transformed it into one of the best-organized armies on the continent. By 1850 it contained 350,000 men and was the third largest after Russia (859,000) and France (570,000).

Before reorganization the army was merely a collection of regiments that were brigaded as needed. Army regiments were organized by the language spoken by the rank and file, including the dialects of the Grenzer (frontier) regiments, composed of men living on the Military Frontier [q.v.] in the south and southeast claimed by both Austria and Turkey. There were ten different *Regimentssprachen* in the line regiments. Officers were usually noblemen or from families of large landowners. Crown Prince Rudolf (1858–1889) was commissioned a colonel and made a regimental proprietor at the age of two days. Few officers, even adult ones, took a serious interest in their profession. They spoke only German, and commands were filtered through interpreters (*Dolmetscher*). In 1862 the journal of the highly bureaucratic army noted that "our officers' ignorance of the language of their men is the Austrian army's single greatest defect."

When Austria-Hungary was formed in 1848, there remained three armies within one state. Services common to both the Hungarian and Austrian armies were known as K. und K. (*Kaiserlich und Königlich*). "K. K." (*Kaiserlich-Königlich*) referred in the strict sense only to Austrian troops; the Hungarian army was known as the K. Ung. (Royal Hungarian) service.

General conscription begun by the law of 5 December 1868 required every male subject between the ages of twenty and thiry-six to serve if called unless he was needed to support a helpless relative. No substitutions were allowed. The same law fixed the number of men on active duty at 457,012 Austrians and 342,988 Hungarians. About 95,000 recruits per year were taken into service. Enlistments of conscripts in regular regiments were for six years in the infantry, ten years for the cavalry, and fourteen years for the artillery. Regiments were composed of one-third volunteers, many of them foreigners, and two-thirds cantonists, conscripts drawn by lot. As in the Russian army [q.v.], soldiers were permitted to earn money doing odd jobs outside the barracks.

The military force of the empire was divided into four parts: the regular army; the reserve; the landwehr [q.v.], which consisted mostly of men who had served ten years in the regular army and reserves; and the landsturm [q.v.], the latter being the *levée en masse* [q.v.] of the entire male population. Service was for twelve years: three years in the standing army, seven years in the reserve, and two years in the landwehr. In the 1880s about 800,000 were in the standing army or the reserve (Hungary contributed 330,000 men) and about 300,000 in the landwehr. In Austria proper and Bohemia, a type of volunteer militia was sometimes used as filler replacements in regular regiments. In wartime the army also used pandours [q.v.].

The emperor, as commander-in-chief, commanded through a minister of war, an inspector general, and the so-called Aulic Council [q.v.]. By the late 1860s professionals, either graduates of military colleges or men who rose from the ranks, dominated the officer corps. The noble dilettantes had been largely swept aside. Cadets, educated mostly at public expense, served for ten years upon graduation from the Military Academy at Wiener Neustadt or the Military Technical Academy at Vienna. The course of study was four years. The commandant at each academy was a major general. In their first months in the army cadets were required to master the duties of privates and noncommissioned officers, to attend for eleven months a school operated by a division, and to pass an examination. Still not commissioned, they performed the duties of officers until vacancies occurred. Noncommissioned officers of sufficient attainments and of good character and antecedents could also obtain commissions by attending one of the cadet schools, of which there were thirteen for infantry, six for cavalry, and one each for artillery, engineers, and pioneers.

Officers in the three arms were promoted by seniority and by merit or selection "out of turn." Up to the grade of captain only one-sixth were promoted by selection; three-quarters of field officers were promoted by selection; the rank of major general (equivalent to American and British brigadier general) was by seniority, but all superior ranks by selection.

In the Napoleonic Wars [q.v.] Austria suffered a series of humiliating defeats. The empire was badly shaken by the Hungarian Revolution [q.v.] of 1848 and rescued only by the intervention of Russia [q.v.]. At the end of the Seven Weeks' War [q.v.] in 1866 a German soldier (Eduard Bartels) wrote: "The history of the Austrian army is a history of defeats. Every time it fights alone against another European Great Power, it loses." By the end of the century the underfunded army threatened Austria's status as a great power.

Austrian Army Ranks.

Feldmarschall (field marshal)	
General of infantry or of cavalry; Feldzeugmeister (for artillery and engineers)	Equivalent to a full general
Feldmarschallleutnant (lieutenant field marshal)	Major general
Generalmajor (major general)	Brigadier general
Oberst	Colonel
Oberstleutnant	Lieutenant colonel
Major	Major
Hauptmann (infantry)	Both ranks as captain
Rittmeister (cavalry and train)	but divided into Class I and Class II
Oberleutnant	First lieutenant
Leutnant	Second lieutenant
Fähnrich (ensign)	

In 1915 the rank of *Generaloberst* was added, a rank just below a *Feldmarschall*. Before 1850 *Hauptmanns* Class II were called *Kapitän-Leutnant*, and from 1850 until 1868 *Fähnrich* were called *Unterleutnant*. The distinction between Class I and Class II *Leutnants* disappeared in 1867, but the two classes of captains remained until 1907.

Austrian Artillery. Before breechloaders became common, the principal manufacturer of artillery for the Austro-Hungarian army was the Artillerie Zeugfabrik in Vienna. In the last half of the nineteenth century the Skoda [q.v.] company of Pilsen became its principal supplier. The Gebrüder Böhler AG also produced weapons beginning about 1890.

In the third quarter of the century Austrian firms produced a popular bronze muzzle-loading rifled field gun in two sizes: a 4-pounder for horse artillery and an 8-pounder for field batteries. The projectiles were not studded but had iron ribs to engage the rifling.

Austrian Knot. A special knot worn in the sleeve braid of Austrian troops. Late in the century it was adopted by the British.

Austrian Weave. A pattern for gold or silver lace used in the Austrian army and early in the century by the British 15th Hussars and other cavalry regiments.

Austro-Italian War (1866). On 20 June 1866, after the outbreak of the Seven Weeks' War [q.v.], Italy declared war on Austria. Four days later in the Second Battle of Custozza [q.v.] an Italian army of 120,000 under Victor Emmanuel [q.v.] was defeated by an Austrian army of 80,000 under Archduke Albert [q.v.]. The Italians retreated across the Mincio River in great disorder. The Austrians soon withdrew to defend Vienna from the Prussians.

Garibaldi, leading a small volunteer army, had some small successes but was ordered to withdraw [see Garibaldi's Alpine Campaign]. The war ended with the Treaty of Vienna on 12 October.

Austro-Piedmontese War (1859). Sardinia-Piedmont, urged on by the French, mobilized. Austria followed and on 26 April 1859 declared war against Piedmont. Three days later an Austrian army under General Franz Gyulai [q.v.] invaded Piedmont. Napoleon III (1808–1873) sent 54,000 troops to Piedmont's aid after the tsar assured him that Russia would remain neutral. French troops, however, came badly prepared. They were sent across the Italian frontier without blankets, tents, and cooking equipment, and some even

Austro-Piedmontese War *Citizens caught in crossfire between Sardinian and Austrian soldiers near Tortona, Italy, 1859*

lacked ammunition. Medical facilities and supplies were inadequate, and shoes had to be borrowed from the Italians. Operating in an area full of waterways and forts, the French brought neither bridging equipment nor siege trains. In spite of the utilization of railroads, the first major use of trains in war, the campaign was a logistical disaster.

Nevertheless, the Franco-Piedmontese army thrust into Lombardy, where on 30 May it defeated an Austrian army at the village of Palestro, 11 miles northwest of Motara, and on 4 June at Magenta [q.v.], forcing the Austrians to abandon Milan and retreat eastward. The Austrians halted at Solferino [q.v.], and here the two armies, each of about 160,000 men, clashed on 24 June. Thanks primarily to the French, the Austrians were routed. They were only saved from disaster by the rearguard actions of General Ludwig von Benedek [q.v.]. Austria sued for peace and was forced to cede Lombardy—once called the richest duchy in Christendom—to Piedmont.

Austro-Prussian War of 1866. See Seven Weeks' War.

Austro-Sardinian War (1848–49). On 22 March 1848 Sardinia declared war upon Austria, and on 29 April Austrian troops crossed the Ticino River at Buffalora, Italy [see Florence Revolt]. King Charles Albert (Carlo Alberto [q.v.]) of Sardinia took command of the Allied Italian forces of about 140,000. In command of the Austrian army eighty-two-year-old General Josef Radetzky [q.v.] with a force of only 70,000 waged a brilliant offensive-defensive campaign. He defeated the Italians in the Battle of Custozza [q.v.], 11 miles southwest of Verona, on 24–25 July, then reoccupied Milan and besieged Venice [q.v.]. On 23 March 1849 he defeated the Italians in the Battle of Novara [q.v.], after which Charles Albert abdicated in favor of his son, Victor Emmanuel II (1820–1878). On 9 August a peace treaty was signed, and northern Italy came under the heel of Baron Julius von Haynau (1786–1853), who became noted for his cruelty.

Automobiles. Although the first successful gasoline-driven motor vehicle reached a speed of 9 mph in 1885 and improvements were continuous, automobiles played no part in any nineteenth-century battle. In 1895 in his first report as commanding general Nelson A. Miles [q.v.] of the American army recommended an experimental regiment of "motor wagons," but his proposal was not acted upon. The first motorcar in the British army appeared at Aldershot in 1902 for the use of the general officer commanding, Sir John French [q.v.]. Armies found no significant use for motorcars until World War I. [see Armored Cars.]

Autosee, Battle of (29 November 1815), Creek War. A force of 1,000 Georgia militia and 400 friendly Indians commanded by Brigadier General John Floyd [q.v.] attacked a Creek settlement on the Tallapoosa River 20 miles above its confluence with the Coosa and burned it down.

Autosight. A direct fire sight invented in Italy about 1875. It was used in coastal defense guns where the height of the gun above sea level allowing for the variation of the tides was known quite precisely, and thus the angle of elevation or depression was known for any range. It was widely used with the British 4-inch coastal defense guns.

Autun. An ancient town in France in the department of Saône-et-Loire that was the scene of hostilities between Giuseppe Garibaldi [q.v.] and German forces during the Franco-Prussian War [q.v.].

Aux Champs. Music played on drums and fifes, introduced into Napoleon's army in 1802 as a general salute for senior officers or to honor others and as the signal for troops to move toward the battlefield.

Auxiliary Forces. Those forces other than the regular or standing army that were available to a nation or an army. In the British service these included the yeomanry, militia, and volunteers [qq.v.]. In 1884 these numbered 15,078 officers and other ranks in the yeomanry, 139,619 in the militia, and 168,751 in the volunteers, including 1,458 permanent staff. In colonial wars both the British and French employed local forces, sometimes tribemen or other irregulars, as auxiliaries.

Ava, Army of. See Anglo-Burmese War, Second.

Avay / Avahy / Avaí, Battle of (December 1868), War of the Triple Alliance. About 4,000 Paraguayans under General Bernardino Caballero [q.v.], later president of Paraguay, were cut to pieces by Brazilian cavalry near this town in west-central São Paulo, Brazil, 20 miles northwest of Bauru. Caballero was captured but escaped and with others joined the remainder of the Paraguayan army for the Battle of Lomas Valentinas [q.v.].

Averasboro, Battle of (16 March 1865), American Civil War. During the Carolinas Campaign [q.v.] a Confederate corps under General William Joseph Hardee [q.v.], positioned on a ridge between Cape Fear River and a swamp near Averasboro, North Carolina, was attacked by an advancing Federal corps under General Henry Warner Slocum [q.v.]. The Federals struck the Confederate right, driving it back to a second line of defense. Darkness halted the attack; Hardee withdrew during the night, and the Federal advance continued toward Bentonville [q.v.]. Federal losses were 678; Confederate losses were 865 men and a three-gun battery.

Averell's Raid on Lewisburg, West Virginia (1–8 November 1863), American Civil War. On 1 November 1863 Federal Brigadier General William Woods Averell (1832–1900) with a brigade of all arms left Beverly, West Virginia, and a few days later, uniting with another brigade under Brigadier General Alfred Napoleon Alexander ("Nattie") Duffié (1835–1880), marched on Lewisburg to cut the East Tennessee & Virginia Railroad. At Droop Mountain on 6 November, about 20 miles north of Lewisburg, Averell encountered and defeated a mixed brigade under Confederate Brigadier General John Echols (1823–1896). The next day the Federals entered Lewisburg but, failing to cut the railroad, returned to their stations.

Avitabile, Paolo de (1791–1850). An Italian soldier who at age sixteen joined the Neapolitan militia. Three years later he joined the French artillery and served under Marshal Joachim Murat [q.v.], then king of Naples. After Murat was defeated and fled, Avitabile, like many soldiers of that era, served kingdoms whose destinies were uncertain. He served at the siege of Gaeta [q.v.], where he was wounded, and was for six years in the Persian army. In 1827 he entered the service of Ranjit Singh, the Sikh ruler of the Punjab. In December 1829 he was appointed governor of Wazirabad, and in 1835 governor of Peshawar, which was in an anarchic state, with murder, robbery, and other outrages being common daily occurrences.

It was said at the time that he was "a perfect monster of cruelty, who has added European refinements of torture and execution to the already long Asiatic list; passionate and vengeful; unscrupulous in gratifying his lusts . . . unmerciful and unforgiving; an immoderate drinker and a scoffer of anything sacred and divine" (C. Grey, *European Adventurers in Northern India* [Lahore: 1929]). He was, then, perhaps well suited to rule in Peshawar. He began by hanging 50 subjects, and hangings became an almost daily occurrence. His cruelties were credited with bringing order to this rough frontier city.

In 1843 he consolidated his considerable assets, disbursed his large harem, and returned to Europe. In London the Honourable East India Company gave him a banquet and presented him with a sword of honor worth 300 guineas for his services to the company, particularly during the First Afghan War [q.v.]. He died in Italy, where he had retired. Quarrels among relatives assured that most of his assets ended up in lawyers' hands.

Awkward Squad. A group of soldiers who have difficulty understanding or performing drill movements and need additional instruction.

AWOL. See Absent without Official Leave.

Axamitowski, Vincent (1760–1828). A Polish artillery officer who entered the French service in 1800. He commanded the artillery of the grand duchy of Warsaw in 1807 and later served on the staff of General Joachim Murat [q.v.]. In 1813 he commanded a cavalry brigade, and in 1825 he became the senior artilleryman in the new kingdom of Poland.

Axe War (1846–47), also known as the Seventh Kaffir War. In Cape Colony, South Africa, British authorities arrested and took to Grahamstown for trial a Xhosa accused of stealing an ax from a frontier store at Fort Beaufort, a village in a loop of the Kat River. On 16 March 1846 a party of armed Xhosas rescued the prisoner as he was being transferred under escort. In the process they killed the colored prisoner to whom he was manacled, and one of the rescuers, the prisoner's brother, was shot and killed by the police.

On 11 April troops under Colonel Harry Somerset (1794–1862) invaded the country of the Xhosas, then under Ngquika [q.v.], in three columns. In an attack on Somerset's base camp Xhosa warriors captured 65 wagons loaded with baggage and supplies that included fine wines, some excellent sporting guns made by some of Britain's finest gunsmiths, and all the regimental silver of the 7th Dragoon Guards, which was never recovered. The British were repulsed in the Battle of Amatola [q.v.], and on 30 April the Xhosas invaded Cape Colony and attacked and besieged a Mfengu [q.v.] settlement near Fort Peddie in Eastern Province de-

fended by a detachment of the 91st Foot and some dragoons. The Xhosas lost 92 men killed but made off with 4,000 head of cattle.

On 8 June, on the banks of the Gwanga River, they suffered a defeat that cost them 300 men. Their initial successes were over. In the end, after nearly two years of warfare, the Xhosas were driven out of Cape Colony, and a section of their lands was annexed.

Axis of Advance or line of advance. The routes leading to the enemy, often a road or group of roads.

Axis of Communication. See Communication, Line of.

Aya-Bassi. A noncommissioned officer grade (equivalent to corporal) in the Turkish corps of janissaries [q.v.].

Ayacucho, Battle of (9 December 1824), Peruvian War of Independence. Although Peru declared its independence in 1821, the Spanish continued to control some sections of the interior. On 9 December 1824 General José de La Serna y Hinojosa [q.v.], the Spanish viceroy, with 9,300 men and 10 guns attacked the rebel leader, Antonio José de Sucre [q.v.], with 5,800 men and 2 guns in the small, elevated (11,600-foot) valley of Ayacucho near the village of La Quinua, 375 miles southeast of Lima, Peru. Sucre's left and center managed to contain the attack while cavalry on his right turned La Serna's left flank. When Sucre threw in his reserve division, the Spanish army crumpled.

La Serna fell with six wounds, and the following day his successor, General José Canterac [q.v.], capitulated. Spanish losses were 1,400 killed and 700 wounded. The battle is sometimes called the Battle of the Generals; 14 Spanish generals were captured. The so-called republican forces under Sucre lost 300 killed and 600 wounded.

The battle ended Spain's hold on South America. Under the terms of capitulation, all Spanish forces left Peru. On 6 August 1825 Sucre established in what had been a part of Peru the republic of Bolivia, named after Simón Bolívar [q.v.]. Sucre became its first president.

Ayda Katti. A broad and heavy knife with a wooden hilt used by natives of the Coorg region of India. It was curved, single-edged, and sharp on the concave side.

Ayerbe-Huesca, Battle of (11 October 1811), Peninsular War. A large guerrilla force under Spanish General Francisco Espoz y Mina [q.v.], seeking to make a diversion in favor of Captain General Joachim Blake's [q.v.] defense of Valencia [q.v.], attacked the French garrison at Exea, but the French cut their way clear and joined a battalion of Italian infantry. This force was surprised by Espoz y Mina's guerrillas near Ayerbe in Huesca Province in northeastern Spain and in a running fight was exterminated. French and Italian casualties were 200 killed, and 600 taken prisoner; Spanish casualties are unknown.

Espoz y Mina marched his prisoners 200 miles across Navarre, Álava, and Biscay to deliver them to a British frigate at Motrico on the Bay of Biscay, 21 miles west of San Sebastián, and then marched back to Valencia without being intercepted, an illustration of the weakness of French control at this time.

Ayub Khan (1855–1914). After the death of Shere Ali [q.v.], amir of Afghanistan (1863–78), Ayub Khan, his youngest son, took possession of Herat. In 1880 he invaded Afghanistan and in the Battle of Maiwand [q.v.] defeated a British army under Brigadier General George Reynolds Scott Burrows (1822?–1913). He was in turn defeated by General Frederick Roberts [q.v.] in the Battle of Kandahar [q.v.] on 1 September 1880 and by Abd-er-Rahman Khan [q.v.], the amir of Afghanistan, in the following year. He took refuge in Persia (Iran) and in 1887 made another unsuccessful attempt to conquer Afghanistan.

Azimghur, Battle of (15 April 1858), Indian Mutiny. A British column of three infantry regiments and three Sikh cavalry regiments—about 2,500 men—under Sir Edward Layard marched to relieve the small British force at Azimghur besieged by the Dinapur mutineers, 5,000 strong, under Kur Singh (d. 1858). Layard defeated and dispersed the besiegers. Kur Singh was mortally wounded in the battle.

Aztec Club of 1847. A club formed by American army officers in Mexico City on 13 October 1847 at the end of the Mexican War [q.v.]. Major General John Anthony Quitman (1798–1858) was the first president. Membership was extended to all officers who had served in the final campaign of the war after Veracruz [q.v.]. The club first met in the home of Sr. Boca Negro, onetime Mexican minister to the United States. It grew to 160 members before its rolls were closed on the evacuation of Mexico City. Opened to descendants, it is still extant.

B

Bachi. See Bashi / Bachi / Baschi.

Back Edge. See False Edge.

Backpiece. On edged weapons, the metal part of the hilt that closes the grip at the top and back.

Backsword. A heavy, straight sword with one sharp edge, usually with a basket hilt; basically a cutting weapon.

Bac-le, Battle of (23 June 1884), Sino-French War. Chinese troops defeated a French force at this place (Backli or Pakli), 13 miles northeast of Kumyan, during the undeclared Sino-French War [q.v.] of 1883–85.

Bacler d'Albe, Louis Albert G. (1761–1824). Napoleon's chief topographical engineer. A painter by profession, he enlisted in the army in 1793. In 1809 he was made a baron of the empire, and in 1813 he was promoted general of brigade. He later served the Bourbons and retired in 1820.

Bacninh, Attack on (12 March 1884), Sino-French War. French forces captured this stronghold of the Black Flags [q.v.], 16 miles northeast of Hanoi, after having taken Santay [q.v.] on 10 December 1883.

Badagri / Badagry, Battle of (4 December 1893), Franco-Dahomey War. French Colonel Alfred Dodds [q.v.], led a French force that defeated the Dahomeans near this Benin town, 38 miles west of Lagos.

Badajoz / Badajos, Sieges of. Peninsular War. Badajoz was a strongly fortified town in Estremadura, western Spain, sitting on the high bluffs of the left bank of the Guadiana River, 200 miles southwest of Madrid and 4 miles from the Portuguese frontier. During the Peninsular War [q.v.] it sustained three sieges.
  First Siege (26 January–9 March 1811). French Marshal Nicolas Soult [q.v.] assembled an army of 21,000 infantry, 4,000 cavalry, and 48 guns and marched on Badajoz. After the commander of the fort was killed, Soult audaciously de-

Bacninh *Chinese print of General Tchung and his troops at the Battle of Bacninh, 1884*

manded that the Spanish surrender, and they meekly complied, apparently under the impression the Soult was stronger than he really was.

Second Siege (6 May–12 June 1811). General Wellesley (later Duke of Wellington) ordered General William Carr Beresford [q.v.] to recapture the town, but it was ably defended by French General Armand Philoppon [q.v.] with 4,900 French, Germans, and Spaniards, and the effort was abandoned. Beresford marched off to fight the Battle of Albuera [q.v.].

Third Siege (16 March–6 April 1812). This was one of the most famous, or infamous, sieges of the nineteenth century. Badajoz was garrisoned by 5,000 French, German, and Spanish troops loyal to Napoleon. Beginning in late March 1812, the Allies maintained a continual artillery attack on the city walls, and on the night of 5–6 April four divisions, about 15,500 men, made simultaneous assaults. On the afternoon before the attack Colonel (later General) Sir Thomas Picton [q.v.] addressed his regiment, the 88th Foot: "Rangers of Connaught, it is not my intention to expend any powder this evening. We'll do this with cold iron." Although the first storming parties were annihilated by hidden mines in the ditch surrounding the fortifications, the walls were breached in three places.

Some 1,410 Allied soldiers fell during the preparatory stage of the siege, and 3,350 in the actual assault; the French lost 1,350. The assault was said to have spawned the greatest slaughter in the smallest space of any battle in the century.

Brigadier (later Lieutenant General) Robert Long (1771–1825) wrote to his brothers on 20 April: "Those, whose faces gladden to the capture of Badajoz should have stood on the breach the day after the assault and have contemplated the scene of desolation that will occasion so much joy."

Badajoz *The storming of Badajoz by the British under Colonel Sir Thomas Picton*

Once in possession of the town, the Allied soldiers, particularly the British, it would seem, indulged in a three-day drunken rampage. All discipline evaporated, and outrages were so horrendous that British Major R. M. Barns, an eyewitness, labeled them the "most discreditable incidents in the history of the army." Another British officer called the soldiers "a pack of hell hounds vomited up from the infernal regions for the extirpation of mankind." Dr. James McGrigor [q.v.], Wellington's chief surgeon, wrote: "I was told that very few females, old or young, escaped violation by our brutal soldiery, mad with brandy and with passion."

Bad Axe, Battle of (2 August 1832), Black Hawk War. The war's chief battle was fought on the banks of the Bad Axe River near its confluence with the Mississippi in Wisconsin Territory. Chief Black Hawk [q.v.], leading bands of Fox and Sauk Indians, was defeated by a force of 1,341 regulars from the 5th and 6th U.S. Infantry and 5,368 Illinois militia under Brigadier General Henry Atkinson (1782–1842). The soldiers were aided by the gunboat *Warrior*, which caught the Indians in the middle of the river and shot up their rafts with 6-pounders.

More than 150 Indians were killed or driven into the river, and about 40 were captured. Atkinson lost 6 killed and 18 wounded. Many of the Indians who succeeded in crossing the river were killed by Sioux. Black Hawk and a few other survivors were captured by the Winnebagos and turned over to the army. They were escorted to Jefferson Barracks, Missouri, by Second Lieutenant Jefferson Davis [q.v.], later president of the Confederacy, and Second Lieutenant Robert Anderson [q.v.], Union commander at Fort Sumter [q.v.] in April 1861.

Baden Insurrection (May–June 1849). Revolutionaries in the duchy of Baden, joined by people in the free city of Rastadt, rose in a revolt led by Ludwik Mieroslawski [q.v.]. Prussian troops entered Baden in early June, and the revolt was suppressed on 15 June 1849. [See Kandern, Battle of; Friedrich Hecker.]

Baden-Powell, Lord, Robert Stephenson Smyth (1857–1941). A British soldier and the founder of the Boy Scout movement, who was educated at Charterhouse, where he distinguished himself neither as a scholar nor as an athlete, preferring to act in theatricals and to draw cartoons.

On 11 September 1876, at age nineteen, without benefit of any military education, he was commissioned as a lieutenant directly into the 13th Hussars and proceeded to join his regiment in India. There he made a name as an actor in amateur theatricals, a creator of humorous cartoons, a polo player, and a pigsticker. In 1883 he won the Kadir Cup for pigsticking (highest accolade for the sport); he later wrote a book on the subject.

In 1888 he was appointed aide-de-camp to an uncle serving in South Africa and took part in the Zulu War of that year [see Zulus and Zulu War]. In 1892 he was promoted major and rejoined his regiment, then in Ireland. He took part in the Ashanti War of 1895–96 and was made a brevet lieutenant colonel [see Ashanti War, Third]. In 1896 he served as a special service officer in Matabeleland and received a brevet colonelcy for his scouting skills.

After two years as commander of the 5th Dragoon Guards, he was sent to South Africa to raise two regiments for the defense of Matabeleland and Bechuanaland. When the Second Anglo-Boer War [q.v.] began, he was at Mafeking [q.v.] with a force of only 1,251 men. He was besieged there on 12 October 1899 by a Boer force of about 9,000 under Piet Cronjé [q.v.]. The "plucky" and sometimes witty messages he was able to send out endeared him to those in England. When Mafeking was relieved on 17 May 1900 after a siege of 217 days, London went wild with joy, adding the verb "to maffik" to the language. "B-P," as he was called, was proclaimed the "Hero of Mafeking" and promoted major general, at age forty-three the youngest in the army. He then formed the South African Constabulary, a semimilitary force used to pacify and control conquered Boer territory.

Although he subsequently took part in the unsuccessful attempts to trap Boer General Christiaan de Wet [q.v.], he saw little further action. In 1907 he was promoted lieutenant general, and in 1908 he published *Scouting for Boys*, the most influential of some thirty books he eventually wrote. Scout troops immediately began to form. The following year 11,000 Scouts assembled at the Crystal Palace. In 1912, at the age of fifty-five, he married Olive Soames, the twenty-three-year-old daughter of a wealthy brewer, who bore him two daughters and a son.

Badges, Union Army Corps. In 1862, during the American Civil War, General Philip Kearny [q.v.], commanding the 3rd Division in III Corps of the Union army, ordered his men to wear a red diamond-shaped patch as identification. This is believed to have been the first use of a distinctive device to identify a military unit larger than a regiment.

In 1863, when Joseph Hooker [q.v.] took command of the Union Army of the Potomac [q.v.], he ordered each corps to wear an individual badge. General Daniel Butterfield [q.v.] is said to have designed them. Stamped out of flannel, they were about one and one-half inches wide and were worn on the cap. Corps badges were adopted by the western armies in 1864:

I	Disk
II	Trefoil
III	Lozenge
IV	Triangle
V	Maltese cross
VI	St. Andrew's cross
VII	Crescent and star
VIII	Six-pointed star
IX	Shield crossed with anchor and cannon
X	Square bastion
XI	Crescent
XII	Five-pointed star
XIV	Acorn
XV	Cartridge box
XVI	Crossed cannon
XVII	Arrow
XVIII	Trefoil cross
XIX	Maltese crosslike figure
XX	Star
XXII	Pentagon cross

U.S. army corps badges in the Civil War

XXIII	Shield
XXIV	Heart
XXV	Lozenge on a square

Badges to designate units were not used in the Confederate army.

Badi Agha (fl.1830s). A Sudanese soldier in the Egyptian army of Muhammad Ali [q.v.] and one of the few Sudanese to hold officer rank. He was a private in 1822 and a sergeant in 1836 when he was commissioned a mulazim [q.v.] and fought in the Egyptian-Turkish War in Syria.

Bad Time. In the American army, bad time was the time lost from duty through a soldier's own misconduct—e.g., contracting a venereal disease or being absent without leave. The number of days so lost was added to the length of a soldier's enlistment.

Baduli-ki-Serai, Battle of (8 June 1857), Indian Mutiny [q.v.]. Marching on Delhi at the beginning of the mutiny, Sir Henry Barnard (1799–1857) encountered a large force of mutineers near this northern India village. He defeated it and captured all its guns.

Bag. The flattened colored cloth that hung from the top of a busby. Simply decorative, it served no useful purpose.

Bagh-nakh / Wagh-nakh / Wahar-nuk / Nahar-nakh. An Indian weapon whose name means "tiger claw," which it resembled. Four or five steel claws on a bar were attached to rings, which were slipped on the fingers of the hand.

Bagpipes. Musical wind instruments with valves, three or four sounding pipes, and a bag. In Scotland the instruments became an integral part of the clan legends, and they were played at dances, funerals, and weddings and to rouse Scotsmen to battle or rebellion. Sir Walter Scott said, "Twelve Highlanders and a bagpipe make a rebellion." The traditions of the pipes were carried into Highland regiments of the British army. They were never issued, but in all Highland regiments they were purchased and maintained by the officers. By 1845 pipers were officially on the rolls of all existing Highland regiments. They played their troops into battle with pibrochs (martial airs) and even took part in assaults. [See Findlater, George.]

Bagration, Prince Pëtr Ivanovich (1765–1812). A Russian soldier of a noble Georgian family, who was commissioned in 1782 and served under Aleksandr Vasilievich Suvorov [q.v.] (1729–1800) at the siege of Ochakov in 1788 and in the Polish campaigns of 1792 and 1794. He campaigned in Italy and fought at Hollabrünn. He made a name for himself at Austerlitz in 1805 and at Eylau and Friedland [qq.v.] in 1807. In 1808 in the Russo-Swedish War he made a forced march across the frozen Gulf of Finland to capture the Aaland Islands. He further distinguished himself in the Russo-Turkish War [q.v.] of 1809–10. In Napoleon's Russian Campaign [q.v.] of 1812 he was defeated in western Ukraine at Mogilev Podolski [q.v.], also known as Mogilev-on-the-Dniester, on 23 July 1812 by Marshal Louis Davout [q.v.]. He was mortally wounded commanding the left wing in the Battle of Borodino [q.v.] on 7 September of the same year.

Baiclakar. A color-bearer in the Turkish army.

Bail. An iron yoke that fitted tightly over the ends of the trunnions and was placed over heavy guns. It was attached by pins to the axis of the trunnions so that the gun could be raised or lowered by means of a gin pole.

Bailan / Beilan. A mountain pass through the Amanus Mountains in southern Turkey where Egyptian troops defeated Turks in 1832 [see Turkish-Egyptian War].

Bailén / Baylen, Battle of (19 July 1808), Peninsular War. In 1806, when Napoleon replaced Charles IV of Spain (1748–1919) with his brother Joseph Bonaparte (1768–1844), the country seethed with revolt. In 1808 Pierre Dupont de l'Étang [q.v.], charged by Napoleon with the pacification of Andalusia, sacked Córdova and then found himself facing an angry uprising of Spaniards throughout Spain. His army of 22,250 men and 18 guns was attacked by a Spanish army of 29,770 and 24 guns under Francisco Castaños [q.v.] near Bailén, a small town 20 miles north of Jaén. Dupont was not only clearly outnumbered but also outmaneuvered and defeated, the Spaniards taking 17,635 prisoners. Although Napoleon was to claim the Spaniards were "picked men," most were raw conscripts. The promise of a safe conduct to France for the prisoners was at once violated. Many were butchered on the spot. Surviving rank and file were thrown into prison hulks. Few ever saw their homes in France again; only 1 in 7 survived the ordeal; French officers, however, were paroled. Dupont de l'Étang was disgraced and imprisoned for six years.

Although most of the French soldiers were raw conscripts and their commander was enjoying his first independent command, the Spanish boasted that they had defeated "the victors of Jena and Austerlitz," and the legend of French invincibility was badly shaken.

This Spanish victory over a Napoleonic army caused a sensation in Europe, and Napoleon, incensed by what he regarded as Dupont's incapacity, raged: "Has there ever, since the world began, been such a stupid, cowardly business as this?" Dupont's defeat, followed by the defeat of General Jean Junot's [q.v.] army at Vimiero [q.v.] on 21 August, led the French government in Madrid to withdraw northeast behind the Ebro River and convinced Napoleon that he himself must take a hand in the war on the Iberian Peninsula.

Bailey. An enclosed space inside a castle or fortification. Sometimes called a ward. If there were two lines of fortifications, there would be an inner and an outer bailey. (The name of London's Old Bailey is derived from its location, which was once inside the city's fortifications.)

Bailey, Joseph (1827–1867). A Union general in the American Civil War who was one of only 15 army officers to receive the Thanks of Congress. He was credited with engineering feats that saved Nathaniel Banks's [q.v.] fleet during the Red River Campaign [q.v.]. Two years after the war he

was killed while serving as sheriff of Newton County, Missouri.

Bairakdar. An ensign or second lieutenant in the Turkish army.

Baird, Sir David (1757–1829). A Scottish soldier, commissioned in 1772, who saw much service in India (1780–1799), where he particularly distinguished himself leading the forlorn hope [q.v.] at Seringapatam in May 1799. He campaigned in Egypt in 1801–02; he was a lieutenant general when he commanded the force that captured the Cape of Good Hope [q.v.] from the Dutch in 1806 [see Blaauwberg/Blueberg/Blue Mountain, Battle of]. He participated in the Battle of Copenhagen [q.v.] in 1807. The following year in the Peninsular War [q.v.] he was second-in-command to Sir John Moore [q.v.] in Spain, where in 1809 he lost an arm at Corunna [q.v.]. He was made a baronet in 1810 and a full general in 1814. He finished his military career as commander-in-chief in Ireland in 1820–22.

Baker, Edward Dickinson (1811–1861). An English-born American soldier and politician. He served as a U.S. senator and was a close friend of Abraham Lincoln, who named his second son after him. During the Mexican War [q.v.] Baker was a colonel of Illinois volunteers and commanded a brigade after the Battle of Cerro Gordo [q.v.]. He was offered general's stars in the Union army during the American Civil War but declined because he could not by law be a general and a senator. He accepted instead the command of the 1st California and the rank of colonel, which allowed him to retain his Senate seat. (The regiment was largely recruited in New York among men who had once lived in California. It was later renamed the 71st Pennsylvania.) On 21 October 1861 he was the battlefield commander in the Battle of Ball's Bluff [q.v.], which he badly mismanaged. Because he was killed in that battle, the blame for the Union defeat unjustly fell upon Brigadier General Charles P. Stone [q.v.].

The Union defeat in the Battle of Ball's Bluff prompted the forming of the meddlesome Joint Committee on the Conduct of the War [q.v.].

Baker, Lafayette Curry (1826–1868). A Union general and a noted spy during the American Civil War. In 1856 he was a member of the San Francisco Vigilance Committee. Later he became a detective for the U.S. State Department. In July 1861, during the Civil War, General Winfield Scott [q.v.] sent him to Richmond to gather intelligence. There he so fully gained the confidence of the authorities that they sent him north to spy for the Confederacy. On 5 May 1863 he was commissioned a colonel in command of the 1st District of Columbia Cavalry. In that capacity he was sent on security missions for the War Department, to which he reported directly. He organized the pursuit of John Wilkes Booth (1838–1865), Abraham Lincoln's assassin, and he was present at his capture and death. On 26 April 1865 he was made a brigadier general of volunteers.

He is reputed to have been a liar and a scoundrel who lined his own pockets in the corruption of wartime Washington.

Baker Pasha, Valentine (1827–1887). A British soldier who served in the Kaffir War of 1852–53 in South Africa and in the Crimean War [qq.v.]. He had been a highly respected cavalryman and colonel of the 10th Hussars for thirteen years when, on 2 August 1875, he was convicted of "indecently assaulting a young lady in a railway carriage" and sent to prison. On his release he repaired to Turkey, where he entered the sultan's service and was made a pasha. As a general he fought in the Russo-Turkish War [q.v.] of 1877–78. In the Battle of Tashkessan (Tashkent) in 1885 he was said to have conducted "one of the most successful rearguard actions on record."

In 1882 he accepted an offer to take command of the British-controlled Egyptian army, but when he arrived in Cairo, the offer was withdrawn. In its place he was offered and accepted the lesser command of the gendarmerie. On 4 February 1884 his force of 3,500 Egyptians was defeated by a Dervish force of fewer than 1,000 under Osman Digna [q.v.] at the wells of El Teb [q.v.], near Suakin. He retained command of the gendarmerie until his death in Cairo on 17 November 1887.

Baker Pasha was the brother of explorer Sir Samuel White Baker (1821–1893).

Baker Rifle. A muzzle-loading flintlock rifle invented by London gunmaker Ezekiel Baker and approved for issue in the British army in February 1800 after tests at Woolwich. It was 46 inches long, weighed 9.125 pounds, and had a 30-inch barrel with seven grooves making only a quarter turn. When it was introduced, it was the most accurate British weapon. Various calibers were produced, and with minor variations, the rifles were used by British and German troops during the Napoleonic Wars [q.v.]. Many were issued to Portuguese caçadores [q.v.] in the Peninsular War [q.v.]. They remained in service until replaced by the Brunswick Rifle [q.v.] in 1838.

Baker rifle

Baker's Creek, Battle of. See Champion's Hill, Battle of.

Bakhit Bey Batraki (1830?–1885). A Sudanese soldier in the Egyptian army. He enlisted as a private and rose to be quartermaster sergeant in the Sudanese battalion sent to Mexico in 1863–67 under Marshal Achille Bazaine [q.v.] to support Emperor Maximilian [q.v.] [see Mexico, French Invasion and Occupation of]. On his return he was commissioned *mulazim* (lieutenant) and transferred to the Sudan, where he served in Equatorial Province and was promoted *quimmaqam* (lieutenant colonel). In 1876 he was made governor of Makraka. Although suspended in 1878, he was rein-

stated by Emin Pasha [q.v.], then the governor of Equatoria, about 1880.

In 1882 he went to Khartoum as second-in-command and later, with the rank of *miralai* (colonel) was commandant of a Sudanese regiment there. He was killed during the siege of Khartoum [q.v.] while defending the eastern fortifications from a Dervish assault.

Bakufu. In Japanese: tent government. The headquarters of the Inner Palace Guards (Konoefu) who were responsible for guarding the Japanese emperor. The term came to be applied to the military government of the shogunates, for in the nineteenth century the military largely replaced the civil bureaucracy.

Balaclava, Battles of (1854–55), Crimean War. Two battles were fought near Balaclava (Balaklava), a seaport town on the southwest coast of the Crimean Peninsula, eight miles southeast of Sevastopol, which was besieged by British, French, Turkish, and Sardinian forces.

1. 25 October 1854. In an effort to raise the Allied siege of Sevastopol [q.v.] Russian General Pavel Petrovich Liprandi (1796–1864), one of the ablest of the Russian generals, leading 25 battalions of infantry, 35 squadrons of cavalry, and 78 guns, about 25,000 in total, advanced at about 5:00 A.M. on the British base near the town of Balaclava. Before dawn the Russians captured six redoubts on Causeway Heights, routing the Turks who held them.

Some 3,000 Russian cavalry advancing on the Fedyukhin Heights were stopped in their charge by the 93rd Highlanders under Colin Campbell [q.v.], whose line was described by William Howard Russell [q.v.] for the *Times* of London as "A thin red streak tipped by a line of steel," later corrupted to "A thin red line." The Russian cavalry was then thrown back by the 4th Dragoon Guards of the Heavy Brigade of British cavalry under James Scarlett [q.v.] in a creditable charge against a force eight times larger than they. The battle was claimed as a British victory in spite of the disastrous charge against 30 Russian guns made by the British Light Brigade of cavalry under James Thomas Brudenell, seventh Earl of Cardigan [q.v.]. [See Crimean War; Light Brigade, Charge of.]

Balaclava *Uniforms of the British army, Crimean War*

2. 22 March 1855. The besieged Russians in Sevastopol made a desperate sortie in which they were repulsed with a loss of some 2,000; the Allies lost about 600.

Balaclava. A close-fitting hood, often knitted, that covered all of the head except the face. It was said to have been devised and used by British soldiers at the siege of Balaclava during the Crimean War [q.v.].

Balangiga Massacre (28 September 1901), Philippine insurrection. On this date, a Sunday, on the island of Samar in the Visaya chain southeast of Luzon, bolo-swinging insurrectionists attacked 74 unarmed American soldiers of Company C, 9th U.S. Infantry. Almost all were slaughtered. Of those captured, 1 was boiled alive; others were disemboweled; others had limbs hacked off. Not even the company's dog escaped. His eyes were gouged out and replaced with stones.

Baldissera, Antonio (1838–1917). An Italian soldier who was commissioned in the Austrian army in 1857 after completing his studies at the military school at Wiener Neustadt. When his native town of Padua was ceded to Italy, he transferred to the Italian service and commanded the 7th Regiment of Bersaglieri. In 1887 he was posted to Eritrea, where he commanded a brigade and clashed with Mahdist forces at Kassala [q.v.] in the eastern Sudan. After the Italian disaster at Adowa [q.v.] on 1 March 1896, he superseded Oreste Baratieri [q.v.] and in 1897 organized the relief of Kassala, which had been invested by Amir Ahmad Fadil Muhammad (d. 1899) [see Italian-Mahdist Conflict].

Baldwin, Frank Dwight (1842–1923). An American soldier who was twice awarded the Medal of Honor [q.v.], the only officer other than George Custer's brother Thomas Ward Custer [q.v.] ever to be awarded the medal twice. A lightning rod salesman before the American Civil War Baldwin was commissioned a second lieutenant on 19 September 1861 in the Michigan Horse Guards of the Union army. He won his first medal for his gallantry at Peach Tree Creek [q.v.], Georgia, on 20 July 1864. He emerged from the war as a captain and remained in the service as a first lieutenant.

He distinguished himself in five successive engagements with Indians. On 6 November 1874, while leading 35 white scouts near McClellan Creek, Texas, on the Staked Plain (Llano Estacado), the extensive high plateau in southeastern New Mexico and western Texas, he attacked a camp of hostile Indians, dispersing them and rescuing two young white girls, Adelaide and Julia Germaine, who had been captured by renegade dog soldiers [q.v.] who had attacked their wagon train. For this he received a second Medal of Honor. For bravery in other engagements he won two brevets. After serving with distinction in Cuba and the Philippines, he retired as a brigadier general in 1902.

Bali Insurrection (1846). When the raja of Karang Asen and the raja of Bulelang (or Buleleng or Boelelang) on the north coast of Bali reasserted their former "right" to confiscate the cargoes of wrecked ships, the Dutch, who claimed supremacy, sent an expedition against them. The rajas came to terms but later returned to their old ways.

Balk. A joist-shaped spar or stringer resting between the cleats upon the saddles of two pontoons [q.v.] and connecting them. They support the chess, or flooring of a pontoon bridge.

Balkan Revolts. The Balkan states—Slovenia, Croatia, Serbia, Dalmatia, Bosnia, Herzegovina, Montenegro, Rumania, Bulgaria, Greece, Albania, and European Turkey—were conquered by the Ottoman Turks in the fourteenth and fifteenth centuries. In the nineteenth century many became infused with a fervid nationalism, and the ramshackle condition of the Ottoman Empire encouraged them to revolt. The unsuccessful Serbian Revolt of 1803 was the first of a series in the Balkans whose persistent problems came to be called the Eastern Question [q.v.].

Nineteenth-century cartoon of the continuous Balkan crisis

In Bosnia and Herzegovina countless revolts flared. After an uprising in September 1875, sparked by oppressive governors and excessive taxation, Sultan Abdul Aziz (1830–1876), under pressure from Austria, promised reforms; when these were not effected, hostility mounted, and in 1876 the sultan was deposed. A few days later he killed himself. A revolt in May 1876 encouraged the Bulgarians, Serbs, and Montenegrans to rebel, but they were crushed. In Bulgaria the insurrection was followed by the Bulgarian Atrocities [q.v.], in which the Turks killed some 12,000 Christians [see Bulgarian Revolution]. In 1878 the Treaty of San Stefano, which ended the Russo-Turkish War of 1877–78, combined Bosnia and Herzegovina into a single province under the control of the Austro-Hungarian government.

Ball, Duchess of Richmond's. On the night of 15 June 1815, the eve of the Battle of Quatre Bras [q.v.], Georgiana Lennox [q.v.], the wife of General Sir Charles Lennox, fourth Duke of Richmond and Lennox (1764–1819), gave a celebrated ball in Brussels, where, according to legend, the Duke of Wellington first learned of Napoleon's imminent intentions.

In fact, Wellington had received the news of Napoleon's movements at about ten o'clock, just before leaving for the ball, but apparently to relieve anxieties, he decided to attend it. There was no mad exit from the ball, as has been claimed, although many were taken by surprise at its close by the news of Napoleon's near approach, and Lieutenant General Sir Thomas Picton [q.v.] fought and died in the battle dressed in the civilian evening clothes he had worn to the ball.

The ball was held not in the Hôtel de Ville, as is usually reported, but in the depot of a coachmaker on the Rue de Blanchissière.

Ball Cartridge / Ball Ammunition. A small-arms cartridge that consisted of a projectile and a propellant charge in a case or shell. The term "ball" refers to the spherical and rifle bullets of the early nineteenth century but

Ball cartridge

it continued to be used when bullets were no longer balls [see Minié Ball]. All kinds of shot and bullets for small arms were occasionally called by the collective name ball.

Balle D. A French rifle bullet of copper-zinc alloy introduced in 1898 for the 8 mm Lebel rifle [q.v.]. It was the first pointed, boat-tailed bullet adopted as standard in any army. The shape reduced the air drag and improved its accuracy. It remained the French army standard for forty years.

Ballesteros, Francisco (1770–1832). An Austrian general who, during the Peninsular War, after being routed at Bilbao [q.v.] in 1809, was active in the fighting in southern Spain. When he objected to the appointment of Wellington as commander-in-chief in 1812, the Spanish Cortes discharged him.

Ballistics. A branch of gunnery dealing with the motion of projectiles. Interior ballistics is concerned with the projectile while still in the gun; exterior ballistics is concerned with the motion of a projectile after it has left the muzzle.

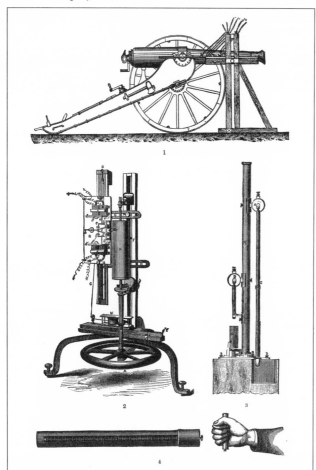

Ballistics *(1) velocimeter, Marine Artillery Service; (2) Bashforth chronograph; (3) Le Boulengé chronograph; (4) telemeter*

Ballivián, José (1804–1852). A Bolivian soldier who fought under President Antonio Sucre [q.v.] and Andrés Cruz (1792?–1865) in the Bolivian war against Peru. In 1841 he won the Battle of Ingaví [q.v.], and he served as president of Bolivia from 1841 until 1848. His son, *Adolfo* (1831–1871), also a soldier, was briefly president in 1873–74.

Balloons. The first practical balloons were manufactured in 1783 by two Frenchmen: Joseph Michel Montgolfier (1740–1810) and his brother Jacques Étienne (1745–1799). The first ascent was made by Jean François Pilâtre de Rozier (1756–1785) on 15 October of that year. Two years later a manned balloon crossed the English Channel.

The French army formed *aérostatier* companies equipped with balloons as early as 1794 and made the first use of an observation balloon in a pitched battle in the Battle of Fleurus on 25 June of that year. Although Napoleon used balloons for reconnaissance purposes in Egypt in 1799, he soon disbanded his balloon companies. In 1807 the Danes attempted to build a dirigible propelled with air oars with which they hoped to bombard the British fleet off Copenhagen. The following year they used free balloons to carry propaganda leaflets into southern Sweden. In 1808 a French Major L'Homond proposed invading England with a vast fleet of *montgolfiers* (hot-air balloons), each 300 feet in diameter and capable of lifting 1,000 men with rations for fifteen days, two guns with caissons and limbers, twenty-five horses, and enough wood to keep the fires burning under the bag. The invasion was never attempted. In 1811 an inventor who arrived in Paris with a scheme for bombarding an enemy with explosive balloons was dismissed as a crank. In 1814 Lazare Carnot [q.v.], defending Antwerp, put aloft a balloon to observe his besiegers, but military men as a whole were slow to realize the balloon's utility. Swiss military strategist Antoine Henri Jomini [q.v.] pointed out one of its advantages: "An observer is doubtless more at his ease in a clock tower than in a frail basket floating in mid-air, but steeples are not always at hand in the vicinity of battlefields, and they cannot be transported at pleasure" (*Précis de l'art de la guerre*, 1838).

Explosive balloons were first used in 1849 by the Austrians against Italian insurgents in Venice [see Venice, Siege of]. In the French campaign in Italy in 1859 [see Austro-Piedmontese War] a few observation balloons were employed in the Battle of Solferino [q.v.].

The Union army during the American Civil War became the first army to make extensive use of balloons for intelligence gathering. The most ardent proponent of their use was a young American, "Professor" Thaddeus Sobieski Coulincourt Lowe [q.v.]. On 18 June 1861 he demonstrated their value to President Abraham Lincoln (1809–1865) by ascending in a tethered balloon and telegraphing a description of the countryside for 50 miles around, a feat hailed as the "first dispatch ever telegraphed from an aerial station." Lincoln was so impressed that in August he assigned Lowe as a civilian to work for the Army of the Potomac [q.v.]. Lowe immediately set fifty seamstresses to work sewing together gored sections of pongee in double thicknesses. The sections on the outside of the balloons were covered with layers of varnish; those on the inside with neat's-foot oil. A netting was thrown over the whole, and from it was suspended a wicker gondola with a steel floor plate. A field-portable hydrogen gas generator, designed by Lowe, was used to inflate the balloons. By the end of 1861 he had produced seven, each named and highly decorated. All towered several stories high; the largest could accommodate several passengers. In use they were tethered, and telegraph lines connected the gondolas with the ground.

Lowe saw much service in George McClellan's [q.v.] Peninsular Campaign, and he claimed, with some justice, to be the most shot-at man in the war. Generals, for the most part, declined to venture in balloons; only four ever made an ascent.

On 3 May 1862 Second Lieutenant George Armstrong Custer [q.v.] ascended in a balloon and was the first to detect the abandonment of Yorktown by the Confederate army and its retreat up the peninsula [see Peninsular Campaign].

In April 1863 balloonists were placed under the Corps of Engineers, but there seemed no place in the tables of organization for them, and Lowe quarreled with those placed over him who failed to understand his requirements and abilities. When his pay was cut from ten dollars per day to six dollars, he resigned, and the balloon corps soon collapsed.

In South America in 1867, during the War of the Triple Alliance [q.v.], two Americans using balloons were able to map part of Paraguay for the Allies and to spot the Paraguayan batteries in the Battle of Ypacarai [q.v.].

During the siege of Paris [q.v.] in the Franco-Prussian War balloons were used to carry messages and to transport people out of the besieged city. On 26 September 1870 the city inaugurated a regular postal service, balloons leaving two or three times a week. Léon Michel Gambetta (1838–1882), the minister of the interior in the Government of National Defense, made a dramatic escape from the city by balloon on 8 October. A total cargo of 10,675 kilograms as well as 164 passengers, 5 dogs, and 384 pigeons [see Pigeons] was sent out of Paris in sixty-five balloons.

The German army bought two "war balloons" from England in 1870, and detachments trained at Cologne; but the tests were not considered successful, and it was not until after the Franco-Prussian War [q.v.] of 1870–71 that balloons became part of the permanent establishment. The French used balloons in Indochina in 1884–85. There was a British balloon detachment in the Sudan, and in 1884 General Charles Warren [q.v.] carried a balloon to South Africa for his Bechuanaland Expedition [q.v.]. In Cuba, on 1 July 1898, during the Spanish-American War, in the battles of El Caney and San Juan Hill [qq.v.] American forces used an observation balloon with a 24-man detachment. War correspondent Stephen Crane (1871–1900) described it as "huge, fat, yellow, quivering." Before it was shot down, observers verified that the Spanish were in force on the San Juan heights and identified a trail that offered the American infantry an alternative attack route.

The possibilities of balloons in warfare were never fully explored. They were scorned by most generals, and some soldiers believed their use unfair. The International Peace Conference, held at The Hague in 1899, prohibited the dropping of projectiles from balloons. [See Zeppelin, Ferdinand von.]

Balloting. The bounding movement of a cannonball inside the bore of a gun.

Ball's Bluff, Battle of (21 October 1861), American Civil War. Union Brigadier General Charles Stone [q.v.] ordered Colonel Edward Baker [q.v.] to make a raid on a supposed Confederate camp near Leesburg, Virginia. Although the camp did not exist, the Federal force encountered troops under Colonel Nathan Evans [q.v.], and a battle ensued. Each side contained about 1,700 men, but the deployment of the Union forces at the top of a high, steep bluff with their backs to the Potomac was egregious, and they were soundly defeated, losing 921 men, including Baker and 48 others killed; 158 were wounded (some mortally), and 714 were captured or missing. The Confederates lost 149.

Several southern civilians joined the fight, notably Elijah Viers White (1832–1907), who later (4 February 1863) commanded the 35th Virginia Cavalry Battalion.

Ball Tuft. The ball of colored cotton or wool sometimes worn on the front of the shako.

Balogun. The military chief of the Yorubas in West Africa. The civil chief was a *bali*.

Balta, José (1816–1872). A Peruvian soldier and politician who, although he supported Mariano Ignacio Prado [q.v.] and served in his cabinet (1865–67), led a revolution that deposed him in 1868. Balta then became president and served until he was assassinated in an army mutiny.

Baltimore, Attack upon (12–14 September 1814), War of 1812. After British troops under Major General Robert Ross [q.v.] had won the Battle of Bladensburg [q.v.] and burned the public buildings in Washington, D.C., on 24 August 1814, they were reembarked on 30 September and transported by ships under Admiral Alexander Forrester Inglis Cochrane (1758–1832) north to a point about 12 miles from Baltimore, where on 12 September about 3,500 disembarked. After a march through thick woods to the city, they found 6,000 militia drawn up to protect it. Ross, who had promised his wife this would be his last campaign, was mortally wounded, and the attack was eventually abandoned. The British lost 46 killed and 300 wounded; the Americans lost 20 killed, 90 wounded, and 200 taken prisoner.

It was the naval bombardment of nearby Fort McHenry [q.v.], Maryland, that inspired Francis Scott Key [q.v.] to write the poem "The Defense of Fort McHenry," which was set to music and became "The Star-Spangled Banner" and eventually the national anthem [see Congreve, William; "Star-Spangled Banner, The"].

Baltimore Riot (19 March 1861), American Civil War. Massachusetts and Pennsylvania Union militia en route to Washington were required to march through Baltimore from one railroad station to another. On this date, as they marched

Balloons *Balloons during the siege of Paris, 1870–71*

through the city, they were set upon by a secessionist mob throwing stones. A few pistol shots were fired. The soldiers answered by firing indiscriminately into the throng. Four soldiers and 12 civilians were killed, and an unknown number wounded.

Bam, Occupation of (1801), Afghan-Persian conflicts. In 1719 the Afghans captured Bam, a town in the province of Kerman, Persia (Iran), 120 miles southeast of Kerman on the western edge of Dasht-i-Lut, the great salt desert 3,600 feet above sea level. They fortified the town, erecting a strong citadel, but in 1801 the Persians recaptured it and expelled the Afghans.

Ban. Persian word synonymous with the German *Markgraf,* meaning lord or master, and the title of some of the military chiefs who ruled banats and guarded the southern and eastern boundaries of Hungary. In 1868 Croatia and Slavonia were reunited with Hungary, and a special administration was made responsible for internal affairs; the head of this bureau was called the ban. The title and function were abolished in 1918. [See Military Frontier; Austrian Army.]

Bancal. A curved French sword used in the first quarter of the nineteenth century.

Banca Tin. A brand of English tin, noted for its purity, much used in the manufacture of cannon. The best came from the islands of Banca and Billotin in the Malayan archipelago.

Banda, Battle of (19 April 1858), Indian Mutiny. A force of about 1,000 British troops under Colonel George Cornish Whitlock defeated some 7,000 mutineers under the nawab of Banda at this place about 70 miles south of Cawnpore.

Bandanna. A neckerchief often worn by U.S. cavalrymen and cowboys in the West. It could be pulled over the nose and mouth to protect them from dust, tied down over the hatbrim to keep ears warm in winter, or tied around the neck to absorb sweat. Its uses were myriad: It was employed to wash, polish, dry, bandage, even to filter foul water.

Bandar Abbas, Revolt at (1868). Formerly known as Gombroon or Benderabbas, this port city on the north side of the Gulf of Ormuz in the Persian Gulf was ruled by the sultans of Muscat until a successful revolt in 1868 expelled the sultan and Persia (Iran) gained control.

Banderet. The title of the commander-in-chief of the troops of the canton of Bern, Switzerland.

Banderole. Sometimes written "bandrol" or "bannerole."
 1. A small flag used to mark out a camp or fortification, to convey signals, or to mark the position of the flanks of a unit deploying.
 2. A streamer on a lance.

Bandolier / Bandoleer. A broad belt worn across the chest and over the shoulder to carry charges, cartridges, or other items or as part of a ceremonial uniform.

Bandolier *Boer commandos with ammunition in bandoliers for single-shot breechloaders, 1875–85*

Bands, Military. At the beginning of the nineteenth century military bands were small, usually not more than 10 or 12 bandsmen. They were first officially recognized in the British army in 1803, when an order limited their size to not more than 1 private from each troop or company and 1 noncommissioned officer to serve as "Master of the Band." The Coldstream Guards was the first unit to import an entire band, 10 bandsmen from Germany. [See Bandsmen.]

Bands, Military *U.S. army regimental band*

Bandsmen. Musicians in a military band. Until 1832 bandsmen in the American army were outfitted at regimental expense, officers contributing one day's pay a month to support the band, which was under the adjutant but not a separate unit, the men remaining on the rolls of their companies. After 1832 colonels of regiments were allowed 10 musicians. Similar regulations applied to most British regiments throughout the nineteenth century.

When American troops under General Winfield Scott [q.v.] made their amphibious landing at Veracruz [q.v.] on 29 March 1847, bandsmen on the decks of the troopships played them over the side. In the American Civil War Philip Sheridan [q.v.] ordered them to "play the troops into action," as was the custom of pipers in the Scottish regiments of the British army. At the storming of the heights of Dargai [q.v.] during the Tirah Campaign [q.v.] a Scottish piper, George Findlater [q.v.], won the Victoria Cross [q.v.] for steadfastly piping his troops although he was badly wounded and under heavy fire.

In both the American and British armies boys as young as

twelve served as drummers or fifers. Such youngsters were permitted in the American army until 1864 [see Drummers and Fifers].

Bandsmen in some armies, including the American, were trained as medics, or were supposed to be, and in battle were used as stretcher-bearers. During the American Civil War some volunteer musicians resented this duty and refused to perform it.

Bangalore Torpedo. A device for exploding mines and later for cutting wire entanglements first used at the siege of Bangalore in India in 1799. It usually consisted of an iron pipe filled with an explosive with a detonating cap and a long fuze.

Bange, Charles Valérand Ragon de (1833–1914). A French artilleryman who in 1877–81 reorganized the French army's artillery. He was also the first to use effectively the screw principle for breechblock mechanisms on breech-loading guns.

Banks, Nathaniel Prentiss (1816–1894). An American politician who became a Civil War general. Although of little formal education, he was admitted to the bar at age twenty-three. After failing seven times, he succeeded in obtaining a seat in the Massachusetts legislature and eventually became speaker of the house. He became a member of Congress (1853–57) and then governor of Massachusetts (1858–61).

Although he had no military experience whatsoever, in January 1861 Lincoln appointed him a major general of volunteers, an appointment much resented by professional officers, who failed to realize the importance of politics and politicians in war, particularly in civil wars.

Banks proved to be a disaster in the field. He lost 30 percent of his force and was driven out of the Valley of Virginia by Thomas ("Stonewall") Jackson in the course of his famous Valley Campaign [q.v.]. In August 1862 he was again defeated by Jackson in the Battle of Cedar Mountain [q.v.]. He launched costly and unnecessary assaults at Port Hudson [q.v.], which he eventually captured and for which he received the Thanks of Congress [q.v.]. Succeeding Benjamin Butler [q.v.], he commanded the ill-fated Red River Campaign [q.v.] in 1864. After being superseded by Edward Canby [q.v.], he resigned from the army on 24 August 1865 and was at once elected to the first of six terms as a U.S. congressman.

Bannock-Paiute War (30 May–12 September 1878), American Indian Wars. Bannock Indians, encountering famine and receiving no government assistance, left their reservation, Fort Hall, on the Snake River in Lincoln Valley in southeastern Idaho. Joined by the Northern Paiutes, to whom they were related, they began to raid white settlements. Brigadier General Oliver Otis Howard [q.v.] led an expedition against them, defeating them in southern Idaho at Bennett Creek on 9 August and at Henry's Lake on 27 August. On 12 September, in a battle at Charles Ford on the Snake River near Big Wind in present-day Wyoming, some 140 Bannocks and Paiutes were killed. The remainder surrendered and returned to their reservations.

Banquette. 1. The step of earth within a parapet that enabled defenders to stand on it and fire over the parapet, then step down to reload in safety. Later called a fire step.

2. A gun platform behind a defensive wall or parapet.

Banzai. Literally, "ten thousand years." An enthusiastic cheer given by Japanese soldiers.

Bapaume, Battle of (2–3 January 1871), Franco-Prussian War. An indecisive battle in northern France claimed as a victory by the French. General Louis Faidherbe [q.v.], the French commander, won some tactical advantage in this fight against Germans under General August Karl von Goeben [q.v.], but on 19 January Faidherbe's army was virtually destroyed by Goeben at St. Quentin [q.v.], a city on the Somme in northern France. The Germans lost 52 officers and 698 men; the French lost 53 officers and 1,516 men killed and wounded and 550 taken prisoner. Faidherbe was forced to abandon his attempt to lift the siege of Péronne [q.v.], which fell soon after.

Bapedi Wars. In northern and eastern Transvaal, beginning in 1846, Bapedi tribesmen waged a series of wars against the Boers that resulted in the tribe's defeat and submission. In September 1861, led by Sekukuni [q.v.], the tribe rebelled against the Transvaal government. Their revolt was not suppressed until 1879, when a military expedition under British General Sir Garnet Wolseley [q.v.] succeeded in subduing them.

Baptism of Fire. A figurative term for the first experience of battle. [See Elephant, to See the.]

Bar. 1. A small rectangular piece of metal attached to the ribbon of medals in the British and some other services. The bar to a war or campaign medal usually gave the name or date of the campaign or engagement. The bar to a gallantry medal indicated a second award of that medal.

2. American insignia for company officers. Originally one silver bar for a first lieutenant and two for a captain. Later a gold bar was made the insignia of a second lieutenant. In the Confederate army a second lieutenant wore one bar, a first lieutenant two bars, and a captain three bars on the collar.

Baraguay / Barraguey d'Hilliers, Achille (1795–1878). A French soldier, son of Louis d'Hilliers Baraguay [q.v.], who was commissioned into the 9th Dragoons in 1809. He served in Napoleon's later campaigns before his first abdication but remained loyal to the Bourbons during the Hundred Days [q.v.]. He served in the force France sent to help Spain suppress the revolt of 1823 [see French Intervention in Spain] and in 1830 was with the expeditionary force that invaded Algeria [see Algeria, French Conquest and Occupation of]. Later that year he was promoted colonel, and from 1833 to 1841 he was commandant of St. Cyr [q.v.]. From 1841 to 1844 he was again in Algeria, where, serving under General Thomas Bugeaud de la Piconnerie [q.v.], he was removed from command for being a martinet. In 1849–50 he commanded the French expedition to Rome [see Rome Expedition, French]. During the Crimean War he commanded the French force that was sent to the Baltic, and on 16 August he captured the Russian fortress of Bomarsund [q.v.]. Soon after he was made a marshal of France. He played a leading role as commander of a corps in the Battle of Solferino [q.v.] in the Austro-Italian War [q.v.].

Baraguay d'Hilliers, Louis (1764–1812). A French soldier who was one of Napoleon's generals in Italy, Egypt, and Spain. His son, *Achille* [q.v.], became a marshal of France.

Baraka. An Arabic word roughly translated as "good luck" or "lucky." Belief in luck as a preternatural gift bestowing success and protection was not confined to the native-born of North and West Africa; it was held by many Europeans in the area. It was considered highly desirable, if not essential, for officers commanding Islamic troops to be thought to have baraka.

Baratier, Albert Ernest Augustin (1864–1917). A French officer who as a captain took part in the Marshand Expedition [q.v.] to Fashoda in 1898. He became a general of division in the First World War and died in the frontline trenches at Rheims on the western front.

Baratieri, Oreste (1841–1901). An Italian soldier who served under Giuseppe Garibaldi [q.v.] in Sicily in 1860–61. He joined the regular army and fought in the Battle of Custozza [q.v.] on 24 June 1866. In 1891 he was commander of troops in East Africa, and in 1892 he was appointed governor of Eritrea and fought the Abyssinians [see Italo-Abyssinian War]. In 1893 he was promoted major general. On 17 July 1894 he captured Kassala [q.v.] from the Dervishes [q.v.], but at Amba Alagai [q.v.] on 7 December 1895, at Mahalle on 21 January 1896, and at Adowa [q.v.] on 1 March 1896 he suffered humiliating defeats for which he was tried and exonerated by a military tribunal at Asmara. Nevertheless, he retired to the Tyrol soon after.

Barbacena, Marquês de, Filiberto Caldeira Brant Pontes (1772–1841). A Brazilian soldier and statesman who commanded the Brazilian army in the war against Argentina and Uruguay. He was defeated at Ituzaingó [q.v.] on 20 February 1827 and relieved of his command. Two years later he was appointed prime minister of Brazil (1829–30).

Barbed Wire. Twisted wire armed with barbs was first used by cattlemen in the American West. There were many designs. Between 1868 and 1885 no fewer than 306 patents for the wire were issued. The chief manufacturer came to be Joseph Farwell Glidden (1813–1906), who in 1874 obtained a patent for his barbed wire (sometimes called devil's rope or thorny fence). By 1883 his company in De Kalb, Illinois, was producing 600 miles, 100 tons, of wire per day. Although by 1900 the United States manufactured 200,000 tons annually, its value in static defense was not readily apparent to military tacticians. It was first used militarily in the 1890s by the Spanish in Cuba. Brigadier General Joseph Wheeler [q.v.] was impressed when he rode into Santiago soon after its surrender. "They were not merely lines of wire," he noted, "but pieces running perpendicularly, diagonally, horizontally and in every other direction, resembling nothing so much as a huge thick spider's web with an enormous mass in the center." It was used in the same period by the Boers in front of entrenchments at Magersfontein [q.v.] during the Second Anglo-Boer War [q.v.].

Barbee's Crossroads, Cavalry Affairs at. In the American Civil War three cavalry actions took place at this crossroads southeast of Manassas, Virginia. The first and most significant occurred on 5 November 1862, when 3,000 Confederate cavalry under Wade Hampton [q.v.] were attacked by about 1,500 Union cavalry under Alfred Pleasonton [q.v.]. The Confederates withdrew, having suffered 36 casualties; the Union cavalry, which lost 15 men, did not pursue.

A small action occurred on 25 July 1863, and one on 1 September 1863, in which Lieutenant Colonel Elijah Viers White (1832–1907) with 150 men of the 35th Virginia Cavalry Battalion ambushed a detachment of the 6th Ohio. The Federals managed to fight their way clear with a loss of 30.

Barbette. 1. A terrace of earth or stone raised behind a parapet high enough for a gun to be fired over. It was used in fixed fortress artillery. A gun was said to be in barbette when it was in a position to fire over a parapet.

2. A protected gun mounting concealed in an emplacement so that only the gun muzzle and upper shield, if any, were exposed.

Barbette *Union Sergeant John Carmody fires the barbette guns during the attack on Fort Sumter, 1861.*

Barbican / Barbacan. 1. A watchtower in a fortification.
2. Advanced works of a fort.
3. A fort or outwork at the entrance to a tower or bridge.

Barcelona, Capture of the Castle of (1808). During the Peninsular War a French force under Philibert Guillaume Duhesme (1766–1815), pretending to be a party of wounded, was allowed to enter the castle of Barcelona, which it quickly captured. The castle was retained as a French base, in spite of being intermittently besieged, until 1814.

Barcelona, Revolts of.
1. (1841–42). A revolt against Queen Isabella II (1830–1904) of Spain by Carlists in Barcelona was not put down until the town was bombarded and captured by Baldomero Esparto [q.v.] in December 1842 [see Carlist Wars].
2. The citadel was destroyed in 1868 in the Second Carlist War.

Barclay de Tolly, Mikhail Bogdanovich, Baron (1761–1818). Called by the Russians Michael Andreas, Prince Bogdanovich. He joined the Russian army as a private in 1776. He fought against the Turks and was commissioned about 1790. Later he fought in campaigns against the Swedes and Poles and in the winter campaign of 1806–07. He distinguished himself at Pultusk on 26 December 1806 and at Eylau [qq.v.], where he was wounded, on 8 February 1807. He recovered sufficiently to accompany General Pëtr Bagration [q.v.] in his capture of Aaland Island in 1808. In 1810 he became minister of war, and in 1812 he was also made commander of the Army of the West. He introduced numerous reforms and modernized the army.

During the 1812 campaign [see Russian Campaign, Napoleon's] he was defeated at Smolensk [q.v.] and superseded as commander in chief by Mikhail Kutusov [q.v.]. He commanded the right wing at Borodino [q.v.] and resigned after the battle. However, the following year he led a new Russian army into Silesia and linked up with the Prussian army. He then fought at Bautzen, Dresden, Kulm, and Leipzig [qq.v.]. In 1814 he commanded the Russian forces in France and occupied Paris. After Napoleon's escape from Elba [see Hundred Days] he set out with a Russian army for France, but the Battle of Waterloo was fought before he arrived.

By the time of his death the former Russian private was a prince and a field marshal.

Bareilly, Battle of (6 May 1858), Indian Mutiny. A British force of 8,000 under Colin Campbell [q.v.] defeated a force of 36,000 rebels, including 6,000 cavalry, with 40 guns under Khan Bahadur II. A notable feature of the battle was an attack by 130 ghazis (Islamic religious fanatics), who held back the British advance until all were killed. The bulk of the rebel force proved timid, and most fled without fighting.

Bärentatzen. The German name (literally, bear's paw) for a fringed lace loop worn on the cuff of Hungarian regiments in the Austrian army.

Baril Ardent. A fire in a barrel used for illumination. It was made of layers of tarred chips mixed with powder into which a fuze was fixed.

Baril Foudroyant / Baril d'Artifice. A baril ardent equipped with explosives between layers of tarred chips. They were used to defend a breech by being rolled down on the attackers.

Barisan. Native infantry in the army of the prince of Madura (Madoera), an island off the northeast coast of Java in what was the Dutch East Indies.

Bark Creek, Skirmish at (18 December 1876), American Indian Wars. A small cavalry affair between American troops and Sioux Indians near the head of Red Water Creek in Dakota Territory.

Barksdale, William (1821–1863). An American soldier and politician who served in the Mexican War [q.v.]. When Mississippi seceded from the Union, he was named quartermaster general of the Mississippi army. In March of that year he was elected colonel of the 13th Mississippi, a regiment he led at First Bull Run, at Ball's Bluff, and in the Peninsular Campaign [qq.v.]. On 29 June 1862 at Savage's Station [q.v.] he was given a brigade, which he commanded at Antietam, Fredericksburg, Chancellorsville, and Gettysburg [qq.v.].

At Fredericksburg he and his brigade particularly distinguished themselves by successfully delaying the Federal river crossing at a cost of 29 killed, 151 wounded, and 62 missing. At Chancellorsville his brigade held off repeated attacks until it was overpowered by superior numbers, losing 43 killed, 208 wounded, and 341 missing. At Gettysburg on 2 July 1863 he was mortally wounded and died the next day.

Barlow, Francis Channing (1834–1896). An American who in 1855 was graduated first in his class at Harvard. He was admitted to the bar three years later and was practicing law when the American Civil War began. He enlisted as a private in the 12th New York Militia, a three-month regiment [q.v.], and married the same day. Eleven days later he was a first lieutenant. He was mustered out in August at the expiration of his three months. On 9 November he was commissioned a lieutenant colonel of the 61st New York Volunteers. On 14 April 1862 he was promoted colonel, and he was present at Yorktown, at Fair Oaks [q.v.], and in the Peninsular Campaign [q.v.]. On 17 September he was severely wounded at Antietam [q.v.]. Two days later he was promoted brigadier general. He recovered to command his brigade at Chancellorsville [q.v.]. He commanded a division in the Battle of Gettysburg [q.v.] and on the first day was again severely wounded, this time by a bullet that temporarily paralyzed his arms and legs. Left for dead, he was found by Confederate General John Gordon [q.v.], who gave him water and had him carried from the field. Gordon also arranged for Barlow's wife, a nurse with the Union forces, to pass through the lines to attend him.

Barlow was exchanged but did not rejoin the army until Grant's Overland Campaign, in which he commanded a corps. On 12 May 1864, in the Battle of Spotsylvania [q.v.], his corps, together with that of David Birney [q.v.], made a spectacular capture of 3,000 Confederates, including 2 generals; also taken were 30 colors and 20 guns. For this action he was made a brevet major general. After the investment of Petersburg [q.v.], he took an extended sick leave in Europe. He returned to the war in time to take part in the Battle of Sayler's Creek [q.v.] and the closing engagements in Virginia.

After the war he returned to practicing law and was one of the founders of the American Bar Association. He entered politics, and as attorney general for New York he prosecuted William Marcy ("Boss") Tweed (1823–1878).

Barnard, Henry William (1799–1857). A British soldier educated at Sandhurst [q.v.] who was commissioned into the Grenadier Guards [q.v.] in 1814. The following year he was with the Allied army that occupied Paris. He saw service in Jamaica and as a major general fought in the Crimean War [q.v.], serving as chief of staff. In April 1857, on the death of General George Anson (1797–1857), he was placed in command of the force that in May of that year, during the Indian Mutiny, marched on Delhi. He died of cholera on 5 July during the siege.

Barnard, John Gross (1815–1882). An American officer who was graduated number two from the West Point class of 1833 and so served in the Corps of Engineers. He spent his career in construction. At the beginning of the American Civil War he was charged with building Washington's defenses. He became chief engineer of the Army of the Potomac [q.v.], a post he filled until Grant took command. After the war he restructured the entire coastal defense system to cope with iron warships.

Barong. A heavy knife with a spatulated, double-edged blade used in Borneo and the Philippines. [See Parang.]

Barrackpore Mutiny (1824). During the First Anglo-Burmese War [q.v.] the 47th Bengal Native Infantry regiment of the Honourable East India Company at Barrackpore, 15 miles north of Calcutta, was scheduled to embark for Burma (Myanmar), but its troops refused to leave, protesting that they would lose caste by "crossing the dark waters." They were bombarded with artillery and fled under fire. The ringleaders were caught and hanged, others were imprisoned, and the regiment was disbanded.

Barracks. 1. In a general sense, any post, camp, station, or fort where soldiers are stationed, including the quarters, stables, messes, shops, offices, and other buildings.

2. In a narrower sense, permanent or semipermanent buildings used in garrisons for housing soldiers. Although the first barracks for troops in Britain were erected for the Foot Guards [q.v.] in 1660, all other British troops, until the nineteenth century, were billeted in civilian homes, a practice so unpopular that the Americans specifically protested it in their Declaration of Independence and made a point of prohibiting the practice when they became independent. By 1805 there were 203 British barracks, but serious health problems developed when overcrowding became so severe that men slept two to four in a bed. The first bath was not installed in a British barracks until 1855. The mortality rate of soldiers in Britain in the nineteenth century was 17.5 per 1,000, which compared unfavorably with the rate of 9.2 for males in civil life. In 1861, following a commission's report on barracks, 600 cubic feet of air space became standard.

In the American army as late as 1870 only 39 out of 146 army posts met the British standard. General William Tecumseh Sherman [q.v.], after inspecting the barracks at Fort Sedgwick in eastern Colorado in the 1870s, called them "hovels in which a negro would hardly go" and added that if southern slaveholders had used such quarters, "a sample would, ere this, have been carried to Boston and exhibited as illustrative of the cruelty and inhumanity of masters."

By 1895 most of the American barracks had iron bunks, but neither sheets nor pillows were issued. Every two men were, according to regulations, given 44 pounds of straw per month, and a cord of wood for heating was issued to every six men.

[See Women in Barracks.]

Barrel. The metal tube in firearms that contains the projectile and charge and serves as the projectile's initial path. Sometimes called the tube.

Barrel, Powder. Barrels built to contain 100 pounds of powder and large enough to allow space for the powder to move when rolled to prevent caking.

Barrel Drill. The American name for a punishment that required a soldier to stand on a barrel for a specified length of time, sometimes with a placard proclaiming his offense. He was sometimes required to wear a "barrel overcoat," a barrel with the ends removed, suspended from the shoulders by straps.

Barricades. Mounds formed of trees, earth, overturned vehicles, or any other item to bar a street, road, or any passageway.

Barracks used by the Prussian army in 1866.

Barracks at Giesboro depot, July 1865

Barricades *Citizens of Altenberg erecting barricades during the German Revolution of 1848*

Barringer, Rufus (1821–1895). A Confederate soldier and politician who was elected a captain in the 1st North Carolina Cavalry at the outbreak of the American Civil War. He served with distinction in all the campaigns of the Army of Northern Virginia [q.v.] and was three times wounded. Although he was by his first marriage the brother-in-law of both General D. H. Hill [q.v.] and T. J. ("Stonewall") Jackson, he remained a captain until after Gettysburg, after which he rose rapidly to end the war as a brigadier general.

Barrios, Justo Rufino (1835–1885). A Guatemalan soldier and political leader who was commander-in-chief of the Guatemalan army from 1871 to 1873, when he and Miguel García Granados (1809–1878) led a revolution that toppled the government. Granados became president but retired after two years. Barrios succeeded him. In an attempt to unite Central America he invaded El Salvador and was killed on 2 April 1885, leading an army in the Battle of Chalchuapa [q.v.].

Justo Rufino Barrios, Guatemalan general (1835–1885)

Barrosa, Battle of (5 March 1811), Peninsular War. Some 15,000 Spanish and British troops under General Thomas Graham [q.v.] in southwestern Spain marched from Tarifa upon Cádiz, which was being besieged by French General Claude Victor [q.v.]. Near the village of Barrosa, southeast of Cádiz, they encountered 7,000 French under General Jean François Leval. British losses were 50 officers and 1,160 men out of 4,000 engaged; French losses were about 2,000 killed and wounded, including 2 generals, and 400 taken prisoner, plus six guns. A large Spanish force stood idly by and took no part in the engagement.

It was at this battle that Sergeant Patrick Masterson [q.v.] of the British 87th Regiment captured the eagle of the French 87th Regiment of the Line from Sous-Lieutenant Edmé Guillemin. This first capture of a French eagle invigorated Britain. At least three popular prints depicted the action.

Barry, Dr. "James" (1799?–1865). A female British military surgeon whose sex was not discovered until after her death. Her parents are unknown. She gave her birth year as 1799, but she entered Edinburgh University in 1810 and after qualifying M.D. and passing as a man, she entered the army as a hospital assistant on 5 July 1813, giving her age then as eighteen. Two years later she was an assistant surgeon and began her progress through the various grades to become inspector general of army hospitals.

Standing only five feet tall, she was delicately built. Her complexion was pale, and her hair described as reddish.

She served at Malta and in South Africa, where she fought a duel with an aide-de-camp of the governor-general, in which neither was scratched. Quarrelsome and brash, she was several times placed under arrest but never court-martialed. She was once described as "the most skillful of physicians and the most wayward of men."

In 1829 she was transferred to Mauritius, where her superior noted that she had an unfortunate manner, was tactless and impatient of control. When informed of his evaluation, she promptly boarded ship and returned to England. There she reported to Sir James McGrigor [q.v.] and, when asked why she had left her post without permission, ran her fingers through her hair and answered, "I have come home to have my hair cut." Thinking her tetched, McGrigor granted her a year's leave.

She later served in the Caribbean and at St. Helena, where she complained of lack of supplies and quarreled with the commissary. When she complained directly to the secretary of state for war in London, she was court-martialed but acquitted. A quarrel with the governor over pay led to her being ordered back to England under arrest. Dispatched back to the West Indies, she was stricken by yellow fever, the first time in thirty-two years of foreign service she had ever reported sick. She placed the doctor who tended her under orders to bury her in her clothes immediately if she died and not to allow her body to be inspected.

When permission to serve in Crimea during the Crimean War was denied, she took leave and went there anyway. In Turkey she met Florence Nightingale [q.v.] and, according to Miss Nightingale, scolded her in public and "behaved like a brute." After Barry's death she referred to her as "the most hardened creature I ever met."

Barry was forced to retire in 1859, and she died on 25 July 1865. It never occurred to the surgeon who signed her death certificate to check her sex; he had known Dr. Barry as a "brother officer" for many years. Her sex was discovered by the woman summoned to lay out her body, who declared that not only was she a woman but that the striae gravidarum on her abdomen attested that she had had a child. It has been suggested that she may have been a hermaphrodite; the truth will never be known.

Barry, John Decatur (1839–1867). A Confederate soldier in the American Civil War who enlisted in the 18th North Carolina and on April 1862 was elected captain. He fought through the Seven Days' Battles, Second Bull Run, and Antietam [qq.v.]. He was a major at Chancellorsville [q.v.], and it was he who, refusing to believe that Stonewall Jackson and his staff were not Federal cavalry, ordered his men to fire; Jackson was struck by three bullets; others with him were killed or wounded.

This error did not influence Barry's career. He rose to be a colonel and temporarily led a brigade until wounded at Cold Harbor [q.v.]. He led his regiment in Pickett's Charge at Gettysburg and survived the war.

Barry, William Farquhar (1818–1879). An American officer who was graduated from West Point in 1838 and served in the Mexican War and in the Second Seminole War [qq.v.]. At the beginning of the American Civil War he was a major in the 5th Artillery and commanded the Union artillery in the First Battle of Bull Run [q.v.]. During the Peninsular Campaign [q.v.] he commanded the artillery in the Army of the Potomac. He later served as William Sherman's [q.v.] chief of artillery and distinguished himself in the Atlanta Campaign [q.v.] in 1864. On 1 September 1864 he was promoted substantive colonel and a major general of volunteers. He remained in the army after the war and in 1867 reorganized the artillery school of practice [q.v.] at Fort Monroe. He commanded the school for ten years.

Bar Shot. A projectile consisting of two cannonballs or half balls connected by an iron bar.

Bar-sur-Aube, Battle of (27 February 1814), Napoleonic Wars. In northeastern France after the French victory at Montereau [q.v.] on 18 February 1814, Allied forces under Karl von Schwarzenberg [q.v.] retreated eastward beyond the Aube River, pursued by a French force under Marshals Nicolas Charles Oudinot and Jacques Macdonald [qq.v.]. On 27 February, however, Russians and Bavarians launched a counterattack that struck Oudinot when he was poorly positioned astride the Aube. Outmaneuvered and outnumbered, he fell back defeated upon Troyes.

Bartizan. A small overhang or corbel from the wall of a fort or castle used as a sentinel's post.

Bartlett, William Francis (1840–1876). A Union soldier in the American Civil War who was a student at Harvard College when the war began. On 4 April 1861 he enlisted as a private in a Massachusetts infantry battalion, and on 8 August he was elected captain. He fought at Ball's Bluff [q.v.] and elsewhere until he lost a leg in the Battle of Yorktown [q.v.] and was mustered out on 12 August 1862. Fitted with an artificial leg, he organized and led other Massachusetts regiments and was wounded three times more: twice at the siege of Port Hudson and again in the Battle of the Wilderness [qq.v.]. He was promoted a brigadier general on 20 June 1864 at the age of twenty-four and for a time commanded a division. At Petersburg [q.v.] he was captured when his cork leg was shattered. At war's end he was brevetted a major general. He never fully recovered from his wounds.

Barton, Clarissa (Clara) Harlowe (1821–1912). An American Civil War hospital worker and later founder of the American Red Cross. From 1836 to 1854 she taught school in Oxford, Massachusetts, and for two years she worked in the Patent Office in Washington, D.C. During the Civil War she solicited funds for medical supplies, which she distributed to the Union army at Fredericksburg, Antietam [qq.v.] and elsewhere. In June 1864 she was officially appointed superintendent of nurses for the Army of the James. Although she never married, she required affection. For a time she enjoyed an affair with a married officer, and she had affectionate relationships with many patients and friends. In 1870 she traveled to Europe and, working for the International Red Cross, gave aid to sick and wounded in France during the Franco-Prussian War. She was appalled by the "mischief and misery that the armies strew in their paths."

In 1877 she helped organize the American National Committee, which became the American Red Cross [q.v.], whose first president she became, serving from 1882 to 1904. She successfully campaigned to have the United States sign the Geneva Agreement in 1882, and in 1885 she was responsible for the "American Amendment" to the Geneva Convention, allowing the Red Cross to provide relief at times of natural disasters as well as in wartime. At the age of seventy-seven she took to the field during the Spanish-American War. In her final years as president of the Red Cross she was subjected to severe criticism for her authoritarian management style.

Clara Barton as an unofficial field nurse with the Army of the Potomac

Baryatinski / Bariatinsky, Prince Aleksandr Ivanovich (1814–1879). A Russian soldier born into a noble family related to the Romanovs and a childhood companion of the tsarevich. Handsome, tall, rich, and privileged, as a young guards officer he was known for his seductions of women rather than his military skills, but he won fame in the Caucasus, where on 1 January 1856 he was made commander-in-chief of the tsar's Caucasian army. In the next four years he conducted three successful campaigns against rebellious tribes. His crowning achievement was the storming of Gounib in western Daghestan, ending the resistance of the Muslim mountain tribes to Russian rule, and the capture of Shamyl [q.v.], the imam of the Lezghians of Daghestan. His reward was a field marshal's baton and a gold sword. In 1853 he was appointed chief of staff.

Bascom Affair (1860–61), American Indian Wars. In October 1860 Coyotero Apaches raided John Ward's ranch in the Sonoita Valley in south Arizona about 25 miles north of Nogales, making off with his oxen and his six-year-old stepson, a mixed-blood son of an Apache warrior and Ward's Mexican wife, herself a former captive. Because Ward thought (mistakenly) that the raiders were Chiricahua Apaches in Cochise's [q.v.] band, Second Lieutenant George Nicholas Bascom (1836–1862) with one company of the 7th Infantry mounted on mules rode out in January 1861 to meet with Cochise and demand the return of the oxen and the boy. At Apache Pass in southeast Arizona, about 25 miles east-northeast of Willcox, on 4 February Cochise, with his brother, two nephews, a woman, and a child, appeared at Bascom's camp and denied responsibility for the raid. Unconvinced, Bascom tried to seize them all as hostages. There was a struggle, and firing ensued. Cochise escaped, leaving the others in Bascom's hands.

Cochise then seized a stagecoach employee and two hapless travelers and offered to trade hostages. In a dramatic confrontation Bascom refused to bargain unless the boy and the oxen were included in the trade. In reply, Cochise blockaded Apache Pass, on the immigrant route to California, attacked a wagon train and set it afire after tying the wagoners to their wagon wheels, massacred and mutilated his hostages, and fled to Mexico.

When the bodies were discovered, three of the Chiricahua hostages and three Coyoteros were hanged from a scrub oak over the graves of the murdered whites. This exchange of barbarities plunged Arizona into twenty-five years of hostilities between the settlers and the Chiricahua Apaches.

The stepson of John Ward survived to become a famous Arizona character known as Mickey Free [q.v.].

Base Line. 1. The place or line where magazines and supply depots were maintained.

2. The line on which troops in column moved.

Base of Operations. A secure line of frontier or an area from which forward movements could be made, supplies collected, and upon which a retreat might be made.

Bashi / Bachi / Baschi. A Turkish suffix, or often a prefix, to a title indicating head, chief, superior, or officer. Among the most prominent:

Balik-bashi = corporal
Bashbugh = a Turkish commander-in-chief
Bimbashi = a rank equivalent to major
Boluck-bashi = colonel of a regiment (boluck) of 1,000 militia
Bostanji-bashi = chief of the Bostanji [q.v.]
Chorbaji-bashi = Literally, "head soup dispenser." The title of the commander of the janissaries [q.v.]
Dukigi-bashi = second-in-command of a battery of Turkish artillery
Konadschjy-bashi = quartermaster general
Oda-bashi = company officers who supervised drill
Solacki-bashi = subcommander of the archers
Sandschjack-dalars-bashi = chief of the 50 color-bearers
Toptschjy-bashi = general of artillery and inspector of forts

Bashi-Bazouks. Literally, "cracked heads." Irregular Turkish cavalry, usually Albanians, Circassians, and Kurds, from the wilder areas of the Ottoman Empire. They were noted for their lack of discipline, their cruelty, and their plundering of friend and foe. During the Crimean War [q.v.] the British hired a contingent but were unable to infuse any discipline into them. During the war Richard Francis Burton (1821–1890), the explorer and writer, served with them briefly. [See Bulgarian Revolts.]

Bashkir. Asian light cavalry in the Russian army.

Basket Hilt. A sword hilt designed to give protection to the whole hand.

Bassi, Ugo (1800–1849). An Italian who, disappointed in love, became a monk in the Barnabite order at the age of eighteen and eventually became a noted preacher. In 1848 he joined the division of the papal army under Giovanni Durando [q.v.] as a chaplain. When Pope Pius IX (1792–1878) fled, Bassi joined Giuseppe Garibaldi [q.v.] in fighting the French, who had been sent to reestablish the temporal power, and he gained a reputation for bravery in tending the wounded under fire. He was captured near the fortified commune of Comacchio in northern Italy and turned over to the Austrians, who shot him.

He was said to have had a "gentle unselfish soul" and an "almost childlike nature" (*Encyclopaedia Britannica*).

Bastille Day (14 July). This day, memorializing the date in 1789 when the Bastille in Paris was stormed by a mob, was first celebrated in France as a national holiday in 1880. Then and subsequently it was marked by a grand review of the Paris garrison in the Bois de Boulogne. In the first review new regimental colors were presented, mostly to units that had lost theirs at Metz or Sedan [qq.v.] in the Franco-Prussian War [q.v.].

Bastinado. A common punishment in the Turkish army in which the soles of the offender's feet were beaten with a cane or the flat of a sword.

Bastion. 1. Any fortified position or stronghold.

2. A fortification consisting of two faces and two flanks, all the angles being salient, projecting from the main fort or earthwork. The faces of a bastion were those parts exposed to enfilade fire by ricochet batteries and to being battered until breached.

Bastions could be protected by galleries of mines; by demilunes or ravelins and lunettes outside the ditch; and, if the ditch was inundated, by palisades. Two bastions were connected by a curtain, which was screened by the angle made by the prolongation of the corresponding faces of the bastions.

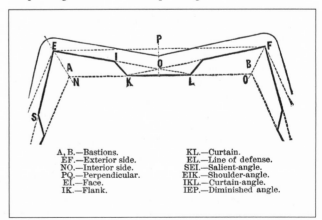

A, B.—Bastions.
EF.—Exterior side.
NO.—Interior side.
PQ.—Perpendicular.
EI.—Face.
IK.—Flank.
KL.—Curtain.
EL.—Line of defense.
SEI.—Salient-angle.
EIK.—Shoulder-angle.
IKL.—Curtain-angle.
IEP.—Diminished angle.

Bastion

Bastionet. A small bastion, usually in masonry.

Basuto Wars (1822–1884). The Basutos were a tribe made up of the remnants of the many tribes scattered by the wars and raids of Shaka [q.v.], king of the Zulus, in the first two decades of the nineteenth century. They were brought together by Moshesh [q.v.], who, about 1822, became their paramount chief and in 1832 established a stronghold on the summit of flat-topped Thaba Bosigo [q.v.]. Although frequently attacked by the Boers, Zulus, and other tribes, the stronghold remained impregnable.

Through his substantial military and political skills, Moshesh was able to hold off both the Boers and the British. He soundly defeated a force of British soldiers, Boers, and a native contingent sent against him in 1852 at Berea, Basutoland, as well as a large Boer commando that attacked him in 1857–58. In 1863 Johannes Hendricus Brand (1823–1888), president of the Orange Free State, began a long, intermittent, and inconclusive war with the tribe.

On 15 August 1865 a Boer commando under Louw Wepener [q.v.] attempted to take Thaba Bosigo by storm. Although the commando was beaten back and Wepener was killed, the Orange Free State acquired a large piece of Basutoland by the Treaty of Thaba Bosigo, signed on 3 April 1866.

On 12 March 1868 the British annexed the country, and it was administered by the British government in Cape Colony. In 1879 British authorities foolishly attempted to disarm the Basutos, whose resistance resulted in the Gun War [q.v.], which dragged on for several years. All diplomatic and military efforts to end it failed until 1884, when Basutoland was made a separate territory, still under a paramount chief but administered by a resident British commissioner reporting directly to London.

During the Second Anglo-Boer War [q.v.] the Basutos remained neutral, and in general, their neutrality was observed by both sides.

Bataillon Carré. See Bataillon Encadré.

Bataillon de Canonniers Sédentairs. A battalion of foot artillery kept up at Lille, France, in remembrance of its siege in 1792.

Bataillon Encadré. A deployment of troops developed by Napoleon in which a battalion or other unit is framed in by others on its right and its left. It is sometimes called a *bataillon carré*. Military historian Basil Liddell Hart (1895–1970) described its overall effect as "a widespread net whose corners are weighted with stones; when one of the enemy's columns impinged on it the net closed in round the point of pressure and the stones crashed together on the intruder."

Batardeau. A strong dam of masonry built across an outer ditch of a fort to sustain the pressure of water when one part of the ditch is dry and another full.

Batavia, Capture of (August 1811), Java War. A British force of 10,000 under Sir Samuel Auchmuty [q.v.] landed in Java and on 8 August occupied Batavia (today Djakarta), which had been abandoned by the Dutch. The Dutch under General Herman Daendels [q.v.] retreated to a strong position at nearby Fort Cornelis. The British stormed it on 28 August, and although its defenders put up a stubborn resistance, a gallant charge by General Rollo Gillespie [q.v.] carried the day. British losses were 872 killed and wounded.

Samarang (Semarang) in north-central Java saw the final Dutch resistance. When it fell on 8 September, the Dutch governor surrendered. On 17 September the Dutch signed the capitulation of Samarang in which they ceded Java, Timor, Palembang, and Macassar to the British.

Bat d'Af. Popular name for the French penal battalions of light infantry whose official name was Bataillions d'Afrique. [See Infantrie Légère d'Afrique.]

Bâteau Gribeauval. The basic bridging unit of the Napoleonic army. Each boat or pontoon was 36 feet long, slightly more than 4 feet high, and weighed more than two tons. As the name Gribeauval's boats implies, they were named after General Jean Baptiste Vaquette Gribeauval (1715–1789), an artilleryman who in the eighteenth century made French artillery the finest in Europe.

Batetelar Uprising (1895–1901). Sometimes referred to as a mutiny because Batetelar troops from the Congo on an 1897 expedition in the southern Sudan mutinied, killed some of their Belgian officers, and bolted. In 1895 the tribe, located in the area of the Lomami and Lulua rivers in the Congo Free State, revolted against Belgian rule, but their revolt was soon suppressed. In September 1897 the tribe again revolted, killed 3 officers and 200 men at Ungula, and this time seized a large area of the eastern Congo. The Belgians organized a considerable force under Baron François Dhanis [q.v.] and advanced against them, but it was not until October 1899 that they were able to put down the rebellion. The tribe was not completely crushed until November 1901.

Bath, Order of the Knights of. A high British order of chivalry, formally constituted on 11 October 1399, that prior to 25 May 1847 was awarded only to military and naval officers. The order has three classes, and the numbers admitted to each are restricted: The Knights Grand Cross (KGB), excluding the royal family and foreigners, is limited to 50 military personnel and 25 civil servants; the Knights Commander (KCB), exclusive of foreigners, is limited to 102 military personnel and 25 civil servants; the Companions (CB) is restricted to 525 military officers and 200 civilians. Although all members of the order are permitted postnominal letters, only those in the first two classes are allowed the title Sir before their first names.

No officer can be nominated unless his name has been mentioned in the *London Gazette* for distinguished services. In the nineteenth century the order was never bestowed upon an officer below the rank of major in the army or commander in the navy.

Batman. Originally a man in charge of a pack animal (French: *cheval de bât*). From tending to the animal the batman progressed to responsibility for the owner's other personal possessions. By the early nineteenth century he had become the servant of an officer; later the term was restricted to the soldier servants of warrant officers (U.S. usage: senior noncommissioned officers). The term "servant" applied to those soldiers who performed similar functions for an officer. In the American service a batman was called a striker; in the French army, *brosseur*.

Batoche, Battle of (9–12 May 1885). The Canadian revolutionary Louis Riel [q.v.] made his headquarters at this village in central Saskatchewan, 40 miles south-southwest of Prince Albert, after his second failure to provoke a general uprising among the Métis (French-Indian half-breeds) and Indians [see Red River Expedition]. In still another attempt at rebellion his able lieutenant Gabriel Dumont [q.v.] won a first small victory over government forces in the Battle of Duck Lake [q.v.] on 26 March 1885, but Riel's popularity among the local people rapidly ebbed.

General Frederick Dobson Middleton [q.v.] with 5,000 Canadian militiamen went to Saskatchewan via the newly built Canadian Pacific Railway. On 11 May near Batoche Middleton fought a pitched battle with Riel's force of Métis under Dumont. Middleton's force suffered a loss of 54 killed and wounded. Riel's force lost 224, of which only about a dozen were killed. Dumont escaped, taking his wife with him, but Riel was captured on 15 May; he was tried, convicted, and on 16 November hanged for treason at Regina. An attempt at rescue by the faithful Dumont was aborted.

Baton. 1. A short, thick truncheon, highly decorated, presented as the symbol of authority to a field marshal. An emblem of authority in Roman times, the baton first appeared in modern times when it was presented to Henry III of France (1551–1589), then still a prince, on his being made generalissimo of the army of his brother, Charles IX (1550–1574) in 1569. Napoleon created a marshalate in 1804 and gave batons to 18 of his generals. Later he presented batons to 8 others. Capped with gold at both ends and covered with blue velvet embellished with gold eagles, they were approximately 18 inches long and 2 inches in diameter.

German, Russian, and other Continental armies had field marshals in the seventeenth century, but the first British field marshal's baton was awarded to a British general only in 1736. Wellington was the first Briton in the nineteenth century to be presented with one. The rank badge of British general officers was and is a baton crossed over a sword; the insignia of a field marshal was, and is, two crossed batons. [See Marshal, Field.]

2. A staff carried by drum majors in the bands of infantry regiments.

Baton Rouge. Battle of (5 August 1862), American Civil War. After failing to capture Vicksburg, Mississippi, in their first attempt, Federal forces on 26 July 1862 fell back upon Baton Rouge, Louisiana, which they had first occupied on 12 May. The city was defended by Union Brigadier General Thomas Williams [q.v.], who commanded some 2,500 effectives in seven regiments. Confederate Major General Earl Van Dorn [q.v.] ordered Major General John Cabell Breckinridge [q.v.] to attack the town with about 6,000 picked men and three batteries of artillery. The attack on 5 August, which was to have been supported by gunboats on the river including the ironclad *Arkansas*, failed, the Confederates losing 453 out of 2,600 actually engaged. The Federals lost 383. Williams, who conducted a brilliant defense, was killed by a rifle bullet in the chest.

Batta. An extra allowance paid to soldiers, officers and other ranks, in the Indian armies for service in the field or outside their normal area. Originally it was only occasionally given,

but it grew to be an expected part of a soldier's compensation, and there were occasions when soldiers became turbulent when the batta was reduced. This was particularly true on 29 November 1828, when Lord William Cavendish Bentinck (1774–1839), the governor-general, reduced the full batta of all regiments serving at stations relatively near the Bengal presidency to half batta. The government refused to back down, and the troops were left to grumble. [See Allowances.]

Battalion. A unit in European and American armies larger than a company and smaller than a regiment. It usually consists of 500 to 1,000 men in two to twelve companies, troops, or batteries commanded by a major or a lieutenant colonel. Although usually a unit within a regiment [q.v.], in the nineteenth century it sometimes acted independently within a larger unit. In the British service a battalion often constituted an entire regiment. In the Confederate army during the American Civil War the word almost always designated a unit smaller than and not a part of a regiment.

Battalion *Swiss battalion in Andermatt, 18 August 1861*

Battalion Men. Soldiers in an infantry regiment except those in the flank companies.

Battenberg, Prince Alexander of (1820–1893). An officer in the Hessian army who in 1879 was elected to be the first prince of the newly formed principality of Bulgaria. In 1885 he annexed eastern Rumania after an uprising there, an action that provoked the hostility of Serbia, whose army he defeated in a two-week campaign. His attack on Serbia offended Russia, and the following year he was abducted from his palace in Sofia by pro-Russian army conspirators and forced to abdicate. Although freed within a few days, he retired to Darmstadt, Austria, where he lived as Count Hartenau.

Batterie en Rouage. An enfilading battery when directed against an enemy battery.

Battering Train. A collection of heavy artillery such as mortars and howitzers of large caliber, used solely for besieging fortified places. [See Siege Train.]

Battery. 1. An artillery unit of two or more cannon, usually four to six, and all necessary animals and gear; an administrative and a tactical unit. In the British and American armies artillery units were originally called companies. The term "bat-

Battery *Lieutenant Bayard Wilkeson holds his battery, 4th U.S. Artillery, at Gettysburg.*

tery" was first employed during the Crimean War [q.v.]. In 1859 all British artillery companies were officially renamed batteries, a change that did not take place in the American army until after the Civil War. In the American army the battery was the smallest administrative artillery unit and was commanded by a captain. In the field and horse artillery each gun and limber or caisson and limber was pulled by a six-horse team.

2. Guns in place and ready to fire.

3. The position of a gun's barrel when ready for action. In firing a muzzle-loading gun, the recoil jolted it out of line; consequently it had to be put back into battery before it could be refired.

Battery Boxes. Square or rectangular chests or boxes filled with earth or stones and used in place of gabions.

Battery Wagon. A long-bodied cart attached to a limber. Boxes carrying tools, supplies, and replacement parts were fixed to its sides, and in the rear was a rack for carrying forage. One accompanied each field battery of artillery.

Battery Wagon *Battery wagon, Petersburg, Virginia, September 1864*

Battle. 1. As a noun, a general hostile engagement between two or more opposing armed forces.

2. As a verb, to engage in conflict; to contend.

In the nineteenth century war was a series of battles, sometimes only two, as in the Gwalior Campaign [q.v.]. On the eve of the Battle of Leipzig (15 October 1813) Napoleon said: "Between a battle lost and a battle won, the distance is immense and there stand empires."

Battle above the Clouds. See Chattanooga Campaign; Lookout Mountain, Battle of.

Battle Array. The disposition of forces prepared for battle.

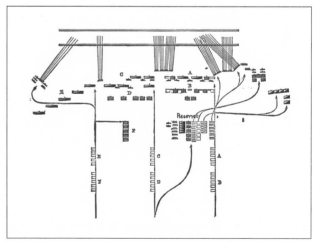

Battle Array *Diagram of exercise for line of battle*

Battlefield. The area where a battle is fought; sometimes referred to simply as the field. The German writer Jean Paul Richter (1763–1825) wrote in *Titan* (1803): "A battlefield is at once the playroom of all the gods and the dancehall of all the furies."

Battle Flag, Confederate. The first Confederate flag, the Stars and Bars [q.v.], too closely resembled the Stars and

Stripes of the Union flag. After the First Battle of Bull Run [q.v.] on 21 July 1861 General Pierre Beauregard [q.v.] designed or had designed a more distinctive flag to be carried in battle. From this evolved the Confederate battle flag, a blue cross of St. Andrew's edged with a narrow white band bearing thirteen five-pointed white stars on a red field. It is this flag that most people associate with the Confederacy.

Battle Flag, Confederate *6th Virginia Cavalry battle flag displaying the St. Andrew's cross*

Battle Honors. In the American army colored streamers inscribed with the names of (usually) successful campaigns or battles are attached to the staff of the regimental or unit flag. In the British army the principal battle honors are stitched onto the regiment flag or painted on the sides of its drums. They can also adorn accoutrements, regimental crests, buckles, cap badges, etc. On regimental crests symbols are sometimes used in place of the names of battles or campaigns—e.g., a sphinx for the Egyptian Campaign of 1801 or a Chinese dragon for units that served in China during the First Opium War [q.v.] in 1839–42.

"Battle Hymn of the Republic." A famous song of the American Civil War. Written by Julia Ward Howe (1819–1910), it first appeared as a poem in the February 1862 issue of the *Atlantic Monthly*. Sung to the melody of a hymn composed in 1852 by William Steffe, a Virginian, it became instantly popular in the North. Soldiers had previously set the words of "John Brown's body lies a-moldering in his grave, but his soul goes marching on" or "We'll hang Jeff Davis to a sour apple tree" to the same hymn.

Battlements. Machiolated walls. Notched or indented parapets in fortifications. The rising parts are called merlons or cops; the lower spaces between them are called crenels or embrasures. The purpose of battlements was to permit soldiers to shoot through the crenels while being shielded by the merlons.

Battleworks. Trenches, breastworks, or earthworks [qq.v.] designed to protect soldiers in battle. [See Revetments.]

Baudens, Jean Baptiste Lucien (1804–1957). A French surgeon, educated in Paris, who joined the forces that in-

vaded Algeria in 1830 [see Algeria, Conquest and Occupation of]. He spent nine years practicing surgery and teaching in Algiers, earning such a reputation that when he returned to France, he was made a member of the council of Santé des Armées and was named chief surgeon at the Val de Grâce. He claimed to have been the first (in 1830) to have the patient survive the opening of an abdomen for the repair of the intestines. He served with distinction in the Crimean War but died soon after.

Baulois. Punk used in firing a saucission or a powder train.

Bautzen, Battle of (20–21 May 1813), Napoleonic Wars. An indecisive battle in which Napoleon, with 115,000 men and 150 guns, engaged Prussian and Russian armies totaling 96,000 with 450 guns under Ludwig Wittgenstein [q.v.] at this walled cathedral town, also called Budissin or Baudissin, on the Spree River, 32 miles east-northeast of Dresden. The French lost about 20,000 men; the Allies, about 13,500.

For Napoleon it was a Pyrrhic victory. He was robbed of the decisive victory he had hoped to achieve, for although he had directed Michel Ney [q.v.], who had an additional 85,000 men, to close the gap in the line that was to have enveloped the Russian and Prussian armies, Ney misunderstood and marched his army to another position. Both sides agreed to an armistice on 4 June.

Bavarian Lighting. The popular name of a single-shot cavalry pistol developed by Johann Werder [q.v.] and adopted by the Bavarian army in 1870. It fired an 11 mm center-fire cartridge.

Bavins. Small bundles of kindling in which one end (the bush end of brushwood) had been dipped into an inflammable composition and then dried.

Baxter Springs, Battle of (6 October 1863), American Civil War. Union Brigadier General James Gilpatrick Hunt [q.v.], commanding the Army of the Frontier [q.v.] and escorted by 100 Federals, was moving his headquarters from Fort Scott to Fort Smith when his convoy was attacked at Baxter Springs in southeast Kansas by Quantrill's raiders [q.v.], wearing Federal uniforms. The Federals lost 65 men killed. It was alleged that corpses were mutilated.

Bay. The space between two pontoons of a pontoon bridge [q.v.].

Bayard, George Dashiell (1835–1862). An American soldier who was graduated from West Point in 1856 and served in the cavalry in the West, where he suffered a poison arrow [q.v.] wound in his face. During the American Civil War he proved an excellent Union cavalry commander and fought at Dranesville, against Stonewall Jackson in the Shenandoah Valley, and at Cedar Mountain [qq.v.]. While commanding a brigade of cavalry, he was mortally wounded in the Battle of Fredericksburg [q.v.]. He died on 14 December 1862.

Bayberry Tallow. A product made from wax myrtle used to lubricate bullets.

Baylen, Battle of. See Bailén / Baylen, Battle of.

Bay of Islands War. See Maori Wars.

Bayonet. 1. A blade with a hollow handle and shoulder designed to be fixed to the end of the barrel of a rifle or musket and used in hand-to-hand combat. It is said to have been invented in Bayonne, France, in the mid-seventeenth century. In 1688 Sébastien Vauban [q.v.] developed the ring and socket bayonet that slotted into a stud on the barrel of a musket instead of being inserted into it. It was said to have been used in battle for the first time by the victorious French in the Battle of Marsaglia, near Turin, on 24 September 1693, but first use has also been claimed in the Battle of Spires (Speyer) in Bavaria in November 1703. The Grenadier Guards, the first British regiment to be armed with bayonets, was equipped with them at least as early as 1693.

Bayonet

The length of the blade and its shape varied in different armies at different times; it could be narrow, broad, triangular, trowel-shaped (a trowel-bayonet), or flat-bladed (a sword-bayonet). In the 1820s, when the saw-backed blade was suggested for the British army, Sir George Murray (1772–1846), the master general of ordnance, rejected it as "an improper weapon to be used in civilized warfare," but it was adopted in 1843.

Many nineteenth-century generals placed greater faith in the bayonet than in their firearms. The Russians were attached to it and frequently quoted a maxim of General Aleksandr Vasilievich Suvorov (1729–1800): "*La balle est folle; la baionette est sage* [The bullet is a fool; the bayonet is wise]." Austrian General Josef Radetzky [q.v.] in 1837 told his officers that "modern infantry can trust only in cold steel."

In the Battle of Sobraon [q.v.] on 10 February 1846, when General Sir Hugh Gough [q.v.] was told that his guns were running out of ammunition, he cried, "Thank God! Then I'll be at them with the bayonet!"

Although it was so prized as a weapon, there were few actual bayonet fights. Bayonet charges were common enough, but they succeeded only when enemy morale was already made fragile by musketry or artillery, and they were ordered only when it was expected that the enemy would flee. Out of 250,000 Union wounded treated during the American Civil War, only 922 were from edged weapons, such as bayonets, sabers, and lances, and of these a goodly number were the result of brawls and private quarrels. General John Gordon [q.v.] wrote: "The bristling points and the glitter of the bayonets were fearful to look upon as they were leveled in front of a charging line; but they were rarely reddened with blood. The day of the bayonet is passed" (*Reminiscences of the Civil War*, 1904).

The emergence of breech-loading rifles marked what ought to have been the end of the bayonet's utility in combat. In 1878 General William Tecumseh Sherman [q.v.] suggested to General Philip Sheridan [q.v.] that the bayonet ought to be replaced with something more practical, but the American army continued, as it still does, to issue bayonets. The tactical manual used during the Spanish-American War, published in 1891, devoted seven pages to bayonet exercise.

As late as 1906 a Russian officer, writing in the prestigious *Revue militaire des armées étrangères,* maintained that the bayonet charge was the essence of combat and "it is force of morale that will bring victory."

2. In the plural, a synonym for infantry—e.g., "a thousand bayonets." [See Saber.]

Bayonet Boss. A short lug on the muzzle of some muskets and rifles that fitted into a groove in the handle of a bayonet.

Bayonne, Siege of (1814), Peninsular War. This city in southwestern France at the confluence of the Adour and Nive rivers was invested by Wellington's Peninsular army on 14 January 1814. On 27 April French General Pierre Thouvenot [q.v.], the military governor, led a sortie that, although at first successful, driving through the Allied siege lines, was finally beaten back by the reserve Brigade of Foot Guards. The British suffered 838 casualties, including the wounding and capture of Lieutenant General Sir John Hope [q.v.]; the French lost 905.

This was the last military engagement of the Peninsular War. Napoleon had already abdicated on 6 April. When the news reached Bayonne on 27 April, Thouvenot surrendered.

Bayou. In military terms, a branch of a trench in a fortification.

Baza, Battle of (1810), Peninsular War. At this commune in southern Spain, 53 miles northeast of Grenada, the French under Marshal Nicolas Soult [q.v.] defeated an Allied force under Joachim Blake [q.v.] and Gómez de Andrade (1752–1817).

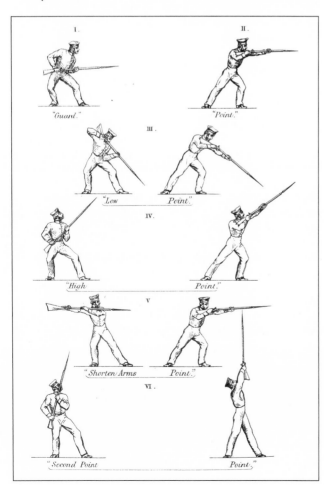

I. | II.

"Guard." | "Point."

III.

"Low | Point."

IV.

"High | Point."

V.

"Shorten Arms | Point."

VI.

"Second Point | Point."

Bayonet exercise

Bazaine, Achille (1811–1888). A French soldier who, after failing his entrance examination for the École Polytechnique [q.v.], in March 1831 enlisted as a private in the 37th Infantry Regiment. He served in Algeria, was commissioned in 1833, and transferred to the Foreign Legion [q.v.]. In 1840 he was one of the few survivors of the siege of Miliana [q.v.]. In the Crimean War he commanded a brigade, taking part in the final assault on Sevastopol [q.v.] on 6 September 1855. He fought with distinction in the corps of Achille Baraguay d'Hilliers [q.v.] at Solferino [q.v.] on 24 June 1859. He commanded a division in the French army sent to Mexico in 1862 and won a victory at Puebla [q.v.] on 17 May 1863. In July 1863 he was made commander of the expeditionary force in Mexico [see Mexico, French Invasion and Occupation of]. In 1864 he became a marshal of France, and in February 1865 he besieged Oaxaca. In the Franco-Prussian War he commanded the main French army and was wounded at Colombey-Borny [q.v.]. Defeated at Vionville and Gravelotte–St. Privat [qq.v.], he retreated into Metz, where he was soon besieged by a Prussian army under Prince Frederick Charles [q.v.] . He attempted to break out but was defeated in the Battle of Bellevue [q.v.].

Success in colonial wars and in subordinate commands had not prepared him for high command, and at Metz his incompetence was evident. On 27 October 1870, after a siege of fifty-four days, he surrendered his entire army of 173,000 men, an act for which three years later he was court-martialed and sentenced to death and degradation. The death sentence was commuted to twenty years' seclusion, and the degradation was not administered. He was secluded on Île Ste. Marguerite, near Cannes, from which, with his wife's help, he escaped on 9 August 1874. He fled to Italy, then to Spain, where he lived out his life in exile.

Bazeilles, Massacre at (31 August–1 September 1870), Franco-Prussian War. In the course of the Battle of Sedan, at this town in the Ardennes, two miles east of Sedan, a sharp clash occurred between French and Prussian troops in which an old woman, whose husband and son had been killed, fired on and killed 2 Bavarian soldiers. The following day the enraged Bavarians burned the village and ran amok. Of the 2,000 inhabitants, only 50 survived. The survivors declared there had been no provocation; the Germans disputed the number killed.

Bazinger. A black slave serving as a soldier, usually in a private army of a slaver in the Sudan and Chad areas.

Beach, Thomas Miller. See Le Caron, Henri.

Beachhead. A section of a hostile seashore held to enable additional forces to land, the beginning of an inroad into enemy territory. [See Bridgehead.]

Beach Master. An officer appointed to superintend the disembarkation of an attacking force. He held plenary powers and his orders could not be questioned. He often led the storming party.

Beal, Richard Lee Turberville (1819–1893). A politician and a Confederate soldier in the American Civil War. A graduate of the University of Virginia, he was commissioned a first lieutenant in May 1861 and was a lieutenant colonel in the 9th Virginia Cavalry in the Peninsular Campaign, Second Bull Run [qq.v.], and the invasion of Maryland. Although he fought well, he was discontented for unknown reasons and three times tried to resign, saying that he wanted to form a company of rangers or to serve as a private. Instead, he was promoted to colonel in April 1862 and led the 9th in the Battle of Fredericksburg. In September 1863 he was severely wounded in a cavalry affair. His troops were among those who killed Ulric Dahlgren [q.v.] during the Kilpatrick-Dahlgren Raid [q.v.] and found the controversial Dahlgren Papers [q.v.]. Late in 1864 he was promoted brigadier general and given a brigade. After the war he practiced law and was elected to Congress in 1878.

Beall, John Yates (1835–1865). A Virginian who studied law, but never practiced. At the beginning of the American Civil War he enlisted as a private in the Confederate army and fought in First Bull Run [q.v.]. In October 1861 he suffered a bullet wound in the lung, ending his career in the army. When he had recovered sufficiently, he was appointed a master in the Confederate navy and engaged in a series of successful raids in the Chesapeake Bay until on 1 November 1863 he and his men were captured and jailed at Fort McHenry as pirates. After he was exchanged on 5 May 1864, he went to Canada. In the same year he led an abortive attempt to seize a Union warship on Lake Erie holding Confederate prisoners of war. He was captured on 16 December while trying to rescue prisoners on a train in New York and was hanged as a spy on 24 February 1865.

Beall, Lloyd James (1812?–1887). An American soldier who was graduated from West Point in 1830. He served in both the infantry and dragoons, fought in the Black Hawk War [q.v.], and studied at the French cavalry school at Saumur [q.v.]. In 1844 he transferred to the paymaster's department. He was a major when the American Civil War began, but he resigned to become a Confederate colonel. On 23 May 1861 he was appointed commandant of the Confederate States Marine Corps, a corps never more than regimental size that was scattered from Virginia to Texas. Beall was its first and only commandant.

Beall, William Nelson Rector (1825–1883). An American soldier and West Point graduate, class of 1848, who rose to the rank of captain in the 1st Cavalry before resigning on 20 August 1861 and accepting a commission as colonel in the Confederate army. He served in Arkansas and was promoted brigadier general on 11 April 1862. He commanded a brigade at Port Hudson until he surrendered on 9 April 1863.

After imprisonment in the Union prison on Johnson's Island [q.v.] in Lake Erie, he was paroled to act as the Confederate agent charged with arranging the exchange of prisoners and handling supplies for Confederate prisoners of war from an office in New York City. As a result of a peculiar agreement between the belligerents, he was permitted to sell cotton, which was allowed to pass through the Federal blockade and to use the profits to buy clothing, blankets, and other necessities for Confederate prisoners. After the war he became a general commission agent in St. Louis.

Bean's Station, Battle of (15 December 1863), American Civil War. At this settlement during the Knoxville, Tennessee, Campaign, Confederate General James Longstreet [q.v.] attempted unsuccessfully to capture three Federal cavalry brigades. They escaped with little loss. Longstreet blamed General Evander Law [q.v.] and Lafayette McLaws for his failure and soon after relieved them of their commands.

Beardslee Magneto-Electric Field Telegraph Machine. A mobile military telegraph system developed by George W. Beardslee and adopted by Albert James Myer [q.v.], the Union army's chief signal officer in the American Civil War. The Beardslee telegraph did not use a key for transmissions but a device with a dial and pointer. Operated by hand-turned magnetos, it transmitted messages for nearly 10 miles. The first attempt to use the telegraph in the field was on 24 May 1862, during the Peninsular Campaign, but its first tactical success was by Ambrose Burnside [q.v.] in the Battle of Fredericksburg [q.v.] on 13 December 1862. However, on 10 November 1863 Myer was ordered by Secretary of War Edwin Stanton (1814–1869) to turn over all of the Signal Corps's telegraph equipment to the Military Telegraph Service, and the Beardslee system was abandoned. Only about seventy sets were manufactured, and these were scrapped.

Bear Flag War. See Black Bear Revolt.

Bear Paw Mountain, Battle of (30 September–5 October 1877), Nez Percé War. In Montana 30 miles from the Canadian border, U.S. forces engaged Nez Percé Indians in a five-day battle that ended with the Indians' surrender to Colonel (brevet Major General) Nelson Miles and Brigadier General Oliver Otis Howard [qq.v.]. The battle ended the Nez Percé War [q.v.]. During the final negotiations, Miles ordered Chief Joseph to be seized, but any plans to hold him were nullified when the Indians seized Lieutenant Lovell Hall Jerome (1849–1935). The Americans lost 24 men killed, including 2 officers, and 50 wounded. The Indians lost 17 killed and 418 made prisoner. About one-third of the Nez Percés managed to escape and find sanctuary in Canada.

Bear River, Battle of (29 January 1863), American Indian Wars. On the banks of the Bear River, 140 miles north of Salt Lake City, near present-day Preston, Idaho, 300 volunteer soldiers from California with two howitzers under Colonel Patrick E. Connor (1820–1891) defeated a force of Shoshoni Indians, killing 224, some of whom were women and children, for a loss of 68. Among those killed was Bear Hunter, the most militant of the Shoshoni chiefs. Connor was rewarded with a promotion to brigadier general.

Bearskins. The tall fur caps made of bearskins worn by grenadiers or guards units in some European armies, including all Foot Guards [q.v.] in the British army. The pelts were imported from Canada. Grenadiers in Napoleon's army in Russia sometimes converted them to muffs.

Beast Barracks. The area at the United States Military Academy where plebes [q.v.] were quartered and trained during initial indoctrination. The term applies to the entire process of introducing new cadets to life at the academy.

Beating Orders. In the American and British armies, these were orders given an officer authorizing him to recruit, or to "raise men by beat of drum."

Beating Up Recruits. A British expression referring to the beating of a drum at fairs, in markets, or before public houses to attract the attention of potential recruits to the persuasions of the recruiting sergeants. Sometimes: "Beating for recruits."

Beauharnais, Eugène de (1781–1824). A French soldier whose general father was guillotined in 1794 and whose sister was Napoleon's first wife. He served Napoleon in Italy and Egypt and was present at the Battle of Marengo on 14 June 1800. In 1805 he was appointed viceroy of Italy and was adopted by Napoleon. In 1809 he was made commander of the Army of Italy. He was defeated by the Austrians at Sacile on 16 April and at Caldiero, near Verona, on 29–30 April, but on 14 July he won a notable victory at Raab [q.v.], or Györ. He fought at Wagram [q.v.], and during the Russian Campaign [q.v.] he led IV Corps, made up mainly of Italians, at Borodino on 7 September 1812 and at Maloyaroslavets [qq.v.] on 24–25 October. During the retreat he commanded the army as of 18 January 1813, after Joachim Murat had fled to Naples. On 2 May he played a major role in the Battle of Lutzen [q.v.]. In Italy on 8 February 1814 he won a victory at the Mincio River [q.v.], but on 16 April was forced to sign the armistice of Schiarino-Rizzino with Naples and Austria, which ended the war in Italy. He then retired to the court of his father-in-law, the king of Bavaria, and fought no more. Napoleon once remarked: "Eugène never caused me the least chagrin."

Beaumont, Battle of (30 August 1870), Franco-Prussian War. At Beaumont-en-Argonne, near the Meuse River, 12 miles south-southeast of Sedan, a part of the French army of General Marie MacMahon under Pierre de Failly [qq.v.], vainly trying to reach Metz, was retreating before the Germans under the crown prince of Saxony when it was surprised, defeated, and driven across the Meuse.

French losses in men, guns, and matériel were heavy, including 4,800 killed and wounded, 7,000 taken prisoner, and 42 guns lost. The Germans, mostly Bavarians, lost about 3,500. The French were pushed to their ultimate defeat at Sedan [q.v.].

Beaumont, William (1785–1853). An American army assistant surgeon who had been briefly apprenticed to a doctor in St. Albans, Vermont. During the War of 1812 [q.v.] he served as a surgeon's mate in the 6th Infantry. After four years of private practice he rejoined the army as an assistant surgeon and was stationed at Fort Mackinac, an island on the frontier in northern Michigan. When a nineteen-year-old voyageur [q.v.] and trapper named Alexis St. Martin (1803?–1880) suffered a gunshot wound that exposed and punctured his stomach, a gastric fistula refused to close, enabling Beaumont to examine the workings of the stomach. For ten years he observed the internal processes of a living man and performed 238 experiments upon him: He tied various types of food to threads and placed them in St. Martin's stomach, removing them from time to time for examination; he also removed gastric fluid several times and had it analyzed. When transferred to another post, he persuaded the unfortunate man to go with him. In about 1833 St. Martin tired of it all and left. He went on to sire seventeen children. In 1833 Beaumont, whose work on gastric physiology had been strongly supported by the surgeon general, Joseph Lovell [q.v.], published his findings in a book, *Experiments and Observations on the Gastric Juice and the Physiology of Digestion,* which revolutionized theories of the physiology of the stomach and the chemistry of gastric digestion.

Beaune-la-Rolande, Battle of (28 November 1870), Franco-Prussian War. From this village in the Loire, the French Army of the Loire, 60,000 men under Louis Jean Aurelle de Paladines (1804–1877), attempted to march toward Fontainebleau to relieve Paris. It was met and defeated by 90,000 Germans under Prince Frederick Charles [q.v.]. French casualties, as reported by the Germans, were 1,000 dead, 4,000 wounded, and 1,700 prisoners; German losses were 37 officers and 817 men. The French defeat led to the German capture of Orléans.

Beauregard, Pierre Gustave Toutant (1818–1893). An American soldier from Louisiana who was graduated second in his class of forty-five at West Point [q.v.] in 1838. During the Mexican War [q.v.] he served as a captain of engineers on the staff of General Winfield Scott [q.v.], receiving two wounds and earning two brevets for his conduct at Contreras, Churubusco, and Chapultepec [qq.v].

In January 1861 he was, for a few days only, superintendent of West Point. He was transferred when he told a Louisiana cadet that if Louisiana seceded, he would go with his state. On 20 February he resigned, and on 1 March he was appointed a brigadier general in the Confederate army and sent to Charleston, South Carolina. There he supervised the reduction of Fort Sumter [q.v.], the first engagement of the Civil War, and was heralded as the "Hero of Fort Sumter."

On 1 June 1861 he took command of the Confederate forces at Manassas Junction, in northeast Virginia. He commanded the line there on 21 July, during the First Battle of Bull Run [q.v.], called the Battle of Manassas by the Confederates, while his superior, General Joseph Johnston [q.v.], in overall command, pushed forward reinforcements for him and shifted troops from the right to the left of the line.

He was promoted general on 31 August to rank from 21 July and sent west. In the Battle of Shiloh [q.v.], on 6 April 1862, he was second-in-command to Albert Sidney Johnston [q.v.] and took command when Johnston was killed. Placed in charge of defending the Georgia and South Carolina coastline, he successfully defended Charleston from attacks in 1863 and 1864. Returning to Virginia, he defeated Benjamin Franklin Butler [q.v.] in the Battle of Drewry's Bluff [q.v.] and bottled him up in the Bermuda Hundred, an area on a peninsula in central Virginia between the James and Appomattox rivers. In July he fought off the Petersburg mine assaults [see Petersburg Mine] and later was again second-in-command to Johnston in the Carolinas Campaign [q.v.].

After the war he refused offers to be chief of staff of the Egyptian army or to be a general in the Rumanian army. In time he became president of two railroads. From 1870 to 1888 he was the supervisor of the drawings for the Louisiana Lottery, and from 1888 he was commissioner of public works in New Orleans. He also wrote articles and books on military subjects.

Beaver Dam Station, Raid on (9–10 May 1864), American Civil War. Also known as Sheridan's Richmond Raid. On 9 May the 1st Michigan Cavalry, leading George Armstrong Custer's [q.v.] brigade, entered Beaver Dam Station, Virginia, about 30 miles north-northwest of Richmond, and destroyed 2 locomotives, more than 100 railroad cars, and 10 miles of track belonging to the Virginia Central Railroad. Destroyed too were medical stores and 504,000 bread and 915,000 meat rations. The cavalrymen also freed 378 Union prisoners of war.

Bebut. A Caucasian dagger with a curved blade similar to a kama [q.v.]. It was issued to some artillery units in the Russian army.

Bechlis. Elite Turkish light cavalry composed of picked men and horses.

Bechuanaland Border Police. A paramilitary force established in 1885 after the British annexation of Bechuanaland in 1884 by Sir Charles Warren [q.v.], ostensibly to prevent annexation of the Transvaal by Germany. It was absorbed into the British South Africa Police [q.v.] in 1889.

Bechuanaland Expedition (1884–85). When conflicts between Boers and black Africans created chaos in Bechuanaland, where the Boers had established the republics of Goshen and Stellaland, the British dispatched a force of 4,000 men under Sir Charles Warren [q.v.] to restore order. By threats of punitive action the Boers were forced to capitulate and to return land they had taken from the natives. On 30 September 1885 Bechuanaland was taken under British protection; the portion to the south of the Molopo River was declared a crown colony and ten years later was annexed to Cape Colony.

Beck-Rzikowsky, Friedrich (1830–1920). An Austrian soldier who at age sixteen was enrolled in the *Pionierschule* (Pioneer Academy) near Vienna. In 1848, during the Hungarian Revolution [q.v.], he became a second lieutenant in the Duke of Baden Infantry Regiment No. 59 and was sent to Italy to join the army of Field Marshal Josef Radetzky [q.v.] where he took part in the storming of Brescia [see Brescia Uprising]. He attended the newly formed *Kriegsschule* (War College), graduating fourth in his class in 1854. In June 1859 he distinguished himself at the Battle of Magenta [q.v.], where he was wounded in the left knee and was awarded the Order of the Iron Crown Second Class [q.v.].

In 1863 he was appointed to the adjutant general's office, and in 1864 he assisted General Ludwig von Gablenz [q.v.] in preparing plans for the Schleswig-Holstein War [q.v.]. He was head of the military chancellery from 1867 to 1881, making it by 1875 the focal point of power in the army. Together with General Archduke Albert [q.v.] he fought against the administrative changes of General Franz Freiherr Kuhn von Kuhnenfeld [q.v.], the war minister, and in June 1874 Kuhn was replaced.

In May 1878 Beck was promoted major general, and in

1881 he assumed personal direction of the general staff, a post he retained until 1906. when he was forced to retire. During his tenure he made the general staff responsible for all military planning. He institutionalized the elite general staff, and his principal officers came to dominate the thinking of not only the Austrian-Hungarian army but that of most modern military institutions. He was a promoter of staff rides and war games [qq.v.] as practical supplements to field exercises. In 1884 he conducted the army's first corps-level exercises.

Beck rose to the rank of *Feldzeugmeister* (lieutenant general), and he was a pivotal figure in the transformation of the inept Hapsburg army into the modern military force that fought in World War I. He was said to have been the favorite general of Emperor Franz Josef (1830–1916), who in 1906 created him a count and bestowed upon him the Hungarian Order of St. Stephen.

Beckwith, George (1753–1823). A British soldier who fought in the American Revolutionary War and was the brother of Sir Thomas Sydney Beckwith [q.v.]. In 1797 he was appointed governor of Bermuda and commander of troops there. He became governor of St. Vincent in 1804. In 1805 he was promoted lieutenant general, and in 1808 he was governor of Barbados. In 1809 he conquered Martinique [q.v.] and sent back to England captured French eagles (given as standards by Napoleon to his regiments), the first to be seen there, for which he received the Thanks of both houses of Parliament and was created a Knight of the Bath. The following year he captured Guadeloupe [q.v.], the last French possession in the West Indies. When he returned to Britain, he was made general. From 1816 to 1820 he commanded the troops in Ireland.

Beckwith, John Charles (1789–1862). A British soldier, nephew of George and Thomas Sydney Beckwith [qq.v.], who took part in the Hanover Expedition, the Expedition to Denmark, and the Battle of Copenhagen [q.v.]. He was with the Walcheren Expedition [q.v.] and in 1810, during the Peninsular War [q.v.], went with his regiment, the 95th Rifles, to Portugal, where he took part in all the engagements in 1811 against French General André Masséna's [q.v.] retiring army. As brigade major he was present at the battles of Ciudad Rodrigo, Badajoz, Salamanca, Vitoria, Nivelle, the Nive, Orthez, and Toulouse [qq.v.]. In 1815 he fought in the Battle of Waterloo, where he lost his left leg. He was promoted lieutenant colonel and awarded the CB. In 1820 he retired on half pay. He never served again, but under the peculiar British promotional system, he rose in rank to become a major general.

He became an advocate of the peasants of the anti-Catholic Waldenses (today called Vaudois), descendants of the oldest of the heretical medieval sects, who lived in poverty in the Italian Piedmont southwest of Turin. He lived among them for thirty-five years, marrying a Waldenses girl in 1850 and establishing 120 schools in the district.

Beckwith, Thomas Sydney (1772–1831). A British soldier; brother of George Beckwith and uncle of John Charles Beckwith [qq.v.], who was commissioned in the 71st Regiment in 1791 and the following year was present at the siege of Seringapatam in India. In 1800 he commanded a company in an experimental rifle regiment raised by Colonel Coote Manningham, who commanded a brigade in Sir John Moore's [q.v.] army in the peninsula [see Peninsular War]. As a captain in what became the 95th Rifles he accompanied the expedition to Copenhagen [q.v.] in 1801. In July 1808 he went to Portugal as commander of the 95th Rifles and was present in the Battle of Vimeiro, Talavera [qq.v.], and numerous smaller engagements. When the famous Light Division was formed, he commanded one of its brigades. He has been called "one of the finest leaders of light infantry ever known" (*Dictionary of National Biography*). He was quartermaster general in Canada, and in the War of 1812 [q.v.] he commanded the forces in the attack on Ocracoke Island off the central North Carolina coast. He became a major general in 1814, and in 1829 he was appointed commander-in-chief at Bombay, India, where two years later he died of a fever.

Bee, Barnard Elliott (1824–1861). An American soldier, a West Point graduate (class of 1845), who fought in the Mexican War [q.v.], where he was wounded and won two brevets for his bravery at Cerro Gordo and Chapultepec [qq.v.]. During the American Civil War he was appointed a brigadier general in the Confederate army on 17 June 1861, and in the First Battle of Bull Run [q.v.] he commanded a brigade before he fell mortally wounded. He is best remembered for immortalizing Thomas Jackson with the words "There stands Jackson like a stone wall." It was said that he had "a capacity for command that was not usual in the early days of the war" (*Dictionary of American Biography*).

Beecher Island, Battle of (17–25 September 1868), American Indian Wars. On 24 August 1868 Major General Philip Sheridan [q.v.], then the newly appointed commander of the Department of the Missouri, which included more than half the United States, ordered the formation of a mobile mounted unit of 50 "first class hardy frontiersmen." Recruited from Kansas settlements of the high plains, many were Civil War veterans. Technically civilian scouts hired by the Quartermaster Department, they operated directly under two regular army officers. Their pay was generous: seventy-five dollars a month if they provided their own horses and fifty dollars if they did not. Major (Brevet Brigadier General) George Alexander ("Sandy") Forsyth [q.v.], 9th Cavalry, was placed in command of the unit. Second-in-command was First Lieutenant Frederick Henry Beecher (1841–1866), 3rd Infantry, a nephew of the famous preacher Henry Ward Beecher (1813–1887).

Forsyth rashly led his small command far up the Republican River in the shortgrass prairie of the central plains in what is today Colorado. At dawn on 17 September they were attacked by about 450 Arapaho, Sioux, and Cheyenne dog soldiers [q.v.]. They retreated to a small, sparsely vegetated sandbar island at the Arickaree fork of the river. (The island was later named Beecher's Island after Lieutenant Beecher, killed in the attack. It disappeared in a flood on Labor Day 1935.) The Indians made several attacks but were beaten back each time by the seven-shot Spencer repeating rifles and Colt revolvers of the unit [see Spencer Rifle; Colt Revolvers]. In one of the attacks Roman Nose [q.v.], the famous Cheyenne warrior, was killed.

The fighting ended at nightfall, but the Indians laid siege to the island. During the night two of Forsyth's men, Pierre Trudeau (d. 1869) and Simpson Everett ("Jack") Stillwell [q.v.], managed to slip away unobserved. They reached Fort Wallace, Kansas, nearly 125 miles away on the night of 21 September. Four days later relief arrived: Company H of the 10th Cavalry found the party in desperate condition. Forsyth lost 5 killed and 18 wounded and all his horses. He himself suffered multiple wounds, including a slug in his leg that he had removed with his razor. The Indians lost 9 killed and an unknown number wounded. [See Tucker, H. H.]

This small battle had an emotional impact and acquired a fame beyond its import. General Nelson A. Miles [q.v.] called it "one of the most remarkable affairs with Indians in the history of the American frontier." Colonel George Armstrong Custer [q.v.] called the battle "a wonderful exhibition of daring courage, stubborn bravery, and heroic endurance under circumstances of the greatest peril and exposure. In all probability there will never occur in our future hostilities with the savage tribes of the West a struggle of the equal of that in which were engaged the heroic men who defended so bravely Beecher's Island." The battle called attention to the need for more troops on the plains and increased the pressure to transfer the Indian Bureau to the War Department.

Beecher's Bibles. The name given to shoulder weapons sent to Kansas by abolitionists inspired by such preachers as Henry Ward Beecher (1813–1887) during the five years of civil war between slaveholders and abolitionists following the passage of the Kansas-Nebraska Bill in 1854 [see Border War]. The weapons were said to have acquired their name when George Washington Deitzler (1826–1884), a Kansas farmer, realtor, and staunch free stater, bought some Sharps rifles while on a trip East and shipped them to Kansas in crates marked "Bibles." In another version the name was said to be derived from the professed belief of abolitionists that rifles "possessed more moral power than a hundred Bibles."

Beecher's Bibles, rifles used by border ruffians in the 1850s

Beefeaters. A popular name for the Warders of the Tower of London and sometimes applied to the Yeomen of the Guard [q.v.].

Beer Money. An addition of a penny a day given from 1800 to 1873 to privates and noncommissioned officers of the British army when they were on home service. The payment, a substitute for the issue of beer or spirits, was begun at the suggestion of the Duke of York [see Frederick Augustus, Duke of York and Albany] when he was commander-in-chief of the British army.

Beetles. Large wooden hammers used for driving down the posts of palisades and other such purposes.

Beffroy. A temporary tower structure built by besiegers to reach the top of an enemy's walls.

Behanzin (fl.1880s). A son of King Gelele, who became king of Dahomey in West Africa and who in the 1880s fought the French. His army was notable for its corps of amazons [q.v.] and its military organization. [See Franco-Dahomean Wars.]

Behmaru / Beymaroo Heights (23 November 1841). First Afghan War. Afghans (Kohistani tribesmen) occupied the Behmaru heights overlooking the British cantonment at Kabul, and a weak attack by the British on 22 November failed to drive them away. At 2:00 A.M. on the 23rd a larger force, consisting of the 44th Regiment, two regiments of sepoys, and two squadrons of cavalry, with a single gun, all under Colonel John Shelton (1786?–1845), initiated a surprise attack upon the heights. One detachment lost its way, the gun became overheated, and some soldiers refused to follow their officers. Just as the Anglo-British force was about to bolt, the Afghan leader was assassinated and the Afghans fled. It was, by chance, a British victory, but a poor one.

Beilerbeg. Turkish title for a governor of a province. Three horsetails were his badge of rank.

Bel Air, Battle of (30 August 1814), War of 1812. British naval Captain Peter Parker (1785–1814) sailed up the Chesapeake Bay and landed near Bel Air, Maryland, 22 miles northeast of Baltimore. With 134 seamen and marines he launched an attack upon American militia but was repulsed with a loss of 41 killed, including himself.

Beleaguer, to. To invest a town or fortress; to besiege.

Belém, Occupation of. In the Peninsular War a Portuguese port city (today a suburb of Lisbon) occupied by the French in November 1807. As French troops entered the town, the Portuguese royal family was at the quay, embarking for Brazil.

Belfort, Sieges of. 1. (1814). This French fortified commune 88 miles east-northeast of Dijon dominated the Burgundian gate between the Vosges and the Swiss Jura Mountains. It was unsuccessfully besieged by the Allies during the Napoleonic Wars.

2. (3 November 1870–15 February 1871). During the Franco-Prussian War a German siege corps of 10,000 men and 24 guns under General Hermann von Tresckow laid siege to the town to which Helmuth von Moltke the Elder [q.v.] attached greater significance than to Metz [q.v.]. The original fortifications, designed by the famous military engineer Marquis Sébastien le Prestre de Vauban [q.v.], were thought to be antiquated, and the Germans assumed that the place would soon fall, but its commander, Colonel Pierre Marie Philippe Aristide Denfert-Rochereau (1823–1878), a veteran of the Crimean War and of fighting in Algeria, was a clever engineer who, in his six years there, had laid out formidable defenses. During the siege he utilized all available strength, including the national guard and volunteers, for a total force of 17,600 men. The Germans found Belfort a nut impossible to crack.

After the victory of German General Karl Werder [q.v.] over General Charles Bourbaki [q.v.] at the Lisaine [q.v.], the Germans were able to increase their besieging force to 17,600 infantry, 4,700 artillery, and 1,100 engineers with 34 field guns, and the investment was more closely maintained. By 8 February 1871 they had captured two redoubts and their success seemed certain, but Denfert-Rochereau held out until he received a direct order from his government to surrender; Belfort was included in the 15 February armistice. Its garrison received the full honors of war [q.v.], marching out under arms with flags flying and with all its baggage.

In the 105-day siege the Germans lost about 2,000 men; the French, 4,750 plus 336 civilians.

Belgian-Dervish War (1897). In February 1897 a small Belgian military expedition from the Belgium Congo under François Dhanis [q.v.] reached the Nile at Rejaf in Equatorial Province of the Sudan. It successfully defeated the Dervishes [q.v.] and occupied the towns of Wadelai and Lado. It had reached the Bahr-el-Ghazal region by August, when, on the news of the Batetelar uprising [q.v.], it returned to the Congo.

Belgian Revolution (1830–33). Belgian discontent with Prince William of Orange, who had assumed the throne as William I (1772–1843) in 1815, stemmed from his attempt to substitute Dutch for French as the official language. On 25 August 1830, following a performance in Brussels of *La Muette de Portici (The Dumb Girl of Portici),* an opera by Daniel Auber (1782–1871), based on a Neapolitan uprising against Spanish oppressors in 1647, with a libretto by Augustin Scribe (1791–1861) that is replete with calls for liberty, a riot occurred that shook the royal authorities. This was followed by uprisings throughout Belgium. War broke out in earnest when the Dutch sent an army of 50,000 to retake the country, but attempts to quell the disturbances with troops failed.

On 4 October the revolutionaries proclaimed Belgium independent of the Netherlands. In November Belgian nationalists captured Antwerp, but the Dutch commander, Lieutenant General Baron David Hendryk Chassé [q.v.], remained in control of the citadel and bombarded the town [see Antwerp, Sieges of]. The French intervened, sending 63,000 troops to assist Belgian patriots, and on 23 December Chassé surrendered to French Marshal Count Maurice Gérard [q.v.].

On 20 January 1831 Belgian independence was confirmed by the great European powers. Peace was fully restored on 21 May 1833, and Belgium eventually regained its independence, although it was not until 19 April 1839 that the Netherlands recognized it.

Belgian Rifle. See Albini-Braendlin Rifle.

Belgrano, Manuel (1770–1820). An Argentine soldier who led patriot forces that defeated Spanish royalists in the battles of Tucamá [q.v.] in 1812 and Salto in 1813. However, he was defeated in campaigns in Bolivia in 1813, and in 1814 José de San Martín [q.v.] replaced him as commander.

Belknap, William Worth (1829–1890). An American soldier and politician who fought in the Union army during the American Civil War in the western theater, taking part in every battle. On the recommendation of W. T. Sherman [q.v.] he became a brigadier general of volunteers on 30 July 1864. He was made a major general in 1865 and commanded a division in Sherman's "March to the Sea" [q.v.]. He was often commended for his bravery.

In 1869 he became secretary of war in President Grant's [q.v.] cabinet, but in 1876 he was impeached by the Senate for malfeasance in office (accepting bribes from a sutler) and resigned.

Bell, James Franklin (1856–1919). An American soldier, an advocate of physical fitness and marksmanship, who after graduation from West Point in 1878 served in the 7th Cavalry. As an instructor he was the first American officer to use a sand table to illustrate problems in minor tactics, and he was the first American to draw up a set of rules governing maneuvers. In the Philippines in 1900 he personally conducted all negotiations with Emilio Aguinaldo [q.v.]. On Luzon, while serving as chief of scouts for the division commanded by Major General Arthur MacArthur [q.v.], he earned the Medal of Honor [q.v.] and was promoted from captain to brigadier general for his gallantry.

He commanded and revitalized the Command and Staff School at Fort Leavenworth (1902–06), became army chief of staff (1906–10), and commanded a division in the First World War.

Belle Alliance. See La Belle Alliance.

Bellegarde, Count Heinrich Joseph Johannes von (1756–1845). An Austrian soldier and statesman who transferred from the Saxon to the Austrian army in 1771 and distinguished himself in the Austro-Turkish War of 1788–89, the Netherlands campaigns of 1793–94, and the campaign in Germany in 1799. In 1800 he was a general and chief of staff of the Austrian army in Italy. In 1805 he was president of the Aulic Council [q.v.]. By 1813 he was a field marshal and commander-in-chief of the Austrian forces in Italy, where on 8 February 1814 he was defeated in the Battle of the Mincio [q.v.]. Later that year he became governor of Lombardy and Venetia. In 1820 he was again president of the Aulic Council. He retired in 1825.

Belle Isle Prison. A Confederate prison during the American Civil War for Union enlisted men on an island in the James River at Richmond, Virginia. It was established after First Bull Run [q.v.], and by the end of 1863 it held some 10,000 men. Because there were several attempts to free the prisoners, notably the Kilpatrick-Dahlgren raid [q.v.], and because they strained the city's food distribution system, all were moved to Andersonville [q.v.], Georgia.

Bellevue, Battle of (18 October 1870), Franco-Prussian War. Marshal Achille Bazaine [q.v.] tried to break through the German lines investing Metz [q.v.] but was driven back with a loss of 64 officers and 1,193 men; the Germans lost 75 officers and 1,703 men.

Belligerent. As a noun, a nation, an army, or organized revolutionaries at war; as an adjective, to be or threaten to be engaged in hostilities.

Bell Mouth. A widening of the muzzle of a muzzleloader. It made the gun easier to load and reduced cracks around the muzzle by reducing the pressure on the tube's thinnest part.

Bell of Arms. A building or tent in which small arms are stored.

Bells. In the eighteenth century and perhaps earlier the bells of a town (or their cash equivalent) captured by British artillery became the perquisite of the officer commanding the artillery. However, during the Walcheren Campaign [q.v.], when the town of Flushing was so taken in 1809, the magistrates of the town refused to hand over its bells or their equivalent and appealed to the Duke of Portland (1738–1809), then prime minister, who disallowed these "ancient rights."

Bell Sharp. A mule in a packtrain trained to follow a mare with a bell and to line up before its own packsaddle at the sound of a bell. [See Shavetail.]

Belmont, Battle of (7 November 1861), American Civil War. Brigadier General U. S. Grant from his base in Cairo, Illinois, personally led 3,114 troops with six guns south. All were loaded on four transports on the Mississippi River protected by two gunboats. His move was intended only as a demonstration to menace Belmont, a village in southeast Missouri held by the Confederates, but when he heard (incorrectly) that the Confederates were moving troops into Missouri, fearing they would attack a weaker Federal column in the south of the state, he turned his demonstration into an actual attack.

At 6:30 A.M. on 7 November he landed and, leaving five companies to guard the transports, moved on Belmont with the remainder. Driving through thick woods, he routed six Confederate regiments, their survivors fleeing to the banks of the river where they were protected by the guns of Columbus, Kentucky, on the opposite shore. While the Union troops paused to loot and burn the captured Confederate camp, Confederate Major General Leonidas Polk [q.v.] ferried 10,000 men across the Mississippi below Belmont and attempted to cut Grant off from his transports. Grant, however, was able to withdraw, taking with him six captured guns, some horses, and a few prisoners.

In this running fight, which continued until sunset, Grant lost 607 and the Confederates 642. This was the first battle in the western theater and the first battle of the war fought by Grant.

Belmont, Battle of (23 November 1899), Second Anglo-Boer War. The British under Paul Sandford, Lord Methuen [q.v.], advancing to the relief of Kimberley, encountered a Boer commando of about 3,000 strongly entrenched in hills 55 miles south of the town, near a small village of Belmont. The Boer position was taken by a frontal attack, but at a cost of 28 officers and 250 men; the Boers were said to have lost about 300 in killed and wounded, although the actual number was probably less, and 50 taken prisoner.

Belt, Sam Browne. An officer's sword belt invented by Samuel James Browne, VC [q.v.], who as a young officer lost his left arm in 1858 during the Indian Mutiny [q.v.]. The belt, which makes it easier to draw and replace a sword in its scabbard, consists of a thin strap crossing the chest diagonally from the right shoulder to a broad belt around the waist. It was adopted by the British, American, and many other armies. Browne's original belt is now in the National Army Museum in London.

Bem, Jósef (1795–1850). A Polish soldier educated at a military school in Warsaw who joined the French army as an artillery officer and took part in Napoleon's Russian Campaign [q.v.] of 1812. He distinguished himself in the defense of Danzig in 1813. He returned to Poland and served briefly in the Russian army before joining the Polish revolutionary army. In 1831 he commanded the artillery at Igany and distinguished himself in the Battle of Ostrolenka [qq.v.]. After taking part in the bitter battle for Warsaw [q.v.] on 6–7 September 1831, he fled to Paris [see Polish Revolution].

In 1848 he took part in the Vienna insurrection and joined the Hungarian army [see Hungarian Revolution of 1848]. He was given command of the Army of Transylvania, composed mostly of Szeklers [q.v.], and in February 1849 he defeated the Austrians at Piski [q.v.], driving them into Walachia. Although he won the Battle of Orsova [q.v.] on 16 May, his army was almost annihilated by a superior Russian force at Schussburg [q.v.]. He escaped only by feigning death. He commanded in the Battle of Timişoara [q.v.], the last major battle of the revolution, in which he was severely wounded and defeated. With the collapse of the revolution, he fled to Turkey, became a Muslim, and took the name Murad Pasha. He was appointed governor of Aleppo in what was then Syria, where, during an émeute, he risked his own life to save the Christians there from being massacred. He died at Aleppo on 16 September 1850.

Benavente, Battle of (29 December 1808), Peninsular War. When Sir John Moore [q.v.] was retreating toward Corunna [q.v.] from Sahagún, Spain, Napoleon sent General Charles Lefebvre-Desnouëttes [q.v.] with 600 *chasseurs-à-cheval* to harass his rear. Near Benavente, Spain, 35 miles north of Zamorra, the French forded the Esla River, and there they were lured into an ambush and cut up, losing about 150, of whom some 100 were taken prisoner, including a wounded Lefebvre-Desnouëttes. The British lost perhaps a dozen.

Napoleon himself watched the rout of his cavalry, which enabled Moore to get his rear guard clear and press on toward Astorga and Corunna.

Benavides, Óscar Raimundo (1876–1945). A Peruvian soldier who served in the French army before joining the Peruvian army in 1894. He became chief of staff in 1913 and president twenty years later.

Benedek, Ludwig August von (1804–1881). An Austrian soldier who was graduated from the Maria Theresa Military Academy in 1822. In 1846–49 he served in campaigns in Galicia, Italy, and Hungary. In 1859 during the Italian Wars of Independence he commanded the Austrian VIII Corps at Solferino [q.v.], where he conducted a brilliant rearguard action. The following year he commanded the army in Venetia and the Alpine provinces. In 1860 he was governor of Hungary. At Sadowa [q.v.] on 3 July 1866, during the Seven Weeks' War [q.v.], he suffered a crushing defeat at the hands of the Prussians, after which he was relieved of his command and court-martialed.

He favored the bayonet over firepower and had no faith in staff work, which he distrusted: "I conduct the business of war according to simple rules and I am not impressed by complicated calculations."

Benét, Lawrence Vincent (1863–1948). An American engineer and inventor, educated at Yale University, who became interested in the manufacture of machine guns. His father was Brigadier General Stephen Vincent Benét (1847?–1895), who was chief of ordnance from 1874 to his retirement in 1891, and he was the uncle of the poet, novelist, and editor William Rose Benét (1886–1950) and the poet Stephen Vincent Benét (1898–1945). During the Spanish-American War [q.v.] he served as an ensign in the U.S. Navy. He was for fifty years associated with the Hotchkiss Company in France, and he made numerous improvements in the Hotchkiss machine gun [q.v.].

Bengal Army. Until 1833 the governor of the presidency of Bengal had his own army and commander-in-chief, as did the governors of the presidencies of Madras and Bombay. In 1833 the governor of the presidency of Bengal became the governor-general of India, and the head of his army became commander-in-chief, India. Although nominally in charge of all three presidency armies, he in fact commanded only the Bengal army, the largest of the three. [See Indian Army; Honourable East India Company; Indian Mutiny.]

Two sons of Benedict Arnold (1741–1801), the famous American traitor of the American Revolutionary War, served in the Bengal army.

Benin Expeditions (1897 and 1899). A British punitive expedition of 1,200 men—a naval brigade and some Hausas—under Admiral Sir Harry Holdsworth Rawson (1843–1910) landed at the mouth of the Benin River in Dahomey on 12 February and advanced upon the city of Benin, which, five days later, after considerable fighting, was captured. One Dahomean chief was exiled, and six were executed. A further punitive expedition was undertaken in 1899, and in 1914 the area became part of southern Nigeria.

Benjamin, Judah Philip (1811–1884). An American politician who during the American Civil War became attorney general of the provisional Confederate government on 25 February 1861 and secretary of war on 17 September of the same year. He served until 18 March 1862, when he became secretary of state. After the war he fled to England.

Bennigsen, Levin August (1745–1826). A German soldier who entered the Russian service in 1773 and fought the Turks in 1774. He distinguished himself in the Polish War of 1793–94 and in the Persian War of 1796. In 1801 he was part of the conspiracy that resulted in the assassination of the

Russian Tsar Paul I (1754–1801). In the Napoleonic Wars he fought at Pultusk on 26 December 1806 and commanded the Russian forces in the Battle of Eylau [qq.v.] on 7–8 February 1807. He was badly defeated at Friedland [q.v.] on 14 June 1807. In the Battle of Borodino [q.v.], the major engagement of Napoleon's Russian Campaign he commanded the center of the Russian line. At Tarutino [q.v.] in 1812 he defeated Marshal Joachim Murat [q.v.]. In October 1813 the tsar made him a count on the battlefield in recognition of his conduct in the Battle of Leipzig [q.v.], in which he commanded the Russian army on the right wing. He led Russian forces in northern Germany and besieged Marshal Louis Davout [q.v.] at Hamburg from 18 December 1813 until 10 May 1814.

Benning, Henry Lewis ("Rock") (1814–1875). An American lawyer and Confederate soldier who was part Cherokee Indian. Before the American Civil War, as an associate justice of the Georgia Supreme Court, he handed down a decision that the state court was not bound by the U.S. Supreme Court on constitutional questions. When war was declared, he became colonel of the 17th Georgia, a regiment he led at Malvern Hill and Second Bull Run [qq.v.]. He commanded a brigade at Antietam and Fredericksburg [qq.v.] and was promoted brigadier general to rank from 17 January 1863. Under John Bell Hood [q.v.], he commanded his brigade at Gettysburg, Knoxville, and Chickamauga [qq.v.]. Under Charles Field [q.v.], he fought at the Wilderness [q.v.], where he was severely wounded. He recovered to fight again at Petersburg and Appomattox [qq.v.]. After the war he returned to the practice of law.

Benteen, Frederick William (1834–1898). A brave and efficient officer who rose from lieutenant to lieutenant colonel during the American Civil War. Although he disliked George Armstrong Custer from their first meeting, he served as a captain in Custer's 7th Cavalry after the war. Two months after the Battle of Washita [q.v.] Benteen wrote anonymously to the *St. Louis Democrat,* blaming Custer for the loss of a detachment of a lieutenant and 19 men in the fight, although it would seem that Custer had acted judiciously given the conditions on the field.

At the Battle of the Little Bighorn [q.v.] Benteen played a conspicuous role. He had been dispatched by Custer to reconnoiter hills some five miles away from the main column, but he returned to join Major Marcus Albert Reno [q.v.], who was engaged in fighting on a hill some distance from the main battle area, where Custer was making his last stand. He was wounded but not incapacitated in that battle.

Bengal Army *The Bengal army on the march, 1845*

Benteen saw action against the Nez Percés in an inconclusive action at Canyon Creek [q.v.], Montana, in 1877. He became a hard drinker, and in 1887, while commanding at Fort Duchesne, Utah, he was court-martialed for being too drunk to perform his duty. He was insubordinate to the court and was sentenced to be cashiered. Because of his distinguished services, President Grover Cleveland (1837–1908) reduced the sentence to one year's suspension; however, he never served again. At the end of his suspension he retired on 7 July 1888.

Bentinck, Lord William Cavendish (1774–1839). A British soldier and governor-general of India. He was born the second son of the third Duke of Portland and was commissioned an ensign in the Coldstream Guards in 1791. In 1794 he was promoted lieutenant colonel of the 24th Light Dragoons and served on the staff of the Duke of York [q.v.] in the Netherlands. He was attached to the Austrian forces in northern Italy and was present at the battles of Trebbia, Novi, Savugliano, and Marengo [q.v.]. In 1803 he was appointed governor of Madras but was recalled three years later after the Vellore Mutiny [q.v.]. While serving in India, Bentinck had been promoted major general, and on his return to Europe in 1808 he was sent to Portugal [see Peninsular War]. He commanded a brigade at the Battle of Corunna [q.v.] and as a lieutenant general commanded a division in the army of the future Duke of Wellington [q.v.]. He raised a German unit, which he commanded in Sicily and Spain, but was defeated at Ordal and Villafranca on 12 and 13 September 1813 by Marshal Louis Suchet [q.v.]. Bentinck has been described as a man with a "violent and haughty nature" in whose judgment Wellington lost confidence.

In 1828 Bentinck assumed the office of governor of Bengal, and in 1833 he became the first governor-general of India, but he made himself unpopular with army officers by reducing the batta [q.v.] and with many Indians by his abolition of suttee. In 1835, just before leaving India, he wrote a minute in which he deplored the spread of knowledge among Indians and the bad influence of the press.

On his return to England he spent most of the remainder of his life as a member of Parliament.

Bentonville, Battle of (19–21 March 1865), American Civil War. Federal forces under General Henry Warner Slocum [q.v.], constituting the left wing of the army under General William Tecumseh Sherman, advancing from Averasboro, North Carolina, were attacked by Confederate forces under General Joseph Johnston [qq.v.] near the village of Bentonville, North Carolina, 37 miles southeast of Raleigh. Initially successful, the Confederates gave a severe check to the Federals, but they were unable to exploit their success and withdrew toward Raleigh. This was Johnston's last battle. Of the 16,127 Union troops engaged, 1,646 were casualties; of the 16,895 Confederates engaged, 2,608 were casualties. Among the dead was the sixteen-year-old son of Confederate General William Joseph Hardee [q.v.], fighting his first and last battle.

Sherman, continuing his advance on a broad front, reached Goldsboro, North Carolina, 46 miles southeast of Raleigh, on 23 March.

Battle of Bentonville, North Carolina, 19 March 1865

Berber, Captures of. This Sudanese town on the Nile, about 210 miles northwest of Khartoum, was captured by Egypt in 1820, taken by the Dervishes [q.v.] on 26 May 1884, and reconquered on 6 September 1897 by the Anglo-Egyptian forces commanded by Horatio Kitchener [q.v.].

Berdan, Hiram (1823?–1893). An American soldier and inventor who commanded the 1st U.S. Sharpshooters in the American Civil War. Before the war he had invented a repeating rifle and patented a musket ball. During the war he won a brevet for his services at Chancellorsville and a brevet to major general for Gettysburg [qq.v.], but he never served as a general officer. He resigned on 2 January 1864 to devote himself to the design of firearms and ammunition. Among his inventions of this period was a distance fuze for shrapnel. In 1867 and 1868 he worked with two Russian officers to develop a suitable .42-caliber metallic cartridge for a rifle he had designed. This was introduced into the Russian army as a Berdan No. 2 or Model 1870 rifle and popularly known as a Berdanka.

Many of those who dealt with Berdan found him excessively aggressive. Alexander Brydie Dyer (1815–1874), who commanded the Springfield Armory, thought him "thoroughly unscrupulous and unreliable." He was credited with being one of the best rifle shots in the country.

Berea, Battle of (20 December 1852), Basuto Wars. In Basutoland, near Berea, a British force under Sir George Cathcart, governor and commander-in-chief in Cape Colony, South Africa, was defeated by Basutos under Moshesh [q.v.].

Berea was also the scene of a conflict in 1865 between Boers of the Orange Free State, under Commandant J. J. Frick, and the Basutos.

Beresford, Charles William de la Poer (1846–1919). A British naval officer and the son of a marquess who became a naval cadet at the age of twelve. He was present at the bombardment of Alexandria in 1882 and was sent ashore as provost marshal and chief of police to restore order, as he did with efficiency, ordering those caught looting to be flogged and those caught setting fires to be shot. [See Arabi's Revolt.] In 1885 he was a captain in the Royal Navy and commanded a naval brigade in the Gordon Relief Expedition [q.v.]. With a small group of sailors he accompanied the desert column under Sir Herbert Stewart [q.v.] to take charge of any of Gordon's steamers that might be found at Metammeh. He therefore took part in the Battle of Abu Klea [q.v.], in which the Dervishes broke the British square. He became a full admiral and commanded first the Mediterranean Fleet and then the Channel Fleet. As a member of Parliament [1885–89, 1898–1900 and 1910–16] he was a vociferous critic of the Royal Navy.

Beresford, William Carr (1764–1854). A British soldier, natural son of the first Marquess of Waterford, who entered the army in 1785 and served in Nova Scotia (where in 1786 he lost an eye in a hunting accident) and in Egypt in 1801–03. He was present at the taking of the Cape of Good Hope [q.v.] in January 1806, and later that year he captured Buenos Aires. Soon after he was himself captured by the Argentines, but after six months he managed to escape and return to England. [See Río de la Plata, British Expedition to].

During the Peninsular War [q.v.] he was promoted major general, and on 2 March 1809, having become fluent in Portuguese, he was made a marshal in the Portuguese army, which he reorganized. He was present in the Battle of Badajoz and was severely wounded in the Battle of Salamanca [qq.v.]. His independent command ended after the Battle of Albuera [q.v.]. He commanded the center of the army in the battles of the Nive and Orthez [qq.v.]. After the fall of Napoleon he sailed to Brazil to aid the king of Portugal in suppressing rebellions, but he tired of the undertaking. Having twice refused the supreme command, he returned to Britain. In 1823 he was promoted general, and in 1828 Wellington appointed him master general of ordnance.

Berezina / Beresina River, Napoleon's Crossing of (26–28 November 1812), Napoleon's Russian Campaign. By 22 November 1812 Napoleon's army, retreating from Moscow and Smolensk and now in Byelorussia about 45 miles northeast of Minsk, was in pitiful condition. Only some 49,000 men remained under arms with 250 guns; a tail of 40,000 stragglers followed. On this day Napoleon learned that Russian General (and Admiral) Pavel Tshitsagov [q.v.] had reached the Beresina River with 34,000 men, had destroyed the bridge at Borisov [q.v.], and was blocking his road to Poland and safety. Two other Russian armies were closing in on the remains of the once-proud French Grande Armée: General Ludwig Wittgenstein [q.v.] with an army of 30,000 was advancing from the northeast, and only 30 miles behind the French rear guard,

Berezina River *Napoleon's troops crossing the Berezina River.*

General Mikhail Kutusov [q.v.] with 80,000 men was advancing from the east.

The Berezina River, normally frozen solid at this time of year, had been turned into a torrent by an unseasonable thaw. Only a few days earlier Napoleon had ordered his pontoon train to be burned, but one of his commanders, General Jean Baptiste Eblé [q.v.], had saved from it two forges, two wagons of charcoal, and six wagons of pioneer and sapper tools. With available wood, bridges could be built. A reasonably shallow ford was found near the village of Studienk (Studenki), nine miles north-northwest of Borisov. Nicolas Oudinot [q.v.] made a feint that drew off Tshitsagov, Kutusov was dilatory, and by dint of soldiers working up to their armpits in frigid water, two makeshift 300-foot-long bridges were built by the afternoon of 26 November and troops began to cross.

Tshitsagov, learning that he had been deceived, hastened back toward Studienk. However, Oudinot was able to check him, and Marshal Claude Victor [q.v.] repulsed the first at-

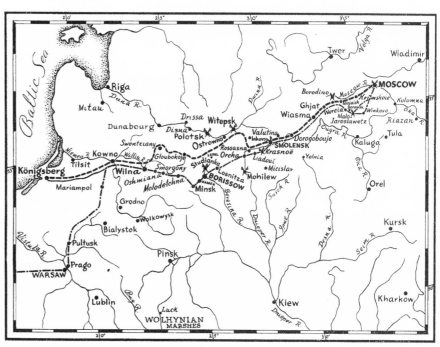
Berezina River *Map of Napoleon's Russian campaign and the crossing of the Berezina River.*

MARCH TO MOSCOW -----   RETREAT —·—·   BATTLES ⚔

tacks of Wittgenstein. About 4:00 P.M. on the 27th the largest bridge broke down, causing some panic, but it was repaired, and by the next morning all the combatants of two corps had crossed safely, except for one division in Victor's corps that had lost its way in the night and was compelled to surrender. Most of the stragglers and camp followers had refused to trust themselves to the rickety bridges at night, and it was now too late for them to cross.

The 28th was a day of fierce combat. The French faced ever-growing Russian forces, but the French line, although thinned, held firm. The bridges came under fire from the Russian guns, however, and one was destroyed. Nevertheless, the rear guard of Victor's corps managed to cross by one o'-clock on the morning of the 29th. The stragglers and camp followers again refused to cross until daylight, but at 9:00 A.M. Eblé ordered the bridge set on fire. In the ensuing panic thousands died in the crush or were drowned in the river. When the Cossacks came upon the scene, they butchered an estimated 10,000.

Napoleon had crossed the Berezina, leaving his foes behind. He had suffered a loss in battle of about 25,000 men and about 30,000 noncombatants. The Russians claimed to have recovered 36,000 bodies from the river.

Bergen op Zoom, Battle of (8 March 1814), Napoleonic Wars. British troops under Thomas Graham [q.v.], sent to Holland to cooperate with the Prussian army of Friedrich von Bülow [q.v.], made a night attack upon this fortified southern Netherlands town and were repulsed. Wellington's only comment on Graham's failure was: "Night attacks on good troops are seldom successful."

Bergmann. The common short form for the firm of Theodor Bergmann Waffenfabrik of Shul, Thuringia. This company, founded by Theodor Bergmann (d. 1915), produced pistols and later machine guns, most of which were designed by Louis Schmeisser [q.v.], who in conjunction with a Swiss watchmaker from Szegedin took out his first patent for a pistol in 1893. The first Bergmann machine gun, patented in 1900, was probably his work.

Berhampore Mutiny (1824). The 24th Bengal Native Infantry at Berhampore, a town in West Bengal, 110 miles north of Calcutta, was ordered to Burma (Myanmar) to take part in the First Burma War [q.v.], but its men refused to go by sea, claiming that to cross the "black water" was against their religion. They were then ordered to march by land and again refused because no transport was available. The troops were eventually dispersed by artillery. Several ringleaders were hanged; others were sent to prison in chains. The remainder were dismissed, and the regiment was disbanded.

Berk, Fëdor Fëdorovich (1793?–1874), German name: Friedrich Wilhelm Rembert Berg. A Russian soldier who distinguished himself in the Russo-Turkish War [q.v.] of 1828-29 and in the suppression of the Polish Revolution [q.v.] of 1830. From 1854 to 1861 he was governor of Finland, and in 1863 he played a major role in the suppression of the Poles. In 1865 he was made a field marshal.

Berlin Decree (21 November 1806). An order issued by Napoleon that forbade the importation of British goods and denied port facilities to any neutral vessel that had touched at a British port. [See Continental System.]

Berlin Uprising (18 March 1848). An unexpected, unplanned, and leaderless uprising in Berlin that began when King Frederick William of Prussia (1840–1861) authorized troops to clear his discontented subjects from the square around the royal palace. Citizens erected barricades in the streets, and General Karl von Prittovitz (1790–1871) informed the king that he was unable to clear the city block by block. The uprising shook the king and overnight routed the military autocracy. Frederick William was forced to grant a constitutional government.

Berm. A narrow path around fortifications between the rampart and the ditch.

Bermuda Line (17 May–14 June 1864), American Civil War. After the failure of Union General Benjamin Franklin Butler [q.v.] at Drewry's Bluff [q.v.], in early May 1864, he drew his forces into the Bermuda Hundred, an area between the James and Appomattox rivers in Virginia. There he found himself bottled up and was soon facing Confederate earthworks that came to be known as the Bermuda Line. [See Ware Bottom Church, Battle of.]

Bern. The common short form for the Eidgenossiche Waffenfabrik Bern, the Swiss government arsenal at Bern.

Bernadotte, Jean Baptiste Jules, Prince de Ponte Corvo, King of Sweden (1763–1844). Born in Pau, in southwestern France, Bernadotte began his military career at the age of seventeen, when he enlisted in the French army as a private in the Régiment Royal-Marine; eight years later he was a sergeant major. After saving his colonel from a Marseilles mob, he was commissioned in November 1791 into the 36th Regiment of the Line. Less than three years later (22 October 1874), he was a general of division. He saw action along the Rhine and in Italy. In August 1798 he found time to marry Désirée-Eugénie Clary, Joseph Bonaparte's sister-in-law, a woman to whom Napoleon had once been engaged. In 1799 he was briefly ambassador to Austria and then minister of war.

On 30 August 1805 he took command of a corps and served well in the Ulm Campaign. He played a small but important role at Austerlitz [q.v.]. He was a good tactician and a brave general, but he could not always be depended upon and was sometimes insubordinate. In 1803 Napoleon appointed him minister to the United States, but he found excuses never to occupy that post, so remote from the action in Europe. In 1806, at Jena and Auerstädt [qq.v.], he infuriated Napoleon by failing to commit his corps, but he conducted an able pursuit of the Prussians and forced Gebhard von Blücher [q.v.] to surrender at Lübeck [q.v.]. In March 1807 he was wounded in the head. In June of the same year he was wounded in the throat and was forced to retire for a time. In March 1809 he again commanded a corps, but he mishandled his troops at Wagram [q.v.]. He developed a reputation as an intriguer, and when he made the mistake of criticizing Napoleon, he was relieved of his command.

King Charles XIII of Sweden had no heir, and on 21 August 1810 the States General elected Bernadotte, who became a Lutheran for the honor of becoming crown prince. Napoleon reluctantly and unwisely gave his blessing to this arrangement. In July 1813 Bernadotte took the lead in the Sixth Coalition against France [see Napoleonic Wars]. On 23 August he took part in the defeat of Nicolas Oudinot [q.v.] at Grossbeeren [q.v.] and two weeks later played an active role in the defeat of Michel Ney [q.v.] at Dennewitz [q.v.].

In 1813 he invaded Denmark [q.v.] and forced that country to cede Norway to Sweden. He refused to join the Seventh Coalition during the Hundred Days [q.v.] and instead occupied Norway.

On 5 February 1818 he became King Charles XIV of Sweden. The royal dynasty he founded still flourishes. He died of apoplexy in Stockholm on 8 March 1844. His last words were aptly "No one has had a career like mine."

The present monarchs of Sweden, Norway, Denmark, and Belgium are his direct descendants through his only son, Oscar I (1799–1859), who ruled from 1844 until 1859.

Bernard, Ribbon Frank (1834–1903). An American soldier who enlisted in the 1st Dragoons on 19 February 1855, rose to be a first sergeant on 14 September 1862, and soon after was commissioned. He took part in many small actions, mostly against hostile Indians in the Southwest. He emerged from the Civil War a brevet colonel. After the war he served as a captain and rose to be a substantive major, taking part in numerous engagements against Indians, including action in the Modoc War [q.v.].

On 4 February 1886, as a major in command of Fort McIntosh, Texas, he moved on the town of Laredo, where civil disorders generated by local politics had caused the deaths of 20. He disarmed all contenders and took control of the town, for which he was later thanked by the citizens and by his superiors.

For his victories in three actions against hostile Indians he received the brevet of brigadier general. He retired on 14 October 1896. He claimed to have fought in 103 battles and skirmishes in the course of his career. He was three times married.

Bernard, Simon (1779–1839). A French military engineer who served in the French army from 1797 to 1814. He became an aide-de-camp to Napoleon and was with him at Waterloo [q.v.]. In 1815 he emigrated to the United States, where on 16 November 1816 he was appointed an assistant engineer with the pay and emoluments of a brigadier general. For fifteen years he designed American coastal defenses, notably at Fort Monroe, Virginia, and around New York City. He resigned on 10 August 1831 and returned to France, where he was made a lieutenant general and in 1836 was appointed minister of war.

Bernese Revolt (1802). Led by Rodolphe Louis d'Erlach (1749–1810), who came from a family of Swiss soldiers, the citizens of Bern, Switzerland, rose in revolt against French rule, imposed in 1798. The revolt was suppressed by General Michel Ney [q.v.], and Bern became part of the French-organized Helvetic Republic of eighteen cantons.

Bersaglieri. Literally sharpshooters. Elite rifle battalions in the Italian army organized in 1836 by General Alessandro La Marmora [q.v.]. By the time of the Crimean War [q.v.] there were ten such battalions (later increased to twelve), two of which served in the Crimea. Bersaglieri battalions were

Bersaglieri of the Italian National Guard in 1849 uniforms

kept together in peacetime but were distributed one to a division in war. They were noted for their excellent battle record, their picturesque green uniforms, their Tyrolean caps with black feathers, and their habit of parading at the trot.

Berthier, Louis Alexandre (1753–1815). A French soldier who became the oldest of Napoleon's marshals and, from 1808 to 1814, his brilliant and seemingly tireless chief of staff. It was said that he was the only man who could read Napoleon's handwriting.

He had won promotion for his valor and meritorious service while a volunteer with the expeditionary force of General Jean Baptiste Donatien de Vimeur de Rochambeau (1725–1807) in North America during the American Revolution. When the French Revolution began in 1789, he was a thirty-six-year-old lieutenant colonel. He supported the Revolution, and Marie Joseph Paul de Motier, Marquis de Lafayette (1757–1834) promoted him colonel. He fought royalists in La Vendée [q.v.] and was wounded there. As minister of war (1799–1808) he organized the Army of the Reserve in 1800 and sent it across the Alps into Italy. On 19 May 1804 he was made one of the eighteen original marshals, and the following year he became chief of staff for the Grande Armée. In 1806 he was made a prince and the Sovereign Duke of Neuchâtel. In 1812 he concentrated the enormous army that Napoleon led into Russia [see Russian Campaign, Napoleon's]. He proved a poor field commander but a brilliant staff officer. In 1808 Napoleon arranged for the fifty-four-year-old marshal to marry the twenty-four-year-old niece of the king of Bavaria. After Napoleon's first abdication in 1814 he abandoned Napoleon and retired to Bamberg, Bavaria.

There is much uncertainty about the cause of his death, which has been attributed to a variety of factors from illness to assassination. The most romantic version is that on 1 July 1815, at the sight of a Russian division moving toward the French frontier, he threw himself from a window to his death.

Bertrand, Comte Henri Gratien (1773–1844). A French general who was with Napoleon in all his campaigns and accompanied him into exile on Elba and St. Helena. In 1809 he directed the construction of the bridges by which the French army crossed the Danube at Wagram [q.v.], and he was credited with saving the army from destruction after the Battle of Leipzig [q.v.]. After Napoleon's death he returned to France, and in 1830 he was appointed commandant of the École Polytechnique [q.v.]. In 1840 he was selected to return Napoleon's remains from St. Helena to France.

Bessières, Jean Baptiste (1768–1813). A French soldier who was elected a cavalry lieutenant in 1793 and two years later was appointed to command the cavalry of Napoleon's guard [see Guides, Les]. He proved to be an outstanding commander of cavalry and in 1804 was made one of the original eighteen marshals. In 1808, during the Peninsular War [q.v.], he saved the French line of communications by defeating a larger Spanish force under Spanish General Gregorio de la Cuesta [q.v.] at Medina del Río Seco [q.v.]. In the Danube Campaign he performed outstandingly at Aspern-Essling [q.v.]. In 1809 he distinguished himself at Wagram [q.v.], where he held Napoleon's center throughout the day, and he was wounded leading some light infantrymen against Austrian artillery. In 1811 he was back in Spain, where he quarreled with André Masséna [q.v.], who accused him of failing to support him at Fuentes d'Oñoro [q.v.]. He was killed at Rippach on the eve of the Battle of Lutzen by a chance cannon shot at the beginning of the 1813 campaign.

He was an intelligent, courageous soldier who took exceptional care of his men. He married his childhood sweetheart, described as angelic, but he squandered his fortune on a dancer and died in debt. Napoleon paid his debts and gave a pension to his widow.

Betioca / Betijoque, Battle of (13 May 1813), Colombian War of Independence. Colombian patriots under Simón Bolívar gained a complete victory over royalist forces at this town in the Andean foothills, 20 miles west of Trujillo, in western Venezuela.

Betwa River, Battle of (1 April 1858), Indian Mutiny. On the banks of this river in central India, about 140 miles south of Agra, a force of 1,200 British under Sir Hugh Rose [q.v.], part of the army besieging Jhansi, defeated some 21,000 rebels and mutineers, most from the Gwalior Contingent [q.v.]. When their flank was attacked by cavalry and their front by a bayonet charge, the Indians fled, leaving 1,000 dead and wounded on the field.

In this battle Lieutenant (later Lieutenant Colonel) Hugh Stewart Cochrane (1829–1884) won the Victoria Cross for capturing a gun and attacking the enemy's rear guard.

Bey / Beg. Both a military and a civil Turkish title that was given automatically to officers holding the rank of mirali [q.v.]. In the strictest usage it applied to the governor of a province. The title could be placed either after the first name or after the full name. One horsetail was a sign of the rank. Bey was the hereditary title of the rulers of Tunis.

Beylan, Battle of (1831), Turco-Egyptian War, also Bailan, Beilan, or Syrian Gates. Egyptians and Syrians under Ibrahim Pasha [q.v.] defeated the Turks near this southern Turkish town just south of Iskenderun, an inlet of the eastern Mediterranean on the southern coast of Turkey near the Syrian border.

Bheestie. Various spellings. An Indian word for a water carrier. Bheesties, carrying water in mussacks [q.v.], were assigned to each regiment, both in barracks and on the march. They were immortalized in English literature by the poem "Gunga Din," written by Rudyard Kipling [q.v.] in 1892, which begins:

> You may talk o' gin an' beer
> When you're quartered safe out 'ere,
> An' you're sent to penny-fights an' Aldershot it;
> But when it comes to slaughter
> You will do your work on water,
> An' you'll lick the bloomin' boots of 'im that's got it.

Bhil Corps. See Mewar Bhil Corps.

Bhoosa. A forage for bullocks in India. A ration consisted of 14 pounds of finely chopped straw mixed with 6 pounds of grain.

Bhurtpore / Bharatpur / Bhurtpoor, Sieges of, Maratha Wars. Bhurtpore was the walled, strongly fortified Jat stronghold, eight miles in circumference, of Jaswant Rao Holkar, maharajah of Indore (d.1811).
First Siege (3 January–28 February 1805). Bhurtpore was besieged by a British force under Gerard Lord Lake [q.v.]. Lake's force consisted of 1,500 European infantry, 7,500 sepoys, 3,000 Indian and European cavalry with six 18-pounder siege guns and eight mortars. The Indians had about 36,000 of all arms but were strongest in their cavalry, which roamed the plain outside the town.

On 7 January Lake opened fire with his heavy artillery. Two days later his 18-pounders created a breach. On the night of 9–10 January an assault was launched but was repulsed with great slaughter. On 21 January a second breach was made, again stormed, and again repulsed. A third attempt on 19 February and a fourth the following day were also unsuccessful. On 24 February Lake raised the siege and withdrew six miles northeast. British casualties were 3,203 killed and wounded.
Second Siege (November–January 1826). The great Jat fortress came to be regarded as a menace to the expanding interests of the Honourable East India Company. To protect those interests, Lord Combermere [see Cotton, Stapleton] with 27,000 men and 102 guns laid siege to the town in November 1825 and on 18 January 1826 forced its surrender. The British then razed the fortifications.

Biacolytes. A Greek military unit charged with preventing excesses against life or property. Its duties were similar to those of the French gendarmes [q.v.].

Bianchi, Vincenz Ferrerius Friedrich, Baron von (1768–1855). An Austrian soldier who was commissioned in the engineers in 1787. He served in the Austro-Turkish War of 1787–91 and in the French Revolutionary Wars of 1792–99. He served at Austerlitz in 1805 and in 1809 distinguished himself at Aspern-Essling [qq.v.]. During Napoleon's Russian Campaign [q.v.] in 1812 he was a major general commanding a division in the corps of Prince Karl von Schwarzenberg [q.v.]. At Dresden [q.v.] on 26–27 July 1813 he commanded a corps. On the second day of the battle he was driven back by the corps of Marshal Claude Victor [q.v.] but was more successful three days later at Kulm [q.v.]. On 16–18 October he fought at Leipzig [q.v.], and in February–March 1814 he led an expedition against Lyons, defeating a small French force at Mâcon on 11 March. In 1815 he commanded the Austrian forces in Italy, where, in the Battle of Tolentino [q.v.] on 3 May, with only 11,000 men, he defeated a strong French force (29,000) under Joachim Murat [q.v.]. This was his last battle.

Bickerdyke, Mary Ann Ball (1817–1901). At the beginning of the American Civil War Mother Bickerdyke, as she was known, visited the various hospital sites in Cairo, Illinois, to distribute supplies that had been collected for the sick and wounded. She was so appalled by the conditions she found that she at once began cleaning, cooking, and caring for the men, work she carried on until a general hospital was organized. After the fall of Fort Donelson [q.v.], Tennessee, she searched the field for wounded. As a Sanitary Commission [q.v.] worker she served in the western theater, on board gunboats on the Mississippi, and with Grant at Vicksburg [q.v.]. At the request of General William T. Sherman [q.v.], she served as the field agent of the Sanitary Commission in XV Corps throughout the Atlanta Campaign [q.v.]. In the Grand Review [q.v.] at the war's end she rode a horse at the head of that corps. After the war she was tireless in her efforts to help needy veterans. In 1886 a grateful Congress awarded her a pension of twenty-five dollars a month.

Bickford Fuze. A slow-burning safety fuze invented by William Bickford, a British engineer, in 1831.

Bicycles. In the last decade of the nineteenth century many European armies experimented with bicycles. They included the Italian army, which for a time converted the bersaglieri [q.v.] into a cyclist corps.

The first bicycle was developed in 1839 by Kirkpatrick Macmillan (1813–1878), an Englishman. Al-though the first pneumatic tire was patented in 1846 by Robert William Thomson (1822–1873), all bicycles tires were solid rubber until 1888, when the pneumatic tire was reinvented by John Boyd Dunlop (1840–1921), a Scottish veterinary, who founded a company to produce the tires.

In 1892 the U.S. army issued a field manual on bicycle mounting and bicycle drill. Several American units tried using bicycles. The 25th Infantry, a black regiment, had a selected

Bicycles *French bicycle troops on the march, carrying bicycles, and in combat position, late nineteenth century*

unit that in 1896 rode 790 miles from Fort Missoula, on the Bitterroot River in Montana, to Yellowstone Park and back at an average speed of 6¼ mph. In 1897 it bicycled 1,900 miles from Fort Missoula to St. Louis, Missouri, and back in forty days. [See Black Troops in the U.S. Army.]

In 1901 there was a small bicycle unit at Sandhurst [q.v.], and at the beginning of the Second Anglo-Boer War [q.v.] the Boers formed the Transvaal Cyclist Corps, which was headed by Danny Theron [q.v.].

Biddulphsberg, Battle of. See Senekal, Battle of.

Bien Hoa, Capture of (15 December 1861). French-Indochinese War. A French naval force captured this fortified town in Indochina (Vietnam) from the Annamites.

Bierce, Ambrose Gwinnett (1842–1914?). An American writer known for his caustic wit. He was one of thirteen children—all with names beginning with *A*—of an impoverished Indiana farmer and had little formal education, but he studied for a time at the Kentucky Military Institute. He was nineteen when he enlisted in Company C, 9th Indiana Infantry, within days of the Confederate attack on Fort Sumter [q.v.]. He was soon a sergeant and served throughout the Civil War. He first saw service in West Virginia and then fought at Shiloh, Perryville, Stones River, Chickamauga, and elsewhere.

He rose to be a first lieutenant, but at Kennesaw Mountain [q.v.] in Georgia on 27 June 1864 a bullet fractured his skull near the temple. After a month in a Chattanooga hospital he was sent home, feeling, he said, as if his skull had been "broken like a walnut." He returned to duty in September but saw no more combat. He resigned on 16 January 1865 and became a journalist. He wrote many stories based upon his war experiences, particularly at Shiloh.

Big Bethel, Battle of (10 June 1861), American Civil War. This first important land battle of the war was fought 10 miles northwest of Fort Monroe, Virginia, when Union General Benjamin Butler [q.v.] sent 4,400 men to attack a Confederate outpost at Big Bethel Church. The Union force was divided into three parts, two of which fired on each other, killing 2 and wounding 21.

The attack was badly managed, and the Confederates, 1,408 men, including the 1st North Carolina under Colonel D. H. Hill [q.v.], forced the Federals to retreat in some disorder. The Federals lost 76 killed and wounded; the Confederates lost 11.

Big Dry Wash / Chevelon's Fork, Battle of (17 July 1882), American Indian Wars. Three troops of the 3rd U.S. Cavalry, three troops of the 6th Cavalry, and some Indian scouts, all under Major Adna Romanza Chaffee [q.v.], defeated an Apache force at this place on the banks of East Clear Creek, Arizona.

Big Foot (1825?–1890), Indian name: Si-tanka. A leader of the Miniconjou Sioux, a band of the Teton Sioux. When the ghost dance [q.v.] craze swept through the western Indian tribes, Big Foot was an enthusiast, although he later renounced it. Under the supervision of Colonel George Alexander Forsyth [q.v.] he was persuaded to settle his people

at Wounded Knee in south-central South Dakota. There, on 29 December 1890, he and 145 of his people were killed in the Battle of Wounded Knee [q.v.].

Big Foot, Sioux chief, killed at the Battle of Wounded Knee

Big Hole Basin, Montana, Battle of (9–10 August 1877), Nez Percé War. Chief Joseph and Chief Looking Glass [qq.v.] and their Nez Percé Indians were caught by surprise by a troop of the 2nd U.S. Cavalry with seven companies of the 7th Infantry, a total of 191 men, under Colonel John Gibbon [q.v.]. Instead of fleeing, as was usual for Indians when taken by surprise, the Nez Percé rallied, and the troops were forced to fall back in the face of accurate rifle fire that killed 22 soldiers and 6 volunteers; 5 officers, 30 enlisted men, and 4 volunteers were wounded, 2 mortally. The fighting continued the next day. By this time the wounded were suffering terribly, and all the men were parched. A stream ran between the opposing forces about 100 yards away from Gibbon's position. Three men volunteered to carry canteens to the stream for water. One soldier, Private Homer Coon, later confessed in a letter that "it was not entirely on account of the wounded that we volunteered . . . we were thinking of ourselves too and the beautiful stream we could see glistening down below." The three reached the stream, and to Private Coon it seemed to take forever to fill the canteens. In the excitement of the danger he forgot to get a drink for himself. The water for which he had risked his life was given to the wounded, while he remained as thirsty as he had been before. Gibbon and his thirsty men were rescued only by the arrival of reinforcements under General O. O. Howard [q.v.] late in the day.

This was the most savage fight of the Nez Percé Campaign. Two officers and 21 enlisted men were killed and 5 officers and 41 others, including Gibbon, were wounded; Indian losses were 89 killed, many of them women and children, and uncounted wounded.

Bigors. Shortened form of French *bigorneau* (sea snail), the colloquial name of colonial artillery in the French service. [See Troupes de Marine.]

Big Will. An enormous 400-pounder cannon developed by and named for William Armstrong [q.v.].

Bilbao, Sieges of (1833–36 and 1872–76), Carlist Wars. This town in northern Spain, seven miles from the bay of Biscay, was besieged by Carlists in both Carlist Wars [q.v.]. In the first, the Carlist Basque General Tomás Zumalacárreguy [q.v.] was mortally wounded.

Bilboquet. A small 8-inch mortar with a bore of only half a caliber that threw a 60-pound shell 400 toises, about 2,400 feet.

Billet. A soldier's indoor sleeping place other than a barracks.

Billeting, Forced. The compulsory quartering of soldiers in private households. The practice was forbidden in the United States in 1791 by the Third Amendment to the Constitution, which states: "No soldier will, in time of peace, be quartered in any house without the consent of the owner, nor in time of war, but in a manner to be prescribed by law."

In Britain a soldier's billet included by law not only a place to sleep but candles, vinegar, salt, the use of utensils for dressing and eating his meat, small beer, and the use of a fire. Cavalrymen had to be provided with forage and stables. All were to be paid for by the government at a fixed rate.

In Scotland, officers were not obliged to pay for their lodgings except in the suburbs of Edinburgh.

Billings, John Shaw (1838–1913). An American army doctor and bibliographer who compiled and analyzed the medical records of military hospitals and barracks. He developed the U.S. army's medical library into one of the largest in the world and served as an adviser on the construction of military hospitals.

Bimbashi. See Bashi / Bachi / Baschi.

Bingham, George Charles, Third Earl of Lucan (1800–1888). An English soldier who, except for service as a volunteer on the Russian staff in the Balkans in 1828, had seen no active service until, as a major general in charge of the cavalry division, he was sent to the Crimean War [q.v.]. His division consisted of two brigades, one light under his detested brother-in-law Lord Cardigan [q.v.], the other heavy under James Yorke Scarlett [q.v.]. Lucan was present in the Battle of the Alma [q.v.], but his cavalry played no part.

When the army laid siege to Sevastopol, the cavalry remained in the Balaclava Valley. It was after the splendid charge of the heavy brigade that Lucan received an order from the British commander-in-chief delivered by an aide who gave him the wrong direction, and as a result the light brigade charged in the wrong direction [see Light Brigade, Charge of]. For this Lucan was censored and relieved of his command. Nevertheless, he was knighted for his service in the Crimea and rose to be a field marshal.

Birkenhead, **Wreck of the**. See Troopship.

Birmingham Small Arms Company. An English company founded in Birmingham, England, in 1861 to manufacture rifle stocks. In 1866 the company obtained a contract to convert 100,000 muzzle-loading Enfield rifles [q.v.] into Snider [q.v.] breechloaders. Soon after, it obtained contracts to produce various small arms for the British army.

Birney, David Bell (1825–1864). A Union army officer, the younger brother of William Birney [q.v.], and the son of James Gillespie Birney (1792–1857), the abolitionist Liberty Party candidate for president in 1840. He began his military career as a lieutenant colonel during the American Civil War and was soon colonel of the 23rd Pennsylvania, raised largely at his own expense, which he led at Falling Waters [q.v.]. On 17 February 1862 he became a brigadier general and led his brigade in Philip Kearny's [q.v.] division in the Peninsular Campaign [q.v.]. When Kearny was killed in the Battle of Chantilly [q.v.], he assumed command of the division and on 20 May 1863 was promoted major general. He commanded a division at Fredericksburg and Chancellorsville and III Corps at Gettysburg [qq.v.] after Daniel Sickles [q.v.] fell wounded. He himself was twice slightly wounded. Grant selected him to command X Corps, but he contracted malaria and died on 18 October 1864.

Birney, William (1819–1907). An American officer, the son of noted abolitionist James Gillespie Birney (1792–1857), and the brother of David Bell Birney [q.v.], who after graduation from Yale spent five years in Europe, taking an active part in 1848 in the violent revolutionary activities there [see Revolutions of 1848]. During the American Civil War he fought as a Union officer in all the campaigns of the Army of the Potomac [q.v.] through Chancellorsville [q.v.]. On 22 May 1863 he was appointed colonel of the 22nd U.S. Colored Infantry and also a brigadier general of volunteers. He raised seven additional black regiments and served with them in Florida. In 1865 he commanded a division of black troops in X Corps and was present at the surrender of Lee at Appomattox. Mustered out as a major general, he practiced law and wrote books on history and biography and articles on religion.

Bis and *Ter*. New French regiments or demi-brigades were sometimes added on to old ones by adding *bis* to the first clone and *ter* to the second. Thus two more regiments could be added to, say, the 20th Regiment and called 20 *bis* and 20 *ter*.

Bisbee, William Henry (1840–1942). A Union soldier in the American Civil War who fought at Shiloh, Murfreesboro, and Jonesboro and in the Atlanta Campaign [qq.v.] Later he fought in the Indian Wars, the Spanish-American War of 1898 and in the Philippine Insurrection of 1899–1902 [qq.v.]. He was made a brigadier general in 1901.

Bishamon. In Japan, the god of war and one of the seven gods of good fortune (*shichifukujin*) in Shinto. He was usually depicted wearing armor and standing over a fallen demon while holding a spear in one hand and a small pagoda in the other.

Bismarck-Schünhausen, Prince Herbert Nikolaus (1849–1904). A German soldier, son of Otto von Bismarck (1815–1898), the Iron Chancellor. He served in the Franco-Prussian War [q.v.], in which he was wounded, and later served in the diplomatic service.

Bisset, John Jervis (1819–1894). A British soldier who saw service in South Africa. He was taken from England to Cape

Colony as a small boy and first saw active service at age fifteen. He served in the Cape Mounted Rifles [q.v.] and fought in the Axe War of 1846–1847 and in the seventh Kaffir War [qq.v.] in 1851–52. He rose to be a lieutenant general and from 1865 to 1867 was lieutenant governor of Natal.

Bite the Bullet. An expression for enduring anything painful or unpleasant. For most of the nineteenth century anesthetics were scarce or unavailable. Kindly surgeons, while performing an amputation or other painful operations, would give soldiers lead musket balls to bite.

Bitter-ender. Those Afrikaners who in the Second Anglo-Boer War [q.v.] continued to fight through the guerrilla phase of the war until the bitter end.

Bivouac. Originally a bivouac was a night watch by an entire army under arms to prevent surprise, but in the nineteenth century it came to mean a temporary camp, usually without tents, except those reserved for senior officers and for head-quarters. Napoleon believed tents were unwholesome.

"Bivouac of the Dead, The." A poem written in 1847 by Theodore O'Hara [q.v.] on the reburial in Kentucky of American volunteers who fell during the Mexican War [q.v.] in the Battle of Buena Vista [q.v.] on 22 February 1847:

> The muffled drum's sad roll has beat
>   The soldier's last tattoo;
> No more on life's parade shall meet
>   That brave and fallen few.
> On fame's eternal camping ground
>   Their silent tents are spread,
> And glory guards with solemn round
>   The bivouac of the dead.
> No rumour of the foe's advance
>   Now swells upon the wind;
> No troubled thought at midnight haunts
>   Of loved ones left behind;
> No vision of the morrow's strife

> The warrior's dream alarms;
> No braying horn, nor screaming fife,
>   At dawn shall call to arms.
> Their shivered swords are red with rust,
>   their plumed heads are bowed.
> Their haughty banner trailed in dust,
>   Is now their martial shroud.
> And plenteous funeral tears have washed
>   The red stains from each brow;
> And the proud forms, by battle gashed,
>   Are freed from anguish now.
> The neighing troop, the flashing blade,
>   The bugle's stirring blast,
> The charge, the dreadful cannonade
>   The din and shout are past;
> Now war's wild note nor glory's peal
>   Shall thrill with fierce delight
> Those breasts that never more may feel
>   The rapture of the fight.
> Like the fierce northern hurricane
>   That sweeps his great plateau,
> Flushed with the triumph yet to gain,
>   Came down the serried foe.
> Who heard the thunder of the fray
>   Break o'er the field beneath,
> Knew well the watchword of that day
>   Was "Victory or Death."
> Long had the doubtful conflict raged
>   O'er all that stricken plain,
> For never fiercer fight was waged
>   The vengeful blood of Spain;
> And still the storm of battle blew,
>   Still swelled the glory tide;
> Not long, our stout old chieftain knew,
>   Such odds his strength could bide.
> 'Twas in that hour his stern command
>   Called to a martyr's grave
> The flower of his beloved land
>   The nation's flag to save.
> By the rivers of their fathers' gore
>   His first-born laurels grew,

Bivouac *Union troops bivouac on the line of battle at Fort Donelson.*

And well he deemed the sons would pour
    Their lives for glory too.
Sons of the Dark and Bloody Ground
    Ye must not slumber there,
Where stranger steps and tongues resound
    Along the heedless air;
Your own proud land's heroic soil
    Shall be your fitter grave;
She claims from war her richest spoil—
    The ashes of her brave.
Rest on, embalmed and sainted dead
    Dear as the blood ye gave;
No imperious footsteps here shall tread
    The herbage of your grave;
Nor shall your glory be forgot
    While Fame her record keeps,
Or honour points the hallowed spot
    Where Valour proudly sleeps.
Yon marble minstrel's voiceless stone,
    In deathless song shall tell,
Where many a vanished age hath flown,
    The story how ye fell;
Nor wreck, nor change, nor winter's blight,
    Nor time's remorseless doom,
Shall dim one ray of glory's light
    That gilds your deathless tomb.
The muffled drum's sad roll has beat
    The soldier's last tattoo;
No more on life's parade shall meet
    That brave and fallen few.
On fame's eternal camping ground
    Their silent tents are spread,
And glory guards with solemn round
    The bivouac of the dead.

This poem was so popular that an Act of Congress required it to be displayed at every national battlefield park, an honor shared with the Gettysburg Address, and at every national cemetery. The latter requirement was not always fulfilled.

Bixby Letter. See Next of Kin.

Bixio, Girolamo Nino (1821–1873). An Italian soldier who commanded Roman soldiers against the French in 1849. He commanded a ship in Giuseppe Garibaldi's [q.v.] Sicilian Campaign of 1860 and captured Regio di Calabria. He became one of Garibaldi's most trusted lieutenants. In 1870 he forced the surrender of Civitavecchia. He was elected to the Chamber of Deputies in 1866 and became a senator in 1870.

Bizerte, Seizure of (April 1881), French conquest of Algeria and Tunisia. Bizerte on the northeast coast of Tunisia was seized and occupied by a French naval force while French land forces moved across the border from Algeria into Tunisia. The bey of Tunis was forced to accept a French protectorate by the Treaty of Bardo on 19 May 1881.

Blaauwberg / Blueberg / Blue Mountain, Battle of (8 January 1806), Napoleonic Wars. A British force of 6,600 troops under Lieutenant General Sir David Baird [q.v.] landed at Saldanha Bay, near Cape Town, South Africa, and defeated a 1,000-man Franco-Dutch force of the Batavian Republic under General Jan Willems Janssens [q.v.], who surrendered on 18 January. British losses were 204; French and Dutch losses were about 300.

Black Bear Revolt / Bear Flag War (1846). In January 1846 American settlers in the Sacramento Valley, California, proclaimed California an independent republic, free of Mexico. At Sonoma on 14 June they captured the headquarters of the Mexican commandant and hoisted a flag bearing a grizzly bear and a red star.

The United States declared war on Mexico [see Mexican War] on 11 May 1846, and on 7 July Commodore John Drake Sloat (1780–1867), an American naval officer commanding the Pacific Squadron, landing sailors and marines, took possession of Monterey and claimed California as an American possession, thus aborting the California republic.

Even before the war had been declared, a military force under Colonel Stephen Watts Kearny [q.v.] had been ordered to occupy an area of Mexico stretching from the Rio Grande to the Pacific. When Kearny learned of the Black Bear Republic, he moved his force from New Mexico toward California. While he was still on the march, Captain John Charles Frémont [q.v.], a young American army officer who had been surveying in California, assumed command of the republican volunteers, joined forces with Kit Carson [q.v.], and marched on Sacramento. Californios, Mexican loyalists moving to block their advance, defeated them in two battles [See San Pedro and San Pasqual battles]. In spite of these defeats, the Americans, with local help, were able to seize control, and when Kearny arrived early in 1847, he found California under the military rule of Frémont and Commodore Robert Field Stockton (1795–1866), who had replaced Sloat. Both Stockton and Kearny claimed command. Frémont, who backed Stockton, refused to obey Kearny's orders and was later court-martialed for insubordination.

California was formally ceded to the United States in 1848, following the Mexican War, and in 1850 was admitted as the thirty-first state to the Union.

Blackburn's Ford, Battle of (18 July 1861), American Civil War. Union forces under General Irvin McDowell [q.v.] advancing on Manassas made a reconnaissance in force with a division under Daniel Tyler [q.v.] that clashed with Confederates at this ford on the banks of Bull Run, a small stream about 25 miles west of Alexandria, Virginia. Tyler was defeated with a loss of 83; the Confederates lost 68.

Union reports referred to this engagement as merely an affair, but for a time the Confederates referred to it as the Battle of Bull Run [q.v.].

Black Flag. To raise the black flag was to declare no quarter—i.e., take no prisoners. In Mexico in 1865 the emperor Maximilian issued a black flag decree in which he announced that all those captured fighting against the government would be executed. Later that year a group of American filibusters [q.v.] crossed the border into Mexico and were captured. When Maximilian threatened to execute them, the United States threatened war.

Black Flags. The name given to Chinese warlords who from the 1860s through the 1880s dominated northern Indochina and the upper reaches of the Red River in southern China. They were so called because each unit of their armies carried a black flag. At times the Black Flags enjoyed official status in Indochina because they controlled the predatory Montagnards, who were not ethnic Vietnamese. [See French Indochina Wars.]

Blackford's Ford, Battle of (19–20 September 1862), American Civil War. After the Battle of Antietam [q.v.] Lee withdrew his army south, crossing the Potomac at Blackford's (or Boteler's) Ford near Shepherdstown (now in West Virginia). Fearing that all his reserve artillery had been or was about to be captured by pursuing Federals, he sent A. P. Hill's [q.v.] division back as a rear guard. At the ford the Confederates clashed with elements of the Union V Corps and drove them back across the river. The Federals suffered the loss of 92 killed, 131 wounded, and 103 missing out of 800 engaged, most of whom were members of the so-called Corn Exchange Regiment (118th Pennsylvania), which had been issued many faulty weapons. Confederate losses were reported as 30 killed and 231 wounded.

Black Hawk (1767–1838). Indian name: Ma-ka-tae-mish-kla-kiak, meaning Black Sparrow Hawk. A Sauk Indian who by age nineteen was an experienced warrior, having successfully fought in and led raids upon the Osage Indians in present-day Illinois. He later defeated the Cherokees in battle. During the War of 1812 [q.v.] he allied himself with the British and enlisted the support of the Winnebagos, Potawatomis, and Kickapoos. He remained troublesome after the war, and in 1831 he and his warriors were defeated in an engagement by Illinois militia, who burned his village. On 30 June 1831 he was forced to sign a treaty by which he agreed to move, and to stay, west of the Mississippi River, but in April 1832 he led his people back across the Mississippi into Illinois, provoking the Black Hawk War [q.v.].

At the end of the war Black Hawk and some of his band

Black Hawk *Chief Black Hawk (right) with his son Whirling Thunder. Painting by John Jarvis, 1833*

fled north, but they were captured by the Winnebagos, who turned them over to the government. Black Hawk was imprisoned for a time at Fort Monroe, Virginia, and then taken on a tour of eastern cities to impress him with the power and grandeur of the whites. After a second tour in 1837 he was allowed to settle on land by the Des Moines River near Iowaville, and there he died.

His corpse was clothed in a uniform donated by Andrew Jackson, and various notables contributed medals, a cane, and other accoutrements for a surface burial, all of which were stolen in 1839, when his bones were taken to St. Louis, cleaned, and moved to Quincy, Illinois; then to the home of the governor of Iowa; and finally to the Burlington (Illinois) Geological and Historical Society, where they were destroyed in a fire in 1855.

Black Hawk War (1832). In April 1832 Chief Black Hawk [q.v.], who had signed a treaty agreeing to move and remain west of the Mississippi River, led some 2,000 Fox and Sauk (or Sac) Indians, of whom about 500 were warriors, out of Indian territory to land east of the Mississippi, where they planted crops, believing they could avoid the white settlers. A force of 900 Illinois militia, including Captain Abraham Lincoln [q.v.], and 400 regulars under Brigadier General Henry Atkinson (1782–1842) was sent against them. Two Sauk Indian envoys dispatched to parlay with Atkinson were shot dead by Illinois militiamen, marking the beginning of a four-month war. On 14 May in the present Ogle County, Illinois, about 40 Indians led by Black Hawk attacked a party of soldiers and killed 12. On 24 June in an indecisive battle Indians attacked Apple River Fort [q.v.], near present-day Galena, Illinois. They defeated the militia at Stillman's Run, about 12 miles south-southwest of present-day Rockford (founded two years later), and then decided to cross into what is now Wisconsin. They were attacked at Wisconsin Heights as they attempted to cross the Mississippi by troops ashore and an armed steamer on the river, but Black Hawk and most of his band escaped.

On 1–2 August the Indians suffered a decisive defeat in the Battle of Bad Axe [q.v.] on the Bad Axe River south of present-day La Crosse, Wisconsin, near the confluence of the Mississippi and Bad Axe rivers, soldiers killing or driving into the river about 150 and capturing 40 for a loss of 6 killed and 18 wounded. Many of the band who succeeded in crossing the river were attacked by the Sioux. Chief Black Hawk fled north and sought protection with the Winnebagos, who refused him shelter and turned him over to the government. On 21 September a treaty was signed by which the Foxes and Sauks agreed to remain west of the Mississippi.

Indian casualties during the war are unknown, but fewer than 150 of the original warriors survived. General Atkinson's force suffered a total loss of 1 officer and 25 enlisted men killed and 4 officers and 35 enlisted men wounded.

This was the last Indian war fought on the northwestern frontier east of the Mississippi.

Black Jack. 1. From the sixteenth century to the early years of the nineteenth century this was the name for a leather jug holding beer or liquor, coated on the outside with tar.

2. An American drink of rum and molasses sometimes drunk with water.

Black Hawk War *The Sauks and Foxes are trapped between the steamship* Warrior *and 1,300 American troops during the brief Black Hawk War.*

3. A weapon with a short shaft and weighted end used as a bludgeon.

(The use of blackjack as a name for the game of vingt-et-un, or twenty-one, was unknown in the nineteenth century.)

Black Mountain Expedition. See Hazara Expeditions.

Black Powder. See Gunpowder.

Blacks in the British Army. Many colonial units used local blacks—e.g., King's African Rifles in East Africa and the West African Defence Force—and for a specific campaign African tribesmen were sometimes formed into temporary regiments of auxiliaries named after the colonels who raised them. However, the only black combatants carried as regulars were the West India Regiments. Raised in the British colonies of the West Indies, they were manned by British officers and used in West Africa and elsewhere. Black troops from these regiments took part in the storming of Fort Petrie in 1814 during the War of 1812 [q.v.] and fought in all three Ashanti Wars [q.v.]. Some West Indians also served as bandsmen [q.v.] in British regiments.

No blacks were used in combatant units on either side during the Second Anglo-Boer War [q.v.] of 1898–1901, which was regarded as a "white man's war," although Lord Kitchener [q.v.] employed many as armed guards in blockhouses [q.v.] along railway lines.

Black Troops in the U.S. Army. Although about a 1,000 blacks had fought in the American Revolution and some free blacks had fought under Andrew Jackson in the Battle of New Orleans [q.v.] in the War of 1812 [q.v.], blacks were not permitted to enlist as regulars in the U.S. army until after the Civil War. The first black unit in the Union army was formed on 27 September 1862 by General Benjamin Butler [q.v.] in

New Orleans as the 1st Louisiana Native Guards; it was mustered out on 12 October.

After the Emancipation Proclamation took effect on 1 January 1863, Lincoln called for four regiments of Negro infantry. In April 1863 Robert Shaw [q.v.] was appointed colonel of the 54th Massachusetts Volunteers, the first regiment of black troops from a free state to be mustered into the U.S. service. In November 1863 former slaves were enlisted by Colonel Thomas Wentworth Storrow Higginson (1823–1911) into a regiment of volunteers, the 1st South Carolina Infantry, which on 8 February 1864 became the 33rd United States Colored Troops. Higginson was the former pastor of the Free Church of Worcester, Massachusetts, and an active abolitionist who in 1854 had passed out axes to a mob and urged them to free a fugitive slave named Anthony Burns.

In all, some 300,000 blacks were organized into sixty-six regiments, and served in the ranks of the Union army in segregated units known as United States Colored Troops (USCT). Only a handful of blacks were granted commissions, and all units were commanded by white officers. Comparatively few units saw action, and even fewer saw more than one battle. In the course of the war 143 white officers with black units and 2,751 black enlisted men were killed or mortally wounded.

The first black regiment to see action was the 79th USCT at Island Mounds, Missouri, on 28 October 1862, and it was first used in a general engagement in the attack upon Port Hudson [q.v.], Louisiana, on 27 May 1863. The highest casualties were sustained by the 55th Massachusetts at Honey Hill, South Carolina, on 30 November 1864. In the last months of the war an entire corps of black troops was formed (XXV Corps), but it saw no action.

The wrath of Confederate soldiers facing blacks in Union uniforms led to excesses and atrocities at Fort Pillow,

Petersburg [qq.v.], Passion Spring, Saltville, and elsewhere. Even among some of the northern troops there were objections to blacks' wearing the same uniform.

From the beginning of the war the Confederate army used black servants and laborers, but it was not until March 1865 that the Confederate Congress authorized 300,000 slaves to be conscripted. In April a few companies were formed, but none fought.

In 1866 Congress authorized for the first time the enlistment of blacks in the regular army and created six (soon reduced to four) black regiments: the 9th and 10th Cavalry and the 24th and 25th Infantry. Integration was suggested by General Ambrose E. Burnside [q.v.] in 1877, when he was a U.S. senator. Other generals recommended it as well. All were ignored.

During the Indian fighting period, from 1866 to 1891, 18 blacks, 11 of them troopers in the 9th Cavalry, won the Medal of Honor [q.v.]. In spite of their generally fine performance—a lower desertion rate and a higher percentage of reenlistments than in white regiments—most of their junior officers came from the bottom of West Point classes prior to 1887, after which some graduates of higher class standings chose the 9th or 10th Cavalry. John Joseph Pershing, who was graduated 29th in a class of 66 in 1886 and became the only general of the armies, served as a first lieutenant in the 10th Cavalry from 1892 to 1898 and for his championship of black soldiers was called Black Jack Pershing. Between 1866 and 1898 only 8 blacks were commissioned, and 5 of these were commissioned as chaplains.

The first black to enter West Point was James Webster Smith of South Carolina in 1870. He attended for four years but never became a first classman. Between 1870 and 1889 12 blacks were admitted to West Point, but half of them failed to survive the first semester. The first black cadet to graduate and receive a commission was Henry Ossian Flipper [q.v.] in 1877. [See West Point.]

Black Troops in the U.S. Army *Black artillerymen in Tennessee drill, 1864.*

Black Watch. Popular name for a Scottish regiment in the British army. From 1758 to 1861 it was the 42nd (the Royal Highland) Regiment of Foot. From 1861 to 1881 it was the 42nd (the Royal Highland) Regiment of Foot (the Black Watch). When in 1881 it was joined with the 73 (Perthshire) Regiment of Foot it became officially the Black Watch (Royal Highlanders).

Black Watch *Black Watch on Sinkat Road during Graham's first campaign from Suakim*

Black Week (December 1899). A period at the beginning of the Second Anglo-Boer War [q.v.] in which the British suffered three major reverses within a week: Stormberg on 10 December, Magersfontein on 11 December, and Colenso [qq.v.] on 15 December. These defeats caused so much alarm in Britain that on 17 December all the first-class British reserves were called to the colors and Field Marshal Lord Roberts, on the verge of retirement, was sent to South Africa to take command.

Blackwell, Elizabeth (1821–1910). The first woman to become a physician in America. Born in England, she was brought to the United States when she was eleven. She earned her M.D. in 1849 from a small medical school in Geneva, New York, and then studied in London and Paris. Returning to the United States in 1850, she founded the New York Infirmary and College for Women in 1854 and was soon joined by her sister, Emily, who had also become a doctor. When the American Civil War broke out, she formed the Ladies Sanitary Aid Institute, which became the National Sanitary Aid Institute and later merged with other women's aid societies to become what was popularly called the Sanitary Commission [q.v.].

After the war she was active both in the United States and in Britain, where she established the National Health Society. She wrote prolifically on medical subjects; some of her publications, such as *The Human Element in Sex,* shocked the profession. Until 1921, what is now Welfare Island off New York City was called Blackwells Island in her honor.

Blackwood, Alicia (née August) (1818–1913). Lady Blackwood, the wife of a Church of England cleric, the daughter of an earl, and the sister of a baron, served as a volunteer nurse during the Crimean War [q.v.]. Having journeyed to Constantinople (Istanbul) at her own expense, she offered her services to Florence Nightingale [q.v.], who put her to work nursing soldiers' wives.

Bladensburg, Battle of (24 August 1814), War of 1812. Near this Maryland town on the Patuxent River only seven miles east-northeast from Washington, D.C., some 6,500 American militia with a handful of regulars under Brigadier General William Henry Winder (1775–1824), and a naval contingent of 400 sailors and marines under Commodore Joshua Barney (1759–1818) with 26 guns were routed after three hours' fighting by 4,500 British regulars and Canadian militia with 3 light guns and some Congreve rockets under Major General Robert Ross [q.v.]. A number of the American soldiers were terrified by the rockets. The 5th and 24th Maryland regiments fled in a panic when they were fired.

Their victory, at a cost of 294 casualties, enabled the British that same evening to enter the American capital, where, in reprisal for the American burning of York [q.v.], Canada, they burned most of the public buildings while U.S. marines guarded cowering congressmen in a Washington hotel.

General Ross later wrote: "So unexpected was our entry and capture of Washington, and so confident was [President] Madison of the defeat of our troops, that he had prepared a supper for the expected conquerors; and when our advanced party entered the President's house, they found a table laid with forty covers."

Blair, Francis Preston, Jr. (1821–1875). A Union soldier and politician, educated at Princeton, who was a U.S. congressman when the American Civil War began. He at once organized volunteer Union troops and was credited with saving Missouri and Kentucky for the Union by ordering, without any authority, the seizure of the St. Louis arsenal. Later he raised several regiments and was appointed a major general in the western theater campaigns. At Chattanooga [q.v.] and in the Atlanta Campaign he commanded a corps.

After the war he served one term in the Senate, where he opposed the government's Reconstruction policies.

Blake, Joachim (1759–1827). A Spanish soldier of Irish extraction who in 1808, during the Peninsular War [q.v.], commanded the Army of Galicia as captain general of the province. He was defeated by French General Jean Baptiste Bessières [q.v.] at Medina del Río Seco [q.v.] on 14 July 1808 and on 31 October by François Lefebvre [q.v.] at Pan Corbo [q.v.]. Later he fought with small forces and guerrillas until January 1812, when he was captured at Valencia. He was generally regarded as a good general with bad luck.

Blake, John Y. Fillmore (1856–1908). An American soldier who, after attending the University of Arkansas, was graduated from West Point in 1880 and served mostly with the 6th Cavalry on the western frontier until he resigned in 1889 and emigrated to South Africa. During the Second Anglo-Boer War he served on the side of the Boers and became the commandant of a unit of Irishmen.

Blakely, Siege of (1–9 April 1865), American Civil War. This battle in the Mobile Campaign was the last important infantry battle of the war. Leading elements in a column of 10,000 infantry and 2,000 cavalry under Union Major

General Frederick Steele (1819–1868) encountered a Confederate outpost held by the 46th Mississippi five miles from Blakely, Alabama, and drove them back to within a mile of Spanish Fort, their defenses at the town. The 46th Mississippi lost its colors and 74 men; the Federals lost only 2 men, one of whom was killed by a land mine (then called a torpedo) that had been placed in front of the Confederate position. The captured Confederates were forced to remove the remaining mines.

The Union force captured Spanish Fort on 8 April and laid siege to Blakely. On the following day the 8th Iowa spearheaded an attack that by 5:30 P.M. had gained it a foothold in the Confederate defenses; by nightfall the place had been captured, and 50 guns and 500 prisoners fell into Union hands. The commander of the fort, Randall Lee Gibson [q.v.], reported 93 killed, 395 wounded, and 250 missing. Most of the defenders escaped to Mobile.

Blakely Gun. An English rifled gun, produced in various calibers, that was imported in small numbers by the Confederates in the American Civil War. John Pelham [q.v.] used one of these guns during his famous stand in the Battle of Fredericksburg [q.v.].

Blakely gun

Blanchisseuse. A washerwoman, one of the *femmes de troupe,* soldiers' wives considered of good character whom each French company was permitted to carry on the strength [q.v.]. After 1804 *femmes de troupe* were entitled to hospitalization in wartime [see Women of the Army]. Sergeant François Lefebvre [q.v.] married a *blanchisseuse* who became a duchess when he became a marshal of France and Duc de Danzig.

Blanco. A cleaning and whitening preparation used on some clothing and accoutrements that began to replace whiting about 1835. It was made from the heat-dried bodies of female cochineal insects found on several species of cactus.

Blanco y Erenas, Ramón, Marqués de Piña Plata (1831–1906). A Spanish soldier and statesman who served in Cuba during the Revolution of 1868–77 and participated in the Spanish annexation of Santo Domingo [see Cuban Revolutions]. After a term as governor of Mindanao in the Philippines, he became colonel general in 1871 during the Second Carlist War [q.v.]. In 1879–81 and again in 1897–98 he was governor-general of Cuba and in 1898 attempted unsuccessfully to resist the invasion by U.S. forces in the Spanish-American War [q.v.].

Blank Cartridge. A cartridge without a projectile.

Blank cartridge

Blasting Powder. An explosive powder similar to gunpowder [q.v.] but containing sodium nitrate instead of potassium nitrate or saltpeter.

Bled. French name for the desert area of North Africa where French forces engaged Arabs in the last half of the nineteenth century.

Bleeding Kansas. See Border War.

Bleibtreu, George (1828–1892). A German painter of battle scenes, especially of the German Wars of Liberation, the Schleswig-Holstein War of 1849, and the Franco-Prussian War [qq.v.] of 1870–71.

Blenker, Ludwig (Louis) (1812–1863). A German-born American soldier who served in the Bavarian Legion and, after taking part in the Revolution of 1848, fled to the United States. During the American Civil War he raised the 8th New York from among Central European emigrants and became its colonel. He later became a major general and commanded a division of foreign-born Americans.

In March 1862, when he was ordered to march his division from north-central Virginia to join John Frémont [q.v.] in northeastern Virginia (present-day West Virginia) in the pursuit of Confederate General Thomas ("Stonewall") Jackson, he lost his way and, thoroughly disoriented, wandered about in northern Virginia with his army. Since he had taken no supplies, his 10,000 men pillaged the countryside. It took twelve days for his division to march fifty miles in the right direction. When he finally joined Frémont in the Shenandoah Valley, he participated in the Battle of Cross Keys [q.v.], but soon after he was summoned to Washington and on 31 March 1862 was honorably discharged. He died seven months later.

Blind. 1. As a noun, a leather hood used to cover the eyes of pack mules while they were being loaded or when their loads were tightened.

2. As a verb, to conceal by means of carpentry or earthworks. [See Blindage.]

Blindage. Usually a siege work, constructed of wood or earth, to conceal powder magazines, trenches, or other military works. Sometimes a shelter from ricochet missiles, crossfire, or grenades.

Blind Shells. Shells that did not explode on impact or when they were intended to explode.

Bliokh, Ivan Stanislavovich. See Bloch, Jean de.

Bliss, Tasker Howard (1853–1930). An officer who was graduated from West Point in 1875 and served in Cuba and Puerto Rico during the Spanish-American War [q.v.]. He became a major general in 1915 and chief of staff in 1918.

Bloch, Jean de (1836–1902). Real name: Ivan (or Jan) Stanislavovich Bliokh. A Polish financier, industrialist, and writer who helped develop Russia's railroads. His highly influential book *The Future of War in Its Technological, Economic and Political Relations* examined the relationship between a nation's socioeconomic infrastructure and its ability to wage war and predicted that war would in time become so expensive that no country would engage in it. First published in seven volumes in Russia in 1898, it was brought out the following year in English in an abbreviated form under the title *Is War Now Impossible?* Many of his predictions proved accurate. He foresaw, for example, that the next large war (World War I) would become a stalemate, in which neither army would be able to get at the other for a decisive victory, that opponents would be separated by a no-man's-land, that the lives of junior officers at the front would be brief, and that submarines would have strategic importance. The arming of nations, he predicted, would result in "slow destruction in consequence of expenditures on preparations for war or swift destruction in the event of war."

Bloch studied the lethality of modern weapons and their effect upon manpower and industry and the impact of total war upon society. He minutely examined the impact of high-velocity bullets upon bone and tissue. He produced statistics on grain production in European countries. Professional officers dismissed his claims as those of an amateur.

Blockhouse. A small fort of stone or logs having sides loopholed for musketry. It was sometimes called a garrison house, and it often formed a corner of a stockade. In the United States it was a common defense against Indians. During the Second Anglo-Boer War [q.v.] prefabricated blockhouses were sent out to South Africa for assembly and used to protect railway lines.

Blockhouse *American Civil War blockhouse near Alexandria, Virginia*

Blood, Binden (1842–1940). A British soldier who was a descendant of Colonel Thomas Blood (1618?–1680), the adventurer who in 1671 attempted to steal the crown jewels. Binden Blood was educated at Addiscombe [q.v.] and in 1860 was commissioned a temporary lieutenant in the Royal Engineers. For the next ten years he specialized in signaling and pontoon bridge construction. In 1870 he became the first commander of a telegraph troop, and the following year he sailed for India, where, except for short periods in Africa to fight in the Zulu War, Arabi's Revolt, and the Second Anglo-Boer War [qq.v.], he spent the next thirty-five years.

In 1877–78 he led an expedition against the Jowacki Afridis in the Northwest Frontier and in 1882 took part in the Second Afghan War [q.v.]. He was promoted brigadier general in 1892, and in 1895 he was chief of staff on the Chitral Expedition [q.v.] and was knighted (KCB). In 1897–98 he commanded the Bruner Field Force, and in 1898 he was promoted major general. He was a lieutenant general in the Second Anglo-Boer War and was made a full general in 1906.

The following year he retired. He lived until age ninety-seven, his name being carried on the Army List for eighty years.

Blood and Iron. This expression was first used by the first-century Roman rhetorician Marcus Fabius Quintilianus, who spoke of *sanguinem et ferrum,* but it is generally associated with Otto von Bismarck (1815–1898), who, in a speech to the Budget Commission of the Prussian House of Delegates on 30 September 1862, said "It is desirable and it is necessary that the conditions of affairs in Germany and of her constitutional relations should be improved, but this cannot be accomplished by speeches and resolutions of a majority, but only by iron and blood [*Eisen und Blut*]."

Blood River, Battle of (16 December 1838). Boers under Pieter Retief [q.v.] and Gerhardus Martinus Maritz (1797–1839), fleeing from British rule, made a pact with King Dingaan [q.v.] of the Zulus on 4 February 1838 that permitted Boer settlement in what is now part of northern Natal in South Africa. Two days later at Dingaan's kraal a Zulu impi [q.v.] fell upon the Boers without warning. Men, women, and children were slaughtered; Retief himself was killed. The Zulus then killed another 282 Boers near present-day Weenen [see Bloukrans Massacre].

A Boer commando sent to retaliate was ambushed. The British force that followed was ambushed and annihilated by some 7,000 Zulus. Later that year the Boers organized a second force, and on 16 December on the banks of the Blood River, a tributary of the Buffalo River in Natal, 20 miles east of Dundee, Boers under Andries Pretorius [q.v.] defeated a huge Zulu force, estimated to be 10,000, under Dingaan. The Zulus were said to have suffered 3,000 casualties. No Boer was killed.

The date of the battle was celebrated each year thereafter as Dingaan Day; today it is called Day of the Covenant because of a promise to God the Boers made to keep the day holy if they were victorious.

Blood's Pontoons. Flat-bottomed boats with light wooden frames covered by layers of cork, canvas, wood, and leather bonded together. Each was 21 feet long and 5 feet 2 inches, wide and weighed 850 pounds. A bridge made of these pontoons could carry a 64-pounder gun.

Bloody Angle. 1. A landmark on the battlefield of Gettysburg [q.v.], Pennsylvania, in the American Civil War, that on 3 July 1863, the third day of the battle, was the scene of much bitter fighting.

2. A section of the battlefield of Spotsylvania [q.v.], Virginia, where on 12 May 1864 some of the most sanguinary fighting of the American Civil War took place between the armies of Grant and Lee. Confederate General Edward Johnson [q.v.] was captured here.

Bloody Lane. Sometimes called Sunken Road, a landmark of the Battle of Antietam

Bloody Lane *The Sunken Road, or Bloody Lane, at Antietam, Maryland*

[q.v.] in the American Civil War that was in the center of Lee's line under D. H. Hill [q.v.].

Bloody Shirt. A metonym for wounds received, as in "waving the bloody shirt." Especially used to typify political oratory using wartime experience as political capital.

Blouberg / Blueberg / Blaauwberg, Battle of. See Blaauwberg.

Bloukrans Massacre (17 February 1838). On Bloukrans Hill, 85 miles northwest of Durban, South Africa, a Zulu impi [q.v.] attacked a Boer laager [q.v.], killing 41 men, 56 women, and 97 children. Many others were wounded. In 1839 a village founded nearby was named Weenen (Weeping) in commemoration. [See Blood River, Battle of.]

Blowing Bags. Bags containing a small charge of gunpowder and coal dust insufficient to explode the shell. Ignited by a fuze, they were used in artillery practice to show where a shell would have exploded. The charges used were called blowing charges.

Blücher, Gebhard Leberecht von, Prince of Wahlstatt (1742–1819). A soldier born near Rostock, Germany, who at the age of thirteen enlisted in a Swedish cavalry regiment and served in three campaigns against the Prussian army of Frederick the Great. In 1760, during the Seven Years' War, he was captured near Friedland and changed sides, becoming a cornet in the Prussian 8th ("Red") Hussars.

In peacetime his wildness and excesses caused him to be passed over for promotion, and (accounts differ) he resigned his commission or was discharged for dissipation and insubordination. He then married and became a farmer in Pomerania, but in 1787 he rejoined the army as a major and fought against the French. In 1794 he commanded the 8th Hussars, and in June was promoted major general (a rank equivalent to brigadier general in the British and American armies). In 1801 he was promoted lieutenant general and in that rank served in the campaign of 1805–06 against Napoleon, notably at Jena-Auerstädt [q.v.], where he commanded the rear guard during the stages of the Prussian retreat.

Napoleon referred to him as "that drunken Hussar." Blücher himself once commented to Augustus Gneisenau [q.v.], his brilliant chief of staff: "Gneisenau, if I had only learned something, what might not have been made of me! . . . Instead of studying I have given myself to gambling, drink and women."

On 7 November 1806, at Ratekau [q.v.], near Lübeck, he was forced to surrender to Jean Baptiste Bernadotte [q.v.]. He did not fight again until he took command of the Prussian forces in the field in Silesia on 28 February 1813. He fought at Lützen on 2 May and Bautzen [qq.v.] on 20 May. He defeated Marshal Jacques Macdonald [q.v.] on 26 August at Katzbach [q.v.] (or Kocaba) and Auguste Marmont [q.v.] at Möcker [q.v.]. He was one of the principal commanders at Leipzig [q.v.], the largest battle of the Napoleonic Wars, where his conduct earned him promotion to general field marshal.

On an 1814 visit to London he remarked, "What a place to plunder!"

In the invasion of France Blücher led his army toward the Marne and Paris, but Napoleon bludgeoned him in the battles of Champaubert on 10 February 1814, Montmirail on the following day, Château-Thierry on 12 February, and Vauchamps [qq.v.] on 14 February before turning south to strike the Austrians at Montereau [q.v.]. However, the march on Paris was resumed after the French defeat at Laon [q.v.] on 9 and 10 March.

On 28 March the Allied armies united at Meaux. Two days later they defeated the armies of Adolphe Mortier [q.v.] and Marmont at Montmartre [q.v.] and occupied Paris, forcing Napoleon's abdication. Blücher, in poor health after a slight stroke, became one of the sights of the city riding about in a barouche wearing a head covering that has been described as a woman's green sunbonnet. The war over, he believed his fighting days were done and retired to his Silesian estate, but on 8 March 1815 when he learned of Napoleon's return from Elba, the old war-horse answered the call to lead the Prussian army in Belgium.

Napoleon, determined to defeat the Allied armies in detail, first attacked the Prussians on 16 June near the village of Ligny [q.v.] and routed them. Blücher tried in vain to stop the rout, even personally leading a cavalry charge, but he was thrown from his horse and ridden over by his own troops. His life was saved by his aide-de-camp, Count Nostitz. That night, as he lay apparently helpless, Gneisenau organized a retreat toward Wavre, but the next day Blücher, bruised and shaken, rose from his bed and, after liberal drafts of gin and rhubarb, announced his determination to support Wellington at Waterloo.

Blücher has not perhaps been given all the credit he deserves for this valiant decision. On 18 June his army threatened the French flank and rear, and Napoleon was forced to use up his reserves to keep him at bay. His action undoubtedly enabled Wellington to deliver the Grande Armée its deathblow. At nine o'clock on the night of the victory Blücher and Wellington met at an inn, La Belle Alliance [q.v.], and it was decided that he would lead the pursuit.

When Napoleon surrendered and was at last secured on St. Helena, Blücher was made Prince of Wahlstadt, and honors were heaped upon him. He chose to retire once more, and he died on his estate in Silesia on 12 September 1819.

Blücher Boots. Hand-sewn leather boots worn by British soldiers until 1913. They were named after German Field Marshal Gebhard von Blücher [q.v.].

Blue and Gray, The. Cognomens, springing from the dress uniform colors, of the Union and Confederate armies in the American Civil War. Although the Union regulars and some volunteers wore blue uniforms, in the first year of the war uniforms of a variety of colors were issued. Some Union soldiers, like those in Massachusetts regiments, wore gray; others dressed as Zouaves [q.v.]. And although gray was the official color of Confederate uniforms, Confederate soldiers too in the early months of the war wore uniforms of various colors; some simply fought in their civilian clothes; in the last years of the war many wore cloth dyed tan, brown, or "butternut."

Thomas ("Stonewall") Jackson [q.v.], who often wore a blue coat, was buried in one, much to the amazement of those who disinterred his body for reburial years later.

Blue Belly. A contemptuous term used by southerners for Union soldiers during the American Civil War.

Blueberg / Blouberg / Blaauwberg, Battle of. See Blaauwberg.

Blue Book. Popular name for *Regulations for the Order and Discipline of the Troops of the United States* by Baron Friedrich von Steuben (1730–1794). The book, first printed in 1779, was often reprinted, even in the nineteenth century.

Blue Flag. Often called the Bonnie Blue Flag. A blue flag with a single white star, it was the unofficial banner of secession for southern states before the American Civil War. Its designer is unknown, but it was first flown in South Carolina, and it flew over the first Confederate Congress in Montgomery, Alabama.

Although the authorship is disputed, it is generally believed that in the spring of 1861 Harry McCarthy, a vaudeville entertainer, wrote a stirring marching song enumerating the reasons for secession. Named "The Bonny Blue Flag," it was set to the tune of "The Irish Jaunting Car" and was enormously popular, rivaling "Dixie." Union authorities in occupied New Orleans banned it. Late in the war McCarthy abandoned the Confederacy and moved to Philadelphia. The tune is used today for the fight song of Georgia Tech.

Blue Light Federalist. During the War of 1812 [q.v.] this name was given to those who failed to support the war, mainly New England bankers who refused to lend money to the American government to pay war expenses and New England merchants who continued to sell supplies to the British army in Canada.

The term derived from the blue lights used by pro-British residents of New London, Connecticut, who on 12 December 1813 signaled a British blockading squadron that American Commodore Stephen Decatur (1779–1820) was trying to slip through the blockade with his squadron.

Blue Mass. Sometimes called blue pills or pills of mercury. This was a common compound of mercury used for the treatment of diarrhea and dysentery during the American Civil War. Often it was merely a combination of metallic mercury and chalk.

Blue Mutiny (1859–62). The name given to an uprising of the peasants on indigo plantations in India, which began in the autumn of 1859 when the ill-used laborers in lower Bengal refused to sow indigo. Its production, the largest private industry in Bengal, was in the hands of British planters. Although a struggle between humanitarians and capitalists pulled the government first one way and then the other, the revolt was suppressed.

Blues, The. Popular name for the British Royal Horse Guards, whose uniform coats were blue.

Blumenthal, Count Karl Albrecht Leonhard von (1810–1900). A Prussian officer who was chief of staff of the Austro-Prussian forces under Frederick III [q.v.] in the Schleswig-Holstein War of 1866, the Seven Weeks' War, and the Franco-Prussian War [qq.v.] of 1870–71.

Blunt, James Gilpatrick (1826–1881). A Union officer who served mostly on the western frontier during the American Civil War. He was promoted brigadier general on 8 April 1862 and was named commander of the Department of Kansas. On 22 October at Old Fort Wayne [q.v.] he defeated a force of hostile Indians led by Confederate Colonel Douglas Cooper [q.v.]. On 28 November of that year he defeated a Confederate force under John Marmaduke [q.v.] at Cane Hill [q.v.] and, united with a force under Francis Herron, defeated Confederate Brigadier General Thomas Hindman [qq.v.] at Prairie Grove [q.v.] on 7 December. Having been made a major general of volunteers on 29 November, he took command of the District of the Frontier on 9 June 1863. On 17 July he defeated a Confederate force under now Brigadier General Cooper at Honey Springs [q.v.]. At Baxter Springs [q.v.] he suffered a humiliating defeat at the hands of Quantrill's raiders [q.v.], but he successfully defeated a portion of the Confederate force under Sterling Price [q.v.], who attempted a raid into Missouri in September–October 1864. This was the last Confederate threat to the West.

Blunt was an overly suspicious man, ever detecting plots against himself or the government. He died in an insane asylum.

Board of Engineers. In the American army, a board of three or more officers appointed by the chief of engineers to plan or revise projects for permanent fortifications or river and harbor improvements.

Board of Ordnance. A British government department that managed all affairs relating to military engineers and the artillery. It was in existence from the time of Henry VIII (1509–1547) but was abolished in 1855 along with the post of master general of ordnance.

Board of Survey. In the American army, officers appointed to fix responsibility for the loss, damage, or destruction of government property or for making an inventory of the government property found in the effects of a deceased officer.

Board of Visitors. An Act of Congress of 16 March 1846, amended by acts of 16 March 1868 and 21 February 1870, established a board consisting of two senators, three representatives, and seven members appointed by the president of the United States to conduct an annual examination and issue an annual report on the condition of the U.S. Military Academy at West Point, New York. The board could also be present for the annual examination of the classes, which occurred on the first day of June unless this fell on a Sunday or a Monday.

Boat Bridge. See Pontoon Bridge.

Boat-Tailed Bullet. A bullet with a tapered base that is less than the maximum diameter.

Bobrikov, Nikolai Ivanovich (1839–1904). A Russian soldier who, as governor of Finland from 1898 to 1903, was ruthless in his attempts at Russification. In 1903 he was granted dictatorial powers. He was assassinated the following year.

Bobtail Discharge. American army slang for a dishonorable discharge as a result of a court-martial sentence. The discharge papers had the section under "character" bobbed (cut out), a certain indication that the recipient had been released under conditions less than honorable.

Bobtail Guard. A colloquialism in the American army for the first turn of guard duty for the night.

Bodeo Revolver. A pistol adopted by the Italian army in 1889 and made in various arsenals and factories in two styles: one with an octagonal barrel, a folding trigger, and no trigger guard issued to privates and one with a normal trigger and guard issued to noncommissioned officers and officers.

Bodmer, Johann Georg (1786–1864). A Swiss inventor among whose most successful inventions was a percussion shell devised in 1805.

Body of a Fortification. Sometimes called the body of the place. The citadel or enceinte of a fort or the main line of bastions and curtains, as distinguished from the outworks.

Boer Wars. See Anglo-Boer Wars.

Bofors. The largest Swedish armament works, founded in 1883, located in Bofors, now an industrial suburb of Karlskoga in south-central Sweden.

Bogue / Boca / Bocca Forts, Capture of (25–27 February 1841), First Opium War. A British expeditionary force in China under Sir Hugh Gough [q.v.] captured these Chinese forts, the keys to Canton (Guangzhou), on the Bocca Tigris (tiger's mouth), the narrow channel between the upper and lower Pearl River. The Chinese admiral was killed, and 459 guns were captured. On 14 September the British demolished the forts.

Bogus Charley (1852?–1881). An English-speaking Modoc Indian chief who acted as interpreter for Captain Jack [q.v.]. He was suspected of being involved in the plot to murder General Edward Canby [q.v.], although he denied the charge. He surrendered on 22 May 1873 and attempted to save himself by turning upon his own tribesmen. He was exiled to the Quapaw Agency in Oklahoma, where he ruled as headman for many years.

Bohemian Brigade. A name Union newspaper correspondents who followed the contending armies in the American Civil War gave themselves.

Bojeleschti, Battle of (1828), Russo-Turkish War. Near this village in Walachia the Russians under General Friedrich von Geismar defeated a superior Turkish force, capturing 7 guns, 24 ammunition wagons, 400 bread wagons, 24 colors, and enough small arms to equip 10,000 men. Cossacks captured 507 prisoners.

Bokhara, Conquest of (1868). Russian conquests in Central Asia. After Tashkent was captured by Russian General Mikhail Chernyaiev [q.v.] in 1864 [see Khokand, Russian Conquest of], the Russians turned their attention to the khanate of Bokhara. In April 1867 Russian General

Konstantin Kaufmann [q.v.] with 7,500 men set out for the city of Samarkand and on 2 May 1868 occupied it against slight opposition at a loss of 2 killed and 31 wounded. Leaving a small garrison in place, Kaufmann pressed eastward and 100 miles from Bokhara met and defeated a Bokharan army. At about the same time Bokharan forces attacked Samarkand, killing 50 and wounding 200 Russian soldiers before Kaufmann could race back to the rescue of the garrison. When its attackers were defeated, the amir of Bokhara surrendered, agreeing to pay a large indemnity and to cede the fertile Zarafsham Valley, which contained the source of Bokhara's water. The amir became a Russian puppet.

Bolívar, Simón (1783–1830). Called El Libertador, Bolívar was the hero founder of five South American republics: Colombia, Venezuela, Bolivia, Ecuador, and Peru. He dreamed of a united Latin America that would stretch from Mexico to Chile. Although hailed as a liberator, he favored government by a president for life—a dictator—and two legislative bodies without any real power.

Portrait of Simón Bolívar

Born in Caracas, Venezuela, to upper-class Creole parents, owners of vast tracts of land and many slaves, Bolívar was orphaned at fifteen. His uncle sent him to be educated in Spain, where he studied law in Madrid and at age eighteen married the daughter of the Marqués of Toro. In January 1803, ten months after his return to Venezuela, his wife died of yellow fever.

The young widower returned to Europe, where, although he admired many of Napoleon's reforms, he was appalled by his formation of a new hereditary peerage. In 1806 he reembarked for Venezuela, determined to free the country from Spanish rule.

He first saw action in 1810, when he fought under Francisco Miranda [q.v.] in a Venezuelan revolt against Spain. Although the revolt was initially successful, Venezuela collapsed into civil war, and Bolívar fled to Colombia, from which he led a new revolt in 1812–13. In a proclamation to his army he wrote: "Our hatred knows no bounds, and the war shall be to the death!"

On 6 August 1813, after fighting six pitched battles and capturing 50 guns within ninety days, he marched into Caracas. But the war was not over. In the ensuing months a series of bloody battles were fought. After his victory in the Battle of Victoria [q.v.] on 12 February 1814, Bolívar ordered the execution of 886 Spanish prisoners. Decisively defeated in the Battle of La Puerta [q.v.], he withdrew to Cartagena, arriving on 25 September 1814. There he led a revolt that captured Bogotá. Again defeated, he fled first to Jamaica and then to Haiti.

On 1 January 1817 he returned to Venezuela to lead yet another revolution, and although defeated by Pablo Marillo [q.v.] in the second Battle of La Puerta [q.v.], he rallied new forces. Operating from the area of the Orinoco estuary, he set out on 25 May with a force of 2,500, largely composed of Irish and English adventurers who had been formed into a foreign legion commanded by a man named Simon B. O'Leary. With these he marched over the Andes and in the Battle of Boyacá [q.v.] on 7 August 1819 decisively defeated a superior royalist army in New Granada (Colombia). On 17 December the Republic of Greater Colombia was proclaimed, composed of present-day Colombia, Ecuador, and Venezuela. Bolívar was made president and given almost supreme powers.

In 1821 he marched south, defeated a royalist force in the Battle of Bombona [q.v.], and joined his capable lieutenant Antonio Sucre [q.v.], who had just won the decisive Battle of Pichincha [q.v.]. The combined force then marched to the seaport of Guayaquil, where on 26 July Bolívar met with José de San Martín [q.v.]. What transpired at this historic meeting is unknown, but San Martín soon after returned to Lima, resigned his position as protector of Peru, then settled in Chile, later in Argentina, never again to take part in the revolutionary movement.

Bolívar sailed south and landed at Callao, Peru, on 1 September 1823. With Sucre he assembled an army and, on 6 August 1824, defeated the Spanish under José La Serna and José Canterac [qq.v.] in the Battle of Junín [q.v.]. After the Battle of Ayacucho [q.v.] on 9 December 1824, won by Sucre, Bolívar was named president (dictator, actually). In 1825 he visited Upper Peru, and on 16 May he proclaimed its independence as the República Bolívar (later Bolivia).

In January 1826 he returned to Peru and then to Caracas. Everywhere squabbles, intrigues, and plots marred the new republics. In 1830 he resigned as supreme chief of Colombia and retired to his estate 3 miles from Santa Marta, about 50 miles east of Barranquilla, where he died on 17 December of that year.

Bolivia-Chile War. See Pacific, War of the.

Bolivian Revolutions (1809–25 and 1868). There were fierce conflicts between Spaniards and Creoles in what is often called the Bolivian War of Independence. No prisoners were taken by either side. In 1825 patriot forces under Antonio José Sucre [q.v.] invaded Bolivia and finally won independence from Spain.

In 1826, after the declaration of a republic, Sucre was chosen president for life of Bolivia, but he agreed to serve for just two years and only if he could retain his 2,000-man Colombian army. He faced continual revolts, and at the end of 1827 he and his Colombians were driven out of the country. Quiet was not restored until 1831. Andrés Santa Cruz [q.v.] became president but was overthrown and fled to Europe after his defeat by Chileans under Manuel Bulges (1799–1866) in the Battle of Yungay [q.v.] in June 1839.

General José Ballivián [q.v.] assumed the presidency, fought the successful Peru-Bolivia War [q.v.], and remained in office until 1848, when he was overthrown in a revolution. Others who succeeded him were in turn brought down by revolutions. In September 1857 Dr. José María Linares (1810–1861) assumed dictatorial powers, but he too was overthrown by a revolution in 1861. His place was taken by Dr. María de Achá, who was deposed in February 1865 by a military revolution led by José Mariano Melgarejo (1818–1871), who became dictator and successfully suppressed revolts in 1865 and 1866 [see Abtao, Battle of].

In January 1871 Melgarejo was deposed by a revolution led by Colonel Agustín Morales, who ruled as president until assassinated in November of the following year. He was succeeded by Colonel Adolfo Ballivián, who died a few months later and was succeeded by Dr. Tomás Friar (1804–1882), who ruled until overthrown by General Helarión Daza (real name: Grosolé, 1840–1894) in 1876. Daza performed so poorly in the War of the Pacific [see Pacific, War of the] that his troops mutinied and he was deposed by General Narciso Campero (1815–1896), who after the Pacific War was succeeded by a series of politicians calling themselves doctors until December 1898, when there was still another revolution headed by Colonel José Manuel Pando (1848?–1917).

Bolster. 1. A block of wood placed on the carriage of a siege gun when it was being moved from place to place.

2. A padded or cushioned part of a saddle.

Bolt Action. The closing of the breech of a firearm by a bolt moving along the prolongation of the barrel's axis. The bolt prevented gas from escaping from the breech, ejected spent cartridges, and inserted fresh cartridges when pushed forward.

Bomarsund, Capture of (16 August 1854), Crimean War. This Russian fort on one of the Ahvenanmaa (Åland) Islands in the Gulf of Bothnia was captured after an eight-day siege by a fleet under Vice Admiral Sir Charles Napier (1786–1860) and 10,000 French troops under Marshal Achille Baraguay d'Hilliers [q.v.]. The Russian governor and 2,400 troops were taken prisoner, and the fort was destroyed.

The first Victoria Cross [q.v.] for a naval exploit was awarded for action in this battle. Mate Charles Davis Lucas (1834–1914) picked up a live shell that fell on the deck of HMS *Hecla* and threw it over the side. Lucas rose to become a rear admiral in the Royal Navy. From 1873 to 1883 he commanded the Ballachulish Corps in Scotland and held the rank of brigadier general.

Bomb. 1. As a noun, an explosive device with a fuse designed to detonate it under certain conditions.

2. As a noun, an explosive artillery shell.

3. As a verb, to attack with bombs.

Bombard, to. To attack with artillery. [See Bombardment.]

Bombardier. Originally a soldier in charge of a bombard, a heavy gun.

1. In the British army, a noncommissioned officer in the artillery equivalent in rank to a corporal.

2. An artilleryman who prepared ammunition and fuzes.

3. The person who loaded and fired mortars and howitzers.

Bombardment. An attack upon a fortified position by means of artillery, rockets, carcasses, or other machines throwing a shower of explosives and incendiaries into a fortification.

Bombardon. The name given to the bass tuba in military bands.

Bombay Army. The Honourable East India Company [q.v.] divided British India into three separate governments called presidencies, Bombay, Bengal, and Madras, each with its own governor and its own commander-in-chief. These divisions were retained when the crown assumed control after the Indian Mutiny [q.v.]. Aden was a part of the Bombay Presidency from 1839 to 1937, and Sind from 1843 to 1937, and troops of the Bombay army garrisoned these areas. [See Bengal Army; Madras Army.]

Bomb Chest. A mine consisting of a chest filled with bombs or gunpowder placed underground to be exploded under an enemy position.

Bombing Trench. An auxiliary trench often dug behind the fire trench close enough to it to permit grenades to be thrown into the fire trench should it be captured by an enemy raiding party.

Bombona, Battle of (7 April 1822), Colombian War of Independence. Simón Bolívar [q.v.], marching with 2,000 men to the assistance of Antonio Sucre [q.v.] near Pasto, in southwest Colombia, was halted in his advance through the mountains of Quito Province by a force of 2,500 royalists, who were routed; Bolívar entered Pasto the following day.

Bombproof. Term used for any dugout or shelter believed capable of resisting the force of a shell's explosion.

Bombshell. A hollow ball of iron loaded with powder and fired from a mortar.

Bonaparte, Napoleon. Emperor of France. [See Napoleon I.]

Bonaparte, Napoleon Joseph Charles Paul, Prince Napoleon (1822–1891). A French soldier known as Plon-Plon, the son of Napoleon's brother Jérôme (1784–1860). He served in the Crimean War [q.v.] and was a corps commander in 1859. He was exiled from France in 1886.

Bonin, Eduard von (1793–1865). A Prussian soldier who served as Prussian war minister from 1852 to 1854 and again from 1858 to 1859.

Bonnet. 1. A small triangular defense work built at salient angles of the glacis or larger work, consisting of only two faces with a parapet about 3 feet high and 10 or 12 feet wide, usually in front of a ravelin. The purpose of the bonnet was to check attackers attempting to make a lodgment. A larger version was called a priest's bonnet or *bonnet à prêtre.*

2. The headgear in various styles of Highland regiments in the British army. They were made at Stewarton, a small town in north-central Ayrshire, and at Kilmarnock, five miles away. Sometimes called a Glengarry.

Bonnette. 1. An addition on the top of a parapet for a short distance to give greater protection against enfilading fire. Bonnettes were often made of sandbags or gabions and were sometimes placed on a parapet between guns in barbette.

2. An earthwork placed before the salient angle of a ravelin.

Bonneville, Benjamin Louis Eulalie de (1796–1878). A French-born American soldier who was graduated from West Point in 1815 and commissioned in the artillery. After serving on frontier posts in Arkansas Territory and Indian Territory, he took leave of the army for two years to lead a party of 110 trappers and traders into the Rocky Mountains. He conducted the first wagon train over the South Pass, and a party sent out by him to reconnoiter made the first crossing of the Sierra Nevada. His expertly executed maps provided the first accurate geographical information about the American Far West.

He served in the Mexican War [q.v.] as a major and saw action at Veracruz, Cerro Gordo, Molino del Rey, Contreras, and Churubusco [qq.v.]. For the latter two actions he was brevetted lieutenant colonel, but he was also court-martialed for "misbehavior before the enemy" and found guilty on three of ten specifications, for which he was "admonished" by the commanding general. In 1855 he became a colonel, and in 1857 he commanded the Gila River Expedition [q.v.] against the Apaches. He retired in 1861 but returned to duty in the Union army during the American Civil War, serving in garrisons and on recruiting duty. He again retired, this time as a brevet brigadier general. In 1871, at age seventy-five, he married a twenty-six-year-old woman. When he died at age eighty-two, he was the oldest retired army officer.

His fame rests upon his journals, which he sold to Washington Irving (1783–1859) for a thousand dollars. Irving edited them with enthusiasm, fleshing them out with conversations he had with Bonneville. His romanticized biography, *The Adventures of Captain Bonneville, U.S.A. in the Rocky Mountains of the Far West* [1837], went through many editions.

Bonnie Blue Flag. See Blue Flag.

Bonus, United States Veterans'. Not a pension but a lump sum paid to all former American servicemen who were veterans of the War of 1812, the Mexican War [qq.v.], and various Indian Wars. American Civil War veterans of the Union army received small bonuses adjusted to length of service. Veterans of the Spanish-American War [q.v.] received none.

Boomerang. A curved throwing stick with one convex edge used as a weapon by Australian aborigines.

Booming Out. A system for constructing pontoon bridges [q.v.]. Onshore a frame with two saddles was prepared and connected by balks. When a pontoon was launched, the frame was lifted and the pontoon was positioned under the first saddle and bolted to it. Meanwhile the balks of a second frame were bolted to a third saddle. The bridge was pushed out—boomed out—and the second pontoon was positioned under a second saddle and again boomed out.

Boomplats / Boomplatz, Battle of (29 August 1848), early South African revolt. On this farm near Jagersfontein, Orange Free State, South Africa, Boers under Andries Pretorius were defeated by a British force under Sir Harry Smith [qq.v.]. There were about 1,000 combatants on each side. The British lost 22 killed and 38 wounded; the Boers lost 14. Many of the defeated Boers migrated north of the Vaal River to establish the South African Republic, popularly known as the Transvaal.

Booneville, Battles of. During the American Civil War there

were two battles fought at this railroad center and river port on the right bank of the Missouri River, 22 miles south of Corinth, Mississippi.

First Battle (17 June 1861). A Confederate force of 2,500 green troops was attacked and routed by 1,700 Federals under General Nathaniel Lyon [q.v.], who two days earlier in a bloodless coup had captured Jefferson City, the state capital. When the Confederate prisoners from Booneville were marched through the streets of St. Louis, a mob of civilians tried to interfere. Lyon ordered his men to open fire, and some two dozen fell.

Second Battle (1 July 1862). Colonel Philip Sheridan [q.v.], commanding a cavalry brigade of 827 sabers, was attacked at Booneville by an estimated 5,000 Confederate cavalry under James Ronald Chalmers (1831–1898). The Federal pickets were driven in, and the brigade appeared on the point of being overwhelmed when Sheridan launched a surprise attack on the Confederates' rear and routed them. Sheridan was promoted brigadier general with rank to date from this battle.

Boots. In spite of the importance of boots to soldiers, particularly infantrymen, little attention was paid to their comfort or quality. In Britain shoes and gaiters [q.v.] were replaced by trousers and half boots in 1823. The boots were manufactured without eyelet holes for laces; these were to be pierced to suit the soldier's feet. Only in 1843 were eyelets provided and boots differentiated for right and left feet. Before this, many regiments required soldiers to alternate boots from the right foot to the left every other day to ensure that they wore more evenly and lasted longer.

Boots and Saddles. A bugle call in the American army, adopted in 1841 as a signal for cavalrymen to mount with their arms and equipment. In the British army it is a cavalry and artillery parade call, sounded a half hour before the call to turn out. Its name is believed to be a corruption of the French *boute-selle* (saddle up).

Booty, Legitimate. In the British service, Parliament spelled out what might lawfully be taken from an enemy. Legitimate booty included arms, ammunition, stores of war, goods, merchandise, and treasure of the state or of any public trading company of the enemy found in any fortress or possession. Such booty was preserved and its value divided between the crown and its captors [see Prize; Prize Agents; Private Property, Military Respect for].

In the Piedmontese army a special staff corps was entrusted with administering booty. French laws made no mention of booty, and during the Napoleonic Wars the French were noted for marauding and despoiling.

In the United States the 58th Article of War provided that "all public stores taken in the enemy's camp, towns, forts and magazines, whether of artillery, ammunition, clothing, forage, or provisions shall be secured for the service of the United States. . . ." There was no division of the booty among those who had done the fighting or bonuses from the sale of captured enemy goods. [See Looting.]

Borchardt Pistol. An early automatic pistol patented by Hugo Borchardt (1850?–1921) in September 1893. Some three thousand were manufactured between 1894 and 1899, when production was suspended. [See Löwe, Ludwig; Luger, Georg.]

Bordel Militaire Controllé / Bordel Mobile de Campagne. Popularly called the BMC. An establishment of prostitutes provided and administered by the French army in North Africa and elsewhere. Facilities ranged from prostitutes housed in tents to elaborate establishments, such as those at Meknès, Morocco, where the BMC area included five hundred buildings with cafés, dance halls, and prophylactic stations. Separate brothels were maintained for European and indigenous troops, and the women employed were given daily medical examinations. Soldiers were required to report to prophylactic stations and were severely punished if they acquired a venereal disease by failing to do so [see Venereal Diseases].

Prostitutes often accompanied French troops on campaign. In 1810 a captured French officer remarked to Wellington: "You, Sir, have an army; we have a travelling brothel." In North Africa troops in remote posts were served by women brought in by government transport. One result of this attention to the sex life of soldiers in the ranks was a lower venereal disease rate in the French army than in the British army. The BMCs remained in operation in some areas until the 1970s.

Border Ruffians. The name given to those in Missouri who crossed over to Kansas to vote for proslavery candidates. Many became guerrillas, who fought in the Border War [q.v.].

Border Ruffians *Missouri border ruffians at the Kansas border*

Border War (1854–59). Name given to the civil warfare in "Bleeding Kansas" between slavery advocates and abolitionists. It began when Congress on 30 May 1854 passed the Kansas-Nebraska Act. Its popular sovereignty principle, designed to ease tensions by allowing residents to decide whether slavery was to be permitted in the state, created chaos instead. The area was soon swamped by adherents of both sides, including half-mad fanatics, such as John Brown [q.v.], who in 1856, with four of his sons and two other men, massacred five unarmed proslavery men on the banks of the Pottawatamie River. There were gunfights at Fort Saunders,

Black Jack, Hickory Point, and Slough Creek. Minor disturbances persisted until the American Civil War.

Citizens of Missouri who crossed the border to vote illegally in Kansas to establish Kansas as a slave state were known as border ruffians [q.v.]. Rifles imported into the state by abolitionists were called Beecher's Bibles [q.v.] after Henry Ward Beecher (1813–1887), an ardent antislavery preacher.

The bloodshed and lawlessness did not end until regular American troops intervened in 1860.

Bore. 1. The part of a piece of ordnance that is bored out; the interior of the barrel of a gun from its muzzle face to the rear of the chamber.

2. The interior diameter of the gun's tube.

Borisov, Battle of (21 or 23 November 1812), Napoleon's Russian Campaign. On Napoleon's retreat from Moscow a Russian army under Admiral (or General) Pavel (Paul) Tshitsagov [q.v.] (or Chichagov), which had captured Minsk on 16 November, turned and marched 48 miles northeast to attack successfully on 23 November a Polish corps under French General Nicolas Oudinot [q.v.] at Loshbitsa [q.v.], near the town of Borisov on the left bank of the Berezina River, a tributary of the Dnieper. Napoleon, who with the main body of his army was falling back on the town, was taken by surprise. The loss was serious, for he had counted on crossing the bridge there, the only bridge on the Smolensk–Vilna road. Although the French retook Borisov two days later, the Russians destroyed the bridge [see Berezina / Beresina River, Napoleon's Crossing of].

Borny, Battle of. See Colombey-Borny, Battle of.

Borodino, Battle of (5–7 September 1812), Napoleon's Russian Campaign. The battle is called by the French the Battle of Moskwa (or Moscow). Near the village of Borodino, the largest of several villages in the area, about 70 miles west-southwest of Moscow, on the Moscow–Smolensk road, Russians under sixty-seven-year-old General Mikhail Kutuzov [q.v.] attempted to defend Moscow from the advancing French under Napoleon. The position, a rugged piece of high ground broken by ravines south of the steep-banked Kalatsha River, was selected by Kutuzov, and there he deployed his 72,000 infantry, 18,000 cavalry, and 640 guns, plus some 17,000 Cossacks and militia.

On 3 September 10,000 Russian *opolchenie* [q.v.] from Moscow began work on fortifications. On 5 September the cavalry of French Marshal Joachim Murat [q.v.] discovered the Russian deployments and made probing thrusts on outlying positions. The following day was a Sunday, and at 2:00 A.M., after making a personal reconnaissance, Napoleon decided that he would wait for more of his artillery to arrive on the field. Neither side made any offensive movements on this day as Napoleon deployed his army of 133,000 men, including 28,000 cavalry, and 587 guns. That afternoon Kutuzov, accompanied by an entourage of priests and the icon of the venerated Black Virgin of Smolensk, made the rounds of his troops and fortifications, exhorting his men to pledge themselves to their "monarch and country in the blood of the aggressor."

At 6:00 A.M. on 7 September the main battle began with a

massive exchange of artillery fire that obscured the field with smoke, the only major artillery duel of the campaign, and with an attack by Marshal Louis Davout [q.v.] on the Russian left. A French infantry assault carried the village of Borodino and sent its defenders, a Russian Lifeguard Jäger regiment, flying. The Russians counterattacked but were repulsed. The French made repeated attacks upon some smaller redoubts, called flèches, some of which changed hands at least four times. Napoleon, who felt ill all day, displayed little of his putative military genius and did little more than launch a frontal attack, which he sustained throughout the day. Near the center of the Russian line on a hilltop south of Borodino was the Great Redoubt (later Raevski's Redoubt [q.v.]), a massive field fortification armed with nineteen 12-pounder guns. A second strongpoint was a pentagonal redoubt on a hill near the village of Shevardino.

The French captured, then lost the Great Redoubt. At about 10:00 A.M. Napoleon brought every available gun to bear upon it, and shortly after 3:00 P.M. it was taken by storm. By noon Kutusov had already committed large numbers of his reserves, and the center of his line became the critical position of the battle. He launched a feint attack with cavalry on his right, which somewhat eased the pressure on his center as the French reacted to a possible flank attack.

Napoleon too quickly used up his reserves, and by 1:00 P.M. he had none but the Old Guard left. Late in the day he was about to send them in, but he accepted the advice of Marshal Jean Baptiste Bessières [q.v.] not to risk them "800 leagues from Paris."

Although the Russians maintained their positions with dogged determination, they were barely able to maintain a coherent line of defense. General Pëtr Dmitrievich Gorchakov (1789–1868) commanded the reinforced division defending the Shevardino Redoubt. It was captured at 8:00 P.M. None of the troops inside it surrendered. All were killed.

The Russians launched a counterattack but withdrew about 11:00 P.M. after sustaining 6,000 casualties. Having heard the reports of his senior commanders, Kutusov decided against making another stand and during the night managed an orderly retreat toward Moscow, a decision that enabled Napoleon to claim a victory.

The losses on both sides were horrendous. Napoleon lost 33,000 men; Kutuzov lost 44,000, including General Pëtr Bagration [q.v.], who received a wound from which he died two weeks later. Dr. Jean Larrey [q.v.], the famous French military surgeon, amputated 200 limbs in twenty-four hours. Napoleon is said to have reconciled himself to his severe losses by saying, "One Paris night will replace them."

Boromo Campaign (1810), Portuguese occupation of Mozambique. A Portuguese force commanded by Villar Boas Truavo (d. 1810) was wiped out by tribesmen on the upper Zambezi River in Portuguese East Africa.

Boshin Civil War (1868–69). In Japanese: *Boshin Senso.* Sometimes called the Restoration War. The Japanese civil war that overthrew the Tokugawa shogunate and helped bring about the Meiji Restoration—i.e., returning authority to the Japanese emperor, then sixteen-year-old Mutsuhito (1852–1912), reigning as Meiji.

After American Commodore Matthew Calbraith Perry (1794–1858) secured for the United States the first commercial treaty with Japan, Japanese authorities yielded to the Western powers' demands for trade, thereby creating great internal unrest.

In November 1867 the shogun Tokugawa Yoshinobu (1837–1913) agreed to give power to the emperor if he led a council of daimyos [q.v.], but on 3 January 1868 rebel forces from Satsuma Province (Kagoshima Prefecture), led by Saigo Takamori [q.v.], and forces from Choshu Province (Yamaguchi), led by Kido Takayoshi (1833–1877), seized the imperial palace at Kyoto. The shibboleth of the rebels was "Revere the emperor; expel the barbarians." On 27 January they won the battles of Toba and Fushimi [q.v.] and proclaimed the imperial restoration (*osei fukko*).

On 4 February of that year U.S. marines landed at Osaka to protect foreign nationals. There was scattered, sporadic resistance in Ueno District and on the northern Honshu Island on 6 November. In October 1868 a French artillery captain,

Borodino *Napoleon at the Battle of Borodino*

Jules Brunet, who had been part of a French military mission to Japan, joined forces with Japanese Vice Admiral Buyo Enomoto (1839?–1909) and proclaimed a rebel republic on the northern island of Hokkaido, but this was soon crushed [see Enomoto Rebellion].

Saigo Takamori negotiated the surrender of Edo (Tokyo) with Katsu Kaishe (1823–1899), the shogun's retainer. The final battle of the war ended with the surrender of the proshogun fleet off Hokkaido Island in June 1869.

The Japanese record that 6,971 people were killed. At the request of the emperor Meiji (1852–1912) the Yasukuni shrine [q.v.] was erected to honor those who had died to reinstate imperial authority.

Boshin Civil War *Meiji Emperor Mutsuhito*

Bosnia and Herzegovina / Hercegovina, Revolts in (1862–75). Bosnia was incorporated with Turkey in 1463; there followed numerous unsuccessful revolts against Turkish rule. Bosnia's first major revolt in the nineteenth century was mounted in 1821 while the Turks were occupied in quelling disorders in Greece. Another was launched by Mustapha Skodra Pasha during the Russo-Turkish War of 1828. A nearly successful uprising in 1831 was led by Hussein Kapetan, known as the Lion of Bosnia. Only with great difficulty did Reshid Pasha (1802–1858), the grand vizier, manage to drive the Lion over the frontier into Croatia. In 1862 the Christians in Bosnia, led by Luka Vukalović, revolted. In September 1875 the Bosnians joined the insurgents in Herzegovina, a

revolt not suppressed until August 1877. Some 100,000 refugees fled to Austria, which invaded Bosnia on 29 July 1878. The Bosnians were defeated in a battle fought between Zepce and Maglal on 7–8 August, and Austrian forces entered the old Bosnian capital (1686–1850) of Travnik, 45 miles northwest of Sarajevo, on 16 August. On the same day the Austrians defeated the Bosnians at Han Belalovic, and two days later at Tegethoff. On 30 August Sarajevo was bombarded, and it was taken by storm on 5 September. Senkovic, a strong fort and arsenal, was taken on 21 September, and by the end of October resistance had almost ceased. On 9 November a general amnesty was issued. Austrian casualties were estimated to be about 5,000; Bosnian losses are unknown.

Herzegovina, ceded to Turkey in 1699 by the Treaty of Carlowitz, was from that time the seat of many revolutions. Ali Pasha Rizvanbegovic, a Herzegovinian chief, who had allied himself with the Turks in earlier revolts, rebelled in 1850 and maintained his independence for a time, but he was effectively suppressed by the odious Omer Pasha [q.v.] in 1851. In the spring of 1875, when, in spite of an almost complete crop failure, the tax collectors demanded their usual extortion from the peasants, discontent and anger swelled. On 1 July peasants in the village of Nevesinje (or Nevesinye) in central Herzegovina, 16 miles east-southeast of Mostar, raised the flag of revolt, and the revolution quickly spread into Serbia and Montenegro. Prince Peter Karageorgevich [q.v.] of Serbia (king of Serbia, 1903–21) was one of its leaders, and the revolutionists were encouraged by the Bulgarian Revolt [q.v.] and by an uprising in Constantinople itself. On 2 October the sultan offered to reduce taxes, permit religious freedom, and allow a regional assembly, but this was rejected; complete independence was demanded. On 30 June 1876 Serbia and Montenegro declared war on Turkey. There was fighting in Mostar, the capital of Herzegovina, on 4 August, but by the end of the month the country was occupied by Austrian troops. At the Congress of Berlin in July 1878 Bosnia and Herzegovina were united into a single province under Austrian control, and in 1909 it was formally annexed by Austria [see Balkan Revolts].

Bosquet, Pierre Jean François (1810–1861). A French soldier who after graduation from the École Polytechnique [q.v.] was commissioned in the artillery in 1833 and on 1 January 1834 was sent to Algeria. On 14 January 1841 he was wounded in the Battle of Sidi Sakdar, and again on 17 July in the Battle of Oued Melah. He became general of brigade on 17 August 1848 and commanded an expedition into the Kabylia in 1852. He was promoted general of division on 10 August 1853, and the following year he took part in the Crimean War. He led the French attack at the Alma, and during the Battle of Inkerman [qq.v.] on 5 November he led two divisions that relieved hard-pressed British troops, earning the gratitude of Lord Raglan [q.v.] and the Thanks of Parliament. At the storming of the Mamelon [q.v.] on 7 June 1855 he personally led his corps in the charge. In the major assault on 8 September, he commanded all the attacking units and was severely wounded in the struggle for the Malakoff [q.v.]. The following year he was created a senator, and on 9 February 1856, a marshal of France.

Bostanji. Turkish foot guards, similar to the Janissaries [q.v.]. At one time their strength amounted to 5,000, but by the 1880s it had diminished to fewer than 600. Their leader, titled Bostanji Bashi, was always chosen from among the personal favorites of the reigning sultan.

Botev, Christo (1847–1867). A Bulgarian revolutionary and poet. In 1864 he studied in Odessa until his involvement in Russian revolutionary movements obliged him to return home. Continued revolutionary activities forced him to flee to Rumania in 1867. On 6 May of that year, with some 200 other revolutionaries, many disguised as gardeners, he boarded and seized the Austrian steamer *Radetzky* and forced it to sail to Bulgaria. There the rebels scattered a force of Turkish irregulars but were surrounded and defeated by Turkish regulars. Botev was killed in the engagement.

Botha, Louis (1862–1919). A South African soldier and politician who first saw action as a fighter with Boer commandos supporting the Zulus in intertribal wars [see Zulu Civil Wars; Zulu-Boer Conflicts]. He cut his teeth as a politician when in August 1884 he became one of the founders of a short-lived New Republic on land ceded to the Boers by the Zulus. Three years later, when the republic was absorbed into the South African Republic (Transvaal) as the District of Vryheid, he entered Transvaal politics.

In the Second Anglo-Boer War [q.v.] Botha was with the Boer army that invested Ladysmith [q.v.]. Upon the death of Piet Joubert [q.v.] on 27 March 1900 he was appointed commandant general of the Transvaal forces. He was largely responsible for the Boer successes at Colenso, Spion Kop, and Val Kranz [qq.v.]. He proved himself both an able general and, at the end of the war, an able negotiator with the British.

In 1907 he became prime minister of the Transvaal, and in 1910 he was elected the first prime minister of the Union of South Africa (today's Republic of South Africa) and served for nine years. He proved to be a loyal British subject, suppressing a mutiny in 1914 and personally leading his army against the Germans in Southwest Africa (Namibia), the only prime minister in the British Empire ever to do so.

Bouching Bits. Instruments used to bore a hole in the vent of field guns to receive the bouch (plug) through which the vent was drilled.

"Boudin." Literally, blood pudding. The marching song of the French Foreign Legion [q.v.]. It became popular after it was introduced during the legion's stay in Mexico in the 1860s [See Mexico, French Invasion and Occupation of].

Bougie, Attacks on (1833 and 1842). This ancient town on the coast of northeast Algeria, 115 miles east of Algiers, was captured by the French on 19 October 1833. On 25 August 1842 the French successfully defended it from Arab tribesmen.

Boulanger, Georges Ernest Jean Marie (1837–1891). A French soldier who after graduation from St. Cyr entered the army in 1856 and served in Algeria, in Cochin China, and in the Franco-Prussian War [q.v.]. In 1882 he was director of infantry. A protégé of Georges Clemenceau's (1841–1929), he was named war minister in January 1886. The major reforms he introduced quickly made him the most popular general in the army. In May 1887 he was given command of a corps. The following year he was deprived of his command for twice going to Paris without leave. A rabble-rouser, he spoke often and heatedly of the need for France to regain Alsace and Lorraine. He was elected to the Chamber of Deputies and became perhaps the leading French political figure, so powerful that many feared he would stage a coup d'état and install himself as dictator. In 1889, threatened with arrest, he fled to England. His popularity waned when it was revealed that he had been financed by royalists who hoped to overthrow the republic. In April 1891 he shot and killed himself on his mistress's grave in Brussels.

Boulenge Chronograph. A device for measuring the velocity of a gun, invented in the 1860s by Belgian Captain Commandant P. L. Boulengé.

Bounty. A subsidy paid by a government to encourage enlistments or reenlistments. Land bounties of from 40 to 160 acres were given American veterans of the Mexican and Indian wars [qq.v.]. From American colonial times through the American Civil War bounties were paid to those who enlisted. A total of six hundred million dollars was paid in bounties to fill Union quotas for the war.

Boulenge chronograph

Bounty Jumping. The practice of enlisting for a bounty [q.v.], then deserting and reenlisting in another unit. One bounty jumper during the American Civil War admitted to having claimed thirty-two bounties.

Bourbaki, Charles Denis Sauter (1816–1897). A French soldier, the son of a Greek colonel, who, after graduating from St. Cyr in 1836, served in Algeria with the Foreign Legion. In 1850 he was a lieutenant colonel in the 1st Zouaves. He commanded a brigade of Algerians in the Crimean War, where he distinguished himself and was wounded in the assault on the Malakoff [q.v.]. After the war he returned to Algeria and in 1857 became a general of division. In the Austro-Piedmontese War he distinguished himself at Solferino [q.v.]. In 1870, during the Franco-Prussian War, he commanded the Garde Impériale [q.v.] at Metz [q.v.]. When his attempt to break through the Prussian lines to relieve the siege of Belfort [q.v.] failed and his army fled over the border to be interned in Switzerland, he tried to commit suicide but succeeded only in wounding himself in the head. His political views being unpopular, he was retired in 1881.

Bourbon, Capture of (8 July 1810), Napoleonic Wars. A combined British naval and military force of about 1,000 under Captain Josias Rowley, RN (1765–1842), captured this island in the Indian Ocean (called Réunion after 1846), about 400 miles east of Madagascar, for a loss of 22 killed and 79 wounded. It remained in British possession until April 1815, when it was restored to France.

Bourbon, Louis Joseph de (1736–1818). A Condé prince and French soldier who distinguished himself in the Seven Years' War. In 1789, during the French Revolution, he fled to

Germany, where he organized the Army of Condé (1792–97), composed of French aristocratic émigrés and Austrians. In 1797 he joined the Russian service, and in 1801, the British army.

Bourdett, Sara (1813–1866). A renowned American camp follower who, during the Mexican War [q.v.], first joined Zachary Taylor's [q.v.] army at Matamoros, Mexico. Carrying two pistols and driving a buggy team, she set up a cook tent and throughout the campaign cooked for officers of the 5th Infantry and 2nd Dragoons. An impressive six feet tall, she was called by the soldiers Great Western after the massive ship that was the second steamer to cross the Atlantic.

Bourges Arsenal. The principal manufacturing arsenal of the French army in the last half of the nineteenth century. It was located at the town of Bourges, 150 miles southeast of Paris. The famous French 75 [q.v.]—75 mm M1897 field gun—was developed here.

Bourgogne, Adrien Jean Baptiste François (1785–1867). A French soldier who enlisted in 1806 and rose to the rank of sergeant, fighting at Jena, Pultusk, Eylau, Friedland, and Aspen-Essling [qq.v.], where he was wounded. He served in Spain during the Peninsular War and in Napoleon's disastrous Russian Campaign of 1812 [qq.v.]. In 1813 he was commissioned into the 145th Regiment of the Line and fought at Lützen and Bautzen [qq.v.]. He was captured by the Prussians on the Elbe and spent two years as a prisoner of war. He is known for his extraordinary *Memoirs*, which vividly described his experiences in the Russian Campaign.

Bourke, John Gregory (1846–1896). An American army officer and ethnologist who, during the American Civil War, ran away from his Philadelphia home and on 12 August 1862, at age sixteen, enlisted in the 15th Pennsylvania Cavalry. Four months later he won a Medal of Honor [q.v.] for bravery in the Battle of Stones River [q.v.], Tennessee. After the war he entered West Point and was commissioned a second lieutenant in the 3rd Cavalry on 15 June 1869.

Bourke saw a great deal of action in the West, serving under George Crook [q.v.] in many of his campaigns, taking part in, among other battles, those on the Rosebud and the engagement at Slim Buttes [qq.v.]. He was a part of the Yellowstone Expedition of 1880, and he was frequently detached to pursue ethnological studies among the Indians. Although he served for thirty-four years in the army, he never rose above the rank of captain.

His books, the outgrowth of his studies, made him better known as an ethnologist than as a soldier. His *Scatalogic Rites of All Nations* was published in Germany with a preface by Sigmund Freud, and his essay "The Urine Dance of the Zuni Indians of New Mexico" earned him a fellowship in the American Association for the Advancement of Science.

His illustrated diary, numbering 128 volumes, is in the library at West Point.

Bourmont, Louis Auguste Victor de, Comte de Ghaisnes (1773–1846). A French soldier who, although an émigré in 1789, returned to serve Napoleon. During Napoleon's invasion of Russia [q.v.] in 1812 he was taken prisoner, but he managed to escape and rejoin the army. In 1813

he was wounded in the Battle of Lützen [q.v.]. In 1814 he was general of division and commanded a division during the Hundred Days [q.v.]. In 1815, just four days before Waterloo [q.v.], he deserted to Louis XVIII. The evidence he gave went far to convict Marshal Michel Ney [q.v.] and send him to the firing squad. In 1829 Bourmont was minister of war, and in 1830 he commanded the expedition to Algeria that captured Algiers [q.v.]. He was created a marshal of France.

In the French Revolution of 1830 [q.v.] he was superseded and left Algeria for France to share in the exile of Charles X (1757–1836).

Bournouse. A long, full Arab outer mantle of wool with a hood. It constituted part of the uniform of some corps of the French army.

Bowie, James (1799–1836). A Texan soldier reputed to have invented the bowie knife [q.v.]. He was born in Tennessee (not in Georgia in 1796, as recorded in the *Dictionary of American Biography*). With his brother, Rezin, he ran a plantation in Louisiana and made a fortune trading in slaves, buying some from the pirate Jean Laffite [q.v.]. In September 1827, after killing a man in a fight with a knife made from a blacksmith's rasp, he decamped for Texas and finally settled in San Antonio (then called Bexar), Texas, where he married and became a naturalized Mexican citizen and a Roman Catholic.

In 1830 he became a colonel in the Texas Rangers [q.v.] and took part in numerous skirmishes with Indians. Noted for his daring, he was a hero to his men. In August 1832 he joined an early rebellion against Mexican authorities at Nacogdoches, 20 miles north of Lufkin in East Texas. In 1833 his wife and two children died of cholera.

When the Texas Revolution began on 2 October 1835, Bowie was a member of the Committee of Safety. He fought in the Battle of Mission Concepción [q.v.] on 28 October and the Grass Fight on 26 November, and he participated in the storming of Bexar on 5–9 December.

In December he became a colonel in the Texan army, and early the following year he joined Colonel William Travis [q.v.] at the Alamo [q.v.]. Although it is widely believed that he was killed in the Mexican attack on the Alamo, he appears to have died there of natural causes. He fell sick during the siege and was found dead on his cot when Santa Anna's troops captured the Alamo on 6 March 1836.

Bowie Knife. A name generally applied to a variety of well-balanced, all-purpose one-edged blades of no set pattern. The original, said to have been invented by James Bowie [q.v.], or perhaps his brother, Rezin P. Bowie, was a heavy knife with a long blade that broadened along the spine until it narrowed abruptly and tapered to a point. Although the main part of the blade was single-edged, it was double-edged near the tip.

The bowie knife

Boxer, Edward Mourrier (1819–1898). An officer in the British Royal Artillery who in 1857 became superintendent of the Royal Laboratory at the Woolwich Arsenal. He was particularly concerned with the development of ammunition and invented the Boxer Improved Diaphragm Shrapnel Shell, the Boxer Parachute Light Ball, several time fuzes, and the Boxer primer and cartridge used with the .577 Snider rifle [q.v.]. The cartridge, which improved accuracy, was made of coiled metal with a percussion cap in the center of its base. It was adopted for service in the British army on 20 August 1866 and was used by several Balkan armies.

Boxer Rebellion (1898–1900). A seemingly spontaneous émeute in China among the peasants of Shantung who took up swords, spears, and muskets not against the corrupt government of the empress Tzu Hsi (1832–1908), China's last Manchu empress, but against the "foreign devils" from the West, mostly Christian missionaries, who, they were convinced, were ruining the country. Their rallying cry was: "Protect the Ch'ing dynasty. Exterminate the foreigners."

The movement was instigated by one of China's many secret societies called the Society of Righteous and Harmonious Fists. Westerners called its members Boxers. They were said to be allied to the White Lotus Society or to be a rebirth of the Nien [qq.v.]. The movement, probably with the encouragement of the regime of the empress, spread rapidly. In 1898 the Boxers began to attack missionaries and other foreigners, killing 231, mostly missionaries, and uncounted numbers of Chinese Christian converts in various parts of China. The imperial Chinese government claimed that the Boxers were beyond its control.

On 31 May 1900 a small force of 337 sailors and marines from the United States, Britain, Italy, Japan, and Russia taken off warships on the China station arrived at Peking (Beijing) to help protect the European legations. They were followed on 3 June by 89 Austrians and Germans. On 10 June, after capturing the forts defending the mouth of the Pei-Ho River, British Vice Admiral Edward Hobart Seymour (1840–1929), with 2,129 men (including 130 Americans) collected from the ships of eight nations, started for Peking. He came within 25 miles of the city before being driven back.

On 19 June all foreign diplomats were ordered to leave Peking within twenty-four hours. The following morning the German ambassador was shot by a Chinese soldier in the street. The first Boxer attack on the legations came that afternoon while imperial Chinese troops stood by. The legations were soon under siege.

The legation area just southeast of the Forbidden City, about three-quarters of a mile square and bound on the southern edge by the ancient 60-foot-tall Tatar City Wall, held some 500 foreigners, including 149 women and 79 children, and about 3,000 Chinese Christians. The ten or twelve legations pooled their military resources, and by unanimous consent, the collective force was placed under the British minister, Sir Claude Macdonald [q.v.], a former soldier. By 3 July one-fourth of the military personnel had been killed or wounded, and by the 13th the foreigners were hard pressed.

On 4 August an international relief force consisting of 2,500 Americans—the 9th and 14th U.S. Infantry, the 6th Cavalry, and a battalion of marines under General Adna Chaffee [q.v.]—8,000 to 10,000 Japanese; 4,000 to 5,000 Russians; 3,000 British, including Indian army units; 800 French; and smaller units of Italians, Austrians, and others, about 25,000 in all, marched out of the river port of Tientsin, 80 miles from Peking. It fought its way to Peking and on 13 August attacked the city, which by this time contained about 140,000 Boxers, including some Chinese army regulars. According to British accounts, troops of the British Indian army were the first to fight their way into the legation area, breaking the siege. According to most American accounts, the Americans were the first troops into the city although they arrived about two hours after the British.

In the course of the siege 76 foreigners had been killed, and 150 to 200 wounded. Chinese Christians were killed or

Boxer Rebellion *Chinese siege of the European legations in Peking during the Boxer Rebellion*

wounded, in uncounted numbers. Many starved to death. Among the 451 U.S. marines who took part in the relief force were two future commandants of the corps: Captain Ben Hebard Fuller (1870–1937), who commanded a battery of artillery, and Smedley Darlington Butler (1881–1940), who was wounded in the chest.

The International Settlement at Tientsin, 30 miles up the Pei-Ho, was also besieged. The first attempt to reach the city by 140 U.S. marines and sailors and 50 Russians on 19–21 June failed, but on 13–14 July it was captured by an international force of 6,500 (about one-sixth American) commanded by British Brigadier General Alfred Gaselee (1844–1918).

A German contingent sent to China under Field Marshal Count Alfred von Waldersee (1832–1904) arrived too late for the liberation of the legations. Perhaps it was as well, for before their departure the troops were addressed by Kaiser William II (1859–1941), who exhorted them: "If you meet the enemy you ought to know: no pardon will be given, no prisoners will be taken. As a thousand years ago the Huns under their king Attila made a name for themselves that lets them even now appear mighty in tradition, so may the name of German be impressed by you on China in such a manner that never again will a Chinese dare to look askance at a German."

The conflict did not end until the Peace of Peking was signed on 7 September 1901. In the meantime, troops looted Peking.

By the Peace of Peking, China was forced to pay heavy indemnities totaling $333 million. Of the $25 million paid to the United States, $18 million was returned as a fund to pay for sending Chinese students to American colleges and universities. The United States awarded fifty-nine Medals of Honor to participants in this action, four to soldiers and thirty-three to marines. Great Britain awarded two Victoria Crosses.

Box Magazine. A metal box holding rifle ammunition that either is a part of the rifle or can be detached from it. The cartridges are forced into the chamber by a spring.

Box Trail. A trail of a cannon in the shape of a rectangular box.

Boyacá, Battle of (7 August 1819). In central New Granada (today Colombia) a force of 2,500 Spanish royalists, including 400 cavalry under José María Barreiro (1793–1819), was defeated by a patriot army under Simón Bolívar [q.v.], who had lost two-thirds of his 7,000 men (including a number of British volunteers) in crossing the cordilleras, a rugged 700-mile march under near-incredible difficulties. With the remnant of his force and some local patriots Bolívar took up a position at Boyacá, a village five miles south of Tunja, cutting off the royalists from their base. The royalists attacked but were routed, losing 1,600 taken prisoner, including General Barreiro. It was, as Bolívar later said, the Waterloo for Spanish rule in this part of South America. Bolívar, who lost only 66 men in the battle, entered Bogotá on 10 August and established the republic of Colombia with himself as president.

Boyaux. Zigzag or winding saps dug by besiegers leading to an enemy's fortified position.

Boyaux of Communication. A trench or branch of a trench leading to a magazine, a latrine, or any other particular point.

Boyd, Belle (1843–1900). An alleged Confederate spy in the American Civil War. As a young Virginia girl, not yet twenty, she aspired to spy for the Confederate army, but there is no evidence, other than her own account, that she ever supplied Confederate commanders with vital information. Although she claimed to have supplied information to Thomas ("Stonewall") Jackson [q.v.], he appears never to have met or corresponded with her. She was twice arrested by the Federals but was released each time. In 1863 she sailed for England, where she became an actress.

Belle Boyd, an aspiring American Civil War spy

Boyd, Gerald Farrell (1877–1930). A British gentleman ranker from a wealthy, well-connected family. In 1895, after failing his entrance examination for Woolwich [q.v.], he enlisted as a private in the Devonshire Regiment. In 1900, after winning the Distinguished Service Medal as a sergeant at Colenso [q.v.] in the Second Anglo-Boer War [q.v.], he was commissioned. He became a captain of mounted infantry and later won the CB, CMG, and Croix de Guerre [q.v.]. At age forty-one he was the youngest major general in the British army.

Boyd, James Parker (1764–1830). An American soldier who was commissioned in the American army in 1784 but five years later resigned and went to India, where he served as a mercenary in the forces of various Indian princes. He returned to the United States in 1801. In 1808 he rejoined the American army as colonel of the 4th Infantry, and on 8 November 1811 he fought in the army of William Henry Harrison [q.v.] in the Battle of Tippecanoe [q.v.]. The following year he was promoted brigadier general. During the War of 1812 [q.v.] he led a brigade in the capture of Fort George on 27 May 1813. He was blamed for the defeat at Chrysler's Farm [q.v.] on 11 November and was removed from command. He was discharged in 1815. He published *Documents* *and Facts Relative to Military Events during the Late War* (1816).

Boyen, Hermann (1771–1848). A German soldier who entered the Prussian army in 1789 and took part in the suppression of the Polish insurrection in 1794–95. In 1803 he joined a military society devoted to army reform headed by Gerhard von Scharnhorst [q.v.], chief of the general staff. On 14 August 1806 he was severely wounded in the Battle of Auerstädt [q.v.]. In January 1808 he was appointed to the Military Reorganization Commission [q.v.]. In 1813 he served as chief of staff to General Friedrich Wilhelm von Bülow [q.v.] and was present at the battles of Grossbeeren on 28 August, Dennewitz on 6 September, Leipzig on 16–18 October, and Laon on 9–10 March 1814 [qq.v.]. Appointed minister of war on 3 June 1814, he supported universal conscription. He was forced to resign in 1819 because of objections to his liberal policies.

Boyer, Jean Pierre (1776–1850). A Haitian general who fought the French. In 1818 he succeeded Alexander Pétion (1770–1818) as president. At first he ruled only in the south, but after the death of Henri Christophe [q.v.] in 1820 he united the country and ruled through army officers who were put in charge of districts. In January 1843 a revolt was mounted against his rule, and he fled the country in March.

Bozeman Trail. Also known as the Powder River Road in the American West, it began at Julesburg, in the northeast corner of Colorado on the South Platte River, and ran to Fort Laramie, Wyoming, on the Powder River and the mining country of Montana. The trail which cut through the foothills of the Bighorn Mountains, the hunting grounds reserved by treaty to the Northern Cheyenne and Arapaho Indians, came to be called, with sufficient justification, the battleground of the Sioux. Early in 1866, to maintain order, Colonel Henry Beebe Carrington (1824–1912), 18th Infantry, was ordered to establish military posts along the trail. He enlarged Fort Connor on the Powder River, renaming it Fort Reno, and in July he established Fort Phil Kearny, Wyoming, in the Bighorn Mountains between the Big and Little Piney forks of the Powder River, just south of the Wyoming-Montana border, and made this his headquarters. A detachment was sent 90 miles farther northwest to establish Fort C. F. Smith in Montana on the Bighorn River, 8 miles above Rotten Grass Creek.

The erection of these forts so enraged the Indians that they became the focus of almost incessant attacks by the Sioux and Cheyennes. There were more than fifty hostile demonstrations, most led by Red Cloud [q.v.], against Fort Phil Kearny alone. By 20 December 1866 the Indians had killed 5 officers, 91 enlisted men, and 58 civilians and had taken some 750 head of cattle. On 21 December there occurred the Fetterman Massacre [q.v.], in which 83 whites were killed. Carrington was relieved of his command. The forts were abandoned after the Fort Laramie Treaty of 1868.

Bozzaris, Marco / Marko Botsares (1788–1823). A Greek patriot who became a hero of the Greek War of Independence [q.v.]. In 1813 he was forced by Ali Pasha [q.v.] to retreat to the Ionian Isles. In 1820 he led 800 expatriate Suliotes against the Turks. He was famous for his defense of Missolonghi [q.v.] against the Turks in 1822–23. He was killed in action fighting the advanced guard of the invading Turkish-Albanian army at Karpenizi [q.v.] (also spelled Carpenisi or Karpenision).

Brackenbury, Henry (1837–1914). A British soldier and writer on military subjects. His schooling was "interrupted by youthful vagaries" (*Dictionary of National Biography*), but he entered Woolwich [q.v.] in 1854 and was commissioned early to serve in the Crimean War [q.v.]. In 1857–58 he served in India during the mutiny [q.v.] and soon after began to write military articles. In 1868 he was appointed professor of military history at Woolwich. During the Franco-Prussian War [q.v.] he headed a relief committee in France for which he was decorated by both belligerents.

During the Ashanti War [q.v.] he served as military secretary to General Garnet Wolseley. In 1878 he helped organize a military police force and remodeled the prisons on Cyprus. The following year he once more served on Wolseley's staff when he was sent to Zululand [see Zulu War]. In 1882 he was in Ireland as undersecretary for police and crime. He again served Wolseley in the Gordon Relief Expedition [q.v.] in 1884–85. During the Second Anglo-Boer War [q.v.] he served as director general of ordnance.

He was knighted KCB in 1894 and became a full general in 1901.

Brady, Mathew B. (1823?–1896). A photographer who sent teams of men he had trained to accompany Union armies during the American Civil War [q.v.]. He had learned to make daguerreotypes from Samuel Finley Breese Morse (1791–1872), and by 1844 he had his own successful commercial studio in New York City. In 1855 he mastered the new wet plate process. Using this process, his trained teams photographed every aspect of the Civil War. He himself covered many of the battles of the Army of the Potomac [q.v.]. A set of two thousand of his photographs was purchased by the government after the war.

Brady's success faded quickly when the war was over. He was ruined by the panic of 1873 and died in a charity ward of a New York City hospital on 15 January 1896.

Bragg, Braxton (1817–1876). An American soldier who, after his graduation from West Point in the class of 1837 served in the Second Seminole War and the Mexican War [qq.v.]. In 1856 he resigned as a lieutenant colonel and became a planter in Louisiana. At the beginning of the American Civil War he was appointed a Confederate brigadier general, and on 12 September 1861, a major general.

He commanded a corps in the Battle of Shiloh [q.v.], and when Albert S. Johnson [q.v.] was killed in that battle, he assumed command. He was made a general to rank from 6 April 1862. Having replaced Pierre Beauregard [q.v.] as head of the Confederate Army of Tennessee [q.v.], he led it on an abortive invasion of Kentucky, where on 8 October 1862 in the Battle of Perryville [q.v.] he came to grief [see Kentucky, Confederate Invasion of]. Pushed back to Chattanooga [q.v.], which he unsuccessfully besieged, he was pushed even farther south into Georgia by General U. S. Grant. He was relieved of command at his own request, and the army was passed to Joseph Johnston [q.v.]. He remained a favorite of Jefferson Davis [q.v.], however, and for a time he was charged "with the conduct of the military operations of the armies of the Confederacy." After Robert E. Lee became general-in-chief, Bragg served in North Carolina under Johnston.

Many soldiers regarded him as a martinet, and many of his officers found him abrasive. Quarrelsome, impatient, stiff, unimaginative, and deceitful, he was arguably the worst Confederate field commander. One of his chiefs of staff described his character as "repulsive."

Bragg's Invasion of Kentucky. See Kentucky, Confederate Invasion of.

Branch, Lawrence O'Bryan (1820–1862). A Princeton-educated Confederate army officer who was promoted brigadier general on 16 November 1861, after commanding the 33rd North Carolina. He commanded the brigade that disputed the advance on New Bern [q.v.] by Union Major General Ambrose Burnside [q.v.] during his North Carolina Campaign [q.v.]. He was then sent to Virginia, where his brigade was attached to A. P. Hill's Light Division. He fought with distinction from Seven Days' through Antietam [qq.v.], where, just at the battle's end, he was killed by a sniper's bullet.

Brandenburg Cuff. A uniform coat cuff worn in several armies with a rectangular flap carrying three buttons.

Branding. A punishment imposed by American, British, and numerous other armies, sometimes a tattooing process rather than a brand with a hot iron. In the U.S. army before the Civil War, culprits were often branded on the forehead, cheek, or hand. During that war a *D* for "desertion" or a *C* for "cowardice" was often branded on the shoulder, hip, or cheek, a practice neither Grant nor Lee permitted in their commands. From the end of the war until 6 June 1870, when branding and tattooing as punishments were made illegal by an act of Congress, deserters were tattooed with a *D* measuring one and one-half inches in height on their left hip or cheek.

In the British service, under the Mutiny Act of 1858, deserters were branded with a *D* not less than one inch high "Two Inches below and One Inch in rear of the Nipple of the Left Breast." Men of "bad character" were both punished and prevented from reenlisting by being branded with a *BC* on the upper part of the right forearm. Branding was abandoned in the British army in 1871.

In France those sentenced to forced labor (*thrives force's*) before 1832 could be branded *TF.* Branding was illegal in the German armies.

Brandschwärmer. A small rocket with a bullet. It could be fired from a gun and was used to set fire to thatch or wooden structures.

Brandwater Basin, Battle of (30 July 1900), Second Anglo-Boer War. At this place Boer General Martinus Prinsloo (d. 1900), defeated by a British force under General Archibald Hunter (1856–1936), surrendered his force of 4,314 Boers as well as 2,800 head of cattle, 4,000 sheep, 5,000 horses, and 2 million rounds of ammunition.

Brandweg. Literally, fire guard. Sentries set by the Boer commandos in the Kaffir Wars and Anglo-Boer Wars [qq.v.].

Brandy Station, Battle of (9 June 1863), American Civil War. Also known as the Battle of Fleetwood Hill, this was the largest and only major cavalry battle of the American Civil War. Indeed, it was the largest cavalry engagement ever held on American soil. Union General Joseph Hooker [q.v.] dispatched the cavalry corps of General Alfred Pleasonton [q.v.], supported by two additional brigades of cavalry and six batteries of artillery—in all, about 12,000 men—from Falmouth, Virginia, near Fredericksburg, toward Culpeper for a reconnaissance in force. Near Brandy Station, Virginia, six miles east-northeast of Culpeper, they clashed with the Confederate cavalry of J. E. B. Stuart [q.v.], about 10,000 men, watching the Rappahannock River and shielding the bulk of the Army of Northern Virginia [q.v.] assembled at Culpeper. The twelve-hour cavalry battle that followed ranged over a wide area.

The Federals withdrew toward the end of the day, leaving the field to the Confederates. Estimated losses on the Confederate side were 523; Federal losses were 866, including 81 killed, 403 wounded, and 382 missing. Both sides claimed victory.

Except for this battle, cavalry suffered far fewer casualties than infantry or artillery during the war. An infantryman's joke asked: "Whoever saw a dead cavalryman?"

Branitzko Pass, Battle of (1849), Hungarian Revolution. A Hungarian army of 10,000 under Richard Guyon [q.v.] defeated an Austrian army under Franz von Schlik (or Schlick) [q.v.] at this pass (Bran) in the Transylvania Alps in southeast-central Rumania between the Piatra-Craiului and Bucegi mountains, 12 miles west-northwest of Sinaia.

Brannan, John Milton (1819–1892). An American soldier who was graduated from West Point in 1841. He served in the artillery during the Mexican War, in which he was wounded and won a brevet to captain. He was appointed a Union brigadier general at the beginning of the American Civil War and commanded an infantry division, first under William Rosecrans [q.v.] in the Tullahoma Campaign and later under George Thomas [q.v.] at Chickamauga [q.v.], where he lost a third of his command. He became chief of artillery in the Army of the Cumberland and took part in the Atlanta Campaign [q.v.].

He was brevetted a major general but remained in the army after the war as a field officer, retiring as a colonel in 1882.

Brass. 1. Empty cartridges of breech-loading cannon.

2. The common use of this term as slang for officers, particularly high-ranking officers, did not begin until World War I, but it was occasionally so used at least as early as 1864.

Brassard. Originally a piece of armor covering the upper arm, but in the nineteenth century and since, a cloth armband often bearing letters or insignia such as *MP* or the red cross worn on the upper sleeve by special aides or soldiers on special duties.

Brass Cannon. Guns so called were actually made of bronze for greater strength and resistance to corrosion.

Braves. American Indian warriors.

Bravo, Nicolás (1787?–1854). A Mexican soldier and political leader who overthrew Agustín Iturbide [q.v.] in 1823. He was vice president of Mexico from 1824 to 1827, when he led an unsuccessful revolt against President Guadalupe Victoria [q.v.]. He was banished in 1828 but again held office under Santa Anna [q.v.]. He was twice acting president and for a few days in 1846 president. [See Mexican Revolutions.]

Brazil–Buenos Aires Conflict (1814–1828). Brazil and Buenos Aires struggled for control of Banda Oriental (Uruguay) until, assisted by Britain, Uruguay declared its independence. [See Uruguayan Revolutions.]

Brazilian Revolutions. In 1807 the Portuguese royal family, fleeing from Napoleon, sailed to Brazil under the protection of the British navy. They arrived at Rio de Janeiro on 7 March 1808. On 16 December 1815 the emperor decreed the Portuguese dominions to be the "United Kingdom of Portugal, Brazil and the Algarves." In 1817 a revolt against Portuguese rule broke out in the city of Pernambuco, and a republic was established that lasted ninety days before being suppressed. A second revolution in 1820 was more successful, and on 7 September 1822 Dom Pedro I (Dom Antonio Pedro de Alcântara Bourbon [1798–1834]), Portuguese regent of Brazil, allied himself with Brazilians against the reactionary policy of the Portuguese. On 7 September 1822 he declared Brazil independent, and on 22 October he was crowned emperor. He was popular for a time but proved to be a despot and was forced to abdicate on 7 April 1831. He was succeeded by his son, Dom Pedro II (Dom Pedro de Alcântara [1825–1891]).

In 1823 the first attempt to establish a republic was made in Bahia; the following year another Pernambuco revolt was suppressed, and in 1825 a revolt in Cisplatine Province (Uruguay) was put down. In 1837 Pará and Rio Grande provinces were in open revolt, but they too were suppressed.

During a revolution beginning on 15 November 1889, in which a republic was proclaimed, a portion of the army mutinied. The empire collapsed, and Dom Pedro and his family fled to Europe. A provisional government was formed by General Manuel Deodoro da Fonseca (1827–1892). In 1891 a United States of Brazil was announced with Fonseca as president, but the army and navy forced him to step down in favor of General Floriano Peixoto (1842–1895). In 1893, when Peixoto announced that Brazil needed a dictator,

Brazilian Revolutions *Soldiers from Bahia, Brazil, 1824*

Admiral Custodio José de Mello (1845?–1902) led a revolution in the navy that was soon joined by revolutionaries in the provinces. The revolts were suppressed with difficulty. Mello surrendered on 16 April 1894, but fighting continued until Peixoto's death in August 1895. He was replaced by Brazil's first civilian president, Prudente José de Morais Barros (1841–1902), whose efforts to govern were hampered by army mutinies and a revolt in Bahia.

Breach. 1. As a noun, a rupture made in an enemy fortification to facilitate an assault.
    2. As a verb, to make such a rupture.

Breastplates. A metal vest or garment fitted with metal plates. Except for cuirasssiers [q.v.], personal armor was little used in the nineteenth century. However, during the American Civil War G. & D Cook & Company of New Haven, Connecticut, offered to Union soldiers a "soldier's bullet proof vest" in two models, a seven-dollar model for officers and a five-dollar one for enlisted men, and for a time early in the war the Atwater Armor Company also in New Haven, produced two hundred per day. Although they were nonregulation in both Civil War armies, a few volunteer regiments were equipped with them. They proved too heavy to be practical, and the increased efficiency of weapons destroyed any value they may have had.

Breastwork. A field fortification breast high, usually of earth, logs, stones, or sandbags.

Breastwork *Ohio volunteers build breastworks before Corinth, Mississippi, May 1862.*

Breckinridge, John Cabell (1821–1875). A Confederate soldier and politician who was a major of volunteers in the Mexican War [q.v.]. At age thirty-five he was vice-president of the United States (1857–61), and in 1860 he was a proslavery candidate for the presidency. For a brief time in 1861 he served in the U.S. Senate. He opposed the war, but when military rule was established in his native Kentucky in September 1861, he accepted a Confederate commission as a brigadier general and soon after was appointed a major general. In 1862 he commanded the reserves at Shiloh and defended Vicksburg [qq.v.]. He failed in an attack upon Baton Rouge, Louisiana, but distinguished himself at Murfreesboro, in the campaign to relieve Vicksburg, and at Chickamauga [qq.v.].

After fighting at Cold Harbor and accompanying Jubal Early's raid on Washington [qq.v.], he was appointed secretary of war by President Jefferson Davis [q.v.].

When Richmond fell, Breckinridge, knowing he was wanted as a traitor, filled a money belt with gold coins and fled with Davis, with whom he parted at Washington, Georgia. After a hair-raising trip through Florida Breckinridge and a few others sailed to Cuba, suffering storms, a shortage of food, and the fear of possible capture. Landing in Cuba, they were greeted as heroes by members of the Confederate colony established there. He eventually reached Europe, where he remained until the amnesty proclamation in 1869, when he resumed his law practice in Lexington, Kentucky.

Bredow, Adalbert von (1814–1890). A Prussian cavalry officer who won fame in the Franco-Prussian War [q.v.] for his pursuit of the defeated Austrians after the Battle of Sadowa [q.v.] on 3 July 1866 and for leading a charge, known as Bredow's Death Ride [see Death Ride], against the French on 16 August 1870 at Mars-la-Tour–Vionville [q.v.]. It was in this charge that Prince Herbert Nikolaus Bismarck-Schönhausen [1849–1904], son of the Iron Chancellor, was severely wounded. Bredow was promoted lieutenant general in 1871.

Breech. The rear of a firearm behind the bore. In muzzle-loading cannon, the solid metal at the rear of the bore, extending to the base ring.

Breechblock. In breech-loading firearms, the block that closes the rear of the bore against the force of the charge and prevents the escape of gas.

Breechloader. Any firearm loaded from the breech as opposed to a muzzleloader [q.v.]. The earliest-known breechloaders were two carbines and two pistols made for King Henry VIII (1491–1547). The carbines used a trapdoor at the base of the barrel that could be lifted to insert an iron tube containing a ball and powder. The powder was ignited by a wheel lock through a vent in the tube. There were other similarly handcrafted breechloaders, but they were not employed

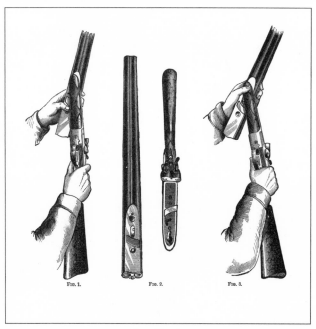

Breechloader

in wartime until 1777, during the American Revolution, when they were used by a special British company in the Battle of Brandywine Creek. In 1819 the United States became the first nation to adopt a breechloader as a standard weapon. This was the Hall carbine [q.v.].

The first successful breech-loading cannon was a 6-pounder manufactured by Krupp [q.v.] in 1851. Shortly thereafter rifled breechloaders were developed by Armstrong and Whitworth [qq.v.] in Britain.

Brescia. The short popular name for the Frabricca National d'Armas in Brescia, Italy, the Italian government arsenal that from the 1880s produced military rifles and the Bodeo service revolver [q.v.].

Brescia Uprising (31 March–1 April 1849), Italian Wars of Independence. On 31 March 1849 in this walled commune in northern Italy, 55 miles northeast of Milan, Italian revolutionaries forced the small Austrian garrison to retreat into the citadel, but a 4,000-strong Austrian force under General Julius von Haynau [q.v.] stormed the town and, fighting from barricade to barricade, soon destroyed all resistance. The Austrians lost 480 killed and many more wounded; losses among the revolutionaries are unknown.

After the battle General Haynau, noted for his fanatical hatred of revolutionaries, ordered so many executions that he became known as the Hyena.

Brevet Rank. An honorary title without the authority, precedence, or pay of substantive rank. Brevets were much used in the American army to reward "gallant and meritorious service." There were no gallantry medals in the American army until the introduction of the Medal of Honor [q.v.] during the Civil War. A brevet was provided for under the 61st and 62nd Articles of War of 1806, but regulations regarding brevet rank were vague. In the United States the Congress frequently changed the rules, giving rise to much confusion and misunderstanding. It did not help when, during the Mexican War [q.v.], Congress passed a bill allowing regular army officers who had won brevets in temporary regiments to "have the benefit of any promotion" when they rejoined their regular regiments.

Brevets could (although not necessarily) become temporarily substantive in detachments and courts-martial composed of various regiments or corps. Article 62 stated that whenever different units of the army, militia, or Marine Corps were joined, "the highest in rank of the line" should command, but few knew exactly what this meant. In 1851 then senator Jefferson Davis [q.v.] wrote that the brevet system had "grown upon our service until it has produced such confusion in the Army that many of its best soldiers wish it could be obliterated." The Civil War left thousands of brevets in its wake. Of 1,978 generals appointed during or soon after the war, 1,700 were brevet brigadier generals or major generals, most of whom were given their brevets on 13 March 1865 at the end of the war. The new Articles of War decreed that "brevet rank shall not entitle an officer to precedence or command except by special assignment of the President; but such assignment shall not entitle any officer to additional pay or allowances." In 1869 the articles were repealed.

In the British army brevets were also given under special circumstances to officers of the rank of captain and above, but not to general officers, and they often included the pay of the higher rank. There were mass brevets of officers above the rank of captain in 1837, 1838, 1841, 1846, 1851, and 1854. In one instance 200 colonels were promoted brevet major general. In 1854 increases of pay were abolished.

Brialmont, Henri Alexis (1821–1903). A Belgian military engineer, regarded as the greatest expert of his time on fortifications, who designed the forts of Liège and Namur in the 1800s. Each city was ringed by forts located on high ground. They were sunk in the ground so that only the cupolas of disappearing guns appeared on the surface. Each was surrounded by a 30-foot-deep moat. He also designed the fortifications of Antwerp, Bucharest, and other cities. He was sometimes called the Belgian Vauban, a reference to Sébastian le Prestre de Vauban [q.v.], the famous seventeenth-French military engineer.

Brice's Crossroads, Battle of (10 June 1864), American Civil War. Near this place in northeast Mississippi a Federal force of 4,800 infantry, 3,000 cavalry, and 18 guns under Brigadier General Samuel Davis Sturgis [q.v.], moving south from Memphis, was attacked by a Confederate force of less than half that number (about 3,500) under Major General Nathan Bedford Forrest [q.v.]. The day was extremely hot, and most of the fighting was done in thick underbrush. The Confederates pushed on both Federal flanks, which gave way about 5:00 P.M. A panic ensued, and Sturgis was unable to stem the rout until fleeing soldiers reached Stubb's Plantation, some 10 miles north of the crossroads.

Federal losses were 223 killed, 394 wounded, and 1,623 captured, for a total of 2,240. Forrest put his losses at 492. The Confederates captured 16 guns and 250 wagons, limbers, caissons, and carts loaded with ammunition, rations, and supplies.

Two weeks later a board was appointed to make a lengthy investigation into the "disaster to the late expedition under Brigadier General Sturgis." Sturgis fought no more battles in this war.

Bricole. 1. A kind of harness worn by men to pull guns, limbers, caissons, or wagons; it was standard equipment in Napoleon's artillery. It consisted of a heavy leather belt to which was attached a five-foot drag rope hooked to the vehicle to be pulled.

2. A cannon was said to have fired *en bricole* when its shot hit a sloping revetment.

Bridgehead. 1. A defensive position at the end of a bridge closest to the enemy.

2. An area organized to defend a bridge, ford, or defile.

3. An advanced position in hostile territory capable of being used for further advance.

[See Tête-de-Pont.]

Bridgeman's Bull Battery. In 1898, during the Philippine Insurrection [q.v.], Battery G of the 6th U.S. Artillery, commanded by Captain Victor Horace Bridgeman (1857?–1934), landed in the Philippines without its horses. Because the local horses were not strong enough to pull the 3.2-inch field guns with their limbers and caissons, more than one hundred Brahma bulls and their Philippine drivers were pressed into service. It was said that the animals performed well and even learned to recognize the pertinent bugle calls.

Bridle. 1. The headgear for governing a horse.

2. A bracing device used in the locks of muzzleloaders to keep the pins rigid against the pressure of the spring.

Brienne-la-Château, Battle of (29 January 1814), Napoleonic Wars. Near this small town, where as a youth (1779–84) he had been enrolled in a military school, Napoleon with 30,000 men pounced on the 25,000 men of an Allied army of Prussians and Russians under Field Marshal Gebhard von Blücher [q.v.]. The Allies were driven from their position, and a night attack by the Russians failed to retake the town. At one point Blücher was almost captured, and Napoleon himself narrowly escaped being taken by Cossacks. The French suffered about 3,000 casualties, the Prussians about 4,000.

Brigade. 1. As a verb, to form a new unit by subsuming two or more others—e.g., a regiment of infantry and a battery of artillery.

2. As a noun, a military unit composed of more than one regiment, usually only two or three with perhaps units of artillery and cavalry added.

3. As a noun, in the British Royal Artillery, a brigade consisted of several batteries (usually seven).

4. As a noun, a general name for some special units, as Brigade of Guards or Brigade of Gurkhas, of no special size.

Brigade *General Samuel Beatty's brigade advances to sustain the Union right near Nashville, Tennessee.*

Brigade Major. In the British army, the principal staff officer in a brigade.

Brigadier / Brigadier General. In the French service a brigadier was (1) a man in charge of baking bread; (2) an assistant wagonmaster; (3) a man in charge of five gendarmes in the Gendarmerie Nationale; or (4) a rank in Napoleon's mounted units equivalent to a corporal.

The French equivalent to the English brigadier was general of brigade, a rank that did not necessarily mean that those holding the title commanded brigades.

In the British army brigadier or brigadier general was a temporary rank between colonel and major general. The rank was never substantive in the nineteenth century. After 1880 it was not used until 1889, when it was revived for the Second Anglo-Boer War [q.v.].

In the American army the term "brigadier" was seldom used alone. The rank, between colonel and major general, was brigadier general. It was always substantive and was equivalent to the rank of commodore in the navy.

In the German armies this rank did not and does not exist. Thus, an American or British brigadier general was and is equivalent to a German major general.

Brigate Estense. A brigade made up of troops from the smaller Italian states that, until 1863, was in the service of the Duke of Modena.

Briquet. A short, slightly curved infantry saber with a two-foot blade and a stirrup hilt.

Brisbane, Thomas (1773–1860). A British soldier and astronomer who entered the army at sixteen and served in Flanders, the West Indies, North America, and Spain. He was promoted major general in 1813. From 1821 to 1825 he was governor of New South Wales in Australia, where he cataloged 7,385 stars, a feat for which he was given the Copley Medal by the Royal Society. Brisbane, the capital of Queensland, was named after him.

Bristoe Station, Battle of (14 October 1863), American Civil War. When General Lee in northern Virginia took the offensive against George Meade, A. P. Hill [qq.v.], commanding Lee's leading corps, impetuously attacked what he assumed to be a single Union corps near Bristoe Station.

When the Confederate division of Major General Henry Heth [q.v.] arrived on the field, its two brigades, under Brigadier Generals John Rogers Cooke (1833–1891) and William Whedbee Kirkland (1833–1915), were at once thrown forward to meet the Federals' crossing of Broad Run east of the railroad station. They ran into a trap, for a second Federal corps lay concealed behind a railroad embankment on their flank. The two Confederate brigades wheeled to meet their fire and were cut to pieces.

Federal losses were 548 men. Hill's rash decision to attack without reconnoitering cost Lee's army about 1,700 casualties; both Cooke and Kirkland were seriously wounded. Lee consoled Hill with the words "Well, well, General, let us bury these poor fellows and say no more about it."

British Army. An army with no permanent infantry or cavalry formation larger than a regiment, which was an administrative, not a tactical, formation. Many infantry regiments contained only one battalion, some had two; rifle regiments had four. Battalions had at different times eight or ten companies, each of about 100 men. All infantry line regiments were numbered except for the 60th, which became the King's Royal Rifle Regiment, and, after Waterloo, the 95th, which became the Rifle Brigade. However, the Regiment of Artillery encompassed the entire arm. Each regiment had its own uniforms and customs and did its own recruiting, usually from a particular region. On his first appointment as commander-in-chief (1798–1809) the Duke of York and Albany [q.v.] introduced for the first time a uniform drill throughout the army.

During the Napoleonic Wars the army contained 120 regiments of infantry, 51 of which served in the Iberian Peninsula between 1808 and 1814 [see Peninsular War]. It normally contained about twenty regiments of cavalry. Between 1840 and 1880 there were just over 10,000 cavalrymen in the line and about 5,000 to 6,000 in India.

In the far-flung wars the army fought, foreign regiments were sometimes established, but these, except for Gurkhas [q.v.], colonial forces, and those in the Indian Army [q.v.] were never retained in peacetime. [See King's German Legion.]

Regiments of the line were numbered prior to 1870, although early in the century many were known by the names of their commanding officers, as was the custom throughout the century when temporary regiments or levies of locals were formed. Guards regiments of infantry were named, not numbered. In the cavalry, except for the 1st and 2nd Life Guards, guards regiments bore names; regiments of the line were numbered, but dragoon guards were numbered separately. Cavalry regiments were formed into two wings, which corresponded to infantry battalions. In the artillery, horse artillery batteries bore letters; others, numbers.

The British army in 1858 contained ninety-nine regiments of regular infantry until the Canadians raised a regiment that was numbered 100. After the Indian Mutiny [q.v.], when the armies of the Honourable East India Company were incorporated into the British army, nine more regiments were added. [See White Mutiny.] In 1881 most infantry regiments were reorganized, and most were given territorial names—e.g., Somerset Light Infantry, instead of numbers. Most were two-battalion regiments, and each had linked battalions of militia and volunteers.

Officers came from the aristocracy and the upper middle classes. They sometimes had two ranks, one within the regiment and another rank in the army when they served outside the regiment. In addition, some carried local or temporary ranks. They wore the insignia of the rank in which they were serving. For most of the century most officers in Guards regiments automatically carried an army rank one grade higher than their rank in their regiment. Most infantry and cavalry officers were graduates of Sandhurst, and most artillery and engineer officers were graduated from Woolwich [qq.v.]. Very few were commissioned from the ranks, and these were usually riding masters or quartermasters.

The other ranks were recruited for the most part from the lower socioeconomic classes, with just enough of the partially educated classes to provide noncommissioned officers. There was never conscription for the regular army or for the Indian army. Although in India recruiting was never a problem, it was always, except during popular wars, a problem in the British regular army, and sometimes crimps [q.v.] were employed to shanghai men. A very large percentage of the army, sometimes as high as 40 percent, was Irish.

The size of the British regular army differed considerably in various years. In 1880 it consisted of 190,600 men, of whom 62,653 were in India. Of these, 7,980 were officers, 16,500 were noncommissioned officers, drummers, and trumpeters, and the rest were rank and file. [See Indian Army.]

Divisions, formed only in wartime, usually consisting of two brigades, each of three or four battalions, with two batteries of artillery, were first used in the British army in the Peninsular War [q.v.], but these formations were not continued after the Napoleonic Wars. Similar units were formed in the Crimean War and the Second Anglo-Boer War [qq.v.] but were broken up at war's end. Brigades were always ad hoc units.

Between the Battle of Waterloo in 1815 and the Crimean War of 1854–55 there were no organic changes except for the Limited Service Act of 1847, which changed the enlistment period from life to ten or twelve years.

When the Crimean War began, army administration was inconceivably complex. The secretary of state for war and colonies sat at the Colonial Office and had vague powers only in time of war. The secretary at war represented the army in Parliament and handled financial affairs. The commander-in-chief was responsible only to the sovereign in matters concerning discipline, patronage, and command in the infantry and cavalry. He was not responsible for the troops in India or the colonies. The master general of ordnance and the Ordnance Board were responsible to no one, but they were expected to supply guns and ammunition; the engineers and artillery officers came under the master general's command. The Commissariat Department was in the Treasury, and until 1852 the militia came under the home secretary. When the blunders of the Crimean War made apparent the need for an improved organization and a reformed army administration, Sidney Herbert [q.v.] revised the entire administration of the army. In 1855 the Colonial Department was separated from the War Department, and the Board of Ordnance was abolished. Finally, there were but two chiefs, the secretary of state for war and the commander-in-chief. In 1870, with the reforms initiated by Edward Cardwell with the help of Colonel Garnet Wolseley [qq.v.], the army became more manageable. Shorter terms of enlistment, the abolition of the purchase system, and many other improvements were made. Cardwell also tried, but without great success, to organize the army into units larger than regiments. The localization of most regiments, attaching them to counties, begun by Cardwell, was completed by his successor, Viscount Haldane (1856–1928), who was secretary of state for war from 1905 to 1912.

British Artillery. Until the middle of the nineteenth century almost all ordnance was manufactured in the arsenal at Woolwich [q.v.], although a few small guns were produced by commercial iron foundries. When the breech-loading Armstrong gun [q.v.] was adopted, many were made in William Armstrong's [q.v.] Elswick Ordnance Works at Newcastle-upon-Tyne. The British army was slow and reluctant to adopt breech-loading guns even though the first had proved satisfactory in China in 1860. As a result, by the end of the century its Boer opponents in South Africa had superior artillery [see Second Anglo-Boer War].

British Civil Disorders. As a result of the enclosures of common lands and the introduction of machinery into previously skilled trades, unrest flared in Britain between 1816 and 1844. There were riotous assemblies, destruction of machinery, and sometimes murders of landowners or factory owners. Troops were frequently called on to overawe malcontents, and Yeomanry [q.v.] were often called out to support the police [see Chartist Riots]. In 1830 gangs roamed about destroying farm machinery, and Yeoman troops faced 500 rioters at Tilsbury. In 1831 Yeomanry and regulars were used to quell rioting in Bristol, where the Bishop's Palace and public buildings were burned to the ground. There were serious riots in South Wales, where a troop of Swansea Yeomanry Cavalry was

surrounded and disarmed. During the Chartist riots [q.v.] in 1837–42 both regulars and Yeomanry were used against rioters. In 1839 Monmouth was attacked by Welsh miners, and the country seemed on the verge of revolution.

The establishment of effective police forces in London in 1829 and in the counties in 1855 resulted in fewer calls upon the army or the Yeomanry to suppress disorders. The last instance of magistrates' calling for the support of the Yeomanry occurred in 1867, when it was called out to overawe food rioters in Devon.

British-Egyptian War (1840). When Muhammad Ali [q.v.], the ruler of Egypt, threatened war against the sultan of Turkey, his nominal master, and advanced on Constantinople (Istanbul), the European powers, particularly Britain, became alarmed. Britain, Prussia, Russia, and Austria signed an agreement in which they offered to make Muhammad Ali's rule hereditary and grant him lifetime possession of Syria if he would give up Egyptian sovereignty over it (Syria then included present-day Lebanon), relinquish Crete and the holy cities of Mecca (Makkah) and Medina (Medinah), and return the Turkish fleet, which had been treacherously surrendered to him.

When he refused, the British launched an expeditionary force under Rear Admiral Sir Robert Stopford (1768–1847). On 9 September 1840 Beirut was shelled, and on the following day sailors and marines landed and captured the town. On 3 November Acre fell after a short bombardment, and Muhammad Ali agreed to give up Syria, Crete, and the Turkish fleet in exchange for heredity rule. He also agreed to reduce his army to 18,000 men and to pay tribute to the sultan of Turkey.

British-Egyptian War *A horse ridden to exhaustion near Suakim, during the British-Egyptian War*

British Legion. A force of British volunteers under General Sir George de Lacy Evans [q.v.] that was sent to help the infant Isabella II (1830–1904) fight the Carlist War [q.v.] in 1833–39. It was raised in haste and was described by one observer as "six or eight thousand ragamuffins." Because Wellington opposed employing regular officers in the legion, it was still untrained when it was shipped off to Spain.

In spite of a disaster to one battalion, the legion managed to defeat the Carlists at Hernani on 5 May 1836 and San Sebastián on 1 October 1836, and to capture Irún on the Bidassoa River in northern Spain in May 1837, but it was badly supported by the Spanish government, and it wasted away through neglect, desertion, and diseases. The remnants were shipped home at the expense of the British government.

British South African Company. A chartered company formed by Cecil Rhodes (1853–1902) and his friends to find and extract minerals in the lands north of the Transvaal in what became Southern Rhodesia (Zimbabwe) and Northern Rhodesia (Zambia). Its avowed purpose included the encouragement of colonization, the extension of the railroad and telegraph northward, and the promotion of trade and commerce. Queen Victoria gave her signature to the charter on 29 October 1889. Broad powers were granted the company. It could "make treaties, promulgate laws, preserve the peace, maintain a police force, and acquire new concessions." It could construct roads and harbors and undertake other public works, own or charter ships, engage in mining or any other industry, establish banks, make land grants, and carry on any lawful commerce, trade, pursuit, or business. Its authorized police force became, in effect, an army that fought the Matabele War [q.v.] and engaged in other conflicts with native tribes. [See Lobengula; Jameson, Leander Starr; Matabele War.]

Broad Arrow. In Britain an arrowheadlike mark on arms, equipment, and other items indicated crown property. Prison uniforms were also often imprinted with this design. The origin of the mark is obscure, but it was in use at least as far back as the seventeenth century.

Broadfoot, George (1807–1845). A British soldier, the eldest of three brothers, all killed in the service of their country. In 1826 he was commissioned in the 34th Madras Native Infantry. He took part in the First Afghan War [q.v.] and was with Sir Robert Sale [q.v.] when he marched to Jelalabad. He was active in the defense of the town when it was besieged, and he was wounded there [see Jelalabad, Siege of]. He was later in the army of retribution under General George Pollock [q.v.]. He was only a major when he was killed in the Battle of Ferozeshah [q.v.] during the Second Sikh War [q.v.].

Brock, Isaac (1769–1812). A British soldier, born in Guernsey, who came to be hailed as the Hero of Upper Canada. In 1785 he entered the army as an ensign in the 8th Foot, and from 1791 to 1793 he served in the West Indies. In 1797 he was promoted lieutenant colonel, and two years later he saw service in northern Holland. In 1802 he was sent to Canada, where three years later he was promoted colonel. From 1806 to 1810 he commanded the garrison at Quebec, and in 1811 he was appointed a major general. During the War of 1812 [q.v.] he crossed the frontier from Canada, and on 16 August 1812 he captured Detroit [q.v.]. He was knighted on 13 October 1812, just before his death in the Battle of Queenston Heights [q.v.].

Bromhead, Gonville (1844–1891). A British soldier commissioned in the 24th Regiment who as a lieutenant was at Rorke's Drift [q.v.] in January 1879, when it was attacked by Zulus during the Zulu War [q.v.]. [See Chard, John Rouse Merriot.] His gallantry there earned him a Victoria Cross [q.v.].

Broncos / Bronco Bucks. 1. Name given by white Americans to hostile Indian warriors, particularly in Arizona.

2. A half-wild horse or pony of the western plains of the United States.

Bronkhorstspruit, Battle of (20 December 1880), First Anglo-Boer War. In the first battle of the First Anglo-Boer War [q.v.] British Lieutenant Colonel Philip Robert Anstruther (1834?–1882?) and 259 men of the 94th Regiment were ambushed by a Boer commando of about 150 men under François Gerhardus Joubert (1827–1903) at this Transvaal village, 38 miles east of Pretoria. The British lost 155 killed and wounded; the Boers lost only 2 killed and 5 wounded.

Brooke, James (1803–1868). A British soldier and adventurer who, after fighting and being wounded in Burma (Myanmar), inherited a fortune and purchased and equipped a 142-ton schooner, *Royalist*, in which he set forth in 1838 to rescue the Malay Archipelago from barbarism. In 1840 he helped the uncle of the sultan of Brunei suppress a rebellion by Dyak headhunters. On 24 September 1841 the sultan appointed him ruler of Sarawak on the island of Borneo, and on 18 August 1842 at Kuching he was formally installed as raja of Sarawak. He proceeded to reform the government and, with some help from the Royal Navy, destroyed the strongholds of Malay and Dyak pirates that flourished in the area and abolished the Dyak practice of headhunting.

In 1849 he was charged in Parliament in London with abusing his powers. He returned to London prepared to defend himself, but a royal commission sitting in Singapore found the charges against him not proven. In 1857 he narrowly escaped death at the hands of rebellious Chinese immigrant residents by diving into the river and swimming under a Chinese junk. He was knighted (KCB) in 1858.

He left Sarawak in 1863 and returned to England, leaving behind as his successor his nephew Charles Arthur Johnston (1829–1917), who had joined him in 1852 and taken the name Brooke. Charles Arthur was in turn succeeded by his son, Charles Vyner (1874–1963), who in 1946 ceded Sarawak to the British crown. It is now part of Malaysia.

Brooke, John Rutter (1838–1926). An American soldier who on 7 November 1861, during the American Civil War, became colonel of the 53rd Pennsylvania. He fought in the Peninsular Campaign, at Antietam, Fredericksburg, Chancellorsville, and Gettysburg [qq.v.], where he was wounded. He commanded a brigade at the Wilderness, Spotsylvania, and Cold Harbor [qq.v.], where he was severely wounded. On 12 May 1864 he was promoted brigadier general and on 1 August brevetted major general.

He became a lieutenant colonel in the regular army in 1866, colonel in 1879, brigadier general in 1888, and finally a regular army major general in 1897. During the Spanish-American War, he commanded a training camp at Chickamauga Park in Georgia, which was cited for its prevailing unsanitary conditions. He later took part in the Puerto Rico Campaign under General Nelson Miles, fighting in a skirmish at Guayama on the southeast side of the island, 32 miles east of Ponce. He was about to attack Cayey when the war ended. He was appointed military governor of Puerto Rico and Cuba. In 1902 he retired from the service.

Brooke Gun. An artillery piece designed during the American Civil War by John Brooke (1826–1904), the

Confederate chief of ordnance and hydrography. It was manufactured in various sizes, the most popular being a 3-inch 10-pounder. It resembled the Parrott Gun [q.v.].

Brooks, William Thomas Harbaugh (1821–1870). An American soldier who obtained an appointment to West Point at the age of sixteen and was graduated in 1841, ranking 46th in a class of 52. He fought in the Second Seminole War and won two brevets in the Mexican War [qq.v.]. He served as an aide to General David Twiggs on frontier duty in the West and was promoted captain in 1851. Ten years later, at the beginning of the American Civil War, he was promoted brigadier general of volunteers in the Federal army and given command of a division.

He fought in the Peninsular Campaign and was wounded during the Seven Days' [qq.v.]. He temporarily led a corps at Antietam, where he was again wounded; he commanded a corps at Petersburg [qq.v.].

Shortly after this disastrous Federal repulse, Major Generals William Franklin and William Smith [qq.v.] wrote directly to President Lincoln, expressing their lack of confidence in their commander Ambrose Burnside [q.v.], declaring that "the plan of campaign . . . already . . . commenced cannot possibly be successful." General John Cochrane (1813–1898) and William Brooks both concurred. Although Lincoln soon fired Burnside, the careers of all four of these senior officers suffered, and Brooks's promotion to major general on 10 June 1863 was revoked on 6 April 1864.

The following month he resigned as a brigadier general of volunteers and as a regular army major. For the next 30 years he farmed near Huntsville, Alabama. Curiously, the ex-Yankee general was accepted, even respected, in this southern community and admired for his "amiable disposition, simplicity of character, and sound common sense" (*Dictionary of American Biography*).

Brothels, Military. See Bordel Militaire Controllé / Bordel Mobile de Campagne; Venereal Diseases.

Broussard. A French term for a soldier considered a good bush fighter, capable of adapting himself to operating in wild, difficult terrain. From *broussaille,* meaning bramble or underbrush.

Brown, George. The name given a loaf of British army bread during the Napoleonic Wars.

Brown, George (1790–1865). A British soldier who was gazetted an ensign in the 43rd Foot at age fifteen. While still in his teens, he took part in the expedition to Copenhagen, the Battle of Vimeiro, and the retreat to Corunna [qq.v.] [see Peninsular War]. In 1809 he was back in the Iberian Peninsula, where his regiment became part of the light brigade, and until June 1811 he took part in all its battles. He was promoted captain just before his twenty-first birthday, and after the battles of Nivelle and the Nive [qq.v.] he was promoted major on 26 May 1814.

He took part in the expedition against the United States during the War of 1812 and was present in the Battle of Bladensburg [q.v.], where he was severely wounded. After his recovery he was promoted lieutenant colonel. For the next twenty-five years he held staff appointments and saw no action. In 1841 he was promoted major general, and ten years later, lieutenant general.

During the Crimean War he was given command of a division and was the first general officer to arrive in Turkey. A martinet, his policy of "pipe-claying, close-shaving and tight-stocking" (according to William Howard Russell [q.v.]) made him highly unpopular. In the Battle of the Alma [q.v.] his horse was shot from under him, and on 5 November 1854, during the fighting before Sevastopol, he was severely wounded in the chest and the left arm.

He refused to go home, but in June he fell ill and was invalided back to Britain. He was promoted full general in September 1855.

Brown, Jacob Jennings (1775–1828). An American teacher, surveyor, and soldier. From 1798 to 1800 he was secretary to Alexander Hamilton (1753?–1804). He then settled beside Lake Ontario, where he founded the town of Brownsville and grew wealthy smuggling goods across the U.S.-Canadian border. He became active in the New York militia and by 1809 was a colonel. A brigadier general at the beginning of the War of 1812 [q.v.], he was given command of the troops on the Canadian frontier. On 3 October 1812 he repelled a British attack upon Ogdensburg [q.v.], New York, a town on the St. Lawrence River 55 miles north-northwest of Watertown. In May 1813 he thwarted a British attack upon Sackets Harbor [q.v.]. He proved to be the best field commander in the American forces, and on 19 July 1813 he was promoted brigadier general in the regular army. He commanded a brigade in the disastrous Montreal Campaign. On 28 January 1814 he was promoted major general and took command at Niagara, succeeding the incompetent Major General James Wilkinson [q.v.]. He attempted another invasion of Canada and captured Fort Erie [q.v.] on 3 July 1814. On 5 July he sent Brigadier General Winfield Scott [q.v.] to attack Chippewa, and on 25 July he commanded the victorious forces at Lundy's Lane [qq.v.], where he was twice wounded. These rare American victories led Secretary of War John Armstrong [q.v.] to write Brown that he had "rescued the military character of your country, from the odium brought upon it by fools & rascals." From 13 August until 21 September he withstood a siege at Fort Erie [q.v.]. He was given the Thanks of Congress for his successes at Chippewa, Niagara Falls, and the capture of Fort Erie, Canada.

In June 1815 Brown became the senior general in the American army, and six years later, on 1 June 1821, the commanding general of the army, an appointment he held until his death on 24 February 1828.

Brown, John (1800–1859). An American insurrectionist and abolitionist fanatic who believed himself to be God's chosen instrument to abolish slavery. After murdering five defenseless slavery advocates near Pottawatomie, Kansas, on 24 May 1856, he fought with proslavery men at Osawatomie in August. In 1859, hoping to spark and lead a slave insurrection, he headed a small band that seized the U.S. arsenal at Harpers Ferry, Virginia (West Virginia) on 17–18 October. No slave joined his "army." Attacked by a small force of Virginia militia, he was forced to hole up in the town's firehouse, and there he was wounded and captured by marines led by Colonel Robert E. Lee with Captain Edward Ord and Lieutenant J. E. B. Stuart [qq.v.]. He was convicted of treason and on 2 December was hanged at Charles Town (West Virginia). [See John Brown's Raid.]

In his last speech at his trial he said: "You may dispose of me very easily: I am nearly disposed of now; but this question is still to be settled—this negro question, I mean."

Brown, John *John Brown's raid at Harpers Ferry*

Brown Bess. The popular name for the British Tower Musket or British long land-pattern musket. Developed in late 1730, it was the best mass-produced musket of the Napoleonic era. It and its many imitations were used by all American and European armies until about 1840. A smooth-bore flintlock musket in caliber .753, it was manufactured at the Enfield Royal Small Arms factory in Middlesex, England, now part of Greater London. Its manufacture ended in 1815, but eighteen years later British ordnance still had 440,000 India pattern Brown Bess muskets (improved by a reinforced cock, which had been introduced in 1809). Many were sold to Mexico and to Central and South American armies.

To "hug Brown Bess" was to enlist or serve as a soldier. Rudyard Kipling [q.v.] in "Brown Bess" wrote:

Though her sight was not long and her weight was not small
Yet her actions were winning, her language was clear;
And everyone bowed as she opened the ball
On the arm of some high-gaitered, grim grenadier.
All Europe admitted the striking success
Of the dances and routs that were given by Brown Bess.

Brown Boy. The tan cotton quilt issued to cadets at West Point. When the color of the quilt changed, it became a "green girl."

Browne, Samuel James (1824–1901). A British soldier born in India who first served in the 46th Bengal Native Infantry. He fought in the Second Sikh War and in 1858 in the Indian Mutiny [qq.v.], during which he commanded the 2nd Punjab Cavalry at Lucknow.

On 31 August 1858 in an engagement against mutinous forces under Khan Ali Khan at Sirpur (Sipura or Seerpura) in northeast Hyderabad, Brevet Major Browne, accompanied only by an orderly, advanced upon a 9-pounder gun commanding the approaches to the enemy position and attacked its gunners. In the hand-to-hand combat he was wounded by a sword cut to his left knee and his left arm was severed at the shoulder, but he managed to kill his adversary and prevent the gun from being used. For this he was awarded the Victoria Cross [q.v.].

Browne remained in the army, was promoted major general on 6 February 1870, and commanded a division of the Peshawar Field Force during the Second Afghan War [q.v.].

He was knighted (KCB) in 1879 and became a general in 1888.

He is best known as the inventor of the Sam Browne belt [q.v.], a device that allowed a one-armed man to draw a sword and return it to its scabbard with ease.

Brownell, Kady (1842–?). A Union army camp follower in the American Civil War, the daughter of a Scottish soldier in the British army, who was born somewhere in Africa. When her husband, Robert, enlisted in the 1st Rhode Island and later, when he served as orderly sergeant in the 5th Rhode Island, she accompanied him. At First Bull Run [q.v.] she carried the regiment's colors. She acquired a rifle and a saber and was said to have become proficient with both. She was with the regiment when it took part in General Ambrose Burnside's [q.v.] expedition to North Carolina. In the Battle of New Bern [q.v.], when the 5th Rhode Island, emerging suddenly from a woods, was mistakenly fired upon by other Union troops, she is reputed to have rushed into the fire, waving its flag. After the battle she nursed her seriously wounded husband and helped with the nursing of other wounded, both Union and Confederate. When her husband was given a medical discharge eighteen months later, she disappeared from history. Although she never had any official capacity, it was said that Burnside himself issued her a discharge.

Browning, John Moses (1855–1926). An American son of a Mormon gunsmith who became one of the world's foremost inventors of firearms. At age thirteen he built his first rifle from scrap metal, and he obtained his first patent—for a breechloader—when he was twenty-four. Guns designed by him were manufactured by Winchester, Colt, Remington, and other firms, but only those weapons manufactured by the Fabrique d'Armes de Guerre of Herdtal, Liège, Belgium, carried his name.

His Model 1900 automatic pistol, sometimes called Old Model, used a recoil spring on the side above the barrel that also served as the mainspring for the firing pin. His first practical machine gun, a gas-operated weapon, was manufactured by Colt as its Model 1895. Browning also designed special ammunition.

Brownrigg, Robert (1759–1833). A British soldier of much experience in many parts of the world who became a lieutenant general in 1808 and served as quartermaster general in the Walcheren Expedition [q.v.] of 1809. In 1811 he was appointed governor and commander-in-chief in Ceylon (Sri Lanka). At that time the British occupied only a few coastal towns; the interior was ruled by the king of Candy (or Kandy), upon whom Brownrigg soon declared war. [See: Candian / Kandian Wars.]

In December 1814 he completed the organization of an army of 3,000 and personally led them inland, occupying Candy, the enemy's capital, on the Mahaweli River, 60 miles east-northeast of Colombo, on 14 February 1815. Four days later the king was captured. On 2 March the kingdom of Candy was annexed. Brownrigg was created a baronet in 1816 and promoted general in 1819. He returned to England the following year.

Brune, Guillaume Marie Anne (1763–1815). An ardent French revolutionist and soldier who joined the National Guard in 1789 and became a captain. He was promoted general of brigade in 1793. In 1797 he was with Napoleon's army in Italy, and in the following year he plundered Switzerland. In January 1799 he was sent to take command in Holland against the Anglo-Russian forces there. In 1800 Napoleon gave him command of an army in Italy, replacing André Masséna [q.v.], an assignment in which he proved a disaster. "À la Brune" became a synonym for hopeless confusion. Napoleon remarked that "the campaign of Italy showed the limits of Brune's talents." Nevertheless, on 19 May 1804 he was one of the first to be given a marshal's baton. In 1807 he was assigned to protect Napoleon's left rear and successfully drove the Swedes from Stralsund [q.v.]. In 1815, after he had plundered northern Germany, he was placed on the inactive list. He was murdered by a royalist mob during the White Terror in Avignon on 2 August 1815, when all who had been prominent under Napoleon were sought out and massacred. Dying, he is said to have exclaimed: "Good God! to have survived a hundred fields and die like this. . . ." His body was torn apart, the pieces thrown into the Rhône River.

Brunswick, Friedrich Wilhelm, Duke of (1771–1815). A German soldier, son of Karl Wilhelm Ferdinand [q.v.], who after the French victory in the Battle of Wagram [q.v.] in July 1809 removed to England until 1813, when restored to his duchy, he took command of a new army. In 1815 he commanded the Brunswick forces in Wellington's army and was mortally wounded in the Battle of Quatre Bras [q.v.].

Brunswick, Karl / Charles Wilhelm Ferdinand, Duke of (1735–1806). A German soldier, nephew of Frederick the Great, under whom he served for a time, who won fame in the Seven Years' War (1756–63). He commanded the army that invaded Holland in 1787 and was commanding general of the Prussian and Austrian army that invaded France in 1792. He was repulsed at Valmy by François Christophe Kellermann and Charles Dumouriez [qq.v.] on 20 September of that year. After further defeats he retired in 1794. In 1806, given command of the largest of the Prussian armies put in the field against Napoleon, he suffered defeat at the hands of Louis Nicolas Davout [q.v.], and on 14 August he was mortally wounded at Auerstädt [q.v.]. He died two months later.

Brunswick Rifle. The original model was German. With variations it was adopted by many armies. Issued to rifle regiments in the British army in 1838, it was the first percussion arm issued to British troops. It differed from the Baker rifle, which it replaced, by being a percussion weapon, using a copper cap, rather than flint and steel with priming powder, by having a two-groove rifling with a steeper twist, and by firing a ball belted to fit in the two deep spiral grooves. Weighing 9.125 pounds, it was 46 inches long with a 30-inch bore, and it was accurate at 100 yards if the weather was good, the charge was properly measured, and the lock remained in good condition. It was difficult to load when the bore became fouled. Originally built with eleven-groove rifling, it was later altered to two grooves for use with belted spherical ball. It remained a standard issue until the arrival of the Enfield rifled musket at the beginning of the Crimean War [q.v.] in 1854. In India the Brunswick remained in service even longer and was issued to loyal Sikh regiments after the Indian Mutiny [q.v.].

There was also a Heavy Brunswick of 20 mm caliber weighing 12 pounds, but this appears to have had limited use.

Brusilov, Aleksei Alekseevich (1853–1926). A Russian soldier who began his career as a cavalry officer in the Caucasus. He distinguished himself by his tactical genius during the Russo-Turkish War [q.v.] of 1877–78. During the First World War he commanded an army in Galicia, and later he became a leading Bolshevik.

Brydon, William (1811–1873). A British surgeon who entered the Bengal army in 1835. In 1842, during the First Afghan War [q.v.], he was severely wounded in the disastrous retreat from Kabul, but he was the only European to reach the safety of the British force under Sir Robert Sale [q.v.] at Jelalabad. He later returned to Kabul with the army of retribution [see Afghan Wars] under General George Pollock [q.v.]. Fifteen years later he was in Lucknow [q.v.] when it was besieged by mutineers, and he again survived. He returned to Scotland in 1859 and joined the Highland Rifles militia regiment (later 3rd Seaforth Highlanders).

Bubna von Litic / Bubna-Littitz, Count Ferdinand (1768–1825). An Austrian soldier who first campaigned against the Turks in 1788 and saw much service in the Napoleonic Wars [q.v.]. In 1809 he was promoted field marshal after the Battle of Wagram [q.v.]. He also served at the battles of Leipzig, Lützen, Bautzen, and Dresden [qq.v.]. In 1818 he was appointed governor of Lombardy.

Bucharest, Occupations of. This Rumanian city was occupied by Russian troops in 1828, 1848, and 1853–54 and by Austrian troops in 1854–57. In 1861 it became the capital of the new Rumania (Romania or Roumania). Between 1885 and 1896 fortifications with a perimeter of 48 miles were constructed around the town, but they failed to stop the Germans in 1916.

Buck and Ball. A cartridge for muskets containing one ball and several buckshot. An American invention, it was said to have been highly effective against the British in the War of 1812 in the Battle of Bladensburg [q.v.] on 24 August 1814, although obviously not effective enough. The British considered its use improper. During the American Civil War three buckshot behind a ball was a common load for Confederates with caliber .69 muskets.

Buck and Gag. A punishment used in the American and French armies in which arms were bound around drawn-up knees with a stick inserted under the knees and over the arms, and a gag, usually a tent peg or a bayonet, inserted crosswise in the mouth. [See Crapaudin.]

Buckland Mills, Engagement at (19 October 1863), American Civil War. A small affair in Northern Virginia in which Confederate cavalry under J. E. B. Stuart [q.v.] surprised and routed Union cavalry under Hugh Judson Kilpatrick [q.v.]. The Confederates called their pursuit the Buckland Races and claimed to have captured 250, but Kilpatrick reported only 150 lost. This was the last significant engagement in the Bristoe Campaign [q.v.].

Buckner, Simon Bolivar (1823–1914). An American soldier who was graduated from West Point in 1844 and served in the Mexican War [q.v.], winning two brevets. He resigned in 1855. At the beginning of the American Civil

War he was the adjutant general of Kentucky. He was offered a general officer's commission by both belligerents but accepted the offer of neither until Federal troops entered Kentucky. On 14 September he then accepted an appointment as a brigadier general in the Confederate army. He commanded a division during Braxton Bragg's [q.v.] invasion of Kentucky [q.v.] and fought at Perryville [q.v.] on 8 October 1863. He fortified Mobile, Alabama (December 1862–April 1863), and then led a corps at Chickamauga [q.v.]. On 20 September he became a lieutenant general and served as chief of staff to Edmund Kirby-Smith [q.v.]. After the war he became a newspaper editor, and in 1887 he was elected governor of Kentucky.

Buckshot. Lead shot usually 160 to 170 to a pound. They were usually made by molding or compression.

Buckshots. See Molly McGuires.

Bucktails. Popular name of the 13th Pennsylvania Reserves in the American Civil War. The regiment was recruited in April 1861 from among woodsmen who were excellent shots and carried their own rifles. Each prospective recruit was required to bring the tail of a buck he had shot as proof of his musketry skills. The tails were then worn pinned to their caps. The regiment was later equipped with Sharps rifles [q.v.] and still later with Spencer repeating carbines [q.v.]. It saw much action throughout the war; two of its colonels were killed in battle.

Budapest, Occupation of (5 January 1849), Hungarian Revolution. The Hungarian capital was captured by Austrian General Alfred von Windisch-Graetz, who drove the Hungarian general Arthur von Görgey [qq.v.] into the mountains north of Budapest. Because Görgey had broken with the revolutionary leader Lajos Kossuth (1802–1894), Henryk Dembiński [q.v.] took command of the Hungarian army, but he was soon defeated in the Battle of Káplona [q.v.].

Budge Barrel. A small copper-bound barrel with one end covered by a leather cap and drawstring. It was used to carry cartridges from magazines to siege batteries or to guns in forts.

Budissin / Baudissin, Battle of. See Bautzen, Battle of.

Buell, Don Carlos (1818–1898). An American officer who graduated 32nd out of 52 in the famous West Point class of 1841, which produced 20 general officers of the American Civil War. On graduation he was posted to the 3rd Infantry and fought against Indians in Florida and in the West. During the Mexican War [q.v.] he was severely wounded in the Battle of Churubusco [q.v.] and won brevets to captain and major. For the next thirteen years he served as a staff officer. In 1861, when the Civil War broke out, he was a lieutenant colonel and adjutant of the Department of the Pacific in San Francisco.

He went to Washington as a brigadier general of volunteers. After U. S. Grant captured Fort Donelson and Fort Henry [qq.v.], Buell led 50,000 men to Nashville without opposition.

On the first day of the Battle of Shiloh [q.v.] on 6 April 1862, he arrived just in time to counter the Confederate assault and save Grant from almost certain defeat. On 22 March 1862 he was promoted major general of volunteers, and in June he advanced to Chattanooga [q.v.] under continual harassment by Confederate cavalry.

In September he moved into Kentucky to counter the invasion by Braxton Bragg and Edmund Kirby-Smith [qq.v.]. He entered Louisville unopposed and on 8 October fought the inconclusive Battle of Perryville [q.v.]. Bragg retreated, and Buell slowly followed. Too slowly, it was thought, and on 30 October he was relieved of his command. After waiting more than a year for a new assignment, he resigned both his volunteer and his regular commission in the summer of 1864. Although Grant recommended his restoration to duty, he was not recommissioned.

Buell was a skillful administrator, organizer, and logistician; he had also shown himself an able, if not brilliant, commander. However, he neglected to take account of the political realities of civil wars. He had a southern wife, he was a friend of George McClellan [q.v.], and his political views were inimical to those of the Republican administration.

After the war he operated a foundry and a coal mine in Kentucky, and from 1885 to 1889 he was a government pension agent.

Buena Vista, Battle of (22–23 February 1847), Mexican War. Near this hacienda in northeastern Mexico, eight miles south of Saltillo, General Zachary Taylor [q.v.] with 4,650 men, only 500 of whom were regulars, was attacked by a Mexican force variously estimated between 15,000 and 22,000 under Antonio López de Santa Anna [q.v.]. Taylor's force was deployed on a series of hills rising from a sunbaked plain. When Santa Anna sent a Prussian officer on his staff to demand his surrender, Taylor's response was: "Go to hell!"

On the afternoon of 22 February there was skirmishing. The main battle on the following day was one of the hardest fought in the war. A regiment of Indiana volunteers blunted a Mexican attack and fought bravely for more than half an hour, but when ordered to withdraw, the men broke and ran. The day was saved by the arrival on the field of the artillery and the Mississippi Rifles, commanded by Colonel Jefferson Davis [q.v.], whose deceased wife had been Taylor's daughter. Taylor is said to have ordered his gunners to "double-shot your guns and give 'em hell!"

The battle was a close-run affair. When Mexican lancers threatened Taylor's rear, he ordered Colonel Davis to stop them. Davis did so with "an appalling fire," then led his

Buena Vista *Charge of Mexican lancers at the Battle of Buena Vista*

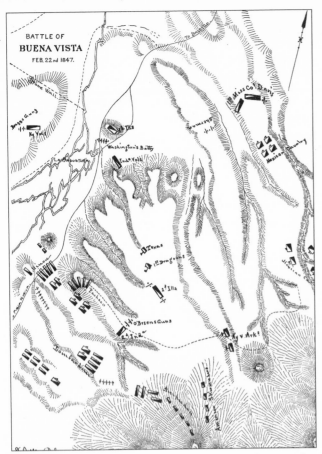

Buena Vista *Map of the Battle of Buena Vista, 22 February 1847*

Mississippians in an attack, shouting, "For the honor of Mississippi and George Washington. . . ." The Mexicans were routed.

Among the American heroes were Colonel Davis, who, wounded and bleeding profusely, refused to leave the field, and artillery Captain and Brevet Major Braxton Bragg [q.v.], who at one point reported that he would have to retreat or lose his guns. "Captain Bragg, it is better to lose a battery than a battle," Taylor said. In reply Bragg's guns "belched forth a storm of iron which prostrated everything in its front."

Taylor, who had vehemently objected to his daughter's marriage to Davis, now greeted him after the battle with "Sir, my daughter was a far better judge of men than I."

Santa Anna retreated the next morning with a loss of 825 dead and 1,360 wounded; the Americans lost 264 killed, 456 wounded, and 23 missing. This battle ended the war in the northern theater, and Santa Anna moved south.

Buenos Aires, British Expedition to (1806–08). Admiral Sir Home Riggs Popham (1762–1820) was in Cape Town when in April 1806 he was told by an American sea captain that the inhabitants of Montevideo and Buenos Aires were groaning under a tyrannical government and would welcome British soldiers as liberators. Borrowing from General David Baird 1,200 soldiers under Colonel William Carr Beresford [qq.v.], Popham sailed for South America and reached the Rio de la Plata in mid-June. He landed his troops and 400 marines near Buenos Aires and on 27 June easily captured the city. He then sailed away to announce the victories in England. The small British force under Beresford left behind was attacked by local militia and citizen volunteers under Santiago de Liniers [q.v.], and Beresford was forced to surrender. British losses were about 250 killed and wounded; Beresford with 1,300 men was taken prisoner. On 12 August Buenos Aires was retaken by the Spanish. British reinforcements were sent out under Sir Samuel Auchmuty [q.v.], who arrived with 4,800 men but was unable to recapture the city. However, he did successfully storm Montevideo on 3 February 1807, although with a loss of 600 men.

The British made a second attempt to liberate Buenos Aires. A force of 7,822 men and 16 guns under Lieutenant General John Whitelocke (1757–1833) landed 30 miles below the city on 28–29 June and marched on it. On 2 July 1807 it drove in Spanish outposts, and advanced elements occupied a southern suburb.

Buenos Aires was then a city of about 70,000 with a garrison of some 6,000. It was unfortified, but the streets were barricaded. The Spanish forces of some 30,000 militia, partisans, and guerrilleros were again commanded by Liniers. At six-thirty on the morning of 5 July the British attacked the town and encountered stout resistance. The British lost 2,500, of whom 1,676 were prisoners.

The following morning Liniers proposed a cease-fire and an exchange of prisoners if Whitelocke would agree to evacuate Buenos Aires and Montevideo within two months. If his terms were not accepted, Liniers warned that he could not be responsible for the safety of his prisoners. To the disgust of his soldiers, Whitelocke accepted the terms. A bitter toast went

Buenos Aires *The taking of Buenos Aires by the British, 1806*

round in officers' messes: "Success to grey hairs, but bad luck to white locks."

Back in England in January 1809 Whitelocke was court-martialed, found guilty of having been "deficient in zeal, judgment and personal exertion," and cashiered.

Buff. In the American army, the leather, usually buffalo hide, from which belts and certain accoutrements were made.

Buffalo Soldiers. The name given by American Indians to black soldiers in the American army, perhaps because their hair reminded them of the curly hair on the heads of buffaloes. It was a name the black soldiers proudly accepted. (In the last session of the 101st Congress in 1991, 28 July was declared to be Buffalo Soldiers Day.) The most famous regiments of buffalo soldiers were the 9th and 10th Cavalry and the 24th and 25th Infantry. [See Black Troops in the U.S. Army.]

Buffalo Soldiers *Buffalo Soldiers during the Indian Wars, by Frederic Remington*

Buffington, Adelbert Rinaldo (1837–1922). An American officer who was graduated from West Point in 1856 and, with William Crozier [q.v.], invented the Buffington-Crozier disappearing gun carriage. On 5 April 1899 he became a brigadier general and chief of ordnance.

Buford, Abraham (1820–1884). An American soldier of a military family who during the American Civil War became a brigadier general in the Confederate army while two of his cousins were generals in the Union army.

He was graduated from West Point in the class of 1841 and during the Mexican War was brevetted for his gallantry in the Battle of Buena Vista [q.v.]. During the American Civil War he was appointed a Confederate brigadier general to rank from 2 September 1862. He took part in the Vicksburg Campaign [q.v.] and commanded a cavalry brigade in Nathan Bedford Forrest's [q.v.] cavalry corps until Forrest's surrender at Selma, Alabama, in April 1865.

After the war he raised racehorses and served in the Kentucky legislature. After suffering financial reverses, he committed suicide.

Buford, John (1826–1863). An American soldier who was the half brother of Union General Napoleon Buford and a cousin of Confederate General Abraham Buford [qq.v.]. He was graduated from West Point in 1848 and commissioned into the 1st Dragoons. He served on the western frontier and took part in General William Harney's [q.v.] punitive expedition against the Sioux in retaliation for the Grattan Massacre [q.v.] and in Albert S. Johnston's [q.v.] expedition against the Mormons in Utah [see Utah Expedition].

In 1862, during the American Civil War, he was appointed a Union brigadier general of volunteers in John Pope's Army of Virginia [q.v.]. He was severely wounded at Second Bull Run [q.v.], but in September he was appointed chief of cavalry for the Army of the Potomac [q.v.]. Major General John Gibbon [q.v.] said of him: "John Buford was the best cavalryman I ever saw." He took part in Stoneman's Raid and commanded a division at Gettysburg [qq.v.], where he greatly distinguished himself.

In November 1863 he was stricken with typhoid fever, and he died on 16 December. His commission as major general was presented to him as he lay on his deathbed.

Buford, Napoleon Bonaparte (1807–1883). An American officer who, like his half brother John and his cousin Abraham [qq.v.], was a West Pointer (class of 1827). All three became generals, he and his half brother in the Union army, his cousin in the Confederate army.

After serving eight years as an artillery lieutenant, he resigned in 1835 to go into business. By 1861 and the beginning of the American Civil War he was bankrupt, but he raised the 27th Illinois and was elected its colonel. On 15 April 1862 he was promoted a brigadier general and fought at Belmont, in the campaign against Island No. 10, at Corinth, and in the early battles of the Vicksburg Campaign [qq.v.]. In 1865 he was made a brevet major general. After the war he held several federal appointments.

Bugeaud de la Piconnerie, Thomas Robert, Duc d'Isly (1784–1849). A French soldier who came from a petite noblesse family so poor that he was reared to be a field hand. He enlisted as a common soldier in 1804 and served in Napoleon's Garde Impériale [q.v.]. He was commissioned in 1806 and served in the Peninsular War [q.v.], where he distinguished himself at the sieges of Saragossa and Pomplona [qq.v.]. He rallied to Napoleon during the Hundred Days [q.v.] and then left the army.

In September 1830 he was restored in rank as a colonel, and on 31 April 1831 he was appointed *maréchal de camp* (brigadier general). Soon after he was elected to the Chamber of Deputies. In April 1834 he directed the harsh repression of the insurrection in Paris. Later that year he killed in a duel a young man who had criticized him.

He made his name in North Africa, where he served from 1836 to 1847, being appointed governor of Algeria in 1840. He waged ruthless, ferocious campaigns against Arabs who rebelled against the expanding French Empire in North Africa, particularly Abd el-Kader [q.v.], whom he finally decisively defeated in the Battle of Isly [q.v.] on 4 August 1844. During his tenure he annexed most of Algeria north of the Sahara. In 1843 he was made a marshal of France. After the French disaster at Sidi Brahim [q.v.], Morocco, on 22 September 1845 he again took the field and was almost constantly on campaign until July 1846. Sacked in 1847, he returned and commanded the army in Paris during the Revolution of 1848 [q.v.]. He was then appointed commander of the Army of the Alps but soon after died of cholera.

Bugle. A treble brass wind instrument, originally without valves, used to sound orders. [See Bugle Calls.]

Bugle Calls. In the course of the nineteenth century bugles gradually replaced drums as instruments for sounding orders. Because absence of valves restricted the bugle to one key, C major, and usually to five notes, the bugle calls in various countries tended to resemble one another. The American and French bugle calls for reveille [q.v.] are identical, and the same call can often have different meanings in different armies. Thus the regimental call of the British 14th Hussars was identical to the American fire call. Varieties of calls increased with the invention of the valved bugle. In the American army there were sixty-seven calls in use by 1880; perhaps the best known is taps [q.v.].

Bugle Calls *A bugle call during the American Civil War*

Buglers. See Drummers and Buglers.

Bukhara / Bokhara, Conquest of (1886–1888). In 1886 a Russian army invaded Bukhara (today a province of Uzbekistan) and crushed the forces of the amir. In 1888 the Russians entered Samarkand and forced the amir to sign a treaty that placed the country under Russian domination.

Bukors. Kettledrums of Swedish cavalry.

Bulawayo, Battle of. See Matabele-Mashona War.

Bulgaria, Invasion of (June–July 1877). During the Russo-Turkish War of 1877–78 [q.v.], a Russian force of thirty-one squadrons of cavalry, ten battalions of infantry, and 32 guns under General Ossip (Joseph) V. Gourko [q.v.] crossed the Danube on 23 June 1877. The main Russian army followed. Because the Shipka Pass, the main pass through the Balkan Mountains in central Bulgaria, was strongly held by the Turks, Gourko shifted his forces east and crossed by way of a smaller, undefended pass, a move that forced the retreat of the Turks [see Shipka Pass, Battle of].

Bulgarian Atrocities. In May 1876 Turkish bashi-bazouks [q.v.] massacred more than 12,000 Bulgarian Christians. The massacres, first reported by American journalist Januarius MacGahan [q.v.], aroused intense anti-Turkish feeling throughout Europe and the United States. [See Bulgarian Revolts.]

Bulgarian Legion. A unit in the Russian army formed in 1877 from volunteers of Bulgarian descent living in Bucharest and Ploesti, led by Russian officers.

Bulgarian Mutiny (March 1887). On 1 March 1887 a mutiny at Silistra against Turkish rule was suppressed the next day, but on 3 March troops mutinied at Rustchuk (Ruse) on the Danube River, 40 miles south of Bucharest. Although it was put down the next day by militia and volunteers, and several ringleaders were shot, Sofia was in a state of siege until relative calm returned at the end of the month. Unease remained, however, and in June 1890, 9 officers were court-martialed, and 1 was sentenced to be shot. Even so, mutineers, supported by many civilians, were not completely quelled until the end of September. Bulgaria was not completely independent of Turkey until 1908.

Bulgarian Revolts (May–September 1876). Sparked by uprisings in Bosnia and Herzegovina, the Bulgarians staged an abortive revolt against Turkish rule that was suppressed with great brutality. In May 1876 bashi-bazouks under Achmet Agha massacred 1,000 Bulgarians who had taken refuge in a church at Batak, a town in southern Bulgaria in the West Rhodope Mountains on a branch of the Maritsa River (today a summer resort). Some 15,000 were reportedly massacred near Philippopolis (Plovdiv) on the Maritsa River north of the Rhodope Mountains. Five monasteries and fifty-eight villages were destroyed. The Bulgarian Atrocities [q.v.] outraged the rest of Europe. The full horror of the massacres was disclosed in vivid dispatches by Januarius MacGahan [q.v.], an American war correspondent, upon whose tomb in New Lexington, Ohio, is inscribed "Liberator of Bulgaria."

Russia, ever eager to attack Turkey, mobilized. In Britain there were protest meetings, and William Ewart Gladstone (1809–1898) railed against the "unspeakable Turk," publishing a widely read pamphlet, *Bulgarian Horrors and the Question of the East*. At the conclusion of the Russo-Turkish War [q.v.] of 1877–78 an autonomous Bulgarian principality (including most of Macedonia) was created by the Treaty of San Stefano on 3 March 1878. On 13 July the Congress of Berlin reduced Bulgaria to less than half the size recognized by the treaty; parts of Macedonia were given to Serbia, but most remained with Turkey, and a large part of Thrace was formed into an autonomous Turkish province known as Eastern Rumelia, which Bulgaria annexed, over Serbia's objections, on 13 November 1885 after an émeute. Bulgaria did not attain complete independence until 1908. [See Balkan Revolts.]

Bulgarian-Serbian War. See Serbo-Bulgarian War.

Buller, Redvers Henry (1839–1908). A British soldier who was commissioned at age nineteen and saw service in India, the Third Opium War [q.v.] in China, and in Canada. He attracted the attention of Garnet Wolseley during the Red River Expedition [q.v.] and became a member of the Wolseley Gang [q.v.]. He accompanied Wolseley in 1873 to West Africa for the Second Ashanti War [q.v.] and in 1879 to Zululand [see Zulu War], where he won the Victoria Cross [q.v.]. During the First Anglo-Boer War [q.v.] in 1881 he served as chief of staff to Sir Evelyn Wood [q.v.], another member of the Wolseley Gang. He took part in the Gordon Relief Expedition [q.v.] and in 1896 was promoted general.

At the outbreak of the Second Anglo-Boer War [q.v.] in 1899 he was appointed commander-in-chief of the British army in South Africa. Young Winston Churchill described him at this time: "Buller was a characteristic British personality. He looked stolid. He said little, and what he said was obscure." His attempt to relieve General Sir George White [q.v.], besieged in Ladysmith [q.v.], Natal, failed. He suffered defeat in the battles of Colenso, Spion Kop, and Vaal Kranz [qq.v.]. After Black Week [q.v.] he was superseded as commander-in-chief by Lord Roberts, but before Roberts could reach South Africa from England, Buller finally had succeeded in relieving Ladysmith.

He returned to England in 1901 and took command at Aldershot [q.v.]. There he became involved in a press dispute, speaking out when he should have held his tongue, and was relieved of his command in October of that year.

Bullet. A projectile fired from small arms, originally round and designated by the number required to make a pound. Although in 1742 it was proved that a conical form was superior, it was not until about 1840 that round bullets were abandoned.

Diverse bullets used by the French, 1870s–90s

Bullet, Explosive. See Dumdum Bullets.

Bullet Extractor. Pincers with claws that, embedded in a bullet, enabled it to be extracted from a bore.

Bulletins of the Army. After the Battle of Marengo [q.v.] on 14 June 1800, Napoleon's first victory as first consul, he began the practice of sending bulletins, some personally dictated, detailing his progress and victories to *Le Moniteur* [q.v.], which was in effect the government's official journal. It was distributed throughout France and throughout the army. On 17 December 1805, in an account of the Battle of Austerlitz [q.v.] *Le Moniteur* reported that a "radiant sun" had looked down upon "one of the century's most valiant deeds of arms on the anniversary of the Emperor's coronation."

Bulletin 19, written on 2 December 1812 at the end of Napoleon's Russian Campaign [q.v.] and published on 17 December, revealed for the first time the hideous losses suffered by the Grande Armée in its retreat from Moscow. It concluded: "His Majesty's health has never been better."

Bullet Probe. An elongated surgical instrument, called a sound, was used to find a bullet in a body. It was usually a soft steel wire with a bulbous extremity.

Bull Run, Battles of. Confederate name: battles of Manassas, but see Battle of Blackburn's Ford. Two major battles of the American Civil War were fought in northeastern Virginia about 25 miles west of Washington.

First Bull Run (21 July 1861). Because the Union army was largely composed of untrained volunteers, senior officers advised against an immediate offensive in Virginia. However, because almost all the volunteers were in three-month regiments [q.v.] and in mid-July their enlistments were about to expire, Brigadier General Irvin McDowell [q.v.] was ordered to attack the Confederates under Pierre Beauregard [q.v.] positioned around Manassas Junction.

McDowell's advance, begun on 15 July, was slow, and it was 18 July before he reached Centreville, about six miles north of Manassas, with his army of 20,000. Had he attacked at once, he would probably have achieved a victory, but there were logistical and disciplinary problems with his green troops. While McDowell loitered, the authorities in Richmond ordered Joseph Johnston to move his 12,000-man army, then near Harpers Ferry, to Manassas to join Beauregard. Johnston managed to get the bulk of his army into action before the battle was over by putting them aboard trains. This was the first use of trains by any army to achieve strategic mobility.

McDowell planned to attack the left flank of the Confederate line; Beauregard planned to attack the left flank of the Union army. The two armies might have moved in a giant turning ballet had not Confederate Lieutenant Colonel (later Brigadier General) Nathan ("Shanks") Evans, warned by signals from Captain Edward Porter Alexander [qq.v.], acted promptly to delay the advancing Federals until Confederate forces could be shifted to meet them.

When Johnston arrived on the field, although senior in rank to Beauregard, he permitted Beauregard to act as battlefield commander while he worked to keep him supplied with troops and ammunition. His troops, arriving a trainload at a time, were shoved at once into the defensive line. Among them was a brigade under Thomas Jackson, who here earned the nickname Stonewall for himself and his brigade.

The battle was hard fought on both sides, but as Johnston later pointed out, when both sides consist of raw, untrained troops, the side on the defensive has the advantage. William Tecumseh Sherman in his *Memoirs* (1875) said of the battle: "It was one of the best-planned battles of the war, but one of the worst-fought." At about four o'clock in the afternoon the

Bull Run *Burnside and Rhode Island volunteers attack Confederate batteries at First Bull Run.*

Federal line began to give way, and the retreat soon became a rout. McDowell failed to rally his men at Centreville, and his defeated troops streamed into Washington, D.C., along with the civilians who had brought picnic baskets to enjoy the battle. The Confederates, who could at this time have captured Washington and perhaps ended the war, failed to pursue.

Of 28,452 Federal troops engaged, an estimated 418 were killed, 1,011 were wounded, and 1,216 were missing for a total of 2,645, according to one reliable source (Livermore, see Selected Bibliography), but others give higher figures (see Casualties]. Confederate strength was 32,232, of whom an estimated 387 were killed, 1,582 wounded and 12 missing, for a total of 1,981. Three days after the battle more than 1,000 wounded were still on the ground; five days after the battle there were still 600; some were not collected for a week.

Second Bull Run (29–30 August 1862). Although Lee had only 55,000 men to face John Pope's 75,000 Federals across the Rappahannock River, he decided to divide his army, and on 25 August he sent Brigadier General Thomas Jackson with 24,000 men, nearly half of his army, including the cavalry of J. E. B. Stuart [q.v.], on a bold giant swing around the right of the Union army. By the night of 26 August Jackson's victorious and hungry men were devouring the edible and potable supplies at the Union's huge supply depot at Manassas Junction; what could not be eaten or carried away was burned or broken.

On 28 August Jackson launched a surprise attack upon a Federal column at Groveton [q.v.], a settlement no longer in existence, about five miles west of Manassas. He then took up strong defensive positions in a railroad cutting from which Pope, with 62,000 men, in a series of badly coordinated piecemeal attacks, failed to dislodge him. About eleven o'clock in the morning on 29 August Lee arrived with James Longstreet's [q.v.] corps and took position on Jackson's right but did not attack. That night Jackson pulled back, leading Pope to think he was retreating.

On the morning of 30 August the Federals, still unaware of Longstreet's presence, launched a strong attack. When Pope's attack was under way, Lee sent Longstreet against the Union left flank, and the Federals fell back with heavy losses. A complete rout was prevented by some Federal units who furnished a strong rear guard.

Union losses have been estimated (Phisterer, see Selected Bibliography) at 7,800; Confederate losses at 3,700.

Bullseye Canteen. A round U.S. army canteen made of tin with nine concentric pressed rings on its side. Although hundreds of thousands were manufactured between 1862 and 1865, it was found that the rings, designed to add strength to the seam area, failed to do so.

Bully Soup. See Panda.

Bulnes, Manuel (1799–1866). A Chilean soldier and politician who commanded the Chilean army in the Battle of Yungay [q.v.] on 20 January 1839, defeating the army of the Peru-Bolivian Confederation under Andrés Santa Cruz [q.v.]. Bulnes was president of Chile for two terms from 1841 to 1851. [See Peru-Bolivian Confederation, War of.]

Bülow, Baron Friedrich Wilhelm von, Count Bülow von Dennewitz (1755–1816). A Prussian soldier of distinguished ancestry who fought in the Napoleonic Wars. He entered the army in 1768 and served in the Rhine campaigns of 1792–95 and the campaign against Napoleon in 1805–06. He became a lieutenant general and commanded a division in 1813. He won several victories over the French, notably at Luckau [q.v.], where, on 23 August 1813, he

Bull Run *Confederate fortifications at First Bull Run, by Harry Fenn*

defeated Nicolas Oudinot [q.v.], and at Grossbeeren [q.v.], where, on 6 September, he defeated Michel Ney [q.v.]. He served with distinction at Leipzig in October and the following year at Laon [qq.v.]. His arrival with a corps at 4:00 P.M. on 18 June 1815 near Waterloo [q.v.] in a position to cut Napoleon's retreat was a crucial element in Napoleon's defeat.

Bulwark. 1. A bastion or rampart.
2. Any shelter that offers protection from an enemy.

Bumf. British army slang for unnecessary paperwork. During the Second Anglo-Boer War many line officers considered all intelligence reports bumf. The term came from British public schoolboy slang: bum-fodder for toilet tissue.

Bummers. 1. A deserter.
2. Union foragers and looters during William Tecumseh Sherman's [q.v.] March to the Sea [q.v.], were often called Sherman's bummers.
3. Shirkers, perhaps from the German *Bummler* (loafer); a hospital bummer was one who pretended to be sick.

Bummer's Roost. American slang for a place behind the battleline where cooks, doctors, chaplains, and other noncombatants stayed. [See Bummers.]

Buonaparte, Napoleone. Original name of Napoleon Bonaparte [see Napoleon I].

Bureau. A large administrative service unit of an army, e.g., Bureau of Ordnance.

Bureaux des Affaires Arabes. A military and civil organization established in Algeria in 1844 by Thomas Bugeaud de la Piconnerie [q.v.] that employed the best officers in the Armée d'Afrique [q.v.]. They functioned as intelligence gatherers and administrators, protecting Arabs from rapacious French colonists attempting to develop commerce and industry at their expense. They were also most useful in helping to suppress Arab revolts.

Burgo / Burgoo. Originally an oatmeal gruel. The name came to be applied to a mixture of molasses and hardtack cooked together or to any thick highly seasoned soup or stew. In 1863 in the Confederate States of America it was the name given to a thick meat and vegetable stew created by Gus Jaubert of Lexington, Kentucky. When available, chicken, small game animals, tomatoes, corn, onions, or other vegetables were added to it.

Burgos, Sieges of (19 September–22 October 1812 and 10–12 June 1813), Napoleonic Wars. This ancient city in north-central Spain, 132 miles north of Madrid, controlled part of the important highway linking Madrid and southern France. In 1808 Napoleon ordered the fortifications strengthened. After the Battle of Salamanca [q.v.] on 22 July 1812, Wellington marched to Madrid and then north to Burgos and laid siege to the town, which was defended by a French garrison of 2,000 under General of Brigade Jean Louis Dubreton (1773–1855).

On 20 September the great hornwork [q.v.] was carried by a coup de main and several mines were exploded, allowing the

Allies to penetrate the lower levels of the main fortress, but the French successfully withstood the siege. Wellington was hampered by a shortage of siege artillery and by heavy rains that flooded his saps. When French relief forces began to assemble north of the town, he launched a final unsuccessful assault on 18 October. Three days later he abandoned the siege. Allied casualties were about 2,000; the French lost 623.

The following summer, just before the Battle of Vitoria [q.v.] on 21 June 1813, another Allied assault was launched against the town. This time it submitted after only two days.

Burgoyne, John Fox (1782–1871). A British soldier, the illegitimate son of General Sir John Burgoyne (1722–1792), who distinguished himself as a brilliant military engineer. He was commissioned at the age of sixteen and in 1800 served in the Mediterranean. In 1807 he served in the Egyptian Campaign. The following year he was with Sir John Moore in Sweden and then in Portugal. He served with distinction throughout the Peninsular War, and in 1813, after the Battle of Vitoria [q.v.] on 21 June, he became Wellington's chief engineer. In the War of 1812 [q.v.] he served at Mobile and in the Battle of New Orleans [q.v.].

He became a lieutenant general in 1851 and was principal engineer in the Crimea [see Crimean War]. For twenty years he was inspector of fortifications. In 1865 he was appointed constable of the Tower of London, and when he resigned in 1868, he was made a field marshal. He died on 7 October 1871, a year after the death of his only son, Captain Hugh Talbot Burgoyne, VC (1833–1870), who was in command of the HMS *Captain* when it sank in the Bay of Biscay.

Burkes Station. See Ream's Station.

Burleigh, Bennet (1840?–1914). A soldier and a war correspondent who, although a British subject, first saw action as a soldier in the Union army during the American Civil War, in which he was twice captured and threatened with execution. As a war correspondent he covered many wars and revolutions, including in 1884 the Suakim Campaign in the Sudan, where he was the first to report on the disaster at El Teb [q.v.]. He accompanied the Gordon Relief Expedition and was wounded in the Battle of Abu Klea [qq.v.]. He was mentioned in dispatches for his part in this battle, the first British war correspondent to be so honored. He covered Lord Kitchener's [q.v.] campaign for the reconquest of the Sudan [q.v.] in 1896–98 for the *London Daily Telegraph*.

Burley. The butt end of a lance.

Burlington Heights, Battle of (5 May 1813), War of 1812. Also known as the Battle of Fort Meigs in Ohio. A British force of 500 regulars, 450 militia, and some 1,500 Indians under Tecumseh [q.v.], with two 24-pounder guns that had been captured at Detroit, all under Colonel Henry Procter, reached Fort Meigs on 12 April. The American fort, made of dirt and logs, sat on a bluff overlooking the rapids of the Maumee River in northwestern Ohio and commanded the best land route to Detroit. By the time Procter dragged his heavy guns into position, it was 1 May.

The garrison of the fort numbered only 1,100 men, commanded by Major General William Henry Harrison [q.v.], the future president of the United States, but reinforcements—

1,200 Kentucky militia under Brigadier General Green Clay (1757–1826)—were expected soon. On 5 May the first regiment of Clay's force arrived, surprised the besiegers, spiked the guns, and abandoned them to chase Indians.

Procter organized his troops and fought a pitched battle in which more than 200 Kentucky militia lost their lives and 500 were taken prisoner; only 170 escaped. The British lost about 50 killed and wounded plus some uncounted Indians.

The American prisoners suffered at least 20 killed and many more wounded when their Indian captors tried to club them to death. Procter did not interfere, but Tecumseh, scornfully calling Procter a squaw, put a stop to the massacre. This was not the last time Procter allowed his prisoners to be killed. [See Raisin River Massacre.]

When the remainder of Clay's force reached Fort Meigs on 9 May, Procter packed up and left, unhindered by Harrison. The Indians, loaded with scalps and booty, had already faded into the forest.

Burlington Hospital. In the first year of the War of 1812 [q.v.] Dr. Joseph Lovell [q.v.] established a large military hospital at Burlington, Vermont, that was a model for its day. Without the benefit of microbiology and long before the bacteriological age, emphasis was placed upon cleanliness, ventilation, and isolation of febrile patients. In the first four months of 1814 there were 2,412 admissions and only 75 deaths.

Burmese Wars. See Anglo-Burmese Wars.

Burnaby, Frederick Gustavus (1842–1885). A British soldier and traveler, said to be the strongest man in the British army, who stood six feet four inches tall. He joined the Royal Horse Guards in 1859. In 1875 he traveled with General Charles ("Chinese") Gordon [q.v.] in the Sudan, and that winter he traveled across the Russian steppes on horseback. He published an account of his hazardous journey the following year (*A Ride to Khiva*). He had a remarkable gift for languages, and in 1877 he commanded a brigade in the Turkish army during the Russo-Turkish War [q.v.]. In 1882 he crossed the English Channel to Normandy in a balloon. In 1884 he accompanied Pasha Baker's [q.v.] disastrous campaign in the eastern Sudan and in the Battle of El Teb [q.v.] fought off Dervish warriors with a double-barreled shotgun. He was killed in action at Abu Klea [q.v.] on 17 January 1885 during the Gordon Relief Expedition [q.v.].

Burnham, Frederick Russell (1861–1947). An American soldier and adventurer who fought Indians in the West and in 1893 distinguished himself as a scout in South Africa during the First Matabele War [q.v.]. He played some part in the Second Matabele War [q.v.] of 1896, and he won the DSO as chief scout for the British army during the Second Anglo-Boer War [q.v.]. He was captured once during that war but escaped. After the war he developed oilfields in California and led an expedition to the Volta River in Africa. He was instrumental in establishing the Boy Scouts of America and became famous as Scout Burnham.

Burns, Alexander (1805–1841). A British soldier and explorer who came to be known as Bokhara Burns after a hazardous trip through Afghanistan to Bokhara, which he reached on 27 June 1832. He took a prominent part in the First Afghan War [q.v.] before he was hacked to death by a fanatical Afghan mob in Kabul.

Burns, John (1789–1872). An American soldier known as "The Old Hero of Gettysburg." He was said to have fought in the War of 1812, the Seminole Wars, and the Mexican War [qq.v.]. At the time of the American Civil War he was a cobbler in Gettysburg, Pennsylvania. He was seventy-four years old when the Battle of Gettysburg began, but on the first day (1 July 1863), carrying his flintlock musket, he joined the fight beside the 7th Wisconsin and later fought in the ranks of the 150th Pennsylvania. In the course of the battle he was three times wounded and once captured and threatened with hanging as a combatant without uniform or insignia.

He was lionized by the Union press. Lincoln met him when he came to Gettysburg to dedicate the cemetery there on 19 November 1863. He was honored by a lengthy poem by Bret Harte (1836–1902), a part of which reads:

> He was the fellow who won renown,—
> The only fellow who didn't back down
> When the rebels rode through his native town;
> But held his own in the fight next day
> When all his townsfolk ran away.

In 1903 a monument was raised in his honor on the battlefield.

Burnside, Ambrose Everett (1824–1881). An American officer who was a tailor's apprentice before receiving an appointment to West Point (class of 1847) at the age of nineteen. He served as an artillery officer during the occupation of Mexico City at the end of the Mexican War [q.v.] and then was stationed in the West, where he was slightly wounded fighting Apaches in 1849.

In 1853 he resigned his commission and established the Bristol Firearms Company in Bristol, Rhode Island, to manufacture a breech-loading carbine he had invented. Only 250

Burnside *General Ambrose Burnside with his famous sideburns*

were manufactured, and the company went bankrupt in 1857. (His creditors reorganized it as the Burnside Arms Company and during the Civil War turned out 22 million rounds of ammunition and 55,567 Burnside carbines of a somewhat improved character.)

Burnside's friend George McClellan [q.v.] found him a job with the Illinois Central Railroad, where he rose to be treasurer. In 1861, at the beginning of the Civil War, he recruited the 1st Rhode Island Infantry, a three-month regiment [q.v.] that was the first to march into Washington.

After First Bull Run, where he commanded a brigade, he was promoted on 6 August 1861 to brigadier general of volunteers. In January he led a successful expedition to North Carolina [q.v.], and on 18 March he was promoted major general.

At Antietam [q.v.] he commanded two corps but proved too timid, even for McClellan. Nevertheless, in November he was chosen to succeed McClellan as commander of the Army of the Potomac [q.v.]. After failing miserably at Fredericksburg [q.v.], he attempted a flank attack upon Lee's Army of Northern Virginia. This aborted movement, known as the Mud March [q.v.], undertaken in spite of the opposition of most of his senior generals, proved to be his last move as commander of the Army of the Potomac. He was replaced by Joseph Hooker [q.v.] and given command of a new Army of Ohio. In Ohio, after successfully stopping John Hunt Morgan's [q.v.] raid, he marched his army south and ably defended Knoxville from attacks by James Longstreet [q.v.]. In the spring of 1864, in command of a corps, he took part in Grant's Overland Campaign and the siege of Petersburg [q.v.]. When a court of inquiry found him accountable for the failure of the Federal mine at Petersburg, he resigned on 15 April 1865.

In his memoirs Grant described him as "an officer who was generally liked and respected. He was not, however, fitted to command an army. No one knew this better than himself."

After the war Burnside prospered in business and was three times elected governor of Rhode Island. In 1871 he organized and became the first president of the National Rifle Association of America. In 1874 he was elected a U.S. senator and commander of the Grand Army of the Republic [q.v.].

His style of whiskers, by anagrammatization, became known as sideburns.

Burnside's North Carolina Expedition. See North Carolina Expedition, Burnside's.

Burnt Corn, Battle of (27 July 1813), First Creek War. In this first battle of the war, fought in Alabama at the confluence of Bashi Creek and the Tombigbee River, Creek warriors led by Jim Boy [q.v.] defeated a militia lieutenant colonel and 25 mounted men. The Creeks called the battle the Skirmish of Bashi Creek.

Burrel Shot. Nails, small shot, stones, small pieces of metal, etc. put into cases to be fired from muzzle-loaded guns. Sometimes called emergency shot.

Burroughs, Edgar Rice (1875–1950). An American writer who in his youth served in the U.S. cavalry and took part in operations against the Apaches until it was discovered that he was underage and he was discharged. His book *Tarzan of the Apes* and its many sequels made him famous.

Busa, Capture of (23 February 1897). French conquests in West Africa. French forces captured Busa, then the capital of Borgu, located in northern Nigeria on the Niger River at the rapids where explorer Mungo Park (1771–1806) drowned. Britain's vigorous protests were ignored.

Busaco. See Bussaco / Busaco, Battle of.

Busby. A small fur cap with a flat top. A cloth "bag," sometimes in the color or colors of the unit's facings, hung from its top on the left side. It was adopted by British rifle regiments in 1873, discontinued in 1878, and adopted again in 1890. Hussars and the Royal Horse Artillery also wore busbies, and the latter still do. The word is sometimes applied (incorrectly) to the bearskin [q.v.] worn by Foot Guards.

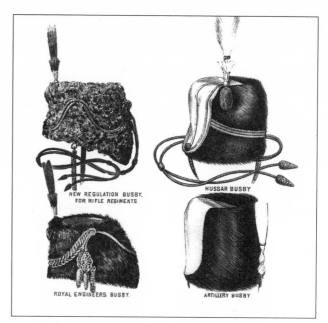

Busby *An assortment of busbies worn by fusiliers, hussars, Royal Engineers, artillery and rifle regiments*

Bushido. Literally, the way of the warrior. The Japanese code of chivalry, codified during the Tokugawa shogunate (1603–1868), that guided the life of the samurai [q.v.]. An ethic of complete loyalty and unhesitating sacrifice, it demanded of its adherents honor, bravery, self-sacrifice, discipline, duty, and loyalty to one's daimyo [q.v.], as well as the development of skill in the martial arts and in the handling of weapons. It was influenced by Zen Buddhism and Confucianism.

Bushire, Battles of (10 December 1856 and 18 January 1857), Anglo-Persian War. A British naval and military force attacked and captured this Persian port on the Persian Gulf for a loss of 9 killed and 36 wounded. In a subsequent battle on 18 January 1857 the 3rd Bombay Light Cavalry in a notable charge broke a well-formed Persian square.

Bushiri's Revolt (1888–90). A revolt of coastal Arab slave traders in German East Africa (now Tanzania), against the German East Africa Company, founded by Carl Peters (1856–1918), which ruled the colony. The revolt was begun by Bushiri bin Salim (d. 1889), a wealthy slave trader. In

December 1899 Hermann von Wissmann (1853–1905), a noted German explorer who had been appointed German commissioner in the colony, stormed Bagamoyo, a major port of the slave traders on the Indian Ocean, with 600 Sudanese troops. The Arabs were defeated, and Bushiri was hanged.

A joint German-British blockade that prevented the export of slaves and the import of guns and ammunition brought a complete end to the revolt.

Bushman's River Pass, Affair at (4 November 1873). Langalibalele [q.v.], chief of the Amahlubis in Natal, South Africa, was ordered to hand over to the government the rifles that his young men had acquired with money earned while working in the South African diamond mines. When he refused and threatened to take his tribe over the Drakensberg Mountains into Basutoland (Lesotho), a campaign was planned to force him to comply. Major Anthony William Durnford [q.v.], a Royal Engineers officer, was dispatched to lead a small force of 2 officers, 6 noncommissioned officers, 45 troopers of the Natal and the Karkloof Carbineers (untrained yeomanry), 25 mounted Basutos, and an interpreter to Bushman's River Pass (now called Langalibalele Pass) in the Drakensbergs, five miles north of Giant's Castle Pass.

After a difficult march, in which the pack animals carrying food and ammunition were lost, they reached the pass and encountered the tribesmen. Durnford, who had just dislocated a shoulder in a fall from his horse, was under orders not to shoot first, a fact the tribesmen soon discovered. Taunting the soldiers, they refused to obey his orders to disperse. As the number of tribesmen increased and their behavior grew increasingly hostile, Durnford attempted an orderly retreat, but his semitrained troopers turned it into a rout. They were saved from destruction largely by the gallant actions of the Basutos. Three carabineers, a Basuto, and the interpreter were killed.

Langalibalele and his tribe made good their escape into Basutoland, but four columns were later sent against him. On 11 December 1873 he and several of his chiefs were captured and brought back to Natal in chains. [See Langalibalele Rebellion.] He was tried and found guilty of treason and rebellion and exiled to Cape Town.

Bushwackers / Bushwhackers. Originally a term for American backwoodsmen, but during the American Civil War it came to mean guerrillas, usually Confederates, such as Quantrill's raiders [q.v.], who fought more for plunder than from patriotism. It was also applied to franc-tireurs [q.v.] who attacked by surprise from cover and quickly fled.

Bussaco / Busaco, Battle of (27 September 1810), Peninsular War. In September 1810 Wellington retired toward the prepared defenses of Torres Vedras [q.v.], 25 miles north of Lisbon, but he paused to deploy a force of 26,000 British and 25,000 Portuguese with 60 guns along a steep-sided ridge, 8 to 10 miles long, called Serra do Bussaco, astride the main Vizeu–Mealhada road 120 miles northeast of Lisbon. Many, perhaps most, of his men were concealed in positions that dominated the road and a nearby secondary road. There he was attacked by a French force of 65,974 men and 114 guns under André Masséna.

Masséna, "the spoilt child of victory," as Napoleon once called him, assuming that he was merely facing a rear guard, underestimated Wellington's strength and failed to make a careful reconnaissance. He also assumed that the Portuguese

troops would either flee or put up minimum resistance. The first of five French attacks began at 5:45 A.M. on 27 September with an attack upon the British right. The leading elements were almost at the crest of the ridge when they were thrown back by a bayonet charge. Two more French assaults were also repulsed and suffered heavy casualties.

Marshal Michel Ney [q.v.], commanding a corps on Masséna's right, was unaware of the failed assaults on his left when he launched his assault at 8:15 on the British left. It was at first successful. Robert Craufurd's [q.v.] Light Division fell back, and the French occupied the village of Sula, but here they were halted by rifle bullets and artillery fire from the British on the crest. The French then threw eleven battalions against the Portuguese in the center of the British line, but they were repulsed, suffering 1,200 casualties. There was scattered fighting until 4:00 P.M., when Masséna, without sending in his reserves, pulled back. Sagely, Wellington did not attempt a counterattack into the valley below him.

Allied casualties were 1,253, of whom 622 were Portuguese, who on this occasion fought well; French casualties totaled 4,486, including more than 250 officers, among them 5 generals killed or seriously wounded.

During the night Wellington pulled back toward Coimbra and then drew his men into the lines of Torres Vedras. By 10 October Masséna found the Allies too strong for him and retreated into winter quarters. After losing some 20,000 men to diseases and British hit-and-run tactics, he retreated into Spain in early 1811, leaving Portugal, except for Almeida, free of French forces.

Bust, to. To reduce in rank. A colloquial expression in both British and American armies from the late nineteenth century.

Bustamante, Anastasio (1780–1853). A Mexican soldier and politician who in 1808 fought in the Spanish army against the Mexican revolutionaries but in 1821 supported the revolt of Agustín de Iturbide [q.v.]. He briefly served as vice president under Vicente Guerrero [q.v.] in 1829, but united with Antonio López de Santa Anna [q.v.] to lead a successful revolt against him. He then became president of Mexico (1829–32) but was in turn driven out of office by Santa Anna. After Santa Anna's downfall in 1836, he was again president (1837–39; nominally until 1841).

Butcher's Bill. A colloquial term for a casualty list.

Butler, Benjamin Franklin (1818–1893). An American army officer and politician whose father died when he was young and whose mother operated a boardinghouse in Lowell, Massachusetts. He was graduated from Colby College in Maine and became a successful criminal lawyer. In 1860, as a member of the Democratic National Convention, he voted fifty-seven times to nominate Jefferson Davis [q.v.] for president of the United States, and he was a member of the group that bolted the convention to vote for John Cabell Breckinridge [q.v.], the states' rights candidate. However, when the American Civil War broke out, he went to war as a brigadier general of the Massachusetts militia, and on 16 May 1861 he became the first major general of volunteers appointed by Lincoln.

He was given command of Fort Monroe, Virginia, and while there declared escaped slaves to be contraband, a term that continued to be used throughout the war. After his defeat

Butcher's Bill *Chelmsford departs from the scene of the grizzly Zulu slaughter of British troops at the Battle of Isandhlwana, January 1879, a particularly apt example of the expression.*

in his first battle, at Big Bethel [q.v.] on 10 June 1861, he commanded a successful expedition to North Carolina [q.v.] in February–April 1862, capturing Roanoke Island and New Bern. In May 1862 he commanded the land forces in the successful attack on New Orleans and was named its military governor.

On his orders William Mumford, a citizen of the town, was shot for lowering the American flag from the New Orleans Mint, and Butler created a furor in both North and South, even in Europe, with his "Woman Order" [see General Orders No. 28]. Before he was recalled in December 1862, it was said that he had managed to enrich himself illegally. The Confederates, who called him Beast Butler, declared him an outlaw and threatened to kill him if he was captured. The inside bottom of some Confederate chamber pots, particularly in New Orleans, carried his visage.

He was not again employed until late in 1863, when he was given command of two corps that became the Army of the James. Through his inept handling, his army was defeated at Drewry's Bluff [q.v.] on 12–16 May and was bottled up in the Bermuda Hundred [q.v.] by a numerically much inferior Confederate force under Pierre Beauregard [q.v.]. After failing in an attack upon Fort Fisher [q.v.], North Carolina, in December, Grant relieved him of command. Receiving no further employment of consequence, he resigned on 30 November. A Union staff officer characterized him as "shrewd, able, without conscience or modesty—overbearing."

In 1866 he was elected to Congress, and he served until 1875. In 1882 he was elected governor of Massachusetts, and in 1884 he was the presidential candidate of the Greenback-Labor Party. [See Butler Medal.]

Butler, Elizabeth Southerden (née Thompson) (1846–1933). Best known as Lady Butler, the most celebrated British painter of military scenes in the Victorian era and the wife of Sir William Francis Butler [q.v.], one of the most literary of Victorian generals, whom she married in 1877. She was the sister of Alice Meynell (1847–1922), the essayist and poet. In 1866 she enrolled in the advanced course

at the Female School of Art in London. She first exhibited at the Royal Academy in 1873 with a painting entitled *Missing,* a depiction of two French soldiers straggling after a battle of the Franco-Prussian War. In May of the following year she exhibited *Calling the Roll after an Engagement in the Crimea,* popularly called *The Roll Call,* a canvas described by the *London Daily Telegraph* as "an honest manly Crimean picture, as full of genius as it is full of industry." *The Times* praised it as exhibiting "no sign of a woman's weakness." It was so intensely admired that it had to be protected from the press of its viewers. Miss Butler wrote: "I awoke and found myself famous." (The canvas was acquired by Queen Victoria and is now owned by Queen Elizabeth II.)

"Thank God," she said later, "I never painted for the glory of war, but to portray its pathos and heroism." Correct in every military detail, her pictures were both spirited and stirring. General Butler was so moved by her depiction of the Battle of Rorke's Drift [q.v.] that he is reported to have said, "One more picture like this and you will drive me mad."

She was the mother of three sons and three daughters, the eldest of whom died in infancy.

Butler, William Francis (1838–1910). A British soldier and prolific author, born in Tipperary, who saw more action than did most officers. Commissioned an ensign in the 69th Foot on 17 September 1858, he spent two years at the regimental depot before joining his regiment in Burma. In 1862 his regiment moved to Madras. He was promoted lieutenant on 17 November 1863. On the return of his regiment to Britain the following year, he was able to spend two days at St. Helena, days "steeped in thoughts of glory and grief," for Butler was a lifelong admirer of Napoleon.

In 1867 he sailed with his regiment to Canada, then threatened by Fenian raids [q.v.] from the United States, and while there he obtained three months' leave to visit Nebraska and "the glorious prairies." In 1869 he returned to Britain, and in 1870 he published his first book, a history of the 69th Foot. When he learned that Colonel (later Field Marshal) Garnet Wolseley [q.v.] was organizing the Red River Expedition [q.v.], he wired: "Remember Butler 69th Regiment." Wolseley had no place for him on his staff, but he dispatched him on a special mission to the Red River by way of the United States. Butler reached Fort Garry well ahead of Wolseley and then traveled back to meet him and give him a full report on his enemy and his destination. From that point on he became a member of the so-called Wolseley Gang [q.v.].

In October 1873 he joined Wolseley in West Africa, where, in spite of his best efforts, he failed to raise a corps of African auxiliaries. [See Ashanti Wars.] Nevertheless, he was awarded a CB and promoted major. He wrote a book about his West African experience, *Akim-Foo: The History of a Failure*.

In 1877 he married Elizabeth Thompson [see Butler, Elizabeth Southerden (née Thompson)], an artist already famous for her paintings of military scenes, particularly *The Roll Call*.

In 1879 he took part in the Zulu War [q.v.] but saw no fighting. He served as Wolseley's staff officer during his expedition to suppress Arabi's Revolt and was present at Tell el-Kebir [qq.v.]. He took part in the Gordon Relief Expedition [q.v.], which he described as "the very first war during the Victorian era in which the object was entirely noble and worthy." After the abandonment of the Sudan, he was left in charge of the Anglo-Egyptian forces at Wadi Halfa with the local rank of brigadier general. When the Dervishes [q.v.] attacked, he commanded one of the two brigades in the Battle of Ginniss [q.v.]. He was invalided home in June 1886 and was knighted KCB on 25 November.

On 7 December 1892 he was promoted major general, and in November 1898 he arrived in Cape Town to assume command of the troops in South Africa. Since Sir Alfred Milner (1854–1925) was absent, Butler was sworn in as acting high commissioner as well. Although Milner had been trying to provoke a war with the republican Boers in the Transvaal and the Orange Free State, Butler sympathized with them and made every effort to keep the peace. When Milner returned in February 1899, Butler was relieved of his civil responsibilities. As might have been expected, he and Milner clashed, the diplomat attempting to foment a war, the general attempting to keep the peace. Two months before the war broke out, Butler returned to Britain, where he was given command of the Western District and played no part in the Second Anglo-Boer War. He retired at age sixty-seven as a lieutenant general.

Butler, William Orlando (1791–1880). An American soldier, lawyer, and politician who was educated at Transylvania College in Lexington, Kentucky, and on graduation in 1812 enlisted in the army for the War of 1812 [q.v.]. He was commissioned on 28 September 1812. He was wounded and captured in the Raisin River Massacre [q.v.] but was exchanged and took part in the capture of Pensacola and the siege of New Orleans [q.v.], earning a brevet to major. In 1816 he served as an aide to General Andrew Jackson [q.v.], but he left the army in 1817 and married a cousin of Mary Todd Lincoln's. He then practiced law and served in the Kentucky legislature and the U.S. Congress until the Mexican War [q.v.], when he returned to the army and was appointed major general and commander of volunteers. He was wounded in the Battle of Monterrey [q.v.] in September 1846 and evacuated to New Orleans. When General Winfield Scott [q.v.] took command of the invasion of Veracruz, Butler was summoned to Washington to take Scott's place as head of the army. He served from February through May 1848 and was honorably discharged on 15 August 1848.

Butler Medal. In the American Civil War Union General Benjamin Franklin Butler [q.v.] ordered two hundred specially designed medals suspended from red, white, and blue ribbons to be awarded to black soldiers for gallantry. The obverse of the medal depicted black troops charging a bastion and carried the inscription "Fero iis libertas prevenient." On the reverse, "Campaign before Richmond" encircled the words "DISTINGUISHED FOR COURAGE." In May 1865, as he was preparing to run for Congress, he presented the first forty-six of these to soldiers of the Union XXV Corps for their bravery in storming the Petersburg siege lines at Market Heights and at Chaffin's Farm on 28–30 September 1864.

Butt. 1. The thick end of the stock of a rifle or musket.

2. The embankment behind the targets on a firing range. The name was sometimes used to include the entire target area of the range.

Butterfield, Daniel (1831–1901). An American soldier of the American Civil War who began his military career as first sergeant of a Union volunteer unit on 16 April 1861; sixteen days later he was colonel of the 12th New York, which on 24 May became the first Union regiment to set foot on Virginia soil. On 7 September he was made a brigadier general of volunteers. On 27 June 1862, during a critical moment in the Battle of Gaines's Mill [q.v.], he seized the colors of the 3rd Pennsylvania Volunteers and was wounded leading the command in a charge under a "galling fire," a feat for which he was awarded the Medal of Honor [q.v.] thirty years later. He was present at Second Bull Run and Antietam [qq.v.]. In the Battle of Fredericksburg [q.v.] he commanded a corps, and on 18 November he was promoted major general. He became chief of staff in the Army of the Potomac under Joseph Hooker [q.v.] and is credited with designing the famous corps patches and of composing the bugle call taps [see Badges, Union Army Corps; Bugle Calls]. While serving as chief of staff under George Meade [q.v.], he was severely wounded in the Battle of Gettysburg. He fought in the Atlanta Campaign [q.v.] until he fell ill and thereafter saw no further action.

In 1865 he received brevets of brigadier and major general in the regular army, in which on 1 July 1863 he had been made a substantive colonel of the 5th U.S. Infantry. He resigned from the army in 1870 and took an active part in a wide variety of business, civic, and military affairs.

Butterflies. The name scornfully applied to American officers who during the War of 1812 [q.v.] left their commands in winter to advance their careers in the warmer and more comfortable climate of Washington, D.C.

Butternut. Slang term for a Confederate soldier. When the South ran out of imported cloth and dyestuffs, soldiers' uniforms or other clothing were often dyed with a solution made by boiling butternut shells or walnut shells with iron oxide or copper. The resulting color ranged from yellow to dark brown.

Buxhöwden, Count Friedrich Wilhelm (1750–1811). A Russian soldier who first distinguished himself as a general during the campaigns in Poland in 1793–94. In 1805 he commanded the Austro-Russian left wing in the Battle of Austerlitz [q.v.], which made the main, but unsuccessful, attack against Napoleon. In 1808–09, after the Treaty of Tilsit [q.v.], he led the Russian army that attacked the Swedes in Finland and occupied Finland as a new Russian possession [See Russo-Swedish War].

Buy Out. See Purchase of Discharge.

Buzenval, Battle of [19–20 January 1871], also called Battle of Mont Valéries. Franco-Prussian War. During the siege of Paris [q.v.], French General Louis Jules Trochu [q.v.] in an early-morning *sortie en masse* of some 90,000 men, about half the Garde Nationale [q.v.], took a position under cover of fog in the Park of Buzenval, between St. Cloud and Bougival, on the left bank of the Seine River. He occupied St. Cloud and held his position for the day, but the next day, finding himself unsupported, he abandoned his positions. French losses were 189 officers and 3,881 men; Prussian losses were 40 officers and 570 men.

Buzzicot. A primitive field range sometimes used in the American army. It was basically a piece of collapsible sheet iron.

Byng, John (1772–1860). A British soldier who saw service in Flanders (1793–95) and was wounded in the Irish uprising of 1798. After service in Hanover, Copenhagen [q.v.], and Walcheren [q.v.], he was sent to the Iberian Peninsula, where he commanded a brigade under Sir Rowland Hill [q.v.] in the Peninsular War [q.v.]. He saw action at Vitoria, Roncesvalles, Nivelle (where he was wounded), Nive, and, as a major general, Orthez [qq.v.]. In the Battle of Waterloo [q.v.], his last battle, he commanded the 2nd Guards Brigade. In 1855 he was made a field marshal, and he was created an earl in 1857.

Byron, George Gordon, Sixth Baron (1788–1824). A British poet who accepted an invitation from Alexandros Mavrokordatos (1791–1865), first president of the Greek National Assembly (1822) and later prime minister of Greece, to aid the cause of Greek independence. Although in his epic *Don Juan* (1819–24) he decried the cruelty and shame of war, in August 1823 he set off for the seat of war in Greece, carrying a large amount of cash and a large supply of medicine. He raised, or at least paid for, a regiment of 500 undisciplined Suliotes (people of mixed Greek and Albanian blood [see Suliot Rebellions]), who soon turned mutinous and killed a Swedish officer. Byron attempted to settle disputes between the various revolutionary factions at Missolonghi [q.v.] and tried to bring order out of the revolutionary chaos, but he lacked the required skills. Less than a year after his arrival he contracted rheumatic fever or malaria (accounts differ). He died on 19 April 1824.

Byron, John Joseph (1864–1935). An Irish-born South African soldier who joined the Australian army and from 1895 to 1899 commanded the Queensland Regiment of Royal Artillery. During the Spanish-American War [q.v.] he was an attaché with the American army in the Philippines, and in the Second Anglo-Boer War [q.v.] he served as an aide-de-camp to Lord Roberts [q.v.] in South Africa. He served for ten years as a senator in the Union of South African legislature, and during the First World War he commanded a brigade in East Africa and Persia.

Caballero, Bernardino (1831–1885). A Paraguayan soldier active in the War of the Triple Alliance [q.v.] of 1865–70 between Paraguay and the combined forces of Brazil, Argentina, and Uruguay. He was taken prisoner in 1870 but was soon released. He later became minister of war and, from 1880 until his death, president of Paraguay.

Caballero y Fernández de Rodas, Antonio (1816–1876). A Spanish general who fought in the Carlist Wars [q.v.] and in 1868 was present in the Battle of Alcolea [q.v.]. In 1869–70 he was governor of Cuba.

Caban. A loose coat, almost a cloak, worn by some French officers from about 1835.

Cabezón, Battle of (12 June 1808), Peninsular War. The 5,500-man Spanish Army of Castile [q.v.] under General Gregorio de la Cuesta [q.v.] was destroyed by a French force of 9,000 near this town in central Spain on the Pisuerga River, seven miles north of Valladolid.

Cabrera, Ramón (1806–1877). A Spanish soldier who commanded Carlist troops in Catalonia in 1833–40 during the First Carlist War and again in the Second Carlist War [qq.v.] of 1868–76. He established a reputation for cruelty. After the defeat of the Carlist forces [see Morella, Battle of] he emigrated to England, where he married a Protestant Englishwoman and soon died.

Caçadores. Light infantry-men in the Portuguese army raised by British General William Carr Beresford [q.v.] when he was a marshal in the Portuguese service. During the Peninsular War [q.v.] they wore brown uniforms and were armed with rifles.

Caçadores, 1866–70

Cáceres, Andrés Avelino (1836?–1923). A Peruvian soldier who fought in the War of the Pacific [q.v.]. He became head of the provisional government in 1883 after the capture of Lima by the Chileans at the end of that war. He led those Peruvians who refused to accept the Treaty of Ancón [q.v.] in 1884 and overthrew President Miguel Iglesias [q.v.], whom the Chileans had supported in the civil war of 1885–86. [See Chilean Civil Wars.] He became president of Peru, serving from 1886 to 1890 and again from 1894 to 1895.

Cacolet. See Ambulance.

Cadence. In marching, the uniform time and pace of troops.

Cadenettes. The tresses of plaited hair hanging from the temples of French hussars in the Napoleonic era.

Cadet. A young man studying or in training for military service in a school providing military education. In the United States Military Academy at West Point, New York, cadets ranked above all noncommissioned officers but below second lieutenants. American warrant officer ranks did not exist in the nineteenth century.

Cadet's College. A British school established in 1858 when the Junior Department of the Royal Military College, Sandhurst, was remodeled. Young men of sixteen to nineteen could apply. Tuition varied from £100 for "the sons of private gentlemen" to £20 for the sons of officers who had "died in the service and whose families were in pecuniary distress." Provision was made for twenty Queen's Cadets, sons of officers killed in action who were educated free of charge. The college was abolished in 1870.

Cádiz, Capture of (3 October 1823), French intervention in Spain. The town was captured by the French, who released

Cadiz *Charge of the chasseurs of Madrid upon the insurgents of Cadiz*

the imprisoned King Ferdinand VII (1784–1833) and held the city until 1828. [See Cádiz Mutiny; Riego y Núñez; French Intervention in Spain.]

Cádiz, Siege of (5 February 1810–24 August 1812), Peninsular War. French General Claude Victor [q.v.] with 60,000 men besieged Cádiz, a major seaport, naval base, and capital of that part of Spain not controlled by Napoleon. Located at the tip of the Isla de León Peninsula which projects into the Atlantic Ocean, Cádiz then had a garrison of 20,000 Spanish and Portuguese and 4,500 British. Supplied by the British, it became the capital of free Spain. The siege was raised by Wellington.

Cádiz Mutiny (January 1820). A mutiny led by Colonel Rafael del Riego y Núñez [q.v.] in Cádiz, the most southerly provincial capital in Spain, which swelled into a revolution that deposed King Ferdinand VII (1784–1833), who was held prisoner at Cádiz. [See Trocadero, Battle of; French Intervention in Spain.]

Cadmean Victory. A victory in which the victor loses as much as the defeated or a victory that involves one's own destruction. The name is a reference to Cadmus, who sowed dragons' teeth that turned into warriors who killed one another.

Cadorna, Raffaele (1815–1897). An Italian soldier and engineer who commanded a volunteer battalion of Sardinian-Piedmontese engineers in 1848–49. During the Crimean War [q.v.] he served in the Sardinian contingent in the Crimea. In 1859 he became minister of war in Tuscany. In 1866 he was military commandant in Sicily and crushed a revolt there. On 20 September 1870 he led an invasion force into the Papal States and captured and occupied Rome. From 1873 to 1877 he was commanding general in Turin.

Cadoudal Conspiracy (1803–04). Georges Cadoudal (1771–1804) was a Breton who in 1799 had led a Chouan uprising and in 1803 hatched a conspiracy to assassinate Napoleon. Some fifty conspirators, including General Charles Pichegru (1761–1804) and perhaps Jean Victor Marie Moreau (1763–1813), were involved. The plan was to kill Napoleon at the Place du Carrousel in Paris during a parade. The plot was discovered, and Cadoudal was arrested on 13 February 1804. He was guillotined on 25 June.

Cadre. The key officers, noncommissioned officers, and specialist soldiers needed to organize and train a unit. Also the permanent staff of a military training institution.

Cadwalader, George (1803–1879). An American soldier and lawyer who served as a brigadier general in the militia and was instrumental in suppressing the chauvinist riots [q.v.] in Philadelphia in 1844. During the Mexican War [q.v.] he served as a brigadier general of volunteers and won a brevet to major general for gallantry at Chapultepec [q.v.]. During the American Civil War he served as a Union major general, and he was in command at Baltimore during rioting there in May 1861. From December 1862 he served on a board appointed

to revise military laws and army regulations. He resigned on 5 July 1865 at the end of the war.

Caesar's Camp Battle of (6 January 1900), Second Anglo-Boer War. One of the British strongpoints in the defenses of Ladysmith in Natal was dubbed Caesar's Camp. A Boer attack upon it was repulsed after heavy fighting.

Cafard. The impulsive neurotic behavior patterns, sometimes violent, springing from combinations of isolation, inactivity, boredom, and loneliness that afflicted French soldiers, particularly soldiers in the French Foreign Legion, in North Africa. It was sometimes called *le saharite* or, south of the Sahara, *nigerite*.

Caffarelli du Falga, Marie François Auguste (1766–1849). A French soldier who served for seven years in the Sardinian army before entering the French dragoons. He fought in the Battle of Wagram and became a general of division in 1805. He was sent to Spain in 1809. In May 1812 he was named commander of the Army of the North, but he was recalled the following January to become one of Napoleon's aides. In 1815 he rallied to Napoleon during the Hundred Days [q.v.], but in 1831 was made a peer of France.

Cagg Keg. An informal pledge to stop drinking or to refrain from becoming drunk for a stated period. This early-nineteenth-century slang expression was used in both the British army, where it originated, and the American army.

Cahaba Prison. A Confederate stockade for prisoners of war in the American Civil War that was opened in early 1864 on the banks of the Cahaba (Cahawba) River in central Alabama. By October 1865 it held 2,000. The prisoners cooked their own food; water, although plentiful, was for a time so badly polluted that many sickened and some died.

Caimi, Pietro (1830–1886). An Italian rear admiral who was in command of the Italian forces that landed at Massaua (Massawa) in Eritrea and ousted the Egyptian garrison there in 1885.

Cairo Mutiny (1815). An unsuccessful mutiny in the Egyptian army, mainly by Albanian units resentful of the modernization efforts of Muhammad Ali [q.v.].

Caisson. 1. A two-wheeled vehicle for carrying artillery ammunition. Drawn by four to six horses, it could be attached to a limber, which was often considered a part of the caisson. Light field batteries had one for each gun; heavy batteries had two.

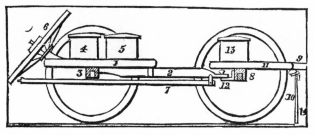

Caisson *Artillery caisson*

2. A large box used to hold ammunition.

3. A hollow box of wood or metal open at the bottom designed to be sunk into water where piers were to be placed. The earliest caissons were those sunk in the Thames in 1738–40 for the construction of Westminster Bridge.

Caking. Gunpowder tended to cake unless the barrels holding it were taken outside the magazine periodically and rolled on boards. Powder that absorbed moisture and became lumpy was called cake powder.

Calabee Creek, Battle of (27 January 1814), Creek War. A band of Upper Creek Indians under Red Eagle [q.v.] surprised and routed a large force of Georgia militia on the banks of this small stream in Alabama.

Calabozo / Calaboso, Battle of (1820), Venezuelan insurrection. Spanish forces were defeated by revolutionaries under Simón Bolívar and José Antonio Páez [qq.v.] at this central Venezuelan town on the left bank of the Guárico River, 123 miles south-southwest of Caracas.

Calabrian Chasseurs. A light cavalry unit of 600 locally recruited Calabrians formed by French General Jean Reynier [q.v.] during the Calabrian War [q.v.]. The volunteers were townsmen rather than peasants, and many were more interested in settling family vendettas than in assisting the French. It was later expanded and called *compagnes frances de guides*.

Calabrian War (1806–11). Calabria is the province that forms the toe of Italy, and in the early years of the nineteenth century its mountains were heavily forested, providing a haven for game and for outlaws. Among the rugged Calabrian peasants Catholicism and brigandage did not seem incompatible, and a number of outlaw bands were led by priests and monks, the most notorious of whom was known as Fra Diavolo [q.v.] (Brother Devil).

On 4 July 1806 French General Jean Reynier [q.v.], who had been sent by Napoleon to seize Calabria, was defeated by an English force of 7,300 under General James Henry Craig (1748–1812) at the Battle of Maida. Craig then retired to Sicily.

The defeat of the French caused revolts in every Calabrian village. Small French garrisons were overwhelmed, and the Calabrian peasants outdid themselves in their cruelties, the worst tortures being reserved for those of their compatriots who had collaborated with the French. At the village of Acri the pro-French officeholders were roasted alive in the public square. Each day at Strongoli a prisoner was taken to the town square, tortured, butchered, cooked, and fed to the other prisoners. When the French arrived, they looted, burned, and massacred a wide swath through the town. The war became one in which no quarter was given by either side.

Reynier was superseded by Marshal André Masséna, who appeared with his latest mistress and reinforcements but soon departed for France, leaving Reynier to fight the rebellion. After a thirty-eight-day siege, the rebel stronghold of Amantea, a base of supplies, fell to the French on 6 February 1807. That summer French forces were increased to 25,000. On 1 February 1808 the French captured Reggio, and on 17 February Scilla, the last rebel stronghold, fell, but brigandage continued unabated. However, the French were now in strong

positions, and one by one the undisciplined brigands, constitutionally unable to cooperate with one another, were hunted down and killed. By the end of 1811 the French were in firm control of Calabria.

At least 20,000 French and their allies died in the war, most, of course, from disease; malaria was endemic in the region.

Calafat, Siege of (February–May 1854), Crimean War. In the first major engagement of the war some 40,000 Russians invested some 30,000 Turks at this Rumanian town on the Danube opposite the Bulgarian fortress of Vidin. Although the Russians made repeated assaults, they were unable to break through the Turkish defenses. Suffering badly from privation and disease, the Russians withdrew, having lost 20,000 men through disease, wounds, and privation. The Turks lost 12,000.

Calatafimi, Battle of (15 May 1860), Italian Wars of Independence. Giuseppe Garibaldi [q.v.] and his 1,000 Red Shirts [q.v.] landed at Marsala, Sicily, 18 miles south of Trapani, on 11 May 1860 and marched inland, rallying more than 1,000 Sicilians to rebel against the kingdom of Naples. At this commune in northwestern Sicily, 21 miles east-southeast of Trapani, Garibaldi defeated a force of Neapolitans for a loss of 18 Red Shirts killed and 128 wounded. He then marched on Palermo, which he took on 27 May.

Calderón Bridge, Battle of (17 January 1811), Mexican Revolution. A Mexican priest, Miguel Hidalgo y Costilla [q.v.], organized a revolt in the northeastern province of Guanajuato and led an ill-organized horde of 80,000 peasants against Mexico City. Near the capital he was turned back by a Spanish force of 6,000 under General Félix María Calleja del Rey [q.v.]. The peasant army fled, pursued by Calleja, who overtook it on 17 January at the bridge at the town of Calderón near Guadalajara, 240 miles west of Mexico City. The rebels suffered a crushing defeat; Hidalgo and his two principal lieutenants, Juan Aldama (1774–1811) and Ignacio Allende (1779–1811), were captured and executed.

The leadership of the revolt was then assumed by José Morelos y Pavón [q.v.]. He was captured and executed on 22 December 1815.

Caldiero, Battles of (30 October 1805), Napoleonic Wars. At this village in northeastern Italy, five miles east of Verona, a French army of 37,000 under Marshal André Masséna [q.v.] attacked 50,000 Austrians, under Archduke Charles Louis [q.v.], who were strongly posted in the village and in the heights above. Masséna carried the heights, but during the night the Austrians succeeded in removing their baggage and guns.

The Austrians lost 3,000 killed and wounded and 8,000 taken prisoner; the French lost about 4,000 in killed and wounded.

Masséna had been defeated at the same place on 12 November 1796 by Austrians under General Josef Alvintzi (1735–1810).

Calhoun, John Caldwell (1782–1850). An American politician who served as secretary of war from 1817 to 1825. He was later vice-president of the United States (1825–32) and secretary of state (1844–45). In the U.S. Senate (1845–50) he was a champion of states' rights and a defender of slavery.

Caliber / Calibre. The diameter of the inside of a gun's bore. The caliber of rifled guns as well as the weight of the projectile it fires is measured from the lands of the rifling.

The measurement of the inside of the bore was expressed in millimeters in continental Europe, except in Germany, where it was expressed in centimeters until after World War II. In the British Empire and in the United States it was usually expressed in inches for artillery and in tenths or hundredths of an inch for hand-held weapons (1 inch = 25.4 mm).

In the first half of the nineteenth century the caliber of small arms was expressed by the number of bullets needed to weigh a pound, as is still the case with shotguns.

In the artillery the size of a field gun was generally expressed by the weight of the projectile, and that of larger guns by the diameter of the bore, but this was not universal, and comparing calibers was complex. The famous Napoleon [q.v.], workhorse of the American Civil War artillery, was a 12-pounder, but it had a larger caliber measured in inches (4.62 inches) than the 30-pounder Parrott gun, which was only 4.2 inches. In 1867 an artillery text published the following conversions for American guns:

6-pounder	3.67 inches	24-pounder	5.82 inches
9-pounder	4.2 inches	32-pounder	6.42 inches
12-pounder	4.62 inches	42-pounder	7.0 inches
18-pounder	5.2 inches		

Calibration. The determination of the muzzle velocity of a gun so that those of similar velocity could be grouped to place shells close together on a target. [See Boulengé Chronograph.]

California Column (1862), American Civil War. On 13 April 1862 a Union column of eleven companies of infantry, two of cavalry, and 2 batteries of artillery, nearly 2,000 men, raised and organized by Colonel James Henry Carleton [q.v.], began a march from southern California, across hostile Indian territory, to New Mexico, which had been invaded by Confederate troops. It reached Santa Fe on 20 September. Although the Confederate invasion of New Mexico had already been repulsed, Carleton's arrival on the scene led the Confederates to retire to San Antonio, Texas [see New Mexico, Confederate Army of]. For three years the column fought not the Confederates but the Apaches and Navajos in the Southwest.

Calladine, George (1793–1837). A British soldier who rose to the rank of colour sergeant [q.v.] and in *The Diary of Colour-Sergeant George Calladine* [1922] wrote of his experiences in the 19th Foot. He served in Ceylon, St. Helena, the West Indies, and Ireland.

Callaghan, George (1852–1920). A British sailor who was captain of the *Endymion* on the China station when the Boxer Rebellion [q.v.] broke out in 1900. He commanded the naval brigade [q.v.] that entered Peking (Beijing). He was promoted admiral in 1917.

Callao, Sieges and Battles of (1825–26, 1866, and 1880). This chief Peruvian seaport on Callao Bay, eight miles west of Lima, was the scene of three major conflicts in the nineteenth century.

1. During the War for Peruvian Independence, Peruvian forces, assisted by troops from Chile and Venezuela, laid siege to the Spanish fortress here. The city fell on 19 January 1826.

2. On 2 May 1866 the city was bombarded by eleven Spanish warships. Peruvian batteries drove them off for a loss of 200 Spaniards and 1,000 Peruvians.

3. In 1880, during the War of the Pacific [q.v.], Chileans took possession of the town.

Calleja del Rey, Félix María, Conde de Calderón (1750–1820). A Spanish general, known as The Butcher because of his cruelties to prisoners. From about 1789 he served in Mexico. In January 1811 he defeated rebel leader Miguel Hidalgo y Costilla [q.v.] at Puente de Calderón [q.v.], and in May of the same year he defeated Hidalgo's successor, José Morelos [q.v.], both of whom he executed. He was viceroy of Mexico in 1813–16. He returned to Spain and in 1820 at Cádiz was imprisoned by his own soldiers. He retired the following year. [See Cádiz Mutiny; French Intervention in Spain.]

Calpee, Battle of. See Kalpi, Battle of.

Calpulálpam, Battle of (20 December 1860), War of the Reform. At this central Mexican town, 8,474 feet above sea level, the Conservative forces of Félix Zuloaga [q.v.] were defeated by the Liberal forces of Benito Pablo Juárez [q.v.], led by General Jesús González Ortega (1824–1881). This battle ended the War of the Reform [q.v.], and Juárez became president.

Caltrop. A four-pronged piece of metal so shaped that in any position one prong is always upright. Numbers were used as a defense against cavalry. Sometimes spelled Calthrop, Caltrap, or Calrop and sometimes called crow's feet.

Caltrop

Cambodian-Siamese War (1831–34). In 1831, after An Chang II (1791–1835) of Cambodia had regained his throne, a Siamese army led by General P'ya Bodin invaded the northern part of the country and soon after defeated the Cambodians in the Battle of Kampong Chhlong (Kompong Chang) in central Cambodia, 50 miles north-northwest of Pnom Penh. An Chang fled to Vietnam and appealed for help. In response the Siamese advanced into Vietnam until they were confronted by a Vietnamese army of 15,000 and forced to retreat. Aided by a general uprising in Laos and Cambodia, the Vietnamese forced a Siamese withdrawal from Cambodia. An Chan was returned to his throne, but the Vietnamese were left in virtual control of the country. [See Cambodian-Vietnamese War.]

Cambodian-Vietnamese War (1841–45). Cambodians, unhappy with the Vietnamese domination of their country, appealed for assistance to their former enemies the Siamese. Siamese General P'ya Bodin led an army into Cambodia, beginning a fierce four-year war. It ended with a compromise peace in which Vietnam and Siam exercised a joint protectorate, with Siam predominating. Cambodians were required to pay for this protection.

Cambridge, George William Frederick Charles, Second Duke of Cambridge (1819–1904). A Hanoverian-born British soldier who was the grandson of George III (1738–1820). In 1837 he entered the Hanoverian army but soon after was sent to England and appointed a colonel in the British army. He served in Gibraltar and Ireland and in 1850 succeeded his father as Duke of Cambridge. As a major general he commanded a division in the Crimean War. He was present at the Alma and at Balaclava [qq.v.], but his generalship was not conspicuous. In 1856 he was promoted a full general and appointed commander-in-chief of the British army, an office he held for forty years. He was a conservative and opposed Cardwell's reforms [q.v.].

Cambridge Asylum. A home for the widows of British soldiers that was established in the 1880s by the second Duke of Cambridge. [See Cambridge, George William Frederick Charles.]

Cambronne, Pierre Jacques Étienne (1770–1842). A French citizen who enlisted as a volunteer in 1792 and was commissioned the following year. He served on the Rhine, in Switzerland, and in the campaigns of 1805–07. In 1809 he was assigned to the Garde Impériale [q.v.], and in 1813 he was promoted general of brigade. He accompanied Napoleon to Elba and led the advance on his return. He commanded part of the Garde Impériale at Waterloo, where he was wounded and captured. When asked to surrender, he is said to have uttered his famous *mot de Cambronne* [q.v.]—*merde* (shit)—which became a part of legend. It was at Waterloo too that he was alleged to have said, "The Old Guard dies, but never surrenders," a journalist's invention. Although he had been sentenced to death in absentia, he was pardoned by the Bourbons and in 1820 commanded a division.

Camden Expedition. See Arkansas Campaign of 1864.

Camel Corps. In the nineteenth century camel corps were formed at various times by a number of armies. The hardihood of the animal offered distinct advantages. Because of its ability to store water and fat, it can travel long distances without water or forage. An Arabian camel could carry twice the load of a mule. A Bactrian camel could carry even greater loads, up to 1,000 pounds or more, although 400 pounds were the average. Its pace was a steady $2\frac{1}{2}$ miles per hour.

The French mounted troops on camels in Egypt in 1800, and in 1843 a camel corps was formed in Algeria, the recruits being selected from those who had suffered least from seasickness on the voyage from France. In 1901 Colonel Henri Laperrine formed 3 companies of Saharans, each with 300 Arabs and 46 Frenchmen, of whom 6 were officers, and 230 of these were infantry. The remainder were mounted on camels to form a *faction mobile*, the first permanent French camel corps.

General Sir Garnet Wolseley formed an ad hoc camel corps during the Gordon Relief Expedition [q.v.], even mounting some kilted Scots in kilts. Camel corps became a permanent part of the Egyptian army and later of the Sudan Defense Force.

In the United States a number of proposals were made to employ camels in the West, but none was seriously considered until Jefferson Davis [q.v.], when secretary of war, recommended their use to the 33rd Congress: "For military purposes, for expresses, and for reconnaissances, and for transportation with troops moving rapidly across the country, the camel, it is believed, would remove an obstacle which now serves greatly to diminish the value and efficiency of our troops on the western frontier." In response Congress appropriated $30,000 to purchase a number of the beasts. Major (later Confederate Brigadier General) Henry Constantine Wayne (1815–1883), who was put in charge of the project, hurried to London to examine camels in the zoo, and then to Pisa, Italy, where the 250 camels owned by the Duke of Tuscany were reputed to perform the work of 1,000 horses. Eventually he bought 3 camels in Tunisia, 9 in Egypt, and 21 in Smyrna (Izmir), Turkey, and hired a group of Arab and Turkish camel handlers. A naval vessel transported them to Indianola, Texas, where they landed on 14 May 1856; 41 more camels followed in a second shipment. In March 1857 the 1st U.S. Camel Corps was formed under the command, curiously, of a naval officer, Lieutenant Edward Fitzgerald Beale (1822–1893). It was tested on an expedition to survey a road from San Antonio, Texas, to Los Angeles. Beale reported: "I have tested the value of the camel, marked a new road to the Pacific, and traveled 4,000 miles without an accident." The War Department requested 1,000 more camels, but the debate in Congress was sidetracked by the American Civil War.

Although popular legend claims that some of Beale's camels ran wild and that the last of their progeny died in 1934, most were sold by auction or died of neglect during the war.

In India the maharajah of Bikaner raised and maintained a camel corps of about 500 recruited on the silladar system [q.v.] as an imperial service unit. The Bikaner Camel Corps still exists. The nizam of Hyderabad also had a camel corps. In the 1890s South African police were mounted on camels in the Kalahari Desert and in Bechuanaland (Botswana).

Camels were used as transport animals, notably by the French in their conquest of Algeria [q.v.]. In 1900–01 during the invasion of the Tuat region of North Africa, French forces requisitioned 35,000 camels, of which 25,000 died of thirst and ill treatment at the hands of inexperienced French camelteers. [See Tuat, French Invasion of.]

Camel Corps *British camel regiments depart from Korti, 30 December 1884.*

Camel Gun. Any lightweight field gun or Gatling gun capable of being carried on the backs of camels, mules, or horses. In the American service the term often referred to the short-barreled Gatling, Model 1874.

Camel Gun *A Gatling-equipped camel corps*

Camera Lucida. An instrument invented by Dr. William Hyde Wollaston (1766–1828) in 1812 for copying and reproducing drawings. Through the use of a prism a virtual image of an object could be made to appear on a paper or other flat surface. Its outlines could then be traced. Aimé Lassitude, a French officer, made improvements for the reproduction of maps and plans.

Camerone, Battle of (30 April 1863), correctly, Camarón (today Villa Tejeda), French conquest and occupation of Mexico. Near this small Mexican village, 50 miles southwest of Veracruz, in the foothills of the Sierra Madre, Captain Jean Danjou (d. 1863), a one-handed veteran of the Crimean War [q.v.], with 2 other officers and 62 enlisted men of the French Foreign Legion [q.v.] was attacked by a Mexican force of about 1,000 foot and 800 horse. Forming square and moving into a walled farmyard of the Hacienda de la Trinidad, about 200 yards east of the village on the road to Palo Verde, the legionnaires, fighting without food or water, held off the Mexicans for nine hours until their ammunition was exhausted. Captain Danjou was killed about noon. About four o'clock only Second Lieutenant Evariste Berg (d. 1864) and four legionnaires were left, and they fixed bayonets and charged. The 3 survivors, Lieutenant Berg and 2 legionnaires, surrendered when surrounded by Mexican bayonets.

The French Foreign Legion still celebrates the valor of this small engagement every year on 30 April, its anniversary, when Captain Danjou's wooden hand, retrieved from the battlefield, is solemnly displayed. *Faire Camerone* came to mean to fight to the last man. Lieutenant Berg was killed in a duel the following year.

Cameron Highlanders. The 79th Regiment of Foot in the British army. After several minor name changes, it became in 1881 the Queen's Own Cameron Highlanders. Raised by Alan Cameron of Erroch (1753–1828) in January 1794, it was a kilted regiment of battalion strength (1,000 men). A second battalion was added in 1804. One and sometimes both battalions saw service in the Peninsular War, Waterloo, the Cape of Good Hope [qq.v.], India, Egypt, Java, Flanders, and Afghanistan.

Cameron Highlanders *79th Foot Cameron Highlanders*

Cameronians. The unofficial name of the 26th Cameronian Highlanders [q.v.], which in 1881 was linked with the 90th Perthshire Light Infantry to form the 1st Battalion of the Cameronians (Scottish Rifles). The name commemorated Richard Cameron, a preacher killed in 1680 by the Moss troopers of Claverhouse. The 26th fought in the Peninsular War [q.v.], China, and Abyssinia. As a two-battalion regiment it fought in the Second Anglo-Boer War [q.v.] in South Africa.

Cameronians *Cameronians, Scottish Rifles*

Camisado / Camisade. 1. An unexpected night attack.

2. A shirt, often colored, worn over a uniform in a night raid or attack to enable those taking part to recognize one another.

Camouflage. Deliberate disguise or pretense.

Camouflage *Painting khaki on scabbards of British Officers' swords, Dundee, 1899*

Camouflet. 1. A small mine employing about 10 pounds of explosive used to suffocate an enemy's miners without disturbing the surface of the ground and creating a crater that could be used to make a lodgment by assaulting infantry.

2. An underground cave caused by an underground explosion.

Camp. 1. As a noun, the ground on which tents or buildings, usually temporary, are provided for troops.

2. As a noun, a body of encamped troops.

3. As a noun, military life or military service.

4. As a verb, to create a camp or to occupy one.

Camp *7th New York at Camp Cameron, Washington, D.C.*

Campaign. A distinct phase or stage of a war involving an interrelated series of military actions, usually in a limited geographic area, designed to achieve a particular objective and usually including several battles. In many European armies, but not in the American, additional allowances or recompense were given for time on campaign. In the French army a year-long campaign was counted as two years' service.

Campaign Hat. In the U.S. army, a wide-brimmed black hat issued in 1872 based upon the Andrews hat [q.v.]. In 1876 it was replaced by a smaller, more durable model.

Campaign Medal. Sometimes called a war medal. A medal suspended by a ribbon of various colors awarded to participants in a battle, campaign, or war. Toward the end of the century a small ribbon on a bar in the color of the ribbon suspending the medal was often worn in lieu of the medal. In India British troops were issued silver medals; native troops were issued medals of the same design but in a baser metal [see Medals]. The practice of national governments' awarding campaign or war medals began in the British army with the issuance of a medal to all ranks who served in the Battle of Waterloo [q.v.]. None was issued to American soldiers in the nineteenth century, but in 1907 a Civil War Medal was authorized by the War Department and issued to 554 veterans.

Campbell, Archibald (1769–1843). A British soldier, commissioned an ensign in the 77th Foot in 1787, who saw much service in India in the Third Mysore War, in which he was present at the siege of Seringapatam, eight miles north of Mysore, in 1792. In 1799, during the Fourth Mysore War, he distinguished himself in the attack upon the same place. In 1808 he went to the Iberian Peninsula with the 71st Highlanders, and in 1809 he helped General William Carr Beresford [q.v.] reorganize the Portuguese army. During the Peninsular War [q.v.] he commanded Portuguese units at Bussaco, Arroyo dos Molinos, and Albuera [qq.v.]. He became a general in the Portuguese army and in that rank fought at Vitoria [q.v.] and in the final battles of the war.

He remained with the Portuguese army until 1820, when he returned to England to serve as a lieutenant colonel. He took the 38th Regiment to India, and in 1824 he commanded the Anglo-Indian forces in the First Anglo-Burmese War [q.v.] [see Kamarut and Kemedine, Battles of]. At its successful conclusion he was made GCB, voted a gold medal, and granted an income of £1,000 a year. In 1826 he was appointed governor of Burma, and he served until 1829. In 1831 he was created a baronet and appointed lieutenant governor of New Brunswick, Canada (1831–37). He was promoted to lieutenant general in 1838. In August 1839 he was appointed commander-in-chief at Bombay but was forced to refuse the appointment because of ill health.

His son, John Campbell (1807–1855), who also became a general, was killed in the Crimean War [q.v.] leading an attack upon the redan [q.v.].

Campbell, Charles Thomas (1823–1895). An American soldier who served as a lieutenant in the Mexican War [q.v.] and later as a captain in the 11th U.S. Infantry. In the American Civil War he served as captain of Battery A, Pennsylvania Light Artillery and later as lieutenant colonel and colonel of the 1st Pennsylvania Artillery, with which he fought at Dranesville, Virginia. In February 1862 he became colonel of the 57th Pennsylvania Infantry, which he led into battle at Seven Pines [q.v.], where he was three times wounded and had a horse shot from under him. Seven months later, with one arm still in a sling, he was so severely wounded in the Battle of Fredericksburg [q.v.] that he was not expected to live. Before he had completely recovered, he was assigned to the Department of the Northwest. He ended the war as a brigadier general.

After the war he was appointed inspector of Indian agencies in Dakota Territory. Then he pioneered a stagecoach line into the Black Hills and founded the town of Scotland, South Dakota, where he built a hotel and was elected mayor.

Campbell, Colin (1792–1863). A British soldier who was the son of John Macliver, a Glasgow carpenter. His mother was a Campbell, and he was educated at her family's expense. When his maternal uncle, a colonel, introduced his fifteen-year-old nephew to the Duke of York [q.v.] as a candidate for a commission, the duke exclaimed, "What! Another of the clan!" Reluctant to correct the duke, his uncle accepted the change in name. "Campbell is a good enough name to fight under," he told the boy, and on 26 May 1808, as Colin Campbell, young Macliver was gazetted an ensign in the 9th Foot.

He soon sailed with the 2nd Battalion of the regiment to Portugal to fight in the Peninsular War [q.v.], and the fifteen-year-old officer received his baptism of fire at Roliça [q.v.] on 17 August 1808. Four days later he saw action again at Vimeiro [q.v.]. The following year he was promoted lieutenant and took part in the disastrous Walcheren Expedition [q.v.] in the Netherlands, where he was "attacked by a fever" (probably malaria) that troubled him for the rest of his life.

Back in the peninsula, he commanded on 5 March 1811 the flank companies of the 9th Foot at Barossa [q.v.], where his gallantry was noted and remembered by General Sir Thomas Graham [q.v.]. After serving for a time with the Spanish army under General Francisco Ballesteros (fl. 1810), Campbell returned to regimental duty and took part in the siege of Tarifa [q.v.] from 19 December 1811 to 5 January 1812. In January 1813 he joined the 1st Battalion of the 9th Foot under Colonel (later General) John Cameron (1773–1844) and fought at Vitoria [q.v.] on 21 June of that year. At the siege of San Sebastián (25 July–31 August 1813) he led a forlorn hope [q.v.] in which he was wounded in the leg and groin and for which he earned a mention in dispatches. Many years later, when he was asked what his thoughts had been at the time, he replied candidly that he hoped he would be promoted captain.

In December 1814 and January 1815 he took part in the disastrous British expedition against the Americans at New Orleans [q.v.]. In 1823 he participated in the suppression of the Demerara insurrection [q.v.] in British Guiana.

On the recommendation of General Graham, he was promoted captain without purchase, awarded a pension of £100 per year, and given a company in the 60th Rifles. The thirty-one-year-old captain had already seen more action than most soldiers saw in a lifetime. On 26 November 1825, while he was serving as a staff officer in Barbados, a generous friend lent him the money to purchase his majority. On 26 October 1832 he managed to pay £1,300 for a lieutenant colonelcy.

He was in command of the 98th Regiment when it was ordered to China to reinforce the army of Sir Hugh Gough [q.v.] in the First Opium War [q.v.]. He left England with a one-battalion regiment of 810, but cholera struck while they were still at sea, and 432 men died between September 1842 and February 1843. In China he once again saw action and was mentioned in dispatches. He was awarded a CB, appointed aide-de-camp to the queen [q.v.], and promoted colonel.

In 1847 he was in India in command of a brigade during the Second Sikh War [q.v.]. For his distinguished services in this war he was knighted (KCB) in 1849. In his journal on 20 October of that year he wrote: "I am growing old and only fit for retirement." But his career was far from finished.

He spent three years in almost constant action on India's Northwest Frontier [q.v.], leading expeditions against the Momunds, Swatis, and other turbulent tribesmen. In 1852 he returned to Britain after an absence of twelve years and went on half pay until he was offered a command in the army destined for the Crimea. During the Crimean War [q.v.] he commanded a Highland brigade and was promoted major general. Of this promotion he wrote that the small additional income it brought was "the only circumstance in which I take any interest."

He distinguished himself in the charge of the Highlanders at the Alma [q.v.], and he directed the repulse of the Russian cavalry by the 93rd Highlanders at Balaclava, the "thin red line" [q.v.]. He quarreled with his superiors, however, and returned to England, where he was made a lieutenant general and sent back to the Crimea. He was there only a month before returning to Britain, where he was appointed inspector general of infantry.

On 11 July 1857 news of the Indian Mutiny [q.v.] reached England, and Campbell was offered the post of commander-in-chief, India. He accepted immediately and left the next day. He arrived in August to learn of the recovery of Delhi [q.v.], the capture of Cawnpore [q.v.], and the preparations for the relief of those besieged in the Residency in Lucknow [q.v.].

After organizing his forces, he took personal command of the army in the field. Leaving a force to occupy Cawnpore, he started for Lucknow on 9 November 1857 with 4,700 men—all British except for two regiments of Sikhs—and 32 guns. Fighting his way into the city, he was able to rescue the garrison plus some 400 women and children. Carrying 1,000 sick and wounded, he returned to Cawnpore, which he reached on 30 November [see Lucknow, Siege of].

The British force left to occupy Cawnpore had been attacked and defeated, but Campbell arrived in time to prevent further damage and established his headquarters there. By 1 March 1858 he had assembled an army of 25,000 for the reduction of the mutineers in Oudh (later the northeast portion of the united provinces of Agra and Oudh). Lucknow was reduced by 19 March, and by the end of May the entire province had been pacified. Campbell was to be the last commander-in-chief, India, personally to take the field.

Ill health caused his retirement, but he was promoted full general and elevated to the peerage as Lord Clyde of Clydesdale. The remainder of his life saw a succession of honors heaped upon the old warrior. His biographer in the *Dictionary of National Biography* says of him: "Lord Clyde has made a reputation in the military history of England absolutely unrivalled in the records of the middle of the nineteenth century."

Campbell, William Bowen (1807–1867). An American soldier and politician who fought as a captain with the 2nd Tennessee Volunteers in the Second Seminole War [q.v.] and as a colonel in the Mexican War [q.v.]. In 1851 he was elected the last Whig governor of Tennessee. During the American Civil War he served briefly as a Union brigadier general.

Campbell-Bannerman, Henry (1836–1908). A British politician who served as secretary for war in 1886 and again from 1892 to 1895. He promoted army reform and the ousting of the Duke of Cambridge [q.v.] as commander-in-chief. During the Second Anglo-Boer War [q.v.] he condemned Britain's use of concentration camps [q.v.], calling their establishment "the methods of barbarism." He was prime minister from 1905 to 1907.

Campbell's Station, Battle of (16 November 1863), American Civil War. Near this hamlet in Knox County, Tennessee, Union General Ambrose Burnside [q.v.] fought a delaying action, withdrawing into Knoxville before superior Confederate forces under General James Longstreet [q.v.]. Federal losses were 318; Confederates lost 174.

Camp Chase. Originally a Union training camp in the American Civil War, located in the western outskirts of Columbus, Ohio. It was named after Salmon P. Chase (1808–1873), the secretary of the treasury and a former governor of Ohio. Converted into a prisoner of war camp, it housed prisoners captured in the West. Conditions were initially lax; Confederate officers who gave their parole were permitted to wander about town, live in hotels, and attend meetings of the state legislature; visitors to the camp paid for tours of the facility. When an overflow of prisoners arrived and the camp was taken over by the federal government, officers were transferred to Johnson's Island [q.v.] in Lake Erie, and the rules at Camp Chase were tightened considerably. Crude barracks were built for 7,000, but the prison population grew to 10,000 before the end of the war. Conditions within the camp deteriorated, particularly the sanitary arrangements. Many died in a smallpox epidemic.

Camp Douglas. Originally a 60-acre training camp south of Chicago. During the American Civil War it was transformed into a prison camp for Confederate prisoners that in time held 30,000. Young Henry Morton Stanley [q.v.], the future African explorer, was a prisoner here.

Campero, Narciso (1815–1896). A Bolivian general and politician who fought in the War of the Pacific [q.v.] in 1879–84.

Camp Fever. A commonly used term for enteric (typhoid) fever.

Camp Followers. Civilians who followed armies. These included sutlers, vivandiers [qq.v.], washwomen, wives, gamblers, bootleggers, prostitutes, etc.—"the rogues and whores who went with the baggage." Armies in India were always accompanied by an immense number of camp followers, who usually exceeded the number of troops. In February 1839, when an Anglo-Indian army of 15,000 troops left Shikarpur in northern Sind for Afghanistan, it was accompanied by 85,000 camp followers. [See Bourdett, Sara; Blanchisseuse.]

Camp Ford. This largest Confederate military prison in Texas was established in August 1863 four miles northwest of Tyler in the northeastern part of the state. By July 1864 the camp held 4,900 Union prisoners. It was an open stockade with no shelter provided, as was the case in most Confederate prisoner of war camps. However, most prisoners were able to construct crude shelters, and a fine stream ran through the camp. Local farmers sold provisions, and meals were cooked over fires fueled by wood collected outside the stockade. In general, exceptionally good health prevailed. The camp was so healthful that there was no need for a hospital until after Nathaniel Banks's [q.v.] Red River Expedition [q.v.], when overcrowding and the resultant diseases made one necessary. Even so, only about 250 men died, a remarkable statistic when compared with other Civil War prisoner of war camps, North and South.

The last prisoners were discharged on 17 May 1865, and two months later the camp was burned.

Camp Grant Massacre. See Apache War of 1871–73.

Camphausen, Wilhelm (1818–1885). A German painter of battle scenes who accompanied the Prussian army during the Schleswig-Holstein War [q.v.]. He is best known for his paintings of the Franco-Prussian War.

Camp Lawton. A Confederate prison camp at Millen, Georgia, consisting of a stockade enclosing 42 acres built in the summer of 1861. By November 1864 it held 10,000 men.

Camp Morton. A Union prison camp, originally a training area for Indiana volunteers, established on the State Fair Grounds just north of Indianapolis, Indiana. After the capture of Fort Donelson [q.v.] it contained 3,000 Confederate prisoners. The camp was personally administered by Governor Oliver Hazard Perry Throckmorton (1823–1877) of Indiana, for whom the camp was named. Deaths at the camp totaled 1,763, of whom 7 were killed trying to escape.

Camp of Instruction. Encampments in war time designed to introduce and habituate newly enlisted troops to drill and to the duties and fatigues of camp life.

Campoos. Infantry regiments of the Mahratta states.

Campos, Arsenio Martínez de (1831–1900). A Spanish soldier who took part in the Moroccan Campaign of 1859–60, and in 1869 was sent to Cuba. In 1872 he was promoted general. On his return to Spain he took part in operations against the Carlists [see Carlist Wars]. In 1893 he commanded the army at Melilla on the north coast of Morocco.

Canada, American Invasion of (1813), War of 1812. A planned two-pronged American attack upon Canada that envisaged the capture of Montreal. One force under General Wade Hampton [q.v.] was to move north from Plattsburg, New York; the second column, led by his personal enemy,

General James Wilkinson [q.v.], was to move down the St. Lawrence River.

On 19 September Hampton led a force of 4,000 men to the Canadian border and met a force of Canadian militia near Four Corners on the Chateaugay River [see Chateaugay, Battle of]. The Americans were routed. Hampton refused Wilkinson's orders to join him and retreated to Plattsburg on 11 November. This was Hampton's first and last battle in the war.

Canadian Army. Canada did not have a standing army, only militia, for most of the century, relying upon the British army for protection against Americans and rebels, a situation that led Benjamin Disraeli (1804–1881) to rail at the anomaly of "an army maintained in a country which does not even permit us to govern it!"

The Canadian army was founded with the formation of a regiment of infantry in 1868, but not until after the Articles of Confederation were signed on 1 July 1870 was serious effort devoted to the formation of a separate army. When formed, it followed the traditions, customs, and doctrine of the British army. In 1876 the Royal Military College of Canada at Kingston, Ontario, was founded. Although Canada engaged in no wars of its own in the last quarter of the century, it contributed volunteers to fight in the Second Anglo-Boer War [q.v.] in South Africa in 1900.

Canadian Revolts (1837–38). In November 1837 Louis Joseph Papineau (1786–1871), a politician in Quebec who believed that under British rule French-Canadian grievances were not being addressed, launched a short-lived revolt. His followers, called *Patriotes,* hoped to establish a French republic on the St. Lawrence River, and there was fighting in the streets of Montreal. Lieutenant General Sir John Colbourne (1778–1863), a veteran of the Napoleonic Wars [q.v.], was appointed governor-general and commander-in-chief. He repaired the fortifications, enlisted veteran soldiers living in Canada, and on 13 December embarked upon a winter campaign from Montreal with 2,000 men. Rebel forces were attacked and dispersed by British troops at St. Denis, St. Eustache, St. Charles, and elsewhere. General Colbourne's

Canadian Revolts *Canadian rebels drilling in North York, Ontario, 1837*

swift and effective action earned him a peerage, and two years later he became the first Baron Seaton.

Almost simultaneous with the revolt in Quebec, on 25 November 1837, William Lyon Mackenzie (1795–1861), a fiery politician in Ontario who had been mayor of Toronto, announced the formation of a provisional republican government and on 4 December appeared at the head of 800 men. His small force was attacked and defeated by British troops at a place called Montgomery's Tavern, near Toronto, on 7 December.

The next serious revolt was an uprising of the Métis in Manitoba [see Red River Expedition; Riel, Louis; Riel Rebellion].

Canalizo, Valentín (1797?–1847). A Mexican soldier and political leader who in 1843, during the absence of Santa Anna [q.v.], was acting president. In 1844 he was impeached and banished. Allowed to return in 1846 to fight the Americans in the Mexican War [q.v.], he was in command of the retreat after the Battle of Cerro Gordo [q.v.].

Canal Worker's Riot (1834). On 29 January 1834 workers on the Chesapeake and Ohio Canal (begun in 1828) struck and rioted. President Andrew Jackson [q.v.] ordered Secretary of War Lewis Cass (1782–1866) to send troops to suppress them. This was the first time American troops were used to put down discontented laborers. [See Civil Disorders.]

Canarder, to. To fire from under cover.

Canby, Edward Richard Sprigg (1817–1873). An American soldier who, after being graduated from West Point in 1839, joined the 2nd Infantry. He fought in the Second Seminole War and in the Mexican War [qq.v.], winning two brevets for his valor in the latter. He then served in the West, seeing action in encounters with Indians. On 14 May 1861, at the beginning of the American Civil War, he was named colonel of the 19th U.S. Infantry and placed in command of the Department of New Mexico. After preventing a Confederate invasion of California [see New Mexico, Confederate Army of], he was appointed assistant adjutant general in Washington. On 31 March 1862 he was made a brigadier general. In August of that year he commanded the troops in New York City that restored order after the draft riots [see Civil Disorders].

On 7 May 1864 he was promoted major general and sent to western Mississippi, where, while on a gunboat on the White River, he was severely wounded by guerrillas. He recovered to lead the assault on Mobile, Alabama, in 1865. In May, six weeks after the surrender of Robert E. Lee at Appomattox, he received the surrender of the last major Confederate forces under Generals Richard Taylor and Edmund Kirby Smith [qq.v.].

After the war he served again with the army in the West. When the Modoc Indians in Oregon and northern California refused to move to a reservation, he joined in prolonged talks seeking a peaceful resolution [see Modoc War]. During a parlay on 11 April 1873 "near Van Bremmer's Ranch," near Siskiyou in northern California, he was assassinated by Captain Jack and Ellen's Man George [qq.v.], two Modoc chiefs.

Canby was the highest-ranking officer and the only general ever killed by North American Indians.

Cancha-Rayada, Battle of (16 March 1818). Argentine War of Independence. A Spanish force of 9,000 under General Mariano Osorio (1777–1819) defeated an insurgent force of 6,000 under José de San Martín [q.v.] at this place in western Argentina. Osorio lost 200 killed and wounded; San Martín lost 120 killed and 22 guns.

Candian / Kandian Wars (1803–15). On 21 February 1803 Candy (Kandy), capital of the Candy kingdom of Ceylon (Sri Lanka), located on the Mahaweli River, 60 miles east-northeast of Colombo, was captured by a British force of about 10,000 with little opposition. The physical difficulties in reaching Candy had been considerable. When the exhausted troops entered the city, they found it suffering from a shortage of food and swept by sickness. It had been deserted by Sri Wikrama Raja Sinha (1780–1832), the king, who had fled with his people and all his valuables. The bulk of the force soon withdrew, leaving behind a garrison of 300 Europeans and 700 Ceylon infantry. On 24 June 1803 these troops, the last to leave, began their march to the coast. They were fallen upon by Candyans and massacred almost to a man.

In September 1804 a second expedition, fitted out by Major General David Douglas Wemyss (1760–1839), was scheduled to move by a number of columns and approach Candy from several directions. It was canceled at the last minute, but one of the column commanders, Captain Arthur Johnston, who had failed to receive the order, moved out with 312 men and after incredible hardships reached Candy, which had again been evacuated. Johnston remained only fifty-six hours and then withdrew under constant harassment, losing 69 men in killed and wounded. Only when they reached Trincomalee, their point of departure, on 19 October did they learn their ordeal had been unnecessary.

In October 1814 the war was renewed, and on 28 February 1815 General Robert Brownrigg [q.v.] sent eight small columns into the interior. On 8 February the Candyan army surrendered. The king, Sri Wikrama, fled with his wives but was captured ten days later. On 2 March Brownrigg received the submission of the chiefs, and Britain soon proclaimed its sovereignty over all Ceylon. Sri Wikrama was exiled to Madras, where he lived comfortably until his death. A rebellion in 1818 and serious riots in Ceylon in 1848 were quickly suppressed.

Canditeer. Brushwood or other material used to conceal and protect miners and sappers and those involved in siege operations. [See Gabion.]

Cane Hill, Battle of (28 November 1862), American Civil War. Learning that a Confederate cavalry force of 8,000 under General John Sappington Marmaduke [q.v.] was located north of the Boston Mountains, a part of the Ozarks in northwestern Arkansas, General James G. Blunt (1826–1881) of the Army of the Frontier [q.v.] marched against it with 5,000 men. Following a 35-mile march, Blunt's force encountered the Confederates and attacked. Caught by surprise, the Confederates retreated into the mountains. After a short pursuit and an aborted Confederate counterattack, a truce was declared, and the dead and wounded were collected. The Federals admitted to a loss of 40 and claimed a Confederate loss of 435.

Cane River Crossing, Battle of (23 April 1864), American Civil War. Also known as the Battle of Monett's Bluff or Monett's Ferry or Cloutiersville, this was one of the final engagements of the Red River Expedition [q.v.] in Louisiana. Union General Nathaniel Banks [q.v.], retreating before a Confederate force under General Richard Taylor [q.v.], fought off an attempt to prevent his forces from crossing the Cane River. Federal losses were about 300; Confederate losses, about 50.

Caneva, Carlo (1845–1922). An Italian officer who served in the Austrian army during the Seven Weeks' War [q.v.] and from about 1867 in the Italian army. He served in the Italian-Abyssinian Campaign of 1896 [see Italo-Abyssinian Wars] and was in command of the Italian garrison at Kassala in 1897, when Lord Kitchener [q.v.], sirdar of the Egyptian army, visited the town and arranged for the withdrawal of the Italians; Kassala was transferred to Egypt on 25 December 1897. Caneva became a lieutenant general in 1902 and commanded the Italian forces in the Libyan Campaign of 1911–12.

Caney, Battle of. See El Caney, Battle of.

Canister. An artillery projectile consisting of a container of tin or sheet iron filled with small iron or lead balls or slugs (usually 27) set in sawdust. When fired, the balls or slugs immediately scattered, giving an effect rather like that of a large shotgun. As a defensive device used at close range—100 to 200 yards—it was most effective. [See Case Shot.]

Cannelure. A groove cut into a bullet into which a lubricant could be pressed or the mouth of the cartridge could be pressed to grip the bullet closer.

Canning. The method of preserving fresh food for long periods by sterilizing them in hermetically sealed containers had a profound effect upon the health and mobility of modern armies, but the process was unknown for most of the nineteenth century. Although a French chef in Paris experimented with canning in 1783–95, its scientific basis was not understood, and it was not until the application of the fermentation studies of Louis Pasteur (1822–1895) in the last years of the century that its military use was appreciated. Although some canned meat was used in the American Civil War, the Second Anglo-Boer War [q.v.] was the first major conflict in which canned (British: tinned) foods, including meats, were issued extensively. "Embalmed beef" [q.v.] was the American soldier's expression for such food.

Cannon. All firearms larger than small arms [q.v.] are cannon, often referred to as guns, mortars, howitzers, or artillery [qq.v.] if mounted on carriages, and, if rifled, sometimes called rifles. Field guns have a comparatively flat trajectory, mortars have a high, arching trajectory, and howitzers have a trajectory somewhere in between.

Large-caliber cannon were used for coastal defenses in permanent installations or in siege trains. Cannon smaller than the usual field guns were used in mountain artillery and were often capable of being broken down for transport on the backs of pack animals. [See Screw Gun; Camel Gun.]

When names are attached to a cannon—Armstrong, James, Parrott, or Blakeley—no specific caliber is indicated, only the type of cannon. [See Artillery; Ammunition; Armstrong, William; Parrott, Robert Parker.]

Cannon *La Joséphine, a huge bronze cannon, defended Paris during the siege of 1870–71.*

Canteen *A trooper takes a drink from his canteen during the Indian Wars. Drawing by Frederic Remington*

Cannonade. An artillery attack with many guns of some continuance; a bombardment.

Cannoneer. An artilleryman who served a cannon.

Cannonière. Originally a tent to shelter four cannoneers, but the term came to be applied to all tents sheltering seven or eight men.

Cannon Lock. A contrivance placed over the vent of a gun to explode the charge.

Canrobert, François Certain (1809–1895). A French soldier, commissioned in 1828 after attending St. Cyr [q.v.]. He served with distinction in Algeria. In 1839 he organized the French Foreign Legion [q.v.] to fight in the Carlist Wars [q.v.]. In 1841 he returned to North Africa and was promoted general of brigade. He was an aide to Louis Napoleon (1808–1873) in 1850 and played a key role in the coup d'état of 2 December 1851. During the Crimean War [q.v.] of 1853–56 he was twice wounded. He took command of the French army in the Crimea on the death of General Jacques St. Arnaud [q.v.] in 1854 and at its conclusion was made a marshal of France. In 1859, in the Austro-Piedmontese War [q.v.], he commanded III Army Corps in Lombardy and distinguished himself at Solferino and Magenta [qq.v.]. During the Franco-Prussian War [q.v.] of 1870–71 he commanded the Army of the Rhine and was taken prisoner by the Germans at Metz [q.v.] on 27 October 1870. In 1876 he was elected a senator.

Canteen. 1. A flask of wood, rubber, or metal for carrying water, wine, or liquor. In the British army canteens were made of wood and held about three pints. Each was painted and inscribed with the number or designation of the unit. [See Bullseye Canteen.]

2. A store or sutling house in which soldiers could purchase necessities or comforts. Wet canteens, where beer was sold, were established before mid-century; dry canteens, where tea, cakes, and extra food were sold, came much later.

In 1894 Major Harry James Craufurd (b. 1848?) of the Grenadier Guards, who was then commanding the Guards Depot, and Surgeon Captain Herbert Murray

American Civil War cloth-covered canteen with filter

Ramsay, in the Scots Guards, established a Canteen and Mess Co-Operative Society with a capital of £400 to provide canteens on army posts. It paid only 5 percent to shareholders; the remainder of the profit was plowed back into capital, which by 1900 had risen to £265,000. [See Sutler; Post Exchange.]

3. In French barracks, a kind of clubhouse for the entire regiment.

4. A small trunk or chest divided into compartments for the plate and table equipage of one or more officers while on campaign. It sometimes contained food and liquor.

Canterac, José (1775–1835). A Spanish soldier of French descent who entered the Spanish army with the officer cadet class of 1805 and took part in the Peninsular War [q.v.]. In 1815 as a brigadier general he was sent to South America, where he fought in several campaigns under José de La Serna [q.v.] against rebels in Upper Peru (Bolivia). In 1821 he was a part of the cabal that deposed Viceroy Joaquín de la Pezuela (1761–1830) in favor of La Serna, who promoted him lieutenant general and appointed him commander-in-chief of the royalist forces in Peru. He was defeated by rebel troops under Simón Bolívar in the Battle of Junín [q.v.], Peru, on 6 August 1824. In the Battle of Ayacucho [q.v.] on 9 December of the same year he commanded the reserves and on La Serna's death surrendered to Antonio de Sucre [q.v.]. Soon after, he returned to Spain, where in January 1835 he was appointed captain general of New Castile. Three days later he was shot by mutinous troops in Madrid.

Canton. 1. As a verb, to disperse troops into winter or summer quarters.

2. As a noun, the top inner quarter of a flag.

Cantonière. In the French army and at times in other armies these were women, selected from the wives of noncommis-

A cantonière

Cap-and-Ball Gun. A single-shot pistol or rifle loaded with a ball and loose powder and fired by a percussion cap. In revolvers a percussion cap was placed on the nipple of the chamber. Both conical and round bullets could be molded.

Caparison. The saddle, bridle, and housing of a military horse.

Cape Mounted Rifles. 1. A unit of Hottentots (Khois) and Coloureds (people of mixed races) led by European officers founded in 1793 in Cape Colony, South Africa, and originally called Pandours. In 1796 it became the Cape Corps and served until 1803, when it was temporarily disbanded. From 1806 to 1817, when it was again disbanded, it was known as the Cape Regiment. It was re-formed in 1827 and served in most of the Kaffir Wars [q.v.] as Cape Mounted Rifles. It was disbanded in 1870.
   2. A semimilitary unit designed for rapid movement established in Cape Colony, South Africa, in 1878. Members were responsible for their own transport and supplies. The unit distinguished itself in the Morosi War, the Gun War, and the Anglo-Boer Wars [qq.v.]. In 1913 it became the 1st South African Mounted Rifles (not to be confused with the unit of Coloured and Khois. See above).

Cape of Good Hope, Capture of (January 1806), Napoleonic Wars. When the Treaty of Amiens [q.v.] restored to the Dutch the Cape of Good Hope, then under French control, the British dispatched a force of 6,000 under Sir David Baird [q.v.] to retake it. Baird landed at Saldanha Bay on 5 January 1806 and three days later near Cape Town defeated the Dutch under General Jan Willem Janssens [q.v.] in the Battle of Blaauwberg [q.v.]. On 10 January Cape Town was taken, and on the 18th Janssens surrendered.

Cape Palmas, Battle of (17 September 1875). Freed American slaves who had been settled in Liberia defeated aborigines near this port town, today called Harper.

Capitulation. 1. A convention, a treaty, or an agreement involving the surrender to an enemy. Depending upon circumstances, honors of war [q.v.] in full or in part might be granted to those surrendering.
   2. The act of surrendering.

Caponnière / Caponier. 1. A covered communications trench running from the enceinte to a detached work.
   2. In fortifications, a casement projecting over a ditch that enabled the defenders to deliver a flanking fire upon attackers.
   3. Any passageway from one part of a fortification to another.

Caponière for ditch defense

Cap Pouch. A small pouch of black bridle leather lined with sheepskin used for carrying percussion caps [q.v.]. It was closed by a flap secured by a brass button.

Capri, Attacks on (1806 and 1808). Napoleonic Wars. This island in the Bay of Naples was captured by Rear Admiral

sioned officers and privates, who were authorized to sell spirits and provisions in garrisons or military units. In the French army their costumes were a combination of female dress and soldier's uniform. They were never part of American or British armies. [See Vivandière.]

Cantonment. 1. In India, a permanent military post, usually near a city.
   2. Elsewhere a group of more or less temporary structures for housing soldiers. Sometimes used to describe troops quartered in houses.
   3. The quartering of troops.

Canyon Creek, Battle of (13 September 1877), Nez Percé War. At this place in present-day Montana elements of the 1st and 7th U.S. Cavalry fought an inconclusive battle with Nez Percé Indians

Canyon de Chelly, Battle of (January 1864). Colonel Kit Carson [q.v.] leading 389 men attacked the Navajos in the Canyon de Chelly in northeast Arizona, the main Navajo stronghold, which Carson described as "the great fortress of the tribe since time out of mind." In a sweep through the canyon, Carson and his men captured 200 sheep, destroyed fruit trees, and fired homes. Faced with ruin, the Navajos capitulated, thus ending the Navajo War [q.v.]. Some 9,000 of the tribe were compelled to move to the Bosque Redondo Reservation, a barren stretch of the Pecos River valley in eastern New Mexico.

Sir (William) Sidney Smith (1764–1840) on 22 April 1806 and retaken by a French force under Maximilien Lamarque (1770–1832) on 4 October 1808. In 1815 it was restored to Ferdinand I (1751–1825), king of Naples and the Two Sicilies.

Caprivi de Caprera de Montecuccoli, Georg Leo von (1831–1899). A German soldier and statesman who entered the Prussian army in 1849 and saw service in the Schleswig-Holstein War and the Seven Weeks' War [qq.v.]. He was chief of staff of X Corps during the Franco-Prussian War [q.v.]. In 1883 he was chief of the Admiralty, and in 1888 he commanded X Corps in Hanover. He succeeded Otto von Bismarck (1815–1898) as imperial chancellor of Germany in 1890, resigning four years later. The Caprivi Strip in southern Africa was named for him.

Caps, Percussion. See Percussion Cap.

Captain. The oldest-known military rank and in earlier centuries a higher one than it is at present.
1. A general designation for the leader of a land force.
2. A rank above a lieutenant and below a major. A captain's command is a company, troop, or battery. He is responsible for its arms, clothing, accoutrements, and all government property issued to his command. The rank is usually abbreviated Capt. or Cpt. In German: *Hauptmann*.

Captain General, often hyphenated. A rank bestowed upon those holding certain positions in government, not used as a regular army rank. The governor-general of Canada carried this title. The Marquess of Wellesley (Wellington) was so designated when in India. It was also used in the Spanish service, the military governors of Cuba and of other Spanish possessions were so styled. In the United States the governors of states were captains general of the militia.

Captain Jack (1837?–1873). A minor chief of the Modoc tribe in the American Northwest. The Modoc Indians had been forced onto the Klamath Reservation in Oregon, which held their traditional enemies, the Klamath Indians. In 1872 Captain Jack and about 50 of his tribe fled the reservation and returned to their homeland on the Lost River in northern California. Some 400 troops were sent to bring them back, and on 29 November 1872 a small battle was fought. One soldier was killed, and 7 were wounded; 8 Modocs were reported slain. Soon after, the survivors killed 14 white settlers and fled into the lava beds in northern California. [See Modoc War.]

General Edward Canby [q.v.] attempted to arrange a peace, but while parlaying with Captain Jack and Ellen's Man George [q.v.], he and a preacher, Eleazar Thomas (d. 1873), were assassinated. Captain Jack was captured on 1 June 1873, tried with 5 other Indians for murder, and with 3 of them was hanged at Fort Klamath, Oregon, on 3 October 1873.

Army surgeon and brevet Major Henry McElderry (1842–1898) retrieved the Indians' heads and, after removing the flesh, sent the skulls to the office of the surgeon general in Washington, D.C.; they were ultimately sent to the Smithsonian Institution, where they remain.

Captain Swing Revolt (1850). A British labor revolt named after a mythical leader, Captain Swing. Machinery was broken, buildings were set afire, and attacks were made upon the gentry. The army was used to crush the uprising, and 1,100 people were transported.

Capua, Siege of (October–November 1860), Italian Wars of Independence. At this town on the Volturno River, 19 miles north of Naples, a besieged Neapolitan force surrendered to Giuseppe Garibaldi [q.v.] on 2 November 1860. Count Luigi Menabrea [q.v.] conducted the siege. Gustave Cluseret [q.v.], who became a general in the Union army during the American Civil War, was wounded leading the French contingent of Garibaldi's army.

Carabao, Military Order of. An unofficial organization formed in November 1900 in Manila by American servicemen during the early days of the American occupation "to foster a high standard of military and social duty and to perpetuate the memories of military service in the Philippines." Later chapters were formed in San Francisco, San Antonio, and Washington, D.C. The water buffalo (carabao) was adopted as the symbol of the organization. Its meetings were known as wallows.

Carabineer. Originally a soldier armed with a carbine [q.v.].

Carabinier à Pied. Elite light infantry in Napoleon's armies.

Carabinieri. An Italian paramilitary force established by Victor Emmanuel I (1759–1824) of Piedmont in 1814 to restore law and order. It is still extant.

Carabobo, Battle of (24 June 1821), Venezuelan War of Independence. This was the last battle in Venezuela's struggle for independence. A revolutionary army of 6,500, led by Simón Bolívar with José Antonio Páez and Antonio José de Sucre [qq.v.] and including 1,500 horsemen and a 900-man British legion, defeated 3,000 Spanish royalists under Miguel de la Torre (d. 1838) at this Venezuelan village, some 20 miles southwest of Valencia and 100 miles west of Caracas. The battle was fought on a plain at the southern exit of the mountain passes. The rebels were aided by two Venezuela caudillos [q.v.]: Santiago Mariño (1788–1854) and José Páez (1790–1873). The British who won the day with a bayonet charge were acclaimed by Bolívar, "*Salvadores de mi Patria!*" Only about 400 royalists managed to reach the safety of the coast. Five days later Bolívar entered Caracas.

Carabinieri *Nineteenth-century Italian carabiniere or military policeman*

Caraguatay, Battle of (10 August 1869), War of the Triple Alliance. A Brazilian force defeated Paraguayans under Francisco López [q.v.] near this town, 50 miles east of Asunción in south-central Paraguay.

Carbine. A short-barreled firearm, lighter than a rifle, fired from the shoulder, chiefly used by cavalry and mounted infantry. The most successful carbine of the nineteenth century was developed by Christopher Miner Spencer [q.v.]. The first breech-loading, rifled repeating carbine, it was 39 inches long, with a tubular magazine holding seven cartridges. When the trigger guard was lowered, the fired cartridge case was extracted and a new cartridge slid into the breech. [See Spencer Repeating Carbine.]

Among the most celebrated carbines were those developed by an American, Christian Sharps [q.v.]. The Sharps model of 1859 and that modified in 1863 were extensively used in the American Civil War.

Carbine *The Joslyn and Maynard carbines*

Carbinier. 1. A trooper in a French heavy cavalry regiment during the Napoleonic Wars.

2. A grenadier [q.v.] in a French light infantry regiment in Napoleon's army.

Carbonari, Italian for charcoal burners. Members of a secret revolutionary society founded in Naples in 1819. One of its early leaders was the revolutionary Filippo Buonarroti (1761–1837), who organized a complex network of local cells and established an elaborate ritual. Many of its members were army officers.

The first uprising promoted by Carbonari occurred in July 1820 in Naples, when troops there mutinied, crying, "God, the king, and the constitution." Troops sent against the mutineers joined them. Ferdinand I (1751–1825), king of Naples and the Two Sicilies, was forced to grant a constitution, which he swore on an altar to preserve, a promise he broke a year later.

The society played an active part in the early-nineteenth-century history of France, where in 1821 Carbonarist uprisings at Belfort, Thouars, La Rochelle, and elsewhere had to be suppressed.

The revolutionary Giuseppe Mazzini (1805–1872) joined the society in 1830, and many Carbonari joined his Young Italy movement. Lord Byron [q.v.] was among a number of Englishmen who belonged. Membership reached a possible peak of 300,000. The society's red, blue, and black flag was the standard of revolution until replaced by the red, white, and green in 1831.

Carbonari were credited with fomenting an uprising in Piedmont in March 1821. It was quickly crushed, and many

of its leaders were executed. An uprising of the Carbonari in Naples was suppressed in August 1828. In 1831 Carbonari in Romagna and the Marches provoked uprisings and overthrew papal authority. Carbonari at Parma and Modena expelled their rulers. With the reunification of Italy the society quickly died out.

Carcano, Salvatori (fl. 1860–1890). An inspection engineer at the Turin, Italy, arsenal who in 1867 designed a rifle for the Italian army. It was a bolt-action, single-shot weapon based upon the Dreyse needle gun [q.v.], using an 11 mm caliber cardboard cartridge and a lead bullet with a hollow base. About 1889 he developed the Mannlicher-Carcano rifle, which used his design for a thumb-operated safety catch.

Carcass. A hollow case filled with combustibles fired from mortars for the purpose of setting fire to an enemy's works. The term was loosely applied to any incendiary or illuminating device, such as a flaming barrel of tar.

Cárdenas, Battle of (19 May 1850), filibuster action in Cuba. Narciso López [q.v.], a filibuster who organized a small force in the United States, landed in Cuba and fought a battle with the Spanish and loyalist troops. Although he was victorious, no Cubans rose to support his revolution, and he returned ingloriously to the United States. Among the wounded in this battle was Theodore O'Hara [q.v.]. [See Filibuster.]

Cardigan, Seventh Earl of, James Thomas Brudenell (1797–1868). A British soldier who entered the army in 1824 by purchasing his commission in the 15th Hussars. By 1830 he was a lieutenant colonel, having acquired all of his promotions by purchase [see Purchase System]. He was an unpopular commander and understandably so: Within two years of command he had arrested 700 soldiers and court-martialed 105. In 1834 he was himself court-martialed and was forced to resign from the army for illegally arresting one of his officers, but in 1836 he managed to return as commander of the 11th Light Dragoons (in 1840 renamed 11th Hussars). On 12 September 1840 he fought a duel with and seriously wounded one of his former officers, for which he was tried in the House of Lords and acquitted on a technicality. In 1847 he was promoted major general. In the Crimean War [q.v.] he commanded the Light Brigade of cavalry. In its famous charge at Balaclava [see Light Brigade, Charge of], which he led, he plumed himself on being the first to enter the Russian lines, although once there he disdained to strike a blow, leaving, he said, such brawling to common soldiers. From 1855 to 1860 he was inspector general of cavalry. In 1861 he became a lieutenant general. The imitation of the knitted woolen sweater he wore in the Crimea, collarless and buttoned down the front, was named for him.

Cardwell, Edward (1813–1886). An English politician and military reformer. In 1864 he was appointed secretary of colonies. In that position he refused to keep British troops in the colonies in peacetime unless the colonies paid for them, and he abolished penal transportation. Although a man with a particular abhorrence of all forms of violence, with no military experience or prior interest in the army, he was in 1868 named secretary for war in Gladstone's cabinet. With the help of Colonel (later Field Marshal) Garnet Wolseley, he instituted a series of radical reforms in the British army, reorganizing it, abolishing the purchase of commissions [see Purchase System], and forming a retirement system for officers. He inaugurated short service, which reduced enlistments to six years with the colors and six with the reserve, thus forming the first veteran reserve; reduced the number of overseas garrisons; abolished flogging in peacetime; and subordinated the commander-in-chief to the war secretary. He localized infantry regiments, linking most with counties, and was instrumental in introducing an efficient breech-loading rifle. [See Cardwell's Reforms.] On the resignation of the Gladstone ministry in 1874, he was elevated to the House of Lords as Viscount Cardwell.

Cardwell's Reforms. The radical reformation of the British army by Secretary for War Edward Cardwell [q.v.] in 1868–74 was carried out in spite of heated opposition from most senior officers. Perhaps his greatest accomplishment was the abolition of the purchase system [q.v.], by which commissions and promotions in the army were bought and sold. Unable to persuade Parliament to abolish the system, he contrived for the change to be made by royal warrant and in effect arranged for the government to buy back the command of the army through the Army Regulation Act, which came into force in July 1871. By the Army Enlistment Act of 1870 he instituted a system known as short service, under which soldiers enlisted for only six years instead of twelve, after which they were placed on the reserve for six more years.

In 1870 the army had 141 battalions of infantry; all but 50 were numbered and more or less independent. In 1857 some regiments had been given two battalions; Cardwell extended this linked battalion system to the entire army. He wished in time to localize most regiments, assigning each to a county, a town, or an area, a plan he could not entirely carry through. It was completed, or nearly so, by his successor, Hugh Culling Eardley Childers (1827–1896).

Cargador. In the American West a cargador was the man responsible for making up packtrains and forming the loads, caring for the mules, repairing aparejos [q.v.] and the like. He was second in importance only to the packmaster [q.v.].

Carignan, Battle of (31 August 1870). Franco-Prussian War. On the plain of Douzy in northeastern France near the small town of Carignan, 12 miles from Sedan, French forces under General Marie MacMahon [q.v.], retreating before the Germans, stopped and made a stand. There followed a severe engagement in which positions often changed hands until the Germans turned the French flanks and forced them to retreat to Sedan [q.v.].

Caripi. A special unit in the Turkish cavalry consisting mostly of renegade Christians or Moors.

Carleton, James Henry (1814–1873). An American soldier who was a militia lieutenant in the so-called Aroostook War in 1839, a bloodless encounter occasioned by a border dispute between New Brunswick, Canada, and Maine. On 18 October of the same year he received an appointment as a sec-

ond lieutenant in the 1st Dragoons. He served in Indian Territory, and in the Mexican War [q.v.] he was a staff officer, winning a brevet to major for gallantry in the Battle of Buena Vista [q.v.]. In 1854, with Christopher ("Kit") Carson [q.v.] as his guide, he operated against Jacarilla Apaches [see Navajo War; Chelly Canyon, Battle of.]

On 14 October 1861, during the American Civil War, he assumed command of the military district of southern California. Soon afterward he organized the California Column [q.v.], and on 26 April 1862 he was promoted brigadier general of volunteers. He spent the war fighting hostile Indians. He remained in the army after the war as lieutenant colonel of the 4th Cavalry.

Carl Gustav Stads Gevarsfaktori. The Swedish government's arsenal at Eskilstuna, Sweden, 50 miles west of Stockholm. Its principal output was the manufacture of Mauser and Ljungman rifles [qq.v.]

Carlist. A supporter of Don Carlos in the Carlist Wars [q.v.].

Carlist War, First (1833–40). Ferdinand VII (1784–1833), king of Spain (1808 and 1814–1833), on 29 March 1830 bequeathed his throne to his newborn daughter, María Isabella Louisa (1830–1904), who upon his death became Isabella II, with her mother, María Christina (1806–1878), as regent. However, Ferdinand's brother, Don Carlos María Isidro de Borbón (1788–1855), claimed to be the heir, as decreed under Salic Law (established in 1713 by Philip V), which prohibited women from inheriting the throne. Those who agreed with him, calling themselves Carlists, raised an army in revolt. His claim was supported by the Catholic Church, Basque conservatives, and Catalonians; he was opposed by Isabella's supporters, known as Cristinos, and by the governments of Portugal, Britain, and France. Britain dispatched a foreign legion of volunteers under Sir George de Lacy Evans [q.v.], and France sent its Foreign Legion [q.v.].

General Tomás Zumalacárreguy [q.v.], a Basque, led the Carlist forces to several victories in the north until, during the unsuccessful siege of Bilbao, he was severely wounded in the leg and, in the hands of incompetent doctors, died soon after. With his death the tide turned, and Cristino forces under General Baldomero Espartero [q.v.], were eventually victorious. On 31 August 1839 the Carlist commander-in-chief, without Don Carlos's approval, conceded defeat and signed the Treaty of Vergara. Don Carlos fled to France, but a small force under Ramón Cabrera (1806–1888) stubbornly fought on for a time, and Carlists continued to be a political force. In 1840 a revolt led by Espartero, who had assumed dictatorial powers, drove María Christina and Isabella from the country. A counterrevolution led by Ramón Narváez [q.v.] in July and August 1843 restored Isabella to the throne.

Carlist War, Second (1870–76). When Queen Isabella II grew to womanhood, she made herself unpopular. Her morals were not of the highest, and the legitimacy of her children was doubted. Her reign was one of turmoil marked by political intrigue, attempted insurrections, and numerous changes of ministries. In 1857 a priest attempted to assassinate her, but his dagger was deflected by the whalebone in her corset.

She was finally deposed in 1868 by a revolution and fled to Paris.

In 1870 the Spanish Cortes (national assembly) voted to accept Duke Amadeo (1845–1890) of Aosta as king of Spain to succeed the deposed Queen Isabella II. However, opposition to him was so strong that he was forced to abdicate in 1873, and the Cortes proclaimed Spain's first republic. The Carlists again rose in revolt, this time in favor of Don Carlos's grandson Don Carlos III (1848–1909). The Spanish army fractured, and the Carlists, with the help of the Basques, seized much territory in northern Spain.

In January 1874 the republic capsized, and Spain dissolved into chaos. A dictatorship established under General Francisco Serrano y Domínguez (1810–1885) was replaced by a monarchy under Isabella's son Alfonso XII (1857–1885). Carlist forces were suppressed in Catalonia and Aragón; Pamplona, after a long siege, capitulated in February 1876; and Carlos fled to France.

Carlo Alberto, Prince (1798–1849), sometimes referred to as Charles Albert. After 1800 he was prince of Savoy and Piedmont, and in 1829 he became Viceroy of Sardinia. In 1831 on the death of his father, Carlo Emmanuel, sixth prince of the Savoy-Carignan line, he succeeded to the throne of Sardinia and set about creating a sizable army. In 1848 he declared war on Austria. He was defeated in the Battle of Custozza [q.v.] on 23 June 1848 by Archduke Albert [q.v.], and again at Novara [q.v.] on 23 March 1849, after which he abdicated in favor of his son Victor Emmanuel II (1830–1878) and retired to a monastery in Oporto, Portugal.

Carney, William H. (1840–1908). An American soldier and former slave who fought in the American Civil War and as a sergeant in the 54th Massachusetts earned the Medal of Honor [q.v.] for his gallantry at Fort Wagner, South Carolina, on 18 July 1863. When his regimental color-bearer was shot down, Carney seized the flag and, although wounded in the chest, right arm, right thigh, and head, retained it through the battle. He was one of only five blacks to win the Medal of Honor in the Civil War. After the war he worked for thirty-two years as a mail carrier. The medal was not presented to him until 23 May 1900.

Carnifex Ferry, Battle of (10 September 1861), American Civil War. At this place in what is today Carnifax Ferry State Park in West Virginia, seven miles southwest of Summerville, Union forces under William Rosecrans [q.v.] attacked a smaller Confederate force under Brigadier General John Buchanan Floyd [q.v.] at the ferry crossing the Gauley River. Floyd drew his force into a strong fortified camp and escaped during the night, destroying the ferry after he had safely crossed the river.

Carnot, Lazare Nicolas Marguerite (1753–1823). A French soldier commissioned in the Corps of Engineers who became a revolutionist and politician, sometimes called *le grand Carnot* to distinguish him from his brother, a famous jurist. In 1793, as a member of the Committee of Public Safety, he voted for the execution of the king. Named minister of war in 1800, he released professional officers from prison, reorganized the French army, and proved to be an able and honest administrator. Napoleon awarded him a pension in 1809, and he retired for a time. In 1810 he published a book on fortifications, *De la Défense des places forte,* which influenced all European armies [see Carnot's Wall]. In 1814 Napoleon appointed him general of division and made him governor of the fortress at Antwerp [q.v.]. He rejoined Napoleon for the Hundred Days and was forced to flee the country after the Battle of Waterloo.

Carnot's Wall. A heavy detached wall in front of a fort, loopholed and high enough to be an obstacle to an attacker. This was a design of Lazare Carnot [q.v.].

Carol I, Karl Hohenzollern (1839–1914). A Prussian officer who in 1866 was elected prince of Rumania. He organized the army along Prussian lines, and in the Russo-Turkish War of 1877–78 [q.v.] he had joint command of the Russian and Rumanian forces. In 1881 Rumania was proclaimed a kingdom, and he became king.

Carolinas Campaign (1865), American Civil War. After William Tecumseh Sherman's March to the Sea [q.v.], General Grant ordered the capture of Fort Fisher [q.v.] and the port of Wilmington on the east coast of North Carolina in order to give Sherman an alternate base from which to be supplied. Fort Fisher fell on 15 January 1865, and a Federal force moved to within 10 miles of New Bern [q.v.], 30 miles west of Pamlico Sound.

Sherman, after threatening Augusta, Georgia, and Charleston, South Carolina, and being delayed by heavy rains, moved north on 1 February with 60,000 troops and reached the Augusta–Charleston Railway on the 7th. Opposing the Federal advance was a scattered Confederate force of less than 23,000 under the overall command of Pierre Beauregard [q.v.], who ordered the evacuation of Charleston and a concentration at Cairo, South Carolina, toward which the Federals were marching. Before any significant action took place, Joseph Johnston [q.v.] was brought out of retirement and placed in command over Beauregard.

Sherman reached Cairo on 3 March; the Confederates under William Hardee [q.v.] had arrived there before him but had dropped back to Fayetteville, in south-central North Carolina. After a series of engagements near Kinston, North Carolina, 25 miles east-southeast of Goldsboro, on 7–10 March, the Confederates fell back in the face of thickening Federal forces. Sherman reached Fayetteville on the 12th and three days later resumed his advance in three columns. On the 16th Union forces attacked Hardee at Averasboro [q.v.], North Carolina, and that night Hardee retreated.

Johnston launched a counterattack, and the largest battle of the campaign was fought at Bentonville [q.v.], 17 miles west of Goldsboro, on 19 March. The Confederates were repulsed; Sherman concentrated his entire force for an attack upon Johnston on the 21st, but the Confederates fell back toward Smithfield. On the 23rd Sherman marched into Goldsboro, where he received reinforcements from General John Schofield [q.v.] that raised the size of his army to 80,000.

Johnston reorganized his army to continue the struggle, but on 13 April, after the surrender of Lee, he realized his position was hopeless and asked for an armistice. Hostilities were never renewed. He surrendered on 26 April 1865.

Carpenisi / Karpenision, Battle of (20 August 1823), Greek War of Independence. A battle fought at the southern end of the Pindus Mountains between Greeks and Turks in which the Greeks were defeated and their hero, Mario Bozzaris [q.v.], was killed.

Carpet Knight. 1. In British usage, a soldier who remained at home during a war or was too accustomed to luxury.

2. During the American Civil War Confederate soldiers sometimes referred to Mosby's Rangers by this name because they were assumed to avoid the hardships of hard marching and primitive camping.

Carr, Eugene Asa (1830–1910). An American soldier who obtained an appointment to West Point at age sixteen, was graduated 19th out of 44 in the class of 1850, and began a military career of forty-three years, most of it spent in the West in the cavalry or mounted infantry.

He was first assigned to the mounted rifles on the western frontier, where on 10 October 1854 near present Limpia, Texas, he was severely wounded by an Apache arrow. In 1885 he transferred to the 1st Cavalry and saw action under General William Selby Harney [q.v.] in a campaign against Sioux Indians. While at Fort Riley, Kansas, he survived his first cholera outbreak.

He was a captain when the American Civil War broke out, and he fought his first battle at Wilson's Creek [q.v.], Missouri, on 10 August 1861. Six days later he was elected colonel of the 3rd Illinois Cavalry. In the Battle of Pea Ridge [q.v.] in southwest Missouri on 7–8 April 1862 he was three times wounded. For conspicuous gallantry in action he won the Medal of Honor [q.v.] and was promoted brigadier general.

By the end of the war he had been brevetted major general in both the volunteer and the regular service, but he reverted to his substantive rank of major. He was in Kansas in 1868 and fought small actions on 18 October and again on 25–26 October against Sioux and Cheyennes on Beaver Creek. Late in that year he was with Philip Sheridan's [q.v.] South Plains Expedition and on 11 July 1869 he commanded at the Battle of Summit Springs [q.v.], where he rescued Mrs. George (Maria) Weichel, who had been captured by Cheyenne dog soldiers.

He became a lieutenant colonel in 1873, and in 1876, after a brief visit to Europe, he commanded the 5th Cavalry in the Sioux Campaign during the summer and fall of that year, taking part in the Battle of Slim Buttes [q.v.] on 9–10 September. In July 1877 he was in Chicago, commanding a squadron of cavalry during the railway strike [q.v.]. He was promoted colonel in 1879 and commanded the 6th Cavalry in Arizona, where his most celebrated action took place in the Battle of Cibicue [q.v.].

In 1890 he took part in the Wounded Knee [q.v.] operations at the Pine Ridge Agency in present-day South Dakota. On 19 July 1892 he became a brigadier general and soon after retired. By this time he had become a living legend in the West, where he had served for thirty of his forty years in the army. He had fought in thirty-seven to forty battles and two sieges, had been wounded by bullet or arrow four times, and had survived four cholera epidemics.

Carrago. A defensive position made by circling wagons around a camp, as was done by Boers in South Africa [see Laager] and by American units and wagon trains in the West.

Carrera, José Miguel de (1785–1821). A Chilean revolutionary who first saw action in the Spanish army during the Peninsular War [q.v.]. In 1810 he and his brothers, Juan José and Luis (both shot as rebels at Mendoza, Argentina, in 1818), joined the revolutionary movement in Chile. In 1811 he led a revolution that overthrew the conservative junta. He dissolved Congress and made himself military dictator. In 1813 he was replaced by Bernardo O'Higgins [q.v.]. In October 1814, after his defeat by royalists in the Battle of Rancagua [q.v.], he fled to Buenos Aires and then to the United States. In 1816 he returned to Buenos Aires and attempted another rebellion, but he was betrayed by his own men, captured, and shot at Mendoza, Argentina.

Carrera, Rafael (1814–1865). A Central American soldier and politician of mixed white and Indian parentage. After the dissolution of the Central American Federation in 1839 he was one of the leaders who formed Guatemala as a separate state. In 1844 the Guatemalan Assembly named him *Benemérito Caudillo y General en Jefe* (worthy leader and general-in-chief). In 1851 he defeated the Federalist forces from Salvador and Honduras at Larada, near Chiquimula, in southeast Guatemala. In the same year he was elected president, and in 1854 he was made president for life. In the struggle for the domination of Central America, he took the Conservative and clerical side against the Liberals. Aided by Costa Rica and Nicaragua, he occupied San Salvador and became the virtual power behind all the Central American governments.

Carriage Department. The Royal Carriage Department was established at Woolwich, England, in 1803 for the manufacture of armaments and specifically gun carriages. It was under the Board of Ordnance until 1855, when it was placed directly under the secretary of state for war, who administered it through the surveyor general of ordnance.

Carrick's / Corrick's Ford, Battle of (13 July 1861), American Civil War. At this ford over the Cheat River in western Virginia a Confederate force under Brigadier General Robert Selden Garnett [q.v.], retreating from Laurel Hill, was attacked by Union troops. The Federals, who lost 53, killed 20 Confederates, wounded 10, and captured 50 men plus 40 wagons and a gun. Among the dead was Garnett, who became the first Confederate officer and the first general on either side to be killed in the war.

Carrier Pigeon. A pigeon used to carry messages. The name frequently was often misapplied to homing pigeons [q.v.] or *pigeons voyageurs* [see Paris, Siege of].

Carroll, James (1854–1907). An Englishman who was taken to Canada at the age of fifteen and at age twenty enlisted in the American army. He rose to be a first sergeant in the 7th Infantry. He grew interested in medicine and in 1883 was promoted to hospital steward. Eight years later he received his M.D. Through his interest in bacteriology he became a friend of Major Walter Reed [q.v.], and in 1900, when Surgeon General George Sternberg appointed the Yellow Fever Board [q.v.], he went as Reed's assistant to Cuba. There he contracted the disease. During his convalescence he came to feel that he had been mistreated and developed a profound hatred for Reed—just at the time that Reed was doing his best to obtain his promotion. He was promoted captain in 1902 and major in 1907, a few weeks before his death. From 1899 until his death he published twenty-seven articles on yellow fever.

Carronade. A short, large-bore iron cannon developed in 1776 at the Carron Iron Works. It fired a heavy ball or grapeshot and was often used to guard the gates of forts. It was still in use in the early nineteenth century.

Carry Arms. A command in the American Manual of Arms [q.v.] directing that muskets or rifles be carried in the right hand with the barrel nearly vertical and resting in the hollow of the shoulder, the arm hanging down with the thumb and forefinger around the guard, and the remaining fingers grasping the stock just under the hammer.

Carson, Christopher ("Kit") (1809–1868). An American scout for armies in the West. At age sixteen he ran away from his home in Franklin, Missouri, and joined a wagon train bound for Santa Fe. He spent the rest of his life on the American frontier, becoming a trapper and hunter, skilled with a rifle and coolheaded in peril. In 1842 he guided John Frémont's expedition over the South Pass of the Rockies in what is today central Wyoming, and the fol-

lowing year he led a second Frémont expedition over the same route.

Although he never learned to read or write, he spoke fluent Spanish, and in February 1843 he married Maria Josefa Jaramello, a member of one of the most prominent families in New Mexico. In 1845 he guided a third Frémont expedition to California. There, after the Battle of San Pascual [q.v.], on the night of 6–7 December 1846, he crawled through investing Californios and summoned aid from San Diego. On 9 June 1847 President James Polk (1795–1849) commissioned him a second lieutenant in the mounted rifles, but on 28 January 1848 the Senate negated the commission.

In November 1849 he led a party of dragoons in a vain attempt to rescue a white woman captured by the Apaches. He served for two years as a dispatch rider for the army, and in 1853 he was appointed an Indian agent.

In 1861, during the American Civil War, Carson became colonel of the 1st New Mexico Infantry. In the autumn of 1862 his troops broke the power of the Mescalero Apaches and forced them onto reservations. In June 1863 he marched with 700 men against the Navajos and defeated them in the Battle of Canyon de Chelly [q.v.]. On 13 March 1865 he was brevetted brigadier general for distinguished service in New Mexico and gallantry in the Battle of Valverde [q.v.] on 21 February 1862. He remained in the army after the war, serving as a lieutenant colonel, and was honorably mustered out on 22 November 1867, just six months before his death.

Cartagena, Sieges of (1815 and 1821), South America revolutions. This walled seaport on the northwest coast of what is today Colombia was captured from the Spanish by Simón Bolívar but only briefly held. It was retaken in 1821.

Carte de Visite. A calling card, $2\frac{1}{4}$ by $3\frac{3}{4}$ inches, which in the latter half of the nineteenth century often bore the donor's photograph. The fashion began in 1857, when the deposed Duke of Parma, Charles II (Charles Louis Ferdinand de Bourbon, 1799–1883) began to attach his picture to his cards. The practice spread rapidly in Europe and the United States, where cards could be purchased for as little as twenty-five for a dollar. During the American Civil War millions were dispersed by soldiers, who most frequently posed for their photographs in uniform, holding weapons. Oliver Wendell Holmes called them "the sentimental greenbacks of civilization." When the government began taxing the cards, their popularity rapidly declined.

Cartel. In military terms, an agreement between belligerents regarding nonhostile relations. It was usually an agreement concerning the exchange of prisoners of war.

Cartel Ship. An unarmed vessel used to exchange prisoners of war or to carry proposals to an enemy.

Carter, Samuel Powhatan (1819–1891). The only American fighting man ever to have been both a rear admiral and a major general. An 1846 graduate of the U.S. Naval Academy at Annapolis, Maryland, he served in the Pacific, Atlantic, and Mediterranean. At the beginning of the American Civil War he was detached to drill Tennessee volunteers for the Union

Carson, Kit *Kit Carson on the cover of the New York Dime Library.*

army. On 1 May 1862 he was made a brigadier general of volunteers; on 16 July he was promoted to lieutenant commander in the U.S. navy.

Carter led the first successful Union cavalry raid in the West into eastern Tennessee [see Carter's Raid]. As an army officer he saw much action in the war; he was brevetted major general in August 1865. After the war he returned to the navy and retired as a commodore in 1881. The following year he was appointed a rear admiral on the retired list.

Carter's Raid (26 December 1862), American Civil War. Brigadier General Samuel Carter [q.v.] led a Union cavalry brigade south from Manchester, Kentucky, and, crossing the mountains east of the Cumberland Gap, entered the upper Tennessee Valley, where he destroyed two strategically important bridges and inflicted 295 casualties at a loss of 3 Union troopers. He returned safely with the remainder to Manchester.

Cartouche. 1. The case or roll of paper holding the charge for a firearm.

2. A leather sling or pouch to carry artillery ammunition from the tumbrel or caisson to the gun.

3. A wooden case containing both musket balls and larger iron balls fired from a howitzer. [See Grape Shot / Grapeshot.]

4. A cartridge case.

Cartridge. 1. A tube of paper or metal, sometimes both, containing a complete charge for a firearm.

2. A case with an explosive charge for blasting.

Cartridge *Central-fire solid-head reloading rifle cartridges*

Cartridge *Central-fire solid-head reloading pistol cartridges*

Cartridge, Bottle. A metal cartridge so called because of its shape. The Henri-Martini rifle [q.v.] used bottle cartridges.

Cartridge, Rimfire. Metal cartridges in which the fulminate was placed in the rim. If the rim was struck at any point, the powder was exploded.

Cartridge Belt. A belt for carrying rifle or pistol cartridges. One such, often used in the American West, carried loops of leather or canvas on its exterior. It was sometimes called a prairie belt.

Cartridge Headspace. The distance between the face of a bolt or breechblock of a weapon and the base of a seated cartridge. It is usually measured in thousandths of an inch in the American and British armies.

Carupaity, Battle of (22 September 1866), War of the Triple Alliance. A victory of the Allied forces of Brazil and Argentina over Paraguayans near the confluence of the Paraná and Paraguay rivers.

Casal Novo, Battle of (14 March 1811), Peninsular War. A battle fought in central Portugal between 11,000 men of the rear guard of Marshal Michel Ney's [q.v.] army and the 12,000 men in the advanced guard of the Allied army under Wellington. Casualties were 130 British, 25 Portuguese, and 55 French. Among the British wounded were George Napier and his brother, William [qq.v.], who was to write the classic history of the Peninsular War.

Casati, Gaetano (1838–1902). An Italian soldier who joined the bersaglieri [q.v.] in 1859, was commissioned, and rose to the rank of captain in the 1866 war with Austria [see Seven Weeks' War.] He retired from the army in 1879 and joined the staff of *L'Esploratore,* a Milanese geographical journal. In 1880 he took service under Romolo Gessi Pasha [q.v.], then governor of Bahr el-Ghazal Province in the Sudan. When Dervishes overran the province, he escaped to Equatoria, where in 1883 he was employed by Emin Pasha [q.v.], the governor. In the following years he embarked upon numerous explorations. In 1886 he was taken prisoner in Uganda but managed to escape. He left Central Africa with Henry Morton Stanley (1841–1904), who led an expedition to "rescue" Emin, then threatened by Dervishes. After reaching the safety of Bagamoyo on the Indian Ocean in 1889, Casati retired to Italy.

Casbah. A North African word for fortress or citadel.

Cascabel. The projection having a short neck and a base called a fillet in rear of the breach of a cannon that facilitated its handling when being mounted or dismounted. It was not found on mortars.

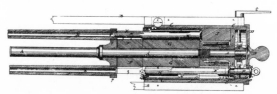

Cascabel *An 1871 revolving battery Gatling gun shows a cascabel plate through which breech bolts are removed.*

Cascans. Well-like holes that served as entrances to galleries in fortifications.

Casemate. A chamber, usually vaulted and bombproof, within a wall or fortified position from which guns could be fired through embrasures.

Casemate *Civil War casemate in Fort Burnham, January 1865*

Casemates Nouvelles. Batteries constructed under the openings of revetments and ramparts. The forts at Cherbourg, Dover, and at Fort Columbus, New York, were erected on this principle.

Caserne. A barracks.

Caseros, Battle of. See Monte Caseros, Battle of.

Case Shot. Antipersonnel artillery ammunition that included grapeshot, canister, and shrapnel [qq.v.].

Cashier. To expel an officer from the service ignominiously, usually as a verdict of a court-martial. It implies more than mere dismissal, for a dismissed officer could be reinstated; a cashiered officer was prohibited from ever again holding a commission. The word was borrowed from the Dutch *casseren,* which carries much the same meaning.

Castalla, Battles of (21 July 1812 and 13 April 1813), Peninsular War. Near this town in eastern Spain, 13 miles southwest of Alcoy, two battles were fought.

First Battle (21 July 1812). A Spanish force of 10,000 infantry and 1,000 cavalry under General Joseph O'Donnell [q.v.], whose mission was simply to contain the French under Marshal Louis Gabriel Suchet [q.v.] in front of him, attempted instead a complicated movement by night followed by a dawn attack. The attack failed, and O'Donnell lost 3,000, including 2,135 taken prisoner, three colors, and two guns. The French lost about 200.

Second Battle (13 April 1813). An Allied force of British, Sicilians, and Iberians that totaled 14,000 infantry and 1,000 cavalry with 30 guns under British General Sir John Murray (1768?–1827) defeated a French force of 11,000 infantry and 1,250 cavalry with 24 guns under General Louis Gabriel Suchet [q.v.]. French losses were 800; Allied losses, 440.

Castaños, Francisco Xavier (Javier) de, Duque de Bailén (1758–1852). A Spanish soldier who saw action in the American Revolution and in the War of the Bavarian Succession in 1778–79. He became a lieutenant general in 1802, and in 1808 he was named captain general of Andalusia. During the Peninsular War [q.v.] his most notable battle was the defeat of French General Pierre Antoine Dupont de l'Étang [q.v.] at Bailén [q.v.] on 19 July 1808. On 23 November he was soundly defeated by French Marshal Jean Lannes in the Battle of Tudela [q.v.]. He fought at Badajoz [q.v.] in March and April of 1812, and he commanded the Spanish army at Vitoria [q.v.] on 21 June 1813.

Soon after, he was relieved by the Cortes in a command reshuffle; however, he remained active in politics. In 1833 he was president of the Council of Castile. In the Carlist Wars [q.v.], as the guardian of Queen Isabella II (1830–1904), he opposed the Carlists.

Castelfidardo, Battle of (18 September 1860), Italian Wars of Independence. At this town in central Italy, 11 miles south of Ancona, Piedmontese forces, 35,000 strong, under Enrico Cialdini [q.v.] defeated the papal army of Pius IX (Giovanni Maria Mastai-Ferretti, 1792–1878), 8,000 strong, under Christophe Léon Louis Juchault de Lamoricière [q.v.]. The town was besieged, and Lamoricière fled with about 300 men to Ancona, which surrendered on 29 September.

The Piedmontese then marched south and linked forces with Giuseppe Garibaldi [q.v.] and the combined force marched southwest against the Neapolitan army.

Castilla, Ramón (1797?–1867). A Peruvian soldier who fought under Antonio de Sucre (1820–26) and in Peruvian civil wars (1841–45). In 1837 he was minister of war, and from 1845 to 1851 he was president of Peru. In 1855 he led a revolution that overthrew President José Acinic (d. 1879) and again became president until 1862. In 1856 he abolished slavery, and in 1860 he proclaimed a new constitution.

Castillejos, Battle of (January 1860), Spanish-Moroccan War. Spanish forces under Juan Prim y Prats [q.v.] defeated an Arab force under Mule Abbas at this northwest Spanish Moroccan town on the Mediterranean, 24 miles south of Ceuta. This was the first decisive action between the Spanish and the "Moors" in North Africa. It opened the road to Tetuán [q.v.] for the Spanish.

Castle Pinckney. An eighteenth-century fort built on a shoal in the harbor of Charleston, South Carolina, and named after Revolutionary War General Charles Cotesworth Pinckney (1750?–1825). It was occupied by Charleston Zouave Cadets on 20 December 1860, the moment South Carolina seceded from the Union. After the First Battle of Bull Run [q.v.] on 21 July 1861, it was converted into a prison. It seems to have been a comfortable one in which the prisoners and their South Carolina Zouave guards enjoyed a hearty camaraderie known as the Castle Pinckney Brotherhood.

Castle Thunder. The name given during the American Civil War to two Virginia tobacco warehouses converted by the Confederates into prisons. One was in Petersburg, and the other in Richmond. The latter, which held many accused of spying or of being politically unreliable, had an unsavory reputation.

Castramentation. The art of laying out military camps in the best locations in the best manner and allotting appropriate quarters for the different troops. An area with good drainage near potable water and firewood was desirable.

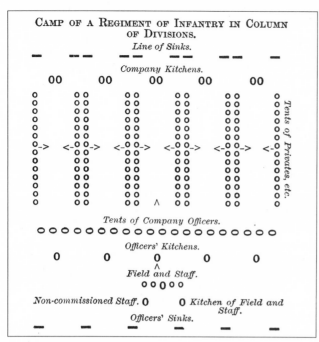

**Castr
 mentation** *Castramentation, or the arrangement of a camp of a regiment of infantry in a column of divisions*

Castro, Cipriano (1858?–1924). A Venezuelan soldier who in 1899 led a successful revolution and became "supreme military leader." His rule was marked by many unsuccessful insurrections, enormous debts, and trouble with the United States when he confiscated American property. He was deposed by a revolution in 1908.

Casualties. All those who after a battle are not present for duty: the killed, captured, wounded, injured, the deserters, the lost, and all otherwise missing in action. In the nineteenth century a distinction was not always made between battle casualties and other losses. Some casualty figures included stragglers and sick and discharged soldiers.

Casualty figures can vary widely because the number depends upon when a count was made: Those wounded and lost sometimes soon return to duty; the captured sometimes escape or are freed; the wounded sometimes die. It also depends upon who makes the count. Some armies keep better records than others, some generals or politicians may have reason to falsify the numbers, but in general the victor's numbers tend to be more accurate than those of the defeated, or at least the victor is usually in a better position to count the casualties. Napoleon's dispatches almost always estimated the enemy's losses as double the real figure and his own at about half. His was a practice continued through the century and well beyond.

No nineteenth-century war's casualties have been studied as carefully as those of the American Civil War, but the three leading authorities almost never agreed. Although Union figures were usually more accurate than Confederate numbers, Thomas L. Livermore (*Numbers and Losses in the Civil War in America, 1861–65* [Boston; Houghton Mifflin Co., 1901]) gives Union casualties for the First Battle of Bull Run [q.v.], or Manassas, as 2,645; Frederick Phister (*Statistical Record of the Armies of the United States* [New York: Charles Scribner's Sons, 1889]) as 2,952; and William F. Fox (*Regimental Losses*

in the . . . Civil War [Albany: Albany Publishing Company, 1898]) as 3,334, a difference of 689 between the highest and lowest numbers of these three experts, Fox's figure being more than 25 percent higher than Livermore's. For battles in the Napoleonic Wars, the difference between varying figures is often in the thousands. It would be fair to say that few, if any, nineteenth-century casualty figures are exact, and all must be regarded as guesses or approximations. Those given in this encyclopedia are those considered by the author to be most plausible.

Casus Belli. The event or action that causes a war or serves as an excuse for war. The justifications for any given war abound. Prince Pëtr Alekseevich Kropotkin (1842–1921) wrote: "War is the usual condition of Europe. A thirty years' supply of the causes of war is always at hand" (*Parole d'un révolté,* 1884). But causes of wars are usually irrelevant to the conduct of the war, the causes frequently change in the course of the war, and when the peace is signed, those causes deemed sufficient to justify the war are often completely forgotten, as was the case with the Americans and the Treaty of Ghent that ended the War of 1812 [q.v.] and with Britain, France, Sardinia, and Turkey in the Congress of Paris that ended the Crimean War [qq.v.].

Cathcart, Charles Murray, Second Earl (1783–1859), styled Lord Greenock (1807–1843). A British soldier, a son of General Sir William Cathcart [q.v.], who was commissioned a cornet in the 2nd Life Guards on 2 March 1800. During the Napoleonic Wars he served on the staff of Sir James Henry Craig (1748–1812) in Naples and Sicily in the campaigns of 1805–06 [see Mediterranean Expedition, British; Calabrian War]. He obtained his majority on 14 May 1807 and took part in the Walcheren Expedition [q.v.] and the Siege of Flushing [q.v.] in 1809. Like most who took part in that ill-advised expedition, he was disabled by "pestilence."

He became a lieutenant colonel on 30 August 1810 and was sent to the peninsula, where he was present at the battles of Barossa, Salamanca, and Vitoria [qq.v.]. In 1815 he fought at Waterloo [q.v.], where three horses were shot from under him.

After the war Lord Greenock was able to find time for his interest in scientific pursuits. In 1841 he discovered a new mineral, greenockite, which was named after him. From 16 March 1846 to 17 June 1847 he was commander-in-chief of British forces in North America.

He was a brother of General Sir George Cathcart [q.v.].

Cathcart, George (1794–1854). A British soldier, a brother of Charles Cathcart [q.v.], who on 10 May 1810 was commissioned a cornet in the 2nd Life Guards. He served as an aide to his father, General Sir William Cathcart [q.v.], in Russia and was present at the chief battles of the Napoleonic campaigns of 1813. On 31 March 1814 he entered Paris with the Allied armies. He was an aide to Wellington in the battles of Quatre Bras and Waterloo [qq.v.] in 1815.

He became a major general on 11 November 1851. The following year he was sent to South Africa as governor-general to establish a colonial parliament and to crush the Basutos and other disaffected tribesmen. In Cape Colony he called the first Cape parliament, granted a constitution, and marched against hostile tribesmen, whom he subdued. He then marched into Basutoland (Lesotho), where in February 1853 Sandilli [q.v.] surrendered to him.

He commanded a division in the Crimean War but quarreled with Lord Raglan [q.v.]. In the confusing Battle of Inkerman [q.v.] he was shot in the chest. His last words were to a staff officer: "I fear we are in a mess."

Cathcart, William, Tenth Baron (1755–1843). A British soldier and the father of the generals George Cathcart and Charles Cathcart [qq.v.]. He fought in the American Revolution, where he commanded an irregular corps known as the British Legion and distinguished himself in the storming of Forts Clinton and Montgomery on 6 October 1777 and in the Battle of Monmouth Court House on 28 June 1778.

He was promoted major general on 3 October 1794 and fought in the Netherlands. From 1803 to 1805 he was commander-in-chief in Ireland. In May 1807 he was appointed commander of an army in the Baltic and commanded the land forces that forced the surrender of Copenhagen [q.v.]. In addition to the many honors bestowed upon him, he and Admiral James Gambier (1756–1833) divided prize money of £300,000, then an enormous fortune.

In July 1812 he was sent to Russia as ambassador to the tsar and British military commissioner to the Russian army. He returned to England in 1820.

Cat-o'-Nine-Tails. Nine pieces of line or cord each bearing three knots at intervals, fastened to a piece of thick rope. It was used for flogging when ordered as a punishment.

Caucasian Corps. A separate autonomous organization in the Russian army that has been likened to the British Indian army. Less stiffly controlled than the rest of the army, the Caucasian Corps was considered a breeding ground for new ideas and experiments. Its troops wore colorful Circassian-style uniforms.

Caucasian Wars. See Murid Wars.

Caudillos. Provincial chieftains in Argentina who in the early nineteenth century based their power on rural gaucho militia.

Caulaincourt, Auguste Jean Gabriel (1777–1812). A French soldier who in 1804 was an aide-de-camp to General Louis Alexandre Berthier [q.v.] and in 1806 was promoted general of brigade. He served in Spain, Portugal, and Russia, where he was killed in the Battle of Moscow. His older brother, the Marquis Armand Augustine Louis de Caulaincourt (1772–1827), was also a soldier and a diplomat who served as minister of foreign affairs during the Hundred Days [q.v.].

Cavagnari, Pierre Louis Napoleon (1841–1879). A British soldier, the son of one of Napoleon's generals and an Englishwoman, he was educated at Addiscombe [q.v.] and in 1857 went as a cadet to India, where he served with the 1st Bengal European Fusiliers during the Indian Mutiny [q.v.]. He became a political officer and took part in several campaigns in the Northwest Frontier. He was knighted (KCB) for his efforts in personally negotiating the Treaty of Gandamak with Muhammad Yakub Khan [q.v.] in Afghanistan on 26 May 1879.

In the same year he was sent to Kabul as British Resident. On 24 July 1879, escorted by a detachment of the Corps of Guides [q.v.], he entered Kabul. There on 3 September in a mutiny of Afghan regiments he and his escort were attacked. All were massacred.

Cavaignac, Louis Eugène (1802–1857). A French soldier who served in Algeria from 1832 to 1848, when he was made governor-general. He was soon recalled to Paris to be minister of war and to make plans to defend the government from insurrection. He was among those responsible for the suppression of the Paris Commune [q.v.]. Serving as de facto president, having been given full powers by the Constituent Assembly, he deported thousands of dissidents and suppressed several newspapers. In 1848 he ran for president but was defeated. In 1852 he refused to take an oath to uphold the imperial constitution and retired from public life.

Cavalier. In fortifications, a cavalier is a work with a parapet that rises from the level ground of a bastion above the rampart, creating a high command of fire.

Cavalier Battery. In siege operations, a battery mounted upon a platform of earth.

Cavalry. The arm of an army designed to fight on horseback. The first modern cavalry was probably the French *compagnies d'ordonnance* organized by Charles XII in 1439. Saxon cavalry was renowned in the early part on the nineteenth century, and Russian Cossacks [q.v.] throughout the century.

There were two major categories of cavalry, light and heavy. The latter rode heavier horses and usually were more heavily armed. Heavy cavalry included cuirassiers and carabiniers (carabineers) [qq.v.], who were mounted on powerful horses and wore breastplates. Napoleon had fourteen regiments of cuirassiers and two of carabiniers.

Dragoons, originally mounted infantry, evolved into regular cavalry, sometimes light cavalry and sometimes heavy cavalry. In the United States before the Civil War horsemen were divided into dragoons and mounted rifles [qq.v.]. The postbellum army contained regiments of dragoons, cavalry, and mounted rifles, although the difference between the first two was not readily apparent and dragoons soon disappeared.

The British army held three classes of cavalry for most of the nineteenth century: (1) household cavalry, which consisted of the 1st and 2nd Life Guards and the Royal Horse Guards (Blues), (2) seven regiments of dragoon guards (heavy cavalry) numbered separately; the 6th Dragoon Guards were called carabiniers, (3) twenty-one regiments of line cavalry: lancers, dragoons, and hussars [qq.v.].

Hussars and lancers were always light cavalry, although hussars tended to grow ever more heavy. Uhlans [q.v.] in the Prussian and Austrian armies and Cossacks [q.v.] in the Russian army were light cavalry.

Cavalry regiments, which were numerically smaller than infantry regiments, were divided into squadrons or wings, which in turn were divided into companies or troops. In Napoleon's cavalry, companies were divided into two *peletons*. In major wars regiments of cavalry were often formed into larger units: brigades, divisions, and, under Napoleon and in the Union army during the American Civil War, into army corps. In the American army the basic unit was called a company until in 1883 it was renamed a troop.

Cavalry *Charge of Russian cavalry*

As the century progressed and the rifle replaced the musket, cavalry became increasingly ineffective until by the American Civil War it was generally restricted to scouting and patrolling or employed as mounted infantry. General William Tecumseh Sherman [q.v.] wrote: "Infantry can always whip cavalry and in wooded or mountainous areas can actually thwart it and even at times capture it."

The machine gun and the clip-fed, breech-loading rifle put an end to all usefulness of cavalry as an arm. Although it remained of some use for reconnaissance and as couriers in battle, the choice of regular cavalry was either to sit in idleness or to launch suicidal charges, such as the Death Ride of General Adalbert von Bredow [q.v.], who led his brigade of uhlans and cuirassiers to destruction in the Battle of Mars-le-Tour–Vionville [q.v.] during the Franco-Prussian War. Yet in 1890 the German army had ninety-three regiments of cavalry, all equipped with lances.

Cavalrymen, as they grew ever less useful, continued to think themselves superior to those who fought on foot.

Cavalry Club. A club founded in 1890 in London at 127 Piccadilly by an officer of the 20th Hussars as a proprietary club. It became a members' club in 1895. Only those who had been commissioned in cavalry and yeomanry regiments or in the Honourable Artillery Company [q.v.] were eligible. (In 1976 it merged with the Guards Club.)

Cavin. A natural hollow large enough for troops to be lodged and protected from enemy fire. A cavin facilitated the construction of trenches.

Cavite Mutiny (1872). On 20 January 1872 some 200 Filipino soldiers in the Spanish army mutinied in this province in southwest Luzon on the south side of Manila Bay in the Philippines. They were quickly and ruthlessly crushed, and the Spanish governor used the mutiny as a pretext to persecute intellectuals who were endeavoring to form an independence movement. Among those publicly executed were three priests, who thus became martyrs of the Philippine independence movement.

Cawnpore / Cawnpur / Cawnpoor / Kanpur (today), Battles of, Indian Mutiny. Cawnpore, a city on the right bank of the Ganges River 245 miles southeast of Delhi, was the scene of a siege and two battles during the course of the Indian Mutiny [q.v.].

First Battle of Cawnpore (26 November 1857). The garrison of Cawnpore, consisting of 1,200 infantry and 100 cavalry with 12 guns under Major General Sir Charles Ash Windham (1810–1870), defeated the Gwalior Contingent [q.v.] of mutineers—2,500 infantry and 500 cavalry under Tantia Topi [q.v.]—and captured 3 of their 6 guns, but in the face of heavy mutineer and rebel reinforcements the garrison was forced to retreat. The British lost about 300 men and abandoned a large quantity of baggage and stores.

Second Battle of Cawnpore (6 December 1857). A British force of 5,000 infantry and 600 cavalry with 35 guns under Sir Colin Campbell [q.v.], after relieving besieged Lucknow [q.v.], turned southwest and defeated a force of 25,000 mutineers and rebels with 40 guns under Tantia Topi [q.v.] just outside Cawnpore. The British lost only 99 men; the mutineers lost 36 guns and suffered heavy casualties. Many who fled were cut down by cavalry who maintained the pursuit for 14 miles. Tantia Topi fled to Jhansi and joined with rebel forces there. This battle was regarded as the turning point in the Indian Mutiny; the British no longer considered themselves in danger of being overcome.

Cawnpore, Siege of (4–27 June 1857). On the night of 4 June 1857 some 3,000 sepoys of the Bengal army under General Sir Hugh Massy Wheeler (1789–1857) stationed here mutinied and were joined by Nana Sahib [q.v.], who became their leader. The 900 European women, children, and troops took refuge in an entrenched position previously prepared, but the defenses were weak, and it was inadequately stocked with supplies.

Cawnpore, Siege of *Comprehensive view of the Cawnpore Massacre combines the killing of surrendering captives on the left with the slaughter two weeks later of others.*

On 6 June the mutineers began a bombardment of Wheeler's position. The defenders made a gallant defense, but hunger, thirst, and extreme heat added to the horrors of the siege, and there were daily losses. Wheeler's wounded son, who was being tended by his sisters and parents, had his head taken off by a round shot.

On 25 June, when Nana Sahib offered terms of capitulation, Wheeler reluctantly accepted them. On the morning of the 27th the survivors, only about 450, were marched to the Ganges River, where they had been promised boats to take them to Allahabad under a safe conduct. But when they arrived at the ghat and began to embark, the mutineers and rebels opened a devastating fire in which Wheeler and his family were among the first to fall. The survivors of this massacre, almost all women and children, were then tortured before being put to death on 15 July.

The next day Nana Sahib's force was defeated by a British force under Henry Havelock [q.v.] at Futtehpore, and on the following day Cawnpore was recaptured. British losses included 99 killed.

Caxias, Duque de, Luiz Alves de Lima e Silva (1803–1880). A Brazilian soldier and diplomat who was the commander-in-chief of the Brazilian forces in the War of the Triple Alliance [q.v.]. He was made a duke by the emperor Dom Pedro I (1798–1834), and he served as prime minister in 1850, 1856–57, 1861–62, and 1875–78.

Cayenne Expedition (11–12 January 1809), Napoleonic Wars. To retaliate for the occupation of Portugal by French troops, the Portuguese, in cooperation with a British force, launched an expedition from Pará, Brazil, to Cayenne Island at the mouth of the Cayenne River in French Guiana. The expedition was led by Portuguese Lieutenant Colonel Manuel, Marquês de Elvas. On 11–12 January 1809 the island was captured. It was returned to France by the Treaty of Vienna in 1815.

Cayuse War (1847–1855). In the Walla Walla Valley east of the Cascades, near present-day Walla Walla, Washington, on 29 November 1847 Reverend Marcus Whitman (1802–1847), a Presbyterian missionary, his wife, and 12 others were murdered by Cayuse Indians, who also captured and held hostage 53 women and children [see Whitman Massacre]. The Indians blamed the missionary, perhaps correctly, if unjustly, for a measles epidemic. Settlers, militia, and regulars rushed to arms, and the Cayuse War was begun. Five captured Cayuse chiefs were tried for murder, convicted by a military court, and on 3 June 1850 hanged. Undeterred, the Cayuses fought on until finally suppressed in 1855.

Cease-Fire. 1. A temporary cessation of a military action by mutual agreement, usually for only a few hours or a few days.

2. An order to stop firing.

Cease-Fire *Cease-fire at the Battle of Talavera, 1809. French and British troops refresh themselves in the same stream.*

Cedar Creek, Battle of (19 October 1864), American Civil War, also known as the Battle of Belle Grove or Middletown, Virginia. Confederate General Jubal Early [q.v.], although outnumbered nearly two to one (30,829 Federals to 18,410 Confederates), launched an early-morning surprise attack upon the eastern flank of Federal forces of Philip Sheridan [q.v.] camped around Belle Grove Plantation on the north bank of Cedar Creek in the Shenandoah Valley near Strasburg, Virginia. The Federals panicked, and one Confederate soldier said, "We were shooting them as fast as we could. . . . It was the worst stampede I ever saw." Early captured 1,300 prisoners and 18 guns. Sheridan, returning from a conference in Washington, was sleeping in Winchester, 13 miles away, when he was awakened by artillery fire. He made a rapid ride to the sound of the guns on his black Morgan gelding, Rienzi, and arrived in time to rally

his men and launch a counterattack on the Confederates, many of whom had broken ranks to loot the Federal camps.

The counterattack drove the Confederates back to Fisher's Hill, eight miles north-northeast of Woodstock, where on 22 September Sheridan had previously defeated Early [see Fisher's Hill, Battle of]. Federal losses were 5,665, of whom 1,591 were missing; the Confederates lost 2,910, of whom 1,050 were missing. Early also lost 25 guns, all of his ambulances, and most of his ammunition, forage, and other wagons. This was the only battle of the Civil War in which the opposing armies each won a major victory against the other on the same day. It was also the last major battle in the Shenandoah Valley.

Sheridan's dramatic return was made famous by a popular poem, "Sheridan's Ride," by poetaster and painter Thomas Buchanan Read (1822–1872), who made the ride the subject of his best-known painting.

Cedar Creek *American Civil War Battle of Cedar Creek, by Alfred Waud*

Cedar Creek, Battle of (21 October 1876), American Indian Wars, also known as the Battle of Big Dry River. At this place in western Montana an American force known as the Yellowstone Command [q.v.], which included the 5th Infantry, under Colonel Nelson A. Miles [q.v.], defeated Sioux Indians under Sitting Bull [q.v.]. Miles's force lost only 2 men and some horses wounded; the Indians lost at least 5 killed. The battle proved the value of infantry as well as cavalry or mounted rifles on the plains.

Cedar Mountain, Battle of (9 August 1862), American Civil War. During the Second Bull Run Campaign, Federal forces numbering 8,030 under General Nathaniel Banks [q.v.], advancing toward Culpeper, Virginia, encountered Confederate General Thomas Jackson [q.v.] with 16,868 men about four miles from the town and immediately launched a furious attack. The Confederates were saved by the timely arrival of A. P. Hill [q.v.], who launched a counterattack on the Federals' east flank. When darkness fell, the Federals retreated in good order.

Federal losses were 314 killed, 1,445 wounded, and 594 missing; Confederate losses were 231 killed, 1,107 wounded, and none missing.

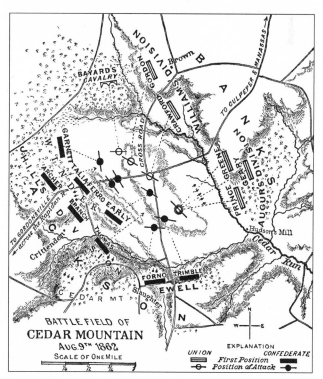

Cedar Mountain *Battlefield of Cedar Mountain, 9 August 1862*

Çelinks. The feathers worn in the turbans of those Turkish janissaries [q.v.] who had distinguished themselves in individual combat.

Cells. Places of short-term confinement (not to exceed 168 hours) in the British army.

Cemetery Hill and Cemetery Ridge. Physical features on the American Civil War battlefield at Gettysburg [q.v.], Pennsylvania. Cemetery Ridge, a low rise south of

Gettysburg, was in the center of the Union line, which was anchored on its northern end by Cemetery Hill, a defensive position with 16 guns. At twilight on 2 July two Confederate brigades charged the hill. It took an hour for them to reach the crest, both brigades taking heavy casualties. Once there, one brigade crumpled, but the other held fast, and there was much confused fighting around the guns before the Confederate survivors abandoned the fight and fled down the hill.

On 3 July General Robert E. Lee ordered an attack on the Union center, and 15,000 Confederates charged toward a clump of trees on Cemetery Ridge. They were mowed down by rifle and artillery fire. Pickett's Charge [q.v.], as it was called, was said to be "the high watermark of the Confederacy."

Cenotaph. A monument erected to the memory of those who are interred elsewhere or whose bodies or bones were not found after a battle.

Censorship. The prohibition against the publication of critical military information and the requirement that all military news sent by soldiers or correspondents be approved by military authorities.

Throughout the last half of the nineteenth century generals of all countries with a free press complained bitterly about journalists who thought it normal and proper to comment upon battle preparations, plans, and the quality of the generalship. Wellington, writing from Cartaxo, Spain, on 20 December 1810, complained in a private letter to the secretary of the admiralty: "The licentiousness of the press, and the presumption of the editors of the newspapers, have gone near to stultify the people of England; and it makes one sick to hear the statements of supposed facts. . . ."

Although censorship has a legitimate use in wartime, it is open to abuse, as when it is used to conceal the deficiencies of generals and ministers of war. Ian Hamilton [q.v.] once noted: "The freest people and press in the world are the most hoodwinked by military regulations for secrecy made in their own War Office!"

During the American Civil War some newspapers North and South were suppressed. In February 1862 the Union imposed telegraphic censorship, but this failed to stop the reporting of war news and military information. Secretary of War Edwin M. Stanton (1814–1869) tried without success to reduce Grant's losses at Petersburg by a third and to claim that the surrender of nearly 12,000 Union troops at Harpers Ferry was a loss of only 4,000.

Occasionally correspondents rebelled. When General George G. Meade [q.v.] ejected from the Army of the Potomac Edward Crapsey, a reporter from the *Philadelphia Enquirer* from whose reports Confederate General Robert E. Lee often gained valuable information, all the northern newsmen conspired to omit Meade's name from their stories and to credit future successes of the army to U. S. Grant. Much of the their resentment came from the manner of Crapsey's expulsion: Bearing a placard around his neck marked "Libeler of the Press" and tied backward on a horse, he was led out of camp by a band playing the "Rogue's March." Union General William Sherman [q.v.] habitually expelled reporters from his camps.

The Confederates were somewhat more successful in their censorship efforts, in part because of a paper shortage. Only 5 percent of America's paper mills were in the South.

Prussian attempts at censorship during the Seven Weeks' War and the Franco-Prussian War [qq.v.] met with some success, in large part because the press was less free. Both Otto von Bismarck (1815–1898) and Helmuth von Moltke [q.v.] proved adept at manipulating not only their own but the foreign press.

During the Franco-Prussian War French authorities declared that all telegrams would be censored and that no journalists would be allowed at the front. French General Edmond Leboeuf [q.v.], having assured Napoleon III that the army was completely prepared "even to the buttons on the gaiters" and loath to have journalists see how wrong he had been, declared, "*On fera du fusilier tous les journalistes.*" Nevertheless, correspondents swarmed over the front with impunity; none was shot. It was said that the Prussian general staff learned the location of all the French forces from French newspapers.

During the Spanish-American War [q.v.] the Spaniards were said to have been kept fully informed of U.S. preparations by the American press. In Britain a War Office memorandum of 12 October 1904 noted that "towards the end of 1898, when the country was believed to be on the eve of war with France [see Fashoda Incident], the newspapers contained exhaustive information concerning our defence and our preparations. The compositions of the garrisons of all of our defended ports were given."

Most generals harbored a disdain for journalists. Sir Garnet (later Lord) Wolseley advocated deliberately lying to them, as he boasted of doing, even arranging elaborate schemes to deceive them. Some feared, with reason, the effects of stories from the front. Even heroes could be hurt. Kitchener successfully conquered the Sudan, but did not escape Queen Victoria's displeasure when she read in the *Times* of his indifference to the suffering of the wounded, and a public outcry followed the report that El Mahdi's tomb had been desecrated and Kitchener had toyed with the notion of having an inkstand made from his skull.

During the Crimean War [q.v.] William Howard Russell [q.v.] of the *Times* provoked an outcry by his revelation of the blunders that had been made by the War Office and the army in their provisions for supplying the needs of the British field army.

Censorship in the modern sense did not exist until the Russo-Japanese War in 1904, when the Japanese, who had practiced censorship of a sort since the Satsuma Rebellion [q.v.] of 1877, successfully imposed a rigid control of information. [See War Correspondent.]

Center Fire. This is said of a cartridge in which the percussion cap is located in the center of the cartridge's base: If the cap is concealed within the cartridge, it is said to be "inside primed."

Central African Mission, French (1898–99). One of the most ruthless and devastating of the nineteenth-century French military expeditions into Central Africa that created France's enormous African colonial empire. Captain Paul Voulet (1866–1899) and Captain Paul Jules Chanoine (1870–1899), who had served together in a ferocious and bloody campaign in the Mossi states in 1897, commanded the expedition, which was composed of 3 other officers, a doctor, 3 noncommissioned officers, 50 Senegalese tirailleurs, 20 Sudanese spahis, and 400 African "auxiliaries." The troops were armed with magazine-fed Lebel rifles [q.v.], bolt-action carbines, and an 80 mm gun. Because there was no money for porters, 800 Africans were conscripted; 12 who tried to escape were killed.

The expedition left Say, on the Niger River southeast of Niamey, in January 1898, and its members were soon raiding villages and devastating a wide area. In one village 101 women, children, and old men were bayoneted; a tirailleur who used his rifle instead of his bayonet was shot for wasting ammunition. Floggings became commonplace. Porters who grew too weak to march were decapitated. When on 13 July 1898, 2 tirailleurs were killed in the assault on a village, 124 women and children were slain in reprisal.

When a lieutenant who had left the expedition carried back to France a report of its depredations, a lieutenant colonel was sent out to recall it and arrest its captains. He was killed by Voulet, who, with Chanoine and the remains of the expedition, set out to build an African empire, Voulet calling himself the chief of sofas [q.v.].

On 16 July 1899 the men mutinied, and the 2 captains were killed. A lieutenant tried to assume command, but after a second mutiny in which 45 tirailleurs and spahis died, the expedition disintegrated. The lieutenant perished on his way back to France.

Central American Conflicts. On 21 September 1821 Nicaragua, Honduras, Guatemala, Costa Rica, and El Salvador declared themselves independent of Spain and allied themselves with Mexico. On 21 July 1823 the five separated from the Mexican Confederation and formed the Central American Federation with Manuel José Arce (1783?–1847) as president. The members soon quarreled among themselves. Arce assumed dictatorial powers and led an army against El Salvador. When it besieged San Salvador, the capital, an army from Honduras under Francisco Morazán [q.v.] came to the city's rescue. Morazán then seized power, and conflicts continued until the federation was dissolved in 1839 by Rafael Carrera [q.v.], an illiterate conservative supported by the Roman Catholic Church. From 1840 to 1869 dictator Carrera, elected president of Guatemala for life in 1854, dominated Guatemala and most of Central America.

The duration of the century saw turmoil: rebellion, assassinations, anarchy, and bloodshed, as well as filibustering expeditions from the United States. [See Filibuster; Walker, William; Miranda, Francisco; Gutiérrez de Lara, Bernardo; Mina, Francisco; López, Narciso; Chalchuapa, Battle of.]

Central Asian Wars (1866–75). In 1839 the Russians sent an expedition under General Basil A. Perovsky (1795–1857) against the khanate of Khiva (now in Uzbekistan) on the left bank of the lower Oxus (Amu Darya) River, an action that ended in disaster. In 1847 the Russians established a fort on the northeastern banks of the Aral Sea at the mouth of the Jaxartes River. In 1864–65 Russians under Mikhail Grigorievich Chernyaiev [q.v.] captured Tashkent, the center of a khanate in an area between southeast Kazakhstan and northern Tadzhik. In May 1866 the khan of Bokhara (Bukhara, now in Uzbekistan) began a war with Russia in which he suffered a series of defeats by forces under Russian

General Konstantin Petrovich Kaufmann [q.v.]. Peace was declared on 11 July 1867, and the khanate was made a Russian protectorate.

On 26 May 1868 after several bitter battles a Russian force under General Kaufmann occupied Samarkand in Uzbek (Uzbekistan). In December 1872 the Russians made a reconnaissance in force toward Khiva and were defeated. In March 1873 a full-scale military expedition was launched, and on 10 June Khiva surrendered and was declared a subject territory in the Russian Empire.

In September–October 1875 Russia fought a war with Khohand (Kokand) in eastern Uzbek, which had come into conflict with other Turkic peoples in Turkistan [see Khohand War].

Centralia Massacre (27 September 1864). One of the nastier episodes of the American Civil War occurred at Centralia, Missouri, 22 miles north-northeast of Columbia, when Confederate William ("Bloody Bill") Anderson (1840–1864), who had left Quantrill's raiders [q.v.] and was marauding with his own band of ruffians, captured a train, whose crew they slaughtered along with 24 unarmed Union soldiers. Civilian passengers who tried to hide their valuables were also murdered. After looting $3,000 found in the express car and setting the train on fire, they rode off. They were soon pursued by three companies of the 39th Missouri and a detachment from the 1st Iowa Cavalry. Anderson's band ambushed them, and of the Union force of 147 men, 116 were killed, 2 were wounded and left for dead, and 6 remained unaccounted for.

One month later, on 26 October, Anderson was killed near Richmond, Missouri, by militia, who decapitated him and mounted his head on a telegraph pole.

Central Plains Campaign (April–July 1867), American Indian Wars. A costly and ineffectual campaign by American army forces led by Winfield Scott Hancock and George Custer [qq.v.] against Cheyenne and Sioux Indians.

Cépeda, Battle of (22 October 1859), Argentine Revolution. Bartolomé Mitre [q.v.], leading the forces of Buenos Aires, was defeated near this Argentine village by forces of the Argentine Confederation under Justo José Urquiza [q.v.]. Buenos Aires was incorporated into the confederation.

Cerro Gordo, Battle of (17–18 April 1847), Mexican War. At this mountain pass, 60 miles northwest of Veracruz, a Mexican army of about 12,000 under Antonio López de Santa Anna and Valentín Canalizo [qq.v.] was defeated by an American army of 8,500 under Winfield Scott, which was marching west toward Mexico City after the capture of Veracruz. Captain Robert E. Lee distinguished himself in the battle by discovering the way to turn the Mexican flank. Mexican losses were about 1,000 killed and wounded, 204 officers and 2,837 men taken prisoner, and 43 guns and 4,000 small arms captured. American losses were 63 killed and 337 wounded. George B. McClellan, who was a lieutenant of engineers in the battle, later described it as a "tactical masterpiece."

The following day Scott advanced 20 miles to Jalapa.

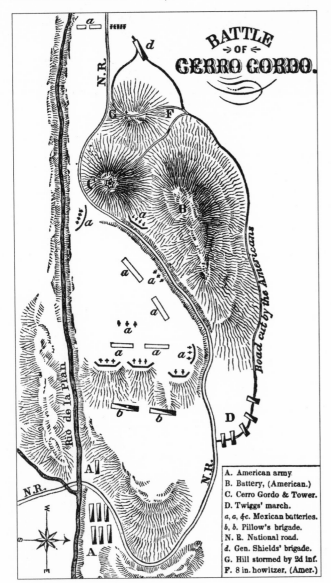

Cerro Gordo *Battle of Cerro Gordo, Mexican War*

A. American army.
B. Battery, (American.)
C. Cerro Gordo & Tower.
D. Twiggs' march.
a, a, &c. Mexican batteries.
b, b. Pillow's brigade.
N. R. National road.
d. Gen. Shields' brigade.
G. Hill stormed by 2d Inf.
F. 8 in. howitzer. (Amer.)

Certificate of Merit. An American certificate for "distinguished service involving peril of life" in the presence of the enemy, signed by the president of the United States, awarded to enlisted men in the American army upon the recommendation of their commanding officers. The handsomely designed parchment certificates were approved by Congress on 3 March 1847, and 539 men received the award for their services in the Mexican War [q.v.]. Between 1874 and 1891 only 59 soldiers in the Indian-fighting army received certificates. Unlike holders of the Medal of Honor, recipients received an extra two dollars a month as long as they remained in service; payment dated from the commission of the deed. [See Medal of Honor.]

By an act of 5 March 1934, any surviving holder of a certificate could, upon application to the War Department, receive a Distinguished Service Cross, still the army's second-highest award.

Cesnola, Luigi Palma di (1832–1904). An Italian soldier who served for three years in an Italian army (1849–52). In 1860 he emigrated to the United States, where he served in the Union army in the American Civil War and won the Medal of Honor [q.v.]. He became a naturalized American citizen in 1865, served as the American consul in Cyprus, where he conducted archaeological excavations, and from 1879 to his death was director of the Metropolitan Museum of New York City.

Cetewayo / Cettiwayo / Cetshwayo / Cetywago / Ketshwayo / Ketchwayo (1827?–1884). A Zulu chief who, to assume the chieftainship of his father, fought an internecine war with his half brother, whom he decisively defeated on 2 December 1856 in the Battle of 'Ndondakusuka, after which he butchered 7,000 of his enemy and some 20,000 of their women and children. In the Zulu War [q.v.] of 1879–80 he sent his impis [q.v.] to fight the invading British but took no personal part in the battles. His warriors destroyed a battalion of the South Wales Borderers in the Battle of Isandhlwana [q.v.] but were soon after defeated in the Battle of Ulundi [qq.v.]. Cetewayo then fled. He was captured on 28 August 1879 and sent to Cape Town as a prisoner. In 1882 he was taken to London, where he was presented to Queen Victoria, who described him in her journal as "tall, immensely broad and stout, with a good-humoured countenance, and an intelligent face." He was soon after returned to South Africa, where on 29 January 1883 he was restored to his throne. In the same year he was defeated in a war against Usibepu [q.v.], a former subordinate, and his kraal was destroyed. He died, possibly of poison, near Ulundi on 8 February 1884.

Cetewayo *Cetewayo, king of the Zulus, in captivity in Cape Town, South Africa*

Chacabuco, Battle of (12 February 1817), Chilean War of Independence. Patriot forces led by José de San Martín of Argentina and Bernardo O'Higgins [qq.v.] of Chile, having left Mendoza, then a town in western Argentina about 60 miles southeast of Aconcagua (destroyed by earthquake and fire on 20 March 1861), and having crossed the Andes into Chile, encountered and defeated at this village just north of

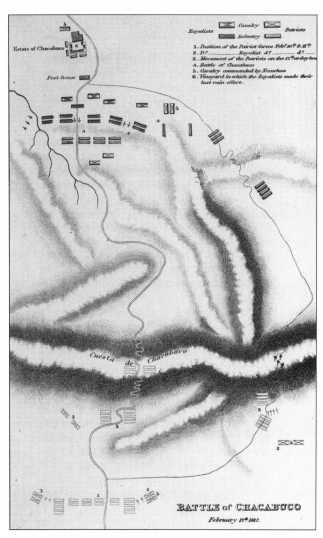

Chacabuco *Battle of royalists against the patriots at Chacabuco, Chile, 12 February 1817*

Santiago in central Chile a Spanish royalist force under General Marco del Pont. The battle was won by a bayonet charge led personally by O'Higgins.

This victory drove the Spanish out of Santiago, and the independence of Chile was proclaimed on the day of the battle. O'Higgins was soon dictator of Chile.

Chad, Conquest of (1897–1901). As Lake Chad in Central Africa was thought to be of economic importance, French explorer Emile Gentil (1866–1914) led an expedition down the Chari River to the lake's southern edge in 1897, made a treaty with the sultan of Baguirmi (Bagirmi), whose territory was just southeast of the lake, and established a French protectorate. In 1900 French forces marched south from Algeria and east from Senegal and Niger to join with Gentil, then governor of Shari (Chari) Province, northwest of Lake Chad, in a war against the forces of Rabah (or Rabih) Zubair (1845–1900), not to be confused with Rahma Mansur Zobeir [q.v.]. Zubair, a slaver and freebooter, had killed a French naval lieutenant in an attack upon a French mission at remote Togba (17°29′N, 10°12′W). On 22 April 1900, in a battle near Lake Chad, Zubair was killed, and his force dispersed, but bloody fighting between the French and tribesmen followed,

continuing well into the twentieth century until the French conquered Chad.

Chaffee, Adna Romanza (1842–1914). An American soldier who on 22 July 1861, during the American Civil War, enlisted as a private in the 6th U.S. Cavalry and soon became a first sergeant. On 13 March 1863 he was commissioned a second lieutenant. In the course of the war he earned two brevets: to first lieutenant for gallantry in the Battle of Gettysburg [q.v.], where he was wounded on 3 July 1863, and to captain for valor in the Battle of Five Forks [q.v.], or Dinwiddie Court House, on 31 March 1865.

He remained in the army after the war and won a brevet to major for his gallant conduct in an engagement against Comanche Indians at Paint Creek [q.v.], Texas, on 7 March 1868, and another to lieutenant colonel on 27 February 1890 for two actions: leading a cavalry charge on rough and precipitous bluffs held by Indians on the Red River in Texas on 30 August 1874 and for action against Indians at Big Dry Wash, Arizona, on 17 July 1882. On 8 May he was promoted colonel of the 8th Cavalry.

On 4 May 1898, during the Spanish-American War, he was promoted brigadier general of volunteers and distinguished himself in the Battle of El Caney [q.v.] on 1 July of that year. This led to promotion to major general of volunteers on 8 July. On 13 April 1899 he was promoted brigadier general in the regular army. He again became a major general of volunteers on 19 July 1900, when he took command of the 2,500 American troops in China during the Boxer Rebellion [q.v.]. He was made a major general in the regular army on 4 February 1901 and appointed military governor and commander of U.S. forces in the Philippines. From 1904 to 1906 he was a lieutenant general and chief of staff.

His son, whose name was the same (1884–1941), accompanied his father to China. He later entered West Point and, following his father's footsteps, became a general.

Chaffin's Farm, Battle of. See New Market Heights.

Chaillé-Long, Charles (1842–1917). An American soldier and adventurer who served first as a noncommissioned officer in a Maryland regiment of the Union army during the American Civil War and rose to the rank of captain. In 1869 he was appointed a lieutenant colonel in the Egyptian army. Later he became chief of staff to Charles ("Chinese") Gordon [q.v.] in the Sudan. Here he was wounded in a battle with slavers on 17 August 1874. He took part in the conquest of Niam Niam country and the occupation of Juba, on the Bahr el Jebel in Equatoria. He was then sent on a secret mission to Uganda, where he explored the Upper Nile Basin. When illness forced his retirement on 31 August 1874, he returned to the United States and studied law at Columbia University. He published *Naked Truths of Naked People* (1876), in which he described his experiences in Uganda, and books on Arabi Pasha, El Mahdi, and Gordon [qq.v.]. He then returned to Egypt, where he was admitted to the practice of law before the international tribunals. In September 1882 he resigned his law practice, and from 1887 to 1889 he was U.S. consul in Korea. There he discovered the source of the Kan (Han) River, which flows west-northwest into the Yellow Sea north of Jinsen. In December 1889 he sailed for the United States, married Marie Amelia Hammond on 16 July 1890, and returned to Egypt in December. From that time he occupied himself in writing accounts of his own experiences and those of adventuresome contemporaries.

Chain of Command. The succession of command and subordination from commanding officer to the lowest subordinate by which military command is exercised. "Command channels" refers to the same command structure.

Chain of Evacuation. The route or chain of posts or areas by which prisoners of war, wounded, and salvageable matériel pass from the battlefield to the rear.

Chain Shot. Two cannonballs connected by a short chain.

Chaka. See Shaka.

Chalchuapa, Battle of (2 April 1885), Central American Wars. Having won their independence from Spain, the Central American republics considered uniting in an isthmian confederation. Honduras and Guatemala were willing, but Costa Rica, El Salvador, and Nicaragua proved recalcitrant. Guatemalan President General Justo Rufino Barrio [q.v.], who envisioned himself the dictator of all Central America, tried to force the union by invading El Salvador. He was decisively defeated in the Battle of Chalchuapa, near the town of the same name in western El Salvador. [See Central American Conflicts.]

Challenge. 1. A sentinel's questions or demands for the countersign [q.v.] of anyone who approaches his post.

2. The call on another person to answer for an alleged offense by fighting a duel.

3. An objection raised by an accused to any member of a court-martial.

4. Any threat.

Chaltin, Louis Napoleon (1857–1933). A Belgian soldier and administrator who was commissioned in the Belgian infantry and in 1890 served in the Congo Free State, where he fought the Arab slave traders in the eastern Congo [q.v.]. In 1896 he took command of a column that in early 1897 defeated Dervish forces under Mahdist Amir Arabi Dada Allah (d. 1916?) at Rejaf on the Bahr el Jebel River in Equatorial Province in the Sudan, forcing them to retreat north.

Chamade. A signal made with a drum for a parley.

Chamber. The part of a gun's bore in which the cartridge explodes. By having the chamber larger than the bore, gunmakers obtained certain ballistic advantages. Muzzleloaders with larger chambers were known as chambered guns.

Chamberlain, Joshua Lawrence (1828–1914). An American soldier who was educated at Bowdoin College and Bangor Theological Seminary. He was a professor at Bowdoin when on 8 August 1862, during the American Civil War, he was commissioned a lieutenant colonel of the 20th Maine. In the course of the war he fought in twenty-four engagements, was wounded six times, had fourteen horses shot from under him, and rose to be a general. For his gallantry in the Battle of Gettysburg he was awarded the Medal of Honor [q.v.]. At

Appomattox Grant gave him the honor of formally receiving the surrender of the Army of Northern Virginia [q.v.]. After the war he was elected governor of Maine and re-elected three times. He then served as president of Bowdoin College.

Chamberlain, Neville Bowles (1820–1902). A British soldier who served his entire career in India and Afghanistan. (He was no relation to later Prime Minister Neville Chamberlain, 1869–1940.) Of his four brothers, one became an admiral and three entered the service of the Honourable East India Company. On 27 February 1837, when he had just turned seventeen, he was commissioned an ensign in the company's army. He first saw action in the First Afghan War [q.v.] when his regiment, the 16th Bengal Native Infantry, became part of the Army of the Indus [q.v.], which reached Kandahar on 27 April 1839. In the march on Kabul he distinguished himself in the fight for Ghazni [q.v.].

The 16th Bengal Native Infantry was relieved in 1841 and was marching back to India when an outbreak of violence at Kabul caused it to be ordered back to Kandahar. It arrived there on 8 November 1841 and remained for nine months in the force under General William Nott [q.v.]. In the frequent skirmishes with Afghans, Chamberlain made a name for himself as a skillful swordsman and an able leader of irregular horse. On 29 May 1842 he was stabbed in the thigh by a Ghazi [q.v.] who sprang upon his horse, and on 12 June 1842 he was wounded in the knee. He was given a gratuity of twelve months' pay by the Honourable East India Company for his wounds.

In August he was sufficiently recovered to accompany Nott's advance upon Kabul and was present for the storming and burning of Istalif [q.v.] on 28 September, a bloody action that he later said made him "disgusted with himself, the world, and above all, with my cruel profession."

After occupying Kabul, Nott's force combined with that of George Pollock [q.v.] and left for India on 12 October. The column was much harassed, and Chamberlain, who was with the rear guard, was twice wounded: by a bullet near his spine on 16 October and by a bullet in his leg on 6 November. In all, he was wounded six times during his four years in Afghanistan. Although he had not yet recovered from his last wound, he took part in the Gwalior Campaign [q.v.] and fought in the Battle of Maharajpore [q.v.] on 29 December 1843.

On 20 February 1845 he left India for sick leave in England and thus missed the First Sikh War, but he returned late in 1848 in time for the Second Sikh War [qq.v.], in which he served as brigade major [q.v.] in an irregular cavalry brigade. Before the British crossing of the Chenab River, he volunteered to swim across and reconnoiter, an operation that would have cost him his life had the Sikhs captured him. On his safe return, Lord Gough [q.v.] dubbed him "the bravest of the brave."

He was present in the Battle of Chilianwala [q.v.] but was with the baggage guard. However, he again distinguished himself in the Battle of Gujerat [q.v.], the final battle of the war. On 1 November 1849 he was promoted captain and awarded a brevet majority. Given civil employment, he organized the police in the Punjab. When he was stricken with malaria and granted a leave of absence for a year, he recuperated by hunting lions in South Africa.

He returned to India in 1854 and was given command of an irregular force in the Punjab. Although only a captain in his regiment, he was brevetted a lieutenant colonel in the army and appointed a local brigadier general. He led an expedition in April 1855 against the Miranzis and in August against the Orakzais on the Northwest Frontier. In the fall of 1856 he led a second expedition against the Miranzis, and in March 1857 he led an expedition into the Bozdar country, where no European had ventured before.

When the Indian Mutiny [q.v.] erupted in May 1857, Chamberlain was given a movable column, which he had to turn over to John Nicholson [q.v.], who was his senior. He then, on 24 June, joined the British army before Delhi. There he took a leading part in repulsing the mutineers' attacks, and on 14 July he was badly wounded by a musket ball in the shoulder. On 11 November 1857 he was awarded the CB. Returned to the Punjab, he aborted a planned mutiny among Sikh troops at Dera Ismail Khan, on the right bank of the Indus River 155 miles south of Peshawar. He led an expedition in December 1859 against the Kabul Khel Waziris and in April–May 1860 against the Mahsuds [see Mahsud Expedition]. On 11 April 1863 he was knighted (KCB).

Late in 1863 he led a force of 5,000 men against the Wahhabi Fanatics near Sitana. This developed into the Umbeyla Campaign [q.v.], in which he was severely wounded in the forearm and returned to Europe to recover. He was promoted major general on 5 August 1864 and in the next ten years received a cornucopia of honors. At Queen Victoria's request, he accompanied the Duke of Edinburgh on a trip to India in 1869. In 1873, at age fifty-three, he married the sixth daughter of a major general. In 1876 he returned to India as commander-in-chief of the Madras army. In February 1881 he left India for England and spent the remaining twenty-one years of his life quietly at his estate near Southampton. His wife died in 1896. The marriage was childless.

Although he served no more, he was promoted general on 1 October 1877 and field marshal on 25 April 1900. His friend Sir Charles Napier [q.v.] referred to him as "the very soul of chivalry."

Chambersburg, Burning of (30–31 July 1864), American Civil War. During Confederate General Jubal Early's Washington Raid [q.v.] he sent two of his brigades, about 2,600 men, under Bradley Johnson [q.v.] and John McCausland (1836–1927) to Chambersburg, Pennsylvania, 50 miles west-southwest of Harrisburg, to demand $100,000 in gold or $500,000 in Federal currency. This, he said, was to indemnify the Virginians whose property had been destroyed by the foray of Union General David Hunter [q.v.] into the Shenandoah Valley in May–June 1864. When the citizens would not or could not raise such a sum, Early ordered its 3,000 inhabitants evacuated and ordered McCausland to burn the town.

Colonel William Elisha Peters (1829–1906) of the 21st Virginia Cavalry refused to obey the burning order and was placed under temporary arrest. Other officers and men also refused, but there were enough obedient soldiers to torch the town and some 400 buildings, 274 of which were private houses. About two-thirds of the town was burned to the ground.

Champaubert, Battle of (10 February 1814), Napoleonic Wars. Near this village, 17 miles south-southeast of Épernay

in northeastern France, Napoleon, after a forced march through difficult country in heavy rain with 30,000 men and 120 guns, fell upon and bowled over 5,000 Russians in the middle of Prussian General Gebhard von Blücher's [q.v.] three divisions marching on Paris. Russian casualties were 4,000; Napoleon lost 200. [See Montmirail, Battle of; Vauchamps, Battle of.]

Champ de Mars. A large open square in front of the Military School in Paris where parades and large meetings were held and where on 10 May 1804 eagles [q.v.] were first distributed to units of the army. On 1 June 1815 a grand fete was celebrated in Paris during Napoleon's Hundred Days [q.v.]. Some 50,000 troops marched in a parade; 600 guns fired salutes; mass was celebrated at an altar erected in the Champ de Mars, where Napoleon, with his brothers in attendance, sat garbed in elaborate robes of purple velvet and white satin. The *acute additionnel aux constitutions de l'Empire,* a new liberal constitution providing liberty of the press, ministerial responsibility, and a parliament, which had been hurriedly drafted by Benjamin Constant (1767–1830), was promulgated, and Napoleon and others took oaths to defend it.

Champigny-sur-Marne, Battles of (30 November and 2 December 1870), Franco-Prussian War. French forces of about 12,000 under General Auguste Ducrot and General Louis Trochu [qq.v.] attempted unsuccessfully to break through the German lines around Paris at the point held by German General Eduard Fransecky [q.v.], then about eight miles south-southeast of Paris.

Champion's Hill, Battle of (16 May 1863), American Civil War, also known as the Battle of Baker's Creek. An engagement in the Vicksburg Campaign [q.v.] in which General U. S. Grant sent two army corps, about 29,000 men, to intercept 22,000 Confederates under General John C. Pemberton [q.v.], who had been ordered to unite his forces with those of Joseph E. Johnston [q.v.]. The armies met at Champion's Hill, Mississippi, 20 miles east of Vicksburg. The Confederates were defeated and retreated to Big Black River, less than 10 miles from Vicksburg, after losing 27 guns and hundreds of men taken prisoner.

Union losses were 410 killed, 1,844 wounded, and 187 missing. Confederate losses were 381 killed, about 1,800 wounded, and 1,670 missing.

Chancellorsville, Battle of (1–4 May 1863), American Civil War. When Robert E. Lee discovered that Federal General Joseph Hooker [q.v.], with 134,000 men, was advancing through the Wilderness on his position at Fredericksburg, he divided his force of 60,000 in the face of the enemy. Leaving only 10,000 under General Jubal Early [q.v.] at Fredericksburg, he advanced with the remainder to meet Hooker's main force. Surprised by this move, Hooker took up a defensive position. Lee then further divided his forces, sending General Thomas Jackson with 26,000 men around the Federal flank. Jackson was in position and began his charge at 6:00 P.M. It was completely successful. The Federals were driven from their positions in great confusion. Later that night Jackson was severely wounded when shot by his own men who mistook him and his staff for Federal cavalry.

J. E. B. Stuart [q.v.] took over Jackson's corps and launched a vigorous attack at dawn on 3 May, driving the Federals farther away. Meanwhile Federal General John Sedgwick [q.v.] attacked Early's positions at Fredericksburg. After four bloody but unsuccessful assaults, the Federals broke through the Confederate line at Marye's Heights [q.v.] and then turned to reinforce Hooker. Again Lee divided his forces. Leaving only 25,000 under Stuart to watch Hooker's 75,000, he turned to face Sedgwick and drove him across the river.

This battle, which has been called Lee's masterpiece, has been much studied and described as the perfect battle. It was, however, a costly victory. Although the Federal forces lost some 17,000 in killed, wounded, and missing, this was only 13 percent of Hooker's force. Lee lost about 12,800, or 22 percent of his force, and in addition, the wounded Jackson soon died.

Chanda, Siege of (May 1818), Third Maratha War. This fortress on an affluent of the Wardha River, 85 miles south of Nagpur, was the stronghold of the bhonsla of Nagpur, who defended it with 3,000 of his troops. It was besieged by a force of 4,000 British infantry, 2,000 irregular horsemen, and 25 guns. On 9 May 1818 after a two-day bombardment it was taken by storm, with a British loss of 14 killed and 56 wounded. More than 200 of the garrison, including its commandant, were killed.

Chandelier. In military terms, a wooden frame containing fascines to form a traverse in sapping.

Chandler, John (1762–1841). An American soldier who as a youth fought in the American Revolution. He was a brigadier general in the War of 1812 [q.v.] and took part in an invasion of Canada in 1813. He was honorably discharged in 1815.

Changarnier, Nicolas Anne Théodule (1793–1877). A French soldier who served in Algeria (1830–48) and became its governor. In 1848 he commanded the troops in Paris during the abortive uprisings. Banished in 1852 for his opposition to Napoleon III, he returned after the amnesty in 1859. During the Franco-Prussian War [q.v.] of 1870–71 he was with Achille Bazaine [q.v.] in Metz [q.v.] when it capitulated in October 1870. In 1875 he was elected senator for life.

Change Front, to. To change the direction in which troops are facing.

Chang Lo-hsing (d. 1863). An illiterate Chinese salt smuggler and bandit who became a leader in the Taiping Rebellion [q.v.], calling himself King of the Great Han with Heavenly Mandate. In 1856, during the Nien Rebellion [q.v.], he joined forces with Li Hsiu-ch'eng [q.v.]. He was finally defeated by Mongol cavalry. He was arrested by his own officers and handed over to General Seng-kuo-lin-ch'in [q.v.] on 23 March 1863. Chang and his wife, daughter, and son were promptly executed.

Changsha, Siege of (11 September–30 November 1852), Taiping Rebellion. A Taiping force under Hsiao Ch'ao-kuei [q.v.] attacked the large port city of Changsha on the right bank of the Siang River, about 45 miles south of Lake Tungting Hu in Hunan Province in south-central China. The city was defended by an imperial force under Tso Tsung-t'ang [q.v.]. The attack failed, and Hsiao was killed.

Chantilly / Ox Hill, Battle of (1 September 1862), American Civil War. After the Second Battle of Bull Run [q.v.] on 29–30 August 1862, Lee sent General Thomas ("Stonewall") Jackson [q.v.] on a wide arc around the west flank of Union General John Pope's [q.v.] army. Jackson struck Federal forces under Isaac Stevens and Philip Kearny [qq.v.] near the Chantilly plantation in Virginia, 20 miles west of Washington. Federal losses were 1,300; Confederate losses were 800. Although Pope had plenty of reinforcements at hand, he withdrew his army into the defenses of Washington.

Both Stevens and Kearny, generally regarded as two of the most promising generals in the Union army, were killed in this battle.

Chanzy, Antoine Eugène Alfred (1823–1883). A French soldier who served mostly in Algeria. He became a general of brigade in 1868 and commanded XVI Corps and later the Army of the Loire during the Franco-Prussian War [q.v.]. In 1873 he was appointed governor of Algeria, and in 1879 he was an unsuccessful candidate for president.

Chape. A metal piece mounted at the end of a sheath or scabbard of a sword or saber as reinforcement.

Chapeau Bras. The cocked hat that was the traditional formal headgear for general officers in several armies. In the United States it was formal wear for generals and certain staff officers. It was eliminated in 1851 but reinstated in 1859.

Chapeau bras

Chapeau Chinois. A musical instrument employed in military bands that consists of small bells on a pole. British soldiers called it a jingling Johnny.

Chaplain General. An appointment established in the British army in 1796 that designated a clergyman chief chaplain and supervisor of the work of all army chaplains. The position was abolished by Wellington soon after the Battle of Waterloo [q.v.] in 1815, but it was revived in 1846 by Mr. Sidney Herbert [q.v.] when he was secretary for war.

Chaplains. Priests, ministers, rabbis, and other religious leaders attached, officially or unofficially, to an army. The spiritual comfort of troops was for the most part not first in the thoughts of nineteenth-century generals, and the position of chaplains was often amorphous. Napoleon, who had no use for them although he allowed them in some of his foreign corps, once remarked: "Theology gives sure rules for spiritual government, but not for the government of armies." All chaplains were withdrawn from the French army in 1880 for fear of clerical opposition to the republican constitution.

There were of course exceptions. Confederate General Thomas Jackson put great store by chaplains and for a time had a Presbyterian minister with no military experience as his assistant adjutant general (chief of staff). Confederate General Leonidas Polk [q.v.] was himself a bishop. Henry Havelock [q.v.], even as a subaltern, took an active part in promoting religion in the British army in India.

The British army, in which Sunday attendance at divine service was compulsory, employed chaplains from 1796, but until 1827, when Presbyterian ministers were admitted, all were Anglican. Roman Catholic chaplains were allowed in 1836, and Wesleyans in 1881. The first Jewish chaplain was not appointed until 1892. Even at the end of the century nearly three out of four chaplains were Anglican. British chaplains were given officer status in 1816, but none was allowed to wear a uniform until 1860 [see Chaplain General].

Between 1818 and 1838 the U.S. Congress did not authorize chaplains for the American army, but some army posts hired their own. Those authorized in 1838 were all Protestant, with the Episcopal Church the most strongly represented until the Mexican War [q.v.] in 1845, when President Polk appointed two Jesuits in an attempt to counter Catholic Mexican sentiment that the war was a religious one. In 1841 army regulations made church service compulsory. The first Jewish chaplain was appointed in 1862, during the American Civil War, after nearly a year of congressional debate. Colonel Guy Vernor Henry (1835?–1899), who won a Medal of Honor for gallantry at Cold Harbor during the Civil War, testified before the House Military Affairs Committee in February 1876: "I am sorry to say, that I think chaplains are not of much account in the army. They are generally old men who do not exert a good influence. . . . [T]he men will have nothing to do with them." He pointed out that at Fort D. A. Russell in Wyoming, which had a garrison of 350 men, he never "saw over ten soldiers in the chapel on any one Sunday."

At West Point six of the first eight chaplains were Episcopalians, and Sylvanus Thayer [q.v.], superintendent from 28 July 1817 to 1 July 1833, made church attendance mandatory. There were no exceptions. Even Alfred Mordecai, a Jew who was graduated at the head of the class of 1823, attended.

In the Confederate armies of the Civil War there were four types of ministerial laborers: a few chaplains who had official commissions from a state or from the Confederate government; army missionaries who acted as chaplains but were under denominational control; army evangelists, who, like the missionaries, served brief terms; and colporteurs who distributed religious literature. Of the some 600 in the Confederate army who served officially, 25 died in service; 14 were killed in battle. In the Union army some 2,300 served, at least 66 died, and 3 won the Medal of Honor [q.v.].

The American army did not pay for churches, chapels, or synagogues, but it was a court-martial offense for a soldier to behave "indecently or irreverently" at any place of worship, and enlisted men could be fined the curious sum of "one-sixth of a dollar" for each offense.

Chappe. 1. A barrel that contained powder.

2. The earth, dung, and wad sometimes used to cover the muzzle of a gun.

Chappé's Semaphore. See Semaphore.

Chapultepec, Battle of (13 September 1847), Mexican War. The penultimate battle of the Mexican War [q.v.]. American General Winfield Scott [q.v.] deployed 7,200 men to the southwest of Mexico City and launched an attack on the castle, perched upon a steep 200-foot hill, Chapultepec (Grasshopper Hill), three miles from the city. The castle held the Mexican military academy and some 1,000 troops of General Antonio López de Santa Anna [q.v.]. An additional 4,000 Mexicans were posted in other fortifications nearby.

The American attack began with an artillery bombardment early in the morning. At eight o'clock two divisions of infantry under Generals John Quitman and Gideon Pillow [qq.v.], carrying pickaxes and ladders, began to climb the heights. An hour and a half later they raised the American flag above the castle. The stoutest defenders had been about 100 young cadets, who earned a place in Mexican history as *los Niños Perdidos* [q.v.]. Their numbers and their deeds—some were said to have thrown themselves from the walls to certain death to avoid capture—have been much embellished and have become a part of Mexican folklore.

American losses were 130 killed, 703 wounded, and 29 missing; Mexican losses are unknown. [See Mexican War.]

Charasiab, Battle of (6 October 1879), Second Afghan War. A force of Afghans, perhaps 15,000, massed on heights six miles south of Kabul to attack a British convoy, was routed by about 4,000 British regulars armed with new Martini-Henry rifles [q.v.] under Sir Frederick (later Lord) Roberts. The Afghan position was skillfully turned, and the Afghans fled, pursued by British cavalry.

The British sustained fewer than 100 casualties; Afghan losses were perhaps 300. It was in this battle that Major (later Field Marshal Sir) George White, who became the commander of besieged Ladysmith [q.v.] in the Second Anglo-Boer War [q.v.], won his Victoria Cross [q.v.].

Chard, John Rouse Merriot (1847–1897). A British soldier who was educated at Woolwich, [q.v.] and commissioned a lieutenant in the Royal Engineers on 15 July 1868. After service in Bermuda he was sent to South Africa. During the Zulu War [q.v.] of 1879 he was the senior lieutenant at Rorke's Drift [q.v.] when on 22 January it was attacked by thousands of Zulus. He was awarded the Victoria Cross [q.v.] for his gallant defense and promoted captain and brevet major to rank from 23 January. He later served with the Royal Engineers in Singapore and Malaya and rose to become a colonel. [See Bromhead, Gonville.]

Charge. 1. As a noun, the act of troops rushing toward an enemy with the intent of causing him to flee, surrender, or fight at close quarters.

2. As a noun, the temporary command of a military unit.

3. As a noun, the quantity of powder with which a cannon or small arm is loaded.

4. As a noun, the position of a weapon in the hands of a soldier about to make a charge.

5. As a noun, the amount of propellant in fixed or semi-fixed ammunition or the amount of explosive in a mine, bomb, or grenade.

6. As a noun, an indictment by a court-martial.

7. As a noun, a round of small-arms ammunition.

8. As a noun, an assigned responsibility for a task or mission.

9. As a noun, an allegation.

10. As a verb, to fill an explosive device.

11. As a verb, to move a round of ammunition into the magazine of a weapon.

Charge *Cavalry charge on the western frontier, 1897, by Frederic Remington*

Charge of the Light Brigade at Balaclava. See Light Brigade, Charge of.

Charger. An officer's horse.

Charivari. See Cherivallies.

Charles Albert, Prince. See Carlo Alberto.

Charles Augustus. See Karl August.

Charles, Louis John, Archduke of Austria and Duke of Teschen (1771–1847), usually referred to as Archduke Charles. The third son of Leopold II (1747–1792) and the brother of his successor, Francis I [q.v.]. He first saw action during the French Revolutionary Wars in the Battle of Jemappes on 6 November 1792. Soon after he was made governor-general of the Austrian Netherlands. He successfully fought off a French invasion and won the Battle of Neerwinden on 18 March 1793, but he was defeated at Wattignes on 15–16 October 1793 and Flexures on 26 June 1794.

In 1796 he became a field marshal and fought brilliant battles against the French generals Jean Baptiste Jourdan and Jean Victor Moreau [qq.v.], driving them out of Germany. After the fall of Mantua on 2 February 1797, he transferred to the Italian theater, where he fought bitter, but usually losing, battles against Napoleon and Jourdan.

Ill health caused him to abandon his military career for a time, although he became minister of war. In 1805 he was again on the Italian front, fighting an indecisive battle against André Masséna at Caldiero [q.v.] on 30 October. In 1806, after the Battle of Austerlitz [q.v.], he reorganized the Austrian army, and three years later he again led it against Napoleon. Although defeated at Eckmühl [q.v.] on 20 April 1809, he successfully checked Napoleon at Aspern-Essling [q.v.]. However, in July he was dealt a serious defeat at Wagram [q.v.], after which he left the field command of the army to Prince Schwarzenberg [q.v.] and retired to write on the theory of the art of war.

An epileptic, Archduke Charles was a courageous soldier and a good tactician and strategist; he was certainly one of Napoleon's most able opponents.

Charleston, Siege of (July 1863–February 1865), American Civil War. On 11 July 1863 a Union army-navy force commanded by Brigadier General Quincy Adams Gillmore (1825–1888), employing eleven warships under Admiral John Adolphus Bernard Dahlgren (1809–1870), attacked Fort Wagner [q.v.], which was defended by 1,200 men under Confederate Brigadier General William Booth Taliaferro [q.v.]. The fort, measuring 250 by 100 yards, sat on the edge of an impassable swamp on Morris Island at the south entrance to the harbor of Charleston, South Carolina. The attack was repulsed with a heavy loss. The 54th Massachusetts, a black regiment with white officers, lost 54 killed, 189 wounded, and 48 missing. Total Union losses were 1,500. The Confederates lost 36 killed, 145 wounded and missing.

Bringing up siege artillery to supply a covering fire, the Federals launched a two-brigade attack (5,264 men) led by Colonel Truman Seymour (1824–1891). A foothold was gained, but the Federals were thrown back; both the brigade commanders were killed, and Colonel Seymour was severely wounded. The Federals lost 1,515; the Confederates 174.

The Federals then began a formal siege, and on the night of 6–7 September 1863 the Confederates abandoned the island. Fort Sumter in Charleston Harbor continued to resist, and Confederate General Pierre Beauregard [q.v.], in overall command, was able to hold Charleston, in spite of the naval blockade, until 17–18 February 1865, when he ordered the city abandoned on the advance of General William Sherman [q.v.].

Charras, Jean Baptiste Adolphe (1810–1865). A French soldier who served in Algeria. In 1848 he was undersecretary for war, but he opposed policies of Louis Napoleon (1808–1873) and was banished after the coup d'état on 2 December 1851.

Chartist Riots (1842). The rejection by the British Parliament of a so-called People's Charter, drafted in 1838, demanding such political reforms as universal male suffrage, a ballot, salaried members of Parliament, and equal constituencies, touched off strikes and riots. Troops were used to protect lives and property in many parts of Britain. On 10 April 1842, 20,000 Chartists met on Kensington Commons to march on Westminster and present an enormous petition to Parliament. The Duke of Cambridge organized the military protection of London; banks and other buildings were fortified; 150,000 people were sworn to act as special constables. The threat of military force discouraged the reformers, and the monster petition was sent to the House of Commons in cabs. Thenceforth the movement declined rapidly.

Chase. The chase of a gun is its entire length.

Chassé, Baron Hendrik (or David Henri) (1765–1849). A Dutch soldier who, after service in the Dutch army (1775–92), served in the French army in Spain in 1808–13, during the Peninsular War [q.v.], becoming a general of division. Napoleon called him Général Baïonette because of his fondness for that weapon. After the abdication of Napoleon in 1814, Chassé rejoined the Dutch army and served in the Battle of Waterloo in 1815. In 1830 during the Belgian Revolution he conducted the defense of the citadel in Antwerp against the revolutionaries and held out until 1832. [See Antwerp, Sieges of; Belgian Revolution.]

Chassepot Rifle. A rifle developed in 1863 by Antoine Alphonse Chassepot (1833–1905), an employee of the French arsenal at St. Thomas d'Aquin (later a hotelkeeper in Nice), and adopted by the French army in 1866. As in the Dreyse needle gun [q.v.], a firing pin was propelled by a spring that was compressed when the bolt was cocked and was released by pulling the trigger. It was superior to the needle gun in that it did not drive the firing pin through the cartridge and it used a rubber seal on the face of the bolt that prevented the escape of gas rearward. It had a rate of fire of six or seven rounds per minute and used an improved cartridge with the percussion cap at the base rather than the center of the propelling charge. By April 1867 some 10,000 had been issued. After the Battle of Mentana [q.v.] in 1867 General Pierre de Failly [q.v.] reported: "The Chassepot has done wonders." By 1870 a million of these rifles, sighted up to 1,600 yards, were available, and in the Franco-Prussian War they proved superior to the Germans' Dreyse needle gun, outranging it by 1,000 yards. The Chassepot remained the standard rifle in the French army until 1874, when it was replaced by the Gras rifle [q.v.], which took metallic cartridges.

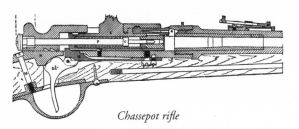

Chassepot rifle

Chasseur à Cheval. French light cavalrymen. Also sometimes called *chevaux-léger*.

Chasseur à Cheval *Prince Eugène de Beauharnais in uniform of Chasseurs à Cheval*

Chasseur à Pied. French light infantrymen.

Chasseurs d'Afrique. A light cavalry unit in France's African army formed by royal ordinance in November 1831 as an all-volunteer regiment of French settlers in Africa and a few volunteers from metropolitan France. They wore a dashing uniform consisting of white gauntlets, a long light blue coat, and red trousers with leather straps. Originally the troopers were armed with lances, but these were given up in 1833.

A mutiny in 1834 resulted in the execution of several men and the court-martialing and cashiering of six officers. The crops was then reformed and eventually came to enjoy so great a social cachet that officers in metropolitan regiments sometimes volunteered to serve in its ranks.

The Chasseurs d'Afrique made a famous charge in the Battle of Isly [q.v.] in 1844, and served with distinction in the Crimean War.

Chateaugay, Battle of (26 October 1813), War of 1812. A battle fought in Canada on the banks of the Chateaugay River, about 15 miles from its confluence with the St. Lawrence and 14 miles above Montreal. Some 800 British and Canadian soldiers barred the advance of Major General

Wade Hampton [q.v.] with 4,000 Americans. Hampton became entangled in a marsh, and British bugle calls sounded to give the impression that he was about to be overwhelmed by a superior force so deluded him that he fell back upon Plattsburg, New York, and went into winter quarters. [See War of 1812; Queenston Heights.]

Château-Thierry, Battle of (12 February 1814), Napoleonic Wars. Blücher's army of Russians and Prussians was retreating after the Battle of Montmirail [q.v.], fought on 11 February, when two of his corps were attacked by Napoleon and Adolphe Mortier [qq.v.]. The Allies lost about 2,800 men (1,300 Prussians and 1,500 Russians); the French lost only 600. The French captured nine guns, many wagons, and much equipment.

Chattanooga Campaign (September–November 1863), American Civil War. Following the Confederate victory at Chickamauga [q.v.] on 19–20 September 1863, Union General William Rosecrans [q.v.] drew his forces into Chattanooga, Tennessee, and Confederate General Braxton Bragg [q.v.] laid siege to the town. Two Union corps under Joseph Hooker [q.v.] were sent to raise the siege. In less than three weeks 20,000 men and more than 3,000 horses and mules were carried 1,157 miles by railroad. Additional reinforcements were dispatched from Memphis, Tennessee, and Vicksburg, Mississippi. By 15 October advance elements, about 17,000 men, arrived at Bridgeport, Alabama, three miles south of the Tennessee border.

In October, when Rosecrans did not, as expected, give up Chatttanooga, Bragg tried to cut his lines of communication and supply [see Cracker Line Operations], and when this failed, he abandoned the siege and sent General James Longstreet's corps to eastern Tennessee to attack Union General Ambrose Burnside [q.v.]. General U. S. Grant, put in command of the newly created Military Division of the Mississippi, arrived in Chattanooga to take personal charge on 23 October. The major battles of the campaign came in the following month at Orchard Knob (or Indian Hill) on 23 November, Lookout Mountain (the so-called Battle above the Clouds) the following day, and Missionary Ridge [qq.v.] on 25 November. All were Federal victories.

The Chattanooga Campaign was a Union victory of great strategic importance, for a vital Confederate east-west line of communications was severed and the stage was set for Sherman's Atlanta Campaign [q.v.] and his famous March to the Sea [q.v.].

Bragg lost a total of 361 killed, 2,106 wounded, and 4,146 missing out of 64,000; Grant lost 753 killed, 4,722 wounded, and 349 missing.

Chausse-Trappe. See Caltrop.

Chauvinism. Excessive love of country and a detestation of foreigners. The word comes from the name of Nicolas Chauvin, a soldier wounded seventeen times in the Napoleonic Wars, the recipient of a sword of honor and a medal, who was fanatically devoted to Napoleon. His pugnacious brand of patriotism was legendary. Popular songs and a number of plays made his name a household word. [See Jingoism.]

Chauvinism was not confined to the French. In April 1816 American naval officer Stephen Decatur (1779–1820), at a banquet celebrating his return from the Barbary Coast, where he had forced a peace upon the Algerians on American terms, made a famous toast: "Our country! In her intercourse with foreign nations may she always be right; but our country, right or wrong!"

Chauvinist Riots (1844). Antiforeigner and anti-Catholic riots in Philadelphia, Pennsylvania, were provoked by the oratory of the American or Know-Nothing Party. The riots were suppressed by militia under Brigadier General George Cadwalader [q.v.], for whom anti-Catholics erected a gibbet. Unable to hang the man himself, they hanged him in effigy.

Chaves, Battle of (11–12 and 20–25 March 1809), Peninsular War. After the embarkation of the British army of Sir John Moore [q.v.] in January 1809 [see Corunna, Retreatto], French Marshal Nicolas Jean de Dieu Soult [q.v.] was ordered to invade Portugal. He reached the Minho River on 8 February and on 16 February tried but failed to cross; it was not until 7 March that he crossed the frontier. In order to clear the road to Oporto, the French II Corps—14,000 infantry, 1,300 cavalry, and 54 guns—attacked Chaves, a forti-

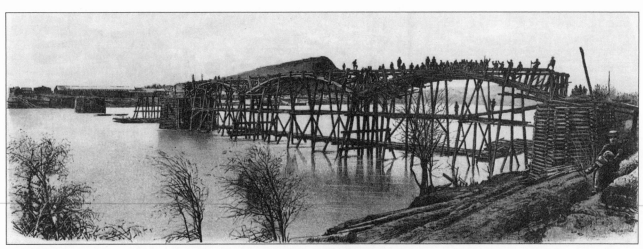

Chattanooga Campaign *U.S. military bridge over the Tennessee River at Chattanooga*

fied town in northern Portugal near the Spanish border, 22 miles north-northeast of Villa Real. It was defended by a Portuguese force of 12,000, most of them irregulars armed with only 6,000 muskets, under Brigadier Francisco da Silveira, the military governor of Trás-os-Montes (now Trás-os-Montes e Alto Douro) Province. Fortifications had not been repaired since the town had been besieged by the Spanish in 1762. Defense was almost impossible, and most fled, but a scratch force of about 4,000 had stayed behind. All were captured the next day. Soult dispersed the Portuguese peasant volunteers and incorporated the Portuguese regulars into a Portuguese legion. He then marched on, leaving behind in the town 1,200 convalescents, the legion, and a company of infantry.

When Silviera learned that Soult had left, he marched back to Chaves with a force of 6,000. The French, only a third of whom were physically fit to fight, retired into the citadel but after five days were forced to surrender. This Portuguese victory induced the peasants in the province to enlist in great numbers.

Cheat Mountain, Operations at (10–15 September 1861), American Civil War. Confederate General Robert E. Lee on his first campaign of the Civil War attempted to regain the portion of western Virginia (West Virginia) that had been captured by Union General George B. McClellan [q.v.] in the summer of 1861. On 10 September, in cold, wet weather, Lee began his advance with six brigades through rough mountain terrain. The following day he made contact with Union forces under Brigadier General Joseph Jones Reynolds [q.v.] near 3,478-foot Cheat Mountain. By the 12th the Union outposts had been driven back to the village of Elk River, seven miles west of Cheat Mountain in what is today northeast-central West Virginia. However, Lee soon found himself in an untenable position in a valley, and on 15 September he withdrew.

Federals claimed to have taken 20 prisoners and to have killed or wounded 100; Union forces suffered 21 killed and 60 taken prisoner, many of whom escaped. Granny Lee, as some now called him, was severely criticized and sent to South Carolina to supervise the construction of fortifications.

Chéchia. A soft fezlike cap worn by some French officers and by Zouaves and tirailleurs in North Africa.

Chef d'État Major. The chief of staff of a division or a corps in the French army.

Chella, Battle of. See Moualok, Battle of.

Chelmsford, Second Baron Frederic Augustus Thesiger. See Thesiger, Frederic Augustus.

Chelsea Hospital. The popular name for the Royal Hospital, Chelsea, situated on the north bank of the Thames River. It was founded by Charles II (1630–1685) as a home for veteran soldiers, an idea inspired by the Hôtel des Invalides [q.v.] in Paris. The first stone was laid by Charles on 19 February 1681. Designed by Christopher Wren (1632–1723), it was completed in 1682. The first pensioners, 476 old soldiers, were admitted in 1689. Organized into six companies commanded by "captains of invalides" who were retired officers, ex-soldiers of good character over the age of sixty-five (or fifty-five if unable to earn a living) were boarded, lodged, and clothed; they were nursed when ill, and received a small weekly allowance.

The uniform of the pensioners (still worn), dating from the eighteenth century, is scarlet in summer and blue in winter. A tricorn hat is worn on special occasions.

Each year on Oak Apple Day (29 May), the anniversary of King Charles II's birth and the date he reached London for his restoration in 1661, his statue in the central square of the hospital is decorated with sprigs of oak, and the pensioners parade carrying oak sprigs, in commemoration of the so-called Royal Oak in which Charles was said to have hidden from his pursuers after his defeat by Oliver Cromwell (1599–1658) in the Battle of Worcester on 3 September 1651. [See Hôtel des Invalides; Soldiers' Homes.]

Chemin de Ronde. A protected footpath, sometimes sheltered by a hedge, a low wall, or a small earthen parapet, at the foot of the exterior or scarp slope or between the ditch and the glacis in a permanent fortification.

Cheng Hsiu-chi (d. 1864). A Chinese soldier usually referred to as simply General Ching. During the Taiping Rebellion [q.v.] he was one of the leaders of Taiping forces, but he changed sides and became a general in the imperial army, distinguishing himself in the recapture of Nanking (now Nanjing). Although he frequently clashed with Charles Gordon [q.v.], commander of the Ever Victorious Army [q.v.], who detested him, he was one of the best of the imperial generals. He was mortally wounded in the attack on Kashing on 20 March 1864 and died on 15 April.

Ch'en Yü-ch'eng (1836–1862). A Chinese soldier who became a general in the Taiping army [see Taiping Rebellion]. In 1856–58 he ably conducted successful operations west of Nanking (Nanjing or Nanxiang). In 1860, in conjunction with Li Hsiu-ch'eng [q.v.], he raised the second siege of Nanking [q.v.] by the imperial forces. In May 1862 he was betrayed and killed by imperialist forces.

Cherivallies. A waist-high overall strapped under the foot, sometimes reinforced with leather, worn to protect horsemen's trousers and boots from dust and mud. The name perhaps derived from *esquavar*, a term for leg covering used by eighteenth-century hussars. Also called charivari.

Chermside Bey, Herbert Charles (1850–1929). A British soldier commissioned a lieutenant in the artillery on 23 July 1870 who served as military attaché on the Turkish side in the Russo-Turkish War [q.v.] of 1877–78. He transferred to the Egyptian army and was governor-general of the Red Sea littoral from 1884 to 1886. Later he was commandant at Wadi Halfa in southern Egypt, military attaché at Constantinople (Istanbul), and British commissioner in Crete. He was promoted major general on 23 November 1898, and in 1900 he commanded a division in the Second Anglo-Boer War [q.v.], fighting in the Orange Free State and later in the Transvaal. He was governor of Queensland, Australia, in 1902–03 and retired in 1907.

Chernaya, Battle of (16 August 1855), Crimean War. During the siege of Sevastopol [q.v.] the French under General

Chernaya *Battle of Chernaya in the Crimea*

Aimable Pelissier were joined by a division of Sardinian troops commanded by the Marchese di La Marmora [qq.v.], and the combined force of 35,000 was placed in the Allied line east of Sevastopol. When the Russians made a major sortie with three divisions under General Prince Mikhail Gorchakov [q.v.] on 16 August, they struck the position held in part by the Sardinians, who, with the British and French, repulsed the attack. Russian losses were 260 officers and 8,000 men; Allied losses were about 1,700. This was the last attempt by the Russians to save Sevastopol.

Chernyaiev, Mikhail Grigorievich (1828–1898). A Russian soldier educated at the Nicholas Staff College and commissioned in 1847 who served in the Crimean War [q.v.] and in Central Asia. In 1859 he led an expedition to support the Kirghiz tribes on the borders of the Sea of Aral against the Khivans. In 1863, now a major general, he made a march across the steppes of Turkestan with 1,000 men and joined forces with a Russian column from Semipalatinsk in Siberia. Together the Russian forces successfully attacked Chimkent. They did not succeed in taking Tashkent, 60 miles farther south, but after wintering in Chimkent, in disobedience of his orders, Chernyaiev captured Tashkent in 1864. For this he was hailed as the Lion of Tashkent and awarded the Cross of St. Anne [see Central Asian Wars; Khokand, Conquest of]. He received no further employment, and in 1867 he resigned from the army and then practiced law in Moscow. In 1876 in the Turko-Serbian War [q.v.] he was given command of the Serbian army by Prince Milan (1864–1901) of Serbia but was soundly defeated by the Turks under Osman Pasha [q.v.]. He resigned his post, and in 1877, while visiting Austria, he was expelled from the country for his Pan-Slavic propaganda. In 1879 he organized an uprising in Bulgaria but was arrested at Adrianople and sent back to Russia. In 1882 he was appointed governor of Turkestan, but after two years his aggressive policies led to his recall. He was then appointed to the War Council in St. Petersburg, from which he was dismissed in 1886 because of his opposition to the Central Asian Military Railway. He died on his estate near Mogilev.

Chernyshëv, Prince Aleksander Ivanovich (1786–1857). A Russian soldier who fought against Napoleon at Austerlitz in 1805 and Friedland in 1807. He again fought against Napoleon in 1813–14. From 1828 to 1852 he was Russian minister of war.

Cherokee Disturbances and Removal (1830–38). The Cherokees, once one of the largest and most powerful Indian tribes in North America, occupied the mountainous areas of Georgia, Alabama, Tennessee, and the Carolinas. During the French and Indian War they fought with the British against the French. During the American Revolutionary War they again allied themselves with the British and attacked many American frontier settlements. In the War of 1812 [q.v.], however, they sided with the Americans, and in the Creek War [q.v.] they aided Andrew Jackson [q.v.] in the suppression of the Creeks.

In 1827 they formed the Cherokee Nation, adopting a constitution based upon that of the United States. In 1830 Congress passed the Indian Removal Acts, giving the president authority to remove all Indians from lands east of the Mississippi River to territories west of the river. The Cherokees and several other tribes at first refused, but in 1838 the U.S. army began their forcible removal. John Ross [q.v.] led them on the long Trail of Tears [q.v.], some 4,000 dying along the way to Indian Territory. There the Cherokees became one of the Five Civilized Tribes.

During the American Civil War Cherokees were divided in their loyalty. One Confederate unit (John Drew's Mounted Rifles) and one Union unit (Watie's Regiment) were formed. [See Drew, John; Watie, Stand.]

Chesney, Sir George Tomkyns (1830–1895). A British soldier and brother of military historian Charles Cornwallis Chesney (1826–1876). He served in India and was wounded during the mutiny [q.v.] at Delhi. He founded and was the first president of the Royal Indian Civil Engineering College. He was the author of several novels and created a sensation when in 1871 he wrote for *Blackwood's Magazine* "The Invasion of Dorking," an imaginary account of a German invasion of England.

Chesnut, James, Jr. (1815–1885). A Confederate soldier who served as an aide to Pierre Beauregard [q.v.] at Fort

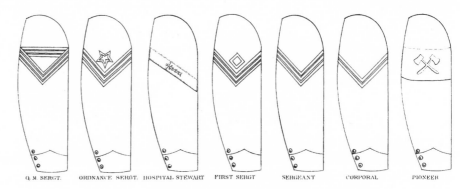

Chevrons *Examples of U.S. army chevrons on uniform sleeves during the Civil War.*

Q. M. SERGT.   ORDNANCE SERGT.   HOSPITAL STEWART   FIRST SERGT   SERGEANT   CORPORAL   PIONEER

Sumter [q.v.] and later on the staff of Jefferson Davis. His wife, Mary Bodkin Chesnut (1823–1886), whom he married when she was seventeen, began a diary on 15 February 1861 in the early days of the Civil War and, with its postwar publication as *Diary from Dixie* [1905], became the best-known diarist of the war. The name is often misspelled Chestnut.

Chesses. The plankings or floorboards of a pontoon bridge.

Chetate, Battle of (6–9 January 1854), Crimean War. On 6 January 1854 some 6,000 Turks under Ahmed Pasha attacked an advanced Russian post with about an equal number of troops. The Turks lost about 1,000, but the Russians lost 3,000 in killed and wounded, and another 1,000 were taken prisoner. The Russians brought up 20,000 reinforcements on 9 January and counterattacked but lost 2,000 before conceding defeat.

Cheval-de-Frise or (pl.) Chevaux-de-Frise (or -Frize). 1. A movable defensive piece usually consisting of thick branches six to eight feet long, often sharpened, from which sharp spikes projected. It could also be constructed of metal. At Badajoz [q.v.] during the Peninsular War [q.v.] chevaux-de-frise were made from sword blades fixed into beams of wood.

Chevaux-de-frise were particularly effective in repelling cavalry. The term, meaning "horse[s] of Friesland," comes from the province in the northern Netherlands where such a device was first used in the sixteenth century against cavalry.

2. A wall or fortification topped by broken glass, nails, or other sharp objects.

Cheval-de-frise in front of Fort Mahone, April 1865

Chevrons. V-shaped insignia, also called stripes, denoting rank, service, or wounds. It is believed that the first sleeve

badges indicating noncommissioned officer ranks were worn by the 43rd Foot in the British army in 1795. In May 1803 a system of sleeve chevrons, points down, was introduced into the British army: four chevrons for quartermaster sergeants and sergeant majors, three for sergeants, two for corporals. However, chevrons did not come into general use in the British service until after the Battle of Waterloo [q.v.] in 1815. Chevrons were worn points down on the upper sleeve until 1869, when the four of the sergeant major were carried on the lower arm with points up.

In the American army chevrons similar to the British were worn from 1821 on the upper sleeve. At West Point, the Virginia Military Institute, and other American military academies, a system of chevrons varying from that of the active services is used to denote cadet ranks.

Chevrons were introduced in the French army in 1777 to indicate long service, a practice the British army adopted in 1836. The stripes were worn on the right forearm. In 1881 they were moved to the left arm and worn point upward.

Cheyenne-Arapaho War (1864–68). Most of the Cheyenne and Arapaho Indians living on a reservation in Colorado abided by a treaty they signed in 1861, but in 1864 some began to steal cattle, and there were a number of Indian-settler clashes that became serious when the Indians began to attack wagon trains, rob stagecoaches, and raid farms.

Not all Indians wanted conflict. Those who did not tried at first to distance themselves from their warlike neighbors, but after Chivington's Raid [q.v.] on 28 November 1864 there were few peaceful Indians on the plains; from Colorado to Texas, Indians rose against white men. Three army columns sent against them met with little success, but the Indians lacked staying power, and the war dragged to an end in 1868.

Cheyenne War (1878). In September 1878 about 300 Cheyenne Indians broke out of their reservation in what is today Oklahoma and returned to what had been their homelands around the headwaters of the Platte River. All were captured, and some were cruelly treated at Fort Robinson, near Crawford, Nebraska, where in bitterly cold weather they were locked up without food, water, or fire.

Chicane, to. To dispute every inch of ground by taking advantage of natural inequalities of the terrain.

Chichagov or Chicagou, Paul Vasiilievich. See Tshitsagov, Pavel.

Chickamauga, Battle of (19–20 September 1863), American

Civil War. ("*Chickamauga*" means "river of death.") In the first battle of the Chickamauga Campaign of August and September 1863 in northwest Georgia and southeast Tennessee, Confederate General Braxton Bragg [q.v.], driven out of his positions north of Chattanooga, Tennessee, wanted to launch another offensive but lacked the means until reinforced.

On 18 September with his reinforced troops now numbering 71,000, Bragg ordered an attack upon the north flank of the Federal Army of the Cumberland, 58,000 men under William Rosecrans [q.v.], a movement that was checked by Federal cavalry. The main battle began the following day, when the two sides, mostly floundering about in thick woods, neither knowing the other's position, lumbered up against each other. In a daylong battle of heavy but confused fighting along a four-mile front east of Chickamauga Creek no decided advantage was obtained by either army.

During the night both sides tried to rearrange their forces: Rosecrans prepared breastworks and took other defensive measures; Bragg prepared to attack. Confederate General James Longstreet [q.v.], who arrived during the night, was placed in command of the left wing of the Confederate army; General Leonidas Polk [q.v.] commanded the right wing. Dawn on 20 September found some units still not in their proper places.

With a mistaken notion of where his units were located, Rosecrans issued orders that left a hole in his line. It was at that exact spot, through blind luck, that Longstreet attacked. When Confederate troops penetrated the defenses, many Federals turned and fled, but because Bragg had failed to provide for a sufficient reserve, he was unable to exploit fully the opening Longstreet had made. While withdrawing his army into the defenses of Chattanooga, Rosecrans was saved from utter destruction by the steadfast performance of General George Thomas [q.v.], who here earned his sobriquet of the Rock of Chickamauga. Union Brigadier General James B. Steedman [q.v.] with the reserve corps of Major General Gordon Granger (1822–1876), ordered by Thomas to cover the retreat, held off repeated Confederate attacks and suffered 44 percent casualties. At the end of the day, with their ammunition exhausted, Steedman's force pulled back, leaving behind the 22nd Michigan and the 21st and 89th Ohio, who were ordered by Granger to hold the position with their bayonets to cover the retreat. Only when the army was safely away did they surrender.

The Confederates held the field, but it was a pyrrhic victory for Bragg, who, out of 66,000 effectives, lost 18,454, including 2,312 dead. The Federal losses were 16,170, including 1,657 dead. In killed and wounded, the Federals lost 19.6 percent; the Confederates reported 2,312 dead, 14,674 wounded, and 1,468 missing, almost 30 percent casualties, making this one of the bloodiest battles of the Civil War. Neither commanding general exhibited any brilliance.

Chickasaw Bluffs, Battle of (29 December 1862), American Civil War. In one of the first moves in the Vicksburg Campaign, Federal troops under General U. S. Grant followed the Mississippi Railroad line toward Vicksburg, Mississippi, while General William Tecumseh Sherman [q.v.] took a force of 32,000 in boats down the Mississippi River to land just above Vicksburg, whose defenses, manned by 6,000 men commanded by Confederate Major General Martin Luther Smith (1819–1866), an engineer officer, were located on a line of steep bluffs running from the river north of the town, some 10 miles northwest.

When Grant's overland march was halted by the Confederate capture of Holly Springs [q.v.] on 20 December, the Confederates were able to reinforce their troops at Vicksburg, achieving a force of 25,000. Sherman's main attack came on 29 December in a cold rain. Dense fog and the difficult terrain deprived the attackers of adequate artillery support, and the attack failed.

Federal losses were 208 killed, 1,005 wounded, and 563 missing; the Confederates reported 63 killed, 134 wounded, and 10 missing.

Chief of Section. The noncommissioned officer in charge of a small group of soldiers or in charge of an artillery piece and its crew.

Chief of Staff. The senior staff officer who works directly for a commander, relieving him of much detail work and coordinating the efforts of the other staff officers. In the United States the army chief of staff is the title of the ranking uniformed officer of the army, the president being the commander-in-chief. During the Napoleonic Wars the brilliant Prussian General Count August von Gneisenau served as chief of staff to Field Marshal Gebhard von Blücher [qq.v.], who said of him, "Gneisenau makes the pills that I administer."

In 1831 Napoleon defined the role of a chief of staff: "The leading qualifications . . . are, to know the country thoroughly; to be able to conduct a reconnaissance with skill; to superintend the transmission of orders promptly; to lay down the most complicated of movements intelligibly, but in a few words and with simplicity."

In divisions, brigades, and regiments of the Confederate and Union armies during the American Civil War the effective chief of staff carried the title of assistant adjutant general.

In 1838 Henri de Jomini [q.v.] wrote that the chief of staff must be "a man of high ability, of open and faithful character, between whom and the commander there may be perfect harmony" (*Précis de l'Art de la Guerre*).

Chihuahua Campaign (1846–1847), Mexican War. On 23 September 1846 Colonel Alexander William Doniphan [q.v.], a lawyer by profession, left Sante Fe, New Mexico, with the 1st Regiment of Missouri Mounted Volunteers and, encountering little opposition, occupied El Paso, Texas, on 27 December with the loss of only 7 wounded. On 8 February 1847 he crossed the Rio Grande and marched south, again meeting with only slight opposition until on 28 February he encountered 4,000 Mexican troops at the Sacramento River. Using only a quarter of his force, he stormed their position and routed them, capturing all their artillery and supplies. Mexican losses were 300 killed; American losses were 1 killed and 11 wounded. On 1 March Doniphan occupied the town of Chihuahua. He then led his men on a 700-mile march to Saltillo, capital of Coahuila State, and eventually back to the Rio Grande, where they were transported by ship to New Orleans and disbanded.

Chikuto. A Japanese fencing sword about 110 cm (43 inches) long made of bamboo with a long, straight hilt.

Children of the Regiment. All European and American armies were burdened with children. Much as the authorities would have liked to ignore them, their plight was all too visible. Soldiers contracted alliances with women, with or without benefit of matrimony or official approval, and if their children survived infancy under what were often primitive and unsanitary conditions, they grew up in posts, camps, and garrisons, sometimes carried on the strength [q.v.] and sometimes not. Orphans too belonged to the regiment and were petted or cuffed by the soldiers. Wearing ragged bits of uniforms, the boys learned to swear mightily and to smoke short clay pipes; many were mischievous. At age eleven or twelve they might become drummer boys or buglers, and at sixteen or so they could enlist.

In Napoleon's armies each regiment was allowed two male orphans, *enfants de troupe,* provided they were twelve years old and born to a *vivandière* or *blanchisseuse* [qq.v.] and sired by soldiers who had been killed in action or died of wounds. The boys were clothed, were given an elementary education, drew half pay, and carried briquets [q.v.].

There was no consistent policy for rearing the children of a regiment in the American army. During the Second Seminole War [q.v.] the 6th U.S. Infantry issued half rations to children who, with their mothers, accompanied the regiment on active service, apparently on no one's authority except the colonel's.

British officers stationed abroad sent their children back to Britain to be educated, often not seeing them for years. The children of American officers usually followed their fathers. Some children growing up in Indian Territory or the Southwest had never seen a tree until their fathers were transferred east or to the West Coast.

In the Russian army soldiers' children (*soldatshie deti*) constituted a juridically defined social category. As early as 1719 and until 1856 both the legitimate and illegitimate children of soldiers and the illegitimate children of their daughters belonged to the military domain (*voennoe vedomstvo*). Until they reached the age of eighteen, they could live with their parents. Then the young men were taken into the army. Daughters of soldiers, unless they married early, led difficult lives. While the sons of soldiers were regarded as a valuable manpower resource, daughters were seen as simply welfare problems. When this status was abolished in 1856, there were 378,000 such children.

Childs, Thomas (1796–1853). An American soldier who was graduated from West Point in 1814 and commissioned in the artillery. During the War of 1812 he distinguished himself in the taking of Fort Erie [q.v.] in July 1814, and during the Second Seminole War [q.v.] he won a brevet to major for his attack upon Fort Drane, in Marion County, Florida, on 21 August 1836. During the Mexican War [q.v.] he fought at Palo Alto on 18 May 1846 and Resaca de la Palma the following day [qq.v.] and led the forlorn hope [q.v.] that captured the Toma de Independencia at Monterrey [q.v.] in September. For his defense of Puebla against the forces of Santa Anna [q.v.] he was brevetted brigadier general on 12 October. From 1852 to his death on 10 August 1853 he was in command of troops in eastern Florida.

Chilean-Bolivian War. See War of the Pacific.

Chilean Civil and Revolutionary Wars. 1. On 18 September 1810 Chile declared its independence from Spain. The war was carried on with varying success until Simón Bolívar [q.v.] won the decisive Battle of Chacabuco [q.v.] on 12 February 1817, but peace was not made with Spain until 1826 [see Chilean War of Independence].

2. Following the ouster of dictator Bernardo O'Higgins [q.v.] in 1823, there was much unrest in Chile springing from the animosity between conservatives, mostly landowners and the Catholic Church, and liberals, mostly the poorer classes, who wanted agrarian reforms and a curtailment of clerical prerogatives. In 1829 civil war erupted, and on 17 April 1830, in the Battle of Licay [q.v.], conservative forces led by General Joaquín Prieto [q.v.] decisively defeated liberal forces led by General Ramón Freire (1787–1851). Prieto became president. In 1841 one of his cabinet appointees, Diego Portales (1793–1837), made himself virtual dictator.

3. In 1826 Spanish royalists and Indians revolted against the government on the Pacific island province of Chiloé (4,700 miles square) off the southwest coast of Chile.

4. A revolt led by Pedro Gallo, begun in December 1858, was suppressed the following April.

5. When President José Manuel Balmaceda (1838–1891) refused to convoke the Assembly but ordered the continued collection of taxes, the navy led a revolution in January 1891. In August 9,000 rebel troops were landed near Valparaiso. Although the army initially remained loyal, many government troops refused to fight, and Valparaiso was easily taken; Santiago, the capital, fell soon after. Balmaceda fled to Argentina and there committed suicide on 19 September.

Chilean-Spanish War (1865–66). A Spanish fleet appeared before Valparaiso on 17 September 1865 demanding satisfaction for Chilean intervention in Spain's war with Peru. When this was refused, the Spanish declared a blockade on 29 September. On 31 March 1866 they bombarded Valparaiso, but on 14 April, their supplies exhausted, they raised the blockade.

Chilean War of Independence (1810–18). When it was learned in Chile that Ferdinand VII (1784–1821) of Spain had been dethroned, the Spanish captain general was deposed, and a revolutionary junta seized power, but the revolutionists were divided between moderates under Bernardo O'Higgins [q.v.] and radicals following José Miguel Carrera [q.v.]. This dissension strengthened the royalists and contributed to the rebel army defeat in October 1814 in the Battle of Rancagua [q.v.].

Carrera and O'Higgins then joined forces with José de San Martín [q.v.], who had spent three years raising and training an army of 5,000 at Mendoza, in western Argentina. Early in 1814 he had crossed the Andes, above 12,000 feet, with artillery and supplies and descended into Chile, a feat never before accomplished. After San Martín dismissed Carrera, he and O'Higgins defeated royalists in the battles of Chacabuco on 12 February 1817 and Maypo [qq.v.] on 5 April 1818. With the aid of Admiral Thomas Cochrane, the British admiral of the Chilean navy, Chilean independence from Spain was accomplished. San Martín then marched his forces to Peru.

Chilianwala / Chillianwala, Battle of (13 January 1849), Second Sikh War. General Sir Hugh Gough [q.v.] with 12,000 Anglo-Indian troops fought a force of 40,000 Sikhs near this village five miles east of the Jhelum River in what is now north West Punjab, Pakistan. The battle is noted for the splendid charge of the 24th Foot, who in dress uniform, including the tall, cumbersome shako, their muskets unloaded, armed only with bared bayonets, advanced steadily in the face of heavy fire in an infantry equivalent of the Charge of the Light Brigade [q.v.], losing 497 out of 960 engaged, of whom 238 were killed. The Sikhs retreated in good order, taking with them two British guns and three regimental colors.

Sikh losses were estimated at 8,000, but this figure is obviously too high; the British lost 26 officers killed and 66 wounded; 731 other ranks were killed and 1,446 wounded. These figures appalled those in Britain unaccustomed to such losses in Asian wars. Gough was castigated for his "Tipperary tactics," and Sir Charles Napier [q.v.] was sent out from England to replace him, but before he could arrive on the scene, Gough won the Battle of Gujerat [q.v.], and the war was over.

Chimborazo Hospital. During the American Civil War this enormous hospital complex, covering 125 acres and capable of accommodating 4,800 patients, was established at Richmond, Virginia. It consisted of five hospitals, each directed by a surgeon, with forty-five to fifty assistant and acting assistant surgeons under each. It was divided into sections by states until amalgamated into the Confederate Medical Corps in 1863.

Chinese Artillery. In the nineteenth century the Chinese produced their own muzzleloaders; their only breechloaders were those captured from the Japanese in the Sino-Japanese War [q.v.] of 1894–95 or those purchased in Europe, notably from Krupp and Schneider [qq.v.].

Chinese Civil Wars. After the suppression of the San Fan Rebellion in 1681, China enjoyed a century of relative internal peace. This was broken by the rise of the White Lotus [q.v.], a secret antigovernment society, in 1796. In the nineteenth century civil wars were endemic. Some were simply accommodated; others, such as the series of rebellions in the 1850s and 1860s, shook the Ch'ing dynasty and revealed China's many military weaknesses. The bloodiest war of the century was the Taiping Rebellion [q.v.], which raged from 1850 to 1865.

Following the end of the Taiping Rebellion, scattered revolts sprang up throughout the empire, one of the worst occurring in the provinces of Kansu, Shensi, and western Sinkiang [see Chinese Turkestan, Conquest of]. Provocations varied: presence of foreigners, Muslims, Christians, or the Manchu. In some there were no provocations, simply warlords or bandits attempting to profit from a country in turmoil. Others were the Miao Rebellion [q.v.] in Keichow, which began about 1855 and did not end until 1872; the Panthay Rebellion [q.v.], which began about the same time and was suppressed in 1873; and the seventeen-year-long Nien Rebellion [q.v.]. It took the Manchu dynasty sixteen years to bring even a semblance of order to China, and this was accomplished only with the aid of the essentially autonomous gentry-led provincial armies, such as the Hunan army raised and led by Tsêng Kuo-fan [q.v.].

Chinese-French War. See Sino-French War.

Chinese-Japanese War. See Sino-Japanese War.

Chinese Light. An illumination shell filled with niter, sulfur, antimony, and other chemicals. It was used as early as the Napoleonic Wars.

Chinese Turkestan, Conquest of. Muslims in Chinese Turkestan (Sinkiang) frequently revolted against their Chinese overlords, and several times they succeeded, notably in 1825, 1830, and 1847, but all were eventually suppressed. In 1857 still another revolt erupted, but in a few months the Chinese took Kashgar (Chinese: Shufu), the chief city of Chinese Turkestan. During the Dzungarian uprising [q.v.] in 1864 the Chinese were again expelled, and the revolt, which began in the east, spread westward. A Muslim adventurer from Central Asia, Yakub Beg [q.v.], who had suffered five wounds fighting the Russians, led an army from Khokand (now Kokand, Uzbekistan) into Chinese Turkestan, ostensibly to restore to the throne the former Muslim ruler, then in exile in Khokand. In January 1865 he crossed the mountains and within two years captured Kashgar and Yarkand (Chinese: Soche), 100 miles southeast. He then proclaimed himself the ruler of "Kashgaria." Fighting his way east and north, he conquered all of Chinese Turkestan as far east as Urumchi, the chief town of Dzungaria on the north side of the Tien Shan range; Turfan, 90 miles to the southeast; and Hami (Qomul), north of the Taklamakan Desert and 1,000 miles from Kashgar.

In 1864 the Russians, under the pretext that the revolt might spread in their direction, sent an army to occupy areas in northern Turkestan around Kuldja and the Ili River. In the following year the Russians signed a commercial treaty with Yakub Beg. In 1873 the British sent a mission and opened a legation.

Yakub Beg's reign lasted until the Chinese had ended the Taiping Rebellion [q.v.] and could spare imperial troops to reconquer the area. In 1876 an imperial army of 100,000 under Tso Tsung-t'ang [q.v.], a general known for his ruthlessness, moved into the area. Urumchi (or Tihwa) in northern Sinkiang was captured on 6 November 1876, and Turfan, 90 miles southeast on 16 May 1877. When the forces of Yakub Beg were defeated near Kashgar, Yakub surrendered and died soon after. By the beginning of 1878 almost all Turkestan had been reclaimed, but the Russians did not give up the territory they occupied until 1881.

Ching, General. See Cheng Hsui-chi.

Chin-t'ien. During the Taiping Rebellion [q.v.] two battles were fought near this village in Kwangsi Province in southeast China.

1. First Battle (4 November 1850). Hung Hsui-Ch'üan [q.v.] and another Taiping were preaching their brand of Christianity in the village of Chin-t'ien when Manchu imperial forces surrounded the village. Hung and his partner quickly armed the villagers with weapons they had hidden in a pond, and the imperial forces were driven off with a loss of about 200.

2. Second Battle (1 January 1851). Taiping forces under Yang Hsiu-ch'ing [q.v.] repulsed two attacks by imperial troops, but on the third attack the Taipings gave way and fled down a narrow path between cliffs. The imperial forces pursued and were ambushed. The imperial troops lost 2,000 before they could extricate themselves.

Chin Y-ching (d. 1862), also known as Sez'-yan Kow, the Four-Eyed Dog. A distinguished Chinese rebel leader in the Taiping Rebellion [q.v.] who was made Ying Wang (Heroic King) by Hung Hsui-ch'üan [q.v.]. He was betrayed to the imperialists, who executed him.

Chios / Scio, Turkish Occupation of (1822), Greek War of Independence. In April 1822 Turkish forces landed on this Greek island, believed by many to be the birthplace of Homer, and massacred or enslaved its entire population. In retaliation, on the night of 18–19 June Greek patriot Konstantinos Kanares (1790–1877) sent fire ships into the Turkish squadron assembled in the harbor and blew up the flagship, killing all on board.

The Massacre at Chios, a painting by Eugène Delacroix (1798–1863) is said to have opened the path from romantic to impressionist art. It also roused sympathy among Europeans for the Greeks in their fight for independence, as did the poetry of Lord Byron [q.v.].

Chippewa, Battle of (5 July 1814), War of 1812. On 3 July 1814 American General Jacob Jennings Brown [q.v.] with 3,500 American troops crossed the Niagara River into Canada and seized Fort Erie at the confluence of the Niagara River and Lake Erie. The British under General Phineas Riall retreated to the Chippewa River, 16 miles north in southeast Ontario. Brown posted his force in a strong position behind Street's Creek, with his right flank on the Niagara River and his left on a swamp. In front of the Americans was a broad plain and, beyond that, the Chippewa River, on the other side of which was the smaller British force, which contained 1,500 regulars. Riall crossed the Chippewa with 600 Indians and some militia, and Brown ordered an attack by the brigade of regulars, about 1,300 men under Brigadier General Winfield Scott. The fight, the first time in the war that the Americans had faced British regulars, lasted only thirty minutes. The British were repulsed with a loss of 137 killed and 304 wounded; the Americans lost 48 killed and 227 wounded.

Because of a shortage of blue dye, men in Scott's brigade were dressed in gray uniforms, leading General Riall to believe that he faced militia, but seeing them maneuver under fire, he exclaimed, "Those are regulars, by God!" It is said that it is in recognition of this victory that cadets at the United States Military Academy at West Point, New York, still wear gray uniforms.

The Americans broke the British line, killing 137 and wounding 375, for an American loss of 48 killed and 227 wounded. The British retreated north and Brown pursued [see Chrysler's / Christler's Farm; Lundy's Lane; War of 1812].

Brown in his official report gave almost all the credit to Scott, saying that "to him more than any other man, am I indebted for the victory of the 5th of July." Scott and his three regimental commanders were given brevet promotions.

Chisolm, John Julian (1830–1903). A Charleston, South Carolina, surgeon, educated in London and Paris, who at the beginning of the American Civil War wrote a *Manual of Military Surgery* for the inexperienced Confederate surgeons. During the war he was engaged in the production of medicine for the army.

Chitral Campaign (1895). In 1889 the British established an agency in Chitral, a mountainous princely state slightly smaller than Wales, on the south slope of the Hindu Kush, where several peaks rise more than 20,000 feet. (The state is now the northernmost province of Pakistan.) Following a palace coup d'état on 4 March 1895, 5 British officers with 400 native troops and about 137 noncombatants were besieged in a ramshackle fort, 80 yards square, commanded by Captain Charles V. P. Townshend [q.v.]. To rescue them, the British dispatched a 16,000-man military expedition under Major General Sir Robert Low (1838–1911). After several battles along the way with local rulers who objected to their intrusion—including the storming on 3 April of the Malakand Pass held by 5,000 Pathans—an advance force under Colonel William Gatacre [q.v.] reached Chitral on 15 May, only to find that the siege had already been raised by a small force from Gilgit led by a middle-aged regimental officer, Lieutenant Colonel James Graves Kelly (his exact age is unknown, but since he was commissioned in 1862 he must have been close to fifty, perhaps older). Kelly's little army consisted of only 382 Sikhs from the 32nd Bengal Infantry (Pioneers) and 34 Kashmiri sappers, some reluctant local porters, and two ancient mountain guns. They had made a near incredible trek of 220 miles through the 12,400-foot Chandur Pass in severe weather without tents and had fought two battles, all within twenty-eight days, reaching Chitral in mid-April. It was, as London newspapers declared, "one of the most remarkable marches in history."

In the month-and-a-half-long siege the Chitral garrison lost 41 killed and 62 wounded; 5 of those killed and 4 of the wounded were noncombatants.

Chivalry. A code embracing the honor, generosity, and courtesy of gentlemen, which included admiration for and even protection of gallant enemies. In the Battle of Barossa [q.v.] in 1811 French Colonel Vigo-Roussilion of the 8me Ligne was restrained by *sentiments de compassion* from cutting down sixty-two-year-old Lieutenant Colonel Sir Thomas Graham [q.v.] because of his age. Chivalry was still much in force during the American Civil War, although it diminished as the war progressed. Confederate General T. J. ("Stonewall") Jackson [q.v.] more than once rebuked officers for shielding gallant Federal soldiers, the very ones, he maintained, who ought to be killed. Confederate guerrilla leader John S. Mosby [q.v.] in his *War Reminiscences* (1887) wrote: "In one sense the charge that I did not fight fair is true. I fought for success and not for display. There was no man in the Confederate army who had less of the spirit of knight-errantry in him, or who took a more practical view of war than I did."

(The idea of chivalry persisted in the military well into the twentieth century. A 1956 U.S. Army Field Manual (FM 27–10) stated that war should be conducted "with regard for the principles of humanity and chivalry.")

Chivalry, Orders of. Soldiers have been rewarded by promotions, brevets [q.v.], medals, gratuities [q.v.], pensions, etc., but in many European armies one of the most common rewards for officers was initiation into one of the many orders of chivalry. The most complex system of such orders was in Britain, where the oldest order was, and is still, the Most Noble Order of the Garter, established at Windsor in 1348 and awarded to certain royal personages and to 25 Knights

Companions. The origin of the Most Ancient and Most Noble Order of the Thistle is obscure; instituted in the seventeenth century, it was rarely awarded in the nineteenth century, although Lord Roberts received it. The Most Illustrious Order of St. Patrick (now moribund) was also infrequently awarded.

Between 1815 and 1837 many British officers were recipients of the Royal Guelphic Order, a Hanoverian order. The Royal Victorian Order, instituted in April 1896, was divided into five classes and could be awarded to any number of men or women in recognition of personal services to the sovereign or the royal family.

The order most commonly awarded to officers was the Most Honourable Order of the Bath, an order with a civil and a military division instituted in about 1399. The highest award in this order is that of Knight Grand Cross, limited to 68 military and 27 civil recipients who use the postnominal letters GCB. Next is Knight Commander (KCB) with 173 military and 112 civil appointments. Both Knight Grand Cross and Knight Commander confer knighthoods, and recipients are henceforth called Sir (first Name). Such awards, particularly the GCB, were usually awarded only to generals. Successful field officers might expect to become a Companion of the Bath (CB), of which there were 943 reserved for the military and 555 for civilians.

On 23 February 1861 Queen Victoria instituted the Most Exalted Order of the Star of India as a reward for service in India, which was awarded to civilians and soldiers and many Indian princes. Its original numbers—36 Knights Grand Commander (GCSI), of whom 18 were British and 18 Indian; 85 Knights Commander (KCSI), and 170 Companions (CSI)—were extended in 1866 and again in 1875 and 1876.

A junior Indian order, the Most Eminent Order of the Indian Empire, was instituted on 31 December 1877. Originally it had only one class, but on 2 August 1886 it was enlarged to include three classes.

The Most Distinguished Order of St. Michael and St. George instituted by the prince regent on 27 April 1818 was originally limited to those serving on the Ionian islands, which in 1815 had been formed into an independent state under British protection. In 1879 the limitations were extended to include service in any British colony and extended again in 1902. Like the Bath, it had three orders.

The now popular Order of the British Empire was not instituted until 17 June 1917.

Belgium and Austria-Hungary each had an Order of Leopold. Bulgaria had an Order of Alexander in six classes; Denmark had the ancient Order of the Elephant, instituted in 1464; Hesse-Kassel had the Order of Military Merit. [See Medals; Golden Fleece.]

Chivington, John Milton (1821–1894). An American Methodist preacher turned soldier who was called the fighting parson for his exploits in New Mexico during the American Civil War. He joined the Methodist Episcopal Church in 1848, made a name for himself as a preacher at camp meetings, and became the presiding elder of the Rocky Mountain Conference of his church. When the 1st Colorado Volunteers was formed in 1861, he was elected its major. His gallantry and military skills in the Battle of Glorieta [q.v.] and other engagements made him a hero. He helped block the March 1862 invasion of New Mexico by Confederate General Henry Hopkins Sibley [q.v.], and on 14 April 1862 he was brevetted colonel and named military commander of the Military District of Colorado. [See New Mexico, Confederate Army of.]

Although he had visions of a brigadier general's star and considered running for Congress, Chivington's Raid [q.v.] and the Sand River Massacre [q.v.], in which peaceful Indians were treacherously massacred, collapsed his dreams of a bright political future. Three official investigations of the affair castigated his conduct. He resigned his commission on 4 January 1865 and escaped all punishment. His formerly promising career in the church went downhill. At the last he had to work as a newspaper reporter.

Chivington's Raid (November 1864), American Civil War. On 26 September 1864 Colonel John Chivington [q.v.], the chief military commander in Colorado, attended a meeting in Denver between the governor of Colorado and several

Chivington's Raid *Colonel John Chivington with the 3rd Colorado Cavalry mounts a surprise attack at Sand Creek.*

Cheyenne chiefs, including Black Kettle (1803?–1868) and White Antelope (1789?–1864), who swore to the desire of their people to live in peace and security. They were instructed to report to Fort Lyon, Colorado, on the Arkansas River, where they were given some rations and ordered to camp at Sand Creek, a tributary of the Arkansas River about 40 miles north of the fort. There some 500 Cheyennes of all ages and both sexes built about 100 lodges. Black Kettle, as he had been instructed to do, erected flagpoles and flew both the American flag and a white flag over his lodge.

Despite the fact that Colonel Chivington was well aware of the Indians' peaceful intent, he organized in late November an expedition of 700 men of the 1st and 3rd Colorado with two howitzers to destroy them. Having reminded his men of the white women who had been tortured and killed by Indians in the past, he informed them that although he would not order them to retaliate in kind, he wanted no prisoners.

He reached Fort Lyon on the morning of 28 November and left that night for Sand Creek. When he reached the encampment on the next day, he ordered an attack without parley. Only about 50 of the Indian men were armed and able to resist. About 150, mostly women and children, were slain. Their bodies were mutilated, and most were scalped. Chivington boasted: "It may perhaps be unnecessary for me to state that I captured no prisoners." First Lieutenant Clark Dunn (1831–1913) asked Chivington if he would object if he killed one of the captured Indians. Chivington said he would not, and Dunn shot the prisoner. (Dunn testified for Chivington in the subsequent hearing.) One of the white men engaged in scalping the dead, two-thirds of whom were women and children, was Harry Richmond (1837–1910), an actor turned temporary soldier in the 100-day service of the 3rd Colorado Cavalry.

Ten troopers were lost. White Antelope was killed, but Black Kettle escaped, and his wife, shot nine times, survived; both were killed four years later by Custer on the Washita River [q.v.].

In testimony before a panel in Washington, D.C., investigating the action, Samuel Marshall Robbins (1832–1878), one of Chivington's staff officers, who had not been present in the attack, testified that his commander was under public pressure to act against the Indians. The people, he said, "wanted some Indians killed. Whether friendly or not, they did not stop long to inquire." On the return of Chivington and his men to Denver the Cheyenne scalps were displayed at the Denver Opera House to wild applause. To the last Chivington maintained that he had won a glorious victory over hostile Indians.

Chiza Katana. A medium-size Japanese sword (about 45 cm) used mostly as a dress sword with court dress, particularly by those in the suite of the shogun.

Chłopicki, Józef (1771–1854). A Polish general who served in the French army under Napoleon, and from 1815 to 1818 in the Russian army. He briefly became dictator of Poland during the Polish Revolution [q.v.] from December 1830 to January 1831 but resigned to join the Polish forces fighting the Russians. He was wounded the following month and retired. He died in exile at Cracow.

Choctaw Resolution (7 February 1861), American Civil War. The General Council of the Choctaw Nation passed a resolution stating that while all hoped that the differences between the North and the South could be peacefully resolved, in case they were not, the chiefs would "follow the natural affections, education, institutions and interests of our people, which indissolubly bind us in every way to the destiny of our neighbors and brethren of the Southern states."

Copies of this resolution were sent to the governors of all the southern states, and a delegation was dispatched to Montgomery, Alabama, then the capital of the Confederacy. Although the delegation was coolly received, the Choctaws ordered a conscription of all males aged eighteen to thirty-five and formed a home guard. This was the first conscription legislation ever passed in North America.

On 25 May 1861 the Chickasaws passed a similar resolution. [See Pike, Albert; Conscription.]

Cholera. One of a number of gastrointestinal diseases that were the scourge of soldiers in the nineteenth century. There was no prophylactic and no cure for cholera. The first symptom was painless diarrhea, followed by vomiting and dehydration. The mortality rate was 50 percent either within hours or, at most, within two days. In India during the first half of the century the mortality rate from the disease among European troops was 69 per 1,000. In June 1845 the 86th Foot, stationed in Karachi, had 410 cases (more than half its strength), of whom 238 died.

The cause of cholera was unknown, but it was generally believed to be bad air until Dr. John Snow (1813–1858), vice-president of the Westminster Medical Society (later the Medical Society of London) discovered in 1855 that contaminated water was the source of the disease. Although Snow was a well-respected doctor—in 1853 he administered chloroform to Queen Victoria when she gave birth to Prince Leopold—no one believed him. The acceptance of the "germ theory" was more than a decade in the future. Not until 1884 did Robert Koch (1843–1910) manage to isolate and cultivate the cholera bacterium (*Vibrio comma*).

The disease was first recognized in the Ganges Delta in India about 1819 and recurred in successive waves in the West for half a century. One such wave struck the armies in the Crimean War [q.v.] and was the principal killer in all four Allied armies in the Crimea. Cholera was the first pandemic since the bubonic plague, the Black Death of the fourteenth century.

Cholera Belts. Strips of flannel or wool worn around the waist next to the skin that were thought to protect the wearer in areas where cholera was prevalent.

Chorrillos, Battle of (13 January 1861), War of the Pacific. At this Peruvian town nine miles south of Lima, in a war between Chile and Peru, the Peruvians were defeated with a loss of 9,000 killed and wounded out of about 22,000. The Chileans lost 800 killed and 2,500 wounded out of 24,000. The Chileans then advanced and captured Lima.

Chouaf. In North Africa, a lookout or scout.

Chouans. A name given to French peasants in Brittany, Maine, and Normandy who in 1793 rose in revolt, demanding the return of the monarchy. They were never completely suppressed. The name comes from Chouan, the sobriquet of four brothers, leaders of royalist revolts, whose family name was Cottereau. Only the youngest brother, René (1764–1846), survived the Revolution and the Napoleonic era. *Chouannerie* came to mean any peasant rising, and *chouanner* became a verb meaning "to carry on a partisan war."

Christian Commission, United States. An organization formed by the YMCA in 1861, during the American Civil War, that worked with the United States Sanitary Commission [q.v.] to provide comforts to Union soldiers.

Christmas, Leon ("Lee") Winfield (1863–1924). An American soldier of fortune who began his career as a locomotive engineer in America. After falling asleep and wrecking a train, he decamped to Honduras and plied his trade there. When a revolution erupted in 1897, he joined the revolutionaries. Ultimately he became a general and was said to have served in that rank in five Latin American countries. He became an internationally known figure, the fabled hero (or villain) of countless exploits.

It was said that at one time, when sentenced to be shot, he requested that his body be left unburied, adding, "Because I want those vultures overhead to eat me and then shit me all over you bastards." He died of acute anemia in New Orleans.

He was said to have been the model for the hero of Richard Harding Davis's [q.v.] *Soldiers of Fortune* (1897). He and the war correspondent / novelist were friends.

Christophe, Henri (1767–1820). A Caribbean revolutionary who was born a slave in Grenada. He was a lieutenant of Toussaint L'Ouverture [q.v.] in the unsuccessful Haitian Revolution of 1791 against the French, and in 1802 he joined the successful uprising of Jean Jacques Dessalines [q.v.]. With independence the country became divided between a mulatto-controlled south, ruled by Alexandre Pétion [q.v.] and a black-controlled north. After assassinating Dessalines, Christophe proclaimed himself Henri I, king of Haiti, although he ruled only in the north. There near Cap Henri (Cap-Haïtien) he built an ornate palace, Sans Souci, now in ruins, and the enormous fortress of La Citadelle Laferrière [q.v.], still standing. His cruelty and avarice generated a rebellion in 1818. In 1820 he shot himself with a silver bullet shortly before a mob set fire to his palace. (Eugene O'Neill's play *The Emperor Jones* [1920] is based on Christophe's life.)

Chrysler's / Christler's Farm, Battle of (11 November 1813), War of 1812. Early in November 1813 American General James Wilkinson [q.v.] led a force of 7,000 to 8,000 from Sackets Harbor on Lake Ontario in northern New York down the St. Lawrence River to capture Montreal. A second force of 4,000 men under Wade Hampton [q.v.], which was to move up the Chateaugay River to support him, failed to do so. Wilkinson sent off a part of his force, about 2,000, under Brigadier General John Parker Boyd [q.v.] to attack a British force of 800, under Colonel J. Whitford Morrison, that threatened his advance. Boyd attacked piecemeal at a place called Chrysler's Farm and was defeated, losing 102 killed, 237 wounded, and about 100 captured. Faced with this defeat and the failure of Hampton to join him, Wilkinson went into winter quarters at French Mills on the Salmon River.

Ch'uan-Chou or Tao-Chou, Siege of (20 May–3 June 1852), Taiping Rebellion. At this fortified town in Kwangsi Province in southern China a Taiping force under Hung Ksiuchan [q.v.] laid siege to imperial Chinese forces. When the town was taken, the Taipings massacred the inhabitants, a deed that extinguished Western sympathy for this "Christian" rebellion.

Church, Richard (1784–1873). A British soldier from a Quaker family who at sixteen ran away from home and enlisted as a private after being expelled from the Society of Friends. Relatives soon purchased a commission for him, and on 3 July 1800 he was gazetted an ensign in the 13th Light Infantry, in which he served in the Egyptian Campaign. On 7 January 1806 he was promoted captain in the Corsican Rangers and led a detachment in the Battle of Maida [q.v.] on 9 July of that year [see Calabrian War].

He was next sent to Capri, where he was conspicuous in the defense of the island against the French and was wounded. In September 1809 he was quartermaster general of the forces sent under Major General Sir John Oswald (1771–1840) to occupy the Ionian islands. There he distinguished himself in the capture of Zante, Cephalonia (Kefallonia), Paxo, and Ithaca and particularly in the taking of Leukas, where his left arm was shattered. [See Ionian Islands, British Occupation of.]

For the defense of the islands, in 1811 he raised a regiment of light infantry from Greek brigands, whose chiefs he made officers. It was disbanded in 1815 at the end of the Napoleonic Wars, and Church was then for a time attached to the Austrian army.

In 1817, with the permission of the War Office, he accepted a position as a major general in the army of King Ferdinand I of Naples (1751–1825) and was placed in charge of two Apulian (Puglian) provinces, where he struggled to suppress brigandage. In 1820 he was made commander-in-chief in Sicily, where he was imprisoned by his mutinous soldiers. He returned to England and was knighted (KCH). In 1827 he was commander-in-chief of the Greek insurgent army, which he led against the Turks [see Greek War of Independence].

In 1832, when Otto I (1815–1867) assumed the Greek throne, Church's appointment as commander-in-chief was confirmed. But because he came to detest the king, he cooperated in the Revolution of 1843, which gave Greece a constitution. He became a Greek citizen, was appointed a senator, and spent the remainder of his life in Athens. In 1854 he was elected a general in the regular Greek army, an honor conferred on no other foreigner.

Churchill, Winston Leonard Spencer (1874–1965). A British soldier and politician who was educated at Harrow and in 1893, after his third attempt, was admitted to Sandhurst [q.v.]. The following year he passed out 20th in order of merit from a class of 130, and on 20 February 1895 he was commissioned in the 4th Queen's Own Hussars. In October, with another subaltern, he took leave and set off to see the insurrection in Cuba. His dispatches from the island were published in the *Daily Graphic* of London. He saw service in India and then in Egypt and Sudan, where on 2 September 1898 he took part in the cavalry charge of the 21st Lancers at Omdurman [q.v.]. In 1899 he resigned his commission to enter politics but was defeated in his first attempt to be elected to Parliament.

At the beginning of the Second Anglo-Boer War [q.v.] he sailed to South Africa as a correspondent for the *London Morning Post*. Having been captured when the Boers ambushed an armored train on which he was a passenger, he made a sensational escape after appropriating another prisoner's plan. After a short period of service in the South Africa Light Horse, he returned to England in 1900 to pursue political and literary careers.

Except for four months as a major in the Oxfordshire Hussars, a Yeomanry regiment, and a brief period as a lieutenant colonel of the 6th Battalion of the Royal Scots Fusiliers in France during the First World War, he served no more as a soldier. He remained in politics, becoming prime minister during the Second World War.

He was the author of *The Story of the Malakand Field Force* (1898), *The River War* (1899), *Ian Hamilton's March* (1900), and many other later works.

Churubusco, Battle of (20 August 1847), Mexican War. At this hamlet on the Churubusco River American forces under General Winfield Scott [q.v.], marching on Mexico City, defeated the Mexican forces of Antonio López de Santa Anna [q.v.] who, entrenched in a fort improvised from a church and a convent, were attempting to defend their capital. The capture of the fort cost Scott 133 killed and more than 900 wounded. The Americans took 3,000 prisoners and 37 guns, but their losses, with those in the Battle of Contreras [q.v.], accounted for 7 percent of Scott's army. Santa Anna, having lost more than a third of his, including 8 generals, requested an armistice, which was granted on 24 August. The negotiations collapsed, however, and on 7 September the fighting was renewed.

Cialdini, Enrico, Duca di Gaeta (1813–1892). An Italian soldier and diplomat who fled Italy in 1830 after the failed insurrection in Parma and in 1834–39 fought against the Carlist rebels in Spain [see Carlist Wars]. He returned to Italy in 1848 and commanded a regiment of Piedmont infantry in the Battle of Novara [q.v.] on 23 March 1849, during the Italian Wars of Independence [q.v.]. In the Crimean War [q.v.] he commanded the 3rd Sardinian Division. At the beginning of the Austro-Piedmontese War [q.v.] of 1859 he organized the Cacciatori delle Alpi (Alpine Hunters), and he defeated the Papal army under Louis Lamoricière [q.v.] at Castelfidardo [q.v.] on 18 September 1860. After a long siege he conquered Gaeta [q.v.] on 13 February 1861, and on 29 August 1862 he defeated the army of Giuseppe Garibaldi [q.v.] at Aspromonte [q.v.]. In 1866 in the war against Austria [see Seven Weeks' War] he occupied Venice. In the same year he was promoted general and chief of staff. He was twice ambassador to France, 1876–79 and 1880–81.

Cibicue / Cibecu Creek, Skirmish at (30 August 1881), American Indian Wars. A small fight northwest of Fort Apache, Arizona. Captain Edmund Clarence Hentig (1842–1881) was ordered by Colonel Eugene Asa Carr [q.v.] to arrest Noch-ay-del-Klinne, a medicine man believed to be preaching incendiary ideas. Despite the hostility of his followers, the arrest was made, but the troops then unwisely camped nearby on the banks of Cibicue Creek. There some of Hentig's Apache scouts mutinied and joined the belligerent tribesmen. Gunfire erupted, and Hentig and a half dozen sol-

diers were killed. Private Henry F. Ofdenkamp later recalled that "there were so many Indians that the bullets put one in mind of a hail storm." Colonel Carr had ordered that if there was any trouble, the medicine man was to be killed. A young bugler shot him with a .45 pistol but failed to kill him. He was finally killed with an ax, before the troopers retreated with their wounded and prisoners during the night.

Three of those captured were hanged on 3 March 1882. One was a mutinous Apache scout named Deadshot. He left behind two orphaned sons, who were adopted by Signal Sergeant Will Croft Barnes (1838–1936).

This disturbance caused Geronimo [q.v.] and other Indian leaders to break out of their reservation with their followers and head for Mexico.

Cieneguilla, Battle of (30 March 1854), American Indian Wars. A detachment of the 1st U.S. Dragoons under Lieutenant John Wynn Davidson (1824–1881) was ambushed by Jicarilla Apaches in the Embudo Mountains, 25 miles south of Taos, New Mexico. The dragoons, outnumbered four to one, fought for three hours to extricate themselves. Davidson, although wounded, managed to get his command back to Taos, but he left 22 dead on the field and the detachment carried 36 wounded. Only 2 men were untouched.

Cienfuegos y Jovellanos, José (1768–1825). A Spanish soldier who served in the Peninsular War [q.v.] and was captain general of Cuba from 1816 to 1819. He returned to Spain, and in 1822 he was appointed minister of war.

Cilliars, Sarel Arnoldus (1801–1871). A Boer leader who served under Andries Hendrik [q.v.] and distinguished himself in the Battle of Vegkop, during a Kaffir War [q.v.], and later in fighting the Zulus in the Battle of Blood River [q.v.]. When the British occupied Natal, he moved to the Orange Free State, where he helped draft that country's constitution.

Cimbres, Battle of (28 April 1862), French invasion and occupation of Mexico. The advance guard of the French expeditionary force in Mexico encountered and defeated a force of 6,000 Mexicans with 18 guns in a defile in the Cimbres Mountains.

Cincinnati, Society of the. A society formed in the United States in 1783 by officers of the Revolutionary Army. Its stated purpose was "to perpetuate our friendship, and to raise a fund for relieving the widows and orphans of those who had fallen during the war." George Washington (1732–1799) was elected president of the society in 1787. Because membership became hereditary, many, including Benjamin Franklin (1706–1790), feared that it contained "the germ of an American aristocracy." The society is still extant.

Cinco de Mayo, Battle of. See Puebla, Battle of.

Cintra, Convention of (22 August 1808). After Wellington's victory over General Jean Junot [q.v.] in the Battle of Vimeiro [q.v.] on 21 August 1808 in the Peninsular War [q.v.] he was superseded by Lieutenant General Sir Harry Burrard (1755–1813), who forbade pursuit of the beaten French. Burrard was in turn superseded by General Sir Hew

Whitfoord ("Dowager") Dalrymple (1750–1830). Burrard and Dalrymple decided to negotiate with the French and signed the Convention of Cintra, which permitted 26,000 French troops with all their baggage, their impedimenta, and even their loot to be repatriated to France in British ships.

When this became known in Britain, there was an uproar. The three commanders were recalled to face a court of inquiry, but they escaped a court-martial.

Cipayes. French sepoys [q.v.] serving in the French possessions in India in the early nineteenth century.

Cipher. Secret writing. "Substitution cipher" substitutes letters or characters for the letter intended. "Transposition cipher" transposes the letters after arranging them in blocks or squares [see Code]. French Commandant Bazaries, a famous cipher expert of the nineteenth century, who deciphered Louis XIV's famous Grand Chiffre and

Cipher disks

is said to have solved the mystery of the man in the iron mask, devised a military cipher of letter square codes based on a key word, using a numeral that changed daily. He later improved on this to make it a double substitution system.

Cipriani, Amilcare (1845–1918). An Italian revolutionary and soldier of fortune who served in the Italian army in the Battle of Solferino [q.v.] and under Giuseppe Garibaldi [q.v.]. During the Franco-Prussian War [q.v.] he served in the French army and was among the revolutionary leaders in the Paris Commune [q.v.]. He was captured, tried, and sentenced to prison at hard labor but was pardoned in 1888. In 1891 he returned to Italy, where he was soon sentenced to imprisonment for three years for his revolutionary activities. During the Graeco-Turkish War [q.v.] he raised a battalion of volunteers that fought for the Greeks.

Circumvallation, also called contravallation or countervallation. Earthworks or other defensive measures erected by a besieging force to protect it from being surprised by a sally from the besieged or from attempts by the enemy to relieve the siege from the outside. Such measures were usually employed only for a long siege.

The most outstanding example in the nineteenth century was the outer circle of redoubts near Sevastopol that in the Crimean War [qq.v.] protected the batteries and sappers from Russian forces in the field. The near disaster to the Allied forces at Inkerman [q.v.] well illustrated the necessity for circumvallations.

Cisalpine Legion. An army formed in 1786 in the Cisalpine Republic (1797–1804) and the kingdom of Italy under Viceroy Eugène de Beauharnais (1781–1824). It was disbanded in 1814.

Cisleithanian Troops. Austrian troops from west of the Leitha River.

Citadel. 1. A strong fort or fortifications commanding the approach to or within a city.

2. Any stronghold.

3. A fort of four or five bastions located in or near a city either to overawe the inhabitants or to provide a place of refuge in case of attack.

4. The Citadel [q.v.] is the name of a military college in Charleston, South Carolina, founded in 1842.

Citadel, The. A state military academy in Charleston, South Carolina, founded in 1842. During the American Civil War the cadets formed part of a cadet battalion that was mustered into the South Carolina militia in November 1861. In the postwar years it was permitted to operate as a nonmilitary school until 1882, when it again became a military academy.

Citadelle la Ferrière. The huge Haitian fortress built on a 3,100-foot high peak outside Cap-Haïtien by the self-proclaimed Henri I, Henri Christophe [q.v.]. Some 200,000 former slaves labored for more than thirteen years (1806–20) to construct it. When completed, it could hold 15,000 people with enough food and water for a year. [See Haitian Wars and Revolts.]

Citation. 1. A narrative description of a meritorious action for which a medal is awarded.

2. A mention in an after-action report or in orders of commendable behavior.

Ciudad Real, Battle of, (27–28 May 1809), Peninsular War. Near this town in La Mancha, south-central Spain, 99 miles south of Madrid, a French force of 10,500 infantry and 2,000 cavalry under General Horace François Sébastiani [q.v.] defeated a Spanish force of 10,000 infantry and 2,500 cavalry under General Cartaojal. The Spanish lost 2,000 taken prisoner and three guns but suffered hardly any killed or wounded; French losses were fewer than 100. The Spanish, forced out of La Mancha, retreated into the mountains.

Ciudad Rodrigo, Peninsular War. In the nineteenth century this fourteenth-century castle on the Agueda River, 53 miles southwest of Salamanca, dominating the Almeida–Coimbra road, was twice besieged.

First Siege (30 May–9 June 1810). In 1810 the castle was garrisoned by 6,500 Spanish troops, mostly militia, under Don Andrés Herrarti, an aging but able general. On 30 May of that year it was invested by the French under Marshal Michel Ney [q.v.]. When the first elements of the siege train arrived on 8 June, the French began a bombardment with heavy mortars. By 25 June they were able to bring 40 guns to bear. On 9 July Ney was personally preparing to lead an infantry attack when Herrarti surrendered. Ney granted the gallant garrison full honors of war [q.v.], but the town was pillaged. The French lost 180 killed and 1,000 wounded; Spanish losses were 61 killed, 994 wounded, and about 4,000 made prisoner. Because Wellington refused to go to the aid of the Spanish commander, British-Spanish relations soured for a time.

Second Siege (8–19 January 1812), Peninsular War. After spending seven months organizing his forces, Wellington renewed his offensive early in 1812. On 8 January, in bitter weather, he arrived before the fortress, which had been captured by the French in 1810. It was garrisoned by 1,937 men with 150 guns under Marshal Auguste Marmont [q.v.]. Of Wellington's five divisions, one was used to conduct the siege with some 38 siege guns that were made available. The British engineers were ably led by Lieutenant Colonel Richard Fletcher [q.v.], of whom Wellington said that his "ability exceeded all praise." On 18 January in a night assault by the 3rd Division and the Light Division the fortress was taken and plundered. The siege cost the Allies some 200 killed and 900 wounded, of whom 568 fell in the final assault. Among the dead was General Robert Craufurd [q.v.], commander of the light division. Wellington next swung south to attack Badajoz [q.v.].

Civil Disorders. The laws of most countries allow the military to be used to support civil authorities when they are unable to maintain order. It is a service most soldiers dislike. It is frightening to face a hostile, unpredictable mob and at the same time unpleasant to fire upon civilians, especially those whose demands may seem justified. General Charles Napier [q.v.], who was charged with suppressing Chartist riots [q.v.] in 1839, had much sympathy for the Chartists' aims. British soldiers, many of whom were Irish, were often called out against civilians in Ireland, and those stationed abroad were frequently employed to maintain order in India and elsewhere in the empire.

In the United States regular troops were first used against civilians in January 1834 in the canal workers' strike. During the American Civil War troops were used to suppress the Molly McGuires [q.v.] in Pennsylvania, and they were called on to suppress the so-called draft riots [q.v.] in New York City in July and August 1863, when masses protested the Enrollment Act of 3 March 1863. Except for the Civil War itself, it was the largest, bloodiest, and most destructive insurrection in American history. The New York rioting began on 11 July, when the first draft numbers were called. Fights erupted with police in the streets, and the Colored Orphan Asylum at 43rd Street and fifth Avenue was burned. The chil-

dren were saved by George Rallings, a quick-witted police officer, who evacuated 260. Only one little girl was killed—by a blow from an ax. The building was burned.

After the war regulars were used against striking workers in eight states during the great railroad strike in July 1877 and more frequently thereafter. In 1894 troops intervened in industrial disputes in eleven states, and 3 times in the 1890s regulars were used in the Coeur d'Alene mining region of Idaho. Between 1870 and the end of the century state troops were called out 150 times to maintain order during strikes.

In France the greatest use of military force against civilians occurred during the Commune [q.v.] in Paris, March–May 1871, when Frenchmen bitterly protested the German occupation of the city. Tens of thousands of civilians died at the barricades or were executed. [See Semaine Sanglant, la]

Civil War. A war between portions of a nation or between groups of differing religious, political, or ideological beliefs. (For the civil wars of particular countries, see the entries for those countries.)

Clam-Gallas, Count Eduard von (1805–1891). An Austrian officer who was commissioned in the cavalry in 1823 and fought in Italy and Hungary in 1848–49 [see Hungarian Revolution of 1848], distinguishing himself in the Battle at Novara on 23 March 1849. He was engaged at Magenta on 4 June 1859 and Solferino [qq.v.] on 24 June. During the Seven Weeks' War [q.v.] he commanded a corps in Bohemia, where he was defeated in the Battle of Podol (near Mladá Boleslav) on 27 June 1866 and at Münchengrätz the following day. He also took part in the disaster at Sadowa [q.v.] on 3 July, for which he was relieved of his command. Cleared of charges of negligence by a military court, he served as a general during the Franco-Prussian War [q.v.].

Civil Disorders *Police charge rioters at the* Tribune *office. New York City, draft riots, July 1863.*

Clarke, George Sydenham, First Baron Sydenham of Combe (1848–1933). A British soldier and colonial administrator who, after being graduated first in his class at the Royal Military Academy, Woolwich, was gazetted to the Royal Engineers in 1868. He took part in the suppression of Arabi [q.v.] in 1882 and served in the Suakim Campaign [q.v.] of 1884, but he saw little action. From 1885 to 1892 he was secretary of the Colonial Defence Committee, and from 1888 to 1890 he was also secretary of the Royal Commission on Navy and Army Administration. It was during his tenure that for the first time in history the British army and navy held a joint discussion of imperial strategy. From 1894 to 1901 he was superintendent of the carriage department at Woolwich Arsenal [q.v.].

Clarke, Henri Jacques Guillaume (1765–1818). A French soldier born to immigrant Irish parents and commissioned in 1781 on graduation from the École Militaire. He fought in the American Revolutionary War, and in 1795 he was promoted general of division. From 1799 to 1804 he was Napoleon's private secretary. In 1807 he replaced Alexandre Berthier [q.v.] as minister of war, serving until 1814. He did not rally to Napoleon during the Hundred Days [q.v.] but remained loyal to Louis XVIII. He was reappointed war minister and was created a marshal of France.

Class. In the Indian army this was the term used toward the end of the century to denote the caste, ethnic, cultural, or religious groupings in the army. There were class regiments, composed entirely of men from the same class, and class company regiments [q.v.], which had a different class in each company. No Indian officer commanded troops of a different class from his own.

Class Company Regiment. A regiment in which each company was composed of men from a single tribe, religion, race, or caste.

Class Corps. In the Indian army a unit drawn from a single race, tribe, religion, or caste.

Clausel / Clauzel, Comte Bertrand (1772–1842). A French soldier who commanded a division in 1802 and served with distinction in the Peninsular War [q.v.]. In the Battle of Salamanca [q.v.] he took command when Marshal Auguste Marmont [q.v.] was wounded and, although defeated, saved the French from the even worse defeat they seemed destined to suffer. He aided Napoleon during the Hundred Days [q.v.] and lived in exile in the United States from 1816 to 1819, when he was permitted to return to France. In 1831 he was made a marshal of France. From 1835 to 1837 he was governor of Algeria, where his attempt to conquer Constantine [q.v.] failed.

Clausewitz, Karl von (1780–1831). A Prussian soldier and military writer who in 1792 began his military career as an *Fahnenjunker Unteroffizier* [q.v.] in the Prussian 34th Infantry and was commissioned the following year at age thirteen. He first saw action in the Rhineland in 1793–94. In 1801 he was assigned to the Kriegsschule in Berlin and became an admirer of the school's founder and director, Gerhard von Scharnhorst [q.v.]. In 1804 he joined the General Staff. He fought at

Auerstädt [q.v.] on 14 October 1806 and two weeks later was captured at Prenzlau. He was not released until the following September. His experience gave him a lifelong dislike of the French and their ways. As one of the Five Reformers [q.v.] he assisted Scharnhorst in remodeling the Prussian army. In late 1811, just before the French invasion of Russia, he, with about 30 other Prussian officers, resigned and joined the Russian army to protest Prussia's role as a puppet of Napoleon. He played a principal part in persuading Prussian General Count Yorck von Wartenburg [q.v.], who commanded the Prussian corps in Napoleon's Grande Armée to desert and proclaim the Prussian army neutral. In 1813 he served on Gebhart von Blücher's [q.v.] staff and was chief of staff to General Johann Thielmann [q.v.] at Ligny [q.v.], just before the Battle of Waterloo. In 1816–17 he was chief of staff to the Prussian occupation forces in the Rhineland. In 1818 he was promoted major general and named director of the Berlin War College (Allgemeine Kriegsakademie). In 1830 he was posted as chief of staff to the Prussian army of observation during the Polish Revolution [q.v.]. He died of cholera in 1831.

Many consider Clausewitz the father of modern strategic thought. His most celebrated work, *Vom Krieg* (On War), a philosophical treatise on the impact of democracy and imperialism on war, is still studied in all armies. Most often quoted is his description of war as "the continuation of policy by other means," but that is not quite what he said. He wrote of the continuation of political intercourse "with the intermixing of other means" (*mit Einmischung anderer Mittel*). War, he said, "admittedly has its own grammar but not its own logic." He defined his well-known phrase the "friction of war" [q.v.] as the accumulation of many elements, large and small, that cause the best of plans to go awry in battle. The key to a successful war, he believed, lies in victorious battles, and he declared decisive victory to be war's supreme moment.

He argued that battles and wars could be won only by commanders seizing the initiative and aiming at the destruction of the enemy's army. He prescribed the use of terror as one of the ways to shorten wars, for he believed terror would cause civilians to pressure their leaders for peace. He also illuminated the human side of war: the fears, confusion, and emotional experiences of combatants at all levels of command.

Clausewitz's scientific approach to war and its practice by the Germans in the Seven Weeks' War [q.v.] led British Colonel (later Field Marshal) Archibald Percival Wavell to write in the fourteenth edition of the *Encyclopaedia Britannica* (1929): "Historians a century hence may write that Clausewitz and his disciple, von Moltke, killed war by making it so serious, so dull and so deadly." It can now, well over a century after the Battle of Sadowa [q.v.] and more than seventy years after Earl Wavell's words, be safely said that despite far more deadly weapons and greater scientific military skills, war seems unlikely to disappear.

Claymore. A basket-handled double-edged broadsword used by Scottish Highlanders.

Clearwater, Battle of (11–12 July 1877), Nez Percé War. On the banks of the Clearwater River in Idaho General O. O. Howard defeated a force of Nez Percé under Looking Glass [qq.v.] for a loss of 13 dead and 22 wounded, 2 mortally. According to Howard, 23 Indians were killed; according to the Indians, they lost 4 killed and 6 wounded. Howard had a battery of howitzers and two Gatling guns, but he opened fire with these too soon and from such long ranges that he merely revealed his position.

Cleburne, Patrick Ronayne (1828–1864). An Irish soldier born on St. Patrick's Day who served three years in the ranks of the 41st Foot of the British army (1846–49) before emigrating to the United States (probably after deserting) in 1849. During the American Civil War he became the only Irishman and one of only two foreign-born officers to reach the rank of major general in the Confederate army. He fought in the western theater, where he earned the sobriquet Stonewall of the West. One admirer said of him "Men seemed afraid to be afraid where he was." He distinguished himself at Murfreesboro [q.v.], and he received the Thanks of the Confederate Congress for saving the baggage and ammunition trains of the Army of Tennessee [q.v.].

He was one of the first to suggest enlisting and arming slaves, reasoning that by doing so, the South would ease its manpower problem and that the sanctioning of black soldiers would help secure European recognition for the Confederacy. His suggestion raised a furor in the South, where he was roundly denounced. He was killed in the Battle of Franklin [q.v.] on 30 November 1864.

Clem, John Lincoln. See Drummer Boy of Chickamauga.

Clery, Cornelius Francis (1838–1926). A British soldier, the son of a wine merchant, who, after graduation from Sandhurst [q.v.] was commissioned into the 32nd Foot on 5 March 1858. He was graduated from the Staff College [q.v.] in 1870 and taught at Sandhurst for four years. In 1875 he wrote *Minor Tactics*, which became the standard infantry text for the next thirty years. It was said that "few British military handbooks can have ever exercised so much influence" (*Dictionary of National Biography*).

In 1882 he served in the Arabi Campaign [see Arabi's Revolt] under Garnet Wolseley [q.v.], and in 1884 he served under Sir Gerald Graham [q.v.] in the Suakim Campaign [q.v.], in which he distinguished himself at El Teb on 29 February and at Tamai [qq.v.] on 13 March. In these latter engagements he spurned the new khaki uniforms and persistently wore a smartly tailored scarlet jacket. In 1885 he took part in the Gordon Relief Expedition [q.v.], and in 1886 he was chief of staff to the army of occupation in Egypt. On 20 December 1894 he became a major general.

During the Second Anglo-Boer War [q.v.], he commanded a division under Sir Redvers Buller [q.v.], but he proved a poor commanding general. In October 1900, in the middle of the war, he returned to England, and he retired in 1901.

Personally vain (he dyed his whiskers and was always smartly arrayed), he was a bachelor noted as an epicure and famed for his hospitality and for his courtesy.

Clery Litter. See Travois; Ambulance.

Clinch, Duncan Lamont (1787–1849). An American soldier who was commissioned a first lieutenant in the 3rd Infantry on 1 July 1808. Five years later he was promoted lieutenant colonel. His principal exploits were the reduction of Negro Fort [q.v.] on 14 August 1813 in the Creek War [q.v.] and the victory over the Seminoles in the Battle of Withlacoochee [q.v.] on 31 December 1835 in the Second Seminole War [q.v.].

He was made a brevet brigadier general on 20 April 1829 and became commander of military affairs in Florida. He resigned in 1836.

Clinometer. An instrument for measuring a degree of incline or the elevation of the barrel of an artillery piece. In the American army this was called a quadrant.

Clinometer

Clinton, Henry (1771–1829). A British soldier and brother of William Henry Clinton [q.v.], who was commissioned into the 11th Foot on 9 March 1788. He served on the staff of the Duke of York during his disastrous campaign in Flanders and was wounded in 1794. He saw active service in India, commanding the right wing in the Battle of Laswari [q.v.] on 1 November 1803. In 1805 he left India and served as military commissioner with the Russian army during the Austerlitz Campaign [see Austerlitz, Battle of].

In 1808, after service in Sicily, he was promoted brigadier general and accompanied Sir John Moore [q.v.], first to Sweden and then to the Iberian Peninsula, where he served as Moore's adjutant general. He was on the famous retreat from Corunna [q.v.] and was promoted major general on 25 July 1810. In October 1811 he joined Wellington as division commander and reduced the forts at Salamanca [q.v.]. Sickness sent him back to Britain, but he recovered in time to take part in the final battles of the Peninsular War [q.v.]. In the Battle of Waterloo he commanded a division on the right center of the line.

Clinton, Henry Pelham Fiennes Pelham, Fifth Duke of Newcastle (1811–1864). A British politician who on 12 June 1854 became secretary for war. He traveled to the Crimea to verify the reports of the deplorable state of the army and resigned after witnessing its sufferings before Sevastopol.

Clinton, William Henry (1769–1846). A British soldier and brother of Henry Clinton [q.v.], who was commissioned into the 7th Light Dragoons on 22 December 1784 and saw service in Flanders. In 1799 he was liaison officer with the army of Aleksandr Suvorov [q.v.] in northern Italy. On 23 July 1801 he led a successful expedition to capture the island of Madeira and became its military governor. In May 1807 he was sent on a secret, apparently successful mission to Sweden, and on 28 April 1808 he was promoted major general.

In 1812 he took command of a division at Messina, Sicily, and then was sent to the Iberian Peninsula. He became a lieutenant general in 1813. In 1825 he was appointed lieutenant general of the ordnance, a post he held until 1829. In December 1826 he took a division of 5,000 men to Portugal to maintain order, and he brought them back the following April. On 22 July he was promoted general, and he retired that same year.

Close Order. The distance of about one and a half paces between men in ranks.

Cloyd's Mountain, Battle at (9 May 1864), American Civil War. On 29 April 1864 Union General George Crook [q.v.], following the orders of General U. S. Grant, advanced with three brigades—6,155 men—into the rugged Allegheny Mountains. His mission was to destroy the Virginia & Tennessee Railroad, which was vital to the Confederacy.

On 9 May Crook encountered a Confederate force of 2,400 under Brigadier Albert Gallatin Jenkins (1830–1864) on wooded bluffs near Cloyd's Mountain, five miles north of Dublin Station (today Dublin) in southwestern Virginia. After a vicious, hard-fought contest, the Confederates were forced to retreat. Confederate casualties were 538, nearly 23 percent of Jenkins's command, and Jenkins himself was wounded and captured; a Union surgeon amputated his arm, but he died on 21 May.

Clubbed (as a unit). Troops thrown into confusion. A clubbed battalion was one in which the commanding officer maneuvering his men was unable to place them in the desired order. "To club a unit" was to throw it into disorder.

Clubbed Muskets or Rifles. 1. The use of the barrel of a firearm as a handle and the stock as a club. An evolution sometimes performed in close fighting when ammunition had become exhausted.

2. Muskets or rifles carried on a march with butts pointed to the rear.

Cluseret, Gustave Paul (1823–1900). A French soldier who was graduated from St. Cyr [q.v.] and won the Legion of Honor [q.v.] for helping suppress insurrectionists in Paris in June 1848. In 1855, after service in Algeria and in the Crimean War [q.v.], he was promoted captain, but he resigned his commission in 1858 to command a French legion in the army of Giuseppe Garibaldi [q.v.] in Italy. He was wounded at the siege of Capua [q.v.] in 1860.

In January 1862 he arrived in the United States and was commissioned a colonel in the Union army, in which he served under John Frémont [q.v.]. He was promoted brigadier general to rank from 14 October 1862 and fought in the Valley Campaign in Virginia. He appears to have been under arrest in January 1863 for reasons that remain obscure. He resigned on 2 March of the same year. In 1867 he returned to Europe. His aid to Fenian rebels led the British to place a price on his head. He joined the Paris Commune [q.v.] and was jailed by the French for revolutionary activities. After his release, he lived in exile in Geneva until 1884, when he returned to France. He was then four times elected to the Chamber of Deputies from Toulon.

Coa, Battle at the (24 July 1810), Peninsular War. A battle on the Spanish-Portuguese frontier between an Allied force of 2,500 British and 1,100 Portuguese infantry with 900 British cavalry and six guns under Brigadier General Robert Craufurd [q.v.] and a French force of 21,000 infantry and 3,000 cavalry under Marshal Michel Ney [q.v.]. The Allied force was forced to retreat. British infantry held back the French while the Portuguese infantry and the artillery escaped across a narrow bridge over the Coa River. Craufurd was able to withdraw in good order.

The British lost 248 casualties; the Portuguese 45; and the French 527. The French victory allowed the French to invest Almeida [q.v.].

Coacoochee. See Wild Cat.

Coalition Wars. See Napoleonic Wars.

Coast Defense. The fortifications erected on land to protect harbors, coastal cities, and other possible land targets from attack from the sea.

Coatee. A waist-length jacket, buttoned across the front with tails in back.

Cochin China and Annam, French and Spanish Invasion of (1858–62). From about 1851 to 1857 there were attacks upon French, Spanish, and other European Christian missionaries in what is today Vietnam. French authorities responded by protests and an occasional bombardment of seaports. In 1858 the murder of a Spanish bishop provoked a joint French-Spanish naval force to bombard and then occupy Tourane, a seaport 50 miles southeast of Hué in Annam. In February 1859 a French-Spanish force of about 1,000 moved to Saigon, and there in March 1860 it was besieged by Annamese troops [see Saigon, Siege of].

The siege lasted almost a year, until February 1861, when it was raised by French Admiral Leonard V. J. Charner after his defeat of the Annamese in the Battle of Chi-Hoa on 25 February 1861. The Annamese sued for peace, and France was ceded three eastern provinces, the beginning of French Indochina.

Tensions persisted. In 1873–74 the French government intervened in an Annamese civil war and seized Hanoi, giving it up only after the Annamese had granted further concessions. In 1882 war was renewed. The French again seized Hanoi, and France was granted a protectorate over still more territory. Between 1885 and 1895 there were numerous uprisings against French rule, but all were suppressed [see Black Flags].

Cochise (1805?–1874). An American Indian chief of the Chiricahua band of the Apaches. Early in life he established his reputation as a warrior in the many forays that made the Apache name feared, both in the American Southwest and in northern Mexico.

On 27 January 1861 at a Sonoita Valley ranch near Fort Buchanan, Arizona, a group of Indians stole some oxen and took hostage a boy (who grew up to become the scout known as Mickey Free [q.v.]). Cochise was suspected, and Second Lieutenant George Nicholas Bascom (1836–1862) with 54 soldiers was sent to apprehend him and rescue the boy. After some inconclusive fighting Cochise and Bascom met to parley at Apache Pass. Cochise denied all responsibility for the raid, insisting that Coyotero Apaches had taken the boy and that he would probably be able to recover cattle and boy in ten days. When Bascom informed him that he would be held hostage until they were returned, Cochise bolted and, although wounded, made good his escape. However, he left behind five of his relatives, whom Bascom seized. When his offer of a captured stagecoach attendant and two passengers in exchange was refused, Cochise went on a rampage. He killed some drovers he came across, attacked some soldiers watering cattle, slaughtered his hostages, and left their hacked remains beside a road before riding off into Mexico.

In retaliation Lieutenant Bascom, urged on by Assistant Surgeon Bernard Dowling Irwin (1830–1917), hanged six

Apache prisoners from a scrub oak. Their bodies were left to dangle and rot. Thus began a war that lasted a decade [see Bascom Affair].

Cochise with his father-in-law, Mangas Colorado [q.v.], chief of the Mimbreño Apaches, began a long series of raids on white settlements and stagecoaches. [see Apache Wars]. In 1868 he met with Captain Frank Perry [q.v.] and expressed a desire for peace but refused to go to a reservation. He told Perry that he had been twice wounded, once in the leg and in 1866 in the neck. Perry thought that he was "a man who means what he says; age is just beginning to tell on him," but the fighting continued until 1872, when Cochise agreed to settle with his people on a reservation in southeastern Arizona. Both a county and a mountain in Arizona are named after him.

Cochrane, Douglas Mackinnon Baillie Hamilton, Twelfth Earl of Dundonald (1852–1935). A British soldier known as Lord Cochrane until he assumed his father's title in 1885. In 1870 he entered the army as a cornet and sublieutenant in the 2nd Life Guards. In 1884 he commanded a contingent of that regiment during the Gordon Relief Expedition [q.v.]. In 1885 he took part in the battles of Abu Klea and Gubat [qq.v.], and he was promoted lieutenant colonel for his services in Egypt and Sudan.

In the Second Anglo-Boer War [q.v.] he commanded the South Natal Field Force under Sir Redvers Buller [q.v.] and took part in the Battle of Colenso [q.v.] and other battles on the Tugela River. He entered Ladysmith [q.v.] with the army that raised its siege on 28 February 1900. Later that year he returned to England and was promoted major general.

In December 1900 he sat on the Yeomanry Reorganization Committee. In 1906 he was promoted lieutenant general, and he retired from the army the following year. At the age of seventy-seven he sailed a fourteen-ton boat across the Atlantic to South America.

Cock, to. To ready a weapon for firing by drawing back the bolt, hammer, or plunger.

Cockade. A round button or disk of metal or cloth rosette, usually in the national colors worn at various times in European armies, usually on the cap or hat.

Cockerill, John (1790–1840). An Englishman who founded a gun-manufacturing and engineering company at Seraing, Belgium, on the Meuse River south-southwest of Liège, in 1817. This was the first Belgian firm to make Bessemer steel, and it is still a center for the manufacture of heavy metal products.

Code. A system of words or symbols arbitrarily used to represent words in secret writing [see Cipher].

Codrington, William John (1804–1884). A British soldier who was commissioned in 1821. He was promoted major general in 1834 and distinguished himself in the Crimean War [q.v.] in the battles of the Alma and Inkerman. From 1859 to 1865 he was governor of Gibraltar.

Cody, William Frederick ("Buffalo Bill") (1846–1917). An American scout, frontiersman, and entertainer, he claimed to have killed his first Indian at age eleven or twelve. At age fifteen he joined a gang of Kansas freebooters who stole cattle in Missouri and sold them in Kansas. In 1862, during the American Civil War, he served as a scout for the 9th Kansas Volunteers, which was serving on the Santa Fe Trail. On 19 February 1864 he enlisted in the 7th Kansas Cavalry (Jennison's Jayhawkers), a unit better known for its freebooting ways than for actual fighting; he was mustered out as a private in September 1865.

After the war he returned to scouting and turned as well to professional hunting under a contract to supply buffalo meat for the Union Pacific Railroad. His boast of having killed 4,280 buffaloes supplied him with his sobriquet. Scouting for the 5th Cavalry on 13 May 1869, he was wounded in the head in a skirmish at Beaver Creek. In one twelve-month period, from 5 October 1868 until 28 October 1869, he took part in 7 expeditions and engaged in 9 fights with Indians. Scouting for the 5th Cavalry, he took part in a total of 14 Indian fights. In April 1872 his bravery in a skirmish in Nebraska earned him a Medal of Honor (it was taken from him in 1916 on the ground that he had been a civilian and thus ineligible for the award; it was posthumously restored in 1989).

Late in 1872 he began his career as an entertainer, and at the same time he occasionally scouted for the 5th Cavalry. On 14 July 1876 on Hat Creek near Montrose, Nebraska, he fought a duel with the Cheyenne chief Yellow Hand or Yellow Hair (1850?–1876), so named for a flaxen-haired scalp he had taken. In Cody's version of the encounter the two, both mounted, met by accident and fired at the same time. Yellow Hand missed, but Cody's shot wounded the Cheyenne and killed his horse. Fighting on foot, both fired again, and Yellow Hand fell mortally wounded. Cody scalped him. This affair, called the First Scalp for Custer, aggrandized in the press, added greatly to Cody's success as an entertainer, a profession to which he returned in 1877 and pursued for the remainder of his life. During a European tour of his show in 1891 he impressed German army officers with his logistical skills as he quickly moved his entire troupe from place to place. In time the German army developed rolling kitchens based upon those he had devised.

At the beginning of the Spanish-American War Cody, age fifty-two, volunteered to raise a company of mounted scouts; the offer was accepted by General Nelson A. Miles [q.v.], but the unit was never formed.

Coehorn Mortar. A small muzzle-loading smoothbore mortar invented by a Dutch soldier, Baron Menno van Coehoorn (1641–1704). It usually had a caliber of $4\frac{3}{5}$ inches and was mounted on a sled or a portable platform. It weighed about 300 pounds and could be fitted with handles so as to be carried by four men. Coehorn mortars were used by the Americans through the American Civil War. Other large-siege mortars were sometimes erroneously referred to as coehorns. [See Mortars.]

Cohesion, Unit. See Unit Cohesion.

Cohort. 1. Originally a unit in the Roman army used in relation to conscription, being the annual manpower increment of men who had reached a certain age.

2. During the First Empire (1804–14) a unit in the French National Guard equivalent to a battalion.

Coigny, Augustin Louis Joseph Casimir Gustave (1780–1865). A French soldier who fought in Spain in 1808–11 and in Russia in 1812. He was a colonel of cavalry in 1814, and in 1830 he was made a marshal of France.

Coimbra, Battle of (10–13 March 1811), Peninsular War. A Portuguese force of 3,000 militia with three guns under Colonel Nicholas Trant [q.v.], governor of Oporto, Portugal, was occupying the town of Coimbra on the north bank of the Mondego River, 108 miles north-northeast of Lisbon, when a French cavalry corps plus one infantry battalion, all under General Louis Pierre Montbrun [q.v.], a part of Marshal André Masséna's [q.v.] Army of Portugal, attempted to force a crossing of the river. The Mondego was at a high level, and the only available crossing was over a partially destroyed bridge that after a small artillery duel on 12 March the French infantry tried unsuccessfully to secure. On the 13th, Montbrun, having received news of Marshal Michel Ney's [q.v.] retreat from Condeixa [q.v.], realized that his position was now untenable and withdrew to the east.

Although this affair was nearly bloodless, it marked a watershed in the Peninsular War. It was thereafter impossible for the French to hold positions in central Portugal, and Masséna was forced to retreat into Spain.

Coimbra, Siege of (December 1864), War of the Triple Alliance. This old fort on the Paraguayan River in southwest Mato Grosso, 65 miles south of Corumbá, Brazil, was held for three days (26–28 December 1864) by Brazilian Colonel Porto Carreira with only 120 soldiers against 3,000 Paraguayans. Porto Carreira surrendered only after his ammunition was exhausted.

Coin. See Quoin.

Colburn, John, First Baron Seaton (1778–1863). A British soldier who served in Egypt in 1801, in Sicily in 1806, in the Peninsular War, notably at Albuera in 1811, and fought in the Battle of Waterloo [qq.v.] in 1815. He became a major general in 1825 and was appointed governor of Lower Canada, where he crushed the revolt of 1837 [see Canadian Revolts]. He became a general in 1854 and a field marshal in 1860.

Cold Burning. A punishment inflicted by soldiers upon comrades who had not lived up to acceptable camp or barracks standards. A cup or pitcher of cold water was poured slowly down the sleeve of an upraised arm.

Cold Harbor, Battles of, American Civil War. Two battles were fought near this place in east-central Virginia about 10 miles east-northeast of Richmond.
1. 27 June 1862. See Gaines's Mill, Battle of.
2. 1–3 June 1864. General Grant with 108,000 men tried to drive his Army of the Potomac [q.v.] through the center of General Lee's 59,000-man Army of Northern Virginia [q.v.] in order to cross the James River and capture Richmond, but Lee's line held, and Grant failed. This was the last battle of the Wilderness Campaign [q.v.] and Lee's last major victory. Grant lost 13,000 men; Lee, 3,000.

At the end of the battle on 3 June, one of the bloodiest days of the war, Grant, repulsed, had lost 12,000 men. In his *Memoirs* he wrote that he had "always regretted that the last

assault at Cold Harbor was ever made." Neither side withdrew, and their lines became stabilized, some within 100 yards of each other, for ten days. It was not until 7 June that Grant requested a truce to collect the wounded and dead between the lines. Total casualties for this engagement were 13,078 Federals and 3,000 Confederates.

After the monthlong campaign the Union forces had lost 50,000 and the Confederates 32,000, but the Confederate loss was more serious, for the South was running short of manpower, while the North had an almost inexhaustible supply.

Colditz, Rearguard Action at (12 October 1813), Napoleonic Wars. At this Saxon town, 30 miles southeast of Leipzig, the French rear guard, commanded by Marshal Joachim Murat [q.v.], successfully held off General Karl von Schwarzenberg's [q.v.] Army of Bohemia and elements of the Russian forces under General Levin Bennigsen [q.v.], allowing the main French army to retire in good order toward Leipzig.

Cold Spring Foundry. See West Point Foundry.

Coldstream Guards. A British regiment of the Household Guards infantry raised in 1650 as Colonel Monck's Regiment of Foot, named after George Monck (1608–1670), its colonel. After the death of Oliver Cromwell (1599–1658), the regiment, then stationed in the border town of Coldstream, Berwick, marched to London to maintain order. It was Monck and his soldiers who were mainly responsible for ensuring the free election of a new Parliament that restored the monarchy. The regiment became the Coldstream Regiment of Foot Guards in 1670 and the Coldstream Guards in 1817. In the nineteenth century it saw action in Egypt, Hanover, the Iberian Peninsula, Waterloo, the Crimea, and South Africa.

Colenso, Battle of (15 December 1899), Second Anglo-Boer War. In the second week of December 1899 General Sir Redvers Buller, VC [q.v.], led a British army of 20,000 in

Colenso *Battle of Colenso, Second Anglo-Boer War, 15 December 1899*

Natal to the relief of besieged Ladysmith [q.v.]. At Colenso [q.v.], a village on the bank of the Tugela River, 16 miles south of Ladysmith, he encountered Boers in about equal numbers under Louis Botha [q.v.] in strong defensive positions on the north bank of the river. Although he knew almost nothing of the Boer strength or position, Buller attacked—or rather, attempted to attack—with two brigades. He was repulsed with a loss of 71 officers and 1,050 other ranks. Boer losses were negligible. The action saw the death of Lieutenant Frederick Roberts, the only son of Field Marshal Lord Roberts [q.v.], mortally wounded while trying to save British guns. He was awarded the first posthumous Victoria Cross [q.v.]. Said Sir Redvers: "It was a very trying day." [See Black Week; Anglo-Boer War, Second.]

Coler, Alwin Gustav Edmund von (1831–1901). A Prussian doctor who greatly improved military hygiene and hospital service. It was Dr. Coler who first introduced antiseptics into military surgery.

Collective Punishment. A system of punishing the tribe, band, clan, or group when an unidentified member was thought to have committed a crime. It was frequently used by white Americans in dealing with Indians, and it was routinely used by the British on India's Northwest Frontier, where tribes were punished by being forced to give up a certain number of muskets or rifles. It was also used within the British army: When the perpetrator of damage to a barracks could not be discovered, members of the company or battalion were required to make good the cost of repairs from their pay.

The Germans used collective punishment in France during the Franco-Prussian War [q.v.]. Hostages were carried on troop trains to prevent their derailment, and localities were held responsible for acts of sabotage within their border. In one case the inhabitants of Fontenoy in northeast-central France were fined ten million francs.

Collector. In British India this was the title of the chief administrative officer of a district.

Colletta, Pietro (1775–1831). A Neapolitan soldier who served under Joseph Napoleon and Joachim Murat and became a general in 1812. After the return of King Ferdinand I (1751–1825) in 1815, Colletta commanded a division. During the 1820 revolution he crushed the separatist movement in Sicily with ruthless severity. In 1821, on the return of the autocracy, he was exiled to Moravia.

Colley, George Pomeroy (1835–1881). A British soldier who at the age of sixteen was commissioned without purchase as an ensign in the 2nd Foot. Two years later he was promoted lieutenant without purchase and joined the headquarters of his regiment in Cape Colony, South Africa. He was sent to China in 1860 and commanded a company at the capture of the Taku Forts [q.v.] and in the advance on Peking (Beijing).

In 1862 he entered the staff college and in only ten months passed with great distinction the course that normally took two years. A man of many talents, he was an accomplished watercolorist and mapmaker; he studied Russian, chemistry, and political science as well as a host of other subjects usually ignored by British officers, and he wrote the long entry "Army" for the ninth edition of the *Encyclopaedia Britannica*.

He accompanied Sir Garnet Wolseley on his Ashanti Campaign [see Ashanti Wars]. In 1876 he was military secretary to the viceroy of India, and in 1879 he was Wolseley's chief of staff during the Zulu War [q.v.]. He returned to India and was knighted (KCSI) in July of that year. On 28 April 1880 he became a major general and was sent to Natal as both high commissioner and commander-in-chief. He was then regarded as one of the brightest soldiers in the British army.

In December 1880 the Boers proclaimed a republic in the Transvaal, and in the following month there were clashes between British and Boers, particularly at Laing's Nek and on the Ingogo River [qq.v.], all British defeats. British reinforcements under Evelyn Wood [q.v.] arrived, and on 28 February 1881 Colley led a force to the top of a prominent mount known as Majuba [q.v.], from which he could look down upon a large Boer laager. He felt himself secure on his summit, but the Boers scaled the heights and fell upon and completely routed his force. Colley was killed in the battle. [See Anglo-Boer War, First.]

Colombey-Borny, Battle of (14 August 1870), Franco-Prussian War, sometimes called the Battle of Colombey-Courcelles or Colombey-Nouilly, nearby towns. French forces under Marshal Achille Bazaine [q.v.], falling back on Verdun, engaged advanced elements (30,000 men) of the German I Corps (100,000) under Karl von Steinmetz [q.v.] at this village three miles east of Metz [q.v.]. The French maintained their positions, but two divisions were badly mauled, and Bazaine's retreat to Verdun was delayed. The French lost about 3,500; the Germans lost 222 officers and 5,000 men. Both sides claimed victory, but the French retreat in the night left the field in the possession of the Germans.

Colombey-Courcelles, Battle of. See Colombey-Borny.

Colombey-Nouilly, Battle of. See Colombey-Borny.

Colombian Revolts. The Spanish name for present-day Colombia was New Granada, and its viceregal capital was at Bogotá, perched on a 8,563-foot-high plateau.

1. In 1810 Bogotá and most other towns in the colony ousted Spanish officials and established juntas. Instead of uniting, the juntas fought among themselves. Although there were some rebel successes under Simón Bolívar, their troops were decisively defeated in 1815 at Santa Marta [q.v.] by Spanish royalist forces under Pablo Morillo (1777–1838), and the country again came under Spanish rule.

2. In 1819 the country was freed by Simón Bolívar with his victory in the Battle of Boyacá [q.v.], after which he became president.

3. In 1860, when the federal government of President Mariano Ospina (1805–1875) tried to increase its power over the states, a civil war erupted. General Tomás Cipriano de Mosquera [q.v.], governor of the state of Cauca, declared his state independent and marched an army into Bogotá; Ospina was deposed and imprisoned, and Mosquera declared himself president.

4. In 1867 Mosquera, who had assumed dictatorial powers, was deposed, imprisoned, and then exiled. The next thirteen years are known as the Epoch of Civil Wars. There were no less than forty armed conflicts, which ended only when Rafael Núñez (1825–1894) became president and strengthened the power of the central government.

5. On 31 July 1900 Vice-President José Manuel Marroquín (1827–1908) ousted President Manuel San Clemente (1820?–1902), and a bitter, bloody civil war erupted that lasted three years, ruined the economy of the country, and cost the lives of an estimated 100,000 Colombians.

Colonel. The word is said to come from the Italian colonello (little column).

1. The highest-ranking field officer, ranking just above a lieutenant colonel and just below a brigadier general or lowest-ranking general officer. The normal command for a colonel was a regiment or demi-brigade. Napoleon once said, "There are no bad regiments; there are only bad colonels."

The insignia for the rank in the British army was (and is) a crown and two stars (pips); in the American army it has been a silver eagle since 1830. In the Confederate army during the American Civil War the insignia was three stars on the collar. In the British army there were relatively few army colonels on active duty. The colonels of line and guard regiments were largely honorary positions given to senior generals or members of the royal family.

2. The first company of a French infantry regiment in Napoleon's army.

Colonel Commandant. An appointment in the British artillery and engineers analogous to that of an honorary colonel in a regiment of British infantry or cavalry.

Colonel General. 1. A rank in some European armies equivalent to a lieutenant general or a full general in the British and American services. In the German army the rank (*General-Oberst*) stood between a general of infantry, cavalry, or artillery and a general field marshal (*General-Feld-Marschall*).

2. An honorary appointment in the Swiss Guards.

Colonel-in-Chief. The honorary commander of the Royal Regiment of Artillery or the Royal Engineers in the British army; always a member of the royal family.

Colonel's Allowance. See Allowances.

Colonial Allowance. An allowance of varying amounts granted to troops in certain British colonies to meet cost-of-living expenses. In 1885 these colonies were Mauritius, Ceylon (Sri Lanka), Straits Settlements, Malaysia, China, West Indies, and Africa, including Cape of Good Hope. [See: Allowances; Batta.]

Colonial Corps, British. From 1794 to 1854 the War Department paid for locally raised troops in British colonies, but after 1854, when the Colonial Office was established, it assumed responsibility for the expenses of colonial defense, and officers were seconded from the regular army.

Before Edward Cardwell [q.v.] decreed that the colonies should be responsible for their own defense in time of peace, a number of small colonial units were paid for out of imperial revenues and considered part of the regular establishment. When these units reached their greatest numbers in about 1860, they were:

West India regiments (later raised to 5)	3,420	Native
Newfoundland Veterans	229	British
Ceylon Rifles	1,585	Native
Ceylon Invalids	163	Native
Cape Mounted Rifles [q.v.]	1,084	Boers and natives
Malta Fencibles	638	Native
Canadian Rifles	1,106	British
St. Helena Regiment	433	British
Gold Coast Artillery	351	Native
Falkland Islands Company	37	British
African Artillerymen	64	Native
Hong Kong Gun Lascars	88	Native

All officers in these units were British except in the Malta Fencibles. By the end of the century only the Malta Fencibles and two West India regiments had survived.

Coloniale, La. See Armée d'Afrique.

Colonial Troops. Troops raised within a European colony. Britain, France, Germany, Italy, Spain, and Portugal all had such forces in the nineteenth century. [See Colonial Corps, British.]

Colorados (Reds). 1. A South American revolutionary group active in Uruguay in the 1860s led by Venancio Flores [q.v.].

2. A tribe of South American Indians whose weapons were the bow and arrow and the pellet blowgun.

Color-bearer. One who carries the colors or standard in battle or on ceremonial occasions, such as formal reviews.

Colored Troops, American. See Black Troops in the U.S. Army.

Color Guard. A guard of honor or ceremonial escort that carries and escorts the colors and standards on ceremonial occasions.

Colors / Colours. The national and regimental flags carried by dismounted troops in the American and British armies. In the American army every regiment, and in the British army every battalion of infantry, carried one of each. The regimental flag bore the name or number of the unit and its crest or motto, if any. In the British service, regimental flags were in the color of the regiments' facings and were inscribed with the principal battles or campaigns in which the regiments had been engaged. In the American army, battle honors were indicated by streamers attached to the staff.

Much sentiment was invested in the regimental colors. French General T. R. Bugeaud [q.v.] wrote: "A man is not a soldier until he is no longer homesick, until he considers his regiment's colors as he would his village steeple; until he loves his colors, and is ready to put hand to sword each time the honor of his regiment is attacked" (*Les Transformations de l'armée française*, 1887).

The flags of mounted units are called standards [q.v.].

Color Salute. A salute rendered by dipping the colors or standard. In the United States the national color is never dipped.

Colour Sergeant. 1. In the British army this noncommissioned officer grade was instituted in 1813, replacing the rank of company sergeant major, and was originally given as an award to senior sergeants. In time it became a rank above a sergeant and denoted the senior noncommissioned officer of a company. The rank was abolished in 1915. [See Sergeant; Sergeant Major.]

2. The noncommissioned officer designated to carry the colors or be in charge of the color guard. Sometimes spelled "color."

Colston, Raleigh Edward (1825–1896). A French-born American soldier who was graduated from the Virginia Military Institute [q.v.] in 1846 and remained there as a professor until the American Civil War in 1861, when he became colonel of the 16th Virginia. On 24 December he was promoted to brigadier general in the Confederate army. Many thought he displayed cowardice at Antietam [q.v.], and even Lee suspected it after his poor performance at Chancellorsville [q.v.]. He was then transferred to Georgia. After the war he was superintendent of a military school in North Carolina until 1874, when he accepted a commission as a mirali (colonel) in the Egyptian army, in which he served for four years on the general staff under former Union Brigadier General Charles P. Stone [q.v.]. He made two exploring expeditions: one into the Nubian Desert and the other into Kordofan Province in the Sudan. During the latter expedition a fall from a camel paralyzed him from the waist down. He retired from the Egyptian service in 1878 and returned to the United States, where he lost all his money in unwise investments, found work as a clerk in the War Department, and died at the Camp Lee Soldiers' Home [q.v.] in Richmond, Virginia.

Colt, Samuel (1814–1862). An American inventor, weapons designer, and manufacturer. He went to sea at age sixteen and it was said that it was on a voyage to India that he conceived the idea for a repeating firearm. He did not invent the revolver, but he was responsible for making the revolver principle practical and its use widespread. To finance his experiments, he toured for a time as "Dr. Coult," taking up collections after giving demonstrations of laughing gas (nitrous oxide). In 1835, when he was only twenty-one, he was granted British and French patents for a revolving breech pistol holding six bullets. The following year he was granted a patent in the United States and at once formed the Patent Arms Manufacturing Company in Paterson, New Jersey. Although the breech-loading revolver rifle he developed was used by Andrew Jackson's [q.v.] soldiers in the Seminole War [q.v.] of 1837, the army showed little interest in his weapons, and the company failed in 1842.

Colt then occupied himself in other fields, including the laying of the first successful submarine cables from Coney Island and Fire Island to New York City in 1843. However, the Mexican War [q.v.] created a demand for his revolvers, and in 1846 the U.S. army officially adopted them, giving him a government order for 1,000, which the Eli Whitney Company produced [see Whitney, Eli]. The following year at Hartford, Connecticut, he established the successful Colt Patent Fire-Arms Manufacturing Company, which became the world's largest private armory.

In 1851 he obtained orders from the British army, and in 1853 he opened an armory in London, but this closed in 1856. His revolvers were produced in several models—Model 1860 and Model 1873, which was his most famous—in various calibers, .36, .38, and .45 being the most popular. His six-shooter was the first firearm that could be used effectively by mounted troops. His Model 1860, a .44 caliber weapon, became the American army's official pistol and the most favored revolver in the American Civil War. Its percussion ignition system was one of the most reliable and efficient ever developed. The New Service .445-inch revolver, designed in 1897, remained popular well into the twentieth century in countries throughout the world.

In 1895 Colt produced a machine gun designed by John Moses Browning [q.v.] that was adopted by both the U.S. army and navy.

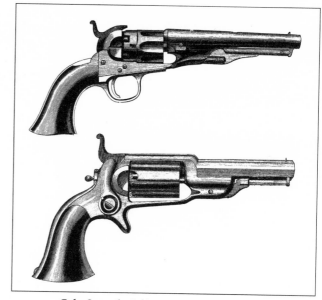

Colt, Samuel *Colt's new patent revolving pistol*

Colt Revolvers. See Colt, Samuel.

Columbia, South Carolina, Capture and Burning of (17 February 1865), American Civil War. Federal troops under General William Tecumseh Sherman [q.v.] drove Confederate forces from Columbia, the capital of South Carolina. After the mayor had surrendered the town and Federal troops had moved in to occupy it, a fierce fire broke out, and half the town was destroyed before the fire could be brought under control.

The responsibility for this disaster is still debated. The Confederate version was given by General Wade Hampton [q.v.], commander of the Confederate rear guard, who claimed that Sherman "burned it to the ground, deliberately, systematically and atrociously." The Federal version, given by Sherman, maintained that Confederates had set fire to bales of cotton to keep them from falling into Federal hands and that a high wind had spread the flames over the city. Federal troops, he said, had fought the fires.

Columbiad. A long, chambered muzzle-loading cannon that could use heavy charges of powder to throw solid shot or shells at high angles of elevation, first used in the War of 1812 [q.v.]. It was invented in 1811 by Colonel George Bumford (1780?–1848), who in 1804 had been the eighth cadet to graduate from the U.S. Military Academy at West Point, where he had studied for nine months. Although cannon of cast brass were first designed and manufactured in the sixteenth century, there were no long-range guns capable of firing hollow projectiles by direct fire until the Columbiad. It was manufactured in 8-, 10-, or 12-inch caliber. The guns were particularly useful as coastal artillery, being capable of defending narrow channels and distant roadsteads.

In 1844 the bore was lengthened and more metal was used, enabling the Columbiad to take larger powder charges. In 1858 the model was again changed by shortening the length of the bore and using a hemispherical chamber. In 1860 Thomas Jackson Rodman [q.v.] made further small improvements, but by the end of the American Civil War the guns were obsolete.

Column. A military formation composed of a mass of soldiers in ranks, which could be of any depth, as opposed to troops in line. Depending upon the density of the column, it was referred to as open or closed. The desirability of having troops in column or in line in action was much debated in the first half of the century. In general, the French preferred the column, and the British the line. The rifle gradually convinced those favoring the column that it was no longer a viable battle formation.

Column of March. The formation that marching troops assumed. It usually included an advanced guard [q.v.] and a rear guard, [q.v.], and often men guarding the flanks of a moving column, usually cavalry. Artillery was usually kept in the rear, where it could set its own pace, for if intermingled with infantry, it was fatiguing for the horses to conform to the pace.

Column of March *A U.S. army column on the march in the Indian Wars, by Frederic Remington*

Comancheros. Traders in New Mexico who exchanged rifles and ammunition for the plunder of Indian raids.

Comanche Wars. Although never a large tribe, few, if any, other American Indians were the source of so many alarms (1,031 depredations between 1812 and 1889) or did so much damage to property ($3,116,169) as the Comanches. The tribe ranged from the Platte River to the Texas border, and its men were renowned as superb horsemen. In 1875, when the Comanches were gathered on a reservation in Oklahoma, they numbered only 1,500.

Comanche Wars *Quanah Parker, leader of the Comanches*

Combatant. Any member of a belligerent force or, specifically, an active fighter or group designated to be actively engaged with an enemy as opposed to members of support units.

Combatant Officer. An officer of the infantry, cavalry, or artillery, line or staff, whose business was concerned with the primary purpose of the unit, as opposed to chaplains, doctors, riding masters, and other nonfighters. In British officers' messes the senior combatant officer acted as mess president, even when a noncombatant officer of higher rank was present.

Combat d'Usure. A battle of attrition.

Combat Strength. See Strength, Unit.

Combermere, First Viscount. See Cotton, Stapleton.

Combined Arms. Infantry, artillery, and cavalry used in combination with one another. Henri de Jomini [q.v.] in 1838 (*Précis de l'art de la guerre*) wrote. "It is not so much the mode of formation as the proper combined use of arms that will ensure victory."

Comblain Rifle. A breech-loading shoulder weapon similar to the Sharps Rifle [q.v.]. At the end of the century Belgian militia were armed with this rifle.

Command. 1. As a noun, a military unit under the orders of an officer who is said to hold command. According to William Tecumseh Sherman [q.v.] in his *Personal Memoirs* (1875): "To be at the head of a strong column of troops, in the execution of some task that requires brains, is the highest pleasure of war." Such sentiments have been held by many officers in all armies.

2. As a noun, the height of an interior crest of a fortification or earthwork above the site, or the height of one such crest above another.

3. As a verb, to govern or to give official orders to subordinates; also, the order itself.

In the nineteenth century confusion frequently arose over who was or who ought to be in command. Officers of the same grade in the same service usually determined their seniority by their date of rank, but in the United States, militia officers ranked below all regular officers of the same rank. In the British service, before reforms late in the century, most officers in guards regiments held double ranks, one while doing regimental duty and a rank one or two grades higher when serving outside their regiments. In India officers in the armies of the Honourable East India Company took seniority below all regular officers of the same rank. In neither army could paymasters, chaplains, or medical officers command troops in the line or staff outside their own responsibilities. The greatest source of rank confusion was caused by brevet ranks [q.v.], particularly in the American army.

In the United States, Congress, but not the president, could designate a junior officer to command a senior.

Command and General Staff College. The name of an American school of application for infantry and cavalry at Fort Leavenworth, Kansas, established in 1881, that evolved into a school for field-grade officers.

Commandant. 1. In the French, Belgian, and Spanish services, a rank (*comandante* in Spanish) equivalent to major in the American, British, and German armies.

2. In the armies of the Boer republics in South Africa, the leader of a commando [q.v.].

3. The head of a school or garrison; a temporary commander.

4. The officer at a military educational institution responsible for military discipline and training.

5. The commander of a regiment of native cavalry in the Indian army under the British.

6. The senior officer and head of the U.S. Marines.

7. A commander.

Commandant de Place. In the French army, the commanding officer of a fort or city. He was usually a field officer or a general officer.

Commandant of Cadets. An officer having command of the cadets at the United States Military Academy at West Point, New York, and his counterpart in other American military colleges responsible for the discipline of the cadets and for strictly military instruction. Under him are assistant instructors in tactics (tactical officers).

Commandeer. The arbitrary or illegal seizure or occupation of property for military purposes.

Commander. The person in charge of the direction, coordination, and control of a military force. In 1838 Henri de Jomini [q.v.] wrote that such a man should be one "of tried bravery, bold in the fight and of unshaken firmness in danger" (*Précis de l'art de la guerre*).

Commander-in-Chief (always hyphenated in the nineteenth century). The person in supreme command of any large army. In the United States only the president is so designated by Article II, Section 2 of the Constitution, but the last president of the United States to exercise his authority to command troops in the field was the fourth, James Madison (1751–1836), in the Battle of Bladensburg [q.v.] in the War of 1812. During the American Civil War President Abraham Lincoln issued military orders for a time, breaking the chain of command.

The uniformed commander of the American army was called by different names at different times. Among the titles used were general-in-chief, commanding general, and major general commanding the army [see Commanding General of the Army].

The uniformed commanders of the U.S. army in the nineteenth century were:

James Wilkinson	June 1800–Jan. 1812
Henry Dearborn	Jan. 1812–June 1815
Jacob Brown (senior officer until 1 June and thereafter commanding general)	June 1815–Feb. 1828
Alexander Macomb (commanding general)	May 1828–June 1841
Winfield Scott	July 1841–Nov. 1861
George B. McClellan	Nov. 1861–March 1862
Henry W. Halleck (commanding general)	July 1862–March 1864
Ulysses S. Grant	March 1864–March 1869
William T. Sherman	March 1869–Nov. 1883
Philip H. Sheridan	Nov. 1883–Aug. 1888
John M. Schofield	Aug. 1888–Sept. 1895
Nelson A. Miles	Oct. 1895–Aug. 1903

In the British army the commander-in-chief was the chief staff officer of the army, but his authority was circumscribed and consisted mostly of personnel and regulatory matters for infantry and cavalry. He had no control over colonial armies or over the armies in India, where each of the three Indian presidencies had its own commander-in-chief, although the commander of the Bengal army was designated commander-in-chief, India.

Flavius Vegetius Renatus, a Roman writer of the fourth century A.D., in his famous treatise on war, *Epitoma rei militaris*, describes a commander-in-chief as a man "to whose fidelity and bravery the fortunes of his countrymen, the defense of their cities, the lives of soldiers, and the glory of the state are entrusted" and as one who should "not only consult the good of the army in general, but extend his care to every soldier in it."

Commanding General of the Army. An appointment given to the senior uniformed officer in the American army beginning in 1821. The title was held by Jacob Brown, Winfield Scott, and Henry Halleck [qq.v.]. In 1864 Congress created the position of commanding general of the armies of the United States. The title was first given to Ulysses S. Grant, who was given the rank of lieutenant general, the only such rank in the Union army at that time. [See Ranks; Commander-in-Chief; General Officers.]

Commando System. In the Boer republics there were no standing armies. The only fully organized, uniformed, full-time soldiers were members of artillery units in the Orange Free State and the Transvaal. In all Boer republics every able-bodied male citizen when called upon was required to assemble with his fighting unit (commando) at a designated place with his horse, saddle, weapons, ammunition, and sufficient food for a stated number of days. One of the staple foods of men on commando was biltong, strips of meat, usually game, dried in the open air.

Commando System *Christiana commando, Transvaal, Boer Republics*

Command Post. A position where a commander and his staff perform their functions in the field. A temporary headquarters.

Commands. In drill or on parade every command phrase contains two commands, the preparatory command and the command of execution. Thus, in the infantry, in the command "Forward march!" the first word, given in ascending tones, is the preparatory command, and the second, more of a bark, the command of execution. In the cavalry, even the command of execution was more or less prolonged.

Commissariat. The organization designed to furnish an army with food, forage, and other daily needs other than arms, ammunition, clothing, and accoutrements. In the greater number of European armies the commissariat was managed for the most part by civilian contractors. In the British army a contractor general was appointed in 1793 to superintend contracts to civilian suppliers of food and forage.

The Crimean War [q.v.] tragically demonstrated the deficiencies of this system. In 1858 and 1859 the commissariat was reorganized as a War Office department under a commissary general-in-chief. In 1870, as part of the reforms of Edward Cardwell [q.v.], the commissariat was merged with other supply departments into a short-lived Control Department under the surveyor general of the ordnance. In 1875 a Commissariat and Transport Department was formed to supply food, forage, lodgings, fuel, and transportation. This was commanded by a commissary general who usually held the rank of major general.

In the United States the commissariat was under the commissary general of subsistence, who had the rank of brigadier general. [See Commissary and Subsistence Department; Intendance.]

Commissary. 1. A place where food and other necessities can be obtained.

2. An officer in charge of supplying subsistence to troops.

3. Sometimes a rank in the American army. In 1862 each cavalry regiment was authorized one such rank. The rank was abolished in 1870 but reinstated in 1899 with one commissary allotted for each cavalry and each infantry regiment.

In the British and American armies, and early in the century in the French army, the term was also applied to officers performing a number of special occupations.

Commissary of Muster. An officer charged with mustering troops into the army and out of it. Used principally in the Union army during the American Civil War.

Commissary of Ordnance. A title given in the Indian army to officers in charge of arsenals. Their duties varied somewhat depending upon the presidency.

Commissary Sergeants. A noncommissioned officer in the British army who assisted the commissary in his duties. The post was regarded as a plum assignment, a reward for long and faithful service. The soldier so appointed had to be well recommended and to have served at least five years in the line with at least three years as a noncommissioned officer.

Commission. A formal, written warrant or letter patent issued to a person authorized to exercise certain powers over subordinates. In armies in which the warrant was issued by a president or sovereign or under his or her authority the recipient usually became a commissioned officer.

Commissary *Commissary Department, Headquarters, Army of the Potomac, February 1864*

Commissionaires, Corps of. A civilian organization formed to provide employment for old, retired, or (originally only) disabled British soldiers established in February 1859 in London and later in Dublin, Manchester, Edinburgh, and other cities by Captain Edward Walter (1823–1904) after his retirement from the 4th Hussars. The corps was run on military lines; commissionaires wore uniforms and their former insignia of rank and could be hired as guards, porters, timekeepers, and messengers. In 1885 Walter was knighted for his services. The corps expanded rapidly and by the end of the century numbered about 3,000. It is still in existence.

Commission Rifle. The popular name for the German army service rifle Model 1888, so named because it was designed by the Military Rifle Testing Commission at the Spandau Arsenal. It had a fixed magazine below the bolt that could hold a clip of five cartridges.

Committee on the Conduct of the War, Joint. On 20 December 1861, in the American Civil War, a joint committee of senators and representatives was organized by the Congress to investigate the Federal disasters in the First Battle of Bull Run and the Battle of Ball's Bluff [qq.v.]. Dominated by Radical Republicans and led by Senator Benjamin Franklin ("Bluff Ben") Wade (1800–1878) of Ohio, it was not dissolved after its original investigation but remained in being until June 1865, becoming a thorn in the side of most senior commanders. As a result of its original investigation, although its members later denied responsibility, Brigadier General Charles P. Stone [q.v.] was arrested and imprisoned for six months. Contrary to the Articles of War [q.v.], no charges were ever leveled against him. When finally released, he was never again given an active command. Eventually every commander of the Army of the Potomac, except U. S. Grant, was investigated, some interrogated as if they were recalcitrant schoolboys. Members of the committee tried to appropriate the right to hire and fire generals, and they meddled in military matters of which they knew nothing, once recommending a reduction in the number of cavalry regiments because cavalry was more expensive than infantry.

Common Time. The length of a marching step. In the United States, this was 28 inches, and the cadence was 90 steps per minute. Common time and the cadence varied in different armies and sometimes in the same army. In the British army, rifle regiments marched to a faster cadence than other regiments, which sometimes made parades difficult.

Commune of 1871. On 8 February 1871 France elected largely monarchist deputies who were in favor of ending the Franco-Prussian War [q.v.], and on 1 March 1871 they accepted Germany's harsh peace terms although the people of Paris and the republican Garde Nationale [q.v.] were bent upon fighting on. Louis Adolphe Thiers (1797–1877), who had been selected as premier, gave orders to the army to disarm the guard. From the beginning things went wrong: The attempt on the night of 17–18 March to seize its cannon parked at Montmartre was bungled, many regular soldiers allied themselves with the guard, two generals were killed, the southeastern quarters of Paris erupted in mass uprisings, and the National Assembly fled to Versailles, leaving Paris in the hands of the rebels.

Commune of 1871 *"Live free, or die!" slogan of the Paris Commune*

A Red Republican insurrectionary government was formed, and on the orders of Charles Théophile Ferré (1845–1871), the chief of police of the Paris Commune, 67 royalist hostages were murdered in cold blood, including Georges Derby (1813–1871), the archbishop of Paris (1863–71). Communards burned the Hôtel de Ville, the Palace of Justice, and the Tuileries along with other government buildings, and they attempted to blow up Notre Dame.

The Germans offered to help the French government, but their offer was refused. Nevertheless, they sped the release of French prisoners of war so that they could return home to fight their countrymen. Paris was bombarded on 2 April, and the uprising was repressed with great brutality by 130,000 troops under Marshal Marie MacMahon [q.v.]. The city was taken at a cost of 873 troops, and it has been estimated that at least 20,000 communards were killed, either in the fighting or in the executions that followed. General Gaston Alexandre Auguste de Galliffet [q.v.], a former spahi officer with a record of repressive campaigns in Algeria and Mexico, was particularly bloody-minded, personally ordering the execution of prisoners without trial. Surviving prisoners were exiled to New Caladonia, an island in the southwest Pacific Ocean. The week of 21–28 May came to be called *la semaine sanglant* [q.v.] (the bloody week).

Uprisings and communes in Toulouse, Lyons, Marseilles, Narbonne, and other French cities were all quickly suppressed.

Communications. The transmission of understandable orders, reports, and information. In all armies this has always been one of the most difficult problems facing commanders and their staffs. Alfred Thayer Mahan (1840–1914) wrote: "Communications dominate war; broadly constituted, they are the most important single element in strategy, political or military." In a broader sense, communications include all the supplies and personnel necessary to keep an army in the field or on the march. [See Line of Communications.]

Communications, Line of. See Line of Communications.

Communication Trench. A trench connecting two other trenches, or saps, or a trench leading to the rear by which ammunition, food, and supplies are brought up.

Commutation Fee. Payment to a government in lieu of performing military service. By such payments families of wealth were sometimes able to save their young men from conscription [q.v.]. Many conscription laws had commutation clauses that permitted such exemptions from service.

Comorn, Siege of (1848–49), Hungarian Revolution. The fortress of Comorn, 48 miles from Budapest, contained 7 miles of entrenchments along the banks of the Danube and Waag rivers, and its citadel was considered the strongest in Europe. It was occupied during the 1848 Hungarian Revolution [q.v.] by the insurgent Hungarians, who were besieged there by Austrian forces from October 1848 until it was forced to surrender in September 1849.

Comoro Insurrection (March 1891). Under French protection since 1886, the Comoro Islands (French: *Îles Comores*), between northeastern Mozambique and northwest Madagascar, were slave-trading centers ruled by Arab chiefs. In March 1891 slaves there rebelled and seized the town of Mutsamudu on the northwest coast of the island of Johanna (Anjouan), 80 miles southeast of Great Comoro Island. In the fighting that followed, atrocities were committed by both sides. Europeans who could took refuge in ships. The insurrection was suppressed by the French with great brutality.

Compagnies Disciplinaires. Disciplinary companies formed by Napoleon I in 1802 and retained after his reign. In 1818 a royal order fixed their number at ten, of which six were fusiliers and four were pioneers. The fusiliers were composed of soldiers convicted of some indiscipline; those who proved to be incorrigible were sent to the pioneers. All served in Algeria in the Armée d'Afrique [q.v.]. Life in such units was severe and unpleasant. Their number was later reduced to seven.

Compagnies Sahariennes. A French camel corps formed in 1894 from a camel-mounted spahi squadron. It was composed entirely of volunteers, who engaged for only four months at a time and provided their own food, clothes, and special riding camels called meharis (usually two or three per man). It was regarded as an elite corps and attracted the most adventuresome French officers.

Company. A military unit larger than a section or a platoon and smaller than a battalion; the smallest administrative unit in a battalion; the basic tactical unit of infantry, artillery, and cavalry, usually commanded by a captain assisted by one or more lieutenants. Cavalry troops and artillery batteries were called companies in the American army until late in the century.

In some armies, companies were numbered, and in others they were lettered sequentially within a battalion or a regiment. In the American army, companies were known by the names of their commanders until 22 May 1816, when Colonel Charles K. Gardner (1790?–1869) instituted the system of designating the companies of each regiment by letters. The letter *J* is never used, probably to avoid confusion with the letter *I* when written by hand.

The size of a company varied in different armies. At the beginning of the American Civil War a full Confederate company numbered 82 men, a Union company 100. Among the largest were those in the German infantry, which held about 250 men under a captain, who was mounted.

Company, the. Popular name for the Honourable East India Company [q.v.]. Also called John Company.

Company Clerk. In the American army, the assistant to the first sergeant of a company, often carrying the rank of corporal or its equivalent. He handles all routine paperwork and helps prepare reports.

Company Fund. In the American army the savings accumulated by an economical handling of ration money (except that earmarked for the purchase of flour) constituted a fund that was used exclusively for the benefit of the enlisted men in a company.

Company Grade Officers. Captains, lieutenants, and other commissioned ranks below the rank of major. [See Subaltern.]

Company Punishment. A minor punishment awarded without a court-martial by the company commander for minor infractions of rules or orders.

Company Q. An American slang term variously used. 1. In the Mexican War [q.v.] and after, it stood for the guardhouse or for imprisonment.

2. During the American Civil War and American Indian Wars it was sometimes used to denote those on the sick list.

3. In the Confederate service, where cavalry supplied their own mounts, those who had lost and could not replace their horses were formed into units called Company Q.

4. In the Union army there were at least two so-called Q companies composed of officers who, having disgraced themselves in action, were given a chance to redeem themselves by fighting as enlisted men. One of these was a unit of the 150th Pennsylvania. Many former officers redeemed themselves and regained their commissions.

Company Street. The area between rows of tents or barracks.

Concentration Camps. A place for detaining and controlling large numbers of people considered undesirable or troublesome. The concentration camps of the nineteenth century, appalling as they were, should not be confused with those of Nazi Germany in the twentieth century. In 1896, in an effort to control insurgency in Cuba, its Spanish captain general, Don Valeriano Weyler y Nicolau [q.v.], inaugurated a *reconcentrado* system. That is, he forced the inhabitants of the four westernmost provinces, where rebellion was most rampant, into fortified areas. There they died in great numbers from neglect, starvation, and disease.

In December 1900, during the Second Anglo-Boer War [q.v.], Lord Kitchener [q.v.] established concentration camps in South Africa for Boer families whose farms his troops had destroyed in an effort to prevent Boer guerrillas from obtaining food, forage, and assistance. Because widespread destruction left women, children, and old men homeless and starving, it was decided to bring them in off the veld and provide for them in protected camps. Initially humanitarian, the effort proved a disaster. By October 1901 there were 118,000 European and 43,000 black South Africans in the camps, which were incompetently administered by the army. Diseases, including a deadly measles epidemic, swept through the camps, and an estimated 20,000 women and children died. Henry Campbell-Bannerman [q.v.], the future British prime minister, called use of the camps "the methods of barbarism."

The dreadful conditions in the camps were exposed by a remarkable woman, Emily Hobhouse (1860–1936), a clergyman's daughter who, after traveling to South Africa to see the camps for herself, reported her findings to the world. Shortly after, a government-appointed committee of women confirmed her report. As a result, responsibility for the administration of the camps was taken from the army and put into civilian hands, and conditions soon dramatically improved.

During the American Civil War similar camps were sometimes established (although not called concentration camps) by Union army commanders for the freed or escaped slaves who followed them and interfered with military operations. The unfortunates in these camps suffered the same appalling death rates as those so confined later in Cuba and South Africa. One such camp reported a 25 percent loss from disease in less than two years.

The American authorities in the Philippines employed concentration camps on the Spanish model in 1900–02.

Concentration Marches. Marches made by units separated from each other but all making for the same location.

Concón, Battle of (21 August 1891), Chilean Civil War. Some 10,000 rebels landed unopposed near this town in central Chile at the mouth of the Aconcagua River, 12 miles north-northeast of Valparaiso, and attacked government forces of President José Manuel Balmaceda (1842–1891). Although aided by fire from three warships, the rebels were repulsed with a loss of 1,648 killed and wounded and 1,500 taken prisoner; the government forces lost 869.

Condeixa, Battle of (13 March 1811), Peninsular War. Near the important crossroads town of Condeixa-a-Nova in north-central Portugal, eight miles south-southwest of Coimbra, Wellington, with an Anglo-Portuguese army of 12,000 British and 6,000 Portuguese, pried the 35,500-man army of André Masséna [q.v.] out of Portugal by an attack on the 5,000-man French rear guard under Marshal Michel Ney [q.v.]. The failure of the French to cross the Mondego River made Ney vulnerable and his retreat inevitable [see Battle of Coimbra]. When he saw his only line of retreat threatened by the Allied 3rd Division, he fell back precipitously to Casal Novo [q.v.].

Conductor. In the British Royal Artillery, a soldier in charge of one or more ammunition wagons in the field.

Conduct Prejudicial to Good Order and Military Discipline. Crimes in the American army that are not specified in the Articles of War but that a court-martial might consider and punish at its discretion.

Conduct Unbecoming an Officer and a Gentleman. A court-martial offense in the American army. Because no definitions of "unbecoming conduct" were ever provided, the court, guided by its own moral sense, could determine what it chose. The vagueness of this Article of War led to abuses. [See Flipper, Henry Ossian.]

Confederate Army. Officially the Army of the Confederate States of America established on 6 March 1861 as the regular army of the Confederacy, but in fact there was never an actual Confederate regular army. A few officers were appointed, and a few companies of cavalry and artillery were formed, but it was never an army in being. The army in the field that fought the war, composed of volunteers, was the provisional army, which was established by acts of the Confederate Congress on 28 February and 6 March 1861. Prior to this, each southern state had its own army.

A confederate soldier of 1862

Until 16 April 1862, when the first Confederate conscription act was passed, men entered the army through their state organizations. The total number of enlistments is unknown, but estimates range from 600,000 to 1.5 million. At the end of the war only 174,223 surrendered. Throughout its existence the provisional army was plagued with desertions. According to the *Richmond Enquirer* of 6 October 1864, President Davis admitted that two-thirds of the army were absent without leave. [See Conscription.] An estimated 133,785 Confederate soldiers died in battle, and many more from disease.

Confederate Soldiers' Homes. See Soldiers' Homes.

Confederate Veteran. A magazine specializing in anecdotes, biographies, and memoirs of former Confederate soldiers, founded by a journalist, Sumner A. Cunningham (d. 1913), who had served as a sergeant major in the 41st Tennessee. It began publication in Nashville, Tennessee, in January 1893 and originally sold for five cents a copy or fifty cents per year. It continued publication until December 1932.

Confederation of the Rhine (1806–13). A confederation of German states organized by Napoleon to act as a buffer between France and its main Continental enemies. The confederation was instituted on 12 July 1806, when, under Napoleon's pressure, the rulers of seventeen states—Bavaria, Saxony, Westphalia, and Württemberg, seven grand duchies, and six duchies—deserted the Holy Roman Empire and pledged their allegiance to France. Other states joined later. The confederated states remained independent in their internal administration but could not pursue their own foreign policy and were required to place their troops at Napoleon's disposal at any time and collectively to provide 258,000 troops in case of war. The confederation was dissolved after Napoleon's defeat in the Battle of Leipzig [q.v.] in October

1813, when Saxony and Württemburg deserted Napoleon and joined the Allies. Other German states followed.

After Napoleon's first abdication this confederation was replaced by the Germanic Confederation in 1815, which in turn was replaced by the North German Confederation in 1886.

Confederatka. A square-topped peakless cap that in 1803 was formalized into a *czapska* or *shapska* [q.v.].

Confidential Reports. 1. In the British army, the reports on all regiments made annually by general officers.

2. The confidential reports on their subordinates submitted annually by British superior officers. These were often quite informal. One cavalry commander wrote: "Personally, I would not breed from this officer."

Congo Rebellion (1892). Arab slavers in the Belgian Congo, angered by the imposition of an export duty on ivory and by other irksome government edicts, revolted against Belgian rule in mid-May 1892 and killed 11 Belgians on the Upper Lomami River. They were defeated by Belgian forces, mostly African, under Belgian Commandant (later Baron) François Dhanis [q.v.] on 22 November.

Congressional Medal of Honor. See Medal of Honor.

Congreve, Walter Norris (1862–1927). A British soldier who served in India in 1885–89 and again in 1893–95. As a captain during the Second Anglo-Boer War [q.v.] he won the Victoria Cross in the Battle of Colenso [q.v.] on 15 December 1899, when he attempted to recover guns whose crews had been swept away by Boer musketry and, although suffering from several wounds, risked his life to bring in the mortally wounded son of Lord Roberts. He was a lieutenant general in the First World War, in which he lost both his left hand and a son, William, who had won the Victoria Cross as well as the Distinguished Service Order and the Military Cross. He became a full general in 1922.

Congreve, William (1772–1828). A British soldier and the inventor of the Congreve rocket. After passing through the Royal Academy, Woolwich, he was attached in 1791 to the Royal Laboratory at Woolwich, where his father was comptroller and superintendent of military machines. In 1806 he invented a military rocket. Thanks to his father's influence and in spite of Wellington's disdain for the weapon, it was ac-

cepted for military use. His rockets were used for the first time at sea in an attack on the harbor of Boulogne when about 400 were discharged in less than a half hour. Although they were not as successful as had been anticipated, the navy used them again in 1807 in the Dardanelles and on 2–4 September 1807, when some 300 rockets were fired at Copenhagen. During the Peninsular War they were used on the north coast of Spain. Congreve was permitted to organize two rocket companies for the British army, one of which saw action in the Battle of Leipzig [q.v.] in 1813. The only British unit to take part in that battle, it terrified 2,500 French soldiers into surrendering. That same year he established a workshop at Woolwich capable of producing 36 rockets per day. In 1814 the British used rockets in their invasion of the United States, frightening the militia in the Battle of Bladensburg [q.v.] and providing the "rocket's red glare" of "The Star-Spangled Banner" [q.v.] in the bombardment of Fort McHenry in Baltimore's harbor. British rocket companies were sent to take part in the Battle of Leipzig and in the Battle of Waterloo in 1815. The Austrians used Congreve's rockets against rebels in 1848–49 and in the Austro-Piedmontese War [q.v.]. As late as 1868 the rockets were employed in Robert Napier's Abyssinian Campaign [q.v.].

In 1814 Congreve succeeded his father as a baronet and stepped into his father's position at Woolwich. He called rockets "the soul of artillery without the body" and predicted: "The rocket is . . . an arm by which the whole system of military tactics is destined to be changed" [see rockets]. Congreve's rocket was not superseded until 1867, when it was replaced by Hale's war rocket [q.v.].

Congreve Rocket. See Congreve, William; Rockets.

Connaught, Duke of, Prince Arthur William Patrick (1850–1942). A British soldier and the third son of Queen Victoria, who was gazetted to the Royal Engineers in 1868. He commanded the Guards Brigade in the Battle of Tell el-Kebir [q.v.] in 1882. From 1886 to 1890 he served in India. He was made a general in 1890 and was commander-in-chief in Ireland from 1900 to 1904, when he was named commander-in-chief in the Mediterranean. From 1911 to 1916 he was governor-general of Canada.

Conolly, Arthur (1807–1842). A British soldier, one of six brothers, orphaned when he was twelve. At age sixteen he joined the Honorable East India Company's army as a cornet.

Congreve, William *Detail of the rocket system, by William Congreve*

In 1829, then a lieutenant, he decided to return to India from leave in England by way of Moscow, the Caucasus, and Persia (Iran). Crossing the 500 miles of the Kara Kum Desert south of Lake Aral from Astrabad to Khiva in disguise, he was captured, robbed, and forced to turn back. He then proceeded to Meshed, 300 miles east, and from there to Herat, which he reached in September 1830. From Herat he made his way slowly 300 miles farther to Kandahar, Afghanistan. There he fell sick and was forced to flee from Islamic fanatics before he was completely recovered. Nevertheless, he reached Quetta, at the head of the Boland Pass in India, on 22 November. From Moscow to Quetta he had traveled 4,000 miles.

With his reputation for traveling in hostile territory confirmed, he was sent in 1841 on a mission to the Central Asian khanates of Khiva, Khokand, and Bokhara. At the latter, when he made a futile attempt to secure the release of a British officer who was being held prisoner, he was himself seized and thrown into a verminous pit, where he lay for months until taken out and beheaded.

Conquest. The military defeat of an army, placing its territory and its people in control of the victors. In 51 B.C. Gaius Julius Caesar (100 B.C.–44 B.C.) wrote in *De bello Gallico*: "War gives the right to the conquerors to impose any condition they please upon the vanquished."

Conscientious Objectors. See Pacifists.

Conscript. A conscripted soldier [see Conscription].

Conscription. The compulsory enrollment of citizens or subjects as soldiers. In the modern sense, conscription began in France in 1798 when General Jean Baptiste Jourdan [q.v.] proposed a *levée en masse* [q.v.] that was adopted on 19th Fructidor (4 September) of that year. Men, registered by age-groups, were called up in annual drafts and divided into five categories. Those called served for a limited time, then were transferred to the reserve. Although the levée allowed numerous exemptions, it made Napoleon's conquests possible, giving him the abundant manpower he required, for he told Prince Klemens von Metternich (1773–1859) at Schönbrunn in 1805, "I can use up 25,000 men a month." Jourdan's system provided Napoleon with 30,000 men in 1800; 60,000 per year in 1801–02–03–04; 210,000 in 1805, by which time about two-thirds of the French army were conscripts; 80,000

in 1806 and 1807; 240,000 in 1808; 76,000 in 1809; 160,000 in 1810; 120,000 in 1811; 237,000 in 1812; and 1,140,000 in 1813. From 1818 to 1870 young men were selected by lot from the age-group liable to provide the number necessary to make up the size of the army fixed by the legislature. Until 1872 those who drew *mauvais numéros* were allowed to provide substitutes, and agencies were established to find them.

The idea of conscription took hold in Prussia, even though initially King Frederick William III [q.v.] feared that conscripts would impair the professionalism of his army. Although the Military Reorganization Commission recommended universal military service on 15 March 1808, a recommendation repeated in December, the king did not agree to conscription in all Prussian lands until March 1813. Unlike the French, the Prussians established universal military service "without distinction of class, or right of exemption by purchase." Only the possession of an advanced education, a rejection by a medical board, or proof that a man was the sole support of a family excused him from service.

As in France until 1872, an adjustment was created for those with advanced education. Under a law of September 1814 sponsored by General Hermann von Boyen [q.v.], the minister of war, the institution of *einjahrigen Freiwilligen* was introduced. This permitted those of a certain standard of education who passed an examination, to enroll as one-year volunteers, who would then pass into the reserves. The volunteers provided their own uniforms, lived outside barracks, and could wear civilian clothes when off duty. The program survived until the dissolution of the imperial army in 1918.

After the Franco-Prussian War, other countries followed the Prussian pattern. The notion that "God marches with the largest battalions" pervaded the strategy of the time. Japan introduced conscription in 1872 under a plan based upon a scheme of Aritomo Yamagata [q.v.] that stripped the samurais [q.v.] of their feudal privileges. All Japanese males between the ages of seventeen and forty could be called up for three years' active service, followed by two years in the first reserve and two years in the second reserve. Minimum height was five feet, and following the French system, there were numerous exceptions, and allowance was made for payment in lieu of service.

Conscription was adopted in Italy in 1873, but emigration, particularly to the United States, drew off so many potential recruits that a law was passed in 1885 forbidding men under the age of thirty-two to leave the country.

Conscription *French conscripts being taken to the army, 1807*

In the Russian army, serfs had been conscripted since the formation of a standing army by Peter the Great (1672–1725) in the early eighteenth century. Service was for twenty-five years—virtually life—and many serfs resorted to self-mutilation to avoid service, although the punishment for doing so was twenty-five to fifty lashes. Cholera epidemics in 1830–31 and 1847 so devastated some areas that temporary exemptions were granted. In January 1813 those living in the areas devastated by Napoleon's armies were similarly exempt.

Few serfs appear to have been physically fit for service. In 1850, of 20,712,756 eligible males, only 6,900,000 were accepted. In 1848, of every 100 possible recruits, 34 were rejected as being too short. It was sometimes necessary to lower height and age norms; in 1812 the minimum height was lowered to 4 feet, 11 ½ inches and the minimum age to twelve. In 1815 these were revised to 5 feet 3 inches and nineteen years of age.

After the emancipation of the serfs on 9 February 1861, even though a random impressment that took men off the street and enrolled them for life persisted for a time, a need, strongly supported by General D. A. Miliutin [q.v.], for universal military service was recognized. A statute, signed by the tsar on 1 January 1874, required all Russian males without regard for class or birth to serve for six years in the regular army and nine years in the reserves. There were many exemptions. Merchants, nobles, and the clergy were exempt, as were men living close to frontiers across which they could flee to escape conscription. Exceptions were based upon education, physical standards, and domestic considerations. This statute endured until 1917. [See Russian Army.]

Lengths of service varied from country to country and often by arm of the service. France required three years' service, later raised to five. Eventually even Russia adopted a more modern system and required three years for infantry and artillery, and four years for cavalry and other services, followed by thirteen to fifteen years in the reserve; Germany and Austria required three years for cavalry and horse artillery and two years for other arms. In every country men passed into the reserves after their terms of active duty, and thus was created the mechanism for creating the mass armies of the twentieth century.

By the end of the nineteenth century, among major nations with standing armies, only Britain and the United States relied entirely upon volunteers. Wellington and Lord Roberts, among other British soldiers, favored conscription, but it was not introduced in Britain until April 1916, during the First World War; it was never used in India or the colonies. Wellington once said: "The conscription calls out a share of every class—no matter whether your son or my son—all must march." Opponents argued that it would bring into the army men of poor physique, that it was unwise to train the populace in arms, as the Paris Commune [q.v.] had shown, and that in any case, Britain's "splendid isolation" made it unlikely that it would ever have to face a Continental army.

Nevertheless, there was a strong movement in favor of what was called national service led by Lord Roberts [q.v.]. Even Lord Wolseley, Roberts's rival for glory, argued that conscription would be "an invigorating antidote against that luxury and effeminacy which destroys nations as well as individuals" and would "keep healthy and robust the manhood of a state."

The first conscription act in North America was passed by the General Council of the Choctaw Nation in 1861 [see Choctaw Resolution]. During the American Civil War the Confederacy passed a conscription act, signed by President Jefferson Davis [q.v.] on 16 April 1862, allowing many exceptions, including one for overseers of fifteen or more slaves [see Fifteenth Slave Law]. The North followed with the Enrollment Act of 3 March 1863, which resulted in the draft riots in New York City in July and August in which an estimated 1,200 were killed or wounded [see Civil Disorders].

Conscription acts in both North and South included commutation clauses. In the South exemption could be purchased for $500. In the North, because a man who could pay the $300 commutation fee was exempt, the shibboleth of the draft rioters was: "A rich man's war and a poor man's fight." Of the 292,441 men whose names were drawn in the first northern draft in August 1863, some 52,000 paid the $300 commutation fee. In the course of the war, 86,724 northern men avoided service by paying the fee; others avoided service by hiring substitutes. All conscription acts lapsed at the war's end.

Conseil de Guerre. A French court-martial [q.v.].

Conseil Supérieur de la Guerre. A board that assisted the French minister of war in matters of mobilization, deployment, supplies, and other matters.

Constable of the Tower. A British general who is in charge of the Tower of London and the Tower Hamlets. He holds his appointment by letters-patent from the sovereign. The position is largely honorary.

Constantine, Grand Duke. See Pavlovich, Konstantin.

Constantine, Sieges of (1836 and 1837), French conquest of Algeria. This fortified Algerian city, the most formidably bastioned in North Africa, 200 miles east-southeast of Algiers, was built by Arabs on rocky heights 800 feet above a riverbed. The first attempt in 1836 by 7,000 French under Bertrand Clausel [q.v.] to capture it failed, the French losing about 2,000.

The second siege on 6–12 October 1837 by 20,400 men under French General Comte Charles Denys de Damremont (d. 1837) finally took the city by assault. Damremont was killed in the action; Algerian casualties were said to be about 5,000.

Constantine *The capture of Constantine, Algeria, 1837*

Contagious Diseases Acts. See Venereal Disease.

Continental System. In the Berlin Decree of 21 November 1806 and later by other decrees, such as the Milan Decree of 1807, Napoleon launched an economic war against Britain.

No person under French control was permitted to trade with Britain, and all smuggled British goods found were confiscated. Britain retaliated by twenty-four orders-in-council [q.v.] forbidding nearly all trade with France and with any nation that complied with Napoleon's decree.

Contingent Allowance. See Allowances.

Contraband of War. The name given arms, ammunition, and various stores used in warfare that neutral countries were forbidden to supply to belligerents. Whether fuel, forage, and food could be so considered was much debated. In Britain a distinction was made between "absolute contraband," such as arms and ammunition, and "conditional and occasional contraband," materials and articles, such as food, fuel, and forage, that were of use in peace as well as war. Not all countries agreed with the distinction, and the matter was not resolved in the nineteenth century.

On 23 May 1861, at the beginning of the American Civil War, three runaway slaves sought protection at Fort Monroe, Virginia, where Major General Benjamin Franklin Butler [q.v.] was in command. When their owner demanded their return, Butler refused, declaring them contraband of war since they had worked to supply the Confederate armies. The term continued as a colloquial expression for freed slaves throughout the war.

The Federal Confiscation Act of August 1861 provided that any fugitive slave who had been employed to advance the Confederate cause was to be treated as a prize of war and set free. [See Concentration Camps.]

Contraband of War *Runaway slaves who join the Union forces become known as contrabands of war.*

Contract Surgeons. In the American army, when there was a need for more doctors than were commissioned, civilian doctors were employed and given the allowance of an assistant surgeon. Although they held no rank, they were entitled to the same respect as commissioned officers.

Contravallation. See Circumvallation.

Contreras, Battle of (19–20 August 1847), Mexican War. During the Americans' march on Mexico City, 4,200 Americans under General Winfield Scott [q.v.], led by General Gideon Pillow [q.v.], launched a surprise attack at dawn near this hamlet eight miles southwest of Mexico City and in seventeen minutes defeated a Mexican force of 7,000 under Gabriel Valencia, who had absented himself at the beginning of the battle. The Americans lost 60 killed and wounded; the Mexicans lost 700 dead. More than 700 were taken prisoner, and vast quantities of supplies fell to the Americans, who also recaptured two guns lost in the Battle of Buena Vista [q.v.].

Convention. A compact between opposing commanders, usually concerning exchange of prisoners or the arrangements for an armistice.

Conventions of War. Certain unwritten rules often called upon to make war less barbaric. A commonly invoked convention regulated the conduct of victorious besiegers, granting the honors of war [q.v.] to a besieged force that voluntarily surrendered and sanctioning pillage only in those cases in which the besieged resisted until conquered.

Convoy. 1. As a noun, troops acting as a protective escort for supplies or people.
    2. As a noun, a group organized to move together.
    3. As a verb, to escort for protection.

Cook, George Smith (1819–1902). An American master daguerreotypist who became known as the photographer of the Confederacy. Although General Pierre Beauregard [q.v.] employed him to reproduce maps and drawings, he was best known for a series of photographs taken at Fort Sumter over a two-year period. His collection of ten thousand photographs is now in the Valentine Museum in Richmond, where Cook lived and worked after the American Civil War.

Cook, John (1847–1915). A bugler in the Union army during the American Civil War who was the youngest "man" ever to receive the Medal of Honor [q.v.]. Before the war Cook was a paperboy in Cincinnati, Ohio. He enlisted on 7 June 1861 and in December was with Company B, 4th U.S. Artillery. He fought at Second Bull Run, Antietam, and Gettysburg [qq.v.]. At Antietam General John Gibbon [q.v.] ordered Cook's battery into action on the Hagerstown pike, where it came under heavy fire. When the battery commander was twice wounded, Cook helped him to the rear. Returning, he found the cannoneer assigned to carry ammunition dead, so he took over the job. When the Confederates charged, he helped man the guns. In all, the battery lost 44 men and 40 horses.

At Gettysburg Cook acted as a runner, carrying messages to the gunners. The battery commander later praised him, saying that "his services were simply invaluable and that he exhibited a degree of bravery that was never equalled by one his age."

After the war Cook became a court reporter in Cincinnati. He married and in 1870 moved to Washington, where he worked as a watchman at the Government Printing Office. It was not until 30 April 1894 that he was awarded the Medal of Honor for his gallantry at Antietam. After his death and burial in Arlington National Cemetery [q.v.], his medal was on display at the Freedom Foundation until August 1987, when it was stolen.

Cook Off. 1. The unintentional firing of a chambered round of ammunition in a gun caused by the heat of the bore. In muzzle-loading guns this could seriously injure the gun crew.

2. The explosion of ammunition in a fire.

Cook Travel Agency. See Thomas Cook & Son.

Cooper, Douglas Hancock (1815–1879). An American soldier who fought in the Mexican War [q.v.] as a captain in the 1st Mississippi Rifles. In 1853 he was appointed U.S. commissioner to the Choctaw Indians. During the American Civil War he and Albert Pike (1809–1891) were sent by the Confederate government to secure alliances with the Choctaw, Creek, Cherokee, Chickasaw, and Seminole Indian tribes. Using cash subsidies, gifts, and their considerable persuasive powers, they achieved a substantial, but incomplete, success.

Cooper raised the 1st Choctaw and the Chickasaw Mounted Rifles and became their colonel. On 2 May 1862 he was promoted brigadier general, and he later commanded an Indian division in the Trans-Mississippi Department. Among other operations, he took part in the pursuit of Upper Creeks under Opothleyohola, a chief who held Unionist sympathies. In 1864 he commanded the Indians during Sterling Price's [q.v.] Missouri operations. At the end of the war he was in command of all Confederate Indian forces west of the Mississippi River. He was defeated at the Battle of Honey Springs [q.v.] on 17 July 1863 by Federals under James C. Blunt.

After the war he successfully pressed Indian claims against the government for losses suffered during the war.

Cooper, Samuel (1798–1876). An American soldier born in New Jersey who was graduated from West Point in 1815. During the Seminole War and the Mexican War [qq.v.] he served mostly in staff functions. He was on the staff in Washington when Jefferson Davis [q.v.] was secretary of war. Married to a Virginian and loyal to Davis, he sided with the Confederacy when Virginia left the Union, becoming one of the few northerners to join the Confederate army. Davis appointed him a brigadier general. On 31 August 1861 he was appointed a full general to rank from 16 May, making him the senior officer in the Confederate army. He served with distinction throughout the war as adjutant general, a post in which he was largely responsible for keeping Confederate armies functioning in the field.

He fled with Davis when the Confederacy collapsed but was captured and paroled. When he fell upon hard times attempting to farm near Alexandria, Virginia, Lee took up a subscription for his financial relief.

Coorg, British occupation of (7 May 1834). This state (sometimes spelled Kurg) in southern India, southwest of Mysore, in a mountainous area on top of the western Ghats had an insane tyrant for a raja. Claiming that it was "the unanimous wish of the inhabitants," the British removed him and placed the state under British "protection."

Copenhagen (1808–1836). A chestnut stallion named to commemorate the siege of Copenhagen [q.v.], purchased as a foal by Wellington from General (later Field Marshal) Thomas Grosvenor, nephew of Richard, first Earl Grosvenor

(1731–1802), the greatest breeder of racehorses in England. General Grosvenor himself was known as "a staunch and respected supporter of the turf" (*Dictionary of National Biography*). When fully grown, Copenhagen stood 15 hands high. Throughout the Peninsular War he was Wellington's favorite mount, and in the Battle of Waterloo [q.v.] he rode him all day. [See Horses.]

After Copenhagen's death the second duke erected a tablet on the paddock at Stratford Saye, the house in Hampshire that had been presented to Wellington by a grateful nation:

Here lies
COPENHAGEN
The charger ridden by
The Duke of Wellington
The entire day at the
Battle of Waterloo
Born 1808, died 1836

God's humble instrument, though meaner clay,
Should share the glories of that glorious day.

Copenhagen, Battle of (2 April 1801), Napoleonic Wars. Although primarily a naval battle between the British and Danish fleets in which Admiral Horatio Nelson (1758–1805) distinguished himself, infantry battalions of the 95th Foot (later the Rifle Brigade) and the 49th Foot served as marines. The 49th suffered 13 killed and 49 wounded. Some 40,000 Congreve rockets were fired during this engagement. Wellington, who was present, was not impressed with them. [See Congreve, William.]

The attack prevented the renewal of the league of armed neutrals established by Denmark, Sweden, Prussia, and Russia.

Copenhagen, Siege of (August–October 1807), Napoleonic Wars. On 16 August 18,000 British and Hanoverian troops under General William Cathcart [q.v.] landed in Denmark and laid siege to Copenhagen. No war was declared, but following the Treaty of Tilsit [q.v.], the British were determined that the Danish fleet not fall into Napoleon's hands. An attempt by the Danes to relieve the city was repulsed by Arthur Wellesley, later Duke of Wellington, on 29 August. A British bombardment of the almost defenseless town on 2–5 September was joined by guns of 27 ships of the line, which moved inshore. On 6 September the Danes surrendered and handed over their fleet of 18 ships. Since the object of the expedition had been achieved, the siege was raised. The last British troops embarked in October.

Coptic Legion. When Napoleon left Egypt, he gave command of the French forces there to General Jean Baptiste Kléber (1753–1800). As reinforcement, Kléber raised a corps of about 600 native Christians (Copts) and armed them as French infantry.

Corbel. An architectural feature in a wall that projects from it, often stepped upward and out.

Corbett, Boston (1822?–1890?). An American soldier who claimed to have shot John Wilkes Booth (1838–1865), President Lincoln's assassin. A religious fanatic, he had castrated himself sometime before the American Civil War. In 1865 he was a sergeant in Company F, 16th New

York Cavalry and one of a detachment of 25 men under Captain Edward P. Doherty (1843?–1897) sent to search for Booth, who was found with a friend, David E. Harold (1842–1865), in a tobacco barn on the farm of Richard H. Garrett, near Bowling Green, about 18 miles south-southeast of Fredericksburg in east-central Virginia. When the barn was surrounded, Harold surrendered (to be hanged on 7 July), but Booth refused to give himself up. The barn was set on fire, and although Doherty had given orders not to shoot, a single shot was fired. A mortally wounded Booth was dragged from the blaze and died on the Garrett porch.

Booth probably shot himself, but Corbett claimed that the shot was his and that he had disobeyed orders because God told him to become the "Avenger of Blood." Although he was arrested for disobedience and taken to Washington, Secretary of War Edwin McMasters Stanton [q.v.] released Corbett with a reward. For a time Corbett went on the lecture circuit. He then became doorkeeper for the Kansas legislature until in 1886 he unaccountably fired two pistols in the legislative chambers. Having been placed in an insane asylum, he escaped and disappeared from history.

Corcoran, Michael (1827–1863). An Irish-born American soldier, son of a British army officer, whose anti-British sentiments led him in 1849 to flee his homeland and emigrate to the United States. He enlisted in the army as a private and rose to become colonel of the 69th New York Militia. Because in 1859 he had refused to turn out his largely Irish regiment to honor the visit of the Prince of Wales (the future Edward VII, 1841–1910), he was facing court-martial charges when the American Civil War began. The charges were forgotten in the demands of war.

Wounded and captured at First Bull Run [q.v.], he was held as one of several field officers whom Jefferson Davis threatened to hang if Lincoln, as he had threatened, hanged captured Confederate privateers, whom he considered pirates. When Lincoln relented, Corcoran was exchanged on 15 August 1862. He then raised a unit known as Corcoran's Legion, composed mostly of Irish immigrants, which saw service in western Virginia before being transferred to Washington after the Battle of Gettysburg [q.v.]. In October 1863 he was made a division commander. On 22 December he was killed when his horse fell on him near Fairfax Court House.

Cordite. A smokeless, slow-burning explosive powder made of nitroglycerin, nitrocellulose, and mineral jelly. It was invented by Frederick August Abel (1827–1902), an English chemist, and John Dewar (1842–1923) a Scottish chemist and physicist, inventor of Dewar's Vessel [q.v.]. On 2 October 1889 the *London Daily News* announced the discovery of "The new explosive, known as 'cordite' on account of its curiously string-like appearance."

Córdoba, José María (1800?–1830). A Colombian soldier who served with distinction under Simón Bolívar and Antonio de Sucre [qq.v.] in the wars fought to free South American countries from Spanish rule. He became a general at age twenty-two and played an important part in the victory over royalist forces in the Battle of Ayacucho [q.v.] in 1824. He was assassinated in a conspiracy.

Cordon. 1. A chain of forts or sentry posts enclosing an area.

2. The rounded coping stone on top of a revetment.

3. A cord or ribbon worn as a badge of honor or as a decoration.

4. The coping of the escarp or inner wall of a trench that protects the top of the trench from water and forms an obstacle for an enemy attempting to scale the wall.

Cordon Sanitaire. 1. A buffer area between two rival nations or forces.

2. A quarantine line to seal off those infected with the plague or other contagious disease.

Córdova, Capture of (8 June 1808), Napoleonic Wars. French troops under General Pierre Dupont de l'Étang [q.v.] easily captured from the Spanish this town in southern Spain on the Guadalquivir River and then ruthlessly pillaged it. Soon after, on 4 July, Dupont was created a count. The town was again pillaged by the French in 1811.

Cordua, Hans (1875?–1900). A German living in the Transvaal during the Second Anglo-Boer War [q.v.]. He hatched a plot to kidnap Lord Roberts [q.v.], the British commander-in-chief in South Africa, which was discovered in July 1900 by the British authorities in Pretoria. Cordua was tried by a military tribunal, found guilty, and shot.

Corduroy Road. A road, often over marshy ground, made by placing logs side by side transversely, creating a ribbed surface resembling corduroy. [See Plank Road.]

Union troops build a corduroy road.

Corinth, Battle of (3–4 October 1862), American Civil War. At 10:00 A.M. on 3 October 1862 Confederate General Earl Van Dorn [q.v.] with 22,000 men attacked Union General William Rosecrans [q.v.] with 23,000 men near Corinth, Mississippi. The Federals fell back to a line of inner works and successfully repelled strong Confederate attacks until early afternoon, when Van Dorn broke off the action and retreated westward along a railroad line to Ripley. Newly arrived Union reinforcements forced him to fight bitter rearguard actions all the way.

Of the 21,147 Federals actually engaged, 2,520 became casualties; the Confederates lost 2,470 killed and wounded and 1,763 missing, at least 300 of whom were prisoners of war.

Van Dorn was court-martialed on charges of dereliction of duty but found not guilty.

Corinth, Union Advance on (29 April–10 June 1862), American Civil War. After the Battle of Shiloh [q.v.] in April 1862, Union General Henry Halleck [q.v.] took command of forces that consisted of Grant's Army of the Tennessee, John Pope's Army of the Mississippi, and Don Carlos Buell's [qq.v.] Army of the Ohio, a force of 110,000 by the time it began its advance to Corinth in northwest Mississippi. Because he had little confidence in Grant, Halleck gave command of his army to General George H. Thomas [q.v.]. Appointed second-in-command, a job with a fine title and little responsibility, Grant determined to ask to be relieved but was persuaded not to by his friend William Tecumseh Sherman [q.v.].

Confederate General Pierre Beauregard [q.v.], who had retired to Corinth with 30,000 veterans of Shiloh, was able to reinforce his army to 66,000 while, in spite of his superior strength, Halleck advanced at a snail's pace. By 25 May, after nearly a month, he had traveled only 20 miles. When he was finally prepared to bombard the Confederate positions, Beauregard wisely pulled back his army on the night of 29 to 30 May and put it into strong defensive positions along the Tuscumbia River. In the Union pursuit Colonel Philip Sheridan [q.v.] distinguished himself as a cavalry commander, but on 11 June Halleck broke off contact and consolidated his position in Tennessee.

Cornelis, Battle of (August 1811), Java War. The British landed unopposed at Chillingcherry, Java, on 4 August 1811, and on the 11th they fought a sharp skirmish in which the advanced guard under Colonel Rollo Gillespie [q.v.] drove back the French and Dutch and laid siege to Fort Cornelis. Admiral Sir Robert Stopford (1768–1847) landed a naval brigade with heavy guns, and on 26 August the fort was successfully stormed. The British captured 246 officers, including 2 generals, and 6,000 other ranks with 280 guns. Java then surrendered unconditionally.

Cornet. 1. A wind instrument of brass or other metal popular with military bands. Originally it did not have keys or stopples and resembled a bugle. Later the cornet-à-pistons, resembling a small tuba, was developed in France.

2. In British cavalry, the lowest commissioned rank, equivalent to ensign or second lieutenant in the infantry. The rank was abolished in 1871 when the rank of sublieutenant was introduced.

3. In the American cavalry, also for a time the lowest commissioned rank, sometimes ranking below a second lieutenant. The rank was abolished in 1800. However, in the Philadelphia City Troop (now Troop A, 1st Squadron, 104th Cavalry of the Pennsylvania National Guard) the rank was retained and is still used (officially since 1921) for the one soldier who acts as an officer without drawing an officer's pay; he is promoted second lieutenant when a position becomes available.

Corning. In the manufacture of gunpowder this was a term for granulating, when powder in cake form was run through rollers and sieves to form the various sizes of grains.

Corona. A woolen saddle pad, often with ornamental borders, set on the back of pack animals before the blanket or aparejo [q.v.] is placed.

Corporal. In the American army, the lowest-ranking noncommissioned officer, ranking above a private first class or marine lance corporal and below a sergeant.

In the British army, except in the Household Cavalry and Royal Artillery, a corporal holds a rank below a sergeant and above a lance corporal but is not considered a noncommissioned officer. The insignia in both armies is two chevrons. [See Bombardier; Lance Corporal; Corporal Major; Corporal-of-Horse.]

Corporal Major. In the British army, there were (and are) no sergeants in the Household Cavalry. A corporal major, the highest-ranking noncommissioned officer in a troop, is the equivalent of a sergeant major of infantry [q.v.].

Corporal-of-Horse. In the British Household Cavalry [q.v.] a rank equivalent to sergeant. In the sixteenth and seventeenth centuries there were no sergeants in the cavalry, the corporal-of-horse serving in that position, a tradition preserved in the three regiments of Household Cavalry—1st and 2nd Life Guards and Royal Horse Guards—but in no other.

Corporal's Guard. A small detachment of men under a corporal or any small group of armed men.

Corps. 1. A part of a nation's military establishment, such as the Marine Corps or Corps of Cadets.

2. An entire arm or service, such as the Corps of Engineers [q.v.] in the American army.

3. A tactical unit, often called a *corps d'armée,* of one or more divisions, usually with auxiliary arms and services. In the nineteenth century the French under Napoleon began to combine divisions to make larger units with permanent staffs. The first such units are believed to have been formed by Marshal Jean Victor Moreau [q.v.] about 1800, when he organized his eleven divisions into four corps. In 1804 Napoleon made *corps d'armée* permanent parts of his army's organizational structure, the building blocks of the Grande Armée.

A typical Napoleonic army corps consisted of three infantry divisions, each with one light infantry and twelve line infantry regiments; a cavalry brigade of three regiments; and about 46 guns, of which 29 were with the infantry divisions and 17 in corps artillery. In all, a Napoleonic corps contained about 28,000 to 30,000 infantry and 1,500 cavalry plus horse and field artillery—an army unto itself. Napoleon declared that a corps "well handled . . . could go anywhere." In 1879 France had nineteen *corps d'armée,* Germany eighteen, and Austria thirteen. Russia had fourteen military districts that resembled corps.

In the nineteenth century the United States had such corps only during the American Civil War. The first were formed under Union General George McClellan [q.v.] in March 1862. The South followed on 6 November 1862, when Robert E. Lee reorganized the Army of Northern Virginia [q.v.] into two corps; a third was added on 30 May 1863. By convention, corps are numbered using Roman numerals.

Corps Artillery. The part of the artillery not assigned to the support of any subordinate unit of a command but kept at the disposal of the officer commanding the artillery to be used as required by the corps commander. Sometimes called the reserve artillery, it consisted of field artillery and sometimes mortars, siege guns, or other heavier guns.

Corps de Chasse. A unit that, after a successful attack, exploits the success by pursuing the fleeing enemy.

Corps of Artillerists and Engineers. A unit of the U.S. army formed at West Point in 1794 by a professional French officer, Lieutenant Colonel Stephen Rochefontaine. It consisted of four battalions of artillery, each with four companies, commanded by engineer officers. This combined arm disappeared on 1 April 1802, when separate corps of arms and services were formed.

Corps of Engineers. This corps became a distinct branch of the American army in 1802. Based at West Point, New York, it consisted of a colonel, a lieutenant colonel, 4 captains, 4 lieutenants, and not more than 8 cadets. The size was later increased to 47 officers, and a separate topographic corps was instituted. In 1846 sappers, miners, and pontoniers were added. Until 1886 it was solely responsible for the U.S. Military Academy, whose superintendent was always an officer in the corps. Considered the elite service, the corps was open to only the top graduates of West Point. All military construction, even seawalls and lighthouses, rivers and harbors, were the corps's responsibility.

Corps of Guides. One of the most famous of the irregular units in the Indian army. It was a unique unit, containing both infantry and cavalry, and was designed to gather intelligence and act as guides on India's Northwest Frontier. The corps did not become a regular part of the Indian army subject to the commander-in-chief, India, until late in the century.

The idea of forming such a unit was first proposed by Henry Lawrence [q.v.], and in 1846 a unit composed of one troop of cavalry and two companies of infantry was formed with Lieutenant Harry Lumsden [q.v.] in command as the sole British officer.

At the beginning of the Indian Mutiny [q.v.] the guides made a famous forced march to Delhi and played a major role

Corps of Guides in India, 1880s

in the siege [see Siege of Delhi]. Out of a strength of 600 at the beginning of the siege, only 250 survived unscathed. The British officers, increased from 2 to 3, had been replaced four times. One officer was wounded six times.

When Sir Louis Cavagnari [q.v.] went to Kabul as British Resident, he was accompanied by 25 guides cavalry and 52 guides infantry, all under Lieutenant Walter Hamilton, VC (1856–1879). There on 3 September 1879 in an attack upon the Residency by mutinous Afghan troops all were killed, the guides fighting to the last man.

Corret de la Tour d'Auvergne, Théophile Malo. See First Grenadier of France.

Corse, John Murray (1835–1893). A Union officer in the American Civil War whose gallant defense of Allatoona Pass in Georgia in October 1864 inspired evangelist Philip Paul Bliss (1838–1876) to write the words for a popular hymn, "Hold the Fort." Corse entered West Point in 1853 but left after two years and read law. When war was declared, he joined the army, and by July 1861 he was a major in the 6th Iowa Infantry. He saw much action in the West. In March 1863 he became a colonel and in that rank distinguished himself in the capture of Jackson, Mississippi, and at Chickamauga [q.v.], where he was badly wounded on Missionary Ridge [q.v.]. At Allatoona he put up a valiant defense in the face of a vastly superior Confederate force and, although badly wounded, refused to surrender, signaling instead to a relief force: "I am short a cheekbone and one ear, but I am able to whip all hell yet!" He was brevetted a major general for this action.

Cortland, Henry Charles (1814–1888). An Anglo-Indian whose father was a British colonel. He was educated in England, and thanks to his father's influence, he was commissioned in the Khalsa [q.v.], the Sikh army in the Punjab. He rose to command two battalions, and in 1843 he saw service in the Hazara district. He changed sides during the First Sikh War [q.v.] and remained with the British. During the Indian Mutiny [q.v.] he raised and commanded a corps of Sikhs and commanded them in clearing the Ferozepur area of rebels and mutineers. He died in London a colonel on full pay.

Corumbá, Battle of (1867), War of the Triple Alliance [q.v.]. This town on the Paraguay River in southwest Brazil, 11 miles from the Bolivian frontier, changed hands several times during the war. In 1867 a Brazilian force attempting to enter Paraguay from the southeast was completely routed here and was pursued for miles by the Paraguayans. A notable feature of the engagement was the presence of a corps of Paraguayan amazons, led by Eliza Lynch, the mistress of Paraguayan dictator Francisco López [qq.v.].

Corunna / La Coruña, Battle of (16 January 1809), Peninsular War. In his famous retreat [see Corunna, Retreat to] Sir John Moore [q.v.], arrived on 11 January 1809 at Corunna on the northwest coast of Spain, 127 miles west of Oviedo, and took up a strong defensive position on a peninsula south of the city to await the British fleet that was to evacuate his ragged army. On 14 January 100 transports, escorted by 12 ships of the line, arrived off the coast, and the embarkation of the cavalry and artillery began at once. On the following day the leading elements of the French army—24,000 men with 36 guns under Marshal Nicolas Soult [q.v.]—appeared on the scene, and brisk skirmishing took place at the village of Piedralonga. Moore by this time had only 15,000 men and 12 guns on land.

On the 16th, a cold winter's day, the French attempted an enveloping movement that failed; by four-thirty in the afternoon they were falling back. It was at about this time that Moore, trying to organize an attack by the Guards Brigade, was struck by a round shot that crushed his right side and shoulder.

Moore's place was taken by Sir John Hope [q.v.], who successfully repulsed the last feeble French attack launched in the twilight. British losses were about 800; French losses, about 1,400.

When the dying Moore learned of his victory, he exclaimed: "I hope the people will be satisfied. I hope my country will do me justice." He died shortly after 8:00 P.M. and was buried by lamplight in an unmarked grave on the ramparts. Soult, who occupied Corunna when the British departed, later raised a monument to his fallen foe.

By the 18th the British expeditionary force was embarked. After surviving a storm at sea, it arrived safely in England. In the total campaigns in Portugal and Spain the British had lost about 7,000 men. Although at the end of the campaign Britain's only field army was in shambles, Moore had succeeded in disrupting Napoleon's plans for the conquest of the Iberian Peninsula. Wellington completed his work.

In 1823, during the French intervention in Spain [q.v.], Corunna was again captured by the French, and in 1836 it fell to the Carlists [q.v.] in the First Carlist War.

Corunna, Battle of *Battle of Corunna, 16 January 1809*

Corunna, Retreat to (December 1808–January 1809), Peninsular War. On 11 October 1808 Sir John Moore [q.v.], in command of a British expeditionary force of 25,000 in Portugal, made a bold advance to Salamanca in western Spain, 107 miles west-northwest of Madrid. Here he learned that Napoleon himself with an army of 250,000 men had entered the country and, having inflicted disastrous defeats on the Spanish army, was advancing on Madrid. As soon as Moore was reinforced, he moved to Sahagún in southwest Spain, 33

miles east-southeast of León, where he hoped to pounce upon the widely separated divisions of Nicolas Soult [q.v.]. However, when he learned that Napoleon, in an effort to trap him, was leading an army from Madrid by way of the 4,151-foot-high Guadarrama Pass south of Segovia, he began on Christmas Day a painful and near-disastrous 250-mile retreat to Corunna (La Coruña) through the Cantabrian Mountains by way of Benaventa, Astorga, Vilafranca, and Lugo. Under appalling winter conditions, with unit cohesion [q.v.] and military discipline badly eroded, and with some 5,000 men falling by the wayside, he still managed to stay just ahead of the pursuing French force of 70,000.

When Napoleon's advance guard reached the Esla River, they found all the bridges destroyed. This action gave Moore a good lead, but at Astorga, where he found a horde of demoralized Spanish troops, billeting arrangements and the distribution of rations and supplies were thrown into confusion. British discipline snapped, and soldiers began looting. The town was soon littered with drunken soldiers, and Moore's army was unable to move.

Fortunately for the British, Napoleon believed that Moore had probably escaped him, and he returned to France on 2 January 1809, leaving Soult to continue the pursuit. Under deplorable weather conditions, in the bitter cold, and over rough mountain roads, pursuers and pursued plodded, the sick and the weak falling by the wayside. A commissary wrote: "A woman fell up to her waist in a bog and as she was sucked down by the slimy, ice-cold water, the man behind her walked over her head." At Lugo, on the Mino River, 45 miles southeast of Corunna, Moore decided to take a stand in an effort to revive morale and gain time, but Soult refused to attack and the retreat continued. Amid the general demoralization of the British army, there were exceptions: the Guards, the Light Division [q.v.], and the so-called Reserve Division maintained their discipline and coherence.

Captain (later Lieutenant General) William Warre (1784–1853) wrote home from Sobrado on 4 January 1809 that even some of the officers were barefoot: "I am not yet really hardened enough to misery and wretchedness not to be unhappy at contemplating the miseries of war in our men and the wretched inhabitants of the country."

On 11 January Moore managed to reach Corunna, only to discover that the fleet that was to have carried his troops off had not yet appeared. With his back to the sea, he was forced to fight the day after the fleet arrived before he could embark all his troops [see Corunna, Battle of]. Moore himself was mortally wounded and was buried in the ramparts of his defenses.

Cosenz, Enrico (1812–1898). An Italian soldier who as a colonel in Giuseppe Garibaldi's [q.v.] Cacciatori delle Alpi (Alpine Hunters) led Garibaldi's third expedition to Sicily in 1860. After Garibaldi seized Naples, Cosenz was briefly appointed minister of war. In 1861 he was given command of a division in the Italian army, and from 1881 to 1893 he was chief of the Italian general staff.

Cossacks. 1. A general term for all Caucasian irregular cavalry in the Russian service.

2. Specifically, males of mixed ancestry living on the south and east borders of the Russian Empire who were members of a military caste. They were given land in exchange for military

service. Leo Tolstoy [q.v.] said of them: "These people live as nature does; they die, are born; intermingle, give birth to children, fight, eat, drink, are happy and die again, and their lives are not conditioned except as nature herself inexorably rules the sun, the grass and the animals, the trees and them" (*The Cossacks,* written in 1854 and published in 1862.)

In 1801 the Don Cossack Ataman Matvei Ivanovich Platov [q.v.] pledged himself and his followers to Tsar Alexander I [q.v.]. Other Cossack hosts followed his example. In 1805 they were grouped into the Don, Ural, and five other military districts on the frontier. They were excused from taxes, but males were liable for twenty years of military service beginning at age eighteen. Cossacks were employed almost constantly in wars with Central Asian peoples. Serving under their own officers, they generally held Russian soldiers in contempt. They were of little use in pitched battles, but riding their nimble Cossack ponies in their own style, they were swift and ruthless raiders. Their favorite weapon was a lance, but they also often carried sabers, pistols, carbines, or rifles without bayonets. Their uniforms were based upon their regional costume, which featured an open-necked caftan called a *cherkesska.*

When Napoleon invaded Russia in 1812 [q.v.], Platov raised an army of 50,000 Cossack cavalrymen with whom he harried the rear of Napoleon's ill-fated army.

For the Russo-Turkish War [q.v.] of 1877–78 Cossacks mobilized 3,672 officers and 140,882 other ranks; this constituted about 70 percent of all Russian cavalry. By 1900 there were 67,000 Cossacks on active duty, and they could be quickly expanded to 190,000. By 1912 there were 40,000 fully equipped and trained Don Cossacks alone.

Cossacks *Circassian Cossacks photographed in the 1890s*

Coston Signal Lights. Flares of red, green, and white lights that could be fired from a signal holder or a pistol.

Cotonou, French Seizure and Defense of (22 February– 4 March 1890), French-Dahomean War. On 22 February 1890 some 360 French soldiers seized Cotonou, Dahomey (Benin), on the west coast of Africa, from the Dahomeans, who counterattacked the following day and were repulsed. On 1 March the fon (ruler) of Dahomey launched a second unsuccessful attack. Three days later the Dahomeans launched a third assault. Although they attacked at dawn and caught the French by surprise, this too failed, and 127 dead were counted within the French lines; about half were women warriors [See Amazons].

Cotton, Stapleton, First Viscount Combermere (1773– 1865). A British soldier from a wealthy family who entered the army as an officer at sixteen and one-half. Four years later, thanks to the purchase system [q.v.], he was a lieutenant colonel commanding the newly raised 25th Light Dragoons. He served in Flanders in 1793–94 and at the Cape of Good Hope in 1796. In India he took part in the Fourth Mysore War against Tipu Sahib (1751–1799), including the siege of Seringapatam in 1799. He was promoted colonel on 1 January 1800 and major general on 30 October 1805 at the age of thirty-two.

In 1808, during the Peninsular War [q.v.], he was posted to Spain in command of a cavalry brigade and for a time commanded all British cavalry in the peninsula. He took part in Moore's campaign [see Corunna, Retreat to] and was present at the Battle of Talavera [q.v.]. On his father's death he inherited his baronetcy, and in January 1810 he returned to England for six months. When he came back to the peninsula, he was given command of a division and subsequently commanded all the Allied cavalry with the local rank of lieutenant general, a rank he reached substantively on 1 January 1812.

After the Battle of Salamanca [q.v.] he was severely wounded in the right arm by the fire of a Portuguese picket. He recuperated in England and returned to the Peninsula just after the Battle of Vitoria [q.v.]. He was again in command of all Allied cavalry, a post he held until the end of the war. In recognition, he was raised to the peerage as Baron Combermere and given a pension of £2,000 for his own and two succeeding lives.

After a variety of commands in France, the West Indies, and Ireland, he was named commander-in-chief, India, where in November 1825 he besieged the great Jat fort at Bhurtpore [q.v.]. On 18 January 1826 he captured it. He was made a viscount in 1827. After serving five years in India, he returned to spend most of the last thirty years of his life with his third wife in "parliamentary and social duties" (*Dictionary of National Biography*).

Couch, Darius Nash (1822–1897). An American soldier who was graduated from West Point in 1846 and saw service in the Second Seminole War and the Mexican War [qq.v.], winning a brevet for his "gallantry and meritorious conduct" in the Battle of Buena Vista [q.v.]. In 1855 he resigned his commission and entered business. On 15 June 1861, at the beginning of the American Civil War, he was named colonel of the 7th Massachusetts. Two months later he was made a brigadier general to rank from 17 May. On 4 July 1862 he was promoted to major general, and in October he was given command of a corps, which he led at Fredericksburg and Chancellorsville [qq.v.]. He later organized home defense forces in Pennsylvania and fought at Nashville [q.v.] and in North Carolina. From 1876 to 1878 he was quartermaster general of Connecticut, and in 1883–84 he was adjutant general.

Coulmiers, Battle of (9 November 1870), Franco-Prussian War. Following the French defeat at Sedan, the fall of the great fortress at Metz, and with Paris [qq.v.] under siege, a "people's army" of about 70,000 was formed at Tours under General Louis Aurelle de Paladines [q.v.]. On 9 November 1870 it marched on Coulmiers, a small town in north-central France 12 miles west of Orléans on the road to Le Mans, where it encountered and, after a hard fight, defeated three cavalry and four infantry brigades of Bavarians (20,000 men with 110 guns) under General Ludwig von der Tann-Rathsamhausen (1811–1881). The Bavarians lost an ammunition column and two guns, 576 were killed or wounded, 800 taken prisoner; French losses were about 1,500. The Germans were forced to abandon Orléans. This was the first and only clear victory for the French army in what was sometimes called the People's War.

Council of Administration. In the American army, a board of three officers that supervised post or unit sutlers [q.v.].

Council of War *Raglan at a council of war at British headquarters in the Crimea*

Council of War. A conference of senior officers called in wartime when a commander wishes to fortify his own judgment by soliciting that of others. General Henri de Jomini [q.v.] called councils of war "a deplorable resource," and Napoleon advised against them, declaring that they led to "the most pusillanimous or . . . the most prudent measure, which in war is almost uniformly the worst that can be adopted." After the Battle of Gettysburg [q.v.] General Henry Halleck advised General George Meade [qq.v.]: "Call no council of war. It is proverbial that councils of war never fight." In a letter of 20 January 1890 to (Henry) Spencer Wilkinson (1853–1937) Helmuth von Moltke [q.v.] wrote: "If a commander . . . feels the need of asking others what he ought to do, the command is in weak hands." In spite of the universal advice of all great generals, many commanders

have weakened and called councils of war.

Count Coup, to. Among certain American Indian tribes, particularly those on the Great Plains, a coup was a successful strike at a foe. It was not essential that the man struck be killed or even injured, but special glory was obtained if the enemy's horse or weapons were taken. The number of coups established the prestige of a warrior.

Counterapproach. A trench dug by the besieged, usually a zigzag, to meet the approaches of the enemy.

Counterattack. An attack made to counter an enemy's attack or, after it has halted, immediately to attack the attackers in order to regain lost ground.

Counterbattery. A battery of artillery used to silence an enemy battery.

Counterfort. Buttresses or ramparts of earth placed inside old walls to increase their strength.

Counterguard. An outwork so placed as to defend the faces of a bastion or ravelin.

Countermand, to. To revoke a command; to annul or prohibit a previous command.

Countermarch. An evolution by which a body of men change front or march in the opposite direction from that which they had previously taken.

Countermines. Underground galleries or chambers dug for the purpose of listening for digging by the enemy—it was said that the sound of a pickax could be heard through the ground at a distance of 60 feet—or for aborting an enemy's mining efforts.

Extensive mining operations were undertaken by the Russians in the siege of Sevastopol [q.v.], and extensive countermining was engaged in by the Allies, particularly the French. When countermining failed to detect the enemy's mining, the results could be catastrophic. [See Petersburg, Siege of; Camouflet.]

Counteroffensive. An attack made by a force that has been for some time on the defensive.

Counterscarp. The outer slope of a trench, the side facing the enemy. The inner slope is the escarp.

Countersign. A watchword or number, usually changed daily, to enable sentinels and pickets to distinguish friend from foe when making a challenge.

Countervallation. See Circumvallation.

Coup de Grace. A finishing or decisive shot or stroke.

Coup de Main. A sudden, vigorous attack in force upon a surprised enemy. Napoleon believed that "The success of a coup de main depends entirely upon luck rather than judgment."

Coup d'État. A sudden and violent overthrow of a ruler or government, as Napoleon's coup d'état of 9 November 1799, in which he overthrew the Directory and became first consul, or as the dissolution of the Assembly of the Second Republic by Louis Napoleon (1808–1873) on 2 December 1851.

Coup d'Oeuil Militaire. The art of rapidly sizing up military situations, opportunities, or problems, quickly grasping the advantages and disadvantages of terrain or deployments. Chevalier Charles de Folard (1669–1752), a French soldier of much experience of war, wrote in *Nouvelles Decouvertes sur la guerre* (1724): "The coup d'oeil is a gift of God and cannot be acquired. . . . To look over a battlefield, to take in at the first instance the advantages and disadvantages is the great quality of a general." Napoleon thought it was "inborn in great generals."

Coupe-gorge. A position so bad that a unit occupying it would be forced to surrender or be cut to pieces.

Courage. This quality was best defined by General William Tecumseh Sherman [q.v.] in his *Memoirs* (1875): "I would define true courage to be a perfect sensibility of the measure of danger, and a mental willingness to incur it." Field Marshal Bernard Montgomery (1887–1976) said much the same thing: "Many qualities go to make a leader, but two are vital—the ability to make the right decisions and the courage to act on the decisions." Courage takes many forms, and as playwright Vittorio Alfieri (1749–1803) once wrote: "Often the test of courage is not to die, but to live."

Courier. A messenger, usually mounted, sent to carry orders or dispatches. The officer receiving the message sometimes initialed the envelope and gave it as a receipt to the courier.

Court, Claude Auguste (1798–1861). A French officer who was graduated from the École Polytechnique in 1813 and commissioned into the 68th Infantry. He resigned in 1818 and, like a number of other French officers, accepted a commission in the Persian army. In 1827 he left the Persian service and was commissioned in the Khalsa [q.v.], the Sikh army of Ranjit Singh [q.v.]. Unlike many of the other Europeans in the Khalsa, Court appears to have been a gentleman. Henry Lawrence [q.v.] said, "M. Court was the most respectable of the French officers in Ranjit Singh's service. A person of high literary attainments and with a cautious and retiring disposition." He was an ordnance expert and worked in the Sikh arsenal. In 1836 he was promoted general. He married a Kashmiri woman, and in 1844 returned to France, where he died.

Court-martial. 1. As a noun, a temporary military court of law consisting of three or more officers appointed to hear a specific case or series of cases of soldiers alleged to have committed an offense or offenses punishable under military law. Officers were tried by officers senior to them.

2. As a verb, to charge a soldier with an offense liable to be tried by court-martial.

In the British army, there were three types of courts-martial: general, district, and regimental. Officers could be tried only by a general court-martial, the sole court permitted to sentence those found guilty to be executed or to be trans-ported. Regimental courts-martial tried minor offenses, and district courts-martial more serious offenses not requiring severe punishments. The system in the American army was similar, the district court-martial's being called a garrison court-martial. There was no lower court until 1891, when a summary court-martial was authorized.

General courts-martial in the American army could legally sentence those found guilty to execution, confinement on bread and water for up to fourteen days, confinement shackled with a ball and chain, hard labor, forfeiture of pay and allowances, dishonorable discharge from the service, a reprimand, or, in the case of noncommissioned officers, reduction to the ranks. Early in the century flogging and branding [qq.v.] could also be ordered. Hospital stewards, commissary sergeants, and ordnance sergeants were, like officers, tried only by general courts-martial. They could be discharged but not reduced in rank. In the early part of the century, no counsel was provided for the accused. If he obtained one, the counsel was not allowed to speak in court.

Garrison courts were seldom used in the American army. In 1896, for example, there were 1,486 general courts-martial and 13,267 summary courts-martial, but only 289 garrison courts-martial.

In most armies only combatant officers could be members of a military court. In the United States, surgeons, assistant surgeons, paymasters, and chaplains were specifically excluded.

Different commanders in different armies at different times took different views of courts-martial and punishment. Field Marshal Prince Aleksandr V. Suvorov [q.v.] believed that "no offense must go unpunished, for nothing can cause the men so much harm as lax discipline." William Tecumseh Sherman [q.v.], however, believed that "too many courts-martial in any command are evidence of poor discipline and inefficient officers." During the American Civil War no general North or South court-martialed as many officers as did General Thomas ("Stonewall") Jackson [q.v.], while his commander, General Robert E. Lee, fought through the war without court-martialing a single officer.

Civil servants, camp followers, or others properly attached to an army were sometimes considered to be subject to military law.

Court-martial *British and Indian officers conduct a court-martial.*

Court of Honor. In the Prussian army, a court that could be convened to uphold the honor of the army or of an individual and to punish officers who had deviated, however slightly, from the code of an officer. It approved or disapproved duels after examining the offense and deciding if an officer's honor had been besmirched [see Dueling.]

Court of Inquiry. The president, a general, or a commanding officer in the American army could order a board of one to three officers and a judge advocate or recorder to examine the nature of any incident, transaction, accusation, or imputation involving any soldier of any rank to determine if any dereliction had occurred. The proceeding was much like a court-martial, except that in some cases the board was required only to determine the facts and not to pronounce judgment. It could sit with open or closed doors, and there was no limitation on the lapsed time since the act was said to have occurred.

Cover. Any protection from observation or from projectiles.

Covered Approach. 1. A route protected from enemy observation or fire.

2. An approach made under the protection of other forces or by natural cover.

Covered Flank. See Flank, Covered.

Covered Way. 1. The area behind the foremost fortification in which a standing man would be unseen by an enemy.

2. An infantry fire step in a trench.

3. A protected line of communications.

Covering Fascines. Fascines made of thick, closely trimmed branches used in place of plank in wooden bridges or as roofs for powder magazines in the field.

Covering Fire. Protective fire by a portion of a unit to enable the rest to advance, such as the fire directed at the walls of a fortification to reduce the fire directed at those attempting an escalade [q.v.].

Cowardice. An absence of the courage or resolution to face a present danger. In nineteenth century armies cowardice was almost never excused, and cowards were frequently shot. Rudyard Kipling [q.v.] wrote:

I could not look on death, which being known,
Men led me to him, blindfold and alone.
("The Coward" in *Epitaphs of the War*, 1919)

The disgrace of cowardice was not easily brushed aside, as A. E. Housman (1859–1936) noted:

Cowards' funerals, when they come,
Are not wept so well at home.
("The Day of Battle" in *The Shropshire Lad*, 1896)

Cow Row (April 1846). A British sentry in the Punjab, annoyed by a herd of cows obstructing a road, slashed some of them with a saber, thus deeply offending the religious sensibilities of the Hindus and Sikhs. The next day the British Resident and senior officers who went into Lahore to explain the incident were pelted with stones. The British demanded punishment for the stone throwers, and Lal Singh (d. 1867),

the chief minister, obliged. The man who incited the incident was hanged, and two others were deported. The soldier who slashed the cows was "warned to be more careful in the future."

Coxwell, Henry Tracey (1819–1900). An English balloonist who, in spite of his pertinacity, was unsuccessful in promoting the increased use of balloons in war. In 1862, in company with the mathematician and astronomer Dr. James Whitbread Lee Glaisher (1848–1928), he soared to the world record height of seven miles. Glaisher lost consciousness, and Coxwell, unable to turn the gas valve with his frostbitten hands, turned it with his teeth, effecting a speedy but safe descent.

Crabb Filibustering Expedition in Sonora, Mexico (1837). Henry A. Crabb (1823?–1847), a lawyer from Tennessee, emigrated to San Francisco, California, in 1849. He played an active role in state politics but was defeated in a bid for the U.S. Senate. His marriage to a daughter of a prominent Mexican family involved him in political feuds in Sonora. For a promise of mineral rights and large tracts of land, he agreed to support Ignacio Pesqueira, a would-be governor of Sonora with an army of American volunteers. Crabb with 90 men was to advance overland and rendezvous near Altar with 1,000 men to be sent by sea, but an adventurer known as General John D. Crosby, who was to recruit the additional 1,000 men, made no effort to do so.

After a hard journey over desert country, Crabb and his men were ambushed on 1 April at Caborca, 80 miles southwest of Nogales, Arizona. The Americans loopholed an adobe building, but a large force of Mexicans arrived with two cannon, and on 6 April the surviving Americans were forced to surrender. The Mexican commander promised that if they gave up their arms, they would be allowed to retreat across the border. Instead all were massacred except for sixteen-year-old Charles Edward Evans. The bodies were left on the ground to be eaten by animals. Crabb's head was severed and pickled.

Meanwhile Pesqueira had managed to become governor of Sonora without the help of Crabb and his men, whom he now denounced. An attempted rescue party of 26 men from the United States was driven back with some loss.

For many years after the Battle at Caborca the citizens of the town held a fiesta on 6 April to commemorate the Mexican victory with feasting and patriotic oratory.

Crab Lice. One of the many varieties of vermin, *Phthiris pubis*, that attach themselves to the pubic area, a common irritant to soldiers.

Cracker Line. An American slang name for the route used to bring up supplies. It is usually associated with the precarious Federal lines of communication and supply into besieged Chattanooga [q.v.] in October–November 1863 during the Civil War. Union steamboats on the Tennessee River opened a route to replace the railroad into Chattanooga that had been cut by the Confederates.

Cracow / Kraków Insurrection (1846). At the third partition of Poland in 1795 the city of Cracow became part of

Austria. In July 1809 it was liberated by the French and the Polish Legion of Marshal Jozef Anton Poniatowski [q.v.] and was absorbed into the grand duchy of Warsaw. However, in 1815 the Congress of Vienna divided what had been Poland among Prussia, Russia, and Austria, except for Cracow (Kraków or Kraau), which remained an independent buffer state. An insurrection led by Jan Tyssowski (1811–1857) against Austria began in Galícia and spread rapidly in February and March 1846. The rebellion reached its apex at Cracow, where it was crushed by Austrian and Russian forces, which occupied the city. In November 1848, as a result of the conference at Vienna, and with the concurrence of Russia and Prussia, Cracow was absorbed into the Hapsburg Empire.

Craig, Henry Knox (1791–1869). An American soldier who was commissioned in the artillery in 1812. He served in the Mexican War [q.v.], and from 1851 to 1861 he was chief of ordnance. He refused to consider supplying the infantry with breech-loading rifles for fear the troops would consume excessive amounts of ammunition. He also argued that the increased rate of fire would lead to decreased accuracy. He was succeeded on 24 April 1861 by James Wolfe Ripley [q.v.], who was almost as old and equally backward in his thinking. On March 1865 Craig was promoted brigadier general.

Crane's Feet. See Caltrop.

Craonne, Battle of (7 March 1814), Napoleonic Wars. While Napoleon was pushing the main Allied army away from the gates of Paris, Prussian Marshal Gebhard von Blücher [q.v.] launched a new attack down the valley of the Marne and was repulsed by the French. As he was retreating across the Aisne River, Napoleon began a pursuit. Blücher planned to make a stand on the Craonne Plateau, about 15 miles southeast of Laon, while at the same time enveloping the right rear of the French with a Russian corps and 11,000 cavalry under Field Marshal Baron Ferdinand von Wintzingerode (1770–1818), but Napoleon struck first, attacking Craonne with 37,000 men on 7 March from the direction of Berry. Although generally credited as a French victory, this was an indecisive battle. It cost Napoleon 5,400 casualties; the Allies lost 5,000.

Crapaud. A British nickname for French soldiers during the Napoleonic Wars. In French, the word means toad, an ugly person, a brat, or a defect in a diamond. It also means the carriage of a mortar.

Crapaudin. A punishment used in the French army, particularly in the Armée d'Afrique [q.v.], in which it was said to have been introduced by François de Négrier in 1881, a flint-hearted officer who took command of the Foreign Legion [q.v.] in 1879. It was similar to the buck and gag [q.v.] used in the American army. Wrists and ankles were tied behind a man's back and joined. Pains in the arms, across the abdomen, in the knees, and in the ankles increased rapidly and became intolerable.

Crater. A depression or hole in the earth caused by an explosion of a mine or shell.

Crater, Battle of the. See Petersburg Mine.

Craufurd, Robert (1764–1812). A British soldier who was commissioned an ensign in the 25th Foot in 1779 at the age of fifteen and at nineteen became a captain in the 75th Foot. He fought in India in the 1790s against Tippu Tib (1749–1799), and in 1798 as a lieutenant colonel he assisted in the suppression of the Irish revolt. Promoted colonel on 28 October 1805, he commanded a brigade in the abortive British expedition to Buenos Aires [q.v.] in 1807. Later that same year he was briefly in the Iberian Peninsula, where he served under Sir John Moore [q.v.] and took part in the retreat to Corunna [q.v.]. In 1809 he returned to the peninsula in command of a brigade, soon expanded to a division, which he was to make famous as the Light Division [q.v.]. Although something of a martinet (he was called Black Bob), he proved to be a brilliant commander of light infantry. He was promoted major general on 4 June 1811. On 19 January 1812, when the walls of Ciudad Rodrigo [q.v.] were breached, Craufurd led the attack and was mortally wounded at the moment of victory. He lingered in agony until 24 January. His men buried his body in the breach.

Cravat. 1. The streamer on top of a standard pole.

2. A pompon around the blade and hilt of a sword to prevent rainwater entering the scabbard.

3. Any neckwear.

Crazy Horse (1840?–1877). Indian name: Tachunca-Uitco. An American Indian chief of the Oglala Sioux who took part in numerous raids against whites and against other Indian tribes. He played a leading role in the Fetterman Massacre on 21 December 1866 and the Wagon Box Battle [qq.v.] on 2 August 1867. Together with Sitting Bull [q.v.], he refused to obey the War Department order commanding all Sioux bands to report to Indian agencies by 1 January 1876. That year he fought in the Battle of the Little Bighorn [q.v.]. He surrendered on 6 May 1877 at the Red Cloud Agency just outside Fort Robinson near Crawford, Nebraska. [See Great Sioux War.]

When it was rumored that he was plotting to go on the warpath, he was arrested and taken to Fort Robinson, commanded by Lieutenant Colonel (brevet Brigadier General) Luther Prentice Bradley (1822–1910). There, on 5 or 7 September 1877, ostensibly while attempting to escape, he was bayoneted in the abdomen by Private William Gentles (1830?–1878) of the 14th Infantry. He died about midnight from internal bleeding.

Crazy Woman Creek, Battle of (25–26 November 1876), American Indian Wars. During the Powder River Expedition, Colonel Ranald Slidell Mackenzie [q.v.] with eleven companies of cavalry and some Indian scouts defeated in sub-zero weather a band of Northern Cheyennes under Dull Knife [q.v.] at Crazy Woman (or Bate's) Creek, near the north fork of the Powder River in Wyoming.

Creagy, Garrett O'Moore (1848–1923). A British soldier who saw service in India. As a captain in the Second Afghan War [q.v.] he won the Victoria Cross on 21–22 April 1879, when, in command of 150 men protecting the village of Kam Dakka, attacked by Muslims "in overwhelming numbers, about 1,500," he took up a defensive position in a cemetery and held it until relieved by Bengal Lancers. He was made a brigadier general in 1899 and commanded a brigade in the Boxer Rebellion [q.v.] in China. In 1907 he became a full general and from 1909 to 1914 was commander-in-chief, India.

Creedmoor Rifle Range. The largest and most complete practice range for small arms in the United States established in 1871 by the National Rifle Association [q.v.] with help from army engineers. It was 10½ miles east of New York City when it was built and was a station on the Long Island Railroad. The area is now in the borough of Queens.

In the first competition held there in 1873 militiamen proved to be better shots than regulars.

Creek War (1812–14). In the nineteenth century there existed in America two geographically separate Creek tribes that shared a common language and culture but little else. The Upper Creeks lived in the valleys of the Alabama, Tallapoosa, and Coosa rivers; the Lower Creeks lived in the area of the lower Chattahoochie and lower Flint rivers. During the War of 1812 [q.v.], when the Upper Creek Indians, a settled agricultural people who sided with the British, became restive, Colonel James Caller (1758–1819) mustered a militia force in Clarke County, Alabama, and marched against them. On 27 July 1813 he fought the Battle of Burnt Corn [q.v.], in which his militia suffered two killed and a number wounded, including Samuel Dale [q.v.], who commanded one of the companies. After the battle the militia mustered itself out and never assembled again. This was the first battle of the Creek War.

On 30 August 1813 Red Eagle [q.v.] led Upper Creek warriors (Red Sticks) in a sudden attack upon Fort Mims [q.v.], a settlement in Alabama at the confluence of the Alabama and Tombigbee rivers, 35 miles above Mobile. Some 550 men, women, and children were at the fort, and most were massacred. The Creeks then took up a strong defensive position at Econochaca in present-day Lowndes County on the Alabama

Creek War *Creek leader William Weatherford surrenders to Andrew Jackson after the battle at Horseshoe Bend*

River, about 20 miles west of present-day Montgomery, Alabama, from which they raided the surrounding countryside.

Andrew Jackson [q.v.], then a major general in the Tennessee militia, took the field and defeated the Creeks at Tallasahatchee on 3 November 1813 and again at Talladega [q.v.], 44 miles east of Birmingham, Alabama, on 9 November.

On 18 November in the same year John Cocke (1772–1854), a Tennessee politician, philanthropist (the University of Tennessee sits on land he donated), and militia major general, took it upon himself to order militia Major General James White (1747–1821) to attack the towns of the Hillabee Creeks in Alabama. By the time White, with 1,000 militia, reached the settlements the Hillabees had already agreed to surrender and were in the process of arranging terms with Andrew Jackson. Nevertheless, White attacked, killing 60, taking 250 prisoner, and burning two towns. The Hillabee Creeks understandably felt they had been betrayed, and the surviving warriors who renewed their attacks proved to be formidable foes.

On 23 December 1813 Brigadier General Ferdinand Leigh Claiborne (1773–1815) led 1,000 Mississippi volunteers in an attack that dispersed them. The Creeks regrouped, however, and on 27 January 1814 they launched an attack on a force of Georgia militia camped at Calabee Creek [q.v.] and routed them.

On 22 January 1814 Andrew Jackson fought a difficult engagement with Creeks on the banks of the Emuckfau Creek in present Tallapoosa County, east-central Alabama, and two days later fought another at a creek crossing near a place called Enitachopco. Jackson lost 20 killed and 75 wounded, some mortally; Creek losses were put at 189 killed.

The war ended only when with 2,000 men Jackson defeated the main Creek band of 900 in the Battle of Horseshoe Bend [q.v.] on the Tallapoosa (or Tohopeka) River on 27 March 1814. Even then, hostile Creeks held out in Florida, where Major Uriah Blue (1799?–1836), leading a large force of soldiers and friendly Indians, scoured the western swamps and woods, killing and capturing large numbers.

Crémaillère. An indented or zigzag line of entrenchments.

Crémaillère line

Crénaux. Holes made in the walls of a fortification that are wider on the inside than on the outside, giving the person shooting from inside a wide arc of fire while presenting a narrow target.

Crenel or Crenelle. See Battlements.

Crenellated. Having battlements [q.v.].

Crescent, Order of the. A Turkish military order, similar to European orders of chivalry [q.v.], founded in 1801.

Crespo, Joaquín (1845–1898). A Venezuelan soldier born in Cuba who led the revolution that deposed President Entozoa Palace in 1892 and became dictator of Venezuela. It was during his dictatorship that the boundary dispute between Venezuela and Britain created a crisis between Britain and the United States in 1895–97.

Crest, Military. See Military Crest.

Cretan Revolts. In 1821, when revolution against Turkish rule broke out in continental Greece, Turkish janissaries [q.v.], noted for their cruelty, began a massacre of Christians on the island of Crete. The archbishop of Candia (Heraklion) and his congregation were slaughtered in the cathedral. In response, Christian Cretans rose in revolt and occupied the countryside; the Turks and Greek Muslims fled to the fortified cities. In 1824 Mohammed Ali [q.v.] of Egypt, at the request of the Turkish sultan, evacuated the janissaries and with his own troops ruthlessly crushed the revolt. The island was not returned to Turkey but was ceded to Egypt until 1840, when it came once more under direct Turkish rule.

In 1856 there was again an insurrection; reforms were promised but not effected. In 1866 another uprising burst forth in both the urban areas and the wild countryside around Sphakia, a coastal town in southwest Crete. A Turkish army sent to repress it was forced to surrender. In revenge the Turks attacked and blew up a fortified monastery in which hundreds of women and children had taken refuge. After cutting wide swaths of destruction, the main Turkish army returned to Turkey, leaving garrisons behind.

Discontent festered, and in 1895 a group of rebellious Cretan leaders met in the mountains and formed an *epitropé* (committee of reform). Its membership grew rapidly, and in April 1896 they invested a garrison town. In May rioting broke out on the north coast, in Canea, the Crete capital since 1841. Greece sent an army to help the Christians, and war was averted only by the intervention of the Great Powers, but sympathy for the Cretans had been aroused, particularly among the Greeks, who declared war on Turkey [see Graeco-Turkish War].

On 4 February 1897 a Greek force landed near Canea and claimed the island for Greece. This inspired the Christians to massacre their Turkish and Greek Muslim neighbors. Again the European powers intervened. European forces occupied Canea, and warships bombarded the insurgent positions. Notes presented to the Turkish and Greek governments demanding the withdrawal of the Greek fleet and the evacuation of Turkish forces from the island. On 20 March Cretan autonomy was proclaimed, but pacification was delayed by Turkish foot-dragging and the inability of the Great Powers to agree on a governor-general. Discontent and Greek-Turkish animosity persisted throughout the next century.

Crew Served. A weapon such as a piece of artillery manned or operated by two or more men.

Crimean War (1853–1856). A war between Russia and the Allied forces of Turkey, France, Britain, and, later, Sardinia. The war began as a Russo-Turkish war, Russia claiming the right to protect the Holy Land and the Christians, particularly Slavic Christians, in the Turkish Empire. The Turks rejected this claim. On 20 March 1853 the Russians crossed the Danube and occupied the provinces of Moldavia and Walachia. Eight days later Britain and France declared war on Russia. In July 1853 Russia invaded Turkish-held Rumania. Britain and France responded by sending fleets to Constantinople (Istanbul). On 4 October 1853 Turkey declared war on Russia and sent an army under Omar Pasha [q.v.] northward. On 4 November the Turks defeated a Russian force at Oltenita [q.v.], the first Turkish victory over

a Russian army in more than a century. From this point on, except for two abortive engagements in the Baltic Sea, the war was fought almost entirely on the Crimean Peninsula in Ukraine.

In June 1854, when an Anglo-French force of 55,000 landed at Varna, a fortified seaport on the Black Sea in northeast Bulgaria, it found that the Russians, at the insistence of Austria, had withdrawn, thus ending the reason for the Allies to go to war. But the war, once begun, continued.

According to General Edward Hamley [q.v.], the British landed in the Crimea knowing "as little . . . as knight errants, heroes of the romances of Don Quixote, knew of the dim enchanted region where, amid vague perils, and trusting so much to happy chance, they were to seek some predatory giant."

From September 1854 to April 1855 the effective strength of the British army was 31,333, but victims of inefficient sanitation, improper clothing, and inadequate quarters, 9,762 men died from diseases, including cholera, at a rate of 235.8 per 1,000. In the better-prepared French army during the same period the average effective strength was 49,150, but deaths from disease numbered 9,523, never higher than 75.5 per 1,000.

In spite of these losses and a serious lack of artillery, cavalry, and, above all, land transport, particularly among the British, Lord Raglan [q.v.], the British commander, was ordered to quit Varna and to cooperate with the French force under

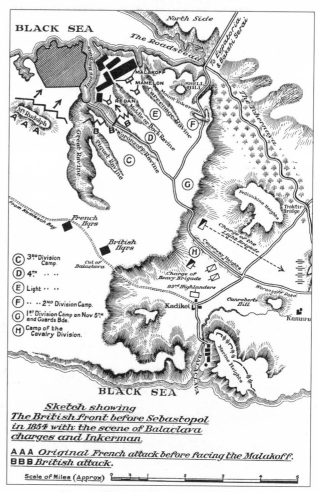

Crimean War *Map showing the British front before Sevastopol in 1854*

Marshal Armand St. Arnaud [q.v.] in an attack on the great Russian naval base at Sevastopol.

On 14–15 September Allied troops landed in Calamita Bay on the Crimean Peninsula. They found their route to Sevastapol blocked by a Russian force under Prince Aleksandr Menshikov [q.v.]. On 20 September on the Alma River the Allies fought and won the first battle of the war [see Alma, Battle of the].

Military intelligence was a neglected discipline in the nineteenth century. The great difficulty the Allied forces faced, as Prince Albert had wisely surmised, was "the absence of all information about the Crimea itself." Undeterred, the French and British forces pushed blindly on to besiege Sevastopol, where they were to be joined by a Turkish force under Omar Pasha.

A rapid advance might well have resulted in a quick capture, but the advance was slow. St. Arnaud died and was replaced by General François Canrobert [q.v.]. When the city was eventually besieged, the besiegers, camping on desolate heights, faced a winter campaign still without adequate preparation for its rigors. In October and November Russian attacks at Balaclava and Inkerman [qq.v.] were repulsed, but diseases, inadequate supplies, and bitter cold weather without sufficient fuel took a hideous toll on the Allies. Alleviation of their sufferings was found by those few sick and wounded fortunate enough to survive and be transported to the hospital established by Florence Nightingale [q.v.] in an old Turkish barracks at Scutari (Üsküdar), across the Bosporus from Constantinople (Istanbul). Of the first 25,000 British troops sent to the Crimea, 18,000 were dead within a year, most felled by diseases. The appalling conditions of the British army in the Crimea were vividly reported by William Russell [q.v.] in the *Times,* and a horrified British public demanded army reform.

In 1855 the Sardinians entered the war, sending a division under the Marchese di La Marmora [q.v.]. On 18 June the main attack on Sevastopol was launched by the French. It failed because French General Aimable Pélissier [q.v.], who had replaced Canrobert, did not wait until he had adequate artillery support.

On 28 June Lord Raglan died. He was replaced by General James Simpson (1792–1868), a good soldier but not up to the responsibilities suddenly thrust upon him.

The final assault was made on 8 September 1855. The French successfully attacked the Malakoff [q.v.] redoubt, and the British made an unsuccessful assault upon the redan [q.v.]. The French fight for the Malakoff was the first time in history that an attack was made at a prespecified moment by officers with synchronized watches. The French victory induced the Russians to abandon the city.

Although the great Russian field army had not been defeated, the fall of Sevastopol virtually ended the war. On 1 February 1856 the preliminaries for peace were begun, and a peace treaty was signed in Paris on 30 March. [See Sevastapol, Siege of; Inkerman, Battle of; Light Brigade, Charge of; Balaclava, Battle of; Malakoff, Attacks on; Redan, British attacks upon; Nightingale, Florence; Soyer, Alexis.]

Crimes, Military. Soldiers in all armies are expected to obey their countries' civil laws and to abide by a long list of specifically military regulations and laws. In the nineteenth century the most serious military offenses were desertion, striking an officer, and sleeping on duty in the face of the enemy.

Among the common but less serious offenses were drunkenness, loss of equipment or accoutrements, petty theft, possession of a dirty musket or rifle, appearing late for parade, contraction of a venereal disease, or being unshaven. "Answering back" was usually considered an offense. In the British army a man could be charged with "dumb insolence" should he not appear sufficiently contrite or submissive when admonished.

In the American army, freedom of speech was considerably impaired in spite of the Constitution. It was a court-martial offense for a soldier to use "contemptuous or disrespectful words" about the president, the vice-president, and the Congress or against the chief magistrate or the governor or legislature of any state in which he was stationed.

Crimp. British slang for a civilian agent or an army recruiter, known as a crimping sergeant, who provided soldiers for the service by kidnapping, drugging, decoying, or other illegal means. Lord St. Vincent (1735–1823) spoke of "the vile crimps who recruit for the foreign regiments in Spain." Crimps also supplied the Royal Navy in the days of impressment—and even much later. During the American Civil War the term was used for bounty brokers, men who for a commission enticed men to enlist and stole their bounty.

Crimping. 1. The process by which a bullet is secured to a cartridge case or a blasting cap to a fuze.

2. The use of illegal means to secure recruits.

Crimping House. A place where young men were entrapped into enlisting in the British army by crimps [q.v.]. On 16 September 1794 a young man was killed while attempting to escape such a house, and the ensuing scandal caused a riot.

Cristinos. The adherents of Queen Isabella II (1830–1904) in the Carlist Wars [q.v.]

Crittenden, George Bibb (1812–1880). An American soldier who was graduated from West Point in 1832 and served in the Black Hawk War in that year. In 1833 he resigned his commission and then studied law. Later he emigrated to Texas, where he joined the Texan army and on the ill-fated expedition to attack Mier [q.v.] was one of those taken prisoner. To deal with their captives, the Mexicans counted into a container one bean for each man; one-tenth of the beans were black. Those who drew black beans were to be shot; the rest were to be imprisoned. Crittenden drew a white bean and

Crimean War *Russian cavalry and Allied infantry in the Crimea*

passed it to a friend. When he drew again, that bean too was white. He returned to the American army in 1846 to fight in the Mexican War [q.v.], in which he commanded a company of Kentucky riflemen and earned a brevet to major.

On 10 June 1861 he resigned as a lieutenant colonel in the mounted rifles to join the Confederate army as a brigadier general. He was soon promoted major general. On 19 January 1862 he attacked with 4,000 men a Union force of about the same strength under George H. Thomas [q.v.] at Mill Springs [q.v.] and was defeated, losing all his guns and baggage. For this he was arrested and censured. He resigned in anger and for the remainder of the war served as a civilian volunteer staff officer. After the war he became state librarian of Kentucky at Frankfort.

He was the older brother of Union General Thomas Leonidas Crittenden [q.v.].

Crittenden, Thomas Leonidas (1819–1893). A Kentucky lawyer and soldier who served in the Mexican War [q.v.] as an infantry lieutenant colonel and aide to General Zachary Taylor [q.v.]. He fought at Buena Vista [q.v.] and was promoted colonel. After the war he returned to Kentucky to practice law, and in 1860 he became a major general in the Kentucky militia. In the first months of the American Civil War he commanded a Union division in the Army of the Ohio. In September 1861 he was promoted brigadier general of volunteers, and on 6–7 April 1862 he distinguished himself in the Battle of Shiloh [q.v.]. In July of that year he was appointed a major general. He commanded a corps at Chickamauga [q.v.] and was one of the four generals upon whom General William Rosecrans [q.v.] tried to shift some of his responsibility for the disaster. All were acquitted, but Crittenden resigned his volunteer commission on 13 December 1864. On 28 July 1866 he was offered and accepted a commission as colonel of the 32nd Infantry. He served in that rank until he retired in 1881.

He was the younger brother of Confederate General George B. Crittenden and a first cousin of Thomas Turpin Crittenden [qq.v.].

Crittenden, Thomas Turpin (1825–1890). An American soldier and lawyer, the son of a senator, who, in the American Civil War, on 19 April 1861 was elected a captain in the 6th Indiana. He fought in the Battle of Shiloh [q.v.] and on 28 April 1862 was promoted brigadier general. On 13 July he was in command of a post at Murfreesboro, Tennessee, when he and all in his vicinity were captured by Confederate General Nathan Bedford Forrest [q.v.]. General Don Carlos Buell [q.v.] said of his conduct there: "Few more disgraceful examples of neglect of duty and lack of good conduct can be found in the history of wars." He was to see no further useful service. He resigned on 5 May 1863 and moved to San Diego, where he became a realtor.

Crockett, David ("Davy") (1786–1836). An American frontiersman, Whig politician, and sometimes soldier of almost no formal education about whom many myths have been woven. He served as a scout for Andrew Jackson (q.v.) in the Creek War (q.v.). He claimed to be a mighty "b'ar hunter" and to have killed 105 bears in 1822 alone. He was elected to the Tennessee legislature and served three terms in Congress, where he tried to abolish West Point. In 1835, when defeated

for election to the House of Representatives, he moved to Texas to join the Texan struggle for independence from Mexico. (see: Texas War of Independence). He died at the Alamo (q.v.) on 6 March 1836.

Davy Crockett fells a Mexican soldier at the Alamo (an unlikely event).

Croghan, George (1791–1849). An American soldier who first saw action as a volunteer aide to General William Henry Harrison [q.v.] in the Battle of Tippecanoe [q.v.] on 7 November 1811, after which, on Harrison's recommendation, he was commissioned a captain in the 17th Infantry on 12 March 1812. A year later, although not yet twenty-two years old, he was promoted major and was placed in charge of Fort Stephenson on the Sandusky River, on the site of present Fremont, Ohio. There on 1–2 August 1813 with about 160 men he repulsed repeated attacks by 1,200 British regulars with several fieldpieces assisted by a troop of Indians commanded by Colonel Henry Proctor and supported by a number of Indian allies [see Fort Stephenson, Attack upon]. The Americans suffered only 1 killed and 7 wounded; British losses were thought to be heavy. Indian losses are unknown. On 3 August the British retreated.

Croghan was hailed as a hero and promoted to lieutenant colonel. On 13 February 1835 Congress belatedly awarded him a gold medal with "suitable emblems and devices in testimony of the high sense entertained by Congress of his gallantry and good conduct in the defense of Ft. Stephenson, Ohio." On 31 March 1817 he resigned from the army and was appointed postmaster of New Orleans. On 21 December 1825 he was commissioned a colonel and appointed inspector general of the army. During the Mexican War [q.v.] he served under General Zachary Taylor [q.v.] and was present at the Battle of Monterrey [q.v.].

Cronjé, Pieter ("Piet") Arnoldus (1840?–1911). A South African soldier and politician who led the Boer forces in the First Anglo-Boer War [q.v.]. In 1881 he distinguished himself as a commandant in the siege of the British at Potchefstroom [q.v.]. At Doornkop on 2 January 1896 he led the commando that forced the surrender of Jameson and his men [see Jameson Raid]. In the Second Anglo-Boer War [q.v.] he commanded on the western frontier, where he initiated the siege of Kimberley [q.v.] and successfully opposed the advance of Lord Methuen [q.v.]. He fought delaying actions at Belmont, at Graspan [qq.v.], and on the Modder River. In December 1899 he completely repulsed Lord Methuen [q.v.] and held him in place for two months until the arrival of Lord Roberts [qq.v.].

Unable to prevent the relief of Kimberley, he tried to retreat eastward with his force, but he was surrounded by superior forces under Lord Roberts at Paardeberg [q.v.] and forced to surrender on 27 February 1900. He was held a prisoner of war on the island of St. Helena in the South Atlantic until the end of the war.

Crook, George (1828–1890). An American soldier who was graduated from West Point in 1852 and initially served in the Northwest, mostly in northern California and Washington, where in 1857 he was wounded by an arrow while fighting the Pit River Indians; he carried the arrowhead to his grave. On 14 May 1861, at the beginning of the American Civil War, he was promoted captain, and on 13 September he was made colonel of the 36th Ohio, which he led in the fighting in western (West) Virginia. He was wounded at Lewisburg on 23 May 1862 but recovered to fight at South Mountain and Antietam [qq.v.], having been made a brigadier general on 7 September. In 1863 he commanded a cavalry division in the Army of the Cumberland and took part in the Chickamauga Campaign. He succeeded General David Hunter [q.v.] as commander of the Army of West Virginia, which he led in Philip Sheridan's [q.v.] Shenandoah Valley Campaign, taking part in the fighting at Winchester, Cedar Creek, and Fisher's Hill [qq.v.]. On 21 October 1864 he became a major general of volunteers.

On the night of 21–22 February 1865 he suffered the humiliation of being captured, not in battle but at the Revere Hotel in Cumberland, Maryland, in a raid by 64 partisans (one of whom was his future brother-in-law); he and General Benjamin Franklin Kelley (1807–1891), captured in the same raid, were taken to prison in Richmond, Virginia. Crook, the highest-ranking Union officer ever captured, was exchanged on 20 March in time to take part in the Battle of Five Forks [q.v.] and the pursuit of Lee to Appomattox [q.v.].

After the war, in the army reorganization of 1866, he became a lieutenant colonel in the 23rd U.S. Infantry and was sent to Idaho, where by his bravery, powers of endurance, and persistence, he succeeded in ending a conflict with Paiute and Pit Indians that had dragged on for years. In June 1871 he was transferred to Arizona, where the Apaches under Cochise, Geronimo [qq.v.], and other leaders were terrorizing white settlements. He was so successful in subduing the Apaches that he was promoted two grades to brigadier general on 29 October 1873.

In 1875 he took command of the Department of the Platte, where, after the discovery of gold in the Black Hills and the invasion of Indian lands by hordes of rapacious prospectors, he was heavily engaged in fighting the Sioux and the Cheyennes under Crazy Horse [q.v.]. All of 1876 was spent in the field [see Great Sioux War]. In March he rode out of Fort Fetterman, located on a sagebrush-covered plateau on the south bank of the North Platte River in Wyoming, to join forces with General Alfred H. Terry [q.v.] on the Yellowstone River. On 17 June at the Rosebud [q.v.] he encountered a force under Crazy Horse that has been estimated at between 1,200 and 6,000 (the former figure is the most probable) and, in a bitterly contested battle, forced the Indians to retire.

Six days later George Custer [q.v.] and his 7th Cavalry met disaster on the Little Bighorn [q.v.] and Crook marched for the battle site. To improve mobility, he took no wagons; supplies ran out, and the trek came to be called the starvation march [q.v.]. Actual starvation was averted only when on 9 September 1876 at a place called Slim Buttes [q.v.] he captured the Sioux village of American Horse (1830?–1876), and his men devoured the Indians' dried buffalo meat.

On 4 September 1882 he was again sent to Arizona and organized and led expeditions against the marauding Chiricahua Apaches under Geronimo [q.v.]. He pursued them deep into the Sierra Madre of Mexico and in 1883 brought them back to the reservation in Arizona. In 1885, when Geronimo and a small band fled and again spread terror among the whites, Crook once more tracked them but was

Crook, George *General George Crook, leader of the Black Hills Expedition*

relieved by General Nelson A. Miles. On 6 April 1888 he was again a major general. He was given command of the Division of Missouri and made his headquarters in Chicago, where he died on 21 March 1890.

He gained a reputation as the best Indian fighter and the most original military thinker the American army produced. He relied upon mule trains rather than wagons to increase his mobility, and he pitted Indian against Indian by his use of Indian scouts. In 1886 he told a reporter: "Nothing breaks them up like turning their own people against them. . . . It is not merely a question of catching them better with Indians, but of a broader and more enduring aim—their disintegration." But Crook was also a champion of Indian rights and harbored a deep antipathy for those whites who cheated or exploited Indians.

Crooked Creek, Battle of (13 May 1859), American Indian Wars. Major Earl Van Dorn [q.v.] led some 500 troops and 58 Indians from the Brazos Reservation in an attack upon Comanches in a deep, bush-covered ravine in the Nascutunga Valley, 15 miles south of old Fort Atkinson, Texas. The Comanches, it was said, "fought without asking or giving quarter until there was but one left to bend a bow." None escaped; 49 Comanches were killed, and 5 wounded; 32 women and the 5 wounded Indians were taken prisoner. Two officers were badly wounded: Captain (later General) Edmund Kirby Smith [q.v.] was shot through the thigh, and Lieutenant (later General) Fitzhugh Lee [q.v.] was struck by an arrow that passed through his body and protruded from his back. In addition, 2 soldiers were killed, and 9 wounded; 2 of the Indian allies were killed, and 2 others mortally wounded.

Croppy. British army slang term for an Irish rebel.

Cross Keys, Battle of [8–9 June 1862], American Civil War. The penultimate battle of Thomas ("Stonewall") Jackson's Valley Campaign was fought against Union General John Frémont [q.v.] near the village of Cross Keys at the southern end of the Massanutten Mountain range in the Valley of Virginia. Jackson had little to do with the battle, which was fought and won by his subordinate, Major General Richard Ewell [q.v.].

Union losses were 114 killed, 443 wounded, and 127 missing; Confederate losses were 41 killed, 232 wounded, and 15 missing. [See Port Republic.]

Cross Keys *Battle of Cross Keys, 1862*

Crowning. Occupying or fortifying a height or a parapet.

Crow's Feet. A popular name for caltrops [q.v.].

Crow-Sioux War. An unrecorded but indisputable conflict that took place in mid-century in which the Sioux Indians took by conquest the lands of the Crow Indians on the American plains (later claimed by the Sioux to be their "ancestral lands"). Crows were always eager to scout for American forces operating against the Sioux.

Crozet, Claude (1790–1864). An army officer, educator, and engineer, born in France and educated at the École Polytechnique [q.v.] in Paris, from which he was graduated in 1807. He was commissioned in the artillery and served in the Napoleonic Wars. For two years he was a Russian prisoner but survived to serve his emperor again during the Hundred Days [q.v.]. In 1816 he emigrated to the United States and, on the recommendation of the Marquis de Lafayette (1757–1834) and others, was appointed assistant professor of engineering at West Point, where he remained for seven years.

In 1823 he resigned to become state engineer of Virginia, a post he held until 1832. When the Virginia Military Institute [q.v.] was organized in 1839, he was appointed to the Board of Visitors and was elected its first president.

Crozier, William (1855–1942). An American soldier and inventor who was graduated from West Point in 1876. After three years fighting Sioux and Bannock Indians on the plains, he became an instructor of mathematics at West Point, where he remained until in 1884 he was appointed superintendent of the Watertown Arsenal [q.v.] in Massachusetts. After studying artillery in Europe, he was given charge of the construction of gun carriages for the army. He was promoted captain in 1890. In 1896, with General Adelbert R. Buffington [q.v.], he invented the Buffington-Crozier disappearing gun [q.v.].

He later served in the Philippines and was chief of ordnance on the staff of General Adna R. Chaffee [q.v.] during the Boxer Rebellion [q.v.] in China. In 1901 he was promoted brigadier general and appointed chief of ordnance. He later became a major general and served in the First World War.

Cry Havoc. The order to take no prisoners in an assault. This expression was little used in the nineteenth century. [See Black Flags.]

Cuautla Amilpas / Cuautla, Battle of (February–May 1812), Mexican War of Independence. Some 6,000 Mexicans and other revolutionaries under José María Morelos [q.v.] repulsed an attack by 7,000 loyalists under Félix María Calleja del Rey [q.v.] near the present resort town of Cuautla in south-central Mexico, 18 miles southeast of Cuernavaca. The loyalists fled, but Calleja was reinforced and returned to the attack on 1 March and laid siege to the town. On the night of 2 May the rebels withdrew. They were attacked, and there was much confused fighting in the dark, after which they dispersed with orders to regroup at Izúcar [See: Izúcar Battle of].

Rebel losses were 500 killed and wounded; loyalist losses were about 1,500.

Cuba, American Invasion of (June–July 1898), Spanish-American War. U.S. troops under Major General William

Crow-Sioux War *Fight between Sioux and Crow forces, drawn by a Crow, 1884*

Rufus Shafter [q.v.] left Tampa, Florida, on 14 June 1898 for Cuba. The expeditionary force consisted of fifteen regiments of regulars (most of the regular army) and three regiments of volunteers, including the Rough Riders [q.v.] under Theodore Roosevelt [q.v.]. On 22–25 June the force debarked without opposition at Daiquirí, near Santiago de Cuba.

After a skirmish at Las Guásimas [q.v.], the Americans fought and defeated the Spanish on 1 July in the battles of San Juan Hill and El Caney [qq.v.]. On 3 July the U.S. navy won a victory in the Battle of Santiago Bay, and on 17 July the Spanish at Santiago, unaware that the Americans were succumbing in large numbers to yellow fever, capitulated.

Cuban Revolutions. Sharp social distinctions between Creoles (those born in Cuba) and the *peninsulares* (those born in Spain) and Cuba's isolation from Spain, particularly during the long Peninsular War [q.v.], led to frequent plotting against Spanish rule and many aborted insurrections.

Between 1849 and 1851 there were three filibustering expeditions from the United States, all aborted [see Filibuster]. Two of these were led by a Spanish general, Narciso López [q.v.]. Between 1850 and 1868 discontent with a particularly ineffective and corrupt government fanned revolts.

The Ten Years' War [q.v.] began on 10 October 1868, when Carlos Manuel de Céspedes (1819–1874), a wealthy landowner, proclaimed a revolution promising reforms, including the gradual emancipation of slaves with compensation to owners. The long war was marked by excesses on both sides; as the government became increasingly repressive, the rebels became more cruel and violent. In January 1878, by the Convention of Zanjón, the government agreed to an amnesty and pledged reforms, including the liberation of slaves. The promised reforms were more superficial than substantive, and the level of discontent increased. There was a Little War [q.v.] in 1879–1880, but it was easily suppressed.

On 23 February 1895 previously accepted constitutional guarantees were suspended and the leaders of the Ten Years' War—among them, Máximo Gómez y Báez, Antonio Maceo, José Julian Martí, and Calixto García y Íñiguez [qq.v.]—again rose in revolt. The Ten Years' War had been fought almost entirely in the eastern provinces, but the renewed fighting extended into the western provinces, where it was at its fiercest.

Here the Spaniards constructed lines of blockhouses and barbed wire and herded people into concentration camps, where thousands died of diseases and starvation [see Concentration Camps].

In the United States, sympathy for the Cuban people was high, and many Americans argued for intervention. When, on 15 February 1898, the USS *Maine* was blown up in Havana Harbor—by whom is unknown—the U.S. government was supplied with an excuse for intervention. The American demand on 20 April that Spanish troops leave Cuba was rejected, and the Spanish-American War began.

Cuban Revolutions *Cubans fight from tree tops.*

Cuesta, Gregorio García de la (1740–1812). A Spanish soldier who became a cadet in 1758 and was commissioned in the Granada Infantry in 1761. He served in the invasion of Portugal and distinguished himself at the siege of Almeida. In 1799 he took part in the early days of the siege of Gibraltar. He then served in the West Indies, and in 1781 he participated in the attack on Jamaica. He helped quell an insurrection in Peru and in 1791 returned to Spain. He first fought the French in 1793, and in 1795 he occupied Cerdagne (Cerdaña) in the eastern Pyrenees. In 1796 he was promoted lieutenant general and commanded the troops in Minorca. In 1808 he was named captain general of Old Castile. He was defeated at Río Seco on 14 July 1808 and again at Medellín [qq.v.] on 28 March 1809. He took part in the Talavera Campaign, but he was unwilling or unable to cooperate fully with Wellington at Talavera [q.v.]. He was paralyzed by a stroke soon after.

He was known as a stubborn and cantankerous curmudgeon, more disliked by his allies than by his enemies.

Cugnot, Nicolas Joseph (1725–1804). A French military engineer who invented a three-wheeled steam-driven artillery carriage. It was capable of a speed of 2 to 3 mph but it failed to gain the interest of his superiors.

Cuirass. A jerkin or vest originally of leather, as the name suggests, that in the nineteenth century was made of metal. It was composed of a backplate and front plate, each with a ridge running down the middle. The plates were fastened to each other at the sides. Cuirasses were worn by heavy cavalry in many European armies and sometimes by sappers digging the leading saps in siege warfare.

Cuirassiers. Heavy cavalry wearing cuirasses [q.v.]. Perhaps the first European army to have cuirassiers was the Austrian army, which had *Kyrissers* as early as 1484. In 1705 it had twenty regiments, but in 1866 they were converted to dragoons. In France a regiment was formed in 1666. Napoleon had fourteen regiments by 1804, and they were imitated in many other European armies. Westphalia and Saxony each had two regiments; the duchy of Warsaw had one regiment. In the British army the Life Guards and Horse Guards [qq.v.] were cuirassiers; in the Russian army, the first rank of cuirassiers in battle was armed with lances.

Cullen Rifle. A rifle with a magazine that could hold up to fifty rounds of ammunition.

Cullum, George Washington (1809–1892). An American soldier who graduated third in his class from West Point in 1833 and served in the American Civil War in staff positions. In September 1864 he was appointed superintendent of the U.S. Military Academy, an institution to which he was devoted. The year after his retirement from the army in 1874 he married the wealthy widow of General Henry Halleck [q.v.], who was also a granddaughter of Alexander Hamilton. He used much of her money to erect a memorial hall at West Point (Cullum Hall) and to compile and publish a register of the academy's graduates. He also helped form an association of graduates that is still in existence.

Culp's Hill. A wooded eminence that was a prominent physical feature on the Gettysburg battlefield in the American Civil War. It towered over Cemetery Hill and Cemetery Ridge [q.v.] and was the anchor for the northeastern end of the Union position. It was attacked on 1 July by a division under Confederate Major General Edward Johnson [q.v.]. Although it was held only by a single Federal brigade under Brigadier General George Sears Greene (1801–1899), one of the oldest field commanders in the Union army, the three Confederate brigades were repulsed.

The struggle for the hill resumed on 3 July. The battle raged for seven hours. Musketry and artillery fire destroyed one of the area's finest oak forests, but the Federals could not be dislodged.

Culp's Hill *Confederate attack on Culp's Hill, Gettysburg*

Cuirassiers
Lieutenant of the 8th Régiment de Cuirassier, France, 1810

Cult of the Offensive. The military doctrine holding that the offensive is always, or almost always, preferable to the defensive. After the Franco-Prussian War [q.v.] this was widely accepted in many European armies, particularly in the French and German armies.

Cumberland, Army of the. A Union army formed in October 1862, during the American Civil War, and led by General William Starke Rosecrans [q.v.] in the Chickamauga Campaign of August–September 1863. In October Rosecrans was replaced by George Thomas [q.v.]. The army, reformed to consist of IV, XIV and XX Corps, about 70,000 men, fought throughout the Atlanta Campaign [q.v.] but was broken up after the fall of Atlanta [see Atlanta, Battle of].

Cumbermere, Viscount. See Cotton, Stapleton.

Cumming, Kate (1835–1909). A Scottish-born Confederate volunteer nurse in the American Civil War. She cared for the wounded at Shiloh, Corinth, Chattanooga [qq.v.], and elsewhere.

Cunette or Cuvette. A small drain at the bottom of a trench or sap to carry off rainwater.

Curare. A dried, aqueous, poisonous extract used by some South American Indians to tip arrows.

Cureton, Charles Robert (1790–1849). One of only a handful of British soldiers who, commissioned from the ranks, rose to high rank and distinction as a combat commander in the nineteenth century. He was commissioned as ensign in the Shropshire militia at the age of sixteen and shortly after was promoted lieutenant. It was said that "his habits were somewhat prodigal," and to avoid arrest, he fled to London. There he enlisted under the name Charles Roberts in the 4th Light Dragoons. In 1809 he was sent to Portugal, where he soon became a noncommissioned officer. During the Peninsular War he participated in the battles of Talavera, Busaco, and Fuentes de Oñoro [qq.v.], where he received a saber slash on his left hand and suffered a fractured skull. He took part in the siege of Badajoz and the battles of Salamanca, Vitoria, Orthez, Tarbes, and Toulouse [qq.v.]. On 1 October 1810 he was severely wounded by a rifle ball in his right leg at the crossing of the Mondego River near Coimbra. In 1814 he was commissioned in the 40th Foot under his real name. In 1825–26 he was in India with the 16th Lancers and took part in the siege and capture of Bhurtpore [q.v.]. In the First Afghan War he took part in the siege and capture of Ghazni [q.v.]. At the Battle of Maharajpore [q.v.] in 1843 he commanded a brigade of cavalry. During the First Sikh War as a major general he commanded the cavalry at the Battle of Aliwal [q.v.] and fought at Sobraon [q.v.]. In the Second Sikh War [q.v.] he was killed at the Battle of Ramnagar [q.v.] on 22 November 1849.

Curtain. A wall or portion of a rampart between two supporting bastions or between a bastion and a gate.

Curtain Angle. The angle formed by the flank of a bastion and the curtain.

Curtis, Samuel Ryan (1805–1866). An American soldier who was graduated from West Point in 1831 and commissioned in the 7th Infantry. He fought in the Mexican War [q.v.] and saw action at Contreras and Chapultepec [qq.v.]. He resigned his commission at the end of the war and became a successful civil engineer. At the beginning of the American Civil War he rejoined the army as colonel of the 2nd Iowa Infantry. On 17 May 1861 he was promoted brigadier general of volunteers, and on 23 March 1862, major general. He commanded the Union army that stopped the Confederates at Pea Ridge [q.v.], Arkansas. After the war he was appointed an Indian commissioner.

Curupayty / Curupaity, Battle of (22 September 1866), War of the Triple Alliance. Allied forces under Venancio Flores [q.v.] attempted to dislodge Paraguayan forces under Francisco Solana López [q.v.] from strongly entrenched positions at a bend of the Paraguay River in northeast Paraguay just west of Ayacucho. There Paraguayan men, women, and children had dug a ditch 6 feet deep and 11 feet wide from Río Paraguay on the west to Lake Méndez on the east. The Allies shelled it with eight ironclads and then landed 11,000

Brazilian and 7,000 Argentine troops, who, caught in a devastating enfilading fire, were forced to retreat. They left behind 9,000 killed and wounded, who were thrown into a lagoon to the crocodiles. Among the Allied dead was the only son of Argentine President Domingo Faustino Sarmiento (1811–1888). Paraguayan casualties were 54. The Argentine army was knocked out of the war. Flores abandoned his army and returned to Montevideo. This was Paraguay's greatest victory in the war; it was also its last.

Cush. 1. A campaign dish of the American Civil War. Typically, morsels of beef were mixed with corn bread or hardtack and fried in bacon fat.

2. In British usage, a weighted weapon similar to a blackjack.

Custer, Elizabeth Bacon (1841–1933). The wife of George Armstrong Custer [q.v.] who jealously guarded the reputation of her hero husband. On 30 August 1879 at West Point some three thousand people were present for the dedication of a statue of General Custer by the artist James Wilson Alexander MacDonald (1815–1891). Mrs. Custer refused to attend because she had not been consulted about its design. By persistent complaints and her considerable influence she managed to have the statue removed in 1884. In 1906 she decided it would be appropriate to have the head and shoulders detached and displayed. Although on 20 June 1906 Brigadier General Albert Leopold Mills (1860?–1916), the superintendent at West Point, assured her that this had been done, no part of the statue can now be found.

Mrs. Custer was the author of *Boots and Saddles* (1885) and other accounts of her life with Custer in Dakota Territory.

Custer, George Armstrong (1839–1876). An American soldier who was graduated at the bottom of his class at West Point in 1861. Three days after graduation he took part in the First Battle of Bull Run, and he went on to fight in every battle but one of the Union Army of the Potomac [q.v.]. A superb cavalry commander, he rose to be a brigadier general at age twenty-three, the youngest in the Union army. After Gettysburg, in which he commanded a Michigan brigade, one of his troopers wrote on 9 July: "He is a glorious fellow, full of energy, quick to plan and bold to execute, and with us he has never failed in any attempt he has yet made."

Taking leave, the young general was married on 9 February 1863 in the Presbyterian church in Monroe, Michigan, to Elizabeth ("Libbie") Bacon [q.v.], the daughter of a judge. Custer was a spendthrift and a gambler, but his wife defended his reputation all her life.

On 15 April 1865 he became one of the youngest major generals. He won brevets for his bravery in the battles of Gettysburg, Yellow Tavern, Winchester, Fisher's Hill, and Five Forks [qq.v.]. Eleven horses were shot from under him, but he himself was wounded only once.

Custer was a man innocent of modesty. In a letter to his wife (1863) he wrote: "I feel that my destiny is in the hands of the Almighty. This belief, more than any other fact or reason, makes me brave and fearless as I am."

Before the end of the war he was well known inside and outside the army. He cultivated newspaper correspondents and was much in the news. Philip Sheridan [q.v.], his commanding officer, said of him: "If ever there was any poetry or romance in war, he could develop it." He remained in the army after the war, and serving as a lieutenant colonel in the 7th U.S. Cavalry, he fought in a muddled campaign against Indians in Kansas under Winfield Scott Hancock [q.v.]. In 1867 he was suspended from the army for a year after a court-martial had found him guilty of being absent without leave from his post at Fort Wallace, Kansas.

On his return to duty he was in command in the Battle of Washita River [q.v.] in November 1868. The 7th Cavalry was disbanded in 1870, but Custer remained in the West and resumed command when the 7th was reorganized in 1874. With a force of 951 men, including 3 newsmen, 1 photographer, 2 prospectors, and 75 Indian scouts, he set out on a campaign against the Sioux. According to the *New York Times,* his was "the best equipped expedition that was ever fitted out for service on the plains."

The expedition assembled at Fort Abraham Lincoln, near the mouth of the Heart River in present-day North Dakota. (It is now a state park.) At 8:00 A.M. on 2 July 1874 ten companies of the 7th Cavalry in sets of four wheeled into column and, as the 16-member band mounted on white horses played "Garry Owen," marched out of the fort. It returned on 7 August, reporting that gold had been found on the upper reaches of French Creek. By the end of 1875 some 15,000 miners had moved into the Black Hills.

In 1876 General Alfred H. Terry [q.v.] led a concentrated offensive against the Sioux [see Great Sioux War], during which Custer was ordered to lead a column south of the

Custer, George Armstrong *General Custer with his chief scout, Bloody Knife*

Bighorn Mountains. On 25 June 1876 he came upon Indians camped along the Little Bighorn River. He attacked prematurely and was killed with most of his men. [See Little Bighorn, Battle of the.]

Custer once said that he wanted to be known "not only to the present but to future generations." His dramatic death in the Battle of the Little Bighorn and the unceasing efforts of his wife, Elizabeth, ensured his lasting fame.

Custer, Thomas Ward (1845–1876). An American soldier and the younger brother of George Armstrong Custer [q.v.]. During the American Civil War, on 21 September 1861, at age sixteen, he enlisted as a private in the 21st Ohio Infantry. On 8 November he was commissioned a second lieutenant in the 6th Michigan Cavalry. He won brevets to major and was the only soldier in the war who was twice awarded the Medal of Honor [q.v.]: the first for the capture of a flag at Namozine Church [q.v.], Virginia, on 3 April 1865 and the second for his gallantry three days later in the Battle of Sayler's Creek [q.v.] when, according to General Philip Sheridan [q.v.], "he leaped his horse over the enemy's works, being one of the first to enter them, and captured two stand of colors, having his horse shot under him and received a severe wound." After turning in the captured colors, he had to be placed under arrest to prevent him from returning to the battle.

After the war, on 23 February 1866, he was given a commission as a second lieutenant in the 1st Infantry, and on 2 July he was promoted first lieutenant in his brother's 7th Cavalry. He was slightly wounded in the right hand in the Battle of Washita [q.v.] on 27 November 1868 and was killed in action with his brother in the Battle of the Little Bighorn [q.v.] on 25 June 1876.

Custer Avengers. The name given to those who enlisted in the United States 7th Cavalry after the Battle of Little Bighorn [q.v.]. The reference is to George Custer [q.v.], who commanded the regiment and was killed in the battle.

Custer's Cavalry Brigade. The brigade commanded by George Custer [q.v.] during the American Civil War. It consisted of the 1st, 5th, 6th, and 7th Michigan Cavalry. Cavalry battles were so rare during the war that the cavalry was the safest arm in which to serve, but Custer's brigade suffered the highest casualties of any cavalry unit in the Union army: 525 killed or mortally wounded.

Custer's Last Stand. See Little Bighorn, Battle of.

Custer's Missing Statue. See Custer, Elizabeth Bacon.

Customs of the Service. In addition to the many rules and regulations observed by soldiers, certain specific customs, an army's common law, were observed by officers. Many of these concerned officers' messes; others, daily living when not fighting. One such custom, common to both the British and American services, frowned upon an officer's carrying an umbrella or pushing a baby carriage.

Custozza, Battles of. Also written Custoza. Two important nineteenth-century battles between Piedmontese and Austrians were fought near this village in northeastern Italy, 11 miles southwest of Verona.

First Battle (24 July 1848), Italian Wars of Independence. After being expelled by rebels from Milan in March 1848, the Austrians withdrew into strong defensive positions known as the Quadrilateral [q.v.]. Some 70,000 Piedmontese and Italian rebels under the prince of Savoy, Charles Albert (Carlo Alberto, [q.v.]), attacked the western side of this position at Custozza and were defeated by 100,000 Austrians under the aged Count Josef Radetzky [q.v.]. The Piedmontese lost about 7,000 men and were driven out of Lombardy. On 6 August the Austrians reoccupied Milan. Piedmont was saved from an invasion largely through intercession by Britain.

News of the Austrian victory caused wild celebrations in Vienna, and Johann Strauss (1804–1849) composed the "Radetzky March," which received three encores when first played. Not everyone was pleased. Karl Marx (1818–1883) called Radetzky a symbol of the counterrevolution.

Second Battle (24 June 1866), Seven Weeks' War. Some 80,000 Italians under the Marchese di La Marmora [q.v.], having crossed the Mincio River, a tributary of the Po, met 74,000 Austrians commanded by Archduke Albert [q.v.], who was covering Verona. The Italians had passed through hilly country in which their columns had become disorganized and they debouched in some confusion onto the plain of Custozza. They were defeated in detail [q.v.] and driven back, retreating across the Mincio in great disarray. Austrian losses were 4,650 killed and wounded; Italian losses were 720 killed, 3,112 wounded, and 4,315 taken prisoner. Soon afterward the Austrian army was withdrawn to help defend Vienna against the Prussians, and after the Austrian defeat at Sadowa [q.v.], Venice was ceded to Italy.

Cut Knife, Battle of (2 May 1885), Second Riel Rebellion. At the Cut Knife Indian Reservation in Manitoba, Canada, 35 miles from Battleford, 390 men, including 100 constables of the Northwest Mounted Police, under Lieutenant Colonel William Dillon Otter (d. 1928) attacked Cree Indians under Chief Poundmaker (d. 1886), believed to be allies of Louis Riel [q.v.]. The attack was repulsed by warriors under their war chief, Fineday (1850?–1941), and Otter and his men were forced to return to Battleford, having lost 8 killed and 14 wounded; Cree losses were 5 dead and a few wounded.

Cutto (from French *couteau-de-chasse,* or hunting knife). A short sword or hanger [q.v.].

Cylinder. The cylindrical metal piece behind the bore of a pistol in which the chambers are bored.

Cynthiana, Battle of (11–12 June 1864), American Civil War. A small engagement at Keller's Bridge near Cynthiana, in northern Kentucky, 27 miles north-northwest of Lexington, which raised ethical and legal problems concerning parole [q.v.].

Brigadier General Edward Henry Hobson (1825–1901) and 300 officers and men of the 171st Ohio were captured by John H. Morgan [q.v.] on 11 June 1864. The men were close to the end of their enlistments, and Morgan did not want to be burdened with prisoners, so he offered them a parole if they would sign an "agreement" stipulating that they would try to effect an exchange and, if they could not do so, would report to Morgan as soon as possible. Hobson and 7 other officers signed. They left under the escort of 3 Confederate officers and 1 private.

At sunset the following day Hobson and his party reached the Union lines at Falmouth, Kentucky, 30 miles southsoutheast of Covington. By that time Morgan had been defeated and driven off by a Union force under Brigadier General Steven Gana Burbridge (1831–1894). Hobson appealed to Burbridge, who was commanding the District of Kentucky, to determine whether he was still under parole since he had not been captured "within the permanent lines of the rebel army."

Although hitherto an officer's word had been good whether or not his captor was subsequently defeated, chivalry was wearing thin by this stage of the war, and Hobson was informed that Burbridge considered "no officers or men prisoners of war except such as Morgan retained and took off with him" (official records). At Burbridge's direction the three Confederate officers and the private of the escort were held as prisoners.

Cyprus, British occupation of. There were serious uprisings on Cyprus against Turkish rule in 1764, 1804, and 1821. All were suppressed. On 4 June 1878 Britain signed a treaty with the sultan of Turkey whereby the British were to rule the island while Turkey was to retain sovereignty and to receive an annual tribute of £92,800. General Sir Garnet Wolseley [q.v.] became the first administrator of the island. Cyprus was formally annexed to Britain after Turkey had declared war against the Allies on 5 November 1914.

Czaikisten. Hungarian pontoon troops.

Czapka. See Shapska.

Czech Revolt (June 1848). In early June 1848 the Czechs convened the first Pan-Slav congress in Prague, arousing feelings of nationalism and resentment of the Austro-Hungarian Empire. On 13 June the populace rose in revolt when Austrian troops under Prince Alfred zu Windisch-Graetz [q.v.] dispersed the congress, but this was quickly suppressed.

D

Some names of people and places that have the following elements will be found under entries for the part of the name following the element: d', da, dal, de, degli, dei, del, de l', de la, de las, dell', della, de los, der, des, di, do, du.

Dabney's Mills, Battle of (6 February 1865), American Civil War, a battle also known as the Battle at Hatcher's Run, Armstrong's Mill, Boydton Plank Road, or Rowanty Creek. A Union force of 35,000 under General Fitz-Henry Warren (1816–1878), 12 miles southwest of Petersburg, Virginia, moving upon Boydton Road, believed to be a Confederate supply route, was attacked by a Confederate force in division strength under General John Pegram [q.v.]. The attack was repulsed, and Pegram was killed. The Confederates, although driven back, inflicted 1,512 casualties, including 170 killed. Confederate casualties are unknown.

Dabulamanzi (d.1886). A Zulu warrior, the half brother of Cetewayo [q.v.], who, in the Zulu War [q.v.] of 1879, commanded two impis at the Battle of Isandhlwana [q.v.] and led the abortive attack on the British at Rorke's Drift [q.v.]. He surrendered later that year and was permitted to return to Zululand. In 1886 he was accused of fraud in the sale of a horse and was summoned to appear before the magistrate at Vryheid. When he refused to appear, he was arrested and shot dead while trying to escape—or so it was said.

Dacoitee. An expedition or foray by dacoits [q.v.] for the purpose of plundering.

Dacoits. The hereditary robbers of northern India who were sometimes employed as mercenaries by Indian sovereigns. According to the Indian penal code, there had to be at least 5 in a band to constitute dacoity. Between 1818 and 1834 one tribe alone carried out 118 dacoitees [q.v.], in which 172 persons were killed and plunder worth more than £100,000 was taken. George Eden, Earl of Auckland (1784–1849), governor-general of India in 1835–41, did much to suppress the dacoits and break up their settlements, but they remained disturbers of the peace until almost the end of the century. Several bands were suppressed in 1879.

The term was also applied to armed gangs in Burma (Myanmar), where, after the defeat of King Thibaw or Thebaw (1858–1916) in November 1885, dacoits carried on a guerrilla war for several years [see Anglo-Burmese Wars].

Dade Massacre (28 December 1835), Second Seminole War.

In an action that marked the beginning of this war Captain and Brevet Major Francis Langhorne Dade (1792–1835) of the 4th U.S. Infantry, 6 other officers, 1 civilian, and about 110 soldiers, marching on the military road from Fort Brooke at the head of Tampa Bay to reinforce brevet Brigadier General Duncan Lamont Clinch [q.v.] at Fort King, were ambushed by about 200 Seminole Indians and 100 blacks 65 miles from Fort Brooke, by Wahoo Swamp and the Withlacoochie River near present-day Ocala, Florida. The Indians are believed to have been led by a Red Stick Creek named Jumper [q.v.], but it was said that Major Dade was killed by the Seminole chief Micanopy [q.v.]. The soldiers were massacred almost to a man; only 2 or 3 escaped.

Counties in both Georgia and Florida were named in honor of Major Dade.

Daendels, Herman Willem (1762–1818). A Dutch soldier who began a career as a lawyer but abandoned it in 1787 to serve in the French Revolutionary army. In 1793 he became a lieutenant general in the army of the Batavian Republic, and in 1799 he opposed the Anglo-Russian invasion. In 1806, after conquering Friesland and Westphalia, he entered the service of the king of Holland and was created a marshal. From 1807 to 1814 he was governor-general of the Dutch East Indies [see Java War]. In 1815 he became governor of the Dutch possessions on the Gold Coast in West Africa, where he died.

Daffadar Major. A noncommissioned officer rank in the Indian army corresponding to sergeant major or first sergeant [see Indian Army].

Dagger. An edged weapon with a handle and a short, pointed blade.

Dahlgren's Raid (February–March 1864), American Civil War. When a message from Elizabeth Van Lew [q.v.], a Union spy in Richmond, Virginia, informed the Union army that the Confederates planned to transport Federal prisoners of war from Richmond to Georgia, a raid was mounted to free them before they could be moved. The raiders, 3,584 cavalry with six guns under Brigadier General Hugh Judson Kilpatrick [q.v.] and Colonel Ulric Dahlgren (1842–1864), crossed the Rapidan River at Ely's Ford, near Chancellorsville, Virginia, at 11:00 P.M. on 28 February 1864. Dahlgren, the son of Admiral John Adolf Dahlgren (1809–1870), who invented the Dahlgren gun, much used by the U.S. navy, had lost a leg in the Battle of Gettysburg but could still ride. The next day, at Spotsylvania, they divided their forces, Kilpatrick taking the main body toward Richmond, which was thought to be protected by only 3,000 militia, and Dahlgren taking 500 men toward Goochland, 30 miles north of Richmond.

The Confederates were alerted on the night of the 29th, and Confederate Colonel Walter Husted Stevens (1827–1867), commander of the Richmond defenses, distributed his 500 men and six guns at the northern approaches to the city. Brigadier General George Washington Custis Lee [q.v.], eldest son of Robert E. Lee, quickly organized a force of mechanics and clerks and deployed them to block any approach from the west.

Kilpatrick arrived before the Richmond defenses on 1 March, decided they were too strong, and fled eastward. Dahlgren arrived on the same day in Goochland. There he detached 100 troopers of the 2nd New York Cavalry and, planning to cross the river and dash into Richmond from the south, led the rest in a march down the north bank of the James River, destroying property as he went. To find a crossing, he impressed a local black boy, Martin Robinson, who, instead of leading him to a ford, led him to a point where crossing was impossible. At Dahlgren's order he was hanged.

That evening, reunited with the New York cavalry, Dahlgren led his force within two miles of Richmond. Encountering increasingly stiff resistance and losing heavily, he began to retreat the next day. About eleven o'clock that night, near King and Queen Court House, his force was ambushed. Dahlgren was killed, and 92 of his men were captured.

William Littlepage, a thirteen year-old boy, found, or claimed to have found, papers on Dahlgren that proved that the raiders planned to kill Jefferson Davis [q.v.] and his cabinet and to burn Richmond. The authenticity of these papers is still argued, but at the time their publication created a furor in the South. Dahlgren's body was subjected to public display and numerous indignities before being thrown into an unmarked grave. (After the war his remains were exhumed by Union sympathizers and returned to Admiral Dahlgren.)

The entire raid cost the Union forces 340 men and 583 horses (103 horses were lost outright, and 480 of those that returned were unfit for further service). Also lost were 90 Spencer rifles, 504 carbines, 516 pistols, and 500 sabers.

Dahomean-French Wars. See Franco-Dahomean Wars.

Dahomey-Yoruba War (1851). A tribal war in West Africa in which King Gezo of Dahomey (Benin) unsuccessfully attacked Abeokuta, about 60 miles north of Lagos, in what was then Yoruba country.

Dahra Cave Massacre (18 June 1845), French conquest of Algeria. A small French force in Algeria under Colonel (later Marshal) Aimable Pelissier, perhaps on the orders of Marshal Thomas Bugeaud de la Piconnerie [qq.v.], herded about 1,000 men, women, and children of the Oulad-Riah tribe into a line of caves, where about half of them were asphyxiated when the French filled the cave entrances with burning faggots and threw in explosives. The outrage was committed as a reprisal against tribesmen who had fired upon a French messenger as he approached with a proposal for a truce.

Daimyo / Daimio. Japanese feudal samurai [q.v.] lords who controlled various Japanese provinces from medieval times until after the Meiji Restoration of 1868 [see Boshin Civil War]. About two-thirds of the lands not ruled directly by the shogun were controlled by 245 daimyos, who were permitted to levy taxes, raise armies, and enforce laws, in return for the military service they owed the shogun. The domains of the daimyos were abolished in 1871.

Dai-sho. The classical set of Japanese weapons, consisting of the long-bladed *katana* and the short-bladed *wakizashi* [qq.v.]. The term *dai-sho* means simply "long and short." It was the *wakizashi* with which the *bushi* (warrior) cut off the head of an honored opponent after killing him or disemboweled himself in the act of seppuku or hara-kiri [q.v.].

Dale, Samuel (1772–1841). An American frontiersman and soldier who served as an army scout from 1783 to 1796, a period in which the Creek and Cherokee Indians were proving troublesome. In the summer of 1813, when the Creek War [q.v.] was about to break out, he was lying low in Mississippi, avoiding U.S. authorities seeking to question him about the illegal importation of slaves and goods from Spanish Pensacola, but he was soon in command of a militia company. On 27 July 1813 he was wounded in the Battle of Burnt Corn [q.v.], the opening battle of the war. Although not completely recovered, he held Fort Madison in the heart of Creek country with only 80 men, even after the Fort Mims Massacre [q.v.].

On 12 November 1813 on the Alabama River just above its confluence with the Tombigbee he gained a hero's reputation in a so-called canoe fight when in the middle of the river he and a handful of others, fighting hand to hand, defeated Creeks who were triple their number.

In 1817 he became a member of the Alabama legislature. The following year found him again in the field against Creeks who had sided with the Seminoles [see Seminole War, First]. On 15 December he was made a brigadier general of Alabama militia for life and authorized half pay. In 1831 he was placed in charge of moving the Choctaws west of the Mississippi. He fell ill on the journey and was unable to finish the mission. An Alabama county is named for him.

Dalhousie, George Ramsay, Ninth Earl (1770–1838). A British soldier, commissioned in 1788, who joined the British army in the peninsula in 1812 as commander of the 7th Division. He played a prominent role in the so-called Battle of the Pyrenees [q.v.], but Wellington was often critical of his performance, particularly his late arrival on the field in the Battle of Vitoria [q.v.]. He was later governor of Canada and commander-in-chief, India.

Dalil-Bashi. Literally, chief of guides in Turkish. An officer in Turkish and Egyptian armies (see Bashi).

Dallas, Battle of. See New Hope Church, Battle of.

Dalmanutha, Battle of (21–28 August 1900), Second Anglo-Boer War. Boers, positioned from Belfast to Machadodorp, protecting the railway to Delgoa Bay, were attacked from the south by General Redvers Buller and from the west by Lord Roberts [qq.v.]. By 28 August 1900, when Buller entered the village of Machadodorp, the Boer seat of government in western Transvaal after the fall of Pretoria, the Boers had been driven from all their positions and Transvaal President Stephanus Johannes Paulus ("Paul") Kruger (1825–1904) had fled the country. The British lost about 500 men; Boer losses are unknown.

Dalton, Battles of (1864), American Civil War. In 1864 three important engagements were fought at this Georgia town 38 miles north of Rome.

1. 24–27 February 1864. In an effort on 24 February to force the Confederate position at Buzzard Roost Gap, just outside Dalton, Federal forces under John McAuley Palmer (1817–1900) drove in the Confederate outposts, but the Confederate position was too strong, and the Federals fell back. Union losses were reported as 345; Confederate losses were reported as 167 but were probably larger.

2. 5–11 May 1864. This battle, marking the beginning of the Atlanta Campaign [q.v.], is often called the Battle of Rocky Faced Ridge. Confederate forces under Joseph E. Johnston [q.v.] occupied a position running north and south along Rocky Faced Ridge protecting Dalton. General W. T. Sherman directed General George Thomas [qq.v.] to make a holding attack while General James Birdseye McPherson [q.v.], commanding the Army of the Tennessee [q.v.], turned the Confederates from the west. Although the maneuver was not as successful as was hoped—McPherson was criticized for his timidity—it did force Johnston to abandon Dalton.

3. 14–16 August 1864. On the afternoon of 14 August Confederate cavalry under General Joseph Wheeler [q.v.] approached Dalton, Georgia, then occupied by Union forces, and demanded its surrender. This was refused. One Union regiment and some convalescents successfully fought off two attacks, suffering about 50 casualties.

Daly, Henry W. (1850–1931). An Irish-born American frontiersman who became a civilian packer for the army in 1880. Noted for his intelligence, imagination, and endurance, he was said to possess all the requisites of a skilled packer, including respect for a good mule, the ability to deal with Indians, and the faculty of managing unruly men of whatever race. He handled the packing for many military expeditions against Indians, including the operations culminating at Wounded Knee [q.v.].

He became chief packer, or packmaster, for the army Quartermaster Corps. During the Spanish-American War [q.v.] he was called on to give advice on packing in several theaters. In 1901 he taught classes in his art at West Point. His *Manual of Instruction in Pack Transportation* was published by the West Point Press. On 7 July 1917 he was made a captain in the Quartermaster Corps, and he finished World War I as a major. He received an honorable discharge on 30 September 1920.

Damascus, Capture of (January 1832), Turko-Egyptian War of 1832–33. Egyptian general Ibrahim Pasha [q.v.] captured Damascus, Syria, then under Turkish control.

Damascus Steel. A kind of steel used in the making of swords in many Asian countries. Strips of iron and steel twisted together were welded into a mass. The result was a steel with a peculiar watered or streaked appearance.

Dame. 1. A piece of wood with two handles used to tamp earth or dirt in a mortar.

2. The dirt that remains after the explosion of a mine.

Damjanich, János (1804–1849). A Hungarian soldier of Serbian origins who fought as a general with the Hungarian revolutionary forces in 1848–49. In April 1849 he commanded one of the three divisions under General Arthur von Görgey [q.v.] that entered Vac (Vácz or Vacs). After the Battle of Világos [q.v.] he surrendered to the Russians and was handed over to the Austrians, who, a few days later, shot him in the marketplace at Arad in western Rumania.

Dana, Napoleon Jackson Tecumseh (1822–1905). An American soldier whose father fought in the War of 1812 [q.v.] and whose grandfather fought in the American Revolution. After graduating from West Point in 1842, he fought in the Mexican War [q.v.], in which he won a brevet. He was so severely wounded in the Battle of Cerro Gordo [q.v.] that he was left for dead on the field until a burial party found him to be still alive two days later. In 1855 he resigned his commission and became a banker in St. Paul, Minnesota, and a brigadier general in the state militia. In the American Civil War he was named colonel of the 1st Minnesota on 2 October 1861 and a brigadier general of volunteers on 3 February 1862. He served through the Peninsular Campaign and was severely wounded at Antietam [qq.v.]. When he returned to duty, he was appointed a major general, to rank from 29 November 1862, and sent to the Department of the Gulf, taking command of a force that landed at the Rio Grande and drove the Confederates back to Laredo, Texas. For a time he commanded a corps in Mississippi and Tennessee. He resigned on 27 May 1865, and until 1871 he acted as the general agent of the American-Russian Commercial Company of San Francisco. For a number of years he was a railroad executive, and from 1893 to 1897 he was deputy commissioner of pensions in Washington, D.C.

Dane Guns. Flintlock muskets were so called in West Africa early in the nineteenth century, when the Danes established trading centers there and sold the muskets to Africans.

Danger. Exposure or liability to injury, pain, or loss. Karl von Clausewitz [q.v.] wrote: "Danger is part of the friction of war. Without an accurate conception of danger we cannot understand war" (*On War*, 1833). Not all men fear danger. René Quinton wrote: "Some men approach danger as a virgin approaches love. They think there are no consequences."

Danger Space. The term employed by Major General Wesley Merritt [q.v.] to describe the ground directly in front of a position being attacked, an area attackers must cross in a final assault. Sometimes called the deadly ground.

Danish-Prussian War. See Schleswig-Holstein War.

Danites. Mormon militia in Deseret (Utah). In 1857–58 they actively opposed the Utah expedition [q.v.] under General Albert S. Johnston [q.v.].

Danjou, Jean (d. 1863). A French soldier who, as a captain in the French Foreign Legion [q.v.], which had been sent to Mexico to help prop up the regime of the emperor Maximilian, became the hero of the Battle of Camerone [q.v.], in which his legionnaires fought almost to the last man and he himself was killed. His wooden hand, fitted after he lost his own in a musket explosion in Algeria, was retrieved from the battlefield. Still preserved, it is the most sacred icon of the legion.

Dannebrog, Order of. An ancient chivalric order in Denmark that was reorganized as an order of merit on 28 June 1808. The medal of the order is gold and bears a white cross edged in red. It is carried on a red-edged white ribbon.

Dannewerk. Literally, Dane's rampart. An ancient rampart of the Danes erected to keep out the Germans. It was begun in the ninth century and extended in the tenth so that it ran from just south of the town of Schleswig for $10\frac{1}{2}$ miles to the marshes of the Trene River near the village of Hollingstedt. After Schleswig and Holstein had become part of Denmark, it fell into decay. In 1848 it was strengthened, and on 13 April 1848 of that year it was attacked by Prussian artillery and successfully stormed [see Schleswig-Holstein War].

In 1850 the rampart was again repaired and strengthened, but in 1864 the invading Prussians marched around it, and on 6 February it was abandoned without a shot's being fired. The Prussians reduced it to rubble.

Danubyu, Battle of (2 April 1825), First Anglo-Burmese War. At this place in Lower Burma on the right bank of the Irrawaddy, 65 miles northeast of Bassein, a Burmese attack upon the British under General Archibald Campbell [q.v.] was broken up primarily by Congreve rockets [q.v.]; the British counterattacked, and the Burmese fled when their general was killed.

Danzig / Gdansk, Sieges of. Danzig (Gdansk), an important port and fortress city on the Baltic coast of Prussia (today in Poland), was twice besieged in the nineteenth century.

1. 1 April–27 May 1807, Napoleonic Wars. Most of the French army went into winter quarters after the Battle of Eylau [q.v.] on 8 February 1807, but Marshal François Joseph Lefebvre [q.v.] with 18,000 French troops was sent to capture Danzig. The garrison there consisted of 14,400 infantry and 1,600 cavalry with 349 guns under Prussian Field Marshal Count Friedrich Adolf von Kalckreuth (1737–1818). The city was well stocked with supplies and strongly fortified, and the garrison made a stubborn defense. Lefebvre called up reinforcements under Jean Lannes [q.v.] and besieged the town. Prussian and Russian efforts to raise the siege failed. When the city finally capitulated on 27 May, the garrison was given full honors of war [q.v.].

2. January–November 1813. After the French retreat from Moscow in 1812 [see Russian Campaign, Napoleon's] about 30,000 French troops under General Jean Rapp [q.v.] held Danzig until in January 1813 it was besieged by 30,000 Allied troops under the Duke of Württemberg. On 29 November 1813 it was forced by starvation and exposure to surrender.

Darbytown, Battle of. See Deep Bottom Run, Battle of.

Darfur, Mahdist Conquest of (1881–83), War in the Sudan. Rudolf Slatin Pasha [q.v.], the Austrian-born Egyptian gover-

nor of the Sudanese province of Darfur, fought twenty-seven engagements against the Mahdist Dervishes [q.v.] from 1881 until December 1883, when he was forced to surrender to the forces of Khalifa Abdullahi [q.v.], the ruler of the Sudan who had succeeded El Mahdi. Slatin remained a prisoner until his escape in 1895.

Dargai, Battle of (20 October 1897), Tirah Campaign. On India's Northwest Frontier the British under Sir William Lockhart [q.v.] encountered Afridi and Orakzai tribesmen in a strong position on the Dargai ridge (6,000 feet above sea level) in the Samana range, about 4 miles west-northwest of Malakand and 38 miles north-northwest of Peshawar. After five hours in which several attempts to dislodge them had failed, the Gordon Highlanders [q.v.] were ordered to attack. The lieutenant colonel commanding the 1st Gordons called his officers and pipers together and told them: "Highlanders, the general says the position must be taken at all costs. The Gordons will take it."

Officers and pipers led 600 cheering Highlanders up the steep slope and carried the heights. General Lockhart wrote a graphic description of the charge: "The bugle sounds the 'advance,' the pipers play. . . . The first division reach the sheltering rocks panting for breath, they shout, the officers waving their swords to those behind, while Piper Findlater, though wounded and unable to move still inspires them with his war-like strains . . . the top is reached . . . the Highlanders rush unopposed and great is the cheering as they realize the enemy is in flight."

The date, 20 October, was ever after celebrated in the regiment as Dargai Day. The British lost 37 killed and 175 wounded. Piper George Findlater [q.v.] was awarded the Victoria Cross.

Dariyah, Siege of (11 March–11 September 1818), Arabian wars. A Turko-Egyptian force under Ibrahim Pasha [q.v.], the eldest son or stepson of Mehmet Ali [q.v.], attacked this capital of the Wahhabis in the Wadi Hanifi, a four-mile-long fertile valley protected on one side by a 100-foot cliff. On the valley's highest point was the citadel of Turaif, containing a mosque and royal residences.

Ibrahim Pasha had 5,000 infantry and 2,000 cavalry plus four 12-pounders, five Turkish guns, a Swedish gun, and a howitzer. The siege, which began on 11 March 1818, slowly strangled the Wahhabis until by September they held only the citadel. It was taken by storm on 11 September. The town was pillaged and then systematically destroyed. The date palms were cut down, the wells filled in, and every building was rendered uninhabitable. Dariyah was never restored, but the modern capital of Riyadh was built not far away.

Dartnell, John George (1838–1913). A Canadian who enlisted in the British army and fought in the Indian Mutiny [q.v.]. He was discharged in 1869 and emigrated to Natal, South Africa, where in 1874 he founded the Natal Mounted Police, which he commanded in the Zulu War of 1879, the Gun War of 1880, and both Anglo-Boer Wars [qq.v.]. He retired in 1903.

Daru, Pierre Antoine (1767–1829). A French soldier who entered the army at age sixteen. He was imprisoned during the Terror, but in 1800 he was made secretary of war industry and intendant general (*intendant-général*) in Prussia and Austria [see Intendance]. In 1805 he was made chief commissary of the Grande Armée [q.v.]. In 1811 he was appointed minister of war. He retired after Napoleon's first abdication but aided Napoleon during the Hundred Days [q.v.].

Dar ul Harb. Turkish: the domain of war.

Date of Rank. The date on which an officer was commissioned or last promoted. Promotions were sometimes backdated to a date in which an officer distinguished himself. Seniority within each grade was, and still is, determined by this date.

Dauphins. Handles, sometimes ornamental, over the trunnions on some brass guns to assist in mounting or dismounting the guns from their carriages. The handles, so called from their resemblance to dolphins, were sometimes cast in their likeness.

David's Day, St. The first day of March. St. David being the patron saint of Wales, his day is celebrated in all Welsh regiments of the British army with parades and festivities. Every soldier wears a leek, the floral emblem of Wales, on his cap or jacket, and old soldiers, if possible, attend.

Davidson, John Wynn (1823–1881). An American soldier who was graduated from West Point in 1845 and fought in the Mexican War [q.v.] with Phil Kearny's [q.v.] Army of the West [q.v.], narrowly missing death in the Battle of San Pasqual [q.v.].

On 30 March 1854 he was severely wounded in a fight with Jicarilla Apaches in the Embudo Mountains, 25 miles south of Taos, New Mexico. In one of the worst defeats the army had suffered at the hands of Indians on the plains to that date Davidson lost 22 men killed. Of the 38 survivors, only 2 were unscathed.

Davidson, a Virginian, chose to remain with the Union during the American Civil War, although his three brothers fought for the Confederacy. He fought in the battles of the Seven Days [q.v.] and was made a brigadier general on 3 February 1862. He held commands in Missouri, Arkansas, and Natchez, Mississippi.

He was mustered out of the volunteers as a major general in 1866 but remained in the army as a lieutenant colonel. From 1868 to 1871 he was professor of military science and tactics at Kansas Agricultural College. On 20 March 1879 he became colonel of the 2nd Cavalry. He died at Fort Custer, Montana, of injuries sustained when his horse fell on him.

Davis, Jefferson (1808–1889). An American army officer who became U.S. secretary of war and in 1861 president of the Confederate States of America. He was born in a log cabin, the tenth child of a Kentucky farmer. In 1824 he entered West Point. He was graduated four years later, ranking 23rd in a class of 32. Future Confederate generals at the academy at the same time included Robert E. Lee, Albert Sidney Johnston, Joseph Eggleston Johnston, and Leonidas Polk [qq.v.].

From 1828 to 1835 Davis served in frontier posts in the West. In 1832 he fought in the Black Hawk War [q.v.]. In 1835 he resigned from the army and eloped with Sarah Taylor, the daughter of Colonel (later General) Zachary Taylor [q.v.]. Within three months of their marriage his bride died of malaria. Davis became a planter near Vicksburg, Mississippi, and in 1845 remarried. He was elected to Congress but resigned to command the 1st Mississippi Volunteers in the Mexican War [q.v.], serving under his former father-in-law. He was severely wounded in the Battle of Buena Vista [q.v.], where his gallantry inspired General Taylor to confess that his daughter had been a better judge of character than he had.

In 1847 he was elected a U.S. senator by the Mississippi legislature, and in 1853 President Franklin Pierce (1804–1869) appointed him secretary of war, a post he held until 1857. An innovative leader, he experimented with camels [q.v.] for the cavalry in the West; turned from wooden to metal gun carriages; approved new infantry tactics; pressed for improved coastal defenses and the construction of a military railway across the continent; and, as he boasted, "secured rifled muskets and rifles and the use of Minié balls." He was, however, frequently at odds with Winfield Scott [q.v.], the ranking general in the army.

From 1857 until he resigned in 1861, he was back in the

Davis, Jefferson *Jefferson Davis is captured by Federal cavalry, 10 May 1865.*

U.S. Senate. On 9 February 1861 the Convention of the Confederate States at Montgomery, Alabama, elected him president of the Confederacy for a six-year term. When he arrived at the new nation's capital in Montgomery, Alabama, on 16 February, the noted political orator William Lowndes Yancey (1814–1863) declared: "The man and the hour have met!" Nevertheless, in the course of the American Civil War many in the Confederate states criticized him for meddling in military affairs, protecting incompetent generals such as Braxton Bragg while quarreling with others, such as Joseph Johnston and Pierre Beauregard [qq.v.]. However, throughout the war he remained a strong supporter of Lee.

On 2 April 1865, threatened by the Union advance, he and some members of his cabinet fled Richmond, then the capital, and established new executive offices in a spacious house in Danville, Virginia. On 5 April he issued a stirring Proclamation of the Confederacy, predicting the South's eventual victory and proclaiming, "I will never consent to abandon one foot of the soil of any of the states of the Confederacy." On 8 April he held the last official meeting of his cabinet. The following day Lee surrendered at Appomattox, and on 10 May Davis and his cabinet attempted to flee by train. He was captured that same day near Irwinville, Georgia, and confined at Fort Monroe, Virginia. He was never tried. After his release on bail on 1 May 1867 he became president of an insurance company and steadfastly refused to take any part in politics. In 1881 he wrote *The Rise and Fall of the Confederate Government*. He died at age eighty-one in New Orleans.

His wife, Varina Howell Davis (1826–1905), said of him: "He did not know the arts of the politician and would not practice them if understood."

Davis, Jefferson Columbus (1828–1879). An American soldier (unrelated to the president of the Confederacy) who volunteered for the Mexican War [q.v.] and served from private to sergeant in the 3rd Indiana Volunteers from 22 June 1846 to 27 June 1847. On 17 June 1848 he was commissioned a second lieutenant in the 1st Artillery, and at the beginning of the American Civil War he was a first lieutenant at Fort Sumter [q.v.]. On 1 August 1861 he became colonel of the 22nd Indiana, and on 10 August he commanded a brigade in the Battle of Wilson's Creek [q.v.]. In May 1862 he was promoted a brigadier general to rank from 18 December 1861.

In August 1862 Davis was in Louisville, Kentucky, under the command of Major General William Nelson (1824–1862), a graduate of the U.S. Naval Academy (1844), who had leaped from lieutenant in the navy to brigadier general in the army on 16 July 1861, and to major general a year later. When Davis, ordered to organize a local defense battalion, did not perform as well as expected, Nelson administered a strong rebuke, to which Davis retorted hotly, and such "high words" ensued that Nelson relieved him of his duty and ordered him out of town.

About a month later, when Nelson had been superseded by Major General Don Carlos Buell [q.v.], Davis returned. Nelson was still in his office at Galt House, a Louisville hotel, and there on 29 September the two men met in the lobby. Davis demanded an apology and, when it was refused, crumpled a visiting card and threw it in Nelson's face. Nelson responded with a slap and called Davis a "damned puppy."

Davis turned on his heel and left. He returned armed with a pistol and finding Nelson still in the lobby, shot him at point-blank range, mortally wounding him.

Although, or perhaps because, Indiana's Governor Oliver Hazard Perry Throckmorton (1823–1877), a close friend of Davis's, was with him at the time, Davis was imprisoned for only a few days. Never tried or punished in any way, he returned to duty as if nothing had happened.

He commanded a division at Stones River and Chickamauga, in the Atlanta Campaign and on the March to the Sea [qq.v.]. On 4 August 1864 he was brevetted a major general. On 1 September 1866 he was mustered out of the volunteer service, but he remained in the army as colonel of the 23rd Infantry.

In 1867 he was in Alaska to receive that territory from the Russians at Sitka, the chief town of Russian Alaska and the future capital of American Alaska, situated on the west coast of Baranof Island. He commanded the territory for two years, during which he provoked numerous Indian-white hostilities.

After the murder of General Edward Canby [q.v.] by Modoc Indians in the lava beds of California on 11 April 1873, he was placed in command of the troops in the Modoc War [q.v.], which he pushed to a successful conclusion.

He died at the age of fifty-one, never having expressed regret for the death of General Nelson.

Davis, Richard Harding (1864–1916). An American war correspondent and novelist noted for his dash and valor in covering wars for British and American newspapers. He reported the Graeco-Turkish War, Spanish-American War, Second Anglo-Boer War [qq.v.], Russo-Japanese War, and, until his death, the First World War.

Davis Boot. A boot introduced into the army when Jefferson Davis was U.S. secretary of war and named after him. The top of the boot came slightly above the ankle and was tied in front by a lace that passed through two pairs of eyes. It was found that "a few standard sizes fit most men." During the Civil War Union army contracts for the manufacture of these boots were fraught with swindles, bribery, and scandals. Some men made fortunes. An enormous surplus was found to exist after the war.

Davis Medal. The Davis Guard, a Houston, Texas, Confederate volunteer infantry unit, was mustered into the 1st Texas Regiment, Heavy Artillery, in the fall of 1861 during the American Civil War. Filled with dockworkers and laborers, mostly Irish, and commanded by a former saloonkeeper, Lieutenant Richard W. Dowling [q.v.], it quickly earned a reputation for rowdiness and lack of discipline, but it showed its mettle in the Battle of Sabine Pass [q.v.] when, largely because of its efforts, the Confederates won their striking victory. President Jefferson Davis [q.v.] (*The Rise and Fall of the Confederate Government*, 1878–1881) called the battle the Thermopylae of the Civil War.

To show their appreciation, the people of Sabine County presented Lieutenant Dowling and each of his 43 men with a medal, the only medals ever awarded in the Confederacy. Made by shaving silver dollars, they bore a Maltese cross and "D. G." on the obverse and the inscription "Battle of Sabine Pass, September 8, 1863" on the reverse. They were worn suspended on a green ribbon.

One was presented to President Davis, who carried it until it was taken from him at Fort Monroe, Virginia, after his capture. On 15 May 1875 at the sixth Texas State Fair one of the battery's three survivors presented him with a replacement.

Davout, Louis Nicolas (1770–1823). A soldier of a noble but impoverished French family who rose to become a marshal of France. At age ten he was admitted to the provincial Royal Military School at Auxerre, and he later attended the military school at Brienne with Napoleon. In 1788 he was commissioned in his father's old regiment.

Although he welcomed the Revolution, his family's background made him suspect. In 1791 he was arrested and resigned his commission; a week later, cleared of suspicion, he commanded a regiment of volunteers. On 25 July 1793 he was promoted general of brigade but was forced to resign when the Assembly decreed that former aristocrats could not serve as officers. He was not long out of service, however, and was soon fighting on the Rhine and the Moselle. He fought in Egypt, where he was captured by the British and released a month later. On 3 July 1800 he was promoted general of division. On 19 May 1804 he was appointed marshal of the empire and colonel general of the Garde Impériale [q.v.]. In September he commanded a corps and fought with distinction in the War of the Third Coalition [see Napoleonic Wars], particularly at Austerlitz [q.v.], where he commanded the right wing of Napoleon's army. On 14 October 1805 he defeated the Duke of Brunswick [q.v.] in the Battle of Auerstädt [q.v.], and in February 1807 he commanded the right wing in the Battle of Eylau [q.v.]. After the Treaty of Tilsit [q.v.] he was appointed governor-general of the grand duchy of Warsaw. The following year he was created Duke of Auerstädt. He

Davout, Louis *Louis Nicolas Davout, one of Napoleon's premier generals, was never defeated in battle*

was soon back in action, serving in the battles of Ratisbon, Wagram, and Eckmühl [qq.v.], where he particularly distinguished himself. He took part in Napoleon's Russian Campaign [q.v.] of 1812 and was wounded in the Battle of Borodino [q.v.]. He was appointed governor-general of the Hanse towns and from Hamburg instituted a regime of oppression. During the Hundred Days [q.v.] he was minister of war. On 22 June 1815, given responsibility for the defense of Paris, he checked the advance of Marshal Gebhard von Blücher [q.v.].

Davout was regarded as a stern, able, loyal, fair, incorruptible soldier who took care of and trained his troops and maintained a strict and exemplary discipline. He was never defeated in battle.

Dead Ground. A hollow or fold in the ground capable of shielding troops from view or from enemy fire.

Deadman. A picket or holdfast sunk in the ground to which a picket line to hold horses was attached.

Dead Shot. An unerring or excellent marksman.

Deane and Adams Pistol. A percussion revolver designed by Robert Adams [q.v.]. Soon after being exhibited at the Great Exhibition in London in 1851, it was adopted by the British army.

Dearborn, Henry (1751–1829). A physician and soldier who served as a battalion and regimental commander in the American Revolution and in 1795 was appointed a brigadier general of militia. He served as a congressman for five years, and in 1801 President Thomas Jefferson (1743–1826) appointed him secretary of war. In this post he introduced new gun carriages and the Whitney musket to the army [see Whitney, Eli] and greatly improved the nation's fortifications. In 1803 he ordered the construction of a fort at "Chikago" that became Fort Dearborn. Because Indian affairs were then the responsibility of the War Department, he obtained millions of acres of land through treaties with the Indians.

The American army at the time was political. Dearborn managed to weed out most of the Federalist officers and, by means of the Military Peace Establishment Act of 1802 [q.v.], which established many new military and civil positions, to fill the army with Jeffersonian Republicans.

In 1809 he left Washington and became collector of customs in Boston. At the beginning of the War of 1812 [q.v.] he reluctantly accepted from President James Madison (1751–1836) an appointment as the army's senior major general and took charge of the northeast sector from Niagara Falls to the Atlantic Ocean.

On 27 April 1813 he launched an attack upon Canada and captured and sacked York (Toronto) in Upper Canada (Ontario), but he sustained such heavy losses that he was unable to pursue the retreating British. A month later he captured Fort George, but here, as at York, the British army was allowed to escape. He then fell too ill to command, and the invasion plan was completely aborted after the British made a successful surprise attack upon his exposed force at Sackets Harbor [q.v.] on 28 May.

He acted as president of the court-martial that tried and condemned General William Hull [q.v.] for surrendering Detroit, but he did not again play an active part in the war.

He was honorably discharged on 15 June 1815. In 1822 he was appointed ambassador to Portugal, and he served there for two years.

Deas, Zachariah Cantey (1819–1882). An American soldier who served in the Mexican War [q.v.] and then made his fortune as a cotton broker in Alabama. During the American Civil War he recruited and equipped at his own expense the 22nd Alabama, paying $28,000 in gold for fine imported Enfield Rifles [q.v.], for which he was reimbursed with Confederate bonds. He commanded his regiment at Shiloh [q.v.], where he was severely wounded, but he recovered in time to take part in the invasion of Kentucky by Braxton Bragg [q.v.] in 1862 [see Kentucky, Confederate Invasion of]. On 13 December 1862 he was promoted brigadier general. In that rank he led a brigade at Murfreesboro and Chickamauga [qq.v.] and took part in all the engagements of the Confederate Army of Tennessee [q.v.]. After the war he became a prominent member of the New York Stock Exchange.

Death Hunters. Civilians who followed armies in order to rob the dead and wounded after a battle.

Death Ride (16 August 1870). One of the last great cavalry charges in European warfare took place in the Battle of Mars-la-Tour–Vionville [q.v.] during the Franco-Prussian War [q.v.]. When the French under General Achille Bazaine [q.v.] were about to launch an attack upon the exhausted German left, General Gustav von Alvensleben ordered General Adalbert von Bredow [qq.v.] to sacrifice his brigade, six squadrons of the 16th Uhlans and the 7th Cuirassiers, to save the infantry. In line of squadron column the troops moved to the crest of a ridge that had concealed their approach until they came within a few hundred yards of the French. Bredow sounded line to the front, but before the order could be carried out, his impetuous troopers charged across 1,200 yards toward lines of French infantry and artillery.

Helmuth von Moltke the Elder [q.v.] described Bredow's charge: "Being received by heavy infantry and artillery fire, he made a determined attack on the enemy's lines, riding down the foremost, breaking through their fire and securing the guns and their drivers. . . . But the triumph and excitement of success carried the small body of horsemen too far, and after an advance of 3,000 paces they found themselves surrounded by the cavalry of the enemy, which attacked them on all sides. . . . [T]he brigade was forced to cut its way back through French infantry, who followed them up with numerous volleys."

Only about half of the brigade survived to return to the German lines, but their charge had given the Prussians time to bring up reinforcements, and the French advance was halted. It was in this charge that Prince Herbert Nikolaus Bismarck-Schönhausen (1849–1904), the eldest son of the great chancellor Otto von Bismarck (1815–1898), was severely wounded.

Deblai. In fortifications, any hollow space or hole in the ground. The earth taken out to make the deblai was called the remblai.

Debouch. As a verb, to come out of a woods, defile, mountain pass, or other confining area into an open area. As a noun, the place where such a movement can be made.

Deccan Prize. At the conclusion of the Third Maratha War [q.v.] a squabble over the distribution of the considerable amount of spoils of war became a celebrated case. Much of the spoils had been acquired by small independent detachments, but the largest portion of the booty had been taken by the Army of the Deccan, commanded by General Sir Thomas Hislop (1764–1843). The Bengal army, under the command of Francis Rawdon, first Marquess of Hastings (1754–1826), which had seen nothing of the fight, demanded to share the prize. The matter eventually reached the Privy Council, which decided that although the Bengal army had been far from the fighting, it had cooperated by its presence and by keeping native powers in check and therefore would share equally with the Army of the Deccan.

The Duke of Wellington, looking upon the bright side, remarked that since Hislop had received a smaller share, a major part of the prize had not vanished into Mexican bonds or Colombian securities, as had Hislop's private fortune. [See Prize; Prize Agents; Talneer, Affair at.]

Decembrist Uprising (December 1825). A Russian revolt against the Romanovs by a group of Freemasons [see Freemasonry], many of them army officers inspired by the Carbonari [q.v.], who wished to establish a republic. On 1 December 1825 the rebellious officers marched their regiments to Senate Square (Decembrist Square) in St. Petersburg and there refused to obey the order of Tsar Nicholas I (1796–1855) to disperse. A cavalry charge failed to rout them, for the horses, improperly shod, slipped and fell on the icy cobblestones. Artillery cleared the square more effectively. The revolt, badly planned and without adequate civilian support, was quickly suppressed, and the Masonic Order was prohibited in Russia. Five leaders were hanged; 100 others were sent to Siberia.

Decembrist Uprising *Decembrists in exile in Siberia*

Deception. A strategic or tactical technique for making an enemy believe that which is not true. As Sun Tzu, the fourth-century A.D. military writer, said, "All warfare is based on deception."

Decimation. Literally, the loss of 1 in 10 of a military force or any group but often used to describe heavy casualties of whatever proportion.

Decisive Battle. An engagement that affects the course of a campaign or war.

Declaration of War. The formal announcement by a government of its intention to make war upon another country. It is, says *Wilhelm's Military Dictionary and Gazetteer* (1881), "a proceeding which is observed among all civilized nations." In the United States, only Congress can declare war.

Decoration Day. A day observed in the United States to honor its military dead. Before the end of the American Civil War several southern states selected a day to remember their fallen soldiers and decorate their graves with flowers and flags; eight southern states still observe Decoration Day, variously on 26 April, 10 May, or 3 June. No such day was fixed in the North until 5 May 1868, when General John Alexander Logan [q.v.], then the commander-in-chief of the Grand Army of the Republic [q.v.], issued a general order designating 30 May of that year as Decoration Day with the hope that it would become a yearly event. In 1971 it was renamed Memorial Day and proclaimed a day to honor the dead soldiers of all American wars.

Decorations. See Medals and Orders, Military.

Decoy. 1. As a noun, a person or persons who lead troops into a trap or ambush.

2. As a noun, an imitation of a person, object, or phenomenon intended to deceive or mislead an enemy.

3. As a verb, to deceive an enemy by leading him into a snare or ambush.

The use of a decoy was a favorite stratagem of American Indians on the plains. It was seldom successful, for personal bravery was valued over group success, and an overeager young warrior almost invariably sprang the trap too soon. That it was rarely successful did not diminish its use. The Fetterman Massacre [q.v.] was a notable exception.

Deep Bottom Run, Battle of (27–29 July 1864), American Civil War, sometimes called Battle of Strawberry Plains, Darbytown, or New Market Road. An indecisive action in Virginia during the Petersburg Campaign, in which about 28,000 Federals under U. S. Grant tried to break through strong Confederate lines under Robert E. Lee. Union losses were 334 killed and wounded; Confederate losses are unknown, but since they were fighting from behind earthworks, they were undoubtedly fewer.

Deep Run. See Franklin's Crossing.

Defaulter. In the British army, a soldier who had committed a military offense or default. The term generally applied to minor offenders.

Defaulter's Sheet. In the British army, a company defaulter's [q.v.] sheet was kept as a record of minor offenses and the punishments given; a regimental defaulter's sheet was kept as a record of all offenses for which punishment exceeding seven days' confinement was awarded.

Defeat in Detail, to. To destroy an enemy force piece by piece, attacking only a portion of the whole at any one time, particularly when the portions are separated.

Defensive Battle. A battle in which an army or military unit chooses a position from which to await an attack and fights for no other purpose than to hold the position and repulse the enemy, as did Confederate General Robert E. Lee's Army of Northern Virginia at Fredericksburg [q.v.]. Karl von Clausewitz [q.v.] believed that "the defensive is the stronger form of making war" (*On War*, 1833).

Defilading or Defilement. The arrangement of defenses so that they cannot be, or cannot easily be, enfiladed or subjected to plunging fire or attack from the rear.

Defile. In a military sense, any narrow passageway, such as a narrow mountain pass or a forest path; a causeway, a bridge, or a village might also be so considered. The word is used as a verb for troops moving on a narrow front or narrowing their front; the opposite of "to deploy."

Degen. Technically a straight-bladed infantry sword, but in popular British usage, any sword.

Degradation. A ceremony sometimes inflicted on officers convicted by a French court-martial in which on parade they were publicly humiliated. Their buttons and insignia were torn off, and their swords broken. An officer so degraded was stripped of all titles, privileges, and decorations.

General Achille Bazaine [q.v.] was sentenced to degradation in 1873 for his failures in the Franco-Prussian War [q.v.], but the ceremony was never carried out. Alfred Dreyfus [q.v.] was less fortunate, and in 1894 his degradation was witnessed by a large crowd that included the actress Sarah Bernhardt (1844–1923).

Degrade, to. To reduce a soldier in rank, status, or grade.

Deig, Battle of. See Dig / Deeg / Deig, Battles of.

Dejean, Jean François Aimé (1749–1824). A general in French Revolutionary armies and a minister of war under Napoleon from 1802 to 1809.

Dekabrist Uprising. See Decembrist Uprising.

De la Rey, Jacobus Hercules (1847–1914). An Afrikaner political and military leader in the Transvaal who rose to be a field cornet and then a commandant before the Second Anglo-Boer War [q.v.]. He first attained prominence in the capture of the Jameson raiders in January 1896 [see Jameson Raid]. During the Second Anglo-Boer War he became a general and distinguished himself in the Battle of Magersfontein [q.v.] and in the retreat of the Boer forces before the advance of the British army under Lord Roberts. In March 1902 his forces captured Major General Lord Methuen [q.v.], the highest-ranking British officer to be captured in the war. In the last half of the war he proved himself a brilliant leader of guerrilla forces.

After the war he was killed by a policeman in Johannesburg

when the car in which he was riding failed to stop for a road-block that had been established to catch gangsters.

Delbrück, Hans (1848–1929). A German professor who saw action in the Franco-Prussian War and was a tutor of Crown Prince Frederick (1856–1936), whose education and career were almost entirely military. For twenty years he taught at the University of Berlin, and from 1883 to 1919 he was editor of *Preussische Jahrbücher* (Prussian Yearbook). He is known as the founder of the scientific study of military history and as a pioneer in the study of armies and their relation to society. His first work, a biography of Count August Neithardt von Gneisenau [q.v.], was published in 1880. His most renowned work, the four-volume *History of the Art of War in the Framework of Political History* (1900–20), relates war to the economic, political, and social life of nations. He divided all military strategy into the strategy of annihilation (*Niederwerfungsstrategie*) and the strategy of exhaustion (*Ermattungsstrategie*), the strategy preferred in the eighteenth century, particularly by Frederick the Great (1712–1786).

Delhi, Battle of (11 September 1803), Second Maratha War. This ancient capital of the Hindu and Mogul empires in northern India was captured by the British during the Hindustan Campaign waged by British General Gerard Lake [q.v.], who led an Anglo-Indian army of 10,500 against a French-trained Maratha force of 43,000 under General Louis Bourquien, a French officer in the Maratha service. In the battle British losses were 478, of whom 137 were from the 76th Highlanders; Maratha losses were said to be nearly 3,000. Lake captured 68 guns as well as considerable treasure, and his occupation of Delhi gave the British control over the entire country between the Jumma and the Ganges rivers.

Delhi, Sieges of. There were two major sieges of this ancient capital of the Hindu and Mogul empires astride the Jumma River in northern India.

1. 7–16 October 1804, Second Maratha War. After the disastrous retreat of Colonel William Monson (1760–1807) from Mokundra Pass [q.v.] in August 1804, Jaswunt Rao Holkar [q.v.] with 20,000 Marathas and 100 guns, continued his march on Delhi, which he reached on 7 October. Colonel David Ochterlony [q.v.], in command of the garrison, made vigorous efforts to shore up its dilapidated defenses. When invested, his troops made a determined sortie that successfully spiked almost all of the Marathas' guns. On 14 October the Marathas launched an assault on the Lahore Gate and were beaten back with heavy losses.

Meanwhile General Gerard Lake [q.v.] was pushing forward a relief force from Agra. As it approached the city, the Marathas drew off and the siege was raised.

2. June–September 1857, Indian Mutiny. Major General Sir Archdale Wilson (1803–1874), leading an Anglo-Indian force of 3,000, besieged Delhi, held by about 30,000 mutineers. Even when reinforced, he was unable completely to invest the city. Although on 8 June he occupied the Badli-ki-Serai ridge, just outside the city walls, his force was too weak to assume the offensive. There was almost daily fighting until 14 September, when, after a three-day artillery preparation, a determined assault led by John Nicholson [q.v.] gained a foothold inside the city walls. Losses in the assault were severe and included Nicholson, who fell mortally wounded. Six days of street fighting followed before the city was finally taken. The British lost about 4,000, half of whom were Europeans. Losses among the mutineers are unknown.

Delhi, Sieges of *Blowing up of the Cashmere Gate at Delhi in 1857*

De Lisle, Claude Jean Rouget (1760–1836). A French engineer captain who, on the evening of 25 April 1792, when news that France had declared war on Austria reached Marseilles, wrote the words and the music to "La Marseillaise," originally entitled "Chant de guerre de l'armée du Rhine." On 20 September of that year it was ordered sung on the battlefield at Valmy. Although it became the national anthem, it was suppressed for a time by Napoleon and again for a time after the restoration of the Bourbons. In spite of the fervor of his song, de Lisle was thought not to be republican enough and was cashiered and even imprisoned.

Deliver Battle, to. An expression taken from the French *livrer bataille,* meaning to enter seriously upon an engagement, usually when the opposing forces are in sight of each other.

Déllis. Bosnian and Albanian horsemen who served without pay in the Turkish army in the hope of plundering and acquiring loot.

Delort, Jacques Antoine Adrian (1773–1846). A French soldier who enlisted as a volunteer in 1791 and was commissioned a lieutenant the following year. As a lieutenant colonel in the Battle of Austerlitz [q.v.] he led his regiment when his colonel was killed. He himself was wounded by a Cossack lance. In 1806 as a colonel he was involved in the bitter fighting in Calabria, Italy [see Calabrian War]. He served in Spain during the Peninsular War [q.v.] and was again severely wounded. In 1811 he became general of brigade, and in 1814 general of division. He was present at the Battle of Waterloo [q.v.], where he was shot in the leg and sabered in the arm. From 1830 he served in the royal army. In 1837 he was made a peer of France.

Del Parque, Don Lorenzo de Villavincencio, Duke of Del Parque and San Lorenzo (1778–1859). A Spanish soldier who became a brigadier general in 1808 and in 1809 commanded the Army of the Left in the Peninsular War [q.v.]. He won a clear victory in the Battle of Tahanes on 18 October 1809 but was defeated in the Battle of Alba de Tormes [qq.v.] and was replaced by Francisco Ballesteros [q.v.].

Dembriński, Henryk (1791–1864). A Polish soldier who entered the Polish army in 1809 and fought under Napoleon in his Russian Campaign and at Leipzig [qq.v.]. He was commander-in-chief of the Polish army in the Polish Revolution of 1830–31 [q.v.] and conducted the retreat of the Polish army through Lithuania in 1831. In 1833 he took service under Mehemet Ali [q.v.]. At the beginning of the Hungarian Revolution of 1848–49 [q.v.] he commanded the Hungarian army. He was defeated by the Austrians in the Battle of Kaplona [q.v.] in eastern Hungary on 26–27 February 1849 and again at Timișoara [qq.v.], or Temesvár, in Rumania, on 9 August. The Hungarian Revolution collapsed soon after the last defeat, and its embers were ruthlessly stamped out. Dembriński fled to Turkey. In 1850 he established himself in France.

Demerara Insurrection (1825). A quickly suppressed insurrection against British rule by the natives of British Guiana.

Demi-Brigade. A unit in the French army equivalent to a regiment. The term was in use from 1792 to 24 September 1803, when Napoleon changed the name to regiment. The unit as devised by General Lazare Carnot [q.v.] consisted of a battalion of experienced regulars and two battalions of recruits raised in response to the *levée en masse* [q.v.]. With the return of the monarchy the designation changed back to *demi-brigade*.

Demi-Lune. See Ravelin.

Demonstration. A show of force made without serious intent in an area or a portion of a front in order to deceive an enemy [see Feint].

Denison, George Taylor (1839–1925). A Canadian soldier and writer who served in the militia that repelled the Fenian Raids [q.v.], launched from the United States in 1866. In 1885 he took part in the suppression of the revolt of the Métis. He was the author of *History of Cavalry*, *The Struggle for Imperial Unity*, and *The Fenian Raid at Fort Erie*. [See Riel, Louis David; Riel's Rebellion.]

Denmark, Swedish Invasion of (December 1813–January 1814; 1815). A Swedish army under Crown Prince Jean Baptiste Bernadotte [q.v.] invaded Denmark and forced that country to cede Norway to Sweden. In the spring of 1815 Bernadotte occupied Norway.

Denmark Vesey Rebellion (1822). A slave rebellion planned by Télémaque ("Denmark") Vesey (1767?–1822), a mulatto carpenter and respected member of the African Methodist Church in South Carolina, who purchased his freedom in 1800 after winning a lottery in Charleston. He was in touch with blacks in Haiti, whom he expected to invade America and assist him, but his plot to seize Charleston was uncovered on 16 June 1822, when he was betrayed by one of the conspirators, and the revolt was suppressed. Vesey and 36 co-conspirators were hanged on 2 July.

Dennewitz, Battle of (6 September 1813), Napoleonic Wars. At this Brandenburg village 42 miles south-southwest of Berlin, General Friedrich Wilhelm von Bülow [q.v.] with an army of 50,000 Germans surprised a force of 58,000 French, Poles, and Saxons under Marshal Michel Ney [q.v.] marching on Berlin and struck the division of General Henri Gatien Bertrand (1773–1844) on the French flank. In fierce fighting both sides more than once drove their enemy from their positions, until Ney finally ordered a retreat. The French retreat was turned into a rout by the arrival on the field of a large army under Jean Baptiste Bernadotte [q.v.], the former French marshal, now crown prince of Sweden, fighting on the side of the Allies. Ney lost 10,000 men and was forced to retreat to Torgau on the Elbe River, 39 miles southeast of Dessau. Allied casualties were about 7,000. For his part in the battle Baron Bülow was raised in the peerage to become Count Bülow von Dennewitz.

Dental Services. No nineteenth-century army included dentists. There was no dentist in the British army until General John French [q.v.] suffered a toothache in World War I. If teeth needed to be extracted, the operation was performed by the regimental surgeon.

Denunciator. A military informer. In the Napoleonic French army, a soldier was rewarded for denouncing anyone, enlisted rank or officer, who had embezzled or misappropriated government property.

Department. 1. A territorial division of the U.S. army, e.g., Department of the West, Department of the Cumberland, or Department of the Ohio. During the American Civil War field armies took their names from the department in which they were operating.
2. The designation of certain large military bureaucracies.

Department of War. See War Department.

Deploy, to. To move troops and equipment into assigned or desired positions; to place them in battle formation or into strategic or tactical positions.

Depon. The rank of general in the army of Nepal.

Depot. 1. Any place—a building or a field—where military supplies were stored or recruits were received. It was often located in the center of a regiment or other unit's recruiting district. Armies, such as the British and French, that had overseas garrisons left behind small detachments to send out supplies and drafts and to train recruits. They were sometimes called depot troops [see Depot, Regimental].
2. The place where military supplies were stored; a storehouse.

Depot, Regimental. The "home" of regiments in the French and British armies. When a regiment went on active service, it left behind in its regimental depot its uninstructed recruits, its recruiters, its sick and wounded, and all paperwork not essential in the field. It was the responsibility of the depot to supply its battalions in the field with the men and supplies they needed. It also acted as a recruiting center and often held the regimental museum.

Deringer. See Derringer.

Derna, Battle of (26 April 1805), Tripolitan War. William Eaton [q.v.], an American "naval agent" in North Africa, led an expedition of 8 marines, 1 midshipman, and about 100 mercenaries on a 600-mile trek across the Libyan Desert to restore the throne of Tripoli to Hamet Karamanli, who had been ousted by his brother, Yusaf Karamanli, a rogue who was holding American seamen hostage. Eaton's force captured Derna on the northeast coast of Libya with a bit of help from some American warships, and he probably would have completed his mission had the American commodore not paid the usurper a ransom of $60,000 for the seamen and then abandoned Eaton's mercenaries and Hamet Karamanli. [See Tripolitan War.]

This was the United States' first overseas military land operation. The war contributed "to the shores of Tripoli" to the lyrics of "The Marines' Hymn."

Derrick, Clarence (1837–1907). An American soldier who was a member of the West Point class that was graduated in June 1861, two months after the start of the American Civil War. He ranked fourth in his class and was commissioned in the Corps of Engineers, but he immediately resigned and joined the Confederate army. During the war he rose to be a lieutenant colonel in the 23rd Virginia. In 1864 he was wounded and captured at Occoquon, Virginia.

In 1873 he sailed for Egypt, where he was appointed chief engineer on the staff of General Muhammad Ratib Pasha [q.v.], the commander of the Egyptian army that invaded Abyssinia (Ethiopia) in 1876. He was present at the rout of that army in the Battle of Gura [q.v.] but escaped unharmed. In 1877 he served on the Egyptian general staff and worked on the staff-prepared map of Africa. He left Egypt in 1878 and returned to the United States, where he was variously occupied as a lawyer, teacher, and planter.

Derringer (deringer and other variant spellings). A short, single-shot percussion pistol, deadly only at short range, invented in 1825 by Henry Deringer (1789–1868), a gunsmith in Philadelphia. He failed

Derringer pistol

to patent his design, and there were so many imitators that any small single-shot pistol came to be so called. A double-barreled model existed in which one barrel was placed above the other; this was called an over-and-under. Although never issued, derringers were sometimes carried by soldiers.

Dervishes. The Persian word for beggars.

1. Members of a Muslim religious fraternity noted for body movements that led to trances (whirling dervishes).

2. Mahdists in the Sudan, followers of Muhammad Ahmad, El Mahdi, and his successor, Khalifa Abdullahi [qq.v.], so called by Europeans.

3. The followers of Muhammad ibin-Abdullah (d. 1920), the so-called Mad Mullah of Somaliland [see Mad Mullah of Somaliland, Operations against].

Dervishes *Mounted amir, first Dervish charge at the Battle of Omdurman, 2 September 1898*

Dervish Pasha, Ibrahim (1817–1896). A Turkish soldier who was a general in the Russo-Turkish War [q.v.] of 1877–78. In 1880 he suppressed a revolt in Albania, and in 1882 he served in Egypt. In 1888 he was an aide-de-camp to the sultan of Turkey, Abdul Hamid II (1842–1918).

Desertion. The deliberate absence of a soldier from a post or duty without the intention of returning. In all armies desertion is severely treated, particularly in time of war. One of the most heinous of military crimes is desertion with arms to the enemy in wartime. The arms and equipment a deserter takes with him are sometimes more valuable than the man himself.

Desertion has always been a problem in all armies. In the U.S. army in 1823 there were 5,424 enlisted men, of whom 668, or 12 percent, deserted. In 1830, 24 percent of its soldiers deserted. In the years between 1823 and 1830, when the average strength of the army was 5,100, deserters numbered 6,952. Between 1830 and 1856 an average of 21 percent per year deserted. In 1855, of the first 500 men enlisted in the newly raised 10th Infantry, 275 deserted before completing their five-year enlistments. Between 1865 and 1891, when the average strength of the army was about 25,000, there were 88,475 desertions. One-third of the men recruited between 1867 and 1891 deserted.

Most desertions occurred in the first months of a soldier's enlistment. Two-thirds of all desertions in the American army occurred in the first year and a half of service. Officers blamed the poor quality of recruits, intemperance, poor living conditions, and low pay. In the 1850s soldiers stationed in California deserted in wholesale numbers to join the gold rush.

During the American Civil War about 278,000 deserted from the Union army, and about 105,000 from the Confederate army. Most of them deserted to go home. In southwestern Virginia an association of deserters was formed. In both armies it was noted that more young men from cities and towns deserted than those from farms or rural communities. Foreign-born soldiers, substitutes, and, of course, bounty jumpers were also prone to desert. In peacetime those convicted of deserting were usually punished by two to five years at hard labor, a dishonorable discharge, and loss of pay and allowances, but on both sides during the Civil War the punishment was often death. Of the 267 men executed in the Union army, 147 were deserters. Of those deserting to the enemy, almost all were enlisted or drafted men. Of some 15,000 Union officers, only 26 deserted to the Confederate cause. The rewards sometimes offered for the return of a deserter grew in size as the war progressed. The Union's initial offer of five dollars was raised by the war's end to thirty dollars.

If caught, a deserter sometimes faced summary punishment. John McCue (1848?–1871) enlisted as a private in the 12th Infantry at Albany, New York, on 20 September 1870. On 21 July of the following year at Beale's Springs, Arizona, he deserted and headed west. At Union Pass he was joined by a number of other deserters. There, with the help of Hualapais Indian trackers, they were found by McCue's company commander, Captain Thomas Byrne (1827?–1881). Five of the group surrendered; McCue, who refused, was shot by Byrne and left on the ground for the vultures. There was no investigation.

In 1889 General Nelson A. Miles [q.v.] stated that desertion was "the principal evil besetting the army." After Congress passed the act of June 16, 1890, that reduced the length of enlistments, increased the vegetable allowance, and permitted men to buy their way out for $100, desertions decreased drastically, dropping to 6 percent in 1891, "less than in any year in the history of the army," according to the secretary of war.

One reason for the exceptionally high desertion rate in the nineteenth-century U.S. army was the ease with which capture could be evaded in a country so large; only one in five deserters was ever caught. In the British army, in which men stationed in Britain were close to home and those posted to the colonies or India seldom had a place of refuge, the desertion rate was below 3 percent, a rate equaled in the American army only by the four black regiments formed after the American Civil War [see Black Troops in the U.S. Army]. British troops in Canada were tempted to desert by the sanctuary afforded by the United States, and desertions were also high in Australia, where, as in the United States, it was easy to begin a new life.

Desgenettes, Nicolas René Dufriche (1762–1837). A French surgeon who served in Napoleon's armies in Italy and Asia. At Jaffa in 1799 in an effort to find a vaccine for bubonic plague he courageously inoculated himself with pus from the sores of victims. At Acre, when Napoleon ordered the mercy killing of the sick, Desgenettes refused to obey. He served in Napoleon's Russian Campaign [q.v.] and was captured, but he was released on orders from the tsar. His last service under Napoleon was at Waterloo. Until 1822 he was senior medical practitioner at the Hôtel des Les Invalides [q.v.] in Paris.

Despard, Edward Marcus (1751–1803). An Irish officer commissioned in the 50th Foot of the British army in 1866 who came from a family of six brothers, all of whom, except the eldest, became army officers. He distinguished himself in the West Indies, where he led expeditions against Spanish possessions. Later, as superintendent of a colony in Yucatán, he exhibited talent as an engineer and rose to the rank of colonel. He returned to England to face false charges that had been brought against him, and he spent some time in prison. Embittered because on release he was not given another command or further employment as an officer, he hatched a plot to seize the Tower of London and the Bank of England and to assassinate George III (1738–1820) as the king made his way to open Parliament. On 16 November 1802, before the plot could be executed, Despard and some 40 Irishmen he had persuaded to join him were seized. On 7–8 February 1803 they were tried for high treason.

Vice Admiral Lord Nelson (1758–1805), who had known Despard intimately in the West Indies, was a character witness at his trial and testified: "Colonel Despard was then a loyal man and a brave officer." Found guilty, Despard was sentenced to be hanged and drawn and quartered—the last man in England to be so sentenced. On 21 February he was hanged and beheaded; further butchering was remitted. His wife witnessed the execution and collected his remains.

An older brother, John Despard (1745–1829), also a soldier, was untainted by his brother's crime and became a major general in 1814.

Despard's Plot. See Despard, Edward Marcus.

Despatch. See Dispatch / Despatch.

Dessalines, Jean Jacques (1758–1806). A black soldier born in Guinea who made himself emperor of Haiti. A former slave, he had taken the name of his master, a French planter. In 1797 he joined Toussaint L'Ouverture [q.v.] in his struggle against French rule, but in 1802 he surrendered to French General Charles Victor Leclerc [q.v.]. In 1803, following the betrayal and deportation of Toussaint, Dessalines renewed the war with France and, aided by the British, drove the French out of the country. In January 1804 he announced that Haiti was a republic, but on 8 October he proclaimed himself Emperor Jacques I. He ruled despotically until assassinated by Henri Christophe and Alexandre Sabès Pétion [qq.v.] in 1806. [See Haitian Revolts.]

Detached Works. Field fortifications or other works constructed beyond the musketry range of the principal work but in a position to exercise an influence in any attack upon the main works. [See Ravelin.]

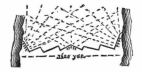

Detached works

Detachment. A fraction of a military unit detached from it for a specific reason or for a specific time.

Detachment *A detachment from General Floyd's command prepares to shell General Rosecrans's camp at Gauley Bridge, American Civil War.*

Detaille, Édouard (1848–1912). A French artist who was a student of Jean Meissonier (d.1891) and was known for his portrayals of Napoleon's battles. Constantly striving for accu-

Detaille, Édouard *The artist at work in his studio*

racy, he acquired a large collection of militaria. During the Franco-Prussian War [q.v.] he enlisted in the 4th Company of the 8th Mobile Battalion and fought at Villejuif and Châtillon.

Detroit, Capture of (16 August 1812), War of 1812. American General William Hull [q.v.], who commanded what was intended to be the western tine of a three-pronged attack on Canada, behaved so timidly that he surrendered Detroit, 2,200 men, and an enormous pile of supplies, to a weaker force of 350 regulars, 400 untrained volunteers, and 600 Indians under Canadian Major General Sir Isaac Brock [q.v.].

Hull was court-martialed and sentenced to be shot but was pardoned because of his record in the Revolutionary War.

Deutsche Waffen und Munitionsfabrik (German Weapons and Ammunition Manufacturing). Popularly called DWM, this German weapons-making company was founded in 1872 as Henri Ehrmann & Cie, a manufacturer of metallic cartridges. After passing through several hands and name changes, it became DWM in 1896, by which time it was manufacturing primers, smokeless powder, detonators, and various weapons. Its telegraphic address was "Parabellum Berlin," and the word "Parabellum" was stamped on all its weapons. Its most famous product was the Parabellum pistol [q.v.], popularly called a Luger.

Deux-Ponts, Christian de Forbach (1752–1813). A French soldier who commanded a regiment in the American Revolution and served with distinction at the Battle of Yorktown in 1781. After the French Revolution, about 1793, he left the French army and commanded a Bavarian unit at the Battle of Hohenlinden [q.v.]. He later returned to the French army and was killed in the Battle of Leipzig [q.v.].

Devens, Charles (1820–1891). A lawyer, politician, and Union soldier in the American Civil War who served initially as colonel of the 15th Massachusetts. He first saw action in the Union debacle at the Battle of Ball's Bluff [q.v.], near Leesburg, Virginia, in October 1861. He was promoted brigadier general on 15 April 1862 and commanded a brigade at Seven Pines [q.v.]. During the Peninsular Campaign [q.v.] he saw action at Fredericksburg and Chancellorsville [qq.v.]. Although his handling of his brigade at Chancellorsville was inept, he was rewarded after the battle by promotion to major general "for highly meritorious service." Later he was given command of a division in the Army of the James.

After the war he became a justice on the Massachusetts Supreme Court and then attorney general of the United States.

Devil Carriage. Sometimes called a *diable*. An early-nineteenth-century four-wheeled wagon for carrying ordnance, usually mortars, for short distances. It had hooks on both ends so that it was unnecessary to turn it around.

Devil's Den. A mass of boulders forming a hill that was a feature on the battlefield at Gettysburg during the American Civil War. On 2 July 1863, held by a brigade and six guns, it was the left-flank anchor of the Union III Corps. At about four o'clock in the afternoon it was attacked by Confederates, who, after bitter fighting, captured it and held it until the end of the battle.

Devil's Den *Dead Confederate sharpshooter in Devil's Den at Little Round Top, Gettysburg, Pennsylvania.*

Devil's Island. French: Île du Diable. One of the Safety Islands off the north coast of what was French Guiana that in the latter part of the nineteenth century became a penal colony for both military and civilian criminals. Captain Alfred Dreyfus [q.v.] was a prisoner here from 1895 to 1898.

Devil's Rope. A colloquial name for barbed wire [q.v.].

De Wet, Christiaan Rudolph (1854–1922). An Afrikaner military and political leader who saw much military action. As a boy he served in Boer commandos during the Basuto Wars of the 1860s. He served in the First Anglo-Boer War [q.v.] of 1880–81 and fought in the Battle of Majuba [q.v.]. He served in the volksraads (legislative bodies) of both the Orange Free State and the Transvaal. At the beginning of the Second Anglo-Boer War [q.v.] of 1899–1902 he served on the Boers' western front as a commandant of an Orange Free State commando under Piet Cronjé [q.v.]. After Cronjé's capture at Paardeberg [q.v.] on 27 February 1900 De Wet became commander-in-chief of the Orange Free State Forces. Exceptionally skillful as a guerrilla leader, he stayed in the field to the end.

In 1914, after leading a rebellion that was suppressed by the South African forces of Prime Minister Louis Botha [q.v.], he was captured and briefly imprisoned.

Dha. The national sword of Burma (Myanmar). It consists of a single edged, slightly curved blade of 12 to 40 inches with a long hilt made of hardwood, horn, ivory, or silver, often carved or engraved. Its scabbard is usually wooden with brass or silver fittings.

Dhanis, François (1861–1909). A Belgian soldier and administrator in the Belgian Congo, who had been educated at the Belgian École Militaire and sent to the Congo in 1887. In 1892–94 he successfully led an expedition against Central African slave traders and was raised to the rank of baron. In 1895 he was given command of the Congo Free State troops at Stanley Falls and was made vice governor. In the following year he led a column composed for the most part of troops recently enlisted from the Batelelar tribe, some of whose chiefs

had not long before been executed for cannibalism. Its purpose was to march to the Upper Nile and annex additional land. In 1897 he occupied Lado and made treaties with surrounding chiefs. The expedition was brought to a halt by the mutiny of his troops, who murdered many of their white officers and bolted [see Batetelar Uprising]. Much of the remainder of 1897 and the year 1898 was spent in breaking up and suppressing bands of mutineers and their rebellious fellow tribesmen. He returned to Belgium in 1899.

Dhuleep Singh (1837–1893). A Sikh ruler at Lahore who was a son and successor of Ranjit Singh [q.v.]. In 1849 he was deposed and pensioned by the British. He became a Christian and until 1886, when he tried, unsuccessfully, to reestablish himself, lived as a Suffolk squire.

Diamond Hill, Battle of (11–12 June 1900), Second Anglo-Boer War. Some 17,000 British troops, divided between forces under Field Marshal Lord Roberts and General Sir Redvers Buller [q.v.], successfully attacked 15,000 Boers who were entrenched in strong positions about 15 miles from Pretoria, capital of the Transvaal. British losses were 25 officers and 137 other ranks killed or wounded; Boer losses are unknown.

Díaz, Juan Martín (1775–1825). A Spanish soldier who distinguished himself as a guerrilla leader known as Empecinado (the Stubborn) in the Peninsular War [q.v.]. In 1814 he became a general, but for his efforts to reestablish the Cortes he was banished in 1818 to Valladolid. In 1820 he joined the Constitutionalists. When the Absolutists won in 1823, he was captured and exposed in an iron cage until stabbed to death by a soldier.

Díaz, Porfirio (1830–1915); his name in full: José de la Cruz Porfirio Díaz. A Mexican mestizo soldier and politician who won fame fighting the Americans in the Mexican War [q.v.] and the French during the occupation of Mexico by the French in 1863–67 [see Mexico, French Invasion and Occupation of]. Between these wars and after them he continually plotted against whoever was in office. Having joined the Oaxaco National Guard, he rose to the rank of general.

As a disciple of Benito Juárez [q.v.] he opposed the dictatorship of Antonio López de Santa Anna [q.v.]. Although Juárez's most effective officer, he was shunned by him in peacetime, and in 1871 he opposed the election of Juárez for a fourth presidential term as unconstitutional. In 1876 he rebelled against Sebastián Lerdo (1825–1889) and was elected president. He remained in office until 1880 and returned to it in 1884. A revolution in 1910 forced him to abdicate in May 1911. He died penniless in exile in Paris on 2 July 1915.

Dibich-Zabalkansky, Count Ivan Ivanovich. See Diebitsch, Count Hans Karl Friedrich Anton von.

Dickman, Joseph Theodore (1857–1927). An American soldier who was graduated from West Point in 1881 and assigned to the 3rd Cavalry. From May 1885 to October 1886 he saw action in the Southwest pursuing Geronimo [q.v.]. In 1899, during the Spanish-American War [q.v.], he served on the staff of General Joseph Wheeler [q.v.] in operations around Santiago, Cuba, and later he served in the Philippines during the insurrection [see Philippine Insurrection against the United States; Aguinaldo y Famy, Emilio]. In 1900, during the Boxer Rebellion [q.v.] in China, he was chief of staff to General Adna Chaffee [q.v.], and in the First World War he commanded first a division and then a corps.

Dickson, Alexander (1777–1840). A British artillerist who passed out of the Royal Military Academy, Woolwich, in 1794. After service in Minorca, Malta, and South America, he was posted to Spain in 1809 during the Peninsular War [q.v.] as brigade major of Wellington's artillery and, although still only a substantive captain, was made chief of all Allied artillery with 8,000 men under his orders. In 1815 he served on the artillery staff in the battles of Waterloo and Quatre Bras [qq.v.]. He died a major general. He was among the first Fellows elected to the Royal Geographical Society.

Dictator. 1. One ruling a country absolutely and arbitrarily, often oppressively. In a number of South American countries, rulers, usually soldiers, who had seized power, assumed this title.

2. The name given a 13-inch seacoast mortar mounted on a railroad car and used by the Union army during the American Civil War on 9–31 July 1864 at the siege of Petersburg [q.v.]. It weighed 8.5 tons and could throw a 200-pound shell 4,325 yards. Soldiers also called the gun the Petersburg Express.

Diebitsch, Count Hans Karl Friedrich Anton von (1785–1831); Russian name: Ivan Ivanovich Dibich-Zabalkansky. A Prussian soldier who was educated at the Berlin cadet school but in 1801 joined the Russian army. He was wounded at Austerlitz, fought at Eylau and Friedland [qq.v.], and was promoted captain. Promotions then came fast. In 1813 he was made a lieutenant general. In 1820 he was chief of staff to Tsar Nicholas I (1796–1855) and served with distinction at Dresden and Leipzig [qq.v.]. In 1825 he quelled a cabal seeking to assassinate the tsar.

During the Russo-Turkish War [q.v.] of 1828–29, he captured Varna [q.v.] after a three-month siege on 12 October 1828 and Silistra in northeast Bulgaria in 1829. He won the Battle of Kulevch [q.v.] on 11 June of the same year and occupied Adrianople on 20 August [see Adrianople, Capture of], winning the surname of Zabalkansky (crosser of the Balkans) and a field marshal's baton. In 1831, commanding the forces fighting the rebel Poles, he won battles at Grochów and Ostrolenka [qq.v.]. He died soon after these victories either from cholera or by committing suicide.

Diesel Engine. This internal-combustion engine was patented by Dr. Rudolf Diesel in 1892, but the first real diesel engine was not built until 1895. At its first public exhibition in Munich in 1898 Austrian senior officers present expressed no interest. Dr. Diesel died when he fell overboard the Antwerp–Harwich steamer on the night of 30 September 1913.

Difaqane. The Sotho word for the *mfecane* [q.v.].

Dig / Deeg / Deig, Battles of, Second Maratha War. Two battles were fought by the British against the Marathas at Dig in east Rajputana, northwestern India, the site of a strong fort built in 1730 and held by the raja of Bhurtpore, an ally of the maharajah of Indore.

1. On 10 December 1804 a British army of 900 European and 7,000 Indian infantry, 1,000 European and 2,000 Indian cavalry, with 10 siege guns and 4 mortars, all under the command of General Gerard Lake [q.v.], laid siege to Dig, which was defended by some 8,000 Marathas under Jaswunt Rao Holkar [q.v.], the maharajah of Indore. Ten days later the artillery made a breach. During the night of 23–24 December three storming parties were formed, and the outer defenses were carried. On the night of the 24th the Marathas decamped. Dig with its numerous guns, large stores of grain, and considerable treasure in specie was in General Lake's hands. British casualties were 43 killed and 184 wounded.

2. On 13 November 1805 a British force of 900 European infantry, 4,200 sepoys, and 700 cavalry under Major General Henry Fraser (d. 1805), who had been detached by General Gerard Lake [q.v.] to reduce Dig, engaged a Maratha force of 14,000 infantry, 3,000 cavalry, and 162 guns again under Jaswunt Rao Holkar. The Marathas were drawn up in front of the fort in a strong position, their left protected by a morass and their right anchored in a village on a height bristling with guns. The battle began in midafternoon with a successful assault on the village. Fraser himself led the 76th Foot in an attack upon the Maratha guns until a cannonball took off his leg. Command then fell upon Colonel William Monson (1760–1807), who completely routed the Marathas, redeeming himself for the disgrace at Mokundra Pass [q.v.] in July–August 1804.

Digna, Osman. See Osman Digna.

Dingaan (d.1843), sometimes Dingane. A Zulu warrior and king who was a half brother of Shaka [q.v.] and one of those who assisted in Shaka's assassination in 1828. Although initially friendly to missionaries and Boer voortrekkers, he treacherously murdered Pieter Retief [q.v.] and a party of Boers in 1838, then sacked a white settlement at present-day Durban in Natal. He was defeated by voortrekkers under Andries Pretorius [q.v.] in the Battle of Blood River [q.v.], after which he became a fugitive, fell out with his brother Panda [q.v.], and fled into Swaziland, where he was murdered.

Dingaan's Day. This principal secular holiday for Afrikaners in South Africa was established on 16 December 1838 in commemoration of the victory of the voortrekkers over Dingaan's [q.v.] Zulus at the Battle of Blood River [q.v.]. In 1952 the name of the day was changed to Day of the Covenant.

Dingiswayo (1770?–1818). A South African warrior, son of a chief, who became chief of the Abatetwas in Natal. A plot to kill his father having failed, he fled from his tribe. Having adopted some European ways, he returned in 1808 riding a horse (never before seen) and carrying a gun. He soon seized power and the chieftainship and then set about shaping his tribal army in an organized manner, aided by a young warrior named Shaka [q.v.]. After Dingiswayo was killed in battle, disturbances broke out throughout the area now containing Natal and Zululand. Under Shaka the Abatetwas were merged with the Zulus.

Dining In. A formal gathering of the officers (sometimes noncommissioned officers) of a unit to dine at the mess and to foster esprit de corps. Guests were often invited.

Dinizulu (1860?–1913). A Zulu chief, one of the sons of Cetewayo. Drawn into a civil war with his brother, Usibepu [q.v.], he called on the Boers in the Transvaal to aid him and with their help became supreme chief. When the British annexed the whole of Zululand in 1887, he revolted. His impis were defeated, and he was captured and exiled for a time to the island of St. Helena. In 1906 he involved himself in the Bambata Revolution and was banished for life to Middleburg in the Transvaal.

Dinwiddie Court House, Battle of. See Five Forks, Battle of.

Diomba. Royal slaves among the Mandes in West Africa, who sometimes served as warriors. They often acquired wealth, wives, arms, and power, and themselves owned slaves.

Diphtheria. This acute infectious disease was a killer of soldiers and civilians alike. Before the discovery of an antitoxin by German bacteriologists in 1894 about one in three victims died.

Diplomacy and the Study of War. Soldiers often complain that diplomats know nothing of war. American General John MacAllister Schofield [q.v.] wrote: "No man can qualify for the duties of statesman until he has made a thorough study of the science of war in its broadest sense. He need not go to military school. . . . But unless he makes himself thoroughly acquainted with the methods and conditions requisite to success in war he is liable to do almost infinite damage to his country" (*Forty-six Years in the Army*, 1897). He was echoed by British General Sir Ian Hamilton [q.v.], who wrote: "The statesman has nothing in his gift but disaster so soon as he leaves his own business of creating or obviating war, and endeavors to conduct them" (*A Staff Officer's Scrapbook*, 1905).

Dippa Negara War. See Java Uprisings.

Direct Fire. Artillery fire in which the gunners can see the target and take direct, visual aim. Until nearly the end of the nineteenth century, all artillery fire was direct fire.

Dirk. A Scottish dagger, long and straight-bladed, usually single-edged, carried by officers and drummers in Highlander regiments in the British army. The officers' dirk, usually worn with sword slings, was $17\frac{3}{4}$ inches long overall, the blade being $10\frac{1}{2}$ inches, and about $1\frac{1}{2}$ inches wide. The dirk of the drummers and sometimes bandsmen was 12 inches long in the blade. [See Skean Dhu.]

Disappearing Gun. A gun that could be raised by counterweights to fire from or over a parapet and then by the force of the recoil controlled by pneumatic brakes sink back behind the parapet. It was used mostly for coastal defenses in the United States.

Disarm, to. 1. To take away the weapons of an armed person.
2. To remove or render harmless an explosive device.

Discharge, to. 1. To fire a firearm.
2. To separate from the army.
[See Bobtail Discharge; Purchase of Discharge.]

Disciplinary Companies. See Compagnies Disciplinaires.

Discipline. Obedience to the orders of those superior in rank or to constituted authority and to the regulations and customs governing soldiers' conduct; the subordination of a soldier's will, pleasure, and inclination to those of higher rank placed over him. Discipline has always been the warp and woof of an army, that which distinguishes it from a mob. As Thucydides (471?–?400 B.C.) wrote in his *History of the Peloponnesian War*, "The strength of an army lies in strict discipline and undeviating obedience to its officers."

Discipline involves the training of a soldier in his duties, responsibilities, and behavior, but it also includes chastisement. Crimes and punishments were set forth in special military rules such as the Mutiny Act [q.v.] in Britain, the Articles of War [q.v.] in the United States, and similar instruments in most other countries. [See Court-martial.]

Diseases. In nearly every European war in the nineteenth century the death rate of soldiers from diseases exceeded that of men of the same ages in civilian life. Death rates among European soldiers in tropical climes were considerably higher. The lightning Franco-Prussian War [q.v.] of 1870–71 and Maori Wars [q.v.] in healthful New Zealand in 1843–48 and 1860–70 were the only wars in the century in which European battle deaths exceeded deaths from diseases. In these wars alone a soldier in the field was less likely to die from disease than was a soldier in barracks in Europe.

For most of the nineteenth century quinine [q.v.] was the only effective medicine known, and the only effective preventive vaccination was that for smallpox.

Dr. Charles Stuart Tripler (d. 1866), appointed medical director of the Army of the Potomac [q.v.] at the beginning of the American Civil War, had served as a doctor on the western frontier, in the Second Seminole War and in the Mexican War [qq.v.], but medical experience was not to be equated with knowledge, for during the Civil War he reported complacently that the Army of the Potomac "must be conceded to have been the most healthy army in the service of the United States." That army had a half million cases of dysentery and diarrhea; bowel diseases alone killed more Union troops than Confederate bullets and shells.

In general and in all armies, young men from the cities fared better than those from rural areas, for many, if not most, had run the gauntlet of childhood diseases—mumps, whooping cough, chicken pox, measles, and scarlet fever—which swept through the rural recruits exposed to them for the first time. In one Confederate training camp during the Civil War, 4,000 out of 10,000 were felled by measles. Military hygiene, if practiced at all, was primitive. Men on the march fared better than those who remained in camps, where contaminated water and food, often by the feces–finger–fly route from camp latrines, ensured a higher rate of dysentery and diarrhea. Whether the soldier was on the march or in camp, mosquito-borne diseases, such as malaria, were, in season, a danger.

Just as the etiology of diseases was unknown, so infections were not understood, although there was an awareness of "zymotic poisons" that caused gastrointestinal diseases and of transfer "agents" for contagious and childhood diseases, such as smallpox. Instruments and dressings were unsterile, and infection was often considered merely a part of the healing process. [See Medicine, Military.]

Disengage, to. To break off contact with an enemy by moving to a new location. This was usually a difficult movement in which a covering force was used to deceive the enemy. One of the most successful of such maneuvers was the disengagement of the Confederate army under Joseph E. Johnston in June 1861 near Harpers Ferry to fight at First Bull Run [q.v.].

Disgarnish, to. To remove guns from a fortification.

Dislodge, to. In a military sense, to force an enemy away from a position he has taken.

Dismissed the Service. When a British officer was dismissed, he was usually told that the sovereign had no further occasion to use his services; when an officer was dismissed specifically, he was said to be cashiered [q.v.] and his dismissal was sometimes attended by marks of degradation [q.v.] and the implication was that he could never serve again.

Dispatch / Despatch. 1. As a noun, a message sent by way of a military courier from one place or person to another. Acknowledgment of its safe receipt was sometimes verified by the recipient's initialing or signing the envelope to be carried back to the sender.

2. As a verb, to send such a military message. [See After-Action Report.]

Dispatch *An American Civil War dispatch bearer*

Displaced. British officers could by their misconduct be forbidden to serve in their regiment (displaced), but they were free to serve in any other regiment or corps that would accept them.

Dispositions. The place and manner in which troops are deployed.

Distinctions. The battle honors awarded to a unit. The names of the battles or wars in which a unit has taken part are displayed on regimental standards or colors, on drums, on streamers attached to the flagpole, or in other fashions.

Distinguished Conduct Medal. A British medal authorized by royal warrant of December 1854 and awarded to noncommissioned officers who had exhibited exceptional bravery in battle. It was originally accompanied by a gratuity that varied according to the rank of the soldier: a sergeant received a one time £15, a corporal £10, and a private £5. Gratuities were abolished in 1862. [See Medals.]

Distinguished Service Order. A British order, commonly referred to as the DSO, instituted on 6 September 1886 and awarded to army and navy officers for "individual instances of meritorious or distinguished service in war." The first investiture was on 17 December and the first officer to receive the award was Deputy Surgeon General Stewart Aaron Lithgow (1833–1899), who had seen much active service in India and Africa. Bars to indicate multiple awards were not authorized until 23 August 1916.

Ditch. An excavation around a fortification. The earth removed was used to construct the rampart and parapet.

Dithakong, Battle of (24 July 1878), Tswana Revolt. Tswana rebels, who had taken up positions on a low ridge overlooking Dithakong, a village in Griqualand, South Africa, were successfully attacked by 300 British colonial troops under Irish-born Colonel William Owen Lanyon (1842–1887).

Divers, Bridget (fl. 1860s), real name: Deaver. During the American Civil War Mrs. Divers, whose husband was in the 1st Michigan Cavalry, accompanied the regiment as a kind of vivandière [q.v.] and later as an agent for the Sanitary Commission [q.v.]. Credited with many acts of valor, she fearlessly ministered to soldiers on the battlefield. At Fair Oaks [q.v.], she was said to have looked up from tending to her mortally wounded husband to urge on his comrades: "Arragh, go in, bhoys! Bate the bloody spaleens and revinge me husband!"

At Cedar Creek she was surrounded but rode through the Confederate lines. She was reputed to be sorry when the war ended but to brighten when she learned that each company of the Indian-fighting army in the West was allowed four laundresses. She soon made her way to the plains and attached herself to a company.

Diversion. Military operations intended to draw the attention of the enemy away from the intended major area of operation.

Division. A military unit containing two or more brigades of cavalry or infantry plus artillery and supporting units. A division was usually the smallest unit containing all arms and services. Although a divisional organization containing all arms was first devised by the Duc de Broglie (1718–1804) in 1759, Napoleon is credited with the development of the divisional concept and the creation of permanent divisions. Other Continental armies followed France's example, but the British did not adopt a divisional structure until 1807, when Wellington formed such units temporarily during the Peninsular War [q.v.]. The division did not become standard in the American army until 1917. Throughout the nineteenth century British and American divisions were always ad hoc arrangements formed only in wartime.

Diwaykarat, Battle of. See Umm Dibaikarat.

Dix, Dorothea Lynde (1802–1887). A philanthropist and hospital reformer who on 29 May 1861, during the American Civil War, was appointed superintendent of female nurses for the Union army. Before the war she had agitated for improved prison conditions and better care for the insane and had been responsible for the formation of model asylums, not only in the United States but in Europe and in Japan.

During the war she recruited nurses, toured hospitals, chastised doctors who were rude to her nurses, and supplied a house in which nurses could rest and recuperate. When the government failed to provide her with sufficient hospital supplies, she collected donations from private citizens.

In recruiting would-be nurses, she set high standards. Applicants had be at least thirty-five years old, but under fifty. "Habits of neatness, order, sobriety, and industry are prerequisites," she wrote. Character references from two "persons of trust" testifying to each applicant's "morality, integrity, seriousness and capacity for the care of the sick" were required. All who were too young or too fetching were rejected; only those who were "plain to almost homeliness in dress, and by no means liberally endowed with personal attractions," were accepted. Dix served without pay for four years; some 6,000 women finally served under her.

She died at eighty-five in the New Jersey State Asylum, one of many she had founded, in Trenton, New Jersey. [See Nurses, Army.]

"Dixie." The rousing song that became the unofficial anthem of the South in the American Civil War was composed by Daniel Decatur Emmett (1815–1904), a popular minstrel singer, who first sang it with his Virginia Minstrels in New York City in 1859. In the following year it was copyrighted, and on 18 February 1861 a march arrangement was played at the inauguration of Jefferson Davis [q.v.] at Montgomery, Alabama.

Dixon, Denham (1786–1828). An English officer and explorer who served with distinction in the Napoleonic Wars [q.v.] and in 1821 joined explorer Hugh Clapperton (1788–1827) in an attempt to discover the source of the Niger River. The two traveled south across the Sahara to Lake Chad, after which Clapperton pushed on alone, but the river's source had eluded them. In 1827 Dixon was appointed governor of Sierra Leone; he died there the following year.

Djunis, Battle of (29 October 1876), Turko-Serbian War. Following the savage suppression of Christian insurrection-ists in Bosnia and Herzegovina in 1875 by the Turks, Serbia and Montenegro declared war on Turkey. At Djunis, Serbia, a Serbian army that included numerous Russian volunteers was defeated by the Turks under Suleiman Pasha [q.v.]. Soon after, Russia declared war on Turkey. [See Turko-Serbian War; Russo-Turkish War; Bulgarian Atrocities.]

Doane Litter. A stretcher made from poles and rawhide invented by Lieutenant George Cheeny Doane (d.1892) of the 2nd U.S. Cavalry.

Doane litter

Doctrine, Military. The accepted body of ideas, as opposed to military theory, concerning an army and its methods of conducting war.

Dodd, David Owen (1846–1864). A seventeen-year-old Confederate spy in the American Civil War who was captured at Little Rock, Arkansas, with incriminating evidence, and tried on 31 December 1863. He was found guilty and sentenced to be hanged, but Union General Frederick Steele (1819–1868), who had captured Little Rock in September, offered to spare his life if he would reveal the names of those who had aided him in gathering intelligence. He refused with the words "I can die, but I cannot betray the trust of a friend." The hanging was bungled; it took eight minutes to kill him.

Dodds, Alfred Amédée (1842–1922). A French soldier born in Senegal of Anglo-French parents who was educated at St. Cyr [q.v.] and commissioned into the Troupes de Marine [q.v.]. He was a company commander in the Franco-Prussian War [q.v.] and was captured at Sedan [q.v.]. In 1872 he was sent to West Africa, where he remained, mostly in Senegal and Upper Niger, except for service in Cochin China in 1878 and Tonkin in 1883.

From 1888 to 1891 he was the colonel commanding troops in Senegal. He led expeditions against the Boal and Kayor tribes in 1889 and against the Serreres in 1890. In April 1892 he commanded a successful expedition to Dahomey (Benin) and annexed the country [see Franco-Dahomey Wars]. He was later inspector general of marine infantry and then of colonial troops.

Dodge, Grenville Mellon (1831–1916). An American soldier who was graduated from Norwich College in 1851. He did engineering work for a railway in Iowa, where in 1856 he formed a militia unit called the Council Bluffs Guards. At the outbreak of the American Civil War he volunteered for the Union army and was soon promoted colonel of the 4th Iowa, serving under John Frémont [q.v.] in Missouri. He fought at Pea Ridge [q.v.] in March 1862 and was promoted brigadier general soon after. In the Atlanta Campaign [q.v.] he commanded a corps. After the war he became chief engineer for the Union Pacific Railroad and served a term in Congress.

In 1898 he was appointed by President William McKinley (1843–1901) to head a commission to investigate the army's logistical performance in the Spanish-American War. The report was published in 1900, and many changes resulted from its findings.

Dog Robber. American army slang for an officer's servant, a striker. Because he could have the food left over from the officer's table, the servant thus could rob the officer's dog of its due.

Dogs, Army. See Pets and mascots.

Dog Soldiers. Members of American Indian warrior societies on the plains who often acted as tribal police. Membership carried both social and military significance. The Cheyenne dog soldiers, one of six warrior societies, formed a separate band renowned for their extreme militancy. During the 1864–69 wars on the plains they stoutly resisted all efforts by peaceful chiefs to accommodate the whites. Their resistance was not broken until they were surprised by seven companies of the 5th Cavalry and three companies of Indian scouts on 11 July 1869 at Summit Springs [q.v.], Colorado.

Dohna, Friedrich (1784–1859). A Prussian soldier who resented and resisted French domination of Prussia in the 1806–11 period. In 1812 he was commissioned in the Russian army, in which he served for three years. He returned to Prussia in time to take part in the Battle of Waterloo [q.v.] in 1815.

His older brother, Friedrich Ferdinand Alexander Dohna (1771–1831), also a determined opponent of Napoleon, was the Prussian minister of the interior from 1808 to 1810 and organized the Prussian landwehr [see Prussian army].

Dolman. The short braided inner jacket worn by hussars.

Dolni-Dubnik, Battle of (1 November 1877), Russo-Turkish War of 1877–78. Russians under General Osip Gurko [q.v.] successfully completed the investment of Plevna [q.v.] in Bulgaria by the capture of this redoubt on the outskirts of the town. The attack on the Turks was made by two divisions of Russian guards.

Dolphins. See Dauphins.

Domaine Extraordinaire. On 30 January 1810 Napoleon established this special department to handle the confiscated properties and war indemnities acquired by his conquests. By this means he helped make past conquests pay for future victories.

Dombrowski, Jan Henryk (1755–1818), more correctly, Dábrowski. A Polish soldier who fought in the Saxon army for four years before joining the Polish army in 1791. He defended Warsaw in 1794 and in 1800 organized the Polish Legion, which fought for France in Italy. After organizing a Polish division at Posen, he fought at Friedland [q.v.] in 1807 and against the Austrians in 1809. In 1812 he took part in Napoleon's disastrous Russian Campaign [q.v.], in which he was wounded at the crossing of the Berezina [q.v.]. In the Battle of Leipzig [q.v.] in 1813 he commanded VIII Corps after the death of General Jozef Poniatowski [q.v.]. In 1815, after the Battle of Waterloo, he returned to Poland. He joined the Russian army and was chosen by the tsar to organize Polish cavalry. He was also appointed senator palatine of the kingdom of Poland.

Domokos, Battle of (17 May 1879), Graeco-Turkish War of 1879. Some 60,000 Turks under Edhem Pasha [q.v.] engaged 40,000 Greeks under the Greek crown prince at this town in central Greece, 17 miles north-northwest of Lamia. The Greeks put up a stubborn defense until their right flank was turned late in the day, upon which they made an orderly retreat. The Turks failed to exploit their advantage. Greek losses were about 600 killed and wounded; Turkish losses were said to be 1,800.

The Graeco-Turkish War [q.v.] of 1879 ended here.

Donabue / Donabew, Battles of (March 1825 and 1853), Anglo-Burmese Wars. Two battles were fought near this Burmese (Myanmaran) town in Pegu Province.

1. On 7 March 1825 Burmese forces successfully resisted an attack by British forces under General Stapleton Cotton [q.v.]. Cotton's force of 700 was too small to succeed, for the Burmese had 12,000 men in three strong stockades. Not until 25 March, when General Sir Archibald Campbell [q.v.] arrived with reinforcements, was the place taken.

2. In November 1853 the British annexed Pegu. [See Anglo-Burmese Wars.]

Donatys. Small copper crosses awarded to Russian privates and noncommissioned officers who had served twenty years in the Russian army.

Donga. The name for a washed-out watercourse or gully in parts of Africa, particularly South Africa.

Dongali, Battle of (26 January 1887), Italo-Abyssinian War. Abyssinian forces under Ras Alula [q.v.], governor of Tigré, attacked and defeated an Italian force of about 500, killing more than 400.

Dongola, Capture of. The Sudanese province of Dongola and the town of the same name (now El Orde) situated on the Nile River about 47 miles above the third cataract were the scenes of three actions between 1812 and 1896.

1. In 1812 Mamelukes who had escaped the fury of Muhammad Ali [q.v.] in Egypt made themselves masters of the province.

2. In 1820 Egyptian forces under Ibrahim Pasha [q.v.] captured the town in the process of conquering the Sudan.

3. In 1885, after the failure of the Gordon Relief Expedition [q.v.], Dongola, which had been used as a base, was abandoned by the British and reoccupied by the Dervishes [q.v.]. On 21 September 1896 General H. H. Kitchener [q.v.], marching up the Nile on his way to Khartoum and Omdurman with an Anglo-Egyptian army, recaptured the town from the Dervishes.

Doniphan, Alexander William (1808–1887). An American lawyer, Missouri legislator, and soldier who, during the so-called Mormon War of 1838, an uprising against the Mormons, was appointed commanding officer of the 1st Missouri Volunteers. When ordered to execute Joseph Smith (1805–1844) and other Mormon leaders who had been tried for treason and sentenced to death, he refused to obey, insisting that to do so would be murder. On the night of 27 June 1844 an enraged mob tore Smith and his brother, Hyrum, from the jail at Carthage, Illinois, and lynched them.

At the beginning of the Mexican War [q.v.] Doniphan enlisted as a private in a volunteer company, but he was soon elected colonel of the 1st Regiment of Missouri Volunteers, a part of the Army of the West under Stephen Watts Kearny [q.v.]. In June 1846 Kearny's force marched out of Fort Leavenworth, Missouri; five weeks and 850 miles later it marched into and occupied Santa Fe, New Mexico.

Kearny, then a brigadier general, divided his army. He took half and marched west to wrest California from Mexico; he left Doniphan in command of the other half with orders to complete the conquest of New Mexico, subdue its Indians, and invade northern Mexico as far as Chihuahua, where he was to link up with General John Ellis Wool [q.v.].

After coercing the principal Navajo into accepting the jurisdiction of the United States, Doniphan set off with his tough but worn command to invade Mexico. On Christmas Day 1846, near the then Mexican town of El Paso, he fought off an attack of some 1,200 Mexican cavalry at a cost of 7 wounded. Mexican losses were 63 killed and about 150 wounded. He occupied the town and did his best to pacify its Mexican citizens. Having learned that they feared the Apaches more than the Americans, he launched a minicampaign to induce the Indians to leave them in peace, then set off on his march to Chihuahua, 4,600 feet high, 200 miles due south as the crow flies, with a desert to cross on the way.

On 28 February 1847 at the Sacramento River just north of Chihuahua he encountered 4,000 Mexicans behind fortifications. In a furious attack he carried the positions, capturing all the Mexican artillery and supplies. Mexican losses were said to be 300 killed; 1 American was killed [see Chihuahua Campaign].

On 1 March he occupied Chihuahua but found no sign of General Wool and his men. The Missourians' one-year enlistments were now expired, and they wanted to go home. Nevertheless, when he finally received orders from General Zachary Taylor [q.v.] to join him at Buena Vista, he and his ragged, footsore men set off for three more weeks of desert marching.

Almost unaided by the American government, Doniphan had led untrained volunteers on a march of 3,600 miles across plains and deserts and fought two successful battles at the cost of 1 man killed and 7 wounded. He had conquered the Southwest for the United States.

After his return he resumed his law practice and again was elected to the legislature.

Donjon. The principal tower or keep of a castle or fortress. Its lower floor or underground portion was used as a prison. Thus, the modern meaning of "dungeon."

Doolie. See Ambulance.

Doornkop, Battle of. See Jameson's Raid.

Dorr Rebellion (1842). More than a half century after the American Revolutionary War, the state of Rhode Island still had not recognized universal male suffrage. In protest, Thomas Wilson Dorr (1805–1854), a lawyer, organized a People's Party that, in a "people's convention," proposed a new, more liberal state constitution. In 1840 a new state government was elected with Dorr as governor. State authorities declared the election illegal, and in 1842 they submitted

their own new constitution, which failed to gain popular support.

Dorr and his people made an unsuccessful attempt to seize the state arsenal at Providence, and armed clashes between "Dorrites" and militia followed. Throughout the conflict the federal government remained aloof. The Dorr government collapsed; Dorr was captured, tried, and sentenced to life in prison at hard labor. A year later he was released under a general amnesty act.

Late in 1842 the state authorities extended the vote to all males.

Dos Mayo Uprising (2 May 1808), Peninsular War. Early in 1808 French Marshal André Murat [q.v.] with 35,000 men occupied Madrid, but he failed to endear himself to the Spanish people. On 2 May (dos Mayo or dos de Mayo) an aroused mob stoned one of his aides in front of the palace, and the French battalion stationed there opened fire.

Rioting spread throughout the city. Murat called up reinforcements and in four hours of considerable bloodshed suppressed the uprising. About 1,000 people were killed, including some 200 French soldiers and the 100 Spanish whom Murat ordered executed the following day. Their executions are the subject of the famous painting by Francisco José de Goya y Lucientes (1746–1828) *3 May 1808.*

Dosser. A stout basket used by soldiers to carry earth on their shoulders from one part of a fortification to another.

Dost Muhammad Khan (1793–1863). An Afghan ruler who assumed the title of amir in 1835. He opposed the attempt of the British to place Shah Shuja-ul-Mulk (1780?–1842) on the Afghan throne and in 1824 established himself on the throne in Kabul. In 1837 he defeated the Sikhs in the Battle of Jamrud and assumed the title of Commander of the Faithful (*Amir ul Mu'minin*). When he made overtures to the Russians and permitted the installation of a Russian agent in Kabul, the alarmed British invaded the country. On 23 July 1839 they sacked Kabul [see First Afghan War] and soon after placed Shah Shuja-ul-Mulk on the throne. Dost Muhammad was held a prisoner in India from 1840 to 1842, when British officials reinstated him as the only prince who could maintain order in the turbulent country. During the Indian Mutiny [q.v.] he kept Afghanistan neutral. In 1862 the Persians invaded Afghanistan and captured Herat, but the seventy-year old Dost Muhammad led his warriors in a campaign that recaptured the city on 26 May 1863 and drove the Persians out of the country.

Dost Muhammad sired twenty-seven sons and uncounted daughters. Two of his sons occupied the throne for short periods before the reign of Shere Ali Khan [q.v.].

Douay, Charles Abel (1809–1870). A French soldier who fought in the Crimean War [q.v.] and distinguished himself in the attack on the Malakoff [q.v.]. He distinguished himself again as a general in the Austro-Piedmontese War at the Battle of Solferino [qq.v.] on 24 June 1859. He was killed in action in the Battle of Wissembourg [q.v.] on 4 August 1870.

His younger brother, Félix Charles Douay (1816–1879), also became a French general in 1863. He distinguished himself at Sedan [q.v.] in 1870, during the Franco-Prussian War [q.v.], and in commanding troops entering Paris during the Commune [q.v.] in May 1871.

Double Action. This is said of pistols that can be fired in either of two ways: by pulling back the hammer to the full cock before pressing the trigger or by using the trigger both to cock and to discharge the pistol. The first method allows for a more deliberate and accurate shot.

Doubleday, Abner (1819–1893). An American soldier who was graduated from West Point in 1842 and served in the Mexican War and the Second Seminole War [qq.v.]. He fired the first gun in the defense of Fort Sumter at the beginning of the American Civil War, and he saw action at Second Bull Run, South Mountain, Antietam, Fredericksburg, and Chancellorsville [qq.v.]. He became a major general, and when Major General John Fulton Reynolds [q.v.] was killed at Gettysburg, he took command of his corps.

Doubleday is often credited with inventing the game of baseball in 1835, while attending school in Cooperstown, New York. This is disputed, but he did do much to promote and develop the game. He retired in 1873 and wrote two books about the Civil War: *Reminiscences of Forts Sumter and Moultrie in 1860–61* (1876) and *Chancellorsville and Gettysburg* (1882).

Double Envelopment. An attack around both flanks of an enemy. The classic example was the maneuver by Hannibal at Cannae in southeastern Italy in 216 B.C.

Double Redan. Two redans side by side and joined. When the outer faces were longer than the inner ones, the work was called a priest's hat [q.v.] or a swallowtail.

Double Shell. A shell used in British 7-inch rifled guns. It was 27 inches long and had a large cavity. To strengthen it against outside pressure, it had three internal longitudinal ribs that projected nearly an inch into the cavity.

Double Shotting. The practice, usually used only in an emergency, of doubling the load of canister or grapeshot in an artillery piece. Occasionally guns were triple-shotted.

Double Time. The fastest marching step. In the American army this was 165 steps, each 33 inches long, taken in one minute. In other armies the pace could be up to 180 steps per minute.

Doughboy. A slang term for an American infantryman in use at least as early as 1859. Only in the First World War did it come to mean any American soldier.

Douglas, Howard (1776–1861). An English soldier commissioned in the Royal Artillery in 1794. He served in Canada and the Netherlands and in the Peninsular War [q.v.]. From 1823 to 1831 he was governor of New Brunswick. From 1835 to 1840 he was lord high commissioner of the Ionian Islands. In 1851 he was promoted general. He wrote about fortifications and bridge construction, and in 1820 he published *A Treatise on Naval Gunnery*.

Douglass, Frederick (1817–1895), real name: Frederick Augustus Washington Bailey. The American son of a female slave and a white man, he escaped from slavery in 1838 and fled to Europe, where he earned enough money to return, buy his freedom, and found a newspaper. During the American Civil War he recruited regiments of blacks for the Union army, and he was later appointed U.S. marshal for the District of Columbia. In 1881 he was named U.S. minister to Haiti.

Doughboy *Doughboys on the march in the Spanish-American War*

Douro, British Crossing of (12 May 1809), Peninsular War. General Wellesley, soon to be Duke of Wellington, crossed the Douro River with 12,000 men and drove Marshal Nicolas Soult [q.v.] with 24,000 out of Oporto, Portugal. The French lost 116 in the action and 5,000 in their retreat; British losses were about 500.

DOW. A common abbreviation for "died of wounds," particularly during the American Civil War.

Dowling, Richard William (1838–1867). An Irish-born owner of several billiards saloons in Houston, Texas, who, at the beginning of the American Civil War, became a first lieutenant in a company calling itself the Davis Guards, a Houston, Texas, volunteer infantry unit that was mustered into Confederate service in the 1st Texas Regiment, Heavy Artillery, in the fall of 1861. Most of its members were Irish dockhands or laborers. Dowling distinguished himself in the recapture of Galveston on New Year's Day 1863, and on 8 September of the same year he won lasting fame in the Battle of Sabine Pass [q.v.], in which he commanded a six-gun battery placed in Fort Griffin, an earth fort situated at a harbor near the mouth of the Sabine River. There his guns beat back a Union force of four gunboats and several transports attempting to invade Texas by way of the river.

Dowling and his men were presented with medals, the only medals ever awarded in the Confederacy [see Davis Medal], received the praise of President Jefferson Davis [q.v.], and the Thanks of the Confederate Congress in Richmond. Dowling himself saw no more action, for he was placed on recruiting duties. He died in a yellow fever epidemic soon after the war.

Down Range. The direction of the targets on a rifle or artillery range.

Doyle, Fanny (fl. 1812). During the War of 1812 [q.v.], in an artillery duel on 12 November 1812 between Americans at Fort Niagara and British and Canadians in Fort George across the Niagara River, Mrs. Doyle, whose husband, an American artilleryman, had been captured in the Battle of Queenstown [q.v.], served one of the Fort Niagara guns with hot shot. On this occasion Fort Niagara was the target of 2,000 solid shot and 180 shells.

Draft. 1. As a noun, a group of recruits or replacements.

2. As a verb, to select or detach soldiers from an army or army post.

3. As a verb, to conscript [see Conscription].

Draftee. In American usage, a conscript.

Draft Riots. See Civil Disorders.

Dragomirov, Mikhail Ivanovich (1830–1905). A Russian soldier and one of the most widely known Russian military writers of the nineteenth century. Born in Ukraine, the son of a veteran of the Napoleonic Wars, he entered the Noble Cadets Corps in 1846 and in 1849 joined the Semenovskii Guards regiment. In 1854 he matriculated at the Nicholas Academy [q.v.], and after graduation he was a student for a time at St. Cyr [q.v.] in France. He investigated the training methods of the French and British armies and in 1859 was an observer at the Austro-Piedmontese War [q.v.]. Throughout the 1860s he occupied the chair of tactics at the Nicholas Academy. He wrote prolifically on military subjects, and his works were translated into German and French. He considered war an art and wrote: "At the present time it will enter no one's head to assert that there can be a military science; it is just as unthinkable as the sciences of poetry, painting and music." A theoretician and a practitioner whose concepts of tactical development reigned for nearly half a century in the Russian army, he favored the "offensive at all costs," particularly a crushing short-range fire followed by a bayonet charge. He railed against a preoccupation with aimed rifle fire and was quoted as saying, "I consider machine guns an absurdity in a field army of normal composition."

Dragomirov was responsible for popularizing the maxim of General Aleksandr Suvorov: "Train the troops only to do that which is necessary in war." Enlarging on the principle, he maintained that men in combat are pulled by two conflicting emotions—self-preservation and self-sacrifice—and that their military education should be divided into indoctrination in loyalty, patriotism, and courage, on the one hand, and, on the other, combat training, such as bayonet drill and related military subjects. Of the two, he considered indoctrination the more important.

He took part in the suppression of the Polish insurrection in 1863–64, the Austro-Prussian War of 1866, and the Russo-Turkish War [qq.v.] of 1877–78, from which he emerged a hero. In the latter war he commanded the division in the van at the crossing of the Danube at Zimnitza (Zimnicea) in southern Rumania. He was wounded soon after at the Shipka Pass [q.v.]. In 1891 he was promoted general of infantry. From 1898 until 1903 he was governor-general of Kiev.

Dragon Musket. See Musketoon.

Dragoon Guards. In the British army, seven regiments of heavy cavalry were for several years so designated and were numbered separately from guards and regular cavalry regiments.

Dragoons. 1. Originally mounted infantry armed with a short musket called a dragon or dragoon because it belched fire. By the nineteenth century the word had no specific meaning. There were sometimes light dragoons and sometimes heavy dragoons and, in the British army, dragoon guards [q.v.].

In the U.S. army the 1st Dragoons was organized in 1832, followed in 1836 by the 2nd Dragoons, an elite service of native-born Americans of specific size and riding ability, standards the army was unable to maintain. In time all cavalry units, except mounted rifles, came to be called dragoons. The term was dropped in 1861, and dragoon regiments became cavalry regiments.

2. The popular name for an early Colt revolver manufactured in various sizes and shapes. All were designed for use by cavalry. The Dragoon Army Model 1848 was a single-action .44 caliber pistol.

Dragoons *French dragoons in the army of Napoleon*

Drawn Battle. An engagement in which neither side wins a complete victory.

Dresden, Battle of (26–27 August 1813), Napoleonic Wars. An Austro-Russian army of 230,000 Austrians, Russians, and Prussians under Prince Karl Philipp von Schwarzenberg [q.v.], accompanied by the tsar of Russia, the king of Prussia, and the emperor of Austria, advanced with 130,000 men upon Dresden, capital of Saxony, over the Bohemian Mountains to the south, 63 miles east-southeast of Leipzig on the Elbe River. Only the French corps of Laurent de Gouvion St. Cyr [q.v.] was in place to protect the city, but Napoleon rushed three additional corps as reinforcements and on 26 August arrived himself to take command. The battle began at once, the French defending with 97,000 troops. The bulk of the first day's fighting fell upon St. Cyr's XIV Corps, but his line held.

On the following day the Allies massed 120,000 men for an attack upon the French center, where Napoleon, intending to attack on both Allied flanks, had left only 50,000 men. At six o'clock in the morning Napoleon opened the battle with attacks by Murat and Victor [qq.v.] on the Allied right flank and soon after attacked on the left, where Ney's [q.v.] columns drove back the Russians. French forces were victorious on both flanks while the Allied forces attacking the French center made little headway. Napoleon expected to continue the battle the next day, but the Allies, having lost 16,000 killed and wounded, 15,000 taken prisoner, and 40 guns, disengaged and retired during the night toward Bohemia. French casualties were 10,000. This was Napoleon's last major victory on German soil.

Dresden Insurrections (1832 and 1849). In 1832 an émeute in Saxony led to the joint regency of Frederick Augustus II (1797–1854) and King Antony (1755–1836). The failure of Frederick Augustus to acknowledge the democratic constitution of the German parliament led in May 1849 to a second insurrection, which was suppressed with the aid of Prussian troops.

Dress, to. To form soldiers in straight lines.

Dressing Station. A medical station directly in rear of the line of battle where wounded soldiers were first seen by a doctor and given field dressings.

Dress Parade. A ceremonial parade in full-dress uniforms.

Dress Sword. A light sword worn by officers in dress or full-dress uniforms.

Dress Uniform. The uniform, often colorful, prescribed for ceremonial use. "Even good men like to make the public stare" (Lord Byron, *Don Juan* III, 1823).

Drew, John (1796–1865). A Cherokee Indian leader who during the War of 1812 [q.v.] fought on the side of the United States against the pro-British Creeks. In 1842 he was captain of a company of Cherokees from Webbers Falls, Indian Territory (on the Arkansas River in eastern Oklahoma), engaged in tracking down runaway black slaves attempting to seek freedom in Spanish-owned Florida. On 4 October

Dresden, Battle of *The death of General Jean Victor Moreau at the Battle of Dresden, August 1813*

1861, during the American Civil War, he was commissioned colonel of a Confederate regiment of Cherokees who formed part of the brigade of Alfred Pike [q.v.] at Pea Ridge [q.v.]. Many of his men tried to defect to the Union army, and fighting flared between the would-be defectors and the Confederate Cherokee regiment of Stand Watie [q.v.].

Drew's regiment was broken up in July 1862. He then produced salt for the Confederacy until the Cherokee lands were overrun by Union forces. He died a poor and saddened man on 25 August 1865.

Drewry's Bluff, Federal Attack upon (6–16 May 1864), American Civil War. In April 1864 General U. S. Grant ordered Major General Benjamin Franklin Butler [q.v.] to move on Richmond, Virginia, from the south with an army of 39,000. Butler moved up the James to Bermuda Hundred, an area between the James and the Appomattox rivers, and built a three-mile long line of entrenchments across the neck of the peninsula, only about two miles from the Richmond &

Dress Parade *The 70th Indiana on dress parade at Camp Burgess, Bowling Green, Kentucky*

Petersburg Railroad. One of his corps commanders, William Farrar Smith [q.v.], strengthened his position by stringing telegraph wire between trees and stumps, the first use in the war of wire entanglements for defense. Butler was unaware that Richmond was then being held by only four brigades of artillery with less than two dozen guns. On 6 May he sent a brigade to reconnoiter in the direction of Petersburg, 23 miles south of Richmond, and it was soon engaged in battle with 20,000 Confederates under General Pierre Beauregard [q.v.].

On the following day Federals launched an attack that reached a junction of the railroad, where they remained long enough to destroy telegraph wires and several hundred yards of track. This battle is sometimes called the Battle of Port Walthall Junction. Federal losses were 289; Confederate losses were 184.

On 9 May Butler moved in strength on Petersburg but was stopped by strong Confederate entrenchments along the banks of Swift's Creek. On 11 May he retreated to his defenses at Bermuda Hundred, and on the following day he began an advance with two corps on Drewry's Bluff (formerly Drury's Bluff), a height, on the right bank of the James River five miles south of Richmond, strongly fortified by Confederates.

The river proved too shallow for the Federal monitors, but Butler received some support from Federal gunboats, although they came under fire from Confederate batteries. Occupied with defending his force, Butler used so many men in his defenses that he had too few for his planned attack.

On 16 May just before five o'clock in the morning Beauregard launched an attack on the Union right with four brigades. He had hoped to demolish Butler's army, but by ten o'clock he had used up his reserves; his subordinates were delayed, and Butler's force retreated in a heavy rainstorm to Bermuda Hundred. By the following morning Butler was, to use Grant's expression, "bottled up."

Drexel Mission, Battle of. See Wounded Knee, Battle of.

Dreyfus, Alfred (1859–1935). A Jew from a wealthy Alsatian family who, after graduation from the École Polytechnique [q.v.], became an officer in the French army. In 1894 in a court-martial he was convicted of treason based on papers forged by Major Marie Esterhazy and Lieutenant Colonel Hubert Joseph Henry [qq.v.], who accused him of writing and passing to the Germans a *bordereau* (memorandum or register) revealing military secrets. He was subjected to public degradation [q.v.] and in 1895 was sent to Devil's Island [q.v.], where he was kept under exceptionally close arrest. In 1898 his case was reopened, thanks in large part to the unremitting efforts of his brother and to the writings of Émile Zola (1840–1902). He was tried by court-martial a second time and again convicted. However, his conviction was set aside by political authorities, who restored him to rank and awarded him the Legion of Honor [q.v.]. He served as a lieutenant colonel in World War I.

The Dreyfus Affair created chaos in the officer corps of the metropolitan French army. Not only were opinions divided and anti-Semitic sentiments openly expressed, but many officers believed that it would somehow stain the honor of the French army to admit that a mistake had been made.

Dreyse Needle Gun (*Zündnadelgewehr*). An 11 mm breech-loaded, percussion-detonated rifle that was the first practical military breech-loading bolt-action rifle and the first to be standardized for use on the battlefield. It was invented in 1836 by Johan Nikolaus von Dreyse (1787–1867), a Prussian inventor, and adopted by the Prussian army in December 1848. Sometimes called a Prussian needle gun, it employed a long, slender, needlelike steel firing pin, propelled by a spring, that passed through the bolt, penetrated a propelling charge of black powder, and detonated a fulminate of mercury primer seated in the base of the bullet. It was the first practical military breech-loading rifle to feature the bolt system of closure. It weighed nine pounds, with a 38-inch barrel, and it fired a 15.43 mm bullet developed by Dreyse. It was 65 percent effective at 300 paces.

The rifle was introduced officially as Model 1841 Percussion Rifle, a clumsy attempt to conceal its method of operation. Not until 1855 was its designation officially changed to needle gun. It was first used in battle, and its effectiveness proved, in the Schleswig-Holstein War [q.v.].

There was worldwide interest in the rifle. In 1866 its comparatively rapid rate of fire proved devastating against Austrian charges in the Seven Weeks' War [q.v.], and *Punch* published a ditty:

The needle gun, the needle gun,
The death defying needle gun;
It does knock over men like fun.
What a formidable weapon is the needle gun!

It was the principal Prussian infantry weapon in the Franco-Prussian War of 1870–71. Although the Prussians won that war handily, they discovered that the French Chassepot [q.v.] was a superior weapon, both in accuracy and in rate of fire. A major disadvantage of the Prussian gun was the fragility of the needle, which had to be replaced after 100 or so shots. Also, the sealing of the bolt soon deteriorated, and flame from the cartridge sometimes burned the face of the firer [see Rifle]. Immediately after the war the Prussian army replaced the gun with the Mauser Model 1871 rifle.

Driefontein, Battle of (10 March 1900). Second Anglo-Boer War. At this place near Bloemfontein 1,500 Boers under De La Rey [q.v.] held off 10,000 British under Field Marshal Lord Roberts for an entire day but were finally forced to retreat. The British lost 82 killed and 342 wounded; Boer losses were more than 100 killed and 22 taken prisoner.

Drift. 1. In South Africa, a ford in a river—e.g., Rorke's Drift [q.v.].
2. The sideways movement of a shell or bullet as it passes through the air resulting from its rotation because of rifling.

Driggs-Seaburg. An American manufacturer of ordnance founded about 1890.

Drill. 1. As a verb, to train or exercise troops in military movements or in the use of weapons.
2. As a noun, the movements or training itself.

Drill *Final movement of a drill to "Prepare to resist cavalry" from a nineteenth-century British military manual*

Drill Jacket. Also known as a shell, fatigue, or stable jacket. This is a plain, short jacket, usually white, best described as a vest (waistcoat) with sleeves.

Drill Sergeant. A noncommissioned officer who drills soldiers and trains them to perform military evolutions.

Drivers. The men attached to horse-drawn artillery companies to drive the horses. In the Napoleonic Wars these were civilians who often bolted when the battle began. In the French army, drivers were not placed under the command of artillery officers until 1817, and men were not enlisted as drivers until 1822.

Drooping. The wearing away from long firing of the muzzle of a smoothbore gun, especially one made of bronze.

Dropping Block. A term for single-shot rifles in which the breechblock moved vertically in guides. An operating lever was used to expose the back of the chamber for loading and unloading.

Drouet d'Erlon, Jean Baptiste (1765–1844). A French soldier in Napoleon's army. In 1803 he was general of division. He distinguished himself at Jena in 1806, Friedland in 1807, and Maya in 1813 [qq.v.]. In 1810, during the Peninsular War, he was posted to Spain as commander of IX Corps. There he served with André Masséna [q.v.] in Andalusia. He recaptured Madrid and fought at Vitoria [q.v.]. He rejoined Napoleon for the Hundred Days [q.v.] and commanded a corps at Waterloo in 1815 [q.v.]. Condemned to death at the second Bourbon restoration, he fled to Bavaria, where he opened a brewery near Munich. In 1825 his death sentence was repealed, and he returned to France and to the army. In 1834 he was appointed governor-general of Algeria, a post in which he served for one year. In the year before his death he was made a marshal of France.

Drouot, Antoine (1774–1847). A French soldier who rose to be a general of division and a senior aide-de-camp to Napoleon. He was wounded in the Battle of Wagram but recovered to distinguish himself in the Battle of Borodino [qq.v.]. He accompanied Napoleon to exile on Elba in 1814. At Waterloo [q.v.] he commanded the Garde Impériale [q.v.]. Napoleon called him *"Le sage de la Grande Armée."*

Druck-punkt Nehmen. German army slang for shirking duty.

Drum. A percussion instrument used in military bands and often employed to transmit orders. After 1858 the British infantry used brass snare drums tuned with screws in place of the earlier ropes and straps and three pounds lighter than previous models. In Germany a copper kettledrum, first used only in elite units, was adopted throughout the cavalry, a practice copied by the British. The bass drum was rarely used.

Drumhead Court-martial. 1. So called from the use of a drum as a field expedient for a table. A court-martial called suddenly by a commanding officer to try soldiers accused of offenses while on the line of march when it was believed necessary to present an immediate example. In such trials the legal niceties were not always observed.

2. Any unofficial court-martial.

Drum Major. The person who commanded and instructed the drummers in a unit and directed the evolutions of the unit's band on parade. In 1881 drum majors in the British army became drum sergeants, wearing on the cuff an insignia of four chevrons pointing upward. The title of drum major was not restored until 1928. The title of fife major was abolished in 1848.

Drummer Boy of Chickamauga. In all American and European armies in wartime there were underage drummers, fifers, and often buglers [see Drummers and Buglers]. In the Union army during the American Civil War one of the youngest was nine-year-old John Lincoln Clem, born John Joseph Klem (1851–1937), who ran away from home in May 1861 and tried without success to join the Union army. Undeterred, he tagged along with the 22nd Massachusetts. He learned to beat a drum, "just the same as a drummer boy," it was said. He performed camp duties, and bore himself as a soldier so well that officers of the regiment clubbed together

Johnny Clem, the hero drummer boy of Chickamauga

to give him a soldier's pay, thirteen dollars a month, until he was formally enrolled on 1 May 1863 as a musician in Company C, 22nd Michigan.

In the Battle of Shiloh [q.v.] in April 1862 his drum was smashed by Confederate artillery. Newspapers dubbed him Johnny Shiloh. In the Battle of Chickamauga [q.v.] in September 1863 he rode into battle on a limber or caisson with a musket trimmed to his size. During the retreat he shot and killed a Confederate officer who yelled, "Surrender, you damned little Yankee!" This too received wide coverage in the northern press, which hailed him as the Drummer Boy of Chickamauga. In October 1863 he was captured when Confederates raided a supply train. He was held captive for two months, and the Confederates seized the opportunity to hold him up as an example of "what sore straits the Yankees are driven, when they have to send their babies to fight us." On 4 January 1864 he was assigned to the headquarters of General George H. Thomas [q.v.], and during the Atlanta Campaign [q.v.], while delivering a message to General John A. Logan [q.v.], he had his horse shot from under him. He was twice wounded in the campaign. By the end of the war he was a lance sergeant.

Still in the army after the war, he tried to obtain an appointment to West Point, but he lacked the academic qualifications. However, a personal appeal to President U. S. Grant won him a commission as a second lieutenant in the 24th Infantry on 18 December 1871. He became a colonel in 1903, and he retired from the army as a brigadier general in 1916, the last Civil War veteran on the rolls.

Drummers and Buglers. Men or boys who played drums or bugles. In the American army, drummers were sometimes called sheepskin fiddlers. Many drummers and buglers were underage, and the majority were the sons of soldiers. In the British and some other armies, the boys were orphans whose

Drummers *Drummer boys of the Union army, by Winslow Homer*

only home was the regiment. When flogging was used as punishment, it was often performed by a drummer while the adjutant stood behind him with a switch to employ if he did not lay on the lashes with a will. Drummers often carried messages, cut hair, and helped surgeons operate.

The Union army during the American Civil War employed 300 drummer boys under the age of fourteen and 25 under ten years of age. Although the U.S. Sanitary Commission [q.v.] complained to President Abraham Lincoln, the practice continued. Albert Woolson, who became a drummer in the 1st Minnesota Artillery when he was less than ten years old, was the last survivor of the war. Orion P. Howe, a fifteen-year-old drummer in the 55th Illinois, won a Medal of Honor at Vicksburg. One of the most famous of the boys was John Lincoln Clem, the Drummer Boy of Chickamauga [q.v.], who grew up to be a brigadier general. Andrew H. ("Andy") Burke (1850–1918), who was a twelve-year-old orphan when he became a drummer in the 75th Indiana, was elected governor of North Dakota in 1890. John Cook [q.v.], a bugler in the Union Army at age thirteen, became the youngest "man" ever to win the Medal of Honor [see Bugle].

Willard Wheeler Nye (1846–1938) served as a drummer boy in the Union army. Enlisting in the 23rd Illinois at age fifteen, he saw much action. After the war he practiced medicine in Hiawatha, Kansas, until his death at age ninety-two.

Drumming Out. A ritual sometimes performed when a soldier was dishonorably "discharged with ignominy and good riddance." The *Times* on 18 May 1863 described the typical British drumming out of a Private Smith: "The sentence upon the culprit was read aloud and he was stripped of his buttons, facings, etc. The battalion then formed a line on either side of the roadway, and, preceded by a corporal and private, and led by a rope attached to his neck by the smallest drummer boy, Smith marched to the gate, the band playing 'The Rogue's March.' On leaving the gate he was supplied with an overcoat, and was taken in charge by an escort which accompanied him to Coldbath-fields Prison, where he will undergo the six months of hard labour" [see Degradation]. To be "drummed out" was sometimes used figuratively to mean dismissal from the service.

Drummond, Thomas (1797–1840). A British soldier who entered the Royal Engineers in 1815 and five years later was a member of the ordnance survey. He invented the limelight, often called a Drummond light, produced by the combustion of oxygen and hydrogen upon a surface of lime [see Searchlight]. Said to have been visible at night for 112 miles, it created a sensation in the scientific world. In 1831 he "glided into politics" (*Dictionary of National Biography*) and became noted for his work in Ireland, of which he became the virtual ruler. He reorganized the constabulary and reduced lawlessness to the point where the number of troops needed to keep order was curtailed from 25,000 to 15,000.

Druse-Maronite Fighting (1860–61). In 1860 the Druses in Lebanon began a series of attacks upon their Maronite neighbors that escalated into massacres of entire families. In the summer of 1860 there began a massacre of Christians of all persuasions in which an estimated 3,000 were killed. In August and September Turkish troops under Mehmet Faud Pasha (1814–1869) with help from French auxiliaries invaded the country, and in January 1861 they quelled the uproar and compelled the Druses to surrender their chiefs.

Duane, William (d. 1835). An American writer and soldier who wrote *Handbook for Infantry* [q.v.] in 1812. It was adopted by the army the following year. In 1813 he wrote *Handbook for Riflemen,* and in 1814 *Handbook for Cavalry.* He served as a colonel in the adjutant general's office from 18 March 1813 to 15 June 1815.

Dubba, Battle of. See Hyderabad, Battle of.

Duberly, Frances ("Fanny") (1829–1903). The wife of Captain Henry Duberly (1822–1891), the regimental paymaster of the 8th (King's Royal Irish) Hussars, who accompanied her husband to the Crimean War [q.v.] and made herself popular with many of the senior officers. Later she accompanied her husband to India, where in the last days of the Indian Mutiny [q.v.] she rode in a cavalry charge. In her old age she complained of the boredom of her life in England.

Duck Lake, Battle of (26 March 1885), second rebellion of Louis Riel. A force of perhaps 200 Métis rebels led by Gabriel Dumont, a lieutenant of Louis Riel [qq.v.], defeated a force of 56 Canadian Northwest Mounted Police and 43 militia and volunteers with a 7-pounder 2 miles from Duck Lake, near a Métis town on the North Saskatchewan River, 83 miles north-northeast of Saskatoon, in present-day south-central Saskatchewan Province. The police and volunteers lost 12 dead or mortally wounded and 11 wounded; the Métis lost 5 dead and 3 wounded, including Dumont, who was slightly wounded in the head.

Ducrot, Auguste Alexandre (1817–1882). A French officer, educated at St. Cyr, who was commissioned in 1840. In 1858 he was promoted general of brigade, and in 1865 general of division. He spent much of his career in North Africa. During the Franco-Prussian War [q.v.] he commanded an army corps at Fröschwiller and Sedan [qq.v.] in 1870. He was captured by the Prussians, and because he refused to accept parole, he was imprisoned at Pont-à-Mousson, from which he soon escaped. During the siege of Paris [q.v.] he commanded the French Second Army. He tried without success to break the siege on 19 September, 21 October, and 30 November 1870 and again on 19 January 1871 [see Buzenval, Battle of]. After the war he took a seat in the National Assembly, where he opposed all democratic ideas. From 1872 to 1878 he commanded the French VIII Corps at Bourges, but he was relieved of his command, accused of inspiring violent articles in *Le Figaro* against the minister of war. He then left the army and occupied himself writing a four-volume work on the defense of Paris.

Dueling. Individual combat between two persons with agreed-upon weapons conducted according to accepted rules at an arranged time and place. The Code Duello, an eighteenth-century formulation of supposed medieval etiquette, was generally observed. Duels were witnessed by seconds, representatives of the two parties, who made the arrangements and oversaw the manner in which the combat took place. Although generally forbidden, duels were not an uncommon method of settling private disputes, particularly among officers, for they involved no social stigma. In overseas garrisons boredom and bad weather sometimes raised temperatures to dueling heat.

In the United States, civil laws varied by state, not all of which outlawed the practice. Some locations became favorite dueling sites. Dueling Oaks in New Orleans and Bloody Island near St. Louis were well known. A "field of honor" [q.v.] at Bladensburg, Maryland, only five miles from Washington, was popular with officers and politicians, for in 1839 Congress outlawed dueling in the District of Columbia, and Virginia also prohibited the practice. From 1818 to the American Civil War more than fifty duels were fought there. The Bladensburg field is now a wedge-shaped grassy area between a cemetery and an International House of Pancakes at Bladensburg Road and 38th Avenue.

American officers were forbidden to duel by the Articles of War adopted in 1806 and in general orders forbidding the practice in 1814. General Zachary Taylor [q.v.] wrote: "I have been in the army 40 years without fighting duels. . . . I will have no dueling men around me if I can help it." Nevertheless, officers persisted in the practice. In one of the most notorious American duels former Vice President Aaron Burr (1756–1836) mortally wounded Major General Alexander Hamilton (1753?–1804) on 11 July 1804 at Weehawken, New Jersey. In 1806 Andrew Jackson [q.v.] killed Charles Dickson, a lawyer whose words had offended him, and himself sustained some broken ribs. In 1810 Winfield Scott suffered a scalp wound in a duel with a fellow army officer, Edmund Pendleton Gaines [qq.v.], and in 1839 he fought another duel with the "Great Pacificator," Henry Clay (1777–1852). On 22 March 1820 in a duel at Bladensburg, naval hero Stephen Decatur (1779–1820) was mortally wounded by James Barron, another naval officer [see Fort Huger, Capture of]. At the same dueling ground navy Midshipman Daniel Key, a nephew of Francis Scott Key [q.v.], was killed by a classmate in 1835.

Duelers were seldom punished. In 1827, when Second Lieutenant David Hunter [q.v.], later a Union major general, challenged his colonel to a duel, he was court-martialed and sentenced to be cashiered, but President John Quincy Adams (1767–1848) remitted the sentence. At Little Rock, Arkansas, when Confederate General John Sappington Marmaduke (1833–1887) made comments that reflected unfavorably upon the courage of Confederate Brigadier General Lucius Marshall Walker (1829–1863), a nephew of President James K. Polk (1795–1849), the two fought a deadly duel at sunrise on 6 September 1863: "pistols at ten paces to fire and advance." Walker was mortally wounded and died the next day. Marmaduke went unpunished.

In England, on 12 September 1840, Lieutenant Colonel Lord Cardigan [q.v.] fought a duel with Captain Harvey Tuckett on Wimbleton Common and wounded him with his second shot. Arrested, he demanded to be tried by his peers. By a legal quibble the House of Lords found him not guilty.

England's most noted duel in which an officer took part was fought by the Duke of Wellington, then prime minister, and George Finch-Hatton, ninth Earl of Winchilsea (1791–1858), a former militia captain and ardent Protestant, who, in denouncing the Catholic Relief Bill of 1829, accused the duke of trying to establish "Popery." Although dueling was not yet illegal in England, Wellington had always opposed the practice, yet at six-thirty on the evening of 20 March 1829 he sent Winchilsea a formal challenge: "I now call upon your Lordship to give me that satisfaction for your conduct which a gentleman has a right to require, and which a gentleman never refuses to give."

The following morning at eight o'clock they met at Battersea Fields. Colonel Henry Hardinge [q.v.] was Wellington's second. Before firing, the duke remarked, "I used to be a good shot but have been out of practice for some years." His shot went wide, and Winchilsea fired into the air.

George Canning (1770–1827), then Britain's foreign secretary, and Viscount Castlereagh (1769–1822), then war minister, met in a duel on Putney Heath in 1809. Castlereagh was slightly wounded. Their quarrel was over who was responsible for the disastrous Walcheren Expedition [q.v.].

Seconds at times contrived to make the duel bloodless. Just before the American Civil War, when an army lieutenant and a sutler's clerk who had quarreled over a poker game at Fort Laramie, Wyoming, met with rifles on the banks of the Platte River on a bitter cold winter's day, Captain (later Confederate General) Henry Heth [q.v.], who was managing the affair, delayed the action so long that the participants' fingers were nearly frozen. Both missed.

Dueling was more common and persisted longer on the European continent, particularly in Germany, Austria, and France, than in Britain and the United States. In Paris the Bois de Boulogne was a popular dueling place. Dueling was so accepted a practice among officers in the Second Empire that one officer who refused to accept a challenge was cashiered. In August 1866, 21 Belgian officers sent their cards and challenges to 21 French officers after the French had been heard to comment unfavorably upon Belgian courage.

In French cavalry regiments the master of arms decided if the pretext for the duel was sufficient. In Germany the military code authorized dueling as a last resort in grave cases. Officers sending or receiving challenges were required to report the circumstances to a council of honor, consisting of three officers, who determined if a duel was justified. Any officer who was offered a challenge and refused to accept it was forced to leave the service.

The famous German student duels (*Mensuren*) were illegal, but widely practiced by dueling societies (*Verbindungen*) and were an accepted part of student life.

In the Austro-Hungarian army [q.v.] dueling was declared *Verbrechen* (a felony) in 1855, and officers who dueled or were seconds in a duel in peacetime could lose their commissions and in wartime could face a death sentence. Nevertheless, dueling continued unabated, for to fail to accept a challenge was a sure loss of a commission [see Ehrennotwehr]. Few officers were indicted, fewer were punished, and sentences were always commuted.

Causes of duels ranged from calling a man a liar to staring fixedly "while playing with a dog whip." Many causes were more trivial in the Hapsburg Empire than in Germany.

In the nineteenth century in various countries there also existed the so-called American duel, where a drawing by lot determined which of two parties would end his own life.

Duffadar. See Daffadar.

Duffié, Alfred Napoléon Alexander (1835–1880). A French soldier who was graduated from St. Cyr in 1854 and fought in the Crimean War [q.v.], in which he is said to have been awarded four decorations. He claimed to have served in Senegal and Algeria, although this seems unlikely, and to have been wounded in the Battle of Solferino [q.v.]. In 1859 he arrived in the United States, married a New York heiress, and resigned his commission in the French army. On 9 August 1861, at the beginning of the American Civil War, he became a captain in the 2nd New York Cavalry. By 23 June of the following year he was promoted brigadier general. For a time he commanded a division under General Alfred Pleasonton [q.v.]. A fellow officer referred to him as "a swaggering and flashy fellow," and he appears not to have been popular with his subordinates. He was captured by Confederate guerrillas in October 1864 at Bunker Hill, (West) Virginia, and was not paroled until the end of February 1865. General Philip Sheridan, who condemned him for allowing himself to be captured, wanted him cashiered, but he was exchanged in April and mustered out on 24 August 1865.

After the war he served as U.S. consul in Cádiz, Spain, where he died of tuberculosis on 8 November 1880.

His nickname, Nattie, is sometimes given as part of his real name.

Dufour, Wilhelm Heinrich (Guillaume Henri) (1787–1875). A Swiss soldier who studied at the French École Polytechnique [q.v.] and served in the French army from 1807 to 1814. After the Battle of Waterloo [q.v.] he returned to Switzerland and founded and taught at a military school at Thun, where Louis Napoleon (1808–1873) was one of his pupils. While there he worked on the thirty-two-year project of creating a trigonometrical survey of Switzerland. In 1831 he was appointed chief of staff of the Swiss army. In 1847 he was made a general, and in that capacity he was involved in the suppression of the revolt of the Catholic cantons [see Sunderbund War].

Dufour *General Dufour as conciliator of the Swiss*

In 1856, during the conflict with Prussia over the possession of Neuchâtel, he was placed in command of the republican army and sent to Paris to obtain the mediation of his former pupil, by then Napoleon III, a mission that was repeated in 1859, when the French annexed Savoy. In 1864 he presided over the international conference that drafted the First Geneva Convention [q.v.] pertaining to the treatment of wounded in time of war.

Dufour was the author of a number of books on fortifications, artillery, and other military subjects.

Duke of York's School. See Military Asylum, Royal.

Dukuza. The name of the principal kraal of Shaka [q.v.] after he became chief of the Zulus in 1818. For a time in Shaka's heyday it had a population of several thousand.

Dulcey y Garay, Domingo, Marqués de Castelflotite (1808–1869). A Spanish officer in the Carlist Wars [q.v.]. In the Revolution of 1854 he was captain general of Catalonia. He was twice governor-general of Cuba: in 1862–66 and again in 1869.

Dull Knife Battle (25 November 1876), Great Sioux War. On 14 November 1876, in a campaign aimed at Crazy Horse [q.v.] and his warriors, General George Cook and Colonel Ranald Slidell Mackenzie [qq.v.] with a force of all arms marched out of Fort Fetterman, a post built in 1867 on a sagebrush-covered plateau on the south bank of the North Platte River near the mouth of Prele Creek in Wyoming [see Powder River Expedition]. They marched north, and Cook, learning of a large force of Northern Cheyennes on the Red Fork of the Powder River, hurried Mackenzie forward with about 1,200 cavalry and some Indian auxiliaries. Scouts located the camp of Chief Dull Knife (1810?–1883), about 100 lodges, and after a 25-mile approach march during the night Mackenzie attacked and routed the Indians on the morning of 25 November.

In the lodges were found clothing and accoutrements of the 7th Cavalry taken from soldiers slain in the Battle of the Little Bighorn [q.v.].

Nearly 100 Indians were killed, including three of Dull Knife's sons. Mackenzie lost about 40, more than a dozen of whom were killed or later died of their wounds. More than 600 ponies were captured.

Dull Knife Outbreak (September 1878–January 1879), American Indian Wars. In 1877 the Northern Cheyennes were removed from their home territory in Montana and settled with Southern Cheyennes on a reservation in Indian Territory (Oklahoma), where they were wretched. On 7 September 1878 two of their chiefs, Dull Knife (1810?–1883) and Little Wolf (1820?–1904), led out about 300 of the tribe to begin a long trek back toward Montana. After they crossed the Platte River, they split into two bands. Little Wolf continued northward, but Dull Knife led his people into Fort Robinson in northwest Nebraska under the mistaken belief that from there they would be settled on northern lands. Instead, they were imprisoned.

In January they escaped, but a third of the band was killed in the pursuit or succumbed to the cold. Dull Knife and remnants of his family found shelter through the winter with white and Indian friends, among them Red Cloud [q.v.] and his Sioux, who gave him a permanent place to live. He died, broken and embittered, near the Rosebud River.

Dum-Dum Arsenal. A British arsenal and headquarters of the Bengal Artillery from 1783 to 1853 located at Dum-Dum in West Bengal, eight miles northeast of Calcutta. It was primarily an ammunition factory; dum-dum bullets [q.v.] were said to have been first manufactured here.

Dum-Dum Bullet, also spelled "dumdum." An explosive or expansive bullet that inflicted gaping wounds, named after the Dum-Dum Arsenal [q.v.], where such bullets (called Mark IV) were said to have been first manufactured. The explosive bullet carried a percussion cap on its head and a small charge of powder in a cavity. Expanding bullets carried soft heads or were filed to make longitudinal slits that expanded when they struck bone.

Later William Ellis Metford [q.v.], an English gunsmith, invented an explosive bullet that his government adopted in 1865. Toward the end of the century strong international sentiment arose against the use of dum-dums because of the ghastly wounds they inflicted, but the British argued that such bullets were needed to stop the "savages" they fought in their many wars, who, they said, could be brought down only by "man-stoppers." Nevertheless, the use of the dum-dum was forbidden by a declaration of the St. Petersburg Convention of March 1869 [see St. Petersburg Convention], an action reaffirmed by the Second Hague Convention [q.v.] on 29 June 1899.

Dumont, Gabriel (1837–1895). A Canadian Métis frontiersman, a crack shot, and an expert buffalo hunter, who was chief lieutenant of Louis Riel [q.v.] during his second rebellion. In 1884 he was among those who urged Riel to end his self-imposed exile in the United States and return to Canada. In March of the following year he joined Riel's second rebellion [q.v.] and was wounded in the head at the Battle of Duck Lake [q.v.]. He commanded the Métis in the Battle of Batoche [q.v.], in which they were overwhelmed by General Frederick Middleton [q.v.]. With the failure of the rebellion and Riel's imprisonment, Dumont fled with his family to the United States and from Montana hatched an elaborate plot to rescue Riel. After collecting money, horses, and men, he set up relay stations from Regina in present-day Saskatchewan Province, where Riel was imprisoned, to Lewiston, Montana, but the rescue attempt failed, and Riel was hanged.

Dumont then drifted from job to job. At one time he was a trick rider and marksman in Buffalo Bill's *Wild West Show.* In his last years, under an amnesty for rebels, he returned to Batoche, where he died.

Dumouriez, Charles François du Périer (1739–1823). A French soldier who rose to the rank of general. In September 1792 he defeated the Duke of Brunswick at Valmy, and in November he defeated the Austrians at Jemappes. But after his defeat by the Austrians at Neerwinden in Belgium on 18 March 1793, he initiated a plot to march on Paris and overthrow the revolutionary government. When his troops refused to support him, he fled to the Austrians. In 1800 he settled in England, and in 1804 the British government granted him a pension of £1,200 a year. He was consulted by Wellington, and he advised the Spanish on guerrilla operations during the Peninsular War [q.v.].

Dunant, Jean Henri (1828–1910). A Swiss philanthropist who dedicated his fortune to charity. In 1859 he was so horrified by the sufferings of the wounded he saw on the battlefield at Solferino [q.v.] that he devoted himself to founding an international organization to aid wounded soldiers. He succeeded in bringing about the Geneva Convention of 1864 [q.v.] and was responsible for the establishment of the International Red Cross [q.v.]. In 1901 he shared the first Nobel Peace Prize with Frédéric Passy (1822–1912), the French economist and statesman who in 1868 had founded the International League of Peace [q.v.].

Dundas, David (1735–1820). A British officer, educated at Woolwich [q.v.], who after much active service was appointed quartermaster general in 1795 and promoted lieutenant general the following year. In 1803 he was appointed governor of Chelsea Hospital [q.v.]. After retiring in 1805, he was selected in 1809 to succeed the Duke of York as commander-in-chief of the British army, and he served until 1811. In that time he devised a new system of tactics based upon the methods of Frederick the Great (1620–1688). Dundas was described as "a tall spare man, crabbed and austere, dry in his looks and demeanor."

Dundee, Battle of. See Talana Hill, Battle of.

Dundhu Panth. See Nana Sahib.

Dundonald, Twelfth Earl of. See Cochrane, Douglas Mackinnon Baillie Hamilton.

Dung. The traditional Tibetan spear from 7 to 12 feet long with a double-edged head. The shaft was often reinforced with metal bands, and the butt was fitted with an iron ferrule.

Dunkard Church at Antietam. A whitewashed brick church of the German Baptist Brethren, known as Dunkards, that was a feature of the battlefield of Antietam [q.v.], near Sharpsburg, Maryland, during the American Civil War. Some of the fiercest fighting took place around it on 17 September 1862. The church was destroyed in a storm in 1921, but a citizen of Sharpsburg saved many of the bricks and boards, and a replica was built.

Dunkard Church *Confederate dead of the battle at the Dunkard Church, Antietam, Maryland, 17 September 1862*

Du Picq, Ardant. See Picq, Ardant du.

Duplex Cartridge. A round for a pistol or rifle that fires two bullets from one cartridge case, the second bullet designed to vary its trajectory slightly. Its purpose was to improve the chance of hitting a random target. Georg Luger [q.v.] patented such a cartridge in 1900.

Dupont de l'Étang, Comte Pierre Antoine (1765–1840). A French soldier who was commissioned in 1784 and became a general of division in 1797. He distinguished himself at Valmy, Marengo, Ulm [q.v.], and Friedland [q.v.]. During the Peninsular War [q.v.] he was wounded and forced to surrender at Bailén [q.v.] on 22 July 1808. He was repatriated, disgraced, and imprisoned from 1812 to 1814, when Louis XVIII (1755–1824) appointed him minister of war, a position in which he served only eight months before being dismissed for incompetence. He fled the country when Napoleon returned from Elba but returned after Waterloo and was named a minister of state.

Du Pont de Nemours, Éleuthère Irénée (1771–1834). A French-born American manufacturer who worked in his father's printing plant in Paris from 1791 until it was closed by French radicals in 1798. The following year he emigrated to the United States, and in 1802–04 he founded a factory for making gunpowder on the Brandywine River near Wilmington, Delaware. Large quantities of his gunpowder were sold to the American government during the War of 1812 [q.v.] and later to South American governments. On his death, his sons, Alfred Victor (1798–1856) and Henry (1812–1889), and then his grandsons and great-grandsons continued the manufacture of explosives.

One of Henry's sons, Henry Algernon (1838–1926), served as an army officer from 1861, through the American Civil War, until 1875. He worked for eleven years in the family firm and then served two terms as a U.S. senator.

Düppel / Dueppel / Dybböl, Battles of, Schleswig-Holstein conflicts. Four battles were fought between Danes and Germans near this small town in Jutland opposite the town of Sönderborg, on the island of Alsen six miles to the southeast.

1. On 28 May 1848 German federal troops were defeated by the Danes.

2. On 6 June 1848 in a battle between Germans and Danes the Germans were repulsed.

3. On 13 April 1849 an indecisive battle was fought between German federal troops under Karl von Prittwitz (d. 1871) and Danes under Bernard von Bülow (1815–1879).

4. In 1864, during the Schleswig-Holstein War [q.v.], the Prussians succeeded in capturing the place from the Danes, and it was not returned until 1920. [See Düppel / Dueppel / Dybböl, Siege of; Schlesweg-Holstein War.]

Düppel / Dueppel / Dybböl, Siege of (13 February–17 April 1864), Schleswig-Holstein War. At this south Jutland town (Dybböl in Danish) on the island of Alsen six miles southwest of Sönderborg, the Prussians and Austrians crushed the Danish army.

In February 1864 the Prussians under Prince Frederick Charles [q.v.] laid siege to the fortress and the Danish fortifications along the Dannewerk [q.v.], a line 3,000 meters long with palisaded ditches backed by small blockhouses and ten redoubts connected by a rifle trench and a few gun pits. On 15 March the Prussian siege train was in position and opened fire, bombarding the Danish defenses with 54 guns, of which 36 were the latest Krupp breechloaders. The investment was complete on 30 March. Although the garrison was armed solely with muzzleloaders, the 22,000 Danes held out for sixty-five days against 18,000 Prussians. Only after a particularly heavy bombardment on 17 April was an infantry assault able to carry the defenses.

Danish losses were 1,800 killed and wounded and 3,400 taken prisoner; German losses were 70 officers and 1,331 men killed and wounded.

The end of the siege was followed by a daring passage of the Alsen Sund by the Prussians in small boats under the guns of Danish warships. On 29 June the entire island was captured. [See Schlesweg-Holstein War.]

Düppel, Battles of *Prussian raise the flag at Düppel during the Schleswig-Holstein War, 1864.*

Durand, Henry Marion (1812–1871). A British soldier, the son of a cavalry officer who had served at Waterloo [q.v.]. He was orphaned at an early age but attended Addiscombe [q.v.] and was commissioned a second lieutenant in the Bengal engineers in June 1828. The following year, at age seventeen, he sailed to India, surviving a shipwreck off the Cape of Good Hope en route. In the First Afghan War [q.v.] he played a prominent part in the capture of Ghazni [q.v.], being in charge of blowing in the city's gate. In 1843 he married the daughter of a major general and was promoted captain. In 1848 he served in the First Sikh War and fought at

Chilianwala and Gujerat [qq.v.]. As a lieutenant colonel he distinguished himself in the Indian Mutiny [q.v.], during which his wife was killed. In 1859 he married the widow of an army officer. In 1867 he was knighted and promoted major general, and in 1870 he was appointed lieutenant governor of the Punjab. He was killed when an elephant on which he was mounted crashed his howdah against the roof of a gateway.

Durando, Giacomo (1807–1894). An Italian soldier who was implicated in revolutionary activities in 1831 and 1832. In the Austro-Piedmontese War [q.v.] he commanded the Lombard volunteers and served as an aide-de-camp to the king. During the Crimean War [q.v.], while General Alfonso di La Marmora [q.v.] led the Sardinian troops in the Crimea, Durando replaced him as war minister. In 1856 he was appointed a lieutenant general, but all his duties were political or diplomatic. His brother was Giovanni Durando [q.v.].

Durando, Giovanni (1804–1869). An Italian soldier who was born in Piedmont but spent his early life abroad. He returned to Italy in 1848 and became the commander of a division of the papal forces. He fought the Austrians in Venetia until the fall of Vicenza, then returned to Piedmont and was made a major general. He later served in the Crimean War and commanded a corps in the Austro-Piedmontese War [qq.v.] of 1859.

D'Urban, Benjamin (1777–1849). A British soldier and colonial administrator who served in the Netherlands, Germany, and the West Indies. In the Peninsular War [q.v.] he distinguished himself as a cavalry commander, particularly at Salamanca [q.v.] on 22 July 1812. In 1813 he was a colonel in the British army and a major general in the Portuguese service.

He was governor of Antigua in 1820, of Barbados in 1825–29, and the first governor of British Guiana in 1831. He was promoted lieutenant general in 1837 while governor of the Cape of Good Hope in South Africa (1834–38), where he fought in the sixth Kaffir War [q.v.] and tried unsuccessfully to extend the colony's eastern borders to include the area occupied by the Xhosas. In 1843 he occupied Natal. From 1847 he was commander of troops in Canada. He died in Montreal.

Durban, Natal, in South Africa was named after him.

Durbar. 1. The court or government of a princely state in India.

2. A loose word for a levee or meeting. It was applied both to the great ceremonial levee held in 1877 to proclaim Queen Victoria (1836–1900) queen empress of India and to the informal meetings of a battalion commander with his Indian troops.

Durnford, Anthony William (1830–1879). A British soldier born in Ireland and educated in Germany until he entered Woolwich [q.v.], from which he was graduated and commissioned in the Royal Engineers in 1848. He served in Ceylon, Malta, and Gibraltar before he was sent to South Africa in December 1871. In July 1872 he was promoted major. He commanded the militia and volunteers at the Battle of Bushman's Pass [q.v.], in which he was wounded, on 4 November 1873. He was killed during the Zulu War at the Battle of Isandhlwana [qq.v.] on 20 January 1879.

Dürnstein or Durrenstein, Battle of (11 November 1805), Napoleonic Wars. An attempt by Russian forces under General Mikhail Kutuzov [q.v.] to oppose a French force under Marshal Mortier advancing on Vienna forced the battle near this village on the Danube in central Lower Austria, four miles west-southwest of Krens. The Russians lost about 4,000 men and had to fall back; the French lost about 3,000.

Duroc, Gérard Christophe Michel (1772–1813). A French soldier who was trained as a gentleman cadet in 1789. In 1793 he was commissioned a lieutenant in the 4th Artillery. In 1796 he was Napoleon's aide-de-camp. He served in Italy and in Egypt, where he was wounded. In 1801 he was made general of brigade and two years later general of division. He then served in Prussia, Poland, and Austria. In 1808 he was created Duke of Frioul. He fought at Essling and Wagram and in Napoleon's Russian Campaign [qq.v.], and he played a part in many confidential and diplomatic missions for Napoleon. He was killed by a cannonball near Görlitz in Silesia on 22 May 1813.

Durnford *Africans who enlisted to fight under Major Anthony Durnford in 1873 photographed in the Drakensberg foothills*

Durova, Nadezhda (1783–1866). A Russian woman who abandoned her husband and child to serve in the tsar's cavalry. She enlisted in 1806, claiming to be a man, and distinguished herself in the Russian Campaign against Napoleon in 1807, earning the St. George Cross, the only woman ever to do so. Although her identity was discovered, the tsar commissioned her in the Mariupol Hussars and allowed her to remain in the service in disguise. Between 1812 and 1814 she fought the French and was wounded in the Battle of Borodino [q.v.]. She rose to the rank of captain before resigning her commission in 1816.

Duryée's Zouaves. A famous regiment of volunteers in the Union army in the American Civil War. The regiment, uniformed to resemble French Zouaves [q.v.], was raised in New York City by Abraham Duryée (1815–1890), a rich merchant, and was made up of "some of the best material in the city and its suburbs." On 9 May 1861 it was mustered into Federal service as the 5th New York Infantry. At Gaines's Mill [q.v.] it suffered 169 casualties out of a strength of 450. The regiment later distinguished itself in the Second Battle of Bull Run [q.v.], where it lost 297 men.

Düsack / Dusägge / Düsägge. Originally a short German saber with a large curved blade and a knuckle guard used in fencing. It was adopted as an infantry hanger and used until the mid-nineteenth century.

Dust Shot. The smallest size of shot made. Often used to describe any small shot.

Duty. In military terms, the actions that are required by military regulations and customs of the service regardless of a soldier's personal likes or dislikes and regardless of danger or duress. Different leaders at different times and in different places have used different words to convince men of the significance and worth of duty. Emperor Meiji of Japan in an imperial rescript to soldiers and sailors in 1883 wrote: "Death is lighter than a feather, duty heavy as a mountain." Andrew Jackson [q.v.], addressing his troops on 8 January 1815, just before the Battle of New Orleans [q.v.], said: "The brave man, inattentive to his duty, is worth little more to his country than the coward who deserts her in the hour of danger." Perhaps the finest definition of the duty of an officer was written by an unknown hand and inscribed on a wall at the Indian Military Academy at Dehra Dun: "The safety, honour and welfare of the country comes [*sic*] first, always and every time; the honour, welfare and comfort of the men you command comes next; your own ease, comfort and safety come last, always and every time."

DWM. See Deutsche Waffen und Munitionsfabrik.

Dybböl, Battle of. See Düppel / Dueppel / Dybböl, Battles of.

Dyer Projectile. A three-inch cast-iron artillery projectile with a soft metal expanding cap (an alloy of lead, tin, and copper) at its base and a corrugated cap at its point to direct the flame of the charge, which escaped over the projectile to ignite the fuze. It was invented by Alexander Brydie Dyer (1815–1874), a Virginian who remained loyal to the Union and on 12 September 1864 became a brigadier

Dyer projectile

general and chief of ordnance, a post he held for nearly nine years. Dyer refused to accept any reward for his invention.

Dynamite. An explosive, often called giant powder in the United States, invented in 1866 by Alfred Bernard Nobel [q.v.], a Swedish engineer. He harnessed the power of nitroglycerin [q.v.], which had been discovered in 1847 and was the most powerful explosive known in the nineteenth century, by mixing it with absorbent diatomaceous earth to create a safe blasting powder that could replace black powder. It sometimes included ammonium nitrate or cellulose nitrate. It was not always safe, however, and because of a number of accidents, its importation into Britain was banned from 1869 until the promulgation of the Explosives Act in 1875.

During the siege of Paris [q.v.] in 1870 French military engineers successfully freed gunboats frozen in the ice of the Seine River below the suburb of Charenton-le-Pont by simply exploding a large quantity of dynamite on the surface of the ice. In England in the summer of 1877 it was successfully used to kill oxen, a use the authorities hailed as an advance.

[See Explosives; Propellant.]

Dynamite *Destruction of railroad train by dynamite during the Spanish-American War*

Dynamite Gun. A gun that used compressed air as a propellant to fire a shell filled in part with dynamite. It was conceived in the 1880s by a Mr. Medford but developed by Lieutenant Edmund Louis Zalinski [q.v.], who had been involved in the initial trials in 1884. While Medford was occupied in devising improvements, one G. H. Reynolds mysteriously took out patents covering Medford's unpatented designs. Zalinski resigned his commission and joined Reynolds to form the Pneumatic Dynamite Gun Company, while Medford disappeared from history. A few guns were installed in harbor defenses, including at least one in New York Harbor, and another, mounted on a gunboat, fired three projectiles at Santiago during the Spanish-American War [q.v.]. The gun was sometimes called the Zalinski dynamite gun. A

Dynamite gun

small dynamite gun known as the Sims-Dudley dynamite gun was mounted on a field carriage and was also used in operations above Santiago, but it fired only twenty rounds. Its commander admitted to "faults in material and construction."

Dynamometer. In military usage, this was a machine for measuring the recoil of small arms.

Dysentery. Sometimes called the bloody flux, it is a disease characterized by an infection of the bowels, causing severe diarrhea, often accompanied by the passing of blood and mucus. Dysentery has been one of the great scourges of armies in all ages.

Dzungarian Uprising (1864–71). On a semidesert plateau in Central Asia, between the Tien Shan and Altai mountains, an Islamic people, variously called Dzungarian, Dzoungarian, Dzhungariyan, Jungarian, Sungarian, and Zungarian, who had paid tribute to China for many years, rose in revolt in 1864, massacred all Chinese residents, and established Abel Oghlan, one of their own, as sultan. Since the Dzungarians made frequent predatory raids upon subjects of the tsar, Russia declared war in April 1871. After a brief campaign in May and June that saw several sharp engagements, in all of which the Russians were victors, the sultan surrendered on 4 July and Russia annexed the country. It was returned to China in 1878 and made part of Sinkiang Province.

Eagle. A gilded ornament in the shape of an eagle mounted at the top of the staff of a French Napoleonic standard with distinctive numbers or insignia. It served as a regimental icon and unit designation.

Eagle Creek, Battle of. See Bear Paw Mountain, Battle of.

Earle, William (1833–1885). A British soldier who joined the army as an ensign in the 49th Regiment in 1851. In 1854–55 he fought in all the British battles of the Crimean War [q.v.]. He became a major general in 1880 and took part in the suppression of Arabi's Revolt [q.v.] in 1882. He commanded the garrison at Alexandria from 1882 to 1884, when he was selected to command the river column during the Gordon Relief Expedition [q.v.]. On 10 February 1885 he encountered Dervishes entrenched at Kirbekan. He attacked and carried the Dervish position but was killed by a ball in his forehead.

Early, Jubal Anderson (1816–1894). A Confederate officer who was graduated from West Point in 1837 and at once went to fight in the Second Seminole War [q.v.] in Florida. He resigned his commission the following year to study law and was admitted to the bar in 1840. He later practiced in Rocky Mount, Virginia. In the Mexican War [q.v.] he served as a major of volunteers but saw little action. During the war he developed a severe case of rheumatism that stooped his back for life.

Although he strongly opposed secession, he joined the Confederate army in 1861 as colonel of the 24th Virginia, which he commanded at the First Battle of Bull Run [q.v.]. He was promoted brigadier general, to rank from 21 July, the date of the battle. From 1862 to 1864 he took part in all the engagements of Lee's Army of Northern Virginia [q.v.]. He was promoted major general from 17 January 1863 and lieutenant general from 31 May 1864.

After the Battle of Cold Harbor [q.v.] Lee sent him to the Shenandoah Valley, where he drove Union General David Hunter [q.v.] westward into the Allegheny Mountains. He then moved north. He crossed the Potomac on 9 July 1864 and defeated General Lewis Wallace [q.v.] in the Battle of Monocacy [q.v.] in Maryland. On 11 July he threatened Washington, D.C. [see Early's Raid]. Although driven back into Virginia, he again struck across the Potomac later that month. His cavalry conducted destructive raids over a wide area, and on 3 July he burned Chambersburg, Pennsylvania [see Chambersburg, Burning of]. However, in September he was defeated by Philip Sheridan [q.v.] at Winchester and Fisher's Hill [qq.v.], and his surprise attack upon Sheridan's force was repelled at Cedar Creek [q.v.] on 19 October. The remainder of his command was destroyed by General George Custer at Waynesboro [q.v.], Virginia, on 2 March 1865.

At war's end he fled to Mexico in disguise, and he later sailed to Canada. For a time he considered emigrating to New Zealand, but in 1867 he returned to Virginia, where he resumed his law practice. He became the first president of the Southern Historical Society and wrote his memoirs. His final years were spent with Pierre Beauregard [q.v.], supervising the drawings of the Louisiana Lottery, and in an acrimonious quarrel with James Longstreet [q.v.], whose reputation he endeavored to destroy. Although a capable general, Early was not loved by his subordinates, for he was a meanspirited man, sarcastic, profane, critical, and caustic.

Early's Raid (27 June–7 August 1864), American Civil War. On 27 June 1864 Maryland was invaded by 14,000 Confederate troops, called the Army of the Valley District, under General Jubal Anderson Early [q.v.]. His dual purpose was to force General U. S. Grant to detach part of his army for the defense of Washington, D.C., and to free 18,000 Confederate prisoners held at Point Lookout [q.v.], Maryland. On 9 July his troops found 6,050 Union troops under General Lewis ("Lew") Wallace [q.v.] behind the Monocacy River east of Frederick. Union forces threw back five Confederate assaults, and at the end of the day Early was forced to fall back [see Monocacy, Battle of]. Federal forces lost 1,880, of whom 1,188 were listed as missing; the Confederates lost fewer than 700.

Early dispatched a cavalry brigade to threaten Baltimore while he drove for Washington, D.C. He reached Silver Spring, Maryland, on the outskirts on 11 July, so close to his goal that he could see the recently completed dome of the Capitol only six miles away. After some heavy skirmishing around Fort Stevens, the Federal defenders were reinforced, and Early drew back on the night of the 12th, recrossed the Potomac at Leesburg, Virginia, on the 14th, and moved west and then south toward Strasburg.

Earnest Gun. A breech-loading rifle with a fixed chamber closed by a movable breechblock.

Earthworks. Battleworks made by constructing trenches, revetments, and other defensive works from soil or sand.

Earthworks *Using rockets in bombardment from earthworks*

Eastern Question. An expression used from about 1822, the date of the Congress of Verona, and subsequently to encompass the international problems brought about by the weakness of the Ottoman Empire and its impending dissolution. The revolt of Mehmet Ali, the Russo-Turkish Wars, the revolts of the Balkan provinces, and the Crimean War [qq.v.] were all part of the problem.

Eastern Tennessee, Army of, American Civil War. This force of about 1,500 Confederate militia, organized in 1861 to occupy eastern Kentucky, fought its principal engagement on 16 March 1863 at Pound Gap, Kentucky, where it was shattered by a Union force under Brigadier General James A. Garfield [q.v.]. [See East Tennessee, Confederate Army and Department of.]

East India Company. See Honourable East India Company.

East Indies Rebellions (1894–96). Unsuccessful rebellions by the Indonesians against Dutch rule.

East Tennessee, Confederate Army and Department of, American Civil War. A Confederate department established on 25 February 1862 after the Confederate defeat on 19 January in the Battle of Mill Spring [q.v.], Kentucky (also known as the Battle of Logan's Crossroads). It comprised initially an area of about 17,000 square miles, including the city of Chattanooga, and the number of troops within it varied from 7,000 in January 1863 to 14,000 three months later. It was commanded at various times by about a dozen generals and technically ceased to exist on 25 July 1863.

Eating Irons. British army slang for eating utensils.

Eaton, William (1764–1811). An American soldier who was graduated from Dartmouth in 1790 and entered the army as a captain in 1792. He saw service under Anthony Wayne (1745–1796) against the Indians in Ohio and Georgia, and in 1797 he was appointed U.S. consul at Tunis. In 1802 he quarreled with the dey and returned to the United States. There he hatched a scheme to free American seamen imprisoned by the Barbary pirates and restore to the throne of Tripoli the rightful ruler, who had been usurped by his brother. To carry out the plot, the American government gave him the title of Navy

Agent to the Barbary States, the only person ever to have such a title. He reentered Tripoli in 1804 and, after locating the deposed pasha in Upper Egypt, put together a force of Greek, Italian, and Arab mercenaries and a squad of U.S. marines. With this force and the help of three American cruisers he captured the port of Derna [q.v.] on 27 April 1805, an exploit commemorated by John Greenleaf Whittier (1807–1892) in his poem "Derne" and by the line "to the shores of Tripoli" in "The Marine Corps Hymn." However, his plan to conquer the country was undercut by American naval negotiators, who recognized the usurper as the legitimate ruler and paid a ransom for the release of the captured American sailors. Disgruntled, Eaton resigned and returned to the United States [see Tripoli, War Against the Pirates of]. In 1806 Aaron Burr [q.v.] attempted to enlist him in his conspiracy to seize Spanish-American territory in the Southwest and create a new nation there. In 1807 Eaton testified at Burr's trial and soon after was given the $10,000 he had long demanded to cover his expenses in Tripoli.

Ebelsberg / Ebersberg, Battle of (3 May 1809), Napoleonic Wars. The French won a costly victory at this town on the Traun River in west-central Austria. The Austrian army, retreating toward Vienna after the battles of Abensberg and Eckmühl [qq.v.], was protected by a strong rear guard of 40,000 men and 70 guns commanded by General Johann Hiller [q.v.]. After some preliminary action on 2 May, French Marshal André Masséna [q.v.] launched a strong frontal attack with about 22,000 men. Hiller failed to counterattack, retreating instead to Enns and then to Krems. The French lost 1,700; the Austrians lost an estimated 2,000 to 3,000 killed and wounded and 4,000 taken prisoner.

Ebenezer Church, Battle of (1 April 1865), American Civil War. A cavalry force of about 9,000 under Union General James Harrison Wilson (1837–1925), raiding into Alabama, encountered some 8,000 cavalry and militia under Confederate General Nathan Bedford Forrest [q.v.] at this church near the village of Mapleville in central Alabama. Wilson routed the militia, and Forrest was forced to retreat. The battle lasted less than an hour. The Confederates lost three guns and 300 to 400 men, most of whom were taken prisoner. The Union forces lost 12 dead and 40 wounded.

Ebira. A type of Japanese quiver of lacquered bamboo worn slung from the left shoulder. It often contained a small drawer in the lower part for extra bowstrings or other small accessories.

Eblé, Jean Baptiste (1758–1812). The son of a gunner, Eblé enlisted in the French army as a gunner in 1773 and was commissioned twelve years later. In October 1793 he was made general of division. In 1806 he fought at Halle and Lübeck [q.v.], and in 1808 he became minister of war for Jérôme Bonaparte (1784–1860) in Westphalia. In 1810 he served under André Masséna [q.v.] in Portugal. In 1812 he commanded the bridging train of Napoleon's army in Russia and saved the remnants of the French army by bridging the Berezina [q.v.].

Éboulement. The crumbling or failing of the walls of a fortification.

Ebro, Crossing of the (June 1813), Peninsular War. When French Marshal Jean Baptiste Jourdan [q.v.] retreated from Wellington's army advancing from Portugal, he fell back behind the 480-mile-long Ebro River in northern Spain, which served as a major line of defense. Wellington, however, successfully outflanked the French and broke the Ebro line, an action that led directly to the Battle of Vitoria [q.v.].

Échauffouré. A surprise attack that causes severe damage to the force attacked.

Echelon. 1. A military formation of troops in successive and parallel lines facing the same direction, each on a flank and to the rear of the unit in front of it. To form echelon from a line, the units forming the line moved off, each directly to its front, in succession, so that the unit on the right was farthest advanced and the unit originally on its left was in left rear.

2. "Echelon" is also used loosely to indicate parts of a force—rear, forward, or reserve echelon—regardless of positions or distances.

3. The level of command—e.g., a regiment is a higher echelon than a battalion.

Eckert, Thomas Thompson (1825–1910). An American telegraph expert and soldier who was chief of the telegraph service in the army of General George McClellan [q.v.] during the Peninsular Campaign [q.v.] of the American Civil War. In September 1862 he was transferred to the War Department and placed in charge of the telegraph office that kept in touch with the field armies. He devised a system of laying telegraph wire by spinning off reels mounted on the backs of mules and was brevetted through the volunteer ranks to brigadier general. He remained in the army until 1867. Later he became president of a telegraph company and then a judge in Texas.

Eckmühl, Battle of (22 April 1809). On a hot afternoon near this Bavarian village (now Eggmühl), south of Regensburg, French, Bavarians, and Württembergers under Napoleon and Marshal Louis Nicolas Davout defeated Austrians under Archduke Charles [qq.v.]. In an attempt to cut Napoleon's line of communication, Charles attacked the left of Davout's force, which was isolated, but the attack was pushed home, and Davout held firm. Early in the afternoon

Napoleon arrived with leading elements of his main force on Davout's right. By midafternoon the Austrians were in retreat, having lost 12,000 men. French losses were 6,000, but Napoleon was unable to pursue, for his men were exhausted.

Later, in exile on St. Helena, Napoleon said, "The greatest military maneuvers I have made, took place at Eckmühl, and were infinitely superior to those of Marengo." However, the superior generalship of Davout did more to assure a French victory than did the maneuvers of Napoleon.

Éclaireurs. 1. Grenadier units in Napoleon's army noted for their swift movements.

2. Light cavalry used in the van or on the flanks to obtain intelligence of the enemy's movements.

3. Scouts.

Éclopé. A French term to describe a sick or wounded soldier (not an officer) temporarily unable to function in the ranks but not so ill as to require hospitalization. The term was also applied to temporarily sick or injured cavalry horses. *Éclopés,* men or horses, marched at the rear of a column.

École de Tir. The French musketry school at Vincennes.

École Polytechnique. This school in Paris is one of the most prestigious of the national *écoles spéciales*. Established as a military school by the National Convention on 28 September 1794, it was reorganized and given its present name on 1 September 1795 (informally it is called X, pronounced "eeks"). On 16 July 1804 Napoleon converted it into a school to train artillery and engineer officers. It was again reorganized in 1816 and thereafter provided engineers for civil organizations as well as the army. In 1814 and again in 1830 its students joined in the defense of Paris. Because of the expressed radical political sentiments of the students, the school was temporarily dissolved in 1816, 1830, and 1832.

All Frenchmen, age sixteen through twenty (or twenty-five if soldiers) were eligible to take the annual examination for admittance. The average number of cadets was 350, and the term was two years. A distinctive feature of the cadets' uniforms was, and remains, the bicorne, the cocked hat.

École Supérieure de la Guerre. An advanced French war college founded in 1878. Its first director was Jules Lewal [q.v.].

Écoute. A small mine gallery designed to listen for enemy mining.

Ecrasite. An explosive impervious to damp, shock, or fire invented by Austrian engineers in 1889.

Ecuador, Revolutions in. The first Ecuadorian revolution against the Spanish was a short-lived one beginning at Quito on 10 August 1809 and ending with the execution of its leaders on 2 August 1810.

A second attempt, beginning on 11 October 1810, was crushed in December 1812. Royalists then remained in control until an army under Antonio Sucre [q.v.] defeated a royalist force in the Battle of Pichincha [q.v.] on 24 May 1822. As the Department of the South the newly independent country united with Venezuela and Colombia in a confederacy called Colombia, but this soon fell apart. In 1834 an uprising was led by Vicente Rocafuerte (1783–1847) against the rule of General Juan José Flores [q.v.], a Venezuelan soldier who had arrived with the liberating army of Simón Bolívar [q.v.], ruling since 1830 as dictator, supported by an army largely composed of foreigners. The revolt was suppressed, and Rocafuerte was briefly jailed. He and Flores then agreed to alternate as president.

There were eighteen presidents of Ecuador between 1830 and 1901. Many were overthrown in revolutions led by army officers; one was assassinated while in office. In those years the constitution was rewritten eleven times.

Eden Commission (1879). A British commission whose purpose, to examine the organization of the Indian army and recommend changes, was much the same as that of the 1859 Peel Commission [q.v.].

Edged Weapons. Hand-held cutting weapons, such as lance, sword, saber, bayonet, or bowie knife [qq.v.]. All these were of questionable value in battle, particularly after the Napoleonic Wars and the improvement in shoulder weapons.

Edhem Pasha (1851–1909). A Turkish soldier who was a brigade commander at the siege of Plevna [q.v.] in the Russo-Turkish War [q.v.] of 1877–78. In the Graeco-Turkish War [q.v.] of 1879 he was the victorious commander in the Battle of Domokos [q.v.] on 17 May 1879. In the Graeco-Turkish War [q.v.] of 1897 he was general-in-chief and won the Battle of Pharsalus [q.v.] on 1 May 1897. In 1909 he was appointed minister of war.

Edmonds, Sarah Emma Evelyn, alias Frank Thompson (1841–1898). A woman who during the American Civil War enlisted under the name of Frank Thompson in a volunteer company that became Company F, 2nd Michigan. She fought at First Bull Run, in the Peninsular Campaign of May–July 1862, and in the Battle of Fredericksburg [qq.v.]. At least twice she acted as a spy "disguised" as a woman. She was with the 2nd Michigan in Kentucky when she was infected with malaria; fearing detection, she deserted and under her own name worked as a nurse for the U.S. Christian Commission.

After the war she married a man named Seelye. In 1882 she was able to secure affidavits from former comrades and apply for a pension. In July 1884 Congress granted her a pension in the name of "Sarah E. E. Seelye, alias Frank Thompson." Shortly before her death on 5 September 1898 she became the only woman to be mustered into the Grand Army of the Republic [q.v.] as a regular member.

Education, Military. The first school for the education of officers was founded in Russia by Peter I (1672–1725) in 1698. By the nineteenth century every country of importance either already had or was in the act of establishing military schools. The Royal Military College, Sandhurst [q.v.] was founded in 1799. Both West Point [q.v.] in the United States and the École Spéciale Militaire in France were founded in 1802, and St. Cyr [q.v.] was established the following year. In the United States a number of states founded military schools, among them The Citadel in South Carolina, in 1842, and the Virginia Military Institute [qq.v.], in 1839.

Edwardes, Herbert Benjamin (1819–1868). An English soldier and statesman who served with distinction in India. By applying directly to a member of the Court of Directors of the Honourable East India Company, he obtained a cadetship without attending Addiscombe [q.v.] or obtaining any military education. He was posted as an ensign in the 1st Bengal Fusiliers in 1841 and within three years passed examinations in Urdu, Hindustani, and Persian. In November 1845 he was made an aide-de-camp to Sir Hugh (later Viscount) Gough, commander-in-chief, India. During the First Sikh War [q.v.] he took part in the battles of Mudki and Sobraon [qq.v.]. He was severely wounded in the Battle of Mudki [q.v.] on 18 December 1845. After the war he entered the civil service under Sir Henry Lawrence [q.v.]. He assisted Lawrence in the suppression of a religious disturbance at Lahore in the spring of 1846 and in the following year led an expedition to Bannu on the Waziri frontier. When two British officers were murdered at Multan on orders of the local ruler, Edwardes raised an army of tribesmen and obtained the support of neighboring Muslim states. He won a victory over a numerically superior force at a small village called Kineyri on 18 June 1848, and he took part in the siege and capture of Multan [q.v.].

In 1850 he returned to England, married, and published *A Year on the Punjab Frontier*. The following year he returned to India. As a commissioner on the Peshawar frontier, when the Indian Mutiny [q.v.] erupted, he secured the neutrality of the amir of Afghanistan and raised a force of Punjabis to assist in the siege of Delhi [q.v.].

Ill health led to his retirement to England in 1860. He was knighted and promoted major general but spent his remaining years in Christian causes.

Edwards, John (fl. 1815). At sixteen years of age he was the trumpeter for General Lord Somerset (Robert Edward Henry Somerset, 1776–1842). In the Battle of Waterloo [q.v.] on 18 June 1815 he sounded the charge that launched the British Heavy Brigade and Union Brigade against the French cuirassiers and the infantry of General Jean Baptiste Drouet (1765–1844). Wellington lost a third of his cavalry in the charge, but it checked a French attack. Young Edwards and his bugle survived the slaughter, and his bugle can be seen today in the museum of the Household Cavalry at Windsor.

Effectives. Soldiers armed, fit, and ready for service or action.

Effective Strength. See Strength, Unit.

Eflaka. Turkish musketeers.

Egba-Igadan War (1850?–70?). In the 1850s and 1860s the Egbas, a division of the Yoruba people of West Africa who had their capital at Abeokuta in southern Nigeria, carried on a long, intermittent war with Ibadan that closed the trade routes to Lagos. From about 1865 the Egbas' interests collided with those of the British, and they came increasingly, if unwillingly, under British influence.

Eggmühl, Battle of. See Eckmühl, Battle of.

Eggnog Riot (24 December 1826). At the U.S. Military Academy at West Point, New York, a group of southern cadets, including Jefferson Davis [q.v.], invited the corps to join them in drinking eggnog. When the party was discovered by tactical officers, Davis was arrested and ordered to his room; the others were ordered to disperse. Davis, as ordered, went to his quarters, but his fellows, instead of dispersing, began to riot. North Barracks was wrecked. Muskets were loaded, and one cadet tried to shoot a tactical officer.

By returning to his quarters, Davis was saved from dismissal, but 19 others were dismissed, including Benjamin Grubb Humphreys (1808–1882), who went on to become a lawyer, planter, and legislator in Mississippi and, in the American Civil War, a colonel of the 21st Mississippi and then a brigadier general.

Egypt, British Expedition to (1807). The British believed they could profit from the three-way quarrel among the Mamelukes [q.v.], Muhammad Ali [q.v.], and the Turks [see Egyptian Civil Disorders]. By dispatching a small force to Egypt, they hoped to assure their supremacy there. Accordingly, on 21 March 1807 a British expeditionary force of 70 light dragoons, 180 artillerymen, and 5,000 infantry under Major General Alexander Mackenzie Fraser (1756–1809) arrived at Alexandria and, unopposed, occupied the city.

Fraser was the sort of commander who has been the despair of more than one government, a likable and well-liked incompetent. A small British force he sent up the Nile was ambushed at Rosetta, on the left bank of the Rosetta mouth of the Nile, and lost 185 killed and 218 wounded—nearly half the force. He then sent a brigade of 2,500 men to besiege the town. Muhammad Ali dispatched a strong force to raise the siege, and on 20 April the British were forced to retire with the loss of some 900 men, including a detachment of 36 officers and 780 men trapped at El Hamid and forced to surrender. The British prisoners were made to walk through Cairo streets lined with stakes holding the heads of 200 of their comrades-in-arms who had been killed at Rosetta. Although Fraser was soon reinforced by 2,000 troops, on 14 September this disastrous British expedition sailed back to England.

Egyptian-Abyssinian Wars. See Abyssinian-Egyptian Wars.

Egyptian Campaign of 1882. See Arabi's Revolt.

Egyptian Civil Disorders (1803–05). In 1802 the sultan of Turkey sent a force to drive the French and the British out of Egypt. In March 1803 the British evacuated the country. Egypt then fell into violent turmoil amid a struggle among the Turks, the Mamelukes [q.v.], and the Arnauts [q.v.]. In 1805 the Albanian Muhammad Ali [q.v.] defeated all rivals in the Battle of Minieh and was recognized as the sultan's viceroy. He ruled Egypt for forty years.

In 1824 a rebellion broke out in Upper Egypt led by Ahmed, a self-proclaimed prophet, from a village just south of Thebes. Some 20,000 to 30,000 followers, mostly unarmed fellahin, flocked to his call. The rebels were soon crushed, however, ending the last serious internal threat to the power of Muhammad Ali [see Egyptian Revolt].

Egyptian Conquest of the Sudan. See Sudan, Egyptian Conquest of.

Egyptian Mutiny (1815). This revolt in the Egyptian army ignited when Muhammad Ali [q.v.] first attempted to reorganize it along European lines. The revolt was quickly suppressed, and by 1823 Turkish and Albanian soldiers had largely been replaced by blacks from the Sudan and Egyptian fellahin who were more amenable to military discipline [see Mamelukes, Massacre of].

Egyptian Revolt (1831–32). When Turkish Sultan Mahmud II (1784–1839) failed to award Muhammad Ali [q.v.] of Egypt with the promised pashaliks of the Morea (Peloponnesus) and Syria for his intervention in Greece on the sultan's behalf, he revolted, and on 1 November 1831 an Egyptian naval and land force under his son, Ibrahim Pasha [q.v.], invaded Syria and besieged Acre, which fell on 27 May 1832. On 9–10 June Ibrahim Pasha defeated the advanced guard of an Ottoman army at Homs and Hamah, and on 15 June his Egyptians were in Damascus. On 17 June he routed the main Ottoman army under Hussein Pasha [q.v.] at the Pass of Beilan (Syrian Gates), which cuts through the Amanus Mountains in southern Turkey south of Iskenderon.

Moving into Anatolia, he crushed a Turkish army under Reshid Pasha on 23 December at Konia [q.v.]. Constantinople (Istanbul) now lay open to him. However, a desperate sultan accepted help from Russia, and on 20 February a Russian squadron entered the Bosporus. As the price of peace, Ibrahim demanded and was given Syria, Adana, and İçel.

Egyptian Sudanese Battalion in Mexico (1863–67). Because European troops supporting the reign of Emperor Maximilian [q.v.] in Mexico [see Mexico, French Invasion and Occupation of] were decimated by diseases, especially yellow fever [q.v.], the khedive of Egypt was asked by Napoleon III to supply black soldiers from the Sudan, who were presumed to be more resistant to tropical diseases. On the night of 6–7 January 1863, 446 troops and a civilian interpreter under Jubara Allah Muhammad boarded a French frigate, *La Seine,* commanded by Frigate Captain (later Admiral) Constant Louis Jean Benjamin Jaurès (1823–1889).

Most of the troops were ex-slave conscripts—i.e., they ceased to be slaves the moment they were conscripted. But some were "recruits" rounded up by the Alexandria police just before the ship sailed. When *La Seine* arrived at Veracruz on 24 February, it had lost 5 soldiers from sickness; 5 more died within a few days of landing. In the first two weeks 52 Sudanese soldiers and French sailors died. On 29 May Jubara Allah Muhammad died of yellow fever and was succeeded by Muhammad Bey Almas [q.v.].

Most of the service of the battalion was in the pestilential coastal area called the Tierra Caliente, a hot flat area of gullies, swamps, and quagmires. The battalion earned a good name, but it lost 133 men, 112 of whom were killed. After four years in Mexico the survivors returned to Egypt by way of Paris, arriving at Alexandria on 27 May 1867. All wore at least one medal, and some bore the Legion of Honor [q.v.]. They were feted and promoted, but the battalion was then disbanded and its members were distributed to other units.

Egyptian-Turkish War of 1831–33. See Egyptian Revolt.

Egyptian-Turkish War of 1839–41. Mahmud II (1785–1839), sultan of Turkey, anxious to regain Syria, which was lost to the forces of Ibrahim Pasha [q.v.], the son of Egyptian ruler Muhammad Ali [q.v.], in the Egyptian Revolt [q.v.] of 1831–32, invaded Syria on 21 April 1839, but on 23 June was crushingly defeated by the forces of Ibrahim Pasha [q.v.] in the Battle of Nizib [q.v.]—also called Nezeb (today Nizip)—about 22 miles east of modern Giziantep in northern Turkey. On 1 July Mahmud II died and was succeeded by a sixteen-year-old lad. The admiral of the Turkish fleet then handed over his fleet to Muhammad Ali at Alexandria.

France, Russia, and Britain persuaded the Porte to agree to make Egypt a hereditary pashalik if the Turkish fleet was returned, an offer Muhammad Ali foolishly rejected. Consequently, the British, after bombarding Beirut and Acre, landed troops and defeated the Egyptian army stationed in Syria. When Alexandria was threatened, Muhammad Ali agreed to return the fleet, withdraw from Syria, and resume his annual tribute to Turkey.

Egyptian-Wahhabi Wars. See Arabian Wars.

Ehrennotwehr. A German or Austro-Hungarian army officer's code of "urgent defense of honor," by which an officer was obliged to defend any implied stain upon his honor instantly, even if by doing so, he disobeyed the nation's laws. In 1855 Paragraph 114 was added to the criminal code of the Austro-Hungarian army: "The *Ehrennotwehr* with the aid of a weapon is legal when the honor of an officer . . . is under attack, without provocation and in the presence of one or more persons." The rule applied only to combatant officers and not to medical officers, judge advocates, accountants, and others who were assumed to have a lower standard of personal honor.

Many officers faced a dilemma because they were required at once to assess the quality of the insulter. If the officer drew his sword and cut down a gentleman, he could be punished for not challenging him to a duel instead [see Dueling]. If he failed to cut down his opponent, who later proved to be unworthy of giving satisfaction, he was likely to be punished for failing to exercise *Ehrennotwehr*.

Ehrhardt, Heinrich (1840–1928). A German gun designer and chief ordnance engineer for Rheinische Metallwaaren und Maschinenfabrik of Sömmerda in central Germany. He developed a number of fieldpieces and mountain guns that from 1895 until the First World War were sold to many countries. The 15-pounder used by the British in South Africa during the Second Anglo-Boer War [q.v.] was principally his design.

Eight Banner System. A Chinese military and administrative bureaucracy first established in 1615 by the Manchu emperor Nurhachi (d. 1626). Each *gushan* (about 7,500 men) was given a colored banner, and the units themselves were called banners. In times of war they were used as soldiers; in peacetime they were used as laborers. By the nineteenth century there were many more than eight banners, but they continued to be called Eight Banners and were the mainstay of the Ch'ing (Qing) dynasty. Their number never exceeded 300,000. They were supplemented by troops of Han origin known as Green Battalions. Following the Opium Wars [q.v.] the leaders of the Eight Banners and Green Battalions became so corrupt that their fighting ability was greatly curtailed.

Einjährigen Freiwilligen. One-year volunteers in the Prussian and German armies. These were young men of education and good character who bought their own uniforms and equipment and served only one year with the expectation that each would be given a commission at its conclusion. [See Conscription.]

Ejector. The device on breech-loading small arms that throws out the metal cartridge case after the bullet has been fired.

Elandslaagte, Battle of (21 October 1899), Second Anglo-Boer War. Sixteen miles north of Ladysmith in Natal in one of the early battles of the war a British cavalry force under Major General John French and infantry under Colonel Ian Hamilton [qq.v.] defeated a Boer force that included some German volunteers under Commandant Johannes Hermanus Michiel Kock (1836–1899). The battle was notable for a charge of the 5th Dragoon Guards and the 5th Lancers that turned the Boer retreat into a rout. The Boers lost 250 killed and wounded, including Kock, who was mortally wounded. About 200 were taken prisoner; the British lost 35 officers and 219 other ranks.

Elands River, Battle of (4–15 August 1900), Second Anglo-Boer War. On 4 August a force of 4,000 Australians on an exposed kopje (hill) was surrounded by about 2,500 Boers with six guns. Although pounded by 1,800 artillery shells, the Australians held out for eleven days until relieved by Lord Kitchener [q.v.] on 15 August. The Australians lost 75 killed and wounded and nearly all their horses.

Elba. An island in the Mediterranean Sea between the northeast coast of Corsica and the mainland of Italy near Piombino, to which Napoleon was sent after his first abdication. The Treaty of Fontainebleau on 12 April 1814 made him the ruler of this 86-square-mile island, which then had a population of about 112,000. Napoleon was carried to the island on HMS *Dauntless,* arriving on 4 May 1814. He was permitted a bodyguard of 400 but actually maintained 600 volunteers from the Old Guard. On the night of 26 February 1815 he and his men clandestinely slipped away in hired feluccas. He landed in Provence on 1 March and then began the famous Hundred Days [q.v.], in a triumphal march to Paris.

El Caney, Battle of (1 July 1898), Spanish-American War. A battle in which 6,600 Americans under General Henry Ware Lawton [q.v.] attacked the Spanish and Cuban forces under Calixto García Iñiguez [q.v.] in eastern Cuba, Oriente Province, just northeast of San Juan Hill [q.v.], which was attacked the same day. A Spanish force of 520 under General Joaquín Vara del Rey y Rubio (1840–1898) held the fortified village of El Caney and fought well, but it suffered 235 killed and wounded, including the mortally wounded Vara del Rey; 120 were taken prisoner. The Americans lost 81 killed and 360 wounded. The battle is sometimes said to have marked the end of Spanish rule in the Western Hemisphere.

Elchingen, Battle of (14 October 1805), Napoleonic Wars. At this town on the Danube River near Ulm in Württemberg French forces under Marshal Michel Ney [q.v.] defeated a portion of an Austrian army (about 20,000 men) under General Baron Karl Mack von Leiberich [q.v.]. The French suffered about 3,000 casualties; the Austrians, about 4,000.

Electro-Ballistic Machine. See West Point Electro-Ballistic Machine.

Elena, Battle of (1877), Russo-Turkish War of 1877–78. Russians under Mikhail Loris-Melikov [q.v.] defeated the invading Turkish army under Mukhtar Pasha [q.v.] at this north-central Bulgarian town (today Yelena) on the northern slope of the Yelena Mountains.

Elephant, to See the. An expression common in the American Civil War meaning to experience battle. It was used earlier, particularly in the American West, as a synonym for seeing the world, the big city, for exposure to vice or glamour, etc. An expanded version was "To see the elephant and hear the owl." The implication was that one who had "seen the elephant" was not a recruit or a country bumpkin.

Elephants, Military. Elephants have been employed in armies since biblical times. In the nineteenth-century Indian army they were used for pulling or carrying heavy artillery and for extricating mired vehicles. An Indian elephant with an average weight of 6,600 pounds stands from 10 to 11 feet high and can carry loads of from 1,680 to 2,240 pounds, exclusive of pads. With its marching pace of 3 to 3 ½ miles per hour it could easily keep pace with marching infantry, and it was considered more surefooted than horses or mules on mountain roads. Because elephants tend to panic under fire, they were usually replaced by bullocks on the battlefield. General Robert Napier [q.v.] carried some Indian elephants to Africa, where they gave good service in the Abyssinian Campaign [q.v.].

Elío, Francisco Javier (1767–1822). A Spanish soldier who arrived in Argentina in 1805 and recaptured Montevideo in 1807. In 1810 he became viceroy of Buenos Aires. In 1812 he was back in Spain as commander of the Catalonian and Valencian army. He became governor of Murcia and Valencia in the following year. He was deposed in 1822 by Liberal insurgents and executed on 4 September 1822.

Elephants, Military *The French use elephants to transport heavy artillery.*

Elite Troops. A unit or units designated or regarded as superior. Napoleon's Old Guard, British Guards regiments, and the Confederacy's Stonewall Brigade are examples.

Elkhorn, Battle of. See Pea Ridge, Battle of.

Elkhorn Tavern, Battle of. See Pea Ridge, Battle of.

Ellen's Man George (d. 1873). A Hot Creek warrior with the Modoc Indians, so named because he had been adopted by Ellen, a woman only a few years older than he, whom he later married. During the Modoc War, in the plot to kill General Edward Canby [q.v.] and the peace commissioners, Ellen's Man George was the backup man who fired into the wounded Canby as he lay on the ground. He was killed on 10 May 1873, taking part in an attack led by Captain Jack [q.v.] upon the bivouac of Captain Henry Cornelius Hasbrouck (1839–1910) at Lake Sorass, California.

Ellison's Mill, Battle of. See Mechanicsville, Battle of.

Ellsworth, Elmer Ephraim (1837–1861). An American soldier who, although he was unable to obtain an appointment to West Point, retained an abiding interest in things military, particularly close-order drill. Using the drill and the uniform of French Zouaves [q.v.], he formed and trained marching and drill units. In 1860 he and his company made a successful exhibition tour of eastern cities, even performing on the White House lawn. When the American Civil War broke out, he organized a regiment of New York firemen and dressed and drilled them as Zouaves. The New York Fire Zouaves, as they were called, with Ellsworth as their colonel, were mustered into service as the 11th New York Infantry in April 1861 and took part in the occupation of Alexandria, Virginia. There, on 24 May, Colonel Ellsworth, seeing a Confederate flag flying over the Marshall House, climbed to the hotel roof and replaced it with the Stars and Stripes. As he descended, the hotel proprietor shot and killed him. One of his young Zouaves, Private Francis E. Brownell (1840?–1894), immediately shot and killed the proprietor, an act for which he was awarded the Medal of Honor in 1877. A reporter for the *New York Times* was present, and his account of the affair did much to inflame martial ardor in the North.

Elmira Prison. During the American Civil War this Union prison for enlisted Confederate prisoners of war on the Chemung River at Elmira, New York, was infamous. Built in May 1864 to hold 3,000, it sometimes held as many as 10,000. Ten percent of the prisoners had no blankets; food was scarce and poor in quality; the death rate averaged 5 percent per month. In February and March 1865 there were 917 deaths. Out of the total of 12,123 prisoners, 2,963 died, the highest death rate for any Union prison. The chief surgeon, Eugene Francis Sanger (d. 1897), boasted that he had killed more rebels than any soldier at the front. The abominable conditions have been compared with the Confederate Andersonville Prison [q.v.]. Punishments for such crimes as eating a dog were brutal. Sweatboxes, hanging by the thumbs, and the buck and gag [q.v.] were frequently employed. Only 17 prisoners managed to escape; 10 of these were men who dug a tunnel 66 feet long and escaped through it on 7 October 1864.

By the end of the American Civil War 25,967, or 12 percent, of the Confederate prisoners held by the North died in captivity, as did 30,218, or 15.5 percent, of Union prisoners of war in Confederate prisons.

El Obeid, Battle of. See Kashgil, Battle of.

El Salvador, Revolts in. 1. December 1822–February 1823. In December 1822 Salvadorians who wanted freedom from Mexican rule rose in revolt and proclaimed their desire to unite with the United States. In the following February the revolt was crushed by Mexican troops under General Vicente Filísola, a Neapolitan soldier in the Mexican service.

2. In 1832 and 1833 unsuccessful Indian uprisings flared in San Vicente and Tejutla.

Elswick Ordnance Company. The company established by Sir William Armstrong [q.v.] to manufacture his guns. Elswick is now a ward of Newcastle-upon-Tyne.

El Teb, Battles of (1884), Egyptian-Dervish conflicts. This halting place in the desert of eastern Sudan, more correctly called Ander Teb, nine miles west of the Red Sea port of Trinkitat, saw two battles during the Mahdiya [q.v.].

1. On 4 February 1884 a heterogenous Egyptian force of 3,800, consisting mostly of a newly formed and ill-trained Egyptian gendarmerie, all under the command of Valentine Baker Pasha [q.v.], marching to relieve besieged Sinkat, was utterly destroyed by an estimated 1,200 Hadendowa Beja tribesmen ["Fuzzy-Wuzzies," q.v.] under Osman Digna [q.v.]. Baker Pasha survived but lost more than 2,000 men. The Hadendowas collected a rich store of Remington rifles, half a million rounds of ammunition, four Krupp guns, and two Gatlings.

2. On 28 February 1884 an Anglo-Egyptian army of 4,000 with 14 guns under Major General Gerald Graham, VC (1831–1899) defeated a Hadendowa force under Osman Digna at this same place. The brunt of the fighting by Graham's force was borne by a battalion of the Black Watch,

which suffered 30 killed and 159 wounded. The Hadendowas lost 825 dead.

Elvas, Siege of (October 1808), Peninsular War. A French garrison stationed at this fortified city in east-central Portugal 10 miles northwest of Badajoz surrendered to a numerically superior Anglo-Spanish force. Elvas contained an arsenal and bombproof barracks that could house more than 6,000 men. It was from this city that the ultimately successful British effort to retake Badajoz was launched in March 1812 [see Badajoz, Sieges of].

Elzey (born Jones), Arnold (1816–1871). A Confederate soldier, born Arnold Elzey Jones in Maryland, who was graduated from West Point in 1837, at which time he dropped his last name (Elzey was the name of his paternal grandmother). He fought in the Second Seminole War [q.v.]. Stationed in what is today Brownsville, Texas, he fired the first shot of the Mexican War [q.v.], in which he was twice brevetted for his gallantry.

At the beginning of the American Civil War he resigned his commission as captain and joined the Confederate army as colonel of the 1st Maryland. He was promoted brigadier general for his services at the First Battle of Bull Run and served in the Valley Campaign of 1862 and in the Seven Days' Battles (in which he was severely wounded) and later as chief of artillery for the Army of Tennessee [qq.v.]. After the war he became a farmer.

Emancipation Proclamation (23 September 1862). A presidential pronouncement during the American Civil War, said by President Abraham Lincoln to be a "military necessity" and "a fit and necessary measure" to suppress the rebellion, providing that as of 1 January 1863, all persons held as slaves within states and parts of states in rebellion "are and henceforth will be, free." No slaves were immediately freed, for as Secretary of State William Henry Seward (1801–1872) said, the government was "emancipating slaves where we cannot reach them and holding them in bondage where we can set them free." Later slaves so freed flocked to the Union forces under General William T. Sherman [q.v.] and proved an encumbrance in his March to the Sea [q.v.].

Emathla. The term for male Creek Indians who had proved themselves warriors and been given appropriately martial names. Until a male Creek had shown his mettle in battle, he had a "baby name" and performed manual labor like a woman.

Embalmed Beef. During the American Civil War Union soldiers used this term for the canned beef supplied by Chicago meat-packers. The expression returned to use during the Spanish-American War [q.v.], when it was applied to the tasteless and tough canned boiled beef supplied to the Cuban Expeditionary Force. Because it began to spoil as soon as the can was opened, it was said, with some justification, to have caused more casualties than did Spanish bullets. The term gained considerable notoriety after the war, when General Nelson A. Miles [q.v.], who is sometimes erroneously credited with having coined the term, claimed that the refrigerated beef sent to Cuba in the last months of the war was actually embalmed—treated with preservatives injurious to the soldiers' health.

El Teb *The Black Watch assaults the Sudanese in the Battle of El Teb.*

Embar. The placing of handspikes for the movement of a piece of heavy artillery and its carriage.

Embarkation. The loading of troops and their supplies onto ships.

Embattle, to. 1. To prepare or arm for battle or to arrange in order of battle.

2. To furnish with embattlements—e.g., to embattle a house, turning it into a temporary fort.

Embattlement. An indented parapet; a battlement.

Embauchage. The crime of enticing or assisting a soldier to desert to the enemy and to serve against his own country.

Embaucheur. One who tries to persuade troops to desert, usually to enlist in another army.

Embrasure. In fortifications this is an opening in the parapet or the mask wall of a casement through which guns are pointed. The bottom of the embrasure was called the sole, and the widening of the embrasure the splay. The mouth was the exterior opening, and the throat the interior opening. The side walls of the embrasure were the cheeks.

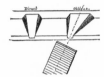

Embrasure, direct and oblique

Émeute. A popular uprising.

Emily, Jules Michel Antoine (1868?–1944). A French naval surgeon in the colonial service who saw active service in the French Sudan before being attached to the Marchand Expedition [q.v.] as medical officer [see Fashoda Incident]. In 1913 he wrote an account of this expedition, *Mission Marchand*. He served throughout the First World War.

Emin Pasha. See Schnitzer, Eduard.

Emir-Achir. The Turkish master of the horse.

Emir-Alem. A Turkish standard-bearer.

Emmet's Insurrection (23 July 1803). Robert Emmet (1778–1803), an Irish revolutionary, led a revolt against British rule in Ireland in the hope of founding a French-style republic along the lines suggested by the Irish revolutionist Wolfe Tone (1763–1798). Almost everything that could go wrong with Emmet's plot did, beginning with the explosion of his arms magazine. On 23 July 1803, dressed in a white and green general's uniform, with about 100 of his followers, he rashly tried to storm Dublin Castle and capture the viceroy. When this failed, he fled to the mountains of Wicklow, where he was captured on 25 August. He was convicted of treason, and his final words from the dock were: "When my country takes its place among the nations of the earth, then, and not till then, let my epitaph be written." On 20 September he was hanged.

Emmett, Daniel Decatur (1815–1904). The American composer who wrote "Dixie" [q.v.]. He was disconcerted when, during the American Civil War, his song was adopted by the Confederacy, for he was a Union man. Before the war, as a musician in the band of the 6th U.S. Infantry, he wrote the army's first drum manual, *Emmett's Standard Drummer*.

Emousser. To cut off the corners of a unit formed into a square so as to make an octagonal formation with unequal sides. Artillery pieces or Gatling guns were often placed on the sides formed at the former corners.

Empecinado, El (The Stubborn). The nickname of Juan Martín Díaz [q.v.].

Empilement. The stacking of shot and shell in a secure and convenient manner, often in a pyramid, as was usual in arsenals and forts.

Emprise. A dangerous attack upon an enemy.

Empty Bastion. See Hollow Bastion.

Enceinte. The continuous inner ring of fortifications around a town, a castle, or another structure, usually including the principal wall or rampart with its curtains and bastions. Sometimes referred to as the body of a place or the main enclosure.

Encipher, to. To use a code or cipher system; to put plaintext into a form unintelligible to those without the cipher key.

Encode, to. To transfer from one system of communication into another.

Encombrer. In fortification, to fill up any hollow place, such as a stagnant pond, with rubbish or dirt.

Encounter Battle. See Meeting Engagement.

Encrypt, to. To use a cryptosystem to convert plaintext into an unintelligible form. N.B.: This term includes the meanings of the words "encipher" and "encode."

Enfant de Troupe. A deceased soldier's child. In Napoleon's army each company carried on its books such children who had no other homes. They were supported by the regiment. Boys received special consideration in gaining entrance to military preparatory schools (*écoles militaires préparatoires*) and other benefits. [See Children of the Regiment.]

Enfants Perdus, Les. See Forlorn Hope.

Enfield Rifle. The first generally issued British rifle and the last muzzleloader. Sometimes called a rifle-musket, the 1853 model, which replaced the Brunswick rifle [q.v.] in the British army, was originally a muzzle-loading, single-shot, shoulder-held percussion weapon manufactured at the Royal Arms Factory in Enfield, England. Based upon the Minié [q.v.], it used a smooth-sided bullet that expanded to fit the three-groove rifling that gave a twist of about one turn in six feet. With a 54-inch-long barrel, the rifle weighed 8.6 pounds, and with bayonet, 9.75 pounds. It was the first rifle in which the

Enfield Rifle *British infantry firing Enfield rifles, 1855*

barrel was held to the stock by bands instead of pins and was sometimes referred to as the three-band Enfield. For its day it was considered reliable, accurate, and durable—more so than the Belgian and Austrian arms imported into the United States during the American Civil War. Enfields were first used in action during the Crimean War [q.v.].

The 1860 model had five grooves and was $48\frac{3}{4}$ inches long. The so-called Enfields used in America during the Civil War were not those from the Enfield factory but came from private contractors in London and Birmingham who lacked the ability to manufacture them with interchangeable parts. They were, however, considered dependable. Each side imported about 400,000.

In 1867 some 150,000 of these were converted by the army to breechloaders by cutting out a section and inserting a hinged-block design of Jacob Snider (d. 1866), an American inventor. These were eventually replaced by the Martini-Henri [q.v.].

Enfilade, to. To fire along an enemy's flank. Banks of earth called traverses were often constructed to prevent parapets or trenches from being enfiladed. In siege operations, saps were dug in a zigzag for the same reason.

Enfilading Batteries. Guns so placed as to secure a raking fire along the terrepleins of a besieged work.

Engagement. Any battle, large or small, or the encountering of hostile parties in combat.

Engagement *Engagement of Union General John Starkweather's brigade at Perryville, Kentucky, American Civil War*

Enghien, Louis Antoine Henri de Bourbon-Condé, Duc d' (1772–1804). A French soldier and the only son of Henri Louis Joseph, Prince de Condé [q.v.]. In 1792 he joined the corps of émigrés assembled on the Rhine, and from 1796 to 1799 he commanded the vanguard. In 1801, after the Peace of Lunéville, he retired to Baden. In 1804, when the Cadoudal conspiracy [q.v.] against Napoleon was discovered, Napoleon chose to believe that he was involved in the plot. Violating the territory of neutral Baden, he had Enghien kidnapped and taken to the prison at Vincennes. In March he was shot in the castle moat, an act that Joseph Fouché (1763–1829), the minister of police, described as being worse than a crime: It was a blunder.

Engineers, Military. Soldiers specializing in military construction work and demolitions. For the greater part of the nineteenth century most armies had only engineer officers who directed the work of infantrymen or civilians in constructing roads, bridges, trenches, barracks, and other military works. They were also often used for scouting and mapmaking [see Topographical Engineers; Pioneers].

In the British army, engineer units did not exist prior to 1772, when a small unit was formed at Gibraltar. Formal rank was not given until 1775, and a corps of engineers was not established until 25 April 1787. In 1802 the chief engineer in England was called the inspector general of fortifications, and until 1855 all engineers came under the master general of ordnance. However, when Lord Raglan [q.v.] died in that post, the Corps of Royal Engineers was formed, and for the first time its commandant reported to the commander-in-chief.

While on the Iberian Peninsula, Wellington so constantly complained of a lack of engineer officers that in 1812 the School of Military Engineering was founded at Chatham, and three years later a brigade of engineers was attached to each division. Military architecture came under the engineers in 1826. Submarine mining was undertaken in 1863 and not taken over by the Royal Navy until forty years later. In 1870 a detachment of telegraphists was formed. The first steam transport unit was created in 1899 and first used in South Africa during the Second Anglo-Boer War [q.v.]. A number of famous British generals began their military careers as engineers, including Robert Napier, Charles ("Chinese") Gordon, and Lord Kitchener [qq.v.].

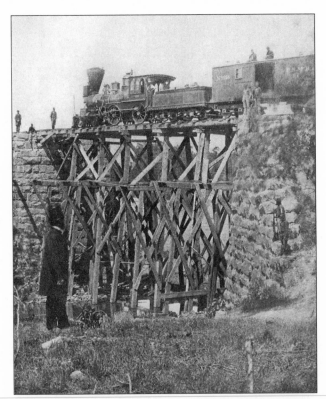

Engineers, Military *Time and again, during 1862–63, bridges on the Orange & Alexandria railroad line were destroyed by both sides in the American Civil War. The Corps of Engineers rebuilt such bridges in but a few hours.*

In the French army the Corps de Génie was established in about 1690 by the famous military engineer Sébastien Vauban [q.v.]. The companies of sappers and miners became classed as *génie* in 1801. The Bureau Topographique, a small staff that made maps, was under the war ministry. Pontoniers, who built bridges, and pioneer units were separate organizations. In 1868 French engineers acquired responsibility for the electric telegraph, and in 1878 they took control of military railways. Most French military engineers were trained at the École Polytechnique [q.v.]

In Prussia, engineer officers were assigned in three separate corps—miners, sappers, and pontoniers—until 1809, when they were amalgamated into a composite corps of engineers and pioneers and restricted to the construction of fortifications and buildings. By the time of the Franco-Prussian War [q.v.] the work of engineers was somewhat expanded, and a pioneer battalion then consisted of three field companies, three fortress companies, a pontoon column, a train section, and a depot company. A balloon detachment was added a few years after the Franco-Prussian War.

In the United States, a corps of engineers was formed during the American Revolution, when three companies of sappers and miners were organized with Brigadier General Louis LeBégue de Portail of the French army as the corps's commandant. It was mustered out of service at the end of the war. Artillerymen and engineers were linked in a single service briefly, but this was discontinued in 1802. A separate Corps of Topographical Engineers [q.v.], created in 1838 to conduct explorations, make surveys, draw maps, and select sites for defenses, was merged with the Corps of Engineers in 1863.

Although there have always been engineer officers in the American army, after the disbandment of the sappers following the Revolutionary War there were no engineer troops until the War of 1812 [q.v.], when a single company of bombardiers, sappers, and miners was created. This was disbanded in 1821, and no new units were formed until a company was raised for service in the Mexican War [q.v.]. In 1861, during the American Civil War, the number of companies was augmented to four and attached to the Army of the Potomac.

The Corps of Engineers became a distinct branch of the American army in 1802. Based at West Point, New York, it consisted of 1 colonel, 1 lieutenant colonel, 4 captains, 4 lieutenants, and not more than 8 cadets. The size of the corps was later increased to 47 officers, and a separate topographic corps was instituted. In 1846 sappers, miners, and pontoniers were added. Until 1886 it was solely responsible for the U.S. Military Academy, whose superintendent was always an officer in the corps. It was considered the elite service, and only the top graduates at West Point could enter it. All military construction, even seawalls and lighthouses, rivers and harbors, were the corps's responsibility.

American military engineers, who could be ordered on duty outside their profession only by special order of the president, have undertaken a wider range of functions than have the engineers in any other country. The Rivers and Harbors Act of 1824 gave the Corps of Engineers control of the nation's seaports and inland waterways. It was also responsible for the construction of dams, exploratory expeditions in the Far West, the construction of monuments and public buildings (notably the Capitol and the Washington Monument in

Engineers, Military *Union Engineers, 1861, American Civil War*

Washington, D.C.), and later the Panama Canal as well as other functions. Robert E. Lee, George B. McClellan, and George Custer [qq.v.], among others, began their military careers as engineer officers.

England, Civil Disorders. See British Civil Disorders.

England, French Army of (1803–05). When France and Britain, after the brief interruption of the Treaty of Amiens, resumed their war on 17 May 1803, Napoleon formed a 160,000-man Army of England, which he massed in a series of encampments along the English Channel. After the Battle of Trafalgar on 21 October 1805, when it became apparent that no invasion of Britain could take place, the army was broken up.

English Rifling. A system of rifling artillery pieces with deep and broad grooves, each of which in firing engages two soft metal circular studs that are attached to the projectile.

En l'Air. Literally, in the air, or unsupported. The term usually refers to a flank that is not anchored by a strong point or protected by an obstacle or that does not have a flank sufficiently refused. It can also refer to a unit too far detached from the main body to receive support or assistance.

Enlist, to. To engage as a soldier.

Enlisted Man. In the American army, a private, or non-commissioned officer; usually referred to in the British army as another rank, or often, as in the German army, by a term relating to his arm—e.g., sapper, gunner, etc. American Colonel William Duane (d. 1835) in 1814 published *A Handbook for Infantry*, in which he wrote: "The humblest bred man who stands in the ranks of an army, is as susceptible of the sentiment of glory, and honor, and shame, as the proudest captain that ever carried a plume." However, in early-nineteenth-century armies the flower of a nation seldom stood in the ranks. Wellington in 1809, on seeing a draft of men sent to him during the Peninsular War [q.v.], is reported to have said: "I don't know what effect these men will have on the enemy, but, by God, they frighten me." In 1813, in a letter to Lord Bathhurst, he wrote: "We have in the service the scum of the earth as common soldiers."

Enlistment. The voluntary enrollment in a military service. In the United States from 15 April 1850 enlistments were for five years. At the beginning of the American Civil War much shorter enlistments were introduced, many for only ninety days.

In England recruiting was in private hands [see Crimp; Crimping; Crimping House] until 1802, and until 1847 a soldier enlisted for life. After that date shorter enlistments were permitted: ten years for infantry and twelve years for cavalry or artillery. At the end of his enlistment a soldier could then leave the army without a pension or reenlist for up to twenty-one years in the infantry and twenty-four years in other arms. The second enlistment entitled the soldier to a pension at the end of his service and, after 1868, an extra twopence a day was added to his pay. In 1870, as a result of Cardwell's reforms [q.v.], soldiers enlisted for twelve years with only six years or less served "with the colours," and the remainder in the reserves.

In Britain the Army Discipline and Regulation Act of 1879 required a recruit to be brought before a magistrate to assure that his enlistment was voluntary. If an apprentice enlisted, his master could recover him under certain conditions, and in some armies, including the American and British, it was usually possible for a soldier with money to buy his way out.

Enomoto Rebellion (1868–69). A Japanese rebellion against the antishogunate forces immediately following the Boshin Civil War [q.v.]. It was led by Vice Admiral Buyo Enomoto (1838?–1909), who, unreconciled to the fall of the Tokugawa shogunate, established a "republic" on Hokkaido. Initial attempts by the imperialists to defeat him were repulsed, but in June 1869 they routed his troops in the Battle of Hakodate. Enomoto surrendered and was imprisoned until 1872, when he was released and appointed vice admiral in the new Japanese navy. In 1874 he negotiated a treaty with Russia in which Japan traded the southern half of Sakhalin for the Kuril Islands.

Ensconce, to. In a military sense, to cover, as a fort.

Ensiform. Having the shape of a sword.

Ensign. 1. Sometimes used as the lowest commissioned rank in an army; the equivalent of a second lieutenant. In the American army ensign was the lowest commissioned rank for an infantry officer until 1800. In the British army it was the lowest combatant rank of commissioned officers until 1871 [see Cornet; Lieutenant]. In the Russian army it was a rank below a second lieutenant.

2. A national flag.

Entire or Rank Entire. A line of soldiers in a continuous row, side by side. When they were in a continuous row behind one another, they were said to be "in file."

Entrench, to. To dig ditches or throw up earthworks to improve the defenses of a position.

Entrenching Tool. A small shovel used for digging trenches and holes.

Entrenchments. Ditches dug or earthworks constructed for defensive purposes. Except in siege operations, soldiers were not usually encouraged to dig trenches, for many officers believed that they would kill the offensive spirit, that it would be difficult, once infantrymen were entrenched, to move them forward to the attack. Henri Jomini [q.v.] wrote in *Précis de l'art de la guerre* in 1838: "To bury an army in entrenchments, where it may be outflanked and surrounded, or forced in front even if secure from flank attack, is manifest folly." And Colonel (later General Sir) John Frederick Maurice (1841–1912), writing in the *United Service Magazine* (March 1895), said: "We fear lest a war of mere entrenchments should reduce armies to a condition in which there will be little of that spirit which nails victories to standards."

Although trenches were much used in the last two years of the American Civil War, European military observers considered their use justified only because the American troops were not disciplined regulars.

Entrepôt. An intermediate depot for arms, ammunition, and stores, usually in a garrison town without an arsenal or magazine.

Envelop, to. To attack an enemy on one or both flanks and sometimes the front as well [see Envelopment].

Envelope. The continuous enceinte in which the counterguards of the bastions are connected to those of the ravelins.

Envelopment. The movement of troops against the flank of an enemy's position, particularly with the intention of obtaining an enfilading fire or to secure positions in the enemy's rear. The word was sometimes used to describe any attack that was not a frontal attack.

Epaule. The shoulder of a bastion or the place where its face and flank meet to form an angle.

Epaulets. Shoulder boards used to indicate the rank of officers. These were first introduced in the Russian army about 1810 and in the German and British armies soon after. In 1853 British officers ceased to wear them. A strap with a fringed pad, an epaulet known as a bear claw [q.v.], was worn in the

American Civil War epaulet

American army by officers and noncommissioned officers until 1851, when its use was discontinued for noncommissioned officers. In the British army and in various others bear claws were often worn by bandsmen. They were worn in the French army until the First World War and are still worn in the French Foreign Legion [q.v.].

Epaulment. In fortifications, an earthwork, such as a rough parapet, usually constructed of gabions or sandbags, used especially as a defense from flanking fire. Siege batteries were usually shielded, at least at one end, by epaul-

ments that formed an obtuse angle with the main line of the battery. The name was sometimes given to an isolated breastwork.

Epinglette. A large iron needle used to pierce the cartridge of any large gun before it was primed.

Epinikian. Pertaining to victory or its celebration, as an epinikian ode.

Epoch of Civil Wars (1863–80). The era of turbulence in Colombian history in which there were more than forty engagements between rival factions for control of the government. The era of disorders ended with the election in 1880 of Rafael Núñez [q.v.].

Épouses Libres. "Free wives" were female prisoners captured by the French forces in their West African and Central African campaigns who were distributed as booty to units of the Senegalese tirailleurs, the French Foreign Legion, and other units, officers usually getting first pick. This was sometimes a wholesale transaction. After the town of Bossé was captured and sacked in July 1854, some 1,200 women were distributed as slaves to the soldiers, the Foreign Legion getting first pick after their French officers. Although the practice was officially forbidden, it continued throughout the nineteenth century, and punishment, if given, was mild. In October 1894 Lieutenant Charles Marie Emmanuel Mangin (1866–1925) was given only thirty days' detention for passing out female slaves to his servants and interpreters. This did not harm his career, for he rose to be a general of division and one of the French heroes of the First World War. In 1921 he became a member of the Conseil Supérieur de la Guerre [q.v.].

Épouvante. A sudden panic that causes soldiers needlessly to flee.

Eprouvette. A small mortar [q.v.] used to test the strength of gunpowder. A very small charge of explosives and a heavy charge of chilled iron that entered only two or three inches into the mortar were fired. The square roots of the ranges (all else being equal) gave the relative power of different gunpowders.

Equerry. Any person—usually an officer—appointed to attend a sovereign or prince of the blood upon outdoor excursions.

Equipage. The necessities of a soldier. The equipage of a private often included his clothing, arms, and accoutrements collectively. Camp equipage included tents, axes, kitchen items, spades, etc.

Equipment. All the articles needed to equip completely a soldier or a military unit [see Matériel].

Equipments, Cannoneers'. In the artillery these included the hausse pouch, cartridge pouches, primer pouches, and thumbstall. The equipments for a field gun included the tampion and strap, vent cover, and tarpaulin.

Equipments, Horse. In the cavalry these included halter, bridle, saddle, watering bridle, saddlebag, saddle blanket, nose bag, lariat, currycomb, brushes, etc.

Escalade *Eight examples of escalades used to scale heights if ladders were unavailable*

Equipments, Infantry. The personal outfit of a soldier. A set of equipments is called a kit [q.v.]. The standard equipments for an infantryman included a knapsack or blanket roll, belts, cartridge box, bayonet scabbard, haversack, and canteen. In some armies at the close of the century an entrenching tool was added.

Erickson Gun. A gun with a solid wrought-iron barrel forged with superior iron and reinforced with a series of thin washers forced on by hydrostatic pressure.

Ericsson, John (1803–1889). A Swedish soldier who became an American engineer and one of the most prolific inventors of the nineteenth century. Born in Värmland, Sweden, he went to work on the Gota Canal at the age of thirteen. At seventeen he joined the Swedish army, was commissioned, and rose to the rank of captain. He later worked for thirteen years as an engineer and inventor in England, where he devised numerous improvements in steam engines, constructed a locomotive, and invented a variety of machines. In 1836 he patented a screw propeller to replace the paddle wheels on ships, and he built the first propeller-driven commercial vessel. In 1839 he sailed to the United States, where he built the first propeller-driven warship, the USS *Princeton.* In 1848 he became an American citizen, and in 1862, during the American Civil War, he built and launched the ironclad *Monitor,* which fought the famous battle at Hampton Roads and opened the age of modern warships.

The revolving turret and many other ordnance devices were also his inventions.

Erie, Fort. See Fort Erie, Battle of; Fort Erie, Siege of.

Erivan / Yerevan / Erevan, Battles of. This ancient Armenian town on the Zanga River, 110 miles south of Tiflis, has been much fought over.

1. Turko-Persian War (1821). Abbas Mirza [q.v.], son of the shah of Persia (Iran), with 30,000 men defeated a Turkish army of 52,000.

2. Russo-Persian War (1827). Russian forces under Ivan Feodorovich Paskievich [q.v.] stormed the town and routed its Persian defenders. The Russians retained possession until it was restored in 1830.

3. Russo-Persian War (1878). The town was again captured by the Russians (and yet again in 1916).

Erivan / Yerevan / Erevan, Siege of (1804), Russo-Persian War. The Russians besieged a Persian force in this ancient Armenian town on the Zanga River, 110 miles south of Tiflis, but it was relieved by a force under Abbas Ali, son of Fath Ali [qq.v.], shah of Persia (Iran).

Ersatzreserve. A reserve component of the German army composed of men whose height was below regulation standards. In wartime they served in depots or as fortress garrisons or acted as replacements if necessary.

Escalade. The scaling of the walls of an enemy fortification, usually by the use of ladders. The system recommended by a British Royal Engineer officer called for ladders 12 feet long that could be fastened together. In India ladders were made of bamboo and were somewhat longer. Government-issue ladders in India were in two sizes: 14 feet and 26 feet.

Separate ladder parties were assigned for each section of the fortification to be scaled. One party every 5 feet was required for the main wall or curtain. Two to four men assigned to each side of a ladder carried it on their shoulders. Other troops were detailed to keep down the fire directed at them, and supports followed at the appropriate interval.

Escarp (or Scarp). In fortifications, the surface of the ditch next to the rampart; the surface on the side facing the enemy is the counterscarp. In permanent fortifications the escarp was usually faced with masonry.

Escarp

Escarp Galleries. Galleries constructed in the escarp in order to flank the ditch caponnière.

Escarpment. Ground cut away vertically from a position to impede an attack.

Escobedo, Mariano (1827–1902). A Mexican soldier noted for his resistance to the French invasion and occupation of his country [see Mexico, French Invasion and Occupation of]. In 1865, after organizing a republican army in San Antonio, Texas, he led it into Mexico, and on 12 February 1867 in the Battle of San Jacinto he defeated Miguel Miramón [q.v.], a Mexican general serving Emperor Maximilian [q.v.]. Escobedo became commander-in-chief of the republican forces, and on 15 May he defeated and captured Maximilian in the Battle of Querétaro [q.v.]. Maximilian was court-martialed, and Escobedo signed the order for his execution on 16 June. He was shot on 19 June.

Escoffier, Auguste (1847?–1935). A French chef who, after service with a Russian grand duke, became the *chef de cuisine* to the Rhine army in the Franco-Prussian War [q.v.]. He later rose to eminence for his cooking at Monte Carlo and at the Savoy and Carlton hotels in London.

Escort. A body of troops assigned to protect an individual, to prevent the escape of a prisoner, or to guard a convoy of stores.

Escort of Honor. A body of troops attending a person of rank as a military compliment.

Escudo. An embroidered shield or plaque awarded to soldiers as an honor by some South American countries. The first was awarded by the government of Buenos Aires to troops who participated in the Battle of Tupizat [q.v.] in Upper Peru (Bolivia) on 7 November 1810.

Eshkenji. The European-trained troops in the Turkish army under Sultan Mahmud II (1785–1839) [see Auspicious Incident; Janissaries]. They were well-drilled, disciplined troops, organized along European lines and with Western-type uniforms.

Esla, Crossing of the (31 May–2 June 1813), Peninsular War. On 31 May 1813 the British corps under General Sir Thomas Graham [q.v.], marching well north of Wellington's main body, encountered the Esla River, a tributary of the Douro River, then in a raging torrent. A ford of sorts was found at Almendra, but several lives were lost in the crossing before a pontoon bridge was constructed. By 3 June Wellington's entire army of 100,000 was united at Toro, north of the Douro, and the French forces in the area retreated. This was Wellington's first strategic triumph in his 1813 campaign.

Esmarch, Johannes Friedrich August von (1823–1908). A German professor of surgery born in Schleswig-Holstein. As a reserve officer he served in the Schleswig-Holstein War [q.v.] of 1848, and in 1864 he served in field hospitals. In the Franco-Prussian War [q.v.] of 1870–71 he was appointed surgeon general to the Prussian army, and later he became consulting surgeon at the great military hospital in Berlin. He invented a rubber bandage that, when wrapped from distal to proximal on a limb, milked out the blood and then acted as a tourniquet, thus keeping a limb nearly bloodless during amputation. He wrote a number of widely read medical books, including *First Aid on the Battlefield* and *The Surgeon's Handbook on the Treatment of the Wounded in War*. He was considered one of the world's greatest authorities on hospital management and military surgery. He is perhaps best known as the devisor of the personal first-aid kit carried by every Prussian soldier in the Franco-Prussian War: a large triangular bandage and a safety pin in a pouch.

Espartero, Baldomero, Conde de Luchana (1792–1879). A Spanish soldier who fought against rebellious subjects in South America between 1815 and 1823 and was captured in the Battle of Ayacucho [q.v.] in 1824. When released,

he returned to Spain, where he supported the infant Queen Isabella II (1830–1904) in the Carlist Wars [q.v.]. In 1836 he was appointed commander-in-chief of the government forces, and after defeating the Carlists, he became regent and virtual dictator of Spain, crushing republican uprisings with severity. When Isabella came of age, he rebelled against her and in 1843 was driven into exile. He regained his honors by royal decree in 1848, and in 1854 he, with Leopoldo O'Donnell [q.v.], led a successful revolution. He then served as prime minister in 1854–56. He was created Prince of Vergara by King Amadeus (1845–1890).

Espinosa, Battle of (11 November 1808), Peninsular War. A badly armed Spanish army of 23,000 men with six guns under Joachim Blake was decisively defeated by a French force under Marshal Claude Victor [qq.v.] near Espinosa de los Monteros in Old Castile, 35 miles west-southwest of Bilbao. The French suffered 1,100 casualties; the Spanish 3,000, including 3 generals.

Espinosa *The French drive back the Spanish at the Battle of Espinosa de los Monteros, 11 November 1808.*

Espionage. The clandestine attempt to gain information about a country and its armed forces for communication to a foreign government. Napoleon operated an efficient spy operation, and the Prussians established an espionage system in mid-century that performed well in the years leading up to the Franco-Prussian War [q.v.]. It has been estimated that in 1870, at the beginning of the war, there were 30,000 German spies in France, although this seems excessive.

Prior to the American Civil War the United States had no formal system for gathering military intelligence. However, in 1860 or early 1861, Thomas Jordan [q.v.], a disloyal infantry captain, established in Washington, D.C., the beginning of a Confederate spy ring that was later directed by Rose O'Neal Greenhow [q.v.]. The first formal secret service was founded in 1862 by the Confederate army as a unit in the Signal Corps. The Union army's first secret service, established soon after, was directed by Allan Pinkerton [q.v.], head of a railroad detective agency, who proved more effective at counterespionage than in gathering information.

Esplanade. In fortifications this was the open area between a town and the glacis of its citadel, designed to prevent an enemy from erecting breaching batteries under cover of the town's houses and shops. It was also used as a parade ground and for exercising troops.

Espontoon. See Spontoon.

Esprit de Corps. The common spirit that unites and animates the members of a unit in enthusiasm, devotion, and strong regard for its honor; military or regimental pride. In 1768 Frederick the Great (1712–1786) defined it as the spirit that exists when a soldier has "a higher opinion of his own regiment than of all the other troops in the country." William Tecumseh Sherman [q.v.] said: "There is a soul of an army as well as the individual man, and no general can accomplish the full work of his army unless he commands the soul. . . ." Perhaps the best description of this spirit was that of John Kincaid, a rank-and-file British soldier in the Peninsular War [q.v.]: "Ours was an esprit de corps—a buoyancy of feeling animating all which nothing could equal. We were alike ready for the field or for frolic, and when not engaged in the one, went headlong into the other."

Essamako, Battle of (21 January 1824), First Ashanti War. Near this village in West Africa, Ashanti tribesmen defeated a company of Royal Africans, some colonial militia, and volunteers under Colonel Sir Charles M'Carthy (1770?–1824), governor of Sierra Leone, who was mortally wounded and captured. After delivering a coup de grace, his captors severed his head to keep his skull as a war trophy.

Essen, Count Hans Henrick von (1755–1824), also known as Jean Henri Essen. A Swedish soldier and statesman, a favorite of and an aide-de-camp to King Gustavus III (1778–1809), who fought in Finland in 1788. In 1795 he became governor of Stockholm, and in 1800 governor of Pomerania. In 1807 he defended Stralsund [q.v.] against the French for eleven weeks, and in 1810 he concluded peace between Sweden and France. He became a field marshal in 1811 and commanded the Swedish army against Norway in 1813 [see Swedish Invasion of Norway]. From 1814 to 1816 he was governor of Norway, and governor-general of Skåne in 1817.

Essling, Battle of. See Aspern-Essling, Battle of.

Establishment. The quota of officers and other ranks in a military unit, often also including its matériel. The peace establishment of a unit or an army was smaller than its war establishment.

Estafette. A courier sent express from one part of an army to another.

Esterhazy, Marie Charles Ferdinand Walsin (1847–1923). A French officer who in 1899 confessed that he had forged the document that was the chief evidence against Captain Alfred Dreyfus [q.v.]. He fled to England, where, calling himself Count de Voilement, he spent the rest of his life living quietly at Harpenden, 30 miles north of London.

Estimates, Army. The budget for the British army presented annually for Parliament's approval.

Estremadura, Army of. During the Peninsular War [q.v.] a Spanish army of 12,848 men with 24 guns.

Étape. 1. The subsistence issued to troops on the march.
2. The halting place of troops at the end of a day's march.
3. The distance between two halting places.
4. The length of a day's march.
5. The regulation distance troops were expected to march in a day under normal conditions, usually 22 to 25 kilometers, or 13 to 15 miles.

Etappen. A Prussian army department first formed in 1867, revised in 1869, which was responsible for the line of communication [q.v.] and was commanded by an inspector of Etappen and railroads. The idea for its formation originated in the Prussian Military Railway Organization. During the Franco-Prussian War [q.v.] the medical department, telegraph organization, post office, and commissariat were all included in the Etappen and became the responsibility of its head. In principle, all operations at the front were the responsibility of the active fighting army, and responsibility for all the support units was that of the Etappen inspector. Following the Franco-Prussian War, the French also established an Etappen.

État Major. The staff of a French army.

États de Service. French army service records.

Etheridge, Anna (fl. 1860s). An American woman known as Michigan Annie during the American Civil War. At the beginning of the war she attached herself as a nurse to the 2nd Michigan and remained with it until the end, often tending men on the battlefield. Although her long dresses were frequently marked by bullet holes, she was wounded only once, a bullet grazing her head. She was awarded the Kearny Cross [q.v.] by General D. B. Birney [q.v.]. After the war she worked in government offices to support her destitute father.

Ethiopian Wars. See Abyssinian Civil Wars.

Eu, Prince Louis Philippe Marie Ferdinand Gaston d'Orléans d' (1824–1922). The eldest son of the Duke of Nemours who entered the Brazilian army and in 1869–70 became commander-in-chief of the Allied forces in the War of the Triple Alliance [q.v.]. He made himself unpopular and was forced to leave Brazil in 1889 on the downfall of the Portuguese empire.

Eugen (Russian: Evgeni), Duke of Württemberg (1788–1857). A Russian soldier born in Prussia who distinguished himself in the battles against Napoleon in Russia and Germany in 1812–13. In 1828, during the Russo-Turkish War [q.v.], he commanded the Russian VII Cavalry Corps. In 1829 he retired to compose music and to write his memoirs.

Eupatoria, Battle of (17 February 1855), Crimean War. Some 40,000 Russians under General Mikhail Gorchakov [q.v.] unsuccessfully attacked the Turks at Eupatoria (Yevpatoriya), a seaport on the west coast of the Crimea 45 miles northwest of Simferopol. Russian losses were said to be 500 to the Turks' 50, but among the latter was Selim Pasha (d. 1855), the commander of the Turkish contingent.

Eureka Stockade, Attack on the (3 December 1854). An uprising of discontented miners in Australia led by Peter Lalor (1823–1889), a local legislator, a mineowner, and the brother of Irish conspirator James Finton Lalor (d. 1849). At a meeting of miners on 29 November 1854 official records were burned, and it was decided to cease paying the government a monthly fee for a license to mine. Near Ballarat, in south-central Victoria, 70 miles west-northwest of Melbourne, dissidents built a stockade, collected muskets, made pikes, adopted a flag (the southern cross on a blue background), and defied the government. About 150 men were manning the stockade when on 3 December, a Sunday morning, it was attacked and taken by 280 soldiers and police. For a loss of 6 government men killed, 22 miners were killed and 125 were taken prisoner. Lalor was struck by a bullet in the arm, which was subsequently amputated.

Some of the instigators were tried for treason, but none was convicted. Although not much of a battle, it was the nearest thing to one ever fought on the Australian mainland.

Eustis, Henry Lawrence (1819–1885). An exceptionally well-educated American officer who was a graduate of both Harvard and West Point, from which he emerged first in his class of 56 in 1842. In 1849 he resigned his commission to become professor of engineering at Harvard, a post he held for the remainder of his life except for two years during the American Civil War, when he served as a colonel of the 10th Massachusetts and later as a brigadier general. He fought at Fredericksburg, Chancellorsville, the Wilderness, Spotsylvania, Cold Harbor, and Gettysburg [qq.v.]. He was forced to resign on 27 June 1864 for neglect of duty, inefficiency, and opium eating. He is believed to be the only Harvard professor to fight in the war.

Evacuation. 1. The process of removing the wounded, injured, and ill to the rear.

2. The clearing of the inhabitants from a given locality, sometimes with their animals and household goods.

Evader. A soldier isolated in hostile country who escaped capture.

Evagination. The unsheathing of a sword.

Evans, George de Lacy (1787–1870). A British soldier who entered the army in India as a volunteer in 1806 and was commissioned in 1807. He first saw action against the Pindaris [q.v.] and later in the capture of Mauritius. He served in the Peninsular War [q.v.], in which he was wounded. In the War of 1812 [q.v.] he fought the Americans in the Battle of Bladensburg [q.v.], in which he had two horses shot from under him, and he took part in the burning of Washington and led 200 light infantry in the seizure of the Capitol. In December 1814 and January 1815 he was present in the Battle of New Orleans [qq.v.], where he was wounded. He returned to Europe and was engaged in the battles of Quatre Bras and Waterloo [qq.v.].

In 1818 he went on half pay and served in Parliament. In 1828 and 1829 he published influential books that argued that Russia had designs on India. Such works sparked the Great Game [q.v.].

In 1834, when Britain suspended the Foreign Enlistments Act, he raised a British Legion [q.v.] of 9,600 men to support the government of Isabella II (1830–1904) of Spain [see Carlist Wars]. On 5 May 1836 he raised the siege of San Sebastián but lost 97 officers and 500 other ranks out of a force that then totaled only 5,000. In spite of insufficient food and general neglect on the part of the Spanish Cristinos [q.v.], the remnant of the legion fought on until June 1837, when it was returned to England at the expense of the British government. Evans was knighted, and in 1846 he was promoted major general.

During the Crimean War [q.v.] Evans commanded a division and was severely wounded in the Battle of the Alma [q.v.]. He rose from his invalid bed to take part in the Battle of Inkerman [q.v.]. He was invalided home in February 1855. In 1861 he was promoted full general.

Evans, Nathan George ("Shanks") (1824–1868). An American soldier who was graduated 36th out of a 38-man class at West Point in 1824. He served as a cavalryman in the Far West, where he distinguished himself as a capable and brave Indian fighter. When the American Civil War began, he was a captain, but he resigned his commission and accepted an appointment as a major in South Carolina's army. He was a lieutenant colonel at First Bull Run [q.v.], and it was in large part due to his initiative that the Union flanking movement was aborted. On 21 October 1861 he was a colonel commanding a brigade on the Potomac near Leesburg, Virginia, when he decisively defeated a Union force that crossed the river at Ball's Bluff [q.v.]. For this action he was promoted brigadier general, given the Thanks of (the Confederate) Congress, and presented with a gold medal by South Carolina.

Although he fought on through the war—Second Bull Run, Antietam, and Vicksburg [qq.v.]—his brigade moving so much it was called the tramp brigade, Evans was never promoted again. He was twice court-martialed—once for drunkenness and once for disobedience—and acquitted both times. After the war he became a school principal.

Evans, Thomas Wiltberger (1823–1897). An American dentist who about 1847 became intimate with Napoleon III (1808–1873). During the Crimean War [q.v.] he visited the troops around Sevastapol and, horrified by the sufferings of those hospitalized, tried without success to improve conditions in French military hospitals. During the American Civil War he arranged the purchase of arms and clothing for the Union army and used his influence with Napoleon to prevent his recognition of the Confederacy. On the outbreak of the Franco-Prussian War in 1870 he organized a field hospital unit. When rioting broke out in Paris, he contrived the escape of the empress to safety in England.

Everest, George (1790–1866). A British soldier who served in India and became superintendent of the trigonometrical survey of the country. From 1830 to 1843 he was surveyor general in India. He completed the survey of the Himalayas in 1841, and he was the first to fix the position and altitude of Mount Everest, which was named after him.

Ever Victorious Army (Chinese name: Chang-sheng-chûn). An army, initially known as the Shanghai Foreign Arms

Corps, raised in 1860 by merchants in Shanghai during the Taiping Rebellion [q.v.]. Its first commander was Frederick Townsend Ward [q.v.], an American adventurer whose second-in-command was a hard-drinking American named Henry Andrea Burgevine (1836–1865). All of the corps's officers were foreigners. Most were Americans, but Germans, Frenchmen, and Spaniards were included. All the rank and file were Chinese, predominantly from the provinces of Kiangsu and Chekiang, areas largely held by the Taipings. The little army was well equipped with Colt revolvers, Sharps carbines, and some light British field guns.

Its first battle was successfully fought on 16 June 1860 against Taiping rebels holding the walled city of Sungkiang, 25 miles southwest of Shanghai on the Hwang Pu River. In spite of a few setbacks, the renamed Ever Victorious Army won eleven victories in four months. In the spring of 1862, by then accepted as part of the imperial army, it won a string of victories, but in September of that year in an assault on the walled city of Tz'u-ch'i on the left bank of the Yangtze, 40 miles west-northwest of Ichang, Ward was mortally wounded by a musket ball in the abdomen.

The British commander at Shanghai, General Charles Stavely [q.v.], asked by the Chinese governor (*futai*), Li Hung-chang [q.v.], to provide a British officer to take Ward's place, selected an engineer, Major Charles Gordon [q.v.], ever after known as Chinese Gordon. Despite his quarrels with his Chinese superiors, Gordon's force fought in thirty-three engagements, capturing walled towns and opening up rich provinces in the silk district. The troops, varying from 3,000 to 5,000, were organized into five or six infantry regiments with two batteries of field artillery and a siege train. British army drill was used, and the words of command were in English so only the most simple evolutions were attempted. Punishment was administered by a rattan cane, as was usual in Chinese armies. For reasons not readily apparent, the troops were paid in Mexican dollars.

An important adjunct to the army, which operated in a country of many streams, was a flotilla of a few small steamers officered by Americans and some Chinese gunboats. Gordon used one of the steamers, the *Hyson,* as his floating headquarters.

In the spring of 1863 Li Hung-chang ordered the execution of some surrendered Taiping leaders at Soochow whose lives Gordon had promised would be spared. Furious at Chinese perfidity, he threw up his command. Although he was then persuaded to return, the war was on its last legs, and in May 1864 the little army was disbanded.

Although the Ever Victorious Army had made a definite contribution to the suppression of the Taiping Rebellion, English accounts have almost uniformly overestimated its importance to the ultimate imperial victory.

Evolutions. The movement of troops in order to change positions—e.g., marching, countermarching, wheeling, changing front, making column or line, defiling, deploying, etc.

Evora, Massacre of (25 July 1808), Peninsular War. At this Portuguese town, 68 miles east by south of Lisbon, a mixed force of Spanish and Portuguese, together with some citizens of the town and some poorly armed peasants, tried to halt the march of the division (7,000 men) of French General Louis Henri Loisson (1771–1816). The French broke their line of

battle and scattered them, then sacked the town and massacred the entire population. Spanish and Portuguese losses were about 2,000; the French lost 290. This atrocity acted as a stimulant to the Spanish insurgents.

Evzones. An elite Greek infantry unit, organized as line infantry, recruited from mountain districts. Their picturesque uniforms consisted of a small red fez with a dark blue tassel; a red waistcoat with a stand collar; a laced jacket; a coat fustanenella; white gaiters; soft yellow leather shoes with black pompons; and a short white skirt. Their dress uniform remains the same today.

Ewell, Richard Stoddert (1817–1872). An American soldier who upon his graduation from West Point in 1840 wrote to his brother that he had "no particular wish to stay in the army but a positive antipathy to starving or to do anything for a living that requires exertion of mind or body." He saw much service in the Far West and in the Mexican War [q.v.], where he won a brevet to captain for gallantry at Molino del Rey, Contreras, and Churubusco [qq.v.]. In 1849 he became a substantive captain and was sent to New Mexico. In 1855 he led a hard campaign against the Mescalero Apaches, and two years later he took part in a campaign led by Benjamin Bonneville [q.v.] against the Coyotero Apaches. In 1860, while in command at Fort Buchanan, 45 miles southeast of Tucson, Arizona, he was successful in trading Indian captives for white women taken by the Apaches.

Still only a captain at age forty-four when the American Civil War began, he declared that at this point in his life he knew everything there was to know about leading 50 dragoons and had forgotten everything else. He resigned his commission in June 1861 and was commissioned a brigadier general in the Confederate army. Four months later he was a major general. In the Valley Campaign [q.v.] he led a division under Thomas ("Stonewall") Jackson [q.v.] and in the Second Battle of Bull Run [q.v.] he lost a leg. In May 1863, after Jackson was mortally wounded at Chancellorsville, he replaced Jackson as commander of II Corps and was promoted lieutenant general. He cleared the Valley of Virginia of Union forces, led the advance into Pennsylvania that culminated in the Battle of Gettysburg [q.v.], and later fought in the Wilderness [q.v.]. At the end of the war he was in charge of the defenses of Richmond. He was captured at Sayler's Creek [q.v.] on 6 April 1865 and imprisoned at Fort Warren in Boston Harbor for four months. After the war he lived on a farm in Tennessee.

Ewing Brothers: Charles (1835–1883), Hugh Boyle (1826–1905), and Thomas Ewing, Jr. (1829–1896). The sons of Thomas Ewing (1789–1871), who was twice a U.S. senator and between terms was secretary of the interior and secretary of the treasury. All the brothers became Union generals during the American Civil War, and all practiced law. Thomas, Jr., who resigned as the first chief justice of the Kansas Supreme Court to join the Union army, later became a congressman. It was Thomas who signed the infamous General Order No. 11 [q.v.] in Missouri. General William T. Sherman [q.v.] was their brother-in-law.

Excelsior Brigade. A Union brigade of six New York regiments recruited at the very beginning of the American Civil

War and initially led by Daniel E. Sickles [q.v.]. This was one of the few units recruited as a full brigade.

Exchange of Prisoners. The exchanging of prisoners of war by belligerents [see Cartel]. A soldier, usually an officer, taken prisoner and paroled could honorably fight again only when an exchange was made for a soldier of the same rank in the enemy's army. In this mutual exchange between belligerents it was sometimes agreed that an officer was the equivalent of a given number of other ranks; privates were usually considered the playing chips. During the American Civil War on 22 July 1862 the North and South agreed that a "general commanding in chief" could be exchanged for 60 privates, a major general for 40, a brigadier general for 20, a colonel for 15, a major for 8, a captain for 6, a first lieutenant for 4, and a second lieutenant or noncommissioned officer for 2 [see Parole; Cartel].

Execution. Facing a firing squad was the normal manner of executing a soldier found guilty by a court-martial and sentenced to death, but at times men were hanged, a death considered more disgraceful, and at times they were blown from guns.

A British corporal in the 32nd Foot in India in the 1840s described standing in a three-sided square to witness the execution of a soldier who had while drunk struck his commanding officer in the face with his hat:

> After the first dawn I could see the party stand with the prisoner, when they were ordered to proceed in the following manner: first the prevost with his arms reversed; then the band and the drummers playing the "Dead March," the drums being muffled with black; next the firing party with arms reversed; then the coffin borne by four men; next to this the prisoner in company of the minister praying, and his comrade on the left of him flanked by a man on either side with swords, the escort following.
>
> They started from the left; the band played the dismal and solemn march which made my blood run cold. As he passed his own regiment he bade his officers and the men fare-

well. . . . The minister had hold of his arm, but he walked with a firm step, keeping the step to the drum and with the party.

Prisoners were often shot while sitting on their coffins. Those blown from guns were strapped over the gun muzzles, and their bodies blown to bits spewed in front of the gun. This method of execution was frequently used during the Indian Mutiny [q.v.].

Exelmans, Rémi Joseph Isidore (1775–1852). A French soldier in the Napoleonic Wars who was a colonel in the Battle of Austerlitz in 1805, a general of brigade at Eylau in 1807, and a general of division in Napoleon's Russian Campaign [qq.v.] in 1812. He was exiled after the Restoration but later returned to duty and in 1851 was created a marshal of France.

Exercise. The maneuvering and drilling of soldiers, particularly drill in the use of arms—e.g., bayonet exercise. This usage goes back at least to the early seventeenth century. A 1619 drill book was dedicated to "yonghe and olde exercised souldiours."

Exon. An officer's rank peculiar to the British Yeomen of the Guard [q.v.].

Expedition, Military. A military force organized and dispatched for a specific purpose [see Expeditionary Force].

Expeditionary Force. A military expedition sent to a distant place, usually in a foreign country.

Expense Magazine. A small powder magazine containing ammunition for present or instant use. Forts usually had one in each bastion.

Exploitation. Taking advantage of a success in battle by attacking an enemy's headquarters, closing escape routes, destroying reserves, or preventing an enemy from reorganizing his forces. This was usually best effected by using previously uncommitted forces.

Explosives. Substances that burn suddenly so as to cause a violent expansion of gases emitting a loud noise and producing violent results, an explosion. Nitroglycerin, the first modern explosive, was discovered by Ascanio Sobrero (1812–1888) in 1847. Soon after, Théophile Jules Pelouzé (1807–1820) discovered nitrosulfates and nitrated paper, which led to the discovery of guncotton. But guncotton (cellulose nitrate) proved unstable. The first factory at Faversham, England, blew up. It was not until 1865, when Frederick Augustus Abel (1827–1902), a chemist in the Royal Navy, patented a process for making a completely stable guncotton suitable for use in shells, that it came into use. In 1872 it was manufactured on a large scale at Waltham Abbey. Cordite [q.v.], invented by Frederick Abel and James Dewar (1842–1923), was first manufactured in 1891.

In 1863 a Swedish chemist, Alfred Nobel [q.v.], invented dynamite [see Propellants]. In 1885 a French chemist, F. E. Turpin, first suggested the use of picric acid (discovered in 1771) as a charge in explosives, and in the same year Paul Marie Eugène Vieille (1854–1934), a French engineer, invented smokeless powder, called *poudre B*.

Execution *Military execution of three sepoys at Peshawar, 1850*

Expugnable. Capable of being assaulted or captured.

Extended Order. A formation for advancing in which the intervals between men was greater than when marching by at least the width of one man.

Exterior and Interior Lines. When an army attempted to surround a fort or an area of any size, its lines of communication [q.v.] were necessarily extended and it was said to operate on external lines. The defender of a fort or territory, who was close to his base of supplies and could move more easily and quickly in any direction, was said to operate on interior lines. In the American Civil War the North operated on external lines, and the South on interior lines.

Helmuth von Moltke the Elder [q.v.] gave a warning about the use of interior lines: "The unquestionable advantages of the interior line of operations are valid only as long as you retain enough space to advance against one enemy . . . gaining time to beat and pursue him, and then to turn against the other. . . . If this space, however, is narrowed down to the extent that you cannot attack one enemy without running the risk of meeting the other who attacks you from the flank or rear, then the strategic advantage of interior lines turns into the tactical disadvantage of encirclement."

Exterior Crest. The top of the exterior slope of a parapet.

Exterior Slope. The forward face of a rampart or parapet.

Eylau, Battle of (7–8 February 1807). At this village in East Prussia, 23 miles southeast of Königsberg, a bloody but indecisive battle was fought in a blizzard between Napoleon with 50,000 men and 200 guns and an Allied force of 67,000 Russians and 10,000 Prussians commanded by Levin Bennigsen [q.v.]. The cold was extreme, and food was scant in both armies. On 7 February a severe general engagement commenced when the head of Napoleon's column, advancing from the southwest, found the outlet of the Grünhöfchen defile blocked by a strong Russian rear guard commanded by Pëtr Bagration [q.v.]. Fighting until ten o'clock at night, the French turned both flanks and the Russians retired through Eylau to the main Allied body.

The action was resumed at eight the following morning, and during the day the French were reinforced by 29,000 men under Louis Davout and Michel Ney [qq.v.]. The battle ended at nightfall with the retreat of the Allied army. The French did not pursue. Losses were about 15,000 French killed and wounded and 10,000 captured; the Allies lost 11,000 killed, 14,000 wounded, 3,000 taken prisoners, and 23 guns.

Eyre, Philip Homan (1832–1885). A British soldier who enlisted as a private in the 38th Foot in 1851 and was commissioned three years later. He served in the Crimean War, the Indian Mutiny, and in Arabi's Revolt [qq.v.], in which he was present in the Battle of Tell el-Kebir [q.v.]. He was a lieutenant colonel with the column commanded by General William Earle [q.v.] during the Gordon Relief Expedition when he was killed in the Battle of Kirbekan [q.v.].

Ezra Church, Battle of (28 July 1864), American Civil War. During the Atlanta Campaign [q.v.], at this place in southwest Atlanta, a Confederate force under General John Bell Hood [q.v.] was repelled by the Union Army of the Tennessee [q.v.] under General William Tecumseh Sherman [q.v.].

Eylau *The Battle of Eylau, East Prussia, 7 February 1807.*

F

Faber du Faur, Christian von (1780–1857). A German soldier and painter of battle scenes. He served as an officer in Napoleon's Russian Campaign [q.v.] in 1812, during which he sketched the sufferings of the army in its retreat. His sketches were later lithographed and published between 1831 and 1843 in Stuttgart. He retired as a general in the Württemberg army.

Fabian Strategy. Avoidance of open battle and use of delaying or harassing tactics in the manner of Quintus Fabius Maximus Verrucocus (d. 203 B.C.), called *Cunctator* (delayer), in his successful operations against Hannibal during the Second Punic War (218–10 B.C.). General Mikhail Kutuzov [q.v.] used fabian tactics to thwart Napoleon's aims in his Russian Campaign [q.v.] and it was a favorite tactic of the Nien rebels [see Nien Rebellion].

Fabrice, Count Georg Friedrich Alfred von (1818–1891). A German soldier who commanded the Saxon forces in Bohemia in the Seven Weeks' War [q.v.]. He became Saxon minister of war and commanded the German army of occupation in France after the close of hostilities in the Franco-Prussian War [q.v.]. He was prime minister in 1876 and minister for foreign affairs in 1882.

Fabrique d'Armes de Guerre. The arsenal at Herstal, Belgium, often referred to simply as FN for Fabrique Nationale. It was founded in 1889 to manufacture Mauser [q.v.] rifles under license for the Belgian army. John Browning [q.v.] joined the arsenal in 1900, and it then began producing automatic pistols under his name.

Fabrizi, Nicola (1804–1885). An Italian soldier and revolutionary who took part in the Modena Insurrection of 1831. With Giuseppe Mazzini (1805–1872) he organized the ill-fated Savoy Expedition. He fought in the Second Carlist War [q.v.] in Spain and was decorated for valor on the field (18 July 1837). He aided Francesco Crispi (1819–1901) in the 1848 insurrection in Sicily. In 1860 he led a force that supported Giuseppe Garibaldi [q.v.], and in 1866 he served as Garibaldi's chief of staff, fighting at Mentana [q.v.] on 3 November 1867. [See Italian Wars of Independence; Seven Weeks' War.]

Fabvier, Baron Charles Nicolas (1782–1855). A French soldier who served in Napoleon's armies, distinguishing himself in the Battle of Borodino [q.v.]. During the Hundred Days [q.v.] he remained loyal to Louis XVIII (1755–1824) but later intrigued against the Bourbons and was forced to flee France. After aiding the Greeks in their struggle to be free of Turkey, he returned to France in 1830. Nine years later he was a lieutenant general, and in 1845 he was made a peer.

Face of a Bastion. Either of the two sides extending from the salient to the angle of the shoulder.

Face of a Map. The side of a piece of paper or other material holding the printed image of a map.

Facings. 1. Distinctive color trimmings on a uniform, usually on the collars, cuffs, and lapels.
2. Drill movements directing soldiers to face in a different direction.

Fahnenjunker-Unteroffizier. A noncommissioned officer who was an officer candidate in the Prussian and German armies.

Fahnrich. In the German army, an ensign or an aspirant officer serving in the ranks.

Faidherbe, Louis Léon César (1818–1889). A French soldier of humble origins who nevertheless was accepted in and was graduated from the prestigious École Polytechnique [q.v.] in Paris. Most of his military career was spent in Africa. Except for two years (1847–49) he served in Algeria from 1844 to 1852, a period in which he took part in numerous military expeditions against various Arab and Berber tribes.

In 1852 he was transferred to Senegal, and two years later he became its governor, a post he held, except for a brief interval, until July 1865. He was promoted general of brigade in 1863.

He greatly expanded the boundaries of Senegal and has been called the founder of modern Senegal. Ambitious to extend French territory across Africa to the Red Sea, he greatly enlarged French territory in West Africa, conquering the country between the Senegal and Gambia rivers. His methods were harsh. In 1856 he established the *école des otages* (school of hostages), in which the children of African notables were placed both to ensure their families' cooperation and to be indoctrinated in French culture. In 1857 he established the Senegalese Tirailleurs, made up in large part from slaves purchased on the open market, in which his son by a Khassonké concubine later became an officer [see Senegalese Tirailleurs].

He was back in Algeria in 1867. At the beginning of the Franco-Prussian War [q.v.] he offered his services to Léon

Gambetta (1838–1882) and was promoted general of division and appointed commander of the Army of the North in Picardy. On 19 January 1871 he was defeated at St. Quentin [q.v.].

He took part in a scientific expedition to Egypt in 1872 and in that same year was elected a senator.

Failly, Pierre Louis de (1810–1892). A French soldier who was graduated from St. Cyr in 1828. He served in the Crimean War [q.v.], becoming a general of division in 1855. He fought at Solferino [q.v.], and he defeated Giuseppe Garibaldi [q.v.] in the Battle of Mentana [q.v.] in 1859. During the Franco-Prussian War [q.v.] he commanded V Corps, but his inactivity at Bitche (Bitsch) on 6 August 1870 occasioned an uproar of indignation in France. Two days after his defeat near Beaumont on 30 August, he was replaced by General Emmanuel de Wimpffen [q.v.].

Fair Oaks and Seven Pines, Battle of (31 May 1862), American Civil War. A battle in the Peninsular Campaign [q.v.] fought seven miles south of Richmond, Virginia, near the Fair Oaks station of the Richmond & York River Railroad and a nearby crossroad with seven loblolly pine trees, landmarks that gave the battle its names. Confederate General D. H. Hill [q.v.] charged the division of Union General Silas Casey (1807–1882), initiating the Confederate attack on the army of General George McClellan [q.v.] in the peninsula (the area between the York and James rivers). Although the Confederates claimed this battle as a victory, General Joseph Johnston [q.v.], the Confederate commander, lost a chance to cripple McClellan's army by failing to communicate his plans to his subordinates and to follow the progress of the battle.

The numbers of troops on each side were extraordinarily close to being identical, 41,797 Federals facing 41,816 Confederates. Casualties were 5,031 Federals and 6,134 Confederates.

Faku (1777?–1867). The paramount chief of the Pondos in southern Africa from the early nineteenth century until about 1820, when he was attacked and defeated by Zulus under Shaka [q.v.]. However, Shaka was unable to overrun the country completely. Later Faku placed himself under British protection.

Falkenhayn, Erich von (1861–1922). A German soldier who served as an adviser with the Chinese army and first gained prominence by his perceptive reports from China during the Boxer Rebellion [q.v.]. He later made a move, remarkable in a German army, from a line regiment to a Guards regiment. He became chief of staff in 1914 but was dismissed in 1917.

Fallback Position. A previously prepared military position to be taken should a retreat become necessary.

Falling Waters, Battles of (2 July 1861 and 14 July 1864), American Civil War. Two battles were fought near the village of Falling Waters south of Harpers Ferry.

1. 2 July 1861. Thomas ("Stonewall") Jackson's first battle in the war, actually little more than a skirmish, was fought against Federal troops making a reconnaissance in force. The Federals pushed back Jackson's inferior force.

2. 14 July 1864. After the Battle of Gettysburg, Lee retreated to Williamsport, Maryland, and then established a defensive position near Falling Waters. His withdrawal was covered by the division of Henry Heth [q.v.], who was attacked by two Union cavalry divisions early on the morning of 14 July. Heth lost two guns and about 500 taken prisoner but was able to withdraw in good order.

Fall Out, to. To withdraw from the ranks or files of a military formation.

False Edge. The sharpened portion of the back near the point of a single-edged weapon. It was sometimes called the back edge.

False Fire. Campfires or lights used to deceive an enemy, often to give an impression of greater than actual numbers or of being still present in a place after having abandoned it.

False Report. A willfully erroneous report of an actual condition, event, situation, or person.

Fame. Renown or popular acclaim achieved by some. William Tecumseh Sherman [q.v.] jocosely defined it as "to be killed on the field of battle and have our names spelled wrongly in the newspapers."

Fanfare. A short and lively military air or call using brass instruments, usually trumpets.

Fanion. A small flag of serge, occasionally in the colors of the livery of the brigade commander. In some armies it was carried at the head of the baggage train of a brigade.

Fannin, James Walker (1804?–1836). A Texan revolutionary who entered West Point under the name of James Walker in 1819 but remained only two years. In 1834 he moved to Texas, where he joined the agitation for independence from Mexico. On 2 October 1835 he fought in the Battle of Gonzales, the first battle of the Texas Revolution, and on 28 October he took part as a captain in the Battle of Mission Concepción [qq.v.]. With a small force of volunteers he had collected, he planned an attack upon Matamoros, Mexico, but instead was attacked himself and captured by a force under Mexican General Antonio López de Santa Anna [q.v.]. Fannin and his men were shot by firing squads on 27 March 1836 [see Goliad Massacre].

Fantabosse / Fantasboehe. A common nineteenth-century French slang term for an infantryman.

Fantassin. An infantryman.

Fanti, Manfredo (1808–1865). An Italian soldier, educated at the military college of Modena, who turned to revolutionary activities in 1831. He was tried and condemned to death but escaped to France, where he became an officer in the French Corps of Engineers. In 1833 he took part in the attempt of Giuseppe Mazzini (1805–1872) to invade Savoy, and in 1835 he went to Spain to serve in the Carlist Wars [q.v.] on the side of the Cristinos and remained there for thirteen years. He returned to France to fight in the Austro-

Sardinian War [q.v.] of 1848–49, in which he commanded a brigade.

During the Crimean War [q.v.] he served in the Sardinian army. In the 1859 Austro-Piedmontese War [q.v.] he commanded a division, contributing to the Piedmontese victories at Magenta [q.v.] and elsewhere. In January 1860 he became minister of war of Piedmont-Sardinia and minister of marine under Camillo Benso di Cavour (1810–1861). In the same year he commanded a Piedmontese army that invaded the Papal States, seized Ancona and other forts, and defeated the papal forces at Castelfidardo [q.v.]. In only three weeks he conquered the Marche and Umbria and captured 28,000 prisoners. After defeating a large Neapolitan force at Mola di Gaeta (Formia), he helped organize the siege of Gaeta [q.v.]. He then returned to the War Office at Turin, until he resigned in 1861 to command VII Corps.

Farik / Fariq. A Turkish or Egyptian commander of a farika or fariqa (division), a rank equivalent to major general or lieutenant general.

Farion. The fez worn by Greek evzones [q.v.]. Made of red felt, it has a black tassel called a founda.

Farmville and High Bridge, Battle of (7 April 1865), American Civil War. Actions at this place in south-central Virginia just north of Appomattox were among the last engagements of the war. The fighting, which lasted from noon to nightfall, was a fatal delay for the Army of Northern Virginia, preventing Lee from reaching his supplies at Appomattox in time.

Farnsworth, Elon John (1837–1863). An American soldier who took part in the Utah Expedition [q.v.] of 1857–58. On the outbreak of the American Civil War he hurried east to join the 8th Illinois Cavalry, which had been raised by his uncle John Franklin Farnsworth (1820–1879).

During his service he took part in all forty-one engagements of his regiment. He was promoted brigadier general just before the Battle of Gettysburg [q.v.], in which he commanded a cavalry brigade and fought at Little Round Top [q.v.]. On the third day of the battle he was ordered to make a charge over rough ground against infantry behind a stone wall. Although he protested the rashness of the maneuver, when General Hugh Judson Kilpatrick [q.v.] gave him a direct order, he led his men in a gallant but disastrous charge in which he fell dead with five bullet wounds.

Farquhar's Farm, Battle of (29 October 1899), Second Anglo-Boer War. At this farm in Natal, South Africa, the main Boer army under Commandant General Petrus Joubert [q.v.] engaged the British garrison of Ladysmith under General Sir George White, VC [q.v.]. The British launched a three-pronged attack but were thrown back with a loss of 317 killed and wounded. Boer losses were small.

Farrier. A noncommissioned officer in a mounted unit responsible for the shoeing and care of horses. In the American army he was originally something of an unlicensed horse doctor, for the army did not establish a Veterinary Corps until 1916. By 1860 there were two farriers in each cavalry troop.

Farrukhabad, Battle of (17 November 1804), Maratha Wars. Near this fortified city (now Farrukhabad-cum-Fategarh), on the right bank of the Ganges River 100 miles west-northwest of Lucknow, British General Lord Lake [q.v.], with a force that was largely cavalry, routed and dispersed the Maratha cavalry under Jeswunt Rao Holkar, who fled into the Punjab. The Marathas lost 3,000; the British lost 2 killed and 20 wounded. Following the battle, Lake marched into Indore and on Christmas Day 1804 captured Dig [q.v.] in East Rajputana. He then turned on the raja of Bhurtpore, who had allied himself with Holkar.

Faschinenmesser. Literally, one who cuts the fascines. A heavy sword with a straight blade carried by German infantry during the Napoleonic Wars.

Fascines. Long, narrow cylindrical bundles of fagots used to support earthworks, fill trenches, or serve in similar functions. Those used to support earth in extensive empaulments were often called *saucissons* (sausages) and were about 18 feet long and 10 inches in diameter; those used in the revetment parapets were 8 or 10 feet long. Fascines were also used to cover wet or marshy ground.

Fashoda Incident (1898). In March 1897 French Captain Jean Baptiste Marchand [q.v.] with a column of 163 men left Brazzaville in the French Congo, determined to reach the Nile River and establish a French presence there. Marchand and his men ascended the Ubangi River in a small steamer. At the headwaters of the Bomu (Mbomu) they dismantled the ship and carried its sections overland to the Sué River, which they descended to the Jur River and thence to the Bahr el Ghazal. On 10 July 1898 they reached the village of Fashoda (Kodok), on the Nile south of Khartoum, where they established a fort, flew the French flag, and fought off a force of Dervishes.

In September an Anglo-Egyptian force of 1,800 under General H. H. Kitchener [q.v.], who had just defeated the Dervishes in the Battle of Omdurman [q.v.], arrived in gunboats and steamers and demanded that they withdraw. With Kitchener obviously in a superior position, Marchand was forced to leave, ending French hopes of establishing a presence on the Nile. The British escorted the little expedition out of Africa by way of Egypt.

During World War I Marchand became a general of division and fought with distinction. One of Marchand's officers on the Fashoda Expedition was Lieutenant (later General) Charles Marie Emmanuel Mangin (1866–1925), who rose to command the Tenth Army Group in World War I.

Fatehpur, Battle of (12 July 1857), Indian Mutiny. British General Henry Havelock [q.v.], marching to the relief of Lucknow [see Lucknow, Siege of] with an Anglo-Indian force of 1,130 men and 8 guns, met and defeated an army of 3,500 and 12 guns under Nana Sahib [q.v.] near this town, 50 miles southeast of Cawnpore.

Fath Ali (1762–1835). The shah of Persia (Iran), who in 1797, the year he ascended the throne, was forced to cede

Derbend (Derbent) in Daghestan to Russia. In the nineteenth century he fought and lost wars with Russia in 1802, 1811–13, and 1826–28 [see Russo-Persian Wars]. Unable to create a modern army to replace his tribal soldiery, he lost Georgia in 1802 and later was forced to cede all of Dagestan and Baku, most of Persian Armenia, and other territory to Russia.

Fatigue Dress. The uniform or clothing worn to perform fatigues.

Fatigue Hat. A brimmed black felt hat that for a time was worn in garrisons and on campaign by all ranks in the American army.

Fatigue hat

Fatigue Jacket. See Drill Jacket.

Fatigues. In the American and British armies the word originally applied to all the common housekeeping chores in barracks and camp: cutting wood, digging latrines, collecting garbage, painting barracks, etc. In the nineteenth century the word applied as well to all nonmilitary activities, such as building roads or quarters.

In America an act of Congress of 2 March 1829 allowed an extra gill of whiskey to those employed on fatigue duty other than housekeeping chores. As of 4 August 1854 in all stations east of the Rocky Mountains, soldiers constructing fortifications, building roads, or other such labor were given an extra twenty-five cents per day if they were laborers or teamsters and forty cents per day if they were mechanics; west of the mountains the pay was, respectively, thirty-five cents and fifty cents.

Fausse Braye / Braie. An advanced parapet in permanent fortifications, usually of earth, placed in front of the main rampart, leaving a chemin de ronde between it and the rampart. It is sometimes described as a lower-level second enceinte outside the main rampart.

Fay, Charles Alexandre (1827–1903). A French soldier and writer who served in the Crimean War and the Franco-Prussian War [qq.v.]. He was made general of brigade in 1879 and general of division in 1885. He was the author of such military memoirs as *Journal d'un officier de l'armée du Rhin* (1871).

Fayetteville, Capture and Recapture (1861 and 1865), American Civil War. This North Carolina town on the left bank of the Cape Fear River housed an arsenal that on 22 April 1861 surrendered to the Confederates, giving them 35,000 stand of arms. The place was retaken by General W. T. Sherman [q.v.] in March 1865.

Fear. The unpleasant emotion, often strong, caused by the presence of or anticipation of danger. Its absence or control has always been demanded of soldiers. General Aleksei Kuropatkin [q.v.] wrote: "The man who conquers in war is the man who is least afraid of death."

Feathers. Many uniform officers' hats included plumes or tufts of feathers. In Britain, colored cock's feathers replaced ostrich plumes in the cocked hats of generals at the beginning of the nineteenth century. Other feathers used in various armies included those of swans and lesser white herons [see Plumes].

February Revolution. See Paris Revolutions of 1848.

Feint. A secondary attack, usually with a small portion of a force, aimed at deceiving an opponent and, by diverting his attention from the main attack, inducing him to shift his reserves or to reveal his strength. A feint differs from a demonstration [q.v.] in that an attack is actually made.

Feldwebel. A sergeant major in the German army.

Feldwebel-Leutnant. A rank in the German army just below a *Leutnant* (lieutenant). It was created in 1877 to alleviate a shortage of junior officers.

Felloes. The parts of an artillery wheel, usually seven, that made up its circumference.

Fencible. 1. As an adjective, capable of being defended.
2. As a noun, a territorial [see Fencibles].

Fencibles. British soldiers who enlisted for the defense of the homeland and were not liable to be sent abroad. Fencible officers ranked as militia officers. Fencible units were usually raised for temporary duty. The only unit bearing the title more or less permanently was the Royal Malta Fencible Artillery.

Feng Tzu-ts'ai (1818–1903). A Chinese soldier who was commander of the Chinese troops in Tonkin when the French invaded in May and June 1884. He was defeated in the Battle of Langson [q.v.] on 13 February 1885 but repulsed a French attack upon his strong position at Chennankuan on 23 March, personally leading a counterattack. The French then withdrew. [See French-Indochina War, Third.]

Fenian Brotherhood. A militant secret revolutionary society, later called the Irish Republican Brotherhood, founded in the United States in 1858 by James Stevens (1825–1901) and John O'Mahony (1816–1877). Members swore "allegiance to the Irish Republic, now virtually established." The name came

Fenian Brotherhood *Fenians meet at Woodford and burn the government proclamation.*

from *fiann* or *feinne,* a legendary band of Irish warriors. The Fenian Raids [q.v.] into Canada were unsuccessful, as was the Fenian uprising in Ireland in 1867.

Fenian Raids (1866 and 1870). The Irish-American Fenian Brotherhood [q.v.] hoped to aid Ireland by attacking Canada and involving Britain in another war with the United States. On 1 June 1866 a Fenian force of 1,500, among them Brigadier General Thomas William Sweeney [q.v.] and many veterans of the American Civil War, calling itself the Irish Republican Army and led by "General" John O'Neil [q.v.], crossed into Canada from Buffalo, New York, and seized the town of Fort Erie. The Canadian volunteer battalion that attacked them was at first repulsed, but three days later, in the Battle of Limestone Ridge, Canadian militia defeated them and drove them back into the United States. A similar raid, launched the following week from Vermont, also failed, as did one from New Hampshire, for the "Inspector General of the Irish Republican Army" was, in fact, a British secret agent [see Le Caron, Henri].

Fenton, Roger (1819–1869). A British photographer who was known for his photographs taken in Russia in 1852 and in the Crimea in 1855 during the Crimean War [q.v.] using the slow wet plate collodion process he had developed in 1851. His photographs could not be published at the time for lack of the necessary technology. In 1862 he gave up photography to become a lawyer.

Fenton, Roger *Fenton's photographic van during the Crimean War*

Fer. The French word for iron was sometimes used figuratively for sword, as in *manier le fer* (to carry a sword), meaning to follow the profession of arms.

Ferdinand, Archduke, Ferdinand Karl Josef d'Este (1781–1850). An Italian prince who was an Austrian army commander during the Napoleonic Wars. At Ulm [q.v.], disliking the plans of General Karl Mack, his superior, he refused to be bottled up, and on 15 October 1805, as the French closed in, he successfully extricated 6,000 cavalry. When the Battle of Austerlitz [q.v.] was fought on 2 December 1805, he

was leading a corps at Iglau, 90 miles away, and attempted in vain to reach the main army in Moravia. However, he had some success over Jozef Poniatowski [q.v.], defeating him in the Battle of Raszyn [q.v.] on 18 April 1809. Having advanced to the outskirts of Warsaw, he was forced to retreat when Russia entered the war on the side of France. By July he had abandoned most of Galicia.

Fère-Champenoise, Battle of (25 March 1814), Napoleonic Wars. A French army of 30,000 under Marshals Auguste Marmont and Édouard Mortier [qq.v.] attempted to stop an Allied army of 110,000 under Field Marshal Prince von Schwarzenberg [q.v.] from advancing on Paris. At the battle near this village in north-central France, 22 miles southwest of Châlons-sur-Marne, the French were defeated and lost some 5,000 men. The disaster might have been greater had not the 9th Regiment of heavy cavalry saved the corps from a complete rout. This was the last major engagement in northern France prior to Napoleon's first abdication.

Fernández de Córdoba y Valeácel, Fernando (1809–1883). A Spanish soldier who was created a field marshal in 1844. He was minister of war in 1847, and in 1849 he led the army sent to Rome to liberate the pope. In 1850 and again in 1870 he was captain general of Cuba. In the Carlist Wars [q.v.] he was a supporter of Queen Isabella (1830–1904), but in 1868 he joined the revolution of Prim y Prats [q.v.] against her. When the republic was proclaimed in 1873, he was once again minister of war.

Ferneyhough, George Thomas (1841–1912). A South African photographer who in 1879 accompanied the British army during the Zulu War [q.v.] and photographed the campaign, including the funeral of Louis Napoleon, the prince imperial [see Napoleon, Eugène Louis Jean Joseph], who, while with the army in an unofficial capacity, was killed by a Zulu impi. In 1882 Ferneyhough was the first to photograph a comet, Finlay's.

Ferozeshah, Battle of (21–22 December 1845), First Sikh War. Beginning at three o'clock in the afternoon on 21 December 1845, near this village in East Punjab, India, 13

Ferozeshah *General Gough confers with his officers after the Battle of Ferozeshah in the First Sikh War, December 1845.*

miles east of Ferozepore and a few miles from the left bank of the Sutlej River, a British force of about 5,674 European and 12,035 Indian troops under Sir Hugh Gough [q.v.] attacked 50,000 strongly entrenched Sikh infantry with 88 guns under Lal Singh (d. 1867) and broke through their first line. It was the shortest day of the year, and nightfall halted the action, but the following morning the second line of entrenchments was stormed and 74 guns were taken. The Sikhs counterattacked but were thrown back with great loss and forced to retreat across the Sutlej. Curiously, Sir Henry Hardinge [q.v.], himself a soldier and the governor-general of India, who was present, volunteered to serve under Gough. He soon regretted stepping down, and the two quarreled as the battle raged.

The Sikhs lost an estimated 7,000; Gough's force lost 694 killed and 1,721 wounded; 103 officers were killed or wounded including 5 aides-de-camp of Hardinge killed and 4 wounded. This was one of the bloodiest battles fought by the British in Asia in the nineteenth century.

Ferrara, Battle of (12 April 1815), Napoleonic Wars. During the Hundred Days, French Marshal Joachim Murat [q.v.], leading an army of 50,000 Italians, tried to cross the Po River in northeastern Italy while facing an Austrian army of 60,000 under General Vicenz Friedrich Bianchi (1768–1855). Murat was repulsed, suffered heavy losses, and was forced to retreat south.

Ferreira, Ignatius Philip (1840–1921). A South African prospector and soldier who served in the Border Police and fought in engagements against the Hottentots (Khois). In the first Sekukuni War [q.v.] he was a field cornet and commanded the defense of Fort Burgers; in the second war he organized and led a mounted unit known as Ferreira's Horse.

Ferrero, Edward (1831–1899). A Spanish-born American soldier who before the American Civil War operated a dancing school established by his father in New York City and taught West Point cadets to dance. Active in the militia, he was a lieutenant colonel when the Civil War began, and on 14 October 1861 he was commissioned a colonel in command of the 51st New York. He fought at Second Bull Run, Chantilly, South Mountain, Antietam, and Fredericksburg [qq.v.]. After fighting at Vicksburg [q.v.] he was promoted brigadier general.

Ferrero is best remembered for the disgraceful role he played in the Petersburg mine explosion [q.v.]: In command of the black 2nd Division, IX Corps, of the Army of the Potomac, he skulked in a bombproof shelter while his troops fought. Nevertheless, he was brevetted major general for the Petersburg and Richmond campaigns.

After the war he managed several large ballrooms in New York City, including Tammany Hall.

Ferrule. 1. A ring that reinforced the grip of an edged weapon.
2. The band on a scabbard or its lower end.

Fessenden, James Deering (1833–1882). A Union soldier in the American Civil War. He is credited with organizing the first regiment of black troops in 1862, but his action was not approved, and the regiment was disbanded. He later served in Tennessee and Georgia and was promoted brigadier general. After the war he became a lawyer and legislator.

He was the brother of Major General Francis Fessenden (1839–1906) and the son of William Pitt Fessenden (1806–1869), who from June 1864 to March 1865 was Lincoln's secretary of the treasury.

Fetterman Massacre (21 December 1866), American Indian Wars. Fort Phil Kearny was built in July 1866 in the Bighorn Mountains between the Big and Little Piney forks of the Powder River, about 15 miles north of present-day Buffalo, Wyoming. It was named after Major General Philip Kearny [q.v.], killed in the Battle of Chantilly [q.v.] on 1 September 1862, and was commanded by Colonel Henry Beebee Carrington (1824–1912). When a woodcutting detail from the fort was set upon by Indians, Carrington sent out to rescue it Captain William Judd Fetterman (1833?–1866) with 2 officers and 80 soldiers accompanied by 2 civilians. The force was lured into an ambush and attacked by 1,500 Sioux under Chief High Backbone (fl. 1860s). All were killed—even the dog that had followed the troops. Fetterman saved his last bullet for himself, as powder burns by his temple testified.

Feu de Joie. A discharge of musketry into the air with blank ammunition, to honor an occasion or salute a person of rank. It was often carried out by lines of riflemen who fired one after the other in rapid succession. When executed by a large number of well-drilled troops, the effect was spectacular.

Feu Rasant. A grazing fire in which the projectiles follow a trajectory low and parallel to the ground.

Fez. A brimless red cap worn by Turkish soldiers, Zouaves, evzones, and others. West Indian troops in the British army wore fezes under their turbans.

Fezzan, Conflicts in. The last of the Beni Muhammad sultans who ruled Fezzan, an area in the southern part of what is today Libya, was killed in 1811 by El-Mukkeni, a lieutenant of Yusef Pasha, the penultimate sovereign of the Karamanli dynasty of Tripoli. El-Mukkeni proclaimed himself sultan of Fezzan and proceeded to enrich himself by carrying out extensive slave raids into the central Sudan, advancing as far as the Baugirmi region, southwest of Lake Chad. In 1831 he was overthrown by Abd-el-Jelil, a chief of the Walid-Sliman Arabs, who, after ten tempestuous years of slave raiding and attacks on other tribes, was killed in a battle against Turkish forces under Bakir Bey. Fezzan was then added to the Turkish Empire.

Fick, Johan Izaak (1816–1892). A South African soldier who as a field cornet fought the British in the Battle of Boomplats [q.v.] in 1848. In 1865, as commandant general of the Orange River State, he fought the Basutos and assumed command of the Boer forces when Lourens (Louw) Jacobus Wepener [q.v.] was killed in the storming of the Basuto stronghold of Thaba Bosigo [q.v.]. The town of Ficksburg in eastern Orange Free State, near Lesotho, was named for him.

Ficqelmont, Count Karl Ludwig von (1777–1857). An Austrian soldier and statesman who took part in campaigns against Napoleon. He was subsequently ambassador to Stockholm, Florence, and Naples.

Field. 1. The locus of combat; a battlefield.
  2. An active theater of military operations.
  3. On campaign—e.g., in the field.

Field, Charles (1828–1892). An American soldier, a graduate of West Point, who saw service in the Far West and as a captain was an instructor of cavalry at West Point before resigning at the beginning of the American Civil War to join the Confederate army. He served under Jeb Stuart [q.v.] until 9 March 1862, when he was appointed a brigadier general and given an infantry brigade. He then fought in the battles of Seven Days, Cedar Mountain, and Second Bull Run [qq.v.], in which he was severely wounded in the hip. His convalescence was long, and he never fully recovered from his wound, but on 12 February 1864 he was promoted major general. In that rank he served under James Longstreet [q.v.] at the Wilderness, Cold Harbor, and the siege of Petersburg [qq.v.].

After the war he engaged in business in Maryland and Georgia until in 1875 he accepted a commission on the general staff of the Egyptian army, whose chief was former American Brigadier General Charles Stone [q.v.]. In 1878 he returned to the United States and became doorkeeper in the House of Representatives. He has been described as a man of "vigorous intellect and indomitable will, of superb physique."

Field Allowance. See Allowances; Batta.

Field Army. An administrative and tactical organization containing a headquarters, support and service troops, and a variable number of corps or divisions operating against an enemy.

Field Artillery. See Artillery.

Field Cornet. A rank in the Boer armies in South Africa below a commandant, responsible for much of the administration of a commando [q.v.].

Field Day. A special day devoted to troop maneuvers and training exercises.

Field Dressing. Individual first-aid kits were introduced into the British army during the Crimean War. They consisted of a piece of calico, some lint, and pins, and they were carried in the knapsack until 1874, when they were transferred to the left breast pocket. In 1884 antiseptic field dressings were added.

During the Franco-Prussian War of 1870–71 German soldiers were issued a triangular bandage and a safety pin.

American soldiers were first issued first-aid packets during the Spanish-American War [q.v.], when 12,000 were presented to brigade surgeons for distribution before the troops sailed for Cuba.

Field Expedient. An improvisation.

Field Fortification. See Fortification.

Field Grade. Officers above the rank of captain and below that of brigadier general—i.e., majors, lieutenant colonels, and colonels. The term originally indicated those with the rank and experience to command a regiment in the field.

Field Hospital. A temporary military hospital sometimes established in existing buildings close to the battlefield.

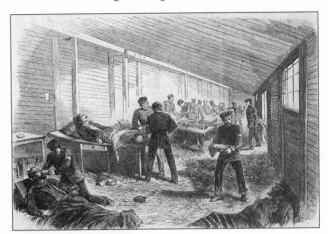

Field Hospital *Temporary Prussian field hospital at Düppel during the Schleswig-Holstein War, 1864*

Field Kitchen. A mobile or temporary kitchen.

Field Marshal. The highest military rank in many European armies. In the French army the rank was marshal of France or marshal of the empire [see Marshal of France]. In Britain the rank was first conferred upon John Duke of Argyll in 1736. On 21 June 1813 the Duke of Wellington became the first British field marshal of the nineteenth century. In the British army the rank was usually bestowed on generals too old to hold active commands in the field. An exception was Field Marshal Lord Roberts [q.v.], who at age seventy was sent to command the imperial forces in South Africa [see Anglo-Boer War, Second] and retrieve British fortunes after the reversals of Black Week [q.v.].

A highly decorated baton [q.v.] indicated the status of a field marshal.

Field Kitchen *Bivouac kitchen in the Crimea, 1853–56*

Field Officer's Court. A lesser court-martial than a general court-martial established in an 1874 revision of the Articles of War in the American army.

Field of Honor. A place where duels were fought.

Field Park. The spare vehicles, reserve supplies of ammunition, tools, and materials for making repairs for the use of an army in the field.

Fieldpiece / Field Piece. A small cannon; a gun in the field artillery.

Field Punishment Number One. A punishment in the American and some European armies in which a soldier was tied spread-eagle onto the wheel of a gun or wagon and left exposed for so many hours or so many days. This form of crucifixion was abolished in the German army in 1918 but not in the British army until 1929. In the American army it was never officially sanctioned, and its use appears to have disappeared in the early nineteenth century.

Field Report. See After-Action Report.

Field Telegraphy. See Telegraph.

Fieldwork. See Fortification.

Fife. A small musical flute in B flat used in the fife and drum units that were the nucleus of military bands. The pitch of the fife was between the concert transverse flute and the piccolo.

Fife *Eurasian boy drummer and fifers, 1800*

Fifteenth Slave Law. A Confederate law passed during the American Civil War that exempted from conscription one white man for every plantation that employed fifteen or more slaves. Its purpose was to ensure sufficient overseers, but because it favored the rich, it was much resented. It was sometimes called the Nigger Law. [See Conscription.]

5th United States Infantry. One of the most renowned regiments in the American army. It was first organized in 1798, but its service was intermittent until the War of 1812 [q.v.]. It subsequently saw service in the Black Hawk War of 1841–42 and the Mexican War [qq.v.] of 1845–48, first under Major General Zachary Taylor and then under Major General Winfield Scott [qq.v.]. It fought in the Seminole War in Florida in 1857 and three years later took part in the Utah Expedition [qq.v.]. In 1860 it was sent to New Mexico, and it remained in the West during the entire American Civil War. The regiment gained its greatest reputation in the Indian Wars, during which, in 1869, it amalgamated with the 37th Infantry under Colonel Nelson Appleton Miles [q.v.].

Fifth Wheel. An American term for the spare wheel that was carried on the rear of an artillery caisson. It was sometimes used to spread-eagle soldiers enduring field punishment number one [q.v.]. During the American Civil War those critical of the Sanitary Commission [q.v.] referred to it as a "fifth wheel to the coach."

Fighting. Contending in battle. Karl von Clausewitz [q.v.] states in *Vom Krieg (On War,* 1833) "War in its literal meaning is fighting, for fighting alone is the efficient principle in the manifold activity which in a wide sense is called war."

Fighting McCooks. The name given the seventeen members of the McCook family of Ohio who served in the Union army during the American Civil War. Ten of the Fighting McCooks were the sons of Major Daniel McCook (1798–1863), who was mortally wounded on 19 July 1863 while leading a home guard unit in an attempt to intercept Confederate raider John Hunt Morgan [q.v.] near Buffington Island, Ohio. He and his sons were known as the tribe of Dan. The remaining McCooks, known as the tribe of John, were mostly his nephews. Six McCooks became generals.

Fiji, Capture of (1874). The search for sandalwood led to European interest in these islands in the Southwest Pacific Ocean. In 1858 a Fiji chief, pressed by a dispute with the United States, offered the island to Britain. Intertribal wars gave cause for Britain to interfere, and in 1874 it was annexed by Britain.

File. A line of soldiers standing one behind the other. Those standing beside each other are in a rank.

File Closers. Officers and noncommissioned officers posted in the rear of a formation to supervise proper behavior and in battle to ensure steadiness by preventing unauthorized flight. In line of battle they usually carried bared sabers or bayonets.

File Leader. The man standing at the head of a file.

Filibuster. 1. A person who made war on a country with which his own was at peace with the intent to overrun and occupy it, claiming a cause.

2. An attack on a country at peace by irregular forces from outside the country or the carrying out of insurrectionist activities in a foreign country.

In the nineteenth century this term was applied to American adventurers and Central or South American exiles who organized military expeditions from the United States against Latin American countries. [See Walker, William; Miranda, Francisco; Gutiérrez de Lara, José Bernardo; Mina, Francisco Javier; López, Narciso.]

Findlater, George (1872–1942). A Scottish soldier who distinguished himself in the Battle of Dargai [q.v.] on 20 October 1897 during the Tirah Campaign [q.v.] on India's Northwest Frontier. Findlater was a piper in the Gordon Highlanders who, although severely wounded in both legs during the Gordon's charge of the heights, propped himself against a rock and, under heavy fire, steadfastly piped the troops into action with the tune "Cock o' the North." He was awarded the Victoria Cross, and his feat captured the imagination of the British public. After his discharge he was hired to pipe the tune in music halls for far more money than he ever made as a soldier.

When army authorities pronounced his enterprise unsuitable for a winner of the Victoria Cross and attempted to end it, the matter was raised in the House of Commons, where Duncan Vernon Pirie (1858–1931), a member of Parliament for North Aberdeen and himself a soldier who had seen active service, rose to ask "whether Piper Findlater V. C. has been offered a post as compensation for forgoing a means of making a living?" The government's ultimate response was the institution of regular annual pensions.

Findlater eventually retired to Cairnhill Farm, Huntley, Aberdeenshire, where he had been born. In 1914 he rejoined the colors and served as sergeant piper in France. He was wounded at Loos in July 1915 and became disabled by aggravation of his "Dargai wounds."

In 1992 his Victoria Cross was offered at auction at Christie's. It was expected to sell for more than £25,000 (about $39,000), but for unknown reasons it was withdrawn before the auction.

Fined Down. An American expression meaning "traveling light;" a soldier or unit marching with only the essential items of equipment.

Finerty, John F. (1846–1908). An Irish-American newspaperman who saw more action than most soldiers. Born in Galway, Ireland, he emigrated to the United States in 1864. In the last months of the American Civil War he served in the 94th New York Infantry. After the war he worked as a newspaper reporter in Chicago, and in 1876 he covered the Sioux Campaign of General George Crook [q.v.]. He went on to cover the Battle of the Rosebud [q.v.] and Crook's campaign in the Black Hills. He also took an active, unauthorized part in the Battle of Slim Buttes [q.v.]. In 1878 he traveled to Mexico, where he became the first American journalist to interview Porfirio Díaz [q.v.]. The following year he accompanied the Sioux Campaign of General Nelson Miles and the campaign against the Utes led by General Wesley Merritt

[qq.v.]. In 1881 he covered the Apache Campaign of Camillo Carr (1842–1914).

In 1882 he married and he founded the *Chicago Citizen*. From 1883 to 1885 he served in Congress. Finerty had the rare distinction of being a newspaper reporter who was liked and respected by army officers.

Fingoes. See Mfecane and Mfengu.

Finland, Invasion of (1808). After the Treaty of Tilsit on 7 November 1807, Russia and France demanded that Sweden end its coalition with Britain. When Sweden refused, Russia invaded Swedish-ruled Finland in February 1808. After a month of desultory fighting, Sweden evacuated the country, and by the Treaty of Frederikshavn on 17 September 1809, Finland and the Aaland Islands were ceded to Russia. Finland then was organized as a "grand duchy in personal union with the tsar." From 1899 it suffered under a Russification policy that took away its constitution along with other rights and sparked civil unrest.

Finley, Jesse Johnson (1812–1904). An American politician and soldier who at the beginning of the American Civil War served as a judge in the Confederate States courts but resigned in March 1862 to enlist as a private in the 6th Florida. Within a month he was elected captain and promoted colonel. He fought in Kentucky, Tennessee, and Alabama. In the Battle of Jonesboro [q.v.] he had his horse shot from under him and was severely wounded. After the war he served in Congress.

Fiodoroivskoy, Battle of (3 November 1812), Napoleon's Russian Campaign. During the retreat of the Grande Armée from Moscow [see Russian Campaign, Napoleon's], the corps of the rear guard, about 20,000 men commanded by Marshal Louis Nicolas Davout [q.v.], was attacked near this village, about 50 miles west of Borodino, by 30,000 Russians, mostly cavalry, under General Mikhail Andreyevich Miloradovich [q.v.]. Davout was cut off from the main body and surrounded, but General Eugène de Beauharnais [q.v.], Napoleon's stepson, sent back two divisions that broke through the encircling Russians and created an escape corridor. Nevertheless, the Russians continued to press until a division of Marshal Michel Ney's [q.v.] corps joined the fight.

Davout's corps, which lost about 4,500 men, was so shaken by this experience that its men did not recover their former morale. Ney's corps took over its rearguard duties.

Fire. The discharge of weapons or an order to discharge weapons. To be "under fire" is to be in battle and vulnerable to the enemy's projectiles.

Firearms. Weapons firing a projectile by exploding gunpowder. The expression usually refers only to small arms, such as rifles and pistols.

Fireball. An illumination shell. During the Napoleonic Wars this was a shell containing rosin, alum powder, sulfur, potassium nitrate, gunpowder, and linseed oil.

Fire Cake. A kind of bread made of flour and water and cooked in hot ashes or on a hot griddle or rack. Sometimes called ash cake.

Fire Discipline or Fire Control. The ability to hold fire for maximum effectiveness, until the enemy was within range, so as not to waste ammunition.

Fire-eater. 1. One who was fond of battle or of dueling.
2. During the American Civil War, a violently partisan southerner.

Firefight. An exchange of musketry. Although thought to be a modern term and little used in the nineteenth century, the word was used in print in mid-century (*Military Review*, February 1853).

Fire for Effect. Artillery fire intended to have a tactical effect upon an enemy, as opposed to fire intended to adjust the azimuth or range of guns.

Fire in the Hole! The traditional warning called out when a demolition charge is about to be ignited.

Firelock. 1. A gunlock which used a slow match to ignite the powder charge or a gun with such a lock.
2. A flintlock.

Firepower. The amount of munitions that a weapon or a military unit can direct to a given target. This term was not used in the nineteenth century, but it is often used in modern accounts of nineteenth-century battles.

Fire Step. See Banquette.

Firestone. A composition of niter, sulfur, antimony, and rosin in a mixture of melted tallow and turpentine that was cast in molds of rocket paper. A priming of fuze composition was driven in a hole. Firestones were used to set structures ablaze.

Fire Swab. Wet rope yarns bunched together and dampened. Used to cool a gun and clean out any grains of powder remaining in a tube after firing.

Fire Tables. Sometimes called tables of fire, these were tabulated figures for each artillery piece that gave the range and time of flight for each elevation, charge of powder, and type of projectile.

Fire Trench. The trench line or parallel most forward in a fortification, siege work, or other defensive position, from which troops could fire hand-held weapons while generally protected.

Fire Unit. Any body of men whose fire could be controlled in action by one man. Toward the end of the century, when improved weapons made it necessary to fight in extended order, the number of men in a fire unit decreased. [See Tactical Unit.]

Firing Line. The positions occupied by troops prepared to fire on an enemy or on a target.

Firing Party. The detail of soldiers that fires three volleys—said to represent the Trinity—at military funerals. Not to be confused with a firing squad [q.v.].

Firing Pin. The part of the firing mechanism that strikes the percussion cap or primer and causes it to ignite the propelling charge.

Firing Range. 1. An area where weapons could be fired for practice or target shooting.
2. The maximum distance a fired projectile would travel.
3. The distance between a weapon and its target.

Firing Squad. A small number of men, usually between 6 and 12, detailed for executions. Frequently one or more rifles fired blanks. In such cases officers loaded the weapons, and no member of the firing squad could be certain that his rifle carried live ammunition until he pulled the trigger. The officer commanding the firing squad usually administered a coup de grace to the victim with a pistol.

The number of such executions ordered tended to decline in all armies prior to the First World War. In the British army, for example, 76 death sentences were pronounced in the period from 1826 to 1835, but from 1865 to 1898 only 44 were awarded, 33 of which were carried out by firing squads. In the First World War, however, the British executed hundreds of their own soldiers.

Firka / Firqa. A division in the Turkish and Egyptian army. In the Sudan it was also the name for the suite of a tribal chief.

Firket / Ferket, Battle of (7 June 1896), reconquest of the Sudan. An Anglo-Egyptian force of 9,500 men under General H. H. Kitchener [q.v.] surprised and defeated a Dervish force of 4,000 under Amir Hamuda Idris al-Baqqari (d. 1896) at this place in the northern Sudan. The Dervishes lost an estimated 1,500 killed and 500 captured. Among the dead was Amir Hamuda, who was killed leading a charge. Kitchener lost 20 killed and 81 wounded.

Firket *Egyptian cavalry pursue the enemy in the Battle of Firket.*

First-Aid Kits. See Field Dressing.

First Call Men. Americans in the North who in May 1861 responded to the call for volunteers to fight in the American Civil War.

First Captain. The senior cadet officer at the U.S. Military Academy, West Point, New York, and at other American military academies. First captains were selected by the tactical officers and the commandant of cadets.

First Grenadier of France. The name given by Lazare Carnot [q.v.]—not, as is often said, by Napoleon—to a man born Théophile Malo Corret who in 1771 adopted as his surname de la Tour d'Auvergne (1743–1800), being descended from an illegitimate member of that famous family. He served in the French army from 1767 to 1791, particularly distinguishing himself in the Battle of Mahon in 1782. He fought in some of the early campaigns of the Revolution until captured by the British in 1795. He returned a captain in 1798 and, refusing all further promotion, served in Switzerland and Germany until he was killed in the Battle of Oberhausen in Bavaria in June 1800. His courage had become legendary. His embalmed heart was carried in a small urn on the cross belts of a chosen grenadier of the 46th Regiment of the Line. Troops marched at attention past his grave, and Napoleon decreed that his name remain on the roll of his regiment. Until 1814 a sergeant responded to his name at roll call with the words *Mort au champ d'honneur!* (killed on the field of honor). In 1889 his remains were interred in the Panthéon.

In addition to his gallantry, he was known for his Spartan simplicity and his chivalrous manners. A scholar who studied Celtic philology, he wrote a book on the Breton language and antiquities.

First Lieutenant. The second-lowest commissioned rank in the American army. The insignia is a silver bar. In the Confederate army it was two bars on the collar. In the British and French armies the rank is simply lieutenant. In the German army it is Oberleutnant.

First Light. Dawn. Technically, the beginning of morning nautical twilight, which occurs when the center of the morning sun is 12 degrees below the horizon.

First Line. 1. The best-trained and -equipped troops.
2. Those troops or fortifications closest to the enemy.

First Sergeant. A rank in the American army of the senior noncommissioned officer in a line company, equivalent to a color sergeant [q.v.] in the British army. Through the American Civil War all sergeants in a company were rated; thus, second sergeants, third sergeants, etc.

Fish Creek, Battle of (24 April 1885), Riel's Second Rebellion. Louis Riel [q.v.] with 280 rebel Métis held a strong position near Fish Creek in present-day Saskatchewan, Canada, where they were attacked by 400 Canadians under General Frederick Middleton [q.v.]. Middleton's force was repulsed, and after losing 50 men, he retreated; the Métis lost 29 killed and wounded.

Fisher's Hill, Battle of (22 September 1864), American Civil War. Following his defeat at Winchester, Virginia [q.v.], on 19 September, Confederate General Jubal Early [q.v.] retreated up the Shenandoah Valley in Virginia and occupied a strong natural defensive position south-southwest of Strasburg astride the Valley Turnpike along a small stream called Tumbling Run. He was pursued by Union General Philip Sheridan [q.v.] with three corps and a cavalry brigade.

One Union corps under General George Crook [q.v.] moved southwest onto Little Run Mountain and then swung eastward to crash into Early's left flank and rout his dismounted cavalry division there. Sheridan then advanced his other two corps in a wild attack on the Confederate front, sending the troops there flying. Early retreated to Waynesboro.

Federal losses were 52 killed and 476 wounded. Early reported a loss of 1,235 infantry and artillery; cavalry losses were said to have been light. Sheridan reported 1,100 Confederates taken prisoner. The Confederates also lost 12 guns.

Fishtail. 1. A ribbon with a V-shaped notch.
2. The garter flash worn on hose by Scottish soldiers.
3. The black ribbon worn on the back of Scottish headdress.

Fishtail Wind. A wind behind a marksman that is variable in direction, thus affecting the trajectory.

Fismes, Battle of (17 March 1814), Napoleonic Wars. When the Allies began to converge upon Paris, Napoleon attempted to strike their line of communication and moved on St. Dizier, a town on the Marne, 39 miles north of Chaumont, but his plans were revealed in a captured letter, and after Field Marshal Gebhard von Blücher [q.v.] defeated Marshal Auguste Marmont [q.v.] at Fismes, 16 miles west northwest of Rheims, the Allies ignored the threat and pressed on to Paris.

Fitness Report. A report on an officer's character and work by a superior in the British army. In the American army, such reports are called efficiency reports. Some nineteenth-century British reports could be terse. One cavalry officer wrote: "Personally, I would not breed from this officer." Another wrote: "This officer has the manners of an organ grinder and the morals of his monkey. I am unable to report on his work as he has done none."

Five Days' Revolt (18–22 March 1848). In Milan, Italy, the killing of a citizen by Austrian soldiers triggered a violent protest against Austrian rule. Some 1,650 barricades were thrown up in the streets and Austrian troops throughout the city were attacked. Austrian Field Marshal Josef Radetsky [q.v.] withdrew his troops, but the Austrians returned with a vengeance a few weeks later and regained control.

Five Forks, Battle of (30 March–1 April 1865), American Civil War. This was the last major battle of the war in Virginia. To turn the Confederates out of their positions at Petersburg [q.v.], Union General Philip Sheridan [q.v.] led three cavalry divisions to Dinwiddie Court House, 15 miles southwest of Petersburg near Five Forks, while two corps advanced on the Confederate right. General Lee sent General George Pickett [q.v.] with 19,000 of all arms to meet the threat. Pickett's cavalry struck Sheridan's right flank and initially forced it back, but Sheridan was strongly reinforced, and Pickett retreated toward Five Forks, creating an opening between him and the main Confederate defenses, a three-mile gap that the Union forces exploited to win a major victory. Confederate losses were more than 5,000. The Federals suffered 634 casualties. The loss of this battle prompted Lee to abandon Petersburg, as he did on the night of 2–3 April. A week later he surrendered at Appomattox [q.v.].

Five Reformers. The members of a Prussian committee formed in 1808 to reorganize the Prussian army. The five were all distinguished generals: Hermann Boyen, August von Gneisenau, Karl von Clausewitz, Karl von Grolman, and Gerhard von Scharnhorst [qq.v.]. They were able to reform officer training and to curb the aristocrats' monopoly of officer rank, but they were unable to push through universal conscription, which they believed was essential for a national army [see Military Reorganization Commission, Prussian].

Fixed Ammunition. A round of ammunition in which the projectile, propellant, igniter, and primer form a single unit.

Fixed Bayonet. A bayonet in place on the muzzle of a musket or rifle.

Flache. A fieldwork consisting of two sides of a salient angle. It resembled a redan but was raised upon a terreplein without a ditch.

Fixed Bayonet *A Prussian infantryman advances with fixed bayonet.*

Flag, Black. See Black Flag.

Flag, Garrison. In the American army this was a national flag, 36 feet fly and 20 feet hoist [see Fly and Hoist]. It was issued only to important posts or those with large garrisons, and it was flown only on special occasions.

Flag, National. A cloth bearing a distinctive design that symbolizes a country. A considerable amount of sentiment, not to say reverence, is often bestowed on a national flag. George Frisbie Hoare (1826–1924), an American, rhapsodized: "I have seen the glories of art and architecture, and mountains and rivers; I have seen the sunset on the Jungfrau, and the full moon rise over Mount Blanc. But the fairest vision on which these eyes ever looked was the flag of my country in a foreign land."

Flag, Post. In the American army this was a national flag, 20 feet fly and 10 feet hoist [see Fly and Hoist], issued to all posts garrisoned by troops. It was flown only in good weather.

Flag, Storm. In the American army this was the national flag, measuring eight feet fly and four feet, two inches hoist [see Fly and Hoist], issued to all military posts and national cemeteries for use in inclement weather. It was also used as a recruiting flag.

Flag Day. An American holiday. The first Flag Day (14 June) was organized in 1861 by the people of Hartford, Connecticut, to show their support for the Union in the American Civil War. Today it is a legal holiday only in Pennsylvania.

Flag of Protection. A flag used to designate a place devoted exclusively to humanitarian or cultural activities in a war zone. In the nineteenth century hospitals were usually designated by a yellow flag.

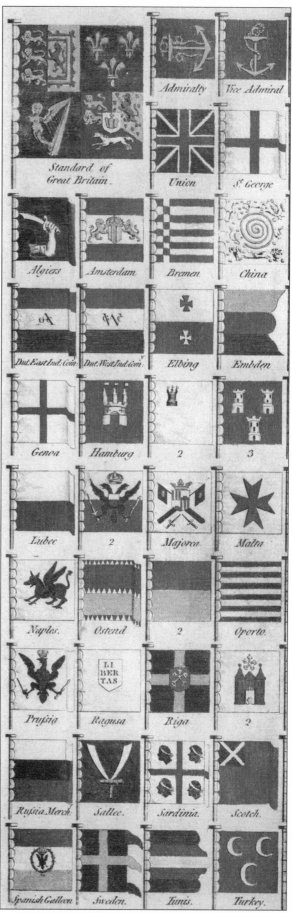

Flag, National *Flags of various nineteenth-century nations*

Flag of Truce. An all-white flag displayed as a signal that one side in a conflict wished to convey information in a non-hostile environment or to surrender. It was usually carried by an officer or sometimes by a soldier accompanying an officer attended by a trumpeter or bugler.

Flahaut de la Billarderie, Comte Auguste Charles Joseph de (1785–1870). A French soldier and diplomat whose putative father was Charles Maurice Talleyrand-Périgord (1754–1838). He lived in exile until 1800, when, at age fifteen, he joined the French army as a volunteer. He was commissioned after the Battle of Marengo on 14 June of the same year. He fought in the Battle of Friedland [q.v.] in 1807 and took part in the Peninsular War and in Napoleon's invasion of Russia [qq.v.]. In 1813 he became general of brigade, and in 1814 general of division. He saw action at Leipzig, Hanau, and Waterloo [qq.v.]. He was minister to Berlin in 1831 and ambassador to Britain in 1842.

Flam. In the British army this was a particular drumbeat directing a unit to make certain evolutions. It was made by two sticks striking the drumhead at almost, but not quite, the same time.

Flank. 1. The right or left side of a body of troops.
2. Any part of a fortification defending another part by fire along the outside of its parapet.

Flank, Bastion. The flank of a bastion is that part between the face and the curtain.

Flank, Covered. The platform of a casement that lay hidden in the bastion.

Flank Attack. An attack upon the left or right side of an enemy line. "Flank attack is the essence of the whole history of war," wrote General Alfred von Schlieffen [q.v.].

Flank Companies. In many European armies these were two companies of picked soldiers, one of which stood on the right flank of a battalion or regiment in formation and one on the left. The left flank company was light infantry, usually short, agile men trained as skirmishers; the right flank company was traditionally a grenadier company of the tallest men.

Flanker. 1. A projecting fortification commanding the flank of an attacking enemy.
2. Often riflemen and light infantry because they frequently functioned on the flank. A flanking party was any body of men sent to operate on the flank.

Flank Files. The men standing on the extreme right and left of each rank of a unit in formation. When the formation consisted of four ranks, they were called a double rank files.

Flanking Position. A defensive position situated to threaten the flank of an advancing army by launching a sally on the enemy's line of communication if it continued to advance. The position occupied by Stonewall Jackson and later by Richard Ewell [qq.v.] at Swift Run Gap in the Blue Ridge Mountains of Virginia during the Valley Campaign [q.v.] in the American Civil War is a classic example. The back of the Confederate force was in a strong defensive position against the Blue Ridge Mountains, over which it could retreat into its own territory, while any Union force that tried to continue south on the Valley Turnpike would expose its flank and line of communication to a sally by the Confederates.

Flank March. A march parallel to or oblique to an enemy's position in order to attack his flank.

Flank Refused. Sometimes called a refused flank. A line of battle in which the ends or flanks are curved back to face any attempt by the enemy to enfilade the line.

Flash. 1. The ribbon used to tie the queue.
2. The ribbons worn on the back of the collars of the Royal Welsh Fusiliers in the British army.

Flash in the Pan. An explosion of gunpowder in a gun when only the primer took fire.

Flats. The flat, uncurled feathers on the Highland bonnet.

Flatters, Paul (1832–1881). A French soldier and African explorer. Orphaned at seventeen, he was graduated from St. Cyr in 1853, ranking 65 out of a class of 230. He served with the Zouaves [q.v.] in Algeria before joining the Arab Bureau [q.v.] in 1856. On 5 March 1880 he led an exploring expedition south out of Ouargla, Algeria, into the Sahara. On 20 April, finding his route barred by hostile Tuaregs [q.v.], he turned back. A second expedition that included 47 tirailleurs had by 18 December 1880 marched 380 miles south of Ouargla when, on 16 February 1881, Flatters was killed in an encounter with Tuaregs.

Flèche, Le Prytanée National de la. A French military school reserved for the sons of French officers, originally only for the sons of officers killed in action, located on the Loire River a few miles north of Angers. Unlike other French military schools, it was entirely free.

Fletcher, Richard (1768–1813). A British military engineer who saw service in the West Indies and against the Turks and who fought in the Battle of Copenhagen [q.v.] before distinguishing himself during the Peninsular War in Portugal, where from 1808 he was the chief engineer of General Wellesley (later Duke of Wellington). It was he who constructed the famous Lines of Torres Vedras [q.v.] near Lisbon in 1808–09. He fought at Bussaco and Ciudad Rodrigo and at Badajoz [qq.v.], where in April 1812 he was wounded in the groin. The following year, while convalescing in England, he was made a baronet and awarded a pension. When he returned to the peninsula, he fought at Vitoria and directed the sieges of Pamplona and San Sebastián [qq.v.]. He was killed in the final assault on San Sebastián on 31 August 1813.

Flintlock. A musket lock or cock with a flint fixed in the hammer for striking a piece of steel (frizzen), creating sparks that ignited the priming powder in the pan, which then fired the charge. It was also the name given the musket itself. This system was invented in the early seventeenth century and was used until superseded by the percussion cap in the early nineteenth century.

Flipper, Henry Ossian (1856–1940). An American soldier who on 14 June 1877 became the first black to be graduated from West Point, ranking 46th in a class of 75. The following year he published *The Colored Cadet at West Point,* an account of his ordeal. In the entire four years no cadet ever spoke to him except in the line of duty. On graduation he was assigned to the 10th Cavalry, stationed at Fort Sill in present-day Oklahoma, one of the two black cavalry regiments in the American army. There he constructed a wagon road from the fort to Gainesville, Texas, and supervised the drainage of a malarial swamp near the post (known as Flipper's Ditch, it was dedicated as a national landmark on 27 October 1977). He served with distinction in the campaign against the hostile Indians under Victorio [q.v.], and his colonel testified to his "efficiency and gallantry in the field." Later he was named quartermaster and commissary of subsistence at Fort Davis, Texas. There he was arrested by Colonel William Rufus Shafter [q.v.], the post commander, and charged with irregularities in his records and with being "careless with accounts." He was court-martialed, and on 30 June 1882 he was dismissed from the service for "conduct unbecoming an officer and a gentleman." This sentence was "corrected" in December 1976, and the West Point Register of Graduates now lists him as "HonDisc [Honorably Discharged] 82."

Flipper became a successful mining engineer, working in Mexico and Venezuela. In 1893 and 1901 he was employed as a special agent for the Justice Department. In 1921 he was assistant to the secretary of the interior for the construction and operation of Alaskan railroads. He never married. He died at the home of his brother, a bishop of the African Methodist Episcopal Church, in Atlanta, Georgia.

Between 1870 and 1889, 23 blacks were nominated for the U.S. Military Academy; 12 were admitted. Flipper and 2 others were graduated: John H. Alexander in 1882 and Charles Young in 1889. Alexander died on duty as a second lieutenant in 1894; Young became a colonel, retired with a disability in 1917, and died in 1922 in Liberia. No other blacks were admitted until World War I, and none was graduated until 1936. All were given the silent treatment meted out to Flipper. [See West Point; Black Troops in the U.S. Army.]

Flissa or Flyssa. A long, single-edged Algerian saber similar to a Yatagan [q.v.] manufactured in Kabyle villages in Morocco and western Algeria. Usually about 40 inches long, it had a double curve and a long point. The blade was frequently engraved and inlaid with brass. The hilt was small and without guards. Emir Abd el-Kader [q.v.] had several in his armory.

Floating Batteries. Guns mounted on rafts or the hulls of ships.

*An ironclad floating battery
near Fort Sumter,
South Carolina, 1861*

Flogging. A punishment by beating with sticks, birches, rope ends, knouts, or whips. It was common in most European armies, particularly the Russian and British, though not in the French army. British General Sir Thomas Picton [q.v.] ordered three of his men flogged on the Waterloo battlefield; one of them, like Picton himself, was killed soon after.

In the British army any of the three levels of courts-martial—general, district or garrison, and regimental—could order any number of lashes, until 1829 when the number was restricted to 500 for a general court-martial and 300 for the others. Beginning in 1834, a British royal commission spent

twelve months investigating the practice. After interviewing seventy-one witnesses, none of whom had ever been flogged, it concluded that flogging was essential for proper discipline. It was, as General Sir Garnet (later Lord) Wolseley said, "cheap, simple, and withdrew the soldier from his duty for the shortest time." It was also often so severe that some men died from its effect. The last British fatality was a Private White, who in 1846 was flogged at Hounslow Barracks.

In 1832 the British army limited the maximum number of lashes to 300, and that number could only be inflicted on order of a general court-martial; lesser courts could order no more than 200. In 1879 the maximum was further reduced to 25. Flogging was abolished altogether in 1881.

In the American army the maximum number of lashes permitted was 100 until 1804, when the number was reduced to 50. However, in 1828 Private Archibald Allison demanded a court-martial for Surgeon John Gale (1792?–1830), who had given him 100 lashes on the bare back, and although a fellow surgeon corroborated Allison's story, Gale was acquitted. All flogging was briefly forbidden until 1831, when the House Committee on Military Affairs recommended its return and Congress, in an act of 2 March 1833, agreed but limited the number of lashes to 50 and then only for desertion. The practice was abolished by the War Department on 5 August 1861, but this was not always observed. In Louisiana in June 1865 George Armstrong Custer [q.v.] threatened to deliver 25 lashes to any soldier in his command who stole from civilians.

In the British army a flogging was executed in the presence of the victim's entire unit. A drummer delivered the beating while the adjutant stood behind him with a cane ready to strike him if the lashes were not laid on vigorously enough. A surgeon was required to be on hand and could stop the proceedings at any time, although not permanently. After a back had healed sufficiently, the remaining lashes were administered.

In the Russian army soldiers were beaten with birches (the lightest punishment), sticks, or the knout. The latter, constructed of dried and hardened strips of rawhide interwoven with wire sometimes hooked or barbed, almost always ended with the death of the victim. Running a gauntlet [q.v.] was common.

In the Turkish army the bastinado, a beating delivered to the soles of the feet by a rod, cord, or whip, was often employed.

In the armies of the Honourable East India Company in India sepoys and sowars [qq.v.] were exempt from flogging after 1820.

Florence Revolt (1859). On 27 April 1859, just before hostilities commenced in the Austro-Piedmontese War [q.v.], an émeute, led by Maschese Fernando Bartolommeo (1821–1869), erupted in Florence against Austrian rule. The troops called out to suppress it refused to fire on the crowds, a defection that led to the overthrow of Grand Duke Leopold II of Tuscany (1797–1870), who had favored the Austrians and refused to make an alliance with Sardinia.

Flores, Juan José (1801–1864). An Ecuadorian soldier and politician who served under Simón Bolívar [q.v.] in the revolts against Spain. In 1829 he won a victory at Tarqui [q.v.]. In 1830, when Ecuador proclaimed its independence from Greater Colombia, he became its first president (1830–35). He was again president from 1839 to 1845. In 1863 he led

Ecuadorian forces against New Granada (Colombia) [see Ecuador, Revolutions in].

Flores, Venancio (1809–1868). A Uruguayan soldier and politician who led the Colorados [q.v.] in a revolt against the government. He was elected president in 1854 but was overthrown the following year. He then crossed to Argentina and joined its army. Aided by Brazil and Argentina, he returned to Uruguay and assumed the presidency in 1866. He was assassinated two years later.

Florida Insurrection (1812). The successful revolt of Spain's American colonies led to American fears that Britain or another European power might seize them. In January 1811 Congress issued a warning to Europe that the United States would not "without serious inquietude" see any part of Spain's former colonies "pass into the hands of any foreign power." In 1812 James Madison (1751–1836), the fourth president of the United States, took advantage of a small insurrection against Spanish rule in western Florida (now part of Louisiana) to seize a part of the territory. The following year he ordered the occupation of the remainder to the banks of the Perdido River.

Florida War. See Seminole Wars.

Flourens, Gustave (1838–1871). A French revolutionary who, after being dismissed from the Collège de France for his evolutionary theories and his revolutionary sentiments, became a guerrilla leader in Crete during that island's insurrection against Turkey. The Greeks themselves kidnapped him and shipped him back to France, where he was seriously wounded in a duel with the noted journalist Adolphe Granier de Cassagnac (1808–1880). During the siege of Paris [q.v.] he commanded five battalions raised at Belleville and then a corps of tirailleurs. On 31 October 1870 with other revolution-minded soldiers, he helped overturn the government. In March 1871, at the beginning of the Paris Commune [q.v.], he was elected to represent the 19th and 20th arrondissements and was made a colonel. In the sortie of 3 April against the Germans besieging Paris he exposed himself too rashly and was captured. While a prisoner, he was killed by a cut from an officer's saber.

Floyd, John (1769–1839). An American carpenter and boatbuilder who was a brigadier general commanding the 1st Brigade of Georgia Militia during the Creek War [q.v.] of 1813–14. He commanded the militia forces and their Indian allies in the Battle of Autosee [q.v.] on 29 November 1813. On 27 January 1814 his force of 1,700 militia and 400 friendly Indians was ambushed by Creeks in the Calabee Valley about seven miles from present-day Tuskegee, Alabama. After hard fighting the Creeks were repulsed and driven into the swamps. Later Floyd served in the Georgia legislature and one term in Congress.

Flügelhorn. A hunting horn in B flat used in light infantry and in military bands. In many countries, including Britain, the hunting horn was used as an emblem for light infantry.

Flushing, Siege of (1809), Napoleonic Wars. During the British Walcheren Expedition [q.v.] 40,000 British laid siege to the seaport of Du Flushing at the mouth of the southern Scheldt River on the south coast of Walcheren Island, 55 miles southwest of The Hague. The defenders put up a stout defense, and although they were eventually forced to surrender, the delay enabled the French to reinforce the defenses of Antwerp and gave time for malaria (Walcheren fever) to weaken the British army.

Fly and Hoist. 1. The measurements of a flag. The fly is usually the length of the flag, at a right angle from the staff. The hoist, attached to the staff, is usually the width.

2. A fly is also the outer canvas of a tent.

Flying Artillery. Horse artillery. Mobile units in which every man was mounted or rode on limbers or caissons and the guns were able to keep pace with the cavalry.

Flying Camp. A strong mobile reserve force to be sent to threatened portions of a line.

Flying Colors. Flags unfurled.

Flying Column. Troops operating independently from the main body.

Flying Sap. In siege operations, when a trench (sap) had been pushed forward to a point in which those digging came under the fire of the enemy's artillery, gabions were brought forward, filled with earth, and placed along the trench to protect the diggers. Excavated earth was thrown over and beyond the gabions. Because this was done speedily, it was called a flying sap.

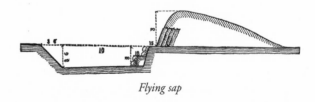

Flying sap

Flying Shot. A shot fired at a person or object in motion.

Flying Telegraph Train. This forerunner of the standard field telegraph train was used by the Union army in the American Civil War. The "train" consisted of two wagons with a Beardslee telegraph [q.v.], wire, portable telegraph poles, and two hand-crank magnetos. About thirty trains were sent to the field in the spring of 1863.

Foch, Ferdinand (1851–1929). A French soldier who on 26 March 1918 during the First World War rose to the chief command of all the Allied armies fighting in France. In 1873 he was commissioned in the French army upon graduation from the École Polytechnique. On 31 October 1894, after graduation from the École Supérieure de Guerre and a tour on the general staff, he became a professor at the École de Guerre and later its director. An official report on his performance rendered by the Securité Nationale stated: "This officer, during his professorship at the École de Guerre, taught metaphysics, and metaphysics so abstruse that it made idiots of a number of his students."

He became famous for his aphorisms: "A battle won is a battle in which one will not confess oneself beaten." And *"Victoire, c'est la volonté"* (Victory is the will [to conquer]). A leader in the development of military doctrine, he advocated in particular a doctrine of the offensive that found favor with the officer corps but that neglected the realities of a battlefield changed forever by the products of the Industrial Revolution. His books—*De la Conduite de la guerre* (1897) and *Des Principes de la guerre* (1899)—were an influence in other countries as well as in France.

In 1907 he was made a general of brigade and appointed commandant of the École Supérieure de Guerre, a post he held for four years. In August 1918 he was made a marshal of France.

Fodder. Any coarse food collected to be fed to domestic animals. In British and American usage this was usually dried herbage, such as hay and straw. [See Forage.]

Fogliardi, Augusto (1818?–1900). A Swiss soldier, born in the canton of Ticino, who saw some fighting in Italy and rose to the rank of colonel in the Swiss army, its highest peacetime rank. In 1863 the Swiss Federal Council sent him to the United States, where, as an observer of the American Civil War, he witnessed the last day of the Battle of Gettysburg and the later fighting in Tennessee. He was a Union partisan and an admirer of General Joseph Hooker [q.v.]. After the war he returned to Switzerland, where in 1867 he resigned his commission.

Fog of War. An expression used by Karl von Clausewitz [q.v.] to describe the confusion of battle and the resultant difficulty in understanding the events taking place on a battlefield as well as their significance. "War," he wrote, "is the province of uncertainty: three-fourths of those things upon which action in War must be calculated are hidden more or less in the clouds of great uncertainty" (*On War*, 1833). Sir William Napier [q.v.] in his *History of the War in the Peninsula* (1828–40) described the fog of war: "He who wars walks in a mist through which the keenest eye cannot always discern the right path."

Fogy or Fogey. 1. A term used by American soldiers for the small increment in pay that was given for each enlistment served and for some medals for which gratuities were awarded.
2. An old or invalid soldier.

Foible or Faible. The upper third of the blade of an edged weapon, ending at the point. The *forte* was the opposite end of the blade, and the *terzo* the middle section.

Fonseca, Manuel Deodoro da (1827–1892). A Brazilian soldier who was active in the War of the Triple Alliance [q.v.]. He was governor of Rio Grande do Sol from 1887 to 1889, when he became a leader in the movement against Emperor Dom Pedro II (1825–1891). He was briefly president of Brazil, from 24 February to 23 November 1891.

Fonteneuille, Paul Amiable de Brian de Fousières (1829?–1864). A French soldier who was graduated from St. Cyr [q.v.] in 1849. Two years later he won the Legion of Honor in Algeria fighting Berbers in the Kabylia. During the Crimean War [q.v.] he was wounded and promoted captain. He fought in Italy and commanded a battalion of the Foreign Legion [q.v.] in Mexico, where, in a rash attack on a hacienda near Santa Isabel in 1864, he was killed.

Food Preservation. As important to the changing face of battle as the development of arms were the advances made in the preservation of food. In 1804 François Nicolas Appert (1749–1841), a Parisian chef, developed a process for preserving vegetables in hermetically sealed containers using the hole and cap method, in which filled tins were capped by a lid with a small hole that after processing was closed by a dab of solder. However, even by the end of the century less than 20 percent of cans so prepared were sterile. In 1810 he devised a system, not entirely successful, for preserving meat.

By 1840 a method of preserving unsalted fish and fresh fruit was discovered. Dried fruits, dried fish, and salted or sun-dried meats had long been known, the latter called jerky in the United States and biltong in South Africa. In 1851 Gail Bordon (1801–1874), an American inventor, produced a meat biscuit, and in 1853 he discovered the secret of making condensed milk, a process he patented in 1856. Malted milk, a product of whole milk, whole wheat, and barley malt, was marketed from 1887.

Meat extracts were developed in Germany by Justus von Liebig (1803–1873) and Max von Pettenkofer (1818–1901) about 1840. About 25 pounds of lean mutton or beef could produce about 1 pound of extract. From Germany also came cognac lozenges and a tablet that dissolved in water to make rum grog. Although these delicacies lacked the alcoholic potency of the real thing, they were said to imitate the flavor.

Contamination in the preservation of food remained a problem until 1864, when Louis Pasteur (1822–1895) discovered how to prevent it. Only then could armies safely stockpile food for long periods. Pasteur's discovery revolutionized military logistics.

Foot. 1. Infantry were often spoken of as foot, as in foot and horse, or as a unit designation, as 11th Foot.
2. A measurement that varied by country:

	METERS
English foot	0.30479
Paris foot (*pied de roi*)	0.32484
Rhenish or German foot	0.31385

Paris foot = 12.78912 inches
Rhenish foot = 12.35652 inches

The Russian foot was equal to the English, but almost every German state used a different length; the Rhenish foot was used in Prussia. The Turin foot, which was about 20 inches, was the longest. The French *pied usual* was one-third of a meter. Fortifications were often measured in *toises*, a French measurement equal to 6.395 English feet, or 2.1315 yards.

Foot Guards. The name given in the British army to infantry regiments in the Brigade of Guards. In the nineteenth century the brigade included the Coldstream Guards, Grenadier Guards, and Scots Guards. In April 1900 the Irish Guards were raised. The Welsh Guards were not raised until 1915. [See Guards Regiments.]

Footlocker. A small trunk at the foot of a cot or bunk in which a soldier could store clothing and personal items. In the nineteenth century it was in use in the American army in a smaller size than the present footlocker.

Forage. 1. As a noun, fodder [q.v.] for the animals used by an army. In early usage the term was applied only to dried fodder, as opposed to grass. A normal ration for a horse was usually considered 14 pounds of hay and 12 pounds of grain.

Forage was a major item of expense. The U.S. army in 1860 had a budget of $7 million, $1.5 million of which was for forage. Much less than half of this amount ($575,000) was budgeted for the subsistence of the soldiers.

2. As a verb, to search for or collect provisions for men or beasts, often by raiding.

Forage *A foraging party of Connecticut volunteers returns to camp near Baton Rouge, American Civil War.*

Forage Cap. A cloth undress head covering worn by all ranks in all European armies. This was sometimes in the shape of a kepi, and it bore unit or corps numbers or insignia. Sometimes it was without a bill and carried a cockade with the national colors. [See Active Service and Peace Maneuvers Forage Cap.]

Forage cap

Foray. 1. A sudden attack, raid, or brief incursion.
2. An attack upon a secondary target.

Forbach, Battle of. See Spicheren, Battle of.

Forbes, Archibald (1838–1900). A British journalist who became one of the most noted war correspondents of his day. He had served for a brief period in the Royal Dragoons before turning to journalism. His first successes as a journalist came in his reporting of the Franco-Prussian War [q.v.] for the *London Morning Advertiser* and *Daily News*. He went on to cover the Second Carlist War in Spain, the Russo-Turkish War of 1876, the Second Afghan War, and the Zulu War of 1879 [qq.v.].

Force. Any body of troops.

Forced Crossing. The crossing of a body of water in the face of enemy opposition.

Forced March. A march at a rapid rate over a long distance requiring more than usual exertion.

Force Majeure. 1. Superior military force.
2. Compelling circumstances.

Ford. In South Africa, a drift.
1. The place where an unbridged river or stream can be crossed. This is usually the widest part of a stream and, by rule of thumb, not deeper than three feet for infantry, four feet for cavalry, two and a half feet for artillery, and less deep in all cases if the current was swift. A gravel bottom was desirable.
2. The act of crossing an unbridged body of water.

Ford *Confederates at a ford near Chambersburg, Pennsylvania*

Ford, John Salmon (1815–1897). An American soldier and frontiersman who was called Rip, said to stand for "rest in peace." He was born in South Carolina but settled in Texas in 1836. Until 1838 he served in the Texas army, in which he was commissioned a first lieutenant. He practiced medicine for six years, served in the Texas Congress, and in 1845 became editor of the *Texas Democrat* in Austin. During the Mexican War [q.v.] he served as adjutant of a regiment of Texas volunteers, earning his nickname by the death notices marked "R.I.P." he sent to next of kin. He later commanded a scout company. In 1849 he was commissioned a captain in the Texas Rangers [q.v.], and in a fight with Comanche Indians on 12 May 1850 he received a troublesome wound. He became a state senator in 1852. In 1858 he was appointed to lead a force against Comanches on the South Canadian River, where on 12 May he killed Chief Iron Jacket (d. 1858), a Comanche medicine man and tribal leader.

At the beginning of the American Civil War he commanded the 2nd Texas Mounted Rifles in the Rio Grande district. In 1862 he became Texas's chief of conscription, but in 1864 he was appointed a brigadier general of state troops and commanded a force organized to recapture the lower Rio Grande Valley. On 13 May 1865 he took part in the Battle of Palmito Ranch [q.v.], perhaps the last battle of the war. On 18 July 1865 he surrendered and was paroled.

After the war he edited a newspaper and became mayor of Brownsville, Texas; from 1875 to 1879 he was again a state senator. One who knew him said he was "the most inveterate gambler and the hardest swearer I have ever met."

Fordable. Said of an unbridged stream capable of being crossed by troops.

Foreign Enlistment Act. In 1819 the British Parliament passed this act, which forbade British subjects to enlist in foreign armies without the permission of the sovereign or Privy Council. The act was suspended in 1835 to permit Colonel George de Lacy Evans [q.v.] to raise the British Legion [q.v.] to fight against the Carlists in Spain [see Carlist Wars].

Foreign Legion. A military force serving a foreign country or a military unit composed of foreigners [see Foreign Legion, British; Foreign Legion, French; King's German Legion].

Foreign Legion, British. On 23 December 1854 the British Parliament authorized the formation of a foreign legion that was to consist of 10,000 Germans, 5,000 Swiss, and 5,000 Italians and was to fight the Russians in the Crimea [see Crimean War]. It was often called the German Legion (*Deutsche Legion*). Hostilities ended before it was completely formed, and in 1885 the corps was disbanded. Many of those discharged accepted a proffered passage to South Africa with the promise of land in Kaffraria and certain cash benefits. Under the leadership of General Carl von Stutterheim [q.v.] some 2,400 men, women, and children emigrated. (Many prominent South African families today are descended from these settlers.)

Foreign Legion, French. French: Régiment Étranger. The French have a long tradition of employing foreign mercenaries, going back to the use of Genoese crossbowmen in the Hundred Years' War in the fourteenth century; Swiss mercenaries in the sixteenth century; and Swiss, German, and Irish units in the eighteenth century. On the eve of the Revolution the French army contained 102 line regiments, 23 of which were composed of foreigners, and in 1803 Napoleon formed the Irish Legion [q.v.]. By far the most famous and most enduring mercenary unit is the French Foreign Legion. Instituted on 10 March 1831 by King Louis Philippe (1773–1850) to absorb some of the flood of refugees who poured into France in 1830, it provided a home for the displaced as well as for social misfits, petty criminals, and adventurers. Recruits were supposed to be between the ages of eighteen and forty, but physical fitness was the only real criterion.

The first battalion sent to Algeria saw its first action on 7 April 1832, when two companies were engaged in an indecisive battle against Algerians. In 1835 the entire Legion, then composed of 123 French officers and about 5,000 foreign enlisted men, was lent to Spain to support Queen Isabella II (1830–1904), who was fighting to save her throne from her uncle [see Carlist Wars]. In spite of the Legion's generally good performance, particularly in the battles of Terapegui, near Pamplona, on 26 April 1836 and Huesca [q.v.], 208 miles northeast of Madrid, on 24 March 1837, Spain treated it badly, as it did the British Legion [q.v.] of Colonel George de Lacy Evans [q.v.]. When it returned to France, fewer than one man in ten of the original force was left in the ranks.

When it was rebuilt, the Legion adopted as its motto: *Legio patria nostra* (The Legion is our country). By the end of 1840 it had five battalions organized into two regiments, and it had found its home, making its headquarters in the walled city of Sidi-bel-Abbès, in northwest Algeria, 40 miles south of Oran. The part it played in the French conquest of Algeria was considerable: Between 1847 and 1852 it fought in twenty-seven engagements, mostly in the Kabylia Highlands and the Aurès Mountains.

The Legion fought well in the Crimean War [q.v.], losing 12 officers killed and 66 wounded; 1,625 legionnaires were

Foreign Legion, French *The French Foreign Legion at l'Ouded–Ada in Algeria, March 1840*

killed or wounded. When Sevastapol [q.v.] was entered, the surviving legionnaires engaged in a monumental orgy of drinking and looting, activities for which they became notorious.

In 1859 the Legion fought in Italy [see Austro-Piedmontese War] and led the French army into Milan, but in 1861 the 1ier Régiment Étranger was disbanded, and enlistments were suspended in the remaining regiment. On 22 March 1864 recruiting was resumed to raise troops to send to Mexico, and the term of enlistment was extended from two years to five. On 10 August 1864 the Convention of Mirimar gave two battalions of the Legion to Emperor Maximilian (1832–1867) with the provision that as long as French troops were present in Mexico, the Legion would remain under French control. When other French troops were repatriated, the legion was to be left and vacancies were to be filled with Mexicans. However, few Mexicans volunteered, and an effort made at the end of the American Civil War to attract former Confederate soldiers was unsuccessful. When French forces began to depart on 13 December 1866, the Legion left with them.

In all, 1,918 officers and other ranks of the Legion died in Mexico, 1,601 from diseases. It was there at a place called Camerone on 30 April 1863 that a small detachment of legionnaires fought so gallantly that the day has been commemorated each year ever after in the Legion [see Camerone, Battle of].

The Legion was reduced from six battalions to four in 1867 and then further reduced to 3,000 men, but it was soon built up again. Although a law of 9 March 1831 prohibited the use of the Foreign Legion in metropolitan France, four battalions fought the Germans on French soil during the Franco-Prussian War [q.v.], and it was employed to fight against Frenchmen in the suppression of the Commune [q.v.].

In March 1875 the *Loi de Cadre,* passed by the French Assembly, fixed the size of the Legion at four battalions, each of four companies. It was later reorganized into two three-battalion regiments.

From 1883 the Legion had units serving in Indochina (Vietnam) as well as various parts of Africa. When legionnaires arrived at Haiphong in Indochina, they were greeted by General François de Negrier with the words "You legionnaires are soldiers in order to die, and I am sending you where you can die."

Foreign Service. Military service in a foreign location.

Foreland. The ground between the wall of a fortification and the moat or ditch.

Foreshore. That part of the seashore between the high- and low-water marks of normal tides.

Forestier-Walker, Frederick William Edward (1844–1910). A British soldier who served most of his career in South Africa. In 1877–78 he served in the Sixth Kaffir War [q.v.], after which he was mentioned in dispatches and promoted colonel. During the Zulu War [q.v.] of 1879 he distinguished himself in the Battle of Inyezane and in the occupation of Eshowe. In 1884 he was with the expedition under Sir Charles Warren [q.v.] that occupied Bechuanaland (Botswana) [see Bechuanaland Expedition]. From 1890 to

1895 he was a major general and commander of troops in Egypt. As a lieutenant general he commanded the line of communications in the Second Anglo-Boer War [q.v.]. In 1902 he was promoted general.

Forey, Élie Frédéric (1804–1872). A French soldier who took part in the coup d'état of 2 December 1851 by which Louis Napoleon (1808–1873) seized power and became Napoleon III. During the Crimean War [q.v.] in 1854–55 Forey commanded a division. He fought in Italy in 1859 [see Austro-Piedmontese War] and was appointed commander-in-chief of the French Expeditionary Force sent to Mexico [see Mexico, French Invasion and Occupation of; La Puebla, Battles of]. He was superseded in Mexico in 1863 by General Achille Bazaine [q.v.]. He ended his life as a marshal of France.

Forges, Comité des. A state-controlled organization formed in France in 1864 to centralize the production and divide the supplies of rough casting and to deal in British steels.

Forlorn Hope. 1. A body of men selected, usually from volunteers, for a dangerous mission, such as leading an assault as a storming party or scaling the walls of an enemy's fortifications. In French such a group is called *les enfants perdus* (the lost children), an expression that goes back at least to the sixteenth century. In German, *die vorlornen Posten;* in Dutch, *verloren hoop.* It did not mean, as often used today, an enterprise with no hope of success.

2. Any desperate enterprise.

Formation. An arrangement of troops in a prescribed manner.

Formosa (Taiwan), French Invasion of (1884–85). In October 1884 the French landed a force of 1,800 men on the north coast of the island at Keelung (Kilung or Chilung) and seized the heights above the town. They advanced 20 miles down the coast to Tanshui before they were repulsed. Cholera and other diseases melted the force away, and by January 1885 the garrison at Keelung had been reduced to 600. Reinforcements landed in March, and another attempt was made on Tanshui. When it was unsuccessful, the French withdrew, having accomplished nothing.

Formosa (Taiwan), Japanese Invasion of (April–October 1874). Citing as an excuse the slaughter by Formosan aborigines of 54 Okinawan seamen who were shipwrecked on Formosa (Taiwan), the Meiji government of Japan (1868–1912) sent a punitive military expedition to the island in April 1874. The expedition, which landed at Keelung (Kilung or Chilung), was badly organized and proved expensive. Assailed by diseases and without medical services, it was forced to withdraw. At the conclusion of the Sino-Japanese War [q.v.] of 1894–95, by the Treaty of Shimonoseki in 1895, Japan finally acquired the island, along with the neighboring Pescadores Islands, which they retained until 1945. When the Chinese residents of Formosa objected to Japanese rule and mounted émeutes, the Japanese subdued the island by force. Periodic insurrections flared for many years.

Formosa *The Japanese take possession of Formosa, 1895.*

Forno, Henry (1797–1866). An American soldier who was born in Louisiana when it was a Spanish possession. After service in the Mexican War [q.v.] he served as chief of police in New Orleans. In the American Civil War he fought for the Confederacy, seeing action in the Seven Days' Battles, Cedar Mountain, and Second Bull Run [qq.v.]. He was so severely wounded in the latter, in which he commanded a brigade, that he was expected to die. He recovered, however, and served out the war. He was killed in a railroad accident less than a year after the war ended.

Forrest, Nathan Bedford (1821–1877). A Confederate soldier of almost no formal education who before the American Civil War had amassed a fortune as a slave trader and planter. During the war, after serving briefly as a private in the 7th Tennessee Cavalry, he raised and equipped a battalion of cavalry at his own expense and was elected to be its lieutenant colonel in October 1861.

After taking part in the defense of Fort Donelson [q.v.], he was elected colonel of the 3rd Tennessee and fought at Shiloh [q.v.]. Two months later he commanded the brigade that captured the Union garrison and considerable Union stores at Murfreesboro [q.v.]. On 21 July he was promoted brigadier general, and in December he cut General U. S. Grant's communications in western Tennessee. He took part in the Chattanooga Campaign [q.v.] but quarreled with General Braxton Bragg [q.v.], his superior, and so was given an independent command in western Tennessee and northern Mississippi. He was promoted major general on 4 December 1863. In April he captured Fort Pillow [see Fort Pillow Massacre], and in June he defeated a numerically superior force at Brice's Crossroads [q.v.]. He fought in the Battle of Tupelo under Stephen Dill Lee [q.v.], and in the last two months of 1864 he commanded the cavalry under John Hood [q.v.] in Tennessee. Just before he was overwhelmed by superior forces at Selma, Alabama [see Selma, Capture of], in April 1865, he was promoted lieutenant general, to rank from 28 February of that year.

After the war he resumed the management of his plantation and was named president of the Selma, Marion & Memphis Railroad. A violent man with an ungovernable temper, in his lifetime he is said to have killed 30 men, at least 2 before the war and 1 after, and not all of those he killed during the war were Federal soldiers. He knifed and killed a Confederate lieutenant who had disagreed with him.

Forsyth, Alexander John (1768–1843). A minister of the Church of Scotland and an inventor, the first to use a fulminate to detonate ordinary gunpowder and the inventor of the Forsyth lock [q.v.], the first percussion lock system and perhaps the most significant innovation in the history of firearms. In 1805 he submitted his idea for the lock to the master general of ordnance, who provided him with facilities in the Tower of London to work on his invention. In 1807 a new master general evicted him, and he returned to his home in Belhelvie, Aberdeenshire. In 1808 he obtained a patent for his lock and formed a company with James Purdy, a well-known gunsmith. The venture was a success, and more than 20,000 of the locks were made. Forsyth was said to have refused an offer of £20,000 from the Napoleonic government of France for his secret.

In 1842 the British government awarded him £200 in recognition of the importance of his invention, and after his death an additional £1,000 was distributed among his heirs.

Forsyth, George Alexander ("Sandy") (1837–1915). An American soldier who fought for the Union in the American Civil War and subsequently became a renowned Indian fighter. On 19 April 1861, at the beginning of the war, he joined the Chicago Dragoons. In September of that year he was a first lieutenant in the 8th Illinois Cavalry. He fought throughout the war and was wounded four times. Mustered out of the volunteer service as a major and brevet brigadier general in 1866, he remained in the army as a major in the 9th U.S. Cavalry. Two years later in the summer of 1868 he enlisted 50 frontiersmen and scouts to operate against the Cheyenne Indians. His first sergeant was another former brevet brigadier general, William H. H. McCall [q.v.]. On 10 September the little force set out on the trail of Indians who had recently attacked a wagon train. On the 17th on the Arickaree Fork of the Republican River in eastern Colorado, just west of the Kansas line, they encountered some 750 Cheyennes, Arapahos, and Brulé Sioux and were forced to fight for their lives. For almost a week Forsyth and his men were besieged on an island in the dry riverbed. Forsyth was wounded three times, and six of his men were killed, including Lieutenant Frederick Henry Beecher (1841–1868), for whom the battle and the island were named [see Beecher Island, Battle of].

From 1869 to 1873 Forsyth was military secretary to Philip Sheridan [q.v.], and in 1875–76 he was with a group of American officers, headed by Brevet Major General Emory Upton [q.v.], appointed to study armies in Europe and Asia. In April 1882 he was colonel of the 4th Cavalry and engaged hostile Chiricahuas led by Geronimo [q.v.] in the Doubtful Canyon area of New Mexico. In 1887 he was named commander of Fort Huachuca at the mouth of Central Canyon in the Huachuca Mountains. He retired on 25 March 1890. In his career he took part in two sieges, sixteen pitched battles, and sixty minor engagements.

Forsyth, James William (1834–1906). An American soldier and West Point graduate (1856) who served in the West until the American Civil War. During the war he served on McClellan's staff in the Peninsular Campaign [q.v.] and in Maryland. He fought at Chickamauga [q.v.] in September 1863 and then served on staff assignments until at the end of the war he was promoted brigadier general.

After the war he remained in the army as a lieutenant colonel. He served as an aide-de-camp to Philip Sheridan [q.v.] from 1869 to 1873 and as his military secretary until 1878. In 1886 he was promoted colonel and given command of the 7th Cavalry. In 1887–90 he organized the School for Cavalry and Field Artillery at Fort Riley, Kansas. On 29 December 1890 he commanded the troops in the Battle of Wounded Knee [q.v.]. He was promoted brigadier general in the regular army in 1894 and major general in 1897, the year he retired.

Forsyth Lock. An invention of Alexander Forsyth [q.v.] that replaced the flint-carrying lock on muskets by a hammer that struck a pin that was driven into the vent, crushing and exploding the powder. Patented in 1808, this was the first percussion lock system, and it revolutionized the manufacture of firearms. Because the lock was shaped like a scent bottle, it was sometimes referred to as the scent bottle lock.

Fort. 1. Any building or entrenchments that could be held against an enemy.

2. A permanent army installation as opposed to a camp. A fort usually had such defenses as a ditch, moat, ramparts, and other fortifications.

3. The land defenses of a harbor.

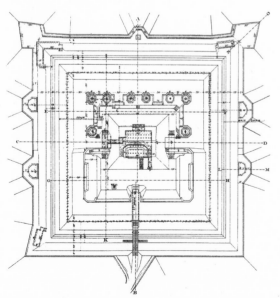

Fort *Diagram of Redoubt B at Fort Mouton, Alabama, June 1865*

Fort Bard, Attack on (21 May–5 June 1800), Napoleonic Wars. An Austrian garrison of 400 grenadiers of the Austrian Kinsky Regiment with 26 guns in this fort d'arrêt successfully delayed Napoleon's Army of the Reserve for four critical days during the final stages of his crossing the Alps by way of the St. Bernard Pass. On the night of 24–25 May Napoleon finally passed infantry and 6 guns around the fort, but the remainder of his artillery and his supply trains were blocked until early June.

Fort Beleaguer. See Fort San Felipe de Beleaguer.

Fort Blakely, Capture of (2–9 April 1865), American Civil War. At this fort in southwest Georgia, 37 miles northwest of Bainbridge, near the Alabama line, Union Brigadier General Edward Richard Sprigg Canby [q.v.] with 45,000 men besieged a Confederate force of 4,000 under Confederate Brigadier General St. John Richardson Liddell (1815–1870). On 9 April an assault by 16,000 Union troops carried the fort at a cost of 105 killed and 466 wounded. The Confederates lost almost 3,200 men taken prisoner.

Fort Brown. See Fort Texas, Attack on.

Fort Buford, Attack on (24–25 December 1866 and 6 November 1867), American Indian Wars. Although it was rare for Indians to attack a fortified position, Sioux Indians under Sitting Bull [q.v.] twice attacked elements of the 31st U.S. Infantry at this fort in northern Dakota Territory near the mouth of the Yellowstone River. Each time they were repelled with difficulty.

Fort Darling, Battles of. See Drewry's Bluff, Federal Attack upon.

Fort d'Arrêt. A detached fort that blocks access to a pass, bridge, channel, or defile.

Fort Dearborn, Evacuation of (15 August 1812), War of 1812. American General William Hull [q.v.] ordered the evacuation of Fort Dearborn (Chicago) and the removal of its garrison to Fort Wayne in present-day Indiana. While this was in progress, the Americans were attacked by Pottawatomie Indians allied with the British. The Indians killed 12 soldiers, 12 militiamen, and 14 women and children. They captured 29 soldiers and 13 women and children. Fort Dearborn was burned.

Fort Delaware. A Union prison for captured Confederates in the American Civil War on Pea Patch Island in the Delaware River near New Castle, Delaware. It was commanded by Polish-born General Albin Francisco Schoepf [q.v.], called General Terror by the prisoners. Although the surgeon general complained that the place was overcrowded, unsanitary, and without proper cooking facilities, Colonel William Hoffman (1808?–1884), the commissary general of prisoners, ignored his promptings to improve conditions. Of the 7,000 prisoners of war at the fort in September 1863, 331 died; when smallpox broke out the following month, the death rate soared. The last prisoners were not released until July 1865.

Fort Donelson, Attack on (12–16 February 1862), American Civil War. When the capture of Fort Henry [q.v.] by Union forces on 6 February 1862 forced Confederate General Albert Sidney Johnston [q.v.] to pull back his forces, he reinforced Fort Donelson, on the Cumberland River in Tennessee, with 12,000 men under Brigadier General John

Floyd (1806–1863). General U. S. Grant's forces camped at Fort Henry until 11 February and then invested Fort Donelson the following day. With the help of the gunboats of Commodore Andrew Hull Foote (1806–1863) the fort was soon in a hopeless position.

General Floyd, who in 1857–60 had been secretary of war under President James Buchanan (1791–1868), feared that if taken prisoner, he would be shot as a traitor, so he passed the command to General Gideon Johnson Pillow [q.v.], who, not wanting to surrender either, at once passed the command to General Simon Bolivar Buckner [q.v.]. Floyd and Pillow with about 3,000 Virginia troops escaped across the river.

Buckner requested terms for surrendering, and it was then that Grant penned his famous unconditional surrender note [see Unconditional Surrender]. The battle forced the Confederates to abandon Kentucky, making it possible for Grant's forces to split the Confederacy by a drive down the Mississippi River.

About 17,000 Federals and 21,000 Confederates were engaged at Fort Donelson. There are unusually wide discrepancies in the casualty figures, but the numbers would appear to be nearly 3,000 Federals and 16,000 Confederates, of whom about 14,500 were taken prisoner or missing. Pillow was subsequently relieved of duty; Floyd was removed by President Davis without a court of inquiry.

Fort Erie, Battle of (13 July 1813), War of 1812. Americans under Jacob Brown [q.v.] captured this fort opposite Buffalo, New York, from the British [see Fort Erie, Siege of].

Fort Erie, Siege of (2 August–18 September 1814), War of 1812. American General Jacob Brown [q.v.], after being checked in the Battle of Lundy's Lane [q.v.] on 25 July 1813, retreated into Fort Erie, a strong fort in Upper Canada (Ontario) on the north shore of Lake Erie across the Niagara River from Buffalo. (Fort Erie is now the name of a town built on the site in southeast Ontario.) Before continuing his retreat, Brown placed Colonel Edmund Gaines [q.v.] in charge of the garrison of 2,000. On 2 August Gaines was besieged by 2,800 British, many of them veterans of the Peninsular War [q.v.], under Lieutenant General Gordon Drummond (1772–1854), a veteran of the British campaign in Egypt.

On 13 August the British brought up siege guns, and after a two-day bombardment they launched a three-pronged assault. Two of the attacking columns were repulsed, but a third, led by General Drummond's nephew, succeeded in capturing a bastion. Before the British could go farther, ammunition in the bastion exploded, killing most of the attack-

ers, and the survivors fled. Later an American sortie led by Major General Peter Buel Porter [q.v.] destroyed the British batteries. The British lifted the siege on 18 September after suffering 609 casualties; American losses were 511. This battle was the first American victory on land against an organized British force in the war.

The fort was evacuated by the Americans on 5 November 1814. The British occupied it the following day.

Fortesque, John William (1859–1933). A British military historian who served as a private secretary to the governor of the Wayward Islands and the governor of New Zealand. He was for twenty-one years librarian of Windsor Castle. He is most famous for his magisterial thirteen-volume *History of the British Army* (1890–1930).

Fort Fisher, Attacks on (1864–65), American Civil War. Fort Fisher, guarding the port city of Wilmington, North Carolina, was on the Cape Fear River, 40 miles north of its mouth. The city was the chief port for Confederate blockade-runners.

1. 18–27 December 1864. General U. S. Grant ordered General Benjamin Franklin Butler [q.v.] to cooperate with the navy and reduce the fort. On 8 December 1864 Butler with 6,500 troops and two batteries moved down the James River in transports to Fort Monroe [q.v.]. On the 18th he was joined by a fleet under Rear Admiral David D. Porter (1813–1891). Confederate reinforcements arrived on the 24th. The

Fort Donelson *Map of the Federal attack on Fort Donelson*

Union forces had already captured some shore batteries, but it was decided that an attack on Fort Fisher would be too costly, and Butler withdrew. Union losses were only 15 wounded; Confederate losses were 300 men and four guns.

2. January 1865. Grant ordered Alfred H. Terry [q.v.] to organize a second expedition, and 8,000 men were assembled on 4 January 1865, at Bermuda Landing, Virginia, where they were joined by Porter's North Atlantic Blockading Squadron of 60 vessels and 627 guns. Storms delayed the ships, and they did not arrive at Fort Fisher until late in the afternoon of the 24th. By this time the 1,200-man garrison had been reinforced by 600 more, and General Braxton Bragg [q.v.], the commander of this area, had sent a division of 6,000 infantry and cavalry north of the fort to oppose a Union landing.

The naval bombardment began on the night of 12 January, and at about three o'clock on the morning of the 13th a division and a half of white troops and one of U.S. Colored Troops began to disembark. The assault, by 1,600 sailors and 400 marines, which began at four o'clock in the afternoon of the next day, was successful, and Fort Fisher was taken; the Confederates' last resistance was offered by a lone battery at about ten o'clock that night. Total Confederate casualties are unknown, but 112 Confederate officers and 1,971 other ranks were captured. Of the 8,000 Union troops engaged, 184 were killed, 749 were wounded, and 22 were missing; the navy's total casualties, including marines, were 686.

On the 15th two drunken sailors seeking loot wandered with torches into an ammunition chamber and exploded 13,000 pounds of powder, killing 25 Union soldiers and wounding 66; 13 men were missing.

Fort Gibson, Siege of (August–September 1864), American Civil War. This fort, located on the left bank of the Neosho River three miles above its confluence with the Arkansas River, was the strongest Union fort in Indian Territory (Oklahoma). In 1857 it had been evacuated and given to the Cherokee Nation. In August 1864, during the American Civil War, it was besieged, but never completely invested, by the Indian brigade of Confederate Brigadier General Stand Watie [q.v.], chief of the pro-Confederate Cherokees. When winter seemed imminent, Watie's brigade simply decamped for Texas. It was some time, however, before those in Fort Gibson realized that they were no longer besieged.

Fort Guaraich, Attack on (2 October 1893), Spanish-Riff War. An estimated 7,000 Riff tribesmen attacked this fort garrisoned by only 300 Spanish troops in northwest Spanish Morocco. The attack was repulsed with difficulty.

Fort Henry, Attack on (6 February 1862), American Civil War. This Confederate fort in northwestern Tennessee near the Tennessee River, commanded by Brigadier General Lloyd Tilghman (1816–1863), was a closed fieldwork on low ground, mounting 17 guns. Behind it was an entrenched camp on a high plateau. Attacked by a force of 15,000 under General U. S. Grant, assisted by a force of seven gunboats under Commodore Andrew Hull Foote (1806–1863), it

surrendered after a short bombardment by the gunboats. Foote lost 11 killed, 5 missing, and 31 wounded; Grant suffered no casualties. The Confederates surrendered 80 artillerymen and 16 hospital patients.

Fort Huger, Capture of (19 April 1863), American Civil War. During the siege of Suffolk [q.v.] a Union army-navy force of 270 men under a navy lieutenant captured this fort on Hardee's Bluff on the James River by a coup de main. At six o'clock in the evening the Federals disembarked without opposition about 400 yards from the fort and landed four boat howitzers. After a brief battle, the garrison—7 officers and 130 other ranks—surrendered the fort and five guns.

This small affair created a bitter altercation between two Confederate commanders, each of whom had assumed that the other had been responsible for picketing the area in which the Federals landed. Colonel John Kerr Connally (1839–1904), commander of the 55th North Carolina, was enraged by a report signed by two captains on the staff of Colonel (later General) Evander McIvor Law [q.v.] that blamed him for the disaster. Connally and his major, Alfred Horatio Belo (1839–1901), challenged the captains to a duel with double-barreled shotguns at 40 yards; one of the challenged, enraged in turn, demanded the more deadly Mississippi rifle [q.v.]. In the double duel no one was seriously injured. One hat was punctured, and one neck grazed [see Dueling].

Fortification. The strengthening of a military position against attack in order to obtain the best advantage for one's own weapons and to prevent the enemy from taking full advantage of his by providing protection from an enemy's missiles and raising obstacles that prevent him from coming to close quarters while holding him under fire for as long as possible.

Fortifications are of two types: permanent and field. The former are usually built in peacetime of enduring materials; the later, sometimes called fieldworks, are temporary and often hastily constructed of earth or available materials.

Soon after the Battle of Waterloo [q.v.] European nations began to take an increased interest in fortifications. The Belgians began to repair and improve a number of bastioned fortresses. About 1830 the French followed suit and, following the German example, began to construct entrenched camps. Paris was surrounded by a bastioned trace without outworks, and three great fortresses were constructed at Belfort, Besançon, and Grenoble. In 1859 the Belgians began the construction of an entrenched camp for 100,000 men at Antwerp with an enceinte nine miles in circumference and detached forts two or three miles in front. At about this same time the British began construction of the land defenses of some of their dockyards.

During the American Civil War the Americans discovered the power of rifled guns against masonry forts in the capture of Fort Pulaski [q.v.]. After the French artillery experiments at Fort Malmaison [q.v.] in 1886 European military engineers began designing permanent fortifications of greater strength to resist the increased power of artillery shells.

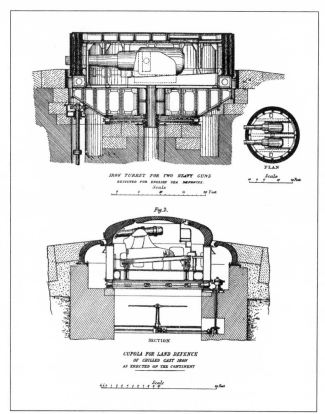

Fortification *Permanent fortifications designed to protect heavy guns*

Fort Loudon. See Fort Sanders, Attack on.

Fort McAllister, Capture of (13 December 1864), American Civil War. During the siege of Savannah, Georgia, which had been fortified and was held by 15,000 Confederates under William Joseph Hardee [q.v.], Union General William Tecumseh Sherman [q.v.] sent one of his divisions under the command of William Babcock Hazen [q.v.] to capture this fort garrisoned by 250 men on the Great Ogeechee River 15 miles from the town. The attack was successful, but the Federals lost 135 men, some to land mines, then called torpedoes. The capture of the fort was of strategic importance, for Sherman was now on the coast and could be supported by the Union navy.

Fort McHenry, Attack on (12–14 September 1814), War of 1812. After the British captured and burned the public buildings in Washington, D.C. [see Washington, D.C., Burning of], they moved on Baltimore, Maryland, with ten ships of the line under Rear Admiral Sir George Cockburn (1772–1853). Because Baltimore's harbor was blocked by scuttled ships, they began a bombardment of Fort McHenry, the fort that defended the city. The fort was stubbornly defended by its garrison of 1,000 men under Major General Samuel Smith (1752–1839), and a British land force of 4,500 men under Major General Robert Ross [q.v.], which moved on Baltimore, was defeated by American militia. The British were forced to abandon their efforts to capture the city.

It was while watching the fort's bombardment that Francis Scott Key [q.v.] conceived the words to "The Star-Spangled Banner" [q.v.], which became the American national anthem. The "rocket's red glare" was produced by British Congreve rockets [see Congreve, William].

Fort Malmaison, Artillery Experiments at (1886). To determine how well fortifications could stand up to the newest in artillery, the French army used Fort Malmaison in northern France, eight miles south-southwest of Laon, as a target for guns firing eight-inch shells containing large charges of melinite, a high explosive similar to lyddite [q.v.] composed chiefly of picric acid. The shells proved astonishingly effective. Magazine casements were destroyed by single shots, revetment walls were overturned, and breaches easily made by two or three well-placed shells. Many thought the tests proved that the days of permanent fortifications were over, but military engineers set about constructing stronger fortifications to meet the threat.

Fort Meigs, Battle of. See Burlington Heights, Battle of.

Fort Mims Massacre (30 August 1813), Creek War. A force of Red Stick Creek Indians under Chief Red Eagle [q.v.], also known as William Weatherford, attacked Fort Mims at the confluence of the Tombigbee and Alabama rivers in southern Alabama, 30 miles north of Mobile, and slaugh-tered more than 500 men, women, and children. The fort was commanded by Daniel Beasley

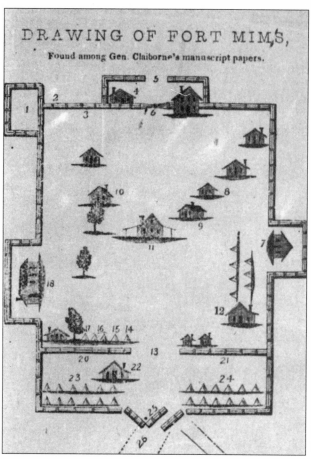

Fort Mims Massacre *Site of the Creek massacre on 30 August 1813*

(d. 1813), a militia officer who had neglected its defenses. Just before the attack he ordered two blacks who had reported seeing Indians in force to be flogged for spreading false reports.

Fort Monroe. A massive granite fort, often called a fortress, begun in 1817 at the tip of the peninsula formed by the York and James rivers in southeast Virginia at the entrance to Hampton Roads. Surrounded by a moat and able to mount 400 pieces of ordnance, it was the largest fortification in the Western Hemisphere. For the thirty years prior to the American Civil War it held the army's Artillery School of Practice. From 1865 to 1867 Jefferson Davis [q.v.] was imprisoned here.

Fort Napier. A military post overlooking Pietermaritzburg in South Africa. It was laid out in 1844 and remained throughout the nineteenth century the headquarters of the British troops in Natal.

Fort Peck Expedition (6 November–13 December 1876), Great Sioux War. After the Battle of Cedar Creek [q.v.], on 6 November 1876, Colonel (later General) Nelson Miles [q.v.] led the 5th Infantry from the Tongue River cantonment at Fort Peck into the wilderness area between the Yellowstone and the Missouri rivers in search of Sitting Bull [q.v.] and his band. The command suffered severely from sub-zero weather and snowstorms. Crossing the Missouri River filled with ice floes proved a for-midable task. In spite of their persistence, no hostile Indians were encountered, and the expedition ended without a fight.

Fort Phil Kearny, Attack on. See Wagon Box Fight.

Fort Pickens, Defense of (1861–65), American Civil War. First Lieutenant Adam Jacoby Slemmer (1829–1868) of the 1st U.S. Artillery was in command at Fort Barrancas and the barracks on Pensacola Bay when on 10 January 1861 Florida seceded from the Union. He promptly moved his small command to Fort Pickens on Santa Rosa Island in Pensacola Harbor and held it until reinforced. This fort, which ensured control of the Gulf of Mexico, remained in Federal hands throughout the war.

Fort Pillow Massacre (12 April 1864), American Civil War. This Union fort, located on the Mississippi River 40 miles above Memphis in Tennessee, was garrisoned by 262 black and 295 white soldiers from Tennessee commanded by Major Lionel F. Booth (1838–1864) when it was attacked by dismounted cavalry under Nathan Bedford Forrest [q.v.]. Booth was killed by a sniper, and his place was taken by Major William F. Bradford (1832?–1864), who refused Forrest's demand that he surrender. After a six-hour battle the fort was overrun by the Confederates, who, maddened by the sight of blacks in Union uniforms, killed them as they tried to surrender. Major Bradford was murdered after he had surrendered. Confederate losses were 14 killed and 86 wounded. Federal losses were 231 killed and 100 seriously wounded. Only 58 blacks survived. Forrest, a successful slave dealer before the war, did not order the massacre, but he was held responsible for not preventing or arresting it.

Fort Pulaski, Capture of (10–11 April 1862), American Civil War. This Confederate fort on Cockspur Island in the harbor of Savannah, Georgia, guarded the sea approach to the port. It was of thick masonry construction with about 40 guns either in casements or in barbette. Union Colonel (later General) Quincy Adams Gillmore (1825–1888) established rifled guns on nearby six-mile-long Tybee Island at the mouth of the Savannah River and at 8:00 A.M. on 10 April 1862 began a bombardment of the fort. It surrendered at 2:00 P.M. the following day. Each side lost 1 man killed and several wounded. Some 360 Confederates were taken prisoner.

    This was the first test of the new rifled guns against masonry forts. The extensive damage they inflicted led to a revolution in the design of American coastal defenses. [See Fortification; Fort Malmaison, Artillery Experiments at.]

Fortress. Any large fort or fortified city. It was sometimes said that "Fortresses are the tombs of armies." This was certainly true of the French at Metz [q.v.] in the Franco-Prussian War [q.v.].

Fort Sanders, Attack on (29 November 1863), American Civil War. Confederate name: Fort Loudon. This Union fort, defended by troops under General Ambrose Burnside [q.v.], was a bastioned earthwork on a hill on the northeast corner of the entrenchments of Knoxville, Tennessee. Named in honor of Brigadier General William Price Sanders (1833–1863), who had

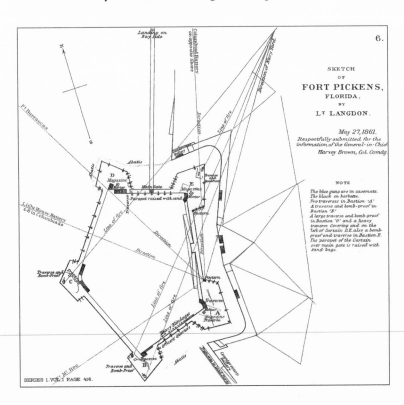

Fort Pickens *Sketch of Fort Pickens, Florida, May 1861*

been mortally wounded nearby eleven days earlier, it was protected by a ditch 12 feet wide and 8 feet deep and by telegraph wire stretched close to the ground around stumps and stakes. It was held by 440 men with 12 guns. On a bitter cold morning, when the ground was frozen hard and the sides of the ditch were covered with sleet, it was attacked by about 1,000 men under General Lafayette McLaws [q.v.] in the corps of Confederate General James Longstreet [qq.v.]. Having no scaling ladders, the attackers gallantly climbed on one another's shoulders, but they failed to take the fort and were forced to fall back. Confederate losses were 813, including 216 missing; Federal losses were 20 killed and 93 wounded. [See Knoxville, Battle of.]

Fort San Felipe de Beleaguer, Capture of (3–7 June 1813), Peninsular War. British Colonel William Prevost [q.v.] was sent with about 1,000 soldiers and marines with three guns to reduce this small French-held fort perched in a nearly inaccessible location near Tarragona. His initial bombardment was unsuccessful, but on 7 June a lucky shot exploded the French magazine, killing or wounding a third of the garrison; the survivors surrendered.

Fort Sitabaldi, Attack on. See Nagpur, Battle of.

Fort Stedman, Attack on (25 March 1865), American Civil War. Confederates under General George Washington Gordon [q.v.] attacked this Union-held fort near Petersburg, Virginia, at 4:00 A.M. and quickly captured it and a number of the surrounding positions. Counterattacks by Federals under John Frederick Hartranft (1830–1889) drove them from their advanced positions back to the fort. About eight o'clock General Lee ordered the force withdrawn, but by that time the line of retreat was being raked by a Union crossfire, and many chose to surrender rather than risk the fire.

The Confederates lost about 3,500, of which nearly 2,000 were taken prisoner. Later in the day Union General George Meade [q.v.] directed an attack on the remainder that brought the total casualties for the day to about 4,500 Confederates and 2,080 Federals.

Fort Stephenson, Attack on (1–2 August 1813), War of 1812. In 1813 twenty-one-year-old American Major George Croghan [q.v.] was placed in charge of Fort Stephenson, garrisoned with 160 men, on the Sandusky River, on the site of present Fremont, Ohio. On 1 August of that year he was attacked by 1,200 British regulars with several fieldpieces assisted by a troop of Indians commanded by Colonel Henry Proctor and supported by a number of Indian allies. The Americans threw back repeated assaults and suffered only 1 killed and 7 wounded; British losses were thought to be heavy. Indian losses are unknown. On 3 August the British retreated.

Croghan was hailed as a hero and promoted lieutenant colonel. On 13 February 1835 Congress belatedly awarded him a gold medal with "suitable emblems and devices in testimony of the high sense entertained by Congress of his gallantry and good conduct in the defense of Ft. Stephenson, Ohio."

Fort Stevens, Attack on (11–12 July 1864), American Civil War. This fort, part of the defenses of Washington, D.C., stood near Seventh Street Road, north of the city, and came under fire from troops under Jubal Early [q.v.]. It was here

that on two occasions President Abraham Lincoln, according to his personal secretary, John George Nicolay (1832–1901), "exposed his tall form to the gaze and bullets of the enemy in a manner to call forth earnest remonstrance." He thus became the only American president to come under enemy fire in wartime while in office.

Fort Sumter, Siege of (12–14 April 1861), American Civil War. This brick fort in the shape of a pentagon, 300 by 350 feet in area with walls 8 to 12 feet thick and 40 feet high, was built in the harbor of Charleston, South Carolina, three or four miles from the city on an artificial island in the middle of the main shipping channel. It was named after General Thomas Sumter (1734–1832), a Revolutionary War soldier. Construction had begun in 1829, but in 1861 it was not yet completed, mounting only 48 of its intended 140 guns. In April that year it was commanded by fifty-six-year-old southern-born Major Robert Anderson [q.v.], who had with him 8 officers, 68 enlisted men, 8 musicians, and 43 civilian workmen.

After South Carolina passed the Ordinance of Secession in December 1860, it demanded that all federal property in the state be given up to the new government. On 10 April 1861 Pierre Beauregard [q.v.] ordered Major Anderson to evacuate the fort at once. Anderson refused. At four-thirty on the morning of 12 April, having nearly surrounded the fort with 30 guns and 17 mortars, Beauregard opened the bombardment with the fire of a 10-inch mortar, whose shell landed in the middle of the parade ground. The American Civil War had begun. Captain (later General) Abner Doubleday [q.v.] fired the first answering round about three hours later.

During the 34-hour bombardment some 4,000 shells fell on the fort, but the Federals suffered not a single casualty. When Anderson ran out of live ammunition, a surrender was arranged that allowed him to depart with his men with the honors of war. Before leaving the fort on 14 April, Anderson saw the American flag ceremoniously lowered and ordered a 100-gun salute. At the 50th round a powder magazine exploded, tearing off the right arm of Private Daniel Hough of

Fort Sumter *Bombardment of Fort Sumter, Charleston, South Carolina*

Battery E, 1st U.S. Field Artillery, who died within minutes of his wound. If the salute can be called a military action, Private Hough was the first casualty of the war. One other soldier was mortally wounded in the accident, and another seriously injured. The remainder of the garrison was evacuated by steamer to New York.

On 14 April 1865, only a few hours before the assassination of President Lincoln, Brevet Major General Robert Anderson (retired) was present when the original flag was raised again over Fort Sumter.

Fort Texas, Attack on (3–9 May 1846), Mexican War. General Zachary Taylor [q.v.], American commander in the Southwest, built this fort (now Brownsville) on the Rio Grande, across the river from Matamoros, Mexico. After a cavalry affair north of the river, a Mexican force under General Mariano Arista [q.v.] crossed and laid siege to the fort, commanded by Major Jacob Brown (1794?–1846). The garrison managed to hold out until Taylor, after defeating the Mexicans at Palo Alto and Resaca [qq.v.], was able to bring up a relieving force. Major Brown was mortally wounded on 6 May, and the fort was renamed Fort Brown in his honor.

Fortunes of War. The uncertain fate of individuals and armies in war. Wolfgang von Goethe (1749–1832) wrote in *Iphigenie auf Tauris* (1787): "The fortunes of war flow this way and that, and no prudent fighter holds his enemy in contempt."

Fort Wagner, Union Attack on and Siege of (10 July–6 September 1863), American Civil War. This South Carolina fort was an isolated fortification extending across the width of Morris Island in Charleston Harbor a mile and a half from Fort Sumter [q.v.]. On 10 July 1863 Union Brigadier General George Crockett Strong (1832–1863) landed his brigade on the southern end of the island. The following day he lost 339 men in a daylight assault upon the fort, which was defended by 1,200 Confederates under General William Taliaferro [q.v.], who lost only 12 men in the engagement.

Fort Wagner *Black troops from the 54th Massachusetts Regiment attack Fort Wagner.*

The Federals brought up two more brigades and siege artillery and on 18 July bombarded the fort with 26 rifled guns and 10 large mortars. At sunset they attacked with two brigades, spearheaded by the 54th Massachusetts Colored Infantry under twenty-six-year-old Colonel Robert Gould Shaw [q.v.]. In the action General Strong was mortally wounded, and all but one of his regimental commanders were killed or wounded, including Colonel Shaw, who was killed. The Federals secured a foothold within the fort but were driven out before they could be reinforced.

Of the 5,264 Union troops engaged, 1,515 were killed or wounded; the Confederates lost 174 out of 1,785 engaged.

The Federals began siege operations, and by 6 September saps had reached the ditch of the fort. An assault was planned for the next day, but during the night the Confederates evacuated the fort and abandoned Morris Island.

Forward Slope. Any slope that descends toward the enemy.

Fosbery, George Vincent (1833–1907). A British soldier with an abiding interest in the design of firearms who was commissioned in 1852 and became a lieutenant five years later. During the Umbeyla Campaign [q.v.] on India's Northwest Frontier he commanded a body of marksmen armed with rifles and ammunition of his own invention. It was in this campaign, on 30 October 1866, that he won the Victoria Cross. He retired as a colonel in 1877 but continued his interest in firearms.

Although he held patents for several breech-loading rifles and cartridges, his name was particularly attached to the Webley-Fosbery automatic revolver, which he patented in 1895. In his original design the barrel and cylinder were movable and slid along the top of the butt frame and cocked the hammer when the pistol was fired. He took out new patents the following year and later assigned his patents to the Webley & Scott Revolver and Arms Company. [See Webley Pistol.]

Foss or Fosse. The ditch or moat around an earthwork or any other fortification from which the earth necessary to construct the rampart, parapet, and banquette is obtained.

Foucauld, Charles de (1858–1916). A French soldier who was graduated from St. Cyr in 1878. After spending a year at the cavalry school at Saumur, he joined the 4th Hussars in Algeria, taking his mistress with him. He took part in the Bou Amana insurrection in 1881. The following year, at age twenty-four, he resigned his commission and set out to explore Morocco. Two years later he returned to France and entered a Trappist monastery in southern France. After taking orders in 1901, he was sent back to the Sahara, where he wrote the first dictionary of Tamahak, or Tamashek, the language of the Tuaregs [q.v.].

Fougasse. A kind of small land mine to be exploded in case of attack that was placed on the perimeter of a position or at a site an attacking enemy might be expected to pass. It was sometimes simply a pit containing gunpowder at its base and filled with stones or other missiles.

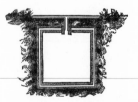

Fougasse, or powder box, used by Russians in Crimea

A more sophisticated fougasse was the powder box used by the Russians at the Siege of Sevastapol [q.v.] during the Crimean War [q.v.]. This was a waterproof box containing 35 pounds of gunpowder on top of which was a glass tube filled with sulfuric acid and coated with a composition of chlorate of potassium, sugar, sulfur, and gum water that ignited when in contact with the acid. It was attached to a flat plate and buried so that the plate was on the surface lightly covered with earth. When stepped on, the tube was crushed, and the gunpowder exploded.

Fouling. The dirtying of the bore of a gun by the action of gunpowder when fired.

Founda. The black tassel on the fez of an evzone [q.v.].

Fouraschka. A Russian field cap.

Fourche. A trident or kind of military pitchfork sometimes carried by sergeants in the early nineteenth century instead of a pike. Grenadier sergeants in some old French regiments carried them as late as 1808. They were said to symbolize the armed peasants who fought in the ranks in eighteenth-century wars.

Fourgon. 1. A tumbrel or ammunition wagon.
2. A French baggage vehicle.

Fourragère. A shoulder cord similar to an aiguillette [q.v.] but usually worn on the right shoulder.

Fourrier. A peculiar rank in Napoleon's armies between a corporal and a sergeant that was not in the normal line of promotion. The fourrier had to be literate and was a combination of company clerk and supply sergeant. Later a duty, not a rank.

Fouta Toro Uprisings (1877 and 1881). Émeutes in Senegal against French rule. They were suppressed by Captain (later Marshal of France) Joseph Gallieni [q.v.].

Fowle, Elida, née Rumsey (1841?–?). An American woman with a remarkably beautiful voice who, during the Civil War, wished to enroll as a nurse but was judged too short, too young, and too attractive to join the nursing corps of Dorothea Dix [q.v.]. Instead, accompanied on the piano by her fiancé, John Fowle, she sang at soldiers' hospitals and gave a concert series to raise money for a soldiers' library and clubhouse. After Second Bull Run [q.v.] the two went onto the field to nurse the wounded. So great was her fame that her marriage to Fowle, after a two-year engagement, took place in the House of Representatives before a joint session of Congress. Mrs. Lincoln made the bride's bouquet. At the end of the marriage ceremony she was asked to sing "The Star-Spangled Banner," and she did, it was said, "with never more fervor in her beautiful voice."

Given her renown, it is curious that nothing is known of her later career or the date of her death.

Fowling Piece. A smooth-bored sporting gun; a shotgun.

Foy, Maximilien Sébastien (1775–1825). A French soldier who served in Napoleon's armies in Spain and Portugal and was badly wounded at Bussaco and again at Orthez [qq.v.] He was promoted general of brigade in 1809 and general of division in 1811, proving himself one of Napoleon's best division commanders. Although accepted by the Bourbons and made an inspector general, he joined Napoleon for the Hundred Days [q.v.]. He fought at Quatre Bras [q.v.] on 16 June 1815 and was wounded two days later at the Château of Hougoumont [q.v.] during the Battle of Waterloo [q.v.]. From 1811 to 1825 he was a member of the Chamber of Deputies, where he defended freedom of the individual and freedom of the press.

Foz do Arouce, Battle of (15 March 1811), Peninsular War. Near this town in central Portugal the advance forces of Wellington's British-Portuguese army of about 10,000 men fought about 9,000 French under Marshal Michel Ney [q.v.], who commanded the rear guard of the Army of Portugal under Marshal André Masséna [q.v.]. The French panicked when part of the 95th Rifles opened fire in their rear. The Allies suffered 71 casualties; the French 250.

Fra Diavolo, properly Michele Pezza (1760–1806). Italian Cardinal Fabrizio Ruffo (1744–1827) proclaimed the Sanfedista (Army of the Holy Faith) and led a revolution against French invaders that in 1799 restored Ferdinand I to the throne of Naples. One of his most able compatriots was Fra Diavolo, a renegade monk who led a band that took part in Ruffo's successful march on Naples. He quickly gained a reputation as leading the most undisciplined, murderous, and thieving band in the Sanfedista. After the revolution he turned to brigandage and led a barbarous band in the Calabrian Mountains. In 1806 he attempted, with British aid, to raise a revolt against French rule, and after the Battle of Maida [q.v.] he played a major role in the insurrections in Calabria [see Calabrian War]. On 12 August 1806 he failed in an attempt to capture Licosa, but the British transported him to Spurlunga, near Gaeta, from which he carried out a number of successful raids. After a defeat by a French column at Itri, he fled to Abruzzi, where he joined with local insurgents, and soon the entire province was in revolt. Although badly wounded in an engagement at Sora, he escaped over the Apennines. However, his luck ran out. He was betrayed and captured on 1 November, taken to Naples, and on 11 November he was hanged in the public square.

In 1830 composer Daniel Auber (1782–1871) wrote an opera, *Fra Diavolo,* with a libretto by Augustin Scribe (1791–1861) based on his exploits.

Fraises. Sharpened poles or palisades laid on the crest of a scarp or counterscarp as an obstacle for those attempting an escalade. To fraise an infantry unit was to arrange the formation so that it bristled with bayonets in every direction to withstand a cavalry charge.

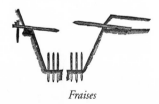

Fraises

Français de Fraiche Date. Literally, Frenchmen of fresh date or a newly made Frenchman. Foreign-born men who after 1889 received French citizenship for having served in the French army.

Franches. Detached bodies of Frenchmen sent to raid and harass the enemy's territory; partisans. They accompanied the main army in war, and in peace they were distributed among garrisons in France. Other European powers also employed such people [see Pandours].

Francia, José Gaspar Rodriguez (1756–1840). A leading Paraguayan revolutionary who became the first president and then the first of many dictators of Paraguay.

Francis, Milly (1802–1848). A Creek Indian girl who was the daughter of a prophet named Josiah Francis. In 1818, during the First Seminole War [q.v.], she saved the life of Sergeant Duncan McKrimmon of the 2nd Georgia Militia near Fort Gadsden, on the east bank of the Apalachicola River in Florida. Sergeant McKrimmon had been captured by Red Stick Creek Indians [q.v.] while fishing. After being questioned, stripped, and tied to a tree, he was about to be tortured to death when comely sixteen-year-old Milly managed to persuade the warriors to spare the young man's life. They ransomed him to the Spanish for seven and one-half gallons of rum.

After the war McKrimmon returned to Florida and found Milly destitute. McKrimmon gave her some money and offered to marry her, but she refused. In 1842 Major Ethan Allen Hitchcock [q.v.] found her living in poverty in Arkansas; her husband and five of her eight children were dead. Hitchcock, after a two-year campaign of entreaty, persuaded Congress to grant her an annuity pension of ninety-six dollars and to strike a medal to commemorate her rescue of McKrimmon. Four years later the government's first installment of the pension arrived, but by then Milly Francis was dying.

Franco-Chinese War. See Sino-French War.

Franco-Dahomean Wars (1889–1890 and 1892–1894). The First Franco-Dahomean War occurred after Britain had ceded the town of Cotonou on the coast of Dahomey (Benin) to the French in 1889. Since the Dahomeans had not been consulted and this was their main port for exporting palm oil, they resisted a French force sent there.

The Dahomean army consisted of about 2,000 to 3,000 male warriors and a corps of about 800 amazons [q.v.], women warriors noted for their ferocity. There was fierce fighting until in October 1890 the French and Dahomean King Behanzin (d. 1906) signed a treaty in which in exchange for an annual subsidy the French were ceded Cotonou and Porto Novo, another coastal town that was the chief city of the Tofa kingdom.

A second war erupted on 27 March 1892, when Dahomean warriors fired upon a French gunboat on the Oueme (Weme) River, which flows into the Gulf of Guinea near Cotonou. Although the gunboat was in Dahomean territory, the French retaliated with a military expedition under Colonel (later General) Alfred Amédée Dodds [q.v.] consisting of 3,450 Senegalese Tirailleurs [q.v.], marine infantry, and Foreign Legionnaires with an 80 mm gun manned by sailors. After a two-and-one-half month campaign Dodds captured Abomey, the Dahomean capital, on 17 November. King Behanzin fled, but he was betrayed and captured on 29 January 1894, ending the independent existence of the Dahomean kingdom. The French annexed the country in 1894.

The war cost the French 11 officers and 70 other ranks killed plus 25 officers and 411 wounded, but an estimated five times that number were felled by disease.

The French faced no further serious threats although small uprisings surfaced until 1899.

Franco-Fulani War (1892). French forces under Louis Archinard defeated the Fulanis on the Upper Niger and captured Segou (or Segu), 120 miles east-northeast of Bamako.

Franco-German War. See Franco-Prussian War.

François, Hugo von (1859–1904). A German soldier who was commissioned in the Prussian army and as a captain was sent to German South-West Africa (Namibia). In 1899 he wrote the book *Deutsche Südwestafrika* (German South-West Africa). He was killed near Ovikokorero during the Herero War. He was the brother of the explorer and soldier Kurt von François [q.v.], who was commander of troops in German South-West Africa from 1889 to 1894.

François, Kurt von (1853–1931). A soldier born in Luxembourg who joined the Prussian army and served on exploring expeditions in West Africa. In 1889–94 he was commander of troops in German South-West Africa (Namibia), where he made war upon the Hereros and the Witboois Hottentots [see Witbooi, Hendrik].

Franco-Mandingo Wars (1885–98). For thirteen years the French in West Africa fought intermittently with the powerful Mande kingdom, ruled by Samory [q.v.] or Samori, which stretched from the sources of the Niger to the Upper Volta basin in present-day Burkina Faso in what is today mostly Ivory Coast.

First Mandingo War (1885–86). The French defeated Samory's warriors and in 1889 established a protectorate.

Second Mandingo War (1894–95). The French were deterred from extending their protectorate into the interior by Samory's successful opposition.

Third Mandingo War (1898). The French succeeded in defeating the Mandingos, and Samory was captured and exiled to Gabon. The final battle was fought on 29 September 1898.

Franco-Prussian War (1870–71). France allowed itself to become provoked into declaring war when the throne of Spain, traditionally held by a Bourbon, was secretly offered by Spanish army insurgents to a prince of the Hohenzollern family. Antoine Alfred Agénor de Gramont (1819–1880), Duc de Guiche and Prince de Bidache, France's foreign minister (January–August 1870), a man Bismarck called "the stupidest man in Europe," decided that war was necessary because a Hohenzollern on the throne of Spain would "imperil the interests and honor of France" and so convinced Napoleon III. Although no Hohenzollern accepted the offer, on 15 July 1870 France declared war before it had the means and ability to wage it.

General Edmond Leboeuf [q.v.], the minister of war, confidently assured Napoleon III of his army's readiness: "So ready are we, that if the war lasts two years, not a gaiter button would be found wanting." This was far from the truth. In the chaotic scramble to mobilize, a great many things besides gaiter buttons were found wanting.

The German states mobilized 850,000 men, 309,000 of whom were sent to field armies; the French initially mobilized 567,000 but were able to send only 200,000 to field armies, although more were brought into action after the Battle of Sedan [q.v.]. French mobilization was slow and disorderly, but an army under Achille Bazaine [q.v.] marched east, and the first battle of the war took place at Weissenburg [q.v.], about 40 miles northeast of Strasbourg, where on 4 August the Germans trounced Marshal Marie MacMahon [q.v.]. This was quickly followed by other French defeats on 6 August 1870 at Spicheren [q.v.], near Saarbrücken, where the French II Corps under General Charles Frossard [q.v.] was repulsed by Germans under General Carl Friedrich von Steinmetz [q.v.], and on the same day at Fröschwiller [q.v.], or Wörth, where the French under Marshal MacMahon were again defeated by Crown Prince Frederick Charles [q.v.] of Prussia. Three German armies invaded France. On 14 August a sharp battle was fought at Colombey-Borny [q.v.]. At Mars-la-Tour and Vionville on 16 August battles were fought on reversed fronts, i.e., with the Germans facing east; the French under Achille Bazaine [q.v.] retreated [see Mars-la-Tour–Vionville]. The South Germans at this point threw in their lot with the Prussians, adding three corps to the German forces.

After a disastrous last stand at Gravelotte–St. Privat [q.v.] on 18 August Bazaine with 170,000 men retreated into the fortress at Metz and was besieged there for fifty-four days by Prince Frederick Charles [see Metz, Siege of].

Marshal MacMahon with the Army of Châlons, marching to the relief of Metz, suffered a disastrous defeat in the Battle of Sedan [q.v.] on 1 September. On the following day 80,000 French troops, including MacMahon and Napoleon III himself, were forced to surrender. On 19 September two German armies began a 135-day siege of Paris [q.v.]. The French Second Empire collapsed; Napoleon III (1808–1873), now a prisoner of the Germans, was deposed; on 4 September a French provisional Government of National Defense was established, and a Third Republic was proclaimed.

On 15 September the Garde Nationale was called up, and the French government managed to scrape together an army of more than half a million. On 27 October the great fortress at Metz fell. The Germans captured 3 marshals of France, 10 generals, 6,000 officers, and 173,000 men plus 800 siege guns, 541 field guns, 100 mitrailleuses, and 300,000 rifles.

In the Battle of Coulmiers [q.v.] on 9 November the French gained their only victory. There was some fighting in the French provinces, but small garrisons and forts fell one by one. An exception was the fort at Belfort [q.v.], which was besieged but holding out gallantly. An army of more than 120,000 men under General Charles Bourbaki [q.v.], sent to its relief, was defeated by a German army of 60,000 on the banks of the Lisaine River [q.v.] on 15–17 January 1871. Bourbaki's army was pushed across the frontier into neutral Switzerland, where 82,000 men with 10,000 horses were interned. (After the war the Swiss demanded eleven million francs for their keep.)

Meanwhile the Paris Commune [q.v.] had been established in March, sparking a short, bloody civil war. The National Assembly met in Bordeaux and sent troops to occupy Paris and suppress the Communards.

Although on 28 January an armistice was signed by the Government of National Defense, fighting continued at Belfort [q.v.] until 26 February. In 180 days the Germans had fought in 156 engagements, large and small, including 17 pitched battles and attacks against 20 fortified places; they had captured 19,316 officers and 613,667 other ranks and 7,441 guns. German losses were 28,208 killed and 88,488 wounded. The French lost 156,000 dead, 17,000 of whom had died of wounds and diseases while prisoners in German hands, and 143,000 wounded; 720,000 were taken prisoner or were interned.

Although the war lasted seven months, German victory was certain after the first two months, but its completeness astonished the world. German losses were 9.4 percent of their forces; the French lost just over 16 percent. The French infantry was armed with the Chassepot rifle, which was superior to the Germans' Dreyse needle gun [qq.v.], but some French recruits had never before seen a Chassepot and did not even know how to load one. Some French artillery was still equipped with muzzleloaders, while the Germans used fine Krupp breechloaders. However, the French were not defeated because German soldiers were braver or had better arms and equipment. German successes were due primarily to the superior organization and the work of the Prussian general staff, which contained the brightest graduates of the Kriegsakademie, under General Helmuth von Moltke [q.v.]. The North German Confederation had been able to mobilize quickly an army of 15,324 officers and 714,950 other ranks; the landwehr had been able to provide 6,510 officers and 201,640 other ranks.

German operations were more disrupted by the Germans' own field commanders than by the French. Particularly exasperating to Moltke was the contrariness and pigheadedness of

Franco-Prussian War Queuing for Rat Meat *caricatures food shortages in Paris during the winter of 1870–71.*

General Steinmetz who was not removed from command of the First Army until September 1870.

The Franco-Prussian War marked a distinct stage in the evolution of European armies. The French army, which before the war had been considered the finest in the world, was composed of long-term regulars who on average had served seven years, but it was augmented by poorly trained conscripts. The victorious German army consisted almost entirely of short-term conscripts who had been intensively trained by professional officers and noncommissioned officers.

Although the Germans resorted to collective punishments [q.v.] during the final stages of the conflict, they were better disciplined than the French and showed a higher regard for persons and property. French peasants came to fear their own drunken, looting troops more than they did the Germans, even though the good behavior of the German army was not uniform. A battalion of Gardes Mobiles [q.v.] that surrendered at Passevant on 29 August 1870 was massacred; a German cavalry patrol burned the village of Voncq; and Remilly was sacked by Hessians.

At the end of the war the Germans demanded a victory parade down the Champs-Élysées. Friedrich von Bernhardi (1849–1930), then a young Prussian cavalry officer, was the first German to pass under the Arc de Triomphe. He later became a general and a military historian. In 1910 he published a widely read book, *Germany and the Next War.*

By the Treaty of Frankfurt, signed on 10 May 1871 and ratified on 23 May, France ceded the province of Alsace and the German portion of Lorraine to Germany and agreed to pay an indemnity of approximately one billion dollars. A German army was to occupy France until it was paid. Making an enormous effort, France paid off the indemnity within three years. The last German soldier left France in July 1873. The humiliation of France led novelist Victor Hugo (1802–1885) to sound the trumpet of revenge and speak of the "sacred anger."

The war united the German states, and William I (1797–1888) of Prussia was proclaimed emperor of Germany—at Versailles. After the signing Victor Hugo wrote: "Henceforth there are in Europe two nations that will be formidable, the one because it was victorious, the other because it is vanquished."

After the war the cause of the catastrophic defeat of the French army was much debated. Perhaps the best summation was made by Prussian General Kolmar von de Goltz [q.v.], who wrote that the French "had always concentrated on material matters. They thought that the offensive power of the enemy would be broken by the defensive action of new and terrible weapons. In that way they ruined the spirit of their army. That is what chiefly weighed in the scale."

Franco-Tukulor Wars (1854–90). From the fourth to the fourteenth century the Tukulor people of West Africa dominated the valley of the Senegal River. They were converted to Islam in the eleventh century, and in the following years their influence extended northward into Morocco. In the fourteenth century they were conquered by the Mali Empire. They remained a subject people until the middle of the nineteenth century, when a charismatic leader, al-Hajji Omar (1795?–1864), founded the Tijaniyya Brotherhood and launched a jihad, seeking to revive their past glory. In his raids

east of the upper Senegal he was successful, but in 1854, when he turned his forces westward, he collided with the French, who checked his expansion. Turning inward, he conquered in 1861 the large Bambara kingdom of Segu in what is today roughly Mali, extending eastward to Timbuktu.

On the death of Omar, dynastic civil wars destroyed the power of the Tukulors. In 1890 the French were able to seize control of the Senegal and Segu without serious fighting.

Franco-Vietnamese Wars. See French Indochina Wars.

Franc-Tireurs. 1. During the Crimean War [q.v.] the name was applied to French sharpshooters posted as snipers.

2. French civilian combatants in the Franco-Prussian War [q.v.] who were usually members of rifle clubs or unofficial military societies formed in eastern France in 1867. Well armed with modern rifles, they wore no uniforms, elected their own officers, and disdained military discipline. In July 1870, at the beginning of the Franco-Prussian War, they were placed under the minister of war, but they did not serve under general officers until November. Some were then incorporated into larger organizations, but many continued to operate as small bands, blowing up culverts, attacking detached German troops, and destroying railway tracks and telegraph lines. Their most famous feat was the destruction of the railway bridge at Fontenoy on 22 January 1871. Although some groups were joined by men more interested in looting than defending their country, most appear to have been patriots. Those who fell into German hands were generally shot out of hand. [See Bushwacker.]

Franke, Victor (1866–1917). A German soldier born in Silesia who as a colonel was the last German military commander in German South-West Africa (Namibia). He fought in the Herero War and against the South Africans in the First World War.

Franklin, Battle of (30 November 1864), American Civil War. Confederates under General John Hood attacked Union forces under Brigadier General John Schofield [qq.v.] at Franklin, Tennessee, 19 miles south of Nashville. In a gallant but foolish charge across 2 miles of open ground, the Confederates broke through the center of the Union line, forcing two Union brigades to retreat in some confusion. In places there was hand-to-hand fighting. The Federals lost eight guns before the Confederates were repulsed. In a separate cavalry action east of the Harpath River, Confederate cavalry under Nathan Bedford Forrest [q.v.] was driven back.

Of 27,939 Union troops engaged, 2,326 were casualties, of whom 1,104 were missing. Of 26,897 Confederates engaged, 6,252 were casualties, including 702 missing. The Confederates lost 32 battle flags and 6 generals killed or mortally wounded, including Patrick Cleburne and States Rights Gist [qq.v.].

The Confederate charge has been compared to Pickett's Charge [q.v.] at Gettysburg. It also has been called mass suicide. General Schofield was given a brevet to major general and awarded the Medal of Honor for his victory. The battle was a clear indication of the power of the defense when armed with the new breech-loading small arms.

Franklin *Map showing the Battle of Franklin, Tennessee, 30 November 1864*

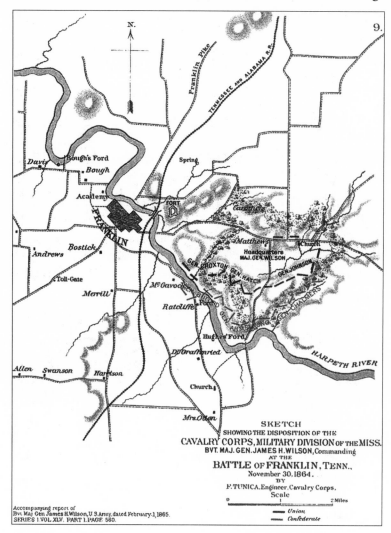

Franklin, William Buel (1823–1903). An American soldier who was graduated first in his class of 39 at West Point in 1843. He served in the Mexican War [q.v.] and won a brevet to first lieutenant for gallantry in the Battle of Buena Vista [q.v.]. In July 1857 he was assigned to Washington, D.C., where, until the outbreak of the American Civil War, he was in charge of the construction of the dome of the Capitol and other public works.

In the First Battle of Bull Run [q.v.] he commanded a Union brigade. In the operations before Richmond he commanded first a division and then a corps. In July 1862 he was promoted major general and in that rank fought at South Mountain and at Antietam [qq.v.]. In the Battle of Fredericksburg [q.v.] he commanded the left grand division of two corps. General Ambrose Burnside [q.v.] later charged him with disobedience and negligence in that battle and tried unsuccessfully to have him cashiered. He commanded a corps in the aborted Red River Campaign [q.v.] of 1864 and was severely wounded in the Battle of Sabine Crossroads [q.v.]. After the war he was for twenty-two years vice-president and general manager of Colt's Patent Firearms Manufacturing Company in Hartford, Connecticut [see Colt Revolvers]. In 1874 he published a pamphlet on the Gatling gun [q.v.]. He was for a time a director of the Panama Railway; he supervised the construction of the Connecticut Capitol, and he served as commissioner general of the United States for the Paris Exposition of 1888. From 1880 to 1890 he was president of the Board of Managers of the National Home for Disabled Volunteer Soldiers.

Franklin's Crossing or Deep Run (5 June 1863), American Civil War. During the Gettysburg Campaign a reconnaissance in force was made by Union General John Sedgwick [q.v.] to determine if the Confederates were withdrawing from Fredericksburg. His attempt to cross the river opposite Deep Run, Virginia, near Fredericksburg, was opposed by Confederate infantry in rifle pits. Federal infantry crossed on pontoon bridges and drove them back, capturing 35 prisoners and suffering 6 killed and 35 wounded.

When Sedgwick reported the Confederates still in place, General Joseph Hooker [q.v.] ordered the cavalry reconnaissance that resulted in the Battle of Brandy Station [q.v.].

Fransecky, Eduard Friedrich von (1807–1890). A Prussian soldier who served under Count Friedrich Wrangel [q.v.] in the Schleswig-Holstein War [q.v.] of 1848 and commanded the infantry in the Battle of Sadowa [q.v.] in 1866. During the Franco-Prussian War [q.v.] of 1870–71 he led II Corps in the Battle of Gravelotte–St. Privat [q.v.] and repelled the attempts of French General Auguste Ducrot [q.v.] to break through the lines at Champigny-sur-Marne [q.v.]. He also took part in the

campaign of General Edwin Manteuffel [q.v.] against French General Charles Bourbaki [q.v.] and his Army of the East in which 82,000 French were pushed over the frontier into internment in Switzerland [see Franco-Prussian War]. From 1871 to 1879 he commanded XV Corps at Strasbourg, then served as governor of Berlin until 1882.

Fraser, Alexander George (1785–1853). A British soldier, and from an early age the 16th Baron Saltoun, who was commissioned an ensign in the 35th Foot on 28 April 1802 and in 1804 transferred to the Grenadier Guards [q.v.]. He served in the Peninsular War [q.v.] under Sir John Moore [q.v.] and was present at the Battle of Corunna [q.v.] on 16 January 1809. Later that year he took part in the disastrous Walcheren Expedition [q.v.]. At Quatre Bras and Waterloo [qq.v.] he commanded the light companies of the 2nd Brigade of Guards, and he accepted the sword of General Pierre Cambronne [q.v.]. At Waterloo his defense of the orchard at Hougoumont and his leading of a bayonet charge ensured his reputation and fame. Wellington once held him up as a pattern to the army, both as a soldier and as a man. In 1841 he commanded a brigade in China during the First Opium War [q.v.]. After the war he succeeded Sir Hugh Gough [q.v.] and remained in China until 1843. In 1849 he was promoted lieutenant general.

Lord Saltoun was also an enthusiastic musician. At the time of his death, which occurred in his shooting box at Rothes, he was president of the Madrigal Society of London and chairman of the Musical Union.

Frayser's Farm, Battle of. See White Oak Swamp, Battle of.

Frederick Augustus, Duke of York and Albany (1763–1827), usually referred to simply as the Duke of York. The second son of George III (1738–1820), who was named both a Hanoverian bishop and a British colonel before he was eighteen. On 1 November 1780 he was sent to Hanover to learn French and German. On 20 November 1782 he was promoted major general. Two years later he was made a lieutenant general and created Duke of York and Albany. In 1793–95 he commanded British troops in Flanders. Although he proved himself an inept commander, his father promoted him to field marshal on 18 February 1795, and on 3 April 1798 he was named commander-in-chief of the British army. A disastrous foray in Holland, which forced him to sign the humiliating Convention of Alkmaer, by which 8,000 French prisoners of war were returned to France, and the public knowledge of his entanglement with a beautiful adventuress who exacted money from officers in return for recommending their promotions forced him to retire on 18 March 1809. He was returned to the post in May 1811.

Although a failure as a field commander, he generally performed well at the Horse Guards [q.v.]. He acted to stop corruption in the quartermaster general's department, and he did much to keep down favoritism in the officer corps. Every Tuesday he held a levée in which any officer might have an audience, and he reduced some of the evils of the purchase system [q.v.], established a military college, and improved the rations, accommodations, and health care of the rank and file. He also ameliorated some of the army's more brutal penal codes. In 1814 and 1815 he was given the Thanks of Parliament [q.v.] for his services. The distinguished military historian John Fortesque [q.v.], writing at the end of the century, considered him to have done "more for the British army than any one man has done for it in the whole of its history."

Frederick Charles, Prince (1828–1885), in full: Friedrich Karl Nikolaus. A nephew of Emperor William I [q.v.] and a Prussian soldier. He served in the Prussian army in the Schleswig-Holstein War [q.v.] of 1848–49 on the staff of General Friedrich von Wrangel [q.v.]. During the Baden Insurrection he was wounded in an engagement at Wiesenthal (Württemberg-Baden) while leading a charge against entrenched infantry. He was promoted colonel in 1852 and major general two years later. In 1861 he became general of cavalry. He commanded the First Army in the Seven Weeks' War [q.v.] in 1866 and the Second Army in the Franco-Prussian War [q.v.] of 1870–71. After the war he became inspector of cavalry.

Fredericksburg, Battle of (13 December 1862), American Civil War. Some 79,000 Confederate troops under General Robert E. Lee with Thomas ("Stonewall") Jackson and James Longstreet [qq.v.] as corps commanders were deployed on a six-mile-long ridge facing the Rappahannock River above the town of Fredericksburg, Virginia, about halfway between Washington, D.C., and Richmond, Virginia. It was a strong position. "A chicken could not live on that field when we open on it," Confederate Colonel E. Porter Alexander told General James Longstreet [qq.v.], describing the position of his Confederate I Corps's artillery on Marye's Heights, where Lee's left was anchored. The Confederate infantry there was protected by a sunken road and a 1,200-foot-long stone wall. Six hundred yards of open field stretched between their position and the town. Packed two ranks deep behind the stone wall, they had a clear field of fire to their front. Shoulder high, the stone wall was an ideal position to defend.

Fredericksburg *The bombardment of Fredericksburg, Virginia, 11 December 1862*

Fredericksburg *Map of the Battle at Fredericksburg, 13 December 1862*

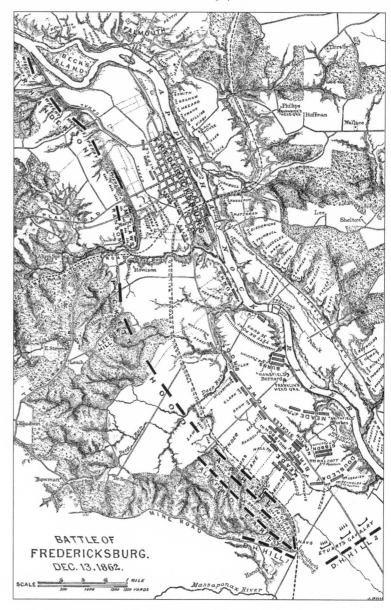

Lee faced a Union army numbering 122,000 under Ambrose Burnside, who had replaced George B. McClellan [qq.v.] on 7 November 1862. Burnside had divided his army into three "grand divisions" of two corps each. The first of these, under Edwin Vose Sumner [q.v.], had arrived at Falmouth, opposite Fredericksburg, on 17 November, to find that the pontoon train needed for the river crossing, which was to have been sent from Washington, had not arrived. Pontoon bridges were eventually put in place, but Sumner's troops in the center and opposite the town of Fredericksburg encountered a withering musketry fire from the buildings and rubble of the town. When the two remaining grand divisions under William Buel Franklin and Joseph Hooker [qq.v.] came up, Union artillery took up strong positions on the heights to cover the river crossing.

Around noon on December 13, 1862, a brigade of blue-coated men filed out of Fredericksburg, formed their battle lines, and charged toward the stone wall. They were cut to pieces by Confederate artillery and fell back before the Georgians behind the wall fired a single volley. Union attacks on the Confederate line were everywhere thrown back, but those attacking Marye's Heights, which Longstreet's corps held, suffered the heaviest casualties. In the long day's fighting not a single Federal soldier succeeded in reaching the stone wall. Seven Union divisions launched fourteen unsuccessful charges.

The Union army lost 12,650 men; the Confederates, 4,200. For the numbers engaged, Fredericksburg was the largest battle of the war. Burnside proposed personally to lead an attack the next day but was dissuaded by his commanders, and on the night of the 15th the entire Union army withdrew.

Frederick III (1831–1888). The king of Prussia and emperor of Germany, nicknamed Unser Fritz, who as crown prince first saw action in the Schleswig-Holstein War [q.v.] when he served on the staff of General Friedrich von Wrangel [q.v.]. Although he strongly opposed the policies of Otto von Bismarck (1815–1898), he fought in the Seven Weeks' War [q.v.] of 1866, commanding an army of four corps with General Karl von Blumenthal [q.v.] as his chief of staff. He played an active part in the arduous operations involved in pushing his army through the mountains from Silesia to Bohemia, fighting four engagements in three days. In the Battle of Sadowa [q.v.] the arrival of his army on the field after a 20-mile march ensured the Prussian victory. During the Franco-Prussian War [q.v.] of 1870–71 he commanded the armies of the German southern states, and again General von Blumenthal was his chief of staff. His troops won the victory at Fröschwiller and took part in the Battle of Sedan and the siege of Paris [qq.v.]. After the war he saw no further action, but remained active in affairs of state.

His father died on 9 March 1888, and he was emperor for only a few months before he died of cancer of the throat.

Frederick William, Crown Prince (1831–1888). See Frederick III.

Frederick William III (1770–1840). The king of Prussia. In 1806 he rashly formed the Fourth Coalition of the Napoleonic Wars [q.v.] and provoked a war with France. After the French victories of Jena and Friedland [qq.v.] and the Treaty of Tilsit [q.v.], he became a client king of Napoleon until 1813, when the army reforms of General August von Gneisenau [q.v.] so raised Prussian capabilities that at Breslau on 17 March 1813 Frederick William issued a proclamation, *An mein Volk,* calling upon the Prussian people to revolt against the French and wage a war of liberation. He joined the Sixth Coalition and was present at the battles of Bautzen, Dresden, and Leipzig [qq.v.]. He entered Paris in the wake of the tsar on 31 March 1814.

Fredonian Rebellion (1826–27). In 1821 Spain permitted Americans to settle in Texas, a policy reaffirmed by the newly independent government of Mexico the following year, when it granted a charter to Hayden Edwards (1771–1849) to establish a colony of about two hundred families on land near Nacogdoches, 20 miles north of present-day Lufkin, where in 1716 a Spanish mission had been established for the Indians [see Mexican Revolutions]. The land had already been settled by Mexicans who, although they could not produce clear titles, were unwilling to give up their holdings. In response to their protests, the Mexican government revoked Edwards's title and ordered him out of Texas. Instead of leaving, Edwards and his settlers, with help from some Cherokee Indians, seized Nacogdoches and on 21 December 1826 adopted a constitution and proclaimed an independent republic, naming it Fredonia. It was short-lived. In January 1827 a large Mexican force overwhelmed the settlers and their Cherokee allies, and the republic ceased to exist.

Free, Mickey (1847?–1915). An American army scout and interpreter in the American West. His Mexican mother was living with an American farmer in the Sonoita Valley of Arizona when, along with some oxen, he was taken by Apache Indians. His abduction precipitated a confrontation between Cochise [q.v.] and Lieutenant George Nicholas Bascom (1836–1862) that resulted in the capture of Indian and white hostages, all of whom were killed [see Bascom Affair].

The boy was taken to the San Carlos River area and raised by Western White Mountain Apaches. Although in his youth he was blinded in one eye, on 2 December 1872, under the name of Mickey Free, he enlisted in the Apache Scouts, and by December 1874 he had become a sergeant and still later first sergeant. Married four times, he fathered two sons and two daughters. In 1883 he served as a member of the Sierra Madre Expedition under General George Crook [q.v.]. He served in the army as interpreter, scout, or spy until July 1893.

Freedmen's Bureau (1865–72). The popular name for the Bureau of Refugees, Freedmen and Abandoned Lands that on 3 March 1865 was established for one year by Congress under the U.S. War Department. Its operation was later extended to 1872. "Freedman" was the term applied to all former slaves after the passing of the Thirteenth Amendment to the U.S. Constitution. The bureau, headed by General Oliver Otis

Freedmen's Bureau *Teaching the freedmen*

Howard [q.v.], who had lost his right arm in the Battle of Fair Oaks [q.v.], operated in sixteen states, the District of Columbia, and Indian Territory, but even at its peak it never numbered more than 900 agents. Its operations in the South were much resented by southern whites because of the arrogance of many of its officials and their encouragement of blacks to seize political power; but the agency was impotent without bayonets to enforce its edicts, and the size of the army of occupation, 15,000 in 1867, reduced to 6,000 in 1876, and a mere 3,000 by 1880, was never sufficient to support it.

Although it was unable to effect a basic change in the social fabric of the South, the bureau established more than 4,000 schools for former slaves, some in government buildings that were no longer needed. By 1870 one in ten of all black children were in school. Howard University, the nation's first for freedmen, founded in Washington, D.C., in 1867, was named after General Howard. During the bureau's short existence it founded more than 100 hospitals, gave medical aid to 600,000 people, distributed 20 million food rations, and settled thousands of former slaves upon confiscated or abandoned lands.

Although General Howard was accused of influence peddling and misuse of funds, he was cleared by a congressional committee on 2 March 1870 and went on to earn a reputation as an Indian fighter.

Freemasonry. A widespread secret fraternal society called Free and Accepted Masons. The grandmother lodge of the world was inaugurated in London in 1717 by four or more older lodges. When Pope Pius VII (1742–1823) threatened to excommunicate Catholic Masons, many dropped out, but papal condemnation did not decrease Freemasonry's popularity. In the nineteenth century numerous European and American army officers, including Napoleon, were Masons, and soldiers' lodges were established in the French, American (including Confederate), British (including the Indian), and other armies. During the ten years of Napoleon's empire the number of lodges in France increased from 300 to 1,000. The wars of the era saw numerous instances of prisoners' being aided or saved from execution by giving the Masonic "sign of distress."

Freire, Manuel (1765–1834). A Spanish soldier who was active in Murcia and Granada in 1810–12 during the Peninsular War [q.v.]. He commanded the Army of Galicia in 1813 and won the Battle of San Marcial [q.v.] on 31 August 1813.

Freire, Ramón (1787–1851). A Chilean soldier and statesman who served in the Chilean War of Independence [q.v.] in 1811–20. After the fall of Bernardo O'Higgins [q.v.] in 1823 he became dictator. When forced to resign, he led an army revolt, but he was defeated in 1830 and banished to Peru.

Freire de Andrade, Bernardino (1764–1809). A Portuguese general who in 1808, during the Peninsular War, organized an army to resist the French occupation forces of Jean Junot [q.v.]. He generally refused to cooperate with the British, but he did lead Portuguese troops in the Battle of Vimeiro [q.v.] in August 1808. He was killed the following year by his own troops, who mutinied during the Battle of Braga in northwestern Portugal.

Freiwillige Jaeger. In Prussian armies of the Napoleonic era, these were companies of middle-class volunteers that served as training units for future noncommissioned officers or officers.

Frémont, John Charles (1813–1890). An American soldier who was the son of an émigré French dancing master and a Richmond, Virginia, housewife who had left her husband to live with him. Frémont attended Charleston College in South Carolina from 1829 until he was expelled in 1831. In 1833 he was hired as a teacher of mathematics on board a sloop of war that cruised off South America for two and a half years. On 7 July 1838 he was commissioned a second lieutenant in the army topographical engineers. In 1841 he married sixteen-year-old Jessie Benton (1824–1902), over the strenuous objections of her father, Senator Thomas Hart Benton (1782–1858) of Missouri. Mrs. Frémont later became a writer of note and the author of *Story of the Guard* (1863), set in the American Civil War; *A Year of American Travel* (1878), set in California; and *Far West Sketches* (1898).

Frémont made a name for himself as an explorer of the Far West. Under congressional authority he led three expeditions to Oregon Territory, earning the honorific of "the Pathfinder." He played a leading role in the conquest of California but was court-martialed, convicted of mutiny and insubordination, and sentenced to be cashiered [see Black Bear Revolt / Bear Flag War]. Although President James Polk (1795–1849) canceled the sentence, Frémont resigned his commission as captain on 15 March 1848. Soon after, enormous quantities of gold were discovered on the 40,000-acre estate he owned on the Mariposa River in the Sierra foothills of California. In a few years he had developed mines that made him a multimillionaire. In December 1849 he was elected one of the first two U.S. senators from California; however, he served less than one year. In 1856 he was the Republican Party's candidate for president.

At the beginning of the American Civil War Lincoln appointed him a major general in the regular army, but he proved to be a controversial army administrator and a failure as a field commander. Appointed on 25 July 1861 to command the newly created Department of the West, he set up headquarters in St. Louis, surrounded himself with a large and resplendently dressed staff and bodyguard [see Frémont's Bodyguard], and passed out contracts with abandon, many to unscrupulous suppliers. On 30 August he established martial law in Missouri and angered Lincoln by freeing the slaves, an emancipation proclamation the president revoked. Frémont was defeated at the Battle of Wilson's Creek [q.v.] on 10 August 1861 and relieved of his appointment on 2 November 1861 by Major General David Hunter [q.v.]. He was sent to what is now West Virginia, but he was unsuccessful in opposing Stonewall Jackson [q.v.] in the Valley Campaign [q.v.], and in the spring of 1862 at his own request he was relieved of his command.

Frémont lost most of his large fortune in unsuccessful railroad ventures, and in 1873 he was convicted, fined, and sentenced in default by the French government for swindles involving a proposed transcontinental railroad from San Francisco to Norfolk. He was saved from poverty by his wife's writings and by his appointment in 1878 as territorial governor of Arizona, a post he held until 1881. He was named a major general on the retired list in 1890.

Frémont's Bodyguard. When John Frémont [q.v.] was appointed to command the Department of the West, which included all the area west of the Mississippi, he made his headquarters in St. Louis, where he gathered a staff of 28 officers, including a director of music who was given the rank and pay of a captain of engineers, 2 private secretaries, and 15 aides. He also formed a bodyguard of 300 men, dressed them in resplendent uniforms, armed them with German sabers and Colt and Beale revolvers, and drilled them under Charles Zagonyi, a Hungarian refugee of whom little is known. The unit fought well at Springfield and Lexington, Missouri, but Frémont was relieved of his appointment on 2 November 1861 by Major General David Hunter [q.v.], and General George McClellan [qq.v.] ordered the unit disbanded on 28 November.

French, John Denton Pinkstone (1852–1925). A British soldier, the son of a naval officer, who was orphaned at an early age and reared by his six older sisters. He was educated at Eastman's Naval Academy at Portsmouth and in 1866 at the age of fourteen entered HMS *Britannia,* passing out as a midshipman two years later. In 1870 he left the navy and four years later managed to pass from the militia to the 8th Hussars. He distinguished himself in the Gordon Relief Expedition [q.v.] under Sir Garnet Wolseley [q.v.] and in February 1885 was made a brevet lieutenant colonel.

In 1890 he commanded the 19th Hussars in India and in 1895 was promoted colonel and appointed assistant adjutant general at the War Office. In September 1899, sent to Natal to command the cavalry under Sir George White, VC [q.v.], he saw action in the early battles of the Second Anglo-Boer War [q.v.]. On 15 February 1900 he gained fame when, leading two cavalry brigades, he drove them through the Boer positions and raised the siege of Kimberley [q.v.]. This was quickly followed by his success in halting 4,000 retreating Boers under Piet Cronjé [q.v.] at Paardeburg [q.v.] on 27 February and in turning the Boer flank at Poplar Grove on 7 March and again at Driefontein [q.v.] three days later. Although he was promoted major general and knighted, his subsequent actions in the war were more mundane.

Not noted for his brains, French was said to have "the mercurial temper commonly associated with Irishmen and cavalry officers." Nevertheless, in March 1912 he became chief of the imperial general staff and in June 1913 was promoted field marshal. His last posting was as the commander of the British Expeditionary Force in France in the First World War.

French, Samuel Gibbs (1818–1910). An American soldier who was graduated from West Point in 1843 and served in the Mexican War [q.v.], in which he was wounded and earned two brevets. He resigned in 1856 and was operating a plantation near Vicksburg, Mississippi, when the American Civil War began. He was commissioned a major in the Confederate army in April 1861 and a brigadier general on 23 October; a year later he was promoted major general. He led a division in the Atlanta Campaign and in Hood's campaign in Tennessee.

French, William Henry (1815–1881). An American soldier who was graduated from West Point in 1837 and served in the Second Seminole War [q.v.]. During the Mexican War he served as an aide-de-camp to General (later President) Franklin Pierce [q.v.] and won two brevets. After the war he commanded a company of artillery in Florida in which Thomas ("Stonewall") Jackson was one of his lieutenants. The two quarreled bitterly, and each attempted to have the other court-martialed.

Captain French was in command at Fort Duncan, at Eagle Pass, Texas, 130 miles west-southwest of San Antonio on the Rio Grande, when the American Civil War began. A loyal Unionist, he marched his garrison down the river to the Gulf of Mexico and there boarded a ship to Key West. He was promoted brigadier general on 28 September 1861 and commanded a brigade through the battles of the Peninsular Campaign, at Antietam, Fredericksburg, and Chancellorsville [qq.v.]. Promoted major general on 29 November 1862, he commanded a corps at Manassas Gap, Auburn, Kelly's Ford, Brandy Station [q.v.], and elsewhere. After the Federal failure at Mine Run [q.v.] in December 1863, for which General George Meade [q.v.] held him responsible, he held no other important commands.

He remained in the army after the war and retired as colonel of the 4th Artillery in 1880.

French Army. Until 1830, when France began its conquest of North Africa, the French army was designed and trained to fight in Europe. Its basic unit was the line regiment or demi-brigade of infantry, which contained one to five battalions. Each battalion had one grenadier company, one voltigeur company, and four fusilier companies. Light infantry regiments were organized similarly, but the center companies were called chasseurs, and a company called carabiniers replaced the voltigeurs.

Napoleonic armies contained large numbers of foreign troops. In 1805 only about half the army consisted of Frenchmen. Of the 467,000 who invaded Russia in 1812, only 187,000 were French. During this period the army also contained many veterans and attained its highest level of maneuverability and steadiness in battle. [See Grande Armée.]

After about 1840 the army became almost as much African as European and consisted of three distinct groups: (1) the *armée métropolitaine,* which was composed mostly of conscripts who served in Europe and garrisoned France; (2) the *armée d'Afrique* [q.v.], which became the major military force in northwest Africa; and (3) *troupes de marine,* which consisted primarily of infantry and artillery responsible to the ministry of the navy, and in 1900 became *troupes coloniales.* For all these entities there was but one general staff.

In 1868 the size of the army was raised to 600,000 men, and the length of service increased from seven to nine years with five years with the colors and four years in the reserve. It was also fixed that 100,000 men would be called up each year, only 70,000 of whom would serve with the colors, the remainder forming part of a First Reserve, which would drill for a specified time in each of five years. All other fit men were to serve five years in the Garde Mobile, a reserve that could be called on in an emergency.

This system, in place when France declared war on Prussia in 1870, proved inefficient, and in July 1872 the French Assembly voted for general conscription. Almost every fit male was required to serve; substitutions were no longer permitted; men remained liable to call from age twenty to age forty. Nevertheless, there were certain exceptions, such as the eldest brothers of orphans, the eldest son of a widow, etc. As in the German system, those of higher education could volunteer to serve for one year, paying their own expenses. They then stood for examinations that, if failed, condemned them to a year in the ranks. Those who passed were given certificates of qualification as noncommissioned officers or officers. [See Conscription.]

In 1875 there was a further reorganization. The army was designed to include 144 infantry regiments of the line, each consisting of four battalions of four companies each plus two depot companies; 30 battalions of *chasseur à pied,* each of four fighting companies and one depot company; and an African corps headquartered in Algeria with 4 regiments of Zouaves, 1 regiment of the Foreign Legion, 3 regiments of Turcos [qq.v.], and five disciplinary companies.

The cavalry consisted of 77 regiments, 26 of which were classed as dragoons [q.v.], 12 cuirassiers [q.v.], 20 chasseurs [q.v.], 12 hussars [q.v.], four *chasseurs d'Afrique,* and three spahis [q.v.]. Nineteen squadrons of volunteers provided the generals with escorts, guides, orderlies, and couriers.

Thirty-eight regiments of artillery were stationed in France, as were three rocket companies and four regiments of sappers and miners.

Officers were selected from the ranks and from military colleges, principally St. Cyr and the École Polytechnique [qq.v.]. Unlike the British, German, Russian, and American armies, a large percentage of the officers always came from the ranks.

French Civil War. See Commune of 1871; French Revolution of 1830.

French Expeditionary Force to Japan. See Japan, French Expeditionary Force to.

French Foreign Legion. See Foreign Legion, French.

French Indochina War, First (1858–63). To protest the abuse of European missionaries in Indochina (Vietnam, Laos, Cambodia) a joint French and Spanish naval force bombarded Toutaine (Da Nang, Vietnam) in the summer of 1858. In 1859 troops landed and seized Saigon (Ho Chi Minh City) in Cochin China (southern Vietnam) and garrisoned it with a Franco-Spanish force of 1,000. The city was soon besieged and remained so for a year until relieved by a French force in February 1861. Attempts to negotiate terms with the Vietnamese ruler, Tu Duc [q.v.], were unsuccessful.

At the end of the Second Opium War [q.v.] French troops were released for duty in Cochin China, where they seized three provinces. In 1862 Tu Duc sued for peace, and in a treaty signed in April 1863 the French were ceded the Poulo Condore Islands in the South China Sea, 50 miles southeast of the mouth of the Mekong River, off the south coast of Cochin China, and the three eastern provinces of Saigon, My Tho, and Bien Hoa. Tu Duc was also forced to open three ports to trade, to allow Christian missionaries to operate, and to pay a substantial indemnity. In the same year the young Cambodian king Norodom (1834–1904), threatened by Siamese expansionism, accepted a French protectorate. In 1867 Siam gave up its claims to Cambodia.

French Indochina War, Second (1873–74). François Garnier (1839–1883), a French explorer, was sent with a small force to Hanoi to arbitrate between a French salt smuggler and local officials. Garnier favored his countryman, and when the Vietnamese refused to comply with his demands, he stormed the fort at Hanoi and went on to capture others in the Red River delta. Reinforcements arrived, and French forces fought regular Vietnamese forces and Black Flags [q.v.]. In a series of disasters Garnier was killed, pro-French Christian towns in Tonkin (northern Vietnam) were destroyed, and French ships were taken. Having suffered heavy losses, the French temporarily withdrew from Tonkin.

The retreat had grave political repercussions in Paris. There was an uproar in the Chamber of Deputies, where the government of Jules Ferry (1832–1893) fell under a hostile vote of 308 to 161, and Ferry himself escaped violent crowds inside and outside the chamber by slipping out a side door. For the first time a policy of colonial expansion toppled a French government.

French Indochina War, Third (1881–85). In 1881, when China invaded Annam (Vietnam) and sent troops down the Red River to seize Tonkin (northern Vietnam), France renewed its expansionist policies [see French Indochina War, Second]. Captain Henri Laurent Rivière (1827–1883), a French naval officer who was the author of novels, plays, and in 1859 a history of the French navy under Louis XV, was dispatched to evict the Chinese and suppress the depredations of the Black Flags [q.v.]. He captured Hanoi and the coast of Nam Dinh in the Red River delta 45 miles southeast, but on 19 May 1883 he and 49 men were ambushed by Black Flags [q.v.] near Hanoi, and all were killed. Their heads were pickled in brine and triumphantly exhibited.

In response, the French organized an expedition under Admiral Amédée Anatole Prosper Courbet (1827–1885) with General of Brigade François de Négrier as second-in-command. On 9 November 1883 a battalion of the French Foreign Legion [q.v.] disembarked at Haiphong and moved up the Red River to Hanoi and, with Tirailleurs Algériens [see Tirailleurs] and other colonial troops, about 5,500 in all, moved on to attack the main Black Flags stronghold at Sontay [q.v.], 30 miles northwest of Hanoi. Although Sontay was a formidable fort with walls of brick 16 feet thick and heavy wooden gates, it was successfully attacked on 16 December by the Foreign Legion battalion. Reinforced, the French moved east on 8 March toward Bac Ninh [q.v.], the second major stronghold of the Black Flags. This fort was taken on 12 March.

At the close of 1884 the Black Flags, led by Liu Yung Fu, a Chinese warlord, were reinforced from China by troops under Feng Tzu-ts'ai [q.v.] and armed with modern rifles, Nordenfeldt machine guns, and some old Krupp field guns. On 26 January 1885 they attacked Tuyen Quang [q.v.], a brick wall fort about 100 miles north of Hanoi that was successfully defended by 390 legionnaires and 200 colonial troops.

On 3 February 1885 twelve French battalions, about 9,000 men, entered the Bôn Mat Mountains and fought their way to Lang Son [q.v.], on the Chinese frontier of Kwangsi, 85 miles northeast of Hanoi. This was a walled citadel, about 425 yards on each side near the village of Ki Lua. The place was captured on 13 February. Feng retreated into his stronghold, where on 23 March he repulsed a French attack.

The war appeared to end on 4 April 1885, when France and China signed the Treaty of Tientsin. China recognized as a French protectorate Laos, Cambodia, and the Vietnamese provinces of Tonkin, Annam, and Cochin China, which together constituted French Indochina. When China renounced the agreement, the French bombarded the Vietnamese capital at Hué and captured Hanoi and Haiphong. The war finally ended with a new treaty signed on 25 August 1885 recognizing all French claims. The country was not completely pacified, however, until 1891.

French Intervention in Spain (1823). Alarmed by the disorders in Spain and the seizure of King Ferdinand VII (1784–1833) by revolutionaries, the monarchs of continental Europe at the Congress of Verona in October 1822 authorized France to intervene. On 17 April 1823 a French army led by Louis Antoine de Bourbon, Duke of Angoulême (1775–1844), and General Nicolas Charles Victor Oudinot [q.v.] crossed the Pyrenees and invaded Spain. A force was sent to besiege San Sebastián while the duke attacked Madrid, then in the hands of the revolutionaries [see San Sebastián, Sieges of]. When the Spanish commander in Madrid secretly capitulated and fled to France, the leaderless garrison surrendered.

The French then marched south to Cádiz, where King Ferdinand was being held by the Cortes. The Spanish were defeated in the Battle of Trocadero [q.v.] on 31 August, and Cádiz, which was held by revolutionaries under Colonel Rafael del Riego y Núñez [q.v.], fell on 23 September. [See Cádiz, Siege of; Spanish Civil War of 1820–21.]

King Ferdinand was restored to his throne and, in spite of a promise of amnesty, ordered ruthless reprisals against the revolutionaries.

French Revolutionary Wars (1792–1800). The general name for the series of conflicts beginning with the French declaration of war on England in 1792 and ending with the final overthrow of Napoleon in 1815. [See Napoleonic Wars.]

French Revolution of 1830. After the restoration of the monarchy in 1815, Charles Philippe, Comte d'Artois (1757–1836), became leader of an ultraroyalist party. On his accession to the throne as Charles X in 1824 he attempted to establish himself as an absolute monarch and in the process grew increasingly objectional to all classes. After appointing ultraroyalist Jules de Polignac (1780–1847) minister of foreign affairs, he asked him to form a new ministry. When the Chamber of Deputies objected, Charles dismissed it in May 1830. On 25 July Polignac promulgated "ordinances" that ended freedom of the press, decreed a new method of elections, reduced the electorate, and completely dissolved the deputies. Outraged Parisians took to the streets, and barricades were manned not only by disgruntled civilians but by army units and former members of the National Guard, which had been disbanded in 1827. Monarchists and imperialists by a coup d'état overturned the government and rejected the ordinances. There was a three-day battle (27–29 July) before the rebels were overpowered by troops led by Marshal Auguste Marmont [q.v.] and order was restored. Although Charles annulled the new ordinances and dismissed Polignac on 30 July, he did not react quickly enough. The people wanted no more of him. On 2 August he abdicated in favor of his grandson. On 14 August he went into perpetual exile; Marmont retired to Vienna. The revolutionaries, who expected to place their choice on the throne, were for a time divided between the Marquis de Lafayette (1757–1834) and Louis Philippe (1773–1850). In the end the bourgeois legislature opted for Louis Philippe.

French-Samory Wars. See Franco-Mandingo Wars.

French 75. In French: the *soixante-quinze,* the popular name for the *Canon de 75 Modèle 1897,* the 1897 Model 75 mm breech-loading field gun that was one of the most famous field guns ever manufactured. Designed by a team of French ordnance experts at Bourges Arsenal, 126 miles south of Paris, it had a Nordenfeldt eccentric screw type breechblock and a novel hydropneumatic axial recoil mechanism developed in great secrecy at the Puteaux Arsenal in a northwestern suburb of Paris. It was this mechanism that made the 75 the parent of all so-called quick-firing field guns of the next half century.

A piston operating inside a hydraulic cylinder was located in a cradle just below the barrel. This was not new, but a companion cylinder, working under compressed air, returned the barrel to battery after it was fired so that while the gun recoiled on the cradle, the carriage remained relatively stationary and was ready to be fired without being relayed. It could thus fire a 16-pound shrapnel shell for 4.3 miles at a rate of about ten rounds per minute. The gun was produced in quantity by Schneider-Creusot.

Frenchtown, Battle of (22 January 1813), War of 1812. British General Henry A. Proctor, leading a force of regulars, Canadian militia, and Shawnee Indians under Tecumseh [q.v.], attacked and defeated an American force under Brigadier General James Winchester (1757?–1826) at this town (now Monroe, Michigan) on the Raisin River. American losses were 197 killed and wounded; 737 were taken prisoner. Many were scalped by the Indians after they had surrendered.

French-Tukulor Wars. See Franco-Tukulor Wars.

French-Vietnamese Wars. See French Indochina Wars.

Friction of War. A term for all the delays, misunderstandings, and unexpected obstacles encountered in carrying out any military operation. General Karl von Clausewitz [q.v.] defined this term: "Everything is very simple in war, but the simplest thing is difficult. These difficulties accumulate and produce a friction which no man can imagine exactly who has not seen war" (*On War*, 1833).

Friction Tube. An artillery ignition system introduced in France about 1830 that soon replaced the slow match, fuze tube, and all other ignition systems. It consisted of a thin tube of copper or brass about two inches long that could be fitted into the vent of a gun barrel. The end of the tube was sealed with wax and pitch, which held in place tightly compressed gunpowder. This could be ignited by a detonator employing a mixture of antimony and saltpeter contained in a smaller copper tube. A thin, flattened copper wire, saw-edged at one end, fitted into the detonating mixture so that when it was pulled hard, the friction ignited the powder. There were a number of variations, but the system was basically the same. It was sometimes called a friction primer.

Friedland, Battle of (14 June 1807), Napoleonic Wars (Fourth Coalition). French forces under Napoleon, after capturing Danzig (Gdansk) on 26 May 1807, defeated a Russian army under General Levin Bennigsen [q.v.] at Friedland (Pravdinsk) in East Prussia (Poland) on the Alle River, 27 miles southeast of Königsberg (Kaliningrad). The main French attack was against the Russian left, which was cramped on a narrow tongue of land between the Alle River and a millstream at the village of Posthenen. Late in the afternoon a division of Marshal Michel Ney [q.v.] drove the Russians to a point where they came under the French guns. Ney's cavalry was driven back, but the French infantry under Pierre Dupont de l'Étang [q.v.] advanced, supported by massed artillery, and the Russian line collapsed. Pushed to the river, the Russians suffered heavy losses from drowning.

French losses were 12,100 (14 percent) out of 86,000 engaged; Russian losses were 10,000 (21 percent) out of 46,000 engaged.

Napoleon then marched 27 miles northeast to occupy Königsberg near the Baltic Sea. After reaching the Neman (Neiman) River, he met with Tsar Alexander I and Frederick William III [qq.v.] of Prussia on a specially constructed raft in the middle of the river near Tilsit (Sovetsk), and there on 7 July the monarchs signed two treaties. This battle effectively ended the Fourth Coalition. [See Tilsit, Treaties of; Napoleonic Wars.]

Friend, The. A newspaper established in Bloemfontein, South Africa, in 1850 that in 1900 was briefly taken over by

Friedland *Napoleon at Friedland, by Meissonier, June 1807*

Rudyard Kipling [q.v.] and other British war correspondents, who turned it into a newspaper for the troops. This was one of the first, if not the first, such army newspaper.

Friendly Fire. This expression, meaning the bullets and shells that kill or wound one's own troops, was not used in the nineteenth century, but friendly fire certainly occurred. Winston Churchill [q.v.], speaking of the reconquest of the Sudan [q.v.] in 1898, wrote: "A certain loss of life is inseparable from war, and it makes little difference whether a man is shot by his own side or cut down by the other. But even the rawest recruit in the moment of extreme agitation has a distinct preference for shooting his enemies rather than his friends."

Frill. An ornamental appendage on the front of a shirt worn with a uniform. Officers' frills usually had a small hole on the top to admit the hook and eye of the uniform coat. Other ranks usually wore frills detached from the coat.

Frimont, Johann Maria Philipp von (1759–1831). An Austrian soldier and the prince of Antrodocco, who in 1776 entered the Austrian army as a trooper in the cavalry and won his commission during the War of the Bavarian Succession in 1778–79. He took part in the Turkish campaigns and against the French Revolutionary armies in Italy. In 1815 he commanded the Austrian troops in Italy and carried his army into France as far as Lyons. In 1821 he suppressed a revolution in Naples, and four years later he was made governor-general of the Lombardo-Venetian kingdom. In 1831 he suppressed uprisings in Modena, Parma, and the papal territories and became president of the Aulic Council [q.v.].

Frizzen. In flintlocks, the steel plate that the flint struck to produce sparks.

Frizzen Pick. A metal pick used to clean the flash holes of flintlocks.

Frock Coat. A coat with long skirts worn as an officer's undress uniform in some armies, including the British and American.

Frog. 1. An attachment to a waist belt designed to hold a sword, bayonet, or tool.
2. An ornamental fastening on the front of a coat or jacket, often consisting of a covered spindle-shaped button and the loop through which it passed.

Frog

Froneman, Christoffel Cornelius (1846–1913). A Boer leader who fought in the Basuto War of 1865 and distinguished himself as a guerrilla leader in the Second Anglo-Boer War [q.v.]. He served under Pieter Cronjé [q.v.] and was with him when he was surrounded in the Battle of Paardeberg [q.v.]. Subsequently he served under Christiaan De Wet [q.v.], distinguishing himself at Saana's Post and in the Brandwater Basin [qq.v.]. By 1901 he was acting commandant general of the Eastern Orange Free State.

Frontal Attack. Although often used to mean an attack upon an enemy's front, as opposed to an attack on a flank or an envelopment, the strict meaning is a simultaneous attack by troops more or less evenly distributed along a front.

Frontier, Army of the. During the American Civil War a Union field force of the departments of Missouri and Kansas that existed from 12 October 1862 until 5 June 1863.

Front Royal, Battles of, American Civil War. During Thomas Jackson's Valley Campaign [q.v.] there were two engagements at the town of Front Royal, 20 miles south of Winchester, Virginia.

1. 23 May 1862. This battle was the most striking Confederate victory in the Valley Campaign. Confederate Major General Thomas ("Stonewall") Jackson moved his force down the Shenandoah Valley toward Strasburg, where the Union army of General Nathaniel Banks [q.v.] was located. He then moved east, crossing the Massanutten Range, and was joined by the forces under General Richard Ewell [q.v.]. Their united force of 16,000 moved down the Page Valley (between the Massanutten and the Blue Ridge) to Front Royal, Virginia, where Jackson pounced upon the 1,063 Federals there, routing them and seizing a vast amount of Union stores and equipment. Union losses were 904; Confederate losses were fewer than 50.

This is sometimes called the Battle of Brother against Brother because the 1st Maryland of the Union army fought the 1st Maryland of the Confederate army [qq.v.].

2. 30 May 1862. Colonel Zephaniah Turner Connor (1811–1866), commanding the 12th Georgia, was left to guard the mountain of supplies captured by Jackson on 23 May [see above]. Attacked by a Union force under Brigadier General Nathan Kimball [q.v.], Connor fled with his men. A pursuit by 1st Rhode Island Cavalry caught 156.

General Jackson was so enraged that he had Connor cashiered.

Fröschwiller / Froeschwiller / Fröschweiler–Wörth, Battle of (6 August 1870), Franco-Prussian War. A French corps of 42,800 infantry, 5,750 cavalry, and 167 guns under Marie Edmé Patrice MacMahon [q.v.] deployed in a defensive position near the villages of Fröschwiller and Wörth in Alsace on a ridge of the eastern slopes of the Vosges was attacked by a German force under Crown Prince Frederick William [q.v.]. The French position was excellent, but all of its artillery pieces were obsolete, and although mitrailleuses—primitive machine guns consisting of twenty-five revolving barrels that could fire about 150 rounds per minute—were available, only one noncommissioned officer in the corps had been trained to use them. The French repulsed a strong German reconnaissance in force, but early the next morning Frederick William built up a strength of 89,000 infantry, 7,750 cavalry, and 342 guns, 232 of which were rifled breechloaders, and attacked. The battle was ended by 4:30 P.M., and that night the French retreated to Châlons-sur-Marne, leaving the road through the Vosges to Lorraine open to the Germans.

The French lost 10,760 killed and wounded and 6,200 taken prisoner. German losses were 8,200 killed and wounded and 1,373 missing. Friedrich Wilhelm Nietzsche (1844–1900), until the war a philology teacher at the University of Basel, was among those returning to Germany escorting wounded from the battle. He wrote to his mother: "With this letter comes a memory of the terribly devastated battlefield, sadly bespattered everywhere with human remains and reeking corpses." More than a decade later he wrote in *Thus Spake Zarathustra* (1883): "You say it is the good cause that hallows even war? I say unto you: it is the good war that hallows any cause."

Frossard, Charles Auguste (1807–1875). A French soldier who was graduated from the École Polytechnique [q.v.] and served in the Crimean War [q.v.] of 1854–55. He was made a general of brigade in 1855 and in 1857 was aide-de-camp to Napoleon III (1808–1873). The following year he was promoted general of division. He was one of the few senior French officers who foresaw and tried to prepare for the war against Germany. During the Franco-Prussian War [q.v.] he commanded II Corps in the Army of the Rhine. On 6 August 1870 he was defeated at Spicheren [q.v.] by Germans under General Carl Friedrich von Steinmetz [q.v.] and retired into Metz. There he took part in the battles around the city but was captured on 28 October 1870 and interned in Germany.

Fry, Birkett Davenport (1822–1891). An American soldier who attended but failed to graduate from West Point, having been found deficient in mathematics. He practiced law for a time before volunteering to join the army in the Mexican War [q.v.]. He was mustered out as a first lieutenant on 31 August 1848. In 1856 he joined the filibustering expedition of William Walker [q.v.] to Nicaragua. When Walker's dreams collapsed, Davenport returned to the United States and was managing a cotton mill in Alabama when the American Civil War began. He was quickly commissioned a colonel of the 13th Alabama and fought in the Army of Northern Virginia [q.v.]. During the Peninsular Campaign [q.v.] he was wounded at Seven Pines. Later an arm was shattered at Antietam, and he was wounded again at Chancellorsville [qq.v.]. At Gettysburg he succeeded to the command of a brigade and was wounded a fourth time and captured in Pickett's Charge [q.v.]. Nine months later he was exchanged and promoted brigadier general. He commanded two brigades at Cold Harbor [q.v.] and was then in charge of the military district of Augusta, Georgia. After the war he spent three years in Cuba before returning to the United States, again to mill cotton.

Fry, James Barnet (1827–1894). An American soldier who after graduation from West Point saw action in the Mexican War [q.v.] and as a Union officer in the American Civil War. He fought at Corinth, Shiloh, and Perryville [qq.v.]. On 17 March 1863 he was promoted colonel and appointed the first provost marshal [q.v.] general. His responsibilities included recruiting and conscription, and among his concerns were bounties, desertions, state quotas, and dealing with draft riots. On April 21 1864 he was promoted brigadier general. Under his direction, 1.1 million men were inducted into the Union army and 76,526 deserters were arrested.

The post of provost marshal was abolished on 27 August 1866, and Fry returned to the adjutant general's department, where he remained until his retirement in 1881.

Fuchi. The ornamental metal collar around the hilt of a Japanese sword or dagger. Its manufacture was a distinct craft, and the craftsmen often signed their work. The fuchi was sold separately and mounted by the weapon's owner.

Fuel and Light Allowance. See Allowances.

Fuentes de Oñoro, Battle of (3–5 May 1811), Peninsular War. On 3 May 1811, in an attempt to relieve Almeida, French General André Masséna [q.v.] with six divisions—34,500 infantry, 1,864 cavalry, and 48 guns—moved from his base at Ciudad Rodrigo and attacked the village of Fuentes de Oñoro, 10 miles south on the Spanish-Portuguese border between the rivers Coa, Turones, and Des Casas. The town was garrisoned by 2,260 British troops, mostly light infantry, and the 2nd Battalion of the 84th Foot. There was bitter fighting around the village all day as the French took it and the British retook it. By the end of the day the French had lost 652 men, and the British 259.

The following day saw only some skirmishing by the outposts, but on 5 May Masséna launched a mass attack at dawn on Wellington's right flank near the village of Nave di Haver, routing the Spanish forces there. Wellington sent the Light Division [q.v.] under General Robert Craufurd [q.v.] to check him, and a new line was formed facing south. Craufurd, opposing a numerically superior enemy, made a masterful withdrawal while Wellington's cavalry kept the French artillery at bay.

That same day Masséna launched four successive major attacks upon Fuentes de Oñoro, but Wellington reinforced the garrison, and each attack was repulsed, although with great difficulty. Men fought with bayonets in the narrow streets, and 100 French grenadiers were killed in one cul-de-sac. At 2:00 P.M. Masséna recalled his troops, and on 10 May he retreated. Wellington, noting the destruction, wrote in his dispatch the next day: "The village of Fuentes de Oñero, having been the field of battle, has not been much improved by the circumstances."

In the three days' fighting the French lost 2,192; the Allies 1,545.

Fuentes de Oñoro *The charge of French cavalry at Fuentes do Oñoro*

Fugitive's Drift. A ford on the Buffalo River in Natal, South Africa, where on 22 January 1879 a handful of survivors of the Battle of Isandhlwana [q.v.] managed to cross and escape the Zulus.

Fugleman. A soldier skilled in drills, such as the manual of arms, who was positioned in front of a unit to give a correct execution of the drillmaster's commands. The term was derived from the German *Flügelmann,* and the spelling is sometimes flugelman, flugleman, or fugelman.

Fukuda, Masataro (1866–1932). A Japanese general who took part in the Sino-Japanese War [q.v.] and the Russo-Japanese War.

Fukushima, Baron Yasumara (1853–1914). A Japanese soldier who commanded the Japanese contingent in China during the Boxer Rebellion [q.v.] in 1900. He was on the general staff during the Russo-Japanese War and became its vice chief in 1906.

Fulani-Hausa Conflict (1804?). In Nigeria about 1804 the Fulanis, a long-headed, thin-nosed, light-skinned race with a considerable intermixture of Bantu blood, conquered the Hausa kingdoms and sustained a precarious reign until the British established protectorates in 1904.

Full-Dress Uniform. Usually the most elaborate of uniforms worn for ceremonial and social occasions. In French: *grande tenue.*

Funeral Honors. Military honors accorded the burial of soldiers. These ceremonies vary from country to country, and within a country there are sometimes variations depending on the rank of the deceased. In many countries, including the United States and Britain, it was, and is still, usual for a firing party to fire three volleys over the casket or the grave. This was said by Christians to represent the Trinity.

Fung Yun-san (d. 1852). A Chinese revolutionary who was a friend of Hung Hsiu-ch'üan [q.v.] and in the Taiping Rebellion [q.v.] was one of the original five wangs: Nan Wang (Southern King). He was killed in action.

Funston, Frederick (1865–1917). An American soldier and adventurer who failed to pass the entrance examination for West Point. His father, a senator, obtained a job for him as a field botanist with the Agriculture Department, and he spent sixteen months in Alaska. On his return he heard a rousing speech by General Daniel Sickles [q.v.] that inspired him to join the insurrectionists in Cuba. Although his sole exposure to artillery was a salute he had once heard fired for President Rutherford B. Hayes (1822–1893) at a Kansas county fair, he received a commission as an artillery captain with Cuban insurrectionists Calixto García and Maximo Gómez y Báez [qq.v.] in August 1896. He fought in twenty-two engagements, was wounded several times, contracted malaria, and rose to the rank of lieutenant colonel before he was captured by the Spanish. Although sentenced to death, he managed to escape, and in January 1898 he returned to the United States.

On 13 May he accepted command of the 20th Kansas Volunteer Infantry, expecting to fight Spaniards in the Spanish-American War [q.v.]. Instead, in November he and his regiment were sent to the Philippines to fight against the insurrectionists there [see Philippine Insurrection against the United States]. On 27 April 1899 he crossed the Río Grande de Pampanga at Calumpit, Luzon, with only 45 men and drove 2,500 insurrectos from their entrenchments, an action for which on 1 May 1899 he was promoted brigadier general of volunteers and later,

on 14 February 1900, was awarded the Medal of Honor [q.v.]. He was wounded in a battle at Lake Tomás, northeast of Lake Taal, and returned home in September 1899.

Back to the Philippines in December, he commanded the 4th District of the Department of Northern Luzon. On 14–25 March 1901 in a brilliant and daring exploit he captured Emilio Aguinaldo [q.v.], the leader of the insurrection, a feat for which he was promoted brigadier general in the regular army. He was in temporary command of the troops in San Francisco on 18 April 1906, when the great earthquake struck. In April 1914 he commanded troops in the invasion of Veracruz, Mexico, and was for a time governor of the town. In 1916 he was involved in the pursuit of the Mexican bandit Pancho Villa (1877–1923). He died of a heart attack in the lobby of the St. Anthony Hotel in San Antonio, Texas, on 19 February 1917. Many believed that had he lived he would have commanded the American Expeditionary Force in France during the First World War.

Furia Francese. Fury of the French. That spirit of the offensive the French believed their soldiers to possess. The expression was much used before the Franco-Prussian War but was seldom heard after it. Its origin went back to the attempt by the Duke of Anjou (1554–1584) to capture Antwerp by storm on 17 January 1587; in a furious battle all his force was killed or captured within an hour.

Furlough. An authorized extended absence for noncommissioned officers and privates. Officers went on leave. It was sometimes used as a verb meaning to allow a soldier to go on furlough.

Furniture, Firearm. The furniture of a firearm consists of its mountings, trigger guard, barrel bands, butt plate, etc.

Fuse. An igniting or explosive device used in blasting and demolition work. [See Fuzes / Fuses.]

Fushimi, Prince Sadanaru (1858–1923). A Japanese soldier and diplomat who was the uncle of Emperor Yoshihito (1879–1926). He served in the Sino-Japanese War [q.v.] of 1894–95 and in the Russo-Japanese War of 1904–05. He rose to be a general and was the emperor's personal representative to the United States in 1904.

Fushimi-Toba, Battle of. See Boshin Civil War; Meiji Restoration.

Fusil. In Napoleon's armies the *fusil infantrie,* issued to all dismounted troops, was a .69 caliber musket firing a one-ounce ball. Sometimes called Charlevilles after the armory where they were manufactured, fusils were light and rugged and had strong firing mechanisms. A short-barreled model was called *fusil des vélites.*

Fusiliers. Infantry armed with a fusil [q.v.] or short flintlock originally used to escort and protect artillery. In the British army fusiliers were first raised in 1685. For most of the nineteenth century they were indistinguishable from regular infantry. In the British regular army only the 7th (Royal Fusiliers, after 1881); Royal Fusiliers (City of London Regiment); 21st (Royal Scots Fusiliers); 23rd (Royal

Welch); the Enniskillen Fusiliers; Royal Irish Fusiliers; Royal Munster Fusiliers; Royal Dublin Fusiliers; and briefly, from 1831 to 1877, the Scots Guards (Scots Fusilier Guards) regiments were so designated.

In the French army the center companies of line battalions or regiments were called fusiliers. In the German army, fusiliers were light infantry.

Fusiliers *Officers of Scots Fusilier Guards, 1855*

Fusillade. A simultaneous discharge of firearms.

Fustanella. A short, full skirt of stiffened linen or cotton worn by Greek evzones [q.v.].

Fuste. A Mexican saddle of wood and rawhide usually having a flat horn.

Fuyard. In French, a soldier who flees the battlefield. *Un corps fuyard* is a regiment that tends to run to the rear.

Fuzes / Fuses. Devices for detonating explosives. A "fuse" was used for demolition blasting, and a "fuze" was a device for exploding ammunition, but this distinction was frequently blurred. There were three general types for artillery ammunition: concussion fuzes ignited by the discharge or impact of a projectile, particularly a spherical shell; percussion fuzes, operated when the impact set off a fulminate and exploded the powder in the shell; and time fuzes, using a wooden or paper tube cut to various lengths containing a combustible substance ignited by the charge of the gun. Until the Franco-Prussian War [q.v.] time fuzes were usually undependable.

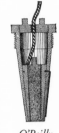

O'Reilly fuze

Fuzzy-Wuzzy. The British soldier's name for a warrior of the Hadendowa tribe in the eastern Sudan. Rudyard Kipling [q.v.] in his poem "Fuzzy-Wuzzy" wrote:

So 'ere's *to* you, Fuzzy-Wuzzy, at your 'ome in the Soudan;
You're a poor benighted 'eathen, but a first-class fightin' man.

[See Osman Digna.]

G

Gabion. A portable hollow cylinder of basketwork or other material measuring from about one to six feet in diameter and from three to six feet in height reinforced with stakes. Filled with earth, they were used as protective barriers in field fortifications or as temporary protection of sappers. A *gabion faci*, or sap roller, was rolled ahead of a sapper. In the last quarter of the century gabions were also made of corrugated iron. [See Jones Gabion; Fascines.]

Gabion *Carrying gabions to make a flying sap*

Gabionade. A work constructed with gabions. Sometimes gabions were used as large building blocks to create a circular ziggurat. Such works were used to protect guns and magazines, particularly from enfilading fire.

Gabionade

Gablenz, Baron Ludwig von (1814–1874). An Austrian soldier who commanded the Austrian forces in the joint Austro-Prussian attack upon Denmark in 1864 [see Schleswig-Holstein Wars]. In the Battle of Sadowa [q.v.], or Königgrätz, in 1866, during the Seven Weeks' War [q.v.], he commanded a corps.

Gadsden, James (1788–1858). An American soldier and diplomat who was graduated from Yale in 1806 and first served in the regular army during the War of 1812 [q.v.] as a lieutenant of engineers. In 1818, as a captain, he served as an aide to General Andrew Jackson [q.v.] and fought the Seminole Indians [see Seminole War, First]. In October 1820 he was promoted colonel and appointed inspector general of the Southern Division. In this capacity he assisted in establishing military posts in the newly acquired areas of Florida. In 1822 he left the army to become a planter, but the following year he was appointed a federal commissioner to supervise the removal of the Seminole Indians from northern to southern Florida. In 1832, when the government attempted to move the Seminoles once again, this time to Oklahoma, they refused to go. When open war broke out in 1838, Gadsden served as quartermaster general of the Florida Volunteers [see Seminole War, Second].

After the war he became a rice planter and railroad president in South Carolina until 1853, when President Franklin Pierce [q.v.] appointed him minister to Mexico. On 30 December 1853, he signed the so-called Gadsden treaty that, among other provisions, added 45,535 square miles of land to present-day New Mexico and Nevada, an acquisition known as the Gadsden Purchase.

Gaeta. A fortified seaport on the Gulf of Gaeta, an inlet of the Tyrrhenian Sea, 41 miles east-southeast of Littoria.

1. 18 July 1806, Napoleonic Wars. The town was captured by Austrian forces under Maximilien Lamarque [q.v.] after a heroic defense by French troops under Marshal André Masséna [q.v.] whose forces included two battalions of Haitian pioneers (*pionniers noires*) who were awarded fifty centimes for every shell they could successfully chase and defuze before it exploded. Later that year these battalions were given to the king of Naples and became the 7th Regiment of the Line.

2. 18 July 1815. Gaeta was soon back in French hands, but during the Hundred Days [q.v.] it was again captured from the French after a three-month siege by the Austrians.

3. November 1848–4 September 1849. Pope Pius IX (1792–1878), fleeing in disguise from Roman revolutions, found refuge in Gaeta.

4. 3 November 1860–13 February 1861, Italian Wars of Independence. Gaeta was the last stronghold of the Neapolitan Bourbons, the last stand of Francis II (1836–1894), king of the Two Sicilies, who had been driven out of Naples

on 7 September 1860 by insurrectionists under Giuseppe Garibaldi [q.v.]. After a long siege directed by Colonel General Enrico Cialdini [q.v.], Gaeta fell on 13 February 1861 to Garibaldi's forces of United Italy, thus ending the Kingdom of the Two Sicilies. Francis II remained in exile for the remainder of his life.

Gaika (1779–1829). A Xhosa chief of the Rarabe clan whose claim to leadership was challenged by his uncle Ndlambe [q.v.]. In 1819, with the help of the British, he defeated his uncle near Grahamstown and became the acknowledged chief.

Gaines, Edmund Pendleton (1777–1849). An American army officer who first saw service in 1795 as a lieutenant in a militia rifle company fighting against Indians. He was a second lieutenant in the regular army in 1797, and in 1804, as a lieutenant in the 4th infantry, he was placed in command of Fort Stoddard, at the confluence of the Alabama and Tombigbee rivers. On 19 February 1807 he apprehended and arrested for treason Aaron Burr (1756–1836), the former vice-president of the United States (1801–05), who had mortally wounded Alexander Hamilton (1853?–1804) in a duel and had conspired to create a new nation in the Southwest. Although Gaines was created a captain ten days after making the arrest, he took an extended leave from the army, during which he practiced law.

He returned to the army as a major to serve in the War of 1812 [q.v.]. In 1813 he was promoted lieutenant colonel. His regiment covered the American retreat after the Battle of Chrysler's Farm [q.v.] on 13 November 1813. He was promoted a brigadier general in March 1814. In August and September of that year he successfully defended Fort Erie [q.v.], for which he was made a brevet major general. In 1815 he commanded the southern frontier with 1,000 men. When hostilities broke out with the Seminole and Creek Indians in 1817, he took part in the First Seminole War [q.v.] of 1817–18. He constructed Fort Scott at the confluence of the Chattahoochee and Flint rivers, not far from Negro Fort [q.v.] on the Apalachicola River in Florida. Negro Fort was later blown up by Lieutenant Colonel Duncan Lamont Clinch [q.v.]. He became commander of a new Western Department in 1821 and took the field in the Black Hawk War [q.v.]. When the Second Seminole War [q.v.] broke out, he was in Louisiana. There he mounted an expedition that was carried by sea to Tampa, Florida. Although Florida was technically in his command territory, Major General Winfield Scott [q.v.] was put in charge. Before Scott could arrive to assume command, Gaines was ambushed on the Withlacoochee River on 26 February and in an eight-day siege lost 5 killed and 46 wounded [see Withlacoochee, Battles on the]. He himself was wounded, a bullet knocking out two teeth.

When Scott arrived, an unseemly dispute arose over who was in command. A court of inquiry later cleared Gaines of misconduct, but it censured both men for failing to cooperate with each other.

In 1836, during the Texas War of Independence [q.v.], Gaines led a force from Louisiana across the Sabine River and occupied Nacogdoches for five months.

At the beginning of the Mexican War [q.v.] he commanded the Western Department. Although he was later court-martialed for calling up without authorization a force of several thousand volunteers to assist Zachary Taylor [q.v.], he was acquitted and given command of the Eastern Department.

He died of cholera in New Orleans on 6 June 1849. Gainesville, Florida, founded in 1854, is named for him.

Gaines's Mill, Battle of (27 June 1862), American Civil War. The third of the Seven Days' Battles [q.v.], it is sometimes called the Battle of the Chickahominy. Here Lee launched a badly managed attack on Federal positions east-northeast of Richmond. General Thomas Jackson [q.v.] was late arriving on the field, and General A. P. Hill [q.v.], who led a gallant but premature attack, was repulsed.

Out of 34,214 Federals engaged, 893 were killed, 3,107 were wounded, and 2,836 were missing. Of the 57,018 Confederates engaged, 8,751 were killed or wounded.

Gaiters. Leggings, a covering of the instep and calf of the leg, usually made of cloth or some stiff material. Those reaching to just above the ankle were called half gaiters.

Galicia, Army of. A Spanish army in the Peninsular War [q.v.] under General Joachim Blake [q.v.]. It contained 37,200 men and 38 guns.

Gall (1840?–1894). A chief of the Hunkpapa Sioux called Pizi by his people. A famous warrior from his youth, he was informally adopted by Sitting Bull [q.v.]. In the Battle of the Little Bighorn [q.v.] on 25 June 1876 he was one of the twenty-five leading chiefs of warrior societies and was later often cited (erroneously) as a more important chief than

Gall *Sioux Chief Gall, one of the leaders in the Battle of the Little Bighorn*

Sitting Bull [q.v.]. After the battle he fled to Canada, but he soon returned. On 1 January 1881 he surrendered to Major Guido Ilges [q.v.] and settled down as a farmer on the Standing Rock Reservation in Dakota. He became an ally of his former enemies, and in 1889 he was appointed a judge of the Court of Indian Affairs. He played no part in the final Sioux uprising of 1890.

Gallabat, Battles of (1885 and 1889), Sudanese-Abyssinian conflicts. Two battles between Sudanese and Abyssinians (Ethiopians) were fought near this town, now in the northeastern Sudan on the Abyssinian border, 90 miles southeast of Galadi.

1. In 1885, after Sudanese Dervishes looted an Abyssinian church, Ras Takla Adal, an Abyssinian chief, invaded the Sudan and defeated the Dervishes near Gallabat.

2. On 12 March 1889 Abyssinians under King Johannes [q.v.] were defeated by a Dervish force under Zaki Tamal [q.v.]. The Abyssinians were winning, thousands of prisoners were taken, and the town was stormed and burned, until Johannes was mortally wounded by a stray bullet and the dispirited Abyssinians quit the field. As they did so, the Dervishes turned and pursued, routing the Abyssinian rear guard and capturing Johannes's corpse, which was sent as proof of their victory to Omdurman, the Sudanese capital under the Mahdists.

Gallery. A passageway cut through earth or masonry in a fortification for communication or, if loopholed, for protected infantry fire.

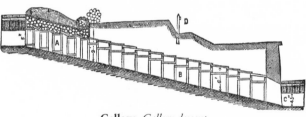

Gallery *Gallery descent*

Gallieni, Joseph Simon (1849–1916). A French soldier who left St. Cyr [q.v.] in August 1870 to fight in the Franco-Prussian War [q.v.]. He was wounded and captured at Sedan [q.v.] on 1 September, and while a prisoner, he learned German. After his release in 1871 he was posted to the island of Réunion and in 1878 to Senegal, where he engaged in several expeditions against African chiefs and empires. From 1882 to 1885 he was stationed in Martinique. In 1886 he was appointed governor of the French Sudan, where he waged war on the Mandingos [see Franco-Mandingo War]. In May 1888 he returned to France and studied at the École Supérieure de la Guerre. In September 1892 he was sent to Tonkin. He returned briefly in January 1896 to France, where he was promoted general of division and put in command of an expedition to Madagascar. There he overturned the government of Queen Ranavalona II (1829–1893), suppressed a revolt of the Merinas in 1895–96, and established a military government with himself as its leader [see Madagascar, Warfare in]. He remained until 1905. His colonial successes were the result of what was known as the *tache d'huile* strategy [q.v.], a French colonial system for expanding control and pacification of an area.

He was a decisive man, some thought too decisive. His chief of staff once spoke of "one of those long conferences he holds on grave issues—they generally last from two to five minutes." He was governor of Paris in 1914 and is best known for rushing reinforcements to the Marne in taxis and other civilian automobiles. He became minister of war in 1915. He died of prostatitis and was created a marshal of France posthumously in 1921.

Galliffet, Marquis Gaston Alexandre (1830–1909). A French soldier who won renown during the Franco-Prussian War by leading a cavalry charge at Sedan [q.v.] on 2 September 1870. News of the charge led William I [q.v.] of Prussia to exclaim: *"O, les brave gens!"* (Oh, the brave people!) He became a general of division in 1875 and later served as president of a cavalry board that revised cavalry regulations and tactics.

Galling Fire. The sustained fire of artillery or small arms that greatly hampers the safe movement of an enemy.

Galloper. A courier or aide.

Galloper Guns. Light, mobile guns of small caliber with shafts for a horse.

Gallwey, Thomas Joseph (1852–1933). A British military surgeon who joined the army as a doctor in 1874 and was promoted surgeon major in 1885. He served on the Gordon Relief Expedition [q.v.] that same year. In 1892 he transferred to the Egyptian army and was principal medical officer on Kitchener's staff during the reconquest of the Sudan [q.v.] in 1896–98. During the Second Anglo-Boer War [q.v.] he served in South Africa.

Galons. Braiding on sleeves to indicate officer ranks, first used by French Zouaves [q.v.] and later by French and Confederate officers.

Galvanized Yankees. The 2,700 Confederate prisoners of war who during the American Civil War agreed to join the Union army to fight Indians in the West. They were formed into the 1st through 6th U.S. Volunteer Infantry. Many served under aliases or changed their names after the war.

These were part of the estimated 100,000 southerners who fought for the Union during the Civil War. Many of them came from western Tennessee and what is now West Virginia, where pro-Union sentiment always prevailed.

After the war the term was also applied to Confederate veterans who enlisted to fight Indians.

Gamarra, Agustín (1785–1841). An ethnic Inca Peruvian soldier who became president of Peru in 1829–33 and later led a revolt against his successor, Luis José Orbegaso (1795–1847). In the War of the Peru-Bolivian Confederation [q.v.] in 1839, he commanded the Chilean reserve division. After the Chilean victories at Yungay [q.v.] on 20 June 1839 he again became president, an office he held until he was killed in the Battle of Ingaví (Yngaví) [q.v.] during the Peru-Bolivia War [q.v.] on 20 November 1841.

Gamelle. A French army mess tin. This was sometimes a large bowl containing the rations for three, five, or seven men.

Gamonal, Battle of (10 November 1808), Peninsular War. At this town in central Spain, six miles west of Talavera, a French force under Marshal Nicolas Soult [q.v.] destroyed a Spanish force under the Conde de Belvedere in a short, bloody fight that left 2,500 Spanish dead or wounded. The French captured 1,000 prisoners, 12 standards, and 16 guns and themselves suffered 65 casualties.

Gandhi, Mohandas Karamchand (1869–1948). An Indian lawyer, politician, and social reformer. During the Second Anglo-Boer War he raised an ambulance corps in Natal and led his men onto the field to collect the wounded. He was mentioned in dispatches and awarded the War Medal. In 1915, during the First World War, he earned the Kaiser-i-Hind [q.v.] medal in gold, the highest order, for his recruiting efforts in India and other "services to the Empire." In World War II, a proclaimed pacifist, he raised a rebellion against British rule.

Gandoura. A Moroccan smock that French troops sometimes wore over their uniforms in North Africa.

Gandzha / Ganja, Battle of (26 September 1826), Russo-Persian War. Some 15,000 Russians under Ivan F. Paskevich [q.v.] defeated 15,000 Persians under Abbas Mirza [q.v.] near this city (present-day Kirovabad, also once known as Elisavetpol) in western Azerbaidzhan, south of the Kura River, 110 miles southeast of Tiflis. The horses of the Turkish cavalry were terrified by the Russian artillery and provoked a rout.

Gantlope or Gantlet. See Gauntlet.

GAR. See Grand Army of the Republic.

García Hernández, Battle of (23 July 1812), Peninsular War. After Wellington's victory at Salamanca [q.v.], Allied cavalry pursued the retreating French. Near this village, seven miles beyond Alba de Tormes, four squadrons (445 men) of heavy dragoons of the King's German Legion [q.v.] under General Eberhardt von Bock (fl. 1812) attacked the rear guard of General Maximilien Foy [q.v.], three battalions of infantry, in a properly formed square. In this rare instance the cavalry broke and scattered the square. In another maneuver the dragoons made a successful uphill charge against a French column. The Allied cavalry suffered a loss of 150; the French lost 1,400.

García Iñiguez, Calixto (1836?–1898). A Cuban revolutionary, lawyer, and soldier who was one of the leaders in the Ten Years' War [q.v.] of 1868–78 against Spain. In 1898, during the Spanish-American War [q.v.], he led the Cuban forces at El Caney [q.v.]. He was widely known in the United States through the immensely popular essay of Elbert Hubbard (1856–1915) *A Message to Garcia* [q.v.].

Garde. Indian soldiers trained in European infantry tactics.

Garde du Corps. A French term used in the German armies for heavy bodyguard cavalry.

Garde Impériale. This French Imperial Guard of Napoleon was one of the most famous guard units in history. It had its beginnings in the Corps of Guides, an escort squadron that accompanied Napoleon during his Italian Campaign of 1796–97 and later accompanied him to Egypt. In 1799, when Napoleon became first consul, he combined this unit and the guard of the Directory to form the Consular Guard, a unit of infantry and cavalry, which took part in the Battle of Marengo on 14 June 1800. In 1804 the Consular Guard became the Garde Impériale. It was then about the size of a division and fought at Austerlitz and Jena [qq.v.].

Chasseurs-à-pied and grenadiers each formed a regiment of two battalions of six companies in the Garde Impériale. In 1806–08 and again in 1811–14 these were expanded to two regiments each. The guard cavalry consisted of grenadiers-à-cheval and chasseurs-à-cheval. There was originally one company of artillery, later expanded to a regiment. Almost from the beginning the guard included velites [q.v.].

In 1805 the Imperial Guard numbered 12,000; two years later a foreign regiment was added. By 1812 the unit had reached a total of 56,169. About 30,000 took part in Napoleon's Russian Campaign [q.v.]; only about 2,000 survived. Rebuilt, by 1814 it numbered 112,482, almost an army in itself.

The Guard was an elite service, and its prerogatives were many: Each grade was equivalent to the next higher grade in the line regiments. The pay was much higher. While a line sergeant drew only 62 centimes per day, a guards sergeant drew 222 centimes. The guards had their own hospital at Gros-Caillou, near Paris. Mounted noncommissioned officers were supplied with civilian grooms and on the march, a line unit encountering a guard unit was required to halt and sound Aux Champs [q.v.], the ceremonial salute, on a drum or trumpet.

The complex organization of the guard often changed as units were added, disbanded, or amalgamated, but there came to be three main sections. The Old Guard was the elite of the elite; no one could belong who had not served five or ten years

Garde Impériale *Napoleon's Imperial Guard from left to right: chasseur-à-cheval and marines*

in the army and fought in two campaigns. The Middle Guard was added in 1806, and finally the Young Guard, made up of the best of the annual conscript class, was formed in 1809. At Waterloo the Garde Impériale fielded a total of twelve infantry and five cavalry regiments and sixteen batteries of artillery, the finest fighting force of the Napoleonic era.

Napoleon's Garde Impériale disappeared after the Battle of Waterloo, but on 1 May 1854 it was revived by Louis III (1808–1873). It then consisted of three regiments of grenadiers, four of voltigeurs, and one of Zouaves [qq.v.]. After the fall of the empire in 1871 there were no longer Guard troops in France.

Garde Mobile. This French military organization, established in 1868, consisted of men of military age who had escaped conscription. Service was for five years with annual training periods of two weeks, served a day at a time under conditions that allowed men to return home every evening. Officers were appointed by the prefects; noncommissioned officers were selected by the army. Unorganized, ill trained, and ill equipped, members of the Garde Mobile tended to be insubordinate and inclined to insurrection.

In July 1870, on the eve of the Franco-Prussian War [q.v.], the Garde Mobile numbered 492,585 men, 120,000 of whom, it was hoped, would be available for service, but this proved unrealistic.

Garde Nationale. Originally a volunteer citizens' militia restricted until 1848 to members of the propertied class. It was established by the Committee of Safety on 13 July 1789, the day before the storming of the Bastille, to provide protection of lives and property during internal disorders. In 1790 provincial battalions were formed, and in 1793 it became a compulsory force of men from sixteen to sixty years old under the direction of civil or municipal authorities. It was soon merged into the Napoleonic armies. Reconstituted by Napoleon, it was returned to its original mission. Reformed by Louis XVIII (1755–1824), it was suppressed by Charles X (1757–1836) in 1827. In 1830, following the July Revolution, it was revived by Louis Philippe. In 1870 it took some part in the fighting against the Germans in the Franco-Prussian War, but its gradual abolition was decreed on 24 August 1871.

Garde Royale. A French military organization formed in 1826 and composed of five French and two Swiss regiments.

Gardiner, John (1801–1877). An Englishman who deserted the British service in India and joined the Khalsa [q.v.], the Sikh army raised by Ranjit Singh [q.v.]. Of the many Europeans who served in the Khalsa, few could have been as odious as Gardiner. He rose in the service and in 1842 commanded an expedition to Sialkat to suppress a mutiny. He gained his name for infamy and a colonelcy by an incident during the tumultuous period of the anarchy in the Punjab [q.v.], when an officer named Jodha Ram offended a Sikh sirdar (chief) and was sentenced to have a thumb, his nose, and his ears cut off. Because Ram was a Brahmin, no one could be found to carry out the sentence until Gardiner came forward and with a razor performed the deed.

Gardner Machine Gun. A type of automatic weapon invented by William Montgomery Gardner (1824–1901), a former officer in the American army during the Mexican War [q.v.] and a former brigadier general in the Confederate army during the American Civil War. The gun was introduced into the army in the 1870s. It had gravity feed, two parallel barrels, and a crankshaft trigger with a handle that opened and closed the breechblocks. The rotating handle drove a crankshaft that pushed the breechblocks and barrels open and shut so that the barrels were fired in turn. The 1879 model had twin air- or water-cooled barrels.

Gardner machine gun on tripod

Gardner machine gun carriage

Garfield, James Abram (1831–1881). American soldier and politician who became the 20th president of the United States. He was an orphan who managed to graduate from Williams College and become a schoolteacher. In 1859 he was elected to the Ohio Senate. During the American Civil War he fought in the Union army as a lieutenant colonel and then as a colonel of the 42nd Ohio. He was soon given a brigade, and on 11 January 1862, on winning a victory at Big Sandy Valley, he was made a brigadier general. He fought at Shiloh and at Corinth [qq.v.], and he served on the military commission that recommended the removal of Fitz-John Porter [q.v.] from the army. He was appointed chief of staff to General William S. Rosecrans [q.v.] and was promoted major general.

After the war Garfield served nine terms as a congressman, and in 1880 he was elected president. He was inaugurated on 4 March 1881. On 2 July in the Washington, D.C., railroad station he was shot by an assassin, Charles J. Guiteau (1840?–1882), a lawyer and disappointed office seeker. He died of his wounds on 19 December.

Garibaldi, Giuseppe (1807–1882). An Italian revolutionary and soldier who was born in Nice. He joined the Sardinian navy and in 1834 became involved in the Young Italy Association of Giuseppe Mazzini (1805–1872). In 1836 he was forced to flee when it was discovered that he was involved in a plot to mutiny and seize Genoa. From 1836 to 1848 he lived in South America and while in Brazil eloped with and married a beautiful Creole, Anita Riveira da Silva. In the War of the Triple Alliance [q.v.] he fought on the side of the Allies and was among the besieged at Montevideo [q.v.].

He later operated as a privateer for the rebellious province of Rio Grande do Sul against Brazil. In 1846 he joined the rebels in Uruguay and formed an Italian Legion, which won the battles of Cerro and San Antonio.

Learning of an incipient revolution in Italy against the Austrians, he returned to Europe. After landing in Nice on 21 June 1848, he offered his services to King Charles Albert, or Carlo Alberto [q.v.], king of Sardinia, and raised for him an army of 3,000 volunteers, telling them: "I offer no pay, no quarters, no food. I offer only hunger, thirst, forced marches, battle, and death. Let him who loves his country with his heart, and not merely with his lips, follow me!"

When Charles Albert was defeated in the Battle of Custozza [q.v.] on 24 July 1848, Garibaldi fled to Switzerland. He then made his way to Rome, where the Roman Republic appointed him commander of the defenses of San Pancrazio. There on 30 April 1849 he gained a victory over the French. In May he dispersed the Bourbon troops at Palestrina, Velletri, and elsewhere. When Rome fell to French forces, he led his troops on a remarkable retreat through central Italy, pursued by the troops of France, Spain, Austria, and Naples [see Palestrina, Battle of]. He finally escaped to Piedmont and then emigrated to the United States, where he became a naturalized citizen. He worked as a candlemaker on Staten Island, New York, until 1854, when he returned to Italy. In the Austro-Piedmontese War of 1859 he briefly commanded a volunteer corps of the Piedmont-Sardinian army known as Cacciatori delle Alpi (Alpine Hunters). On 8 May he defeated an Austrian force at Casale. On 23 May he crossed the Ticino and captured the Alpine territory as far as the Tyrol.

His first wife having died, he briefly left off fighting to marry the Countess Raimondi at Como in northern Italy. He then rushed south, where he organized a volunteer unit known as Red Shirts [q.v.], which on 11 May 1860 landed at Marsala under the protection of two British warships and successfully invaded Sicily, defeating Neapolitan forces at Calatafimi [q.v.]. On 30 May Palermo fell to Garibaldi, and on 6 June he captured 20,000 Neapolitan regulars. Leading his men to the mainland, he defeated the forces of the Kingdom of the Two Sicilies. On 7 September he entered Naples and a month later at Volturno routed the last remnant of 40,000 men of the Bourbon army. On 7 November he accompanied King Victor Emmanuel II (1820–1878) in a triumphant entry into Naples.

After the union of the Kingdom of the Two Sicilies with Sardinia and the proclamation on 17 March 1861 naming Victor Emmanuel king of Italy, Garibaldi retired to his farm on the six-square-mile island of Caprera in the Tyrrhenian Sea, off the northeast coast of Sardinia. He was now an international celebrity. In the American Civil War the Confederates formed a Garibaldi Legion, and in the Union army the 39th New York Volunteer Infantry called themselves the Garibaldi Guard. Although Garibaldi toyed with the idea of fighting on the Union side in the war and was actually offered a major generalcy, he ultimately rejected the offer.

In 1862, angered at the ceding of Nice and Savoy to France, he organized and launched an attack on Rome, but he was defeated in the Battle of Aspromonte [q.v.] on 27 August. After a brief imprisonment he was allowed to return to Caprera. In 1864 he traveled to England, where he was received with great enthusiasm.

When Prussia and Austria went to war in 1866 and Piedmont took the opportunity to attack Austrian forces in Italy [see Seven Weeks' War], he took command of a volunteer army and defeated the Austrians in the Battle of Monte Asello on 3 July, at Lodrone on the 7th, at Darso on the 10th, at Candino on the 16th, at Ampola on the 19th, and Bezzecca on the 21st. He was about to attack Trent when Otto von Bismarck (1815–1898) made it clear that he would not permit the Italian occupation of the Trentine Tyrol. Ordered by General Alfonso Ferrero di La Marmora [q.v.] to halt his victorious march and pull back, he gave his famous laconic reply "*Obbedisco* [I obey]."

In 1867, while planning another march on Rome, he was arrested and escorted back to Caprera, where he was kept under a loose house arrest. He escaped and tried again. On 23 October, at the head of a small army, he entered papal territory at Passo Corese, and on the 25th he captured Monterotondo, but on 2 November his force was routed at Mentana by French and papal troops. He was again arrested and taken back to his island.

During the Franco-Prussian War [q.v.] of 1870–71 he journeyed to France and, commanding the Garibaldi Legion in the French army, defeated German forces at Châtillon, Autun, and Dijon. These were the old warrior's last successful battles. He later was in the debacle of Bourbaki's army at the Lisaine [q.v.].

Giuseppe Garibaldi (the elder)

Garibaldi, Giuseppe (1879–1950). Born in Melbourne, Australia, and called Peppino, he was the son of Ricciotti Garibaldi and the grandson of the elder Giuseppe Garibaldi [qq.v.]. In 1897 he fought at his father's side in the Greek army in the war against the Turks, and in 1901–02 he fought in the Boer army during the Second Anglo-Boer War [q.v.]. In 1904 he fought alongside Venezuelan insurrectionists. In 1913 during the Balkan wars he commanded a brigade in the Greek army, and in the First World War he joined the Italian army and rose to command the Alpine Brigade. An antifascist, he emigrated to New York, where he devoted himself to business.

Garibaldi, Menotti (1840–1903). An Italian soldier born in Brazil who was a son of the elder Giuseppe Garibaldi [q.v.]. In 1859 and again in 1862 he fought beside his father in Italy. He joined the French army to fight in the Franco-Prussian War [q.v.]. Elected to the Italian Parliament, he joined the party of the extreme left.

Garibaldi, Ricciotti (1847–1924). An Italian soldier, born in Montevideo, Uruguay, the son of the elder Giuseppe Garibaldi [q.v.] and a brother of Menotti Garibaldi [q.v.]. He joined the French army and distinguished himself in the Franco-Prussian War [q.v.] in 1870–71. In 1897 he fought the Turks in Greece. During the First World War he organized the Garibaldi Legion to fight for France. After the war he welcomed Benito Mussolini (1883–1845), asserting his Black Shirts to be worthy successors to his father's Red Shirts.

Garigliano, Battle of (October 1850), Italian Wars of Independence. Italian patriots under Colonel Enrico Cialdini [q.v.] defeated Neapolitans under Francis II (1836–1894) on the banks of this river in southeast Latium.

Garland. A wooden rack or framework used to keep round shot in neat pyramids or piles.

Garland, John (1792–1861). An American soldier who was commissioned a first lieutenant in the 35th Infantry in 1813 and saw service in the last part of the War of 1812 [q.v.]. During the Second Seminole War [q.v.] he was castigated by some for inviting Seminole warriors to a feast, plying them with liquor, and then making prisoners of them. He became a colonel in 1849, and in the Mexican War [q.v.] he was cited for his gallantry in four battles and won brevets to brigadier general. In 1853 he was appointed to command in New Mexico, where he took action against the Ute and Mogollon Indians. In 1858 he was succeeded by Benjamin Bonneville [q.v.].

Garlington, Ernest Albert (1853–1934). An American officer who was graduated from West Point in 1876 and joined the 7th Cavalry immediately after the Battle of the Little Bighorn [q.v.]. In 1877 he took part in the Nez Percé War [q.v.] and fought in the Battle of Canyon Creek, Montana, on 13 September. In 1883 he joined the Signal Office and led one of the unsuccessful expeditions attempting to relieve Lieutenant Adolphus Washington Greely [q.v.] who was stranded in the Arctic.

Returning to frontier duty, he won a Medal of Honor [q.v.] for "distinguished gallantry" on 29 December 1890 in the Battle of Wounded Knee [q.v.], where he was shot in the elbow. He was promoted captain in 1891 and was named to a board that revised the cavalry drill regulations.

He served in the Spanish-American War [q.v.] and was present at the surrender of the Spanish forces in Cuba. After serving in the Philippines, he retired as a brigadier general in 1917, only to be recalled for duty the following year for service in World War I.

Garnett, Richard Brooke (1817–1863). An American army officer who was a cousin of Robert Selden Garnett [q.v.]. He was graduated from West Point in 1841 and fought against the Seminoles in 1841–42 [see Seminole Wars]. He did not see active service in the Mexican War [q.v.] but was in command at Fort Laramie, Wyoming, from 1852 to 1854. In 1855 he was promoted captain. He resigned in May 1861 at the outbreak of the American Civil War to join the Confederate army as a major. On 14 November of that year he was promoted brigadier general. He commanded the Stonewall Brigade in the Battle of Kernstown, after which Stonewall Jackson preferred charges against him and placed him under arrest for retreating when his brigade ran out of ammunition. The trial was never concluded, and he was reassigned to Longstreet's corps, in which he saw action at South Mountain, Antietam, and Fredericksburg [qq.v.].

On the third day of the Battle of Gettysburg his brigade of five Virginia regiments led Pickett's Charge [q.v.]. He was killed in the charge, and his body was never recovered. After the war his sword was found in a Baltimore pawnshop.

Garnett, Robert Selden (1819–1861). An American soldier who was a cousin of Richard Brooke Garnett [q.v.], with whom he was graduated from West Point in 1841. He served in the Mexican War [q.v.], earning two brevets, and in the Second Seminole War [q.v.]. In 1855 he led a successful expedition against Puget Sound Indians. In 1858 he conducted a campaign against hostile Indians in which he gained a reputation for indiscriminate attacks against peaceful as well as belligerent tribes.

In April 1861, at the outbreak of the American Civil War, he resigned his commission as a major and joined the Confederate army. He was quickly promoted brigadier general and sent to northwestern Virginia (West Virginia). On 13 July he was killed near Corrick's Ford on the Cheat River while forming a skirmishing line, becoming the first general officer to be killed on either side in the war.

Garnier, Marie Joseph François (1839–1873). A French naval officer who in 1862 was appointed inspector of natives in Cochin China and the administrator of Cholon (today a section of Ho Chi Minh City). In a number of exploring expeditions, some in Indochina and in China, he penetrated territory previously unknown to Europeans, notably in the Mekong River area, where he mapped 3,100 miles of previously unknown territory in Cambodia and Vietnam. In 1870, just before the Franco-Prussian War [q.v.], he returned to France, where he served as a staff officer in the eighth sector during the siege of Paris [q.v.]. After the war he returned to Asia and in 1873 followed the course of the Yangtze Kiang, the principal river of China, to the waterfalls. He was next ordered to establish a new colony in Tongking (Tonkin), and on 20 November 1873 he captured Hanoi, its capital. He was killed by Black Flags [q.v.] the following day. [See French Indochina War, Second.]

Garrison. 1. As a noun, a town, fort, or camp occupied by troops for an extended period.

2. As a noun, the troops so placed.

3. As a verb, to place soldiers into a town or fortifications.

Garrison *The garrison on Fort Sumter, South Carolina, watching the firing on the* Star of the West

Garrison Court-Martial. An American legal military tribunal in which the court itself called all witnesses and questioned them. The accused was permitted to ask additional questions and to make a statement if it was "respectful in character."

Garrison House. 1. A blockhouse.

2. In America any house fortified against attacks by Indians.

"Garry Owen." The name of an Irish drinking song adopted by the U.S. 7th Cavalry, which contained many Irish immigrant soldiers. George Custer [q.v.] and his men rode out to its rollicking tune to fight and die in the Battle of the Little Bighorn [q.v.]. The words of the refrain are:

Instead of Spa we'll drink down ale,
And pay the reckoning on the nail:
No man for debt shall go to jail
From Garry Owen in glory.

Garter, Order of the. The oldest and most renowned of the British orders of chivalry, often awarded to distinguished British generals. It was founded for unknown reasons by Edward III (1312–1377) at Windsor in 1348 with the motto *Honi soit qui mal y pense* (Evil to him who evil thinks). Originally limited to twenty-five knights or dames plus the sovereign, it was enlarged by George III (1738–1820) in the early nineteenth century to include some foreign royalty. The Military Knights of Windsor [q.v.] are an adjunct to the order.

Gas Guns. Small arms using air or gas as propellants. Although there were some Danish experiments with gas guns in 1834, the first to be manufactured was an invention of Henri Giffard (1825–1882), a Frenchman who in 1872 patented a gun using a cartridge of compressed air. In 1873 he obtained an American patent for a gun using a steel container of carbon dioxide. Giffard's gun was manufactured in France and in the early 1890s in London. Although some armies experimented with gas guns, none adopted the idea, and production ceased in 1900.

Gas gun

Gasht. A patrol on India's Northwest Frontier [q.v.].

Gas-Operated. Term used to describe an automatic weapon that utilized part of the gas in the barrel after it was fired to unlock the bolt and actuate the loading mechanism.

Gasser, Leopold (1836–1871). An Austrian gunsmith who in 1862 began the manufacture under license of Beaumont-Adams revolvers. He later designed a new revolver that was adopted by the Austro-Hungarian army. Operating in two factories, he turned out 100,000 revolvers a year for military and commercial sales. On his death, his son carried on the business. Its most famous weapon was an 11 mm long-barreled Gasser Montenegrin revolver, so called because of the allegation that the king of Montenegro, having a financial interest in its manufacture, required every adult male to acquire one. Certainly large numbers found their way to the Balkans.

Gatacre, William Forbes (1843–1906). A British soldier who was commissioned an ensign in the 77th Foot, then in Bengal, in 1862. He passed out of the Staff College in 1875 and in 1884 commanded his regiment. He was a fitness fanatic whose men dubbed him General Backacher. In the Hazara Expedition [q.v.] in 1888 he earned the Distinguished Service Order and high marks for his physical endurance. In 1895 he took part in the arduous Chitral Campaign [q.v.]. For his efforts in fighting an outbreak of the plague in Bombay in 1897 he was awarded the Kaiser-i-Hind [q.v.]. In 1898 with the local rank of major general he took part in the reconquest of the Sudan [q.v.] and was knighted (KCB).

When the Second Anglo-Boer War [q.v.] began in October 1899, he sailed to South Africa with the British expeditionary force as a division commander under Sir Redvers Buller [q.v.]. He proved to be inept. His defeat at Stormberg [q.v.] on 9–10 December 1899 was one of the three disasters of Black Week [q.v.]. When he failed to relieve a beleaguered force at Reddersburg in April 1900, Lord Roberts relieved him of his command.

Gatacre had three sons by his first wife, a daughter of the dean of Limerick, whom he married in India in 1875 and divorced in 1892—a rare event among British officers in the nineteenth century—after she had eloped with another man. He retired on 19 March 1904. While exploring rubber forests in Abyssinia, he caught a fever and died on 18 January 1906.

Gate Pa, Battle of (29 April 1864), Second Maori War. About 1,700 British soldiers and sailors under Major General Sir Duncan Alexander Cameron (1808–1888) unsuccessfully attacked an unknown number of Maori warriors in a New Zealand pa (stockade). A second assault the following day found the Maoris gone, leaving behind 40 dead and wounded. British losses were 14 officers and 98 other ranks killed or wounded. [See Maori Wars.]

Gatewood, Charles Baehr (1853–1896). An American officer who was graduated from West Point in 1877. Posted to the 6th Cavalry in the Southwest, he probably saw more action serving with Apache scouts than any other officer. He served in the Victorio War of 1879–80 [see Victorio] and in many small actions. In 1879 General Nelson Miles [q.v.] selected him to go to Mexico, find Geronimo [q.v.], and persuade him to surrender, a difficult mission he successfully accomplished.

Geronimo remained on a reservation until in 1881, following the Cibicue incident, [q.v.] he and Juh [q.v.] took their people south into the Sierra Madre. Gatewood was with General George Crook [q.v.] in his expedition into the Sierra Madre in 1883 and in the campaign against Geronimo in 1885–86. He served in California and in the Dakotas during the Sioux troubles there [see Ghost Dance Disturbances]. Injured by an explosion of dynamite, he was forced to retire. His only reward for his years of service was burial in Arlington National Cemetery and a belated pension of seventeen dollars a month granted to his widow.

Gatling, Richard Jordan (1818–1903). An American inventor who developed machines for sowing cotton seeds and various grains. In 1849, after studying medicine for two and a half years, he settled in Indianapolis, Indiana, where he married the daughter of a physician and remained for the next twenty years. In 1850 he invented a hemp-breaking machine, and in 1857 a steam plow. In 1862 during the American Civil War he invented the machine gun that bears his name [q.v.]. A naive man, he later said, "It occurred to me that if I could invent a machine—a gun—that would by its rapidity of fire enable one man to do as much battle duty as a hundred, that it would to a great extent, supersede the necessity of large armies, and consequently exposure to battle and disease would be greatly diminished."

Federal authorities were slow to adopt Gatling's gun. Colonel (later Major General) James Wolfe Ripley [q.v.], the Union's chief of ordnance, who was sixty-eight years old when the war began, opposed every innovation in ordnance that was suggested to him in its course. On 9 May 1865 Gatling patented an improved version of his gun, one that used fixed ammunition rather than individually loaded chambers, and in January of that year it was demonstrated to Major General Alexander Brydie Dyer (1815–1874), who had succeeded Ripley. In August 1866 the Gatling gun [q.v.] was officially approved. The army ordered 100. This success was followed by sales to Russia in 1867. Sales to Turkey soon followed. In 1870 Gatling moved to Hartford, Connecticut, where, after further improvements, he sold the rights to manufacture his gun to the Colt Firearms Company. By 1880 most armies were equipped with the weapon. Its first American official use in a major war was in the Battle of Santiago [q.v.] in 1898, but by this time it was almost obsolete, having been surpassed by the Maxim machine gun [q.v.].

In 1893 Gatling had patented an electrically powered gun capable of firing 3,000 rounds per minute that was never adopted. Among his later inventions were a new method for casting cannon and a motorized plow. He was for six years president of the American Association of Inventors and Manufacturers.

Gatling Gun. A crank-operated machine gun with six revolving barrels developed in 1861 and patented on 4 November 1862 by Richard Jordan Gatling [q.v.]. It is said to have been the first practical machine gun. Although not fully automatic—it required an operator to turn the crank—it could deliver heavy bursts of fire at a rate of 250 rounds (some said 500 rounds) per minute. Over forty years it was chambered in more than a dozen calibers. All agree it was first used in the American Civil War, but accounts, all undocumented, differ on how or when. A number are known to have been used in the Battle of Nashville [q.v.] on 15–16 December 1864, but it is said they were first used a few weeks earlier at the siege of Petersburg [q.v.] by General Benjamin Butler [q.v.], who had purchased 12 with his own money for his unit.

In 1865 Gatling offered an improved version that used fixed ammunition. It was 1866 before the U.S. army officially adopted the weapon with an order for fifty .50 caliber and fifty 1-inch. It was then regarded as an artillery piece rather than an infantry support weapon. During the American Indian Wars nearly 500 were purchased, but except for those used in the defense of forts, few were ever fired. The expense of providing ammunition precluded firing practice.

The first documented use of the gun occurred in 1874 in three battles fought by General Nelson A. Miles [q.v.] against Indians. In October 1877 it was used in the Battle of Bearpaw Mountain [q.v.] against the Nez Percés, and in 1878 it was used in the Bannock War [q.v.].

It was first used as an infantry weapon in Cuba, when Second Lieutenant John Henry Parker (1874?–1942) organized the 1st Provisional Machine Gun Company. At the Battle of San Juan Hill [q.v.] one gun fired 18,000 rounds. Colonel Theodore Roosevelt [q.v.] wrote: "Parker deserved more credit than any one man in the entire campaign. . . . [H]e had the rare good judgment and foresight to see the possibilities of the machine guns. . . ."

In 1867 a Russian colonel (later general) Gorloff headed a purchasing commission to the United States that bought 20 Model 1866 guns chambered for .42 caliber infantry cartridges. A second order for 70 was increased to 100 in exchange for a license to manufacture. The guns' brass Gatling plates were then replaced by plates bearing Gorloff's name, giving rise to the Russian belief that Gatling had purloined his invention from Gorloff. These guns were last used at the siege of Port Arthur in the Russo-Japanese War.

Gatling Gun *Model 1865 Gatling gun, one-inch caliber*

In 1870 Turkey ordered from Gatling 200 of his guns, and the Russo-Turkish War [q.v.] of 1877–78 became the first in which Gatling guns were employed by both sides in a battle. When the Canadian army ordered the gun, Lieutenant Arthur Howard of the Connecticut militia, later killed in South Africa in the Second Anglo-Boer War [q.v.], was hired to command a battery. In 1874 the British army, the last European army to acquire the gun, adopted a ten-barrel version in .45 caliber. Two Gatlings saw service in 1879 during the Zulu War in the Battle of Ulundi [qq.v.].

In 1885 American First Lieutenant Edward S. Farrow wrote: "Among the many important and valuable inventions in fire-arms, of which the present century has been prolific, there is none that equals the Gatling gun in originality of design, rapidity of fire and effectiveness." The slang term "gat" for a handgun is derived from Gatling.

Gaulauli, Battle of (22 May 1858), Indian Mutiny. Near this village a column under Sir John Rose [q.v.] engaged 20,000 mutineers and rebels under Tantia Topi, the rani of Jhansi [qq.v.], and others. Although it at first appeared that Rose would be overwhelmed by the great numbers opposing him, he drove his enemies from the field.

Gauntlet. A form of punishment used in many armies, but particularly the Russian army, in which two lines of soldiers, facing each other, armed with sticks, clubs, whips, or other weapons, struck the culprit as he passed between them, sometimes carrying a heavy stone to slow his pace.

Gawilghur, Battle of (15 December 1803), Second Maratha War. Major General Arthur Wellesley (the future Duke of Wellington) with 10,000 men attacked this strong fort on a mountaintop, 170 miles northeast of Aurangabad, garrisoned by about 4,000 Marathas. On 12 December 1803 nine siege guns were with difficulty dragged into position before the north gate of the fort and four more into position at the south gate, where they made practicable breaches by the night of the 14th. The assault was launched on the 15th, and the fort taken at a cost of 14 killed and 112 wounded.

Gazette. 1. Any one of the three British official journals entitled the *London Gazette,* the *Dublin Gazette,* and the *Edinburgh Gazette* published twice a week, on Tuesdays and Fridays. They listed government appointments and promotions, published the names of bankrupts, and recorded other public notices.

2. To be "in the gazette" was to be a bankrupt, but in military usage, "to be gazetted" was to be commissioned as an officer or to be given an award, honor, appointment, or promotion. To be "gazetted out" was to resign.

Gazons. Wedge-shaped pieces of earth or sod covered with grass, usually about a foot long and six inches thick, used to line the exteriors of parapets, ramparts, banquettes, etc., in fortifications.

Gcaleka War (1877–78). On 5 October 1877 Sir Henry Bartle Edward Frere (1815–1884), the governor of Cape Colony and the first high commissioner for the territory of South Africa, announced that he had deposed Sarile [q.v.], the Xhosa chief of the Gcalekas, and that Gcalekaland, on the southeast coast of Africa, was to be invaded. On 17 October a force of 500 police, 1,000 colonial volunteers, and 6,000 Mfengu [q.v.] and Thembu levies under Commandant Charles Duncan Griffith [q.v.] marched into the territory. They were initially unable to bring the Gcalekas to battle, for they had fled eastward with their families and cattle, but with their families and cattle secure, the tribesmen returned and on 2 December about 1,000 attacked police and soldiers at a place called Holland's Shop. They were repulsed with difficulty.

On 13 January the Gcalekas suffered a severe defeat in the Battle of Nyumaga and again on 7 February 1878 in the Battle of Centane, in which they lost some 400 killed. Their spirit broken, they fought no more.

Geary, John White (1819–1873). An American soldier and politician who first saw action while leading a regiment of volunteers in the Mexican War [q.v.], in which he received five wounds in the storming of Chapultepec [q.v.]. In 1850–51 he served as mayor of San Francisco. He was territorial governor of Kansas from 1856–1857 during the Border War [q.v.]. At the beginning of the American Civil War he commanded the 28th Pennsylvania and saw much action, being wounded at Bolivar Heights, near Harpers Ferry, (West) Virginia, and twice more at Cedar Mountain [q.v.]. In March 1862 he was captured at Leesburg, Virginia, but he was soon exchanged and promoted to brigadier general. He commanded a division at Chancellorsville [q.v.], where he was struck in the chest by a cannonball and for weeks afterward was able to speak only in whispers. Transferred to the West, he fought in the Chattanooga Campaign (October–November 1863) under Joseph Hooker [q.v.]. Geary's son died in his arms in the confused night battle at Wauhatchie [q.v.] on 28–29 October 1863. He took part in the storming of Lookout Mountain [q.v.] on 24 November. For a time he was military governor of Savannah, and he served in the Carolinas Campaign [q.v.].

At the end of the war he was brevetted a major general with an unusual citation: "For fitness to command and promptness to execute." After the war he was elected governor of Pennsylvania and was briefly considered as a presidential candidate for the National Labor Reform Party. He was only fifty-three at the time of his death.

Gebelis. An elite corps in the Turkish army famous for its endurance and fighting qualities.

Gebora, Battle of (19 February 1811), Peninsular War. A Spanish and Portuguese army of Extremadura (Estramadura), numbering 12,400, under Lieutenant General Gabriel Mandizabal, attempting to relieve the besieged town of Badajoz [q.v.], was defeated by 7,000 French under Marshal Nicolas Soult [q.v.]. The Allies lost 850 killed and wounded plus 4,000 taken prisoner and 17 guns; the French lost 400.

Gee, John Henry (1819–1876). An American doctor who, during the American Civil War, served as an officer in the Confederate army and commanded the prison camp at Salisbury, North Carolina. On 25 November 1864 there was a mass breakout from the overcrowded prison, and artillery as well as infantry was used to contain it. Casualties were sustained on both sides. At the close of the war, in November 1865, Gee was imprisoned and charged with murder. In August 1866, after a trial that lasted five months, he was, unlike Henry Wirtz [q.v.], acquitted and released. He returned to the practice of medicine and was killed while fighting a fire in Florida.

Geffrard, Nicholas Fabre (1806–1879). A Haitian soldier and politician who led the successful insurrection of 1858–59 that overthrew the "emperor" Faustin, who, as Faustin Élie Soulouque (1785–1867), had been elected president in 1847 and had pronounced himself emperor in 1849. The victorious Geffrard proclaimed a republic and served as president from 1859 to 1867.

Gefreiter. A German army grade above a private but below a corporal. A *Gefreiter* was not considered a noncommissioned officer.

Gelibach. The chief of the gebelis [q.v.] in the Turkish army. He ranked just below the toppibachi, or chief of artillery.

Gendarme. A member of a gendarmerie [q.v.].

Gendarmerie. An armed military force for the maintenance of public order.

Gendarmerie Nationale, La. A French paramilitary constabulary first formed in December 1800–February 1801 from the Maréchausée Royale, a force of literate veterans that had been formed in 1790 to keep public order. Gendarmerie Nationale members, usually specially selected soldiers, received much higher pay than others. In 1802 it was reorganized, and detachments were placed in each commune, where they were active in hunting up those who attempted to escape conscription. After 1812 the Gendarmerie Nationale was itself a source of recruits. In 1885 it contained about 27,000 men.

Gendarmes d'Elite, Les. A part of the French Garde Impériale [q.v.], raised on 19 March 1802 to be responsible for the security of Napoleon's person, particularly on ceremonial occasions. It was disbanded on 23 April 1814 but was briefly revived during the Hundred Days [q.v.].

Gendarmes d'Ordonnance. A unit raised on 23 September 1806 from the sons of returned émigrés. The young aristocrats were unpopular, however, and on 23 October of the following year the unit was disbanded.

General. 1. Any general officer of whatever grade.

2. In many European armies a rank just below field marshal, sometimes referred to as full general. In the American army, stars were used as insignia, as they are still: one for a brigadier general, two for a major general, three for a lieutenant general and four for a general. Grant, Sherman, and Sheridan [qq.v.] were the only full generals in the nineteenth century.

3. In the Confederate army, general was the highest rank, but all Confederate generals of whatever rank wore the same insignia: three large stars within a wreath.

According to General Karl von Clausewitz [q.v.]: "Generals have never risen from the very learned or erudite class of officer, but have been mostly men who, from the circumstances of their position, could not have attained to any great amount of knowledge." [See Generals, Confederate; Generals, Union; Brigadier / Brigadier General; Major General; Lieutenant General; Colonel General; Captain General; General of Brigade; General of Division; Field Marshal; General of the Army; Commander-in-Chief.]

4. A drumroll. To "beat the general" was to call for the assembly of troops.

General Court-Martial. The highest military court in the United States in the nineteenth century. It was capable of pronouncing a death sentence for certain crimes.

General Engagement. A major battle involving all or most of the forces on both sides.

General Hospital. The hospital farthest removed from the line of battle. It received those sick and wounded from field hospitals who required more intensive care.

General-in-Chief. 1. A corps commander in Napoleon's army who was not a marshal.

2. The highest-ranking general in an organization or an area containing more than one major general.

Generalissimo. The commander-in-chief of all of a nation's armed forces. This was a title often used in South and Central American countries.

General of Artillery, Cavalry, or Infantry. A German army rank equivalent to lieutenant general in the British and American armies.

General of Brigade. A rank in the French army between a colonel and a general of division [q.v.] corresponding to a brigadier or brigadier general (major general in the German army). The title did not necessarily imply that the holder of that rank actually commanded a brigade.

General of Division. A French army rank, not an appointment or an assignment, ranking above a general of brigade.

General Officers. All officers above the rank of colonel.

General of the Army. An American army rank given by Congress on 26 July 1866 to General U. S. Grant, who thus became the first American general to wear four stars. Both William Tecumseh Sherman and Philip Henry Sheridan [qq.v.] were subsequently given the rank, but with the retirement of Sheridan in 1888 it was discontinued, and the highest rank again became that of lieutenant general. The rank of major general in the American army was, and is still, the highest substantive rank.

General Orders. 1. Orders from a general officer, usually of a permanent nature, concerning policy or administrative affairs of interest to or affecting the entire command. Praise for troops or actions by courts-martial were also sometimes announced in general orders.

2. In the American army, general orders consisted of a series of permanent orders for all sentries on post [see Special Orders].

General Orders No. 9. See Lee's Farewell to the Army of Northern Virginia.

General Orders No. 11, Missouri (25 August 1863). The most severe order affecting civilians given during the American Civil War. Issued by Brigadier General Thomas Ewing [q.v.] at the insistence of his superior, Brigadier General James Henry Lane (1814–1866), it ordered the depopulation of all areas within one mile of a military post in the Missouri counties of Cass, Bates, and Jackson and parts of Vernon. The 15th Kansas Cavalry was assigned the task of clearing the area, and charges of arson and murder were leveled against its troops. So much was burned that the economy in western Missouri was ruined, and the area was long called the Burnt District. This infamous order was memorialized in 1869 by George Caleb Bingham (1811–1879) in his painting *Orders Number Eleven.*

General Orders No. 28 (15 May 1862). When Union Major General Benjamin Butler [q.v.] imposed military government upon New Orleans, he issued General Orders No. 28, which made him infamous in the Confederacy: "As the officers and soldiers of the United States have been subjected to repeated insults from the women (calling themselves ladies) of New Orleans . . . it is ordered that hereafter when any female shall, by word, gesture, or movement, insult or show contempt for any officer or soldier of the United States, she shall be regarded and held liable to be treated as a woman of the town plying her avocation." This order, often called the Woman Order, created an uproar in the Confederacy and made Butler the most hated of Union generals. [See Military Government.] It also created an uproar in Europe. Prime Minister Lord Palmerston (1784–1865) declared: "An Englishman must blush to think that such an act has been committed by one belonging to the Anglo-Saxon race."

General Orders No. 100. An order issued in 1863 during the American Civil War to the Union army bearing upon the humane treatment of prisoners. It read in part: "Men who take up arms against one another in public do not cease on this account to be moral beings, responsible to one another and to God." [See Lieber, Francis.]

General Reserve. The troops held in reserve under the direct control of the senior commander, as contrasted with reserves of subordinate commanders.

Generals, Battle of the. See Ayacucho, Battle of.

Generals, Confederate. Originally there were only three grades of generals in the Confederate army: brigadier general, major general, and general. The rank of lieutenant general, to rank between general and major general, was added in 1862. Of the 425 men appointed to general officer rank, 146 were West Point graduates, including all the full generals and 14 of the 17 lieutenant generals. Most were young. Although two-thirds had served in the Mexican War [q.v.], the average age of a brigadier general was thirty-six, and major generals averaged only a year older.

The rank of general did not ensure safety. Seventy-seven were killed or mortally wounded in action, 15 died of diseases or were killed in accidents, 2 were killed in duels, 1 was assassinated, and 1 committed suicide. Only 299 were serving in grade when the war ended. The longest lived was eighty-nine-year-old Felix H. Robertson (1839–1928), whose nomination was never confirmed by the Confederate Senate.

(A more detailed account of Confederate generals is given in Ezra J. Warner's *Generals in Gray* [Louisiana State University Press, 1959].)

Generals, Union. Until General U. S. Grant was appointed lieutenant general on 2 March 1864, there were only two general officer ranks in the Union army during the American Civil War: brigadier general and major general. In the course of the war 583 men were appointed to full general officer rank (as opposed to brevet ranks), 374 of whom were serving at the end of the war. Most had had some previous military experience, but 188 had none. There were 217 West Point graduates, 11 others had attended the academy but not been graduated, and 9 were graduates of other military schools in the United States or Europe. In the course of the war 47 were killed in action or died of wounds received and 18 died of accidents or diseases.

In addition to those who served as "real generals," commanding brigades or larger units or holding staff positions calling for a general officer, 1,367 other officers were given brevets as generals. In addition to full rank and brevet rank [q.v.], there were ranks in the regular army (USA) and in the volunteers (USV), so that it was possible for a man to have four different ranks. In the USA there were 9 major generals and 152 brevet (Bvt.) major generals; there were only 2 full brigadier generals, but 165 with that brevet rank. In the USV there were 71 major generals and 242 brevet major generals, 195 brigadier generals, USV, and 1,140 brevet brigadier generals.

(For a more detailed study of Union generals, see Ezra J. Warner's *Generals in Blue* [Louisiana State University Press, 1964].)

Generalship. The art and skill of commanding and leading large bodies of soldiers.

General Staff. A group of officers in a division or larger unit who assisted the commanding general in planning, supplying, coordinating, and supervising the operations of the unit. The generals in most nineteenth-century European armies were served by rudimentary staffs, often composed entirely of noblemen or their sons. The British and Indian armies had only two staff departments, one headed by a quartermaster general and one by an adjutant general.

The first attempt to provide a national general staff as now conceived was made by the Prussians in 1817 to formulate mobilization plans, establish training programs, and prepare the army for war. Its first chief was Gerhard von Scharnhorst [q.v.], who had begun the reorganization of the Prussian army in 1807.

The reorganization of the German Great General Staff undertaken by Karl Müffling [q.v.] in 1821 cast the staff in a mold that remained little changed in the following 120 years. In the nineteenth century it achieved its greatest brilliance under the elder Helmuth von Moltke [q.v.], whose staff work enabled the German armies to achieve such a stunning victory in the Franco-Prussian War. Moltke made the staff elite the brains and the nerves of the army. Officers were chosen by examinations and were educated professionally at the Kriegsakademie [q.v.], where great emphasis was placed upon the study of military history and the study of and adherence to a uniform doctrine. So imbued were officers with the importance of the latter that command could safely be decentralized, and good commanders guided by sound doctrine and good basic planning could be relied upon to make decisions without waiting for orders. Moltke wrote: "A favorable situation will never be exploited if commanders wait for orders. . . . [O]missions and inactivity are worse than resorting to the wrong expedient."

The general staff occupied a semiautonomy within the War Ministry. Entrance to the War College was by competitive examination, and only about one-third of those admitted were graduated. These were assigned to the Great General Staff (Grosser Generalstab) for two years, after which three or four were selected for permanent membership on the staff. They rotated between the Great General Staff and the general staffs of field armies. By 1870 most of the senior Prussian officers had been trained in this way.

The German Great General Staff consisted of a central division that concerned itself with personnel and administrative affairs and eight departmental divisions:

1. Russia and Scandinavia
2. Germany
3. France and Western Europe
4. Fortresses, except Russia's
5. Austria, Italy, and the Balkans
6. Maneuvers, staff rides, transportation, and affairs pertaining to the Kriegsakademie
7. Russian fortresses
8. Britain, America, Asia, Africa, Australia

In 1891 there were 154 officers on the Great General Staff; in 1914 there were 650. Each division had a member of the general staff, and each corps had two or three.

With the exception of Britain, many European countries, notably France, Italy, Austria, and Russia, copied the Prussian system, although in no other country did the chief of the general staff exercise the authority invested in the chief of the German Great General Staff. Neither the British nor the American army had a respectable general staff until the twentieth century. Although the Spanish-American War [q.v.] certainly demonstrated the need, the American army did not begin to develop a general staff until 1903, and then it was only an adjunct of the War College.

Geneva Convention, First (1864). A convention adopted by many countries to improve the care of the sick and wounded in war and to establish medical personnel as nonbelligerents and ambulances and hospitals as neutral ground. It was the direct result of a powerful book, *Un Souvenir de Solferino* written by Henri Dunant [q.v.], a Swiss who was torn by the sufferings of the more than 13,000 untended wounded lying on the field of the Battle of Solferino [q.v.] in 1859. In October 1863 representatives of fourteen nations—including Prussia, Great Britain, France, Switzerland, Austria, and Italy—met in Geneva, Switzerland, in the First Geneva Convention under the chairmanship of Swiss General Guillaume Henri Dufour [q.v.]. One result of their deliberations was the formation of the International Red Cross [q.v.], a society designed to succor sick and wounded soldiers. Although every European power and Persia (Iran) signed the convention, the United States did not sign until 1882. A convention in The Hague in 1899 adapted to war on the sea the principles in the Geneva Convention of 1864.

Gentlemen-at-Arms. Henry VIII (1509–1547), on his accession to the throne in 1509, formed the King's Bodyguard of the Honourable Corps of Gentlemen-at-Arms. Several attempts were made to restrict the guard to pensioned officers of the army or navy, but none was successful until 1862, when membership was restricted to pensioned regular officers who had earned war decorations. However, the office of captain

was political, its holder resigning when the government left office. The corps consisted of a captain, lieutenant, standard-bearer, clerk of the cheque (adjutant), suboffizer, and thirty-nine gentlemen-at-arms.

Gentlemen Rankers. British gentlemen serving in the ranks, some because they had failed examinations or had disgraced themselves socially and some in the hope of so distinguishing themselves that they would win a commission. Rudyard Kipling's [q.v.] poem "Gentlemen-Rankers," written in 1892 and later set to music, is best known to Americans in an altered version as the "Whiffenpoof Song." [See Rankers.]

Geok Tepe, Sieges of, Russian conquest of Central Asia. This fortified town, 40 miles northwest of Ashkhabad, was the main fortress of the Turcoman (or Turkoman) Tekkes. It was surrounded by a wall 3 miles in circumference. The Russians made two assaults upon the fortress.

1. In September 1879 the town was unsuccessfully assaulted by Russian troops, who were driven back across the desert in the worst Russian defeat in Central Asia since an ill-fated military expedition sent by Peter the Great to attack Khiva in 1717.

2. In 1881 Geok Tepe was besieged a second time by Russian forces under General Mikhail Skobelev [q.v.] with an army of 7,000 infantry and cavalry supported by 60 guns and rocket batteries. The Tekkes, making almost nightly sallies, captured 14 Russian guns, but the Russians breached the wall with a mine that blew a 50-yard gap, and on 17 January they launched a four-column assault, one led by Skobelev personally, another by Aleksei Kuropatkin [q.v.]. The fortress was captured, and the Tekkes fled into the desert, pursued by Cossacks. Russian losses were 268 killed and 669 wounded; Turcoman losses were estimated at 15,000. Skobelev was later censored for permitting his men to plunder, rape, and slaughter in the town. [See Tekke Campaign, Russian.]

Georgevsky Banners. See St. George the Martyr, Order of.

Georgia, Army of. In the American Civil War the unofficial name of a Union army commanded by Major General Henry W. Slocum [q.v.] that consisted of XIV and XX Corps and cavalry under Hugh Kilpatrick [q.v.]. This army took part in William Tecumseh Sherman's March to the Sea [q.v.].

Gérard, Comte Étienne Maurice (1773–1852). A French soldier who joined the army in 1791 and was commissioned the following year. He distinguished himself in the battles of Austerlitz, where he was wounded, and Jena [qq.v.]. He was promoted general of brigade in 1806 and fought in the Iberian Peninsula. Promoted general of division in 1812, he fought in the Battle of Bautzen [q.v.]. In the Battle of Leipzig [q.v.] in October 1813 he was again wounded. He rejoined Napoleon for the Hundred Days [q.v.] and fought brilliantly in the Battle of Ligny [q.v.]. From 1815 to 1817 he lived in exile. In 1830 and again in 1834 he was French minister of war. In 1831 he drove the Dutch army out of Belgium, and in 1832 he directed the successful siege of Antwerp [q.v.]. From 1838 to 1842 he commanded the Garde Nationale [q.v.] of the Seine.

German Army. In 1816 the Congress of Vienna united the German states with the German Confederation, and a federal army was formed by drawing upon the individual states. Boasting a regular strength of 452,474 with 100,554 in the reserve and 1,134 guns, this army fought in the Schleswig-Holstein Wars (1848 and 1864). On 24 August 1866, at the end of the Seven Weeks' War [q.v.], both the confederation and the federal army came to an end.

The new German army of the unified Germany that emerged after the spectacular victories in the Franco-Prussian War [q.v.] was organized on the Prussian pattern and guaranteed the independence of the crown from the popular will. It followed Prussian conscription policies and elevated the army to an elite position in both the state and society. It consisted of a guards corps, twelve army corps, and a Hessian division and it had a wartime footing of 12,777 officers and 543,058 other ranks, in addition to garrison and depot troops and 1,212 guns. In 1874 the permanent strength of the army was established by law at 401,659 men; four-fifths of the federal budget was spent on the army.

In 1880 men entered the army at age nineteen, and recruit training lasted six weeks. Most troops were armed with Mauser rifles; there were three cannon for every 1,000 infantry, 120 mm guns with 29-pound shells for siege operations, field batteries of 88 mm guns, and horse artillery with 78.5 mm guns. All these were made of cast steel by Krupp [q.v.], except for mountain batteries, which were equipped with 3-pounder rifled bronze guns.

Nobles, on passing an examination, became officers. Legally a commission was available to all men of "respectable family" and, because of the social status enjoyed by officers, even in the reserve, was much desired. [See Einjährigen Freiwilligen.]

In the 1890s the army had grown to twenty corps, each containing two divisions. Each division included two brigades of infantry, each of two regiments; one regiment of cavalry; one regiment of field artillery, each with six batteries; one or two companies of pioneers; and a pontoon detachment, a medical detachment, and a telegraph detachment. In 1899 this army was increased to twenty-three army corps.

Not included in the German army in the 1890s were about 2,500 African troops from German East Africa (now mainland Tanzania), Kameruns (now part of Cameroon), Togo, and a force of 500 to 600 German colonials, mostly mounted, in German South-West Africa (Namibia). These were trained and commanded by German officers and noncommissioned officers. Service in Africa counted double for the pensions of officers and doctors. [See General Staff.]

German-Danish Wars. See Schleswig-Holstein Wars.

German Legion, King's. An act of the British Parliament of 1794 enabled the embodiment of this unit of 15,000 Germans, a number later doubled. It distinguished itself in several engagements in the Napoleonic Wars. It was disbanded in 1815, and its officers were placed on half pay.

German Revolutions (1848–49). Émeutes flared in many European cities and states in 1848, Paris providing one of the key revolutionary areas [see Revolutions of 1848; Paris Revolutions of 1848]. Although Paris became the stage for ul-

timate decisions in France, revolutionary activity fragmented in the German and Austrian states. Uprisings in Berlin, Frankfurt, Vienna, and elsewhere remained uncoordinated and were usually suppressed with little difficulty, though this was not the case in Baden. The gulf between the army and civilians is generally credited as one of the principal causes of the discontent in Germany, but in Baden almost the entire army joined hands with the revolutionaries.

The Baden Insurrection was led by a thirty-four-year-old Polish revolutionary, Ludwig Mieroslawski [q.v.], who formed a military force of 20,000 consisting of regulars, free corps, people's guard, a group of foreign volunteers, and even a few amazons [q.v.]. A much larger Prussian force, with some Hessians and Mecklenburgers, under Prince William of Prussia (1797–1888) joined him. In the first battle at Waghäusel, north of Heidelberg, Mieroslawski was defeated but retreated in good order. By mid-July 1849 the revolt had been suppressed, largely by Prussian regulars, and all Baden was pacified. Mieroslawski returned to Poland, where he took part in other insurrections.

German Revolutions *Life behind the barricades in Berlin, 18 March 1848*

German War of Liberation. A name given (in German: *Befreiungskrieg*) for the German war waged against Napoleon in his campaign of 1813–14. Russo-Prussian collaboration was established in the Treaty of Kalisch on 28 December 1813, and in the Breslau proclamation *"An mein Volk,"* on 17 March 1814, Frederick William III [q.v.] of Prussia called on his subjects to resist French tyranny and wage a war of liberation.

Gerona, Siege of (1809), Peninsular War. On 24 May 1809, one day after the repulse of Louis Suchet [q.v.] at Alcañiz [q.v.], a French force of 12,000, later increased to 16,000, began a siege of Gerona, a strong fortress, 52 miles northeast of Barcelona, Spain, garrisoned by about 6,000 armed peasants under the command of Mariano Álvarez de Castro (d. 1809).

General Joachim Blake [q.v.] three times tried unsuccessfully to relieve the place. On 12 October the siege operations were taken over by French Marshal Pierre Augereau [q.v.], who managed to deliver a decisive assault on 11 December. Some 3,000 walking skeletons surrendered, and the French gained a demolished, disease-ridden shell of a town. Spanish losses were 7,000 soldiers killed or felled by sicknesses and starvation, including Álvarez de Castro; 6,000 of the 15,000 citizens died. French casualties were 13,000 killed and wounded and 6,000 sick.

Gerona *The Spanish repulse assault on the walls of Gerona, October 1809.*

Geronimo (1829–1909), real name: Goyathly (One Who Yawns). An Apache medicine man who became a war leader in the American Southwest. In 1850 his mother, wife, and three children were murdered by Mexicans. In revenge he joined in numerous bloody raids into Mexico, earning a reputation among the Apaches as a great warrior. Many of his forays were under Juh [q.v.], and he was probably with Juh in the affray at Whetstone Mountains in Arizona on 5 May 1871, when First Lieutenant Howard B. Cushing (1844?–1871) was killed. Geronimo was arrested and imprisoned for a time at the Ojo Caliente Reservation. After being freed, he joined Juh in the Victorio War of 1879 [see Victorio]. Late in that year both surrendered and settled for a time on the San Carlos Reservation in Arizona, a place one Indian described as "nothing but cactus, rattlesnakes, heat, rocks and insects. No game; no edible plants." After the Cibicue [q.v.] skirmish in 1881, they took up arms again and led a band into the Sierra Madre, making their headquarters in Mexico. In the spring of 1882 Geronimo, probably again with Juh, made a daring raid on San Carlos.

In 1884 he surrendered again, but a year later, on 17 May 1885, he bolted, taking numbers of malcontent reservation Indians with him to his lair in the Sierra Madre, from which he launched frequent raids. In March he agreed to surrender to George Crook [q.v.] with the words "Once I moved about like the wind. Now I surrender to you and that is all." But it was not all; he failed to surrender.

It was 4 September 1886 before he and 35 of his warriors surrendered at Skeleton Canyon, just north of the border in Arizona, to Nelson Miles [q.v.], who, to hunt him down, had employed 5,000 men for five months. The actual capitulation was made to a detachment commanded by Captain Henry W. Lawton [q.v.]. Geronimo was shipped first to Fort Pickens, Florida, then to Alabama, and finally in 1894 to Fort Sill, Oklahoma, where he died of pneumonia.

Geronimo was a scowling, unpleasant man, often in ill temper, but one Apache described him as a man who was "intelligent and most resourceful as well as the most vigorous and farsighted. In times of danger he was a man to be relied upon." In the last years of his life he learned something of the white man's curious ways and sold his autograph for twenty-five cents a copy.

Geronimo *An 1886 photograph of Geronimo by Camillus S. Fly*

Gessi, Romolo (1831–1881). An English-speaking Italian soldier and explorer who served as an interpreter for the British army in the Crimea in 1854–55. In the Austro-Piedmontese War [q.v.] in 1859 he served in the Sardinian army under Giuseppe Garibaldi [q.v.]. In 1874 he accompanied Charles ("Chinese") Gordon [q.v.] to the Sudan, where in 1876 he circumnavigated Lake Albert. Piqued that the Egyptian government awarded him only the third-class order of the Majidya for his services, he returned to Italy for a time, but he was soon back in Africa with an exploring expedition under Dr. Pellegrino Matteucci (1850–1881).

In 1878 he again entered the khedival service under Gordon, then governor-general of the Sudan, who appointed him governor of the Bahr el Ghazal, a province in the southwest Sudan. There he mounted numerous campaigns against slavers and in 1879, in one such campaign in southern Darfur, killed Suleiman, the son of Rahma Mansur Zubair Pasha [q.v.]. Although made a pasha, Gessi was ignominiously dismissed by Gordon's successor, Muhammad Rauf Pasha (1832?–1888), on false charges of corruption. He died soon after at Suez.

Getty, George Washington (1819–1901). An American soldier who entered West Point at the age of sixteen and served in the American army for the next forty-eight years. He fought in the Mexican War [q.v.] as an artillery officer and won a brevet. At the beginning of the American Civil War he was an artillery captain; by September 1861 he was a lieutenant colonel in the Union army. He commanded four batteries in the Peninsular Campaign [q.v.], and he was chief of artillery for General Ambrose Burnside [q.v.] at South Mountain and Antietam [qq.v.]. On 25 September he was promoted brigadier general of volunteers and in that rank commanded a division in IX Corps in the Battle of

Fredericksburg [q.v.]. In March 1863 he and his division helped resist the attempt by Confederates under General James Longstreet [q.v.] to capture Suffolk, Virginia, which guarded the approaches to Norfolk and Hampton Roads. On the second day of the Battle of the Wilderness [q.v.] he was severely wounded, but he recovered to take part in the siege of Petersburg [q.v.] and the campaign of Philip Sheridan in the Shenandoah Valley. He was also present in the campaign that culminated in the surrender of General Robert E. Lee at Appomattox. He was brevetted major general of volunteers in August 1864 and a major general in the regular army in March 1865. In 1866 he returned to the smaller, reorganized regular army and was appointed colonel of the 38th Infantry. In 1879 he was a member of the board that exonerated Civil War General Fitz-John Porter [q.v.]. He retired in 1883.

Gettysburg, Battle of (1–3 July 1863), American Civil War. When Union General Joseph Hooker [q.v.] learned that Robert E. Lee and the Army of Northern Virginia [q.v.], about 89,000 men, had crossed the Potomac on 25–26 June 1863, he concentrated his Army of the Potomac, about 122,000 men, in and around Frederick and South Mountain in Maryland, intending to strike at Lee's vulnerable line of communications should he continue to advance north. However, Hooker, exasperated by the interference of Henry Halleck [q.v.], then general-in-chief, asked to be relieved. He was replaced by General George Meade [q.v.] only three days before the battle.

On 28 June a Confederate spy known only as Harrison revealed to Confederate Lieutenant General James Longstreet [q.v.] the disposition of Meade's army. As a result, Lee concentrated his force around the village of Gettysburg, Pennsylvania, a move that probably prevented its annihilation.

On 1 July a Confederate brigade from the corps of A. P. Hill [q.v.], moving on Gettysburg to capture a supply of shoes that was said to be there, encountered a Federal cavalry division under John Buford [q.v.]. Both sides built their strength. The Confederates captured McPherson's Ridge and moved on Seminary Ridge, which the Federals held. After a day of bitter fighting the Confederates appeared victorious. The Union XI Corps had lost 4,000 men captured. Among

Gettysburg *Battle of Gettysburg*

Gettysburg *The dead from both armies strew the field, dawn, 5 July 1863*

Confederate losses was General James Archer (1817–1864), the first general officer to be captured since Lee had taken command.

Meade, with 220 guns, was concerned that his right, or northeast, flank could be turned, but on the second day of the battle Lee, with 172 guns, ordered Longstreet to attack two small rocky hills subsequently known as the Round Tops on Meade's southern flank. Union General Daniel Sickles [q.v.], on the southern end of the Union line, moved forward without permission, creating Sickles Salient, an area that became famous for three physical features of the battle where fighting was particularly violent: the Peach Orchard, the Wheat Field, and Devil's Den.

The fighting on the second day did not seriously begin until four o'clock in the afternoon, when the division of John Hood [q.v.] launched its attack upon the Round Tops. Hood, leading the attack, was seriously wounded, permanently losing the use of one arm. The Confederate fighting was gallant but suffered from poor leadership. A. P. Hill, in the center of the Confederate line, failed to attack soon enough, so that Meade was able to shift his forces. Nevertheless, Sickles's division was pushed back. Confederate General Richard Ewell [q.v.] launched an attack upon the Federal right (north) about six o'clock. Initially successful, it failed to sustain its momentum and was pushed back.

In spite of Longstreet's strong objections, Lee decided to attack again for a third day of battle. His plan was to strike the Union line with ten brigades supported by 159 guns. Since Lee had attacked his flanks on the previous day, Meade divined (correctly) that the attack would be on the center of his line. For reasons not readily understandable, this charge by 15,000 Confederates commanded by Longstreet is known in history as Pickett's Charge [q.v.]. The artillery exchange that preceded the charge was said to produce the loudest noise ever heard on the American continent. People in Pittsburgh, 140 miles away, claimed to have heard it. The attack was a total disaster, and nineteen Confederate regimental flags were taken by the Federals. Facing defeat at the end of the day, Lee said to General Cadmus M. Wilcox [q.v.]: "Never mind, General, all this has been my fault, it is I who have lost this fight, and you must help me out of it the best way you can." The following morning, under cover of a rainstorm, the Confederates began their retreat south.

Of the 75,000 Confederates engaged, 3,903 were killed, 18,735 were wounded or captured, and 5,425 were missing for total casualties of 28,063. Of the 88,289 Union forces engaged, 3,155 were killed, 14,529 were wounded or captured, and 5,365 were missing for a total of 23,049.

Gettysburg *Map of the battlefield at Gettysburg with position of troops, 2 July 1863*

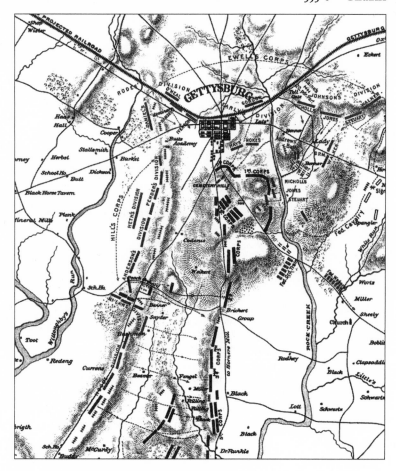

Meade was much criticized by President Lincoln and later by historians for his failure to pursue Lee, and in consequence he has received less than his due for his victory in one of the most critical battles of the Civil War and one of the most decisive in nineteenth-century military history. General Francis A. Walker (1840–1897) once declared: "There is probably no other battle of which men are so prone to think and speak without a conscious reference to the commanding general of the victorious party, as they are regarding Gettysburg." This battle, followed by the surrender of Vicksburg on 4 July, put an end to the Confederate offensive momentum.

Gettysburg Address. Shortly after the Battle of Gettysburg [q.v.], Pennsylvania Governor Andrew Gregg Curtin (1817–1894) directed a local attorney to purchase land for a Union cemetery, and 17 acres adjacent to privately owned Evergreen Cemetery were purchased. The land was laid out in pie-shaped plots, one for each Union state, radiating from a central point. Only about a third of the 3,500 dead had been transferred to the new cemetery when its dedication was held on 19 November in the third year of the war. Lincoln's brief address, listed on the official program as "Dedicating Remarks," was given after an eloquent and moving oration of two hours by Edward Everett (1794–1865), a former Unitarian minister, professor of Greek, ambassador, governor, and senator, whose speech was followed by a hymn.

Speaking slowly and emphatically in a tenor voice of great carrying power, Lincoln delivered the 272 words he had come to say:

> Fourscore and seven years ago our fathers brought forth upon this continent a new nation, conceived in liberty and dedicated to the proposition that all men are created equal. Now we are engaged in a great civil war, testing whether that nation, or any nation so conceived and so dedicated, can long endure. We have come to dedicate a portion of that field, as a final resting place for those who here gave their lives that that nation might live. It is altogether fitting and proper that we should do this. But, in a larger sense, we cannot dedicate—we cannot consecrate—we cannot hallow—this ground. The brave men, living and dead, who struggled here, have consecrated it far above our poor power to add or detract. The world will little note, nor long remember, what we say here, but it can never forget what they did here. It is for us the living, rather, to be dedicated to the great task remaining before us,—that from these honored dead we take increased devotion to that cause for which they gave the last full measure of devotion—that we here highly resolve that these dead shall not have died in vain—that this nation, under God, shall have a new birth of freedom—and that government of the people, by the people and for the people, shall not perish from the earth. [This is the final, revised text, differing slightly from stenographic notes made on the occasion.]

Contrary to popular mythology, Lincoln's speech was carefully drafted and redrafted, and it was so enthusiastically received that it was interrupted by applause five times in the short three minutes of its delivery.

An act of Congress later decreed that copies of the address be displayed at every national battlefield park, an honor it shares with the poem "The Bivouac of the Dead" [q.v.].

Ghazis. Fanatic Islamic religious fighters in Afghanistan who swore to die fighting unbelievers. Ghazis, quick to lead charges, were bold warriors who sometimes seemed to welcome death. [See Afghan War, Second.]

Ghazni, Attacks on. Ghazni, an ancient city protected by massive walls 60 feet high, sits on a high tableland in Afghanistan, 92 miles southwest of Kabul, on the road to Kandahar.

1. 23 July 1839. During the First Afghan War [q.v.] the city, garrisoned by 3,000 Afghans, was captured by British General Sir John Keane (1781–1844) at a cost of 17 killed and 165 wounded. Keane had no siege guns, but a nephew of Dost Muhammad [q.v.] crept into the British lines and gave him valuable information regarding the defenses of the town, including the fact that the town's Achilles' heel was the Kabul gate. The gate was blown in by a party that included Lieutenant Henry Durand [q.v.], and the fortress was stormed by a forlorn hope [q.v.] under Colonel Robert Sale [q.v.]. Afghan losses were said to be 500.

2. 16 December 1841–6 March 1842. Two and a half years later, when the Afghans revolted against the British oc-

cupation, Ghazni, garrisoned by a regiment of sepoys from the Bengal army, was besieged and forced to surrender on 6 March 1842.

3. 6 September 1842. British General William Nott [q.v.], leading an avenging army into Afghanistan, occupied the city without a fight, destroyed its gates and some of its walls, and carried off as a prize the famous Gates of Somnath from the tomb of Mahmud of Ghazni (997–1030).

Ghazni *The fortress and citadel of Ghazni, British target during the invasion of Afghanistan, 1839*

Ghorchana / Ghorchurras. Irregular Sikh Yeomanry who served in the two Sikh Wars [q.v.] against the British.

Ghost Dance Disturbances (1890–91). In the 1870s among the Paiute Indians of western Nevada a new faith arose based on the Ghost Dance. It spread rapidly. The dance, a feature of the religion, was usually performed around sacred trees, and was distinguished by a slow shuffling that seemed to have a hypnotic effect. Many dancers experienced visions. The religion disappeared immediately after the Modoc War [q.v.] but reappeared in 1890 among the Indians of the western plains. Crushed by the white Americans, the Plains Indians dreamed of a redeemer who would drive out their oppressors and usher in a better life. One of the principal leaders of the movement was Short Bull, who was invited by Sitting Bull [qq.v.] to hold the first ghost dance on the Great Plains. Among the Sioux the dance took on bizarre rituals; participants sometimes attached thongs through their skin and were suspended by them. Ghost shirts, usually white, were said to make men invincible to bullets. Bolstered by this belief, the Sioux became increasingly turbulent and hostile to whites. At the Pine Ridge Agency there was a drift toward anarchy as a weak and corrupt agent found himself ignored by his charges. After several panicky appeals for troops, in November 1890 troops appeared, and the Sioux ghost dancers, some 3,000, armed themselves and deployed on elevated land in the northwest corner of the reservation.

On 15 December 1891 the agent sent 43 Indian policemen to arrest Sitting Bull in a dawn raid. They were supported by cavalry, but these were held back so as not to alarm the Indians unduly. Sitting Bull was found in a cabin on Grand River, 30 miles south of the agency, and he was arrested, but there followed some delay in saddling the fine circus horse given to him by Buffalo Bill Cody [q.v.]. Angry Indians

began to swarm around the police. A gun was fired, and a melee erupted. Inspired by the shooting, the horse plunged into the tricks that had formed his act in Cody's show. The cavalry, hearing the shooting, galloped up to find Sitting Bull and 7 of his followers dead on the ground. Inside the cabin were 4 dead and 3 wounded policemen, 2 of whom later died.

After Sitting Bull's death the movement rapidly died out, largely as a result of military and political operations carried out by General Nelson Miles [q.v.]. [See Wounded Knee; Messiah War; Plenty Horses Trial.]

The noted American ethnologist James Mooney (1861–1921) in 1892 gave perhaps the best explanation for the ghost dances: "When the race lies crushed and groaning under an alien yoke, how natural is the dream of a redeemer, an Arthur, who shall return from exile or awaken from some long sleep to drive out the usurper and win back for his people what they have lost. A hope becomes a faith and the faith becomes the creed of priests and prophets, until the hero is a god and the dream a religion, looking to some great miracle of nature for its culmination and accomplishment." (*14th Annual Report of the Bureau of American Ethnology*).

Ghost Dance Disturbances *Ghost dance of the Oglala Sioux*

Gibbon, John (1827–1896). An American army officer who was graduated from West Point in 1847. He took part in operations against the Seminoles and in 1853–54 assisted in their removal from Florida to Indian Territory [see Seminole Wars]. He wrote *The Artillerist's Manual*, published by the War Department in 1860. When the American Civil War began, he was a captain of artillery. Although his wife was from Baltimore and three of his brothers entered the Confederate army, he remained loyal to the Union. Promoted brigadier general on 2 May 1862, he commanded the Iron Brigade [q.v.], which he led at Second Bull Run [q.v.] and in the Maryland Campaign. He was badly wounded at Fredericksburg [q.v.] in December but returned to duty to receive a second wound on the last day of the Battle of Gettysburg [q.v.]. Although he was left with a bad limp, he fought in all the battles of the Wilderness Campaign [q.v.], and on 7 June 1864 he was promoted major general. In the fall he was given command of XVIII Corps, and in January 1865 he commanded the newly created XXIV Corps in the Army of the James. At Lee's surrender at Appomattox he was a surrender commissioner.

After the war he served as a colonel with the 36th and later the 7th Infantry on the plains. He led the force that reached the scene of the Battle of the Little Bighorn two days after Custer's last stand, and his men spent two days burying the dead and moving the wounded. In 1877 he led a small force of combined arms against the Nez Percés, and on 8–9 August fought an action at Big Hole Basin [q.v.] in Montana, on the second day of which he was badly wounded in the thigh. He became a brigadier general in the regular army in 1885, and as commander of the Department of the Columbia he played a major role in quelling the anti-Chinese riots in Seattle in 1886. He retired in 1891. He was regarded as one of the best small-unit generals in the American army. [See American Civil Disorders.] When he died on 6 February 1896, he was commander-in-chief of the Military Order of the Loyal Legion [q.v.]. His *Personal Memoirs of the Civil War,* written in 1885, was not published until 1928.

Giberne. 1. A sack or bag in which grenadiers carried their grenades.

2. A waxed and polished cartridge box of black leather carried by French infantry that held thirty-five cartridges, bullet end up, and a small tin of oil. An outside pocket held a screwdriver (*tournevis*), a bullet extractor (*tire-balle*), spare flints, a greasy cloth, and a heavy needle (*épinglette*) to clean the touchhole. Gibernes carried by grenadiers were ornamented with the "flaming grenade."

Gibson, Randall Lee (1832–1892). A Confederate soldier in the American Civil War. Commissioned a captain in the 1st Louisiana Artillery in 1861, he fought at Shiloh, Perryville, and Chickamauga [qq.v.]. Appointed brigadier general on 11 January 1864, he led his brigade in the Atlanta and Tennessee campaigns. After the war he became a lawyer and politician, serving as a U.S. representative and senator.

Gifford, Maurice Raymond (1859–1910). A British soldier who from 1876 to 1882 served as a sailor on merchant ships. Having left the sea, he was a volunteer during Arabi's Revolt [q.v.] of 1882 in Egypt and a scout for the British during the second rebellion of Louis Riel [q.v.] in Canada. He then emigrated to South Africa, where, during the Matabele War [q.v.] of 1893, he raised two troops known as Gifford's Horse. He distinguished himself in this war, in which he lost an arm. During the Second Anglo-Boer War [q.v.] he served with the Kimberley Mounted Corps and took part in the relief of Mafeking.

Gila River Expedition (1857). An expedition against the Gila Apaches in southwestern New Mexico led by Colonel Benjamin Bonneville [q.v.], then in command of the Military Department of New Mexico. The expedition culminated on 24 May 1857 in the Battle of Canyon de los Muerto Carneros, in which the Indians were defeated. In a later battle on 27 June against Coyotero Apaches 40 Indians were killed or wounded and 45 women and children were captured.

Gillem, Alvan Cullem (1830–1875). An American soldier who fought in a Seminole War [q.v.] and on the Texas frontier. During the American Civil War he rose to be a Union major general of volunteers. On September 1864 in Greenville, Tennessee, forces under his command killed the Confederate raider John Morgan [q.v.]. After the war he became colonel of the 24th Infantry and later of the 11th. He was a personal friend of President Andrew Johnson (1808–1875) and was active in Reconstruction until he was sent back to the Texas frontier. In 1873 he was given command of the forces engaged in fighting the Modoc War [q.v.]. His health soon broke down, and he went on sick leave in January 1875; he died the following December.

Gillespie, Robert Rollo (1766–1814). A British soldier usually referred to as Rollo Gillespie. On 28 April 1783 he was appointed to a cornetcy in the 3rd Irish Horse (later 6th Dragoon Guards). A wild youth, he made a clandestine marriage and killed a man in a duel. In 1788 he was tried for murder but was acquitted when a jury decided it was "justifiable homicide." In 1792 he was promoted lieutenant in the newly raised 20th Jamaica Dragoons. Sailing to the West Indies, he survived a shipwreck, and in Jamaica he survived an attack of yellow fever, thus acquiring immunity. He became a captain in 1794 and that year was present in the Battle of Tiburón on the west coast of present-day Colombia. At Port-au-Prince, Haiti, he swam through enemy fire carrying a flag of truce to demand the town's surrender. In the capture of Port-au-Prince he distinguished himself at the capture of Fort Bizotten and received several wounds in the attack on Fort de Hôpital. After a brief return to Britain he returned to the West Indies, where in 1796 he was promoted major.

It was in the West Indies that he won renown when a gang described as "desperados" broke into his quarters and murdered his "slave-boy." Although he was a small man, he drew his sword and killed six before one shot and wounded him and then fled. Word of his feat preceded him to England, where some years later, on his being presented to King George III at a levee, the king remarked, "Eh, eh, what, what! Is this the little man that killed the brigands?"

In 1801, when as a colonel he left Jamaica, the House of Assembly voted him 100 guineas for the purchase of a sword, but back in Britain he was charged with having signed false returns; tried by a general court-martial, he was acquitted. His next posting was to India, where he was appointed commandant at Arcot in eastern Madras. There on 10 July 1806, as he was out riding before breakfast, he was informed of the mutiny at Vellore [q.v.], 14 miles away. With a squadron of the 19th Light Dragoons and some Indian cavalry, he at once set out for the city, ordering the rest of the dragoons and their galloper guns [q.v.] to follow.

At Vellore Gillespie found that a number of Europeans had been massacred and that the 69th Foot, having shot away all its ammunition, was prepared to make a last stand in the fort. He had himself hoisted into the fort by a rope and took command. It was said that his dragoons and guns killed some 800 mutineers. With Vellore secure, he moved to other disaffected areas and restored order.

In 1811, now a brigadier general, he commanded the advance of General Sir Samuel Auchmuty [q.v.] in Java [see Java War]. Although sick with fever, he directed the attack against the Dutch lines at Cornelis [q.v.]. At the completion of the island's subjugation, Auchmuty appointed Thomas Stamford Raffles (1781–1826) governor with Gillespie as commander of troops. When it was learned that the sultan of Palembang on Sumatra had killed the Europeans there, Gillespie set out with a force, quickly deposed the sultan, replaced him with his compliant brother, and secured the cession of a small island to the British.

When he returned to Java, he found that a confederation of defiant Javanese chiefs had erected a strong stockade at Djakarta and manned it with 30,000 men and 100 guns. With only 1,500 troops, he assaulted the stockade and routed the Javanese.

Soon after, he became embroiled in a series of quarrels with Stamford Raffles that culminated in charges being preferred against Raffles over the sale of land. The Court of Directors of the Honourable East India Company launched a prolonged inquiry into the charges and eventually, after Gillespie's death, found against Raffles.

On 1 April 1812 Gillespie became a major general, and in October he returned to India, where he killed a tiger on the Bangalore racetrack. In 1814 he commanded the Meerut Division of the Bengal troops in the Nepalese War [q.v.] against the Gurkhas [q.v.]. On 31 October he led the attacks upon the strong Gurkha fort at Kalunga [q.v.] in the Himalayas near Dera Dun. There, while trying to rally his men, he was shot through the heart.

Gillmore, Quincy Adams (1825–1888). An American soldier who was graduated from West Point in 1849 and commissioned in the Corps of Engineers. During the American Civil War he was chief engineer in the joint army-navy expedition against Port Royal, South Carolina, in November 1861. In July 1863 he was appointed brigadier general and then major general in the volunteer service. In the same month, with Admiral John A. B. Dahlgren (1809–1870), he launched a campaign in Charleston Harbor that resulted in the capture of Morris Island and Fort Wagner [q.v.] and the destruction of Fort Sumter [see Gillmore Medal]. He sustained severe injuries in the pursuit of Confederate General Jubal Early [q.v.]. In December 1865 he was mustered out of the volunteer service.

After the war he remained in the service as a captain. By 1883 he had worked his way up to colonel.

Gillmore Medal. Until the establishment of the Medal of Honor [q.v.] in December 1861 there were no official American medals to honor valor on the battlefield. Such recognition came only from individuals, organizations, or localities that struck medals. One of these was the bronze medal ordered by Union General Quincy Adams Gillmore [q.v.] from Ball, Black and Company of New York to reward enlisted men who had distinguished themselves in the summer of 1863 in his operations against Charleston, South Carolina, and Fort Sumter. Recipients were those recommended by their regimental commanders, and their names, ranks, and regimental names were engraved on their clasps.

Gingal / Gingaul / Jinjaul. A weapon used by Asian armies, usually in the defense of forts or stockades. It resembled an oversize musket and was fired from a rest. Garnet Wolseley [q.v.] received his first wound from a gingal in Burma (Myanmar).

Ginginhlov, Battle of (2 April 1879), Zulu War. A battle fought when a large Zulu impi attacked a British column under Lord Chelmsford [q.v.] near this place on the Inyezane River in Natal, South Africa. The Zulus were repulsed with a loss of about 700. The British lost 2 officers and 11 other ranks killed and 48 wounded. (British soldiers dubbed the place "Gin, gin, I love ya.")

Ginnis, Battle of (30 December 1885), fighting on the Egyptian-Sudanese frontier. When Abd al Rahman wad al Najumi [q.v.], a Dervish emir, began an advance toward the Egyptian frontier at Dongola, Sir Frederick Stephenson [q.v.] concentrated an Anglo-Egyptian force at Firket [q.v.] and successfully attacked the main Dervish force at Ginnis (Jinnis). The attack was the baptism of fire for the new British-trained Egyptian army.

Gionules. A volunteer Turkish cavalry noted for its horsemanship.

Girón, Pedro Augustín (1788–1842). A Spanish soldier in the Peninsular War [q.v.] who was a nephew of General Francisco Castaños [q.v.] and commanded the Army of Galicia in the Vitoria [q.v.] Campaign. After the Battle of Nivelle [q.v.] on 10 November 1813, he replaced Spanish General Joseph Henry O'Donnell [q.v.] as commander of the Army of Reserve of Andalusia.

Girouard, Edouard Percy Cranwill (1867–1932). A Canadian soldier and engineer who was educated at the Royal Military College, Kingston, Canada. He joined the army in 1888 and served in Egypt and the Sudan, where, although only a young lieutenant, he was put in charge of constructing the military railway across the Nubian desert south of Wadi Halfa to Kerma. In the Second Anglo-Boer War [q.v.] he was director of railways for the British army in South Africa from 1899 to 1902. He later became British high commissioner for northern Nigeria and then governor of the East African Protectorate. In World War I he was chief organizer of the ministry of munitions.

Gislikon, Battle of (23 November 1847), Sonderbund War. At Gislikon (Gisikon), seven miles northeast of Lucerne, Switzerland, on the Reuss River near Lake Zug, about 100,000 Swiss federal troops with 260 guns under General Guillaume Henri Dufour [q.v.] outmaneuvered, attacked, and defeated 79,000 troops of the Sonderbund (Roman Catholic cantons) led by Colonel J. U. Salis-Soglio. Although strongly positioned, the Sonderbund troops had little artillery. Only about 70,000 Federals and 40,000 Sonderbunds were actually engaged. The Federals lost 78 killed and 260 wounded; the Sonderbunds lost 50 killed and 175 wounded. On the following day Dufour entered Lucerne and the war ended. [See Sonderbund War.]

Gist, States Rights (1831–1864). An oddly named American lawyer and soldier from Union County, South Carolina, who fought in the Confederate army and although without previous military training became a brigadier general at the age of twenty-four. He fought in the Carolinas and Virginia before his transfer to Tennessee, where he fought in the battles of Chickamauga and Chattanooga [qq.v.]. He was killed leading his men in the Battle of Franklin [q.v.].

Gitschin. See Jičín / Gitschin, Battle of.

Give Ground, to. To retreat.

Giya. A Zulu war dance.

Glacis. 1. A cleared slope descending from a fortification. 2. A buffer zone.

Glengarry. A soft foldable cap with ribbons attached to the back worn only in Highland regiments of the British army until 1868, when a similar cap without ribbons was introduced for all infantry regiments.

Glinka, Fedor Nikolaevich (1786–1880). A Russian soldier who fought at Austerlitz [q.v.] on 2 December 1805. He also fought Napoleon in 1812–13, and in 1814 in France. In 1853 he became a mystic and won recognition as a poet. He was the uncle of composer Mikhail Ivanovich Glinka (1803–1857).

Glorieta, Battle of (28 March 1862), American Civil War. Confederate forces under Brigadier General Henry Hopkins Sibley [q.v.] and Lieutenant Colonel William R. Scurry (1821–1864), attempting to secure New Mexico for the Confederacy, captured Santa Fe on 4 March 1862, but fourteen days later in this battle in Apache Canyon near La Glorieta Pass in the Sangre de Cristo Mountains in north-central New Mexico, they were defeated by Union forces under Colonel John Potts Slough (1829–1867) and Major John M. Chivington [q.v.] and Confederate hopes were crushed. Just over 1,000 troops were engaged on each side. Confederate losses were 36 killed, 60 wounded, and 25 missing; Union losses were 31 killed, 50 wounded, and 30 missing.

In 1990 the remains of 30 Confederates killed at Glorieta were found in a mass grave near the body of Major John Shropshire, who had been buried separately. Shropshire's body was reburied in Bourbon County, Kentucky, on 5 August 1990.

Sibley's retreat from this battle was arduous. His force, weakened by lack of sufficient food and water, did not reach El Paso until May.

Glory. The honor and fame acquired by military achievements. It has been described by one American soldier as "That precarious splendor which plays around the brows of a warrior, and has been collected by hard service, extraordinary genius, and unblemished integrity; but which may desert the greatest hero through one unfortunate failure, occasioned by the fatality of human imperfection" (Edward S. Farrow, *Farrow's Military Encyclopedia* [New York; privately published, 1885]).

Abraham Lincoln, speaking of glory in the House of Representatives on 12 January 1848, said: "Military glory—that attractive rainbow that rises in showers of blood, that serpent's eye that charms to destroy."

Gluck, Sara (fl. 1900). The doughty British postmistress of the small town of Lady Grey in the Witteberge Mountains of South Africa, 30 miles east of Aliwal North. During the Second Anglo-Boer War [q.v.] Mrs. Gluck won international fame when she defied the order of a Boer commandant to haul down the Union Jack flying over her post office.

Gneisenau, Count August Wilhelm Anton Neithardt von (1760–1831). A German soldier, the son of a Saxon officer, Neithardt, who took the name Gneisenau from the family's lost estates in Austria. He was commissioned in the Austrian army in 1779, but in 1782 he transferred to the army of the Margrave of Baireuth-Anspach and accompanied the German auxiliaries of England to America to fight against the American rebels. In 1786 he returned to Europe and joined the Prussian army, in which he served in Poland from 1793 to 1795.

In 1806–07 he fought against Napoleon and saw action in the Battle of Jena [q.v.] and in the Lithuanian Campaign. Early in 1807, as commandant at besieged Colberg, he held out until the peace brought about by the Treaty of Tilsit [q.v.]. For this he was awarded the order Pour le Mérite [q.v.] and was promoted lieutenant colonel. In 1807–12, with Gerhard von Scharnhorst [q.v.] and others, he was engaged in the reform of the Prussian army, reorganizing the reserves and officer training and helping form the general staff [see Five Reformers; Military Reorganization Commission, Prussian]. He served in the War of Liberation in 1813–14 as a major general and became quartermaster general under General Gebhart von Blücher [q.v.]. In October 1813 he played an important role in the Battle of Leipzig [q.v.]. At Ligny and Waterloo [qq.v.] he served as chief of staff for Blücher, who said of him: "Gneisenau makes the pills I administer." He was appointed governor of Berlin in 1818 and was made general field marshal in 1825. During the Polish Revolution of 1831 he commanded the army of observation on the Polish frontier with Karl von Clausewitz [q.v.] as his chief of staff [see Polish Revolutions]. He died of cholera at Posen.

Count August Wilhelm Anton Neithardt von Gneisenau

Goble, Jonathan. A U.S. marine who, while an enlisted man stationed in China, in or about 1855 invented the rickshaw.

"God Save the Queen [King]." The national anthem of Great Britain, whose tune, in the rhythm and style of a galliard, has been adopted by some twenty countries, including Denmark and Germany ["Heil dir im Siegerkranz!"], as the melody of their official national anthems. The identity of the author and composer of the song as sung today in Britain is obscure, but it has been ascribed to John Bull (1563–1628), who is said to have written both melody and words in 1606 for a dinner given at Merchant Taylor's Hall for James I (1556–1625). It gained its popularity in Britain at the time of the landing of the Young Pretender in 1745. In the nineteenth century it was probably the most widely known tune in the world, but it was not officially recognized in Britain until 1933.

The American version, popularly known from its first line, "My country, 'tis of thee," was the work of the Reverend Samuel Francis Smith (1803–1895), a Baptist clergyman, who set his words to the English tune in 1831. It was first published the following year.

Goeben, August Karl von (1816–1880). A Prussian soldier who was commissioned in the Prussian army at age seventeen. In 1836 he resigned to fight with the Carlist army in Spain [see Carlist War, First]. After five strenuous campaigns, in which he was twice taken prisoner, he returned to Prussia and reentered the Prussian army. In 1834 he was on the staff of IV Corps and there formed a friendship with Helmuth von Moltke [q.v.] the Elder. In 1860 he was present with the Spanish troops in Morocco and took part in the Battle of Tetuán [q.v.] on 4 February [see Spanish-Moroccan Wars]. In 1863 he became a Prussian major general (equivalent to brigadier general in the British and American armies) and commanded a brigade.

In the Seven Weeks' War [q.v.] of 1866 he commanded a division, and in 1870, at the beginning of the Franco-Prussian War [q.v.], he commanded VIII (Rhineland) Corps, part of the First Army under Karl von Steinmetz [q.v.]. On 8 January he took command of the First Army and won the victory at St. Quentin [q.v.] on 18–19 January 1871. After the war he commanded VIII Corps at Coblenz until his death on 13 November 1880.

Goggles. Sand goggles, or sand glasses, were first issued in the British army to the soldiers taking part in the suppression of Arabi's Revolt [q.v.] in Egypt in 1862.

Goito, Battle of (30 May 1848), Italian revolts. The Piedmontese revolt against Austrian rule on 18 March was quickly followed by insurrections in Venice and all Lombardy. The Piedmontese raised twenty-three battalions of infantry and twenty-four squadrons of cavalry. Near this village on the Mincio River, nine miles northwest of Mantua, they engaged an Austrian force of fifteen battalions of infantry, eight squadrons of cavalry, and 33 guns under Field Marshal Josef Radetzky [q.v.] and forced it to withdraw to a position behind the Adige River. The Austrians lost 618; the Italians, 362.

Golanddanzee (various spellings). In India, a term for an artilleryman.

Goldbeater's Skin. The prepared external membrane of the large intestine of an ox. It was often used to protect fuzes and priming from dampness. It was also sometimes used as a covering for balloons [q.v.].

Golden Fleece, Order of the. One of the oldest orders of chivalry, it was established by Philip the Good (1396–1467), Duke of Burgundy, in 1429 in honor of his marriage to Isabella of Portugal (1397–1471). When the Spanish Netherlands became Austrian, and the Bourbons became kings of Spain, the grandmastership of the order was claimed by both the Spanish sovereign and the Archduke of Austria. In the nineteenth century both Austria and Spain conferred the order.

Golden Kites, Order of the. In Japanese: *Kinshi kunsho*. In 1890 Japan instituted this order to honor military men. It was the only such decoration. It was abolished in 1947.

Gold Stick in Waiting. A British officer of the royal household who on ceremonial occasions pays close attendance to the sovereign. The office was instituted in 1678, and until 1820 it was always held by a colonel of the 1st or 2nd Life Guards. In 1820 the honor was extended to the colonel of the Royal Horse Guard. The emblem of office was, and is, an ebony stick with a gold head.

Silver Stick in Waiting is an officer who stands next to Gold Stick "ready to relieve him on occasions."

Gole. A Hindustani word for the main body of an army.

Goliad Massacre (27 March 1836), War for Texan Independence. Some 500 men under Colonel James Walker Fannin [q.v.] were attacked and captured by forces under Mexican General Antonio López de Santa Anna [q.v.], who ordered Fannin and his men to be shot. This was in accordance with a decree of the Mexican Parliament of 30 December 1835 that all prisoners be executed, a decree Santa Anna had sought. The order was reluctantly carried out by Colonel José Urres [q.v.], and 342 were executed. Some 48 were somehow spared or escaped.

Golog. A Malay knife with a heavy single-edge blade and a convex cutting edge. Lengths ranged from 6 to 27 inches.

Goltz, Kolmar von der (1843–1916). A German soldier who was commissioned in 1861 and entered the Kriegsakademie in Berlin in 1864 but left to fight in the Seven Weeks' War [q.v.] and was wounded in the Battle of Trautenau on 27 June 1866. He served as a staff officer during the Franco-Prussian War [q.v.] in 1870–71 and saw action in the battles of Mars-la-Tour on 16 August 1870 and of Noisseville on 31 August and 1 September and at the siege of Metz, 19 August–27 October [qq.v.]. In 1871 he was appointed to the historical section of the general staff and a professorship at the Potsdam cadet school. From 1873 to 1883 he lectured at the Kriegsakademie. He published *Rossbach und Jena,* revised as *Von Rossbach bis Jena und Auerstädt* (1883) and later *Das Volk in Waffen* (A Nation in Arms) in which he says: "We have won our position through the sharpness of our sword not through the sharpness of our mind."

In June 1883 he was sent to reorganize the Turkish army along Prussian lines. He became known as Goltz Pasha and was appointed a mushir (field marshal). He remained in Turkey until 1896. In 1900 he was promoted lieutenant general of infantry in the German army. He retired in 1913 but returned to duty during World War I and conducted the brilliant siege of Kut-al-Amara. He died of cholera or was poisoned by Young Turks on 19 April 1916 in Mesopotamia.

Golymin, Battle of (26 December 1806), Napoleonic Wars. Some 38,000 French troops under Joachim Murat, Pierre Augereau, and (a late arrival on the field) Louis Davout [qq.v.] fought 18,000 Russian troops under General André Gallitzin (fl. 1806) and General Dmitri Sergeivich Doctorov (or Dokhturov) (fl. 1812) just south and east of this Polish village in east-central Poland only 11 miles from Pultusk [q.v.], where another battle was being fought on the same day. The Russians put up a stout fight from good defensive positions but were pushed back, retreating in good order. Each side lost about 800 men.

Gómez y Báez, Máximo (1826–1905). A Cuban soldier who served in the Spanish army in Santo Domingo and Cuba. He then farmed in Cuba until he joined the Revolution of 1868–78 [see Cuban Revolutions]. In the second Revolution of 1895 he was general-in-chief of the Cuban forces. A ruthless man, he believed that the way to rid Cuba of Spaniards was to burn all their plantations and kill all the Cubans who worked for them. In 1898, when the United States intervened [see Spanish-American War], he placed his troops at the disposal of the American army. A Cuban military assembly deposed him from the supreme command in 1899, when he accepted three million dollars from the United States to support the Cuban army.

General Maximo Gómez y Báez

Gomm, William Maynard (1784–1875). A British soldier who was gazetted to the 9th Foot at the age of ten as a tribute and favor to his father, a lieutenant colonel killed in the attack on Guadeloupe in 1794. In 1799 he joined his regiment and fought in Holland under the Duke of York [q.v.]. He served as assistant quartermaster general at Copenhagen, in the Peninsular War, and at Waterloo [q.v.]. He was present at Corunna and later that year at Walcheren [qq.v.]. In 1837 he was promoted major general, and from 1839 to 1842 he commanded the troops in Jamaica. In 1846 he was sent to be commander-in-chief, India, but when he arrived, he found that his appointment had been canceled and the position given to Sir Charles Napier [q.v.]. However, he was again appointed in 1850, and he served until 1855. In 1868 he was made a field marshal, and in 1875 he was appointed constable of the Tower.

Gondar, Battle of (1887), Abyssinian-Sudanese conflict. A Dervish army from the Sudan under Mahdist Emir Abu Anja [q.v.] invaded Abyssinia and defeated an Abyssinian army under Ras Takla Haymanot Adal [q.v.] in a fierce battle on the plain of Debra Sin, near this ancient town, 21 miles north of Lake Tana and 30 miles west of Gondar. Adal himself escaped, but his son was taken prisoner, and when the Dervishes sacked Gondar itself, his wife and daughter were captured.

Gonzales, Battle of (2 October 1835). The first battle of the War for Texan Independence [q.v.] was fought between Texans and Mexicans near this town, 60 miles east of San Antonio. When a force of 100 Mexican troops arrived to capture an old 6-pounder gun in the possession of Texan colonists, they were met by 167 armed Texans. On the morning of 2 October the two sides faced each other. A volley was fired, the Texan cannon discharged a quantity of nails and scrap, and the Mexicans fled.

González, Manuel (1833–1893). A Mexican soldier and political leader who served as president of Mexico from 1880 to 1884.

Good Conduct Badges and Pay. In the British army a private who could keep his name out of the regimental defaulter's book for two years was given the good conduct badge, worn on the sleeve below the elbow, and an extra penny per day. After six years of good conduct, he received twopence per day and a second badge. An additional penny a day was added for the next three badges, awarded after twelve years, eighteen years, and twenty-eight years. Noncommissioned officers were not eligible for the extra pay.

Good Hope. See Cape of Good Hope, Capture of.

Good Offices. The offer of a nonbelligerent government to give unofficial and impartial advice to two or more belligerent governments. This is often a first step toward mediation. It usually is a useful channel of communication into and out of belligerent countries.

Good Templars, International Order of. A temperance organization whose members pledged abstinence from all alcoholic drinks. It originated in 1851 in Utica, New York, and spread through the United States, Canada, and Britain. Good

Templars were found throughout army units, and many commanding officers encouraged their work. The first American lodge established on an army post was formed in 1873 at Camp Baker, Montana, by Lieutenant William B. Nelson. Many lodges provided some form of clubroom where soldiers could play cards and relax.

Goose Step. Originally a drill in which recruits were taught balance by standing on one leg and swinging the other backward and forward. From this developed the straight-legged, stiff-kneed marching step in which the legs are swung high from the hip that is used by some European armies in parades and ceremonies. The step originated in the imperial Russian army and, called *Stechschritt,* was adopted in German armies from the days of Frederick the Great (1712–1786). It came to be associated with extreme militarism. Writer George Orwell (1905–1950) described it as "one of the most horrible sights in the world."

Gora. In India, the name for a white man, such as a British private, who was not a gentleman, not a sahib.

Gorben, August von (1816–1880). A Prussian general who during the Franco-Prussian War [q.v.] distinguished himself in the Battle of Spicheren on 7 August 1870 and at Gravelotte [qq.v.] on 18 August 1870. He succeeded General Edwin von Manteuffel [q.v.] in command of the First Army and won a decisive victory over the French in the Battle of St. Quentin [q.v.] on 18–19 January 1871.

Gorchakov / Gortchakov. The name of a noble Russian family that traced its ancestry back to Vladimir the Great (956?–1015) and in the nineteenth century produced a number of distinguished soldiers:

Prince Aleksandr Ivanovich (1764–1825). He served as a soldier under his uncle General (later Field Marshal) Count Aleksandr Vasilievich Suvorov [q.v.] in Turkey and Poland. In 1798 he became a lieutenant general and distinguished himself during the Napoleonic Wars, especially at Heilsburg and Friedland [qq.v.] in 1807. From 1812 to 1814 he was minister of war, and from 1814 until his death he was a member of the Imperial Council.

Prince Andrei Ivanovich (1768–1855). A brother of Aleksandr who in 1799 served as a major general under Suvorov in Italy. He was present at Friedland in 1807. He commanded a division of grenadiers in the Battle of Borodino [q.v.] in 1812, where he was wounded, and he fought with distinction at Leipzig [q.v.] and in the French Campaign of 1814. He was promoted general of infantry in 1819 and retired in 1828.

Prince Mikhail Dmitrievich (1795–1861). He served in campaigns in Persia in 1810 and against Napoleon in 1812–15. During the Russo-Turkish War [q.v.] of 1828–29 he commanded a division and was present at the sieges of Silistria and Shumla. He fought to suppress the Poles in the Polish Revolution [q.v.] and distinguished himself in the Battle of Grochow, in which he was wounded on 25 February 1831, and in the Battle of Ostrolenka [qq.v.]. From 1839 to 1851 he was governor of eastern Siberia, except for a period in 1849, when he commanded the artillery in the Russian intervention to suppress the Hungarian Revolution [q.v.]. In 1852 he was the Russian army's representative at the funeral

of the Duke of Wellington. In the Russo-Turkish War that began in 1853 he commanded the troops that occupied Moldavia and Walachia. In 1854 he crossed the Danube and besieged Silistria. In 1855 he was commander-in-chief of the Russian forces in the Crimea [see Crimean War]. From 1856 to 1861 he was governor-general of Poland.

Prince Pyotr Dmitrievich (1790–1868). He fought in the Napoleonic Wars in 1807 and again in 1813–14. He also fought in the Caucasus in 1820 and in the Russo-Turkish War [q.v.] of 1828–29, in which he won the Battle of Aidos. From 1843 to 1851 he was governor-general of western Siberia. Although he had retired, he came back into service and commanded VI Corps in the Crimean War [q.v.], fighting the battles of the Alma and Inkerman [qq.v.].

Gordon, Alexander (1786–1815). A British soldier who served as aide-de-camp to his uncle Sir David Baird (1757–1829) in the capture of the Cape of Good Hope [q.v.] in 1806. In 1807 he took part in the Battle of Copenhagen [q.v.]. He then fought in the Peninsular War and took part in the abortive expedition to Buenos Aires [qq.v.]. In 1813 he was promoted lieutenant colonel. During the Hundred Days [q.v.] he served as an aide to Wellington. He was mortally wounded in the Battle of Waterloo [q.v.] and died at Wellington's headquarters while in the next room the duke was writing his famous dispatch announcing his victory.

Gordon, Charles George (1833–1885). A British soldier known as Chinese Gordon and as Gordon Pasha. He served in the Crimean War [q.v.] and was with one of the columns that attacked the redan [q.v.] on 18 June 1855. As an engineer officer he took part in the capture of Peking (Beijing) [q.v.] and the destruction of the Summer Palace [q.v.] in 1860–62. In 1863–64 he commanded the Ever Victorious Army [q.v.] during the Taiping Rebellion [q.v.] and was made a mandarin of the first class. It was this service that established his reputation as a commander and gave him the name Chinese Gordon. At the end of his service in China the *Times* in a leading article said: "Never did soldier of fortune deport himself with a nicer sense of military honour, with more gallantry against the resisting, and with more mercy towards the vanquished, with more disinterested neglect of opportunities of personal advancement, or with more entire devotion to the objects and desires of his own government than this officer, who, after all his victories, has just laid down his sword" (5 August 1864).

In 1874 he was employed by Ismail Pasha (1830–1895), khedive of Egypt, as governor of the equatorial provinces in the Sudan, where he served until 1876, striving unsuccessfully to suppress the slave trade. In 1877 he was appointed governor-general of the Sudan and for nearly three years fought against slavers and worked to establish a sound government. He then returned to the British army, was made a major general, and was given command of the Royal Engineers on Mauritius. In 1883 he spent most of the year on leave studying biblical archaeology in Palestine.

After the disaster to William Hicks Pasha [q.v.] Egypt decided to abandon the Sudan to the Dervishes [q.v.] and called on Gordon to withdraw its garrisons. He was dispatched to Khartoum, where he was successful in withdrawing some 2,500 soldiers and their families before he was besieged by Dervishes on 12 March 1884 [see Khartoum, Siege of]. He

Gordon, Charles George *British troops investigating the steps of the governor's palace where Gordon was killed.*

held out until 26 January 1885, when a determined Dervish assault carried the town and he was killed. A rescue attempt under General Garnet Wolseley [q.v.] narrowly failed to reach him in time [see Gordon Relief Expedition]. In a postscript to his last letter from the besieged city on 29 December 1894, he wrote: "I am quite happy, thank God, and, like [Sir Henry] Lawrence [q.v.], I have *tried* to do my duty."

Gordon, who because of his religious zeal was often called the Christian soldier, was also noted for disobedience to orders. In 1844 an exasperated Lord Cromer (1841–1917), Britain's agent in Egypt, wrote in a letter to Lord Granville (1815–1891), the British foreign secretary: "A man who habitually consults the Prophet Isaiah when he is in difficulty is not about to obey the orders of anyone."

Gordon, George (1770–1836). A British soldier who was also the 15th and last Duke of Gordon. In 1794 he raised the Gordon Highlanders [q.v.] and commanded the regiment in Spain, Corsica, Ireland, and Holland. In the Walcheren Expedition [q.v.] of 1807 he commanded a division.

Gordon, George Henry (1823–1886). An American soldier who entered West Point in the class of 1846. In the Mexican War [q.v.], in which he fought under Winfield Scott, he was twice wounded and won a brevet for his bravery in the Battle of Cerro Gordo [q.v.]. In 1854 he resigned his commission, studied law at Harvard, and was admitted to the bar in 1857. At the outbreak of the American Civil War he raised the 2nd Massachusetts and on 25 May 1861 became its colonel. In the spring of 1862 he served under General Nathaniel Banks [q.v.] in the Shenandoah Valley; on 9 June of that year he was promoted brigadier general. He fought at Cedar Mountain, Chancellorsville, South Mountain, and Antietam [qq.v.]. In 1863 he commanded a division during the siege of Charleston [q.v.]. He was mustered out as a brevet major general. After the war he practiced the law in Boston and was one of the founders of the Military Historical Society of Massachusetts.

Gordon, George Washington (1836–1911). An American soldier who was graduated from the Western Military Institute in Nashville, Tennessee, in 1859. At the beginning of the American Civil War he enlisted in the Confederate 11th Tennessee and by December 1861 was its colonel. He took part in the battles of Murfreesboro, Chickamauga, and Chattanooga [qq.v.]. During the Atlanta Campaign [q.v.] he was wounded in the Battle of Franklin [q.v.]. He was appointed a brigadier general in 1864.

After the war he practiced law and served in Congress, where he became the last surviving Confederate general to serve as a member. At his death he was commander-in-chief of the United Confederate Veterans.

Gordon, John Brown (1832–1904). An American lawyer who became a Confederate general. He attended the University of Georgia but failed to graduate. When the American Civil War began, he was developing coal mines in Georgia. In 1861, although he had no previous military experience, he was elected captain of a company calling itself the Raccoon Roughs. He ended the war as a major general and a corps commander, having taken part in every battle of the Army of Northern Virginia [q.v.] except those in which he was absent because of wounds, of which he suffered eight.

In the Battle of Antietam [q.v.] he was wounded in the head and almost drowned in his own blood. On 1 November 1862 he was promoted brigadier general and in that rank led a Georgia brigade at Chancellorsville and Gettysburg [qq.v.]. Gordon distinguished himself in the Wilderness [q.v.] in May 1864 and soon after, on 14 May, was promoted major general. At Appomattox his men made the last charge of the Army of Northern Virginia [q.v.].

After the war he was three times elected to the U.S. Senate and served four years as governor of Georgia. He was one of the founders of the United Confederate Veterans and was its first commander-in-chief, serving from 1890 until his death.

Gordon Highlanders. One of the most famous regiments in the British army. It was raised in 1794 by the Duke of Gordon [see Gordon, George]. From 1798 to 1861 it was known as the 92nd (Highland) Regiment of Foot. From 1861 to 1881 it was the 92nd (Gordon Highlanders) Regiment of Foot. In 1881 it was amalgamated with the 75th (Stirlingshire) Regiment of Foot to form the Gordon Highlanders.

The regiment, or portions of it, served in the Peninsular War and at Waterloo, the Tirah Campaign, the relief of Chitral, Arabi's Revolt, the Second Afghan War, and the Second Boer Anglo-War [qq.v.]. It was during the Tirah Campaign that a battalion of the regiment made its famous charge on the heights of Dargai [q.v.] and Piper George Findlater [q.v.] won the Victoria Cross [q.v.].

Gordon Relief Expedition (1884–85). An unsuccessful military expedition under Lord Wolseley [see Wolsely, Garnet] that attempted to relieve besieged Khartoum [q.v.] and rescue General Charles ("Chinese") Gordon [q.v.]. There was considerable delay in authorizing the expedition, for which Prime Minister William Gladstone (1809–1898) was later blamed.

Wolseley carried his army up the Nile as far as possible in 800 specially designed boats with 400 imported Canadian voyageurs to help man them. Fighting several small engagements, the army advanced into the Sudan. There an advanced desert column of 73 officers and 1,032 other ranks formed under Herbert Stewart (1833–1885), including a few sailors under Lord Charles Beresford [q.v.], and set off on a dash across the desert, avoiding the great loop of the Nile. It was attacked and its advance halted at Abu Klea, where Frederick Burnaby [q.v.], whom Wolseley had named second-in-command, was killed. At Gubat [q.v.] on 19 January it was again attacked, and Stewart was mortally wounded. It gained the Nile under Sir Charles Wilson (1836–1905) and on the 24th sent an advanced force up the river in steamers that had escaped from Khartoum. On 28 January 1885 it reached Khartoum, just two days after the city had fallen and Gordon had been killed [see Siege of Khartoum]. *Punch* on 14 February 1885 published a sketch of a stricken Britannia holding her forearm across her eyes with the caption "Too Late!" General Wolseley was never again given an independent command.

Gorgas, Josiah (1818–1883). An American soldier who, after graduation from West Point in 1841, spent his entire military career in ordnance work. During the Mexican War he served as chief of ordnance at the army's depot established at Veracruz. During the American Civil War he served as the Confederate chief of ordnance. Struggling under enormous difficulties, he managed to keep the Confederate armies supplied with guns and ammunition. General Joseph Johnston [q.v.] said that he "created the ordnance department out of nothing." In November 1864 he was promoted brigadier general. It has been said, with much justice, that next to Robert E. Lee, Gorgas was the most important officer in the Confederacy.

Gorgas was a thoughtful officer and sometimes questioned the righteousness of the southern cause. After the Confederate defeat at Gettysburg on 3 July 1863 and the fall of Vicksburg the following day he wrote in his journal: "Can we believe in the justice of Providence or must we conclude that we are after all wrong?" Still, he soldiered on.

After the war he managed an ironworks until 1869, when he became a professor at the University of the South. He later became president of the University of Alabama.

Gorgas, William Crawford (1854–1920). An American army surgeon who was the son of Josiah Gorgas [q.v.]. Unable to obtain an appointment to West Point, he became a doctor and then an army surgeon, serving in the West. At Fort Brown, Texas, fighting an epidemic of yellow fever, he was himself infected. Recovered, and thus immune, he devoted himself to the study of the disease. Following Walter Reed's [q.v.] discovery that mosquitoes carry the fever, Gorgas freed Havana of the disease while serving as chief sanitary officer there from 1898 to 1908, during and after the Spanish-American War [q.v.]. Later he was equally successful in Panama. He became surgeon general of the American army and a brigadier general.

Gorge. An opening in the rear of a fortification. The gorge of a redan or a lunette is the open space between the extremities of the flanking walls.

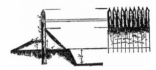

Section and elevation of gorge of stockade

Gorget. Originally a piece of armor worn at the neck, it became in the nineteenth century in some armies an ornamental collar or metal plate, crescent-shaped and decorated, worn on a chain or strap around the neck to indicate officer rank or a special appointment or duty.

Gorget Patches. Sometimes called tabs. Colored patches worn on the collar. In the British army, red was used for generals and staff officers.

Görgey (Görgei), Arthur von (1818–1916). A Hungarian officer who in 1841 as an *Oberstleutnant* (first lieutenant) in the 12th Hussars had to borrow a large sum (2,000 gulden) from his family to purchase the elaborate uniforms and sleek chargers he was required to own. To help pay back his debt, he drank water and ate only army-issue bread. In 1845 he resigned and joined the Hungarian national army as a higher-paid captain. Within a year he was a general and served in the Hungarian Revolution [q.v.] of 1848–49. He was appointed commander-in-chief in February 1849 and won a series of victories, culminating in the capture of Buda on 21 May. He became dictator of Hungary, briefly, succeeding Lajos Kossuth (1802–1894). He was overwhelmed when Russian forces intervened to restore Austrian authority. He surrendered to the Russians under General Fedor Rudiger [q.v.] at Siriak (Világos) on 13 August 1849 and was interned by the Austrians until 1867.

Gorloff Gun. See Gatling Gun.

Gorni-Dubnik, Battle of (24 October 1877), Russo-Turkish War of 1877. The 2nd Division of the Russian Guard under Ossip (Joseph) V. Gourko [q.v.] led the Russian invasion of Bulgaria [q.v.] and successfully attacked Turks under Achmet Hefzi Pasha (d. 1877) at Gorni-Dubnik (Dabnik) in northern Bulgaria, 14 miles west-southwest of Plevna (Pleven). Turkish losses were 1,500 killed and wounded and 53 officers and 2,250 other ranks captured, including Achmet Hefzi Pasha. Russian losses were 3,300 killed and wounded, including 116 officers of the guard.

Goudrons. Small fascines or faggots covered with wax and pitch and used for setting fire to buildings, crops, etc.

Gough, Hugh (1779–1869). A British soldier who in 1793 was commissioned in the newly formed Limerick City Militia, of which his father was lieutenant colonel. At fifteen he was adjutant of the 119th Foot, and on 6 June 1795 he was made a lieutenant in the 78th Highlanders. He was with that regiment in the capture of the Cape of Good Hope in 1796. After transferring to the 87th Regiment (Royal Irish Fusiliers), he served in the West Indies, where he fought brigands at St. Lucia and took part in the capture of Trinidad, the attack on Puerto Rico, and the capture of Surinam. He was promoted captain in 1803 and major in 1805. In January 1809, during the Peninsular War [q.v.], he arrived in Portugal in command of a battalion and was severely wounded in the side by a shell in the Battle of Talavera de la Reina [q.v.] in July. At the request of Wellington he was commissioned brevet lieutenant colonel, to date from that battle. He was thus the first British officer to be brevetted for service in action at the head of his regiment.

He took part in the charge that captured the first French eagle at Barrosa [q.v.] on 5 March 1811, and he defended the breach at the siege of Tarifa [q.v.]. In 1812 he led his battalion at Vitoria. In the Battle of Nivelle [q.v.] on 10 November 1813 he was again severely wounded. On 4 June 1815 he was knighted. His battalion was disbanded on 1 February 1817, and he was placed on half pay until 1819, when he joined the 22nd Foot. In 1826 he was again on half pay, although in 1830 he was promoted major general. In 1837 he was given command of the Mysore Division of the Madras army, in which he served until he was sent to China to take command of the British troops in the First Opium War [q.v.].

On 2 March 1841 he arrived in China, and in May he successfully attacked the forts defending Canton (Guangzhou) in a combined operation with Admiral Sir William Parker (1781–1866). In July he attacked and captured the fortified city of Ching-keang-foo (Chinkiang), 40 miles east of Nanking (Nanxiang or Nanjing) on the right bank of the Yangtze River.

Gough returned to Madras as commander-in-chief of the Madras army. On 11 August 1843 he was appointed commander-in-chief, India. In December of that year he defeated the Marathas in the Gwalior Campaign [q.v.]. In 1845 he led his army in the First Sikh War, and three years later in the Second Sikh War [qq.v.], defeating the Sikhs after hard-fought battles in both wars. His losses in the Battle of Chilianwala [q.v.] in the Second Sikh War so horrified those in England that General Charles Napier [q.v.] was sent out to replace him. Before Napier could arrive, Gough had won the final Battle of Gujerat [q.v.] and accepted the surrender of the Sikh forces.

He saw no more active service, but he was made a viscount, granted a pension, and became a full general in 1854 and a field marshal in 1862. He was said to have commanded in more general actions than any other British officer in the century except Wellington.

Goumiers or Goums. *Goum* is an Arabic word denoting a gathering of the armed and mounted men of a tribe. Such men were formed by the French into irregular Arab posses of about 100 men, part on foot and part mounted, and were used as scouts in Algeria from about 1850 and later in Tunis. Eventually they were incorporated into the order of battle of the French army.

Goundam Massacre (15 January 1894), French conquest of Algeria. On 12 January 1894 French Lieutenant Colonel Eugène Bonnier (d. 1894) led a punitive expedition against the Tuaregs [q.v.], taking about 150 men with some artillery southwest from Timbuktu (now in Mali) to Goundam, near Lake Fabuibine. The following day they surprised a Tuareg camp and captured 500 sheep and a large number of camels. There was some skirmishing on the 14th. At four o'clock on the morning of 15 January the Tuaregs attacked the French camp and killed the entire force with the exception of one officer. The corpses were later returned to Timbuktu by Major (later Marshal) Joseph Joffre [q.v.].

Gour. Wheat cakes mixed with molasses and fed to elephants in India.

Gourgaud, Gaspard (1783–1852). A French officer who served in Napoleon's armies and was one of the three persons chosen to accompany Napoleon to St. Helena in 1815. He remained on the island two years. He wrote *Sainte Hélène, Journal inedédit de 1815 à 1818,* which was published posthumously in two volumes in 1889. He also collaborated with Charles Tristan de Montholon [q.v.] in writing *Mémoires pour servir à l'histoire de France sous Napoléon,* based upon notes dictated by Napoleon, which was published in 1823. Gourgaud returned to France in 1821 and was promoted lieutenant general.

Gourko, Ossip (Joseph) Vladimirovich (1828–1901). A Russian soldier of Lithuanian extraction who entered the imperial bodyguard. At the beginning of the Russo-Turkish War [q.v.] of 1877 he commanded the leading column in the Russian invasion of the Balkans. On 7 July he captured Trnovo (Tirnovo), Bulgaria, on the Yantra River, 60 miles east of Plevna (Pleven), and crossed the Balkan Mountains by way of the Hain Bogaz Pass. On 18 July he captured Shipka [q.v.], a village 7 miles north-north-west of Kazanlik, which the Turks evacuated the following day. He made a series of raids into the Tunja Valley and cut the railroad there in two places. Having checked the advance of the Turkish army, he returned to Russia. In October he was given command of the Allied cavalry and cut the communication lines to Plevna [q.v.]. In December he recrossed the Balkans and occupied Sofia, Adrianople, and Philippopolis [see Bulgaria, Invasion of; Gorni-Dubnik, Battle of]. In 1879–80 he was governor of St. Petersburg, and in 1883 and 1894 governor-general of Poland.

Grade. Rank, usually applied to officers' rank.

Graeco-Turkish War (1897). In this war, foolishly provoked by the Greeks, two distinct campaigns were fought, one in Thessaly and another in Epirus.

Thessaly Campaign. In March 1897 the Turks massed about 58,000 men and 156 guns under Edhem Pasha [q.v.] on the Thessalian frontier on the east-central portion of the Greek peninsula, which had been ceded to Greece in 1881. Opposing them were about 45,000 Greeks with 98 guns. After some skirmishing in early April, Edhem Pasha ordered a general advance on the 18th. The left and right wings of the advancing Turkish army encountered stiff Greek resistance in the mountains near Nezeros (today Kallipeuke, in northeast Thessaly on the slope of lower Olympus), but on the 19th the main body of his army occupied the Meluna Pass.

On the road to Tirnovo (Trnovo or Tyrnovo), 10 miles west of Larissa, the Greeks entrenched, and there was some sharp fighting on the 21st and 22nd. On the 23rd the Turks threatened both flanks of the Greek position, and the Greeks panicked. They could have made a retirement upon Larissa, which was well provisioned and offered a good defensive position, but the terrified soldiers, refusing to halt their flight, streamed south toward present-day Pharsala (Phársalos), near the Enipeus River, where in 48 B.C. Caesar had defeated Pompey. The Turks did not vigorously pursue, and it was 27 April before they entered Larissa. This ended the first phase of the war. A hoped-for uprising against the Turks in Macedonia did not occur.

At Pharsala the mass of the Greek soldiery was halted, their panic cooled, and order established. Recognizing the importance of Velestinon (ancient Pherae) in southeastern Thessaly, 10 miles west of Volos, the Greeks sent a brigade there. But Velestinon was 40 miles from Pharsala, and the numerically inferior Greek army was thus divided. On 5 May the Greeks were driven from their positions before Pharsala, and the following day they fell back in fairly good order upon Domokos (Dhomokos, ancient Thaumaci), 17 miles north-northwest of Lamia. Velestinon was abandoned.

The Greeks entrenched, and the Turks did not attack until 17 May. Although repulsed on their right and center, they succeeded on the left and threatened the Greek line of retreat. This was sufficient for the Greeks to abandon their entire position during the night, and demoralized, they failed to hold the Furka Pass.

Epirus Campaign. At the beginning of the war about 15,000 Greeks under Colonel Manos in Epirus in northwestern Greece occupied a line from Arta, on the Arakhthos River,

Graeco-Turkish War *Greeks bring out the wounded after the Battle of Velestinon, 1897.*

four miles east to Peta. Some 28,000 Turks under Achmet (or Ahmed) Hifsi faced them and on 18 April began a three-day bombardment of the Greek positions. Unable to take the bridge across the Arakhthos River, they fell back, and the Greeks advanced to Pentapolis (Pendapolis or Pentepagadia), seven miles east-southeast of Serrai, but were soon driven back to Arta in a panic. Greek reinforcements were sent up from Athens, but on 12 May the Turks again attacked, and the Greeks were defeated as completely in Epirus as they had been in Thessaly. In response to Greek appeals, the tsar telegraphed the sultan, who ordered an armistice. On 20 May a peace arranged by the European powers gave money and land in Thessaly to Turkey.

Graham, Gerald (1831–1899). A British soldier, educated at Woolwich and commissioned into the Royal Engineers in 1850, who in the Crimean War [q.v.] won one of the first Victoria Crosses. He served in the Opium War [q.v.] in China in 1861–62 and distinguished himself in the attacks on the Taku Forts [q.v.], in which he was wounded in the leg. He was promoted major general in 1881, and in 1882, during Arabi's Revolt [q.v.], he defeated the Egyptians in the Battle of Kassassin and led the assault at Tell el-Kebir [qq.v.]. In 1884–85 he commanded at Suakin in the eastern Sudan and won the Second Battle of El Teb [q.v.] and the Battle of Tamai against the Dervishes of Osman Digna [q.v.]. He became a lieutenant general in 1884.

Graham, John (1778–1821). A British soldier born in Scotland who was commissioned at sixteen into the 90th Foot. In 1806 he was present in the invasion of the Cape of Good Hope [q.v.], and in 1811, on the eastern frontier of Cape Colony, he drove back invading Xhosa forces under Ndlambe [q.v.]. In 1812 he established a camp 75 miles east-northeast of Port Elizabeth, which grew into present-day Grahamstown. After returning to Europe, he took part in the Walcheren Campaign [q.v.]. In 1815 he was back in South Africa, where he became commandant at Simon's Town.

Graham, Thomas, Baron Lynedoch (1748–1843). A British soldier who served with the force that blockaded Malta in 1799–1800. During the Corunna Campaign [q.v.] he was aide-de-camp to Sir John Moore [q.v.]. He commanded a brigade in the Walcheren Campaign [q.v.], and was promoted lieutenant general in 1810. He was commander of the British garrison at Cádiz [q.v.]. In 1811 after defeating Marshal Claude Victor [q.v.] at Barrosa [q.v.], he resigned in pique when the Spanish generals claimed all the credit for the victory. When he finally returned to duty, he commanded a division under Wellington on the Iberian Peninsula in 1812–13, serving at Ciudad Rodrigo and Badajoz [qq.v.]. In 1813 he besieged San Sebastián [q.v.]. After Wellington's crossing of the Bidassoa on 3 October 1813, he retired for a time, troubled by an eye disease, but he returned the following year and commanded the British contingent in Holland. He was promoted general in 1821. He was one of the principal founders of the United Services Club [q.v.] in London in 1815.

Grahamstown, Battle of (6 January 1835), Kaffir Wars. In December 1834 Chief Maqoma [q.v.] led the largest Xhosa army ever assembled across the Fish River in eastern South Africa and began marauding in Cape Colony. Refugees fled to Grahamstown, 75 miles east-northeast of Port Elizabeth, defended by 300 soldiers along with 150 Hottentot hunters who were there by chance, and five guns, all under Colonel Harry Smith [q.v.], who had ridden, it was said, 600 miles in six days to join them. In a battle lasting two and a half hours, the Xhosas lost an estimated 1,000. The defenders of Grahamstown lost 3 killed and 5 wounded.

Grand Army of the Republic. The largest organization of Union veterans of the American Civil War was established in 1865 by Dr. Benjamin Franklin Stephenson (1823–1871), a former surgeon in the 14th Illinois Infantry, with the support of former Union Generals Richard James Oglesby (1824–1899), Stephen Augustus Hurlbut, and John Alexander Logan [qq.v.]. Members of the organization had to have served in the Union army at some time between 12 April 1861 and 9 April 1865 and to have been honorably discharged. The first post was established in Decatur, Illinois. Black veterans were segregated in separate posts; immigrants, particularly Irish, were not always welcome.

In 1866 the GAR, as it was popularly known, held its first "encampment" and elected General Hurlbut its first commander-in-chief. Peak membership, reached in 1890, was 408,489 (or 427,981—accounts differ). The most powerful pressure group in the country, it censored textbooks, intimidated congressmen, and threatened presidents.

Beginning in the 1880s, a fellow feeling for former Confederates developed, and Blue-Gray reunions were inaugurated. The final encampment held in Indianapolis in August 1949 was attended by six of the sixteen surviving members. Its last member, Albert Woolson [q.v.], a former drummer boy, died in 1956.

Grand Divisions. During the American Civil War, when Major General Ambrose Burnside [q.v.] took command of the Union's Army of the Potomac [q.v.] in November 1862, he reorganized it into three grand divisions, each of two army corps plus some cavalry and artillery [see Fredericksburg, Battle of]. The grand divisions were soon after broken up.

Grande Armée. An army created by Napoleon on 18 May 1803 after Britain had repudiated the Treaty of Amiens (27

March 1802). French field armies, like those of most other countries, were named after the areas in which they served. By avoiding this practice, Napoleon gave no clue to his plans. Originally the Grande Armée consisted of 350,000 men divided into seven army corps with a cavalry and an artillery reserve plus the elite Imperial Guard [see Garde Impériale]. By June 1812, as Napoleon made plans to invade Russia, it had grown to 630,000 and was divided into eleven army corps, four reserve cavalry corps, the Imperial Guard, and an independent Austrian corps. The name came to be applied to any of Napoleon's principal field armies.

Technically, the Grande Armée remained in existence until Napoleon's first abdication at Fontainebleau on 6 April 1814.

Grand Quartier-Général Imperial. Napoleon's imperial army headquarters. It consisted of his *maison* (personal staff), the *grand état-major* (army staff), and the *intendance* (administration and supply).

Grand Review, The (23–24 May 1865). A review of 150,000 Union veterans of the American Civil War [q.v.], led by General William Tecumseh Sherman [q.v.] in Washington, D.C. The 23rd, the first day of the review, was the first day the American flag was flown at full mast since the death of President Abraham Lincoln on 15 April.

Grand Rounds. In the American army an inspection by the officer of the day of the guard posts, made at least once in twenty-four hours, when he was accompanied by the non-commissioned officer of the guard and an escort of privates.

Grand Strategy. The part of military planning and operations concerned with the enunciation of war aims, the formulation of key policies, the maintenance of alliances, and the overall organization of an army or a nation for war.

Grand Tactics. The planning for a battle and the employment of the forces on the field.

Grant, Colquhoun (1780–1829). A British soldier who was commissioned into the 11th Foot at the age of fourteen and at eighteen was captured at Ostend in 1798. From 1810 he served as Wellington's intelligence officer in the Peninsular War [q.v.]. He has been called the "first respectable spy." Wellington called him "a very remarkable character." He was adept at breaking French codes, and he often rode behind the enemy's lines, always in full uniform. He was captured near the Coa River in 1812 but escaped at Bayonne and made his way to Paris, from which he relayed much valuable information. He then left France disguised as a sailor and returned to Spain. During the Hundred Days [q.v.] he became the first "head of intelligence." He was the first to discover that Napoleon was advancing directly on Brussels from Charleroi, not, as expected toward Mons, news he tried to send to Wellington. He was foiled by the stupidity of Wilhelm von Dorberg (fl. 1815), a cavalry general who had deserted to the Allies in 1813. Instead of relaying the information to Wellington, Dorberg sent it back to Grant, insisting he was dead wrong. Thus Wellington was unaware of Napoleon's movements until just before the Duchess of Richmond's ball [q.v.].

Grande Armée *Napoleon's Grande Armée retreats from Moscow, 1812.*

In 1821 Grant was promoted colonel of the 54th Foot, and he commanded a brigade in the First Anglo-Burmese War [q.v.]. He should not be confused with another soldier of the same name (1764?-1835) who also fought in Spain and at Waterloo and rose to become a lieutenant general.

Grant, James Augustus (1827–1892). A Scottish soldier and African explorer. He served in the Indian army to the rank of colonel, taking part in the Second Sikh War, the Indian Mutiny, and the Abyssinian Campaign [qq.v.]. His biological collections were notable, and with John Hanning Speke [q.v.] he explored the sources of the Nile River (1860–63).

Grant, James Hope (1808–1875). A British soldier who was commissioned in 1826 and became a captain in 1835. He served in the First and Second Sikh Wars, the Indian Mutiny, and the Opium War of 1860 [qq.v.]. In 1861, as a lieutenant general, he was commander-in-chief of the Madras army, having succeeded General Patrick Grant [q.v.]. He returned to England in 1865, and in 1870 he was in command at Aldershot, where he was largely responsible for the annual maneuvers. In 1872 he was gazetted general.

Grant, Patrick (1804–1894). A British soldier who was commissioned into the Bengal Native Infantry in 1820 and became a captain in 1822. He served in the Gwalior Campaign and the First Sikh War [qq.v.] and from 1856 to 1861 was commander-in-chief of the Madras army. He was promoted lieutenant general in 1862, general in 1870, and field marshal in 1883. In 1885 he was appointed colonel of the Horse Guards and Gold Stick in Waiting [q.v.] to Queen Victoria. He became governor of the Royal Hospital, Chelsea [q.v.], in 1874 and remained in that position for twenty-one years.

Grant, Ulysses Simpson (1822–1885), real name: Hiram Ulysses Grant. An American soldier who, learning that his congressman had entered him in West Point as Ulysses Simpson Grant, simply accepted the new name and was so graduated in 1843, ranking 21 out of a class of 39. He served through the Mexican War [q.v.], under Zachary Taylor and later under Winfield Scott [qq.v.]. He won a brevet of first lieutenant for his gallantry at Molino del Rey and a brevet captaincy for his conduct at Chapultepec. On 31 July 1854 he resigned his commission and tried various business ventures without success. In 1861, at the beginning of the American Civil War, he was working as a clerk in a leather goods store run by his two younger brothers. On 17 June he became colonel of the 21st Illinois Volunteers, and on 31 July he was promoted to brigadier general, to rank from 17 May. He commanded various military districts and on 7 November 1861 was outmaneuvered at the Battle of Belmont [q.v.] by a Confederate force under Leonidas Polk [q.v.]. As the leader of the expedition that captured Fort Donelson [q.v.] he earned the sobriquet of Unconditional Surrender Grant. On 6 February he was promoted major general of volunteers. On 6–7 April 1862 he was surprised by a Confederate attack at Shiloh [q.v.] that he was barely able to repulse. On 4 July 1863, with the seizure of Vicksburg and of 30,000 Confederate troops, he broke Confederate control of the Mississippi. He was promoted major general in the regular army, to rank from 4 July, and received the Thanks of Congress and a gold medal.

When his department was enlarged, he moved against Confederate General Braxton Bragg [q.v.] in Tennessee; there he raised the siege of Chattanooga. On 2 March 1864 he was promoted lieutenant general and placed in command of all the Union armies. He launched a relentless attack upon the Army of Northern Virginia, and in spite of suffering heavy casualties in the battles of the Wilderness, Spotsylvania, and Cold Harbor [qq.v.], he persisted. After a ten-month siege he captured Petersburg [q.v.] and entered Richmond. On 9 April 1865 he received Lee's surrender at Appomattox [q.v.]. On 25 July he was made a full general.

Grant's avowed philosophy was: "Find out where your enemy is. Get at him as soon as you can. Strike at him as hard as you can, and keep moving on." There were people who believed Grant's methods inhumane. To them he replied: "My object in war was to exhaust Lee's army. I was obliged to sacrifice men to do it. I have been called a butcher. Well, I never spared lives to gain an objective; but then I gained it, and I knew it was the only way."

In 1868 Grant was elected president of the United States. He was reelected in 1872. His administrations were marked by numerous scandals, though he himself was blameless. In Europe in 1879, attending a Potsdam military review, he shocked Bismarck by remarking: "I am more of a farmer than a soldier. I take little or no interest in military affairs." In 1880 he lost all his money through an unsuccessful business venture. Although suffering from cancer of the throat, he wrote *Personal Memoirs of U. S. Grant,* hoping to provide for his family. The manuscript was finished on 23 July 1885, only four days before his death. In the spring of that year he had been placed on the retired list as a general.

William Tecumseh Sherman said of Grant: "Each epoch creates its own agents, and General Grant more nearly than any other man impersonated the American character of 1861–5. He will stand, therefore, as the typical hero of the Great Civil War."

General Ulysses S. Grant at Spotsylvania Court House

Grant's Peace Policy. This was a policy initiated by President U. S. Grant to win over the hostile Indians of the plains by applying just, "Christian treatment," to make a "conquest by kindness." The Indian Appropriations Act of April 10, 1869, gave Grant the power to appoint ten men "eminent for their intelligence and philanthropy" to oversee the plan. Churchmen, mostly Quakers, were appointed agents and superintendents. By 1882 there were seventy-three agencies with church-appointed agents. The policy dissolved after the murder of General Edward Canby [q.v.] by Modoc Indians on 11 April 1873 [see Modoc War].

Grant's Tomb. The tomb of Ulysses S. Grant in New York City is the largest mausoleum in the United States. Funded by $600,000 raised by 90,000 Americans, it stands 150 feet tall on a bluff above the Hudson River. It was dedicated on 27 April 1897, the seventy-fifth anniversary of Grant's birth, while warships fired salutes watched by a crowd of thousands. For many years it was one of the principal tourist attractions of the city. By 1996 it had become the most neglected of all tombs of former presidents, and vagrants were using its marble halls as toilets. Since then it has been cleaned and refurbished.

Granulation. A reference to the size and shape of the grains of powder in a propellant.

Grapeshot / Grape Shot. Artillery ammunition composed of a number of small shot, generally nine, arranged around a spindle on an iron disk or, earlier, in a canvas bag. The size of the shot varied with the caliber, but in general it was larger than canister [q.v.]. The effective range of grapeshot was from 300 to 600 yards, and when used, the cannon acted much like a large shotgun.

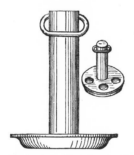

Grapeshot *Stands to hold grape, called lamp-posts*

Graspan, Battle of (25 November 1899), Second Anglo-Boer War. A British division plus a naval brigade, all under Lord Methuen [q.v.], attacked 2,400 Boers in a strong position near this town in western Cape Colony and routed them at a cost of 9 officers and 185 other ranks killed or wounded.

Gras Rifle. The Chassepot [q.v.] rifle as modified by French Major (later General) Basile Gras (1836–1901). The Gras single-shot rifle had slightly diminished grooves and used a metallic center-fire cartridge of 11 mm caliber that Gras invented. It was adopted by the French army in 1874 and was the first French service rifle to use metallic cartridges. In 1876 Lieutenant François Descostes Orsat (d. 1890) in a letter home from West Africa described its effect: "A bullet in the head takes off the skull, a bullet in the chest makes a hole the size of a plate in the victim's back, the limbs are crushed and the bones broken in a horrible manner."

This was the first French service rifle to use metallic cartridges. It remained in service in the French army until 1886, when it was replaced by the Lebel rifle [q.v.], but it continued to be sold in Balkan countries and in Japan, where it was a model for the Murata rifle [q.v.] Model 1881.

Grass Widow. According to *Hobson Jobson* (see bibliography), this was "applied in India, with a shade of malignity, to ladies living apart from their husbands, especially as recreating at the Hill stations, whilst the husbands are at their duties in the plains."

Graticule. 1. A line on a map representing a parallel of latitude or the meridian of longitude.

2. The cross wire or aiming mark in a telescope or aiming device. In American usage this was often called a reticule.

Grattan Massacre (19 August 1854). When a Mormon settler reported to Brevet Second Lieutenant John Lawrence Grattan (1830–1854) at Fort Laramie that a young Miniconjou Indian had killed one of his cows, Grattan persuaded his commanding officer and post commander, First Lieutenant Hugh Brady Fleming (1828?–1895), to dispatch him to arrest the culprit. With 2 noncommissioned officers, 27 privates, a French interpreter, a 12-pounder mountain gun, and a 12-pounder howitzer, Grattan set off for the camp of Chief Conquering Bear. The chief offered to give a horse in exchange for the cow, but this was rejected.

When a forty-five minute parlay failed to produce the cow killer, young Grattan opened fire with his artillery. Conquering Bear was mortally wounded, but most of the guns fired too high. The Sioux swarmed over the soldiers; those who tried to flee were tracked down and killed. Only one survivor limped into Laramie; he too died the next day. After looting a storehouse, the Indians retreated northward.

Two companies of infantry from Fort Riley marched to Laramie, and Lieutenant Fleming was replaced by a more mature major. Nevertheless, for some months violent incidents flared along the Platte River. Finally Colonel William Selby Harney [q.v.], who on Christmas Eve had just returned from leave in Paris, was sent to deal with the situation. The expedition he launched against the Indians culminated in the Battle of Blue Water Creek, Nebraska, on 3 September 1855, in which more than 130 Indians were killed for a loss of 4 soldiers killed and 7 wounded, one mortally.

Gratuities. Extra payment given to British soldiers who reenlisted, were awarded certain medals, earned good conduct badges [q.v.], or agreed on discharge to settle in a British colony.

A French noncommissioned officer on promotion to commissioned officer was given a gratuity called *gratification de première mise d'officier* so that he could purchase the proper uniform and equipment. A similar gratuity was given in the British army. At the beginning of a campaign a gratuity was given to all French officers as an equipment fund.

Gravelotte–St. Privat, Battle of (18 August 1870), Franco-Prussian War. This battle, fought around these villages in northeast France near Metz, was one of the largest and most important of the war. For the first time the bulk of both armies was engaged.

Following the Battle of Mars-le-Tour–Vionville [q.v.], French Marshal Achille Bazaine [q.v.], with an army of 112,800 men and 732 guns, found his way west, toward Verdun, blocked by the Prussian First and Second armies under General Helmuth von Moltke [q.v.], with 188,332 men and nearly the same number of guns. Bazaine drew up his army in a line facing west with his right on the village of St. Privat and his left on the village of Gravelotte. On 18 August the Germans, under the titular command of King William I of Prussia [q.v.], launched a two-pronged attack, the First Army at Gravelotte and the Second Army at St. Privat. The French held their ground, and the First Army was repulsed and retreated in some disorder, losing within twenty minutes 8,000 killed and wounded, more than a quarter of the entire force. The Prussian Guards, an elite unit of 30,000 infantry, suffered much the same fate when, over the strong objections of the commander of the 1st Guards Division, Prince Augustus of Württemberg ordered it to attack strong entrenched French positions over open ground. Within twenty minutes the Guards lost one-third of their infantry—307 officers, 7,923 other ranks, and 2 surgeons killed or wounded—the Chassepot rifle [q.v.] creating the most havoc. In spite of their successes, the French made no counterattack because an acoustical shadow [q.v.] prevented Bazaine from hearing the sounds of battle at his headquarters.

At the same time at St. Privat the Second Army also suffered heavy casualties. By six o'clock that evening the French had repulsed every attack, but at seven-thirty the Prussians were reinforced by fifteen Saxon and Prussian Guards battalions, which launched a determined assault upon the French left flank at Gravelotte. Nine French battalions were crushed, and the French were forced from St. Privat. In this bloody battle the Prussians lost 899 officers and 19,260 other ranks killed or wounded; the French lost 595 officers and 12,698 other ranks killed or wounded. From 2,000 to 5,000 were taken prisoner.

A counterattack by Bazaine might have changed the course of the war, but that night he began the withdrawal of all his forces into the fortress of Metz.

On high ground between Rezonville and Gavelotte King William of Prussia and Helmuth von Moltke, with a staff and foreign observers that included American General William Tecumseh Sherman [q.v.], observed the battle.

Graveur. A person employed by the founders of cannon to repair damaged artillery pieces.

Gray, Raleigh (1860–1936). A British soldier, educated at Durham and Oxford, who was commissioned in 1881. In 1888 he commanded the Bechuanaland Border Police in South Africa. He fought in the Matabele War of 1893 and in the Second Anglo-Boer War [qq.v.].

Grazing Fire. Musketry or artillery fire roughly parallel to the ground and not above the height of a standing man.

Grazing Ricochet. Artillery fire in which the angle of fall of the projectile did not exceed four degrees. This made for a long, flat trajectory.

Greatcoat. An overcoat.

Great Game, The. The British name for the intrigue, spying, and political maneuvering in Central Asia that took place among British and Russian officers and political administrators as Russia began to conquer the khanates north of Afghanistan and Persia (Iran), drawing ever closer to India. It was a cold war that lasted throughout most of the nineteenth and into the twentieth century.

Great Patriotic War. Russian name for Napoleon's invasion of Russia [q.v.] and the successful Russian defense of the homeland.

Great Sioux War (March 1876–December 1877), sometimes called Sitting Bull's War. On 3 November 1875 at a White House meeting in Washington, D.C., President Grant decided that the army would no longer be responsible for keeping white miners out of the Black Hills and that dissident Sioux must move onto reservations. Although notified in December that they must relocate by the end of January 1876, the Sioux refused to leave. In February 1876 the War Department was made responsible for forcing Sitting Bull, Crazy Horse [qq.v.], and their followers onto the Great Sioux Reservation. William T. Sherman [q.v.] wrote: "We must act with vindictive earnestness against the Sioux, even to their extermination, men, women and children. Nothing less will reach the root of the case."

The Great Sioux War, the largest American military operation since the Civil War, eventually required the deployment of 40 percent of the army. It was directed by Lieutenant General Philip Sheridan [q.v.] from his headquarters of the Military Division of the Missouri in Chicago. Under him were Brigadier General Alfred H. Terry [q.v.], who commanded the Department of Dakota with headquarters in St. Paul, Minnesota, and Brigadier General George Crook [q.v.], who commanded the Department of the Platte in Omaha, Nebraska.

The war began in early 1876, when Sioux attacked the 46 people in the stockaded post of Fort Pease, Montana, on the Yellowstone River near the mouth of the Bighorn River, killing 6 and wounding 8 before the fort was relieved on 4 March by a force of the 2nd Cavalry and the 7th Infantry under Major James Sanks Brisbin (1837–1892), known to his men as Grasshopper Jim.

On 1 March General Crook struck north from Fort Fetterman in northern Wyoming into the Powder River region. There the first encounter occurred on 17 March, when a portion of Crook's command under Colonel Joseph Jones (Joshua) Reynolds [q.v.] surprised a village of Northern Cheyennes under Chief Two Moons (1847–1917?) on the Powder River and, thinking it contained Teton Sioux, attacked and burned it. The Indians put up a stiff resistance. The troops suffered 4 killed and 5 wounded; the dead and a wounded man were left on the field; Indian losses were unknown. This affair, which prompted the previously nonhostile Cheyennes to support the Sioux, so infuriated Crook that he court-martialed Reynolds.

On 17 June Crook was attacked by Sioux and Cheyennes in the indecisive Battle of Rosebud Creek [q.v.]. On 25 June General George Custer [q.v.] made his disastrous attack upon the Sioux camp at the Little Bighorn [q.v.]. On 9 September in the Battle of Slim Buttes [q.v.], in what is today northwest South Dakota, Crook defeated a force of mostly Miniconjous led by American Horse [q.v.]. It was the first substantive victory of the war for the whites.

On 14 November Crook left Fort Fetterman with 2,000 men of all arms. On 19 November he sent Colonel Ranald Slidell Mackenzie [q.v.] with 750 soldiers and 350 Indian scouts along the North Fork of the Powder River, and on 25 November they attacked a village of Northern Cheyennes under Dull Knife (1810?–1883), killing about 25, burning the village and its large stocks of food, and leaving the Indians adrift in freezing weather [see Dull Knife Outbreak]. Mackenzie's losses were 1 officer and 5 enlisted men killed and 25 wounded.

A second winter campaign was launched in the same month by Nelson A. Miles [q.v.], who had ordered his men to cut up blankets and buffalo robes to make warm clothing. From 6 November to 14 December his force of 15 officers and 434 infantry with a detachment of a 3-inch ordnance rifle and a 12-pounder Napoleon marched 558 miles. Although they fought only one small battle with hostile Indians, they were able to penetrate the Indians' winter quarters, demoralizing them.

On 8 January 1877 Miles fought Sioux and Cheyennes in the Battle of Wolf Mountain [q.v.] on the Tongue River. Three Indians were killed at a cost of 2 soldiers killed and 7 wounded.

The Indians were at last worn down and unable to continue their resistance. On 6 May Crazy Horse surrendered at Fort Robertson in northwestern Nebraska. On 7 May Miles defeated a force of Miniconjou Sioux on Muddy Creek [q.v.], a tributary of the Rosebud Creek. The battle marked the end of the war [see Rosebud Creek, Battle of].

Total losses for the war were 16 officers and 283 other ranks killed and 2 officers and 123 other ranks wounded. Estimates of Indian losses were 150 killed and 90 wounded, but many hundreds died of hunger or exposure.

Great Tasmania, The. An infamous British troopship overloaded with 1,043 discharged soldiers, mostly Irish, and their families, which sailed from Calcutta provisioned with insufficient water and contaminated food. It carried only one doctor. By the time the ship anchored in the Mersey in March 1860 more than 500 of its passengers had been buried at sea. Some 200 surviving sick were hauled in open carts through chilling rain to a workhouse infirmary. Public outrage demanded an official inquiry into troopship conditions, which remained disgraceful. [See Troopship; White Mutiny.]

Greble, John Trout (1834?–1861). An American soldier who was graduated from West Point in 1854 and as a first lieutenant in the artillery became the first regular army officer to be killed in the American Civil War [q.v.] when, on 6 June 1861, he fell beside his gun near Big Bethel [q.v.]. He was posthumously brevetted captain, major, and lieutenant colonel, all to date from his death.

Greco-Turkish War. See Graeco-Turkish War.

Greek Army. In 1876 the Greek army was divided into a regular army, an army reserve, a militia, and a militia reserve. All Greek men between the ages of nineteen and thirty not serving in the regular army were placed in the regular reserve; those from thirty-one to forty served in the militia, and those from forty-one to fifty in the militia reserve. The estimated strength of the army at this time was 200,000, about 15,000 of which were in the regular army and about 105,000 in its reserve. [See Evzones.]

Greek Fire. An incendiary composition used in projectiles to create fires in the enemy lines.

Greek Revolutions. In 1862 King Otto I (1815–1867), unpopular because of his taxation, his German advisers, his religion, and his wife's meddling in Greek affairs, was deposed by a revolutionary government after a twenty-nine year reign. Replaced by King George I (1845–1913), Otto sought refuge on a British warship and fled to Bavaria. A revolt of Greeks in Crete in 1896 was suppressed by the Turks in 1897. Greece intervened, bringing on the Graeco-Turkish War of 1897 [q.v.]. Crete was occupied by forces of the European powers in 1898. [See Greek War of Independence.]

Greek-Turkish War. See Graeco-Turkish War.

Greek War of Independence (1821–33). The wars to free Greece from Turkish rule began in February 1821, when the Turks brutally suppressed a revolt in Walachia and rejected a Russian demand for the restoration of Christian churches and the right to protect Greek and other Christians in the Ottoman Empire. On 25 March of that year (a day still celebrated as Greek Independence Day) Archbishop Germanos of Patras (1771–1826) gave the signal for the revolution to begin and then led an ill-armed peasant force from Kalavryta to Patras in the Morea (Peloponnesus). Prince Alexander Ypsilanti [q.v.] then entered Moldavia from Russian territory with a small force. This uprising collapsed when the tsar refused to support it.

Later that year, while the Turks were engaged in trying to suppress the recalcitrant Ali Pasha of Jannina [q.v.], there were further outbreaks of rebellion. The long, intermittent conflict that followed may be divided into three periods: the first, from 1821 to 1824, when the Greeks with the help of many European volunteers successfully fought the Turks; the second from the entry of Mehemet Ali [q.v.], who, with his disciplined Egyptian troops, produced Turkish victories; and finally, the autumn of 1827, when the European powers intervened, beginning the final period of the conflict.

The revolt of the maritime communities in the Greek archipelago gave the insurgents control of the sea, and they enjoyed initial success. They were soon joined by Theodorus Kolokotrones [q.v.], a notable brigand who had been persuaded by a vision of the Virgin to ally himself with them. Kolokotrones shortly began a bloodbath when after capturing Karytaina, a town in the central Peloponnesus eight miles northwest of Megalopolis, he slaughtered all the Turks. Within three weeks not a Muslim was left alive in the open country. The Christians of Boeotia and Attica joined the rapidly spreading revolt. By May Athens was captured, and the Muslims there were besieged in the Acropolis.

Wherever Muslims were found, whatever their sex or age, they were killed. On 5 October Greek insurgents captured Tripolitsa (Tripolis or Tripolitza), the main Ottoman fortress in the central Peloponnesus, and slaughtered a reported 10,000 Turks [see Tripolitsa Massacre]. The Turks, equally barbaric, slaughtered Greeks in Turkey, including the Patriarch Gregorios V of Constantinople (1739?–1821), who on Easter, 22 April 1821, was accused of secretly aiding the Greeks. He was hanged by Turkish janissaries [q.v.] at the door of his own church.

On 13 January 1822 Greek independence was declared, but in the spring two Turkish armies moved south. One, under Omar Vrioni, a Muslim Greek of the race of the Palaeologi, marching south along the coast of western Hellas, was held in check by the mud walls of Missolonghi and forced to retreat; the other under Ali Pasha of Drama (called Dramali) marched through Boeotia and Attica, crossed the peninsula, and advanced to the relief of besieged Nauplia. The Greek government at Argos fled at Damali's approach, but the Turks' supply line failed, and in August they retreated. At the Pass of Dervenaki the Greeks waited for them and destroyed them by pouring down an avalanche of stones.

The victorious Greeks, free to pursue their own feuds, began to fight among themselves. A civil war briefly erupted when Kolokotrones led an army against the government forces, but by early 1824 he had been defeated and was imprisoned.

Sultan Mahmud II (1785–1839), at last recognizing the ineptness of his own army, called upon Mehemet Ali of Egypt to assist him, and in January 1824 the Egyptian expeditionary force under Ibrahim Pasha [q.v.] sailed from Alexandria. On 25 February the Egyptian army with 4,000 regular infantry and 500 cavalry landed at Modon (today Methone or Methoni), a port on the Ionian Sea in the southwest Peloponnesus. The Greeks there fled before the first charge. Ibrahim Pasha quickly overran the peninsula north of the Gulf of Corinth and forced the Greek government to flee. In desperation the Greeks released Kolokotrones and appointed him commander-in-chief of their army, but Kolokotrones, whose forte was guerrilla warfare, was powerless to stop the disciplined Egyptian regulars. However, in October 1824 the Greeks annihilated the Turkish garrison on the island of Lesbos in the Battle of Mityelene (Mytilene), and Tripolitsa was retaken and destroyed.

Meanwhile, in the north a Turkish army, led by Reshid ("Kutahia") Pasha of Jannina, invaded Greece and on 7 May 1825 began a year-long siege of Missolonghi [see Missolonghi, Sieges of]. After its fall on 22 April 1826 many Greeks submitted and Reshid marched on Athens, which fell at the first assault on 25 August. Those Greek soldiers who survived were in turn besieged in the Acropolis. The first attempt to relieve them, with the help of some French troops, was checked.

Early in 1827 the Greek government gave command of its navy to former British Admiral Lord Cochrane, later Earl of Dundonald (1775–1860), who had previously commanded the navies of Chile, Peru, and Brazil. Command of the Greek army was given to Sir Richard Church [q.v.]. On 25 April Church led an attack upon the Turks near the Monastery of St. Spiridion. The Albanian troops there held out for two days before surrendering under terms, but as they marched out, the Greeks massacred them.

On May 4 General Church launched an attack on the main Turkish camp that ended in disaster, the Greeks fleeing in panic when attacked by Turkish cavalry. On 5 June the defenders of the Acropolis surrendered, and continental Greece was again in the hands of the Turks. In the parts of Greece still unconquered, rival chiefs renewed their feuds, Greek fought Greek, and anarchy reigned.

Ibrahim Pasha began a systematic destruction of the country until the European powers intervened. A joint British, Russian, and French naval force sailed to Greece and defeated the Turks in the Battle of Navarino on 20 October 1827, but Turkey did not completely yield until after the Russo-Turkish War of 1828–29 [q.v.]. On 22 March 1829 the Treaty of London was signed, making Greece an autonomous tributary state. A second treaty of London on 7 May 1832 made Greece an independent kingdom.

Greek War of Independence *Delacroix painting of Greece dying on the ruins of Missolonghi*

Greely, Adolphus Washington (1844–1935). An American soldier who specialized in laying telegraph lines. His military career began during the American Civil War, when, on 26 July 1861, he enlisted as a private in the 19th Massachusetts. He rose to the rank of captain and brevet major in the Union army and remained in the army after the war as a second lieutenant in the 36th Infantry. In 1876–79 he was in charge of stringing 2,000 miles of telegraph lines in Texas, the Dakotas, and Montana. As a first lieutenant in 1881 he was commander of the post on Lady Franklin Bay, opposite the western coast of Greenland, one of thirteen international circumpolar stations. From there he explored and mapped portions of Greenland and Ellesmere Island, attaining the most northerly point ever reached at that time (83°24′ north, 42°45′ west). Relief ships due in 1882 and 1883 failed to reach the post, and by 1884, when one finally arrived, all except Greely and 6 of the 24 men who had manned the post had starved to death. Greely was accused but eventually absolved of responsibility for the cannibalism that had occurred. Later he was active in establishing telegraph lines to outlying U.S. possessions, and on 3 March 1887 he was made a brigadier general and chief signal officer. He was in charge of constructing telegraph lines in Cuba, China, the Philippines, and Alaska. In 1888 he was one of the founders of the National Geographic Society. He was promoted major general in 1906 and retired in 1908. On 27 March 1935, his ninety-first birthday, he was awarded the Medal of Honor [q.v.], becoming only the second person (after Charles Lindbergh) to receive the medal for peacetime service. He died on 20 October of that year.

Green Battalions. See Eight Banner System.

Green Cross. An international relief committee that assisted prisoners of war during the Franco-Prussian War [q.v.] of 1870–71.

Greene, Edward Mackenzie (1857–1931). A South African soldier who fought in the Zulu War [q.v.] of 1879 and commanded the Natal Carbineers in the Second Anglo-Boer War [q.v.]. He later became minister of railways and harbors.

Greene, George Sears (1801–1899). A long-lived American soldier who was graduated second in his West Point Class of 1823. After serving for thirteen years, he resigned to become a civil engineer. On 18 January 1862, during the American Civil War, he became colonel of the 60th New York in the Union army, and on 28 April of that year he was promoted brigadier general, becoming one of the oldest generals serving with an active field army. He saw action at Cedar Mountain, Second Bull Run, Antietam, and Chancellorsville [qq.v.]. During the attempt to relieve Chattanooga he was severely wounded in the face. He recovered to join Sherman in his Carolinas Campaign [q.v.].

He was brevetted major general for his war services and was mustered out on 30 April 1866. Returning to engineering, he became one of the founders of the American Society of Civil Engineers, which he served as president. When he died, he was the oldest living West Point graduate.

Greenhow, Rose O'Neal (1817–1864). A widow and "lady of fashion" who was also a noted Confederate spy in Washington, D.C., during the American Civil War. Her spying career began in June 1861, when she passed military intelligence to Confederate General Pierre Beauregard [q.v.] just before the First Battle of Bull Run [q.v.]. In August 1861 her espionage was detected by Allan Pinkerton [q.v.], and she was placed under house arrest, but undeterred, she continued to send messages south. In January 1862 she was taken to the Old Capitol Prison and held for five months before being exiled to the Confederacy. In August 1863 she sailed to Europe to plead the southern cause and was presented to Queen Victoria. In September, carrying dispatches from Confederate agents, she embarked to return to the Confederacy, but her ship sank in a storm, and she was drowned, dragged down, it was said, by the $2,000 in gold she was carrying.

Rose O'Neal Greenhow (right), Confederate spy in Washington, D.C., during the American Civil War

Greenock, Lord. See Cathcart, Charles Murray, second Earl.

Gregg, Maxcy (1814–1862). An American soldier and politician who served as a major in the 12th U.S. Infantry during the Mexican War [q.v.] and became a Confederate brigadier general in the American Civil War. He was mortally wounded in the Battle of Fredericksburg [q.v.].

Grenade. 1. A hand-thrown missile filled with explosives causing damage either by flying fragments or by igniting fires. Although in use from at least 1660, grenades were seldom employed in the nineteenth century. Why this was so is a mystery. During the American Civil War the Union army purchased about 100,000, and the Confederates sometimes improvised grenades in bottles, but they did not become a common weapon.

2. Large-explosives projectiles used in some mortars and howitzers.

Grenadiers. Tall long-armed men who were originally throwers of grenades. In the nineteenth century they were often formed into elite units. In Napoleon's army and in others, one company in each infantry regiment was a grenadier company formed of the regiment's tallest men. In the French army they wore large mustaches, and their insignia was a flaming bomb or grenade. In the Garde Impériale [q.v.] the grenadiers wore gold earrings. One of the oldest regiments in the British army is the Grenadier Guards.

In the American army for a decade, from about 1825, each infantry regiment had a flank company called a grenadier company.

Grenadiers *Grenadiers of the Coldsteam Guards, 1812*

Grenfell, Francis Wallace (1841–1925). A British soldier commissioned in 1859. Beginning in 1874, he served five years in South Africa. He was assistant adjutant general for Garnet Wolseley [q.v.] during Arabi's Revolt [qq.v.] in 1882, and during the Gordon Relief Expedition [q.v.] he was a brigadier general in command of the line of communication. From 1885 to 1892 he was sirdar (commander-in-chief) of the Egyptian army, succeeding Sir Evelyn Wood [q.v.]. In 1889 he defeated the Dervish army of Abd al Rahman wad al Nujumi in the Battle of Toski [q.v.].

During his term as sirdar he completely reorganized the Egyptian army and consolidated Egyptian control of Suakim in the eastern Sudan. In 1899 he was made governor and commander-in-chief of Malta. In 1902 he was raised to the peerage. He commanded troops in Ireland from 1904 to 1908 and became a field marshal in 1908.

Grenfell, George St. Leger (1807–1868?). A British adventurer who served without pay as an officer in the Confederate army. His previous experience was said to have been in the French Foreign Legion, with Garibaldi's Red Shirts, and in the British army in the Crimean War and the Indian Mutiny [qq.v.]. It was even claimed that he had fought Barbary pirates. In June 1863 he was arrested for assisting a slave to escape. He was saved by General Braxton Bragg. In September 1863 he joined with Jeb Stuart's cavalry. In November he crossed the lines and took the amnesty oath in Washington, D.C. From there he traveled to Chicago, where he involved himself in a plot to release the prisoners of war at Camp Douglas and to burn Chicago. He was arrested on 6 November 1864, tried, and convicted [see Sweet, Benjamin Gaffer]. He was sentenced to death, but this was commuted to life imprisonment on Dry Tortugas. On 7 March 1867 he and three other prisoners and a bribed guard fled. None was ever seen again, and it was assumed that all drowned.

Grenoble, Napoleon at. See Laffrey, Affair at.

Grenzer Troops. See Austrian Army; Military Frontier; Ban.

Grierson, Benjamin Henry (1826–1911). A bankrupt Illinois store owner and music teacher who in the American Civil War became colonel of the 6th Illinois Cavalry of the Union Army. William Tecumseh Sherman [q.v.] had a profound distrust of cavalry, but he called Grierson "the best Cavalry officer I have yet had."

On 17 April 1863, on orders from General Grant, who wanted to divert attention from his crossing of the Mississippi below Vicksburg, Grierson led 1,700 men of the 6th and 7th Illinois Cavalry and the 2nd Iowa Cavalry on an 800-mile raid, from La Grange, Tennessee, through the heart of the Confederacy. In seventeen days he ruined 2 railroads, demolished immense quantities of stores and property, captured 1,000 horses and mules, destroyed 3,000 stand of arms, killed or wounded an estimated 100 Confederate soldiers, and paroled 500 more at a cost of 3 killed, 7 wounded, 9 missing, and 7 left behind to tend the wounded. He ended his raid on 2 May at Baton Rouge, Louisiana. Grant called it "one of the most brilliant cavalry exploits of the war, and will be handed down in history as an example to be imitated." It was an example, he said, of "what might be done in the interior of an enemy's country without a base from which to draw supplies." As a reward Grierson was promoted brigadier general, to rank from 3 June 1863. In command of a cavalry division, he took part in the Mobile Campaign. He was promoted major general of volunteers on 19 March 1866 and was mustered out of the volunteer service on 30 April.

When the regular army was reorganized in July, he was appointed colonel of the newly raised 10th Cavalry, one of two black cavalry regiments in the American army. He commanded it for nearly a quarter of a century. Most of his postwar service was in the Southwest, operating against the Comanche and Kickapoo Indians in West Texas and against the Mescalero Apaches in New Mexico who were suspected of aiding Victorio [q.v.]. He twice turned back Victorio's incursions from Mexico. On 30 July 1880, although ambushed and trapped with a small escort on Devil's Ridge, north of Fort Quitman, Texas, he managed to withdraw. In December 1888 he was appointed commander of the Department of Arizona, succeeding Nelson Miles [q.v.]. He was promoted brigadier general on 5 April 1890 and retired three months later.

Griffin or Grig. A soldier or other person newly arrived in India and unaccustomed to its ways.

Griffith, Charles Duncan (1830–1906). A British soldier who saw much service in South Africa. He fought in the Axe War [q.v.] of 1846. From 1848 to 1850, as a lieutenant, he led Hottentot levies, and in the Kaffir War [q.v.] of 1851 he served as an inspector of the Armed Mounted Police. In 1877

General Francis Wallace Grenfell reviews Grenadier Guards in Cairo.

he was a colonel in command of all troops in the Transkei. From 1878 to 1881, when he retired, he was British agent and commander of troops in Basutoland, the site of the Gun War [q.v.], fought in 1881.

Griswold and Gunnison. Samuel Griswold and A. W. Gunnison, the largest manufacturers of handguns for the Confederacy in the American Civil War, produced some 3,500 pistols in their factory at Griswoldville, Georgia, until it was destroyed by Union troops on 22 November 1864. Their pistols were copies of the Colt 1851 Navy, although the barrels were round and the frames were of brass.

The second-largest producer of handguns for the Confederate army was the Memphis Novelty Works [q.v.].

Grochow, Battle of (25 February 1830), Polish Revolution. The Treaty of Vienna in 1815 put most of Poland under Russian rule. When Polish patriots in Warsaw, inspired by the 1830 uprisings in Paris, drove the Russians from the city and proclaimed their independence, a Russian army of 110,000 under Count Hans Karl Friedrich Anton von Diebitsch [q.v.] advanced on the city. At the village of Grochow (now a suburb of Warsaw), on the right bank of the Vistula, it fought an indecisive battle with a Polish force of 90,000 under Prince Michael Radziwill (1778–1850). The Poles claimed victory. The Russians were said to have lost between 7,000 and 10,000; the Poles, between 2,000 and 5,000.

Grognard. Literally, a grumbler. In France, an old soldier, an old sweat, especially a French infantryman of Napoleon's army. Originally applied to the Old Guard.

Grolman, Karl von (1777–1843). A Prussian soldier who was commissioned into an infantry regiment when he was barely thirteen. While a subaltern, he became a disciple of Gerhard von Scharnhorst [q.v.]. In 1806, after the Battle of Jena [q.v.], he assisted Scharnhorst in the reorganization of the Prussian army. During the Peninsular War [q.v.] he served as a volunteer with the Spanish forces. Returning to Prussia in 1814, he joined the general staff and served in the campaigns of 1813–14. In 1815 he was appointed quartermaster general on the staff of Gebhard von Blücher [q.v.]. It was he who persuaded August von Gneisenau [q.v.], Blücher's chief of staff, to go to the aid of Wellington at Waterloo [q.v.]. After the peace he served on the general staff, with the war ministry, and as commander-in-chief at Posen.

Grommet. A ring of metal or other stiff material placed inside a visored cap to keep it stiff.

Groove. One of the channels between the lans in the bore of a rifled gun.

Gros Bonnets. Literally, big hats. The French slang term for Napoleon's marshals.

Grossbeeren, Battle of (23 August 1813), Napoleonic Wars. Austria declared war on France on 12 August 1813. Eleven days later, at this village just south of Berlin, a French corps in the army of Marshal Nicolas Oudinot [q.v.] under General Henri Gatien Bertrand (1773–1844), advancing on Berlin, came in contact with a Prussian force of 32,000, many of them raw landwehr, with 32 guns under General Bolesas Friedrich Emmanuel Tauntzien (1760–1824). About three o'clock on the afternoon of 23 August 1813, while these forces skirmished, a French corps of 27,000 Saxons under General Jean Louis Reynier [q.v.] advanced on the village, captured a height just above it, then bivouacked.

Although he had placed a complete division in a square to hold Grossbeeren, Reynier was taken completely by surprise when he was attacked in a heavy rain by 38,000 Prussians under Friedrick von Bülow [q.v.]. The village was captured, and the heights above it were stormed. The French right flank collapsed, and a counterattack failed to retake the heights. Reynier retreated and again bivouacked. After some further confused fighting between a French cavalry division and Prussian hussars, the French and Saxons drew back. Berlin was saved.

The Prussians lost barely 1,000; the French and Saxons lost 3,000 men, 13 guns, and 60 wagons.

Grossgörschen, Battle of. See Lützen, Battle of.

Grouard, Frank (1850–1905). An American army scout who was born in the Society Islands in the South Pacific, the son of a Mormon missionary and a Polynesian mother. He was taken to Utah when he was two. At fifteen he ran away from home. While carrying mail in Montana, he was captured by Sioux near the mouth of the Milk River. In the six years he was with the Sioux he learned their language and absorbed many of the arts of the plainsman. In 1876, as a scout for General George Crook [q.v.], he took part in the battles of the Rosebud Creek and Slim Buttes [qq.v.]. He was at Fort Robinson, Nebraska, when Crazy Horse [q.v.] was killed, and his misinterpretation of Crazy Horses's words may have contributed to his death. He continued to serve as an army scout in Wyoming and Nebraska through the disorders caused by the ghost dance [q.v.].

He was said to have had a "shrewd native intelligence," and Crook praised his skill as a scout.

Grouchy, Marquis Emmanuel de (1766–1847). A French soldier whose family had been part of the French aristocracy since the fourteenth century. His military career began at age fourteen, when he was sent to the artillery school at Strasbourg. At fifteen, he was commissioned in the artillery, but three years later he transferred to the cavalry. In 1786 he was a lieutenant in an elite unit. The following year he left the army. In 1791 he volunteered for service and proved himself, it was said, "a horseman by nature and a cavalry soldier by instinct." Because he was an aristocrat, he was suspended in 1793. He was restored the following year, and by 1795 he was a general of division. He served in Italy, where in the rear guard covering the retreat after the Battle of Novi (15 August 1799) he suffered nine wounds and was captured at Pasturana. When exchanged, he distinguished himself at Jena, Eylau, Friedland, Wagram, and Borodino [qq.v.], suffering twenty-three wounds. He was too badly injured to serve in 1813, but in 1814 he became Napoleon's chief of cavalry, and served until he was disabled by still another wound.

He was quick to join Napoleon for the Hundred Days [q.v.], and in 1815 he was the last of Napoleon's generals to be given a marshal's baton. He helped destroy Field Marshal Gebhard von Blücher [q.v.] in the Battle of Ligny, but at Waterloo [qq.v.], where he initially commanded the cavalry reserve, then the right wing, where he obeyed his orders rather than march to the sound of the guns. Although he managed a skillful retreat on 19 June, he was excoriated by Napoleon for his failure to exhibit the initiative expected of him.

Proscribed by the Bourbons, he sailed to the United States and lived for several years in Philadelphia. He returned to France in 1820, and his marshal's baton was restored to him in 1831.

Ground Arms, to. To lay arms on the ground.

Grover, Cuvier (1828–1885). An American soldier who was graduated fourth in his class at West Point in 1850. In 1853–54 he explored part of what became the route of the Northern Pacific Railroad. He later served in the Utah Expedition [q.v.] and on garrison duties in the West. At the beginning of the American Civil War he was an infantry captain in New Mexico but was soon appointed a brigadier general of volunteers. He fought in the Second Battle of Bull Run [q.v.], in which his brigade suffered 486 casualties. He commanded a division in the Department of the Gulf and then in northern Virginia, where he was wounded in the Battle of Cedar Creek [q.v.]. Although he was brevetted major general in the regular army, in the reorganized army after the war he became a lieutenant colonel in the 38th Infantry and subsequently colonel of the 1st Cavalry.

Groveton, Battle of (28 August 1862), American Civil War. The corps of Thomas ("Stonewall") Jackson [q.v.] ambushed a Union brigade, soon to be known as the Iron Brigade of the West [q.v.], under Brigadier General John Gibbon [q.v.], near this village (no longer extant) about four miles from Manassas, Virginia. The Union brigade suffered 33 percent casualties. One of the survivors observed that while the brigade was always ready for battle, it was "never again eager."

The battle was a prelude to the Second Battle of Bull Run [q.v.] and is sometimes considered part of that battle.

Gruic, Sava (1840–1913). A Serbian soldier and politician who fought against the Turks in 1876. He was minister of war from 1876 to 1879. For most of the years between 1888 and 1906 he was prime minister of Serbia.

Grumbkow Pasha, Viktor von (1849–1901). A German officer who in the late nineteenth century reorganized the Turkish artillery.

Gruson, Hermann (1821–1895). A German armaments manufacturer who in 1855 founded a shipyard on the Elbe River at Buckau, now a suburb of Magdeburg. In 1869 it became the Gruson Works, producing armored turrets, cannon, gun carriages, shells, and other military items. For the United States it produced the Gruson seacoast carriage for large eight-inch guns. Made of cast iron, the Gruson carriage was cheaper but heavier than the steel carriage manufactured by Krupp [q.v.]. The Gruson works were bought by Krupp in 1893.

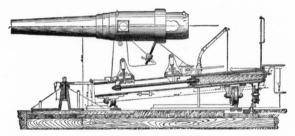

Gruson, Hermann *Gruson seacoast carriage*

Guadeloupe, British Capture of (28 January–5 February 1810), Napoleonic Wars. On 28 January 1810 Sir George Beckwith [q.v.] landed a force on this island in the Leeward Islands, the last French possession in the West Indies, defeated a French force there, and took possession of the island. Although in 1813 Guadeloupe was transferred to Sweden, the British remained. The French tried unsuccessfully to invade in 1814, but the island was not returned to France until 1816.

Guadeloupe Revolution. In the summer of 1795 the French freed many of the slaves on the island of Guadeloupe and armed them to help drive out the British. In 1802 Napoleon, then first consul, sent a military expedition to the island to restore slavery, but the former slaves stoutly resisted, many preferring to commit suicide rather than return to their former status. Slavery was not abolished until 1848.

Guad el-Ras, Battle of (23 March 1860), Spanish-Moroccan War. Marshal Leopoldo O'Donnell [q.v.] with 25,000 Spanish troops defeated 40,000 Moors strongly entrenched behind the Guad el-Ras River and ended the short war in what is today Spanish Morocco.

Guam, Capture of (June 1898), Spanish-American War. Marines and sailors on the USS *Charleston* landed and captured this largest and most populous of the Marianas Islands. By the Treaty of Paris of 10 December 1898 it became a U.S. possession. Government was entrusted to the navy, which appointed its first naval governor in the spring of 1899.

Guantánamo Bay, American Seizure of (7–11 June 1898), Spanish-American War. Some 1,500 American marines landed almost unopposed on the shore of Guantánamo Bay, on the southeast coast of Oriente Province, Cuba, on 7 June 1889. The next day they were attacked by 2,000 Spanish infantry. The battle, continued sporadically for the next few days until at last the Americans prevailed. In 1903 the United States leased 30 square miles to use as a naval base.

Guard. 1. As a noun, a person or a group assigned to protect a person, place, or thing.

2. As a verb, to watch over and prevent escape.

3. As a noun, a soldier in a regiment of guards; a guardsman.

Guard

Guardhouse. The building occupied by the guard of a military base. It was also used to confine prisoners temporarily.

Guardia Civil. A paramilitary police force formed in 1844 to police rural areas of Spain. Members wore patent leather hats and green uniforms. In spite of its proclaimed moral code—"The Guardia Civil must not be fearsome, except to those who do evil. It must not be feared, except by enemies of order"—it was greatly feared by Basques, Gypsies, and others whose political views did not match those of the government in power. The Guardia still exists and still wears its patent leather hats.

Guardiola, Santos (1812–1862). A Honduran general and politician who was known as The Tiger of Central America. In 1855, after leading a revolt that ousted the president, he proclaimed himself president. He governed from 1856 to 1858 and was murdered in 1862.

Guard of Honor. Soldiers in a ceremonial formation representing an honor to a person of distinction.

Guards Regiments. Almost all European and some South American nations formed elite units of guards. Napoleon formed the Garde Impériale [q.v.] in 1804. In 1807 the Prussians formed the 1st Regiment of Foot Guards, composed of men of superior physique who were drawn from every area of the kingdom. On parade they wore grenadier hats copied exactly from those worn in the era of Frederick the Great (1712–1787). In Britain the oldest regiments of guards infantry were, and are, the Coldstream Guards and the Grenadier Guards. The former was the only regiment retained from the parliamentary infantry after the Restoration. The Grenadier Guards, raised by Charles II (1630–1685) in Bruges in 1656, was known as the 1st Regiment of Foot Guards until after the Battle of Waterloo [q.v.], when in recognition of its defeat of the French Imperial Guards, it became the 1st, or Grenadier, Regiment of Foot Guards.

These two regiments and the Scots Guards, originally formed in 1660 as the Scots Regiment of Foot Guards, were the only regiments of foot guards in the nineteenth-century British army until in April 1900 the Irish Guards was formed to recognize the "bravery shown by Irish regiments . . . in South Africa."

A number of British cavalry regiments were given the guards title: the 1st and 2nd Life Guards, the Royal Horse Guards, and seven regiments of dragoon guards. Only the first three counted as household cavalry. Until 1871 officers in guards regiments held titles in the army higher than their regimental titles. Ensigns were lieutenants in the army, lieutenants were captains, and captains were lieutenant colonels, a regulation highly unpopular with line officers.

In the Russian army [q.v.] each arm—infantry, artillery, cavalry, and engineers—had its own guards regiments. They were given special equipment, higher pay, and other privileges.

Guards Regiments *French Imperial Foot Guards accompany Napoleon in Spain.*

Guásimas, Las, Battle of. See Las Guásimas.

Guastadours. Pioneers in the Turkish army. They were usually Greeks or Armenians.

Guatemalan War (1885). In 1871 liberals led by Miguel García Granados (1809–1878) and Justo Rufino Barrios [q.v.] captured Guatemala City after a ninety-day campaign. Granados served as president for two years and was succeeded by Barrios, the commander-in-chief of the army. In 1876 Barrios tried, unsuccessfully, to unite the Central American states peacefully with himself as president. In 1885 he tried again to establish a Central American government, this time by force. After invading El Salvador, his forces were defeated, and he himself was killed in the Battle of Chalchuapa [q.v.] on 2 April 1885.

Gubat, Battle of (19 January 1885), Gordon Relief Expedition, also known as the Battle of Abu Kru. In northern Sudan a British force of 1,500 men and three guns under Sir Herbert Stewart was attacked by a greatly superior force of Dervishes two days after the Battle of Abu Klea [q.v.]. The British formed square, repelled all attacks, and moved in formation to the Nile. British losses were 23 killed, including Stewart, who was mortally wounded, and 82 wounded; Dervish losses are unknown.

Gudda. See Gurry.

Guémou, Battle of (28 October 1859), Franco-Tukulor War. In West Africa a French force of 320 Europeans and 760 Africans defeated a numerically superior Tukulor force under Umar bin Said Tall [q.v.].

Guerre à Outrance. All-out war; war of extermination.

Guerre Preta. A second-line Portuguese force in Angola raised by tribal chiefs on the coast upon being bribed or threatened by the Portuguese.

Guerrero, Vicente (1783–1831). A Mexican soldier and politician who joined in the war for independence under José María Morelos y Pavón [q.v.] in 1810 and became a leader of Mexican guerrilla forces. He became vice-president of Mexico (1824–28) and president from March to December 1829. A successful revolution against him was led by Anastasio Bustamante and Antonio López de Santa Anna [qq.v.]. In February 1831 he was captured and shot.

Guerrillas / Guerillas. Those who engage in irregular warfare, usually in small bands that harass and sabotage. Antoine Henri de Jomini [q.v.], who served in Spain during the Peninsular War, wrote: "No army, however disciplined, can contend successfully against such national resistance un-less it be strong enough to hold all the essential points, . . . cover its communications, and . . . furnish an active force sufficient to beat the enemy wherever he may present himself."

Karl von Clausewitz [q.v.] specified five conditions necessary for successful guerrilla operations: The war must be fought in the interior of a country; battles must be decided by single blows; the theater of operations must be large enough for the guerrillas to move about and hide; the terrain must be rough and not easily traversed by regular forces; and the national character must be such that this type of warfare is appealing. Such conditions prevailed in Spain during the Peninsular War [q.v.], in Calabria during the Calabrian War [q.v.], in Russia during Napoleon's Russian Campaign [q.v.], and in Mexico during the French occupation [see Mexico, French Invasion and Occupation of]. Wellington derived much valuable intelligence from Spanish guerrillas, who were noted for their cruelty. One in four French casualties in the Iberian Peninsula was inflicted by guerrillas.

Spanish guerrillas followed French columns at a distance, picking off those who through wounds, disease, or fatigue fell behind. Women accompanying the guerrillas were said to fall upon them and, with scissors and knives, stab out their eyes and devise other cruel tortures. A witness has said that they seemed to exult at the sight of blood.

In Italy that uncompromising revolutionary Giuseppe Mazzini (1805–1872), in his *General Instructions for Members of Young Italy* (1831), wrote: "Guerrilla warfare opens a field of activity for every local capacity, forces the enemy into an unaccustomed method of battle, avoids the evil consequences of a great defeat, secures the national war from the risk of treason, and has the advantage of not confining its activities within any defined and determinate basis of operations. It is invincible, indestructible."

The most successful Russian guerrilla bands were led by regular army officers, but a Private Chertvertakov, a Russian dragoon captured in the Battle of Borodino [q.v.] who managed to escape, organized hundreds of peasants, whom he led in raids on the retreating French. Because Chertvertakov and his men behaved so barbarously, General Mikhail Kutuzov [q.v.] tried to curb them, but did not succeed.

John S. Mosby [q.v.], writing in 1887 of his experience as a Confederate guerrilla in the American Civil War, said: "It is as legitimate to fight an enemy in the rear as in the front. The only difference is in the danger."

There is an ever-present risk that guerrillas will become mere brigands, as was the case with William Quantrill [q.v.] and his band during the American Civil War, with many of the Chinese during the Nien Rebellion [q.v.], and with the guerrillas in the Mexican War [q.v.].

At the Peace Conference of 1899 rules were adopted determining the conditions under which guerrillas should be recognized as legitimate belligerent forces. They were required to serve under leaders who were responsible for their subordinates, to wear distinctive badges, to carry arms openly, and to conform in their operations to the customs and laws of war. Although the rules were confirmed at the London Conference of 1907, they were largely ignored by guerrillas themselves, most of whom were unaware of the niceties of the international conventions.

Guerrillas *Confederate guerrillas shoot at Federal boats on the Mississippi, 1862.*

Guiana, Attack on (September 1803), Napoleonic Wars. British Commodore Samuel Hood (1762–1814) landed a force that captured the country from the Dutch. It became British Guiana, a British colony in 1814.

Guichet. A small door made in the gate of a fortified place. It was usually not more than four feet high so that a person using it had to stoop.

Guides. Since maps were rare and often inaccurate, marching armies generally employed local people to assist them in finding their way.

Guides, Corps of. A unique unit in the Punjab Frontier Force [q.v.]. It was formed by Henry Lawrence [q.v.] and contained both cavalry and infantry. It served mostly on the Indian Northwest Frontier.

Guides, Les. Veteran cavalry units in the French army that formed the bodyguards and escorts of generals. A unit raised by Napoleon in June 1796 and commanded by Captain (later Marshal) Jean Baptiste Bessières [q.v.] became the cadre for the *chasseurs-à-cheval* of the Garde Impériale [q.v.].

Guidon. 1. Small-unit flag. In the United States guidons are swallow-tailed flags in the corps colors that identify companies, batteries, and troops.

2. The soldier who carries the guidon.

Gujerat, Battle of (22 February 1849), Second Sikh War [q.v.]. In the final battle of this war in northeast Punjab, on the west bank of the Chenab River, about 70 miles north of Lahore, British General Hugh Gough [q.v.] with 24,000 men and 84 guns defeated a Sikh force of 50,000 to 60,000 and captured 53 guns. British losses were 92 killed and 682 wounded; Sikh losses are unknown. It was here that anesthetics were used for the first time on British soldiers on a battlefield.

Gumbai Uchuia. A type of battle fan used in Japan from the eleventh century as a war standard.

Gun. The general term for any tubular weapon from which a projectile is launched by means of an explosive. When applied to artillery, it is sometimes used to distinguish pieces with flatter trajectories and higher muzzle velocities than howitzers and mortars [see Artillery].

Gun, Evening. The ritual firing of a blank shell in a gun at the end of a day on an army post.

Gun Cap. The percussion cap used to ignite the powder charge of cap-and-ball rifles or pistols.

Gun Carriage. The framework supporting an artillery piece. For mobile guns it is equipped with wheels.

Gun Carriage *Making Confederate gun carriages at the Tredegar Iron Works, Richmond, Virginia*

Guncotton. Cellulose nitrate. Cotton intensively treated with a mixture of nitric and sulfuric acids. It was extensively used in conjunction with nitroglycerin in the making of cordite [q.v.] and other smokeless gunpowders [see Gunpowder].

Gundet, Battle of (17 November 1875), Abyssinian-Egyptian War. Near this village in the Abyssinian highlands, 30 miles northeast of Axum, west of Massaua (Massawa), near the Egyptian border, Abyssinians under King Johannes [q.v.], aided by Walad Michael, hereditary chief of Bogos, defeated an invading Egyptian force of 2,500 led by Søren Adolph Arendrup [q.v.], who was killed in the battle.

Gun Emplacement. The firing location of an artillery piece.

Gunflint. A small, sharp flint used to ignite the priming in a flintlock weapon.

Gungunhana (d. 1907). The paramount chief of Gazaland in Mozambique in the last half of the nineteenth century who resisted the Portuguese expansion into his lands. In September 1894 an expedition under Portuguese Colonel Mousinho d'Albuquerque [q.v.] defeated his forces and captured him. He was exiled to Angola, where he died.

Gunhouse. That part of a turret visible above a barbette.

Gunmakers Company. One of the liveried companies of the City of London, which received its charter in 1637. It tested small-arms gun barrels for safety and marked them as tested, a task that since the early nineteenth century it shared, as it still does, with the Birmingham Proof House. It is still located at 48–50 Commercial Road in London.

Gunmetal. A kind of bronze used in the making of cannon. Hard bronze for gunmetal consisted of eight or nine parts of copper to one of tin.

Gunner. 1. A member of the crew that operates a cannon. Specifically, the soldier who fires a cannon.

2. Any soldier in the artillery.

Gunner's Chant. Sometimes called the gunner's doxology. Before watches became common, this was a chant used by artillery noncommissioned officers when firing salutes in order to time the intervals between rounds and keep them uniform. It began:

Fire!
If I had good sense I wouldn't be here.
Fire!
I'd like to slip off for a pail of beer.
Fire!

Gunner's Coin. A metal wedge used to elevate a cannon or mortar.

Gunnery. The science concerned with the flight patterns of projectiles and the study of the most effective use of guns.

Gunpowder. An explosive powder similar to blasting powder but using a mixture of saltpeter or potassium nitrate, charcoal, and sulfur that was often called black powder. Broadly, any of a variety of powders used in guns as propellant charges. During the Peninsular War [q.v.] British gunpowder was 75 percent saltpeter, 10 percent sulfur, and 15 percent charcoal. French and Swedish gunpowders had somewhat less sulfur and somewhat more charcoal. In 1882 the Germans developed a powder for large charges composed of about 78 percent saltpeter, 3 percent sulfur, and 19 percent charcoal. The charcoal was made from straw roasted to a brown color.

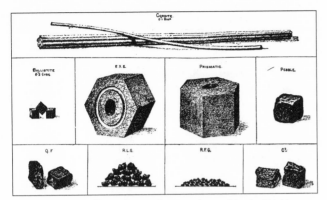

Gunpowder *Different shapes of gunpowder used by the British army*

Gunrei. The power to command the army, one of the two great powers of the Japanese emperor as decreed in 1885. This included military planning, strategy, training, discipline, and the deployment of troops. It was formalized in Article 12 of the Meiji Constitution (*kempo*) of 1889. [See Gunsei.]

Gunsei. The power to control military administration, one of the two great powers of the Japanese emperor as decreed in 1885. This included the power to determine the size of the army, regulate conscription, and determine the kinds and amount of arms and supplies. It was formalized in Article 13 of the Meiji Constitution (*kempo*) of 1889. [See Gunrei.]

Gunsmith. One who manufactures or repairs small arms.

Gun War (1879–83). A war between the British and Basutos in southern Africa that began in December 1879, when the British, who had exercised jurisdiction over the Basutos since 1868, ordered them to give up their firearms [see Basuto Wars]. Many Basutos refused to comply. Led by a son and grandson of Moshesh [q.v.], they launched attacks upon British and colonial columns of troops and laid siege to magistracies. The war ended with negotiations and with the Basutos retaining their guns.

Günzburg, Battle of (9 October 1805), Napoleonic Wars. At and near this town at the confluence of the Günz and Danube rivers in Swabia, western Bavaria, the French VI Corps under Marshal Michel Ney [q.v.] seized the three bridges over the Danube and drove off the Austrians under General Karl Freiherr von Leiberich Mack [q.v.] with a loss of 300 killed and wounded and 1,000 prisoners. The Austrians lost 2,000 and retreated to Ulm, where Mack was forced to surrender on 20 October with most of his army.

Gura, Battle of (7 March 1876), Abyssinian-Egyptian War. After the Abyssinian victory over the Egyptian army under Søren Adolph Arendup [q.v.] at Gundet [q.v.] on 17 November 1875, an Egyptian force of 14,000 under Muhammad Ratib Pasha [q.v.], sirdar of the Egyptian army, with American staff officers who included former Confederate General William Wing Loring and former Confederate Colonel Samuel Henry Lockett [qq.v.] invaded Abyssinia from Mussawa. On a plateau near Gura in central Eritrea 5 miles south of Decamere and 20 miles south-southeast of Asmara, it was soundly defeated by an Abyssinian force under Walad Michael, the hereditary chief of Bogos. Ratib Pasha blamed his defeat upon his American staff officers and retained his post as sirdar.

Gurkhas. A people living in the mountains of eastern Nepal whose young men have since 1817 served as mercenaries in the Indian and British armies in specially formed units and, after the Indian Mutiny [q.v.], in separately numbered battalions. The Nepalese government, which from 1846 to 1951 was controlled by the Rana family, who held a hereditary premiership, remained loyal to an alliance with Britain and India.

Gurkha War. See Nepalese War.

Gurko, Iosip (Joseph) Vladimirovich (1828–1901). A Russian soldier who served in the Crimean War [q.v.] in 1854–56 and in Poland in 1863. As a lieutenant general he commanded an army in the Russo-Turkish War [q.v.] of 1877–78. In June 1877 he led the advanced force toward Trnovo and took part in the defense of the Shipka Pass [q.v.] against Suleiman Pasha [q.v.]. Subsequently he defeated the Turks in the Battle of Philippopolis (Plovdiv [q.v.]) on 17 January 1878. From 1882 until he retired as a field marshal in 1894 he was commander of the Warsaw Military District.

His son, **Vasily Iosifovich** (1864–1937), was commissioned in the Grudno Hussars in 1885 and rose to became a general in World War I.

Gurry. A small fort in India, often made of mud.

Gurwood, John (1790–1845). A British soldier who was commissioned in 1808 and served in the Peninsular War [q.v.], distinguishing himself in the Battle of Ciudad Rodrigo [q.v.] in 1812. He later served under the Prince of Orange in the Netherlands. He was severely wounded (for the third time) in the Battle of Waterloo. He served for many years as Wellington's private secretary and engaged in the preparation of *Wellington's Despatches*.

Gurry

Gusoku. A style of Japanese armor produced in the Tokugawa period (1603–1867), particularly in the nineteenth century. There were many variations, with their own names, but in each the main pieces were formed of overlapping metal plates or lames of lacquered iron. In the last quarter of the nineteenth century many were made entirely of lacquered leather. The armor was sometimes called *tosei gusoku*.

Gusoku Bitsu. In Japan, a box in which armor was kept. It was usually of wood but occasionally of papier-mâché.

Gutherie Ambulance Cart. See Ambulance.

Gutiérrez de la Concha, José (1809–1895). A Spanish soldier and politician who was captain general of the Basque provinces in 1843–46 and three times governor of Cuba: 1850–52, 1854–59, and 1874–75. In 1863 he was minister of war. During the Carlist Wars [q.v.] he was a partisan of Queen Isabella (1830–1904), and in 1868 he was forced to leave Spain.

Gutiérrez de Lara, José Bernardo Maximiliano (1780–1843). A Mexican blacksmith who in 1810 joined the insurrectionists fighting against Spanish rule. In 1811 he was sent to the United States to request aid, which was refused by the American government. At Nacogdoches, on the Louisiana-Texas border, he met Lieutenant William Magee [q.v.], who resigned his commission in the American army to become colonel of a revolutionary "army" of about 60 men. On or about 12 August 1812 the little army crossed the Sabine River, invaded Spanish-ruled Texas, and occupied La Bahia (Matagorda Bay). A strong Spanish force arrived, and for four months it laid siege to the place before falling back to Bexar (San Antonio). Although on 10 March 1813 Magee died of disease, his force, greatly strengthened by recruits, successfully attacked and captured Bexar. The Spanish officers who surrendered were murdered.

A provisional state was established with Gutiérrez as governor and commander-in-chief. On 17 June the insurrectionists won another victory, but without Magee's leadership they grew increasingly undisciplined. They rejected Gutiérrez, who fled to New Orleans, thus escaping the fate that befell his erstwhile army, which on March 15 1814 was soundly defeated and lost 1,000 killed in the Battle of San Antonio [q.v.]. Gutiérrez went on to take part in several raids into Mexico, and after independence had been achieved, he became a general and governor of Tamaulipas.

Guyon, Richard Debaufre (1803–1856). An English soldier of fortune who was the son of a British naval officer. He was educated for the army and at an early age was commissioned in the Surrey militia. He later studied at an Austrian military academy and in 1823 was commissioned in the 2nd Hungarian Hussars, in which he rose to the rank of captain. In November 1838 he married the daughter of an Austrian field marshal and soon after retired to manage her estate near Pest.

When the Hungarian Revolution [q.v.] began, he was asked by the Magyars to take command of the landsturm and honveds [qq.v.]. He won his first victories over the Austrians in the Battle of Tyrnau [q.v.] on 29 September 1848 and in the Battle of Schwechat [q.v.] on 30 October. He was made a general, but with the defeat of Arthur von Görgey [q.v.] at the hands of the intervening Russians under General Fedor Vasilievich Rudiger [q.v.] at Vilàgs on 13 August 1849, the revolution collapsed, and Guyon fled to Turkey. In 1853 he joined the Turkish army. Sent to Damascus as a liwa (lieutenant general) and made a pasha, he became the first Christian to hold a command under the sultan.

During the Russo-Turkish War [q.v.] of 1853–55 he fought in Anatolia, but he was soon defeated and placed on half pay. He died of cholera on 12 October 1856.

Guzmán Blanco, Antonio (1829–1899). A Venezuelan soldier and dictator. He was vice-president from 1863 to 1868, then led a successful revolution and was "president" from 1870 to 1889, when Congress deposed him.

Gwalior (Fortress), Capture of. A famous rock fortress of the maharajahs of Sindhia that rose 300 feet out of a plain 35 miles south of Agra. It was three times captured by the British: 1780, 1805, and 1858. After the last capture on 19 June 1858, in which it was believed that the rani of Jhansi [q.v.] was killed, it was retained in British hands until December 1885, when it was restored to the Sindhia family.

Gwalior Campaign (December 1843). Sometimes called the Forty-Eight-Hour War. Gwalior in north-central India was one of the five major Indian states, its northern and northwestern boundaries formed by the Chambal River. Since the early eighteenth century it had been the dominion of the Sindhia family of Marathas, which had resisted the expanding British raj. In a two-battle war, both fought on the same day (29 December 1843), the Marathas were defeated by Anglo-Indian forces under the overall command of Hugh Gough [q.v.], commander-in-chief, India, who commanded on the field in the Battle of Maharajpore [q.v.], and Major General John Grey (1780?–1856), who engaged 12,000 in the Battle of Punniar [q.v.].

Gwalior Contingent. The army of the Maratha state of Gwalior—seven regiments of infantry, three of cavalry, and five batteries of artillery—trained by British officers, joined with the mutineers during the Indian Mutiny [q.v.] in 1857. The maharajah of the state, who remained loyal, was forced to seek British protection.

The British considered the well-disciplined contingent one of the most formidable of the mutineer forces they faced.

Gymnasterka. A Russian military blouse with a standing collar buttoning at the side. It was worn outside the trousers with a leather belt at the waist.

Gyn. A portable crane used for lifting artillery pieces on or off their carriages or beds. It consisted of three sheer legs and a lifting tackle with several handling blocks.

Gyulai, Franz, Count von Matros-Németh und Nádaska (1798–1868). A Hungarian aristocrat who in 1846 was promoted major general and appointed commandant of Trieste. In 1848, at the beginning of the Hungarian Revolution [q.v.], he took command of the Austrian naval vessels in the Adriatic and maintained a strict coastal defense. Later that year he was named minister of war, and a year later he was promoted *Feldzeugmeister* (full general) and appointed commander-in-chief of the Austrian army in the Austro-Piedmontese War. He was a martinet whose orders were often ridiculous. In Italy he ordered every soldier to wear a black mustache. This was often possible only with the aid of shoe polish, and rain created a disaster for uniforms, particularly white ones. He retired after the Austrian defeat in the Battle of Magenta [q.v.] on 4 June 1859.

H

Habaki. The metal ferrule that covered the base of the blade of a Japanese sword. It helped hold the blade steady in the scabbard and protected the blade from exposure.

Hackery. A two-wheeled bullock cart used in India.

Hackle. A tuft of short feathers worn on a Highland headdress.

Hacquet Wagon. A four-wheeled wagon used in the Prussian army to carry pontoons. The underframe was designed to enable the wagon to turn easily.

Haft. The hilt of a sword, dagger, or knife.

Hague Conference (1899), the first peace conference. On 28 August 1898 Tsar Nicholas II (1868–1918) suggested to the diplomatic representatives of the Great Powers that the time had come to seek some means of maintaining peace and "above all of limiting the progressive development of existing armaments." The following year representatives of twenty-six nations, including the United States, convened at The Hague in the Netherlands. Certain conventions were signed, among them those forbidding the use of dum-dum bullets [q.v.] or asphyxiating gases as well as "the discharge of projectiles and explosives from balloons or by any other new methods of a similar nature." A permanent court of arbitration was established. The conference produced no diminution of the pace of the arms race then in progress.

A second Hague Conference, convened in 1907, was attended by forty-six nations.

Haig, Douglas (1861–1928). A British soldier who was commissioned into the 7th Hussars in 1885. He was a captain in 1891 and passed through the staff college at Camberley. In 1898, serving in the Egyptian army, he took part in the reconquest of the Sudan [q.v.], earning a brevet majority. During the Second Anglo-Boer War [q.v.] he served first as a staff officer in Natal and then as chief staff officer of the cavalry division under General John French [q.v.]. During the guerrilla phase of the war he commanded a column, earning a brevet to colonel.

Although David Lloyd George said of him (eight years after his death), "He was devoid of the gift of intelligible and coherent expression," in World War I he rose to command the British Expeditionary Force in France.

Hailshot. Grapeshot [q.v.].

Hair. For reasons not always discernible or sensible, almost all armies in all eras have been preoccupied with hair. Moustaches and beards were sometimes required, sometimes forbidden, and the length of hair has been persistently regulated. Powdered hair had largely disappeared by the beginning of the nineteenth century, but in the first years of the century the powdered queue was a perennial subject for debate.

When Tsar Alexander I [q.v.] assumed the throne in 1801, his first order to the army abolished powdered hair and the powdered queue, and troops were ordered to cut their hair. The Austro-Hungarian army abolished hair powder in 1804, and the French army the following year, although in some units it continued to be worn for a few years longer. Marshal Jean Baptiste Bessières [q.v.] persisted in wearing his powdered queue with "dog ears" until his death in 1813. The Prussian army abandoned the queue in 1806, and finally the British in 1808.

Brigadier General James Wilkinson [q.v.], the senior officer of the American army, who believed "the less hair about a soldier's head, the neater, and cleaner will he be," in an order of 30 April 1801 directed that "for the accommodation, comfort and health of the Troops the hair is to be Croped [*sic*] without exception." Colonel Thomas Butler (1755?–1805), the army's second-ranking officer, calling the order "a wanton act of Despotism," refused to obey. He was court-martialed at Frederickstown, Missouri, in 1803 and found guilty but was given only a mild rebuke. Because he still refused to part with his queue, he was again court-martialed in New Orleans in October 1804 for "Willful, obstinate, and continued disobedience" and "Mutinous Conduct." He was again found guilty and this time was sentenced to be suspended from the army without pay for twelve months. Two weeks before the sentence could be confirmed, he died of yellow fever, still wearing his queue. When Wilkinson was told of his death, he said, "Butler has defected."

It was said that Butler's defiance extended beyond his death and that a hole was cut in his coffin through which his queue protruded, a tale immortalized by Washington Irving (1783–1859) in his *History of New York . . . by Diedrich Knickerbocker* (1809).

"Thus ends the contest," wrote Colonel Henry Burbeck (1752?–1848), chief of artillery, "and I hope it will rest with him—and that the Army will never again be disturbed with a dispute so destructive to order and Military discipline." However, on 30 January 1805 the U.S. Senate received a complaint from 75 Tennessee militiamen who protested against a general order "regulating the cut of the hair."

In India in the Sikh armies and later in Sikh units of the

Indian army, soldiers' hair was traditionally allowed to grow to any length if tucked under a turban. The Vellore Mutiny [q.v.] in 1806 was sparked in large part by orders to sepoys to cut their hair. In Japan topknots were not abandoned until 1871. In China keeping the hair long was a sign of rebellion against the Manchu dynasty [see Nien Rebellion].

Haircloth. A cloth of horsehair that was laid upon the floor of magazines and laboratories to prevent accidental explosions. It was usually made up of strips 14 by 11 feet, each weighing about 36 pounds.

Hair Trigger. A trigger on a handgun so delicately adjusted that a light touch will fire the weapon.

Haitian-Dominican Conflicts. In 1802 the French conquered Spanish Santo Domingo and held it for seven years until colonists overthrew the French government and reestablished Spanish control in 1809. In 1822 Haitian forces invaded and ruled the country until 1844, when another revolution, led by Pedro Santana [q.v.], turned them out and established independence. In November 1855 some 30,000 Haitians invaded the country again but were defeated in the battles of Santomé and Cambronal. Frontier clashes continued throughout the century.

Haitian-French War (1801–03). When Pierre Dominique Toussaint L'Ouverture [q.v.], a black, seized power in Haiti, Napoleon dispatched his brother-in-law General Charles Victor Emmanuel Leclerc [q.v.], to restore French rule. On 29 January 1802 a French fleet carrying 12,000 soldiers prepared to land on the island, then called St. Domingue by the French.

Within a month the French were in control of the seacoast, but the blacks burned their towns and retreated into the hills. When the French tried to move inland, they faced heavy opposition, particularly from the forces of Toussaint L'Ouverture, Henri Christophe, and Jean Jacques Dessalines [qq.v.], which roamed through the country, leaving behind them burning plantations and white corpses.

Toussaint L'Ouverture's safe area in the rugged Grands Cahos Mountains had at its main entrance a large fort called Crêt-à-Pierrot. In March the French advanced and after hard fighting and at a cost of 2,000 men captured the fort; the blacks lost half that number.

Soon after, Dessalines and Christophe with most of their followers deserted to the French and helped subdue black and mulatto (*gens de couleur*) guerrillas. On 6 May Touissant, tricked into entering the French camp at Le Cap-François (Cap-Haïtien) in northern Haiti, was treacherously seized. After being transported to France, he died in a French prison. Meanwhile, on 27 April 1802, Napoleon had issued a decree reestablishing slavery. On learning of this, Dessalines and Christophe revolted.

In spite of his successes, Leclerc faced major problems. His men were dying of diseases, mostly yellow fever [q.v.], and in spite of some reinforcements, by September his army had been reduced to 8,000. He himself seemed to be losing his hold on reality. In late August 1802, when the 7th Colonial Brigade attempted mutiny, he ordered every man in it to be executed—after they had been forced to witness the public execution of their wives. This atrocity induced the 8th Colonial Brigade to desert en masse and join the rebels in the mountains. On 13 October three black regiments mutinied. Among the new rebel leaders at this time was an able general, Alexandre Pétion [q.v.], who led an attack upon Le Cap François.

Leclerc, suffering from yellow fever, appears to have totally lost his mind. He ordered hundreds of loyal black soldiers and their wives to be drowned in the harbor of Le Cap François, where their floating decomposing corpses brought on more pestilence.

On 2 November 1802, while some 10,000 rebel soldiers surrounded Le Cap François, garrisoned by only 2,000 French, Leclerc died. He was succeeded by his second-in-command, General Donatien de Rochambeau [q.v.], who had considerable experience in the West Indies. In November, having received reinforcements of 10,000 French, he drove back the rebels and launched a counteroffensive. Believing that the former slaves had been "freedom infected," he had 6,000 taken out to sea, where they were bayoneted and thrown overboard. On one of the ships a black general who had been loyal to the French was tortured to death along with his entire family.

On 27 March 1803 Napoleon sent 15,000 more troops, and the French imported from Cuba killer dogs trained to attack blacks, but before a new offensive could be mounted, the Treaty of Amiens was shattered and British attacks in the West Indies cut off French supplies. Rochambeau concentrated his

Haitian-French War *Revenge taken by the black army for the cruelties practiced on them by the French*

army at Le Cap François, and Port-au-Prince was evacuated; Le Cap François was soon after also abandoned, and the French army left Haiti. Most of the resident Europeans fled to Cuba. Only 92 whites remained at Port-au-Prince. Dessalines hanged them.

On 1 January 1804 independence was proclaimed, and Dessalines was named governor-general for life in a newly named Haiti, an Indian word meaning "mountainous." On 8 October he proclaimed himself Emperor Jacques I, but he reigned less than two years. [See Haitian Revolts.]

Haitian Revolts (1806–20). When Spain ceded its part of the island of Santo Domingo (the future Haiti) to France in 1795, Pierre Dominique Toussaint L'Ouverture [q.v.], a black who in 1791 had taken a prominent part in a successful slave insurrection, led a revolt and seized power. In October 1801 in a ruthless suppression of a mutiny led by some of his generals he ordered some 2,000 men killed. One unfortunate general was "fettered in a cruel manner," according to a bystander, "and his cries are heard a long distance. Ingenuity is at work, contriving torments for the poor wretch."

The mutiny suppressed, Toussaint faced new problems, for Napoleon was determined to restore French rule [see Haitian-French War]. The resulting war ended disastrously for the French, and badly for Toussaint, who was captured, sent to France, and died in a French prison. At the war's end it was Jean Jacques Dessalines [q.v.] who was in control. On 1 January 1804 he made himself governor-general for life, and beginning in March, he set out to kill every white person in the country. On 8 October he pronounced himself Emperor Jacques I. Two years later he was assassinated.

After Dessalines's death, civil war broke out, and Haiti was divided between Henri Christophe, who ruled in the north, and Alexandre Pétion [qq.v.], who ruled in the south. In June 1811 Christophe proclaimed himself emperor of all Haiti. In 1820 he shot and killed himself with a silver bullet. Jean Pierre Boyer (1776–1850), a mulatto, who then became president, unified the country, but corrupt and financially irresponsible, he was driven out by another revolution in 1843. His ouster was followed by nearly five years of instability and oppression until Faustin Élie Soulouque (1776–1867), a former slave, assumed power in 1849 and, naming himself Emperor Faustin I, established an elaborate court. His repressive reign was marked by a general massacre of mulattoes and several failed attempts to conquer the Dominican Republic [see Haitian-Dominican Conflicts]. In 1859, overthrown in a

bloody revolution, he fled into exile. He was succeeded by one of his generals, Nicholas Fabre Geffrard [q.v.], whose regime was constantly racked by revolts. Although his government was recognized by the United States in 1862, he was ousted and forced into exile in 1867. The country then collapsed into chaos with revolutions in 1870, 1874, 1876, and 1888–89. Hostility between blacks and mulattoes remained a problem.

Hakimdar. An Arabic word used in the Sudan as the title of an officer in command of a garrison, guard, or police post.

Hakodate Rebellion. See Enomoto Rebellion.

Halbstiefel. A short boot, usually unlaced, adopted by German infantry in 1819.

Hale's War Rocket. A rocket invented by an American engineer, William Hale, in 1840 that superseded the Congreve

Hale's war rocket

rocket [see Congreve, William]. It had three vents in the rear, the jets impinging upon vanes that caused the rocket to spin and thus stabilized it. A 24-pound rocket had a range of about 2,000 yards. It was first used in action by Americans in the Mexican War [q.v.]. The British used some in the Abyssinian Campaign [q.v.] in 1867. It was eventually adopted by the American, British, Russian, and Austrian armies.

Half Merlon. The merlon at the end of a parapet.

Half Pay. In the British army this was a kind of retainer fee to officers not on active duty because of casual sickness, disbandment of their unit, or other recognized reasons. One such officer was William Hambley (b. 1792), who as a young man served in the Peninsular War, fighting in eighteen battles and suffering five wounds. When the war was over and his battalion disbanded, he was placed on half pay and remained on half pay for more than thirty-five years until the Crimean War [q.v.], when, at the age of sixty-two, he was recalled for duty. After the abolition of purchase [q.v.], officers with twenty-five years of service could demand half pay, and in this sense it served as a pension.

Half-Sunken Battery. A battery of artillery having its interior space (terreplein) below the surface behind a parapet made of the excavated earth.

Halkett, Colin (1774–1856). A British soldier who from 1792 to 1795 served in the Dutch Foot Guards. In 1805 he took command of the 2nd Battalion of the King's German Legion [q.v.] and served in Ireland, Hanover, and Spain and in the Walcheren Expedition [q.v.]. He was promoted lieutenant general in 1830. He served much time in India, becoming commander-in-chief, Bombay, in 1831–32. In 1849 he was made commander of Chelsea Hospital [q.v.].

Halkett, Hugh von (1783–1863). A Hanoverian general and a British colonel born in Scotland who distinguished himself in the battles of Copenhagen in 1807, Albuera in 1811, and Salamanca in 1812 and in the siege of Burgos in 1812 [qq.v.]. He commanded two brigades of Hanoverian militia in the Battle of Waterloo [q.v.] in 1815.

Haitian Revolts *Fighting in St.-Domingue during the Haitian Revolts*

Hall, John. A British army doctor who entered the medical service as a hospital assistant in June 1815 and was sent to the army in Flanders. He served in several British colonies in the West Indies, and from 1847 to 1851 he was principal medical officer in Kaffraria, South Africa. During the Crimean War [q.v.] he was principal medical officer in the Crimea from June 1854 to July 1856, heading a department that was in organizational disarray. Doctors in general were looked down upon by combatant officers, and Hall was given no information about troop movements or expected casualties. He had no control over regimental surgeons, base hospitals, medical supplies, or any of the medical staffs. Although he was much criticized for the failure of the medical services to provide adequate care of the sick and wounded, he was awarded a knighthood (KCB), and the French awarded him the Legion of Honor.

After the war he retired on half pay. In 1857 and 1858 he published pamphlets in which he defended the medical officers in the Crimea and attacked the reforms of the Sanitary Commission [q.v.]. [See Nightingale, Florence; Medical Services.]

Hall Carbine. In 1819, when the United States adopted the Hall carbine, it became the first nation to employ a breech-loading firearm as standard. Manufactured on an assembly-line principle with interchangeable parts, it had a removable breech and lock unit, and its chamber was hinged at the rear so it could be tipped up for loading. Although hot gases tended to erode the joint between the barrel and the chamber and to leak into the firer's face, the Hall carbine remained in service for nearly fifty years.

Halleck, Henry Wager (1815–1872). An American soldier who as a boy ran away from home because he hated farming. His maternal grandfather, who came to his rescue, provided him with an excellent education. He was graduated from West Point in 1839, third in his class, and was commissioned in the Corps of Engineers.

In 1846 he published *Elements of Military Art and Science,* in which he defended the profession of arms, submitting that "The Bible nowhere prohibits war. In the Old Testament we find war and even conquest positively commended, and although war was raging in the time of Christ and his Apostles, still they said not a word of its unlawfulness and immorality." During the Mexican War [q.v.] he served in California, and in 1850 he helped draft the constitution of the new state. After studying law, he resigned from the army in 1854 to head the leading California law firm. In the next few years he refused seats on the state supreme court and in the U.S. Senate, wrote several books, acquired a fortune, and married a granddaughter of Alexander Hamilton.

At the beginning of the American Civil War he was appointed a major general in the regular army, to rank from 19 August 1861, leaving only Winfield Scott, George B. McClellan, and John C. Frémont [qq.v.] senior to him. After administrative successes and battlefield failure in the West, he was summoned to Washington to be general-in-chief, but in spite of the promise of his early successes and accomplishments, he failed to impress those in high places. Gideon Welles (1802–1878) when secretary of the navy (1861–69), declared that Halleck "originates nothing, anticipates nothing . . . takes no responsibility, plans nothing, is good for nothing." Lincoln considered him "little more than a first rate clerk." Demoted to chief of staff when Grant took command of the Union armies, he chronically exasperated subordinates and superiors alike. Nevertheless, he remained in the army after the war and served in administrative posts in California.

Hallue River, Battle of the (23 December 1870), Franco-Prussian War, sometimes known as the Battle of Amiens. German General Edwin von Manteuffel [q.v.] with 22,500 men and 108 guns attacked 40,000 French with 8 guns under General Louis Léon César Faidherbe [q.v.], who were entrenched at Pont à Noyelles in heights above the Hallue, a small river 5 miles east-northeast of Amiens, 72 miles north of Paris. An intensive seven-hour battle ended inconclusively. Although the French slept on the field, they were forced to abandon Amiens the next day. Faidherbe, writing soon after the battle, spoke disparagingly of his troops: "My army is 35,000 strong, of whom half fight seriously. They decrease at every encounter. The rest are only useful for making a show on the battlefield."

French losses were 1,383 killed and wounded plus 1,300 taken prisoner or missing; Prussian losses were 76 officers and 1,216 other ranks.

Halyard. The rope used for raising and lowering a flag. It was sometimes written "halliard."

Hamburg, Siege of (30 May 1813–27 May 1814), Napoleonic Wars. When Napoleon retired from Germany he left Marshal Louis Davout [q.v.] with about 25,000 men isolated at Hamburg. Besieged by a Russian force under Count Levin Bennigsen [q.v.], Davout put up a spirited defense, maintaining it even after Napoleon's abdication. He did not capitulate until King Louis XVIII (1755–1824) sent him a personal message.

Hamdam Abu Anja (1835?–1888). A principal amir in the Mahdist state in the Sudan who saw more fighting than any other amir. In 1883 he was given command of the black riflemen, and he helped defeat the army of General William Hicks Pasha [q.v.] in the Battle of Kashgil [q.v.] on 1–5 November of that year. In 1885 during the siege of Khartoum [q.v.] he captured the fort at Omdurman. He fought against those who rebelled against the rule of Abdullahi [q.v.] and against Abyssinians on the Abyssinian frontier. In 1887 he invaded Abyssinia, defeated an Abyssinian army near Gallabat, and sacked Gondar [qq.v.]. He died at Gallabat, perhaps from cholera or typhoid fever or, as some believed, from poisoned medicine.

Hamidye. Turkish special militia.

Hamilton, Frank Hastings (1813–1886). A surgeon who served in the Union army during the American Civil War and wrote the influential *Military Surgery and Hygiene* (1862) and *Principles and Practice of Surgery* (1872).

Hamilton, Ian Standish Monteith (1853–1947). A British soldier and son of a British officer who, after passing out of Sandhurst in 1872, was posted to the 12th Foot. After eighteen months in Ireland, he transferred to the 92nd Highlanders in India, where his father had recently commanded the regiment.

He took his profession seriously, and unusual for a British officer of that era, he had a flair for painting and a delight in poetry. An avid sportsman, he shot the largest markhor on record in 1876.

He first saw action in 1879 during the Second Afghan War [q.v.], during which he was twice mentioned in dispatches. Early in 1881 his battalion was sent to Natal, where he took part in the First Anglo-Boer War [q.v.], receiving a wound in the left hand in the Battle of Majuba Hill [q.v.] that left it crippled for life. His conspicuous gallantry at Majuba earned him another mention in dispatches.

In 1882 he accepted a position as aide-de-camp to Lord Roberts, then commander-in-chief in Madras. Two years later he took leave to go to Egypt, where he at once rushed to the Sudan to take part in the Gordon Relief Expedition [q.v.]. He was present in the Battle of Kirbekan [q.v.] and was again mentioned in dispatches and promoted brevet major.

In 1886 he returned to Lord Roberts, now commander-in-chief, India, and served with him during the final pacification of Burma (Myanmar). Here he was again mentioned in dispatches and won a brevet to lieutenant colonel. During the campaign for the relief of Chitral [q.v.] he served on the line of communication. In the Tirah Expedition [q.v.] he commanded a brigade, but he broke his leg just before the campaign began and did not return to duty until after the fighting.

During the Second Anglo-Boer War [q.v.] he so distinguished himself in the Battle of Elandslaagte [q.v.] that he was recommended for the third time for a Victoria Cross [q.v.]. It was denied him because he was then a colonel commanding a brigade and the medal had never been awarded to such a high-ranking officer. When Lord Roberts assumed command in South Africa, Hamilton was appointed a lieutenant general and commanded a division. He returned to England with Lord Roberts but was soon back in South Africa as Lord Kitchener's chief of staff.

He later became quartermaster general; he was an observer during the Russo-Japanese War of 1904–05, and in World War I he commanded the Anglo-French force that landed at Gallipoli. He bore the brunt of the blame for this disaster, although most of the causes lay elsewhere.

Hamley, Edward Bruce (1842–1893). A British soldier who served in Ireland and Canada and in the Crimean War [q.v.]. He wrote *Operations of War* (1866), which became a standard textbook. From 1870 to 1877 he was commandant of the War College. He served in Egypt during Arabi's Revolt [q.v.] of 1882 but saw no action.

Hammerless Gun. A misleading term for a weapon in which the firing mechanism, including the hammer, is inside the gun and the locks are automatically cocked when the gun is opened. The first such gun was patented in Britain in 1875.

Hammond, William Alexander (1828–1900). An American army surgeon who at the age of twenty was graduated from the Medical School of the University of the City of New York and after a year in a Philadelphia hospital became an assistant surgeon in the army. He served for three years with troops in New Mexico before taking leave to recover his health and study medical practices in Europe. He served for a time at West Point, in Florida, and with troops operating against the Sioux in Kansas. In 1857 he won the American Medical Association Prize for his studies on nerves.

In 1860 he resigned his commission to become a professor at the University of Maryland, but at the beginning of the American Civil War he returned to the army, and in the spring of 1862 he was appointed surgeon general of the United States. He was soon upending the tradition-bound Medical Department and organizing it to meet the unprecedented difficulties of the war. He redesigned the army field hospitals, using pavilion types of tents that reduced the mortality rate; wrote a volume on military hygiene and commissioned other volumes on gunshot wounds, camp diseases, etc.; established medical laboratories; developed a system for the employment of female nurses; and supported the work of Jonathan Letterman [q.v.]. He established the army Medical Museum and permanent boards of examination, which enforced rigid standards for surgical procedures. However, his assertive personality clashed with that of Secretary of War Edwin Stanton [q.v.], and in 1864 he was court-martialed and cashiered, a sentence overturned in 1878, when he was put on the retired list as a brigadier general. By this time he was America's foremost specialist on neurology. He later founded a postgraduate medical school and edited six professional journals.

Hammond was also the author of romantic novels and a noted collector of flora, fauna, and geological specimens as well as a student of local cultures. He became a noted ornithologist. Hammond's flycatcher was named after him.

Hampton, Wade (1751?–1835). An American soldier and politician whose father, mother, a brother, and a nephew all were killed by Cherokee Indians. Although he had little formal education, he served as a cavalry colonel in the Revolutionary War, particularly distinguishing himself in the Battle of Eutaw Springs on 8 September 1781.

After the Revolution, through shrewd investments and three marriages within eighteen years to well-dowered and socially well-connected women, he became enormously wealthy. In October 1808 he reentered the army as a colonel and was promoted brigadier general the following February. In December 1809 he took command of the garrison in New Orleans and reported to Washington its shocking condition and high mortality rate, a revelation that prompted a congressional investigation and provoked the enmity of his predecessor, Brigadier General James Wilkinson [q.v.]. On 2 March 1813, during the War of 1812 [q.v.], he was made a major general and sent to command the Lake Champlain frontier, making his headquarters at Plattsburg, New York. General Wilkinson, still smarting from Hampton's New Orleans report, held him responsible for the failure of the two-pronged American expedition against Montreal, one of the great fiascos of the war [see Canada, American Invasion of].

After presiding over the court-martial of General William Hull [q.v.], Hampton resigned in April 1814 and devoted himself to the management of his estates in South Carolina, becoming, it was believed, the largest landholder in North America. He was the grandfather of Confederate General Wade Hampton [q.v.].

Hampton, Wade (1818–1902). An American soldier, politician, and wealthy landowner and the grandson of General Wade Hampton [q.v.], who fought in the American Revolution and in the War of 1812 [q.v.]. He served in both houses of the South Carolina legislature while continuing to manage the vast estates he had inherited from his father. At the beginning of the American Civil War he raised Hampton's Legion [q.v.] for the Confederacy and equipped it largely at his own expense. Although he had no previous military experience, he was elected its colonel. The legion fought well in the First Battle of Bull Run [q.v.], in which he was wounded. During the Peninsular Campaign [q.v.] he commanded an infantry brigade. On 23 May 1862 he was appointed brigadier general, and in July he was given command of a cavalry brigade under J. E. B. Stuart [q.v.]. He was severely wounded in the Battle of Gettysburg [q.v.]. He was promoted major general as of 3 August 1863. He succeeded to the command of the cavalry corps and distinguished himself in the fighting around Richmond and Petersburg [see Hampton-Rosser Cattle Raid]. In January 1865 he was sent to the Carolinas to serve under General Joseph Johnston [q.v.], and the following month he was promoted lieutenant general, becoming one of only three civilians without military training to attain that rank in the Confederate army. The other two were Nathan Bedford Forrest and Richard Taylor [qq.v.]. At the end of the war he took part in an abortive attempt to help Jefferson Davis [q.v.] escape to Texas.

After the war he served as governor of and then as senator from South Carolina. From 1893 until 1899 he was commissioner of Pacific railways.

Hampton-Rosser Cattle Raid (14–16 September 1864), American Civil War. As the Union army in Virginia tightened its siege of Petersburg [q.v.], food grew scarce in the Confederate lines. When an alert sergeant reported a large herd of cattle within the Union lines, Major General Wade Hampton [q.v.] immediately advanced a plan to capture it. The herd, guarded by 150 men of the 13th Pennsylvania Cavalry and the 1st District of Columbia Cavalry, pastured at Coggin's Point, on the south bank of the James River six miles below City Point. Hampton and Brigadier General Thomas Lafayette Rosser [q.v.], commanding the Laurel Brigade [q.v.], led 4,000 Confederate horsemen on a circuitous route to Coggin's Point and at 5:00 A.M. on 16 September attacked and routed the Union cattle guards, killing, wounding, or capturing 219 within thirty minutes. Union forces were slow to react, and Rosser fought a successful four-hour rearguard action while Hampton pushed the herd of 2,486 cattle into the Confederate lines, completing the largest cattle-rustling episode in American history.

Hampton's Legion. At the beginning of the American Civil War Wade Hampton [q.v.], an immensely wealthy South Carolina landowner, raised for the Confederacy and equipped, largely at his own expense, a "legion" [q.v.] that consisted of six companies of infantry, four companies of cavalry, and a battery of artillery. Its ranks included sons of some of the wealthiest families in the state. Led by Hampton, the legion infantry fought in the First Battle of Bull Run [q.v.]. Out of some 600 engaged, it suffered 121 casualties, including Hampton, who was wounded. He ceased to command the unit when he was promoted brigadier general on 23 May 1862. The cavalry and artillery were separated from the legion, but the infantry, essentially a battalion, retained the name and fought both in Virginia and in the West, earning a reputation for bravery and endurance.

Hanau, Battle of (30–31 October 1813), Napoleonic Wars. An army of 43,000 Bavarians and Austrians with 28 guns

under General Prince Karl von Wrede [q.v.], attempting to cut off the retreat to France after the Battle of Leipzig [q.v.] of a French army of 90,000 with 50 guns under Napoleon, was soundly defeated at this Prussian town on the Main River, 11 miles east of Frankfurt-am-Main. The French lost about 5,000; the Austrians and Bavarians, about 9,250, including Wrede, who was seriously wounded.

Hancock, Cornelia (1839–1926). A volunteer nurse in the American Civil War and a Quaker who regarded war as "a hellish way to settle a dispute." Although rejected by Dorothea Dix [q.v.] for her corps of nurses because she was too young and pretty, she refused to be deterred and, seating herself in the train scheduled to take the nurses to the seat of war, declined to move. She served at Brandy Station, the Wilderness, Fredericksburg, the Peninsular Campaign, and Petersburg [qq.v.] and quickly earned a reputation as a capable nurse and a good organizer. Her letters home, written between 7 July 1863 and 13 May 1865, were published in 1937 as *South after Gettysburg*.

After the war she founded the Laing School for Negroes, and a decade later she helped found the Society for Organizing Charity and the Children's Aid Society.

Hancock, Winfield Scott (1824–1886). An American soldier who was graduated from West Point in 1840, ranking 18th of 25 graduates, and joined the 6th Infantry in Texas. During the Mexican War [q.v.] he served under General Winfield Scott [q.v.] and won a brevet to first lieutenant for his services at Churubusco and Molino del Rey [qq.v.]. He served in Florida, helped suppress disturbances in Kansas, and served on the western frontier. At the beginning of the American Civil War he was promoted brigadier general of volunteers. He fought in the Peninsular Campaign and the Battle of Antietam [qq.v.]. In November 1862 he was promoted major general. He distinguished himself at Fredericksburg, Chancellorsville, the Wilderness, Spotsylvania, Petersburg, and Gettysburg [qq.v.], where he was severely wounded.

He remained in the army after the war and saw service in the West, where he ordered the court-martial of George Custer [q.v.] for, among other offenses, being absent without leave and ordering deserters shot without trial. In 1867 he led an expedition against the Cheyennes and other tribes on the central plains. As a major general he saw varied service, ultimately commanding the Department of the East. In 1880, as the Democratic Party's candidate for president, he narrowly lost the election to James Abram Garfield [q.v.].

Handarm. A weapon such as a pistol (handgun), sword, bayonet, or knife used with one hand, as distinguished from a shoulder weapon.

Handbook for Infantry. A manual written in 1812 by William Duane [q.v.] and adopted by the American army in 1813. It was the first American manual to provide doctrine and the first new drill manual since 1779, when General Frederick von Steuben (1730–1794) wrote *Regulations for the Order and Discipline of the Troops of the United States,* known as the *Blue Book* [q.v.]. Duane's handbook was revised in 1815 by a committee headed by General Winfield Scott [q.v.].

Handspike. A stout wooden pole shod with iron, usually about six feet long, used to shift the trail of an artillery piece or to elevate its breech.

Handsupper. During the Second Anglo-Boer War [q.v.] this was the name Boers contemptuously gave to those who surrendered to the British.

Hand-to-Hand Combat. Individual soldiers fighting close enough to use bayonets, knives, clubbed muskets, or fists. As the century progressed, improvements in firearms made this an increasingly rare action.

Hand-to-Hand Combat *Hand-to-hand combat in Cuba during the Spanish-American War*

Hanger. A short sword, usually slightly curved.

Hangfire. A brief delay in the function of a round of ammunition, usually an unwanted delay in the ignition of the propelling charge.

Hanoi, Capture of (20 November 1873), French Indochina War. French forces under Marie Joseph François Garnier [q.v.] captured this capital of Tonkin from the Black Flags [q.v.]. Garnier was killed the following day. [See French Indochina War, Second.]

Hanover Court House, Battle of (27 May 1862), American Civil War. Near this town in east-central Virginia Union General Fitz John Porter [q.v.] with a provisional corps engaged 4,500 Confederates under General Lawrence Branch [q.v.] and drove them west to Ashland. The Federals lost 355; the Confederates lost 200 killed and 730 taken prisoner.

Hanoverian Expedition (1805–06). When in 1805 news reached London that Napoleon had broken up his camp at Boulogne and was marching across Germany, it was decided to send a large army under General William S. Cathcart (1755–1843), 10th Baron Cathcart, to Hanover (Hannover) to create a diversion in favor of Austria. Lord Cathcart established his headquarters at Bremen and fought a small battle at

Hanoi *The French take Hanoi, Indochina, November 1873.*

Munkaiser, but made no attempt to fall upon the French flank. Early in 1806 after the French victory in the Battle of Austerlitz [q.v.] he and his army were recalled.

Hanover Junction, Battle of. See North Anna, Battle of.

Hanseatic Legion. On 20 March 1813, just two days after they were liberated by the Russians, the cities of Hamburg and Lübeck were asked to raise a corps for the Allies. In response the Hanseatic Legion was formed, consisting of three infantry battalions, two batteries of artillery, and two Jäger companies, a total strength of about 3,800. Although Hamburg and Lübeck were reoccupied by the French, the legion remained with the Allied Army of the North.

Hara-kiri. Ceremonial suicide by disemboweling practiced by Japanese samurais [q.v.] and officers who were disgraced or were in danger of capture. (*Hara* = belly; *kiri* = cut.) The Japanese also frequently use the Chinese word for this: *sepukku.*

Harar, Occupation of (1875–1887), Egyptian-Abyssinian Wars. An Abyssinian province that was occupied by the Egyptians in 1875. The garrison was withdrawn during the Mahdiya [q.v.], and a former emir was installed as ruler. In January 1887 the province was captured and held by Abyssinian forces.

Harassing Fire. Musketry or artillery fire, sometimes into rear areas, not required for an attack or defense but designed to annoy, worry, or anger an opponent. Today often called interdiction.

Hardee, William Joseph (1815–1873). An American soldier who was graduated from West Point in 1838 and studied at the French cavalry school at Saumur. Just before the Mexican War [q.v.] he was stationed along the disputed Mexican-Texas border under the command of General Zachary Taylor [q.v.] when he and a detachment of the 2nd Dragoons were captured on 25 April 1846 at the Carricitos ranch just north of the Rio Grande. When President James Polk (1795–1849) heard of the affair, he drafted his war message, which on 10 May proclaimed that Mexicans had "shed American blood upon American soil." Although criticized for surrendering, Hardee was cleared by a court of inquiry.

During the Mexican War Hardee won two brevets. In 1855 he published *Rifle and Light Infantry Tactics*, commonly called *Hardee's Tactics* [q.v.], which became the standard textbook, replacing the *Infantry Tactics* of Winfield Scott [q.v.].

He was a lieutenant colonel and commandant of cadets at West Point when he resigned on 31 January 1861 to join the Confederate army, becoming a brigadier general on 17 June and major general on 7 October. He took part in the Battle of Shiloh [q.v.] and in the Chattanooga and Atlanta campaigns. An outstanding corps commander, he earned the sobriquet of Old Reliable. He surrendered in North Carolina in April 1865 and became a planter in Alabama.

Hardee Hat. A broad-brimmed black felt hat with a tall, round crown, the brim usually rolled up on the right side and fastened with a pin in the shape of an eagle. The left side of the crown was decorated with a black plume. The hat was regulation headgear for the U.S. cavalry from 1855 until just prior to the American Civil War. It was said to have been inspired by the Hungarian Kossuth hat and was believed to have been designed by Major William J. Hardee [q.v.], although he was merely on the board of officers who approved the design. It was sometimes called the Davis hat because Jefferson Davis [q.v.] was secretary of war at the time it was approved.

Hardee's Tactics. The popular name for *Rifle and Light Infantry Tactics,* a manual written by Major (later Confederate Lieutenant General) William J. Hardee [q.v.]. Improvements in firearms since the Napoleonic Wars made necessary a new drill emphasizing speed and flexibility. In November 1853 Hardee began his work, based upon a French manual, *Ordonance de roi sur l'exercices les manoeuvres des bataillons de chasseurs à pied* (1848). Eight months later he submitted it to the War Department, and in 1855 it was published at government expense and used as a textbook. It was reprinted numerous times and during the American Civil War it was copied without any major changes by the Confederates.

One of the most interesting aspects of Hardee's manual is his concept of installing in small units a "comrades in battle" formation composed of groups of four men who trained and fought together and gave mutual support in battle.

Hardinge, Henry (1785–1856). A British soldier who was gazetted an ensign at the age of fourteen in the Queen's Rangers, a small corps in Upper Canada (southern Ontario). By means of a series of changes and purchases of rank he was a captain by the age of nineteen. In the Peninsular War he fought in the battle of Roliça on 17 August 1808 and on 21 August in the battle of Vimeiro [qq.v.], in which he was severely wounded. He took part in the retreat to Corunna and in the Battle of Corunna [qq.v.] and was at the side of Sir John Moore [q.v.] when he was fatally wounded. In 1809 he obtained his majority. In 1811 he was a lieutenant colonel serving as deputy quartermaster general of the Portuguese army. He was present in the battles of Bussaco and Albuera, the first and second sieges of Badajoz, and fought in the battles at Salamanca and at Vitoria [qq.v.], where he was again badly wounded. In the Battle of Ligny [q.v.] he was with the Prussians and was wounded so severely that his left hand had to be amputated at the wrist.

From 1828 to 1830 and again from 1841 to 1844 he was secretary of war. On 21 March 1829 he acted as Wellington's second in his duel with Lord Winchilsea [see Dueling; Wellington, Arthur Wellesley, first Duke of]. On 22 July 1830 he became a major general, and on 22 November 1841 lieutenant general, lower on the roll than Hugh Gough [q.v.], who was promoted to the same rank on the same day.

On 22 July 1844 he arrived in India as governor general, replacing his brother-in-law, Edward Law, first Baron Ellenborough (1750–1818). One of his first acts was the restoration of corporal punishment in the Indian army; it had been abolished in 1833 by Lord William Cavendish Bentinck (1774–1839), the first governor-general.

On 11 December 1844 the Sikh army crossed the Sutlej River, invading the territory of the Honourable East India Company and thus beginning the First Sikh War [q.v.]. During the war Hardinge took the extraordinary step of volunteering to serve as second-in-command to Hugh Gough, his commander-in-chief, and in that capacity he fought the war, although he did not always agree with Gough and undoubtedly regretted his decision. At the war's end he was raised to the peerage as Viscount Hardinge of Lahore and was granted a pension of £3,000 a year for his own and two succeeding lives. In addition, the East India Company gave him a pension of £5,000 a year.

Hardinge increased the pensions awarded to wounded Indian soldiers, established the first hill sanitarium, and encouraged the establishment of a home for soldiers' children. He left India on 12 January 1848, predicting (wrongly) that "it would not be necessary to fire a gun again there for seven years to come."

On his return to England he was appointed to succeed Wellington as commander-in-chief of the British army. In 1854 he was made a full general, but the following year was demoted to field marshall, having been blamed for the poor state of preparedness at the outbreak of the Crimean War.

Hardinge married in 1821. His eldest son, Charles Stuart (1822–1894) was undersecretary of state for war in 1858–59, another son, Arthur Edward (1828–1892), became a general and commanded the Bombay army from 1881 to 1885.

Hardtack or Hard Bread. A hard biscuit or cracker about three inches square and nearly a half inch thick made from unleavened and unsalted flour. It was thoroughly baked and would keep for some time.

Fifty-pound box of hardtack and a piece of hardtack

Harka. An Arab war party in Algeria.

Harney, William Selby (1800–1889). An American who was prepared for a naval career but on 13 February 1818 was commissioned in the 1st Infantry. He was a captain in 1825 and in 1827 took part in a campaign in southern Wisconsin against Red Bird [q.v.] and his Winnebago warriors. He fought in the Black Hawk War [q.v.] in 1832 and was present at the Battle of Bad Axe [q.v.]. In 1836 as a lieutenant colonel in the newly raised 2nd Dragoons he fought in the Second Seminole War [q.v.]. He was a ruthless enemy. He once threatened to hang a group of Indian children unless their mothers gave him the information he needed, and after one battle he ordered captured Seminoles to be hanged. Stephen Watts Kearny [q.v.] paid him a backhanded compliment in a letter to a friend on 6 May 1841: "You know the opinion I have of Col. Harney, that he has no more brains than a Greyhound. Yet I consider that by his stupidity and repair in action, he has done more to inject the Indians with a fear of us and the desperate state of their cause than all the other commanders."

In July 1839 he opened a trading post on the Caloosahatchee River and there was attacked by Indians, who killed 11 dragoons; Harney with his slave and 8 soldiers escaped. Two years later he attacked a party of Seminoles and killed 4 who had taken part in the post raid and hanged 5 others.

On 30 June 1846 he was promoted colonel. He fought in the Mexican War [q.v.] but clashed with General Winfield Scott [q.v.], who mistrusted his judgment and relieved him of command. He was restored to command by President James Polk (1795–1849) and was brevetted brigadier general for his services. In 1855 he led a punitive expedition against Sioux Indians, announcing, "By God, I'm for battle. No peace." In the Battle of Ash Hollow [q.v.] he killed 85 Brulé Sioux, wounded 5, and captured 70 women and children. From 1855 to 1858 he fought in the Third Seminole War [q.v.].

On 14 June 1858 he was promoted brigadier general and given command of the Department of Oregon. In 1859 he seized San Juan Island in Puget Sound, an act that almost provoked a war with Britain [see Pig, War of the]. He was promoted major general, but he saw no action in the American Civil War although on 25 April 1861 he was taken prisoner when Confederates captured the train he was on. He was placed under house arrest at the home of Virginia's governor and asked to change sides. When he refused, he was released.

He was then given command of the Department of the West in St. Louis and almost instantly relieved from command on the suspicion (false) that he was a southern sympathizer. He resigned in 1863.

Harper's Farm, Battle of. See Sayler's Farm, Battle of.

Harpers Ferry. At the confluence of the Shenandoah and Potomac rivers in what is today the easternmost point in West Virginia, the United States built an arsenal in 1796. In 1859 the arsenal was attacked by John Brown [q.v.], and on 18 April 1861, at the beginning of the American Civil War, Union troops abandoned it after setting fire to its shops and the building where 17,000 finished muskets were stored. Much of the machinery for making muskets and rifles was salvaged and shipped south by the Confederates who entered and occupied the town.

Harpers Ferry, sometimes written Harper's Ferry, was the scene of several engagements, the most noteworthy of which was the successful attack on 12,000 Union troops under Colonel Dixon S. Miles (1804–1862) on 13–15 September 1862 by Confederate forces under General Thomas ("Stonewall") Jackson [q.v.].

Although 1,300 Federal cavalry made their escape on the night of 14 September [see Harpers Ferry, Federal Cavalry Escape from], the surrender of more than 10,000 Union troops was the largest surrender of an American garrison prior to World War II. Colonel Miles was mortally wounded in the final hour of the siege.

Harpers Ferry, Federal Cavalry Escape from (14 September 1862), American Civil War. When Federal troops at Harpers Ferry under Colonel Dixon Stansbury Miles (1804–1862) were surrounded by forces under Thomas ("Stonewall") Jackson [q.v.], 1,300 cavalry made an escape by night, captured the 97-wagon ammunition reserve train of General James Longstreet [q.v.] and its 600-man escort, and reached the safety of the Union lines at Greencastle, Pennsylvania, without the loss of a single man.

Harpers Ferry Rifle. See Mississippi Rifle.

Harrison, Benjamin (1833–1901). An American soldier and politician who began his military career during the American Civil War as a second lieutenant in the Union army on 14 July 1862. By 7 August he was a colonel, but he was not always popular with his troops. He was brevetted brigadier general in 1865. After the war he reentered the practice of law and soon entered politics. In 1881 he became a senator, and in 1889 the twenty-third President of the United States.

Harrison, William Henry (1773–1841). An American soldier and politician. He entered the army as an ensign in 1791 and resigned as a captain in 1798. From 1800 to 1813 he was governor of Indiana Territory, and in 1811–12 led a mixed force of regulars and militia against hostile Shawnee Indians, whom he defeated in the Battle of Tippecanoe [q.v.] on 7 November 1811. During the War of 1812 [q.v.] he commanded the Army of the Northwest with the rank of brigadier general. He was placed on the defensive after his left wing, under General James Winchester (1755?–1826), was captured in the Battle of Raisin River [q.v.] in Michigan Territory on 22 January 1813. At Fort Meigs (Maumee, Ohio) at the mouth of the Maumee River he suffered two sieges, the first on 1–9 May and the second on 21–28 July 1813 [qq.v.]. However, after the victory of Captain Oliver Perry (1785–1819) near Put-in-Bay on Lake Erie on 10 September 1813 and the receipt of reinforcements from Kentucky, he was able to recapture Detroit, which had been captured by British General Isaac Brock [q.v.], and invade Lower Canada (Ontario). He was promoted major general after his successful campaign, but he resigned in early 1814. He served in Congress and in 1836 ran unsuccessfully for president. In 1840 he ran again with John Tyler (1790–1862) as his running mate and won with the slogan "Tippecanoe and Tyler too!" On 4 March 1841 he became the eleventh president of the United States, and on 4 April he died of pneumonia, becoming the first president to die in office.

He was the grandfather of Benjamin Harrison [q.v.].

Hartington Committee. A British government committee, officially the Royal Commission on Naval and Military Administration, convened under Lord Hartington (1833–1908) on 7 June 1888 to consider improvements in the army and to establish some contact between the army and navy. On 3 July 1890 it made a number of radical recommendations, including the abolition of the office of commander-in-chief and the appointment of a general officer, commanding in Great Britain; the establishment of a joint naval and military council; and the formation of a promotion board. Every one of its recommendations was objected to by the Duke of Cambridge [q.v.], the commander-in-chief at the Horse Guards. None was accepted. However, five years later, in 1895 a Naval and Military Council, headed by the eighth Duke of Devonshire (1833–1908), established the first link between the Royal Navy and the British army.

Hartmann, Jules (1774–1856). A German soldier who served under Wellington during the Peninsular War and in the Battle of Waterloo [qq.v.]. He became a lieutenant general in 1836 and retired in 1850.

His son, *Julius,* also a soldier, commanded the German 1st Cavalry Division in the battles around Metz [q.v.] in the Franco-Prussian War [q.v.]. In January 1871 he successfully besieged Tours. After the war he became governor of Strasbourg.

Hasan Pasha (1855–1888). The third son of the khedive Ismail I (1830–1895) and a soldier. He was educated at Oxford and briefly served as a lieutenant in a German hussar regiment. Returned to Egypt, he served on the general staff and took part in the Abyssinian-Egyptian War [q.v.] of 1876, being present at the Battle of Gura [q.v.]. In October 1876 he served briefly as sirdar of the Egyptian army, and in November he was made minister of war.

Hasegawa, Yoshimichi (1850–1924). A Japanese soldier and nobleman who in 1868 during the Boshin Civil War [q.v.] served in the forces of the Choshu clan. In 1871 he joined the new government army as a captain, and in 1877 he was a major commanding a regiment during the Satsuma Rebellion [q.v.], taking part in the fighting at Kumamoto Castle [q.v.] on 14 April. In 1885 he spent a year in France studying the French army. On his return to Japan he was promoted major general. He commanded a brigade in the Sino-Japanese War [q.v.] of 1894–95 and distinguished himself in the Battle of Pyongyang [q.v.] on 15 September 1894. In the Russo-Japanese War of 1904–05 he commanded a division under General Tamemoto Tamesada (1844–1923). In 1915 he was promoted field marshal.

Hashin, Battle of (20 March 1885), British campaigns in the Sudan. In the eastern Sudan 8,000 British troops under General Gerald Graham [q.v.] defeated a part of the Dervish force of Fuzzy-Wuzzies under Osman Digna [qq.v.]. The British lost 48 killed and wounded; the Dervishes lost about 1,000, it was said.

Haslach, Battle of (11 October 1805), Napoleonic Wars, Third Coalition. Near this village on the north bank of the Danube south of Frankfurt an entrenched French army of 6,000 under General Pierre Dupont de l'Étang [q.v.], a part of Marshal Michel Ney's VI Corps, was marching on Ulm when it was threatened by an Austrian army of 25,000, including 10,000 cavalry, under Archduke Ferdinand [q.v.]. Dupont seized the village of Haslach and fortified it. With great élan, he boldly attacked the Austrians and then held off counterattacks. He retreated after dark toward Brenz, taking with him 4,000 Austrians as prisoners.

Hastings, Francis Rawdon (1754–1826). A British soldier and peer (first Marquess Hastings and, in the Irish peerage, second Earl Moira) who fought with distinction against the American colonists in the American Revolutionary War. From 1813 to 1822 he was governor-general of Bengal and commander-in-chief, India. He carried on a war against the Gurkhas (see Nepalese War) in 1814–16 and against the Pindaris and Marathas in 1817 [see Maratha Wars; Pindari War]. From 1824 until his death he was governor of Malta.

Hasty Attack. An attack in which little time is spent in preparation in order to move speedily upon an objective to exploit an opportunity.

Hatch, John Porter (1822–1902). An American soldier who was graduated from West Point in 1845 and commissioned a brevet second lieutenant in the 3rd Infantry. He took part in the occupation of Texas and during the Mexican War [q.v.] served in the mounted rifles, earning two brevets. In 1857 he took part in the expedition against the Gila Apaches [q.v.] and in 1858 in operations against the Navajos.

At the beginning of the American Civil War he was promoted brigadier general and commanded an infantry brigade until he was severely wounded in the Battle of South Mountain [q.v.]. He earned a brevet of major general but fought no more. In the postwar army he became a major in the 4th Cavalry. Having risen to colonel in 1881, he retired in 1886.

Hatcher's Run, Battle of. See Dabney's Mill, Battle of.

Hats and Helmets. See Busby; Kepi; Shako; Tarleton; Forage Cap.

Hatvan, Battle of (2 April 1849), Hungarian Revolution. Some 15,000 Austrians under General Franz von Schlik [q.v.] attacked the Hungarian VII Corps (15,000 troops) at this commune 30 miles east of Budapest and were totally defeated. Casualties were about 5,000.

Haupt, Herman (1817–1905). An American soldier who was graduated from West Point in 1835 at age eighteen and was said to have been the youngest graduate of the Military Academy. He resigned his commission one month later to become a draftsman and still later became a railroad engineer famous for building truss bridges. In 1851 he published *General Theory of Bridge Construction,* a text that was widely used at engineering schools, including West Point. By this time he was superintendent of the Pennsylvania Railroad; he was later on its board of directors. In April 1862, at the beginning of the American Civil War, he was asked to take charge of all military railroading for the Union, and on 18 August he was given authority to seize and operate all railroads and to utilize any needed equipment. He soon demonstrated his skill, building with 300 soldiers in nine days a 400-foot bridge, 80 feet high at its midpoint, over Potomac Creek. President Lincoln thought it was "the most remarkable structure that human eyes ever rested upon," for it seemed to be constructed only of "beanpoles and cornstalks." Haupt not only ran the North's railroads efficiently, but built blockhouses to protect his lines and yards, and he greatly improved the telegraph system. He insisted that all trains run on time, that cars be unloaded immediately after arriving at their destination, and that he alone would be responsible for what trains moved where and when. On 5 September he was promoted brigadier general, but he refused the appointment and was forced by Secretary of War Edwin Stanton [q.v.] to resign on 14 September 1863. He thus became, he claimed, the only man "ever guilty of the crime of refusing to be made a general." After the war he managed the Northern Pacific Railroad, built the first crude oil pipeline, and developed a superior pneumatic drill. He died in his son's arms aboard a train on 14 December 1905, the last surviving member of his West Point class.

Hauptmann. A German rank equivalent to captain.

Hausse-Col. A gorget [q.v.].

Hautpol, Jean Joseph Ange (1754–1807). A French soldier who was commissioned in 1777. A leader of the heavy cavalry, he became a general of brigade in 1795. After the Battle of Stockach on 17 March 1799 he was accused by General Jean Baptiste Jourdan [q.v.] of disobeying an order and was court-martialed but acquitted. He distinguished himself in the Battle of Hohenlinden and in the Battle of Austerlitz [qq.v.], where he led a charge that drove in the right center of the Allied line. He fought in the Battle of Jena, was present at the fall of Lübeck, and was mortally wounded in the Battle of Eylau [qq.v.].

Havelock. A piece of white cloth fastened to the back and sides of headgear to protect the neck from the sun. It was named after British General Henry Havelock [q.v.], a hero of the Indian Mutiny [q.v.].

Havelock, Henry (1795–1857). A British soldier who entered the Middle Temple in 1813 but was forced by poverty to abandon the law the following year. Thanks to his older brother, William (1793–1848), who had distinguished himself in the Peninsular War and at Waterloo [qq.v.], he was commissioned a second lieutenant in the 95th Foot on 30 July 1815 and was posted to the company of Harry Smith [q.v.]. He was promoted lieutenant in 1821, and the following year he exchanged into the 13th Foot, then commanded by Major Robert Sale [q.v.], and sailed for India.

He fought in the First Anglo-Burmese War [q.v.] of 1824–26 but had to be invalided back to India. When he recovered, he returned to Burma (Myanmar), where he saw much action in the final days of the war.

Havelock was a deeply religious man who formed prayer groups and temperance societies wherever he was stationed. In 1829 he married the daughter of a British missionary in India.

After twenty-tree years' service as a subaltern because he was unable to purchase higher ranks, he was finally promoted captain at age forty-three, having been, he said, "purchased over by two fools and three sots." He served in the First Afghan War [q.v.] and wrote a two-volume book on the campaign. He was with Robert Sale at Jalalabad during the disastrous retreat of the British army from Kabul, and he accompanied the army of retribution under General George Pollock [q.v.]. He was brevetted major for his services and in 1843 obtained a regimental appointment as major without purchase.

He took part in the Gwalior Campaign and was present in the Battle of Maharajpore [qq.v.]. In the First Sikh War he fought at Mudki and Ferozeshah, and he had a horse shot from under him in the Battle of Sobraon [qq.v.]. He was serving as a staff officer in Bombay when the Second Sikh War [q.v.] broke out and so did not participate, but his brother Colonel William Havelock was killed in the Battle of Ramnuggar [q.v.].

After twenty-six years' continuous service in India, Havelock's health broke down. He returned to England in 1849 but three years later was back in India. In 1854 he was promoted a lieutenant colonel and made a brevet colonel. In the same year he became adjutant general of the queen's troops in India.

In 1857 he commanded a division under Sir James Outram [q.v.] in the Persian-British War [q.v.] and led the successful attack upon Mohumra on 26 March. During this campaign he had as his aide-de-camp his eldest son Henry Marshman Havelock (later Havelock-Allen, 1830–1897), who subsequently won the Victoria Cross [q.v.]. On returning to Bombay, he learned of the mutiny in the Bengal army [see Indian Mutiny], and on 12 June he embarked on the *Erin* for Calcutta. Although shipwrecked en route, he arrived on 17 June and was soon given command of a column with instructions to quell all disturbances in Allahabad and destroy all mutineers. He was then to go to Lucknow to support Sir Henry Lawrence [q.v.].

On 3 July he learned of the massacre of the garrison at Cawnpore [q.v.]. With 2,000 infantry, some volunteer cavalry, and six guns he at once set off and by forced marches in the hottest time of the year marched 126 miles in nine days. On 12 July he reached Futtehpore (Fatehpur), 50 miles southeast of Cawnpore, and defeated a rebel force there. On the 15th he defeated a rebel force at Aong [q.v.], and on the 17th he entered Cawnpore.

Cholera and dysentery struck his little army, and he was forced to leave many behind as he pushed on toward Lucknow [q.v.], where by this time the garrison and its defendants were besieged in the Residency at Lucknow. He crossed the Ganges on 25 July and on the 29th defeated two forces of mutineers. Three other enemy strongpoints remained to be taken before Lucknow could be reached; cholera was killing his men; he was running out of ammunition and supplies. He decided that he could not go on. However, he marched to Bithur, 11 miles north-northwest of Cawnpore, and there defeated a force of 4,000 rebels before falling back on Cawnpore.

On 15 September Sir James Outram arrived at Cawnpore, having been made chief commissioner and commander of troops in Oudh, where Havelock was operating and had been in command. Outram then made what has been called "one of the most memorable acts of self-abnegation recorded in military history (*Dictionary of National Biography*)." He waived his superior rank and accompanied the march for the relief of Lucknow in his civil capacity and as a military volunteer.

On 19 September Havelock marched from Cawnpore with 3,000 men of all arms. Fighting a daily running battle, his force reached Lucknow on the 25th and reinforced the garrison in the Residency, but it was not strong enough to bring away the women and children. Thus the relieving force added to the garrison's firepower but increased the number of mouths to be fed. Lucknow was finally relieved seven weeks later by Sir Colin Campbell [q.v.] with a force strong enough to bring away the garrison and its noncombatants, although not strong enough to retake the town.

The relieving force brought word that Havelock had been knighted for his services and promoted major general, but on 20 November, just as the British were withdrawing from Lucknow, he was attacked by diarrhea. He died on the 24th. On the day of his death he told his son, "See how a Christian can die."

Before his death was known in Britain, he was raised to the rank of a baronet. The baronetcy was allowed to pass to his eldest son, Henry Havelock-Allen, who was later killed by Afridis in the Khyber Pass.

Haversack. 1. A shoulder bag of coarse linen for carrying an infantryman's rations or other necessities. It was usually suspended from the right shoulder and carried on the left hip.

2. A leather bag used in the artillery to carry ammunition from an ammunition chest to a gun.

Havildar. A rank in the Indian army equivalent to sergeant.

Havildar *A havildar (left) and a sepoy, 1850*

Havildar Major. A rank in the Indian army equivalent to sergeant major or first sergeant.

Havoc. To cry havoc was to signal permission to kill, pillage, and destroy; it was sometimes taken to mean that no quarter would be given. The expression is probably best known from Shakespeare's *Julius Caesar* (act III, scene 1), written in 1599: "Cry 'Havoc,' and let slip the dogs of war."

Hawaiian Wars and Revolutions. During the latter part of the eighteenth century the Hawaiian Islands, a group of twenty islands covering 6,407 square miles 2,090 miles west-southwest of San Francisco, were ruled by a number of island warlords who fought one another. In 1782 King Kamehameha I (d.1819), called "the Great," gained control of the island of Hawaii and set out to gain control of all the islands. By 1800 only the islands of Kauai and Niihau were outside his kingdom. His attempted invasion was driven back by a storm at sea, but he tried again in 1804. However, an epidemic, perhaps cholera, killed so many of his warriors that he abandoned his plans of conquest and began peaceful negotiations that led in 1810 to a consolidation of all the islands under his rule. He managed to thwart Russian designs on the islands in 1815–16 and to expel Spanish pirates in 1818. After his death there was violent dissension between progressives, who wanted to adopt Western ways and the Christian religion, and conservatives, who wanted to keep the old ways and worship the old gods. In a bloody battle on 20 December 1819, the progressives were victorious, and the following year Christian missionaries began to descend upon the islands. In 1889 an armed insurrection of conservatives was suppressed.

On 30 January 1893 Queen Lydia Kamekehi Liliuokalani (1838–1917), famous as the composer of "Aloha Oe" (Farewell to Thee), was deposed by annexationists. These were primarily American plantation owners, spurred on by John L. Stevens, an American minister who had formed a "Committee of Safety" that was aided by a contingent of U.S. marines, which had landed on 16 January. Hawaii was proclaimed a republic with Sanford Ballard Dole (1844–1926), an American lawyer and the son of a missionary, as president. Those who remained loyal to the queen revolted on 8 December, but their revolution was quickly suppressed. In the same month President Grover Cleveland (1837–1908), who wished to restore the monarchy, appealed to Congress, advising it "that the only course for our government to pursue was to undo the wrong that had been done by those representing us and to restore as far as practicable the status existing at the time of our forcible intervention." Congress rejected his plea. On 12 August 1894, under Cleveland's successor, William McKinley (1843–1901), Hawaii was annexed as a possession of the United States by a joint resolution of Congress. It became the fiftieth state on 21 August 1959 by presidential proclamation.

On 27 October 1993 the U.S. Senate voted, 65 to 34, to issue a formal apology to the islanders "to provide a proper foundation for a reconciliation between the United States and the native Hawaiian people." Four weeks later this was signed by President William Clinton (1946–).

Haxo, François Nicolas Benoît (1774–1838). A French military engineer commissioned in 1792. In 1807 he aided the Turks in the construction of fortifications on the

Dardanelles. In 1808 he was in Spain and took part in the sieges of Saragossa [q.v.] and Lerida. In June 1810 he was made general of brigade and in 1812 fought at Smolensk and Borodino [qq.v.]. During the retreat from Moscow he was stricken by typhus. He recovered, only to be wounded and taken prisoner at Kulm [q.v.].

He rallied to Napoleon during the Hundred Days [q.v.] and fought at Waterloo [q.v.]. In 1831 he was senior engineer in the Army of the North when it invaded Belgium. In 1832 he besieged the citadel at Antwerp [q.v.], which fell after a twenty-four-day siege. He retired in 1833.

Hayago. A Japanese powder flask manufactured of various materials in a variety of shapes.

Hayes, Edward Mortimer (1842–1912). An American soldier who enlisted as a musician at age fourteen and with the 5th Cavalry took part in a number of actions against Indians in the West. During the American Civil War he served in the military telegraph service and ended the war with a brevet as major. He remained in the army after the war as a second lieutenant and returned to the frontier, where he fought Indians in Kansas, Colorado, and Indian Territory.

He was present on 11 July 1869 in the Battle of Summit Springs [q.v.], in which Colonel Eugene Asa Carr [q.v.] called on his bugler to sound the charge for an attack upon a village of hostile Cheyennes. The terrified bugler struggled vainly to produce a sound until Hayes, the former musician, took the bugle from him and blew a perfect call. He retired as a brigadier general in 1903.

Hayes, Rutherford Birchard. An American soldier and politician who was graduated from Harvard Law School and practiced law in Lower Sandusky and Cincinnati, Ohio, before the American Civil War. During the war he served as major of the 23rd Ohio and on 24 October 1862 became its colonel. He served in the Shenandoah Valley and at South Mountain [q.v.], where he received the first of four wounds. Although he commanded a brigade and later briefly a division and was brevetted brigadier general and major general, he never served in a substantive rank higher than colonel. Of those who left the seat of war to enter politics, he said, "An officer fit for duty who in this crisis would abandon his post to electioneer for a seat in Congress ought to be scalped," but he himself was nominated in 1864 and elected to the House of Representatives the following year. He was later governor of Ohio and in 1877, after a close election with contested returns, entered the White House as the nineteenth president of the United States by an electoral college vote of 185 to 184.

Speaking of the war years long afterward to a group of veterans, he described them as the "best years of our lives."

Hayfield Fight (1 August 1867), American Indian Wars. Near Fort C. F. Smith, on the Bighorn River in northern Montana, which had been established on 12 August 1866, 12 civilians were working mowing machines protected by 19 soldiers under Second Lieutenant Sigismund Sternberg (1840?–1867) when on the morning of 1 August 1867 they were attacked by Indians. All sought protection behind the foundation logs of a corral, but Sternberg remained standing and was killed. Al Colvin, one of the civilians, took charge. The Indians, outnumbering the whites by at least 20 to 1, charged three times, twice while mounted and once on foot, but were driven off each time by the fire of the soldiers' newly issued Springfield rifles [q.v.]. Only in late afternoon, after the battle had been in progress for six hours, did a relief force arrive from Fort C. F. Smith and drive off the Indians. Colvin's force sustained losses of 3 killed and 2 wounded.

The Wagon Box Fight [q.v.] took place the following day at Fort Phil Kearny under similar circumstances. Both were thought to have been planned by Red Cloud [q.v.].

Haynau, Julius Jacob (1786–1853). An Austrian soldier who entered the Austrian army as an infantry officer in 1801 and saw much service in the Napoleonic Wars [q.v.], and rose to the rank of field marshal. He had a fanatical hatred of revolutionaries and was noted for his cruelties to those he captured. In 1848, fighting against Italian and Hungarian revolutionaries, he suppressed them with such ferocity that he earned the sobriquet of the Butcher. After capturing Brescia in Lombardy on 30 March 1849, he outraged world opinion and won the title Hyena of Brescia by ordering women flogged. In the same year he became virtual dictator of Hungary after the suppression of the revolution [see Hungarian Revolution] but was dismissed the following year for excessive violence. So evil was his repute that he narrowly escaped the wrath of a mob in Brussels, and on a visit to the brewery of Barclay and Perkins in London he was attacked and beaten by the firm's draymen.

Hays, John Coffee (1817–1883). An American soldier who migrated to Texas in 1836, arriving soon after the Battle of San Jacinto [q.v.]. After serving four years as a scout with the Texas army, he was appointed a captain of the Texas Rangers, then little more than partisan bands. Hays brought a sense of discipline to his unit, and it performed better than most. He is credited with introducing the Colt "six-shooter" revolver to the West, and he used it in many engagements against the Indians [see Colt Revolvers]. In August 1840 he was present in the Battle of Plum Creek against the Comanches, a fight that effectively destroyed the Indians' influence in the vicinity of San Antonio.

During the Mexican War [q.v.] he became a colonel of the 1st Texas Volunteers, serving under Zachary Taylor [q.v.], and particularly distinguished himself in the Battle of Monterrey [q.v.] on 20–24 September 1846. He later served under Winfield Scott [q.v.] in the campaign that captured Mexico City. He was discharged in 1848, and the following year he led a party of gold seekers to California, where from 1850 to 1853 he was sheriff of San Francisco County. He became a large landholder and is said to have laid out Oakland, California.

Hazara Expeditions (1852 and 1868–69). Two successful British punitive expeditions sent into the Black Mountains on India's Northwest Frontier to punish Hassmezia tribesmen. In the first of these Robert Napier [q.v.] commanded a column; William Lockhart [q.v.] took part in the second.

Hazen, William Babcock (1830–1887). An American soldier who was graduated from West Point in 1855. He served in the Pacific Northwest, where he fought Rogue River and Klamath Indians, and in Texas, where he scouted against hostile Mescalero Apaches. In 1859 he was severely wounded in a fight with Comanches. Shortly after the outbreak of the American Civil War he was promoted captain, and on 29 October 1861 he was promoted colonel of the 41st Ohio. On 29 November of the following year he was appointed brigadier general. Among other battles, he fought at Perryville, Chickamauga, and Chattanooga, and he took part in Sherman's March to the Sea [qq.v.]. By the end of the war he was a major general and had received brevets through major general in the regular service. He remained in the army as a colonel of the 38th Infantry and saw much active service in the West. With William Tecumseh Sherman [q.v.] he was an American observer of the Franco-Prussian War [q.v.] of 1870–71.

Hazen was involved in numerous controversies, and he was instrumental in the impeachment for malfeasance of Secretary of War William Worth Belknap [q.v.]. In December 1880 he was promoted brigadier general and chief of the Army Signal Corps, which included the Weather Bureau. In this capacity he was openly critical of Robert Todd Lincoln (1843–1926), then secretary of war, for his failure to authorize promptly the rescue of the stranded Arctic expedition of A. W. Greely [q.v.]. In 1885 Hazen was court-martialed—General Winfield Scott Hancock [q.v.] was president of the court—and censured for "unwarranted and captious criticism" of his superior, a finding that did nothing to harm his career since most people agreed with him. Ambrose Bierce (1842?–1914), who knew him well, described him as "aggressive, arrogant, tyrannical, honorable, truthful, courageous—a skillful soldier, a faithful friend and . . . the best hated man I ever knew."

Hazing. An American term for the mistreatment of plebes by upperclassmen at American military academies. All attempts to suppress this evil failed.

Head, Francis Bond (1793–1875). A British soldier and colonial administrator who served as an officer in the Royal Engineers in Malta and the Ionian Islands. In 1815 he was assigned to the command of Count Hans Ernst Karl von Ziethen [q.v.] of the Prussian army. He took part in the Battle of Quatre Bras, and the following day he was present at the Battle of Waterloo [qq.v.]. From 1835 to 1837 he was lieutenant governor of Upper Canada, where he successfully resisted the attempts of Canadian republicans and Americans to break Canadian ties to Britain.

Headquarters. Any place where the head of an army or commander of a smaller unit establishes himself and his staff to exercise his command.

Headquarters *Union headquarters of General Grant at Vicksburg, Mississippi, 3 July 1863*

Head Space. The distance between the face of a fully closed bolt in a small arm and the cartridge-seating shoulder of the chamber.

Heavy Artillery. Guns of large caliber, such as siege guns and large guns in fixed positions, the term often including the troops who serve them.

Heavy Cavalry. Cavalry units mounted on large horses as opposed to light cavalry [q.v.].

Heavy Metal. Large-caliber artillery pieces. An army with larger guns than its opponent was said to have heavier metal.

Hecker, Friedrich Franz Karl (1811–1881). A German revolutionary who tried to establish a German republic. On 12 April 1848 he called on all men in the Black Forest area who could bear arms to come to Donaueschingen, a town in Baden on the Brigach River just above its confluence with the Breg, seven miles south-southeast of Villingen, "at midday on the 14th with arms, ammunition and provisions for six days." Although he expected 70,000, only a few thousand appeared. Eight days later the troops of Baden and Hesse commanded by General Friedrich Baldwin von Gagern (1794–1848) defeated him near the village of Kandern [q.v.] on the west slope of the Black Forest, seven miles north of Lörrach. Hecker escaped to Switzerland and then to the United States.

He returned in 1849 to take part in the second rising in Baden. When this was also repressed, he sailed back to the United States, where for a time he farmed near Belleville, Illinois. During the American Civil War he raised a Union regiment and served as its colonel.

Heel Plate. A metal plate on the butt of a gunstock. Sometimes called butt plate.

Heilsberg, Battle of (10 June 1807), Napoleonic Wars. Near this town (now called Lidzbark Warminski) on the Lyna River, near Königsberg in northern Poland, an inconclusive battle took place between 30,000 French under Marshals Joachim Murat and Nicolas Jean de Dieu Soult [qq.v.] and some 80,000 Russians under General Count Levin Bennigsen [q.v.]. Murat made a precipitous attack with his cavalry and was repulsed with a loss of about 8,000. Had it not been for the timely arrival of French reinforcements under Marshal Jean Lannes [q.v.], the battle might have been a severe French defeat. French losses were about 10,600; Russian losses about 8,000.

Heintzelman, Samuel Peter (1805–1880). An American soldier who was graduated from West Point in 1826, ranking 17th in a class of 41. He served in the Second Seminole War [q.v.] and in Michigan and Missouri and later surveyed some of the Great Lakes. After twelve years' service he was promoted captain. He served in the Mexican War [q.v.] under General Winfield Scott [q.v.] and earned a brevet to major. After the war he was engaged in operations against Indians in California. On 27 November 1850 he founded what became in 1852 Fort Yuma. While in service, he was involved in several businesses, none of which prospered. He was promoted major in 1855 and fought Indians and Mexican bandits in Texas.

At the beginning of the American Civil War he was made brigadier general of volunteers and commanded a division at First Bull Run [q.v.], where he was severely wounded. During the Peninsular Campaign [q.v.] he commanded a corps. On 5 May 1862 he was promoted major general. He took part in the Seven Days' Battles [q.v.] but thereafter saw little action. Although personally brave, he tended to magnify difficulties and lacked initiative.

Heligoland / Helgoland, Capture of (31 August 1807), Napoleonic Wars. This small (one-quarter square mile) island (German: Helgoland) in the North Sea, 28 miles off the west coast of Schleswig-Holstein, was captured from the Danes by the British in a small expedition under the command of Vice Admiral Thomas Macnamara Russell (1740?–1824). It was ceded to Germany in 1890.

Heliograph. 1. An instrument for signaling invented by Sir Henry Mance (1840–1926) that used the sun's rays reflected from a mirror to transmit messages in code.

2. A signal made by such an instrument.

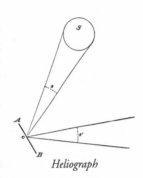
Heliograph

The British began using heliographs with circular mirrors mounted on tripods in India about 1875. They were first used in action during the Second Afghan War [q.v.] in 1878. In the same year the first American experiments were made with mirrors of plate glass four and a half inches square backed by cardboard and supported by sheet brass. The instruments were introduced in the Far West by General Nelson A. Miles [q.v.] and were widely used in the American Indian Wars.

Heliographs had a working range of up to 30 miles and in the hands of a good operator could transmit five to twelve words per minute. The British found them particularly valuable in the clear air of the high veld in South Africa during the Second Anglo-Boer War [q.v.]. Rudyard Kipling [q.v.] recorded their use in his poem "Chant Pagan," in which a discharged English volunteer compares the vapid life he has returned to in England with the spirited life he knew on the veld.

> Me what 'ave watched 'arf a world
> 'Eave up all shiny with dew,
> Kopje on Kop to the sun,
> And as soon as the mist let 'em through
> Our 'elios winkin' like fun—

Heme War (1891). A war between the German East Africa Company and the Heme tribe in Tanganyika (mainland Tanzania). German machine guns finally prevailed over the primitive weapons of the tribesmen.

Henderson, Archibald (1783–1859). An American marine said to be the father of the U.S. Marine Corps. He was appointed a second lieutenant in the Marine Corps on 4 June 1806 and was promoted first lieutenant the following March. During the War of 1812 [q.v.] he commanded the marines on board the USS *Constitution* and took part in the engagement

that resulted in the capture of two ships. For his part he received a brevet majority.

In 1817 he joined with other officers in boldly charging Lieutenant Colonel Franklin Wharton (1778?–1818), commandant of the corps, with neglect of duty and conduct unbecoming an officer, a charge of which he was acquitted. Wharton died soon after and was succeeded by Brevet Major Anthony Gale, an Irish-born officer who assumed office on 3 March 1819 and was cashiered on 18 October 1820 after an evening of drinking and whoring in which he swore at some of his officers and proclaimed that he "did not care a damn for the President, Jesus Christ or God Almighty."

On 21 January 1821 Henderson became lieutenant colonel commandant of the corps. In 1837 he collected a regiment and personally led it against Indians in Alabama, Florida, and Tennessee, for which he was brevetted brigadier general in 1843, to rank from 27 January 1837. During the Mexican War [q.v.] he again offered the marines to the army, but they saw little action until the final days, when they participated sufficiently to justify the later inclusion of the "Halls of Montezuma" in "The Marines' Hymn." Henderson commanded the corps for thirty-eight years and died at the Commandant's House at the Marine Corps Barracks in Washington, D.C.; his wife followed him thirteen days later.

Henningsen, Charles Frederick (1815–1877). An Anglo-Swedish soldier of fortune who was born in England of Swedish parents. He served with the Carlists in the First Carlist War [q.v.], with the Russians in Circassia, with the Hungarians during the Hungarian Revolution [q.v.], and with William Walker [q.v.] in Nicaragua. During the American Civil War he commanded a Confederate brigade. After the war he was superintendent of a firm that manufactured Minié rifles [q.v.]. In between wars he wrote books, including *The White Slave* (1845) and *The Past and Future of Hungary* (1852).

Henry, Benjamin Tyler (1821–1898). An American gunsmith. When Oliver Winchester [q.v.], a prosperous textile manufacture, bought the assets of the bankrupt Volcanic Rifle Company [q.v.] in New Haven, Connecticut, and established the New Haven Arms Company, he hired Henry, who had been apprenticed to a gunsmith as a young man and had proved he had a talent for the trade, to improve the rifle that the company had been producing. In October 1860 the Henry rifle [q.v.] was patented. In commemoration of Henry's pioneering achievement, every rimfire cartridge manufactured by Winchester has had impressed on its base the letter *H*. (Not to be confused with his contemporary Alexander Henry [d. 1900], also a gunsmith and codesigner of the Martini-Henry Rifle [q.v.].)

Henry, Hubert Joseph (1846–1898). A French army officer who, while in charge of the French army's intelligence department, forged papers that were used to convict Captain Alfred Dreyfus [q.v.] of treason. He eventually confessed his guilt and on 31 August 1898 killed himself.

Henry Rifle. An American lever-action, 15-shot, repeating rifle that used a metallic .44 caliber rimfire cartridge patented in October 1860 by Benjamin Tyler Henry [q.v.]. Total production was about 13,000, of which the U.S. government bought 1,731. During the American Civil War several states armed their troops with this rifle. It was later improved by the Winchester Repeating Arms Company [q.v.], which to this day stamps an *H* (for Henry) on each rimfire cartridge.

Henty, George Alfred (1832–1902). A British war correspondent who first experienced war while serving in the purveyor's department in the Crimea [see Crimean War]. He later reported on the Austro-Italian War of 1866 [q.v.], accompanied Giuseppe Garibaldi [q.v.] on his Tyrolese Campaign, and covered the Abyssinian Campaign [q.v.] of Robert Napier [q.v.] and the Second Ashanti War [q.v.] with Sir Garnet Wolseley [q.v.]. During the Franco-Prussian War [q.v.] he survived the hardships and hunger of the siege of Paris and then traveled south to cover the Second Carlist War [qq.v.] in Spain. He witnessed the Russian campaign to conquer Khiva [see Khiva, Russian Conquest of] and the Turko-Serbian War [q.v.].

Henty is best known for the adventure books for boys based upon historical events, mostly military, that he began writing in 1868, in his middle years. His last of eighty books was published in 1904, two years after his death on his yacht.

Heppa. A fort or stockade built by the Maoris in New Zealand. Sometimes spelled hippa or pah or simply pa. [see Maori Wars.]

Herat, Sieges of. This ancient city in northwest Afghanistan sits on the Hari Rud River on the trade route from India to Persia (Iran), Mesopotamia, and Europe. It was notable for its huge walls and earthworks. [See Persian-Afghan Wars.]

1. In the nineteenth century Herat was besieged, but never completely invested, from 23 November 1837 to 9 September 1838, by a Persian force led by Muhammad Shah (1810–1848). The first prisoner of war to be captured was bayoneted in his presence. The Afghan defenders were greatly assisted by Lieutenant Eldred Pottinger [q.v.] of the Indian army, who happened to be present. The Persians were assisted by Russian advisers, who devised a heavy artillery barrage followed by a five-pronged attack that was launched on 24 June 1838. It was beaten back with a loss of 1,700, and the courage of Pottinger during a crucial moment is said to have saved the city. On 9 September an armistice was negotiated, and the Persians, under British pressure, withdrew.

2. On 25 October 1856 the Persians captured Herat after a short siege. Britain protested and declared war on Persia on 1 November [see Anglo-Persian War]. The victorious British under General James Outram [q.v.] forced the Persians to evacuate the city and to sign a pledge not to interfere in the affairs of Herat and Afghanistan.

3. On 26 May 1863 Dost Muhammad [q.v.] at the head of an Afghan force captured Herat from the possession of rebel Afghan forces and incorporated it into his realm.

Herbert, Percy Egerton (1822–1876). A British soldier and the second son of the Earl of Powis who served in the Kaffir War of 1851–53 [see Kaffir Wars]. During the Crimean War [q.v.] he served as quartermaster general in the Crimea, and during the Indian Mutiny [q.v.] he held commands in the fighting around Cawnpore. He became a lieutenant general in 1875.

Herbert, Sidney (1810–1861). A British politician who served three times as war minister: 1845–46; 1852–55, during the Crimean War [q.v.]; and 1859–60. It was at his invitation that Florence Nightingale [q.v.] took a contingent of nurses to Turkey. After the war he led the movement to reform the War Office. He did much to improve education, living conditions, food, pay, and sanitation in the regular army, and he was active in promoting the volunteer movement. After the Indian Mutiny [q.v.] he amalgamated the Indian armies of the three presidencies with the imperial forces [see Indian Army].

Herero-Namas Wars (1863–70 and 1880–90). In Southwest Africa (Namibia) the Hereros, under Chief Samuel Maherero (d. 1890), fought a seven-year war, ending in 1870, to free themselves from the rule of the Namas, a cattle-breeding tribe closely related to the Hottentots. A second conflict between the two peoples beginning in 1880 lasted ten years.

Hernani, Battles of. During the First Carlist War [q.v.] this town in northern Spain on the Urumea River four miles south of San Sebastián was the scene of two battles.

1. 29 August 1836. The British Legion [q.v.], under General George de Lacy Evans [q.v.], fighting for Queen Isabella (1830–1904) of Spain, was defeated by Carlist forces.

2. 15–16 March 1837. The British Legion and a small contingent of Cristinos, all under General Evans, encountered some 17,000 Carlists and on 16 March drove them from their positions on the Venta heights above the town. The following day the Carlists were reinforced, and Evans was forced to retreat.

Hero. An illustrious soldier or warrior; someone who has exhibited exceptional courage. To risk one's life to save another or for a noble cause has always excited admiration, particularly among soldiers. British Major General J. F. C. Fuller [q.v.] wrote (1933): "War is, or anyhow should be, an heroic undertaking; for without heroism it can be no more than an animal conflict, which in place of raising a man through an ideal, debases him through brutality." [See Heroism.]

Heroes of America, Order of the. See Peace Societies.

Heroism. The superlative courage sometimes exhibited on a battlefield or elsewhere. In a speech in New York on 29 May 1882 Robert Green Ingersoll (1833–1899), who had served as a colonel in the American Civil War, dramatically defined its nature: "When the will defies fear, when duty throws the gauntlet down to fate, when honor scorns to compromise with death—this is heroism."

Herrán, Pedro Alcantara (1800–1872). A Colombian soldier and statesman who served from 1824 to 1826 in the republican army under Antonio Sucre [q.v.] in Ecuador, Peru, and Bolivia. In 1824 he distinguished himself in the Battle of Ayacucho [q.v.]. From 1841 to 1845 he was president of New Granada (Colombia).

Herrera, Battle of (23 August 1837), First Carlist War. Carlists under Don Carlos María Isidro de Borbón (1788–1855), marching on Madrid, attacked and defeated Cristinos before they could effect a junction with General Baldomero Espartero [q.v.]. The Cristinos lost 50 officers and 2,600 killed, wounded, and missing.

Following this victory, Don Carlos marched to within 12 miles of Madrid before Espartero with 12,000 Cristinos forced him to fall back [see Huesca, Battle of].

Herrera, José Joaquín (1792–1854). A Mexican soldier and political leader who supported Agustín de Iturbide [q.v.] when in 1821 he proclaimed himself Emperor Agustín I. Although he opposed the war with the United States [see Mexican War], Herrera fought as second-in-command under Santa Anna [q.v.]. Twice acting president of Mexico (1844 and 1844–45), Herrera was president from 1848 to 1851. His attempts to establish a more liberal government were generally unsuccessful.

Herron, Francis Jay (1837–1902). An American soldier who was captain of an Iowa militia company at the beginning of the American Civil War. Mustered into the Union army as a captain in the 1st Iowa, he served in that capacity in the disastrous Battle of Wilson's Creek [q.v.] under Nathaniel Lyon [q.v.]. In September 1861 he became a lieutenant colonel. In the Battle of Pea Ridge [q.v.] on 7–8 March 1862 he exhibited such extraordinary gallantry that he was promoted brigadier general of volunteers, to rank from 16 July 1862. Thirty years later he was awarded the Medal of Honor [q.v.] for his heroism on this occasion.

In December 1862 he was in command of two divisions with which he marched in freezing weather without tents or equipment, 125 miles in three days, from Wilson's Creek to Prairie Grove, Arkansas, arriving in time to ensure a Union victory [see Prairie Grove, Battle of]. For this he was appointed major general of volunteers, to rank from 29 November 1862, making him, at age twenty-five, the youngest major general on either side. He was with Grant at the siege of Vicksburg [q.v.] and took part in the expedition that captured Yazoo City on 13 July 1863.

After the war he served for a time (1867–69) as U.S. marshal in Louisiana. When he died on 8 January 1902 in a "tenement" on West Ninety-ninth Street in New York, his circumstances had declined, and his death certificate listed his occupation as "None."

Hersillon. A strong log or beam bristling with spikes that was thrown by the besieged into a breach made by an enemy in a fortification as an obstacle to attacking enemy infantry.

Hertzog, James Barry Munnik (1866–1942). A South African soldier and statesman who was a judge of the Supreme Court of the Orange Free State from 1893 until the outbreak of the Second Anglo-Boer War [q.v.] in 1899. As a Boer general he made daring raids into Cape Colony. After the war he served in the cabinet of Louis Botha [q.v.]. He was prime minister from 1924 to 1939. He remained hostile to the British and during the Second World War sided with Adolf Hitler (1889–1945).

Herwarth von Bittenfeld, Karl Eberhard (1796–1884). A Prussian soldier who, in the Schleswig-Holstein War [q.v.], captured Als (German: Alsen [q.v.]), a 124-square-mile island off the east coast of South Jutland. He was commander of the Army of the Elbe in the Seven Weeks' War [q.v.] in 1866 and invaded Saxony and Bohemia. At Sadowa [q.v.] he commanded the right wing of the Prussian army. In 1870 he was appointed governor of the Rhine provinces. He was created a field marshal in 1871.

Herzegovina and Bosnia Revolts (1875). In July 1875 Christians in these Turkish provinces rose in revolt against the Ottoman Empire. They were crushed with such ruthless cruelty that strong Russian dissent was aroused, creating a break in relations that led to the Russo-Turkish War of 1877 [q.v.].

Hess, Heinrich Hermann Joseph von (1788–1870). An Austrian soldier who joined the army in 1805 and in 1831, after distinguished service in the Napoleonic Wars [q.v.], became chief of staff for General Josef Radetzky [q.v.] in Italy. From 1834 to 1848 he was employed in Moravia and Vienna. At the beginning of the Revolution of 1848 [see Hungarian Revolution of 1848] he returned to Italy as Radetzky's chief of staff, and the following year he was chief of staff to the emperor. During the Crimean War he commanded the Austrian forces. He was promoted field marshal in 1860.

Hess, Peter von (1792–1871). A German artist born in Düsseldorf who specialized in military subjects. Many of his best-known paintings were scenes from the Napoleonic Wars, among them *Crossing the Berezina* and *Battle of Smolensk.* He is also known for his forty frescoes in the Hofgarten in Munich commemorating the struggles for Greek independence.

Hessian Boots. A light boot ending below the knee with a V notch in front and sometimes decorated with lace. It was often worn by light cavalry. One variety was called a hussar boot.

Hetaeria Philike. A secret Greek revolutionary society that helped foment Greek hostility to Turkish rule.

Heth, Henry (1825–1899). A soldier in the Confederate army during the American Civil War. He was said to have been the only officer in the Army of Northern Virginia [q.v.] whom General Robert E. Lee addressed by his first name. Graduated at the bottom of his West Point class in 1847, he served in the Mexican War and later in campaigns against the Indians on the western frontier, including the Sioux Campaign of 1855. In April 1856 he provoked an outbreak of the Cheyennes when he was sent to arrest 3 warriors involved in a dispute over a horse trade. In the fracas that followed, 1 was killed, 1 arrested, and the third escaped. The Cheyennes responded with a series of depredations along the emigrant road.

Heth, who had been promoted captain in 1855, was still a captain in 1861, when the Civil War began. He resigned his commission and joined the Confederate army, becoming a brigadier general in January 1862. He commanded a division in the invasion of Kentucky by Braxton Bragg [q.v.]. He commanded a brigade in the division of A. P. Hill [q.v.] in the Battle of Chancellorsville [q.v.] and was promoted to major general rank as of 24 May 1863. He succeeded Hill after that battle. Heth was credited with initiating the Battle of Gettysburg [q.v.] when, contrary to his orders, he advanced four brigades against the cavalry of General John Buford [q.v.]. He was severely wounded in the battle but recovered sufficiently to take part in the remaining battles in Virginia and to be paroled at Appomattox. After the war he was engaged in the insurance business.

Hetman. See Ataman.

Heyman, Herman Melville (1859–1935). A Rhodesian soldier born in Gibraltar who journeyed to South Africa in 1877 and joined the Cape Mounted Rifles. He fought in several Kaffir Wars, including the Gun War [qq.v.]. In 1890 he was with the British South Africa Company police and in the Battle of Macequece [q.v.] drove out the Portuguese, who were trying to get a foothold in Rhodesia. In the Matabele War [q.v.] he rose to the rank of colonel. Later he held several important government posts in southern Africa. During World War I he commanded the Rhodesian Reserve Regiment.

Heywood, Charles (1839–1915). An American marine who was commissioned a second lieutenant in 1858. At the beginning of the American Civil War he commanded the marines who took part in the destruction of the Norfolk Navy Yard on 20 April 1861. He was given the brevet of lieutenant colonel for his part in the Battle of Mobile Bay on 5 August 1864, in which he led the boarding party that captured the Confederate ship *Tennessee*.

In 1877, in command of a small force of marines, he broke railroad strikes in Baltimore and Philadelphia. In 1885 he commanded the marines who landed in Panama to restore order and protect American lives and property [see Panama Expedition]. In January 1891 he was made colonel commandant of the Marine Corps. When the commandant's statutory rank was raised to brigadier general in March 1899 and to major general in July 1902, he became the first Marine Corps officer to achieve those ranks, Archibald Henderson [q.v.] had held only brevet rank as a brigadier general when he commanded the corps. Heywood retired in 1903.

Hiberian Military School, Royal. A British school established in Dublin in 1815 that educated 350 sons of military officers at the state's expense. It closed in 1922. [See Military Asylum, Royal.]

Hickenlooper's Battery. Popular name for the 5th Ohio Independent Battery, Light Artillery of the Union army, which was raised by twenty-four-year-old Andrew Hickenlooper (1837–1904). Perhaps no other battery saw as much action in the American Civil War and so distinguished itself. It was particularly outstanding in fighting on contested ground at Shiloh and Corinth [qq.v.]. In spite of its record, only 5 of its members were killed in action.

Hickok, James Butler (1837–1876), called Wild Bill. American scout and frontiersman. About 1856 he joined James Henry Lane's [q.v.] Free State Army of the North in Kansas and presumably took part in the raids on proslavery districts there. He earned his name from a gunfight near Fairbury, Nebraska, on 12 July 1861 in which he killed David McCandles (1828–1861) and wounded, perhaps mortally, two others; he was arrested and tried but acquitted. With the American Civil War in progress, he enlisted as a civilian scout for the Union army and fought at Wilson's Creek [q.v.] on 10 August 1861. It was said that among other battles, he later fought at Pea Ridge [q.v.]. After the war he scouted for army expeditions in the West, sometimes served as a marshal, and toured with the road show of William ("Buffalo Bill") Cody [q.v.]. In his lifetime he was known to have killed at least

seven men, and though it was said that he killed only in self-defense, he seems to have found frequent occasions for defending himself. He himself was killed by a shot in the back while drinking in a saloon in Deadwood, South Dakota.

Hicks Pasha, William (1830–1883). A British soldier who was commissioned an ensign in the Bombay army in 1849 and served during the Indian Mutiny [q.v.]. He was promoted captain in 1861 and served in the Abyssinian Campaign [q.v.] of 1867–68. He became a lieutenant colonel in 1875 and an honorary colonel in 1880. He was retired from the Indian army when, on the recommendation of Valentine Baker Pasha [q.v.], he was sent in February 1883 to command the Egyptian army in the Sudan and to suppress the revolt of El Mahdi [q.v.] and his Dervishes [q.v.]. He enjoyed some initial successes, driving the Dervishes out of Sennar Province, but El Mahdi's influence continued to grow until his forces numbered in the tens of thousands.

On 9 September 1883, with 7,000 infantry, 1,000 cavalry, and 2,000 camp followers, Hicks left Omdurman for El Obeid, the capital of Kordofan, which the Dervishes had taken. The army first marched up the Nile. On 20 September it left the river and marched westward across the waterless wastes of Kordofan. On 5 November Hicks and the main body of his army were ambushed. In a three-day battle, known as the Battle of Kashgil [q.v.], they were utterly destroyed.

Hidalgo, Bartolomé (1788–1822). A Uruguayan soldier, politician, and poet who fought for Uruguayan independence under José Artigas [q.v.]. He became famous as the originator of *género gauchesco* (gauchoesque poetry).

Hidalgo y Costilla, Miguel (1753–1811). A Mexican priest and revolutionary. On 16 September 1810 he led an army of ill-armed peasants who seized the prison at Dolores (Dolores Hidalgo), 30 miles northeast of Guanajuato, and proclaimed a revolt against Spanish rule. He then captured Guanajuato and Guadalajara. Supported by Ignacio José Allende (1779–1811) and Juan Aldama (d. 1811), Mexican army officers, he marched upon Mexico City with an army, untrained but numbering 80,000. In spite of his initial success, he was defeated on 7 November by Spanish forces under Félix Calleja [q.v.] and forced to fall back. He was again defeated and routed on 17 January 1811 by Calleja at Calderón Bridge [q.v.] over the Santiago River, near Guadalajara. He was captured fleeing north, degraded from the priesthood, and shot, as were Allende and Aldama.

Higginson, Thomas Wentworth Storrow (1823–1911). An American Unitarian minister, army officer, and writer who before the American Civil War was active in the antislavery movement. During the war he served as colonel of the 1st South Carolina Volunteers, the first black regiment in the Union army (1862–64). After the war he devoted himself to writing biographies, particularly of poets.

High Bridge, Battle of (6 April 1865), American Civil War. A force of about 900 Union troops under Lieutenant Colonel and Brevet Brigadier General Theodore Read (d.1865) attempted to destroy this 60-foot-high bridge near Farmville, Virginia, which lay on the line of Lee's retreat toward Appomattox. Read drove off a small force of dismounted Confederate cavalrymen under Thomas Rosser [q.v.], but in a counterattack the Confederates were victorious, capturing 780 Federals. Among the dead was Read; Rosser was slightly wounded.

High Command. 1. The supreme headquarters of an army. 2. Those who occupy the highest positions in an army.

Highlanders. In the British army seven regiments were recruited from among the Celtic inhabitants of the Highlands of Scotland. These were the 42nd (Black Watch [q.v.]), 71st, 72nd, 74th, 78th, 92nd, and 93rd. Each wore uniforms based on traditional Highland dress, and each wore a distinctive tartan. The Highland Light Infantry, despite its name, was not recruited from Highlanders.

Highlanders *The Highlanders during the reconquest of the Sudan, 1896–98*

High Port. The position in which a rifle or musket is held diagonally across the soldier's body, the butt to the right.

High Tide of the Confederacy. The term was applied to the most advanced point reached in the Confederate charge on the third day of the Battle of Gettysburg [q.v.] known as Pickett's Charge [q.v.].

Hill, Ambrose Powell (1825–1865). An American army officer who was graduated from West Point in 1847, a year behind his entering class because of gonorrhea he contracted on leave in New York City. After serving in the Mexican War [q.v.] and against the Seminoles [see Seminole Wars], he resigned on 1 March 1861, at the beginning of the American Civil War, to join the Confederate army as colonel of the 13th Virginia. He was appointed a brigadier general on 26 February 1862, and after the Peninsular Campaign [q.v.] he was promoted major general on 26 May 1862. Under Thomas ("Stonewall") Jackson [q.v.], with whom he frequently quarreled, he commanded a so-called light division, the largest division in the Army of Northern Virginia [q.v.].

In the Battle of Chancellorsville [q.v.], he took command of Jackson's corps when Jackson fell. When he himself was wounded, the command passed to J. E. B. Stuart [q.v.]. From 24 May 1863 Hill was a lieutenant general. He commanded a newly organized III Corps at Gettysburg and through most

of the Wilderness Campaign [q.v.]. He was killed by a Union straggler on the Petersburg lines on 2 April 1865.

Hill, Daniel Harvey (1821–1889). An American soldier and educator who was graduated from West Point in the class of 1842 and earned two brevets fighting in the Mexican War [q.v.]. In 1849 he resigned to become professor of mathematics at Washington College (today Washington and Lee University) at Lexington, Virginia, and from 1854 to 1859 at Davidson College in North Carolina. In 1859 he became superintendent of the North Carolina Military Institute. At the beginning of the American Civil War he joined the Confederate army as colonel of the 1st North Carolina Infantry. On 10 July 1861 he was appointed a brigadier general, and on 26 March 1862 he was promoted major general. He distinguished himself as a division commander in every battle of the Army of Northern Virginia [q.v.]. After the Battle of Antietam [q.v.] he was given command of the Department of North Carolina. On 11 July 1863 he was promoted lieutenant general and sent to serve under Braxton Bragg [q.v.] in the Army of Tennessee [q.v.]. He commanded a corps at Chickamauga, where he was openly critical of Bragg's generalship.

He once declined a soldier's request to be transferred to a band by saying, "Shooters are more needed than tooters."

After the war he published a newspaper before becoming president of the University of Arkansas (1877–84) and then president of the Middle Georgia Military and Agricultural College, where he remained until his death.

Hill, Rowland (1772–1842). A British soldier who entered the army in 1790 and by 1804 was a major general. He served in the Peninsular War [q.v.] from 1808 to 1810, when he fell ill. He returned to England to recuperate but was back the following year. After the Battle of Salamanca [q.v.] on 22 July 1812 he commanded the right wing of Wellington's army and in that year was promoted lieutenant general. In 1813 he fought with distinction in the battles of Nive and Nivelle [qq.v.]. In the Battle of Waterloo [q.v.] he led the charge against the Garde Impériale [q.v.] and swept them from the field. He was made a general in 1825, and in 1828 he became general commanding-in-chief. He served until his death.

Hilliers, Louis Barraguey (1764–1813). A French soldier who was commissioned in 1787 and rose to be a general of brigade in 1793. In 1804–05 he commanded dragoons in Italy and Spain. In 1812 he was appointed governor of Smolensk. Given command of a division under Marshal Claude Victor [q.v.], he was so badly defeated during the retreat from the Battle of Jelna that he was relieved of command and sent home. He died of a "nervous fever" on his way back to France.

Hilt. The handle of a sword.

Hindenburg, Paul von (1847–1934), full name: Paul Ludwig Hans Anton von Beneckendorff und von Hindenburg. A German soldier who as a young man fought at Sadowa (Königgrätz) [q.v.] and in the Seven Weeks' War in 1866. He won the Iron Cross [q.v.] in the Franco-Prussian War of 1870–71 [q.v.] in which he fought in the battles of Gravelotte–St. Privat and Sedan and in the siege of Paris [qq.v.]. In 1877 he became a member of the general staff, and in 1889 he was named head of the Infantry Bureau at the War Department. He was promoted major general (equivalent to brigadier general in the American service) in 1897 and lieutenant general (major general) in 1900.

During the First World War he commanded the army in East Prussia and won the Battle of Tannenberg. He was awarded the Pour le Mérite [q.v.], became a field marshal, and was elected president of Germany (1925–34).

Hindersin, Gustav Eduard von (1804–1872). A Prussian soldier who entered the Prussian artillery at age sixteen. In 1841, although still a subaltern, he was appointed to the Great General Staff and later was appointed chief of its topographical section. In 1849 he took part in the crushing of the Baden insurrection [see Hecker, Friedrich Franz Karl]. In the Schleswig-Holstein War [q.v.] of 1864 he directed the artillery. Appointed inspector general of artillery, he began the arming of the Prussian army with rifled guns. After the Seven Weeks' War [q.v.] he established a school of gunnery. It was due to Hindersin's efforts that the German artillery outgunned the French in the Franco-Prussian War [q.v.]. In that war he was present at Gravelotte, Sedan, and the siege of Paris [qq.v.].

Hindman, Thomas Carmichael (1828–1868). An American soldier, a graduate of Princeton College in 1846, who distinguished himself as a junior officer in the Mexican War [q.v.]. After the war he was admitted to the Mississippi bar and was twice elected to Congress. At the outbreak of the American Civil War he joined the Confederate army as a colonel of the 2nd Arkansas. On 28 September 1861 he was made a brigadier general, and on 14 April 1862 a major general. In the Battle of Prairie Grove [q.v.] on 7 December 1862 his attack on Union forces was repulsed. He commanded a division at Chickamauga [q.v.]. In Sherman's drive on Atlanta he was severely wounded in the eye and fought no more.

After the war he fled to Brazil but returned to Arkansas in 1868 to practice law. He was murdered in his home at Helena, Arkansas, on 28 September of that year.

Hindon, Oliver John ("Jack") (1874–1919). A British and Boer soldier who in 1888 went with his regiment to South Africa as a drummer boy and deserted in Zululand. He fled to the Transvaal, where he worked in the goldfields before becoming a contractor. He became a naturalized burgher and during the Second Anglo-Boer War [q.v.] fought on the side of the Boers, earning a reputation as an outstanding scout and guerrilla leader. Tales of his derring-do made him and his associate, Daniel Theron [q.v.], Afrikaner heroes.

Hinged Frame. A type of revolver in which the cylinder and barrel form a movable unit that is hinged to the frame.

Hintsa (1789–1835). A Xhosa chief of the Gcelecas in South Africa. He was the father of Sarili [q.v.] and the grandson of Gcaleka (d.1778). In 1835 he waged war upon Cape Colony until he was hunted down by Sir Harry Smith [q.v.] and shot to death while trying to surrender. His ears were cut off as trophies.

Hispañiola Revolts. In Hispañiola in 1802 a revolt against the French was led by Jean Jacques Dessalines [q.v.], who in 1804 declared the island independent and himself ruler over its entirety although from 1807 to 1821 the Spanish ruled the eastern part of the island. Jean Pierre Boyer [q.v.] brought the entire island under his control from 1822 to 1843, when he was driven out by a revolution in Santo Domingo (Dominican Republic) led by Pedro Santana [q.v.], who divided the island into two countries. [See Haitian Revolts.]

Hissar Massacre (1857). During the Indian Mutiny [q.v.] the inhabitants of this town and district in the Punjab, about 100 miles west-northwest of Delhi, rose in revolt under hereditary chiefs and murdered all Europeans who did not flee.

Hitch. A popular American word for a soldier's term of enlistment.

Hitch, Frederick (1856–1913). A British soldier who as a twenty-two-year-old private in the 2nd Battalion of the 24th Foot won the Victoria Cross [q.v.] in the Battle of Rorke's Drift [q.v.] on 22–23 January 1879. He later took his discharge in London and became a cabdriver. Only after his death at Chiswick did his friends and acquaintances learn of his heroism. His funeral was attended by men of his old regiment (by then the South Wales Borderers) and by fifteen hundred London cabdrivers.

Hitchcock, Ethan Allen (1798–1870). An American soldier who was graduated from West Point in 1817, ranking 16th out of a class of 19. He served for four years as commandant of cadets at West Point and for three was stationed at Fort Crawford (Prairie du Chife) in Wisconsin Territory. He served in the Second Seminole War [q.v.] under General Edmund P. Gaines [q.v.] and testified on his behalf at the court of inquiry in Gaines's dispute with General Winfield Scott [q.v.]. He served for three years in the Pacific Northwest, and in 1841 he conducted an investigation into the War Department's handling of funds for the Cherokee Indians.

A lieutenant colonel at the beginning of the Mexican War [q.v.], he served first under General Zachary Taylor [q.v.] and then under General Winfield Scott, earning brevets to colonel and brigadier general. In 1851 he was promoted colonel, given command of the 3rd Infantry, and made commander of the Division of the Pacific.

In 1854 he ordered the seizure of a ship loaded with supplies for the Nicaragua filibustering expedition of William Walker [q.v.], an act disapproved of by Secretary of War Jefferson Davis [q.v.]. Hitchcock resigned a few months later.

At the beginning of the American Civil War he was appointed a major general of volunteers. Secretary of War Edwin Stanton [q.v.] later offered him command of the Army of the Potomac, replacing George B. McClellan [q.v.], but he refused it. He served on commissions for the exchange of prisoners and on the establishment of a military code and as a special adviser to President Lincoln. He was mustered out in October 1867.

Hitchcock was interested in Hermetic philosophy and was the author of a number of books on a wide variety of subjects ranging from Spinoza to alchemists to fairy tales. An autobiography, *Fifty Years in Camp and Field,* was published posthumously.

Hiu uchi Bukuro. A Japanese flintlock fire lighter fitted into a round case of tinder and used to fire the match of a gun.

Hlobane, Battle of (28 March 1879), Zulu War. Colonel Evelyn Wood and Lieutenant Colonel Redvers Buller [qq.v.] attempted the destruction of a stronghold of the abaQulusis, a Nguni clan allied with the Zulus, located on a mountain called Hlobane, but found more warriors than anticipated and were forced to retreat.

Hoa Moc, Battle of (1885), Tonkín Campaign. A French victory over Chinese forces in present-day Vietnam. It was almost a Pyrrhic victory, for the French lost 78 killed and 408 wounded out of about 2,000. [See French-Indochina Wars.]

Hobhouse, Emily (1860–1926). An Englishwoman, the daughter of a clergyman, who made public the deplorable conditions in the concentration camps [q.v.] operated by the British army in South Africa during the Second Anglo-Boer War [q.v.]. When she died, she was given a state funeral by the government of the Union of South Africa and buried at the foot of the Women's and Children's Memorial in Bloemfontein.

Hobson-Jobson. 1. A term used by British soldiers in India to describe any native festival.

2. The title of "a glossary of Anglo-Indian colloquial words and phrases and of kindred terms," compiled by Colonel Sir Henry Yule (1820–1889) with Arthur Coke Burnell (1840–1882). It was first published in 1886 and frequently republished until at least 1968.

Hodson, William Stephen Raikes (1821–1858). A British soldier who was the son of an archdeacon and, most unusual for a nineteenth-century British soldier, a graduate of Trinity College, Cambridge. In 1845 he obtained a commission in the Indian army and fought in the First Sikh War [q.v.] of 1845–46. Although a brave soldier and a good organizer, he had what has been described as "the defects of his qualities."

In 1847 he was named adjutant of the Corps of Guides [q.v.], and in 1852 he was given command of that corps and civil charge of the Yusafzai area on the Northwest Frontier. In this capacity he was charged with wrongfully imprisoning a Pathan chief, with brutality in his treatment of Indians, and with dishonesty in connection with regimental accounts, which were said to have been "calculated to screen peculation and fraud." He was removed from command in 1855. When he appealed, a second inquiry exonerated him in the matter of his accounts.

During the Indian Mutiny [q.v.] he raised a body of horsemen that became famous as Hodson's Horse. Hearing a rumor that an Indian named Bisharat Ali (d. 1857), to whom he owed money, had become a rebel, he rode with a body of sowars to his village near Delhi and attacked it, killing Bisharat Ali and several members of his family. For this he was never punished.

He took part in the siege of Delhi [q.v.] and the day after it fell rode with 50 of his men to the tomb of the onetime Mogul emperor of Delhi Humayun (1508–1556), then six miles outside the city, where he seized Bahadur Shah II (1768?–1862), last of the Mogul emperors, and took him prisoner into Delhi. The following day he returned with 100 men and seized the 3 Shahzadah princes, who surrendered without a fight. When a large, angry mob collected, fearing, he claimed, that a rescue would be attempted, he took a carbine from one of his men and shot and killed the princes in cold blood. "The capture of the king and his sons," he wrote later, "however ultimately creditable, has caused me more envy and ill-will than you would believe possible." In spite of general disapprobation, he suffered no punishment for his murders.

In the attack on the Begum Kotee at Lucknow [see Lucknow, Siege and Relief of] in March 1858, while searching for mutineers at the begum's palace, he was shot in the chest. He died the next day.

Hofer, Andreas (1767–1810). A Tyrolean soldier and innkeeper from St. Leonhard, an Alpine valley southwest of Innsbruck. In 1797 he enlisted as a sharpshooter in the Alpine campaigns of the Austrians against the French and rose to the rank of captain. In 1805, by the Treaty of Pressburg, the Tyrol was transferred from Austria to Bavaria, then a French puppet state. In 1809, encouraged by the Austrians, who pledged to support him, Hofer led a rebellion against the Bavarian government of the Tyrol. His revolutionaries defeated a Bavarian army at Iselberg (Isel), a hill just south of Innsbruck, and he entered Innsbruck in triumph. Although Francis II (1768–1835) of Austria assured Hofer and the Tyrolese that their land would never again be Bavarian, the Tyrol and Vorarlberg were yielded to Bavaria in the Armistice of Znaim on 12 July 1809. Some 40,000 French and Bavarian troops under Marshal Joseph Lefebvre [q.v.] marched into the Tyrol, and the country again rose in revolt. Hofer was elected *Oberkommandant* and for two months ruled in the name of Francis II. On 29 September the emperor sent him a chain and medal of honor, but thirteen days later, by the Treaty of Schönbrunn, the Tyrol was again ceded to Bavaria. The rebels were amnestied by the treaty, but misled by rumors of Austrian victories, Hofer again mounted a revolt. This time regular troops defeated him in November, and he was forced into hiding. He was betrayed and captured by Italian troops on 27 January 1810. On 18 February he was shot at Mantua. Nine years later the Viennese government that had abandoned him ennobled his family. In 1823 his remains were removed to a Franciscan church in Innsbruck.

Hofkriegsrath. See Aulic Council.

Hog Ranches. Places just outside American army posts where unauthorized liquor sellers provided liquor and usually gambling facilities and prostitutes. The whiskey was usually the worst, the gambling was likely to be crooked, and the whores were usually diseased. It was said that when a prostitute had sunk to the nadir of her career, she went to a hog ranch. Every post of any size in the West had at least one such place, which produced more casualties than all the Indian tribes combined.

Hohenlinden, Battle of (3 December 1800). In the early summer of 1800 French General Jean Moreau [q.v.] with about 90,000 men was moving slowly on Munich. Following a brief armistice (15 July–13 November) the Austrian army of about 83,000 was placed under the command of the youthful Archduke John [q.v.]. The two armies clashed at Hohenlinden in miserable weather: mud, snow, and sleet. The French army moved faster and was well handled. Portions of the Austrian army were cut off, and Archduke John's forces were soundly defeated. On Christmas Day the Austrians sued for peace.

Hohenlohe, Hermann, Prince of Hohenlohe-Langenborg (1832–1913). A German soldier who served in the armies of Württemberg, Austria, Baden, and Prussia. From 1871 to 1880 he was a member of the Imperial Reichstag. A founder of the Deutsche-Kolonialgesellschaft (German Colonial Club), he was its president from 1887 to 1894. From 1894 to 1907 he served as governor of Alsace-Lorraine.

Hohenlohe, Régiment de. See Légion Royale Étrangère.

Hohenlohe-Ingelfingen, Kraft Karl August Eduard Friedrich (1827–1892). A Prussian aristocrat who entered the Prussian Guards artillery in 1845 and fought in the Battle of Sadowa [q.v.] on 3 July 1856. During the Franco-Prussian War [q.v.] he commanded the Guard Corps artillery brigade, winning distinction at Gravelotte–St. Privat on 10 August 1870 and at Sedan [qq.v.] on 1–2 September. During the siege of Paris [q.v.] he directed the artillery against the city. He became a full general in 1873 and retired six years later.

Hohenlohe-Ingelfingen, Prince Friedrich Ludwig (1746–1818). A Prussian soldier who entered the army in 1768 and fought in the campaigns on the Rhine in 1794. In 1806 he commanded an army that was nearly destroyed by Napoleon in the Battle of Jena [q.v.]. A fortnight later, on 28 October, he surrendered the remnant at Prenzlau. After two years spent as a French prisoner, he retired to his estates.

Hohenlohe-Waldenburg-Bartenstein, Ludwig Aloysius (1765–1829). A German soldier who entered the service of the Palatinate in 1784. In 1792 he left to take command of a regiment raised by his father for the emigrant princes of France in the Army of Condé formed by Louis Joseph de Bourbon [q.v.] [see Légion Royale Étrangère]. He fought in the unsuccessful campaigns of 1792–93 and then entered the Dutch service, where he was again defeated by the French. Napoleon offered to restore his principality if he would adhere to the conditions of the Confederation of the Rhine. When he refused, it was joined to Württemberg.

After Napoleon's fall in 1814, he raised a regiment for France, which he commanded, and he fought in Spain in 1823 [see French Intervention in Spain]. In 1827 he was created a marshal and peer of France.

Hoist. See Fly and Hoist.

Hoke, Robert Frederick (1837–1912). An American soldier, educated at the Kentucky Military Institute, who at the beginning of the American Civil War joined the Confederate army as a second lieutenant in the 1st North Carolina and fought at Big Bethel, the Seven Days' Battles, Second Bull Run, Antietam, Fredericksburg, Chancellorsville (where he was wounded), Cold Harbor, Petersburg, Fort Fisher, and Bentonville [qq.v.]. He was promoted brigadier general on 17 January 1863 and major general on 20 April 1864.

Holdich, Thomas Hungerford (1843–1929). A British soldier who in 1862 passed out of Woolwich [q.v.] into the Royal Engineers. He took part in the Bhutan Expedition of 1865, the Abyssinian Campaign of 1867, the Second Afghan War [qq.v.], and several military expeditions on India's Northwest Frontier [q.v.]. In 1891 he was promoted brevet colonel, and from 1892 to 1898 he was superintendent of the frontier surveys in India.

In 1898 he was Her Majesty's commissioner for determining the Persian-Baluchistan boundary and in 1902–03 he was named to the Argentine-Chile boundary commission. In 1916–18 he was president of the Royal Geographical Society.

Holding Attack. Aggressive action designed to fix an enemy in his position in order to prevent his sending reinforcements elsewhere or maneuvering.

"Hold the Fort." A message said to have been sent on 5 October 1864 by General William T. Sherman to General John Murray Corse, who was being attacked by Confederates under John Hood [qq.v.] at Allatoona Pass [q.v.]. What Sherman actually signaled was "Hold fast; we are coming."

Hollabrünn, Battle of (16 November 1805), Napoleonic Wars, sometimes called the Battle of Oberhollabrünn. After capturing Vienna on 13 November 1805, Napoleon, with an army of 110,000, turned south in an attempt to cut off a Russian force of 40,000 under Mikhail Kutuzov [q.v.] in Lower Austria that was retreating after the Battle of Ulm [q.v.]. French cavalry under Marshals Lannes and Soult [qq.v.] attacked the 7,000-man Russian rear guard under Russian General Bagration [q.v.] near this town, 25 miles north of Vienna. Bagration was ordered to delay the French, and he did so, not retreating until he had lost half his army. This temporary check enabled Kutusov to withdraw safely to the east and regroup. French losses were about 1,200.

Hollow Bastion. See Empty Bastion.

Hollow Square. A formation in which soldiers formed a square or a rectangle to repel an attack. Baggage, supplies, and animals were gathered in the center.

Holmes, John (1790?–1848). An Anglo-Indian soldier who began his military career as a trumpeter in the Bengal Horse Artillery. In 1829 he deserted and joined the Khalsa, the Sikh army in the Punjab. In 1834 he took part in the capture of Peshawar. In 1835 he was appointed kardar (governor) of Gujarat. He took part in several expeditions against hill tribes and in the First Sikh War [q.v.] in 1845–46. In October 1848 his troops mutinied, and he was slain by his own troops, who cut off his head.

Holmes, Oliver Wendell (1841–1935). American soldier and jurist. During the American Civil War he fought as a lieutenant in the Union army at Balls Bluff, where he was wounded in the chest; Antietam, where he was wounded in the neck and left for dead; and Fredericksburg [qq.v.]. He ended the war a lieutenant colonel. He was admitted to the bar in 1867, and in 1909 he became an associate justice of the Supreme Court.

Holster. Originally a piece of horse furniture but later a pocketlike compartment to hold a handgun and worn on a belt or harness.

Holster

Homing Pigeons. See Pigeons.

Honduran Revolts. From 1890 to 1899 Honduras was in constant turmoil as local generals tried to seize power. In 1894 Honduran insurrectionists were aided by forces from Nicaragua. Other foreigners became involved. They included Lee Christmas [q.v.], a former American locomotive engineer who aided the rebels.

Honeycomb. A defect in artillery pieces that resembled a wax honeycomb caused by imperfect casting or by long exposure to damp weather.

Honey Springs, Battle of (17 July 1863), American Civil War. The Federal Army of the Frontier under Major General James G. Blunt (1826–1881) defeated a Confederate force of 5,000 men under Brigadier General Douglas H. Cooper (1815–1879), a former Indian agent, in the largest engagement to take place in Indian Territory. Indians fought on both sides. Federal losses were 13 killed; Confederate losses were 134 killed and 47 taken prisoner.

Honor. Officers have always laid claim to the title of gentleman and most have adhered to a code of integrity and decency. General Karl von Clausewitz [q.v.] wrote (1832): "The soldier trade, if it is to mean anything at all, has to be anchored to an unshakable code of honor. Otherwise, those of us who follow the drums become nothing more than a bunch of hired assassins walking around in gaudy clothes . . . a disgrace to God and mankind." The West Point motto is "Duty Honor Country."

Honorable Discharge. A formal release from a military service honestly and faithfully performed.

Honors of War. Privileges sometimes given by the conquerors of a fortified place to those who have capitulated, allowing them to surrender with some dignity. These varied according to negotiated terms but usually permitted the defeated to leave their fortifications with their arms, flags flying, and drums beating. Officers were sometimes permitted to keep their sidearms.

During the Franco-Prussian War, in the formal surrender of the French army at Sedan [q.v.], the French asked for an "honorable capitulation," permitting them to march out with their arms, baggage, and full honors, but General Helmuth von Moltke [q.v.] and Prince Otto von Bismarck (1815–1898) refused, declaring that what might have been appropriate for the surrender of a garrison was inappropriate for the surrender of a national army. At the end of the siege of Metz, French General Achille Bazaine [q.v.] was offered but refused the honors of war.

Honourable Company of Artillery. A unique unit, the oldest regiment in the British army, it originated in a group of citizen archers known as the Guild of St. George, formed by letters patent on 25 August 1537 as the Fraternity or Guild of Artillerie of Longbows, Crossbows and Handguns. Members were to be "overseerers of the science of artillerie." Over the years it was called by various names, such as Gentlemen of the Artillery Garden, but it evolved into what by the nineteenth century and since has been the Honourable Company of Artillery. Since 1842 the officers have been appointed by the sovereign, and on 1 June 1883 it was given precedence directly after the regular forces. It did not become part of the regular service until 1908, when, by a special act of Parliament, it was included under the Territorial Forces Act. It was larger than a company—it contained 1,200 members in 1803 and 800 in 1860—not entirely or always artillery, and although it called itself Honourable since 1686, it was not officially so designated until Queen Victoria's reign. Members were elected, paid annual fees, and purchased their own uniforms and equipment. Until 1842 members elected their own officers, although the sovereign was always the captain general. In 1888, when its officers and others refused to vote £500 to pay for the adjutant and sundry expenses, it was disarmed on 18 December by the War Office. However, the company resumed drilling on 17 January 1889.

Despite its long history, it never engaged in actual warfare until the Second Anglo-Boer War [q.v.]. Since 1642 the organization's headquarters have been at Armoury House on City Road in London.

Honourable East India Company. Popularly called John Company, this was a company chartered by Queen Elizabeth I (1563–1603) on 31 December 1600 to trade in India and the East Indies. Being ejected by the Dutch from the East Indies after the massacre of Amboina in 1623, the company established a foothold in Bengal, where it grew steadily. In the eighteenth century it was divided into three parts, called presidencies, Bengal, Madras, and Bombay, each with its own governor, army, and commander-in-chief. By force and diplomacy the amount of territory it directly controlled and the number of dependent princely states grew rapidly in the nineteenth century. Its armies fought Marathas, Sikhs, Pindaris, and numerous tribes on the Northwest Frontier. Criticism of the company's administration led to a number of restrictive Government of India acts. In 1813 it lost part of its trading monopoly. In 1833 it ceased to be a trading company, and its functions were completely administrative and political. In 1858, at the end of the Indian Mutiny [q.v.], the crown assumed full responsibility for India. The company survived as a hollow entity until 1873, when it was completely dissolved.

Honvéd. 1. A member of the Honvédség, a volunteer Hungarian military force similar to the landwehr [q.v.]. The Honvéds supported the revolution in 1848–49, but in 1868, when the independence of Hungary was promised, offered a loyal address to the emperor-king.

2. Hungarian infantry.

Hood, John Bell (1831–1879). An American soldier who was graduated from West Point in 1853 and saw service in California and Texas. At the outbreak of the American Civil War he resigned as a first lieutenant on 17 April 1861 and joined the Confederate army, in which he enjoyed the most spectacular rise of any Confederate officer. A liar, schemer, and backbiter, he possessed a bold, impetuous, and ruthless nature. He had an overweening ambition and an almost pathological need for praise.

He was made brigadier general in March 1862 and commanded the Texas Brigade. On 10 October of the same year he was appointed major general and in that rank fought in nearly all the battles in northern Virginia. He was severely wounded in the arm at Gettysburg and lost his right leg at

Chickamauga [qq.v.]. He was promoted lieutenant general, to rank from 20 September 1863, and temporarily general from 18 July 1864. After replacing Joseph Johnston in 1864, he suffered a series of defeats at the hands of William Tecumseh Sherman [q.v.], and in May 1865 he surrendered at Natchez, Mississippi.

After the war he became a commission agent in New Orleans and at first prospered, but then he fell upon hard times. He married in 1868 and sired eleven children (including three sets of twins) in ten years. He died of yellow fever in 1879 together with his wife and one of their children. The Hood Orphan Memorial Fund was established for the surviving children, and in 1880 the fund published his memoirs, *Personal Experiences in the United States and Confederate States Armies.*

Hood's Sorties. See Atlanta Campaign. For Hood's first sortie, see Atlanta, Battle of; for his second sortie, see Peach Tree Creek, Battle of.

Hooker, Joseph (1814–1879). An American soldier who was graduated from West Point in 1837. As a staff officer during the Mexican War [q.v.] he won brevets to captain, major, and lieutenant colonel. In 1853 he resigned his commission to become a farmer, but an unsuccessful one, near Sonoma, California.

On 17 May 1861, during the American Civil War, he was commissioned a brigadier general of volunteers in the Union army, and he saw much service in northern Virginia. After the Battle of Fredericksburg [q.v.], in which he commanded a grand division [q.v.], he criticized General Ambrose Burnside

General Joseph Hooker at Chancellorsville

[q.v.], his commander, and was himself given Burnside's command of the Army of the Potomac. He skillfully moved his army of 135,000 men across the Rapidan and Rappahannock rivers and was about to crush Lee when Stonewall Jackson by clever maneuvering crashed into his right flank and rolled it back. Hooker was forced to retreat. Three days before the Battle of Gettysburg, he was supplanted by General George C. Meade [q.v.].

Moved to the West, his troops drove a lightly held Confederate line off Lookout Mountain in a battle celebrated as the Battle above the Clouds [q.v.]. At Atlanta he asked to be relieved when General Oliver Otis Howard [q.v.] was appointed to command the Army of the Tennessee [q.v.]. Sherman obliged. Hooker retired as a major general in 1868.

Legend says that the term "hooker" for a prostitute derives from the class of women who frequented Joseph Hookers' headquarters, where, it was averred, "no gentleman cared to go and no lady could go." The derivation is disputed.

Hooker Jim (1825?–1879), also known as Hooka or Ha-karjim. A Modoc Indian leader who took a prominent part in the Modoc War [q.v.] of 1872–73. It was he who led the warriors who slaughtered 14 settlers after the Battle of the Lost River on 29 November 1872, and he was one of the assassins of General Edward Canby [q.v.] on 11 April 1873. After quarreling with Captain Jack [q.v.], he surrendered in May of that year. He then became one of the army's Modoc Bloodhounds, who scouted for hostile Indians, and he was a prime government witness at the trial of Captain Jack and five other Modoc ringleaders. In 1873 he and 153 other Modocs were sent to Indian Territory. He died there at the Quapaw Agency.

Hope, John, Fourth Earl of Hopetoun (1765–1823). A British soldier who served as adjutant general under Sir Ralph Abercomby [q.v.] in the West Indies in 1796 and in the Mediterranean in 1800. He was wounded in Holland in 1799 and again, quite severely, in the Battle of Aboukir [q.v.] in Egypt. He was promoted major general in 1803 and lieutenant general in 1808. In the peninsula he was a division commander at Corunna [q.v.] and took command of the army after the death of Sir John Moore [q.v.]. In 1810 he became ill and left to recuperate in England, but he returned in 1811 and commanded the army's southern wing, operating independently for much of 1811–12. He played important roles in all battles subsequent to the Battle of Salamanca [q.v.] on 22 July 1812. He commanded a division in the Battle of Nivelle on 10 November 1813, and in the Battle of the Nive [qq.v.] on 9–12 December 1813 he was severely wounded. At Bayonne on 14 April 1814 he was again wounded and taken prisoner. Wellington called Hope "the ablest man in the Peninsular army." He was made a full general in 1819.

Hopkins, Juliet Ann Opie (1818–1890). An American woman, married to a justice of the Alabama Supreme Court, who during the American Civil War superintended the Alabama section of the Chimborazo Hospital [q.v.] until it was merged into the Confederate Medical Department in 1863. She was a resourceful and efficient administrator. Alabama honored her by using her likeness on twenty-five-cent coins and fifty-dollar bills. She died in Washington, D.C., and was buried with full military honors at Arlington National Cemetery [q.v.].

Hore-Ruthven, Alexander Gore Arkwright (1872–1955). A British soldier and statesman who won the Victoria Cross [q.v.] on 22 September 1898 while a captain in the Camel Corps. He later won the Distinguished Service Order and Bar and the Croix de Guerre [qq.v.]. He attained the rank of brigadier general and was raised to the peerage as first Baron Gowrie. From 1836 to 1845 he served as governor-general of Australia.

Hornwork. 1. In fortifications, an outwork of two demibastions connected by a curtain. It was often connected to works in the rear by long, almost parallel wings.

2. A defensive work to protect a bridge or some other point with a bastioned front and long flanks extending back to a river or some other obstacle.

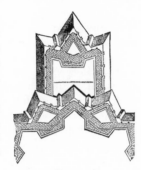

Hornwork

Hors de Combat. Out of the battle. A term applied to a person who was wounded or otherwise incapacitated and unable to fight.

Horse. Often used to mean cavalry or a body of men mounted on horseback. Often part of the name of an irregular unit, e.g., Hodson's Horse.

Horse Equipments. See Equipments, Horse.

Horse Guards. 1. In the British army, the mounted regiments of the Brigade of Guards, which in the nineteenth century consisted of three regiments—the Royal Horse Guards and the First and Second Life Guards.

2. The Palladian-style building, constructed in 1750–58 that until 1872 was the headquarters of the commander-in-chief of the British army in Whitehall, London. Thus the colloquial name for the British army headquarters in Britain.

Horseholder. When cavalry or mounted infantry dismounted to fight on foot, one man in four held four horses in the rear, usually in a protected location. The term was often applied to anyone who sought a position free of danger.

Horses. Almost all nineteenth-century armies were dependent upon horses to move men, supplies, and guns. Much time and energy were expended in the breeding, training, selecting, feeding, doctoring, and general care of horses. In Europe in the early nineteenth century horses bred in the German state of Mecklenberg and on the offshore island of Rügen were much prized. In every army mature horses were considered the ideal. Napoleon preferred horses five years old without docked tails. Cavalry horses were trained to respond to the various pressures of a rider's legs and to recognize certain trumpet calls. A wise horse learned to keep its ears flat when the trumpet blew the charge.

In China the preferred horses were those from outside the Great Wall. Those from Manchuria and Inner Mongolia were far stronger than horses from South China. The capture of such horses was considered a great prize by the Nien [q.v.].

When armies suffered hardships and casualties, so did their horses. Napoleon is believed to have lost between 130,000 and 175,000 in Russia in 1812.

The horses of many generals became famous. Wellington's favorite mount was Copenhagen [q.v.], named after the battle. Lord Roberts's horse, Veronel, an Arab named after a Lushai chief (Roberts had served in the Lushai Expedition [q.v.]), was given the campaign medal after the Second Afghan War [q.v.]. Robert E. Lee rode Traveller. Thomas ("Stonewall") Jackson rode a horse that he named Fancy but that is known to all as Little Sorrel [q.v.], whose body, artfully mounted, is still to be seen at the museum of the Virginia Military Institute in Lexington, Virginia. U. S. Grant rode Cincinnati. General George Meade's [q.v.] bay, called Baldy, four times wounded, was faithfully maintained by the general after the war; Baldy lived to follow the general's hearse in 1872. Sheridan [q.v.] rode Winchester. Philip Kearny [q.v.] was killed at Chantilly [q.v.] riding a light brown horse named Bayard. Napoleon rode a horse named Marengo, after his famous victory over the Austrians in Italy on 14 June 1800; the

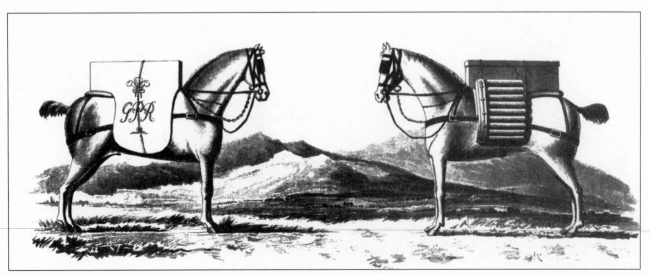

Horses *Ammunition horses, 1814*

horse's skeleton became one of the odder exhibits at the British Army Museum in Chelsea.

John Hammond (d.1889), who rose from private to brevet brigadier general during the American Civil War, rode his horse, Pink, in thirty-four battles and eighty-six skirmishes. A monument to Pink stands in his owner's hometown, Crown Point, New York.

Horseshoe Bend, Battle of (27 March 1814), Creek War. Some 2,000 men, mostly Tennessee militia, under Major General Andrew Jackson [q.v.] attacked and defeated in a seven-hour battle some 900 Creek Indians under Menewa [q.v.] at a place in present-day Tallapoosa County, eastern Alabama, called Horseshoe Bend [q.v.], or Tohopeka, on the Tallapoosa River. A bayonet charge led by the regulars routed the Creeks, who were ruthlessly hunted down and killed. Only some 100 warriors, including the wounded Menewa, survived. Jackson later reported: "I regret that two or three women and children were killed by the accident." Jackson's losses were 49 killed and 157 wounded. This was the final battle in a six-month campaign.

When Menewa recovered sufficiently from his wounds, he killed the medicine man whose prophecy had led him to make a bad deployment of his warriors. Jackson was appointed a major general in the regular army. The remaining hostile Creeks fled to Spanish Florida.

Horseshoe Ridge. A physical feature on the battlefield of Chickamauga [q.v.] on 20 September 1863 during the American Civil War. The western end of Snodgrass Hill, an extension of the Lookout Mountain range in the northwestern quadrant of the battlefield, it was the scene of some of the day's most vicious fighting.

Horseshoe Roll. The American name for a blanket rolled, tied at the ends, and worn over a shoulder. Personal items were often rolled inside the blanket.

Horsetail. A Turkish badge of rank. A sultan rated seven horsetails, his vizier five, and pashas, depending on their grades, one, two, or three. Mounted on staffs, horsetails were carried in front of the dignitary on the march and stood in front of his tent in camp.

Horstmann Brothers & Company. An American firm that supplied uniforms and equipment to American officers. It was founded in 1815 by Wilhelm H. Horstmann of Cassel, Germany, who had learned silk weaving in France. He introduced the Jacquard machine into the United States, and he used machines for the manufacture of gold lace before they were operated in Europe. After his death his sons, William J. and Sigmund, continued the business and built a factory in Philadelphia. By 1890 the third generation of Horstmanns was managing the business.

Horton, James Africanus Beal (1835–1883). A native of Sierra Leone who was educated in missionary schools, King's College, London, and Edinburgh University (1853–59). He became an army doctor in 1859, and he retired as head of the British Gold Coast medical services. He strove to introduce Western ideas, technology, and values to West Africa.

Hose. In the British army this referred to the close-fitting, knee-high leg coverings worn by Scottish regiments from the eighteenth century. They were originally red and white, but in the 1830s red and green hose (Rob Roy) appeared. Cloth hose, called *cath d'atch* in Scottish, were worn until about 1848, when stockings or knitted hose appeared.

Hospital Corps. In March 1887 the U.S. Congress authorized a corps to assist army doctors. Recruits were given four months' training in "litter bearing, ambulance work, tent pitching, field cooking, establishment of dressing stations, application of emergency bandages and tourniquets and the care and use of draft and saddle animals." Ten years later the corps contained 98 hospital stewards [q.v.], 99 acting stewards, and 513 corpsmen. [See Hospital Stewards.]

Hospital Stewards. Druggists and clerks in American army hospitals who were given this title in 1887. They ranked as noncommissioned officers with three classes and drew higher pay than first sergeants in combatant units. To become a steward, a man had to serve for a year as an acting steward and pass oral and written examinations.

Horseshoe Bend *Battle plan records the location of Andrew Jackson's troops against the Creeks.*

A. Branches' Reg't.
B 39th Regiment.
C Militia.
DD Russell's Spies
EE Coffee's command
F & G Friendly Indian's

H Women and children
JJ Creek Warriors
KK Breast Work.
L Cabins.
M Covered Ravine.

Hostage. A person held as a pledge that a certain agreement or set of terms will be fulfilled.

Hostiles. The formal designation given by the U.S. War Department to Indians living west of the Mississippi who were not on reservations and who attacked or were likely to attack settlers, miners, and soldiers.

Hotchkiss, Benjamin Berkeley (1826–1885). An American who spent his early years working with Samuel Colt [q.v.]. A rifled field gun he designed was used in the Mexican War [q.v.]. During the American Civil War he was in charge of the New York City Arsenal. In 1867 he sailed to France, where he manufactured a metallic cartridge he had designed. After the Franco-Prussian War [q.v.] of 1870–71 he designed a revolver cannon, which resembled a five-barreled Gatling gun [q.v.], and in 1875 he established a company to manufacture it in various calibers. In the spring of 1876 it was demonstrated at the Centennial Exposition in Philadelphia. His firm later developed some of the first quick-firing artillery pieces using metallic cartridges.

In the 1870s Hotchkiss developed a bolt-action rifle that the Winchester Company manufactured in the United States, producing in 1878 the Winchester-Hotchkiss rifle that was adopted by both the U.S. army and navy. In the early 1880s he developed a breech-loading 3-pounder, 47 mm caliber, with a sliding breechblock that fired fixed round ammunition.

The Hotchkiss machine gun [q.v.] was not invented by Hotchkiss but was developed after his death by another American, Lawrence V. Benét [q.v.].

Hotchkiss, Benjamin Berkeley *This revolver-type machine gun invented in 1871 by Hotchkiss resembles an oversized Gatling gun.*

Hotchkiss, Jedediah (1828–1899). An American educator, cartographer, and soldier who became famous as the mapmaker for General Thomas ("Stonewall") Jackson [q.v.] during the American Civil War.

Hotchkiss Machine Gun. A gas-operated machine gun developed by Lawrence V. Benét [q.v.], an American, combining certain of Hotchkiss's designs with those of Captain Baron Adolph von Odkolek (fl. 1890s) of the Austro-Hungarian army. A gas piston operated the bolt. It was adopted by the French army in 1897, and in 1899 the Japanese army purchased large quantities, which in the Russo-Japanese War of 1904–05 were pitted against the Russians' Maxims [q.v.].

Hôtel des Invalides. A hospital for old and disabled veterans in the Faubourg St. Germain, Paris, on the left bank of the Seine. Designed by Libéral Bruant (d.1697) and built on orders of Louis XIV (1638–1715) between 1671 and 1676, it could accommodate 5,000 men and is believed to be the first institution of its kind in the world [see Soldiers' Homes]. In 1840 Napoleon's remains were brought back to France from St. Helena, and on 3 April 1861, protected by six sarcophagi, the outer one of red porphyry, they were placed in a crypt in the Invalides chapel [see Napoleon's Remains].

The Invalides once housed hundreds of standards captured by Napoleon's armies, but when the Allies entered Paris in 1814, the governor of the hospital, General Jean Mathieu Philibert Sérurier ordered fifteen hundred to be burned. The building was also the headquarters of the military governor of Paris.

Hot Shot. Solid shot that had been heated in a fire for use in a muzzle-loading cannon. Used against wooden ships or fortifications, it was capable of setting its targets afire. Before it was inserted into the bore, the gun was cleaned, the powder charge was loaded, and a sabot and one or more wads of hay (the outer one damp) were thrust in. When the hot shot was inserted, the gun was fired immediately.

Hot Shot *The hot shot furnace at Fort Moultrie, American Civil War*

Hottentot Wars (1893–98). Hottentot was the popular name for the yellow-skinned Khoi people of southern Africa, but by the nineteenth century there had been such a mixture of Bantu, Bushman, and white blood that few pure-blooded Khois remained.

In the late nineteenth century there were numerous clashes between Germans and so-called Hottentots in German South-West Africa (today Namibia). On 12 April 1893 German Major Kurt von François [q.v.] with 200 troops attacked the Hottentot stronghold of Hendrik Witbooi [q.v.]

and slaughtered great numbers, including women and children. On 10 August 1897 Germans were repulsed by Hottentots in Damaraland. The following month the Germans ordered all tribes to register their guns. This was resisted by the Hottentots and other tribes. All were repressed with great brutality in a short campaign, the Germans suffering only 11 killed.

Hotze, Henry (1833–1887). A journalist who worked as a Confederate propagandist during the American Civil War. Born in Switzerland, he became a naturalized American in 1856. After serving briefly in the Mobile Cadets, a militia unit later absorbed into the 3rd Alabama, he was sent to England to muster support for the southern cause. His stories and articles appeared in numerous newspapers, first in Britain and then on the Continent. For a time he published a pro-Confederate newspaper. After the war he returned to Switzerland.

Hougoumont, Château of. A structure successfully held by the British and a feature of the Battle of Waterloo [q.v.]. The fighting that took place there is generally regarded as the fulcrum of the battle and the key to the Waterloo victory.

The "château" was, in fact, merely a gray stone farmhouse in an enclosure with several other buildings about 400 yards in front of the right center of Wellington's forces deployed along four miles of a low ridge called Mont St. Jean. The enclosure was originally garrisoned by a few companies of Scots and the Coldstream Guards under Lieutenant Colonel James Macdonell. Early in the battle they were reinforced by some Hanoverians and then by the remainder of the Scots and Coldstream Guards and in the evening by the 52nd Foot (later the Oxfordshire Light Infantry). With difficulty Macdonell and his men repelled repeated attacks. Although by midafternoon buildings in the enclosure were burning, including the roof of the farmhouse, Macdonell held fast.

One of the feats of the battle was the closing of the great heavy wooden gate of the enclosure. It had been broken open, and French infantry were inside, but Macdonell himself, with the help of some of his men, managed to close and bar it in the face of onrushing French attackers. It was, said the great duke, "a damn fine thing." Several years later the will of a clergyman left a substantial sum of money to be given to the bravest man in England. Wellington, when asked who that might be, named Macdonell, who generously shared his new wealth with two survivors of those who had helped him that bloody day at Hougoumont.

Hourd. A wooden gallery extending outside the battlements of a fortification.

Household Troops. Troops with a special mission to guard the sovereign. In the British service this was, and is, the Guards infantry and cavalry, known collectively as the Brigade of Guards.

House-to-House Fighting. Fighting in an urban setting against a determined foe.

Housewife. A small sewing kit sometimes carried by soldiers.

Houston, Samuel (1793–1863). An American soldier and political leader who was born in Rockbridge County, Virginia. In his teens he ran away from home to live with the Cherokee Indians, abandoning his widowed mother and eight siblings. He was adopted by a chief known as John Jolly and learned the language and customs of the tribe. In 1813 he joined the army and took part in the Creek War [q.v.]. He was seriously wounded in the Battle of Horseshoe Bend [q.v.] but so distinguished himself that he impressed General Andrew Jackson and in 1814 was given a commission.

On 3 February 1818 he was severely reprimanded by Secretary of War John C. Calhoun (1782–1850), who thought it inappropriate that a lieutenant in his army should appear before him dressed in a breechcloth, blanket, and turkey feathers. He resigned his commission, became a lawyer, was elected to Congress (1823–27) and then to governor of Tennessee (1827–29). In January 1829 he married Eliza Allen. Three months later, for unknown reasons, she left him and returned to her parents; a divorce was later secured. Houston then resigned his governorship and moved to Indian Territory, where he lived on the banks of the Arkansas River in the Cherokee Nation (Oklahoma), married an Indian woman, Tiana Rogers Gentry, and was given a new Cherokee name, Oo-Tse-Tee-Ardee-tah-Skee—in English: big drunk. Although true to his name, he frequently drank himself into insensibility, he championed Indian rights in Washington, where he at one time assaulted Congressman William Stanbery (1788–1873) of Ohio for accusing him of corruption.

In November 1835 he emigrated to Texas and established a practice of law in Nacogdoches. When Texans revolted against Mexico on 4 March 1836, he was appointed commander-in-chief of the forces of the provisional government. On 21 April 1836 he met and defeated a numerically superior Mexican force under Santa Anna [q.v.] in the Battle of San Jacinto [q.v.]. Although he was seriously wounded in the right ankle, he captured Santa Anna the following day. On 1 September he was elected the first president of Texas, winning 80 percent of the votes. He served until 1838 and again from 1841 to 1844.

Houston, Samuel *Lieutenant Sam Houston fighting the Creeks at Horseshoe Bend, 1814, apparently oblivious to an arrow embedded in his thigh.*

When Texas was admitted to the Union in 1845, Houston was elected to the U.S. Senate (1846–59). He married a woman half his age and by her sired eight children. Margaret Lea Houston persuaded her husband to give up liquor, to attend meetings of the local temperance society, and to join the Baptist Church. In 1859 he was elected governor of Texas but was removed from office in 1861 when he refused to take an oath of allegiance to the Confederacy. He retired to his farm in Huntsville, Texas.

Hova Rebellion (1896). When the Hova people of Madagascar revolted against French rule, Joseph Gallieni [q.v.], with Louis Hubert Gonzalve Lyautey (1854–1934) as his chief of staff, was sent from Tonkin to suppress the émeute. He succeeded, but 80 percent of his French troops died on the campaign, most from diseases.

Hovey, Alvin Peterson (1821–1891). An American soldier and lawyer who commanded volunteers in the Mexican War [q.v.], but saw no active service. In 1854 at the age of thirty-three he was named to the Indiana Supreme Court, the youngest justice ever appointed up to that time. At the beginning of the American Civil War he was commissioned in the Union army as a colonel of the 24th Indiana. He fought at Shiloh [q.v.], where his gallantry earned him a promotion to brigadier general, and at Vicksburg [q.v.]. In 1864 he was brevetted major general. He spent most of the war recruiting, and because he enlisted only unmarried men, his recruits were known as Hovey's Babies. After the war he served as a congressman and as governor of Indiana.

Howard, Oliver Otis (1830–1909). An American army officer who was graduated from Bowdoin College and then from West Point in the class of 1854. In 1857 he saw some action against the Seminole Indians [see Seminole Wars]. When the American Civil War began, he was a first lieutenant of ordnance. He resigned his commission and was elected colonel of the 3rd Maine of the Union army. In the First Battle of Bull Run [q.v.] he commanded a brigade of four regiments, and although his brigade was routed, he was promoted brigadier general as of 3 September 1861. Ambrose Bierce [q.v.] derided him as "a consummate master of the needless defeat."

In the Peninsular Campaign he lost his right arm in the Battle of Fair Oaks [q.v.]. At Antietam [q.v.] he succeeded to the command of a division. He was promoted major general on 29 September 1862, and on 31 March he took command of XI Corps after General Franz Sigel [q.v.] had resigned in a huff.

In spite of an order from General Joseph Hooker [q.v.] to guard his exposed flank at Chancellorsville, he failed to do so, and his corps was routed by Thomas ("Stonewall") Jackson. For his services in the Battle of Gettysburg he was given the Thanks of Congress. He later served under General W. T. Sherman [q.v.], who gave him command of the Army of the Tennessee [q.v.]. He was appointed a brigadier general in the regular army at the close of the war and, always a zealous abolitionist, was appointed the first commissioner of the Bureau of Refugees, Freedmen and Abandoned Lands, popularly called the Freedmen's Bureau [q.v.]. In 1869 he became the founder and first president of

Howard University in Washington, D.C. He was also the director of a bank for blacks, which suffered heavy financial losses.

In 1872 President U. S. Grant appointed him a special Indian commissioner and sent him to the Southwest. There he was successful in his negotiations with many of the chiefs, among them Cochise [q.v.], whom he persuaded to take his people onto a reservation. From July 1877 to 1880 he commanded the Department of the Columbia and took the field in the Nez Percé War [q.v.] of 1877. He was also in overall command of the operations against the Bannocks and Paiutes in 1878.

From June 1881 to 1 September 1882 Howard was superintendent of the U.S. Military Academy at West Point. He then served as commander of the Department of the Platte until 1886. In March of that year he was promoted major general and given command of the Department of the Pacific for two years, placing him in overall command of the final phases of the operations against Geronimo [q.v.]. From 1888 until his retirement on 8 November 1894 he was commander of the Division of the East. Belatedly he was awarded the Medal of Honor [q.v.] in 1893 for his bravery in the Battle of Fair Oaks [q.v.] in which he had lost his arm thirty-one years earlier.

Howard *General Oliver Howard tries to rally his troops, American Civil War.*

Howdah. A chair or framed seat carried by an elephant.

Howitzer. A short-barreled artillery piece capable of a high angle of fire—above forty-five degrees—at low velocity. Howitzers fire heavier shells at lower velocity than do guns. [See Artillery.]

Howitzer *Perspective view of a field howitzer*

Hsiao Ch'ao-Kuei (d.1851). One of the best of the Taiping [q.v.] generals who was appointed Western King. While attacking Changsha [q.v.] in Hunan Province (central China), he was killed by a sniper.

Hualapais / Walapais War (1867–68). An American Indian War in northwestern Arizona in which the government forces were led by General John Irvin Gregg (1826–1892), a veteran of both the Mexican and American Civil wars [qq.v.].

Huang Hsing (1873–1916). A Chinese soldier educated at Tokyo University and active in revolutionary plots against the Manchus. He was a member and a founder of the Kuomintang.

Huesca, Battle of (24 March 1837), First Carlist War. Some 20,000 Carlists under Don Carlos (1758–1865) drove 12,000 Cristinos and British and French Foreign legionnaires under General Irribarreu (d.1837) from the field at this commune, 208 miles northeast of Madrid. The French Foreign Legion [q.v.] distinguished itself, but the British Legion [q.v.] behaved unsteadily. The Cristinos lost more than 1,000 killed and wounded, 227 of whom were from the British Legion.

Huger, Benjamin (1805–1877). An American soldier who was graduated from West Point in 1825 and, as chief of ordnance under Winfield Scott [q.v.] during the Mexican War [q.v.], won brevets to major, lieutenant colonel, and colonel. At the beginning of the American Civil War he resigned his commission and was appointed a brigadier general in the Confederate army. On 7 October he was appointed major general. He fought at Fair Oaks and in the Seven Days' Battles [qq.v.], but he did not make a good field commander. He was relieved on 12 July 1862 and appointed inspector of artillery and ordnance, a post for which he was well qualified.

Hughes, Sam (1853–1921). A Canadian soldier and politician who in 1870 served with the volunteer militia that repelled the Fenian Raids [q.v.] from the United States. In 1873 he was gazetted to the 45th Regiment, but he later turned to journalism and was elected to the dominion parliament. During the Second Anglo-Boer War [q.v.] he served in South Africa. In 1911 he became minister of militia and defense. He was made a major general in 1915.

Hulche. A Mexican throwing stick with two finger holes, enabling an arrow to be thrown more swiftly and more accurately.

Hu Lin (Hun Linyi) (1812–1861). A Chinese soldier and official who in 1847, when in charge of Kweichow (Guizhou) Province in South China, between the tributaries of the Yangtze and Si rivers, raised a militia force to combat bandits and secret societies [see White Lotus Society]. When Taiping rebels threatened neighboring Hupeh (Hubei) and Hunan provinces, he led a small force to aid General Tsêng Kuo-fan [q.v.]. [See Taiping Rebellion.] In 1855 he captured the strategic city of Wuchang on the south bank of the Yangtze, 425 miles west of Shanghai. (In October 1911 the city was again a center of rebellion against imperial rule.) In 1861 he successfully repulsed Taiping attacks, enabling Tsêng's Hunan army to recapture Anking (Hwaining or Nganking or Anqing), the Taipings' supply center on the north bank of the Yangtze, 280 miles west-southwest of Shanghai, which the Taipings had captured in 1852.

Hulin, Pierre Augustin (1758–1841). A French soldier of the Revolutionary and Napoleonic periods. He took part in the storming of the Bastille on 14 July 1789, served in the Italian Campaign, and aided General André Masséna in the defense of Genoa [q.v.] in 1800. In 1804 at the Château de Vincennes he presided at the court-martial that tried for treason the Duc d'Enghien (Louis Antoine Henri de Bourbon-Condé, only son of the last Condé prince, 1772–1804). The duke was not allowed a defense and was convicted and shot, an act that, according to the wily Joseph Fouché (1759–1820), was "more than a crime—it was a mistake." As a general of brigade Hulin distinguished himself at Jena [q.v.] in 1806, and the following year he was promoted general of division. In 1808 he was made governor of Paris, and in 1812 he suppressed the conspiracy led by General Claude François de Malet [q.v.].

Hull, William (1753–1825). An American soldier who served as an officer in the Revolutionary War and was governor of Michigan Territory from 1805 to 1812. Having been appointed a brigadier general at the beginning of the War of 1812 [q.v.], he led an abortive attack from Detroit into Canada in July of that year but was outmaneuvered and defeated. After retreating to Detroit, he surrendered it on 16 August 1812 without a fight [see Detroit, Capture of]. He was carried a prisoner to Canada, where he was soon paroled. Upon his return to the United States he was immediately arrested, and in 1814 he was court-martialed, convicted of neglect of duty, and sentenced to be shot, the only general officer in American history so sentenced for a military failure. However, his life was spared in consideration of his record in the Revolutionary War.

Humaitá, Battles of (1866–67), War of the Triple Alliance. At this town in southern Paraguay on the Paraguay River above its confluence with the Paraná, 19 miles southwest of Pilar, the Paraguayans under Francisco López [q.v.] built strong fortifications.

    1. May 1866. The fortifications at Humaitá were first attacked, unsuccessfully, and with heavy losses, by Argentines under Bartolomé Mitre [q.v.].

    2. February 1868. When a flotilla of Brazilian gunboats tried to force the passage of the river, the entire flotilla was sunk by Paraguayan shore batteries.

    3. 1869. The Allies (Brazil, Argentina, and Uruguay) were

able to field overwhelming numbers. Asunción, the capital of Paraguay, was abandoned. Unsupported, the remaining garrison of 3,000 men at Humaitá could no longer escape or hold out. On 2 August 1869 they surrendered.

Hume, John Robert (1781?–1857). A Scottish doctor who was Wellington's personal physician through most of the Peninsular War [q.v.] and for a time after the war. In 1836 he became a fellow of the College of Physicians and was appointed a commissioner in lunacy.

Hump (1848?–1908). An American Indian, chief of the Miniconjou Sioux, who played a leading part in the Fetterman Massacre and the Battle of the Little Bighorn [qq.v.]. He and about 550 of his tribe fled with Sitting Bull to Canada, and he was one of the last of the party to surrender to the American authorities. He and his people took part in the ghost dance disturbances [q.v.], but on the advice of a trusted white friend, Captain Ezra Philetus Ewers (1837–1912), he retired with his band to the Pine Ridge agency and refused to join those demanding revenge for the slaying of Sitting Bull. On 29 December 1890, after the Battle of Wounded Knee [q.v.], he journeyed to Washington to seek (unsuccessfully) a relaxation of the government's restrictive policies toward Indians.

Humphreys, Andrew Atkinson (1810–1883). An American soldier who was graduated from West Point in 1831 and served in the Topographical Engineers. He saw action during the Second Seminole War [q.v.], but most of his service before the American Civil War was devoted to surveying and other engineering duties. At the beginning of the war in 1861 he became an aide to Union army General George B. McClellan [q.v.], and in April 1862 he was promoted brigadier general. He served in the Peninsular Campaign and the Seven Days' Battles [qq.v.]. In September 1862 he commanded a division in V Corps. He served with distinction at Antietam, Fredericksburg, Chancellorsville, and Gettysburg [qq.v.] and for a time acted as chief of staff for George Meade [q.v.]. In November 1865 Grant gave Humphreys command of II Corps, which he led until the surrender at Appomattox [q.v.].

He was made a brigadier general after the war and became chief of engineers, a post he held until his retirement in 1879. In the course of a military career that spanned fifty-two years, he took part in seventy engagements.

Hunan Braves. A counterinsurgent force raised during the Taiping Rebellion [q.v.] by Chinese General Tsêng Kuo-fan [q.v.]. It was later commanded by Hsi Pao-t'ien, who in 1864 defeated the breakaway army of Shih Ta-k'ai [q.v.].

Hundred Days. The time from Napoleon's return from exile on Elba until the collapse of the restored empire in the Battle of Waterloo [q.v.]. It was in fact 116 days.

On 1 March 1815 Napoleon, with 1,000 followers, disembarked on the shore of the Gulf of Juan, near Cannes, and marched on Paris by way of Grenoble and Lyons. His first challenge came at Grenoble, where troops under Jean Gabriel Marchand [q.v.] barred his way. It was here that Napoleon bared his chest and challenged any soldier to shoot his emperor. Cheering, the troops joined him, as others did subse-

quently in a march that became triumphal. Marshal Michel Ney [q.v.] had promised to bring Napoleon to Paris in a cage, but at Auxerre, 96 miles southeast of Paris, he too submitted, and Napoleon entered the Tuileries in triumph on 20 March. Louis XVIII (1755–1824) and the other Bourbons fled to Ghent.

There was consternation among the representatives of the Allies gathered for the Congress of Vienna, then in session. Napoleon was declared "the enemy and disturber of the peace of the world," and Austria, Prussia, Britain, and Russia pledged to raise armies and find funds to maintain them until he was permanently crushed.

By June Napoleon had raised an army of 200,000. He himself led 125,000 men north, where two Allied armies—124,000 Prussians under General Gebhard von Blücher [q.v.] and 105,710 British, German, Dutch, and Belgians with 204 guns under Wellington—had assembled in southern Belgium, waiting only for the arrival of the Russians and Austrians before launching a major offensive. Napoleon had hoped to divide the two armies and destroy them in detail [see the battles of Tolentino, Ligny, Quatre Bras, and Waterloo], but with his defeat at Waterloo on 18 June 1815, his days as ruler of France and commander of great armies ceased.

The term "Hundred Days" is sometimes used to refer to the period in which Louis XVIII (1755–1824) was absent from Paris, from Napoleon's arrival on 20 March 1815 until 28 June 1815.

Hungarian Army. The first autonomous Hungarian army with distinct uniforms was formed during the Hungarian Revolution [q.v.] in 1848–49. [See Austrian Army.]

Hungarian Revolution of 1848. After the revolt in Paris in February 1848 [see Paris Revolutions of 1848] similar rebellions broke out throughout Europe, particularly in the Austro-Hungarian Empire, where economic conditions had deteriorated. The revolt against the Hapsburg Empire began on 3 March 1848 in the provincial Hungarian Diet, meeting in Debreczen. Spurred by Lajos Kossuth (1802–1894), the editor of a Magyar journal, Pesti Hirlap, who delivered a fiery speech denouncing the Hapsburg government under Emperor Ferdinand I (1793–1875), the Diet proclaimed Hungarian independence from Austria. Kossuth was elected "responsible governor-president."

A rising of the Czechs in Prague followed, and on 13 March an initially peaceful demonstration in Vienna turned violent. At nine o'clock that evening Prince Klemens Wenzel Nepomuk Lothar von Metternich (1773–1859), Austrian chancellor and symbol of European stability and the suppression of liberal ideas, was forced to resign. He fled to England. Although on 15 March Emperor Ferdinand promised a liberal constitution, the reverberations of a revolt in Milan on 18–22 March [see Milan Uprising] forced him to abdicate in December. Hungarian rebels seized the strong fort at Comorn [q.v.], 48 miles from Budapest, but they were besieged there by the Austrians from October 1848 until they were forced to surrender in September 1849.

On 5 January 1849 the new emperor, Franz Josef (1830–1916), a nephew of Ferdinand, sent troops to occupy Budapest. The great Austro-Hungarian Empire seemed on the verge of dissolution. The Czech rebellion was quickly suppressed in June by General Prince Alfredzu Windisch-Graetz [q.v.], but in September workers rioted in Vienna. In the uproar Croatia, which, although not hostile to the Hapsburg Empire, entertained strong anti-Magyar sentiments, saw an opportunity to separate from Hungary. Austrian General Josip Jelačić od Bužima [q.v.], appointed ban of Croatia on 22 March, united the southern Slavs with the imperial army and on 11 September crossed the Drave River with 36,000 Croatian troops and advanced to Lake Balaton, 55 miles southwest of Budapest. On 6 October the government arsenal in Budapest was seized by mobs. Count Theodor Latour (1780–1848), the minister for war, was actually torn to pieces on the Budapest bridge by a mob, an action that so frightened the imperial family that it fled to Olmütz (Olomouc), a small town in Moravia. However, the revolution lacked adequate leaders and failed to organize a force to stand against regular imperial troops. Armies under Jelačić, who on 2 October had been made commander-in-chief of the Austrian forces, and Windisch-Graetz marched on Vienna, which they besieged. Their bombardment of the city killed some 4,000 people.

On 31 October the Austrians defeated the Hungarians in the Battle of Schwechat [q.v.] and occupied Vienna the following day. On 29 November the burghers of Vienna formally thanked Windisch-Graetz for freeing them from the "chains of terror-rule." On 5 January 1849 Budapest was recaptured, and numerous Hungarian leaders who failed to flee were executed or imprisoned. Nine generals were hanged, and four were shot.

Hungarian forces under Arthur von Görgey [q.v.], who commanded on the upper Danube, had at first been victorious, driving Windisch-Graetz out of Hungary. In Transylvania, Hungarian forces under Joseph Bem [q.v.], together with Kossuth, held off all Austrian armies, but Austrian Premier Felix zu Schwarzenberg (1800–1852) requested help from the Russians, and a Russian army of 100,000, fortified by the watchwords of Tsar Nicholas I (1796–1855) "Submit yourselves, ye peoples, for God is with us," marched into Hungary on 17 June 1848. Görgey was forced to withdraw into the mountains north of Budapest. General Henryk Dembiński [q.v.], who attempted a rescue, was defeated in the Battle of Kapolna [q.v.] on 26–27 February 1849 and had to retreat behind the Theiss (or Tisza) River. He was again defeated in the Battle of Temesovar (Timişoara [q.v.]), near the Timis River in what is now southwestern Rumania, on 9 August.

The Hungarian revolutionists were now much divided. On 13 August Görgey surrendered his entire army to the Russians, and the revolution was practically over. On 6 October 1849, 13 Hungarian generals were shot or hanged at Arad by General Haynau [q.v.], who succeeded Windisch-Graetz. In all there were 114 executions, and some 2,000 were imprisoned. Kossuth, Bem, and Dembiński fled to Turkey.

Hungary did not obtain a degree of autonomy until 1867.

Hunger. Keeping large armies in the field supplied with sufficient food was a problem never satisfactorily solved in the nineteenth century. Consequently, hunger was a persistent problem, for, as Wellington wrote from Spain (August, 1809), "A starving army is actually worse than none. The soldiers lose their discipline and their spirit. They plunder even in the presence of their officers."

Hunger could also be used as a weapon, as Russian General Aleksandr Suvorov [q.v.] well knew when he wrote: "The first art of a military leader is to deprive the enemy of subsistence." American General William Tecumseh Sherman [q.v.] also understood this principle [see March to the Sea].

Hung Chen-kan (d.1864). A Taiping wang, he was a cousin of Hung Hsiu-ch'üan [q.v.]. During the Taiping Rebellion [q.v.], which he joined in 1859, he was made Kan Wang (Shield King). He was well acquainted with foreigners and spoke English. He was executed after the fall of Nanking [see Nanking, Siege of].

Hung Hsiu-ch'üan (1813?–1864). A name adopted in 1837 by Hung Huo-hsiu, a former Chinese schoolteacher and student of Christianity who was the instigator of the Taiping Rebellion [q.v.], which raged in China from 1850 to 1864. It is now spelled Hong Xiuquan.

In 1837 he failed to pass the official examination that would have given him the *sheng-yüan* degree and admitted him to the privileged status of the Chinese gentry. Perhaps as a result of his failure, he became critically ill. When he recovered, he seemed to have undergone a personality change and to harbor enlarged liberal views. In 1843, after failing the examination once again, he became interested in Christianity through a pamphlet he had been given. In 1847 in Canton (Guangzhou) he became a convert of Issachar T. Roberts, an American Southern Baptist missionary. He soon began to experience religious visions in which he saw himself as the younger brother of Jesus Christ who had been given a mission to rid the world of demons. In Kwangsi Province in southeastern China he became a leader of a mystic society of God worshipers, which adopted many Protestant rites and beliefs. In about 1849, his following having multiplied, he began to have visions that told him he must create a heavenly kingdom of great peace (*T'ai-p'ing T'ien-kuo*). In 1850, calling himself T'ien-wang (Heavenly King) and his movement Taiping, or T'ai-p'ing (Great Peace), he declared an open rebellion against the Manchu dynasty. Making his headquarters at Nanking (Nanxiang or Nanjing), he raised armies that initially were everywhere successful. [See Taiping Rebellion.] As time passed, he exercised less and less authority over the enormous revolution he had created and demonstrated less and less interest in the world outside his palace filled with wives and concubines. Without his leadership his generals fell into struggles for power, and his once-victorious armies were defeated on all fronts. With the fall of Nanking, seeing disaster overtake him, he poisoned himself.

Hung Ta-ch'üan (1823–1852). A Chinese rebel who, when he failed to pass the civil service examination, joined the anti-Ch'ing (antigovernment) secret Heaven and Earth Society and soon became its leader. In 1851 he merged most of his followers with the Taiping Rebellion [q.v.]. He played a key role at the siege of Yungan (Yong'an) in 1852, but he was captured a few months later, taken to Peking (Beijing), and executed.

Hunt, Henry Jackson (1819–1889). An American soldier who was graduated from West Point in 1839, a son and grandson of soldiers, and an older brother of General Lewis Cass Hunt (1824–1886). During the Mexican War [q.v.] he fought as an artilleryman under General Winfield Scott [q.v.] and won brevets to captain and major. He was later a member of a three-man board that revised the system of tactics for light artillery; the board's report was adopted in 1860, and the revised system was used by both sides in the American Civil War.

As a Union officer Hunt played a prominent part in the First Battle of Bull Run [q.v.]. In the winter of 1861–62 he was appointed chief of artillery for the Washington defenses. He won renown for his handling of the artillery in the battles of Malvern Hill and Fredericksburg [qq.v.]. He also served with distinction in the Battle of Antietam [q.v.] and on 15 September 1862 was promoted brigadier general. On the final day of the Battle of Gettysburg, he deployed the 77 guns that destroyed Pickett's Charge [q.v.]. In June 1864 he was in charge of all siege operations at Petersburg [q.v.]. For work at this siege he was brevetted major general. After the war he reverted to his permanent rank of lieutenant of the 3rd Artillery. In 1869 he was promoted colonel, and he retired in that rank fourteen years later. He then became governor of the Soldiers' Home [q.v.] in Washington, D.C.

A bill to retire Hunt as a major general, giving him an increased pension, passed both houses of Congress but was vetoed by President Chester Arthur (1830–1886).

Hunter, Archibald (1856–1936). A British soldier who after passing out of Sandhurst was gazetted to the 4th Foot (King's Own) in June 1874. He was promoted captain in 1882 and saw his first active service in Upper Egypt in 1884. He was seconded to the British-controlled Egyptian army and served in Egypt and the Sudan for fifteen years.

In December 1885, in the Battle of Giniss [q.v.], in which a Dervish advance was checked, he was badly wounded and won the Distinguished Service Order [q.v.] [see Mahdiya]. He was again wounded in the Battle of Toski [q.v.] on 3 August 1889. For nearly two years (1892–94) he was governor of Suakim and the Red Sea littoral. He became a major general in November 1896 and took part in General Herbert Kitchener's expedition for the reconquest of the Sudan [q.v.] in 1896–98. In 1899 he was briefly in command of the division at Quetta in India, but later that year he was sent to be chief of staff to Sir George White, VC [q.v.] in South Africa. There, during the Second Anglo-Boer War [q.v.], he was besieged with White at Ladysmith [q.v.] Shortly after the relief of the town (1 March 1900) he was promoted lieutenant general. He was given command of the 10th Division and defeated the Boers in the Battle of Rooidam on 5 May 1900. On 30 July he effected the surrender of 4,314 Boers at Brandwater Basin [q.v.]. After the war he held commands in Britain, India, and Gibraltar. During the First World War he commanded at Aldershot.

When, at the age of seventy-four, he married for the first time, Lord Kitchener was his best man. Hunter was a well-liked soldier. It was said of him that he "never spoke ill of any man, was always seeking to do others kindnesses, and never forgot a friend."

Hunter, David (1802–1886). An American soldier who was graduated from West Point in 1822. He resigned in 1836 to speculate in real estate in Chicago, but six years later he returned to the army as a paymaster with the staff rank of major. In 1860 he was stationed in Fort Leavenworth, Kansas, where he began a correspondence with the newly elected president, Abraham Lincoln, who invited Hunter to accompany him on the inaugural train to Washington in February 1861. At the outbreak of the American Civil War Lincoln promoted him

brigadier general of volunteers, to rank from 17 May, and on 13 August he became a major general.

He fought at First Bull Run, where he was wounded, and at Secessionville [qq.v.], South Carolina. Placed in command of the Department of the South, he issued an order on 9 May 1862 abolishing slavery in his department, an order revoked by Lincoln ten days later. He organized a regiment of South Carolina slaves, an act that was upheld by Congress but denounced by Confederates, who declared him a "felon subject to be executed if captured." In September 1862 he presided over the court-martial that cashiered Fitz John Porter [q.v.], a sentence later revoked. In 1864 he led a raid up the Shenandoah Valley to Lexington, Virginia, where he fired the buildings of the Virginia Military Institute [q.v.]. After Lincoln was shot, he presided over the military commission that tried the alleged conspirators and sent 4 to the gallows. He retired as a colonel in 1866.

Hunza-Nagar Expedition (1891). Hunza and Nagar were two small independent states inhabited by people of the Dard race of the Yeshkun in the mountainous northwest corner of India's frontier bordering Kashmir. They became pawns in the Great Game [q.v.] when Russian conquests in Central Asia pushed the Russian frontier ever closer to India. On 1 December 1891 an Anglo-Indian force of about 1,000 Gurkhas, Kashmiri regulars, and some Indian pioneers, all under Colonel Henry Durand [q.v.], crossed the Hunza River by an improvised bridge and invaded Hunza. In its first battle Durand's force attacked a stone fort at Nilt. After blowing in the gate, the fort was captured for a loss of 6 killed; about 80 Hunza tribesmen were killed. Two young British officers were later awarded Victoria Crosses for their gallantry in this action. The next obstacle was a hill covered by stone sangers behind which lay some 4,000 tribesmen. These were routed by 100 Gurkhas and Kashmiris, and a third British officer was awarded the Victoria Cross for this feat. Hunza was taken, but the amir escaped with his wives and treasure. Hunza and Nagar were annexed.

Hurdles. A framework of woven willows or other wood used to hold earth in defensive works. They were similar to gabions [q.v.] except that the pickets were in a straight line, not a circle.

Hurlbut, Stephen Augustus (1815–1882). An American soldier and lawyer who served in the South Carolina militia during the Second Seminole War [q.v.]. At the beginning of the American Civil War he was appointed a brigadier general of volunteers in the Union Army. He commanded a division in the Battle of Shiloh and in September 1862 was promoted major general. He was mustered out in June 1865. He was one of the organizers of the Grand Army of the Republic [q.v.], and in 1866 he was elected its first national president.

Husarka. See Attila.

Hussars. Originally Hungarian and Croatian light cavalry, first formed by Mátyá Hollós Matthias Corvinus (1459–1490), king of Hungary, to fight the Turks. The name, style, and distinctive uniform were copied by light cavalrymen in Prussian, French, British, and other European armies. All Rumanian cavalry wore hussar uniforms. The first French hussars were authorized by Louis XIV in 1692. The first

British hussar regiment was established in 1805 when the 7th Light Dragoons was converted to hussars. The 1st and 2nd Hussars in the Prussian army, the famous Totenkopfe (Death's-Head) Hussars, wore black uniforms. Even their sabretaches were of black leather without ornamentation, and their insignia was a skull and crossed bones.

The hussar uniform, with its tight dolman [q.v.] and breeches, swinging pelisse, plumed shako or busby [qq.v.], light boots with jingling spurs, and a dangling sabretache [q.v.], created a dashing image that many tried to live up to. Lord Byron (1788–1824) wrote of "The young hussar,/ The whisker'd votary of waltz and war. . . ." It was said that the hussar was "in every land dearly beloved by the wife, hated by the husband." Professor Dennis H. Mahan [q.v.] spoke of a hussar as "the epitome of military impudence."

Hussars *A member of the 7th Queen's Own Hussars, 1833*

Hussein Auni Pasha (1819–1876). A Turkish soldier and statesman who served as a general against the rebels in Montenegro in 1859–60 and against the Greeks in Crete in 1867–69. In 1869–71 he was minister of war. In 1874 he was made grand vizier but the following year was demoted to governor of Smyrna. In 1876 he was one of the leaders in the plot that deposedSultan Abdul-Aziz (1830–1876) and placed Murad V (1840–1904) on the throne. Hussein himself was soon after assassinated.

Hyderabad, Battle of (24 March 1843), conquest of Sind, sometimes called the Battle of Dubba or Dabo. An Anglo-Indian force of 5,000, including 1,500 cavalry and 19 guns, under General Sir Charles Napier [q.v.] defeated 26,000 Baluchis with 11 guns under Amir Shir Muhammad, known as the Lion of Mirpur, near the village of Dubba, on the east bank of the Indus River, not far from the city of Hyderabad, then the capital of Sind (Pakistan). British losses were 39 killed and 231 wounded; Baluchi losses were probably overestimated at 5,000.

General Napier, for the first time in British history, named in his after-action report not only officers who had distinguished themselves but also other ranks, both Indian and British.

Hygiene, Military. The importance of cleanliness was little understood or appreciated in nineteenth-century armies, and bathing was frequently regarded as a dangerous exercise. In the British 7th Dragoons in 1823 orders were issued for "every dragoon to wash his private parts at least once a week," and in 1832 the 15th Hussars had standing orders to "wash their feet every Sunday morning before parade," and "in summer their bodies also." This regiment seems to have been particularly fastidious, for men were also required to don clean drawers every other Sunday.

Hythe School of Musketry. In the first half of the nineteenth century, when men fired in volleys, little attention was paid to marksmanship, but the increasing use of the rifle, with its longer range and greater accuracy changed this. In 1853 Colonel (later Major General) Charles Crauford Hay (1805?–1873) of the 19th Foot formed this school on the coast of Kent to train instructors in musketry.

Ibrahim Aga. See Keith, Thomas.

Ibrahim Bey (1735?–1817). An Egyptian soldier and ruler who was born in Slovakia and sold as a slave to a leading Egyptian Mameluke, who freed him and later made him governor of Cairo. He became co-ruler of Egypt with Murad Bey (1750–1801) and fought against Napoleon in the Battle of the Pyramids and at Heliopolis, but after the evacuation of the French he was unable to sustain his authority. He survived the massacre of the Mamelukes [q.v.] in 1811 but died in obscurity.

Ibrahim Muhammad Husain (1834–1874). The sultan of Darfur, an independent kingdom in the western Sudan. In 1874 the private army of Zubair Pasha Rahma Mansur [q.v.], invading from the south, and the regular forces of Ismail Pasha Aiyub [q.v.], the governor-general of the Sudan, invading from the east, defeated his forces in the Battle of Manawashiand. He was killed by Zubair Pasha.

Ibrahim Pasha al-Wali (1789–1848). An Egyptian soldier and viceroy who was the son or stepson of Mehemet Ali [q.v.], ruler of Egypt. In 1816 he succeeded his brother Tusun [q.v.] as commander of the Egyptian army in Arabia, and in a two-year campaign he destroyed the power of the Wahhabis [see Arabian Wars]. He westernized the Egyptian army, employing a French officer to teach European drill and tactics. In 1821 he organized the expedition under Muhammad Bey Khusraw al-Daramali [q.v.] that conquered northern and central Kordofan in the Sudan. In 1824 Mehemet Ali appointed him governor of the rebellious Morea (Peloponnesus peninsula). He landed at Modon (present-day Methone or Methoni) in southwest Peloponnesus with an army of 17,000 on 26 February 1825 and easily defeated rebel Greeks in open battle. He then laid siege to Missolonghi [q.v.], which, although costly, ended in its capitulation on 24 April 1826. When the Greeks resorted to guerrilla warfare,

*Ibrahim Pasha, son or stepson
of the viceroy of Egypt*

he ravaged the country and sent thousands to Egypt as slaves, measures that stirred the wrath of the Great Powers and led to their intervention. On 20 October 1827 the Turkish and Egyptian fleet was destroyed in the Battle of Navarino by British, French, and Russian fleets, and a French expeditionary force landed in Greece. Ibrahim was forced to evacuate the country on 1 October 1828.

In 1831, angered that he had not been adequately rewarded by Sultan Mahmud II (1785–1839) for suppressing the Greeks, he led an Egyptian army into Syria. On 27 May 1832 he took Acre [q.v.] after a short siege. On 8 July he defeated a Turkish army at Homs and on 29 July another Turkish army at Bailan [see Turko-Egyptian War]. He invaded Asia Minor and on 21 December routed the grand vizier at Iconium [q.v.]. He was then made governor of Syria.

In 1839 the Turks initiated a second war against Ibrahim Pasha, who won a great victory in the Battle of Nizib [q.v.] on 24 June 1839 but was compelled by Britain and Austria to abandon Syria in February 1841. In 1848 he became viceroy for his senile father until his own death.

Ibutho. Plural: Amabutho. A Zulu fighting unit smaller than an impi [q.v.]. Roughly of battalion or regimental strength.

Icheriden, Battle of (24 June 1857), Kabylia Campaign, French conquest of Algeria. Berber tribesmen gathered at this small village located on the edge of a steep ravine in the mountainous coastal region of the Kabylia in Algeria and built a series of defensive walls. The French attacked and captured the place with a battalion of the French Foreign Legion, some Zouaves, and a regiment of line infantry.

Ichido, Hyoe (1855–1931). A Japanese soldier who became a probationary lieutenant in 1876 and in the following year distinguished himself in the Satsuma Rebellion [q.v.], in which he was wounded. In the Sino-Japanese War he commanded the advanced guard for the Oshima brigade in the Battle of Songwa on 29 July 1894, and he was a brigade commander in the Battle of Pyongyang [q.v.] on 15 September. He later fought in the Russo-Japanese War of 1904–05.

Ichi-no-ashi. In Japan, the lockets for the sling on the scabbard of a tachi [q.v.].

Iconium, Battle of (21 December 1832), Turko-Egyptian Wars. Egyptians under Ibrahim Pasha [q.v.] completely defeated a Turkish army led by Reshid Pasha (1802–1858), the grand vizier, near this town (later Konieh, Konia, or Konyah) on the shores of Lake Trogitis about 100 miles inland from the Mediterranean Sea.

Igany, Battle of (8 March 1831), Polish Revolution of 1830–31. Near this village Poles under General Jan Skrzynecko [q.v.] defeated a Russian force under General Ivan Paskevich [q.v.].

Iglesias, Miguel (1822–1901). A Peruvian soldier and politician. After the War of the Pacific [q.v.] he was elected president of Peru in 1883 but was forced to resign by a revolution in 1886 led by Andrés Avelino Cáceres (1836?–1923).

Ignatiev, Nikolai (1832–1908). A Russian soldier and diplomat who served as military attaché in London in 1857–58. In 1858 he was sent on a secret mission to Central Asia to discover the extent of British influence in the area, the ability of the khanates to wage war, and the navigability of the Oxus (Amu Darya) River. In 1859 he was sent to Peking (Beijing), where he secured the Amur region by the Treaty of Aigun. For this he was made a general and given the Order of St. Vladimir. From 1864 to 1877 he was ambassador to Constantinople (Istanbul) and took a leading part in the diplomatic maneuvers preceding the outbreak of the Russo-Turkish War [q.v.] of 1877–78.

Ijichi, Kosuke (1855–1917). A Japanese soldier who served as an officer in the Sino-Japanese War [q.v.] of 1894–95, taking part in the fighting at Port Arthur (Lüshan), and in the Russo-Japanese War.

Ikhanda. Plural: Amakhanda. A Zulu military kraal, a kind of barracks.

Île-de-France. See Mauritius, British Capture of.

Ilges, Guido Joseph Julius (1835–1918). A Prussian-born American soldier who practiced law in Indiana before the American Civil War. During that war he rose to the rank of captain in the Union army, earning brevets to lieutenant colonel for gallantry at the Wilderness and at Spotsylvania [qq.v.]. He remained in the army after the war and served in the Southwest.

In 1875 Ilges became a major. He took part in the Nez Percé War [q.v.], fighting a pitched battle at Cow Creek Canyon, Montana, on 25 September 1877. In 1881 he fought the Sioux and captured Gall [q.v.], the great Sioux chief. He was promoted lieutenant colonel of the 18th Infantry, but he was court-martialed and dismissed from the service on 31 October 1883 for financial irregularities, although he was not, it seems, accused of dishonesty.

In 1867 he had rescued a boy named Ernest Amelung (1860–post 1912), who had been captured by the Apaches, and had taken him as his ward and sent him to live with his aunt in San Francisco until he was able to take him to an uncle he had found living near Frankfurt, Germany. About 1882, when Amelung was twenty-two, he returned to the United States, where he eventually secured work as an interpreter in the War Department, and began a long search for Ilges, whom he finally found in 1912 in Cincinnati, Ohio. For eighteen years Ilges had worked as a journalist for German-language newspapers in Cincinnati and then as a weight master at a hay market. In 1917 he applied for a pen-

sion, testifying that he was crippled from injuries and nearly blind. Finally granted one of thirty dollars per month, he died a few days before the first check arrived.

Ili, Conquest of (1871). In 1871 the Muslim country of Ili, lying adjacent to and northeast of present-day Sinkiang, revolted against Chinese rule and declared itself independent. A Russian army under General Konstantin Kaufmann [q.v.] invaded the country, defeated a force twice its size, and on 24 June entered the capital of Kuldja or Kulja (Chinese: Ining, formerly Ningyuan), on the Ili River 320 miles west of Urumchi.

Chinese demands for the return of this territory were rejected at the time, but ten years later Russia restored the greater part of it.

Images d'Épinal. In the eighteenth century craftsmen in the commune of Épinal on the Moselle River in northeastern France were licensed to make what are today called posters. They were at first primitive woodcuts and later lithographs depicting religious themes or popular myths and were sold mostly to colporteurs and small merchants in rural areas. Piety proved profitable. In 1836 the firm of Pellerin employed forty engravers and produced hundreds of thousands of posters each year. By this time the number of themes had expanded, and many of the *images* depicted patriotic or martial scenes. One popular print celebrated the apotheosis of Napoleon. Each war produced new military themes and new heroes. Pellerin continued well into the twentieth century. Among its last productions was a series following the rise of Charles de Gaulle (1890–1970) from military school to the presidency.

Imboden, John Daniel (1823–1895). An American officer who was educated at Washington College (now Washington and Lee University) and during the American Civil War rose to the rank of brigadier general in the Confederate army. He fought at First Bull Run [q.v.], and he served under General Thomas Jackson [q.v.] in his Valley Campaign [q.v.]. In April and May 1863 he was one of the leaders of a successful raid into present-day West Virginia [see Jones' and Imboden's Raid]. He commanded a cavalry brigade that covered Lee's advance into Pennsylvania and his retreat from Gettysburg. In the fall of 1864 Imboden was stricken with typhoid fever. When he recovered, he was posted to prison duty in South Carolina. After the war he devoted himself to the development of Virginia's mineral resources and to his wives, of whom he had five.

Immortals. The nineteenth-century name given to cadets at the bottom of their class at the U.S. Military Academy at West Point, New York.

Immunes. An American brigade of 10,000 men believed to be immune to tropical diseases, particularly malaria, formed during the Spanish-American War [q.v.] because of the high casualty rate from diseases suffered by troops in Cuba. It consisted of ten regiments, six of southern whites and four of black soldiers.

Impedimenta. The baggage and gear carried by an army that impeded its march or rapidity of movement. Excess baggage was a problem often complained of by commanders. Union General William Tecumseh Sherman said that "an army is efficient for action and motion in inverse ratio of its *impedimenta*."

Imperial Guard, French. See Garde Impériale.

Imperial Guard, Japanese. A military organization of samurai [q.v.] created in 1871 and originally drawn from the three leading clans. Its first commander was Saigo Takamori [q.v.], one of the principal heroes of the Boshin Civil War [q.v.]. This was the beginning of the first national Japanese army.

Imperial Japanese Army.   See Japanese Army.

Imperial Light Horse. A South African military unit raised on 21 September 1899 to fight on the British side in the Second Anglo-Boer War. It was equipped at the expense of Alfred Beit (1853–1906), the diamond merchant and capitalist who, with Cecil Rhodes (1853–1902), was cofounder of Southern Rhodesia (Zimbabwe).

Imperial Military Railways. In South Africa during the Second Anglo-Boer War [q.v.] this was the name given to the captured railway system of the Boer republics: the Netherlands South African Railway Company and the Orange Free State Railways. They were placed under the control of Edouard Percy Girouard [q.v.] and later absorbed into the Central South African Railways.

Imperial Rescript to Soldiers and Sailors. The Japanese code of conduct that placed the military forces under the emperor and supposedly freed them of the influence of political parties.

Impi. A Zulu army or regiment of indeterminate size. Its warriors could not marry until they reached a certain age or until they had "washed their spears" in the blood of an enemy.

Incident. A brief clash or other temporary military disturbance not resulting in protracted hostilities. [See Affair.]

Incursion. 1. A raid.
  2. An invasion without conquest.
  3. A hostile intrusion into a territory.

Indemnification. French and British armies usually allotted payments for personal losses as a result of military service as well as payments for unusual expenses. In the American army the loss of an officer's charger in battle could be indemnified by a payment of not more than two hundred dollars. [See Allowances; Gratuities.]

Indent, to. In British usage, to requisition stores or equipment.

Independent Line of Sight. A system for aiming cannon in which the elevation of the sights on the gun were independent of the elevation of the gun's barrels, enabling changes in elevation to be made without moving the azimuth sight off the target or aiming stakes. It was developed by the French in 1897 for their 75 mm field guns [see French 75].

Indian Affairs, Bureau of. A bureau in the American War Department organized in 1824 to handle relations with American Indians. In 1849 it was transferred to the newly created Department of the Interior.

Indian Army. A regular armed land force that was first organized by the British in Madras in 1748. Before the Indian Mutiny [q.v.] of 1857–58 the Indian army was a convenient abstraction, for it was actually three armies. The name was used to encompass the armies of the three presidencies—Bengal, Bombay, and Madras—into which British India was divided. Each had its own governor, bureaucracy, and army with its own commander-in-chief. Each developed its own style, traditions and, in particular, recruiting methods [see Martial Races]. Each contained all three arms until after the mutiny, when the crown took over the armies from the Honourable East India Company. At that time all Indian artillery units, except for a few mountain batteries in the Punjab Frontier Force [q.v.], were disbanded, and the employment of artillery was placed completely in the hands of British gunners. The separate armies were abolished in 1895.

No substantive combat unit larger than a regiment ever existed in the nineteenth-century Indian armies, and most were composed of Indian or Gurkha troops, all of whom were without exception volunteers. All officers were British. The Bengal army contained a few regiments of European troops, which with some difficulty were transferred to the British army by an act of Parliament on 1 November 1858 [see White Mutiny]. After the Nepalese War [q.v.], Gurkhas [q.v.] from Nepal served in units composed only of Nepalese hillmen, who were dressed and trained as rifle regiments, uniquely uniformed and separately numbered.

British officers in the Indian army had to learn at least one Indian language, usually Hindustani, and those in Gurkha regiments learned Gurkhali as well. They were commissioned and promoted in the army of their own presidency (Madras, Bengal, or Bombay) until 1891, when the fiction was created that all officers belonged to an Indian Staff Corps [q.v.] and were carried on a single promotion roll. Seniority was then within the entire Indian army. Until the rule was abolished soon after the Indian Mutiny, officers in the Indian army ranked below all officers of equal rank in the British army. This was a source of much discontent among officers in the Indian army.

Indian privates in the infantry were known as sepoys and in the cavalry as sowars. Only four grades of noncommissioned officers existed. In the infantry these were lance naik, the equivalent of lance corporal in the British service; naik, the equivalent of corporal; havildar, the equivalent of sergeant; and havildar major, the rough equivalent of an American first sergeant or a British sergeant major. In the cavalry the ranks were unpaid lance, lance daffadar, daffadar, and daffadar major.

A peculiarity of the Indian army was a special level of authority known as native officers until the crown assumed control after the Mutiny, a viceroy was appointed, and they became known as viceroy's commissioned officers. All received salutes and were entitled to carry swords. There were three grades, and their insignia was the same as that of second or sublieutenant, captain, and major in the British army. The lowest, in both infantry and cavalry, was jemadar. The highest in the infantry was subedar and subedar major, and in the cavalry, rissaldar and rissaldar major. All ranked below the most junior British officer. No Indian held a sovereign's commission until 1918 except for Indian doctors, some of whom were commissioned in 1912.

Until 1884 the Indian army had no transport service. When a unit was ordered to move, it had to contract locally for animals and carts.

Before the mutiny some cavalry units were organized on the irregular or silladar system [q.v.]. After the mutiny all were so organized.

Until the Penjah Incident [q.v.] in 1885 frightened the British into believing the Russians were coming, it was assumed that the Indian army would be employed only to fight poorly armed tribesmen and to suppress internal disorders. Its weapons were therefore usually hand-me-downs from the British army, adequate for fighting most Asian armies, but unsuitable for a European war.

British army units posted to India were not part of the Indian army; these composed what was known as the British army in India.

Indian Army *Types of the 36th Sikhs (left to right): jemadar, havildar, sepoy in poshteen, bugler*

Indian File. Single file; people in a row following each other.

Indian Mutiny (1857–1858). On 10 May 1857 three regiments of Bengal Native Infantry stationed at the cantonments at Meerut (Mirath) mutinied, shot and killed their officers, released military prisoners, and marched on Delhi, 40 miles to the southwest.

The causes of the mutiny, which was contained within the Bengal presidency, were complex. India had seen an increase in the number of Christian missionaries, and this gave rise to heightened fears (largely justified) among both Hindus and Muslims that the British would like to see India converted to a Christian country. In the Bengal army, which had seen a growing distance between British officers and their men, the spark that fanned religious fears into the flame of mutiny was the introduction of new cartridges for the Minié rifle [q.v.]. These were covered by greased paper, which had to be torn open with the teeth, and word spread rapidly that the grease used was pig fat (abhorrent to Muslims) and cow fat (abhorrent to Hindus). As subsequent investigation proved, some cartridges had indeed been so greased. British arrogance and

insensitivity had never been so blatant or caused such a holocaust. Throughout the Bengal presidency mutinies flared in cantonment after cantonment, and a few discontented princes in central India and Oudh (Awadh) who had hopes of turning the mutiny into a full-scale rebellion aided the mutineers.

Mutineers from Meerut, joined by the mutinous garrison at Delhi, called upon the last mogul ruler, living in the city on a British dole, to lead them. Soon every European who could be found in Delhi was murdered. At the arsenal a small band of Britons held out as long as possible, then blew up the ammunition magazine and themselves.

The mutiny outraged Britons everywhere, although perhaps none so much as Colonel John Nicholson [q.v.], who, in a letter to Herbert Edwardes [q.v.], wrote: "Let us propose a Bill for the flaying alive, impalement or burning of the murderers of women and children at Delhi. The idea of simply hanging the perpetrators of such atrocities is maddening."

Delhi was the magnet for mutineers, who arrived daily in increasing numbers. They sought a leader, but none of sufficient stature appeared. As Karl Marx rightly wrote, "A motley crew of mutineering soldiers who have murdered their officers, torn asunder the ties of discipline, and not succeeded in discovering a man in whom to bestow supreme command are certainly the body least likely to organize a serious and protracted insurrection" (*The First Indian War of Independence*, 1859).

The British were slow off the mark, but on 17 May a column under General George Anson (1797–1857), the commander-in-chief Bengal, who had been recovering from an illness at Simla, set forth from Umballa (Ambala), 120 miles north-northwest of Delhi. Ten days later, when the column reached Karnal, still 75 miles from Delhi, Anson died of cholera. His place was taken by General Archdale Wilson (1803–1874), who fought his way to Delhi and on 8 June established his army on the Bandli-ki-Serai ridge, then on the edge of the city [see Delhi, Siege of].

Meanwhile the British found themselves besieged in other Bengali cities, notably at Cawnpore and Lucknow [qq.v.]. General Henry Havelock [q.v.] marched 2,500 men 126 miles in nine days in the hottest season of the year, defeating the forces of Nana Sahib [q.v.] at Fatehpur on 12 July and at Aong [qq.v.] on 15 July. The following day he entered Cawnpore, where the hacked and mutilated bodies of European men, women, and children lay. Here he was forced to wait for reinforcements. When these arrived with Sir James Outram and Henry Havelock [qq.v.] at their head, the combined force fought its way to Lucknow [q.v.], where a small British garrison and more than 100 women and children were besieged in the Residency [q.v.]. Not strong enough to bring them away to safety, Havelock's force joined the besieged, increasing their firepower, but adding to the food shortage.

The Residency was not completely relieved until a column under Sir Colin Campbell [q.v.] pushed through on 16 November and extricated the besieged. With the help of 10,000 troops supplied by the kingdom of Nepal, Campbell captured the city itself on 16 March.

Meanwhile Wilson had stormed and taken Delhi in September. Soon most of the major cities of Bengal were again in British hands. "Movable columns" had been making their way through the presidency, disarming regiments suspected of disloyalty and fighting with mutineers who were in open re-

Indian Mutiny *Mutineers about to be blown from cannon at Peshawar*

bellion. The threat of losing India, which had been real enough, disappeared, and mopping-up operations began.

Of the seventy-four regiments of infantry in the Bengal army, forty-five mutinied and twenty-four others were disbanded. In the Bombay presidency only two regiments were affected, and none in the Madras presidency.

Sir Hugh Rose [q.v.] with two brigades from the Bombay army launched a whirlwind campaign that on 3 February 1858 relieved the British besieged in an old Maratha fort at Saugor, 180 miles north of Nagpur. On 21 March he invested

Indian Mutiny *British infantry fights hand to hand in Delhi, 1857.*

the stronghold of the rani of Jhansi [q.v.] and took it by assault on 3 April, then went on to defeat the forces of the rebel Tantia Topi [q.v.]. In the Battle of Gwalior on 19 June 1858 he killed the rani of Jhansi.

Smaller operations took place throughout northern Bengal for many months. Mutineers were hanged, shot from the mouths of cannon, and bayoneted. In August Parliament passed the India Act, which transferred all the authority of the Honourable East India Company to the crown. A new cabinet post was created, secretary of state for India, and the governor-general was replaced by a viceroy. The largest army ever controlled by a private company disappeared from history.

There were 182 awards of the Victoria Cross [q.v.] for gallant actions during the mutiny; 43 were for actions around Delhi.

Indian Reservations. American troops were frequently employed to force Indians to move to reservations set aside for them. The first of these was created by a policy inaugurated in 1786, and ultimately more than 200 were established in forty states. In 1887 Indians held some 137 million acres of land; by 1960 this had shrunk to about 54 million acres.

Indian Soldiers, American. American Indians fought as allies or auxiliaries or individually as scouts in the War of 1812 and in the Seminole Wars [qq.v.], and volunteer units fought on both sides in the American Civil War. Stand Watie [q.v.], a three-quarter–blood Cherokee, became a Confederate general [see Regiment of Mounted Rifles, John Drew's; Watie Regiment; Ross, John]. In 1862 the Union army raised three regiments of home guards from among the Creeks, Seminoles, Washitas, and Cherokees. These wore no special insignia or uniforms. Both the Confederate and the Union army attempted with mixed results to raise regular regiments of Indians.

Indian soldiers were not regularized until about 1870, when the Indian Scouts were formed. They were then given uniforms and organized into regular companies. Their arm of service badge displayed crossed arrows with the initials *U.S.S.* above. In 1891 an effort was made to include Indians in regular army units. General Order 28, issued on 9 March 1891, authorized a company of 55 Indians in each of twenty-seven infantry and cavalry regiments. (The two black infantry regiments and the two black cavalry regiments were excluded.) Although 1,485 men were authorized, only 780 were ever recruited, and only one company—Troop L, 7th Cavalry—served out a full enlistment to 1897 [see: I-See-O].

Indian Staff Corps. In 1891 the armies of the three presidencies in India—Madras, Bombay, and Bengal—were brought under a central command for the first time, and until 1903, when the army was named the Indian Army, all British officers, including regimental officers exercising command, were considered members of the Indian Staff Corps. Opportunities for promotion were thus equalized since seniority was no longer determined in the individual presidencies but army-wide. [See Indian Army.]

Indian Wars, American. Between the Battle of Tippecanoe [q.v.] in Indiana on 7 November 1811 and a skirmish in the mountains near Lang's ranch in Arizona on 16 May 1896 there were few years in which American soldiers were not fighting Indians, and from 1847 to 1893 not a year passed without clashes, but the common perception of the Indian Wars encompasses those campaigns, battles, and skirmishes that took place in the American West, often called the frontier, between 1865 and 1896, when 941 engagements were fought between regulars and Indians. Virtually every major engagement in the years following the American Civil War involved trying to force reluctant Indians onto newly created reservations or attempting to make them return to reservations from which they had fled. By the time the Indian Wars ended in the 1890s there had been twenty-four military operations officially classified as wars, campaigns, or expeditions and nearly two-thousand armed conflicts.

The U.S. army, which in 1865 numbered more than a million men, was reduced to 37,313 by 1869 and to 26,859 by 1885, and these were scattered in dozens of small posts over a vast area. It was a portion of this small army that over the last years of the century engaged an estimated 100,000 hostile Indians in more than a thousand named engagements in an area of about a million square miles. Major General George Crook [q.v.] characterized these wars as being for the American army "the most dangerous, the most thankless, and the most trying."

Most of the major campaigns against the Indians were planned and ordered executed by Philip H. Sheridan [q.v.], who was in charge of the enormous Division of the Missouri from 1869 to 1883 and thereafter of the entire American army until his death in 1888. Among the most notable of the campaigns were those against the Sioux, Cheyennes, Apaches, Navajo's, Nez Percés, and Modocs. Most engagements were unreported in the press, but some could not be ignored and shook even eastern Americans; among these were the Fetterman Massacre near Fort Phil Kearny in northern Wyoming on 21 December 1866 and the Wagon Box Fight [qq.v.] on 2 August 1867. In 1870 and 1871 army units were engaged in serious fighting with the Apaches in New Mexico and Arizona. The Modoc War [q.v.] of 1872–73 and the resultant murder of Major General E. R. S. Canby [q.v.] left a bitter taste in the mouth of many white Americans. In 1876–77 the Great Sioux War [q.v.] raged and occasioned such notable engagements as the Battle of Slim Buttes, the Battle of Rosebud Creek, Custer's last stand in the Battle of the Little Bighorn, and the Battle of Wolf Mountain [qq.v.]. In 1877 the Nez Percé War was fought, and the following year the Bannock-Paiute War [qq.v.]. In 1879 soldiers fought the Northern Cheyennes, the Sheep-eaters, Paiutes, and Bannocks. In 1885–86 Generals George Crook and Nelson A. Miles [qq.v.] waged war against Geronimo [q.v.] and his Apaches. The early 1890s witnessed the Ghost Dance Disturbances [q.v.], the killing of Sitting Bull [q.v.], and the last major battle of the Indian Wars, the Battle of Wounded Knee [q.v.].

Indian culture emphasized individual deeds of daring in warfare, and Indian chiefs often lacked the authority to control their glory-hungry warriors or to carry out a battle plan. The Plains Indians have been called the finest light cavalry in the world, but they were not cavalry. They were splendid horsemen and often brave, but they lacked discipline, unit cohesion, and organization, and it was these qualities in their enemies that ultimately defeated them. They were often accused of treachery, but as one officer wryly remarked, "Strategy, when practiced by Indians, is called treachery."

William Tecumseh Sherman [q.v.], who understood the position of the Indian, spoke of him as being "hemmed in" and said, "[S]o the poor devil naturally wriggles against his doom." Few whites were so forbearing. In July 1852 a Methodist minister in San Francisco informed Colonel (later General) Ethan Allen Hitchcock [q.v.] that God intended the extermination of the Indians and that he thought it would be a "good thing to introduce the smallpox among them."

The Indian warriors of the plains were indeed savage. They neither gave nor expected to receive quarter. They tortured and mutilated living and dead captives in gruesome ways and took no adult male prisoners.

The number of soldiers killed fighting Indians and the number of Indians killed is unknown, as is the number of women and children of all races killed in the course of the fighting. There were 423 Medals of Honor [q.v.] and 59 Certificates of Merit [q.v.] awarded.

Although fighting Indians was the main occupation of the American army for most of the nineteenth century, not a single course, not a single class, at the U.S. Military Academy was devoted to Indian culture, habits, or language or to the skills needed to fight hostile Indians. Many believed that western volunteers made better Indian fighters than army regulars. One such was Congressman Thomas Hart Benton (1782–1858), who declared in 1855 that the Indian would never be conquered by "school-house officers and pot-house soldiers."

In the end it was not the white soldiers who defeated the Indians, but the vast numbers of whites with their superior technology and resources, which the Indian was incapable of fending off or destroying.

Indian Wars *Custer's party finds corpses of the men of the 7th U.S. Cavalry at Beaver Creek, 1867.*

Indirect Artillery Fire. Guns shooting at targets unseen by the gunners, who laid on an aiming point and then shifted their fire by a calculated angle to bring the shells onto the target. This method could not be used until recoil systems were developed at the end of the century that obviated the need to relay guns completely after each firing. [See Independent Line of Sight; French 75.]

Indochina, French Invasion and Occupation of (1858–93). In retaliation for the persecution of Catholic missionaries, the French bombarded Da Nang in 1858 and captured Tourane, the port of Hué. In February 1861 they seized Saigon, and by

Indochina *Death of Commander Rivière of the French marines, 19 May 1883*

a treaty of 5 June 1862 the three eastern provinces of Cochin China were ceded to France by the Annamese. In 1867 the French seized the remainder of Cochin China, the southernmost province of Annam [see Tonkin Campaign].

France gradually expanded its holdings in Indochina. Although hostilities were suspended for a time during the Franco-Prussian War [q.v.], in 1873 Marie Joseph François Garnier (1839–1873), a French explorer and adventurer, attacked and captured Hanoi. He then sent for reinforcements and successfully attacked five other fortresses in the Red River delta. This provoked the Tonkinese to ask help of the Chinese Black Flags [q.v.], who attacked several French-held villages near Hanoi. Garnier was killed fighting them. The French then withdrew from a large area, a move that resulted in the massacre of the Christian converts there.

In 1882 Henri Laurent Rivière (1827–1883), a French naval officer, was sent with a small force to open up a route between Cochin China and Yünan. His campaign followed almost exactly that of Garnier, and he was killed on 19 May. In 1883 a French naval force captured Hué, and in August of that year the king of Annam recognized the French protectorate. The French then advanced on Sontay [q.v.], which was captured on 16 December.

In 1884 the French took control of the lower delta but found themselves fighting Chinese regulars. In May the French consul at Tientsin arranged for the Chinese to be withdrawn from northern Tonkin, and in a treaty signed at Hué the Chinese recognized the French protectorate. A misunderstanding over the date of the Chinese withdrawal led the French to dispatch an expedition to occupy Langson, 85 miles

northeast of Hanoi. It collided with the Chinese regulars and was routed. However, another French expedition defeated the Chinese and captured Chu, 10 miles southeast of Langkep.

In January 1885 large French reinforcements arrived, and an advance was made upon Langson by François de Négrier. On 13 April it was taken [see Langson, Battle of], but in the end the French were forced to retreat. The news of this disaster caused the fall of the government in Paris. Peace was eventually restored, but France persisted in its aggression and in 1893 compelled Siam (Thailand) to renounce its claims to the left bank of the Mekong River.

Indonesian War. See Java War.

Induna. A Zulu general.

Indus, Army of the. The name given the Anglo-Indian army of 21,000 under Sir John (later first Lord) Keane (1781–1844) that invaded Afghanistan in 1838 and overthrew Dost Muhammad [q.v.]. [See Afghan War, First.]

Inert Ammunition. Shells, rockets, cartridges, etc. in which the explosive agent has been removed.

Infanterie de Marine. Infantry under the command of the French navy. They were transferred to the French army in 1900 and became the Armée Coloniale [q.v.].

Infanterie Légère. Penal battalions of light infantry in the French Armée d'Afrique popularly called "Bat d'Af," short for Bataillon d'Afrique (African Battalion). Their members were sardonically called *les joyeux* (the joyous). Units of the Bat d'Af were sometimes confused with the *compagnies disciplinaires* or the *section d'exclus* [qq.v.] or with the Foreign Legion [q.v.], whose uniforms were similar, except for their insignia: that of the Legion, a seven-plumed grenade; that of the *infanterie légère* the hunting horn, always the symbol of light infantry.

The first battalions were formed from three categories: soldiers who had served their time in disciplinary companies but still had time to serve before their enlistments were complete; men who had served prison sentences of not more than three months; and, curiously, volunteers who were attracted by the romance of serving in Africa and by the tough image of the Bat d'Af, which had a reputation for brutality in combat and turbulence in barracks. Only volunteers who had committed some misdemeanor were accepted.

The discipline was ferocious, the living conditions were Spartan, the long marches exhausting, and the food was execrable, but there was always a wine ration. Although much of

Indochina *French forces in forts and gunboats battle Chinese infantry near Hanoi, 1884.*

the time of *les joyeux* was spent building roads and forts in Algerian deserts and mountains, they earned a reputation for their endurance and bravery in the Algerian campaigns and in the Franco-Prussian War [q.v.].

Infantry. 1. Men armed, equipped and trained to fight on foot.

2. Units of such soldiers.

Infantry was often classified as light, heavy, or mounted, or as grenadiers, voltigeurs, sharpshooters, fusiliers [qq.v.]. Units were sometimes designated as rifle regiments at the time when most regiments were armed with muskets, a distinction that remained in the British army long after all were armed with rifles.

Colonel Henry Lee Scott (d. 1886) in his *Military Dictionary* (1881) rhapsodized about the infantry, stating that "it is the principal force and lever of power in time of war; it can act alone; other arms move to second it; thus good infantry is the true strength of nations; every one in an army feels its importance; its posts guard the army; its duties are, of all others, the most constant, the most simple, the most easily regulated; and the most certain and most important."

British Field Marshal Sir Archibald Wavell (1883–1950)

Infantry *Four studies of infantrymen of the Army of the Potomac, by Winslow Homer*

wrote ("The Training of the Army for War," February 1933): "One well-known Brigadier always phrases his requirements of the ideal infantryman as 'athlete, stalker, marksman.' I always feel inclined to put it on a lower plane and say that the qualities of a successful poacher, cat burglar, and gunman would content me."

Infernal Machine. 1. Any explosive device.

2. An explosive device for the wrongful destruction of life or property.

Infiltration. The movement of troops through gaps in their enemy's lines.

Ingalls, James Monroe (1837–1927). An American soldier who began his career as an enlisted man in the 16th Infantry in 1864 and was commissioned in 1865. He became a ballistics authority and in 1882 founded the Department of Ballistics at the U.S. Army Artillery School at Fort Monroe, Virginia. He retired in 1901 as a lieutenant colonel.

Ingaví / Yngaví, Battle of (20 November 1841), Peru-Bolivia War. In August 1841 General Agustín Gamarra [q.v.], president of Peru, with an army of 5,200 invaded Bolivia and attempted to annex the province of La Paz, but in this battle at Ingaví Mountain, south of La Paz, 3,800 Bolivians under General José Ballivián [q.v.] defeated the invaders. Gamarra was killed, and Peru was plunged into civil war.

Inglis, John Eardley Wilmot (1814–1862). A British soldier who was born in Nova Scotia, the son of a bishop. In 1833 he was commissioned in the 32nd Foot, in which all his regimental experience was passed. He served in Canada and in the Punjab. He fought in the Second Sikh War [q.v.] and led the attack on Multan [see Multan, Siege of]. In 1857, when the Indian Mutiny [q.v.] erupted, he commanded his regiment at Lucknow and was besieged in the Residency there. When Sir Henry Lawrence [q.v.] was mortally wounded on 1 June 1857, he took command and held the Residency for eighty-seven days against superior enemy forces [see Lucknow, Siege of]. With him were his twenty-three-year-old wife, Julia (1834–1904), née Thesiger, daughter of the first Lord Chelmsford, and their three children. For his gallant stand he was knighted and promoted major general. In 1860 he commanded the British troops in the Ionian Islands.

Inglis, William (1764–1835). A British soldier who was commissioned in the army in 1781, saw service in America and Flanders, and took part in the capture of St. Lucia. In 1809 he commanded a brigade in the Peninsular War [q.v.] and fought at Bussaco and the first siege of Badajoz [qq.v.]. Wounded during the Battle of La Albuera [q.v.], he called out to his vastly outnumbered regiment, the 57th Foot (later the Middlesex Regiment): "Die hard, 57th!" They did. Of a strength of 579 officers and men, 23 officers and 415 other ranks were killed or wounded. In commemoration the regiment was ever after known as the Die Hards. Inglis recovered, saw further service, and became a major general.

Ingogo, Battle of (8 February 1881), First Anglo-Boer War. In western Natal a British force of four companies of infantry with a small mounted unit and four guns under Colonel Cromer Ashburnham (commissioned 1855) attacked Boers under Nicolas Jacobus Smit (1837–1866) in positions on Schuin's Hoogte, the heights above the Ingogo River. They were repulsed with a loss of 7 officers and 69 men killed and 3 officers and 64 men wounded. Boer casualties were 8 killed and 6 wounded.

Ingraham, Prentiss (1843–1904). An American soldier of fortune who fought on the Confederate side in the American Civil War and was twice wounded. After the war he fought in Mexico under Benito Juárez [q.v.] in the War of the Reform [q.v.]. He is said to have fought in the Franco-Prussian War [q.v.] and in Africa, Crete, and Cuba, where he was arrested by the Spanish as a filibuster [q.v.]. He escaped, narrowly avoiding execution, and settled in London, where he became a prolific writer of adventure stories. Later he returned to the United States, where he met and became a close friend of William ("Buffalo Bill") Cody [q.v.]. He died at the Beauvoir Confederate Home in Beauvoir, Mississippi.

Inhlazatye Mountain, Battle of (2 April 1879), Zulu War. General Lord Chelmsford [q.v.], leading a British force toward the Zulu capital of Ulundi, repulsed an attack by a strong Zulu impi. The Zulus lost at least 700; the British lost 2 officers and 11 other ranks killed or wounded.

Inhlobane Mountain, Battle of (28 March 1879), Zulu War. About 1,300 British troops under Colonel Redvers Buller [q.v.] attacked a strong Zulu kraal holding an estimated 15,000 Zulus. The attack was repulsed with heavy losses.

Iñiguez, Calixto García. See García Iñiguez, Calixto.

Initial Velocity. The speed with which a projectile leaves a weapon, usually expressed in the number of feet or centimeters passed in a second.

Inkerman, Battle of (5 November 1854), Crimean War. A Russian force of 16,000 under Prince Aleksandr Menshikov [q.v.], augmented by a force of 19,000 that made a sortie from Sevastopol, launched a double attack at dawn in fog and heavy mist against the Allied forces besieging the city. The brunt of the attack fell upon the British holding a ridge overlooking the Chernaya River near the Tatar village of Inkerman, on the eastern extremity of Sevastopol Harbor. In the initial assault the British were overwhelmed and the Russians were able to bring up artillery, but the thick fog and mist prevented the guns from effective firing, and the British with French help were able to drive the Russians back.

The commanders on both sides fed troops into the battle piecemeal and lost control of the action. The dying words of English General Sir George Cathcart [q.v.] were: "I fear we are in a mess." The result was a classic soldier's battle [q.v.], and there was much hand-to-hand fighting. The arrival of a French division under General Pierre Bosquet [q.v.] saved the day for the Allies. The struggle was particularly fierce around a position known as Sandbag Battery. General Bosquet, viewing the position after the battle exclaimed, "*Quel abattoir!* [What a slaughterhouse!]"

Of the 8,500 British engaged, 2,357 were killed or wounded; the French lost 939 out of some 7,000 engaged. The Russians were said to have lost 11,000 out of 35,000.

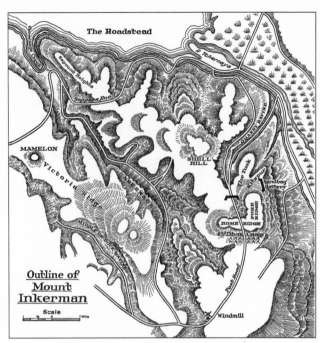

Inkerman *Outline of Mount Inkerman*

Inkos / Inkos Enkhulu. Inkos was the title of a Xhosa chief. An Inkos Enkhulu was a paramount chief.

Inkovo, Battle of (8 August 1812), Napoleonic Wars. As Napoleon advanced on Smolensk [q.v.], French General Horace Sébastiani [q.v.] with 3,000 cavalry engaged about 5,000 Cossacks under Russian General Matvei Ivanovich Platov [q.v.] near this village. Although the French suffered most from this inconclusive engagement of their Russian Campaign, it seems to have shaken the resolve of Russian General Mikhail Barclay de Tolly [q.v.], and his consequent hesitation gave time for Napoleon to cross the Dnieper River on a 15-mile front.

Inkpaduta (1815?–1879?). An American Indian leader of Sioux in Minnesota. In 1848 he attacked rival Sioux living on the Wakpekute River and killed their chief and 17 warriors while they slept. On 8–9 March 1857 he led the attack of about 20 warriors upon white settlers near Spirit Lake, killing 34 and taking 3 women as prisoners. In the next few days the band captured still another woman and killed another man, and two weeks later they killed more whites at Springfield (near present-day Jackson, Minnesota). Two of the captured women were ransomed; 2 were slain. Although Little Crow [q.v.], chief of the Kaposia division of the Mdewakanton Sioux, for reasons of his own, found and killed some of Inkpaduta's warriors, Inkpaduta himself eluded capture. He was later reported to have been present at the engagements at Fort Abercrombie on 3–6 September 1862; in the Battle of Big Mound, in present-day South Dakota, on 24 July 1863; at Dead Buffalo on 26 July 1863 and at Stoney Lake two days later; at Whitestone Hill, near present-day Ellendale, North Dakota, on 3 September 1863; and in the attack upon Marcus Reno [q.v.] in the Battle of the Little Bighorn [q.v.]. He died somewhere in Canada, still free.

Inlying Picket. A body of men kept in camp or quarters ready to turn out or march at once if called upon.

Inniskillen Dragoons and Enniskillen Fusiliers. The 6th (Inniskillen) Dragoons, a famous cavalry regiment in the British army, and the Enniskillen Fusiliers were named for the town of Inniskillen in County Fermanagh, Ireland, where in 1689 the forces of William III (1650–1702) defeated the army of James II (1633–1701). Originally recruits for these regiments came from the town.

Inorodtsy. Russian "native troops," mostly from the Caucasus. In wartime the Caucasus could contribute 23,500 men.

Inoue, Hikaru (1851–1908). A Japanese soldier who took part as an officer in the Boshin Civil War [q.v.] of 1868, which resulted in the Meiji Restoration, the Satsuma Rebellion of 1877, and the Sino-Japanese War of 1894–95 [qq.v.].

Inoue, Ikutaro (1872–1965). A Japanese soldier who fought in the Sino-Japanese War of 1894–95 [q.v.] and later in the Russo-Japanese War.

Inquiry, Board (or Court) of. A panel of officers assembled to determine the facts concerning a person or event. In the American army the board had the same authority as that of a court-martial to summon witnesses and examine them under oath, but it had no power to punish. In the British army a court of inquiry had no power to compel witnesses to appear.

Insignia (in the singular, sometimes insigne). A distinctive device or symbol worn to identify a soldier's nationality, rank, unit, or branch of service.

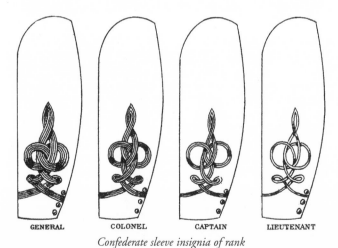

GENERAL   COLONEL   CAPTAIN   LIEUTENANT

Confederate sleeve insignia of rank

Inspection. 1. A formal look at the state of preparedness of a soldier or a military unit.

2. A ceremonial review of a unit, often an honor guard, by a visiting dignitary.

Inspection *British reinforcements undergo kit inspections after landing in Cape Town, South Africa, during the Boer War.*

Inspector General. A staff officer whose duty is to investigate and report on recruiting, administration, accountability for money or property, training, etc. and to see that all activities are conducted according to army regulations. In the French army a certain number of generals were annually designated to make inspections.

Insubordination. The willful defiance of lawful authority. This, one of the most heinous of military offenses, has always been punishable. It could be committed by striking or offering violence to a superior officer, disobeying his command, or using threatening or abusive language to him. Most armies deemed it a capital offense to strike an officer. However, in 1817 on St. Helena Napoleon mused that "insubordination may only be the evidence of a strong mind."

In Support of. Term used to describe a position of one unit or formation whereby it can assist or protect another such body.

Insurgents. Those who try to overthrow a constituted government by subversion or armed conflict.

Insurgents *A family of insurgents protect a barricade during the French Revolution of 1848.*

Insurrection. An uprising of a people against their rulers. Karl von Clausewitz [q.v.] wrote (*On War* [1833]): "In a national insurrection the center of gravity to be destroyed lies in the person of the chief leader and in public opinion; against these points the blow must be directed."

Insurrectos. Filipino guerrillas who, not liking American rule any better than Spanish rule, fought unsuccessfully for their freedom [see Philippine Insurrection].

Intelligence, Military. The Duke of Wellington wrote, "The whole art of war consists in getting at what lies on the other side of the hill, or, in other words, separating what we do not know from what we do," but for most of the nineteenth century the systematic collection and analysis of military intelligence were almost unknown. What passed for intelligence could for the most part be classified as news or rumors supplied by cavalry, spies, balloons, newspapers, refugees, private letters, prisoners of war, defectors, and, at the end of the century, wiretapping. Karl von Clausewitz [q.v.] wrote: "Many intelligence reports in war are contradictory; even more are false, and by far the greatest part are of a doubtful character. . . . In short, most intelligence is false."

Although by the end of the century the ability of armies to collect information had increased enormously, military intelligence was still viewed with suspicion. In the British army the intelligence branch remained a small unit in the Department of the Quartermaster General until 1904.

In the United States the first professional intelligence agency was the Bureau of Military Information, formed in November 1862, during the American Civil War when Major General Joseph Hooker [q.v.] ordered Colonel George Henry Sharpe (1827–1900), his deputy provost marshal, to organize the bureau. It functioned much like a modern military intelligence unit, drawing on information from a wide variety of sources, analyzing it, and providing concise and generally accurate intelligence. It was the most efficient intelligence agency of the time, but it was dissolved after the war.

In 1885 a Military Information Division was formed as part of the Miscellaneous Branch of the U.S. Adjutant General's Office. Its purpose was to collect "military data on our own and foreign armies which would be available for use by the War Department and the Army at Large," but by 1897 it contained only 11 officers and was so ineffective that it was unable even to supply maps of Cuba for use in the Spanish-American War [q.v.].

Intendance Militaire. One of the most important military administrative branches of the French army. Although it has been described as a superpowerful quartermaster corps, it operated almost independently of the command structure until reformed in 1882. It was responsible for supplying food, forage, bedding, transportation, clothing, equipment, and pay. It promulgated regulations and exercised control over most of the army's budget, and prior to 1882 it even had to approve all requests made by doctors and pharmacists. Its lowest officer grade was *adjoint à l'intendance,* the equivalent of captain.

Following the disastrous defeat of the French army in the Franco-Prussian War [q.v.] in 1870–71 the Intendance was heavily criticized for its inefficiency, particularly for its han-dling of the medical arrangements. Whereas the Germans had 1 doctor for every 290 men, the French had only 1 for every 740. Many sick and wounded French soldiers survived only because they were fortunate enough to be captured and treated by German doctors.

On 16 March 1882 the Intendance was relieved of its directive functions, army officers were given the right to command all the troops under their control, and doctors were permitted to give orders to nurses and pharmacists.

Interdiction. An action that denies an enemy's access to an area, a road, or supplies.

Interior Economy. In a military sense, this is the management of the affairs of a regiment or other unit. It involves the handling of the various funds, the library, amusements, band, messes, and everything pertaining to the good order and welfare of a military unit.

Interior Lines. See Exterior and Interior Lines.

International Law. The sum of the treaties, agreements, and customs among sovereign states, many of which pertain to wars and armies. The so-called father of international law was Hugo Grotius (1583–1645), who in 1625 wrote *De jure belli ac pacis* (*The Law of War and Peace*), in which he argued that it was possible to create an international law code applicable to every place at any time, a concept that influenced all subsequent thinking on the subject.

International League of Peace. A pacifist organization founded in 1868 by Frédéric Passy (1822–1912), a French economist and a member of the Chamber of Deputies from 1874 until 1889. In 1901 Passy shared with Jean Henri Dunant [q.v.] the Nobel Peace Prize.

Intervene, to. To come between combatants or to be a third party to a conflict. [See French Intervention in Spain.]

Intervention. The act of interference with force in another nation's internal affairs, usually to compel or prevent an action.

In the Field. An expression used when an army or some part of it is engaged in offensive or defensive operations against an enemy or those suspected of hostile intentions.

Invalid Corps. A Union army unit organized in April 1863, during the American Civil War, to utilize men who were or had been in the army but were physically unable to fight. Organized into companies and regiments, it was used to man garrisons and work in hospitals. On 18 March 1864 it was renamed the Veteran Reserve Corps. Between its inception in 1863 and its disbandment in 1866 some 60,000 men served in the corps.

In 1864 the Confederacy formed a loosely organized invalid corps, some serving only until they were able to return to their units.

Invalides, Des. See Hôtel des Invalides.

Invalid Establishment. An institution in the Indian army for transferring British officers who were no longer fit into an invalid battalion if they were still capable of garrison duty or to the Indian Pension List if they were incapable of any duty—"Provided their conduct and habits are such as not to affect the character of that Institution, which is designed as an honourable retreat to the worn-out or disabled but deserving officers."

Invasion. The entry by a hostile armed force into a country or region for the purpose of conquering it or plundering it. Karl von Clausewitz [q.v.] defined invasion (*On War* [1833]) as "the occupation of an enemy's territory, not with a view to keeping it, but in order to levy contributions upon it or even to devastate it."

Henri Jomini [q.v.] warned (*Précis de l'art de la guerre* [1838]): "Remoteness is not a certain safeguard against invasion."

Investment. A siege.

Investment, Lines of. The trenches and earthworks created by besiegers of a fort or fortified position.

Inworks. The inner defenses of a fortification.

Iodine. An antiseptic first discovered in 1812 by a manufacturer of saltpeter in Paris. Armies did not begin to use it until late in the century. It was given its English name in 1814 by Sir Humphry Davy (1778–1829), the chemist who in 1799 discovered the exhilarating effect of nitrous oxide when inhaled. It was known in France as *iode* from the color of its vapor, but Davy, who thought the word would be confusing in English, dropped the *e* and added *-ine*, as in *chlorine* in British pronunciation. Iodine, bromine, and chlorine waters were used as wound antiseptics.

Ionian Islands. Under the Treaty of Campo Formio (17 October 1797) France acquired the Ionian Islands from the republic of Venice, and Napoleon made a commitment never to abandon them. However, in 1798 a combined Russian and Turkish force occupied the islands, and an independent Septinsular Republic, or republic of Seven Islands, was established under the protection of Russia. In the Treaty of Tilsit [q.v.] in July 1807 the tsar restored the islands to France, and in 8 August they again became a part of the French Empire. In 1809 British forces under Sir John Oswald (1771–1840) seized the Ionian islands of Zante, Cephalonia, Itaca, Paxo, and Cerigo. In March of the following year with a force of 2,000 men Oswald attacked the remaining French garrison at Leukas, and after an eight-day siege it surrendered. From 1815 to 1864, when they were given to Greece, the islands formed an independent state under British protection.

Iquique, Battle of (November 1879), War of the Pacific. At this seaport town 235 miles north of Antofagasta in present-day Peru, Chileans defeated a combined Peruvian-Bolivian force. Only two years before, the town had been nearly destroyed by an earthquake, a fire, and a tidal wave. It was ceded to Chile by treaty on 20 October 1883.

Irish Insurrections. 1. Robert Emmet (1778–1803) and his band of insurrectionists in an attempted uprising against

British rule tried without success on 23 July 1803 to kidnap the British viceroy. They then launched a series of violent acts that inspired riots in the streets. All were easily suppressed. Emmet went into hiding but was betrayed and captured on 25 August. He was tried by a special court and on 20 September was hanged.

2. In 1848 an insurrection led by William Smith O'Brien (1803–1864) ended with his arrest at the railway station at Thurles, County Tipperary. The arrest itself touched off a near riot. O'Brien was tried and sentenced to death. His sentence was later commuted to transportation to Tasmania, and he was pardoned in 1856.

3. In 1867 an attempted insurrection in the south and west of Ireland was frustrated by an informer named John Joseph Corydon [see Fenian Brotherhood].

Irish Insurrections *Irish riots at Belfast*

Irish Legion. An Irish unit in Napoleon's army. It was formed in 1803 and given a green flag in addition to a tricolor. It was hoped that the legion would provide officers for regiments to be formed after the capture of Ireland. In 1806 it was converted to a regular regiment, and by 1809 it had three battalions.

Irish Soldiers. Throughout the nineteenth century young Irishmen were found in armies throughout the world, most notably in the British army, which in 1830 consisted of 42.2 percent Irish. Before 1817 Irish Catholic officers could not serve outside Ireland. Most Irish officers, such as Charles Napier, Garnet Wolseley, and Lord Roberts [qq.v.] were Protestant Anglo-Irish.

Irishmen served in the Spanish army and in South American armies fighting for independence. Simón Bolívar [q.v.] was an admirer of their fighting qualities. In the Mexican Civil War, [q.v.] they fought for the Americans, although the San Patricio Battalion [q.v.] in the Mexican army, made up of American deserters, contained 40 percent Irish. There were Irish units in Napoleon's army and in the pope's army in 1860. Irish-born men fought on both sides in the American Civil War, although most were in Union armies. There were Irishmen fighting on both sides in the Second Anglo-Boer War [q.v.]. In the British army they so distinguished themselves that Queen Victoria decreed that the shamrock, previously forbidden, could be worn on St. Patrick's Day, and in 1900 the Irish Guards was established.

Iron and Blood. An expression based on an oft-quoted speech by Otto von Bismarck (1815–1898) to the Prussian parliament: "Germany does not look at Prussia's liberalism but at her power. . . . The great questions of the age are not settled by speeches and majority votes . . . but by iron and blood."

Iron Brigade of the West. One of the most famous units in the Union army in the American Civil War and the only all-western brigade in the Army of the Potomac. Formed in the autumn of 1861 and originally called the Black Hat Brigade after the black slouch hats its men wore, it was composed of the 19th Indiana and the 2nd, 6th, and 7th Wisconsin under Brigadier General Rufus King [q.v.]. The 24th Michigan was added just before the Antietam Campaign, and in May 1862 John Gibbon [q.v.] took command. In its first engagement, on 28 August 1862 the brigade distinguished itself at Groveton [q.v.], where it suffered 33 percent casualties when it was ambushed by troops under Confederate General Thomas ("Stonewall") Jackson. In five battles in one three-week period in 1862 it lost 58 percent of its original strength. Its gallant conduct in the Battle of South Mountain [q.v.] on 14 September 1862, in which it lost 25 percent of its strength, inspired a newspaper correspondent to dub it the Iron Brigade. It fought at Fredericksburg, Chancellorsville, and Gettysburg [qq.v.], and on the first day of the latter battle, in the struggle for Seminary Ridge [q.v.], it lost 1,212 out of 1,883 (65 percent of its effectives). The 24th Michigan lost 399 out of 496.

Iron Cross. The most famous German medal. Black and edged in silver, it is in the shape of a Maltese cross. It was originally a Prussian medal, instituted on 10 March 1813 for

Kaiser Wilhelm I wearing the Iron Cross.

heroism in battle or for victorious senior commanders. It was later discontinued, then revived in 1870 for the Franco-Prussian War [q.v.]. In 1871, when the king of Prussia became also the emperor of Germany, it became a medal of the German Empire. In 1895 survivors of the Franco-Prussian War who had received the Iron Cross twenty-five years earlier were awarded a white metal oak-leaf cluster with the number 25 that was to be worn just above the ring of the cross.

The medal originally had only two classes, second and first; after the Battle of Waterloo [q.v.] a Grand Cross was created for Marshal Gebhard von Blücher [q.v.], but it was rarely awarded thereafter. No categories were added in the nineteenth century. (Hitler added grades, and by the end of World War II there were eight, including the *Brillianten,* the Knight's Cross with Golden Oak Leaves, swords, and diamonds.)

Iron Crown, Order of the. In Milan, Italy, on 23 May 1804 Napoleon had himself crowned king of Italy using the sixth-century jewel-bedecked gold crown called the Iron Crown because it was believed to have incorporated in it a nail from the True Cross. On 5 July of the same year he instituted a new order, the Order of the Iron Crown, to reward distinguished military or political service. Although this was an Italian order, its arched crown bore an inscription in French: "*Dieu Me L' a-Donnée, Gare A Qui Y Touchera* [God gave it to me, woe to him who touches it]," a statement Napoleon had repeated at his coronation. In 1809 the inscription was changed into Italian.

Irregular Forces. Armed groups not a part of an established army, gendarmerie, police, or other security forces. They often engaged in guerrilla warfare [q.v.].

Irún, Battle of (18 May 1837), First Carlist War. A British and Cristino force of 10,000 under British General Sir George de Lacy Evans [q.v.] appeared before Irún in northern Spain nine miles east of San Sebastián, near the French border, and demanded its surrender. The Carlists refused. The town was taken by assault with small loss after an eleven-hour battle.

Isabella, Order of. A Spanish order of knighthood established in 1815 as an award for loyalty and for the defense of Spanish possessions in America, later extended as an all-purpose reward.

Order of Isabella

Isandhlwana, Battle of (22 January 1879), Zulu War. On 11 January 1879 Frederic Thesiger, Viscount Chelmsford [q.v.], led an army of 5,000 British troops and 8,200 Africans into Zululand in three widely dispersed columns. On 22 January, while he was absent with a portion of his force seeking out the Zulus, his central column of about 1,800 British and 1,000 Africans, notably six companies of the 2nd Battalion of the 24th Regiment, which was camped at the base of a tall craig called Isandhlwana, 28 miles east-northeast of Dundee in what became the semiautonomous state of KwaZulu, was attacked by a Zulu impi of about 20,000 men. All but 55 British and about 300 Africans were slaughtered. No prisoners were taken.

Isandhlwana *The 24th Foot faces a Zulu charge at Isandhlwana in 1879.*

Lord Chelmsford admitted: "We have certainly been seriously under-rating the power of the Zulu army." Among the acclaimed heroes of the battle were Lieutenant Josiah Aylmer (1852–1879) and Lieutenant Teignmouth Melville (1842–1879), who were killed while trying to cross the Buffalo River carrying the regimental colors of the 24th Foot. In 1907 both were awarded posthumous Victoria Crosses [see Zulu War].

Isaszcq, Battle of (6 April 1849), Hungarian Revolution. In a battle near this town in central Hungary on the Rakos River, 15 miles east of Budapest, 42,000 Hungarians under General Arthur von Görgey engaged 27,000 Croats under General Josef Jelačić od Bužima [qq.v.], the ban of Croatia. One Hungarian corps was driven from the field, but the remainder held their ground, and both sides bivouacked on the field. The following day the Croatians withdrew, and the Hungarians claimed a victory.

Isa wad al-Zain (1860?–1947). A Dervish amir who campaigned in Darfur against tribes rebelling against Mahdist rule. He was wounded in a battle near El Fasher, the capital of Darfur. In 1863 he was made chief amir of Kordofan. In the Battle of Omdurman [q.v.] he led a force of riflemen and cavalry against the victorious Anglo-Egyptian force under General H. H. Kitchener [q.v.]. He escaped unscathed from this battle and from the Battle of Umm Dibaikarat (Diwaykarat) [q.v.] as well, living to retire to the village of Umm Hayaya, near Kosti.

Ischia, Siege and Capture of (June 1809). Napoleonic Wars. On 11 June Sir John Stuart (1759–1815) with Vice Admiral Cuthbert Collingwood (1750–1810) and 11,000 men sailed from Messina bound for the Bay of Naples. Although delayed by calms, the expedition arrived on 24 June 1809. The next day Stuart landed on the 18-square-mile island of Ischia in the Tyrrhenian Sea between the Bay of Naples and the Gulf of Gaeta and carried by assault all but the castle, which he besieged. It surrendered on 30 June. Because Collingwood feared that his ships would be attacked in the Ischia harbor, Stuart reembarked his men and returned to Messina.

I-See-O (1851?–1927). A Kiowa scout who in 1867, while still in his teens, engaged in a raid against the Navajos in New Mexico. On 12 July 1874, under Lone Wolf [q.v.], he took part in a successful fight against Texas Rangers led by John B. Jones [q.v.]. On 26–28 September of the same year, on the Red River, near Tute and the Palo Duro canyons, Lone Wolf and his band were defeated in an engagement with eight companies of the 4th Cavalry. On 25 February 1875 I-See-O and the remainder of the band surrendered at Fort Sill, Texas.

I-See-O then served as a scout, working out of Fort Sill, where he became friends with Captain Hugh Lenox Scott [q.v.], whom he helped to quell a local outbreak of ghost dance [q.v.] hysteria. In 1891, when the all-Indian Company L of the 7th Cavalry was formed, he enlisted and became its first sergeant [see Indian Soldiers, American]. When the company was disbanded in 1897, he enlisted again and served for five years as a scout and as courier for Nelson Miles [q.v.]. After the Spanish-American War [q.v.] he retired and lived with his family at Big Bend on the Washita River.

In 1915 he was part of a delegation to Washington, D.C., where he again met Scott, now army chief of staff. Scott persuaded the secretary of war to make I-See-O a sergeant for life, and on 1 February 1915 Scott wrote to Colonel Granger Adams (1858?–1928), commanding at Fort Sill, ordering him to "let him [I-See-O] live on the reservation or out among his people, as he elects, and see that he gets pay, clothing and rations . . . until he dies. He is old . . . his mind is back in the middle ages and he has simply been stunned by civilization. I do not see how he survived this long. When the government needed him, he was supremely loyal, against the wishes of his own people." The army provided for him until in January 1927 he contracted pneumonia. I-See-O, the last Indian scout, died at Fort Sill.

Isijula. A Zulu stabbing spear, an assegai. It had a broad 9-inch blade and a haft of about 14 inches.

Iskakote, Battle of (18 May 1852), Northwest Frontier. Colin Campbell [q.v.] with 2,500 men and seven guns led a punitive expedition against Swat tribes north-northeast of Peshawar, defeating a force of 6,000 Swatis.

Island No. 10. See New Madrid and Island No. 10.

Isly River, Battle of (14 August 1844), French conquest of Algeria. On this river in northeastern Morocco on a day when the temperature was said to have reached 60°C, a French army of 8,500 infantry, 1,400 cavalry, and 400 friendly Arabs with 16 guns under General Thomas Bugeaud [q.v.] defeated a force of 45,000 Moroccans and Algerians under Abd el-Kader [q.v.] and Abdur Rahman (1778–1859), sultan of Fez and Morocco. Abd el-Kader and Abdur-Rahman lost 800 men; the French, 30.

Ismail Haqqi Pasha (1818–1882). An Egyptian soldier of Kurdish ancestry. In 1853 he was for a few months governor-general of the Sudan but was recalled for alleged misdeeds. During the Crimean War [q.v.] he commanded the Egyptian infantry brigade before Sevastopol. He was later sirdar (commander-in-chief) of the Egyptian army. In 1863 he was appointed treasurer of the royal household of the khedive.

Ismail Kamil Pasha (1795–1822). An Egyptian soldier and the third son of Muhammad Ali Pasha [q.v.]. In 1813 his father sent him to Constantinople (Istanbul) to present to the sultan the keys of the city of Mecca (Makkah), which Egyptian troops had captured from the Wahhabis [see Arabian Wars]. In 1820 he was given command of a small army, which he led in an invasion of the Sudan. In November of that year he fought battles with Shaiqiya Arabs at Korti, on the left bank of the Nile, 30 miles south-southwest of Merowe, and at Dairut (Deirut or Dayrut), 33 miles south-

Ismail, Kamil Pasha *Ismail's army encamped on the shores of the Nile, 1821*

west of Asyût. On 12 June 1821 after great difficulties he entered Sennar, but his army was so weakened by sickness and he himself was so ill that he began a withdrawal to Egypt. At Shendi, a town on the right bank of the Nile 100 miles above present-day Khartoum, he was burned to death by Arabs he had offended.

Ismail Pasha Aiyub (18??–1884). An Egyptian soldier and official who was said to have been born a Kurd or Circassian. He commanded one of the columns that went to the relief of Kassala in 1865 when it was besieged by Sudanese mutineers. After serving in a number of administrative posts he was appointed governor-general of the Sudan in 1873. In 1874 he led an army into Darfur and annexed that land to Egyptian-held Sudan. During Arabi's Revolt [q.v.] he sided with Arabi Pasha [q.v.], but he later managed to disassociate himself so successfully that he was appointed to the commission that tried the leaders of the revolt.

Istalif / Istaliffe, Battle of (28 September 1842), First Afghan War. General William Nott [q.v.] led an Anglo-Indian force that stormed and burned this Afghan town 22 miles north northeast of Kabul on the slope of Paghman Mountain.

Itagaki, Count Taisuke (1837–1919). A Japanese samurai who joined with Saigo Takamori [q.v.] and others in the overthrow of the Takugawa shogunate (1603–1867) and in the Meiji Restoration [q.v.] [see Boshin Civil War]. He then founded the first major political party in Japan.

Italian Army. An Italian national army formed after the unification of Italy. In 1861 the army of Piedmont was amalgamated with the armies of Lombardy, Parma, Modena, Emilia, and Naples. Many officers of Garibaldi's Red Shirts [q.v.], men of little formal education who were in the Neapolitan army, were discharged with six months' pay after failing to pass examinations. In 1870 there occurred another purging of the officer corps to weed out the inefficient, the ill, or those otherwise unsuitable.

On 30 September 1873 Italy was divided into seven military commands or army corps and on 22 March 1877 into eighty-eight military districts, each commanded by a colonel. The entire army consisted of just over 400,000 regulars, about 180,000 *mobile milizia* (landwehr) and 280,000 *milizia territoriale*. Almost from the beginning Italy introduced conscription with service of twelve years, three of which were on active duty (five years for cavalry), followed by five years in the reserve and the remainder in the *mobile milizia*. By 1877 service had been extended to nineteen years, from the beginning of the twenty-first year to the end of the thirty-ninth year, usually, as before, with three years on active duty.

Officers for the infantry and cavalry were educated at Modena; those for the artillery and engineers, at Turin, where there was also a staff college. With the exception of university graduates, no officer who had not passed through one or more of the military academies was commissioned. Promotions were by examination, and any lieutenant who failed the examination for captain was forced to remain in grade for twenty-five years.

Italian-Mahdist Conflict (1893–94). In 1893 Mahdist Dervishes in the Sudan threatened the Italian colony of Eritrea but were driven back by Italian forces that won a victory in the Battle of Agordat [q.v.] in 1893 and occupied Kassala [q.v.] in 1894.

Italian Wars of Independence (1848–70). Until 1848 Italy was divided into nine states, all dominated to a greater or lesser degree by the Austrian Empire. Hatred of Austrian rule led to increasingly numerous revolts. In 1820 an insurrection led by General Guglielmo Pepe [q.v.], a Carbonarist, forced Ferdinand IV (1751–1825) of the Two Sicilies to grant a liberal constitution, which he soon repudiated [see Carbonari]. An Austrian army occupied Naples, and Pepe was defeated and banished. In 1831 there was an unsuccessful uprising in Modena, and in 1847 in Leghorn.

On 3 January 1848 an uprising in Milan [q.v.] began with a clash between the Milanese and the Austrian garrison. In late March the Austrians, driven out of the city, withdrew into the fortresses of the Quadrilateral [q.v.]. In Venice workers at the arsenal rioted and killed the proprietor, and on 22 March Venice declared itself a republic. Carlo Alberto [q.v.], Prince of Savoy and Piedmont, allied himself with the rebels and declared war on Austria, but the Piedmontese, badly led and poorly supplied, were defeated by Field Marshal Josef Radetzky [q.v.] in the First Battle of Custozza [q.v.] on 24 July 1848.

On 12–27 January 1849 there was an uprising in Palermo. On 9 February, with the support of Giuseppe Garibaldi [q.v.], who had raised an army of 4,700 Red Shirts [q.v.], a Roman republic was proclaimed with executive power placed in the hands of a triumvirate. French General Nicolas Oudinot [q.v.], at the head of an army of 86,000 French, Spanish, Austrian, Tuscan, and Neapolitan troops, moved against the rebels. In a battle on 30 April Garibaldi inflicted heavy losses upon Oudinot and was himself wounded. On 3 June he launched a costly attack upon the French, but he was forced to evacuate Rome in early July.

The tide had turned against the revolutionaries. Rome was returned to Pope Pius IX (1792–1878), and Garibaldi fled the country. Venice, blockaded since July 1848, capitulated on 22 August 1849.

No further serious challenge to Austrian rule surfaced in Italy until in 1859 King Victor Emmanuel II (1820–1878) of Piedmont and his premier, Count Camillo di Cavour (1810–1861), met secretly with Napoleon III, who agreed to support the unification of Italy even if it meant war with Austria. Piedmont mobilized in March 1859, and in April Austrian forces invaded. Napoleon III dispatched French troops, and in the battles of Palestro on 30 May, Magenta on 4 June, and Solferino on 24 June [qq.v.] the Austrians were defeated.

On 11 July Napoleon III met with Emperor Franz Josef (1830–1916). An agreement was reached in which Piedmont retained Lombardy while Venetia remained under Austrian rule. Piedmont ceded the provinces of Nice and Savoy to France in return for its help. These arrangements did not please many Italians, and in 1852 an uprising flared in Mantua, the following year in Milan, in 1857 in Genoa—all instigated by Giuseppe Mazzini (1805–1872) and all crushed without great difficulty by Austrian troops.

In 1860 Sicilian authorities aborted a revolt against Bourbon rule. Garibaldi, returned from his exile, organized an army of a 1,000 Red Shirts at Genoa, and on 5 May he sailed for Sicily. Having landed at Marsala on 11 May, he marched inland, gathering recruits as he marched, and on 15 May he defeated a Neapolitan force at Calatafimi [q.v.]. On 6 June he captured Palermo and, with British help, crossed the Strait of Messina and on 7 September captured Naples.

On 17 March 1861 Italy was declared a united kingdom under Victor Emmanuel of Piedmont's house of Savoy, but the country was still not unified. Nice, Savoy, and Rome were in French hands; Austria held Venetia.

On 20 June 1866, while Austria was attempting to fight off an invasion by Prussia [see Seven Weeks' War], Italy declared war on Austria. An army under the Marchese di La Marmora [q.v.] crossed the Mincio River, and at Custozza [q.v.] on 24 June Italians again met Austrians, this time under Archduke Albert [q.v.]. They were again defeated. Nevertheless, on 3 July the Austrians agreed to cede Venetia to Italy. In 1867 Napoleon III agreed to remove French troops from Rome, and in 1870 Rome became the capital of a united Italy.

Italian Wars of Independence *The tricolor flag of a united Italy is carried by Giuseppe Garibaldi.*

Italo-Abyssinian Wars. In the 1870s the Italians acquired a foothold on the Abyssinian coast that they steadily expanded. In January 1885 they seized Beilul, a fishing port on the Red Sea, 25 miles west-northwest of Assab (Aseb), and in February they occupied Massawa (Massaua) on the Gulf of Massaua, an inlet of the Red Sea. They purchased Assab from a local Eritrean prince and began to move inland. The Abyssinians were slow to react, but on 26 January 1887 the chieftain of

Italo-Abyssinian Wars *A procession of Abyssinians comes through the Faluk Gate at Harrar during the 1890s campaign.*

Shoa (Shewa)—attacked a detachment of 500 Italian troops at a place called Dongali [q.v.] and killed more than 400. In response, reinforcements were sent from Italy, and by April 1888 more than 20,000 Italian troops were on the northeast coast of Africa. They saw little fighting but were decimated by diseases. Following the death of his father in the Battle of Gallabat [q.v.] on 12 March 1889, the chieftain of Shoa, took the throne as Menelek II [q.v.], and on 2 May 1889 he signed the Treaty of Uccialli, by which the Italians retained a small coastal colony they called Eritrea. When the Italian and Amharic versions of the treaty were found to differ, Menelek again took to the field.

Italians under Colonel Oreste Baratieri [q.v.] crossed the frontier from Eritrea and defeated the Abyssinians in the battles of Kotit and Senafe on 13–15 January 1895, but having pushed too far south, they were defeated by the Abyssinians in the Battle of Amba Alagai [q.v.] on 7 December 1895 and at Makalle on 21 January 1896, after which they retreated.

In February 1896 Italian reinforcements arrived, and Baratieri took the field with about 20,000 men, but by that time Menelek had assembled an army of 90,000 and occupied a strong position at Abba Garima, a mountainous area near Adowa, 80 miles south of Asmara. On 1 March the Italians attacked and were soundly defeated [see Adowa/Aduwa/Adua, Battle of]. When more reinforcements arrived, the Italians occupied Adigrat, just east of Adowa, and the Abyssinians withdrew. On 26 October the Italians and Abyssinians signed the Treaty of Addis Ababa [q.v.], in which the Italians recognized Abyssinian independence. Italy was left with a small bit of the coast in Eritrea that was reduced in 1900 to about 80 square miles.

Itá-Ybaté, Battle of. See Loma Valentinas, Battle of.

Iturbide, Agustín de (1783–1824). A Mexican Creole landowner and Catholic who became a revolutionary. He had fought for the royalists against the revolt of peasants led by Miguel Hidalgo y Costilla [q.v.] in 1810 and against the revolt of Vicente Guerrero [q.v.] in 1820 [see Mexican Revolutions]. However, he soon joined Guerrero in his struggle with Spain, and in 1821 the Spanish government was forced to capitulate and sign the Treaty of Córdoba, assuring Mexican independence. Iturbide, who became head of the provisional government, a few months later proclaimed himself emperor of Mexico as Agustín I. His government was op-

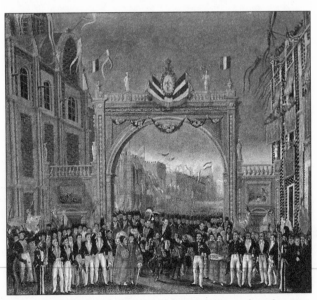

Iturbide *A victorious Iturbide leads his army through the arch of triumph in Mexico City, 1821.*

pressive, and he was overthrown by a revolution led by Guerrero and General Antonio López de Santa Anna [q.v.] in which the army turned against him. On 19 March 1823 he was forced to abdicate. He went into exile in Europe but a year later, hoping to regain power, returned. He was soon captured and on 19 July 1824 was shot.

Ituzaingó, Battle of (20 February 1827), Brazil–Buenos Aires War. After Argentina broke away from Spain and Brazil broke away from Portugal, the territory between the two on the Paraná River 50 miles west of Pasadas was taken over by Brazil in 1821 and called the Cispalatine Province. In 1825 its people rose against Brazilian control. About 8,000 Argentine and Cispalatine troops under General Carlos María de Alvear [q.v.] eventually won a signal victory over a force of an equal number of Brazilians, Portuguese, and Germans under General Filiberto de Barbacena [q.v.]. Casualties were fewer than 500 on each side. The Cispalatine became the separate country of Uruguay in 1828.

Iuka, Battle of (19 September 1862), American Civil War. At Iuka, Mississippi, 20 miles east southeast of Corinth, some 9,000 Union troops under General William Rosecrans [q.v.] were attacked by a Confederate force of 14,000, part of General Sterling Price's command under General Lewis Henry Little (1817–1862). After two hours of heavy fighting, the Confederates were repulsed. Little was killed when a bullet passed under Price's arm and struck him in the forehead.

Ivanov, Nikolai Yudovich (1851–1919). A Russian officer who served in the Russo-Turkish War of 1877–78 [q.v.], the Russo-Japanese War, and subsequent wars.

Ixcaquixtla, Battle of (1 January 1817). At this central Mexican town (officially San Juan Ixcaquixtla), 50 miles southeast of Puebla, Spanish troops crushed one of Mexico's many revolutions.

Izard, George (1776–1828). An American soldier born in England and educated in England, France, and Germany. In 1794, while attending the French engineering school [École du Génie] at Metz, he was commissioned a second lieutenant of artillery in the U.S. army. He returned to the United States in 1797 and served until 1804. On the outbreak of the War of 1812 [q.v.] with Britain, he returned to the army as a colonel in the artillery and on 12 March 1813 was promoted brigadier general and placed in charge of the defenses of New York City, then considered in danger. On 21 January 1814 he was promoted major general and found himself the senior officer on the Canadian frontier in command of some 4,000 regulars. In early September 1814 he was ordered to move toward Sacket's Harbor, New York, on Lake Ontario, but then, on 10 September, he received a request from Major General Jacob Brown [q.v.] to support him at Fort Erie [q.v.]. Izard made a difficult march of 400 miles in foul weather and on the night of 10 October bivouacked 2 miles from Fort Erie. Taking command of the entire force of 8,000 regulars and militia, he moved on the British forces under Lieutenant General Gordon Drummond (1772–1854), a veteran of the fighting against the French in Egypt, and forced the British to retreat north of the Chippewa River. On 13 October he again moved against Drummond, and although he inflicted heavy losses, at a cost of 12 killed and 54 wounded, he retreated to Fort George and Burlington Heights and soon after marched back to Buffalo, New York, where he went into winter quarters. He was much criticized for this, and on 18 December 1814 he submitted his resignation. It was not accepted, but he saw no further action.

From 1825 to his death Izard was governor of Arkansas Territory.

Izinti. A Zulu throwing spear.

Izucar, Battle of (24 February 1812), Mexican Revolution. Mexican insurgents under Mariano Matamoros (1770?–1814), a priest, defeated a Spanish force at this town in south-central Mexico, now named Izucar de Matamoros. In the Battle of Puruarán on 5 January 1814 Matamoros was captured, and on 3 February 1814 he was executed at Valladolid.

J

Jackboots. Heavy cavalry boots reaching above the knee, made of heavy leather that had been jacked, a process using wax and tar to produce a hard shiny surface.

Jackman. A cavalryman.

Jackson, Andrew (1767–1845). An American soldier and politician called Old Hickory. He first saw action in the American army during the American Revolution, when on 1 August 1780 at age thirteen he took part in the Battle of Hanging Rock. The following year he was orphaned and captured by the British. While a captive, he was slashed on the hand and head with a saber by an irate British officer whose boots he refused to polish.

After the war, although he had very little formal education, he studied law and in 1787 was admitted to the bar in North Carolina. The following year he was appointed prosecuting attorney of the western district (now Tennessee) and moved to Nashville. In 1791 he married Mrs. Rachel Robard (née Donelson), who, it was later discovered, had not yet been divorced. When her divorce became legal, he married her again.

In 1795 he fought a duel with another lawyer, Colonel Waitstill Avery (1745–1821). Neither was injured. In 1796 he helped write the constitution for the new state of Tennessee and was elected to Congress; in 1797 he was appointed to the Senate. In 1798 he resigned to accept a judgeship on the Tennessee Supreme Court. In 1802 he was elected major general of the Tennessee militia. In 1806 he fought a second duel in which he killed a man named Charles Dickinson, with whom he had had a long and bitter quarrel, and himself received a wound from which he never completely recovered.

In the War of 1812 [q.v.] he was made a major general of volunteers and ordered to take his Tennessee militia to New Orleans, where he would be under the command of Major General James Wilkinson [q.v.], a man he despised. At Natchez he received orders to cancel his mission, and he and his men were dismissed. After marching his men back to Tennessee, he embroiled himself in a tavern brawl with Thomas Hart Benton (1782–1858) and his brother Jesse and was shot in the shoulder.

He was recovering when word reached him of the Fort Mims Massacre [q.v.], perpetrated by Creek Indians. He promptly assembled his militia and marched to the upper Coosa River in Alabama. Although he won a victory at Talladega [q.v.] on 9 November 1813, Creek power remained unbroken. When needed supplies failed to reach him and disputes flared over the terms of service, his men turned mutinous. He effectively curbed them by summarily hanging two

ringleaders. In February 1814 reinforcements began to arrive, including a regular army infantry regiment, and by March Jackson had an army of 5,000. With this force he attacked the Creeks on 27 March and won a decisive victory in the Battle of Horseshoe Bend [q.v.], for which he was promoted major general on 28 May. On 9 August he concluded the Treaty of Fort Jackson, by which the Creeks ceded twenty-three million acres of land to the government.

Jackson was promoted major general in the U.S. army and marched upon a British force that had landed at Mobile. When it retreated, he pursued it to Pensacola, then a Spanish possession, and on 7 November successfully attacked the town, but before he could attack the nearby fort the British occupied, they sailed away [see War of 1812]. Fearing that New Orleans would be the next British target, he rushed there. Arriving on 2 December, he declared martial law and issued a proclamation stating in part: "The individual who refuses to defend his rights when called by his government, deserves to be a slave, and must be punished as an enemy of his country and friend to his foe."

The British had indeed planned an attack, using an unguarded waterway leading to the town, and by 23 December they were within seven miles of their goal. The Battle of New Orleans [q.v.], a British disaster that made Jackson a national hero, was fought on 8 January 1815. Neither the Americans nor the British knew that on 24 December 1814 the Treaty of Ghent had been signed, ending the war. With the peace, civil law was restored in New Orleans, and a local judge who had opposed the imposition of martial law fined Jackson a thousand dollars for contempt of court. In 1844 Congress ordered the sum repaid with interest.

When the American army was divided into two commands, northern and southern, Jackson was given the latter with its headquarters established at his hometown, Nashville, Tennessee. In November 1817 the Seminole Indians in Florida were provoked into attacking an army boat on the Apalachicola River, and the following month Secretary of War John C. Calhoun [q.v.] declared war [see Seminole War, First].

In March 1818 Jackson invaded Florida. He captured St. Mark's, a Spanish town in northwestern Florida, 20 miles south-southeast of Tallahassee, near the mouth of the St. Mark's River on Apalachee Bay. He then marched east toward a large Seminole community on the Swannee River, burning all the Indian villages in his path and hanging several Seminole leaders. After destroying his objective, he marched back to St. Mark's and hanged two British subjects, Alexander Arbuthnot and Robert Ambrister, whom he accused of inciting the Indians, an execution that provoked an outcry in Britain [see Arbuthnot and Ambrister Affair]. From St. Mark's he moved on Pensacola, which he captured on 24 May.

In 1821 Spain ceded Florida to the United States. In the same year Congress reduced the size of the army, making it imperative that either Jackson or Jacob Jennings Brown [q.v.] be demoted. Both were popular and powerful generals. President James Monroe (1758–1831) solved the problem by persuading Jackson to resign his commission in June and serve as governor of Florida. However, in October Jackson gave up his governorship and returned to Tennessee.

In 1824 he ran unsuccessfully for the presidency. Four years later he ran again and was elected. He served two terms and became the first person to lend his name to an era of American history. An outstanding accomplishment of his administration was the complete paying off of the national debt.

Jackson, Andrew *The Creek chief Red Eagle surrenders to Andrew Jackson in Alabama, March 1814*

Jackson, Thomas J. ("Stonewall") (1824–1863). An American soldier born in what is now West Virginia and orphaned at an early age. Although he had little formal education, he was appointed to West Point and by diligent study was graduated in 1846. He distinguished himself as an artilleryman in the Mexican War, serving under Winfield Scott and winning brevets to major for his bravery. After the war he served as a lieutenant in Florida, where he quarreled with his commanding officer, Captain (later Union Major General) William French, whom he did his best to have court-martialed. In 1851, he accepted a position as a professor at the Virginia Military Institute at Lexington, Virginia, resigning his commission in February 1852. Although a poor teacher, he remained at VMI until the beginning of the American Civil War.

In 1861, when Virginia seceded from the Union, Jackson was commissioned a colonel and put in charge of the defense of Harpers Ferry. He was superseded there by General Joseph Johnston but was soon promoted brigadier general. He earned the animosity of his men, even many of his most senior officers, by pushing them through a punishing, futile midwinter campaign, but he distinguished himself in the First Battle of Bull Run and won the sobriquet of "Stonewall" when General Barnard Elliot Bee (1824–1861) called out to his troops, "There is Jackson standing like a stone wall! Rally behind the Virginians!"—or words to that effect. The name stuck, though it seems inappropriate when applied to a man who proved one of the South's most aggressive generals.

In the spring of 1862 Jackson fought his brilliant Valley Campaign [q.v.], which brought him his greatest fame, for he performed best as an independent commander. Here he proved himself a brilliant strategist, and his attack upon Front Royal and Winchester drove the Union army of Nathaniel Banks across the Potomac and out of Virginia. Although he pressed his men relentlessly, he earned their respect, for troops will endure much for those generals who provide victories.

Serving directly under General Robert E. Lee in the Army of Northern Virginia, he took part in the Seven Days' Battles, where he was less than his best, his judgment and mettle blunted by fatigue and above all by an overpowering need for sleep.

In August 1862 he advanced against Union General John Pope, capturing and destroying the Union army's principal supply depot in Virginia at Manassas and driving the Union army out of the state. He played a notable part in the Second Battle of Bull Run and defeated the Union forces at Chantilly. He commanded a corps in the invasion of Maryland, and it was he who captured some 12,000 Union troops at Harpers Ferry, a number not equalled until the Japanese capture of the American army in the Philippines in World War II.

At Antietam he ably commanded a corps on the left of the Confederate line; at Fredericksburg he held fast on the right of Lee's line. At Chancellorsville he executed a key flanking maneuver and attacked with great élan the right of the line of General Joe Hooker, resulting in one of the most remarkable victories of inferior over numerically superior forces in the history of warfare. But there on the night of 2 May 1863, while he was making a personal reconnaissance with a staff, his knot of horsemen was mistaken for enemy cavalry, and he was shot by Confederate soldiers. His shattered arm was amputated, but he died eight days later of pneumonia.

Like Lee, Jackson was a bold, aggressive soldier. Unlike most Civil War generals, he did not try to aggrandize himself

Jackson, Thomas J. *Stonewall Jackson in advance of his line of battle, Chancellorsville, Virginia*

and he was so secretive that he refused to reveal his plans even to key members of his staff, a policy that would have proved disastrous had he ever succeeded to a higher command. A stern disciplinarian, he held his officers to exacting standards, and no general North or South court-martialed or tried to cashier so many of his subordinates.

An austere man, deeply religious, he did not drink, gamble, or smoke, and his years as an artilleryman had left him partially deaf, a severe handicap to a lively social life. He was by nature a reserved man, but not a cold one. His few intimates found him a warm friend, and he was a loving, even playful husband to two wives, both of whom were the daughters of Presbyterian ministers who were college presidents.

He died at an early age, not yet forty, at the pinnacle of his reputation, which has proved enduring.

Jacob, John (1812–1858). An English soldier, educated at Addiscombe [q.v.], who entered the Bombay artillery in 1828. As commandant of the Sind Horse and political superintendent of Upper Sind he pacified the Upper Sind Frontier from 1841 to 1847. The town of Jacobabad, 200 miles north of Hyderabad in present-day Pakistan, was named for him.

Jacob's Staff. A pole that provides a firm support for a compass or other instrument. It was used by military engineers to measure heights and distances.

Jacqueminot, Jean François (1787–1865). A French soldier who served in Napoleonic armies at Austerlitz, Aspern-Essling, Wagram, Napoleon's Russian Campaign, and Waterloo [qq.v.]. In 1838 he became a lieutenant general and commanded the Paris Garde Nationale [q.v.]. In 1842 he commanded the Garde Nationale of the Seine, and his indecision at a critical moment made the 1848 Revolution possible. A variety of rose is named in his honor.

Jäger. German light infantry. Originally these were men conscripted from forest regions (the name means hunter or gamekeeper) and formed into rifle regiments.

Jäger *A battalion of Austrian Jägers at the railroad station in Vienna*

Jaghire / Jagir / Jaginder. The revenue of a district or estate in India often given as a reward to successful generals in the early nineteenth century. The holder of a jaghire was called a jaghirdar.

Jahn, Friedrich Ludwig (1778–1852). A German pedagogue and soldier often called *Turnvater* (father of gymnastics). A student of theology and philosophy, he joined the Prussian army in 1808 after the Battle of Jena [q.v.]. He believed it was possible to restore German morale, crushed by the defeats inflicted by Napoleon, by the physical and moral vigor gained through exercise. In 1811 he opened the first open-air gymnasium (*Turnplatz*) in Berlin. At Breslau in 1813 he raised a battalion of volunteers, which he commanded. He was often involved in espionage, the exact nature of which is unknown. After the peace of 1815 he wrote *Die Deutsch Turnkunst* (German gymnastic skills) (1816). He became one of the founders of the patriotic fraternities (*Burschenschaften*) that were hostile to the existing order, and he was imprisoned for a time. In 1840 he was awarded the Iron Cross for his service in the Napoleonic Wars [q.v.].

Jalalabad, Siege of (November 1841–April 1842), First Afghan War. At this frontier town in eastern Afghanistan west of the Khyber Pass, 70 miles east of Kabul and 80 miles west of Peshawar, Brigadier General Robert Sale [q.v.] with 2,000 men, including the 13th Foot, was besieged by 6,000 Afghans under Akbar Khan [q.v.], a son of Dost Muhammad.

On 13 January 1842 Dr. William Brydon [q.v.], wounded and exhausted, appeared at Jalalabad, the sole European to survive the march from Kabul undertaken when the British garrison there was withdrawn. On 23 January Sale learned that troops sent from India to his relief had been forced back, the Khyber Pass closed, and the fort of Ali Musjid abandoned. On 19 February a severe earthquake destroyed all the fortifications Sale and his men had been able to construct. On 28 February and again on 2 and 4 March Afghans led by Akbar Khan attacked the town and were repulsed. The garrison made several successful sallies on 1 and 24 March and on 1 April, when they captured a flock of 500 sheep. On 7 April Sale made a full-scale attack, driving the Afghans from their entrenchments and capturing several guns, ammunition, horses, and supplies of all kinds. The Afghans then drew off. On 16 April Jalalabad was completely relieved by a British force under General George Pollock [q.v.] that had forced the Khyber Pass. After destroying the town's fortifications, Pollock brought out what Lord Ellenborough (1790–1871), governor-general of India, called "that illustrious garrison."

The 13th Foot (later the Somersetshire Light Infantry) added the name Jellalabad, (so spelled) to its regimental crest. Sale was ever after known as Fighting Bob.

Jamaican Revolts (1831 and 1864). When the British abolished the slave trade in 1807, there were 319,351 slaves in Jamaica. In 1831 many of them, thinking they had been emancipated, revolted. A number of Europeans were killed and much property was destroyed before they were pacified.

All slaves were emancipated in 1833, but most continued to live in poverty. On 11 October 1864 former slaves in the Morant Bay area (southeast Jamaica), unemployed in a depressed economy, rose in revolt. The courthouse was burned; at least 20 Europeans, including the chief magistrate of the parish were killed; and atrocities were committed against whites throughout the area. On 12 October martial law was imposed by the British governor, Edward John Eyre (1815–1901). Mustering all available force, he crushed the rebellion in eleven days. By his orders 450 rebels were executed, and some 600, including some women, were flogged; 1,000 houses belonging to rebels were burned. Eyre's actions were applauded in the West Indies, but they occasioned a public outcry in Britain, and in 1866 he was removed. Representative government was not restored until 1884.

Jamaican Revolts *Jamaican rebels attack the courthouse at Morant Bay, October 1864.*

Jambiya. A short, thick, curved Arabian dagger with a rib down the middle used in the Ottoman Empire, Persia, India, and elsewhere.

James, Army of the. A Union army of two army corps and a cavalry division organized in April 1864, during the American Civil War, to operate against Richmond from south of the James River while the Army of the Potomac [q.v.] attacked Confederate forces under Robert E. Lee from the north. After the failure of the first assaults at Petersburg [q.v.], the corps commanders, William Farrar Smith [q.v.] and Quincy Adams Gillmore (1825–1888), were replaced by David Bell Birney and Edward Otho Ord [qq.v.]. In August the army consisted of 17,000 infantry and 2,300 cavalry.

Jameson, Leander Starr (1853–1917). A Scottish physician, administrator, and statesman in South Africa. He was a close friend of Cecil Rhodes (1853–1902), and in 1889 and 1890 he undertook three missions for Rhodes to Lobengula [q.v.], king of the Matabeles, confirming the concessions of the British South Africa Company. In 1891 he was appointed administrator of Mashonaland (which became part of Rhodesia), and it was under his administration that the Matabele War [q.v.] of 1893 erupted, for the British took exception to the traditional raiding of the Mashonas by the Matabeles.

In December 1895 he led the famous (or infamous) Jameson Raid [q.v.] into the Transvaal in an effort to spark an uprising among foreigners, mostly miners and mineowners, against the Boer government in Johannesburg. In a sharp fight on 2 January 1896 he was captured by the Boers and turned over to the British, who sent him to England to be tried. In

July he was sentenced to fifteen months in prison, but he was released in December. He returned to South Africa and during the Second Anglo-Boer War was among the besieged at Ladysmith [q.v.] but took no active part in its defense. In 1900 he was elected to the Cape Colony Parliament and finally became prime minister of Cape Colony (1904–08). In 1911 he was made a baronet.

Jameson Raid (29 December 1895–2 January 1896). The foreign miners and speculators, called *uitlanders,* in Johannesburg, Republic of South Africa (popularly called the Transvaal), planned a revolt against the Boer government to begin on 28 December 1895. Their sympathizer, Cecil Rhodes (1853–1902), prime minister of Cape Colony and director of the British South Africa Company, shipped rifles and ammunition to them and posted his friend Dr. Leander Starr Jameson [q.v.], administrator of Rhodesia, at Pitsani Potluko, a small Bechuanaland (Botswana) town on the Transvaal border. With 511 mounted company police and volunteers, 150 African drivers, and three guns, he was to rush to Johannesburg as soon as the uprising began. However, the uitlanders never screwed their courage to the point of actually revolting, and on 29 December Jameson, tired of waiting and without Rhodes's permission, crossed the frontier and raced for Johannesburg.

He was intercepted on 2 January 1896 by a Boer commando under Piet Cronjé [q.v.] at Doornkop, near Krugersdorp, 20 miles west of Johannesburg, and in a short, sharp battle was forced to capitulate. He and his surviving raiders were turned over to the British, and Jameson was tried in England. On 20 July 1896 he was sentenced to fifteen months in prison. Rhodes, who accepted full responsibility, resigned as prime minister. Many in Britain sympathized with Rhodes, Jameson, and the uitlanders, and all Britain was incensed when the German kaiser William II (1859–1941) sent a telegram to President Paul Kruger (1840–1926) congratulating him on repelling the invaders "without having to appeal to friendly powers for assistance" [see Kruger Telegram].

James River Bridge. On 16 June 1864, during the Petersburg Campaign [q.v.] in the American Civil War, in order to facilitate the movement of the Army of the Potomac [q.v.] south to attack Petersburg, Union forces built a pontoon bridge between Wyanoke Landing on the north side of the James River in eastern Virginia and Fort Powhatan on its south side. It is believed to have been the longest continuous pontoon bridge ever built in any war. The James at this point was then 2,100 feet wide and 15 fathoms deep in midstream, with a strong tidal current. Working from both banks of the river under the supervision of Captain George Henry Mendell (1846?–1902), 450 men used 101 pontoons with three schooners, anchored in the deepest water in the middle of the stream, to complete the construction of the bridge, in eight hours, not counting the time necessary to prepare the approaches. The Union army completed its crossing at 7:00 P.M. on 18 June, and the bridge was then broken down to construct three rafts that were floated downriver that night to City Point (then a village, now part of Hopewell, Virginia).

Janbiyya. The general name for a variety of Moroccan daggers.

Jangees or Janghers. Short drawers worn by sepoys in the eighteenth and early nineteenth centuries.

Janissary. A soldier of an elite corps of Turkish troops formed as a select bodyguard in the fourteenth century by Sultan Orkhan, the Ottoman ruler who reigned from 1326 to 1359 or 1360. With members drawn from Christian prisoners of war, slaves, and young soldiers from the European part of the Ottoman Empire, it became the first regular infantry ever maintained in constant employment by any European ruler. Over the years the corps became politically as well as militarily powerful until, as Edward Gibbon (1737–1794) wrote, "even the Turks themselves were excluded from all civil and military honours; and a servile class, an artificial people, was raised by the discipline of education to obey, to conquer, and to command."

Janissaries were not allowed to marry or grow beards, but they were known for their "cruel and furious mustaches," as well as for their brightly colored uniforms and white felt brimless hats. Their military ranks were peculiar, all being based upon culinary terms. Their commander was the *chorbaji-bashi*, or head cook; the second-in-command was the *asci-bashi*, or head soup distributor. On parade each unit (*orta*) carried a soup cauldron. An *orta* that lost its cauldron in battle was so disgraced that it was no longer allowed to parade in public.

The janissaries were followers of an Islamic sect known as Bektasi, an order of Dervish mystics that held relaxed views of some Islamic sins. They drank wine and associated freely with women. They considered themselves soldiers of Allah but refused to fight except in defense of their interests. They frequently ignored their officers. Not only was their independence tolerated, but some rose to high positions, even becoming provincial satraps.

In the nineteenth century they grew ever more turbulent and lawless. A revolt in Serbia in 1804–05 was largely against the misrule of a local janissary. In 1806 in Constantinople (Istanbul) the janissaries attacked the grand vizier's house and, after destroying it, marched on the sultan's palace. They were stopped only when shelled by artillery that killed 600.

Six sultans were dethroned or murdered by janissaries. In 1807, when Sultan Selim III (1761–1807) attempted to replace them with a modern army and improve the administration of the government, they killed him and installed Mustafa IV as sultan. Mustafa Bairakdar (1755–1808), pasha of Rustchuk, marched on the city, occupied the palace, deposed Mustafa, executed the assassins of Selim, and installed on the throne Mustafa IV's brother Mahmud II. Demanding the restoration of Mustafa, janissaries stormed the palace. When defense was hopeless, Bairakdar garroted Mustafa with a bowstring, threw his head to his enemies, then blew himself up.

As their military prowess declined, the janissaries became more political. In the words of Stratford Canning (1786–1880), British minister to Turkey, they were "the masters of government, the butchers of their sovereigns and a source of terror to all but the enemies of their country."

In 1825 Sultan Mahmud II (1785–1839) formed the *eshkenjisa* (singular: *eshkenji* [q.v.]), a military unit of well-drilled, disciplined troops organized along European lines and dressed in Western-type uniforms. The following year, when

he moved to organize the janissaries in the same fashion, they revolted, an event for which Mahmud had prepared. In early June janissaries began to collect at the Et Meidan Square in Constantinople, the center of the district they inhabited, bringing with them their cooking pots, which they upturned as a sign that they would no longer accept the sultan's rations or his authority. When they began to pillage and rob, the sultan deployed his *eshkenjisa* and surrounded the square. The sacred standard of the Prophet was unfurled, and the janissaries were offered and refused a last chance to surrender. On 15 June 1826, a date known in Turkish history as the Auspicious Incident [q.v.], they were mowed down by muskets and cannon. No quarter was given; those who surrendered were butchered. Turkish mobs joined the fray, and into the following day the janissaries were hunted through the streets and slaughtered, their corpses thrown into the Bosphorus. Estimates of the number killed range from 6,000 to 20,000. Their barracks was burned, and a proclamation of 17 June 1826 declared the force forever dissolved and the name janissary banned.

Janissary *Officer of the Turkish janissaries, 1826*

Janssens, Jan Willem (1762–1838). A Dutch soldier and colonial administrator who in 1802 was appointed governor at the Cape of Good Hope after the cape was returned to Holland by the British under the Treaty of Amiens [q.v.]. When the war resumed, the British landed an expeditionary force, and Janssens was defeated in the Battle of Blaauwberg [q.v.]. He later served as governor of the Dutch East Indies, where he was again defeated by the British in 1811 [see Java War].

Japanese Army. In the nineteenth century prior to the Meiji Restoration [q.v.], Japan had no national army. Private armies of samurai [q.v.] operated under some 250 daimyos [q.v.], each of whom ruled over his own few square miles and swore allegiance to the Tokugawa shogun. The myth was preserved that he ruled on behalf of the emperor, who was in fact a virtual prisoner at Kyoto, then the capital.

For the first half of the nineteenth century the sword and the bow and arrow remained the principal weapon, "bow and arrow" and "war" being synonymous in Japanese. The governor of Nagasaki, Takashima Shuhan, purchased through Dutch sources some small arms and field guns and, having trained men in Western drill and musketry, demonstrated their military skills at Yedo (Tokyo) to senior conservative officials. He was thrown in prison for his pains.

In mid-century the Tokugawa shogun Iyesada (1824–1858) attempted to form a more modern army with cavalry, infantry, and artillery. He organized 13,600 men into three divisions of all arms, but most remained equipped with old muskets and swords, and only about a quarter of the infantry were given rifles and light infantry training by a French military mission. Many of the samurai refused to exchange their swords for firearms.

After the Boshin Civil War [q.v.] in 1868–69 and the Meiji Restoration, which returned power to the emperor, Japan began to create a truly modern army (Dai Nippon Teikoku Rikugan) based upon European models. General Taro Katsura [q.v.], who made a methodical study of European armies, was particularly impressed by the Prussian army. Nearly 100,000 rifles were imported, many of them leftovers from the American Civil War, but a considerable number were British-made weapons bought through Jardine, Matheson & Company in Hong Kong.

An imperial army was formed in 1871, and four (later six) garrisons were strategically stationed to weaken the power of the daimyos, many of whom retained their private armies of samurai. In 1872 conscription, including men from non-samurai classes, was introduced, ending the samurai's unique

place in Japanese society. Many samurai refused to stand in ranks with peasants and clerks or to take orders from plebeian officers. That same year a second French military mission arrived, and in 1873 the Toyama military school was established to train noncommissioned officers. In 1875, after the Japanese invasion of Formosa [q.v.], a military academy modeled after St. Cyr [q.v.] was founded.

In 1876 the samurai lost their right to wear swords, and in 1877 Saigo Takamori [q.v.] led an unsuccessful samurai revolt [see Satsuma Rebellion]. In August 1878 members of the elite Imperial Guard [q.v.], who believed themselves inadequately rewarded for their services in the Satsuma Rebellion, mounted a mutiny that was quickly suppressed.

A general staff, separate from the War Ministry, was established in 1878 with Aritomo Yamagata [q.v.] as chief of staff. The emperor commanded the country's armed forces [see Gunsei; Gunrei; Imperial Rescript to Soldiers and Sailors], but only on the advice of the chief of staff and senior officers, who were accountable to no one. In 1879 service in the reserves was extended from four to seven years. Japan then maintained an army of about 200,000, or 100 per 100,000 inhabitants.

In 1880 Japan began the manufacture of the first Japanese rifle, a design of Major Tsuneyoshi Murata (1838–1921), after whom the single-shot rifle was named [see Murata Rifle]. In 1882 the 8 mm Type 20, 47.5 inches long and weighing 8.68 pounds, was adopted. This was the standard infantry rifle used in the Sino-Japanese War [q.v.] of 1894. In 1897 the Meiji rifle [q.v.], with an overall length of 49 inches and weighing 8.25 pounds, was adopted.

Most of Japan's artillery was imported, and most guns were manufactured by Krupp until the first arsenal to build modern artillery weapons was established at Osaka in 1882. From it came the first Japanese breechloaders. A staff college was founded in 1887 with Gentaro Kodama [q.v.] as commandant, and an army service corps was created in 1888. A German military mission introduced German methods.

In 1890 the new army flexed its muscles. When Japan's first

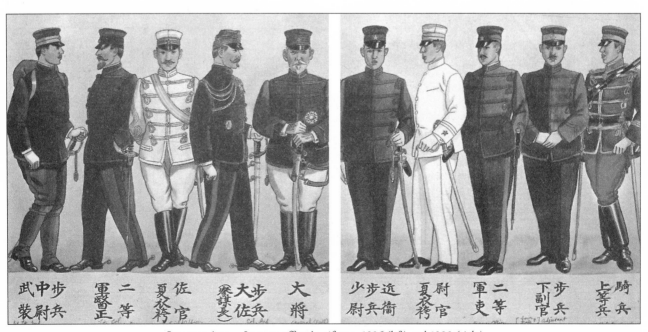

Japanese Army *Japanese officers' uniforms, 1886 (left) and 1890 (right)*

Diet rejected the military budget, it was quickly dissolved. In the spring of that year the army went on display in grand maneuvers at Nagoya. European observers were impressed. The following year all military strongpoints were connected by railways. The Sino-Japanese War [q.v.] of 1894 marked the beginning of Japan's entry onto the world stage as an imperial power.

In 1896 Japan adopted a ten-year plan to increase the size of its army from 200,000 to 600,000, and the period of conscription was extended to twelve years and four months of active and reserve service.

In its final act of the nineteenth century the army fought in concert with American and European troops during the Boxer Rebellion [q.v.] in China. The Japanese army entered the twentieth century with an excellent infrastructure founded on Western principles.

Japanese Blades. Japanese sword and knife blades were manufactured in identical fashion and in identical shape, but in different lengths. The most characteristic lengths were Jin Tachi, 33 inches or longer; Katana and Tachi, 24 to 30 inches long; Chisa Katanga, 18 to 24 inches; Wakizashi, 16 to 20 inches; Tanto and Aikuchi, 11 to 16 inches; Yori and Toshi, 9 to 12 inches; and Kwaiken, 3 to 6 inches.

Japanese-Korean War. See Korean-Japanese War.

Japanese Rifle. See Murata Rifle.

Jasoos. Name for a spy in India.

Java Uprising (1825–29). When Java was returned to the Dutch in 1816, they faced a rebellious people. An uprising beginning in 1825 led by Dippa Negara (or Dipo Negoro [1785?–1855]), the eldest son of the third ruler of Jogjakarta, coincided with the revolt in Europe of the Belgians against Dutch rule [see Belgian Revolution]. Dippa carried out aggressive guerrilla operations until 1828, when the Dutch began to establish strongholds about the country, connecting them with good roads over which flying columns of troops could operate. In 1829 two of Dippa's top aides deserted him, and he agreed to negotiate with the Dutch. In spite of a promise of safe conduct, he was seized and deported to the Celebes. The uprising had been bloody, and the Dutch lost some 15,000 soldiers. This rebellion is sometimes referred to as the Great Java War or the Dippa Negara War.

Java War (1811–12). In 1808 the Dutch completed their conquest of Java. To protect it from the British during the Napoleonic Wars [q.v.], Herman Willem Daendels [q.v.], governor-general of the Dutch East Indies, fortified the island. Nevertheless, after Sir Gilbert Elliot-Murray-Kynynmound, later the first Earl of Minto (1751–1814), captured the French islands of Bourbon (Réunion) and Mauritius in the Indian Ocean and the Dutch East Indian possessions of the Amboina (Ambon) and the Molucca Islands, a British expeditionary force of 5,344 European troops and 5,777 Indian sepoys under Major General Samuel Auchmuty [q.v.] in 57 transports, escorted by 33 warships under Rear Admiral Robert Stoppford (1768–1847), set sail for the island. It arrived at Batavia, the capital of the Dutch East Indies, on the northwest coast of Java, on 4 August 1811, and the invasion force under Colonel Rollo Gillespie [q.v.] landed at Chillingcherry, 10 miles east of the town. Five days later the British occupied Batavia unopposed. The Dutch force of 16,500 Dutch and Javanese plus 500 French voltigeurs, all under the command of General Jan Willem Janssens [q.v.], retreated 7 miles south of Batavia to a well-fortified position with 280 guns at Fort Cornelis protected by a strong outpost at Weltewreeden just in front of the fort's main fortifications. On 11 August the French-Dutch force at Weltewreeden was driven out with a loss of 500. Heavy guns and mortars were brought up from the ships, and a bombardment of Fort Cornelis was begun on 24 August. By this time sickness had reduced the Dutch defenders to about 14,000 and the British to about 8,000. When a Dutch deserter showed the British an opening on the Dutch flank, a dawn assault on 26 August led by the intrepid Gillespie collapsed the Dutch line. Lord Minto, who witnessed the attack, wrote: "The slaughter was dreadful, both during the attack and in the pursuit. . . . We have upwards of 5,000 prisoners, including all the Europeans left alive. . . . There never was such a rout."

The Dutch lost some 4,000 killed and 5,500 surrendered. Janssens retreated with about 800 to Samarang (Semarang) on the north coast of Java, 225 miles east of Batavia. British battle losses for the campaign were 865 killed and wounded.

On 10 September 1812 the British occupied Samarang without loss, and on 18 September Janssens formally surrendered. The Dutch ceded to the British not only Java but Timor, Palembang in Sumatra, and Macassar (Makasar) in the Celebes. Thomas Stamford Raffles (1781–1826) was appointed lieutenant governor of Java, a position he held until 1816.

Although the Dutch had been subdued, the Indonesian princes remained hostile. On Sumatra the sultan of Palembang ordered the killing of all Europeans. In response, in March 1812, Colonel Gillespie took a force to Palembang and, after deposing the sultan, placed the sultan's brother on the throne and secured cession of the island of Banca to the British. When a confederation of Javanese chiefs built a strong stockade equipped with 100 guns manned by 30,000 men at Djokjokarta (Djakarta), Gillespie successfully assaulted it with 1,500 men.

In 1816, at the end of the Napoleonic Wars, all the islands were returned to the Dutch.

Jawan. Literally, youth or youngster. A soldier in the Indian army. The name began to replace sepoy [q.v.] informally in the late nineteenth century. It was roughly the equivalent to the French *poilu* or the American "doughboy."

Jawra Alipur, Battle of (20 June 1858), Indian Mutiny. After the defeat of the rebel force under Tantia Topi [q.v.] by Sir John Rose [q.v.] on 16 June at Morar [q.v.], Tantia Topi and the remnants of his army were pursued by 800 British under General Charles Napier [q.v.], who caught up with 4,000 near this town 60 miles west-southwest of Bhopal. He immediately attacked with his entire force. After a brief resistance Tantia Topi and his force fled after losing 400 men, 25 guns, and all stores, elephants, and ammunition.

Jayhawker. The name given to American antislavery guerrilla fighters active in Kansas and Missouri during the Bloody Kansas period in the 1850s. They fought the proslavery Border Ruffians [q.v.]. During the American Civil War many became Union guerrillas. Dan Anthony, the brother of women's suffrage advocate Susan Brownell Anthony (1820–1906), was also a Jayhawker.

Jelačić od Bužima, Josef (Josip) (1801–1859). A Croatian soldier and statesman who entered the Austrian army in 1819 and saw service in Bosnia in 1845. On 19 March 1848 he was appointed ban of Croatia and promoted lieutenant general. Ambitious to disassociate Croatia from Hungary, he promoted the separatist movement in the Croatian diet. On 11 September 1848 he led his troops across the Drava (or Grave or Brau in German) River and attacked Hungarian forces rebelling against Austrian rule [see Hungarian Revolution of 1848]. In 1855 he was created a count and placed in command of the expedition against Montenegro.

Jehad. See Jihad.

Jelalabad. See Jalalabad, Siege of.

Jemadar. The lowest-ranking Indian officer in the Indian army [q.v.].

Jena, Battle of (14 October 1806), Napoleonic Wars. Near the towns of Jena and Auerstädt on the banks of the Saale River, 25 miles east of Erfurt, Napoleon, pressing north on a 30-mile front to sever the Prussian communications with Berlin, met the Prussian and Saxon armies under the overall command of Karl Wilhelm Ferdinand, the duke of Brunswick [q.v.]. Near Jena, Napoleon with 54,000 men and 70 guns attacked and defeated General Friedrich Ludwig, Prince of Hohenlohe (1746–1818) with 50,000 men and 120 guns, while at the same time French Marshal Louis Davout [q.v.] was defeating the main German force near Auerstädt. The defeated armies, falling back by different routes upon Weimar, were pursued by French cavalry and suffered further losses [see Auerstädt, Battle of].

The two battles are often considered one and called the Battle of Jena-Auerstädt. Prussian and Saxon casualties at Jena were about 25,000 killed, wounded, and taken prisoner. French losses were about 4,000 killed and wounded. Twenty German generals were killed, wounded, or captured. At Auerstädt the Prussians and Saxons lost 11,000 killed and wounded. Among the dead was the Duke of Brunswick.

It was at Jena that Marshal Joachim Murat [q.v.], armed with only his riding crop, led an unauthorized charge of French dragoons and Marshal Michel Ney [q.v.] ordered his troops to advance with the words "The wine is poured and we must drink it."

Napoleon's victories caused some in Britain to despair, fearing that Britain would soon be left to fight the French alone. William Wordsworth (1770–1850) lamented in "November, 1806":

Another year!—another deadly blow!
Another mighty empire overthrown!
And we are left, or shall be left, alone;
The last that dare to struggle with the foe.

Jenifer Saddle. A saddle with a flat English-style seat designed by Captain (later Confederate Colonel) Walter Hanson Jenifer (1823–1878) and patented in 1860. It was the official saddle of the Confederate army during the American Civil War and was manufactured by the firm of C. A. Farwell of Mobile, Alabama. It was also used by many Union officers.

Jenkins, Micah (1835–1864). An American soldier educated at the South Carolina Military Academy, where he was graduated at the head of his class in 1854. He was one of the founders of the King's Mountain Military School at Yorkville, South Carolina, and at the beginning of the American Civil War he was colonel of the Confederate Palmetto Sharpshooters. He fought at the Seven Days' Battles [q.v.] and was promoted brigadier general on 22 July 1862. He was severely wounded at the Second Battle of Bull Run [q.v.] but recovered in time to take part in the Battle of the Wilderness [q.v.], where on 6 May 1864 he was accidentally shot and mortally wounded by his own men while riding with James Longstreet [q.v.].

Jenneval, Pseudonym of Hippolyte Louis Alexandre Dechet (1801–1830). A French actor, poet, and soldier who in 1830 left La Comédie Française to join the Belgian patriots fighting the Dutch. There he wrote the words of "La Brabançonne," which later became the Belgian national anthem. He was killed in action near Lierre (or Lier), just south of Antwerp.

Jerez, Máximo (1818–1881). A Nicaraguan soldier and political leader. A lawyer and student of the classics, he was obsessed with the idea of unifying Central America but failed in every attempt. He fought against the forces of the American filibuster William Walker [q.v.] and later in El Salvador fought without success on the side of reformer Justo Rufino Barrios (1835–1885). In 1876, with Guatemalan support, he tried to invade Nicaragua, but his army evaporated before it fought a single battle.

Jericho Mills / Bridge / Ford, Battle of. See North Anna River, Battle of.

Jesup, Thomas Sidney (1788–1860). An American soldier who was commissioned a second lieutenant in the 7th Infantry in 1808. He was a major by the end of the War of 1812 [q.v.], and by 1818 he was a brigadier general and quartermaster general of the army. [See Battles of Chippewa, and Lundy's Lane.] In 1828 he was brevetted major general for serving ten years in grade. On 19 May 1836 he was given a field command in Alabama, where he acted against the Creeks. He then moved on to Florida to fight the Seminoles [see Second Seminole War].

After establishing a detention camp for tribesmen near Tampa, he tried to push depots ever deeper into the interior. On 2 June 1837 Osceola [q.v.], a Seminole leader, with about 200 warriors attacked the camp at Tampa and liberated about 700 of his tribesmen. In retaliation Jesup seized a group of Seminole chiefs, including Micanopy [q.v.], whom he had enticed to join him for talks, an action many Americans thought despicable. In October of the same year he assembled 900 men, the largest army ever mustered for the Seminole Wars. Undeterred, the Seminoles fell upon a column led by Jesup himself, killing 7 and wounding 31, including Jesup, whose cheek was laid open. In May 1838 he was relieved by General Zachary Taylor [q.v.]. He returned to his desk as quartermaster general in Washington, a post he held until his death.

Jetersville, Battle of. See Amelia Springs, Battle of.

Jezail. A long-barreled Asian matchlock with a smooth or rifled bore and a slender butt. It often had an A-shaped bipod fastened to a lug on the forestock. It usually took two men to man the weapon.

Jhansi, Battle of (March-April 1858), Indian Mutiny. In June 1857 mutineers and rebels seized this town and fort, 130 miles south of Agra. In March 1858 it was invested by a force under British General Sir Hugh Rose and was taken by assault on 2 April [see Jhansi, Rani of].

Jhansi, Rani of (1827?–1858). An Indian woman of a good but humble Maratha family who in 1842 married Gangadhar Rao (d.1853), the raja of Jhansi, a Maratha principality whose capital was Jhansi, a Mogul fort 142 miles south of Agra, constructed in 1613 and conquered by the Marathas in 1742. Her given name was Manakarnika, but on her marriage to her much-older groom she took the name of Lakshmibai.

Because the marriage was childless, her husband on the day before his death adopted a five-year-old boy. When the British refused to recognize the boy as his heir, the rani left purdah and began to run the little state herself with great efficiency. Nevertheless, she was expelled by the British, a deed that instilled in her a bitter hatred.

An Englishman who knew the rani just before the Indian Mutiny [q.v.] described her as "a woman of about middle size, rather stout, but not too stout. Her face must have been very handsome when she was younger, and even now it had many charms. . . . The expression also was very good and very intelligent. The eyes were particularly fine and the nose very delicately shaped."

During the mutiny the rani enjoined her people to support the mutineers, and on 12 June 1857 the 12th Bengal Native Infantry stationed at Jhansi mutinied and murdered a number of their officers. The surviving British officers and officials with their families took refuge in the fort, where they held out for several days. Promised they would be spared if they laid down their arms and left the fort, they surrendered, only to be immediately fallen upon. Some 30 men, 16 women, and 20 children were slaughtered. The rani's responsibility for this massacre is in dispute, but at the time she was given full blame.

When a neighboring raja, taking advantage of the turmoil of the mutiny, seized one of her forts and proclaimed himself maharajah of Jhansi, the rani sent her forces—10,000 local levies, 1,100 mutinous sepoys, and 400 sowars with about 35 guns—against him. She defeated him in two battles and imprisoned him at Jhansi, now converted into a military camp.

On the morning of 21 March 1858 General Sir Hugh Rose with a strong force reached Jhansi, and two days later the place was completely invested. Rose began siege operations and by 31 March had made a breach. He was preparing for an assault when that evening he received word that Tantia Topi [q.v.] with a rebel army of 22,000 was marching from the north to the relief of the town. Rose did not abandon the siege but sent a force of 1,500 to meet the advancing rebel army. They met at the Betwa River [q.v.] on 1 April, and the rebels were defeated and forced to retreat. British losses were 15 killed and 66 wounded, 4 mortally.

On 3 April Jhansi was successfully assaulted, but the rani escaped. She reached Kalpi, 45 miles west of Cawnpore and 100 miles from Jhansi on the fifth. There she persuaded Tantia Topi to advance with his army to meet the British, who were marching on the town. The armies met near the village of Kunch, 45 miles south of Kalpi, on 7 May, an exceptionally hot day on which the thermometer registered 115° F in the shade. Sunstroke and heat exhaustion felled soldiers on both sides. The rebels were routed and fled back to Kalpi, losing some 500 in the battle and in the British pursuit. On 22 May Rose captured Kalpi for a loss of 24 killed and 43 wounded.

Following the rani's advice, Tantia Topi advanced upon Gwalior, one of the most formidable fortresses in India, 60 miles south of Agra. The peshwa of Gwalior, loyal to the British, marched out to fight, but his troops deserted him, thus presenting to the rebels and mutineers what became known as the Gwalior Contingent [q.v.], a British-trained force that was among the most formidable the British had to face.

General Rose, reinforced, marched upon Gwalior with a siege train, and on 17 June he soundly defeated the rebels, who had sallied out to meet him. In the course of the battle the rani, dressed as a cavalry leader, was killed. Accounts of her death varied, but it was probably at the hand of a trooper of the 8th Hussars in a cavalry charge.

Jibbah / Jibbeh. A long cloth robe with long, wide sleeves worn by Muslims in Egypt and the Sudan. Randomly patched in various colors, it became the uniform of the Mahdist Dervishes [see Mahdiya]. Later Dervish robes came to be elaborately decorated with colored squares.

Jičín / Gitschin, Battle of (29–30 June 1866), Seven Weeks' War. Prince Frederick Charles [q.v.] with 16,000 Prussians defeated 30,000 Saxons and Austrians under General Count Eduard von Clam-Gallas [q.v.] near the northeast Bohemian walled town of Jičín (German: Gitschin). The Austrians lost 184 officers and 4,714 other ranks killed and wounded; the Saxons lost 27 officers and 586 other ranks killed and wounded. The Prussians lost 71 officers and 1,482 other ranks. Among the wounded Prussian officers was Lieutenant General Ludwig Karl von Tümpling, who received a congratulatory telegram from Prince Frederick Charles: "It is fine when a Prussian general bleeds. It brings the army luck." General von Tümpling's reaction to this stroke of luck is unrecorded.

Jiddah Revolt (1855–56). When the firman from the sultan of Turkey banning the slave trade was read at the Red Sea port of Jidda (Jedda or Gedda), 45 miles west of Mecca (Makkah), the people rose in a revolt that spread until the entire Hejaz was in rebellion. The insurrection was quelled only by a cholera epidemic in 1856.

Jihad / Jehad. An Islamic holy war against those considered infidels. The Koran (ii, 214–15; viii, 39–42; ix, 5–6, 29) declares it to be a religious duty to wage war on those who do not accept the tenets of Islam. However, Yasir Arafat (1929–) has defined it as "the reconstruction of mankind."

Jim Boy (1790?–1851). A Creek Indian chief, also known as High Head Jim or Tustenaggee Emathia, who commanded the Creeks in the Battle of Burnt Corn [q.v.] on 27 July 1813, the battle that began the Creek War of 1813–14. He may also have taken part in the Fort Mims Massacre [q.v.]. In 1818 he fought in the First Seminole War [q.v.], serving in the U.S. army under William McIntosh [q.v.]. In 1835, during the Second Seminole War [q.v.], at the request of Major General Thomas Jesup [q.v.], he raised a regiment of Creeks. He fought in the Second Battle of Wahoo Swamp [q.v.] on 17–21 November 1836 and in the Battle of Lake Monroe on 8 February 1837.

Although General Jesup, had promised him that his family and possessions would be protected in his absence, Jim Boy returned home to find that his family had been transported to Indian Territory and all his possessions destroyed. Four of his 9 children were among those killed when the emigration ship *Monmouth* sank, drowning 236 Creeks.

Jingasa. A low-crowned Japanese war helmet of wood or metal, padded on the inside. Padded flaps hung down at the sides.

Jingling Johnny. See Chapeau Chinois.

Jingo. A British patriot eager for war. This word for aggressive patriotism came from a music hall song introduced on the London stage by a singer billed as the Great McDermott during the Russo-Turkish War [q.v.] of 1878. Its refrain was:

We don't want to fight, but, by jingo if we do,
We've got the ships, we've got the men, we've got
    the money too.

Jirón, Battle of. See Tarqui, Battle of.

Jitgurgh, Battle of (14 January 1815), Nepalese War. Near this village in southern Nepal British Major General John S. Wood (1770?–1851) with three guns and 4,500 troops, 400 of whom were Europeans, marching to attack a stockade, was led by a treacherous guide into an ambush manned by 1,200 Gurkhas under Umur Singh Thapa (d. 1816). Wood was forced to retreat.

Jochmus, August Giacomo, Baron von Cotignola (1808–1881). A German general and soldier of fortune who served as a general in the British Foreign Legion during the Carlist War [q.v.] of 1835–38. He was chief of staff of the combined British, Austrian, and Turkish forces in Syria in 1840–41. In 1848 he served briefly in the Turkish War Ministry, then returned to Germany. In 1849 he was minister of foreign affairs and of the navy. In 1859 he was promoted field marshal.

Joffre, Joseph (1852–1931). A French officer whose studies at the École Polytechnique were interrupted by the Franco-Prussian War [q.v.], during which he took part in the defense of Paris. He served in the Far East, participating in the French occupation of Formosa in the Sino-French War [q.v.] in 1885. For three years he was chief of engineers at Hanoi in Indochina. In 1892 he was posted to Senegal to build a railroad from Kayes to Bafoulabe. On 27 December 1893 Joffe, now a major, began a memorable march of 500 miles from Ségou over difficult terrain to fabled Timbuktu (today in Mali),

arriving on 12 February 1894. A few years later he was sent to Madagascar [q.v.] to serve as fortifications officer under General Joseph Gallieni [q.v.]. There he established the French base at Diégo-Suarez. Posted back to France, he was assigned to a railroad regiment.

He was promoted a general of brigade in 1900 and a general of division in 1905. In 1911, at the age of only fifty-nine, he became the designate wartime commander-in-chief. It was Joffre who designed the disastrous Plan XVII, completed in April 1913, that failed so miserably in August 1914.

Johanne, Yohannes, or John IV (1839–1889). Abyssinian soldier and king. He was ruler of the province of Tigre when he assisted the British under Robert Napier [q.v.] by providing supplies during the Abyssinian War [q.v.] of 1868. By 1872 he ruled all Abyssinia and was crowned king of kings at the religious center at Aksum (Axum) in Tigre Province, 12 miles west-southwest of Adowa (Aduwa).

When war broke out with Egypt in 1875 [see Abyssinian-Egyptian Wars], he lured two Egyptian armies into the highlands of Eritrea and defeated them at Gundet on 13 November 1875 and at Gura on 25 March 1876 [qq.v.]. In 1879 General Charles ("Chinese") Gordon [q.v.] negotiated a peace treaty for Egypt with Johannes, who in 1884 agreed to assist in the withdrawal of the Egyptian garrisons in the Sudan along the Abyssinian-Sudan frontier where Mahdist power was growing [see Mahdiya]. The withdrawal was only partially successful.

Johannes was killed by a chance shot in the Battle of Gallabat [q.v.] just as he seemed to be on the point of winning.

John, Archduke, Johann Baptiste Joseph Fabian Sebastian (1782–1859). An Austrian soldier who, although not yet nineteen years old, commanded the Austrian army in Bavaria in 1800, during the Napoleonic Wars [q.v.], and was defeated by Jean Moreau [q.v.] at Hohenlinden [q.v.] on 3 December. In 1805 he commanded the Austrian army in the Tyrol but was pushed back by the Bavarians. In 1809 he encouraged the rising in the Tyrol [see Tyrolean Revolt] led by Andreas Hofer [q.v.]. He was defeated in the Battle of Raab [q.v.] in Hungary on 14 June 1809. In January 1815 he again contacted Tyrolean dissidents and attempted to foster a national uprising, a move which led to his being placed under house arrest by Klemens von Metternich (1773–1859), the Austrian foreign minister. After the campaign on the Rhine in 1815 he returned to private life. He was chosen regent of the Austrian-Hungarian Empire in 1848 by the German National Assembly.

John Brown's Raid (17–18 October 1859). John Brown [q.v.], an American abolitionist fanatic, believed himself to be God's chosen instrument to abolish slavery. After killing unarmed proslavery settlers in Kansas [see Border War], he concocted a plot to capture and hold the U.S. arsenal at Harpers Ferry, Virginia (now West Virginia), believing that if he did so, Virginia slaves would rise up against their masters and join his "army." On the night of 17 October 1859 Brown, with 21 followers, seized the undefended arsenal without difficulty after mortally wounding a Baltimore & Ohio Railroad watchman, Heyward Shepherd, a free black who attempted to sound a warning. A number of white hostages were taken.

On the morning of the 18th an exchange of fire with Virginia militia resulted in a few casualties. Not a single slave joined Brown, and he and his surviving men were forced to flee for shelter to a brick firehouse. When Colonel Robert E. Lee, aided by Lieutenant J. E. B. Stuart [q.v.], arrived by railroad from Washington with a company of marines, the firehouse was stormed. In the action several of the raiders were killed, and Brown was wounded and captured. He was tried, convicted, and on 2 December 1859 hanged at Charlestown, Virginia (now West Virginia).

John Company. Colloquial name for the Honourable East India Company.

John Drew's Regiment of Mounted Rifles. A Confederate regiment raised during the American Civil War from Cherokee Indians loyal to John Ross [q.v.] and led by John Drew, Ross's nephew by marriage. In March 1862 the regiment fought in the Battle of Pea Ridge [q.v.] in Arkansas, in which some Union soldiers were scalped, provoking an outcry against the use of Indians [see Indian Soldiers, American]. Drew's men signed up for one-year enlistments, but few served that long. Many were members of a secret pro-Union and antislavery society called Keetoowahs, and desertions were so high that the regiment was effectively disbanded in 1862 [see Watie Regiment]. It was the only Confederate regiment to lose almost its entire complement through desertions.

Johnnycake. An American flat corn cake usually baked on a griddle or on hot stones.

Johnny Newcombe. A British soldier colloquialism used during the Napoleonic era for a new soldier.

Johnny Shiloh. See Drummer Boy of Chickamauga.

Johnson, Bradley Tyler (1829–1903). An American soldier and politician who was graduated from Princeton University and during the American Civil War was commissioned a major in the 1st Maryland Regiment of the Confederate army. He fought in Jackson's Valley Campaign and at Gaines's Mill [qq.v.] and he commanded a brigade at Second Bull Run, Antietam, and the Wilderness [qq.v.]. On 28 June 1864 he became a brigadier general of cavalry under General Jubal Early [q.v.], and on 30 July, on Early's orders, he burned Chambersburg [q.v.], Pennsylvania. He fought against Union General Philip Sheridan in the Valley of Virginia until in November 1864 he was sent to Salisbury, North Carolina, to become commandant of prisons.

After the war he practiced law and served in the Maryland legislature.

Johnson, Edward (1816–1873), called "Allegheny" Johnson. An American officer who was graduated from West Point in 1838 and fought in the Second Seminole War [q.v.], on the western frontier and in the Mexican War [q.v.], during which he earned two brevets. He resigned as a captain on 10 June 1861 and joined the Confederate army as colonel of the 12th Virginia. Promoted brigadier general on 13 December, he led the small (2,500-man) but grandly named Army of the Allegheny in what is today West Virginia. On 8 May 1862 he

was severely wounded in the Battle of McDowell [q.v.]. On 28 February he was promoted major general and commanded a division in the Battle of Gettysburg [q.v.]. He fought in the Wilderness [q.v.] and in the Battle of Spotsylvania [q.v.], where he was captured at the Bloody Angle [q.v.]. After being exchanged, he took part in the invasion of Tennessee under John Bell Hood [q.v.] until he was captured at Nashville. After the war he became a farmer.

Johnson, Richard Mentor (1780–1850). An American soldier and politician who during the War of 1812 [q.v.] raised a regiment of mounted riflemen and in the summer of 1813 joined the army of William Henry Harrison [q.v.] in northern Ohio. In the Battle of the Thames [q.v.] on 8 October 1813, in which he was severely wounded, he led the charge that carried the day for the Americans, and he was credited by some as having personally killed Chief Tecumseh [q.v.].

In the 1836 presidential elections he was the running mate of Martin Van Buren (1782–1862), who became the eighth president of the United States. For the first time in American history there was no clear majority among the four candidates for the vice presidency. Johnson was elected by the Senate.

Johnson's Island. During the American Civil War this 300-acre island in Sandusky Bay at the western end of Lake Erie, a mile from the mainland and two and a half miles from Sandusky, Ohio, was leased to the government for $500 per year as a Union prison camp. Two-story barracks buildings were built inside an enclosure of about 16 acres surrounded by a high fence, and the 128th Ohio Volunteer Battalion, commanded by a former mayor of Sandusky, was formed to provide guards. The first prisoners, a group of officers and enlisted men, arrived on 10 April 1862. The enlisted men were soon transferred to Camp Chase outside Columbus, Ohio, and the prison camp thereafter held only officer prisoners.

There were several escapes. On one bitter cold night three prisoners crossed the ice to the mainland. In 1863 a Confederate captain escaped and managed to reach Canada. Using the information he supplied, the Confederates made an unsuccessful attempt to free the prisoners. Confederate naval Captain John Yates Beall [q.v.], chosen to lead the rescue, was captured, tried by a military court as a spy, and in February 1865 hanged.

More than two dozen general officers were imprisoned on the island at one time or another, as were several former congressmen and governors who had become Confederates. Designed to hold 2,500, by the end of the war it held some 3,000, but it remained a remarkably healthy prison camp by Civil War standards; only 206 prisoners died. Fishing and sometimes bathing in the lake were allowed, and reading material, including newspapers, was abundant. Assisted by the YMCA, a library of some six hundred books was on hand. A sutler [q.v.] was allowed to sell food and other items until the spring of 1864, when in retaliation for the hardships suffered by Union prisoners in Confederate prisons, the food ration was cut, and the sutler forbidden to sell edibles. In February 1865 prisoner exchanges were resumed, and the camp thinned out. The island was returned to its owner, Leonard B. Johnson, on 8 June 1866.

Johnsonville Raid, Forrest's (19 October–9 November 1864), American Civil War. On 19 October 1864

Confederate Major General Nathan B. Forrest [q.v.] led his cavalry from Corinth, Mississippi, on a twenty-three-day raid. After marching northwest through Jackson, Tennessee, to the Big Sandy River, then turning sharply east, he reached Paris Landing on the Tennessee River on 28 October. On 1 November, having captured two Federal steamers, he steamed downriver. "Forrest's cavalry afloat" seized the town of Johnsonville and set about destroying Union supplies and property. Union losses were 4 gunboats, 14 steamboats, 17 barges, 33 guns, 70,000 tons of supplies, and the capture of 150 prisoners. Forrest and his men safely reached their own lines on 9 November.

Johnston, Albert Sidney (1803–1862). An American soldier who was graduated from West Point in 1826 and first saw action in the Black Hawk War [q.v.]. In 1834 he resigned his commission and farmed in Missouri. In 1836, when his wife died, he emigrated to Texas, where he enlisted as a private in the Texan revolutionary army. Within a year he was senior brigadier general and commander-in-chief [see Texas War of Independence]. He was seriously wounded in a duel with Samuel Houston [q.v.] but served from 1838 to 1840 as secretary of war for the Republic of Texas. This was not a desk job, for in 1839 he led an expedition against the Cherokee Indians in East Texas. After Texas became a state in 1845, he served as a colonel of the 1st Texas Rifles in the Mexican War [q.v.] and fought at Monterrey. In 1849 he rejoined the American army and was soon colonel of the 2nd Cavalry. In 1858–60 he commanded the Utah Expedition [q.v.] and was brevetted brigadier general for his services.

On 10 April 1861, at the start of the Civil War, he resigned his commission, rejecting an offer of a command second only to Winfield Scott [q.v.], and joined the Confederate army as a full general. Given command of all Confederate forces west of the Allegheny Mountains, he concentrated an army at Corinth, Mississippi, and on 6 April 1862 he nearly succeeded in defeating the army of Union General U. S. Grant when he launched a surprise attack at Shiloh [q.v.]. He was wounded in the leg in the battle and bled to death on the battlefield before anyone realized the wound was serious. It was said that "with him went one of the greatest hopes of the Confederacy." President Jefferson Davis [q.v.] noted of Johnston that he was "the greatest soldier, the ablest man, civil or military, Confederate or Federal, then living," but Grant thought him overrated, for he found him "vacillating and undecided in his actions."

Johnston, Joseph Eggleston (1807–1891). An American army officer who was graduated from West Point in 1829 and was a classmate of Robert E. Lee. He served with distinction in the Second Seminole War [q.v.], winning a brevet to captain, and in the Mexican War [q.v.], in which he won brevets to major and lieutenant colonel. He was severely wounded in the Battle of Cerro Gordo [q.v.] "under the enemy's works while on reconnoitering duty."

On 22 April 1861, at the beginning of the American Civil War, he resigned his commission and joined the Confederate army as a brigadier general. For his performance in the First Battle of Bull Run [q.v.] he was promoted to full general. He opposed Union General George B. McClellan [q.v.] in the Peninsular Campaign [q.v.] until, after being severely wounded in the Battle of Seven Pines [q.v.] in May 1862, he was replaced by General Robert E. Lee. On his recovery he was given command of the Department of the West. In November 1863, after the debacle of General Braxton Bragg [q.v.] at Chattanooga, he was given command of the Army of Tennessee [q.v.]. His strategic withdrawal before Sherman's march on Atlanta exasperated President Jefferson Davis [q.v.], who replaced him with John Bell Hood [q.v.]. In February 1865 he was assigned by Lee to oppose Sherman's march north. Soon after Lee's surrender to Grant, he surrendered to Sherman on 26 April 1865.

After the war he served in Congress and as U.S. commissioner of railroads.

Johnston, Richard Mentor (1780–1850). A Kentucky militia leader and politician who was born in Beargrass (Louisville), Kentucky. He served six terms in Congress and was a leading War Hawk, arguing for war against Great Britain [see War of 1812]. In 1812 he raised a battalion of mounted Kentucky militia and the following year obtained permission to raise 1,000 more. In the summer of 1813 he led his militia through more than 700 miles of the Northwest Territory, eroding the confidence of the Indians in the protection the British could provide.

After a brief respite he and his men joined the army of William Henry Harrison [q.v.], which on 5 October 1813 defeated the British and Indians in the Battle of the Thames [q.v.], in which Johnson was wounded while distinguishing himself by leading a charge that routed his enemies. He never contradicted those who claimed that he had personally killed Tecumseh [q.v.] in this battle.

Johnson was a lifelong bachelor, but by a mulatto slave he had inherited from his father he sired two daughters, whom he openly acknowledged and educated. Although this breaking of a racial taboo cost him the electoral votes of Virginia, the Senate elected him the ninth vice president of the United States, the only American vice president ever to have been so placed in office.

Joint Committee on the Conduct of the War. A joint committee of the U.S. Congress headed by Ohio Senator Benjamin Franklin Wade (1800–1878). Originally proposed in December 1861 to investigate the Union disasters in the battles of Ball's Bluff and First Bull Run [qq.v.], it expanded its horizons to query all aspects of the conduct of the war, and interrogated every general except Grant. It was this committee that made Charles P. Stone [q.v.] the scapegoat for the Union disaster at Ball's Bluff [q.v.]. It remained in existence until June 1865.

Jointed Gun. See Screw Gun.

Joinville, François Ferdinand d'Orléans, Prince d' (1818–1900). A French naval officer who served in the French navy from 1834 to 1848. During the American Civil War he served on the staff of General George B. McClellan [q.v.]. He was exiled from France in 1870 but returned in disguise in 1871 to take part in the Franco-Prussian War [q.v.]. Joinville was elected a deputy to the National Assembly and served until 1875.

Jollies. The popular name for the British Royal Marines.

Jomini, Baron Antoine Henri de (1779–1869). A Swiss soldier born in the canton of Vaud and a writer on military affairs who helped organize the army of the Helvetic Confederation. He was working in a bank when excited by Napoleon's victories, he set out to discover "the fundamental principles, . . . independent of the kind of weapons, of historical time, and of place" that accounted for the victories. He volunteered for the French army and became an aide to Marshal Michel Ney [q.v.], serving with him as a volunteer in the Battle of Ulm [q.v.] in 1805. His first major work, *Traité des grande opérations militaires (Treatise on Large Military Operations)*, was published in four volumes in 1804–05.

He was transferred to Napoleon's general staff in 1806 and was with him at Jena on 14 October 1806 and at Eylau [qq.v.] on 7–8 February 1807, winning the Legion of Honor [q.v.]. He later became chief of staff in Ney's corps and served in the Peninsular War [q.v.]. On 7 December 1810 he was promoted general of brigade. During Napoleon's Russian Campaign [q.v.] he fought at Smolensk, the crossing of the Berezina, Lützen, and Bautzen [qq.v.]. Ney recommended him for promotion, but after a quarrel with Marshal Louis Alexandre Berthier [q.v.], he left the French service, and on 15 August 1813 he joined the Russian army to become a lieutenant general and an aide-de-camp to Tsar Alexander I [q.v.]. He wrote extensively on military matters, emphasizing the importance of mobility and concentration of force. His theories were later oversystematized and oversimplified by his epigones.

Beginning in 1823, he served for six years as military instructor to the tsarevich who became Alexander II [q.v.]. During the Russo-Turkish War [q.v.] of 1828–29 he took part in the siege of Varna [q.v.]. In 1838 he published in Paris his most famous book, *Précis de l'art de la guerre (The Art of War)*, two volumes, in which he argued that all human experience, even war, could be subjected to the immutable principles of reason. He is most widely known for his statement "War is not a science, but an art." In 1848 he retired from the Russian army and settled at Passy, France, near Chamonix. He was a contemporary of Karl von Clausewitz [q.v.].

He predicted in 1836 that railroads would lead to "a bloody and most unreasonable struggle between great masses equipped with weapons of unimaginable power."

Jones, Adrian (1845–1938). A British soldier and sculptor. At the age of twenty-one he passed the examinations of the Royal College of Veterinary Surgeons, but he never practiced as a veterinarian. In 1867 he was commissioned in the Royal Horse Artillery and subsequently in the 3rd Hussars, the Queen's Bays, and the 2nd Life Guards. He served in the Abyssinian Campaign of 1868, the First Anglo-Boer War in 1881, and the Nile Campaign [qq.v.]. After twenty-three years' service he retired in 1890 as a captain. While in the service he began his work as a sculptor, and he first exhibited at the Royal Academy in 1884. He continued exhibiting until 1935 and became famous for his war memorials.

Jones, John (1834–1881). An American soldier and Texas ranger. He enlisted as a Confederate private in Terry's Rangers during the American Civil War and rose to be adjutant of

the 15th Texas and then assistant adjutant general of a brigade. After the war he traveled in Mexico and South America, seeking without success to locate sites suitable for establishing colonies of ex-Confederates. He was appointed major in the Texas Frontier Battalion on 2 May 1874 and on 10 July to the command of six companies of Texas Rangers, with 75 men per company. Most of these were stationed along the Rio Grande to restrain Indians and discourage outlaws. His first notable engagement with Indians occurred at Lost Valley near Jacksboro in north-central Texas on 12 July 1874, when with 28 men he was attacked by some 100 Kiowas, Apaches, and Comanches. He lost 2 killed and 2 wounded.

Jones established a reputation for efficiency in settling feuds, capturing train robbers, and generally establishing peace. In January 1879 he was appointed Texas adjutant general, a post he held until his death.

Jones, William Edmonson (1824–1864). An American soldier who was graduated from West Point in 1848 and served with the mounted rifles on the western frontier until he resigned in 1857 to become a farmer. In May 1861 he was commissioned a major in the Confederate army and assigned to train cavalry. In September he was elected colonel of the 7th Virginia Cavalry and with it fought at Cedar Mountain, Groveton, and Second Bull Run [qq.v.]. On 19 September 1862 he was appointed brigadier general and in that rank served under J. E. B. Stuart [q.v.] although the two developed a mutual antipathy. Jones, known as Grumble Jones to differentiate him from another Confederate general, Neighbor Jones (1825–1863), distinguished himself in the Battle of Brandy Station [q.v.], in which his brigade bore the brunt of the fighting and suffered the greatest number of casualties. In April and May 1863 he led a successful raid into western Virginia [see Jones and Imboden Raid]. He served in the Gettysburg Campaign under Stuart until the two quarreled and Jones was transferred to eastern Tennessee to serve under James Longstreet [q.v.]. In the spring of 1864 he returned to Virginia, and on 5 June he was killed in the Battle of Piedmont [q.v.].

Jones and Imboden Raid (April 1863), American Civil War. A successful Confederate raid carried out by separate forces under William ("Grumble") Jones and John Imboden [qq.v.] in what is today north-central West Virginia. Jones was able to destroy a considerable amount of railroad property, including several bridges.

Jonesboro, Battle of (31 August–1 September 1864), American Civil War. In this two-day battle during the Atlanta Campaign, attacking Confederate troops under John Bell Hood [q.v.] were repulsed by Union forces under General William T. Sherman [q.v.] at Jonesboro, a small town in northwest-central Georgia. On 31 August Federal forces lost 179 out of 14,170 engaged; the Confederates lost 1,725 out of 23,811 engaged. On 1 September the Federal forces lost 1,274 out of 20,460 engaged; the Confederates perhaps lost an equal or larger number.

Jones Gabion. A gabion [q.v.] constructed of ten sheets of galvanized iron worked over twelve wooden pickets and fastened at the ends.

Jordan, Thomas (1819–1895). An American soldier who in 1840 was graduated from West Point, where he was a roommate of William T. Sherman [q.v.]. He served in the Second Seminole War and the Mexican War [qq.v.]. On 21 May 1861, at the beginning of the American Civil War, after having served thirteen years as a captain, he resigned his commission and joined the Confederate army as a lieutenant colonel. Before leaving Washington, he established a southern spy ring in the city. All his war service was on staff, first as adjutant general on the staff of General Pierre Beauregard and later on the staffs of Braxton Bragg and Albert S. Johnston [qq.v.]. He was appointed brigadier general on 14 April 1862.

After the war he turned to journalism, and in 1866 he became editor of the *Memphis Appeal.* Three years later he joined the insurrectionists in Cuba, first as chief of staff and then as a commander. In 1870 the Spanish government in Cuba placed a price of $100,000 on his head. When his movement collapsed, he returned to journalism in the United States.

Jörgensen, Jögen (1779–1844). A Danish adventurer, son of a watchmaker, who served on a whaler and then on a privateer in the American Revolutionary War. On 21 June 1809 he landed in Reykjavik with a small group of armed men and, after seizing the Danish governor, declared Iceland independent with himself as "protector." On 9 August a British armed sloop captured him and brought him to London in chains. After being freed, he lived in London for several years until, after a conviction for robbery in 1820, he was transported to Tasmania. He was sometimes called the King of Iceland.

Jong. A Tibetan fort.

Joseph, Chief (1840?–1904), Indian name: Hin-mah-too Yah-lat-kekt (Thunder Rolling in the Mountains). His father, one of the first of his tribe to become converted to Christianity, gave him at age five the baptismal name Joseph. From 1871 he was a leader, although not a war leader, of the Nez Percés, one of the largest and most powerful tribes in the American Northwest. For six years he resisted the efforts of white men to move his band of nontreaty Indians from the Wallowa Valley of the Snake River in Oregon to an Idaho reservation where the treaty Nez Percés had been established. In 1877, when General O. O. Howard [q.v.], acting on instructions, ordered him and his band with all their livestock to proceed on their own to the reservation or be driven there by cavalry, Joseph led his followers, about 350 in all, including 191 fighting men, to join other nontreaty bands in camps along Whitebird Creek and the Salmon River.

Depredations by some young Nez Percé warriors, including the killing of unarmed white settlers, led to the Battle of Whitebird Canyon [q.v.] on 17 June 1877 and the beginning of the Nez Percé War [q.v.]. With his tribe Joseph embarked on a 1,700-mile hegira from Whitebird Canyon across Idaho and present-day Yellowstone Park until on 1 October he was captured by General Nelson Miles [q.v.] while under a flag of truce. He was released in exchange for Lieutenant Lovell Hall Jerome (1849–1935), who had been captured by the Nez Percés. Four days later, on 5 October 1877, 431 of the tribe surrendered at Bear Paw Mountain in Montana, and Joseph uttered his famous words, "Hear me, my chiefs! I am tired. My heart is sick and sad. From where the sun now stands, I will fight no more forever."

Joseph and his people were sent to a reservation in Oklahoma, where many soon sickened and died. In 1883 and 1884 most of the survivors were allowed to return to Oregon, but Joseph and 150 of his band were transported to the Colville Reservation in Washington, where he died.

Although a brave warrior, Joseph was not a war chief. He spoke English and possessed great diplomatic skills and was recognized as the spokesman for the Nez Percés, but he was not the Indian Napoleon legend has made him. Other Nez Percé chiefs, such as Looking Glass [q.v.] exercised equal, if not greater, influence upon the tribe's fighting strategy. [See Nez Percé War.]

Chief Joseph, 1898

Joubert, Petrus ("Piet") Jacobus (1834–1900). A Boer soldier and politician who opposed British annexation of the Transvaal. In the First Anglo-Boer War [q.v.] he was commandant general of the Boer forces. In 1881 he led 2,000 into Natal and defeated the British under George Colley [q.v.] at Laing's Nek and at Majuba [qq.v.]. He was instrumental in procuring from Krupp [q.v.] and other European makers of armaments some of the most modern artillery for the Transvaal *staatsartillerie,* the only standing army the Boers possessed. In 1899, at the beginning of the Second Anglo-Boer War, as the nominal commander-in-chief of the Boer forces in Natal, he defeated the British under Sir George White [q.v.] at Talana on 15 October, Elandslaagte on 21 October, and Nicholson's Nek on 30 October [qq.v.] and forced them into Ladysmith [q.v.], where they were bottled up and besieged. A bad fall from his horse and ill health forced him to resign on 25 November 1899. He died on 27 March 1900.

Joubert, Piet *The Transvaal commander-in-chief breakfasts with his staff outside Ladysmith. His chaplain sits cross-legged in front of him.*

Jourdan, Jean Baptiste (1762–1833). A French soldier who enlisted as a private in 1778 and in 1779 fought in the American Revolution in the Régiment d'Auxerrois before Savannah. During the French Revolution he became a captain of the Garde Nationale [q.v.] at Limoges in 1791, and two years later he was a general of division. He fought in September 1793 at Hondschoote, where he was wounded, but he recovered to win the Battle of Wittignies in October. On 26 June 1794 he won his greatest success at Fleurus. In 1798 he was the major architect of the conscription law [see Conscription; Levée / Levy en Masse]. He was appointed inspector general of infantry and cavalry in 1800. In 1804 he commanded the Army of Italy and on 19 May 1804 was named one of the first marshals. He fought in Spain, and in June 1813 he commanded the Army of the Center in the great French defeat at Vitoria [q.v.], where his marshal's baton was captured. It was sent to London as a present for the prince regent.

Jourdan again held active command only in 1815. He rallied to the Bourbons but returned to Napoleon's side during the Hundred Days [q.v.] and led the Army of the Rhine. After Waterloo [q.v.] in which he played no part, he again changed sides. He was appointed president of the military court that was to try Marshal Ney [q.v.], a task he evaded by insisting that Ney, a peer, had to be tried by other peers. His last post was as governor of the Hôtel des Invalides [q.v.] in Paris.

Jovellar y Soler, Joaquín (1819–1892). A Spanish soldier who served as a captain in Cuba (1842–51) and was promoted brigadier general in 1863. By 1872 he was a lieutenant general. The following year he returned to Cuba as governor and served until 1874 and again from 1876 to 1878. Between those terms he returned to Spain, where he commanded an army against the Carlists and became minister of war. His second term in Cuba saw the end of the Ten Years'

War [q.v.] and the Convention of Zanjón on 10 February 1878.

Joyeuse, les (the Joyous). The sardonic popular name for members of the Infanterie Légère or Bat d'Af [qq.v.], the African disciplinary battalions that were full of toughs possessing all the faults of the Foreign Legion [q.v.] without its panache.

Juárez, Benito Pablo (1806–1872). A Mexican leader of Zapotec Indian parentage who in 1847 became governor of Oaxaca. In 1853 he was exiled by Antonio López de Santa Anna [q.v.]. He returned two years later and joined the revolution led by Juan Álvarez [q.v.] that toppled Santa Anna. In 1857 he became minister of justice. From 30 June 1861 to 1865 he was president of Mexico. Reelection was made impossible by the French invasion [see Mexico, French Invasion and Occupation of]. After waging a successful war against the invaders, he was again elected president for two terms (1867–72), successfully crushing numerous insurrections. He died in office on 18 July 1872.

Jugdulluk, Battle of (12 January 1842), First Afghan War. At this mountainous pass in eastern Afghanistan the remnants of the army of British General William Elphinstone (1782–1842), retreating toward India from Kabul, made its last stand. Dr. William Brydon [q.v.] was the only European who survived to reach safety at Jalalabad [q.v.].

Juh (1825?–1883). An Apache Indian who became a war leader. He fought both Mexicans and Americans and is thought to have killed Lieutenant Howard B. Cushing (1844?–1871) and two others in the Whetstone Mountains of Arizona on 5 May 1871. He took part in the Victorio War [q.v.] in southern New Mexico and perhaps in the skirmish of Cibicue [q.v.]. He was noted for his leadership and his cruelty.

July Revolution, French. See French Revolution of 1830.

Jumper (1796?–1838), also known as Otee Emathla or Onselmatche. A Red Stick Creek Indian who became a Seminole leader and fought against Andrew Jackson [q.v.] in the First Seminole War [q.v.] of 1816–18. He was one of the leaders, if not the chief leader, in the Dade Massacre [q.v.]. He took a major role in the Second Seminole War [q.v.] and was one of those heading the attack on General Edmund Gaines [q.v.] in the so-called eight-day siege of Fort Izzard at the Withlacoochee River in late February 1836, in which the Americans lost 5 killed and 46 wounded, including Gaines, who was wounded in the face. On 27 January 1837 Jumper took part in the Battle of Hatcheelustee. When he and 63 of his followers finally surrendered on 19 December 1837, they were sent to New Orleans and confined at Fort Pike on the island of Petite Coquille. He died there a few months later.

June Days. See Paris Revolution of 1848.

Jungay, Battle of. See Yungay, Battle of.

Jung Bahadur (1816–1877). Nepalese soldier and ruler. During the Indian Mutiny [q.v.] he resisted all attempts of the Indian rebels and mutineers to enlist his support. Instead he sent a column of 8,000 Gurkhas to assist the British in the recapture of Lucknow. When he died, three of his widows immolated themselves on his funeral pyre.

Junín, Battle of· (6 August 1824), Peruvian War of Independence. Near this Peruvian town on Lake Junín, about 95 miles northeast of Lima, a Spanish royalist army of 9,000, including 2,000 cavalry, under General José Canterac and Viceroy José de La Sernay Hinojosa [qq.v.] was decisively defeated by a revolutionary army of about the same strength that included 4,000 Peruvians under Simón Bolívar and Antonio Sucre [qq.v.].

The battle was fought entirely by the cavalry, most armed with sabers, and it was said that not a shot was fired. The insurgents lost about 150; the Spanish royalists about 250. The battle marked the turning point in the struggle for Peru.

Junior Officer. 1. A company grade officer—i.e., below the rank of major.

2. An officer junior in rank to another. When two officers held the same rank, the junior was usually he who had served the least time in grade.

Junker. A member of the Prussian landed aristocracy. Junkers dominated the Prussian officer corps. In 1847, 77 percent of the officers were Junkers, and in 1860, 65 percent. Many Guards regiments had not a single commoner among their officers.

Junot, Jean Andoche, Duc d' Abrantes (1771–1813). A French soldier who served under Napoleon in the Italian and Egyptian campaigns. He enlisted as a private in 1790 and was wounded in the Battle of Longwy in 1792 and again the following year. He was commissioned in 1794. In August 1796 he killed six men in individual combat and was himself severely wounded. In Egypt he was promoted general of brigade

Junot, Jean Andoche *March of General Junot and his troops in the Sierra de Goze gorges, Portugal, 1807*

and was wounded in a duel after he challenged an officer who was critical of Napoleon. He became a general of division in 1801 and in 1807 commanded the army that invaded Portugal and captured Lisbon, just missing the departing Portuguese fleet that carried the king and court to Brazil. After his defeat by General Arthur Wellesley (later Duke of Wellington) at Vimeiro [q.v.] on 21 August 1808 he was forced to quit Portugal. Back in Spain he was made commander of VIII Corps and later III Corps in the army of André Masséna [q.v.], and he conducted the siege of Saragossa [q.v.], but he left the peninsula after the Battle of Fuentes de Oñoro in May 1811. He later served in the Russian Campaign [q.v.] and fought at Smolensk [q.v.], where he was criticized for his failure to cut off the Russian retreat. He was briefly governor of Illyria. Suffering from insanity, he committed suicide on 29 July 1813 by throwing himself out of a window.

His widow, Laure, née Permon (1784–1838), whose relations with her husband were tempestuous and who for a time was the mistress of Klemens von Metternich (1773–1859), the reactionary Austrian statesman, wrote the bitter but colorful *Souvenirs historiques sur Napoléon la Revolution, le Directoire, le Consulat, l'Empire et la Restoration* (1831–35).

Junta. A dictatorship by a council of officers, usually following a more or less violent coup. In Spanish the word means simply council or committee.

Just War. The notion that war was more than a feud among chieftains and that "might making right" was not ethically sound was introduced by early Christians. The first to deal with it at some length was St. Augustine (354–430). He and later St. Thomas Aquinas (1225–1274) noted that even God had ordained war, citing St. Luke (Luke 3:14); therefore war in itself was not evil.

Aquinas set forth three requirements for a just war (*bellum iustum*): a just cause, a legitimate authority to conduct the war, and righteous intentions (*Summa theologica, II*). Franciscus de Vitoria (1485?–1546) added that to be just, a war must not cause more suffering than the evil it hoped to correct.

Niccolò Machiavelli (1469–1513) held different views: "Where the very safety of the country depends upon the resolution to be taken, no consideration of justice or injustice, humanity or cruelty, glory or shame should be allowed to prevail" (*Discorsi, III*).

These two views, the religious and the secular, are still being debated today. Most nations believe, or want to believe, that their cause is just, even when, as with Britain in the Opium Wars [q.v.], it patently was not. Islamic countries had no trouble justifying any war against unbelievers; wars between Islamic countries were usually justified by different interpretations of the Koran, as in the Arabian War [q.v.].

Although declaring a war to be just is a popular propaganda slogan, there is no evidence that any nation or peoples ever desisted from making war because they believed their cause unjust.

K

Kabayama, Sukenori (1837–1922). A Japanese who in the course of his career became both a general and an admiral. He fought in the Boshin Civil War [q.v.], which restored the Meiji emperor to power in 1868, and in the Sino-Japanese War [q.v.] of 1894–95.

Kabbade. A sleeveless coat, usually of wool, fastened by a girdle around the waist, worn by Greek soldiers.

Kabul, Battle of (14 September 1842), First Afghan War. Following the disaster to the army of General William Elphinstone (1782–1842) in Afghanistan in January 1842, British General George Pollock [q.v.] forced the Khyber and attacked Kabul, defeating Akbar Khan [q.v.] and destroying part of the city in retribution. On orders from London he retreated in October.

Kabul *Alexander Burnes is murdered by an Afghan mob in Kabul, 2 November 1841. The incident, among others, led to the First Afghan War the following year.*

Kabul to Kandahar March (August 1880), Second Afghan War. Following the defeat of the British army under Brigadier George Burrows (1822?–1898) at Maiwand by Ayub Khan [q.v.], the British retreated into Kandahar and were there besieged. To relieve the city, Sir Frederick (later Lord) Roberts with 10,000 men marched from Kabul to Kandahar, a distance of 313 miles over difficult terrain, in twenty-two days. The city was relieved, and Roberts defeated Ayub Khan in the Battle of Kandahar [q.v.] on 1 September 1880.

Kabuto. A Japanese military helmet.

Kabyle Gun. A conventional term for the guns extensively used by the Berbers in North Africa. They were exceptionally long, measuring 70 inches or more, and most were flintlocks. During the first half of the nineteenth century many were manufactured for the Arab trade in Liège, Belgium, where they were called Mahomet trade guns.

Kabylia Campaigns (1850s–71). French invasion and occupation of Algeria. In the mountainous coastal area of Algeria between Algiers and Philippeville (Annaba) fiercely independent Berbers known as Kabyles offered desperate resistance to the French invaders from the 1850s until the suppression of the last insurrection in 1871.

Kaffir Wars (1781–1879). The word "kaffir," originally used by Arab slavers to denote unbelievers or heathens, came to be used in nineteenth-century South Africa to refer to any Bantu, particularly a member of the Xhosa tribe. Today in South Africa the word is pejorative. The long series of wars known as the Kaffir Wars were fought between 1781 and 1879 on the eastern frontier of Cape Colony between whites of European origin, principally Dutch and British, and black Africans, mostly Xhosas and Basutos. Most of these wars were numbered from one to nine, but authorities are not in agreement on which numbers apply to which wars, and the Axe

Kabylia Campaigns *Submission of Kabylia to the French in Algeria, 1871*

448

War [q.v.] in 1846–48, although a Kaffir War, is seldom numbered.

Eric Rosenthal in *Encyclopedia of South Africa* (1961) counts only eight numbered wars, all in the nineteenth century–the first in 1811–12; the second in 1818; the third in 1819; the fourth in 1834–35; the fifth in 1850–53; the sixth in 1858; the seventh, also known as the Gcaleka War [q.v.], in 1877–78; and the eighth, also known as the Tamboekie War in 1879—but others have counted differently.

Kaffrarian Rifles. A South African military unit raised in East London, southeast Cape Colony, on 20 December 1883. It fought in the Langeberg Campaign in 1897, throughout the Second Anglo-Boer War [q.v.], including the siege of Mafeking [q.v.], and in both world wars.

Kagoshima, Battle of (18 August 1877), Satsuma Rebellion. Japanese rebel forces under Saigo Takamori [q.v.] were surrounded at Enotakeon on the west coast of Kagoshima Bay near this Japanese seaport town in southern Kyushu, which had been long a castle city of a powerful daimyo of the Satsuma clan. The rebels broke through the imperialist lines and seized the city, but after ten days of fighting they were driven out. The imperial army under Prince Taruhito pursued them, and they retreated to Shirogama, where on 14 September Takamori, cornered and wounded, ordered a samurai to behead him or was killed in battle or committed hara-kiri (accounts differ). Unknown but large losses were sustained by both sides.

Kaiping, Battle of (10 January 1895), Sino-Japanese War. A Japanese force under General Maresuke Nogi [q.v.] drove the Chinese from their strongly entrenched positions near this town in northeast Hopei Province in northeast China north of Tientsin. The Japanese suffered about 300 casualties in a three-hour battle.

Kaiser-i-Hind Medal. A British decoration instituted in April 1900 to be awarded to any person who distinguished himself or herself by important or useful service in the advancement of the public good in India. The medal had three classes in gold, silver, and bronze. In 1915 Mohandas Gandhi (1869–1948) was awarded the gold medal for his aid in recruiting for the Indian army.

Kalai. A Turkish fortress. The term was usually applied to stockades and similar structures.

Kala Jugga. Literally, dark place. At British military balls in India this was a secluded area arranged near the ballroom "for the purpose of flirtation" (*Hobson-Jobson* [q.v.]).

Kalckreuth, Friedrich Adolf von (1737–1818). A Prussian soldier who served in the Seven Years' War and distinguished himself at the siege of Mainz in 1793. In 1805 he became commander-in-chief of the Pomeranian army. He served with distinction in the unsuccessful defense of Danzig in 1807 and that year was promoted field marshal. Thereafter he served successively as governor of Königsberg, Berlin, and Breslau.

Kalerges (Kalergis), Demetrios (1803–1867). A Greek soldier and politician who was born in Crete. He served in the Greek War of Liberation in 1821 and in the insurrection of 1843 that forced King Otto I (1815–1867) to shed his Bavarian advisers. He was forced into exile in 1845 but was recalled for the Crimean War [q.v.] and served as minister of war in 1854–55. In 1861 as Greek minister in Paris he negotiated for the accession of Prince George of Denmark (1845–1913) to the Greek throne.

Kalifa Abdullahi. See Abdullahi, Khalifa.

Kalmuk. Asian light cavalry in the Russian army.

Kalpi, Captures of (1851 and 1858). This town on the Jumma River in India, 45 miles southwest of Cawnpore, was first captured by the British in 1803. During the Indian Mutiny [q.v.] it was occupied by the mutinous Gwalior Contingent [q.v.], and on 10 May 1858 it was besieged by Sir Hugh Rose [q.v.]. The garrison made two unsuccessful sorties, but on 23 May 1858, the queen's birthday, the British captured the town [see Kunch, Battle of].

Kalsa. See Khalsa.

Kalunga, Siege of (October–November 1814), Nepalese War. Nepalese troops (Gurkhas) with six guns occupied this fort of logs and earth, sheltering about 600 men, women, and children, on an isolated, jungle-covered hill about 500 feet high. It was attacked by an Anglo-Indian force of 2,500, of whom 300 were European, with eight guns under General Robert Rollo Gillespie [q.v.]. Although the British brought up heavy guns and finally reduced the fort to rubble, it never surrendered. After holding out for more than a month, some 60 Gurkhas fought their way clear and escaped, leaving the British with a worthless fort filled with wounded.

The Gurkhas lost about 520; the British lost 31 officers, including General Gillespie, who was killed, and 750 other ranks. This was the first important engagement of the war, and the tenacity and courage of the Gurkhas made a deep impression upon the British officers.

Kama. A straight, double-edged Caucasian dagger ending in a point. Its length varied from 4 to 20 inches. It was favored by Cossacks.

Kamaiakan (1800?–1877). The principal chief of the Yakima Indians and the confederated tribes of the eastern part of the state of Washington who, beginning in September 1855, waged war on the whites. On 4–5 October 1855 near Toponish in the Simcoe Valley he defeated a force of 85 soldiers of the 4th Infantry under Major Granville Owen Haller (1819–1897), a victory that sparked a general rising of the tribes in the area. On 17 May 1858 warriors under Kamaiakan defeated a force of dragoons and infantry under Colonel Edward Steptoe [q.v.] near Spokane Lake, not far from present-day Colfax, Washington. However, on 10 September, in a battle at the Okanogan River, he was defeated by a force under Colonel George Wright (1801 [or 1803]–1865). Kamaiakan was wounded in the battle but refused to sue for peace and fled to British Columbia.

Kamarut, Battle of (8 July 1824), First Anglo-Burmese War. A small British force under General Archibald Campbell [q.v.] stormed Burmese stockades held by 10,000 men under Tuamba Wangyee (d. 1824). The position was carried, and 800 Burmese, including Tuamba Wangyee, were killed.

Kambula, Battle of (29 March 1879), Zulu War. Colonel (later Field Marshal) Evelyn Wood [q.v.] with a force of 400 Europeans and about 1,500 African auxiliaries invaded Zululand, where he was attacked by an estimated 20,000 Zulus. They were beaten off after a four-hour battle in which Wood lost a quarter of his effectives, including 81 British killed or wounded.

Kamenskoi, Aleksandr (1731–1807). A Russian officer who as a general had served with distinction under Aleksandr Suvorov [q.v.] but who in December 1806, as a marshal, failed to delay the advance of Napoleon's army on Warsaw and barely escaped being surrounded. He was assassinated by a peasant on 9 January 1807.

Kamio, Mitsoumi (1856–1907). A Japanese soldier who served in the Sino-Japanese War [q.v.] and in World War I commanded the Japanese force that captured Tsingtao from the Germans in September 1914.

Kammerling, Gustave (fl. 1860s). A German-born American soldier who fought with distinction in the Union army during the American Civil War, becoming colonel of the 9th Ohio. At Chickamauga he led a bayonet charge to recapture a battery of artillery. For this feat he was offered a promotion to brigadier general, an advance he refused, saying that he preferred to stay with his regiment.

Kanawha, Army of the. In the American Civil War, a Confederate command established in June 1862 to operate in the Kanawha Valley of western Virginia (today West Virginia).

Kandahar, Battle of (1 September 1880), Second Afghan War. After the British defeat by Afghans under Ayub Khan [q.v.] at Maiwand [q.v.], General Frederick Roberts [q.v.] made in 22 days a famous forced march of 313 miles from Kabul to Kandahar [q.v.]. There he defeated 11,000 Afghans under Ayub Khan, who had taken up a strong position two miles northwest of the city. Afghan losses were 1,200; British losses were 40 killed and 228 wounded. This decisive victory ended the Second Afghan War [q.v.].

Kandern, Battle of (20 April 1848), Baden insurrection. Near this town in southern Baden, seven miles north of Lürrach on the southwest slope of the Black Forest, troops from Baden and Hesse under General Friedrich von Gagen defeated Black Forest insurgents under Friedrich Hecker [q.v.]. [See Mieroslawski, Ludwik; Baden Insurrection.]

Kandian Wars. See Candian / Kandian Wars.

Kane, Thomas Leiper (1822–1883). An American politician and soldier who was the brother of Arctic explorer Elisha Kent Kane (1820–1857). He was a diminutive man: five feet, four inches tall and weighing only ninety-five pounds.

Although never a Mormon, he maintained a thirty-year friendship with Brigham Young (1801–1877), one of whose wives, Mary Ann Angel Young, had nursed him through "swamp fever" when he was a young man in Illinois. In the Mexican War [q.v.] he helped raise the Mormon Volunteers [q.v.]. In 1857, during the so-called Mormon War [see Utah Expedition] he rose from a sickbed in Philadelphia and by way of Panama, San Francisco, and an overland route reached Utah, where he was instrumental in bringing into agreement Brigham Young and Albert Sidney Johnston [q.v.], thus averting a possible conflict of major proportions.

During the American Civil War he organized the 13th Pennsylvania Reserves, known as the Bucktails [q.v.], one of the most celebrated units in the Union army, and served as its major until promoted lieutenant colonel on 25 November 1861. On 6 June 1862 he was wounded and captured at Harrisonburg, Virginia. He was promoted a brigadier general on 7 September 1862 while he was still a prisoner. He was paroled the following August, and in May 1863, just after the Battle of Chancellorsville [q.v.], he fell ill of pneumonia. Before he had fully recovered, he returned to his brigade on the second day of the Battle of Gettysburg [q.v.], although he was too ill to command it. He resigned on 7 November 1863, and in the omnibus brevet promotions awarded on 13 March 1865 he was brevetted major general. He lived the remaining twenty years of his life as a semi-invalid.

In the rotunda of the Utah State Capitol a statue was erected to his memory as "The Immortal Friend of Utah and Its People." A duplicate was erected in Kane, Pennsylvania, the town he founded in 1859.

Kapikulu. Slave soldiers of the sultan of Turkey.

Káplona, Battle of (26–27 February 1849), Hungarian Revolution. Hungarian troops under General Arthur von Görgey [q.v.] were forced to retreat into the mountains north of Budapest. At this town in central Hungary southwest of Eger, General Henryk Dembrinski [q.v.] with 45,000 men attempting to relieve him was defeated by 15,000 Austrians under General Prince Alfred Candidus Ferdinand zu Windisch-Graetz [q.v.].

Kaptkulu Süvarileri. Turkish household cavalry.

Karageorge (or Karadjordje) (1762–1817), original name: Djordjé Pétrovic. A Serbian soldier and revolutionary known as Crni Djordje (Black George) who, although born the son of a peasant, founded the Serbian dynasty of Karageorgevich. As a young man he served under a Turkish brigand, but after killing a fellow brigand, he enlisted in the ranks of the Austrian army, became a sergeant, and fought in the Russo-Turkish War of 1788. In 1791 he deserted and for a while dealt in pigs. At the same time he joined in the guerrilla fighting against the Turks. In 1804 at the outbreak of the Turko-Serbian War [q.v.] he was elected supreme leader of the Serbs. He fought with considerable success until the signing of the Treaty of Bucharest in 1812 enabled the Turks to use their entire strength against the insurgents. He was then decisively defeated in 1813 and forced to flee to Hungary. He returned to Serbia in 1817 and put himself at the head of a new revolt. He was murdered in his sleep at Radovis, 14 miles southeast of Stip, probably on the orders of his rival, Milos Obrenović

(1780–1860). His severed head was sent to Constantinople (Istanbul).

In a violent time Karageorge was a man of extraordinary violence. When his father refused to accompany him into exile, he killed him in a fit of rage. He hanged his brother for rape and refused to permit his mother to mourn. He was known to have killed with his own hands at least 125 men unfortunate enough to have provoked him.

Karageorgevich, Peter (1844–1921), Serbian: Petar Karadjordjević. A Serbian soldier and king who was trained in French military schools and fought in the French army in the Franco-Prussian War [q.v.]. During the Bosnian revolt against Turkey in 1875 he commanded a corps [see Bosnia and Herzegovina / Hercegovina, Revolts in]. After the assassination of Alexander I of the house of Obrenović (1876–1903), he became King Peter I of Serbia, until 1918, when he became king of the Serbs, Croats, and Slovenes, over whom he reigned until his death.

Karaïskakes (Karaïskakis), Georgios (1782–1827). A Greek insurrectionary leader in the Greek War of Independence [q.v.] who helped raise the first siege of Missolonghi [q.v.] in 1823 and tried unsuccessfully to raise the second siege in 1826. He commanded the patriot forces in Rumelia and gained some success in fighting the Turks, although he failed to cooperate with other Greek chieftains. In 1827 he took part in the unsuccessful efforts to raise the siege of Athens and was killed in action on 4 May 1827.

Karam Allah Muhammad Kurkusawi (d. 1903). A Dervish emir in the Sudan who in his youth worked for slavers but in 1882 joined the Mahdist cause. He led the Dervish army that conquered Bahr al-Ghazal Province and captured its governor, Frank Lupton Bey [see Lupton, Frank], whose place he took. He later led a force that suppressed with ruthless and bloody efficiency a rebellion of the Rizaiqat tribe in Darfur. In 1896 he fought in the Battle of Firket [q.v.], where he was wounded. After the collapse of the Mahdist regime he took refuge in Darfur with Ali Dinar [q.v.], who, mistrusting him, had him killed.

Karica, Tamemoto Tamesada (1844–1923). A Japanese soldier who fought for the Satsuma clan during the Boshin Civil War [q.v.] and in 1872 joined the new imperial army as a captain. During the Satsuma Rebellion [q.v.] in 1877 he was a lieutenant colonel. He distinguished himself as a lieutenant general in the Sino-Japanese War [q.v.] of 1894–95 and was created a baron for his services. He also commanded in the Russo-Japanese War, winning the first battle on the Yalu River.

Karl August (Charles Augustus) (1757–1828). A German soldier and ruler who was Grand Duke of Saxe-Weimar from 1758 to 1815. He joined the Prussian army in 1786 and remained in it until the Battle of Jena [q.v.] on 14 October 1806. He joined the coalition against the French and was influential at the Congress of Vienna [see Napoleonic Wars].

Karpenizi, Battle of (21 August 1822), Greek War of Independence. With a force of only 300 men, Greek patriot leader Marco Bozzaris [q.v.] attacked at night the advance guard of a Turkish army invading the peninsula north of the Gulf of Corinth. Surprised, some 4,000 Turks fled. Bozzaris was killed in this battle.

Kars, Battles and Sieges of (1828, 1855, and 1877), Russo-Turkish Wars. This city, the capital of an independent Armenia in the ninth and tenth centuries, was built on a mountain spur in the mountainous area of northeastern Turkey, a region that has been invaded by Seljuk Turks, Russians, Kurds, Kabardins, Mongols, Circassians, and others. In the nineteenth century the city was three times stormed and captured by Russians.

On 5 July 1828 a Russian army of 12,000 under General Ivan Paskievich [q.v.] defeated 18,000 Turks under Emin Pasha and captured the city's sixteenth-century citadel. Russian losses were 600 killed and wounded; Turkish losses were 3,500 killed and wounded and 1,500 taken prisoner.

During the Crimean War a Russian army of 25,000 under General Mikhail Muravyov [see Muravyov Family] attacked the city, which was defended by a Turkish garrison under British Major General and Turkish Ferik (Lieutenant General) William Fenwick Williams Pasha [q.v.]. After an unsuccessful assault on 16 June the Russians established a blockade and besieged the town. On 29 September a Turkish force stationed on the heights above the town was defeated in what was called the Battle of Kars. The survivors retreated to the town, where the garrison held out until food was completely exhausted. On 29 November 1855 their Russian besiegers permitted them to march out with the honors of war [q.v.]. In accepting the surrender General Muravyov paid tribute to Williams: "You have made yourself a name in history and posterity will stand amazed at the endurance, the courage and the discipline which this siege has called forth in this remnant of an army."

In the Russo-Turkish War of 1877–78 [q.v.] a Russian army on the night of 17 November 1877, under nominal command of Grand Duke Mikhail Nikolaevich (1832–1909) with General Count Mikhail Loris-Melikov [q.v.] as his chief of staff, again assaulted and captured Kars, garrisoned by 24,000 Turks. Russian losses were 2,273; Turkish losses were 2,500 killed, 4,500 wounded, and 17,000 captured along with 303 guns. The Turkish commander of the area, Ahmed Mukhtar Pasha [q.v.], was forced to withdraw to Erzurum in northeastern Turkey.

At the end of the Russo-Turkish War of 1878 the entire vilayet was transferred to Russia. It was not returned to Turkey until 1921.

Kashgar Rebellion. See Chinese Turkestan, Conquest of.

Kashgil, Battle of (5 November 1883), sometimes spelled Kashgal or called the Battle of Shaikan or of El Obeid. Mahdist revolt in the Sudan. An Egyptian army of 7,000 infantry, 1,000, cavalry and 2,000 camp followers led by William Hicks Pasha [q.v.], who had been a colonel in the Indian army before he entered the service of the khedive of Egypt, was surrounded and attacked by a large Dervish force in the wastes of Kordofan, in the western Sudan, 30 miles south of El Obeid and 220 miles southwest of Khartoum. Only 300 survived. Hicks Pasha was killed by a spear thrust of Khalifayt Muhammad Sherif [q.v.], the son-in-law of the El Mahdi [see Muhammad Ahmed]. This was Egypt's last major effort to defeat the forces of El Mahdi.

Kashmir, Sikh Capture of (1819). The Sikh army of Ranjit Singh [q.v.] conquered this state in northwest India on the boundary of Tibet and Sinkiang. In 1846, after the Sikh Wars [q.v.], the province was held by the raja of Jammu as part of British India.

Kassala, Battle of and Siege of (1894 and 1897), Italian-Dervish conflicts. In 1885 this fortified town, 250 miles east of Khartoum near the border of Eritrea, was captured by the Dervishes. On 17 July 1894 Italian Colonel Oreste Baratieri [q.v.] with 2,600 men in a surprise attack drove them out and occupied the town. He then garrisoned it with local levies under Italian officers commanded by Carlo Caneva [q.v.].

In 1897 Mahdist forces under Emir Fadil Muhammad (d. 1899) invested Kassala, but it was relieved by an Italian force under General Antonio Baldissera [q.v.].

Kassala Mutinies (1864 and 1865). Egyptian troops at this fortified town on the border of Eritrea had long been unpaid, and their officers were corrupt. In October 1864 some 500 soldiers mutinied, seized a stock of arms and ammunition, and vented their rage by sacking the village of Sabdarat. They were finally brought back to duty when a prominent religious notable, al-Hassan Muhammad 'Uthman al-Miirghani (d. 1869), persuaded them to give in.

In July 1866 there was a second mutiny when Sudanese troops, mostly Dinkas, learned that they were to be part of a battalion formed to replace the Sudanese battalion then in Mexico [see Egyptian Sudanese Battalion in Mexico]. Miralai (Colonel) Hasan Ali Pasha Arnaût (d. 1865), an Albanian in the Egyptian service, had arrived to take command. With about 150 loyal troops he held the citadel and was able to fight off all attacks until a relief force arrived in August and September. The mutiny was then crushed with great ruthlessness: In the fighting and the massacre that followed 1,637 mutineers were killed. Among the loyal troops, 312 were killed and 83 wounded. Rotting corpses so polluted the area that disease ran rife, and in the ensuing epidemic Hasan Ali died.

Kassassin, Battle of (28 August 1882), Arabi's Revolt. At this place in northern Egypt a British force under General Gerald Graham [q.v.] was attacked by Egyptian forces under Arabi Pasha [q.v.]. Graham remained on the defensive most of the day, repulsing Egyptian assaults; late in the afternoon he counterattacked with his cavalry, and the Egyptians broke and fled. British losses were 11 killed and 68 wounded [see Tell-el-Kebir, Battle of].

Katabasis. Retreat; a backward march.

Kataha. The specially fused steel bar from which Japanese sword and knife blades were forged.

Katana. A Japanese fighting sword with a wooden grip. This was regarded as the most important of the Japanese swords. Scabbards were usually made of lacquered light magnolia wood (*honoki*) and decorated with the owner's crest. Blades, required to be capable of cutting off a man's head at a single stroke, were sometimes tested on criminals condemned to death or on corpses. Various types of cuts with the sword were sometimes perfected in the same way.

Katana-Kake. A Japanese sword rack, used not only for the katana but for other swords as well.

Katipunan. A secret society formed in the Philippines in 1896 by Andrés Bonifacio (1863–1897) to oppose Spanish rule. Two years later the society came into the open and called for an armed rebellion [see Philippine Insurrection against the Spanish].

Katsina, Battles for (1807–14), West African conflict. This Nigerian town, 85 miles northwest of Kano, was capital of the ancient kingdom of Katsina, one of the earliest Hausa states. It was a part of the Sokoto Empire when it was attacked by the Fulahs in 1807, beginning a seven-year war. The town was captured only through its near destruction.

Katsura, Taro (1847–1913). A Japanese soldier and statesman who fought in the Boshin Civil War [q.v.] for the Meiji Restoration and who, in 1870 and again in 1884, was sent to Europe at government expense to study its armies. He was so impressed by the Prussian army, particularly its general staff, that when Aritomo Yamagata [q.v.] appointed him to report on the performance of Japan's conscript army during the Satsuma Rebellion [q.v.], he stressed the need for a general staff, or staff bureau, in the Japanese army. In 1886 he was appointed vice-minister of war, and in 1891 he commanded a division. In the Sino-Japanese War [q.v.] he commanded the left wing of the Japanese army, making in 1894–95 a remarkable winter march from the northeast shore of the Yellow Sea to Haicheng, 80 miles southwest of Mukden in Manchuria, and finally occupying Newchwang, on the Liao River about 30 miles from its mouth, where he joined with II Army Corps and moved up the Liaotung Peninsula. He was minister of war from 1898 to 1900, after which he became premier.

Katzbach / Kocaba, Battles of (22 and 26 August 1813), Napoleonic Wars. When seventy-one-year-old Prussian General Gebhard von Blücher [q.v.] with 95,000 troops moved westward from Breslau (Wroclaw) on 14 August 1813, Napoleon concentrated 150,000 troops that stopped his progress and on 22 August threw him back behind the Katzbach River northwest of Breslau in southwest Poland. Napoleon then left Marshal Jacques Macdonald [q.v.] in charge while he himself saw to the Austrian front. Macdonald, disobeying orders, crossed the Katzbach in three places on 26 August and in a blinding rainstorm was attacked and routed by Blücher. French losses were 15,000 men and 100 guns.

This reverse, combined with subsequent reverses by subordinate commanders, undermined Napoleon's successful defense of Dresden and hastened the evacuation of his forces in Central Europe.

Kaufmann, Konstantin Petrovich (1818–1882). A Russian soldier who first saw service as an engineer at the siege of Kars [q.v.] in 1855. In 1867 he became governor of Turkestan, and in 1868 he gained fame by his conquest of Samarkand. In continued campaigns in Central Asia between 1868 and 1875 he captured the khanates of Bokhara, Khiva, and Kokand [qq.v.], extending the Russian frontier to the border of Afghanistan and greatly alarming the British [see Great Game, the; Central Asian Wars]. During the Russo-Turkish War of 1878–79 [q.v.] he readied a 30,000-man army to invade India if Britain entered the war on the side of Turkey. In 1880 and 1881 he sent Mikhail Skobelev [q.v.] against the Akhal Tekkes [see Geok Tepe]. He was scheming to add Merv to the Russian Empire when he died suddenly on 15 May 1882.

Kaulbars, Nikolai Vasilievich (1842–1905). A Russian soldier and cartographer who made the first Russian maps of South America, Australia, and Africa. With his brother Baron Aleksandr Vasilievich Kaulbars (1844–1920) he explored the Tien Shan Mountains and Amu Darya River in Central Asia in 1869–73. He was chief of a divisional staff in the Russo-Turkish War of 1877–78 and also served in the Russo-Turkish War of 1878–79 [qq.v.]. In 1882–83 he was war minister in Bulgaria. Later he served in China and Odessa. In the Russo-Japanese War of 1904–05 he was an army commander. He was a brother of General Nikolai Vasilievich Kaulbars (1842–1905).

Kautz, August Valentine (1828–1895). A German-born American soldier who in 1846 enlisted as a private in the 1st Ohio Infantry and fought under Zachary Taylor [q.v.] in the Mexican War [q.v.]. In 1848 he entered West Point and was graduated four years later. He served in Washington and Oregon territories and in October 1855 was wounded in a skirmish with hostile Indians. Less than five months later, near Puget Sound, he was again wounded. In 1857 he made the first recorded ascent of Mount Rainier (14,408 feet). One of the mountain's twenty-six glaciers is named for him.

A captain when the American Civil War erupted, he fought in the Union army in the 6th Cavalry in the Peninsular Campaign [q.v.]. On 2 September 1861 he was promoted colonel of the 2nd Ohio Cavalry, and on 26 July 1863 he took part in the capture of John Hunt Morgan [q.v.] and his raiders. He rose to command a cavalry division, being brevetted brigadier general on 7 May 1864 and major general in October. During May and June 1865 he was a member of the military commission that tried those accused of assassinating Abraham Lincoln.

After the war he remained in the army as a lieutenant colonel and served in the Southwest, where he organized several expeditions against the Mescalero Apaches. On 7 July 1874 he was promoted colonel of the 4th Infantry. His tour of duty in the Southwest was marred by abrasive encounters with John Philip Clum (1851–1932), a member of the Dutch Reformed Church and the Indian agent for the San Carlos Apaches, who had an unconcealed contempt for all army officers. He became a brigadier general on 20 April 1891 and commanded the Department of the Columbia until he retired on 5 January 1892. He wrote several books on the customs of the service, and he kept a voluminous diary.

Kavanagh, Thomas Henry (1821–1882). A British minor civil servant in India who became the first civilian to win the Victoria Cross [q.v.]. During the Indian Mutiny [q.v.], with his wife and fourteen children, he was among those besieged in the Residency at Lucknow [q.v.]. Without telling his wife, he volunteered to carry maps and information from the Residency to Sir Colin Campbell [q.v.], commanding the relieving force, at the Alumbagh, a large walled garden just outside Lucknow. On 9 November 1857, disguised as an Indian, he managed to slip through the rebel lines and reach Sir Colin, a feat for which he won the award.

He died in Gibraltar, and a memorial was erected to him in the North Front Cemetery there.

Kawakami, Soroku (1848–1899). A Japanese soldier who was born to a samurai family in a Satsuma fife in southern Kyushu and fought as a Satsuma samurai in the Boshin Civil War [q.v.] of 1868. In 1871 he was commissioned a lieutenant in the new national army, and in 1877 he fought in the Satsuma Rebellion [q.v.]. In 1884 and 1885 he traveled in Europe and the United States, studying military affairs. On his return he was promoted major general and appointed assistant chief of staff. He spent 1887 in Germany studying the German military system. In 1898, the year before he died, he was promoted general and made chief of the general staff.

Kawamura, Kageaki (1850–1926). A Japanese soldier who in 1868 fought against the shogunate in the Boshin Civil War [q.v.] and in 1871 joined the new imperial army as a sergeant. He was commissioned a year later and fought in the Satsuma Rebellion [q.v.] in 1877. In 1891 he was promoted major general, and in the Sino-Japanese War [q.v.] of 1884–85 he commanded the Imperial Guard Division. He was a full general in the Russo-Japanese War of 1904–05.

Kearny, Philip (1814–1862). An American soldier, nephew of Stephen Watts Kearny [q.v.]. In 1836, three years after he was graduated from Columbia University, he inherited a million dollars on the death of his grandfather. He was commissioned a second lieutenant of dragoons in 1837 and in 1839 attended the French cavalry school at Saumur. In 1840 he saw action with the Chasseurs d'Afrique in Algeria in an expedi-

Kearny, Philip *Death of General Kearny, 1 September 1862*

tion against the Milianah. He was promoted captain in 1846 and served in the Mexican War [q.v.], winning a brevet to major for distinguishing himself in the battles of Contreras and Churubusco [qq.v.]. In the latter battle his left arm was shattered and had to be amputated. General Winfield Scott [q.v.] called him "the bravest man I ever knew and a perfect soldier." He resigned in 1851 and served in the French army in Italy in 1859, fighting at Magenta and Solferino [qq.v.] and winning the French Legion of Honor [q.v.]. On 17 May 1861 he was made a brigadier general of volunteers in the Union army and saw service in the Peninsular Campaign and at Second Bull Run [qq.v.]. He was promoted major general of volunteers as of 4 July, but he was killed in the Battle of Chantilly [q.v.] on 1 September 1862 before receiving word of his promotion.

Kearny, Stephen Watts (1794–1848). An American soldier who was appointed a first lieutenant on 12 March 1812 and fought well in the War of 1812 [q.v.], distinguishing himself in the Battle of Queenston Heights [q.v.], in which he was wounded and taken prisoner. He was paroled in 1813. On 1 April of that year he was promoted captain, a rank he retained for ten years until brevetted major in 1823, an automatic promotion after ten years in grade. In June 1846 he was promoted brigadier general for the Mexican War [q.v.], and he won a brevet to major general for capturing Santa Fe, New Mexico. He was then posted to California, where on 6 December 1846 he fought the Battle of Pasqual [q.v.] against Mexican Californians (Californios) and contended with John Frémont [q.v.] over which was in command of the California land forces.

In April 1848 he joined the expeditionary army of General Winfield Scott [q.v.], which invaded Mexico [see Mexican War] and was commander at Veracruz [q.v.], when he succumbed to yellow fever.

He was the uncle of Philip Kearny [q.v.].

Kearny Medal and Kearny Cross. In November 1862, during the American Civil War, officers in the 1st Division of II Corps of the Union Army of the Potomac decided to create a medal for officers who had "honorably served under Major General Kearny and whose military record was unstained." General Philip Kearny [q.v.] had been killed on 1 September in the Battle of Chantilly [q.v.]. The medal was manufactured by Bell, Black & Co. of New York City, which was required to post a bond as a guarantee against unauthorized copies. It was in the shape of a Maltese cross on which was superimposed a circle with the words "Dulce et decorum est pro patria mori." It was to be worn suspended by a ribbon. The medals cost fifteen dollars each, and 317 were distributed.

General David Bell Birney (1819–1864), who succeeded Kearny, directed on 13 March 1863 that a "cross of valor" be awarded to others who had distinguished themselves. The bronze cross had "Kearny Cross" on the obverse and "Birney's Division" on the reverse. Among the first recipients were two women: Anna Etheridge and Marie Tebe [qq.v.].

Kecherklechi. A corps of personal guards to the king of Persia formed in the eighteenth century. They were armed with large-caliber muskets.

Keep. The self-defensible citadel or inner defenses of a forti-

fication to which the garrison could retire if the outer ramparts were taken.

Kehla. A headring worn by married Zulu male warriors as a sign of status. It was usually made of resin and worked into the hair.

Keith, Thomas (d. 1815), Turkish name: Ibrahim Aga. A Scottish soldier born in Edinburgh who was a gunsmith with the 72nd Highlanders when he was captured at Rosetta, Egypt, in 1807 during the disastrous attempt by the British to overthrow Mehemet Ali [q.v.]. [see Egypt, British Expedition to]. In captivity he was made a slave of Tusun [q.v.], Mehemet Ali's son. He proved to be brave, loyal, and an able soldier and rose to become chief of cavalry and then a high court official. In the Arabian Wars [q.v.] he distinguished himself in the battles against the Wahhabis. He was for a time governor of the holy city of Medina, certainly one of the most curious offices that a Scot ever attained. He was killed in battle fighting the Wahhabis.

Keitt, Laurence Massillon (1824–1864). An American politician who was a rabid defender of states' rights in the U.S. Congress and a foe of Jefferson Davis [q.v.] in the Confederate Congress. On 11 January 1862, during the American Civil War, he raised the 20th South Carolina and was its colonel. He was mortally wounded at Cold Harbor on 2 June 1864 and died two days later.

Kelat. See Khelat, Battle of.

Kellermann, François Christophe (1735–1820). A French soldier from Alsace who was awarded the Order of St. Louis during the Seven Years' War. He earned the title Duc de Valmy on 20 September 1792 after he led the ragtag French Army of the Moselle, which, in the rain-soaked Battle of Valmy, held back the advance of the Allies on Paris. During the Terror he was imprisoned for more than a year but was finally acquitted and returned to the army. Napoleon made him one of his first marshals on 19 May 1804. He took no part in the Hundred Days [q.v.]. Louis XVIII (1755–1824) made him a peer.

Kellermann, François Étienne (1770–1835). A French soldier and the son of François Christophe Kellermann [q.v.]. Commissioned in 1785, he became general of brigade in 1797. He led the decisive charge in the Battle of Marengo in 1800 and was promoted general of division. He commanded the cavalry in Portugal, distinguished himself at Austerlitz, took part in Napoleon's Russian Campaign, and fought at Waterloo [qq.v.].

Kelly-Kenny, Thomas (1840–1914). A British soldier, born Thomas Kelly, who took the additional surname of Kenny in 1874. In 1858 he was commissioned into the 2nd Foot (later Queen's Regiment), and in 1860 he took part in the Second Opium War and was present at the capture of the Taku forts [q.v.]. In 1866 he served in the Abyssinian Campaign [q.v.] as a captain. In 1882 he commanded the second battalion of his regiment. As a major general in South Africa during the Second Anglo-Boer War [q.v.] he served under Lord Roberts and took part in the relief of Kimberley. He rose to become a full general and retired in 1907.

Kemble, Gouverneur (1786–1875). An American arms manufacturer. He was graduated from Columbia College in 1803 and, interested in literary pursuits, became a friend of Washington Irving (1783–1859). During the War of 1812 [q.v.] he was U.S. consul in Cádiz, where he observed the Spanish method of casting cannon. When he returned to the United States, in Irving's words, he "turned Vulcan and began foraging thunderbolts." In 1818 he founded the West Point Foundry at Cold Spring, New York, across the Hudson River from West Point, where he manufactured and continually improved the best cast cannon in America. During the American Civil War he was the chief supplier of artillery for the Union army, producing more than 3,000 guns and 1.6 million projectiles. His successor at the foundry was his brother-in-law Robert Parker Parrott [q.v.].

Kemendine, Battle of (10 June 1824), First Anglo-Burmese War. A British force of 3,000 under Major General Archibald Campbell [q.v.] drove a Burmese force of equal strength from their stockades at Kemendine, near Rangoon (Yangon), Burma (Myanmar).

Kemp, Christoffel Greyling (1872–1946). A South African soldier who fought in campaigns against native tribes and distinguished himself as a Boer commando leader during the Second Anglo-Boer War [q.v.], rising to a general. In 1912 he became an officer in the Union Defense Force (South Africa's army), but he joined the Boer rebellion in 1914. Nevertheless he later became a cabinet minister.

Kempeitai. A Japanese military police force founded in 1881 to ferret out dissidents. It later became the most repressive instrument in the Japanese military government.

Kemper, Reuben (d. 1827). An American adventurer who attempted to overthrow the Spanish government in Florida. He led unsuccessful expeditions to capture Baton Rouge in 1804 and moved on Pensacola and Mobile, then part of Florida, in 1810.

Kempt, James (1764–1854). A British soldier who fought in Egypt in 1800–01 and served in Canada from 1809 to 1811, when he joined Wellington and fought in the Peninsular War [q.v.]. He was severely wounded at the siege of Badajoz [q.v.]. In the Battle of Waterloo [q.v.] he assumed command of the division of Lieutenant General Sir Thomas Picton [q.v.] when Picton was killed leading a charge. Later he became successively governor of Nova Scotia and, from 1828 to 1830, governor-general of Canada. From 1834 to 1838 he was master general of ordnance.

Kendrick, Henry L. (1811–1891). An American soldier who was graduated from West Point in 1835 and fought in the Mexican War [q.v.], winning a brevet to major for his gallantry in the defense of La Puebla [q.v.] in 1847. From 1849 to 1857 he served on the American frontier, commanding Fort Defiance, New Mexico, from 1852 to 1857, when he returned to West Point as professor of chemistry, mineralogy, and geology, a post he held for twenty-three years.

Kenesaw Mountain, Battle of (27 June 1864), American Civil War. Confederates under Joseph Johnston [q.v.] were entrenched on this mountain, about two and a half miles long and about 700 feet high four miles from Marietta, Georgia. After a six-day bombardment by the Federal artillery of William T. Sherman [q.v.] the Federals attacked on 27 June 1864 and were repulsed. Confederate losses were 270 killed and wounded and 172 missing out of an estimated 17,733 engaged; Federal losses were 1,999 killed and wounded and 50 missing out of 16,225 engaged.

Kennerly, James (1792–1840). A sutler for the American army who was in business at Fort Atkinson, Nebraska, on the Missouri River about 15 miles from present-day Omaha in 1823, when Colonel Henry Leavenworth [q.v.] commanded there. Kennerly was one of the best of a class of citizens frequently vilified [see Sutler]. When a paymaster was shot and robbed, he paid the troops; he lent money to needy officers; and he held money and valuables for men when they went on leave. He owned two slaves and paid his other help partly in liquor. When Fort Atkinson was abandoned on 6 June 1827, he moved to Jefferson Barracks, Missouri.

Kentage. Unserviceable military hardware, such as condemned guns and cannonballs.

Kent, Jacob Ford (1835–1918). An American soldier who was graduated from West Point in 1861. During the American Civil War he fought for the Union in the First Battle of Bull Run [q.v.], where he was wounded three times and captured. After more than a year in prison he was exchanged and fought at Antietam and Fredericksburg [qq.v.]. He was then appointed a temporary lieutenant colonel and served on the staffs of IX and VI corps.

After the war he served for four years as a professor at West Point and then for nearly thirty years in the South and West. Although he did not receive his majority until 1885, he was a colonel at the beginning of the Spanish-American War [q.v.] and was soon a brigadier general. In Cuba he saw no action until 1 July 1898, when he took part in the capture of San Juan Hill [q.v.], for which he was promoted major general. After brief service in the Philippines he retired on 15 October 1898.

Kent Bugle. An early cornet or key bugle with pistons and six keys developed early in the nineteenth century and named after the Duke of Kent (1767–1820), Queen Victoria's father.

Kentucky, Confederate Invasion of (August–October 1862), American Civil War. On 24 August 1862 two corps of the Confederate Army of Tennessee [q.v.] under General Braxton Bragg [q.v.] crossed the Tennessee River above Chattanooga. On 13 September they entered Glasgow, Kentucky.

Kentucky *Bragg's invasion of Kentucky, 1862*

Munfordville [q.v.] was captured on 14–17 September. Bragg then pressed farther north. Federal troops under General Don Carlos Buell moved on him and in the Battle of Perryville [q.v.] defeated him, though not decisively. He retreated in good order to Tennessee.

Kentucky Rifle. Sometimes called the American long rifle or the Pennsylvania rifle. A muzzle-loading rifle with a long barrel developed by German settlers in Pennsylvania in the eighteenth century. It was manufactured in various calibers from .32 to .60. Although first a flintlock, it developed into a percussion rifle.

Keogh, Myles Walter (1840–1876). An Irish-born soldier of fortune who fought in papal armies before coming to the United States in 1862 and serving as a captain in the Union army. He won brevets to lieutenant colonel for his conduct at Gettysburg [q.v.] and Dallas, Texas. He remained in the army after the war as a second lieutenant and then as a captain in the 7th Cavalry. He is said to have fought in more than a hundred engagements. He was killed in the Battle of the Little Bighorn [q.v.].

Kepi. A visored military cap of French origin worn in several armies, including the American during the American Civil War and the Russian from 1864. It was close-fitting and featured a flat, round top that sloped forward.

Keppel, George Thomas, Sixth Earl of Albemarle (1799–1891). An Englishman who was so idle at Westminster School that when he was sixteen, the headmaster pronounced him unfit for any learned profession. His family then purchased an ensigncy in the 14th Foot for him. He joined his battalion in Belgium two months before the Battle of Waterloo [q.v.], in which he fought. In 1821 he was promoted lieutenant in the 22nd Regiment, and in 1825, after service in India, he was promoted captain. He obtained a majority on half pay in 1827, and although he served no more, he rose in rank to full general (on half pay of his former commission) in 1874. He became a member of Parliament and paid a visit to the Russo-Turkish War of 1828–1829 [q.v.]. In 1854 he was appointed a trustee of Westminster School, a post he held until his death at the age of ninety-two.

Kerana. A Persian trumpet shaped like an old-fashioned speaking trumpet. It was played with other instruments at sundown or retreat.

Kernstown, Battles of. During the American Civil War there were two important battles fought at this town four miles south of Winchester, Virginia.

1. 23 March 1862. Confederate General Thomas Jackson [q.v.], retreating up the Shenandoah Valley before the superior army of Union General Nathaniel Banks [q.v.], received information that the Federals were withdrawing. He reversed course in the hope of attacking the Federal rear guard. Instead he found himself faced with a numerically superior force under General James Shields [q.v.]. Although Shields was badly wounded before the battle got under way, the Union forces, ably led by Nathan Kimball [q.v.], carried the day. Jackson resumed his retreat up the Shenandoah Valley.

Of about 9,000 Federals engaged, some 600 were killed or wounded. The Confederates lost about 700 out of 4,200 engaged.

2. 24 July 1864. Two Federal divisions under General George Crook [q.v.] encamped near Kernstown were attacked and routed by Confederates under General John Breckinridge [q.v.]. Federal losses were 1,185, including 479 captured.

Kettledrum. A percussion instrument with a parchment head stretched over a hollow brass or copper hemisphere, it is the only drum with a definite musical pitch. In many European armies kettledrums were used in pairs by cavalry and horse artillery, but they were never adopted by the American army. Because they were sometimes used in camps as a temporary table for tea or drinks, the word came to mean, particularly in India, an informal party given by officers.

Kettledrum

Key, Francis Scott (1779–1843). An American lawyer and poet who during the War of 1812 [q.v.] wrote the verses of "The Star-Spangled Banner" [q.v.] after anxiously watching the British bombardment of Fort McHenry [q.v.], one of the forts defending Baltimore, Maryland, on the night of 13–14 September 1814. Earlier he had visited the British fleet, then in the Chesapeake Bay, to plead for the release of a friend, Dr. William Beanes, who had been captured. The British were willing to release their prisoner, but he and Key were detained on board a British ship in the Patapsco River near Baltimore until after the attack. Some years after he had written it, Key's four-stanza verse was put to the tune of a British drinking song, "To Anacreon in Heaven." It became an immediate success and was generally considered the American national anthem, although it was not so declared officially by Congress until 3 March 1931.

For eight years (1833–41), under three presidents, Key was U.S. attorney of the District of Columbia and, as far as is known, never wrote the lyrics to another song. The earliest-known version of the words is on a yellowed sheet of paper owned by the Maryland Historical society.

Keyes, Erasmus Darwin (1810–1895). An American officer who was graduated from West Point in 1832 and later taught cavalry and artillery there. During the American Civil War he commanded a Union brigade at First Bull Run, a division that winter, and IV Corps of the Army of the Potomac from March 1862 through the Peninsular Campaign [qq.v.]. He was promoted major general on 5 May 1862. His participation in diversionary movements around Richmond during the Gettysburg Campaign led to a bitter controversy with General John Adams Dix (1798–1879), who accused him of retiring from a position at Baltimore Store (Tallysville), Virginia, while facing inferior numbers of Confederates. He resigned on 6 May 1864 and moved to California, where he farmed, mined for gold, and engaged in banking.

Keyserlicks. A colloquial name for Austrian soldiers.

Khaki. From the Hindustani word meaning dust-colored. The word was applied to the color of light yellowish brown

twilled cotton cloth that was first used in 1848 in field uniforms by the Corps of Guides [q.v.] in India. Sir Charles
Napier [q.v.] declared, "The Guides are the only properly
dressed Riflemen in India." Although khaki was later the
color of the uniforms worn in the Sudan campaigns and
in South Africa during the Second Anglo-Boer War [q.v.],
the color did not meet with widespread approval. An article in
the *Pall Mall Gazette* (25 March 1892) spoke disdainfully of
cotton khaki uniforms: "Khaki is not showy enough except
when it is new and well made up, and if constantly worn it
tends to promote slovenliness." Khaki-colored twill was
adopted by the American army in 1898 as the field service
uniform and was worn during the Spanish-American War
[q.v.], but it was not universally adopted by the British army
until 1902. Many other armies eventually switched to khaki
uniforms.

Khalassi. In India a man who pitches tents, but the word
was often employed to designate any camp follower.

Khalsa. The Sikh army in the Punjab, India. The word is
also often taken to mean the entire Sikh government or religion. Before the rise of Ranjit Singh [q.v.] the Sikh states in
the Punjab were a series of loosely confederated clans, called
misls, that fought with each other and with their Muslim
neighbors. Ranjit Singh by his genius, cunning, and daring
welded the clans into a state. He created an army on European
lines by hiring European officers, mostly French, and British
deserters. By 1833 his army was one of the best on the Indian
subcontinent.

Khama (1837–1922). A member of the Bamangwato
tribe in present-day Zimbabwe (formerly Rhodesia) who
became chief in 1872. He was said to be "one of the
greatest men the Black races have produced." He embraced
Christianity in 1860 and, on becoming chief, banned all
liquor in the lands he controlled. He successfully fought
off attempted encroachments by the Matabeles and Boers.
He was friendly to the British and assisted Cecil Rhodes
(1853–1902) in the establishment of Rhodesia. In 1895
he visited England, where he was received by Queen
Victoria.

Khanda. A traditional Indian sword used by the Marathas
and Rajputs and the state weapon of Orissa. Its straight, broad
blade widened toward a blunt point. It was usually, but not always, single-edged.

Khanger. Any Eastern or Middle Eastern dagger. Also
spelled khanjar, kanjar, kinjal, and handshar.

Khartoum, Siege of (12 March 1884–26 January 1885),
Mahdist uprising. British General Charles ("Chinese")
Gordon [q.v.], who was appointed governor-general of the
Sudan and sent to save and repatriate the Egyptian garrisons
threatened by the Dervishes [q.v.], arrived at Khartoum, capital of the Sudan, at the confluence of the White Nile and
Blue Nile rivers on 18 February 1884. He had managed to
evacuate about 2,500, mostly women and children, before he
was besieged in the city by Mahdist forces. On 26 January

Khartoum *Punch magzine was so sure Khartoum had been relieved that on 7 February 1885 it depicted Gordon greeting his rescuer (left).*
But the following week it showed a Britannia, grief-stricken upon learning that Gordon was dead (right), crying "Too late!"

1885, after a siege of 317 days, Khartoum was taken by a Dervish assault and Gordon was killed. An advanced element of the relief expedition under General Garnet Wolseley [q.v.], which had set off from Cairo in October 1884, arrived just two days too late [see Gordon Relief Expedition].

Khasgi Paga. Regular cavalry that formed the Maratha household cavalry.

Khedive. The principal title of the viceroy or ruler of Egypt, a tributary of the sultan of Turkey. Ismail Pasha (1830–1895), who became viceroy in 1863, was the first to be given the title of khedive by the Turkish government on 8 June 1867.

Khelat, Battle of (13 November 1839), First Afghan War. A British punitive expedition was sent against Mehrab Khan (d. 1839) of Khelat (Khalat or Kelat), 88 miles south of Quetta. His Baluchi warriors had earlier annoyed the British army advancing to Kabul. With only 1,166 men Brigadier General Thomas Willshire (1789–1862), a veteran of the Peninsular War [q.v.] and of Kaffir Wars against Xhosas in South Africa, advanced upon the formidable citadel at Khelat. Pushing his guns to within 200 yards, he blew in the main gates, through which his infantry dashed. British losses were 37 killed and 107 wounded; Baluchi losses were 400 killed, including the khan, and 2,000 prisoners taken.

Willshire was made a baronet for his victory. At the time he was childless, but at age fifty-nine he married and sired two sons and three daughters.

Khiva, Russian Conquest of (1839–73). Khiva was the capital of a khanate of 35,700 square miles on the left bank of the lower Oxus (Amu Darya) River in Central Asia. The Russians first attempted to conquer it in November 1839 when General Basil A. Perovsky (1795–1857) with 5,200 troops and a camel train of 10,000 left Orenburg (Chkalov) on the Ural River (across the Caspian Sea from Baku) to move against it. The expedition encountered severe snowstorms, and many of the troops fell victim to snow blindness; food, particularly fresh food, was in such short supply that scurvy broke out. By January 1840 some 200 men had died; camels began to expire at the rate of 100 per day; wolves plagued the survivors. On 1 February 1840 the expedition turned to retrace its steps. By the time it reached Orenburg more than 1,000 men and 1,500 camels had died.

In 1869 the Russians built a fort on the eastern shore of the Caspian and made it a military base. Early in 1873 three Russian columns, all under General Konstantin Kaufmann [q.v.], moved out from Tashkent (captured by the Russians on 15 June 1865). On 29 May 1873 the khan fled and Kaufmann entered Khiva, which was soon annexed [see Khokand, Russian Conquest of].

Khojak Pass, Battle of (28 March 1842), First Afghan War. British Brigadier General Richard England (1793–1883) marched a small force of 500 men into the Khojak Pass in a western ridge of the Sulaiman Mountains in Afghanistan between Quetta and Chaman, to relieve the besieged garrison at Kandahar. He was repulsed by the Afghans with a loss of one-fifth of his force and retired to Quetta. On 12 April he returned with four battalions of infantry and a battery of horse

artillery, to which on 4 May was added a support column sent out by General William Nott [q.v.] from Kandahar. The pass was cleared.

Khokand, Russian Conquest of (1864–76). From about 1780 the khanate of Khokand (Kokand) in Central Asia was a semiautonomous state that acknowledged the sovereignty of China, but in 1812 the ruling khan unsuccessfully rebelled, and the khanate became merely a tributary. Beginning about 1817, the khan began to enlarge his state and to build forts along the Syr Darya River as protection against Kirghiz nomads. This brought the khanate into conflict with Russia, which, starting in 1847, tried unsuccessfully to destroy the forts. However, in 1853 General Basil A. Perovsky (1795–1857) captured the fortress of Ak-Mechet on the Syr Darya.

In 1864 Russians seized the oasis towns of Chimkent and Turkestan, about 75 and 140 miles respectively north of Tashkent, and several small forts belonging to Alim Kul (d. 1865), the current khan. While Alim Kul was warring with the khan of Bokhara (Bukhara), Major General Mikhail Chernyaiev [q.v.], largely on his own initiative, moved with 1,900 men and 12 guns on Tashkent, his capital, then the richest city in Central Asia with a population of about 100,000 protected by 16 miles of crenellated walls. Chernyaiev arrived before the city on 8 May 1865 and took it by storm at first light on 15 June. Russian losses were 25 killed and 89 wounded.

Tashkent was incorporated into a new state of Turkestan, and General Konstantin Kaufmann [q.v.] was appointed governor-general.

The khanate was not completely subjugated, however. In 1875 a rebellion erupted against Russian rule. Kaufmann took the field and on 22 August routed a rebel army. Four days later he entered Khokand. On 4 September he defeated a rebel force of 30,000. After further fighting the towns of Osh and Andijan fell, and part of the khanate was folded into Turkestan. In October a Russian garrison of 300 at Andizhan was surprised and massacred [see Andizhan / Andijan Uprising]. On 30 January 1876 the khan's forces were defeated at Assake [q.v.], and on 29 February the entire khanate was annexed as Fergana, but minor uprisings continued. In 1924 it was merged into Uzbek.

Khushab / Khoosh-ab, Battle of (8 February 1857), Anglo-Persian War. A battle fought near this walled village on the Jhelum River three miles northwest of Sargodha in what is today Pakistan between a British force of 4,000 infantry and 400 cavalry with 18 guns under General Sir James Outram [q.v.] and a Persian force of 6,000 infantry and 800 cavalry with 18 guns under the Persian commander-in-chief, Shuja-ul-Mulk. A Persian attack launched about midnight on 7 February was repulsed. The next morning the two armies faced each other. A charge of the 3rd Bombay Light Cavalry broke a Persian square, and led by their commander-in-chief, the Persian army fled in great disorder, leaving some 700 dead on the field. British losses were 19 killed and 64 wounded.

Khyber Knife. A straight, single-edged blade that was the traditional knife of the Afridis and other tribes on what was India's Northwest Frontier (now Pakistan).

Khyber Pass. The most practicable of the four passes through mountains of the Safed Koh range on the Northwest Frontier of India (today Pakistan). The Khyber Pass, 33 miles long with its eastern entrance just over 10 miles from Peshawar, was the scene of protracted fighting in the two Afghan Wars [q.v.] and between British and Afridi tribesmen in the nineteenth century. The British built forts at Ali Masjid in the center of the pass and at Landi Kotal at the Afghan border, the highest point (3,370 feet). With the help of forts, bribes, and the enlistment of Pathans into special units such as the Khyber Rifles [q.v.] the British managed to control the pass for most of the century.

Khyber Rifles. A unit of Frontier Scouts that enlisted Afridi tribesmen and employed them on India's Northwest Frontier (now Pakistan), mainly in the Khyber Pass [q.v.].

Kibee. A flaw in the bore of a gun caused by a shot striking it.

Kigoshi, Yasutsama (1854–1932). A Japanese soldier who took part in the Satsuma Rebellion [q.v.] in 1877 and served as a general in the Sino-Japanese War [q.v.] of 1894–95 and the Russo-Japanese War of 1904–05.

Kiheitai. Japanese shock troops in the *shotai* [q.v.], formed in 1864. In the core units most were radical Choshu samurai, but they were purposely surrounded by units of commoners.

Kilij Saber. A term used for several types of Middle Eastern and Caucasian swords with a blade double-edged at the point.

They were popular in Turkey and were issued to Cossack regiments in the Russian army, where they were called *kylch*.

Killa. In India, a fort or castle. The commandant or governor of such a fort was called the *killadar*.

Killdeer Mountain, Battle of (28 July 1864), American Civil War. In the Killdeer Mountains, a series of lofty buttes rising 600 feet above the plain and extending for 10 miles in what is today western North Dakota, Union General Alfred Sully and Lieutenant Colonel Minor Thomas [qq.v.], at the head of 2,200 men, encountered a force estimated by Sully to be 6,000 Sioux warriors (the Sioux said 1,600), many under Inkpaduta [q.v.], near the Knife River. The Indians were routed, losing perhaps 100 (the Sioux said 31). Sully lost 5 killed and 10 wounded. Although Sully was credited with the victory, he was ill on the day of battle, and the troops were actually commanded by Thomas.

Killed in Action. A casualty killed in battle or one who dies before reaching a medical treatment facility.

Kilmainham Hospital. An institution near Dublin housing about 250 wounded or pensioned officers. It was founded in 1675 by Charles II (1630–1685). The general commanding the forces in Ireland was considered the master of the hospital and had his residence on the grounds.

Kilmallock, Attack on (5 March 1867). Some 200 armed Fenians attacked the police barracks at this Irish town 18 miles south of Limerick [see Fenian Brotherhood]. For three

Killdeer Mountain *General Alfred Sully's troops attack Lakota Sioux warriors at the Battle of Killdeer Mountain, 1864.*

hours the barracks was defended by 14 police constables, who finally made a sally and drove off the attackers.

Kilmarnock. A type of military bonnet worn by English soldiers from 1812 to 1874 and by Scottish soldiers from at least 1800 and throughout the century. The name came from the town of Kilmarnock in southwest Scotland, 12 miles northeast of Ayr, where the bonnets were made.

Kilpatrick, Hugh Judson (1836–1881). An American Civil War soldier who was graduated from West Point in the class of May 1861 and on 9 May became a Union army captain in the 5th New York Infantry. On 10 June 1861 he was wounded in the Battle of Big Bethel [q.v.], the first regular officer to be wounded in action. In September he was promoted lieutenant colonel and colonel in December 1862. On 14 June 1863 he was promoted brigadier general, in which rank he took part in every major engagement in the eastern theater. In February 1864, with Ulrich Dahlgren [q.v.], he led an aborted cavalry raid on Richmond that resulted in Dahlgren's death [see Dahlgren's Raid]. In April he was sent to take command of a cavalry division in the army of William T. Sherman [q.v.], and in mid-May he was severely wounded in the Battle of Resaca [q.v.].

In August 1864 he led a raid on Lovejoy Station, 20 miles southeast of Atlanta, an action he claimed was a substantial success, although in fact he accomplished little [see Kilpatrick's Raid].

Kilpatrick neither drank nor gambled, but he was vain, a womanizer, and given to telling lies about his accomplishments. He was described by another cavalry officer as "of a highly excitable and nervous temperament." In November 1864 Sherman, just before his famous March to the Sea, said of him: "I know that Kilpatrick is a hell of a damned fool, but I want just that sort of man to command my cavalry in this expedition." For his command of the cavalry Kilpatrick won promotion to major general of volunteers and brevet major general, U.S. army.

At the end of 1865 he gave up his commissions and was appointed minister to Chile, where he served until 1868 and again in 1881 until his death.

Kilpatrick-Dahlgren Raid. See Dahlgren's Raid.

Kilpatrick's Raid (18–22 August 1864), American Civil War. Two brigades of cavalry (4,000 men) and two batteries of horse artillery under Brigadier General Hugh Kilpatrick [q.v.] left Sandtown, Georgia, on 18 August to raid Confederate railroads. After destroying a small section of track belonging to the Atlanta & West Point Railroad the raiders moved on to Lovejoy Station, about 20 miles southeast of Atlanta, where more damage was done. At Jonesboro in northwest-central Georgia they destroyed large quantities of stores but damaged little track. On his return to the Union lines Kilpatrick boasted that he had done enough damage to keep the Macon Railroad out of operation for ten days. In fact, the line was in operation within two days. The raid confirmed the low opinion of cavalry held by General W. T. Sherman [q.v.].

Kilt. The early kilt was simply the lower part of the plaid girded around the waist. The modern version, a separate skirt extending from the waist to the knees and pleated at the back and sides, worn by Highland regiments of the British army, seems to have been devised about 1727 by Thomas Rawlinson, an English industrialist who was seeking an appropriate costume for his Scots workers. In 1775 the British Parliament banned the wearing of kilts, but this seems never to have been enforced; it may even have encouraged the wearing, for the Scots then adopted the kilt as their national costume.

Kimball, Nathan (1823–1898). An American doctor who fought as a volunteer in the Mexican War and in the American Civil War served as colonel of the 14th Indiana. He fought in the battles of Cheat Mountain and Greenbriar. He was serving in the division of James Shields [q.v.] in the Shenandoah Valley when on 22 March 1862 Shields was severely wounded by a shell from one of the guns of Turner Ashby [q.v.]. Kimball assumed command of the division and the following day defeated the force under Thomas ("Stonewall") Jackson [q.v.] at Kernstown [q.v.]. On 15 April he was promoted brigadier general and in that rank fought at Antietam and Fredericksburg [qq.v.], where he was wounded. He later fought at Vicksburg and in the Atlanta Campaign [qq.v.]. On 1 February 1865 he was brevetted major general, and on 24 August he was mustered out. After the war he entered politics in Indiana and later in Utah.

Kimberley, Siege of (15 October 1899–15 February 1900), Second Anglo-Boer War. For 133 days about 8,000 Boers under Commandant Martinus Wessels Pretorius and later General Pieter Cronjé [qq.v.] besieged this town, the center of diamond-mining operations in Cape Province, South Africa. British forces in the town, commanded by Colonel (later Major General) Robert George Kekewich (1854–1914), numbered fewer than 4,000 regulars and volunteers, including armed townspeople. An indignant and impatient Cecil Rhodes (1853–1902), besieged with a number of fellow directors of the De Beers Company, proved more troublesome to Colonel Kekewich than did the Boers. The British lost 18 officers and 163 men, mostly from Boer artillery fire. Kimberley was relieved by a cavalry force commanded by General Sir John French [q.v.].

Colonel (later Field Marshal) Douglas Haig [q.v.], one of the relievers of the town, wrote to a friend: "The people in Kimberley looked fat and well. It was the relieving force which needed food."

"Kimi ga Yo." Japanese: "His Majesty's Reign." A song of praise to the emperor, expressing the hope that his reign will last a thousand years. Most Japanese consider this their national anthem, although the Diet has never so declared it. The text, which originated in an anonymous poem written in the tenth century, was set to music by the nineteenth-century composer Hayashi Hiromori. It was first performed publicly on the birthday of the emperor Meiji on 3 November 1880.

Kineyre, Battle of (18 June 1848), Second Sikh War. In April 1848 when the governor of the ancient city of Multan in southwestern Punjab (today in Pakistan) revolted and ordered the two resident British officers killed, young

Lieutenant Herbert Edwardes [q.v.], on his own initiative, raised a force of 3,000 Pathans and enlisted the help of the Muslim nawab of Bhawalpur, who took the field with 12,000 men. Multan was defended by about 6,000 Sikhs, who took positions near the neighboring village of Kineyre. The initial attack by the Bhawalpuris was repulsed, but a second attack, launched when Edwardes arrived with his Pathans and some artillery, routed them.

The victors lost about 300 men; the Sikhs at least 500.

King, Charles (1844–1933). An American soldier who was graduated from West Point in 1866 and saw much action against hostile Indians in Arizona. He lost most of the use of his right arm after being wounded in a fight with Apaches at Sunset Pass, not far from present-day Flagstaff. He later fought at Slim Buttes and in the Nez Percé War [qq.v.]. After thirteen years' service he was promoted captain, but he retired six weeks later. During the Spanish-American War [q.v.] he served under General Henry Lawton [q.v.] in the Philippines, and in 1899 he became a brigadier general of volunteers. Serving in the Wisconsin National Guard, he helped train troops for World War I. King became famous for his more than seventy books about soldiering and was hailed as "the first novelist of the army." His purpose, he said, was "making the army known to the people." Among his novels were *The Colonel's Daughter* (1833); *A War-Time Wooing* (1888); and *Under Fire* (1894).

At age eighty-nine he died from injuries after tripping over a rug.

King, Richard ("Dick") Philip (1813–1871). An English-born South African wagoneer who achieved lasting fame during the First Anglo-Boer War [q.v.]. In 1842 when a British force at Congella (today a southern suburb of Durban in Natal) was besieged by the Boers and was in desperate straits, King volunteered to ride for help to Grahamstown, 600 miles away in southeastern Cape Province. Accompanied only by a Zulu named Ndongeni (d. 1911), he crossed Durban Bay by boat and began a wild ride on his horse, Somerset, through land held by hostile tribes. In just ten days he delivered his message. A relief force was sent by ship from Port Elizabeth. King was rewarded for his heroism and stamina with a gift of £15.

King, Rufus (1814–1876). An American engineer, a newspaper editor, the attorney general of New York, and a member of the Board of Visitors of the U.S. Military Academy at West Point. He was a grandson of Rufus King (1755–1827), a signer of the Constitution, and a nephew of James Gore King (1791–1853), who was assistant adjutant general during the War of 1812 [q.v.]. In 1861 he was appointed minister to the Vatican, but before he sailed to take up his post, the Battle of Fort Sumter [q.v.], opened the American Civil War. He promptly declined the appointment and joined the Union army. After raising the Iron Brigade [q.v.] in Wisconsin, he became its brigadier general. When his brigade was surprised at Groveton, Virginia, by General Thomas ("Stonewall") Jackson [q.v.]. King, who suffered from epilepsy, was not on the field. When he failed to appear in the Second Battle of Bull Run [q.v.]. General John Pope, thinking he was drunk, had him court-martialed. He was found guilty of disobedi-ence and of exercising poor judgment. Curiously, following his own court-martial, he served on the commission that tried General Fitz-John Porter [q.v.] in December 1862–January 1863. On 20 October 1863 he resigned from the army and was then reappointed to the Vatican. There he discovered John H. Surratt (1844–1916), one of the alleged conspirators in the Lincoln assassination, serving in the Papal Zouaves. He arranged for his extradition to the United States in 1897. Surratt's trial resulted in a hung jury, and he was nolle prossed.

King, William Shakespeare (1815?–1895). An American physician who joined the army as an assistant surgeon in 1835 and became a major in 1856. An observant man, he noted, while serving in California, the prevalence among the inhabitants of "the extreme tendencies to functional disturbances of the brain. . . . Insanity, it is well known, is very frequent in California" (*Statistical Report on the Sickness and Mortality of the United States* [1852]).

King served in the Union army during the American Civil War, earning brevets to lieutenant colonel and colonel for his war services in North Carolina. He became a lieutenant colonel in 1876 and colonel in 1880. He retired two years later.

King's African Rifles. A unit established by the British Colonial Office in 1891 as the main defense force in British East Africa, which included Kenya, Uganda, British Somaliland (Somalia), and Nyasaland (Malawi). With a peacetime strength of about 5,000, it consisted of battalions of black African askaris (soldiers) who enlisted to serve in any part of the world for three-year periods, total service not to exceed eighteen years. It was led by regular British officers seconded to the corps, and a high standard of discipline and efficiency was maintained. It served in the campaign against the Mad Mullah of Somaliland [q.v.] in 1898 and later in both world wars.

King's German Legion. A British army unit raised in 1803 mostly from Hanoverian soldiers whose own army had been disbanded in July of that year; other former German soldiers joined later. The legion consisted of five regiments of cavalry, considered the best in Wellington's army in the Peninsular War [q.v.]; several regiments of infantry, including two of light infantry; and both horse and foot artillery. In 1814 all were discharged except the Hanoverians who were intended to become the new Hanoverian army. However, the return of Napoleon from Elba delayed the transfer and the King's German Legion fought its last battle at Waterloo [q.v.].

King's (or Queen's) Commissioned Officers. Officers in the British service who held their commissions directly from the sovereign as opposed to "company officers," who served in the army of the Honourable East India Company [q.v.]. Until the government of India was taken over by the crown after the Indian Mutiny [q.v.], an officer holding the sovereign's commission outranked all other officers of the same rank in the company's service.

Kingtehchen, Battle of. See Chin-t'ien, Battle of.

Kiöge, Battle of. See Copenhagen, Battle of.

Kiowa War (1874). The Kiowas were a militant tribe of American Indians living in the Staked Plain, or Llano Estacado, an extensive plateau 1,000 to 5,000 feet high in southeastern New Mexico and West Texas. Their winters were spent in deep canyons created by tributaries of the Red River, where they found protection from severe weather and grass for their ponies. In late September 1874 U.S. army columns attacking the main Kiowa village found it all but deserted. When a scout discovered their secret refuge in Pala Duro Canyon, an early-morning attack routed them. Most of their pony herd was captured, and the ponies were killed. This engagement, while it did not completely destroy the tribe, marked the beginning of the end for them [see Red River War].

Kiowa War *Kiowa Chief Big Bow*

Kipinga. A Central African throwing blade consisting of several sharpened blades welded to an axis.

Kipling, Rudyard (1865–1936). An English writer born in India whose work included novels, short stories, and poems about the British army, particularly about the men in the ranks. Although Kipling was never a soldier and had limited contact with the British military rank and file, his voice was so accurate that he became their troubadour. Writing about them as human beings, he touched a chord of sympathy for the private soldier both in and out of the army that had not been sounded before.

During the Second Anglo-Boer War he traveled to South Africa, and in 1900 he helped edit the *Friend* [q.v.], probably the first newspaper edited exclusively for troops in the field.

Sir George Younghusband believed that Kipling had created the British soldier: "I myself had served for many years with soldiers, but had never heard the words or expressions that Rudyard Kipling's soldiers used. Many a time did I ask my brother officers whether they had heard them. No, never. But sure enough, a few years later the soldiers thought, and talked, and expressed themselves exactly like Rudyard Kipling's soldiers. . . . Rudyard Kipling made the modern soldier" (*A Soldier's Memories in Peace and War* [1917]).

Kirbekan, Battle of (10 February 1885), Gordon Relief Expedition. An Anglo-Egyptian column of about 1,000 men under Major General William Earle (1838–1885) attacked about 9,000 entrenched Dervishes on the Upper Nile River and routed them. General Earle was killed in the battle by a bullet in his forehead. British losses were 60 killed and wounded.

Kirby, Edmund (1840–1863). An American soldier who was a grandson of Major General Jacob Brown [q.v.]. He was graduated from West Point in May 1861 and served as an artilleryman in the American Civil War at First Bull Run, at Ball's Bluff, in the Peninsular Campaign, and at Fredericksburg [qq.v.]. At Chancellorsville [q.v.], while he was trying to save some guns from capture, his thigh was fractured by a piece of case shot. The wound became infected, and although his leg was amputated, the surgeons informed him that he would die. He met the sentence courageously, fearing only how his sister and widowed mother would fare without his support. On 23 May Lincoln on a visit to the hospital was so touched by his suffering and distress that standing at his bedside, he commissioned him a brigadier general of volunteers, thus assuring a handsome pension for his family. General Kirby died five days later. He was the only American, perhaps the only soldier anywhere, to be promoted from first lieutenant to brigadier general in one day while serving in the same army.

Kirby Smith, Edmund (1824–1893). An American soldier born in Florida who was graduated from West Point in 1845 and won brevets to captain in the Mexican War [q.v.] for his gallantry at Cerro Gordo and Contreras. Later he taught mathematics at West Point and served on the Texas frontier. On 6 April, when Florida seceded from the Union, he resigned his commission as a major and joined the Confederate army as a lieutenant colonel. He served under Joseph E. Johnston [q.v.] in the Shenandoah Valley. On 17 June 1861 he was appointed brigadier general and four days later was severely wounded in the First Battle of Bull Run [q.v.]. He was promoted major general in October and in that rank took part in Braxton Bragg's invasion of Kentucky [q.v.]. He was promoted lieutenant general, to rank from 2 October 1862, and given command of the Trans-Mississippi Department. On 19 February 1864 he became a general of the provisional army, and soon after he repelled the Red River Expedition [q.v.] of Nathaniel Banks [q.v.]. On 26 May 1865 he surrendered to E. R. S. Canby [q.v.]. He was almost the last Confederate commander to lay down his arms.

After the war he became president of a telegraph company and then of a military school and eventually chancellor of the University of Nashville. From 1875 to his death eighteen years later he taught mathematics at the University of the

South. When he died on 28 March 1893, he was the last of the Confederate full generals.

Kirkee, Battle of (5 November 1817), Third Maratha War. Forces acting under Baji Rao II (1795–1818), the last Maratha peshwa, attacked and burned the British Residency at Poona. When the British force of 2,800 stationed at Kirkee (today a suburb of Poona) moved out of their entrenchments, they were attacked by a Maratha force estimated to be 25,000 cavalry and 10,000 infantry. The British stood firm, and the attack was repulsed. Some 500 Marathas were believed killed; the British lost 86 killed and wounded.

Kirovabad, Battle of (26 September 1826), Russo-Persian War. A decisive victory in the first major battle of the war was won by 15,000 Russians under General Ivan Paskievich [q.v.] over 30,000 Persians under Prince Abbas Mirza [q.v.] at this town 110 miles south of Tiflis.

Kisaki. The point of the blade of a Japanese sword or knife.

Kit. The personal articles necessary for a soldier.

Kitchener, Horatio Herbert (1850–1916). A British soldier who passed out of the Royal Military Academy, Woolwich, and was commissioned in the Royal Engineers in 1871. In 1884–85 he served under Garnet Wolseley as an intelligence officer in the Gordon Relief Expedition [q.v.]. In 1886 he was commander of forces in the eastern Sudan, and in 1892 he was sirdar (commander-in-chief) of the Egyptian army. In 1898 he led an Anglo-Egyptian army into the Sudan,

Kitchener as sirdar (commander-in-chief)
of the Egyptian army

defeating Dervish forces in the Battle of Atbara and decisively at Omdurman [qq.v.]. He then went south to dislodge a French expedition that had attempted to establish a French presence on the Nile at Fashoda (Kodok) [see Fashoda Incident; Marchand, Jean Baptiste].

He served briefly as governor-general of the Sudan and then was sent to South Africa, where he served as second-in-command to Lord Roberts in the Second Anglo-Boer War [q.v.]. After Roberts returned to England, Kitchener served as commander-in-chief during the final guerrilla phase of the war, creating the blockhouse system, laying waste farms, and establishing concentration camps [q.v.]. After the war he served as commander-in-chief, India.

He became a field marshal in 1909 and secretary of state for war in 1914. In 1916 he was lost at sea when the cruiser HMS *Hampshire* was sunk while carrying him to Russia.

Kites. In the 1890s the American army experimented with remote-controlled cameras on kites. They were not a success.

Kittel. A loose upper garment sometimes worn in arsenals and for drill by German and Russian soldiers.

Kiuiang, Capture of (18 February 1853), Taiping Rebellion. After the fall of Wu-hsüeh on 15 February 1853, Taipings under Shih Ta-k'ai [q.v.] captured this port city on the south bank of the Yangtze River in southeast China.

Kiziltepe, Battle of (25 June 1877), Russo-Turkish War. A Russian force under General Mikhail Loris-Melikov [q.v.] was defeated by a numerically superior Turkish force under Mukhtar Pasha [q.v.] near this town (also called Kochisar) in southwest Turkey 11 miles southwest of Mardin.

Klapka, György (1820–1892). A Hungarian soldier who became a lieutenant general in the Austrian army but commanded the Northern Hungarian Army against the Austrians in the Revolution of 1848–49 [see Hungarian Revolution of 1848]. In the Battle of Káplona [q.v.] and at Komárno he fought with distinction under Arthur von Görgey [q.v.]. He went into exile in 1849, but in 1859 with Lajos Kossuth (1802–1894), he organized a Hungarian Legion that served in Italy and in 1866 in Upper Silesia. After the amnesty in 1867 he returned to Hungary and served in the Hungarian Parliament.

Kleist von Nollendorf, Count Friedrich Heinrich Ferdinand Emile (1762–1823). A Prussian soldier who commanded a corps in 1812 and 1813. He fought at Dresden and in the Battle of Leipzig [q.v.]. He was defeated in the Battle of Étoges but distinguished himself in the Battle of Laon [q.v.] in 1814.

Klicket or Klinket. A small postern or gate in a fort for the passage of a sallying force.

Kluck, Alexander von (1846–1934). A German soldier born in Münster who first saw action as a junior officer in the Seven Weeks' War [q.v.] of 1866 and later in the Franco-Prussian War [q.v.] of 1870–71. During the First

World War he served on the western front as an army commander and played a key role at the Battle of the Marne in 1914.

Kmety, György (1810–1865). A Hungarian soldier who took part in the Hungarian Revolution [q.v.] in 1848–49 and who, following the surrender of Arthur von Görgey [q.v.] at Világos [q.v.] on 13 August 1849, fled to Turkey. There he embraced Islam and as Ismail Pasha became a general in the Turkish army. During the Crimean War [q.v.] he fought to defend Kars [q.v.] from the Russians.

Knapsack. A pack, often covered with canvas, leather, or other water-shedding material, carried on the back. It was used to hold clothing and other necessities but usually not rations or accoutrements.

Knesebelk, Baron Karl Friedrich von der (1768–1848). A Prussian general who in 1831 succeeded August von Gneisenau [q.v.] as commander of the army of observation on the Polish frontier. He was promoted field marshal on his retirement in 1847.

Knapsack

Knife, Swiss Army. A pocketknife with several blades and tools developed by Carl Elsener, the fourth son of a hatter, who in 1884 established a cutlery shop in Switzerland. The knives were first purchased by the Swiss army in October 1891 as *schweizer Offiziresmesser,* for officers only. A more elegant version that was lighter and included a corkscrew and an extra blade appeared in 1897.

Knife Bayonet. A bayonet with a handle and a blade capable of being used as a knife or dagger.

Knights of St. John of the Hospital, Military Order of. A Christian military order established on Malta in 1530. Its members were pledged to fight the infidel and to maintain difficult strategic positions on the frontiers of Christendom. They were led by their grand master, who recognized only the pope as his superior in authority.

Knights of the Golden Circle. A secret society in the midwestern United States organized in the 1850s whose members promoted the extension of slavery and, during the American Civil War, sympathized with the Confederacy. Members encouraged Union soldiers to desert, interfered with the functioning of the draft, and resisted enlistment. Its peak membership was about 200,000. In 1863 its name was changed to Order of American Knights, and in 1864, under "Supreme Commander" General Clement Laud Vallandigham (1820–1871), it was again changed, this time to Sons of Liberty. Late in 1864 authorities made wholesale arrests of members and seizures of the organization's property. Three of the society's leaders were sentenced to death by a military court. The sentence was suspended, and in 1866 they were released under an order of the Supreme Court. The society was dissolved soon after.

Knobkerrie / Knobkierrie. A stout knobbed stick carved from a single piece of hardwood used as a war club by many African warriors, particularly the Zulus.

Knollys, William Thomas (1797–1883). A British soldier who was commissioned at age sixteen and at once sent to join Wellington's army in the peninsula. In 1855–60 he organized the new military camp at Aldershot [q.v.]. In 1861 he became president of the Council on Military Education, and in 1862 treasurer and comptroller of the household of the Prince of Wales, a post he held for fifteen years. From 1877 until his death he was gentleman usher of the Black Rod.

Knout. A scourge of plaited thongs interwoven with wire wielded as a frequent punishment in the Russian army until abolished by Tsar Nicholas I (1796–1855), who substituted the *pleti,* a kind of lash without wires. The nobility were legally exempt from punishment by the knout.

Knoxville, Battle of (29 November 1863), American Civil War. Confederate General Braxton Bragg [q.v.], confident of the strength of his positions on Lookout Mountain and Missionary Ridge at Chattanooga [qq.v.], Tennessee, detached James Longstreet [q.v.] with 15,000 men, including 5,000 cavalry, to besiege about 6,000 men under Ambrose Burnside [qq.v.] at Knoxville. Although Longstreet was unable to invest Burnside completely, the Federals were starving when on 29 November 1863 Longstreet, with troops under Lafayette McLaws [q.v.], launched an attack on a salient known as Fort Sanders [q.v.]. He was repulsed with a loss of 813 men to the Federals' 113.

After this failure Longstreet withdrew northeast and went into winter quarters at Greenville, Tennessee.

Knuckle Bow. The part of the guard on a sword that protected the knuckles.

Kocaba, Battle of. See Katzbach / Kacaba, Battles of.

Kochisar, Battle of. See Kiziltepe, Battle of.

Kodama, Gentaro (1852–1906). A Japanese soldier who at the age of sixteen fought in the Boshin Civil War. In 1870 he entered the new imperial army as a private but within a year was a first lieutenant. He studied staff work under German Major Jakob Meckel, and in 1887 he became the first commandant of the Japanese Army Staff College. He was promoted major general in 1889 and was governor of Taiwan [q.v.] in 1898. He later served as a senior staff officer in the Russo-Japanese War.

Koegas Atrocities (1879). In the northwestern part of Cape Colony in South Africa a Boer commando sent to suppress a rising of Korana Hottentots (Khois), killed a number of Hottentots being held in custody. Five members of the commando were later arrested, tried for murder, and acquitted. Their acquittal gave rise to considerable controversy and was discussed in the House of Commons, to no avail.

Kohat Pass, Capture of (February 1850), Northwest Frontier fighting. Anglo-Indian forces under Colin Campbell [q.v.] captured this pass (13 miles long and from 400 yards to $1\frac{1}{4}$ miles wide) on India's Northwest Frontier (today in Pakistan) from Adam Khel Afridi tribesmen with a loss of 19 killed and 74 wounded.

Kokand. See Khokand, Russian Conquest of.

Kolokotrones (Kolokotronis), Theodoros (1770–1843). A brigand who in 1821, during the Greek War of Independence [q.v.], turned patriot. Although in 1823 he was commander-in-chief in the Peloponnesus, he was cashiered and imprisoned briefly for using guerrilla tactics and for marauding. After the Greek disaster in the Battle of Krommydi [q.v.] he was restored to rank. Later he conspired against the regency governing for King Otto I (1815–1867) and in 1834 was condemned to death for treason, a sentence commuted to imprisonment. When Otto assumed the throne in 1835, he was pardoned and restored to the rank of general.

Kolokotrones *Theodore Kolokotrones, commander-in-chief of the Greek troops in the Peloponnesus*

Komárno, Battle of (26 April 1849), Hungarian Revolution. Komárno (Komorn), a key fort, was besieged by the Austrians until two Hungarian corps under General Arthur von Görgey [q.v.] surprised their entrenched camp, captured six guns and took 200 prisoners. The Austrians retreated, and Komárno was relieved, but the Hungarians failed to pursue.

Königgrätz, Battle of. See Sadowa, Battle of.

Königswartha, Battle of (19 May 1813), Napoleonic Wars. Near this former capital of East Prussia (later Kaliningrad, Russia) on the Pregel River, 80 miles east-northeast of Danzig (Gdansk), a Russian army of 15,000 under General Mikhail Barclay de Tolly [q.v.] attacked the 8,000 troops in the Italian Division of the French army. The division lost some 2,000 men and might have been totally destroyed had not Marshal Michel Ney [q.v.] and his cavalry corps arrived to save it.

Konoefu. The Inner Palace Guards of the Japanese emperors.

Konya, Battle of (21 December 1832), Egyptian-Turkish War. Mehemet Ali [q.v.], viceroy of Egypt, demanded that the Turkish sultan Mahmud II (1785–1839) give him Syria as a reward for Egyptian help in suppressing Greek rebels [see Greek War of Independence]. When the sultan refused, Mehemet sent an army under his son Ibrahim Pasha [q.v.] to invade Syria. In the summer of 1832 Acre, Damascus, and Aleppo were taken by the Egyptians, who then invaded Armenia. A Turkish army under Reshid Pasha [q.v.] sent to repel the invaders suffered a crushing defeat at this Anatolian town (ancient Iconium; sometimes spelled Konia or Konieh or Koniah) on the edge of the central Turkish plateau. Only the intervention of Russia and other powers prevented the overthrow of the Ottoman Empire.

Koonguel, Battle of (14 March 1886), Senegambian War. In the Senegal-Gambia (Senegambia) area of West Africa a force of about 1,500 African warriors under Mahmadou Lamine [q.v.] attacked 600 French troops. After a four-hour battle the French fled in great disorder, many leaving their arms and ammunition behind. The French lost 10 killed and 36 wounded.

Korean Civil Disorders. In 1882 the father of the king and former regent of Korea, the Tai-wan-Kun, led an anti-Japanese and antiliberal revolt in which the Japanese legation was attacked and numerous Japanese were killed. It was quickly suppressed. In May 1894 there was an uprising of the Tonghak, a fanatically nationalist religious sect supported by Japanese ultranationalists even though it sought the expulsion of all foreigners from Korea. China, which claimed suzerainty, landed 2,000 troops on 10 June. Japan also sent troops and, ignoring Chinese demands that they leave, soon had 12,000 troops in Korea, occupying the capital and the treaty ports. On 23 July Japanese troops successfully attacked the royal palace and after further fighting ejected the Chinese from the country. The Korean king was forced to renounce Chinese suzerainty, and the Japanese took control of the government. This quarrel between Japan and China over the control of Korea provoked the Sino-Japanese War [q.v.].

On 8 October 1895, at the end of the Sino-Japanese War,

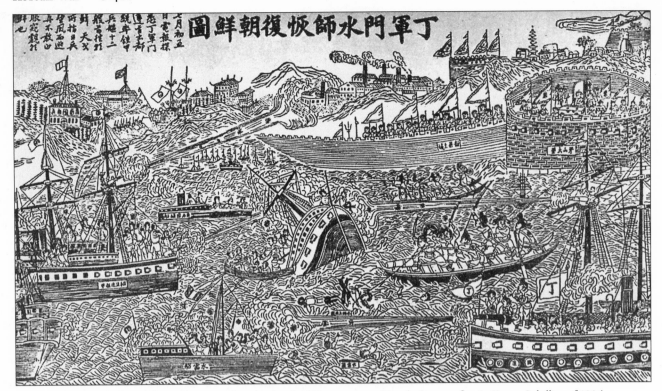

Korean Civil Disorders *Chinese woodcut showing the Chinese navy crushing the Japanese fleet in Korean Rebellion of 1894. In reality the Japanese were victorious.*

the Tai-wan-Kun, leading Korean soldiers backed by the Japanese, captured the palace at Seoul, assassinated the queen, and took the king prisoner. Four months later the king escaped to the Russian legation, there was a revolt against Japanese influence, and in 1897 the king returned to power and proclaimed himself emperor.

Korean War (1871). In the spring of 1871 U.S. Secretary of State Hamilton Fish (1808–1893) ordered an expedition against Korean "barbarians," and on 16 May the Asiatic Squadron under Rear Admiral John Rogers (1810–1882) sailed from Japan with 1,230 sailors and marines equipped with Remington breech-loading carbines and 85 guns, including 7 mobile howitzers. Eleven days later it landed at Kanghwa (Kanghoa or Kangwha) Island, in the Yellow Sea at the mouth of the Han River, 30 miles northwest of Seoul, and stormed its fortifications. The Americans took two of its small forts in early June and the citadel, a fort on a 150-foot-high conical hill, on 11 June. One of the first over the ramparts was naval Lieutenant Hugh H. McGee (1844–1871), who was mortally wounded by a spear thrust. The Americans lost 3 marines and sailors killed and 10 wounded. The Koreans lost 243 killed; many of their wounded were cremated when the place caught fire. Only 20 surrendered. The Americans captured 50 flags and 481 guns of various calibers.

On 14 June the force on land was withdrawn, and on 3 July the Asiatic Squadron sailed away. The *New York Herald* headlined its account of the action as OUR LITTLE WAR WITH THE HEATHENS. The Medal of Honor was awarded to 9 seamen and 6 marines, including Lieutenant McGee.

Koregaon / Korygaum, Battle of (1 January 1818), Third Maratha War. At this village (sometimes spelled Korygaon),

12 miles east of Satara and 120 miles southeast of Bombay, an entrenched British force of 500 men of the 1st Bombay Native Infantry with two 6-pounders, all commanded by Captain (later Lieutenant Colonel) Francis French Staunton (1779?–1825), under attack by 20,000 Marathas led by Baji Rao [q.v.], held out all day until reinforcements arrived after dark. Five of the 8 British officers were killed.

Kornspruit, Battle of. See Sanna's / Sannah's Post, Battle of.

Koul. A soldier in a special corps of the king of Persia's (Iran's) household troops, consisting of nobles and men of note. The commander, the *kouler-agasi*, was usually the governor of a province.

Koummya. A North African knife carried in a baldric sheath slung over the right shoulder.

Kounguel, Battle of (14 March 1886), Senegambian War. On 13 March 1886 the village of Mahmadou Lamine [q.v.], Goundiourou, was raided by the French. Thirty-four wives, children, and relatives were captured, and his household and treasury were looted. The next day the French were routed in the first major encounter of the war, which was carried into the Guidimaka area, a region not controlled by the French. Here the French suffered many losses from sickness.

Kousseri, Battle of (22 April 1900), French conquests in Central Africa. When 50 French tirailleurs and their cadres were killed in July 1899 at Togbao, near Fort Archambault, in southern Chad, 300 miles southeast of present-day N'Djamena, the French launched a three-pronged advance into southern Chad. One column, led by Émile Gentil

(1866–1913), moved north from the Congo; Major François Lamy [q.v.] moved south, fighting off Tuareg tribesmen; a third column under Captain Paul Voulet (d. 1900) ended in disaster, turning into a rogue force that enslaved Africans and killed the French officer sent to replace Voulet, who was finally murdered by his own troops.

The combined French forces of Gentil and Lamy linked at N'guigmi on the northwest shore of Lake Chad, 280 miles west of Zinder, and moved on Kousseri (later Fort Foureau) on the left bank of the Logone River near its confluence with the Shari. There they attacked the local ruler, Rabah (d. 1900), who had been responsible for the July massacre of the tirailleurs. Both Lamy and Rabah were killed on the field. After the battle the victorious French set about the slaughter of the inhabitants.

The survivors of Rabah's force, led by his son, were finally crushed in August 1907.

Kpinga. A throwing knife of the Azande in present-day northeast Congo.

Kraft, Karl August Eduard Friedrich, Prince of Hohenlohe-Ingelfingen (1827–1890). A Prussian soldier who fought in the Crimean War, at Sadowa in the Seven Weeks' War, and in the Franco-Prussian War [qq.v.]. He rose to become a full general and wrote extensively on military subjects.

Krag, Ole H. J. (1837–1912). A Norwegian soldier and gun designer who joined the Norwegian artillery in 1857 and in 1880 was director of the Kongsberg Arsenal in southern Norway. In 1895 he became master general of the ordnance, a post he held until he retired in 1902. He took out patents for many rifle and pistol mechanisms, but his name is usually joined with that of Erik Jörgensen, the works superintendent of the Kongsberg Arsenal. The Krag-Jörgensen bolt-action military rifle, caliber 8 mm, with a five-shot magazine and sighted to 2,200 yards was adopted by the Danish army in 1889. A .30 caliber version was adopted by the American army in 1892, and a 5.5 mm version by the Norwegian army in 1894. Although the Americans later replaced this rifle with the Springfield 1903 [q.v.], the Danes and Norwegians continued its use until the end of the Second World War.

Krag-Jörgensen Rifle. See Krag, Ole H. J.

Krakow Insurrection. See Cracow / Kraków Insurrection.

Krankentrager. A corps of stretcher-bearers in the German army composed of uniformed Landwehr and students from hospitals who were trained to give first aid and remove the wounded. Its members were not uniformed, but all wore the Red Cross brassard. They were mostly men who had served for at least two years and were intelligent and of good character.

Krasnoi, Battle of (17 November 1812), Napoleon's Russian Campaign. During Napoleon's retreat from Moscow, Russian General Mikhail Kutusov [q.v.] with some 50,000 men sent a corps under General Mikhail Barclay de Tolly around the corps of Marshal Michel Ney [qq.v.] to place itself in front of the retreating French and bar their road. The two forces collided at Krasnoi, (Krasnoye Selo), just southwest of St. Petersburg, and 30 miles west of Smolensk, a city on the left bank of the Dnieper (Dnepr) River, 210 miles west of Moscow. After a running all-day battle Ney's corps, which held only 9,000 men, was reduced to 800 effectives. Napoleon managed to assemble such fit men as he had at hand and, with the help of the corps of Marshal Louis Davout [q.v.], repulsed the Russians. French losses were 5,000 killed and wounded and 8,000 missing out of some 25,000 engaged.

Kray von Krajowa, Baron Paul (1735–1804). An Austrian soldier who commanded in the Netherlands against the French and fought in Napoleonic battles. In 1799 in the Italian Campaign he won victories at Verona, Legano, Magnano, and Mantua. In 1800 he succeeded Archduke Charles Louis [q.v.] as commander in Germany, but he proved a failure and was relieved of his command.

Kreli (1818?–1893). A Xhosa chief and son of Hintsa [q.v.] who gained fame in 1845, when he first defeated the Tembus. He led his tribe to war against them again four years later and still again in 1873. From 1850 to 1852 he was at war with the British and Boers in South Africa. Although he was defeated, he went to war against them in Cape Colony, where he was again defeated and driven back into Bomvanaland in the Transkei [see Kaffir Wars].

Krieg Mobile. German mobilization order.

Kriegsakademie. The German military school founded in Berlin in 1810. Every officer selected to attend had to have commanded a military unit for at least one year. The curriculum included statistics, military history, tactics, fortifications, surveying, communications, economics, law, geography, French, and (optional) Russian, Polish, and English. Of the 400 who annually attended, only about 120 took the final examinations, and of those who passed, only 6 or 8 were assigned to the general staff.

Kriegsraison. The justification or perceived necessity for waging war. American jurist Francis Lieber [q.v.] laid down that "To save the country is paramount to all other considerations. . . ." Otto von Bismarck (1815–1897) asked rhetorically, "What head of government would allow his state and its citizenry to be conquered by another state just because of international law?"

Kriegsspiel. A war game invented by a German civilian, Herr von Reisswitz, and much improved upon by his nephew, a Prussian artillery officer. It became popular in the 1820s and was continually improved. When General Karl von Muffling [q.v.], chief of the Prussian general staff, saw it played, he exclaimed, "It's not a game at all! It is training for war." It was used in German military schools to train officers in tactics and strategy. It was a favorite of the generals who won the Schleswig-Holstein War of 1866 and the Franco-Prussian War of 1870–71 [qq.v.]. Helmut von Moltke [q.v.] himself belonged to a society devoted to the game. Skill at the game became almost a requirement for advancement in the Prussian army. After the Franco-Prussian War it was introduced into Britain.

A similar game, called Strategos [q.v.], was invented by American army Lieutenant Charles Adelle Lewis Totten (1848?–1908) in the 1870s. Major William Livermore (1844–1918) in 1879 published the first American book on war gaming, *An American Kriegsspiel*. He used American Civil War statistics, mathematical tables, and the use of such details as the state of morale and training; he also used dice to introduce the element of chance. A naval version was employed at the Naval War College in 1887.

Kris. A Malay knife or dagger with a wavy ("flaming") blade. It was sometimes made more lethal by being dipped in poison. There were more than a hundred varieties, each associated with a particular area, and they were called by more than fifty names: creese, cressit, krees, etc.

Kritzinger, Pieter Hendrik (1870–1935). A South African who became a Boer commando leader and served under Christiaan de Wet [q.v.] in the Second Anglo-Boer War [q.v.]. In 1900–01 he carried out a long, daring raid into Cape Colony.

Krnka, Karel (1858–1926). A Bohemian gunmaker who served in the Austro-Hungarian army, reaching the rank of captain. While in service, he designed a "quick loader" for single-shot military rifles that made it easier for a soldier to reload from a prone position. In 1887, with his father, Sylvester, he designed a bolt-action rifle with a detachable magazine that the Austro-Hungarian army refused to adopt. He then retired from the army and moved to England, where he became chief engineer of the Gatling Arms and Ammunition Company in Birmingham. When that company was liquidated in 1890, he returned to Bohemia, where he worked as a patent agent for eight years until he joined George Roth [q.v.] and manufactured ammunition. After Roth's death in 1909 he was employed by other gun and ammunition companies.

Krommydi, Battle of (19 April 1825), Greek War of Independence. An Egyptian force of 2,400 under Ibrahim Pasha [q.v.] defeated a Greek force that included some Albanians and Bulgarian irregular cavalry. Egyptian losses were light; the Greeks lost about 600. In response to this fiasco the frightened Greek government released from prison Theodoros Kolokotrones [q.v.], the former guerrilla leader, and placed him at the head of its army.

Kropatschek, Alfred (1838–1911). An Austro-Hungarian soldier who joined the army as a cadet in 1854 and became a designer of weapons. In 1874 he developed a repeating rifle mechanism using the Gras turn bolt action. The French adopted this rifle with modifications as the Gras-Kropatschek in 1878, and it was subsequently adopted by the Hungarian and several Balkan armies. Kropatschek later developed artillery pieces for the Austro-Hungarian army.

Kruger, Stephanus Johannes Paulus (1825–1904), usually referred to as Paul Kruger. An Afrikaner leader who fought in wars with natives in South Africa and was commandant general of the South African Republic (Transvaal) from 1863 to 1873. In 1883 he became president and re-

mained president during the Second Anglo-Boer War [q.v.] until driven into exile in 1900.

Krugersdorp, Battle of. See Jameson Raid.

Kruger Telegram (3 January 1896). After the Jameson Raid [q.v.] into the Transvaal in an attempt to provoke a revolt against the Boer government, Kaiser William II (1859–1941) of Germany telegraphed Transvaal President Stephanus Kruger [q.v.]: "I express to you my sincere congratulations, that, without appealing for the help of friendly powers, you and your people have succeeded in repelling with your own forces the armed bands that had broken into your country, and in maintaining the independence of your country against foreign aggression." The telegram created an uproar in Britain, where it was regarded as an unfriendly act.

Krukowiecki, Count Jan (1770?–1850). A Polish soldier who became president of the insurrectionary Polish government in 1830 but surrendered Warsaw to Russian General Ivan Paskevich [q.v.] on 7 September 1831 [see Warsaw, Battle of].

Krümper System. A system (sometimes written *Krümpersystem*) for keeping an army small, while training many. It was devised in 1808 by General Gerhard von Scharnhorst [q.v.], then the director of the Prussian War Department. After the Prussians' defeat at Jena [q.v.] they were allowed by the Treaty of Tilsit [q.v.] on 7 and 9 July 1807 an army of only 42,000 men, a number the French gave permission to increase to 75,000 in 1812. Using the Krümper system, the Prussians managed to pass many recruits through the army's ranks by keeping the entire available manpower as a cadre. As soon as a man was trained, he passed into the reserve. At the outbreak of the wars of liberation, a well-trained army took the field with a strength of 33,600 men over the stipulated limit and the new Prussian army proved most successful. A Prussian reservist of 1808–12 was called a *Krümper*.

Krupp Gustahlfabrik. Napoleon, having cut off all British imports, thus depriving his armies of English cast steel, offered a 4,000-franc reward to any Continental manufacturer who could produce steel equal in quality to that produced by the British. Hoping to claim the reward, Friedrich Krupp (1787–1826) and a partner, Friedrich Nicolai, bought a small forge in the Prussian town of Essen on the Ruhr River in the middle of a coal-bearing region and about the year 1810 formed a company "for the manufacture of English cast steel and all articles made thereof." Cast steel was composed of puddled steel and wrought iron. Although Krupp and his partner used the best European hematite ores for the iron and the locally mined spathic ore of Siegen, 50 miles east of Cologne, for the steel, they did not win the prize, and their business did not prosper initially. After Krupp's death the firm was carried on by his widow and their son, Alfred Krupp (1812–1887), who dropped out of school at age fourteen to help manage the business.

In 1845 the firm employed only 122 workmen and profits were slim, but in 1850 Krupp began to make seamless tracks for German railroads, and in 1851 he exhibited at the Great Exhibition in London a flawless solid two-ton ingot of cast

Krupp *Ahmed Mukhtar Pasha sights a Krupp gun in the redoubt at Erzerum, Russo-Turkish War.*

steel. The Krupp Gustahlfabrik became famous and prospered. In 1856 it made guns for the Egyptian army and then began production of ordnance on a large scale. In 1857 Krupp manufactured a three-inch muzzle-loading gun of cast steel. He sold his guns to the Belgian army in 1861 and to the Russian army in 1863. The breech-loading rifle he developed was adopted by the Prussian army in 1861. In the 1860s his company developed a sliding breech mechanism, and throughout the decade it continued to advance the development of breech-loading artillery. In 1865 Krupp adopted the system of William Armstrong [q.v.], building up gun barrels by shrinking hoops around them. Krupp's greatest success came after the Franco-Prussian War [q.v.], in which the superiority of his artillery was demonstrated. Called the Cannon King, he reequipped the German army and navy as well as many foreign armies, and his factory expanded every year until by 1880 the Krupp works at Essen covered 500 acres and employed 20,000 people.

When Alfred Krupp died on 14 July 1887, he was succeeded by his only son, Friedrich Alfred Krupp (1854–1902), who devoted himself to the financial side of the business. By 1914 the firm employed 80,000 and by 1918, 167,000. F. A. Krupp's daughter, Bertha (1886–1957), gave her name to the enormous Big Bertha (*die dicke Berta*), which shelled Paris in the First World War.

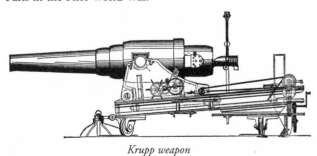

Krupp weapon

Kryzanowski, Wladimir (1824–1887). A Polish-born American soldier who, after taking part in the failed Polish Revolution of 1846 as a young man [see Polish Revolutions], emigrated to the United States, arriving without money, skills, letters of introduction, or knowledge of English. Thanks to hard work and the generosity of other Polish exiles, he com-

pleted his education and became an engineer. He married the daughter of the West Point graduate and prominent engineer Ward Benjamin Burnett (d. 1884) in 1854. At the beginning of the American Civil War he served as colonel of a regiment of Poles and Germans he had raised, which became the 58th New York. As part of the army of General John C. Frémont [q.v.] the regiment fought in the Battle of Cross Keys and in the Second Battle of Bull Run [qq.v.], where Frémont's horse fell and he was thrown and landed on his head; he later heard himself eulogized during a Sunday mass in Washington as one of the dead. At Chancellorsville the 58th was overwhelmed by Thomas J. ("Stonewall") Jackson [q.v.]. On 29 November 1862 Kryzanowski was appointed a brigadier general, an appointment not confirmed by the Senate because, as one senator said, "We cannot confirm the nomination of a man whose name no one can pronounce." He fought at Gettysburg and at Chattanooga and was finally brevetted brigadier general of volunteers on 2 March 1865. He was mustered out in October.

After the war he worked for the Internal Revenue Service in parts of Florida and Georgia. On unfounded charges of fraud he was fired in 1874. He moved to San Francisco and with borrowed money opened a casino and tavern that initially was successful, but in 1877 he filed for bankruptcy. He was given a government job in Panama, where he became overwhelmed by fevers and died.

Ksars / Ksours. Fortified villages in the Sahara, some of which resembled medieval castles.

Kshetriya. The Hindu warrior caste. It ranked socially below Brahmans (priestly caste), but above Vaishus (traders) and Sudras (cultivators and artisans). Untouchables were outside the caste system.

Kueffner, William C. (d. 1893). A German-born American soldier who at the beginning of the American Civil War moved north from Texas to serve in the Union army, first as a sergeant in the 9th Illinois and later as colonel of the 149th Illinois. He participated in 110 engagements, giving him the longest combat record of any soldier, North or South. He was wounded four times, severely at Shiloh and Corinth [qq.v.]. At war's end he was brevetted brigadier general.

His name is variously spelled, sometimes Küffner or Kneffner.

Kufit, Battle of (September 1885), Abyssinian-Sudanese War, variously spelled Kuft, Krift, Qift, Quft, etc. Abyssinian forces under Ras Alula [q.v.] defeated a Dervish army under Osman Digna [q.v.] at this place on the east bank of the Nile, 13 miles south-southeast of Qena.

Kuhn, Franz, Baron Kuhn von Kuhnenfeld (1817–1896). An Austrian soldier who in the Austro-Piedmontese War [q.v.] of 1859 served as chief of staff under General Franz Gyulai [q.v.]. He later served as war minister (1868–74) and in 1873 became master of ordnance. From 1874 to 1888 he commanded forces in Styria, Carinthia, and Carniola.

Kukri. A curved knife with a forward angled blade carried in a sheath housing one or two smaller knives used by Gurkhas [q.v.] from Nepal [see Nepalese War].

Kulevcha, Battle of (11 June 1829), Russo-Turkish War. Russian General Count Hans Diebitsch [q.v.] with an army of 50,000, after seizing the fortress at Silistra on the right bank of the Danube, marched south toward the Balkan Mountains. At the Kulevcha mountain pass, 40 miles west of Varna, he won a victory over 40,000 Turks under the grand vizier Mustafa Reshid Pasha [q.v.], killing or wounding 5,000. On 20 August he occupied Adrianople [see Adrianople, Capture of] at the junction of the Martitsa and Tundzka rivers. However, his army was too weakened by diseases to go further.

Kulm, Battle of (30 August 1813), Napoleonic Wars. Following the Battle of Dresden [q.v.] on 26–27 August 1813, a French force of 32,000 under General Dominique Joseph René Vandamme [q.v.] attempted to block the retreat of the Allied army of 44,000 Prussians, Russians, and Austrians under Field Marshal Karl von Schwarzenberg, General Aleksandr Ivan Ostermann-Tolstoi, and General Friedrich von Kleist [qq.v.]. At this town in the mountains of Erz Gebirge, 25 miles south of Dresden, Vandamme's force engaged the force led by General Ostermann-Tolstoi. Vandamme was holding his own until on the arrival of 10,000 Prussians under General von Kleist, he found himself almost surrounded. Nearly half his force was killed or taken prisoner. The Allies lost 11,000, but the battle gave their troops a tremendous morale boost after their defeat at Dresden.

Kumamoto, Battle of (22 February–14 April 1876), Satsuma Rebellion. Imperial government forces numbering about 50,000, mostly conscripts, under General Tani Tateki [q.v.] held the massive seventeenth-century castle (built 1601–08) at Kumamoto, one of the strongest in Japan, which even today has forty-nine towers, eighteen gatehouses, and three main buildings. Rebel forces of about 40,000 traditional samurai under Saigo Takamori [q.v.] besieged the castle and made frequent unsuccessful assaults, destroying part of the ramparts. It was here that the last hand-to-hand combats took place in Japan. The rebels nearly destroyed the castle but were forced to withdraw.

Kumasi, Siege and Relief of. See Ashanti War, Fourth.

Kunch, Battle of (6 May 1858), Indian Mutiny. At this town, 85 miles west-southwest of Cawnpore, a British force of 4,000 under General Hugh Rose [q.v.], marching on Kalpi [q.v.], was halted 42 miles south of its goal by some 10,000 rebels and mutineers under Tantia Topi [q.v.]. On an exceedingly hot day the British drove off their enemies for a loss of 62 killed and wounded in battle and 45 casualties from sunstroke. An estimated 600 rebels and mutineers were killed, and 15 guns were captured.

Kuropatkin, Aleksei Nikolaevich (1848–1921). A Russian soldier educated at the Paul Junker Academy and in the 1st Cadet Corps who entered the army in 1864. In 1874 he was graduated from the Nicholas Academy [q.v.], and in 1875 he took part in operations in Turkistan, Khokand, and

Samarkand [see Khokand, Russian Conquest of; Central Asian Wars]. He distinguished himself in the Russo-Turkish War [q.v.] of 1877–78 as chief of staff to Mikhail Skobelev [q.v.]. In 1880 he returned to Central Asia with Skobelev, and in 1881 they captured Geok Tepe [q.v.]. From 1890 to 1898 he commanded the Russian army in the Transcaucasia. He was war minister from 1898 to 1904. In the Russo-Japanese War he was defeated at Mukden and relieved of command.

Kurram Punitive Expeditions (1856 through 1897). The Kurram Valley was, and is, a beautiful valley of the Kurram River south of the Safed Koh on what was India's (now Pakistan's) Northwest Frontier [q.v.]. The Turis, one of the tribes that inhabited it, paid tribute to the Afghan government in Kabul every four or five years when a military expedition was sent to collect it. In 1880, after the Second Afghan War [q.v.], in which the Turis were helpful to the British, they were rewarded by being given their independence from Afghanistan, but they were a turbulent people and often led raids into territory under British protection, particularly in the Kohat district.

In 1897, amid uprisings all along the Northwest Frontier, Orakzais from the valley attacked British camps. A British force of 14,230 again fell upon the Kurram Valley and severely punished the tribesmen, burning fruit trees and destroying crops.

In 1900 the British formed two battalions of Kurram militia to police their own people.

Kurta. A blouse or loose frock worn in India. It reached to the knees, and the neck was open to the waist.

Kurtka. A Polish lancer jacket used by cavalry in several armies.

Kurtshi. A militia cavalry composed of Persian nobles and lineal descendants of the Turkish conquerors.

Kutusov, Mikhail Ilarionovich Golenischev-Kutusov (1745–1813). A Russian soldier who entered military service as an engineering cadet at age twelve. He served in Poland in 1764–69 and fought against the Turks in 1770, 1771–72, and 1811–12, losing an eye at Alushta in the Crimea and later suffering a second wound to the head. In the Napoleonic Wars he commanded Russian armies from 1805 to 1812. Having grown too fat to sit a horse, he rode about the battlefields in a buggy. After defeats at Austerlitz and Borodino [qq.v.] he ordered his army back through Moscow toward Kaluga, saying, "Napoleon is a torrent which as yet we are unable to stem; Moscow will be the sponge to suck him dry." During Napoleon's retreat from Moscow he won a victory of sorts over Ney and Davout in the Battle of Smolensk [q.v.], for which he was created Prince of Smolensk.

Kutuzov was a shrewd man, said to be lazy and cautious and known as a prevaricator, claiming Borodino [q.v.] to be a Russian victory and ever failed to mention that it was the French who won at Austerlitz [q.v.].

Kylch. See Kilij Saber.

Kyle, John Gowdy (1846?–1877). An American soldier

who was graduated from West Point and commissioned a second lieutenant in the 1st Cavalry in 1870. He performed well in the Northwest, taking part in several actions against Indians, and was twice wounded. From January to November 1876 he was confined to a government insane asylum in Washington, D.C., but on 3 September of that year, while officially insane, he was promoted first lieutenant. This appears to be the only instance in history of the promotion of a certified insane officer. He died on 30 May 1877.

L

Laager. In South Africa, an encampment in which wagons were drawn together in a rough circle for protection.

LaBarge, Joseph (1815–1899). An American riverboat captain whose father and both brothers were also riverboat captains. He first saw action on 2 August 1832 at the age of seventeen, when with a party of traders he took part in the Battle of Bad Axe [q.v.] against Sac and Fox tribes under Black Hawk [q.v.]. In 1833, when he was an apprentice on the steamboat *Yellowstone* plying the Missouri River, the boat was attacked by Sioux. One white man was killed and three wounded; soon after, the captain and the pilots succumbed to cholera, and young LaBarge, taking charge, brought the boat safely to Fort Atkinson (in present-day Nebraska near Council Bluffs). At age nineteen he received his pilot's license and built his own steamboat, the first of fifteen [see Missouri River Steamboat Company].

La Bédoyère, Charles Angélique François Huchet (1786–1815). A French soldier who served as an aide-de-camp to Marshal Jean Lannes [q.v.] in 1807–09. He was the first senior officer to rally to Napoleon during the Hundred Days [q.v.], turning over to him the garrison at Grenoble. He became a general of division and an aide to Napoleon. After the Battle of Waterloo [q.v.] and the second Bourbon restoration, he was arrested for treason and was shot.

La Belle Alliance. An inn near the field of Waterloo, Belgium, on the high road to Brussels, about two miles from Mont St. Jean. Here Surgeon Dominique Jean Larrey [q.v.] established his main dressing stations on 18 June 1815, and from here Napoleon marshaled his Guards for a last effort. And here Wellington and Blücher [q.v.] met at nine o'clock that evening after the battle, Blücher's greeting being *"Mein lieber Kamerad! Quelle affaire!"* (My dear Conrad! What an affair!) It was here decided that Blücher would lead the pursuit of the beaten French.

Laboratory. In military usage, a powder magazine; a building; or, in the field, a large tent in which ammunition and pyrotechnics were made up. To avoid sparks, nothing made of iron or steel was employed, and soldiers working here wore shoes without nails.

Laborde, Henri François de (1764–1833). A French soldier who fought in the French Revolution, was present at the siege of Toulon in 1793, and in 1799 was with the Army of the Rhine. He fought in the Peninsular War and Napoleon's Russian Campaign [qq.v.]. He rallied to Napoleon during the Hundred Days [q.v.] and after Waterloo went into exile.

Labram, George (1860–1900). An American engineer who in 1894 emigrated to South Africa, where on 8 October 1896 he was appointed chief mechanical engineer for the De Beers Consolidated Mines. With Cecil Rhodes (1853–1902) he was trapped in Kimberley throughout its siege [q.v.] during the Second Anglo-Boer War [q.v.]. Although he had no experience of artillery and no knowledge of ballistics, using the facilities of the De Beers workshops there, he built in just twenty-four days a breech-loading rifled cannon with a 4.1-inch bore capable of firing 28-pound shells. Called Long Cecil after Rhodes, it was first fired on 20 January 1900 and in the course of the siege fired 225 shells, which Labram had also designed. As *The Times History of the War in South Africa* noted, "The production of this gun must be considered one of the most remarkable events in the history of beleaguered garrisons." Labram also devised an iron carriage for the gun, a system of watchtowers connected by telephones, a searchlight, and an enormous refrigerator.

On 9 February 1900, as he was dressing to have dinner with Rhodes, a Boer artillery shell, the last of the day, exploded in his room and killed him.

Lace. Ornamental braid of woven silk or worsted used to decorate uniforms. It was often used to indicate officer status.

Ladder Bridge. A temporary bridge made by running a wagon, cart, or gun limber into a shallow stream and securing it. Ladders running from each bank were rested on it, and planks were then laid over the rungs.

Ladmirault, Louis René Paul de (1808–1898). A French soldier who fought in the Battle of Solferino [q.v.], commanded IV Corps at the beginning of the Franco-Prussian War [q.v.], and was engaged at Rezonville [q.v.]. He commanded I Corps during the suppression of the Paris Commune [q.v.] and was subsequently military governor of Paris.

Ladrones. Outlaw Navajos or Apaches who could not be controlled by the tribal political structure. In mid-century they raided New Mexico settlements and *ricos* (peaceful Apaches who had wealth in sheep and other possessions).

Ladysmith, Siege of (2 November 1899–28 February 1900), Second Anglo-Boer War. This town on the Klipp River in northern Natal was named after the Spanish wife of Sir Harry Smith [q.v.], the governor of Cape Colony in 1847, and here 12,000 British troops under General George White, VC, were besieged in 1899 for eighty-eight days by Boers, initially under Petrus Joubert, later under Louis Botha [qq.v.].

For the most part the Boers were content to bombard the town with their heavy guns. The besieged suffered only about 60 killed until on 6 January a Boer force made an attempt to storm the British lines at strongpoints called Wagon Hill and Caesar's Camp. Although hard pressed, the British repelled all assaults in a daylong battle. Of the 89 British officers and 805 other ranks killed in action during the siege, most fell on this day.

On 19 February 1900 Sir Redvers Buller, VC, [q.v.], who had lost 1,896 men in killed and wounded in repeated and unsuccessful attempts to relieve Ladysmith, managed to break through the Boer lines with a force of about 25,000 men after the capture of the commanding height called Hlangwana enabled him to secure crossings over the Tugela River. On 27 February Buller attacked along a three-mile front. He entered Ladysmith the following day.

La Fayette, Marie Joseph Motier (1757–1834). A French marquis and officer who in 1777 offered his services to the American rebels. After his return to France he became commandant of the Garde Nationale [q.v.] on 15 July 1789. He took no part in government under Napoleon, but in 1830 he again commanded the Garde Nationale.

La Fère–Champenoise, Battle of (25 March 1814), Napoleonic Wars. Near this commune in northern France an Allied army under Prince von Schwarzenberg [q.v.], marching on Paris, defeated two French corps, about 30,000 men, under Marshals Adolphe Mortier and Auguste Marmont [qq.v.]. French casualties were about 5,000. This was the last action fought in France before Napoleon's first abdication.

Laffite (Lafitte), Jean (1780?–1826?). A French pirate and smuggler who operated in the Barataria Bay region of the southeastern Louisiana coast. During the War of 1812 [q.v.] the British offered him a commission and £30,000, but he cast his lot with the Americans and fought by their side in the Battle of New Orleans [q.v.], where his men distinguished themselves, particularly as artillerymen. Although he and those of his men who had taken part in the battle were subsequently pardoned for their former depredations by President James Madison (1751–1836), Lafitte gathered nearly 1,000 followers and resumed his buccaneering off the coast of Texas, basing his operations at the site of present-day Galveston.

Laffrey, the Affair at (7 March 1815), Napoleonic Wars. At the beginning of the Hundred Days [q.v.], soon after landing in France from Elba, at this small town 25 miles south of Grenoble, Napoleon and his escort encountered the French 5th Infantry Regiment, which had been sent to arrest them. Sensing the mood in the ranks, Napoleon faced them, opened his coat, and invited them to fire on their emperor. The men of the 5th broke ranks and rushed forward to hail him. He entered Grenoble to the cheers of the populace. "Before Grenoble I was an adventurer," he said; "at Grenoble I was a

prince." At Auxerre on 16 March the 14th Infantry also joined him.

Lagholuat, Battle of (December 1853), French conquest of Algeria. Three French columns converged on this oasis in northern Ghardaia territory in the Atlas Mountains and after stiff fighting occupied the place and then moved east to occupy Touggourt and Ouargla. Aimable Pélissier commanded one of the columns, and Marie MacMahon [qq.v.] another.

La Glorieta, Battle of. See Glorieta, Battle of.

La Haye Sainte. A walled farm that was a feature of the Battle of Waterloo [q.v.] on 18 June 1815. Roughly in the center of the main position and somewhat in front of the main line, it was held by 376 riflemen of the King's German Legion [q.v.], who were reinforced to 400 after repelling the initial French attack. The farmhouse was finally taken by the French at about six-thirty that evening. Of the original 376 men, only 38 were still alive.

Laing's Nek, Battle of (28 January 1881), First Anglo-Boer War. A British force of 1,000 under Sir George Colley was defeated by Boers under Petrus ("Piet") Joubert [qq.v.] at this pass in the Drakensberg near the Transvaal-Natal border. The British lost 83 killed, including 7 officers, and 111 wounded; Boer losses were 14 killed and 27 wounded.

Lai Wen-kuang (1827–1868). An educated Chinese soldier who joined the forces of the Taipings in 1850 [see Taiping Rebellion]. After the fall of Anking [q.v.] in 1861 he convinced the Taiping leaders that they should form an alliance with the Niens [q.v.], and he led an army north, fighting numerous battles with government forces. In the spring of 1861 he was summoned back to protect the threatened celestial capital, Nanking (Nanxiang or Nanjing), but the city fell before he could reach it.

Closely pursued by government forces, he merged his remaining troops with the Niens, who welcomed him. He tried to introduce stronger organizational structures and to inculcate political ideas similar to the Taipings. It was Lai who introduced the tactic of wearing out an opposing force before turning to destroy it. However, when superior government forces freshly armed with modern weapons appeared on the field, he was defeated. He fled to Yangchow (Kiangtu), where he surrendered to the local governor. He wrote a confession of more than a thousand words before he was executed.

Lake, Gerard (1744–1808). A British soldier who at age fourteen was commissioned in the Foot Guards. He served in Germany from 1760 to 1762, in America in 1781, and in the Low Countries in 1793–94. He routed Irish rebels at Vinegar Hill in 1798, and in 1800 he was appointed commander-in-chief, India. He was made a full general in 1802 and commanded British forces in northeastern India in the Second Maratha War [q.v.], capturing Agra and Delhi and winning the battles of Laswari on 1 November 1803 and Farrukhabad on 17 November [qq.v.]. He was superseded as commander-in-chief by Lord Cornwallis (1738–1805) in July 1805, but Cornwallis died while on his way to take command, and Lake pursued Jaswant Rao Holkar [q.v.], the Maratha leader, into the Punjab and forced his surrender at Amritsar in December of that year. He was created a baron in 1804 and a viscount in 1807.

Lake Erie Conspiracy. See Johnson Island.

Lake Okeechobee, Battle of (25 December 1837), Second Seminole War. At this lake on the north end of the Everglades, about 40 miles west-northwest of present-day West Palm Beach, Brigadier General Zachary Taylor [q.v.], commanding in Florida, found a hostile Seminole Indian stronghold with about 500 men under Wild Cat [q.v.] (also known as Coacoochee), and attacked with about 1,000 men, half of them untrained volunteers. Taylor carried the day for a loss of 26 killed and 112 wounded; Indian losses were 11 killed and 14 wounded. Although organized Seminole resistance was temporarily crushed, the Indians began a guerrilla war that lasted for many years.

Lakh (Lac, Lack, Lak, etc.). In India the number 100,000. In the nineteenth century the word was usually used in connection with money, as in a lakh of rupees. In Java and Malaya it signified 10,000.

Lal Bazaar. The area in or near a cantonment in India that contained approved, regularly inspected houses of prostitution, often within the lines of British regiments. Although the prostitutes were Indian, British military police turned away all male Indians. In the last years of the nineteenth century the virtuous in Britain raised a clamor, demanding that they be closed. [See Venereal Disease; Bordel Militaire Controllé / Bordel Mobile de Campagne.]

Lallemand, Frédéric Antoine (1774–1839). A French baron and soldier who fought in the French Revolutionary and Napoleonic Wars. After the Battle of Waterloo he and some companions fled to Texas, where they endeavored to establish a colony. Spanish opposition doomed the attempt.

La Macta. See Maacta, Battle of.

La Marmora, Alberto Ferrero, Conte di La Marmora (1789–1863). An Italian who served as a general in the army of King Carlo Alberto [q.v.] of Sardinia. He was the brother of Alessandro and Alfonso La Marmora [qq.v.].

La Marmora, Alessandro Ferrero, Cavaliere di La Marmora (1799–1855). An Italian soldier and the elder brother of Alfonso La Marmora [q.v.]. As a general of brigade he is credited with organizing the bersaglieri [q.v.], which became an elite corps in the Italian army.

La Marmora, Alfonso Ferrero di, Marchese di La Marmora (1804–1878). An Italian soldier who entered the Sardinian army in 1823. He served in the Austro-Sardinian War [q.v.] of 1848–49 and distinguished himself at the siege of Peschiera in May 1848. As minister of war between 1848 and 1859 (with a few interruptions) he reorganized the Sardinian army. In January 1855 he led the Sardinian expeditionary force to the Crimea [see Crimean War]. During the Austro-Piedmontese War [q.v.] he commanded the Sardinian army and fought in the Battle of Solferino [q.v.] on 24 June 1859. During the Seven Weeks' War [q.v.] he commanded a

corps and was defeated in the Battle of Custozza [q.v.] on 24 June 1866. He was twice prime minister of Sardinia (1859–60 and 1864–66). In 1866 he was named chief of staff.

Lamarque, Maximilien (1770–1832). A French soldier who campaigned in Italy and in 1806 captured Gaeta [q.v.]. He served under Napoleon at Wagram [q.v.] in 1809. A member of the Chamber of Deputies from 1828 until his death, he was an outspoken critic of the French government. His funeral on 5–6 June 1832 was an occasion seized upon by republicans for an insurrection in Paris [see July Revolution, French].

"La Marseillaise." See "Marseillaise, La."

Lame Deer, Battle of (7 May 1877), Great Sioux War. After the Battle of Wolf Mountains, many Sioux and Cheyenne warriors and their families came into the various Indian agencies to give themselves up or, like Sitting Bull, took refuge in Canada. But in May 1877 Lame Deer, a Minieconjou Sioux, proclaimed his defiance and swore that he would continue to hunt in the Powder River country in Montana. Colonel Nelson Miles [q.v.] with six companies of cavalry and six of infantry launched a campaign against Lame Deer and his band. He found them in fifty-one lodges on Little Muddy Creek, a small tributary of Rosebud Creek in Montana. After a night approach march he attacked. Lame Deer and 14 other Indians were killed, as were 4 soldiers; 9 other soldiers were wounded. In this engagement, 5 soldiers won the Medal of Honor [q.v.]. About 600 horses were captured and were used to mount the 5th Infantry. It was the last significant battle of the Great Sioux War [q.v.].

Fast Bull, Lame Deer's son, and 225 others escaped and eluded Miles all summer, but with the coming of cold weather they finally surrendered.

Lame Deer The Lame Deer Fight, *1877, by Frederic Remington*

Lamine, Mahmadou (1838?–1887), also known as Muhammad al-Amin Demba Debassi. A religious, political, and military leader who founded the Sarakole (Sarrakule) Empire in West Africa. In the process of leading the Sarakoles in a struggle to free them from French and Tukulor political authority and occupation, particularly from the French, who from 1876 became aggressively expansionist, he created an empire that extended over Bambuk, Bondu, Guoy, Khasso, and the emirates of Diafounou Guidimaka.

About 1868 Lamine left home to make the haj. He then spent seven years in Mecca (Makkah), Constantinople (Istanbul), and elsewhere in the Middle East. On his return to West Africa he was imprisoned for seven years (1878–85) because he offended Ahmadu [q.v.], the Tukulor ruler at Ségou (Segu), capital of the Tukulor Empire, located on the Niger River, 120 miles east-northeast of Bamako in present-day Mali.

When freed, he returned to his native village of Goundiour, southwest of Timbuktu, and at once announced a jihad to drive both the French and the Tukulors from the Senegambia region. A charismatic figure, he soon had thousands of adherents and by February 1886 he had built up the core of his empire. The size of his volunteer army have ranged from 3,000 to 12,000. Opposed to him were the forces of Ahmadu of Ségou and the Tukulors allied with the French against him [see Senegambian War]. Most of the French soldiers were Africans in the Tirailleurs Sénégalais [see Senegalese Tirailleurs]. Although French forces probably did not exceed 4,000, they were better disciplined and better armed than Lamine's warriors. On 13 March 1886 the French raided Lamine's village and captured members of his family as hostages. The following day some 600 French were defeated by 1,500 warriors near Kounguel, with a reported loss of 10 killed and 36 wounded.

The French who had been engaged in fighting with Samori [q.v.] turned to face Lamine and concentrated their forces at Bakel, in what is today East Senegal on the left bank of the Senegal River, 300 miles east of Dakar. The battle for Bakel began on 1 April, when Lamine's forces were repulsed, but on 4 April he launched a two-pronged attack that led to much confused street fighting. After he was again repulsed, Lamine surrounded Bakel, cut telegraph lines, and made hit-and-run raids. In December 1886 Colonel Joseph Simon Gallieni [q.v.] arrived to take charge of the French forces. Gallieni waged an aggressive campaign, and Lamine was killed in a battle with the French in December 1887 at Toubakouta (Touba), 70 miles west of Séguéla. His death marked the end of the Sarakole nationalist movement in the Senegambia.

Lamoricière, Louis Christophe Léon Juchault de (1806–1865). A French soldier who was present in the Battle of Isly [q.v.] on 14 August 1844. He was temporary governor-general of Algeria when in 1847 he effected the capture of Abd el-Kader [q.v.]. In June of the same year he quelled rioting in Paris. As a member of the Legislative Assembly from 1849 to 1851 he vigorously opposed the intrigues of Louis Napoleon (1808–1873). Briefly war minister, he was arrested and banished after the coup d'état of 1851. He then entered the papal army as a general. On 18 September 1860 he was defeated by General Enrico Cialdini [q.v.] at Castelfidardo [q.v.], and he capitulated at Ancona.

Lamy, François (1858–1900). A French soldier who at age ten was sent to the military preparatory school of Prytanée National de la Flèche [q.v.] and from there straight to St. Cyr [q.v.] in 1876. He was graduated in 1879, fifth in a class of 340. He chose the Algerian Tirailleurs rather than a more elite unit, and he was with the force that invaded Tunis in 1881. In 1895 he led 1,500 Algerian troops to Madagascar to fight the Hovas [see Madagascar, Warfare in]. French losses to disease in this campaign were horrendous, but Lamy was one of the few who remained in good health, not even contracting malaria.

In 1897 he was promoted major and appointed aide-de-camp to President François Félix Faure. On 5 March 1898 he received official approval and a half million francs to "join Algeria to Chad." On 20 September of that year, on what was purported to be a scientific expedition, he left Blida for Ouargla in the northern Sahara, leading 212 tirailleurs, 13 spahis, two 42 mm Hotchkiss guns provided with 200 rounds of ammunition, and 1,004 camels to carry equipment and supplies. On 23 October the expedition left Ouargla for Lake Chad, 2,000 miles away. They were repeatedly attacked by Tuareg and Chaambi tribesmen, and they were near starvation by December. In one week in February 1899, 97 camels died. On 18 February Lamy met up with the French Central African Mission [q.v.] on the banks of the Chari River near its entrance into Lake Chad, but he was probably unaware of the hostility that mission had aroused in its bloody and ruthless trek into central Africa. He was killed in a battle by the bazingers [q.v.] of Rabih Fadl Allah (Ribih Zubair Pasha) near what later became Fort Lamy (today N'Djamena, Chad).

Lance. A weapon consisting of a long shaft of wood with a metal point used by some cavalry. Although an ancient weapon, it was introduced to nineteenth-century armies by the Poles in about 1801, and soon every army in Europe included lancers [q.v.]. French lances in the Napoleonic era were 276 cm long; a Polish lance was 6.25 cm longer. British lances that were 16 feet long in 1816 were reduced in 1829 to 9 feet 1 inch. In the British service the shaft of the lance was originally ash impregnated with a mixture of tar and linseed oil; in 1868 it was changed to male bamboo.

Lance Bombardier. A rank above a private and below a corporal. The rank was, and is, unique to the British artillery.

Lance Corporal. 1. The lowest-ranking noncommissioned officer in the British infantry and in the U.S. Marine Corps, ranking above a private but below a corporal. The badge of rank is a single chevron.

2. An acting corporal, but with the pay of a private.

Lancers. Cavalry troopers armed with lances. The Russian army had lancers from 1803 and from 1882 to 1910 two guards regiments of lancers. Lances were also carried by many Cossacks and was said to have been their favorite weapon. In the Turkish army the Guard Lancers were considered among the elite. Prussia armed its uhlans [q.v.] with lances. In 1811 Napoleon converted nine regiments of dragoons into lancers and later armed some with both lance and carbine. Mounted Californios (Mexican loyalists in California) fought the Americans under John Frémont [q.v.] with lances [see Black Bear Revolt / Bear Flag War; San Pasqual, Battle of]. The British first formed regiments of lancers after seeing their successful use in the Battle of Waterloo [q.v.]. A general order of 19 September 1816 converted the 9th, 12th, 16th, and 23rd Light Dragoons into lancers. In 1822 the 17th Light Dragoons was also converted. In 1859 the 5th Dragoons, which had been disbanded in 1799, was re-formed as the 5th Lancers. British lancers fought in the early stages of the

Lancers *A Mexican lancer, from the sketches of William Meyers, a U.S. navy gunner who fought in California in the Mexican War.*

Second Anglo-Boer War [q.v.]. In 1927 all were abolished except for ceremonial purposes, although the name persisted. In Japan the lance was only carried by the guards cavalry for ceremonial purposes. [See Lance; Uhlans; Elandslaagte, Battle of; San Pasqual, Battle of.]

In America a number of volunteer cavalry units, including Turner Ashby's [q.v.] horsemen, possessed lances at the beginning of the Civil War, but there were never any lancers in the regular cavalry of the U.S. army.

Lancers *A British lancer during the Boer War, 1899–1902*

Lance Sergeant. In the British army a corporal acting in the capacity of a sergeant but drawing the pay of a corporal.

Landells, Robert Thomas (1833–1877). A British war artist who worked for the *Illustrated London News* covering the Crimean War, Schleswig-Holstein War, Seven Weeks' War, and Franco-Prussian War [qq.v.].

Landeshiet, Battle of. See Landshut, Battle of.

Land Force. A military force organized to fight on land.

Land Grant Act. See Morrill Act.

Landi Kotal. A fort built in mid-century by the British at the Afghan entrance to the Khyber Pass [q.v.].

Land Mines. Explosive devices hidden in the ground and designed to be exploded under men or carriages. In the nineteenth century they were usually called torpedoes. They were thought to have been invented during the Second Seminole War [q.v.] by Gabriel James Rains [q.v.], an American officer. As a brigadier general under D. H. Hill [q.v.] during the American Civil War Rains perfected his mines, and while falling back from Yorktown [q.v.] before McClellan's army in May 1862, he planted large quantities of 8- or 10-inch artillery shells capped with nipple fuzes filled with fulminating powder. Union General George McClellan [q.v.] wrote that his entry into Yorktown was "much delayed by the caution made necessary by the presence of these torpedoes. I at once ordered that they should be discovered and removed by Confederate prisoners."

There was much discussion both North and South over the morality of using land mines, although not over the use of prisoners to defuze them. Confederate General James Longstreet [q.v.] prohibited their use, pronouncing them "not a proper or effective means of war." Their use outraged Union General William Tecumseh Sherman [q.v.], who declared that when mines were found, the area should be walked over by "wagon-loads of prisoners, or . . . citizens implicated in their use." Nevertheless, they were subsequently used by both sides.

European armies were slow to adopt land mines, and they were not used in the Franco-Prussian War [q.v.].

Lands. The raised portion between the grooves (spiral channels cut in the bore) of a rifle or cannon.

Landshut, Battle of (21 April 1809), Napoleonic Wars. At this town (also known as Kamienna Gora, Landeshut, or Landshiet) on the Bobr River, 52 miles southwest of Wroclaw and 35 miles northeast of Munich, French forces under Marshal Jean Lannes [q.v.] defeated a numerically inferior Austrian force under Baron Johann Hiller that narrowly escaped encirclement. Hiller's losses were 9,000 men and all his guns and baggage.

Landsturm. The third reserve in the German and Austrian armies; a militia, consisting of all men between seventeen and forty-five, whether or not they had previously served, who were then not serving in the regular army, landwehr, or reserves. Not all were fully fit. Soldiers in the German army after serving three years in the regular army, four in the reserve, and five in the landwehr, passed into the landsturm. A bill passed in 1874 allowed the emperor to draft men in the landsturm into the landwehr.

Landwehr. The second reserve in German and Austrian

armies, which was usually made up of recently discharged soldiers.

Lane. Soldiers in two ranks facing each other. Called *haie* (hedge) in French. A lane was sometimes formed as a guard of honor for persons of rank to pass through.

Lane, James Henry (1814–1866). An American soldier and politician who during the Mexican War [q.v.] served as colonel of the 3rd and later the 5th Indiana Volunteers. In 1855 he moved to Kansas and identified himself with the free state movement, leading an Army of the North that raided proslavery districts in Kansas. In 1858 he killed a neighbor in a duel but was not punished. On 18 December 1861, during the American Civil War, he was appointed a Union brigadier general of volunteers, an appointment that was canceled on 21 March 1862, when he became a U.S. senator. In the Senate he urged emancipation of slaves and advocated the arming of blacks. In July 1866 he committed suicide.

Langalibalele (1818?–1889). Chief of the Amahlubi tribe in Natal, South Africa, who lived on the left bank of the Buffalo River until 1848. When driven out by the Mpandes, he and his people fled across the river into the Klip River country. The government moved the tribe to arable lands in central Natal just north of Giant's Castle, one of the most prominent features of the Drakensberg range. Here the tribe grew, with accretions from other tribes, from 7,000 in 1850 to nearly 94,000 in 1873.

After the so-called Langalibalele Rebellion [q.v.] in 1873, Langalibalele fled to Basutoland (Lesotho). He was tracked down at Leribe, a village near the Orange Free State border, on 11 December and taken in chains for trial with several of his chief followers to Pietermaritzburg, Natal. There he was sentenced to banishment for life on Robben Island. This island, five miles from the mainland in Table Bay, was used from 1846 to 1931 to confine lepers, lunatics, and political undesirables. However, thanks to pleading by Anglican Bishop John William Colenso (1814–1883), Langalibalele's sentence was reduced, and in 1886 he was allowed to return to Natal, where he settled in the Swartkop Location.

Langalibalele Rebellion (1873). In 1871, when Kimberley was founded in the north of Cape Province in South Africa, many young men of the Amahlubi tribe, led by Chief Langalibalele [q.v.], worked in the diamond mines there and used the money they earned to purchase firearms. When the local magistrate called upon Langalibalele to order his men to give up their arms, he refused. In October 1873 a force of 200 regulars, 300 Natal volunteers, and 6,000 African auxiliaries with two guns was mobilized to force him to comply. Sir Theophilus Shepstone (1817–1893), the secretary for native affairs, and Sir Benjamin Chilley Campbell Pine (1813–1891), the newly appointed governor of Natal, accompanied the expedition. The chief's deserted kraal was found, but Langalibalele had fled to Basutoland (Lesotho). He was tracked down on 11 December 1873, and he and his followers were heavily punished [see Bushman's River Pass, Affair at].

Langensalza, Battle of (29 June 1866), Seven Weeks' War. When Hanover sided with Austria against Prussia, Prussian forces invaded Hanover, and a battle was fought at this place, 19 miles west-northwest of Erfurt. Initially, each side had about 12,000 men, and the Hanoverians under General Alexander von Arentschildt [q.v.] threw back the Prussians, who lost about 1,400 killed and wounded and 900 taken prisoner for a Hanoverian loss of 1,329. However, Prussian General Eduard Vogel von Falckenstein pushed forward 30,000 reinforcements and captured the entire Hanoverian army. Hanover surrendered. On 20 September the kingdom was extinguished, and the country was annexed to Prussia. This was the last battle fought by independent Hanoverian forces.

Langeron, Andrault (1763–1831). A French officer who entered the Russian service. He was a general of division at Austerlitz [q.v.] in 1805, and he distinguished himself at Leipzig [q.v.] in 1813. In 1814 he stormed Montmartre and entered Paris with the Allies. In 1822 he was governor-general of New Russia.

Langiewicz, Marjan (1827–1887). A Polish patriot and soldier who, after entering the Prussian landwehr and serving in the Royal Guard, went to Paris in 1860 and briefly taught school before going to Italy to take part in the Neapolitan Campaign of Giuseppe Garibaldi [q.v.]. Langiewicz then taught for a time in a military school until, at the outbreak of the Polish insurrection on 22 January 1863, he hurried back to Poland and took command of the armed bands in the district of Sandomierz. He enjoyed some successes in clashes with the Russians, and on 10 March 1863 his troops proclaimed him dictator of Poland. Eight days later his force was almost annihilated, and he fled to Austria, where he was arrested and imprisoned. In 1865 he was released and took refuge in Switzerland and France, using the name Langle. He finally entered the Turkish army as Langlie Bey and died at Constantinople (Istanbul).

Langlois, Hippolyte (1839–1912). A French soldier who upon graduation from the École Polytechnique [q.v.] was appointed a sublieutenant in the artillery in 1858. During the Franco-Prussian War [q.v.] he served at Metz. In 1888 he became professor of artillery at the École de Guerre [q.v.] and published *L'Artillerie de campagne* (1891–1892), which became an artillery classic. In 1907 he founded the *Revue militaire générale*.

Langlois, Jean Charles (1789–1870). A French soldier and painter famous for such battle panoramas as *Bataille de la Moskova, Incendie de Moscou,* and *Prise de Malakot.*

Langrage. Artillery ammunition that consisted of odd pieces of metal, sometimes bolted together or enclosed in a canister.

Langson, Battle of (13 February 1885), French conquest and occupation of Indochina. A column under Colonel François de Négrier was attacked by Black Flags [q.v.] near this town in northeast Tonkin, 85 miles northeast of Hanoi, and was forced to retreat. The vigorously pursued colonial policy of Prime Minister Jules Ferry (1832–1893) in Indochina was much criticized and this misadventure, for the first time, brought down a French government.

Languet. A small piece of metal on the hilt of a sword that hangs over the scabbard.

Lannes, Jean, Duc de Montebello, Prince de Siévers (1769–1809). A French soldier in the French Revolutionary and Napoleonic armies who was the son of a poor farmer in the former royal province of Gascony. His brother, a priest, taught him to read, write, and cipher, and he began life as an apprentice dyer. He ran away from his apprenticeship to become a soldier and, in spite of his lack of a formal education, had risen to be a colonel by 1795. Two years later Napoleon promoted him general of brigade. General Louis Desaix (1768–1800) described him at this time as being "bravest of the brave, young, fine appearance, well-built, face not very pleasing, riddled with wounds, elegant, has fine horses and carriages, the finest in Italy, married a has-been in Rome." There, when the pope put out his hand to be kissed, Lannes seized it and squeezed it heartily.

After serving in Egypt, in 1799 he returned to France as a provisional general of division and divorced his wife, who had begun her family without waiting for his return. He won his first battle and his first title in the Battle of Montebello on 9 June 1800, when, with 6,000 men and later the help of General Claude Victor [q.v.] with another 6,000, he defeated 17,000 Austrians with 35 guns under General Peter Carl Ott (1738–1809), inflicting some 4,000 casualties while sustaining a loss of only 500.

On 19 May 1804 he was promoted marshal, one of the first. In 1805 he fought at Ulm and Austerlitz [qq.v.]. On 10 October 1806 he won the Battle of Saalfeld [q.v.]. He later fought at Jena, Pultusk, the siege of Danzig (Gdansk), and Friedland [qq.v.]. He served in the Peninsular War [q.v.], defeating General Francisco Castaños y Aragón [q.v.] in the Battle of Tudela [q.v.] and participating in the siege of Saragossa [q.v.].

In 1809 he was back in Germany, taking part in the battles of Abensburg, Landshut, Eckmühl, Ratisbon, and Aspern-Essling [qq.v.]. In the latter engagement a cannonball shattered both his legs. Although they were quickly amputated by Dr. Dominique Jean Larrey [q.v], he died nine days later, the first of Napoleon's marshals to die of wounds. He had fought in sixty battles and had been wounded ten times, more than any other senior Napoleonic commander.

Napoleon wept at his death, for he regarded him as perhaps his finest battlefield commander and his friend, the only man permitted to address him with the familiar *tu*. He once said of him: "No man has ever been or still is more attached to me than Lannes is at heart. He has made a rampart of his body in my defense."

By his second wife Lannes produced five children. One son became a diplomat of note, and another, *Gustave Olivier Lannes* (1804–1875), a soldier and an aide-de-camp to Napoleon III. He commanded a French corps in the occupation of Rome in 1862–64 and a cavalry division in the Garde Imperiale [q.v.] from 1865 to 1869.

Lanterne. A large ladle or scoop for pouring gunpowder into a muzzle-loading cannon.

Lanyard. 1. A cord worn around the neck and attached to a whistle, pistol, or knife.
   2. A strong cord with a hook at one end for firing cannon.
   3. An aiguillette.

Laon, Battle of (9–10 March 1814), Napoleonic Wars. On 9 March near this town, 77 miles northeast of Paris, Prussian General Hans Yorck von Wartenburg, serving under General Gebhard von Blücher, surprised and routed a French force under Marshal Auguste Marmont [qq.v.]. In this action the Russian General Matvei Platov [q.v.], hetman of the Don Cossacks, distinguished himself. Only the arrival of the guard saved Marmont from total destruction. That night the French camped on the field, but Blücher launched a night attack that drove Marmont toward Rheims. Napoleon summoned reinforcements, and Blücher, who was sick, broke off all pursuit.

French losses were about 6,000 killed and wounded out of 47,000; Allied losses were about 4,000 out of 85,000. However, the road to Paris was now open to the Allies.

Laos, French Pacification of (1893–95). Beginning in 1893, France made Laos, a kingdom of about 90,000 square miles in Southeast Asia, a French protectorate, and General Joseph Gallieni [q.v.] and General Louis Gonzalve (1854–1934) pacified a region as large as France containing sixteen million people.

Lapel. Sometimes written "lapelle." The facings of a coat. In the British army prior to the introduction of epaulets in 1812, a coat with a white lapel indicated a lieutenant.

Laptot. A Wolof word meaning sailor that came to be applied to West African soldiers who had formerly been slaves [see Sofa].

La Puebla, Battles of. This city in central-southeast Mexico, 80 miles southeast of Mexico City, now called La Puebla de Zaragoza, has an altitude of 7,150 feet and is one of the oldest and most beautiful cities in Mexico. There were three military actions here in the nineteenth century.

1. 14 September–12 October 1847, Mexican War. Mexican forces besieged La Puebla, then held by the Americans, but were driven off by American reinforcements from Veracruz.

2. 5 May 1862, French invasion and occupation of Mexico. Sometimes called the Battle of Cinco de Mayo. A French force of 7,500 men under General Charles Lorencez [q.v.] unsuccessfully attacked a ridge near the city that was held by 12,000 Mexicans under Generals Ignacio Zaragoza and Porfirio Díaz [qq.v.]. French losses were 456 killed and wounded.

3. 4–17 May 1863, French invasion and occupation of Mexico. French General Élie Forey [q.v.] with 25,000 men laid siege to the city protected by a garrison of 18,000. It was captured on 17 May 1863. This left the road to the capital open.

La Puebla *French forces storm Fort San Guadalupe at La Puebla, 5 May 1863.*

La Puerta, Battles of. During the struggle for Venezuelan independence from Spain two battles were fought near this western Venezuelan town on a spur of the Andes Mountains, 16 miles south-southwest of Valera.

1. 15 June 1814. Revolutionary forces under Simón Bolívar [q.v.] were defeated by royalist forces of Venezuelan plainsmen under Spanish General José Tomás Boves (d. 1821?), who then entered Caracas, where he inaugurated a harsh regime and massacred 3,500 suspected rebels.

2. 15 March 1818. Simón Bolívar was again defeated here, this time by royalist forces under Pablo Morillo [q.v.]. Bolívar was wounded in this engagement.

Laramie Loafers. Colloquial name for American Indians who became totally dependent upon government gifts and services. Other Indians called them stay-around-the-fort people.

Largeau, Victor Emmanuel Étienne (1866–1916). A French soldier who as a captain took part in the Congo-Nile Expedition led by Jean Baptiste Marchand [q.v.] that sparked the Fashoda Incident [q.v.]. He took a leading part in the campaign against the Masalit sultanate, which had destroyed a French column at El Geneina, 100 miles west of El Fasher in Darfur Province of the Sudan. He died of wounds received in the fighting around Verdun in the First World War.

Lariat. 1. A lasso for catching animals.

2. In the U.S. cavalry, a 30-foot long rope, $1\frac{1}{4}$ inches in cir-

cumference, made of Indian hemp, used to picket horses while grazing.

La Rochejacquelein, Comte de. See Vergier, Auguste.

La Rochejaquelein, Louis Du Vergier, Marquis de (1777–1815). A French soldier who emigrated during the Revolution but returned to France in 1801 and in 1813 headed the royalist revolt in the Vendée. In 1814 he commanded the army of the Vendée, and during the Hundred Days [q.v.] he maintained the royalist cause with the support of the British. He was killed in action near St. Gilles on 4 June 1815.

La Romana, Pedro Caro y Sureda (1761–1811). A Spanish soldier who served as a general in the Peninsular War [q.v.]. In 1807–08 he commanded the Baltic Corps. He replaced Joachim Blake [q.v.] as commander of the Galician forces and aided Sir John Moore [q.v.] in his retreat to Corunna. He was defeated at Mansilla on 30 December 1808 by Marshal Nicolas Soult [q.v.]. Late in 1809 he replaced General Don Lorenzo del Parque [q.v.] as commander of the Army of the Left. In January 1810 he tried unsuccessfully to save Seville, but he campaigned effectively in Portugal and Estremadura until he died of a heart attack while trying to relieve besieged Badajoz [q.v.]. He was generally considered the best of the Spanish commanders in the war. Henry Crabb Robinson (1775–1867), the first war correspondent for the *Times,* thought La Romana, who was usually unkempt, resembled a Spanish barber more than a general.

La Rothière, Battle of (1 February 1814), Napoleonic Wars. Prussian Field Marshal Gebhard von Blücher [q.v.] with 53,000 men attacked Napoleon with just over 40,000 near this village in northeastern France. Late in the afternoon Blücher captured the village, but he was driven out by the Young Guard [see Garde Imperial]. Toward evening the French retreated from the field. Each side lost about 6,000.

Although this was a drawn battle, Blücher claimed victory, and in an after-action report written on 2 February in idiosyncratic English he wrote: "The grate Blow has been struck, yesterday I totally defeated the Emperor Napoleon, he is in full Retreat on Paris we may soon get a peece, for he can face us no longer."

Larrey, Dominique Jean (1766–1842). A French military surgeon who qualified at Toulouse, where his uncle was surgeon-in-chief at a local hospital. After serving briefly as a surgeon in the French navy and leading medical students in the storming of the Bastille, he worked for two years as an assistant surgeon a the Hôtel des Invalides [q.v.], then joined the army and accompanied Napoleon to Egypt and Syria. There he did forward resuscitation, evacuation, and surgery during the battle.

He designed the first custom-built ambulance and organized ambulance units of about 300 men with vehicles, horses, and medical and surgical supplies, which he brought onto the battlefield for the evacuation of the wounded (*ambulance volante*).

In 1802 he was chief surgeon of the Garde Imperiale [q.v.].

During the Austrian Campaign of 1805 he became the first doctor to amputate the hip joint. He won fame and the Legion of Honor for his surgical skills in the Battle of Aspern-Essling [q.v.], where of 1,200 guardsmen wounded, half were returned to duty within a few months, 250 were evacuated to France, and only 45 died. After the Battle of Wagram [q.v.] he was made a baron. He was with Napoleon's army on the march to Moscow, and following the Battle of Borodino [q.v.], he performed 200 amputations in twenty-four hours. On 12 February 1812 he was appointed surgeon-in-chief of the Grande Armèe.

In the Battle of Waterloo [q.v.] he sited his main dressing station at La Belle Alliance Inn [q.v.] but was forced to flee. He encountered a patrol of Prussian uhlans and tried to cut his way through, but he was sabered down, suffering cuts on his head and left shoulder, and captured. He survived to become surgeon-in-chief at the Hôpital de Gros-Caillou and Hôtel des Invalides. Napoleon called him "the most virtuous man I have ever known." [See Medicine and Surgery, Military.]

Lasalle, Comte Antoine Charles Louis de (1775–1809). A French soldier who had a distinguished record as a cavalry commander. In the Battle of Rivoli on 14 January 1797 he captured an entire battalion of Austrians. A colonel of the 10th Hussars in 1800, he was said to have broken seven swords and had two horses killed from under him in a single battle. He was a general of brigade at Austerlitz [q.v.] in 1805. The following year, in the pursuit after the Battle of Jena [q.v.], in command of only 600 hussars and with no artillery, he panicked the commander of the fortress of Stettin, 75 miles northeast of Berlin, into surrendering [see Stettin, Capture of]. For this he was promoted general of division. In the Peninsular War [q.v.] he defeated the army of Castile. He was killed in July 1809 leading a charge in the Battle of Wagram [q.v.].

Lascar. In the Indian army a low-caste artilleryman or tent pitcher. In the artillery, sometimes called a gun lascar.

Las Cruces Pass, Battle of (30 October 1810), Mexican Revolution. Some 60,000 rebellious Mexican peasants under Father Don Miguel Hidalgo y Costilla and José Ignacio Allende defeated 7,000 Spanish loyalist forces under Agustín Iturbide [qq.v.] The Mexicans suffered a loss of 5,000 killed and wounded to the loyalists' 1,000.

La Serna y Hinojosa, José de (1770–1831). A Spanish soldier who in 1816 was a major general commanding in Upper Peru (Bolivia). He was viceroy of Peru from 1821 until he was captured with his entire army by General Antonio de Sucre [q.v.] in the Battle of Ayacucho [q.v.] on 9 December 1824.

Las Guásimas, Battle of (24 June 1898), Spanish-American War. About 17,000 American regulars and volunteers under General William Shafter [q.v.] sailed from Tampa, Florida, in thirty-two transports on 14 June and landed—"higgledy-piggledy," according to Lieutenant Colonel Theodore Roosevelt [q.v.]—on 22 June at Daiquirí, Cuba, 14 miles east of Santiago de Cuba. A force commanded by sixty-one-year-old Major General Joseph Wheeler [q.v.], a former Confederate general, with 1,000 regulars and Theodore Roosevelt's Rough Riders [q.v.], not counting war correspondents Stephen Crane (1871–1900) and Richard Harding Davis [q.v.], moved inland and fought the first land battle of the campaign at Las Guásimas, a fortified gap in the hills just east-southeast of Santiago de Cuba in southern Oriente Province. Some 800 Cuban patriots under General Calixto García [q.v.] were to have supported them, but they proved ineffective; it was said that they slept through the engagement. In a sharp fight that lasted just over an hour the Spanish were driven from their positions with a loss, officially reported, of 9 killed and 27 wounded; American casualties were

Las Guásimas *Wounded Rough Riders walk into Siboney after the Battle of Las Guásimas, 24 June 1898.*

16 killed and 52 wounded. The Rough Riders suffered proportionately the heaviest losses: 8 killed and 34 wounded. These were the official figures; the actual number of wounded was much higher, but only those requiring sustained hospitalization were counted as wounded. This was a preliminary to the battles of El Caney and San Juan Hill [qq.v.] and the taking of Santiago.

Roosevelt viewed the battle from a personal viewpoint: He considered the battle "really a capital thing for me, for practically all of the men had served under my actual command, and henceforth felt enthusiastic belief that I would lead them aright."

Lashkar. An ad hoc tribal army on the Northwest Frontier [q.v.] of India (today Pakistan).

Last Post. The last bugle call at night in the British service. A signal for lights to be extinguished. It is also played at funerals and memorial services. In the American service a call with an identical usage is taps [q.v.].

Last Stand. 1. The final defensive position taken by a unit facing overwhelming odds, as in Custer's last stand [see Custer, George Armstrong; Camerone, Battle of].

2. A decision to fight to the death. Those of one's own side who make such decisions are called heroes; those of the enemy who make such decisions are called fanatics.

Laswari, Battle of (1 November 1803), Second Maratha War. At this village in Rajputana, northwest India, 20 miles east of Alwar and about 78 miles south-southwest of Delhi, British General Gerard Lake [q.v.] with 10,500 men, mostly Indians, defeated a Maratha army of 4,000 to 5,000 cavalry and 9,000 infantry commanded by Pierre Cuillier, a French adventurer. Lake's infantry fought after having marched 65 miles in forty-eight hours. British losses were 838, including 82 Europeans killed and 248 wounded; Lake's son, a lieutenant colonel, was severely wounded. Maratha losses were estimated to be 7,000 killed, wounded, or dispersed, and 2,000 taken prisoner. The British took 72 guns and a large quantity of stores.

In his after-action report Lake wrote: "I never was in so severe a business in my life or anything like it. . . . [T]hese fellows fought like devils, or rather like heroes."

Latane, William (1833–1862). A Confederate soldier killed in the American Civil War and made famous by a painting of his funeral. He was graduated from the medical department of Hampton-Sydney College in Virginia in 1853, but was serving as a cavalry captain under General J. E. B. Stuart [q.v.] when he was killed near Hanover Court House on 14 June 1862. He was buried at Summer Hill, the home of William Brockenbrough Newton. Mrs. Newton, who had four sons in the army, read the burial service. From a newspaper account John Reuben Thompson [q.v.], an editor and poet, wrote a poem, "The Burial of Latane," lauding the fallen captain and Mrs. Newton and her granddaughters, who had arranged the burial. The poem, published in the *Southern Literary Messenger* in the summer of 1863, was believed to have inspired a young painter, William Dickenson Washington (1833–1870), who in 1869 became the chairman of the newly created art department at the Virginia Military Institute, to paint *The Burial of Latane,* his most famous picture, from which hundreds of engravings and lithographs were made. The painting itself disappeared for nearly sixty years but in 1930 turned up in the home of a family in New Jersey who were ignorant of its provenance. It is now owned by a Virginia judge.

Lateral Route. A route that runs generally parallel with the line of battle.

Latigo Strap. A strong leather strap, tapering at one end, used with the aparejo cinch to tighten the aparejo [q.v.].

Latin American Wars of Independence. The early nineteenth century was marked by a series of revolutionary wars waged in Mexico, Central America, and South America by local inhabitants, many of them criolos or Creoles (first- or second-generation French and Spanish) against European domination. The most notable of the revolutionary campaigns were those carried out against the Spanish by Símón Bolívar of Venezuela and José de San Martín [qq.v.] of Argentina, who saw in the fall of Spain to France in the Peninsular War [q.v.] an opportunity to rid Spanish colonies of the Spanish yoke.

La Tour d'Auvergne, Théophile Malo Corret. See First Grenadier of France.

Latrine. Communal toilets, sometimes called sinks, particularly in British usage, used in camps and barracks. It was often a receptacle or a pit or trench in the earth. In the British army as late as 1910 flush toilets were a rarity even in permanent barracks. For most of the nineteenth century the usual urinal for night use in the barracks of all armies was a wooden tub, often leaking, in an unlit squad room. Much of the sickness that attended armies in barracks and in the field resulted from defective or ill-made latrines.

Laudable Pus. A type of suppuration of a treated wound that was considered healthy and a sign of healing. It was said to have a particular thick, creamy appearance. It was usually due to staphylococcal infection with local abscess but was not usually septicemia and thus could be regarded as a good sign. However, a serosanguinous pus was usually caused by streptococcal infection and often led to septicemia and death.

Laurel Brigade. A Confederate unit in the American Civil War composed of the 7th, 11th, and 12th Virginia Cavalry Regiments and the 35th Virginia Cavalry Battalion. From February 1864 members wore laurel leaves on their hats.

Lauriston, Jacques Alexandre Bernard Law (1768–1828). A French soldier who was Napoleon's comrade at artillery school. In 1800 he was an aide-de-camp to Napoleon. He served at Austerlitz [q.v.] and captured Ragusa in 1807. In 1809 he distinguished himself at Wagram [q.v.], and he took part in the retreat from Moscow [see Russian Campaign, Napoleon's]. However, at the Bourbon restoration he rallied to the Bourbon cause. In 1817 he was created a marquis, and in 1821 he was made a marshal of France.

Laussedat, Aimé (1819–1907). A French officer and geodesist. He pioneered in the use of the camera lucida [q.v.] in the preparation of maps, drawings, and plans and is credited with the invention of photogrammetry. He also invented several astronomical instruments.

Lava Beds, Battle of (17 January and 26 April 1873), Modoc War. On 17 January 1876 in a land of ice caves, ravines, and lava beds that made a natural fortress near Tule Lake in northern California 75 Modoc Indian warriors under Captain Jack [q.v.] with about 150 women and children held off 400 American soldiers under General Edward Canby [q.v.], killing 9 and wounding about 30, including 3 officers. Canby drew back and was reinforced to more than 1,000. No Modocs were killed or wounded.

During peace talks Canby was treacherously killed. In a second battle, on 26 April, an American force under Jefferson Davis [q.v.] fought its way into the lava beds and eventually routed the Indians at a loss of 4 officers and 18 enlisted men killed and 1 officer and 16 men wounded [see Modoc War]. Captain Jack was captured with four others and hanged at Fort Klamath on 3 October 1873.

Lavalette, Antoine Marie Chamans (1769–1830). A French soldier and politician who served in the Alps and was an aide to Napoleon. He became a general and was French minister to Saxony. After the Bourbon restoration in 1815 he was condemned to death but escaped by changing clothes with his wife.

Laveran, Charles Louis Alphonse (1845–1922). A French military physician and parasitologist who was professor of medicine and epidemic diseases at the military college of Val de Grâce from 1874 to 1878 and again from 1884 to 1894. He studied malaria in Algeria and in 1880 discovered the blood parasite that causes the disease. For this he was awarded the Nobel Prize, the eighth person to receive it. From 1896 until his death he was at the Pasteur Institute in Paris.

La Victoria, Battle of (February 1814), Venezuelan Wars of Independence. Simón Bolívar [q.v.] won a victory over royalist forces at this northern Venezuelan town, 32 miles southwest of Caracas.

Lavure. The grains, metal dust, and pieces of metal that fall off during the casting of cannon.

Law, Evander McIvor (1836–1920). An American soldier who was graduated from the South Carolina Military Academy (the Citadel) in 1856. He taught school and aided in the founding of the Military High School at Tuskegee, Alabama. At the beginning of the American Civil War he was elected a lieutenant colonel of the 4th Alabama and fought at the First Battle of Bull Run [q.v.], in which he was wounded. When he recovered, he was elected colonel of the regiment, which he led in the Battle of Seven Pines and in the Seven Days' Battles [qq.v.]. Commanding brigades or divisions, he fought at Gettysburg, Chickamauga, the Wilderness, Spotsylvania, and Cold Harbor [qq.v.], where he was again wounded. In the final days of the war he commanded a cavalry unit in the Carolinas.

After the war he helped found the educational system of Florida and was active in veterans' affairs.

Lawrence. The family name of three brothers, sons of an English army officer, all of whom distinguished themselves as soldiers and administrators in India.

George St. Patrick Lawrence (1804–1884) took part in the First Afghan War and commanded forces in Rajputana during the Indian Mutiny [qq.v.].

Henry Montgomery Lawrence (1806–1857) was commissioned in the Bengal artillery at age sixteen and first saw action in Burma (Myanmar) in 1824. He took part in the First Anglo-Burmese War of 1828, the First Afghan War in 1838 and 1842, and both Sikh Wars [qq.v.]. While commissioner of the province of Oudh, he was mortally wounded defending the residency at Lucknow [q.v.] during the Indian Mutiny [q.v.]. Before he died, he dictated a much admired epitaph: "Here lies Henry Lawrence who tried to do his duty. May the Lord have mercy on his soul."

John Laird Mair Lawrence (1811–1879) became in 1853 lieutenant governor of the Punjab, where he did much to curb the oppression of the chiefs. During the Indian Mutiny [q.v.] he disarmed mutineers in the Punjab and dispatched loyal Sikhs to the relief of Delhi. He was viceroy of India from 1863 to 1869, and he opposed the intrigues that led to the Second Afghan War [q.v.] in 1878.

Laws of War. Rules of behavior for states and those engaged in war agreed to by civilized states. They generally consist of rules for the protection of noncombatants, neutrals, and wounded. The first codification of the laws of war was by Francis Lieber [q.v.], an American, in 1863. [See Lieber Code; Hague Convention; Geneva Convention.]

Lawton, Henry Ware (1843–1899). An American soldier who at age eighteen enlisted in the 9th Indiana at the beginning of the American Civil War and fought in more than twenty engagements, including Shiloh, Murfreesboro, and Chickamauga [qq.v.]. He was a tall man, standing six feet four inches, and possessed a commanding presence. He won the Medal of Honor for heroism at Atlanta. In November 1865 at his discharge he was a twenty-two-year-old lieutenant colonel. For a time he studied law at Harvard, but in July 1866 he accepted a commission as a second lieutenant in the regular army. In the same year, as part of the Indian-fighting army on the southwestern frontier, he doggedly pursued Geronimo [q.v.], leading a column for more than 1,300 miles through the Sierra Madres. He was credited by many for Geronimo's surrender. During the Spanish-American War [q.v.] he served as a brigadier general of volunteers in Cuba, leading the advance from the beachhead at Daiquirí [q.v.]. He captured El Caney [q.v.] and was appointed military governor of Santiago de Cuba when it was captured. For his services he was brevetted major general.

In January 1899 he was sent to help put down the insurrection in the Philippines [see Philippine Insurrection against the United States; Aguinaldo y Famy, Emilio]. He operated north of Manila, capturing Santa Cruz on 10 April and San Isidro on 15 May. In June he pushed the insurgents from Cavite, south of Manila, and in December he took charge of an expedition to the east. He was killed in action leading an attack on San Mateo, just east of Manila, on 19 December.

Lay. 1. As a verb, to aim an artillery piece at a target or from an aiming point.

2. As a verb, to plan or project a course.

3. As a noun, the setting of the range, direction, or elevation or all these of a weapon.

Lazaret. A Russian field hospital.

Lazaretto. A hospital for patients with contagious diseases.

Leadership. The qualities necessary to motivate, care for, and direct soldiers. Perhaps the best description of leadership offered by a nineteenth-century officer was given by Wellington in his general order of 15 May 1811 during the Peninsular War [q.v.]: "The quality which I wish to see the officers possess, who are at the head of the troops, is a cool discriminating judgement when in action, which will enable them to decide with promptitude how far they can go and ought to go, with propriety; and to convey their orders and to act with such vigour and decision, that the soldiers will look up to them with confidence in the moment of action, and obey them with alacrity."

Leaf Sight. An elevating rear sight on a rifle that consisted of several hinged leaves of different heights so that the sight could be adjusted for the range.

League. A measurement frequently encountered in military accounts and one that was frequently misunderstood in the nineteenth century, particularly during the Peninsular War [q.v.], when four different measurements were used. The most common was the Spanish league, which was 4.21 miles; the Castilian league was 2.63 miles; the maritime league was 3.49 miles; and the geographical league was 4 miles, sometimes referred to as the league on the king's highway (*legales del camino real*).

Leaguer. A camp, usually of a besieging army.

Lea, Homer (1876–1912). An American who twice became a Chinese general. Because he was frail and had a hunched back and poor eyesight, he was rejected when he tried to enlist in the American army, but he retained from his youth a deep interest in military affairs and military history. As a young man he became fascinated with things Chinese and applied himself to the study of the country's language and culture. A student at Stanford University when the Boxer Rebellion [q.v.] erupted, he abandoned his classes in July 1899 and sailed to China. His courage and military acumen impressed the Chinese, particularly the reformer Kang Yu-wei (1858-1927), who laid plans to free Emperor Kung Hsu (1871–1908) from the domination of his aunt, the regent empress dowager. Lea was made a general and took command of a group of revolutionary volunteers. When the plot was discovered in 1900, he fled to Hong Kong, where he met the revolutionary leader Sun Yat-sen (1866–1925). He returned to the United States in 1901, but nine years later was back in China as a military advisor to Sun with the rank of lieutenant general. He was present at the ceremony announcing the overthrow of the Manchu dynasty.

In 1909 he published *The Valor of Ignorance*, in which he predicted a war between Japan and the United States that would begin with a Japanese attack upon Hawaii, the subsequent fall of the Philippines, and the formation of an Anglo-American alliance that would counterbalance the power of Russia in a struggle for world domination. In a second book he predicted the downfall of the British Empire. While he was preparing a third book, he suffered a stroke that left him blind and paralyzed. In the spring of 1912 he returned to the United States and lingered in agony until his death on 1 November, just before his thirty-sixth birthday.

Leap over the Sword. An informal marriage ceremony sometimes performed by British soldiers that endured into the early nineteenth century. The couple to be married joined hands before a sword placed on the ground and jumped over it as a senior noncommissioned officer present intoned: "Leap rogue and jump whore, and then you are married forevermore." Such marriages were often considered binding. Rudyard Kipling [q.v.] alluded to the practice in his poem "The Sergeant's Weddin'."

Lear, Genrikh Antonovich (1829–1904). A Russian soldier educated in St. Petersburg who began his military career in an engineer battalion in the Caucasus. From 1852 to 1854 he studied at the Nicholas Military Academy [q.v.], where after 1858 he served as adjunct professor of tactics. In 1865 he became a professor of military tactics and strategy. From 1889 to 1898 he was commandant of the academy. He was an admirer of Napoleon and measured all other campaigns against his. His textbook *Strategy* went through six editions between 1867 and 1898.

Leatherneck. A colloquialism for a U.S. marine. For a twelve-year period beginning about 1880 the collar of the marine dress uniform had a leather lining that often became slimy with sweat in summer and in winter cracked with the cold and chafed the neck of the wearer.

Leave. 1. Permission.

2. An authorized absence from duty. The Duke of Wellington once granted a mere forty-eight hours' leave to an officer because, he said, "that is as long as any reasonable man can wish to stay in bed with the same woman."

In the American army, officers were given leave; enlisted men were granted furloughs [q.v.].

Leavenworth, Henry (1783–1834). An American soldier who left the practice of law to accept a commission during the War of 1812. He distinguished himself in the Battle of Chippewa on 5 July 1814 and the Battle of Lundy's Lane [qq.v.] on 25 July. After the war he was elected to the New York legislature. In 1818 he accepted a commission as lieutenant colonel of the 5th Infantry and served first on the Northeast Frontier and then in the Southwest. In 1823 he led a successful punitive expedition against the Arikara Indians, who on 2 April of that year had attacked a party of fur traders led by William Henry Ashley (1778?–1838). Leavenworth was brevetted brigadier general in July 1824 and a regular colonel in December. On 8 May 1827 he established a cantonment on the west bank of the Missouri River in present-day Kansas. Six months later, on 8 November, it was designated Cantonment Leavenworth. On 8 February 1832 it was renamed Fort Leavenworth.

In 1834 he was appointed to the command of the entire southwestern frontier. He died of illness on 21 July of that year while leading the newly formed 1st Dragoons in a show of force at the Pawnee and Comanche villages on the Arkansas River.

Lebel, Nicolas (1838–1891). A French officer who designed the small-caliber gun named after him. He was originally an infantry officer and in 1876 commanded a battalion. When he was assigned to command a small-arms training school, he became interested in the design of small arms. The Lebel rifle [q.v.] and the cartridge he designed were adopted in 1887 and remained the French standard until the 1920s. Lebel, promoted colonel, was given command of the 120th Infantry, a command he held until his death.

Lebel Rifle. This 8 mm magazine-fed French service rifle, designed by Lieutenant Colonel Nicolas Lebel [q.v.], a member of the French small-arms committee, was adopted by the French army on 22 April 1887 and modified in 1893 and 1898. It was the first service rifle to use smokeless propellent cartridges. It had a turning bolt action and weighed 4.18 kilograms. From 1886 to 1919 nearly four million were manufactured by Manufacture d'Armes at Châtellerault, St Étienne, and Tulle. A modified version was passed to the reserves in 1945.

Leboeuf, Edmond (1809–1888). A French soldier who was graduated from the École Polytechnique [q.v.] and served in Algeria and in the Crimean War [q.v.]. In the Austro-Piedmontese War [q.v.] of 1859 he distinguished himself in the Battle of Solferino [q.v.] by his skillful use of new rifled artillery. He was an aide-de-camp to Napoleon III (1808–1873) and in 1869–70 was minister of war. In 1870 he was made a marshal of France. When war with Prussia became imminent, he assured Napoleon III: "So ready are we, that if the war lasts two years, not a gaiter button would be found wanting." In fact, when the Franco-Prussian War [q.v.] began, it was immediately obvious that the French army was almost totally unprepared. He served as chief of staff of the army on the Rhine and then commanded III Corps in the battles around Metz. After the fall of Metz he became a prisoner of war in Germany. Following his release, he lived in retirement in France.

Le Boulengé, Paul Émil (1832–1901). A Belgian artilleryman noted for his discoveries in the science of ballistics and for inventing a chronograph for measuring the time of flight of projectiles.

Le Bourget, Battle of (27–30 October 1870), Franco-Prussian War. During the siege of Paris the French made a sortie and captured the village of Le Bourget, six miles east of Paris. They held their positions until driven back by the Prussian Guards attacking in open order. The French lost more than 1,200 men; the Prussians lost 34 officers and 344 men.

Le Caron, Henri (1841–1894). A British-born soldier and secret agent whose real name was Thomas Miller Beach. In 1861 he emigrated to the United States, where he enlisted in the Union army under the name Henri le Caron. In 1864 he married a young woman who had helped him escape capture by Confederates, and by the end of the war he had risen to the rank of major.

From 1865 to 1889 he lived in Detroit and other northern American cities, where acting as a secret agent for the British army he spied on the Fenian Brotherhood [q.v.] and established himself as an intimate of their leaders. In 1870 his information was instrumental in turning the planned Fenian invasion of Canada into a disaster [see Fenian Raids]. In 1871 he supplied information that led to the capture of Louis Riel [q.v.].

Leclerc, Charles Victor Emmanuel (1772–1802). A French soldier who in 1797 distinguished himself in the Battle of Rivoli by leading a cavalry charge to clear the Osteria Gorge. In that same year he married Napoleon's sister and served under Napoleon in Egypt. Ordered to capture Santo Domingo in the Caribbean, he sailed from Brest on 14 December 1801 and in February 1802 landed in present-day Haiti. There he soon captured Toussaint L'Ouverture [q.v.] and sent him a prisoner to France. He died in Haiti of yellow fever [q.v.] on 2 November [see Haitian-French War].

Lecolle Mill, Battle of (30 March 1814), War of 1812. An American force of 4,000 under Major General James Wilkinson [q.v.] was repulsed by a British force of 200 at this village near the Richelieu River, 17 miles south-southwest of St. Jean in present-day Quebec. This was Wilkinson's last battle.

Lee, Fitzhugh (1835–1905). An American soldier who was a grandson of Henry ("Light-Horse Harry") Lee (1756–1818) and a nephew of Robert E. Lee. He was graduated from West Point in 1856, ranking 45th in a class of 49. In 1861 he resigned to join the Confederate army. He was a cavalry commander in the Peninsular Campaign and fought at Chancellorsville and Spotsylvania Court House [qq.v.]. From 1886 to 1890 he was governor of Virginia, and from 1896 to 1898 the American consul general in Havana, Cuba. During the Spanish-American War [q.v.] he served as brigadier general and major general of volunteers in Cuba, and in 1899 he was military governor of Havana. He retired in 1901 as a regular army brigadier general, one of only two Confederate generals later to become an American regular army general. The other was General Joseph Wheeler [q.v.].

Lee, George Washington Custis (1832–1913). An American soldier who was a son of General Robert E. Lee and was graduated from West Point in 1854. In 1861 he resigned to join the Confederate army. In 1863 he was promoted brigadier general, and in 1864 major general. Almost all his service was as a staff officer, as aide-de-camp to Jefferson Davis. He saw no action until the closing months of the war, when he organized the clerks and mechanics of Richmond to try to defend the capital. He retreated with the corps of General Richard Ewell [q.v.] and was captured at Sayler's Creek [q.v.] on 6 April 1865. Soon released, he later that year became a professor at Washington College (now Washington and Lee University) in Lexington, Virginia, and succeeded his father as president in 1871. He remained until 1897.

Lee, Henry (1787–1837). An American soldier and politician who was a son of Henry ("Light-Horse Harry") Lee (1756–1818) and an older brother of General Robert E. Lee. He served in the War of 1812 and wrote military biography and history, including a biography of Napoleon and works defending his father's war record.

Lee, James Paris (1831–1904). A Scottish-born American gunsmith who in the 1860s established the Lee Firearms Company and in 1879 patented the first rifle with a removable box magazine beneath a bolt action. The American navy contracted for it, but his financial backers sold out, and the contract went to Remington. Lee then joined Remington, for which he developed a number of handguns using his magazine and bolt action. In 1888 the British army adopted his system, producing the Lee-Enfield and the Lee-Metford [qq.v.] from his designs. In 1895 the U.S. navy adopted his 6 mm caliber rifle with a straight-pull bolt.

Lee, Robert Edward (1807–1870). Robert Edward Lee was born in Virginia, the fifth child of Henry ("Light-Horse Harry") Lee (1756–1818), of Revolutionary War fame, by his second wife. In 1829 he was graduated second in his class at West Point without having incurred a single demerit in his four years there. Commissioned in the Corps of Engineers, he served as a captain under General Winfield Scott [q.v.] in the Mexican War [q.v.], in which he distinguished himself in the battles of Veracruz, Churubusco, and Chapultepec [qq.v.]. He was slightly wounded in the war and earned three brevets to colonel. General Winfield Scott [q.v.] declared him to be "the very best soldier that I ever saw in the field."

In 1852 he was appointed superintendent of West Point. Three years later, with the approval of Jefferson Davis [q.v.], then secretary of war, he transferred as a lieutenant colonel to the newly raised 2nd Cavalry and served in West Texas.

Although John Brown's raid [q.v.] on the U.S. arsenal and armory at Harper's Ferry, Virginia (West Virginia), in October 1859 occurred while Lee was on extended leave at his home in Arlington, Virginia, he was placed in command of a detachment of marines and, with Second Lieutenant J. E. B. Stuart [q.v.], captured Brown and his band.

On 20 April 1861, at the outbreak of the American Civil War, he resigned his commission. In a letter to his sister he wrote: "With all my devotion to the Union, and the feeling of loyalty and duty of an American citizen, I have not been able to make up my mind to raise my hand against my relatives, my children, my home." In his letter of resignation, sent to General Winfield Scott, he spoke of "the struggle it has cost me to separate myself from a service to which I have devoted the best years of my life and all the ability I possessed. . . . Save in defense of my native State, I never desire again to draw my sword."

Three days later he was appointed by Governor John Letcher (1813–1884) of Virginia to be commander-in-chief of the military and naval forces of the state. When Virginia's troops were transferred to the Confederate service, he became, on 14 May 1861, a brigadier general, the highest rank then authorized. Soon after, he was promoted to full general, to rank from 14 June.

Lee's first field command was in the western part of the state (now West Virginia), where he failed to hold back invading Union forces in an area in which there was strong pro-Union sentiment. He was recalled to Richmond, and from March 1862 he was military adviser to President Davis. From this position he was able to influence some operations, notably those of General Thomas ("Stonewall") Jackson [q.v.] in his Shenandoah Valley Campaign [q.v.].

When General Joseph E. Johnston [q.v.] was wounded in the Battle of Seven Pines [q.v.] on 31 May 1862, Lee took command of what became the Army of Northern Virginia [q.v.]. He successfully repulsed the efforts of Union General George McClellan [q.v.] in the Peninsular Campaign [q.v.], concluding with the Seven Days' Battles: Oak Grove, Mechanicsville, Gaines's Mill, Golding's Farm, Savage's Station and Allen's Farm, White Oak Swamp, and Malvern's Hill [qq.v.]. Victories were won through Lee's aggressiveness and daring in the face of McClellan's timidity rather than by any comprehensive generalship on Lee's part, for he was unable to exercise control over his subordinate commanders, and the individual battles were tactical defeats.

On 29–30 August 1862 he defeated General John Pope [q.v.] in the Second Battle of Bull Run [q.v.], but his invasion of Maryland was checked on 17 September at Antietam [q.v.] by Union forces under McClellan. Here, even after the bloodiest day of the entire war, Lee held on and was willing to fight on the same field another day. On 13 December he defeated General Ambrose Burnside [q.v.] at Fredericksburg [q.v.], where he made the remark to General James Longstreet [q.v.] that many of his admirers have tried to explain away: "It is well war is so terrible—we would grow too fond of it." Lee loved fighting a war.

Lee's most brilliantly fought battle was the defeat of Joseph Hooker [q.v.] at Chancellorsville [q.v.] on 1–4 May 1863. It is one of the most elemental rules of generalship, indeed, one might believe it elemental common sense, that the general of a numerically inferior force refrain from dividing that force in the face of his enemy. Yet Lee had done that just before Antietam, detaching Jackson to capture Harpers Ferry, and at Chancellorsville he did it not merely once, leaving part of his army at Fredericksburg, but twice, for he detached Jackson with the larger portion of his remaining force to come in on the Union right flank while Lee stood with only two divisions in front of the massive Federal army. Such actions seemed so unthinkable to Hooker that he could not take them in. He paused to think about them, and the pause was fatal. The courteous, calm Lee was daring to the point of rashness.

Again invading the North, he was again checked, this time at Gettysburg, where his rashness in insisting on what became known as Pickett's Charge [q.v.], a massed infantry assault across a wide plain, cost the South dearly. The rifle, which had largely replaced the musket in the Union armies, had made such attacks hopeless. Lee failed to recognize the effect of improved weapons.

From the Battle of the Wilderness [q.v.] in May–June 1864 until the siege of Petersburg [q.v.], from July 1864 to April 1865, Lee fought what was essentially a rearguard action. By an act of 23 January 1865 signed by President Davis on 6 February 1865 he was appointed general-in-chief of the armies of the Confederate States, but by that time the Confederates had lost the war.

Lee, Robert *Lee and Stonewall Jackson in council on the night of 1 May 1863 before Chancellorsville*

Lee has been charged with being too bloody-minded, of fighting on even when he must have known that his cause was lost. Viewed realistically, this was certainly true, but what the mind knows the heart cannot always accept. Lee was not alone in failing to admit defeat in a cause to which he was emotionally attached. He fought to the bitter end, and that end came on 9 April 1865 at Appomattox Court House in Virginia when he surveyed his position and said, "Then there is nothing left for me but to go and see General Grant, and I would rather die a thousand deaths." That afternoon of Palm Sunday Lee surrendered to General U. S. Grant in the front parlor of the home of Wilmer Mclean, a man who had moved his family from Manassas to this quiet corner of the state, where he thought "the sound of battle would never reach them."

After the war Lee became president of Washington College (today Washington and Lee University) in Lexington, Virginia. He applied to have his citizenship restored, but the application was mislaid. (It was found in 1970 and granted.) He died in Lexington of heart disease on 12 October 1870. His last words were said to have been "Strike the tent."

In American history, perhaps in the history of the world, no general who failed so often has been so revered by friends and enemies alike.

Lee, Robert *Lee returns to Richmond, 15 April 1865.*

Lee, Stephen Dill (1833–1908). An American soldier, distantly related to the Lees of Virginia, who was graduated from West Point in 1854 and commissioned in the 4th Artillery.

During the Third Seminole War [q.v.] of 1856–57 he saw limited action as a staff officer. On 20 February 1861 he resigned his commission as a lieutenant and joined the Confederate army, first as a captain and an aide-de-camp to General Pierre Beauregard [q.v.]. He served through all the campaigns in Virginia and commanded an infantry battalion at Antietam [q.v.]. He particularly distinguished himself in the Second Battle of Bull Run [q.v.], where he commanded the artillery in the corps of General James Longstreet [q.v.]. On 6 November he was appointed a brigadier general and sent to Vicksburg, where he was made prisoner after the surrender of that place on 4 July 1863 [see Vicksburg, Siege of]. He was exchanged soon after and on 3 August 1863 was promoted major general. On 23 June 1864, when thirty years old, he became the youngest lieutenant general in the Confederate army and commanded a corps under Hood.

After the war he was named the first president of Mississippi Agricultural and Mechanical College (later Mississippi State University) and helped establish the Vicksburg National Military Park. He was active in the United Confederate Veterans, of which he was the head from 1904 until his death.

President Jefferson Davis [q.v.] called Lee "one of the best all-round soldiers which the war produced." Union General William Tecumseh Sherman [q.v.] considered him "the most enterprising of all in their army."

Lee, William Henry Fitzhugh (1837–1891). A soldier and a son of Robert E. Lee, he was known as Roony Lee to distinguish him from his first cousin Fitzhugh Lee [q.v.]. He attended Harvard and in 1857 was commissioned directly into the U.S. army, but he resigned two years later to farm in Virginia. During the American Civil War he rose to colonel of the 9th Virginia Cavalry and fought under J. E. B. Stuart [q.v.]. On 15 September 1862 he was promoted brigadier general and the following June was badly wounded in the Battle of Brandy Station [q.v.]. While recuperating, he was captured. He was not exchanged until March 1864, and the following month he was promoted, becoming at twenty-eight the youngest major general in the Confederate army.

After the war he returned to farming, and in 1887 he was elected to Congress, a seat he held until his death on 15 October 1891.

Leech & Rigdon Revolvers. See Memphis Novelty Works.

Leech Lake Uprising (4–7 October 1898), American Indian Wars. The last Indian uprising in the United States was by Sioux near Leech Lake in north-central Minnesota. It was a minor disturbance easily suppressed by the U.S. 3rd Infantry.

Lee-Enfield. A British bolt-action repeating rifle, caliber .303, with a detachable ten-round magazine adopted by the British army in 1895 to replace the Lee-Metford [q.v.], which tended to wear out with the change to cordite propellant. The two rifles were basically the same, differing only in that the Lee-Enfield had a deeper rifling with five square-shouldered grooves. The name unites the name of the designer, James Paris Lee [q.v.], with the town of Enfield, on the New River, 10 miles north of London, where the rifle was manufactured by the Royal Small Arms Factory.

Lee-Metford Rifle. A rifle designed by the Scottish-born American gunsmith James Paris Lee [q.v.] using narrow seven-grooved rifling (one turn in 10 inches) designed by William Ellis Metford [q.v.] that resisted fouling. Sighted to 1,600 yards and fitted with a detachable box magazine that could hold eight rounds of .303 black powder cartridges, it had a turning bolt action and weighed 5.5 pounds. The British army adopted it on 12 December 1888 as Magazine Rifle Mark I. In 1891 a cordite cartridge was introduced, and this tended to wear out the barrel. In 1895 a new model used a box magazine holding ten rounds, each of which had to be loaded singly into the magazine. It remained the standard service rifle until replaced by the Lee-Enfield [q.v.] in 1895.

Lee's Farewell to the Army of Northern Virginia (10 April 1865). The day after he surrendered to U. S. Grant at Appomattox Court House, Robert E. Lee issued General Orders No. 9, his farewell to his troops:

After four years of arduous service, marked by unsurpassed courage and fortitude, the Army of Northern Virginia has been compelled to yield to overwhelming numbers and resources. I need not tell the survivors of so many hard-fought battles, who have remained steadfast to the last, that I have consented to this result from no distrust of them; but, feeling that valour and devotion could accomplish nothing that could compensate for the loss that would have attended the continuation of the contest, I have determined to avoid the useless sacrifice of those whose past services have endeared them to their countrymen. By the terms of the agreement, officers and men can return to their homes and remain there until exchanged. You will take with you the satisfaction that proceeds from the consciousness of duty faithfully performed; and I earnestly pray that a merciful God will extend to you His blessing and protection. With an increasing admiration for your constancy and devotion to your country, and a grateful remembrance of your kind and generous consideration of myself, I bid you an affectionate farewell.

R. E. Lee, General.

The following morning Lee ate a small breakfast, mounted his horse, Traveller, and with a small honor guard, set off for home.

Lefebvre, Pierre François Joseph (1755–1820). A French soldier, the son of a miller in Alsace, who always spoke French with a German accent. He received some education from his uncle, a village priest, and entered the army at age eighteen. In 1789, on becoming a sergeant major, he married Catherine Hubscher, a laundress (*blanchisseuse*) in his company. In 1792 he was made a captain, in 1793 a general of brigade, and the following year he was promoted general of division. By 1797 he commanded the equivalent of an army corps. In 1799 the Directory placed him in command of the Paris garrison, but he joined Napoleon in his coup d'état to "throw the lawyers into the river."

Although on 19 May 1804 he was elevated to be one of Napoleon's first marshals, his voice and his manners remained those of a drill sergeant. In 1809 Napoleon complained that there was such "imbecility in his correspondence that I cannot understand it." Nevertheless, he successfully besieged Danzig (Gdansk) and won praise for his command of the Saxon and Polish troops. When Napoleon raised him to the peerage as the Duc de Danzig, his wife, the former laundress, now a duchess, retained the simplicity, frankness, and naiveté of her origins. Although she was proud to wear her jewels, she as proudly displayed her *blanchisseuse* apron. Victorien Sardou (1831–1908), made her the heroine of a comedy, *Madame Sans-Gêne*.

In 1809 Lefebvre suppressed the Tyrolean revolt [q.v.] of Andreas Hofer [q.v.], and in Napoleon's invasion of Russia [q.v.] he commanded the infantry of the Old Guard [see Garde Impériale]. The death of his son on the retreat from Moscow so devastated him that when Napoleon summoned him to command the Old Guard in January 1813, he responded: ". . . all is lost for me. I go to hide myself. . . . I take with me my wife, who has totally lost her wits. . . . I don't want to see another soldier. . . . Pardon my scribble."

Yet he did return and even after Waterloo called for one more battle. At the restoration Louis XVIII appointed him a peer of France.

Lefebvre-Desnouëttes, Charles (1773–1822). A French soldier who became a general of brigade in 1807. He fought in the Peninsular War [q.v.] and in Russia. In 1813, having distinguished himself at Bautzen [q.v.] and elsewhere, he was promoted general of division. During the Hundred Days [q.v.] he rejoined Napoleon and fought at Waterloo [q.v.].

After the Battle of Waterloo he emigrated to the United States and lived for a time in Alabama. In 1822, while returning to Europe, he was drowned in a shipwreck off the coast of Ireland.

Le Flo, Adolphe Emmanuel Charles (1804–1887). A French soldier and diplomat who was a general of brigade in 1848 and minister of war during the Franco-Prussian War [q.v.] of 1870–71. From 1871 to 1879 he was ambassador to Russia.

Left, Army of the. An Allied army in the Peninsular War [q.v.] formed in the autumn of 1809 under Don Lorenzo del Parque [q.v.], who was soon replaced by Pedro Romana [q.v.].

Left Division. During the War of 1812 [q.v.] this was an American division commanded by General Jacob Brown [q.v.] in the Niagara Campaign of 1814. Composed of two brigades of infantry and a brigade of specially trained volunteers, it fought and won the battles of Chippewa, Lundy's Lane, and Fort Erie [qq.v.] and became the most famous army unit of the war.

In his *History of the United States* (nine volumes, 1889–91) Henry Adams (1838–1918) wrote: "So famous did Brown's little army become that details of its force and organization retain an interest equalled only by that which was attached to the frigates and sloops of war."

One of the regular brigades was commanded by Brigadier General Winfield Scott [q.v.]. Because of a shortage of blue dye, many of Scott's men were dressed in gray militia uniforms, which in the Battle of Chippewa on 5 July 1814 at first deceived their enemy until the British commander, observing the polish of their evolutions, cried out, "Those are regulars, by God!" West Point cadets are said to wear gray today as a commemoration of the incident.

Left / Right Bank. That bank of a river or stream that is on the left (or right) side of the stream's flow or of an object floating on the surface.

Legend. The explanation of symbols used on a map, often as an inset.

Leggings. Coverings for the calves of legs, full or partial, usually of leather or canvas. In the British army they were worn by all dismounted troops from 1860.

Legion. A special purpose organization such as the French Foreign Legion or the King's German Legion [qq.v.], often with mixed arms, such as the Hampton Legion in the Confederate army. The United States Legion under General Anthony Wayne defeated the Maumee Indians in the Battle of Fallen Timbers on 20 August 1794.

Legion of Honor. French: *La Légion d'Honneur*. A French award instituted by Napoleon on 9 May 1804. When Antoine Thibaudeau (1765–1854), an old revolutionary, denounced decorations as "baubles," Napoleon replied: "It is with baubles that men are led." Although the medal was frequently redesigned, the first to be issued was in the shape of a five-pointed star with ball finials suspended by a red ribbon. The gold obverse bore the seal of Napoleon until 1814. The first distribution was to old soldiers and the wounded on 1 July 1804 in a splendid ceremony at *the Hôtel des Invalides* [q.v.] in Paris. On 16 August Napoleon distributed many more at the Camp de Boulogne. An estimated 50,000 awards were made before his final abdication in 1815. Until 1852, when Médaille Militaire was instituted, the Legion of Honor was the only French award for gallantry.

French Cross of the Legion of Honor

The original order consisted of three classes—grand officers, commanders, and knights—organized into thirteen cohorts of 350 legionnaires each. After the Bourbon restoration in 1815 the order was remodeled into four classes—grand officers, grand crosses, commanders, and knights—and was extended to include civilians as well as soldiers. As the century progressed, they were ever more freely distributed. Even Mark Twain (1835–1910) received the decoration and wrote: "The cross of the Legion of Honor has been conferred upon me. However, few escape that distinction" (*A Tramp Abroad* [1880]).

Legrand, Claude Juste Alexandre (1762–1815). A French soldier who enlisted in 1777 and was a sergeant major by 1786. In 1790 he joined the Garde Nationale as a private, but in two years he was a lieutenant colonel. He distinguished himself on the Rhine and in 1799 was a general of division. In 1805 he fought in Austria, participating in the battles of Hollabrunn and Austerlitz [qq.v.]. In 1807 he fought at the battles of Eylau and Heilsberg, and in 1809 he took part in the Battle of Aspern, in which he was wounded, and the battles of Wagram and Znaim [qq.v.]. In 1812 he served in Napoleon's invasion of Russia [q.v.] and was seriously wounded in the crossing of the Berezina [q.v.]. He never truly recovered, and on 9 January 1815 he died as a result of the wound.

Leib, Edward Henry (1840?–1892). An American officer who enlisted in a Pennsylvania regiment at the beginning of the American Civil War. He was soon commissioned and rose to the rank of lieutenant colonel of volunteers while fighting in the eastern theater. On 31 March 1865 he was severely wounded in the Battle of Five Forks [q.v.]. He remained in the army after the war and served in Indian Territory, taking part in several engagements against hostile Indians, including the Battle of Slim Buttes [q.v.] on 9 September 1876. For unknown reasons, he was dismissed from the service on 9 May 1877 and became a special agent in the Office of the Commissioner of Pensions.

Leibhusaren Regiment. One of the oldest regiments in the Prussian army, having been raised in Brandenburg in 1741 as the 5th Hussar Regiment. It was one of three hussar regiments to wear the *Totenkopf* (death's-head design on the headgear).

Leibrock. A German army dress coat or cavalry coat.

Leipzig, Battle of (16–19 October 1813), Napoleonic Wars. The largest battle of the Napoleonic War—indeed, the largest battle in European history up to that time—was the only battle in which Napoleon was wholly on the defensive. It was sometimes called the Battle of the Nations because the Allied force included 130,000 Austrian, 110,000 Swedish, 270,000 Prussian, and 78,000 Russian troops, together with 1,400 guns and a British rocket battery. After twice failing to capture Berlin, Napoleon on 24 September 1813 fell back west of the Elbe River to concentrate his army at the Saxon city of Leipzig on the Elster River, 74 miles west of Dresden and 100 miles southwest of Berlin. Leipzig was then a city of about 30,000 surrounded by old and crumbling fortifications, beyond which were numerous suburbs. On 3 October General Gebhard von Blücher [q.v.] crossed the Elbe at the village of Wartenburg, eight miles east-northeast of Wittenberg, and the Swedish crown prince and former French marshal Jean Bernadotte [q.v.] bridged the river downstream. They then descended upon Leipzig from the north and northeast. Meanwhile, Prince Karl von Schwarzenberg [q.v.] moved on Leipzig from the southeast. On 15 October Napoleon had an army of 122,000 in the Leipzig area.

On 16 October Schwarzenburg sent Russian General Mikhail Barclay de Tolly [q.v.] to attack Napoleon's southern defenses, but the attack was ill organized, and when it failed, the French counterattacked and drove him back. The same day French Marshal Auguste Marmont [q.v.], in the northern end of the French perimeter with a corps of about 25,000 men, successfully repelled an attack by 54,000 under Blücher.

There was little fighting on 17 October. Napoleon was able to reinforce his army to 195,000 with 700 guns, and the Allies were able to increase their armies at Leipzig to 350,000 men with perhaps 1,500 guns. On the following day the Allies launched a massive, bloody assault on all sectors that, although unsuccessful in gaining much ground, convinced Napoleon that he could not long sustain such heavy losses. That night he began to withdraw southwest toward Erfurt, crossing the Elster River by the single stone bridge just west of Leipzig. In the early hours of 19 October the bridge was prematurely blown up, leaving his rear guard of some 20,000 men under Marshal Józef Poniatowski [q.v.] stranded. Poniatowski was killed trying to cross the river on horseback, and two French generals were captured. In all, the French lost 38,000 killed and wounded and another 30,000, including 15,000 abandoned in Leipzig hospitals, taken prisoner. Allied casualties were about 54,000.

Leipzig *Battle of Leipzig*

The British rocket battery, the only British unit in the battle, for the first time in land warfare fired Congreve rockets [see Rockets; Congreve, Walter Norris].

The Bavarians changed sides in the course of the battle, and Napoleon lost control of Germany.

Lejeune, Louis François (1775–1848). A French soldier who served in the French Revolutionary and Napoleonic wars [q.v.] and became a painter, especially of battle scenes. He is credited with introducing lithography into France.

Le Mans, Battle of (10–12 January 1871), Franco-Prussian War. After the Germans had destroyed the French regular army, several improvised armies sprang up. One of these "civilian" armies that took the field following the French disaster at Sedan [q.v.] was the Army of the Loire, 150,000 men commanded by General Antoine Chanzy [q.v.], assembled at Le Mans, 77 miles southwest of Chartres and 117 miles southwest of Paris. The numerically much smaller but well-disciplined German Second Army—50,000 men in four corps plus four cavalry divisions—under Prince Frederick Charles [q.v.] advanced on Le Mans and in a three-day battle inflicted 10,000 casualties and captured 22,000 prisoners and 17 guns.

Chanzy's army was destroyed; its remnants retreated westward. Prussian losses were 200 officers and 3,200 other ranks.

Le Marchant, John Gaspard (1766–1812). A British soldier born in Guernsey who was commissioned in the British army in 1781 and by 1797 was a lieutenant colonel. In 1801 Parliament approved his plans for a school of instruction to train army officers that became the Royal Military College, Sandhurst [q.v.]. He then developed plans for other military schools, and from 1801 to 1810 he was lieutenant governor of the schools. In the Peninsular War [q.v.] he commanded a heavy cavalry brigade. He was mortally wounded leading a charge in the Battle of Salamanca [q.v.] on 22 July 1812.

Le Mat, Jean François Alexandre (1824–1883). A French-born American, a designer of hand-held weapons who claimed to be a doctor and later a colonel but was probably neither. His first patent was issued in 1856. He was made famous by his Le Mat revolver [q.v.].

Le Mat Revolver. A single-action, double-barreled pistol in which a cylinder revolved around a shotgun barrel. It could fire nine successive .40 caliber bullets, followed by a single burst of 12 gauge buckshot. It was developed by Jean François Alexandre Le Mat [q.v.] of New Orleans. It became a favorite of Confederate generals, including J. E. B. Stuart and Pierre Beauregard [qq.v.], who in 1856 had been Le Mat's partner. At the outbreak of the American Civil War Le Mat negotiated a contract to manufacture 5,000 pistols for the Confederates, but he was unable to obtain the machinery he needed. Boarding the British mail steamer *Trent* in November 1861, he sailed to Europe, and in France he licensed C. Girard & Co. to manufacture his pistols and carbines. Because the first to be produced were faulty, the man-

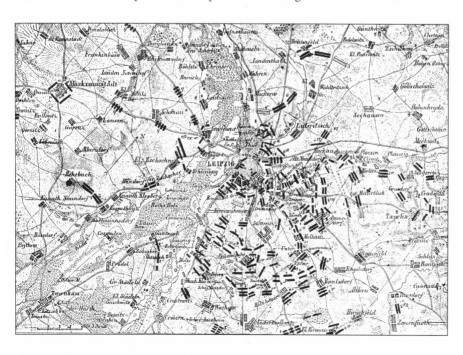

Leipzig *Map of the Battle of Leipzig*

ufacturing was moved to Birmingham, England. About 1,500 were imported by the Confederacy.

Leopard Skin. British officers of hussars used leopard skins as part of their horse furniture. The Dress Regulations for 1894 list twelve regiments so distinguished. In British infantry regiments, leopard skins were sometimes worn by bass drummers. Tenor drummers sometimes wore them as aprons.

Leopold, Maximilian Joseph Maria Arnulf (1846–1930). A Bavarian prince and soldier who entered the Bavarian army in 1861 and served in the Seven Weeks' War and the Franco-Prussian War [qq.v.]. From 1891 to 1913 he was inspector general. He was promoted field marshal in 1905.

Leopold I (1790–1865), originally named Georges Chrétien Frédéric. An uncle of Queen Victoria who was a general in the Russian army and served from 1805 to 1814 in the Napoleonic Wars [q.v.], in which he saw action at the battles of Lützen, Bautzen, and Leipzig [qq.v.]. He was elected king of Belgium in 1831 on its separation from Holland.

Lermontov, Mikhail Yurievich (1814–1841). A Russian soldier, poet, and novelist who was graduated from the school of cadets in 1834 and joined a guards regiment. On the death of the Russian poet Aleksandr Pushkin (1799–1837) he addressed an impassioned ode ("On the Death of the Poet") to the tsar in which he denounced the tsar's courtiers. For this he was court-martialed, expelled from the guards, and assigned to a line regiment in the Caucasus. There he fought and survived several duels, but in 1841 he quarreled with a former schoolmate over a woman; they met at Pyatigorsk, and he was killed.

Leslie, Armand (1843–1883). A British doctor who from 1868 to 1872 was medical officer to the Poti & Tiflis Railway Company in the Caucasus. In 1876–77 he worked in Serbia for the British National Society for Aid to the Sick and Wounded in War. During the Russo-Turkish War of 1877–78 [q.v.] he was principal medical officer for a society tending to the Turkish wounded. In 1883 in Egypt he attended victims of a cholera outbreak. When an army was formed under General Valentine Baker [q.v.] to fight the Dervishes of Osman Digna [q.v.] on the Red Sea coast of the Sudan, he accompanied the force as principal medical officer and was killed in the First Battle of El Teb [q.v.].

Letterman, Jonathan (1824–1872). An American army surgeon who in 1849 was graduated from Jefferson Medical College in Philadelphia and in June of that year was appointed assistant surgeon in the Army Medical Department. He saw service in the Third Seminole War [q.v.] in Florida, and from 1854 to 1859 he saw action against Apaches in New Mexico Territory. In 1860–61 he took part in a campaign against the Ute Indians in California. In the American Civil War he served as medical director of the Army of the Potomac [q.v.] from 1862 to 1864 with the rank of major. A superb organizer, he completely reorganized the medical service in the field and devised a superior ambulance system for collecting the wounded. He assigned surgeons in an echeloned system from first aid to definitive surgery with elements of a system of triage, and he pioneered the evacuation of the wounded by train. In the Battle of Antietam [q.v.] in September 1862 he developed a field medical supply and depot system. After the

Battle of Fredericksburg [q.v.] in January 1863 he installed a medical inspector system and required reports. Throughout his time in the army he insisted persistently on field sanitation and preventative medicine. Without any conceptual change, his methods are still used in every North American and European army.

Letterman was the first to obtain medical control of the entire combat medical system. This did not happen in Germany until the 1880s, Britain until 1898, and France until about 1918. He resigned in December 1864 and became a businessman in San Francisco, but two years he later returned to medical practice. From 1867 to 1871 he was the elected coroner of San Francisco. Letterman General Hospital at the Presidio in San Francisco, California, was named in his honor.

Levée en Masse. Universal conscription or the mass raising of the population. In effect, the imposition of the obligation of every male within certain age limits and with certain exceptions to perform military service. The first such levée occurred in August 1793 during the French Revolution when the Committee of Public Safety decreed the conscription of the entire male population of France [see Levy].

Leventhorpe, Collett (1815–1889). An English-born soldier who served as a Confederate brigadier general in the American Civil War. At age seventeen he was commissioned in the British 14th Foot, but he resigned as a captain in 1842 and emigrated to the United States, settling in North Carolina. He fought at Gettysburg, where he was severely wounded and captured.

Levy. 1. As a verb, to conscript soldiers [see Levée en Masse].
2. As a noun, conscripted soldiers.
3. As a verb, to call the militia into service.
4. As a verb, to call upon one unit to support another.

Lewal, Jules Louis (1823–1908). A French soldier who in 1870 served on the staff of General Achille Bazaine [q.v.] and after the Franco-Prussian War [q.v.] aided in the training of the new French army. In 1878 he was appointed the first commandant of the École Supérieure de la Guerre [q.v.].

Lewanika (1843?–1917), original name: Lobosi. Paramount chief of the Barotses or king of Barotseland in what is today western Zambia. From 1830 to 1865 the Barotses were under the rule of the Makololos, but in 1865 in a well-organized revolt the Barotses nearly exterminated the Makalolos in a single night. An uncle of Lobosi, who then became chief, was overthrown after an eleven-year tyrannical rule. His place was taken by Lobosi, who changed his name to Lewanika. He too was a tyrant, and in 1884, after he had ordered the torture and execution of his brother, tribal members rose in an open rebellion in which he barely escaped with his life. A cousin was proclaimed chief, but a year later Lewanika organized his forces, seized the throne, and wreaked a ruthless revenge upon his enemies.

In 1890 he acknowledged the supremacy of the British South Africa Company established by Cecil Rhodes (1853–1902) and gave the company mineral rights. In 1897 Barotseland was thrown open for European settlers. In 1902 Lewanika attended the coronation of Edward VII as the guest of the British government.

Lewis, Isaac Newton (1858–1931). An American soldier

and inventor who was graduated from West Point in 1884 and entered the coast artillery. The inventor of numerous military mechanical and electrical instruments, he patented in 1891 a range finder and in 1911 the Lewis machine gun, which became the first machine gun ever fired from an aircraft (7 June 1911). He originated the American Artillery Corps organization that was adopted in 1902.

Lewis, Meriwether (1774–1809). An American army officer who with William Clark (1770–1838) led the Lewis and Clark Expedition, the most significant transcontinental journey in American history. The expedition left St. Louis on 14 May 1804 and reached Fort Clatsop (or Kitsap) at the mouth of the Columbia River in present-day Washington State on 15 November 1805, completing the first crossing of the continent from east to west. It returned to St. Louis on 23 September 1806. From 1807 until his death Lewis was governor of Louisiana Territory. On 11 October 1809, while traveling to Washington, he died on a farm in central Tennessee. The manner of his death is disputed. He was ill, perhaps suffering from syphilis acquired from a Shoshone woman, and was believed to have committed suicide, though some suspected murder. No money was found on his body, and his watch later surfaced in New Orleans.

Lewis, Meriwether *The great explorer in frontiersman's garb, 1806*

Lewis, Morgan (1754–1856). An American lawyer and soldier who served in the American Revolution and became governor of New York. In the War of 1812 [q.v.] he was a major general. He was not an effective general, but he donated large sums of his own money to procure the release of American prisoners in Canada. He was president of the Society of the Cincinnati [q.v.] from 1839 until his death.

Lewis, William Henry (1825?–1878). An American soldier who was graduated from West Point in 1845. He served with the 5th Infantry in Texas, took part in the Utah Expedition in 1857–58 and fought in the Third Seminole War [qq.v.]. During the American Civil War he served in the Union army in New Mexico Territory and won a brevet for his gallantry in the Battle of Apache Pass [q.v.]. He was a lieutenant colonel when on 27 September 1878 at Punished Woman's Fork of the Smoky Hill River he was mortally wounded by Dull Knife's Cheyennes [see Dull Knife Outbreak].

Lexington, Siege of (12–20 September 1861), American Civil War. After the Federal defeat in the Battle of Wilson's Creek [q.v.] Confederate General Sterling Price [q.v.] with 7,000 men moved north and besieged Lexington, Missouri, a town of 1,000 overlooking the Missouri River, garrisoned by 2,800 men under Colonel James Adelbert Mulligan (d. 1864). Although Mulligan suffered only 159 casualties, he capitulated on 20 September, giving the Confederates 3,000 rifles, 750 horses, and seven guns.

L'Héritier, Samuel François (1772–1829). A French soldier who became a grenadier in 1792 and was commissioned to rank as of 1796. In 1800 he was wounded in the Battle of Marengo but recovered to become a renowned cavalry commander. He served in Austria, Poland, and Prussia between 1805 and 1812, and in 1809 he was wounded in the shoulder in the Battle of Aspern-Essling [q.v.]. That same year he was promoted general of brigade. In 1812 he was in Russia and fought at Polotsk [q.v.]. In 1813 he became general of division and helped defend the Rhine crossings. During the Hundred Days [q.v.] he rallied to Napoleon and was again wounded at Waterloo [q.v.]. In 1819 he became inspector of cavalry, and he retired in 1828.

Liaison. The contact or intercommunication between units for mutual understanding and rapport.

Liaison Officer. An officer from one unit sent to another to facilitate communications.

Libby Prison. During the American Civil War an infamous Confederate prison for Union officers on the James River in Richmond, Virginia. The three-story brick building built in 1845 had been the warehouse of Libby & Son, Ship Chandlers and Grocers. More than 45,000 prisoners were held here in the course of the war. Of the few escapes recorded, the most famous was Colonel Thomas Ellwood Rose (1830–1907) of the 77th Pennsylvania, who was captured on 20 September 1863 in the Battle of Chickamauga [q.v.]. He engineered a fifty-foot tunnel, and on the night of 9 February 1864, 109 officers made their escape, 48, including Colonel Rose, were recaptured and 2 were drowned. In May of that year the authorities, worried by threatened Federal raids, moved the prisoners to Macon, Georgia.

Libby Prison *Libby Prison, Richmond, Virginia, April 1865. Photograph by Alexander Gardner*

In 1889 Libby Prison was dismantled, and the entire structure moved to Chicago, where it became a museum. (Not quite all the parts arrived safely, for on 6 May a train carrying some of the building was derailed near Springdale, Kentucky, and local people scavenged for souvenirs.) The prison was rebuilt on Wabash Avenue between 14th and 16th streets in Chicago and was opened to the public on 20 September. Later the facade was retained when the rest of the building was torn down to make way for the Chicago Coliseum. In 1982, when the Coliseum was torn down, the facade was moved to the Chicago Historical Society.

Liberty Place, "Battle" of (14 September 1874). In New Orleans, Louisiana, 8,700 Confederate veterans and members of the Democratic White League, commanded by, among others, former Confederate General James Longstreet [q.v.], in an attempt to wrest control of the government from the hands of carpetbaggers and blacks, battled police and militia. Radical Republican Governor William Pitt Kellogg (1831–1918), a Civil War Federal brigadier general, was forcibly removed from office and took refuge in the customhouse. Before order was restored by regular troops who arrived the next day, 11 police and militia were killed, and 60 wounded; the White League suffered 21 killed and 19 wounded. In 1891 an obelisk to commemorate the event was erected on the site. In 1995 blacks demanded its removal.

Li Chao-shou (d. 1882). A cruel and wily Chinese leader who was immensely rich. He joined the Nien [see Nien Rebellion] and plundered villages. Although arrested several times, he freed himself by bribing his jailers. In 1855 he merged his Nien force with the Taipings [see Taiping Rebellion]. In 1858 he surrendered to the government because his mother and other relatives were in the government's hands. His 17,000 followers were organized into a unit called the Victorious Army of Hunan. He then changed his name to Li Shih-chung, meaning "loyal for generations." In 1859 he

successfully attacked the Taipings across the river from Nanking (Nanxiang or Nanjing), and he was soon granted the title of a provincial commander-in-chief.

He set himself up as a warlord, and Tsêng Kua-fan [q.v.] in September 1862 submitted a memorial to the throne saying that Li was ruling cities like a king, selling salt (a government monopoly) for his own profit, and establishing customhouses, but nothing was done to curb him. He bought modern weapons and several gunboats, but instead of fighting the Taipings, he used his troops to guard his personal property. He was finally investigated by General Seng-ko-lin-ch'in [q.v.] and was forced to give up his gunboats, cities, and customs collecting.

In retirement he was still a very rich man and he spent his money lavishly, not only on himself but on charity and in good works for the government. He traveled about with a bevy of a hundred beauties and actresses from his three troupes. But the authorities found him hard to tolerate, and on the pretext that he had illegally arrested a local scholar the governor of Anhwei seized him and on 4 February 1882 had him executed.

Lieber, Francis (1800–1872). A German-born American writer who assisted the Greek rebels and spent six months in confinement in Berlin on charges of political disaffection before emigrating to the United States in 1827. Between 1829 and 1833 he founded and edited the *Encyclopedia Americana* in thirteen volumes. For twenty-one years he was a professor of history and political economy at South Carolina College (now the University of South Carolina) before moving to a similar position at Columbia University in 1857. In 1863 he wrote the famous Lieber Code [q.v.], *A Code for the Government of Armies,* the first code of military law and procedure in the world. During the American Civil War his eldest son was killed fighting for the Confederacy; two other sons fought in the Union army. One of his surviving sons, Guido Norman Lieber [q.v.], became a distinguished military jurist.

Lieber, Guido Norman (1837–1923). A soldier and military lawyer who was a son of Francis Lieber [q.v.]. He was graduated from South Carolina College (now the University of South Carolina) in 1856, received his LL.B. from Harvard Law School in 1858, and practiced in New York until the beginning of the American Civil War, when in 1861 he was commissioned a first lieutenant in the 11th U.S. Infantry. He served as an infantry officer during the Peninsular Campaign [q.v.] and on 27 June 1862 was brevetted captain for "gallant and meritorious service" in the Battle of Gaines's Mill [q.v.]. In November 1862, after fighting at Second Bull Run [q.v.], he was appointed judge advocate of volunteers and promoted major. He took part in the Red River Campaign [q.v.], and at the end of the war he was brevetted lieutenant colonel.

He elected to remain in the army after the war. In 1881 he was assistant to the judge advocate general, Brigadier General David Gaskill Swaim (1840?–1897), and in 1885, when General Swaim after a fifty-two-day trial was convicted of "conduct prejudicial of good order and military discipline" for giving to the secretary of war "evasive, uncandid and false" reports regarding various billings and was sentenced to be deprived of rank and duty for twelve years, Leiber became de facto adjutant general. In 1894, when Swaim's sentence was remitted, he at once retired. Lieber was promoted brigadier general and officially appointed advocate general, a position he held until he retired on 21 May 1901 after forty years in the army, sixteen as head of the Judge Advocate General's Department, the longest tenure ever there.

Lieber wrote *Remarks on the Army Regulations* (usually referred to as Lieber on Army Regulations) and *The Use of the Army in Aid of the Civil Powers*.

Lieber Code. The short name for *A Code for the Government of Armies* by Francis Lieber [q.v.], a German-born American jurist who in 1863, at the request of President Lincoln, devised this code of forty-eight articles that constituted the first modern rules for conducting land warfare among civilized nations. His manuscript was submitted to the army and examined by five generals, who made only a few changes. On 20 February 1863, in the midst of the American Civil War, it was submitted to General Henry Halleck, the general-in-chief of the Union army, and on 23 April 1863 it was promulgated to the army, as General Orders No. 100, *Instructions for the Government of the Armies of the United States in the Field.*

Lieber's code was a distillation of the best practices in European armies and of European thought. He was obviously influenced by Jean Jacques Rousseau (1712–1778), who wrote in the *Social Contract* (1762) that in time of war "individuals are enemies only accidentally, and not as men, nor even as citizens, but as soldiers." Paragraph 15 of General Orders No. 100 reads: "Men who take up arms against one another in public war do not cease on that account to be moral beings, responsible to one another and to God."

One of the most arresting sections of the code, particularly in view of the deliberate devastations of the later years of the Civil War, is set forth in paragraph 16: "Military necessity does not admit of cruelty—that is, the infliction of suffering for the sake of suffering, nor of maiming or wounding except in fight, nor of torture to extort confessions. It does not admit of the use of poison in any way, nor of the wanton devastation of a district. It admits of deception, but disclaims acts of perfidy; and, in general, military necessity does not include any act of hostility which makes the return to peace unnecessarily difficult."

Lieber's Code had a great influence on the drafters of the Hague Convention [q.v.] in 1899.

Liechtenstein, Johann, Prince of (1780–1836). An Austrian soldier in the Napoleonic Wars who commanded the cavalry on the right of the Allied line at Austerlitz [q.v.] and on the day after the battle was sent to arrange a cease-fire. In 1809 he distinguished himself at Aspern-Essling and Wagram [qq.v.]. On 12 July he was appointed commander-in-chief and was again given the task of making peace. After three years as governor of Upper and Lower Austria, he returned to the army and fought at Leipzig [q.v.].

A holder of vast estates and the owner of a baroque palace on Vienna's Herrengasse, he was reputedly the richest man in the Austrian Empire. From 1805 he was the ruler of the principality of Liechtenstein, although in the thirty-one years of his reign he never set foot in the country.

Lie on (or under) Arms to. To remain ready for action. Soldiers were sometimes said to "sleep on their arms," meaning to sleep with their weapons handy.

Lieutenant. In German: *Leutnant;* in Spanish: *teniente;* in Italian: *tenente.*

1. Any assistant or second-in-command.

2. In most armies there are usually two grades, the lower being an ensign, cornet, sub or second lieutenant; in France, *sous-lieutenant.* The higher grade in the American service is a first lieutenant, ranking just below a captain; in German, *Oberleutnant.* In the nineteenth-century American and British armies the lowest lieutenant did not wear insignia of rank. In the American army the present gold bar insignia for second lieutenants was not introduced until World War I.

In the British army cornets and ensigns commissioned after 1 August 1871 became sublieutenants. In 1877 the title was changed to second lieutenant, but this was abolished in 1881 and re-created in January 1888.

Lieutenant Colonel. A field officer ranking above a major and below a colonel.

Lieutenant General. A rank above a major general and below a full general in the British and American armies. In the German army the equivalent rank is colonel general. [See General.]

In the American army this rank was first given by an act of Congress to George Washington (1732–1799) in 1798. After his death the rank was not again bestowed until 29 March 1847, when it was revived as a brevet rank for General Winfield Scott [q.v.]. On 2 March 1864 a special act of Congress gave the rank to General U. S. Grant. When Grant was promoted to the new American rank of general on 25 July 1866, William Tecumseh Sherman [q.v.] was promoted lieutenant general. On 4 March 1869, when Sherman became a full general, the title passed to Philip Sheridan [q.v.]. On 6 June 1900 Nelson A. Miles [q.v.] was promoted lieutenant general.

Life Guard Preobrajenski Regiment. The senior regiment in the Imperial Russian Foot Guards, dating from 1683.

Life Guards. Name of the two numbered regiments of British household cavalry.

Life Guards *British standard-bearer, 1st Regiment, Life Guards, 1829*

Life Guard *Member of the famous Russian Preobrajenski Regiment talking with civilians.*

Light Bobs. A colloquial name for British light infantry [q.v.].

Light Brigade, Charge of (25 October 1854), Crimean War. An incident in the Battle of Balaclava [q.v.] in which the commander of British cavalry, General George Charles Bingham, third Earl of Lucan (1800–1888), misunderstanding several muddled orders from the commander-in-chief, Fitzroy James Henry Somerset, first Baron Raglan [q.v.], ordered a charge by the Light Cavalry Brigade under James Thomas Brudenell, seventh Earl of Cardigan [q.v.], toward wrongly identified Russian artillery positions at the end of a long, heavily defended valley instead of toward undefended guns elsewhere. The final, fatal vague order was delivered to Lord Cardigan by Captain Lewis Edward Nolan (1820?–1854) of the 15th Hussars, who, when Cardigan seemed not to understand where he was to charge, gestured wildly in a direction thought by Cardigan to be the end of the valley and called out: "There,

my Lord! There is your enemy! There are your guns!" Nolan was killed at the very beginning of the charge. A shell fragment from the first Russian gun to fire tore open his chest to the heart.

The suicidal charge down the valley was not in the direction Raglan intended, but the charge, once started, could not be recalled. Although the Russian guns at the end of the valley were reached, the remnants of the brigade were unable to occupy the position and were pushed out with heavy losses. French General Pierre Bosquet [q.v.], who witnessed the charge, is reputed to have said, "*C'est magnifique, mais ce n'est pas la guerre* [It's magnificent, but it's not war]."

The Light Brigade of British cavalry consisted of 673 men in the 4th and 13th Light Dragoons, the 8th and 11th Hussars, and the 17th Lancers. Only 198 returned unscathed. In the 17th Lancers only 35 out of 145 returned from action. Most of the horses were killed or had to be destroyed. The *Times* correspondent William Howard Russell [q.v.] wrote: "A more fearful spectacle was never witnessed than by those who, without the power to aid, beheld their heroic countrymen rushing to the arms of death."

The action was made famous by the poem "The Charge of the Light Brigade," by Alfred, Lord Tennyson (1809–1892), published in 1854, soon after the action. The poem, popular at the time and memorized by later generations of schoolchildren, immortalized a minor and uninfluential action as an example of fruitless but heroic sacrifice.

Light Cavalry. Cavalry mounted on lighter horses than heavy cavalry. Lancers, light dragoons, uhlans, and hussars were usually considered light cavalry.

Light Division. 1. A famous unit of the British army fighting in Spain and Portugal in the Peninsular War [q.v.]. Originally a light brigade of infantry that included the 43rd and 52nd regiments and one battalion of the 95th Regiment (later the Rifle Brigade). It won renown by marching 62 miles in twenty-six hours in a fruitless effort to play a part in the Battle of Talavera [q.v.], which was won before it arrived. The division also distinguished itself in the battles of Bussaco and Fuentes d'Oñoro [qq.v.]. It was commanded by General Robert Craufurd [q.v.] until his death at the storming of Ciudad Rodrigo [q.v.] on 19 January 1812.

2. The division commanded by General A. P. Hill [q.v.] in the Army of Northern Virginia [q.v.] during the American Civil War was also so called. Larger and more diverse than most Confederate divisions, it contained brigades from Virginia, Georgia, North and South Carolina, Tennessee, and Alabama. It was prominent in the Seven Days' Battles, at Antietam, Gettysburg, the Wilderness, and Petersburg [qq.v.].

Light Horse. Light cavalry.

Light Infantry. In the British army, lightly equipped foot soldiers trained for rapid evolutions and used as skirmishers and for special missions. In the French army they were called *chasseurs à pied* (hunters on foot), and their insignia was a hunting horn.

Light Marching Order. A soldier carrying only his weapons, ammunition, canteen, and haversack was said to be in light marching order.

Lignards. Members of line regiments in the French army.

Ligne. Literally line, but in France often used to mean a regiment of the line—e.g., the 1ᵉʳ Ligne would be the 1st Infantry Regiment of the line.

Ligny, Battle of (16 June 1815), Napoleonic Wars. On 14 June 1815 Napoleon crossed the Belgian frontier and seized Charleroi, thus driving a wedge between the Allied armies of Field Marshal Gebhard von Blücher [q.v.] and Wellington. Marshal Michel Ney [q.v.] was sent with 77,000 men and 218 guns to take Quatre Bras, on the road to Brussels, while Napoleon, with 80,000 men and 218 guns, attacked Blücher, who, with 84,000 Prussians and 224 guns, was stretched along a series of low ridges north of the village of Ligny, a commune 14 miles northwest of Namur. The battle began at about two-thirty on the afternoon of 16 June, and in most places the Prussians were pushed back, but Count August von Gneisenau [q.v.], Blücher's chief of staff, later called it one of the most obstinate combats ever recorded. At seven-thirty Napoleon launched an attack by the Guard, and Blücher's line crumbled. Blücher himself, while leading a charge, was thrown from his horse and ridden over by his own cavalry. He was carried away half conscious from the field.

The Prussians, who lost 23,000 men, including 12,000 who deserted that night, retreated north toward Wavre.

Napoleon suffered 11,500 casualties, but he was satisfied that he had destroyed the fighting capability of the Prussian army and pushed it away from Waterloo. However, the badly bruised Blücher and his army were still able to give Wellington effective support. [See Hundred Days; Waterloo, Battle of.]

Li Hiu-ch'eng (1824–1864). A Chinese rebel who, although conscripted as a private, rose to become one of the most distinguished of the Taiping generals in the later part of the Taiping Rebellion [q.v.]. He was elevated to be Chung Wang (faithful king) by Hung Hsiu-chüan [q.v.]. He was executed by the imperialists on 7 August 1864. [See Shanghai, Attack on.]

Li Hsu-pin (1817–1858). A Chinese soldier who joined the Hunan militia, known as the Hunan Braves [q.v.], during the Taiping Rebellion [q.v.] and rose to be its commander. In December 1856 he won distinction by a successful attack upon the Taiping stronghold at Wuchang, a city in southeast China on the south bank of the Yangtze River, 425 miles west of Shanghai. He then moved down the Yangtze Valley and captured the port of Kiukiang on 19 May 1858. He was killed soon after while leading an assault upon Luchow (Hofei), just north of Lake Chao Hu.

Li Hung-chang (1823–1901). A Chinese soldier and administrator who in the 1850s raised a regiment of militia to fight the Taiping rebels [see Taiping Rebellion]. This brought him to the attention of General Tsêng Kuo-fan [q.v.], who

Li Hung-chang *Photograph of Li Hung-chang*

promoted him. With the support of the Ever Victorious Army [q.v.] under British Major Charles Gordon [q.v.], he captured Soochow (Wuhsien) and Nanking (Nanxiang or Nanjing), for which he was decorated with the yellow jacket and made governor of Kiangsu Province. He angered Gordon when he ordered the beheading of the Taiping wangs captured at Soochow, brushing aside Gordon's promise to them that their lives would be spared.

In 1866 he took the field against the Nien [q.v.] in Shantung and Hunan. In 1870 he was appointed to the viceroyalty of the province of Chih-li, where for twenty-four years he was active in suppressing antiforeign sentiments. In the Sino-Japanese War [q.v.] of 1894 he was in supreme command in Korea, but his efforts to repel the Japanese were thwarted by the dishonesty, incompetence, and cowardice of his subordinates. In 1895, at the end of the Sino-Japanese War, he represented the emperor at the Shimonoseki Conference. While these negotiations were in progress, he was wounded by a would-be assassin. During the Boxer Rebellion [q.v.] he led a group of provincial governors in refusing to make war on the foreigners, and he helped negotiate a peace treaty with the Western powers. He died soon after. Some called him the Bismarck of Asia.

Lij Kassa. See Theodore of Abyssinia.

Li K'ai-feng (d. 1855). A Chinese Taiping general whose military career paralleled that of Lin Feng-hsiang [q.v.].

Limber. 1. As a noun, the forward detachable two-wheeled carriage to which the trail of an artillery piece or a caisson was attached for transport. It often carried ammunition for immediate use in a box mounted on the axle. The box could form the seat for two cannoneers.

2. As a verb, to attach the horses and limber to a gun carriage or a caisson.

Limber chest. The ammunition box or tool chest mounted on the limber of a fieldpiece.

Limestone Ridge, Battle of (4 June 1866), Fenian invasion. Canadian militia defeated a force of Fenians who had invaded Canada from the United States at this place near Fort Erie, Ontario [see O'Neil, John; Fenian Brotherhood; Fenian Raids].

Lincoln, Abraham (1809–1865). An Illinois lawyer and politician who was a captain of volunteers in the Black Hawk War [q.v.]. In 1860, after serving in the Illinois legislature (1834–41) and in Congress (1847–49), he was elected president of the United States, in which capacity he was also commander-in-chief. When the American Civil War erupted in 1861, he became the only president ever actually to give strategic orders to generals in the field in time of war, work for which he proved ill fitted. He was shot at Ford's Theater in Washington, D.C., on 14 April 1865 and died the following day.

Lincoln, Abraham *Abraham Lincoln from an ambrotype, 20 May 1860, two days after his first nomination.*

Lincoln Rifles. Any of the shoulder weapons issued to pro-Unionist militia in Kentucky during the spring of 1861, when the state was embroiled in a passionate struggle to determine whether or not it would secede.

Lincoln Shingles. A colloquial American army name for hardtack or hard bread. The term originated during the American Civil War but was still used long after by soldiers in the Indian Wars [q.v.].

Lindenau, Battle of (16 October 1813), Napoleonic Wars. While the principal engagements of the Battle of Leipzig were taking place north and south of the city, Austrian General Ignatius Gyulai (1763–1831) advanced with 30,000 troops to attack the fortified village of Lindenau (today a western suburb of Leipzig), which guarded the bridge over the Elster River. By noon he had broken into the town. The garrison commander called for help from General Henri Gatien Bertrand (1773–1844), who was marching his IV Corps to reinforce the French forces in the south. Bertrand answered the plea, and two of his divisions drove off the Austrians.

Line. 1. In the British and French armies, regular infantry and cavalry that were not guards units. Line troops [q.v.].

2. Applied to combatant officers, as distinguished from staff officers.

3. Applied to the regular army, as opposed to militia or sometimes to volunteers.

Linear Tactics. The deployment of troops into successive lines to meet an enemy in battle. The lines themselves, usually two or three, made up the line of battle.

Line of Battle. 1. Any front line.
2. The leading formations of infantry on a front.
3. The linear deployment of opposing forces facing each other.

Line of Battle *The halt on the line of battle at the Second Battle of Bull Run*

Line of Communications. All the routes by land or water that connect a military force in the field with bases of operation. Supplies, munitions, and reinforcements move forward along such a line, and the wounded and prisoners of war move back along it. It is also usually the line of retreat.

In his *War Reminiscences* (1887) John Mosby [q.v.], the famous Confederate guerrilla, wrote: "The line that connects an army with its base of supplies is the heel of Achilles—its most vital and vulnerable point."

Line of Defense. 1. A natural or artificial barrier that is a defense against attack.
2. A nation's military forces, of which the first line is the standing army. Additional lines are composed of various classes of reserves.

Line of Departure. That place from which troops begin their attack. It is usually the closest place to the enemy where protection or concealment can be obtained.

Line Officers. 1. Officers in the chain of command, as opposed to staff officers.
2. Officers in combatant arms, as opposed to officers in service units. [See Line.]

Line of Fire. The course of projectiles in flight.

Line of March. 1. The route selected or taken by a military unit.
2. The disposition of the various units during a march.

Line of Operation. The routes taken by an army ahead of the line of communications. [See Exterior and Interior Lines.] An accidental line of operations [q.v.] was not a route taken by accident but merely a route that differed from the original plan.

Line of Retreat. The route taken, to be taken, or that might be taken should there be a need to fall back. It would commonly be along the line of communications [q.v.].

Line of Skirmishers. Dismounted soldiers at staggered intervals in front of the main line of battle [see Skirmish; Skirmishers].

Lines of Torres Vedras. See Torres Vedras, Lines of.

Line Troops / Regiments. Regular army units other than guards, grenadiers, gendarmes, militia, Yeomanry, fencibles, or special-purpose units, such as supply or labor battalions.

Linevich, Nikolai Petrovich (1838–1908). A Russian soldier who commanded the Russian contingent in China during the Boxer Rebellion [q.v.] in 1900. During the Russo-Japanese War he commanded the left wing in the Battle of Mukden, and in 1905 he was commander-in-chief of the Russian front in the Far East.

Lin Feng-hsiang (d. 1855). A Chinese soldier who joined the Taipings and made the march into the Yangtze Valley in 1852–53. He was co-commander with Li K'ai-feng (d. 1855) of the force that captured Peking (Beijing) and in the failed attempt to capture Kaifeng, 340 miles northwest of Nanking (Nanxiang or Nanjing) in the valley of the Hwang Ho River. In October 1853 the two unsuccessfully besieged the port of Tientsin, 80 miles southeast of Peking. The following year both were captured by imperial cavalry under General Seng-kuo-lin-ch'in [q.v.].

Ling-che. "A slow and ignominious death." A Chinese sentence frequently pronounced upon captured enemy commanders, who were tortured before being beheaded. Such cruelties were often condoned by Europeans: "What might be exquisite torture to the nervous vascular European is something much less to the obtuse-nerved Turanian; and it may be safely affirmed that the Chinese penal code . . . is, considering the nature of the people, not a whit more severe than that of any European country. Every doctor who has had to perform operations on Chinamen, knows how little they suffer in comparison with more sensitive races" (Andrew Wilson, *"The Ever Victorious Army"* [1868]).

Liniers, Santiago (or Sebastian) Antonio María de (1756–1810). A French-born Spanish naval officer who in 1806 wrested Buenos Aires from the British and was installed by popular acclaim as viceroy. In 1808 he was confirmed as provisional viceroy, but in 1809 the Spanish central junta dismissed him. In May 1810 he joined a revolutionary movement that attempted to reestablish Spanish royal authority, but he was captured and executed by a firing squad on 26 August of the same year.

Linstock. A pole with a clamp or slot at one end that held the quick match that was applied through the touchhole to the powder in a loaded cannon to fire it. The opposite end of the linstock had a point, usually of metal, to stick into the ground. Early in the nineteenth century the linstock was replaced by the friction tube [q.v.].

Lin Tse-hsü (1785–1850). A Chinese soldier and administrator known as Commissioner Lin. In Canton (Guangzhou) in 1838 he destroyed six million dollars' worth of opium owned by foreign, mostly British, merchants, thus precipitating the First Opium War [q.v.] of 1839–42. Later he was active in the suppression of the rebels in the Taiping Rebellion [q.v.].

Liquor Ration. It was common practice in most European armies to issue a ration of spirits of some sort. In the United States a whiskey ration was issued until a money substitute replaced it by General Orders No. 72 on 8 December 1830. Two years later the cash was replaced by a ration of sugar and coffee. (The U.S. navy continued to issue liquor until 1862 and the Royal Navy issued rum until 1979.)

Lircay, Battle of (17 April 1830), Chilean Revolution. Near this mountain town (altitude 8,900 feet) in south-central Peru, 26 miles east-southeast of Huancavelica, during the Chilean Revolution of 1829–30, conservative forces under General Joaquín Prieto (1786–1854) decisively defeated liberal forces under General Ramón Freire (1787–1851).

Lisaine, Battle of (15–17 January 1871), Franco-Prussian War. In bitter cold weather, over roads choked with snow, French General Charles Bourbaki [q.v.] with an army of 150,000 marched to the relief of besieged Belfort [q.v.], the only important French fort still resisting in the east. On the Lisaine River, a small stream that rises in the Vosges northwest of Belfort and flows into the Doubs River at Montbéliard, Bourbaki attacked and threw on the defensive some 60,000 German besiegers under General August von Werder [q.v.]. Some 40,000 German reinforcements under Edwin von Manteuffel [q.v.] swung the tide of this three-day battle. The French suffered one of the worst defeats ever to overtake a European army. This was the last attempt by the French to raise the siege of Belfort.

French losses were more than 6,000; German losses were fewer than 1,900. It was a humiliating defeat. In one instance 3,000 French soldiers surrendered to a single battalion of Germans. Giuseppe Garibaldi [q.v.] with an Italian contingent was on the scene, but gout kept the old warrior confined to a carriage, and he was ineffectual. General Bourbaki, in despair, tried to kill himself, but the shot he fired only grazed his head. Six days later on 23 January he was replaced by General Justin Clinchchant (1820–1881). On 1 February at Pontarlier, a commune on the Doubs near the Swiss border, 29 miles south-southeast of Besançon, 80,000 of his demoralized army were driven over the frontier into Switzerland and were interned.

Lisbon, French Occupation of (30 November 1807), Peninsular War. General Andoche Junot [q.v.] with only 1,500 French troops marched 300 miles in fourteen days and entered Lisbon without firing a shot. However, on 13 December rioting erupted in the town, and mobs attacked French soldiers. Junot put down the uprising and ordered the dissolution of the Portuguese army.

Lischine Tent. A Russian hospital tent with an iron frame the sides of which were covered with thin boards that overlapped in the manner of venetian blinds. The roof was of canvas.

Lischine tent

Litter. A stretcher for carrying sick and wounded. [See Ambulance; Doolie.]

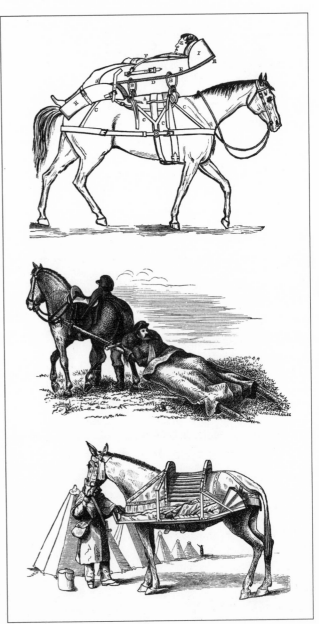

Types of Litters

Little Bighorn, Battle of the (25 June 1876), Great Sioux War. Lieutenant Colonel and Brevet Major General George Armstrong Custer [q.v.] set out on an Indian hunting expedition with 647 men: 31 officers and 566 enlisted men of the

7th Cavalry (twelve companies), the rest scouts, guides, and civilian employees. Of the cavalrymen 30 percent were German and Irish immigrants, and 20 percent had little or no experience. The cavalrymen were armed with the newly issued model 1873 trapdoor Springfield carbine [see Springfield Rifle and Carbine].

It was a Sunday when they came upon an Indian village of Sioux and Cheyenne spread along the banks of the Little Bighorn River on the Crow Reservation in what is today southern Montana. It was the largest Indian village ever seen on the plains, about 7,000 people, of whom 2,000 to 3,000 were warriors under such renowned leaders as Gall, Crazy Horse, Rain-in-the-Face, Inkpaduta, and Sitting Bull [qq.v.].

Not realizing or not caring that he faced such a large force, Custer foolishly divided his men into three groups. Captain Frederick William Benteen [q.v.] was sent with three companies on a scout to his left, and Major Marcus Albert Reno [q.v.] was sent with two companies to attack the village at its upper end. Custer himself attacked with five companies (211 men). Although taken by surprise, the Indians reacted quickly. Custer and all the men with him were annihilated, including his nephew, his brother-in-law, and a brother, Thomas Wade Custer [q.v.], a two-time winner of the Medal of Honor.

Custer was struck by a bullet near his temple and another in his ribs below the heart. His left thigh was slashed to the bone, a finger was cut off, and an arrow shaft was stuck in his penis. Later, when Benteen viewed his corpse, he sneered: "There he is, God damn him. He will never fight anymore."

Reno with 112 men was driven across the river, where he took up a defensive position on some high bluffs. There he was later joined by Benteen and his men. For the remainder of the day and all of the next day they held off persistent attacks, suffering 53 killed and 52 wounded before they were rescued by General Alfred Howe Terry [q.v.], leading a column of cavalry.

Indian losses were unknown, but Custer's command lost 268 killed, including 3 mortally wounded. Another 50 were wounded.

Four Gatling guns [q.v.] had been available to Custer for this expedition, but he had refused to take them, contending that they would slow his movements. There is some indication that he believed their use would cause him to lose face with the Indians.

News of Custer's defeat, the worst military debacle since the American Civil War and the American army's worst defeat in the long history of wars with the Indians, reached the East Coast just as the nation was about to celebrate its centennial. Few events in American history have so profoundly shocked the citizenry. Some former southern officers even volunteered to reconstitute their Confederate units to join the fight. Walt Whitman was moved to write "A Death-Sonnet for Custer" (*New York Tribune*, 10 July 1876) eulogizing him as "Desperate and glorious—aye, in defeat most desperate, most glorious." Not everyone felt this way. President Ulysses Grant [q.v.] stated publicly: "I regard Custer's massacre as a sacrifice of troops brought on by Custer himself, that was wholly unnecessary—wholly unnecessary."

In terms of nineteenth-century battles this was a small affair, and strategically, in the historic conflict between whites and Indians, it was of no importance whatsoever. It was the completeness of the Indians' victory—not a single man with

Custer survived—that struck Americans so forcefully during the centenary of the country.

Congress, acting quickly, authorized in July a 2,500-man increase in the size of the army, although it balked at replacing the 4th Cavalry's Springfield rifles with the superior lever-action, magazine-fed Winchesters.

In 1886 the site of Custer's last stand at the Little Bighorn was made into a national cemetery.

Little Bighorn Custer's Last Stand against the Sioux at the Battle of the Little Bighorn, *by Frederic Remington*

Little Crow (1803?–1863). An American Indian chief of the Kaposia division of the Mdewakanton Sioux. From 18 July until 4 August 1857 he led the pursuit of Inkpaduta [q.v.], the man responsible for the Spirit Lake Massacre [q.v.] in March of that year. Although he killed some of Inkpaduta's band, most escaped to the West. In 1862 in Minnesota, Little Crow led the great Sioux Uprising [q.v.]. After his defeat at Wood Lake on 23 September by a volunteer force under Henry H. Sibley [q.v.] he fled to Canada with some 200 of his followers. For reasons unknown, he soon returned and, while picking berries near Hutchinson, Minnesota, was killed by a farmer named Nathan Lampson and his son Chauncey, who were awarded $500 from the state treasury. Little Crow's body was thrown on the refuse heap of a local slaughterhouse. Later his skeleton was placed on public exhibition. It was in the custody of the Minnesota Historical Society until 1971, when it was turned over to some of his numerous descendants (he fathered twenty-two children by six women), who buried it near Flandreau, South Dakota.

Little Round Top. A rock-strewn, partly wooded hill 650 feet high, a feature of the Battle of Gettysburg [q.v.] during the American Civil War that lay on the south flank of the Union army under General George G. Meade [q.v.]. On 1 July 1863 the hill was occupied by the Federals, but it was not fortified and was used as a Union signal station. Late in the afternoon of 2 July, after the Confederates had launched an attack upon the Union III Corps under Major General Daniel E. Sickles [q.v.], who had made an unauthorized advance to the Peach Orchard [q.v.]—high ground in a shallow valley between Cemetery Hill and Cemetery Ridge [q.v.]—Little Round Top was seen to be of great tactical importance, and Confederate General Robert E. Lee, in spite of the objections of General James Longstreet [q.v.], ordered an attack. For three hours the two sides contended for its possession. At the bitter battle's end the Union forces still held it.

An acknowledged Union hero of this engagement was

Colonel Joshua Chamberlain of the 20th Maine, who, for his stout defense and gallant behavior, was awarded the Medal of Honor—thirty years later, in August 1893.

Little Round Top *View from the position of Hazlett's Battery on Little Round Top*

Little Sorrel. The favorite mount of Thomas ("Stonewall") Jackson [q.v.] was bred by Noah Collins of Somers, Connecticut, east of Enfield, who sold him to the U.S. army. In 1861, at the beginning of the American Civil War, the horse, which was on a train at Harpers Ferry, was captured by Confederates and then purchased from the Confederate government by Jackson, who found him to have a gait "as easy as the rocking of a cradle" and wonderful powers of endurance. After the war Jackson's widow presented Little Sorrel to the Virginia Military Institute (VMI), where he was permitted to roam the parade ground and was much petted. When he died at the age of thirty-six, his body was mounted. For a time it was kept at the Confederate Soldiers' Home in Richmond. It is now at the VMI Museum in Lexington, Virginia.

On 13 July 1991 in Somers, Connecticut, a street was named in commemoration of Little Sorrel. [See Horses.]

Little War. See Cuban Revolutions.

Liu K'un-yi (1830–1902). A Chinese soldier who, during the Taiping Rebellion [q.v.], joined the Hunan army under General Tsêng Kuo-fan [q.v.] and rose rapidly to the rank of general. After the Taiping Rebellion was crushed in July 1864, he commanded the force that operated against the Nien rebels [see Nien Revolt] in northern China. In 1872, when Tsêng died, he became commander of the Hunan army.

During the Sino-Japanese War [q.v.] of 1894–95 he commanded the garrison at the Shanhai Pass (Shanhaiguan) between Manchuria and northern China. In 1900, during the Boxer Rebellion [q.v.] he ignored the imperial government's declaration of war against the Western powers and suppressed the Boxers in southern China. He also advised the government to accept the Boxer Protocol of 12 September 1901, humiliating as that was to China.

Liu Yung-fu (1837–1890?). A Chinese bandit leader of Black Flags [q.v.] in Indochina. Born of poor parents in Kwangtung Province and orphaned in 1853, he joined a gang of bandits and soon became their leader. In 1865 he formed his own band of Black Flags in Vietnam and at first aided the government in fighting the Montagnard hill tribes, but his army soon grew stronger than the government's and he became a law unto himself. During the Franco-Vietnamese War [q.v.] of 1883–89 he fought the French.

Live Ammunition. Service ammunition containing cartridges filled with explosives and with a projectile, as opposed to blank cartridges or inert drill shells.

Liverpool, Robert Banks Jenkins, Second Earl of (1770–1828). British political leader who as foreign minister played an active role in framing the Treaty of Amiens [q.v.] in 1802. He was secretary for war and colonies from 1809 to 1812 and prime minister from 1812 to 1827.

Liwa or Liva. Literally, a flag. In the Turkish, Egyptian, and some Arab armies it was a unit the equivalent of a brigade and was commanded by a mirliwa or mirliva.

Liziere. A narrow path around field fortifications between the parapet and the ditch.

Load. 1. As a noun, the charge of a weapon.
2. As a verb, to charge a gun with ammunition or powder.

Löbau, Battle of. See Aspern-Essling, Battle of.

Lobau, Georges Mouton, Comte de Lobau (1770–1838). A French soldier who in 1799 was aide-de-camp to General Barthélemy Catherine Joubert (1769–1799), general-in-chief of the French army in Italy, and in 1805 to Napoleon. In 1807 he became general of division, and the following year he was given a command in Spain [see Peninsular War]. He later fought at Landshut, Aspern-Essling, and Ligny [qq.v.]. He was taken prisoner in the Battle of Dresden [q.v.] but was with Napoleon in the Battle of Waterloo [q.v.]. In 1830 he was commander of the National Guard, and the following year he was appointed a marshal of France and a peer.

Lobengula (1833–1894). King of the Matabeles and son of Moselekatze (d. 1868)—also known as Silkaats or Umsiligasi—whom he succeeded in 1868. After quelling a rebellion set in motion by his elder half brother, he established his capital at Gubulawayo, near present-day Bulawayo, Zimbabwe. He was on good terms with white hunters, explorers, and missionaries, and he granted mineral rights to Cecil Rhodes (1853–1902) and his associates, but in 1893 he came into conflict with the chartered British South Africa Company [q.v.] when he attempted to assert his traditional authority over the Mashonas, whom his tribesmen were accustomed to enslaving. Because Europeans now lived in Mashonaland and employed the Mashonas, the Matabeles created chaos with their raiding parties. In the Matabele War [q.v.] that resulted, he was crushingly defeated by the superior weapons, including machine guns, of the Europeans. He was driven from his capital and died in the bush near the Zambezi River.

Lobosi. See Lewanika.

Local Rank. 1. A rank conferred on an officer for the performance of a specific duty or in a specific location.

2. Sometimes the brevet rank of an officer assigned to a particular duty.

Loch, Henry Brougham (1827–1900). A British soldier and statesman who began his career in the Royal Navy but in 1842 obtained a commission in the Bengal light cavalry. During the First Sikh War [q.v.] he served on the staff of Sir Hugh (later Viscount) Gough [q.v.]. In 1852 he was second-in-command of Skinner's Horse [q.v.]. In 1854, at the beginning of the Crimean War [q.v.] he left India to raise a body of irregular Bulgarian cavalry, which he commanded in the Crimea. In 1857, during the Second Opium War [q.v.], he was in China and was present at the capture of Canton (Guangzhou). He carried to England the Treaty of Yedo and then returned to China as secretary of the newly opened embassy. With Harry Smith Parkes (1828–1885) he negotiated the surrender of the Taku forts [q.v.].

In the Second Opium War [q.v.], during the advance on Peking (Beijing), Loch and Parkes, under a flag of truce, with a small party of officers and an escort of Sikh cavalry, rode forward to negotiate a peace at Tungchow (later Nantung), on the north side of the Yangtze estuary, 65 miles northwest of Shanghai. Having been informed that the Chinese were plotting an attack upon the British, Loch rode back to give warning; then, still under a flag of truce, he rejoined Parkes and the rest of the party. When the Chinese learned of this, they arrested the entire party and escorted them to Peking. There Loch and Parkes were put in irons; the remainder were tortured. Most died as a result of their usage or succumbed to infections. The survivors were released after three weeks, a mere ten minutes before orders were received from the emperor to kill them. Loch never completely recovered from his ordeal.

After the war he served in several diplomatic posts. In 1889 he was appointed governor of Cape Colony and high commissioner of South Africa, where he was a strong supporter of Cecil Rhodes (1853–1902). In 1895 he returned to Britain and was raised to the peerage as first Baron Loch.

Lochus. A Greek army unit, the equivalent of a company, consisting of between 100 and 200 men. It was commanded by a lochage.

Lock. 1. As a noun, the firing mechanism of a gun. The mechanism used to explode a charge or cartridge of a firearm.

2. As a noun, a safety device on a firearm that could be turned on to prevent the weapon from firing.

3. As a verb, to make a loaded weapon safe by setting the lock.

Lockahatchie / Loche-Hachee, Battle of (24 January 1838), Second Seminole War. An American column in Florida, consisting of seven companies of the 2nd Dragoons, eight companies of the 3rd Artillery, and two of the 4th Artillery, led by Major General Thomas Sidney Jesup [q.v.], was attacked by Seminole Indians. Before the Indians were driven off, the column lost 7 killed and 31 wounded, including Jesup, wounded by a bullet that broke his glasses and laid open his cheek.

Lock Chains. Chains used to prevent the wheels of gun carriages from moving.

Lockett, Samuel Henry (1837–1891). An American soldier who was graduated from West Point in 1859 second in his class. He served in the Confederate army during the American Civil War, rising to become a colonel of engineers. In 1875 he was one of a group of former officers who joined the Egyptian service. Most of his work was topographical, but he was present at the Battle of Gura [q.v.] on 25 March 1876. He returned to the United States in 1878 and taught at the University of Tennessee. He later worked on the construction of the pedestal of the Statue of Liberty under Charles P. Stone [q.v.], who had been chief of staff of the Egyptian army. Still later he worked as an engineer in South America, and he died in Bogotá, Colombia.

Lockhart, William Stephen Alexander (1841–1900). A British soldier who fought in the Indian Mutiny of 1857–58, the Bhutan Campaign of 1864–65, the Abyssinian Expedition of 1867–68, the Hazara Black Mountain Expedition of 1868–69, the Second Afghan War in 1878–79, and the Third Anglo-Burmese War of 1886–87 [qq.v.]. From 1890 to 1895 he commanded the Punjab Frontier Force [q.v.]. In 1896 he became a full general and commanded the Anglo-British forces in the Tirah Campaign [q.v.] of 1897. Two years later he was appointed commander-in-chief, India.

Lockspit. A small cut or trench made with a spade to mark the beginning of a field fortification.

Locomotive Chase in Georgia. See Andrew's Raid.

Lodge. An Indian dwelling in North America. It could be a simple buffalo skin tent or a stout house.

Lodging Allowance. See Allowances.

Lodgment. 1. A footing or hasty entrenchment made inside an enemy's fortifications.

2. Any place used as quarters by soldiers.

Loftcha, Battle of (3 September 1877), Russo-Turkish War of 1877–78. A Russian force of 5,000 men, increased during the battle to 9,000, under Mikhail Skobelev [q.v.] attacked and defeated 15,000 Turks under Adil Pasha near this Bulgarian town. Turkish losses were 5,200; Russian losses, 1,500.

Logan, John Alexander (1826–1886). An American soldier and politician who had no schooling until he was fourteen. Eleven years later, in 1851, he was graduated with a law degree from Louisville University. He was a second lieutenant in an Illinois volunteer regiment during the Mexican War [q.v.] and later served in the Illinois legislature and in Congress. In the American Civil War he fought as a civilian volunteer in a Michigan regiment at First Bull Run [q.v.], then raised the 31st Illinois, which he commanded as a colonel. He was wounded at Fort Donelson [q.v.] and promoted brigadier general to rank from 21 March 1862. On 13 March 1863 he was made a major general. For his gallantry in the siege of Vicksburg [q.v.], in which he led his men in a desperate assault, he was awarded the Medal of Honor [q.v.]. He commanded a corps in the Atlanta Campaign [q.v.] and was wounded at Dallas, Georgia, in June 1864. When

General James Birdseye McPherson [q.v.] was killed in front of Atlanta on 22 July, Logan took command of the Army of the Tennessee [q.v.]. He was generally considered one of the best of the political generals.

After the war he served as a U.S. representative or senator almost continuously until his death. He was instrumental in the formation of several veterans' societies, including the Grand Army of the Republic [q.v.], and he promoted veterans' interests in the Congress. It was while serving as commander of the Grand Army of the Republic in 1868 that he instituted Decoration Day [q.v.], which has become Memorial Day. In 1884 he was an unsuccessful Republican nominee for vice president.

Logistics. The planning and carrying out of the procurement, movement, maintenance, and distribution of men, matériel, facilities, and supplies. Baron Henri de Jomini [q.v.] defined logistics as comprising "the means and arrangements which work out the plans of the strategy and tactics. Strategy decides where to act; logistics brings the troops to this point" (*Précis de l'art de la guerre* [1838]). Frederick the Great (1712–1786) considered the primary duty of a general was "to procure nourishment for the soldier wherever you assemble him and wherever you wish to conduct him" (*Instructions to His Generals* [1747]). Wellington in the Iberian Peninsula in 1811 wrote: "It is very necessary to attend to this detail and to trace a biscuit from Lisbon into a man's mouth on the frontier and to provide for its removal from place to place by land or by water, or no military operation can be carried out." In more colorful language, Winston Churchill [q.v.] wrote: "Victory is the beautiful, bright-coloured flower. Transport is the stem without which it never could have blossomed" (*The River War* [1899]).

The most revolutionary advancements of logistics in land warfare were the development of the telegraph and the railroad [qq.v.] and the improvements in methods of preserving certain foods by canning, bottling, and pasteurization.

Log Paper. Thin drawing paper used in the manufacture of paper fuzes.

Loigny-Pouprey, Battle of (1 December 1870), Franco-Prussian War. Near the present village of Loigny-la-Bataille, 17 miles north-northwest of Orléans, a Prussian force of 34,000, advancing behind a military band, routed the French Army of the Loire (90,000 men) under General Louis Jean Baptiste d'Aurelle de Paladines (1804–1877). French losses were 18,000 men and nine guns; Prussian losses were 4,200.

Lomas Valentinas, Siege of (21–27 December 1868), War of the Triple Alliance. Near low hills called Lomas Valentinas, not far from Asunción, Paraguay, some 3,000 to 8,000 Paraguayans under General Francesco Solano López [q.v.] were besieged by about 27,000 Brazilians and Argentines in semicircular lines. The Paraguayans were forced to surrender, but López escaped. Allied casualties were about 4,000; Paraguayan casualties were more than 2,000. The siege is also known as the Battle of Itá-Ybaté.

Lomoro Xujang (1853–1912). A man of the Lotuxo tribe of Tirrangore in Equatoria Province of the Sudan who entered the warrior class in about 1873 and won such prestige that he was appointed chief in 1892. By fighting, but chiefly by bluff, he extended his authority over most of the Lotuxos and many neighboring tribes. He wisely cooperated with the Uganda government, which in 1898 sent an expedition under Colonel (later Major General Sir) James Ronald Leslie Macdonald [q.v.] into Lotuxo country. In 1912 during a coup he was killed by a spear thrust, and his kingdom was divided.

Londonderry, Charles William Stewart (Vane), Third Marquess of (1778–1854). A British soldier and diplomat who joined the army and served in the Netherlands in 1794, in Germany in 1795, in the Irish rebellion of 1798, and in Holland in 1799, reaching the rank of colonel. In 1808, during the Peninsular War [q.v.], he was given a cavalry command in Spain and promoted major general. He became Wellington's adjutant general and was present at the capture of Ciudad Rodrigo [q.v.]. At the beginning of 1812 he was invalided home. He later served in a number of diplomatic posts in Europe.

Lone Wolf (1820?–1879). A chief of the Kiowa Indians who was one of nine signers of the Medicine Lodge Treaty of 1867, by which the Kiowas agreed to live on a reservation. The death of his son in a Texas raid in 1873 kindled his hostility to whites. He led a raid into Lost Valley, Texas, and fought at the Second Battle of Adobe Walls [q.v.] on 27 June 1874 in present-day Hutchinson County, Texas. In the spring of 1875 he surrendered at Fort Sill (Oklahoma). He was confined at Fort Marion (St. Augustine, Florida), for three years.

Long, Stephen Harriman (1784–1864). An American soldier who was educated at Dartmouth College and in 1814 was commissioned a second lieutenant of engineers. He taught briefly at West Point and in 1816 was promoted captain and transferred to the topographical engineers [q.v.], then a separate branch of the army. He explored, mapped, and wrote articles about the American West, and it was he who labeled the area between the Platte and Arkansas rivers the "Great American Desert." In 1847 he was a member of the court-martial that tried and convicted John C. Frémont [q.v.] of mutiny and insubordination.

Long Cecil. See Labram, George.

Longa, Francisco (1770–1831). A successful Spanish guerrilla leader in the Peninsular War [q.v.] who was given regular commands and particularly distinguished himself in the Battle of San Marcial [q.v.] on 31 August 1813.

Long Gray Line. The cadets and graduates of the U.S. Military Academy at West Point, New York.

Longmore, Thomas (1816–1895). A British military surgeon educated at Guy's Hospital who became a regimental surgeon in the 19th Foot. Serving in the Crimea during the Crimean War, he complained vociferously about the lack of medical supplies, ambulances, and drugs and railed against contract surgeons who were excessively paid. To a friend he wrote that he was "one of the troublesome medical officers of the army." After the war, in 1860, he was appointed the first professor of military surgery at the newly created Army Medical School at Chatham. In 1861 he published an article on gunshot wounds that was widely distributed in the United States during the American Civil War. He became interested in eye diseases and in 1863 published *Army Medical Officers Ophthalmic Manual.* In 1869 he published *A Treatise on the Transport of Sick and Wounded Troops,* which was reprinted in 1893.

He was a British representative at the first Geneva Convention [q.v.] in 1864 and was a member of the committee that settled the terms of the convention. He was a friend and admirer of Florence Nightingale [q.v.]. In 1880 he urged more attention in the British service to the antiseptic treatment of wounds.

In 1876 he was placed on the retired list, but he was allowed to continue teaching at the school for a further fifteen years.

Long Roll. The drumbeat for soldiers to assemble.

Long Service Chevrons. Insignia to denote years of service. In the French army these were small chevrons worn point up on the upper left arm and called *chevrons d'ancienneté*. In the American army they were half chevrons, colloquially called hash marks. The British did not use chevrons but instituted a Long Service and Good Conduct Medal in 1830.

Longstreet, James (1821–1904). An American soldier who was graduated from West Point in 1842. He served in several Indian campaigns and won two brevets in the Mexican War [q.v.], in which he was seriously wounded in the Battle of Chapultepec [q.v.]. He was a paymaster with the rank of major when he resigned on 1 June 1861, at the beginning of the American Civil War [q.v.]; sixteen days later he was appointed a brigadier general in the Confederate service. He fought at the First Battle of Bull Run [q.v.] on 21 July 1861 and was promoted major general on 7 October. He fought in the Peninsular Campaign, at Second Bull Run and at Antietam [qq.v.], where, when he arrived at Sharpsburg, Maryland, Lee greeted him with "Here is my war horse at last." As of 9 October 1862 he was a lieutenant general and distinguished himself in the Battle of Fredericksburg [q.v.], where he commanded I Corps in Lee's Army of Northern Virginia [q.v.]. At Gettysburg [q.v.] he commanded the right wing of Lee's army, and after the war he was unjustly blamed for his delayed attack on the second day. He was largely responsible for the Confederate victory at Chickamauga [q.v.], but he failed in an attempt to take Knoxville, Tennessee. In the Battle of the Wilderness [q.v.] he arrived on 6 May 1864 in time to repulse a Federal attack and launch a brilliant counterattack. Soon after, he received a severe wound from friendly fire that kept him out of action until the closing months of the war. He surrendered with Lee at Appomattox.

After the war Longstreet settled in New Orleans and became a Republican and a personal friend of U. S. Grant, who in 1880 appointed him the American minister to the Porte in Constantinople (Istanbul), Turkey. In 1881 he returned home and served as a U.S. marshal until 1884. From 1897 to 1904 he was commissioner of Pacific railroads. In 1896 he published his autobiography, *From Manassas to Appomattox.*

Long Tom. A name often applied to large guns, such as the 30-pounder Parrott gun captured by the Confederates at First Bull Run [q.v.] during the American Civil War, the famous large gun in the Cumberland Gap, and a gun that fired a 94-pound shell manufactured by Schneider of Le Creusot and used by the Boers in the Second Anglo-Boer War [q.v.] at the sieges of Ladysmith, Mafeking, and Kimberley [qq.v.]. The name was also applied to a long-barreled, large-caliber rifle used mostly to shoot buffalo in the American West.

Long Tom *Long Tom rifles on the firing line.*
Print by Frederic Remington

Looking Glass (1823?–1877). A Nez Percé chief. Although Looking Glass took no part in the Battle of White Bird Canyon [q.v.], General O. O. Howard [q.v.] sent troops to arrest him on his reservation in Idaho. Eluding them, Looking Glass joined the hostile Nez Percés on the south fork of the Clearwater River and helped lead them into Montana, where, believing they were safe, they relaxed their vigilance [see Nez Percé War]. In August 1877 at Big Hole Basin [q.v.] they were attacked by 238 soldiers and volunteers under Colonel John Gibbon [q.v.]. The whites suffered more than 20 killed and more than 40 wounded; the Nez Percés lost between 60 and 90 killed, including some women and children.

The surviving Nez Percés resumed their anabasis, moving toward Canada. Looking Glass, now in command, slowed down the movement so that his people could rest and his young men could hunt. This proved fatal. On 30 September 1877 they were camped in the Big Bear Paw Mountains of Montana when they were attacked by 383 soldiers under Colonel Nelson A. Miles [q.v.]. The fighting continued off and on until 5 October. Looking Glass was killed when he was struck in the forehead by a bullet fired by a Cheyenne scout, and with his death the Nez Percés gave up their long struggle to escape. The Battle of Bear Paw Mountain [q.v.] was the last battle of the Nez Percé War.

Lookout Mountain, Battle of (24 November 1863), American Civil War. A part of the Battle of Chattanooga, sometimes called the Battle above the Clouds, in which Union troops under Major General Joseph Hooker [q.v.] drove off a lightly held Confederate skirmish line of Lieutenant General James Longstreet [q.v.]. General U. S. Grant called this action "one of the romances of the war. There was no such battle and no action even worthy of being called a battle on Lookout Mountain." As for being above the clouds, the *New York Tribune* reported: "There were no clouds to fight above—only a heavy mist."

On the day after the action a party of the 8th Kentucky scaled the height, which rises 1,100 feet above the Tennessee River, and planted the American flag where it was plainly visible to Grant's troops in the valley below.

Lookout Mountain *Point of Lookout Mountain, Tennessee*

Loophole. An aperture in a wall or stockade through which defenders could fire small arms with minimum exposure to enemies. Ideally, a loophole was larger on the inside than the outside.

Loose Ammunition. Ammunition divided into two or more components, such as projectile and propellant, as opposed to fixed ammunition.

Looting. Robbery in wartime. The word "loot" or "looting," from the Indian word *lootie*, meaning a gang of robbers, did not enter the English language until the early 1840s. The stealing of food, liquor, or articles of value, while generally deplored, was common enough in nineteenth-century armies. Napoleon said, "Nothing will disorganize an army more or ruin it more completely than pillage" (*Maxims of War* [1831]). He was speaking, of course, of the undisciplined and uncoordinated looting by troops. However, looting was sometimes carried out with the permission of commanders, as in China when the Winter Palace [q.v.] was looted by British and French forces with their officers foremost among them. The first Pekinese dog seen in England was sent to Queen Victoria from China and aptly named Lootie.

In the British and Indian armies prize agents were appointed

after a victory to secure the assets of the conquered, as well as the loot acquired by individuals and to sell it, sometimes by auction. The proceeds were divided among the troops involved in the battle or campaign. In such cases the largest share went to the general commanding; lesser sums went to lesser ranks, the private often receiving a very small share indeed.

Looting *Jackson's troops pillage the Union depot of supplies at Manassas Junction.*

López, Francesco Solano (1827–1870). A Paraguayan soldier and dictator, the son of Carlos Antonio López (1790–1862), the dictator of Paraguay from 1844 until his death in 1862, at which time Solano López became president

López, Francesco *Francesco Solano López, 1865*

and assumed dictatorial powers. As a young man he had been sent to Paris to buy arms and hire officers to train the Paraguayan army. He returned home with an Irish mistress and a shipload of fine china services, elegant furniture, a piano, lavish gowns, and seventy pairs of handcrafted leather boots garnished with silver, all with elevated heels, for he was short and stout. His ambition to dominate all South America led in 1885 to the War of the Triple Alliance [q.v.], in which Brazil, Argentina, and Uruguay allied themselves against him and in which his mistress, Eliza Lynch [q.v.], organized a corps of women warriors [see Amazons]. Although initially successful, he was eventually defeated, and Paraguay was devastated.

López possessed an inordinately suspicious nature, which prompted him to kill thousands of his own people, even some of his own relatives. According to Richard Francis Burton (1821–1890), who visited Paraguay during the war, López's paranoia was exacerbated by an addiction to "port-wine and piety, to mass-going and hard drinking."

He was finally hunted down and killed by Brazilian troops. His body, surrounded by those of his generals, was eventually interred in the Paraguayan National Pantheon of the Heroes in the center of Asunción.

López, Narcisco (1799–1851). A Spanish soldier who entered the army at an early age and was a colonel at age twenty-one. He distinguished himself in the Carlist Wars [q.v.], rising to the rank of major general. In 1843 he was sent to Cuba, where he took part in an unsuccessful revolt, and in 1849 he fled to the United States, from which he organized three filibustering expeditions to Cuba. The first one, in August 1849, was aborted by U.S. marshals before it sailed. He tried again the following year with 450 followers, including Rob Wheat and Theodore O'Hara [qq.v.], who later wrote "Bivouac of the Dead" [q.v.]. The band landed at Cardenas in late April and after a three-hour battle killed or captured all of the garrison for a loss of 14 killed and 30 wounded. López then issued a call for local volunteers. When none came forward, he despaired of success, reembarked his troops, and sailed to Key West. In 1850 he made a final filibustering attempt, using volunteers from Kentucky, Tennessee, and Mississippi, including "Colonel" William Logan Crittenden (1815?–1851), a West Point graduate of the class of 1839. This time López was captured by the Spanish authorities, and on 16 August 1851 he was shot, as were Crittenden and 50 of his men.

López Domínguez, José (1829–1911). A Spanish soldier and statesman who, under the republic, became captain general of Burgos in 1873 and captured Cartegena. He was promoted to lieutenant general and in 1893 was minister of war. In 1905 he was president of the Senate, and in 1906 he was premier of Spain.

Lorcha War. See Arrow War.

Lord Lieutenant. In England prior to the Army Regulation Act of 1871, the officer appointed to take charge of the militia.

Lorencez, Charles Ferdinand Latrille de (1814–1892). A French soldier and grandson of Marshal Nicolas Oudinot [q.v.] who distinguished himself in the Crimean War [q.v.] of 1854–55. In 1862 he commanded the French expeditionary force to Mexico [see Mexico, French Invasion and Occupation of], but following his repulse before La Puebla [q.v.] he was replaced by General Achille Bazaine [q.v.]. During the Franco-Prussian War he commanded the 3rd Division in IV Corps until captured at Metz [q.v.] and interned in Germany.

Lorenz Rifle Musket. An Austrian weapon much used by Confederate forces in the American Civil War. It was issued in calibers from .54 to .59, the former especially favored by the Confederate Army of Tennessee.

Lorimer. A maker of bits, spurs, and other horse gear. In England lorimers were formed into a special guild in 1712. In 1830 the Court of Sessions declared it to be a gross violation of the exclusive privileges of lorimers for others to manufacture horse gear with a view to silver-plating them.

Loring, William Wing (1818–1886). An American soldier who first saw action in the Second Seminole War [q.v.], when he joined the militia and fought on the Withlacoochee River in February and March 1836 and at Wahoo Swamp on 26 November. He later became a lawyer and served in the Florida legislature until the beginning of the Mexican War [q.v.], when he was commissioned a captain in the Mounted Rifle Regiment. In February 1847 he was promoted major and later distinguished himself at the battles of Contreras on 19–20 August and Chapultepec [qq.v.] on 13 September, in which he lost an arm and earned a promotion to lieutenant colonel.

After the war he served in Oregon and Texas, where he saw considerable action fighting the Cheyennes and Comanches and was promoted colonel. He took part in the Utah Expedition [q.v.] of 1857–58. In May 1861, at the outbreak of the American Civil War, he resigned his commission and was appointed a brigadier general in the Confederate army. With Brigadier General Thomas ("Stonewall") Jackson [q.v.] he took part in the Bath-Romney winter campaign. After quarreling with Jackson, he was transferred to the West, where during the Vicksburg Campaign (October 1862–July 1863) he commanded a division under John C. Pemberton [q.v.] at Champion's Hill on 16 May 1863. From May to the end of August, during the Atlanta Campaign [q.v.], he commanded a corps in the Army of Mississippi. He became John Hood's [q.v.] second-in-command in the Army of the Tennessee [q.v.] and fought at Franklin and Nashville [qq.v.]. With General Joseph Johnston he surrendered to William T. Sherman [qq.v.] on 18 April 1865.

After the war he worked briefly in a New York bank until in 1869 he accepted an appointment as inspector general of the Egyptian army with the rank of mirliwa (brigadier general). In 1875 he was in charge of Egyptian coastal defenses. He took part in the Abyssinian-Egyptian War [q.v.] and fought in the Battle of Gundet [q.v.] on 13 November 1875. He became a pasha and was promoted fariq [q.v.] but resigned in 1879 and returned to the United States.

Loris-Melikov, Mikhail Tarielovich (1826–1888). A Russian soldier and statesman of Armenian descent who was educated at the Lazarev School of Oriental Languages and at the Guards Cadet Institute. In 1847 he joined a hussar regiment and was ordered to the Caucasus, where he spent most of the next twenty years. He commanded a regiment in the Crimean War [q.v.] and became a major general in 1856 and a lieutenant general in 1863. During the Russo-Turkish War [q.v.] of 1877–78 he commanded a separate army corps with which he invaded Armenia. There he captured the fortified town of Ardahan (*Russian: Ardgan*), 45 miles north of Kars, besieged Kars [q.v.], which he took by storm, and besieged and captured Erzurum. For these services he was created a count. In 1879 he was briefly governor of the lower Volga area, where he tried without success to contain an outbreak of the plague. In 1880 he was chairman of the Imperial Administration Commission charged with combating nihilism. He was about to be appointed minister of the interior when Tsar Alexander II [q.v.] was assassinated. When Alexander's successor adopted a more reactionary policy, Loris-Melikov resigned and retired to Nice, France.

Loshnitsa, Battle of (23 November 1812), Napoleon's Russian Campaign. As the disintegrating French army fell back from Smolensk [q.v.], Russian Admiral Pavel Tshitsagov [q.v.] captured Borisov, 50 miles northeast of Minsk, and the only bridges over the Berezina River [q.v.]. On 23 November French forces under Marshal Nicolas Oudinot [q.v.] defeated a portion of Tshitsagov's army on the plains of Loshnitsa, capturing more than 1,000 prisoners and many supplies. Oudinot then occupied Borisov, but the vital bridges remained in Russian hands. [See Borisov, Battle of; Berezina / Beresina, Napoleon's Crossing of.]

Lost Order. On 9 September 1862, just before the Battle of Antietam [q.v.], in the American Civil War, General Robert E. Lee issued Special Order No. 191, splitting his army into two parts: Thomas ("Stonewall") Jackson [q.v.] to move on Harpers Ferry and James Longstreet [q.v.] to move toward Hagerstown. Four days later a copy of this order wrapped around some cigars was found in a field by soldiers of the 27th Indiana. Although the order was quickly passed up to General George McClellan [q.v.], he failed to move fast enough to take advantage of the information it contained. How this copy of the orders came to be lost and how it came to be in a field are unsolved mysteries.

Loudoun Rangers. A Virginia unit of irregular volunteer cavalry recruited from Union sympathizers, including a number of Quakers, in Loudoun County, Virginia, during the American Civil War. It was the only Virginia unit to fight for the Union. Most of their engagements were against Mosby's Rangers [q.v.] and the 35th Virginia Cavalry, composed of Loudoun County citizens under Colonel Elijah Viers White (1832–1907). On 5 April 1865, in one of the last battles of the war, Mosby's Rangers in a brief melee captured nearly the entire unit: 65 men and 81 horses.

Louis Ferdinand. See Louis Frederick Christian.

Louis Frederick Christian (1772–1806), usually called Prince Louis Ferdinand. A Prussian prince and soldier who distinguished himself in 1792–95 in campaigns against the French. He was killed in the Battle of Saalfeld [q.v.] on 10 October 1806 by a French soldier in the 10th Hussars. He has been referred to as the Alcibides of Prussia, for he was a pianist and composer, a patron of the arts, and a friend of Ludwig van Beethoven (1770–1827).

Lovell, Joseph (1788–1836). An American military surgeon who received his M.D. from Harvard Medical School in 1811 and in the spring of the following year became a regimental surgeon. During the War of 1812 [q.v.] he served in a number of hospitals in the Northeast. On 13 April 1818, largely at his urging, Congress passed a reorganization act, and Lovell, not yet thirty years old, became the first surgeon general of the newly formed permanent Army Medical Department. In that capacity he instituted regular reports on health and sanitation and required doctors to collect data on the weather in order to determine the relative salubrity of army camps and posts. Regulations issued in 1825 required examinations for candidates to be army surgeons, but they were not enforced until in 1832 Lovell insisted on them; he required candidates to pass rigorous examinations, both oral and written and to take others at given intervals. He encouraged vaccination against smallpox, which, although ordered by the secretary of war on 26 May 1812, was often regarded as logistically difficult to comply with. He also suggested that vegetables be included in army rations and began the collection of books around which the National Library of Medicine was later formed. He strongly supported the physiology studies of Assistant Surgeon William Beaumont [q.v.], who could not have accomplished his great work without such support.

Lovell, Mansfield (1822–1884). An American soldier who was born in Washington, D.C., where his father, Joseph Lovell, was U.S. surgeon general. He was graduated from West Point in 1842 and commissioned in the 4th Artillery. During the Mexican War [q.v.] he served first under General Zachary Taylor [q.v.] in southern Texas and in May 1846 took part in the battles of Palo Alto and Resaca de la Palma [qq.v.]. In September of the same year he was wounded at Monterrey. The following year he transferred to the army of General Winfield Scott [q.v.] and on 13 September 1847 took part in the Battle of Chapultepec [q.v.], in which his gallantry won for him a brevet to captain. He was wounded in the fighting at Belén Gate (*Garita de Belén*), just outside Mexico City.

In 1854 he resigned from the army to join Cooper & Hewitt's Iron Works in Trenton, New Jersey, and in 1858 he was appointed deputy street commissioner in New York. At the beginning of the American Civil War he joined the Confederate army, and on 7 October 1861 he was appointed a major general and assigned to the command at New Orleans. With too few men and guns to defend the town, he was forced to evacuate it after Union troops under Union General Benjamin Butler [q.v.] were landed. Lovell took part in the Battle of Corinth [q.v.], but in December he was relieved of his command and criticized for his abandonment of New Orleans. Although eventually cleared by a court of inquiry, he never held another major command.

Lovell Musket. A percussion musket designed by George Lovell, a British government inspector of small arms, and first produced in caliber .753. It was first used in action by the 55th Foot in the Battle of Amoy [q.v.] on 26 August 1841. It did not, however, replace the Brunswick rifle [q.v.], which had been introduced into the British service in 1838.

Lowe, Hudson (1769–1844). A British soldier, commissioned at the age of eleven, who saw much service during the Napoleonic Wars, particularly in the Ionian Islands, and was for a time attached to the Prussian army under Gebhard von Blücher [q.v.]. When Napoleon was sent to St. Helena, Lowe became his custodian and from 1815 to 1821 maintained a strict surveillance, for which he was publicly attacked by Barry Edward O'Meara [q.v.], a British naval surgeon who was assigned to be Napoleon's physician. From 1825 to 1844 Lowe was commander of troops at Ceylon.

Löwe, Ludwig (1837–1896). A German engineer who formed a machine tool company in Berlin in the 1860s and, following a visit to the United States, began the production of sewing machines. During the Franco-Prussian War [q.v.] he made weapons components. In the late 1870s he obtained a license to produce Smith & Wesson [q.v.] .44 caliber revolvers, which he manufactured for the Russian army. In the 1890s he was producing Mauser rifles [q.v.] for the German and other armies.

In 1892 he hired Hugo Borchardt (1850?–1921), who designed the Borchardt pistol [q.v.], which was developed into the Luger pistol or Parabellum [q.v.]. Löwe retired in 1896, and his company, with others, was amalgamated to become the Deutsche Waffen und Munitionsfabrik. [See Luger, Georg.]

Lowe, Thaddeus Sobieski Coulincourt (1832–1913). An American military balloonist who called himself "Professor" Lowe. He fabricated his first balloon in 1858 and made an ascent at Ottawa, Canada, as part of the celebration of the laying of the Atlantic cable. On 19–20 April 1861, during the American Civil War, he sailed by balloon from Cincinnati, Ohio, to Unionville, South Carolina, where he was promptly arrested as a spy. When released, he hurried to Washington and offered his services to the Union army. He impressed President Lincoln, who in August appointed him chief aeronaut with the pay of a colonel. On 24 September he became the first aerial observer to supply fire direction to artillery on the ground [see Balloons].

He devised mobile coal gas generators and took the field with General George McClellan [q.v.] in the Peninsular Campaign [q.v.], sending his messages to the ground by means of a telegraph wire. Under his direction seven balloons were constructed, ranging in size from 15,000 to 32,000 cubic feet. His most famous, *Intrepid,* was one of his largest.

He was out of action with malaria for a time, but he served in the Battle of Fredericksburg [q.v.], and in all, his little balloon corps made more than 3,000 ascensions. However, when General Joseph Hooker [q.v.] took command of the Army of the Potomac [q.v.], Lowe's status, pay, staff, and materials were reduced; he was placed under the Corps of Engineers and was so hampered in his work that he resigned on 8 May 1863.

Lowe went on to invent an ice-making machine, reputedly the first in the United States, and to build an electric railway up a California mountain, but he did no more work for the army.

Had General Hooker employed balloons at Chancellorsville, observers probably would have detected the corps of Thomas ("Stonewall") Jackson [q.v.], which crashed into his right flank and routed it.

Lowell Machine Gun. A gun similar to a Gatling [q.v.] developed in 1875 by De Witt Farrington and named for its place of manufacture, Lowell, Massachusetts. It had four barrels in a circular frame and a crank-driven bolt mechanism. All shots came from one barrel until it became too hot; then a fresh barrel was rotated. [See Machine Gun.]

Lowell machine gun

Löwenberg, Battle of (21 August 1813), Napoleonic Wars: Leipzig Campaign. Napoleon with a force of 120,000 advanced on Gebhard von Blücher [q.v.] with 80,000 near this town, now in Poland (Polish name: *Lwowek Slaski*). Blücher retired behind the Haynau River, but not before losing 2,000 men.

Loyalist. A soldier or civilian who adheres to the existing sovereign or the constituted government.

Loyal Lusitanian Legion. A unit of irregular light infantry raised in Portugal in 1808 by Sir Robert Wilson [q.v.] during the Peninsular War [q.v.]. It consisted of three 1,000-man infantry battalions of ten companies each, a battery of artillery, and a few horsemen. The legion played an active part in the defense of Castile and at Almeida, Ciudad Rodrigo, and Seville [qq.v.]. In 1811 it was disbanded, and the three infantry battalions became the 7th, 8th, and 9th Caçadores.

Loyal Volunteers. British militia, the first unit of which was formed in 1798 as protection against a possible French invasion. The government provided pay while men were on duty and some equipment. Units were usually commanded by the local squire or a prominent merchant. After 1803 the volunteers came under stricter military control, but their small numbers and scattered dispositions made it difficult to train and discipline them. After the Napoleonic Wars most of these units were merged into local militias.

Lübeck, Battle of (6–7 November 1806), Napoleonic Wars.

On 6 November 1806 French Marshals Nicolas Soult and Jean Baptiste Bernadotte pushed Prussian General Gebhard von Blücher [qq.v.] into Lübeck, 35 miles northeast of Hamburg, and then stormed and captured the town. Blücher escaped with part of his army to nearby Ratkow but surrendered the next day.

Lucan, Third Earl of. See Bingham, George Charles.

Luchau, Battle of (23 August 1813), Napoleonic Wars. Prussians under General Friedrich von Bülow defeated a French force under General Nicolas Oudinot [qq.v.] near Luchau, a commune in Brandenburg, Germany, 45 miles south-southeast of Berlin.

Luck. Chance plays such a large part in any battle that many soldiers become superstitious. It is said that when any commander was recommended for promotion, Napoleon invariably asked if he had luck. Arab soldiers in North Africa were reluctant to serve under officers who did not have *barakka* (luck). However, Field Marshal Helmuth von Moltke the Elder [q.v.] declared: "Luck in the long run is given only to the efficient."

Lucknow, Siege of (1 July–19 November 1857), Indian Mutiny. Indian mutineers and rebels besieged British men, women, and children and a few loyal Indians in the Residency at Lucknow on the right bank of the Gumti River, 270 miles east-southeast of Delhi. The Residency, a cluster of offices and homes of officials within a 37-acre area, had been hastily fortified under the direction of Henry Lawrence [q.v.], the British chief commissioner. Lawrence was mortally wounded at the beginning of the siege, and his last orders were "Entrench, entrench, entrench . . ." The command devolved upon forty-three-year-old Lieutenant Colonel John Inglis [q.v.], commander of the 32nd Foot, the only English regi-

Lucknow *The interior of the Residency at Lucknow. Photograph by Felice Beato*

ment in the Residency. On 25 September a relief force under the command of James Outram and Henry Havelock [qq.v.] arrived, but it was not strong enough to bring out safely the nearly 500 women and children. In fighting its way to Lucknow, it had lost 535 men. By this time the defenders of the Residency had lost 483 killed. With the arrival of the remains of the relief force the garrison had increased its firepower but added mouths to feed. Starvation seemed to threaten until Colonel (later General) Robert Napier [q.v.] discovered that one of the compound's buildings held a large store of food not known to have existed. On 19 November, after a three-week campaign, Sir Colin Campbell [q.v.] with some 4,700 men and 32 guns, including a naval brigade with heavy guns, effected the relief of the Residency and brought all out. The town was not wrested from the mutineers until 21 March 1858.

Luddite Riots (March 1811–January 1813). Disorders directed against English textile manufacturers who displaced workers with machines. The riots began in Nottinghamshire, where gangs under a mythical "King Ludd" or "General Ludd" destroyed knitting frames, which were credited with allowing manufacturers to swamp the market with cheap products. In the following months Luddites, as they were called, burned factories and destroyed cotton power looms and other machinery in Lancashire and Cheshire. The government reacted harshly. The burning of knitting frames was made a capital offense, and rioting was suppressed by British regulars. After some of the rioters had been shot, public opinion swung to the Luddites, but in 1813, after a mass trial, all the leaders were hanged or transported. Nevertheless, in 1816 and later there were sporadic outbreaks, all of which were easily contained by local authorities.

Ludhiana, Battle of (21 January 1846), First Sikh War. British forces under Sir Harry Smith [q.v.] defeated a Sikh force under Runjur Singh near this town in East Punjab, near the Sutlej River, 100 miles east-southeast of Lahore.

Luetzow, Adolf (1782–1834). A Prussian soldier who entered the army in 1795 at the age of thirteen. During the "war of liberation" in 1813 he obtained permission to form a free corps (*Freikorps*) of infantry, cavalry, and Tyrolean sharpshooters, known as the Black Jäger, to operate in the rear of the French forces, but at Kitzen, near Leipzig, the corps was annihilated as a fighting force. Luetzow and a few survivors cut their way free. Reorganized, the corps fought at Gadebusch and Göhrde (where Luetzow was wounded) and took part in the siege of Jülich. In 1815 he was captured leading the broken charge of the 6th Uhlans in the Battle of Ligny [q.v.]. He escaped on the day of the Battle of Waterloo [q.v.].

In one of the last acts of his life he issued a challenge (ignored) to Field Marshal Gebhard von Blücher [q.v.] for making disparaging remarks about the disastrous charge of the 6th Uhlans at Ligny.

Lugard, Frederick John Dealtry, First Baron, (1858–1945). A British soldier and colonial administrator, born in Madras, India, who served in the Second Afghan War of 1879–80, the Gordon Relief Expedition of 1885, and the Third Anglo-Burmese War [qq.v.]. In May 1888 he was seriously wounded while leading an expedition organized by

British settlers in Nyasaland (Malawi) against Arab slave traders on the shores of Lake Nyasa. In April 1889 he joined the Imperial British East Africa Company, and in 1890, after some severe fighting, he secured British predominance in Uganda. While administering Uganda, he made extensive explorations of the region.

In 1894, sent to Bornu (today a province of Nigeria) by the Royal Niger Company, he secured treaties with local chiefs, beating out French and German rivals. In 1896–97 he led an expedition to Lake Ngami for the British West Charterland Company. He was recalled by the government to raise a force of native troops for the protection of the hinterland of Nigeria from French aggression. From 1897 to 1899, although only a major, he commanded the West African Frontier Force [q.v.], which he raised. He is best known for his work in Nigeria, where he was high commissioner and commander-in-chief of Northern Nigeria from 1900 to 1906. After a five-year stint as governor of Hong Kong, he returned to be governor of Northern and Southern Nigeria and finally governor-general of Nigeria from 1914 to 1919. He was raised to the peerage as a baron in 1928.

Luger, Georg (1849–1923). An Austrian who became a cadet in the Austro-Hungarian army in 1865 and was commissioned but resigned in 1872 to marry and become a railway engineer. In 1875 he collaborated with Ferdinand Mannlicher [q.v.] in designing a magazine rifle. In 1891 he joined the firm of Ludwig Löwe [q.v.] as a consultant designer, and there he met Hugo Borchardt (1850?–1921) and, with his help, improved his pistol design to produce the Parabellum [q.v.] or Luger pistol.

Luger Pistol. See Parabellum.

Lumsden, Harry Burnett (1821–1896). A British soldier who was commissioned in the 59th Bengal Native Infantry in 1838. He fought in both Sikh Wars, the Second Afghan War, the Indian Mutiny [qq.v.], and various campaigns on India's Northwest Frontier [q.v.]. In 1846, when he was a political agent under Sir Henry Lawrence [q.v.] and stationed at Peshawar, he was ordered to raise a corps of trustworthy Pathans "who could at a moment's notice act as guides to troops in the field and collect information." This expanded into a unique corps of cavalry and infantry that distinguished itself during the Indian Mutiny and evolved into an elite corps on the frontier with Lumsden as its commander.

In 1860 he led an expedition against the Waziris, and from 1862 he commanded the Gwalior Contingent [q.v.]. He left India in 1869 and rose to become a lieutenant general in 1875. He is credited as the initiator of the khaki uniform.

Lundy's Lane, Battle of (25 July 1814), War of 1812. This battle, fought within sight and sound of Niagara Falls, has also been called the Battle of Niagara, or Niagara Falls, or Bridgewater. After the American victory in the Battle of Chippewa [q.v.] on 5 July 1814, the British army of 1,500 regulars and 600 militia, aided by some Indians, all under the direct command of British Major General Phineas Riall [q.v.], fell back to the vicinity of Niagara Falls, where Riall was soon reinforced by additional troops, including many veterans of the Peninsular War [q.v.], under General Gordon Drummond (1772–1854), American General Jacob Brown [q.v.] followed

the retreating British as far as Queenston, where he halted to await the arrival of the fleet of Commodore Isaac Chauncey (1772–1884). After waiting two weeks for Chauncey, who failed to participate in the campaign, Brown drew back to Chippewa, intending to strike out across country to Ancaster, a village seven miles west of Hamilton in southern Ontario, by way of a small road known as Lundy's Lane, from which he could reach the British rear.

As Brown withdrew, Riall sent forward about 1,000 men along Lundy's Lane. A part of Brown's force, about 1,000 men, led by twenty-eight-year-old Winfield Scott [q.v.] encountered a larger force of about 1,800 British near the crossroads of the lane and the Queenston road, named River Road. There followed one of the fiercest land battles of the war and one of its most stubbornly contested engagements. Both sides were reinforced, Scott by Brown and Riall by Major General Thomas Drummond [q.v.], and the five-hour battle lasted into the night. Scott and Brown were each twice wounded; Riall lost an arm and was captured.

Casualties were heavy on both sides. The Americans lost 171 killed, 572 wounded, and 110 missing. The British lost 84 killed, 559 wounded, and 235 captured or missing. Both sides claimed victory, but the Americans pulled back in the night to Fort Erie, which they had captured on 13 July [see Fort Erie, Battle of].

Lunette. Sometimes called conserve, silton, or envelope.

1. A redan with flanks or wings extending from the arms of the V.

2. Fieldworks that flank a ravelin, one face being perpendicular to the face of the bastion and the other to the face of the ravelin.

3. Any V-shaped or semicircular fieldwork. During the American Civil War lunettes were often named after their battery or brigade commanders.

4. The iron ring at the end of the trail of a gun carriage. In limbering up the gun, the lunette was placed over the pintle hook.

5. The hole through the iron plate on the underside of the stock of siege guns through which the pintle of the limber was passed when the gun was limbered.

6. An officer's telescope.

7. Any crescent-shaped or semicircular shaped object.

Lupton, Frank Miller (1854–1888). A British sailor who left the sea and in 1879 rode from Suakin to Berber and then sailed up the Nile to Khartoum, where he joined the staff of Charles Gordon [q.v.], the governor-general of the Sudan. The following year Lupton became a deputy to Emin Bey (Edouard Schnitzer [q.v.]), governor of Equatoria Province. Soon after, he was made a bey and appointed governor of the Bahr al-Ghazal Province in succession to Romolo Gessi [q.v.]. From 1882 he resisted the Dervishes and their Dinka allies, who were encroaching upon Bahr al-Ghazal from the north, but Dervishes under Karam Allah Muhammad Kurkusawi [q.v.] finally conquered the province and captured Lupton, who was led in chains to Khartoum, where he was so cruelly treated that he died in delirium. He left behind his Abyssinian wife, a former slave by whom he had had two daughters.

Lurton, Horace Harmon (1844–1914). An American jurist who, although he had served in the Confederate army during the American Civil War, became an associate justice of the U.S. Supreme Court from 1910 until his death.

Lushai Expedition (1890). In 1840 Lushai tribesmen invaded the mountainous district of Assam in northeastern India and in 1849 made their first attack upon British territory. They grew increasingly troublesome. After they had kidnapped a small British girl named Mary Winchester, an arduous but successful expedition was launched against them and the little girl was restored to her friends.

Lusitanian Legion. See Loyal Lusitanian Legion.

Lützen, Battle of (2 May 1813), Napoleonic Wars. Southeast of this Saxon town a Prussian army under General Gebhard von Blücher [q.v.] and a Russian army under General Ludwig Wittgenstein [q.v.], totaling 120,000 men, not realizing Napoleon's strength, attacked Napoleon. Blücher was wounded, and his place taken by General Johan Yorck von Wartenburg [q.v.]; Russian reserves were late reaching the field, and Napoleon threw his Young Guard and Old Guard at the Allied center [see Garde Impériale]. The village changed hands several times during the day. At eight o'clock that evening, over Blücher's objections, the Allied armies retreated. The Allies lost about 20,000, the French 18,000, and Allied morale was shaken. Marshal Bessières was killed in this battle.

Lü-ying. Chinese professional soldiers of the imperial army. Their units were called Green Banner battalions. The term was used to distinguish these regulars from the troops raised by provincial governors, such as Tsêng Kuo-fan [q.v.].

Lyddite. A high explosive composed chiefly of picric acid (trinitrophenol) first demonstrated in 1885 in France. It derived its name from the town of Lydd in southwest Kent, England, on the coast of the Strait of Dover, because it was developed at a nearby military camp. The first operational use of Lyddite shells was against the Mahdist Dervishes in the Battle of Omdurman [q.v.] on 1 September 1898.

Lynchburg, Battle of (18 June 1864), American Civil War. Union General David Hunter [q.v.], having moved up the Shenandoah Valley in Virginia, attempted to capture Lynchburg, but was repulsed by two brigades under Confederate General John Breckinridge [q.v.]. Hunter retreated into western Virginia, leaving General Jubal Early [q.v.] free to march down the valley on his way to attack Washington.

Lynch, Eliza (fl. 1870s and 1880s). The Irish mistress of Francisco Solano López [q.v.], dictator of Paraguay. Considered both beautiful and intelligent, she had been the wife of a French surgeon before meeting López. During her sixteen years in Paraguay she bore López seven children. She sometimes accompanied him on campaign, and in the Battle of Corumbá [q.v.] during the War of the Triple Alliance [q.v.] she led a corps of women soldiers she had organized. In the Battle of Villeta, south of Asunción, she is said to have led the cavalry charge that turned the tide of battle. At the end of the War of the Triple Alliance and after López's death, she fled to Paris, taking her jewels.

Lynedoch, Thomas Graham (1748–1843). A Scottish soldier who in 1794 raised the 90th Regiment of Foot (later the Perthshire Regiment) and served with it in Minorca. In 1800 he besieged Valetta, Malta. During the Peninsular War he was an aide to General Sir John Moore [q.v.] at Corunna [q.v.] in 1809 and took part in the disastrous Walcheren Expedition [q.v.]. In the Peninsular War [q.v.] he fought at Barrosa, Ciudad Rodrigo, Badajoz, and Salamanca [qq.v.]. In 1813 he commanded the left wing in the Battle of Vitoria [q.v.], and captured Tolosa and San Sebastián [q.v.]. He was victorious at Merxem (then in the Netherlands but now part of Belgium), but failed to take Bergen op Zoom [q.v.] in 1814. In that same year he was created Baron Lynedoch of Balgowan. In 1817 he was one of the founders of the Senior Service Club [see United Service Club].

Lyon, Nathaniel (1818–1861). An American army officer who was graduated from West Point in 1841. He fought in the Second Seminole War [q.v.] and served throughout the Mexican War [q.v.] on the western frontier. In February 1861 as a captain commanding the U.S. arsenal in St. Louis he rendered powerless the secessionist threat to that city by seizing a pro-Confederate militia camp established by Missouri's secessionist governor at Camp Jackson. In May he was promoted brigadier general. In an effort to drive Confederate forces out of the state, he captured Jefferson City on 15 June and Boonville on 17 June. He was killed on 10 August in the Battle of Wilson's Creek [q.v.] while leading a final charge.

He bequeathed almost all he possessed, about $30,000, to the U.S. government.

M

Maacta, Battle of (28 June 1835), French conquest of Algeria. A French column of 2,000 men, including three and a half battalions of infantry (mostly Foreign Legion), four squadrons of cavalry, and some artillery under General Camille Trézel, was attacked by Arabs under Abd el-Kader [q.v.] at a mountain pass in Algeria. The French panicked and lost 262 killed and 308 wounded. This was the first major battle fought by the French Foreign Legion [q.v.] in Algeria.

MacArthur, Arthur (1845–1912). An American soldier who at age seventeen, having failed to obtain an appointment to West Point, enlisted in the Union army at the beginning of the American Civil War. A few weeks later, on 4 August 1862, he was first lieutenant and adjutant of the 24th Wisconsin. He first saw action in the Battle of Perryville and then at Stone's River [qq.v.], where his gallantry earned him a mention in dispatches. During the Battle of Chattanooga [q.v.], when his regiment's color-bearer was shot down at a critical moment, he seized the colors and, shouting, "On, Wisconsin!," led the regiment in a charge in the Battle of Missionary Ridge [q.v.], where he planted the flag on the captured earthworks in front of what had been Confederate General Braxton Bragg's headquarters. MacArthur's action was witnessed by General Philip Sheridan, and on 30 June 1890, after years of pleading and appeals, he was awarded the Medal of Honor [q.v.] for his "coolness and conspicuous bravery" on Missionary Ridge. On 25 January 1864 he was promoted major, and when his commanding officer was wounded in the Battle of Resaca [q.v.] on 15 May 1864, two days after his nineteenth birthday, he took command of the regiment. In the Battle of Kennesaw Mountain [q.v.] he was twice wounded. He received a third wound in the Battle of Franklin [q.v.] on 30 November 1864 while leading an audacious charge. On 13 March 1865, for "gallantry and meritorious service" in several battles, he was made a brevet lieutenant colonel.

He was mustered out of the volunteers on 10 June 1865 but returned to the army as a lieutenant in the 17th infantry on 23 February 1866 and was promoted captain on 28 July of the same year. He then remained a captain for twenty-three years, during which he saw much service in the Southwest. In 1885 he took part in the campaign against Geronimo [q.v.]. In 1875 he married a woman he had met in New Orleans, and five years later a son was born: Douglas MacArthur

(1880–1964). On 26 May 1896 the elder MacArthur attained the rank of lieutenant colonel.

During the Spanish-American War [q.v.] he served in the Philippines, taking part in the capture of Manila on 13 August 1898. He became a brigadier general on 2 January 1900 and participated in the suppression of the insurrection led by Emilio Aguinaldo [q.v.] [see Philippine Insurrection against the United States]. On 6 May 1900 he was appointed military governor of the Philippines. He was promoted major general on 5 February 1901, and on 15 September 1906 he became a lieutenant general, then the highest rank in the American army. Disappointed that he was not appointed chief of staff, he retired in 1909.

McCall, George Archibald (1802–1868). An American soldier who was graduated from West Point in 1822. He served in the Second Seminole War [q.v.] and for five years was an aide to General Edmund P. Gaines [q.v.]. He was a captain in the 4th Infantry when the Mexican War broke out, and he won two brevets for gallantry at Palo Alto and Resaca de la Palma [qq.v.] fighting under Zachary Taylor [q.v.]. He resigned his commission in 1858, but at the beginning of the American Civil War he was appointed major general of Pennsylvania volunteers on 15 May 1861. Two days later he was appointed a brigadier general of U.S. volunteers. He fought in the Peninsular Campaign [q.v.] and was captured on 30 June 1862. On 16 August he was exchanged for Confederate General Simon Bolivar Buckner [q.v], who had been captured at Fort Donelson [q.v.]. He at once went on sick leave until he retired on 31 March 1863. He was one of the oldest West Point graduates to serve in the field during the war.

McCall, William H. H. (1838–1883). An American soldier who during the American Civil War enlisted as a sergeant in the 5th Pennsylvania and rose to become a brevet brigadier general. He particularly distinguished himself in the attack on Fort Steadman [q.v.], which he retook after it had been captured by Confederate General John B. Gordon [q.v.].

In 1868 he enlisted as first sergeant in the body of scouts that Brevet Brigadier General George Alexander Forsyth [q.v.] had put together. Forsyth said of him that "like many another good man of either army, [he] had drifted West since the close of the war, been unsuccessful, became a bit dissipated." With Forsyth he fought the Battle of Beecher's Island [q.v.], where he was wounded. Later he turned to mining in Arizona, where in October 1877 he was a member of a posse that ran down and shot two outlaw gunmen. He married in 1878 and fathered two children.

McCallum, Daniel Craig (1815–1878). A Scottish-born American engineer who in 1851 designed the first arched truss bridge. In 1862, during the American Civil War, he was made military director and superintendent of railroads with emergency war powers. He was brevetted brigadier general in 1864 and major general in 1865.

McCausland, John (1836–1927). An American soldier who was graduated from the Virginia Military Institute in 1857 and in 1861 was commissioned in the Confederate army. By May 1864 he had risen to become a brigadier general in command of a brigade of cavalry. In the Shenandoah Valley he opposed a superior force under Union General David Hunter [q.v.] and managed to hold it in check until the arrival of General Jubal Early [q.v.] with a corps that drove Hunter from the valley. He played a conspicuous part in Early's raid on Washington [q.v.] when he was sent to threaten Chambersburg, Pennsylvania [q.v.], and burn it unless it paid a ransom. He refused to surrender at Appomattox but was captured soon after. When released, he went abroad for two years and then settled in Virginia.

McCawley, Charles Grymes (1827–1891). An American who was commissioned in the Marine Corps in 1847 and fought in the Mexican War [q.v.], winning a brevet to first lieutenant at Chapultepec. He did not become a substantive first lieutenant until eight years later. In the American Civil War on 10 May 1862 he commanded a detachment of 200 Federal marines that reoccupied the Norfolk Navy Yard in Norfolk, Virginia. He became a major in 1864 after taking part in several engagements. In June 1871 he took command of the marine barracks in Washington, D.C., and in November 1876 he was promoted colonel and appointed commandant of the U.S. Marine Corps, a post he held until he retired in January 1891. In 1882 he inaugurated the policy of appointing new Marine Corps officers from among the graduates of the Naval Academy.

McCleave, William (1823–1904). An Irish-born American soldier who enlisted in the 1st Dragoons on 7 October 1850 and ten years later was first sergeant. On 23 August 1861, at the beginning of the American Civil War, he was commissioned a captain in the 1st California Cavalry (by 1 May 1863 he was a major). In March 1862 he and nine men were captured by Confederates near Tucson, in what is now Arizona. He was paroled four months later. When he received his $582.50 back pay, he returned it to the government, saying that in "times like these when the government is engaged in such a desperate struggle I can but render my humble assistance in the noble work."

From January 1863 on, McCleave was engaged in fighting Indians. He was with Kit Carson [q.v.] at the first Battle of Adobe Walls [q.v.] on 25 November 1864. He finished the war with brevets to lieutenant colonel and was mustered out of the volunteer service on 19 October 1866.

He remained in the army as a second lieutenant and on 10 August 1869 was made a captain in the 8th Cavalry. He retired ten years later and settled in Berkeley, California. He was

married and sired six children; two of his sons became army officers.

McClellan, George Brinton (1826–1885). A brilliant young man who was given special permission to enter West Point two years before he reached the minimum age. He was graduated in 1846, ranking second in his class. He served through the Mexican War [q.v.] in the Corps of Engineers, earning brevets to first lieutenant and captain. In 1855–56 he studied military operations abroad, including the Crimean War. Among his recommendations on his return was the adoption of a saddle that he had designed and that came to bear his name [see McClellan Saddle]. On 16 January 1857 he resigned his commission to become chief engineer and subsequently vice-president of the Illinois Central Railroad, one of whose lawyers was Abraham Lincoln [q.v.]. When the American Civil War began, McClellan was president of the Ohio & Mississippi Railroad.

On 23 April 1861 he was commissioned in the Union army as a major general of Ohio volunteers and three weeks later was given the same rank in the regular army. In June, on his own initiative, he launched a campaign into northwestern Virginia (today West Virginia), winning small but significant battles at Philippi, Rich Mountain, and Carrick's Ford [qq.v.]. On 16 July the House of Representatives gave him and his men formal thanks for "the series of brilliant and decisive victories which they have recently achieved by their skill and bravery over traitors and rebels in arms on the battlefields of western Virginia."

After the Union fiasco at First Bull Run [q.v.] on 21 July 1861, McClellan, only thirty-five years old, was called to Washington as general-in-chief to take direct command of what came to be called the Army of the Potomac [q.v.]. He was successful in creating a fine army under enormous difficulties, but his handling of that army in the Peninsular

McClellan, George Brinton *President Lincoln in General McClellan's tent at Antietam after the battle there*

Campaign [q.v.] in March and August 1862 was hesitant, uncertain, even timid. Lincoln said of him: "[He] is an admirable engineer, but he seems to have a special talent for the stationary engine."

On 17 September 1862, the bloodiest day of the war, McClellan defeated General Robert E. Lee's Army of Northern Virginia [q.v.] at Antietam [q.v.] but he failed to press forward and permitted Lee to retreat into Virginia. On 5 November he was relieved of his command and replaced by Ambrose Burnside [q.v.].

In 1864 McClellan ran unsuccessfully for the presidency on the Democratic ticket. He resigned his commission on election day. He was later engaged in several large engineering enterprises and served two terms as governor of New Jersey.

McClellan Cap. A tailor-made kepi-style cap favored by General George B. McClellan [q.v.] and some other Union officers during the American Civil War.

McClellan Saddle. A saddle designed by Captain (later General) George B. McClellan [q.v.] in the 1850s and adopted by the American army in 1859. It was modeled on a Hungarian style and was used by American cavalry as long as it had horses. It featured an open seat covered with rawhide, wooden stirrups, and a thick harness leather skirt. It replaced the Grimsley or dragoon saddle of 1847.

McClernand, John Alexander (1812–1900). An American lawyer and legislator in Illinois who served briefly in the Black Hawk War [q.v.] and who at the beginning of the American Civil War was commissioned a Union brigadier general. He became one of the most successful of the so-called political generals. In 1862 he was promoted major general. He commanded a corps in the Vicksburg Campaign [q.v.], although he was chagrined at being placed under U. S. Grant. He ran afoul of Grant and was relieved by him for saying that he had not been properly supported in an unsuccessful assault. He later took part in the Red River Expedition until he contracted malaria and returned to Illinois.

McCook Family. See Fighting McCooks.

McCulloch, Ben (1811–1862). An American soldier who fought in the Texas War for Independence, the Mexican War, and the American Civil War. He also served with the Texas Rangers [q.v.] and was a U.S. marshal. A close friend of David Crockett and Samuel Houston [qq.v.], he escaped death in the siege of the Alamo [q.v.] by a fortunate attack of measles that delayed him en route to San Antonio. When he recovered, he joined the Texas army and won a battlefield commission in the Battle of San Jacinto [q.v.]. In the American Civil War he became the first civilian to obtain a general's commission in the Confederate army. In the spring and summer of 1861 he commanded all the Confederate forces in Indian Territory. He was killed by a sniper in the Battle of Pea Ridge [q.v.].

Macdonald, Claude Maxwell (1852–1915). A British soldier and diplomat educated at Sandhurst [q.v.] who entered the 74th Highlanders in 1872 and distinguished himself in

the Arabi's Revolt [q.v.] of 1882 and in the eastern Sudan in 1884–85. In 1891 he became the first commissioner and consul general of the Oil River Protectorate in West Africa, and in 1895 he took part in the Brass River Expedition [see Nigerian Uprising]. In 1896 he was appointed British minister at Peking (Beijing), China, and during the Boxer Rebellion [q.v.] he was elected by the other foreign emissaries to commanded the defense of the legations there. In 1905 he became the first British ambassador in Tokyo.

Macdonald, Hector Archibald (1853–1903). A British soldier, the son of a crofter, who enlisted in the ranks but was commissioned after distinguished service in Afghanistan. He served in Egypt and the Sudan, particularly distinguishing himself in the Battle of Omdurman [q.v.] in 1898. He later served in the Second Anglo-Boer War [q.v.] as a major general. While serving as commander of troops in Ceylon (Sri Lanka), he was accused of engaging in homosexual acts with schoolboys. On the advice of the governor he traveled to London to consult with the military authorities. After hearing the charges, Lord Roberts ordered a court of inquiry, which would have almost certainly led to a court-martial, to be held in Ceylon. Macdonald began the journey back but got no farther than Paris. There he shot and killed himself in his hotel room. Only after his death was it discovered that he was married and had a grown son in Scotland.

Macdonald, Jacques Étienne Joseph Alexandre, Duc de Taranto (1765–1840). A French soldier of Scottish descent who began his military career as an enlisted man in Légion Irlandais in 1784. The following year he transferred to a French regiment raised for service in Holland. In October 1791 he was commissioned a lieutenant, and three years later, at the age of twenty-nine, he was a general of division.

He served in the French Revolutionary Wars and became general of brigade in 1794 and a general of division two years later. In 1799 he commanded the Army of Naples. He was severely wounded in a minor skirmish and then defeated in the Battle of Trebia on 17–19 June 1799 by Russian Marshal Aleksandr Suvorov [q.v.]. In 1809 he captured Laibach (Ljubljana), and he served with distinction in the Battle of Wagram [q.v.] on 5–6 July, leading the assault that broke the left center of the Austrian line, an act rewarded by a marshal's baton. He served in Catalonia in 1810–11 during the Peninsular War [q.v.]. In Napoleon's Russian Campaign [q.v.] he commanded a corps of Poles, Prussians, and assorted Germans. In the Battle of Lützen [q.v.] he led an attack on the Russo-Prussian left, and he exhibited great courage in the Battle of Leipzig [q.v.].

He supported the restoration of Louis XVIII (1755–1824) and escorted him into Belgium during the Hundred Days [q.v.]. After the Battle of Waterloo [q.v.] he supervised the dispersal of the remaining units of Napoleon's army. He was made a peer and from 1816 was chancellor of the Legion of Honor.

Macdonald, James Ronald Leslie (1862–1927). A British soldier who passed out of Woolwich [q.v.] at the head of his class in 1882. Commissioned in the Royal Engineers, he was sent to India and first saw action in the Hazara Expedition of 1888. In 1891 he went to Uganda to survey a projected railroad from Mombasa to Lake Victoria. He had just completed his survey when he was ordered back to Uganda, where civil war had erupted. For the next two years he was engaged in military expeditions in Unyoro against slave traders and the Wavumas. In 1893 he was promoted major general and made acting commissioner of the Uganda Protectorate, as it then was. He returned in 1894 to India and two years later to England.

In 1897 he was ordered to lead an expedition from Mombasa, in East Africa, to Fashoda (Kodok), on the Nile in the Sudan. He arrived in Mombasa in July but was unable to set out because of a mutiny among the Sudanese troops in his command and a revolt of Buganda Muslims. For several months he was engaged in operations against the rebels and mutineers. He captured the fort at Usoga in October 1897, defeated Mwanga (1866?–1903), king of Buganda, at Ankole on 19 January 1898, and then conducted successful operations against rebels near Lake Choga until at last the protectorate was again peacefully under British protection. By this time General Kitchener [q.v.] had pried the French out of Fashoda [see Fashoda Incident; Marchand, Jean Baptiste], and Macdonald's expedition there was canceled.

During the Second Anglo-Boer War [q.v.] he was in charge of the balloon factory at Aldershot, and at the outbreak of the Boxer Rebellion [q.v.] he was sent to China as director of balloons. He was soon given larger responsibilities as director of railways for the China expeditionary force. After the war he returned to India, where in 1904 he commanded the military escort of Sir Francis Younghusband (1863–1942) on his expedition to Tibet. In 1908 he was promoted major general and commander of troops in Mauritius. He retired in 1912.

Macdougall, Patrick Leonard (1819–1894). A British soldier who served in Canada and from 1865 to 1869 was adjutant general of the Canadian militia. In 1869 he returned to England and served in the War Office as head of the intelligence branch. In 1877 he returned to Canada as commander of troops in North America.

McDowell, Battle of [8 May 1862], American Civil War. Union Major General John Frémont was leading an army south through western Virginia (West Virginia) in the hopes of attacking Nashville, Tennessee, when leading elements of his force—3,500 infantry, 250 cavalry, and four batteries of artillery—under General Robert Schenk and Robert Milroy, encountered an almost equal force under Thomas ("Stonewall") Jackson, led by General Edward Johnson [qq.v.]. Although the Confederates occupied the high ground near the village of McDowell, 25 miles west-northwest of Staunton, Virginia, in west-central Virginia, the Union forces attacked. When Johnson was wounded, his place as battlefield commander was taken by William Taliaferro [q.v.]. Although the Union attacks were successfully repulsed, the defenders lost more men than did the attackers. Union losses were 28 killed and 225 wounded; Confederate losses were 75 killed and 428 wounded.

McDowell, Irvin (1818–1885). An American soldier educated in France until his appointment to West Point in 1834 at the age of sixteen. He was graduated four years later. From 1841 to 1845 he taught tactics at West Point. He served in the Mexican War [q.v.] on the staff of General John Wool [q.v.] and earned a brevet to captain for his gallantry in the Battle of

Buena Vista [q.v.]. At the outbreak of the American Civil War he was a major with more than twenty years of experience, all in staff positions. For a time he was an aide to General Winfield Scott [q.v.]. On 14 May 1861 he was promoted brigadier general and placed in command of the Department of Northern Virginia. He commanded the Union troops that were defeated in the First Battle of Bull Run [q.v.] on 21 July 1861. He was superseded by George McClellan [q.v.] in March 1862. In the Second Battle of Bull Run [q.v.] he commanded a corps, but his conduct in that battle was criticized, and he was never again given a command involving operations.

He testified against General Fitz John Porter [q.v.], who was court-martialed for his alleged delinquencies in the battle. On 1 July 1864 McDowell was sent to command the Department of the Pacific, and he saw no more active service. On 25 November 1872 he had acquired enough seniority to be promoted major general. He retired in 1882.

McElderry Mule Litter. A litter capable of being mounted on the back of a mule. It was devised by surgeon Henry McElderry (1845?–1898) during the Modoc War [q.v.], when it was found difficult to remove wounded from the lava beds. "It is used upon the aparejo. It is well-balanced, and has no tendency to make the animal's back sore." [see Farrow in bibliography.]

McElderry mule litter

Maceo, Antonio (1848–1896) and his brother José (1846–1896), both Cuban patriots, and leaders of rebel forces, fought together during the Ten Years' War [q.v.] of 1868–78. In 1895 they again joined forces and in the same year defeated Spanish forces at Jobito.

Macequece / Masikesi. In 1888 the Portuguese occupied this town in west-central Mozambique to safeguard their claim to Manicaland. They were driven out by a South African force under Colonel Herman Melville Heyman [q.v.].

MacGahan, Januarius (1844–1878). An American war correspondent who covered the Franco-Prussian War, the Russian conquest of Khiva, the Russo-Turkish War of 1877–78, and a Carlist War in Spain [qq.v.]. He investigated Turkish atrocities in Bulgaria [q.v.], and his reports from Bulgaria created so great a sensation that he was credited with turning world sympathy from the Turks to the Bulgarians. On his tombstone in New Lexington, Ohio, are carved the words "Liberator of Bulgaria."

McGarry, Edward (1823?–1867). An American soldier who on 1 April 1847 was commissioned a second lieutenant in the 10th Infantry and promoted to first lieutenant on 13 September. In California on 21 August 1848 he resigned his commission. At the beginning of the American Civil War he was commissioned a major in the 2nd California Cavalry. He earned a reputation as an Indian killer, summarily executing prisoners and those "trying to escape." He fought in the Battle of Bear River [q.v.] on 27 January 1863, and on 29 November he was promoted colonel. He ended the war as a brevet brigadier general and remained in the army after the war as lieutenant colonel of the 32nd Infantry. Assigned the subdistrict of Santa Cruz in southern Arizona, he launched punitive expeditions against the Apaches, ordering: "No prisoners are to be brought back." General Irvin McDowell [q.v.] canceled his orders with the words "No killing in cold blood will be authorized."

In 1867 McGarry, who had a severe drinking problem, was relieved of his command. He returned to California, where in a San Francisco hotel room he cut his throat.

MacGregor, Gregor (1786–1845). A Scottish soldier of fortune who in 1811, after service in the British army, journeyed to Venezuela, where he became a commandant of cavalry and a brigadier general in the revolutionary army of Simón Bolívar. In 1817, with the design of liberating Florida from Spanish rule, he collected a band of adventurers and in June of that year captured Amelia Island, a sea island that is separated from the mainland of northern Florida by salt marshes and extends south from the St. Mary's River. On 23 December he and his men were driven off by U.S. sailors, soldiers, and marines [see Amelia Island Affair].

MacGregor proceeded to Nassau in the Bahamas, where he devised a scheme to enlist British veterans of the War of 1812 [q.v.] to organize the Indians of Florida, establish a settlement at Tampa Bay, and then march overland to capture St. Augustine. He sent ahead Robert Chrystie Ambrister, an English former royal marine who was familiar with Spanish Florida, to select a site and enlist the Indians, but Ambrister was captured by Andrew Jackson [q.v.], who accused him of inciting Indians to rebel and after a drumhead court-martial ordered his execution. [See Arbuthnot and Ambrister Affair; Jackson, Andrew.] Unnerved, McGregor abandoned the scheme. He appears to have been active in revolutionary circles in the Caribbean and in Central America for several years but finally withdrew to Caracas, where he was again appointed a general.

McGrigor, James (1771–1858). A British army surgeon who became a regimental surgeon by purchase on 13 September 1793 and served with what became the 88th Foot or Connaught Rangers in Flanders. In 1795 and 1796 he served in the West Indies. In 1799 he was in India, and in 1801 he was with the British army in Egypt. He took part in the disastrous Walcheren Expedition [q.v.] of 1809, in which 11,296 men, most stricken by malaria, had to be evacuated. On 25 August 1809 he was promoted inspector general of hospitals.

On 10 January 1812 he landed at Lisbon to be chief of the medical services of Wellington's army in the Iberian Peninsula and served from the Battle of Ciudad Rodrigo [q.v.] to the end of the Peninsular War [q.v.]. In all, 95,348 men passed through his hospitals. After the siege of Badajoz [q.v.], when medical officers were for the first time mentioned in dispatches, his name was one of the first to be included. Wellington said of him: "He is one of the most industrious, able and successful public servants I have ever met with." On 13 June 1815 he was named director general of the British army's Medical Department, a post he held until 1851.

In 1816 he founded the Army Medical Friendly Society, for the aid of the widows of army medical officers, and in 1820 the Army Medical Benevolent Society to assist the orphans of medical officers.

McGuire, Hunter Holmes (1835–1900). An American doctor from Winchester, Virginia, who in the American Civil War served as medical director to Thomas ("Stonewall") Jackson [q.v.] and amputated his arm when it was shattered by bullets at Chancellorsville [q.v.]. After Jackson's death he served under Richard Ewell [q.v.]. He was captured in March 1865 and released at the end of the war.

Machicolations. The openings between corbels of a structure of a projecting parapet or in the floor for discharging missiles on attackers below; a parapet or gallery with such openings. [See Battlements; Corbel; Machicoulis.]

Machicoulis. A projecting gallery from the second story of a structure that enabled the building's defenders to fire down upon attackers. Sometimes called a machicolation.

Machilla. A hammock suspended from a pole and carried by bearers in parts of South Africa and Mozambique.

Machine Gun. An automatic gun firing small-arms ammunition at a continuous rate. The first practical machine gun was the invention of Richard Jordan Gatling [q.v.], an American who was issued a patent on 4 November 1862. In 1870 the French introduced an improved model, but both the French and American models were cumbersome machines operated by turning cranks that rotated barrels. The American model was first used in action in the American Civil War. In 1884 Hiram Maxim [q.v.], an American, invented the first true machine gun in which the energy of the recoil was used to load, fire, extract the cartridge case, and reload. It could fire six hundred .45 caliber bullets in a minute. Maxim's first saw action in the Riel Rebellion [q.v.] in 1885, and it proved its deadly efficiency in 1893 in the Matabele War [q.v.]. The first gas-operated gun was designed by John Browning (1855–1926), another American.

John Ellis, a perceptive modern historian, notes: "The machine gun was an essentially American invention. Not simply because the four greatest names of machine gun history—Gatling, Maxim, Browning and Lewis—were Americans, but also because it was in America that were first developed the material conditions that made automatic fire a feasible proposition" (*The Social History of the Machine Gun* [1975]).

Machine Gun *A Maxim machine battery at St. Gotthard, Switzerland, 1896*

Although there were many other designs, most European armies equipped themselves with the Maxim gun. The Japanese, however, chose the Hotchkiss [q.v.] in 1899 and used it effectively in the Russo-Japanese War.

Machine Gun *Maxim machine gun, demonstrated by Hiram Maxim's assistant Louis Silverman, 1886*

McIntosh, Archie (1834–1902). The son of a Scottish father and a Chippewa mother who became a famous American army scout. His father, employed by the Hudson's Bay Company, was killed in an ambush by Indians in British Columbia. He, his mother, and his siblings escaped to Fort Vancouver. They were taken in by a Scottish doctor who provided the boy with a good education, even sending him to study for two years in Edinburgh. When he returned to North America, he acted as scout and interpreter on many army expeditions. George Crook [q.v.] thought so highly of him that he took him along when he was transferred to Arizona. In 1880 McIntosh was instrumental in arranging the surrender of Chief Juh, Geronimo [qq.v.], and 100 of their followers. He served for a time on the San Carlos Indian Reservation until in 1884 he was found to be diverting supplies from the Indians to his own ranch and was dismissed from government service.

MacIntosh, Charles (1766–1843). A Scottish chemist who invented waterproof fabrics by bonding two layers of india rubber by means of naphtha. His invention, called mackintosh and patented in 1823, was much appreciated by soldiers.

Mackall, William Whann (1816?–1891). An American soldier who was graduated from West Point in 1837 and fought in the Second Seminole War [q.v.], in which he was ambushed and wounded at River Inlet on 11 February 1839. In the Mexican War [q.v.] he won two brevets, and in the Battle of Chapultepec [q.v.] he was again wounded. At the beginning of the American Civil War he resigned his commission and became assistant adjutant general under Confederate General Albert S. Johnston [q.v.]. On 6 March he was appointed brigadier general to rank from 27 February. He fought at Island No. 10 and commanded a brigade in Tennessee. During the Atlanta Campaign [q.v.] he was chief of staff to Joseph E. Johnston [q.v.]. After the war he farmed in Virginia.

Mackensen, August von (1849–1945). A German soldier who served in the 2nd Life Hussars during the Franco-Prussian War [q.v.] and in 1880 was assigned to the Great General Staff. He became a field marshal and was one of the few successful German generals in World War I.

Mackenzie, Ranald Slidell (1840–1899). An American soldier who in 1862 was graduated first in his class of 28 from West Point and immediately plunged into the American Civil War. He fought at Second Bull Run, Fredericksburg, Chancellorsville, Gettysburg, Petersburg, and Cedar Creek [qq.v.]. General U. S. Grant considered him "the most promising young officer in the army." In the course of the war he suffered six wounds, including the loss of two fingers on his right hand; Indians later called him Bad Hand. At the end of the war he was brevetted a brigadier general in the regular army and a major general of volunteers. He was twenty-four years old.

In 1867 he reverted to the rank of captain of engineers, but was soon promoted colonel of the newly formed 41st Infantry, the first black unit in the regular army. The regiment saw good service on the Texas frontier in 1867–69, and in 1869 it was amalgamated with the 38th Infantry to form the 25th Infantry with Mackenzie as its colonel. On 25 February 1871 he took command of the 4th Cavalry and pursued Comanches and Kiowas who had left their reservation at Fort Sill to raid. On 30 June 1871 on the Staked Plain (Llano Estacado) in West Texas he received a painful seventh wound, from a Comanche arrow, that troubled him for the rest of his life. In 1873 he led a daring raid into Coahuila State in Mexico to attack and destroy the villages of renegade Apaches, Kickapoos, and other Indians who had been raiding into the United States. In 1876 he commanded the cavalry in the Powder River Expedition [q.v.] and defeated the Northern Cheyennes under Dull Knife [q.v.] at Crazy Woman Creek [q.v.] on 25–26 November in sub-zero weather, winning the biggest battle of the Red River War [q.v.]. In August 1881 he supervised the removal of more than 1,400 Utes to a new reservation in Utah.

In 1883 he was given command of the Department of Texas. There he courted Florida Tunstall Sharpe, a thirty-two-year-old army widow with a twelve-year-old son, and wedding plans were announced, but before the wedding date arrived, he began to exhibit irrational behavior and, although previously abstemious, to indulge in drunken binges. He was relieved of his command and placed in the Bloomingdale Asylum in New York. On 24 March 1884 he was honorably retired as a brigadier general. He was eventually released from the asylum and died at his sister's home on Long Island. He was forty-eight.

Mackenzie's Revolt. See Canadian Revolts.

McKinstry, Justus (1814–1897). An American soldier who was graduated from West Point in 1838 and served in the Mexican War [q.v.], where he won a brevet to major. Most of his career was served in the Quartermaster's Department, and at the beginning of the American Civil War he was promoted brigadier general of volunteers and appointed chief quartermaster in the Department of the West under Major General John Frémont [q.v.] in St. Louis, Missouri, an appointment he found to be highly remunerative, as did the contractors he employed. One admitted to a profit of $280,000 on sales to the government of $800,000. The firm of Child, Pratt & Fox in St. Louis sold the government goods for a 300 percent profit. One grateful contractor gave McKinstry a horse and buggy, Mrs. McKinstry was presented with a $3,000 silver service, and still another contractor gave a pony to their son.

Ezra J. Warner, the modern authority on Civil War generals, describes General McKinstry (*Generals in Blue* [1986]) as "one of the most thoroughgoing rogues ever to wear a United States uniform." Not only did McKinstry pay high prices, but he accepted shoddy goods: Boots fell apart, and blankets unraveled. Of 400 horses he purchased, 5 died within a few hours; most of the remainder were blind, too old, or otherwise unsuitable. When General David Hunter [q.v.] assumed command of the department, McKinstry was replaced by Philip Sheridan [q.v.], and his peculations were investigated. When arrested, he complained of a "foul conspiracy against me." After a year under arrest, he was court-martialed, and on 28 January 1863 he was cashiered for "neglect and violation of duty to the prejudice of good order and military discipline." No other general officer, North or South, received such a sentence in the war. He later became a stockbroker in New York and a land agent in Missouri.

Mackintosh, William (1775?–1825). An American soldier born in Florida to a Scottish father and a Creek Indian mother. During the War of 1812 he was a leader of the Lower Creeks and given the rank of major by the Americans. He was responsible for the massacre of 200 anti-American Creeks at Atasi (Autoosee or Auttose) on 29 November 1813 and played a leading part in the Battle of Horseshoe Bend [q.v.] against the Red Stick Creeks (Upper Creeks) on 27 March 1814. In the Second Seminole War [q.v.] he was commissioned a brigadier general of volunteers and served with General Andrew Jackson [q.v.]. When he negotiated treaties that ceded Creek lands to whites, a band of 50 Creek warriors, angry at his betrayal, surrounded his house on the Chattahoochee River in Carroll County and murdered him on 1 May 1825.

McKrimmen, Duncan. See Francis, Milly.

Mack von Leiberich, Baron Karl (1752–1828). An Austrian soldier who first earned distinction in the wars against Turkey. He occupied Rome for the king of Naples but was forced to conclude a treaty with the French and was driven by riots in Naples to seek refuge with them. Taken to Paris as a prisoner, he escaped in 1800. In 1804 he was appointed quartermaster general of the Austrian army and hastily tried to prepare for war with France. He commanded the Austrian army in southern Germany in 1805 and was forced to capitulate with 20,000 men to Napoleon at Ulm [q.v.] on 20 October 1805, a failure for which he was court-martialed and condemned to death. This sentence was commuted to twenty years in prison, but he was released in 1809.

Mack had no faith in firepower and once insisted that "infantry should always advance in closed formation, neither skirmishing nor halting to fire volleys. March quickly to the enemy and fall upon him, for salvo firing and skirmishing cost men and decide nothing."

MacMahon, Patrice Edmé Maurice de (1808–1893). A French soldier who first won distinction during the French conquest of Algeria, where in October 1837 he took part in the storming of Constantine [q.v.]. During the Crimean War as general of division he led the French assault on the Malakoff [q.v.] on 8 September 1855. In 1859, during the Austro-Piedmontese War [q.v.], he turned defeat into victory in the Battle of Magenta [q.v.] by pushing his guns forward to cover the attack on the Magenta Bridge. At the end of this war he was created marshal of France and Duc de Magenta. From 1864 to 1870 he was governor of Algeria and fought campaigns against the Kabyles. During the Franco-Prussian War he commanded I Corps and in an attempt to relieve General Achille Bazaine [q.v.] was defeated at Weissenburg and Fröschwiller [qq.v.]. Before the Battle of Sedan [q.v.] he boasted: "If they attack us, so much the better; we shall be able, no doubt, to fling them into the Meuse." Instead he himself was captured. The German attack that followed was a disaster for French arms.

He later played a major role in the brutal suppression of the Paris Commune of 1871 [q.v.], in which 873 troops and an estimated 20,000 Communards were killed. On 24 May 1873 he became the second president of the Third Republic and in that office experienced the continual struggle between monarchists and republicans. He resigned on 28 January 1879.

MacMahon had a distrust of military theory and threatened not to promote any officer who wrote a book.

McLaws, Lafayette (1821–1897). An American soldier who was graduated from West Point in 1842. He fought in the Mexican War [q.v.] but did not win any brevets. In March 1861 he resigned and was appointed a colonel in the Confederate army, and in September he was promoted brigadier general. He served in the Peninsular Campaign [q.v.] and in May 1862 was promoted major general. He performed poorly in the unsuccessful assault on Fort Sanders and was relieved of his command "for lack of confidence" by his West Point classmate James Longstreet [q.v.]. He was restored to command by President Jefferson Davis [q.v.] and sent to Georgia to serve under General Joseph Johnston [q.v.].

After the war he became a collector of internal revenue and postmaster of Savannah, Georgia.

Mclean, Wilmer (fl. 1860s). In 1861, after his farm had become part of the Bull Run [q.v.] battlefield, he moved his family to central Virginia, "where the sound of battle would never reach them." However, it was in the parlor of his brick house at Appomattox Court House [q.v.] that General Robert E. Lee surrendered to General U. S. Grant on 9 April 1865.

Macodou, M'Baye (1870–1948). An African soldier who was born in Senegal and at age twelve entered the École des Enfants des Troupe, a school for the children of African soldiers, at St. Louis, Senegal. At eighteen he joined the *Tirailleurs Sénégalese* [see Senegalese Tirailleurs] and distinguished himself in campaigns under Colonel Alfred Almédée Dodds [q.v.], rising to the rank of sergeant. In

1894 he became one of the few Africans to be commissioned in the French army. He retired in 1918 after thirty years' service.

Macomb, Alexander (1782–1841). An American officer who was commissioned a cornet [q.v.] in the light dragoons on 10 January 1799 at the age of sixteen and a second lieutenant on 2 March, when he was not yet seventeen. He was discharged on 15 June 1800 and reentered the army on 16 February of the following year as a second lieutenant in the 2nd Infantry. He served as an aide to General James Wilkinson [q.v.] on a mission to treat with Indian tribes in the Southeast. On 12 October 1802 he was promoted first lieutenant in the newly created Corps of Engineers at West Point, New York. In 1809 he published *A Treatise of Martial Law and Courts Martial.*

At the beginning of the War of 1812 [q.v.] he was a lieutenant colonel but was soon promoted colonel and given command of the newly raised 4th Artillery. He saw some action on the northeast frontier and on 24 January 1814 was promoted brigadier general, taking command at Plattsburg, New York. On 11 September, with only 4,500 men, he stalled a British force of 14,000 while Captain Thomas Macdonough (1783–1825) destroyed the British supporting fleet on Lake Champlain. Macomb was brevetted major general for his services.

In 1815, with the war ended, the American army was reduced from 60,000 to 10,000, and the officer corps from 2,271 to 489. Macomb remained a substantive brigadier general, but in a further reduction of the army in 1821 he was reduced to colonel. In February 1828 he was promoted major general and appointed general-in-chief of the army. The move infuriated General Winfield Scott [q.v.], who at first refused to recognize the appointment and at one point called for Macomb's arrest. Macomb handled Scott's insubordination with forbearance and tact and remained the uniformed head of the army until 1841, gathering increasing power over the military bureaucracies and in 1830 even court-martialing an insubordinate adjutant general. He abolished the liquor ration to troops, revised and modernized army regulations, and improved the artillery.

McPherson, James Birdseye (1828–1864). An American soldier who at the age of thirteen, when his father, an unsuccessful blacksmith, lost his mind, went to work in a backwoods store in Sandusky County, Ohio. The store's owner took an interest in him and sent him to the Literary, Scientific and Military Academy at Norwich, Vermont, for two years. At the advanced age of twenty, he won an appointment to West Point, from which in 1853 he was graduated first in his class, enabling him to be commissioned in the prestigious Corps of Engineers.

He worked on harbor and coastal defenses on both coasts and supervised construction of the fortifications on Alcatraz Island. On the outbreak of the American Civil War he was a first lieutenant; on 6 August 1861 he was promoted captain; on 12 November he was made a lieutenant colonel; on 1 May 1862 he was promoted colonel, and on 15 May a brigadier general of volunteers; on 8 October he was made major general of volunteers and given command of a division.

In January 1863 he commanded XVII Corps in the Vicksburg Campaign [see Vicksburg, Siege of], earning praise from both U. S. Grant and W. T. Sherman [qq.v.]. He was with the Union army before Atlanta [see Atlanta Campaign] and, accompanied by a single orderly, was returning from Sherman's headquarters to his own when he was killed by skirmishers. Sherman openly wept when he saw McPherson's body laid out on a door used as an improvised stretcher. McPherson had earlier requested leave to marry his fiancée in Baltimore, but the leave had been refused by Sherman, who considered him indispensable.

McQueen, Peter (1780?–1819?). One of the most important of the Creek leaders in the Creek War [q.v.] of 1813–14, waged against the United States. He played a leading role in the Battle of Burnt Creek and the Fort Mims Massacre [qq.v.]. After the war he migrated with about 1,000 other Creeks to Florida. There he fought on the side of the Seminoles in the First Seminole War [q.v.]. He was defeated in the Battle of Escombia in April 1818.

Macta. See Maacta, Battle of.

Madagascar, Warfare in (1810–97). In 1811 British troops occupied Tamatave, a port town on the east coast of Madagascar. In exchange for abolishing slavery and allowing missionaries to enter his country, the Hova king, Radama I (d. 1828), received from the British arms, ammunition, and soldiers to train his troops. On his death the throne was seized by one of his wives, Queen Ranavalona I (d. 1861), who in 1835 declared Christianity illegal and expelled all British missionaries. The next twenty-five years saw general unrest and numerous rebellions, all of which were brutally suppressed. All foreigners were finally expelled. Upon her death Ranavalona was succeeded by Radama's son Radama II (d. 1863), who was soon assassinated and replaced by his widow, Queen Rasoherina (d. 1868), who then married the prime minister. During Rasoherina's brief reign missionaries were permitted to return, and the Hova army of 30,000 to 40,000 men was again trained at first by British noncommissioned officers and later by commissioned officers. Rasoherina was succeeded by her cousin Ranavalona II (d. 1893), who was also married to the prime minister. The British were happy with the Hova government. The French were not.

In 1840 French forces seized the island of Nossi-be (Nosy-Be), 113 square miles off the northwest coast of Madagascar, inhabited by the Sakalava people, and they claimed in addition a vague protectorate over some of the adjacent mainland, claims that were generally allowed to lapse until renewed with vigor in 1882. In May 1883 the French sent an ultimatum to Queen Ravanalona II, demanding recognition of their territorial claims. When this was refused, they bombarded the port town of Tamatave on the east coast and occupied it with the 4ème Infantrie de Marine. Hova forces skirmished with the French, and the French captured Diégo-Suarez (Antsirane) on the north coast. The war progressed in a desultory fashion until the Hova government on 17 December 1885 signed a treaty giving the French control of their foreign relations, agreed to a French resident in the capital, and gave France the port of Diégo-Suarez and surrounding territory.

Queen Ranavalona II was succeeded by her niece Razafindrahety, who assumed the throne as Ranavalona III (d. 1917). In 1890, in return for concessions on Zanzibar, Britain recognized the French protectorate. Nevertheless, the Hova army continued to be trained by British officers. In 1894 the French demanded complete control of the government and, when this was refused, sent an expeditionary force of about 18,000 men under General Joseph Gallieni [q.v.] to Madagascar. The chief ports were occupied, and a French force moved inland toward Tananarive, the capital in east-central Madagascar.

A separate expedition under General Jacques Charles René Achille Duchesne (1837–1918) seized Diégo-Suarez and marched inland. It was in this expedition that Duchesne gave his famous admonition to the French Foreign Legion: "March or die!"

On 30 September 1895 Duchesne had reached the heights north and east of Tananarive and combined with Gallieni's army. The city was bombarded on 30 September 1895 and surrendered that afternoon. That evening the French marched into the capital. The French suffered only 25 battle deaths out of 4,613 total deaths, about 70 percent from malaria.

Gallieni was made governor, and the queen was initially allowed to retain her throne, but numerous rebellions flared against French rule throughout the island, and on 6 August 1896 she was forcibly removed by the French and sent into exile, first to the island of Réunion (called Bourbon until 1848) and then to Algeria. Hova rule ended, and Madagascar became a French colony.

Madagascar *The French conquest of Madagascar, about 1895*

Madeira, Capture of (24 December 1807), Peninsular War. Troops under British General William Carr Beresford [q.v.], transported to Madeira by Admiral Sir Samuel Hood (1762–1814), captured the island, which the British then held in trust for the Portuguese royal family, who had fled from Napoleon's armies to Brazil. The island was restored to the Portuguese in 1814.

Mad Mullah of Somaliland, Operations against (1899–1920). There were many Mad Mullahs in the nineteenth century, but probably the most famous, and certainly the most able and elusive, was Muhammad ibn Abd Allah (Abdullah) Hasan (1856–1920), leader of a militant Sufi brotherhood called Salihiyah, in what is today Somalia. Beginning in 1899, and operating mainly from a base about 50 miles southwest of Berbera, he raided in all directions for twenty-one years. British, Italians, and Abyssinians sent military expeditions against him, but none succeeded. His raids ended only with his natural death in 1920.

The Mad Mullah became a folk hero, and when Somalia gained its independence, a monument in his honor was erected in front of the parliament building in Mogadishu.

Madrid, Fighting at (1808), Peninsular War. The capital of Spain was captured by the French in March 1808, but on 2 May the citizens of Madrid rose up and attempted to expel them, as depicted in *El Dos de Mayo,* painted in 1808 by Francisco José de Goya y Lucientes (1746–1828), which portrays the populace assaulting French cavalry at the Puerta del Sol. Curiously, Goya was at first a Josefina, one of the Spaniards who sided with King Joseph I (Joseph Bonaparte). When the French left, Goya was forced into hiding for three months to escape the fury of the populace. The rebellion was suppressed with great slaughter. Many of the rebels were executed by firing squads, also portrayed by Goya, in the canvas *Los Fucilamientos del 3 Mayo.*

Madriers. Long, broad wooden planks used to support the earth in mining, making caponiers, galleries, and such in siege operations. They were also used to cover the mouths of petards after they were loaded.

Mafeking, Siege of (13 October 1899–17 May 1900), Second Anglo-Boer War. A British force of 1,251 effectives under Colonel Robert Baden-Powell [q.v.], together with numbers of African and European men, women, and children, was besieged by some 9,000 Boers under Piet Cronjé [q.v.] at this town on the border of the Transvaal and Bechuanaland (Botswana). After an unsuccessful initial attack, only one other assault was made on the town. It too failed, and the besiegers settled down into a more or less continual bombardment. Baden-Powell managed to send out a stream of cheery dispatches, the most famous being "All well, four hours' bombardment. One dog killed." The siege was raised by the arrival of a column of British cavalry under Major General Bryan Mahon (1862–1930). In the 217 days of the siege British losses were 273.

When news of the relief of Mafeking reached London, men, women and children took to the streets in a tremendous spontaneous celebration so riotous that a new verb was created to stand for uproarious rejoicing or any extravagant demonstration: "to maffick."

The queen sent Baden-Powell a personal message of congratulations, and he was promoted major general, the youngest in the army. Although Bryan Mahon became a general and had a distinguished career as a statesman, he was always known as the man who relieved Mafeking.

Magazine. 1. A storehouse for supplies, particularly gunpowder and ammunition.

2. The holder of cartridges in breech-loading rifles. The magazine was often detachable.

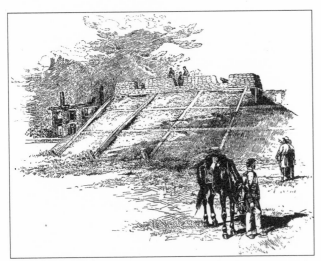

Magazine Confederate battery on the terraced magazine commands the land approach to the Gosport navy yard in Virginia.

Magazine Guns. Small arms with a magazine capable of holding several cartridges.

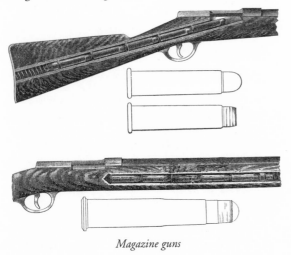

Magazine guns

Magdala, Capture of (10–13 April 1868), Abyssinian Campaign. A British army under General Robert Napier [q.v.], sent to rescue and avenge captured Europeans, arrived before Magdala, the stronghold of King Theodore [q.v.], a fortified town (now called Amba Maryam) 9,110 feet above sea level in north-central Abyssinia (Ethiopia) on 10 April 1868. An Abyssinian attack at Aroghee [q.v.], three miles north of Magdala, was repulsed with great slaughter on 11 April. On the following day, in an attempt to appease the British, all the prisoners were released. Nevertheless, on 13 April (Easter Sunday) Napier stormed the citadel. Even though it was discovered that gunpowder and scaling ladders had been left behind, a drummer boy scampered up a wall

and assisted others. The place was captured with a loss of only 2 killed and 13 wounded. King Theodore committed suicide by shooting himself.

The British razed the citadel and marched back to their ships. Napier was given the Thanks of Parliament and raised to the peerage as Baron Napier.

The British losses were 2 killed and 20 wounded; Abyssinian losses were about 500 killed and wounded. On 17 April the British razed Magdala.

Magdala Abyssinian King Theodore commits suicide (upper left) after British capture Magdala, April 1868.

Magdeburg, Siege of (20 October-11 November 1806), Napoleonic Wars. After the battles of Jena and Auerstädt [qq.v.] this Prussian fortress on the Elbe River, 82 miles westnorthwest of Berlin, was one of the few to offer resistance to the French. Its commander, Prince Hohenlohe-Ingelfingen [q.v.], after rejecting Marshal Joachim Murat's [q.v.] order to surrender, withdrew from the fortress, leaving a garrison of 25,000 in the command of the aged Field Marshal Friedrich von Kleist [q.v.]. Although besieged by a force of only 18,000 French, Kleist soon surrendered, and Magdeburg was annexed by the French to the kingdom of Westphalia. It was restored to Prussia in 1814.

Magee, Augustus William (1789–1813). An American soldier who was graduated from West Point in 1809 and served in the artillery in Louisiana. On 22 June 1812 he resigned his commission and joined José Bernardo Gutiérrez de Lara [q.v.] in his invasion of Texas. The expedition crossed the Sabine River into Texas on or about 12 August 1812, and Fort Bahía (known as Goliad since 1829) was captured on 14 November. On 10 March 1813 Magee died of an illness.

Magenta, Battle of (4 June 1859), Austro-Piedmontese War. After the failure of the Italian revolutionary movements in Italy in 1848 and 1849, many Italians looked to the kingdom of Sardinia-Piedmont for deliverance from Austrian rule. On 10 December 1858 Louis Napoleon (1808–1873) of France was asked to help free northern Italy from Austria. The following spring 49,500 French and Piedmontese troops under General Marie MacMahon [q.v.] pushed eastward across the Ticino River into Austrian-held Lombardy and met 53,000 Austrians under General Eduard von Clam-Gallas [q.v.] near this Lombardy commune 14 miles west of Milan. In the battle that followed generals on both sides behaved ineptly. The Austrians failed to attack the French army as it marched northward across their front, and neither side took advantage of the available railroads. After much confused fighting the Austrians were pushed back. Both sides slept on the field, but early the next morning the Austrians retreated eastward. French and Sardinian losses were 4,000 killed and wounded and 600 missing; Austrian losses were 5,700 killed and wounded and 4,500 missing. MacMahon was made Duc de Magenta.

A brilliant crimson aniline dye, discovered soon after this bloody battle, was named magenta. That same year a bluish pink dye was developed and named solferino after the Battle of Solferino [q.v.], fought on 24 June 1859 in the same war.

Magersfontein, Battle of (11 December 1899), Second Anglo-Boer War. At this place in western Orange Free State a British force under Lord Methuen [q.v.], marching to the relief of besieged Mafeking and Kimberley [qq.v.], was repulsed by a Boer force under Piet Cronjé [q.v.]. The Highland Brigade, under Major General Andrew Wauchop (1846–1899), suffered the most: Of total British casualties of 971, the brigade lost 23 officers and 182 other ranks killed, including General Wauchop. As one Highlander put it, "We were led into a butcher's shop and bloody well left there."

This was the second of the three British defeats in what came to be called Black Week [q.v.].

Magistral. The crest line of the parapet in field fortifications.

Magistral Line. In field fortifications, a line traced on paper or marked on the ground from which the position of all other works was determined.

Magnam, Bernard Pierre (1791–1865). A French officer who served at Waterloo [q.v.] in 1815, Spain in 1823, and Algeria in 1830. He was promoted general of brigade in 1839 and six years later was promoted general of division. In 1849 he suppressed the uprising in Lyons. On 2 December 1851 he helped ensure the success of the coup d'état that transformed Prince Louis Napoleon (1808–1873) into Napoleon III, and a few weeks later he was created a marshal of France and a senator. In 1859 he was commander of the Army of Paris.

Magongo, Battle of (January 1840), South African Wars. To overthrow the Zulu chief Dingaan [q.v.], Boers allied themselves with his brother Panda [q.v.], also called Umpanda or Mpanda. In a battle at this place on the Umkuzi River in Natal the forces of Dingaan were defeated.

Magruder, John Bankhead (1810–1871). An American soldier who was graduated from West Point in 1830. In the Mexican War [q.v.] he so distinguished himself as a battery commander that he won three brevets. Immediately before the outbreak of the American Civil War, although a substan-

tive captain, he was exercising command in his brevet rank of lieutenant colonel. On 17 June 1861 he resigned his commission and was appointed a brigadier general in the provisional Confederate army. On 7 December he was promoted major general. He fought in the Peninsular Campaign, notably distinguishing himself at Yorktown and in the Seven Days' Battles [qq.v.]. He was then assigned to the Southwest and captured Galveston, Texas.

At the end of the war he did not surrender but took refuge in Mexico, where he was appointed a major general in the imperial army of the emperor Maximilian [q.v.]. When that regime collapsed, he returned to the United States and made his home in Houston, Texas. Although as a younger man he had been called Prince John because of his love of high living, he died in comparative poverty and obscurity.

Mahan, Dennis Hart (1802–1871). An American soldier and educator who was graduated first in his class from West Point in 1824 and who from 1832 until his death was professor of military and civil engineering and of the science of war at the Military Academy. He also helped organize the Virginia Military Institute [q.v.] in Lexington, Virginia, where until 1860 the summer encampment was called Camp Mahan. The author of textbooks on advanced guard and outpost duties, military engineering and geometry, he was best known for the 1847 book called by generations of West Point cadets Mahan's *Outposts*, the first American study of war. (Its full title is *An Elementary Treatise on Advanced Guard, Outpost and Detached Service of Troops, and the Manner of Posting and Handling Them in the Presence of the Enemy. With a Historical Sketch of the Rise and Progress of Tactics, etc.*) His lessons greatly influenced the cadets who later served as officers in the Mexican War and became the generals in the American Civil War [qq.v.]. He preached the importance of surprise, boldness, and mobility, telling his students that "celerity is the secret of success." In 1871, because of his age (sixty-nine), the West Point Board of Visitors recommended his retirement. This made him so despondent that on 16 September he threw himself off a Hudson River steamer and drowned.

He was the father of Alfred Thayer Mahan (1840–1914), author of *The Influence of Sea Power upon History, 1660–1783* (1890) and *The Influence of Sea Power upon the French Revolution and Empire, 1793–1812*, 2 vols. (1892).

Maharajpur / Maharajpore / Maharajpoor, Battle of (29 December 1843), Gwalior Campaign. British General Sir Hugh Gough [q.v.] with 14,000 men and 40 guns defeated the Maratha army of Gwalior, 16,000 men with 100 guns, at this village 11 miles northeast of Chhatarpur. This was one of the two battles of the Gwalior Campaign [q.v.], both fought on the same day; the second was the Battle of Punniar [q.v.], fought and won by General Charles Grey (1780?–1856).

General Gough, who had not anticipated a hard campaign, had invited a party of ladies to accompany him, including his wife and daughter; the wife of his commissary general, Lady Ellenborough (wife of the governor-general of India); and the beautiful Spanish wife of Sir Harry Smith [q.v.]. The ladies had an exciting day. Their elephants, frightened by an exploding powder magazine, ran away with them; the Maratha infantry shot at them; and just as they were about to calm themselves with tea served in a captured tent, a battery of artillery concealed in a field of millet opened fire on them. In his afteraction report Gough wrote: "I thought I should have a mob without a leader, with the heads at variance. I found a well-disciplined, well-organized army, well-led and truly gallant."

The British lost 787 killed and wounded. The Marathas lost some 3,000 and 56 guns.

Mahdi, El. See Muhammad Ahmed.

Mahdists. See Dervishes.

Mahdiya (1885–98). The period in the Sudan that began after the British and Egyptians had been driven out by the Dervishes [q.v.] and the Sudan became the only African state ever to free itself from European rule solely by its own arms and valor. It lasted until Anglo-Egyptian forces led by Horatio Kitchener [q.v.] reconquered the country and established the Anglo-Egyptian Condominium [see Sudan, Reconquest of the]. Although the era was named after El Mahdi [see Muhammad Ahmed], it was, for most of its duration, presided over by his successor, the khalifa Abdullahi [see Abd Allahi Muhammad Turshain], who turned the state into a military dictatorship [see Abyssinian-Sudanese Conflict].

Maherero (d. 1890). Chief of the Herero tribe in Southwest Africa (Namibia) who, in the Herero-Namas Wars [q.v.], freed his people from the rule of the Namas.

Mahidpur / Mehidpur, Battle of (21 December 1817), Third Maratha War. General Thomas Hyslop with 5,500 men defeated a Maratha force of 30,000 horse, 5,000 infantry, and 100 guns near this town on the Sipra River, 22 miles north-northwest of Ujain, in present-day west-central Madhya Bharat. The British lost 778; the Marathas an estimated 3,000.

Mahmadou Lamine. See Lamine, Mahmadou.

Mahmud Shevket Pasha (1855– or 1858–1913). A Turkish general born in Baghdad who in 1909 deposed Sultan Abdul-Hamid II (1842–1918).

Mahon, Bryan Thomas (1862–1930). An Irish-born British soldier who served in the Second Anglo-Boer War as a major general and distinguished himself by leading a column of cavalry to the relief of besieged Mafeking [see Mafeking, Siege of]. He also served in the First World War. Although Mahon became a lieutenant general and had a distinguished career as a statesman, he was always known as the man who relieved Mafeking.

Mahon, Charles James Patrick (1800–1891), known as The O'Gorman Mahone. An Irish politician, adventurer, and soldier. His father was an Irish revolutionary, and his mother was a daughter of one James O'Gorman. In 1819 he matriculated at Trinity College, Dublin, and was graduated with a Master of Arts degree in 1826. In 1821 he was a justice of the peace, and on 17 August 1830 he was elected a member of Parliament, in which he was unseated after a charge of bribery. He became a captain of militia and was called to the Dublin bar but never practiced. From 1835 to 1846 he traveled over Europe and to parts of Africa and South America. In about 1853 he again set out on foreign travels. He was an intimate of Talleyrand (1754–1838) in Paris and a favorite at the French court; the tsar commissioned him a lieutenant in his guards, and he hunted bears in Finland with the tsarevich; he served in the Turkish and Austrian armies; he traveled to China and fought the Tatars; he became a general in a civil war in Uruguay, commanded a Chilean fleet, and was a colonel in the Brazilian army; and he served in the Union army during the American Civil War. In 1866 he obtained a colonelcy in a regiment of French chasseurs. In 1871 he returned to Ireland and took part in the Home Rule Conference of 1873. In 1887 he was in Berlin, where he became intimate with Otto von Bismarck (1815–1898) and the crown prince. He was elected a member of Parliament for County Clare in 1879 and reelected the following year; he served until 1885, and he was again elected in 1887. He served until his death in Chelsea, London, on 15 June 1891. In his lifetime he fought thirteen duels, the results of which are unknown, but his dueling pistol bore two notches.

If most of The O'Gorman's military career and social life strain one's credulity, the story is told, one presumes as gospel, by Frederic William Whyte in the magisterial *Dictionary of National Biography*, in which The O'Gorman is described as "one of the last of the old race of dare-devil Irish gentlemen."

Mahone, William ("Little Billy") (1826–1895). An American soldier who was graduated from the Virginia Military Institute in 1847, then taught at the Rappahannock Military Academy while he studied engineering. When the American Civil War broke out, he was superintendent of the Norfolk & Petersburg Railroad, a position he left to join the Confederate army as colonel of the 6th Virginia, which he led in the capture of the Norfolk Navy Yard. On 16 November 1861 he was promoted brigadier general. Except when recuperating from a wound suffered at Second Bull Run [q.v.], he took part in all the battles of the Army of Northern Virginia [q.v.] from Seven Pines until the war's end. He fought at Fredericksburg, Chancellorsville, Gettysburg, the Wilderness, and Spotsylvania [qq.v.]. His brigade is said to have been "the most renowned shock troops of the army." On 30 July 1864 he was promoted major general for his performance at the Petersburg crater [q.v.]. After the war he became a railroad president and then a U.S. senator.

Mahout. The driver and caretaker of a working elephant.

Mahsud Expedition (April–May 1860). In February 1860 the Mahsuds made a daring raid on Tank, 40 miles west of Dera Ismail Khan, on India's Northwest Frontier (today Pakistan). In early April the British responded by assembling at Tank under General Neville Chamberlain [q.v.] a force of 5,000 men that included eleven battalions of native infantry, three regiments of cavalry, and four batteries of artillery. On 17 April this force entered Mahsud territory. On 23 April Chamberlain's camp was attacked. Although he repelled the attack, he lost 63 killed and 166 wounded, as well as a large number of animals.

On 4 May Chamberlain attacked the Mahsuds in strongly held positions guarding the Berara Pass, which had never been forced. He succeeded in forcing it but sustained casualties of several hundred men. Entering Mahsud country, the expedition burned villages and crops, cut down fruit trees, and finally levied fines the tribesmen were forced to pay by yielding up their firearms.

Maida, Battle of (6 July 1806), Calabrian War. When Napoleon deposed the king of Naples and put his elder brother on the throne, Britain sent an expeditionary force of 5,400 men with ten 4-pounder mountain guns, four 6-pounders, and two howitzers under General John Stuart [q.v.], the British commander of troops in Sicily, to Calabria in southern Italy. It was reinforced by 200 Calabrian peasants, to whom the British gave arms. A French force of 6,440 with only four mountain guns under General Jean Reynier [q.v.], sent to oppose it, was attacked by the British near this village 7 miles inland from the Gulf of Santa Euphemia (Eufemia) and 12 miles southwest of Catanzaro.

The French attacked in column, and the British in line were able to pour a devastating fire on the advancing French, who were unable to respond adequately. The French columns broke and were routed by a fierce bayonet attack, but the British lacked cavalry to pursue. Reynier was disgusted by the poor performance of his veteran troops and in his after-action report complained: "My soldiers lacked the vigor for which I had hoped from soldiers of such established reputations."

French losses were at least 500 dead and more than 1,100 taken prisoner; British losses were 45 killed and 282 wounded. [See Calabrian War; Naples, Anglo-Russian Expedition to.]

Maidan, Battle of (14 September 1842), First Afghan War. A British force under General William Nott [q.v.] attacked 12,000 Afghans on heights commanding the route to Kabul, Nott's destination, and drove them off.

Maiden. A fortress that has never been captured.

Maid of Saragossa. See Saragossa, Maid of.

Mailed Fist. An expression of brute force, probably from the German *gepanzerte Faust*. The term was used by Kaiser William II (1848–1918) in 1897, when he advised the showing of a mailed fist to those who questioned Germany's right to protect its interests in the Far East.

Main Work. In fortifications, the principal defensive work, as opposed to the outworks.

Maipo / Maipú, Battle of. See Maypo, Battle of.

Maison. The French word for house. In the French army, the official household or personal staff of a general officer. Napoleon's *maison* consisted of his personal staff, aides-de-camp, the governor of pages, and several general officers.

Maison, Nicolas Joseph (1771–1840). A French soldier who served in the French Revolutionary army of 1792 and under Napoleon. In August 1812 he was promoted general of division. He did not rally to Napoleon during the Hundred Days [q.v.], and in 1817 he was created a marquis. In 1828 he commanded a French expedition to the Peloponnesus (Morea) and was made a marshal of France. He served in several diplomatic posts and was minister of war in 1835–36.

Maitland, Perigrin (1777–1854). An English soldier who was appointed an ensign in the 1st Foot Guards (Grenadier Guards) on 25 June 1792. He served in Flanders in 1798, in the failed descent upon Ostend in the same year, and in Spain during the Peninsular War [q.v.]. In 1814 he was promoted major general. He commanded the Brigade of Guards at Quatre Bras and Waterloo [qq.v.]. From 1818 to 1828 he was lieutenant governor of Upper Canada. He was commander-in-chief of the Madras army from 11 October 1836 to Christmas 1838, when he resigned because the Honourable East India Company failed to enforce the order exempting Christians from compulsory attendance at Hindu and Muslim religious festivals.

From 18 March 1844 to 27 January 1847 he was commander-in-chief and governor of Cape Colony in South Africa. He was promoted general in 1846.

Maître d'Armes. A fencing master. Nearly every regiment of the metropolitan French army had one. [See Master of the Sword.]

Maiwand, Battle of (27 July 1880), Second Afghan War. At this place, 33 miles west of Kandahar and 10 miles northeast of Kushk-i-Naklud, an Afghan force of 20,000 under Ayub Khan [q.v.] defeated a British force of 2,565 men with six guns under Brigadier General George Reynolds Scott Burrows (1822?–1899). British losses were 962 killed and 161 wounded, 44 percent of the strength. Also lost were 1,676 camels and more than 1,000 horses, donkeys, bullocks, and other animals. Afghan losses are unknown.

It was in this battle that about 100 men of the 66th Foot, who had been valiantly fighting a rearguard action, found themselves in a small enclosure surrounded by the entire Afghan army. None survived.

Maiwand was one of the few pitched battles won by Asians over an army commanded by Europeans. (It was in this battle that Sherlock Holmes's companion Dr. Watson was said to have been wounded.)

Major. A rank in many armies (Italian: *maggiore;* Spanish: *mayor*) between a captain and a lieutenant colonel. In the American army this is the lowest-ranking field officer. In the French army major was never a rank but a function of an officer in charge of administration; sometimes used to indicate the head or the best of something.

Majuba, Battle of (27 February 1881), First Anglo-Boer War. During the night of 26–27 February a British force of 647 soldiers and sailors under General George Colley [q.v.] climbed to the top of Majuba (Amajuba) Hill, a height in northwest Natal, 75 miles north of Ladysmith, which overlooked a Boer laager of General Petrus Joubert [q.v.], and unfurled its colors. (This was the last occasion in which British colours were carried uncased into battle.) Colley felt completely secure and failed to take precautions, but the Boers, instead of retreating, climbed the height, surprised the British, and drove them off with slight loss to themselves. British losses were 223 killed and wounded, including General Colley, who was killed, and 50 taken prisoner. Soon after, the British concluded a peace signed by Colonel (later Field Marshal) Evelyn Wood [q.v.].

Majuba *British rout at the Battle of Majuba Hill, February 1881*

The psychological effect of the battle was far-reaching. Ian Hamilton [q.v.], who was badly wounded in the hand in the battle, described it as "a sort of Bunker Hill in Afrikander history." In South Africa its anniversary was celebrated each year as Majuba Day until 1900, during the Second Anglo-Boer War, when the Boers surrendered after the Battle of Paardeberg [q.v.] on the same date.

Makhwanpur, Battle of (27 February 1816), Nepalese War. Major General Sir David Ochterlony [q.v.], who had marched on the Nepalese capital of Katmandu with 20,000 men and one gun, was attacked by an estimated 2,000 Gurkhas [q.v.] at this village, his most advanced outpost, where he had 2,000 men and the gun. The British were hard pressed until reinforcements arrived and the Gurkhas were driven off. British losses were 220, and Gurkha losses were estimated at twice that. This was the last battle of the war.

Malakand, Battle of (3 April 1895), Chitral Campaign. An Anglo-Indian army of 15,000 under Sir Robert Cunliffe Low (1838–1911), marching to the relief of besieged Chitral [q.v.], a fort on the southern slope of the Hindu Kush, found its path blocked at the Malakand Pass in southern Swat, 40 miles north-northeast of Peshawar, by 12,000 Pathans [q.v.] entrenched on some heights. Low stormed their positions and drove them off. British losses were 8 officers and 61 other ranks killed and wounded. The Pathans were said to have lost about 500.

Malakand Campaign (1897–98). In 1895, after the Battle of the Malakand [q.v.], during the campaign for the relief of Chitral [q.v.], the British built a fortified camp in the Malakand Pass on the Northwest Frontier of India (now in Pakistan) to guard the route to Chitral. In 1897 it was unsuccessfully attacked by Pathan [q.v.] tribesmen from Swat. About 700 tribesmen were killed in the action. Another 2,000 fell at an adjacent post at Chakdara. Tribal unrest spread until British military force under General Binden Blood [q.v.] succeeded in suppressing what had grown into massive uprisings. Lieutenant Winston Churchill [q.v.] wrote a book about this campaign, *The Story of the Malakand Field Forces* (1898).

Malakoff, Attacks on (17–18 June and 8 September 1855), Crimean War. The Malakoff, standing on a hill in southeast Sevastopol [q.v], was the city's chief fort, and the key to its defenses. On 17–18 June 1855, after a three-day bombardment, the French and British launched a combined assault, which was repulsed with heavy loss by the Russian garrison.

After closely observing the Malakoff for several days, French General Aimable Pélissier [q.v.] confirmed that Russian forces were relieved at the same time each day and that for a few minutes their defenses were unmanned. To exploit this period of vulnerability, he placed his forlorn hope [q.v.] as close to the fort as he dared with orders to rush forward at the crucial moment. The work was captured in a matter of minutes. The storming party was immediately reinforced by 30,000, and the fort secured before the Russians could mount a counterattack. By nightfall it was in French hands. This was the most perfectly planned operation of the war, and it is believed to be the first time in history that an assault was governed by a synchronization of watches.

The French lost 3,338 killed and wounded. Among the wounded was Sergeant Muhammad Ouled al-Haj Kadour, who lost both arms in the attack and was awarded the Legion of Honor [q.v.], the first Algerian tirailleur to be so honored. General Pélissier was created the Duc de Malakoff.

A British attack on the redan [q.v.] that same day failed.

Malaria. See Quinine.

Malegnano, Battle of (8 June 1859), Second War of Italian Independence. Near this commune, 10 miles southeast of Milan, three French divisions under Marshal Baraguay d'Hilliers [q.v.] in three hours of heavy fighting defeated an Austrian force of about equal strength. The Austrians lost heavily, including 1,000 taken prisoner; the French lost 850 killed and wounded.

Malet, Claude François de (1754–1812). A French soldier who rose to the rank of general, even though he was known to have been in and out of prisons and insane asylums. On 23 October 1812 he announced that Napoleon had died in Russia [see Russian Campaign, Napoleon's] and proclaimed the formation of a provisional republican government. A large number of officers believed his story and were prepared to follow his lead until he shot and killed the military governor of Paris, who had challenged him for proof. He was arrested, tried, and, with 14 accomplices, was shot on 29 October.

Malingerer. A soldier who avoids or attempts to avoid duty in a disreputable manner, often by feigning illness.

Malleson, George Bruce (1825–1898). A British officer and military writer who on 11 June 1842 was given a direct commission as an ensign in the Bengal Army and posted to the 66th Bengal Native Infantry. He first saw action in the Second Anglo-Burmese War [q.v.]. While still a lieutenant, he wrote *The Mutiny of the Bengal Army*, known as the Red Pamphlet, predicting that the poor administration of the Bengal army and the annexation of the province of Oudh could lead to a mutiny. It was published anonymously in 1857, just before the outbreak of the Indian Mutiny [q.v.]. In 1869 he was appointed guardian of the young maharajah of Mysore, a post he held until 1877, when he retired as a colonel. He completed and edited *The History of the Indian Mutiny*, 6 vols. (1878–80), which had been begun by Sir John William Kaye (1814–1876).

Maloyaroslavets, Battle of (24 October 1812), Napoleon's Russian Campaign. Napoleon evacuated Moscow on 19 October 1812 and marched southwest toward Kaluga, preceded by 15,000 French under General Eugène Beauharnais [q.v.]. At this village, 35 miles north-northeast of Kaluga and 60 miles southwest of Moscow, a Russian force of 20,000 under Field Marshal Prince Mikhail Kutuzov [q.v.] tried to cut off Beauharnais. Five roads converged here at a bridge over the Lutsa River, and during a day of bitter fighting in which both sides were reinforced, the village and the bridge changed hands seven times. With difficulty the Russians were driven back. French losses were 5,000 to the Russians' 6,000. Although tactically the French won, the Russians gained strategically, for the victory multiplied the problems of the French retreat. Napoleon changed direction and moved northwest through Smolensk, a more difficult route, which he had hoped to avoid.

Napoleon, who spent the night at Gorodnya, only five miles north of Maloyaroslavets, narrowly escaped capture by Cossacks.

Malta Militia. In May 1852 the governor of Malta introduced the formation of a local militia of male Maltese volunteers sixteen to thirty years old. Eighteen drills were held a year, and the words of command were in English. However, because there was no pay, the force dwindled and died in 1857.

Malta Mutiny (4–12 April 1807). A locally raised force of mostly Corsicans and Greeks launched a mutiny that ended when the mutineers inadvertently blew themselves up by setting fire to a magazine containing more than four hundred barrels of gunpowder.

Malvern Hill, Battle of (1 July 1862), American Civil War. The final battle of the Seven Days' Battles [q.v.]. After failing at White Oak Swamp [q.v.] to strike the retreating army of Union General George B. McClellan [q.v.], General Robert E. Lee tried again at Malvern Hill near the James River southeast of Richmond, where the Union forces were in an exceptionally strong position with well-placed artillery. Although the Confederate command was confused and there

was much bungling, the Union force retreated during the night to Harrison's Landing, where they entrenched. Federal losses were 3,214; Confederate losses were 5,355.

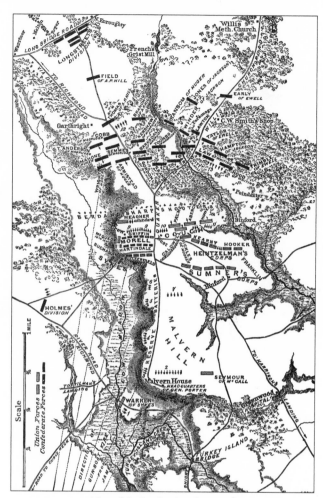

Map of the Battle of Malvern Hill

Mamelukes. Originally Turkish and Circassian slaves who in about 1260 formed the bodyguard of the sultan of Egypt. They soon advanced one of their own corps to the throne, a practice they continued until 1517, when Egypt became a Turkish province. Turkish beys then hired them, and although they filled the corps's ranks with renegades from various foreign countries, the Mameluke chiefs (with the title of beys) maintained their power. When Napoleon conquered Egypt, 24 Mameluke beys, nominally under a Turkish viceroy, were virtual rulers of their own fiefedoms, and even though they lost much of their power after Napoleon's victory in the Battle of the Pyramids on 21 July 1798, they remained formidable. On 21 October 1801 Napoleon, impressed with their fighting qualities, ordered the formation of a squadron of up to 150 Mamelukes, who retained their Eastern dress but were commanded by French officers. The formation was disbanded in 1814.

With the downfall of the French in Egypt the Mamelukes with some help from the Arnauts [q.v.] reclaimed their power in Egypt. On 1 March 1811 all the Mameluke notables—24 beys, 60 *kalifs* (lieutenants), and 400 of lesser rank—were invited by Mehemet Ali [q.v.], the Turkish pasha, to come to the citadel in Cairo for a ceremony in which Mehemet's favorite son, Tuson, was to be given a special pelisse and the command of the army that was soon to set forth to fight the Wahhabis [see Arabian Wars]. Bringing with them their retinues, all but one of the beys assembled. At Mehemet Ali's orders they were led into a narrow street and set upon. No quarter was given. Only one of the 485 Mamelukes escaped; he fled by leaping his horse over a wall onto rocks sixty feet below. Orders were sent to governors of provinces throughout Egypt, and a general slaughter of the Mamelukes ensued. Some managed to flee to Nubia, where in 1812 Ibrahim Pasha, Mehemet Ali's eldest son, successfully campaigned against them.

Mamelukes *A Mameluke bey mounted on an Arab stallion. Drawing by Carle Vernet*

Mamooty. In India, a digging tool shaped like a hoe with the shaft at an acute angle from the blade. Also spelled mamoty, momatty, and other variations.

Man. 1. As a noun, an enlisted or conscripted soldier, not an officer.
2. As a verb, to have enough men effectively to operate, as in to man a gun.

Manassas, Battles of. See Bull Run, Battles of.

Mandarin. In Chinese, *kwan.* One of nine grades of high public officials or officers. Each grade was distinguished by a different colored ball or button on top of round brimless hats, by particular embroidery on their jackets, and by distinctive clasps on their girdles. Military mandarins also commanded provincial armies and militia. The term was applied by foreigners to any Chinese senior officer.

Mandingo-French Wars. See Franco-Mandingo Wars.

Mandora, Battle of (13 March 1801), Napoleonic Wars. A British expeditionary force under Sir Ralph Abercromby [q.v.], dispatched to drive the French out of Egypt, debarked at Marmarica Bay under heavy fire on 8 March 1801. On the 13th Abercromby began a march on Alexandria in three columns, and on the same day near the village of Mandora he was attacked by the French under Napoleon. The British routed the attackers at a cost of 6 officers and 153 other ranks killed and 66 officers and 1,936 other ranks wounded; French losses are unknown but were believed to be heavy. [See Abukir, Battle of.]

Mandrel. A mold used in making cartridge cases. (The same word is used today for the inner configuration of the solid propellants used in rocket motors.)

Maneuver. British: manœuvre. 1. A movement of men and weapons from an established position to a different location with respect to the enemy in the hope of gaining an advantage, often aiming at an enemy's flanks or line of communication. Colonel Charles Ardant du Picq [q.v.] wrote: "Maneuvers are threats; he who appears most threatening wins" (*Battle Studies* [1880]).
2. A tactical exercise carried out in time of peace in imitation of a wartime situation.
3. A principle of war that emphasizes the importance of locating forces for optimum results on a field of battle.

Maney, James Allison (1855–1920). An American soldier, the son of a Confederate general, who was graduated from West Point in 1877 and assigned to the 15th Infantry at Fort Bayard, New Mexico. While still a second lieutenant, he played a major role in the Victorio War [q.v.]. On 23 September 1885 he was promoted first lieutenant. On 30 October 1893, while still a first lieutenant, he quarreled with and killed Swedish-born Captain Alfred Hedberg (1844?–1893). For this he was court-martialed but was found not guilty. He was finally promoted captain in 1897, took part in the Boxer Rebellion [q.v.] in China in 1900, and retired as a colonel in 1911.

Mangas Coloradas (1795?–1863). An Apache chief, known as Red Sleeves, who was generally credited as being the most intelligent and most talented Apache in the nineteenth century. About 1837, through his personal qualities and exceptional abilities, he became the leader of the Eastern Chiricahua Apaches. He led his warriors on widespread and devastating raids upon Mexican ranches and villages. With the discovery of gold in the Pinos Altos area, just north of present-day Silver City, New Mexico, in the heart of his territory, white miners and his warriors were soon in a conflict in which the miners came off second best. He took a leading part in the Battle of Apache Pass [q.v.] on 14 July 1852. Soon after, he was seriously wounded in a skirmish with a white soldier. His followers carried him to a Mexican doctor whom they threatened with death if he died.

In 1863 he was finally captured by soldiers and, it seems, goaded into trying to escape. He was killed in the attempt.

Mangus (1846–1901). A son of Mangas Coloradas [q.v.] who became leader of the Mimbres Apaches. For a time he fought at the side of Victorio and with Geronimo [qq.v.]. He surrendered in 1886 and was eventually settled at Fort Sill, Oklahoma. He married a daughter of Victorio, and his son enlisted in the 12th Infantry as a scout.

Manifest Destiny. A reference to a statement attributed to Andrew Jackson [q.v.] declaring that the United States was "a country manifestly called by the Almighty to a destiny which Greece and Rome . . . might have envied."

Maniglions. The two handles on the back of the barrel of an artillery piece.

Manila, Battle of (9–13 August 1898), Spanish-American War. On 9 August 1898 American Major General Wesley Merritt [q.v.], with 10,700 regulars and about the same number of irregular Philippine forces under Emilio Aguinaldo [q.v.], launched an attack upon 13,000 Spanish troops under General Fermín Jáudenes near Manila in the Philippines. On 13 August the city itself was assaulted and was taken after only token resistance.

Manin, Daniele. (1804–1857). A Venetian lawyer and patriot who was the leader of the Venetian Revolution against Austrian rule in 1848. When Austrians were forced to leave the city on 26 March, he became president of a short-lived Venetian Republic and quickly organized a defense force and instituted a provisional government. In August the Venetians moved to ally themselves with Piedmont, but after the defeats of the Piedmontese in Lombardy by the Austrians, they were abandoned. When Carlo Alberto [q.v.] of Piedmont was defeated by Austrians at Novara [q.v.] on 23 March 1849, the Venetian Assembly voted "Resistance at all costs!" and Manin was granted unlimited powers. But as Austrian forces closed in on the city, food became scarce. On 19 June a powder magazine exploded. In July cholera broke out. Austrian batteries shelled the city, and when the Sardinian fleet left the Adriatic, Venice was bombarded by sea as well. On 24 August Manin negotiated a treaty in which the Austrians promised amnesty to all Venetians except him. On 27 August he left for France. His wife died at Marseilles, and he arrived in Paris broken in health and nearly destitute. There he became a leader of the Italian exiles. He died on 22 September 1857. In 1868, two years after the Austrians had departed, his remains were returned to Venice and accorded a public funeral.

Manipur, Rebellion in (1891). This small state in northeastern India southeast of Assam was a quasi-independent British protectorate ruled from 1834 by Chandra Kirti Singh (1832–1866). On his death his sons and other relatives formed numerous parties, each contending for the throne. In the midst of general unrest, on 24 March 1891 the British political agent and other resident British officials were murdered, and the residency in Manipur was attacked.

The small surviving band of loyal sepoys was led to safety in India by Ethel St. Clair Grimwood, the wife of the slain political Resident. The British sent troops into the country and, after several encounters with the 3,000-man Manipuri army, finally restored order. The offending princes were hanged or transported to the Andaman Islands [q.v.]. Mrs. Grimwood was awarded the Royal Red Cross.

Manitoba, Fenian Attack upon (12 October 1871). A planned attack by Irish Fenians [q.v.] on Manitoba, Canada, from the United States that was easily aborted by American troops.

Mannlicher, Ferdinand von (1848–1904). An Austrian engineer who first became interested in firearms after seeing the displays of them at the world exposition in Philadelphia in 1876. Associated with the Steyr Waffenfabrik [q.v.] in Austria, he became a prolific inventor, who developed a repeater rifle and a self-loading pistol. In 1885 he patented a short-recoil rifle capable of automatic fire. Other automatic rifles were developed in 1894, 1895, and 1900. Between 1876 and his death he designed more than 150 weapons. [See Mannlicher Automatic Pistol; Mannlicher Carbine; Mannlicher Rifle.]

Mannlicher Automatic Pistol. The Mannlicher 7.63 automatic pistol Model 1900 was manufactured by the Steyr Waffenfabrik [q.v.] in Austria. It weighed 29 ounces, had an overall length of eight and three-quarter inches, and featured a magazine with an eight-round capacity. This pistol and the

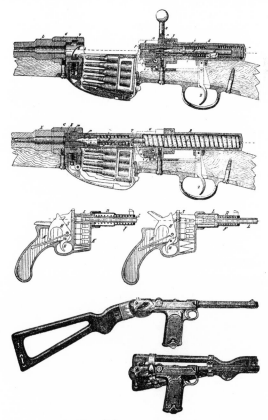

Mannlicher automatic pistols

Spanish imitations of it required a 7.63 mm cartridge with a straight side case. [See Mannlicher, Ferdinand von.]

Mannlicher Carbine. The Mannlicher 8 mm carbine Model 1890 was the first weapon featuring a straight-pull rotating bolt to enter the Austrian army. It weighed 6.9 pounds, and its overall length was 39.5 inches. A magazine carried five rounds. It was manufactured by the Steyr Waffenfabrik in Austria. [See Mannlicher, Ferdinand von; Steyr.]

Mannlicher Rifle. A bolt-action 11 mm automatic rifle designed by Ferdinand von Mannlicher [q.v.] in 1884 and patented and adopted by the Austrian army the following year.

Man on Horseback. A military dictator to whom people turn in the hope of obtaining honest and efficient government. The expression was first used in 1860 by Caleb Cushing (1800–1878) in a speech warning that the American Civil War might end with a man on horseback, such as Napoleon, in power. The term was applied to Ulysses S. Grant during the 1868 presidential campaign.

Mansfield, Joseph King Fenno (1803–1862). An American soldier who was graduated from West Point in 1822 and commissioned in the Corps of Engineers. At the outbreak of the Mexican War [q.v.] in April 1846 he was a captain and chief engineer on the staff of Zachary Taylor [q.v.]. He built Fort Brown (today Brownsville, Texas) opposite Matamoros and was brevetted major for his role in the defense of that place on 3–9 May 1846. He earned two more brevets for his conduct in the battles of Monterrey on 20–24 September and Buena Vista on 22–23 February 1847 [qq.v.]. During the American Civil War he built the forts that surrounded Washington, D.C., and in May 1862 took part in the occupation of Norfolk and Suffolk, Virginia. He was promoted major general of volunteers and in July was given command of XII Corps. He was killed in the Battle of Antietam [q.v.] on 17 September 1862.

Mansilla, Battle of (30 December 1808), Peninsular War. At the town of Mansilla de la Mulas in León Province, northwest Spain, Spanish General Pedro La Romaña [q.v.] with 3,000 men encountered and was defeated by a French force under Marshal Nicolas Soult [q.v.].

Man Stoppers. See Dum-Dum Bullets.

Manta. A waterproof canvas used as a pack cover, usually five feet square.

Mantatisi (d. 1830). A South African chieftainess of the Batlokua who possessed great military abilities. She organized a large horde of warriors, who, in her honor, called themselves Mantaties. Her army so preyed upon her neighbors that she was responsible for depopulating most of what is today the Transvaal and Orange Free State.

Manteuffel, Edwin Hans Karl (1809–1885). A Prussian soldier who in 1827 entered the Guards Cavalry in Berlin. In 1853 he was a colonel in command of the 5th Uhlans, and four years later he was promoted major general (equivalent to American and British brigadier general). He served in the

Schleswig-Holstein War of 1864 and the Seven Weeks' War of 1866 [qq.v.], in which he commanded a division and forced the Hanoverians to capitulate. For this he was awarded the order *Pour le mérite* [q.v.].

When a liberal official named Carl Twestern accused him of helping to create "an atmosphere of distrust and hostility between the army and civil society," Manteuffel challenged him to a duel and shot him in the arm. He then demanded that he himself be punished, so he was given a mild detention in a fortress at Magdeburg. He was returned to duty when the king complained to General Albrecht Roon: "To have him hounded out of my presence by the triumph of democracy . . . there are things that can rob me of my senses."

In the Franco-Prussian War [q.v.] of 1870–71 he led first I Corps and then the First Army. In January 1871 he commanded the newly formed Army of the South, which he led through the Côte d'Or and over the plateau of Langres to cut off the 80,000-man army of French General Charles Bourbaki [q.v.], which was forced to cross the frontier into Switzerland and internment. In 1871–73 he led the Prussian army of occupation in France, a difficult assignment for which he was rewarded by being created a field marshal and endowed with a large sum of money. In 1879 he was an unpopular governor of Alsace-Lorraine.

Mantlet. 1. A wooden screen, sometimes on wheels, used to protect diggers at the head of a sap.

2. A covering for embrasures or portholes to protect gunners between shots.

3. A shield to protect snipers.

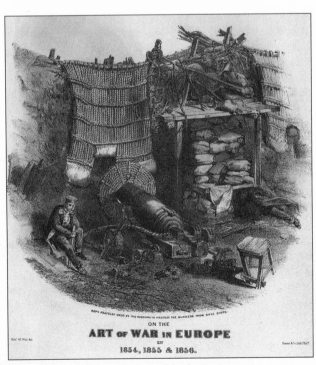

Mantlet *Rope mantlet used by the Russians to protect the gunners from rifle shots, 1854–56*

Manton, Joseph (1766?–1835). An English gunmaker in London who patented improvements in guns. He was instrumental in the introduction of the percussion system.

Mantonets. Pegs of wood or iron in French soldiers' quarters for hanging clothes or accoutrements.

Manual. A military reference book.

Manual for Courts-Martial. A manual, first published in 1895, that described the proper procedures for conducting courts-martial. It was written for the U.S. army by Lieutenant (later Major General) Arthur Murray (1850?–1925), an artillery officer.

Manual of Arms. The prescribed handling of a weapon, usually a musket or a rifle, in drill or for a ceremony.

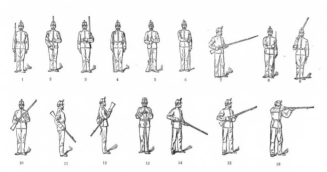

Manual of arms (sixteen figures), United States infantry: The positions are: 1. the shoulder, 2. the present, 3. the support, 4. the order, 5. stand at ease, 6. fix Bayonet, 7. charge Bayonet, 8. unfix Bayonet, 9. the Slope, 10. the port, 11. the secure, 12. reverse arms, 13. rest on your arms reversed, 14. ready, 15. prime, 16. aim.

Manuelito (1819?–1893). A Navajo chief who, as a young man, took part in the defeat of Mexican and Pueblo forces at Washington Pass in northwestern New Mexico in 1835. When, after years of hostility between Navajos and whites, the Indians were forced to move to the Bosque Redondo Reservation on the Pecos River, Manuelito refused to go. On 30 April 1860, in a rare instance of Indians' attacking a military post, he led an assault of 1,000 Navajos on Fort Defiance, at the mouth of Cañon Bonito on the west side of Black Creek, 35 miles northwest of Gallup. The Indians were driven off after killing 1 white and wounding 2 for a loss of 12 Navajos killed. In 1866 Manuelito and some 50 of his followers surrendered and were put in a reservation. From 1870 to 1884 he was head chief. He also served from 1872 as commander of the native police force. In 1876 he visited President Grant in Washington, D.C.

Maori Wars. Wars between the British in New Zealand and the native Maoris. All the conflicts involved disputes over land.

First Maori War (1843–47). Sometimes called the Bay of Islands War, it may be said to have begun when Europeans in New Zealand broke the Treaty of Waitangi, by which the Maoris retained possession of their land. Maoris' wrath burst out on 17 June 1843 in the Wairau Massacre, which left 23 whites dead. In July 1844 Hone Heke (fl.1840s), a Maori chief who ruled in the northern Bay of Islands off North Island, attacked Russell, a small white settlement established in 1829 as a whaling port 115 miles north-northwest of Auckland. This first attack accomplished only the destruction of the British flagstaff, but in March of the following year Heke led his followers on a raid that sacked the town. The efforts of colonial forces to suppress him failed, and aided by other chiefs, he proceeded to attack other towns farther north.

In mid-1845 Sir George Grey (1812–1898), the new governor-general, took personal charge of the troops, and a year later he brought a peace to New Zealand that lasted until 1860.

Second Maori War (1863–70), also called the Taranaki Wars. A Maori subchief, without the authority of his tribe, sold land on North Island to Europeans who were repulsed when they tried to claim the land. The British called up troops and set about attacking Maori pas (forts). Major General

Maori Wars *Maori Chief Tamati Waka Nene signs the Treaty of Waitangi, 6 February 1840*

Duncan Alexander Cameron (1808–1888), commanding a force of just under 4,000 men, defeated the Maoris on 4 January 1863 on the Katikara River. On 12 July Cameron crossed the Maungatawhira River, and on 29 October he occupied Meri-Meri (Meremere). In the same year Sir George Grey built a military road into the Waikato River area on North Island, which was coveted by European settlers. On 29 November 1863 Cameron defeated a Maori force at Rangaria (Rangiriri), but on 29 April 1864 he was repulsed with considerable loss at Gate Pa [q.v.]. In January 1865 he refused to attack Weroroa Pa, considering it too strong, and Grey himself took command. The pa was reduced in three days. Cameron returned to England, British troops were gradually withdrawn, and from 1865 the war was fought with locally raised forces.

A truce was arranged that allowed the Maoris to keep the land still in their possession, but small actions and skirmishing continued. The situation has been compared with the Indian wars on the plains in the American West.

· The Maoris resorted to guerrilla tactics, and a religious-military cult, called Ringatu, sprang up, but by 1872 the Europeans held most of the land they wanted and some 50,000 Maoris, about 54 percent of their population, had died. It became evident to them that they had no hope of preserving their land and their culture. Not until the twentieth century did they begin to recover their population and some prosperity.

This and the Franco-Prussian War were the only wars in the nineteenth century in which more soldiers were killed by enemy weapons than by disease. This does not reflect the deadliness of the weapons used, but it is testimony to the healthful climate of New Zealand. British soldiers fighting there had a better chance of staying alive than those stationed in Britain, whose death rate from 1830 to 1836 was 15.3 per 100,000. While exact comparisons cannot be made, the death rate among soldiers fighting in New Zealand from 1846 to 1855 was 8.55 per 100,000.

Map. A representation, usually on paper, of a portion of the earth's surface, usually including both natural and artificial features and, where possible, drawn to scale. Good military maps were a rarity in the nineteenth century.

Maqoma / Makoma (1798–1873). The second son of Ngqika [q.v.], chief of the amaRarabe Xhosas in South Africa, and an older brother of Sandile [q.v.]. In November 1818 he led a Xhosa army against Ndlambe (d. 1828), a rival for the chieftainship, whom he defeated in the Battle of amaLinde, in which Ndlambe was mortally wounded. In December 1834 he led an attack upon European settlements in eastern Cape Colony that resulted in much damage and loss of life.

Marabout. 1. A North African religious leader. Marabouts often exerted considerable secular authority and fomented rebellion against French rule.

2. A tomb of a Muslim saint or holy man.

Maratha Wars (1775–82, 1803–05, and 1817–18). A lack of a strong central government during the decay of the Mogul Empire in the seventeenth century encouraged the Marathas (Mahrattas), a warlike and ruthless people, whose principal rulers, united only in a loose confederacy, were members of the Sindhia (Scindia) family. By the early eighteenth century they had extended their empire from Gwalior, about 26,000 square miles, to an area of 900,000 square miles in south-central India. The British waged three wars against the Marathas, four if one counts the Gwalior Campaign [q.v.] of 1843, but since it was over in a day, it was scarcely a war. The First Maratha War was waged from 1775 to 1782.

Second Maratha War (1803–05). By the Treaty of Bassein, signed on 31 December 1802, Baji Rao II (1775–1851), the seventh and last peshwa (ruler), placed himself under the protection of the Honourable East India Company's government. The various rulers in the confederacy of five clans of Marathas and their territories resented British interference and raised an army to oust the Europeans. The largest contingent of the combined Maratha army was supplied by Doulet (Daulet) Rao [q.v.].

The war began on 6 August 1803. Richard Colley Wellesley, the second Earl of Mornington (1760–1842), governor-general of India, deployed two field armies, one under General Gerard Lake [q.v.] in the north and a second under his younger brother, Major General Arthur Wellesley (later Duke of Wellington), in south-central India. Wellesley captured Poona on 20 March 1803 and Ahmadnagar on 11 August. Maratha forces were decisively beaten at Assaye on 23 September and Argaon on 29 November [qq.v.]. General Lake captured Agra, won the Battle of Aligarth [q.v.] on 4 September, captured Delhi on 16 September, and won the Battle of Laswari [q.v.] on 1 November.

On 17 November 1804 British forces defeated the Marathas at Farrukhabad [q.v.] and then took Indore. In January–April 1805 the British under Lake tried unsuccessfully to take Bhurtpore [q.v.]. Nevertheless, Maratha forces were pursued into the Punjab, and Doulat Rao was forced on 30 December 1805 to sign the Treaty of Sarji Anjangaon, by which he ceded to the British all the land between the Jumma and Ganges rivers.

Third Maratha War (1817–18). The peshwa of the Marathas united with the princes of Nagpur and Indore in waging war against the British, a war sometimes called the Pindari War after the hordes of outlaws and freebooters known as Pindaris [q.v.] who were employed by the princes. Often supported by Maratha chiefs, they carried out widespread depredations throughout central and southern India. In the Northern Circars alone they destroyed 339 villages

Maratha Wars *General Wellesley leads the bayonet charge at the Battle of Assaye.*

and attacked British garrisons. Two British forces totaling 20,000 men took the field against them: the Army of the Deccan, 5,500 men under Sir Thomas Hyslop, and the Grand Army under Lord Francis Rawden-Hastings of Hastings and Moira (1754–1826), the governor-general of Bengal and commander-in-chief, India. The Pindaris were hunted down, and the Marathas defeated decisively in the Battle of Mahidpur (Mehidpur) [q.v.] on the Sipra River in what is today west-central Badhya Bharat on 21 December 1817. The surrender of the peshwa of the Marathas on 2 June 1818 ended the war.

There was a quarrel between the Bengal and Madras armies on the distribution of the spoils of war, which were considerable. [See Deccan Prize.]

Maraud, to. To rove in search of plunder.

Marbot, Jean Baptiste Antoine Marcelin de (1782–1854). A French soldier who rose from the ranks of the 1st Bercheny Hussars. He served as an aide to five different marshals in his career, including General Pierre Augereau [q.v.] at Austerlitz, Jena, and Eylau [qq.v.]; Jean Lannes [q.v.] at Saragossa in the Peninsular War [q.v.]; and André Masséna in the Battle of Wagram [q.v.]. During the Hundred Days [q.v.] Napoleon promoted him general of brigade, and he fought at Waterloo, where he was wounded. Under the July Monarchy he was present at the siege of Antwerp [q.v.]. He was promoted lieutenant general in 1832, and from 1835 to 1840 he took part in several military expeditions in Algeria. In 1845 he was made a peer of France.

His elder brother Antoine Adolphe Marcelin de Marbot (1781–1844) also served in Napoleon's campaigns from 1808 to 1812 and again during the Hundred Days. He returned to the army after 1830.

March. 1. As a noun, the movement of a body of men on foot or on horseback or by other conveyance from one place to another.

2. As a noun, the distance marched over—e.g., a march of twenty miles.

3. As a verb, to cause a man or group to move in a military manner.

4. As a noun, a musical composition in a regularly accented meter that enables troops more easily to march in cadence.

5. As a verb, to walk steadily with a measured stride, sometimes with music.

March, Flank. A march parallel to or oblique to an enemy's position with the purpose of going around or attacking an enemy's flank.

March, Forced. A hard march, usually one exceeding 20 miles in a day. [See March, Route.]

March, Route. An ordinary march of a body of troops usually not exceeding 20 miles in a day. [See March, Forced.]

March, Strategic. A march to a position from which an attack is to be made or to a position from which an attack is expected to be made.

March, Tactical. A march in the immediate vicinity of an enemy, often when the enemy can observe the march. These were usually made without the encumbrance of wagons or camp followers.

Marchand. See Fashoda Incident.

Marchand, Jean Baptiste (1863–1934). A French soldier and African explorer who was commissioned after four years in the ranks. In 1889 he saw active service in Senegal, where he was twice wounded and won the Legion of Honor [q.v.]. He traced the Niger River to its source and explored the region from the Ivory Coast to Tengrela, about 180 miles east of Kankan. His name is best known for his expedition of 1897–98 across Africa from the west coast to the Nile, in which he precipitated a crisis in Anglo-French relations when he planted the French flag at Fashoda (Kodok) on 10 July 1898 [see Fashoda Incident]. From December 1898 to May 1899 he marched through Abyssinia (Ethiopia) to Djibouti. During World War I he rose to command a division and saw much action on the western front.

Marchand, Jean Gabriel (1765–1851). A French soldier who in 1791 became a captain of volunteers and from 1792 to 1799 served in Italy. He became a general of brigade in 1799 and general of division in December 1805. He fought at Jena and Friedland [qq.v.], and in 1808 he was posted to Spain and fought in the Peninsular War [q.v.] under Marshal Michel Ney [q.v.]. In 1812 he took part in Napoleon's Russian Campaign [q.v.], fighting at Smolensk and Borodino [qq.v.]. He remained in service after Napoleon's abdication and was court-martialed but acquitted for having given up Grenoble to Napoleon at the beginning of the Hundred Days. He retired in 1825.

Marchand, Louis Joseph Narcisse (1791–1876). Napoleon's valet. His mother was one of three *berceuses* (cradle rockers) for Napoleon's son. He was twenty when he joined the personal staff, and he remained with Napoleon through his exiles until his death. Napoleon created him *comte* on his deathbed.

Marching Order. Troops are said to be in marching order when they are in the proper uniform and carrying the arms, accoutrements, and kit necessary for a march. In the British army, "service marching order" included some provisions and campaign necessities.

Marching Regiment. A British term for a regiment liable to be sent to another station at any time.

March-Past. A filing by; a parade past a reviewer; a procession.

March to the Sea (15 November–21 December 1864), American Civil War. The march made by a Union army of 55,000 infantry, 5,000 cavalry, and 2,000 artillerymen with 65 guns under General William Tecumseh Sherman [q.v.] through Confederate territory from Atlanta, Georgia, to the Atlantic Ocean.

On 19 October 1864 Sherman wrote to General U. S. Grant: "I propose to abandon Atlanta . . . to sally forth to ruin Georgia and bring up on the seashore." In the process he promised to "make Georgia Howl!" With his plan approved by Grant and Lincoln, he proceeded to destroy the military resources and industrial capabilities of Atlanta [see Atlanta Campaign], and on 15 November 1864, after amassing rations for twenty days, he began his march on Savannah, Georgia, taking with him only 600 wagons and ambulances and 2,500 ammunition wagons. His army was divided into two wings: the right wing, the Union Army of the Tennessee [q.v.] under Major General O. O. Howard [q.v.], and the left wing, later known unofficially as the Army of Georgia [q.v.], under Major General Henry Slocum [q.v.]. The only Confederate force in the field to oppose him numbered some 13,000 troops near Lovejoy, 21 miles south of Atlanta. It could only retreat, fighting a rearguard action with Howard's dismounted cavalry on 16 November.

Major General William Hardee [q.v.], sent by the Confederate high command to take command in Georgia, ordered the strengthening of the defenses of Savannah while small forces tried futilely to slow Sherman's advance. There were skirmishes at Griswoldville, 10 miles east of Macon, on 22 November; at Ball's Ferry on 24–25 November; and at Sandersville on 26 November. On 27–29 November there were cavalry skirmishes in the neighborhood of Waynesboro, and in the first week of December there were almost daily skirmishes. Sherman was not to be stopped. Largely living off the land, his men confiscated or destroyed all property in a 60-mile swath that could be of any possible use to the Confederacy. Although in orders issued on 22 November General Howard threatened to shoot any soldier found burning or robbing private property, there were frequent excesses.

On 10 December Sherman reached Savannah, and on 13 December Fort McAllister was taken in a fifteen-minute assault that began at 4:30 P.M. Sherman now had the support of the Union navy. Hardee evacuated Savannah and withdrew his forces across the Savannah River.

Sherman had completed the most destructive raid in the history of North America. Abandoning his line of communications, he had cut a giant swath through the heartland of the Confederacy, destroying most the South's remaining capacity to wage war at a cost of fewer than 2,200 casualties.

March to the Sound of the Guns. The movement of a force by its commander who, without specific orders and on his own initiative, marches toward a battle in progress. According to Field Marshal Aleksandr Suvorov [q.v.], "The safest way of achieving victory is to seek it among the enemy's battalions." However, as Captain Basil Liddell Hart (1895–1970) pointed out, the drawback to marching to the sound of the guns is that "it may serve to nullify a higher commander's strategical plan" (*Thoughts on War* [1944]).

Marcy, Randolph Barnes (1812–1887). An American soldier who was graduated from West Point in 1832 and spent most of the next fourteen years on the Wisconsin and Michigan frontier. In 1846 he was a captain and served in the Mexican War [q.v.], in which he fought at Palo Alto and Resaca de la Palma [qq.v.]. After the war he served in the American Southwest and took part in the Utah Expedition [q.v.].

Drawing on his experience, he wrote a guidebook on travel in the West, giving details of more than thirty overland trails.

Published by the War Department in 1859 as *The Prairie Traveller*, it became something of a best seller.

In May 1861, at the outbreak of the American Civil War, he became chief of staff to his son-in-law General George B. McClellan [q.v.], and on 28 September he was promoted brigadier general of volunteers. He served most of the war and into the postwar era as inspector general, and from 12 December 1878 with the staff rank of brigadier general. He retired in 1881.

Marcy, William Learned (1786–1857). An American politician who served in the militia in the War of 1812 [q.v.]. He served as a justice of the New York Supreme Court, as a U.S. senator, and as a governor of New York before being named in March 1845 secretary of war. He coined the term "spoils system" in a speech in which he said he could "see nothing wrong in the rule that to the victor belong the spoils." As secretary of war (1845–49) he had a staff consisting of nine clerks, two messengers, and a handyman. The army consisted of eight regiments of infantry, four of artillery, and two of dragoons. All were undermanned. When General Zachary Taylor [q.v.] was sent to the Texas frontier, on the eve of the Mexican War, Congress refused to increase the size of his army, acting only after Taylor was attacked. With the country ill prepared to fight a war on foreign soil, Marcy performed his duties as well as could be expected, and he acted as a buffer between President James Polk (1795–1849) and General Winfield Scott [q.v.]. From 1853 to his death he was secretary of state.

Maréchal. A blacksmith, veterinarian, corporal, or field marshal in the French army. A master farrier carried the grand title of *brigadier maître maréchal ferrant* and ranked as a corporal.

Maréchal de Camp. A rank in the French army equivalent to a brigadier general. The rank was abolished in 1792 and reintroduced in 1814.

Maréchal de France / Maréchal d'Empire. French field marshal. The latter title was that used under the first empire. In the Napoleonic period it was more of a dignity than a rank. The highest substantive rank was general of division, which corresponds to a major general in the American and British services. [See Marshalate.]

Maréchal des Logis. A French noncommissioned officer ranking with a cavalry, artillery, or engineer sergeant.

Marengo, Battle of (14 June 1800), Napoleonic Wars. Napoleon, after assembling on army of 30,000 in Switzerland, made a secret march through the St. Bernard Pass and entered Milan on 2 June, cutting the Austrian line of communication. He then advanced on a broad front and encountered the entire Austrian army under General Michael Friedrich Benedikt von Melas [q.v.], near this village in southeast Piedmont. Melas immediately attacked. The French were saved only by the arrival of troops led by General Louis Charles Desaix (1768–1800), commanding the reserves, who marched to the sound of the guns [q.v.]. The Austrians were driven from the field with a loss of about 9,000. The French lost about 4,000, including General Desaix who was killed in the fighting.

Marengo *Death of French General Louis Charles Desaix at the Battle of Marengo, 14 June 1800*

María, Battle of (15 June 1808), Peninsular War. Near this village 12 miles from Saragossa, a French army of 7,500 infantry and 800 cavalry with 12 guns under General Louis Suchet [q.v.] attacked a Spanish army of 12,000 infantry and 600 cavalry with 16 guns under General Joachim Blake [q.v.]. The battle was a disaster for Blake, who lost 1,000 killed, more than 3,000 wounded, and all but two of his guns; French casualties were about 800.

Mariage à la Mode des Pays. Literally, marriage in the custom of the country. French officers and cadre noncommissioned officers in the Armée d'Afrique [q.v.], when serving away from garrison towns or barracks, would often, and were usually expected to, contract semipermanent liaisons with local women. The procedure was institutionalized with an agreed financial arrangement, a kind of marriage ceremony, and the bestowal of the man's surname upon the woman. Although such marriages were not always considered acceptable in nonmilitary colonial social circles, they persisted until the 1850s in many parts of the French Empire, particularly in West Africa and Indochina. Officers often contracted such liaisons with daughters of prominent local families, and it was thought the relationships gave the army an important link with the community, the marriage being a kind of community relations project. [See Mistresses.]

Marias Massacre (23 January 1870), American Indian Wars. American Major Eugene Mortimer Baker (1837?–1884) with four companies of cavalry and 55 mounted infantry was ordered to lead a punitive expedition against the inveterately hostile Piegan band of Blackfoot Indians under Mountain Chief (d. 1872). By mistake, Baker fell upon a camp of friendly Piegans under Heavy Runner (d. 1870) on the Marias River in Montana. In the attack 173 were killed and the camp was fired. About 140 women and children were taken captive and held until the camp was reduced to ashes, when they were released in sub-zero weather without protection or supplies.

Maria Theresa, Military Order of. An Austrian award for officers instituted on 18 January 1757 and conferred for brav-

ery or for successful initiative in battle. It became famous as the only medal that could be awarded to an officer who disobeyed an order and succeeded in battle by doing so. In the nineteenth century the order had three classes, the highest being grand cross for generals; commander for other senior officers; and knight for lesser acts of bravery by any officer. Holders of the order were automatically created *Freiherr* (baron). Unlike the American Medal of Honor and the French Legion of Honor, this medal was never at any time awarded haphazardly and thus retained its esteem intact. It was awarded until October 1931. Its counterpart for noncommissioned officers and other ranks was the Medal for Bravery in 1879 in gold and silver.

Marie-Louises. The name of Napoleon's second wife was colloquially given to fifteen- or sixteen-year-old conscripts pressed into service in Napoleon's army in 1813–14 following his disastrous Russian Campaign [q.v.], in which his losses were crippling.

Marignano, Battle of. See Malegnano, Battle of.

Marine Corps, United States. The U.S. Marines came into being on 10 November 1775, when the Continental Congress authorized two battalions of marines decreeing that "no Marines be commissioned or enlisted unless they are good seamen, or so acquainted with maritime affairs as to be able to serve to advantage by sea when required." It became a permanent autonomous force within the Department of the Navy as the Marine Corps by Act of Congress on 11 July 1798.

On 30 June 1834 Congress placed the corps under the direction of the secretary of the navy but also authorized the president to direct marines to serve under the army if he thought fit to do so. This provision allowed a small marine unit to serve with General Winfield Scott [q.v.] during the Mexican War and accounts for the inclusion of the "halls of Montezuma" in "The Marines' Hymn."

When the marines served with the army, they were subject to army regulation, and after 1812, when flogging [q.v.] was abolished in the army, they could not be flogged while in its service. However, on shipboard they came under navy regulations and, until 1850, when the practice was abolished in the navy, could be flogged.

Marine Corps, U.S. *Marine uniforms: 1899 dress (left) and field (right)*

Marines. Infantry and often artillery serving on ships or in association with a nation's navy [see Marines, Royal; Marine Corps, United States; Troupes de Marines]. In the U.S. service marines could also serve with the army. The British service established in 1664 was the earliest. The Dutch formed a corps of marines the following year. The U.S. Marine Corps was formed in 1775 and first saw action against the British the following year. Not until the 1890s did Germany establish sea battalions, one of which was permanently stationed at Kiau-Chou, China. French marines reestablished in 1803 fought most of France's colonial wars.

Marines, French. See Troupes de Marine.

Marines, Royal. British marines were constituted in 1664 as the Admiralty Regiment. On 1 May 1802 they were styled Royal Marine Forces. In 1803 there were 12,000 Royal Marines, raised to 31,400 during the Napoleonic Wars in the peak years of 1810–12, and averaging about 9,000 for the first half of the nineteenth century. In the early years of the century enlistments were for life. By 1827 marines had taken part in 106 engagements. They were employed, usually in small numbers, in every major Victorian war and in many small actions, usually as part of a naval brigade, fighting on-shore in Malaya in 1874–75, in Zanzibar in 1875, in the Congo in 1875–76, in Samoa in 1876, and in the Niger in 1876–77. They sometimes served far from the sea, as they did in the Indian Mutiny and in the Second Anglo-Boer War [qq.v.].

Originally the marines were all infantry, but in 1804, at the suggestion of Lord Nelson (1758–1805), companies of artillery were formed. These were ordered disbanded in 1832, but two were retained. From 1862 to 1923 the force was divided into separate corps: Royal Marine Light Infantry and Royal Marine Artillery. Their officers were then carried on separate lists.

The Marquess of Anglesey [see Paget, Henry William], speaking at Portsmouth on 5 August 1841, said of the Royal Marines: "It is a Corps which never appeared on any occasion or under any circumstances without doing honour to itself and its country." Nevertheless, not until December 1882 were officers of the Royal Marines made equal in rank with those in the army and navy.

Marketenden / Marketenderin. A German sutler.

Marksman. One skilled in hitting a target by shooting a hand-held or shoulder weapon.

Marksmanship. Skill in hitting a target with a weapon, which in the nineteenth century was usually a musket or a rifle. General Gerhard von Scharnhorst [q.v.] in an 1812 memorandum wrote: "Good marksmanship is always the most important thing for the infantry." This had not always been true, and probably few other senior officers agreed with him at that time. In the eighteenth century, when muskets were inaccurate, it was more effective to fire in volleys in the general direction of the enemy. As shoulder-held weapons improved and more open formations were adopted, more and more emphasis was placed upon marksmanship.

Marksmanship

Marmaduke, John Sappington (1833–1887). An American soldier who attended Yale and Harvard before going to West Point, from which he was graduated in 1857. He took part in the Utah Campaign [q.v.] and was serving on the frontier at the beginning of the American Civil War. On 17 April 1861 he resigned his commission as a second lieutenant and became a colonel in the Confederate militia. He rose to be a brigadier general and to command the 3rd Missouri in the Battle of Shiloh [q.v.] and the cavalry in the raid of Sterling Price [q.v.]. On 6 September 1863 he fought a duel with Brigadier General Lucius Marshall Walker (1829–1863), whose courage he had impugned, and mortally wounded him. He was himself wounded and taken prisoner at Mine Creek, a tributary of Marais des Cygnes, in Kansas on 25 October 1864. While a prisoner, he was promoted major general, the last Confederate so appointed. When he was released from prison in July 1865, he settled in St. Louis. In 1884 he was elected governor of Missouri, as his father had been before him.

Marmite. A camp kettle.

Marmont, Auguste Frédéric Louis Viesse de, Duc de Raguse (1774–1852). A French soldier commissioned in 1790. He first distinguished himself in northern Italy, where he led a cavalry charge in the Battle of Lodi on 10 May 1796 and at Castiglione on 5 August. He served in Napoleon's army in Egypt and was a general of brigade by the age of twenty-six. After the Battle of the Pyramids on 21 July 1798 he commanded at Alexandria. He later served as commander of the artillery in the Battle of Marengo [q.v.] on 14 June 1800. On 16 September 1802 he became inspector general of all French artillery and as such standardized the calibers of guns and developed uniform artillery tactics. He abolished 4-pounder guns, introduced a 6-pounder as the standard for field artillery, and adopted improved limbers and wagons. In June 1803 he became Napoleon's chief of artillery, and led the II Corps at Austerlitz [q.v.]. From 1805 to 1809 he was governor of Illyria (Dalmatia), where with only 6,000 French he repelled a Russo-Montenegrin army of 16,000 in the Battle of Old Ragusa on 30 September 1806. On 17 May 1809 he was slightly wounded in a skirmish at Gradschatz in Croatia. He fought at Wagram [q.v.], where he distinguished himself.

On 12 July 1809 he was created a marshal of the empire. In 1811 he was sent to Spain to succeed André Masséna [q.v.]. He lost an arm in the Battle of Salamanca [q.v.] on 22 July 1812 but was back in action in 1814. Napoleon criticized his conduct, in his last battle, at Laon [q.v.] on 9 March 1814, saying that he had behaved like a second lieutenant. In response he deserted to the Allies with an entire corps of 12,000 men. Napoleon struck his name from the list of marshals, but after the victory of Waterloo the Bourbons lavished honors and wealth upon Marmont, and he lived extravagantly. During the Revolution of 1830 [q.v.] he tried but failed to quell the Paris mob that rose against the Bourbons. The last twenty-two years of his life were spent in exile, mostly in Venice. He was pointed out wherever he went as the man who had betrayed Napoleon.

Maroon. A firework consisting of a cardboard cube filled with gunpowder and wrapped with two or three layers of twine. The explosion imitated the report of a cannon.

Marr, John Quincy (1825–1861). A graduate and instructor at the Virginia Military Institute [q.v.] in Lexington, Virginia, who raised a company of Confederate troops that at the outset of the American Civil War was stationed at Fairfax Court House in northern Virginia. Early in the morning of 1 June 1861 in a skirmish with troopers of Company B, 2nd U.S. Cavalry, he became the first Confederate soldier killed in the war.

Marriage Roll. A register of those noncommissioned officers and privates who married with permission. Soldiers in most nineteenth-century armies, including the American and British, were forbidden to marry without the permission of their commanding officers. Usually several years of service with good conduct were required before such permission was granted. Women who had married with permission in the British army were said to be "on the strength" of their husband's unit. Only such wives were permitted to set themselves up as laundresses in the unit or to work as servants to officers and their wives or to be considered if permission was given for a certain number of women to accompany a unit sent overseas.

"Marseillaise, La." The French national anthem. Its title when first published in Strasbourg was "Chant de guerre de l'armée du Rhin" (war song of the Army of the Rhine). It was written on 25 April 1792 by a French captain of engineers, Claude Joseph Rouget de Lisle (1760–1836), who, suspected of being a too moderate republican, was cashiered and imprisoned for a time. It became the French national anthem on 14 July 1795, but it was repressed for a time by Napoleon, who considered it too rabble-rousing. He tolerated and even exploited its use in 1814 and again in 1815. After the restoration, of course, the Bourbons banned it, but in 1830 Louis Philippe (1773–1850) restored it and even granted a small pension to its composer. It was again banned by Napoleon III (1808–1873), but in 1879 it was again and has since remained the French national anthem.

Marsh, Grant (1834–1916). An American riverman who began his career on riverboats as a cabin boy at the age of twelve. In 1852 he was a deckhand, and by 1858 he was first mate on the *A. B. Chambers No. 2,* on which Samuel Clemens (Mark Twain) had served as a pilot. During the American Civil War Marsh worked with the Union fleet on the lower Mississippi until 1864. After the war he manned commercial boats on the river until 1873, when he moved to Yankton, South Dakota, and became a captain for the Missouri River Transportation Company [q.v.], often called the Coulson Line, which transported troops and supplies on the frontier. By the time of the disaster to the 7th Cavalry on the Little Bighorn [q.v.] on 25 June 1876 Marsh was said to be the "most popular steamboat captain on the upper Missouri," a man "always ready to take any chances when the services of the government demanded them."

During the Great Sioux War [q.v.] of 1876 his 190-foot boat the *Far West,* with a passenger capacity of thirty, was leased to the government for $360 a day. When fully loaded, it drew only 20 inches of water. After Custer's debacle, in what was described as "an amazing piece of maneuvering," he took the steamer above the mouth of the Little Bighorn and carried off the wounded, whom he transported 710 miles downstream in only fifty-four hours. He arrived at Bismarck with his flag at half-mast and his boat draped in black, bringing the first news of the disaster. In 1881 he led a flotilla of steamers that carried 1,500 surrendered Sioux from Montana to agencies in Dakota.

Marshal. 1. As a noun, the highest military rank in many armies [see Field Marshal].

2. As a verb, to assemble the men and equipment needed for a military operation.

3. As a noun, a dignity in the French army [see Marshal of France / Marshal of the Empire].

Marshal, Field. See Field Marshal.

Marshal, Provost. See Provost Marshal.

Marshalate. 1. The collective name for the men created marshals by Napoleon, creating a rough "battlefield nobility" [see Marshal; Marshal of France / Marshal of the Empire].

2. The period in France from 1873 to 1879, when Marshal Marie MacMahon was the second president of the Third Republic.

Marshal of France / Marshal of the Empire. The title of marshal (*maréchal*) was used in the Middle Ages. In 1788 marshal of France (*maréchal de France*) was the highest dignity in the French army, which then had twenty marshals, but the title was suppressed in 1793 during the French Revolution. On 18 May 1804 it was revived by Napoleon as marshal of the empire (*maréchal de l'empire*) by Article VI of the *senatus consultum,* the law that inaugurated the Napoleonic Empire. The following day Napoleon, who had recently proclaimed himself emperor, announced the names of the first eighteen marshals; an additional seven were later created. Marshal of the empire was not a rank but a dignity, a title of honor, with pay and privileges that distinguished the holders from generals of division, the highest rank. Their status was indicated by a baton about eighteen inches long and two inches in diameter, gold-capped at both ends and covered with blue velvet embroidered with gold eagles. Although the marshals were Napoleon's favorites and formed the nucleus of the imperial aristocracy he created, barely one-third of them rallied to him during the Hundred Days [q.v.]. After the Bourbon restoration in 1815 the title was returned to the original marshal of France, and the numbers of those holding it were gradually reduced. After 1870 there were no new creations until General Joseph Joffre [q.v.] was given the title and rank in 1916. [See Baton; Field Marshal; Marshalate.]

Mars-la-Tour–Vionville, Battle of (16 August 1870), Franco-Prussian War. After the Battle of Colombey-Borny [q.v.] on 14 August 1870 the French army of 80,000 men under General Achille Bazaine [q.v.] resumed its retreat westward and fell back across the Moselle River. The Prussian Second Army, two corps under Prince Frederick Charles [q.v.] totaling 67,000 men with 222 guns and operating between Metz and Verdun, intercepted the retreating French in an area around two Lorraine villages, Mars-la-Tour and Vionville, in northeast France southwest of Metz.

The French scored an early advantage over the leading Prussian corps under General Konstantin von Alvensleben [q.v.], but Bazaine failed to exhibit sufficient energy and allowed the Prussians to build up their strength until his road to the west was blocked. There followed an enormous cavalry battle involving 5,000 horsemen. Helmuth von Moltke [q.v.] called it the "greatest cavalry battle of the war." After twelve hours of fighting, in which each side tried to turn the flank of the other, the French turned back toward Metz [see Rezonville, Battle of]. French losses were 877 officers and 16,128 other ranks; Prussian losses were 711 officers and 15,097 other ranks.

It was in this battle that the Prussian 1st Guards Dragoons, led by Adalbert von Bredow [q.v.], made the celebrated Death Ride [q.v.] in which Prince Herbert von Bismarck-Schönhausen (1849–1904), eldest son of the great chancellor Otto von Bismarck (1815–1898), was severely wounded.

After this battle Bazaine established a new defensive line from St. Privat to Gravelotte [see Gravelotte–St. Privat, Battle of].

Mars-la-Tour–Vionville *Prussian 1st Guards Dragoons on their "Death Ride" at Mars-la-Tour*

Marsouins. French: dolphins. Colloquial name for colonial infantry in the French service. [See Troupes de Marine.]

Martello Towers. Small, round stone towers about 40 feet high with walls $5\frac{1}{2}$ feet thick and vaulted ceilings, built between 1803 and 1812 along the eastern and southern coasts of England and Ireland as deterrents to French invasions, which were feared. Their ground floors were magazines, and the two rooms above housed the garrisons.

The name is a corruption of Mortella, the name of a cape in Corsica where a fort of similar size and construction commanded the Gulf of San Fiorenzo. On 8 February 1794 it was attacked by three British warships and 1,400 troops, and although defended by only 33 men with three guns, it put up such a gallant resistance that the British were deeply impressed by the value of such small, strong structures.

Martello towers were also built in Ontario and Halifax, Canada. Of the five built to protect Halifax Harbor between 1796 and 1804, one remains preserved in Point Pleasant Park and is believed to be the oldest in the former British Empire.

Martial. Of or pertaining to war, warriors, armies, or military life; warlike.

Martial Law. 1. Law administered in an occupied area or nation by the occupying army.

2. Law administered by military authorities when the civil authority collapses or is unable to function and maintain order through normal law enforcement agencies. In 1866 the U.S. Supreme Court decreed in Ex Parte *Milligan* that martial law could not be declared where the civil courts were functioning [see Posse Comitatus Act]. In Britain martial law was only authorized twice in the nineteenth century, in 1803 and 1833.

Martial law is applied to civilians, as opposed to military law, which applies only to those in military service or to those serving with an army and subject to the articles of war or similar military rules.

Martial Races. In the nineteenth century both the British in India and the French in Africa subscribed to a belief that men of certain tribes, castes, races, or communities were more warlike or soldierly than others. The notion that some classes or races of people make better soldiers is ancient. Flavius Vegetius, a fourth-century Roman, wrote: "Peasants are the most fit to bear arms for they from their infancy have been exposed to all kinds of weather and have been brought up to the hardest labor. They are able to endure the intense heat of the sun, are unacquainted with the use of baths, and they are strangers to the other luxuries of life. They are simple, content with little, inured to fatigue, and prepared in some measure for military life" (*Epitoma rei militaris* [A.D. 378]).

British Indian regiments kept detailed family genealogies, making almost a science of selecting recruits by certain characteristics. They preferred to enlist Sikhs, Gurkhas, and Dogras, among others, and rejected Bengalis; the French in West and Central Africa preferred men from the savanna area, especially those from the Bambara tribe and Tukulors, and rejected Wolofs and coastal tribesmen. In both instances those rejected were usually the most educated and socially sophisticated. The British scorned the Bengali babu (an Indian clerk who wrote English) as superficially cultivated and effeminate; the French rejected the Wolof as being "a 'Rights-of-Man' nigger." A British officer described the type of recruit desired as "the wilder the better." A French officer described the sought-after Bambara as "an uncouth fellow who possesses all the strong warrior's virtues, but who did not unfortunately show much intelligence."

In other parts of Africa the Zulus, Yaos, Masais, Sudanese, and Wakumas were among those whose men were considered "more virile" than their neighbors.

Martí, José Julián (1853–1895). A Cuban patriot and lawyer who was for a time the consul in New York for Argentina, Paraguay, and Uruguay. In 1892 he founded the Cuban Revolutionary Party. In 1895 he inspired a revolt and with a few companions landed in Cuba to lead the rebels. On 20 May 1895 he was killed when he and his troops were ambushed by Spanish troops at Dos Ríos, a village in Oriente Province, forty miles northwest of Santiago de Cuba. A monument to him stands there. Radio Martí was named in his honor.

Martinet. An overly strict officer or noncommissioned officer, a rigid disciplinarian. The word has no such connotation in French, where it's most common meaning is the bird that in English is called a martin or swallow. Its English usage derives from Colonel (later General) Jean Martinet (d. 1672), a French officer in the army of Louis XIV (1638–1715) who devised a new drill that bore his name.

Martínez, Tomás (1812–1873). A Nicaraguan soldier and politician who in 1856–57 fought against William Walker [q.v.], the filibuster. For eight years, beginning in 1857, he was the first president of Nicaragua. He was defeated in a war with Honduras and El Salvador.

Martínez de Campos, Arsenio (1834–1900). A Spanish soldier and statesman who served in Morocco in 1859, Mexico in 1861, and Cuba in 1869–72. In 1874–75 he helped restore the monarchical government in Spain that seated Alfonso XII (1857–1885) on the throne, and in 1876 he helped defeat the Carlists [see Second Carlist War]. In 1878 he suppressed a Cuban revolution and the following year was premier of Spain. From 1881 to 1884 he was minister of war. He served in the Senate until 1895, when he again commanded Spanish troops fighting Cuban revolutionaries. When he proved unable to defeat the rebels, he was replaced in 1896.

Martini-Henry Rifle. In 1871 the British army adopted a rifle with a breech action developed by Frédéric de Martini (1832–1897), a Hungarian inventor and gunsmith working in Switzerland, and in 1877 it adopted the rifling system of Alexander Henry (d. 1900), a Scottish gunsmith who founded the Henry Rifled Barrel Company. It weighed eight pounds four and a half ounces, and was 49 inches long. The resultant single-shot Martini-Henry Mark II was the rifle used in the Battle of Rorke's Drift [q.v.] in the Zulu War [q.v.]. Originally in caliber .45, it was rebored in 1890 for the new .303 caliber cartridge.

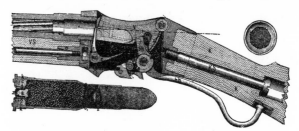

Martini-Henry rifle

Martinique, British Conquest of (January–July 1809), Napoleonic Wars. Sir George Beckwith [q.v.] led a British expedition of 11,000 men that sailed from Carlisle Bay, the open roadstead in southwest Barbados, on 28 January 1809 in ships commanded by Alexander Forrester Inglis Cochrane (1758–1832) and disembarked at the Caribbean island of Martinique two days later. French resistance was not strong, and the British took 2,000 prisoners. The conquest was completed on 24 July, and Beckwith sent back to England captured French eagles [q.v.], the first seen there. In 1814 the island was restored to France.

Marye's Heights. A steep ridge above the town of Fredericksburg, Virginia, which became a feature of the Battle of Fredericksburg [q.v.] during the American Civil War. The bloodiest fighting of the battle took place here on 13 December 1862 as Union forces tried to dislodge Confederates under General Robert E. Lee [q.v.]. Marye's Heights was also a prominent feature in the Battle of Chancellorsville [q.v.] the following May.

Marye's Heights *The stone wall at Marye's Heights immediately after the position was carried by a Union assault in the Battle of Chancellorsville.*

"Maryland, My Maryland." See Randall, James Ryder.

MAS. The common abbreviation for the Manufacture Nationale d'Arms de St. Étienne at St. Étienne, France, an arsenal in operation since 1669 that has manufactured numerous firearms of all types. The town itself, located on the Loire 32 miles southwest of Lyons, has had gunmaking factories since 1535.

Mascots. See Pets and Mascots.

Masked Battery. 1. Concealed artillery, usually protected by breastworks, whose position was not revealed until guns were fired.

2. A battery unable to fire because friendly troops or some other deterrent stand in the line of fire.

Mask Wall. The scarp wall of casements in permanent fortifications.

Mass. 1. As a verb, to concentrate troops or guns—e.g., to mass the fire of guns.

2. As a noun, a large number of troops or guns.

3. As a noun, the concentration of men and weapons at a critical place and time for optimum strength.

Massed artillery is sometimes referred to as being hub to hub, but this is not to be taken literally. Muzzle-loading cannon could be served only by men moving back and forth from front to rear, movements that hub-to-hub guns would make impossible.

Massacre. The slaughter of a large number of people unable adequately to defend themselves.

Massacre Hill. See Fetterman Massacre.

Masse. The rebel Calabrian army [see Calabrian War].

Massed Fire. The firing of a number of weapons at a single target. Napoleon said: "In a battle, like in a siege, skill consists in converging a mass of fire on a single point: Once the combat is opened, the commander who is adroit will suddenly and unexpectedly open fire with a mass of artillery on one of these points, and is sure to seize it."

Masséna, André (1758–1817). A soldier who was born in Nice, then a part of the kingdom of Sardinia, and raised by an uncle who was a soap manufacturer, until at age thirteen he ran away from home and became a cabin boy. At age seventeen he joined the Royal Italian Regiment in the French service. He was promoted sergeant when only nineteen. Seven years later he was a sergeant major. In 1789 he was discharged and turned to smuggling and fruit peddling at Antibes. He is said to have married a surgeon's daughter with a large dowry, enabling him to develop a taste for high living. In 1791 he joined the National Guard, and in February 1792 he was elected lieutenant colonel of the Volunteers of Vars. For the next six years he served in the Army of Italy, where his leadership earned him promotion to general of brigade in August 1793 and to provisional general of division the following December, a promotion confirmed nine months later. In March 1796 he served under Napoleon, winning distinction in every battle of his Italian Campaign. In April 1799 he took command of the French forces in Switzerland, where he defeated Russian General Aleksandr Suvorov [q.v.] in the Second Battle of Zurich on 25 September 1799. In 1800 he became commander of the Army of Italy, but he was soon besieged at Genoa by Austrian General Michael von Melas [q.v.] and forced to capitulate on 4 June 1800. He fought at Marengo [q.v.] and on 19 May 1804 was one of the first marshals of the empire to be created [see Marshal of France / Marshal

of the Empire]. Napoleon said of him: "Masséna was at his best and most brilliant in the midst of the fire and disorder of battle; the roar of the cannon used to clear his ideas. . . ."

Masséna captured Verona and fought an inconclusive battle at Caldiero. In December 1806 he invaded the Bourbon kingdom of Naples; he captured Gaeta and Capua, later Calabria [see Calabrian War]. An inveterate looter, he amassed a huge fortune by plundering Naples, even though Napoleon confiscated much of his loot. He was next dispatched to command a corps in Germany. Speaking of Napoleon's marshals, Wellington once said: "Masséna gave me more trouble than any of them." He distinguished himself at the battles of Landshut, Eckmühl, Aspern-Essling, and Wagram [qq.v.], where his leg was badly injured when his horse fell on him. In 1808 he was blinded in his left eye in a hunting accident at Fontainebleau.

In 1810 Napoleon sent him to the Iberian Peninsula, where he won battles at Ciudad Rodrigo and Almeida [qq.v.] but was repulsed by Wellington in the Battle of Bussaco [q.v.]. Masséna may have been somewhat distracted by the presence of his mistress, Henriette Renique Libertine (fl. 1810), known as Madame X, a sister of one of his aides-de-camp, who enjoyed riding about dressed as a dragoon cornet and wearing a Legion of Honor [q.v.]. Her charms were blamed for delaying his arrival on the field and thus contributing to his repulse at the Lines of Torres Vedras [q.v.].

In March 1811 Masséna was forced to begin a retreat from Portugal to Spain. When he was defeated by Wellington in the Battle of Fuentes de Oñoro [q.v.] on 5 May 1811, Napoleon relieved him of command. He retired with his wealth and his mistresses to the south of France and refused to join Napoleon during the Hundred Days [q.v.]. In 1815 he commanded the Garde Nationale [q.v.] in Paris.

Massenbach, Christian Karl August Ludwig von (1758–1827). A Prussian soldier who became an officer in the Württemberg army in 1778 but left this service in 1782 to join the army of Frederick the Great (1712–1786). In the first decade of the century he played a major part in the reorganization of the Prussian army. In 1805 he was made quartermaster general (equivalent to chief of staff) to Prince Hohenlohe [q.v.], and it was through Massenbach's bad advice that the battles of Jena and Auerstädt [qq.v.] were lost. He then retired to his estate, where he occupied himself writing pamphlets and memoirs.

Massen-Drieckebergertum. A German expression for mass skulking on the battlefield.

Master General of the Ordnance. In the British army this was the head of the Board of Ordnance, and all details of the Regiment of Artillery were his responsibility. The title originated in the fifteenth century but was abolished when Lord Raglan [q.v.], the last master general of the ordnance, died in the Crimea in 1855.

Master Gunner. In the British service this was a pensioned artillery sergeant placed in charge of the ammunition and supplies stored in towers and small forts. There were three classes of master gunner; the lowest received three shillings per day, the second class three shillings and sixpence, and the first class five shillings.

Master of the Sword. An American citizen employed at West Point to instruct cadets in the use of the sword and bayonet. Although without rank, he wore a uniform generally similar to that of a lieutenant with the letters *M.A.* in silver encircled with a gold wreath on his cap, and he was entitled to the "pay, allowances and emoluments" of a mounted first lieutenant. This title was in use from 1881; previously, at least as early as 1857, the official title was sword master. In 1901 the master of the sword also became responsible for "military gymnastics and physical culture." Fencing is no longer a required subject at West Point.

Masterson, Patrick (fl. 1811). An Irish sergeant of the 87th Foot who became a British hero when in the Battle of Barrosa on 5 March 1811 he captured the eagle standard of the French 87th Regiment of the Line from French Sous-Lieutenant Edmé Guillemin (d. 1811). Masterson's exploit was celebrated in poems and pictures and depicted in at least three popular prints.

MAT. The abbreviation for the Manufacture Nationale d'Armes de Tulle, a French arsenal since the seventeenth century. The town of Tulle is located in south-central France, 47 miles south-southeast of Limoges.

Matabele Wars. The Matabeles (now called Ndebeles or, more correctly, Amandebeles) were a southern African tribe, originally a branch of the Zulus. About 1818, when their leader, Moselekatse (1796?–1868)—also known as Mzilikazi, Umsiligaas, or Silkaats—failed to pay tribute to Shaka [q.v.], king of the Zulus, Shaka sent a punitive expedition against him. To escape, Moselekatse led his people to safety westward across the Drakensberg range into land that was to become the Orange Free State and the Transvaal. There they made raids on other Bantu tribes and came into conflict with Boers (Afrikaners), who in 1836 defeated them in battles at Vegkop and Mosega. Moselekatse then led his people north across the Limpopo River into what was to become Southern Rhodesia (Zimbabwe), where he made the local tribe, the Mashonas, subservient to him.

When Moselekatse died, power passed to Lobengula [q.v.]. By this time Europeans were coming into the area in increasing numbers [see British South Africa Company], and in 1893 they demanded that the Matabeles cease making their accustomed raids upon the Mashonas. In July of that year when a defiant Matabele impi attacked Mashonas near Fort Victoria, the British South Africa Company launched an expedition against them: 1,200 men, some volunteers from South Africa, led by Dr. Leander Starr Jameson [q.v.]. On 24–26 October 1893, thanks largely to Jameson's Maxim machine guns, one of the first operational uses of the guns, Lobengula's army of about 5,000 was defeated in a battle on the Shangani River and again on 1 November in the Battle of Imbembese, on the banks of the Bembesi River. Lobengula fled, and his capital, Bulawayo, was occupied on 4 November. There continued to be small fights between whites and Matabeles, but the war was soon over [see Shangani Patrol]. Lobengula fled, and before he could be captured, he died "of a fever," probably smallpox, on 23 January 1894 while in flight. Cecil Rhodes (1853–1902) paid for the education of three of his sons. In February most of the Matabele army surrendered.

In March 1896 the Matabeles again revolted against the authority of the British South Africa Company in what is now celebrated in Zimbabwe as the First War of Independence. In Matabeleland 141 European men, women, and children were slain; 103 more were killed in Mashonaland. In the following months large numbers of isolated settlers and their families were murdered [see Mazoe Party]. Even after the British sent troops under Colonel (later Field Marshal) Herbert Plumer [q.v.], the suppression of the Matabeles proved difficult. They retreated into the stronghold of the Matopos, the granite hills 50 miles long near Bulawayo, and their defiance ended only when Frederick Russell Burnham [q.v.] found and murdered their chief prophet and Cecil Rhodes boldly walked unarmed into the their stronghold and persuaded them to lay down their arms. The war ended in October 1897.

Matagorda, Siege of (23 February–22 March 1810), Peninsular War. At this small fort in southern Spain contiguous to Cádiz 140 British troops were posted on 22 February 1810. They were attacked the next day and shelled by field artillery but refused to surrender. Beginning on 22 March and continuing for thirty hours, the fire of 48 guns and mortars was directed against them. The garrison capitulated after suffering 64 casualties.

Matamoros, Mariano (1770?–1814). A Mexican priest and revolutionary who in 1811–14 served under José Morelos [q.v.]. He was captured in the Battle of Puruará on 5 January 1814 and was executed by firing squad on 3 February. The Mexican town of Matamoros, opposite Brownsville, Texas, on the Rio Grande was named in his honor.

Matchlock. 1. A slow-burning cord that ignites the charge in a musket when lowered over the breech.
2. A musket equipped with a matchlock.

Matériel. All the weapons, carriages, and implements of war, as opposed to personnel. Often written without the accented *e*.

Matron. A woman employed to assist in a hospital by washing, cleaning, etc. Usually the wife of a well-behaved soldier, she was generally selected by the surgeon and worked under his direction.

Matross. In the early nineteenth century a low-ranking artilleryman, ranking below a gunner. The term passed out of usage in about 1820.

Matucanas, Battle of (18 September 1828), Peru-Colombia War. Peruvians defeated a Colombian army at this Peruvian town 45 miles east-northeast of Lima. (A cross erected on the site to commemorate the battle unaccountably bears the wrong date: 1836 instead of 1828.)

Maude, Frederick Francis (1828–1900). A British officer who served in the Gwalior Campaign of 1843 and the Crimean War of 1855–56 [qq.v.]. As an artillery captain during the Crimean War he won the Victoria Cross [q.v.] on 8 September 1855 by holding a portion of the redan [q.v.] with only 9 or 10 men against overwhelming force until felled by a severe wound. He later led military expeditions on the Northwest Frontier [see Afridi Tribes, Military Expeditions Against].

Mauritius, Capture of (28 November–3 December 1810), Napoleonic Wars. British troops under Sir Gilbert Elliot-Murray-Kynynmond, later first Earl Minto (1751–1814), sailed into Mapon Bay in Mauritius, the French island in the Indian Ocean, on 28 November 1810 and stormed French positions near Port Louis. By 3 December the entire island was in British hands.

Maury, Dabney Herndon (1822–1900). An American soldier, the nephew of famed oceanographer Matthew Fontaine Maury (1806–1873), who was graduated from West Point in 1846. During the Mexican War [q.v.] he won a brevet and was wounded in the Battle of Cerro Gordo [q.v.]. He was a brevet captain when on 25 June 1861, at the beginning of the American Civil War, he was dismissed from the service on the charge that he "entertained and had expressed treasonable designs." He joined the Confederate army as a cavalry captain and on 12 March 1862 was promoted brigadier general; on 4 November he was promoted major general. He fought at Pea Ridge, Corinth, and Vicksburg [qq.v.]. After the war he became a teacher in Richmond, Virginia, and in 1868 founded the Southern Historical Society. He also served as a diplomat in Colombia.

Mauser Brothers. The Mauser brothers—*Peter Paul* (1838–1914) and *Wilhelm* (1834–1882)—were German inventors and gunsmiths who in 1865 designed an improved needle gun [see Dreyse Needle Gun] at the Royal Württemberg Arms Factory in Oberndorf, a small town 11 miles north-northwest of Salzburg. In 1867 they left the firm and established themselves in Liège, Belgium, where they perfected the bolt-action 11 mm breech-loading military rifle, which became the Gewehr (musket or rifle) 71 when it was adopted by the Prussian army in 1871. The brothers formed Gebrüder Mauser & Cie. and purchased an arsenal at Oberndorf that remained in operation until bombed by Allied planes in 1945. After Wilhelm's death, Peter Paul developed a rifle with a tubular magazine that was adopted by the German army as Gewehr 84. It was replaced four years later by the Reich Kommission 7.92 mm rifle, Gewehr 88. In 1889 Mauser developed a 7.65 mm rifle with a magazine holding five rounds. In 1893 a 7 mm version was adopted by the Spanish army. In 1898 an improved 7.92 mm version was

adopted by the German army as Gewehr 98; it remained in service until 1945. In 1896 he designed the so-called broomhandle Mauser pistol in caliber 7.63 mm and 9 mm, the first true automatic pistol with a self-loading magazine. These went into production in 1897.

Maxim, Hiram Stevens (1840–1916). An American-born inventor who avoided the Civil War by going to Canada. His mechanical ingenuity led to many inventions; his first patent was issued in 1866 for a hair-curling iron. In 1878 he became chief engineer of the United States Electric Light Company. Three years later he emigrated to England, where in 1884 he founded the Maxim Gun Company, which four years later merged with the Nordenfeldt Company and in 1896 became Vickers' Sons and Maxim. In 1900 he became a naturalized British subject, and in 1901 was knighted by Queen Victoria.

The best known of his many inventions—he obtained more than 250 patents in the United States and Great Britain—was the recoil-operated machine gun. It was a water cooled 7.69 caliber weapon capable of firing 500 rounds per minute. It was first used in action by the British in 1893 in the Matabele War [q.v.].

His brother **Hudson** [q.v.] was also an inventor and an explosives expert. Sir Hiram's son **Hiram Percy** (1869–1936), still another prolific inventor, was best known for his invention of the Maxim silencer in 1908.

Maxim, Hudson (1853–1827). An American inventor whose original first name was Isaac. He was the younger brother of inventor Hiram Maxim [q.v.]. He had little formal education but took a keen interest in chemistry. In 1888 he began experiments with explosives and just two years later opened a dynamite and powder factory at Maxim, New Jersey. There with Dr. R. C. Schupphaus he developed the Maxim-Schupphaus smokeless powder, the first to be manufactured in the United States and the first to be adopted by the government. This was followed by the invention of a smokeless cannon powder with cylindrical grains perforated to burn more rapidly. In 1897 he sold his factory and his inventions to E. I. du Pont, but he remained on as a consulting engineer. He then invented maximite, a high-explosive blasting powder and a delayed-action detonating fuze and later a highly stable new smokeless powder called motorite. During the First World War he donated several of his patents to the government.

Maximilian I (1832–1867), in full: Ferdinand Maximilian Joseph. An Austrian archduke, brother of the emperor, who was trained for the naval service and in 1854 was in command of the Austrian navy. From 1857 to 1859 he was viceroy of the Lombardo-Venetian kingdom. In July 1863, when the French had partially conquered Mexico, a group of Mexican notables meeting under French auspices decided their country should have an emperor. The throne was offered to Maximilian, who accepted on 10 April 1864, with the proviso, to which Napoleon III (1808–1873) agreed, that he be supported by French troops. Maximilian and his wife entered Mexico City on 12 June. There remained considerable Mexican opposition to French rule, but with the aid of French troops, the

Mauser rifle

Mexican forces of Benito Pablo Juárez [q.v.], who had been president, were driven over the border into the United States [see Mexico, French Invasion and Occupation of]. On 10 October 1865 Maximilian issued a black flag decree, proclaiming that anyone taking up arms against his government would be shot [see Black Flag].

On 12 February 1866 the American government, which refused to recognize Maximilian's empire, demanded the withdrawal of the French troops. Napoleon III, breaking his pledge, complied, in spite of a personal appeal by the empress, who went to Paris to plead for continued support. At the departure of the French, Juárez, with American help, returned to the attack. Maximilian was besieged at Querétaro, 160 miles northwest of Mexico City, by General Escobedo Mariano [q.v.], and on 13 May 1867 he was forced to surrender. He was tried by court-martial, and on 19 June he was shot.

Maximilian I *Maximilian before a firing squad of Mexican republicans, 19 June 1867*

Maxims of War. General principles regarding the management of armies and the conduct of war. Those said to have originated from Napoleon are the most widely known. Historian Barbara Tuchman (1912–1989) wrote: "Nothing so comforts the military mind as the maxim of a great but dead general" (*The Guns of August* [1962]). War is so filled with unknowable factors that commanders always search for certainties. However, there is probably no maxim of war that has not been successfully ignored. One of the soundest lays down the rule that a general with a numerically inferior force should not divide it in the face of the enemy, a tactic Robert E. Lee successfully adopted more than once, most notably before the Battle of Antietam [q.v.] and at Chancellorsville [q.v.], where he not only divided his numerically inferior force once but further divided one of its portions to give to Thomas J. Jackson [q.v.] for his movement around the Union right flank.

Maxwell Pasha, John Grenfell (1859–1929). A British soldier who was commissioned in 1879 and first saw action in Egypt during Arabi's Revolt [q.v.] of 1882 in the Battle of Tell el-Kebir [q.v.]. He took part in the Gordon

Relief Expedition [q.v.]. In 1886 he was seconded to the Egyptian army, in which he served three years in Upper Egypt and, commanding the 2nd Egyptian Brigade, took part in the reconquest of the Sudan [q.v.]. Under the Anglo-Egyptian Condominium he was the first governor of Khartoum in 1898–99. He served in the Second Anglo-Boer War [q.v.], and from 1908 to 1912 he commanded the British troops in Egypt. He was promoted full general in 1919.

Maya, Battle of (25 July 1813), Peninsular War. One of the battles of the so-called Battles of the Pyrenees [q.v.]. Wellington placed forces to guard the passes over the Pyrenees to prevent the French from attempting to relieve besieged forces at Pamplona and San Sebastián [qq.v.], their last garrisons in Spain. Marshal Nicolas Soult [q.v.] planned a double breakthrough: one at Roncesvalles [q.v.] to relieve San Sebastián and one at the gorge between Bidassoa and Nivelle called Maya to relieve Pamplona. General Jean Baptiste Drouet [q.v.], with a corps of three divisions and some national guardsmen—perhaps 20,000 men—sent toward Pamplona, found his way blocked at the gorge by a British division under Lieutenant General William Stewart (1774–1827). There was stiff fighting, particularly over four Portuguese guns, which fell into French hands when the British, after suffering 1,347 casualties and inflicting upon the French about the same, were forced to fall back. In his dispatch Wellington spoke with some asperity of the loss of those Portuguese guns. Of more importance, the French were able to resume their march to Pamplona.

Maynard, Edward (1813–1891). An American dentist who practiced in Washington, D.C., from 1836 to 1891 and invented many improvements in firearms, especially in breech-loading rifles. In 1845 he patented the Maynard Tape Primer. This consisted of a strip of tape studded with pellets of fulminate of mercury. The strip was coiled in the magazine, and a pellet was brought into position each time the hammer was cocked, as in a cap pistol. Rain made the primer useless, and the army discontinued its use in 1861.

He also developed a breech-loading percussion carbine 36¾ inches long weighing about six pounds, which was the first weapon to use the expansion of the cartridge to check the escape of gas. The federal government bought 20,202 during the American Civil War. Just before the war Georgia, Florida, and Mississippi bought 2,369 in calibers from .35 to .50 from the Massachusetts Arms Company.

Maypo, Battle of (5 or 6 April 1818), Chilean War of Independence. A Chilean army of 9,000 under José de San Martín and Bernardo O'Higgins [qq.v.] crossed the Andes from Argentina and on the banks of the Maypo "Maipú" or Maipo) River, a few miles south of Santiago de Chile, defeated a force of 6,000 Spanish royalists under General Manuel Osorio (1777–1819). Each side lost about 1,000 killed and wounded; the patriot forces captured 2,350 men and 12 guns. Osorio, who escaped, retreated into Peru and died soon after in Havana, Cuba. The battle virtually assured the independence of Chile, but a small Spanish garrison remained on the remote island of Chiloé until 1826.

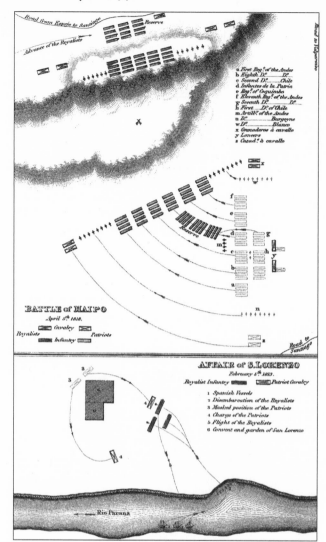

Maypo *Plan of the Battle of Maypo, April 1818*

Mazoe Party (1896). An incident in the Matabele War [q.v.] of 1896. A number of European settlers, men and women, in Southern Rhodesia (Zimbabwe), many from the Alice Mine near Mazoe, 20 miles north of Salisbury (Harare), finding themselves cut off by a band of Matabele warriors, devised a desperate measure. A wagonette, which earlier had been sent out from Salisbury to bring in the women, was covered with sheets of iron from the mine. Dragging the wagon with the women inside, the men fought their way through the Matabeles and, although a number were killed and wounded, managed to reach help. Two telegraphists had remained behind to send out calls for help, but the line was cut, and they were killed before they could be rescued.

Mbholompo, Battle of (27 August 1828), Kaffir War. On the Umtata River in eastern Cape Colony in South Africa a force of 500 soldiers and burgher volunteers with some 26,000 friendly Bantus defeated a force of perhaps 20,000 Ngwanes.

Meade, George Gordon (1815–1872). An American soldier who was graduated from West Point in 1835 and resigned the following year. After an unsuccessful pursuit of a career in civil engineering, he returned to the army on 19 May 1842 as a second lieutenant in the Topographical Engineers.

During the Mexican War [q.v.] he was present at the battles of Palo Alto, Resaca de la Palma, and Monterrey [qq.v.], earning a brevet to first lieutenant. He was a captain when the American Civil War began, and in August 1861 he was promoted brigadier general of volunteers and given command of a Pennsylvania brigade.

Meade's family was much divided by the war. He had a sister in Mississippi who was a rabid secessionist; another was the wife of a Confederate naval officer. Three other sisters were married to Union officers, and a brother was a Union naval officer. Numerous nephews fought on both sides.

General George Gordon Meade

Meade took part in the Peninsular Campaign [q.v.] and was twice severely wounded. He was only partially recovered when he led his brigade at Second Bull Run [q.v.]. In the battles of South Mountain and Antietam [qq.v.] he commanded a division in I Corps under General Joseph Hooker [q.v.]. Soon after the Battle of Fredericksburg [q.v.] in December 1862 he received command of V Corps, which he led at Chancellorsville [q.v.].

On 28 June 1863, only three days before the Battle of Gettysburg [q.v.], he was given command of the Army of the Potomac. Although he won the battle, he was roundly damned by some for allowing Lee's Army of Northern Virginia [q.v.] to "escape." When he received a message from General Henry Halleck expressing President Lincoln's "dissatisfaction," he offered to resign. He was not only retained but made a brigadier general in the regular army, to rank from 3 July 1863, and he received the Thanks of Congress.

When Grant became a lieutenant general in the spring of 1864, he made his headquarters with the Army of the Potomac, and Meade became his subordinate. In this capacity he fought through the battles of the Wilderness, Spotsylvania, and Cold Harbor and the siege of Petersburg [qq.v.]. He was finally made major general in the regular army on 18 August 1864.

After the war he commanded districts and divisions in the South and East.

Meagher, Thomas Francis (1832–1867). An Irish-born American revolutionary and soldier who in 1849 was transported to Tasmania for his political activities in Ireland. He escaped and in 1852 made his way to California and thence to New York City, where his abilities as a speaker and his Irish patriotism made him popular among Irish-Americans. At the beginning of the American Civil War he raised a company of Zouaves that became part of the 69th New York Militia commanded by Michael Corcoran [q.v.]. He fought at First Bull Run [q.v.] as a major, and the following winter he organized an Irish Brigade in New York City. He was appointed a brigadier general, to rank from 3 February 1862, and he led his brigade in all the battles of the Army of the Potomac from Second Bull Run to Chancellorsville [qq.v.]. He later served under Sherman [q.v.] in the West. In 1865 he was appointed territorial secretary of Montana, where, in the absence of a governor, he was acting governor for more than a year. On 1 July 1867 he was taking part in a drunken spree aboard a steamer on the Missouri River near Fort Benton, Montana, when he fell or was pushed overboard. His body was never found.

Meal Powder. An unglazed black powder of very fine granulation that has been treated with alcohol, causing it to burn readily and quickly.

Meat Biscuit. A biscuit in which the nutritive qualities of meat were preserved. It was developed in 1851 by Gail Borden (1801–1874), an American.

Large slabs of meat were covered with water and slowly boiled. The fat was skimmed off and the water allowed to evaporate until the liquid was reduced to the consistency of syrup. It was then mixed into flour, rolled, cut into desired sizes, and baked. One part of a biscuit contained about five soluble parts of meat. Although they could be eaten as ordinary biscuits, they were usually boiled in water with seasoning and eaten as a soup.

Neither the American nor any other army fully realized the advantages of having such nutritive food in a compact form.

Mechanicsville, Battle of (26 June 1862), American Civil War. This was the second of the Seven Days' Battles [q.v.]. Union General George B. McClellan [q.v.] had placed his army astride the Chickahominy River in east-central Virginia when he was attacked by Robert E. Lee's Army of Northern Virginia [q.v.]. In the piecemeal battle, "Stonewall" Jackson was late arriving on the field and A. P. Hill [qq.v.] launched an ill-considered attack that proved suicidal.

Although tactically indecisive, the battle was clearly a Confederate disaster: Of 15,631 Union troops engaged, 49 were killed, 207 were wounded, and 105 were missing, a total loss of 361; Confederate losses were about 1,400 out of 16,356 engaged.

Médaille Militaire. A French decoration instituted in 1852 and awarded to naval ratings and army noncommissioned officers and privates for acts of bravery in which they had been wounded; it was also given to generals commanding armies and admirals commanding fleets when they had attained the Grand Croix of the Legion of Honor [q.v.]. Recipients received a small pension. The design of the medal changed several times, but the original was silver with a gilt medallion within a silver wreath of laurel. It was suspended by a yellow ribbon with a green border.

Medal of Honor. The highest decoration awarded by the United States and its only national medal for valor or military merit in the nineteenth century. Because it is customarily bestowed by the president "in the name of the Congress," it is frequently and erroneously called the Congressional Medal of Honor.

Before the American Civil War the United States, unlike all European nations and most South American countries, had no standard medals of any description. On 7 August 1782, during the Revolutionary War, George Washington (1732–1799) authorized the award of a Purple Heart. This was not a medal but a cloth badge of purple silk edged in lace. There is no record of more than three ever having been awarded. General Washington was presented with a medal (manufactured in Paris) for driving the British out of Boston in March 1776, and John Paul Jones and Horatio Gates were each given one-of-a-kind medals. Chambers of Commerce, citizens, and groups of officers sometimes awarded medals, but no national medals or criterion for awarding them was established. Officers were usually rewarded with brevet rank [q.v.]. During the Mexican War [q.v.] and later, enlisted men who distinguished themselves in battle were given the Meritorious Service Citation Certificate, commonly called the Certificate of Merit [q.v.].

In 1861 Lieutenant Colonel Edward Davis Townsend (1830?–1893), assistant adjutant general in Washington, recommended the creation of a medal for valor. General Winfield Scott [q.v.], although noted for his love of military finery, rejected the idea, saying that the awarding of decorations was "contrary to the spirit of American institutions." But the navy liked the idea, and on 9 December 1861 Senator James W. Grimes (1816–1872) of Iowa, chairman of the Committee on Naval Affairs, proposed it. The bill passed both houses, and on 21 December Lincoln signed it into law. The act authorized 200 "medals of honor" for sailors, and on 15 May 1862 the mint was ordered to make 175. The original medal was made of copper coated with bronze, which gave it a somewhat reddish cast, and the cost was $1.85 each.

On 17 February 1862 Senator Henry Wilson (1812–1875) of Massachusetts, chairman of the Senate Committee on Military Affairs, proposed a similar medal for the army, and this bill was signed into law on 12 July. The medal was to be awarded "to such noncommissioned officers and privates as shall most distinguish themselves by their gallantry in action, and other soldierlike qualities, during the present insurrection." The original purpose of the medal was "to improve the efficiency" of the troops, and acts of bravery were not necessarily required.

The army ordered 2,000 at a cost of two dollars each in November 1863. The first were presented to the surviving six members of the Andrews's Raid [q.v.] by Secretary of War Edwin Stanton [q.v.].

Army officers did not become eligible until an act of Congress in March 1863, but the award was made retroactive to the beginning of the war. However, the revision was largely ignored. In the postwar era three had been awarded to officers, but they received the award for service while enlisted men. There were many late awards, particularly in the 1890s, when the politically powerful Grand Army of the

Republic [q.v.] demanded that more medals be presented. After Arthur MacArthur [q.v.] managed successfully to press his claim in 1890, other officers applied for the medal, and between 1891 and 1896 there were 67 awards to officers for gallantry during the Civil War, 45 of whom were still on active duty. Not until 1915 were naval officers entitled to the award. The army and navy medals were similar but carried different designs.

The high value later attached to the medal was not attributed to it originally; many were passed out haphazardly. During the Civil War 1,520 were awarded, 1,196 of which were given to soldiers and 17 to marines. During the first two weeks of April 1865 awards were made to 155 men. There were many instances of what were later considered abuses.

The most egregious distribution occurred in the awarding of the medals to 309 men of the 27th Maine, none of whom had ever heard a shot fired in anger. The 864 men in the regiment had enlisted for nine months only, and on 30 June 1863 they were all to be discharged [see Ninety-Day Regiments]. Four days before this date, and five days before the Battle of Gettysburg, they were asked to stay at their post, guarding Washington, D.C. All refused until they were offered the Medal of Honor. With this bribe 309 agreed to remain. In the event, their extended tour was only four days, and they were not required to fight at Gettysburg [q.v.] or anywhere else.

Nevertheless, they had been promised the medal, and orders were issued to give it to every member of the regiment. The governor of Maine was sent 864. After distributing medals to the 309 who had remained, he refused to distribute any others. The remainder were stashed in his barn and disappeared when it was subsequently broken into. In 1917, under the provisions of section 122 of the Act of Congress of 3 June 1916 (39 Stat. L.214), 911 awards of the Medal of Honor were revoked by direction of a board of officers, including all those awarded to soldiers of the 27th Maine.

Only one woman was ever awarded a Medal of Honor: Mary Walker [q.v.], who had worked as an army surgeon. Her medal was among those canceled in 1917, although political pressure from women's groups caused it to be posthumously restored in 1977. The medal awarded to William ("Buffalo Bill") Cody was also canceled. In the Civil War 24 black Americans earned the award (8 sailors and 16 soldiers). One, William Carney [q.v.], who saved the flag of the 54th Massachusetts in a failed attack on Fort Wagner [q.v.], South Carolina, on 10 July 1863, did not receive his award until 1900.

Sergeant Llewellyn Norton of the 10th New York Cavalry was recommended for the award for his heroism in the Battle of Sayler's Creek [q.v.] on 6 April 1865. The award was promptly approved on 5 July, but he learned of it only twenty-three years later, when he read his name among a list of recipients in *Appleton's Cyclopedia*. He contacted the War Department and was given his medal.

Only 5 soldiers ever received the Medal of Honor twice in the nineteenth century (19 as of 1997). One of these was Thomas Ward Custer [q.v.], younger brother of George Custer [q.v.]; both brothers died in the Battle of the Little Bighorn [q.v.]. Another was to Frank Dwight Baldwin [q.v.], a lightning rod salesman before he took to soldiering in the Civil War. No one has earned it three times. Unlike the British Victoria Cross [q.v.] and the French Legion of Honor [q.v.], the medal was not supposed to be awarded to foreigners, but 714 have been made to men born outside the United States, and it is doubtful that all were citizens at the time.

On 26 June 1897 new regulations were adopted for awarding the medal. Claimants were required to supply War Department records or eyewitnesses. After 1 January 1890 claims could not be submitted by the claimant, and recommendations had to be made within one year of the performance of the act.

In the nineteenth century, in addition to the 1,520 awarded during the American Civil War, 15 were awarded for gallantry in the Korean War of 1871, 109 for the Spanish-American War, and 59 for the Boxer Rebellion [qq.v.]. Like the Victoria Cross, the Medal of Honor became with time increasingly more difficult to earn, and the esteem given its recipients increased dramatically. President Harry Truman (1884–1972) said: "I would rather have that medal than be president of the United States," and General George Patton (1885–1945) said: "I'd give my soul for that decoration."

Not everyone approved of the medal's being award to civilians. When Charles Lindbergh, was awarded the medal, Ernest Williams, a former Marine Corps officer who had won a Medal of Honor in the Dominican Republic in 1916, swore never to wear his medal again, and although he lived until 1940, he kept his vow.

Medals and Orders, Military. A medal is a piece of metal bearing a design given as an award for bravery or other meritorious service; for commemoration of an event; for war service; or for long service and good conduct. It is usually suspended by a piece of colored cloth, called a ribbon, and pinned to the breast of a coat or jacket, but some medals are worn on ribbons around the neck. Military medals were rare before the nineteenth century, when they proliferated in European armies [see Médaille Militaire; Legion of Honor; Victoria Cross]. The United States had no medals or badges of any description until the Medal of Honor [q.v.] was instituted in 1861; no others were created in the nineteenth century.

War or campaign medals [q.v.] are issued to those participating in a particular war, campaign, or battle. In Britain a medal was issued to all those who took part in the Battle of Dunbar in 1650, and the Honourable East India Company issued medals to the victors, both British and Indian, who took part in the storming and capture of Seringapatnam in 1799. The first British nineteenth-century war medal issued to all ranks was the Waterloo Medal, issued in 1816 to all who participated in the 1815 Battle of Waterloo [q.v.]. In 1848 a general service medal was issued with appropriate clasps bearing the names of battles from 1793 to 1814, but the participants in the Battle of Maida [q.v.] on 4 July 1806 had to wait forty-two years for theirs, and those who fought at Albuera [q.v.] on 10 May 1811 waited thirty-seven years. By that time few were alive to receive them.

The practice of giving a medal for service in a war or campaign and adding inscribed clasps or bars for each battle came into being after the Second Sikh War [q.v.] of 1848–49.

Some medals, such as the Victoria Cross, have always been awarded only for acts of bravery in war. Others, such as the French Legion of Honor and the American Medal of Honor, were at one time awarded to civilians as well as soldiers and sailors and for services other than gallantry in action. Some medals too are divided into two or more classes, but never more than five. Medals or orders initiated in one country have sometimes become the medal or order of another. The Order of St. Stanislas, originally a Polish order instituted in 1765, became in 1831 a Russian order in three classes. In many orders the number of living recipients was limited for each class.

Most ribbons have been square or rectangular. The practice of folding the ribbons of breast badges into triangular shapes began in Austria in the 1830s, and by 1860 it was common practice in many countries, although never in Britain or France. Ribbons were sometimes decorated with stars, clasps, or other devices and, rarely, jewels.

Some grades of chivalric orders carry medals, but the higher classes of the order wear metal and enamel, sometimes jeweled, stars in various shapes, unsuspended, often with sashes and special robes.

In many countries medals awarded by certain other countries have been and are authorized. The Turkish Order of Medjidie [q.v.] was issued to many British, French, and Sardinian officers after the Crimean War and to British officers after Arabi's Revolt [qq.v.]. An Egyptian medal was authorized for all those who took part in the reconquest of the Sudan [q.v.].

Medellín, Battle of (29 March 1809), Peninsular War. At this town on the Guadiana River in Badajoz Province, Spanish General Gregorio de la Cuesta [q.v.] with 20,000 infantry, 3,000 cavalry, and 30 guns was defeated by a French force of 17,000 infantry, 5,000 cavalry, and 60 guns under Marshal Claude Victor [q.v.]. The Spanish lost 8,000 dead and 2,000 taken prisoner; also lost were nine standards and 20 guns. Estimates of French losses vary from 300 to 2,000 but were probably about 1,000.

Medicine and Surgery, Military. For most of the nineteenth century the practices, preparations, and substances used in treating and preventing diseases in all armies were more often deleterious than beneficial. Some drugs administered were actually toxic; strychnine and turpentine were both in the pharmacopeia. A standard treatment for almost any internal ailment, even diarrhea, was a purgative. Calomel (mercurous chloride, Hg_2Cl_2) and blue mass [q.v.] were favorites. The work of Louis Pasteur (1822–1895) in France in the 1860s proved the germ theory, while Robert Koch (1843–1910), a pioneer bacteriologist in Germany, was a leader among those who proved that specific bacteria caused specific diseases.

Although, by reason of the general lack of accurate medical knowledge, much could be excused army doctors, the conditions under which soldiers lived, even in peacetime, were notoriously unhealthy. General William Tecumseh Sherman once complained that slaves were better housed than soldiers. In 1850 the death rate among American civilians was 1 in 576. Although during the War of 1812 James Tilton [q.v.] was appointed "Physician and Surgeon General" in 1813 and a Medical Department of the Northern Army was established, the U.S. army did not have a proper and permanent medical department until 1818. The death rate among soldiers was 1 in 108 in 1821, and nearly forty years later it was 1 in 142. The army's most disastrous exposure to disease was suffered by the 1st Infantry stationed at Baton Rouge, Louisiana, which between 1819 and 1824 had a mean strength of 284 and a death rate of 20 percent per year and an average sick rate of 400 percent.

In 1854 British infantry regiments lost 20.8 percent of their strength through men invalided out of the service. A royal commission appointed in 1857 to inquire into conditions in barracks and hospitals revealed an alarming mortality rate, nearly double the civilian death rate. In British line infantry regiments, 18 per 1,000 died each year. In the British Foot Guards stationed in London, where guardsmen in barracks were given fewer cubic feet of air than were prisoners in cells, the rate was 20.5 per 1,000.

Although in 1800 Dr. Benjamin Waterhouse (1754–1846), a Boston doctor, introduced Jennerian cowpox vaccination, many doctors were unconvinced of its benefits or did not understand how best to administer the vaccine. The first tetanus antitoxin was produced in Berlin only in 1890 by Emil von Behring (1854–1917) with Shilbasaburo Kitazato (1852–1931); it was not widely used until the twentieth century. In the same year a diphtheria antitoxin was produced. Malaria was the only disease effectively treated, the benefits of quinine [q.v.] being known, but it was not always available or properly dispensed.

Special scourges affected some parts of the world and made them more dangerous than others. Soldiers stationed in India and other parts of Asia were frequently stricken by cholera [q.v.], and it was not until 1855 that Dr. John Snow (1813–1858), vice-president of Westminister Medical Society and the world's first M.D. anesthesiologist (he once gave Queen Victoria chloroform during a birthing), discovered it was transmitted by contaminated drinking water; the beautiful Caribbean was soaked in yellow fever; West Africa was known as the white man's grave because of malaria and a host of exotic diseases. In time of war, of course, conditions worsened.

In war, surgeons saved more lives than medical doctors did, although the unsanitary conditions under which they usually operated created their own problems. Napoleon complained that "the inexperience of surgeons does more harm to the army than the enemy's batteries." During the Napoleonic Wars the chance of surviving a major wound was not better than one in three. In the American Civil War, hospital gangrene, pyemia (pus in the blood), or erysipelas resulted from 20 percent of all operations. Only 3 percent survived pyemia. The treatment of wounds was confined to trying to control bleeding, removing bullets, shrapnel, and shell fragments; splinting bones; and amputating limbs. Most wounds to the head and torso were fatal. Of the wounded seen by surgeons in the Union army during the American Civil War, 71 percent were leg or arm wounds, probably because those wounded in the head or torso died before they could see a doctor.

A major problem in all nineteenth-century wars was the difficulty of removing wounded from the field. In the United States, army bandsmen were required to lay down their musi-

Medicine and Surgery *Medicine pannier, surgeons' field companion, ambulance and medicine wagons, American Civil War*

cal instruments and become stretcher-bearers. This system did not work well, but it was in place until the Second World War. A much-improved system for forward surgery and forward evacuation was devised by army surgeon Jonathan Letterman [q.v.] during the American Civil War, but not until 11 March 1864 did Congress create an Army Ambulance Corps with assigned enlisted men under medical control. Even so, quartermasters, not medical personnel, usually controlled ambulances and horses.

In Europe, Dominique Larrey [q.v.] developed the flying ambulance during the Napoleonic Wars, and during the Franco-Prussian War the Germans developed an excellent evacuation program using railroads.

Chloroform was developed as an anesthetic in 1847 by Sir James Simpson (1811–1884), a Scottish obstetrician, and the anesthetic properties of ether were discovered in 1842 by Crawford Williamson Long (1815–1878) of Jefferson, Georgia, who performed eight operations using it between 1842 and 1846. Two years later a Connecticut dentist, Horace Wells (1815–1848), used nitrous oxide (laughing gas) in removing teeth.

Ether was first used in war in 1847 at Veracruz during the Mexican War. Many doctors refused to use it even when available. Dr. (later Sir) John Hall [q.v.], principal medical officer and inspector general of hospitals in the Crimea [q.v.], issued a memorandum to army doctors cautioning them against the indiscriminate use of chloroform, saying that "the smart of the knife is a powerful stimulant." Nevertheless, some surgeons continued its use.

Hippocrates wrote: "War is the only proper school for a surgeon" (*Wounds of the Head* [c. 415 B.C.]). Certainly war gives surgeons ample practice. In the nineteenth century they learned to work rapidly, and it was said that an exceptionally able surgeon could remove a leg in thirty seconds. One cynical wag reported a particularly rapid surgeon who also removed the patient's left testicle and two fingers from the hand of an assistant holding the patient down. After the Battle of Borodino [q.v.] French army surgeon Larrey was said to have performed two hundred amputations in twenty-four hours, an average of about seven minutes per operation, if one assumes there were no breaks in his schedule.

Most army doctors were held in low esteem, even by other doctors. Dr. James McGrigor [q.v.], principal medical officer on Wellington's staff during the Peninsular War [q.v.], regarded many of his colleagues as little more than apothecaries and "druggists' apprentices." Doctors rarely acquired army officer rank and, even when commissioned, were regarded as second-class officers in the mess. In the British army in 1882 the pay was so low that no doctors could be recruited.

For most of the century medical services in most armies were in the hands of civilians or regimental surgeons who were responsible only to regimental commanders. In the British service a Hospital Corps was formed in 1857, not until 1873 were doctors removed from regimental organizations, and doctors did not command hospitals until 1877. In 1884 a Medical Staff Corps was formed with officers and other ranks, but there was no fully integrated medical service until 1889, and the Royal Army Medical Corps was established only in 1898. There were no dentists until World War I.

In all armies throughout the nineteenth century most of the nursing was done by male orderlies or soldiers, principally because in peace and war a large percentage of the patients in any military hospital suffered from venereal diseases [q.v.], and it was considered unseemly that women should be exposed to such men or administer the treatments considered necessary. Even as late as 1821 the London Hospital refused to accept any more female students because instructors found it difficult to teach "certain unpleasant subjects of medicine."

There were no professional nurses in American armies, but on 10 June 1861, at the beginning of the American Civil War, Dorothea Lynde Dix [q.v.] was appointed superintendent of women nurses, all of whom were volunteers. Dix was strict and had her own standards, turning away would-be nurses who were pretty or under thirty and accepting only those who were "plain to almost homeliness in dress, and by no means endowed with personal attractiveness." Her nurses were not allowed to wear ribbons, jewelry, or hoop skirts.

In the Confederate army nursing was not considered a respectable vocation for women other than nuns, and sick and wounded soldiers in army hospitals were tended by soldiers, male civilians, or slaves.

Medina, Siege of (October–November 1812), Arabian War. A Turkish-Egyptian army under Ahmad Bonaparte (fl. 1810), an Albanian general, laid siege to the holy city of Medina (Medinah) in Arabia, held by the Wahhabis. In mid-November 1812, while the Wahhabis were attending midday prayers, a Turkish mine was exploded, blowing a large hole in the city wall. The Arnauts [q.v.]—Albanians in the Egyptian service—led by Thomas Keith [q.v.], a former soldier in the ranks of the 72nd Highlanders and now a trusted soldier in the forces of Tuson, the son of Mehemet Ali [q.v.], swarmed through the breach. Some 1,000 Wahhabis were killed, for a loss of 50 of the attackers. The city was plundered, and Ahmad Bonaparte built a tower of Wahhabi heads on the road to Yenbo in the Hejaz.

Medina del Río Seco, Battle of (14 July 1808), Peninsular War. At this Galician village, 25 miles northwest of Valladolid on the Sequillo River, an Allied force of 21,900 infantry and 600 cavalry with 20 guns under Spanish General Gregorio de la Cuesta and General Joachim Blake [qq.v.] were defeated by a French force of 14,000 infantry and 1,200 cavalry with 40 guns under Marshal Jean Baptiste Bessières [q.v.]. The Spanish lost 400 dead, 500 wounded, and 1,200 taken prisoner; 10 guns were lost. French losses were 105 killed and 300 wounded.

Medina del Río Seco *Battle of Medina de Río Seco, 14 July 1808*

Mediterranean Expedition, British. See Naples, Anglo-Russian Expedition to; Calabrian War.

Medjidie. 1. A Turkish military and knightly order in five classes instituted in 1852 by Sultan Abd ul Medjie (1823–1861). The three highest classes wore the medal, in a distinctive size for each, suspended by a ribbon around the neck. After the Crimean War [q.v.] the order was conferred upon many French and British officers.

2. The name of a Turkish coin worth twenty piasters that was first coined in 1844.

Meeanee, Battle of. See Miani, Battle of.

Meerut, Mutiny at (May 1857). At this Indian town, 42 miles northeast of Delhi, the Indian Mutiny [q.v.] began on 10 May 1857, when the sowars and sepoys of the garrison there murdered their officers and every European they encountered before marching off to Delhi.

Meeting Engagement. A battle that occurs when a moving force deployed for battle engages an enemy unexpectedly, before either side has adequate time to plan to attack or defend. Sometimes called an encounter battle.

Mehemet Ali (1769–1849). An Egyptian soldier and ruler of Albanian parentage. He served as a junior officer in the 6,000-strong army of Albanians (known as Arnauts) sent by the sultan of Turkey to Egypt, and in 1799 he fought against Napoleon in the Battle of Aboukir (Abukir). By 1803 he was second-in-command. After the French and British left, he suppressed a mutiny among the Arnauts and became their commander. In 1805 the sheikhs of Cairo made him a pasha, and in the same year the sultan recognized him as his viceroy in Egypt. In the next few years he strengthened his position, and after massacring the Mamelukes [q.v.] in 1811, he was left without rivals. Between 1811 and 1818 he made war on the Wahhabis [see Arabian Wars]. In 1819 he prepared an expedition to conquer the Sudan, and the following year his son Ibrahim Pasha [q.v.] led an army south. From 1820 through 1822 he extended his power up the Nile, conquering Nubia and Kordofan, and in 1822 he laid the foundation for Khartoum. He then crossed the Gazira of Sennar and conquered the decadent Funji kingdom.

In 1822 the sultan of Turkey persuaded him to aid in suppressing a Greek rebellion. In 1827 Ali lost his fleet in the Battle of Navarino, but in 1830 he gained possession of Crete. Feeling himself inadequately rewarded for suppressing the Greeks, he sent Ibrahim Pasha in 1831 to conquer Syria, then a Turkish province. The Turks were completely routed in the

Mehemet Ali, viceroy of Egypt, 1830s

Battle of Nizib [q.v.] on 24 June 1839, but Mehemet Ali was prevented by the European Great Powers from conquering Constantinople (Istanbul) and was forced to content himself with a hereditary vice-royalty of Egypt conferred in 1841. During his last years his mind gave way, and Ibrahim Pasha was appointed viceroy.

Mehemet Ali Pasha (1827–1878), real name: Karl Detroit. A German-born Turkish soldier who emigrated to Turkey in 1843 and became a protégé of Mehemet Ali (1815–1871), the grand vizier. He attended a Turkish military school, adopted Islam, and was commissioned in the Turkish army in 1853. He served in the Crimean War and in 1865 was promoted brigadier general. During the Russo-Turkish War [q.v.] of 1877–78 he commanded the Turkish army in Bulgaria until he was forced to retreat and was replaced by Suleiman Pasha [q.v.]. On 7 September 1878 he was mobbed and killed by insurgents in Albania.

Mehemet Ali Revolt. See Egyptian Revolt; Mehemet Ali.

Mehtar. In India, a sweeper or scavenger.

Mehter. A Turkish military band.

Meigs, John Roberts (1841?–1864). An American soldier and the son of General Montgomery Meigs [q.v.], who was graduated from West Point in 1863, ranking first in his class. In his brief career as an army engineer in the Union army during the American Civil War he won brevets to major before he was killed on 3 October 1864 at Dayton, Virginia, near Harrisonburg. At the time it was believed that he was killed by Confederate guerrillas, and in retaliation General Philip Sheridan [q.v.], on whose staff he was serving, ordered the destruction of all houses within a five-mile radius of the town. Only after the war was over was it learned that he was killed not by guerrillas but by a Confederate scout while trying to avoid capture.

Meigs, Montgomery Cunningham (1816–1892). An American soldier who attended the University of Pennsylvania and was graduated from West Point in 1836. He worked on numerous engineering projects, including the construction of the House and Senate wings and the dome of the Capitol in Washington, D.C. On 14 May 1861 he was promoted from captain of engineers to colonel of the 11th Infantry. The following day he was appointed quartermaster general of the U.S. army with the rank of brigadier general. He served as quartermaster general throughout the American Civil War and until he retired in 1882. In his long tenure he did much to contain dishonesty and to tighten the enforcement of army regulations regarding procurement. On 5 July 1864 he was brevetted major general.

After his retirement he served as a regent of the Smithsonian Institution and was the architect of the palatial Pension Office Building in Washington, D.C., built between 1882 and 1887 at 401 F Street Northwest, into the cast-iron columns of which, curiously, he stuffed newspapers, war records, construction manuals, and building plans. On 4 January 1892, two days after his death, general orders were issued stating in part: "The Army has rarely possessed an officer . . . who was entrusted by the government with a greater variety of weighty responsibilities, or who proved himself more worthy of confidence."

Meiji Restoration, War of. See Boshin Civil War.

Meiji Rifle. See Arisaka Rifle.

Mejía, Tomás. A Mexican general of native descent who supported the emperor Maximilian [q.v.] and was executed with him at Querétaro on 19 June 1867.

Melas, Michael Friedrich Benedikt von (1729–1806). An Austrian soldier who commanded the Austrian army in Italy in the 1790s. He was defeated by Napoleon in the Battle of Marengo [q.v.] in 1800 and in 1801–03 was commanding general in Bohemia.

Mêlée. A confused struggle often involving hand-to-hand fighting. (Now usually written without diacritical marks.)

Melegnano, Battle of (8 June 1859). Austro-Piedmontese War. After the Battle of Magenta [q.v.] on 4 June 1859 some 18,000 Austrians under Field Marshal Ludwig August von Benedek [q.v.] entrenched themselves in this commune, then called Marignano, 10 miles southeast of Milan, where they were attacked and driven from their positions by 16,000 French under Marshal Achille Baraguay d'Hilliers [q.v.]. Austrian losses were 1,400 killed and wounded and 900 taken prisoner; French losses were about 850 killed and wounded. Before retreating, the Austrians massacred many of the commune's inhabitants.

Melénite. An explosive developed by a French chemist, M. Turpin, which was approved for use by the French war minister in December 1886. On 17 June 1891 Turpin and a French army captain were fined, imprisoned, and then exiled for "receiving money for communications concerning melénite to foreigners."

Memoir. In military usage, a plan involving military matters offered by officers to their government or senior commanders.

Memorial Day. See Decoration Day.

Memphis, Confederate Raid on (20 August 1864), American Civil War. In a raid on this Tennessee town Confederate General Nathan Bedford Forrest [q.v.] attempted without success to capture Federal Generals Stephen A. Hurlbut [q.v.] and Cadwallader Colden Washburn (1818–1882). Only Washburn's uniform was taken. Federal losses in the short affair were 15 killed, 65 wounded, and 112 missing; Confederate losses were 9 killed and 24 wounded.

Memphis Novelty Works. A factory, initially located in Memphis, Tennessee, operated first by Thomas S. Leech, a former cotton broker, and later joined by Charles H. Rigdon (1823–1866), an engineer and small manufacturer. A newspaper advertisement in the *Memphis Appeal* on 18 September 1861 stated that the firm was "Established primarily for the Manufacture of Army cutlery and brass castings of all kinds." It offered swords, knives, and "bayonets for shotguns and rifles." The business was at first limited to the production of edged weapons.

In May 1862 the company moved to Columbus, Mississippi, where the Confederates established the Briarfield Arsenal and Armory and "Memphis" was dropped from the firm's name. Soon after, it appears, the company began to manufacture for the Confederacy 1,500 copies of Colt's six-shot .36 caliber Navy Model 1851 revolver pistol. Still later, it moved to Greensboro, Georgia. It became the second largest Confederate manufacturer of handguns after Griswold and Gunnison [q.v.]. The partnership was dissolved in December 1863. Little is known of Leech, who after the war returned to being a cotton broker.

Menabrea, Luigi Federigo (1809–1896). An Italian soldier and statesman who in 1859 was chief of engineers in the Piedmont-Sardinian army. In the Italian Wars of Independence [q.v.] he directed the sieges of Ancona, Capua, and Gaeta [qq.v.]. In 1861–62 he was minister of marine, and from 1867 to 1869 he was premier.

Menelek II (1844–1913). An Abyssinian warrior and ruler who was the son of Haile Melikot (1825–1855), king of Shoa, and grandson of Sahale Selassie (1795–1847), king of Shoa and Galla. He succeeded to the throne of Abyssinia (Ethiopia) in 1889 and signed a treaty that in its Amharic version said he *could* ask for Italian protection but that in the Italian version placed him and his country under the domination of Italy. In 1893 he abrogated the treaty and in the Battle of Adowa [q.v.] on 1 March 1896 soundly defeated an Italian army. In 1898 he sent a force under General A. K. Boulatovich, a mercenary Russian soldier, to occupy the Lake Rudolf region and another to plant the Abyssinian standard at the confluence of the White Nile and Sobat rivers. From 1910 to his death he was unable to rule because of apoplectic attacks.

Menelek II, king of Ethiopia

Méneval, Claude François de (1778–1850). Napoleon's private secretary, who served him from 1802 to 1813.

Menewa (1765?–1865). A leader of the Lower Creek Indians in Alabama. During the War of 1812 [q.v.] Tecumseh [q.v.] traveled to Alabama and persuaded Menewa and others

to side with the British, thus beginning the Creek War [q.v.]. Menewa acted as war chief, but in the Battle of Horseshoe Bend [q.v.] on 27 March 1814, he listened to the prophecies of the medicine man, who was also a head chief, and disposed his men accordingly. The battle proved a disaster for the Creeks. Menewa himself received several wounds but survived to kill the medicine man.

Menewa opposed the ceding of Creek lands to the United States that had been agreed to by his rival, William McIntosh [q.v.], and he led the band of warriors who killed McIntosh. In 1826 he led a delegation to Washington to protest the treaty but met with no success. His portrait, now owned by the Smithsonian Institution, was painted while he was there.

In 1836, during the Second Seminole War [q.v.], when a number of Creeks sided with the Seminoles, he led warriors against them and in consideration for his services was promised that he and his people could remain in Alabama. Nevertheless, about 1840 they were transported to Indian Territory.

Menotti, Ciro (1798–1831). An Italian patriot who led an unsuccessful short-lived insurrection against the Austrians at Modena, Italy, in February 1831. He was hanged on 26 May.

Menou, Jacques François de (1750–1810). A French officer in Napoleonic armies who was with Napoleon in Egypt and appointed governor of Rosetta. He became a Muslim and married the daughter of a keeper of a bathhouse. After the assassination of General Jean Baptiste Kléber (1753–1800) on 14 June 1800 he commanded the French army in Egypt. On 21 March 1801 he was defeated by the British in the Battle of Abukir [q.v.]. Later that year he returned to France and held no further commands but served in a number of administrative positions. He was governor of Venice when he died.

Mensdorff-Pouilly, Alexander von (1813–1871). An Austrian soldier and statesman who became a general in 1850 and from 1864 to 1866 was minister of foreign affairs.

Menshikov, Aleksandr Sergeivich (1789–1869). A Russian soldier who was the great-grandson of Field Marshal Aleksandr Danilovich Menshikov (1660?–1729). He became a general during Napoleon's invasion of Russia [q.v.]. He fought in the Russo-Turkish War [q.v.] of 1828–29 and was wounded in the siege of Varna [q.v.]. In 1831 he was governor-general of Finland, and in 1836 he was minister of marine. He later served as ambassador to Turkey, where his overbearing behavior was thought to have provoked the Crimean War [q.v.]. He commanded Russian forces in the battles of Alma and Inkerman [qq.v.] and commanded at Sevastopol [q.v.] until forced by illness to retire in 1855.

Mentana, Battle of (3 November 1867), Italian Wars of Independence. At this commune, 10 miles northeast of Rome, 5,000 French plus 1,500 Papal Zouaves under General Pierre Louis de Failly [q.v.] soundly defeated a 10,000-man patriot army under Giuseppe Garibaldi [q.v.]. General de Failly reported that "the chassepot rifles [q.v.] did wonders." The Allied forces lost 182, mostly Papal Zouaves. Garibaldi lost 1,100 killed or wounded and 1,000 taken prisoner. He himself escaped, but he was captured soon after and exiled to the island of Caprera, off northern Sardinia.

Not until August 1870, when the French withdrew from Italy to fight in the Franco-Prussian War [q.v.], did patriot forces take Rome and make it the capital of the kingdom.

Mention in Dispatches. A method in the British service of conferring an honor upon soldiers. In his dispatch after a battle the general in command included the names of officers who had distinguished themselves. In his dispatches from Sind in 1842 General Charles Napier [q.v.] was the first to list common soldiers as well as officers, even including the names of Indian soldiers whose behavior had been outstanding.

Menuki. Metal ornaments on the sides of the hilt of a Japanese sword or dagger.

Mercenaries. 1. Men serving merely for money, loot, or other advantages.

2. Men serving in the army of a nation not their own.

In the nineteenth century France, Prussia, Naples, the Papal States, and Great Britain all employed mercenaries. The French in particular have always generously permitted foreigners to donate their blood and lives for French causes, a tradition going back to the twelfth century. Napoleon had battalions or regiments of Irish, Welsh, Greek, Egyptian Copts, Poles, Austrians, Italians, Hungarians, Swiss, and other nationalities, particularly in the period between 1806 and 1813. In 1809 about one-third of the French army consisted of foreigners, as did more than half of the army Napoleon led into Russia in 1812 [see Russian Campaign, Napoleon's].

In 1813 Britain had an army of 52,000, of whom one-fifth were foreigners. The British enlisted Gurkhas from Nepal after 1816, and in the Peninsular War and the Crimean War [qq.v.] they enlisted Germans into special units. Local corps were also trained in many African colonies. Both British and French vied for Swiss recruits during the Crimean War.

Except during major wars, most of the American regular army was made up of foreign-born soldiers, but these were not considered mercenaries.

The Swiss served in many foreign armies. In 1859 Switzerland passed a law forbidding its citizens to serve as mercenaries, but the practice continued. From 1855 to 1861 the French Foreign Legion [q.v.] had a Swiss regiment, the last time that Swiss were incorporated as a separate unit by a French government. The Swiss Guards at the Vatican remain the last completely Swiss military unit outside Switzerland.

Mercenaries have often been excoriated and seldom admired. The Italian poet Giacomo Leopardi (1798–1837) wrote: "Wretched is he who is killed in battle not in defense of his native land, but by another's enemies and for another people" (*All'Italia* [1818]). But the British poet A. E. Housman (1859–1936) in his "Epitaph on an Army of Mercenaries" (*Last Poems* [1922]) saw them in a different light:

These, in the day when heaven was falling,
  The hour when earth's foundations fled,
Followed their mercenary calling
  And took their wages and are dead.

Their shoulders held the sky suspended;
  They stood, and earth's foundations stay;
What God abandoned, these defended,
  And saved the sum of things for pay.

Mercenaries *Alexander Gardner, Irish-American mercenary and commander of Indian artillery in battles with the Afghans*

Mercury Fulminate. A gray crystalline solid, $Hg[CNO]_2$, extremely sensitive to shock, friction, or a spark, used in the manufacture of percussion caps and detonators. It was sometimes called fulminate of mercury. In 1823 a German chemist, Justus von Liebig (1803–1873), became the first to succeed in isolating fulminic acid.

Merit, Certificate of. See Certificate of Merit.

Meritorious Service Medal. A British medal instituted in 1845 and awarded to sergeants for meritorious service or gallantry. The medal came with an annuity and was colloquially known as the Sergeants Medal. Eligibility was expanded to include others during the First World War.

Merkin. A mop used to clean a cannon.

Merlin. A handspike.

Merlon. The space between the crenels of a battlement [q.v.].

Merritt, Wesley (1834–1910). An American soldier, the seventh of eleven children, who was graduated from West Point in 1860 and after brief service in Utah returned east to take part in the American Civil War. On 29 June 1863, leaping over the heads of many more senior officers, he became a Union brigadier general of volunteers in command of a cavalry brigade. By 1 April 1865 he was a major general of volunteers, and he was one of the three commissioners who received Robert E. Lee's capitulation at Appomattox. A staff officer of Philip Sheridan [q.v.] described Merritt as "tall, slender and intellectual looking. He had a constitution of iron, and underneath a rather passive demeanor concealed a fiery ambition."

After the war he became a lieutenant colonel in the 9th Cavalry, one of the two black cavalry regiments (the other being the 10th Cavalry), and in 1876 colonel of the 5th Cavalry. He was again a brigadier general in 1887 and in 1895 a major general. In his thirty-three years of service following the Civil War he served on the western frontier, took part in the Nez Percé War [q.v.], commanded several departments in the West, and was superintendent at West Point from 1882 to 1887. During the Spanish-American War [q.v.] he commanded the first expeditionary force to the Philippines, where he captured Manila on 13 August 1898. He retired on 16 June 1900 after giving forty years to the service of his country.

Merthyr Tydfil Riots (1831). Miners and ironworkers in Merthyr Tydfil in Glamorganshire, South Wales, suffering under poverty and falling wages and incited by the ferment aroused by the Reform Bill, rose in rebellion and seized the town, which they held for three days until troops were called in. A confrontation in front of the Castle Hotel resulted in 16 dead. One of the leaders of the uprising, Richard Lewis (1807/8–1831), known as Dick Penderyn, was convicted of wounding a soldier and publicly executed at Cardiff on 31 August 1831. Many in South Wales, convinced of his innocence, turned him into a folk hero.

Mesolóngion. See Missolonghi, Sieges of.

Mess. 1. As a verb, to dine.

2. As a noun, an arrangement among soldiers to eat together and share costs. Unmarried officers of a regiment dined together, and even married officers were expected to dine at the mess at specified periods. In the French army, subalterns messed separately from captains, and field officers also usually dined alone.

3. As a noun, in the British service the home of bachelor officers in a regiment or other military unit, which on permanent bases often included recreational facilities.

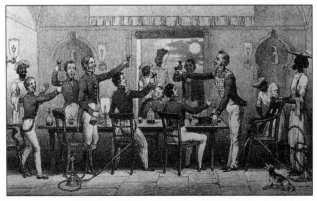

Mess *British officers' mess in India*

"Message to Garcia, A." In April 1898 American army Lieutenant Andrew Summers Rowan [q.v.], a graduate of the West Point class of 1881, was sent on a secret mission to Cuban insurgent General Calixto García y Iñiguez [q.v.]. Despite many obstacles, Rowan made his way through the Spanish blockade and on 1 May 1898 met with García and obtained valuable information. He returned with his mission accomplished. He was made famous by the widely read essay "A Message to Garcia," written by Elbert Hubbard (1856–1915) and published in 1899. Hubbard used Rowan's feat to illuminate a manifesto that struck a chord: "It is not book learning young men need, but a stiffening of the vertebrae which will cause them to be loyal to a trust, to act promptly, concentrate their energies, do a thing—'carry a message to Garcia.'" That the message was *from* García was inconsequential to Hubbard's theme.

An estimated hundred million copies of the essay were sold. Industrialists presented copies to their workers, teachers distributed copies to their students, and parents gave copies to their children. During the Russo-Japanese War of 1904–05 translations were issued to soldiers on both sides.

Rowan was awarded the Distinguished Service Cross for his exploit and was made a lieutenant colonel of volunteers in the Spanish-American War [q.v.]. He served in the Philippines, where he earned the Silver Star Certificate and was wounded. He retired as a regular army major in 1909. Hubbard was one of the 128 Americans who died when the *Lusitania* was sunk by a German submarine off the coast of Ireland on 7 May 1915.

Mess Beef. An American name for jerky, strips of meat dried in the sun or over a fire [see Biltong].

Mess Dress. Sometimes called a mess kit. A uniform worn by British officers for evening dinner or for formal parties. In the 1820s a shell jacket [q.v.] came to be worn in Indian army messes, and the fashion spread to Britain, finally becoming subject to regulation. It was not worn by other European armies.

Messedaglia, Giacomo Bartolomeo (1846–1893). An Italian soldier who in 1859 enlisted in the Sardinian-Piedmontese army and six years later was promoted sergeant. He fought in the Austro-Piedmontese War [q.v.] of 1859 and received a medical discharge in 1869. In 1876, after working for a time in Asia Minor, he journeyed to Egypt, where he found work with the Egyptian general staff. In 1878 Charles Gordon [q.v.], then governor-general of the Sudan, appointed him governor of Dara in the province of Darfur, which had been conquered by Egypt in 1874. The following year, after fighting with some but not complete success against the rebellious Muhammad Harun al Rashid Saif el-Din [q.v.], he was appointed governor of Darfur with the rank of *miralai* [q.v.]. In 1880 he was discharged and charged with irregularities. He was tried in Cairo and acquitted of all charges. In 1882 he made an inspection trip in the Sudan with Lieutenant Colonel John Donald Hamill Stewart (1843?–1884), soon to be killed by Arabs trying to reach Egypt after escaping from besieged Khartoum. In 1884 Messedaglia was chief of intelligence in the Red Sea coastal expedition of Valentine Baker [q.v.], in the course of which he was wounded in the Battle of El Teb [q.v.]. After working in intelligence during the Gordon Relief Expedition [q.v.], he retired from the Egyptian service. In 1887 he returned to Upper Egypt as a correspondent for *La Riforma* of Rome. In 1891 he returned to Italy, and two years later he died at Pisa.

Messiah War (1890–91). A Paiute Indian medicine man named Wovoka [q.v.], or Jack Wilson, originated the ghost dance that inspired a creed involving the arrival of an Indian Messiah. It became distorted as it was embraced by the plains tribes, particularly the Sioux, who turned it into faith in the eventual Indian conquest of the white men [see Ghost Dance Disturbances], a belief that inspired an uprising on the Black Hills Reservation. A military expedition led by General Nelson A. Miles [q.v.] moved against the Teton Sioux, and a short war culminated in the defeat of the Indians in the Battle of Wounded Knee [q.v.] in North Dakota.

Mészáros, Lázár (1796–1858). An Hungarian soldier and politician who in 1848 was a colonel in the army of Austrian General Josef Radetzky [q.v.] in Italy. Later in the same year he became briefly Austrian minister of war. In 1849 he organized a revolutionary Hungarian army, but after defeats at Szreg and Timioşara [q.v.] he fled to Turkey. [See Hungarian Revolution.]

Meteorological Register. A record of the weather. Throughout the nineteenth century it was widely believed that weather conditions had an effect upon diseases. Therefore, in the American army, beginning in 1814 under Surgeon General James Tilton [q.v.], surgeons at every military post were required to file monthly reports on the weather, including temperatures taken three times daily, winds, amount of cloudiness, barometric pressures, amount of rain or melted snow, etc. Beginning in 1826, these were published. In 1870 the task of collecting weather data was transferred to the Army Signal Service, but army medical officers continued to collect and forward weather information until 1890, when the U. S. Weather Service took over the task.

Metford, William Ellis (1824–1899). An English inventor and gunsmith who in the early 1850s developed an improved theodolite. In 1857 he accepted an appointment with the East India Company Railways and arrived at Monghyr, a city on the Ganges 235 miles north-northwest of Calcutta, on 18 May 1857, just as the Indian Mutiny [q.v.] erupted. He worked energetically to build up the defenses of the town, but his health gave way, and after a year he returned to England. There he invented an explosive rifle bullet, which in 1863 was adopted by the government.

Metford was a pioneer of shallow grooving in rifles and the use of hardened cylindrical bullets, which he patented in 1865. In 1875 he developed his first breech-loading rifle. His bore, combined with a bolt action and detachable magazine developed by American inventors James P. Lee [q.v.] and James Ellis Metford (1824–1899), produced the .303 caliber Lee-Metford rifle, which was adopted by the British army in 1888.

Methuen, Paul Sanford, Third Baron (1845–1930). A British soldier who was commissioned in the Scots Guards in 1863. He took part in 1864–65 in the Bechuanaland Expedition [q.v.] of Sir Charles Warren [q.v.] but saw no action. He first saw action serving under Sir Garnet Wolseley [q.v.] in the Second Ashanti War in 1873–74 [q.v.] and in 1882 in suppressing Arabi's Revolt [q.v.] in Egypt. In 1897–98 he was press censor on the Tirah Expedition and later filled the same function in the Gordon Relief Expedition [qq.v.]. In 1899–1902, during the Second Anglo-Boer War [q.v.], he commanded the division that was defeated at Magersfontein [q.v.] by Pieter Cronjé [q.v.], and in 1902 he was captured by the Boers at Tweebosch, the only British general to fall into Boer hands. From 1907 to 1909 he was commander-in-chief in South Africa.

Métier, Armée de. A standing army of long-term professional soldiers.

Métis. French-speaking Catholics in Canada's Northwest Territories of mixed French and Indian blood who called themselves Bois-Brûlés (burnt wood). In 1870 and again in 1885, led by Louis Riel [q.v.], they unsuccessfully rebelled against British Canadian rule. [See Red River Rebellion; Riel's Rebellion.]

Metropolitan Army. An army based on a nation's own soil, as opposed to separate armies serving in colonies and possessions.

Metz, École d'Application de l'Artillerie et du Genié at. The French army's school of application for artillery and engineers, the counterpart of the British Royal Military Academy, Woolwich, was established at Metz in 1802. Combining two existing schools, it gave practical training to graduates of the École Polytechnique [q.v.] and educated artillery noncommissioned officers aspiring to hold commissions.

Metz, Siege of (19 August–27 October 1870), Franco-Prussian War. Metz and Strasbourg were the two great French fortresses in northeast France on which were based the entire system of defense guarding the traditional German invasion routes. Because the railroad from Saarbrücken to Rheims, Châlons, and Paris ran through Metz, the city was one of the Germans' prime objectives. After the Battle of Mars-la-Tour–Vionville [q.v.] Marshal Achille Bazaine [q.v.] fell back to Metz, taking up a strong position on a ridge west of the city. The Prussians attacked and defeated the French in the Battle of Gravelotte [q.v.], and Bazaine drew his forces into the fortress. In August 1870 the 154,481 French troops garrisoned there were besieged by a German army of 170,000 under General Prince Frederick Charles [q.v.]. Several attempts to break out were frustrated, and the defeat in the Battle of Sedan [q.v.] of the French marching to relieve the place ended any hope of swift relief. Metz had been inadequately provisioned, and on 4 September the authorities began to issue horsemeat to soldiers and civilians; on 13 September food for civilians was rationed; and on 20 September army rations were reduced three-fourths. On 23 September the mysterious Edmond Régnier appeared, encouraging false hopes in the breasts of the generals there [see Régnier Affair]. By 10 October there were 19,000 sick within the fortress; typhus and smallpox cases had appeared.

The Prussians offered no terms, but they did offer to permit the French to surrender with the honors of war [q.v.]. Curiously, Bazaine refused, saying merely that the weather was too bad for a ceremony. He finally capitulated on 27

October, giving the Prussians an unprecedented victory. The French surrendered 3 marshals of France, 10 generals, 6,000 other officers, 173,000 soldiers and civilians, 53 eagles and other regimental colors, 541 field guns, 876 siege guns, 72 mitrailleuses, and 300,000 rifles. *Le Combat,* a newspaper published by the revolutionary Félix Pyat (1810–1889), printed a black-edged announcement of the pourparlers that led to the surrender.

Metz *A Prussian battery before Metz*

Meuse, Army of the. The appellation given the German Fourth Army under Crown Prince Albert [q.v.] during the Franco-Prussian War [q.v.] of 1870–71. It consisted of XII Army Corps (Saxons), the Prussian Guard Corps, and IV Army Corps (Prussian Saxony). The Army of the Meuse was the point on which the entire German army wheeled in pursuit of French General Patrice MacMahon [q.v.], who commanded the French I Army Corps. It defeated the French in the Battle of Buzancy on 29 August 1870 and the Battle of Beaumont [q.v.] the following day.

Mewar Bhil Corps. A unit raised by the British in India in 1840–44 from among the primitive Bhils of the northwestern Deccan. It was one of the few Hindu regiments to remain loyal during the Indian Mutiny [q.v.]. Originally an irregular unit, it was given its colors in 1863.

Mexican Revolutions. During the nineteenth century revolutions were endemic in Mexico: against the Spanish, against the French, and against successive Mexican regimes, which were all military. In 1810–11 Miguel Hidalgo y Costilla [q.v.], a fifty-seven-year-old Catholic priest, led a revolt against Spanish rule and marched on Mexico City. He was joined by Ignatio José Allende (1779–1811), but their forces were defeated in the Battle of Calderón [q.v.]. Both men were captured in January 1811, and both were shot.

In 1820 Agustín Iturbide [q.v.] persuaded the Spanish viceroy, Juan Ruíz de Apodoca (1783–1824), to give him command of 2,500 troops to crush the rebel force of Vicente Guerrero [q.v.], who, after a few skirmishes, was persuaded by Iturbide to join him in a War of Independence (18 January–12 May 1821) to free Mexico from Spain. On 24 February 1821 the two issued the Plan of Iguala calling for an independent Mexican monarchy. Their army, under Iturbide's command, swept away Spanish royalist resistance. The Treaty of Córdoba, signed by Iturbide and the new Spanish viceroy, Juan O'Donoju, established Mexican independence. Iturbide was proclaimed emperor and on 19 May 1822 as Agustín I placed the crown on his head with his own hands.

Iturbide was extravagant, and his soldiers went unpaid. General Antonio López de Santa Anna [q.v.] took control of the army and called for a republic. He was joined by General Guadalupe Victoria (1780–1843), who formed a junta that included Nicolás Bravo [q.v.], Santa Anna, and Guerrero. Their Plan de Casa Mata was issued in February 1823. Even conservatives such as Anastasio Bustamante (1780–1853), who commanded 6,000 men, joined the cause. Iturbide, forced to abdicate on 19 May 1823, fled the country; when he returned a year later, he was captured, and on 19 July 1824 he was shot. Guadalupe Victoria was installed as president, and he held the office until 1827, when an insurrection led by Bravo overthrew his government.

The so-called War of Reform [see Reform, Mexican War of] was fought in 1857–60 between Liberals under Benito Pablo Juárez and Conservatives under Miguel Miramón [qq.v.]. It ended in a Liberal victory that established Juárez as president [see Calpulálpam, Battle of]. From 1861 to 1867 war was waged against French invaders [see Mexico, French Invasion and Occupation of]. After the French were driven out, Juárez again assumed the presidency. Serving from 1867 to his death, he successfully suppressed numerous insurrections. After he died, the country fell into chaos until 1877, when General Porfirio Díaz [q.v.] clawed his way to the presidency. He governed with some degree of moderation until he was overthrown in 1911.

Mexican Spy Company. In the Mexican War [q.v.], during the march on Mexico City by General Winfield Scott [q.v.], American Lieutenant Colonel Ethan Allen Scott (1795?–1871), a West Point graduate (class of 1817) and a grandson of Revolutionary War hero Ethan Allen (1738–1789), recruited a notorious Mexican bandit, Manuel Domínguez (fl. 1850s), and his gang to scout, guard the supply line, and supply information about the nature of the terrain. Named the Mexican Spy Company (it was actually formed into three companies), the unit did good service. Its members were evacuated to New Orleans after the war.

Mexican War (1845–48). The United States inherited a boundary dispute with Mexico when it annexed Texas in 1845. The 150-mile-wide strip of land between the Nueces River and the Rio Grande was claimed by both Texas and Mexico. To establish the American claim, President James Knox Polk (1795–1849) ordered sixty-one-year-old General Zachary Taylor [q.v.] to take a force of 2,700 men across the Nueces to the Rio Grande.

On 7 July 1845 at the town of Monterey, California, John Drake Sloat (1781–1867), an American naval officer in command of the U.S. Pacific Squadron, acting under orders, claimed the Mexican territory of California for the United States. Two days later a subordinate, John Berrien Montgomery (1794–1869), captured San Francisco. Sloat was succeeded by Commodore Robert Field Stockton

(1795–1866), son of U.S. Senator Richard Stockton (1769–1828), who, with the help of John Frémont [q.v.], captured Los Angeles on 13 August.

On 12 April 1846 Mexican troops crossed the Rio Grande and ambushed an American cavalry reconnoitering party. Taylor's little army on 8 May defeated a Mexican force of 6,000 in the Battle of Palo Alto and the next day routed the Mexicans in the Battle of Resaca de la Palma [qq.v.]. President Polk announced that Mexican troops had "invaded our territory and shed American blood on American soil," and on 13 May Congress formally declared war, voted ten million dollars to prosecute it, and authorized an increase in the size of the army from 7,500 to 50,000 men by enlisting volunteers.

On 14 September 1846 General Antonio López de Santa Anna [q.v.] took command of the Mexican army and led 10,000 men to confront General Taylor. In the Battle of Monterrey [q.v.] in northwestern Mexico the Mexicans were defeated by Taylor's army of 6,600 on 24 September after a three-day battle.

On 15 November Tampico fell to U.S. naval forces, and the following day Taylor captured Saltillo, capital of the state of Coahuila.

Reluctantly, because he did not wish to see another Whig general become a hero, President Polk agreed to a plan formulated by General Winfield Scott [q.v.] to attack the port city of Veracruz (originally Villa Rica de Vera Cruz) and march on Mexico City, 230 miles away. On 9 March 1847 an unopposed amphibious landing, in which not an American soldier was lost, was made by 10,750 men near Veracruz. The defenses proved less formidable than had been supposed, and the city was occupied after a brief siege [see Veracruz, Siege of].

Scott's army moved inland about 30 miles and won its first battle at Cerro Gordo [q.v.] on 18 April, thanks in large part to the efforts of Captain Robert E. Lee, who found a flanking mountain trail. By 15 May Scott had reached Puebla, 75 miles from Mexico City, where he called a halt. He had to return 4,000 men whose enlistments had expired and await reinforcements. On 7 August, in a daring move, he abandoned his line of communication to Veracruz and, leaving some 3,000 sick and a small garrison at La Puebla, resumed his march on the Mexican capital with about 11,000 men.

On 20 August the Americans won twin victories at the battles of Contreras and Churubusco [qq.v.]. The Mexicans suffered 4,000 casualties, including 8 generals, two of whom were former presidents.

On 25 August an armistice was declared and peace proposals were discussed, but the talks broke down, and on 6 September Scott continued his advance. On 8 September he won the Battle of Molino del Rey [q.v.], but it was a costly victory, and his effectives were reduced to 7,500. Nevertheless, he pressed on, and the Castle of Chapultepec [q.v.], on a steep 200-foot-high hill, then just outside Mexico City, was stormed and taken on 13 September after a day-long bombardment. Lieutenants U. S. Grant and Thomas

Mexican War *Scenes from the Mexican War (clockwise from upper left): Resaca de la Palma; Churubusco; General Scott entering Mexico City, 17 September 1847; and Buena Vista.*

"Stonewall" Jackson [qq.v.] particularly distinguished themselves in this battle. Mexico City was entered the next day, and for the first time the American flag flew over a foreign capital.

Peace negotiations dragged on for months but the Treaty of Guadalupe Hidalgo was signed on 2 February 1848. By its terms the United States received an area today encompassing California, Nevada, and Utah; most of Arizona and New Mexico; and parts of Wyoming and Colorado. Mexico was paid fifteen million dollars.

Altogether the United States mustered 60,000 volunteers, 12,000 militia, and 42,587 regulars to fight the war with Mexico. Total American losses were 12,876. Of these 1,192 were killed in action, 529 died of wounds, and the rest of disease and accidents. About 20 percent of those admitted to a hospital died there. Losses in the volunteers from disease were nearly twice as high as those among the regulars.

Not everyone approved of the war. Grant considered it "one of the most unjust ever waged by a stronger against a weaker nation" and in later life wrote: "I do not think there ever was a more wicked war than that waged by the United States in Mexico. I thought so at the time, when I was a youngster, only I had not moral courage enough to resign" (*Personal Memoirs* [1885]).

Mexico, French Invasion and Occupation of (1861–67). On 30 June 1861 Benito Pablo Juárez [q.v.] was elected dictator by the Mexican Congress, which on 17 July decided to suspend all payments of debts to foreigners for two years. Ten days later France and Britain broke diplomatic relations with Mexico, and on 31 October the governments of Britain, Spain, and France signed a convention in which they agreed to combine in hostile operations against Mexico. On 15 December the Mexican Congress dissolved after conferring full powers upon Juárez.

On 8 December Spanish troops landed near Veracruz, and on the 17th the city surrendered. On 7–8 January 1862 a British naval force and a French military force under General Charles Ferdinand Latrille de Lorencez [q.v.] arrived at Veracruz and landed troops and sailors. The combined invasion met with resistance. Juárez refused to capitulate, and the Allies quarreled among themselves. Representatives of the three European powers met with Mexican representatives of the Spanish government at La Soledad. The Spanish and British quickly came to an accommodation and quit the country. The French stayed and on 16 April declared war.

French forces under Lorencez were reinforced to about 3,000 and moved inland. On 5 May 1862 they were defeated at Fort Guadalupe near La Puebla [q.v.] and fell back to Orizaba to await orders from Paris. Lorencez was replaced by General Élie Forey [q.v.], who arrived with 2,000 more troops on 28 August. On 24 February 1863 Forey began his march toward Mexico City. La Puebla [q.v.] was captured after bitter fighting on 3 April.

On 5 June French forces of the Armée d'Afrique [q.v.] under General Achille Bazaine [q.v.] captured Mexico City. General Forey entered the city five days later. On 1 October he resigned and sailed for France. Left in charge of French land forces, Bazaine began to occupy key Mexican cities. On 27 February 1864 Mexican General Antonio López de Santa Anna [q.v.], a former president, arrived at Veracruz and, hoping to reestablish himself, professed loyalty to the new government. He was dismissed by Bazaine.

Over the objections of Britain and Spain, France moved to establish a monarchy in Mexico with the aid of some "Mexican notables," offering the title of emperor to Archduke Maximilian [q.v.] of Austria, who accepted it on 10 April 1864, after being promised that he would be supported by French troops. On 29 May he and his wife landed at Veracruz, and on 12 June they entered Mexico City. Meanwhile, Juárez established his republican capital at Monterrey.

There remained considerable Mexican opposition to French rule, but with the aid of French troops, the Mexican forces of Juárez were driven over the border into the United States. On 9 February 1865 General Bazaine captured Oaxaca. On 10 October Maximilian issued a black flag decree, proclaiming that anyone taking up arms against his government would be shot. Two weeks later several of Juárez's generals were executed. By this time there were 30,000 French troops in Mexico.

On 12 February 1866 the American government, which refused to recognize Maximilian's empire, demanded the withdrawal of the French troops. Napoleon III, breaking his pledge, complied, in spite of a personal appeal by the empress, who traveled to Paris to plead for continued support. French troops began to embark on 10 February 1867, and the last load of troops left on 12 March. Among the last to leave was the depleted Egyptian Sudanese battalion [q.v.].

With the departure of the French, Juárez returned to the attack. Maximilian was besieged at Querétaro, 160 miles northwest of Mexico City, by General Escobedo Mariano [q.v.] and on 13 May 1867 was forced to surrender. He was tried by court-martial and on 19 June was shot. Mexico returned to its normal chaotic state.

Meyer, Lucas Johannes (1846–1902). A Boer soldier who fought in both Anglo-Boer Wars [q.v.] and became a general in the second. He first came into prominence when he led a Boer commando that backed Dinizulu [q.v.] in an intertribal war. In return for their support, Dinizulu presented the Boers with a large tract of land on which they founded a state called New Republic with Meyer as president. In 1887 it was merged with the Transvaal.

Mfecane and Mfengu. In the 1820s the wars of the turbulent Zulus against their neighbors in South Africa gave rise to distant ripples of fighting and disorders as powerful tribes plundered weaker ones in widening circles of devastation. These troubled times were called the *mfecane* (the Crushing), and the tens of thousands driven from their traditional homelands were called *mfengu* or *amafengu* (homeless wanderers) or, by most Europeans, Fingos.

Miani, Battle of (17 February 1843), conquest of Sind. Near this village, sometimes spelled Meeanee, on the banks of the Falaili River in Sind (Pakistan), six miles north of Hyderabad, General Charles Napier [q.v.] with 2,200 troops and 12 guns defeated forces of the Sind amirs, who had an estimated 27,000 Beluchis and 18 guns. British losses were 6 officers killed, and 13 wounded, 3 Indian officers wounded, 54 other ranks killed, and 177 wounded.

The main English component of Napier's force was the

The battle of Miani

22nd Foot (later the Cheshire Regiment), which ever after celebrated 17 February as its regimental day.

Miao Rebellions (1855–72). The Miao tribes were the original inhabitants of mountainous areas of southwestern China. Dissension arose in the eighteenth century, when Chinese colonists began to move into the area. In 1733 and again in 1735–37 the Miaos rose up against the Manchu government and were crushed. An even more serious and prolonged insurrection beginning in 1795 embracing the provinces of Hunan, Kwangsi, Yunnan, and Kweichow was not suppressed until 1806.

Further revolts during the Taiping Rebellion [q.v.] were led by Chang Hsiu-mei, a former herb peddler, with help from the White Lotus Society [q.v.], whose members were distinguished by various colored headgear and jackets. Most of the Miaos supported Shih Ta-k'ai [q.v.], a former Taiping general who broke away from the rebel army and with 200,000 followers overran Kweichow Province in September 1859.

After Shih's defeat by the Hunan Braves [q.v.] under Hsi Pao-t'ien, Chang Hsiu-mei fought on, even invading Hunan Province, but he was finally surrounded and defeated by imperial and provincial forces. The Miao rebels retreated into the mountains and carried on guerrilla activities until 1872. Casualties, including civilians, were estimated at one and a half million.

Micanopy (1780?–1849). A Seminole who in 1810 became hereditary chief of his tribe. A rich man, he owned large herds of cattle and horses, and 100 black slaves. He supported Osceola [q.v.] in his determination to resist the resettlement of his tribe and to remain in Florida. Neither signed the 23 April 1835 agreement to emigrate. Instead the warriors of the tribes sent their families deep into the interior, armed themselves, and sacked the farms of the white settlers along the border. Troops were summoned, and the Second Seminole War [q.v.] began. On 28 December 1836 Major Francis Dade (1792–1835) was ambushed, and it was believed that Micanopy personally killed him [see Dade Massacre]. In 1837 Micanopy, under a white flag, entered the camp of Major General Thomas S. Jesup [q.v.] to arrange a treaty. On Jesup's orders he was seized and held. He was sent first to South Carolina and then with 200 of his followers to Indian Territory. There he remained until his death.

Michael. Russian: Mikhail. The name of three Russian grand dukes. *Mikhail Nikolaevich* (1832–1909) was a general who for a time commanded all Russian cavalry. *Mikhail Mikhailovich* (1861–1929) was an officer in the Russo-Turkish War [q.v.] of 1877–78 who took up residence in England after being exiled in 1891 for contracting a morganatic marriage with Countess Sophie Nikolaevna (b.1868). *Mikhail Aleksandrovich* (1878–1918) was an officer who became an army commander in World War I and in 1917 refused the throne of Russia.

Michael and St. George, Order of. A British order of chivalry established on 27 April 1818. Originally it was confined to "natives of the United States of the Ionian Islands [garrisoned by British troops from 1809 to 1863], and of the island of Malta and its dependencies, and such other subjects of His Majesty as may hold high and confidential situations in the Mediterranean." In 1879 the limitations of the order were extended. It has three classes: grand cross, knight commander, and companion.

Michelberg Heights, Battle of (16–17 October 1805), Napoleonic Wars. Marshal Michel Ney [q.v.] captured the heights of Michelberg, Bavaria, while Marshal Jean Lannes [q.v.] carried the Frauenberg, driving the Austrian forces into Ulm [see Ulm, Battle of].

Middleton, Frederick Dobson (1825–1896). A British soldier who passed out of Sandhurst [q.v.] and was commissioned in 1842. He fought in the Maori Wars [q.v.] in New Zealand and in the Indian Mutiny [q.v.]. In 1867 he sailed with the 29th Foot to Canada, where he remained for three years. Fourteen years later he returned to Canada as a major general to command the 5,000 Canadian militia. In 1885 he suppressed the second Riel's Rebellion [q.v.], and a grateful Canadian Parliament awarded him £4,000. On his return to England he was promoted lieutenant general and made a knight commander of the Order of Michael and St. George [q.v.].

Mier Expedition (December 1843). A force of 300 Texans attempting to invade Mexico in December 1843 were all killed or captured on the 26th of that month by Mexicans under General Pedro de Ampudia [q.v.] near the town of Mier on the Rio Grande opposite present-day Roma, Texas, 90 miles northeast of Monterrey. The captives were to be taken to Mexico City, but on the march one large group escaped. Many of them became lost in the mountains, and weakened by hunger and thirst, 176 were recaptured. In punishment each was forced to draw a bean from a box in which one bean in ten was black. Those who drew black beans were shot. One captive, Erwin Cameron, although he drew a white bean, was also shot.

George Bibb Crittenden [q.v.], a West Pointer from Kentucky, drew a white bean, handed it to a fellow Kentuckian, and drew another, fortunately also white. Crittenden lived to become a Confederate major general.

The survivors of the Mier Expedition were taken to Perote Prison near Mexico City. A few tunneled to freedom; more died in captivity. They were finally released late in 1844 through the good offices of Daniel Webster (1782–1852). They were not, however, returned to the United States but simply turned out of the prison. The exact number who survived the experience is unknown.

Mier Expedition *Texan prisoners draw beans to determine which of them will die.*

Mieroslawski, Ludwik (1814–1878). A Polish revolutionary who took part in the Polish Revolution of 1830–31 and subsequent revolutionary movements in Poland in 1846, 1848, and 1863 [see Polish Revolutions; Baden Insurrection].

Miguelite Wars (1826–34), Portuguese civil wars. Sometimes called the Wars of the Two Brothers. In 1823, during the drafting of a democratic constitution, monarchial absolutists, opposing King John VI and the formation of a Cortes or national assembly, staged two unsuccessful insurrections.

In 1826 Miguel Maria Evaristop de Bragança, usually known as Dom Miguel (1802–1866), the third son of King John VI (1769–1826), began a revolution against his father. He was supported by royalists protesting the drafting of a democratic constitution. The revolutionaries occupied Lisbon, and Miguel was acclaimed king by his military supporters, but the Portuguese populace rebelled, King John regained his throne, and Dom Miguel was exiled to Vienna.

King John reestablished the Cortes but retained succession rights to the thrones of both Brazil and Portugal vested in his son Dom Antonio Pedro de Alcántara, known as Dom Pedro (1798–1834), emperor of Brazil. When John died in 1826, Pedro succeeded him as Pedro IV and promulgated a parliamentary charter based upon the British parliamentary system. Choosing to remain in Brazil, where he ruled as Pedro I, he abdicated the Portuguese throne in favor of his infant daughter Maria da Gloria (1819–1853). Dom Miguel, appointed regent during her minority, married her from Portugal by proxy, swearing to accept the constitution. Nevertheless, he wasted no time in replacing moderate governors and army officers with aristocrats and supplanting the Cortes with a tame assembly. None of this was accomplished peacefully. Civil war erupted between the absolutist supporters of Miguel, known as Miguelites, and constitutionalists, who were supported by General John Carlos de Oliveira e Daun Saldanha [q.v.]. In December 1826 the British sent a 5,000-man force under General William Henry Clinton (1769–1846) to assist the constitutionalists and maintain order. The British remained until April 1828, when Dom Miguel again agreed to abide by the constitution and was again named the regent of Maria, who was then en route from Brazil. However, he once more rejected democratic rule, and in May the Cortes, at his direction, proclaimed him king of Portugal. Maria's ship was intercepted and diverted to England.

Constitutionalists and others who supported Pedro and Maria revolted, but their forces were defeated by Miguelites near Coimbra on 24 June 1828. On 11 July Miguel was crowned king, and his followers waged a bloody war of reprisal, taking all Portugal except the Azores [q.v.], which were captured by the British and held in Maria's name. In April 1831 King Pedro landed in the Azores, having abdicated his Brazilian throne in favor of his son, and began to assemble, with British support, an expeditionary force to conquer Portugal.

In February 1832 his army landed at Oporto and captured the city, but then it endured a yearlong siege by the Miguelites, who finally recaptured the city with the help of French General Auguste Victor de Bourmont (1773–1846). However, the Miguelite naval forces were defeated at Cape St. Vincent on 5 July 1833 by a so-called Liberation Fleet commanded by English Admiral Sir Charles Napier (1782–1853), and on 24 July Lisbon fell to the constitutionalists.

Because Miguel had taken sides in the Carlist War [q.v.] in Spain, sheltering Don Carlos (1788–1855), an army of Spanish Cristinos (those loyal to Queen Isabella) invaded Portugal. To preserve constitutionalism and counter the Holy Alliance of Russia, Prussia, and Austria, the Quadruple Alliance was formed with Britain, France, Spain, and Portugal. With Spanish aid, the constitutionalist forces won a series of battles against the Miguelites, culminating in the

Battle of Santarém [q.v.] on 18 February 1834. Ten days later Dom Miguel surrendered, gave up his claims to the throne, and departed for Germany. Pedro reinstated the 1826 constitution, and Maria was declared of age and as Maria II was crowned queen.

Mikhnevich, N. P. (1849–1927). A Russian soldier noted as a strategist. In 1891, when the concept of operational theory was just emerging, he wrote the definition of military operations [q.v.] for the *Encyclopedia of the Military and Naval Sciences.* In 1892 he was professor of the history of Russian military art at the Staff Academy.

Milan Uprising (1848). On 17 March 1848 an armed uprising of Italians in Milan, triggered by the death of a citizen at the hands of Austrian soldiers, surprised the city's Austrian rulers. Some 1,650 barricades were thrown up in the streets, and Austrian troops throughout the city were attacked. Austrian General Josef Radetzky [q.v.] reported: "The character of the people has altered as if by magic, and fanaticism has taken hold of every age group, every class, and both sexes."

The Austrian forces in Milan withdrew and in their retreat burned the villages of Melegnano [q.v.] and Castelnuovo and massacred their inhabitants. Venice also revolted [see Manin, Daniele], and 20,000 Italian troops in the Austrian army mutinied. King Charles Albert [q.v.] of Sardinia invaded Lombardy but was defeated by the Austrians in the Battle of Custozza [q.v.]. The Austrians regained control and on 7 August reentered Milan without opposition.

Milazzo, Battle of (18 July 1860), Italian Wars of Independence. Giuseppe Garibaldi [q.v.] with 2,500 Red Shirts [q.v.], drove the Neapolitans out of northwestern Sicily and pursued them to Milazzo, a fortified seaport on the Tyrrhenian Sea 17 miles west of Messina, where, with some help from local volunteers, he routed 7,000. On 22 August he crossed the Strait of Messina to Italy proper [see Sicily, Garibaldi's Invasion of].

Miles, Nelson Appleton (1839–1925). An American soldier who was born on a Massachusetts farm. Although he received little formal education, he attended night classes and took military instruction from a former French colonel while clerking in a Boston store. On 9 September 1861 he was commissioned a first lieutenant in the 22nd Massachusetts Volunteers of the Union army and served in the Peninsular Campaign [q.v.], in which he was wounded. He distinguished himself in the Battle of Seven Pines [q.v.] and was promoted lieutenant colonel of the 61st New York. He commanded a regiment at Antietam [q.v.] and was promoted colonel. He was again wounded in the Battle of Fredericksburg [q.v.] in December 1862. At Chancellorsville [q.v.] on 3 May 1863 he distinguished himself "while holding a line of abatis [q.v.] and rifle pits against a strong force of the enemy until severely wounded." (He was shot in the abdomen and temporarily paralyzed.) For his services in that battle he was brevetted brigadier general in the regular army and awarded—but not until 1892—the Medal of Honor [q.v.]. He recovered from his wounds in time to command a brigade at the Wilderness and Spotsylvania [qq.v.]. At the siege of Petersburg he commanded a division, and received his fourth wound. On 21 October 1865 he was made a brevet major general of volunteers, and by war's end, not yet twenty-six years old, he was a corps commander.

After the reorganization of the army in July 1866 he was appointed colonel of the newly formed 40th Infantry. Two years later he married a niece of William Tecumseh Sherman [q.v.]. For fifteen years he fought an assortment of Indian tribes on the plains and in the Far West. In 1874–75 he fought the Comanches, Kiowas, and Southern Cheyennes. In 1876–77 he launched a winter campaign against the Sioux, pursuing Sitting Bull [q.v.] to the Canadian border [see Great Sioux War]. In September 1877 he fought the final battle in the Nez Percé War [q.v.] in the Bear Paw Mountains [q.v.].

On 15 December 1880 Miles was promoted brigadier general. He commanded the Department of the Platte until 1886, when he succeeded General George Crook [q.v.] as commander of the Department of Arizona. In September 1886 he accepted the surrender of Geronimo [q.v.]. Two years later he commanded the Department of the Pacific. In 1890 he returned to the plains and directed the operations against the Sioux that ended with the Battle of Wounded Knee [q.v.]. On 5 April 1890 he was promoted major general. Five years later he was commanding general of the army, the last to hold that appointment (his successors were called chief of staff). During the Spanish-American War he directed recruitment and training and personally led the operation that captured Puerto Rico. On 6 June 1900 he was appointed a lieutenant general, then the highest rank in the American army. He retired on 8 August 1903. In Washington, D.C., on 15 May 1925 he took his grandchildren to Ringling Brothers Circus and there, as the national anthem was being played, he died, the last survivor of the full-rank major generals of the Civil War.

Miles was a brave man and a capable commander, but he was vain, quarrelsome, sensitive of his lack of formal education, particularly among West Pointers, inordinately ambitious, and often callous to the needs of others.

Miles, Nelson *General Miles charges a Nez Percé camp.*

Milhaud, Édouard Jean Baptiste (1766–1833). A French soldier who served in the Bourbon army and the Garde Nationale [q.v.] and in 1800 was a general of brigade. He commanded light cavalry in Italy, at Austerlitz and Eylau [qq.v.]. He was made general of division in 1806 and served in Spain in 1808, taking part in the fighting at Talavera and Ocaña [qq.v.]. In 1812 he took part in numerous actions in Germany, commanding a corps of cavalry at Hanau [q.v.]. In January 1813 he retired, but he returned during the Hundred Days and commanded a division of cuirassiers in the cavalry reserve at Ligny and Waterloo [qq.v.].

Miliana, Siege of (1840), French conquest of Algeria. In the summer of 1840 at this commune in northern Algeria, 60 miles west-southwest of Algiers, a battalion of the French

Foreign Legion [q.v.], a battalion of the 3rd Light Infantry, 45 artillerymen, and a detachment of engineers—1,232 men in all—were besieged by thousands of hostile Arabs. Temperatures reached 120° F, and sicknesses felled most of the defenders. When relief reached them on 4 October, only some 600 had survived, and of these, only about 150 were fit enough to fight. Two months later only 70 of those rescued remained alive. One of these was Captain (later Marshal) Achille Bazaine [q.v.].

Militarism. The glorification of war and of military virtues was common in all countries in the nineteenth century. Theodore Roosevelt [q.v.], speaking at the Naval War College on 2 June 1898, said: "No triumph of peace is quite so great as the supreme triumphs of war. The courage of the soldier, the courage of the statesman who has to meet storms which can be quelled only by soldierly virtues—this stands higher than any quality called out merely in time of peace." Lieutenant General Adna R. Chaffee [q.v.] wrote in 1902: "An occasional fight is a good thing for a nation. It strengthens the race. . . . Let war cease altogether and the nation will become effeminate."

Military. 1. As an adjective, pertaining to soldiers, armies, and wars.

2. As a noun, the entire body of fighting men of a country.

Military Academies. Schools designed to train officers or to train young men to be officers. In the nineteenth century such schools proliferated. The United States had only a single federal school, the United States Military Academy at West Point [q.v.], New York. Many states had state military schools, of which two remain: The Citadel in Charleston, South Carolina, and the Virginia Military Institute in Lexington, Virginia [qq.v.].

Britain had the Royal Military Academy, Woolwich, to train officers for the engineers and artillery, and the Royal Military College, Sandhurst, to train officers for the cavalry and infantry [qq.v.]. A Staff College was established at Camberley in 1858, and it provided a two-year advanced course for officers. The Honourable East India Company had its own "seminary" in England at Addiscombe [q.v.] to train officers for the Indian army.

There were, and still are, two primary military academies in France: École Polytechnique in Paris and St. Cyr near Versailles [qq.v.]. The former provides not only officers for the engineers and artillery but also engineers for civil government organizations.

The Prussian (later German) system, unlike the American, British, and French systems, aimed at giving all officers a good professional education. Six junior academies were established at Bensburg, Potsdam, Ploem, Kulm (Chelmno), Oranienstein, and Wahlstatt, and a senior school at Berlin. Graduates then passed to one of eight divisional schools.

The Austrian *Kriegsschul,* based on the Prussian *Kriegsakademie,* was founded in 1852 and took students at a very early age. Boys were pledged to the military service by their parents when eleven years old and were sent to one of four cadet houses. At fifteen they advanced to a service academy and emerged four years later as an officer in the engineers, artillery, infantry, or cavalry. The most fortunate entered the staff school for two years.

Russia had twenty-two military colleges and an imperial staff college.

Military Asylum, Royal. A British school established at Chelsea for the education of the children of British soldiers, popularly known as the Duke of York's School. It opened in 1803 and offered free board, uniforms, and tuition for seven hundred boys and (originally) three hundred girls, mostly orphans. Girls were excluded in 1850 because, it was said, they "brought discredit upon the school in afterlife."

The school was organized along military lines, and between 1803 and 1830 it provided 1,500 recruits for the army, many of whom became noncommissioned officers. Those who chose not to enlist were apprenticed to a trade.

The school was moved in 1909 to Dover, where it continues to exist as the Duke of York's Military School. A similar school was established in Dublin as the Royal Hibernian Military School.

Military Attaché. An army officer sent to a foreign country for the purpose of gathering information about its military capabilities. Prussia was the first to establish a military attaché system. The general order establishing it, published on 14 April 1816 by General Karl von Grolmann [q.v.], stated: "The purpose of the assignment of these officers is accurate knowledge of states from the purely military viewpoint. Their purpose is absolutely apolitical, and they must avoid meddling in politics and must, above all, observe the utmost caution and circumspection in their behavior."

Military Crest. The top line of a slope from which maximum observation is possible, but behind the true crest so that the terrain offers some protection.

Military crest

Military Discipline. The obedience to and compliance with all orders designed to enhance the good management of an army or any of its parts.

Military Exhibition, Royal. A British exhibition at Chelsea opened by the Prince of Wales on 7 May 1890 to promote an increase in the number of soldiers' institutes. It displayed industrial work by soldiers, articles of military equipment as well as pictures, paintings, and objects of military interest. It also featured military sports and drills and, on several days beginning on 10 May, the ascension of a "war balloon."

Military tournaments, with profits going to military charities, were held annually in May, from 1879 to 1905, in the Agricultural Hall (no longer extant) in Islington, North London, and later elsewhere.

Military Frontier. A narrow strip of land, about 7,500 square miles, between Turkey and the Austro-Hungarian Empire, which until 1873 formed a separate "crown land" and was governed by a special military constitution. It came into being in 1527, when the Austrians, threatened by the Ottoman conquest of Hungary, built a string of forts in the zone and organized a military force from the Croats, Serbs, and Vlachs who had fled from the Turks and settled there. By 1766 its territory stretched from the Adriatic to Moldavia. In 1869 it had a population of 690,300, and all males of military age were armed to defend it. Residents had the use but not the ownership of their land until, on 4 March 1849, in gratitude for their assistance in the crushing of the Revolution of 1848 [see Hungarian Revolution of 1848], they were given the land, not as individuals but as families. The oldest member of the family, the *Hausvater,* and his partner, the *Hausmutter,* ruled equally in its management.

In 1868 Croatia and Slavonia were reunited with Hungary, and a special administration headed by the ban [q.v.] was made responsible for the district's internal affairs. Although by 1881 most of the area had come under normal civil administration, many of the traditions survived, and in the Austro-Hungarian army there were separate units of *Grenzers* (frontiersmen), as soldiers from the area were called (German: *Militärgrenz*).

Military Geography. The natural and man-made physical features that affect the planning and conduct of military operations.

Military Government. The government imposed by a conquering army upon a city, province, or country. In 1807 French Marshal François Lefebvre [q.v.] notified the inhabitants of a Franconian town he was occupying: "We come to give you liberty and equality. But do not lose your heads about it. The first person who stirs without my permission will be shot." Such were generally the sentiments of those administering military government.

When Union Major General Benjamin Butler [q.v.] imposed military government upon New Orleans during the American Civil War, he issued General Order No. 28 [q.v.], which made him infamous throughout the Confederacy: "As the officers and soldiers of the United States have been subjected to repeated insults from the women (calling themselves ladies) of New Orleans . . . it is ordered that hereafter when any female shall, by word, gesture, or movement, insult or show contempt for any officer or soldier of the United States, she shall be regarded and held liable to be treated as a woman of the town plying her avocation."

Military Information. See Intelligence, Military.

Military Justice. All countries make special provisions for military courts (courts-martial) and provide special laws for the governing of soldiers' conduct. In the nineteenth century military justice in all cases was characterized by allowing the death penalty for more crimes than civilian laws allowed.

Military Knights of Windsor. An adjunct to the Most Noble Order of the Garter [q.v.], established soon after its founding by King Edward III (1312–1377). Originally a charity known as the Poor Knights of Windsor or the Alms Knights, it received its present name from William IV (1765–1837) in 1833. Its members were limited to twenty-four, later raised to twenty-six, officers who had rendered distinguished military service.

Military Law. A code devised for military discipline that in wartime was sometimes applied to civilians as well as soldiers. In Britain the articles listing offenses and punishments were originally attached to the Mutiny Act [q.v.], but these were separated by the Army Act of 1881.

Military Merit, Order of. A French order instituted in 1759 in three classes for foreign Protestant officers in the French army. The ribbon, originally blue, was changed to red in 1814.

Military Occupation. A state of affairs in which a country or territory is effectively under the control of and ruled by a foreign armed force.

Military Order of the Loyal Legion of the United States. Union officers, veterans of the American Civil War, fearing that insurrection would reemerge, met in Philadelphia in 1865 to form a society pledging loyalty to the federal government. Rebellion did not reoccur, and the Loyal Legion became a fraternal veterans' organization, open to former Union officers and their descendants and collateral descendants.

Military Peace Establishment Act of 1802. An act drafted by President Thomas Jefferson (1743–1826) and Henry Dearborn [q.v.], his secretary of war, ostensibly for creating a smaller standing army, but in fact a scheme to fill the officer ranks with Republicans and crowd out the Federalists. It was passed in March 1802. Under its terms the army was reduced from 3,600 to 3,289. Although 81 of the 230 army officers were removed, positions were created for 20 new (and Republican) officers.

This act also created the U.S. Military Academy at West Point, New York. Joseph Gardner Swift [q.v.], the first graduate of the academy, was personally interrogated about his politics by President Jefferson.

Military Police. Soldiers selected to help preserve order in camps and garrisons and to prevent desertions during battles. These were usually not organized into a separate corps in the nineteenth century but were simply infantry operating under the provost marshal, who exercised exceptional powers in wartime. [See Gendarme.]

Military Reconstructions Acts. In March and July 1867 the U.S. Congress passed these acts over the veto of President Andrew Johnson (1808–1875). The acts created five military districts in the former Confederacy in which army generals supervised civil officials, voter registration, and constitutional conventions.

Military Reorganization Commission, Prussian. A military committee formed in 1808 by Prussian General Gerhard von Scharnhorst [q.v.] to reform and reorganize the Prussian army. Its members—Hermann Boyen, August von Gneisenau, Karl von Clausewitz, Karl von Grolmann [qq.v.], and Scharnhorst—came to be known as the Five Reformers. Officer training was reorganized, and the monopoly by aristocrats was curbed, but the commission was unable to push through universal conscription, which it believed essential for a national army.

Military Science. The study of the ways and means of making war. Its status as a science has been disputed. Dame Rebecca West (1892–1983) once wrote: "Before a war military science seems like a real science, like astronomy, but after a war it seems more like astrology."

Military Secretary. An appointment in the British army to the staff of a general. The military secretary to the commander-in-chief was himself a general. He was in charge of all important correspondence, especially that of a confidential nature, such as that dealing with promotions, awards, and appointments.

Military Service Institution. An organization founded in

September 1878 on Governor's Island, New York, by a group of officers for "the promotion of the military interests of the United States." It was based upon the Royal United Service Institution [q.v.], which had been formed in 1831 in London. About a quarter of all officers joined at once, and General Winfield Scott Hancock [q.v.], one of the founders, was elected its first president. In 1880 it began publication of a quarterly journal.

Military Train. The wagon companies that brought forward food, ammunition, forage, and supplies. In Britain a corps of this name, organized into six battalions, each with 166 horses, was established after the Crimean War to replace the Land Transport Corps; it was later renamed the Army Service Corps.

Militia. A part of a nation's defense force that consists of men who drill irregularly and are called into service only in a national emergency. Sometimes it includes all able-bodied men regardless of lack of training. In the United States the Militia Act of 1792, in force throughout the nineteenth century, included in the militia every able-bodied male citizen between the ages of eighteen and forty-five, as well as aliens in the age-group who declared their intentions to become citizens. Militiamen were required to furnish their own weapons and equipment, but there was no penalty for noncompliance. No provision was made for training, organization, or accoutrements.

The Constitution gave Congress power for "calling forth the militia to execute the laws of the Union, suppress insurrections, and repel invasions." However, as George Washington (1732–1799) informed the president of the Congress on 24 September 1776, "To place any dependence upon militia is assuredly resting upon a broken staff." Nevertheless, many Americans evinced a strong aversion to a standing army and an even greater aversion to paying for one. In 1799 Thomas Jefferson (1743–1826) wrote: "I am for relying, for internal defense, on our militia solely, till actual invasion . . . and not for a standing army in time of peace." Soon after, however, Jefferson changed his mind and helped draft the Military Peace Establishment Act of 1802 [q.v.].

In Britain the Assize of Arms in 1181 gave statutory recognition to the militia. In the sixteenth century it was placed under the lord lieutenants. The Militia Act of 1757 empow-

ered the government to conscript all males of military age for three years, but only a few battalions were so raised. The militia continued to exist until the establishment of the Territorial Army in 1909. [See Yeomanry; Landsturm; Landwehr; Opolchenie; Ordenança; Franc-Tireur; Garde Nationale.]

Militiaman. A member of a militia.

Miliutin or Milyutin, Dmitri Alekseevich (1816–1912). A Russian soldier who was educated at Moscow University and in 1833 became an artillery officer candidate in the Life Guards. He was commissioned within six months and three years later was graduated from the Nicholas Military Academy [q.v.]. He was posted in 1837 to the Guards general staff, and two years later to the Caucasus, where, in the Murid Wars [q.v.], he was seriously wounded in the right shoulder. After ten months of recuperative leave, he returned to duty in the Caucasus. In 1845, as a lieutenant colonel, he was assigned to the faculty of the Nicholas Military Academy, where he remained for more than ten years. In 1856 he was a major general and again posted to the Caucasus, where he helped capture Shamyl [q.v.]. In 1860 he returned to Moscow, and from 1861 to 1881 he was war minister. He then presided over a series of far-reaching reforms that touched every aspect of the Russian army. All administration was subordinate to him, and he was the chief military adviser to the tsar. He simplified the ministerial organization and reduced its workload by nearly half. He also laid the foundation for the Imperial Russian Main Staff. He was created a field marshal in 1888. He was a brother of *Nikolai Alekseevich Miliutin* (1818–1872), a Russian statesman who in 1866–68 was secretary of state for Poland.

Milk River, Skirmish at the (17 July 1879). A small fight at the Milk River in Montana in which seven companies of the 2nd Cavalry, nine companies of infantry (six from the 5th Infantry) and some Indian scouts, all under Nelson A. Miles [q.v.], routed a war party of Sioux Indians.

Mill. American slang for the post guardhouse. "Ten days in the mill" was a common punishment for drunkenness.

Milledgeville Armory. Sometimes called the Georgia Armory. A state arsenal and armory established early in the American Civil War in an old state penitentiary at this town, the capital of Georgia from 1805 to 1868, 30 miles northeast of Macon. It was burned in the autumn of 1864.

Miller, Stephen (1816–1881). An American who began his military career in 1861 as a lieutenant colonel of the 1st Minnesota Infantry of the Union army at the beginning of the American Civil War. He later commanded the 7th Minnesota, which came into being to fight the rampaging Sioux in Minnesota [see Minnesota, Sioux Uprising in]. After the uprising was suppressed and 36 Sioux were hanged, he was promoted brigadier general on 28 October 1863. He resigned the following January to become governor of Minnesota.

Miller, William (1795–1861). A British soldier who served as an assistant commissary in the Peninsular War [q.v.]. In 1815 in North America, during the War of 1812 [q.v.], he served in the operations in the Chesapeake Bay and in the Battle of New Orleans [q.v.]. After the war he resigned his po-

Militia *Texas militiamen, 1842*

sition and traveled for two years in Europe. He then sailed to La Plata (Argentina), where he involved himself in revolutionary activities and became an intimate of Simón Bolívar. He organized and commanded a battery, the Buenos Ayres Artillery, and distinguished himself in the struggle to free Chile and Peru from Spanish rule. In 1818 he served as a major commanding marines. In 1823 he was made general of brigade in the Peruvian army, and on 1 September he was made general of division. He led a cavalry charge in the Battle of Ayacucho [q.v.] on 9 July 1824.

In 1826 he returned to Europe, having fought in every battle against the Spanish royalists in Peru and Chile. He was much feted on the Continent and in Britain, where he was given the Freedom of the City of Canterbury. He later returned to Peru, where he was named grand marshal under Andrés Santa Cruz [q.v.]. In 1834 he was commander-in-chief of the army and put down an insurrection led by Agustín Gamarra [q.v.], but in 1839 he was banished. In 1843 he was made British consul general of the Pacific.

Mills, Anson (1834–1924). An American soldier who spent a year and a half at West Point but did not graduate. In 1857 he migrated to West Texas, where he worked as a surveyor, helping to lay out the city of El Paso, then mined for gold in New Mexico. During the American Civil War he returned to the North and was commissioned a first lieutenant in the 18th Infantry of the Union army. He emerged from the war a captain with brevets to lieutenant colonel. He remained in the army and saw much action against hostile Indians. He won a brevet to colonel for his gallantry in the Battle of Slim Buttes [q.v.] on 9 September 1876. On 16 June 1897 he was promoted brigadier general, and he retired one week later.

Mills was an inventor and designed accoutrements for soldiers and sportsmen. He invented a looped webbed belt that was adopted by the American army in 1879, and in 1881 he designed a sturdy canvas cartridge belt for field use that was also adopted by the army. After his retirement from the army he established a business and accumulated a fortune. He sold his business in 1905.

Mill Springs, Battle of (19 January 1862), American Civil War, also known as the Battle of Fishing Creek, Somerset, and Beech Grove, Kentucky. A reinforced Federal brigade (about 4,000 men) under General George Thomas [q.v.] attacked Confederates under General Felix Zollicoffer [q.v.] in entrenched positions in the angle formed by Fishing Creek and the Cumberland River. Zollicoffer was killed, and the Confederates were routed, abandoning all their guns and supplies. The Federals suffered 246 casualties; Confederate casualties are unknown, but many Confederate troops were demoralized and deserted.

Milner, Moses Embree (1829–1876). An American army scout known as California Joe. During the American Civil War he served with the 1st U.S. Sharpshooters in the Army of the Potomac [q.v.]. After the war he was an army scout, much of his time with George Custer [q.v.]. He was discharged in 1875 but reenlisted the following year in the 5th Cavalry. Soon after, he was shot in the back by a civilian with whom he had quarreled.

Miloradovich, Mikhail Andreevich (1771–1825). A Russian soldier who commanded a division at Austerlitz [q.v.] in 1805. He fought with distinction in the Battle of Guirgevo in 1807 in the Russo-Turkish War of 1806–12. As a general of infantry he commanded a corps during Napoleon's invasion of Russia and in the Battle of Borodino [q.v.] in 1812, he commanded the rear guard after the battle. His corps was one of the most active in harassing the French during their retreat from Moscow. In 1813 he fought at Lützen [q.v.]. He led a combined Russian-Prussian force in the Battle of Leipzig [q.v.] and in the campaign of 1814. From 1819 to 1825 he was governor of St. Petersburg. He was killed in Senate Square on 26 December 1825 while trying to suppress the Decembrist uprising [q.v.].

Miloš (1780–1860). A prince of Serbia, of the house of Obrenovich, who led the Serbians in their war of liberation in 1815 and became ruler of Serbia in 1817. In 1827 he was declared hereditary prince, and in 1830 he was recognized by the sultan of Turkey. He abdicated in 1839 in favor of his son Milan (1819–1839), who died the same year. Michael (1825–1868), another son, then succeeded. Miloš is regarded as the creator of modern Serbia.

Milroy, Robert Huston (1816–1890). An American lawyer and soldier who in 1843 was graduated from the military academy established by Captain Alden Partridge [q.v.] at Norwich, Vermont. At the beginning of the American Civil War he was colonel of the 9th Indiana. After taking part in the Western Virginia Campaign of General George B. McClellan [q.v.], he was promoted brigadier general of volunteers on 3 September 1861 and major general on 10 March 1863, to rank from 29 November 1862. In that rank he fought at the battles of McDowell and Second Bull Run [qq.v.]. In June 1863 he commanded about 7,000 men at Winchester, Virginia, a force almost totally destroyed by troops under Confederate General Richard Ewell. Although Milroy escaped, he was not given another command until near the end of the war.

Mina, Francisco Espoz y (1781–1836). A Spanish soldier and guerrilla leader in the Peninsular War [q.v.] of 1808–14 who was promoted general in 1813 but was in exile from 1815 to 1820 because of his democratic and radical views. In 1820 he returned to Spain to fight for the liberals of Galicia, León and Catalonia, and in 1823 he played an active part in defending Barcelona from the invading French [see French Intervention in Spain]. In 1830 he was involved in the unsuccessful insurrection against King Ferdinand VII (1784–1833) and was again exiled. In 1835 he was recalled from exile to command the Spanish army fighting the Carlists [see Carlist War, First]. However, success eluded him, for by this time his health was giving way, his many old wounds ached, and he was opposed by Tomás Zumalacárreguy [q.v.], a highly skilled guerrilla fighter.

Mina, Francisco Javier (1789–1817). A nephew of Francisco Espoz y Mina, sometimes called Mina the Younger, who was a successful Navarrese guerrilla fighter in the Peninsular War [q.v.] until he was captured in 1810 by troops under French General Louis Suchet [q.v.] and imprisoned in

Vincennes until 1814. After his release he took part in an unsuccessful revolution in Spain and was forced to flee to the United States. On 15 April 1817 he left New Orleans with 270 men and landed at Soto la Marina, Mexico, 60 miles east of Ciudad Victoria. He proposed to start a revolution against Spain, and he was initially successful, but his Mexican allies betrayed him, and with 25 of his men, he was executed on 11 November 1817.

Minangkabau War. See Padri War.

Minard, Charles Joseph (1781–1870). A French military engineer and graphics designer whose statistical graph depicting Napoleon's Russian Campaign [q.v.], drawn in 1869, has been described as "the best statistical graph ever drawn." Elegantly simple, it is both a data map and a time series, plotting the size of the army at various locations, its direction of march, and the temperature on significant dates in the retreat.

Mines. See Land Mines; Rains, Gabriel.

Minhla, Battle of (17 November 1885), Third Anglo-Burmese War. At this fort on the right bank of the Irrawaddy, 15 miles south-southeast of Magwe in Upper Burma (Myanmar), General Harry North Dalrymple Prendergast (1834–1913) with a force of 9,000 troops and 67 guns, supported by fifty-five river steamers and barges manned by 600 sailors, attacked an estimated 20,000 Burmese under Thibaw (Thebaw) Min (1858–1916). In spite of stiff resistance, the British carried the fort (still extant).

Minié Ball. This was not in fact a ball, but a cylindrical-conoidal–shaped lead bullet with a hollow base into which an iron thimble was sited. When fired, the thimble drove into the bullet, expanding the lead walls into the rifling. It was invented by French Captain Claude Étienne Minié (1814–1879) in 1849 and was soon, with minor variations, the standard rifle bullet for muzzle-loading rifles in Europe and the United States, for it improved the accuracy, increased the range, and enabled its users to increase their rate of fire. In the United States any bullet fired from a rifled musket was called a Minié ball.

Captain Minié, an officer who rose from the ranks and became a colonel, also invented the Minié rifle [q.v.].

Minié Rifle. A rifle designed by French Captain Claude Étienne Minié (1814–1879) that was put into production in 1849 and quickly adopted by the French, British, Austrian, Danish, and other armies. The Enfield factory, located in what is now part of Greater London, was given the first order for 500 in October 1851. The British version, a .702-inch caliber weighing 10 pounds $8\frac{3}{4}$ ounces had a 39-inch-long barrel rifled with four grooves making a half turn in its length. It was the first British service rifle sighted up to 1,000 yards and was more accurate than its predecessors. It was used in Kaffir Wars [q.v.] in South Africa. In the Crimean War [q.v.] three of the four British infantry divisions were armed with the Minié rifle. [See Minié Ball.]

A defect of the rifle was what is called the parabola effect. The Minié bullet would rise, at medium distance pass over the heads of the enemy, and return to the lethal level after 250 meters. Thus, attacking troops could sometimes run under the fire of the defenders. The effect was of course magnified if ill-trained troops fired high, as was often a tendency.

Mining, Military. The digging of underground galleries for the purpose of planting and detonating explosives (mines) under an enemy's entrenchments or fortifications, one of the oldest forms of siege warfare. At the siege of Sevastopol during the Crimean War [qq.v.] more than five miles of galleries were driven from both sides, and the French alone used more than 130,000 pounds of powder.

One of the most famed mines of the nineteenth century was that placed by Union forces under Confederate lines at Petersburg, Virginia [q.v.], on 30 July 1864. Evidence of the crater is still extant.

Countermines designed to blow in an enemy's gallery without disturbing the surface were called camouflets [q.v.].

Minnesota, Sioux Uprising in (1862). Minnesota became a territory in 1849 and a state in 1858. On 18 August 1862, during the American Civil War, Sioux living in Minnesota, inflamed by the usurpation of their lands and the failure of the American government to live up to treaty obligations, depressed by poor crops, and aware that the whites were fighting each other, rose in revolt. The spark that ignited the uprising was the gratuitous killing of 4 whites by young Indians on 17 August 1862 near the village of Acton. At first light the next day Sioux warriors, led by Little Crow [q.v.], swept through the Redwood Agency and spread out through the farms of the whites, killing and burning. By evening some 400 whites had been slaughtered in an orgy of savagery rarely equaled in the history of the Indian Wars. There were instances of children nailed to doors, babies hacked to pieces, their limbs flung in the faces of their mothers, and families burned alive in their cabins. Hundreds of farmers and their families fled to the settlements and to Fort Ridgely, a post established in 1853 just north of the Minnesota River at the mouth of the Rock River, about 20 miles above New Elm. Both the settlements and the fort were attacked, and there was bitter fighting. The ravages extended for more than 200 miles along the valley of the Minnesota River, and an estimated 800 whites were slain.

Colonel Henry Hopkins Sibley [q.v.] of the state militia organized 1,619 volunteers and promised to attack the Indians and "sweep them with the besom of death." As he advanced up the Minnesota River, the Sioux appeared to be falling back before him, but on 23 September they attempted an ambush at Wood Lake, just below the Yellow Medicine Agency. They were decisively defeated, and the surviving Sioux, including Little Crow, scattered; several hundred were captured.

A military commission of dubious legality tried those believed to be guilty of the most heinous behavior, and by 3 November 303 Sioux had been sentenced to be hanged. The sentences were reviewed by President Lincoln, and over the vociferous protests of the Minnesota authorities, the number to be hanged was reduced to 38. A large scaffold was constructed at Mankato, 65 miles south-southeast of Minneapolis, and on the day after Christmas, a cold winter day, all were hanged in the largest mass execution in North American history.

Minnesota *Sioux uprising in Minnesota, 1862*

Minute Gun. 1. A gun fired every minute as a signal of distress.

2. A gun fired every minute as a token of mourning, as during the funeral procession of a great soldier.

Minuteman. During the American Revolution in the eighteenth century this was the name given a group of armed male citizens pledged to take the field at any minute. The term was revived in the South in the days just before the outbreak of the American Civil War and applied to various groups of armed southerners who proclaimed themselves instantly ready for battle.

Miquelets. Originally bandits who infested the Pyrenees. In 1808 Napoleon organized these armed mountaineers into a corps of Miquelets Français, who were said to provide good service.

Miqueletti. A small body of mountain men formed into fusiliers in the Neapolitan army.

Mir. A commander or prince in the Turkish and Egyptian services.

Miraflores, Battle of (15 January 1881), War of the Pacific. Chileans under General Manuel Baquedano (1826–1880), marching on Lima, Peru, encountered and defeated Peruvians under Andrés Avelino Cáceres [q.v.] at this seaside town, now a suburb of Lima. The Peruvians lost about 3,000 killed and wounded; the Chileans lost 500 killed and 1,625 wounded. On 17 January the Chileans occupied Lima, ending the war.

Miralai. An Egyptian or Turkish commander of a regiment, the equivalent of a colonel.

Miramón, Miguel (1832–1867). A Mexican soldier who in 1859 headed a revolutionary political faction and commanded the Mexican forces fighting against Benito Pablo Juárez [q.v.]. He was defeated on 22 December 1860 and fled into exile. In 1866 he returned to Mexico and supported the government of Emperor Maximilian [q.v.]. He was captured and shot with the emperor.

Miranda, Francisco de (1752–1816). A Venezuelan who served for ten years in the Spanish army and became a general of division in French Revolutionary armies. In the American Revolution he fought under Jean Rochambeau (1725–1807). In 1805 he bought a ship, *Leander*, in London and sailed to New York, where he collected about 200 men and in 1806 embarked for Venezuela with the intention of starting a revolution. The expedition was aborted. He tried again in December 1810 and led an initially successful patriot army. On 5 July 1811 he was made commander-in-chief of the Venezuelan army, and in April 1812 he became dictator of the country. On 25 July he was defeated in battle by the Spanish royalists, and the following day he was forced to sign the Treaty of Victoria, which returned the country to Spain. He had capitulated only after being promised that he would be deported to the United States. Instead he was sent in chains to Spain, where he died in prison.

Mirliton. A tall felt cap worn by French light cavalry, particularly hussars.

Mirliwa. The commander of a liwa or liva (brigade) in the Egyptian and Turkish armies. It was a rank equivalent to a brigadier general.

Misfire. 1. As a noun, the failure of a weapon to fire or an explosive charge to explode.

2. As a noun, the failure of a primer or propellant to function properly.

3. As a verb, to fail to fire or to fire improperly.

Missionary Ridge, Battle of (25 November 1863), American Civil War. An unexpected Union victory in the Chattanooga Campaign occurred when Union troops under General George H. Thomas [q.v.] drove Confederate forces under General Braxton Bragg [q.v.] from rifle pits at the foot of this ridge, which runs northeast to southwest of Chattanooga, Tennessee. Without orders, Thomas and his troops scrambled up the west side of the ridge and burst through the second and third Confederate lines of defense. Captured Confederate guns were turned on their former owners, and Union troops led by General Philip Sheridan drove the Confederates from the ridge.

Mission-Type Order. An order to lower units of a command that included an explanation of what was to be accomplished by the entire mission. This was a concept founded by General Helmuth von Moltke the Elder about 1860 and called an *Auftragstaktik*. (Today the expression indicates an order in which the mission is specified but not the means of accomplishing it.)

Mississippi, Confederate Army of. There were three Confederate armies by this name in the American Civil War. The first was formed by General Pierre Beauregard [q.v.] on 5 March 1862. Just before the Battle of Shiloh it was added to the Central Army of Kentucky. The new Army of Mississippi, commanded by Albert S. Johnston [q.v.], which totaled just over 40,000, ceased to exist on 20 November, when it was merged with the Army of Kentucky and became the Army of Tennessee [q.v.] with General Braxton Bragg [q.v.] as its commander.

On 7 December 1862 a third Confederate Army of Mississippi was created under General John Pemberton [q.v.] from what had been the Army of West Tennessee. It numbered about 22,000 before it was defeated by Grant. Its name disappeared in January 1863.

On 12 May 1864 General Leonidas Polk [q.v.] adopted the name for his corps, but after his death on 14 June it ceased to be used.

Mississippi, McClernand's Union Army of the. A short-lived Union army in the American Civil War under John McClernand [q.v.], which existed only from 4 January to 12 January 1863.

Mississippi, Pope's and Rosecrans's Union Army of the. A Union Army organized by John Pope [q.v.], which was in existence from 23 February to 26 October 1862 and was commanded by W. S. Rosecrans [q.v.] from 26 June. It numbered about 19,000, and it captured Island No. 10 [q.v.] in the Mississippi River.

Mississippi Rifle. A colloquial name for the standard U.S. Rifle, Model 1841. Sometimes called the Jäger rifle, it weighed 9.75 pounds, had a 33-inch barrel, and fired a .54 caliber half-ounce ball wrapped in leather or tallow-soaked cloth. It was first used in action in the Mexican War [q.v.], where it was made famous by Colonel Jefferson Davis [q.v.] and his 1st Mississippi Rifles. After the .58 caliber Minié ball [q.v.] was introduced in the United States in 1849, many of these guns were rebored to take them.

The rifle later came to be called the Harpers Ferry rifle, for between 1846 and 1855 the arsenal at Harpers Ferry, (West) Virginia, manufactured 25,296. During the American Civil War production of the rifle was discontinued in favor of the Model 1861, but the Confederates continued to use the 1841 model though the war.

Missolonghi, Sieges of (1822–23 and 1824–26). During the Greek struggles to be free of Turkish rule this city, 20 miles southwest of Patras, sometimes called Misolóngion, was besieged twice. Located in west-central Greece on the north side of the Gulf of Patras, it guarded the entrance to the Gulf of Corinth. Lord Byron [q.v.], who came to assist the Greeks, died here of malaria on 19 April 1824 between the two sieges.

First Siege. From July 1822 to February 1823 the city, invested by 11,000 Turkish troops, was successfully defended by Marco Bozzaris [q.v.], who was killed in a sortie.

Second Siege. Although by 1823 the Turks had subdued most of the countryside, Missolonghi remained unsubdued, and a second siege began on 27 April 1825. After bribing the Albanians to remain neutral, the Turks, reinforced by an Egyptian army under Ibrahim Pasha [q.v.], first attacked on 7 May 1825, but the Greeks put up a firm resistance until the city was taken by assault on 23 April 1826. Of the 7,000 defenders, few escaped. France, Britain, and Russia intervened to secure a peace.

Missolonghi *Second Siege of Missolonghi, April 1826*

Missouri River Transportation Company. Often called the Coulson Packet Line, this was the leading steamboat company on the Missouri River in the 1870s. The river steamers were an important part of the line of communications for the American army in the West, carrying troops and government supplies to the forts along the western rivers. In 1864 there were forty-seven steamers on the Missouri; by 1880 there were about seventy-five.

Formed in 1872 by Sanford B. Coulson and some associates, the Missouri River Transportation Company had eleven steamboats in operation by 1877. The line carried freight for nineteen and one-half cents per 100 pounds and 100 miles on the Yellowstone and for seventeen and one-half cents on the Missouri, but freight rates tended to increase as river levels dropped late in the season. In 1879 the company charged twenty-four dollars to carry officers and seventeen dollars to carry enlisted men the 706 miles from Bismarck to Terry's Landing [in 1883 this became Terry, Montana, on the Yellowstone River, 40 miles northeast of Miles City]. Civilians were charged thirty-five dollars for officer accommodations.

The line's most famous steamboats were the *Far West, Big Horn,* and *Josephine*. On 27 June 1876 the *Far West* was at the mouth of the Little Bighorn River when its captain, Grant

Marsh [q.v.], learned of the defeat of the 7th Cavalry under George Custer [q.v.] two days earlier. After ferrying some troops and taking on the wounded, he steamed for Bismarck (North Dakota), the base of upper Missouri River transportation, traveling 700 miles down the Yellowstone to the Missouri. He arrived at Bismarck in only fifty-four hours, a feat that made him the most famous steamboat captain in Yellowstone River navigation.

Steamboat travel was seldom comfortable for the troops who were packed on board. In a letter to his mother Captain Simon Snyder (1840?–1895?) described a trip with some 5th Infantry on the Yellowstone River in June 1876: "The weather is very warm, it being now 98 in the shade. The officers occupy the cabin, which is very small, while the men, 350 in number, are crowded on the upper deck in the boiling hot sun all day long, and at night to [*sic*] for that matter. The upper deck is 208 ft. long and 25 ft. wide. The lower deck [has] . . . 100 horses and mules . . . with army wagons, etc."

Not all of those transported by the steamboats were willing passengers. In June 1881, 1,712 Sioux were carried in five steamboats, including the government-owned *General Sherman*, from Fort Keogh at the confluence of the Yellowstone and Tongue rivers in Montana to the Standing Rock Indian Reservation south of Bismarck.

Missouri State Guard. In 1861 this state unit was formed in support of the South in the American Civil War, but although allied with the Confederate army, it was not controlled by Confederate authorities. In the first year of the war most Missouri soldiers fighting for the South were not Confederate soldiers.

Mister. Subalterns were so addressed in the British and American armies in the nineteenth century.

Mistresses. Almost all officers found themselves at some time in their careers stationed at points distant from their homes, and a great many in such cases took mistresses. Even Napoleon did so during his Russian Campaign [q.v.], although the practice was usually confined to the younger officers. In the Austrian and Prussian armies it was regarded as almost de rigueur, and in the French armies in Africa it was almost codified [see Mariage à la Mode des Pays].

In the eighteenth and early nineteenth century it was common enough for British officers to take native mistresses when stationed in remote corners of the empire, an arrangement that was thought to facilitate the learning of the local language and to give the officers a closer appreciation of the local mores.

When he was stationed in the Ionian Islands, Colonel (later General) Charles Napier [q.v.], the conqueror of Sind, had a Greek mistress by whom he had two daughters. Even though she deserted him for a Greek officer, he raised the children and supported her parents. The practice of taking a local mistress by officers in India disappeared early in the century, when memsahibs (British ladies in India) became more common. In Burma (Myanmar) the practice seems to have persisted somewhat longer than in India.

In the United States, although mistresses were forbidden by a general order of 22 May 1797, the practice was openly indulged in on the western frontier and in Mexico. General Richard Ewell [q.v.] wrote that "Many officers have Cherokee

Mistresses. . . ." Lieutenant Philip Sheridan [q.v.], when stationed in the Northwest, lived with a Rogue River Indian woman who taught him the Chinook language. At the end of the Mexican War [q.v.] Second Lieutenant John Pope [q.v.] and another officer lived openly with two girls, one of whom was said to have been only fourteen.

Whatever the advantages of having mistresses, they could create problems. The charms of Mme. Henriette Renique Libertine, the sister of an aide to General André Masséna [q.v.], were held responsible for delaying the arrival of the general on the field before the Lines of Torres Vedras [q.v.], and she annoyed the command by riding about dressed as a cavalry officer and sporting the medal of the Legion of Honor.

In 1842 Major Charles Wickliffe (1818?–1862), a West Point graduate of the class of 1839 who was with the 1st Dragoons at Fort Gibson in Indian Territory (Oklahoma), killed in a rage a civilian carpenter who had beaten his own Cherokee mistress, with whom Wickliffe was enamored. As punishment he was "dropped," but in 1847 he returned to the army as a captain in the 14th Infantry. During the American Civil War he joined the Confederate forces and became colonel of the 7th Kentucky. He was mortally wounded in the Battle of Shiloh [q.v.] on 7 April 1862.

The Chinese under the Manchus appear to have had a higher moral code, for during the Taiping Rebellion [q.v.] General Shung Pow (d. 1864), a warrior who delighted in reading poetry, drinking wine, and in sexual pleasures, was given the silken cord with which to strangle himself for introducing concubines into his camp.

Mitraille. Metal debris, such as nails and bits of iron, loaded into a muzzle-loading gun.

Mitrailleuse. A French forerunner of the machine gun based upon the Gatling [q.v.]. It was said to have been developed by Joseph Montigny, a Belgian engineer. Experiments began about 1859 in French arsenals, and full production began in great secrecy in 1866. It had thirty-one rifled barrels in a single jacket loaded by a plate at the breech. It could be fired simultaneously or in sequence. The gun, capable of firing 250 rounds per minute a distance of 2,000 yards, was operated by turning a crank that rotated twenty-five barrels enclosed in a cylindrical case. By 1870 and the beginning of the Franco-Prussian War [q.v.], the French army had 190, but they had been kept such a secret that few knew how to operate them.

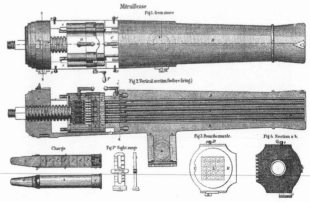

Mitrailleuse *French mitrailleuse of 1870, twenty-five barrels, caliber 13 mm*

In one division on the eve of the Battle of Fröschwiller [q.v.] it was found that only one noncommissioned officer had been trained in their use.

Mitre, Bartolomé (1821–1906). An Argentine politician, writer, and soldier whose insurrectionary activities during the regime of Juan Manuel de Rosas [q.v.] forced him to flee the country and find work as a journalist in Uruguay, Bolivia, Chile, and Peru. He returned to Argentina to support the revolution of Justo Urquiza [q.v.], and he commanded the artillery in the Battle of Monte Caseros [q.v.] on 5 February 1852. With the success of the revolution, he then returned to active political life in Buenos Aires. However, he turned against Urquiza and in 1861 led a revolt against him, defeating him on 17 September in the Battle of Pavón [q.v.]. In 1862, in a rigged election, he became president of Argentina and remained in power until 1868. When Argentina formed an alliance with Brazil and Uruguay, to defeat Paraguay in the War of the Triple Alliance [q.v.] in 1865–70, he was in command of all the Allied forces for a time. In 1874, after losing an election for the presidency, he launched an unsuccessful revolution.

A prolific writer, Mitre wrote poetry, history, and biography and founded in Buenos Aires, *La Natión,* which soon became one of the most successful newspapers in South America. It is still in existence.

Mixed Force. A force containing units of more then one arm or a force containing both army and naval units.

Mixed Order Tactics. The simultaneous deployment of troops in columns, lines, and skirmishers.

Mobile Bay, Battle of (3–23 August 1864), American Civil War. A Union force of 5,500 men under General Robert Seaman Granger (1816–1894) was landed on Dauphine Island in Mobile Bay, Alabama, and within twenty days reduced the bay's three forts, Gaines, Powell, and Morgan, capturing 1,464 men and 104 guns.

Mobilization. The assembly of all the available armed forces of a nation, including the reserves, and the execution of all necessary preparations for war, including the provision of resources to support the forces in the field and at sea. In mid-century Prussia, using railroads and telegraphs, led the way in rapid and efficient mobilization, the effectiveness of which was proved in the Franco-Prussian War [q.v.]. In 1870 Germany mobilized most of its forces in nine days and eight days later deployed 400,000 soldiers and 1,200 guns on the French frontier.

So important did speed of mobilization become in European armies in the last quarter of the nineteenth century that mobilization in itself was considered an act of war, an opening of hostilities.

Modder River, Battle of the (28 November 1899), Second Anglo-Boer War. A British army of 15,000 under General Lord Methuen [q.v.], advancing northward in South Africa for the relief of besieged Kimberley [q.v.], encountered 9,000 Boers under General Pieter Cronjé [q.v.] at the Modder River, an eastern tributary of the Vaal in Cape Province. The Boers were driven from their positions for a loss of about 500. The British lost 24 officers and 461 men killed or wounded.

Modèle d'Ordonnance Revolver. From 1892 to 1935 this was the official French revolver, often called Modèle (Mle) 1892. It was an 8 mm revolver in which the cylinder swung out to the right, the only revolver made in quantity that did this.

Modoc War (1872–73). In what is now southern Oregon and northern California the American government tried to force a band of unwilling Modoc Indians under leaders known as Captain Jack, Scarface Charlie, Hooker Jim, and Ellen's Man George [qq.v.] to move onto the Klamath Reservation. On 29 November 1872 Troop B of the 1st Cavalry attacked Captain Jack's village near Lost River, Oregon. Shots were exchanged, and the Indians fled. One party crossed Tule Lake in boats while another under Hooker Jim filed around the east side of the lake, killing all the white settlers they encountered.

On the south side of the lake, in a wild, boulder-strewn area of black lava, about 80 Modoc warriors settled with their families and animals. It was territory they knew well, containing sufficient patches of grass to sustain their cattle. As the American troops soon discovered, it could not safely be penetrated, bombarded, or besieged. In the first battle of the lava fields on 17 January 1873, 9 soldiers were killed, and 3 officers and 24 enlisted men were injured.

In a standoff that focused national attention, the Modocs held out for four months. The government then decided to try negotiation, and three peace commissioners, escorted by troops under General Edward R. S. Canby [q.v.], were dispatched to the area. Captain Jack agreed to meet with the commissioners peacefully, but he was unable to withstand the taunts of Hooker Joe, who pressed for their slaughter. On 11 April 1873 Captain Jack, Hooker Joe, and other Modoc leaders, all carrying concealed weapons, entered the conference tent erected near the lava beds, where General Canby and the commissioners awaited them. At an agreed signal, they drew their weapons and fell upon the defenseless men. One of the four escaped; the other three were shot, stabbed, and stripped. One, though grievously wounded, later recovered. General Canby was killed, the only regular army American general on active duty to be killed by Indians.

The slaying of Canby and the peace commissioners did much to throw a damper on President Grant's Peace Policy [q.v.]. As many newspapers proclaimed and citizens repeated, this was evidence that Indians were treacherous and untrustworthy; neither kindness nor reason affected them.

Canby was replaced by Jefferson Columbus Davis [q.v.], and the war continued. On 26 April a reconnaissance force of 5 officers and 59 enlisted men commanded by Captain Evan Thomas [q.v.], a son of Lorenzo Thomas [q.v.], entered the lava bed area. They were fallen upon by the Modocs. In the fight that followed the troop lost all 5 officers and 20 enlisted men killed and 16 wounded. On 7 May 1873, in another attempt, 5 officers and 18 enlisted men were killed or mortally wounded, and about 18 others wounded. The area came to be called Captain Jack's stronghold.

Morale of the troops at the lava beds was sinking, and soldiers tended to see a hostile Modoc behind every rock. They were often right. Corporal Charles Buff Hardin of the 1st Cavalry described an attack upon the camp of three companies of his regiment on 10 May: "I saw a line of Modocs pop up their heads and fire a volley. This at first caused some confusion. Men rolled over behind saddles and bundles of blankets—no covering however small being ignored, fastening on belts and pulling on boots under a hail of bullets. . . . There was a possibility of a panic, but this was happily averted by Sergeant Thomas Kelly of our troop, who sprang up and shouted, 'God Damn it, let's charge!'"

Although the Modocs appeared invincible, they began to quarrel among themselves and broke into factions. On 22 May a party of 65, including several of the leaders, surrendered; later others dribbled in. On 1 June Captain Jack and the last of the Modocs surrendered to Captain Joel Graham Trimble of the 1st Cavalry. Captain Jack and other Modoc leaders were taken to Fort Klamath, near the northern end of Klamath Lake Valley. After a trial by a military court Captain Jack and five others were hanged on 3 October 1873. Their heads were then cut off and sent to the Army Medical Museum in Washington.

The villainous Hooker Joe, probably the worst of the lot, escaped punishment by becoming the government's prime witness in the trial. He and 152 other Modocs were sent to Indian Territory.

Modoc War *Captain Jack and his troops in the lava bed near Tule Lake, California*

Moggins. Footless hose worn in Scottish regiments in the early nineteenth century.

Mogilev / Mohilev, Battle of (23 July 1812). Napoleon's Russian Campaign. In June 1812 French forces crossed the Niemen River and began their advance on Moscow; Russian troops fell back, refusing a major engagement, but when the French right wing reached Minsk and threatened to isolate the Russian Second Army, 48,000 men under General Prince Pëtr Ivanovich Bagration [q.v.] struck north to attack French forces of about 23,000, a part of the corps under Marshal Louis Davout [q.v.], who held Mogilev on the Dnieper River, 112 miles east of Minsk. In spite of their numerical superiority, the Russians were repulsed with a loss of about 4,000; the French lost about 1,000.

Mohammed. See Muhammad.

Mohammerah, Battle of (26 March 1857), Anglo-Persian War. At this town (today Khorramshahr) in western Iran at the confluence of the Kurun River and the Shatt-al-Arab, north-northwest of Abadan, a British force of 4,000 under Lieutenant General James Outram [q.v.] defeated a Persian force of 13,000 under Prince Khanzler Mirza with the help of gunboats of the Indian navy. British losses were 41; Persian losses were about 300 men and an enormous amount of supplies.

This was the last battle of the war. It was also the last foreign war fought by an army of the Honourable East India Company. The Indian Mutiny followed soon after, and the Indian armies were brought under the crown.

Mohrungen, Battle of (25 January 1807), Napoleonic Wars. Some 10,000 French under Marshal Jean Baptiste Bernadotte [q.v.] attacked 14,000 Russians under General Levin Bennigsen [q.v.] at this Polish town (Morag) in East Prussia 30 miles southeast of Elbing in an indecisive action in which each side sustained about 2,000 casualties.

Moineau. A small, flat bastion raised in front of an intended fortification as a protection against the fire of small arms.

Molded Powder. Gunpowder in which each grain was separately molded, causing it to burn at an increasing pace, thus easing the strain on the gun at the instant of combustion. General Thomas Jackson Rodman [q.v.] conceived this idea.

Molina de Rey, Battle of (21 December 1808), Peninsular War. Near this village a French army of 18,000 under General Laurent Gouvion St. Cyr [q.v.] defeated a Spanish army of 14,000 to complete the siege of Barcelona [q.v.]. The Spaniards lost 1,500, most of whom were taken prisoner, and all 25 of their guns; French losses were slight.

Molino del Rey, Battle of (8 September 1847), Mexican War. About 10,000 Mexican troops under General López de Santa Anna [q.v.], occupying buildings by this name (king's mill) southwest of Mexico City, were defeated by American forces under General Winfield Scott [q.v.]. The battle, which lasted all day, was fought by 3,447 Americans under General William Jenkins Worth [q.v.]. The Americans suffered 787 killed and wounded, including 59 officers. Mexican losses were 2,000, including 700 taken prisoner.

Battle of Molino del Rey, September 1847

Molitor, Gabriel Jean Joseph (1770–1849). A French soldier in French Revolutionary and Napoleonic Wars who distinguished himself in the Battle of Aspern-Essling and at Wagram [qq.v.] in 1809. In 1811 he was named governor-general of Holland. In 1815 he retired. Recalled to service three years later, he commanded a corps in the French expedition to Spain [see Spain, French Intervention in]. In 1824 he was created a marshal of France and a peer.

Molly Maguires. The name of a secret society formed in Ireland in 1843 and said to be named after an Irishwoman who distinguished herself in shooting the agents of landlords. An organization of the same name, originally known as Buckshots, was formed by rebellious Irish-Catholic anthracite coal miners in Pennsylvania and later in West Virginia, who, beginning in 1862, during the American Civil War, protested

Molly Maguires *The strike in the coal mines, meeting of the Molly Maguires*

the draft by murdering or beating mine managers and owners who cooperated with government officers serving draft notices. In the same year in Schuylkill County, Pennsylvania, Molly Maguires stopped a train filled with recruits and volunteered to protect any who deserted. The violence escalated until in November 1863 the War Department sent the 10th New Jersey, a veteran regiment, to the Schuylkill coalfields. Nearly 100 miners were arrested; some were fined and some sent to prison.

The organization itself survived and was particularly active in Schuylkill and Carbon counties, where Mollies got themselves elected to public office and manipulated public funds in the interests of their organization. By 1877 it dominated the miners and forced a general strike in support of the striking railroad men [see Railroad Strike of 1877, American]. In response, Franklin B. Gowen (1836–1889), president of the Reading Coal and Iron Company, hired the "operatives" of detective Allan Pinkerton [q.v.], who penetrated the organization. After twenty members were convicted of murder and sent to the gallows, the movement began to fade. It completely died out in 1879.

Moltke, Helmuth von (1800–1891). A German soldier, born into a poor Mecklenburg Junker family, who is known to history as Moltke the Elder to distinguish him from his nephew of the same name. His father was an officer in the Danish army. At age eleven Helmuth was sent to the cadet school in Copenhagen. In 1819 he entered the Danish army as a lieutenant; two years later he transferred to the Prussian army as a lieutenant in a *Leibgrenadier* regiment, and he remained a second lieutenant for twelve years. From 1828 he served as an instructor or on staff assignments.

In 1832 he agreed to translate Edward Gibbon's *Decline and Fall of the Roman Empire* into German for £75, because he wanted to buy a horse. He had finished nine of the twelve volumes in eighteen months when the publisher canceled the publication plans. He was paid about £25.

In 1833 he was assigned to the general staff in Berlin, and in 1835 he was promoted captain. He enjoyed his stay in Berlin, where he could enjoy music and the theater and learn to dance the mazurka. From 1835 to 1839 he was, with official permission, in the Turkish service, and in the war with Mehemet Ali [q.v.] he witnessed the defeat of the Turks in the Battle of Nezib [q.v.] on 14 June 1839. He returned to Berlin soon afterward, and in 1841 he married Marie von Burt (1825–1868), his stepsister's daughter by an English father; he was forty-two, she was sixteen. In 1843 he wrote *Considerations in the Choice of Railway Routes*.

He was promoted major general in 1856, and in 1858, although he had never commanded a unit larger than a company, he was appointed chief of the Prussian general staff, an unprecedented step. In his first five years he reorganized the Prussian army. He was one of the first senior military officers in Europe to realize the military potential of the telegraph and railroads. He directed the successful strategies that won the Schleswig-Holstein War in 1864 against Denmark, the Seven Weeks' War in 1866 against Austria, and the Franco-Prussian War [qq.v.]. On mobilization day in 1870 such detailed plans were in place that he had only to order them to be executed, and he was found reclining on a sofa reading, *Lady Audley's Secret* (1862), the most popular work of British novelist Mary Elizabeth Braddon (1837–1915). (This novel of a golden-haired murderess had stirred controversy when first published in 1862 because it dealt with bigamy and madness as well as murder.) In 1871 he was created a field marshal.

Moltke was always resentful of political interference in military affairs or the intrusion of politics in matters he considered strictly military. Political obedience, he said, "is a principle, but man is above principles." Otto von Bismarck (1815–1898), the Iron Chancellor, had great confidence in him and once described him as "unconditionally reliable and at the same time cold to the very heart."

Count Helmuth von Moltke (the Elder), 1889

Moltke, Helmuth von (1848–1916). Known historically as Moltke the Younger to distinguish him from his famous uncle of the same name. He became chief of the German general staff in 1909, and in 1914 he lost the first Battle of the Marne.

Molucca Islands Revolt (May–November 1817). The inhabitants of these islands in the Malay archipelago between the Celebes and New Guinea rose in revolt against Dutch rule. The revolt was put down with difficulty.

Monagas, José Tadeo (1784–1868). A Venezuelan general and politician who fought under Simón Bolívar from 1812 to 1821. When the union of Venezuela and Greater Colombia dissolved in 1830, he became the military leader of Venezuela. In 1846 he was chosen by José Antonio Páez [q.v.] to be president, but in 1847 he broke with Páez, who then led an unsuccessful revolution against him. Monagas remained in office until 1851 and returned to the presidency as a virtual dictator from 1855 to 1858, when he was overthrown in a revolution and banished. Restored to power in 1868, he died in office that year.

Moncey, Bon Adrian Jeannot de, Duc de Conegliano (1754–1842). A French soldier in the French Revolutionary and Napoleonic Wars who enlisted in 1769 and was commissioned ten years later. His original name was Jeannot (variously spelled), but in 1789, after purchasing the old Moncey estate, he added "de Moncey." He dropped the "de" when it became unfashionable, not to say dangerous, to suggest nobility. He was a captain in 1791, a general of brigade in February 1794, and a general of division the same year. Commanding the Army of the Western Pyrenees, in the Peninsular War [q.v.] he won a number of victories over the Spanish. In 1804 he was created a marshal of France and four years later was made a duke. In 1808 he returned to the Peninsular War and proved himself an able mountain fighter.

In 1814 he commanded the Paris Garde Nationale that defended the city, but he did not rejoin Napoleon for the Hundred Days [q.v.]. He was briefly arrested for refusing to preside over the trial of Marshal Michel Ney [q.v.] but was reinstated and created a peer of France by Louis XVIII. In 1823 he commanded a corps in the French expedition to Spain [see French Intervention in Spain]. In 1834 he was appointed governor of the Hôtel des Invalides [q.v.], where six years later he received Napoleon's body.

Moncrieff, Alexander (1829–1906). A British soldier and inventor, educated at Edinburgh and Aberdeen universities, who worked as a civil engineer. In April 1855 he was commissioned in the Forfarshire Militia artillery unit and obtained permission to go to the Crimea, where on 6 June of that year he witnessed the bombardment of the Mamelon, part of the Russian outer defenses, which led him to consider means by which guns might be raised to fire over a parapet and then lowered to be reloaded behind the parapet. He conceived the idea of mounting guns on curved elevators so that when fired, they would recoil back and downward, the force of the recoil lifting a counterweight that could easily be used to raise the gun again. For several years at his own expense he carried out experiments on this "disappearing gun" using a 7-pounder. From 1867 to 1875 he was attached to the Royal Arsenal at Woolwich [q.v.], where he worked out the details for mounting heavier guns and devised a method for laying and sighting them when mounted on his carriage. The government awarded him £10,000 for his disappearing gun carriage and any improvements. In 1878 he was promoted colonel, and in 1890 he was knighted (KCB).

Moncrieff acquired great wealth and was a man of many interests. He hunted game in South Africa and Canada, exhibited his paintings at the Scottish Academy. He was captain of the Wimbleton Golf Club and a director of two banks.

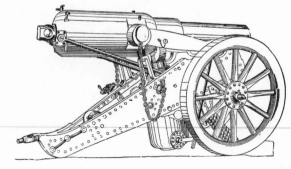

Moncrieff "disappearing gun" carriage

Monge, Gaspard (1746–1818). A French mathematician and physicist, a confidant of Napoleon, and one of the founders of the École Polytechnique [q.v.]. He is considered the inventor of descriptive geometry. In 1792 and 1793 he was minister of marine.

Moniteur. In full: *Le Moniteur universel La Gazette national ou Le.* A French national gazette founded on 24 November 1789 and published by Charles Joseph Panckoucke (1736–1798). It published, among other items, all decrees and military bulletins. "Capitaine Buonaparte" was first mentioned on 14 October 1793 as an officer who had distinguished himself at Toulon. The publication was continued by the founder's son, Charles-Louis-Fleur (1780–1844). From 28 December 1799 it became Napoleon's official propaganda organ. Copies were sent to armies in the field and to foreign capitals as well as to schools, where teachers were ordered to read it aloud to students at mealtimes. Napoleon himself sometimes wrote articles that appeared anonymously. By 1811 it was one of only four newspapers allowed to be published in Paris. It was published under the Bourbons until 1868, when it was replaced by *Le Journal officiel.*

Monobloc. A gun barrel made from a single piece of metal.

Monocacy, Battle of (9 July 1864), American Civil War. A Confederate force of about 10,000 infantry and 4,000 cavalry under General Jubal Early [q.v.], advancing through Maryland in the direction of Washington, D.C., encountered a Union force consisting of a brigade of infantry and a brigade of cavalry under General Lewis Wallace and a division under General James Ricketts [qq.v.] on the banks of the Monocacy River just southeast of Frederick. The numerically inferior Federals were routed, but the battle delayed Early long enough for the Federals to summon reinforcements to defend Washington.

Early did not make a vigorous pursuit, for he did not want to be encumbered with prisoners. Of the 6,050 Federals engaged, 1,880 were casualties, most taken prisoner; of the 14,000 Confederates, fewer than 700 were casualties.

Montbrun, Louis Pierre (1770–1812). A French soldier who enlisted in the cavalry in 1789 and was commissioned in 1794. He saw much service in Germany and fought at Austerlitz [q.v.]. He was promoted general of brigade soon after that battle. In 1809 he was made general of division and fought at Eckmühl [q.v.]. In 1810 he commanded the cavalry in the Peninsular War [q.v.], in which he fought at Almeida, Bussaco, and Fuentes de Oñoro [qq.v.]. He took part in Napoleon's Russian Campaign [q.v.] and was killed in the Battle of Borodino [q.v.].

Montebello, Battle of (9 June 1800). See Lannes, Jean.

Montebello, Battle of (20 May 1859), Italian Wars of Independence. At this northern Italian village, five miles east of Voghera, a French and Sardinian army of 8,000 under General Élie Frédéric Forey [q.v.] attacked an equally strong Austrian force under Field Marshal Graf Stadion and drove it back to Stradella. Austrian losses were 1,423; the French and Sardinians lost 723.

Monte Caseros, Battle of (3 February 1852), Argentine civil wars. At this village 100 miles up the Uruguay River, 80 miles south-southeast of Mercedes, an Allied force of some 20,000 men, mostly Argentine but including some Uruguayans and Brazilians, under Justo Urquiza [q.v.], then governor of Entre Ríos Province, defeated 25,000 Argentine federal troops, mostly gauchos, under Juan Manuel de Rosa [q.v.]. The Allies lost 600; Argentine troops lost 1,500 killed and wounded and 7,000 taken prisoner. Rosas fled to England, and Urquiza became the first constitutional president of Argentina.

Montereau, Battle of (18 February 1814), Napoleonic Wars. After checking the Allied advance on Paris in the Marne Valley, Napoleon moved south and successfully attacked the Allied force under Prince von Schwarzenberg [q.v.] at this village at the confluence of the Seine and the Yonne. The Allies lost 6,000 men and 15 guns; Napoleon lost about 2,500.

Monterrey, Battle of (21–25 September 1846), Mexican War. Some 6,000 Americans under Zachary Taylor [q.v.] defeated 7,000 Mexican regulars and 3,000 militia under General Pedro de Ampudia [q.v.] at this city in northeastern Mexico. After sustaining 367 casualties, the Mexicans surrendered and were allowed the honors of war [q.v.]; American losses were 488, including 120 killed.

The battle inspired a number of songs and poems, including one by Charles Fenno Hoffman (1806–1884), a well-known journalist:

> We were not many—we who stood
> Before the iron sleet that day;
> Yet many a gallant spirit would
> Give half his years, if he could
> Have been with us at Monterrey.

Three years later Hoffman was placed in an institution for the insane, where he died.

Montevideo, British Capture of (3 February 1807). British forces under General Sir Samuel Auchmuty [q.v.] stormed and captured Montevideo, capital of what was then called Banda Oriental (Uruguay), suffering 600 casualties out of 4,800 engaged.

Montevideo, Siege of (1843–51), Uruguayan revolution. In the 1830s political parties in Banda Oriental (Uruguay), which had revolted from Brazil in 1825 and had just been recognized as a separate state in 1828, were polarized between the conservative Blancos (Whites), who drew their support from ranchers, merchants, and the clergy, mostly in the interior, and the liberal Colorados (Reds), whose support came from Montevideo and the coastal area. In 1843, after the withdrawal of the French forces, which had supported the Uruguayan president General José Fructuoso Rivera [q.v.], a Colorado, the city of Montevideo was besieged by forces under General Manuel Oribe [q.v.], a Blanco who had allied himself with the Buenos Aires dictator Juan Manuel de Rosas [q.v.]. One of the leading defenders of the city was the Italian patriot Giuseppe Garibaldi [q.v.]. On 8 October 1851 Justo Urquiza [q.v.] led a combined force of Colorados, Brazilians, and Paraguayans in an assault on the besiegers. Oribe was defeated, and the long siege was lifted.

Montholon, Charles Tristan de (1783–1853). A French soldier in the Napoleonic Wars who served as an aide-de-camp to the French marshals Jean Baptiste Joubert, Pierre Augereau, Jacques Macdonald, and Louis Alexandre Berthier [qq.v.]. Although Montholon later claimed to have risen to the rank of general of division, he probably did not rise higher than colonel. In the Battle of Waterloo [q.v.] he served as an aide to Napoleon, whom he also accompanied into exile on the island of St. Helena. He remained there until Napoleon's death and then acted as executor of his will. In 1840 he joined Louis Napoleon (1808–1873) as his "chief of staff" in his unsuccessful coup d'état. He was captured at Boulogne and imprisoned until 1847. In 1849 he was elected to the Constituent Assembly.

He was the author, aided by General Gaspard Gourgaud [q.v.], of *Mémoires pour servir à l'histoire de France sous Napoléon, écrits sous sa dictée* in 1823. In 1847 he published *Récits des la captivité de Napoléon à Sainte-Hélèna* ("An Account of the Captivity of Napoleon on St. Helena").

Montmartre, Action at (30 March 1814), Napoleon's 1814 campaign. Some 107,000 Allies advanced on Paris with only about 23,000 French forces under Marshals Édouard Adolphe Mortier and Auguste de Marmont [qq.v.] at Belleville and Montmartre to oppose them. The final action of the 1814 campaign took place at two o'clock in the morning of 30 March. Soon after, Marmont on Montmartre opened negotiations with the Allies, a decision that led to the first abdication of Napoleon.

Montmirail, Battle of (11 February 1814), Napoleon's 1814 campaign. After defeating the middle division of the army of Prussian General Gebhard von Blücher [q.v.], Napoleon, marching westward on the north bank of the Petit Morain with 10,500 men and 36 guns, encountered near this village, 14 miles south-southwest of Château Thierry between the Marne and Seine rivers, 18,000 Russians under Russian General Dmitri Osten-Sacken [q.v.]. In the ensuing battle Napoleon was reinforced to 20,000 and delivered the Russians a resounding defeat. French losses were about 2,000, and Russian losses at least twice that.

Montpensier, Antoine Marie Philippe d'Orléans, Duc de Montpensier (1824–1890). A French soldier and the fifth son of King Louis Philippe (1773–1850), who from 1842 to 1845 fought in North Africa. After his marriage to the daughter of Queen Isabella II (1830–1904) of Spain, he lived in Spain and served in the Spanish army from 1847 to 1859.

Montreal Campaign (October–November 1813), War of 1812. The unsuccessful attempt of the Americans to capture Montreal, Canada, has been officially described as "one of the worst fiascos of the war." It was planned as a two-pronged attack with about 6,000 men under Major General James Wilkinson [q.v.] coming down the St. Lawrence River from Sacket's Harbor and 4,000 men under Brigadier General Wade Hampton [q.v.] moving from Plattsburg on Lake Champlain. Neither was strong enough to capture the city without the help of the other, but the two generals detested each other, and each had the lowest opinion of the other's competence. About halfway down the Chateaugay River Hampton had a brief encounter with the British. He immediately retreated back to Plattsburg and resigned from the army. When part of Wilkinson's force, about 2,000 men, was soundly defeated just north of Ogdenbug, on the St. Lawrence River, he too turned back and retreated to Plattsburg.

Mont Valérien, Battle of. See Buzenval, Battle of.

Moochi. A loincloth made of animal skins or tail hairs worn by Zulu warriors.

Moonshee. A native instructor in Oriental languages, such as Hindustani, Urdu, and Persian, was so called by British officers in India, all of whom were required to learn at least one Indian language.

Moore, John (1761–1809). A British soldier commissioned in 1776. From 1779 to 1783 he served in North America fighting the rebellious American colonists. In 1794 he took part in the reduction of the French garrisons in Corsica, and in the next seven years he served in the West Indies, Ireland, Holland, and Egypt. Early in 1808 he was sent to the Baltic to assist King Gustavus IV of Sweden in his quarrel with Napoleon. Gustavus ordered him arrested when he refused to acquiesce in his plans, but Moore managed to escape from the country in disguise. On his return to England he was at once sent to Portugal with 10,000 men to expel the French from the Iberian Peninsula. In August 1808, after the Convention of Cintra [q.v.], he was given the chief command. He was surprised by this promotion and wrote: "How they came to pitch upon me I cannot say, for they have given sufficient proof of not being partial to me." In early November he moved across the frontier into Spain with 30,000 men and made for Valladolid, but the apathy of the Spanish, the intrigues of his own countrymen, and French successes elsewhere placed him in a difficult position. He soon discovered that Napoleon with 70,000 men had occupied Madrid and cut off his retreat to Portugal. He was thus forced to make a disastrous retreat for 250 miles from Astorga through the mountains in the depth of winter to Corunna [q.v.]. On 16 January 1809, when the remnants of his army arrived on the coast and had just begun to embark, it was attacked by a French force under Marshal Nicolas Soult [q.v.]. The French were defeated, losing about 2,000, but at the moment of victory Moore fell mortally wounded. "I feel myself so strong," he said. "I fear I shall be a long time in dying." Indeed, not until 24 January did he die in great agony. He was buried in the ramparts of Corunna.

In 1817 Charles Wolfe (1791–1823), an Irish clergyman, published a poem, "The Burial of Sir John Moore," which became famous. It contained the lines:

We carved not a line and we raised not a stone
But we left him alone with his glory.

Moral. Used in a military sense, the word has nothing to do with morality. It means the capability, motivation, and performance of a unit. It was in this sense that Napoleon used the word when he said, "The moral is to the physical as three to one."

Morale. The mental and emotional attitudes of soldiers toward the tasks assigned to them and toward their officers and comrades; a sense of common purpose with their unit. Napoleon said: "In war everything depends upon morale; and morale and public opinion comprise the greater part of reality."

Morales, Agustín (1810–1872). A Bolivian soldier who became a general and in 1871 president of Bolivia. He was assassinated the following year.

Morales, Bermúdez Remicio (1836–1894). A Peruvian soldier who became a general and in 1890 president of Peru. He died in office.

Morand, Charles Antoine Louis Alexis (1771–1835). A French lawyer who became a captain of volunteers in 1792 and saw service in Germany, Italy, and Egypt. In 1800 he was promoted general of brigade. He distinguished himself at Austerlitz [q.v.] and in 1805 was promoted general of division. The following year he was wounded at Auerstädt and again at Eylau [qq.v.]. He fought at Abensberg, Eckmühl, Ratisbon, and Wagram [qq.v.], where he was again wounded. During Napoleon's Russian Campaign [q.v.] he was severely wounded in the Battle of Borodino [q.v.]. In 1813 he returned to duty and fought at Lützen, Bautzen, Dennewitz, and Hanau [qq.v.]. During the Hundred Days [q.v.] he served as an aide to Napoleon, and in the Battle of Waterloo [q.v.] he commanded part of the Garde Impériale.

Morant Bay Rebellion. See Jamaica Revolts.

Morar, Battle of (16 June 1858). Indian Mutiny. A rebel force of 8,000 under Tantia Topi [q.v.] attempted to bar an Anglo-Indian force of 4,000 under Sir Hugh Rose [q.v.], which was marching to take part in the siege of Gwalior [q.v.]. The rebels were put to flight and were vigorously pursued by light dragoons.

Morazán, Francisco (1799–1842). A Central American soldier who, after Honduras had gained independence in 1821, turned to politics. In 1828 he led an army to victory over reactionaries in El Salvador, and the following year he again defeated such forces in Guatemala. In 1830 he was elected president of the Central American Confederation, but ten years later his attempts to keep the countries of the confederation united failed, and he fled to Peru. He returned to Central America two years later, organized an army, and invaded Costa Rica, but he was captured, court-martialed, and on 15 September 1842 shot.

Morazzone, Battle of (20 May 1848), Italian Wars of Independence. At this northern Italian commune near Kovara, Giuseppe Garibaldi [q.v.] with 1,500 volunteers fought an eleven-hour battle with 5,000 Austrians under General d'Aspre but was forced to retreat to Arona.

Mordecai, Alfred (1804–1886). An American soldier who was graduated from West Point first in his class in 1823 and commissioned into the Corps of Engineers. He was an instructor at West Point for nine years and later assisted in the construction of Fort Monroe in Virginia. In 1832 he was promoted captain in the Ordnance Department, in which he served for more than a quarter of a century. He commanded several important arsenals and carried out extensive research on weapons and ammunition. He was a member of the original Ordnance Board [q.v.] when it was established in 1839 and remained a member until the eve of the Civil War. He was responsible for most of the work on the *Ordnance Manual* [1841], the first ever published by the American army, and he was solely responsible for the second edition in 1850. He took an active part in the formulation of a comprehensive system for the artillery, the details of which were published in 1849 as *Artillery for the United States Land Service, as Devised and Arranged by the Ordnance Board*. During the Crimean War [q.v.] he was sent to Europe to study military developments, primarily organization and weapons. He is credited with the adoption of the 12-pounder howitzer known as the Napoleon [q.v.], which became the most widely used fieldpiece of the American Civil War. Speaking of his work, he wrote: "My ability consists in a knowledge and love of order and system, and in the habit of patient labor in perfecting and arranging details; and my usefulness in the Army arises from the long continued application of these qualities to the specialties of my habitual business."

Because he had conflicting interests North and South, he resigned his commission on the outbreak of the Civil War. Refusing attractive offers from both the Union and Confederate sides, he spent the war teaching mathematics in Philadelphia. After the war he served briefly as assistant engineer of the Imperial Mexican Railway. From 1866 until his death he served as treasurer and secretary of the Pennsylvania Canal Company.

Moreau, Jean Victor Marie (1763–1813). A French soldier in French Revolutionary and Napoleonic armies. In 1789 he formed an artillery company in the Rennes Garde Nationale and served as its captain. In 1791 he was a lieutenant colonel in the Army of the North, and in 1795 he commanded that army. In 1799 he commanded the army in Italy, and the following year he distinguished himself in the Battle of Hohenlinden [q.v.] on 3 December. Napoleon described him as an "excellent soldier, personally brave . . . but an absolute stranger to strategy." He was also an inept conspirator. Having intrigued with royalists and headed a plot to overthrow Napoleon, he was arrested on 15 April 1804, imprisoned, and then exiled. From 1804 to 1813 he lived at Morrisville, Pennsylvania, across the Delaware River from Trenton, New Jersey. He returned to Europe in 1813 to be a military adviser to Tsar Alexander I [q.v.] and was mortally wounded in the Battle of Dresden [q.v.], fighting against his own countrymen. A cannonball shattered both his legs, which were amputated. He died five days later, and his last words were said to have been: "Rest easy, gentlemen. It is my destiny."

Morella, Battle of (23 May 1840), First Carlist War. At this town, a Carlist stronghold in eastern Spain, 32 miles west-northwest of Vinaroz, some 20,000 Cristinos under General Baldomero Espartero [q.v.] besieged 4,000 Carlists under General Ramón Cabrera [q.v.]. A first attempt by the Carlists to break out failed, but Cabrera managed to cut his way free in a second attempt. Morella was the last Carlist stronghold to fall.

Morelos y Pavón, José María (1765–1815). A Mexican priest and revolutionary who in 1810 joined the insurrection of Miguel Hidalgo y Costilla [q.v.] and succeeded as rebel leader after Hidalgo was executed. On 6 November 1813 he issued a declaration of independence from Spain. He was finally defeated and captured by Agustín de Itúrbide [q.v.]. On 22 December 1815 he was shot.

Morés, Antoine Amédée Vincent Manca de Vallombrosa de (1868–1896). A French soldier, farmer, and Mahdist sympathizer. A graduate of St. Cyr and the cavalry school at Saumur, he left the army while a young man, married an American heiress, and emigrated to New York. In 1883 his father-in-law bought him a 26,000-acre ranch in South Dakota, and he moved there to operate it. An excellent shot with a hot temper, he provoked numerous duels and made himself further unpopular in ranching country by stringing barbed wire on the range. He finally sold out and went to Southeast Asia, where he tried, unsuccessfully, to construct a railroad from Tonkin to Yunnan. In 1888 he returned to Europe and allied himself with the political schemes of General Georges Boulanger [q.v.], who wanted to change the French constitution and avenge the French disaster in the Franco-Prussian War [q.v.]. Although he occasioned several duels by making anti-Semitic statements, he gained a considerable following.

On 20 March 1898 he arrived in Tunis with a small band of disciples and set off across the desert to join the Dervishes in the Sudan. He succeeded in avoiding the French outposts and patrols that tried to stop him, but he was set upon and killed by Tuareg Arabs intent upon booty. His death aroused strong anti-Arab feelings in France. Thousands attended his funeral, where the archbishop of Tunis proclaimed: "France, who in 1830 purged the Mediterranean of the Barbary pirates, must now eliminate the pirates of the desert."

L'affaire Morés, as it was called, shattered the French policy of Arab diplomacy and commercial penetration of the Sahara.

Morgan, George Washington (1820–1893). An American soldier who at age sixteen left college to go to Texas, where he obtained from Sam Houston [q.v.] a commission in the Texas army. He later attended West Point but did not graduate. He was practicing law at the beginning of the Mexican War [q.v.] when he was given command of a regiment of volunteers under General Zachary Taylor [q.v.]. On 3 March 1847, at the age of twenty-six, he was commissioned a colonel in the 15th Infantry and served under General Winfield Scott [q.v.]. He was twice wounded and won a brevet to brigadier general. In 1848 he was honorably discharged, and in the next thirteen years he was a farmer, lawyer, and consul at Marseilles. At the beginning of the American Civil War he was minister to Portugal, a position he left to accept a commission as brigadier general in the Union army. He cleared the Confederates from Cumberland Gap and served under William Tecumseh Sherman [q.v.], but when blacks were accepted as soldiers, he resigned in protest on 8 June 1863.

In 1865 he was defeated as a candidate for governor of Ohio, but he was three times elected to Congress, where he vigorously opposed Reconstruction measures.

Morgan, John Hunt (1825–1864). An American soldier who first saw active service in the Mexican War [q.v.]. After the war he became a merchant in Lexington, Kentucky, where in 1857 he organized the Lexington Rifles. When the American Civil War began, he marched the unit to Bowling Green, where it was taken into the Confederate army. On 4 April 1862 he became colonel of the 2nd Kentucky Cavalry, and on 11 December he was promoted brigadier general. He made daring raids into Kentucky, Tennessee, and Ohio. In 1863 he was captured in Ohio and imprisoned. He managed to escape and upon his return to the South was given command of the Department of Southwestern Virginia. On the night of 3–4 September 1864 he was surprised by a detachment of Union cavalry at Greenville, Tennessee, and was killed while trying to escape.

Morgan, John Tyler (1824–1907). An American lawyer, legislator, and soldier. In 1861, at the age of thirty-seven, he enlisted as a private in the Confederate army; in 1863 he rose to be a brigadier general. He saw much service, fighting at First Bull Run, Stones River, and Chickamauga [qq.v.]. In 1876 he was elected a U.S. senator from Alabama and so served until his death thirty-one years later.

Morillo, Pablo, Conde de Cartagena (1777–1838). A Spanish general in South America who defeated Simón Bolívar at the Second Battle of La Puerta [q.v.] on 15 March 1818 but was in the end defeated by him. In 1826 he wrote memoirs of his campaigns.

Mormon Volunteers. During the Mexican War [q.v.] General Winfield Scott directed Stephen Kearny [qq.v.] to raise from 500 to 1,000 Mormon volunteers to be commanded by their own officers with a commander selected by Kearny; they were to receive their discharge in California. The project was approved by President James Polk (1795–1849) and Brigham Young (1801–1877), and General Kearny selected Captain James Allen (d. 1846), who, with the help of Thomas Leiper Kane [q.v.], raised a battalion of 585 Mormons who were mustered in at Council Bluffs, Iowa, on 16 July 1846. The battalion arrived at Sante Fe in early September. When Captain Allen died of "congestive fever" on 23 August, he was replaced by Captain (later Major General) Philip St. George Cooke (1809–1895), who sent the sick and most of the families that had accompanied the volunteers into winter camp near what is today Pueblo, Colorado. The rest marched on, reaching Tucson on 14 December; the Mexican force there fled. They trudged on, reaching San Diego on 29–30 January 1847; most were by then shoeless, and some nearly naked. By the time of their discharges the battalion had dwindled to 317. The Mormons engaged in no battles, and none was killed or wounded.

Mormon War. See Utah Expedition.

Morosi War (1878). Morosi (d. 1878), the chief of the Baphuti clan of the Basutos in South Africa, established a stronghold in the mountains that were the headwaters of the

Orange River. In the 1830s he was a supporter of Moshesh [q.v.]. In 1878, when the government tried to disarm the Basutos, he refused to give up his weapons, and the Boers sent an expedition against him. On 20 November 1878 his stronghold was stormed, and he was killed.

Morrill Act (1862). A bill sponsored by Representative Justin Morrill (1810–1898) of Vermont and passed by Congress on 2 July 1862 that became law after the American Civil War. It provided that proceeds from the sale of federal land be used to endow one college in each state. These came to be called land-grant colleges. Among other provisions was the requirement that such colleges provide instruction in military science and tactics, a program that later developed into the Reserve Officer Training Corps (ROTC).

Morris, John Ignatius (1842–1902). An Englishman who was commissioned in the Royal Marines in 1859 and in 1883–84 was assistant adjutant general of the Suakin Field Force in the eastern Sudan. He became a major general and deputy adjutant general of the Royal Marines.

Mortar. A muzzle-loaded, short-barreled artillery piece with a high angle of fire, usually 45 to 60 degrees.

Mortar *Mortar dictator, front of Petersburg, Virginia, October 1864. Photograph by Alexander Gardner*

Mortar *The great mortar Sevastopol at Theodore, Ethiopia*

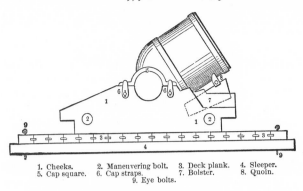

1. Cheeks. 2. Maneuvering bolt. 3. Deck plank. 4. Sleeper.
5. Cap square. 6. Cap straps. 7. Bolster. 8. Quoin.
9. Eye bolts.

Mortar battery

Mortara, Battle of (21 March 1849), Italian Wars of Independence. An Austrian army under Josef Radetzky [q.v.] attacked the northern Italian commune of Mortara, 22 miles west-northwest of Pavia, and routed the Piedmontese under the Duke of Savoy (later King Victor Emmanuel II [1820–1878]). The Austrians lost 300; the Piedmontese lost 500 killed and wounded and 2,000 men with five guns captured.

"Mort au champ d'honneur." Literally, dead on the field of honor. Captain Théophile de la Tour d'Auvergne [q.v.], a man of exceptional bravery whom Napoleon called the First Grenadier of France [q.v.], was killed in the Battle of Oberhausen on 27 June 1800. Thereafter, in every morning roll call in his regiment, his name was called and answered by a sergeant with "Mort au champ d'honneur." The custom was later adopted in other regiments to honor the dead who had been known for their valor.

Mortier, Édouard Adolphe Casimir Joseph, Duc de Trévise (1768–1835). A French soldier in French Revolutionary and Napoleonic armies who enlisted as a volunteer in 1791 and was elected a captain. A large man, standing six feet six inches tall, he was a colonel in 1795 and a general of brigade in 1799. In 1804 he was made a marshal by Napoleon. He particularly distinguished himself in the Battle of Friedland [q.v.] in 1807 and in the Peninsular War [q.v.] in 1808–09. He took part in Napoleon's Russian Campaign [q.v.] and in the last battles in the defense of France.

In 1834 he became minister of war. On 25 July 1835, while standing at the side of Louis Philippe (1773–1850), he was mortally wounded by an infernal machine fired by Joseph Maria Fieschi (1790–1836), a Corsican conspirator. The explosion killed 18 people in all, but spared Louis Philippe, the assassin's target.

Morton, James St. Clair (1829–1864). An American soldier who at the age of fourteen entered the University of Pennsylvania, where he studied for four years before entering West Point, from which he was graduated second in his class in 1851. On 4 April 1863, during the American Civil War, he was promoted brigadier general of volunteers in the Union army with his rank to date from 29 November 1862. He was mustered out of the volunteer service, it is not clear why, but he continued to serve in his capacity of regular army major. He was chief engineer of the Army of the Cumberland and was responsible for the fortification of Nashville and Chattanooga. He was killed at Petersburg, Virginia, while reconnoitering the ground in preparation for an attack. He was posthumously promoted brevet brigadier general in the regular army.

Mosby, John Singleton (1833–1916). An American lawyer and Confederate guerrilla leader who during the American Civil War first served on the staff of General J. E. B. Stuart [q.v.] in the Peninsular Campaign [q.v.]. For most of the war he commanded an independent cavalry unit known as Mosby's Rangers that operated in Northern Virginia, raiding small units and seizing supplies. At Fairfax Court House on 9 March 1863 he captured General Edwin Henry Stoughton [q.v.]. After the war he resumed the practice of law, and from 1878 to 1885 he was U.S. consul at Hong Kong.

Colonel John S. Mosby

Moscow, French Retreat from. See Russian Campaign, Napoleon's.

Moselekatse (1795?–1870), also known as Umsiligasi or Sikaats. A Zulu warrior and first king of the Matabeles. He was born in Zululand and distinguished himself as a military leader under Shaka [q.v.]. About 1824, after quarreling with Shaka, he fled across the Drakensberg with several thousand followers and established a new kingdom north of the Vaal River, in the process destroying most of the tribes living between the Orange and Limpopo rivers. When he came in conflict with the Boers, he and his followers were driven across the Limpopo River, where they conquered most of the Mashonas and established the Matabele kingdom [see Matabele Wars].

Moselle Line. A string of French forts built after the Franco-Prussian War on the upper Moselle between the fortresses of Épinal and Belfort.

Moshesh / Moshweshwe / Moshoeshoe (1796?–1870). The paramount chief of the Basutos who managed to hold off both Boers and British after he established his stronghold on top of a flat-topped mountain known as Thaba Bosigo [q.v.] in Basutoland (Lesotho) in 1832 [see Basuto Wars]. In the Basuto War of 1865 Orange Free State forces under Louw Wepener [q.v.] stormed the mountain and were beaten back. Wepener was killed. Moshesh's Day, 12 March, is celebrated annually as a public holiday in Lesotho.

Mosin-Nagant Rifle. A bolt-action rifle, caliber 7.62 mm, adopted by the imperial Russian army in 1891. It had an overall length of 51.37 inches and weighed 9.62 pounds. The bolt action was designed by Colonel S. I. Mosin (1849–1902), a Russian artillery officer, and the five-round magazine by Émile Nagant, a Belgian gunsmith, who, with his brother, Léon, had produced at Liège the 9 mm Belgian service revolver of 1878.

In 1883 the Russian Rifle Test Commission began extensive tests for a new service rifle. The commissioners were taken by Colonel Mosin's bolt action, but they also liked M. Nagant's magazine. They therefore decided to create a new rifle incorporating these features, and the result was the Model 1891.

Mosquera, Tomás Cipriano de (1798–1878). A Colombian soldier and political leader who was president of New Granada from 1845 to 1849. In 1859–61 he led an insurrection that resulted in his seizure of power. He called a national assembly, which created the United States of Colombia and gave him dictatorial powers. In 1869 he was deposed and banished.

Mossi Expedition (1896–97). An exceptionally brutal and destructive French military expedition in West Africa that conquered the Wagadugu (Ouagadougou) empire, often called the five Mossi states, in what became Upper Volta (Burkina Faso).

Mot de Cambronne. Literally, Cambronne's word. During the Battle of Waterloo [q.v.] Napoleon's Garde Impériale, commanded by General Comte Pierre Cambronne [q.v.], surrounded by the British, was called on to surrender. The general's reply, considered apocryphal, was said to be: "*La garde meurt il ne se rend pas.* [The guard dies; it does not surrender]." Although these words are engraved on the monument erected to him at Nantes, it is generally believed that his actual *mot* was "*Merde!* [shit!]," and it is this word that is known as the *mot de Cambronne.*

Moualok, Battle of (19 May 1881), French conquest of Algeria. A French column searching for Arab rebels under Abu Amana in Algeria found them holding a pass 500 meters wide called Moualok. The rebels attacked the column's rear guard, overwhelmed it, pillaged the baggage, then fled, leaving 72 French dead, 12 missing, and 15 wounded.

Moulinet. A circular movement with a saber.

Mount. 1. As a verb, to make all preparations for a campaign or a military expedition.

2. As a verb, of a guard, to place or prepare to place sentinels.

3. As a noun, a carriage or stand on which a weapon is placed.

4. As a verb, to seat oneself on a horse.

5. As a noun, a horse.

Mountain Gun. A light gun or howitzer, usually capable of high elevation, designed for use in mountainous country. It could be disassembled, and the parts carried by men, mules, or elephants. [See Screw Gun; Pack Howitzer.]

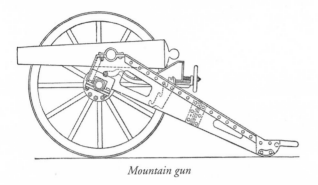

Mountain gun

Mountain Meadows Massacre (11 September 1857). Incited by John Doyle Lee (1812–1877), a Mormon bishop, Paiute Indians attacked a wagon train with 140 emigrants who had left Fort Smith, Arkansas, in late March 1857 bound for California. In a valley known as Mountain Meadows in southwest Utah, 40 miles from Cedar City, the emigrants drew their wagons into a circle and held off their attackers for several days until a group of white men, led by William H. Dame (1819–1884), president of the Parowan stake of the Mormon Church and colonel of the local military district, appeared and offered to escort them to safety if they would surrender their arms. When they had done so, Dame and his group disappeared while the helpless party was massacred by the Indians. Only 17 infants were spared.

Although the Mormons admitted responsibility, it was not until 1874 that Lee was arrested and tried for the murders. He was executed by a firing squad on 22 March 1877 at the site of the massacre. Dame was unpunished.

Mounted Infantry. Troops who were mounted on horses but fought on foot with carbines or musketoons.

Mounted Rangers. In December 1831 Senator Thomas Hart Benton (1782–1858) introduced a bill to raise six companies of mounted volunteers to defend the western frontier. They were to enlist for one year, furnish their own horses and weapons, and receive as pay a dollar a day. The bill passed both houses, and on 18 January 1832 President Andrew Jackson [q.v.] signed it. On 15 June the unit came into being. The idea proved to be less of a success than anticipated, and a new bill, passed through Congress and signed on 2 May 1833, authorized the discharge of the rangers and the establishment of a regiment of 1,832 dragoons, essentially mounted infantry. The 1st Dragoons was commanded by Colonel Henry M. Dodge (d. 1867) with Lieutenant Colonel Stephen Watts Kearny [q.v.] as second-in-command.

Mounted Riflemen. A regiment of the American army authorized by act of Congress on 19 May 1846 specifically for duty on the Oregon Trail but immediately sent to Mexico to fight in the Mexican War [q.v.]. It did not begin duty on the Oregon Trail until 1849. In 1861 its designation was changed to 3rd Cavalry.

Mousqueton. A French carbine used in Napoleon's armies. Its range was three-quarters that of the *fusil infanterie* [q.v.]. It was issued to hussars, *chasseurs à pied*, gendarmes [qq.v.], and others. [See Musketoon.]

Mouton, François Henri (1804–1876). A French soldier who served as a volunteer from 1822 to 1826. In 1830 he was commissioned a lieutenant of cavalry and was promoted captain five years later. In 1837 or 1838 he left the French army, and in 1839 he was commanding the cuirassiers in the Khalsa [q.v.], the army of Ranjit Singh [q.v.] in the Punjab. He took part in operations against tribesmen in Mandi and the Kulu hills in northern Punjab. He played an active role in the Second Sikh War [q.v.], and he is said to have built the earthworks at Ferozeshah [q.v.]. In 1846 he was captured by the British, who deported him.

Mouton rejoined the French army and served as a colonel on the staff during the Crimean War [q.v.]. He retired in 1865.

Mouton, Georges. See Lobau, Georges Moutoun, Comte de.

Mower, Joseph Anthony (1827–1870). An American soldier who attended Norwich Academy in Vermont in 1843–45, then became a carpenter. In 1846 he enlisted in the army as a private and served in the Mexican War [q.v.]. In 1855 he obtained a commission as a second lieutenant of infantry. During the American Civil War he was brevetted brigadier general in the Union regular army and a major general of volunteers, compiling a record of promotions, brevets, and official commendations that was scarcely matched in the war. After the war he remained in the army as colonel of the 39th Infantry. He was commander of the Department of Louisiana when he died in New Orleans on 6 January 1870.

Muawin. A military rank in the Turkish and Egyptian armies just below *bimbashi* [q.v.], equal to the rank of captain. In 1880 the rank was abandoned in Egypt.

Muddy Creek, Battle of. See Lame Deer, Battle of.

Mudir. A governor, often a military governor, in the Sudan, Egypt, and other Arab countries.

Mudki, Battle of (18 December 1845), First Sikh War. General Sir Hugh Gough [q.v.] with 10,500 to 12,000 Anglo-Indian troops and 42 guns advancing into the Punjab in India encountered a force of 16,000 to 22,000 Sikhs with 22 guns at this village, 18 miles southeast of Ferozepore. After an initial setback Gough triumphed, driving the Sikhs from the field and capturing 17 of their guns. Gough suffered 872 casualties, among them Sir Robert Sale [q.v.], a hero of the First Afghan War. The Sikh army was said to have lost heavily.

Mud March (19–24 January 1863), American Civil War. After his defeat in the Battle of Fredericksburg in January 1863 Union Major General Ambrose Burnside [q.v.], over the objections of most of his subordinate generals, attempted to cross the Rappahannock River above Fredericksburg and again attack the Army of Northern Virginia [q.v.]. Two days of heavy rain turned the movement into what was called, even in some official correspondence, a mud march. "An indescribable chaos of pontoons, vehicles and artillery encumbered all the roads," noted one Union officer, "supply wagons upset by the roadside, guns stalled in the mud, ammunition trains ruined . . . and hundreds of horses and mules buried in the liquid mud." The movement was abandoned, and Burnside was relieved of his command soon after.

Müffling, Baron Karl von (1775–1851). A Prussian soldier who was the quartermaster general in the army of Field Marshal Gebhard von Blücher [q.v.] in 1813–14 and served as Prussian attaché at Wellington's headquarters at Waterloo [q.v.]. In 1821 he was chief of the Prussian general staff, and in that position he devoted himself to the improvement of military maps and the advancement of military cartography. In 1829 he negotiated the peace between Russia and Turkey [see Russo-Turkish Wars].

Mufti. Ordinary civilian street clothes when worn by an officer.

Mufu. In China, the term for the headquarters of a general officer.

Muhafiz. A Turkish or Egyptian officer commanding troops in a province.

Muhammad Ahmed (1848–1885). Name in full: Muhammad Ahmed ibn al-Seyyid Abdullah, called El Mahdi (the Messiah). A militant Sudanese Islamic religious reformer whose armies swept the Egyptian and European rulers from the Sudan. As a young man he was noted for his piety and asceticism. In May 1881, having gained a considerable following, he revealed that he was El Mahdi and began preaching a return to fundamental Islam. Combining elements of the Wahhabi and Senusi sects, he opposed music, alcohol, tobacco, the veneration of saints, pilgrimages to tombs, and all foreign influences (including Turkish).

His male followers (Dervishes), dressed in jibbas—white robes with colored patches—became a formidable force. Government troops in ever-larger numbers sent to arrest him were repeatedly repulsed. With each victory his fame and the number of his followers grew. In 1882 his Dervish forces massacred a government army of 7,000 [see Kashgil, Battle of]. Town after town in the Sudan surrendered to him, and tribe after tribe pledged its support.

Prevented from retaliating or taking vigorous action by Arabi's Revolt [q.v.], which was then convulsing Egypt, the Egyptian government began withdrawing its garrisons. British Major General Charles ("Chinese") Gordon [q.v.], sent to evacuate all the Egyptians in the Sudan, was trapped at Khartoum and killed when the besieged town fell to the Dervishes on 26 January 1885 [see Khartoum, Siege of]. Except for a few isolated garrisons, El Mahdi's forces then controlled the entire Sudan, nearly a million square miles of Africa. El Mahdi died of natural causes soon after the fall of Khartoum, and his place was taken by Abdullahi [q.v.].

Muhammad Ali. See Mehemet Ali.

Muhammad al-Sharif (d. 1899). A son-in-law of El Mahdi [see Muhammad Ahmed], who appointed him fourth khalifa. He was said to have personally killed William Hicks Pasha [q.v.] in 1883 [see Kashgil, Battle of]. He took part in the siege of Khartoum [q.v.]. In 1889 he tried unsuccessfully to oppose the military dictatorship of Abdullahi [q.v.]. In 1898 he surrendered to the Anglo-Egyptian government. In 1899, suspected of collecting a force to rejoin Khalifa Abdullahi, he was arrested. An attempt to rescue him failed; he was court-martialed and shot.

Muhammad Bey Ahmed (1845–1931). A Sudanese soldier born in Suakin who joined the Egyptian army and saw much service fighting the Dervishes. He earned a commission and took part in the reconquest of the Sudan [q.v.]. He was promoted *qaimmaquam* [roughly, senior lieutenant colonel] and in 1900 assisted in the capture of Osman Digna [q.v.].

Muhammad Bey Almas (1825?–1880). A Sudanese soldier who entered the ranks of the Egyptian army in 1834 and became a commissioned officer. He was second-in-command of the Sudanese battalion sent to Mexico to assist the French [see Egyptian Sudanese Battalion in Mexico]. In 1863 he was promoted *bimbashi* (major or lieutenant colonel) and became its commander [see Mexico, French Invasion and Occupation of]. In Mexico he was decorated with the imperial decoration of Our Lady of Guadalupe, and on the return of the battalion to Europe in 1867 he was awarded the Legion of Honor [q.v.]. On his return to Egypt he was promoted *miralai* (colonel) and in 1869 he commanded the 2nd Sudanese Infantry Regiment in the Sudan.

Muhammad Bey Khalil Zughal (d. 1903). A Sudanese who was a cousin of El Mahdi, Muhammed Ahmed [q.v.]. He began his career as a humble merchant, and became an Egyptian government official in Darfur. In 1879, as governor of what was then called the Shaqqa District, he assisted in the suppression of the revolt of Sulaiman wad Zubair. In 1882 he was made a bey and governor of Dara. When Darfur was isolated by Dervish forces, he was sent by Rudolf Slatin [q.v.], then governor of Darfur, to arrange with El Mahdi terms for the surrender of Slatin and his province. Converted to El

Mahdi's brand of Islam, he was then appointed governor of Darfur. Upon El Mahdi's death in 1885 Abdullahi [q.v.], who distrusted Muhammad Bey, assumed control, and in 1889 he was accused of plotting rebellion and banished to Rejaf. He was released when the Belgians occupied the town in 1897, and after the Battle of Omdurman [q.v.] and the end of the Mahdiya he returned to Darfur. There he excited the suspicions of Ali Dinar [q.v.], then the sultan of Darfur, who had him killed.

Muhammad Bey Khusraw al-Daramali (d. 1833). A Rumelian Turkish soldier who in 1821, given command of an Egyptian army by Mehemet Ali [q.v.], invaded Kordofan, then ruled by the sultan of Darfur. In a short campaign he defeated the Darfurian army and killed the governor of the province. As a reward, Mehemet Ali then appointed him governor of Kordofan, where he quickly proceeded to lay the foundation of a military government. He raided the Nubian hills for slaves, he quelled an uprising in the Nile Valley in 1823 with great brutality, and he defeated the forces of Nimr Muhammad Nimr, last of the Jali kings of Shendi, forcing him to flee to Abyssinia. Leaving a path of massacred people and burning villages behind him, Muhammad Bey arrived at Sennar in June 1823. He then turned upon the Hadendowas [see Kipling's "Fuzzy-Wuzzy"] and devastated large tracts of their territory. In September 1824 he was succeeded by another officer and returned to Cairo. In 1825 he was appointed minister of war.

He was an excellent organizer and took exceptionally good care of his troops. He was said to have been educated, handsome, and courtly, but he was remembered for his cruelty.

Muhammad Harun al-Rashid Saif al Din (d. 1880). A son of the royal family of Darfur in the Sudan who became sultan of Darfur in 1875, when his father was killed in battle. He succeeded to the leadership of the rebellion against Egyptian rule and enjoyed some initial successes. In 1877 he occupied Umm Shanka al-Fasher as well as other towns. He was defeated by an Egyptian army near al-Fasher and retreated to Jebel Marra, where he was decisively defeated by Egyptian forces under Rudolf Slatin [q.v.], who was then governor of Dara. Undeterred, he raised a new army, but in 1880 he was ambushed by government forces and killed.

Muhammad Ratib Pasha (d. 1920). A Circassian in the Ottoman army who received his military education in Cairo and in France and was sent to Egypt from Constantinople (Istanbul) about 1863. In 1864 he was appointed liwa (brigade commander), and in 1867 sirdar (commander-in-chief), of the Egyptian army. In 1874, after the disaster to the Egyptian army in Abyssinia under Søren Adolph Arendrup Bey [q.v.], the khedive sent him with a larger army to conquer the country. From Massawa he advanced inland to the Hamasien (Asmara) highlands in Eritrea, where he was defeated in the Battle of Gura [q.v.] in March 1876. Refusing to accept responsibility, he blamed his American staff officers and thus retained his command. In 1879 he was promoted field marshal. In 1888 he was appointed minister of war and marine.

Mujahideen. Various spellings. Muslims who take up the sword for a religious cause. Although twentieth-century journalists translated this word as "freedom fighter," that was not its meaning in the nineteenth century and is probably not the meaning mujahideen understand today. [See Ghazi.]

Mukhtar Pasha, Ahmed (1832–1919). A Turkish soldier who during the Russo-Turkish War [q.v.] of 1877–78 commanded at Erzurum. In 1878 he suppressed an insurrection in Crete, and the following year he commanded the Turkish forces on the Greek frontier. In 1885 he was high commissioner in Egypt, and in 1912 he was briefly grand vizier of Turkey.

Mulazim. 1. A Turkish or Egyptian lieutenant.
2. A member of the Dervish bodyguard of Khalifa Abdullahi [q.v.] during the Mahdiya [q.v.] in the Sudan.

Mules. These animals were much prized as carriers of baggage and mountain guns in mountainous or rough country. An American sergeant in the 1870s, after a long trek through Sioux territory, was heard to remark: "Not a bad trip, sir. We lost a couple of the recruits but none of the mules."

Muller, Hendrik (1865–1945). An Afrikaner leader in South Africa who fought in several battles with tribesmen in the Orange Free State. He began the Second Anglo-Boer War [q.v.] as a corporal in the Boksburg Commando, and before the end of the war he rose to be a general. His best-known feat was the capture at Helvetia, in the eastern Transvaal, of the

Mules *Six-Mule team complete, harnessed and hitched to U.S. army wagon*

heavy British Gun that had been christened Lady Roberts, in honor of Lord Roberts's wife. After the war he became a banker and a legislator.

Multan, Battle of. See Kineyre, Battle of.

Multan, Siege of (July 1848–22 January 1849), Second Sikh War. In July 1848 British Lieutenant Herbert Edwardes [q.v.] raised a local force and besieged the Sikhs in the strong fortress of Multan in southwestern West Punjab (today in northwest Pakistan). He was unable completely to invest the place, and a bombardment was ineffectual, so on 22 September he was forced to raise the siege. On 27 September it was renewed when a force of regulars under General William Sampson Whish (1787–1853) arrived before the town. On 2 January 1849 most of the town was taken by storm, and the Sikh garrison retreated into the citadel, where it surrendered twenty days later. British losses were 210 killed and 910 wounded. Prize agents and looting soldiers seized gold and silver estimated at £5 million.

Muncheel. A hammock suspended from a horizontal pole and carried by two men. It was used to carry the wounded in the Madras and Bombay armies. [See Doolie.]

Münchengrätz, Battle of (28 June 1866), Seven Weeks' War. At this northern Bohemian town, also known as Mnichovo Hradiště, 40 miles northeast of Prague, a Prussian army of 140,000 under Prince Frederick Charles [q.v.] defeated an Austrian army of 20,000 under General Eduard von Clam-Gallas [q.v.]. The Austrians lost about 300 killed and 1,000 taken prisoner; Prussian losses were small.

Mundir. A Russian officer's tunic.

Munfordville, Battle of (14–17 September 1862), American Civil War. During his invasion of Kentucky [q.v.] on 16 September 1862 Confederate General Braxton Bragg [q.v.] surrounded and demanded the surrender of 4,133 Union troops near Munfordville, a town in central Kentucky on the Green River about 45 miles north of the Tennessee state line. The Union commander, Colonel John Thomas Wilder (1830–1917), could see no way out of his plight but was loath to surrender. What followed was one of the most bizarre episodes of this or any other war.

Wilder had been a businessman and was without any military education; it was only the previous year that he had been elected lieutenant colonel of the 17th Indiana. He knew that the commander of the Confederate force surrounding him was General Simon Bolivar Buckner [q.v.], a West Point graduate and, he had been told, a gentleman. Under a flag of truce he proceeded to Buckner's headquarters and requested his advice. Buckner, a gentleman indeed, declined to give him any. Wilder then asked if he might see the force surrounding him and count the number of guns. Buckner, amused and convinced of his naiveté and integrity, obliged him. Satisfied at last that resistance would be hopeless, Wilder confided, "I be-

lieve I'll surrender." He did so the next day, 17 September, giving up his garrison and all its artillery and 5,000 stand of arms.

Munitions. All military stores, equipment, ammunition, and arms.

Theodore R. Davis

Munitions *Bridgeport, Connecticut, munitions factory after the American Civil War. Production changed from hand work to machine work to meet demands of European nations at war*

Munro, Thomas (1761–1827). A British soldier educated at the University of Glasgow who arrived at Madras, India, as a cadet on 15 January 1780. In the next twenty-seven years he saw much active service, cultivated an interest in internal Indian administration, and developed a close friendship with the future Duke of Wellington. He returned to England in 1807. In 1814 he was back in India in a civil capacity, but at the outbreak of the Second Maratha War [q.v.] he was made a brigadier general and performed with distinction. George Canning (1770–1827) said of him: "Europe never produced a more accomplished statesman, nor India, so fertile in heroes, a more skilful soldier." In 1819 he became governor of Madras, in which post he served for eight years. He was much opposed to a free press, saying that "the tenure with which we hold our power never has been and never can be the liberties of the people." He was created a baronet for his services in the First Anglo-Burmese War [q.v.]. He died of cholera on the eve of his retirement.

Murata, Tsuneyoshi (1838–1921). A Japanese sumurai whose father was a retainer of the Satsuma clan. He became interested in rifles when the head of the clan began the manufacture of small arms in 1858. He distinguished himself in the Boshin Civil War [q.v.] in 1868 and in suppressing the revolt of Saigo Takamori [q.v.] in 1877. After making a study of European rifles, he designed the Murata rifle [q.v.]. In 1890 he was appointed a member of the House of Peers.

Murata Rifle. An 11 mm rifle developed by Japanese Major Tsuneyoshi Murata [q.v.] and adopted by the army in 1881. This was the first Japanese service rifle, but it was largely a copy of the French Gras rifle [q.v.]. It had an overall length of 50.25 inches and weighed nine pounds. The rifle was improved in 1885 and replaced in 1889 by the Type 13, an 11 mm rifle with a tube repeater.

Murat, Joachim (1767–1815). A French soldier in the Napoleonic Wars who in 1799 aided Napoleon in his coup d'état and the following year married Napoleon's sister Maria. In 1804 he was made a marshal of the empire, one of the first, and the following year was created a prince and high admiral. Perhaps Napoleon's greatest cavalry officer, he commanded the cavalry at Austerlitz, Jena, Eylau, and Friedland [qq.v.] and in 1808 was made king of Naples, in which capacity he captured the isle of Capri from the British [see Capri, Attacks on]. He joined Napoleon during the Hundred Days [q.v.] and was defeated by an Austrian army at Tolentino on 2–3 May 1815. On 8 October he tried to raise a rebellion in southern Italy and landed in Calabria, where he was soon captured. On 13 October he was shot by a Neapolitan firing squad at Castello di Pizzo, himself giving the command to fire.

Joachim Murat

Murat's eldest son, Napoleon Achille Murat (1801–1847), emigrated to the United States in 1821 and settled on an estate near Tallahassee, Florida.

Muraviëv Family. A famous Russian military family, the name sometimes spelled Mouraviev or Mouravieff, in which a father and five sons all served in tsarist armies.

Nikolai Nikolaevich Muraviëv (1768–1840). From 1797 to 1823 he was commandant of the Russian military school for staff officers, a period interrupted by service against Napoleon in 1812–14. He was the father of five sons, all of whom became soldiers and three of whom became generals of note:

Aleksandr Nikolaevich Muraviëv (1792–1864). He became a major general and fought in the Crimean War.

Nikolai Nikolaevich Muraviëv (1794–1866). He engaged in the suppression of the Polish Rebellion [q.v.] of 1830, became a major general, and served in the Crimean War.

Mikhail Nikolaevich Muraviëv (1796?–1866). He took part in the suppression of the Polish rebellion and was known for his cruel severity. On 28 November 1855 he captured Kars [q.v.].

Nikolai Nikolaevich Muraviëv-Amurski (1809?–1881). A representative of another branch of the Muraviëv family who at age seventeen was already an ensign and had been mentioned in dispatches five times. In the Russo-Persian War [q.v.] he traveled behind the Persian lines disguised as a Muslim pilgrim. In 1819 he was sent as a spy on the route to Khiva and was for a time imprisoned by the khan. He became commander-in-chief in the Caucasus and from 1848 to 1861 was governor-general in eastern Siberia. In the latter capacity he conquered the Amur region, which was ceded by China to Russia in 1858.

Murfreesboro, Battle of 1. 7 December 1864, American Civil War. Two cavalry divisions of Confederate General Nathan Bedford Forrest [q.v.], raiding in Tennessee, encountered a strong Union force under Lovell Harrison Rousseau [q.v.] centered on the town of Murfreesboro in central Tennessee, 32 miles southeast of Nashville. The Confederates, after burning a railway station and destroying railroad property, withdrew for a loss of 19 killed and 73 wounded. The Federals reported the capture of 197 prisoners and two guns and sustained a loss of 22 killed and 186 wounded.

2. Action of 31 December 1862–2 January 1863. [See Stones River, Battle of.]

Murid / Murad Wars (1830–59). For twenty-nine years the Lesghian people in the mountains of Dagestan struggled unsuccessfully to be free from Russian rule. Circassia had been under Turkish rule until the end of the Russo-Turkish War [q.v.] of 1828–29, when, under the terms of the Treaty of Adrianople (16 September 1829), it passed to Russia, which tried to subdue its turbulent peoples.

In 1830 the first imam declared a holy war, preaching his own brand of Islam, which had strong Sufi elements and was known as muridism. Its followers called themselves murids [q.v.]. Shamyl [q.v.], who in 1834 became the third imam of Dagestan, proved the most able, ruthless, and enduring of the murid leaders, and by uniting the tribes in the Caucasus, he forged a union fiercely resistant to Russian rule that extended from the Caspian Sea to the Black Sea.

Increasingly larger Russian forces were sent to the Caucasus, and in June 1839 after a two-month siege Shamyl was forced to surrender at the mountain fort (*aoul*) of Akhulgo. He was compelled to give up his son as a hostage, and the boy was sent to St. Petersburg to receive a Russian education. Even so, Shamyl refused to go into exile, and within two years he had raised another murid army.

In 1845 the Russians sent a 10,000-man army under General Mikhail Vorontsov [q.v.] to the Caucasus. Shamyl lured him deep into the mountains and then cut his supply line. By the time a rescue column arrived, Vorontsov had lost a third of his army. Undeterred, the Russians built roads and bridges into the mountains, developed new tactics, equipped their army with better weapons, and found that Cossack regiments proved their best troops for mountain fighting. In 1859 three Russian armies converged on Dagestan, and Shamyl's allied tribesmen began to desert him. An oft-quoted Caucasian proverb ran: "When will blood cease to flow in the mountains? When sugarcane grows in the snows." However, on 25 August 1859, at a mountain *aoul* called Gounib, the last murid stronghold, Shamyl and the remnants of his followers were surrounded by superior Russian forces, and on 7 September he surrendered to General Aleksandr Ivanovich Baryatinsky [q.v.].

Shamyl expected to be executed, but in Russia he received what amounted to a hero's welcome. He was given a tour of the country, met Tsar Alexander II (1818–1881), and was settled comfortably with his family at Kaluga, about 90 miles from Moscow.

Murids. Fanatical "fighting monks" in the army of Shamyl, [q.v.] the third imam of Dagestan. Their leaders were called *naibs*. [See Murid / Murad Wars.] They gained even the admiration of their enemies for their fighting abilities and powers of endurance. Mikhail Lermontov [q.v.] wrote: "They don't seem to know when they ought to die. Indeed, these villains can hardly ever be killed. They are people without the slightest idea of propriety" (*A Hero of Our Time* [1840]).

Musa Bagh, Battle of (19 March 1858), Indian Mutiny. Some 4,000 British troops under Lieutenant General James Outram and Major General Henry Havelock [qq.v.] defeated about 10,000 rebels and mutineers under the begum of Oudh and her son at this fortified palace and gardens four miles northwest of besieged Lucknow.

Music, Military. It is easier to advance bodies of men if they move in step and keep cadence. Because music assists in this process and steadies and inspires men, it has played a role in all civilized and in many uncivilized armies. Homer three thousand years ago wrote: "Noble and manly music invigorates the spirit, strengthens the wavering man, and incites him to brave and worthy deeds" (*Iliad*).

Some musical instruments, notably drums and bugles, were used to give commands. In the British army drums were abol-

ished for this purpose, and bugles were adopted. In the French army a distinction was made between field music (*grande batterie*) and the full band (*la musique*). The former was made up of the regiment's drummers, led by the regimental drum major (*tambour maître*). Bugles or trumpets came into the British service in the eighteenth century but were not used in the French army until 1822. Scottish regiments were renowned for their use of bagpipes although they were never authorized for issue. Most regimental bands were supported by subscriptions from the officers. In the British army regimental bands were not officially recognized until 1856.

In the U.S. army most companies included a drummer and a fifer. The Marine Corps Band, the nation's first marching ensemble, established in 1798, won renown under its great leader John Philip Sousa [q.v.] in the last half of the nineteenth century. In 1832 Congress authorized a ten-member band for each regiment. In 1869 it increased this number to sixteen (later twenty) and a chief musician. The band did not form a separate unit, however; its members were detached from companies [see Bandsmen]. In battle bandsmen became stretcher-bearers. During the American Civil War Union regimental brass bands were officially sanctioned by the War Department in May 1861, but in July 1862 they were ordered disbanded.

Musket. A shoulder weapon loaded from the muzzle with powder and projectile separate.

U.S. flintlock musket with bayonet

Musketoon. A standard U.S. infantry musket shortened for cavalry use that replaced the Hall carbine in 1849. It was a smoothbore, 49 inches long, caliber .69, weighing six pounds two ounces. According to Major General Zenas Randall Bliss (1832?–1900), it "kicked like blazes, and had neither range nor accuracy, and was not near as good as the musket, and was only used because it could be more conveniently carried on horseback." None was manufactured after 1856, but in 1858 Enfield in Britain began the manufacture of a similar weapon called a musketoon. A few (less than 1,000) were imported to the United States during the Civil War.

In the Napoleonic Wars a similar weapon, issued to dragoons, called a mousqueton, was sometimes also known as a dragoon musket although it was also issued to foot artillery, pioneer regiments, and sometimes voltigeurs.

Musketry. 1. Skill in using small arms.
2. The firing of small arms.

Musketry Schools. It was not until mid-century and the improvement in rifles that much attention was given to training soldiers to shoot straight. Austria, to save money, allowed its infantrymen only 20 rounds of ammunition per year for target practice. Consequently, as Austrian General Julius Haynau in 1849 remarked, the Austrians "shot like pigs." The Prussians, their adversary in the Seven Weeks' War [q.v.] of 1866, allowed 100 rounds per man each year. In Britain musketry schools were established at Hythe in southeast England, 10 miles west-southwest of Dover, and at Fleetwood in Lancashire, 20 miles north of Blackpool, in 1854; the latter was closed in 1867. The French established a school of musketry at Vincennes.

Muskrat Cap. On 12 March 1879 Montgomery Meigs [q.v.], the quartermaster general of the American army, authorized the issue of fur hats made from the skins of this aquatic rodent (*Ondatra zibethica*) found in the United States and Canada. It had earflaps, cape, and visor and was lined with brown chintz or silesia.

Muslim Rebellion in South China. See Panthay Rebellion.

Mussack or Mussuck. In India, a leather water bag made of the entire skin of a large goat, stripped of its hair and dressed. It was carried by a bheestie [q.v.].

Mustang. A colloquial name for an American regular army officer who had not been educated at West Point.

Muster, to. 1. To gather troops together for inspection or roll call.

2. To enlist.

Muster, to *Militia muster, Switzerland, 1824*

Muster Roll. The list of members of a unit.

Mutilation of Corpses. The practice of disfiguring the corpses of fallen foes followed by some American Indians, African tribesmen, and others in order to collect trophies, such as scalps and sexual organs, or to increase the terror they hoped to inspire.

Mutiny. 1. As a noun, the willful refusal to obey lawful military authority. Exactly what constitutes mutiny was much debated, as it still is. Article 8 of the U.S. Articles of War, approved on 10 April 1806, defined mutiny as "a combined or simultaneous resistance, active or passive, to lawful military authority." A British legist in 1851 defined mutiny as an act beginning with "a murmuring and muttering" that tended "to raise ill-humour or passions," thus implying that one person could commit mutiny. American legal thinking, in the first half of the century at least, also leaned toward the view that mutiny was not necessarily a collective insubordination, but Colonel H. L. Scott in his *Military Dictionary* (1861) wrote: "The best authorities admit that a single person, without pre-

vious combination or concert with others, cannot commit mutiny."

Mutiny, if confined to the rank and file, is usually put down quickly and often violently. Mutiny by officers has a better chance of success, particularly if they can carry their men with them.

2. As a verb, to commit the offense of mutiny.

[See Indian Mutiny; Malta Mutiny; White Mutiny; Mutiny in the 19th Hussars.]

Mutiny Act. In Britain an act that provided for the "discipline, regulation and payment of the army," including punishment for mutiny and desertion. The first such act was passed in 1689 to deal with disaffected troops at Ipswich and was effective for only six months. It was reenacted with many changes almost annually until 1879. Because it provided for punishments in peacetime, it legalized the existence of a standing army. In 1757 the militia was included, and in 1803 it was extended to troops outside the dominions. In 1879 it was replaced by the Army Discipline and Regulation Act, and after 1881 by annual Army Acts.

The modern version is the Army Act of 1955, which is confirmed by Parliament every five years.

Mutiny in the 19th Hussars (4–12 April 1807). British soldiers in this cavalry regiment, then stationed at the Curragh Camp, near Dublin, protested the extra duties imposed upon them. Six of the ringleaders were court-martialed and given sentences to penal servitude ranging from five to eight years.

Muzzle. The end of the bore of a gun from which the projectile emerges.

Muzzle Burst. The premature explosion of a shell at or near the muzzle.

Muzzle Droop. Distortion of a cannon barrel from overheating.

Muzzleloader. Guns, whether artillery or small arms, loaded from the mouth or muzzle of the bore.

Muzzle Swell. The gradual increase in the contour of an artillery piece barrel close to the muzzle adopted in the 1890s but soon abandoned.

Muzzle Velocity. The speed of a projectile as it leaves the muzzle of a gun. It is normally expressed in the number of feet or centimeters per second. Muzzle velocity depends upon the weight of the projectile, the amount and quality of the explosive, and other factors.

Myer, Albert James (1827–1880). An American soldier who developed an interest in communications while working among the deaf in medical school. He joined the army as an assistant surgeon in 1854, and in 1860, as a major, he was as-

Muzzleloader *Muzzle-loading gun drill of the British artillery*

signed to organize and command a signal corps, a command he filled throughout the American Civil War, winning brevets to brigadier general. He invented the flag semaphore system and worked with "Professor" Thaddeus Lowe [q.v.] in creating observation balloons. At the end of the war he returned to his rank as major. In 1866 he was promoted colonel and chief of the Signal Corps. In this capacity he established the U.S. Weather Bureau. Fort Myer, Virginia, is named in his honor.

Myrmidon. A soldier who blindly carries out orders. The term is often applied to soldiers carrying out brutal orders without questioning them. In Greek mythology Myrmidons were the fierce and devoted Thessalian followers of Achilles in the Trojan War.

Mzilikazi. See Matabele Wars.

Nachod, Battle of (27 June 1866), Seven Weeks' War. The Prussian V Army Corps under General Karl Friedrich von Steinmetz [q.v.], which was directed by telegraph from Berlin by Helmuth von Moltke the Elder [q.v.], defeated an Austrian force under General Ludwig von Benedek [q.v.] in a sharp engagement at this Bohemian town on the Silesian border in the Sudeten foothills. In this prelude to the Battle of Münchengrätz [q.v.] the Prussians won a remarkable victory. A notable feature of the battle was the victory of the Prussian uhlans [q.v.] over the numerically superior Austrian cavalry. The Austrians suffered heavy casualties, including 2,000 taken prisoner, and the loss of five guns; the Prussians lost 900 men.

Nagamaki. A Japanese two-handed sword, long-bladed and without a hilt guard.

Naggur. The principal drum in Asian armies, particularly in India.

Naginata. 1. A kind of Japanese halberd. A sharp, curved blade, one to three feet long mounted on a wooden pole four to eight feet long. During the Tokugawa shogunate (1603–1867) the weapon became associated with women of the samurai class.
    2. A martial art that is still taught.

Nagpur, Battle of (21–24 December 1817), Third Maratha War. At this town, 265 miles north of Hyderabad, a Maratha army of 7,000 infantry, 14,000 cavalry, and 64 guns under Apa (Appa or Napa) Sahib (Shahib), the bhonsla (ruler) of Nagpur (1788–1816), and the Maratha chief Baji Rao II (d. 1854) attacked a small British force of chiefly 1,300 Madrasi and Bengali troops of the Honourable East India Company. The British occupied nearby Fort Sitabaldi and were besieged there but successfully held out until reinforcements of about 3,500 under Brigadier General John Doveton (1768–1847) arrived. On 21 December 1817 the bhonsla's army, which included 3,000 Arab mercenaries, attacked Doveton as he approached Nagpur. The British scored a victory, capturing 75 guns and forty elephants at a cost of 200 killed and wounded. The next day Apa Sahib capitulated, but his men refused to surrender and held the town. An unsuccessful assault cost Doveton 300 casualties. Before he could launch a second attack, his enemies fled, and by 24 December the town was clear.

Nagy-Sarlo, Battle of (19 April 1849), Hungarian Revolution. In this town (Nagy-Szöllös or Vel'ký Sevluš) just west of Chust, now in Ukraine, 10,000 Austrian troops, trying to prevent Hungarians from constructing bridges over the Gran River, were attacked and defeated by 25,000 Hungarians under General Arthur von Görgey [q.v.].

Naik. An Indian or Gurkha noncommissioned officer in the Indian army equivalent to an army corporal. The rank was marked by two chevrons pointed downward on the upper sleeve.

Nail Ball. Round shot with an iron pin projecting from it to prevent its turning in the bore.

Najafgarh, Battle of (24 August 1857), Indian Mutiny. Brigadier General John Nicholson [q.v.] with 2,500 men and 16 guns, on his way to reinforce the British camped before Delhi [see Delhi, Siege of], encountered entrenched mutineers 2 miles from this village, 15 miles west-southwest of Delhi. Nicholson at once attacked and forced them to retreat. He took prisoner or killed some 800 and captured all their artillery at a cost of 23 killed and 70 wounded.

Nakago. The tang of a Japanese blade.

Namas-Herero War. See Herero-Namas War.

Namozine Church and Willicomack Creek, Battle of (3 April 1865), American Civil War. After the Union victory in the Battle of Five Forks [q.v.] a brigade of cavalry under Colonel George Custer [q.v.] led the pursuit and attacked a brigade of Confederate cavalry under General Rufus Barringer [q.v.] on the banks of Willicomack Creek in south-central Virginia. The Union cavalry fought dismounted and drove the Confederates into Namozine Church. Barringer and most of his men were captured. Union losses were 95.

Nana (1800?–1896). An important Mimbres Apache war leader who followed Victorio [q.v.] but escaped his fate at Tres Castillos. When he was more than eighty years old, Nana led Apache raids into southwestern New Mexico, killing more than 30 whites, capturing 2 women and 200 horses and mules, and absconding into Mexico. He later served with Geronimo [q.v.] and did not surrender until March 1886, when he finally submitted to General George Crook [q.v.], who considered him "the brains of the hostile bands." He died at Fort Sill, Oklahoma.

Nana Sahib (1825?–1860?), real Name: Dandhu Panth. The adopted son of the last Maratha peshwa (ruler), Baji Rao II (d. 1854), he was embittered when he was given neither position nor a pension by the British, who had deposed his father. In 1857, at the outbreak of the Indian Mutiny [q.v.], he allied himself with the mutineers and assumed the leadership at Cawnpore, where, after promising safety to the British garrison and other Europeans if they would capitulate, he treacherously murdered them all, men, women, and children [see Cawnpore, Siege of]. His forces later suffered several defeats at the hands of the British, and in 1859 he was finally driven into the jungles of Nepal. He is assumed to have died there.

Nancy, Capture of (12 August 1870), Franco-Prussian War. After the retreat of French General Marie MacMahon [q.v.] the garrison at Nancy, a city of about 100,000 on the Meurthe River, 178 miles east of Paris, expecting the arrival of the Prussian army, surrendered to four uhlans [q.v.].

Naning War (1831–32). In 1829 the ruler of Naning, a Malay state, refused to deliver to the Honourable East India Company one-tenth of the state's crop as tribute, as it had done previously for the Dutch East India Company. A British expedition sent against the state in 1831 was defeated, but the following year a second expedition crushed the Naning forces [see Padri War].

Nanking, Sieges of (1853 and 1864). During the Taiping Rebellion [q.v.] there were two sieges of this city (now Nanxiang or Nanjing), of about one million people on the south bank of the Yangtze River, 150 miles northwest of Shanghai.

First Siege (8–20 March 1853). On 8 March 1853 some 100,000 Taiping soldiers under Shih Ta-k'ai [q.v.] attacked Nanking. Working night and day to establish a breach in the 40-foot-thick walls, they finally secured one on 19 March. The city was taken the next day, and in an orgy of destruction they massacred 50,000 Manchu soldiers who had opposed them, tore down all the national monuments, and destroyed many of the public buildings. Nanking then became the rebel capital, and Hung Hsui-chüan [q.v.], leader of the Taipings, quickly ensconced himself there in an ornate palace with a bevy of wives and concubines.

Second Siege (30 May 1862–19 July 1864). Regional army forces under Tsêng Kuo-fan [q.v.] besieged Nanking, China's second-largest city, which the Taipings had made their capital since its capture by Shih Ta-k'ai [q.v.] on 19–20 March 1853. On 8 July 1864 the Taipings attempted a sortie but were driven back. On 19 July after the explosion of an enormous mine, said to have included 20 tons of gunpowder, the city was taken by storm. Taiping General Li Hsiu-cheng [q.v.], the chung wang (faithful king), was captured, and on 7 August 1864 he was beheaded; his head was later displayed in several cities "in order to gratify the public mind."

In his report to the throne Tsêng claimed 100,000 dead in three days: "The Ch'in-huai creek was filled with bodies. Half of the false wangs, chief generals, heavenly generals and other heads were killed in battle, and the other half drowned themselves in dikes and ditches or else burned themselves. The whole of them numbered about 3,000 men. The fire in the city raged for three days and nights. . . . Not one of the 100,000 rebels in Nanking surrendered themselves when the city was taken but in many cases gathered together and burned themselves and passed away without repentance. Such a band of rebels has rarely been known from ancient times to the present."

Tsêng probably exaggerated the fatalities, but Nanking had indeed become a desolate and devastated city. The acting British consul in Chinkiang paid a visit after its fall and in a dispatch on 29 July 1864 wrote: "Words cannot describe the utter desolation of everything within the walls. . . . I saw a great number of unburied bodies."

The few Taiping leaders who managed to escape were soon caught and executed. Although some rebels fled north and joined the Nien [q.v.], the last major Taiping force was annihilated on 7 February 1866, when 10,000 were killed and 50,000 surrendered. This was proclaimed the official end of the Taiping Rebellion.

Nanking *Nanking rebel chiefs and soldiers engaged in Taiping rebellion of 1853*

Nansouty, Étienne Marie Antoine Champion (1768–1815). A French soldier who commanded cavalry in Napoleonic armies. From 1792 to 1801 he served in the Army of the Rhine, being promoted general of brigade in 1799. He was general of division in 1803. He fought at Wertingen, Ulm, and Austerlitz [qq.v.]. He took part in the campaign in East Prussia and Poland and in 1807 fought at Eylau and Friedland [qq.v.]. In the Danube Campaign of 1809 he fought in all the major battles, including Aspern-Essling and Wagram [qq.v.]. In Napoleon's Russian Campaign [q.v.] he was wounded in the knee in the Battle of Borodino [q.v.]. In July 1813 he was given command of the Imperial Guard Cavalry and fought at Dresden, Leipzig, and Hanau [qq.v.], where he was again wounded. He distinguished himself in the Campaign of France in 1814. He died in Paris on 12 February 1815, missing the Battle of Waterloo [q.v.].

Nan Wang. See Fung Yun-san.

Napier, Charles James (1782–1853). A British soldier, the son of Colonel George Napier (1751–1804), who had served on the staff of Sir Henry Clinton (1738?–1795) during the American Revolution. Although very shortsighted, he was a bright lad and was commissioned an ensign in the 33rd Foot on 31 January 1794 at the age of twelve; on 8 May he was promoted lieutenant in the 89th Foot. In 1808, during the Peninsular War [q.v.], he was sent to Portugal, where he commanded a battalion under Sir John Moore [q.v.] and took part in the retreat to Corunna [q.v.], in which his leg was broken by a musket ball, his head was slashed by a saber, he was bayoneted in the back, and clubbed on the head with the butt of a musket, and his ribs were broken by a gunshot. Taken prisoner, he was kindly treated by French Marshals Michel Ney and Nicolas Soult [qq.v.]. He was paroled on 20 March 1809 but not exchanged until January 1810. He then returned to the war and in the Battle of Bussaco [q.v.] was shot in the face; his jaw was broken, and an eye was injured. His wound affected his breathing, and throughout his life he suffered periodic bouts of near suffocation. He recovered to fight at Fuentes de Oñoro and the second siege of Badajos [qq.v.]. In June 1811 he was promoted lieutenant colonel and returned to England.

In 1813 he commanded a brigade in Bermuda, from which, during the War of 1812 [q.v.], he took part in raids against the Americans in Virginia and the Carolinas. In 1814 he returned to England and in December was placed on half pay.

In 1819 he was appointed inspecting field officer for the Ionian Islands, and from 1822 to 1833 he was military Resident on the island of Cephalonia, where he took a Greek mistress by whom he fathered two daughters, whom he reared and educated after their mother eloped with a Greek captain. He met Lord Byron [q.v.] in 1823 and through him became involved with the Greek revolutionaries fighting the Turks, but he declined an offer to become commander of the Greek army.

In 1833 he suffered a severe attack of cholera. In 1837 he was promoted major general and knighted (KCB) the following year. In 1839 he was in charge of a district in England comprising eleven northern counties and was actively engaged in suppressing Chartist outbreaks, although he had much personal sympathy for the Chartists [see Chartist Riots].

In 1841 he accepted a regional command in India, and in September he took command of the troops in Upper and Lower Sind (today part of Pakistan). Shortly after his arrival he was severely wounded in the leg by an errant exploding rocket. He soon determined that since the various amirs who ruled in Sind were violating treaty obligations and plotting against the British, it would be best to annex the entire region. On 12 January 1842 he seized the Baluchi fortress of Imamghar and destroyed it. On 17 February he fought and won the Battle of Miani, and on 24 March he won another victory in the Battle of Hyderabad [qq.v.]. This ended the campaign: Sind was annexed, and Napier was made governor. In 1844–45 he waged an arduous but successful campaign against the hill tribes on the northern frontier of Sind.

On 9 November 1846 he was promoted lieutenant general. The following July he resigned the governorship of Sind, and on 1 October 1847 he sailed for Europe. The heavy losses suffered by the British in the Battle of Chilianwala in the Second Sikh War [qq.v.] provoked a public outcry in Britain against General Hugh Gough [q.v.], and Napier was selected to replace him as commander-in-chief, India. (Gough fought the Battle of Gujerat [q.v.] and won the war while Napier was still at sea.)

Napier's relations with the governor-general of India, Lord Dalhousie (1812–1860), were initially amicable but later soured to such an extent that he resigned. In 1851 he was back in England, where in spite of illness, he acted as a pall-bearer at the funeral of the Duke of Wellington and caught a severe cold. He never regained his health. He died on 29 August 1853.

Napier, George Thomas (1784–1855). A British soldier who, unlike his older brother Charles Napier [q.v.], was regarded as a dunce in school but nevertheless was appointed a cornet in the 24th Light Dragoons on 25 January 1800. In 1803 he was a captain in the 52nd Light Infantry. He served under Sir John Moore [q.v.] in the peninsula, where he was wounded in the Battle of Bussaco [q.v.] [see Peninsular War]. He lost his right arm in the storming of Ciudad Rodrigo [q.v.] on 19 January 1812. He returned to England to recuperate, married, and rejoined his regiment in January 1814.

In 1837 he was promoted major general and appointed governor and commander-in-chief at the Cape of Good Hope, a position he held until 12 December 1843. He became a full general in 1854.

Napier, Robert Cornelis (1810–1890). A British soldier, born in Colombo, Ceylon (Sri Lanka), the son of a British artillery major. His middle name commemorated the storming of Fort Cornelis [q.v.], in which his father had taken part on 26 August 1810 in the Java War [q.v.], less than four months before his birth. In 1824 young Robert entered Addiscombe [q.v.], and on 15 December 1826 he was commissioned a second lieutenant in the Bengal engineers. He arrived in Calcutta, India, in November 1828 as a lieutenant. He did not see action until he fought in the Battle of Mudki in the First Sikh War [qq.v.]. He was severely wounded in the Battle of Ferozeshah on 21 December 1845 but was able to take part in the Battle of Sobraon [qq.v.] on 12 February 1846. In the Second Sikh War he was in charge of the siege operations at Multan and was again wounded, but he recovered to fight in the Battle of Gujerat [qq.v.] on 21 February 1849. In December 1852 he took part in the Hazara Black Mountain Expedition [see Hazara Expeditions]. In November 1850 he was part of similar expedition against the Bori clan of the Jawaki Afridis in the Peshawar district. During the Indian Mutiny [q.v.] he participated in the unsuccessful efforts of Henry Havelock and James Outram [qq.v.] to relieve the siege of Lucknow [q.v.], and he was badly wounded there just as the second relief force under Sir Colin Campbell [q.v.] arrived. He recovered to serve as second-in-command under Sir Hugh Rose in the battles against Tantia Topi and the rani of Jhansi [qq.v.]. For his services during the mutiny he was knighted (KCB).

In 1860 he commanded a division in China during the Second Opium War [q.v.], and he was promoted major general on 15 February 1861. In 1865 he was appointed commander-in-chief of the Bombay army and in 1867 was promoted lieutenant general and selected to command the troops in the Abyssinian Expedition [see Abyssinian Campaign, British]. On the successful completion of this campaign and the destruction of Magdala, the Abyssinian capital, Prime Minister Benjamin Disraeli (1804–1881), addressing the House of Commons, declaimed: "They brought the elephant of Asia to convey the artillery of Europe to dethrone one of the kings of Africa, and to hoist the standard of St. George upon the mountains of Rasselas."

Medals and honors were lavished on Napier, and he was created Baron Napier of Magdala. On 1 April 1874 he was promoted general and appointed commandant general of the Royal Engineers. Two years later he was made governor of Gibraltar. In 1883, when he retired from that post, he was made a field marshal.

Napier was a man of many interests. He had a great love of poetry, and he painted in watercolors. At the age of seventy-eight he took lessons in a new method for mixing colors. He loved children, of whom he had many: three sons and three daughters by his first wife and six sons by his second wife.

Napier, Robert *General Napier directs the storming of Magdala, Abyssinia, 1868.*

Napier, Thomas Erskine (1790–1863). A British soldier, the brother of Charles and George Napier [qq.v.], who at the age of fifteen was commissioned an ensign in the 52nd Light Infantry and was with that regiment in the Battle of Copenhagen [q.v.] in 1807. He served as an aide to Sir John Hope [q.v.] in the expedition to Sweden in 1808 [see Copenhagen, Siege of] and saw service under Sir John Moore [q.v.] in Spain. In 1809 he was promoted captain in the Chasseurs Britannique, a British Foreign Legion, with which he served in Sicily and in the Peninsular War [q.v.]. On 10 December 1813 he was slightly wounded and on the following day lost his left arm. He saw no more active service but rose to be a general in 1861.

Napier, William (1785–1860). A British soldier and a brother of Charles, Thomas, and George Napier [qq.v.] who on 14 June 1800, at the age of fourteen, was commissioned in the Royal Irish Artillery and ten months later was promoted lieutenant in the 62nd Foot. He fought under the future Duke of Wellington at the siege of Copenhagen [q.v.] and under Sir John Moore [q.v.] in the Peninsular War [q.v.]. He was in England in February 1809 but soon returned to the war, in which he distinguished himself and was seriously wounded. He retired from the active list in 1819 and devoted

himself to painting, sculpture, and history. In 1823 he began his *History of the Peninsular War,* the first volume of which was published in 1828; in 1840 he completed the sixth and final volume. From 1842 to 1847 he was lieutenant governor of Guernsey.

Naples, Anglo-Russian Expedition to (November 1805–January 1806), Napoleonic Wars. A British contingent of 7,300 men, sent to the Mediterranean to preserve the independence of Naples, joined forces with about 11,000 Russian troops stationed in the Ionian Islands. The combined force was under the command of General Maurice Lacy (1740–1820), a Russian of Irish descent who spoke English with a broad Irish brogue. The British contingent was commanded by Lieutenant General Sir James Henry Craig (1748–1812), a veteran who had fought in the American Revolution and been wounded in the Battle of Bunker Hill. In late November the Russians landed directly at Naples; the British landed across the bay at Castelamari di Strabia, 16 miles southeast of the city. They did not long remain. On 7 December, Craig learned of the Allied disaster in the Battle of Austerlitz [q.v.] five days earlier. In January 1806 he reembarked and took his force to Sicily, which became a base of operations from which the British repulsed all French attempts to dislodge them. Sickness decimated the ill-equipped Russian force, and they also left Italy. The French soon occupied southern Italy. [See: Naples, French Conquest of; Calabrian War; Maida, Battle of.]

Naples, Army of. A French army formed by Napoleon in January 1806 for the conquest of the Kingdom of the Two Sicilies [see Naples, French Conquest of]. It consisted of three corps, about 40,000 men, under the nominal command of his brother Joseph Bonaparte (1768–1844). The largest corps was that of Marshal André Masséna; the other two were under Laurent Gouvion St. Cyr and Jean Reynier [qq.v.]. It assembled at Terracino, south of Rome, and at the end of January moved south.

Naples, French Conquest of *Surrender of the Neapolitan troops at Soveria, Calabria*

Naples, French Conquest of (1806–11). In January 1806 Napoleon created the Army of Naples [q.v.] under Joseph Bonaparte (1768–1844), which invaded the Neapolitan territory at the end of January 1806. As it moved down the west coast, it encountered little opposition, the Neapolitans usually fleeing at first sight of the French advance guard. On 11 February the queen fled Naples and joined her husband in Sicily, where the British had established a strong base.

Only the fortified seaport of Gaeta, located on a narrow rocky peninsula, held out and refused to surrender. While General André Masséna [q.v.] laid siege to Gaeta, General Jean Reynier [q.v.] was sent to conquer Calabria [see Calabrian War; Maida, Battle of]. It proved a difficult task, and not until 1811 was the southern Italian mainland firmly in French control.

Naples Revolution. See Neapolitan Revolt.

Napoleon. The common name for a light 12-pounder, muzzle-loaded, smoothbore field gun first used in action by the French in the Crimean War [q.v.]. It was named not after Napoleon Bonaparte but after his nephew Napoleon III (1808–1873), known as Louis Napoleon, under whose auspices it had been developed. The American version, a light 12-pounder field gun, Model 1857, made of bronze with a caliber of 4.62 inches and a tube weighing 1,227 pounds, was the workhorse of the armies on both sides in the American Civil War. The maximum range of the gun, firing solid shot at five-degree elevation, was 1,680 yards, but its effective range was about 900 yards. It was most effectively used firing canister in close support of infantry. An efficient crew of 4 or 5 cannoneers could fire two rounds of shot or shell or four rounds of canister in a minute.

At the outset of the American Civil War the American army had only 5 Napoleons, but in the course of the war the Union acquired 1,127. The Confederates made or acquired at least 481, including an iron version, with a tapered muzzle and a banded breech, manufactured at the Tredegar Iron Works [q.v.] in Richmond.

Napoleon, Eugène Louis Jean Joseph (1856–1879). Known as the Prince Imperial, the only son of Napoleon III (1808–1873), he was educated at the Royal Military Academy, Woolwich [q.v.], from 1872 to 1875. In 1879 he induced the British military authorities to allow him to join the British army engaged in the Zulu War [q.v.]. Senior British officers did their best to keep him out of harm's way, but he was killed by Zulus who attacked a routine patrol he was accompanying in what was thought to be a safe area.

Napoleon I (1769–1821). Until 1796 he used his Italian name, Napoleone Buonaparte; in about 1797 he dropped the *u* from his last name and the final *e* from his first. He was born at Ajaccio, Corsica, the son of an impecunious lawyer who died when he was fifteen. He was educated at military schools at Brienne le Château from 1779 to 1784 and at the École Militaire in Paris in 1784–85, after which he was commissioned into the La Fère regiment of artillery, in which he remained until 1791. He first distinguished himself at the siege of Toulon in 1793 and was promoted general of brigade. He was briefly imprisoned after the fall of Robespierre in 1794, but on 5 October 1795 he was used to protect the Convention in the Tuileries, and he blew a royalist Parisian mob from the streets with a "whiff of grapeshot."

He was rewarded by the newly formed Directory with command of the Army of the Interior. In February 1796 he was given command of the Army of Italy, and just before leaving for the seat of war, he married Joséphine de Beauharnais, née Marie Joséphine Rose Tascher de la Pagerie (1763–1814). In Italy Napoleon succeeded in defeating a succession of Austrian generals, won the Battle of Lodi, occupied Milan, and in 1797 captured Mantua. He then negotiated the Treaty of Campo Formio on 17 October, by which Austria ceded the Austrian Netherlands (Belgium) and Lombardy; accepted French possession of the Ionian Islands and Corfu; and recognized the Cisalpine Republic.

Napoleon's next campaign was in Egypt, which he regarded as a first step toward India. On 19 May 1798 his Army of the Orient, accompanied by a distinguished group of "savants" intending to study the country's treasures and ruins, sailed from Toulon and, after pausing to capture Malta on 12 June, arrived on 1–3 July. Marching up the left bank of the Nile, he defeated the Mamelukes in the Battle of the Pyramids on 21 July and entered Cairo the next day. He pursued the Egyptian forces into Syria, capturing El Arish on 14–15 February 1799 and Jaffa on 7 March; Acre was invested on 17 March. A Turkish army was defeated in the Battle of Mount Tabor on 17 April, but Acre steadfastly resisted, and when the plague broke out in his camps, Napoleon retreated, reaching Cairo on 14 June. The following day an 18,000-man Turkish army, escorted by a British fleet, landed at Aboukir. Assembling all available troops, about 6,000, Napoleon advanced to the delta and on 25 July destroyed the Turkish army. French losses were about 900 killed and wounded. The citadel at Aboukir surrendered on 2 August, but on that day British Admiral Horatio Nelson (1758–1805) defeated the French fleet in Aboukir Bay. Only two frigates escaped, and the Army of the Orient's ties with France were severed. On 22 August 1799, accompanied by his savants and handpicked officers, Napoleon secretly embarked for France, narrowly escaping capture en route. (Cairo was surrendered to the British in July 1801, and the debris of the French army was given free passage back to France.)

In France Napoleon found himself a hero. With two other conspirators he carried out the *coup d'état de Brûmaire* (9 November 1799). The Directory was overthrown, the Council of Five Hundred was dispersed, and Napoleon became one of three consuls in a provisional government. On 9 November he made himself first consul and soon persuaded his collaborators to resign. He was the de facto ruler of France.

Napoleon I *Napoleon with the savants in Egypt*

To assist General André Masséna [q.v.], fighting the Austrians in northern Italy, he raised the Army of the Reserve in 1800, placed himself at its head, and marched it over the Alps via the St. Bernard Pass to take the Austrian army in the rear. In the valley of the Po River, in the Battle of Marengo on 14 June, Napoleon was able to turn near defeat into a victory thanks to the timely arrival on the field of the division under General Louis Desaix (1768–1800).

The Austrians signed the Peace of Lunéville on 8 February 1801, and Britain signed the Treaty of Amiens [q.v.] on 27 March 1802. For the first time in a decade France was at peace. Napoleon negotiated a concordat with Pope Pius VII (1742–1823), radically reorganized government administration, instituted the Code Napoléon, secured Louisiana from Spain, and in 1803 sold it to the United States. On 2 December 1804 he became emperor. Although Pius VII was brought to Paris for the coronation, Napoleon insisted on placing the crown on his head with his own hands. In 1805 he assumed the title of king of Italy and, with his newly christened Grande Armée, launched a campaign in Bavaria and Austria. In response Britain, Russia, and Austria formed the Third Coalition to crush him [see Napoleonic Wars]. It failed to do so.

Napoleon amassed 150,000 men along the Atlantic coast and planned an invasion of Britain, but this was seen to be impossible after the victory of Admiral Nelson at the Battle of Trafalgar on 21 October 1805. Napoleon then turned his armies inland and captured Vienna. At the Battle of Austerlitz [q.v.] on 2 December he delivered a stunning defeat to the Allied armies arrayed against him. The Peace of Pressburg that followed forced Austria to give up its German and Italian possessions to France.

The Fourth Coalition against Napoleon, formed by Britain, Russia, and Prussia, came to ruins in Napoleon's victories at the battles of Jena and Auerstädt on 14 October 1806, which were followed by the winter campaign that culminated in the ruin of the Russian forces at Eylau on 2 February 1807 and nearly complete destruction at the Battle of Friedland [qq.v.] on 14 June. The map of Europe was redrawn at the famous meeting of Napoleon and the tsar on the raft in the Niemen (Neman) River at Tilsit [q.v.] on 7–9 July 1807.

Napoleon, with an empire stretching from the Atlantic Ocean to the Oder River, now began an economic war against Britain with his Continental System [q.v.]. To close Portugal to British trade, he sent General Jean Junot [q.v.] to conquer the country and to force the abdication of the king of Spain, whom he replaced with his brother Joseph (1768–1844). However, the British sent an army to defend Portugal, and the Spanish people rose in revolt against French rule. Thus began the Peninsular War [q.v.], which was so disastrous for France.

Austria and Britain formed the Fifth Coalition, and Austria invaded Bavaria, a French satellite. But the Russians were defeated at Eckmühl and decisively at the Battle of Wagram [qq.v.] on 5-6 July 1809. Austria made peace, and Napoleon agreed to marry the Archduchess Marie Louise (1791–1847) after disposing of the barren Joséphine, as he did in 1810.

In June 1812 Napoleon launched his disastrous Russian Campaign [q.v.]. As the Russians advanced, Prussia and Sweden sided with them. Although Napoleon won victories at Lützen on 2 May 1813, Bautzen on 20–21 May, and Dresden [qq.v.] on 26–27 August, he was decisively defeated at the Battle of Leipzig [q.v.], on 16–19 October, and Wellington was winning the Peninsular War and about to invade France.

Although Napoleon did the best with the inferior forces at hand from January to April 1814, he was faced with vastly superior Allied forces, and on 6 April 1814 he abdicated and was exiled to Elba [q.v.].

In early March 1815 Napoleon with about 1,000 followers landed in France and began a triumphal march to Paris, gaining support as he progressed. On 20 March he entered Paris, and the unpopular Bourbons fled. He was again the dictator of France. Thus began the Hundred Days [q.v.].

It was not until the Sixth Coalition that Napoleon was finally crushed. On 18 July 1815, near the village of Waterloo [q.v.], he fought his last battle. Within three weeks, on 22 June, he was again forced to abdicate. The Allies entered Paris on 7 July, and on 15 July, on board HMS *Bellerophen*, Napoleon surrendered. He was transferred to HMS *Northumberland* and taken to St. Helena [q.v.], an island in the South Atlantic. He landed in mid-October 1815 and remained there until he died, on 5 May 1821. In 1840 his remains were returned to France and were eventually reinterred at the Hôtel des Invalides [q.v.] in Paris [see Napoleon's Remains].

Napoleon and Wellington were without doubt the foremost European generals in the first half of the nineteenth century, when traditional seasonal wars gave way to all-weather wars. It has been asserted that Napoleon fought in more battles than Alexander, Hannibal, and Caesar combined. Certainly he became a superb field commander. Modern land

Napoleon Bonaparte in 1808

warfare began with him. Blücher is reputed to have said that Napoleon's presence on a battlefield was worth 40,000 men. He had an extraordinary talent for deceiving and confusing his enemies, and this talent was combined with remarkable organizational and administrative skills. His concept of an army corps, which contained virtually all arms and services, enabled him to create armies within armies, the larger force being almost indestructible on the field. He was one of the few generals of his era to understand the importance of good staff work, particularly logistics. In tactics and strategy he was perhaps the most inventive and imaginative general of the nineteenth century, leading one Prussian officer of his day to complain that "the whole system of his tactics is monstrously incorrect." But he distrusted improvisations outside the area of land warfare. He knew little about naval affairs; he rejected the ideas of Robert Fulton (1765–1815) for the use of submarines and mines at sea, and he disbanded the French balloon companies.

Napoleonic Wars (1792–1815). The almost continuous series of hostilities between France and other European countries following the French Revolutionary Wars. [See Napoleon I; Peninsular War; Russian Campaign, Napoleon's.] European monarchies, threatened by the menace of the French army, formed a series of alliances, seven in all, aimed at defeating the French. The resulting conflicts are often called the Coalition Wars although the first, begun when Napoleon was a mere boy, is more properly called a Revolutionary War. The accession of Napoleon as first consul on 9 November 1799 is generally assumed to divide the wars of the French Revolution and the Napoleonic Wars.

A striking feature of Napoleon's campaigns was the frequency with which battles were fought, far more than the campaigns of the eighteenth century.

War of the First Coalition. In response to the French declaration of war against the king of Bohemia (a subordinate title of the emperor of Austria) on 20 April 1772, Prussia and Austria formed the First Coalition on 26 June of that year. It resulted in the French victories at Valmy and Jemappes. After the execution of Louis XVI (1754–1793) on 21 January 1793, Britain and, soon after, Spain joined the coalition. But French successes in northern Italy and on the Rhine, combined with a lack of cohesion among the Allies, caused the coalition to collapse, and on 17 October 1797 France and Austria signed the Peace of Campo Formio.

On 2 July 1798 Napoleon landed in Egypt, after a delay en route to capture Malta. His campaign there did not meet with the complete success of which he had dreamed. To protect himself politically, he left his army and returned to Paris, arriving on 16 October 1799, after having been absent for 531 days, but he quickly established himself as first consul and virtual dictator of France.

War of the Second Coalition. The Second Coalition against the French was completed on 22 June 1799 with Britain, Austria, Naples, Russia, and Turkey participating. In the war that followed, except for the Egyptian Campaign and the British war at sea, there were three main areas of conflict: the Netherlands, where an Anglo-Russian army led by the Duke of York [q.v.] tried unsuccessfully to expel the French; northern Italy, where a Russo-Austrian army under Aleksandr Suvorov [q.v.] engaged the French; and Germany, where an Austrian army under Archduke Charles [q.v.] took the field

against Marshal Jean Baptiste Jourdan [qq.v.]. Although by the end of the year France had lost almost all its territory in Italy, it had triumphed elsewhere. The Allies were badly coordinated, and the tsar withdrew his armies and quit the coalition.

Napoleon assembled an Army of the Reserve around Dijon and on 15 May 1800 began to cross the Alps from Switzerland to invade Italy. His troops made an appallingly difficult march over icy terrain and descended into the plain of Lombardy. On 4 June André Masséna [q.v.], who had been besieged at Genoa, was forced by starvation to surrender to Austrian General Peter Carl Ott (1738–1809), who was himself then defeated five days later by French General Jean Lannes [q.v.] at Montebello. At Marengo, a village in northwestern Italy, on 14 June 1800 Napoleon unexpectedly bumped into the Austrian army under Michael von Melas [q.v.] and found himself facing odds of two to one. He was saved by the opportune arrival of General Louis Desaix [q.v.], who turned the tide of battle. The Austrians were routed, and on the 15th Melas surrendered. In Germany a French army under Jean Victor Moreau [q.v.] won a series of quick victories over the Austrians: Stockach on 3 May 1800, Möskirch on 5 May, Ulm on 16 May, and Hochstadt on 19 June. After a brief armistice Moreau defeated the Austrians at Hohenlinden on 3 December, and on Christmas Day the Austrians sued for peace. A treaty was concluded at Lunéville on 9 February 1801.

Britain carried on the war alone at sea, but on 27 March 1802 the Peace of Amiens [q.v.] was signed between Britain and France. It lasted fourteen months, providing the only year of peace in Europe from the French Revolution until the Battle of Waterloo [q.v.] in 1815.

War of the Third Coalition. A general desire to limit French expansionism and Britain's particular desire to recover Hanover led Austria, Russia, Sweden, and some of the princely German states to form the Third Coalition on 11 April 1805, effective on 9 August. The Allies planned to destroy the army of André Masséna [q.v.] in northern Italy and then invade France, but Napoleon moved first, crossing the Rhine on 26 September and reaching the Danube on 6 October, moving in a wide arc that cut off from its supports the Austrian army under General Karl Mack von Leiberich [q.v.], which had invaded Bavaria on 2 September. On 17 October 1805 Mack was forced to surrender his entire army of 20,000 at Ulm [q.v.].

Napoleonic Wars *Napoleon enters Berlin through the Brandenburg Gate, October 1806. Painting by Charles Meynier*

Although the Russians under Mikhail Kutuzov [q.v.] fought delaying actions at Dürrenstein on 11 November and at Hollabrünn on 15–16 November, Napoleon occupied Vienna and drove the Russians before him. In Italy, Masséna defeated Archduke Charles [q.v.] at Caldiero [q.v.]. Continuing his advance, Napoleon defeated the Allies again at Austerlitz [q.v.]. The Austrians surrendered unconditionally on 4 December, and the tsar withdrew his mauled army into Russia. By the Treaty of Pressburg on 26 December, Austria yielded territory in Germany and Italy to France. The coalition collapsed.

War of the Fourth Coalition. Russia and Britain, which had remained in the war, were joined by Prussia, which formerly had remained on the sidelines but was now alarmed by Napoleon's formation of satellite German states into a Confederation of the Rhine [q.v.]. Saxony joined with Prussia, and the new coalition became effective on 6 October 1806, when Napoleon launched a swift invasion of Prussia. The French under General Jean Lannes [q.v.] scored a victory at Saalfeld [q.v.] on 10 October. Napoleon routed another Austrian force at Jena [q.v.] on 14 October, and on the same day at Auerstädt [q.v.] the main Prussian army was swept away by French forces under Louis Davout and Jean Baptiste Bernadotte [qq.v.]. Napoleon captured Berlin on 24 October, and on 24 November the last Prussian force, under General Gebhard von Blücher [q.v.], surrendered near Lübeck.

To forestall any Russian attempt to come to Prussia's aid, Napoleon at once marched into Poland and occupied Warsaw. He intended to destroy the Russian field army there under General Levin Bennigsen [q.v.], but Bennigsen fought a bloody rearguard action at Pultusk [q.v.] on the west bank of the Narew River and escaped. After an indecisive battle at Eylau [q.v.] on 8 February 1807, both sides went into winter quarters.

In the summer of 1807 Bennigsen lunged at Napoleon but was checked at Heilsberg [q.v.] on 10 June. Four days later he crossed the Alle River and was soundly defeated at Friedland [q.v.]. In July the Treaties of Tilsit [q.v.] were signed on a raft in the Niemen (Neman) River, and Russia and Prussia were forced to accept humiliating terms. Napoleon now firmly controlled northeastern Europe. Prussia gave up all its Polish territory, which became the Duchy of Warsaw and a French satellite. All Prussian territory between the Elbe and the Rhine was handed over to the Confederation of the Rhine, and Prussia itself was occupied by a French army until an indemnity of 140 million francs, an enormous amount for the time, was paid. Russia was forced to recognize the Duchy of Danzig and to form an alliance with France against Britain, its former ally.

War of the Fifth Coalition. The Fifth Coalition came into existence on 9 April 1809, when Austria, encouraged by Britain, instigated a revolt in the Tyrol against Bavaria, Napoleon's principal German ally, and an Austrian army under Archduke Charles [q.v.] invaded the country, while a second Austrian army invaded Italy [See Tyrolean Revolt; Andreas Hofer]. Britain's contribution was the disastrous Walcheren Expedition [q.v.]. The Austrians entered Italy by way of the Julian Alps and on 16 April repulsed a French assault at Sacile [q.v.].

Napoleon, who had been in Spain, hurried to Germany and reorganized his forces there. Taking the offensive, he crossed the Danube and on 19–20 April engaged the Austrian forces in the Battle of Abensberg [q.v.] and split them in two. He pursued the left wing under Austrian General Johann Hiller (1754–1819), which managed to escape his attempted encirclement in the Battle of Landeshut [q.v.] on 21 April. Napoleon then moved to attack the Austrian right wing under Archduke Charles, which was being held in place by French Marshal Louis Davout [q.v.]. However, at Eckmühl, Archduke Charles attacked Davout's numerically inferior force, which was saved only by Napoleon's timely arrival.

On 13 May Napoleon occupied Vienna. Nine days later, in the Battle of Aspern-Essling [q.v.], he suffered his first real defeat. On the night of 4–5 July he again crossed the Danube, and on 5–6 July at Wagram [q.v.] he decisively defeated the Austrians after two days' fighting. On 10 July Austria sued for peace, which was concluded on 14 October 1809, by the Treaty of Schönbrunn, by which Austria ceded vast tracts of land and was forced to join Napoleon's Continental System [q.v.]. Napoleon now dominated Central Europe.

Napoleonic Wars *Napolean in defeat, the Russian Campaign, Winter 1812*

War of the Sixth Coalition. When in June 1812 Napoleon invaded Russia [see Russian Campaign, Napoleon's], Russia and Britain, along with Spain and Portugal, became allies in the Sixth Coalition. On 27 February 1813 Prussia turned against Napoleon and joined the coalition. Austria, followed by Sweden and some German states, joined after the battles of Lützen on 2 May 1813 and Bautzen [qq.v.] on 20–21 May. After the Battle of Leipzig [q.v.] on 16–19 October, the French were driven back over the Rhine, and early in 1814 the Allies invaded France. The Treaty of Chaumont on 9 March bound the Allies together with common aims, and on 6 April 1814 Napoleon abdicated. The Bourbons returned to France.

The Congress of Vienna was in session to design a new Europe free of the French menace when, in early March 1815, the news was received that Napoleon had left Elba, to which he had been exiled. On 1 March he landed on the French mainland to begin the famous Hundred Days [q.v.]. Increasingly larger forces sent against him melted away, mostly to join their old emperor, for the Bourbons had quickly managed to make themselves highly unpopular. On 7 March he arrived at Grenoble; on 10 March he reached Lyons; on 15 March he was at Chalon-sur-Saône; and at nine o'clock in the evening he was back in Paris and was its de facto ruler with Louis XVIII in flight. The Allies now formed the last coalition.

War of the Seventh Coalition. This was a short war. Napoleon on 15 June threw his Army of the North across the Sambre at Charleroi and on the 16th fell upon the Prussian army of Gebhard von Blücher at Ligny [q.v.]. On the same day Marshal Michel Ney fought an indecisive battle against Wellington at Quatre Bras [q.v.]. On the 18th the Battle of Waterloo [q.v.] put an end to Napoleon's ambitions, and he was sent to end his days on the island of St. Helena in the South Atlantic, 1,200 miles off the west coast of Africa. HMS *Northumberland* landed him at Jamestown, the island's capital, at seven-thirty on the evening of 17 October. He never again disturbed the peace of Europe.

Napoleon's Remains. Napoleon, believed by many to have been the preeminent general of the nineteenth century, died at St. Helena on 5 May 1821 and was buried in the Slane Valley there. His body was clothed in the uniform of a colonel with a green coat, white kerseymere breeches, and heavy army boots. His breast bore his decorations, and his hat rested on his knees. His knife, fork, and metal plate were buried with him, and some coins bearing his effigy were strewn about on the white satin padding of his coffin. The corpse was not embalmed; only some creosote was sprinkled over it before it was placed in a vault of ashlar and cement held together by iron clamps and flat slabs of stone and layers of pebbles. In 1840 the body was exhumed and brought to Paris to be interred in a crypt under the gilded dome of the chapel of the Hôtel des Invalides [q.v.], where it was hermetically sealed in six massive caskets, one of zinc, one of mahogany, two of lead, one of oak, and one in red porphyry.

Every year hundreds of requests are made to examine the corpse, but it has not been looked upon since 1840, when twenty-five officials and appointed delegates viewed the remains, then reduced to bones covered by dusty bits of uniform and decorations.

Narbonne, Peter Remi (1806–1839). A French-Canadian rebel who took an active part in the 1837 uprising of Louis Riel [q.v.] and subsequently made a number of raids from the United States into Canada until he was captured by loyalists at Odeltown Church on 9 November 1838. He was taken to Montreal, tried for high treason, and hanged on 15 February 1839. [See Red River Expedition; Canadian Revolts.]

Narváez, Ramón María (1800–1868). A Spanish soldier and statesman who supported Queen Isabella II (1830–1904) and in 1834–36 fought against the Carlists in Catalonia [see Carlist Wars]. In 1840 he took part in an unsuccessful insurrection against the government of Baldomero Espartero [q.v.] and fled to France. In 1843 he led a republican rebellion that drove Espartero out of Spain, and in 1844 he became a virtual dictator. In 1851 he temporarily lost power, but he was prime minister in 1856–57, 1864–65, and 1866–68. He once said, "I do not have to forgive my enemies, I have had them all shot." But he must have missed some, for he was overthrown with Isabella in the Revolution of 1868. He was known as a notorious womanizer.

Nashville, Battle of (15–16 December 1864), American Civil War. In this battle about 50,000 Union troops under General George H. Thomas [q.v.] attacked some 31,000 Confederates under General John B. Hood [q.v.] near Nashville, a port city on the Cumberland River in north-central Tennessee. Thomas concentrated on Hood's left flank, which was weak because he had sent Nathan Bedford Forrest [q.v.] to make a raid near Murfreesboro. Hood's army soon disintegrated into a fleeing rabble. Thomas lost 387 killed, 2,562 wounded, and 112 missing. Hood reported his losses as "very small," but they have been estimated at more than 5,000, and he lost about 50 guns. Thomas is known to have captured 4,462, including 3 Confederate generals. The Union victory ended Hood's Tennessee Campaign and eliminated all organized Tennessee resistance.

Nashville, Tennessee, from the southeast, 1860s

Nasib, Battle of. See Nezib, Battle of.

National Association for the Employment of Ex-Soldiers. A British organization founded in 1885 that grew to be the largest employment agency in the United Kingdom.

National Cemeteries, American. President Lincoln established the first national cemeteries in 1862 "for the soldiers who shall die in the service of their country." By 1999 more than two and a half million veterans or family members were buried in 130 national cemeteries in thirty-nine states; of these, 59 were filled. Each grave is dug 5 feet wide, 10 feet long, and 7 feet deep. The government supplies each with a 230-pound marble tombstone. [See Arlington National Cemetery.]

National Guard. 1. The designation of volunteer militia or reserve units in several countries. [See Garde Nationale.]

2. In the United States the term was first used on 16 August 1824, when to honor the visit of the Marquis de Lafayette (1757–1834), the 7th Regiment of New York Militia adopted the name. (The marquis had commanded the Garde Nationale in 1789.] During the American Civil War some states formed home guard militia units, some of which were called National Guards. The present National Guard, federally funded and equipped, came into existence with the Militia (Dick) Act of January 1903, but earlier volunteer militia units, raised in most states, were often called the National Guard. Officers were elected, training was inadequate, and equipment was deficient. Until the Spanish-American War [q.v.] militia were used principally to intervene in labor disputes.

National Rifle Association. An American organization founded on 24 November 1871 to promote interest in marksmanship. With help from army engineer officers, a model firing range was laid out at Creedmoor on Long Island [see Creedmoor Rifle Range], and the first competition was held in 1873, in which militia teams beat all regular army teams. The first president was General Ambrose Burnside [q.v.]. He was followed by George Wood Wingate [q.v.], a New York lawyer who was instrumental in the association's foundation, then served for twenty-five years as its president.

National Service. The concept that the youth of a nation should serve the state in the army or navy for a set time period. A euphemism for conscription or *levée en masse* [qq.v.].

Nations, Battle of the. See Leipzig, Battle of.

Nat Turner's Insurrection (1831). An American slave named Nat Turner (1800–1831), a house servant in Southampton County, Virginia, claiming divine inspiration, exhorted fellow slaves to accept his leadership in rebellion. On the night of 21–22 August 1831 he and six other slaves entered the bedroom of his master, Joseph Travis, who was killed along with his entire family. Securing horses, guns, and liquor, Turner then aroused neighboring slaves and, joined by a few, killed in a short time a total of 57 whites, including 15 women and 29 children. Turner himself is believed to have killed only 1 person, Mrs. Margaret Whitehead. After slashing at her with a dull sword, he crushed her skull with a fence post.

Troops were summoned, and Fort Monroe was reinforced. Turner went into hiding while 2,800 militia and regulars swept through the county, killing more than 100 blacks. Turner was captured single-handedly by Benjamin Phipps, a civilian, on 30 October 1831. He was tried, convicted on 5 November, and on 11 November 1831 hanged by Deputy Sheriff Edward Butts along with 16 others. This was the bloodiest slave rebellion in North American history. It was attributed to abolitionists and led to the enactment of stricter slave laws.

Nautical Twilight. The time after the sun sets or before it rises when objects on the ground can be seen at 400 yards.

Navajo War (1863–64). During the American Civil War a small band of Mescalero Navajo Indians in New Mexico and Nevada attacked trains, launched raids, and proved so difficult for the army to subdue that on 23 June 1863 Brigadier General James Henry Carleton (1814–1873), commanding the Department of New Mexico, ordered all Navajos who wished to be considered friendly to move by 20 July to the reservation established at Bosque Redondo, more than 400

Nat Turner's Insurrection *Nat Turner and his followers killed 57 white Virginians, 1831.*

miles from their homeland. After that date, he warned, "every Navajo that is seen will be considered as hostile and treated accordingly." To hunt down the hostiles, a regiment commanded by Christopher ("Kit") Carson [q.v.] was concentrated at newly established (22 October 1862) Fort Wingate, located at El Gallo, near present-day San Rafael, New Mexico. In addition to the troops, other Indians, particularly the Utes and Zuñis, who knew that the Navajos could be plundered with immunity, joined the hunt. The greatest devastation was carried out by Carson in the Canyon de Chelly [q.v.] in January 1864. Although he killed only 23 Navajos, he destroyed their crops, livestock, and fruit trees. Within three weeks some 3,000 surrendered. Eventually 11,468 were held at Fort Canby. The march, made in batches, to Bosque Redondo is known in Navajo history as the Long Walk. Perhaps as many as 3,000 died on the journey, and perhaps another 2,000 died soon after reaching the 40-square-mile reservation.

Navajo War *A Navajo scout for the army. Photo by Ben Wittick*

Naval and Military Administration, Royal Commission on. See Hartington Committee.

Naval Brigade. The name given by the British to an ad hoc unit of any size composed of sailors and marines that fought on land, often, as in the Indian Mutiny and the Second Anglo-Boer War [qq.v.], far from the sea. They usually manned naval guns mounted on carriages or, as in the Crimean War [q.v.], shore batteries.

During the Indian Mutiny a naval brigade of about 500 sailors and marines under navy Captain William Peel [q.v.], third son of the statesman Sir Robert Peel (1788–1850), manned six 24-pounders, two bullock-drawn eight-inch howitzers, and two rocket tubes mounted on carts.

Nave. The part of the wheel of gun carriages in which the arms of the axletree move and into which the spokes are driven and supported.

Neamathla (fl. 1812–1826). A Creek Indian who became a Seminole chief. William Pope Duval (1784–1854), governor of Florida, described him as "bold, violent, restless, unable to submit to a superior or to endure an equal." His followers, he said, were the most "lawless and vile" in Florida. Neamathla played an active part in the First Seminole War [q.v.] but finally entered a reservation where he died sometime before 1832.

Neapolitan Revolt (1820–21). At Nola, a commune 16 miles east-northeast of Naples, soldiers and their officers, who had previously served under Joachim Murat [q.v.] when he was king of Naples, rebelled on 1 July 1820 against the reactionary government of Ferdinand I (1751–1815), king of the Two Sicilies. When other troops refused to move against the mutineers and civilians cried for reform, a frightened Ferdinand agreed to a constitution, and in October a new Neapolitan Parliament dispatched forces under General Pietro Colletta (1775–1831) to crush the revolt. When Palermo, Sicily, also revolted, the Holy Alliance of European powers met and called for imperial troops to intervene. In March 1821 Austrian forces under General Johann Frimont [q.v.] marched south, and the rebel forces fled. Ferdinand resumed his autocratic ways, renounced the constitution, and ruled despotically, protected by imperial forces, which remained as an occupation force until 1827.

Neck of a Cascabel. The part which joined the knob to the base of the breech of a muzzle-loading artillery piece.

Needle Gun. See Dreyse Needle Gun.

Neelam / Leelam / Nilam. In India, the auction of the personal effects of a deceased European officer. It was held soon after the death occurred, particularly in the case of an officer in the field. The money so raised was sent to the deceased's family.

Negro Fort, Attack on (27 July 1816), War of 1812. When Andrew Jackson [q.v.] drove the British out of Pensacola, Florida, on 7 November 1814, they retreated up the east bank of the Apalachicola River in Georgia with "about 100 Negro slaves" and there built an earthen fort around which the former slaves settled. Before sailing away after the war, the British commander, marine Lieutenant Colonel Edward Nicholls (fl. 1814–15), turned the fort over to Seminole Indians, leaving them 700 pounds of gunpowder and other munitions. They were displaced, however, by the black settlers, reinforced with others, about 400 in all, who kept Indians and whites alike at bay. General Edmund Pendleton Gaines [q.v.] ordered the demolition of the fort, called Negro Fort, and a small force under Lieutenant Colonel Duncan Lamont Clinch [q.v.], 4th Infantry, moved in boats up the river from newly completed Fort Scott on the Flint River near its confluence with the Chattahoochee. Clinch was fired upon from the fort, and he returned the fire with a red-hot cannonball that exploded the fort's powder magazine, killing outright some 270 people, mortally wounding another 50, and dispersing the survivors. The black commander of the fort, who was among the survivors, was killed by Seminoles.

Neill, James George Smith (1810–1857). A Scots soldier who organized a Turkish contingent in the Crimean War [q.v.]. He was in India in 1857 at the outbreak of the Indian Mutiny [q.v.] and was colonel of the 1st Madras Fusiliers in Benares. When he learned that on 4 June 1857 at Allahabad, a holy Islamic city in northwest Hindustan, mutinous sepoys of the 6th Bengal Native Infantry had murdered their officers, including 7 newly arrived youthful cadets, and every European civilian they could find, Colonel Neill marched promptly. He reached Allahabad on 11 June in time to save a small band of Europeans and loyal Sikhs sheltering in the fort. He at once suppressed the mutiny there with great severity, hanging hundreds.

He then marched to Cawnpore and made a famous march from there to join the assault upon Lucknow, where he was killed in action.

Nélaton, Auguste (1807–1873). A French army surgeon known for his operating skills who invented a probe used in searching for bullets.

Nelson, Edward W. (1855–1934). An American soldier, the son of a butcher and a former army nurse, who won renown as a naturalist. After graduation from a Chicago high school he spent the summer and autumn of 1872 observing and collecting birds in the Rocky Mountains and in California. He then attended and was graduated from the Cook County (Illinois) Normal School in 1875. At age twenty-two he was offered a chance to go to Alaska to record weather observations with time to study natural history if he was willing to enlist in the Army Signal Corps. He enlisted and was sent to Fort Myer, Virignia, for training, but because he "lacked enthusiasm for the school of the soldier," he was soon excused from duty.

In April 1877 he arrived in Alaska. During his four-year tour he traveled 4,000 miles by dogsled and kayak. He acquired an enormous collection of Eskimo artifacts, the largest and best extant. In 1899 he published a 518-page monograph on the Eskimos. In 1983 the Smithsonian Institution mounted a major exhibition of his finds.

In 1890 he joined the U.S. Biological Survey. He became its chief in 1916.

Nelson's Farm. See White Oak Swamp, Battle of.

Nemours, Louis Charles Philippe Raphaël d'Orléans (1814–1896). The third son of King Louis Philippe (1808–1873) who served as a soldier in Algeria in 1836–37 and distinguished himself in the capture of Constantine in 1837. He was soon after made a general. He lived in England from 1848 to 1870, when he returned to France. He was expelled from France in 1886.

Nepalese War (1814–16), sometimes called the Gurkha War. A war fought between the troops of the British Honorable East India Company and the Gurkhas, the ruling ethnic group of Nepal. In October 1814 Lord Moira (1754–1826), the governor-general of India, sent an ultimatum to the Nepalese rulers who had refused to accept the frontier between Nepal and British India determined by the East India Company. When the ultimatum was rejected, the British entered Nepal on 1 November 1814 and began erecting forts along the new frontier; the Gurkhas responded with ambushes and skirmishes. When British columns entered the country through four mountain passes, a peace was arranged, and a treaty signed, but disputes soon arose over its terms. In January 1816 the war was resumed, and an Anglo-British army under Sir David Ochterlony [q.v.] fought its way into Nepal and engaged Nepalese forces under Umar Singh Thapa (d. 1816).

The principal engagements of the war were the siege of Kalunga [q.v.] in October–November 1814 and the battles of Jitgurgh on 14 January 1815, Almorah on 25 April 1815, and Makhwanpur on 27 February 1816 [qq.v.]. The war ended on 28 November 1816 with the Treaty of Sagauli, by which the Nepalese agreed to withdraw from Sikkim, Simla, Kumaun (Kumoan), and other border territories and several frontier districts and permit Gurkhas to enlist in Gurkha battalions of the Indian army.

From the beginning the British had been so impressed with the fighting qualities of the Gurkhas that even before the fighting stopped, they had enlisted hundreds of captured Gurkhas who later formed a unique and discrete unit in the Bengal army. Gurkhas and British never again met as enemies. During the Indian Mutiny [q.v.] the Nepalese even sent a sizable army to assist the British in suppressing the rebels and mutineers.

Netley Hospital. The shortened form of the Royal Victoria Hospital at Netley, a village in Hampshire, England, three miles southeast of Southampton. Queen Victoria laid its cornerstone on 19 May 1856. With provisions for a thousand patients, it served as a military hospital, ministering to invalids returning from foreign service as well as those from neighboring areas. Netley also became the headquarters for the female nurses of the army.

Neuchâtel Insurrection (1856–57). The Congress of Vienna (1814–15) gave Neuchâtel a dual status as a canton in the Swiss Confederation and as part of the dominion of King Frederick William IV of Prussia (1795–1861). In 1848, the year of riots and revolutions throughout Europe, the dissatisfied commoners of Neuchâtel announced that henceforth their country was to be solely a republic in the Swiss Confederation. The aristocrats protested, and European nations chose sides and mobilized their armies. No blood was shed, however, for a compromise was reached to remove Neuchâtel from the dominion of Prussia while Frederick William retained the title of Prince of Neuchâtel for life.

Neutrality. The status of a nation that takes no part in an existing war and claims immunity from invasion or exploitation by belligerents.

Neutral Rights. The claims of a neutral country to remain at peace with and to trade with belligerents.

Neuville, Alphonse de (1836–1885). A French painter of battle scenes, particularly of the Crimean War [q.v.]. In the Franco-Prussian War [q.v.] during the siege of Paris he served as an auxiliary engineer officer in the Belleville section of the city. One of his most famous canvases, *Le Bourget,* painted in 1878, memorializes an incident of 30 October 1870, when victorious Prussians stood aside at the battered door of a church as its last defenders filed out. His *The Defence of Rorke's Drift* now hangs in the art gallery of New South Wales in Sydney, Australia.

New Bern, Battle of (14 March 1862), American Civil War. In the nineteenth century the name was variously spelled Berne, Newberne, or Newbern. Near this port town at the confluence of the Neuse and Trent rivers in North Carolina, which had been fortified by the Confederates under Brigadier General Lawrence Branch (1820–1862), Union troops under General Ambrose Burnside [q.v.] won a victory after a five-hour battle and then captured the town. Union losses were 471, of whom 91 were killed; Confederate losses were 578. This was the first town in the Deep South to be captured by Union forces, and it remained in Union hands throughout the war.

New Bern, Raid on (1–2 February 1864), American Civil War. Since the capture of New Bern, North Carolina, by Federal forces in 1862 [see New Bern, Battle of], the Federal presence there had been an irritant to the Confederacy. In an effort to retake the town, General Robert E. Lee sent 13,000 troops under Major General George E. Pickett [q.v.] to make a two-pronged attack from the southwest and northeast. The commanders of both forces found their objectives too strong, and the Confederates were forced to withdraw after sustaining small losses.

Captured in the raid were 22 former Confederate soldiers in Union uniforms. After a drumhead court-martial, all were hanged for desertion, creating a cause célèbre.

New Caledonia, Revolution in (1878). In French: *Nouvelle Calédonie.* This island in the southwest Pacific, 248 miles long and 31 miles wide, was discovered in 1774 by Captain James Cook (1728–1879) and was captured by the French on 20 September 1853. In June 1878 many of the native tribes revolted, burning towns and villages. About 90 Europeans were killed, including the French military commandant. The insurrection was not put down until the end of the year. Soon after, a French penal settlement was established on the island.

Newcastle, Fifth Duke of. See Clinton, Henry Pelham Fiennes Pelham.

New Hope Church, Battle of (25–27 May 1864), American Civil War. Also known as Dallas, Pumpkin Vine Creek, Allatoona Hills, and Burned Hickory. At Altoona Pass in Georgia Union General William Tecumseh Sherman [q.v.] attempted to go around the defenses of Confederate General Joseph E. Johnston [q.v.], but his move was anticipated. Not realizing that he faced Johnston's entire army, Sherman ordered XX Corps under General Joseph Hooker [q.v.] to attack. The attack was repelled with heavy Federal losses.

The following day there was only skirmishing, but on 27 May Sherman ordered an attack by General Oliver O. Howard [q.v.] upon the Confederate right. This attack also failed, the Federals losing about 2,000 to the Confederate's 500. Sherman then moved eastward, maneuvering Johnston out of his defensive positions. Total Federal losses were about 7,000; Confederate losses about 2,000.

New Madrid and Island No. 10 (March and April 1862), American Civil War. After the fall of Fort Donelson [q.v.] Confederate General Leonidas Polk [q.v.] withdrew from western Kentucky, and Confederates took up positions near the village of New Madrid, Missouri, on the Mississippi River 28 miles north of Caruthersville, and at Island No. 10, near the corner of Tennessee. Both positions, containing 7,000 men in all, were under the command of General John Porter McCown (1815–1879). Union General Henry Halleck ordered General John Pope [qq.v.] to organize a corps and attack both. On 3 March Pope arrived before New Madrid. Seeing the strong Confederate position with 50 heavy guns, he sent for siege guns and began constructing approaches. On 13 March he began a bombardment, and at once McCown ordered a withdrawal of the troops at New Madrid across the Mississippi into Tennessee, a much-criticized move for which he was relieved of command and succeeded by General William Whann Mackall (1817–1891). General Pierre Beauregard [q.v.] said of McCown's action that it was "the poorest defense made by any fortified post during the whole course of the war."

Pope then cut a canal through swampy land to enable gunboats to avoid the batteries on Island No. 10 and to provide protection for his river crossing. The canal was completed on 4 April, and four regiments were ferried across the river to Tiptonville, Tennessee, to cut off the Confederates' line of retreat. Mackall surrendered his position and 3,500 men, nearly half of whom were sick; 500 escaped through the swamps.

This victory opened the Mississippi to Federal forces as far south as Fort Pillow, Tennessee, 60 miles downriver.

Newman, Daniel (1780?–1851). An American soldier who was educated at the University of North Carolina and in 1799 was commissioned in the 4th Infantry. He resigned in 1802, but he fought in the Creek War [q.v.] of 1812–14 as colonel of a regiment of Georgia volunteers, which in 1812 he led in an invasion of Spanish Florida, penetrating 100 miles. There, in an attack on King Payne (d. 1812) and his Alachua Seminoles, he was caught in a running fight, lasting from 27 September until 11 October, in which his command barely escaped annihilation. In 1817 he became a major general of the Georgia militia. He held several public offices and served a term in Congress.

New Market, Battle of (15 May 1864), American Civil War. One mile north of this small town in Virginia's Shenandoah Valley a Federal corps of 6,500 under General Franz Sigel [q.v.], advancing from Cedar Creek, Virginia, faced a force of 5,000 Confederates, including 258 cadets from the Virginia Military Institute [q.v.], all under General John Breckinridge [q.v.]. In spite of superior numbers, the Federals were routed with a loss of 831; Confederate losses were 577, including 10 cadets killed or mortally wounded and 47 wounded. A museum owned by the Virginia Military Institute now sits on the field.

New Market Heights, Battle of (29 September 1864), American Civil War. On the night of 28–29 September 19,639 Federal troops under Major General Benjamin Butler [q.v.] crossed the James River on pontoon bridges at two locations in Virginia, Deep Bottom and Aiken's Landing, and drew up before Confederate positions defended by a brigade of infantry and a brigade of cavalry on New Market Heights, a cliff that dominated the terrain. The next morning the Federal attack was led by a brigade of U.S. Colored Troops [q.v.], which, after floundering through swampy ground and wading across a creek, was stopped by an abatis. Confederate musketry riddled the brigade, which disintegrated. A second attack by another Union brigade was also repulsed. A third attack carried the heights, but the bulk of the Confederates had already withdrawn. Butler suffered 3,300 casualties; Confederate losses were estimated at 2,000.

For their bravery in this engagement 37 Union soldiers received the Medal of Honor [q.v.]. Of these, 14 were awarded to blacks, the largest number ever given to blacks for a single engagement. Butler also ordered 197 special silver medals for the black troops, inscribed in part "Distinguished for courage, Campaign before Richmond, 1864."

New Mexico, Confederate Army of. During the American Civil War a Confederate force of 3,700 men, sometimes called Sibley's Arizona Brigade, commanded by Brigadier General Henry Hopkins Sibley [q.v.], was formed on 14 December 1861 and sent to capture New Mexico Territory, which then extended from Texas to California. Sibley marched his force up the Rio Grande to Valverde (Val Verde), Texas, where on 21 February 1862 he encountered and defeated a Federal force of 3,810 men under Colonel Edward Richard Sprigg Canby [q.v.] [see Valverde, Battle of]. Sibley went on to capture Albuquerque, Santa Fe, and Tucson, but Canby, reinforced by Colorado volunteers, defeated him in the Battle of Glorieta [q.v.] on 26–28 March. Canby then retreated to Texas.

New Model Guns. In the United States this referred to artillery pieces manufactured after 1861. They were characterized by a lack of ornamentation, having an outline of gentle curves as far as practicable. The bottom of the bore was semi-ellipsoid.

New Orleans, Battle of (23 December 1814–8 January 1815), War of 1812. On 26 November 1814 a force of 7,500 British troops, most of them veterans of the Peninsular War [q.v.], under Major General Sir Edward Pakenham [q.v.], sailed from Jamaica. On 13 December they landed near Lake Borge, an inlet of the Mississippi near New Orleans. Andrew Jackson [q.v.], leading an army of 800 regulars, some Tennessee and Kentucky volunteers, volunteer militia from the city, and a band of pirates led by Jean Laffite [q.v.]—in all, some 3,100 effectives plus 2,000 badly armed and equipped, untrained Louisiana militia who were kept in reserve—organized the defense of the city, laying out defensive positions along the Rodrigues Canal, an abandoned and dry former waterway south of the city. Because the Creole population was anti-American, Jackson declared martial law, an act for which he was later fined by an irate New Orleans judge.

On the night of 23–24 December, Jackson launched a surprise attack but was repulsed with a loss of 24 killed, 115 wounded, and 74 missing; British losses were 46 killed, 162 wounded, and 64 missing. This action caused the British to pause and gave Jackson more time to prepare his defenses. On 28 December the British launched a probing frontal attack and an attack on Jackson's left flank; both failed. An attempt to sail up the Mississippi and outflank Jackson was thwarted by the successful resistance of Fort Philip, 65 miles downstream.

On 1 January the Americans lost 262, of whom 42 were killed in an artillery duel. British losses were 406, of whom 94 were killed. On 8 January 1815 the British attacked in force and were repulsed with a loss of 2,044: 293 killed, 1,267 wounded, and 484 taken prisoner. Pakenham himself was mortally wounded, and his two most senior generals were killed; the survivors retired to their ships. Jackson lost 13 killed; 39 wounded, 19 mortally; and 19 missing. When he learned that Pakenham had been mortally wounded at the head of his troops, Jackson said: "When our intellect fails us, we have to become heroes."

This battle was of no political consequence. Although none of the participants could know, the war had been ended by the signing of the Treaty of Ghent on 24 December 1814.

New Orleans Uprising (17 September 1874). Federal troops were used to suppress an uprising in New Orleans led by the White League, an organization consisting mostly of Confederate veterans, who attempted to overthrow the local government, then led by blacks and carpetbaggers. [See Liberty Place, "Battle" of.]

Newport Uprising (1839). In Great Britain, textile workers in Montgomeryshire and miners and ironworkers of Monmouthshire and Glamorganshire protested working conditions and marched on Newport, 20 miles west-southwest of Bristol. Soldiers fired into the mob, killing several.

News Walkers. In the American Civil War soldiers who walked from campfire to campfire after a battle, gathering and dispensing news, rumors, and opinions, were called news walkers. They were often good judges of the state of morale and shrewd forecasters of the days ahead.

Newton, John (1823–1895). An American soldier who was graduated from West Point in 1842. All his service before the American Civil War was in the Corps of Engineers. His only field experience was on the Utah Expedition [q.v.] of 1858. On 23 September 1861 he was named a Union brigadier general of volunteers. In that rank he fought at Antietam, Fredericksburg, Chancellorsville, and Gettysburg (where he assumed command of I Corps) and throughout the Atlanta Campaign [qq.v.]. After the war he returned to the Corps of Engineers, and on 6 March 1884 he became chief of engineers. He retired two years later. From 1888 to 1895 he was president of the Panama Railroad Company.

Newtonia, Battles of. American Civil War. Two engagements took place at Newtonia, a village in the Ozark Mountains of southwest Missouri, 10 miles from Neosho.

First Battle of Newtonia (30 September 1862). On 27 September the Confederates established an outpost of 200 men at Newtonia. Two days later, from his headquarters at Sarcoxie, 15 miles away, Union Brigadier General Friedrich Salomon (1826–1897) sent 150 men and a howitzer to rout them. The following day the small fire fight was enlarged into a battle as both sides received reinforcements, including for the Confederates several units of Choctaw and Chickasaw Indians. The Federals were forced to retreat after suffering a loss of more than 400; Confederate losses were reported as 12 killed, 63 wounded, and 3 missing.

Second Battle of Newtonia (28 October 1864). Confederate Major General Sterling Price [q.v.], retreating from his failed raid into Missouri, halted to rest just south of Newtonia and there was attacked by two brigades under Union Major General James G. Blunt [q.v.]. Price successfully repelled the attacks, and Blunt was about to retreat when he was reinforced by three brigades and six guns under Brigadier General John Sanborn [q.v.]. Seeing himself now outnumbered, Price made an orderly retreat.

Next of Kin. In the nineteenth century there was no direct, formal method for notifying relatives of a soldier who was wounded or killed. Although lists were sometimes posted or published, close relatives were usually notified, if at all, by other soldiers. Governments did not send regrets. An exception was the letter sent by President Abraham Lincoln [q.v.] on 21 November 1864 to Mrs. Lydia Bixby, a widow living in Boston:

Dear Madam:

I have been shown in the files of the War Department a statement of the adjutant general of Massachusetts that you are the mother of five sons who have died gloriously on the field of battle. I feel how weak and fruitless must be any words of mine which should beguile you from the grief of a loss so overwhelming. But I cannot refrain from tendering you the consolation that may be found in the thanks of a Republic they died to save. I pray that our heavenly Father may assuage the anguish of your bereavement, and leave you only the cherished memory of the loved and lost, and the solemn pride that must be yours to have laid so costly a sacrifice upon the altar of freedom.

The letter was copied by the Massachusetts adjutant general and sent to Boston newspapers, and it was soon in newspapers across the Union. It was widely reprinted in magazines and textbooks. It was subsequently learned that only two of Widow Bixby's sons had in fact been killed. One was a prisoner of war, and the other two had deserted.

Ney, Michel (1769–1815). A French soldier in French Revolutionary and Napoleonic armies. He enlisted in a hussar regiment in 1787 and four years later was a sergeant major. In 1792 he was commissioned, and by 1799 he was a general of division, commanding the army on the Rhine. In 1802 he commanded the French armies in Switzerland. The most loyal of Napoleon's subordinates, he was created one of the first of Napoleon's marshals in 1804. For his victory at Elchingen [q.v.] on 14 October 1805 he was created Duc d'Elchingen. He fought at Jena in 1806, Eylau and Friedland in 1807, in the Peninsular War from 1808 to 1811, and at Borodino in 1812 [qq.v.]. He was created Prince de la Moskova and commanded the rear guard in the retreat from Moscow. In 1813 he was engaged in the Battles of Lützen, Bautzen, and Leipzig [qq.v.]. In 1814 he took part in the campaign for the defense of France.

Upon the Bourbon restoration he swore allegiance to the king and was created a peer. When Napoleon returned from Elba, Ney vowed to capture him and carry him to Paris in an iron cage, but he soon changed his mind and rallied to him during the Hundred Days [q.v.]. He commanded in the Battle of Quatre Bras [q.v.], where he opposed and killed Frederick William, Duke of Brunswick (1771–1815), and he commanded the Old Guard in the Battle of Waterloo [q.v.] on 18 June 1815. After the second restoration Ney was tried for high treason by the Chamber of Peers, convicted on 4 December, and on 7 December 1815 shot to death in the Luxembourg Gardens. It was said that he reproved one of the firing squad for having an incorrectly buttoned uniform.

On 7 December 1853 a monument was raised on the spot where he fell. Three of his sons and two of his grandsons became French army officers.

Ney, Michel Aloys (1835–1881). A grandson of Marshal Michel Ney [q.v.] who became a soldier and served in Maximilian's [q.v.] army in Mexico in 1863 [see Mexico, French Invasion and Occupation of]. He was promoted general in 1875.

Ney, Napoleon Paul (1849–1900). A grandson of Marshal Michel Ney [q.v.] who served in the French colonial armies and during the Franco-Prussian War [q.v.] took part in the defense of Paris.

Nezib Battle of. See Nizib, Battle of.

Nez Percé War (June–October 1877). One of the last and the most extensive of the American Indian Wars was waged against the Nez Percé (Perce) Indians. It began on 13–14 June 1877, when three hotheaded young Nez Percé warriors, attempting to prove their manhood, killed several white settlers on the Salmon River near Whitebird, Idaho, about 20 miles southwest of Grangeville. On 17 June Captain David Perry (1841–1908), commanding Company F, 1st Cavalry, with 109 men, including some volunteers, retaliated by attacking the Nez Percé camp in Whitebird Canyon [q.v.]. The camp held 130 Indian warriors, but many were suffering from hangovers after drinking liquor looted from a local store and were hors de combat. Nevertheless, Perry's force was repulsed and suffered 40 casualties. In this first battle of the war no Nez Percés were killed, and only 3 or 4 were wounded. The band then retreated into the mountains, where they were joined by a band headed by Chief Looking Glass [q.v.].

On 3 July a detachment of 10 troopers under Lieutenant Sevier McClellan Rains (1850?–1877) was wiped out by Nez Percés near Craig's Mountain, Idaho. On 11–12 July troops under General O. O. Howard [q.v.] engaged the hostiles, now numbering about 300 warriors and 500 women and children, on the banks of the Clearwater River [q.v.] and lost 15 dead or mortally wounded and 25 wounded. Indian losses are unknown.

The surviving Indians moved down the Lolo Trail into Montana, then up the Bittersweet Valley, and on 6 August they crossed the Continental Divide. The following day they were on the shores of the Big Hole River, where, against the advice of other chiefs, Looking Glass decided to rest the weary band. At dawn on 9 August they were attacked by 191 men under Colonel John Gibbon [q.v.], but the troops were forced to fall back in the face of accurate rifle fire that killed 22 soldiers and 6 volunteers; 5 officers, 30 enlisted men, and 4 volunteers were wounded, 2 mortally. The Indians lost 89 killed, many of them women and children, and uncounted wounded [see Big Hole Basin, Montana, Battle of].

The surviving Nez Percés turned, recrossed the Continental Divide, and descended into the Lehmi River valley in Idaho. In their path frightened settlers formed militia companies and clustered in towns. They had reason to be fearful. Warriors plundered freight wagons, stole horses, and killed at least 10 whites they encountered. Ten separate army columns at different times attempted to find them, but they were pursued most closely by General Howard. On 22 August the Indians entered the newly declared (1872) Yellowstone Park. Plans laid to intercept them were thwarted by careful Nez Percé reconnaissance.

The band sacked the village of Coulson (Billings), Montana, and made for Canada. Again following the advice of Looking Glass, they slowed their pace, giving time for General Nelson Miles [q.v.] with a new force of mounted infantry and cavalry and two guns, plus some Cheyenne and Sioux allies, to get in front of them. By this time the Nez Percés had followed a circuitous route that had taken them about 1,700 miles. On 30 September they were only 40 miles from the Canadian border and camped between Bear Paw and Little Rocky Mountains when they were attacked by Miles's column. The troops suffered a loss of 22 killed and 38 wounded and were forced to draw back [see Battle of Bear Paw Mountain]. Miles then laid siege to the Indians. On 1 October he called for a parlay, during which Chief Joseph [q.v.], who met with him on behalf of the band, was treacherously seized by Miles, who mistakenly believed that he was the war chief. The Nez Percés in turn immediately seized an army lieutenant, and Miles was forced to release his hostage. From 1 October to 5 October there was only desultory firing. Whites and Indians alike suffered from the cold and the five inches of snow that fell on them. On 5 October Miles joined Howard, and the Indians decided to make a run for Canada, but before the move could be made, Looking Glass was killed by a bullet in his forehead. In a meeting arranged with Miles and Howard, Joseph was promised by Miles that in return for a cessation of hostilities the band could spend the winter on the Yellowstone and in the spring return unharmed to the reservation in Idaho. Joseph accepted the terms with the words "I am tired of fighting. Our chiefs are killed . . . the old men are all dead. It is the young men who say yes and no. . . . It is cold and we have no blankets. The little children are freezing to death. . . . Hear me, my chiefs! I am tired. My heart is sick and sad. From where the sun now stands I will fight no more forever."

About 400 surrendered, but 98 warriors with about 200 women and children who did not surrender managed to reach the camp of Sitting Bull [q.v.] in Canada.

In spite of the promises of General Miles, the Nez Percés were sent to a reservation in Oklahoma, where many fell ill and died. In 1883, 33 women and children were allowed to return to their homeland in Idaho and 118 others were permitted to return in 1885. Chief Joseph was not among them.

Ngqika (1778–1829). A Xhosa chief, father of Sandile [q.v.], who at age seventeen led a successful war party against the amaGcalekas which captured the young Hintsa [q.v.].

Niagara / Niagara Falls, Battle of. See Lundy's Lane, Battle of.

Nicaragua, British Occupation of (1895). On 15 March 1895 Great Britain demanded £15,500 as reparations for damage to the property of British subjects during the 1893 Nicaraguan Insurrection [q.v.]. When President José Zelaya [q.v.] refused to accede and proposed an impartial arbitration, Britain dispatched three warships, which arrived at Corinto on 22 April. Two days later Zelaya was informed that the reparation must be paid within three days. When their terms were again refused, the British occupied Corinto unopposed on 26 April and the following day installed a navy captain as governor. In response Zelaya declared the republic under martial law. However, the indemnity was paid, and the British evacuated the country on 4 May.

Nicaraguan Insurrections (1893 and 1897–98). On 11 May 1893 Nicaraguan rebel forces led by José Zelaya [q.v.] captured Fort San Carlos and Fort Castillo and were joined by former President Adam Cardenas (d. 1899). On 20 May they defeated government forces, and negotiations for peace were begun. A new government was formed on 30 May, and on 6 June the revolutionists entered Managua. The port of Corinto fell to the rebels in July, and Zelaya became president. He ruled until 1909.

One of Zelaya's first acts was to seize Mosquitia, an autonomous Indian reserve on the Caribbean coast. In February 1897, in response to a revolt in the northwestern part of the country and after the occupation of the port of Corinto by the British [See Nicaragua, British Occupation of], Zelaya declared himself dictator and took the field, defeating the rebels at Mateare and Nargote. In March he defeated rebel forces at Matapa and Mora. On 8 February 1898 the rebels were again defeated at Rivas, but the country remained unsettled until the rebel leaders surrendered to British and American naval officers. [See Walker, William; Nicaragua, British Occupation of.]

Nicholas, Grand Duke (1831–1891). Russian: Nikolai Nikolaevich. The third son of Tsar Nicholas I [q.v.], he commanded the Army of the Danube in the Russo-Turkish War of 1877–78 [q.v.].

Nez Percé War *Surrender of Chief Joseph, 5 October 1877*

Nicholas I (1796–1855). Russian: Nikolai Pavlovich. Tsar of Russia who succeeded to the throne in 1825 and at once put down a mutiny with vigor and cruelty [see Decembrist Uprising]. He quelled a revolution in Poland in 1830–31 and aided Austria in suppressing the Hungarian Revolution of 1848 [qq.v.]. His designs upon Constantinople (Istanbul) provoked a war with Turkey in 1853 into which other European powers were drawn [see Crimean War].

Nicholas Military Academy. The Russian military college established by Nicholas I [q.v.]. In 1855 it was renamed the Nicholas Academy of the General Staff.

Nicholson, John (1821–1857). A British soldier who at seventeen was commissioned an ensign in the Bengal Native Infantry and took part in the First Afghan War [q.v.] of 1839–42, in which he was captured at Ghazni but escaped. He fought in the First Sikh War [q.v.] and then served as an instructor to the troops of the maharajah of Kashmir. In 1848, shortly after his promotion to captain, he suppressed a rebellion and a mutiny of troops in Simalkand, and was wounded in one of the skirmishes. He took an active part in

Tsar Nicholas I, 1840

the Second Sikh War [q.v.] and was brevetted major. After leave in Europe, he was appointed administrator of Bannú on the south-central Northwest Frontier, a land of bloodthirsty people whom he reduced to law-abiding subjects, inspiring in them such respect that in 1848 a band of fakirs began to worship him as a demi-god, Nikkul Seyn. Although Nicholson ordered his devotees flogged and imprisoned, the cult persisted until 1858; the last of the original believers dug his own grave and died in Hazara.

Nicholson was a lieutenant colonel when the Indian Mutiny [q.v.] broke out in May 1857. He was quickly appointed brigadier general and given charge of a movable column. After attacking mutinous troops in the Punjab and disarming those thought to be on the verge of mutiny, he marched his column to Delhi to join the besiegers. Fighting along the way, he arrived on 14 August. On 14 September, while leading an attack upon Delhi, he was shot in the chest. He died in agony eight days later. The Honourable East India Company awarded his mother a pension of £500 per annum.

Nicholson's Nek, Battle of (30 October 1899). Second Anglo-Boer War. Sometimes called the Battle of Farquhar's Farm. A battle fought near Ladysmith in Natal, South Africa, in which a British force under General Sir George White, VC [q.v.], was defeated by a Boer Force under Christiaan De Wet [q.v.]. The British lost 317 killed and 1,068 missing, including 850 taken prisoner; Boer losses were slight.

Nickerson, Azor Howitt (1837–1910). An American soldier who in 1861, at the beginning of the American Civil War, was commissioned a second lieutenant in the 8th Ohio. He rose to the rank of captain and won a brevet to major for his gallantry in the battles of Antietam and Gettysburg [qq.v.]. He was wounded in battle four times and at Gettysburg was so severely wounded that he was left for dead. After the war he served as a lieutenant in the 14th Infantry, rising to the rank of major in 1878. He served on the staff of General George Crook [q.v.] for ten years and saw much action against Indians in the Far West.

His first wife died, and he remarried in 1870. In 1882, while his second wife was out of the country, he tried to divorce her in order to marry a third time, but she returned to contest the divorce, and there was a national scandal. In 1883 he resigned from the army and fled to Canada, where, when his divorce was finally granted, he married the third woman and disappeared from history.

Nicks, Sally (fl. 1830s–1840s). After her sutler husband, John Nicks, died on New Year's Day 1832 at Fort Gibson, Oklahoma, Sally Nicks took over his business and made a success of it, becoming the first woman sutler in the American regular army. Washington Irving (1783–1859) described her as a "plump, buxom dame" who, as a result of having acquired a small fortune, became "the object of desires of all the men."

Nieh Shih-chéng (d. 1900). A Chinese general who took action against Boxer guerrillas, capturing and killing large numbers in spite of opposition from pro-Boxer elements in the imperial court, but at Tang Ts'u [q.v.] on 26 June 1900 he repulsed the first attempts of a 2,000-man international force under British Admiral Edward Hobart Seymour (1840–1899) to relieve the foreign legations besieged in Peking (Beijing).

He was killed soon after in the fighting around Peking. [See Boxer Rebellion.]

Niel, Adolphe (1802–1869). A French soldier who distinguished himself in the storming of Constantine in Algeria [see Constantine, Sieges of] and in the Crimean War [q.v.], especially in the siege of Sevastopol [q.v.] in 1855. He became an aide-de-camp of Napoleon III (1808–1873) and fought at Magenta and Solferino [qq.v.]. In 1859 he became a marshal of France. From 1867 to 1869 he was minister of war.

Nien Rebellion (1851–68). A Chinese social upheaval that was the result of a series of natural disasters and the inefficiencies of a weak and corrupt central government.

It began in the north and central plain along the Hwei River (Hwei Ho or Hui Ho or Huai Ho) and the lower valley of the Yellow River (Hwang Ho) and in the border region of Shantung, Hunan, Anhwei, and Chihli. When repeated flooding of the Yellow River created famine among those living in its valley, many of the young men joined gangs of outlaws that for decades had ravaged the provinces of Shantung, Hunan, and northern Anhwei. Because the Manchu government, preoccupied by the Taiping Revolution in the south and with the Second Opium War [qq.v.], was unable to provide effective protection, communities sought to protect themselves by building earth walls and forming protective alliances with other earth wall communities. Bands, which came to be called Nien, first emerged from such towns as local defense forces. By the 1850s they had become a regional power with their heartland in the area between the Shara and Hwei rivers and were in open rebellion against the imperial government.

The word *nien* denoted twisted paper slips that were dipped in oil and set on fire as torches; why this curious name was adopted is obscure, although perhaps the symbol of the flame explains the reason members dyed their beards red. The movement itself is believed to have had its roots in the Red-Beard Bandits and the White Lotus Society [q.v.].

The numerous Nien bands, numbering from a dozen men to several thousand each, were scattered and led by family or clan leaders, but after the Taipings captured Anking [q.v.] in February 1853, Nien activity increased, and the banner of rebellion was formally raised when the most powerful of the Nien leaders met and formed the League of the Great Han (Ta Han meng-chu). They swore allegiance to Chang Lo-hsing [q.v.], the best of the Nien leaders. They organized under five major units, termed banners, that were known by the color of their flags—red, white, black, yellow, and blue—each led by commanders called lords (*ch'i-chu*). Each banner was in turn subdivided into units bearing a smaller version of its flag with a different colored border. These were led by vice lords (*fu-ch'i-chu*). Chang Lo-hsing, given the name Great Han Prince with the Heavenly Mandate, commanded the yellow banner personally, yellow being a royal color. The Nien initially made their headquarters at Wuyang, south of the Hwei River.

As the number of Nien increased, their organization became more sophisticated, but remained fluid. There were three types of units: banners (*ch'i*), large units for campaigning; forts or walled communities (*yü*) (the word *yü* originally meant an embankment or dike to protect rice paddies); and bands (*ku*), which were primarily local defense units, but they supplied detachments to make up banners.

From about 1855 to 1857 the Nien allied themselves with the Taipings [see Taiping Rebellion], and by 1858 Chang was said to command 100,000 men. But the nature of the Nien organization prevented any effective cooperation with others. With no dynastic aspirations, they never remained in the areas the bands had overrun. Their armies usually sallied forth for loot, mostly in the form of grain and horses, which they brought back to their earth wall communities and later in the era to starving people in border areas. Although they were accused of forcing men to join them, they had no need to compel or threaten as long as they could afford to feed them, and from the beginning the Nien paid close attention to their food supply. It was Nien policy to store enough of plundered foodstuffs to supply both old and new adherents. Eventually the Nien overran eight provinces holding more than 100 million people, raiding twice each year in the spring and autumn for fifteen years. Because most Nien were farmers, the movement never abandoned its agricultural base and initially never raided during the harvest season.

The Nien often enjoyed wide popular support in large part because the lawless behavior of the imperial government troops embittered the people. The Nien robbed, but not as thoroughly or as brutally as the government soldiers. Because of the weakness of the central government and its inability to protect the people from bandits or rebels, provincial armies sprang up. The best of these was the Hunan army, sometimes called the Hunan Braves, led by Tsêng Kuo-fan [q.v.], the ablest general of the provincial armies. He reported that the people in the earth wall communities in Hunan, Shantung, and north Anhwei "hated the government soldiers, considering them deadly foes."

About 1862 the imperial government began to devote some attention to the Nien in the troubled north. Initially the imperial armies sent against them were not entirely successful, although Chang was captured and executed. A favorite tactic of the fast-moving Nien, particularly after 1856, when their cavalry became formidable, was to allow an imperial army to chase them as they moved in a seemingly random pattern until the government troops, slowed by carrying cannon and wagon trains of impedimenta, were worn down. The Nien would then choose a good defensive position from which to fight or would turn and attack their weakened pursuers. It was in this fashion that in May 1865 they defeated and killed the Manchu prince San-ko-lin-ch'in [q.v.], the best imperial general. In the later years of the rebellion the Nien were always on the move and, unlike the Taipings, did not try to defend particular cities or areas. General Tsêng listed as a weakness of the Nien that they used too many donkeys and mules to carry their families and provisions.

After San-ko-lin-ch'in's death the task of suppressing the Nien was given to Tsêng Kuo-fan. When he failed, he was relieved of his command. Li Hung Chan [q.v.], who succeeded him, also failed. In all, twenty Chinese officials campaigned against the insurgents. In 1863 Tsêng again took the field. He instituted a two-pronged policy, political and military, that enjoyed some success. He laid down the plan that was eventually successful.

Previous imperial commanders had regarded the Nien as merely roving bandits, calling them *Nien fei*. Tsêng recognized that while they had devastated land and property around their area, they had a deep attachment to their "nests," which provided all the comforts of home. He did not try to destroy their earth wall communities but tried to convert the chiefs and people of the Nien nests into loyalist supporters, thus detaching the followers from their leaders. He succeeded in large part. He also attempted to curb the roving Nien forces with stationary armies and to encourage the strengthening provincial armies in areas traditionally ravaged by the Nien. Firearms had been little used, but in 1865 the Hwei army imported 30,000 to 40,000 rifles as well as European instructors to teach their use. Four batteries of artillery were also formed, and more cavalry was used. In 1868 the Nien were finally crushed, and the earth wall communities brought under government control.

On 27 August 1868 sacrifices were offered in the ancestral temples and in the temple of the god of war to mark the end of this seventeen-year rebellion which had afflicted eight provinces. Civil and military casualties have been estimated at four million. [See Chinese Civil Wars; Panthay Rebellion; Muslim Rebellion in South China; Chinese Turkestan.]

Nigerian Uprising (1895). Repressive measures by the British Royal Niger Company led on 27–28 January 1895 to an uprising of West African tribes near Brass, then an important trading center on the Brass River, a channel of the Niger Delta. A number of Christians, black and white, were killed at nearby Akasa. Sir Claude Macdonald [q.v.] managed to hold Brass until reinforcements arrived in early February and the uprising was suppressed, but Brass was not reopened for trade until 25 April.

Nigerian Uprising *Mounted Bornu warrior from northern Nigeria, late nineteenth century*

Nigerite. See Cafard.

Night Attack. Although a few nineteenth-century battles, like the Battle of Lundy's Lane and the Battle of Cedar Mountain, lasted until after nightfall, almost all were fought in daylight, the reason being, as Thucydides wrote, "In a night engagement who could be certain of anything?" Major General Karl von Clausewitz [q.v.] in 1832 noted that

schemes for night attacks were "put forward by those who have neither to lead them nor accept responsibility for them. In practice they are very rare." However, General Garnet Wolseley made a successful night approach march to attack at Tell el-Kebir [q.v.], the columns advancing on the objective being led by naval officers with compasses.

Nightingale, Florence (1820–1910). An English nurse, hospital reformer, and philanthropist who was born of prominent and wealthy parents. From childhood she showed an interest in tending the sick. As a young woman, looking for a more active life than was usual for women of her class, she began visiting hospitals in England and abroad. In 1851 she went through the four-month course of nurses' training in the Kaiserwerth Institute near Düsseldorf. On 12 August 1853 she accepted the post of superintendent of the Hospital for Invalid Gentlewomen founded in London in 1850. In 1854, stirred by newspaper accounts of the Crimean War and the sufferings of the sick and wounded, she accepted the proposal of her friend Sidney Herbert [q.v.], secretary of state for war, that she supervise the hospitals of Scutari (Üsküdar), Turkey. Moving expeditiously, she was ready to embark with thirty-eight handpicked nurses within a week. With the official title of Superintendent of the Female Nurses in the Hospitals of the East, she installed her headquarters in the Scutari barrack hospital near Constantinople (Istanbul), where she found patients covered with vermin and lying in filth. Working under the most difficult conditions and resented by medical and military authorities, she and her nurses within a year managed to bring cleanliness to the wards and order to the administration. In 1855, when typhus and cholera raged through the hospital, her constant appeals to the War Office for improved sanitation moved it to order the Scutari Sanitary Commission to carry out reforms. Thanks largely to her efforts, deaths from cholera, dysentery, and typhus fell from about 50 to 2 percent. Because she permitted no other nurse than herself on the wards at night, when they were manned by orderlies, she became known among her patients as "the lady with the lamp."

Although peace was declared in March 1856, she remained until the last hospital was closed. It was August before she slipped quietly into England, avoiding the fanfare and adulation awaiting her. Queen Victoria sent her a brooch designed by the prince consort, and by 1860 the Nightingale Fund for founding a training school for nurses had reached £50,000, and the Nightingale School and Home for Nurses was established, the only official recognition to which she would consent.

Although weakened health caused her to lead a retired life, she threw herself into her work, writing confidential reports on army medical conditions and publishing papers and books. Her *Notes on Nursing*, published in 1860, went through numerous editions. In 1863 the government submitted to her a report on the sanitary state of the army in India, and she turned her attention to that country, pressing for sanitary reform, publishing papers and pamphlets on such subjects as native education, irrigation, and famine. Her parliamentary testimony, aggressive and skilled political operations, and numerous writings led to the formation of an army medical school and hospital, improved standards and pay for medical officers, official attention to hygiene in barracks, recreational outlets other than that provided by prostitutes, and an increased public awareness of the needs of the rank and file.

Nightingale, Florence *An improved ward in the Barrack Hospital, after the arrival of Florence Nightingale.*

Miss Nightingale was the first woman to receive the Order of Merit and the second to be given the freedom of the City of London. Among her foreign honors were the French gold medal of Secours aux Blessés Militaires, the badge of honor of the Norwegian Red Cross society, and the German order of the Cross of Merit.

She died at the age of ninety and by her wish was not buried in Westminster Abbey, as had been offered, but in her family burial plot. She was carried to her grave by six army sargeants. In 1858 American poet Henry Wadsworth Longfellow (1807–1882) had memorialized her in a poem, "Santa Filomena":

A Lady with a Lamp shall stand
In the great history of the land,
A noble type of good,
Heroic womanhood.

Nikko, Battle of (May 1868), Japanese Civil War. At this mountain town (altitude 2,000 feet) in Honshu, 7 miles east of Lake Chuzenji, followers of the shogun under Otori Keisuke were defeated by the army of Saigo Takamori [q.v.] and fled to Wakamatsu Castle in north-central Honshu. The town now stands in the middle of Nikko National Park (Nikko Kokuritsu), which covers 543 square miles.

Nikopoli / Nicopolis, Battle of (14–16 June 1877), Russo-Turkish War of 1877–78. The Russian IX Army Corps under General Nikolai Krüdner captured this town, now in Bulgaria, on the south bank of the Danube 24 miles north-northeast of Plevna, after a two-day bombardment. The 7,000 Turks holding the town surrendered; the Russians lost 1,300 in killed and wounded. The battle was a prelude to the siege of Plevna [q.v.].

Niksich, Capture of (7–8 September 1877), Montenegrin rebellion. This strong Turkish fortress in Montenegro had often withstood sieges, but undermanned by the Turks, it was captured by rebellious Montenegrins. [See Turko-Montenegrin Wars.]

Nile Expedition. See Sudan, Reconquest of.

Nimcha. An Arab saber used mostly in Morocco. The blade was usually curved slightly and was wider than most saber blades. The grip was often made of a single piece of buffalo or rhinoceros horn, although sometimes of a hard wood.

Ninety-Day Regiments. In 1861, at the beginning of the American Civil War, Abraham Lincoln called for 75,000 men to suppress "the insurrection." Volunteer regiments were formed, and men enlisted for only ninety days. Such units were called ninety-day regiments.

Ningpo, Battle of (10 May 1862), Taiping Rebellion. A force of British and French, together with the Foreign Rifle Corps—later called the Ever Victorious Army [q.v.]—under Frederick T. Ward [q.v.] attacked and defeated the Taiping rebels at this port city (now Ninghsien) for a loss of 200. The Taipings lost about 1,000. In August, under the Treaty of Nanking (Nanjing or Nanxiang), Ningpo was made a treaty port.

Niños Perdidos, Los. Also referred to as *Los Niños Heroicos*. At the time of the Mexican War [q.v.] the Mexican military academy was located in the Castle of Chapultepec, then just outside Mexico City. When the castle was stormed by the Americans on 13 September 1847, the cadets fought beside the Mexican regulars [see Chapultepec, Battle of]. Stories of their bravery abound. Six died rather than surrender, and one is said to have leaped from the walls with his body draped in the Mexican flag.

Nishi Kanjiro (1846–1912). A Japanese soldier who fought with distinction in the Boshin Civil War, the Satsuma Rebellion, and the Sino-Japanese War [qq.v.]. He later fought as a general in the Russo-Japanese War.

Nitrate War. See War of the Pacific.

Nitrocellulose. A explosive used in the manufacture of smokeless propellants. [See Guncotton.]

Niños Perdidos, Los *Battle of Chapultepec, Los Niños Perdidos*

Nitroglycerin. An explosive and poisonous liquid—$C_3H_5[ONO_2]_3$—made by nitrating glycerol. It was used in making dynamite. It was discovered in 1847 by Ascanio Sobrero (1812–1888), an Italian chemist, who named it *pyroglycérine*.

Nive, Battle of the (9-13 December 1813), Peninsular War. After pushing the French out of Spain and crossing the Pyrenees and after forcing the Nivelle [q.v.], Wellington with 64,000 men was faced by 63,000 French under Marshal Nicolas Soult [q.v.] in strong positions along the Nive River. On 9 December 1813 General Sir Rowland Hill [q.v.] led five divisions across the Nive while the rest of the Allied army made distracting demonstrations and feints elsewhere. On 10 December Soult launched a surprise attack upon Hill, and there was a desperate battle until British reinforcements arrived; Soult continued intermittent attacks over the following days. Each side lost about 1,600 men.

Nivelle, Battle of the (10 November 1813), Peninsular War. After his defeat at the Bidassoa River on 7 October 1813, French Marshal Soult [q.v.] with about 62,000 men fell back across the Pyrenees into southwestern France, 82,000 Allied infantry under Wellington at his heels. A new French defensive line was established from St. Jean de Luz on the Bay of Biscay to St. Jean Pied de Port in the interior. Soult placed a third of his force on the coast, where an attack was most expected, but Wellington decided to straddle the Nivelle River

and proceed up its valley, overcoming French strongpoints. The French lost 4,265 men, including about 1,200 taken prisoner, and 51 guns; the Allies suffered 2,694 killed and wounded.

Nizib / Nezib, Battle of (24 June 1839), Turko-Egyptian War. An Egyptian army under Ibrahim Pasha al-Wali, a son of Mehemet Ali [qq.v.], defeated a Turkish army of 30,000 under Hafiz Pasha at this place (now Nizip) in southern Turkey, 22 miles east of Aintab. Ibrahim had the most artillery, and its fire so demoralized the Turks that they fled when the infantry charged.

Nobel, Alfred (1833–1896). A Swedish manufacturer and inventor who was educated in St. Petersburg and in the United States, where he studied mechanical engineering. In 1866 he invented dynamite, and in 1888 ballistite, one of the first smokeless powders. In his lifetime he received patents for more than 100 inventions, including a wide range of explosive compounds and devices. He acquired immense wealth through the manufacture in various parts of the world of dynamite and other explosives and through his interests in the Baku oilfields in Russia. He bequeathed $9,200,000 for Nobel prizes in a variety of fields, including a Peace Prize, the first of which was awarded in 1901 to Jean Henri Dunant [q.v.], who inspired the founding of the International Red Cross [q.v.] and Frédéric Passy (1822–1912), who in 1867 founded the International Peace League.

No-Dachi. An enormous Japanese sword, sometimes six feet long, which could be wielded only by exceptionally strong soldiers.

Nodzu, Michitsura. See Nozu / Nodzu, Michitsura.

Nogi, Maresuke (1849–1912). A Japanese soldier who was born the son of a Choshu samurai. During the Satsuma Rebellion [q.v.] his regiment lost its battle standard, and he was restrained from killing himself only by a direct order from his superior. Years of drunkenness and debauchery followed as he brooded on his future, but his spirits revived after a tour of duty in Germany in 1887, and in the Sino-Japanese War of 1894–95 [q.v.] he commanded a brigade in the battles of Kinchow and Port Arthur [q.v.]. He subsequently distinguished himself in the Russo-Japanese War, in which he lost both sons. He and his wife committed hara-kiri on 30 July 1912 upon the death of Emperor Meiji (1859–1912). His house in Tokyo is now the Nogi Shrine and is visited by thousands each year.

Nogi, long considered the embodiment of the traditional bushido standards of the samurai [q.v.], served as an inspiration to the kamikaze pilots of the Second World War.

Noisseville, Battle of (31 August–1 September 1870), Franco-Prussian War. The French army under General Achille Bazaine [q.v.], besieged at Metz [q.v.], attempted to break out but was checked in this battle about three miles east of Metz by Prussians under Prince Frederick Charles [q.v.] and forced back into the city. The following day the attempt to break out was renewed and again failed. In all, the French lost 145 officers and 3,379 other ranks; the Prussians 126 officers and 2,850 other ranks.

On 27 October Metz capitulated.

Noncombatants. Civilians who take no part in a war. The distinction between combatants and noncombatants was seldom clear-cut in the case of nurses, surgeons, chaplains, vivandiers, sutlers, and others who served armies but did not fight. [See Hague Convention.] Noncombatants snug at home were often accused of harboring more rancor against the enemy than combatants felt. Poet Arthur Rimbaud (1854–1891) once spoke of "the notable ferocity of noncombatants," and journalist Charles Edward Montague (1867–1928) noted that "Hell hath no fury like a noncombatant."

Noncommissioned officer. French: *sous-officiers;* German: *Vinter-offizieren* or *Unter-offizieren*. A soldier holding a rank below a commissioned officer and above a private. Often abbreviated in American usage as NCO. "But the backbone of the Army is the non-commissioned man!" Rudyard Kipling wrote ("The 'Eathen" [1896]). "Baron" Friedrich von Steuben (1730–1794), who prepared *Regulations for the Order and Discipline of the Troops of the United States Army* (1779), the so-called *Blue Book*, wrote: "The choice of non-commissioned officers is an object of the greatest importance: the order and discipline of a regiment depends so much upon their behaviour that too much care cannot be taken in preferring none to that trust but those who by their merit and good conduct are entitled to it. Honesty, sobriety and a remarkable attention to every point of duty, with a neatness in their dress, are indispensable requisites." [See Sergeant; Corporal.]

Noneffectives. Men unfit or otherwise unavailable for duty.

No Quarter. A command specifying that no prisoners of war were to be taken; those captured to be slain. Such an order was sometimes given when it was inconvenient to handle prisoners or when they might be a threat in the rear of a fighting force. [See Black Flag; Cry Havoc.]

Nordenfelt Breechblock. An eccentric screw type of breechblock that was a feature of the French 75 [q.v.].

Nordenfelt Machine Gun. A gun invented in 1879 by a Swedish engineer, Helge Palmkrantz. It held from two to twelve barrels which fired in volley when a lever was pushed back and forth, loading and firing all barrels [see Machine Gun]. It was named after Torsten Wilhelm Nordenfelt (1842–1920), the Swedish banker who financed Palmkrantz and established the Nordenfelt Gun and Ammunition Company with factories in Sweden, Britain, and Spain.

Nordenfelt machine gun

Norman, Henry Wylie (1826–1904). A British soldier who first saw action in the Second Sikh War [q.v.]. In 1857 in the Indian Mutiny he served at the siege of Delhi, the relief of Lucknow, and the capture of Cawnpore [qq.v.]. From 1862 to 1870 he was first secretary to the Indian government in the Military Department, and from 1878 to 1883 he was a member of the consul in India. He was later governor of Jamaica (1883–89) and governor of Queensland, Australia (1889–95). He was promoted field marshal in 1902.

Norman Cross Prison. The informal name for the British Depot for Prisoners of War at Cross, built in 1797. It held as many as 7,000 prisoners, mostly French, until the survivors were sent back to the Continent in 1814 after Napoleon's first abdication. It was demolished in 1816.

A group of several hundred prisoners was aptly known as *les Misérables*. Having gambled away all their possessions, even their clothes and future rations, they lived in total nakedness, begging from other prisoners and raking through garbage. About 1,770 died in this prison.

North Anna River, Battle of the (23–27 May 1864), American Civil War. Also known as Mills's Ford, Mill's Bridge, Hanover Junction, Jericho Mills, and Taylor's Bridge. Union troops under General U. S. Grant attacking Confederate entrenchments along the North Anna River held by General Robert E. Lee were repulsed for a loss of 642. Grant withdrew on the night of 26–27 May. The next major engagement took place at Cold Harbor [q.v.] on 31 May–3 June.

North Carolina Expedition (February–July 1862), American Civil War. A military expedition organized by Union General Ambrose Burnside [q.v.] to make an amphibious landing on the North Carolina coast with naval support from Admiral Louis Malesherbes Goldsborough (1805–1864). The armada of nineteen warships, a flag steamer, and sixty-five troopships entered Pimlico Sound and on the morning of 7 February 1862 approached Roanoke Island. Troops and sailors landed at Ashby's Harbor and on 8 February defeated a Confederate force, which lost 149 killed and wounded and 2,500 taken prisoners for a loss of 278 Union soldiers and sailors.

Leaving a garrison on Roanoke Island, Butler attacked New Bern [q.v.], which he captured on 14 March, suffering a loss of 471 to the Confederates' 578. On 11 April he laid siege to Beaufort, which he took on the 26th. Norfolk and Suffolk in Virginia were threatened, but the attack was aborted on 3 July, when Burnside with 7,500 men was ordered to Fort Monroe to reinforce McClellan.

Northern Rhodesia Regiment. A British regiment formed in 1894 by Harry Johnston (1858–1927), a British explorer and administrator, from 200 Sikh volunteers from the Indian army, 40 Zanzibaris, 40 Arabs, 69 Makuas from Mozambique, and other Africans from a number of tribes. The regiment was used to combat slave traders in Nyasaland (Malawi).

Northern Virginia, Army of. A Confederate army under General Robert E. Lee that opposed the Union Army of the Potomac [q.v.] and, briefly, the Army of Virginia under John Pope [q.v.]. Its name dates from 1 June 1862, when Lee assumed command in Virginia after the wounding of General Joseph Johnston [q.v.]. During the Peninsular Campaign [q.v.] it consisted of eleven infantry divisions, a cavalry brigade of eleven regiments under J. E. B. Stuart [q.v.], and six brigades of artillery. The principal infantry commandeers were James Longstreet and Thomas ("Stonewall") Jackson [qq.v.]. After the Battle of Antietam [q.v.] the army was divided into two corps commanded by Jackson and Longstreet, all artillery was assigned to divisions except for some corps reserve, and Stuart's cavalry was formed into a corps of two divisions. A fourth corps was formed in late 1864 under General Richard Anderson [q.v.].

Northrop, Lucius Bellinger (1811–1894). An American soldier who entered West Point in 1827, two months before his sixteenth birthday, and graduated second in his class in 1831. He served on the western frontier and in the Second Seminole War [q.v.], in which he was severely wounded. He was placed on permanent sick furlough and studied to become a doctor. During the American Civil War he resigned his commission to become commissory general of the Confederate army. A contentious man, he quarreled with Pierre Beauregard, whom he called a charlatan, and with Joseph Johnston [qq.v.], whom he called a liar. General Thomas Jordan (1819–1895), Beauregard's assistant adjutant general, regarded Northrop as "so eccentric and full of mental crotchets as to be . . . of unsound intellect and unfit for the management of his own small affairs." President Jefferson Davis [q.v.] appointed him a brigadier general on 26 November 1864, but the appointment was not confirmed by the Confederate Senate. In June 1865 he was arrested on charges of having deliberately starved prisoners of war, but he was released in October. He spent the remaining years of his life on a farm near Charlottesville, Virginia.

Northwest Frontier. The barren, mountainous area (Safed Koh range and Hindu Kush) in nineteenth-century India (today in Pakistan) that borders Afghanistan. It was the site of numerous British battles with Pushtu-speaking Pathan tribesmen who lived in an area about 400 miles long and 100 miles wide and acknowledged no laws but their own. A British administrator described them as "men of predatory habits, careless and impatient of control." The Afridi tribe, about 30,000 people with its numerous clans, was the largest and most turbulent. The Mahsud clan of the Wazir tribe was officially recognized as "the earliest, most inveterate and most incorrigible of all the robbers of the border."

Britain tried to control the important passes, such as the Khyber and Bolan, by building forts, bribing tribal leaders, and enlisting local tribesmen into irregular units. There were forty-two major campaigns involving British soldiers on the frontier from 1847 until the end of the century. [See Punjab Field Force; Pathan Rebellion; Khyber Rifles; Malakand Field Force; Punjab Frontier Force; Punjab Irregular Force; Tirah Expedition.]

Northwest Insurrection. See Riel's Rebellion.

Norway, Swedish Invasion of (1814). By the Treaty of Kiel, signed by Britain, Sweden, and Denmark on 14 January 1814, Norway was given to Sweden. The disposal was unpopular in Norway, and on 17 May the Norwegians declared their independence. On 16 July Swedish troops under Jean Baptiste Bernadotte [q.v.], then the crown prince of Sweden, invaded Norway. On 10 October Charles Frederic, Duke of Holstein (1768–1839), who had been elected king of Norway, abdicated. On 4 November, King Charles XIII (1748–1818) of Sweden was proclaimed king by the Storting. He accepted the constitution that declared Norway a "free,

independent, indivisible and inalienable state, united to Sweden." Perhaps one must be a Scandinavian to understand this. Norway did not really become completely independent until 1905.

Norwich College. Founded in 1819 at Norwich, Vermont, by Alden Partridge [q.v.], it was the first private military college in the United States. In 1898 the state of Vermont named the school the Military College of Vermont. It is now Norwich University in Northfield, Vermont.

Nose Warmers. Colloquial name for the short-stemmed clay pipes smoked by British soldiers.

Nossi Bé, Capture of. See Madagascar, Warfare in.

Nostalgia. A longing to return home, sometimes called homesickness. It may take extreme forms, and a soldier suffering from it may refuse to eat and lose interest in his health. The phenomenon was identified and named in the seventeenth century.

Nott, William (1782–1845). A British soldier who was the son of a farmer and innkeeper. In 1800 he obtained a cadetship in the Bengal army. On his way to India his ship was captured by a French privateer. Not wanting to be bothered by prisoners, the French transferred him and the other British passengers to a small Arab vessel that carried them to India. On 28 August 1800 he was made an ensign. In 1801 he was promoted lieutenant, and in 1804 he took part in an expedition against tribes on the west coast of Sumatra. On 16 December 1815 he was promoted captain. Seven years later he was promoted major, and an augmentation of the army gave him a lieutenant colonelcy. In the following year he took command of the 20th Bengal Infantry.

In 1838, at the beginning of the First Afghan War [q.v.], he was promoted major general. Soon after, his wife, who had borne him fourteen children, died. He commanded at Quetta and Kandahar and later marched on Ghazni and Kabul, being one of the few senior commanders in that war to distinguish himself. He was given a sword of honor, the Thanks of Parliament, and appointed Resident at Lucknow with the title of envoy to the king of Oude. He was unable to occupy his office for long; ill health forced him to return to England, where he died.

Novara, Battles of. Two nineteenth-century battles were fought near this Piedmontese town, 28 miles west of Milan between the Agogna and Terdoppio rivers.

First Battle of Novara (8 April 1821), Piedmontese Revolt of 1821. A combined royalist Austro-Sardinian army under Prince Carlo Felix (1765–1831) defeated a Piedmontese army under Carlo Alberto [q.v.].

Second Battle of Novara (23 March 1849), Italian Wars of Independence. Seven months after the armistice with Austria on 12 March 1849 Prince Carlo Alberto [q.v.] of Sardinia, often called Charles Albert, renounced the agreement. The veteran Austrian commander in Lombardy Field Marshal Josef Radetzky [q.v.] promptly seized Mortara and prepared to deal with the larger Piedmontese army at Novara. There, on 23 March, for the second time in eight months, the Piedmontese under Carlo Alberto were overwhelmed by the more disciplined Austrians and driven from the field in disorder. The battle lasted from midmorning until late in the evening. Alberto was able to bring only a part of his 100,000-man army onto the field to face 70,000 Austrians. The Austrians lost 396 killed and about 1,850 wounded; the Piedmontese lost more than 3,000 killed and wounded, about 3,000 more were taken prisoner, and 27 cannon were captured. This defeat led to Carlo Alberto's abdication and ultimately to a peace treaty by which the Austrians received a large indemnity.

Novelty Works. See Memphis Novelty Works.

Noxious Effluvia. A medical term for the odors of a camp that were believed to cause sickness.

Nozu / Nodzu, Michitsura (1841–1907). A Japanese soldier who took part in the Boshin Civil War [q.v.] and in 1871 was commissioned a major in the new imperial army. During the Satsuma Rebellion [q.v.] he served as chief of staff in an infantry brigade. In the years before the Sino-Japanese War [q.v.] he traveled in Europe and the United States. During the war he commanded a division and on 15 September 1894 played a major role in the Battle of Pyongyang [q.v.] (the city, then in China and called Heijo, is now the capital of North Korea). In December of that year he took command of the First Army when Marshal Aritomo Yamagata [q.v.] fell ill. Soon after he was promoted general. He played a major role in the Russo-Japanese War of 1904–05, commanding the Fourth Army, and was promoted field marshal.

Nueces River, Affair at the (10 August 1861), American Civil War. Large settlements of German immigrants in central Texas were pro-Union and antislavery, and on the outbreak of the American Civil War they organized themselves into the Union Loyal League [q.v.]. Confederate Brigadier General Paul Octave Hébert (1818–1880), commanding the Department of Texas, considered the league a threat. He placed the entire state under martial law and demanded that all adult males swear allegiance to the Confederacy. On 4 July 1862 about 500 men from the German settlements gathered at Bear Creek, near Fredericksburg, 63 miles west of Austin, and formed themselves into three armed companies under Fritz Tegener (d. 1861). When threatened by Confederate military authorities, Tegener disbanded his men but spread the word for them to assemble on 1 August at Turtle Creek, from which they would strike out for Mexico. With the 68 who responded he moved south. When camped about a day's ride from the Rio Grande, near the Nueces River, they were attacked at about two o'clock on the morning of 10 August by 95 Confederates. After putting up a stout fight until daylight, the Germans scattered. Nineteen were killed outright, and 9 wounded, including Tegener. The captured wounded were all shot in the back of the head; 8 more were killed trying to cross the Rio Grande. Only 11 reached safety. They enlisted in the 1st U.S. Cavalry Volunteers.

The Texas Confederates lost 2 killed and 18 wounded. They buried their own dead but left the Germans on the ground. Their remains were not buried until August 1865, when the bones were placed in a common grave at Comfort, Texas, about 45 miles northwest of San Antonio. The monument, known as *Treue Der Union* (true to the Union), raised in their honor on the town's High Street, is said to be (erroneously) the only monument to Union soldiers south of the Mason-Dixon Line; it is however, the southernmost union monument.

Nugent von Westmeath, Laval (1777–1862). An Austrian soldier born in Ireland who became chief of the Austrian general staff in 1809. In 1813 he conquered Croatia, Istria, and the Po region. In 1815 he was given command of all Austrian forces in Italy. He besieged Rome and defeated French Marshal Joachim Murat [q.v.] at Ceprano and San Germano. In 1816 he was made a prince of the Holy Roman Empire, and in 1846 he was made a field marshal. In 1848 and 1859 he supported General Josef Radetzky [q.v.] against the Piedmontese.

Nuits, Battle of (18 December 1870), Franco-Prussian War. A Badenese force under General August von Werder [q.v.] after five hours' fighting captured this small fortified town, used as an arms depot by the French, located north-northeast of Beaune in a region noted for its Nuits St. Georges burgundy. French losses were about 1,000 killed and wounded and 700 taken prisoner; German losses are unknown but were said to be heavy.

Nujeeb. An Indian sepoy serving in one of the armies of an independent Indian state. Such troops were usually poorly trained and badly disciplined.

Nurses, Army. For most of the nineteenth century military nursing was in the hands of males. Although some British female nurses, privately funded, were sent to Natal in 1879 during the Zulu War [q.v.], to Egypt in 1882 [see Arabi's Revolt], and the noble work of Florence Nightingale [q.v.] and her nurses in Turkey during the Crimean War [q.v.] brought attention to the work that could be done by female nurses in war, their work produced no permanent corps of female nurses in the military. There was a general consensus that it would be unseemly for women to nurse venereal disease cases, with which all military hospitals were at all times filled.

During the American Civil War Dorothea Dix [q.v.] was appointed superintendent of nurses and selected about 60 percent of some 10,000 women who served in the war, but they were all discharged at war's end. In the Spanish-American War [q.v.] 1,200 women served under contract with the armed forces, but no permanent staff of trained female nurses came into being in any nineteenth century army, nor were they given commissions. [See Medicine and Surgery, Military.]

Nyasaland, British Wars with Arab Slavers in (1885–98). In what is today the country of Malawi the British battled Arab slave traders in the longest-lasting of the many colonial wars waged in Africa against slavers. Harry Johnston (1858–1927), a British explorer and administrator, assembled a force consisting of mostly Indian troops, which in the 1890s largely suppressed the slavers [see Northern Rhodesian Regiment]. From 1878 until it was declared a British protectorate in 1891 Nyasaland was ruled by the African Lakes Company of Glasgow, Scotland.

Oak Hills, Battle of. See Wilson's Creek, Battle of.

Oak Leaves. A device in the shape of clustered oak leaves that attached to certain German medals to establish a separate and higher order of the award. (It does not, as in modern American medals, indicate an additional award of the medal.) It was first established as an addenda to the Order of the Red Eagle [see Red Eagle, Order of] on 18 January 1811 by King Friedrich Wilhelm III of Prussia (1770–1840) in memory of his wife, Queen Louisa of Mecklenburg, who died on 19 July 1810 at age thirty-four. From 10 March 1813 oak leaves could also be attached to Pour le Mérite [q.v.].

Oaxaca, Siege of (November 1812–August 1813), Mexican Wars of Independence. Rebels under Father José María Morelos y Pavón [q.v.] besieged Oaxaca de Juárez, a fortified town in southeast Mexico held by royalists. On 30 August 1813 the town was stormed and taken.

O'Bannon, Presley Neville (1776–1850). An American marine commissioned a second lieutenant in January 1801. During the Tripolitan War [q.v.] of 1800–05 he served with the naval squadron in the Mediterranean. In 1804 he commanded the marine detachment aboard the *Argus* and in November of that year went ashore in Egypt with 7 marines to accompany William Eaton [q.v.] in his expedition against the city of Derna [q.v.], now in northeast Libya. In March and April he made the arduous trek across the desert and distinguished himself in the attack on and capture of Derna, over which he raised the American flag, the first ever to fly over a captured foreign town. His exploit later adding the phrase "the shores of Tripoli" to "The Marines' hymn." In 1807 he retired, and he lived the rest of his life quietly in Kentucky.

Obassa, Battle of. See Fourth Ashanti War.

Obedience. A trained and disciplined soldier of whatever rank knows that whatever the circumstance he must obey the orders of his superiors. Sir Charles Napier [q.v.] wrote: "Soldiers must obey in all things. They may and do laugh at foolish orders, but they nevertheless obey, not because they are blindly obedient, but because they know that to disobey is to break the backbone of their profession." Robert E. Lee in an 1865 circular to the Army of Northern Virginia wrote: "Men must be habituated to obey or they cannot be controlled in battle, and the neglect of the least important order impairs the proper influence of the officer."

Oberhollabrunn, Battle of. See Battle of Hollabrunn [q.v.].

Obidos, Battle of (15 August 1808), Peninsular War. This small skirmish at the Portuguese village of Obidos three miles south-southwest of Caldas da Rainha involved four companies of British riflemen from the 60th and 95th regiments and the rear guard of a French division. It was the first successful engagement of the British army in the Peninsular War [q.v.].

Obitori. The suspension rings on the lockets of the Japanese tachi scabbard.

Oblique Order. A type of attack, sometimes called the progressive or echelon attack, in which one flank is refused so that the other flank, heavily reinforced, is the first to engage the enemy. This was a type of attack much favored by General Antoine Henri Jomini [q.v.] in his treatise *Grand Military Operations*. It is thought to have been first used by Epaminondas of Thebes (418?–362) against the Spartans in the Battle of Leuctra in July 371 B.C. During the Seven Years' War Frederick the Great (1712–1786) successfully used it in the Battle of Leuthen on 5 December 1757, and it was much favored by Confederate generals, particularly Robert E. Lee, even though at Seven Pines, Gaines's Mill, Malvern Hill, the second day at Gettysburg [qq.v.], and elsewhere the result was generally poor. Braxton Bragg [q.v.] tried the maneuver at Chickamauga [q.v.] and John Hood [q.v.] at Peach Tree Creek [q.v.], both without success.

Obruchev, Nikolai Nikolaevich (1830–1904). A Russian officer who as a youth had become involved in the revolutionary movement Land and Liberty and appears to have retained his revolutionary spirit. He came under an official cloud when he refused to take part in quelling the Polish Rebellion [q.v.] in 1863. His military career was saved by General Dmitri A. Miliutin [q.v.], whom he later replaced as an instructor at the staff academy and as assistant editor of a military journal. He became a major general and a leading influence in Russian military thinking, particularly in the area of manpower and mobilization planning.

Observation Post. A place from which military observations are made.

Observation Post *Observation post at Montfermeil, 1894*

Observer Sergeants. In the United States in peacetime, sergeants in the Signal Corps were posted in large towns and commercial centers to give timely warning of the approach of storms and river risings and to forward other important weather news.

Obstacles, Military. Any natural or man-made obstruction that delays, restricts, diverts, hinders, or prevents the movement of troops, weapons, or impedimenta.

Obturation. The sealing of the breech of a gun to prevent the escape of unwanted gas.

Ocaks. The corps of Turkish janissaries [q.v.]. [See Auspicious Incident / Event.]

Ocaña, Battle of (19 November 1809), Peninsular War. When General Arthur Wellesley, the future Duke of Wellington, drew his army back into Portugal after the Battle of Talavara [q.v.], the Spanish formed an Army of the Center, consisting of 54,000 men and 60 guns under General Carlos Areizaga [q.v.], which advanced from Sierra Morena to La Guardia, near Aranjuez in New Castile, and there halted. French Marshal Nicolas Soult [q.v.] with 30,000 men advanced on Areizaga, who, believing his flanks threatened, at once retreated and pulled his force onto the south bank of the Tagus River. Soult followed and at Ocaña, eight miles from Aranjuez, forced him to fight. A large cavalry engagement was a feature of this battle in which the Spanish were routed. The

Army of the Center was destroyed, and southern Spain was opened to the French. The French suffered 1,700 casualties; the Spanish lost 4,000 killed and wounded and 15,000 taken prisoner. The French captured thirty standards, all the baggage, stores, and 50 guns. The victory gave them the whole of Andalusia.

Occupation Army. The military force that remains in a conquered country until a formal peace is signed and an indemnity paid. Armies of occupation were generally fed at the expense of the conquered.

Occupation of a Position. The movement of troops into an area and its preparation as a battle position.

Occupied Territory. Territory under the authority of and effective control of a belligerent armed force.

Ocean Pond, Battle of. See Olustee, Battle of.

Ochterlony, David (1758–1825). A British soldier born in Boston, Massachusetts, the son of an American Tory. He was commissioned in 1778 as an ensign in the 24th Bengal Native Infantry. In India he fought against Haidar Ali (1722–1782), the Muslim ruler of Mysore, in the Second Mysore War (1780–84) and was for a time a prisoner. He was promoted major in 1800 and lieutenant colonel in 1803, serving under General Gerard Lake [q.v.]. On 11 September 1803 in the Second Maratha War [q.v.] he took part in the Battle of Delhi [q.v.], in which the Marathas under a French soldier of fortune, Louis Bourquin, were defeated. Ochterlony was then appointed Resident at the court of Shah Alam, the titular emperor of the Mogul Empire. When Jaswant Rao Holkar, the Maratha ruler, marched on Delhi with 20,000 men and 100 guns and laid siege, Ochterlony organized the defenses and held the town from 7 October to 16 October 1804. Breaches had been made in the walls, and Holkar was preparing to attack when a relief force arrived under General Lake.

Ochterlony was promoted colonel in 1812 and major general in 1814. In the Gurkha War [q.v.] of 1814–16 he commanded one of the invading columns and was the most successful of the British generals. He was rewarded with a knighthood (KCB), a baronetcy, the Thanks of Parliament, and a pension of £1,000 a year. He also distinguished himself in the Third Maratha War [q.v.] of 1817–18 and participated in the reconstruction of central India. When his orders calling together a force to defend the raja of Bahadarpur were countermanded by the governor-general, he resigned in a huff. He died before his resignation could be accepted.

O'Connor, John (fl. 1861–64). A bounty jumper who during the American Civil War admitted to enlisting in the Union army, collecting a bounty, and deserting thirty-two times. He was court-martialed in Albany, New York, and found guilty in March 1865 but was given an exceptionally lenient sentence of four years in prison. [See Bounty Jumping.]

Oda. 1. In Turkish: a room in a harem.
2. Among the janissaries [q.v.], a military unit about the size of a company, 100 to 200 men commanded by an *oda bashi*.

O'Donnell, Henry Joseph (1769–1834). A Spanish soldier of Irish descent who during the Peninsular War [q.v.] played a prominent role in fighting the French in Catalonia. In 1810 he won a small victory at La Bispal in Catalonia but was defeated by French Marshal Nicolas Soult [q.v.] in April of that year near Lerida. From 1812 he commanded the Reserve Army of Andalusia until in 1818 he was appointed governor of Cádiz. During the French invasion of 1822 he was in charge of the defenses of Madrid against the forces of Jean Baptiste Bessiéres [q.v.], but when accused of treachery by his own officers, he fled to France, where he died [see French Intervention in Spain].

O'Donnell y Joris, Leopoldo (1809–1867). A Spanish soldier who supported the infant Queen Isabella (1830–1904) against her uncle in the First Carlist War [q.v.]. During the war he married a widow, much older than he, who exerted great influence over all aspects of his life. After the war he sided with the moderates against Baldomero Espartero [q.v.] and was forced to flee to France after the abortive coup of October 1841. However, he soon returned and was appointed governor-general of Cuba. From 1843 to 1848 he exercised a high-handed, harsh rule and amassed a fortune. In 1854 he was named minister of war by Espartero, and in 1856 in a coup d'état he supplanted Espartero as prime minister. Three months later he was replaced by Ramón Narváez [q.v.]. In 1858 he returned to power, and the following year he led a successful campaign against the Moors in Morocco and was created Duke of Tetuán [see Tetuán, Battle of]. He was again prime minister in 1863 and 1865, but in 1866 his government was overturned by Narváez.

Ofen, Siege of (4–21 May 1849), Hungarian Revolution. Austrian forces holding the fortress at Ofen (Buda, which in 1873 united with Pest to become Budapest) were attacked by Hungarians on 4 May 1849. The attack failed, as did several further assaults, but the fortress was taken by storm on 21 May.

Offensive, Cult of the. The military doctrine that the tactical offensive would usually prevail over the defensive, which began to win over the minds of military thinkers in all major European countries in the 1880s. It was a doctrine untempered by military reality. Even as increasingly improved machine guns, breach-loading artillery with effective recoil mechanisms and ever more accurate magazine-fed rifles made the tactical offensives ever less probable, the notion prevailed until it died an agonizingly slow death on the western front in the First World War.

Officer. A person who holds a commission [q.v.] of trust or command from the ruler, viceroy, or highest elected official of a country and exercises authority over those of lesser rank. Officers commanding troops in one of the arms of a service are combatant officers; others, such as chaplains, doctors, paymasters, and commissaries, are noncombatant officers. In the American army those holding ranks below captain are called company or troop officers. In the British army they are called subalterns. Field officers are those above the grade of captain but below general officers. Staff officers are those officers serving on the staff of a commander of a battalion or higher organization.

Emory Upton [q.v.], writing in *The Military Policy of the United States* (1904), says: "In every military system which has triumphed in modern war the officers have been recognized as the brains of the army, and to prepare them for their trust, governments have spared no pains to give them special education and training."

Officer of the Day. In the American army, the officer appointed temporarily to be always on duty, commanding the guard and accountable for prisoners and the routine operations of a military unit. In the French service this is the officer of the night; in British usage, the orderly officer.

Officer Patrol. A patrol led by an officer.

Official Records. Popular name for *War of the Rebellion: A Compilation of the Official Records of the Union and Confederate Armies.* In 1863, with the American Civil War still in progress, General-in-Chief Henry Halleck [q.v.] recommended gathering and preserving documents and reports. In consequence, Senator Henry Wilson (1812–1875) of Massachusetts, chairman of the Committee on Military Affairs, introduced a joint resolution "to provide for the printing of the official reports of the armies of the United States." This was adopted by the House and Senate on 19 May 1864 and signed by President Abraham Lincoln the following day.

The project came to a halt for several years for lack of funding. The first 18 volumes were distributed in July 1881, and the completed work—128 volumes plus a separate atlas with 1,006 maps and sketches—did not appear until 1901. The total cost was more than three million dollars.

The American Civil War was the first war to generate massive amounts of paper, and tons were collected and sifted. Between 1885 and 1897 an average of 6 officers and 69 clerks labored on the project. Although several people were in charge of the project over the years, it was Lieutenant Colonel Robert Nicholson Scott (1837–1887), a former aide to General Halleck, who contributed most to the success of the project. He formulated the rules for acceptance and resisted all attempts to amend what had been written at the time. As a result, the Official Records remain the most complete, unbiased, and accessible records of the war. For wars of the nineteenth century no comparable collection exists.

Officier de Fortune. French for officer of fortune. An officer in the French army promoted from the ranks for bravery on the field or for a long term of competence. Such officers rarely rose above the rank of lieutenant [see Rankers; Mustang].

Officier d'Ordonnance. An orderly officer in the French army, usually a lieutenant or a captain, who carried messages, conducted inspections, and collected information. Napoleon had 12 such officers.

Off Reckoning. In the British army early in the nineteenth century this was the allowance given to colonels of regiments and captains of companies taken from the sum allotted for clothing their men, the amount of the allowance depended on the surplus available after clothing had been provided for the regiment. Captains were later excluded and the money was paid only to the colonels of regiments. About 1860 a new computation was made and an average of 30 years was taken. This then became a fixed amount known as a colonel's allowance [see Allowances].

Ogive. 1. The curved or tapered pointed nose of a bullet, rocket, or other projectile.

2. The ornamental S-shaped molding on some cannons, mortars, and howitzers. Sometimes written "ogee."

O'Hara, Theodore (1820–1867). An American soldier of fortune, lawyer, and journalist who in 1846 was commissioned a captain and in the Mexican War [q.v.] was brevetted major for conspicuous conduct at the battles of Contreras, Churubusco, and Chapultepec [qq.v.]. He was mustered out in October 1848. In late 1849, having volunteered to serve under Narciso López [q.v.], the Venezuelan filibuster, he led a battalion of Kentuckians ashore in Cuba. He was wounded in the Battle of Cárdenas [q.v.] on 19 May 1850. From 1852 to 1855 he was editor of the *Louisville Times* in Kentucky. From March 1855 to December 1856 he was a captain in the 2nd Cavalry. In the American Civil War he served as a colonel in the Confederate army.

After the war he became a cotton merchant in Georgia. He is best known as the author of a single poem, "The Bivouac of the Dead" [q.v.], written in 1847 to commemorate the reburial in Frankfort, Kentucky, of Kentuckians killed in the Mexican War.

O'Higgins, Bernardo (1778–1842). A Chilean soldier and politician who came to be called the Liberator of Chile. He was the natural son of Ambrosio O'Higgins (1720?–1801), a Spaniard of Irish descent who became Marqués de Orsono and viceroy of Peru. From about 1810 O'Higgins was a leader of Chilean rebels, and in 1813 he was made commander of a rebel army. After he and José Carrera [q.v.] were defeated by royalist forces from Peru in the Battle of Rancagua [q.v.] on 7 October 1814, he fled to Argentina. There he joined forces with José de San Martín [q.v.] and with the newly created Army of the Andes [q.v.] marched across the Andes and decisively defeated the Spanish forces in the Battle of Chacabuco [q.v.] on 12 February 1817. From 1817 O'Higgins was dictator of Chile until in 1823 he was overthrown in a revolution and retired to Peru.

Okeechobee, Battle of. See Lake Okeechobee, Battle of.

O'Kelly, James (1845–1916). An Irish soldier, war correspondent, and politician who served as a soldier in the French Foreign Legion [q.v.] in Mexico and as a captain in the French army during the Franco-Prussian War. As a correspondent of the *New York Herald* covering a Cuban revolution he was captured by the Spanish and sentenced to be shot. He was spared partly through the efforts of Isaac Butt (1813–1879), an Irish politician. Still working for the *Herald,* he covered the Great Sioux War of 1876–77 [q.v.] in the United States.

He became embroiled in Irish politics and from 1880 to 1892 and again from 1895 to 1916, he was a member of Parliament for Roscommon. As war correspondent for the *London Daily News* he covered the revolt of El Mahdi in the Sudan [see Sudan, Reconquest of].

Okolona, Battle of (21–22 February 1864), American Civil War. At this town in northeastern Mississippi, 18 miles south of Tupelo, Confederate General Nathan Bedford Forrest [q.v.] with 2,000 to 3,000 men encountered 7,000 Federals under William Sooy Smith (1830–1916) moving south in a raid from Memphis, Tennessee. In spite of their inferior numbers, the Confederates defeated Smith's force and drove it back into Tennessee.

Oku, Yasukata (1846–1830). A Japanese officer who was a samurai of the Kokura clan. He joined the imperial army in 1871 and took part in the suppression of the Satsuma Rebellion [q.v.] in 1877. In 1885 he was promoted major general. He commanded a division in the Sino-Japanese War of 1894–95 [q.v.] and played a key role in the Russo-Japanese War of 1904–05. He was promoted field marshal in 1911.

Okubo, Haruno (1846–1915). A Japanese officer who saw service in the Sino-Japanese War of 1894–95 [q.v.] and the Russo-Japanese War of 1904–05.

Okubo, Toshimichi (1830–1878). A Japanese leader who participated in the Boshin Civil War and the Satsuma Rebellion [qq.v.]. He was assassinated on 14 May 1878.

Old Abe. The eagle mascot of Company C, 8th Wisconsin Volunteers of the Union army during the American Civil War. As a very young bird he had been bought from Flambeau Indians and kept as a pet. At the beginning of the war he was presented to C Company and served with it through forty-two battles and skirmishes in which he habitually flew screeching over the Confederate positions. Many southern soldiers tried to shoot the "Yankee Buzzard," and there were several attempts to kidnap him, but he survived the war and was presented to the state of Wisconsin, where he occupied a cage in the state capitol. He was frequently displayed in public appearances, and his molted feathers were sometimes sold for charitable causes. On 28 March 1881 he died of smoke inhalation when the capitol caught fire. His body was then mounted and put on display in the capitol's Memorial Hall until it was consumed when fire swept through the building.

Old Fuss and Feathers. The sobriquet of General Winfield Scott [q.v.], referring to the general's love of military pageantry.

Old Glory. A popular name for the U.S. flag [see "Star-Spangled Banner, The"].

Old Goose (1844?–1886?). The most widely known army mule in the American army. It accompanied Stephen Watts Kearny [q.v.] on his overland march to California during the Mexican War [q.v.] and was bearing Captain Benjamin D. Moore (1815?–1846) when he was killed in the Battle of San Pasqual [q.v.] on 6 December 1846. When General William Tecumseh Sherman [q.v.] visited the West Coast in 1883, he saw Old Goose being used as a pack mule and ordered that "this faithful servant be pensioned." It was done, and in retirement Old Goose was given "regular rations" at the re-mount station near Alameda, California.

Old Guard. 1. See Garde Impériale.

2. In the American army the name taken by the 3rd Infantry after General Winfield Scott [q.v.] so referred to it during the Mexican War [q.v.].

Old Rough and Ready. The sobriquet of General Zachary Taylor [q.v.], which he acquired during the Second Seminole War [q.v.] because of his physical prowess and his disdain of formal military dress. The nickname won votes for him in 1848, when he was a candidate for the presidency.

Old Woman's Gun, Battle of. See San Pedro, Battle of.

Olhão Revolt (16 June 1808), French invasion of Portugal in the Peninsular War. The revolt of this Portuguese fishing village, five miles east of Faro, against the French invaders was the signal for the rest of the province to rise. The local French governor and 70 of his men were captured, and the rest, some 1,200, retreated to Mertola. Soon the French occupying force was limited to the environs of Lisbon [see Portugal, French Invasion of].

Oliver, Paul Ambrose (1830–1912). An American soldier who was commissioned a second lieutenant in the Union army in 1861 during the American Civil War. He ended the war as a brevet brigadier general of volunteers. In 1892 he was awarded the Medal of Honor [q.v.] for an action on 15 May 1864 during the Battle of Resaca, Georgia [q.v.], when, while commanding a brigade, he "assisted in preventing a disaster caused by Union troops firing into each other." He was also an inventor whom some credited with the invention of dynamite and black powder explosives contemporaneously with and independent of Alfred Nobel and Johann Schultze [qq.v.]. His enterprise was bought out by the Du Pont Company of Delaware.

Olivier, Cornelius Hermanus (1851–1930). A Boer leader in the Orange Free State who became a general in the Second Anglo-Boer War [q.v.]. A prominent farmer in the Rouxville district, he was elected to the Volksraad (Boer parliament) in 1893. At the beginning of the war with Britain he led the Taba 'Nchu commando and fought in northern Cape Colony and in the Orange Free State. He fought to the end and was regarded as a trusted and able leader.

Olivier, Jan Hendrik (1848–1924). A Boer leader in the Second Anglo-Boer War [q.v.] who gained fame by his defeat of British General William Gatacre [q.v.] in the Battle of Stormberg [q.v.] on 10–11 December 1899 [see Black Week]. He later carried out a skillful retreat along the border of Basutoland without the loss of a man. In August 1900 he and two of his sons were captured at Winburg. After the war he settled down as a farmer.

Oltenita / Oltenitza, Battle of (4 November 1853), Crimean War. On 4 October 1853, three months after the occupation of the provinces of Walachia and Moldavia by the Russians, Turkey declared war and Omar Pasha [q.v.] was sent north with an army over the Danube. At Oltenita (ancient Constantiola) in eastern Rumania, at the confluence of the Arges and Danube rivers, Omar defeated the Russians, giving a tremendous boost to Turkish morale, for this was the first time in nearly a century that the Turks had defeated the Russians in battle.

Olustee, Battle of (20 February 1864), American Civil War. The only battle of the war fought in Florida; sometimes called the Battle of Ocean Pond. In northeast Florida, 45 miles southwest of Jacksonville, Confederate General Joseph Finnegan (1814–1885) with about 5,000 men and 12 guns decisively defeated a Union force of 5,500 effectives under Brigadier General Truman Seymour (1824–1891). The Union suffered 1,860 casualties; the Confederates lost 946.

Omar, Saidou Tall (1797–1864). A Tukulor Islamic holy man who in 1850 began a war against the French in Senegal that was continued by his son. The French were unable to end it until 1893.

Omar (Omer) Pasha (1806–1871). A Turkish general born in Croatia and christened Michael Latas who served in an Austrian frontier regiment [see Grenzer Troops] until, accused of embezzlement, he deserted in 1828 and fled to Bosnia. He became a Muslim and joined the Turkish army. He was appointed writing master to Abdul Medjid (1823–1861), who, when he became sultan of Turkey in 1839, appointed him a colonel and made him a pasha. In 1842 he was appointed governor of Lebanon, where he suppressed several revolts. From 1843 to 1847 he ruthlessly suppressed revolts in Albania, Bosnia, and Kurdistan. He was cruel, dishonest, and unscrupulous, and regularly pocketed money intended to purchase food for his soldiers, but he was a good organizer and disciplinarian; he proved a better general than most Turks. During the Crimean War he defeated the Russians at Oltenita and forced them to raise the siege of Silistra [qq.v.]; he commanded the Turkish army in the Crimea. From 1857 to 1859 he was governor of Baghdad. In 1861 he again suppressed revolts in Bosnia and in Herzegovina. In 1862 he suppressed a revolt in Montenegro, and in 1867 another in Crete. He was made a marshal in 1864.

Omdurman, Battle of (2 September 1898), Reconquest of the Sudan. General H. H. Kitchener [q.v.], advancing up the Nile with an Anglo-Egyptian army of 26,000 men with 44 guns defeated a Dervish army estimated to be 50,000 on the left bank of the Nile 7 miles north of the city of Omdurman (now Umm Durman), about 1,000 miles south of Cairo. The Dervishes suffered 15,000 casualties, of whom about 11,000 were killed; the British lost 56 killed and 150 wounded; Egyptian losses were 36 killed and 300 wounded. No Dervish came within 200 yards of the Anglo-Egyptian line. Kitchener, well pleased and thinking the battle over, remarked to his staff, "I think we've given them a good dusting, gentlemen." As he started to put his troops into columns for marching upon Omdurman, a Dervish force of some 20,000 fell upon his rear guard, a brigade of Sudanese under Hector MacDonald [q.v.]. MacDonald skillfully maneuvered his troops and drove them off, saving the day for Kitchener.

A feature of the battle was the charge of the British 21st Lancers against Hadendowa tribesmen of Osman Digna [q.v.] in which Winston Churchill [q.v.] participated. It is some-

Omdurman *Charge of the British 21st Lancers at Omdurman, 1898*

times said (erroneously) that this was the last cavalry charge ever made.

George W. Steevens [q.v.], the correspondent of the *London Daily Mail,* said of the battle: "It was the last day of Mahdism and the greatest. They could never get near and they refused to hold back . . . . It was not a battle but an execution." After the battle the Dervish wounded were left on the ground to die or recover if they could. Some, it seems, were put out of their misery by British or Egyptian troops. Lieutenant Churchill wrote to his mother: "I shall merely say that the victory at Omdurman was disgraced by the inhuman slaughter of the wounded and that Kitchener was responsible for this."

The khalifa escaped but was later pursued, brought to battle, and killed [see Battle of Umm Dibaikarat / Diwaykarat].

O'Meara, Barry Edward (1786–1836). An Irish doctor who served as an army surgeon until 1808, when he was cashiered for taking part in a duel. He was a ship's surgeon on board HMS *Bellerophon* when Napoleon surrendered in 1815. Because he could speak both French and Italian, he was asked to accompany the emperor to his exile on St. Helena as his personal physician. He became his patient's partisan, helping him communicate with sympathizers in London and taking his part in his quarrels with Hudson Lowe [q.v.], who was responsible for the conditions of Napoleon's exile. In 1818 Lowe had him dismissed when O'Meara claimed that Lowe had tried to poison Napoleon.

O'Meara opened a dental surgery on Edgewater Road, London, and in his window displayed one of Napoleon's wisdom teeth. He persisted in his attacks on Lowe in letters and in a book, *Napoleon in Exile; or A Voice from St. Helena*

(1822). Lord Byron [q.v.], a supporter, wrote of him in "The Age of Bronze":

> The staff surgeon who maintained his cause
> Hath lost his place—but gained the world's applause.

O'Meara, Walter Alfred John (1863–1939). A British soldier born in India who was commissioned in the Royal Engineers in 1883 and served in the Third Anglo-Burmese War [q.v.]. In 1891 he laid the first telephone line from London to Paris. In the Second Anglo-Boer War [q.v.] he served as chief staff officer during the siege of Kimberley [q.v.]. Later he commanded the Orange River Colony's mounted police, and in 1900, after the fall of Johannesburg in the Transvaal, he became government commissioner and mayor of Johannesburg. He resigned from the army in 1902.

Omura, Masujiro (1824–1869). A Japanese soldier and statesman who was one of the few military leaders of the era not of samurai background. He studied Western military methods and organization and trained and reorganized the Choshu forces. During the Four Borders War (June–July 1866) he successfully led a unit of his retrained samurai against invading Tokugawa forces. He served in the Boshin Civil War [q.v.] and fought in the Battle of Ueno [q.v.]. He was later appointed to a post involving military affairs in the new imperial government. In October 1868 he was appointed vice-minister of military affairs. He was assassinated soon after.

One-Horse Litter. See Travois.

One Hundred Days. See Hundred Days.

O'Neil, John (1834–1878). An Irish soldier and Fenian leader who came to the United States in 1848. In 1866 and again in 1871 he led raids into Canada from Buffalo, New York. He styled himself "General," and his force the Irish Republican Army. In his first attempt he seized the town of Fort Erie, and the Canadian volunteer battalion that attacked him was repulsed. However, three days later, on 4 June 1866 in the Battle of Limestone Ridge [q.v.], Canadian militia defeated O'Neil's army and drove it back into the United States. A similar raid, launched the following week from Vermont, also failed, for the "Inspector General of the Irish Republican Army" was in fact a British secret agent. After his second attempt he was arrested. He tried again in 1871 and again failed. [See Fenian Raids; Fenian Brotherhood; Sweeny, Thomas William.]

Onslow, George Thorp (1859–1921). A British soldier who entered the Royal Marines in 1876 and was promoted captain in 1884. He served at Suakim in the Sudan in 1884–85 and in the Second Anglo-Boer War [q.v.]. In 1906 he was appointed colonel commandant of the Royal Marines.

Ontario. This large Canadian province was known as Upper Canada until 1841, when it united with Lower Canada. Many loyalists settled there at the time of the American Revolution. The desire of many Americans to join it to the United States was one of the causes and purposes of the War of 1812 [q.v.]. It became one of the four provinces of the Dominion of Canada in 1867.

On the Strength. A British expression used for certain civilians, such as soldiers' wives and children, who were entitled to accompany troops abroad. Wives on the strength were entitled to certain privileges, such as permission to take in the washing of officers' families, serve as officers' servants, and sometimes to accompany a unit deployed overseas. [See Troopship.]

Ooolooballong / Ulu Balang. In Malaya, a chosen warrior, a champion.

Oosthuizen, Sarel François (1862–1900). A Transvaal Boer who fought in the First Anglo-Boer War [q.v.] and in several campaigns against tribal chiefs [see Kaffir Wars]. In the Second Anglo-Boer War [q.v.] he became a general. He was fatally wounded while leading a charge against a British position near Krugersdorp.

Open Battle. Troops on both sides fight from standing, uncovered positions.

Opequan Creek, Battle of. See Winchester, Third Battle of.

Operations, Military. The process of carrying out a military action of any sort, including the maneuvering, supplying, attacking, or defending of any thing or place.

Operations Theory. The notion of operations as a stage between strategy and tactics. In 1891 it was defined by General (later Field Marshal) N. P. Mikhnevich [q.v.] in his *Encyclopedia of Military and Naval Sciences:* "Each war consists of one or several campaigns, each campaign of one or several operations, which represent by themselves a known, finite period, from the strategic deployment of an army on the departure line of the operation to the final decision of the latter by way of victorious battle on the field of engagement. . . ."

Opium War, First (1839–42). The imperial Chinese government attempted to prevent the importation of opium, which the Chinese called a devil drug, and other narcotics. Foreign merchants objected. The British Empire was the world's largest producer of opium, and it was a profitable trade for the Honourable East India Company. In 1837 Commissioner Lin Tsê-hsü [q.v.], governor of Hunan and Hupeh provinces, ordered the destruction of six million dollars' worth of opium owned by foreign merchants, mostly British. When the Chinese government refused to pay compensation, Britain declared war.

In June 1840 a British expeditionary force, 4,000 men in twenty warships, arrived at Tinghai, a port on the south end of Chu Shan Island. The Chinese were ill armed, but Sir Hugh Gough [q.v.] judged them "neither wanting in courage nor bodily strength to make them despicable as a foe in a defensive system of warfare."

On 16 February 1841 the Bogue forts [q.v.], on the Pearl River approaches to Canton (Guangzhou or Duangzhou), were captured. Canton was bombarded and fell on 24 May. Moving north up the coast, the British took Amoy on 26 August and Ninghsia on 13 October. Shanghai was captured on 19 June 1842, followed by Chingkiang two days later.

In a report to the emperor Chinese General Kee Shen wrote: "It appears to your majesty's slaves that we are very deficient in means, and have not the shells and rockets used by the barbarians. We must, therefore, adopt other methods to stop them, which will be easy as they have opened negotiations." However, the British proved hard bargainers. The war ended with the Treaty of Nanking (Nanjing or Nanxiang), arranged by Henry Pottinger [q.v.] on 29 August 1842 aboard HMS *Cornwallis* before Nanking. By the terms of the treaty the Chinese agreed to pay Britain an indemnity, to cede the island of Hong Kong for 150 years, and to open five so-called treaty ports (Nangpo, Foochow, Canton, Amoy, and Shanghai) to British traders. In another treaty the following year it was agreed that British subjects were no longer subject to Chinese laws.

Opium War, Second (1856–60). Also called the Arrow War. In 1856 the lorcha *Arrow* with an all-Chinese crew under British registry was seized by the Chinese while lying in the Pearl River. Using this as a pretext, Britain declared war on China. France, claiming offense when a French missionary was killed, allied itself with Britain. The Chinese were soon defeated, but the government refused to sign a treaty that would extend European trading rights in China. A joint French and British force of 18,000 occupied Canton (Guangzhou or Duangzhou) in December 1857. Then, as they moved north, the Taku forts [q.v.], 37 miles east of Tientsin (Tianjin), were captured but not held in May 1858.

Negotiations between China, Britain, France, Russia, and the United States produced a brief peace, and by the treaties of Tientsin, signed on 26–29 June, China agreed to open

Opium War, First *The firepower of British gunboats overwhelms Chinese ships, 1842.*

more treaty ports, permit missionaries to set up missions in the interior, legalize the importation of opium, establish a foreign-inspected maritime customs service, and permit legations in Peking (Beijing). China had already, in May, ceded the left bank of the Amur River to Russia by the Treaty of Aigun.

China soon abrogated its treaties with Britain and France and refused to allow legations in Peking. The British dispatched a force under Admiral James Hope (1808–1881). In June 1859 he bombarded the Taku forts and then launched a land attack against them. He was repulsed with heavy loss and withdrew with the help of an American naval force that chanced to be in the area.

In May 1860 an Anglo-French force assembled at Hong Kong. It included 11,000 British under Lieutenant General James Hope Grant [q.v.] and 7,000 French under General Charles Guillaume Marie Apollinaire Antoine Cousin-Montauban, Comte de Palikao [q.v.]. On 1 August Pei-Tang was occupied without opposition, and on 21 August the Taku forts were successfully assaulted. The expedition moved upriver to Tientsin and then up the Peiho (Han) River toward Peking, the British marching on the right bank and the French on the left. The Chinese pleaded for an armistice, and on 18 September Sir Harry Smith Parkes (1828–1885) was sent with a party to parlay, but he and his party were seized, imprisoned, and tortured; only half survived.

After two victories over Chinese forces, the expeditionary force arrived before Peking on 26 September. On 8 October the Summer Palace [q.v.] was occupied. Peking was captured on 12 October 1860 [see Fatsan Creek, Battle of]. A peace was signed when the Chinese agreed to return the survivors of Parkes's party, cede the Kowloon Peninsula, three square miles on the mainland opposite Hong Kong, to the British for ninety-nine years, and pay a large indemnity. When General Grant learned of the mistreatment of Parkes and those with him, he ordered the Summer Palace burned, and this was done on 24 October after the palace had been looted by both British and French forces. Except for a garrison left at Tientsin, the expedition then withdrew from China.

Russia, taking advantage of China's weakness, seized the maritime provinces where the port of Vladivostok was founded.

Opium War, Second *Storming ladders and dead defenders in a Taku fort, 1860*

Opolchenie. A Russian militia or home defense force that was raised by a ukase of 15 July 1812 and largely paid for by private contributions. Each province was responsible for assembling, clothing, and arming a certain number of men who had been exempt from conscription or had completed their military service and were under the age of forty. Officers were chosen from among civil servants, retired officers, and young gentry. They wore a variety of uniforms, but each wore an *opolchenie* cross and the royal cipher on his headdress. They were generally used as pioneers, stretcher-bearers, and guards, and they sometimes replaced regulars.

Oporto, Battles of (1809), Peninsular War. In 1809 the French captured this seaport in northwest Portugal, 170 miles northeast of Lisbon, from the Portuguese [see Portugal, French Invasion of] and then lost it to the British.

First Battle (26 March 1809). After the remnants of the British army of Sir John Moore [q.v.] were evacuated in January 1809, few British troops were left on the Iberian Peninsula. In March the French under Marshal Nicolas Soult [q.v.] with 13,000 infantry and 3,000 cavalry marched on Oporto and attacked newly prepared fortifications manned by 2,000 Portuguese regulars and 18,000 *ordenança* [q.v.]. The French scored a decisive victory and captured the city when they broke the Portuguese center and the Portuguese fled in terror. French losses were 430 killed and wounded; estimates of Portuguese losses, including many civilians, range from 4,000 to 20,000.

Second Battle (12 May 1809). In April 1809 General Arthur Wellesley (soon to be the Duke of Wellington) assumed command of the British forces in the peninsula and with 30,000 men marched north from Lisbon. He crossed the Douro River at night on barges supplied by townspeople who had fled before the French occupation and on 12 May surprised Soult at Oporto. He captured the city and inflicted 6,000 casualties on the French with small loss to himself. Soult was forced to withdraw through the mountains into Spanish Galicia. The French never returned to this part of Portugal.

Oporto and Lisbon Uprisings (1820). After the British had defeated the French in the Peninsular War [q.v.], they established a regency to rule Portugal, for King John VI (1769–1826) lingered in Brazil, to which he had fled when the French invaded Portugal. William Carr Beresford [q.v.], the English commander-in-chief of the Portuguese army, sailed to Brazil to try to persuade the king to return. While he was absent, Portugal was subject to considerable unrest, doubtless stimulated by the beginning of the Spanish Civil War [q.v.] of 1820–23 [see French Intervention in Spain]. On 24 August 1820 members of the Jacobin Club of Oporto with a number of senior Portuguese officers, including two colonels with their troops, staged a successful coup d'état and established a junta.

On 15 September a similar coup occurred in Lisbon, where the regency was evicted, the Cortes was called into session, and the British troops stationed there ordered out. King John returned to Portugal in 1821 to rule as a constitutional monarch [see Portuguese Civil War].

Opperman, Jacobus Daniel (1861–1901). A Boer leader in the Transvaal who took part in fights with the Zulus in 1884 and in 1893 was appointed police lieutenant in Swaziland (Botswana). In the Second Anglo-Boer War [q.v.] he enlisted many of the Boers in Swaziland and led them in action. He became a general and was killed in action at Bankop, near Ermelo in the southeastern Transvaal.

Oranges, War of the (1801). Napoleon demanded that Portugal cede large sections of its country to France and close Portuguese ports to British ships [see Continental System]. Portuguese reluctance to comply brought an invasion in April 1801 by the French in conjunction with reluctant Spanish forces [see Portugal, French Invasion of]. The Spanish troops were led by Manuel Godoy (1767–1851). He defeated the Portuguese near Olivenza, a fortified commune near the border, 15 miles southwest of Badajoz. When Godoy sent a report of his victory to the queen, he included with it newly picked oranges from nearby Elves—thus the war's name. Portugal was forced to sign the Peace of Badajoz, which gave Olivenza and trade privileges to France, and promised war reparations.

Orchard Knob, Battle of (23 November 1863), American Civil War. In the initial engagement of the Battle of Chattanooga [q.v.] Union troops under General Philip Sheridan [q.v.] captured this low ridge halfway between the lines.

Ord, Edward Otho Cresap (1818–1883). An American soldier who entered West Point at the age of sixteen and was graduated in 1839. He was commissioned in the artillery and was promoted first lieutenant after the Second Seminole War [q.v.] for his gallantry in action. In 1855–59 he served in several campaigns against Indians in the Northwest, including those against the Yakima in 1855, the Rogue River Indians in 1856, and the Spokane Indians in 1858 [see Yakima War; Rogue River War]. In 1859 he was transferred to Fort Monroe, and in October he was with the small force under Robert E. Lee that captured John Brown [q.v.] at Harpers Ferry. In May 1862, during the American Civil War, he was promoted major general of volunteers. In October of that year he was badly wounded while serving in Mississippi. In June 1863 he commanded XIII Corps in the Army of the Tennessee [q.v.] and took part in the siege and capture of Vicksburg. In the siege of Petersburg [q.v.] he was again severely wounded. He returned to duty to take part in the final encounters that led to Lee's surrender at Appomattox [q.v.]. He remained in the army after the war and retired in December 1880. Soon after, by a special act of Congress, he was made a major general on the retired list.

Ordenança. Portuguese militia.

Ordener, Michel (1755–1811). A French soldier who enlisted in the army as a dragoon in 1773 and was commissioned in 1793. In August 1799 in Switzerland he suffered eight saber cuts, three bullet wounds, and one wound from a cannonball. In 1803 he was promoted general of brigade. He was again seriously wounded in the Battle of Austerlitz [q.v.]. On 25 July 1805 he was promoted general of division; the following May he resigned because his wounds rendered him unfit for field service.

Order. Any communication, given orally, in writing, or by signals, from a superior to a subordinate; a command.

Order-in-Council. In Britain, an order given by the sovereign with the advice of the Privy Council. Such orders were used in the nineteenth century to avoid parliamentary discussion of controversial issues. They had the force of law until superseded by acts of Parliament. Cardwell's reforms [q.v.] of the British army were notable examples.

Orderlies. Noncommissioned officers and privates, usually mounted, who were on hand to convey the orders of commanding officers or senior staff officers or to perform routine tasks.

An orderly at headquarters, American Civil War

Orderly Officer. See Officer of the Day.

Orderly Room. The room(s) or tent used as the headquarters of a company or higher unit.

Orderly Sergeant. This was usually the first sergeant of a unit. When a drumbeat or trumpet called for orders, the orderly sergeant reported to the adjutant, wrote down the orders, and delivered them to his company commander; he then alerted the other ranks for duty.

Order of Battle. The list of the units and strength of a military force intended for action or taking part in action, ideally including its dispositions, armament, and equipment.

Order of March. The order and formation of troops on the march. This was commonly an advance guard, main force, baggage and ambulances, and rear guard.

Orders of Chivalry. See Chivalry, Orders of.

Ordnance. All guns, explosives, pyrotechnic and other stores, such as ammunition, grenades, shells, and flares. The term was sometimes used to include tools, machinery, horse equipment, etc.

Ordnance, Board of. 1. In Britain, a board formed by the master general of ordnance and others that was charged with responsibility for the supply of arms and ammunition to the services and for the maintenance of barracks and fortifications. The master general of ordnance was the commander-in-chief of the artillery and engineers. In 1855 the board was merged with the War Office.

2. In the United States, a board established in 1813 to standardize and systemize U.S. army ordnance. It approved the development of new ordnance and directed the design, testing, and evaluation of all ordnance.

Ordnance Department. In the American army this was a military department under the secretary of war established by Congress on 8 February 1812 to test, purchase, and maintain all arms and ammunition. The first chief of ordnance was Colonel Decius Wadsworth [q.v.], whose assistant was Lieutenant Colonel George Bomford (1792?–1848). The creation of the department inaugurated a major effort to standardize weapons, but on 2 March 1821 the department was virtually abolished and artillery officers staffed the department. No new ordnance officers were commissioned until 1832.

Ordnance, Board of *A French ordnance officer from the Commissary of Ordnance, 1841*

The Ordnance Department was remarkably slow in adopting new weapons. Breech-loading repeating rifles using rimfire cartridges were available before the American Civil War, but few were used. The 1889 Springfield, a single-shot rifle that used black powder ammunition, was finally adopted and was in use as late as 1898. The army did not adopt the Gatling machine gun [q.v.] until 1866—after the Civil War was over.

Ordnance Sergeants. In the American army these were, from 1832, selected sergeants of at least eight years' service who received and maintained arms, ammunition, and other ordnance stores at posts under the direction of the post commander. They are not to be confused with sergeants of ordnance, who were sergeants in detachments assigned to arsenals and armories.

O'Reilly, John Boyle (1844–1890). An Irishman and Fenian who in 1863 enlisted in the British army with the intent to incite a mutiny. In 1866 he was arrested, court-martialed, and sentenced to be hanged. The sentence was commuted to twenty years of penal servitude, and in 1868 he was deported to Australia. The following year he escaped and made his way to the United States, where he became a naturalized citizen. In 1870 he was a journalist with the *Boston Pilot*. From 1876 to 1890 he was the newspaper's proprietor and editor.

Organ Gun. A piece of ordnance in which barrels were placed side by side and were capable of being fired simultaneously.

Oribe, Manuel (1796?–1857). A Uruguayan general and political leader who as a boy entered the patriot Army of the Río de la Plata and was later one of the "thirty-three immortals" who liberated Uruguay from Brazil in 1825. From 1833 to 1835 he was minister of war. In 1835 he was president. In 1838 he was deposed and fled to Buenos Aires. Allied with Juan de Rosas [q.v.], he began a long civil war (1842–51). He was the leader of the conservative Blancos, who were defeated by the liberal Colorados combined with Brazilians and Argentine revolutionists under Justo Urquiza [q.v.].

Orillon. In fortifications, a semicircular projection at the shoulder of a bastion to protect the guns and gunners on the flank.

Orillon

Orléans, Ferdinand Philippe Louis Charles Henri, Duc d' (1810–1842). A French soldier, the eldest son of Louis Philippe, the "Citizen King," he distinguished himself at the siege of Antwerp [q.v.] in 1832 and until 1835 took part in the French conquest of Algeria. [see Algeria, French Invasion and Occupation of]. He was killed in a carriage accident, a blow to the future of the dynasty.

Orléans, Louis Philippe Albert d' (1838–1894). The pretender to the crown of France who lived in England. During the American Civil War he served as a captain of volunteers on the staff of General George McClellan [q.v.] and took part in the Battle of Yorktown and the Seven Days' Battle [qq.v.]. He resigned on 15 July 1862.

Ormolu. A variety of brass that most resembles the color of gold and was used in the ornamentation of swords and other weapons. It was made of 25 percent zinc and 75 percent copper.

Ornaments. The parts of a soldier's uniform intended for distinction or appearance.

Ornano, Philippe Antoine d'Ornani (1784–1863). A Corsican soldier in the French army who distinguished himself in the Napoleonic Wars, particularly at Austerlitz in 1805, Jena and Lübeck in 1806, and Borodino in 1812 [qq.v.]. During the Hundred Days [q.v.] he rallied to Napoleon and was exiled in 1815 at the second restoration of the Bourbons. He returned to France in 1818 and to the army in 1828. In 1861 he was created a marshal of France.

Oropesa, Battle of (10–11 October 1811), Peninsular War. At this town, 18 miles west of Talavera, Neapolitan troops in the

Ornaments Embroidered ornaments, American Civil War

army of French Marshal Nicolas Suchet [q.v.], marching toward Sagunto, found the main coast road blocked by two small towers that General Joachim Blake [q.v.] had garrisoned as part of the defense of Valencia. The first tower was easily taken on 10 October, and its garrison of 215 men was made prisoner. The following day HMS *Magnificent* sent in boats and rescued the 150 men in the second tower.

Orphan Brigade. A Confederate brigade in the American Civil War composed mostly of men from Kentucky, a Union state. When the Confederate army was forced out of the state, the brigade also left, never to return [see Kentucky, Confederate Invasion of]. Commanded by Brigadier General Joseph Horace Lewis (1824–1904), it fought at Shiloh, Corinth, Vicksburg, and Chickamauga and all through the Atlanta Campaign [qq.v.]. It finished the war with only about 500 of its original 4,000 men.

Orsova, Battle of (16 May 1849), Hungarian Revolution. At this Rumanian town, near the Timis River on the Serbian border, Austrian forces were defeated by Hungarians under Jósef Bem [q.v.].

Orthez, Battle of (27 February 1814), Peninsular War. After the Battle of the Nive [q.v.], Marshal Nicolas Soult [q.v.] abandoned Bayonne and, fighting a rearguard action, retreated across the Luy de Béarn, a headstream of the Luy River, to this town in southwestern France, 25 miles northwest of Pau. There he formed a line of 48 guns on a ridge with 44,000 troops. The Allies launched parallel attacks to the center and routed them. The French lost 4,000, including 1,350 taken prisoner, and six guns; Allied casualties numbered 2,164, including Wellington, who, although wounded when a bullet hit his sheathed sword hilt and drove it into his thigh, insisted on staying on his horse until the end of the battle [see Personal Presence of the Commander].

Osako, Naotoshi (1844–1927). A Japanese soldier who fought in the Boshin Civil War [q.v.] with his clan against the Tokugawa shogunate. In 1871 he joined the newly formed imperial army and fought against the Satsuma rebels in 1877 [see Satsuma Rebellion]. He was a major general in the Sino-Japanese War [q.v.] and commanded a brigade of infantry in the fighting around Haicheng in December 1894. From 1898 to 1900 he was vice-chief of the army general staff, and as a lieutenant general he fought in the Russo-Japanese War of 1904–05. He retired and was made a viscount in 1908.

Osceola (1804–1838). A chief of the Seminole Indians in Florida who was sometimes called Billy Powell, for his father was an Englishman. He was about fourteen when, during the First Seminole War [q.v.], he and his mother were captured by American troops. In 1830 he was among the Seminole chiefs who resisted the Removal Bill, ordering all Indians moved west of the Mississippi, and retreated into the Wahoo Swamp of the Withlacoochie River.

On 26 December 1835 he led the band that ambushed Major Francis Dade [q.v.] and began the Second Seminole War [q.v.]. After carrying on a guerrilla war for almost two years, he turned himself in to the American authorities at Fort

Osceola *The Seminole leader Osceola defies the whites.*

Melon, near Lake Monroe in May 1837, but fled back to the swamps when the Americans allowed slavers to come into Florida and capture blacks and Seminoles. In October of that year he was lured out of the Everglades by the promise of American Brigadier General Thomas Jesup [q.v.] to honor his flag of truce and to attend a conference. Instead, on Jesup's order he was treacherously seized by Joseph Marion Hernandez (1793–1857), a militia officer and politician, and jailed at Fort Moultrie, near Charleston, South Carolina. There he died of malaria on 30 January 1838.

Osei Bonsu (1801–1824). King of the Ashantis on the Gold Coast [see Ashanti Wars].

Oshima, Hisanao (1848–1928). A Japanese soldier who fought in the Boshin Civil War [q.v.] and was commissioned a lieutenant in the imperial army in 1871. He commanded a battalion in the Satsuma Rebellion and a brigade in the Sino-Japanese War [qq.v.]. He commanded a division in the Russo-Japanese War of 1904–05. He twice served as commandant of the army staff college.

Oshima, Yoshimasa (1850–1926). A Japanese soldier who was educated at the Osaka Youth School (later the Military Academy) and was commissioned a captain in the imperial army in 1871. He commanded a battalion in the Satsuma Rebellion and a brigade in the Sino-Japanese War [qq.v.], where he distinguished himself in the Battle of Pyongyang [q.v.]. In 1898 he was promoted lieutenant general. He won considerable fame for his victories in the Russo-Japanese War of 1904–05.

Oshkosh (1795–1850). A Menominee Indian warrior who with about 100 of his tribesmen sided with the British in the War of 1812 [q.v.], taking part in the capture of Fort Mackinaw in July 1812, the unsuccessful attack upon Fort Sandusky, Ohio, in 1813, and perhaps other military actions.

He became a chief in 1827 and in 1832 allied himself with the Americans in the Black Hawk War [q.v.]. Although considered a good warrior and chief, he was addicted to alcohol and killed at least one man while drunk. He himself was killed in a drunken brawl at Keshena, Wisconsin, on 20 August 1850.

Osman Digna (1836–1926). A Sudanese chief whose proper name was Uthman Abu Bakr Diqna; he was often mistakenly believed to be a Frenchman named Georges Nisbet from Rouen. His father was thought to have been of Kurdish origin, but his mother was a Sudanese woman of the Hadendowa Beja tribe, and it was as a leader of Hadendowa tribesmen (called Fuzzy-Wuzzies by British soldiers and Rudyard Kipling) in the Red Sea hills of the eastern Sudan that he earned his fame. He was converted to Mahdism in 1883 and was appointed an emir. In the Mahdist conquest of the Sudan he besieged and destroyed the garrison of Sinkat in 1884, and in the Battle of El Teb [q.v.] his warriors butchered the Egyptian gendarmerie under Valentine Baker [q.v.].

He was present in the Battle of Omdurman [q.v.] in 1898 but appears not to have taken an active role. To escape the victorious British, he fled to the Red Sea hills but was captured there on 19 January 1900 and imprisoned until 1908. He devoted the last years of his life to religious contemplation and made the pilgrimage to Mecca (Makkah) as an old man in 1924. He died two years later at Wadi Halfa, Egypt.

Osman Nuri Pasha (1832–1900). A Turkish soldier who was educated at the Turkish military academy in Constantinople (Istanbul) and entered the cavalry. He served in the Crimean War [q.v.], and in 1860 he campaigned in Lebanon. He campaigned in 1866–68 against rebels in Crete and in 1871 against rebels in Serbia and Montenegro [see Turkish-Serbian War], distinguishing himself in the Battle of Alexinatz [q.v.]. He commanded the army on the frontier during the Russo-Turkish War [q.v.] of 1878–79. When the

Osman Digna *Sudanese chief and Mahdist commander*

Russians crossed the Danube, he retreated into the fortress at Plevna [see Plevna, Siege of]. After the war he served four times as war minister.

Ossetian Military Road. A military road built in 1889 by the Russians over the Caucasus Mountains by way of the Mamison Pass (altitude 9,230 feet), just south of the Adai Khokh on the boundary between North and South Ossetia, the latter being part of Georgia.

Osten-Sacken, Dimitri von der (1793–1881). A Russian general who in 1855, during the Crimean War [q.v.], was commandant of besieged Sevastopol [q.v.].

Osterhaus, Peter Joseph (1823–1917). A Prussian-born soldier who was educated in German military schools. He became embroiled in the revolutionary movements that swept through Europe in 1848–49 and was forced to flee to the United States. For a time he was a clerk in a store in Belleview, Illinois. He later moved to St. Louis, where he found a welcome in its large German community. At the beginning of the American Civil War he was a major in a battalion of Missouri volunteers taken into the Union army. He fought at Wilson's Creek [q.v.] in August 1861 and was promoted colonel in December. He commanded a division in the Battle of Pea Ridge [q.v.], and in June 1862 he was promoted brigadier general. He served at Vicksburg [q.v.] and was wounded at

Big Black River on 17 May. He recovered to fight at Chattanooga and in the Atlanta Campaign [qq.v.].

Generally regarded as the best of the foreign-born generals, he was promoted major general of volunteers on 23 July 1864. After the war he alternated between homes in France, where he was American consul at Lyons, and St. Louis, where he carried on a hardware business. By an act of Congress on 17 March 1905 he was placed on the retired list as a brigadier general. He died in Coblenz just three months before the United States declared war on his homeland.

Ostermann-Tolstoy, Aleksandr Ivanovich (1770–1837). A Russian soldier who served with distinction at Eylau, Friedland, Borodino, and Bautzen [qq.v.]. Commanding in the Battle of Kulm [q.v.], he defeated French General Dominique Vandamme [q.v.].

Österreichische Waffenfabrik Gesellschaft. See Styr.

Ostroleka, Battle of (26 May 1831), Polish Revolution. After the Polish victory at Grochow [q.v.] on 20 February 1831, the Polish army under General Jan Skrzynecki [q.v.] encountered and was defeated by a much larger Russian army led by Hans Diebitsch [q.v.] at this commune on the banks of the Narew River, 62 miles northeast of Warsaw. The Poles fell back on Warsaw, the only place still in open revolt.

Earlier, during the Napoleonic Wars, French forces defeated a Russian army here on 16 February 1807.

Ostronovo, Battle of (25–26 July 1812), Napoleon's Russian Campaign. While Napoleon was moving forward between the Dvina and Dnieper rivers, seeking to engage Russian forces under General Mikhail Barclay de Tolly [q.v.] near Vitebsk, French Marshal Joachim Murat [q.v.] and his cavalry were strongly opposed near Ostronovo, on the banks of the Dvina, 90 miles northeast of Mogilev. This led Napoleon to believe that the retreating Russians had turned at bay, and he delayed a day to wait for the main body of his army to appear. While he delayed, Barclay de Tolly retreated on 27 July toward Smolensk in an attempt to join forces with General Pëtr Bagration.

Ostrów / Ostrowo / Ostrów Wielkopolski, Battle of (25–26 July 1812), Napoleon's Russian Campaign. At this Polish commune, 62 miles southeast of Poznan, Russian troops under General Aleksandr Ostermann-Tolstoy [q.v.] attacked French corps under Marshal Michel Ney and Joachim Murat [qq.v.]. After a two-day battle the Russians were repulsed with a loss of 3,000 killed and wounded, 800 taken prisoner, and eight guns lost; French losses were comparable.

Other Ranks. A British term for those soldiers below the rank of the lowest commissioned officer. Enlisted men in American usage. [See Rank and File.]

Otis, Elwell Stephen (1838–1909). An American soldier who was graduated from Harvard Law School in 1861 and in September of the following year was commissioned a captain in the 140th New York Infantry to fight for the Union in the American Civil War. He took part in all of the engagements of V Corps of the Army of the Potomac [q.v.]. He received promotions to lieutenant colonel and took command of his regiment in the Battle of Spotsylvania [q.v.]. In 1865 he was mustered out, receiving brevets to colonel and brigadier general.

In the same year he entered the army as a lieutenant colonel of the 22nd Infantry and until 1880 saw service on the northwestern plains, fighting in Indian campaigns, including the Great Sioux War [q.v.] of 1876–77. In 1880 he was promoted colonel of the 20th Infantry, and the following year he was directed to establish a school for young officers at Fort Leavenworth. It was opened in November 1881 with Otis as commandant. An intellectual, he made profound contributions to military training. In 1890 he was assigned to head the recruiting service, and three years later he was promoted brigadier general. In May 1898 he was appointed a major general of volunteers, and in July he sailed to the Philippines. He soon succeeded Wesley Merritt [q.v.] as military governor and commander of the Department of the Pacific. In 1899 he launched a campaign against the Philippine insurrectionists [see Philippine Insurrection against the United States]. When in May 1900 he was succeeded by General Arthur MacArthur [q.v.], he returned to the United States and was promoted major general in the regular army. He retired in 1902.

Otis, George Alexander (1830–1881). An American army surgeon who served in the American Civil War and thereafter. In 1864 he became the second curator of the Army Medical Museum, serving until 1881. He developed the museum into a research institution and the first public medical museum. He was widely known and respected for his surgical writings, but he was interested in all aspects of army medicine. In 1877 he wrote *Report to the Surgeon General on the Transport of Sick and Wounded by Pack Animals*. He edited *Medical and Surgical History of the War of the Rebellion* (vol. 1 [1870]; II [1876]).

Otis, Harrison Gray (1837–1917). An American soldier and journalist who served through the American Civil War and the Spanish-American War, being promoted to brigadier general and brevet major general in 1899. Between wars he settled in California, where he edited the *Santa Barbara Press* (1876–79) and the *Los Angeles Times* (from 1882), which under his leadership violently opposed labor unions. On 1 October 1910 the *Times* building was dynamited, and 21 employees were killed.

Ottoman War with Serbia and Montenegro. See Turko-Serbian War.

Oudinot, Nicolas Charles (1767–1847). A French soldier of the Revolutionary Wars. The son of a brewer, he enlisted in 1784 in the infantry, in which he served for three years. By 1789 he was a captain of a cavalry troop. He fought in the armies of the Rhine and the Moselle and distinguished himself in the battles of Austerlitz in 1805, Friedland in 1807, and Wagram in 1809 [qq.v.]. In 1809 he was made a marshal and the Duc de Reggio. He took part in Napoleon's Russian Campaign and fought at Bautzen in 1813 [qq.v.] and in the defense of France in 1813–14. An exceptionally brave man, he was wounded thirty-four times, more than any other senior officer in Napoleon's armies, although perhaps some of his wounds were incurred in café brawls, for which he was noted. Before each battle his servant, confident that he would be

wounded, laid out bandages and a medical kit. During the Hundred Days [q.v.] he offered his services to Napoleon but was rebuffed. In 1823 he led a French corps into Spain [see French Intervention in Spain]. For a time he was governor of Madrid. His last position was as governor of Hôtel des Invalides [q.v.].

Oudinot, Nicolas Charles Victor (1791–1863). A French soldier who was the son of Napoleon's Marshal Nicolas Oudinot [q.v.]. In July 1849 he led the French expedition against the Republic of Rome that defeated Giuseppe Garibaldi [q.v.].

Outbar, to. To shut out by fortifications.

Outfit Allowance. In the British army this was a sum paid to a newly commissioned officer from the ranks [see Ranker]. In the late nineteenth century it amounted to £150 for cavalry and £100 for infantry.

Outflank. A maneuver in which an attacking force succeeds in going around and behind the flank of its enemy.

Outgeneral, to. To gain victory or some military advantage through superior strategic or tactical skills.

Outpensioner. A veteran attached to a military hospital, such as Chelsea [q.v.], but permitted to live elsewhere.

Outposts. 1. Detachments of soldiers placed at a distance from a camp or bivouac to prevent troops from being surprised by an enemy. Sir Garnet Wolseley [q.v.] wrote: "The most arduous, while at the same time the most important duties that devolve upon soldiers in the field are those of outposts. . . . All concerned should feel that the safety of the army and the honour of the country depend upon their untiring vigilance and activity." [See Mahan, Dennis Hart.]

2. Military installations located far from their national homelands for the purpose of protecting territories or possessions, as in "an outpost of empire."

Outposts *Spanish outpost near Remedios, Cuba*

Outram, James (1803–1863). A British soldier and colonial administrator dubbed by Sir Charles Napier [q.v.], who later became his bitterest enemy, the Bayard of India, an accolade that was inscribed on his tomb in Westminster Abbey. In 1818 he joined the Bombay native infantry and in 1825 organized a corps of Bhil tribesmen, which he led for ten years. He was a political agent in Gujrat from 1835 to 1838 and then took part in the Afghan War [q.v.] of 1839–42. In 1840 he was political agent in Sind, and in 1843 he successfully defended the British Residency in Hyderabad from an attack by 8,000 Beluchis. In 1857 he commanded the British forces in the Persian War [q.v.]. During the Indian Mutiny [qq.v.] he accompanied the force of Sir Henry Havelock [q.v.] as a volunteer and as chief commissioner of Oudh in the expedition to relieve the besieged Residency at Lucknow [q.v.]. The force succeeded in reaching the Residency, but, too weak to bring out the women and children safely, it became itself besieged. Outram took command and held out until the Residency was relieved by General Colin Campbell [q.v.]. He later sat on the Supreme Council at Calcutta. He retired to England in 1860.

Outrance. The final extremity. Usually used in the French sense of *se battre à outrance* (to fight to the last man).

Outrank, to. To be senior to other soldiers because of holding a higher rank than theirs or a rank awarded earlier than others of the same rank or because of being in an army or corps in which officers outrank all officers of equal rank in other armies or corps—for example, regular officers outranking militia officers of the same rank or guards outranking line officers. Before the crown took over the Indian army after the mutiny, all British regular officers outranked all company officers of the same grade.

Outwall. The exterior wall of a fort or building.

Outwing, to. To extend the flanks of an army or line in action.

Outworks. Fortifications or other works between the enceinte and the glacis of a fortress.

Overage in Grade. Said of an officer who was too old to serve in his present rank. Such officers were common in most armies between major wars. It was not a cause for retirement in all armies. In 1855 the average age for a major in the British army was forty-nine. Some were as old as fifty-two, and all had served for at least twenty-six years.

Overalls. In British usage, the tight-fitting trousers strapped under the instep worn by cavalrymen.

Overland Campaign (4 May–12 June 1864), American Civil War. A campaign that began when Union Lieutenant General U. S. Grant and Major General George Meade [q.v.] with 120,000 troops crossed the Rapidan River south into central Virginia with the Army of the Potomac [q.v.], to attack Robert E. Lee's Army of Northern Virginia [q.v.] with 60,000 troops. The fighting continued for forty days almost without respite, General Grant stating that he proposed to "fight it out on this line if it takes all summer." He lost men at the rate of 2,000 per day and failed to capture Richmond, but he seriously reduced the effectiveness of Lee's army.

Overslaugh, to. To hinder or to halt by some unexpected act. Officers were sometimes overslaughed when expecting a promotion or appointment that was given to another, sometimes junior in rank.

Over the Hill, to go. A common expression in the American army, meaning to desert.

Ox Hill, Battle of. See Chantilly, Battle of.

Oyama, Iwao (1842–1916). A Japanese soldier who fought in the Boshin Civil War of 1868 and the Satsuma Rebellion of 1877 [qq.v.]. Between these wars he studied European military methods, particularly those of France, from 1870 to 1874 and thus witnessed the disastrous defeat of that country in the Franco-Prussian War [q.v.]. He became a general in 1891 and commanded the Second Army in the Sino-Japanese war of 1894–95 [q.v.], capturing Port Arthur and Weihaiwei [qq.v.]. He was promoted to field marshal in 1898 and commanded the Manchurian army in the Russo-Japanese War of 1904–05, defeating the Russians in the battles of Liaoyang, Shaho, and Mukden.

Ozanian, Andranik (1863–1927). An Armenian rebel in northeast Turkey who in 1895 joined a guerrilla band near the Russian border and soon became its leader, fighting Turks and Kurds. He later took part in the Balkan War of 1912 and fought with the Russians against the Turks in World War I. When his dream of an Armenian state evaporated, he emigrated to the United States and died in Fresno, California.

Pa / Pah. A Maori fort in New Zealand consisting of a rectangular palisade about 50 by 90 yards behind which was a maze of covered entrenchments.

Paardeberg, Battle of (18–27 February 1900), Second Anglo-Boer War. On 18 February 1900 a fleeing force of about 5,000 Boers, including families, under Pieter Cronjé [q.v.] was surrounded in the riverbed of the Modder River in western Orange Free State, 23 miles south of Kimberly, by British forces under General (later Field Marshal) John French [q.v.]. Lord Kitchener [q.v.] then took command. After more than 1,000 casualties were sustained in unsuccessful British assaults, Lord Roberts took personal command and through less costly siege operations forced Cronjé's surrender on 27 February. Total British losses were 98 officers and 1,437 other ranks; Boer losses were about 1,000 killed and wounded and 4,000 taken prisoner.

Paardekraal. The name of the South African farm near Krugersdorp where on 16 December 1880 thousands of Transvaal burghers, unhappy with a British plan to annex the Transvaal, met to listen to antiannexation speeches and to place stones in a symbolic heap with a pledge to recover their independence. This marked the beginning of the First Anglo-Boer War [q.v.]. A monument was later erected over the cairn to commemorate the event.

Pacific, Army of the. A loosely knit American military force during the American Civil War that fought Apaches and Navajos in the American Southwest from 1862 through 1864. It consisted of a brigade of California volunteers under Brigadier General James H. Carleton [q.v.] and two regiments of New Mexican volunteers.

Pacific, War of the (1879–84). A war fought by Chile against Bolivia and Peru, sometimes called the Nitrate War. All three countries wanted control of the Atacama Desert, an area in present-day north-central Chile extending north from Copiapó to the northern part of Atacama Province near María Elena. It is a completely barren land with borax lakes, saline deposits, and rich deposits of nitrate, the value of which had been discovered in the 1860s. In 1866 Bolivia, which then had access to the sea, and Chile established their borders at the twenty-fourth parallel. On 6 February 1873 Bolivia and Peru secretly formed an alliance to protect their interests in the Atacama. In 1875 Peru seized the Chilean nitrate companies in what it considered its territory, and three years later Bolivia did the same. On 14 February 1879

Chilean President Anibal Pinto (1825–1884) sent 200 Chilean troops to occupy Antofagasta, 680 miles north of Santiago, and on 5 April he declared war on Bolivia and Peru.

The early stages of the war were fought at sea. Chileans bombarded and seized Callao, Peru, and they blockaded the harbors and occupied the entire coast of Bolivia. Peru sent its ironclad ship commanded by Admiral Miguel Grau (1838–1879) to harass the Chileans, but it was destroyed on 8 October 1879 off Antofagasta, and Grau was killed. Chilean land forces moved north and seized Tacna [q.v.] on 26 May and Arica on 8 June 1880. In November Chile defeated the combined Peruvian-Bolivian forces near Iquique [q.v.], 235 miles north of Antofagasta.

The Bolivians were soon knocked out of the war. General Helarión Daza (original surname: Grosolé [1840–1894]), president of Bolivia, led his army so poorly that his troops mutinied; he was overthrown in a revolution in 1880. But the Peruvians fought on until a Chilean army of nearly 25,000 landed at Pisco, Peru, and marched on Lima. Efforts to mediate by the United States, beginning in October 1880, were unsuccessful. On 4 January 1881 the Chileans stormed Lurín, and they again defeated the Peruvians at Chorrillos on the 13th and at Miraflores [qq.v.], now a Lima suburb, two days later. Entering Lima unopposed, they instituted a reign of terror, laying ruin to buildings, looting the university, and destroying the national archives. They remained in occupation for two years, until 20 October 1883. Peru ceded Tarapacá Province with the provision that it was to hold Tacna and Arica for ten years, after which a plebiscite would determine ownership. The war with Bolivia ended on 4 April 1884 with the Treaty of Valparaiso, which deprived Bolivia of all access to the Pacific Ocean.

Pacifists. Aside from certain religious groups, notably the Society of Friends (Quakers), the nineteenth century saw little objection to wars as such, although at times some unorganized objection to particular wars was voiced. Religious pacifists were sometimes employed in noncombatant roles such as wagoneers. The nonreligious conscientious objectors of twentieth-century wars did not exist or if they did, they failed to make their views known, although many objected to conscription [q.v.]. Of the smaller religious sects, the Dunkards, Amanists, Shakers, and Schwenkfelders suffered for their pacifist beliefs during the American Civil War and in Russia the Doukhobars (Dukhbors or Doukhobors), who rejected both religious and civil authority, were persecuted.

Packet, Full or Half. In British army argot, a full packet was a punishment of 168 hours of hard labor; a half packet was, incongruously, 96 hours.

Pack Howitzer. A short-barreled artillery piece that could be easily and quickly dismantled and carried on mules with pack saddles. [See Mountain Gun; Screw Gun; Camel Gun.]

Packmaster. A person in charge of a packtrain [q.v.]; an expert at loading pack animals [see Cargador].

Packtrain. An army caravan of mules, usually about fifty in the American West, with its complement of muleteers and equipment under a packmaster [q.v.].

Padri War (1821–37), a religious war in Sumatra. About 1815 some Muslim pilgrims, having returned from Mecca (Makkah), inaugurated a fundamentalist reformation of the Islamic culture that had long existed in the Minangkabau region in west-central Sumatra. The sect gained in influence, and its adherents became known as Padris (whites) because of the white clothes they habitually wore. Local chiefs, who, contrary to Islamic law, inherited their positions through the female line, found the Padris a threat and attempted to suppress them. When they failed, they called upon the Dutch for assistance. The Dutch responded by laying partial siege to the Padri capital at Bondjol, 20 miles north-northwest of Bukittinggi, for fifteen years. Even though the Padris officially surrendered in 1837, some continued to wage guerrilla warfare in the mountains. An indirect result of this war was Dutch annexation of Minangkaibau.

Paducah, Battle of (25 March 1864), American Civil War. Confederate General Nathan B. Forrest [q.v.] with 2,800 men moved from Columbus, Mississippi, into western Tennessee to recover deserters, break up guerrilla bands, and enlist recruits. Part of his command defeated a Federal force at Union City, Tennessee, while he pushed forward with the remainder to Paducah, Kentucky, which he captured at midday on 25 March, although 665 Union soldiers occupying earthworks west of town refused to surrender. After burning a number of bales of cotton and a steamboat on the Ohio River, Forrest withdrew, taking with him 50 prisoners and 400 horses and mules. Union forces lost 14 killed and 46 wounded; Confederates lost 10 killed and 40 wounded.

Páez, José Antonio (1790–1873). A Venezuelan soldier and political leader who fought against the Spanish from 1810 to 1822, winning victories that were chiefly responsible for bringing Venezuela into the new republic of Greater Colombia. In 1829 he led a successful revolt against Simón Bolívar [q.v.], and from 1831 to 1846 he ruled as the first president of the new republic of Venezuela, before becoming dictator. Forced to resign, in 1847 he led the conservatives in a revolt against President José Tadeo Monagas [q.v.]. He was captured and imprisoned until 1850, when he was allowed to go into exile. He returned to Venezuela in 1858 and in 1860 was named minister to the United States. In 1861 he was again proclaimed dictator, but he was forced to resign in 1863 and again was sent into exile.

Page, Richard Lucian (1807–1901). An American naval officer and a nephew of Robert E. Lee, who during the American Civil War became a commander in the Confederate navy until March 1864, when he was commissioned a brigadier general and put in command of the outer defenses of Mobile, Alabama [see Mobile Bay, Siege of]. He held out until 22 August 1864, when he surrendered to General E. R. S. Canby [q.v.]. He was held prisoner until September 1865. After the war he was superintendent of public schools in Norfolk, Virginia.

Paget, George Augustus Frederick (1818–1880). A British soldier and son of Henry William Paget, First Marquess of Anglesey [q.v.], who fought with distinction in the Crimean War [q.v.], in which he commanded the third line in the charge of the Light Brigade [q.v.] at Balaclava. He was promoted general in 1877. He was the author of *Crimean Journal* (1875).

Paget, Henry William (1768–1854). A British soldier who became First Marquess of Anglesey. In 1793 he raised the 30th Foot from among the tenants on his father's estate in Staffordshire and became its lieutenant colonel. He served in Flanders in 1794 as a brigade commander and in Holland in 1799 as commander of a brigade of light cavalry, and in 1808, in the Peninsular War [q.v.], he commanded a cavalry division. On his return to England he abandoned his wife and eloped with the Duke of Wellington's sister-in-law. Consequently he received no appointment under Wellington in the peninsula, but in 1809 he commanded an infantry division in the Walcheren Expedition [q.v.]. At Waterloo [q.v.] he commanded the cavalry and horse artillery and lost a leg to a round shot. He was later lord lieutenant in Ireland and in 1846 became a field marshal.

Pagri. See Pugri / Puggari / Paggi.

Pahang Civil War (1857–63). A family feud over the sultanate of the Malay state of Pahang broke out on the death of Sultan Bendahara Tun Ali in 1857. The eldest son, Tun Mutahir (d. 1863), was supported by the sultan of Johore and by the British; a younger son was supported by a rival sultan and by the Siamese. Both sides engaged in raids, ambushes, and occasional small fights until the death of Tun Mutahir.

Paint Creek, Battle of (7 March 1868), American Indian Wars. In Texas, Captain (later General) Adna Chaffee [q.v.] led three companies of the 6th U.S. Cavalry in a successful charge against Comanche Indians camped along Paint Creek, an action that earned Chaffee a brevet majority.

Paiute War (January 1867–August 1868), American Indian Wars. American soldiers under Lieutenant Colonel (later Major General) George Crook [q.v.] fought hostile Paiute Indians in southeastern Oregon and southwestern Idaho until they were subdued and forced onto reservations. Two years later the Paiutes instituted the ritual ghost dance [see Ghost Dance Disturbances].

Paixhans, Henri Joseph (1783–1854). A French artillery officer who invented the Paixhans gun, one of the earliest cannon to throw explosive shells. In 1848 he was promoted general of brigade.

Pajol, Claude Pierre (1772–1844). A French soldier who enlisted in 1791 and was commissioned the following year. He served in Napoleon's armies, winning distinction at the battles of Austerlitz, Jena, and Wagram and in Napoleon's Russian Campaign [qq.v.]. He was promoted to general of brigade in 1807 and general of division in 1812. At Borodino [q.v.] he charged at the head of a light cavalry division and was severely wounded. He fought at Lützen, Dresden, and Leipzig [qq.v.]. He rallied to Napoleon during the Hundred Days and fought at Waterloo [qq.v.] in 1815. He took an active part in the French Revolution of 1830 [q.v.] as an insurgent leader and was subsequently appointed a peer of France and governor of Paris.

Pakeha. The Maori word for white soldiers and settlers [see Maori Wars].

Pakenham, Edward (1778–1815). An Irish soldier who was commissioned in the 92nd Foot at the age of sixteen and four years later, thanks to the purchase system [q.v.], became a major and a year after that, at age twenty-one, the lieutenant colonel of the 62nd Foot. In 1801 he was posted to the West Indies, and in 1803 he was wounded in the capture of St. Lucia [q.v.]. He returned to England and then took part in the Battle of Copenhagen [q.v.] before returning to the West Indies in 1809 for a short time. In 1812–13 he served as deputy adjutant general under Wellington in the Peninsular War [q.v.] and subsequently commanded a division. He was killed in the Battle of New Orleans in the War of 1812 [qq.v.] on 8 January 1815.

Pala. A Turkish saber with a large, heavy, relatively short (usually 27-inch) blade.

Palafax y Melzi, José de (1780–1847). A Spanish soldier who during the Peninsular War commanded the defenders of Saragossa [q.v.] from July 1808 to February 1809. He was captured by the French at the fall of the city and remained a prisoner until 1814. During the First Carlist War [q.v.] he was a prominent Cristino. In 1841 he was made captain general of Aragón.

Palanka. A permanent entrenched camp attached to Turkish frontier forts.

Palestrina, Battle of (9 May 1849). Italian Wars of Independence. At this small town east-southeast of Rome some 4,000 Italian patriots under Giuseppe Garibaldi [q.v.] were defeated in a three-hour battle with 7,000 Neapolitan troops under King Ferdinand II (1810–1859). Garibaldi was seriously wounded.

Palestro, Battle of (30 May 1859), Austro-Piedmontese War. Piedmontese under General Enrico Cialdini [q.v.], assisted by a French army under the personal command of Napoleon III (1808–1873), defeated an Austrian force near the town of Palestro, 11 miles north of Martara. The Austrians attacked as the Allies were crossing the Sesia River but were thrown back. The Allied armies then invaded Lombardy.

Palestro *Battle of Palestro, May 1859*

Palikao, Charles Guillaume Marie Apollinaire Antoine Cousin-Montauban, Conte de (1796–1878). A French soldier who was commissioned in 1815 and in 1823 took part in the French expedition to Spain [see French Intervention in Spain]. In 1831 he was sent to Algeria, where he spent the next twenty years. On 23 December 1847 he personally received the surrender of Abd el-Kadir [q.v.], and in 1855 he was promoted general of division. After a tour of duty in France (1857–60) he was sent to China to command the 7,000 French troops there in the Second Opium War [q.v.]. In conjunction with British General James Hope Grant [q.v.] he took part in the storming of the Taku (Dagu) forts [q.v.] and the capture of Peking (Beijing).

In August 1870 on the outbreak of the Franco-Prussian War [q.v.] he was commanding a corps at Lyons but was soon appointed prime minister and minister of war. When the Second Empire was demolished by republican forces, he retreated to Belgium and served no more.

Palisade. 1. As a noun, a fence of a fort made from stakes, often about 10 feet long, triangular in shape and sharpened at the upper end. The blunt end was buried in a ditch. When planted upright side by side and arranged in a square, they formed a fort. The palisades of some forts were slanted slightly outward.

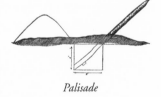

Palisade

2. As a verb, to construct such a fence.

Paliser, William (1830–1882). A British cavalry officer who in 1862 invented a method for converting smoothbore cannons to rifled ones and later developed chilled cast-iron shot.

Pallasch. A German-style backsword with a straight, heavy blade suitable for making cuts, used by heavy cavalry in many armies. It was usually single-edged with a knuckle guard.

Palma, Tomás Estrada (1835–1908). A Cuban revolutionist who participated in Cuban revolutions from 1868 to 1877. He was captured and imprisoned for a year, after which he lived in exile until the Cuban Revolution of 1898 [see Spanish-American War]. In 1902 he was elected the first president of Cuba and served until 1906. Although reelected in May 1906, he resigned in September.

Palmer, Arthur (1840–1904). A British soldier who entered the Indian army in 1857 and served in campaigns on the Northwest Frontier and in the Abyssinian Campaign [qq.v.] in 1868. In 1885 he was with the Indian contingent that took part in the Suakim Campaign in the Sudan [see Sudan, Reconquest of]. In 1899 he was promoted general and appointed commander-in-chief, India.

Palmer, Innis Newton (1824–1900). An American soldier who on graduation from West Point in 1846 during the Mexican War immediately left for Mexico, where he served under General Winfield Scott [q.v.]. He took part in the battles of Contreras, Churubusco, and Chapultepec [qq.v.] and earned two brevets. He later served on the western frontier, where he fought in Indian campaigns in Texas in 1852–54. During the American Civil War he commanded the Union cavalry at First Bull Run and fought in the Peninsular Campaign and the war in North Carolina, including the Battle of New Bern [qq.v.]. He became a major general of volunteers but after the war reverted to his regular army rank of lieutenant colonel. He retired as a colonel in 1879.

Palmer, John McCauley (1817–1900). An American lawyer, politician, and soldier who served in the American Civil War from the rank of colonel of the 14th Illinois through major general. He commanded a division at Chickamauga and a corps at Chattanooga [qq.v.]. While with the army of General W. T. Sherman [q.v.] before Atlanta, he was involved in a dispute with General John M. Schofield [q.v.] over their relative ranks as major generals, and at his own request he was relieved of command on 7 August 1864. He was mustered out on 1 September 1866. In 1896 he was an unsuccessful presidential candidate of the Gold Democrats.

Palmetto Arsenal / Armory. In 1850 the legislature of South Carolina appropriated $300,000 for the purchase of arms for the state militia. One contract, dated 15 April 1851, was issued to William Glaze and Benjamin Flagg of the Palmetto Iron Works in Columbia for the manufacture of 6,000 muskets, 1,000 rifles, 2,000 pistols, and 2,000 swords. Although the plant came to be called an armory, Glaze and Flagg, after purchasing the necessary equipment from northern industries, actually converted it into an arsenal, and when the American Civil War began, South Carolina was better armed than any other southern state. The arsenal produced ammunition and other vital material until 1865, when it was almost gutted by Union troops in the Carolina Campaign [q.v.]. Rebuilt, it continued to operate well into the twentieth century.

Palmetto Musket. A .69 caliber smoothbore musket manufactured in the 1850s by William Glaze & Company of Columbia, South Carolina. It was a virtual copy of the U.S. Model 1842 percussion musket [see Percussion Cap]. South Carolina equipped its militia with this weapon, and it saw considerable service in the American Civil War.

Palmito Ranch, Battle of (12–13 May 1865), American Civil War. Last battle of the war and the last Confederate victory. This battle, 12 miles from Brownsville, Texas, was initiated by Union Colonel Theodore Harvey Barrett (d. 1900), an inexperienced and ambitious officer, who, disregarding direct orders not to initiate military action, led a force of 800 troops, including soldiers from his own 62nd Colored Infantry, in an attack upon about 350 ragged Confederate cavalrymen under Colonel John Salmon ("Rest in Peace") Ford [q.v.]. Barrett's force was routed and pursued as it fled toward Brazos Island. The Federals lost 13 killed and wounded, and 113 were taken prisoner; Ford gave his casualty figures as 5 slightly wounded. Ten months later, for reasons not readily apparent, Barrett was brevetted brigadier general.

Palo Alto, Battle of (8 May 1846), Mexican War. In this first major battle of the war, General Zachary Taylor [q.v.] with 2,300 men defeated a Mexican force of 6,000 under General Mariano Arista [q.v.] at this town, 12 miles northeast of Fort Texas (Brownsville, Texas). The battle began at 2:00 P.M. and lasted five hours. The superior firepower of American rifles and artillery dissolved Mexican cavalry attacks and Arista retreated, having lost an estimated 300 killed and 380 wounded, mostly from artillery fire. American losses were 9 killed and 47 wounded.

Pamplona, Blockade of (30 June–31 October 1813), Peninsular War. After the Battle of Vitoria [q.v.] on 21 June 1813 the main French forces moved into the Pyrenees, but left strong garrisons at Pamplona and San Sebastián. Wellington sent Spanish General Henry Joseph O'Donnell [q.v.] with 11,000 men to blockade Pamplona, which was defended by only 3,000. On 27 July the French made a sortie that so panicked O'Donnell that he spiked his guns. Only the timely arrival of General Carlos José d'Espignac España (so called) (1775–1839) drove the French back. On 28 July Wellington arrived on the scene and fought the Battle of Sorauren [q.v.] almost within sight of Pamplona. The blockade was reestablished under España, and on 31 October 1813 the French capitulated, yielding the last major French post on Spanish soil.

Pan. The small dish-shaped container fitted to the lock of a musket that held the priming powder.

Panada. A hot gruel, sometimes called bully stew, panda, or ginger panada, fed to hospital patients. It was believed to have been created by Eliza Harris (d. 1867), a field worker for the U.S. Sanitary Commission [q.v.], and was usually made of cornmeal, crushed hardtack, wine, and ginger boiled in water. A variation, using sugar and whiskey, was credited to Clara Barton [q.v.].

Panama Expedition, American (2 April–1 May 1885). On 2 April 1885 when a revolution was in progress in Panama [see Panamanian Revolutions] Commander (later Rear Admiral) Bowman H. McCalla (1840?–1915) of the U.S. navy received orders to transport a force of marines and sailors to Panama to protect American lives and property—particularly the trans-isthmus railroad, opened that year, whose Aspinall (Colón) railway terminus had been destroyed. Although the force he landed was not large—280 sailors and 460 marines—it was the largest armed U.S. intervention into Latin America in the nineteenth century and the largest foreign military operation carried out by the United States between the Mexican War in 1846–47 and the Spanish-American War of 1898 [qq.v.]. The marines were led by Major and brevet Lieutenant Colonel Charles Heywood [q.v.], and they manned six 3-inch guns and three Gatling guns. The first contingent of 125 landed at Panama City on 18 April. All departed on 1 May. The expedition proved effective; no American lives were lost.

Panamanian Revolutions. In 1821 Panama declared itself independent of Spain, but it was soon absorbed by Colombia. In the 1830s three unsuccessful revolutions were mounted against Colombia. Between 1850 and 1900 Panama underwent forty political administrations, five riots, and five more attempts to secede from Columbia. The United States intervened thirteen times, but never with a major force [see Panama Expedition, American]. Panama did not gain its independence until 1903.

Panda (d. 1872), also known as Umpande or Umpanda. A brother of the Zulu king Dingaan [q.v.], who in 1839, after quarreling with Dingaan, fled Zululand with his followers and sought the protection of the Boers across the Tugela River. In January 1840, aided by a Boer commando, he went to war against his brother and in a final battle on the Umkuzi River decisively defeated Dingaan's forces. On 10 February 1840 Commandant General Marthinus Wessels Pretorius [q.v.] installed Panda as the king of the Zulus, and in 1843 the British recognized him as an independent king.

Panda / Ginger Panda. See Panada; Bully Soup.

Pande / Pandy. An epithet used by British soldiers and others for mutineers in the Bengal army during the Indian Mutiny [q.v.], derived, it is said, from the name of Sepoy Mangal (Mungal) Pande of the 34th Bengal Native Infantry, who on 29 March 1857 in an attempt to touch off a mutiny wounded the regimental adjutant and the subedar major. He was executed on 8 April.

Pandours. Austrian irregular soldiers. In 1741 Baron Franz von der Trenck (1711–1749), an Austrian soldier, organized for the army of Maria Theresa (1717–1780) an irregular regiment of Croatian peasants, called pandours (a Croatian word for guards, constables, or the armed retainers of large landowners) as a defense against Turks on the Austrian border. By the nineteenth century they had formed a corps of irregulars in which only the officers and noncommissioned officers were paid. They were considered to have plunder rights, and they took no prisoners. Their name became synonymous with brutality, marauding, cruelty. The name was finally applied to Croatian soldiers generally.

In India, Maratha armies had similar groups called *pendhari* or Pindaris [see Third Maratha War].

Panduks. Turkish sharpshooters.

Panjdeh / Pendjeh Incident (1885). Panjdeh, a village in Central Asia on the east bank of the Kushka River near its junction with the Murghab, halfway between Merv and Herat, lying astride the strategic approach to Herat, was claimed by Afghanistan, a claim supported by Great Britain but contested by Russia. On 30 March 1885 there occurred near the village a clash between Afghan and Russian forces. The Russians refused a demand that they leave and sent the Afghans an ultimatum that expired the following day. After

trying unsuccessfully to incite the Afghans to fire the first shot, the Russians advanced and, at a cost of 40 killed and wounded, seized the town; Afghan losses were said, improbably, to be 800.

This small engagement shook the peace of the world, for in the Great Game [q.v.] played out in Central Asia by Britain and Russia, the British believed that Russia must not so easily score an advantage. India itself seemed threatened. The British Parliament voted £11 million for war, the largest sum so voted since the Crimean War [q.v.], and the Royal Navy was placed on full alert. Headlines in the *New York Times* thundered, IT IS WAR, and the news rocked Wall Street and world markets.

The Panjdeh incident came at an apposite time for Prime Minister William Ewart Gladstone (1809–1898), known affectionately as the Grand Old Man. The Gordon Relief Expedition [q.v.] had just ended in failure, but popular sentiment, not shared by Gladstone, was for keeping the British forces in the Sudan, perhaps to reconquer it. The attack on Panjdeh, which he dubbed an "unprovoked aggression," provided him, as he later confessed, "a heaven sent excuse" for withdrawing from the Sudan. However, as one member of Parliament remarked, "I don't object so much to the Grand Old Man always producing the ace of trumps from up his sleeve, but I do object to his saying that the Almighty put it there."

Faced with British opposition, the Russians pulled back. In 1887 the Afghans exchanged the village for a strategic mountain pass farther west.

Panthay Rebellions (1855–61 and 1863–73). In South China during the disorderly state of affairs in the Manchu Empire during the Taiping Rebellion [q.v.] a number of smaller rebellions of discontented peoples flared throughout the empire against Manchu rule [see Nien Rebellion; Miao Rebellions; Chinese Turkestan, Conquest of; Chinese Civil Wars]. In the Chinese province of Yunnan (Yünnan), in South China, south of Sikang and Szechwan, Muslims (Panthays) established their own state under a sultan in 1855. They were crushed in 1861 but rose again in 1863. When the Taiping Rebellion was suppressed, the imperial government moved to reassert its control, and in February 1873 Tungchow (Tali), the capital of the rebellious Panthays on the west shore of Erh Hai, was captured. Many of the town's inhabitants were massacred, and the sultan committed suicide, effectively putting an end to the independence of the state.

Panzerny. Polish light cavalry.

Papachka. The tall fur cap worn by Cossacks [q.v.].

Papal States, Troubles in the. Pope Innocent III (1161–1216), whose papacy began in 1198, established rights of sovereignty over much of central Italy, including Ancona, Ravenna, Ferrara, and Spoleto. Other provinces were added in the seventeenth century. In 1797 Napoleon seized Romagna (a Papal State that now forms the Italian provinces of Ferrara, Bologna, Ravenna, and Forlì) and incorporated it into the Cisalpine Republic. The following year the French occupied Rome, and the Papal States became the Roman Republic. In 1800 Pope Pius VII (1742–1823), who in 1804 was to crown Napoleon, briefly obtained possession of the Papal States, but they were retaken by the French. In 1830–31 the people of Romagna rose in revolt [see Romagna, Insurrection in]. They were put down by Austrian troops. In 1848 there was an insurrection in Rome; Pope Pius IX (1792–1878) fled to Gaeta, and a republic was proclaimed. Following the defeat of Garibaldi in the Battle of Palestrina [q.v.] on 9 May 1849, Pius was restored, and his subjects were reduced to submission by the arms of France, Austria, Naples (Kingdom of the Two Sicilies), and Spain. The French occupied Rome until 1870. The Austrians remained in Romagna until July 1859. At their departure the Romagnese people threw off the papal authority and proclaimed their annexation to Sardinia. Rising discontent and unrest in the Papal States led the Piedmontese in September 1860 to cross the frontier. After defeating papal forces in the Battle of Castelfidardo [q.v.] on 18 September, they marched south to unite with Giuseppe Garibaldi's Red Shirts [q.v.]. The French troops occupying Rome prevented an Italian attack upon immediate papal territory, but other Papal States rose in revolt, and by 1870 all were occupied by the Italians. On 2 October they were declared part of the kingdom of Italy under King Victor Emmanuel II (1820–1878).

Pappenheimer. A sword deriving its name from Gottfried Heinrich, Count of Pappenheimer (1594–1632), a German cavalry general in the Thirty Years' War. It had a large cut-and-thrust blade and a knuckle guard with side bars.

Parabellum. A clip-loaded pistol, initially in 9 mm caliber, designed by Georg Luger [q.v.] in the 1890s and from 1898 manufactured by Deutsche Waffen und Munitionsfabrik (DWM). In 1900, manufactured in 7.65 mm caliber, it was taken into service for the first time when the Swiss army adopted it. In 1904 it was restored to 9 mm. In 1908 it was adopted by the German army. Its name evolved from DWM's telegraph address, PARBELLUM, derived from the Latin motto *Si vis pacem para bellum* (If you want peace, prepare for war). Commonly called a Luger, it became the most famous military pistol of the twentieth century.

Parabola Effect. See Minié Rifle.

Parade. 1. As a noun, the ceremonial formation of troops for inspection by a senior officer or civilian dignitary.
2. As a noun, a public procession.
3. As a noun, the grounds where soldiers drill.
4. As a verb, to cause troops to assemble, march, or maneuver.

Parade *Parade at Falmouth, Virginia, of the 110th Pennsylvania Volunteers*

5. As a verb, to march in a procession; troops usually marching in step.

Paradeanzug. German full-dress uniform.

Parade Officer. An officer who pays close attention to military minutiæ but is not noted for his knowledge of fighting battles and leading his men.

Parade Order. A military unit drawn up with the ranks open and the officers in front.

Paradiddle. A basic drumbeat made by beating with alternate drumsticks.

Paradomania. The obsession of Russian tsars and their military retainers for rigid uniformity and blind adherence to drill regulations. The so-called goose step was a Russian invention.

Parados. A mound, an embankment, or a rearward parapet erected in a fortification to protect defenders from a rear or ricochet fire [see Traverse].

Paraguayan Independence. On 14 May 1811 Paraguay became the first South American country to free itself from Spanish viceroyalty. Its independence was recognized by the Argentine Confederation in 1852 and by Great Britain in 1858. It quickly became a dictatorship. [See Triple Alliance, War of; López, Francesco Solano.]

Paraguayan War. See Triple Alliance, War of the.

Parallels. Trenches dug in siege operations roughly parallel to the fortification being attacked in siege operations, affording the attackers protection from the projectiles of the besieged. Three, connected by zigzag saps, were usually constructed with the third parallel closest to the enemy's walls.

The system was the conception of Sébastien de Vauban [q.v.], whose ideas concerning the defense of a position and of attack upon a fortification were still much respected and studied in the nineteenth century.

Paraná, Battle of (2 May 1866), War of the Triple Alliance. Paraguayan forces under Francisco López Solano [q.v.] attacked the Allied army under General Porto Algre as it was crossing the Paraná River. The Paraguayans were repulsed.

Parang. A name applied to a wide variety of Malay jungle knives whose blades generally widened near the point.

Parapet. 1. Breastwork, walls, bulwarks of earth, wood, stone, or other material behind which a soldier is protected and over which he can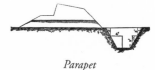

Parapet

fire. The parapets of fieldworks are always of earth, which has many advantages: It is usually readily obtainable, it is easily handled, and it provides good protection, for a strike produces no splinters or flying fragments. The command of parapet is the height of the interior crest above the site.

2. The battlement around a flat roof and the railings of a bridge are also called parapets.

Pardo, Manuel (1834–1878). A Peruvian political leader and banker. The first civilian elected president in Peru (1872–76), he signed the treaty with Bolivia in 1873 that led to the War of the Pacific [q.v.].

Paredes y Arrillaga, Mariano (1797–1849). A Mexican soldier and leader of extreme conservatives. He supported General Antonio López de Santa Anna [q.v.] in 1841, but later revolted against him, and in 1845 he led the attack against José Joaquín Herrera [q.v.]. From January to July 1846 he was president of Mexico. His actions were largely responsible for the war with the United States [see Mexican War]. In 1847 he went into exile.

Paris, Battle of (30 March–1 April 1814), Napoleonic Wars. In March 1814 four Allied columns under Prince von Schwarzenberg [q.v.] converged on Paris and French Marshal Auguste de Marmont [q.v.] fell back on the city. At first light on 30 March three columns attacked French positions at Vincennes, Belleville, and Montmartre [q.v.] while a fourth moved to outflank the Montmartre positions. Early on 1 April, with the Allies on the flank of the Montmartre line, the French surrendered, having lost 4,000 men. The Allies had lost twice that number, but Napoleon was persuaded that the end had come. Five days later he abdicated.

As the Allies approached Paris, the director of the Hôtel des Invalides, Marshal Jean Mathieu Philibert Sérurier [q.v.], ordered the destruction of some 1,500 captured battle flags.

Paris, Siege of (20 September 1870–28 January 1871), Franco-Prussian War. On 20 September 1870, after Napoleon III (1808–1873) was overwhelmed at Sedan and while Metz was still under siege [see Sedan, Battle of; Metz, Siege of], 146,000 Germans under General Helmuth von Moltke [q.v.] surrounded Paris, then a city of 2 million people, which was garrisoned by 220,000 men under General Louis Trochu [q.v.], plus 300,000 untrained and unreliable Garde Nationale [q.v.]. The siege was expected to be brief. Otto von Bismarck (1815–1898) estimated that "eight days without café au lait" would bring Parisians to their knees.

The eight days came and went. On 8 October 1870 Léon Gambetta (1838–1882), minister of the interior and a member of the Government of National Defense, in the futile hope of organizing France for defense, made a spectacular escape from Paris in a balloon. On 31 October a mutiny among the Garde Nationale was put down by regulars.

Moltke wished to wait patiently for the Parisians to surrender, but Bismarck insisted they be shelled into submission, and on 27 December nearly 200 guns were targeted on the city. Siege guns were brought up, and the first shell, fired on 5 January 1871, wounded a baby in a cradle and a schoolgirl in the Luxembourg Gardens. In the following three weeks an estimated 20,000 shells fell on the city, and 97 people were killed, 278 were wounded, and 1,084 buildings were damaged.

Among the besieged were of course some irrepressible souls. Small boys collected and sold shell fragments. The painter Édouard Manet (1832–1883), who had joined an artillery unit of the Garde Nationale, wrote to his wife,

Suzanne: "My soldier's knapsack is filled with everything essential for painting and soon I am going to start making some studies from life."

As food supplies diminished, people ate cats, dogs, and even animals from the zoo, including Castor and Pollux, two beloved elephants. Monkeys escaped slaughter, perhaps, mused an English journalist, because of "a vague and Darwinian notion that they are our relation." While Germans at Versailles dined on "pheasant and sauerkraut boiled in Champagne" and "a wild boar's head and a compote of raspberry jelly and mustard," Parisians ate an estimated 65,000 horses, 5,000 cats, and 1,200 dogs. An estimated 10,000 Parisians died of malnutrition and disease. The winter turned exceptionally cold, and in the week of 14–21 January 1871, the last week of the siege, 1,084 people died of pneumonia and other respiratory diseases. The only foreign envoy to remain in the city was Elihu Washburne (1816–1885) of the United States. Contact with the outside world was maintained by the use of carrier pigeons and balloons [qq.v.].

There were several unsuccessful attempts by General Trochu to break out [see Buzenval, Battle of; Villiers, Battle of]. The last one, a disaster, was on 19 January 1871. Trochu blamed General Auguste Ducrot [q.v.], who brought his corps onto the field two hours late. Whatever the cause, confusion and incompetence combined to ensure failure. The Garde Nationale even fired on its fellow soldiers. A staff officer, Captain Maurice d'Herisson, later wrote: "The drummers beat the charge; the colonel gave the word of command, 'En avant!' the regiment shouted, 'Vive la République!' and—no one stirred. That went on for three hours."

On 23 January 1871 Jules Favre (1809–1880), the foreign minister, donned his best clothes, put on his top hat, and in a leaky rowboat crossed the Seine to talk with Bismarck. Favre spoke airily of the valiant resistance of the people of Paris, but Bismarck cut him short. He set forth harsh terms: Germany wanted the provinces of Alsace and Lorraine and five billion francs in reparations. He also demanded a two-day occupation of Paris, with a triumphal parade through the Arc de Triomphe [q.v.] and down the Champs Élysées.

On 28 January Paris capitulated, having suffered 28,450 military casualties. The Germans captured 602 field guns, 177,000 rifles, 1,362 siege guns, and a garrison of 7,456 officers and 241,686 other ranks. Some 12,000 men of the Garde Nationale were permitted to keep their arms to preserve public order.

Ten days earlier William I of Prussia (1797–1888) had been proclaimed emperor of a united Germany in the Hall of Mirrors at Versailles. A German army of occupation remained in France and did not leave until 1873. The last German soldier crossed the frontier on 16 September.

Paris Commune. See Commune of 1871.

Paris Revolutions of 1848. Rioting in Paris in February 1848 generated the dismissal of an unpopular minister, François Guizot (1787–1874), and the abdication of the unpopular King Louis Philippe (1773–1850) when government troops sent to suppress the rioters not only refused to fire on them but in some cases actually joined them. In an attempt to meet the demands for national elections, a right-to-work law, the establishment of national workshops, etc., the Chamber of Deputies appointed a Committee of Public Safety. Guided

Paris Revolutions of 1848 *Women on the barricade with flag "Bread or Death"*

by Alphonse de Lamartine (1790–1869), it eventually produced a democratic constitution.

A second insurrection erupted on 23 June, when the national workshops were shut down and there was a general concern that the largely monarchist Constituent Assembly would undo the gains made in February. Thousands of workers and the Garde Nationale [q.v.] manned barricades, but in contrast with the February riots, the army remained loyal to the regime. Troops under General Louis Cavaignac [q.v.] were called in, and the revolt was crushed in three days. Some 1,500 rebels were killed, 11,000 were arrested, and 4,500 were jailed or deported. This is sometimes referred to as the June Days.

Paris Revolutions of 1848 *The barracade at the entrance of the Rue du Fanbourg St. Antoine*

Park. The space used to park or store wagons, artillery, carriages, powder, provisions, engineering materials, stores of all description of an army. An artillery park usually included the reserve guns of an army.

Parke, John Grubb (1827–1900). An American soldier who was graduated from West Point in 1849, ranking second in his class, and served most of his career as a military engineer. During the American Civil War he rose to the rank of major general in the Union army and fought at Antietam,

Fredericksburg, Vicksburg, and Petersburg [qq.v.], serving as a division and labor corps commander. From 1866 to 1869 he was with the Northwest Boundary Commission. He retired in 1889.

Parkes, Edmund Alexander (1819–1876). An English physician who in 1842 became assistant surgeon of the 84th Foot and spent three years in India before retiring from the army in 1845. During the Crimean War [q.v.], in 1855–56, he was superintendent of a civil hospital in the Dardanelles. On his return to England he organized a new method of instruction at the Army Medical School, then at Chatham and later at Netley. It was at Netley that he made his reputation. He became known internationally for his teaching and writings on military hygiene in the days before the acceptance of germs as causes of illnesses and earned a reputation throughout Europe. Among his many medical articles was "Treatment of Pneumonia by Wine and Ammonia." In 1864 he published *Manual of Practical Hygiene*.

He served on numerous government advisory committees, and in 1861 he was made a Fellow of the Royal Society. On his death Baron Mundy, professor of military hygiene at the University of Vienna, wrote: "All the armies of the Continent should, at parade, lower their standards tied with crepe, if only for a moment, because the founder and best teacher of military hygiene of our day, the friend and benefactor of every soldier, is no more."

Parlementaire. The bearer of a flag of truce who on behalf of his commander enters an enemy's lines to negotiate openly and directly with the enemy commander.

Parley. A meeting under a flag of truce with an enemy, usually to discuss terms of surrender.

Paroi. A stout wooden frame with horizontal spikes placed on parapets to repel scaling parties.

Parole. 1. A watchword given only to the officers of the guard. In this it differs from the countersign, which is given to all members. The parole was usually the name of a person, such as a senior officer; the countersign was usually the name of a place or a battle.

2. A declaration made on his honor by an officer in circumstances in which only his honor restrains him from breaking his word. "To break *parole* is accounted infamous in all civilized nations, and an officer who has so far forgotten his position as a gentleman, ceases to have any claim to the treatment of an honorable man, nor can he expect quarter should he again fall into the hands of the enemy he has deceived" (Edward S. Farrow, *Farrow's Encyclopedia*). Captured officers were frequently set free on parole with the condition that they were not free to join their units or fight again until they had been exchanged for officers of equivalent rank or until the war had ended [see Cynthiana, Battle of; Cartel]. During the Mexican War [q.v.] two Mexican officers who broke their parole and were later again taken prisoner were shot.

Parr, Henry Hallam (1847–1914). A British soldier who was commissioned into the 13th Light Infantry in 1865. He saw action in the First Anglo-Boer War and in Arabi's Revolt [qq.v.]. In 1883 he was seconded to the Egyptian army and commanded the 9th Sudanese Battalion. In 1884 he was commandant at Suakim and was present in the Battle of Tamai [q.v.]. During the Gordon Relief Expedition [q.v.] he served on the line of communication. From 1885 to 1888 he was adjutant general and second-in-command of the Egyptian army. He retired in 1902.

Parrott, Robert Parker (1804–1877). An American soldier who was graduated from West Point in 1824 and commissioned in the 3rd Artillery. He saw some action in fighting Creek Indians, but he resigned in 1836 to devote himself to designing ordnance. From 1836 to 1867 he was the superintendent of the West Point Iron and Cannon Foundry [q.v.] at Cold Spring, New York. In 1861 he invented, and patented, a method of strengthening cast-iron guns by shrinking wrought-iron hoops on the breech. In the same year he invented an expanding projectile for rifled cannon. The Parrott gun fired an elongated shell similar to the design of the Minié bullet. Parrott's 12-pounder guns were used by Union artillery throughout the American Civil War.

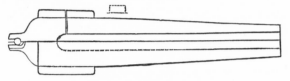

Parrot, Robert Parker *Parrot gun*

Parry. A defensive movement with a sword or bayonet to ward off a blow or slash.

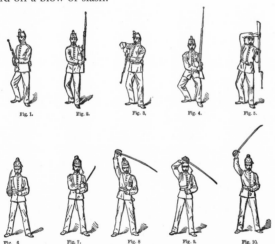

Parry *Ten steps showing the parry movements in bayonet and saber exercises, United States cavalry*

Parsons, Charles (1855–1923). A British soldier who served in the First Anglo-Boer War in 1881 and in Arabi's Revolt [qq.v.] in 1882. In 1897 he was governor and commander of troops at Suakim in the Sudan. In 1898 he defeated the Mahdist Dervishes in the Battle of Gedaref in the eastern Sudan, then entrenched and beat off a counterattack. He fought in the Second Anglo-Boer War [q.v.], and from 1902 to 1906 he was commander of the regular British forces in Canada.

Partida. A group of soldiers; the name was sometimes given to a Spanish guerrilla unit during the Peninsular War [q.v.].

Partisan. 1. A long-handled weapon resembling a halberd [q.v.], but with a lateral cutting projection on the blade. It was originally carried by infantry in the sixteenth and seventeenth centuries. In the nineteenth and twentieth centuries in the British service it was, and is, carried, in addition to their swords, by the Queen's Body Guard of the Yeomen of the Guard [q.v.].

2. A soldier armed and sometimes properly uniformed, operating under a constituted command, who is a member of a unit that operates apart from the main body for the purpose of destroying communications or making inroads into enemy-occupied territory [see Franc-tireur; Guerrillas].

3. A member of a guerrilla group operating behind the enemy's lines.

Partouneaux, Louis (1770–1835). A French soldier who in 1791 was a grenadier in the Paris volunteers and the following year was commissioned in the infantry. In 1799 he was promoted general of brigade. On 15 August of that year he was wounded and taken prisoner in the Battle of Novi. In 1812 he took part in Napoleon's Russian Campaign [q.v.] and at the crossing of the Berezina [q.v.] was ordered to hold off Matvei Platov and Ludwig Wittgenstein [qq.v.]. To Napoleon's fury, Partouneaux bungled his work. He himself was captured and his men surrendered. When he returned to France, he received no further appointments. In 1816 the Bourbons made him a count, and he launched into a new military and political career.

Partridge, Alden (1785–1854). An American military educator educated at Dartmouth College (1802–05) and at West Point, where he taught and in January 1815 became the superintendent. He proved to be a poor administrator, and in the summer of 1817, while he was on leave, he was superseded by Major Sylvanus Thayer [q.v.]. On his return he tried to wrest control from Thayer and in consequence was arrested, court-martialed, and convicted of neglect of duty and insubordination. He was about to be cashiered when his sentence was remitted by President James Madison (1751–1836). The following April he resigned and, after a brief tour of surveying in the Northeast, founded the Literary, Scientific and Military Academy at Norwich, Vermont, which opened in September 1820 with 100 cadets. This was the beginning of the present Norwich University [q.v.], now located at Northfield, Vermont. He later formed similar military schools in Virginia, Pennsylvania, Delaware, and New Hampshire. He is regarded as the founder of secondary-grade military schools.

Pas d'Âne. Either of two rings below and at right angles to the quillons of a sword to guard the forefinger.

Pas de Sours. The steps leading from the bottom to the top of a ditch in permanent fortifications.

Pasha. A title in the Ottoman Empire bestowed on civilians, sailors, and soldiers of high rank. It had three grades, each denoted by the number of horsetails that in the military were displayed on a pole on the march or before a tent. The lowest grade ranked one horsetail; the highest, such as that awarded the grand vizier, rated three. The title, like that of bey [q.v.], followed either the first or last name.

Paskevich, Ivan Fyodorovich (1782–1856). A Russian soldier who was educated at the imperial institution for pages and commissioned in 1800. He fought the French in 1805 and in Napoleon's Russian Campaign [q.v.]. He took part in the Russo-Persian War [q.v.] of 1825–28, in which, in 1827, he conquered Persian Armenia. He was promoted field marshal in 1828, and in 1828–29, he led two campaigns against the Turks, capturing Kars and Erivan [qq.v.]. In 1830 he temporarily suppressed the rebels in Dagestan [see Murid War; Shamyl], and in 1831 he put down the Polish Revolution [see Polish Revolutions]. He was made Prince of Warsaw and was appointed governor of the portion of Poland that was incorporated into Russia. In 1848 he led the Russian army that intervened in the Hungarian revolt [See Hungarian Revolution of 1848] and received the Hungarian surrender at Világos [q.v.]. In April 1854 he commanded the Russian army on the Danube against the Turks at the beginning of the Crimean War [q.v.], and he was wounded in the unsuccessful siege of Silistra [q.v.] on 9 June 1854. He retired to Warsaw, where he died on 13 February 1856. He was known as a rigid and unimaginative man.

Pasley, Charles William (1780–1861). A British soldier and engineer born in Scotland who in 1811 introduced a course of instruction in engineering for noncommissioned officers at the British military engineering school at Chatham. He was director of the school until 1841 and the author of several treatises on military engineering. He was promoted general in 1860.

Paso de Patria, Battle of (24 May 1866), War of the Triple Alliance. An Allied army of 45,000 Brazilians and Argentines crossed the Paraná River and advanced into Paraguay. An attack by 25,000 Paraguayans under Francesco Solano López [q.v.] was repulsed, and the Allies surrounded López on three sides. The result was a near massacre, the Paraguayans losing 13,000 to the Allies' 8,000. The Allied forces failed to follow up their attack, however, and López was able to reorganize.

Passage of Lines. A difficult maneuver that enabled embattled and battered front lines of infantry to retreat in good order behind a second line and to re-form behind it.

Passive Defense. A defense of a place in which no effort is made to sally out or to harass the attackers or besiegers.

Pass-parole. An order passed from front to rear of an army by word of mouth.

Passports, Military. Passes given by a military commander to permit bearers to travel within his lines or to pass out or into his lines, usually at designated points. They were similar to safe conducts.

Pastry War (1838). In December 1828, during one of Mexico's innumerable revolutions, there were four days of fighting and even more days of looting in Mexico City. The demands of property owners for restitution were ignored, but many were foreigners, who protested to their consuls. The French demanded 600,000 pesos, 1,000 of which were due to a pastry cook whose premises had been wrecked by drunken army officers. The Mexican government refused to pay, and there the matter seemed to end until in April 1838, almost a decade later, a French fleet appeared at Veracruz and demanded payment. General Anastasio Bustamante [q.v.], then president, refused.

On 16 April 1838 the French bombarded and then seized Fort San Juan de Ulúa, which guarded the harbor of Veracruz. There was desultory fighting on land, and on 5 December the French captured the entire Mexican navy. The Mexican land forces were led by Antonio López de Santa Anna [q.v.], who had seized command of the Mexican army. In the last days of the French occupation of Veracruz Santa Anna was hit by grapeshot and his left leg was amputated.

Eventually Bustamante promised payment in full, and on 9 March the French sailed away. Whether the French pastry cook ever received his 1,000 pesos is unknown, but Santa Anna's spirited opposition to the French at Veracruz reestablished his political reputation, lost after his disgraceful defeat by Sam Houston [q.v.] in the Battle of San Jacinto [q.v.] on 21 August 1836.

Patagonian Expedition (May 1881). Argentine troops under Julio Argentino Roca (1843–1914) conquered Patagonian Indians in southwestern South America. Their territory was occupied and became the province of Río Negro.

Patcharée. See Petta / Pettah.

Pathan. A tribesman of the principal ethnic group in Afghanistan and on India's (Pakistan's) Northwest Frontier [q.v.]. One or more of the tribes in this group were frequently in conflict with Anglo-Indian forces. [See Malakand Field Force; Afghan Wars; Afridi Tribes, Military Expeditions against; Tirah Campaign; Ghazi.]

Patoo / Patu. 1. A short war club used by the Maoris in New Zealand.

2. A kind of battle-ax used in Polynesia.

Patra. A long flat-bladed sword, usually double-edged, used by the Marathas in India.

Patridge Sight. A type of sight invented by one E. E. Patridge in 1898. (The name is frequently misspelled "partridge.") The foresight had a rectangular blade with a vertical face; the rear sight was a blade with a rectangular notch. To aim, the flat top of the front sight was aligned centrally in the notch of the rear sight and level with the top of the rear sight notch.

Patriotic Fund Asylum, Royal Victoria. During the Crimean War [q.v.] a solicitation for funds raised £200,000 to build on the common at Wandsworth (a borough of metropolitan London) an asylum to accommodate 300 orphaned daughters of fallen soldiers [see: Patriotic Funds]. The first stone was laid by Queen Victoria on 11 July 1857. It was the only institution of its kind. An earlier effort to assist such girls at the Royal Military Asylum, Chelsea [q.v.], was abandoned when it was learned that after leaving, many of the girls became prostitutes.

Patriotic Funds. Charitable funds established in Britain "to encourage the army and navy in times of war." The first was established on 20 July 1803 by the subscribers (names) of Lloyd's "to animate the efforts of our defenders by sea and land." The money was to be used for the relief of wounded soldiers and sailors and the widows and orphans of those who fell [see Patriotic Fund Asylum, Royal Victoria] and to grant "pecuniary rewards and badges of distinction for valour and merit." Between 1803 and 1826, £629,823 14s 1d was received.

Through the century other funds were established, including one for the relief of British subjects who suffered in the Indian Mutiny [q.v.] and another for those who fell in the Russo-Turkish Wars [q.v.]. The Soldiers' Families Fund was opened at the beginning of the Second Anglo-Boer War and was strongly supported by Rudyard Kipling [q.v.], who wrote his "Absent Minded Beggar," first published in the *London Daily Mail* on 31 October 1899, as a plea for funds. Actress Helen Maud Holt (1863–1937), Mrs. Herbert Beerbohm Tree, recited the poem daily from the stage of the Palace Theatre in London and raised £70,000. Alleged maladministration of the funds was brought to the notice of the House of Commons on 9 August 1890, but not until 11 August 1903 was royal assent given for the Patriotic Fund Reorganization Act.

Patriotic Societies. Organizations formed to commemorate historic events, usually of battles or wars, and to foster a patriotic spirit. In the nineteenth century these were formed in many countries, but they were especially numerous and often politically influential in the United States. The Aztec Club, still extant and open to descendants, of 1847 [q.v.] was formed in Mexico City by American officers who had served in the Mexican War [q.v.]; the Sons of the Revolution was formed in 1876; the Sons of Veterans in 1879; the Daughters of the Revolution in 1890; the Society of Colonial Wars in 1893; the Daughters of the Confederacy in 1894; the Sons of Confederate Veterans in 1896; and the largest and most politically potent organization, the Grand Army of the Republic [q.v.], commonly referred to as the GAR, consisting of Union Army veterans, in 1866.

Patriotism. A love of one's country. When carried to extremes, it becomes chauvinism [see Chauvinism; Chauvinist Riots]. French writer Guy de Maupassant (1850–1893) wrote that "Patriotism is the egg from which wars are hatched" (*My Uncle Sosthenes*).

Patriot's War. A Canadian name for the War of 1812 [q.v.].

Patrol. 1. As a noun, a detachment of cavalry or infantry sent to obtain information respecting the nature of the terrain or the movements or positions of the enemy.

2. As a verb, to perform such a task.

Patterson, Francis Engle (1821–1862). An American soldier, the son of General Robert Patterson [q.v.], who served as a lieutenant in the Mexican War [q.v.] and remained in the army until he resigned as a captain in 1857. He returned to the Federal army at the beginning of the American Civil War and on 15 April 1862 was promoted brigadier general. In early November he had advanced to Catlett's Station in Virginia when, hearing a rumor (false) that Confederate forces were close by at Warrenton Junction, he ordered a retreat. This unauthorized movement was about to be investigated when he was discovered in his tent dead by his own hand.

Patterson, Robert (1792–1881). An Irish-born American soldier who began his military career in the War of 1812 [q.v.], serving from captain to colonel between October 1813 and June 1815. From July 1846 he served as a major general of volunteers in the Mexican War [q.v.], distinguishing himself in the Battle of Cerro Gordo [q.v.]. He was also briefly a general in the American Civil War but was mustered out on 27 July 1861 after he failed to prevent Confederate General Joseph Johnston from reinforcing General Pierre Beauregard [qq.v.] in the First Battle of Bull Run [q.v.]. He had failed to engage Johnston, he said, because he had not received orders to attack. He was the father of Francis Engle Patterson [q.v.].

Paul, Gabriel René (1813–1886). An American soldier who was a son and a grandson of Napoleonic soldiers. He was graduated from West Point in 1834 and fought in the Second Seminole War [q.v.], in the Southwest, and in the Mexican War [q.v.], in which he won a brevet. Serving in the Union army in the American Civil War, he soon became a brigadier general. He fought at Fredericksburg, Chancellorsville, and Gettysburg [qq.v.]. On the first day of Gettysburg he was severely wounded by a rifle bullet that entered his right temple and passed out his left eye, leaving him totally blind. He survived for another twenty years.

Pavía y Albuquerque, Manuel (1828?–1895). A Spanish soldier who was commissioned in 1846 and became a major in 1862. In 1865 he was on the staff of General Juan Prim y Prats [q.v.] and engaged with him in the revolution of 1868 that dethroned the queen [see Carlist War, Second]. In 1874 he used his troops to gain control of the turbulent political situation in Madrid and to turn over power to Marshal Francisco Serrano y Domínguez [q.v.] to form a coalition government. In 1880 he served as president of the Supreme Council of War.

Pavía y Lacy, Manuel (1814–1896). A Spanish soldier who in 1833 was commissioned a lieutenant in the Guards. In the Carlist War of 1833–40 [q.v.] he became a general. In 1852 he was captain general of the Philippines, where in 1857 he crushed a formidable insurrection. He commanded the queen's troops in the insurrection against the tempestuous and authoritarian Queen Isabella II (1830–1904) but was defeated at the bridge of Alcolea [q.v.] on 28 September 1868, and in that battle he was badly wounded in the face.

Pavlovich, Constantine (1779–1831). A Russian grand duke and soldier who was governor of Poland in 1815 and was said to have provoked the rebellion of 1830–31 [see Polish Rebellions]. He is reputed to have said: "I detest war. It ruins armies."

Pavlovsky Regiment. A regiment in the Russian army that distinguished itself in the Battle of Friedland [q.v.] on 14 June

1807. In recognition of its valor, Alexander I [q.v.] decreed that the headgear of the regiment be retained and worn exactly in the state it appeared at the end of the battle "as a visible mark of its bravery and of Our grace." More than six hundred were still so preserved and worn at the empire's end. The regiment became a Life Guard regiment in 1813.

Pavón, Battle of (17 September 1861), Argentine Revolution. General Bartolomé Mitre [q.v.] led a successful revolt against the federal government that culminated in this battle, 27 miles south-southwest of Rosario. Justo José Urquiza [q.v.], then governor of Entre Ríos, with 4,000 men was nearby but, seeing Mitre victorious, withdrew without fighting. In May 1862 Mitre was elected president of Argentina. He took office on 12 October.

Paysandú, Battle of (2 January 1865), War of the Triple Alliance. After a heavy bombardment Brazilian troops captured this town (now in Uruguay) on the Uruguay River, 55 miles north-northeast of Fray Bentos and 200 miles north-northwest of Montevideo.

Peabody-Martini Rifle. The American name of the British Martini-Henry Rifle [q.v.], adopted by the British in April 1871. During the Russo-Turkish War of 1877–78 the Providence Tool Company of Rhode Island manufactured more than a half million for the Turkish army.

The trigger mechanism for a Peabody-Martini rifle

Peabody Rifle. In 1862 Henry O. Peabody of Boston patented a type of breech closure on rifles in which a block in prolongation of the barrel axis was hinged at the rear so that it could be lowered at the front for loading.

The American army did not accept the rifle, but in 1865 the Canadian government bought 3,000. Several other countries purchased it, including Rumania, which bought 30,000 between 1867 and 1869, and France, which purchased 39,000 for use in the Franco-Prussian War [q.v.]. It was subsequently improved by Frédéric de Martini (1832–1897), an Hungarian inventor and gunsmith working in Switzerland [see Peabody-Martini Rifle].

Peace. An accord, written or simply accepted, between governments or between a government and some of its citizens in which they agree that they are not for the moment at war with each other. Universal peace has not, as far as is known, ever existed. Thucydides in the fifth century B.C. described peace as "an armistice in a war that is continuously going on" (*History of the Peloponnesian War* [c. 404 B.C.]).

Periods of peace are often dangerous for national states. Political leaders and citizens are frequently lured into a false sense of security and fail to prepare for the inevitable wars that lie unseen but certain in the future. In 1808 Prussian Field Marshal August von Gneisenau [q.v.], reflecting on the hurried mobilization of Prussia that led to the Prussian disasters in the battles of Jena and Auerstädt [qq.v.], said: "In times of peace we have neglected much, occupied ourselves with frivolities, flattered the people's love of show and neglected war."

There have always been those who entertain the notion that if war is not studied, it will not occur and those who believe that for one reason or another war in a future time will not exist. Writing in 1849, Ralph Waldo Emerson (1803–1882) predicted: "War is on its last legs; and a universal peace is as sure as is the prevalence of civilization over barbarism, of liberal government over feudal forms. The question for us is only how soon?" In 1898 Jean de Bloch [q.v.] published a seven-volume work demonstrating that

Peace *Generals Harney and Sherman at peace talks at Fort Laramie, Wyoming, 1868, during the American Indian Wars.*

war had become so destructive and expensive that no civilized nation would in future enter upon it. Richard Gatling [q.v.] thought that his machine gun would be so deadly that nations would not dare go to war. Although wars have since grown ever more destructive and expensive, such predictions have proved delusive, and there is no indication that universal peace will ever be achieved.

Peace Establishment. The reduced size of a nation's regular army in times of peace; the number of troops and guns, and the amount of matériel authorized for an army whose country is not at war. [See War Establishment.]

Peace Policy, Grant's. A policy initiated by American President U. S. Grant to solve the difficulties with the Indians on the plains through a "conquest by kindness." In his inaugural speech Grant stated that he would "favor any course for them which tends to their civilization and ultimate citizenship." The Indians were to be civilized through education, exposure to Christianity, and the adoption of agricultural self-support systems. The Indian Agency was to be purged of corrupt incompetents and replaced with Quakers and other religious leaders. The Indian Appropriations Act of 10 April 1869 gave the president the power to appoint ten men "eminent for their intelligence and philanthropy" to serve without pay and monitor the appropriations of the act. By 1872 there were seventy-three agencies in the hands of religious leaders.

The policy, however, did not eliminate corruption on the reservations, nor did it secure peace on the plains. Indian outrages such as the Salt Creek Massacre and the Modoc War [qq.v.] put an end to the policy.

Peace Societies, Confederate. Soon after the outbreak of the American Civil War societies of people loyal to the Union sprang up in the South. They assisted Confederate deserters and even succeeded in electing representatives to the Confederate Congress who called for ending the war. The most successful were the Peace Society, the Peace and Constitutional Society, and the Order of Heroes of America, the latter being the best organized. The Confederate societies proved more disruptive than were similar societies of copperheads in the North.

Peace Treaties with Indians. The Indian Appropriations Act of 3 March 1871 barred the American government from ever again signing a treaty with Indians.

Peach Orchard, Battle of. See Savage's Station, Battle of.

Peach Tree Creek, Battle of (20 July 1864), American Civil War. Confederate General Joseph Johnston [q.v.], who had been skillfully withdrawing before the superior forces of Union General William Tecumseh Sherman [q.v.], was in position just a few miles from Atlanta, Georgia, on the south bank of Peach Tree Creek, when he was relieved of command and replaced by General John Bell Hood [q.v.]. This change in command delighted Sherman, who said, "At this critical moment the Confederate Government renders us a most valuable service." The battle, in which about 20,000 on each side were engaged, was sometimes called Hood's First Sortie. It

ended in a Confederate defeat. Federal losses were 1,600; Confederate losses were 2,500.

Pea Ridge, Battle of (7–8 March 1862), American Civil War. A battle, also known as the Battle of Elkhorn Tavern, fought in Benton County in northwest Arkansas. In early February 1862 Union Brigadier General Samuel Ryan Curtis [q.v.] with 11,000 men launched a campaign to drive the 8,000 Confederates under Brigadier General Sterling Price [q.v.] out of Missouri. As Curtis advanced toward Springfield, Missouri, where the Confederates had wintered, Price retreated and joined his forces with those of Benjamin McCulloch [q.v.]. The combined force halted in the mountains of Fayetteville, where Major General Earl Van Dorn [q.v.] took command. Reinforced for a total strength of about 14,000, they prepared to attack Curtis, who had also been reinforced and now had 17,000 men. When Curtis was informed of the Confederate advance by one of his scouts, James ("Wild Bill") Hickok [q.v.], he concentrated his forces and entrenched on Pea Ridge. Van Dorn's men were hungry, rations were in scant supply, the weather turned cold, and the troops had just completed a march of 55 miles through wet snow when they were ordered to attack. Van Dorn himself was ill and directed the battle from an ambulance. An all-day battle earned meager results, but Van Dorn launched a second attack the following day. It was repulsed, and a Union charge drove the Confederates from the field. Union casualties were 1,384; Confederate losses, about 800.

A controversy developed after the battle over the brigade of Indians who fought for the Confederacy under General Albert Pike [q.v.]. It included a Creek regiment, a Creek-Seminole regiment, a Choctaw-Chickasaw regiment, and two regiments of Cherokees, including one led by Stand Watie [q.v.]. The Federals found 30 scalped soldiers, and there was an outcry against employing Indians to kill whites.

Peel Commission (1859). A British committee headed by Major General Jonathan Peel (1799–1879) appointed in 1859 at the end of the Indian Mutiny [q.v.] to "Inquire into the organization of the Indian Army." It included the Duke of Cambridge [q.v.] and Lord Stanley (1826–1893), commissioner for Indian affairs and later secretary of state for India. Among its recommendations were the strengthening of British government control over the army and an increase in the number of qualified British officers in Indian units. Of major importance was its recommendation that "the Native Army be composed of different nationalities and castes, and as a general rule, mixed promiscuously through each regiment." In other words, there would be no single regiment composed of men all of one caste or community. An exception was made for the Gurkhas [q.v.].

Peel, William (1824–1858). A British naval officer who distinguished himself in battles on land. He entered the Royal Navy in 1838 and was promoted captain in 1849. In 1850–51, while on half pay, he went exploring in Africa, the interior of which was then little known. In the Crimean War he served with the naval brigade before Sevastopol [q.v.] commanded by Captain Stephen Lushington (1803–1877) and won one of the first Victoria Crosses to be awarded. During the Indian Mutiny [q.v.] he formed a naval brigade in Calcutta and on 14 August 1857 moved inland with 450 sailors and marines and 10 eight-inch guns. At Allahabad on 20 October he was reinforced by 120 men and from then on took an active part in most of the principal operations of the army. On 8 March 1858, during the second relief of Lucknow [q.v.], he was gravely wounded in the thigh by a musket ball. He was ordered back to England to recover, but on the way he contracted smallpox and died at Cawnpore on 24 April 1858.

Pegram, John (1832–1865). An American soldier who was graduated from West Point in 1854. He served on the western frontier, as an instructor at West Point, and was with the Utah Expedition [q.v.]. After a two-year leave of absence spent in Europe, he returned to Indian fighting. At the outbreak of the American Civil War he resigned as a first lieutenant on 10 May 1861 and was commissioned a lieutenant colonel in the Confederate army. Although defeated by General George McClellan [q.v.] in western Virginia (West Virginia), he was promoted brigadier general on 7 November. He was wounded in the Battle of the Wilderness [q.v.] in May 1864 but returned to duty in July. On 19 January 1865 he was married to Hetty Carry of Baltimore, and on 9 February he was killed in the Battle of Hatcher's Run [q.v.].

Pegu, Captures of (June and November 1852), Second Burmese War. British troops under Major Stapleton Cotton [q.v.] (later First Viscount Combermere) captured this town, a provincial capital in Burma (Myanmar), 47 miles northeast of Rangoon (Yongan), on 3 June 1852. It was then abandoned. On 21 November Pegu was recaptured by General Thomas Godwin (1784–1853). The province of Pegu was annexed on 20 January 1853.

Peiwar Kotal, Battle of (2 December 1878), Second Afghan War. At this pass from India (Pakistan) into the Kurram Valley, 60 miles southeast of Kabul in the Safed Koh range, an Anglo-Indian army of 3,200 men with 13 guns under General (later Field Marshal) Frederick Roberts [q.v.] won a victory against an Afghan force of 18,000 with 11 guns under Sher Ali Khan [q.v.]. British casualties were 20 killed and 28 wounded; Afghan losses were said to have been heavy.

Peking, Capture of. See Opium War, Second; Boxer Rebellion.

Pelet-Clozeau, Paul Jacques (1777–1858). A French soldier who enlisted in 1799 and was commissioned in the engineers in 1801. He served in Italy and in the Danube Campaign. He fought at Aspern-Essling and Znaim and in Napoleon's Russian Campaign [qq.v.]. In April 1813 he was promoted general of brigade and fought in the battles of Dresden and Leipzig [qq.v.]. During the Hundred Days [q.v.] he rallied to Napoleon and fought at Ligny and Waterloo [qq.v.]. In 1830 he was a lieutenant general and commandant of the staff college. He pursued a political as well as a military career until severely injured by a bomb in 1835.

Pelham, John (1838–1863). An American soldier who left West Point in May 1861, just before he was to be graduated, to join the Confederate army. Along with 21 of the 33 graduates of the class of 1861 he fought in the First Battle of Bull Run [q.v.], after which he was promoted captain in the artillery. On 9 August 1862 he was promoted major. In the Battle of Fredericksburg [q.v.] he held up a Union division with only 2 guns. When only 1 was left to him and 24 Union guns were aimed at him, he stood firm fighting his gun. General Robert E. Lee observed, "It is glorious to see such courage in one so young." Often identified as "the gallant Pelham," he was killed in the Battle of Kelly's Ford on 17 March 1863. On 4 April 1863, after his death, he was promoted lieutenant colonel to rank from 2 March. He was a handsome young man, and it was said that on his death three young women went into mourning.

Pelischat, Battle of. See Plevna, Siege of.

Pelisse. A hussar's short outer jacket, braided and fur-trimmed, worn over the left shoulder.

Pélissier, Aimable Jean Jacques (1794–1864). A French soldier who served in Spain in 1823 and in the Morea in 1828. In 1830 he took part in the initial conquests in Algeria, and in 1845 he acquired a degree of notoriety by suffocating some 500 Arabs in a cave at Dahra [see Dahra Caves Massacre]. In 1848 he was governor of Oran. In 1850 he was promoted general of division, and he supported the coup d'état of 2 December 1851. In the Crimean War he commanded a corps before succeeding François Certain Canrobert [q.v.] in the chief command of the French army

Pélissier *The Allied commanders, Crimean War, 1855, from left to right: Lord Raglan, Omar Pasha, and General Pélissier*

before Sevastopol [q.v.]. For his success in storming the Malakoff [q.v.] on 8 September 1855 he was made a marshal and created Duc de Malakoff. In 1860, after a stint in London as ambassador, he became governor of Algeria, a post he held until 1864.

Pelloux, Luigi (1839–1924). An Italian soldier and politician who served in East Africa from 1885 to 1889. In 1891 he was promoted lieutenant general and minister of war; he served until 1893 and again from 1896 to 1897. He was premier from 1898 to 1900.

Pelote. A French punishment, officially forbidden, but frequently employed, in which the offender, carrying a fully loaded knapsack or a heavy stone, ran a gauntlet of noncommissioned officers armed with clubs or whips.

Peloton. 1. A platoon.
2. A pennon or lance flag.

Pember, Phoebe Yates (1823–1913). A southern woman, born into a wealthy Jewish family who early in the American Civil War, after she had been widowed by the death of her husband from tuberculosis, was named chief matron of the Chimborazo Hospital [q.v] in Richmond, Virginia. She directed the care and dietary needs of some 10,000 soldiers and was a strong advocate of chicken soup. After the war she remained at the hospital until it was taken over by the federal government. Her book *A Southern Woman's Story* (1879) is the best first-person account of life in a Confederate hospital.

In 1994 the U.S. Postal Service honored her in a thirty-two-cent stamp.

Pemberton, John Clifford (1814–1881). An American soldier, born in Philadelphia, who was graduated from West Point in 1837 and commissioned in the artillery. He took part in the First Seminole War [q.v.]; served as an aide to General William Jenkins Worth [q.v.] in the Mexican War [q.v.], winning two brevets; and in 1857–58 served in the Utah Expedition [q.v.]. In April 1861, at the outbreak of the American Civil War, he resigned to accept a commission as a lieutenant colonel in the Confederate service. (He had two brothers who fought for the Union, but his wife was a Virginian.) The following month he was promoted colonel, and the next month a brigadier general. In February 1862 he was promoted major general, and in October he was a lieutenant general. He was in command at Vicksburg, Mississippi, when it was besieged, and he was taken prisoner when he surrendered the city on 4 July 1863 [see Vicksburg, Siege of]. After he was exchanged, he resigned his commission, but he served as ordnance inspector and as colonel of artillery in the defense of Richmond.

Peña de Cerredo, Battle of (21 June 1838), First Carlist War. About 19,000 Cristinos under General Baldomero Esparto [q.v.] attacked this Carlist fort, 12 miles northeast of Riaño, Spain, manned by 3,000 men [see Carlist Wars]. After a seven-hour bombardment the Cristinos stormed the fort and dispersed the Carlists, 600 of whom were captured.

Pender, William Dorsey (1834–1863). An American soldier who won an appointment to West Point at the age of sixteen and was graduated in 1854. He saw action against Indians on the Pacific coast. In 1861, at the outbreak of the American Civil War, he resigned his commission as a first lieutenant to join the Confederate army as a colonel and commander of a North Carolina regiment. He was promoted brigadier general as of 3 June 1862 and commanded a brigade in the division of A. P. Hill [q.v.], taking part in all the battles of the Army of Northern Virginia [q.v.]. On 27 May 1863 he was promoted major general. He commanded a division in the Battle of Gettysburg [q.v.], in which he was wounded in the leg by a shell fragment. Infection set in, and the leg was amputated, but he died on 18 July.

Pendhari. See Pandours.

Pendleton, William Nelson (1809–1883). An American soldier and clergyman who was graduated from West Point in 1830 and commissioned in the artillery. In 1833 he resigned to become a professor of mathematics and to study for the ministry. In 1853 he was the pastor of the Protestant Episcopal church in Lexington, Virginia. In May 1861, at the outbreak of the American Civil War, he was elected captain of a battery of artillery, and in July he was commissioned a Confederate colonel. In April 1862 he was promoted brigadier general and served on the staff of General Robert E. Lee as chief of artillery. After the war he returned to his parish.

Peninsular Campaign (March–July 1862), American Civil War. When Confederate General Joseph Johnston [q.v.] pulled his army back from Manassas in March 1862 to form a line along the Rappahannock River, Washington, D.C., seemed somewhat safer, and President Abraham Lincoln, having been assured by General George McClellan [qq.v.] that it would be adequately protected, permitted him to begin his planned amphibious invasion of the South with Richmond, Virginia, capital of the Confederacy, as his objective. With a well-trained and well-equipped army of 110,000 McClellan advanced up the peninsula between the James and York rivers. He had intended to include in the campaign McDowell's force, then at Manassas, but Lincoln soon discovered how small and ill trained a force McClellan had deemed adequate to guard the nation's capital and directed that McDowell remain in his position at Manassas. This seriously interfered with McClellan's plans. On 31 May and 1 June McClellan fought the Battle of Fair Oaks [q.v.], just 10 miles from Richmond, but he failed to capture the city. Confederate General Joseph Johnston [q.v.] was wounded in the battle, and his place was taken by General Robert E. Lee, who took the offensive when McClellan, having badly overestimated the size of the Confederate force opposing him, drew his army back to the protection of Union gunboats on the James River. After the Seven Days' Battles [q.v.] McClellan and his army withdrew.

The principal battles of the Peninsular Campaign were: Oak Grove on 25 June; Mechanicsville [q.v.] on 26 June; Gaines's Mill [q.v.] on 27–28 June, and Garnett's and Golding's Farm on the same day; Savage's Station [q.v.] on 29

Peninsular Campaign *Federal ships unloading supplies, White House, Pamunkey River. Drawing by Alfred R. Waud*

June; White Oak Swamp [q.v.] on 30 June; and Malvern Hill [q.v.] on 1 July.

Peninsulares. Those Cubans at the close of the century who wanted to retain close ties with Spain. They resented American political pressure and feared annexation by the United States.

Peninsular War (1807–14). A Napoleonic War between France and the Allied armies of Portugal, Spain, and Great Britain fought on the Iberian Peninsula and, at the end, in southern France. The war consisted of two distinct parts. In the initial phase the British attempted to obtain a toehold on the Continent. This phase ended with the British victory in the Battle of Vimeiro [q.v.] on 21 August 1808; the British then began their campaign to free Spain.

Portugal had infuriated Napoleon by remaining true to its alliance with Britain and refusing to bow to his threats or be seduced by his promises. When it refused to comply with any part of his Continental System [q.v.], essentially a boycott of British goods that he sought to impose upon all Europe, he determined to bring it into line by military force. With Spanish permission, he was able to move on Portugal by way of Spain, and on 17 October 1807 Marshal Nicolas Oudinot [q.v.] with 24,133 troops stepped onto Spanish soil and on 19 November passed through Alcántara on the Tagus River and into Portugal.

Portuguese resistance was swept aside, and on 30 November General Jean Junot [q.v.] entered Lisbon, only to discover that the royal family, numerous dignitaries, the state treasure, and the Portuguese navy, guarded by a British squadron, had sailed for Brazil. Portugal was occupied by French troops, and with Spanish permission, French troops were garrisoned in key Spanish towns from Bayonne to the Portuguese frontier, supposedly to maintain a line of communication, actually to facilitate French intervention in Spain's affairs, which, with French diplomatic help, were drifting toward chaos.

On 16 February 1808 Napoleon, proclaiming his intention to bring order to the country and settle disputes that had arisen in the royal family, seized forts and key positions in northern Spain. French Marshal Joachim Murat [q.v.] with 18,000 men marched on Madrid, which he occupied on 24 March. Although his troops at first had been cheered, an anti-French riot erupted in the city on 1 April. It was followed on 2 May by more alarming riots, which were suppressed with great brutality [see Dos Mayo Uprising]. Undeterred, early that month Napoleon summoned the disputants of the Spanish royal family to a conference in Bayonne, where within a week he settled their quarrels by installing his brother Joseph on the throne. Spanish resentment against the French soared. Before the end of the month Valencia, Seville, and the Asturias were the scenes of riots. By mid-June émeutes had taken place in every province, and the junta of Seville had sent an appeal for help to Britain.

The French moved to suppress what had become a major rebellion. They were initially successful; the Spanish forces, scattered and badly armed, could offer little effective opposition, but on 1 August 1808 Lieutenant General Arthur Wellesley, the future Duke of Wellington, commanding more than 10,000 troops, landed in Portugal at Mondego Bay, 110 miles north of Lisbon. Moving south, he defeated the French under General François Delaborde (1764–1813) at Obidos and Roliça [qq.v.] and took up a position at Vimeiro [q.v.] to cover the landing of more British troops under General Sir Harry Burrard (1755–1813). Here on 21 August Wellesley defeated a French force under General Jean Junot; he would have captured the entire force if Burrard had not arrived and, as senior officer, taken command. Within twenty-four hours Burrard was superseded by General Sir Hew Whitefoord Dalrymple, who declined to pursue the beaten French and on 31 August signed the Convention of Cintra, which allowed the 26,000 French troops with all their arms and impedimenta to be evacuated in British ships. The agreement set off a furor in Britain. Dalrymple was recalled and replaced by General Sir John Moore [q.v.].

Meanwhile, in Spain on 21 July, Spanish forces had scored a major victory in the Battle of Bailén [q.v.] and had driven the French behind the line of the Ebro River. In response, Napoleon set out across the Pyrenees with 80,000 men and on 6 November took personal command of the 200,000 troops in Spain. By 4 December he had swept away Spanish opposition and occupied Madrid. There he learned that Moore was advancing to attack the division of Marshal Jean Soult [q.v.]. Leading an army across the mountains in a blizzard by way of the Guadarrama Pass, he moved to attack Moore, who, realizing his danger, began an arduous retreat over the mountains to Corunna [q.v.], where his force could be evacuated by British ships. When Corunna was finally reached, no British ships were in sight. Two days passed before the first sail appeared, giving the pursuing Soult time to arrive. On 16 January 1809 in the ensuing Battle of Corunna [q.v.], Moore's army narrowly escaped destruction, and Moore himself was killed.

On 22 April 1809 Wellesley assumed command of the 22,000 British troops on the Iberian Peninsula. In the interim, French forces had again invaded Portugal, taken Oporto, and were in the process of subjugating Galicia. In early May Wellesley moved north and cleared the French from Oporto, effectively driving them from Portugal. Counting on Spanish support, he led an army into Spain. On 27–28 July he defeated the French in the Battle of Talavera [q.v.] and was raised to the peerage as Viscount Wellington. But failing to get the support he had expected from Spanish General Gregorio de la Cuesta [q.v.] and threatened by a large French force under Soult, he withdrew into Portugal.

In 1810 he resumed his Spanish Campaign and defeated André Masséna, Michel Ney, and Jean Andoche Junot [qq.v.]. In the same year he was created Duke of Wellington. As Masséna retreated, Wellington pursued and defeated him in the Battle of Fuentes de Oñoro [q.v.]. Wellington then sent a force under Lieutenant General Sir Thomas Graham [q.v.] to help the Spanish government besieged in Cádiz. Graham won the Battle of Barrosa [q.v.] outside Cádiz on 15 March 1811, but he resigned in a fit of pique when Spanish generals claimed most of the credit.

Wellington meanwhile reorganized his army into permanent divisions and integrated into his own army a newly raised Portuguese army supplied, armed, trained, and largely commanded by British officers under Lieutenant General Sir William Carr Beresford [q.v.]. Beresford won a signal victory over Marshal Nicolas Soult [q.v.] at Albuera [q.v.] on 16 May 1811 and besieged Badajoz [q.v.], but the French were reinforced, and he was forced to abandon the siege. He then moved north and laid siege to Ciudad Rodrigo [q.v.], which was eventually captured by Wellington in January 1812. In April the British won a bloody victory at Badajoz [see Badajoz, Sieges of].

Just as Napoleon was withdrawing troops from the peninsula for his invasion of Russia [q.v.], Wellington prepared a major campaign in Spain. After much maneuvering around the Tormes River, on 12 July he won the Battle of Salamanca [q.v.], defeating Marshal Auguste de Marmont [q.v.]. He then marched toward Madrid but turned north to besiege Burgos [q.v.] from 19 September to 22 October 1812. However, unable to capture the city, he returned to winter quarters in Portugal.

After receiving reinforcements and fresh supplies, Wellington resumed the offensive and trounced the French forces in the Battle of Vitoria [q.v.] on 21 June 1813, causing the French to abandon their control of southern and eastern Spain. However, they were not yet ready to abandon the peninsula. Even after the British had taken San Sebastián and Pamplona [qq.v.], Marshal Soult fought stoutly in the Pyrenees.

Peninsular War *The French flee during the siege of San Sebastián in the Peninsular War.*

On 7 October 1813 Wellington crossed the Bidossoa River and stepped onto French soil. Soult fell back to a defensive line on the Nivelle River [q.v.]. Major engagements were fought at the Nivelle and Nive rivers and at St. Pierre and farther east at Orthez, Tarbes, and Toulouse [qq.v.]. The fighting at Toulouse took place before word reached the front that Napoleon had abdicated.

The Peninsular War, which Napoleon came to call the Spanish ulcer for its drain upon his military resources, was in large part responsible for the collapse of his empire. It cost France nearly 240,000 casualties, an average of almost 100 men per day, about a quarter of the losses at the hands of Spanish guerrillas, and it placed an enormous financial strain upon the country.

Historians familiar with the history of Spain found the resistance of the Spanish people to the French as difficult to fathom as did Napoleon, for the Spanish guerrillas were not liberals but Catholics and monarchist peasants. However, among the guerrillas the line between banditry and patriotism was often difficult to discern.

The British won nineteen major battles as well as many smaller engagements, captured four fortresses, and drove the French out of both Portugal and Spain at a cost of about 40,000 British dead. The end of the war freed much of Wellington's army to cross the Atlantic and fight the Americans in the final stages of the War of 1812 [q.v.].

It has been estimated that more people, soldiers and civilians, lost their lives in this war than in any other in the Napoleonic era.

Pennon / Pennant. A narrow flag, frequently with a swallowtail, often hung from lances.

Pennon

Pennsylvania Rifle. See Kentucky Rifle.

Pennypacker, Galusha (1844–1916). An American soldier who at the beginning of the American Civil War enlisted in the Federal army as a volunteer at age sixteen and by age twenty was a colonel. On 15 January 1865 he led a charge at Fort Fisher and fell wounded after planting the colors of his regiment across a traverse. For this he was awarded the Medal of Honor [q.v.]. Brigadier General Alfred Terry [q.v.] declared that without his valor the fort could not have been taken. Just before his twenty-first birthday he was promoted brigadier general, becoming not only the war's youngest general but the youngest man ever to become a general in the U.S. army. On 13 March 1865 he was brevetted major general. He resigned from the army in April 1866 but rejoined as a regular army colonel of the 34th Infantry on 28 July, becoming at age twenty-two the youngest colonel ever to command a regiment of regular infantry. In 1869 he transferred to the 16th Infantry, a regiment he commanded in the South and from 1877 on the western frontier until 3 July 1883, when he retired and settled in Philadelphia. He remained ever active in veterans' affairs.

Pensacola, Capture of (7 November 1814), War of 1812. This town, in what was then Spanish Florida, became a base for British forces, who were supplying their Creek Indian allies. The United States, fearing that Spain might enter the war, avoided attacking the town, but when a British-Creek attack mounted there struck Fort Bowyer, Alabama, at Mobile Point at the entrance to Mobile Bay, General Andrew Jackson [q.v.], without authority, invaded Spanish Florida, seized Pensacola, and occupied it.

Penthouse. A shedlike structure built to protect a gun and its carriage from the effects of weather.

People's War. That part of the Franco-Prussian War [q.v.] fought outside besieged Paris after the fall of Metz on 27 October 1870. It was so called because the French force was largely composed of untrained volunteers. The bulk of the regular forces had been captured or were besieged. [See Coulmiers.]

Pepe, Florestano (1780–1851). An Italian soldier and brother of Guglielmo Pepe [q.v.] who in 1809, during the Peninsular War [q.v.], served in the French army under Marshal Joachim Murat [q.v.] in Spain. In 1812 he took part in Napoleon's Russian Campaign [q.v.], and in 1814–15 he fought in Italy [qq.v.]. In 1815 he was promoted lieutenant general, and in 1820 he commanded the Bourbon troops sent to quell a Sicilian uprising. The following year he retired to private life.

Pepe, Guglielmo (1783–1855). A Neapolitan soldier and Carbonarist [see Carbonari], who led a liberal revolution in Italy in 1820. He was defeated by the Austrians in the Battle of Rieti [q.v.] on 7 March 1821 and banished under penalty of death. In 1848 he commanded the Neapolitan troops sent to Lombardy to fight the Austrians, but the troops were withdrawn. In 1849 as a volunteer he took part in the defense of Venice [see Venice, Siege of]. He was the younger brother of Florestano Pepe [q.v.].

Perak War (1875–76). In 1874 the British government sent its first Resident to Perak, one of the Malay States, now in northwestern Malaysia, and he at once began to interfere with such important matters as revenue collection and slavery. Unhappy with him, the sultan of Upper Perak and other Malay chiefs arranged his murder. In response the British promptly dispatched a military force to deal with the situation. The sultan was deposed, other chiefs were punished, and the British increased their already considerable influence in Malaya.

Percussion Cap. A device for setting off an explosive charge by friction, a blow, or pressure. In the nineteenth century the percussion cap or primer was usually a cap, paper or metal tube, quill, or wafer filled with an explosive charge that was used to fire the charge of powder in a weapon. It was usually a small metal cover inlaid with fulminate of mercury or other explosive, which was placed on the nipple of a rifle or revolver. When the hammer struck the cap, the powder exploded and ignited the charge. Between 1818 and 1823 British, French, and American inventors all laid claim to its invention [see Forsyth, John]. Although by 1827 it had come into general use for sporting guns, it was slow to be accepted by European armies. The French were perhaps the first to experiment with the cap for military use, but the French army was slow to adopt it. The British Board of Ordnance [q.v.] did not approve it until 1834. A percussion carbine that replaced the flintlock, after being on trial for three years, was approved in

1843. In the United States one of the first percussion caps was the tape primer, invented by Dr. Edward Maynard [q.v.], an American dentist, in 1845.

Perdriel, Battle of (5 September 1806), British intervention in Argentina. British General William Beresford [q.v.], who in June and July had tried unsuccessfully to seize Buenos Aires, was defeated by an Argentine force at this town in the Mendoza River valley, 13 miles south-southwest of Mendoza, Argentina.

Pered, Battle of (21 June 1849), Hungarian Revolution. Some 16,000 Hungarians under General Arthur Görgey [q.v.] were attacked by 25,000 Austrians and Russians under Prince Alfred zu Windisch-Graetz [q.v.] and were driven from their positions with a loss estimated to be about 3,000.

Pérignon, Catherine Dominique (1754–1818). A French soldier in the Napoleonic Wars [q.v.] who was first commissioned in 1780. In September 1803 he was recommended to be a general of brigade, and three months later he was a general of division. On 19 May 1804 he was made a marshal. A good administrator, he took part in none of the major battles. He did not rally to Napoleon during the Hundred Days [q.v.], and Napoleon struck his name from the list of marshals.

Periscope. An optical instrument for observing surroundings while remaining hidden. Essentially a tube holding two mirrors set at an angle of 45 degrees and facing in opposite directions, it was developed by E. H. Marie-Davy in 1854. In 1872 prisms replaced mirrors. In the late nineteenth century the instruments were used in fortifications for surveillance and gunnery control.

Permanent Rank. A substantive rank in a military service that does not change with a change in duty or circumstances and from which an officer can not be reduced without a court-martial. Used in distinction to temporary, personal, local, brevet, or volunteer rank. In the American army the highest such rank was, and is, major general.

Perrin, Claude-Victor (1764–1841), commonly called Victor, as if it were his last name. A French soldier who fought in French Revolutionary, Napoleonic, and restoration armies. He left home and enlisted at the age of fifteen as a musician, for he could play the clarinet. He bought his discharge in 1791, married, and found a job. Nine months later he reenlisted and from that time rose rapidly. In 1792 he commanded a battalion, and within a year he was general of brigade. In 1797 Napoleon promoted him general of division. In 1807, after his distinguished service in the Battle of Friedland [q.v.], he was made marshal, the first to be named after the original fourteen [see Marshal; Marshalate]. From 1808 to 1812 he served in Spain and fought in the Peninsular War [q.v.]. During Napoleon's Russian Campaign [q.v.] he commanded the line of communications and distinguished himself in commanding the rear guard in the crossing of the Berezina [q.v.].

During the Hundred Days [q.v.] he did not rally to Napoleon but fled with Louis XVIII (1755–1824). After the Battle of Waterloo [q.v.] he was covered with honors and as-

signed to purge the French army, a task he seemed to enjoy. He was known for his quick temper and his cruelty.

Perry, Frank W. (1845?–1876). An American soldier who at the age of sixteen enlisted in the 14th Infantry. In 1862, during the American Civil War, he was commissioned a second lieutenant in the Federal army. Before the age of twenty-one he had taken part in twenty-five engagements, including all the battles of the Army of the Potomac [q.v.], and had won brevets to major. In the reorganized army after the war he was a captain and for the next five years fought against hostile Indians in Oregon, Idaho, and Arizona.

On 2 June 1871 Perry was tried by general court-martial on three charges: drunk on duty, conduct unbecoming an officer, and conduct prejudicial to good order and military discipline. Colonel Abner Doubleday [q.v.] was president of the court that convicted him of having been drunk on duty thirteen times. He was sentenced to be cashiered, but the sentence was reduced to suspension of rank for eighteen months and of pay for the same period except for fifty dollars a month. On 1 February 1873 he resigned his commission and began a fruitless search for work. His obituary in 1876 stated that he had died of "wounds and disease contracted in the war."

Perryville, Battle of (8 October 1862), American Civil War. At this central Kentucky town 40 miles southwest of

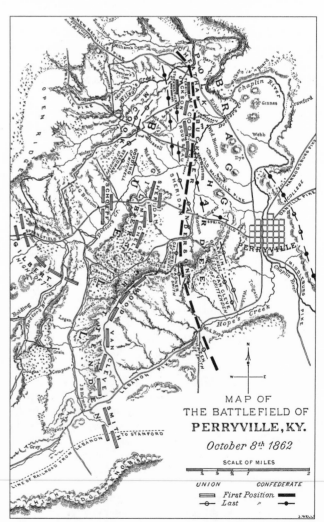

Perryville *Map of the Battlefield of Perryville, Kentucky, 8 October 1862*

Lexington, Confederate General Braxton Bragg [q.v.], commanding the 22,500-man Army of Tennessee [q.v.], fought an indecisive battle with seven divisions of Union troops (36,940 effectives) under General Don Carlos Buell [q.v.]. The next day Bragg retreated into Tennessee; Buell, who failed to pursue, was relieved of his command.

Bragg's losses were 510 killed, 2,635 wounded, and 251 missing; Buell lost 845 killed, 2,851 wounded, and 515 missing.

Pershing Rifles. An American military honor society in American colleges. It began in 1892 when Second Lieutenant (later General of the Armies) John Joseph Pershing (1860–1948), a professor of military science at the University of Nebraska, formed a winning drill team from Reserve Officer Training Corps (ROTC) cadets. It was named the Pershing Rifles in 1894, and the organization spread to most colleges and universities where military science was taught [see Morrill Act].

Persian-Afghan Wars. In the eighteenth century two wars were fought between Afghanistan and Persia (Iran), the first in 1726–38 and the second in 1798. There were three wars between these Asian powers in the nineteenth century. [see Herat, Sieges of.]

Persian-Afghan War of 1816. Persian troops of Fath Ali [q.v.], shah of Persia, marshaled at Ghorian (Ghurian), then a Persian town (today in northwestern Afghanistan), near the left bank of the Hari Rud River, with the intention of attacking Herat, 40 miles west in Afghanistan. Fath Ali was bought off by the governor of Herat, a measure that displeased the vizier of Afghanistan, who had the governor seized and deported, upon which Fath Ali then advanced upon the city. To halt his advance, the ruler of Afghanistan agreed to Persian demands and as punishment blinded the vizier, whose relatives then seized the throne. Persian troops failed to capture Herat, but Persian rulers continued to covet it.

Persian-Afghan War of 1836–38. Muhammad Shah (1810–1848), ruler of Persia, moved with an army upon the city of Herat and laid siege to it from 23 November 1836 until he was forced by the British to withdraw on 28 September 1838.

Persian-Afghan War of 1855–57. In 1855 the Persians again invaded Afghanistan. The Afghans called on the British, who went to war with Persia [see Anglo-Persian War].

Persian-British War. See Anglo-Persian War.

Persian-Turkish War. See Turko-Persian Wars.

Personal Presence of the Commander. In nineteenth century wars it was considered important that soldiers in battle see their commanding general and know that he was with them. Charles Ardant de Picq [q.v.] wrote: "When the battle becomes hot, they must see their commander, know him to be near. It does not matter even if he is without initiative, incapable of giving an order. His presence creates a belief that direction exists, and that is enough" (*Battle Studies* [1880]).

Personal Salutes by Artillery. The firing of guns using blank cartridges or without projectiles to honor civil, diplo-

matic, and military personages of high rank. All civilized countries defined the occasions and the persons to be so honored, but the prime concern was and is the number of shots fired, always expressed as the number of guns [see Gunner's Chant]. In the United States the president as the commander-in-chief receives the maximum, 21 guns. So does a serving foreign sovereign, his or her heir apparent, and consort. The vice president receives 19; members of the cabinet, the chief justice, the speaker of the House of Representatives, generals in chief, field marshals, admirals, and governors of states and territories, 17; lieutenant generals and vice admirals, 15; major generals and rear admirals, 13; brigadier generals and commodores, 11. No other officers receive personal salutes, but consuls general of states accredited to the United States receive 9, the lowest number.

Other governments had similar rules. In India under the British the number of guns received by the hundreds of Indian princes was closely regulated because it indicated to them their standing, their importance to the Raj. At the end of the century only five were accorded 21 guns: the maharajahs of Hyderabad, Mysore, Jammu and Kashmir, Baroda, and Gwalior. More than 300 minor rulers were not entitled to personal salutes.

Peru-Bolivia Confederation, War of the (1836–1839). In 1835 Bolivian dictator Andrés Santa Cruz [q.v.], having invaded Peru to end an army mutiny there, proposed a confederation of the two countries. This was opposed by Chile and Argentina, who feared a shift in the balance of power in the area. Diego Portales (1793–1837), a Chilean politician, urged war to prevent the union, and on 11 November 1836 war was declared. An invasion effort by the Chileans in 1837 resulted in a standoff. Mutinous soldiers murdered Portales, an act that only stimulated martial patriotic emotions, and when Santa Cruz made a peace offering, it was rejected. In 1838 a Chilean army under Manuel Bulnes [q.v.] invaded Peru and captured Lima. A few months later it was recaptured by the forces of Santa Cruz. On 20 January 1839 Chilean and Peruvian-Bolivian forces under Bulnes met at Yungay [q.v.], Chile, southeast of Concepción, and the confederation's force was decisively beaten. Santa Cruz was forced to flee to Ecuador, and the confederation was dissolved. Agustín Gamarra [q.v.], a Peruvian who had served in the Chilean army, became president of Peru.

Peru-Bolivia War (1841). General Agustín Gamarra [q.v.], president of Peru, took advantage of political unrest in Bolivia and in August 1841 invaded the country and attempted to annex the rich province of La Paz. The city of La Paz, defended by General José Ballivián [q.v.], president of Bolivia, was besieged but never taken. The Peruvians were routed on 18 November 1841 in the Battle of Ingavi [q.v.], a mountain south of La Paz, in which Gamarra was killed. Ballivián then invaded Peru, but Chile intervened, and in June 1842 a peace was signed.

Peru-Colombia War (1828–29). A short war in which the main event was the Battle of Jirón [q.v.] on 28 February 1829. Peace was signed on 23 September.

Peruvian Revolutions. Bolivian General Andrés Santa Cruz [q.v.], who had been active in the Peruvian War of

Independence [q.v.] from Spain in 1820–23, became president of Bolivia in 1829. In 1836 he invaded Peru, defeating the army of General Agustín Gamarra [q.v.] and making himself head ("Protector") of a Peru-Bolivia Confederation. Chile, which sided with Gamarra, sent troops into Peru under General Manuel Bulnes [q.v.]. After three years of war Santa Cruz was defeated in the Battle of Yungay [q.v.] in June 1839, and Gamarra became president.

After the death of President Gamarra there erupted a series of almost continuous civil wars. In early 1843 Manuel Ignacio Vivanco, who called himself the Regenerator, seized power. Supported by the army, he ruled as a dictator. He ignored the constitution, refused to convene the Congress, and executed all who opposed him. In 1845 General Ramón Castilla [q.v.] led a successful revolution, seizing Lima during Vivanco's absence. In the Battle of Carmen Alto on 22 July 1844 Vivanco was decisively defeated, then forced into exile. Castilla became president, and until 1862 he maintained a fragile era of order. In 1865 Mariano Ignacio Prado [q.v.] made himself dictator, but his reign was overturned by José Balta [q.v.], who became president in 1868.

On 22 July 1872 Tomás Gutiérrez (d. 1872), minister of war, led a successful revolution and ordered that President Balta [q.v.] be shot. Unsupported by the people or the army and unrecognized by foreign powers, Balta attempted to flee but was caught by a mob and hanged from a lamppost.

In 1874 Manuel Pardo (1834–1878), the first civilian president of Peru, was overthrown by a revolution stirred up by Colonel Nicolás de Piérola [q.v.] and replaced by Mariano Ignacio Prado. In 1879, after the War of the Pacific [q.v.], Piérola engineered another revolution, overthrew the government of Prado and became dictator. Smaller revolutions continued throughout the century.

Peruvian War of Independence (1820–25). In 1820, after the Chilean War of Independence [q.v.], José de San Martín [q.v.] loaded 4,000 troops onto transporters at Valparaiso, Chile, and, protected by the Chilean fleet under Admiral Thomas Lord Cochrane (1775–1860), sailed to Peru. After landing at Pisco, he established a camp at Huacho, where he attracted a considerable number of Peruvian recruits. In July 1821, when the Spanish governor left Lima for a trip into the interior, San Martín entered the city at its invitation and declared Peru (including Bolivia, then a part of the country known as Upper Peru) independent. Needing military assistance, he called on Simón Bolívar [q.v.], the other great South American liberator. On 26–27 July 1822 the two revolutionary leaders met at Guayaquil. No one knows exactly what took place at this famous meeting, but soon after, San Martín turned over his army to Bolívar and retired from all further military and revolutionary activity.

Two years later, with General José de Sucre [q.v.], Bolívar led an army of 19,000 against a royalist army under José Canterac [q.v.], wining a victory in the Battle of Junín [q.v.] on 6 August 1824. On 9 December Sucre pushed on and decisively defeated another royalist force under José de La Serna y Hinojosa [q.v.] in the Battle of Ayacucho [q.v.].

The revolutionaries in Upper Peru (Bolivia) were reinforced by Sucre, and the Spanish driven out of this area.

Peru, War of Independence *Spaniards clamber up the rugged mountain at the battle of Ayacucho.*

Pesh Khana / Pesh Khidmat. In India, the tents and accompanying retinue sent in advance of a unit on the march so that the commander would have quarters or headquarters in place on his arrival at the new campsite. Usually two complete *pesh khanas* were maintained; one of them went ahead each night [see Quartering Party].

Peshwa. The title of a Maratha ruler.

Petard. Originally an explosive device used to blow open gates or blow holes in stockades. They were dangerous to use, and as Shakespeare noted, a man could be "hoist with his own petard." The device was not used in the nineteenth century, but the word was sometimes used as a verb: To petard was to blow up.

Peterloo Massacre (16 August 1819). In Britain the 15th Hussars, Cheshire Yeomanry, and an untrained civic guard, in support of the civil authorities, attempted to arrest Harry Hunt (1773–1835), as he spoke in an open-air meeting of more than 50,000 people at St. Peter's Fields, Manchester. Hunt and his supporters were demanding parliamentary reform and a repeal of the Corn Laws, and to the local authorities the meeting "bore the appearance of insurrection." In the charge of the troops into the mob, 11 civilians were killed and more than 400 were injured. Hunt was arrested and imprisoned for thirty months.

As political scandals in the United States that followed

Watergate were often called -gate, so this affair, only four years after the Battle of Waterloo, was called Peterloo.

Petersburg Campaign (June 1864–April 1865), American Civil War. Petersburg, Virginia, a vital Confederate railway center 20 miles south of Richmond, was besieged by the Union Army of the Potomac [q.v.] in the longest sustained military operation of the war.

On the night of 12–13 June 1864 Union troops in and around Cold Harbor left their trenches fronting Robert E. Lee's Army of Northern Virginia [q.v.] and moved south. Crossing the James River by a newly constructed pontoon bridge [see James River Bridge], they marched on Petersburg, then defended by only 2,500 troops under General Pierre Beauregard [q.v.]. Through a series of mishaps and errors on the part of Union generals U. S. Grant and George Meade [qq.v.] and good generalship on the part of Beauregard, the Union troops failed to take the city. Lee soon moved his army to Petersburg and faced Grant and Meade from defensive positions, mostly trenches. In unsuccessful assaults the Union forces lost 4,000 men.

As the troops on both sides dug into the earth, the siege was fought from trenches and field fortifications. The explosion of the Petersburg mine [q.v.], a Union attempt to get through the Confederate lines, and the bungled Union attack that followed became one of the most dramatic episodes of the campaign—indeed, one of the most bizarre episodes of the war.

The final assault on Petersburg took place on 2 April 1865. The Union II Corps, attacking the Confederate left flank, captured the Confederate position at what was called the Crow Salient. During that night the Confederates withdrew toward Amelia Court House. Union casualties in the assault were about 4,000; Confederate losses are unknown. Two weeks later General Lee surrendered the Army of Northern Virginia at Appomattox [q.v.].

Petersburg Campaign *Union forces explode the Petersburg mine in a failed attempt to breach the Confederate fortifications.*

Petersburg Mine (July 1864), American Civil War. One of the most remarkable features of the Petersburg Campaign [q.v.] was the explosion on 30 July 1864 of an enormous Union mine under the Confederate defenses, followed by a Union infantry assault, sometimes known as the Battle of the Crater.

The 48th Pennsylvania Infantry was a regiment composed largely of coal miners. Its commander, Lieutenant Colonel Henry Pleasants (1833–1880), a mining engineer who later took an active role in breaking up the Molly Maguires [q.v.] in the Pennsylvania coal fields, convinced General Ambrose Burnside [q.v.] that his men could dig a mine and blow a hole in the Confederate defenses large enough to facilitate an assault. Although Grant was not enthusiastic about the project, he gave his approval, and on 23 June 1864 the work was begun. The main shaft of the mine ran 511 feet to a point 20 feet below the Confederate battery at a position known as Elliott's Salient. Two lateral galleries extended for a total of 75 feet under the Confederate trenches. The whole was ventilated by a system that drew out the stale air by fire through a chimney near the shaft's mouth. Fresh air was introduced through a wooden tube along the floor of the tunnel. On 23 July the digging was completed, and the excavated area under the Confederate position was filled with 320 kegs containing 8,000 pounds of black powder. Tamping was provided by filling 38 feet of the tunnel with earth, and a fuze was improvised.

Burnside had selected a black division commanded by Spanish-born General Edward Ferrero [q.v.] to lead the assault. These troops had been brought forward and given special training for their role. However, the day before the assault was to take place Meade informed Burnside that he feared the political repercussions of using black troops for such a perilous mission. Grant concurred. The order for the black troops to lead the assault was canceled, and three commanders of white divisions drew straws to see which would replace them. The decisive straw was drawn by General James Hewitt Ledlie (1832–1882), whose unfortunate men had little notion of what was to happen or what they were expected to do. Their task was made more difficult by the failure of the Federal commanders to provide them passages through their own obstacles. At 3:30 A.M. on 30 July the fuze was lit, but no explosion followed; it sputtered out at a splice. An hour and some minutes later a lieutenant and a sergeant bravely crawled into the tunnel and relit it. At 4:45 the mine exploded, creating a crater 170 feet long, 60–80 feet wide, and 30 feet deep. At least 278 Confederate soldiers, mostly from South Carolina, were killed or wounded. The Union infantry attack, however, was a failure. General Ledlie had chosen not to lead it but to remain behind with a jug of rum in a bombproof shelter [see Personal Presence of the Commander]. By eight o'clock some 15,000 troops, Union and Confederate, were milling about in the crater. Some of the assaulting Federal soldiers, stunned by the magnitude of the explosion, had stopped in their tracks to help free half-buried Confederates.

When the Confederates recovered and counterattacked, Ferrero's division was sent into the fight. It advanced without Ferrero, who had joined the boozing Ledlie in the bomb shelter. By one o'clock the Confederates had driven back or captured the Union attackers. The Federals lost 3,798 of 20,708 engaged; the Confederates lost about 1,500.

"The effort was a tremendous failure," wrote General Grant. Ignoring his own responsibility, he added, "and all due to the inefficiency on the part of the corps commander and the incompetency of the division commander who was sent to lead the assault."

Pétion, Alexandre Sabès (1770–1818). A well-educated Haitian mulatto general and revolutionary who fought in the rebellion led by Toussaint L'Ouverture and André Rigaud [qq.v.] and who from 1802 to 1806 served under General Jean Dessalines [q.v.]. In 1807 he became president of a

Haitian southern republic, and from 1811 to 1818 he was at war with General Henri Christophe [q.v.], a conflict that ended when Christophe shot and killed himself with a silver bullet.

Petites Postes. Outposts [q.v.].

Pets and Mascots. Animals of all sorts, chickens, cats, bears, antelopes, deer, goats, even a Tibetan wild ass, but particularly dogs, and particularly mongrel dogs, have been part of most Western armies either as individuals' pets or as unit mascots. Soldiers of all ranks in British and American armies were especially fond of animals, and no picture of soldiers on parade, on the march, or in cantonments is complete without at least one dog of some description.

Lieutenant Colonel Theodore Roosevelt [q.v.] acquired a dog he named Cuba during the Spanish-American War [q.v.]. On the American western frontier coursing hounds were popular. George Custer [q.v.] frequently hunted with his. Wellington took a pack of hounds to the Iberian Peninsula during the Peninsular War [q.v.].

Dogs took part in many battles. One named Pip, belonging to a British officer in Company G, 2nd Battalion, 24th Infantry, was present in the Battle of Rorke's Drift [q.v.] and during the Battle of the Alma [q.v.]. Toby, a Maltese terrier who had been adopted by the drummers of the Coldstream Guards, persistently chased rolling cannonballs. A mongrel named Bobby of the 66th Foot, although wounded in the neck and back in the Battle of Maiwand [q.v.] in the Second Afghan War [q.v.], still managed to work his way back to his unit at Kandahar, 50 miles distant. Upon the regiment's return to England, Queen Victoria personally presented him with his campaign medal. Bobby failed to survive the rigors of city life; eighteen months after his return he was run over and killed by a hansom cab. The regiment had his body mounted and, with his medal hanging from his neck, preserved in a glass case. He may still be seen at the regimental museum of the Berkshire Regiment at Brock Barracks, Reading.

During the American Civil War the 102nd Pennsylvania brought to war a spotted bull terrier, named Jack, who, it was claimed, knew all the bugle calls and helped seek wounded soldiers on the battlefield. In 1863 Jack was captured by the Confederates at Salem Church, Virginia, but after six months was exchanged for a Confederate prisoner at Belle Isle Prison [q.v.]. He was wounded in the back and shoulder in the Battle of Malvern Hill [q.v.] but recovered. He disappeared on the night of 23 December 1864, and it was believed that he was taken by thieves who coveted a silver collar that had been recently awarded to him.

A variety of animals have been made official mascots. In 1844 Queen Victoria herself presented the Rifle Brigade with two red deer, and from 1844 she kept the Royal Welch Fusiliers supplied with a mascot goat, selected from the royal herd presented to her by the shah of Persia (Iran). The Derbyshire Regiment had a series of rams as mascots, all called Derby, each in succession distinguished by roman numerals; ram XII was presented to the regiment in 1913 by the Duke of Devonshire.

Horses too old to serve were sometimes treated as honored pets. Bob, a horse that had charged with the Light Brigade at Balaclava [q.v.], was at one time the oldest horse in the British army. When he died at age thirty-three, he was buried with full military honors. A horse named Old Times in the British 10th Hussars had been a prize-winning jumper until badly wounded on the Northwest Frontier; thereafter he was allowed to roam the barracks as he pleased. Little Sorrel, the favorite horse of General Thomas ("Stonewall") Jackson, was kept as a pet at the Virginia Military Institute [q.v.] after the American Civil War. Vionel, ridden by Lord Roberts in the Second Afghan War, made the famous march from Kabul to Kandahar [q.v.] and was duly awarded the campaign medal with suitable clasps [see Horses].

An eagle named Old Abe [q.v.] was a mascot of Company C, 8th Wisconsin, in the American Civil War. During the Spanish-American War [q.v.] the famous Rough Riders [q.v.] carried along two pets: an eagle named Teddy and a young mountain lion, Josephine.

Pets and Mascots *Two soldiers of the 29th Maine with Major, their regimental mascot.*

Jack, mascot of the 102nd Pennsylvania Infantry

Petta / Pettah. In India, a cottage in the rear of barracks or a fort where a sepoy could keep his family. A group of such cottages often formed a small village. In 1839 Miss Julia Charlotte Maitland, writing from Madras, informed those at home: "The English ladies told me this pettah was 'a horrid place—quite native!' and advised me never to go into it; so I went next day, of course, and found it *most curious—quite native.*"

Pettigrew, James Johnston (1828–1863). An American soldier who entered the University of North Carolina at age fifteen and immediately after his graduation was appointed an assistant professor at the Naval Observatory. He later practiced law and served in the South Carolina legislature. At the beginning of the American Civil War he was elected colonel of the 12th South Carolina, and soon after, he was promoted brigadier general. In the Peninsular Campaign [q.v.] he was severely wounded and captured in the Battle of Seven Pines [q.v.]. Two months later he was exchanged. He fought at Gettysburg [q.v.], took part in Pickett's Charge [q.v.], and commanded a portion of the rear guard during the retreat. On 14 July 1863 he was mortally wounded in a dashing attack made by Federal cavalry at Falling Waters, Maryland.

Pezza, Michele. See Fra Diavolo.

Pharsalus, Battle of (6 May 1897), Graeco-Turkish War. During a dispute over the control of Crete, three divisions of Turkish troops under Edhem Pasha [q.v.] invaded Thessaly. On 6 May they attacked Greek positions before this town (now Pharsalos or Pharsala) in northeastern Greece and drove the Greeks out at a cost of 230 casualties; Greek losses were about the same. In the treaty signed on 20 September Turkey was indemnified for its losses, and Crete was placed under international control.

Phelps, John Wolcott (1813–1885). An American soldier who was graduated from West Point in 1836. He took part in the war against the Creeks and Seminoles in 1836–39 and fought in the Mexican War [q.v.]. During the American Civil War he became a Union brigadier general of volunteers on 17 May 1861 and cooperated with Admiral David Farragut (1801–1870) in clearing the lower Mississippi of Confederate forces. In New Orleans he organized the first black troops for service in the Federal army. He resigned on 21 August 1862, when the government disavowed his act and ordered him to disband the troops and use them as laborers. In 1880 he was the American Party's unsuccessful candidate for president.

Philip, King (1776?–1839). A Seminole chief, prominent in the Second Seminole War [q.v.], who was married to the sister of Chief Micanopy [q.v.]. In December 1835 his bands raided sugar plantations south of St. Augustine. On 8 February 1837 he led 200 warriors in an attack upon Fort Mellon at the head of Lake Monroe in Florida. Captain Charles Mellon (1792?–1837) was killed, and 17 of his men were wounded. On 8–9 September 1837 Philip's camp south of the Tomoka River was surrounded by 170 men under Brigadier General Joseph Hernandez (1793–1857), a militia officer. Philip and 11 of his people were captured. He died while being escorted to Indian Territory.

Philippi, Battle of (3–4 June 1861), American Civil War. Union General George B. McClellan [q.v.] with 20,000 troops from the Department of the Ohio moved eastward toward Maryland and at Philippi (now in West Virginia), 19 miles east-southeast of Clarksburg, collided with a 5,000-man Confederate army under Robert Garnett [q.v.] moving north.

In an enveloping attack, 15 Confederates were killed or wounded; 2 Union soldiers were wounded. This battle, the first in the war, has been sometimes derided as the Philippi Races because of the speed with which the Confederates decamped.

Philippine Insurrection against Spain (1896–98). In 1896 Katipunan, a secret society opposing Spanish rule, was formed in the Philippines by Andrés Bonifacio (1863–1897). When the Spanish authorities discovered its existence, Bonifacio called for an armed rebellion on 26 August 1898. Spanish troops won their battles with the rebels, but Filipino resistance stiffened after the public execution of José Rizal (1861–1896), a patriot whose writings had done much to inspire the desire for independence.

Much of the fighting occurred in Cavite Province, where Bonifacio had a rival for the leadership of the rebels in the person of Emilio Aguinaldo [q.v.], the mayor of Cavite, who finally accused him of treason and ordered him shot. The rebellion ended on 15 December 1898 with the Pact of Biak-na-bato, in which the Spanish promised substantial social and governmental reforms. Upon the guarantee of a payment of 400,000 pesos Aguinaldo and other rebel leaders agreed to go into exile in Hong Kong.

Philippine Insurrection against the United States (1899–1901). The United States acquired the Philippine Islands from Spain at the conclusion of the Spanish-American War [q.v.] by the Treaty of Paris on 10 December 1898. A rebellion against American authority in the Philippines led by Emilio Aguinaldo [q.v.] had already begun in September, and a Philippine republic was declared on 20 January 1899. The first exchange of shots took place near Manila on 4 February. The Filipinos retreated, but on 22–24 February a rebel army under General Antonio Luna (1866–1912) launched an attack upon Manila. It was beaten back by American forces under General Arthur MacArthur [q.v.]. On 31 March the Americans captured the rebel capital of Malolos, and Aguinaldo was forced to move his headquarters to Tarlac, 65 miles north of Manila. When this town was taken, the rebels dissolved their army and began a guerrilla campaign. On 31 March 1901 Aguinaldo was captured through a stratagem devised by General Frederick Funston [q.v.]. Although the rebellion was effectively ended by Aguinaldo's capture, it was not officially ended until 4 July 1902. Some 1,000 Americans

Philippine Insurrection against Spain *A group of Philippine Muslims*

were killed and 3,000 wounded in the conflict; rebel Filipino casualties are unknown. A civil government was established under American control with William Howard Taft (1857–1930) as the first American governor.

Philippon, Armand (1761–1836). A French soldier who enlisted in 1778 and was a sergeant major in 1790. Two years later he was a captain of volunteers serving in Spain. He later fought at Austerlitz, Talavara, and the siege of Cadiz [qq.v.]. From March 1811 he was governor of Badajoz [q.v.], successfully defying the first siege attempts of William Beresford and Wellington [qq.v.]. He finally surrendered the town after being wounded in the second siege and was carried to England, where he escaped to fight at Kulm [q.v.] in August 1813.

Philippopolis, Battle of. See Plovdiv, Battle of.

Philippoteaux, Paul (1846–1923). A French painter of cycloramas of historical battle scenes. His first, painted with his father, was *The Defense of Fort d'Issy*, completed in 1871. In the next ten years he completed six more based on wars in Europe, North Africa, and the Balkans. In 1881 he visited the battlefield at Gettysburg [q.v.], Pennsylvania, where he sketched and took photographs. In what he later described as the greatest effort of his life he completed in 1884, with the help of five assistants, *The Battle of Gettysburg*, painted on individual panels 27 feet high, the whole measuring 360 feet in circumference. The vantage point of the viewer is from the Union line. In 1885 it was shown commercially in Boston and was so successful that Philippoteaux made three exact copies, which were displayed in other American cities. Nineteen years after the artist's death in Paris, the American government purchased one copy, probably his second version, which is now restored and on display at the Gettysburg National Battlefield Park. A privately owned copy is believed to be in storage.

Philippoteaux, Paul *The French artist's depiction of General Grant at Fort Donelson*

Philippovich von Philippsberg, Josef (1818–1880). An Austrian soldier of Bosnian descent who served under Jelačic od Bužima [q.v.] against Hungarians in 1848–49 [see Hungarian Revolution]. He also fought against Prussia in the Seven Weeks' War [q.v.] in 1866. He had strong pan-Slav sympathies and commanded the 82,000-man Austro-Hungarian army that invaded Bosnia and Herzegovina in 1878 [see Herzegovina and Bosnia Revolts].

Pibroch. (Gaelic: *piobaireachd*.) A set of martial or mournful airs played on a Scottish bagpipe.

Pichegru, Charles (1761–1804). A French soldier who became a general and a hero in the French Revolutionary armies. In 1797, at the height of his fame, he conspired to return Louis XVIII (1755–1873) to the throne and took part in the attempted coup of 18 Fructidor (4 September 1797). His complicity was suspected, but he was allowed to retire in disgrace. In August 1803 he went secretly to Paris with George Cadoudal to lead a royalist uprising against Napoleon [see Cadoudal Conspiracy]. On 28 February 1804 he was arrested, and on 5 April he was found strangled in his cell.

Pichincha, Battle of (24 May 1822), Ecuadorian War of Independence. A patriot force of 2,000 troops from Argentina, Colombia, and Peru under Antonio José de Sucre [q.v.] decisively defeated a royalist force of 2,500 under General Melchos de Aymeric on the side of this 15,713-foot-high active volcano northwest of Quito. The royalists were driven down the mountain into Quito. The Spanish lost 400 killed, 190 wounded, and 14 guns; Sucre lost 200 killed and 140 wounded.

Pickelhaube. A Prussian army headgear composed of a leather helmet decorated with a spike on top for infantry and a ball for artillery. It replaced the shako.

Picker. A small pointed brass wire for cleaning the vent of a musket.

Pickering / Piqueering / Pickerooning. A small hit-and-run skirmish made by marauders or troops detached to pillage or to make a raid just before a major battle.

Picket. 1. One or more soldiers detached from the main body to guard against a surprise attack [see Picket Line].

2. A form of punishment in which one foot was raised so that a man's entire weight fell on the other.

Picket *On picket duty, American Civil War. Drawing by Alfred R. Waud*

3. A pointed stake that, used with others, provided a defensive barrier.

Picket Line. 1. Small bodies of men placed at intervals to guard a place or body of men.

2. A secured rope to which horses were tied overnight or while being groomed.

Picket line

Picket Pin. A pointed metal stake with an attached ring. Driven into the ground, it secured a horse tethered to the ring and allowed it to graze in a circle.

Pickett, George Edward (1825–1875). An American soldier who was graduated from West Point in 1846 at the bottom of his class. During the Mexican War [q.v.] he was twice brevetted for bravery; at Chapultepec [q.v.] he was the first man over the wall. He later served on the Texas frontier from 1849 to 1855 and in Washington Territory from 1855 to 1861. At the beginning of the American Civil War he joined the Confederate army, becoming a brigadier general in February 1862 and a major general in October. He was severely wounded in the Battle of Gaines's Mill [q.v.] but rejoined his command to fight in the Battle of Fredericksburg [q.v.]. He is best remembered for the charge bearing his name made by his division and others in the Battle of Gettysburg [q.v.] on 3 July [see Pickett's Charge]. He was one of the defenders of Petersburg and was defeated in the Battle of Five Forks [qq.v.] by Philip Sheridan [q.v.] on 1 April 1865. After his defeat in the Battle of Sayler's Creek [q.v.] General Lee relieved him of command, but he remained with the army until Lee's surrender at Appomattox [q.v.]. After the war he became an insurance agent in Norfolk, Virginia.

Pickett's Charge (3 July 1863), American Civil War. This Confederate charge on the third day of the Battle of Gettysburg [q.v.] is frequently referred to as the "high water mark of the Confederacy." General Robert E. Lee, against the advice of Lieutenant General James Longstreet [q.v.], ordered Major General George Edward Pickett [q.v.], commanding a small division, to charge Cemetery Ridge [q.v.] in the center of the Union line. Pickett did not actually lead the charge, nor did his men constitute even half of the attackers, but on Longstreet's orders (Longstreet was actually in charge) Pickett formed the brigades for the attack into three lines as they came onto the field. The charge, gallantly made by about 14,000 Confederates in the face of heavy small-arms and artillery fire, crossed more than half a mile of open ground, descended into a valley between two ridges, and mounted the opposite side. The point of attack, Cemetery Ridge, was defended by 77 Union guns skillfully deployed by General Henry Hunt [q.v.] on and around Little Round Top [q.v.]. More than 2,000 men fell or were captured on each side. To the Confederate survivors Lee said simply: "The task was too great," a point they had discovered for themselves. Pickett never forgave Lee, declaring, "[T]hat old man . . . had my division massacred."

Picq, Charles Jean Jacques Joseph Ardant du. See Ardant du Picq, Jean Jacques Joseph.

Picquart, Georges (1854–1914). A French soldier who played an important role in the defense of Alfred Dreyfus [q.v.], for which he was retired from the army in 1898. Upon Dreyfus's vindication, Picquart was restored to active service and commissioned a general of division. From 1906 to 1909 he was minister of war.

Picton, Thomas (1758–1815). A British soldier who entered the army as an officer in 1771 and distinguished himself in 1796 at the captures of St. Lucia, St. Thomas, and Trinidad. In 1797 he was appointed governor of Trinidad. He was promoted brigadier general in 1801, and in 1803 he was appointed commandant of Tobago but was immediately recalled to London to stand trial at the court of King's Bench on charges of having permitted, as was allowed under old Spanish laws, a mulatto woman suspected of theft to be tortured. In 1806 he was found guilty, but he was acquitted on appeal. In

Pickett's Charge from a wartime sketch from the Union position

1809 he took part in the Walcheren Expedition [q.v.] and was made governor of Flushing. From 1810 he was one of Wellington's principal subordinates in the Peninsular War [q.v.], doing good service at the siege of Badajoz, where he was severely wounded, and in the battles of Fuentes de Oñoro, Ciudad Rodrigo, Bussaco, Vitoria, and Toulouse [qq.v.]. In 1815 he was wounded in the Battle of Quatre Bras [q.v.] but hid the fact. He went straight from the Duchess of Richmond's ball [q.v.] to the battlefield at Waterloo and fought in his civilian clothes until struck down and killed by a bullet through his top hat and into his head.

Picton, Thomas *Picton's division in action, the Battle of Toulouse, France, 10 April 1814*

Piece. A cannon. Sometimes used to include a gun and its carriage, with or without its limber.

Piecemeal Attack. 1. Portions of a force that attack as they become available.
2. An uncoordinated attack.

Piedmont, Battle of (5 June 1864), American Civil War. Union General David Hunter [q.v.], in charge of Federal operations in the Shenandoah Valley of Virginia in the summer of 1864, moved with about 16,000 men south from Strasburg up the valley toward Staunton, where he encountered 8,500 Confederates under General William ("Grumble") Jones [q.v.] entrenched near Harrisonburg. Hunter circled eastward to avoid the Confederates, but Jones with about 5,000 men moved to intercept him. At the village of Piedmont, seven miles southwest of Port Republic, Hunter delivered a crushing blow. Jones was killed, and some 600 other Confederates were killed or wounded; 1,000 were taken prisoner. Hunter then occupied Staunton and the following day captured its storehouses and the track of the Virginia Central Railroad. Union losses totaled about 780.

Piedmontese Revolt of 1821. Nobles with liberal ideas allied themselves with the Carbonari [q.v.] in the Piedmont area of northwestern Italy, then a part of the kingdom of Sardinia, to rebel against the rule of King Victor Emmanuel I (1759–1824) of Sardinia, who had refused to accept a constitution. The rebels were supported by Prince Carlo Alberto [q.v.], also known as Charles Albert, of Savoy and Piedmont, the heir designate to the throne. Victor Emmanuel was forced to abdicate, and the throne was assumed by his brother Carlo Felix (1765–1831), but in Carlo Felix's absence, Carlo Alberto became regent and proclaimed a constitution. Carlo Felix opposed its adoption, and on 8 April a combined Austro-

Sardinian army defeated a Piedmontese army at the First Battle of Novara [q.v.].

The army was purged of constitutionists; three of the leading conspirators were shot, others jailed. Carlo Alberto was later reconciled with Carlo Felix.

Piegan Massacre (23 January 1870), American Indian Wars. Colonel Eugene Mortimer Baker (1822?–1885) with four troops of the 2nd Cavalry and four companies of the 23th Infantry attacked a Piegan Indian village on the Marias River in Montana and slaughtered 173 people, including 53 women and children, many prostrated by smallpox. Another 140 women and children were taken prisoner, though later released. Among the dead was Heavy Runner, a Blackfoot chief who had always been a determined friend of the whites. Baker had been ordered not to molest his people, but the lodges of the Blackfoot had mixed with those of the Piegans. As soon as the troops were seen, Heavy Runner had dashed toward them, holding aloft a "paper." He was the first to fall.

Pieper, Henry (1840–1898). A German gunmaker who in 1866 established a factory at Liège, Belgium, to make rifled barrels for rifles. In 1886 he developed a gas seal for revolvers. His company, Établissements Pieper, S.A., continued under his son, Nicolas.

Pierce, Franklin (1804–1869). An American politician who in the Mexican War [q.v.] enlisted as a private and rose to serve as a brigadier general. He took part in the advance on the Mexican capital under General Winfield Scott [q.v.]. In the Battle of Contreras [q.v.] he was thrown from his horse and suffered painful injuries. Nevertheless, he insisted on joining the fight the next day, and in the midst of the battle he fainted, an incident, variously interpreted, that was used both for and against him when he ran for the presidency against General Scott. In 1854 he became the fourteenth president of the United States (1853–57).

Piérola, Nicolás de (1839–1913). A Peruvian soldier and political leader who stirred up revolts against both Manuel Pardo and Mariano Prado [qq.v.] and assumed the presidency when Manuel Pardo left office. He strengthened the army and fought in the War of the Pacific [q.v.], but the defeats of the Peruvian army in that war drove him from office. In 1894 he overthrew the government of Andrés Cáceres [q.v.] and was again president (1895–99).

Pieter's Hill, Battle of (27 February 1900), Second Anglo-Boer War. The final battle waged by British General Sir Redvers Buller [q.v.] in his struggle to relieve Ladysmith [q.v.], besieged since 1 November 1899. On 19 February the British captured Hlangwane, an important height that gave Buller command of the Tugela River crossing. His advance was delayed by the strong Boer positions on Pieter's Hill near Ladysmith, which he finally took by assault at a cost of 1,896 killed and wounded. Besieged General George White [q.v.] in Ladysmith was relieved the day after the battle.

Piffer. The colloquial name for a member or a unit of the Punjab Frontier Force [q.v.].

Pig, War of the (1846). In June 1846 American and British negotiators defining the boundary between the United States and Canada extended the forty-ninth parallel westward from the Rocky Mountains to the Pacific Ocean, the line making a slight dip to give Vancouver Island to the British. The agreement failed to make clear the ownership of the tiny island of San Juan, one of a small group of islands lying between Haro and Rosario straits, southwest of Bellingham, at the north end of Puget Sound. There the Hudson's Bay Company had a settlement near several American farms. Trouble began when an American farmer shot and killed a company pig that had damaged his fence and grubbed about in his garden. Attempts to settle peacefully the resulting contretemps failed. When Canadian authorities attempted to transport the farmer to British Columbia for trial, American General William S. Harney [q.v.], commanding the Oregon Department, with the support of Secretary of War John Buchanan Floyd (1806–1863), sent American troops to the island, an action that created an international furor. In response the British dispatched a warship. General Winfield Scott [q.v.], charged by President James Buchanan (1791–1868) to settle the affair, negotiated a truce that allowed one company of American soldiers on the island and one British warship in the waterways. The fate of the farmer is unknown. The island is now part of the United States.

Pigeons. These birds, carrying messages fastened to their legs, were used in many armies. Messages, printed in columns, were photographed and reduced to microscopic size, then read by the use of magic lanterns. Eventually the system became so perfected that a single pigeon could carry 3,000 messages. Early in the nineteenth century the Dutch established a regular civil and military pigeon post in Sumatra and Java, and in 1882 the Dutch army in northern Sumatra established one at Achin for birds flying to Olehlek-Segli, about 60 miles distant. During the siege of Paris [q.v.] in 1870–71, 382 homing pigeons were sent to Paris by balloon to carry messages from the city. Only 57 survived. The Germans used trained hawks to bring them down.

Pigeons *French carrier pigeons of the 1870s to 1890s*

Pigtail War. The name most American newspapers applied to the Sino-Japanese War of 1894–95 [q.v.].

Pike. A stout rod 12 to 14 feet long carrying a sharp-edged blade of some description at one end. In the British army pikes or half pikes were carried by sergeants until 1830. At the beginning of the American Civil War the Confederate army, short of firearms, bought 7,099 for five dollars each. The shafts were of white oak, ash, or hickory with tips of well-tempered steel. They were never used. In 1861 the city of Baltimore ordered 2,000 or 3,000 to repel "northern invaders." These too were not used.

Pike, Albert (1809–1891). An Arkansas lawyer, planter, publisher, and poet who served as a captain of volunteers in the Mexican War [q.v.]. As a lawyer he gained the trust of many Indians through his successful representation of Creek Indians in American courts. During the American Civil War he was appointed a Confederate brigadier general and given command of a newly created Department of Indian Territory. He persuaded the Creeks to ally themselves with the Confederacy and led a brigade of Indians at the Battle of Pea Ridge [q.v.]. After quarreling with his superiors, he resigned in 1862. He then became a teacher, poet, journalist, and staunch, active Freemason [see Freemasonry]. After the war he was indicted for treason but never tried, and his civil rights were restored.

Pike, Zebulon Montgomery (1774–1813). An American soldier and explorer who was commissioned a first lieutenant in 1799. Between 1805 and 1807 he explored the headwaters of the Mississippi River and the Arkansas and Red rivers. He reached the site of present-day Pueblo, Colorado, and discovered the peak now named in his honor. In 1813, during the War of 1812 [q.v.], he was promoted brigadier general. He was adjutant and inspector general of the American force that attacked York (now Toronto) Canada. On 27 April 1813, leading the assault, he was mortally wounded.

Pile Arms. A command given to stand three or more rifles or muskets with barrels uppermost so that they mutually support one another.

Pillage. See Looting.

Pillbox. From about 1887 this was used to describe a certain round hat with straight sides and a flat top used in some regiments. (It was not used as a term for a circular low concrete fortification before the First World War, 1914–18.)

Pillow, Gideon Johnson (1806–1878). An American soldier and politician who was graduated from the University of Nashville in 1827 and practiced law in Columbia, Tennessee, with James Knox Polk (1795–1849), later president of the United States (1845–49), as his partner. In 1846 he was appointed a brigadier general of volunteers by Polk and served in the Mexican War [q.v.]. He fought in the battles of Contreras, Churubusco, and Chapultepec [qq.v.], was twice wounded, and was promoted to major general. He quarreled with General Winfield Scott [q.v.] over Pillow's claim, made to a newspaper reporter, that he had been "in charge of all of the forces engaged" in the fights that led to the capture of Mexico City, and he created a postwar scandal when he appropriated a number of captured cannon to decorate the lawn of his mansion. The owner of vast tracts of land, he was by 1860 the third-largest slaveholder in Tennessee and the sixth-largest in Arkansas.

During the American Civil War he was appointed senior

major general of the Tennessee army, and on 6 July 1861 he was named a brigadier general in the provisional Confederate army. His military career plummeted after the Battle of Fort Donelson [q.v.], when he ignominiously abandoned his troops by passing on the command to General Simon Buckner [q.v.] before fleeing to avoid capture. After the Battle of Murfreesboro [q.v.] on 7 December 1864 he was accused of cowardice. Although charges were prepared, he was never prosecuted. Thereafter he saw little action. He died of yellow fever on his Arkansas plantation, his fortune gone and his reputation besmirched.

Pindari War. See Third Maratha War.

Pinfire. A cartridge, developed by a French gunsmith, B. Houllier, in 1846, that was ignited by a percussion cap within the cartridge itself and struck by a pin that formed part of the cartridge. When it was loaded, the pin was exposed and was struck by a hammer to fire the cartridge. This was the first completely self-contained cartridge for small arms and was the prototype of the rimfire and center-fire cartridges.

Ping Pu. Chinese for war board. A department analogous to a war ministry or war department in other countries.

Ping Yang, Battle of. See Pyongyang.

Pinkerton, Allan (1819–1884). A Scottish-born American detective who in 1852 established in Chicago Pinkerton's National Detective Agency, the first private detective agency in the United States. His agency had a contract to protect the Illinois Central Railroad when George B. McClellan [q.v.] was a vice-president of the railroad, and in August 1861, at the beginning of the American Civil War, Pinkerton became the head of what was called the secret service in the Army of the Potomac, McClellan's command. He performed better in counterintelligence operations in Washington, D.C., and later in breaking up the Molly Maguires [q.v.] in Pennsylvania than he did in gathering intelligence about Confederate forces in the field, whose numbers he greatly exaggerated. When McClellan was relieved of his command on 5 November 1862, Pinkerton resigned and took his detectives back to Chicago.

Pioneer. 1. A military laborer in a pioneer unit that was used to build roads, make bridges, and perform other construction work. The distinction between pioneer units and military engineer units was not always clearly defined in nineteenth-century armies.

2. In the French, British, and some other armies pioneers were designated men in each company who were capable of turning their hands to any sort of work. They often marched at the head of a regiment, carrying shovels, axes, or other tools, and sometimes they were permitted to wear beards and to be distinctively dressed. Some wore leather aprons.

Pipe Clay. A highly plastic grayish white clay used in making pipes and to scour and whiten leather and webbing. Hundreds of thousands of nineteenth-century infantrymen spent hundreds of thousands of hours using pipe clay to keep their accoutrements gleaming white. In even a light rain it worked into clothing. "There was," as one British officer once

admitted, "absolutely no advantage attending its use." Leather straps in their natural state were not used because it was said that they could not all be kept exactly the same color. Blanco [q.v.] and similar preparations began to replace pipe clay about 1835, but the transition was not complete until the twentieth century.

Pirna, Battle of (26 August 1813), Napoleonic Wars. Near this Saxon town on the Elbe River, 11 miles southeast of Dresden, 40,000 French troops under General Dominique Vandamme [q.v.] defeated 12,000 Allied troops under Eugen (Evgeni), Duke of Württemberg [q.v.], who were guarding the right flank of the main Allied army. Eugen asked for help, and 26,000 men under General Aleksandr Ivanovich Ostermann-Tolstoy [q.v.] were diverted. Vandamme was defeated at Kulm [q.v.].

Pirot, Battle of (25–28 November 1885), Serbo-Bulgarian War. At this town, 45 miles northwest of Sofia, some 40,000 Serbs under Milan I (1854–1901), falling back into Serbia after the Battle of Slivnica [q.v.] on 19 November 1885, were attacked by 45,000 Bulgarians under Alexander I [q.v.]. The Bulgarians captured the town on 25 November 1885; they were ejected the following morning but recaptured it later in the day. The diplomatic intervention of Austria halted the fighting on 28 November. Each side suffered about 2,000 to 2,500 casualties. On 3 March 1886 peace was formally concluded between Bulgaria and Serbia.

Piski, Battle of (9 February 1849), Hungarian Revolution. Hungarians rebelling against Austrian rule serving under General Jósef Bem [q.v.] defeated a numerically superior Austrian army near this village on the Muras River in southern Transylvania.

Adams (top) and Allen pistols

Pistol. A short firearm intended to be fired with one hand. [See Revolver.]

Pistol-Carbine. A pistol for cavalry so designed that a butt piece could be added or attached, enabling it to be used as a shoulder weapon.

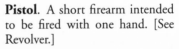

Pistol-carbine

Pitched Battle. 1. In the nineteenth century an engagement in which belligerent forces had firm or fixed positions, as opposed to a skirmish [q.v.].

2. Any intensely fought battle in which hostile forces were closely engaged.

Pitched Fascines. Faggots bundled together and covered with pitch or other incendiary materials. They were used to set buildings afire or to provide light.

Pitt-Rivers, Augustus Henry (1827–1900). An English officer and archaeologist who served in the Crimean War [q.v.]. He changed his name from Lane Fox to Pitt-Rivers upon inheriting the estate of his great-uncle George Pitt, Second Baron Rivers. After his retirement from the army he assembled a notable collection of weapons and other instruments and conducted excavations at British battle sites.

Pittsburg Landing. See Shiloh, Battle of.

Pivot Gun. A gun mounted on a pivot so as to fire in any direction.

Place du Moment. A fortified place not intended to be permanent, but more than transitory. A fort or series of forts intended to last an entire campaign.

Place of Arms. A place in a fortification, often an enlarged area of the covered way, in which troops could be assembled for a sortie.

Plaid. A woolen shawl of a tartan pattern worn by Scottish troops in Highland regiments of the British army.

Plash. The interweaving of branches to make gabions, fascines, or similar items.

Plastron. 1. A cushion or stuffed pad worn on the shoulder to sustain the recoil of a musket.

2. A piece of cloth, sometimes in the facings of the regiment, worn on the front of a shirt or jacket.

Platoon. A subdivision of a company; a unit of two or more squads. The term was little used in the nineteenth century except to apply to a squad of recruits in training or as a vague term for a small group of men.

Plastron

Platov, Matvei Ivanovich (1751–1818). A Russian soldier born in Azov who served in the Russo-Turkish War of 1770–71 and in 1801 was named by the tsar hetman of the Cossacks of the Don. He commanded with a style all his own; a sorcerer he retained on his staff was once flogged for permitting a bullet to pass too close to him.

On 12 January 1801 Tsar Paul I (1754–1801) launched 22,000 Don Cossacks led by Platov on a harebrained expedition across Central Asia to attack India. Fortunately Paul died three weeks after the start of the expedition, and Platov was recalled. In Russian campaigns against the French from 1805 to 1807 he distinguished himself. He fought in the Battle of Borodino [q.v.], and he became internationally famous when he directed his hosts against the rear guard of the French army retreating from Moscow in 1812–13 [see Russian Campaign, Napoleon's]. In June 1814 he visited London, where he was feted and given a diamond-studded portrait of the prince regent. The Platov cap, a fur cap (*kolpak*) of black lambskin with a colored bag, became a leading fashion item with London ladies. He played a major role in the defeat of the French at Laon [q.v.] and

captured Nemours in 1814. He entered Paris with the victorious Allied army.

Playing the Old Soldier. An American expression defined by one soldier as "gracefully shirking work, pretending to do something and doing nothing."

Pleasonton, Alfred (1824–1897). An American soldier who was graduated from West Point in 1844. He won a brevet to first lieutenant for gallantry during the Mexican War [q.v.] and later served on the western frontier and in the Third Seminole War [q.v.]. During the American Civil War he became a major general of volunteers on 22 June 1863. He fought in the Peninsular Campaign, and in the battles of Fredericksburg and Chancellorsville [qq.v.]. In the Battle of Brandy Station he commanded 10,000 Union cavalry, and he commanded the cavalry in the Battle of Gettysburg [qq.v.]. At the end of the war he was brevetted major general in the regular army, but in the reorganization of the army in 1866 he reverted to his prewar rank of major. He soon resigned.

He was a short, slender man whom a newspaper correspondent described as "keen eyed" and "polished and affable," but his fellow officers considered him a self-promoting liar. One called him a tyrannical, cruel disciplinarian given to "illegal exercise of military authority," and another spoke of him as "notorious as a bully and a toady."

Plebe. A cadet serving his first year at the U.S. Military Academy at West Point, New York, and at other American military schools.

Plenty Horses' Trial (April 1891). On 7 January 1891 First Lieutenant Edward Wanton Casey (1850?–1891), leading a detachment of Cheyenne scouts, was shot in the back of his head by a Brulé Sioux Indian named Plenty Horses (b. 1869) during a parley at the White Clay Creek settlement in South Dakota. Plenty Horses explained why: "I was lonely. I shot the lieutenant so I might make a place for myself among my people. Now I am one of them." His trial in a federal court at Sioux Falls, South Dakota, began on 23 April 1891. Legal history was made and American justice suffered a severe blow when he was acquitted on the ground that he was a combatant during a state of war.

Plevna / Pleven, Siege of (20 July–10 December 1877), Russo-Turkish War of 1877–78. On 20 July 1877 Russian forces, having crossed the Danube River, reached the outer defenses of Plevna (Pleven), a Bulgarian town on an important road junction 20 miles south and 80 miles northeast of Sofia. Newly fortified by 14,000 men under Turkish Marshal Osman Nuri Pasha [q.v.], it was guarded by mainly small, square infantry redoubts with parapets 10–15 feet high and 14 feet thick connected by 4-foot-deep trenches and protected by artillery, 72 guns in separate positions. The fortifications were defended by 30,000 Turkish infantry, many of whom had been issued two rifles: a single-shot Martini-Peabody rifle [q.v.] with 100 rounds for long distance shooting and a repeating .44 caliber Winchester carbine for close work. Both were weapons of American origin. However, not all Turkish troops were armed with the same weapons, and William

Herbert, an Englishman fighting with the Turks, was surprised one day to discover that a shipment of ammunition contained none that fitted any firearm on hand.

Three major Russian assaults by General Nikolai Pavlovich Krüdner on 20 July, 30 July, and 11 September were beaten back at a cost of 20,000 Russian and Rumanian casualties to 5,000 Turkish. On 24 August the Russians were reinforced by a Rumanian corps of 32,000 with 108 guns commanded by Prince Carol (1839–1914), later the first king of Rumania, bringing their strength to 70,000 infantry, 10,000 cavalry, and 440 guns under General Franz Eduard Todleben [q.v.]. On 30 August, in an unsuccessful sortie by 25,000 men, the Turks suffered losses of about 3,000 to the Russians' 1,000. On 3 September a Russian force of 20,000 under Mikhail Skobelev [q.v.] cut the Turkish line of communications, and on 24 October Plevna was completely invested. Osman Nuri, in desperation, tried to break out on 9–10 December, crossing the Vid River to the west with 25,000 men and carrying 9,000 sick and wounded in carts. He was forced back into Plevna, having suffered 5,000 casualties and been himself severely wounded. On 10 December, after a siege of 143 days, he was forced to capitulate. The Russians carried on their advance into the Balkans, but Plevna had cost them 38,000 casualties.

The 43,000 captured Turks were marched off to Russia without adequate clothing or sufficient food. Only 15,000 survived, and of these, only 12,000 ever lived to return to Turkey.

Plevna *Hand-to-hand fighting before Plevna*

Pliley, Allison J. (1844–1917). An American soldier and scout who in 1863, during the American Civil War, enlisted in the 15th Kansas Cavalry. He took part in actions against Confederates in Missouri and against hostile Indians in western Kansas. While acting as chief scout, he was twice wounded in the Battle of Beaver, or Prairie Dog, Creek on 21–22 August 1867. In September of 1868 he was one of the 50 plainsmen enlisted by George Forsyth [q.v.]. He fought in the Battle of Beecher's Island [q.v.], and when hopelessly surrounded, he and another scout, John Donovan (d. 1892), volunteered to go for help. Wearing the moccasins of dead Indians, they slipped away in the night. After four days of subsisting on half-rotten horsemeat, they reached a ranch on the stage road and found assistance at Fort Wallace at the junction of Pond Creek and the south fork of the Smoky Hill River in present-day Kansas.

Pliley was named captain in the 19th Kansas Cavalry and saw service under Philip Sheridan and George Custer [qq.v.] on the south plains. On 20 March 1869, while with Custer, he helped rescue two captive women, Anna Brewster Morgan (1844–1902) and Sarah Catherine White (1850–1939), from Cheyennes. He volunteered for Custer's 1876 campaign but was not taken. He finally settled in Kansas City, where he cut ice in winter and sold sand to contractors in summer.

Plongée. 1. In fortifications, this is the slope, normally one in six, toward the front of a position from the top of the parapet.

2. The path of an artillery shell from its highest point to the ground.

Plovdiv, Battle of (17 January 1878), Russo-Turkish War of 1877–78. After the fall of Plevna [q.v.] on 10 December 1877, Russian forces under General Osip Gurko [q.v.] attacked the fortified town of Plovdiv (Philippopolis) on the Maritsa River, 100 miles northwest of Adrianople (Edirne). The outnumbered Turks, commanded by Suleiman Pasha [q.v.], put up a stiff resistance, but the Russians broke into the town at a cost of 1,300 casualties; the Turks lost 5,000 killed and wounded, 2,000 taken prisoner, and 114 guns. The main Turkish force then began a full retreat down the Maritza Valley toward Constantinople (Istanbul), pursued by Russians under General Mikhail Skobelev [q.v.]. The war was brought to a close when the Turks were forced to sign the humiliating Treaty of San Stefano.

Plumage. An edging of white feathers around the brims of hats worn by Prussian generals from 1741 to 1806.

Plumer, Herbert Charles Onslow (1857–1932). A British soldier who served in the Sudan in 1884, the Matabele Campaign [q.v.] in South Africa in 1897, and the Second Anglo-Boer War [q.v.] of 1898–1902, in which he led the Rhodesian relief force to Mafeking [see Mafeking, Siege of] in 1900. In the First World War he commanded the British Second Army in France and was made a field marshal in 1919.

Plumes. The large feathers of birds or knots of buffalo hair worn as ornaments on military headgear. In the U.S. army in the last years of the nineteenth century the general-in-chief wore three ostrich feathers; all other generals and officers of the general staff, except those in the Signal Corps, wore two such feathers. American dragoons at the beginning of the Civil War wore black ostrich feathers on the left sides of their hats, three for field officers, two for company officers, and one for enlisted men.

Plumes *U.S. infantry officer's dress cap with plume, 1872–81*

Rules for the wearing of feathers were sometimes intricate. In the British army, field marshals and generals wore red and white swan feathers 10 inches long. Certain named colonels wore the same, but 8 inches long; certain other staff officers and those holding certain appointments wore the same but 6 inches long. Equerries to the royal family and certain other officers, such as those at the Royal Military Hibernian School in Dublin, wore feathers 5 inches long. Still others wore plumes of different colors and from different birds of different specified lengths. Distinctions were also made on whether the plume drooped outward or inward, etc.

Plunder. Goods taken from an enemy by pillage or open force. Pursuit of plunder often prevented the pursuit of the enemy. In the American Civil War Thomas ("Stonewall") Jackson [q.v.] was denied the use of most of his cavalry while they plundered a Union wagon train before the Battle of Winchester [q.v.]. During the Peninsular War [q.v.] Wellington wrote in a general order published on 5 March 1814: "No reliance can be placed on the conduct of troops in action with an enemy, who have been accustomed to plunder."

Plunging Fire. Direct fire from an artillery piece mounted in an elevated position so that its fire strikes the target at a high angle and does not ricochet.

Podol, Battle of (26 June 1866), Seven Weeks' War. The Prussians sent three armies into Bohemia. One of these, led by Prince Frederick Charles [q.v.], defeated the Austrians under General Eduard von Clam-Gallas [q.v.] at Podol (Podebrady), on the Elbe River, 15 miles north-northwest of Kutna Hors. The Austrians suffered heavy casualties, and 500 were taken prisoner; Prussian losses are unknown. The battle was a prelude to the Battle of Münchengrätz [q.v.] two days later.

Poinsett, Joel Roberts (1779–1851). An American diplomat who in 1825–29 was the first U.S. minister to Mexico. From 1837 to 1841 he was secretary of war. He introduced the tropical woody poinsettia, so popular at Christmastime in the United States, and it is named in his honor.

Point Blank. Term used for a gun barrel that is laid horizontally and pointed directly toward the object or person intended to be struck at a range at which no elevation of the weapon is required and the trajectory is almost a straight line. The gun's being so close to its target, it is almost impossible to miss.

Point d'Appui. Literally, support point. Any definite translation in English is contextual.
  1. The base for a military operation. A fort, village, forest, or other more or less permanent place from which direction can be given.
  2. Any particular point or body of men upon which troops were formed or by which they marched.
  3. Physical features, such as lakes, swamps, thick woods, streams, or steep declivities on a battlefield, that would give shelter, support, or protection to the troops stationed there.
  4. A strongpoint or choke point.

Point Lookout. During the American Civil War an army hospital and a prison camp were established at Point Lookout, Maryland, a low peninsula at the confluence of the Potomac and Patuxent rivers. Before the war the peninsula had held a summer resort with a hotel and about 100 cottages. An army general hospital, named United States Hammond General Hospital after Surgeon General William Alexander Hammond [q.v.], opened there on 20 July 1862. Sophrina Bucklin, one of the first nurses, described the place as "one of the loveliest points that reach their slender green arms out into the shimmering waters of the Atlantic." Over the objections of Dorothea Dix [q.v.], Mrs. Abigail Hopper Gibbons (d. 1893), whom Dix regarded as a threat to her own position, was placed in charge of the nurses. The first patients were 218 men recently released from the Confederate prison on Belle Isle [q.v.], near Richmond. By the end of the war the hospital had grown to twenty buildings serving sick and wounded soldiers from both sides.

On 1 August 1863 the federal government established the largest prison camp in the North at Point Lookout. The Confederate prisoners, at times as many as 20,000 enlisted men, lived in pup tents. Water, wood, and food were scarce, and living conditions were appalling. Catching rats was both a recreation and a source of protein. One former prisoner, captured in 1864, described life in the camp: Many of the tents were "but a few inches above ordinary high tide, and [the camp] was visited in winter by blasts whose severity caused death. . . . The case of the prisoners was pitiable indeed."

Black troops were employed as guards, and there was much animosity between guards and prisoners. One prisoner averred that Union officers offered as much as ten to fifteen dollars for every prisoner shot by a guard on duty.

Point of Passing. In a parade or formal review, the point where troops march past the reviewing officer or other dignitary.

Point of War. A drumbeat, loud and impressive, which was beaten when a unit charged. Its execution was said to require "great skill and activity."

Poison Wells and Poison Gas. To deny an enemy water by poisoning wells was a tactic sometimes used by primitive warriors, but it was frowned upon by all European nations. During the Crimean War [q.v.], when it was suggested that sulfur fumes be used against the defenders of Sevastopol, the British rejected the idea with the words "no honourable combatant would use such means."

Pokalem / Polakem. A squat, pie-shaped undress Russian military hat, often with flaps to let down over the ears and neck.

Poker Joe (d. 1877). A Nez Percé warrior who joined the fleeing Nez Percés under Chief Looking Glass [q.v.] and advised them on trails and terrain in Montana [see Nez Percé War]. He was a leader in the Battle of Big Hole Basin [q.v.] but was forced to yield command to Chief Looking Glass [q.v.], who was jealous of his success. He was killed the first day of the Battle of Bear Paw Mountain [q.v.], shot by mistake by a Nez Percé.

Pole Trail. The trail of a field gun mounted centrally on the axle directly beneath the gun.

Police, Military. A body of soldiers, usually acting under the orders of a provost marshal [q.v.], who act much as civilian police and also maintain military order, arresting soldiers out of bounds without passes, unauthorized civilians in a camp, drunk or disorderly soldiers, etc. [see Gendarme; Gendarmerie]. In neither the British nor the American army was there a permanent corps of military police.

Police, to. To clean a camp, garrison, or any area.

Polignac, Camille Armand Jules Marie, Prince de (1832–1913). A French soldier who served with the French 4th Hussars in the Crimean War [q.v.] but resigned his commission in 1859 to study botany in America. At the beginning of the American Civil War he offered his services to the Confederacy, and on 16 July 1861 he was appointed a lieutenant colonel and chief of staff to General Pierre Beauregard [q.v.]. He distinguished himself at the battles of Shiloh and Corinth [qq.v.], and on 10 January 1863 he was promoted brigadier general and commanded a brigade under General Richard Taylor [q.v.]. On 13 June he was made a major general.

In March 1865 he was sent to France to seek the assistance of Napoleon III (1808–1873). He was there when he learned of the surrender of Robert E. Lee, and he simply retired to his estate. He returned to the French service for the Franco-Prussian War [q.v.], in which he commanded a division. When he died on 15 December 1913, he was the last surviving Confederate major general.

Polish Legions. After the third partition of Poland [see Polish Revolutions] many officers and other ranks from the army of rebel patriot Tadeusz Kosciuszko (1746–1817) emigrated to Italy, where in 1796 they formed units under Jan Dombrowski [q.v.] that in the next ten years fought Napoleon's battles all over Europe, in Egypt, and even in the West Indies.

Polish Revolutions. In August 1772 Russia, Prussia, and Austria divided one-third of Poland among them. A second partition occurred in January 1793, when Russia bit off another piece, a move that incited an unsuccessful insurrection led by Tadeusz Kosciuszko (1746–1817). In October 1795 the remainder was taken by the three autocracies, and Poland as a country ceased to exist. Prussia controlled Warsaw and all of northern Poland, Austria controlled Cracow and the southern region, and Russia took control of Lithuania and Ukraine.

In 1807 Napoleon established the Duchy of Warsaw. In 1815 the Treaty of Vienna gave most of Poland to Russia. The Russian administration was particularly abhorrent to Poles, and a secret society, the National Association against Russia, formed by Polish officers, conspired to rebel. On 29 November 1830 Polish members of the Warsaw Training School, believing they would be aided by the French, raised the standard of revolution. Russian troops and the residence of the unpopular Russian Grand Duke Constantine [see Pavlovich, Constantine], the tsar's brother and the viceroy of Warsaw, were attacked, and Polish regiments, citizens, and freed prisoners joined in creating a state of anarchy. General

Józif Chlopicki [q.v.] briefly became dictator (December 1830–January 1831) but resigned to be active in fighting the Russians. Initially the rebels were successful, winning several small battles, but a Russian army under Count Hans Diebitsch [q.v.] advanced until halted in the Battle of Grochow [q.v.] on 25 February 1831, after which it went into winter quarters. When it emerged in the spring, the Poles won a victory at the Battle of Wawz [q.v.] on 31 March and again at Zelicho on 6 April. Then, on 26 May, the Russians decisively defeated troops under Jan Skrzynecki [q.v.] in the Battle of Ostroleka [q.v.], and on 7 September Polish General Jan Krukowiecki [q.v.] surrendered Warsaw to Russian General Ivan Fyodorovich Paskevich [q.v.]. The following day Russian troops entered Warsaw, ending the rebellion.

In 1846 there was a revolt when on 6 November Austria annexed Cracow; it was quickly suppressed. In 1848 there was an outbreak in Posen against Germans and Jews. This too was easily crushed.

On 22 January 1863, just eight days after the announcement of a new decree aimed at conscripting young rebels, mostly students, there was open rebellion, and on 19 February Ludwik Mieroslawski [q.v.] announced himself the leader of the insurgents. The revolution spread rapidly throughout Poland and into Lithuania. The tsar's offer on 12 April of an amnesty to all those who laid down their arms did nothing to stem the tide. Because they could not raise an effective army, the Poles resorted to guerrilla warfare, and for almost two years guerrilla bands harassed the Russians, but, ill disciplined and poorly equipped, they were no match for trained troops, and by May 1864 the rebellion had been crushed and its leaders executed or sent to Siberia. In 1868 most of Poland was made a Russian province, and in 1876 the Russian language became obligatory in the schools, and Polish was banned from courts of law and public offices.

Polish Revolutions *Russian peasants disarm Polish fugitives during the Second Polish Revolution, 1863.*

Politicians in War. In the nineteenth century the military's aversion to politicians who interfered with matters martial almost equaled their distaste for newsmen [see War Correspondents; Censorship]. The soldier's view was well expressed by General Helmuth von Moltke the Elder [q.v.], who wrote: "The politician should fall silent the moment mobilization begins, and not resume his precedence until the strategist has informed the King, after the total defeat of the enemy, that he has completed his task."

During civil wars politicians often become soldiers. In the American Civil War both the Union and Confederate governments, seeking known leaders, turned to politicians, and some became instant generals. Professional soldiers often scorned these so-called political generals.

Polk, Leonidas (1806–1864). An American soldier who was graduated from West Point in 1827 but resigned his commission in 1831. He received holy orders in the Episcopal Church and in 1838 was consecrated missionary bishop of the Southwest. From 1841 to his death he was bishop of Louisiana.

In 1860 he founded the University of the South in Sewanee, Tennessee. As a Confederate major general [1861] he fought at Belmont, Shiloh, Murfreesboro, and Corinth [qq.v.]. In October 1862 he was promoted lieutenant general and conducted the retreat from Kentucky. After the Battle of Chickamauga [q.v.], in which he commanded the right wing, he was relieved of command, but in December 1863 he resumed command and attempted unsuccessfully to stop the advance of General William T. Sherman [q.v.]. He was killed while reconnoitering at Kennesaw Mountain [q.v.] on 14 June 1864.

Polkownick. A colonel of a Polish regiment.

Pollock, George (1786–1872). A British soldier who entered the army of the Honourable East India Company in 1803 and took part in the siege of Bhurtpore in 1805, the Nepal War of 1814–16, and the First Burmese-Anglo War of 1824–26 [qq.v.]. In 1838 he was promoted major general. On 31 March 1842, during the Afghan War [q.v.], he forced the Khyber Pass and two weeks later relieved General Robert Sale [q.v.], besieged at Jalalabad. He then pushed on to capture Kabul and effect the release of 135 British prisoners.

In 1846 he returned to England, and from 1854 to 1856 he was a director of the Honourable East India Company. In 1870 he was made a field marshal and the following year was appointed constable of the Tower of London. [See Pollock Medal.]

Pollock Medal. The medal commemorating Major General George Pollock [q.v.] and sixteen guineas were awarded at Addiscombe Seminary [q.v.] each year to "the most Distinguished Cadet of the season." Addiscombe closed in 1861, but the following year the award was instituted at the Royal Military Academy, Woolwich [q.v.], to "the most Distinguished Cadet" at the academy. The sixteen guineas were reduced to ten.

Polotsk, Battle of (17–18 August 1812), Napoleonic Wars. At this town on the right bank of the Dvina River in present-day Belarus two French corps (35,000 men) under Marshal Nicolas Oudinot and General Lauren Gouvion St. Cyr [qq.v.] attacked the Army of Finland (35,000 men) under Field Marshal Ludwig Wittgenstein [q.v.] and drove it back over the Dvina. Ouidinot was badly wounded on 17 August. Russian losses were 3,000 killed, 1,500 wounded, and 14 guns; the French lost about 1,000 killed and wounded.

Polytechnique, L'École. See École Polytechnique, L'.

Pommel. 1. The knob on the hilt of a sword.
2. The protuberant part of a saddle bow.

Pommelion. See Cascabel.

Pom-Pom. A 37 mm quick-firing gun firing a one-pound shell developed by Hiram Maxim [q.v.], so called because of the sound it made when fired. Originally designed for use by the Royal Navy, it was put into production in the 1890s. Although it had been rejected by the British army, the Boer republics in South Africa purchased a number and used them effectively against the British in the Second Anglo-Boer War [q.v.].

Pompon. An ornamental tuft of wool or other material sometimes worn on the front of military headgear.

Poncha Pass, Battle of (28 April 1855), American Indian Wars. At this pass (altitude: 9,010 feet) in central Colorado at the northern tip of the Sangre de Cristo Mountains, just west of Salida, two companies of regulars and two companies of volunteers, about 500 men under Colonel Thomas Turner Fauntleroy (d. 1883) made a night attack upon 150 Utes, who were, he said, "swept away like chaff." The battle marked the collapse of Ute resistance.

A highway leading to the San Luis Valley now goes through the pass.

Poniatowski, Jozef Antoni (1763–1813). A Polish soldier who was trained in the Austrian army and saw service in the Russian army in the Russo-Turkish War of 1787–92. In 1789 the Polish Assembly appointed him commander of the Army of the South, and in 1792 he was successful in battles against the Russians in Ukraine. In 1806, when the Grand Duchy of Warsaw was created by Napoleon, he was made minister of war and commander-in-chief. Early in 1807 he was appointed commander of the 1st Polish Legion in Napoleon's army. On 18 April 1809 he was defeated in the Battle of Raszyn [q.v.] by Archduke Ferdinand [q.v.]. In 1812 he commanded a corps of Polish and Saxon troops in Napoleon's Russian Campaign [q.v.], distinguishing himself at Smolensk, Borodino, and the crossing of the Berezina River [qq.v.], where he was wounded. On 16 October 1813 he was made a marshal of France. Two days later, in the Battle of Leipzig, [q.v.], while covering the French retreat, he was wounded four times and drowned trying to cross the Elster River.

Ponsonby, Frederick Cavendish (1786–1837). A British soldier first commissioned in 1800, who fought in the Peninsular War [q.v.], serving with distinction in the battles of Talavera and Barrosa [qq.v.]. He was wounded in the Battle of Waterloo [q.v.]. In 1820 he went on half pay, but in 1825 he was promoted major general and appointed governor of Malta, a post he held for ten years.

Ponsonby, William (1772–1815). A British soldier who served in the Peninsular War [q.v.], commanding a cavalry brigade in the Battle of Vitoria [q.v.]. As a major general in the Battle of Waterloo [q.v.] he led the charge of the Union Brigade, which shattered the corps of General Jean Baptiste Drouet [q.v.]. He was killed in the battle by French lancers.

Pontmain, The Vision at. Famous in nineteenth-century France was the vision that occurred outside the village of Pontmain near Laval, a cathedral town in northeastern France. In the winter of 1870 during the Franco-Prussian War

Pontoons *Pontoon bridges across the Rappahannock, May 1863. Photograph by Alexander Gardner*

[q.v.] the village was in the path of the advancing German forces when five peasant children on a clear night saw the Virgin Mary in a blue robe with a black veil and a gold crown. She urged them to pray and assured them that God would answer their prayers. When the children reported the event, villagers, nuns, and priests assembled on the spot to pray for the safety of the village and its fighting men. Pontmain was spared the boots of the invaders, and all its men lived to return to it after the war. Army chaplains and the local commanding general signed a statement affirming their belief that a miracle had taken place.

Pontoniers. Soldiers in bridging units, particularly those who constructed bridges of pontoons [q.v.]. In most countries they were under the command of engineer officers, but some armies, notably the Austrian, had a distinct corps of pontoniers (German: *Pontoniern.* French: *pontonniers*). In the French army under Napoleon pontoniers were part of the artillery.

Pontoons. Flat-bottomed boats or floats over which planking is laid to construct a bridge. [See Booming Out.]

Pontvalent. A light portable bridge that could be carried forward to cross a narrow moat or ditch in siege operations. Sometimes called a flying bridge.

Pope, John (1822–1892). An American soldier who was graduated from West Point in 1842, a class that supplied the Union and Confederate armies with 17 full-rank generals in the American Civil War. On graduation he was commissioned a brevet second lieutenant; he did not become a substantive second lieutenant until 1846. In the Mexican War [q.v.] he served under Zachary Taylor [q.v.] and won brevets to first lieutenant and captain for his bravery. After the war he served in the Topographical Engineers until the Civil War, when on 14 June 1861 he was promoted from captain to brigadier general of volunteers. He was promoted major general on 22 March 1862, and in June he was given command of the newly formed Army of Virginia [q.v.]. He was badly defeated at Second Bull Run [q.v.] and retreated into the defenses of Washington, D.C. After this fiasco he was sent to handle the Sioux uprising in Minnesota [q.v.].

After the war Pope acquired considerable experience directing the campaigns against Indians on the plains. He retired in 1886 and died six years later in Sandusky, Ohio.

Porlier, Juan Díaz, Marqués of Matoarosa (1783–1815). A Spanish guerrilla leader in the Peninsular War [q.v.] who was nicknamed El Marquésito and became famous for amphibious raids in conjunction with British Rear Admiral Home Riggs Popham (1762–1820). Later, disillusioned with Ferdinand VII (1784–1808), he was one of the leaders of a rebellion against the king. He was captured and hanged at Corunna.

Port Arms. A position in the manual of arms [q.v.] in which the musket or rifle is carried diagonally across the chest, the barrel sloping upward at an angle of 45 degrees.

Port Arthur, Siege of (24 October–19 November 1894), Sino-Japanese War. Marshal Iwao Oyama [q.v.], in command of the Japanese Second Army, consisting of 26,000 troops and

Port Arthur *Japanese soldiers advance toward Port Arthur in the Sino-Japanese War of 1894.*

13,000 auxiliaries, was landed on 24 October 1894 at Pitzuwo (Sinkin, Sinchin, or Hsin-chin), just north of Port Arthur (Ryojunin in Japanese and Lüshunkow in Chinese), at the southern tip of the Liaotung Peninsula, 55 miles northeast of Dairen on Korea Bay. He then marched on Port Arthur, encountering little opposition, and began siege operations against what was then the chief Chinese naval base. On 19 November the port city was bombarded by Japanese warships and successfully assaulted at dawn by a force led by Maresuke Nogi [q.v.]. The 10,000 Chinese defenders offered only feeble resistance. After the war Port Arthur was returned to the Chinese.

Porte-Drapeau. A color-bearer in the French army, sometimes an *officier de fortune* [q.v.].

Porter, Fitz John (1822–1901). An American soldier who was graduated from West Point in 1845. (His first two names are often mistakenly hyphenated.) He served with distinction in the Mexican War [q.v.], winning brevets to captain and major. From 1849 to 1855 he was an assistant instructor of artillery at West Point, and from 1857 to 1860 he served under Albert Sidney Johnston [q.v.] and was his adjutant on the Utah Expedition [q.v.]. At the beginning of the American Civil War he was promoted colonel of the newly formed 15th Infantry but was soon appointed a brigadier general of volunteers. During the Peninsular Campaign he served first as a division and then as a corps commander in the army of General George McClellan, and he became an admirer of McClellan. After the Battle of Malvern Hill [q.v.] Porter was promoted both a major general of volunteers and a brevet major general in the regular army.

Porter, like many of McClellan's admirers, detested Major General John Pope [q.v.] and made no secret of his feelings, but Pope became his superior. In the Second Battle of Bull Run [q.v.] Pope, not properly understanding the situation, issued impossible orders to Porter and then accused him of disloyalty, disobedience, and misconduct in the face of the enemy. After the Battle of Antietam [q.v.], in which Porter again served under McClellan, he stood trial on Pope's charges. In November 1862 he was relieved of command, and on 21 January 1863 he was cashiered and "for ever disqualified from holding any office of trust under the Government of the United States."

In 1869 he was offered but declined an appointment as chief of staff in the Egyptian army, a position later accepted by Charles P. Stone [q.v.]. The remainder of his life was spent attempting to restore his good name. Sixteen years after the court-martial a board headed by Major General John M. Schofield [q.v.], a man whom, as a cadet at West Point, Porter had voted to expel for disciplinary reasons, completely exonerated him of the charges brought against him and recommended that he be reappointed to his former rank. Nevertheless, it was not until President Grover Cleveland signed the bill on 5 August 1886 that Porter was restored to the army, not in his former rank but as colonel, to rank from 14 May 1861.

Porter, Horace (1837–1921). An American soldier, the grandson of Andrew Porter (1743–1813), of Revolutionary War fame, who was graduated from West Point in 1860 and served in the Union army through the American Civil War, mostly in the Ordnance Department. In 1863 he was chief of ordnance for the Army of the Cumberland [q.v.], and on 20 September 1863, at a critical moment during the second day of the Battle of Chickamauga [q.v.], he rallied enough fugitives to enable a train of wagons and batteries to make its escape. For this he was awarded the Medal of Honor in 1902. In 1864–65 he served as an aide to General U. S. Grant, and after the war he served as President Grant's secretary until 1872. In December 1873 he resigned his commission and became vice-president of the Pullman Palace Car Company. In 1897 he was appointed ambassador to France, a post he held until 1905. On 9 May 1906 he was given a unanimous vote of thanks by both houses of Congress for conducting at his own expense a search for the remains of the naval hero John Paul Jones (1747–1792), who had died and was buried in Paris, and for returning his body to the United States.

Porter, Peter Buel (1773–1844). An American congressman and militia general who fought with distinction at Chippewa, Lundy's Lane, and Fort Erie [qq.v.] in the War of 1812 [q.v.]. In testimony to "the high sense entertained by Congress" of his services in the war he was awarded a gold medal and a sword by a joint resolution of Congress on 3 November 1814. In 1815 President James Madison (1751–1836) offered him the chief command of the army, but he declined. In 1828–29 he was secretary of war.

Portfire. A variety of slow match for firing muzzle-loading cannon. It consisted of a paper tube, 12 to 20 inches long, filled with a highly flammable but slow-burning composition (usually niter, sulfur, and mealed powder in different proportions). When lit, it produced a flame that could not be extinguished by water.

Port Gibson, Battle of (1 May 1863), American Civil War. The first of the unsuccessful attempts by the Confederates to halt General U. S. Grant's invasion of Mississippi [see Vicksburg, Campaign and Siege of]. Grant attacked Port Gibson, Mississippi, a crossroads village about 10 miles east of the Mississippi River and 22 miles southwest of Vicksburg, with two corps, about 24,000 men. The town was inadequately defended by 5,164 Confederates under Brigadier General Martin Edwin Green (1815–1863).

Federal losses were 131 killed, 719 wounded, and 25 missing; Confederate losses were reported as 68 killed, 180 wounded, and 384 missing and presumed captured.

Port Hudson, Battle of (14 March–9 July 1863). American Civil War. Here on the right bank of the Mississippi River, 25 miles north of Baton Rouge, Louisiana, the Confederates raised strong fortifications to guard the river traffic. In the first action on 14 March gunboats of Admiral David Farragut (1801–1870) shelled the fortifications, and the Confederate guns sank the USS *Mississippi*. In a second assault from the river on 8–10 May the Confederate batteries were silenced. Union General Nathaniel Banks [q.v.], leading the Army of the Gulf, then moved to attack. On 26 May he encountered Confederates on the Bayou Sara Road 4 miles from Port Hudson and forced them to retreat. The next day his troops made an unsuccessful assault upon the fort. He then put it under siege. Two additional unsuccessful assaults were launched on 11 and 14 June. Vicksburg surrendered on 4 July, and on 9 July Port Hudson capitulated [see Vicksburg, Siege of]. Banks lost 3,000 men in the siege; the Confederates lost 7,200, including 5,500 prisoners, and 60 guns, two steamers, 150,000 rounds of small-arms ammunition, and nearly 23 tons of gunpowder.

This battle marked the first use of black Union troops in a general engagement. Two regiments of the Louisiana Native Guards, made up of free men of mixed racial ancestry from the New Orleans area and runaway slaves who had found protection in the Union lines, took part. The 76 black officers in the Native Guards, some of whom where killed in the battle, constituted the largest group of black officers serving in combatant arms. General Nathaniel Banks [q.v.] said of the black soldiers that "their conduct was heroic; no troops could be more determined or daring."

Portmanteau. A valise. A carrying case with spare clothing and small articles often strapped behind a saddle.

Port Republic, Battle of (9 June 1862), American Civil War. The final battle of Confederate General Thomas Jackson's Valley Campaign [q.v.] was fought at this small town at the southern end of the Massanutten range in the Shenandoah Valley. About 4,000 Federals under Brigadier General Erastus Barnard Tyler [q.v.], a part of the division of Major General James Shields [q.v.], engaged a portion of Jackson's Confederates, who were fed into the battle piecemeal, but the Federals were beaten back. Federal losses were 1,018; Confederate losses were more than 800. [See Cross Keys, Battle of.]

Portugal, British Invasion of (August 1808), Peninsular War. After the invasion of Portugal by the French in November 1807 [q.v.] the British formed an expeditionary force under the future Duke of Wellington to drive them out. In August 1808 the British landed at Mondego Bay and in the Battle of Vimeiro [q.v.] on 21 August defeated an attacking French force under General Jean Andoche Junot [q.v.]. This was the beginning of the end for the French, and Napoleon was soon to complain of the drain on his resources in the Iberian Peninsula, referring to the war as his Spanish ulcer.

Portugal, French Invasions of (1802, 1807–08, and 1810), Peninsular War. In the first Napoleonic invasion of Portugal in 1802 the invading Franco-Spanish army was forced by British intervention to retreat. In November 1807, when the Portuguese refused to cooperate with Napoleon's Continental System [q.v.], a French army under General Jean Andoche Junot [q.v.] invaded Portugal from Spain, with Spanish approval. The Portuguese royal family escaped from Lisbon on a ship for Brazil just hours before Junot's arrival [see Oporto, Battles of]. In August 1808 the French were driven out of the country by the British [see Portugal, British Invasion of; Peninsular War; Olhão Revolt].

In April 1810 a 65,000-man French army under Marshal André Masséna [q.v.] invaded Portugal for the third time. After victories at Ciudad Rodrigo and Almeida [qq.v.], Masséna marched on Coimbra. He was intercepted and suffered a bloody repulse by Wellington's Anglo-Portuguese army at Bussaco [qq.v.] on 27 September. He retreated to Salamanca, having lost 25,000 men, including 8,000 taken prisoner.

When on 11 October 1810 Masséna arrived before the Lines of Torres Vedras [q.v.] with 60,000 men, he was taken completely by surprise, for these formidable works had been constructed in secrecy. He realized that the position was impregnable, so after vainly hoping that Wellington would emerge from his lines and fight, he retreated toward the Mondego River.

Portuguese Civil Wars. See Miguelite Wars.

Port Walthall Junction, Battle of. See Drewry's Bluff, Battle of.

Posse Comitatus Act (18 June 1878). An Act of the U.S. Congress that, among other things, placed restrictions on the use of federal troops to aid civil authorities. Military forces were barred from direct enforcement of civil laws [see American Civil Disorders]. This remained in force until 1989, when, through a bit of sophistry, illegal drugs were declared a threat to national security.

Postern. An underground communications tunnel made in a fortification or its outworks.

Post Exchange. A store on an American military post in which a soldier could buy nonissue necessities and small luxuries. For most of the nineteenth century these items were purchased from sutlers [q.v.], but in 1880 officers in the 21st Infantry stationed at Vancouver Barracks in Washington Territory opened a canteen [q.v.] similar to those operated in the British service. Other units followed this example. By General Order No. 11, dated 8 February 1892, these canteens became officially post exchanges and today, greatly enlarged, are commonly called PXs.

Post Flag. See Flag, Post.

Postnominal Letters. In the British army, soldiers, usually officers, who were knighted or received the Victoria Cross added the initials of the order or *VC* after their names. In the American army, officers added the initials of their arms or services to their names. Thus a British VC was the holder of a Victoria Cross, and an American officer with the postnominal letters *VC* was a member of the Veterinary Corps.

Post of Honor. 1. The advanced guard in an advance; the rear guard in a retreat.

2. The right of a line or formation on parade. The second most honored position is the left of the line or formation.

Post Trader. See Sutler; Post Exchange.

Potato Digger. Soldier slang name for the Colt machine gun [see Colt, Samuel].

Potato Revolution (21–24 April 1848). In Berlin on 21 April 1848 a mob of mostly impoverished artisans and unemployed journeymen plundered the food stands in a public market square. Troops were called out, but it took three days to quell the rioting.

Potchefstroom, Siege of (1881), First Anglo-Boer War. In this southern Transvaal town on the Mooi River, 75 miles southwest of Johannesburg, a small British force under Lieutenant Colonel Richard William Winsloe (1835–1917) in a tiny fort 25 yards square was besieged by Boers. The garrison, after loosing a third of its men, surrendered on 19 March. Ten days after the fort surrendered it was learned that an armistice had been signed: the Treaty of Pretoria on 5 April 1881.

Potgieter, Andries Hendrik (1792–1852). A Boer voortrekker leader who demonstrated great skills as a commander while serving as commandant general of the Transvaal in wars against the Matabeles and other tribes in the Orange Free State. In 1838 he become one of the founders of Potchefstroom. He was the father of Pieter Potgieger [q.v.].

Potgieter, Pieter Johannes (d. 1854). A Boer who in 1853 succeeded his father, Andries Potgieger [q.v.], as commandant general of the South African Republic (Transvaal). He was killed during a punitive expedition under Paul Kruger (1825–1904) while leading an attack on the stronghold of Chief Makapan (Mokopane, d. 1854) in the northern Transvaal.

Potgun. A mortar used for firing salutes.

Potomac, Army of the. A Union army created during the American Civil War on 25 July 1861, four days after the First Battle of Bull Run [q.v.]. By the end of the year, under the command of General George B. McClellan [q.v.], it numbered 138,000 men. Its mission was to guard Washington, D.C., and it was the principal opponent of Confederate General Robert E. Lee's Army of Northern Virginia [q.v.], formed on 1 June 1862. After McClellan's poor performance in the Peninsular Campaign [q.v.] it was commanded successively by Ambrose Burnside, Joseph Hooker, and George Meade [qq.v.]. In addition to the Peninsular Campaign, the army took part in the Seven Days' Battles, Antietam, Gettysburg, and Lee's surrender at Appomattox [qq.v.]. (In the army's final days U. S. Grant was with Meade and was the actual commander.)

Pottawatamie Massacre. See Border War.

Pottinger, Eldred (1811–1843). A British soldier and diplomat who was educated in the Honourable East India Company's military college at Addiscombe [q.v.] and in 1827 entered the Bombay artillery. After a short regimental tour he transferred to the political service and in 1837 obtained permission to travel in Afghanistan disguised as a horse trader. Soon after his arrival in Herat in September of that year the city was invested by a Persian army accompanied by Russian advisers [see Herat, Sieges of]. Lieutenant Pottinger then threw off his disguise and offered his professional services to the Afghan commander. It was largely through his efforts that the city offered such a stout resistance. British protests to Persia (Iran) caused the siege to be lifted in September 1838.

The governor-general of India thanked Pottinger as one who, "under circumstances of peculiar danger and difficulty, has by his fortitude, ability and judgment honourably sustained the reputation and interests of his country." In 1841 he was again in Afghanistan, this time when the Afghans were protesting the British imposition of the unpopular Shah Shuja (1780?–1842) on the Afghan throne. In November, with a battalion of Gurkhas, he was besieged by Afghan troops at Charikar, 35 miles north of Kabul. He was severely wounded there, and, although he managed to escape the massacre that

followed the Afghan assault, he became one of the British officers held hostage by the Afghans until rescued by the army of General George Pollock [q.v.] on 17 September 1842. He died soon after in Hong Kong.

Pottinger, Henry (1789–1856). A British soldier, diplomat, and colonial administrator who was an uncle of Eldred Pottinger [q.v.]. In 1803 he went to India, where in 1809 he was promoted lieutenant in the Bombay army. In 1810–11 he traveled in disguise in Baluchistan and Afghanistan. In 1817–18 he took part in the Third Maratha War [see Maratha Wars]. In 1820 he married Susanna Maria Cooke (1800–1886), by whom he had three sons. In 1821 he was promoted captain. In 1840, during the First Opium War [q.v.], he was sent to China as British envoy and plenipotentiary and negotiated the Treaty of Nanking, signed on 29 August 1842. On 5 April 1843 he was appointed the first governor of Hong Kong. On 28 September 1846 he was appointed governor of the Cape of Good Hope (Cape Colony) in South Africa. He returned to India in 1847 as governor of Madras, a post he held until 1854. In 1851 he was promoted lieutenant general. He died in Malta on 28 March 1856.

Pour le Mérite, Orderen. An order of chivalry founded on 8 May 1667 by Prince Frederick, later Frederick I, of Prussia (1657–1713), as the Order of Générosité, also known as the Grace Cross. On 6 June 1740, under Frederick the Great (1712–1786), it was renamed the Order of Merit and became both a civil and a military award. On 27 September 1750 Voltaire (1694–1778) became the 310th to receive the award and the 3rd civilian; he was also the first to receive the award "with brilliants."

As of 1810 it became exclusively a military order. It was never given posthumously and only to officers. In the nineteenth century 2,607 were awarded, 453 of which were bestowed in 1807, 585 in 1813, and 948 the following year. On 10 March 1813 oak leaves [q.v.] were established as a separate and higher degree of the order. Between 1806 and 1811, of the 590 awards of Pour le Mérite, 243 went to Prussians.

On 31 May 1842 Frederick William IV (1795–1861) added a civil class (with a different badge) for distinguished work in the arts or sciences. On 26 May 1875 the American Poet Henry Wadsworth Longfellow was awarded this medal.

On 18 July 1844 a crown emblem was awarded as an addendum for all surviving recipients of the award who had held it for fifty years or longer. On 18 September 1866 a grand cross of the order was established, but only five were ever awarded, including the one the kaiser awarded himself. In the Franco-Prussian War [q.v.] and in the First World War the Pour le Mérite was the highest German award for bravery in action. The medal changed its design several times, but it was always in the form of a Maltese cross. In its latest form it was in blue enamel with golden eagles between the limbs and was always worn suspended from a ribbon around the neck (in World War I slang it was called the Blue Max). On 9 November 1918 all imperial orders were abolished with the abdication of the kaiser.

Powder Barrel. See Barrel, Powder.

Powder Box. See Fougas.

Powder River, Battle of (16 March 1876), Great Sioux War. In a dawn attack Colonel Joseph Jones Reynolds [q.v.] of the 3rd Cavalry with 900 men from the 2nd and 3rd Cavalry and the 4th Infantry charged into 100 Indian lodges clustered along the Powder River in southeastern Montana Territory. The attack took the Indians by surprise, but they fought back. Robert E. Strahorn (1852–1944), a correspondent for the *Rocky Mountain News,* accompanied Reynolds and reported: "These Indians may be cowardly, but they have a queer way of showing it."

A herd of some 700 horses, ponies, and mules was captured, but because Reynolds neglected to place a guard on the animals, they were retaken by the Indians the following morning. The troops burned the lodges, scattering their contents, even the dried meat, of which the soldiers were in need. When the Indians organized their defenses and killed 4 soldiers and wounded 5, Reynolds beat a hasty retreat, leaving behind his dead and a wounded private, whom the Indians "promptly cut . . . limb from limb."

Reynolds imagined he was charging Sioux under Crazy Horse [q.v.]. Instead he had attacked previously friendly Cheyennes, who had taken no part in the Great Sioux War [q.v.] and never been hostile. As a result of this attack, the Cheyennes became the allies of the Sioux. Brigadier General George Crook [q.v.], under whom Reynolds was serving, was outraged by this bungling; Reynolds was court-martialed and sentenced to lose his rank and command for a year, but he chose to resign.

Powder River Expedition. See Great Sioux War; Powder River, Battle of.

Powder Train. A line or chain of gunpowder to obtain a timed explosion.

Powell, Billy. See Osceola.

POWs. Prisoners of war [q.v.].

Prado, Mariano Ignacio (1826–1901). A Peruvian soldier and political leader who fought under Ramón Castilla [q.v.] in the revolution of 1854. He disagreed with the policy of President Antonio Pezet (1810–1879), who favored compromising with the Spanish, and in 1865 he overthrew Pezet, becoming himself dictator and declaring war on Spain. In 1868 he was forced to leave the country, but he returned and was elected president in 1876. He served until his forces were defeated in the War of the Pacific [q.v.] in 1884. Thereafter he spent most of the rest of his life in Europe.

Prague, Bombardment of (17 June 1848), Hungarian Revolution. When the Czechs rose in revolt against Austrian rule, Prague was bombarded, and the city seized by Austrian troops under Alfred zu Windisch-Graetz [q.v.], who then put all of Bohemia under martial law [see Hungarian Revolution].

Prague Maneuver. The rupture of an enemy's line that allowed attacking troops to pour through the gap, widening the gap's shoulders and securing objectives in the enemy's rear. It is so called from the successful penetration of the Austrian lines by Frederick the Great (1712–1786) in the Battle of Prague on 6 May 1757.

Prairie Belt. A cartridge belt of leather or canvas with loops attached to hold cartridges. It was never an issued item in the American army, but it was often worn by soldiers in the American West in the 1870s and 1880s. It was sometimes called a fair-weather belt.

Prairie Grove, Battle of (7 December 1862), American Civil War. After the indecisive Battle of Cane Hill [q.v.], Union Brigadier General James Gilpatrick Blunt [q.v.] with 7,000 men remained in an exposed position 20 miles southwest of Fayetteville, Arkansas. On 3 December 1862 a Confederate force of 11,000 under General Thomas Hindman [q.v.] moved north from Van Buren to destroy him. Blunt, aware of this move, reported it to General Samuel Ryan Curtis [q.v.], commanding the Department of the Missouri, and Curtis ordered Brigadier General Francis Herron [q.v.], near Springfield, Missouri, to reinforce Blunt.

On the evening of 6 December, a cold night, Hindman, who had driven in Blunt's pickets, turned to attack Herron, leaving only a cavalry screen in front of Blunt. At about midnight Herron's exhausted men started arriving at Fayetteville after a 25-mile march, but Hindman, instead of attacking, went into a defensive position. On the morning of 7 December Herron attacked and was repulsed. Hindman ordered a counterattack, then discovered that an entire regiment of newly raised Arkansas troops had deserted. Herron launched two more unsuccessful attacks, and each time Hindman tried to counterattack, but his troops refused to move.

About eleven o'clock that morning Blunt, hearing the sounds of the fighting, marched to the sound of the guns and, after a short bombardment, attacked and rolled up the Confederate flank, but his men were driven back by Confederate cavalry under General Joseph Orville Shelby [q.v.]. The Confederates clung to their positions until nightfall and then successfully withdrew without being detected.

Federal burial parties found unwounded men who had died of the cold and exposure and wounded who had burned to death in haystacks. They also discovered that many of Hindman's Arkansans, who had been conscripted to fight, had removed their bullets before firing their cartridges. There were about 10,000 actually engaged on each side. The Federals lost 1,251; the Confederates 1,317.

Pratt, Richard Henry (1840–1924). An American soldier and Indian educator who served in the Union army in the American Civil War and was commissioned a second lieutenant of cavalry in the regular army in 1867. He served on the frontier until 1875. In 1879, with government approval and aid, he organized the first nonreservation Indian school at Carlisle Barracks, Pennsylvania, which developed into the Carlisle Indian Industrial School. Pratt remained as the head of the school until he retired, a brigadier general on the retired list, in 1904.

Precedence. 1. Priority in rank in almost all armies was and is determined by the date of an officer's commission or by the standing of the unit to which he belongs.
   2. Precedence of units was usually by the age of the unit, but guards regiments were usually given precedence over line regiments. [See Post of Honor; Rank; Rank, Substantive.]

Premier Aide-Major Général. French assistant chief of staff.

Preobrazhensky Guards. An ancient Russian regiment and a favorite of the tsars until in June 1906 a battalion mutinied in St. Petersburg.

Preradovic, Petar (1818–1872). A Croatian soldier in the Austrian army who rose to the rank of general and wrote lyric and epic poetry. His early works were written in German, but his later works in Croat; he came to be regarded as one of the greatest of Croatian poets.

Present Arms. A command to troops to hold their shoulder weapons in a prescribed manner for saluting or paying a military compliment.

Presidio. 1. A garrisoned fortified place, usually a settlement or military post that was or had once been under Spanish or Mexican control. Spanish soldiers often lived with their families in presidios, where they also raised crops to augment their subsistence.

2. The guardhouse of a garrison.

Preston, John Smith (1809–1881). An American lawyer, politician, and soldier. An ardent secessionist, he served on the staff of Confederate General Pierre Beauregard [q.v.] in the battles of Fort Sumter and First Bull Run [qq.v.]. He commanded prison camps and conscript camps, and from 30 July 1863 he was superintendent of the Bureau of Conscription. On 10 June 1864 he was promoted brigadier general.

Pretorius, Andries Wilhelmus Jacobus (1799–1853). A South African leader and general. He was one of the Boer leaders in the Great Trek into Natal in 1837, and in December 1838 he defeated the Zulu force of Dingaan [q.v.] at the Blood River [q.v.]. In 1847 he led a revolt against the British annexation of the Orange River Republic, but he was defeated in the Battle of Boomplaats [q.v.] on 29 August 1848 by a British force under Sir Harry Smith [q.v.]. He then migrated to the Transvaal, where he took the lead in concluding on 17 December 1852 the Sand River Convention, in which Britain recognized the independence of emigrant farmers north of the Vaal River (Transvaal). His death in 1853 came soon after he had been named commandant general. The town of Pretoria was named for him.

Pretorius, Marthinus Wessels (1819–1901). A Boer leader and soldier who in 1853 succeeded his father, Andries Pretorius [q.v.], as commandant general of the South African Republic (Transvaal) and in 1857 became president. As a young man he had fought the Zulus and British, serving under his father. In 1865 he led a punitive expedition against the Basutos. He died during the Second Anglo-Boer War [q.v.].

Prevesa / Preveza / Prebeza, Attack on (18 April 1897), Graeco-Turkish War. Greeks unsuccessfully attacked this seaport town, lying at the entrance to the Ambracian Gulf, and then unsuccessfully besieged the Turks who held the town.

Prevost, George (1767–1816). The governor-general of British North America who during the War of 1812 [q.v.] made an unsuccessful attack upon Sackets Harbor, New York [q.v.], in 1813 and was repulsed by Americans at Plattsburg in 1814.

Price, Sterling (1809–1867). An American politician and Confederate soldier known as Old Pap who fought in the Mexican War [q.v.] as colonel of the 2nd Missouri Volunteers and later as a brigadier general of volunteers. From 1853 to 1859 he was governor of Missouri. In May 1861 he was appointed commander of the Missouri militia. In the Battle of Wilson's Creek [q.v.] he combined his force with that of General Ben McCulloch [q.v.] to defeat Union forces under General Nathaniel Lyon [q.v.]. He captured the town of Lexington, taking 3,000 prisoners, but was forced to withdraw and retreat into Arkansas by Union General Samuel Ryan Curtis [q.v.]. He fought unsuccessfully in Arkansas, but after the Battle of Pea Ridge [q.v.], in which he participated, he was appointed a Confederate major general to rank from 6 March 1862.

In 1864 he was ordered by General Edmund Kirby Smith [q.v.] to "rally the loyal men of Missouri" and capture St. Louis. In September 1864 he led a ragtag force of 12,000 to 14,000, some without weapons, into Missouri. On 27 September he attacked Fort Davidson, a hexagonal field fortification just west of Fredericksburg, manned by 1,050 men under Brigadier General Thomas Ewing (1829–1896), but three assaults failed. Price lost 1,500 casualties. Ewing, having suffered a loss of 225, escaped during the night, abandoning the fort. Price was unable to reach St. Louis but moved west toward Kansas City. On 23 October he was defeated at Westport and fled south. He reached Laynesport, Arkansas, on 2 December. Price reported that the results of his raid were "of the most gratifying nature."

When the end of the war found him with his command in Texas, he crossed into Mexico to join the army of the emperor Maximilian [q.v.]. In 1866, on the fall of Maximilian's government, he returned to Missouri, where he died a year later.

Priest Cap / Priest Bonnet / Swallowtail. In fortifications, when the faces of a redan are so placed that the flank approaches could not be well guarded, the main face is indented, affording a crossfire on the ground in front. [See Bonnet; Double Redan.]

Prieto, Joaquín (1786–1854). A Chilean political leader who in 1829–30 led the Conservatives in a revolt that ousted Liberal dictator Ramón Freire [q.v.]. In 1831 he became president, and he served for ten years. Working with Diego Portales (1793–1837), minister of war, he created a rare peaceful era in Chilean history, except for a quickly suppressed revolt in 1836 and the War of the Peru-Bolivia Confederation [q.v.] in 1836–39.

Prima Plana. A senior noncommissioned officer in the Austrian army.

Primary Stations. The closest first-aid stations to the front. Field hospitals, which could be two miles behind the lines, sometimes sent assistant surgeons forward with orderlies and medical supplies to provide temporary primary stations just out of musket or rifle range.

Prime, to. To insert a small amount of explosive (primer) into a weapon as a detonator for the main charge [see Primer].

Primer. 1. A percussion cap [q.v.], particularly in British usage.

2. Any highly explosive material used to detonate a weapon's main charge.

Priming Horn. A small horn containing fine gunpowder to prime the pan of a flintlock.

Priming Pan. A shallow pan in the lock of a matchlock or a flintlock musket that held a small quantity of priming powder.

Prim y Prats, Juan (1814–1870). A Spanish soldier who opposed Baldomero Espartero [q.v.] and in 1839 was exiled from Spain but who returned in 1843 and defeated Espartero. In 1847 and 1848 he was captain general in Puerto Rico. In 1859–60 he led a successful campaign against the Moors in Morocco [see Spanish-Moroccan Wars]. In 1866 he led an unsuccessful revolution in Spain, after which he fled first to England and then to Brussels, where he engineered the revolution that in 1868 overthrew Queen Isabella (1830–1904) and General Ramón Narváez [q.v.]. He was shot and killed by an unknown assassin, perhaps as a result of gambling debts, for he was known as an inveterate gambler.

Prince Imperial. See Napoléon, Eugène Louis Jean Joseph.

Principle of the Exterior Line. The strategy of the American army on the western frontier in which forts were constructed and manned at strategic locations, on waterways, and on Indian trails. When the area became reasonably secure for farmers and artisans, the forts were abandoned, and a new line was constructed.

Principles of War. Axioms considered fundamental for the successful conduct of a war. The major military theorists who wrote of the principles of war in the nineteenth century were Karl von Clausewitz and Baron Antoine Henri de Jomini [qq.v.].

Prior, Melton (1845–1910). A British war artist and illustrator who at an early age joined the *Illustrated London News* and in its employment accompanied British troops in twenty-four wars and revolutions.

Prisoners of War. In German: *Kriegsgefangener*. Soldiers captured by an enemy in wartime. Napoleon wrote: "There is but one honorable way of being made a prisoner of war; that is by being taken separately and when you can no longer make use of your arms. Then there are no conditions—for there can be none consistent with honor—but you are compelled to surrender by absolute necessity."

One of the first agreements, perhaps the first, between nations concerning the treatment of prisoners of war was embodied in a treaty of friendship between Prussia and the United States in 1785. Among other items it stipulated that prisoners of war would neither be confined in civil convict prisons nor be fettered and that they were to have the same rations as their captors. The provisions of this treaty were never invoked. In 1863, during the American Civil War, the Union government issued Instructions to the Armed Forces that condoned the killing of prisoners of war in an emergency [see Lieber Code].

Military prisoners were often exchanged or paroled [qq.v.] or, if held captive, were usually repatriated at the end of hostilities [see Cartel]. The Duke of Wellington once wrote to a friend: "When the war is concluded, I am definitely of the opinion that all animosity should be forgotten, and that all prisoners should be released."

During the American Civil War Federal forces captured between 215,000 and 220,000 prisoners, excluding those captured at the close of hostilities; Confederates captured between 200,000 and 211,00 prisoners. Neither side was adequately prepared to handle prisoners of war, and conditions in most of the camps North and South were execrable. An estimated 26,500 Confederates and 22,600 Federals died in prison.

In the nineteenth century the status of captured guerrillas, franc-tireurs, partisans, vivandiers, sutlers [qq.v.], and other camp followers was never defined, and there were no agreed-upon conventions as to their treatment. During the American Civil War sutlers were sometimes captured and exchanged like soldiers.

Prison Hulks. Old warships stripped bare and used to house prisoners. During the Napoleonic Wars [q.v.] the British stuffed 35,000 prisoners of war into fifty hulks moored at Portsmouth, Plymouth, and Chatham. Prisoners who broke rules were put into six-foot-square cells in the bottom hold. Only privates, noncommissioned officers, and officers who had broken their paroles were so confined.

Prisons, Military. Most countries established places of confinement for those soldiers convicted of serious crimes and sentenced by courts-martial to long terms in confinement. The U.S. Military Prison at Fort Leavenworth, Kansas, was established in 1874. It housed prisoners in austere quarters and enforced strict discipline. Prisoners were required to work without pay, and prison shops supplied the army with a large portion of its harnesses, cooking utensils, shoes, and other needed items. When a prisoner had served his term, he was discharged and given five dollars to launch him on a civilian career.

The chief British prison was at Millbank, on the bank of the Thames at Chelsea; the French used Devil's Island (Île du Diable) off the north coast of French Guiana (Guyane Française); and the Russians used Siberia.

Private. In the U.S. army this was the lowest rank in all arms and services. In Britain it was, and is, the lowest rank in the infantry, except in rifle regiments. Cavalrymen were sometimes called troopers. The equivalent rank in the British army in rifle regiments was, and is, rifleman; in the engineers, sapper; in the artillery, driver or gunner. In the Indian army the lowest rank was sepoy in the infantry and sowar in the cavalry. In the German army, as in the French, there was no single rank, and the title depended upon the arm—e.g., *Kanonier, Jäger, Grenadier*.

Private Property, Military Respect for. See Retribution and Retaliation.

Prize. Property captured from the enemy or an enemy's property captured from a neutral in time of war. In Britain the distribution of prize money for the army was regulated by an act of Parliament in 1832. Earlier there had been squabbles about who was or was not entitled to shares; perhaps the most celebrated concerned the Deccan Prize [q.v.] at the conclusion of the Third Maratha War [q.v.].

Prize Agents. Officers of an army in the field appointed to collect all property of the enemy that had been taken by the victors. In British usage this property was usually converted to money and distributed among the victors according to rank, the commanding general receiving the largest share. After the Battle of Waterloo, Wellington's share of the prize money came to £61,000; other generals received £1,275; each private received £2 11s 4d.

Proclamation of Amnesty and Reconstruction. Two proclamations [q.v.] issued by President Abraham Lincoln on 8 December 1863, during the American Civil War, that offered conditional pardons to most southern citizens. Exceptions included high-ranking officers and civil officials.

Proctor, Redfield (1831–1908). An American lawyer, politician, and soldier. As colonel of a Vermont regiment he fought for the Union at Gettysburg [q.v.] in July 1863. In 1869 he became president of the Vermont Marble Company. From 1879 to 1880 he was governor of Vermont, from 1889 to 1891 he was secretary of war, and from 1891 until his death he was a U.S. senator.

Few secretaries of war in the nineteenth century had as profound an effect upon the U.S. army. Ably supported by General John Schofield [q.v.], Proctor worked for an increased food ration that included fresh vegetables, reduced the enlistment period from five to three years, and established near railway stations permanent army posts that contained large, airy barracks with adequate washing facilities; some even had indoor plumbing.

Profession of Arms. 1. The study and practice of the art and science of war.

2. The profession of a career military officer.

Projectile. In a military sense, an object, usually a bullet, cannonball, shell, or rocket intended to be thrown by a weapon to strike a distant object.

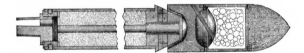

Projectile *A MacDonald's Hale Rocket*

Prolonge. A heavy rope, often with a hook at one end and a toggle at the other, that was attached to the trail of a field gun; the other end tied to a limber so that guns could be dragged short distances without being limbered.

Prome, Battle of (30 November–2 December 1825), First Anglo-Burmese War. After beating off a Burmese attack on 10 November 1825, General Archibald Campbell [q.v.] on 30 November launched a British attack with two columns, supported by a flotilla on the Irrawaddy River, on Prome, located on the left bank of the river 150 miles north of Rangoon (Yangon). After nearly three days of intense fighting, the Burmese army crumbled, and the British continued their advance up the river to a point near Yandabu (Yandabo), about 70 miles from Ava and 40 miles west of Mandalay. It was here that the Burmese sent peace envoys and on 24 February 1826 signed the Yandabu Treaty, by which the king of Ava abandoned all claim to Assam, Arakan, and the Tenasserim coast.

Promote to. To elevate a person to a higher rank or to a more important position.

Proof of Ordnance. All guns were proved (tested) before being issued by firing bullets or shells larger and with a greater powder charge than that which they would fire in ordinary usage. Defective barrels were not uncommon. Of the barrels tested in the American gun factory at Harpers Ferry (West Virginia) between 1823 and 1829, about a quarter were defective. Those that passed the test were given identifying proofmarks. In Britain each maker's proofmark was distinctive.

Propellants. Explosives with low speeds of explosion, such as cordite, gunpowder, and ballistite, were used in the manufacture of cartridges for small arms and ordnance. Until the discovery of nitroglycerine and nitrocellulose in 1845 by Christian Friedrich Schömbein [q.v.], gunpowder, which when fired produced much smoke and revealed the position of the weapon, was the only practical and available propellent. Smokeless powder [q.v.], introduced late in the century, increased the range of the gun and concealed its location but caused faster erosion of the bore. Cordite [q.v.], used by the British, was highly corrosive. The Germans developed a safer propellent called trinitrotoluene, better known as TNT [q.v.], which was adopted in 1902. [See Explosives.]

Protected Barbette. A system designed by Sir William Armstrong [q.v.] in the 1870s for employing coastal defense guns in a semicircular concrete parapet, with the gun carriage mounted to pivot on the center of the semicircle. The gun could be lowered and loaded without exposing the cannoneers to enemy fire.

Protecting Power. A state selected by one or both belligerents in a war to look after their interests in the other's territory or in their own territory if occupied by the enemy. During the Franco-Prussian War [q.v.] of 1870–71 Britain looked after French interests, while the United States, Switzerland, and Russia acted as protecting powers for German states. In the Sino-Japanese War [q.v.] of 1894–95 the United States acted as protecting power for both sides.

Proveditor. A person employed to procure supplies for an army; a purveyor.

Proving Ground. An area used for testing weapons.

Provost. 1. A provost marshal [q.v.].

2. A temporary prison in which prisoners are confined by military police [q.v.].

Provost Marshal. An officer appointed in every army in the field to command those serving as military police and to secure prisoners. He usually had the authority to inflict corporal punishment on the spot without trial to anyone caught red-handed in a felony. During the American Civil War each Union army had its own provost marshal until 17 March 1863, when James Barnet Fry [q.v.] was promoted colonel (later, on 21 April 1864, promoted general) and appointed provost marshal general for the entire Union army. Under his direction 76,526 deserters were arrested. The position was eliminated on 27 August 1866.

Provost Marshal *Provost marshal's office, Aquia Creek, Virginia, February 1863.*

Prussian Army. The German kingdom of Prussia began to take a dominant role in Europe about 1688, but in the eighteenth century King Frederick William (1713–1740) merged a semi-militia into the state structure, and in the later part of the century the belligerent policies of Frederick I (1740–1786), known as the Great, led to an invasion of Silesia, involvement in the War of Austrian Succession (1740–48), and the Seven Years' War (1756–63). Prussia retained a well-trained, well-disciplined, and largely victorious army until it became involved in French Revolutionary and Napoleonic Wars.

After suffering defeats at the hands of Napoleon's armies in 1806, Prussia reformed its army. In July 1807 a Military Reorganization Commission [q.v.] was established by Gerhard von Scharnhorst [q.v.], and as a result of its recommendations, officer schools were opened to young men of the middle classes as well as the nobility, the savage code of discipline was abolished, and army administration was centralized under the minister of war. In 1813 a landwehr [q.v.] was created by Friedrich Ferdinand Alexander Dohna [q.v.], the minister of war. This was a citizen militia organized and armed separately from the regular army. The system of army corps was adopted at about this time. By the Defense Law of 3 September 1814 every Prussian was "bound in duty to the defense of the Fatherland"—i.e., subject to conscription. From age twenty Prussian men served three years in the army, two in the reserve, and then until age forty in the landwehr. The Defense Law, revised by the Landwehr Law of 21 November 1815, was often called Boyen's law, after Hermann von Boyen, who was minister of war from 1814 to 1819.

In 1820 the term of service for the rank and file was reduced from three years to two and a half, and the officer corps was again restricted to the rich and aristocratic. By midcentury the bulk of the officers were Junkers. In 1859 two-thirds of all lieutenants, three-fourths of all senior officers, and 9 out of 10 generals were noblemen. Plebeian officers served mostly in the technical or logistical branches.

In December 1859 when General (later Field Marshal)

Albrecht von Roon [q.v.] became minister of war, a post he held until 1873, he made reform his central objective and strove to create a cadre army that could rapidly train masses of conscripts.

One of the most radical innovations was introduced by General Edwin von Manteuffel [q.v.]: a "royal military cabinet" that was responsible only to the king and thus bypassed the War Ministry, which was responsible to the Diet. An army bill of 1860 that passed the Prussian Diet voted a "provi-

Prussian Army *Prussian Guard Cavalry at the time of the Franco-Prussian War*

sional" money bill giving the king the power to use the army as he liked, thus making Prussia an absolute and a military state, which it remained until the end of the First World War. It also doubled the number of infantry battalions, increased the artillery by 25 percent, augmented the cavalry, and raised the number of annual recruits from 40,000, the number called since 1815, to 63,000. The terms of service were raised to three years for infantry and four years for cavalry. This was followed by four or five years in the reserve. New and improved small arms and artillery added strength. Thus was created the army that defeated the Danes in the Schleswig-Holstein War [q.v.] and the Austrians and their allies in the Seven Weeks' War of 1866 [q.v.] and that in 1870–71, under Helmuth von Moltke the Elder [q.v.], so easily defeated the French army in the Franco-Prussian War [q.v.].

Prussian-Danish War. See Schleswig-Holstein War.

Prytanée National de la Flèche. A military school for the sons of officers. It was founded about 1760 at La Flèche, a commune on the Loire 24 miles south-southwest of Le Mans, and replaced a Jesuit college, where from 1604 to 1612 René Descartes (1596–1650) was educated.

Puebla, Battles of. See La Puebla, Battles of.

Puenta de la Reina, Battle of (6 October 1873), Second Carlist War. Some 50,000 Carlists defeated 9,000 republicans near this town 12 miles west of Pamplona. The Carlists lost only 113 men; republican losses were assumed to be greater.

Puerto Rico, American Invasion of (July 1898), Spanish-American War. On 25 July 1898 American forces under General Nelson Appleton Miles [q.v.] landed on the Caribbean island of Puerto Rico (105 miles long and 25 miles wide), then a Spanish possession. On 28 July the seaport town of Ponce, then the island's largest municipality, surrendered and Spanish resistance ceased.

Pugri / Puggari / Pagri. Cloth wound around the head or a headdress in India and other Eastern countries. Such cloths were part of the uniform of many Indian army units. The way in which they were worn and their colors identified the wearer's regiment or tribe. Government attempts to change the design or restrict the use of turbans often occasioned considerable discontent among the sepoys [see Vellore, Mutiny at].

Puja / Pujah. A Hindi word for worship, used in the Indian army for any ceremony or rite; thus, "*puja* of the flag" was a trooping of the colors.

Pultusk, Battle of (26 December 1806), Napoleonic Wars. After the Battle of Jena [q.v.], Napoleon pushed eastward, and at this Polish town, 32 miles north of Warsaw on the Narew River, 20,000 troops under Marshal Jean Lannes [q.v.] attacked 37,000 Russians under General Levin Bennigsen [q.v.]. In an indecisive battle Lannes's attempt to cut the Russian lines of communication failed, and the Russians retreated during the night to Ostroleka. The French claimed 5,000 Russian casualties to 1,500 French, but the Russians claimed 8,000 French casualties.

Punishments, Military. Punishments for soldiers in all armies were more ferocious than for civilians, and the number of crimes for which the death sentence could be given was greater. Not all commanders agreed with the Duke of Wellington, who said: "I consider all punishment to be for the sake of example and the punishment of military men in particular is expedient only in cases where the prevalence of any crime, or the evils resulting from it, are likely to be injurious to the public interest."

Although punishments in the American and British armies were perhaps less severe than in the armies of other countries, there were, even at the end of the nineteenth century, fourteen offenses for which a British soldier could be shot, and in 1821 an American colonel was only lightly disciplined for cropping the ears of two enlisted men as punishment. In 1842 American General Winfield Scott [q.v.] found it necessary to issue orders condemning officers for illegal punishments [see Flogging; Buck and Gag; Crapaudine; Branding]. Zachary Taylor, when colonel of the 1st Infantry, used to punish by wooling, or grabbing a soldier by his ears and shaking vigorously.

Punjab, Anarchy in the (1839–45). On the death in 1839 of Ranjit Singh [q.v.], ruler of the Sikhs in the Punjab (then the northwest corner of British India), there were a great many claimants to the throne. The only legitimate heir was Kharak Singh (1802–1841), Ranjit's son by his second wife, but he was said to be intellectually feeble as a result of drink, drugs, and "immoral vices." He was soon deposed, and his successor murdered. Bribery and corruption were rampant as contenders and their supporters vied for power. Private armies came into being as soldiers sought the highest bidder for their services. As the soldiers sank into indiscipline their sense of greed sharpened, and they formed *panches* (soldiers' councils) to bargain with those seeking power. All the remaining European officers were dismissed in 1844.

At Lahore, the Sikh capital, the stench of dead bodies exposed to the sun caused the soldiers to tear down wooden houses and build huge funeral pyres on which the bodies were thrown. The wounded too, after being robbed and stripped, were thrown in the fires. In rampages through the city, all who appeared to be clerks—not considered real workers with calloused hands—were murdered. The anarchy spread into the Kulu and Mandi districts in the northeast Punjab. Soldiers became gangs of robbers; old feuds were settled in blood; the only law was the will of the strongest.

In April and May 1845 an outbreak of cholera [q.v.] carried off an estimated 20,000 people, including many soldiers, but the anarchy continued. When the last claimant for the throne was strangled, the soldiers tried to auction the throne (wazirate), but no one could meet their demands. In 1845 the soldiers were persuaded to invade the territory of the Honourable East India Company, and on 8 December 1845 they crossed the Sutlej River near Ferozepur, thus beginning the First Sikh War [q.v.].

Punjab Frontier Force. An Anglo-Indian force on India's Northwest Frontier [q.v.] established in June 1849 as the Punjab Irregular Force. Its members were soon called Piffers, and its first commander was Captain John Coke, who recruited a large number of its men from "fighting tribes" [see Martial Races]. The force was in action within a year of being raised, and it soon built a reputation as an efficient unit. It originally contained five cavalry regiments, five infantry battalions, and three mountain batteries. In 1851 four battalions of Sikhs were added. In 1866 its name was changed to Punjab Frontier Force. The unit was abolished in 1903.

Punjab Irregular Force. See Punjab Frontier Force.

Punjab Frontier Force Members of the Punjab Irregular Force in the 1850s

Punji / Pungi Sticks. Sharpened bamboo stakes concealed in pits or trenches, particularly used in Southeast Asia. They were often placed beside paths so that enemies diverted from the paths would fall on them.

Punniar / Pannier, Battle of (29 December 1843), Gwalior Campaign. One of the two battles fought on the same day in this one-day two-battle war in central India. At Punniar a Maratha force of 12,000 with 40 guns was routed by the British under General John Grey (1780–1856). The second battle of the war was fought and won by Sir Hugh Gough [q.v.], at Maharajpur [q.v.].

Punta de Calderón, Battle of. See Calderón, Battle of.

Pup Tent. A small tent for two prone men invented during the American Civil War. It consisted of two shelter halves, each man carrying one half.

Purchase of Discharge. In the American and British armies it was sometimes possible in peacetime to buy out of the army after a specified term by paying a lump sum of money.

General Orders No. 80, Headquarters of the Army, issued on 16 June 1890 allowed an American enlisted man who had completed three years of service to take a three-month furlough, after which he could return to duty or take an honorable discharge. This remained in effect, except in wartime, until 7 April 1952. Under the same orders, a soldier could purchase his discharge after one year's service by paying $120 or later a payment based on length of service; the longer the service, the lower the price of a discharge.

Purchase System. A method used in the British army by which commissions and commissioned ranks through that of lieutenant colonel could be purchased in most infantry and cavalry regiments. No rank above lieutenant colonel could be purchased, and the system did not apply to the marines, engineers, artillery, 19th to 21st regiments of cavalry, or 101st or higher numbered regiments of infantry. The practice dated

from the first formation of the regular army in Britain from the reign of Queen Anne (1665–1714), and although briefly forbidden from 1711 to 1720, the system was in place thereafter until it was abolished by royal warrant from 1 November 1871, the bill for this purpose having been rejected by the House of Lords [see Cardwell Reforms].

Before the Duke of York [see Frederick Augustus, Duke of York and Albany] made reforms during his years as commander-in-chief (1798–1808 and 1811–27), it was possible for an officer with money to purchase up to the rank of lieutenant colonel within a month. The duke increased the number of free commissions and required two years' experience for promotion to captain and six years for higher rank.

The value of each rank was determined by regulation, which varied somewhat over the years and was more expensive for more socially prestigious regiments, but the following may be taken as typical:

Lieutenant colonel	£4,500
Major	3,200
Captain	1,800
Lieutenant	700
Cornet, ensign, or Sublieutenant	450

Under this system a lieutenant colonel who wished to sell his rank would be paid by the major purchasing it £1,300 plus the £3,200 the major would receive by selling his own rank. In practice, commissions and promotions were sold "over regulation,"—that is, for more than the official going rate. A kind of auction house in London made these arrangements. Commissions and promotions in the guards and other elite regiments always cost more than those of ordinary county regiments.

Vacancies by death, or through augmentation, or by the promotion of a lieutenant colonel to a higher rank were not purchased but generally were given to the next senior officer. Lieutenant colonels threatened with promotion sometimes scrambled to get out of the army before they lost the value of their commissions.

The advantage of the system was pointed out by the Duke of Wellington, who wrote: "It is promotion by purchase which brings into the service . . . men who have some connection with the interests and fortunes of the country." Its disadvantages were pointed out by General Henry Havelock [q.v.], who, before being promoted captain at age forty-three, noted that in his career he had been "purchased over by two fools and three sots."

The abolition of purchase did not basically change the complexion of the British officer corps [see Ranker]. As late as 1891 out of 373 cadets at Sandhurst, 237 entered from the leading public (United States: private) schools, led by Wellington, Eton, and Harrow; 34 came from universities; and the remainder from "Private schools and Tutors." Most possessed private incomes, necessary if an officer was to buy the expensive uniforms, pay mess bills, and keep up the traditions of his regiment. At the end of the century an officer in a line regiment of infantry required a private income of at least £100 and in a cavalry regiment at least £600.

In the eighteenth century the French also had a purchase system, but in 1776 they began to phase out the system, and in the nineteenth century France had the most equal-opportunity system for obtaining commissions in the world. More of its officers came from the ranks than in any other army. This opportunity for promotion was expressed in the adage that every man carried a marshal's baton in his knapsack.

Pursuit. The following of an enemy force in order to overtake, capture, kill, or defeat it, to destroy its morale, to prevent its reorganizing to fight again. Pursuit was one of the principal functions of cavalry. General Karl von Clausewitz [q.v.] wrote: "Next to victory, the act of pursuit is the most important in war." Field Marshal Aleksandr Suvorov [q.v.] wrote: "Do not delay in the attack. When the foe has been split off and cut down, pursue him immediately and give him no time to assemble or form up . . . spare nothing. Without regards for difficulties, pursue the enemy day and night until he has been annihilated." Effectively to pursue a beaten enemy was, and is, to turn his withdrawal into a decisive defeat, for as Winston Churchill [q.v.] told General Archibald Wavell (1883–1950) after his victory in the Libyan desert (13 December 1940), "It is at the moment when the victor is most exhausted that the greatest forfeit can be exacted from the vanquished." But even Napoleon was seldom able to mount an effective pursuit. Only at Austerlitz, Jena, and Eckmühl [qq.v.] and earlier at Rivoli (14 January 1797) did he manage to pursue a beaten foe with the ruthlessness and vigor needed for complete success.

Although generals of all nations and in all ages have stressed the importance of pursuit, it has often been neglected. The tendencies of tired victorious generals and privates alike to enjoy the fruits of victory have frequently overcome the necessity to pursue. Perhaps the failure to pursue was never more dramatically illustrated than the decision by Pierre Beauregard and Joseph Johnston [qq.v.] not to pursue the beaten Federals at the First Battle of Bull Run [q.v.], when Washington itself could have been occupied by the Confederates and the American Civil War might have ended differently. Union General George McClellan [q.v.] was also criticized for not pursuing Robert E. Lee after Antietam [q.v.], and General George Meade [q.v.] for failing to pursue Lee after Gettysburg [q.v.].

Putnik, Radomir (1847–1917). A Serbian soldier who was commissioned in 1866 and fought in the Turko-Serbian War [q.v.] of 1876, distinguishing himself in the battles of Alexinatz and Djunis [qq.v.]. He then served in the Russo-Turkish War of 1877–78 and in the Serbo-Bulgarian War in 1889 [qq.v.]. He was the first holder of the title of voivode [q.v.]. He became deputy chief of the general staff and a professor at the military academy in Belgrade. After the military revolution in 1903 he was appointed general and chief of the general staff. He was later three times war minister and played a leading role in Serbia in World War I.

Puttee / Puttie. A word adapted from the Hindi word for bandage, *patti*. Long, narrow pieces of cloth wound around the legs and fastened by a tape. They could be used as bandages or as slings in case of need, and by the end of the nineteenth century they were in use by infantry in the armies of Britain, the United States, Germany, and France. As an article in *The Times* of London (24 December 1900) stated, "The Puttee leggings are excellent for peace or war, on foot or on horseback."

Put to the Sword, to. To slay.

Pyongyang, Battle of (15 September 1894), Sino-Japanese War. A Japanese army of 20,000 under General Michitsura Nodzu [q.v.] defeated 14,000 Chinese defending Pyongyang, an ancient walled stronghold in northwest Korea (North Korea), on the north bank of the Daido River, that dominated the road through northern Korea to Manchuria (the town was then a part of China and called Heijo). The Japanese suffered only 630 casualties; Chinese losses are unknown. The Chinese then retreated to the Yalu River.

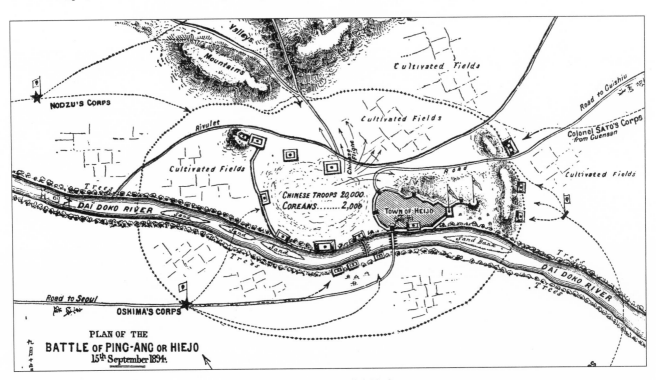

Pyongyang *Plan of the battlefield of Pyongyang*

Pyongyang *After the Battle of Pyongyang, September 1894*

Pyrenees, Battle of the (1813), Peninsular War. The British under Wellington laid siege to San Sebastián [q.v.] in the Bay of Biscay. In the summer of 1813 between 25 July and 2 August French Marshal Nicolas Soult [q.v.] fought a series of battles in unsuccessful attempts to relieve the beleaguered town. These engagements—principally at the pass at Maya and at Roncesvalles [qq.v.]—are known collectively as the Battle of the Pyrenees.

Pyrrhic Victory. A victory nearly as disastrous for the winner as for the loser. The expression refers to the victory of King Pyrrhus of Epirus (318?–272 B.C.) in the Battle of Asculum in 279 B.C. over an equal force of Romans under Sulpicius Saverrio. Pyrrhus had come from Greece to southern Italy to support the Greeks who had settled in Magna Graecia, bringing with him 20,000 infantry, 3,000 cavalry, and 20 elephants. Both sides lost heavily in the battle, about 15,000 men in all, but Rome could supply replacements more easily. According to Plutarch, when congratulated, Pyrrhus remarked, "One more such victory over the Romans and we shall be utterly ruined."

During the Second Anglo-Boer War [q.v.] it could be said that every Boer victory was pyrrhic, for Britain had such vast human and material resources to replace losses compared with the Boers, whose numbers and wealth were limited.

QF. Quick firing [q.v.].

Quadrant. See Clinometer.

Quadrate, to. To position a gun properly on its carriage.

Quadrilateral. An Austrian defense system based on a group of four fortresses in northern Italy that guarded the approaches to the most important Alpine passes to southern Austria: at Verona, Mantua (the military and administrative center for Austria's rule of northern Italy), Peschiera sul (del) Garda (on an island in the Mincio River), and Legano. They constituted the chief bulwark of Austrian rule in northern Italy until the Austrian cession of Venetia in 1866. They were used by the Austrian armies fighting Italian revolutionaries, particularly in 1848–49, when General Josef Radetzky [q.v.] drew his forces into the Quadrilateral to give him time to organize his army to defeat the Piedmontese in the Battle of Custozza [q.v.] in July 1848. Even after the Austrian disasters at Magenta and Solferino [qq.v.] Austria retained the Quadrilateral.

Quaker Gun. An American term for an imitation artillery piece, sometimes no more than a painted log. It was so called because of the opposition of Quakers to war. The term is associated with the American Civil War, but it was in use at least as early as 1809.

Quantrill, William Clarke (1837–1865). "The bloodiest man in American history." A Confederate guerrilla leader who before the American Civil War was a gambler, schoolteacher, farmer, and desperado in Kansas. In 1861 and 1862 he was chief of an irregular band of about 150 operating in Kansas and Missouri. In 1862 he was mustered into the Confederate army first as a captain and later as a colonel, but Union forces declared him an outlaw. In October 1863 he and his men defeated a Federal cavalry unit and killed all those captured, including some noncombatants [see Quantrill's Raids]. In 1864 he lost control of the band, and his force was reduced to fewer than 20 men. Mortally wounded by Union troops near Taylorsville, Kentucky, in May 1865, he died in the Louisville prison. His mistress, Kate Clarke, inherited $500 in gold, which she used to open a brothel in St. Louis.

Quantrill's Raiders (1861–65), American Civil War. A band of pro-southern killers and robbers under William Clarke Quantrill [q.v.] that was mustered into the Confederate service as guerrillas in 1862. They raided and pillaged communities in Missouri and Kansas and attacked isolated Union detachments. Among those in the band were Cole Younger [q.v.], William Anderson (d.1864), and Frank James (1843–1915). In 1864 Jesse James (1847–1882) joined. It was said that for a time the band also included the notorious Belle Shirley, better known as Belle Starr (1848?–1889), the outlaw who in 1881 harbored Jesse James.

Quaker Gun *Quaker guns, Centreville, Virginia, March 1862*

Some of the band's most notorious raids were on Independence, Missouri, on 11 August 1862; Olathe, Kansas, which was looted and burned on 6 September 1862; Lawrence, Kansas, on 21 August 1863, when about 180 men, women, and children were shot and the town was burned; Baxter Springs, Kansas, on 6 October 1863, when a Union force of about 100 soldiers was defeated and all the captives, including non-combatants, were murdered.

There was a rivalry for leadership of the band between Quantrill and his principal lieutenant, George Todd [q.v.], and in 1864 it splintered. Quantrill, with only 13 of his loyal followers, rode to Kentucky, where they were tracked down by Union troops and Quantrill was mortally wounded [see Border Ruffians].

Quantrill's Raiders *Ruins of Lawrence, Kansas, after Quantrill's raid*

Quarter. 1. As a noun, Mercy. The sparing of the life of a vanquished enemy. "To give no quarter" was to take no prisoners.

2. As a verb, to provide housing or shelter.

Quarter Allowance. See Allowances.

Quarter Guard. In British usage, the guard of a camp or cantonment, usually placed near the center.

Quartering Party. Officers and men sent ahead to a new campsite or area of operation to prepare for the arrival of the main body. [See Pesh Khana / Pesh Khidmat.]

Quartermaster. In armies, an officer or a noncommissioned officer in charge of stores, rations, equipment, etc. In the British army the title and duties were reserved for noncommissioned officers of exceptional merit. In French armies for most of the century all supplies were handled by the Intendance Militaire [q.v.], a separate service.

In 1802 quartermaster sergeants in the British army wore four chevrons points down on the right sleeve above the elbow. In 1869 they were worn below the elbow. In 1881 they were worn with points upward. A regimental quartermaster also wore an eight-pointed star until World War I. The quartermaster general of an army was, with the adjutant general, one of the two key staff officers and responsible for all matters other than those pertaining to personnel and discipline.

Quarter of Assembly. A rendezvous point where troops were assembled prior to a march.

Quarters. The place where soldiers are lodged when not on duty; housing for military personnel.

Quarters of Refreshment. A place where troops who had seen hard service on a campaign could be sent to refurbish and rest.

Quarters Winter / Summer. The camp of a campaigning army in northern climes when snow and cold made fighting difficult or impossible or in tropical countries where heat created such conditions.

Quarters Winter / Summer *Quarters at Corinth, Mississippi, occupied by the 52nd Illinois Volunteers during the winter of 1862–63*

Quarter-to-Ten Gun. British soldiers' nickname for a 9.45-inch Skoda howitzer M1898. It weighed 8.5 tons and fired shells weighing 280 pounds. Its maximum range was 7,060 meters. In 1900, during the Second Anglo-Boer War [q.v.], the British bought eight of these guns and sent them to South Africa for use in the siege of Pretoria, but they arrived too late. In 1902 some were sent to China, but none ever saw action. They were returned to England and in 1920 were declared obsolete.

Quarter Upon, to. To force civilians to take in soldiers and provide them with lodging and sometimes food as well.

Quatre Bras, Battle of (16 June 1815), Napoleonic Wars. A preliminary engagement to the Battle of Waterloo [q.v.]. Seeking to drive a wedge between Wellington and Field Marshal Gebhard von Blücher [qq.v.] and to gain control of Flanders, Napoleon successfully attacked Blücher at Ligny [q.v.] and sent Marshal Michel Ney [q.v.] on the French left with 25,000 troops toward Quatre Bras, a Belgian village and important crossroad 20 miles south-southeast of Brussels and 7½ miles northwest of Fleurus. On the afternoon of 16 June 1815 Ney encountered and drove back an Anglo-Dutch detachment of 37,000 near Quatre Bras, but victory was snatched from him by the arrival on the field of a British division under Sir Thomas Picton [q.v.]. Darkness ended the fighting. French losses were 4,300 to the Allies' 4,700.

Although the battle was indecisive, it slowed the French advance, giving the Allies under Wellington an opportunity to retire to defensive positions on a low ridge near Waterloo [see Waterloo, Battle of; Ligny, Battle of].

Quatre Bras *The death of the Duke of Brunswick at Quatre Bras*

Quay, Matthew Stanley (1833–1904). An American politician and soldier who won the Medal of Honor in the American Civil War for heroism in the Battle of Fredericksburg [q.v.]. He was a U.S. senator from 1887 to 1899 and from 1901 to 1904.

Queen's Colours. In line regiments of the British army, the Union Jack, usually with such devices as a regiment's name, number, and battle honors, was so called.

Queenston Heights, Battle of (13 October 1812), War of 1812. By the beginning of October 1812 Major General Stephen Van Rensselaer [q.v.], an American militia general of no military experience, had assembled some 2,300 militia at the village of Lewiston, New York, on the Niagara River seven miles north of Niagara Falls. Stationed at Buffalo, New York, were 1,650 regulars and 400 militia under Brigadier General Alexander Smyth (1765–1830), a regular army general who refused to serve under or to cooperate with a militia general such as Van Rensselaer. Another force of about 1,300 was assembled at Fort Niagara, built in 1796 on a point of land where the Niagara River flows into Lake Ontario.

Opposite Van Rensselaer's camp was the Canadian city of Queenston. It was protected by about 300 men and a battery deployed on top of a steep-sided height between the town and the Niagara River. In the early hours of 13 October 1812 in a heavy rain Van Rensselaer began to cross the river. His men found an unguarded path to the top of the height and surprised their enemy and drove them into Queenston. The British counterattacked but were repulsed, with the loss of British Major General Isaac Brock [q.v.]. Van Rensselaer had won a decided victory, but he lacked the means of holding the ground he had won. Half his men refused to cross the river, and Smyth refused to come up with reinforcements. British and Canadians under General Roger Sheaffe [q.v.] rushed to the defense of the town. The militia on the American side stood idly by while their comrades were overwhelmed.

American losses were 250 killed and wounded and 700 made prisoner. The British lost 14 killed, including Brock, and 96 wounded. After this disaster Van Rensselaer resigned. He was succeeded by General Smyth, who lasted only three months. In 1824 Van Rensselaer founded the Rensselaer Polytechnic Institute in Troy, New York.

Querétaro, Battle of (14 May 1867), Mexican resistance to European rule. The emperor Maximilian [q.v.] with 8,000 men was defeated by rebels under Mariano Escobedo [q.v.] near this town 110 miles northwest of Mexico City. Maximilian was captured here and executed on 19 June [see Mexico, French Invasion and Occupation of].

Questa de Los Angeles, Battle of (22 March 1880), War of the Pacific. A Chilean army of 12,000 men under General Narciso Campero [q.v.] landed at Ilo, at the mouth of the Moguegua River, 37 miles southwest of the town of Moguegua, and moved inland. At the village of Questa de Los Angeles the Chileans encountered an Allied army of 9,000 Peruvians and Bolivians under General Manuel Baquedano, which was defeated at a cost of 687 men; Allied losses were 530.

Queue. 1. A pigtail hairstyle, usually powdered [see Hair].
2. A plug of tobacco shaped like a queue of hair.
3. A line of persons or vehicles.

Quiah War (March 1861–February 1862). A West African war that began in early March 1861, when Timmanies (or Temnes) from the Quiah country plundered a British store on the small island of Tombo just off the coast of Guinea. (It is now connected to the mainland by a bridge.) The British launched a punitive expedition with the 2nd Battalion of the West African Regiment and the Sierra Leone Militia, but the latter behaved so badly that they were returned to Freetown and "disbanded in disgrace for mutinous conduct." After several indecisive battles at Songo, Robea, Waterloo, and Machonia, the Timmany chiefs sued for peace on 1 February 1862. It was concluded at Freetown, Sierra Leone.

Quick Firing. A term, often abbreviated as QF, applied to guns manufactured in the last years of the nineteenth century that had a mechanical absorption of the recoil by the use of brakes, buffers, or recuperators. Such guns did not have to be run back into place and laid again after each firing. [see French 75.]

Quick Match. A quick-firing fuse made of cotton wick saturated with gummed brandy or whiskey, soaked in a paste of starch and gunpowder, and then dried. One yard burned in the open air for about thirteen seconds.

Quick Time. The normal rate of march in formations in most units. This varied in different armies but was usually between 105 and 120 paces per minute.

Quillon. One of the two rings forming the cross guard of a sword; the bar at the base of the hilt that keeps the hand from sliding onto the blade.

Quilted Grape. A form of grapeshot used by muzzle-loading artillery. A round iron plate with an iron pin in the center was surrounded by small shot in quilted canvas so that it took the shape of a bunch of grapes.

Quinine. One of the malignant diseases that attacked soldiers in the tropics was malaria, until an effective treatment was found in the active alkaloid from the powdered bark of the cinchona tree, native to South America. In 1820 Pierre Joseph Pelletier (1788–1842) and Joseph Bienaimé Caventou (1795–1877), French chemists, isolated its chief ingredient and found a method of extracting sulfate of quinine from the cinchona bark. To meet the strong demand, the Dutch in mid-century began the cultivation of the cinchona in the Dutch East Indies (Indonesia).

During the Second Seminole War [q.v.] army surgeons were able for the first time to conduct large-scale trials of the use of quinine and confirmed the value of large doses in the treatment of malaria. Major Benjamin Franklin Harney (1814–1858), the medical director of the army in Florida, gave 10 to 30 grains of "sulphate of quina at all stages of the disease." The surgeon general's report noted the value of large doses "during the intermission of intermittent and remission of remittent fever; and, also, of the exhibition of that remedy in the febrile stages of these diseases."

Quinine remained the best treatment until synthetic replacements were developed, beginning in 1925 with Atabrine (British Mepacain), which was widely used through World War II.

Quitman, John Anthony (1798–1858). An American lawyer and politician who in 1836 led a company of volunteer fencibles [q.v.] to Texas but saw no action in the revolution there. This was his only military experience until the Mexican War [q.v.], in which he served first under General Zachary Taylor, then under Winfield Scott [qq.v.] and, as a brigadier general of volunteers, won a brevet to major general. After leading the troops that captured Chapultepec [q.v.], he was appointed governor of Mexico City, where he was the founder of the Aztec Club [q.v.]. In 1850–51 he was governor of Mississippi, but was indicted by the federal government for aiding a filibustering expedition to Cuba. He was a congressman in 1855–58.

Qui Vive? The challenge of a French sentry; the equivalent of the American "Who comes here?" or "Who goes there?"

Quoin. A wooden block sometimes with a handle used for elevating the barrel of a cannon. Each gun had a set of such blocks of different thicknesses.

R

Raab, Battle of (14 June 1809), Napoleonic Wars. General Eugène Beauharnais [q.v.], Napoleon's brother-in-law, with 33,000 men attacked and defeated 40,000 Austrians under Archduke John (1782–1859) at Raab (Györ) in southwest Hungary, 67 miles west-southwest of Budapest. The Austrians were driven successively from the villages of Kismegyer and Szabadhegy. After losing 5,000 men to the French 3,000, John retreated in the night. Napoleon called this battle "a granddaughter of Marengo and Friedland."

Rabah Zubair. See Rabih Fadl Allah.

Rabih Fadl Allah (1845–1900), better known as Rabah Zubair or Zubier Pasha. A Sudanese slaver and freebooter. As a young man he attached himself to Zubair Rahma Mansur [q.v.], one of the greatest freebooters in central Africa. He was with Zubair's son, Suleiman, in 1879, when Suleiman Pasha [q.v.] was defeated and killed by Romolo Gessi [q.v.] in Darfur. With about 700 *bazinger*s [q.v.] he fled westward and in 1880 founded a sultanate in the country of the Azande. In 1885 he made himself master of Kreich and Dar Banda, areas west and southwest of Wadai (in present-day Central African Republic). Although his forces were defeated by the sultan of Wadai, he moved westward and established himself in Bagirmi, a state southeast of Lake Chad (in present-day Chad). In 1891 he massacred the French mission of explorer Paul Crampel (1864–1891), who was attempting to unite French Congo (Congo) with French Sudan (Central African Republic). In 1893 he overthrew the sultan of Bornu, but he gave little trouble to the Royal Niger Company. In 1897 he made an unsuccessful attempt to capture Kano (in present-day Nigeria), the chief city of the Fulahs, who had captured it about 1800. In 1899 he destroyed a second French mission under a French naval lieutenant at Togbao. The French then took steps to eliminate him. He was killed by a French expedition led by Émile Gentil (1866–1914) on 22 April 1900. French Major François Lamy [q.v.] was also killed in this battle.

The French then engaged Rabih Zubair's sons and killed two. A third son, Fader-Allah, threw himself upon the protection of the British and in 1901 with 2,500 riflemen led a raid into French territory. The French pursued him into British Nigeria and mortally wounded him in a battle at a village called Gujba.

Rachat System. The French practice of purchasing slaves to serve as soldiers in West Africa. It was a practice continued even after the French emancipation of slaves in 1847.

Before 1857, when the Senegalese Tirailleurs [q.v.] were formed, the system was almost the sole source of recruits in Africa. It was continued to some extent through the nineteenth century.

Rackensackers. During the Mexican War [q.v.] a colloquial name used by American troops for Arkansas volunteer cavalry, which acquired a reputation for being more troublesome than the Mexican army.

Radetski, Fëdor Fëdorovich (1820–1890). A Russian general who distinguished himself in the Russo-Turkish War of 1877 [q.v.] by his defense of the Shipka Pass in August and September.

Radetzky, Josef Wenzel (1766–1858). A Prussian soldier born of an old Hungarian family in Bohemia who joined the army as a cadet in 1784 and was commissioned in 1787. He saw much service and in 1800, at the age of thirty-four, was a lieutenant colonel. After the Battle of Wagram [q.v.], in 1809, he was chief of the general staff until 1812. In 1810 he was awarded a commandership in the Order of St. Theresa. In 1813 and 1814 he served with distinction as chief of staff for Prince Karl Philip von Schwarzenberg [q.v.].

In 1816 he faced financial ruin through the extravagance of his wife, a woman eight years his junior, whose many debts forced him to sell his estate and to give up half his pay to his creditors.

In 1830 he took command of the Austrian armies in Lombardy and Venezia, about 62,000 men. He failed to reconcile the Italians to Austrian rule, and in 1848 serious uprisings flared in Milan [q.v.], in Venice [q.v.], in Vincenza, and elsewhere in northern Italy. The uprising in Milan that began on 17 March was not quelled until 7 August, after his victory over the Piedmotese-Sardinian forces at Custozza [q.v.] on 22 June 1848 [see Quadrilateral].

A move in the Reichstag to give Radetzky a vote of public thanks was killed by Czech and Polish representatives. However, Johann Strauss the Elder (1804–1849) composed "The Radetzky March" in his honor, although Emperor Franz Josef I (1830–1916) refused to allow it to be played at court balls.

On 23 March 1849 in the Battle of Novara [q.v.] Rodetzky again crushed the Piedmontese-Sardinian forces, and rebellious Venice surrendered on 28 August. Until 1857 Radetzky was both commander of the Austrian army in Italy and governor-general of Lombardy-Venetia, which he ruled with an iron fist. Hated by the Italians, he was esteemed by his own troops, who referred to him as Vater Radetzky. He improved the soldiers' food, reduced punishments, introduced training maneuvers, and, the master of five languages, tried each day to speak to at least 100 soldiers in the ranks of his multilingual army [see Austrian Army]. He was promoted field marshal at age seventy and was still active and energetic at age eighty-two.

Radowitz, Joseph von (1797–1853). A Prussian soldier and politician who in 1813 entered the Westphalian army and in the same year was wounded and taken prisoner in the Battle of Leipzig [q.v.]. In 1823 he entered the Prussian army, and in 1830 he was appointed chief of the artillery staff. He became an adviser to the crown prince, later Frederick William IV (1795–1861), and an advocate for a united Germany under Prussian leadership. He was foreign minister in 1850, and in August 1852 he was appointed director of military education.

Raevski Redoubt. A feature on the battlefield of Borodino [q.v.], the principal battle of Napoleon's Russian Campaign [q.v.]. An earthwork on the right center of the Russian line holding 18 guns, it was named after General Nikolai Raevski, commander of VII Corps, who had distinguished himself in the Battle of Smolensk [q.v.]. It had initially been called simply the great redoubt.

Rafferty, William Augustus (1842–1902). An American soldier who was graduated from West Point in 1865, a class in which all who entered the Corps of Engineers or the infantry were promoted at once to the rank of first lieutenant. Rafferty, however, who was commissioned in the 6th Cavalry, was one of the fifteen who remained second lieutenants. He saw much service in Kansas, Colorado, Arizona, and Indian Territory. Promoted colonel of the 5th Cavalry on 18 October 1899, he commanded the only mounted cavalry in Cuba during the Spanish-American War [q.v.]. He was killed by a fall in the Philippines.

Rag. British army slang for a house of prostitution or a place where prostitutes congregated.

Raglan, Fitzroy James Henry Somerset, First Baron (1788–1855). A British soldier, the eighth son of the Fifth Duke of Beaufort, who entered the army in 1804 and from 1808 to 1812 served as an aide on Wellington's staff in the Peninsular War [q.v.] and for the next two years as his military secretary. In the Battle of Waterloo [q.v.] his sword arm was so badly injured that it had to be amputated. As it was being carried away for disposal, he cried, "Hallo! Don't carry away that arm until I've taken off my ring." After years spent in the War Office he was again Wellington's military secretary from 1827 to 1852, when he succeeded Wellington as commander of the forces and was raised to the peerage.

Although he had never held an active command, he led the British army to the Crimea in the Crimean War. *The Times* (London) correspondent William Howard Russell [q.v.] wrote from the Crimea to a friend: "He is a good brave soldier, I am sure, and a polished gentleman, but he is no more fit than I am to cope with any leader of strategic skill." After the British victory in the Battle of Inkerman [q.v.], for which

he could claim little credit, he was made a field marshal in 1854. Ten days after the repulse of British and French forces at the redan and the Malakoff [qq.v.] he died of natural causes.

The raglan overcoat, with sleeves extending to the neck without a shoulder seam, is named for him.

Raglan *Lord Raglan, First Baron, an English army officer who lost an arm at the Battle of Waterloo in 1815 and commanded British forces in the Crimea, where he died of natural causes.*

Ragusan Republic, Conquest of (1808), Napoleonic Wars. The independent republic of Ragusa (Dubrovnik) in Dalmatia was captured by French troops in a short campaign in 1808 and became part of Napoleon's vassal Italian kingdom.

Raid. A sudden attack or brief foray by forces, usually small, upon a part of the enemy's territory or armed forces, often undertaken to obtain or destroy resources, gain information, or disrupt lines of communication. Successful raids end with planned withdrawals.

Railhead. In civilian usage, the end of a railroad line, but in military usage, it was, and is, the most distant point en route to their destination to which troops and supplies can be carried by rail.

Railroads in Wars. In 1840 there were only 5,500 miles of railroad in the world, half in the United States, but growth in Europe and North America proceeded rapidly. By the end of the century there were 466,000 miles of track.

The Germans were the first to realize the importance of a railway system that could serve the needs of armies, and they developed railway systems that were in accordance with strate-

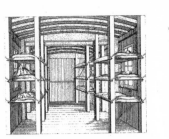
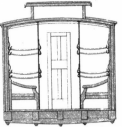

Railroads in Wars *Hospital cars (interior and transverse) on the Orange and Alexandria Railroad*

Railroads in Wars *Sherman's troops destroy a railroad.*

gic as well as economic needs. In 1843 General Helmuth von Moltke the Elder [q.v.] wrote: "Every new development of railroads is a military advantage . . . a few million spent on the completion of our railroads is far more profitably employed than on our new fortresses." Just five years later, in 1848, the Austrians were able to move a corps of 12,000 men with their horses, guns, and impedimenta to Cracow, Poland, 156 miles south-southwest of Warsaw by rail. The first extensive troop movements brought French and Austrian troops to the battlefield of Solferino in June 1859. By 1850 Germany had 3,638 miles of track; by 1870, on the eve of the Franco-Prussian War [q.v.], it had 11,600 miles. By the end of the century German railroads boasted 31,174 miles of track, and the network continued to expand. With military use in mind, main trunks were laid on an east-west axis.

The railroad added a new dimension and opened a new era in warfare. Troops, quickly moved to their destinations, arrived in good physical condition, wounded could be evacuated more quickly, supply problems were simplified, and troops, well supplied, could remain longer in the field.

The United States with its vast land area was the country in which the railroad provided the greatest benefits to civilians and soldiers alike. In 1830 the Baltimore & Ohio Railroad, the first passenger railroad in the country, began operations. By 1860, just before the American Civil War, the country, North and South, contained 30,000 miles of railroads, more than the rest of the world combined. (Great Britain in 1860 had 10,410.) On 10 May 1869, only four years after the end of the war, the last spike was driven in the Union Pacific's great transcontinental railroad. The importance of the event was evident to all: People cheered, and church bells rang. (The Canadian Pacific did not reach Vancouver until 23 May 1887.)

At the beginning of the American Civil War two-thirds of the track lay in the North; about 4,000 miles were added during the war. The South, which lacked the capacity to produce the tracks and engines, added almost none.

The value of railroads was demonstrated early in the war, on 21 July 1861, when Confederate General Joseph Johnston [q.v.] moved his army of 12,000 from the Blue Ridge Mountains to the battlefield of Manassas to reinforce General Pierre Beauregard [q.v.] in the First Battle of Bull Run [q.v.]. Some of the troops detrained while the battle was in progress and were at once deployed. These reinforcements turned the tide of the battle, changing the course of the war.

As the war progressed, the railroads became increasingly important, particularly for the North, which was fighting on exterior lines. In the spring of 1864 twenty-four trains a day left Nashville with food and supplies for the army of William Tecumseh Sherman [q.v.]. Without this logistical support Sherman could not have remained in the field.

After the war Sherman, a railroad enthusiast, was delighted and proud that the first Union Pacific locomotive, a 22-ton engine, bore his name. In 1867 he saw the railroad as "the solution of the Indian problem," and indeed it could be argued that the railroads, more than any other single factor, ended Indian dominance over the Great Plains. In 1873 the railroads carried 73,000 troops, compared with 2,000 by wagon or stagecoach. On at least one occasion the Indians also used the railroad. In 1879, during a Ute uprising, two Indians with rifles boarded a train and, when asked, said they were going to

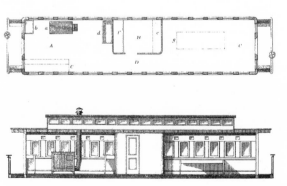

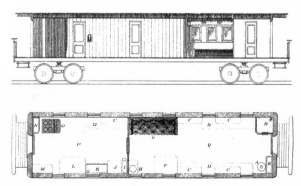

Railroads in Wars *Clockwise from lower left: kitchen car, Army of the Cumberland, longitudinal section; horizontal plan; Surgeon's car, Army of the Cumberland, longitudinal section; kitchen and dispensary car, Army of the Potomac, horizontal plan*

catch the Union Pacific to Wyoming to fight the army. No one stopped them.

By 1890 the United States had 125,000 miles of track to Britain's 20,073 miles and Germany's 26,136 miles.

Although railways were of less strategic importance in England, within days of the opening of the Liverpool & Manchester Railway in 1830, a battalion of infantry was carried between those cities in just two hours—instead of a two-day march.

By 1900 European Russia had 41,515 versts (27,500 miles) of track and an additional 4,900 miles in Central and East Asia. To aid its Central Asian conquests, it began in 1880 a trans-Caspian railroad that by 1888 had reached Bokhara and Samarkand. Since this was primarily a military railroad, many British regarded it as a threat to India, and British General Frederick Roberts [q.v.], commander-in-chief, India, urged the construction of more roads and railroads, declaring, as had Moltke, that they were more valuable than forts.

After the American Civil War all land-grant railroads were required by law to furnish transportation to the army, but as the level of comfort for the troops was not specified, troop trains were as crammed and almost as uncomfortable as troopships [q.v.].

In the Anglo-Egyptian reconquest of the Sudan [q.v.] in 1898 it was the railroad Kitchener pushed into the desert that was the weapon that smashed the Mahdist regime. In Japan the first railroad was not constructed until 1872, when a line of 17.4 miles was built between Tokyo and the port of Yokohama.

Railroad Strikes of 1877, American. The depression that followed the panic of 1873 led to the first major labor strikes in American history. The first occurred in New York and West Virginia in July 1877, ignited by a series of wage cuts by the railroad companies. Unrest spread quickly to Chicago, Baltimore, Philadelphia, Pittsburgh, and other industrial centers. The four great trunk lines between the Atlantic coast and the western states came to a halt, newspapers compared the situation with the recent Paris Commune, and the strikers were named Communists. The strike—called an insurrection by Thomas A. Scott, president of the Pennsylvania Railroad—extended to thirteen of the thirty-seven states. Some brakemen and switchmen were demanding as much as two dollars a day. Governors called out militias, and these failing, President Rutherford B. Hayes (1822–1893) called on federal troops to maintain order and suppress the strikers.

The U.S. army was small and scattered over a wide area. It was with difficulty that sufficient troops were concentrated in West Virginia, Maryland, and Pennsylvania, for the troops had to move by train and strikers sometimes stopped troop trains. Some sailors were also pressed into service as strikebreakers. At Altoona, Pennsylvania, militia were surrounded and disarmed. Track was torn up; bridges were burned. At Reading on 23 July militia troops fired on the mob, killing 10 and wounding 40.

In some places, however, militia refused to fire, and some deserted to join the strikers, while others just walked home. The strike continued to spread, and at Scranton it shut down the large Lackawanna Iron and Coal Company. Miners of the Delaware and Hudson Canal Company joined in. In Chicago police fired on a mob and killed three, but in another action

on Halstead Street police fled in panic from an infuriated mob and were saved only by the arrival of a troop of cavalry.

In East St. Louis a passenger train was stopped, and three women passengers fainted before it was allowed to proceed. In most cases the strikers allowed the mail to go through, and sometimes passenger trains, but never freight. In St. Louis there were monster meetings of sympathy for the strikers and calls to burn down the offices of unfriendly newspapers. Roving mobs destroyed machinery and forced workers to leave their shops and factories. Blacks working on the levees forced steamboat company officers to sign pledges promising wage increases. Stores closed, and groups of citizens organized to drill and protect themselves and their property.

Violence tends to breed violence, and there were disturbances that were completely unrelated to the railroad strike. In San Francisco there was an outbreak against Chinese, and the greatest violence of all occurred in the coal fields of Pennsylvania, where the Molly Maguires [q.v.] spread chaos.

In the end the strikers failed. No great leader emerged to lead them, and they were politically naive. The railroad owners, with the police, militia, regular army, and all the power of the federal government behind them, soon prevailed. The strikers went back to work at their reduced wages, and the regular army went back to fighting Indians.

Rainbow (d. 1877). A Nez Percé chief who won distinction in intertribal battles. He joined the hostile Nez Percés after the Battle of Clearwater Canyon [q.v.] and was one of the leaders of the band that on 3 July 1877 wiped out the command of Second Lieutenant Sevier McClellan Rains (1851–1877) near Craig's Mountain, killing Rains, 10 soldiers, and a civilian scout [see Nez Percé War]. He himself was killed on the first day of the Battle of Bear Paw Mountain [q.v.].

Rain in the Face (1835–1905). A Hunkpapa Sioux warrior who made his reputation as a fighter in intertribal wars. He took part in the Fetterman Massacre [q.v.] on 21 December 1866 and in skirmishes with cavalry under George Custer [q.v.]. In 1873 he killed a veterinarian and a sutler who had strayed too far from an army column. Lamed by wounds received in the Battle of the Little Bighorn [q.v.], he followed Sitting Bull [q.v.] to Canada, where he remained until 1880, when he surrendered at Fort Keogh, Montana, on the right bank of the Yellowstone River just west of Miles City. He had seven wives, the last of whom was found in his tepee with her throat slit.

Rains, Gabriel James (1803–1881). An American soldier who was graduated from West Point in 1827. He was brevetted major for his gallantry in the Second Seminole War [q.v.], and on 5 June 1860 he was promoted lieutenant colonel in the 5th Infantry. He resigned on 23 September 1861 to accept an appointment as brigadier general in the provisional Confederate army in command of a brigade in the division of A. P. Hill [q.v.].

He had always been interested in explosives, and by the beginning of American Civil War he had invented a pressure sensitive fuze that detonated under seven pounds of pressure and a friction timer set off by a trip wire. In front of McClellan's command in the Peninsular Campaign [q.v.] he laid a large number of land mines [q.v.].

General Hill berated him for his failure to make a charge

during the Battle of Seven Pines [q.v.], and in December 1862 he was removed from his command and placed in charge of the Volunteer and Conscript Bureau. In June 1864 he was named head of the Torpedo Bureau, and he spent the balance of the war arranging for mines to be placed around such threatened points as Mobile, Richmond, and Charleston. After the war he worked as a government clerk.

Raise an Army, to. To incorporate a large number of men into military units. This was accomplished by accepting voluntary enlistment or by conscription [q.v.] or by some combination of these methods.

Raise a Siege, to. To raise or lift a siege or blockade is to abandon or terminate operations designed to capture a place.

Raisin River Massacre (22 January 1813), War of 1812. In mid-January 1813 a force of American troops, including three companies of the 17th Infantry, a company of the 19th Infantry, and some volunteers, all under General James Winchester [q.v.], moved from a camp at the Maumee Rapids (above the site of present-day Toledo, Ohio) to recapture Frenchtown (Monroe, Michigan). On 22 January, at the mouth of the Raisin River, near Frenchtown, they were attacked by a combined British and Indian force under Colonel Henry Procter. The Americans were defeated and laid down their arms after the colonel promised to protect them from the Indians. But he failed to keep his promise. The Indians fell upon the unarmed soldiers and killed more than 100. This was not the first time Procter's Indians had been permitted to slaughter prisoners of war. He had done the same after the Battle of Burlington Heights [q.v.] on 5 May 1812. The Raisin River Massacre became a rallying cry of the Americans for the duration of the war.

Raiya. A unit of about 2,000 men in the Dervish army in the Sudan. It consisted of four rubas [q.v.] and was commanded by an amin [q.v.].

Rajput / Rajpoot Sepoy. A Hindu soldier in the Indian army from a subcaste claiming descent from Kshetryias [q.v.]. *Hobson Jobson* [q.v.] says of Rajputs: "The great race in India, the hereditary profession of which is that of arms. The name was probably only an honorific assumption; but no race in India has furnished so large a number of princely families."

Rake, to. To enfilade or to fire effectively upon the enemy; to sweep a column of troops.

Rally. 1. As a verb, enthusiastically to enlist support; to unite for a cause, or to restore order to troops who have dispersed or panicked. The call "Rally 'round the flag!" is attributed to Andrew Jackson [q.v.] in the Battle of New Orleans [q.v.].

2. As a noun, during the American Civil War a rally in soldier slang was the raiding and looting of the tent or wagon of a sutler.

3. As a verb, to return troops to order and duty; to halt or slow a retreat. To accomplish this usually involves the personal example and force of character of the commander. An outstanding example was that of Marshal Jean Lannes in the French attack upon Ratisbon [q.v.] (Regensburg) when after two attacks on the walls had failed, he personally carried one of the ladders in a successful third attack.

Ram Home, to. To thrust home the charge in a firearm.

Rammer. 1. A ramrod.

2. A staff made of hardwood with a cylindrical or conoidal head used as a ramrod for artillery pieces. In the field artillery a sponge was often attached to the other end of the staff, and the instrument was called a sponge and rammer.

Ramnagar, Battle of (22 November 1848), Second Sikh War. Opposite this walled town, 62 miles northwest of Lahore, British cavalry under General Hugh Gough [q.v.] attempted to cross the Chenab River and was repulsed by 35,000 Sikhs.

Ramorino, Girolamo (1790–1849). An Italian soldier who rose to be a general in the Piedmontese army. He took an active part in the military campaigns of 1848 and in the first

Rajput *Bombay Light Cavalry with the Rajput Field Force*

month of 1849, but he was held responsible for the Piedmontese defeat in the Battle of Novara [q.v.] on 23 March of that year and was executed.

Rampart. In fortifications, a broad embankment, usually surmounted by a parapet. Loosely, any protective barrier.

Rampart *View of Charleston, South Carolina, from the rampart of Castle Pinckney*

Ramrod. 1. A metal or wooden rod with a suitable head used in the artillery to ram a charge home.

2. A slim metal rod used with a piece of cloth to clean a musket or rifle. Ramrods could be lethal if fired by mistake, as sometimes happened in the heat of battle or in the hands of ill-trained recruits. In 1808, during maneuvers at Leghorn, a French soldier accidentally killed a civilian by firing a ramrod from his musket. He was saved from punishment when it was discovered that the victim was sought for brigand.

3. Colloquially, in the United States, the first sergeant of a company.

Ramrod Bread. Dough plastered on the end of a ramrod and held over a fire.

Ramsay, George. See Dalhousie, George Ramsay, ninth Earl.

Ramseur, Stephen Dodson (1837–1864). An American soldier who was graduated from West Point in 1860. On 6 April 1861 he resigned and accepted a Confederate commission as a captain of the Ellis Light Artillery under General John Magruder [q.v.]. He served with distinction during the Seven Days' Battles [q.v.] and was severely wounded at Malvern Hill [q.v.]. On 1 November he was promoted brigadier general and was again wounded in the Battle of Chancellorsville [q.v.]. He was wounded a third time in the Battle of Spotsylvania Court House [q.v.]. On 1 June 1864, the day after his twenty-seventh birthday, he was promoted major general, the youngest West Pointer to attain that rank in the Confederate army. While trying to stem an attack by Philip Sheridan [q.v.] at Cedar Creek [q.v.] on 19 October, he was shot through both lungs and captured. He was carried to Sheridan's headquarters near Meadow Mills, where he died the next morning. He had been married less than a year, and on the night before the battle he had learned of the birth of his daughter.

Ram's Horns. A low-profile earthwork in the ditch of a fortification.

Rancagua, Battle of (1–2 October 1814), Chilean War of Independence. Spanish loyalist forces from Peru under General Mariano Osorio defeated Chileans under Bernardo O'Higgins and José Carrera [qq.v.] near this town in the Andean foothills, 48 miles south of Santiago, in central Chile. O'Higgins behaved gallantly, but Carrera failed to support him, and he was forced to flee to Argentina. The Spanish reestablished their control of Chile.

Rancheria. 1. In the American Southwest the term was applied to an Apache encampment, and in California to any Indian camp.

2. The headquarters of a large ranch.

Randall, George Morton (1841–1918). An American soldier who at the beginning of the American Civil War enlisted in the Union army in the 4th Pennsylvania and in October 1861 was commissioned a second lieutenant. He saw much action, won two brevets for gallantry in three engagements, and ended the war a lieutenant colonel. In 1865 as an infantry captain he served under General George Crook [q.v.] in Arizona, winning brevets for campaigns against Apaches. When Crook moved to command the Department of the Platte, Randall became his chief of Indian scouts. He took part in the Battle of the Rosebud [q.v.] on 17 June 1876 and in the Battle of Slim Buttes [q.v.] on 8–9 September. He was promoted colonel in 1898, brigadier general in 1901, and major general in June 1905. He retired less than four months later.

Randall, Horace (1833–1864). An American soldier who, after being graduated from West Point in 1854, fought Indians on the frontier. He commanded the cavalry at Lincoln's inaugural parade. On 27 February 1861 he resigned his commission to join the Confederate army. Refusing the offer of a second lieutenancy, he fought as a private until named colonel of the 28th Texas. He rose to command a brigade and was mortally wounded at Jenkins Ferry, Arkansas, on 30 April 1864.

Randall, James Ryder (1839–1908). A Maryland journalist and songwriter who, during the American Civil War, was a strong southern sympathizer. In April 1861, after learning that several Baltimore citizens (among them a former classmate) had been killed resisting the passage of Massachusetts troops through the town, marching from one railroad station to another, he wrote the poem "Maryland, My Maryland" [q.v.]. Originally sung to the tune of "Lauriger Horatius," the song became popular throughout the South when set to the tune of "Tannenbaum, O Tannenbaum." Its popularity declined sharply after the failure of the Confederate campaign in western Maryland, in which the confidently expected recruits failed to materialize and little sympathy was shown by western Marylanders for the southern cause.

Range. 1. The distance between a weapon and a target.

2. An area equipped with targets, often called a firing range.

3. The maximum distance a weapon can fire a projectile.

Range Finder. An instrument used in the artillery for finding the range of a target. The first is believed to have been developed by two American artillery officers about 1870. By 1880 the firm of Barr and Stroud in Britain had begun manufacturing range finders, and a more accurate stereoscopic instrument was being pioneered in Germany.

Ranging. Finding the range and azimuth necessary to hit a target by firing a series of trial shots and making corrections.

Rangoon, Battle of (12–14 April 1852), Second Anglo-Burmese War. A British expeditionary force of 6,000 under Major General Henry Thomas Godwin (1784–1853) captured Martaban, Burma (Myanmar), at the mouth of the Salween River opposite Moulmein, on 5 April. On 12 April it attacked Rangoon (Yangon), where 20,000 Burmese with 90 guns occupied the Shwe Dagon Pagoda complex. After a heavy bombardment the British attacked and drove out the Burmese. In three days of fighting the British lost 17 killed and 132 wounded.

Rangoon, Occupation and Siege of (May 1824–February 1825), First Anglo-Burmese War. In April 1824 an Anglo-British expeditionary force under General Sir Archibald Campbell [q.v.] was assembled on the Andaman Islands, from which it was transported to Burma (Myanmar). It occupied Rangoon (Yangon) without opposition on 1 May, but the troops were soon ravaged by disease and then besieged by Burmese troops. Although the British were reinforced, the siege continued. On 1 December the Burmese launched a determined but unsuccessful assault in which the Burmese commander was killed. In February 1825 the British began an advance up the Irrawaddy River, and the siege was lifted.

Rani of Jhansi. See Jhansi, Rani of.

Ranjit Singh Sukerchakia (1780–1839). A maharajah and founder of a Sikh kingdom in the Punjab. Before Ranjit Singh the Sikhs formed a theocracy of turbulent coteries of semi-

independent *misls* (clans) owing nominal allegiance to the amir of Afghanistan. They were mostly engaged in fighting one another or neighboring Muslim states or tribes and were roughly associated with Afghanistan.

The Sikhs lived by a rough code. Ranjit's father, the chief of the small Sukerchakia *misl*, had killed his mother, and when Ranjit was seventeen, he killed his mother. In 1792 he succeeded his father.

Ranjit's first foray was against the Chattas, a Muslim tribe whose chief he killed with his own hands. He absorbed the chief's treasures and followers. In 1798, using daring, strategy, and cunning, qualities in which he excelled, he captured the fort and city of Lahore, and in 1799 he was appointed governor by the king of Afghanistan. In 1802 he annexed Amritsar. By his own personality and genius he developed a state, and with the help of European adventurers he created one of the most powerful armies on the subcontinent, known as the Khalsa. His successes aroused the enmity of other clans, some of whom united against him, but they were defeated in battle and nearly annihilated.

Further expansion brought him into conflict with the expanding empire of the Honourable British East India Company [q.v.]. In 1809 he signed a treaty establishing a boundary between the two empires at the Sutlej River and thereafter loyally supported the British. Multan was captured in 1819, Kashmir in 1820, and Peshawar in 1823. The area between the Sutlej and the Indus rivers, most of the Punjab, was consolidated into his Sikh kingdom.

In 1833 when Shah Suja, the erstwhile ruler of Afghanistan, sought refuge in his court, Ranjit Singh took the occasion to relieved him of the Koh-i-noor diamond, which in 1849 came into the possession of the British crown. After his death he was succeeded by his only legitimate son, Dhuleep Singh [q.v.], who was soon deposed. The country fell into anarchy [see Punjab, Anarchy in the].

Rangoon, Occupation and Siege of *British regulars launch an amphibious assault on Rangoon, 1824, during the First Anglo-Burmese War*

Rank. 1. As a noun, a line of soldiers standing side by side.

2. As a noun, the relative position or degree of subordination in an army. Rank and grade are synonymous [see separate entries for Field Marshal, General, Brigadier or Brigadier General, Colonel, Major, Captain, Lieutenant, Noncommissioned Officers, Sergeant, Corporal, Corporal-of-Horse, Private]. Rank among officers of the same grade was usually determined by an officer's date of rank, although regular officers usually outranked all officers of equal rank in the militia. In the British army for most of the century officers of the regular army outranked all those of the same grade in the Indian army and Royal Marines, and officers in Guards regiments had two ranks, a rank in the regiment and a higher rank in the army, so that when serving outside his regiment, a Guards officer exercised a higher rank. In addition to his substantive rank, an officer could have local, brevet, or temporary rank [see Brevet Rank]. British officers seconded to the Egyptian army after 1882 served two grades higher than their substantive rank.

3. As a verb, to outrank. The condition of having a higher rank than another, as a captain ranks a lieutenant. Marshal Ferdinand Foch (1851–1929) was once asked who among officers of equal rank should salute first, and he replied, "The most polite."

Equivalent ranks in different armies can be confusing. In the German army a major general (*Generalmajor*) was and is the equivalent of a brigadier general in the American army and sometimes in the British, which also used, as today, brigadier. A German lieutenant general (*Generalleutnant*) was and is the equivalent of an American or British major general; a German general was and is the equivalent of an American and British lieutenant general; and a German colonel general was and is the equivalent of a full general in the American and British service.

Although marine ranks generally follow the army system, naval ranks in the nineteenth century were different and varied from present-day naval ranks. Relative ranks in the American service were:

Second lieutenant	Ensign
First lieutenant	Master
Captain	Lieutenant
Major	Lieutenant commander
Lieutenant colonel	Commander
Colonel	Captain
Brigadier general	Commodore
Major general	Rear admiral
Lieutenant general	Vice admiral
General	Admiral

Generals of whatever rank were addressed as General, lieutenant colonels as Colonel, and in the British and American services second lieutenants or their equivalent were addressed as Mister.

Rank, Substantive. A rank with all the pay, command, and authority of that rank; a rank from which an officer could not be demoted without a court-martial, in contrast with brevet, local, or temporary rank. In the American army there has never been a substantive rank higher than major general.

Rank and File. Privates and noncommissioned officers. The reference sometimes is simply to those below the rank of sergeant or of corporal.

Rankers. 1. Officers who have been commissioned from the ranks. The practice of giving commissions to enlisted men was rare in nineteenth-century British armies, except in the case of riding masters, bandleaders, and other noncombatant positions. In 1877–78, for example, only 2.2 percent of all British officers were commissioned from the ranks, and nearly all of these were riding masters or quartermasters. Outstanding exceptions were Gerald Farrell Boyd, Hector Macdonald, and William Robertson [qq.v.], all of whom rose from the ranks and became generals. In the Prussian and Russian armies it was almost impossible for a common soldier to be commissioned, but rankers were common in French Napoleonic armies. During the Second Empire two-thirds of all French officers had risen from the ranks. Except in time of war, few American soldiers were commissioned from the ranks. In 1855–56, for example, of the 982 officers in the American army, only 26 had been promoted from the ranks.

2. Men of the middle class who were unable to get commissions in the regular way and who then enlisted in the hope of so distinguishing themselves that they would earn commissions. In both the British and the French armies there were gentlemen rankers (*soldat-gentilshommes*), but the chance to rise was slim indeed in the British army.

Rankling Arrow. An arrow with a loose barbed head that tended to remain in the wound after the shaft had been extracted.

Rapp, Jean (1772–1821). A French soldier who enlisted in the cavalry in 1788, was twice wounded in 1793, and was commissioned in 1794. He was wounded several times more before being appointed an aide to General Louis Desaix [q.v.], whom he accompanied to Egypt, where he was again wounded. Back in Europe he took part in the Battle of Marengo, in which General Desaix died in his arms. The next day he was appointed an aide to Napoleon, and in 1803 he was promoted general of brigade. At Austerlitz [q.v.] in 1805 he led a charge that routed the Russian Imperial Guard and, although again wounded, captured Russian General Nikolai Grigorievich Repnine-Volkonsky (1778–1845). In December of the same year he was promoted general of division. He fought at Jena, Golymin (wounded), Aspern-Essling, and Napoleon's Russian Campaign, including the battles of Smolensk and of Borodino (four new wounds) and the crossing of the Berezina River [qq.v.]. Throughout 1813 he defended Danzig [q.v.]. Forced to surrender, he was imprisoned in Ukraine until 1814. He rallied to Napoleon during the Hundred Days [q.v.]. After the Battle of Waterloo [q.v.] he went into concealment until 1817, but he was welcomed in the monarchy and made a peer.

Rappel. A drumbeat that called soldiers to arms.

Ras Kasa. See Johannes IV.

Raszyn, Battle of (19 April 1809), Napoleonic Wars. Near this Polish town (now a suburb of Warsaw, six miles from the city center) 20,000 French and Poles under Josef Poniatowski [q.v.] attempted to defend Warsaw against 30,000 Austrians under Archduke Ferdinand [q.v.]. After a stubborn fight in woods and marshes, Poniatowski was driven back upon Warsaw with a loss of 2,000 killed and wounded. To save

Warsaw from being bombarded, he surrendered a few days later.

Ratatouille. This now-fashionable side dish was named for a coarse, unappetizing stew that was a staple in the French army. The word comes from *ratatouiller* (to mix or stir), and army ratatouille was simply a mixture of whatever vegetables were available.

Ratekau, Battle of (7 November 1806), Napoleonic Wars. Gebhard von Blücher [q.v.] with a remnant of the Prussian army retreating from Auerstädt [q.v.] was forced to surrender to French forces under Jean Baptiste Bernadotte [q.v.] at this town in Schleswig-Holstein, six miles north of Lübeck.

Rate of Fire. The number of rounds of ammunition fired in a unit of time, usually expressed as rounds per minute.

Ration. 1. As a noun, the food and drink authorized for one person or one animal for one day. In 1857 a ration for a soldier in the U.S. Army consisted of ¾ pound of pork or bacon or 1¼ pounds of fresh or salt beef and 18 ounces of bread or 1¼ ounces of cornmeal or 12 ounces of hard bread. Not until 1890 was 1 pound of vegetables added. However, for each 100 rations there were 8 quarts of peas or beans or 10 pounds of rice; 6 pounds of coffee, 12 pounds of sugar, 6 quarts of vinegar, and 2 quarts of salt. To this was added 1½ pounds of tallow and 4 pounds of soap.

The British army was even more parsimonious. As late as 1877 the ration was 1 pound of bread and ¾ pound of meat—this was usually bully beef by the end of the century—and some coffee. All else had to be purchased by the men.

In Prussia at this period about half a soldier's pay was withheld to pay for his food, the amount of which varied in peacetime between garrison ration and marching or fatigue ration. In the latter the amount of meat was increased from 6 ounces to 8.2 ounces with a similar increase of vegetables. The bread ration remained unchanged: 26.5 ounces, the same as in the French army. Austrian soldiers were given the most bread: 31 ounces. The French soldier was given the most meat, 10.6 ounces, and more vegetables than soldiers in any other army. The Russian soldier had the worst of diets. There were 196 days in which he was given 7 ounces of meat, but there were 169 fast days, in 52 of which he ate only peas and gruel. In the Indian army, sepoys and sowars were given 16 ounces each of flour and rice, 4¼ ounces of peas, some salt, and vegetable oil or butter.

Food in all armies was noted for its sameness, lack of taste, and lack of nutrition. Spirits of some sort were part of the ration in most armies: beer for the British, wine for the French, and whiskey for the Americans. However, the U.S. Congress by an act of 5 July 1838 substituted an allowance of coffee and sugar in place of whiskey.

2. As a verb, to supply with food.

3. As a verb, to distribute in an equitable manner.

4. As a verb, to limit the amount of food or supplies.

Ration Strength. The number of soldiers present in a unit who must be fed.

Ratisbon, Battle of (23 April 1809), Napoleonic Wars. After the Battle of Eckmühl [q.v.], Napoleon pursued the army of Archduke Charles [q.v.], which was escaping to the north bank of the Danube through the walled town of Ratisbon (Regensburg), 65 miles north-northeast of Munich. Rejecting the idea of a siege, Napoleon ordered Marshal Jean Lannes [q.v.] to assault the town, defended by an Austrian rear guard of 6,000. The first assault, led by General Charles Étienne Gudin de la Sablonniére (1768–1812), failed. There was a four-hour pause, during which Napoleon was wounded in the right ankle by a spent ball. Late in the afternoon two more assaults were attempted, but both failed. In a third attempt Lannes himself helped carry a ladder to scale a wall, and the attack succeeded. By 7:00 P.M. the city was in French hands. The victory cost Napoleon 1,000 men.

Archduke Charles had nevertheless made his escape except for one corps under General Johann Hiller (1754–1819) still south of the Danube. Napoleon moved on Landshut [q.v.].

Robert Browning (1812–1889) imagined Napoleon at Ratisbon in "Incident of the French Camp":

> Just as perhaps he mused, "My plans
>   That soar, to earth may fall,
> Let once my army-leader Lannes
>   Waver at yonder wall,"

Raupenhelm. In German armies, a crested helmet.

Ravelin. In fortifications, a work built beyond the main ditch to protect the curtain and shoulders of a bastion or the gate of a fort. It also favored sorties. It consisted of two faces that formed a salient angle toward the enemy, with two demi-gorges formed by the counterscarp and surrounded by a ditch. Even if taken by an enemy, it was difficult to make tenable because its rear was exposed to fire from the enceinte. It was also sometimes called a demi-lune.

Rawlinson, Henry Creswicke (1810–1895). A British soldier, diplomat, and Assyriologist. In 1827 he entered the service of the Honourable East India Company, and from 1833 to 1839 he helped reorganize the Persian army while studying cuneiform inscriptions. After serving as political agent at Kandahar and Baghdad, he became a member of the Council of India in 1868. He was the author of books on cuneiform writing and "the Russian question."

Raw Troops. Inexperienced or untrained soldiers.

Razzia / Razou. A sudden raid or destructive attack or intrusion, often upon civilians.

Ream's Station (23 August 1864), American Civil War. At this settlement in central Virginia a corps under Confederate General A. P. Hill [q.v.] won a victory over three divisions and a brigade under Winfield Scott Hancock [q.v.]. Federal losses were 2,742, of whom 2,073 were taken prisoner; Confederate losses were 720.

Rear Area. An area behind the fighting line not usually subject to enemy fire.

Rear Guard. A detachment of troops designated to protect the rear of a larger force often on the march. Frederick the Great (1712–1786) wrote: "Rear guards are the safety of armies and often they carry victory with them" (*Instructions for His Generals* [1747]).

Rebecca Riots (June 1839 and 1842–43). Bands of tenant farmers in rural Carmarthenshire, southwestern Wales, attacked and destroyed turnpike gates to protest an increase in toll charges, inequitable land tenure, high rents, etc. Their name and inspiration were taken from Genesis 24:60 ("And they blessed Rebecca and said to her '. . . may your descendants possess the gate of those who hate them!'"). The leader of each band was known as Rebecca, and followers, known as his daughters, often dressed as women while attacking. Although they destroyed 120 tollgates, they seldom harmed the gatekeepers. The magistracy invoked army aid in suppressing them.

Rebellion. An open, organized, and usually armed resistance to constituted authority. Of larger extent than a revolt or insurrection, it is often aimed at a specific local grievance rather than against a form of government. H. L. Mencken (1880–1956) rightly noted: "It doesn't take a majority to make a rebellion; it takes only a few determined leaders and a sound cause" (*Prejudices* [1919–27]).

Rebel Yell. A prolonged, high-pitched yell given by Confederate soldiers when attacking during the American Civil War.

Recoil. 1. As a noun, the rearward movement of a gun when fired. Because the amount of recoil is proportionate to the ratio of shot weight to gun weight, generally the larger the gun, the less the recoil.

2. As a verb, to move backward as a result of something seen, heard, or felt.

Reconnaissance. A military survey, a personal reconnoitering, to gain information concerning an enemy's territory and forces. "Knowledge of the country is to a general what a musket is to an infantryman," wrote Frederick the Great (1712–1786). "If he does not know the country he will do nothing but make gross mistakes. Without this knowledge his projects, be they otherwise admirable, become ridiculous and often impracticable" (*Instructions to His Generals* [1747]). In the nineteenth century accurate maps were rarities. "Time spent on reconnaissance is seldom wasted," according to the British army's Field Service Regulations (1912).

Reconnaissance in Force. An advance with some strength to test an enemy's strength and disclose the disposition of his forces. The term has also been used to lessen the disappointment of a failed attack.

Reconquest of the Sudan. See Sudan, Reconquest of.

Recruit. 1. As a noun, a newly enrolled soldier.

2. As a verb, to persuade civilians to enlist in a military service.

Recruiting. The process of persuading civilians to enlist in a military service. In countries that did not raise their armies by conscription, recruiting, particularly in peacetime, was always a difficult task. Britain in the nineteenth century did not con-

script men for its army, nor did it ever conscript men for its Indian army. In the United States conscription was resorted to only in the middle of the Civil War. The problem of recruiting was smartly spelled out by Florence Nightingale in 1858: "It has been said by officers enthusiastic in their profession that there are three causes which make a soldier enlist, viz. being out of work, in a state of intoxication, or jilted by a sweetheart. Yet the incentives to enlistment, which we desire to multiply, can hardly be put by Englishmen in the nineteenth century in this form, viz. more poverty, more drink, more faithless sweethearts."

In Japan the problem of finding recruits for the army was complicated by a shortage of men caused by the practice of *mabiki* (thinning out), in which the second or third sons of the poor were killed at birth. (Daughters could be sold as servants or prostitutes.) To prevent this from happening in France, Napoleon, knowing that male orphans often became soldiers and looking to future recruits, ordered in 1811 that all foundling homes be equipped with turntable devices in or by their doors so that infants could be left anonymously.

In Britain the early-nineteenth-century practice of paying civilians who provided recruits led to press gang tactics and to the deliberate intoxication of young men who were then turned over to recruiting sergeants [see Crimp; Crimping; Crimping House]. In all countries recruiting was easier in hard times. This was particularly true during the panics of 1873, 1877, and 1893–94.

In almost all European armies, enlistments were for long periods, sometimes for life or for twenty years, which was much the same. Often the length of service depended upon the arm, artillerymen and cavalrymen serving longer terms.

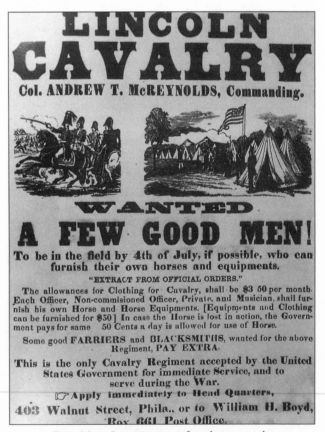

Recruiting *Recruiting poster for volunteer cavalry for the Mexican War, 1846–48*

During wartime, enlistments were sometimes accepted for the duration of the war.

In the United States in peacetime, except for the period from 1833 to 1838, when three-year enlistments were possible, enlistments were for five years. The army relied heavily upon immigrant recruits, the majority of whom were Irish; the next largest number was German. Included was a sprinkling of deserters from British troops in Canada. On 1 August 1894 Congress decreed that recruits must be U.S. citizens and be able to speak, read, and write English. Recruiting plummeted, and the law was soon changed. Although there were volunteer units of American Indians during the Civil War, later efforts to enlist them in regular units failed. Not until after the war were blacks included in the regular army, and the two black regiments of infantry (24th and 25th) and the two black regiments of cavalry (9th and 10th) had the lowest desertion rates and the highest reenlistment rates [see Black Troops in the U.S. Army].

In Britain there was never a central recruiting system. Each regiment did its own recruiting. This was also true in the United States until 1825, when the army established the General Recruiting Service to help the regiments.

The British-officered Indian army never suffered a lack of recruits; the problems of recruiting involved only picking the best and keeping out undesirables, for soldiering carried prestige and, more important, an opportunity to be clothed, fed, and paid regularly.

In all armies efforts were made to keep out drunkards and felons, and a generally halfhearted effort was made to discourage those too young. The physical qualities desired in a recruit have changed little since Roman times. Flavius Vegetius Renatus (fourth century A.D.) described the ideal: "The young soldier should have a lively eye and carry his head erect; his chest should be broad, his shoulders muscular and brawny; his fingers long, his arms strong, and feet wiry rather than fleshy. When all these qualities are found in a recruit, a little height may be dispensed with" (*Epitoma rei militari* [A.D. 378]).

In both the British and American armies soldiers could, if they had sufficient funds, purchase their release from military service. While it was rare for a soldier to save enough for his discharge, those whose families had the wherewithal sometimes paid to have sons discharged [see Purchase of Discharge].

Redan. In fortifications, a salient work of two faces that form a salient angle, a V. The most famous in nineteenth-century history was the redan that during the Crimean War [q.v.] formed part of the defenses of Sevastopol [see: Redan, British Attack upon].

Redan, British Attack upon the (8 September 1855), Crimean War. The redan constructed by the Russians south of Sevastopol at the beginning of the siege [see Sevastopol, Siege of] was initially simply a salient earthwork mounting seven guns with a shallow dry ditch in front of it and earthen embrasures. On the flanks of the battery position were parapet and banquette and a shallow ditch. By constant effort the whole was made formidable with reinforced parapets, gun platforms, bombproof shelters, and deep ditches. Frequently attacked by the British, it was always stoutly defended. On 8 September 1855, in the most determined attack of all, the assault was made by a party of 1,000 with a covering party of 200 and a ladder party of 320. This was followed by a working party of 200. Thousands of other troops were on hand to hold the position once taken. However, the men lost all cohesion in the advance and balked at following their officers inside the work. The first supports, 1,500 men, joined them but could not carry them forward. As General Sir James Simpson [q.v.] wrote in his dispatch, "The fight was maintained for nearly an hour; but the Redan, being open in rear, was difficult to hold; the Russians brought up strong reserves. . . . [T]he troops abandoned the work and fell back." The British suffered a loss of 2,184 killed and wounded. However, the French had successfully captured the Malakoff [q.v.] on the same day, and the Russians abandoned Sevastopol a few days later.

Redan *Assault on the Russian redan, 1855, in the Crimean War*

Red Bird (1788–1828). A Winnebago war chief. He directed a number of attacks upon whites, including an attack upon a Mississippi River boat in which 4 whites were killed and 2 wounded; the Indians lost 8. Troops arrested Red Bird; he was convicted, but died before he could be sentenced.

Red Cloud (1822–1909), Indian name: Makhpiya-luta. A leader of the Oglala Sioux who, although not a chief, wielded great influence as a war leader and whose reputation as a warrior drew numerous other warriors into his band. He took his first scalp at age sixteen in a fight with Pawnee Indians. In a

Recruiting *American Civil War recruiters seek volunteers for the Bucktail Regiment in Philadelphia*

raid on the Crows he killed a boy herding horses, and the following day he killed the chief of the pursuing Crows. In a subsequent attack on the Pawnees he killed 4 men. In a demonstration of the callous cruelty for which he became known, he once pulled a drowning Ute from a stream by his hair, scalped him, and dropped him back into the water. In 1854 he took part in the Grattan Massacre [q.v.]. In June 1866 he met with government representatives at Fort Laramie, Wyoming, but on learning of the government's determination to open up the last large Sioux hunting grounds to white settlers and miners, he withdrew and began what has been called Red Cloud's War.

He concentrated his efforts on obstructing the use of the Bozeman Trail [q.v.] guarded by three major army posts: Fort Reno (originally called Fort Connor), Wyoming, 180 miles northwest of Fort Laramie, on the Powder River; Fort Phil Kearny, Wyoming, on the Piney Fork of the Powder River in the foothills of the Bighorn Mountains; and Fort C. F. Smith, Montana, on the Bighorn River. His warriors harassed soldiers, settlers, and travelers at every opportunity, and he was credited with being the mastermind of the ambush that became the Fetterman Massacre, the Hayfield Fight, and the Wagon Box Fight [qq.v.], the last in which he is known to have participated.

So successful were he and his allies that the Bozeman Trail was closed in 1868. On 4 November of that year he and about 125 other prominent Indian leaders met at Fort Laramie and signed a peace treaty. In late May 1870 with several chiefs he was taken to Washington, D.C., the first

Red Cloud, Oglala Sioux, 1880

of his seven trips; he also visited New York, where he received a royal welcome.

Red Cloud came to be regarded, at least by the whites, as a kind of elder statesman. He was blind and nearly ninety when he died.

Red Cross, International. An organization initially established to relieve the suffering of wounded soldiers. The idea for such an institution came from the book *Un Souvenir de Solférino*, published in 1861 in Geneva, Switzerland. It was written by Henri Dunant [q.v.], who had witnessed the bloody Battle of Solferino [q.v.] and had been appalled by the sight of wounded soldiers left to die on the battlefield. At his urging the idea was taken up by the Société Genevoise d'Utilité Publique and a committee headed by General Wilhelm (or Guillaume) Dufour [q.v.], head of the Swiss army, was formed to investigate how the position of wounded soldiers could best be improved. This committee became the International Red Cross Committee (Comité International de la Croix Rouge), whose efforts in due time led to the formation of a conference in Geneva attended by representatives of twenty-six nations on 8 August 1864. The outcome of what came to be called the Geneva Convention [q.v.] was a set of agreed-upon principles: Wounded were to be treated with respect; military hospitals were declared neutral; medical personnel and materials were to be protected; and the symbol of this protection would be the Swiss flag in reverse colors, a red cross on a white background.

Red Cross societies were established in countries around the world. Many German states were among the first, establishing the Württemberg society in 1863, Hessian and Prussian societies in 1864, the Baden and Saxon in 1866, and the Bavarian in 1868. The Italian Red Cross was established in 1864; the Norwegian, Swedish, and Portuguese societies in 1865. The British Red Cross was not formed until 1870, and the Japanese not until 1877. The French organization was splintered into three groups, the earliest of which was the Société de Secours des Blessé Militaire, founded in 1864. The American Association of the Red Cross [q.v.], thanks to the efforts of Clara Barton [q.v.], was finally formed in 1881.

The Turks formed a similar organization called the Red Crescent, a symbol more acceptable to Muslims than the cross.

The first opportunity for the society's work occurred in the Schleswig-Holstein War [q.v.] of 1864, when the German Red Cross sprang into action on the German side. The Danes were without a Red Cross; their society was not founded until 1876. In the Seven Weeks' War of 1866, the Franco-Prussian War of 1870–71 [qq.v.], and subsequent European wars the societies in the belligerent countries provided ambulances, hospitals, and nurses.

Red Eagle (1780–1824). A Creek Indian leader who appeared more European than Indian and was often called William Weatherford. On 30 August 1813 he led Upper Creeks, known as Red Sticks, in an attack on Fort Mims [q.v.], where some 500 whites were massacred. He then occupied a strong position at Econochaca, on the Alabama River, from which he and his men raided the countryside. On 23 December 1813, 1,000 mounted Mississippi volunteers under Brigadier General Ferdinand Leigh Claiborne (1773?–1815) successfully attacked their town and burned it, but most of the Red Sticks escaped, and Red Eagle regrouped. On 27 January 1814 he led an attack upon a body of Georgia militia at Calabee Creek that was repulsed with difficulty. Although he was not present in the Battle of Horseshoe Bend [q.v.], which ended the Creek War [q.v.], he surrendered soon afterward. He then settled on a farm near Little River, Alabama.

Red Eagle, Order of. A Prussian order of chivalry that originated in 1705 as the Order de la Sincérité of Brandenburg-Beyreuth. It passed through many modifications and embellishments. In 1792 it was established as the second Order of the Kingdom of Prussia. In 1811 oak leaves [q.v.] could be added, the first use of oak leaves to designate a higher order. In 1851 a special badge was designed for non-Christians. In 1861 a Grand Class was added.

Rediger, A. F. (1853–1918). A Russian soldier who, as an officer on the general staff, was a specialist in military administration. From 1905 to 1909 he was war minister.

Redinha, Battle of (12 March 1811), Peninsular War. At this small village in west-central Portugal, 23 miles north-northeast of Leiria, there was a bridge over the Soure River. Defending it, a French rear guard of 5,500 infantry successfully prevented Wellington's Anglo-Portuguese army (12,650 British and 6,600 Portuguese) from attacking the main body of the French army under André Masséna [q.v.]. Wellington sustained 205 casualties; French losses were 227.

Red Leg. American army slang for an artilleryman.

Redoubt. 1. A closed, independent fortification, square, circular, or polygonal, without bastions.

2. An earthwork outside a main fortification, usually placed on the route of a possible attacker.

Red Pamphlet, the. See Malleson, George Bruce.

Red River Campaign (10 March–22 May 1864), American Civil War. In Louisiana, Union General Nathaniel Banks [q.v.] with 17,000 men advanced to the Bayou Tech to join with 10,000 men under General Andrew Jackson Smith [q.v.] sent by General William T. Sherman [q.v.]. Troops supposed to have been sent from Arkansas failed to arrive in time [see Arkansas Campaign of 1864]. On 10 March Smith left Vicksburg and was escorted up the Red River by a formidable force of rivercraft, including thirteen ironclads, under Admiral David Dixon Porter (1813–1891). On 14 March he captured Fort De Russy, near Simsport, and on 18 March he entered Alexandria, 95 miles northwest of Baton Rouge, without opposition.

Red River Campaign Union and Confederate positions, 12 April 1864, after the Battle of Sabine Cross Roads.

On 24 March Banks arrived in person at Alexandria, and there was some skirmishing with cavalry and artillery dispatched by Confederate General Richard Taylor [q.v.], an engagement sometimes called the Battle of Henderson Hill or of Bayou Rapides. Undeterred, Banks moved toward Shreveport, but on 8 April his troops were routed in the Battle of Sabine Cross Roads [q.v.], and 2,500 were taken prisoner. The following day in the Battle of Pleasant Hill, a Confederate attack was repulsed with heavy losses.

Both sides pulled back, and Banks, abandoning his attempt to take Shreveport, retreated toward Alexandria, his rear guard harassed by 4,000 Confederate cavalry and 1,200 infantry. In the meantime Porter on the Red River had lost several of his ships. Banks reached Alexandria on 25 April, but Taylor's cavalry got in Banks's rear and from 4 to 13 May effectively blocked the river. On 16 May the Federals had to fight their way through a Confederate position, and both Banks and Porter were much harried. On 21–22 May, Smith's corps left to return to Vicksburg, and the remainder of Banks's command reached Donaldsonville, Louisiana.

There ensued much finger pointing among the northern commanders over this debacle. Banks was relieved of his command, faced a congressional investigation, and was officially censored.

Red River Rebellion (1869–70). The name sometimes given to the first rebellion of Louis Riel [q.v.] in western Canada. In 1869 Riel seized Fort Garry (Winnipeg) and established a provisional rebel government. Colonel (later Field Marshal) Garnet Wolseley [q.v.] led an expedition of British regulars and Canadian militia against him, a journey of more than 1,000 miles, made more remarkable because none of his

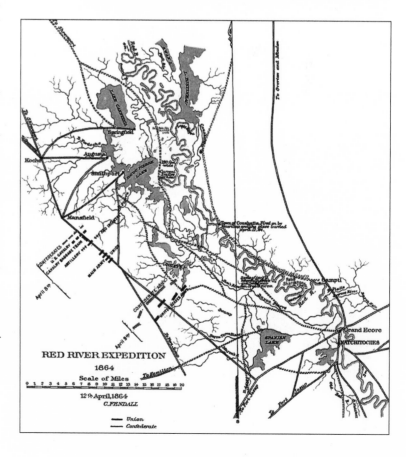

RED RIVER EXPEDITION
1864
Scale of Miles
0 1 2 3 4 5 6 7 8 9 10 11 12 13 14 15 16 17 18 19 20
12ᵗʰ April, 1864
C. FENDALL

— Union
— Confederate

men died of disease. He arrived at Fort Garry in September 1870 only to find that Riel and his people had fled to the United States.

Red River War (1874–75). A war between the United States and the Kiowa, Cheyenne, and Comanche Indians in Texas. About 2,000 Comanches, 1,800 Cheyennes, and 1,000 Kiowas assembled, with a total of perhaps 1,200 fighting men, and moved in large bodies among the forks of the Red River in the Texas Panhandle. In June 1874 at Adobe Walls [q.v.] Cheyenne and Comanche Indians led by Lone Wolf [q.v.] attacked a party of hunters and ambushed a detachment of Texas Rangers [q.v.] near the site of the Salt Creek Massacre [q.v.] of 1871. Soldiers swarmed into the area. In the war that followed, twenty-five engagements, including fourteen pitched battles were fought, all but five in Texas. The climax came on the morning of 27 September 1874, when General Ranald Mackenzie [q.v.] discovered and attacked the Indians' winter camp hidden in the Palo Duro Canyon, south of present-day Amarillo, Texas. Although only a few Indians were killed, all the supplies they had laid in for winter were destroyed. By the spring of 1875 most of the Kiowas and the once-powerful and feared Comanches had surrendered. This campaign completed the subjugation of the tribes on the southern plains. General Philip Sheridan [q.v.] called the Red River War the "most successful of any Indian campaign in this country since its settlement by the whites."

Red Shirts. 1. The red-shirted soldiers in the army of Giuseppe Garibaldi [q.v.] in Sicily and Italy in the 1860s during the Wars of Italian Independence.

2. Pathan rebels in Peshawar.

Red Sleeves. See Mangas Coloradas.

Red Sticks. Upper Creek Indians in Georgia who fought on the side of the British in the War of 1812 [q.v.].

Red Tomahawk (1853?–1931). A Teton Sioux who became a sergeant in the Indian police at the Standing Rock Agency in South Dakota. In 1890, when orders were issued to arrest Sitting Bull [q.v.], Lieutenant Bull Head (d. 1890), Red Tomahawk, and 43 Indian police descended on his camp on Wounded Knee Creek, where after agreeing to surrender, Sitting Bull balked and attempted to escape. In the firing that followed, Red Tomahawk killed Sitting Bull, and Bull Head and a number of the police fell at the hands of Sitting Bull's followers. In the hand-to-hand fighting Red Tomahawk took command of the police and held off the attackers until backup cavalry under Colonel James Forsyth [q.v.] arrived [see Wounded Knee, Battle of]. Red Tomahawk emerged from the battle unscathed and lived to a ripe old age.

Red Turban Revolt (1854–56). A major revolution in China against the imperial government. On 4 July 1854 the rebels, identified by their red turbans, seized the great city of Fatshan (Fo-shan), just south of Canton. By 20 July Triads were on three sides of Canton, and rebellion spread north of the capital [see Triad Society]. There was a lack of unit cohesion, and as food became scarce, rival gangs of rebels quarreled among themselves. By September the movement had begun to fall apart. Imperial junks bombarded Fatshan, and the

rebels melted back into the countryside. In January 1855 Fatshan was recovered by imperial forces, and on 7 March the last major Red Turban force was defeated at Whampoa, on the south side of the Pearl River, 12 miles below Canton.

It is claimed that a half million people died in the aftermath of the revolution as "unreliable elements" were eliminated daily. In Canton alone 250 were beheaded every day. Military commanders produced boxes of ears as proof of their vigor in hunting down rebels.

Reduce a Place, to. To force a town or fortification to capitulate.

Reduce a Square, to. To restore or bring back a unit that had formed a hollow square to a line or column.

Reduce to the Ranks, to. To demote an officer or noncommissioned officer to private or its equivalent.

Red Wing (1750?–1825). A name assumed by a succession of chiefs of the Khemichan band of the Mdewakanton Sioux. This one was, like his father, an ally of the British in the War of 1812 [q.v.]. He fought against the Americans in actions at Sandusky, Ohio; Mackinac, Michigan; and Prairie du Chien, Wisconsin. In 1814 he changed sides and allied himself with the Americans.

Reed, Walter (1851–1902). An American army surgeon who obtained a medical degree from the University of Virginia in 1869 and a second M.D. from Bellevue Hospital in New York in 1872. He was appointed to and entered the army Medical Corps in 1875. In 1893, after fifteen years on the frontier, he was promoted major, named curator of the Army Medical Museum, and appointed a professor of bacteriology and microscopy at the Army Medical School in Washington, D.C. In 1898 he headed the Typhoid Fever Board, which established the carrier state of typhoid and pointed up the failure of line officers to enforce sanitation. In 1900 he was appointed by Surgeon General George Miller Sternberg [q.v.] to head a board to study the cause and mode of transmission of yellow fever in Havana, Cuba [see Yellow Fever Board]. Proving by controlled experiments that the disease was carried by mosquitoes, notably *Aëdes aegypti*, he made possible the virtual elimination of yellow fever in the country. Walter Reed Army Medical Center and the Walter Reed Army Institute of Research, both in Washington, D.C., are named for him.

Reeve, Isaac van Duzer (1813?–1890). An American soldier who was graduated from West Point in 1835. He took part in the Second Seminole War [q.v.], the removal of the Winnebagos in 1840, and the Mexican War [q.v.], where he won two brevets. In Texas when the American Civil War began, he was made a prisoner of war through the treachery of General David E. Twigg [q.v.] and was not exchanged until 20 August 1862. At the end of the war he was a colonel and brevet brigadier general.

Reformado. 1. An officer deprived of command because of reorganization or similar cause who retained his rank and seniority and received full or half pay.

2. A volunteer who served as an officer but did not hold a commission.

Reform, War of the (1858–61). A civil war in Mexico generated by conservative opposition to liberal political and religious reforms. Liberal president Ignacio Comonfort (1812–1863) was overthrown in 1858 by Conservative General Félix Zuloaga [q.v.] and forced to flee to the United States. Zuloaga briefly assumed the presidency in Mexico City until replaced by Miguel Miramón [q.v.]. Meanwhile, the Liberal Party led by Benito Juárez [q.v.] on 4 May 1858 established a separate government at Veracruz that was recognized by the United States on 6 April 1859. In the war that followed, Juárez's Liberal army under General Santos Degollado (d. 1861) lost every major battle, including Tacubaya on 11 April 1859 and Celaya in November. Miramón's attempt to eject Juárez from Veracruz failed when his army was stricken by diseases in the lowland, and Degollado's attempt to capture Mexico City was aborted by his defeat at Chapultepec [q.v.]. By seizing church property, Juárez raised enough money to buy better arms and equipment, and under a new general, Jesús González Ortega (1824–1881), the Liberal army fared better, winning victories near Guadalajara and at Calderón.

There was dissension in the ranks of the Conservatives, and Zuloaga overthrew Miramón. On 20 December 1860 Ortega decisively defeated the Conservative army of Zuloaga in the Battle of Calpulálpam [q.v.] and opened the way to Mexico City, which Juárez entered on 11 January 1861. Miramón fled the country, and in 1861 Juárez was elected president of Mexico.

Réfracteur. A Frenchman who had evaded conscription.

Refugees. 1. People who because of real or imagined danger move of their own volition to places they believe safer.

2. People who are driven from their homes and forced to move elsewhere.

Refugees *Southern refugees in the woods near Vicksburg, Mississippi, 1861–65*

Refused Flank. See Flank Refused.

Regiment. A military unit larger than a battalion but smaller than a brigade, usually commanded by a colonel. During the American Civil War a Union regiment of infantry at full strength averaged about 1,000 men and was divided into ten companies; Confederate regiments were smaller.

Most British regiments consisted of two battalions, but many had only a single battalion of about 800; rifle regiments, however, had four. All the artillery in the British army constituted a single regiment, the Royal Regiment of Artillery. The French often called regiments demi-brigades after 1794. During the First Republic these consisted of infantry and artillery.

Regimental Agent. In the British service, a man authorized to handle the monetary affairs of a regiment, applying monthly at the War Office for the money required by a regiment.

Regimentals. The uniform worn by the soldiers of a regiment or corps.

Regimental Schools. Schools in British regiments designed to teach soldiers and their children reading, writing, and arithmetic. The Duke of Wellington liked his soldiers to be illiterate and opposed such schools, but in 1844 regiments were obliged to establish them. Boys were taught by a sergeant schoolmaster, and girls by a civilian schoolmistress. Two years later a corps of schoolmasters was formed. Soldiers were encouraged but not compelled to attend. Few did. In 1857, 20.5 percent of British soldiers were illiterate, and 16.8 percent more could read some but could not write or could barely sign their names.

The French army supported *écoles régimentaires*, regimental schools in which soldiers were taught reading, writing, and arithmetic.

In Prussia there were garrison schools (*Garnisons Schulen*) to teach soldiers' children and battalion schools (*Bataillons Schulen*), in which soldiers were taught reading, writing, orthography, arithmetic, and how to fill out official forms.

Régiment / Bataillon de Marche. A regiment or battalion made up of men belonging to various units. These ad hoc units were sometimes formed to carry replacements forward to regiments in the field or to form composite units for a campaign or special purpose.

Régiment de la Tour d'Auvergne. A regiment of the French army formed in 1805 and first commanded by a nephew of Théophile Malo Corret de la Tour Auvergne, the "First Grenadier of France" [q.v.]. The regiment was intended to enlist former royalists and Chouans.

Régiment / Bataillon Mixte. A colonial regiment or battalion in the French army with both French and indigenous personnel.

Régnier Affair (1870), Franco-Prussian War. A curious incident in the German siege of Metz, in which the mysterious Edmond Régnier, said to have been a businessman or an official of the Red Cross [q.v.], appeared on the stage of history as a gate-crasher into the realms of high diplomacy and the commands of armies. As France's fortunes were sinking, he wrote to the empress Eugénie (1826–1920), then in Hastings, England, urging her to rally the French people and army and denounce the newly formed revolutionary government. Eugénie did not respond, but the young Prince Imperial [see Napoleon, Eugène Louis Jean Joseph] was persuaded to write a few words of greeting to his father, Napoleon III, then a prisoner of the Germans, on the back of a picture of the

Hastings seashore. With this as a passport Régnier reached the headquarters of the German army, then at Ferrières, on 20 September 1870. His powers of persuasion must have been extraordinary, for he was given a pass to visit Otto von Bismarck (1815–1889) at Wilhelmshöle. There he convinced Bismarck that he could persuade the generals at Metz to surrender in the name of Napoleon III (1808–1873). The French emperor would then declare the revolutionary Government of National Defense overthrown, resume the reins of government, and negotiate for peace. Régnier was supplied with a safe passage to Metz. Once there he persuaded General Achille Bazaine to send General Charles Bourbaki [qq.v.] to the empress in England.

Bourbaki left Metz for England in disguise on 25 September, but the empress refused to have anything to do with the scheme, and on 29 September he announced his failure. Régnier returned to England and is said to have ended his days as the manager of a laundry in Ramsgate.

Regular Army. A permanent army maintained in peace as well as war; a standing army. It did not include reservists or militia [Armée de Métier].

Regulars. Professional soldiers, as opposed to militia or volunteers. Napoleon once said, "When defending itself against another country, a nation never lacks men, but too often, *soldiers.*" American General Emory Upton [q.v.] echoed these sentiments: "Regular troops engaged for the war, are the only safe reliance of a government, and are in every point of view, the best and most economical" (*The Military Policy of the United States* [1904]).

Regulars *A uniform of the U.S. regulars, 1861*

Regulations. The rules that govern the management and procedures of an army. In the nineteenth century it was not always easy to persuade officers, particularly aristocratic ones, to obey regulations. The Duke of Wellington once complained: "Nobody in the British Army ever read a regulation or an order as if it were to be a guide for his conduct, or in any other manner than as an amusing novel."

Reich's Kommission Revolver or Reichrevolver. A Model 1879 pistol, obsolete from the beginning, that was manufactured to the specifications of a Prussian committee. It was a single-action, solid-frame revolver with a 183 mm barrel with an effective range of 70 meters and a weight of 1.02 kilograms. A Model 1883 had a 126 mm barrel. Both remained in service even after World War I. [See Revolver.]

Reid, Whitelaw (1837–1912). An American war correspondent and diplomat. He covered the Union side of the American Civil War [q.v.] from 1861 to 1865 for the *Cincinnati Gazette.* In 1898 he was a member of the American commission that negotiated peace with Spain at the end of the Spanish-American War [q.v.]. His wife, Elizabeth, was acting head of the nursing division of the American Red Cross during that war.

Reid, William (1791–1858). A British soldier, colonial administrator, and meteorologist. From 1810 to 1814 he served as an engineer in the Peninsular War [q.v.], and in 1815 he took part in the Battle of New Orleans [q.v.]. He served as governor of Bermuda (1839–46), the Windward Islands (1846–48), and Malta (1851–58). He was promoted major general in 1856. As a meteorologist he contributed to the development of the circular theory of hurricanes.

Reille, Honoré Charles Michel Joseph (1775–1860). A French soldier who served under Napoleon at Jena and Friedland [qq.v.] in 1806. In 1808 he was Napoleon's aide-de-camp. In 1809 he distinguished himself at Aspern-Essling and Wagram [qq.v.], as well as in the Peninsular War [q.v.]. He rallied to Napoleon during the Hundred Days [q.v.] and commanded a corps at Waterloo [q.v.]. In 1847 he was made a marshal of France. He supported the coup d'état of 2 December 1851 that made Louis Napoleon (1808–1873) a dictator, and the following year, when Louis Napoleon became Napoleon III, Reille was made a senator.

Reims, Battle of. See Rheims, Battle of.

Reinforcement. Strength added to an existing military unit or army. Napoleon said: "A seasonable reinforcement renders the success of a battle certain, because the enemy will always imagine it stronger than it really is, and lose courage accordingly."

Reitz, Deneys (1882–1944). A South African soldier, writer, and statesman who at seventeen joined the Boer forces in the Second Anglo-Boer War [q.v.] and fought to the end. After the war he worked for a time as a transport rider in Madagascar. He returned to South Africa in 1904 and became a colonel in the British army in World War I. After this war he entered Parliament and served in a number of cabinet positions.

He wrote the best personal memoir of the Second Anglo-Boer War, *Commando* (1929), and later two other autobiographical works: *Trekking On* (1933) and *No Outspan* (1943).

Relief. 1. A person or unit that replaces another person or unit at a duty station or post.
2. A force that causes a siege to be lifted.

Relieve of Command, to. To dismiss an officer from the appointment he holds as a commander. A major factor in the relief of a commander is the availability of someone better to replace him. In the Russo-Turkish War [q.v.] of 1877–78 Suleiman Pasha was not only relieved of command but imprisoned when he retreated before the Russians in Bulgaria [q.v.].

Remblai. The earth removed from a hole or ditch in a fortification and usually added to the mass of a rampart, parapet, or banquette; the excavation itself was the *deblai.*

Remington, Eliphalet (1793–1861). An American firearms manufacturer who began his commercial career as a barrel-maker but in 1826 turned to the manufacture of flintlock rifles in what is now Ilion, New York. In about 1845 he purchased the manufactory of Ames & Company in Springfield, Massachusetts, contracted for government work, and from 1847 manufactured pistols, becoming in a few years, after Colt, the second-largest producer.

Philo Remington (1816–1889). A son of Eliphalet who was associated with his father in the firearms business and was named president of what became E. Remington & Sons. The business expanded into typewriters and sewing machines, but in 1886, having encountered financial difficulties, it was taken over by financiers. In 1888 it became the Remington Arms Company. Specializing in shoulder weapons, the firm made rifles for the armies of Denmark, Egypt, Mexico, and many other countries.

Remount. 1. As a noun, a horse purchased by the government for the cavalry or artillery. Also, a horse raised on a government stud farm.

2. As a verb, to replace horses that were disabled, killed, or cast.

3. As a verb, to get back in the saddle.

Rendezvous. 1. As a noun, a prearranged meeting at a given time and place.

2. As a verb, to meet by prearrangement at a certain time and place.

Rennenkampf, Pavel Karlovich (1854–1918). A Russian soldier who was commissioned in 1873 and in 1882 was appointed to the general staff. In 1900 he was promoted general. He had an undistinguished career in World War I, being defeated at the Battle of Tannenberg in 1914. He was killed by the Bolsheviks.

Reno, Jesse Lee (1823–1862). An American soldier who was graduated from West Point in 1846. His class included George B. McClellan, Thomas ("Stonewall") Jackson, and George Pickett [qq.v.]. He won two brevets for gallantry in the Mexican War [q.v.]. Later he was chief of ordnance on the Utah Expedition [q.v.]. In January 1861 he was forced to surrender the arsenal at Mount Vernon, Alabama, to state forces. On 12 November he was appointed a Union brigadier general, and on 30 August 1862 he fought in the Second Battle of Bull Run [q.v.]. He was mortally wounded in the Battle of South Mountain [q.v.] on 14 September 1862. Reno, Nevada, is named for him.

Reno, Marcus Albert (1834–1889). An American soldier who was graduated from West Point in 1857. He served in the Army of the Potomac [q.v.] during the American Civil War and was brevetted brigadier general. After the war he served in Washington Territory, and on 26 December 1868 he was promoted major in the 7th Cavalry. In 1876 he accompanied George Custer [q.v.] on his last expedition, and he was a survivor of the Battle of the Little Bighorn [q.v.].

When Custer came upon the Indians, he ordered Reno to take three troops, cross the Little Bighorn and attack them, adding that he would support him. Reno crossed the river but encountered more Indians than he had anticipated. He tried to make a stand but was soon forced to retreat back across the river to some bluffs, later called Reno's Hill. Here he was joined by Captain Frederick William Benteen [q.v.], who,

having been sent by Custer to reconnoiter hills five miles away, was just returning. He was also joined by the pack team. The little force held out until late the following day, when it was relieved by General Alfred Terry [q.v.].

Reno faced a barrage of charges, none substantiated. He was accused of being panicky, of being drunk, of failing to go to the help of Custer, of charging the Indians at the wrong point, and so on.

He was court-martialed in March and April 1877, not for his actions at the Little Bighorn but for making improper advances to the wife of Captain James Montgomery Bell. Although Mrs. Bell was said to have had "a rather unsavory reputation," Reno was convicted and sentenced to dismissal. President Rutherford Hayes (1822–1893) reduced the sentence to suspension without pay for two years. Immediately four officers, including Captain Bell, accused Reno of being drunk on duty and striking a junior officer, but General Terry disagreed, and the secretary of war ordered the charges dropped.

In 1880 additional charges were brought against him. He was accused of being drunk on duty, striking a junior officer, and being a "peeping Tom." One historian described him as "a besotted, socially inept mediocrity." He was court-martialed, found guilty, and on 1 April 1880 dismissed from the service. Reno spent the rest of his life trying unsuccessfully to clear his name. He died of cancer on 1 April 1889.

In the mid-1960s, at the behest of descendants, the army reexamined the evidence and found the charges against Reno unsubstantiated. They were dismissed, and Reno was restored to rank. In 1967 his remains were exhumed from Glenwood Cemetery in Washington, D.C., and reburied at the Custer Battlefield National Cemetery in Montana with full military honors.

Rensselaer, Stephen Van. See Van Rensselaer, Stephen.

Repatriate. 1. As a verb, to return a person to his native country—for example, to repatriate those taken prisoner after a war is concluded.

2. As a noun, a person so returned.

Repeating Firearm. A pistol, carbine, or rifle that can be fired several times without reloading.

Repington, Charles A'Court (1858–1925). A British soldier and military writer who served in Afghanistan, Burma, the Sudan, and South Africa before becoming involved in an affair with another officer's wife. Forced to resign, he became military correspondent for several London newspapers. He acquired fame for his reporting in *The Times* on the Russo-Japanese War and World War I.

Reprisal. Retaliation on an enemy because of injuries received, by inflicting equal or greater injuries. Napoleon referred to such acts as "a sorry recourse." During the American Civil War President Lincoln jailed and threatened to hang as pirates the crew of a captured Confederate privateer. President Jefferson Davis responded by transferring the highest-ranking prisoners of war to a common jail in Richmond and swore he would hang them in reprisal if the privateers were executed. Tempers later cooled, and no one was hanged.

Reputation. The prestige of a commander. The reputation of a commander in the eyes of an enemy can be a powerful factor either for or against an army. In the 1830s, when Russia was attempting to subdue the tribesmen of the Caucasus, Aleksis Yermolov [q.v.], known as the Lion of the Caucasus, said: "I desire that the terror of my name shall guard our frontiers more potently than chains or fortresses." Napoleon's reputation appears to have sometimes affected his enemies.

Requisition. 1. As a noun, a demand or request for services, supplies, or personnel.

2. As a verb, to make such a request. In British usage, to indent.

Réquisitionnaire. A French recruit.

Resaca, Battle of (13–16 May 1864), American Civil War. Confederate Joseph E. Johnston [q.v.], commanding an army of 70,000 at Rocky Face Ridge in northwest Georgia, became aware of an attempt by William T. Sherman [q.v.], with 98,000 men, to threaten his rear. In response, he moved his army to new positions just west of Resaca (called Dublin until renamed after the Battle of Resaca de la Palma [q.v.] in 1846).

On the afternoon of 14 May 1864 Sherman attacked the center of the Confederate line but was repulsed and suffered heavy losses. Johnston then attacked the left flank of the Union line with the corps commanded by Lieutenant General John B. Hood [q.v.]. The attack was enjoying some success until it was arrested by the arrival on the field of a division under Major General George H. Thomas [q.v.]. Meanwhile, on the Union right, Federal troops captured a hill that commanded the railroad bridge over the Oostenaula River, thus threatening the Confederates' line of communication. Heavy fighting continued the following day, and during the night the Confederates retreated. Their losses were about 5,000; Union losses, about 6,000.

Cadets from the Georgia Military Institute, dressed in their cadet uniforms, were engaged in this battle, but none was killed or wounded.

Resaca de la Palma, Battle of (9 May 1846), Mexican War. General Zachary Taylor [q.v.] with only 1,700 troops defeated a Mexican force of 5,700 under General Mariano Arista [q.v.] that had taken a position in this ravine, which crossed the Matamoros road four miles north of present-day Brownsville, Texas. Dense underbrush prevented the effective use of the American artillery so that the battle was primarily an infantry fight. Nevertheless, the Mexican army, demoralized and disorganized by its defeat at Palo Alto [q.v.] the day before, fled to Matamoros. In this battle Captain Charles A. May (d. 1864) of the 2nd Dragoons distinguished himself by calling out to his men, "Remember your regiment and follow your officers!" and leading them in a charge.

Mexican losses were 262 killed, 355 wounded, and 150 captured; American losses were 39 killed and 83 wounded.

Rescript. An order, decree, edict, or official announcement [see Imperial Rescript to Soldiers and Sailors].

Reserve Artillery. See Corps Artillery.

Reserve Officer Training Corps. Military education to train officers for the army at American land-grant colleges and some private colleges. Usually known by its initials (ROTC), the program was created by Congress with the Morrill Act of 1862 [q.v.]. Named for Justin Morrill (1810–1898), then a senator from Vermont (1867–98), who introduced it.

Reserves. Those troops held back from the front lines of a battle so that a commander can use them to exploit a success, to counterattack, or to prevent a rout. Charles Ardant du Picq [q.v.] wrote: "The system of holding out a reserve as long as possible for independent action when the enemy has used his own, ought to be applied downward. Each battalion should have its own, each regiment its own, firmly maintained." A maxim attributed to Napoleon was that a commander should "throw in his last man, because on the day after a complete success there are no more obstacles in front of him." This advice was ignored by Napoleon himself, both in the Battle of Borodino and at Waterloo [qq.v.]. Karl von Clausewitz [q.v.] wrote: "Fatigue the opponent, if possible, with few forces and conserve a decisive mass for the critical moment. Once this decisive mass has been thrown in, it must be used with the greatest audacity" (*On War* [1833]).

Reshid Pasha, Mustafa Mehmet (1802–1858). A Turkish soldier and statesman. He was defeated by Ibrahim Pasha [q.v.] in the Battle of Konya [q.v.] in 1832. In the Russo-Turkish War [q.v.] of 1828–29 he was defeated by Russians under Count Hans Diebitsch [q.v.]. In the Crimean War he commanded the Turkish forces. He served as grand vizier from 1837 to 1838 and from 1846 with a few interruptions.

Reshire, Battle of (7 December 1856), Anglo-Persian War. When the Persians invaded Afghanistan and besieged Herat, Britain declared war on Persia (Iran) on 1 November 1856 [see Herat, Sieges of]. In December an Anglo-Indian expeditionary force of 5,670 men under Sir James Outram [q.v.] landed in Persia and five miles south of Bushire found a Persian army of about 5,000 holding the village of Reshire (Rishahr), which had once been an important port. Although the Persians were in strong positions among old walls and ruins, they were driven out. They made a last stand at the ruins of an old Dutch fort from which they fled when it was stormed by one British and two Bombay infantry regiments. The British lost 9 killed and 31 wounded. Bushire was then occupied without further opposition.

Resident. A British or Dutch government representative at the court of an Asian ruler. Residents, often army officers or former officers, were sometimes the virtual rulers of the existing rulers.

Ressala / Rissala. In India, a troop of irregular cavalry.

Rest. A device on which to place a hand or shoulder weapon for carrying or to facilitate aiming.

Retief, Pieter (1780–1838). A Boer leader in South Africa. He fought in frontier wars against Bantu tribes and in 1822 was appointed a commandant. He took part in the Great Trek, leading an expedition across the Drakensberg into Natal. He and others with him were murdered by Dingaan [q.v.], chief of the Zulus [see Blood River, Battle of].

Retire, to. 1. To move away from a hostile force although not engaged.

2. To leave active duty after serving a number of years [see Retirement].

Retired Flank. See Flank Refused.

Retirement. 1. A movement away from the battlefield; a retreat.

2. Giving up a career in the army. Most armies for most of the nineteenth century had no retirement programs. Consequently many officers remained in the army long after they were fit to serve. When a retirement program was proposed in the United States in 1851, Congressman Joshua Giddings (1795–1864) warned: "Sir, when the retired military list shall once be established, it will remain an incubus upon the people while the Government shall exist." Not until 1861 was there a retirement system for American officers, and on 30 June 1882 a federal law set the age of retirement at sixty-four. This prompted the retirement of William Tecumseh Sherman, Montgomery Meigs [qq.v.], and the surgeon general Joseph K. Barnes (1810?–1883).

Retreat. 1. As a noun, a bugle call.

2. As a noun, a flag lowering ceremony.

3. As a verb, to move away from the enemy, implying a forced withdrawal and often, but not always, accompanied by considerable disorder [see Withdrawal; Disengage; Retirement]. The "line of retreat" is the route taken or planned to be taken by a retreating force, usually back along the line of communication [q.v.].

Suleiman Pasha [q.v.] was removed from command and imprisoned for retreating, but retreat is not always considered dishonorable. An orderly retreat is often commended. William Napier [q.v.] wrote: "Honourable retreats are no ways inferior to brave charges, as having less fortune, more of discipline, and as much valour." (*Peninsular War* [1810]). No soldier in British military history was more revered than Sir John Moore [q.v.], noted for his retreat before Napoleon's forces to Corunna in the Peninsular War.

Retreat *Retreat over the stone bridge, Second Bull Run, 30 August 1862*

Reveille. A signal such as a bugle call or drumroll marking the beginning of a soldier's day, sometimes accompanied by a formal ceremony, such as raising the flag. Although the word is used in the same way in the British, American, and French armies, the pronunciation differs: British, revally; American ré-ve-lee; and French, written *réveille*, re-vay-eh. In German the call is *Wecken*, and in Spanish *torque de diana*.

Revere, Joseph Warren (1812–1880). A grandson of Paul Revere (1735–1818) who was first a naval officer, entering the American navy as a midshipman at age sixteen. He was promoted lieutenant in 1841 and took part in the conquest of California during the Mexican War [q.v.]. He resigned in 1850 after twenty-two years in the service and then served as an artillery instructor for the Mexican army. In 1853 he left that post and served as a military adviser to various governments. At the outbreak of the American Civil War he joined the Union army as colonel of the 7th New Jersey. He took part in the Peninsular Campaign [q.v.] and on 25 October 1862 was promoted brigadier general. He commanded a brigade at Fredericksburg [q.v.]. In the Battle of Chancellorsville he retreated without orders, "for the purpose," he said later, "of reorganizing and bringing them back to the field comparatively fresh." For this he was court-martialed and sentenced to be cashiered. President Lincoln revoked the sentence, and he was permitted to resign, effective 10 August 1863.

Reverse Slope. The side of a hill or earthwork furthermost from the enemy.

Revetment. A retaining wall, often of stone or masonry, in permanent fortifications that retain the earth sides of a trench or parapet.

Review. 1. As a noun, formal inspection in which troops march past the inspecting official.

2. As a verb, to honor a person or persons in a ceremony that includes a march past those to be honored.

Revolax, Battle of (27 April 1808), Russo-Swedish War. Some 8,000 Swedes surprised a Russian column of 4,000 and routed it. Only about 1,000 escaped. This was one of the few Swedish successes in the war.

Revolt. A revolution of short duration. An insurrection or émeute [qq.v.].

Revolution. A mass uprising of citizens who attempt to replace one governing body of their country or one form of government with another. Antoine Henri de Jomini [q.v.], who had witnessed the French Revolution, wrote: "The spectacle of a spontaneous rising of a nation is rarely seen. Though there be in it something grand and noble which commands our admiration, the consequences are so terrible that, for the sake of humanity, we ought to hope never to see it" (*Précis de l'art de la guerre* [1838]).

Revolutionary Wars, French (1792–1802). The series of French military adventures in which the revolutionary government of France fought its neighbors began on 20 April 1792, when the Legislative Assembly declared war on the "king of Bohemia"—i.e., the emperor of Austria. It may be said to have ended with the signing of the Treaty of Amiens on 25 March 1802. The peace lasted only fourteen months and was followed by the Napoleonic Wars [q.v.].

Revolutions of 1848. Revolutions of a democratic or nationalistic character swept through Europe in 1848, affecting nearly every country and transforming the political life of each. Only Russia, the Scandinavian countries, and Spain were spared domestic upheavals.

Revolution first erupted in January 1848 in Sicily and then flared in France, followed by an uprising in Ireland and the Chartist riots [q.v.] in Great Britain. In Italy a revolt against Austria was led by the king of Piedmont-Sardinia. The insurrectionary spirit was particularly virulent in Paris, Vienna, Frankfurt, Venice, and Berlin [see Paris Revolution of 1848; Venetian Revolution of 1848–49]. Eventually all were suppressed by the use of regular troops. Russia sent troops to the aid of Austria [see Hungarian Revolution].

Revolver. A pistol with a cylinder of several chambers holding bullets that are successively brought into line with the barrel and discharged with the same hammer. Revolvers first became popular when exhibited in 1851 at the Great Exhibition in London. Samuel Colt [q.v.], the exhibitor, obtained contracts to manufacture them for both the British army and navy. He later manufactured them for the American army during the Civil War. Eli Whitney, [q.v.], inventor of the cotton gin, manufactured a .38 caliber revolver.

All these were percussion guns. Loaded and prepared combustible cartridges, containing the bullet and powder charge wrapped in paper or collodion, were inserted from the front of the cylinders and pushed home by using a loading lever pivoted beneath the barrel. The powder was lit by the spark from a percussion cap on a nipple behind each chamber in the cylinder. (See Robert Adams.)

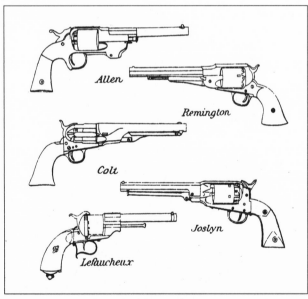

Civil War revolvers

Rey, Louis Emmanuel (1768–1846). A French soldier who was commissioned in 1792 and was a general of brigade four years later. From 1808 he served in Spain during the Peninsular War [q.v.]. In 1811 he was appointed governor of San Sebastián [q.v.] and endured a siege lasting from late June 1813 until he was forced to surrender on 9 September. While he was still a prisoner, Napoleon promoted him general of division. In May 1814 he returned to France and was appointed governor of Valenciennes during the Hundred Days [q.v.].

Reynier, Jean Louis Ebénézer (1771–1814). A French soldier who was with Napoleon in Egypt as a general of division. He distinguished himself at Heliopolis in 1800, but Napoleon held him responsible for the defeat at Alexandria [q.v.], and he was sent back to France in disgrace. After killing another general in a duel, he was exiled from Paris [see Dueling]. He again distinguished himself in Italy in 1805, and in 1808 he became minister of war and marine for the kingdom of Naples under Joachim Murat [q.v.]. In 1810 he fought in the Peninsular War [q.v.] in Spain until 1812, when he took part in Napoleon's Russian Campaign [q.v.]. He fought at Bautzen, Dresden, and Grossbeeren [qq.v.]. At Leipzig [q.v.] he commanded a corps, but his Saxon troops deserted to the Allies, and he was taken prisoner. He was exchanged in February 1814 but died two weeks later.

Reynolds, John Fulton (1820–1863). An American soldier who was graduated from West Point in 1841. After four years of garrison duty on the East Coast, he was ordered to Texas. During the Mexican War [q.v.] he won brevets to captain and major. He fought in the Rogue River War and took part in the Utah Expedition [qq.v.]. When the American Civil War broke out, he was commandant of cadets at West Point. In May 1861 he was promoted lieutenant colonel and in August brigadier general. He took part in the Peninsular Campaign [q.v.] and was captured on 27 June 1862. He was exchanged on 8 August. (N.B. The *Dictionary of American Biography* states that he was exchanged for Confederate General William Barksdale [q.v.], but Barksdale was never captured.) He commanded a division at the Second Battle of Bull Run [q.v.] and a corps in the "Grand Division" of Major General William Franklin [q.v.] in the Battle of Fredericksburg [q.v.], having been promoted major general just a few days before. He was killed by a Confederate sniper on 1 July 1863, the first day of the Battle of Gettysburg [q.v.].

Reynolds, Joseph Jones (1822–1899). An American soldier who was graduated from West Point in 1843. After some service in Texas he was assigned to West Point, where he taught for eight years. He then served in Indian Territory until he resigned as a first lieutenant in 1857. He taught engineering at Washington University in St. Louis and was for a time in the grocery business. At the beginning of the American Civil War he was at first a colonel of the 10th Indiana Militia but was soon appointed a brigadier general. He fought at Cheat Mountain [q.v.] in September 1861 but resigned in January 1862 on the death of his brother, with whom he had a business partnership. He returned to the army in September as a brigadier general and on 29 November was promoted major general of volunteers. He commanded a division at Chickamauga [q.v.], and in July he was given command of XIX Corps and organized the campaign against Mobile [q.v.], Alabama.

After the war he remained in the army as colonel of the 26th Infantry. He later transferred to the 3rd Cavalry. In 1871 he was elected a U.S. senator from Texas, but his seat was successfully contested by General Andrew Jackson Hamilton (1815–1875). On 17 March a portion of his command attacked a Cheyenne village on the Powder River [see Powder River, Battle of] that was wrongly believed to be the village of Crazy Horse [q.v.]. General George Crook [q.v.] court-martialed Reynolds, and in a trial lasting from 6 to 23 January 1877 he was found guilty of several charges and sentenced to be suspended from rank and command for a year. President Grant remitted the sentence, in view of his "long and faithful service," but Reynolds chose to retire on 25 June.

Rezonville, Battle of (16 August 1870), Franco-Prussian War. The German Second Army under Prince Frederick Charles [q.v.], moving north across the Metz–Verdon road, collided with French forces under General Achille Bazaine [q.v.], and a series of engagements resulted in a drawn battle. Cavalry charges were made by both armies, and as in the Battle of Brandy Station [q.v.] in the American Civil War, masses of horsemen mingled in a mad melee. Frederick Charles then launched his infantry in an attack along his entire front and pushed into the village of Rezonville, just west of Metz. That night both armies bivouacked on the field. German losses were 17,000; French losses were 16,000. This indecisive battle was the bloodiest and hardest-fought of the war. It is often considered part of the Battle of Mars-la-Tour–Vionville [q.v.], fought nearby on the same day.

Rheims, Battle of (13 March 1814), Napoleonic Wars. Following his defeat at Laon [q.v.] on 10 March 1814, Napoleon fell back upon Soissons on the Aisne River, 50 miles northeast of Paris. There, learning that on 12 March the Allies had taken Rheims, 40 miles away, he made a rapid march and attacked with 10,000, routing the Russian force of 14,500 there and recapturing the town at a cost of 1,000 casualties to the Russians' 3,000. This was Napoleon's last victory of the war, for he was then northeast of Paris between two numerically superior Allied armies.

Rheinische Metallwaaren und Maschinenfabrik. A German weapons firm (later called Rheinmetall) that was founded in 1889 to make ammunition for Mauser rifles. It soon expanded into the design and manufacture of field artillery. The British army adopted its 15-pounder quick-firing gun in 1901.

Rhine, Confederation of the (17 July 1806). A confederation designed by Napoleon of western and southern German states, notably Hesse-Darmstadt, Baden, Bavaria, and Württemberg, to form a French satellite. Under its provisions the confederation was to supply 63,000 troops to Napoleon's army. The confederation collapsed after the French debacle in the Battle of Leipzig in 1813.

Riall, Phineas (1775–1850). A British soldier who was commissioned an ensign on 31 January 1794 in the 92nd Foot. Thanks to the purchase system [q.v.], he was promoted lieutenant in February, captain in May, and major in December. In 1809–10 he took part in expeditions under Sir George Beckwith [q.v.] against Martinique and Guadeloupe [qq.v.]. In 1810 he became a lieutenant colonel, and three years later he was promoted major general and sent to Canada, where he took part in the War of 1812 [q.v.]. He led an invasion of the United States, during which he burned Buffalo and other villages in northern New York, but was defeated in the Battle of Chippewa and at Lundy's Lane [qq.v.]. In the Battle of Fort Erie [q.v.] he lost an arm. In 1816 he was appointed governor of Canada. He was promoted lieutenant general in 1825 and a full general in 1841.

Ribauld / Ribalde / Ribauldequin. A number of muskets or gun barrels joined together in a bundle or side by side and fired simultaneously. A Danish ribauld, called an *orgelespignål*, was used as late as the Schleswig-Holstein War [q.v.] of 1864.

Ricasso. The blunted or squared underside of the blade of a sword, dagger, or knife beneath the tang and the grip. Swordmakers sometimes engraved their mark here.

Richardson, John Soame (1834–1895). A British soldier commissioned in 1854 in the 12th Foot. He served in the Crimean War and in two Maori Wars [qq.v.]. In 1876 he was appointed to command the forces in New South Wales, Australia, and in 1884 he led a New South Wales force to the Sudan to fight the Mahdist Dervishes in the Red Sea area [see Mahdiya].

Richmond and Lennox, Fourth Duke of (1764–1819). A British soldier who in 1789 fought a duel with the Duke of York [see Frederick Augustus, Duke of York and Albany]. He served in the Leeward Islands and in 1795 became a colonel. In 1805 he was promoted lieutenant general, and from 1807 to 1813 he was lord lieutenant in Ireland. He became a full general in 1814, and on the eve of the Battle of Waterloo he and his wife, Georgiana, gave a famous ball in Brussels [see Ball, Duchess of Richmond's]. He was present in the Battle of Waterloo [q.v.] but did not hold a command. In 1818 he was appointed governor-general of Canada.

Richmond, Kentucky, Battle of (29–30 August 1862), American Civil War. Two Federal brigades, 6,500 men, mostly recruits, held Richmond, Kentucky, 22 miles south-southeast of Lexington, on which an attack was expected. On 29 August 1862 there was some skirmishing, and the Confederates were pushed back, but during the night they were reinforced, and under the command of Confederate General Edmund Kirby Smith [q.v.] they attacked the Federal left and then right flanks, both of which collapsed. The Federals were routed.

Federal losses were 206 killed, 844 wounded, and 4,303 missing. Out of 6,000 Confederates, 78 were killed, 372 wounded, and 1 was missing.

Richmond Raid. See Beaver Dam Station, Raid on.

Rich Mountain (11 July 1861), American Civil War. Union General William Starke Rosecrans [q.v.] led four regiments of infantry and some cavalry around the left flank of the Confederate position astride the Buckhannon–Beverly road in what is today northeast-central West Virginia. The surprise attack was successful, and the Federals captured about 600 Confederates under Lieutenant Colonel John Pegram [q.v.].

Ricketts, James Brewerton (1817–1887). An American soldier who was graduated from West Point in 1839 and commissioned in the artillery. He fought in the Second Seminole War and the Mexican War [qq.v.]. During the American Civil War he commanded a Union Battery in the First Battle of Bull Run [q.v.] in which he was wounded four times and captured. He was exchanged in January 1862 and promoted brigadier general of volunteers. He commanded a division in the Battle of Cedar Mountain and in the Second Battle of Bull Run [qq.v.]. In the Battle of Antietam [q.v.] he was badly injured when his horse was shot from under him. When only partially recovered, he sat on the court-martial of General Fitz John Porter [q.v.]. As a division commander he took part in Grant's Overland Campaign toward Richmond, fighting in the battles of the Wilderness, Spotsylvania, Cold Harbor, and Petersburg [qq.v.]. After the latter he was hurriedly sent north with 3,350 men when Confederate General Jubal Early [q.v.] threatened Washington, D.C. [see Early's Raid]. His division lost 595 men in the Battle of Monocacy [q.v.]. In the Battle of Cedar Creek he was shot in the chest and disabled for life. Retired from active duty, he continued to serve on courts-martial until 1869.

Ricochet. The action of a bullet or shell that bounces, skips, or flies off after it hits an object or surface.

Ricochet Battery. A battery of guns that could include howitzers and mortars that used small powder charges and just enough elevation to fire solid shot over a parapet. The shot when so fired rolled among columns of infantry or troops of cavalry and could be very destructive. This sort of firing was devised by the great French military engineer Sébastien le Prestre de Vauban [q.v.].

Ricochet Fire. Round shot fired at low angles so as to bounce one or more times after striking the ground.

Ricotti-Magnani, Cesare (1822–1905). An Italian soldier who from 1856 to 1859 was director of the artillery school and in 1864 became general of division. In the Seven Weeks' War [q.v.] of 1866 he fought the Austrians and stormed Borgoforte to open a passage for the army of Enrico Cialdini [q.v.]. In 1872 he was named minister of war and in that capacity worked on army reform based on lessons learned in the Franco-Prussian War [q.v.]. The length of service was shortened, conscription was extended to all able-bodied males, a standing army and a militia were created, and weapons were updated. In 1890 he became a senator, and in 1898, after the disastrous Battle of Adawa [q.v.] in East Africa, he formed a ministry, retaining the War Ministry for himself. He is considered the creator of the modern Italian army.

Ridgely, Defense of (20–22 August 1862), Sioux uprising in Minnesota. Two lieutenants with 153 enlisted men, 25 civilians, and three howitzers successfully defended this fort on the north side of the Minnesota River from repeated attacks by some 800 Sioux. Among the defenders, 3 were killed and 13 wounded; an estimated 100 Indians were killed or wounded. [See Minnesota, Sioux Uprising in].

Riego y Núñez, Rafael de (1785–1823). A Spanish soldier and politician who as a young man played an active part in fighting the French in the Peninsular War [q.v.]. As a colonel in 1820 and one of the principal leaders of the Revolution of 1820–23 he captured the cruel and tyrannical king Ferdinand VII (1784–1833). In 1822–23, as president of the Cortes, he resisted the intervention of the Holy Alliance [see Spanish Civil War of 1820–23; French Intervention in Spain]. His army was defeated on 31 August 1823 in the Battle of Trocadero [q.v.] near Cádiz; he was captured and executed as a traitor.

Riel, Louis David (1844–1885). A Canadian Métis who led rebellions in what is now Saskatchewan, Canada. When the Northwest Territory was incorporated into Canada in 1869, the Métis, a seminomadic people of mixed French and Indian blood, many of whom were hunters and trappers, feared a loss of their land titles and traditional way of life. In October of that year a party led by Riel turned back the newly appointed governor. Under Riel's leadership the Métis established their own government in the valley of the Red River with headquarters at Fort Garry (Winnipeg). When a military expedition under Colonel (later Field Marshal) Garnet Wolseley moved against him, Riel fled to the United States. Wolseley occupied Fort Garry on 24 August 1870 [see Red River Rebellion]. In October 1873 Riel became a member of the dominion Parliament for Provencher. He traveled to Ottawa and took the oath but did not sit. On 16 April 1874 he was expelled; in September he was reelected. On 10 February 1875 he was outlawed.

In 1877–78 he spent more than a year in an asylum for the insane in the United States. Discharged, he moved to Montana and became a schoolteacher. In June 1884 a delegation of Métis, who had moved farther west into present-day Manitoba, came to beg him to lead them in another rebellion to obtain what they perceived to be their rights. Riel consented, and in this rebellion blood was shed [see Riel's Rebellion; Duck Lake, Battle of; Batoche, Battle of; Cut Knife Hill, Battle of]. On 15 May 1885 Riel was captured, and although an elaborate scheme to rescue him was hatched by his lieutenant, Gabriel Dumont [q.v.], he was convicted of treason on 1 August and hanged in Regina on 16 November 1885.

Riel's Rebellion (1885). A rebellion of the Métis of Manitoba, Canada, led by Louis Riel [q.v.], sometimes called the Northwest Insurrection. The Métis, people of mixed French and Indian blood, and their Indian allies, fearing a destruction of their seminomadic way of life and the loss of title to their lands by the westward movement of Canadians, had unsuccessfully rebelled in 1868–69 [see Red River Rebellion]. After moving westward into present-day Manitoba, they again rebelled under their earlier leader Louis Riel [q.v.]. On 16 March 1885 in the Battle of Duck Lake [q.v.], the first battle of the rebellion, Northwest Mounted Police, militia, and volunteers were defeated by Métis under Gabriel Dumont [q.v.]. Soon after, nine white men were massacred at Frog Lake by Métis and allied Indians, and about three dozen hostages were taken at Fort Pitt, where on 23 April Inspector Francis Dickens (a son of writer Charles Dickens) and 24 constables of the Northwest Mounted Police had been forced to flee in a leaking scow to Battleford, at the confluence of the North Saskatchewan and Battle rivers. There the Northwest Mounted Police had built a ramshackle fort in which some 500 people had taken refuge. On 24 April Lieutenant Colonel (later Major General) William Dillon Otter (d. 1928) arrived with 750 men. On 1 May Otter set out with a force of 390 men, none of them regulars, and the following morning he lost the Battle of Cut Knife [q.v.].

In spite of this defeat, a few days later Riel and his followers were overwhelmed. At Qu'Appelle, 30 miles east of Regina, the Canadian government had assembled under Major General Frederick Dobson Middleton [q.v.] some 3,000 men, mostly militia, many of whom had been rushed westward over the still-incomplete Canadian Pacific Railroad. On 9–12 May Middleton defeated Riel in the Battle of Batoche [q.v.]. A number of the rebels were sentenced to prison. Riel was hanged.

Riel's Rebellion *A Canadian battery goes to the front in Riel's Rebellion, 1885.*

Rieti, Battle of (7 March 1821), Italian Wars of Independence. The entire reign of Ferdinand IV (1751–1825) of Naples (who was also Ferdinand III of Sicily and Ferdinand I of the Two Sicilies) was tyrannical. In 1820, when a revolution forced him to flee, he sought help from Austria, which supplied an army of 80,000 regulars. Some 10,000 Italian troops under General Guglielmo Pepe [q.v.] were defeated by the Austrians at Rieti, a town 42 miles northwest of Rome, on 7 March 1821. On 23 March the Austrians marched into Naples, and Ferdinand was restored to his throne.

Riff War (1893). Berber tribesmen in the Riff Mountains of North Africa made frequent incursions into Spanish Morocco and gathered in force around Melilla, a Spanish presidio and the most important Spanish port in North Africa. The town was besieged on the land side, but its port remained open. In November 1893 Spain sent a 25,000-man expeditionary force under Leopoldo O'Donnell [q.v.] that drove the tribesmen away.

Rifle. A shoulder-fired weapon with rifling [q.v.]. The first rifles were muzzle-loaded muskets with rifled bores. Because the bullet had to be rammed down against the grooves, its rate of fire was slower than that of a musket. Such rifles were in use in many countries from 1850 to 1890, but the invention of the Minié bullet and breechloaders gradually supplanted them. In addition to the advantage of a faster rate of fire, the

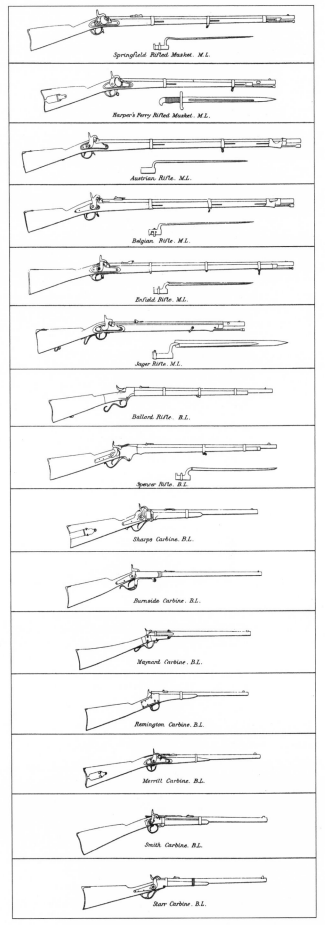

Rifle *Rifles of the American Civil War*

new rifles did not require those firing them to stand erect when loading. The German army adopted the Dreyse needle gun [q.v.] in 1841. It was succeeded by the French Chassepot rifle [q.v.] of 1866, which had a superior breech-loading mechanism. The development of metallic cartridges in the 1860s and the invention of smokeless powder and magazine loading made the rifle a formidable weapon in the hands of infantry and made cavalry as a fighting arm almost obsolete. Jean de Bloch [q.v.], who predicted that wars had become so deadly and destructive that they would cease, wrote: "The outward and visible sign of the end of war was the introduction of the magazine rifle" (*Is War Impossible?* [1899]).

Rifle Green. A very dark green, though not as deep as invis-ible green, was said to have been the color favored by huntsmen [*Jäger* in German and *chasseurs* in French] and thus the color of the uniforms of many rifle regiments, including in Britain the Rifle Brigade and the King's Royal Rifle Corps [see Rifle Regiments]. The color was also worn by Gurkha regiments.

Rifleman. A soldier armed with a rifle and trained as light infantry. In the British army, rifle regiments wore green rather than red blouses, marched faster than line regiments, and never shouldered their rifles. [See Rifle Green.]

Rifled Musket. A musket converted to a rifle by making the barrel rifled. The .58 caliber Model 1855 became the mainstay of the infantry in the American Civil War.

Rifle Pits. Holes dug in the ground and used as protection from enemy fire. Now called foxholes.

Rifle Range. A place where the firing of small arms can be practiced.

Rifle Range *British infantrymen at rifle practice, Rangoon, Burma, 1857*

Rifle Regiments. When rifles or rifled muskets first came into general use in the late eighteenth century, many countries established rifle units. In the United States, Section 11 of the act of March 3, 1799, authorized the formation of a battalion

of riflemen, but it was not formed until 12 April 1808, the first of four. They served only until 1821.

In Britain the King's Royal Rifle Corps was founded during the American Revolutionary War as the Royal Americans. The British also formed the Rifle Brigade (a regiment in spite of its name), and both rifle regiments adopted a dark green uniform with black buttons and trained as light infantry [see Rifle Green].

Riflery. Target practice with a rifle. [See Musketry.]

Rifling. 1. The process or act of making helical grooves in gun barrels.

2. The helical grooves cut into the bore of a gun to impart a spin in the projectile that gives it a gyroscopic stability. The number of grooves depends upon the caliber, usually six grooves for each 25 mm of caliber.

Rigaud, André (1761–1811). A Haitian soldier who opposed Toussaint L'Ouverture [q.v.] and, when defeated, sailed to France. He returned to Haiti with General Charles Leclerc [q.v.] in February 1802, but in a disagreement was imprisoned by the French. After escaping, he aroused Haitians to rebel against the rule of General Alexandre Pétion [q.v.] in 1810 and was again defeated.

Riley, Bennet (1787–1853). An American soldier who was commissioned an ensign of riflemen [see Rifle Regiments] in 1813 during the War of 1812 [q.v.] and served on both the eastern and western fronts. Following a successful fight against Arikara Indians in Dakota Territory, he was brevetted major. He served in the Black Hawk War of 1831–32 and in the Second Seminole War [qq.v.]. During the latter, in the Battle of Chokachatta, Florida, on 2 June 1840, he distinguished himself and was promoted colonel. During the Mexican War [q.v.] he commanded the 2nd Infantry and was brevetted brigadier general for his gallantry in the Battle of Cerro Gordo [q.v.] on 18 April 1847. In the Battle of Contreras [q.v.] on 20 August he led his brigade in a spectacular charge down a slope and fell upon the enemy's rear, a feat for which he was brevetted major general. After the war, in 1848, he was made military governor of California and commander of the Department of the Pacific. In September 1849 he convened a constitutional convention at Monterey, and in December he turned over executive authority to the new state government. Illness forced his retirement. Fort Riley, Kansas, was named for him.

Rimfire Cartridges. A metallic cartridge in which the fulminate is in the rim surrounding the head. When the rim is struck at any point, the powder is exploded.

Rim of a Cartridge. A circular area around the base of a cartridge case. It seats the cartridge while loading and provides a grip for the extractor.

Ringatu. A religiomilitary cult that sprang up among the Maoris in New Zealand during the Maori Wars [q.v.].

Ringgold, Samuel (1800–1846). An American soldier who was graduated from West Point in 1818 and was commissioned in the artillery. In 1836 he took part as a captain in the Second Seminole War [q.v.] in Florida. In poor health, he took leave to sail to Europe and study at the École Polytechnique and at Woolwich [qq.v.]. In 1838, ordered to establish a horse artillery company at Carlisle Barracks, Pennsylvania, he organized, equipped, and trained Company C of the 3rd Artillery, the first horse artillery in the American army. It consisted of six guns, six caissons, two battery wagons, and two forges, each pulled by six horses; 12 mounted cannoneers rode with each gun. Horse artillery, in which all artillerymen rode horses rather than limbers, caissons, or wagons, was then called flying artillery [q.v.] and Ringgold was to become known as the father of flying artillery.

In 1846 he joined the "Army of Occupation" in Texas and was severely wounded by a six-pound cannonball while directing a battery in the Battle of Palo Alto [q.v.] on 8 May. He died three days later, the first West Point graduate to be killed in the Mexican War [q.v.].

Río de la Plata, British Expedition to (1806). This "river of silver" between Argentina and Uruguay is not a river but an estuary, and there is no silver in the area. In June 1806 a British fleet under Commodore Sir Home Riggs Popham (1762–1820) sailed into the estuary and on 25 June landed 1,600 men, including a marine battalion, near Buenos Aires.

Popham, after leading a successful expedition that captured the Cape of Good Hope on 10 January 1806, had been told in April by the captain of an American merchant ship docked at Cape Town that the inhabitants of Buenos Aires and Montevideo were suffering under tyrannical governments and would be delighted if they could be liberated by the British. Fired by these words, he persuaded General Sir David Baird [q.v.], the commander of troops in Cape Colony, to give him 1,200 soldiers under Brigadier General William Carr Beresford [q.v.] and sailed for Argentina. There he encountered little Spanish opposition. The governor fled to Córdoba, and Buenos Aires was occupied on 2 July, but the citizens of the town, led by a French-born soldier, Santiago Liniers [q.v.], took up arms and on 12 August overwhelmed Beresford's troops and made them prisoners. Popham could do nothing but blockade the ports until reinforcements arrived in October, when he was superseded. In 1807 a larger force dispatched from England was also defeated and forced to retire.

Río Seco, Battle of the. See Medina del Río Seco, Battle of.

Riot. In the United States officially defined as the "tumultuous disturbance of the public peace by three or more persons assembled together and acting with a common assent." Riots are normally handled by police; when they are thought to be unable to restore order, militia or regular troops are called up. [See Peterloo Massacre; Chartist Riots; Railway Strike of 1877, American.]

Ripley, Eleazer Wheelock (1782–1839). An American soldier and politician who in 1800 was graduated from Dartmouth College, which had been founded by his grandfather. He became an attorney and served in the Massachusetts legislature. On 12 March 1812, during the War of 1812, he was appointed a lieutenant colonel and commander of the 21st Infantry. He took part in the invasion of Canada and fought in the Battle of York [q.v.]. On 15 April 1814 he was promoted brigadier general and fought under Jacob Brown [q.v.] at Chippewa and Lundy's Lane [qq.v.] as part of the Left Division [q.v.]. He was severely wounded at Fort Erie [q.v.]. Brown considered him too slow and replaced him with Brigadier General Edmund Gaines [q.v.], but Congress voted Ripley a gold medal. He resigned in 1820, resumed the practice of law in New Orleans, and in 1835 was elected to Congress.

Ripley, James Wolfe (1794–1870). An American soldier who was graduated from West Point in 1814, the 102nd graduate of the U.S. Military Academy. He had studied there for little more than a year. He then fought at Sackets Harbor during the War of 1812 and in the First Seminole War [qq.v.]. From 1833 to 1842 he commanded the Kennebec Arsenal in Maine, and for the next twelve years he was the superintendent of the Springfield Arsenal [q.v.]. He was retired and in Europe when the American Civil War began but at once returned. When a friend remarked to the sixty-six-year-old soldier "that his country needed him," he replied: "It can have me and every drop of blood in me." Men spoke like that then.

On 23 April 1861 he was named head of the Ordnance Department and on 3 August was promoted brigadier general. Honest, zealous, and devoted to his duty, he was at the same time unimaginative and excessively conservative. He opposed every suggested innovation and waged a determined fight against breech-loading guns. "A great evil now prevalent in regard to arms for the military service is the vast variety of new weapons, some in my opinion unfit for use as military weapons and none as good as the United States musket," he said. President Lincoln and Edwin Stanton [qq.v.], the secretary of war, finally forced Ripley out of office on 15 September 1863. However, he was brevetted major general in 1865 and continued to serve until 1869 as "Inspector of Armament of Forts on the New England Coast."

He was the uncle of Roswell Sabine Ripley (1823–1887), who became a Confederate general.

Riposte. An attack or blow made in response to a blow or attack.

Rise, to. In a military sense, to make a hostile attack. For rank and file to rise against their officers was mutiny; for citizens to rise against their government was revolution.

Risorgimento. The Italian word for revival or resurrection came to mean the revolutionary movement in the nineteenth-century struggle to unite Italy and banish all Austrian rule. With the surrender of Gaeta [q.v.] on 13 February 1861, Italian independence became a realistic goal. [See Italian Wars of Independence; Garibaldi, Giuseppe; Red Shirts; Austro-Piedmontese War; Verdi, Giuseppe.]

Rissildar. See Indian Army.

Riva Agüero, José de la (1783–1858). A Peruvian soldier and politician who was one of the early leaders in the struggle for Peruvian independence from Spain. In 1821 he joined the rebel army of José de San Martín [q.v.] and in the following months was twice imprisoned. In 1823, from February to June, he was the first president of Peru, but he was forced to resign by Simón Bolívar and Antonio de Sucre [qq.v.].

Rivarola, Cirilo (d. 1871). A Paraguayan soldier and politician who fought in the War of the Triple Alliance [q.v.]. In

1870 he was elected the first president of the republic of Paraguay. He was assassinated after holding office for only a few months.

Rivera, José Fructuoso (1790?–1854). A Uruguayan soldier of gaucho descent who served under General José Artigas [q.v.] and was one of the so-called Thirty-three Immortals who freed Paraguay. In 1830 he led a successful revolution and became the first president of Uruguay, a post he held for five years. He supported Manuel Oribe [q.v.], who had been his minister of war, to succeed him as president, but in 1838 he led a revolt that deposed Oribe and was again established as president. He served until 1851, when a nine-year civil war erupted. He was the leader of the besieged Colorados in Montevideo [see Montevideo, Siege of]. After the Battle of Indio Muerta in 1845, in which he was defeated by Justo Urquiza [q.v.], he fled to Brazil. In 1853 he was one of three chosen to administer the provisional government of Uruguay. He died the following year.

River Crossings. Rivers were major obstacles to the movement of armies. Bridges could be destroyed or stoutly defended. Pontoon bridges took time to build, and in any case those on the opposite shore often had clear shots at vulnerable men constructing them, as in the Battle of Fredericksburg [q.v.]. The most costly river crossing of the century in terms of lives and matériel was Napoleon's crossing of the Berezina River [q.v.] during his disastrous retreat from Moscow. Some 25,000 men and 30,000 followers were lost. Even after a river had been crossed and a bridgehead established, it was not always easy to maintain, as was the case in the Battle of Ball's Bluff [q.v.] in the American Civil War. Streams sometimes appeared to be greater obstacles than they in fact were. General Ambrose Burnside lost many men and valuable time trying to cross a stone bridge over Antietam Creek when his men could have waded across elsewhere [see Antietam, Battle of].

River War. The name given by Winston Churchill [q.v.] to the Anglo-Egyptian reconquest of the Sudan [q.v.] in 1898.

River Warfare. Land warfare was often facilitated if the line of communication was a river or a canal. Supplies could be brought forward, and the wounded could be evacuated more easily and more comfortably by boat. Such was the case in the Second Anglo-Burmese War [q.v.], in which the future Lord Wolseley [q.v.], then a wounded lieutenant, was evacuated by riverboat. Union wounded from the Battle of Ball's Bluff [q.v.] were evacuated via the Chesapeake and Ohio Canal. The early victories of General U. S. Grant were facilitated by naval action and steamboats on the Mississippi River. Troops and supplies moved on riverboats in the American western frontier, and surviving wounded from the Battle of the Little Bighorn [q.v.] were evacuated by steamboat. [See Steamboats; Missouri River Transportation Company.]

"Roast Beef of Old England, The." The traditional tune that announces dinner is served in British messes. It was written by Richard Leveridge (1670?–1758), a composer and a bass singer in London theaters.

Robert, Henry Martyn (1837–1923). An American soldier who was graduated from West Point in 1857. During the American Civil War he worked as a military engineer on the defenses of Washington and Philadelphia. In 1901 he was promoted brigadier general, but his chief claim to fame is his authorship of *Pocket Manual of Rules of Order,* which came to be called *Robert's Rules of Order,* first published in 1876.

Roberts, Frederick Sleigh (1832–1914). A British soldier born in India, the son of an Indian army general. In 1851 he entered the Bengal artillery. He saw much action in the Indian Mutiny [q.v.] and the subsequent mopping-up operations, winning the Victoria Cross [q.v.] at Khudaganj in 1858. He served as assistant quartermaster general in the Abyssinian and Lushai campaigns [qq.v.]. In the Second Afghan War [q.v.] he forced the Afghan positions at the Peiwar Kotal [q.v.] and captured Kabul in 1879. In 1880 he made his memorable Kabul to Kandahar march [q.v.] to relieve the besieged garrison at Kandahar, and the following year he was appointed commander-in-chief, Madras. He served in that post until 1893, when he was made commander-in-chief, India. In 1892 he was raised to the peerage as Lord Roberts of Kandahar and Waterford. In 1895 he became a field marshal and was appointed commander-in-chief, Ireland, which was usually a final post for a distinguished officer, but in 1899, following Black Week [q.v.] in South Africa at the beginning of the Second Anglo-Boer War [q.v.], he was sent to command the army in the field there. He relieved besieged Kimberley [q.v.], compelled Boers under Piet Cronjé [q.v.] to surrender at Paardeberg [q.v.], advanced to Pretoria, annexed the Orange Free State and the Transvaal, and was everywhere successful. He returned to England in 1901 and was created an earl.

He retired in 1904 but continued his interest in improving the army and in pressing for conscription. He died while visiting British troops in France during the First World War.

Roberts and Garnet Wolseley were the two foremost generals of the Victorian era, but although they were contemporaries, there is no record that they ever met. There was a rivalry between the admirers of each, and Wolseley is known to have spoken critically of Roberts, while Roberts scarcely spoke of Wolseley at all; in his two-volume autobiography, *Forty-one Years in India* (1897), he made only three passing references to him. The two men operated in different spheres. Roberts was very much a child of the Indian army who in his autobiography recalled with nostalgia marching through the Bolan Pass from Afghanistan to India: "I fancy myself crossing and recrossing the river that winds through the pass [Bolan River]; I hear the martial beat of drums and plaintive music of the pipes; and I see Riflemen and Gurkhas, Highlanders and Sikhs, guns and horses, camels and mules, with the endless following of the Indian army, winding through the narrow gorges, or over the interminable boulders which make the passage of the Bolan so difficult and wearisome to man and beast."

Robertson, Beverly Holcombe (1826–1910). An American soldier who was graduated from West Point in 1849 and from 1851 to 1859 fought hostile Indians in Nebraska, New Mexico, and Dakota Territory. On 8 August 1861, at the outbreak of the American Civil War, he was dismissed from the army for "having given proof of his disloyalty." In November he was elected colonel of the Confederate 4th Virginia Cavalry. In May–August he commanded a cavalry division in the Army of Northern Virginia [q.v.]. On 9 June 1862 he was promoted brigadier general and in that rank served under Thomas ("Stonewall") Jackson at Cedar Mountain and Antietam and under J. E. B. Stuart at the Second Battle of Bull Run [qq.v.]. Stuart distrusted him, and he was sent to South Carolina in October 1863. He surrendered with General Joseph Johnston [q.v.]. After the war he entered the insurance business in Washington, D.C.

Robertson, George Scott (1852–1916). The son of a pawnbroker who became an army surgeon and Anglo-Indian administrator. He was educated at the Westminster Hospital Medical School and in 1878 entered the Indian medical service. He served as a medical officer in the Second Afghan War [q.v.]. In 1894 he became British Resident at Gilgit, where in less than a year the mehtar (ruler) died. In the bloody scramble among the claimants to the throne that followed he found himself besieged at Chitral in a ramshackle fort, 80 yards square. With him were 5 British officers; 400 native troops, commanded by Captain Charles V. P. Townshend [q.v.], later famous, or infamous, for his surrender of Kut-al-Amara in World War I; and about 137 noncombatants, including the youngest legitimate male survivor of the ruling family. The siege, which began on 4 March, lasted until 20 April, when the fort was relieved [see Chitral Campaign]. In 1895 Robertson was knighted (KCSI). In 1899 he retired, and in 1906 he was elected a member of Parliament.

Robertson, Jerome Bonaparte (1815–1891). An American whose parents apprenticed him to a hatter but who managed to be trained in medicine by a doctor. He emigrated to Texas and fought in the revolution. He remained in Texas as a legislator and Indian fighter. During the American Civil War he rose from captain to brigadier general in the Confederate army, commanding a famous Texas brigade in Longstreet's corps.

Robertson, William Robert (1860–1933). A British soldier from a poor family who enlisted as a private and rose to become a field marshal, the only British subject ever to do so. Although his mother told him she would rather see him dead than wearing a red coat, he enlisted in the 16th Lancers in 1877 at the age of seventeen. He rose to be a troop sergeant major, and ten years after his enlistment, encouraged by his officers, he took and passed the examination for a commission. In 1888 he was gazetted an officer in the 3rd Dragoon Guards, then in India.

It was not an easy path for a poor man. As he wrote in his memoirs, *From Private to Field Marshal* (1921), "It is not altogether agreeable to be seen drinking water in the mess when others are drinking champagne." Because those who passed language examinations earned extra money, he taught himself Urdu, Hindi, Gurkhali, Persian, Pushtu, and Punjabi. In 1892 his linguistic skills earned him a post in the Intelligence Department at Simla, the Indian army's headquarters. As intelligence officer he accompanied the expedition for the relief of Chitral [q.v.], in which he was severely wounded and won the Distinguished Service Order.

He was promoted captain and, while recovering from his wounds, studied for the Staff College, to which he was admitted in 1896. He became the first ranker ever to be graduated. During the Second Anglo-Boer War [q.v.] he was sent to South Africa, where he served as intelligence officer at Lord Robert's headquarters. He advanced rank by rank up the promotion ladder, always as a staff officer, becoming quartermaster general of the British Expeditionary Force in 1914 and chief of staff in January 1915. From December 1915 to 1918 he was chief of the Imperial General Staff.

After the war, in 1919 and 1920, he was commander-in-chief of the British army on the Rhine. In 1920 he was made a field marshal. In 1926 he wrote *Soldiers and Statesmen, 1914–18.*

Robinson, John Cleveland (1817–1897). An American soldier who attended West Point (1835–38), but was not graduated, having been dismissed for violating a regulation and lying about it. However, on 27 October 1839 he received a direct commission as a second lieutenant in the 5th Infantry. He served in the Mexican War and the American Civil War. In April 1861 he commanded Fort McHenry and by his firmness cowed South-sympathizing rioters. In September he was appointed colonel of the 1st Michigan and the following spring was promoted brigadier general. He fought in the Peninsular Campaign and at Fredericksburg, Chancellorsville, and Gettysburg [qq.v.]. He was wounded at Laurel Hill, West Virginia, and lost his left leg at Spotsylvania [q.v.]. He won brevets to major general. A monument marks the spot on the battlefield at Gettysburg where he successfully defended his position against Confederate attacks.

After the war he directed the Freedmen's Bureau [q.v.] in North Carolina. In 1869 he retired from the army, and from 1872 to 1874 he was lieutenant governor of New York. In 1894 he was awarded the Medal of Honor for his gallantry at Spotsylvania. He was blind in the last years of his life.

Robres, Attack on Guerrillas at (April 1812), Peninsular War. At this Spanish village, thanks to the treachery of a subordinate guerrilla chief, the French were able to make a surprise attack upon Francisco Espoz y Mina [q.v.], an effective Spanish guerrilla who prevented thousands of French troops from joining the fight against Wellington. Espoz y Mina and a few of his men fled to La Rioja, but it had been a narrow escape. He later had the pleasure of hanging the chief who had betrayed him along with three alcaldes who had failed to warn him of his danger.

Rochambeau, Jean Baptiste Donatien de Vimeur (1725–1807). A French soldier who entered the army in 1742, served in the Battle of Maestricht (Maastricht), and distinguished himself in the Battle of Minorca in 1756. In 1780 he led a force of 6,000 to America to help the rebel Americans. In 1791 he was made a marshal of France. In 1803 he led a force to Haiti [q.v.] to quell a rebellion there [see Haitian Revolts].

Rockets. A missile propelled by hot gases ejected rearward by a burning charge. Rockets had been used in the Middle Ages and in China and India, but a British officer, William Congreve [q.v.], made a science of the weapons, which he described as "ammunition without ordnance, it is the soul of artillery without the body." His rockets were first used in combat in November 1805, when they were fired from a warship attacking Boulogne. Gale winds and rough seas made the effort a failure, but in September 1807 some 300 rockets were

Rockets
Details of the rockets employed in the system of William Congreve, 1814

fired effectively at Copenhagen [q.v.], and on 16 October 1813 one of Britain's two rocket batteries, commanded by a horse artillery captain, took part in the Battle of Leipzig [q.v.], where they were the only British on the field. During the War of 1812 [q.v.] British rockets scattered the Americans in the Battle of Bladensburg [q.v.] and when fired on Fort McHenry [q.v.] provided the "rocket's red glare" in the national anthem [see "Star-Spangled Banner, The"].

The Congreve rocket was versatile; it could carry solid shot, flares, shrapnel, or carcasses. Congreve made 12-pound, 18-pound, and 32-pound rockets, the largest having a maximum range of 3,500 yards. Eventually every European country, Egypt, and the United States had rocket units. Although Congreve predicted that the rocket was "an arm by which the whole system of military tactics is destined to be changed," there were serious disadvantages to nineteenth-century rockets; the behavior of the rockets, guided by a wooden stick at their base, was unpredictable. Naval Captain William Peel [q.v.], who had rockets with his naval brigade in India during the mutiny [q.v.], asked to comment on their effectiveness, said, "Well, you know rockets are rockets. If the enemy are only half as much afraid of them as we who fire them, they are doing good service."

Rock of Chickamauga. See Thomas, George Henry.

Rocky Face Ridge, Battle of. See Dalton, Battles of.

Rodman, Thomas Jackson (1815–1871). An American soldier who was graduated from West Point in 1841 and served in the Ordnance Department. In the 1840s he developed, in addition to the Rodman gun [q.v.], a pressure gauge for determining the pressure of explosive gas inside the bore of a gun and a black powder with improved propellant quality. During the American Civil War he commanded the Watertown Arsenal, and from 1865 to his death the Rock Island Arsenal.

Rodman Gun. An artillery piece whose barrel was cooled from the inside and coated with successive layers of metal, a process that greatly strengthened it and could be used in mak-

ing both smoothbores or rifled guns in a variety of calibers. The largest Rodman gun had a 20-inch bore, weighed 117,000 pounds, and fired a cast-iron shot weighing half a ton. Only two were made [see Columbiad]. The process was devised by an American army officer, Thomas Jackson Rodman [q.v.], in the 1840s, but was not officially adopted by the American army until 1859. Some of the guns were still in service in the 1890s.

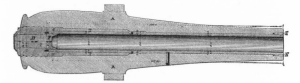

Rodman Gun *Ten-inch smoothbore Rodman gun*

Rogue River War (1850–56). In Oregon resistance to white settlers flared among the Indians settled in the Rogue River and Pitt River areas, chief among them the Umpquas, Modocs, and Klamaths. There were numerous Indian attacks upon campers, miners, and farmers and attacks by white settlers upon Indians. In August 1852 Modocs attacked an emigrant train of 33 people, killing them all. In response a volunteer company from California under Benjamin Wright [q.v.] and a volunteer company from Oregon under William Ross marched into Modoc country. After saving one wagon train besieged by Indians and killing a dozen of the besiegers, Wright took command of the combined force, which unsuccessfully scoured the country for Indians. Finally, in November, he sent a captured Indian woman to the chiefs with an invitation to peace talks and a feast. Those who accepted came under a flag of truce. After talk they sat down to feast on meat laced with strychnine, and when this seemed to have no effect, Wright pulled out his pistol and shot 2 of his guests. At the same time his men opened fire and killed 38; only 10 Indians escaped. When Wright and his men returned to the mining town of Eureka, California, they were given a hero's welcome, and the California legislature agreed to pay them for their services. The editor of the *Oregonian* probably reflected the views of many when, speaking of the Indians, he wrote (20 October 1855): "These inhuman butchers and bloody fiends must be met and conquered, vanquished—yes, EXTERMINATED." Wright's treachery has been credited with being the cause of the Modoc War [q.v.] that followed.

"Rogue's March, The." A tune played when an American or British soldier was drummed out of the service for dishonorable conduct [see Degradation].

Rockets *Early nineteenth-century rockets and rocket car.*

Roguet, François (1770–1846). A French soldier, the son of a locksmith, who enlisted in an infantry regiment in 1789. He was commissioned in 1793, and in 1803 he was promoted general of brigade. Early in 1807 he was wounded and captured in the Battle of Guttstadt. He was released after the Battle of Friedland [q.v.] on 10 June of the same year. He served briefly in Spain during the Peninsular War [q.v.] but was recalled to France to command the 2nd Grenadiers of the Imperial Guard. In 1809 he fought at Aspen-Essling and Wagram [qq.v.] and then returned to Spain, where he served from 1809 to 1812, being promoted general of division in 1811. In 1812 he took part in Napoleon's invasion of Russia [q.v.]. He was wounded at Dresden [q.v.] in August 1813. He rallied to Napoleon during the Hundred Days [q.v.] and fought at Waterloo [q.v.]. From 1815 to 1830 he was not employed, but from 1830 to 1839 he served on the general staff.

Rolfe, Ernest Neville (1847–1909). A British naval officer who in 1873 saw action in the Second Ashanti War [q.v.] and in 1874–76 on the Congo and Niger rivers. He commanded a naval brigade in the Sudan, serving under General Gerald Graham [q.v.], and fought in the Second Battle of El Teb [q.v.] on 29 March 1884. In 1885 he accompanied Admiral William Nathan Wright Hewett (1834–1888) on a mission to Abyssinia (Ethiopia) to arrange for the evacuation through that country of Egyptian garrisons in the eastern Sudan. Rolfe became a rear admiral in 1899 and retired as a full admiral in 1907.

Roliça, Battle of (17 August 1808), Peninsular War. In the hills above this central Portuguese town, 7 miles south-southwest of Caldas da Rainha and 40 miles north of Lisbon, Lieutenant General Arthur Wellesley, the future Duke of Wellington, won his first victory in the war. Commanding a British force of 13,500 and a Portuguese force of 1,350, he defeated French General Henri François Delaborde (1764–1833) with 4,400 men and five guns who had taken up a position barring the road to Lisbon. It was not, however, a well-fought battle by the British. One battalion commander misunderstood his orders and attacked alone; he was killed, and his battalion was cut to pieces. The Portuguese failed to come into action. The French withdrawal was skillful. The Allies lost 485 men; the French lost about 700 and three guns.

A feature of the battle was the first land use of shrapnel [q.v.], then called spherical case shot.

Roll Call. A calling out of the names of those in a unit followed by a response from those present. Roll calls after a battle determined the number of casualties. The most famous picture painted by Lady Butler [q.v.], *Roll Call*, depicts wounded and weary men at a postbattle roll call.

Roll of Honor. In 1862 the Congress of the Confederate States of America passed a law calling for a Roll of Honor to be published after every battle. The names of those who distinguished themselves were to be read on parade, included in official records, and published in newspapers, but this was seldom done.

Romagna, Insurrections in (1830–31 and 1859–60). The Papal State of Romagna (now comprising the Italian provinces of Folì, Ravenna, Bologna, and Ferrara) revolted in 1830, attempting to throw off the temporal authority of the pope. The revolt was suppressed by Austrian forces in 1831.

In July 1859, when the Austrian troops at last departed, the populace at once rose in revolt and sought to ally itself to the new Italy under Victor Emmanuel II (1820–1878). It was accepted in March 1860 and was added to the province of Emilia.

Romana, Marqués of La. See La Romana, Pedro Caro y Sureda.

Roman Nose (1830?–1868). A Cheyenne of the Crooked Lance warrior society whom Allison Plily [q.v.], an American soldier and scout, once described as "the finest specimen of manhood I ever saw." In battle Roman Nose wore a bonnet with a single horn rising over the center of his forehead and a long tail of eagle feathers falling behind, made for him by White Bull (1834–1921), a noted Cheyenne chief and medicine man. One of the prophecies associated with the bonnet warned that if he ever ate food that had been touched by metal, he would die in the next battle.

Roman Nose was generally peaceful until the Sand River Massacre [q.v.] in November 1864, after which he made numerous raids upon white settlers, stage lines, and work parties constructing the roadbed and laying track for the Union Pacific Railroad. He was among the Indians in the Battle of Beecher's Island [q.v.], although he refused to take part in their first charges, for he had learned that a few days earlier he had unknowingly eaten food that had touched metal. He finally agreed to lead one of their last charges and fell, mortally wounded.

Rome, Attacks on (29–30 April and 3–30 June 1849), Italian Wars of Independence. On 9 February 1849, after the pope had fled Rome, a republic of Rome was declared. To restore papal rule, the French dispatched 6,000 men under General Nicolas Charles Victor Oudinot (1791–1863), son of Marshal Nicolas Oudinot [q.v.]. The force landed at the port of Civitavecchia, 39 miles northwest of Rome, on 24 April and five days later attacked the city. It was repulsed by republican defenders under Giuseppe Garibaldi [q.v.] and lost 1,000 men.

After receiving 10,000 reinforcements, Oudinot attacked again on 3 June and was once more thrown back, although Garibaldi had only 8,000 to oppose him. He then laid siege and on 30 June attacked the Porta San Pancrazio. He was again repulsed, losing 300 killed or wounded and 500 taken prisoner; Garibaldi lost 120. The Italians held out for another month until 2 July, when after making terms, Garibaldi surrendered and marched 5,000 men out of the city, ending the Roman republic. Marching northward, Garibaldi's army was attacked and dispersed by Austrian troops.

Roncesvalles, Battle of. See Maya, Battle of.

Rondel / Rondelle. In fortifications, a round tower sometimes located at the foot of a bastion.

Ronin. Japanese samurai [q.v.] who had either lost or left their daiymos [q.v.] and served as soldiers of fortune.

Roon, Albrecht Theodor Emil von (1803–1879). A Prussian soldier and statesman who was commissioned in

1821 on graduation from the Berlin Cadet School. From 1824 to 1827 he attended the Kriegsakademie in Berlin. He was minister of war from 1859 to 1873 and became famous as one of the architects of the efficient Prussian army and made possible its rapid mobilization for the Seven Weeks' War and the Franco-Prussian War [qq.v.]. He was made a field marshal in 1873.

Roosevelt, Theodore (1858–1919). An American politician and soldier who in 1897–98 was assistant secretary of the navy, a post he resigned at the outbreak of the Spanish-American War [q.v.] in order to form a volunteer cavalry regiment that came to be known as Roosevelt's Rough Riders [q.v.], although initially he served as a lieutenant colonel under Colonel Leonard Wood [q.v.]. In Cuba the Rough Riders saw action at Las Guásimas and won fame by charging on foot up San Juan Hill [qq.v.], actually nearby Kettle Hill. After the war he became successively governor of New York, vice president, and president of the United States. During World War I, in spite of his age, Roosevelt tried again without success to serve as a soldier.

Root, Elihu (1845–1937). An American lawyer and statesman who was secretary of war from 1899 to 1904. He found the War Department in a chaotic state with much conflict between the various bureaus. He established order, developed a system of promotion by merit, and put in place efficient administrative systems. He created a general staff and established the Army War College. Root's shibboleth was: "If you want peace, prepare for war." He later became a senator, then secretary of state; he won the Nobel Peace Prize in 1912 and occupied himself with numerous public-spirited activities, including leading a mission to Bolshevik Russia during World War I.

Rooty. In India, British soldier slang for bread. From the Urdu word *roti*.

Rorke's Drift, Battle of (22–23 January 1879), Zulu War. In a mission station at a drift (ford) of the Buffalo River 25 miles southeast of Dundee in South Africa, the British army invading Zululand had established a small hospital defended by 139 British soldiers, 35 of whom were sick. (A mission station still stands there, but the original structures have been demolished.) Attacked by a Zulu impi 4,000 strong led by Dabulamanzi (d. 1886), a half brother of Cetewayo [q.v.], the small force withstood repeated assaults for twelve hours until the exhausted Zulus withdrew. [see Zulu War; Isandhlwana, Battle of; Chelmsford, Second Baron Frederick Augustus.]

No fewer than 11 men were awarded the Victoria Cross [q.v.] for their bravery here, the largest number ever awarded for a single action. Among the recipients were the 2 officers present: Lieutenant John Rouse Merriot Chard [q.v.], an Engineer officer, and Lieutenant Granville Bromhead [q.v.] of the 24th Foot (later South Wales Borderers). Nine Distinguished Conduct Medals were also awarded. The British lost 17 killed and 10 wounded; the Zulus an estimated 400.

Rorke's Drift *The scene after the defense of Rorke's Drift by Lieutenants Chard and Bromhead during the Zulu War*

Rosas, Juan Manuel de (1793–1877). An Argentine soldier and dictator. He left his parents at an early age and became a vaquero, or cowboy. He later purchased a cattle ranch and because of the chaotic condition of the country following independence from Spain, he was given permission to arm his gauchos (cowboys of mixed European and Indian descent). Under his direction they were molded into the most efficient fighting force in the country, and with this small army Rosas became the dominant figure in the province of Buenos Aires. He was elected governor in 1829 and served until 1831. In 1835, after conducting a successful campaign against indigenous Indians in Patagonia, he was again elected governor, and from 1839 to 1852 he retained power without the formality of elections. After the other Argentine provinces had joined Buenos Aires in a loose confederation, he, while nominally the governor of only Buenos Aires, managed to wield power over all of them through calculated terror, ruling the confederation as if it were a large plantation and he its owner. Allying himself with General Manuel Oribe [q.v.], the exiled president of Uruguay, he tried to conquer all Uruguay but was unable to capture Montevideo [see Montevideo, Siege of]. Through his tyranny he provoked Justo Urquiza [q.v.], his former lieutenant, whom he had made governor of Entre Ríos Province, to revolt. Urquiza formed an alliance with Brazil and defeated Rosas on 3 February 1852 in the Battle of Caseros [q.v.]. Rosas fled to England and settled on a farm at Swaythling (now a residential suburb of Southampton), where he remained from 1852 to his death on 17 March 1877.

Rosas, Siege of (7–26 November 1808), Peninsular War. French and Italian forces under Laurent St. Cyr [q.v.] besieged and captured the fort of Rosas, on the northeast coast of Spain south of Cape Creus. The fort was defended by 3,000 Spanish and supported by the Royal Navy, but siege batteries destroyed the defenses.

Rosebud Creek, Battle of (17 June 1876), Great Sioux War. In the northern Bighorn Mountains, along Rosebud Creek, a 100-mile-long stream in southeast Montana that flows into the Yellowstone River, near present-day Sheridan, Wyoming, about 1,500 hostile Indians, mostly Sioux and Cheyennes, under Crazy Horse [q.v.] and other Indian leaders, attacked 1,200 troops (elements of the 4th and 9th Infantry and the 2nd and 3rd Cavalry) and 250 Crow and Shoshone auxiliaries, all under General George Crook [q.v.]. After six hours of hard fighting over a broad area of rugged terrain the Indians withdrew in good order. Crook did not pursue but retreated to his base camp along Goose Creek in Wyoming for fresh supplies. He lost 10 killed and 34 wounded; Indian losses were 39 killed and 63 wounded.

Crook claimed a victory, but he was much criticized for his poor generalship in this battle, and many even blamed him for Custer's defeat eight days later in the Battle of the Little Bighorn [q.v.], claiming his retreat had raised Indian morale.

Rosecrans, William Starke (1819–1898). An American soldier who had little formal education but was an avid reader and gained an appointment to West Point, from which he was graduated in 1842, fifth in his class. After serving ten years in the Corps of Engineers on routine frontier duties, he resigned from the army in 1854 and went into business. In 1861, at the outbreak of the American Civil War, he was manager of a kerosene refinery in Cincinnati, Ohio. In June of that year he was made colonel of the 23rd Ohio and then a brigadier general, to rank from 16 May. In the same year he succeeded General George McClellan [q.v.] as commander of the Department of West Virginia. In 1862 he was promoted major general of volunteers and succeeded General John Pope as commander of the Army of the Mississippi. He defeated the Confederate forces in the Battle of Murfreesboro [q.v.] on 31 December 1862 and 2 January 1863, but he was defeated in the Battle of Chickamauga [q.v.] the following September and was relieved of his command. He resigned from the army in 1867 and served as U.S. minister to Mexico (1868–69), member of Congress (1881–85), and registrar of the U.S. Treasury (1885–93). He then retired to his ranch near present-day Redondo Beach, California, where he complained of oil seeping into his well water, little realizing the wealth it foretold.

Rose, Hugh Henry (1801–1885). A British soldier who was born in Berlin and received military instruction from Prussian officers. He was commissioned in the British army in 1820, and from 1824 to 1833 he earned a reputation by suppressing illegal activities in Ireland. In 1840 he was military

attaché to the Turkish army, and from 1841 to 1848 he was consul general for Syria. He was chargé d'affaires in Constantinople (Istanbul) in 1853, when General Aleksandr Menshikov [q.v.] demanded that Turkey sign an agreement giving Russia control over Christians in the Turkish Empire. Rose was informed and called for the British fleet, precipitating a crisis that helped bring on the Crimean War [q.v.], during which he served as a liaison with French headquarters.

In 1857 he was sent to India on the outbreak of the Indian Mutiny [q.v.] and there defeated Tantia Topi [q.v.], captured Jhansi, and virtually reconquered central India. In 1860 he succeeded Lord Clyde (Colin Campbell [q.v.]) as commander-in-chief, India, a post he held for five years. In 1865 he was promoted lieutenant general and made commander-in-chief, Ireland, where he successfully suppressed Irish Fenians for five years. In 1866 he was raised to the peerage as Baron Strathnairn. He was made a general in 1867 and a field marshal the following year.

Ross, John (1790–1866), Indian name: Koweskoowe. An American Indian chief, who was the son of a Scottish father and a part Cherokee Indian mother. He was president of the national council of Cherokees in 1819–26, and from 1829 to 1839 he was chief of the eastern Cherokees. He served with Andrew Jackson in the Creek War [q.v.]. Although he resisted the removal of the Cherokees to Indian Territory west of the Mississippi River, in December 1838 he led the last party of his tribe to the territory; 4,000 died en route [see Trail of Tears]. From 1839 to his death he was chief of the United Cherokee Nation.

During the American Civil War he tried to remain neutral, but in October 1861 he signed a treaty with the Confederacy. The following year he allied himself with the Union, and in March 1862 he led his warriors against Confederates in the Battle of Pea Ridge [q.v.]. In retaliation for his defection from the Confederacy his house was burned by Colonel Stand Watie [q.v.].

Ross, Robert (1766–1814). A British soldier who attended Trinity College in Dublin and in 1789 was commissioned an ensign in the 25th Foot. In 1799 he saw action in Holland and was wounded in the Battle of Krabbendam (Zyper Sluis). In 1801 he was in Egypt and distinguished himself leading a bayonet charge against the French at Alexandria [q.v.] on 25 August. In November–December 1805 he served under Sir James Henry Craig (1748–1812) in the abortive Anglo-Russian expedition to Naples [q.v.]. In 1808 he served in the Corunna Campaign [see Corunna, Battle of] of Sir John Moore [q.v.], and from 1812 to 1814 he served under Wellington in the Peninsular War [q.v.]. In June 1813 he was promoted major general. When he was wounded in the Battle of Orthez [q.v.] on 27 February 1814, his wife, Elizabeth, whom he had married in 1802, made her way from Bilbao over snow-filled mountain passes to nurse him.

Three months later, promising his wife that this would be his last campaign, he left for the West Indies and America to command the expeditionary force in cooperation with Admiral Sir Alexander Forrester Inglis Cochrane (1758–1832), which, during the War of 1812 [q.v.], made forays on the coasts of the United States. The purpose of the expedition, the chancellor of the exchequer told the House of Commons, was "to retaliate upon the Americans for the outrages they have committed upon the frontiers."

On 19 August 1814 Ross with 4,500 soldiers and marines landed at Benedict, Maryland, a fishing village on the Patuxent River, 33 miles southeast of Washington, D.C. He defeated the Americans in the Battle of Bladensburg [q.v.] on 24 August, and that night and the following day he burned public buildings in Washington, D.C. [q.v.]. He was mortally wounded on 12 September in a skirmish with American militia at North Point (now Fort Howard Park in Greater Baltimore), Maryland, then a village 12 miles southeast of Baltimore. A monument to him, raised at public expense, was placed in St. Paul's Cathedral in London. The prince regent gave his widow and all direct descendants through the male line the distinction of calling themselves Ross of Bladensburg "as a memorial of his loyalty, ability and valour." (The last descendants so entitled died in the 1960s.)

Rosser, Thomas Lafayette (1836–1910). An American soldier appointed to West Point in 1856. On 22 April 1861, two weeks before graduation, he resigned to be commissioned a first lieutenant in the Confederate army. In the First Battle of Bull Run he commanded a battery. After recovering from a wound received in the Battle of Mechanicsville [q.v.], he was appointed colonel of the 5th Virginia Cavalry on the strong recommendation of General J. E. B. Stuart [q.v.]. He was again wounded at Kelly's Ford but retained his command and was promoted brigadier general to rank from 28 September 1863. He replaced Beverly Robertson [q.v.] as commander of the Laurel Brigade [q.v.]. On 1 November 1864 he was promoted major general. His former classmate George Custer [q.v.] defeated him at Cedar Creek [q.v.] and Tom's Brook, but he made two successful raids into West Virginia, and in the spring of 1865 he was at Petersburg, Virginia [see Petersburg Campaign; Hampton-Rosser Cattle Raid]. He fought at Five Forks [q.v.] and was in the retreat to Appomattox. There he refused to surrender and cut his way clear. He was captured on 2 May near Hanover Court House but was soon paroled.

After the war he acquired considerable wealth and was named chief engineer of the Northern Pacific and Canadian Pacific railroads. He later became a gentleman farmer near Charlottesville, Virginia. At the beginning of the Spanish-American War, on 10 June 1898, he was commissioned a brigadier general of volunteers but was mustered out on 31 October.

Rostopchin, Fëdor Vasilievich (1763–1826). A Russian soldier, politician, and writer who served as an aide to Tsar Paul I (1754–1801) and as a general was made grand marshal of the palace. He was disgraced in 1801 for opposing the alliance with Napoleon but was restored to favor nine years later. In 1812 he was governor of Moscow and is believed by some to have given the orders for the city to be burned when Napoleon entered, although he denied this [see Russian Campaign, Napoleon's]. He wrote a number of historical memoirs and plays.

Rough Rider. 1. In the British cavalry and artillery, a non-commissioned officer whose duty it was to break refractory horses and assist the riding master. He wore a spur badge on his arm.

2. In the American service, a member of the volunteer regiment [see Rough Riders] formed for the Spanish-American War [q.v.].

Rough Riders. Officially the 1st United States Cavalry Volunteers. The unit was raised at the outbreak of the Spanish-American War [q.v.] by Theodore Roosevelt [q.v.], who became its first lieutenant colonel and later its colonel. The Rough Riders were composed of cowboys, hunters, sportsmen, and adventurous athletic college students, whose motto was: "Rough-tough, we're the stuff! We want to fight and we can't get enough!" They were led to Cuba by Colonel Leonard Wood [q.v.]. Because there was no room on the ships for horses, they were left behind. The unit first saw action in the Battle of Las Guásimas [q.v.], in which it suffered 8 killed and 34 wounded. In the course of the war in Cuba it suffered 87 casualties. It became famous for its charge up Kettle Hill, a small height in front of the San Juan ridge, an action that made headlines across the United States as the charge up San Juan Hill [see San Juan Hill, Battle of]. The unit held annual reunions until 1969, when only 3 Rough Riders were left and 2 of them were too feeble to celebrate.

Rough Riders *Although this popular print depicts Lieutenant Colonel Theodore Roosevelt of the Rough Riders at San Juan Hill, he and his men fought dismounted at Kettle Hill.*

Round. 1. A single unit of ammunition, including projectile and propellant.

2. A single shot fired by a soldier or by each man in a unit.

Round, Gentleman of the. In British usage, a disbanded or discharged soldier who had taken to begging.

Rousseau, Lovell Harrison (1818–1869). An American lawyer, legislator, and soldier. One of the leading lawyers in Louisville, Kentucky, and a member of the state legislature, he fought successfully to keep his state in the Union during the American Civil War. He was commissioned colonel of the 3rd Kentucky on 9 September 1861, and on 1 October he was promoted brigadier general. A year later he was a major general. During the Atlanta Campaign [q.v.], on 9–22 July 1864, he left Decatur, Alabama, with 2,500 cavalry, and at Opelika, in eastern Alabama, destroyed the rail junction linking Montgomery, Alabama, and Columbus, Georgia. He returned safely to the Union lines at Marietta by way of Carrollton, Georgia. He resigned on 30 November 1865 to become a U.S. representative. In 1867 he returned to the army as a brigadier general and was sent to Alaska to receive the territory recently purchased from the Russians. He died on active duty as commander of the Department of Louisiana.

Roustam, Raza (1780–1845). An Armenian who became Napoleon's valet and bodyguard. He had been kidnapped at the age of seven and sold as a Mameluke slave. In June 1799 the leading sheikh in Cairo presented him to Napoleon, along with a black stallion. For fifteen years he remained at his master's side always dressed in Mameluke costume. At Napoleon's first abdication at Fontainebleau, he deserted and went into hiding. He later married a French woman, lived for a time in London, and appeared in Paris on 14–15 December 1840 for the interment of Napoleon's remains [q.v.] in the Hôtel des Invalides [q.v.] when they were brought back from St. Helena.

Rout. 1. As a noun, a disastrous defeat, a debacle in which the defeated flee in confusion. As Homer put into the mouth of Ajax, "When soldiers break and run, good-bye glory, good-bye all defenses" (*Iliad*, xv).

2. As a verb, to inflict a defeat that causes the enemy to flee in disarray.

Route March. 1. An ordinary march, usually of less than 20 miles for infantry.

2. A march in which troops are allowed to march in route step.

Route Step. A relaxed manner of march in which soldiers are not required to keep in step. They can talk, sing, smoke, and hold their weapons in the most comfortable or convenient way, but relative positions are maintained.

Rovigo, Duke of. See Savary, Anne Jean Marie René.

Rowan, Andrew Summers (1857–1944). An American soldier who was graduated from West Point in 1881 in the bottom third of his class and later earned lasting renown as the man who carried "The Message to García" [q.v.]. From his graduation to 1889 he served on the frontier. In 1890 he was promoted first lieutenant and in that year made a covert reconnaissance of the Canadian Pacific Railroad, collecting information on the line and on the countryside. In 1891–92 he did survey work in Central America for the Intercontinental Railway Commission. In April 1898 he was appointed military attaché in Chile but was immediately detached to carry a message to Cuban insurgent General Calixto García y Iñigues [q.v.], inquiring how much support American forces could expect from the rebels if there were an American invasion of Cuba.

Lieutenant Rowan left Washington in civilian clothes on 8 April 1898 and sailed first to Jamaica, from which, guided by Cuban rebels, he set out in a fishing boat on the 100-mile voyage to Torquino in Oriente Bay, which he reached on 24 April, two days after the U.S. declaration of war. He was thus the first American soldier to land on hostile soil in the Spanish-American War [q.v.]. He was met by guides who took him inland by a jungle trail; at one point he nar-

rowly escaped capture or death at the hands of Spanish soldiers. On 1 May 1898 he reached Bayamo, on the Bayamo River, 27 miles east of Manzanillo, and there met fifty-eight-year-old García and received his reply, promising support. Rowan at once started back, carrying with him a rebel delegation. Sailing from Manatí Bay in a leaky boat on 5 May, the little party reached Andros Island in the Bahamas two days later. A sponging schooner sent word to the American consul in the Bahamas, and they were soon on their way to Key West, which they reached on the 13th. Two days later they were in Washington, D.C.

Rowan was decorated with the Distinguished Service Cross, the second-highest American award for bravery and was made famous by Elbert Hubbard (1856–1915) who, in his "Message to García," used Rowan's exploit as an example of persistence in the face of difficulties. Hubbard's essay sold an estimated one hundred million copies in twenty languages.

During the Spanish-American War [q.v.] Rowan served as a lieutenant colonel of volunteers. During the Philippine insurrection [q.v.] he was awarded the Silver Star Certificate for his gallantry in an attack upon Sublon Mountain, in which he was wounded. In 1909, because of ill health, he resigned with the rank of major.

Rowanty Creek, Battle of. See Dabney's Mill, Battle of.

Rowtee / Routee. A small tent with a pyramidal roof, closed at one end with a flap to keep out rain. It was frequently used by officers in India.

Royal Blue. The color of the facings of royal regiments in the British army. It was a deep blue, almost blue-black.

Royal Cambridge Asylum for Soldiers' Widows. A favorite charity of the Duke of Cambridge [q.v.], who for nearly forty years was commander-in-chief of the British army. It was founded in 1891 with contributed funds of £26,000 and is still flourishing, receiving funds from the Royal Tournament [q.v.], which was held annually at Olympia until 1906 and now takes place at Earl's Court Exhibition Hall in London.

Royal Hospital, Chelsea. See Chelsea Hospital.

Royal Humane Society Medal. A medal awarded for saving a life while exposed to danger. It has been given since 1774, the year the Humane Society was formed in London. In the nineteenth century it was "recognized" by the War Office and could be worn by soldiers but, unlike all other medals, on the right breast only.

Royal Military Academy, Woolwich. A British military college established in what is now a metropolitan borough of London by royal warrant signed on 30 April 1741 by King George II (1683–1760) to instruct "inexperienced people . . . in the several parts of Mathematics necessary to qualify them for the service of Artillery, and the business of Engineers." Those who were graduated in the top third of their class became engineers, and the remainder passed into the artillery. It was usually referred to as simply Woolwich or The Shop. From 1828 to 1849 Michael Faraday (1791–1867), famous for discoveries in electricity and magnetism, lectured there.

In 1836 the first Sword of Honour was awarded to the top cadet for "exemplary conduct." In 1897 the first Queen's Medal was bestowed on the cadet best qualified in military subjects and, after the Addiscombe Seminary [q.v.] had been abolished, its Pollock Medal [q.v.] was annually awarded to an outstanding Woolwich cadet. In 1947 Woolwich merged with the Royal Military College, Sandhurst [q.v.], to become the Royal Military Academy, Sandhurst.

Royal Military College, Sandhurst. A British military college founded by royal warrant of King George III (1738–1820) on 24 June 1801 to train officers for the infantry and cavalry. Before the college buildings were completed in 1812 at Sandhurst, Berkshire, the school was opened in 1802 at High Wycombe and Great Meadow. Originally there were two departments, junior and senior, but in time the senior department separated and became the staff college.

Cadets were drawn from the upper and middle social classes from the beginning. Prince Albert (1819–1861) approved. In 1836 he wrote: "The suggestion that I recommend is, therefore, to get gentlemen with a gentleman's education from the public schools and do away with your military schools for boys as a competing nursery for the army. Test their qualifications and give them two years at a military college." His suggestion was adopted. In 1891 of 373 cadets, 237 came from leading public schools: 37 from Wellington, 29 from Eton, 16 each from Marlborough and Harrow. Only 34 came from universities and 33 came from "private schools and tutors."

The "gentlemen cadets" in the junior department were known at times to be fractious. In 1862, protesting the bad food, they mutinied and barricaded themselves for three days, throwing rock-hard bread rolls at attackers. The Duke of Cambridge [q.v.], commander-in-chief of the army, came down from London to persuade them to return to their studies.

Unlike the classes at West Point, the courses were short, usually one or two years at most, and the accent was upon military subjects, although, except for horsemanship, most of the teaching was in the classroom. Rifle shooting was not compulsory until 1891.

In 1890 the first Sword of Honour was presented to an outstanding cadet, and in 1897 the Queen's Medal was awarded to the cadet best qualified in military subjects, following the custom at the Royal Military Academy, Woolwich [q.v.]. In 1947 the college merged with the Royal Military Academy, Woolwich, to become the Royal Military Academy, Sandhurst.

Royal Niger Company. A large trading company in Nigeria chartered in 1886 by George Goldie (1846–1925). It had its own administration and its own army, which fought small wars with West Africans. Although not a commercial success, it expanded British influence in West Africa. Its charter was withdrawn in 1900.

Royal Sappers and Miners. A British corps formed in 1772 to build fortifications at Gibraltar. It was absorbed into the Royal Engineers in October 1856. The unit was a collection of specialists in many fields—stonecutters, masons, carpenters, miners, smiths, and gardeners—and it never operated as a body.

Royal Tournament. A British military show begun in 1870 as a training competition to promote proficiency in military skills. It became so popular with the public that by the end of the century a committee had been formed to coordinate the spectacle, which included tent-pitching contests and displays of swordsmanship. It remains an annual event, held until 1906 at Olympia and now at Earl's Court Exhibition Hall in London.

Ruba. A unit of about 500 men in the Mahdist army in the Sudan [see Mahdya]. It was commanded by an amin [q.v.].

Rudiger, Fëdor Vasilievich (1784–1856). A Russian general who fought in the wars against Napoleon in 1812 and 1814, and in the Russo-Turkish War of 1828–29 [q.v.]. He aided in the suppression of the Polish Revolution [q.v.] in 1830–31, and when Russia, at Austria's request, helped suppress the Hungarian Revolution [q.v.] in 1849, he received the surrender of Arthur von Görgey [q.v.] at Világos [q.v.], an action that broke the backbone of the revolution.

Ruffin, François Aimable (1771–1811). A French soldier who enlisted in 1792 and two days later was elected a captain. A month later he was a lieutenant colonel. In 1805 he was promoted general of brigade and fought at Austerlitz [q.v.]. In 1807 he became general of division and was sent to Spain to fight in the Peninsular War [q.v.]. He fought in the battles of Somosierra and Talavera [qq.v.] and was mortally wounded and taken prisoner in the Battle of Barrosa [q.v.] on 15 March 1811.

Ruffles and Flourishes. A method of honoring dignitaries. A ruffle is a low, vibrating drumbeat, and a flourish is a short bugle call.

Ruger, Thomas Howard (1833–1907). An American soldier who was graduated from West Point in 1854 but resigned after one year and became a lawyer in Wisconsin. On 29 June 1861, at the beginning of the American Civil War, he reentered the service as lieutenant colonel of the 3rd Wisconsin; he became its colonel in September. He served under Nathaniel Banks [q.v.] in the Shenandoah Valley of Virginia, and on 17 September he was wounded in the Battle of Antietam [q.v.], in which he commanded a brigade. He recovered in time to take part in the Battle of Chancellorsville [q.v.]. He was promoted brigadier general, to rank from 29 November 1862, and at Gettysburg [q.v.] he commanded a division. In August he took part in re-storing order during the draft riots [q.v.] in New York City. Transferred to the western theater, he commanded a division in the bloody Battle of Franklin [q.v.], in which his gallantry earned him a brevet to major general of volunteers. In the closing battles of the war he served under General William Tecumseh Sherman [q.v.]. After the war he served as colonel of the 33rd Infantry, and from 1871 to 1876 he was superintendent at West Point. He was promoted brigadier general in 1886 and major general in 1895. He retired in 1897.

Rugga-Rugga. Carriers (porters) for troops in East Africa, some of whom were given military training.

Rumanian Mannlicher Rifle. A bolt-action 6.5 mm rifle that was first adopted by the Rumanian army in 1862. The

Dutch Mannlicher Model 1895 was almost a copy of the improved Rumanian 1893 model. Both had nondetachable box magazines that carried five rounds.

Rum Rebellion (1808–10). John MacArthur (1767–1834), an English-born former British army officer, emigrated to Australia with his wife and son in 1789 and settled in New South Wales, where he virtually created the wool trade and established the Australian wine industry. Trouble began when, in August 1805, Captain William Bligh (1754?–1817), famous as the survivor of the mutiny on his ship HMS *Bounty,* was appointed captain general and governor of the colony. He launched a crusade against the liquor traffic and ordered distilleries closed. This was more than a hardship for drinkers and liquor merchants, for there was a shortage of currency in the colony, and rum was often used as a medium of exchange. In 1807 MacArthur was the instigator of a rebellion against the government's laws on rum. He was arrested and on 25 January 1808 tried in Sydney and acquitted, but his cause was joined by British soldiers stationed in New South Wales, and on the day after the trial Major George Johnson of the 102nd Foot arrested Bligh, who was imprisoned for more than two years; he was not released until March 1810. Remarkably the rebellion ended without bloodshed, although in 1811 Major Johnson was court-martialed and cashiered.

Runner. A soldier or civilian who acts as a messenger.

Running Battle. A battle that continues as one side retreats while the other advances.

Running Fire. A feu de joie [q.v.].

Ruse-de-Guerre. A stratagem or trick to deceive the enemy as to one's intentions. Sun Tzu, the legendary sixth-century Chinese general and first military writer, most accurately described a ruse-de-guerre:

Runner *An African runner given a message to deliver during the Boer War*

"When capable, feign incapacity; when active, inactivity. When near, make it appear that you are far away; when far away that you are near. Offer the enemy a bait to lure him; feign disorder and strike him. When he concentrates, prepare against him; where he is strong, avoid him. Anger his general and confuse him. Pretend inferiority and encourage his arrogance. Keep him under strain and wear him down. When he is united, divide him. Attack where he is unprepared; sally out when he does not expect you. These are the strategist's keys to victory." (*The Art of War*)

In more modern times ruses often involve deceiving journalists or one's own troops, as did Garnet Wolseley in Egypt during Arabi's Revolt [q.v.]. In *The Soldier's Pocket Book* (1869) Wolseley wrote: "We are bred up to feel it is a disgrace even to succeed by falsehood . . . we will keep hammering along that honesty is the best policy, and that truth always wins in the long run. These pretty little sentiments do well for a child's copy-book, but a man who acts on them had better sheathe his sword forever."

Rusk, Jeremiah McLain (1830–1893). A man of many parts who, before the American Civil War, was a stagecoach driver, construction foreman on a railroad, tavern keeper, and sheriff, among other things. A coroner when the war broke out, he joined the Union army, was made an officer, and won a brevet to brigadier general. After the war he became successively a congressman, governor of Wisconsin (1882–89), and finally U.S. secretary of agriculture from 1889 until his death.

Rusk, Thomas Jefferson (1803–1857). A Texan politician and soldier. In 1836 he was secretary of war of the provisional government of Texas. He fought in the Battle of San Jacinto [q.v.] and commanded the army after Sam Houston [q.v.] was wounded. In December 1838 he became the first chief justice of Texas and in that position took an active part in furthering the annexation of Texas by the United States. In 1839 he commanded the troops that expelled the Cherokees from Texas. In 1843 he was appointed a major general in the militia. From 1846 to 1857 he was a U.S. senator from Texas. Despondent after the death of his wife, he committed suicide.

Russell, George William (1790–1846). A British soldier, the second son of the Duke of Bedford. He entered the army in 1806 as a cornet in the 1st Dragoons, and in 1808 he fought in the Peninsular War with his regiment. In 1812 he became aide-de-camp to Wellington and took part in the battles of Vitoria, Orthez, and Toulouse [qq.v.]. In 1824 he obtained command of the 8th (Royal Irish) Hussars. He retired on half pay in 1828, but his retirement did not end his advancement, and he became a major general in 1841. The remainder of his career was in the diplomatic service.

Russell, Thomas (1767–1803). A British soldier and Irish revolutionary. After serving for a time in India, he returned to Ireland and helped organize the United Irish Party in Dublin, for which he was arrested and imprisoned. In 1803 with Robert Emmet (1778–1803) he attempted unsuccessfully to incite an uprising [see Emmet's Insurrection]. Both men were convicted of high treason and hanged.

Russell, William Howard (1820–1907). An Irish war correspondent who joined *The Times* (London) in 1843. He became famous for his dispatches from the Crimea [see Crimean War], in which he revealed the suffering of British soldiers as a result of poor planning and red tape. He covered the Indian Mutiny [q.v.], and in 1860 he established the *Army and Navy Gazette,* for which he covered the American Civil War, the Seven Weeks' War, the Franco-Prussian War, and the Zulu War [qq.v.].

Russian Army. The first Russian standing army was established in the early eighteenth century by Peter the Great (1672–1725). At the same time conscription of serfs was introduced. Landowners were required to furnish a quota, usually one per so many chimneys, or families, a system that not only produced recruits but enabled estate owners to rid themselves of undesirables. Service was for twenty-five years in the infantry, and only one in three conscripts survived to retire.

Throughout the nineteenth century the Russian army was the largest in Europe. Military colleges were established, and a military bureaucracy worked reasonably well, but Tsar Nicholas I [q.v.], and his two leading generals—Hans Diebitsch and Ivan Paskevich [qq.v.]—were overly conservative, and in 1810, when Baron Barclay de Tolly [q.v.] was appointed war minister, he found an army supplied with obsolete equipment and guns, practicing tactics that were unsuited to an era of superior weapons. The new war minister immediately began an overhaul, and by 1812, when Napoleon began his Russian Campaign [q.v.], Barclay de Tolly had accomplished much, particularly in the infantry, where the raw material was excellent. British Major General Sir Robert Wilson [q.v.] had only praise for the Russian infantrymen. They were, he said, "inured to the extremes of weather and hardships . . . accustomed to laborious toils and the carriage of heavy burdens; ferocious, but disciplined; obstinately brave . . . devoted to their sovereign, their chief, and their country."

In all nineteenth-century armies diseases killed far more men than enemy bullets, but such losses in the Russian army were the greatest. In 1851, out of an army of 994,317 men, 40,450 died. Of these, 247 were suicides, 347 were killed in battle or died of wounds, and 39,831 died of diseases.

The serfs were liberated on 9 February 1861, but the necessary military reforms resulting from the act were not implemented until a decree of 1 January 1874 established that all Russian males over the age of twenty were obligated to perform military service [see Conscription].

A large number of Prussian, French, and other foreigners served as officers in the Russian army for most of the century, but by 1880 a strong prejudice had developed against non-Russian officers and non-Russian ways. By 1882 the entire army was uniformed in the "Russian peasant" style, with baggy trousers tucked into knee-high boots.

In peacetime the army acted as such for only four to six months a year. In the remaining months its soldiers were scattered about in villages and were permitted to take odd jobs. It was a religious army. Each company had its own icon and established an icon fund to pay for repainting and for candles. There were prayers twice a day, and mass was said every Wednesday and Sunday. It was a clean army for its time. A soldier was required to wash his hands and face once a day, shave every third or fourth day, and bathe once a week. Discipline was ferocious, but an officer beating a soldier with a stick could not legally deliver more than twenty-five blows in one day. Private soldiers addressing officers had to kneel.

Most of the officers were nobles, and few were trained for their profession. Although some came from military schools and a cadet corps (abolished in 1863) and a few from deserving noncommissioned officers, most were simply the ill-educated offspring of the Russian nobility. In 1863 fewer than 6 percent were not ennobled.

Among special units were the *opolchenie* [q.v.], a militia that, although it was essentially a labor corps, did good service at Borodino [q.v.]; the Cossacks [q.v.], a unique element in the army, particularly useful in the Caucasus and in harassing the French army in its retreat from Moscow in 1812 [see Russian Campaign, Napoleon's]; and so-called native troops

(*inorodtsy*), which were made up mostly of tribesmen from the Caucasus or Central Asia.

At the beginning of the nineteenth century Russia was, as it is still, geographically the largest country in the world, and in the course of the century it grew larger, thanks to its military activity, principally in the Caucasus and Central Asia. In 1800 Georgia was annexed and through almost continuous fighting, by 1870 the remainder of the Caucasus [see Murid War; Shamyl; Russo-Turkish Wars; Russo-Persian Wars] had been added to the empire. Bessarabia was acquired in 1812, and in the 1840s and 1850s Russia conquered the lands of present-day Kazakhstan, Uzbekistan, and Tadjikistan; and in 1881 Turkmenistan [see Bokhara, Conquest of; Kaufmann, Konstantin Petrovich; Great Game, the; Khiva, Russian Conquest of; Khokand, Russian Conquest of; Tekke Campaign, Russian] was incorporated. Finland came under Russian control in 1809, and the duchy of Warsaw in 1815. The only Russian land given up was Alaska, sold to the United States in 1867.

Russia's population and thus its military manpower resources also increased dramatically from about 30 million in 1800 to about 70 million in 1850 to 124 million by 1897. Even by 1900 some four-fifths were peasants, who made the best infantry for the era.

Russian Campaign, Napoleon's (May–December 1812). In the spring of 1812 Napoleon's Grande Armée, concentrated in Poland between Danzig and Warsaw, consisted of nearly 450,000 men, fewer than half of whom were French; the remainder were Germans, Austrians, Poles, and Italians. They were organized into four main bodies: a main striking force of 382,000 men, commanded by Napoleon himself; a flanking force of 32,000 men, mostly Prussians, under Marshal Jacques Macdonald [q.v.], on the left or northern flank; another force of 33,000 under Prussian Field Marshal Karl Philip von Schwarzenberg was on the south or right flank; and a reserve of 226,000 men east of the Oder River. In all, about 675,000 men and 1,393 guns.

The greatest organizational concept of Napoleon was the army corps, each almost a self-contained army in itself. The largest and best prepared for the Russian Campaign was that of Marshal Louis Davout [q.v.], which achieved a remarkable degree of self-sufficiency. It consisted of 72,000 men of all arms. In his knapsack each man carried spare clothes, housewives, cleaning equipment, bandages, sixty rounds of ammunition, biscuits, flour, and bread. The corp's transport also carried supplies sufficient for twenty-five days. Each regiment had its own masons, millers, tailors, gunsmiths, carpenters, and other artisans and specialists.

In the whole of the French army there were 107 infantry regiments of the line, mostly armed with 1777 pattern flintlock muskets fitted with triangular-shaped socket bayonets. Some of the thirty-one regiments of light infantry were armed with somewhat more accurate rifles. In the cavalry, commanded by Marshal Joachim Murat [q.v.], there were sixteen regiments of cuirassiers and carabiniers armed with long, heavy swords and two pistols each. The line cavalry, called dragons (dragoons), also carried swords but were armed with short-barreled muskets instead of pistols. The basic artillery piece in 1812 was the 12-pounder, but the army included a wide variety of calibers, from the light 4-pounders of the horse artillery to 6-inch howitzers.

Russian Campaign, Napoleon's *French troops fighting off Cossack raiders during the retreat from Moscow*

Napoleon realized that north of the great Pripet Marshes, where he intended to launch his invasion of Russia, the major natural obstacles on their line of march were the Russian rivers: Niemen, Berezina, Dvina, Moskva, Dnieper, and many lesser streams. To cross these, the Grande Armée contained about 5,000 engineer and pioneer troops under General François Chasseloup-Laubat (1754–1833), whose main task was to build bridges, for which 2,000 horses were allotted to pull wagons carrying 200 pontoons, other engineering equipment, and tools. Twenty-six transport battalions were formed with 4,530 four-horse wagons, 2,400 light carts, and four battalions of ox-drawn heavy wagons.

On 22 June Napoleon issued a proclamation: "Soldiers! The second Polish war has opened; the first ended at Friedland and Tilsit. . . . Russia is carried away by fatality; her destiny must be accomplished. . . . She places us between war and dishonor, and there can be no doubt as to our choice. Let us advance, then, across the Niemen." Three pontoon bridges were built just north of Kovno (Polish: *Kowno*) in Lithuania, and on 24 June Napoleon himself crossed the Niemen River and launched the invasion of Russia.

The following day Tsar Alexander I [q.v.] issued a ringing proclamation to his troops: "Warriors! You defend your religion, your country, and your liberty. I am with you. God is against the aggressor." (Since most of his troops were conscripted serfs, virtually serving for life, many must have wondered whom their tsar had in mind when he invoked the defense of liberty.)

To meet Napoleon's juggernaut, the Russians had managed to assemble in the west only about 260,000 men and to form only two field armies: 48,000 men under General Pëtr Bagration [q.v.] in the south and 27,000 in northwest Russia under Mikhail Barclay de Tolly [q.v.]. Napoleon advanced between the two, intending to defeat them in detail.

On 28 June Napoleon entered Vilna. His first major success came when troops in the corps of Marshal Davout won a victory over Bagration on 23 July near Mogilev, a city straddling the Dnieper, 112 miles east of Minsk [see Mogilev / Mohilev, Battle of]. This temporarily prevented Bagration from joining Barclay de Tolly. However, on 3 August the two armies managed to link up near Smolensk. Napoleon crossed the Dnieper south of the city and moved to turn the Russian flank. Some bloody but indecisive battles were fought at Smolensk [q.v.] on 17 August, and on 17–18 August at Polotsk [q.v.], on the right bank of the Dvina River, Laurent Gouvion St. Cyr [q.v.] won his marshal's baton for his generalship after Marshal Nicolas Oudinot [q.v.] was wounded.

Napoleon had planned to winter at Smolensk, but he had not delivered the decisive defeat he had first intended. As the Russians retreated eastward, he followed, his already tangled lines of communication stretched ever longer, requiring more and more troops to defend them. By the end of August these losses to the main striking force combined with the losses from illness, wounds, deaths, and desertion had reduced Napoleon's main striking force from 382,000 to about 155,000.

Exasperated by the Russian withdrawal, Napoleon sought a decisive battle. The tsar too wanted one, and Barclay de Tolly was replaced as commander-in-chief by sixty-seven-year-old Field Marshal Mikhail Kutusov with General Levin Bennigsen [qq.v.] as his chief of staff. Kutusov arrived at army headquarters on 29 August, and his appearance bolstered sagging morale. He at once prepared to make a stand 70 miles west-southwest of Moscow near the village of Borodino [q.v.], and on 7 September the great battle of the campaign was fought. It was bloody but not decisive. The French slept on the field, but the Russians pulled back their battered forces in good order to Kaluga, on the left bank of the Oka River, 90 miles southwest of Moscow. On 15 September Napoleon entered Moscow, religious capital of Russia, and took up residence at the Kremlin.

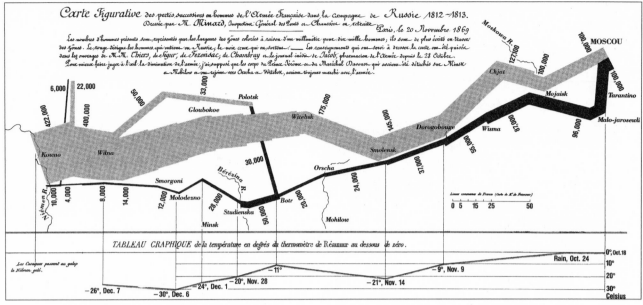

Russian Campaign, Napoleon's *Classic 1869 chart by the French engineer C. J. Minard shows Napoleon's losses en route to Moscow (light band) and on his retreat (dark band). At bottom are the Celsius temperatures during the retreat.*

The city had been evacuated and set afire. In Kutuzov's words, "The loss of Moscow is not the loss of Russia. My first obligation is to preserve the army, to get nearer to those troops approaching as reinforcements, and by the very act of leaving Moscow to prepare inescapable ruin for the enemy. . . . I will play for time, lull Napoleon as much as possible and not disturb him in Moscow. Every device that contributes to this object is preferable to the empty pursuit of glory." Napoleon described the burning city as "the most grand, the most sublime and the most terrible sight the world ever saw."

The tsar ignored Napoleon's peace overtures, and Napoleon, running desperately short of food and with winter approaching, decided to retreat to Smolensk, but first he wanted to destroy the 110,000-man army still intact under Kutusov. He attacked at Maloyaroslavets [q.v.], north of Kalunga, on 24 October, but was repulsed.

Napoleon had already lingered too long in central Russia, waiting futilely for the tsar to sue for peace. Surrounded by Russian forces, regular and irregular, his supply arrangements in disarray, and the morale of his troops plummeting, he ordered Moscow abandoned on 18 October and, as winter set in, began his long retreat. Separate French corps fought off the frequent Russian attacks, and Smolensk was finally reached on 12 November. Instead of halting there as intended, he changed his mind, and the retreat continued.

Kutusov sent a corps around the French to bar their road back, and the French found them at Krasnoi (Krasnoye Selo), just south-southwest of St. Petersburg, on 17 November [see Krasnoi, Battle of]. There 16,000 elite French guards completely routed 34,000 Russians and the road to the west remained open. (This French victory is sometimes cited as justification for Napoleon's decision not to throw in his elite guards at Borodino.)

Harassed along the way by thousands of Cossacks under General Matvei Ivanovich Platov [q.v.] and buffeted by the ferocious Russian winter, much of the French army disintegrated into a disorganized mob. Only 49,000 effectives with

250 guns remained as a fighting force; some 40,000 stragglers were strung out behind, and between the remnants of the French army and Poland and freedom lay the Berezina River. Russian Admiral Pavel Tshitsagov [q.v.] reached the river first and burned all the bridges and available boats [see Berezina / Beresina River, Napoleon's Crossing of]. In the bitter fighting Napoleon lost some 25,000 men and 30,000 noncombatants before finally crossing the river.

Learning of the conspiracy of General Claude Malet [q.v.] in France, Napoleon deserted his troops on 5 December and made a quick return to Paris. By the time the remnants of his army recrossed the Niemen, he had lost 570,000 men, 200,000 horses, and 1,000 pieces of artillery.

Russian-Japanese Conflict (1807). A tentative Russian incursion into Japanese territories on the island of Hokkaido was repulsed by a Japanese daimyo of the Matsumi family.

Russian Leather. A durable leather treated with birchbark oil. It was used for the sword belts of British generals and certain other officers.

Russo-Persian Wars (1805–13). In 1805 Napoleon attempted to enlist Persia (Iran) in a scheme to invade India, promising to give Georgia to Persia after he had defeated Russia. The meeting between the tsar and Napoleon at Tilsit [q.v.] at which the two made peace removed that possibility, but Shah Fath Ali [q.v.] still lusted after Georgia, which Russia had annexed in 1800, and in 1812 he attempted unsuccessfully to wrest it from Russia by force. The Russians then invaded Armenia and laid siege to Erivan [q.v.], 110 miles south of Tiflis, abandoning the siege when their line of communications became too harassed to maintain it. But the Russian victory in the Battle of Aslanduz ended the war, and Fath Ali sued for peace. By the Treaty of Gulistan on 12 October 1813 Persia gave up all claims to Georgia and ceded to Russia Dagestan, Baku, and neighboring territories.

Russian-Japanese Conflict *Japanese cavalry scouts during war with Russia*

Twelve years later Fath Ali tried again, but after some initial successes the Persian troops were swept away by Russian artillery. A small Russian force under Aleksis Yermolov [q.v.] invaded Persia in November 1825, capturing Tabriz and the Persian army's entire artillery park. After the Persians under Abbas Mirza [q.v.] had scored some successes, Yermolov was superseded by Ivan Paskievich [q.v.], who administered a series of defeats on the shah's troops. In the Battle of Gandzha [q.v.] on 26 September 1826 Russian artillery panicked the horses of the Persian cavalry and caused a rout. The shah was forced in 1828 to sign the Treaty of Turkomanchai, by which Persia agreed to pay a crippling indemnity and established the Aras River as the boundary between Russia and Persia, giving up most of Persian Armenia.

Russo-Swedish War (1808–09). The Treaty of Tilsit [q.v.] in July 1807 created the alliance of France and Russia, and both demanded that Sweden give up its membership in the Fourth Coalition and declare war on Britain [see Napoleonic Wars]. Sweden's King Gustavus IV (1778–1837) refused, and in February 1808 a Russian army under Field Marshal Friedrich Wilhelm Buxhöwden [q.v.] and General Karl Federovich Bagavut (1761–1812) invaded Finland, which had been part of Sweden since the twelfth century. The Swedes resisted most strongly at positions near the mouth of the Sikajoki River on 18 April and even more strongly at the island fortress of Sveaborg [q.v.] (*Suomenlinna* in Finnish), in the harbor of Helsinki, but they were forced to surrender on 3 May 1808. Six days later the tsar proclaimed Finland to be a Russian grand duchy. Gustavus was overthrown in a coup

d'état on 13 March 1809 and replaced by King Charles XIII (1748–1818) [see Swedish Military Coup d'État]. However, Swedish troops held out on the shores of the Gulf of Bothnia until 17 September, when the Treaty of Frederikshavn was signed, giving Finland and the Åland Islands (Ahvenanmaa) to Russia. Buxhöwden was appointed military governor.

Russo-Turkish Wars. There were four major conflicts between Turkey and the Russian Empire in the nineteenth century. Russia believed it had a duty to protect Christians within the Ottoman Empire, and this coincided with its aspirations to expand Russia's borders in the south.

1. *The Russo-Turkish War of 1806–12.* Ottoman Sultan Selim (1761–1808), charging the Russian-supported governors of Walachia and Moldavia with inciting émeutes in these principalities, dismissed them and in 1806 declared war on Russia. In June 1807 the Turkish navy was defeated in the Battle of Lemnos, and there was much skirmishing on land, but in August Napoleon negotiated an armistice, and the Russians withdrew their troops from Moldavia and Walachia. However, skirmishing and hostile incidents continued. The British mediated the quarrel, and the Treaty of Bucharest (Bucuresti) on 28 May 1812 recognized Turkish control of Walachia and Moldavia but set the Russian frontier along the Prut (German: *Pruth*) River, giving Bessarabia to Russia.

2. *The Russo-Turkish War of 1828–29.* On 28 April 1828, in nominal support of Greek independence, Russia declared war on Turkey and attacked on two fronts: in the Caucasus and in the Balkans. The latter army, led by Tsar Nicolas (1796–1855) himself, besieged Brăila in Walachia and then crossed the Danube to capture the forts at Ruschuk (Ruse) and Widden (Vidin). Varna [q.v.], besieged for three months by another Russian army, fell on 12 October 1828. In the Caucasus the Russians besieged Kars [q.v.] and on 5 July 1828 captured it. On 27 August they were victorious in the Battle of Akhalzic [q.v.]. The following year they won the Battle of Erivan (Yerevon), [q.v.] and they captured Adrianople [q.v.] on 20 August. When Constantinople (Istanbul) was threatened, Turkey sued for peace, which Prussian General Karl von Müffling [q.v.] helped negotiate. The Treaty of Adrianople, by which the Russians retained the mouth of the Danube and the eastern shore of the Black Sea, was signed on 16 September 1829. The treaty also made Walachia and Moldavia semi-autonomous states; in 1862 these Danubian states joined to form Rumania.

3. *The Crimean War of 1853–56.* This began as a Russo-Turkish war but came to involve Great Britain, France, and Piedmont-Sardinia [see Crimean War].

4. *The Russo-Turkish War of 1877–78.* In 1875 Turkish troops in Bosnia and Herzegovina crushed a revolt of Christian Slavic peasants against their Muslim landlords. In the spring of 1876, when the Turkish province of Bulgaria revolted, the Turks sent bashi-bazouks [q.v.] to put down the revolt, and this they did with a brutality that shocked the world when their atrocities were revealed by an American newspaper correspondent with the improbable name of Januarius MacGahan [q.v.]. In England the Bulgarian Atrocities [q.v.] were denounced in dramatic terms by William Ewart Gladstone (1809–1898).

In April 1877 Russia, filled with brotherly feeling for the Christian Serbian Slavs, demanded reforms and autonomy for Bulgaria. When these were not forthcoming, Russia declared war on Turkey on 24 April. On 15 June a Russian army of 250,000, led by an advance force under Major General Mikhail Ivanovich Dragomurov [q.v.], forced the passage of the Danube. By 1 July four Russian corps, 257,000 men, were south of the Danube in Bulgaria. An advance force under General Osip Gurko [q.v.] seized the Khainkoi Pass, forcing the Turks to abandon the strategic Shipka Pass [q.v.]. Mehemet Ali Pasha [q.v.], who had commanded the 135,000 Turks in Bulgaria was relieved of his command and replaced by Suleiman Pasha [q.v.], who, when he also was forced to retreat, was charged with treason and imprisoned for a time. Army officials then became diverted by the siege of Plevna [q.v.], heroically defended for 143 days by the Turks under Osman Nuri Pasha [q.v.]. After the fall of Plevna on 10 December 1877 and the Turkish disaster in the Battle of Plovdiv [q.v.], Turkish field armies were defeated in a series of engagements in the Balkans when General Gurko launched a winter campaign.

In Asia Minor 120,000 Turks led by Ahmed Mukhtar Pasha [q.v.] faced a Russian army of 190,000 men under Grand Duke Mikhail Nikolaivich (1832–1909) with Mikhail Loris-Melikov [q.v.] as his chief of staff. The Russians attacked the Turks and besieged Kars [q.v.], which surrendered on 18 November 1877. By the end of January 1878 a Russian army under Mikhail Skobelev [q.v.] was almost at the gates of Constantinople (Istanbul). On 3 March the Turks were forced to sign the humiliating Treaty of San Stefano, in which they yielded large chunks of territory, but this was modified, and Russian demands were reduced by the Congress of Berlin in the same year. Nevertheless, Serbia and Rumania were given their independence, Bulgaria was enlarged and became autonomous under Russian authority, and Kars was lost to the Russians and not returned until 1921.

Ruth, Samuel (1818–1872). A Union spy during the American Civil War. As a young Pennsylvanian mechanic he had moved to Virginia in 1839 and rose to become superintendent of the Richmond, Fredericksburg, & Potomac Railroad. In the beginning of the war he is said to have deliberately slowed the movements of men and supplies. General Robert E. Lee's requests that he be removed were ignored. He was unquestionably a spy in 1864 and 1865, passing on much valuable information and helping escaped prisoners of war. He is said to have worked with Elizabeth Van Lew [q.v.] in Richmond.

Ryot. 1. In the Ottoman Empire, a Christian subject who was not liable for conscription, but had to pay a poll tax instead.

2. In India, a tenant farmer or small cultivator.

S

Saalfeld, Battle of (10 October 1806), Napoleonic Wars. Near this town in Thuringa, 29 miles south-southeast of Erfurt and 65 miles southwest of Leipzig, Prince Louis Ferdinand of Prussia [q.v.], who had crossed the Saale River with 9,000 Saxon and Prussian troops, was attacked by 14,000 French under Marshal Jean Lannes [q.v.] and driven under the walls of the town. In a fruitless attempt to retrieve the situation, Louis Ferdinand led a cavalry charge in which he was killed. His Prussian-Saxon army lost 900 killed, 1,800 prisoners, and 33 guns. The victorious Lannes then crossed the Saale to join Napoleon in the Battle of Jena [q.v.].

Saarbrücken, Battle of (2 August 1870), Franco-Prussian War. An inconclusive skirmish between units of the German First Army and the French II Corps at this town on the Franco-German frontier, 39 miles southeast of Trier, that was a prelude to the first battle of the Franco-Prussian War at Spicheren [q.v.].

Saber / Sabre. A cavalry sword having a guard and a curved blade. In 1882 General Philip Sheridan [q.v.] correctly pronounced the saber obsolete. Others maintained that it was still a viable weapon, and it was issued in most armies well into the twentieth century.

Sabine Affair (1805–06), American-Mexican border controversy. In October 1805 the Spanish established two small outposts on the east side of the Sabine River in territory claimed by both Mexico and the United States. In response Secretary of War Henry Dearborn [q.v.] ordered Major Moses Porter (1757?–1822), commandant at Natchitoches, Louisiana, to expel the Spanish and to extend patrols in that area. These orders reached Porter on 24 January 1806, and on 1 February he ordered a captain and 60 men to march on the Spanish outposts. When ordered to evacuate, the Spanish protested but complied.

Saber Rich presentation saber for cavalry officers, American Civil War

Sabine Crossroads, Battle of (8 April 1864), American Civil War. During the Red River Campaign [q.v.] Union General Nathaniel Banks [q.v.] with 25,000 men was moving west toward Shreveport, Louisiana, 18 miles from the Texas border, when at Sabine Crossroads, 40 miles south of Shreveport, he was attacked by Confederate General Richard Taylor [q.v.] with 8,800 men and pursued them. Banks retreated toward Alexandria, Louisiana. A rearguard action at Pleasant Grove the next day delayed the pursuing Confederates, enabling him to retreat in good order. Union losses at Sabine Crossroads and Pleasant Grove were 2,900; Confederate losses were 1,000.

Sabine Pass, Battle of (8 September 1863), American Civil War. A battle in Texas described by President Jefferson Davis [q.v.] as the "Thermopylae of the Civil War." Lieutenant Richard William Dowling [q.v.], a former saloon-keeper commanding 43 members of the Texan Davis Guard, manned a small fort at the mouth of the Sabine River. On 8 September 1862, when General Nathaniel Banks [q.v.] launched an invasion of southern Texas by moving his men up the river in small boats, they were blown out of the water by the six guns of Dowling's fort. Some 400 Federal prisoners were taken, and Banks's invasion was stalled for a month. Dowling and his men were presented by local citizens with the Davis Guard Medal [q.v.], the only Confederate medal for valor ever awarded.

Sabot. In a military sense, this was (1) a disk of wood in fixed ammunition to which were attached the cartridge bag and projectile or (2) the metal device attached to the base of a projectile for a rifled gun to take the grooves of the bore.

Sabots for gun canisters, mountain howitzer shells, spherical case shot and canister had two grooves. All the grooves were 0.3 inch wide and 0.15 inch deep

Sabretache. A flat leather satchel, usually decorated, worn by light dragoon and hussar officers, suspended on the left side by long straps from the sword belt. "A useless square accoutrement which dangles against the legs of officers in some cavalry regiments" (*Farrow's Military Encyclopedia*, 1885). In Britain, heavy cavalry officers wore sabretaches from 1812 until 1831. The word is derived from the German *Säbeltasche*.

Sabretache

Sabugal, Battle of (3 April 1811), Peninsular War. A French army corps under General Jean Reynier, part of the army of Marshal André Masséna [qq.v.], holding the salient angle of the French positions along the Coa River in north-central Portugal near the town of Sabugal, 16 miles southeast of Guarda, was attacked and driven back by three

British divisions under Wellington. The French lost 760; the British 179.

Sacile, Battle of (16 April 1809), Napoleonic Wars. Near this commune in northeastern Italy, 23 miles northeast of Udine, at the head of the Adriatic Sea, a French army of 37,000 men under Eugène de Beauharnais clashed with an Austrian army of 40,000 under Archduke John [qq.v.]. Neither commander exhibited great leadership. When the Austrians threatened the French line of retreat, Beauharnais drew his forces back behind the Piave River.

Sack. Unrestricted pillage.

Sack Coat. A loose-fitting, four-button fatigue coat in use in the American army from the 1830s through the American Civil War.

Sacken, Dimitri Osten (1790–1881). See Osten-Sacken, Dimitri von der.

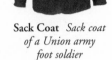
Sack Coat *Sack coat of a Union army foot soldier*

Sackets Harbor, Battle of (28–29 May 1813), War of 1812. A British force under Sir George Prevost [q.v.], governor-general of British North America, crossed Lake Ontario from Kingston, and attacked Sackets Harbor, 11 miles east of Watertown, New York, which was defended by 400 regulars and 750 militia under Brigadier General Jacob Brown [q.v.] of the New York Militia. The British landed under heavy fire to find facing them a double line of infantry and a fortified battery of artillery. The British charge broke through the first line and pressed the second back into prepared fortifications, but there the Americans held. Brown then sent a force to threaten the rear of Prevost's right flank, and fearing to be cut off, the British reembarked and sailed back to Canada.

Sacramento, Battle of (28 December 1861), American Civil War. In this skirmish near a small village in west-central Kentucky, in which few were engaged, there were four present or future generals—Nathan Bedford Forrest [q.v.], James Streshly Jackson (1823–1862), Thomas L. Crittenden [q.v.], and Eli Huston Murray (1849–1896)—as well as four future colonels and a future governor. Forrest, who was leading about 150 Confederates, was apprised of the presence of a small Federal force, by Mary S. ("Mollie") Moorehead (1843–1870), a pretty eighteen-year-old southern sympathizer who met him "with untied tresses floating with the breeze." Forrest was repulsed in his first charge on the 45 Federals commanded by eighteen-year-old Major Eli Huston Murray. A second charge successfully routed them.

Major Murray was to finish the war as a brevet brigadier general. After the war he became a successful journalist and was appointed governor of Utah.

Sacramento River, Battle of (28 February 1847), Mexican War. Along this river near Chihuahua an American force of 900 men under Alexander Doniphan [q.v.] defeated a much larger force of Mexicans. Mexican losses were 600; American losses were 7.

Sacramento River *The Americans decisively defeated the Mexicans here in February 1847*

Sadowa / Königgrätz, Battle of (3 July 1866), Seven Weeks' War. Prince Frederick Charles [q.v.], leading a Prussian army of 220,984 men with 792 guns, crossed the Bohemian Mountains and faced 206,000 Austrians and Saxons with 770 guns under Hungarian-born Austrian Field Marshal Ludwig von Benedek [q.v.], with Major General Gedeon Krismanic (1817–1876) as his principal adviser.

After losing 30,000 men in small battles, the Austrians had withdrawn southeast toward Königgrätz (Czech: *Hradec Králové*) in northeast Bohemia on the Upper Labe (Elbe) River, 65 miles east of Prague. Frederick Charles did not intend to attack the numerically superior Austrians but merely to hold them until the Prussian Second Army, 100,000 strong, under Crown Prince Frederick William [q.v.], could come up from Silesia. However, a rash attack by one of his division commanders, General Eduard Fransecky [q.v.], on the dull and rainy morning of 3 July 1866 brought on a general engagement. In the hills just southeast of the village of Sadowa (Sadová), 8 miles northwest of Königgrätz, about 450,000 men were eventually engaged on a battlefield measuring less than 8 square miles.

The Austrians launched a determined counterattack, and for a time the outnumbered Prussians were in danger of being overwhelmed, but in the early afternoon the Prussian Second Army arrived on the field and soon decided the battle. The Prussians carried a hill near the village of Chulm (Chlumec nad Cidlinou) that was vital to the Austrian position, and an Austrian counterattack failed to recover it. By four-thirty in the afternoon the Austrians were in full retreat. Benedek retired under the fire of his artillery with the Austrian cavalry fighting a rearguard action. Against tremendous odds the artillerymen fought their guns heroically. Within five minutes one battery was destroyed; its captain, August von Groeben, fell mortally wounded along with 53 men and 68 horses. (Near the site of the battery's position today is a crude monument with the inscription in German: "The Battery of the Dead.") The Austrian cavalry—uhlans, cuirassiers, and dragoons—also behaved with gallantry, throwing the Prussian cavalry into some confusion and holding up the infantry for a precious half hour, at a cost of 64 officers, 1,984 other ranks, and 1,681 horses. Benedek retreated with his beaten army to the fortress at Olmütz (Olomouc) and was soon ordered to Vienna, where an armistice was arranged.

The Prussian victory was one of the most decisive in the

Sadowa *Austrian and Saxon artillerymen fight a heroic rearguard action against a superior Prussian army.*

history of European warfare. Prussian losses were 360 officers and 8,812 other ranks killed, wounded, or missing; Austrian and Saxon losses were 1,372 officers and 43,500 other ranks, half of whom were taken prisoner. Some 150 Austrian guns were captured. This battle ended the Seven Weeks' War [q.v.].

The Prussians forces were better trained, better organized, much better led, and, in the case of their infantry, better armed, fighting with modern breech-loading Dreyse needle guns [q.v.], while the Austrians were still armed with muzzle-loaders. Noting this, the French army soon after adopted the Chassepot [q.v.], an improvement over the needle gun. The battle has been said to be the beginning of modern warfare, in which amateur commanders gave way to military professionals.

Sadulapur, Battle of (3 December 1848), Second Sikh War. After the British failure in the Battle of Ramnagar [q.v.] on 22 November 1847, General Hugh Gough [q.v.] sent a force of 8,000 under Major General Joseph Thackwell [q.v.] to cross the Sutlej River higher up. Thackwell found a ford and crossed to the right bank of the river. He took up a position near the village of Sadulapur, where he was attacked by Sikhs at noon on 3 December. There was no close fighting, and the Sikhs drew off in the night.

Although Gough claimed a victory, the Sikhs retired only to take up strong positions at Chilianwala on the Jhelum River, which Gough did not feel strong enough to attack without reinforcements [see Chilianwala / Chillianwala, Battle of].

Safa. A turban.

Safe Conduct. A pass issued to those traveling inside the area controlled by the commander signing the safe conduct. It

was sometimes issued to permit goods to be admitted to a militarily controlled area.

Safford, Mary J. (fl.1861–1862). A young and pretty woman, called the Angel of Cairo, who during the American Civil War cared for the Union wounded in Cairo, Illinois. Exhaustion caused by nursing the numerous wounded of the Battle of Shiloh in April 1862 combined with a spine injury forced her to give up the work. A wealthy brother sent her to Paris to recover.

Sagunto, Siege of (23 September–26 October 1811), Peninsular War. Fresh from victories at Tarragona [q.v.] and Tortusa, French Marshal Louis Suchet [q.v.] with 22,000 men was marching on Valencia [q.v.] when he was delayed at the crumbling fort of Sagunto 16 miles north-northeast of the city. The ancient fort, called Murviedro by Arabs, a name it retained until 1877, was in the process of being refurbished. It was manned by 3,000 Spanish soldiers with 17 guns under Spanish Colonel (later Field Marshal) Luis María Andriani (1775–1856). When the French attacked on 23 September 1811, they were repulsed with a loss of about 200; the Spanish lost 15 dead and 20 wounded. The French then instituted a siege in which the Spanish lost nearly 500 men.

On 25 October a Spanish force under Joachim Blake [q.v.], which tried to raise the siege, was routed in about ten minutes by Louis Suchet [q.v.]. The disheartened garrison surrendered on the 26th.

Sahagún, Battle of (21 December 1808), Peninsular War. At this small town, 33 miles east-southeast of León, in appalling winter conditions, a British cavalry force of 1,200 sabers and four guns under Lieutenant General Henry William Paget [q.v.] surprised a French cavalry force of 800. The French lost

120 killed and 167 taken prisoner; British losses were 2 killed and 23 wounded.

Saharite. See Cafard.

Said Pasha, Husain al-Jimi'abi (1830?–1884). An Egyptian commander of bashi-bazouks [q.v.] who, while fighting Mahdist Dervishes [q.v.] on the White Nile in the Sudan in 1883, was seized by his own troops when he attempted to betray them to the enemy. He was tried by court-martial for murder and treachery, convicted, and executed. [See Mahdiya.]

Saigon, Siege of (March 1860–25 February 1861), French-Indochinese War. French and Spanish forces in Indochina totaling about 1,000 were besieged by Vietnamese at Saigon (Ho Chi Minh City) on the eastern coast of the Indochinese peninsula until a French relieving force under Admiral Léonard V. J. Charner arrived and defeated the Vietnamese in the Battle of Chi-hoa on 25 February 1861. King Tu Duc [q.v.] then sued for peace, and France annexed three eastern provinces of Cochin China.

Saigo Takamori (1827–1877). A Japanese samurai and patriot who, after holding several positions in Satsuma (Kagoshiga Prefecture) moved to Edo (Tokyo) in the service of a daimyo [q.v.]. In 1858, during the Ansei purge of those who threatened the power of the Tokugawa shogunate (1663–1867), he fled to Kagoshima but was captured and exiled to the island of Amami (Oshima) for three years. In 1866 Saigo and Okubo Toshomichi [q.v.] played major roles in the secret alliance formed by the provinces (*Satcho Domei*) of Satsuma and Choshu (Yamaguchi) to overthrow the Tokugawa shogunate. Choshu forces led by Kido Takayoshi (1833–1877) and the Satsuma force led by Saigo were instrumental in overthrowing the Tokugawa and restoring the power of the emperor. [See Boshin Civil War.]

In 1867 the shogun raised an army and attempted to regain power, but he was defeated by Saigo in the battles of Toba, in southern Honshu, and Fushimi (now a suburb of Kyoto). Under the Meiji Restoration Saigo organized and was the commander of the 10,000-man Imperial Guard. In 1872 he was made a field marshal and given command of all armed forces. Troubles in Korea spurred him to argue for an invasion, for he feared Russian expansion in Asia. When he was overruled, he resigned and retired to Kagoshima. He was joined there by many disgruntled samurai, and in 1877 he led the Satsuma Rebellion [q.v.] against the imperial government. When his attempt to capture Kumamoto Castle [q.v.] failed, he ordered a samurai to behead him on 14 September 1877, or in another version, he committed hara-kiri, or in still another, he was killed in a final sortie attacking imperial forces besieging him at Shiroyama. He was posthumously pardoned by the emperor.

Saigo's allegiance to the samurai spirit served as an inspiration for many Japanese soldiers through World War II. At Kagoshima a monument was erected to the Satsuma Loyal Retainers, and a Saigo Takamori museum was established.

St. Albans, Raid on (19 October 1864), American Civil War. The northernmost engagement of the war took place at this small Vermont town near the Canadian border. Bennett H.

Young (1843–1919), a young man from Kentucky, was authorized by the Confederate government to recruit from prisoners who had escaped to Canada a party to raid in the United States. Young and 20 others swept down upon St. Albans at two-thirty in the afternoon and in a half hour robbed three local banks, taking a total of $201,522. A Union officer on leave organized a small force of citizens, and in the fire fight that followed 1 civilian and 1 raider were killed and 1 civilian and 4 raiders were wounded. Young took 14 hostages. A posse that captured some of the party after they had crossed the frontier was forced to give them up to Canadian authorities, who apprehended the remainder. The Canadian courts ruled that they were soldiers under orders and released them on bond as internees, occasioning an outcry in the United States. Only about $86,000 of the stolen money was recovered.

St. Anne, Order of. The most frequently issued decoration in the Russian army. Among its recipients were soldiers in a combatant service who had achieved twenty years of irreproachable service. The order came with a pension and an exemption from the poll tax when or if its recipient retired. Only the tsar or the commander-in-chief could deprive a soldier of the order. After 1838 it endowed the recipient with freedom from arbitrary corporal punishment without trial.

St. Arnaud, Jacques Leroy de (1801–1854), true name: Armand Jacques Leroy. A French soldier who entered the army in 1817 and retired ten years later. At age thirty he reentered the army as a sublieutenant and took part in the suppression of an émeute in the Vendée. He served for a time on the staff of General Thomas Bugeaud de la Piconnerie [q.v.], but debts and scandals in his private life forced him to transfer as a captain in the Foreign Legion [q.v.] in Algeria. There he won the Legion of Honor at the siege of Constantine [q.v.]. In 1840 he returned to France and changed his name to the more aristocratic St. Arnaud.

During the uprising against Louis Philippe (1773–1850) in the 1848 Revolution he was in command of a brigade in Paris [see Paris Revolutions of 1848]. After the revolution he returned to Algeria and led an expedition against the Berbers in Little Kabylia. In 1851 he was promoted general of division and returned to France as war minister, a post he held until 1854. He played an active role in the coup d'état of 2 December 1851 that brought Louis Napoleon to power as Napoleon III (1808–1873), and he was rewarded with a marshal's baton and, it was said, enough money to pay off his enormous gambling debts. When a fellow general made this assertion publicly, St. Arnaud challenged him to a duel, in which he killed him. He resigned as war minister in 1854, to take command of the French army in the Crimean War [q.v.]. He died in the Crimea on 29 September 1854, soon after the Battle of the Alma [q.v.].

St. Chamond. Common name for Compagnie des Forges et Acier de la Marine et d'Homecourt located at St. Chamond, France, seven miles northeast of St. Étienne. The firm began as a foundry in the early nineteenth century, then made steel, and in the 1880s began to produce arms and ammunition. Although most of its work was for the navy, it produced many field guns, one of which was adopted by the Mexican army in 1902.

St. Charles, Battle of (25 November 1837), Canadian revolt. At a stockade in this town, 14 miles west-northwest of St. Hyacinthe, rebel followers (*patriotes*) of Lewis Joseph Papineau (1786–1871) were defeated by Canadian troops and loyalists under Lieutenant Colonel Charles Wetherall (1788–1868) at a cost of 21 loyalists killed. Wetherall's troops burned down the town.

St. Cyr, Claude Carra (1760–1834). A French soldier commissioned in the infantry in 1774 who fought in the American Revolution under General de Lafayette (1757–1834). He left the army for health reasons in 1792 but returned after a few months and in 1795 was promoted general of brigade. He was wounded in Italy but recovered to fight in the Battle of Marengo [q.v.] in 1800. In 1804 he was promoted general of division. He distinguished himself in the Battle of Aspern-Essling [q.v.] in 1809 but was disgraced by Napoleon for losing a battle near Hamburg in March 1813. He was soon reemployed, and from 1814 to 1819 he was governor of French Guiana. He retired in 1832.

St. Cyr, École Espéciale Militaire de. A French military school for the training of cavalry and infantry officers in a village now called St. Cyr l'École, six miles west of Versailles. In 1686 Madame de Maintenon (1635–1719) established a convent school there for highborn girls of little means. It was closed in 1792, and on 1 May 1802 First Consul Napoleon took over the convent's buildings and, adding others, established a military school. Napoleon personally reviewed the detailed curriculum. The course usually lasted two years, after which the brighter students passed to the staff school and eventually served in the *état-major* (army or general staff). The rest were commissioned in the infantry or cavalry.

The school supplied Napoleon with about 4,000 officers, some 700 of whom were killed, the first at Austerlitz [q.v.] on 2 December 1805, the last at Waterloo in 1815. From 1820 the school provided courses in Arabic, providing officers with useful knowledge when France undertook the conquest of Algeria in 1830.

St. Cyr, Laurent de Gouvion (1764–1830). A French soldier who, although abstemious and constrained, joined the notoriously wild Parisian sans-culottes battalion in 1792. Two years later he was made a general of division, and he distinguished himself in fighting on the Rhine in 1800, in Germany, and in Italy in 1865. An intellectual who played the violin and was skilled at chess, he did not consort with fellow officers, who called him the Owl. He was inclined to be insubordinate and twice angered Napoleon by leaving his command without permission. In 1812 he commanded a Bavarian corps in Napoleon's Russian Campaign [q.v.] and on 27 August 1812 was made a marshal for his victory at Polotsk [q.v.] on 18 August. In 1813 he capitulated at Dresden [q.v.] and was held a prisoner for about a year. When released, he gave his loyalty to King Louis XVIII (1755–1824). He was minister of war in 1815, from February to September 1817 he was minister of marine and of the colonies, and he was again minister of war in 1817–19. He retired in 1819 and devoted himself to agriculture and the writing of his memoirs.

St. Dizier, Battles of (29 January and 26 March 1814). Napoleon twice defeated Allied armies near this town on the Marne River in northern France, 39 miles north of Chaumont.

St. Eustache, Battle of (14 December 1837), Canadian revolt. At this town on the Lake of the Two Mountains, 15 miles west of Montreal, on the Mille Îles River, government troops under General Sir John Colborne (1778–1863), the lieutenant governor of Upper Canada (Ontario), defeated a rebel force (*patriotes*) that had taken up a position in a stone church. When the church was shelled and set on fire, the rebels surrendered and the revolt ended.

St. Eustatius, Capture of (1801 and 1810). The French held this Dutch seven-square-mile West Indian island just northwest of St. Kitts from 26 November 1781 until the British captured it in 1801. The British soon abandoned it, but in 1810 they recaptured it from the Dutch. It was restored to Holland in 1814.

St. George the Martyr, Order of. The only Russian order, with one exception for a short period, given solely for bravery. It was established on 26 November 1769 by Catherine the Great (1729–1796) for "exceptional prowess displayed for the greater glory of Russian arms," and its statutes specified that past service, social position, or wounds were not to influence its bestowal. In the nineteenth century it was the most coveted of all Russian orders.

The order was divided into four classes. By imperial ukase of 11 April 1864 officers awarded any class were granted hereditary nobility. Rank and file were awarded higher pay and pensions and after 1838 could not be given corporal punishment without a court-martial. Names of all the members were engraved on marble plaques in Georgevsky Hall of the Grand Imperial Palace in Moscow.

Banners decorated with the colors of the order, and known as Georgevsky banners, were sometimes awarded to regiments that had distinguished themselves. The first were awarded in 1799 to four guards regiments. (The Communists converted this order into the Soviet Order of Glory, preserving the tsarist black and orange ribbon.)

St. Helena. A 47-square-mile island in the South Atlantic (15° 55′ 26″ S by 5° 42′ 30″ W). A British possession under the care of the Admiralty until 1922, it was the place of exile for Napoleon, several Zulu chiefs, a former sultan of Zanzibar, Boer prisoners of war and others. During the Second Anglo-Boer War thousands of Boer prisoners of war were sent there.

St. Lucia, Capture of (21–23 June 1803). During the Napoleonic Wars a seaborne British force under Commodore Samuel Hood (1762–1814), with Lieutenant General William Grinfield commanding the troops, captured this French island in the Leeward Island group, 43 miles north-northwest of St. Kitts. Hood then moved on to capture other French and Dutch possessions: the island of Tobago and Demerara, Essquibo, and Surinam on the South African mainland.

St. Petersburg, Declaration of (29 November and 11 December 1868). In the belief that the "progress of civilization should have the effect of alleviating as much as possible the calamities of war," representatives of the principal European governments met in St. Petersburg, Russia, and drafted a document declaring that prisoners of war must be treated humanely, that their personal property must be preserved, and that they were not to be placed in civilian jails except under certain conditions. It prohibited the use of poisons, the execution of prisoners of war, and the ordering of no quarter. Belligerents also agreed not to pillage, improperly use flags of truce, attack undefended towns or buildings, or supply projectiles or materials calculated to cause unnecessary suffering. Signatories assented to attempt to "preserve buildings dedicated to art, religion, science or charitable purposes, hospitals, historic monuments." Neither the United States nor Bavaria signed the convention.

St. Privat, Battle of. See Gravelotte–St. Privat, Battle of.

St. Quentin, Battle of (19 January 1871), Franco-Prussian War. In 1871 a French army of 40,000 under General Louis Faidherbe [q.v.] was the last French army remaining in the field, and it was hoped that it could divert some of the German forces besieging Paris. On 19 January it engaged 35,000 Prussians under General August von Goeben [q.v.] in northern France near this town on the Somme River, and although the French outnumbered the Prussians, morale was low, there were many desertions, orders went awry, and Faidherbe was decisively beaten. French losses were 3,500 killed and wounded and 9,000 taken prisoner; Prussian losses were 96 officers and 2,304 men. Although the French had almost no prospect of relieving a besieged Paris [q.v.], their last glimmer of hope disappeared with this defeat, and Paris surrendered nine days later.

St. Thomas, Capture of (21 December 1807), Napoleonic Wars. A combined British naval and military force under Admiral Alexander Forrester Cochrane (1758–1832) and General Henry Bowyer captured this island in the West Indies from the Danes.

Salamanca, Battle of (22 July 1812), Peninsular War. On 13 June 1812, after the capture of Ciudad Rodrigo and Badajoz [qq.v.], towns that dominated the main corridors between Portugal and Spain, Wellington invaded northern Spain with an Allied army of 48,000 men and 60 guns: 28,000 British, 3,000 Spanish, and 17,000 Portuguese. On 17 June he reached Salamanca, a university city on the Tormes River, 107 miles west-northwest of Madrid, surprising a slightly larger French force of about 50,000 with 78 guns under Marshal Auguste de Marmont [q.v.], who was under the mistaken impression that Wellington was retreating to Ciudad Rodrigo. After much marching and countermarching as each side sought a favorable position, Wellington took up a position just southeast of the city and facing east, with most of his army concealed. A narrow stream separated the two armies. A nine-hour artillery duel ended when a thunderstorm struck. Marmont, who thought he was facing only a rear guard, moved the bulk of his army across the face of the Allied front to prevent Wellington's escape. Seeing this, Wellington remarked to Spanish General Miguel de Alava (1771–1843): *"Mon cher Alava, Marmont est perdue!"* At four forty-five in the afternoon, when the two sections of the French army were widely separated, he attacked and drove in a French flank.

Marmont was seriously wounded, leaving General Bertrand Clausel [q.v.] to try to save the situation. Although the French launched a counterattack and fought well, the British victory was nearly complete. A cavalry charge was followed by an infantry assault, and within forty minutes a quarter of the French army was broken beyond repair. By nine-thirty that evening the battle was over.

The Allies suffered 5,200 casualties, about 3,129 of whom were British, including Lieutenant Colonel J. G. Le Marchant [q.v.], the founder of British military educational establishments, who was killed. The French lost 14,000, including 7,000 taken prisoner, and 20 guns.

The destruction of Marmont's army might have been complete had the Spanish force under General Carlos José d'Espignac España (1775–1839), who had been ordered to hold the bridge over the Torme River at Alba de Torme [q.v.], 13 miles southeast of Salamanca, not abandoned its positions, allowing the French, retreating in disorder, to escape. Even so, it was an important victory for Wellington, and it destroyed French control of northern and central Spain. British losses were 6,000; French losses were 15,000, and Marmont himself was forced to return to France to recover from a severe wound. Wellington was bitter over España's failure, but on 12 August he rode in triumph through cheering crowds in Madrid.

This was Wellington's greatest victory in Europe to this date. French General Maximilien Foy [q.v.] wrote: "This battle is the most cleverly fought, the largest in scale, the most important in results of any the English have won in recent times."

Salamanca *Battle of Salamanca, 22 July 1812*

Salamanca y Negrete, Manuel (1831–1891). A Spanish general who was governor of Cuba from 1889 to 1890.

Salaverry, Felipe Santiago (1806–1836). A Peruvian soldier who in 1834 successfully led a force against General Agustín Gamarra [q.v.], president of Peru. Salaverry became president in the following year, but in 1836 he was defeated in the Battle of Socabaya [q.v.], captured, and shot by General Andrés Santa Cruz [q.v.], the president of Bolivia.

Saldanha, Duque de, João Carlos de Oliveira e Daun (1791–1876). A Portuguese soldier and statesman who during the Peninsular War fought in the Battle of Bussaco [q.v.] in 1810 and held diplomatic posts in Brazil from about 1811 to 1822. In 1825 he was minister of foreign affairs, and in 1826–27 he was governor of Oporto. During the Portuguese Civil War [q.v.] he supported the infanta Maria II (1819–1853) against her usurping uncle Dom Miguel (1802–1866), and in 1834 he was named a marshal [see Miguelite War]. On 14 February 1834 he defeated the rebels in the Battle of Santarém [q.v.]. In 1835 he was named minister of war and president of the council, serving until 1836, when he instigated an unsuccessful counter revolution against the Septembrists. He was exiled but returned in 1846 to become premier until 1849. He was again premier in 1851–56 and in 1870.

Sale, Lady Florentia (1790–1853). An Englishwoman, the daughter of George Wynch, Esq., who married Lieutenant Robert Sale [q.v.] at Trichinoply, India, a few months after he arrived with his regiment on 24 July 1809. In August of the following year he left for Mauritius, and it was five years before they met again.

She was at Kabul, Afghanistan, and her husband, now a major general, was 80 miles away in Jalalabad when the Afghans revolted against the British forces occupying their country [see First Afghan War]. In January 1842 she took part in the disastrous retreat from Kabul [see Brydon, William] and did what she could to lessen the sufferings of the women, children, and wounded soldiers. In the constant attacks upon the column her clothes were ripped by bullets, and she was twice wounded, once receiving a bullet in her wrist. With her was her youngest daughter, who had been married the previous August in Kabul to a young engineer officer who was mortally wounded on the retreat. When Akbar Khan [q.v.] offered his protection to the women and 15 children of the column, his offer was accepted. With 17 European soldiers and 20 male civilians they were shuttled from place to place, robbed of their baggage and other possessions, and made virtual prisoners. Although their treatment was harsh, Lady Sale was permitted to correspond with her husband, and she was able throughout the ordeal to keep a journal, which was published in 1843. After nine months the captives succeeded in gaining their freedom by distributing official-looking papers and were making their way back to Kabul when they were met by Sir Richmond Shakespear [q.v.] and General Sale leading rescue parties.

Lady Sale remained in India after her husband had been killed in the Battle of Mudki [q.v.] in the First Sikh War [q.v.], and she was granted a pension of £500 by Queen Victoria. In 1853 she sailed to Cape Colony in South Africa for her health, but she died a few days after her arrival at Cape Town.

Colonel Robert Hamilton Vetch (1842?–1910?), writing of her in the *Dictionary of National Biography*, recorded that she was "*par excellence* 'a soldier's wife.' She was the companion and friend of her husband throughout a life of military vicissitude, sympathizing with him in all that concerned his profession, quick in perception, self-reliant and practical."

Sale, Robert Henry (1782–1845). A British soldier who was commissioned an ensign at the age of twelve in the 36th Foot and promoted lieutenant two years later. In January 1798, at age fifteen, he transferred to the 12th Foot, then in Madras, India. He arrived there on 1 March and on 22 July set out with his regiment on his first campaign, an expedition against Tippu (Tippoo or Tipú) Sultan (1749–1799). In the

next ten years Sale saw much action against freebooters and hostile tribesmen and for a time served under the future Duke of Wellington.

In 1809 he married nineteen-year-old Florentia Wynch [see Sale, Lady Florentia] in Trichinopoly. His wife was destined to see little of him in the first years of their marriage. In August 1810 he sailed with his regiment to take part in the capture of Mauritius [q.v.], and he remained on the island until April 1813, when he moved to the island of Bourbon (Réunion); when Bourbon was restored to France, Sale returned with his battalion to Mauritius. On 10 November 1815 he was back in England and, after an absence of five years, reunited with his wife. In March 1818 his battalion was disbanded, and he, a junior major, was placed on half pay.

Three years later he was returned to duty with the 13th Foot and on 1 January 1823 set sail for India. He fought in the First Anglo-Burmese War [q.v.], in which he distinguished himself and was twice mentioned in dispatches. His commanding general, Sir Archibald Campbell [q.v.], reported that he was "an officer whose gallantry has been most conspicuous on every occasion since our arrival at Rangoon." He killed the Burmese commander-in-chief in personal combat and took from him a gold-hilted sword and scabbard. Soon afterward he was severely wounded in the head at Malown. He was promoted lieutenant colonel in 1825 on the same day that his brother George was promoted to the same rank in the 4th Dragoons, and he was given the Companion of the Bath for his services.

For thirteen years he was in garrisons in India. In 1838 he was made a brevet colonel and given command of a brigade in the First Afghan War [q.v.]. After an arduous march he reached Kandahar, 300 miles southwest of Kabul, on 26 April 1839. He took part in the storming of Ghazni [q.v.], where the fifty-seven-year-old officer, although slashed in the face by an Afghan saber, split his assailant's skull.

In 1839 Sale was given the local rank of major general and was knighted (KCB). He spent the winter with his troops in Jalalabad, an ancient walled town in eastern Afghanistan, west of the Khyber Pass on the Kabul River near its junction with the Kunar, 70 miles east of Kabul and 80 miles west of Peshawar.

In the autumn of 1840 Dost Muhammad [q.v.] had once more mobilized his troops and was raising the countryside against the British. In September Sale, back in Kabul, took his brigade on a punitive expedition to Kohistan, the hill country north of Kabul, where he successfully attacked and disabled a number of forts. On 2 November he defeated Dost Mohammed near the village of Parwan. Muhammad soon after surrendered at Kabul.

Although persistent Afghan aggression compelled the British to mount punitive expeditions every month, the country now seemed safe enough for officers to send for their families in India. Among them were Lady Sale and her youngest daughter, who in August 1841 was married in Kabul to Lieutenant J. L. D. Sturt (d. 1842), an engineer officer. But the safety of the countryside proved illusory. When, to save £4,000, the bribes paid to the hill tribes for good behavior were eliminated, the hillmen rose and cut off the passes to India. In October 1841 Sale was ordered to clear the passes to Jalalabad. He was wounded in the first fight by a bullet in his ankle, but by 30 October he had reached Gandamak, 26 miles west-southwest of Jalalabad on the road to Kabul. On 10

November he learned of the revolution in Kabul on 2 November and of the murder of Sir Alexander Burns [q.v.], the British representative there, who was hacked to death by an Afghan mob. With the news came orders to march his men back to Kabul, where, among others, his wife, daughter, and son-in-law were at the mercy of the Afghans. After holding a council of war, he decided to ignore his orders, march to Jalalabad, and make a stand there. Its defenses had fallen into a sorry condition, and Major George Broadfoot [q.v.] was put in charge of making the place defensible. Sale's force consisted of about 2,000 men, of whom 700 were in the 13th Foot.

On 14 November a successful sortie cleared the area of hostiles, and supplies were gathered in, but by the end of the month Sale was besieged by 6,000 Afghans [see Jalalabad, Siege of]. He made so active a defense that he came to be called Fighting Bob and had largely defeated his besiegers when, on 16 April 1842, General George Pollock [q.v.] arrived with a relieving force.

Sale held out at Jalalabad while the government of India tried to decide what should be done. At the end of July Pollock moved his division to Fatehabad, 14 miles west-southwest on the road to Kabul, and a month later the two joined forces and moved toward the city. On 8 September Sale found Afghans strongly entrenched on heights near the village of Jagdalak, 40 miles west of Jalalabad, and was wounded while driving them off. On 15 September, having driven the Afghans from height to height, the force reached Kabul. There it was learned that British captives, among them Sale's wife and daughter, had been taken to Bamian 60 miles north-northwest. Sir Richmond Campbell Shakespear [q.v.] with 600 horses was sent to liberate them, and Sale with the infantry followed to give support. On 17 September the captives, who had managed to induce their guards to release them, met Shakespear. They were in Sale's camp the next day.

Medals and honors were showered upon Sale. He received the Thanks of the Government of India and of both houses of Parliament, Wellington himself proposing the vote in the House of Lords. After a brief visit to England he returned to India in 1844 as quartermaster general of the queen's troops in the East Indies. In 1845, when the First Sikh War [q.v.] began, he was appointed quartermaster general to General Sir Hugh Gough [q.v.]. In the Battle of Mudki [q.v.] on 18 December his left thigh was shattered by grapeshot and he died from the effects of the wound on 21 December.

Salem Church Battle of (3–4 May 1863), American Civil War. In the Chancellorsville Campaign, Union General John Sedgwick [q.v.], after capturing Marye's Heights [q.v.] above Fredericksburg, Virginia, moved west on the morning of 3 May to unite with General Joseph Hooker [q.v.]. The next day he was stopped by four Confederate brigades sent by Robert E. Lee. In a battle that lasted until dark, Sedgwick was unable to break through. The next day Lee reinforced McLaws, who late in the day attacked Sedgwick. The battle was fought well into the night, a rare occurrence in the nineteenth century. The Confederates were unable to break the Union line, and Sedgwick escaped annihilation by withdrawing his force northwest and across the Rappahannock River near Bank's Ford.

Salem Cloth. Cloth manufactured in Salem, Oregon, and much used in American military uniforms.

Salient. 1. Bulges in a line of battle.
2. In fortifications, an angle projecting outward.

Salinas Pass, Engagement at (9 April 1812), Peninsular War. Francisco Espoz y Mina [q.v.], the most renowned of the Spanish guerrillas, after eluding all French efforts to destroy him, moved into Navarre, where, at the Salinas Pass on the road between Vitoria and Mondragón, he surprised a huge French convoy escorted by 2,000 troops. A Polish regiment in the French service on its way to Russia suffered 500 killed, and 150 prisoners were taken. Some 450 Spanish prisoners of war were rescued, and an enormous quantity of booty fell into Espoz y Mina's hands.

Salisbury Prison. An abandoned cotton factory in Salisbury, North Carolina, was converted during the American Civil War into a Confederate prison and originally used for spies, Confederate soldiers awaiting court-martial, and deserters. The first Union prisoners arrived in December 1861; by the following March the prison held 1,500. Food was ample, and prisoners lived in adequate quarters until 1864, when some 10,000 more were crowded in. Although from December 1861 to March 1862 there had been only 1 death, from October 1864 to February 1865 there were 3,419.

Sally. A sortie [q.v.].

Sally Port. A passageway, usually vaulted, that permitted sorties from a fortification. At West Point and other American military academies the archways from the barracks to the parade ground are so called.

Salm-Salm, Agnus Elizabeth Winona Leclerq (née Joy). See Salm-Salm, Felix Constantine Alexander Nepomuk, Prince.

Salm-Salm, Felix Constantine Alexander Nepomuk, Prince (1828–1870). A Prussian soldier of fortune who was educated at the cadet school in Berlin and served in the Prussian cavalry during the Schleswig-Holstein War [q.v.]. He then joined the Austrian army but resigned for financial reasons. In 1861, at the beginning of the American Civil War, he sailed to the United States, where he offered his services to the Union army. During the war he served first as an aide to General Ludwig Blenker [q.v.], then as colonel of the 8th New York and subsequently of the 68th New York before he was brevetted brigadier general.

In 1862 he married Agnes Elizabeth Winona Leclerq Joy (1840–1912), a beautiful, charming, and intelligent young woman of uncertain background who had at one time found employment as a circus performer and an actress in Cuba. The bride followed her husband in the field and became celebrated for her ministrations at the hospital at Bridgeport, Tennessee.

After the war Salm-Salm was mustered out on 30 November 1865, and he and his wife voyaged to Mexico, where he offered his sword to the emperor Maximilian [q.v.] and served as his chief of staff and commander of the French Foreign Legion. His life was spared when Maximilian was captured and executed, and with his wife he returned to Europe, where he again served as a major in the Prussian army. He was killed in the Battle of Gravelotte–St. Privat on 18 August 1870 in the Franco-Prussian War [q.v.].

In this war Princess Agnes formed a hospital brigade, and in 1899–1900, during the Second Anglo-Boer War [q.v.], she twice visited the United States to raise money for a Boer ambulance corps. She lived in Germany thereafter, having remarried in 1876 one Charles Heneage.

Saloman, Louis Étienne Félicité (1820–1888). A Haitian soldier and politician who from 1855 to 1859 was commander-in-chief of the Haitian army. He then spent ten years in exile before returning in 1879 to serve as president until his death. [See Haitian Civil Wars.]

Salta, Battle of (20 February 1813), Argentine War of Independence. Argentine forces under General Manuel Belgrano [q.v.] defeated Spanish forces at Salta, a town in northern Argentina, 140 miles northwest of Tucumán.

Salt Creek Massacre (May 1871), American Indian Wars. A large party of Kiowas led by Santanta (d. 1875) ambushed a wagon train of ten freight wagons with 12 teamsters at Salt Creek Prairie, an open stretch of road between Fort Griffin and Fort Richardson, Texas, near present-day Jacksboro. Only 5 whites escaped alive. The rest were killed, and their corpses mutilated. The wagons were plundered and burned, and the raiders made off with 41 mules.

Salting Boxes. Round boxes about four inches high and two and a half inches in diameter that were used in the artillery for holding mealed powder, which was sprinkled on fuzes of shells so that they might take fire from the explosion of the powder in the chamber.

Saltoun, Lord. See Fraser, Alexander George.

Salt River, Battle of (26 December 1872), Apache Wars. An American army force under Colonel (later General) George Crook [q.v.] undertook a winter campaign against hostile Apache Indians led by Geronimo and Cochise [qq.v.]. Crook found the Indians in a canyon along the Salt River in what is today south-central Arizona. He won a decisive victory, and the survivors were herded onto reservations.

Apaches under Geronimo resumed hostilities in 1885 but were forced to surrender to Crook's successor, Nelson Miles [q.v.], in 1886.

Saltville Massacre (2 October 1864), American Civil War. Federal Brigadier General Stephen Gano Burbridge (1831–1894) with 3,600 troops, 400 of whom were black, launched an attack upon Saltville, a town in southwestern Virginia, 32 miles northeast of Bristol. Barricaded behind stone and log breastworks were some 2,800 Confederates, including men from a brigade under Brigadier Felix Huston Robertson (1839–1928) and a company of bushwackers under Captain Champ Ferguson [d. 1865]. Burbridge retreated, leaving some 350 killed and wounded on the ground. The following morning the Confederates moved over the battlefield, killing all the wounded blacks, more than 100.

Two months later Federal forces occupied and destroyed much of the town. Ferguson was captured, convicted of murder, and hanged on 20 October 1865. Robertson escaped punishment and lived until 29 April 1928. At the time of his death he was the last surviving Confederate general.

Salute. 1. A military mark of deference made by raising the hand in a prescribed manner to the forehead, headgear, or firearm or by raising the sword in a proscribed manner. It is given by soldiers to commissioned officers and by commissioned officers to officers of higher rank and is usually returned by them. Both soldiers and officers salute civilians of high rank. There seems to have been no prescribed rules in the British army for this prior to 1844.

2. The consecutive firing of guns without projectiles to honor personages of high rank, the number fired depending upon the status of the person being honored. In the United States the highest salute is twenty-one guns reserved for the president and ruling sovereigns [see Personal Salutes by Artillery].

3. The lowering of a flag is another salute. In Britain a flag can be lowered to the ground; in the United States the flag could be dipped or flown at half-mast but is never allowed to touch the ground.

Salute in marching past in slow time, British army c. 1868

Salvo. 1. The simultaneous firing of a number of pieces of artillery.

2. The consecutive firing of artillery at measured intervals, often as a salute [see Personal Salutes by Artillery].

Samarkand, Russian Occupation of (1868), Russian wars in Central Asia. In 1868 Russian General Konstantin Petrovich Kaufmann [q.v.] after a bitter struggle captured and occupied Samarkand, an ancient city in the fertile valley of Zeravshan, 180 miles southwest of Tashkent, now in Uzbekistan.

Sam Browne Belt. See Belt, Sam Browne.

Samé. The skin of various types of small sharks and rays used in Japan to cover the hilts or scabbards of swords or daggers. Skilled samé workers were called *sameshi*.

Samejima, Shigeo (1849–1928). A Japanese soldier who fought in the Boshin Civil War of 1868, the Japanese invasion of Formosa (Taiwan) in 1874, the Satsuma Rebellion in 1877, the Sino-Japanese War [qq.v.] of 1894–95, and the Russo-Japanese War in 1904–05.

Samoan Civil Wars. Intratribal warfare was almost endemic in Samoa, a group of islands under native rulers in the southwest-central Pacific Ocean north of Tonga Island. In 1878 the United States established a coaling station at Pago

Pago on Tutuila Island and began to contend for commercial and naval rights with Britain and Germany, causing international and internal dissension. At times three Samoan chiefs, each encouraged by one of the rival powers, all with warships in the harbor of Apia, competed for local domination.

Civil War of 1880–81. In 1880 Germany, Britain, and the United States agreed to recognize Malietoa Talavou (d. 1880) as king. When he died soon afterward, civil war broke out among factions seeking power. After eight months of turmoil Malietoa Laupepa (d. 1898) secured the throne and was recognized by the three powers, to whom he granted special privileges by treaty in return.

Civil War of 1887–89. The German trading company on Samoa collected taxes, a practice much resented by the Samoans, who revolted. In response a German warship landed troops in 1887 and supplanted Malietoa Laupepa with a local chief, Tamasese (fl.1880s), who was proclaimed *tafaifa*, king of all Samoa. King Malietoa Laupepa was exiled.

In September 1888 Mataafa (d. 1899), a powerful chief, led a second rebellion. With the aid of the German consul at Apia, on the island of Upola, Samoan warriors under King Tamasese, attacked the insurgents, but were defeated and driven back to Mulinu'u Point, where they were protected by a German gunboat, which shelled the rebel villages, an action protested by British and American officials. When Mataafa's warriors began plundering German plantations and wiped out a small German detachment, the German consul declared martial law and requested two companies of marines, a request denied for fear of American intervention. A tense situation was somewhat eased by a hurricane on 15–16 March 1889 that destroyed three German and three American ships; a British warship fled. Later that year the American, British, and German governments agreed to restore Malietoa Laupepa to the throne, and a neutrality pact was concluded in which all three powers jointly supervised the islands.

Civil War of 1892–94. In the spring of 1893 Mataafa (d. 1899) rebelled against King Malietoa Laupepa. Robert Louis Stevenson (1850–1894), who was living in Samoa, wrote to Henry James (1843–1916): "You don't know what news is, nor what politics, nor what the life of man till you see it on so small a scale." To Mark Twain (1835–1910) he wrote of "severed heads and men dying in hospital." British and German warships arrived and quelled the fighting. Mataafa surrendered and was taken to the Marshall Islands.

Civil War of 1898–99. In 1898, when King Malietoa Laupepa died, his rival, Mataafa, was brought back from exile in the Marshall Islands and installed as king. Because he was virtually a German puppet, the Americans and British strongly opposed him and supported the former king's son. There was bitter fighting between Samoan factions in January 1899. Apia, the capital, was plundered, and buildings were burned. On 15 March American and British warships shelled the town. American and British troops landed and took command of coastal roads, but fighting raged on in the interior. On 13 May a commission of the three foreign powers arrived, and control of the islands was divided among them. Germany was given the western islands, and the United States the remainder, when Britain exchanged its rights for Tonga and the Solomons.

Samory / Samori Touré (1830?–1900). A Mandingo warrior who from 1870 ruled as a king in Guinea. In 1865 he helped the Sisés conquer the Bèrètés. By 1880 he had founded a state with an efficient administration and a regular army east of the upper Niger River. By 1884 he ruled a large portion of West Africa. After coming into conflict with French expansionist ambitions in 1889, he sent selected men to enlist in French colonial units to learn new training methods and the use of new weapons. He bought arms from both British and French traders and recruited widely, seeking out former soldiers of British and French colonial armies and giving freedom to captured young men in exchange for military service. When the French launched an offensive against him in 1891, he was able to resist for seven years. No other African leader lasted so long in a struggle with European colonizers. He was finally taken by surprise on 29 September 1898 by Captain (later General) Henri Joseph Gouraud (1867–1946) at Guelemou, Ivory Coast, on the upper Cavally River and sent into exile on the island of Ndjole in the Ogooué River in Gabon. With his defeat the entire western Sudan came under French dominance [see Mandingo-French Wars].

Samsonov, Aleksandr Vasilievich (1859–1914). A Russian soldier who was graduated from the cavalry school in St. Petersburg and served in the Russo-Turkish War [q.v.] of 1877–78. In 1884 he was graduated from the general staff college and appointed to the general staff. From 1896 to 1904 he was commandant of the cavalry school at Elizavetgrad. In the Russo-Japanese War he led a division of Siberian Cossacks. In World War I, after the disastrous Battle of Tannenberg, in which he commanded the defeated Russian army, he shot himself.

Samurai. A member of a warrior class or military gentry in Japan that arose in the Heian era (794–1185) whose members ruled Japan until the Meiji Restoration [see Boshin Civil War]. Many served as military retainers of a daimyo [q.v.]. Samurai were particularly powerful on east-central Honshu Island and were often organized into military units called *Bushidan*. They lived by the code of bushido, the fundamental virtues of which were frugality, fealty, and filial piety. They despised money and those who pursued it, priding themselves on their stoicism and powers of endurance. As symbols of their position, they wore their hair in distinctive topknots and carried two swords. At the time of the Meiji Restoration they constituted only 6 percent of the population, but they monopolized military and political power and enjoyed hereditary salaries. The restoration saw the decline of their powers and privileges. In 1873 universal military service was instituted, opening military status to peasants. Reductions in samurai privileges led to a samurai revolt in 1877, but it was soon crushed [see Satsuma Rebellion]. In 1885 they were forbidden to wear swords.

Samurai Swords. Samurai carried two swords: a short sword, the *wakizashi,* and the *katana,* a long fighting sword at least two feet long and usually longer. The latter was slightly curved and hatchet-tipped with a long hilt. Both swords were carried through an obi or fastened to a *koshiate* (sword belt). Their blades were never touched with the bare hands. Of the sixteen recognized cuts, the most difficult was crosswise through the hips. Cuts were sometimes practiced on the bodies of criminals.

San Antonio, Battle of (7 December 1835), Texas War of Independence. Texans, led by Benjamin Rush Milam (1788–1835), successfully attacked San Antonio, which was defended by Mexican General Martín Perfecto de Cós (1800–1854). Milam, a Texas hero, was killed.

Sanborn, John Benjamin (1826–1904). An American lawyer and soldier who in the American Civil War commanded the 4th Minnesota. Later he led a brigade under Union General W. S. Rosecrans [q.v.]. In the Battle of Iuka [q.v.] he suffered 558 casualties out of 2,200 engaged. He later fought at Corinth, at Vicksburg [qq.v.], and against Indians on the western frontier. After the war he returned to the practice of the law and to politics.

Sandbags. Bags of canvas or gunnycloth filled with earth sometimes used in constructing protection for artillery or in mending a breach made by enemy fire.

Sand Creek Massacre. See Chivington's Raid.

Sandeman, Robert Groves (1835–1892). A British soldier who was educated at Perth and St. Andrews University. In 1856 he was commissioned in the 33rd Bengal Native Infantry. He fought in the Indian Mutiny [q.v.], and in 1857, as adjutant of the 11th Bengal Lancers, he took part in the final capture of Lucknow [q.v.]. After the mutiny he became a political officer and as district officer of Dera Ghazi Khan extended British influence to independent Baluchi tribes beyond the border. During the Second Afghan War [q.v.] his influence with the tribesmen enabled him to keep open a line of communication with Kandahar and to control the Baluchis after the disastrous defeat of the British in the Battle of Maiwand [q.v.]. He was knighted in 1879. In 1889 he occupied the Zhob Valley and opened the Gomal Pass through Waziri country to caravans.

Sandhurst. See Royal Military College, Sandhurst.

Sandilands, Gordon (1865–1922). A Scots soldier who was commissioned in the Royal Scots and took part in the Bechuanaland Expedition [q.v.] in 1884–85. In 1895 he retired from the army and settled in South Africa, where he took part in the Jameson Raid [q.v.]. During the Second Anglo-Boer War [q.v.] he raised the Transvaal Scottish Volunteer Battalion and commanded it as lieutenant colonel.

Sandile / Sandilli (1823?–1878). A Xhosa who became a chief about 1850. He quarreled with Sir Harry Smith [q.v.], the Cape governor, and waged local wars against the British in eastern Cape Colony and against other tribes. Although at first neutral in the Kaffir War of 1877–78, he soon became involved. He was killed in a skirmish by two random bullets in 1878 [see Kaffir Wars].

San Gabriel, Battle of (8 January 1847), Mexican War. The army and naval force of Brigadier General Stephen Watts Kearny [q.v.] defeated the main Mexican army in California in the San Gabriel Valley just outside Los Angeles.

Sangar. A stone breastwork parapet or strongpoint. The term was usually used in reference to warfare in Afghanistan and on India's Northwest Frontier [q.v.].

San Isidro, Battle of (10 April 1870), War of the Triple Alliance. In one of the final battles of the War of the Triple Alliance [q.v.], Francisco Solano López [q.v.] and his remaining Paraguayan followers were driven into the mountains by the Brazilians.

Sanitary Commission, Royal. The short title for the Royal Commission appointed to inquire into the "Regulations affecting the Sanitary Condition of the Army, the organization of Military Hospitals and the Treatment of the Sick and Wounded." It was founded shortly after the Crimean War [q.v.], at the demand of Florence Nightingale [q.v.], who politicked, cajoled, and hounded politicians until it was established. The chairman was Miss Nightingale's political friend Sidney Herbert [q.v.].

Among other abuses, the commission found nearly every barracks was overcrowded and had insufficient ventilation. Although 600 cubic feet of air was thought to be the minimum requirement for health, the average was actually 450. It pronounced the food inedible and found the hospitals filled with venereal disease cases: 206 per 1,000 in the cavalry and 250 per 1,000 in the infantry [see Venereal Disease].

In spite of the commission's findings, the British army did little to improve sanitation. Lord Wolseley in his *Soldier's Pocket Book* wrote that there was no need for a sanitation officer except in fixed bases. In South Africa during the Second Anglo-Boer War [q.v.] Lord Roberts had no sanitary officer although thousands died from preventable diseases. Not until 1903 was there even a lecture at the British Staff College on the importance of diet, clean water, and the removal of excreta. The subject of sanitation and hygiene was not introduced at West Point until 1906.

In 1863 Florence Nightingale, as a member of the Royal Commission on the Sanitary State of the Indian Army, wrote: "If the facilities for washing were as great as those for drink, our Indian army would be the cleanest body of men in the world."

Sanitary Commission, United States. A civilian organization established during the American Civil War in June 1861 as the Commission of Inquiry and Advice in Respect of the Sanitary Interests of the United States Forces with Frederick Law Olmsted (1822–1903) as chief executive officer. Working with the Union army, it aided in the care of sick and wounded soldiers and their families. Its president, Dr. Henry Whitney Bellows (1814–1882), of All Souls Unitarian Church in New York City, established his headquarters in Washington, D.C., with main branches in ten of the largest northern cities. The organization expanded its services as the war progressed. It distributed food, medicine, and clothing; built convalescent camps; distributed stamps; and writing paper; telegraphed relatives of the seriously ill; and established lodgings near railroad stations that in the course of the war provided a million night's lodgings. It collected funds, raising more than a million dollars, and distributed some fifteen million dollars' worth of donated supplies.

Much of the money and many of the donations were collected at sanitary fairs, the first of which was held in Chicago from 27 October to 7 November 1863. Schools, businesses, and courts closed for its opening day. President Abraham Lincoln contributed the original draft of the Emancipation Proclamation [q.v.], which was sold at auction for three thousand dollars and donated to the Chicago Soldiers' Home. [See Blackwell, Elizabeth].

Sanitary Commission *Quarters of the Sanitary Commission, Brandy Station, November 1863. Photograph by Alexander Gardner*

San Jacinto, Battle of (21 April 1836), Texas War of Independence. In a battle that lasted less than twenty minutes, fought on a coastal plain on the west bank of the San Jacinto River where it empties into Galveston Bay, former Tennessee Governor Sam Houston [q.v.], commander-in-chief of the Texas army, leading 743 volunteers, defeated a Mexican force of 1,536 regulars under General Antonio López de Santa Anna [q.v.]. The Texans lost 16 killed and 24 wounded, including Houston, who was wounded by a musket ball that fractured both tibia and fibula; Santa Anna lost 630 killed, 208 wounded, and 729 taken prisoner. He himself surrendered the following day. This was the last major engagement of the Texas War of Independence [q.v.].

It has been suggested that the outcome of the battle might have been different had Santa Anna at the time of the attack not been "dallying" with a beautiful mulatto slave he had captured.

A 567.31-foot obelisk, 12 feet taller than the Washington Monument and the world's tallest column, now stands on the battlefield to commemorate the victory. It was begun in 1936, the centenary of the battle, and completed three years later.

San Jacinto, Battle of (12 February 1867), Mexican revolt against Maximilian's rule. Forces of the emperor Maximilian under Miguel Miramón [qq.v.] were defeated by Mexican constitutionalists under General Mariano Escobedo [q.v.] near the San Jacinto River. Miramón's army surrendered, and he narrowly escaped capture.

San Juan, Benito (1775?–1808). An unfortunate Spanish general who during the Peninsular War [q.v.] took up a position on the road to Madrid at Somosierra Pass in the Sierra de Guadarrama with 9,000 men and 16 guns to stop Napoleon's triumphant march toward Madrid [see Somosierra, Battle of]. San Juan failed to rally his troops when they broke and bolted. When they finally stopped their flight at Talavera, they turned on him and hanged him from an elm tree.

San Juan Hill, Battle of (1 July 1898), Spanish-American War. San Juan Hill, 3,792 feet high, near Santiago de Cuba, in south-central Cuba, was successfully attacked by Americans under Brigadier General Hamilton Smith Hawkins (1831–1910), a nongraduating West Pointer, who took command after the obese Major General William R. Shafter [q.v.] became too ill to command and had to retire.

Spanish General Arsenio Linares y Pombo (1848–1914) had placed 520 men at the nearby town of El Caney under Colonel Vara del Rey y Rubio and 10,400 on and near San Juan Hill. The latter was not in the main defense line of Santiago but an outpost. Among the 8,400 American troops taking part in the attack were the dismounted Rough Riders [q.v.], under Lieutenant Colonel Theodore Roosevelt [q.v.], who seized Kettle Hill, northeast of the main heights. Charging with the Rough Riders were the black soldiers of the dismounted 9th and 10th Cavalry. (Captain John Pershing, future general of the armies, who commanded the American Expeditionary Force in France in 1917, served in the 10th Cavalry.)

The Rough Riders lost 89 killed and wounded out of 490 engaged. Roosevelt was recommended by General Leonard Wood for the Medal of Honor, but it was not awarded. War correspondent Richard Harding Davis [q.v.] described the assault. The attackers, he wrote, "had no glittering bayonets, they were not massed in regular array. There were a few men in the advance, bunched together, and creeping up a steep, sunny hill, the tops of which roared and flashed with flame." In the *New York Herald* Davis's story was headlined COLONEL ROOSEVELT LED THE MEN THROUGH THE LINES OF THE REGULARS AT SAN JUAN AND THEIR MAGNIFICENT CHARGE INSPIRED THE ARMY. And so the legend was formed.

In this battle Lieutenant John Henry Parker (1872?–1942), commanding a detachment of Gatling guns, distinguished himself. San Juan was taken nine minutes after his guns

San Juan Hill *Field hospital at the "Bloody Ford" of San Juan Creek, 1898*

opened fire. Roosevelt said of him: "Parker deserved more credit than any other one man in the entire campaign. . . . [H]e had the rare good judgement and foresight to see the possibilities of the machine guns, and thanks to the aid of General Shafter he was able to organize his battery." Total casualties were 1,460. Santiago de Cuba surrendered on 17 July 1898. [See Las Guásimas, Battle of; El Caney, Battle of; Spanish-American War.]

Sankolinsin. See Seng-ko-lin-ch'in.

San Marcial, Battle of (31 August 1813), Peninsular War. French Marshal Jean de Dieu Soult [q.v.], in a last effort to raise the Allied siege of San Sebastián [q.v.], on the Bay of Biscay, launched a two-pronged attack upon Wellington's positions on the ridge of San Marcial, which runs parallel to and a mile south of the Bidassoa River. The assaulted positions were defended by the Spanish division of General Francisco Longa [q.v.]. The fighting ended in mid-afternoon, when a major storm broke over the field. The French were repulsed and fell back in some disorder. Spanish losses were 1,700; French losses were 2,500.

San Martín, José de (1778–1850). A South American soldier and revolutionary who was born in Yapeyú on the Uruguay River in what is today Argentina. He was educated at a military school in Madrid and served in the Spanish army, fighting against the Moors in northwestern Africa and against the French in the Peninsular War [q.v.]. In 1812–13, having joined the South American revolutionary movement, he helped Buenos Aires gain independence from Spain. In 1814 he succeeded Manuel Belgrano [q.v.] as commander-in-chief of the patriot army and with Bernardo O'Higgins [q.v.] organized an army in Cuyo Province, Argentina. In January 1817 he led the army over the Andes to Chile and defeated the Spanish in the Battle of Chacabuco [q.v.]. The following year he was again victorious in the Battle of Maipo [q.v.]. After establishing an independent Chile, he sailed for Peru and in July 1821 entered Lima. There, having proclaimed the country independent, he assumed the title Protector of Peru. Unable to defeat Spanish forces in the Peruvian central highlands, he

In 1817 José de San Martín leads his army through the Upsalata Pass of the Andes.

turned to Simón Bolívar [q.v.] for help. On 26–27 July 1822 the two men met at Guayaquil, Ecuador. No one knows what was discussed or concluded, but San Martín resigned on 20 September, retired to Europe, and fought no more. His work made possible Bolívar's later victories at Junín and Ayacucho [qq.v.] in 1824. He died in Boulogne-sur-Mer, France.

San Miguel, Duque Evaristo (1785–1862). A Spanish soldier and statesman who played an active part in the Spanish revolt of 1820 [q.v.] led by Colonel Rafael del Riego y Núñez [q.v.]. In 1823 he was Spain's minister of foreign affairs, but with the return of King Ferdinand VII (1784–1833) to the throne he was exiled from 1824 to 1834 and lived in Paris and London. On his return to Spain he was made a field marshal and minister of war. He was in retirement from 1843 to 1854, when he became president of the Madrid defense junta.

San Millán de la Cogolla, Battle of (18 June 1813), Peninsular War. A French force of 5,000 was discovered at this town in northern Spain 24 miles west-northeast of Logroño by scouts of the King's German Legion [q.v.]. An Allied force of 5,000 infantry and 1,000 cavalry attacked and routed the French, who suffered the loss of 300 men and all their baggage; the Allies sustained 110 casualties.

Sanna's / Sannah's Post, Battle of (30 March 1900), Second Anglo-Boer War. At this station, 23 miles east of Bloemfontein [q.v.], Orange Free State, a Boer commando of 1,500 men under General Christiaan De Wet [q.v.] surprised and routed a British force of 1,900 men with 12 guns under Brigadier General Robert George Broadwood (b. 1862). Boer losses were 2 men wounded; the British suffered 19 officers and 136 other ranks killed or wounded, 428 taken prisoner, and the loss of 7 guns, 117 wagons, and an enormous amount of supplies.

A distinguishing feature of the battle was the gallant stand of Q Battery, Royal Horse Artillery, which fought its guns until only 10 men were left standing.

San Pasqual / Pascual, Battle of (7–8 December 1846), Mexican War. In California at this place, 40 miles northeast of San Diego, mounted Mexican-Californians (Californios) carrying 10-foot lances and led by Andrés Pico (1810–1876), a prosperous landowner, defeated in about fifteen minutes an American force of 1,700 under General Stephen Watts Kearny [q.v.]. The lancers under Pico were, according to Kearny, "admirably mounted and the best riders in the world, hardly one that is not fit for the circus." The Californios lost 1 killed and 12 injured; the Americans lost 18 killed and 15 wounded, 3 mortally. Only 2 Americans were killed by gunfire, the remainder by lances. Kearny was stabbed twice in the arm and once in the buttock. After the battle Kit Carson [q.v.], with a Delaware Indian and navy Lieutenant Edward Fitzgerald Beale (1822–1893), crept through the Mexican lines to carry news of Kearny's desperate position to Commodore Robert Field Stockton (1795–1866), who sent reinforcements. Before they could arrive, the Californios retreated.

This and the Battle of San Pedro [q.v.] were the only two engagements in the Mexican War in which the Americans were defeated.

San Patricio Battalion. During the Mexican War, American General Winfield Scott [q.v.], most of whose soldiers were volunteers, suffered 9,207 desertions. Some of the deserters joined the Mexican army and took up arms against their former comrades. About 700 were formed into the San Patricio (St. Patrick) Battalion, led by Irish-born John Riley, a former soldier in the 5th Infantry. Although not all of its members were Irish, Riley designed for the battalion an emerald green ensign with an image of St. Patrick, an Irish harp, and a shamrock.

Sixty-nine members of the battalion were captured in the Battle of Churubusco [q.v.] on 20 April 1857. Those who had deserted before hostilities began on 26 April 1846 were lashed and imprisoned; some were branded. Thirty who had deserted after the hostilities were sentenced to be hanged. The execution was arranged by Colonel William S. Harney [q.v.], and on 13 September 1847, the day of the Battle of Chapultepec [q.v.], the condemned, including one who had lost both his legs at Churubusco, were placed on mule wagons under their gallows with ropes around their necks. When the American flag was raised in triumph over the Castle of Chapultepec, the mules were whipped, and the 30 members of the San Patricio Battalion were left dangling in the air.

Riley, who had deserted before the war began and thus escaped death, was sentenced to be flogged and branded and to wear a ball and chain for the duration of the war. He was branded with a *D* on both cheeks because in the first branding the *D* was upside down.

In the Plaza San Jacinto in San Angel, Mexico, a plaque gives the names of the 71 soldiers of the battalion who were killed: 48 appear to have been Irish and 13 German.

San Patricio Battalion *Deserters from the San Patricio Battalion about to be hanged*

San Salvador, Wars of. San Salvador in Central America successfully rebelled against Spanish rule in 1821 and joined the Mexican confederation. Two years later it seceded and became an independent country. In 1863, aided by Honduras, it went to war with Guatemala but was overwhelmed when Nicaragua allied itself with Guatemala.

San Sebastián, Sieges of. This important fortified Spanish seaport on the Bay of Biscay, 48 miles east of Bilbao, was twice besieged in the nineteenth century.

Peninsular War (20 July–8 September 1813). Wellington laid siege to French-held San Sebastián, and the bombardment began on 20 July 1813. The first assault on 25 July failed with heavy loss. By 26 August heavy siege guns were creating breaches in the walls. On 31 August an all-out attack was made, and the town was captured but at a cost of 2,376 casualties. Five days of uncontrolled British excess followed as they sacked the town. Much of it was burned. The French, under the command of General Louis Rey [q.v.], retreated into Monte Urgullo, a strong citadel on top of nearby Monte Marcial [see San Marcial, Battle of]. After an agreed surrender, the French were allowed to march out with the full honors of war. Total British casualties were about 3,700.

First Carlist War (February–June 1836). In February 1836 Carlists besieged Cristinos and a small detachment of the British Legion [q.v.] in San Sebastián until driven off in June by an army of 10,000 Spanish and British troops under British General George de Lacy Evans [q.v.].

San Sebastián *British assault of San Sebastián, 1836*

Santa Anna / Ana, Antonio López de, (1794–1876). A Mexican soldier and revolutionary who in 1810 entered the Spanish colonial army as a cadet. During the Mexican War of Independence he was initially loyal to Spain, but he joined the rebels to support in turn Agustín de Iturbide in 1822, Vicente Guerrero in 1828, and Anastasio Bustamante [qq.v.] in 1832. He led revolts against each. Although he had earned a reputation as a corrupt and ruthless politician, a gambler, and an opium addict, he was elected president of Mexico and served from 1833 to 1835. In 1836 he attempted to crush the Texan Revolution and succeeded in seizing the Alamo [q.v.] on 6 March, but on 21 April, in the Battle of San Jacinto [q.v.], he was defeated and captured by Sam Houston [q.v.]. In 1837 he returned to Mexico and retired to his hacienda until illegally taking command of the Mexican army, he led it against the French, who had made an incursion at Veracruz [see Pastry War]. In the hostilities, which lasted from April 1838 to March 1839, he lost a leg. Although the Pastry War was of little historical importance, it marked the return of Santa Anna as a force in Mexican politics, and in 1841 he seized power as dictator. He was deposed and exiled in 1844, only to be recalled in 1847, when he was named provisional president and given command of the Mexican forces fighting the American invaders, a war in which he lost every battle and was driven out of Mexico City [see Mexican War]. Having been exiled again in 1848, he was recalled from Jamaica in 1853 and was installed as president. He served until 1855, when he was exiled yet another time. He tried to make common cause with the emperor Maximilian [q.v.], but his intrigues failed. In 1867, after Maximilian's death, he attempted to effect a landing in Mexico, but he was captured in the endeavor and, although sentenced to death, was allowed to remove to New York. In 1874 he returned under an amnesty to Mexico City, where he died in poverty, blind, and neglected.

Santa Anna *General Antonio López de Santa Anna*

Santa Cruz, Andrés (1792?–1865). A Bolivian soldier and political leader who fought in the War of Peruvian Independence from Spain in 1820–23. From 1829 to 1839 he was president of Bolivia, and he led the Allied forces in the War of the Peru-Bolivia Confederation [q.v.]. He was defeated by General Manuel Bulnes [q.v.] of Chile in the Battle of Yungay [q.v.] in 1839 and overthrown.

Santa María, Domingo (1825–1889). A Chilean soldier and political leader who was president of Chile from 1881 to 1886. In 1883 he brought to a successful conclusion the War with Peru and Bolivia [see Pacific, War of the].

Santana, Pedro (1801–1864). The leader of the Dominican revolution that in 1844 separated Santo Domingo (Dominican Republic) from Haiti on the island of Hispaniola. He was three times president of the republic: 1844–48, 1853–56, and 1858–61.

Santander, Francisco de Paula (1792–1840). A soldier and politician of New Granada (Colombia), often regarded as the country's founder. On 7 August 1819, during the Colombian War of Independence, he commanded a divi-

sion under Simón Bolívar [q.v.] in the Battle of Boyacá [q.v.]. He served as vice-president from 1821 to 1828 and, during the absence of Simón Bolívar, was acting president from 1821 to 1826. His political activities led to his banishment from 1829 to 1832, when he returned and became president.

Santarém, Battle of (18 February 1834), Miguelite Wars. In 1828, two years after the infanta Maria II (1819–1853) became queen of Portugal following the abdication of her father, her uncle Dom Miguel (in full: Miguel Maria Evaristo de Bragança [1802–1866]) usurped the throne. Loyalist forces mobilized, and near this commune on the right bank of the Tagus River, 43 miles northeast of Lisbon, the forces of Dom Miguel were defeated by an army under the Duke of Saldanha [q.v.]. Dom Miguel was forced to give up all claims to the throne.

Santarosa, Conte Santorre di, Annibale de Rossi di Pomarolo (1783–1825). An Italian revolutionary and soldier who was a subprefect of La Spezia under Napoleon from 1812 to 1814. In 1815 he was a captain in the Sardinian army. He became a leader in the Piedmontese liberal movement, and in 1821 he organized a conspiracy against the Austrians that failed. He was condemned to death but fled into exile. He was killed at Spakteria, Greece, fighting for Greek independence from Turkey.

Santo Domingo Revolts. See Hispaniola Revolts; Haitian Dominican Conflicts; Santana, Pedro.

Sap. 1. As a verb, to undermine a wall, a trench, or any other defensive structure.
2. As a noun, a narrow trench, usually zigzag in design and often covered to provide protection from enemy fire, used to approach a besieged place.
3. As a verb, the act of creating such a trench.
4. As a noun, any trench forming part of a field fortification.
A sap whose dirt is thrown during digging to only one side is called a single sap; if thrown on both sides, it is called a double sap. If the sap was built under fire, gabions were used to protect the diggers and the gabion was pushed forward as the work progressed; the work was then called a flying sap.

Sap Battery. Guns placed at the head of a sap.

Sap Faggot. A fascine about three feet long placed vertically between gabions to protect sappers.

Sap Head. The end of a sap, which could be made to form an exit for an assaulting party or from which parallels could be dug.

Sapper. 1. One who digs saps.
2. In British and French (*sapeur*) usage, any engineer soldier or member of a unit of sappers and miners.

3. In British usage, the lowest rank of an engineer soldier.

Sapper *French sapper (left) and a gunner of the foot artillery*

Sap Roller. A large wicker cylinder similar to a gabion. It was filled with stones and logs and used to protect those digging saps.

Sap Roller *A sap roller ready for use at Vicksburg, Mississippi, 1863*

Saragossa, Maid of. On 4 July 1808, during the Peninsular War [q.v.], at a crucial moment in a French attack upon the Portillo Gate during the siege of Saragossa [q.v.], a young Spanishwoman named Agostina, or Manuela Sánchez, sprang to her lover's place after he was killed or wounded and helped serve a cannon, thus saving the day. She was celebrated by

Saragossa, Maid of *The Maid of Saragossa, July 1808*

Lord Byron [q.v.] in the Spenserian stanzas of his poem *Childe Harold's Pilgrimage* (I, liv–lvi [1812]).

Saragossa, Sieges of (1808–09), Peninsular War. The citizens of Saragossa, a city of about 60,000 on the Ebro River in northeast-central Spain, 170 miles northeast of Madrid, rebelled when Napoleon installed his brother Joseph on the throne of Spain. On 15 June 1808 some 6,000 French troops under General Charles Lefebvre-Desnouëttes [q.v.] attempted unsuccessfully to storm the city, which was ably defended by General José Palafox y Melzi [q.v.], later Duke of Saragossa, with only 1,500 men, 900 of whom were volunteers. Having lost 700 men and several guns, the French fell back and laid siege. On 4 July they made another attack with six columns but were repulsed with a loss of 500, thanks in part to the efforts of the Maid of Saragossa [see Saragossa, Maid of]. On 4 August the French commander called upon Palafox to surrender and received the defiant reply "War to the knife!" In response the French launched a third attack, in which they were repulsed with a loss of about 2,000. The following day Spanish reinforcements reached the beleaguered city. On 17 August the French raised the siege.

The Spanish strongly reinforced the city, but on 20 December Marshals Adolphe Mortier and Bon Adrian Moncey [qq.v.] with 45,000 troops, including 3,000 sappers and 144 guns, 52 of which were siege guns, reimposed the siege and within a month had mined and blasted their way past the outer defenses. French Marshal Jean Lannes [q.v.] assumed command of the siege and on 27 January broke through the defenses, but the garrison put up a stout defense, and the French had to fight street by street to advance through the city. When the surviving 8,000 defenders capitulated on

20 February 1809, a third of the city was in total ruins. The victory cost the French 4,000 killed and 6,000 wounded; the Spaniards lost an estimated 54,000 soldiers and civilians, mostly from diseases.

Sarah Sands, Sinking of the. See Troopship.

Sarawak, Chinese Insurrection at (17–18 February 1857). The Chinese in Sarawak, in northern Borneo, rose in rebellion against the rule of Sir James Brooke [q.v.], who narrowly escaped capture in Kuching by jumping out a window and swimming across the Sarawak River. He returned with a force of Malays and drove out the insurgents, killing 2,000.

Sardar. A Maratha feudal lord [see Maratha Wars].

Sardinian-Austrian War. See Austro-Piedmontese War.

Saricas. Turkish irregulars.

Sárkány, Battle of (30 December 1848), Hungarian Revolution. Austrian forces under Prince Alfred zu Windisch-Graetz [q.v.] defeated and drove off in disorder rebel forces holding a defile near this village (now Cerci) in central Rumania, seven miles east of Fagarar, forcing rebel General Arthur von Görgey [q.v.] to retreat from the positions he had chosen to defend.

Sarmiento, Domingo Faustino (1811–1888). An Argentinean soldier and political leader who opposed the regime of Juan Rosas [q.v.] and was in exile in Chile from 1835 to 1852. He helped Justo Urquiza [q.v.] defeat Rosas. From 1868 to 1874 he was president of Argentina. While in office, he brutally suppressed a rebellion by the last of the old caudillos [q.v.] and his armed gauchos, saying later: "I did not try to economize with gaucho blood. . . . Blood is the only thing they have that is human." He terminated the War of the Triple Alliance [q.v.] against Paraguay.

Sash. A mark of distinction worn for different reasons in different armies by officers and sometimes cadets and noncommissioned officers either around the waist or diagonally across the chest and back.

Sashimono. A Japanese emblem worn on the back or on a small extended flag on the back to indicate the daimyo [q.v.] a samurai was serving. The practice was introduced into Japan in the sixteenth century and persisted until the Meiji Restoration in the 1860s.

Saskatchewan Rebellion. See Riel Rebellion.

Satsuma Rebellion (1877). A Japanese rebellion led by Saigo Takamori [q.v.], a leader of the Satsuma (Kagashima Prefecture) forces that overthrew the Tokugawa shogunate in the Boshin Civil War [q.v.] of 1867–68. The rebellion was a protest against the reforms being made by "evil counselors" of the Meiji emperor, particularly those restricting the feudal privileges of the samurai [q.v.], and the rejection of Saigo Takamori's plan to invade Korea.

When the imperial government, suspecting rebellion, sent troops to remove ammunition stored at Kagoshima, a city on an inlet on the south coast of Kyushu, the southernmost of the four main Japanese islands, they were attacked by young samurai. Saigo Takamori had not anticipated the attack, but once it had occurred, he raised the standard of revolt on 29 January 1877. On 17 February with an army of 40,000 samurai he set out from Kagoshima in a snowstorm to attack Kumamoto Castle, one of the strongest in Japan, located near the mouth of the Shirakawa River. The garrison consisted mostly of conscripts [see Japanese Army]. After an unsuccessful fifty-day siege, the rebels withdrew [see Kumamoto, Siege of].

The besieged imperial forces, led by Yamagata Aritomo [q.v.], had superior firepower: Krupp field guns, Gatling guns, and mortars. They were also better organized and with better communications. The war virtually ended on 14 September, when Saigo Takamori, wounded and cornered, ordered a samurai to behead him. Other versions record that he committed hara-kiri or was killed in battle.

Saucisson. The French name (meaning sausage) for long, narrow fascines, usually about 18 feet long and 10 inches in diameter. Often made of cloth or leather, they were filled with gunpowder and used to explode military mines.

Saud ibn 'Abd al 'Aziz (1769–1814). A Wahhabi leader and chief of the house of Saud. He conquered the Hejaz and fought the Egyptian army of Mehemet Ali [see Arabian Wars].

Saugor / Sagar, Siege of (3 February–3 November 1858), Indian Mutiny. Some 170 European women and children and 68 European artillerymen were besieged by mutineers for ten months at this town, 180 miles north of Nagpur, until relieved by the army of General Sir Hugh Rose [q.v.].

Saussier, Felix Gustave (1828–1905). A French soldier who during the Franco-Prussian War [q.v.] was captured at Metz [q.v.] in 1870. He escaped and in 1871 commanded a brigade in the Army of the Loire. In North Africa in 1881 he commanded the expeditionary force in Tunis. He was military governor of Paris from 1884 to 1886.

Savage, Arthur William (1857–1938). An American arms manufacturer and inventor. He was born in Jamaica, came to the United States in 1886, and was naturalized in 1895. In 1893 he founded the Savage Arms Company in Utica, New York. He invented a dirigible torpedo and devised improvements in magazine rifles.

Savage's Station, Battle of (29 June 1862), American Civil War. The third in the Seven Days' Battles [q.v.] of the Peninsular Campaign [q.v.]. In the late afternoon at this place east of Richmond, Virginia, Confederate General John Magruder [q.v.] launched an attack with two and a half brigades against the forces under Union General Edwin Sumner [q.v.] and was repulsed. The Union forces then counterattacked, the 5th Vermont with great élan. Darkness and a severe thunderstorm ended the fighting, and the Federals withdrew in the night, leaving large amounts of supplies and 2,500 men in a hospital.

Had General Thomas ("Stonewall") Jackson [q.v.] arrived on time, the Federals would doubtless have suffered a severe defeat, but he did not appear until 3:00 A.M. the next day.

The battle is sometimes known as Allen's Farm or Peach Orchard. Federal losses were 1,590; Confederate losses were 626.

Savannah, Siege of (9–21 December 1864), American Civil War. Union General William Tecumseh Sherman [q.v.] laid siege to Savannah, Georgia, the ultimate objective of his March to the Sea [q.v.]. Sherman had 68,000 troops available to him; the Confederates under Major General William Joseph Hardee [q.v.] at Savannah numbered only 15,000. Hardee at first refused to surrender the city, but when Sherman brought up siege guns and prepared to invest it, Hardee retreated before his lines of communication were cut. The eastern states of the Confederacy were then sliced in two.

Savantvadi / Sawantwadi, Disorders in. This Maratha state of less than 1,000 square miles in the south Bombay area of India was subjugated by the British in 1819 but remained under local chiefs. Rebellions against the British flared in 1828, 1832, 1838, and 1844–45. The last was suppressed only after hard fighting by Lieutenant Colonel (later General Sir) James Outram [q.v.].

Savary, Anne Jean Marie René (1774–1833). A French soldier, the son of a French officer, who was commissioned in the cavalry in 1791. After service on the Rhine he became in 1797 an aide to General Louis Desaix (1768–1800), serving under him in Egypt and until 14 June 1800, when Desaix was killed in the Battle of Marengo [q.v.]. He then became an aide to Napoleon and was promoted general of brigade in 1803. In 1803–04 he was engaged in counterintelligence, playing a role in the abduction of the Duke of Enghien (1772–1804) and his execution on 21 March 1804. At Austerlitz [q.v.] he carried out special missions to the tsar for Napoleon. In 1807 he was temporarily in command of a corps in Poland and fought at Ostrolenka [q.v.]. The following year Napoleon created him Duke of Rovigo. In 1810 he succeeded Joseph Fouché (1759–1820) as minister of police, a position he held until April 1814. After Napoleon's final surrender, he fled to Turkey, but he was eventually pardoned and for a few months in 1831–32 commanded the French forces in Algeria.

Savov, Mikhail (1857–1928). A Bulgarian soldier and statesman who commanded a wing of the Bulgarian army in its victory over Serbians in the Battle of Slivnitza [q.v.] during the Serbo-Bulgarian War [q.v.] of 1885. From 1891 to 1897 he was minister of war. He was commander-in-chief in the first two Balkan Wars (1912–13).

Saya. In Japan, the scabbard for a sword or the sheath for a knife.

Sayler's Creek, Battle of (6 April 1865), American Civil War. Also known as the Battle of Harper's Farm. On 5 April 1865 Lee's hungry, exhausted, and retreating Army of Northern Virginia reached Amelia Court House, a village in southeast-central Virginia, where Lee expected but did not receive much-needed supplies. He then moved southwest toward Rice Station, but Grant moved to block him. When two Union divisions pressed against the rear of Confederate General Richard Ewell [q.v.], he deployed along Little Sayler's Creek, where he was soon attacked. Caught in a double en-

velopment, the Confederates suffered a major defeat, and Ewell himself, with at least five other Confederate generals, was captured.

Total Confederate casualties were between 7,000 and 8,000; Federal losses were reported as 1,180, of whom only 166 were killed. Confederate prisoners, at almost 7,000, were second only to Federals captured by Stonewall Jackson at Harpers Ferry on 16 September 1862. Lee, learning of his losses, is said to have cried out: "My God! Has the army dissolved?"

On the Federal side there was a liberal dispersion of honors after the battle. Fifty soldiers were given the Medal of Honor [q.v.] for capturing enemy flags.

Scabbard. A sheath for a sword, a bayonet, or any other pointed weapon.

Scaling Ladders. Ladders carried forward in an attack in order to cross ditches and scale the walls of an enemy fortification [see Escalade].

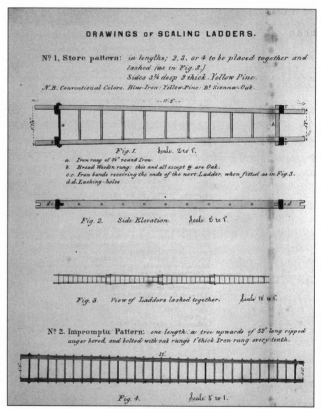

Drawing of scaling ladders from a British military manual

Scalping. A practice among many American Indian tribes of cutting from a fallen foe a circular patch of the scalp with hair attached. John Richardson, a British officer who served in Canada during the War of 1812 [q.v.], described seeing an Iroquois scalp an American he had killed: He "proceeded to make a circular incision throughout the scalp. This done, he grasped the bloody instrument between his teeth, and placing his knees on the back of his victim, while at the same time he fastened his hands in the hair, the scalp was torn off without much apparent difficulty, and thrust still bleeding in his bosom." To preserve the scalp, the loose flesh was scraped off, and the skin stretched over a frame and dried.

White Americans too sometimes scalped. In the War of 1812 [q.v.] Brigadier General Alexander Smyth (d. 1830) offered forty dollars—equal to several months' pay for a private—for each Iroquois scalp. Some of the volunteers who took part in Chivington's Raid [q.v.] scalped the fallen.

Scalping, although painful if the victim was alive, was not itself usually fatal. Prisoners were sometimes scalped to increase their agony before being killed. Sometimes the victim was allowed, as an act of defiance or bravado, to return to his tribe without his scalp.

Scarface Charlie (1851?–1896), Indian name: Chic-chack-am, Lulal-kuel-atko. A Modoc leader who became a noted warrior. On 29 November 1872, when Second Lieutenant Frazier Augustus Boutelle (1840?–1905?) came to arrest him, he fired the first shot of the Modoc War [q.v.]. In the lava beds into which the Modocs retreated, he emerged as one of their leaders and in that capacity took part in the first parlays with General Edward Canby [q.v.]. On 11 April 1873, when it was decided to assassinate Canby during a parley, he refused to take part although he promised not to interfere. On 26 April he laid the ambush that destroyed Lieutenant Evan Thomas [q.v.] and his men, killing or mortally wounding 5 officers and 18 enlisted men. Many more were wounded. The fight ended when Scarface Charlie shouted: "All you fellers that ain't dead better go home! We don't want to kill you all in one day."

Because the soldiers who had fought him believed that he had killed no one except in fair fight, he went unpunished upon the Modocs' surrender, and after the execution of Captain Jack [q.v.], he was appointed chief. With the survivors of the tribe he was herded into the Quapaw Agency in Oklahoma, where he died of tuberculosis.

Scarlett, James Yorke (1799–1871). In the nineteenth century it was rare for a British soldier of any rank to have attended a university, but Scarlett was educated at Eton and Trinity College, Cambridge. From 1840 to 1853 he commanded the 5th Dragoon Guards. In the Crimean War [q.v.] he was appointed a brigadier and commanded the heavy brigade of cavalry, 900 sabers, which at Balaclava on 25 October 1854 he led in a momentous charge against an estimated 2,000 Russian horsemen, routing them. For this he was promoted major general. Subsequently he was given the local rank of lieutenant general and commanded all the cavalry in the Crimea. From 1860 to 1865 he was adjutant general, and from 1865 to 1870 he commanded at Aldershot [q.v.].

Scarp. See Escarp.

Scent Bottle Lock. See Forsyth Lock.

Schapska. A cap originally worn by Polish lancers that bore a distinguishing badge and flared into a high, four-sided flat top that was usually in the facing color. It was adopted with modifications by lancers in other European armies.

Scharnhorst, Gerhard Johann David von (1755–1813). A German soldier who was the son of a tenant farmer who had been a sergeant major in the Hanoverian artillery. He studied at the prestigious military academy of Count Friedrich Wilhelm Ernst zu Schaumburg-Lippe-Bückeburg and was commissioned in the Hanoverian cavalry in 1778. He fought under the Duke of York and Albany [q.v.] in the Netherlands, taking part in the Battle of Hondschoote on 8 September 1792 and in the Battle of Menin (Meenen) on 27–30 April 1793. He edited three journals and wrote two books, establishing himself as a military scholar and theorist. In 1801 he transferred to the Prussian army and taught at the Berlin War Academy. He helped found the Militärische Gesellschaft, the first military society devoted to the study of war, and he reorganized the Berlin Institute for Young Officers.

He was wounded slightly at Auerstädt [q.v.] on 14 October 1806 and with General Gebhard von Blücher [q.v.] was taken prisoner near Lübeck [qq.v.]. Released, he was awarded the Pour le Mérite [q.v.], Prussia's highest medal, for his gallantry in the Battle of Eylau [q.v.] on 7–8 February 1807.

Soon after the Treaty of Tilsit [q.v.] in July 1807 he was promoted major general and appointed to head the Military Reorganization Commission [q.v.]. In this capacity, with four other senior officers, known as the Five Reformers [q.v.], he began the reorganization of the Prussian army. Between 1808 and 1810 he increased the number of trained troops by shortening the length of service, abolished harsh punishment, provided improved musketry training, and encouraged the commissioning of soldiers from the ranks. A supporter of conscription, he declared that "each citizen is a defender of the state." In 1812 he became chief of staff to Blücher. He was wounded in the foot at Lützen [q.v.]; the wound became infected, and he died at Prague a month later (8 June 1813). His army reforms were completed by August von Gneisenau [q.v.].

Scheepers, Gideon (1878–1902). A Boer soldier who joined the South African Republic (Transvaal) State Artillery in 1894 as a heliograph operator. He was later seconded to the Orange Free State to organize a heliograph service there. At the beginning of the Second Anglo-Boer War [q.v.] he served as a scout, but he rose to be a commandant and to lead a commando of Cape rebels. In 1901 he was captured by the British and charged with murder, flogging a British subject, exposing prisoners of war in a firing line, and other crimes. He was convicted and shot on 17 January 1902. He is regarded as an Afrikaner hero.

Schenck, Robert Cumming (1809–1890). An American soldier and politician who served for eight years in the U.S. House of Representatives (1843–51) and for two years as minister to Brazil (1851–53). In 1861, at the beginning of the American Civil War, he was appointed a brigadier general of volunteers in the Union army. He was engaged in the First Battle of Bull Run and was wounded in the arm in the Second Battle of Bull Run [qq.v.]. Between those two battles he saw service in the Shenandoah Valley against Confederate General Thomas ("Stonewall") Jackson [q.v.]. In 1862 he was promoted major general and placed in command at Baltimore. In 1863 he resigned and returned to Congress. Later he was minister to Great Britain. Among his other accomplishments, he was an authority on draw poker.

Schill, Ferdinand Baptista von (1759–1809). A Prussian

soldier who, although commissioned in the Prussian cavalry at the age of twelve, was still a subaltern thirty-five years later, when he fought in the Battle of Auerstädt [q.v.] on 14 October 1806. After the Treaty of Tilsit [q.v.] in July 1807 he was given command of a regiment of hussars. In 1809 he led a revolt against French domination, marching his regiment from Berlin to the Elbe River. On 5 May of that year he fought a skirmish with the Magdeburg garrison, after which he retreated northward, hoping for British support, which was not forthcoming. Near Wismar, a seaport 19 miles north of Schwerin, he was surrounded by 5,000 Danish and Dutch troops. After a sharp fight at Damgarten on 24 May he escaped to Stralsund, 88 miles northwest of Stettin, but there the Danes and Dutch hemmed him in and on 31 May overwhelmed him. He was killed in the fighting.

Schipka Pass, Battle of. See Shipka Pass, Battle of.

Schleswig-Holstein Revolt (1848). These two duchies were claimed by both Frederick VII (1808–1863) of Denmark and the Duke of Augustenburg, the latter's claim supported by Prussia. When Frederick took the throne in 1848, he attempted to absorb Schleswig, which, like Holstein, although under the Danish monarch, was not part of Denmark. The act sparked an émeute in both duchies, for the population of Holstein was predominantly German and Schleswig had a large German minority. In April–May Prussian forces under General Friedrich von Wrangel [q.v.], commissioned by the German Confederation, occupied the duchies, provoking protests from Sweden, Russia, and Britain, all of which feared the expansion of Prussian power into the Baltic and North seas. Prussia was pressured to withdraw, and in 1850 Denmark's rights were assured [see Schleswig-Holstein War].

Schleswig-Holstein War (1864). These two duchies with large German-speaking populations (Holstein was predominantly German, and the population of Schleswig included a large German minority) were ruled by the king of Denmark although neither was part of that country. Both had unsuccessfully revolted in 1848, when Denmark tried to incorporate Schleswig [see Schleswig-Holstein Revolt]. In January 1864, sixteen years after Denmark's rights had been reestablished, Prussian troops under Field Marshal Friedrich von Wrangel [q.v.], with some Austrian forces under General Ludwig von Gablenz [qq.v.], invaded and overran the duchies. Since Wrangel was an octogenarian whose complete sanity was in some doubt and his chief of staff was the incompetent General Vogel von Falkenstein, they were soon replaced by Prince Frederick Charles and Helmuth von Moltke [qq.v.].

The Prussians won the first battle of the war, although their casualties, 193, exceeded those of the Danes, 127. The Prussians were armed with the new Dreyse rifle [q.v.], the so-called needle gun, while the Danes fired slow-loading Minié rifles [q.v.], but Wrangel's bull-at-the-gate tactics were crude: a frontal attack against Danish entrenchments. "*In Gottes Namen, d'ruf!* [In God's name, get 'em!]," he shouted. On 3 February an Austrian brigade of Ukrainians, Hungarians, and Slovaks carried the important heights of Oberselk-Jagel. The Austrians won another victory in the Battle of Oeversee,

but only after three bloody bayonet charges against well-entrenched Danes. An Austrian staff officer described the final charge, with troops "pushing ahead dauntlessly, stepping over the corpses of the fallen and whooping, drunk with victory." The Austrians lost 21 officers and more than 300 other ranks. The emperor personally commended Gablenz on his "death-defying battle."

Near Vejle, a seaport on the southeast Jutland Peninsula, the Danes occupied a strongpoint on a hill that was protected by trenches, stone walls, and the Vejle Fjord. Here the Austrians suffered their first defeat. Their headlong frontal attacks were repeatedly beaten back until it occurred to General von Gablenz to have his men wade the fjord and attack the Danish right flank.

On 15 March 1864 Frederick Charles invested Dybböl [q.v.], and on 15 April he carried it by assault. There was a truce from 25 April to 25 June while Britain tried to bring about a peace, but its efforts were thwarted by Otto von Bismarck (1815–1898). On 26 June the fighting resumed, and on 29 June the Prussians surprised and captured the island of Als (German: *Alsen*) off the east coast of South Jutland, taking the batteries there and capturing 2,500 Danes. An armistice was agreed to on 18 July, and on 1 August Denmark sued for peace. In the peace treaty signed in Vienna on 30 October Denmark gave up all rights to the duchies to Prussia and Austria. (In 1920 the northern part of the old duchy of Schleswig, now known as South Jutland, was returned to Denmark.)

Schleswig-Holstein War *Prussians capture a fort during the Schleswig-Holstein War*

The victors, Prussia and Austria, soon fell out between themselves, and in 1866 Prussia's supremacy was confirmed in the Seven Weeks' War [q.v.].

Schlichting, Sigismund von (1829–1909). A German soldier who became one of the most important officers in the army of imperial Germany. He entered the cadet school at Wahlstatt at age eleven. In 1847 he joined the 7th Grenadier Regiment as an officer candidate, and he first saw combat in 1848 against Polish insurgents. He served as a company commander in a Guards regiment in the Seven Weeks' War of 1866 and as a battalion commander in the Franco-Prussian War [qq.v.] in 1870–71, in which he won the Iron Cross, Second Class [q.v.]. After the war he attended the Russian maneuvers in 1875 and later the Italian maneuvers. He became known for his incisive reports, and his writings on military affairs commanded attention.

In 1888 he was chairman of a committee that produced new infantry regulations that abolished the battlefield formations left over from the days of Frederick the Great (1712–1786), encouraged initiative in junior officers, and restated the doctrine of Helmuth von Moltke the Elder, who had rejected the old Napoleonic tactics and preached that hesitation and inactivity were greater sins than mistakes. As a corps commander from 1888 to 1896 Schlichting incorporated his views in the training of his troops, stretching Moltke's views of strategy to the lowest tactical unit. He argued that an attack on a prepared defense could succeed not by a headlong frontal dash but by a prepared attack.

Not everyone agreed with his views. Among those who opposed him was the illustrious General Kolmar von der Goltz [q.v.], who argued that Napoleonic tactics were still applicable. Schlichting was appointed commanding general in Karlsruhe but was forced to retire in 1896 as, he said, "a sacrifice to the mechanical brains of the army." In retirement he wrote his magnum opus, *Taktische und strategische der Gegenwart* [Modern Tactics and Strategy] (1898) and articles critical of Alfred von Schlieffen [q.v.], chief of the Great General Staff.

Schlieffen, Alfred von (1833–1913). A German soldier, son of a Prussian officer, educated at a Hutterite (Christian Anabaptist) school at Niesky and at the Joachimstal Gymnasium in Berlin. From 1853 to 1858 he served in the Uhlan Guards, and from 1867 to 1869 he was military attaché in Paris. He was a staff officer during the Franco-Prussian War [q.v.], and from 1876 to 1884, when he joined the Great General Staff, he commanded the Potsdam Guards. From 1891 to 1905 he was chief of the Great General Staff and drew up what is generally known as the Schlieffen Plan to attack and defeat France, a plan that violated Belgian neutrality and showed a reckless contempt for international law. As early as 1900 he informed the Foreign Office that in case of a two-front war the army would not "be limited in its options by existing international treaties." He retired in 1906 but continued to write on strategy and other military subjects.

After his wife's death in 1872 he became cold and distant, and he was frequently sarcastic with associates.

Schlik / Schlick, Franz von (1789–1862). An Austrian general who during the Hungarian Revolution [q.v.] was defeated by the Hungarian rebels in the Battle of Hatvan [q.v.]

on 4 April 1849. He commanded the Austrian Second Army in the bloody but inconclusive Battle of Solferino [q.v.] on 24 June 1859.

Schmeisser, Louis (1849–1917). A Swiss gunmaker whose early years were spent as a journeyman gunsmith in France, Germany, and Austria. He finally established his own workshop at Jena in Thuringia. After designing several weapons, he entered into a partnership with Theodor Bergmann (d. 1915) for the production of those weapons and of any future designs. By agreement, the Schmeisser name disappeared, and all his designs became known as Bergmanns [q.v.].

Schmidt, Karl von (1817–1875). A Prussian cavalry commander who during the Franco-Prussian War [q.v.] commanded a brigade and was wounded at Mars-la-Tour on 16 August 1870 [see Mars-la-Tour–Vionville, Battle of]. He later commanded a division in the fighting on the Loire. After the war he took a leading part in the reorganization of German cavalry.

Schmidt-Rubin Rifle. A 7.5 mm rifle (and later a carbine) introduced in 1889 and designed by Colonel Rudolf Schmidt, director of the Swiss arsenal at Bern, and a Major Rubin, director of the military laboratory at Thun. Schmidt's contribution was a twelve-round box magazine and the bolt action, which was slightly modified in 1893 to provide smoother action.

Schneider-Creusot Company. In 1782 William Wilkinson (d. 1808), an English ironmaker who was a brother of John Wilkinson [q.v.], established the Forges et Fonderies du Creusot at Le Creusot, a commune in east-central France, to exploit the deposits of ore found in the region. There he made cannon of iron using coal instead of coke and developed a superior method for boring guns. He prospered during the French Revolutionary Wars and the American Revolutionary War. The French said of him that he "taught them how to bore cannon in order to give liberty to America." In 1837, thirty years after his death, the ironworks was purchased by two brothers, Adolphe (d. 1845) and Joseph Eugène Schneider (1805–1875), who expanded the plant and concentrated on railroad equipment and river steamers. In 1874 they began the manufacture of weapons, and the company developed into the largest steel-manufacturing and munitions plant in the world. Although badly damaged in World War II, it is still extant.

Schnitzer, Eduard Carl Oscar Theodor (1840–1892), known as Emin Pasha. A German born of Protestant Christian parents of Jewish descent who trained as a physician and emigrated to Turkey, where he became a Muslim. In 1875 he arrived penniless in Khartoum, but he was assisted in setting up a practice by the European community there. In 1876 Colonel Charles ("Chinese") Gordon [q.v.] invited him to the Equatorial Province (Equatoria), where he was governor, to serve as medical officer. Gordon liked him and in time made him chief medical officer of the province. He also employed him in administrative duties and dispatched him on missions to Uganda and Unyoro. In 1878 Emin was appointed governor of Equatoria, a post he held until 1889. As the forces of El Mahdi [q.v.] swept through the Sudan, the Sudanese provinces capitulated one by one until with the fall of Khartoum and the death of Gordon in January 1885, Emin was completely isolated from the outside world, a condition that did not seem to bother him, for he was intensely interested in natural science, and the flora and fauna that surrounded him engrossed him. He commanded a small native army, but had the Dervishes made a determined effort it would have been easily swept aside.

When it became known in Europe that he was still alive, a massive effort was made to rescue "the last of Gordon's lieutenants," and an expedition commanded by Henry Morton Stanley (1841–1904) was dispatched. After near-incredible hardships and the loss of hundreds of lives, Stanley reached Emin, only to find him reluctant to be rescued. Nevertheless, Stanley carried him off to safety. When they arrived at Bagamoyo in German East Africa (mainland Tanzania), the resident German officers and officials gave them a celebratory banquet, marred only when Emin fell off a balcony and injured his head. When he was discharged from the hospital, he joined the German service, returned to Central Africa, and was soon murdered by Arab slavers.

Schoepf, Albin Francisco (1822–1886). An Austrian soldier born of an Austrian father and a Polish mother who was educated at a military academy in Vienna and served in the Austrian army to the rank of captain. In 1848 he joined the revolutionary army [see Hungarian Revolution], and after the collapse of the revolution he fled to Turkey, where he served in the Turkish army. In 1851 he emigrated to the United States and was working as a porter in a Washington hotel when he came to the attention of Joseph Holt (1807–1894), the commissioner of patents, who gave him a clerkship. When Holt became secretary of war in January 1861, he took Schoepf with him into the new office. On 30 September of that year, at the beginning of the American Civil War, Schoepf was commissioned a brigadier general of volunteers and sent to Kentucky. There in October he repulsed an attack on his fortified camp by Confederate General Felix Kirk Zollicoffer [q.v.] but was later driven out by Zollicoffer, his men fleeing in a panic that came to be known as the Wild Cat Stampede. He commanded a division in the Battle of Perryville [q.v.] but ended the war as superintendent of the Federal prison at Fort Delaware [q.v.].

After the war he returned to the Patent Office and became chief examiner.

Schofield, John McAllister (1831–1906). An American soldier who was graduated from West Point in 1853 and at the beginning of the American Civil War was appointed a brigadier general of volunteers in the Union army. He was chief of staff to General Nathaniel Lyon at the Battle of Wilson's Creek [q.v.] on 10 August 1861. In May 1863 he was promoted major general. He commanded an army in the Atlanta Campaign [q.v.] and defeated Confederate General John Hood [q.v.] in the battles of Franklin and Nashville [qq.v.]. In November 1865 he was sent on a secret mission to France to inform Napoleon III (1808–1873) of the adamant opposition of the United States to the French troops that were propping up Emperor Maximilian [q.v.] in Mexico. In 1868, during the impeachment crisis, when President Andrew Johnson (1808–1875) attempted to replace Secretary of War

Edwin Stanton, Schofield was briefly secretary of war. He then commanded several departments in the West until in 1876 he was appointed superintendent of the U.S. Military Academy at West Point, where he served until 1881.

He was commanding general of the army, succeeding General Philip Sheridan [q.v.], from 1888 to 1895, when he was made a lieutenant general and retired. During his tenure he introduced examinations for the promotion of officers and lineal instead of regimental promotions and he gave strong support to service schools. He reduced desertions by making enlisted life more attractive through better terms of enlistment, better rations, and the establishment of post exchanges, schools, and gymnasiums. He also streamlined army administration, removing the odd mix of divisions and departments. His autobiography, *Forty-Six Years in the Army*, was published in 1897.

Schönbein, Christian Friedrich (1799–1868). A German chemist who in 1839 first discovered ozone. In 1845 he added nitric acid to cotton and produced guncotton (nitrocellulose) and from it collodion, a viscous solution of pyroxylin used as a coating for wounds.

Schoolmaster, Army. A nineteenth-century rank in the British army just below a sergeant major. Those holding the rank taught soldiers and their children rudimentary knowledge and skills. In 1865 there were 214 army schoolmasters [see Army Schools].

School of the Soldier. That body of knowledge, the basic drill, which every individual soldier needs to master. In the nineteenth century, because many soldiers were illiterate, much was taught by rote and practical experience.

Schools of Practice / Schools of Application. In the U.S. army these were schools for the teaching of special military skills, especially for officers, e.g., the Artillery School of Practice established at Fort Monroe in 1821, the Cavalry School established at Carlisle Barracks in 1838 by Captain (later Major General) E. V. Sumner [q.v.], and a Marine Corps School of Application established on 1 May 1891 at Washington, D.C., under Captain Daniel Pratt Mannix (d. 1894), who had served four years as an adviser to the Chinese navy.

Schumann System of Armored Fronts. A permanent defensive system developed in 1889–92 in Germany that eschewed forts entirely and relied upon the fire of guns and howitzers in protected cupolas surrounded by thornbushes or wire entanglements.

Schurz, Carl (1829–1906). A Prussian-born American soldier and politician who, after his involvement in the revolutionary movements that swept through Europe in 1848–49 [see Revolutions of 1848], fled to the United States in 1852. He became a lawyer, campaigned for Lincoln in 1860, and, when the American Civil War broke out, was minister to Spain. Although he had no military experience, he was made a brigadier general of volunteers in the Union army in June 1862 and fought at Second Bull Run, Chancellorsville, and Gettysburg [qq.v.], becoming a major general in 1863. After the war he became a journalist, a U.S. senator, secretary of the interior, an editor, and an author.

Schützen. 1. As a noun, units of sharpshooters in nineteenth-century German armies.

2. As a verb, to protect or support by firepower.

3. As a noun, a German rifleman.

Schütztruppe. A colonial unit composed of Zulus, Sudanese, Somalis, and coastal Arabs established in German East Africa (mainland Tanzania) in 1891 as a "protective force." Enlistment was for five years and could be renewed. Known as askaris [q.v.], the soldiers of the unit were encouraged to feel superior to the local Africans. A native batman or servant was provided for every two soldiers.

The use of nonlocal Africans was based upon a fear that a mutiny of local troops could lead to a full-scale revolt. Because the Germans kept no regular forces in their colonies—unlike the British in India—local troops were employed only to a scale needed for police actions.

Schwarzenberg, Karl Philip, Prince von (1771–1820). An Austrian soldier commissioned in 1788, he first distinguished himself in the Austro-Turkish War and then against the French in the Austrian Netherlands. He was promoted brigadier general in 1796. In 1805 he escaped from the doomed army of General Karl Mack [q.v.] in the Battle of Ulm and rallied the survivors. In 1812 he commanded an Austrian corps in Napoleon's Russian Campaign [q.v.]. In August 1813, when Austria declared war on France, he was made commander-in-chief of the armies of the Sixth Coalition [see Napoleonic Wars]. Although defeated at Dresden, he led his armies to victory at Leipzig [qq.v.]. In 1814 he led the Army of Bohemia into France. In 1817 he was paralyzed by a stroke. He died three years later.

Schwarzlose, Andreas William (1867–1936). An Austrian artilleryman who was graduated from the Ordnance College with distinction and in 1892 developed his first automatic pistol. This was never produced, but in 1897 he set up a factory at Berlin to produce a locked-breech pistol using the 7.63 mm Mauser cartridge. Production ended in 1904, and most of those remaining were sold to Russian revolutionaries. In 1900 Schwarzlose developed a heavy, water-cooled machine gun that was adopted by the Austro-Hungarian army.

His factory was dismantled in 1919, and he spent the remainder of his life as a consultant.

Schwatka, William Frederick (1849–1893). An American soldier and Arctic explorer who was graduated from West Point in 1871. After seven years on frontier duty, in which he fought battles against Yavapais and Apaches in the Southwest and Sioux in Nebraska and Wyoming, including the Battle of Rosebud Creek [q.v.] against Crazy Horse [q.v.], he took leave in 1878 to accompany William Henry Gilder (1838–1900) on an Arctic expedition in search of lost explorer Sir John Franklin (1786–1847). In the course of the search, which yielded only the wreckage of one ship and the graves of expedition members, Schwatka and his party traveled 3,251 miles by sleigh, the longest such trek on record. He completed the journey in 1880 and returned home in good health and without injury, only to slip on an icy sidewalk and break his leg.

In 1882 he served as an aide-de-camp to General Nelson Miles [q.v.], and in 1883–84 he explored the course of the Yukon River. He resigned from the army in 1885, and in 1886 he led the *New York Times* Alaskan Expedition.

Schwechat, Battle of (30 October 1848), Hungarian Revolution. Hungarian honved militia revolting against Austrian rule marched on and occupied Vienna. At Schwechat, now a southeastern suburb of Vienna, rebel sympathizers within the city threw up barricades, but the Hungarians were defeated by Austrian regulars under Prince Alfred Zu Windisch-Graetz [q.v.], who bombarded and then occupied Vienna the next day [see Vienna, Siege of].

Scorched Earth Policy. The destruction of the military supports and economic resources of an enemy. Although the term was not used in the nineteenth century, the policy was often employed. It was frequently used by the British on the Northwest Frontier [q.v.] against recalcitrant tribes and by Union forces during the American Civil War in the Shenandoah Valley and in Sherman's March to the Sea [q.v.].

During the American Civil War General Ulysses S. Grant's instructions on 5 August 1864 to General Philip Sheridan [q.v.] illustrate the policy: "In pushing up the Shenandoah Valley . . . it is desirable that nothing should be left to invite the enemy to return. Take all provisions, forage and stock wanted for the use of your command. Such as cannot be consumed, destroy."

Scots Greys. A British cavalry regiment raised in 1678. Its uniform facings were stone gray, and its mounts were gray. The regiment was called the Royal North British Dragoons from 1751 to March 1877, when it was renamed the 2nd Dragoons (Royal Scots Greys). It earned battle honors in the Crimean War, the Battle of Waterloo, and the Second Anglo-Boer War [qq.v.]. Napoleon was said to have referred to it as *ces terribles chevaux gris* (those terrible gray horses).

Scott, Hugh Lenox (1853–1934). An American soldier who was graduated from West Point in 1876 and served on the frontier, taking part in the Nez Percé War [q.v.]. He studied Indian sign language and served as negotiator in dealings with several Indian tribes. He did much to quell the Ghost Dance Disturbances [q.v.] in Oklahoma. In 1892 he became the first commander of Company L, 7th Cavalry, a unit composed entirely of Kiowa, Comanche, and Apache Indians. Although he saw no fighting in the Spanish-American War [q.v.], he took part in the military occupation of Cuba (1899–1902), serving as adjutant general, and he was later governor of the Sulu Archipelago in the Philippines, where he abolished the slave trade. He was chief of staff of the army in 1914–17 and then saw action in France.

Scott, Winfield (1786–1866). An American soldier who after studying law was commissioned a captain of artillery on 3 May 1808. He had the misfortune to serve under the egregious General James Wilkinson [q.v.] in Louisiana. He was soon court-martialed for calling his commanding officer a liar and a traitor and maintaining that serving under him was like being married to a whore. He was sentenced to be suspended for a year without pay.

At the beginning of the War of 1812 [q.v.] he returned to the army as a lieutenant colonel. He distinguished himself in the Battle of Queenstown Heights [q.v.] on 13 October 1812 but was captured. When exchanged, he was appointed adjutant general on the staff of General Henry Dearborn [q.v.]. He drew up the plans for the attack on Fort George, near Lake Ontario, and led the attack. In March 1814, at the age of twenty-seven, he was promoted brigadier general, the youngest in the army. He served under General Jacob Brown [q.v.] at the battles of Chippewa on 5 July 1814 and Lundy's Lane [qq.v.] on 25 July. On 3 November 1814 Congress awarded him a gold medal. President James Madison (1751–1836) in a message to Congress in September 1814 praised Scott and others as heroes who "triumphantly tested the progressive discipline of the American soldiery."

After the war Scott wrote a manual on infantry tactics that was used for many years. In 1832 he took part in the Black Hawk War [q.v.], and while on duty in South Carolina in 1833, he faced the nullifiers, who opposed the protective Tariff Acts of 1828 and 1832, declaring that the state had the right of nullification when the federal government exercised powers not specifically given it by the Constitution. By 1833 the movement had gained so many adherents that the South Carolina legislature adopted an Ordinance of Nullification, in which both tariff laws were declared "null and void." Secession and armed resistance were threatened. Exercising great tact, Scott defused the potentially explosive political situation.

In 1837 he supervised the removal of the Cherokees to the Southwest, and in 1838–39, stationed on the Canadian border, he prevented conflict with Canada over a border dispute. On 5 July 1841 he was made general-in-chief of the army, a position he held for more than twenty years. During the Mexican War [q.v.] he led an army that landed in Veracruz in 1847 and fought its way to Mexico City, defeating the Mexican army under Santa Anna [q.v.] at Cerro Gordo in April, Contreras and Churubusco in August, and Molino del Rey and Chapultepec [qq.v.] in September. He occupied Mexico City on 14 September 1847 and returned from the war a hero. The Duke of Wellington pronounced him "the greatest living soldier." He was given the Thanks of Congress and another gold medal and promoted lieutenant general, the only one at the time holding that rank, to date from 29 March 1847. In the same year he stood as the Whig candidate for president, but he was defeated by General Franklin Pierce (1804–1869), who had been one of his subordinates in the war.

Although a Virginian, Scott strongly opposed secession, and in the American Civil War he remained loyal to the Union, correctly predicting the strategy for strangling the South that eventually won the war, the sneered-at Anaconda Plan [q.v.]. Nevertheless, McClellan said of him "He understands nothing, appreciates nothing, and is ever in my way," and he was forced to retire on 1 November 1861.

He was nicknamed Old Fuss and Feathers because of his delight in military pageantry and uniforms, but he was indisputably the foremost American military leader between the era of George Washington (1732–1799) and that of Grant and Lee in the 1860s.

Scout. 1. As a verb, to explore an area, to spy on the enemy, or to determine the nature of a route or area.

2. As a noun, a man or small group of soldiers sent for this purpose.

Scout Master General. The officer responsible for all the scouts and messengers in an expedition or campaign.

Scovell, George (1778–1861). A British soldier commissioned in 1798 who went to the Peninsular War [q.v.] a captain, saw much action, and distinguished himself by breaking French codes. In 1815 he took part in the Waterloo Campaign as assistant quartermaster general and was knighted (KCB). In 1818 he was placed on half pay, but in March 1829 he was appointed lieutenant governor of the Royal Military College, Sandhurst [q.v.], a post he held until 2 February 1837, when he was promoted major general and made governor of the college, where he remained until 31 March 1856, when he retired. He was promoted lieutenant general in 1846 and full general in 1854.

Scout *American Indian soldier in the Crow Scout Corps, by Frederic Remington*

Screen. 1. As a noun, anything used to shield a unit or operation from an enemy.

2. As a verb, to use forces to prevent an enemy from gaining information.

Screw Gun. A jointed gun with separate breech and muzzle sections that could be joined by a screw collar. The guns were transported by mules or camels and were much used by the British and Indian mountain artillery. They were extolled in Rudyard Kipling's [q.v.] poem "Screw-Guns," whose last lines read:

> Jest send in your Chief an' surrender—it's worse if you fights or you runs:
> You may hide in the caves, they'll be only your graves,
> but you can't get away from the guns!

Scylla, Siege of (12–28 July 1806), Napoleonic Wars. British under General Sir John Stuart (1759–1815) successfully besieged a French garrison in the castle of Scylla (Scilla), which sat on a headland projecting into the Strait of Messina from the coast of Reggio di Calabria in southern Italy [see Calabrian War].

Seacoast Defenses. The forts and artillery employed for the defense of the entrances to rivers and harbors. The guns were usually of heavy caliber and mounted in permanent installations [see Martello Towers].

Sea Fencibles. In 1813 the U.S. army organized ten such companies for the defense of ports and harbors. No field officers were appointed, and the companies were disbanded in 1815.

Sealed Orders. Secret or confidential orders issued to a commander in a sealed envelope with instructions not to open until a specified time or at a specified place or after a specified action.

Sealed Pattern. In Britain, the pattern of an arm, an accoutrement, or a uniform part, approved by a board of officers and sealed with the wax of the Board of Ordnance, which set the standard to be used by manufacturers.

Searchlight. About 1822 Lieutenant Thomas Drummond [q.v.], a British officer with the Ordnance Survey, invented the limelight. An automatic-feed carbon arc lamp was invented by W. E. Straite in 1846. By 1874 it had been amplified sufficiently to produce a searchlight of 11,000 candlepower. Searchlights were first used in land warfare in the Second Anglo-Boer War [q.v.].

Seat of War. The country or area in which war is being waged.

Seattle, Attack upon (26 January 1856), Yakima War. Yakima Indians attacked Seattle, Washington, but were repulsed by 55 local defenders and 120 sailors from the USS *Decatur* under Commander Israel Sterrett.

Sébastiani, Horace François Bastien de la Porta (1772–1851). A French soldier born in Corsica who became one of Napoleon's most devoted partisans. Commissioned in the infantry in 1789, he served in Italy and fought in the Battle of Marengo [q.v.] in 1800. He was wounded at Austerlitz [q.v.]. During the Peninsular War [q.v.] he commanded an army corps in Spain. He distinguished himself in 1812 in Napoleon's Russian Campaign, in which he commanded the cavalry, and in 1813 at Leipzig [qq.v.], where he was wounded by a lance in the chest. He returned to Napoleon's side in the Hundred Days [q.v.], but after the Battle of Waterloo [q.v.] he withdrew to England. Returning to France in 1830, he was twice in the ministry, and in 1840 he was made a marshal of France. Under both Napoleon and the Bourbons he served as an ambassador to various countries.

Secessionville, Battle of (16 June 1862), American Civil War. Union Brigadier General Henry Washington Benham (1813–1884) was stationed with 9,000 men on James Island, just southwest of Charleston, South Carolina, with orders not to initiate any offensive operations. On the morning of 16 June, over the objections of his division commanders, he launched an attack upon a Confederate fort near the hamlet of Secessionville commanded by Nathan George ("Shanks") Evans [q.v.]. Three assaults were repelled for a Union loss of 683 men to a Confederate loss of 204. Benham was relieved of his command, arrested for disobeying orders, and Lincoln revoked his appointment as a brigadier general of volunteers.

Seckendorff, Götz Burkhard von (d. 1883). A German soldier who was attached to the staff of General Robert Napier [q.v.] during his Abyssinian Campaign [q.v.] and later wrote an account of his experiences. In 1883,

while with William Hicks Pasha [q.v.] in the Sudan, he was killed in the Battle of Kashgil [q.v.]. His servant Gustav Klootz, who deserted to the Mahdists on the day before the battle, died in 1886 at Gallabat in the Sudan, north-northwest of Lake Tana, while trying to make his way to Abyssinia (Ethiopia).

Secondary Attack. A feint.

Second-in-Command. The person designated to take command of an army or smaller unit should the commander be unable to exercise his authority. The second-in-command might or might not have other responsibilities. Wellington, in a letter (2 December 1812) to General William Carr Beresford [q.v.], wrote: "I have always felt the inutility and inconvenience of the office of a second-in-command. It has a great and high sounding title, without duties or responsibilities of any description; at the same time it gives pretensions. . . . Every officer in an army should have some duty to perform. . . . The second-in-command has none that any body can define; excepting to give opinions for which he is no way responsible."

Seconding / Secunding. In the British army, the posting of officers for duty outside the regular military establishment. After the British suppression of Arabi's Revolt [q.v.] in 1882 a number of officers were seconded to the Egyptian army, where they enjoyed ranks two grades higher than their ranks in the regular British army. In India officers could be seconded to the political service to administer districts or to perform other political or administrative duties. Artillery and engineer officers who accepted civil employment under the crown were seconded after six months, losing pay but retaining rank, seniority, or promotion in their corps. After ten years of such employment—building canals, administering provinces, taking part in explorations, and the like—they had to decide whether to return to duty or retire.

Secord, Laura (1775–1868). A Canadian heroine who in 1813, during the War of 1812 [q.v.], carried the warning of an American surprise attack to the British and Canadian troops and their Indian allies at Beaver Dam, between Stony Creek and the Niagara River, enabling them to defeat and capture the invaders.

Secretary of / at / for / War. In the United States the secretary of war was a cabinet officer in charge of the War Department, which was responsible for supplying the army with its needs, including transportation of men and supplies and the keeping of records. His naval counterpart was the secretary of the navy.

The British secretary at war was primarily responsible for the financial needs of the army. There was also a secretary for war until February 1855, when the two posts became one and assumed responsibility for the Yeomanry, artillery, and engineers, the Medical Department, and almost all other military affairs except those of the infantry and cavalry, whose discipline, training, and promotion were the responsibility of the commander-in-chief.

SECRETARIES OF WAR IN THE UNITED STATES
IN THE NINETEENTH CENTURY

Samuel Dexter	June 1800–Jan. 1801
Henry Dearborn	March 1801–March 1809
William Eustis	March 1809–Jan. 1813
John Armstrong	Jan. 1813–Sept. 1814
James Monroe	Sept. 1814–March 1815
William H. Crawford	Aug. 1815–Oct. 1816
George Graham	
(ad interim)	Oct. 1816–Oct. 1817
John C. Calhoun	Oct. 1817–March 1825
James Barbour	March 1825–May 1828
Peter B. Porter	May 1828–March 1829
John H. Eaton	March 1829–June 1831
Lewis Cass	Aug.1831–Oct. 1836
Benjamin F. Butler	Oct. 1836–March 1837
Joel R. Poinsett	March 1837–March 1841
John Bell	March 1841–Sept. 1841
John C. Spence	Oct. 1841–March 1843
James M. Porter	March 1843–Jan. 1844
William Wilkins	Feb. 1844–March 1845
William L. Marcy	March 1845–March 1849
George W. Crawford	March 1849–July 1850
Charles M. Conrad	Aug. 1850–March 1853
Jefferson Davis	March 1853–March 1857
John B. Floyd	March 1857–Dec. 1860
Joseph Holt	Jan. 1861–March 1861
Simon Cameron	March 1861–Jan. 1862
Edwin M. Stanton	Jan. 1862–May 1868
Ulysses S. Grant	
(ad interim)	Aug. 1867–Jan. 1868
	May 1868–June 1868
John M. Schofield	June 1868–March 1869
John A. Rawlins	March 1869–Sept. 1869
William T. Sherman	
(ad interim)	Sept. 1869–Oct. 1869
William W. Belknap	Oct. 1869–March 1876
Alphonso Taft	March 1876–May 1876
James D. Cameron	May 1876–March 1877
George W. McCrary	March 1877–Dec. 1879
Alexander Ramsey	Dec. 1879–March 1881
Robert T. Lincoln	March 1881–March 1885
William C. Endicott	March 1885–March 1889
Redfield Proctor	March 1889–Nov. 1891
Stephen B. Elkins	Dec. 1891–March 1893
Daniel S. Lamont	March 1893–March 1897
Russell A. Alger	March 1897–Aug. 1899
Elihu Root	Aug. 1899–Jan. 1904

In the French, Prussian, and many other armies the chain of command from the ruler to the serving army was through a military minister, who was usually a general.

Secret Line. See Signal and Secret Service Bureau.

Secret Service. 1. During the American Civil War Allan Pinkerton [q.v.] organized what he called a secret service, which supplied intelligence and counterintelligence for the Union army. It was discontinued after General George McClellan [q.v.] was removed from the senior command [see Signal and Secret Service Bureau].

2. A branch of the American Treasury Department acti-vated in 1864 with a brigadier general in charge of a volunteer force to detect smugglers, counterfeiters, and bootleggers. After Lincoln's assassination it also supplied protection for the president and his family.

Secret Service Fund. In the United States the informal name for the Contingent Fund for Foreign Intercourse, established by Congress on 1 July 1790, which enabled a president to disperse funds for spies or others whose identity and mission could plausibly be denied.

Section. 1. A part of a battery or company of artillery, usually one or two guns.

2. An infantry unit larger than a squad but smaller than a platoon.

3. A military unit of indeterminate size having a specific function.

Section d'Exclus. A unit of the French Armée d'Afrique consisting of soldiers considered unworthy to bear arms and fit only to be punished and humiliated. They were usually employed in building roads or other pioneer work and were never armed.

Secunderbagh, Battle of (16 November 1857), Indian Mutiny. During the second attempt to relieve Lucknow [q.v.] General Sir Colin Campbell [q.v.] encountered a strong rebel force outside this town in a walled enclosure (*bagh*). After an hour's bombardment the 93rd Highlanders and the 4th Punjabis successfully assaulted the place. The rebels lost 2,000, it was said.

Secure, to. To take possession of an area or position or to take steps to prevent its destruction or loss to an enemy.

Sedan, Battle of (1–2 September 1870), Franco-Prussian War. After French Marshal Patrice Bazaine [q.v.] withdrew his troops into the fortress of Metz [q.v.] on 19 August 1870 and was besieged there, Napoleon III (1808–1873) took personal command of the Army of the Meuse, 130,000 men with 564 guns under Marshal Patrice MacMahon [q.v.] at Châlons-sur-Marne and marched eastward to his relief. Near Sedan, a town on the Meuse River 11 miles east-southeast of Mézières and 55 miles northeast of Rheims, he was trapped by two German armies: the Prussian Third Army and the Meuse Army of the North German Confederation, 200,000 men with 774 guns under Helmuth von Moltke [q.v.]. General Auguste Alexandre Ducrot [q.v.], one of the few competent French generals in the war, summed up the French position in a particularly Gallic manner: "*Nous sommes dans un pot de chambre, et nous y seron emmerdés* [We are in a chamber pot, and are about to be shit upon]."

On 1 September 1870, in an unsuccessful attempt to fight their way out toward Carignan, the French suffered a loss of 38,000 men, 21,000 of whom were taken prisoner. The army dissolved into a mass of fleeing soldiers, who were saturated by the fire of German guns deployed in a semicircle on the hills above Sedan. Prince Kraft Hohenlohe-Ingelfingen [q.v.] later wrote: "Our superiority over the enemy was so overwhelming that we suffered no loss at all. The batteries fired as if at practice." Not even the famous cavalry charge of Gaston Galliffet [q.v.] could reverse France's fortunes.

From a clearing on the heights of Frébois above Sedan the battle was observed by the kaiser, the German high command, a host of aristocrats and foreign dignitaries, including Lord Kitchener, General Mikhail Kutuzov, General Philip Sheridan, and the famous correspondent of *The Times* (London), William Russell [qq.v.].

MacMahon, who had been wounded in the battle, was replaced by General Emmanuel Félix de Wimpffen [q.v.], who surrendered the next day, delivering a further 85,000 men into German hands.

The Germans lost 2,320 killed, 5,980 wounded, and 700 missing; French casualties were 3,000 killed, 14,000 wounded, and more than 103,000 others taken prisoner, including both MacMahon and Napoleon III. The Germans also captured more than 1,000 wagons, 6,000 horses, and 414 guns, including 70 mitrailleuses, 139 siege guns, 66,000 rifles, and much other war matériel.

The French disaster at Sedan sparked a revolution in Paris, and the Third Republic was proclaimed with General Louis Trochu [q.v.] as president. The Battle of Sedan was one of the most crushing defeats ever suffered by French arms. The Germans marched on Paris, and Napoleon III abdicated; the Second French Empire crashed and was replaced by the Third Republic. Later Léon Gambetta (1838–1882), one of the founders of the Government of National Defense and a future prime minister, told the French people: "*N'en parlez jamais; pensez-y toujours* [Never speak of it; always think of it]." The anniversary of the victory became the first of the new and popular patriotic festivals of the new united Germany.

Sedan *Battle of Sedan, 1 September 1870*

Sedgwick, John (1813–1864). An American soldier who was graduated from West Point in 1837 and served in the Second Seminole War [q.v.]. He was part of a command that escorted the Cherokees from Georgia to Indian Territory [see Trail of Tears]. During the Mexican War [q.v.] he served first under Zachary Taylor and then under Winfield Scott [qq.v.], winning brevets to captain and major. In 1855 he became major of the newly raised 1st Cavalry Regiment, whose colonel was Robert E. Lee and whose lieutenant colonel was William J. Hardee [qq.v.]; in 1861, when his superiors defected to the Confederacy, Sedgwick commanded the regiment for a few months until he was promoted brigadier general of volunteers.

In the Peninsular Campaign [q.v.] he commanded a division until he was wounded in the Battle of White Oak Swamp [q.v.] on 30 June 1862. He was promoted major general in

July. In the Battle of Antietam [q.v.] he was wounded three times and carried unconscious from the field, but within three months he was back on duty and commanding a corps. He fought at Chancellorsville and was in reserve at Gettysburg [qq.v.]. During the Battle of Spotsylvania [q.v.] on 9 May 1864, when his aides asked him not to expose himself, he assured them, "They couldn't hit an elephant at this distance." Within minutes he fell dead from a sharpshooter's bullet that struck him just below his right eye. Grant, on hearing of Sedgwick's death, said, "His loss to this army is greater than the loss of a whole division of troops."

See the Elephant. An expression first used by American settlers moving west across the plains, a metaphor for exposure to the dangers and hardships of the journey. During the American Civil War and afterward, to see the elephant was to experience battle, to undergo a baptism of fire [q.v.]. The original expression was "I've heard the owl and seen the elephant," meaning I'm not a greenhorn.

Segauli, Treaty of (4 March 1816). The treaty that ended the Nepalese War [q.v.].

Segbans. Turkish horsemen responsible for the care and protection of the baggage of cavalry regiments.

Segesvár, Battle of (31 July 1849), Hungarian Revolution. General Jósef Bem [q.v.], a Pole in the Hungarian service, was decisively defeated by converging armies of Austrian General Julius von Haynau and Russian General Ivan Paskevich [qq.v.] at Segesvár (Sighişoara; German: *Schässburg*), in the Transylvania region, 45 miles northeast of Sibiu. Bem, with the remnant of his force, joined the army of Arthur von Görgey [q.v.] for a last stand at Timişoara [q.v.] on 9 August 1849.

Seğmens. Turkish sharpshooters.

Segu Bambara. A large military state in West Africa that existed from the mid-seventeenth century until it was crushed by the forces of Umar ibn Said Tal [q.v.] in 1861. It was founded and maintained by state-owned warrior slaves (*sofas*), and its chief export was slaves, mostly unfortunates captured in the Bambara's many wars with its neighbors.

Ségur, Philippe Paul (1780–1873). A French soldier who served under General Jacques Macdonald [q.v.] in Grisons in 1800–01 and was an aide to Napoleon. He saw action at Ulm in 1806 and at Leipzig in 1812 [qq.v.]; he was twice wounded. Because he had rallied to Napoleon during the Hundred Days [q.v.], he was retired until 1818. Until the Revolution of 1830 he took no part in politics. He wrote *Histoire de Napoléon et de la Grande Armée en 1812* (1824) and *Histoire de Russie et de Pierre le Grand* (1829). His unflattering portrait of Napoleon in his first book provoked a duel in which he was wounded. In 1831 he was promoted lieutenant general and made a peer. After the Revolution of 1848 he lived in retirement [see Paris Revolution of 1848; Revolutions of 1848].

Sekukuni (d. 1882). A chief of the Bapedis in South Africa who in 1876 rebelled against Boer rule and attacked farmers at Lydenburg. In February 1877 he was found and fined, but he refused to render payment. In the same year, when the British annexed the Transvaal, he refused to recognize British authority. When he attacked some progovernment tribal bands, British General Sir Garnet Wolseley [q.v.] organized a force against him that defeated him in a battle on 28 February 1879 [see Bapedi Wars]. He surrendered to Commandant Ignatius Ferreira [q.v.] on 2 December and was sent as a prisoner to Pretoria. After the First Anglo-Boer War [q.v.] in 1881 he was set free. In August 1882 he was murdered by his half brother.

Selma, Capture of (2 April 1865), American Civil War. Union General James Harrison Wilson [q.v.] with a cavalry corps of 13,500 was sent to Selma, Alabama, a munitions and manufacturing center 40 miles west of Montgomery, to destroy the factories and the major Confederate supply depot there. An attempt by Nathan Bedford Forrest [q.v.] with 3,000 cavalry to delay him failed. Forrest fell back to Selma, where he was reinforced by 4,000 local militia. Selma was ringed by earthworks, but Wilson's cavalrymen assaulted it on foot and captured the town. Forrest and a handful of his men escaped.

Union casualties were 400; Confederate losses, including prisoners, numbered 4,000. Wilson then rampaged through central Georgia, capturing thousands, including the fleeing President Jefferson Davis.

Semaine Sanglant, La (21–28 May 1871). "The bloody week" in the French Commune of 1871 [q.v.]. After the Army of Versailles entered Paris, there was violent fighting in the streets. Thousands of prisoners were taken, and many slaughtered. General Gaston Galliffet [q.v.] was particularly ruthless. By the end of May the Commune had been crushed, but reprisals and punitive measures continued until 1875 [see Paris Commune].

Semaphore. A system of signaling that revolutionized long-distance communication developed by the French engineer Claude Chappe (1763–1805) with help from one of his four brothers, Ignace Urbain Jean Chappe (1760–1828). Called an aerial telegraph, it was officially endorsed by the French government in 1793 and continued in use until about 1850.

A tower with a 30-foot mast supported a movable 14-foot crosspiece that pivoted at its top. At each end of the crosspiece was a 6-foot indicator. The crosspiece had four positions: horizontal, vertical, or a 45-degree incline right or left. Thus 196 combinations were possible. Changes were made by a system of pulleys and cables. Stations were arranged every 10 or 12 kilometers, and in good weather a short message could be sent from Paris to Lille, a distance of 130 miles, in five minutes. Napoleon used the system, and in Portugal Wellington had five semaphore stations along the first line of the Lines of Torres Vedras [q.v.] and four in the second line. After Waterloo [q.v.] the system was extended to Toulon and Bayonne.

Chappe was driven by financial difficulties to commit suicide by throwing himself down a well in January 1805, but the business was carried on by his brothers.

Seminole Wars. Seminole Indians were Creeks who as *simanó-li* (separated or renegade) moved to Florida, then to Spanish territory, sometime in the eighteenth century. Florida was a haven for runaway slaves, deserters, escaped felons, and other renegades, many of whom were accepted by and intermarried with the Seminoles, who were known to make raids into Georgia and then flee back to the safety of Florida, which Spain was unable to govern effectively.

First Seminole War (1816–18). During the spring and summer of 1817 Andrew Jackson [q.v.], aided by 1,600 Creek Indians, crossed the frontier and won several small victories over the Seminoles. He also captured two Spanish towns, St. Mark's and Pensacola. At the latter town he installed one of his officers as governor and established U.S. revenue laws. The war ended with the Adams-Onís Treaty [q.v.], by which the United States purchased Florida for five million dollars. The treaty was ratified by the Senate in February 1818 [see Wright Affair]. Within a week Congress, ignoring the wishes of Secretary of War John C. Calhoun [q.v.], reorganized the army, reducing it in size from 12,664 to 6,183. Less than three weeks after the reduction, the army was ordered to occupy Florida, an operation that nearly stripped the garrisons of army posts elsewhere.

It was in this war that Andrew Jackson created a furor in Britain by arresting and executing two British subjects, Alexander Arbuthnot and Robert Ambrister, Indian traders who, according to Jackson, had incited the Indians [see Arbuthnot and Ambrister Affair].

Seminole War, Second (1835–42). In 1819 the United States purchased for five million dollars all Spanish territory east of the Mississippi River. In 1832 the Seminole Indians signed the Treaty of Payne's Landing, in which they agreed to leave Florida within three years and settle in Indian Territory (Oklahoma). However, at the end of the three years many refused to leave. The war began on 28 December 1835, when Captain and Brevet Major Francis L. Dade (1792?–1835), leading an escort for a supply column from Tampa Bay bound for Fort King, was ambushed by Indians. Dade and 107 officers and men were killed [see Dade Massacre]. Soon after, Congress authorized a second regiment of dragoons to be raised and dispatched it to Florida, where at Fort Mellon, near Tampa, on 6 February 1837 it was attacked, unsuccessfully, by Seminoles under Coachoochee, better known as Wild Cat [q.v.]. In October of the same year Seminole Chief Osceola [q.v.] was lured out of the Everglades and, while under a flag of truce, was treacherously seized by American Brigadier General Thomas Jesup [q.v.]. Imprisoned in North Carolina, Osceola soon died. In August 1842 the war, the longest and most expensive Indian war in North America, was officially declared ended.

It was in this war that Captain (later General) Gabriel James Rains [q.v.] was said to have invented land mines, which he later introduced in the American Civil War.

Although 75 percent of the 1,600 deaths in the war were the result of disease, in the course of the war army surgeons were able for the first time to conduct large-scale trials of the use of quinine [q.v.] and confirmed the value of large doses in the treatment of malaria.

Seminole War, Third (1855–58). Florida became a state on 3 March 1845. The remaining Seminoles refused to part with their lands and resisted the encroachment of the whites. From 1855 to 1858 a determined effort was made to hunt them down and pry them from their homes in the Everglades. The war involved no major fights, but many small skirmishes.

A small band remained secluded in the swamps and did not make peace until 1934.

Seminole Wars *U.S. soldiers at Tampa Bay, 1835*

Senapati. Name for the commander-in-chief of the Manipuri army [see Manipur Rebellion].

Sénarmont, Alexandre Antoine de (1769–1810). A French soldier who became a bold artillery commander in Napoleon's army. He was commissioned in the artillery in 1785 and fought at Marengo [q.v.] in 1800. He distinguished himself at Jena, Austerlitz, and particularly Friedland [qq.v.], where, in a daring dash forward with 36 guns, he blasted open a hole in the Russian lines through which French infantry poured. He was promoted general of brigade in 1806 and became commandant of the artillery school at Metz. In 1808 he was made general of division, and two years later he commanded a division in Spain during the Peninsular War [q.v.]. He was killed by an 8-pounder howitzer shell during the siege of Cádiz.

In the Battle of Waterloo [q.v.] Napoleon is reported to have said, "Ah! If I but had Sénarmont!"

Sencero. The bell mare of a packtrain used by the American army in the West. The mare carried no loads, only a bell. Pack mules were trained to follow her lead on the trail and to graze near her at night.

Senegalese Tirailleurs. West African soldiers in France's colonial army. The Tirailleurs Sénégalais came into being when Napoleon III signed the authorization decree on 21 July 1857, and they were formed into a standing force by General Louis Faidherbe [q.v.]. Reasonably well disciplined and well armed, they fought in all subsequent West African wars, as well as in Madagascar and the West Indies. Originally all recruits were from Senegal, then a French colony, but by 1880 most were from the Bambara tribe or other ethnic groups of the western Sudan; many came from Tukulor subject groups or were former slaves. Many, in fact, were slaves purchased by the French from their masters on the open market under a system called *rachat* [q.v.]. Like the British in India, the French came to believe that some communities produced better soldiers than others, and Bambara and Tukulor tribesmen came to be much preferred [see Martial Races]. Some of the recruits, like the illegitimate son of General Faidherbe [q.v.], rose to become junior officers. In 1889 a pension was granted to soldiers who had served twenty-five years [see Tirailleurs].

Senegambian War (1886–87). Africans in the Senegambian region of West Africa, led by Mahmadu Lamine [q.v.], made war on the French and their African allies. Lamine's followers were mostly fanatical religious devotees rather than warriors. His army probably did not exceed 4,000 poorly armed men, many of whom were deserters from the Senegalese Tirailleurs [q.v.]. The French had a well-armed force of about the same numerical strength, and some artillery.

Lamine began the war by using guerrilla tactics. On 13 March 1886, he suffered a severe loss when his village, Goundiourou, was raided, 34 of his wives, many of his children, and his relatives were captured, and his household and treasury looted, but the next day, in the Battle of Kounguel [q.v.], the first major encounter of the war, the French were routed. The war was carried into the Guidimaka area, a region controlled by the Tukulors, and there the French suffered great losses from sickness.

In October Lieutenant Colonel (later Marshal) Joseph Gallieni [q.v.] arrived to take command. On 12 December 1886 he sent two columns against Lamine's base at Dianna. On 25 December the columns joined and swept into the settlement to find that Lamine had hastily evacuated it and drawn back into the interior. On 12 May 1887 Gallieni signed a treaty with Ahmadu [q.v.], ruler of the Tukulor Empire, under which both the French and the Tukulors agreed to fight Lamine. They first attacked Lamine's son Soybu, who was captured by the French, "court-martialed," and sentenced to death by shooting, a mode of execution for which he thanked Gallieni, saying he could then "go home to Allah with dignity."

Although Lamine tried to avoid a pitched battle, he was finally forced into one in which he was defeated and killed at Toubakouta (Touba), 70 miles west of Séguéla, in December 1887.

Senekal, Battle of (29 May 1900), Second Anglo-Boer War. Boers occupied strong positions near this Orange Free State town, 10 miles northeast of Bloemfontein. When a British column under General Leslie Rundle (1856–1935) approached, the Boers ignited large brushfires through which the column had to pass. Rundle drove out the Boers, although he lost 7 officers and 177 other ranks killed or wounded. Many of the wounded burned to death.

Seng-ko-lin-ch'in (d. 1865). A Mongolian prince who was one of the most energetic generals in the imperial army that fought the Taiping and Nien rebels and the British [see Taiping Rebellion; Taku Forts, Capture of; Opium Wars; Nien / Nienfei Rebellion]. British soldiers referred to him as Sam Collinson.

He had been educated for the Buddhist priesthood in Peking (Beijing), where he came to the notice of the emperor, who had him trained as a soldier. He rose rapidly to general officer rank. In 1853 he led the Tatar cavalry that drove back the Taipings as they attempted to take Peking. In 1858, when he was commander of all the forces in the northeast, he defended the Taku (Dagu) forts against the British [see Second Opium War], but he suffered a decisive defeat in September 1860 at Pauch'iao Bridge near Peking.

Sent to attack the Nien, he enjoyed some initial success, killing Chang Lo-hsing [q.v.], the leading Nien chief, but his inability to understand Chinese put him at the mercy of interpreters. In the autumn of 1864 in the Battle of Lo-shan he suffered a crushing defeat, losing 12 of his principal commanders. In May 1865 he was ambushed and killed at Ts'ao-chou (Tsaochwang or Tsao-Chuang) in southwestern Shantung.

A French doctor described him as "tall and stout, with a very energetic eye, just like Louis Napoleon's."

Seniority. In almost all armies, certainly in peacetime, seniority, though not always promotion, was based upon length of service in grade [see Purchase System]. Many officers long past their prime still served, for as Captain Basil Liddell Hart (1895–1970) once said, "It is a military convention that infallibility is the privilege of seniority" (1933).

Senior Service. A country's oldest armed service. In the United Kingdom this is the navy; in the United States it is the army.

Senova, Battle of (8–9 January 1878), Russo-Turkish War of 1877–78. Russian General Mikhail Skobelev [q.v.], concentrating his forces south of the Shipka Pass in central Bulgaria, encircled and captured the entire Turkish army of Vessil Pasha, some 36,000 men.

Sentinel. A soldier posted to watch or guard. A sentry.

Sentry. A soldier standing guard at a passing point, such as a gate, a road, or an entrance to a military post.

Sentry *A Turkish sentry in a fort at Silistria, 1854*

Sentry Box. A shelter for a sentry, usually a small structure large enough for only one man.

Sepoy. 1. An Indian infantryman of the lowest rank in the British-led Indian armies.

2. Any Indian soldier, not an officer, trained and dressed in the European manner.

The first battalion of sepoys raised and trained by the British was formed under Robert Clive (1725–1774) in 1757 during the Seven Years' War (1756–1763).

Sepoy Mutiny / Rebellion. See Indian Mutiny.

Serbian Revolts (1803–83). Serbia became part of the Ottoman Empire in 1459, and over the centuries Serbs were much oppressed by the Turks and their janissaries [q.v.]. An 1803 revolt against the Turkish dahis, or military chiefs, was quickly and brutally suppressed, but the following year a revolt coalesced under the leadership of George Petrović Karageorge [q.v.]. In August 1805 Serbs decisively defeated the pasha of Bosnia in the Battle of Mišar, and in December they stormed the citadel of Belgrade (Serbian: *Beograd*). The Turks were soon ejected from the entire pashalik of Belgrade, and Karageorge, serving as commander-in-chief and chief of state, faced the task of forming a nation. In 1807 he negotiated a convention with Russia, and in the Russo-Turkish War of 1806–12 [q.v.] he fought as a Russian ally. At the war's end the Treaty of Bucharest (Bucureşti) gave international recognition and a limited autonomy to Serbia, but permitted Turkish garrisons in Belgrade and in other forts.

In the summer of 1813 the Turks turned their attention toward suppressing the fledgling state. By October they had reconquered Serbia, and Karageorge had fled. Reinstalling the worst features of the old regime, the new Turkish pasha, Suleiman Skopljak, lost no time in beheading or impaling some 200 Serb notables. In consequence, a new revolt, led by Miloš Obrenović (1780–1860), erupted on Palm Sunday 1815. By August Serbia was almost free. In secret negotiations with the Ottoman sultan, who made him supreme chief (*vrhovni knez*), virtually a prince, Obrenović promised to assassinate Karageorge, a pledge he kept when Karageorge, thinking to head the government again, returned from exile. Thus began a long and bloody feud between two dynasties.

Declared an hereditary prince in 1827, Obrenović grew increasingly tyrannical and avaricious until in 1839 he was forced to abdicate in favor of his eldest son, who soon died. His second son, Michael (1825–1868), who succeeded, was unpopular and was abandoned by the army. In a surprise move the Skupština (Serb legislature) summoned to the throne Alexander Karageorge or Karageorgevich (1806–1885), the son of George Karageorge.

In 1856 the Treaty of Paris brought Serbia closer to independence, allowing it autonomy in administration, legislation, trade, and religion, but Turkish troops still garrisoned the country.

In December 1858 the Skupština deposed Alexander and recalled Miloš Obrenović who in 1860 was again succeeded by his son Michael. Michael, who in the interim had been an officer in the Russian army, lost no time in installing a French officer as minister of war and completely reforming the Serbian army. In 1862, when the Turks in the fortress of Belgrade bombarded the town, Michael persuaded the European powers to pressure the Porte to remove the Turkish troops from Serbia. In 1868 Michael was assassinated by adherents of the rival Karageorge dynasty, but they failed to place a Karageorge on the throne. Michael was succeeded by his young cousin Milan Obrenović (1854–1901), who did not come into his majority until 1872.

In May 1876 Serbia allied itself with Montenegro and supported the revolt of Bosnia and Bulgaria, declaring war upon Turkey [see Turko-Serbian War]. Although its ranks were swelled by many Russian volunteers and it was led by a Russian general, the Serbian army was defeated in the Battle of Alexinatz [q.v.], and Serbia sought the tsar's protection. After the Russo-Turkish War of 1877–78, Serbia, which had joined the fight on Russia's side on 15 December 1877, five days after the fall of Plevna [q.v.], was given full independence but little else.

On 22 February 1882 the Skupština proclaimed Serbia a kingdom. An attempt was made upon Milan's life later that year, followed in 1883 by an abortive revolt at Zaječar in eastern Serbia, on the Bulgarian border. Although Serbian political life remained chaotic, in part through the personal behavior of Milan with his queen and mistress and the rash and unprovoked attack upon Bulgaria in 1885 [see Serbo-Bulgarian War], the country remained sovereign until the First World War.

Serbo-Bulgarian War (November 1885–March 1886). Bulgaria had a separate existence only after 1879, at the end of the Russo-Turkish War [q.v.] of 1877–78. On 18 September 1885 a revolution broke out against Turkish rule among the Bulgarian population in Philippopolis, capital of eastern Rumelia. The following day Prince Alexander of Battenberg [see Alexander I, king of Bulgaria] proclaimed himself king of a united Bulgarian kingdom.

On 13 November 1885 Serbia, alleging Bulgarian aggression and demanding compensation for the Bulgarian annexation of East Rumelia, declared war upon Bulgaria and at once invaded at four points. Bulgaria, expecting an attack from Turkey, not Serbia, had deployed on the wrong frontier. The small forces left on the Serbian border put up a fierce resistance, but the Serbs soon occupied Zaribrod and the Dragoman Pass. After some desperate fighting, the Serbs captured Raptcha on 15 November, and the Bulgarians fell back to Slivnitza [q.v.], 19 miles northwest of Sofia, and there stopped the advancing Serbs and forced them to retreat. On 17 November the Serbs counterattacked, driving off the Bulgarians, but on 19 November the Bulgarians attacked the

Serbs at Slivnitza and forced them back across their frontier. On 21–22 November the Bulgarians again defeated the Serbs at the Dragoman Pass, near Zaribrod, the Serbs losing an estimated 6,000 in killed and wounded. On 24 November the Serbs retreated to Pirot [q.v.] in southeastern Serbia, on the Nišava River, 33 miles east-southeast of Niš and 45 miles northwest of Sofia. There on 26–27 November they were attacked and defeated by the Bulgarians, who occupied Pirot. On 28 November Austria intervened, and hostilities ceased. On 3 March 1886 a peace treaty was signed. The war accomplished nothing.

Serbo-Turkish War. See Turko-Serbian War.

Sergeant. A noncommissioned officer ranking in almost all armies just above a corporal. There were usually several grades of sergeant, such as staff sergeant, color sergeant, farrier sergeant, etc. [see Sergeant Major]. Gunnery Sergeant Daniel Daly (1873–1937) spoke for many when he said: "Any officer can get by on his sergeants. To be a sergeant you have to know your stuff. I'd rather be an outstanding sergeant than just another officer."

Sergeant, White. See White Sergeant.

Sergeant Major. The highest-ranking noncommissioned officer in a unit of the British army; an appointment in the American army held by a master sergeant.

Sergeant's Medal. See Meritorious Service Medal.

Serrano y Domínguez, Francisco, Duque de la Torre (1810–1885). A Spanish soldier and statesman who served under Queen Isabella (1830–1904) in the First Carlist War [q.v.] in 1834–39. He became a field marshal and captain general of Valencia in 1840 and of Granada in 1848. In 1856 he took part in the successful Spanish revolution of Leopoldo O'Donnell y Joris [q.v.], and from 1859 to 1862 he was governor of Cuba. After O'Donnell's death in 1867 Serrano became the leader of the Union Liberal Party and in 1868, with Juan Prim y Prats [q.v.], he dethroned the queen. From 1869 to 1871 he was regent, and under King Amadeus (1845–1890) he was a military leader.

Serrell, Edward Wellman (1826–1906). An English-born American engineer who, as a Union engineer during the American Civil War, served in 126 engagements in Virginia, Georgia, and South Carolina. He was brevetted brigadier general of volunteers at the end of the war. After the war he worked as an engineer on railroads and canals.

Sérurier, Jean Mathieu Philibert (1742–1819). A French soldier who served in the Seven Years' War and later in Portugal and was promoted general in 1795. After his failure to check Aleksandr Suvorov [q.v.] in 1799 he held only administrative posts. He was made a marshal in 1804, and from 1804 to 1815 he was governor of the Hôtel des Invalides. On 13 March 1814, as Paris was about to fall to the Allies, he ordered the destruction of fifteen hundred captured flags.

Serbo-Bulgarian War *Bulgarians storm the Serbian town of Pirot, 27 November 1885*

Serve a Piece, to. To load and fire a cannon.

Service. 1. The entire armed forces of a nation.

2. One of the major components of an armed force, as army or navy.

3. A unit or an organization that supports another.

4. Time spent in an armed force.

Service Uniform. The uniform worn in the field, as opposed to the dress uniform for ceremonial purposes.

Serving the Vent. An operation in the loading of a muzzle-loading artillery piece in which to prevent air from passing through the vent and thus igniting any bit of cartridge, a cannoneer placed his thumb or a mechanical stopper over it. The cannoneer's thumb was sometimes protected by a thumb stall [q.v.].

Set Piece Battle. An anticipated battle fought in the main battle area with both sides prepared and ready for battle.

Setter. A round stick used in the artillery to drive fuses or any other composition into paper cases.

Sevastopol / Sebastopol, Siege of (28 September 1854–8 September 1855), Crimean War. After the Allied victory at the Alma [q.v.] on 20 September 1854, the French and British armies, about 60,000 men, marched south toward Sevastopol, a fortified Russian city and naval base on the southwest coast of the Crimean Peninsula, on an inlet of the Black Sea, one of the finest natural harbors in the world. On 28 September the Allies mounted a siege but had too few men to invest the place completely. Under the direction of General Franz Todleben [q.v.], the military engineer, the Russians strengthened their defenses. The besiegers—particularly the British, who were inadequately prepared and supplied—endured a severe winter, in which they suffered greatly from the cold and from disease. Russian attempts to drive them off resulted in the battles of Balaclava, Inkerman, and Chernaya [qq.v.]. A British assault on the redan [q.v.] south of the city on 18 June 1855 proved a costly failure, and not until 8 September, when the French captured the vital strongpoint known as the Malakoff [q.v.] southeast of the city, did the Russians complete the demolition of their fortifications, explode their ammunition, and on 11 September withdraw from the city and port.

The Russian withdrawal virtually ended the war. Although the main Russian field armies remained undefeated, Tsar Alexander II [q.v.] signed the peace terms at the Congress of Paris on 30 March 1856.

Seven Days' Battles (25 June–1 July 1862), American Civil War. Those battles of the 1862 Peninsular Campaign [q.v.] between Union Major General George B. McClellan and Confederate General Robert E. Lee [qq.v.] that included Mechanicsville on 26 June, Gaines's Mill on 27 June, Savage's Station on 29 June, White Oak Swamp on 30 June, and Malvern Hill on 1 July [qq.v.]. Taken together, they constituted the first prolonged engagement of the war. Federal forces numbered about 90,000; Confederate forces, 72,000. Federal forces lost 1,734 killed, 8,062 wounded, and 6,053 missing, most of whom were prisoners; Confederate losses were 3,478 killed, 16,261 wounded, and 875 missing.

Although the heavier loss was sustained by the Confederates, Lee pushed the Federals away from Richmond and back to the coast, where they were protected by their navy.

Seven Pines, Battle of. See Fair Oaks.

Seven Weeks' War (June–July 1866). After the defeat of Denmark in the Schleswig-Holstein War [q.v.] the victors, Prussia and Austria, quarreled over the fruits of their victory, the two duchies. On 7 June 1866 Prussian General Edwin Hans Karl von Manteuffel [q.v.] led a Prussian army of 12,000 men into Holstein, forcing out a weaker Austrian force. One week later, on 14 June, Austria, along with Bavaria, Saxony, Hanover, and several minor German states pressured by Austria, declared war on Prussia.

Prussia had an army of 350,000 plus large reserves and could put 254,000 troops against Austria. Although Austria had an army of 320,000, because of its need to maintain forces in Italy, it could field only 240,000 against Prussia. However, allied troops, such as 25,000 from Saxony and perhaps 150,000 from Bavaria and other German states, could be added to the strength. Because the Austrian conscript served for eight years against the Prussians' three or four, it was widely believed that the Austrian army was superior and would prevail, but to save money, many Austrian conscripts were furloughed after serving only one or two years; the Prussian army, through the efforts of General Albrecht von Roon [q.v.], proved to be better organized, better trained, and better led, and its infantry was better armed with the superior breech-loading Dreyse needle gun [q.v.] against the Austrian muzzleloaders. There were other factors: Most of the Austrian officers spoke only German, while most of their troops spoke only one of at least ten other languages of the Austro-Hungarian Empire; their educational level was low, and some were ineducable, for the army had an astonishingly high incidence of cretinism and other sociomedical problems.

The brilliant Prussian Field Marshal Helmuth von Moltke the Elder [q.v.], although his title was chief of staff, controlled the action. The Austrians were commanded by Hungarian-born Field Marshal Ludwig August von Benedek [q.v.], who, aware of his own limitations, accepted the post of commander-in-chief reluctantly. He was advised by Major General Gedeon Krismanic (1817–1876), whose ideas for warfare were those of the eighteenth century.

On 27 April the Austrians mobilized; Prussia followed a week later. The railway system and the telegraph greatly aided the rapid mobilization of the Prussian army, which was organized into three field armies on a 250-mile front. From 16 May to 6 June the Prussian soldiers were carried to the frontier by train, the largest movement of troops by rail ever made up to that time. By 8 June two Prussian armies were poised on the border of Bohemia. The order to advance was delayed because of the reluctance of King William I [q.v.] to appear as the aggressor. Not until 23 June was Moltke able to give the order to cross the frontier.

On 24 June the forces of Piedmont-Sardinia, which sided with Prussia, were defeated in the Battle of Custozza [q.v.]. However, the Prussians surrounded the entire Hanoverian army, which capitulated after the Battle of Langensalza [q.v.] on 29 June; Bavaria was isolated. On the same day an

Austrian army, in strong defensive positions at Gitschin [q.v.], was forced to retreat with heavy losses. There were smaller actions at Trautenau, Schweinschadel, and Prausnitz, but the fate of the German confederacy was decided by the Prussian victory in the Battle of Sadowa [q.v.]. On 30 June Benedek ordered the Austrian army to fall back on Königgrätz. At this point the Austrians had already lost 30,000 men, and many of the survivors seemed demoralized; the Prussians had lost fewer than 8,000 and advanced confidently.

In the hills just southeast of the village of Sadowa (Sadová) in southern Bohemia, eight miles northwest of Königgrätz, the Austrian army passively awaited attack. The Prussians obliged and won a stunning victory, one of the most decisive in the history of European warfare. The Prussians lost 1,935 killed and 7,237 wounded; the Austrians lost 40,000, including 13,000 killed and 18,000 wounded [see Sadowa / Königgrätz, Battle of]. Benedek drew his surviving army to the fortress of Olmütz (Olomouc) on the March (Morava) River, 40 miles northeast of Brno (Brünn). There he was ordered to take the army to Vienna, where two corps had been brought north from Italy to defend the Austrian capital. On 22 July Austrians and Prussians were facing each other outside Vienna when an armistice was arranged. This was followed by peace on Prussia's terms, signed at the Blue Star Hotel in Prague on 23 August. Prussia then replaced Austria as the undisputed head of the German confederacy.

The war was a clash between traditional mass maneuver on the part of the Austrians and the more open formations of the Prussians armed with more modern weapons. The former proved suicidal in the face of the latter.

Sève Pasha, Octave Joseph Anthelme (1788–1860). Also known as Suleiman Pasha al-Faransawi. A French soldier who was a lieutenant in the army of Napoleon. In 1816, after the Battle of Waterloo [q.v.], he sailed to Egypt, where he was employed by Muhammad Ali [q.v.] to create an army on the Western model. This new army, called *nizam al-jadid,* gave a good account of itself in the wars in Syria and Greece. Several of its regiments were composed of Sudanese slaves who later saw service in the Sudan [see Sudan, Egyptian Conquest of].

Sgian. See Skean Dhu.

Shabraque / Shabrack. The saddle cloth of a cavalry horse. It was sometimes of sheepskin or leopard skin and sometimes ornamented. The horses of the 10th Hussars wore scarlet cloth shabraques with the bridle crupper and breastplate ornamented with small seashells.

Shafter, William Rufus (1835–1906). An American soldier who fought in the American Civil War, serving in every grade from private to brevet brigadier general. He was awarded the Medal of Honor [q.v.] for gallantry in the Battle of Fair Oaks [q.v.]. After the war he served as a lieutenant colonel in the newly formed 24th Infantry, one of four regiments of blacks with white officers, and for a decade served on the turbulent West Texas frontier [see Black Troops in the U.S. Army]. In 1876 he led a successful combined arms expedition against Lipan and Kickapoo Indians who lived in Mexico but raided into Texas. In 1879 he was promoted colonel and given command of the 1st Infantry, stationed in the Northwest. In 1898

he was promoted major general of volunteers. By this time he weighed more than 300 pounds, and William Randolph Hearst (1863–1951) described him as "massive as to body— a sort of human fortress in blue coat and flannel shirt." During the Spanish-American War [q.v.] he commanded the successful American expeditionary force to Cuba, and although Colonel Theodore Roosevelt [q.v.] called him "criminally incompetent," he received the surrender of the city of Santiago de Cuba on 17 July 1898. He retired in 1899.

Shahin Pasha, Kinj (d. 1879). A Turkish soldier and Egyptian statesman who during the Crimean War [q.v.] served as second-in-command of an Egyptian infantry regiment. In 1855 he was promoted *mirlai* (colonel). In 1866 he was governor of Cairo. In the same year, as part of a military mission to France to study ways in which the Egyptian army could be modernized, he was present at the review that welcomed back from Mexico the Sudanese battalion that had been sent there to prop up the emperor Maximilian [q.v.] [see Egyptian Sudanese Battalion in Mexico]. Later in the year he traveled to the Sudan to inquire into the causes of the mutiny of Sudanese troops at Kassala [q.v.] in December 1864. In 1869 he became minister of war. In 1875 he was appointed one of the directors of the Sudan railway that was being built from Wadi Half south toward Dongola. In 1879, when the European powers forced Khedive Ismail I (1830–1895) to resign, he accompanied him into exile and died soon after in Rome.

Shaikan, Battle of. See Kashgil, Battle of.

Shaka / Chaka (1787–1828). A South African warrior, born the illegitimate son of a minor chieftain, who became chief of the Zulus and, having developed an army of skilled and disciplined warriors, in a space of only twelve years conquered a vast territory.

Generally recognized as the founder of the Zulu Empire, Shaka officially became a chief in 1818 on the death of Zulu Chief Dingiswayo [q.v.], but he had been de facto chief before then. He revolutionized warfare in South Africa by introducing both the short, heavy-bladed stabbing assegai (*i-klwa*), to replace the throwing spear, and new tactics based upon speed and double envelopment. His army in fighting formation was likened to the head of an ox: From either side of the main body came "horns," troops who ran out ahead to envelop the enemy. He organized his regiments by age-groups, and no man was allowed to marry until he had washed his assegai in the blood of an enemy. Footware was forbidden, and to make sure his warriors' feet were tough, they danced before him on a thorn-strewn field; those whose dancing was not vigorous enough were clubbed to death. In an ever-expanding empire Shaka absorbed land and people and, it is estimated, was responsible for the deaths of more than a million.

The turbulent Zulus' wars against their neighbors gave rise to distant ripples of fighting and disorders as powerful tribes plundered weaker ones in widening circles of devastation. These troubled times were called the *mfecane* (crushing) [q.v.].

When white settlers arrived in Natal, Shaka established good relations with them, even presenting them with large tracts of land. After the death in October 1827 of his mother, to whom he was strongly attached, his cruelty increased, and his rule grew more arbitrary. He was assassinated by his half brothers, led by Dingaan [q.v.], who succeeded him.

Shaka *Imaginative depiction of the South African warrior and chief of the Zulus. He holds the spear, which warriers had once hurled at their enemies. In line with Shaka's new method of warfare, the spear would be shortened for hand-to-hand combat.*

Shakespear, Richmond Campbell (1812–1861). A British soldier and colonial administrator whose mother was Emily Thackeray (1780–1824), an aunt of novelist William Makepeace Thackeray (1811–1863). He was born in India and went to school in England. In 1828 he was graduated from Addiscombe [q.v.] and commissioned a second lieutenant in the Bengal artillery. He served in the First Afghan War [q.v.] in the 6th Field (camel) Battery.

Serving as a political officer, he was ordered in June 1840 to Khiva (now in Uzbekistan), upon which the Russians were advancing. After an arduous 700-mile trip from Herat, he reached Khiva and persuaded the khan to negotiate with the Russians, who were only three days' march away. At his suggestion the khan offered to release all the Russian captives he had enslaved if the Russians would agree to withdraw to their border. The terms were accepted, and Shakespear began the process of collecting the slaves, who were scattered about the khanate and not easy to find. By 14 August he had rounded up 416. These he escorted across the Turkestan desert in defiance of the wild tribesmen there and delivered them to the Russian authorities at Orenburg. He then traveled to Moscow and St. Petersburg, where he was received by the tsar. From

there he carried dispatches to London, where he was knighted, the only time in his career after leaving Addiscombe that he was ever in England. He soon returned to India, where he was appointed military secretary to Major General George Pollock [q.v.].

He distinguished himself during Pollock's forcing of the Khyber Pass to relieve Sir Robert Sale [q.v.], who was besieged at Jalalabad [see Jalalabad, Siege of; First Afghan War; Pollock, George]. In September 1842 after the relief of Sale, he was dispatched with 700 Kazlbach horsemen to rescue the European captives held by Afghans in a northern fort. The captives, including Sale's wife, Florentia Sale [q.v.], had managed to release themselves through the use of false but official-looking documents, but Shakespear escorted them through dangerous territory to the safety of General Sale's camp. During the Gwalior Campaign [q.v.] he served as an aide to General Hugh Gough [q.v.] in the Battle of Maharajpur [q.v.] on 29 December 1843. On 1 May 1846 he was promoted captain.

He fought in the Second Sikh War [q.v.] and commanded a battery of heavy guns in the battles of Chilianwala and Gujerat [qq.v.], in which he was wounded. When he recovered, he returned to duties as a political officer. He died from bronchitis in 1861.

Shakespear had married in 1844 in Agra and was survived by his widow, three sons, and six daughters.

Shako. A stiff, peaked, cylindrical military hat, often worn with a plume. The hat was adopted by British infantry in 1800 and by the French in 1806, replacing the bicorn.

Shakudo. A Japanese alloy composed of copper, with gold and antimony in various proportions, used for sword mountings.

Shamyl / Schamyl / Shamil (1797?–1871). A Caucasian leader born into the Avar tribe in Dagestan who in 1834 became the third imam of Dagestan. As both a spiritual and military leader he carried on the Murid War [q.v.], begun in 1830, when the first imam proclaimed a *ghazavat* (holy war) against the Russians. He forged a union with other mountain tribes in the Caucasus stretching from the Black Sea to the Caspian, but in 1839 Russian successes forced him to give up a son as a hostage to be reared and educated in St. Petersburg. Shamyl himself refused the safety of exile and fought on. By 1842 he had recaptured Dagestan.

In 1845 the Russians sent a 10,000-man army under General Mikhail Semenovich Vorontsov [q.v.] to the Caucasus. Shamyl lured the Russians deep into the mountains and then cut their lines of communication. Vorontsov lost a third of his command before a relief column rescued him. During the Crimean War [q.v.] the Allies supplied Shamyl with arms and money, but by 1859 three large Russian armies were converging on Dagestan. Deserted by his allies, Shamyl was forced to surrender at the fortress of Gounib to Russian General Aleksandr Ivanovich Baryatinsky [q.v.] on 25 August 1859. He expected to be executed; instead he was treated as a hero and was even presented to the tsar. Surrounded by his family, he settled into a comfortable exile at Kaluga, a town 90 miles southwest of Moscow.

In 1870 he was permitted to make the haj to Mecca (Makkah), and his journey was a triumphal one. The sultan of

Turkey offered him a palace, and in Mecca he was so overwhelmed by admirers that special hours had to be arranged for him to pray while police kept back the crowds. He died on 4 February 1871 while en route to Medina (Medinah). One of his sons was commissioned in the Russian army, and the other in the Turkish army.

Shangani Patrol, Destruction of the (4 December 1893), Matabele War. In Southern Rhodesia (Zambia) Major Allan Wilson [q.v.] led a patrol of 33 men along the shores of the Shangani River, a tributary of the Zambezi River in pursuit of Lobengula [q.v.], the defeated chief of the Matabeles. At a point about 84 miles northwest of Shiloh, on the bank of the river, then in flood, the patrol was attacked by a large force of Matabeles. Refusing to surrender, singing "God Save the Queen," they fought until all were killed, although an American known as Tex Long claimed to be a survivor. The heroism of the patrol was commemorated by a monument at World's Rest in the Matopos.

Shanghai, Attack on (17 May 1862), Taiping Rebellion. Taiping rebels under Li Hiu-ch'eng [q.v.] launched an attack upon Shanghai, one of the treaty ports. The city was defended by 12,000 imperial troops from Anhwei brought to the area by the British navy. These were supported by 427 British sailors and 950 British soldiers, 690 sepoys, and 775 French soldiers and sailors, plus 1,000 European-trained Chinese troops under the command of Frederick T. Ward [q.v.], an American adventurer [see Ever Victorious Army; Shanghai Foreign Arms Corps], The battle was fought at Nantao (Nantou, now a suburb of Shanghai). The French admiral was killed in the attack, and to avenge him, the victorious French massacred every man, woman, and child in Nantou. The Taipings retreated, and Li Hiu-ch'eng took his forces to Nanking (Nanjing or Nanxiang).

Shanghai Foreign Arms Corps. A private army of Chinese officered by Americans, Europeans, and Filipinos that was raised by the merchants of Shanghai in 1860 during the Taiping Rebellion [q.v.]. Its first commander was Frederick Townsend Ward [q.v.], an American adventurer. Later it became the Ever Victorious Army [q.v.], commanded by British Major Charles Gordon [q.v.].

Shapska. See Schapska.

Sharovary. The baggy trousers worn by Cossacks.

Sharps, Christian (1811–1874). An American designer of small arms. In 1848 he patented a falling-block rifle, accurate up to 600 yards, that used a paper or linen cartridge. The breechblock was lowered by pushing forward a lever that also acted as a trigger guard [see Sharps Rifle]. Rifles and carbines of this design enjoyed a commercial success; an estimated 100,000 were used in the American Civil War and in the Indian-fighting army that followed. In 1849 Sharps produced a small four-barreled pistol and a number of small-caliber percussion revolvers.

Sharpsburg, Battle of. See Antietam, Battle of.

Sharpshooter. A good marksman with a musket or rifle. One of the best was Sergeant Isaac Putnam Smith (d. 1908), who served in Company G, 84th New York, during the American Civil War. After the war he toured the world as Colonel Ike Austin, shooting apples from his wife's head and potatoes from her mouth until through overindulgence his aim became too shaky and his wife left him. He died in poverty in Sydney, Australia.

Units of sharpshooters were formed in some armies after the rifle became the standard shoulder weapon. During the American Civil War Hiram Berdan [q.v.] was authorized on 14 June 1861 to raise a regiment of sharpshooters for the Union army. To join, a recruit had to be able to hit a 10-inch circle from 200 yards ten times. A second regiment was authorized on 28 September 1861. Members wore uniforms of regulation cut made of dark green cloth, the color worn by Gurkha and British rifle regiments [see Rifle Green; Gurkhas]. Both regiments saw considerable action. Of the original 1,392 men in the 1st United States Sharpshooters, 564 became casualties. In the second regiment, 462 out of 1,178 became casualties.

In the American army, by General Orders dated 20 February 1884, "sharpshooter" became a formal rating, above "marksman" but below "expert."

Sharps Rifle. An early breech-loading rifle developed by Christian Sharps [q.v.]. The chamber was fixed, and the barrel was closed by a vertical block that moved at a nearly right angle to the axis. It was loaded by depressing the trigger guard, which opened the breech.

Shashka. A Circassian saber for slashing and thrusting much favored by Cossacks. It had no guard, and the narrow hilt had a large pommel. The scabbard was usually of wood covered with leather. The 1881 pattern became standard for all mounted troops in the Russian army after 1882.

Shavetail. 1. An American army mule.

2. In nineteenth-century American slang, a recruit; in later usage, a new second lieutenant.

Shaw, Robert Gould (1837–1863). An American soldier who attended Harvard for three years and in April 1861, at the beginning of the American Civil War, enlisted as a private in the Union army. He was commissioned in May and in August 1862 was promoted captain in the 2nd Massachusetts. In April 1863 he was appointed colonel of the 54th Massachusetts Volunteers, the first regiment of black troops from a free state to be mustered into the U.S. service. All previous black units had been formed from former slaves in Union-occupied southern areas. Shaw was killed at the head of his troops in the assault upon Fort Wagner [q.v.] in South Carolina on 18 July 1863. Confederates, enraged that blacks had been enlisted to fight against them, threw his body into a common grave with his men. Shaw's parents, when told of this, declared it was what their son would have wished.

Sheaffe, Roger Hale (1763–1851). A Boston-born British soldier who joined the British army as an ensign in 1780. After service in Canada and Europe he returned to Canada during the War of 1812 [q.v.], serving from July 1812 to

November 1813. In the Battle of Queenston Heights [q.v.] on 14 October 1812 he assumed command upon the death of Sir Isaac Brock [q.v.] and defeated the Americans. On 27 April he successfully defended York (Toronto), causing the Americans to sustain losses that exceeded the total British force engaged.

Sheikabad, Battle of (10 May 1866), Afghan Civil War. A battle in Afghanistan at this site located between Kandahar and Kabul fought between the forces of Amir Shere Ali and those of his nephew Abdur Rahman Khan [qq.v.], who defeated his uncle and became amir. [See Afghan Civil Wars.]

Sheinovo, Battle of (28 December 1877), Russo-Turkish War of 1877–78. In a thick fog, while Russian bands played, Russian troops under Mikhail Skobelev [q.v.] successfully attacked Turks under Vessil Pasha and captured 33,000. Russian losses were about 5,000, of whom 1,103 were killed.

Shelby, Joseph Orville (1830–1897). An American rope manufacturer who was one of the wealthiest men in Missouri at the beginning of the American Civil War. He became a prominent cavalry commander in the Confederate army and cooperated with General Sterling Price [q.v.] in the western theater. He was promoted brigadier general in 1864. After the war he led his men to Mexico, but he soon returned to Missouri. A popular man, he refused all political offices until 1893, when he became a U.S. marshal.

Shell. 1. A projectile filled with an explosive as opposed to shot, which is a solid projectile.
2. A cartridge for a shotgun.

Shell *Manufacture of artillery shells*

Shell Fragments. A piece of metal from an exploded shell. In modern usage, frequently referred to erroneously as shrapnel [q.v.].

Shell Jacket. 1. A sleeveless overjacket.
2. Any undress military jacket.

Shell Shock. A psychological disorder unknown or unrecognized, certainly unnamed, in the nineteenth century. The term was not used prior to World War I [see Stress, Combat].

Shelter Half. One half of a two-man shelter tent, called a dog or pup tent [q.v.]. The two halves buttoned together to provide minimum shelter for two men.

Shenandoah Valley Campaign of Jackson (May–June 1862), American Civil War. A successful Confederate campaign waged by General Thomas ("Stonewall") Jackson [q.v.] intended to hold the fertile Shenandoah Valley, a source of provisions known as the "Breadbasket of the Confederacy," and to divert Federal forces from aiding the Peninsular Campaign [q.v.] of Union General George B. McClellan [q.v.]. With about 10,000 men Jackson faced an army of about 18,000 under Major General Nathaniel Banks [q.v.].

In a short winter campaign (1861–62) Jackson drove out, but failed to capture, isolated Union forces at Romney and Bath (Berkeley Springs), both now in West Virginia. He then established his headquarters at Winchester, Virginia.

In March 1862 Banks marched up the Shenandoah Valley and occupied Winchester, which Jackson had evacuated on 11 March. On 23 March Jackson fought and lost the Battle of Kernstown [q.v.], but he won all subsequent battles of the campaign. Banks made a cautious advance up the valley while Jackson retreated before his superior force and established a position at Swift Run Gap in the Blue Ridge Mountains that put him on the flank of any Union force attempting to advance past Harrisonburg.

The division of General Richard Ewell [q.v.] was given to Jackson, and his force increased to 17,000. Leaving Ewell at Swift Run Gap, he took the remainder of his force east across the Blue Ridge to Mechum's River Station, where waiting trains carried his infantry west to Staunton. There he plunged into the Appalachian Mountains and joined forces with General Edward Johnson [q.v.]. Although he took no direct part in the Battle of McDowell [q.v.], fought and won mainly by Johnson's army on 8 May, Jackson gave credit to God, leaving others to credit Jackson for the victory.

Jackson then marched up the Shenandoah Valley, but he abruptly altered course and moved east across the Massanutten range to the Luray Valley, where he joined forces with Ewell, and on 23 May with 16,000 men made a surprise attack upon Banks at Front Royal [q.v.]. Banks retreated toward Winchester, and Jackson launched an attack upon his rear guard that would have destroyed Banks had not his undisciplined cavalry under Colonel Turner Ashby [q.v.] preferred loot to pursuit. However, Jackson pushed his infantry forward and on 25 May defeated Banks at Winchester. Banks retreated to Martinsburg and crossed the Potomac at Williamsport on 26 May.

Jackson pressed north, and on 29 May he was at Halltown, three miles from Harpers Ferry. His successes so panicked the Union leaders in Washington that Lincoln himself began to direct military operations. Jackson, who wanted to retain control of the head of the valley for as long as possible, lingered almost too long. Two armies converged on his line of retreat: A Union force under James Shields [q.v.] advanced from the east and a force under General John Frémont [q.v.] from the west with the aim of cutting Jackson off at Strasburg. Had these forces acted more expeditiously they might have destroyed Jackson, who narrowly escaped by making forced marches. By noon on 1 June his army, with 2,000 prisoners of war, and a seven-mile-long wagon train of supplies had cleared the Strasburg choke point and were headed south up the Shenandoah Valley.

Frémont followed Jackson, and Shields's force moved up the Luray Valley to cut off his escape east over the Blue Ridge. Ashby, who brought in stragglers and fought an excellent rearguard action in the retreat, was killed in a skirmish on 6 June. The next day Jackson, now at Port Republic at the foot of the southern end of the Massanutten range, knew that both Frémont and Shields were close. On 8 June Ewell fought a successful battle against Frémont at Cross Keys [q.v.], just west of Port Republic, and Jackson, in a badly fought battle, managed to beat off Shields's advanced guard just northeast of the town [see Port Republic, Battle of]. Jackson then made good his escape over the Blue Ridge through Brown's Gap (no longer passable) to join Lee in the Seven Days' Battles [q.v.].

Jackson had been unable to keep permanent control of the Shenandoah Valley, but he had succeeded in diverting Union forces from joining McClellan.

Shenandoah Valley Campaign of Sheridan

(7 August 1864–2 March 1865), American Civil War. In early August 1864 Union Major General Philip Sheridan [q.v.] with 48,000 effectives occupied the lower (northern) end of the Shenandoah Valley in and around Harpers Ferry. Facing him was Confederate Major General Jubal Early [q.v.], who had some 23,000 men at Moorefield (West Virginia). On 10 August Sheridan advanced south to Berryville and Early retreated to Strasburg. In the objectives of the generals on both sides and in many of their movements, the campaign resembled the Shenandoah Valley Campaign of Jackson [q.v.] in 1862.

On 19 September Sheridan defeated Early in an engagement at Winchester, but Sheridan's victory was not decisive, and Early retreated to Fisher's Hill, below Strasburg. Sheridan followed and in the battle there on 22 September again defeated him. [See Fisher's Hill, Battle of.]

Early took his shattered forces to Brown's Gap in the Blue Ridge Mountains, and Sheridan advanced to Harrisonburg. On 6 October Sheridan began to withdraw toward Winchester, but he destroyed as he went, burning crops and cutting fruit trees, acting under the same orders that had earlier been given by Grant to General David Hunter [q.v.]: "In pushing up the Shenandoah Valley . . . it is desirable that nothing should be left to invite the enemy to return. Take all provisions, forage, and stock wanted for the use of your command; such as cannot be consumed, destroy. It is not desirable that buildings be destroyed—they should rather be protected. . . ."

When Confederate cavalry began to harass Sheridan, he ordered his cavalry commander, Alfred Torbert [q.v.], "Either whip the enemy or get whipped yourself." Thus goaded, Torbert attacked and defeated the Confederates in the Battle of Tom's Brook [q.v.].

In his report to Grant, Sheridan wrote: "I have destroyed over 2,000 barns filled with wheat, hay and farming implements; over 70 mills filled with flour and wheat; have driven in front of the army over four herd of stock and have killed

The Shenandoah Valley, where in 1862 the campaign of Confederate General Jackson and in 1864–5 the campaign of Union Major General Sheridan were waged.

and issued to the troops not less than 3,000 sheep. This destruction embraces the Luray Valley and Little Fort Valley as well as the main Valley." Summing up his successful tour of destruction, he wrote: "A crow would have had to carry its own rations if it had flown across the valley."

Believing that he had cleared the Shenandoah Valley of Confederates, Sheridan sent an army corps east to Grant. However, Early returned in force and on 19 October, although numerically inferior, attacked Sheridan's army and in the Battle of Cedar Creek [q.v.] drove back the Federals. Sheridan, returning from a summons to Washington, had reached Winchester when he heard of the attack. After a bold night ride he arrived on the scene in time to rally his troops and defeat Early in a counterattack. On 2 March General George Custer [q.v.] annihilated the remnants of Early's army at Waynesboro [q.v.].

Sherbrooke, John Coape (1764–1830).

An English soldier who was commissioned an ensign in 1780 and served in Nova Scotia and the Netherlands, taking part in the retreat from Holland to Bremen in 1794. He served in Cape Colony in 1796 and later in India, where he took part in the Mysore War of 1799 and commanded a column in the assault on Seringapatam. In the Peninsular War [q.v.] he was second-in-command to Wellington in 1809, and he particularly distinguished himself in the Battle of Talavera [q.v.], in which he led a division in a bayonet charge. Later Wellington said of him: "Sherbrooke was a very good officer, but the most passionate man, I think, I ever knew."

In 1811 he was promoted lieutenant general, married a rector's daughter, and was appointed governor of Nova Scotia. During the War of 1812 [q.v.] he led a successful expedition up the Penobscot River and captured an American brigade. In 1816 he was appointed captain general and governor-in-chief of Canada. In 1818 he suffered a paralytic stroke and retired from active duty. His incapacity did not delay his promotions, and in 1825 he was promoted full general.

Shere / Sher Ali Khan (1825–1879). An Afghan amir, the third son of Dost Muhammad [q.v.], who from 1866 to 1869 quarreled savagely with his brothers and nephews over the throne of Afghanistan and, with the help of his son Yakub Khan [q.v.], overpowered them all. In 1878, when the British failed to guarantee his sovereignty, he refused to receive a British mission, a rebuff that led to the Second Afghan War [q.v.] of 1878–81. In 1879 Yakub Khan rebelled against his father and was captured and imprisoned by him. Shortly afterward, when Shere Ali, forced to flee to Turkestan, died at Mazar-i-Sharif, Yakub Khan succeeded to the throne. [See Afghan Civil Wars.]

Sheridan, Philip Henry (1831–1888). An American soldier who was graduated from West Point in 1853, a year later than his class. He was set back for threatening Cadet Sergeant (later Union General) William Rufus Terrill (1834–1862) with a bayonet and then attacking him with his fists. After graduation he was posted to the Northwest and in 1855 joined in a long but fruitless campaign in Oregon against the Yakima Indians in which he narrowly escaped death in 1856 while recapturing a blockhouse. Later he spent several years on the Grande Ronde Indian Reservation in northeast Oregon, where he lived with a Rogue River Indian woman who taught him her language.

At the beginning of the American Civil War he was an infantry captain, but on 25 May 1862 he was made colonel of the 2nd Michigan Cavalry. On 13 September of the same year he was promoted to brigadier general of volunteers, to rank from 1 July. After distinguishing himself at Perryville and Murfreesboro [qq.v.], he was promoted major general on 16 March 1863, with rank to date from 31 December 1862. He commanded a division in the Battle of Chickamauga [q.v.], and soon after, General U. S. Grant gave him command of all the cavalry in the Army of the Potomac [q.v.]. He fought at the Wilderness, Spotsylvania, and Cold Harbor [qq.v.], and in May 1864 he raided the Confederate lines of communication around Richmond [see Sheridan's Richmond Raid].

After the raid of Confederate General Jubal Early [q.v.] on Washington, D.C., in July 1864, Sheridan was given command of the Army of the Shenandoah, about 42,000 men, and ordered to close the "back door on Washington" [see Shenandoah Valley Campaign of Sheridan]. In September he drove back Early's army at Fisher's Hill [q.v.], but his army was taken by surprise when Early attacked at Cedar Creek [q.v.] while Sheridan, having been called to Washington, was temporarily absent. He was on his return journey, preparing

to spend the night in Winchester, when he heard the sound of guns and made a ride in the night to rescue his command, retrieving victory from defeat, an action made famous by a poem, "Sheridan's Ride," written by Thomas Buchanan Read (1822–1872), a Pennsylvania poetaster and minor painter whose best-known painting depicted the ride. For his feat Sheridan received the Thanks of Congress and was promoted major general in the regular army.

In his campaign Sheridan, perhaps the most antisouthern of the Union generals, turned the fertile Shenandoah Valley, known as the "Breadbasket of the Confederacy," into a wasteland. He then rejoined the Army of the Potomac before Petersburg and played a major role in the operations that led to the surrender of General Robert E. Lee at Appomattox [q.v.].

After the war Sheridan was commander of the military district that included Texas and Louisiana, and by concentrating 52,000 men along the Rio Grande, he was instrumental in forcing the withdrawal of French support for Emperor Maximilian [q.v.] of Mexico. He also gave both moral support and supplies to the rebel army of Benito Pablo Juárez [q.v.]. From 1867 to 1869 he commanded the Department of the Missouri with headquarters at Fort Leavenworth. It was he who sent Colonel George Forsyth [q.v.] into the field with 50 frontiersmen, a unit that met with disaster in the Battle of Beecher's Island [q.v.]. In 1868 he organized and directed a campaign on the South Plains that resulted in the attack by George Custer [q.v.] upon the camp of Black Kettle (1803?–1868) on the Washita River in Indian Territory [see Washita, Battle of]. Although he always denied the words, Sheridan was widely credited with saying, "The only good Indian is a dead Indian."

In 1869 he was promoted lieutenant general by President Grant and assumed command of the Division of the Missouri, an area of a million square miles from Canada to the Mexican border. In 1870–71 he was in France as an observer on the German side of the Franco-Prussian War [q.v.] and witnessed the French disaster in the Battle of Sedan [q.v.]. Back in the United States he did much of the planning and organized the preparation for the Great Sioux War of 1876–77 [q.v.]. On 1 November 1883 he became commanding general of the army, succeeding W. T. Sherman [q.v.], and on 1 June 1888, two months before his death, he was made a full general.

Lincoln described Sheridan as "a brown chunky little chap, with a long body, short legs, not enough neck to hang him, and such long arms that if his ankles itch he can scratch them without stooping." He was energetic, brusque, profane, loyal, and demanding. Captain Alfred Barnitz, who served under him, wrote: "Like Grant, Sheridan is a man of few words, but he always *looks* very animated, and although he really does not say very much, you came away with the impression that you have had quite a prolonged and interesting conversation with him!"

Sheridan's Richmond Raid (9–24 May 1864), American Civil War. With Grant's permission, General Philip Sheridan [q.v.] made a raid around Lee's army, destroying vital Confederate communications and supplies. With 10,000 cavalry and horse artillery he defeated the Confederates in four battles: at Beaver Dam Station [q.v.] on 9–10 May; Yellow Tavern [q.v.] and Ground Squirrel Bridge on 11

May; and Meadow Bridge on 13 May. It was in the Battle of Yellow Tavern that Confederate General Jeb Stuart [q.v.] and General James B. Gordon (1822–1864) were mortally wounded.

Sherman, William Tecumseh (1820–1891). An American soldier, one of eleven children of a justice of the Ohio Supreme Court who in 1829, upon their father's sudden death, were distributed among friends and relatives. William was taken in and raised by Thomas Ewing (1789–1871), a U.S. senator and later cabinet minister whose daughter he later married. Ewing appointed Sherman to West Point, from which he was graduated in 1840. During the Mexican War [q.v.] he was stationed in California, where he earned a brevet to captain. He resigned from the army in 1853 and became a banker. When his bank failed, he took up the law, practicing unsuccessfully in Leavenworth, Kansas. In 1859 he accepted a position as superintendent of the Louisiana State Seminary of Learning and Military Academy at Pineville (now Louisiana State University at Baton Rouge).

At the beginning of the American Civil War he submitted his resignation, stating: "On no earthly account will I do any act or think any thought hostile . . . to the . . . United States." For a few months he was head of a street-car company in St. Louis, but on 14 May 1861 he was made colonel of the newly formed 13th Infantry, and on 7 August he was promoted brigadier general and sent to save Kentucky.

His animosity toward newspaper correspondents led to his vilification in the press, even to the suggestion that he was mentally deranged. On 11 December 1861 the *Cincinnati Commercial* published an article with the headline *General William T. Sherman Insane* [see War Correspondents]. Sherman was briefly relieved of his command, but he commanded a division in the Battle of Shiloh [q.v.], and on 1 May 1862 he was promoted major general. He commanded a corps in the campaign that captured Vicksburg [q.v.] and took part in relieving the army of W. S. Rosecrans [q.v.] in the Chattanooga Campaign [q.v.]. After his good friend U. S. Grant assumed the supreme command, Sherman was given command of all the troops in the western theater. Using his numerical superiority, he pried Confederate General Joseph Johnston [q.v.] out of every position in his march toward Atlanta, which he captured. In September 1864 Grant wrote to him: "You have accomplished the most gigantic undertaking given to any general in this war, and with a skill and ability that will be acknowledged in history as unsurpassed if not unequalled." From Atlanta Sherman began his March to the Sea [q.v.], cutting a 40-mile swath of destruction through the heartland of the South. Jefferson Davis [q.v.] called Sherman "The Attila of the American continent." (*The Rise and Fall of the Confederate Government* [1881]).

In the course of the war Sherman twice earned the Thanks of Congress. Unlike most officers who remained with the army after the war and accepted lower ranks in the reorganization of the army in 1866, Sherman became a lieutenant general and in 1868 a full general in command of the army. On 4 February 1884 he was placed on the retired list at his own request.

Sherman is frequently credited with saying, "War is hell." At a convention of the Grand Army of the Republic [q.v.] in Columbus, Ohio, on 11 August 1880, he is quoted as saying:

"There is many a boy here who looks on war as all glory, but, boys, it is all hell. You can bear this warning voice to generations yet to come. I look upon war with horror."

Sherpur, Battle of (23 December 1879), Second Afghan War. A British army of 6,500 under Lieutenant General Sir Frederick Roberts [q.v.] occupied a fortified cantonment area north of Kabul, Afghanistan. Forewarned of an attack, Roberts was prepared when an estimated 100,000 Afghans launched a predawn assault. The British threw up starshells to illuminate the field, and their superior weapons repelled the attackers, who suffered a loss said to be 3,000. British losses were 3 killed and 30 wounded.

Shields, James (1806–1879). An Irish-born American politician and soldier who fought in the Mexican War [q.v.] and was brevetted major general of volunteers for his gallantry in the Battle of Cerro Gordo [q.v.]. In 1849 he was appointed governor of Oregon Territory, and he later served as a U.S. senator from Illinois, Minnesota, and finally Missouri. At the beginning of the American Civil War he was commissioned a brigadier general of volunteers in the Union army. After an undistinguished career fighting against Thomas ("Stonewall") Jackson [q.v.] in the Shenandoah Valley, he resigned his commission on 28 March 1863 and moved to Missouri, where he returned to politics.

Shih Ta-k'ai (1821–1863). A Chinese rebel who, like Hung Hsiu-Ch'üan [q.v.], the Taiping leader, had failed the official examinations, a necessary step to becoming one of the scholar class gentry. On 1 January 1851 he joined the Taiping Rebellion [q.v.], and in September the Taipings captured their first walled city, Yungcheng, in northwest Anhwei. On 17 December Hung Hsiu-Ch'üan named him I Wang (assistant king), one of the original five Taiping wangs.

One of the best of the Taiping generals, in March 1853 he captured the great city of Nanking (Nanjing or Nanxiang), which became the capital of the Taipings [see Nanking, Siege of]. On 3 April 1855 he captured Wuchang, on the Yangtze River in southeastern Hupeh Province, and then harassed the forces of Tsêng Kuo-fan [q.v.].

In 1857 Shih quarreled with Hung Hsiu-Ch'üan and, taking many of the Taiping troops and some of their best commanders, set himself up as a warlord in Szechuan (Sichuan) Province. In 1858 his army was said to number several hundred thousand. When the Manchu government learned of his defection, it directed Tsêng Kuo-fan to negotiate terms for his surrender, an overture he rejected. In 1863 he was trapped on the banks of the Tatu River in Szechwan. After several unsuccessful attempts to break out, he surrendered, and on 6 August 1863 he was executed at Ch'engtu (Chengdu).

Shilling Fund. During the Second Anglo-Boer War [q.v.] the *Daily Telegraph*, an English newspaper founded on 29 June 1855, began a Shilling Fund to aid the soldiers fighting in South Africa as well as their widows and children. By 1 January 1901 it had collected £236,000 from more than seven million donors.

Shiloh, Battle of (6–7 April 1862), American Civil War. Also called the Battle of Pittsburg Landing. General U. S. Grant with 42,000 men was concentrated around the Shiloh

Methodist Church, on the west bank of the Tennessee River 25 miles north of Corinth, Mississippi, at Pittsburg Landing, Tennessee, waiting for Brigadier General Don Carlos Buell [q.v.] to join him with 20,000 more men. His plan was then to advance upon Corinth, but before Buell could arrive, Confederate General Albert Johnston [q.v.] launched a surprise attack that was initially successful, the Confederates steadily pushing back the Federals all through the day. Johnston fell mortally wounded about two-thirty in the afternoon and was ably replaced by General Pierre Beauregard [q.v.]. Buell arrived during the night, and the next day (7 April) Grant counterattacked. The fighting was particularly heavy around Shiloh Church. At two-thirty in the afternoon Beauregard ordered a retreat.

The battle was later succinctly described by General Grant as "A case of Southern dash against Northern pluck and endurance." The Federals lost 1,754 killed, 8,408 wounded, and 2,885 missing; the Confederates lost 1,723 killed, 8,012 wounded, and 959 missing. The Confederates never regained the strategic initiative in this theater, and Corinth was abandoned on 29 May.

Shiloh *The Battle of Shiloh, Tennessee. Above this ravine the Federal artillery checked the Confederate advance at sunset, 6 April 1862.*

Shinpei, Eto (1834–1874). A Japanese samurai who fought in the Boshin Civil War [q.v.] to restore power to the emperor and became a member of the Meiji government after the restoration. In the 1870s he broke with the government and led an unsuccessful revolution that led to his execution.

Ship Island. A seven-mile-long sandy island in the Gulf of Mexico off the southeast coast of Mississippi used as a British naval base in the War of 1812. In 1847, during the Mexican War [q.v.], it was reserved for military purposes, and in the American Civil War it was for a time a Confederate prison camp. In 1878 a quarantine station was established on the island, and a year later a lighthouse.

Shipka Pass, Battle of (August 1877–January 1878), Russo-Turkish War of 1877–78. While besieging Plevna [see Plevna, Siege of], the Russians dispatched a column of 7,000 Russians and Bulgarians under General Fëdor Radetski [q.v.] into the Balkan Mountains of central Bulgaria. On August 21 1877 it seized the 17-mile-long Shipka Pass, lying 4,376 feet high between Gabrovo and Kazanlik, about 60 miles northeast of Plovdiv. It was soon retaken by 27,000 Turks under

Suleiman Pasha [q.v.], commander of the Turkish force in Bulgaria. Radetski was reinforced by a division under Mikhail Dragomirov [q.v.], raising the Russian-Bulgarian force to 13,000, but by 26 August the battle had ended in a stalemate, each side occupying roughly the same position held five days earlier. The Russians had suffered about 4,000 casualties, and the Turks perhaps twice that number.

On 16 September Suleiman, reinforced to about 40,000, assaulted Radetski's key position on Mount St. Nicholas and was repulsed with a loss of 3,000; Russian losses were 31 officers and 1,000 other ranks. There was no further action until Plevna fell to the Russians on 10 December. The Russians were then able to put 50,000 men in the pass. General Osip Gurko [q.v.] took command and on 8 January 1878 launched a massive assault. The following day the Turks, having suffered 4,000 casualties, were overwhelmed, and 36,000 were taken prisoner; Russian casualties were 3,640 killed and wounded. The Russians then had an almost open road to Constantinople (Istanbul).

Shipka Pass *Turkish assault on Russian positions in the Shipka Pass*

Shipp, Scott (1839–1917). An American soldier and educator who was graduated from the Virginia Military Institute [q.v.] in 1859 and remained there as an assistant professor until the beginning of the American Civil War. He was commissioned a major in the Confederate service and saw action in western Virginia (West Virginia) until January 1862, when he was ordered to return to VMI as commandant of cadets with the rank of lieutenant colonel. On five occasions during the war he led cadets into the field, most notably on 15 May 1864 in the Battle of New Market [q.v.], in which he was wounded at the head of 260 cadets. After the war he remained at VMI as commandant of cadets, and in January 1890 he became superintendent, a post he held until he retired in June

1907. In 1890 he served on the Board of Visitors at West Point, and in 1894 at the Naval Academy.

Shirt Wearer. Any head warrior among the Sioux Indians, not a chief, but one whose influence depended upon his abilities. Red Cloud [q.v.] of the Oglala Sioux was such a person.

Shoeburyness. A cape on the coast of Essex, England, where ordnance tests were made and later a gunnery school was established.

Shoes. In all countries throughout the nineteenth century soldiers marched in ill-fitting footware. In the American army as late as 1885 shoes were issued in two widths, A and B, and in only two styles: post shoes with calf uppers and field shoes with "wax" uppers. All were made in the military prison at Fort Leavenworth, Missouri. Not until near the end of the century were right and left shoes differentiated. In the British army for a time soldiers were required to alternate shoes on the feet so they wore evenly.

Shogunates. Japanese military governments headed by a shogun, the short form for *seii tai shogun* (barbarian-subduing generalissimo). Three shogunates ruled Japan from the late twelfth century until the Boshin Civil War [q.v.] of 1867–68, after which the office was abolished and the power of the emperor restored. The last shogunate was the Tokugawa, which had ruled since 1603.

Sholapur, Battle of (10 May 1818), Third Maratha War. Near this town, 170 miles west of Hyderabad, some 4,000 Anglo-Indian troops, mostly cavalry, under General Theophilus Pritzler [d. 1839] attacked and defeated 7,500 Marathas and Arab mercenaries, the retreating remnants of the peshwa's army under Gompat Rao, a Maratha chief. The British lost 97 killed and wounded; Maratha losses exceeded 800.

Shop, the. Colloquial expression for the Royal Military Academy, Woolwich [q.v.].

Short Bull (1845?–1915). A Sioux medicine man who was one of the leaders in the Ghost Dance Disturbances [q.v.] among the Sioux. In 1890 he and two others were delegated to visit Wovoka [q.v.], the founder of the movement, at Pyramid Lake, Nevada. There he became a devotee, later even proclaiming that he himself was the Messiah. In 1891 he was imprisoned at Fort Sheridan, Illinois. He was later permitted to join the *Buffalo Bill Wild West Show* [see Cody, William] and appeared in the show for several years, including the tour through Europe. He converted to Congregationalism and died at the Rosebud Reservation in South Dakota.

Short Service. See Cardwell's Reforms.

Short Shell. 1. An artillery shell that inadvertently falls among friendly troops, civilians, or nontargeted installations. Sometimes called merely a short.
 2. A defective shell that falls short of its target.

Shot. 1. The discharge of a weapon.
 2. The distance traveled by a fired projectile.
 3. A collective term for all projectiles fired from guns.
 4. A solid projectile, fired by muzzleloaders, as opposed to shell.
 5. The pellets in a cartridge fired by a shotgun.

Shotai. Japanese rifle units formed in 1864 in the army of Choshu led by Shinsaku Takasugi [q.v.]. The units held both samurai and commoners. Its shock troops were called *kiheitai*. Aritomo Yamagata [q.v.], who more than any other Japanese commander shaped the new imperial army after the Meiji Restoration, was a *shotai* officer.

Shotal. An Abyssinian sickle-shaped edged weapon.

Shot from Guns. A type of execution in which the victim was tied across the muzzle of a cannon that was then discharged, spewing body parts. It was widely used by the British against captured mutineers during the Indian Mutiny [q.v.].

Shot Garland. A square framework of wood or iron into which round shot for muzzleloaders could be placed. Layers could then be added to make a pyramid.

Shotted Gun. A cannon loaded with live ammunition and ready to be fired.

Shoulder Arms. A command to place a musket or rifle on the shoulder in a prescribed way. (British: slope arms.)

Shoulder Knots. Epaulets made of ornamental knots of gold or silver cords. They usually indicated rank and often the arm or service.

Shoulder of a Bastion. The meeting of the flank and the face of a bastion.

Shoulder Scale. An epaulet made of overlapping metal plates.

Shoulder Straps. 1. Pieces of cloth, frequently colored, sewn onto the shoulders of shirts or coats and often indicating rank.
 2. Epaulets.

Shoulder Weapon. A weapon fired from the shoulder, as a musket, carbine, shotgun, or rifle.

Show the Flag, to. To send troops or ships to make the presence of power known to people of a given area.

Shoulder Straps *U.S. regulation officers' shoulder straps, from top: colonel, general-in-chief, lieutenant-colonel.*

Shrapnel. 1. The original shrapnel, invented by British Major Henry Shrapnel [q.v.] in about 1785, was an explosive shell filled with musket balls with a fuze that could be cut to time the shell to explode in the air, showering the target with lead balls. It was adopted by the British army in 1803 and was used successfully in Surinam in 1804. It was first used on land in Europe in the Battle of Vimeiro [q.v.] during the Peninsular War. In the American Civil War it was usually referred to as spherical case shot. Present usage, introduced by ignorant war correspondents in World War II, includes fragments from any munition, but this meaning was not attached to the word in the nineteenth century nor in World War I.

2. The musket balls scattered by the explosion of shrapnel.

Shrapnel, Henry (1761–1842). A British soldier who was commissioned in the artillery in 1779. In 1784 at his own expense he began to experiment in making spherical projectiles filled with bullets and explosive charges, experiments that ultimately led to his invention of the type of shell that bore his name [see Shrapnel]. In 1802 he became a major, and in the following year, a lieutenant colonel. In 1804 he was appointed first assistant inspector of artillery at Woolwich, where he made numerous improvements to howitzers and mortars, invented a brass tangent slide, compiled range tables, invented fuzes, and improved small arms and ammunition.

In 1813, having developed his shell primarily with his own money, he asked the Board of Ordnance for some compensation but was told that the board had "no funds at their disposal for the reward of merit." Eventually he was granted a pension of £1,200, and in 1819 he was promoted major general. He retired from active duty in 1825 and was promoted lieutenant general in 1837.

Shuvalov, Count Pavel Andreyevich (1830–1908). A Russian soldier and diplomat who served in the Crimean War and in the Russo-Turkish War [qq.v.] of 1877–78. In 1866 he was made head of the Secret Service. In 1873 he was sent on a secret mission to London to arrange for the marriage of the Duke of Edinburgh to the only daughter of Tsar Alexander II [q.v.]. From 1885 to 1894 he was Russian ambassador to Germany, and in 1896 he was named to the Imperial Council.

Siamese-Cambodian War. See Cambodian-Siamese War.

Siamese-Laotian War (1826–28). In 1826 Laotian forces attacked Siam (Thailand) and threatened Bangkok, coming to within 30 miles of the city before being repulsed by the Siamese. In the following year Siamese forces invaded Laos, decisively defeated the Laotians in the weeklong Battle of Nong-Bona-Lampon, on the Mekong River, and captured and destroyed the Laotian capital of Vientiane. In 1828 Siam annexed Laos.

Siaou Chi-kwei (d. 1852). A Chinese rebel in the Taiping Rebellion [q.v.] who was appointed Si Wang (western king), one of the five original wangs. He was killed in the Siege of Nanking [q.v.].

Sibley, Henry Hastings (1811–1891). An American merchant, public official, and soldier. In 1829 he was employed by the American Fur Company, and in 1834 he went west as its agent. In Mendota on the Minnesota River he built the first stone house in what is today Minnesota. In October 1848 he was a delegate to Congress, and in May 1858 he took office as the first governor of the state and served until 1860. In August 1862, following the Sioux Uprising in Minnesota [q.v.], he was commissioned a colonel of a volunteer militia assembled at Fort Snelling, which had been built in 1819 at the confluence of the Minnesota and Mississippi rivers. On 3 September he relieved a detachment of soldiers who had been besieged at Birch Coulee near Fort Ridgely, about 20 miles above New Ulm. Having discovered a Sioux plot to ambush him, he thwarted and decisively defeated the Sioux in the Battle of Wood Lake [q.v.] on 23 September. Six days later he was promoted brigadier general of volunteers. In June 1863, in conjunction with General Alfred Sully [q.v.], he set out with a large force to pursue the Sioux in the Dakotas. He defeated bands at Big Mound in what is now Kidder County, North Dakota, on 24 July; at Dead Buffalo Lake on 26 July; and at Stoney Lake two days later (both in Burleigh County). In November 1865 he was brevetted major general. He was mustered out in April 1866 and settled in St. Paul, where he developed many business interests. In 1880 he ran unsuccessfully for Congress.

Sibley, Henry Hopkins (1816–1886). An American soldier who was graduated from West Point in 1838. He took part in the Second Seminole War, the Utah Expedition, the Mexican War [qq.v.], in which he was brevetted for his gallantry, and the 1860 campaign against the Navajos [see Navajo War]. On 13 May he was promoted major in the 1st United States Dragoons, but on that date he resigned his commission. Three days later he was commissioned a colonel in the Confederate army, and on 17 June he was promoted brigadier general. He was put in command of an expedition designed to secure New Mexico for the Confederacy, but although he was victorious in the battles of Valverde and La Glorieta [qq.v.], he was forced to retreat, for his command could not subsist off the country. In May 1862, after near-incredible hardships, he reached El Paso, Texas. He then retired to San Antonio and made no further contribution to the Confederate war effort.

In 1869 he joined other former Confederate and Union officers in the Egyptian army, in which former Union General Charles P. Stone [q.v.] was chief of staff. Sibley returned to the United States in 1873. His last years were spent in ill health and comparative poverty. Sibley died in Fredericksburg, Virginia.

Sibley's main claim to fame was his invention of the Sibley tent and the Sibley stove [qq.v.].

Sibley Stove. An American army portable, cone-shaped space-heating stove, 18 inches in diameter, which could be easily assembled, invented by Captain Henry Hopkins Sibley [q.v.] for use with the Sibley tent [q.v.]. It remained an army issue until at least 1941.

Sibley Stove *Christmas in a Sibley tent, around a Sibley stove, by Frederic Remington*

Sibley Tent. A light, bell-shaped American army tent supported by an upright center pole. The tent could hold 10 to 20 men, sleeping with their feet to the center. It was patented on 22 April 1856 by American Captain Henry Hopkins Sibley [q.v.] and was an army issue throughout the remainder of the nineteenth century.

Sibley Tent

Sicily, Garibaldi's Invasion of (May–July 1860). In 1847, 1848, and 1849 Sicilians rose in unsuccessful revolts against the rule of Ferdinand IV of Naples (1835–1908), who in 1815 had assumed the title of King Ferdinand I of the Two Sicilies. In 1860, with the covert support of King Victor Emmanuel II of Piedmont (1820–1878) and his premier, Camillo Cavour (1810–1861), Giuseppe Garibaldi [q.v.] and his 1,000 Red Shirts [q.v.] sailed from Genoa on 5 May and landed at Marsala, Sicily. Marching inland, he gained supporters, and on 15 May he defeated Neapolitan forces at Calatafimi [q.v.]. On 27 May he took Palermo, and on 20 July he again defeated the Neapolitans at Milazzo [q.v.], near Messina. On 22 August, with some help from the British, he crossed the Strait of Messina to Italy proper and in a successful campaign freed Sicily from the kingdom of the Two Sicilies and made it a part of the Italian kingdom.

Sick Call. A signal made by bugle, trumpet, or drum alerting those requiring medical attention to assemble for examination by a doctor.

Sickles, Daniel Edgar (1825–1914). An American politician and soldier. In 1852 he married the beautiful sixteen-year-old Teresa Bagiola, already pregnant. Seven years later in Lafayette Square, almost within the shadow of the White House, Congressman Sickles shot down and killed his young wife's lover, Captain Philip Barton Key, an attorney and the son of Francis Scott Key [q.v.]. In the "trial of the century" that followed, Edwin McMasters Stanton [q.v.], one of the country's leading attorneys and later wartime secretary of war, argued that Sickles had acted "in a transport of frenzy" and won an acquittal on the plea—used successfully for the first time in an American court—of the "unwritten law." Sickles then outraged friends and critics alike by forgiving his errant wife.

At the beginning of the American Civil War he organized a brigade for the Union. He was appointed a brigadier general on 3 September 1861 and commanded his brigade in the Peninsular Campaign. On 29 November of the following year he was promoted major general. In the Battle of Gettysburg [q.v.], in which he commanded a corps, he disobeyed orders (perhaps in another "transport of frenzy") by advancing his men to the Peach Tree Orchard, creating a salient that was subsequently overrun by the corps of Confederate General James Longstreet [q.v.]. Sickles himself was severely wounded, losing his right leg, the shattered bones of which were later displayed at the Army Medical Museum (now the National Museum of Health and Medicine) at Walter Reed Army Medical Center. After the war he was sent on a diplomatic mission to Colombia and served as military governor of South Carolina. In 1869 he was retired with the rank of a major general in the regular army and was appointed by President Grant minister to Spain, where he served until 1873. He was elected to a term in Congress (1893–95) and was for many years chairman of the New York State Monuments Commission. In 1912 he was dismissed for alleged peculation.

(N.B. In old age Sickles advanced the date of his birth by several years, and the date given in the *Dictionary of American Biography* is incorrect.)

Side Arm. A weapon carried at the side or hanging from a belt such as a pistol, sword, or bayonet.

Sidi-bel-Abbès, Capture of (1 January 1848), French conquest of Algeria. An old walled Algerian town, 40 miles south of Oran, that was captured by the French. From 1875 it was for nearly a century the headquarters and main depot of the French Foreign Legion [q.v.].

Sidi Brahim, Battle of (22 September 1845), French conquest of North Africa. A French defeat at the hands of Berber tribesmen 20 miles south-southeast of Mazagan, in southwest Morocco.

Sieges. A siege is a blockade of a city, a castle, or any fortified place or defended position in an effort to compel surrender either by military action or by starvation.

Sieges have been undertaken since ancient times. In the fifteenth century, when the power of artillery increased, it was for a time comparatively easy for besiegers to blow in a gate or a wall, but guns and improved small arms in the hands of the defenders made it increasingly dangerous for the attackers. Siege warfare then changed, and no one contributed more to its transformation than Sébastien le Prestre, Marquis de Vauban [q.v.], a seventeenth-century genius of siege operations in attack or defense. The fortifications he designed were extant in the nineteenth century, and more important, his method for conducting sieges by means of saps and parallels was still the standard.

Saps (trenches) were driven forward in a zigzag pattern toward the place to be attacked, aiming to get close enough to blow in a gate or create a breach in a wall. Because the head of the sap was the most vulnerable and most important position of the attackers and the target of the most concentrated fire of the besieged, parallel trenches were dug out on each side and manned to protect the sappers. Traditionally there were three parallels, each closer to the place to be attacked. Sappers were also protected by gabions and fascines. The system was first used at the siege of Maestricht, successfully conducted by Vauban in 1673. Mining of course was also a common feature of sieges [see Mining, Military].

Many professional soldiers hated sieges, as did Napoleon—and with reason. They were time-consuming and expensive. Not only was there danger from shot and shell, but no other form of warfare was as likely to produce epidemics as siege warfare, in which immobile armies, besieged and besiegers alike, lived amid their own wastes. Ian Hamilton [q.v.], that happy warrior, said: "Sieges are horrible things. A good fight in the open—that is another matter."

A siege does not mean that a place is completely surrounded or completely cut off from supplies. The siege of Balaclava (September 1855–April 1856) during the Crimean War [qq.v.] left the city open to the receipt of supplies by sea, and the siege of Delhi (June–September 1857) during the Indian Mutiny [qq.v.] was scarcely a siege at all, for the British merely occupied a ridge on one side of the city. Some other nineteenth-century sieges of note were the third siege of Badajoz (March–April 1812) during the Peninsular War, one of seventeen in that war; Vicksburg (May–July 1863) during the American Civil War; Paris (September 1870–January 1871) and Metz (August–October 1870) during the Franco-Prussian War; Plevna (July–December 1877) during the Russo-Turkish War of 1877–78; and Mafeking (October 1899–May 1900) and Ladysmith (November 1889–February 1900) during the Second Anglo-Boer War [qq.v.].

Siege Train. The weapons, usually heavy large-caliber guns needed to attack a strongly fortified place. (The use of "train" comes from the French *traigner* [to tow or drag along].)

Siemens Company. In 1847 Ernst Werner von Siemens (1816–1892), a Prussian soldier who was commissioned in the artillery in 1838 and in 1848 laid the first German telegraph line between Berlin and Frankfurt-am-Main. He resigned his commission, and with J. G. Halske formed a company, Siemens & Halske, in Berlin for the manufacture of telegraph equipment. The firm expanded to manufacture a variety of electrical equipment for civilian and military use

and to direct major electrical engineering projects. Siemens's brother (Karl) William Siemens (1823–1883) established a branch in England, where in 1859 he became a naturalized subject and eventually was knighted. The brothers, both of whom invented numerous electrical devices, joined with another brother, Alexander (1847–1928), and formed Siemens Brothers. One of the firm's major efforts was a 2,750-mile telegraph line from Prussia to Teheran. In the two world wars of the twentieth century the companies supplied both sides with critical equipment.

Sierra Leone, Revolt in (1898). Africans in Sierra Leone in West Africa rebelled against the British collection of a hut tax. The rebellion originated in the Karene District in the northeast and was taken up by the Mendis in Mendiland. It was suppressed with difficulty.

Sigel, Franz (1824–1902). A German-born American soldier who was educated at the Karlsruhe Military Academy, from which he was graduated in 1843. During the 1848 Revolutions in Europe he acted as minister of war for the German rebels. When they were overthrown by the Prussians, he fled the country. In 1852 he arrived in the United States. During the American Civil War he organized a Union regiment of foreign-born troops, mostly from Germany and other Central European nations, and became their colonel. He was promoted brigadier general on 7 August 1861 and major general in March 1862. He fought well at Pea Ridge [q.v.], but thereafter less well, particularly while serving under John Frémont [q.v.]. After the war he became publisher and editor of *New Yorker Deutsches Volksblatt*.

Sight. 1. As a noun, a device for guiding the eye when one aims a firearm.
   2. As a verb, to take aim.
   3. As a verb, to adjust the sights of a firearm. [See Sight, Line of; Sight, Angle of.]

Peep sight

Sight, Angle of. The angle between the line of sight and the axis of the gun.

Sight, Line of. The imaginary line between a gun and its target.

Signal and Secret Service Bureau. A Confederate agency established at Richmond in May 1862 during the American Civil War. It provided lines of communication with the various field commands and operated the Secret Line, a network of agents, couriers, and spies who kept contact with sympathizers in the North and carried messages and military information. The bureau was operated by Colonel William Norris, a Yale graduate, class of 1840, who had been a lawyer and businessman. Little is known of its workings, for all its papers were lost or destroyed.

Signal Corps, American. The U.S. Army Signal Corps was established in 1860, but it was not given official status until 1863 during the American Civil War. The Signal Corps included the Weather Bureau until 1890, when it was transferred to the Department of Agriculture. The Signal and Secret Service Bureau [q.v.] of the Confederate Army was established in 1862.

Signal Flags. Dr. Albert James Myer, an army assistant surgeon, and Captain Edward Porter Alexander [qq.v.] developed in the late 1850s a system of wigwag signaling with flags or torches. Myer was appointed chief signal officer, the army's first, with the rank of major. Alexander, who became a Confederate officer during the American Civil War, used the system to warn of the Federal flank attack in the First Battle of Bull Run [q.v.].

Signal Flags *Signaling the main command during the Indian Wars*

Sikajoki River, Battle of the (18 April 1808), Russo-Swedish War. Russians under General Friedrich Wilhelm Buxhöwden [q.v.] attempted to outflank Swedes by moving onto the ice at the mouth of the Sikajoki River while simultaneously making a frontal attack, but both attacks were repulsed after an eight-hour battle. Swedish losses were about 1,000; Russian losses are unknown but believed to have been heavy. Sweden ceded Finland to Russia in 1809.

Sikh Wars. Toward the end of the seventeenth century the Sikhs, a monotheistic Hindu sect in the Punjab, began to change their character. At first they were associated in a number of clans who warred among themselves as well as against their neighbors. In the later part of the eighteenth century they became a rough confederacy with a political-military force known as the Khalsa [q.v.]. Ranjit Singh [q.v.], who succeeded his father as ruler of the Punjab in 1792, united the various Sikh clans and developed a formidable military establishment that posed the last serious threat to the British Raj in India.

First Sikh War (1845–46). On 11 December 1845 a Sikh army of 2,000 infantry and 10,000 cavalry crossed the Sutlej River, which divided Sikh lands from those of the Honourable East India Company, and on 13 December seized Ferozepore. It was met by a 10,000-man Anglo-Indian army under General Sir Hugh Gough [q.v.]. Late in the afternoon of 18 December the Sikhs attacked Gough near the mud village of Mudki [q.v.], 20 miles from Ferozepore, and were defeated. In his after-action report Gough wrote: "Their whole force was driven from position to position, with great slaughter, and the loss of seventeen pieces of artillery, some of them of heavy calibre; our infantry using that never failing weapon, the bayonet."

On 21 December the British successfully attacked strong Sikh entrenchments at Ferozeshah [q.v.] in one of the most bitterly fought battles in British India. The following day after making a halfhearted attack that was easily repulsed, the Sikhs withdrew across the Sutlej.

In January 1846 a Sikh army again crossed the Sutlej. It was defeated by a British force under General Sir Harry Smith [q.v.] at Ludhiana on 21 January and in the Battle of Aliwal [qq.v.] on the 28th. Soon after, on 10 February, Gough led an army of 20,000 across the Sutlej and defeated a Sikh army of 50,000 near the village of Sobraon [q.v.], 45 miles southeast of Lahore on the south bank of the river. On 11 March the Sikhs signed the Treaty of Lahore, and the Punjab became a British protectorate.

Lieutenant William Hodson [q.v.] wrote that the campaign was a "tissue of mismanagement, blunders, errors, ignorance and arrogance." However, Gough and his soldiers won, and in war winning is everything.

Second Sikh War (1848–49). The murder of two British officers by Sikh soldiers on 20 April 1848 at Multan [q.v.]

A Sikh soldier

sparked an uprising that spread rapidly through the Punjab [see Edwardes, Herbert Benjamin]. The British sent an army to besiege Multan, and another army of about 15,000 was raised with some difficulty by General Hugh Gough [q.v.] and marched to Lahore, arriving on 13 November to face a Sikh army twice its size. On 22 November Gough's cavalry was repulsed in a skirmish near the village of Ramnagar [q.v.] when it tried to cross the Chenab River. The British lost 26 killed and 59 wounded.

There was a lull while Gough sorted out his commissary arrangements and quarreled with the governor-general, but in January 1849 he advanced and, near the village of Chilianwala [q.v.], now in northwest Pakistan, five miles east of the Jhelum River, fought a bloody, indecisive battle that resulted in 2,357 British casualties—about 1 of every 5 engaged. Henry Havelock [q.v.] described it as "one of the most sanguinary ever fought by the British in India and the nearest approximation to a defeat of any of the conflicts of that power in the East." When those in England read the butcher's bill, they were appalled, and General Sir Charles Napier [q.v.] was sent out to replace Gough as commander-in-chief, India. The war was over before he could arrive.

Reinforced by the army that had finally successfully besieged Multan, Gough with 24,000 men had decisively defeated 50,000 Sikhs and their Afghan allies in the Battle of Gujerat [q.v.] on 22 February 1849. British losses were 96 killed and 700 wounded. The Sikhs and Afghans lost an estimated 2,000. The British annexed the Punjab.

Sikkah el Hamra, Battle of (6 July 1836), French conquest of Algeria. French forces under General Thomas Bugeaud [q.v.] defeated an Arab force under Abd el-Kader [q.v.] near this Algerian village.

Sikkim Expedition, British (1850). In the later part of 1849 British botanist Sir Joseph Dalton Hooker (1817–1911), traveling with Dr. A. Campbell, superintendent of the Darjeeling (Darjiling) sanatoria, was studying the flora of Sikkim when the two men were arrested and imprisoned by the Sikkim authorities. The British launched a military expedition that freed them and annexed the Sikkim *tarai* at the foot of the hills as well as some hills beyond.

Silistra, Siege of (20 March 1854–22 June 1855), Crimean War. After the Russian occupation of Moldavia and Walachia

Silistra *Victorious sally by Turkish garrison of Silistra, 14 June 1854*

in 1853, Russian Field Marshal Ivan Paskievich [q.v.] on 20 March 1854 crossed the Danube River to besiege the fortress of Silistra, 70 miles west of the Black Sea, now in Bulgaria. The Turks resisted, and Paskievich, after losing some 10,000 men, retired over the Danube.

On 27 March 1854, while the siege was still in progress, France declared war on Russia and was followed the next day by Britain, beginning the Crimean War [q.v.].

Silladar System. A method by which, following the Indian Mutiny [q.v.], most cavalry regiments in the Indian army were raised. Originally, members of irregular cavalry supplied their own horses. Later each regiment was assigned so many slots or places, called *asami*s, the right to supply a man and a horse. There were usually about eight hundred. For each of these the Indian government (sirkar) paid a certain sum each month that covered the cost of food and forage with something left over for a wage to the owner, who might be the sowar (Indian cavalryman) himself or a retired soldier, a soldier's widow, or a moneylender who held the *asami* as an investment. Sometimes a native officer would own several *asami*s and would mount his sons and nephews.

Silver Stick in Waiting. See Gold Stick in Waiting.

Simm's War Car. See Armored Cars.

Simple / Single Line of Operation. An army or other unit moving in a given direction with all its parts united or within supporting distance.

Simpson, James (1792–1868). A British soldier educated at the University of Edinburgh and commissioned an ensign and lieutenant in the Grenadier Guards in 1811. In 1812, during the Peninsular War [q.v.], he was sent to Spain, where he took part in the siege of Cádiz [q.v.] and the relief of Seville. He was soon invalided home and took no further part in that war, but he fought in the 1815 campaign and was severely wounded in the Battle of Quatre Bras [q.v.]. On 10 June 1826 he was appointed lieutenant colonel of the 29th Foot. He took that regiment to Mauritius, where he served for two years. In 1842 he took his regiment to India but soon left it to serve as second-in-command to General Sir Charles Napier [q.v.] in a campaign against hill tribes. In 1846 he returned to Britain, and in 1851 he was promoted major general. In February 1855 he was sent to the Crimea as chief of staff with local rank as lieutenant general [see Crimean War]. He landed at Balaclava on 15 March where upon the death of Lord Raglan [q.v.], on 28 June, he took command of British land forces. As a reward for his failed attack on the redan [q.v.], he was promoted general and received the GCB. On 11 November he gave up his command; he returned to England and retired from the army.

Sind, Conquest of (1843). On 15 February, resenting humiliating demands by the British, 8,000 Baluchis in Hyderabad, in what is now southern Pakistan, attacked the British Residency there. Its small group of defenders under James Outram [q.v.] escaped with difficulty. Moving with expedition, British forces of fewer than 5,000, mostly sepoys, under General Sir Charles Napier [q.v.] attacked and defeated

Baluchi chiefs in the Battle of Miani on 17 February and the Battle of Hyderabad [qq.v.] on 24 March.

The campaign secured for the British the great Indus waterway. At its conclusion Napier is alleged to have telegraphed a one-word report: "*Peccavi* [I have sinned]"; both the pun and the telegram were the creation of an editor of *Punch.*

Single Action. Term used to describe a type of small arm in which the hammer had to be cocked by hand before firing. Double-action weapons cocked and fired with the pulling of the trigger.

Sinkiang, Conquest of. See Chinese Turkestan, Conquest of.

Sino-French War (1883–85). An undeclared war resulting from French expansion in Tonkin. Chinese troops sent from Yunan were ousted by the French from Sontay, 25 miles west-northwest of Hanoi. The French occupied the valley of the lower Black River, and on 23 June 1884 they were defeated by Chinese troops in the Battle of Bac-le [q.v.], 25 miles northeast of Kumyan. The French responded by sending a naval squadron, which on 23 August entered the harbor at Foochow and destroyed a Chinese naval squadron and land fortifications. The squadron then sailed to Formosa (Taiwan), and on 23 October it began a bombardment of the forts at Chi-lung (Keelung or Kilung), 15 miles east-northeast of Taipei. The Chinese defenders surrendered in March 1885, and the French briefly occupied the forts.

In the meantime, the French had launched a major offensive in Tonkin. They captured Langson [q.v.], 85 miles northeast of Hanoi, on 13 February 1885, but six weeks later, after suffering a severe defeat, they abandoned the area, leaving behind a wealth of matériel. In France popular support of the government's expansionist strategy in Indochina collapsed, and the government fell. The new government on 9 June 1885 negotiated the Peace of Tientsin, by which France re- stored the area of Formosa it occupied and the Pescadores, which the French navy had captured.

Sino-Japanese War (1894–95). The war between China and Japan, sometimes referred to as the Pigtail War, began with a quarrel over who would control Korea, a semi-independent vassal of China. In June 1894 civil unrest, fomented by the Japanese, led to a Korean request to China to restore order [see Korean Civil Disorders]. China answered by sending troops by sea to Asan, some 40 miles southwest of Seoul. In response Japan dispatched troops to Seoul through Chemulpo (Inchon). Although the Koreans settled their own disorders, the Chinese and Japanese remained, and on 20 July the Japanese seized control of the government.

On 25 July the Japanese sank a British-registered ship, *Kowshing,* which had been chartered to carry Chinese troops, and four days later Japanese troops under General Yoshimasa Oshima [q.v.], commanding the Japanese troops in Seoul, advanced toward Asan and defeated the Chinese at Söngchon, 30 miles northeast of Pyongyang. The Japanese suffered about 700 casualties; the Chinese, about 6,000. On 1 August 1894 Japan and China declared war on each other, and both sides rushed troops to Korea.

Although the Chinese appeared to have an enormous army, it was actually a paper tiger. An American naval intelligence report estimated it had only 12,000 effective personal weapons with usable ammunition. Some of its soldiers were armed with bows and arrows or carried colorfully decorated lances. By contrast the Japanese were well armed with modern weapons and had been properly trained. When General U. S. Grant visited Japan in 1879, he remarked that Japanese soldiers were so well armed and trained that 10,000 could march against all odds back and forth across China.

On 15 September 20,000 Japanese under General Michitsura Nozu [q.v.] easily defeated 14,000 Chinese under Li Hung-chang [q.v.] in the Battle of Pyongyang [q.v.]. The

Sino-Japanese War *Depiction of a Japanese attack on a Chinese fort.*

Chinese then withdrew to the Yalu River, where they received reinforcements and supplies.

On 17 September the fleets of the two belligerents met near the mouth of the Yalu. In the action that followed, the Chinese fleet suffered heavy damage and the loss of five ships; the Japanese sustained considerable damage but lost no ships. General Nozu advanced to the Yalu, where he was reinforced, and the combined troops organized as the First Army under Marshal Aritomo Yamagata [q.v.]. On 24–25 October it crossed the Yalu unopposed and advanced into Manchuria.

At the same time, the Japanese Second Army— 26,000 troops and 13,000 auxiliaries under General Iwao Oyama [q.v.]—moved down the Liaotung Peninsula to attack Port Arthur (Lushun), the fortified port city at its tip. On 19 November General Maresuki Nogi [q.v.] successfully led a dawn attack on the fortifications, defended by only 10,000 Chinese.

When the Japanese entered the city, they were greeted by the severed, mutilated heads of captured Japanese soldiers suspended by cords. American war correspondent James Creelman (1859–1915) witnessed the Japanese reprisal upon the Chinese civilians. They "killed everything they saw," he reported. "Unarmed men, kneeling in the streets and begging for life, were shot, bayoneted or beheaded. . . . [T]he town was sacked from end to end, and the inhabitants were butchered in their own homes." He estimated that some 2,000 were slaughtered.

Sino-Japanese War *A Japanese Lieutenant climbs the Genbu Gate wall at Pyongyang, 1894.*

Creelman's report, first published in the *New York World* on 11 December 1894, stunned most readers, for European and American sentiment had favored Japan. The *Illustrated London News* had pronounced the conflict "worthy of a first-class European war" and asserted that the Japanese "sent a thrill of admiring wonder through the military world." So many Americans, including aging Civil War veterans, had attempted to volunteer to fight for Japan that federal officials thought it necessary to issue a circular discouraging them.

With the news from Port Arthur, Americans and Europeans alike reversed themselves. Overnight the Japanese became "sly and evil little people."

While the Port Arthur Campaign was under way, Yamagata fought and won a series of engagements in Manchuria, including on 30 November a particularly hard-fought battle at Tsao-ho-ku [q.v.], 170 miles northeast of Port Arthur. Plagued by supply problems and by increasingly severe weather conditions in December 1894 and January 1895, his army had difficulty defending its main base at Haicheng, 80 miles southwest of Mukden, from attack by Chinese General Sung Ching, but on 21–23 February Sung Ching was defeated in the Battle of Taping-shan [q.v.].

In January the Japanese formed a Third Army, which included some units of the Second Army, under General Iwao Oyama, and transported it by ship to the eastern tip of the Shantung Peninsula, about 20 miles from the main Chinese naval base at Weihaiwei. The landing on 10 January 1895 was unopposed, and Oyama at once marched upon Weihaiwei while Japanese naval forces engaged the fortifications there from the sea. On 31 January, after two days of fighting in bitter cold weather, Weihaiwei was taken, and the main Chinese fleet destroyed. The Chinese admiral committed suicide. Even though they had suffered heavy casualties, the Japanese restrained their troops, and no atrocities were reported. Public opinion in Europe and the United States again swung toward Japan.

In February the Japanese First Army, now under General Nozu, advanced farther into Manchuria, defeating the Chinese in the Battle of Tapingchaun, 50 miles west of Ussuriysk. The last major effort of the Chinese to halt the invaders failed on 9 March at Yingkow (Newchwang), a city on the left bank of the Liao River, 120 miles north of Darien, and until 1907 the only port city in Manchuria.

While the Japanese waited only for good weather to march on Peking (Beijing), the Chinese, defeated in every battle, sued for peace, and Li Hung-chang [q.v.], the "Bismarck of Asia," was sent to Japan to negotiate a treaty. On 17 April the Treaty of Shimonoseki was signed. China agreed to recognize Korean independence, to pay an enormous indemnity (300 million tael, about $150 million), to open four more ports to Japanese merchants, and to cede Formosa (Taiwan), the Pescadores Islands, and the Liaotung Peninsula to Japan. The terms would have been even harsher had not France, Germany, and Russia intervened and coerced Japan to relinquish its demand for land on the Chinese mainland.

Sioux Uprising of 1862. See Minnesota, Sioux Uprising in.

Sioux War of 1876–77. See Great Sioux War; Crook, George; Fetterman Massacre; Wagon Box Fight; Red Cloud.

Sioux War of 1890–91. See Messiah War; Sitting Bull; Wounded Knee.

Sirdar / Sardar.

1. The commander-in-chief of the Egyptian army. After the British suppression of Arabi's Revolt [q.v.] by the British in 1882 the sirdar of the Egyptian army was always British.

2. In India, a leader or officer. Sirdar Bahadur was a military distinction, not a rank.

Siria, Battle of (13 August 1849), Hungarian Revolution. At this town (Hungarian: *Vilàgos*) now in western Rumania, 15 miles northeast of Arad, the Hungarian revolutionary army under Arthur von Görgey [q.v.] was soundly defeated and surrendered to the Russians under General Fëdor Rudiger [q.v.] at Siria on 13 August 1849.

Sirkar. Indian name for the government of India under the British.

Sirsuwari. In Arabic, the commander of a regiment of irregular cavalry, roughly equivalent to colonel.

Sitabaldi, Battle of. See Nagpur, Battle of.

Sitana Fanatics. See Umbeyla Campaign.

Sitting Bull (1834–1890). Indian name: Tatanka Yotanka. A Hunkpapa Sioux medicine man and chief. At the age of fourteen he accompanied his father, called Jumping Bull, in raids upon the Crows and even counted coup [q.v.]. In the 1860s he took an active part in the wars on the plains. On 24–25 December 1866 he led a raid upon newly built Fort Buford, on the left bank of the Missouri River just below the confluence of the Yellowstone, in present-day North Dakota. This post, located in the heart of the buffalo country,

Sitting Bull, 1885

was particularly offensive to the Sioux. From 1869 to 1876 Sitting Bull led raids on Crows, Shoshones, and other Indian tribes as well as on whites. Although he has been credited with being one of the leaders in the Battle of the Little Bighorn [q.v.], he was perhaps at the time in the hills "making medicine."

After raiding on the northern plains and harassing troops in Montana, on 20–21 October 1876 he held an inconclusive conference with General Nelson A. Miles [q.v.], whose demand that Sitting Bull and his people relocate to a reservation he rejected [see Great Sioux War]. When talk proved futile, the troops advanced on the Indians, and in a two-day running battle near Clear Creek, Montana, 2 soldiers were wounded and 5 Indians were killed. On 27 October about 2,000 Sioux surrendered, but Sitting Bull, with Chief Gall [q.v.] and others, escaped and for some months moved about in the region of the upper Missouri River and its tributaries. In the spring of 1877 they crossed into Canada, where they were given fair treatment by the newly formed Northwest Mounted Police. In 1881, under a pledge of amnesty, Sitting Bull returned to the United States only to be held for a time at Fort Randall, in present-day South Dakota.

On 6 June 1885 he signed a contract to appear in *Buffalo Bill's Wild West Show* [see Cody, William Frederick] for four months for $50 a week, a bonus of $125, and the right to sell his photograph and his painfully traced signatures.

In 1888, at his invitation, Kicking Bear organized the first ghost dance at the Standing Rock Agency, in southern North Dakota [see Ghost Dance Disturbances]. On 15 December 1890, on the pretext that Sitting Bull was responsible for the Ghost Dance Disturbances, the Standing Rock agent sent 43 Indian policemen to arrest him in a dawn raid on his cabin on the Grand River, 30 miles south of the agency. The police were supported by two troops of the 8th Cavalry, which, to avoid unduly alarming the Indians, were held back out of sight.

The arrest was made without incident, but some delay in saddling the highly trained circus horse presented to Sitting Bull by Cody gave time for angry Indians to swarm around the police. A gun was fired, and in the resultant melee, amid the smoke, dust, and shouting, the horse reared back on his haunches and began its repertoire of tricks. The cavalry, hearing the shooting, galloped up to find Sitting Bull and 7 of his followers, including his seventeen-year-old son, dead on the ground. Inside the cabin were 4 dead and 3 wounded policemen, 2 of whom later died.

Those there that night witnessed a gruesome spectacle, described by one Sergeant George B. DuBois of the 8th Cavalry in a letter to a friend three days later: "The scenes around the camp were awful. I saw one [Indian policeman] go up to old Bull and cut him across the face with an axe. One cut him with a knife till his own squaw wouldn't know him. The dead looked horribly cut and shot."

The Battle of Wounded Knee [q.v.] on 29 December 1890 developed out of the ensuing turmoil.

Sitting Bull's War. See Great Sioux War.

Sixt von Armin, Friedrich (1851–1936). A German soldier who fought in the Franco-Prussian War [q.v.] of 1870–71 and was severely wounded in the Battle of St. Privat [see Gravelotte–St. Privat, Battle of]. He served on the general staff and was named director of the General Department of War in the Prussian army in 1903. In the First World War he commanded a corps.

Sjambok. A short whip, usually of rhinoceros or hippopotamus hide, used in South Africa for driving oxen.

Skalitz, Battle of (28 June 1866) Seven Weeks' War. A single Prussian corps under General Karl von Steinmetz [q.v.] defeated an Austrian corps near this Slovakian town, also called Skalica or Szakolca, 16 miles northeast of Breclav, capturing 3,000 men and 11 heavy guns.

Skean-dhu / Skene-dhu / Sgian-dubk. In Gaelic: black knife. The traditional small knife carried in a sheath in the right stocking by officers in full dress in Highland regiments of the British army. Various patterns were used, but the knife was generally short with a flat grip. The earliest depiction of a Scotsman with a knife in his hose is a portrait of Colonel Alistair Macdonald of Glengarry painted in 1812 by the fashionable Edinburgh portrait painter Henry Raeburn (1756–1823).

Skillygalee. Crumbled hardtack fried in animal fat, eaten by troops in the American Civil War.

Skinner, James (1778–1841). An Anglo-Indian soldier whose father was a Scottish officer in the Indian army and whose mother was a Rajput who in 1790 killed herself in despair when her daughter was removed from her and sent to school. Skinner was educated at a Calcutta boarding school and in 1796 was apprenticed to a printer. He at once ran away. His godfather, an English officer in the Indian army, introduced the young man to a French general in Sindha's Maratha army who gave him a commission. In the next ten years he took part in a number of military expeditions, including in 1798 the capture of Delhi and in 1799 the storming of Hânsi, the stronghold of George Thomas [q.v.], the Irish soldier of fortune.

Dismissed during the Second Maratha War [q.v.] of 1803–05, he went over to the British, who put him in command of an irregular cavalry unit composed of deserters from the Maratha army. This unit, soon called Skinner's Horse, greatly distinguished itself in the campaign against Holkar and in the Third Maratha War of 1817–19 [qq.v.]. Skinner was present at the storming of Bhurtpore [q.v.] in 1826 and was rewarded by the government with grants of land in the newly acquired territory. This property, combined with others he had acquired, gave him a large estate. Having become a Christian, he built the Church of St. James in Delhi, which was consecrated in 1826. In 1828 he was commissioned a lieutenant colonel and awarded a CB.

He is said to have had at least 14 wives. He left 5 sons, 2 of whom also became officers in the Indian army. Although his cavalry unit became the 1st Bengal Cavalry, it continues to be called Skinner's Horse to the present day. Upon his death in 1841 his remains were deposited in the church he had built in Delhi.

Skinner's Horse. One of the oldest cavalry regiments in the Indian army; its uniforms were yellow [see Skinner, James].

Skirmish. A brief military engagement by relatively few men, usually in extended order [see Skirmisher]. A skirmish can be an isolated action or part of a larger engagement.

Skirmisher. A soldier detached from the main body and sent forward to delay or harass the enemy or posted on the flanks to prevent surprise. Skirmishing by light infantry was the usual prelude to a battle. In European armies after 1808 there was a tendency to use ever greater numbers of troops as skirmishers. The Prussians sometimes used up to a third of their force.

Skirmisher *Skirmishers advance in front of the main body of troops. Sketch by Winslow Homer*

Ski Troops. Northern European countries employed soldiers capable of moving on skis. Such troops were added to the armies of France and Italy in 1902. The duties of ski troops were much the same as those of mounted infantry: scouting, communications, and the seizure of advanced positions.

Skobelev / Skobeleff, Mikhail Dmitrievich (1843–1882). A Russian soldier whose grandfather had been a serf, but whose father was an army officer. He entered the army in 1863. In 1868, after his graduation from the General Staff Academy in St. Petersburg, he fought against the Polish revolutionaries. From 1871 to 1875 he took part in the conquest of Khiva and Khokand [qq.v.], winning the coveted Cross of St. George the Martyr [q.v.]. As a major general in the Russo-Turkish War of 1877–78 [q.v.] he played a conspicuous role at Loftcha, Plevna, Sheinovo, Shipka Pass, and Adrianople [qq.v.]. Because he habitually wore a white uniform and rode a white horse, he came to be known as the White General.

In 1880–81 he commanded an army that attacked the Tekke-Turkomans in Central Asia, and in 1881 he successfully stormed Geok Tepe [q.v.] and occupied it [see Tekke Campaign, Russian]. His conquest of Transcaspia led to the construction of a strategic railroad that the British regarded as a threat to India [see Great Game].

In 1882 Skobelev's enormously successful life fell into ruin within a few months. He favored a militant Pan-Slavism, and in a speech given in Paris—he spoke five languages—he declared that war between Slavs and Germans was inevitable, a statement his government was quick to repudiate.

His mother raised a large sum of money to aid the oppressed Bulgarians [see Bulgarian Atrocities], but while traveling to Bulgaria to distribute the funds, she was robbed and murdered by the officer accompanying her, a man personally selected by Skobelev. Soon after, in June, Skobelev died mysteriously in a Moscow hotel room.

Skoda. A manufacturing company founded in 1859 at Pilsen, then part of the Austro-Hungarian Empire. In 1866 the firm was taken over by Emil von Skoda (1839–1900), a Czech engineer and industrialist, and under his direction it became the principal supplier of artillery and other matériel to the empire, enjoying a relationship with the government similar to that of Krupp with the German government. It sold arms to other countries as well, including China, Turkey, and Britain. Later in the century it produced machine guns, railroad equipment, bridges, and other heavy engineering materials and goods. Emil Skoda's son, Karl (1879–1929), became director in 1909.

Skoda Machine Gun. A machine gun with a hopper feed weighing about 25 pounds, made in calibers from 6.5 mm to 11 mm. It was patented in 1888 by Field Marshal Archduke Karl Salvator (d. 1892) and Colonel Ritter von Dormus and was adopted by the Austrian army in 1893 and produced by Skoda. It first saw service during the Boxer Rebellion [q.v.] when employed by the Austro-Hungarian detachment among the defenders of the legation in Peking (Beijing). The original model, which had an overhead hopper, was altered in 1909 to take a cloth belt feed. It remained in use until after the First World War.

Skoptsi, Suppression of. This Russian secret religious society, to which many army and naval officers subscribed, first came to the attention of the authorities in 1771, when a peasant named Andrei Ivanov in the Orel region, about 200 miles south of Moscow, was found to have castrated himself and to have persuaded 13 other peasants to do the same. All were whipped and sent to Siberia. One, who claimed to be the son of God incarnate in the person of Tsar Peter II (1728–1762), escaped. The sect grew until 1847, when 515 men and 240 women were sent to Siberia. In 1872 trials of members took place all over Russia. In 1874 it numbered at least 5,444 men and 1,465 women, 863 of whom had mutilated their genitalia. To escape persecution, some fled to Rumania, where they were known as Lipovans. The sect was still extant in the twentieth century.

Skrzynecki, Jan (1787–1860). A Polish soldier who in February–August 1831 was commander-in-chief of the Polish army in rebellion against Russia. He was defeated in the Battle of Ostrolenka [q.v.] on 26 May 1831 and relieved of his command in August.

Slagter's Nek Rebellion (1815). Frederick Cornelius Bezuidenhout (1773–1815), an Afrikaner farmer who lived in the valley of Baviaan's River, in eastern Cape Colony, South Africa, was charged with cruelty to a Hottentot (Khoikhoi) servant and was ordered to appear in court at Graaff-Reinet in 1813. He refused to comply and ignored several warnings. In 1815, when Lieutenant Frans Rossouw with 12 Hottentots was sent to arrest him, he retreated with a few companions to a cave near Slagter's Nek. For a time they held the troops at bay, but when Rossouw was fired upon, a fire fight erupted in which Bezuidenhout was killed. In the end several of his companions were arrested, tried, and sentenced to be publicly hanged. The hangings were bungled; a rope broke, and the executioners were successful only after a second attempt. The affair gave rise to great indignation among the Boers, many of whom thought it absurd to punish a man merely for abusing a Hottentot.

Slatin, Rudolph Carl von (1857–1932). An Austrian-born soldier who entered the service of Egypt and Britain. In 1878 he took service under General Charles ("Chinese") Gordon [q.v.] in the Sudan, and in 1881 he was made governor of Darfur. He waged war on slavers and hostile Arabs until 1884, when he was captured by the Dervishes [q.v.] and became the personal slave of El Mahdi, Muhammad Ahmed [q.v.]. In 1895 he escaped and was made a pasha by the khedive of Egypt. From 1896 to 1898 he served as a colonel in the British army, taking part in expeditions against the Dervishes and in General H. H. Kitchener's [q.v.] 1898 reconquest of the Sudan [q.v.], in which he fought in the Battle of Omdurman [q.v.]. He became a British major general and was inspector general in the Sudan from 1900 to 1914. During the First World War he was head of the Austrian Red Cross. He described his experiences as a prisoner of El Mahdi in *Fire and Sword in the Sudan* (1896).

Slave Revolts. See Nat Turner's Insurrection; Haitian revolts.

Sleeman, William Henry (1788–1856). A British soldier who was commissioned in the Bengal army in 1809 and served in the Nepalese War [q.v.]. In 1839 he was appointed commissioner for the suppression of thuggi (thuggery) and dacoity [see Dacoits]. By hanging, imprisoning, or deporting hundreds of thugs, one of whom confessed to having murdered more than seven hundred people, he succeeded in stamping out the practice.

Slightly Wounded. This usually indicated, as it does now, the wounds of a casualty who is still able to sit or stand.

Slim Buttes, Battle of (9 September 1876), Great Sioux War. In mid-August 1876 Colonel (later General) George Crook [q.v.] with elements of the 4th and 5th Cavalry, about 1,500 men; 450 men of the 4th, 9th, and 14th Infantry; 45 white volunteers; and 240 Snake and Ute Indians moved to attack hostile Sioux in the Black Hills of South Dakota.

Food gave out, and the march became famous as Crook's Starvation March [q.v.]. On 8 September he ordered Captain Anson Mills [q.v.] to take 150 men and look for food and hostile Indians. At a place called Slim Buttes, near present-day Reva, South Dakota, 80 miles north-northeast of Deadwood, Mills discovered thirty-seven lodges of American Horse (1840?–1908) and a band of mostly Miniconjou Sioux. Although his troops were in near collapse, Crook attacked the camp at dawn the next day and routed the Indians. His starving men, after devouring the dried buffalo meat found in the camp, torched it. Late in the afternoon some 200 warriors, perhaps sent by Crazy Horse [q.v.], counterattacked. They were driven off, but with difficulty. Perhaps as many as 18 Indians were killed; Crook lost 3 killed and 12 wounded. This was the army's first substantive victory in the Great Sioux War [q.v.].

Slivnitza, Battle of (17–19 November 1885), Serbo-Bulgarian War. At this town (now Slivnica) of about 1,000 inhabitants in western Bulgaria, 19 miles northwest of Sofia, Bulgarian forces of about 15,000, under Stefan Stambolov (1855–1895) and Alexander I [q.v.], repulsed 22,000 invading Serbians, personally led by Milan I (1854–1901), king of Serbia, and drove them back across their border.

The battle was fought under execrable weather conditions. Snow, ice, and fog added to the confusion of battle. Although inferior in numbers, the Bulgarians had an advantage in their artillery: modern Krupp guns against the Serbians' obsolete Russian artillery. The Bulgarians were reinforced, and the Serbs were driven back with a loss of about 3,000 men; the Bulgarians lost about 2,000. This was the first defense of its territory by the new nation of Bulgaria.

Slocum, Henry Warner (1827–1894). An American soldier who was graduated from West Point in 1852. In August 1861, early in the American Civil War, he became a brigadier general of volunteers in the Union army. On 25 July 1862 he was promoted major general, becoming at the time the second youngest in the army, after General Alexander McCook [q.v.]. He served in the Peninsular Campaign, helped cover the retreat of General John Pope [q.v.] after the Second Battle of Bull Run, fought at Chancellorsville, and in the Battle of Gettysburg [qq.v.], on 2–4 July 1863, commanded the extreme right of the Union line. He was with W. T. Sherman [q.v.] in his March to the Sea [q.v.] and northward through the Carolinas. He resigned his commission in 1865 and twice served in the House of Representatives.

Sloper. American army slang denoting a deserter. It was used during the American Civil War and later. To slope was to desert.

Slow Match. A match or fuze capable of burning slowly and evenly used for firing cannon. If made of hemp or flax, slightly twisted and soaked in strong lye, it would burn about four or five inches an hour. Well-twisted cotton rope could be used as a slow match without soaking.

Smala, Battle of (10 May 1843), French conquest of Algeria. The French under the Duke of Aumalé (1822–1897) defeated Abd el-Kader [qq.v.] at this village in North Africa.

Small Arms. Hand-held weapons, such as pistols, rifles, carbines, shotguns, or muskets. Swords and bayonets were sometimes also considered small arms. The American Civil War in 1861–65 and the Franco-Prussian War in 1870–71 [qq.v.] were watersheds in the development of small arms, marking the transition from muzzle-loading arms to breech-loading weapons and the increasing use of self-contained cartridges loaded at the breech.

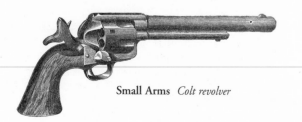

Small Arms *Colt revolver*

Smalley, George Washburn (1833–1916). An American war correspondent educated at Yale and Harvard Law School. In 1861, at the beginning of the American Civil War, he became a correspondent for the *New York Tribune*. He scored a triumph when he personally brought to New York a firsthand account of the Battle of Antietam [q.v.], in which he had carried orders for General Joseph Hooker [q.v.] and had been at his side when Hooker was wounded. In 1866 Smalley covered the Seven Weeks' War [q.v.] as a correspondent on the Prussian side, and the following year he organized the London bureau of the *New York Tribune*. He distinguished himself in his accounts of the Franco-Prussian War [q.v.] in 1870–71. In 1895 he became the American correspondent for *The Times* (London), a position he held until 1905.

Smart Money. 1. In the British army, money paid for wounds and injuries received in the service.

2. In Britain, a sum paid, usually twenty shillings, by a recruit at attestation before a magistrate to free himself from military service. A recruit could not be attested until twenty-four and one-half hours after he had taken the sovereign's enlistment shilling [see Crimping].

Smith, Alexander (1798–1872). A British army surgeon who was graduated M.D. on 1 August 1819. He entered the army as a hospital mate two weeks later. In 1821 he was sent as a hospital assistant to Cape Colony, South Africa. He remained there for sixteen years, rising to become staff surgeon. In 1834–36 he led an expedition into Central Africa and prepared reports on Bushmen and Zulus. He was instrumental in Natal's becoming a British colony. In 1837 he returned to England and on 27 February was appointed inspector general and superintendent of the army Medical Department. During the Crimean War [q.v.], when the sordid state of the hospitals at Scutari was revealed, he was accused of dereliction of duty in the press and elsewhere, but the British system was such that he had no authority over either the hospital medical service or the regimental surgeons. In 1859 he was knighted (KCB).

Smith, Andrew Jackson (1815–1897). An American soldier who was graduated from West Point in 1838. During the American Civil War he served under General Henry Halleck [q.v.] in the Corinth Campaign in 1862. He was promoted brigadier general of volunteers in March 1862 and major general in May 1864.

In December 1862 he commanded a division at Chickasaw Bluffs, and in May–July 1863 he was at the siege of Vicksburg [qq.v.]. In the spring of 1864 he took part in the Red River Campaign [q.v.] of General Nathaniel Banks [q.v.]. On 14 July 1864 he defeated Nathan Bedford Forrest [q.v.] in the Battle of Tupelo [q.v.] in Mississippi. He fought at Nashville, Tennessee, and Mobile, Alabama [qq.v.].

After the war he served briefly as colonel of the 7th Cavalry but resigned to become postmaster in St. Louis. During the strikes in 1877 he commanded a brigade of militia.

Smith, Charles Ferguson (1807–1862). An American army officer who was graduated from West Point in 1825. He later served on the staff at West Point and was commandant of cadets when Grant and Sherman were cadets there. He acquired an enviable reputation during the Mexican War [q.v.]

winning brevets to major, lieutenant colonel, and colonel. He commanded the Red River Expedition of 1856 and served with the Utah Expedition [q.v.] in 1860–61. During the American Civil War he served under Grant in operations against Fort Henry and Fort Donelson [q.v.] in Tennessee. While commanding a division at the siege of Fort Donelson, he personally led a charge that was largely responsible for the surrender of the place. He was named a major general in March 1862. While in command of a force sent up the Tennessee River, he abraded his shin while jumping into a rowboat; the wound became infected, and he died at Grant's headquarters in Savannah on 25 April.

Grant considered Smith the beau ideal of a soldier and believed that had he lived he would have so distinguished himself that no one would ever have heard of Grant or Sherman.

Smith, Edmund Kirby (1824–1893), sometimes called Kirby Smith. An American soldier whose father had fought in the War of 1812 [q.v.]. After he was graduated from West Point in 1845, he served in the infantry in the Mexican War [q.v.], winning brevets to first lieutenant and captain. From 1849 to 1852 he taught mathematics at West Point, then served on the Texas frontier. He was a major when the American Civil War began. When his native state of Florida seceded, he joined the Confederate army as a lieutenant colonel, and on 17 June 1861 he was promoted brigadier general. He was wounded in the First Battle of Bull Run [q.v.]. He commanded the Confederate forces in the Cumberland Gap region and in 1862 took part in the invasion of Kentucky [see Kentucky, Confederate Invasion of] under General Braxton Bragg [q.v.]. As commander of the Trans-Mississippi Department, from February 1863 to the end of the war, he instituted a system of blockade running and defeated the Red River Expedition [q.v.] under Union General Nathaniel Banks [q.v.].

He surrendered in May 1865, the last Confederate general to do so. After the war he served as president of the Atlantic and Pacific Telegraph Company, president of the Western Military Academy, and chancellor of the University of Nashville. From 1875 to his death he taught mathematics at the University of the South.

Smith, Francis Henney (1812–1890). An American soldier and educator who was graduated from West Point in 1833. In 1839 he became the first superintendent of the Virginia Military Institute [q.v.] and so remained until 1888. During the American Civil War he was in the Confederate service but saw no action.

Smith, Giles Alexander (1829–1876). An American soldier in the American Civil War who served in the regiment of his brother Morgan Smith [q.v.] and succeeded him as colonel when the latter was promoted in July 1862. G. A. Smith took part in the siege of Vicksburg [q.v.] and was promoted brigadier general in August 1863. He served under William Tecumseh Sherman [q.v.] in his march through the Carolinas [see March to the Sea]. He was promoted major general in November 1865 and mustered out in 1866.

Smith, Henry George Wakelyn (1787–1860). An English soldier, the fifth of thirteen children of a surgeon on the isle of Ely, six of whose seven sons became officers. Harry (always so called) was educated privately. He was commissioned an ensign in the 95th Foot (later the Rifle Brigade) in May 1805 and promoted lieutenant three months later. Few soldiers saw as much active service as Harry Smith, and fewer still fought on five continents.

In June 1806 he embarked for service under Sir Samuel Auchmuty [q.v.] in South America, and in January 1807 he took part in the capture of Montevideo and in the fruitless attacks upon Buenos Ayres (Aires). He returned with his battalion to England in December 1807 and within a year was in Spain, fighting under General Robert Craufurd [q.v.] in the Peninsular War [q.v.]. He was severely wounded in the Battle of Coa [q.v.] on 24 July 1810, but in March of the following year he commanded a company in engagements against Marshal André Masséna [q.v.]. He took part as a staff officer in the Battle of Fuentes d'Oñoro on 5 May 1811 and in the siege and storming of Ciudad Rodrigo [qq.v.] on 19 January 1812. On 28 February of that year he was promoted captain and in that rank was present at the siege and storming of Badajoz [q.v.] on 6 April.

On the day after the assault Smith and another officer were approached by two distressed young wellborn Spanish women who implored their protection. They had been beset by drunken British soldiers who had robbed them and ripped their earrings from their ears. The elder was the wife of a Spanish officer; the younger was her sister, Juana María de los Dolores de León (1798–1872), only fourteen years old but so beautiful that soldier and writer John Kincade (1787–1862) said "to look at her was to love her." The women were escorted to safety, and Smith proposed at once to Juana. Two days later they were married with Wellington himself giving the bride away.

Juana accompanied Smith throughout the war, sharing the hardships of campaigning as he fought his many battles, including those at Salamanca, Vitoria, Orthez, and Toulouse [qq.v.]. At the end of the war he embarked for the War of 1812 [q.v.] in North America, where as assistant adjutant general under General Robert Ross [q.v.] he took part in the Battle of Bladensburg and the occupation and burning of Washington [qq.v.]. He was carrying dispatches to England when Ross was killed near Baltimore. On 29 September 1814 he was promoted brevet major and then joined the force under Sir Edward Pakenham [q.v.] before New Orleans on Christmas Day [see Battle of New Orleans]. After Pakenham's death and the British defeat, he arranged a two-day truce. On news of the end of the war, he returned to England in time to join Wellington in Belgium. He took part in the Battle of Waterloo [q.v.] and was with the army that entered Paris.

He returned to England in 1818 and served with his regiment in England, Ireland, and Nova Scotia. In November 1826 he became quartermaster general of the forces in Jamaica. At the end of 1834 he was sent to South Africa as a colonel on the staff, commandant of the regular and burgher forces, and second-in-command in the colonies. He arrived in Cape Town during a Kaffir War [q.v.] on 1 January 1835 and at once set off for Grahamstown, then under siege. He accomplished the 700-mile ride in six days [see Grahamstown, Battle of] and took command of all available forces. With 1,100 men he waged a successful campaign against the Xhosas between the Fish and Keiskama rivers in eastern Cape Colony. He established the Kei River as the southern boundary of the native reserve and built a line of forts along it.

On 6 March 1840 he was appointed adjutant general of the queen's army in India. In December 1843 he took part in the Gwalior Campaign [q.v.]. For his services in the Battle of Maharajpur [q.v.] he was knighted and thereafter called Sir Harry. In 1845–46 he fought in the First Sikh War [q.v.] as a temporary major general. After taking part in the early battles and being mentioned in dispatches for his "unceasing exertions," he commanded the troops in the Battle of Aliwal [q.v.] on 6 January 1846. He himself led a charge that drove the Sikhs across the broad Sutlej River. In the House of Lords the Duke of Wellington lauded him: "I never read an account of any affair in which an officer has shown himself more capable than this officer did of commanding troops in the field." Smith commanded a division in the decisive British victory in the Battle of Sobraon [q.v.] and the occupation of the Sikh capital at Lahore. He was made a baronet, given the Grand Cross of the Order of the Bath, and promoted major general.

Smith returned briefly to England in 1847 and then was sent as governor to the Cape of Good Hope. There he again expanded the limits of the colony, taking in the land between the Orange and Vaal rivers, and in so doing aroused the wrath of many Boers. Led by Andries Pretorius [q.v.], the Boers established themselves at Bloemfontein, removed the British Resident, and declared a republic. Smith organized a force, marched against them, and decisively defeated them in the Battle of Boomplats [q.v.] on 29 August 1848. In December there was another invasion by the Xhosas, who were joined by Hottentots (Khois) along the Kei River. Smith crushed this movement with difficulty and was relieved by the home government for not having done so more speedily.

He returned to England, where he was a standard-bearer at Wellington's funeral on 18 November 1852. He was promoted lieutenant general in 1854, but he fought no more. He died childless on 12 October 1860 in London. His widow lived on for another twelve years. The town of Ladysmith in Natal was named in her honor.

Smith, James Francis (1859–1928). An American soldier and jurist who left his law practice in San Francisco to serve in the American army in the Philippines during the Spanish-American War, becoming a brigadier general of volunteers in April 1899. He was appointed military governor first of Negros and then of Visayas. After the war he served as associate justice of the Philippines (1901–03) and as governor-general from 1906 to 1909. From 1910 to his death he was an associate justice of the U.S. Court of Customs Appeals.

Smith, Morgan Lewis (1821–1874). An American soldier in the American Civil War who raised and commanded a Missouri infantry regiment for the Union. He fought at Fort Donelson, Shiloh, and Corinth [qq.v.]. In July 1862 he was promoted brigadier general of volunteers, and in 1863 he commanded a brigade at the siege of Vicksburg [q.v.].

Smith, Persifor Frazer (1798–1858). An American soldier who entered the College of New Jersey (Princeton) in 1815. He practiced law in New Orleans and was active in the militia, becoming adjutant general of the state. In 1836 he raised a regiment of volunteers and for the next two years served under General Edmund P. Gates [q.v.] in the Second Seminole War [q.v.]. In May 1846 he was commissioned colonel of volunteers and in that rank served in the Mexican War [q.v.], where he first distinguished himself under General Zachary Taylor [q.v.] in the Battle of Monterrey [q.v.] on 20–24 September 1846. Brevetted brigadier general, he served under General Winfield Scott [q.v.] in all the battles from Veracruz [q.v.] to Mexico City. In October 1847 he was named a member of the armistice commission and appointed military governor of Veracruz. In 1849 he was brevetted major general of volunteers, and in December 1856 he was promoted brigadier general in the regular army. He was appointed to command the Department of Utah but died at Fort Leavenworth, Kansas, before he could assume command.

Smith, William (1796–1887), known as Extra Billy Smith. An American lawyer who started a stagecoach business and earned his nickname from the extra mail charges he habitually exacted from the government. He was active in politics and was governor of Virginia from 1846 to 1849. At the beginning of the American Civil War he refused an appointment as a brigadier general and fought in the First Battle of Bull Run [q.v.] as colonel of the 49th Virginia. He led his regiment in the Peninsular Campaign and at Antietam [qq.v.]. On 23 April 1863 he accepted a promotion to brigadier general, to rank from 31 January 1863, and in August he was promoted major general. In May of that year he was once again elected governor of Virginia but delayed taking office until after the Battle of Gettysburg [q.v.]. After the war he farmed near Warrenton and sat in the state legislature when he was eighty.

Smith, William Farrar (1824–1903). An American soldier known as Baldy who was graduated from West Point in 1845. In Florida he contracted malaria, which periodically troubled him all his life. During the American Civil War as a Union army officer he fought at First Bull Run and in the Peninsular Campaign; he commanded corps at Antietam and Fredericksburg [qq.v.]. He was chief engineer in the operations around Chattanooga, Tennessee, in 1863 and was engaged at Cold Harbor and Petersburg [q.v.]. While he was absent on leave, General U. S. Grant deprived him of his command. He resigned from the volunteers in 1865 and from the regular army in 1867. Until 1881 he was president of the Board of Police Commissioners in New York City. From 1881 he worked as a civilian for the army Corps of Engineers.

Smith-Dorrien, Horace Lockwood (1858–1930). A British soldier who served in the Zulu War, Arabi's Revolt, and the Gordon Relief Expedition [qq.v.] and from 1893 to 1896 in Bengal and the Punjab. He fought in the Second Anglo-Boer War [q.v.] and served again in India until 1907. He was promoted major general in 1899 and became a full general in 1912. He commanded a corps and then the British Second Army in France during World War I until relieved of his command in 1915 and given command of the East African forces. After the war he was for five years governor of Gibraltar.

Smith and Wesson Revolver Company. An arms-manufacturing firm that grew to become the world's largest producer of handguns. Founded in 1854 in Springfield, Massachusetts, by inventors Horace Smith (1808–1893) and Daniel Baird Wesson (1825–1906), the partnership became a company in 1857. Both men had worked for the manufacturer of the Volcanic rifle and pistol [see Volcanic Arms Company] before leaving to develop their first revolver, patented on 8 August 1854.

In 1857 the company became the first to manufacture a revolver that fired a metallic cartridge, an innovation the American army rejected, although both the Turkish and Mexican armies placed orders. Between 1870 and 1878 the firm produced 215,704 pistols of .44 caliber with barrels six and one-half inches long for the imperial Russian army.

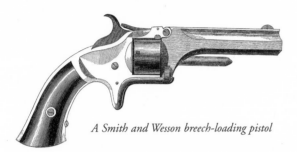

A Smith and Wesson breech-loading pistol

Smokeless Powder. Powders, sometimes called colloidal powders, that, when used in firing guns, did not give off clouds of smoke. The French claim that smokeless powder was discovered by Paul Vieille (1854–1934), a French chemist, who in 1884 introduced B powders. The Germans claim that it was discovered by Max von Duttenhofer in 1883. In 1889 British chemist Frederick Augustus Abel (1827–1902) developed a smokeless powder at the British Royal Laboratory; this was a mixture of nitrocellulose (guncotton) and nitroglycerine and was named cordite [q.v.]. Smoke powder was last used in the Graeco-Turkish War of 1897 [q.v.].

Smoke Screen. The use of smoke to conceal military movements or to hinder the movement of an enemy. In the nineteenth century such screens were created by setting fire to fields or woods or by throwing damp straw on large fires. It was not until 1915 that a way was found to project smoke on an enemy on a battlefield.

Smoliani, Battle of. See Polotsk, Battle of.

Smoothbore. An unrifled firearm. Prior to about 1860 most military firearms were smoothbores.

Smuts, Jan Christiaan (1870–1950). A South African lawyer and statesman who as a Boer general in the Second Anglo-Boer War [q.v.] led a commando that invaded Cape Colony. After the war he was largely responsible for forming the Union of South Africa. In 1914 he was active in the suppression of the revolt led by Christiaan De Wet [q.v.], and in World War I he became a British lieutenant general and commanded in the East African Campaign. After the war he was elected prime minister, and during World War II he was made a field marshal.

Smuts, Tobias (1861–1916). A South African politician and soldier. During the Second Anglo-Boer War [q.v.] he distinguished himself in the fighting around Ladysmith [q.v.]. After the Battle of Colenso [q.v.] he was appointed *veg generaal* (fighting general). He defended Carolina and led the Boer counterattack on Machadodorp. After the war he retired to his farm.

Snap Shot. A quick shot from a small arm made without taking deliberate aim.

Snare Drum. A small military double-headed drum with a catgut string or strings stretched across its lower head for greater resonance.

A snare drum

Snelling, Josiah (1782–1828). An American soldier who was commissioned a first lieutenant in the 4th infantry in 1808 and promoted captain the following year. He took part in the Battle of Tippecanoe [q.v.] under General William Henry Harrison [q.v.] on 7 November 1811. In the War of 1812 [q.v.] he won a brevet majority for his conduct in the Battle of Brownstown on 9 August 1812 during the abortive invasion of Canada under General William Hull [q.v.], and he was in Detroit when it was surrendered by Hull on 16 August [see War of 1812; Detroit, Capture of]. In April 1813 he was exchanged and served most of the rest of the war under General Winfield Scott [q.v.] on the Niagara frontier. In February 1814 he was appointed lieutenant colonel of the 4th Riflemen, and in April he was promoted colonel and named inspector general. He took part in the Battle of Chippewa on 5 July and the Battle of Lundy's Lane [qq.v.] on 25 July.

In June 1819 he was promoted colonel of the 5th Infantry and stationed at Council Bluffs in Missouri Territory. He was responsible for the establishment of a fort at the confluence of the Mississippi and Minnesota rivers and one near St. Paul and Minneapolis, which he commanded until his death.

Snider Rifle. In 1864 gunmakers were asked to submit to a British army committee proposals for improving the 1853-pattern Enfield rifle. Of the fifty suggestions, the committee selected that of an American, Jacob Snider (d. 1865), who died one year before his conversion was adopted on 18 September 1866. In his design the breechblock swung up and to the right. A firing pin passed through the block, and a spring held the pin to the rear so that its end protruded toward the hammer. When the trigger was pulled, the hammer drove the pin forward, and its point struck the percussion cap. The rifle used a cartridge made of coiled metal with a percussion cap in the center of its base, invented by an artillery officer, Lieutenant Colonel Edward Mourrier Boxer [q.v.].

The Snider Mark III was a single-shot rifle, 54 inches long, caliber .577, with five-groove rifling. British soldiers used it in only two campaigns: the Abyssinian Cam-paign in 1868 and the Second Ashanti War [qq.v.] of 1873–74. However, the rifles were widely used by the Indian army until the end of the century.

Sniper. A soldier who shoots at detached enemy soldiers from long range or a hidden position, especially when not in battle.

Snowbirds. The name given to American soldiers in the War of 1812 [q.v.] who enlisted in the autumn and deserted in the spring, when jobs were more plentiful. The expression was carried over and used in the Indian-fighting army.

Confederate sniper

Snow Excluder. The name given to the first low-cut overshoes, issued to the American army in 1874.

Soapsuds Row. The colloquial American term for the quarters on a military post occupied by married enlisted men, many of whose wives took in washing.

Sobraon, Battle of (10 February 1846), First Sikh War. British General Sir Hugh Gough [q.v.] had invaded the Punjab with a force of about 16,000 British and Indian troops with 100 guns. Near the village of Chota Sobraon, 45 miles southeast of Lahore on the south bank of the Sutlej River below its confluence with the Beas, he encountered an army of 20,000 Sikhs with 70 guns entrenched in a bend of the river with their backs to the river.

The battle opened with a two-hour artillery duel. When Gough was told that his guns were almost out of ammunition, he exclaimed: "Thank God! Then I'll be at them with the bayonet!" He launched a direct frontal attack in which the Sikh positions were taken, as he ordered, at the point of the bayonet. In his after-action report he wrote that it was "a gentlemanlike battle, a mixing of all arms and laying on, carrying everything before us by weight of attack and combination, all hands at work from one end of the field to the other."

British casualties were 2,283—nearly 1 in 7 of those engaged—320 of whom were killed, including 13 British officers. Sikh dead were said to be 3,125, and total casualties may have reached 10,000. The British captured 67 guns. This was the last battle of the First Sikh War [q.v.]; peace was signed at Lahore on 11 March.

Socabaya, Battle of (7 February 1836), Peruvian-Bolivian conflict. In 1835, when a factional war broke out in Peru, Bolivia sent troops under General Andrés Santa Cruz [q.v.]. At this town in the province of Arequipa, Santa Cruz won a victory over the rebel Peruvian forces of General Felipe Santiago Salaverry [q.v.], who was captured and shot.

Sofa. A slave soldier in West Africa [see Diomba; Bazinger; Senegalese Tirailleurs].

Sola / Solar Helmet. Headgear offering protection from the sun, sometimes worn by troops in tropical areas. The Hindi word *sola* is used for the pith from the *Aeschynomene aspera* plant from which sun helmets or topees were made. Sometimes called pith helmets.

Soldat-Gentilshomme. In the French army, a gentleman ranker [q.v.].

Soldier. 1. As a noun, a person engaged in military service designed to fight on land. General Sir Ian Hamilton [q.v.] wrote: "Boys are soldiers in their hearts already—and where's the harm? In the Bible Paul bade Timothy to be a good soldier. Christ commended the centurian. Milton urged teachers to fit their pupils for all the offices of war. The very thought of danger and self-sacrifice are inspiration" (*The Soul and Body of an Army* [1921]). Such a view was not confined to the nineteenth century. Samuel Johnson (1709–1784), who never served as a soldier, wrote: "Every man thinks meanly of himself for never having been a soldier or never having been at sea." The word is sometimes used to mean only enlisted men or conscripts but generally refers to all ranks.

2. As a verb, to serve as a soldier.

3. As a noun, in the expression "to play the old soldier," meaning to malinger, to make a pretense of working.

4. As a verb, to persevere in spite of hardships, loss of zeal, or difficulties, as in "to soldier on."

Soldier of Fortune. A man who pursues a military career for profit, adventure, pleasure, or a cause without regard to nationality.

Soldiers and Sailors Families Association. A British organization founded in 1885 by Major (later Colonel) James Gildea of the Royal Warwickshire Regiment to help widows and orphans of soldiers.

Soldiers' Asylums. See Soldiers' Homes.

Soldiers' Battle. A battle such as Inkerman in the Crimean War or the Wilderness or Shiloh in the American Civil War [qq.v.] in which the senior commanders are able to exercise minimal or no control and the fate of the battle is determined by the initiative of the individual soldiers actually engaged.

Soldiers' Homes. The first institution to care for old, sick, mutilated, or destitute soldiers is believed to be the Hôtel des Invalides [q.v.], constructed in Paris in 1670, followed by the Chelsea Hospital [q.v.] in London in 1682. In the United States, Congress authorized a home for veterans of the American navy in 1811. In 1848 General Winfield Scott sent the secretary of war $118,791.19, a part of the payment levied on Mexico after the Mexican War [q.v.], and requested that it be set aside for an asylum for old soldiers. In 1851 Senator Jefferson Davis [q.v.] introduced legislation that resulted in the U.S. Congress's authorizing, but not funding, a soldiers' home, which was eventually erected in Washington, D.C., on about 470 acres three and a half miles from the Capitol. Serving soldiers were required to contribute 25 cents each month, reduced to 12 ½ cents in 1859, when the pay of a private was $13 per month, to support it. Branches were established later in Louisiana, Kentucky, and Mississippi.

In the 1880s and 1890s, twenty-eight states in the North established soldiers' homes with the aid of a per capita subsidy provided by National Homes for Disabled Volunteer Soldiers, a federal agency. Similar institutions were established in the South, but without the help of federal government funds. One of the first Confederate soldiers' homes was Lee Camp Home in Richmond, Virginia, which opened in 1885. These homes survived well into the twentieth century. (The soldiers' home in Washington, D.C., is still in existence.)

Soldier Societies. Among many of the Indian tribes on the American western plains, warrior societies of young men acted as police on hunts and in war. The most noted societies were those of the Cheyennes, of which there were several, the dog soldiers being perhaps the best known.

Soldier's Thigh. An empty purse. When soldiers wore tight breeches, they were smooth because the pockets had nothing in them, a reference to the notorious poverty of soldiers.

Soldiery. 1. Soldiers collectively; the military.
2. The technique and art of soldiering.

Solferino, Battle of (24 June 1859), Austro-Piedmontese War. The Austrian army of 120,000 men and 451 guns under the personal command of Emperor Francis Joseph (1830–1916) retired eastward after its defeat at Magenta [q.v.] on 4 June 1859. It took up defensive positions five miles west of the Mincio River near the village of Solferino in southeast Lombardy, between Brescia and Mantua, four miles southeast of Castiglione delle Stiviere. There on a sweltering day they were attacked by an almost equal number of Piedmontese and French (118,000), the Piedmontese under Victor Emmanuel II (1820–1878) and Alfonso Ferrero di La Mamora [q.v.] and the French under Emperor Napoleon III (1808–1873) and General Marie de MacMahon [q.v.]. This was the first major battle in which extensive movements were made to the front by train. After bitter fighting the Allies broke the Austrian center, and at about four o'clock in the afternoon, when the oppressive heat was broken by a severe thunderstorm, Francis Joseph retreated across the Mincio, leaving behind some 3,000 killed, 10,800 wounded, and 8,600 missing. Many of the casualties were caused by French artillery, firing newly designed rifled guns. The losses of the victors were almost as high, including 2,491 killed, 12,512 wounded, and 2,292 missing. Horrified by the butcher's bill, Napoleon III concluded a separate peace with Austria, whereby France received Lombardy, which he shortly afterward ceded to Piedmont in return for Savoy and Nice.

Jean Louis Ernest Meissonier (1815–1891), a French painter, saw the battlefield after the fighting: "Terrible indeed was it to see the wounded, some rigid with pain, others weeping uncontrollably, victors and vanquished disarmed by suffering, dying side by side." The piteous suffering of the abandoned wounded was brought to public attention by Jean Henri Dunant [q.v.], another horrified witness of the battlefield. Upon the publication of his book *Un Souvenir de Solferino*, sixteen nations met in Geneva, Switzerland, in 1864 [see Geneva Convention, First]. From their conference came standards for the humane treatment of the wounded and prisoners of war and the establishment of the International Red Cross [q.v.].

In a curious tribute to the battle, a newly developed bluish pink dye was named solferino.

Solferino *Battle of Solferino, Italy, 1859*

Somatenes. Spanish levies hostile to the French during the Peninsular War [q.v.].

Somerset, Fitzroy James Henry. See Raglan.

Somerset, Robert Edward Henry (1776–1842). A British soldier, the third son of the Fifth Duke of Beaufort, commonly known as Lord Edward Somerset, who was commissioned in the 10th Light Dragoons in 1793 and was a captain the following year. He served in Holland in 1799 as an aide-de-camp to the Duke of York and Albany [q.v.]. In 1809 in the Peninsular War [q.v.] he was sent to Portugal, where he commanded the 4th Dragoons at Talavera and Bussaco [qq.v.]. In the Battle of Salamanca [q.v.] he took part in the charge of the heavy brigade, capturing five guns. In June 1813 he was promoted major general, and until the end of the war he commanded a brigade of hussars. In the Battle of Waterloo [q.v.], in which he distinguished himself, he commanded the brigade of Household Cavalry. He was promoted lieutenant general in 1825 and general in 1841.

Somosierra, Battle of (30 November 1808), Peninsular War. Napoleon, marching on Madrid, was held up at the Somosierra Pass, 4,757 feet high in the Sierra de Guadarrama in central Spain and the last physical obstacle between him and the capital, by a Spanish force of 15,000 under General Benito San Juan [q.v.]. Four batteries of artillery formed roadblocks in the rocky defile. A probing attack on the evening of 29 November was repulsed. The following morning Napoleon ordered General François Ruffin [q.v.] to make an infantry charge but, impatient with the delay in mounting the attack, turned to his personal escort, a squadron of 88 Polish lancers and ordered them to charge the guns. Charging over 2,500 yards of open ground, they were for 400 yards exposed to the fire of 16 guns. No lancer came closer than 30 yards; only 4 of the 88 remained unscathed. Napoleon awarded 17 Legion of Honor medals to those who participated in the charge, taking one from his own breast to place on the tunic of a lieutenant who lay dying from eleven wounds.

Ruffin's infantry attack carried the day, and 1,000 cavalry routed the Spaniards. French success led to the capture of Madrid, which Napoleon entered on 4 December.

Sonderbund War (November 1847). In 1844 it was proposed in the Swiss Diet that all Jesuits be expelled from the country. No official action was taken, but Protestants formed a small army called a Free Corps and launched an unsuccessful invasion of Catholic cantons. In response, on 11 December 1846 the seven Catholic cantons—Lucerne, Uri, Unterwalden, Valais, Zug, Schwys, and Fribourg—formed a separate alliance, the Sonderbund (special-purpose society). On 20 July 1847 the Diet declared it illegal and ordered it dissolved. When the cantons refused to comply, a federal army marched against them. After several skirmishes the Sonderbund forces were defeated by federal forces under General Guillaume Henri Dufour [q.v.] in the Battle of Gislikon [q.v.] near Lake Zug on 23 November 1847. The war lasted twenty-four days. Dufour adopted a strategy of minimum violence and instructed his troops: "You must emerge from this fight not only victorious but also without reproach." Losses on both sides totaled 93 killed and 510 wounded.

In 1848 a new constitution was adopted that established a strong central government while preserving the local cantonal governments, a system that still prevails.

Sonderbund War *Federal troops in the Sonderbund War in Switzerland, 1847*

Sonno Joi. The Japanese doctrine to revere (*sonno*) the emperor and drive out the barbarians (*joi*). The first Japanese scholar to elaborate this doctrine was Aizawa Seishisia (1782–1863) in *New Proposals* (*Shinron* [1825]). It became the shibboleth of those in the southern provinces of Satsuma and Choshu, which became the center of rebellion against the Tokugawa shogunate [see Boshin Civil War].

Sontay / Son-Tai, Battle of (14–16 December 1883), French invasion and occupation of Indochina. On 9 November

1883 two battalions of the French Foreign Legion [q.v.] under Lieutenant Colonel Jacques Charles René Achille Duchesne (1837–1918) disembarked at Haiphong and moved up the Red River to Hanoi. Joined by Tirailleurs Algérien [q.v.] and other colonial troops, about 5,500 in total, plus eight river gunboats, all under Admiral Amédée Anatole Prosper Courbet (1827–1885), they moved on to attack the main Black Flag (organized Chinese bandit army) stronghold at Sontay [q.v.], 30 miles northwest of Hanoi on the Red River [see Black Flags]. China, unhappy that the Vietnamese had accepted protectorate status, sent a force estimated at 15,000 from Yunan under General Lin Yung-ku to assist the estimated 10,000 Black Flags. Sontay was a formidable fort with walls of brick 16 feet thick pierced with heavy wooden gates. On 14 December 1883 the French captured its outer defenses and drove the defenders into the citadel. During the night a Chinese sortie was repelled after heavy fighting. On the 16th the citadel was stormed by 7,000 French troops supported by seven river gunboats.

French casualties were 92 officers and 318 other ranks killed and wounded; the Chinese lost an estimated 1,000. Reinforced, the French moved east on 8 March toward Bac Ninh [q.v.], the second major stronghold of the Black Flags, which was taken on 12 March.

Sontay *The Battle of Sontay, December 1883*

Soochow, Capture of (4 December 1863), Taiping Rebellion. The Ever Victorious Army [q.v.] under Charles ("Chinese") Gordon [q.v.] captured this Taiping city (later Wuhsien) in eastern China on the Grand Canal near the eastern shore of Tai Hu.

Sorauren, Battles of (28 and 30 July 1813), Peninsular War. Marshal Nicolas Soult [q.v.], with 35,000 men attempting to relieve French troops blockaded in Pamplona, defeated small Allied forces at Maya and Roncesvalles [qq.v.]. Wellington with about 24,000 men hastily moved to intercept him. On 28 July, near Sorauren, a village on a branch of the Arga River, Soult attacked with 25,000 men, and Wellington was able to hold his position only with great difficulty. Fortunately a fresh British division came in on the French flank and saved the day. Thereafter it was, Wellington said, "bludgeon work, a second Bussaco." The Allies lost 2,600; the French lost 4,000.

On 29 July Soult, instead of retiring northward, marched west, but the movement was detected, and in two actions on the next day the French were repulsed. On 2 August, Soult withdrew across the frontier into France. Pamplona fell two months later.

Sortie. A sudden attack made from a fortified place or a defensive position. Sometimes called a sally.

Sortie Passages. Narrow openings in a fortification made through the crest of the glacis to enable communication with the outside without opening a main gate [see Sally Port].

Sotnia. A Russian army unit of about 100 Cossacks [q.v.]. A cavalry regiment contained 6 *sotnii*. At the beginning of the Russo-Turkish War of 1877–78 [q.v.] the Russians had 130 *sotnii*.

Souham, Joseph (1760–1837). A French soldier who enlisted as a royal cuirassier in 1782 and was elected lieutenant colonel ten years later. In 1793 he was promoted general of division. He distinguished himself in the French Revolutionary Wars and served as a division commander in Catalonia during the Peninsular War [q.v.]. He was wounded at Vich, northeast of Barcelona, in 1810, but returned to duty the following year. In 1812 he commanded the Army of Portugal that raised the siege of Burgos [q.v.]. He later served in the east and was seriously wounded at Leipzig [q.v.]. He did not join Napoleon during the Hundred Days [q.v.] and was reemployed after the second Bourbon restoration in 1815.

Soukiers. See Sutlers.

Soulé, Pierre (1801–1870). A Frenchman educated in Jesuit colleges who was exiled from France for antigovernment activities. After living as a shepherd in the Pyrenees, he returned to France and worked as a journalist until he was jailed in 1825 for his radical opinions. He escaped and made his way first to England, then to Haiti and finally to the United States, where he taught himself English and became a lawyer in Louisiana. From 1847 to 1853 he was a U.S. senator and in 1853 was named minister to Spain. He was recalled in 1855, when he called for American annexation of Cuba with or without Spain's consent. He then practiced law in New Orleans until the beginning of the American Civil War, during which, on behalf of President Jefferson Davis [q.v.], he undertook several voyages to Europe, attempting to enlist European support for the Confederacy.

After the Union occupation of New Orleans, Soulé was a thorn in the side of General Benjamin Franklin Butler [q.v.], the military governor, who in June 1862 had him arrested and confined at Fort Lafayette. General Nathaniel Banks [q.v.] wanted to have him shot. He escaped, however, and joined the staff of General Pierre Beauregard [q.v.] and was made a brigadier general, a rank not confirmed. In 1864 he ran the Union blockade and sailed to Europe, where he tried unsuccessfully to raise a foreign legion for the Confederacy. After the war he fled to Cuba, but eventually he returned to his law practice in New Orleans and attempted in vain to establish a colony for Confederate veterans in Sonora, Mexico.

Soulouque, Faustin Élie (1785–1867). A Haitian Negro general and political leader. He was elected president of Haiti in 1847, and in 1849 he proclaimed himself emperor as

Faustin I. In 1858 he was deposed, and from January 1859 he lived in exile.

Soult, Nicolas Jean de Dieu (1769–1851). A French soldier who enlisted in the infantry in 1785 and was a sergeant in 1791. He was commissioned in 1792. In 1794 he became general of brigade and in April 1799 general of division. He fought in Italy and was taken prisoner after the siege of Genoa in 1800. In May 1804 he was one of the first of Napoleon's generals to be created marshal. At Austerlitz [q.v.] he commanded the right wing and stormed the Pratzen Heights. In the Battle of Jena [q.v.] he commanded the French right. He fought at Pultusk, Eylau, and Heilsberg [qq.v.], and in June 1808, after the Treaty of Tilsit [q.v.], he was created Duke of Dalmatia. Napoleon proclaimed him "the best tactician in Europe."

Much of the next six years was spent in fighting the Peninsular War [q.v.], and from 1809 to 1811 he was commander-in-chief of Napoleon's armies there. He drove the British army under Sir John Moore [q.v.] out of Spain and invaded Portugal. He dreamed of becoming king of Portugal, but his hopes were dashed by his defeat at the hands of Arthur Wellesley (soon to be Duke of Wellington) in the Battle of Oporto [q.v.] on 12 May 1809. However, he defeated the Spanish in the Battle of Ocaña [q.v.], and in May 1810 he invaded Andalusia and captured Seville, Olivençia, and Badajoz. A year later he was defeated in the bloody Battle of Albuera [q.v.].

Exasperated by the interference and obstinacy of Joseph Bonaparte (1768–1844), he asked for his own recall. He was given command of the Garde Impériale [q.v.] upon the death of Jean Baptiste Bessières [q.v.] while repulsing the Allied crossing of the Rippach, near Weissenfels, on 1 May 1813 [see Weissenfels, Battle of]. Soult fought at Bautzen [q.v.], but on learning of the French defeat in the Battle of Vitoria [q.v.], Napoleon sent him back to Spain, where on 12 July 1813 he took command of the French forces in the peninsula. He reorganized the troops, reinvigorated them, and led them in the Battle of the Pyrenees [q.v.]. His forces won at Maya and Roncesvalles [qq.v.] but failed in the Battle of Sorauren [q.v.], making it impossible for him to raise the sieges of Pamplona and San Sebastián [q.v.]. Pursued by Wellington, he withdrew into France, where he was defeated at Orthez in February 1814 and at Toulouse on 10 April [qq.v.].

He rallied to Napoleon in March 1815 during the Hundred Days [q.v.]. After the Battle of Waterloo [q.v.] he took command of the army's survivors at Laon but decided that further resistance was futile. In January 1815 he was exiled and established himself in Düsseldorf.

He returned to France in 1819, and in 1820 he was restored to rank. In 1827 he was made a peer. From 1830 to 1834 he was minister of war. In 1838 he attended the coronation of Queen Victoria and for the first time met Wellington. In 1839 he was minister of foreign affairs and from 1840 to 1845 was again minister of war. On 15 September 1847 he retired from public life and eleven days later was proclaimed marshal general of France, an honor awarded only three times previously: to Henri de La Tour d'Auvergne, Viscomte Turenne (1611–1675); Duc Claude Louis Hector de Villars (1653–1734); and Comte Hermann Maurice de Saxe (1696–1750).

Soult was a heavy, square-built man with extremely bowed legs accentuated by a limp, the result of a severe leg wound received at Genoa. A firm disciplinarian, he took good care of his troops, who called him Iron Hand. He was one of Napoleon's most capable commanders and so skilled a looter that Napoleon compared him with Charles Talleyrand (1754–1838) in his ability to "make money out of anything."

Soumenlinna, Battles of. See Sveaborg, Battles of.

Sousa, John Philip (1854–1932). An American bandmaster and composer who came to be known as the March King. From 1880 to 1892 he was the bandmaster of the U.S. Marine Corps Band. He then organized his own band and toured the United States and Europe with great success. He was musical director for the American army in the Spanish-American War [q.v.] and in World War I.

He made significant improvements in instrumentation and in the quality of band music. Among his more than one hundred compositions were marches such as "Semper Fidelis" (1888), "Washington Post March" (1889), and "Stars and Stripes Forever" (1897).

Sous-Lieutenant. See Lieutenant.

South African War. See Anglo-Boer War, Second.

Southampton Slave Revolt. See Nat Turner's Insurrection.

South, Army of the. A French army formed on 15 July 1811 during the Peninsular War [q.v.] by Marshal Nicolas Soult [q.v.]. It consisted of 90,186 men, 68,827 of whom were effectives.

South Mountain, Battle of (14 September 1862), American Civil War. General Robert E. Lee's Army of Northern Virginia [q.v.] was spread out over 25 miles and divided by the unfordable Potomac River. General George B. McClellan [q.v.], commanding a much larger Union army, had a copy of Lee's orders and knew his dispositions [see Lost Order], but it took him two days to move 10 miles from Frederick, Maryland, to the passes over South Mountain, where Confederates delayed him long enough for Lee to concentrate a portion of his army on a low ridge near the town of Sharpsburg along a creek called Antietam [see Antietam, Battle of]. Each side lost about 2,500 men at South Mountain.

South West Africa, German Campaigns in [late nineteenth century]. In German South West Africa (Namibia) Reichskommissar Dr. Heinrich Göring, father of the future Nazi *Reichsmarschall*, was unable to persuade the followers of Hendrik Witbooi [q.v.] to accept German "protection." He therefore dispatched a German force under Landeshauptmann (national captain) Kurt von François [q.v.] to persuade them by force. On 11 April 1891 the Germans launched a surprise attack upon Witbooi's followers at Hoornkranz, 90 miles southwest of Windhoek. The Germans fired 16,000 rounds with repeating rifles and lost one man; Witbooi's followers lost 85 killed, 78 of whom were women. In May the Germans, with African allies, made a second attack. German reinforcements arrived in July.

On 1 January 1894 François was replaced by Major Theodor Leutwein (1849–1921), a veteran of the Franco-Prussian War [q.v.], who built a series of forts and pursued a vigorous campaign against Witbooi until on 9 September 1894 he surrendered.

In March 1896 the Germans launched a campaign against the Herero and Nama tribes east of Windhoek. They captured the tribes' horses, shot several prisoners they described as rebels, and returned with women to be used as prostitutes. The Hereros, only temporarily subdued, revolted again in 1903.

Sowar. A soldier in the Indian army cavalry with the rank equivalent to private or sepoy.

Sowar *Sowars feed horses in the camp of the Bengal Lancers, Egypt, 1882.*

Soyer, Alexis Benoît (1809–1858). A famous French chef who after the 1830 uprising in Paris [see French Revolution of 1830] went in 1831 as a refugee to Britain. In 1839 he became chef at the Reform Club in London. During the Crimean War [q.v.] he sailed to the Crimea, where he undertook to improve the food given to British soldiers. He invented a field stove and wrote an army cookbook containing recipes for such dishes as "Turkish pilaf for one hundred men" and "Cheap plain rice pudding for campaigning," including instructions such as "How to soak and plain boil the rations of salt beef and pork on land or at sea." For hospital kitchens he recommended the preparation of sago jelly, arrowroot panda, and "Soyer's cheap Crimean lemonade." There was, sadly, no lasting improvement in the diets of British soldiers.

Spade. 1. A kind of shovel used for digging.

2. The end of the trail of a cannon pointed to limit movement of the gun in recoil.

Spadroon. A light, straight-bladed sword.

Spahi. 1. Any mounted soldier in the French Armée d'Afrique [q.v.].

2. An indigenous North African cavalry regiment in the Armée d'Afrique.

3. An irregular Turkish cavalryman. Spahi units in the Turkish army were replaced by regular cavalry in 1826.

Spahi *Spahi, light cavalry of French Algeria, in spirited charge against hostile tribesmen*

Spahi Mutiny (1871). In January 1871 a French Spahi regiment stationed near Souk Ahras, in northeast Algeria, south of Bône, mutinied when ordered to France to fight in the Franco-Prussian War [q.v.]. This was followed by considerable unrest in urban areas of Algeria, and in March a chieftain in Constantine proclaimed a war of liberation. In April the war became a jihad when a venerated holy man (marabout) joined the rebels. With perhaps 100,000 Arabs and Berbers in rebellion, France was forced to return to Algeria those elements of the Armée d'Afrique [q.v.] that had been sent to France to fight the Germans and to reinforce them with metropolitan troops. It took nine months to suppress the rebellion. The French suffered 2,700 casualties, mostly from disease.

Spain, French Intervention in. See French Intervention in Spain.

Spandau Firing School. A Prussian school established in 1854 to give training in the use of muskets. It also tested the weapons of other nations and experimented with new inventions.

Spanish-American War (1898). The 112-day war was sparked by the Cuban insurrection of 1895 [see Cuban Revolutions]. Although a number of filibustering expeditions had sailed to Cuba or Central America from the United States [see Filibuster] and in New York City a rebel Cuban "junta" had sold bonds and disseminated propaganda while the Ten Years' War [q.v.] had struggled through its bloody decade, nothing had stirred the American public as had the Cuban Revolution in 1895. In 1896 William McKinley (1843–1901) was elected the twenty-fifth president on a platform that included a demand for Cuban independence.

The United States needed only a pretext for intervention, and this was provided on 15 February 1898 by the explosion from unknown causes of the USS *Maine* in the harbor of Havana, in which 2 officers and 258 other seamen were killed. Spain was blamed, and Congress recognized Cuban independence on 19 April. Diplomatic relations with Spain were broken on 21 April, and the following day Congress passed the Volunteer Army Act and voted fifty million dollars for national defense without a single dissenting vote. On 25 April 1898 war was formally declared. Army mobilization had already begun on 9 March.

Between the end of the American Civil War in 1865 and the beginning of the Spanish-American War of 1898 the American army had been used only to enforce Reconstruction, quell civil disorders, break strikes, and fight hostile Indians. It had not waged a conventional war in thirty-three years, it had not fought a foreign foe in a more than a half century, and it had shrunk to only 28,000 men widely scattered in small posts throughout the country, mostly in the West. President McKinley called for 125,000 men, and nearly a million responded. The Spanish had about 150,000 troops in Cuba.

On 10 June, 647 marines invaded the island by way of Guantánamo Bay and after some hard fighting captured the area around the bay [see Cuba, American Invasion of]. Four days later 16,887 American troops—fifteen regiments of regulars and three of volunteers, including the Rough Riders [q.v.]—left Tampa, Florida, singing "There'll be a Hot Time in the Old Town Tonight." They were commanded by William Rufus Shafter [q.v.], a Medal of Honor winner in the Civil War, now nearly sixty-three years old and weighing more than 300 pounds.

On 22 June the expeditionary force landed without opposition at Siboney, a town just east of Santiago de Cuba, and Daiquirí, a barrio on the coast 14 miles east of Santiago Bay, where the Rough Riders [q.v.] raised a silk flag that had been given to them by the Women's Relief Corps of Phoenix, Arizona. The Americans fought their first battle at Las Guásimas [q.v.] on 24 June.

The United States had hoped that the conflict would be fought primarily at sea, where its navy would have important tactical advantages, but the Spanish fleet under Admiral Pascual Cervera y Topete (1839–1909) sailed into the harbor of Santiago de Cuba, and the American Atlantic fleet under Admiral William T. Sampson (1840–1902) was fully engaged blockading it from May to July 1898.

In the Pacific, American Admiral George Dewey (1837–1917), commanding the Asiatic Squadron—five cruisers and two gunboats—sank the Spanish squadron in Manila Bay on 1 May and imposed a blockade. Guam surrendered to the cruiser USS *Charleston* on 20 June. On 30 June General

Wesley Merritt [q.v.] arrived in the Philippines with 10,000 regulars and volunteers, and on 13 August Manila [q.v.] was taken.

In Cuba the battles of San Juan Hill and El Caney [qq.v.] were fought on 1 July. The victorious Americans had few maps, but they did have an observation balloon, although this was soon shot down. The Spanish fleet ventured out and on 3 July was utterly devastated. Santiago capitulated on 17 July, the Spanish being unaware that the American land force was being rapidly wiped out by malaria, yellow fever, and dysentery.

In a separate operation General Nelson A. Miles [q.v.] landed 5,000 men in Puerto Rico on 25 July and in four weeks eliminated all Spanish opposition [see Puerto Rico, American Invasion of].

Hostilities ended on 13 August, and the war ended with the Treaty of Paris, signed on 10 December 1898. "It has been a splendid little war," Secretary of State John Milton Hay (1838–1905) wrote to Theodore Roosevelt [q.v.], "begun with the highest motives, carried on with magnificent intelligence and spirit, favored by that fortune that loves the brave." Although the shortest declared war in American history, it made the United States a colonial power, procuring for it the Philippines, Guam, Puerto Rico, and Hawaii. Spain gave Cuba its independence. The treaty by which Spain ceded these possessions was ratified by the U.S. Senate in a close vote after heated discussions of imperialism. In March 1901, in an amendment to the army appropriation bill, Cuba was declared a protectorate.

The effective enemies of the Americans in this war were not the Spaniards, who inflicted few casualties—there were only 379 battle deaths—but diseases, which killed 5,400 of the 306,000 soldiers mustered into the service. Although there were those in the invasion force who knew of the epidemic that had destroyed the European armies in the Caribbean in the eighteenth and early nineteenth centuries and knew the effects of malaria and yellow fever, no one envisioned the magnitude of the disaster.

The expeditionary force was crippled by fevers in Georgia and Florida before it embarked. By the end of the first week of July 1898, a yellow fever epidemic was raging among U.S. troops in Santiago. Before the end of the month General Shafter ordered a withdrawal in an effort to save the army from the endemic tropical diseases. Before the campaign had begun, the surgeon general recommended the use of regiments made up of men, black and white, from the American South, hoping that they would enjoy some immunity, particularly from yellow fever. They were called the immunes [q.v.], but 20 percent were soon laid low by typhoid in the training camps, before they could reach Cuba.

It was not just in the Caribbean that the army suffered from disease. In all, between 1 May 1898 and 30 April 1899 thousands died in the training camps in the United States. It was also said, but without any factual confirmation, that many at home and abroad died from eating contaminated tinned meat.

Spanish-Chilean War. See Spanish-Peruvian War.

Spanish Civil War of 1820–23. The refusal of Spanish King Ferdinand VII (1784–1833) to accept the liberal constitution of 1812 and his inept rule generated much dis-

content, particularly among senior army officers. In January 1820 troops assembled at Cádiz for an attempt to reconquer the South American colonies mutinied. Led by Colonel Rafael del Riego y Núñez [q.v.], they seized their commander and marched to nearby San Fernando. When Riego issued a pronunciamento calling on the army to support the constitution of 1812, the mutiny escalated into a revolution. As Riego and his followers prepared to march on Madrid, Ferdinand capitulated and on 7 March 1820 agreed to a liberal constitution. In this heady political atmosphere political factions of all persuasions strove for power, and civil war flared in Castile, Andalusia, and Toledo. The army garrison in Madrid mutinied, and the country began to dissolve into chaos. Ferdinand appealed to the Holy Alliance (Russia, Prussia, and Austria), which declined to come to his aid, leaving him to become a virtual prisoner when the royal palace was attacked by revolutionaries. In October 1822, alarmed by the spreading disorder, the Quadruple Alliance (Britain, France, the Netherlands, and Austria), meeting at the Congress of Verona, gave France a mandate to reseat Ferdinand on his throne and restore order [see French Intervention in Spain].

On 17 April 1822 a French army of 100,000 under General Louis Antoine de Bourbon invaded Spain, captured Madrid and drove rebel forces south to Seville and Cádiz. On 31 August 1823 the rebels were defeated at the Trocadero near Cádiz and on 23 September Cádiz was taken and Ferdinand, who was being held there, was freed. Although he had promised no reprisals if restored to power, Ferdinand was ruthless in his revenge upon opponents, and he rushed to revoke the constitution and establish a despotic government.

Spanish Civil War of 1840–43. Following the First Carlist War [q.v.] of 1834–39, María Christina (1806–1878), who was regent during the minority of her daughter, María Isabella Louisa, Queen Isabella II (1830–1904), attempted to abolish the constitution of 1837, which had granted a considerable degree of independence to Spanish cities, but when the central government attempted to name key local officials, urban uprisings forced her to retreat. General Baldomero Espartero [q.v.], a hero of the First Carlist War [q.v.], refused to crush the rebels, a popular move that resulted in his being named ministerial president. Reforms that limited María Christina's powers so enraged her that in October 1841 she departed for France, taking the future queen with her. From that vantage point she strove to incite insurrections against Espartero, who assumed dictatorial powers. Uprisings were suppressed in Pamplona in October 1841 and in Barcelona in December 1842, but in 1843 Colonel Juan Prim y Prats [q.v.], aided by María Christina's agents, succeeded in leading a rebellion in the south, and the government toppled when troops led by General Ramón María Narváez [q.v.] marched from Valencia and seized Madrid. Espartero fled to England. In November 1843 the thirteen-year-old Isabella was declared of age and was made head of the government. Narváez was named president of the ministry.

Spanish Civil War of 1868. A military junta led by General Francisco Serrano [q.v.] deposed Isabella II, and Serrano became regent until the accession in 1870 of Amadeus I of Savoy (1845–1890).

Spanish Mauser Rifle Model 1893. A 7 mm modified-bolt-action Mauser rifle with a fixed magazine that was flush with the stock and a muzzle velocity of 2,650 feet per minute. It had an overall length of 48.6 inches and weighed 8.8 pounds. In 1895 a shorter, lighter carbine version was produced.

Spanish-Moroccan Wars (1859–60). To maintain their foothold on the northwest corner of Africa, the Spanish were forced to fight off the surrounding Berbers, who came down from the Riff (Rif) Mountains. In 1860 a major expedition was organized by General Leopoldo O'Donnell [q.v.], Spain's premier, who led a 40,000-man army to North Africa. Although his army was attacked by cholera and hampered by bad roads, O'Donnell was victorious in the Battle of Tetuán [q.v.] on 4 February 1860 and defeated the Berbers in the Battle of Guad el-Ras; General Juan Prim y Prats [q.v.] was victorious in the Battle of Castillejos [q.v.]. The Spanish secured the region between the Spanish enclaves of Ceuta and Melilla, which became the protectorate of Spanish Morocco.

Spanish-Moroccan Wars *Moors and Spaniards in hand-to-hand fighting*

Spanish-Peruvian War (1864–66). When Peruvian laborers assaulted Basque laborers on the hacienda of Talambo in Peru, Spain demanded compensation, which was refused. On 14 April 1864 Spain seized the guano-rich Chincha Islands, 12 miles off the coast of west-central Peru. On 27 January 1865 Spain and Peru concluded a treaty whereby Peru paid a three-million-peso indemnity to the Spaniards of Talambo and Spain returned the Chincha Islands. Peruvians were incensed, and the government was overthrown by Mariano Ignacio Prado [q.v.], who made himself dictator and on 14 January 1866 declared war on Spain. Chilean President Joaquín Pérez (1800–1890), fearing a return of Spanish rule, joined with Prado; defensive alliances were made with Bolivia and Ecuador. Spanish ships bombarded the Chilean port of Valparaiso on 31 March 1866 and the Peruvian port of Callao on 2 May. The ships were then withdrawn. In 1879 the United States negotiated a peace treaty.

Spanish Remington Rifle Model 1871. A single-shot 11 mm rifle with an overall length of 50.3 inches. It weighed 9.3 pounds.

Sparks, Harry (1856–1918). A South African soldier who first encountered war when he and his entire family were captured in the Gcaleka War [q.v.] in 1877. In 1878 he joined the Durban Mounted Rifles and fought in the Zulu War of 1879 and the First Anglo-Boer War in 1880–81 [qq.v.]. During the Second Anglo-Boer War [q.v.] he fought on the side of the British and commanded the Natal Mounted Rifles. After the war he became one of the founders of a successful cold storage company.

Spatterdashes. A type of legging intended to keep stones and dirt out of boots and to keep legs dry.

Spear. A blade at the end of a shaft capable of being thrown. It was widely believed in the last quarter of the nineteenth century that the single-shot, nonrepeating, breech-loading rifle was superior to all "native" weapons, such as the spear, but the disaster to the Egyptian forces inflicted by spear-throwing Abyssinians (Ethiopians) in 1876 in the Battle of Gundet [q.v.] and the defeat of the British by Zulus in 1879 in the Battle of Isandhlwana [q.v.] proved that this was not always the case.

Special Orders. In the American army, orders affecting individuals or small groups [see General Orders].

Special Service Officer. In the British army, an officer detached from his normal unit or command for special duty elsewhere.

Speed. One of the great principles of war is the obligation of a general to act with alacrity. Sun Tzu in *The Art of War,* written about 500 B.C., said, "Speed is the essence of war," and this has been echoed by great commanders in every age since. Dennis Hart Mahan [q.v.] wrote: "Speed is one of the chief characteristics of strategical marches as it is of ordinary movements on a battlefield. In this one quality reside all the advantages that a fortunate initiative may have procured; and by it we gain in the pursuit all the results that a victory on the field has placed in our hands" [*Outposts* [1847]].

Speke, John Hanning (1827–1864). A British soldier and African explorer who entered the Indian army in 1844 and during the Indian Mutiny [q.v.] served under Sir Colin Campbell [q.v.] in the Punjab. While on leave, he explored in the Himalayas and crossed into Tibet. In 1854 he joined Richard Francis Burton (1821–1890) in an expedition to Somalia, where in April he was wounded in an attack upon their camp by Somali tribesmen. During the Crimean War [q.v.] he served with a regiment of Turks. In 1856 he again joined Burton in an expedition into the African interior, in the course of which he discovered Lake Victoria. In 1860–61 he made another expedition with Captain (later Colonel) James Augustus Grant [q.v.]. In 1864 he accidentally killed himself while hunting.

Spencer, Christopher Miner (1833–1922). An American gunsmith who began his career as a millwright before going to work for Samuel Colt [q.v.]. He invented an automatic silk-spinning machine and a lever-action repeating rifle with a tubular magazine holding seven cartridges that was inserted into the butt. The breech was closed by a block that rotated backward when the underlever was cocked [see: Spencer Repeating Rifle]. Soon after, he founded the Spencer Repeating Rifle Company and developed the Spencer carbine in .56 caliber, which was accepted by the Union army in the American Civil War; more than 60,000 were manufactured [see Spencer Repeating Carbine]. Manufacturing ceased in 1869, and Winchester [q.v.] purchased the remaining stock. [See Spencer Rifle.]

Spencer Repeating Carbine. The first successful breech-loading magazine rifle was patented in 1860 by Christopher M. Spencer [q.v.], an American. It was in .52 caliber and had the same characteristics as the seven-shot Spencer rifle [q.v.], but it measured only 39 inches long and weighed 8.25 pounds. Its tubular magazine held seven cartridges. When the trigger guard was lowered, the fired cartridge case was extracted and a new cartridge slid into the breech. During the American Civil War it was widely believed that one man with this carbine was equal to seven using muzzleloaders, for it could be fired seven times in nine seconds and could maintain a sustained rate of fifteen aimed shots per minute. By the end of the war it was the most widely used carbine in the service.

In January 1865 Major General James H. Wilson [q.v.] reported to the chief of ordnance: "There is no doubt that the Spencer carbine is the best firearm yet put in the hands of the soldier, both for economy of ammunition and maximum effect, physical and moral."

Spencer Rifle. A breech-loaded, seven-shot, .56 caliber repeating rifle weighing 10 pounds developed by Christopher M. Spencer [q.v.] about 1860. The seven cartridges were carried in the butt of the gun, which held the tubular magazine. An underlever rotated the breechblock and picked up a cartridge from the magazine. When the lever was returned, the metal cartridge (usually copper) was chambered, and the breech locked. To fire, an external hammer struck a firing pin in the breechblock that struck the rimfire cartridge. It was effective up to 2,000 yards. A carbine was also developed [see Spencer's Repeating Carbine]. Both weapons were much used in the American Indian Wars [q.v.].

Spencer Saddle. A saddle patented in 1862 by Robert Spencer of Brooklyn, New York, in which the raised saddle-bow prevented the rider from being thrown forward over the saddle. It was used by some during the American Civil War.

Spent Ball. A projectile from a firearm that reaches an object but no longer has the power to penetrate it.

Sphere of Influence. A term that came to be applied in the late nineteenth century to a country or an area where one major power was dominant and intrusion by other powers was regarded as hostile. The dominant power was assumed to have special interests that were held to be paramount over the claims of national sovereignty. The term entered common usage in 1882, when the "scramble for Africa" began.

Spherical Case Shot. See Shrapnel.

Spicheren / Spickeren, Battle of (6 August 1870), Franco-Prussian War. Sometimes called the Battle of Forbach, a village just west of Spicheren. At this French village, 3 miles south of Saarbrücken in Lorraine, the opening battle of the Franco-Prussian War [q.v.] began when the French II Corps of the Army of the Rhine, 28,000 men with 90 guns under Charles Auguste Frossard [q.v.], advancing to capture Saarbrücken, was defeated by 35,000 Germans with 108 guns under Karl Friedrich von Steinmetz [q.v.]. The main French army was pushed back because the commanders of troops within supporting distance failed to march to the sound of the guns. The Prussians suffered a loss of 850 killed, 3,650 wounded, and 400 missing; the French lost 1,982 killed and wounded and 2,000 captured and were forced to fall back upon Metz, 32 miles west. Although the German losses exceeded the French, they continued to push forward. General Frossard, while undefeated, thought that he had been defeated, and so indeed he came to be. The Prussians, while nearly defeated, refused to believe they were and so were not. There lay the secret of the Prussian victory.

A feature of the battle was the feat of a German company of the 39th Regiment and four companies of the 74th that stormed and captured a position known as Rote Berg and, in the face of vastly superior French forces, held on throughout the afternoon, even after their commander had been killed.

On this same day another French force was defeated in the Battle of Fröschwiller [q.v.] or Wörth.

Spiked Helmet. A helmet with a spike on its crown was in use in most European armies and in the American army for a short time. The German *Pickelhaube* [q.v.] remained in service for German infantry into World War I.

Spike Guns, to. To render artillery pieces incapable of use. Lieutenant Edward Samuel Farrow (1854?–1871) wrote specific instructions for disabling a smoothbore cannon: "To spike a gun drive into the vent a jagged and hardened steel spike with a soft point, break it off flush with the vent field, and clinch it in the bore with the rammer; a nail without a head, a piece of ramrod, or even a plug of hard wood may be used in the absence of a spike. To prevent the spike from being blown out, make a projectile fast in the bottom of the bore by wrapping it with cloth or felt, or by means of iron wedges driven in with a rammer or with an iron bar. . . . When it is expected to retake a gun, use a spring spike with a shoulder to prevent it coming out too rapidly" (*Military Encyclopedia*). A spring spike was one that sprang open after the head entered the bore to prevent withdrawal.

Breech-loading guns were disarmed by removal of the breechblock or the firing pin. The French 75 [q.v.] and guns with similar recoil mechanisms could be disabled by removing the pin that attached the barrel to the recoil mechanism and firing the gun.

Spion Kop, Battle of (19–24 January 1900), Second Anglo-Boer War. General Redvers Buller, VC [q.v.], with an army of about 25,000, while attempting to relieve besieged Ladysmith [q.v.], in Natal, South Africa, was blocked by about 8,000 Boers under General Louis Botha [q.v.]. On 19 January 1900 Buller's men fought their way to the north bank of the Tugela River, and troops under General Sir Charles Warren [q.v.] seized a precipitous height called Spion Kop [q.v.], 24 miles west-southwest of Ladysmith and 20 miles west of Colenso [see Colenso, Battle of]. On 23 January Botha's men climbed to the attack. Because the slope was too steep for artillery to scale, the daylong battle was waged between riflemen at close quarters. The Boers triumphed, and Buller fell back across the Tugela.

The Boers lost about 335 in killed and wounded. The British lost 243 killed and wounded and about 300 captured.

Spirit Lake Massacre (1857), American Indian Wars. In Minnesota in 1855 Henry Lott, a bootlegger and horse thief, killed the brother and family of Sioux leader Inkpaduta [q.v.], an atrocity that turned Inkpaduta against all white men. On 8–9 March 1857 Inkpaduta and his band of perhaps a dozen warriors killed 34 settlers—men, women, and children—near Spirit Lake in northwestern Iowa and took 3 women prisoner. Soon afterward they killed a male settler and captured another woman. Two weeks later they attacked Springfield, near present Jackson, Minnesota, and killed more whites. Two of the 4 female prisoners were killed, 1 was set free, and 1 was ransomed. Although troops pursued the band, Inkpaduta was not caught.

Spoiling Attack. An attack upon an enemy force that is itself in the process of organizing an attack. Its purpose is to confuse, delay, or thwart the attack of the enemy.

Spoils of War. What the victorious army takes from the vanquished [see Loot; Prize; Prize Agents; Deccan Prize].

Spontoon. A short pike or half-pike; a pole arm that in the eighteenth and early nineteenth centuries was regularly issued to sergeants in line regiments and in many volunteer units in the British army. The 1800 pattern was nine feet long with a broad blade. The regiment's name or initials were often inscribed down the cheeks, or langets, that protected the top of the shaft.

In the Russian army, spontoons were carried by junior officers in the early nineteenth century.

Spotsylvania Campaign, Battle of (7–20 May 1864), American Civil War. After the Battle of the Wilderness [q.v.] Grant resumed his advance on Richmond with an army of 111,000 until checked by Robert E. Lee's Army of Northern Virginia [q.v.], numbering 63,000, just north of the village of Spotsylvania Court House, 11 miles southwest of Fredericksburg, Virginia. The heaviest fighting occurred in a salient of the Confederate line, later named the Bloody Angle.

Casualties were high: Grant lost 14,267; Lee lost about 10,000. Lee was unable to do more than delay Grant's steady advance.

Spotted Tail (1823–1883). A Brûlé Sioux Indian leader who was said to have won his first wife in a knife duel with a sub-chief. He initially distinguished himself in the endless war with the Pawnees. He then turned on the whites and was instrumental in the killing of Lieutenant John L. Grattan and his men near Fort Laramie, Wyoming, on 19 August 1854 [see Grattan Massacre]. He later led a band that destroyed a mail coach on its way to Salt Lake City, Utah. In the Battle of Ash Hollow [q.v.] in Nebraska on 3 September 1855 he received two bullet wounds and two saber cuts. On 18 October of that year he and several other warriors, painted and dressed in complete war tenue and singing their death songs, rode into Fort Laramie and surrendered. They were taken to Fort Leavenworth, where they were pardoned on 16 January 1856. Having seen something of the power of the white men, Spotted Tail became a member of the peace faction in his tribe, made several trips to Washington, and became an archenemy of Red Cloud [q.v.].

On 5 August 1873 he and a band hunting along the Republican River encountered and attacked a band of Pawnees, killing about 100. This was his last fight. In 1876 he signed perhaps under duress a treaty that gave away the Black Hills to white men. In 1877 he was said to have been instrumental in persuading Crazy Horse [q.v.] to surrender.

On 5 August 1881 at the Rosebud Agency he was murdered in a dispute with another Brûlé chief, Crow Dog (1833?–1910?). Although Crow Dog's people agreed to pay blood money, Crow Dog was arrested, tried in Deadwood, South Dakota, in 1882, convicted, and sentenced to be hanged. His case was appealed, and in December 1883 the U.S. Supreme Court ruled that Dakota courts had no jurisdiction over crimes committed on Indian reservations by one Indian against another and that by the payment of blood money the murder had been settled by tribal custom. Crow Dog was freed and returned to the Rosebud Reservation.

Springfield Armory. An American armory and arsenal founded in 1794, when General George Washington ordered Henry Knox (1750–1806), his chief of artillery, to establish an arsenal to manufacture guns and ammunition. Knox chose Springfield, Massachusetts, on the Connecticut River. In its first year it produced 245 handmade muskets. By 1825 it was turning out 15,000 muskets yearly as well as pistols and carbines. One of its most famous products, the trapdoor rifle [q.v.], developed in 1868, converted muzzleloaders to breechloaders. The back of the barrel was cut off, and a hinged block inserted that could be lifted and hinged forward so that a .45 cartridge could be inserted into the breech. Inside the block a firing pin was aligned with the cartridge when the block closed and an external hammer fired the gun.

The management of the arsenal by the Ordnance Department was always conservative, resisting most design changes for weapons. It continued to manufacture muzzleloaders when breechloaders were obviously superior because of a distrust of "the common soldier's ability to conserve ammunition." Although in the Battle of Washita [q.v.] the troops under George Custer [q.v.] had fought their way free because they were armed with repeaters, these weapons were replaced soon after by single-shot Springfields, with which they fought the Battle of the Little Bighorn [q.v.].

In 1833 there was a strike at the arsenal that was successfully mediated by Colonel and Brevet Brigadier General John Ellis Wool [q.v.]. Springfield is perhaps the only arsenal ever to be immortalized in a poem by a major poet. In 1841 Henry Wadsworth Longfellow (1807–1882) wrote "The Arsenal at Springfield." It begins:

This is the Arsenal. From floor to ceiling
Like a huge organ, rise the burnished arms;
But from their pipes no anthem pealing
Startles the village with strange alarms.

The arsenal was closed in December 1967 and is now a museum. [See Arsenal / Armory.]

Springfield Musket. A single-shot, muzzleloader, caliber .58, that was in use in the American Civil War. It was 56 inches long and weighed 9.9 pounds.

Springfield Rifle. After the American Civil War the muzzleloading, .58 caliber Springfield rifles, firing the conical Minié ball, were standard in the American army until 1869, when the last were retired, replaced by breech-loading, single-shot Springfields, which were manufactured in .50 caliber until 1873, when the caliber was changed to .45 to achieve better ballistics. The 1873 rifle (and carbine) remained standard issue until replaced by the Krag-Jörgensen in 1892. In 1889, during the Spanish-American War [q.v.], the muzzleloaders were issued to volunteers, one of whom claimed that it could knock down two men, the one it hit and the one who fired it.

Spring Spike. See Spike Gun.

Spun Grass. Grass spun into tight ropes to reduce bulk forage when on campaign.

Spy. 1. As a noun, a person who clandestinely obtains and reports on the numbers, activities, and plans of an enemy. If caught in wartime, spies were usually executed.
2. As a verb, to act as a spy.

Squad. A small group of soldiers, especially a tactical unit that could be easily directed on a field. It usually consisted of 8 to 12 men commanded by a corporal or a sergeant.

Squad *A new Union squad, 1861*

Squadron. A subunit of a cavalry regiment, equivalent to a battalion in an infantry regiment. Sometimes called a wing.

Squadron *A model squadron-over-hurdles in line, late nineteenth century. Illustration by Frederic Remington*

Squad Room. In the American army, the sleeping quarters in permanent barracks.

Square. A defensive formation formed by infantry, usually with fixed bayonets, to repel attacks. Baggage, supplies, and transport animals were usually placed in the center, and guns or machine guns at the corners. Squares formed by one to three lines of infantry with bared bayonets were often successful in repelling attacks by cavalry.

Squib. A small pyrotechnic device that, unlike a detonator, does not explode but fires an igniter.

Stable Jacket. See Drill Jacket.

Stack Arms. 1. As a verb, to place rifles in a group, leaning against one another, with their butts on the ground.
2. As a noun, the command to do so.

Staff. 1. As a noun, the officers assigned to assist a commanding officer in exercising his command [see Staff Officer].
2. As a verb, to provide personnel for a unit or organization.

Staff College. An educational institution for the training of the staff officer [q.v.] and those expected to hold high command.

Staff Officer. A commissioned officer who assists a commander, serving on his staff. Brigadier General Edward Porter Alexander [q.v.] wrote: "An army is like a great machine, and in putting it into battle it is not enough for the commander to merely issue the necessary orders. He should have a staff ample to supervise the execution of each step, & to promptly report any difficulty or misunderstanding."

In the British army almost all staff work at the higher levels of command was handled by two senior officers: an adjutant general, who handled all matters pertaining to personnel and the issuance of orders, and a quartermaster general, who handled everything else, including transportation. Britain did not have a general staff until 1906; the United States not until 1903 [see General Staff].

In the French and German armies staff officers formed a distinct and separate corps and on special missions took precedence over all other officers of equal rank. Regimental officers sometimes served on the staff, but only until a trained staff officer could be found.

The senior general in the Confederate army during the American Civil War was Samuel Cooper [q.v.], the adjutant general. In both the Union and Confederate forces the person who performed the functions of chief of staff in army corps and smaller units was designated assistant adjutant general.

Staff Rides. A study of past and possible future battle sites by staff officers and commanders actually riding over the field and solving various problems. This type of study was initiated by the Prussian general staff and imitated by other European armies in the nineteenth century.

Stance, Emanuel. A black American soldier and former sharecropper who enlisted in the 9th Cavalry in October 1866. He was a diminutive man, barely five feet tall, but because he could read and write, he was promoted sergeant within ten months. In his first two years of service he had five encounters with hostile Indians.

In May 1870 a punitive expedition in which his company took part set out from Fort McKavett, at Laredo, Texas, to punish Kickapoo Indians for outrages against local settlers. With a detachment of 10 privates Stance fought off a band of Indians and captured their ponies. The next day he attacked a band that was about to ambush a wagon train. When later in the day he was attacked by the same band, he turned his men about and drove them off.

On 24 July 1870 he was awarded the Medal of Honor [q.v.] for his deeds near Kickapoo Springs, becoming the first black to be so honored in the post–Civil War period.

Standard. A relatively small flag carried by mounted troops.

Stand Fire, to. To receive the fire of an enemy and not give ground.

Standing Army / Force. An army in being, ready for action even when there is no immediate threat of war; a regular army; a professional army or unit, as opposed to militia, volunteers, and auxiliaries. In the nineteenth century and earlier there were sometimes strong objections to a standing army. American statesman Elbridge Gerry (1744–1814) is said to have compared a standing army with an erect penis: "an excellent assurance of domestic tranquility but a dangerous temptation to foreign adventure."

Standing Orders. More or less permanent orders that remain in force until amended or canceled.

Stand of Arms. See Arms, Stand of.

Stand of Colors. A single color or flag.

Stanton, Edwin McMasters (1814–1869). An American lawyer who was secretary of war from January 1862 to May 1868 and thus guided the War Department through the American Civil War. When Andrew Johnson (1808–1875) succeeded to the presidency upon the death of Lincoln, Stanton opposed him and his policies and intrigued with groups of congressmen against the president. In August 1867 Johnson suspended him, but he was restored by an act of the U.S. Senate in January 1868. On 21 February Johnson discharged him, but he refused to leave office and was supported by the Senate. When impeachment charges against Johnson failed, Stanton resigned.

Star of India. The Most Exalted Order of the Star of India was a decoration instituted in June 1861 to reward loyal Indian princes and officers of the army, navy, and civil service who had rendered important services to the Indian Empire. The order originally consisted of the sovereign, a grand master (the viceroy of India), and 36 knights grand commander (half British and half Indian), 85 knights commander, and 170 companions. The badge of the order was an onyx cameo with the effigy of Queen Victoria set in gold and bore the motto of the order: "Heaven's Light our Guide."

Star of India

Starr Arms Company. An arms-producing company in Binghamton, New York, founded in 1850 by the Starr family, which had manufactured swords and muskets in the early days of the century. The company was founded when Eben Townsend Starr, one of the sons, obtained a patent for a .38 self-cocking percussion revolver. Between 1858 and 1861 some 2,500 were supplied to the American army. At the beginning of the American Civil War the Union army bought 47,000 more. Financial difficulties caused the closing of the company in 1867. Several thousand surplus pistols were sold to France in 1870, and most fell into German hands at the conclusion of the Franco-Prussian War [q.v.].

Stars and Bars. The first national flag of the Confederate States of America was first raised on 4 March 1861 [see American Civil War]. In the upper left-hand corner was a blue field bearing seven white stars in a circle. The main body of the flag consisted of two broad horizontal red bars separated by a white bar. In May 1863 it was altered to the Stainless Banner: pure white with the Confederate battle flag [q.v.] in the canton. However, because this too closely resembled a flag of truce or surrender, a broad vertical red bar was added across the end farthest from the staff on 4 March 1865. This was the last flag of the Confederacy.

Stars and Stripes. The popular name for the flag of the United States of America. It was adopted by Congress in 1783, at the end of the Revolutionary War. Originally it consisted of thirteen white stars on a blue field in the canton and thirteen alternating red and white stripes on the body.

The stars were not arranged in any agreed order until 1912. When Vermont and Kentucky were admitted as the fourteenth and fifteenth states in 1791 and 1792, two new stripes were added, but in 1818 the flag reverted to its original thirteen stripes.

Starshells. A shell that on bursting gave off a shower of brilliant stars. It was used for signaling and for illuminating a battlefield, as in the Battle of Sherpur [q.v.] in Afghanistan on 23 December 1879.

"Star-Spangled Banner, The." The lyrics of this song, which became the American national anthem by act of Congress on 3 March 1931, were written on the morning of 14 September 1814, during the War of 1812 [q.v.] by Francis Scott Key [q.v.] as a four-stanza poem entitled "The Defence of Fort McHenry" [see Fort McHenry, Attack on]. Within weeks it was published as "The Star-Spangled Banner" and set to the tune of "To Anacreon in Heaven," an old English drinking song whose melody was better known as that of a patriotic song, "Adams and Liberty," written in 1798 by Robert Treat Paine (1731–1814), a Boston minister and jurist.

The huge flag with fifteen stars and fifteen stripes, that flew over Fort McHenry, and inspired Key was hand sewn in 1813 by Mary Pickersgill, a Baltimore seamstress, and her thirteen-year-old daughter, Caroline. It had been commissioned by Major George Armistead [q.v.] commanding Fort McHenry. Armistead said that he wanted a flag large enough for the British to see when they retreated. The flag survived the bombardment, and in 1907 the Armistead family presented it to Smithsonian Institution in Washington, D.C. It was kept folded in a special case in the Arts and Industries Building until in 1963 it was hung in a special room in the National Museum of American History. Thirty-five years later, in December 1998, it was taken down after eighteen million dollars had been raised for its cleaning and renovation, a work expected to last three years.

Starvation March, Crook's (August–September 1876), Great Sioux War. General George Crook [q.v.], determined not to hamper his mobility with a supply train, set off with a column of infantry and cavalry for the Black Hills to locate and attack the hostile Sioux and Northern Cheyennes in Montana or South Dakota. The column carried two weeks' rations of only hard bread, bacon, beans, coffee, sugar, and salt on the backs of mules and horses; no supply wagons or ambulances were taken. Moving south from the head of Heart River, Crook was hampered by heavy rains. On 17 August the column arrived at the confluence of the Yellowstone and Powder rivers. Thirty-four sick and disabled men were put on board the *Far West,* a steamboat on the Yellowstone, and the rest marched on to find themselves impeded by heavy rains and out of food three weeks before they reached the Black Hills. First Lieutenant Walter Scribner Schuyler (1846?–1932) tried to describe the misery of the infantry in a letter to his father: "I have seen men so exhausted they were actually insane. . . . I saw men who were very plucky sit down and cry like children because they could not hold out." The last small allowance of coffee, hardtack, and salt pork was issued on 7 September, the date on which the fattest cavalry horses were slaughtered. Men sat up all night roasting and

broiling the meat, preparing it for the march. The next day about 150 cavalry under Captain Anson Mills [q.v.] were sent ahead to forage and to search for Indians. At Slim Buttes, near present-day Reva, South Dakota, they discovered the village of Oglala Sioux Chief American Horse (d. 1876), and early on the morning of 9 September Crook's emaciated troops attacked, dispersed the Indians, and repelled an attempt to retake the village [see Slim Buttes, Battle of].

Soldiers found dried buffalo meat in the Indian lodges and wolfed down most of it before torching the camp, killing their prisoners, including a number of women and children, and resuming their march. The Indians continued to snipe at their rear guard.

On 12 September they marched 36 miles on a meager ration of dried buffalo meat, horseflesh, and one and a half tablespoons of beans per man. At the end of the march, weak and despondent, some simply dropped on the ground and slept without cover. At ten o'clock their misery was complete when it began to rain. The expedition was saved from complete disaster by the arrival of a supply train from Deadwood. The campaign came to an inglorious end, and the troops dispersed to winter quarters.

The march lasted forty days, and it had rained on twenty-two days. Surgeon Bennett A. Clements (1833?–1886), the chief medical officer with the column, stated in his official report that the troops had "reached the limits of human endurance . . . and it is unpleasant to contemplate the probable consequence of another march like that of September 12, 1876."

Static Defense. A purely defensive position without offensive operations.

Stavely, Charles William Dunbar (1817–1896). A British soldier who was the son of a lieutenant general and educated at the Scottish Military and Naval Academy at Edinburgh. In 1835 he was commissioned in the 87th Foot, and for three years beginning in 1840 he served as an aide-de-camp to the governor of Mauritius. In 1847 he was an aide to the governor-general of Canada. Because he was a talented draftsman, his sketches proved useful in settling the Oregon boundary dispute with the Americans. In 1854 he was sent to the Crimea and took part in the Battle of the Alma and the siege of Balaclava [qq.v.]. In 1857 he went to India, where he was stationed in Madras and took no part in the suppression of the Indian Mutiny [q.v.]. In 1860 he was sent to China, where he was present at the capture of the Taku forts [q.v.] in the Second Opium War [q.v.]. In 1862 he was in command of the troops still remaining in China. In April of that year, when the Taiping rebels approached Shanghai, he led an Anglo-French force of 2,000, about two-thirds sailors and marines, against them and drove them out of several towns [see Taiping Rebellion]. Asked by Li Hung Chang [q.v.] to recommend a British officer to take charge of the Ever Victorious Army [q.v.], he named Major Charles George Gordon [q.v.], whose brother was married to his sister.

In 1865 Stavely was knighted (KCB) and sent to command a division in the Bombay army. On 25 September 1867 he was promoted major general, and he commanded a division in the expeditionary force led by General Robert Napier [q.v.] to Abyssinia (Ethiopia) and organized the army's base at Annesley Bay [see Abyssinian Campaign, British]. On the march inland he conducted the battle on the Arogye plain that preceded the capture of Magadala [q.v.].

From 1874 he was for four years commander-in-chief of the Bombay army. In 1875 he was promoted to lieutenant general and in 1877 to general.

Steamboats. In the United States the beginning of efficient steamboat service, commercially introduced in 1807, freed waterborne transportation from reliance upon currents and winds and had an enormous effect upon the settlement of the West and the logistics of the Indian-fighting army. In 1818 Secretary of War John C. Calhoun approved a project initiated by Brevet Major Stephen Harriman Long [q.v.] of the Topographical Engineers in which a team of scientists and explorers were to be conducted west to explore the area and describe the flora and fauna. To transport them, Long designed and had built the *Western Engineer,* the first stern wheel steamer used in the West. During the Mexican War [q.v.] he supervised the construction of a number of other steamboats for the army, which eventually had a small flotilla plying the western rivers, carrying troops, supplies, and sometimes Indians. So great was the demand that commercial steamers were used as well [see Missouri River Transportation Company; River Warfare].

One of the army's greastest tragedies was the sinking of the *Sultana* [q.v.].

Steam Gun. Among the weapons that failed to win the support of any army was the steam gun invented by Thomas Winans [q.v.] of Baltimore, Maryland. It was a large-caliber gun in which the shot fell from a hopper into a breech chamber and was projected by a sudden emission of steam under great pressure. Being a southern sympathizer during the American Civil War, Winans attempted unsuccessfully to ship his gun to the Confederacy.

Winans steam gun

Steam Tractors. Cross-country tractors driven by steam were first used in war by the British during the Crimean War [q.v.]. Moving on "footed wheels," they were the first military vehicles to be propelled by something other than the muscle power of man or beast. When it was suggested that perhaps they could be armored and armed with a cannon, Lord Palmerston (1784–1865), then prime minister, rejected the idea as "uncivilized."

Steedman, James Blair (1817–1883). A printer who after service in the Texas army served in the Ohio legislature. At the beginning of the American Civil War he was named colonel of the 14th Ohio. He fought at Perryville, Stones River, and Chickamauga [qq.v.], where he commanded a division. In that battle he lost 20 percent of his command within twenty minutes, and his horse was shot from under him. Shaken and bruised, he remained on the field and, before personally leading a charge, enjoined a staff officer to make sure his name was spelled correctly in the obituaries: Steedman, not Steadman. On 20 April 1864 he was promoted major general. After the war he again served in the legislature and was active in public affairs.

Steevens, George Warrington (1869–1900). A British war correspondent who began his career as a classical scholar. In 1893 he was elected a fellow of Pembroke College, Oxford, and in the same year decided to become a journalist. In 1897 he covered his first war, the Graeco-Turkish War [q.v.] in Thessaly, and in 1898 he went to Egypt for the *London Daily Mail* and covered the reconquest of the Sudan [q.v.] by the Anglo-Egyptian army under H. H. Kitchener [q.v.]. In 1899 he covered the second trial of Captain Alfred Dreyfus [q.v.] in France. He next sailed to South Africa for the Second Anglo-Boer War [q.v.], which had just begun, and was besieged with General George White [q.v.] at Ladysmith [q.v.]. He died of enteric fever during the siege.

Steinmetz, Carl Friedrich von (1796–1877). A Prussian soldier who while in his teens fought through the 1813–14 campaign to subdue Napoleon [see Napoleonic Wars]. He was promoted general of infantry in 1864, and in the Seven Weeks' War [q.v.] of 1866 he defeated the Austrians at Náchod and Skalitz. In the Franco-Prussian War [q.v.] of 1870–71 he commanded the First Army on the right wing of the German advance, fighting at Spicheren, Colombey-Borny, and Gravelotte–St. Privat [qq.v.]. After the latter he was relieved (September 1870) and appointed governor-general of Posen and Silesia. He was made a field marshal in 1871.

Stephenson, Sir Frederick Charles Arthur (1821–1911). A British soldier who obtained his commission without purchase by virtue of his having been a page of honor at the coronation of William V on 6 September 1831. He joined the Scots Guards as a lieutenant in 1837, and by 1854 he was a lieutenant colonel. He fought in the Crimean War [q.v.], and in 1857 he was shipwrecked off the coast of Banca while on his way to China in the ship *Transit* [see Troopships]. In China he was appointed assistant adjutant general and took part in the Second Opium War [q.v.], including the capture of Canton (Guangzhou) on 5 January 1858 and the storming of the Taku forts [q.v.] on 22 August 1860. He was promoted major general in 1868 and commanded the Brigade of Guards from 1876 to 1879. In 1878 he was promoted lieutenant general.

In May 1883 Stephenson was named commander of the British army of occupation in Egypt. After the Dervish defeat of Valentine Baker [q.v.] at El Teb [q.v.] on 4 February 1884, he organized the army under General Gerald Graham [q.v.] for the relief of besieged Tokar and the defense of Suakin in the eastern Sudan. On 30 December 1885 he defeated the Dervishes in the Battle of Ginnis [q.v.]. He resigned his command in 1887 and returned to England. In 1898 he was made constable of the Tower of London.

Sternberg, George Miller (1838–1915). An American physician who joined the Union army at the outbreak of the American Civil War in 1861 and served as a doctor in the Union Army of the Potomac [q.v.]. He was captured in the First Battle of Bull Run [q.v.] on 21 July, but managed to escape in time to take part in the Peninsular Campaign [q.v.], in the course of which he contracted typhoid fever and was sent north to recuperate. Upon his recovery he served in the Red River Campaign [q.v.]. After the war he served in several Indian campaigns, including the Nez Percé War [q.v.], and he contracted and recovered from yellow fever, thus acquiring immunity. In 1875 he was promoted major. In 1879 he was detailed to the Havana Yellow Fever Board and took the first photomicrographies of the tubercle bacillus. In 1892 he wrote the first textbook of bacteriology.

From 1893 to his retirement in 1902 he was U.S. surgeon general. He established the Army Medical School, Dental Corps, and Nurse Corps. In 1900 he organized the Yellow Fever Commission [q.v.], headed by Major Walter Reed [q.v.], which discovered the transmission of yellow fever by the *Aëdes aegypti* mosquito.

Stettin, Capture of (30 October 1806), Napoleonic Wars. The strong fortress at this Polish city (*Szczecin* in Polish) on the Oder River has the distinction, probably unique, of being a fortress that surrendered to a brigade of light cavalry. The Prussian defeat at Jena and Auerstädt [qq.v.] so panicked the garrison that when a French cavalry brigade, consisting of the 5th and 7th Hussars, arrived—about 600 men and no artillery—the brigade commander, General Antoine Charles Louis Lasalle [q.v.] was able to cozen the fortress commander into surrendering without a fight.

Stevani, Francesco (1840–1917). An Italian soldier who fought in the Piedmontese army against the Austrians and rose to be colonel of the Bersaglieri [q.v.]. He fought in East Africa, defeating a Dervish force at Tukruf, and in 1885 occupied Kassala.

Stewart, Charles William (Later Vane), Third Marques of Londonderry (1778–1854). A British soldier and diplomat who served in the Netherlands in 1794, on the Rhine and Danube in 1795, in the Irish Rebellion of 1798, and in Holland in 1799. In 1807 he was undersecretary of war. In the Peninsular War [q.v.] he was a cavalry commander and, from 1808 until he was invalided home in 1811, Wellington's adjutant general. He then served in diplomatic posts in Berlin, St. Petersburg, and Vienna. In 1819 he took the name of Vane when he married the heiress of Sir Henry Vane-Tempest, who held vast estates in Ireland and Durham. He was the half brother of the diplomat Lord Castlereagh.

Stewart, Donald Martin (1824–1900). A British soldier who entered the Bengal army in 1840 and served on the Northwest Frontier in campaigns against the Mohmands in 1854 and the Aka Khel and the Basi Khel tribes in 1885. During the Indian Mutiny [q.v.] he distinguished himself, taking part in the siege of Delhi, the relief of Lucknow [qq.v.], and operations in Rohilkhand. In 1868 he commanded the Bengal brigade in the Abyssinian Campaign [q.v.] under Robert Napier [q.v.]. In 1869 he reorganized the penal colonies on the Andaman Islands [q.v.] and became the commandant.

During the Second Afghan War [q.v.] he led a force through the Boland Pass and in January 1879 occupied Kandahar. After fifteen months there he marched to Kabul and took command over Sir Frederick (later Lord) Roberts. In 1881 he was appointed commander-in-chief, India. In 1894 he was promoted field marshal, and in 1895 he was appointed governor of Chelsea Hospital [q.v.].

Stewart, Herbert (1843–1885). An English soldier who was commissioned in 1862 and fought in the Zulu War in 1879 and in the war against Sekukuni [qq.v.]. During the First Anglo-Boer War [q.v.] he was captured by Boers in the Battle of Majuba [q.v.] in 1881 but was released in a month. He was with Lord Wolseley during the suppression of Arabi's Revolt [q.v.], and after the Battle of Tell el-Kebir [q.v.], on 13 September 1882, he took possession of Cairo. In 1884 he commanded the cavalry under General Sir Gerald Graham [q.v.], at Suakin in the eastern Sudan and took part in the Gordon Relief Expedition [q.v.]. He was leading a column pushed forward across the desert when, on 17 January 1885, he was attacked by Dervishes at Abu Klea [q.v.] and in the battle was mortally wounded. Three days later, as he lay on his deathbed, he was promoted major general.

Stewart, John Donald Hamill (1843–1884). A British soldier who was commissioned in the 11th Hussars in 1865. In 1882, while serving in Egypt, he and Giacomo Messedaglia [q.v.], the former governor of Darfur, traveled to the Sudan and prepared a report on the Mahdist uprising of Muhammad Ahmed [q.v.]. In February 1884, now a lieutenant colonel, he accompanied General Charles ("Chinese") Gordon [q.v.] to Khartoum, where he was wounded in the course of the siege [see Khartoum, Siege of]. In September, on Gordon's order, he and Frank Power (d. 1864), a correspondent for *The Times* (London), with other Khartoum residents left the city in the steamer *Abbas*. When it ran aground between Abu Hamad and Merowe, he and Power were among those killed by Manasir tribesmen.

Steyr. Short for the Österreichische Waffenfabrik Gesellschaft of Steyr, on the Steyr River in Upper Austria, founded in 1853 by Johann Werder [q.v.], who, after studying production methods in the United States, established workshops that converted 80,000 Austrian army muskets to breechloaders. He then received an order for 100,000 breech-loading rifles. By 1880 Steyr was producing 13,000 rifles a week, an output exceeding any other arms manufacturer. After World War I the company became Steyr-werke AG and diversified into the production of automobiles and other machinery.

Stilwell, Simpson Everett (1849–1903). A scout for the American army on the western frontier. At age fourteen he joined a wagon party for Santa Fe. He remained in New

Mexico until in 1867 he became an army scout. On 28 August he joined the company of 50 scouts under Major George A. Forsyth [q.v.], who set out from forts Harker and Hays in Kansas to find hostile Cheyennes. When camping on an island (later named Beecher Island and no longer in existence) in the then-dry Arikaree fork of the Republican River, the party was attacked by a large band of hostile Cheyennes [see Beecher Island, Battle of; Roman Nose]. On the first night of the battle Stilwell and Pierre Trudeau (d. 1869) slipped away to seek help. With only rotting horsemeat to eat, they reached a fort after five days, and troops were sent to rescue the remnants of the party.

In the next thirteen years Stilwell served as a scout for George Custer, Nelson Miles, and Ranald Mackenzie [qq.v.]. He later became a U.S. deputy marshal in Oklahoma, then a police judge, and a U.S. commissioner at Anadarko. He read the law and became a lawyer. In 1898 he moved to the ranch of William F. Cody [q.v.], near Cody, Wyoming, where he died.

Stinkpot. A shell charged with combustibles that, when exploded, gave off a foul smell and suffocating smoke. It was much used by the Chinese, who used earthenware devices that were also filled with inflammatory material.

Stock. 1. As part of a military uniform, a close-fitting band of stiff leather fastened about the neck. In the tropics many men fainted and some died from "stock apoplexy."
2. The wooden part of a musket, rifle, or pistol.

Stockade. 1. A fort made by driving stout posts side by side into the ground in order to enclose an area [see Palisade].
2. Any enclosure or pen made with posts and stakes.
3. An enclosure for keeping prisoners.

Stoddard, Amos (1762–1813). An American soldier who served in the American Revolutionary War and in 1804 was the first civil and military governor of Upper Louisiana. In the War of 1812 [q.v.] he took part in the defense of Fort Meigs [q.v.].

Stone, Charles Pomeroy (1824–1887). An American soldier who was graduated from West Point in 1845 and served as an ordnance officer in the Mexican War [q.v.], winning two brevets. After five years as chief of ordnance on the Pacific coast, he resigned and worked as a mining engineer in Mexico. In 1861, at the beginning of the American Civil War, he returned to service as a volunteer in the Union army and briefly served as inspector general of the District of Columbia militia. He was soon appointed colonel of the 14th Infantry and then a brigadier general of volunteers in command of three brigades on the upper Potomac. Unfortunately one of his principal subordinates, Colonel (and U.S. Senator) Edward D. Baker (1811–1861), a close friend of President Abraham Lincoln, through rashness and incompetence lost the Battle of Ball's Bluff [q.v.]. Stone was blamed for the disaster and on the night of 8 February 1863 was arrested. For 189 days he was confined in forts in New York Harbor without any charges ever being made against him. He was released on 8 August, but nine months passed before he was given employment. He then served on the unfortunate Red River Campaign [q.v.]. On 13 September 1864 he resigned. After the war he worked as a mining engineer until 1870, when he accepted a position as chief of staff of the Egyptian army, which he held until 1883. When he returned to the United States, he became construction engineer for the building of the base of the Statue of Liberty in the same New York Harbor where he had been unjustly imprisoned. He died soon after the statue's dedication.

Stoneman, George (1822–1894). An American soldier and politician who was graduated from West Point in 1846. During the Mexican War [q.v.] he served as quartermaster of the Mormon Battalion [see Mormon Volunteers], which made an arduous march from Fort Leavenworth, Missouri, to San Diego, California. After the war he served on the Southwest frontier. At the beginning of the American Civil War he refused to surrender to his superior, David Emmanuel Twiggs [q.v.], who had immediately joined the Confederate army. Rapidly promoted, Stoneman was soon a brigadier general and chief of the cavalry in the Army of the Potomac [q.v.]. He was promoted major general in March 1863, to rank from 29 November 1862. He commanded a corps in the Battle of Fredericksburg [q.v.] and from 13 April to 2 May 1863 led some 10,000 cavalry on a raid into the Virginia countryside that aroused considerable apprehension in Richmond but accomplished little else. During the Atlanta Campaign [q.v.] he commanded the Union cavalry corps until he was captured on 31 July 1864. He was exchanged in October of the same year.

After the war he served as colonel of the 21st Infantry and commanded the Department of Arizona. He retired because of disability in 1871 and moved to a lavish estate in California. There he served as a railroad commissioner and as governor for a four-year term from 1883 to 1887.

Stones River, Battle of (31 December 1862–2 January 1863), American Civil War. After the Battle of Perryville [q.v.] a stalemate existed in the central Kentucky-Tennessee theater. In an effort to break it 34,000 men of the Confederate Army of Tennessee [q.v.] under General Braxton Bragg [q.v.] fought a drawn battle 25 miles southeast of Nashville against the 44,000-man Army of the Cumberland [q.v.] under Major General William Rosecrans [q.v.].

Casualties were 12,906 Federal and 11,740 Confederates. Bragg was not beaten, but conscious that the Federals were being reinforced and that the Stones River, which divided his force, was rising, he retreated south to the Tennessee River. This battle is sometimes called the Battle of Murfreesboro, the name also applied to Nathan Bedford Forrest's first raid into Tennessee.

Stoney Creek, Battle of (6 June 1813), War of 1812. After opposing an American landing at Fort George, Ontario, on 27 May 1813, a British force of 704 under General John Vincent withdrew toward Hamilton. The Americans slowly followed with a force of about 2,000 under Generals John Chandler (d. 1841) and William Widner. At Stoney Creek in southeast Ontario, at the west end of Lake Ontario, on the night of 6 June the British turned and attacked. The Americans were routed; both generals were captured, and all their artillery was lost. Casualty figures are unknown.

Stores, Military. Weapons, ammunition, provisions, clothing, and other items needed by an army or any part of it.

Storm. 1. As a noun, a violent assault upon a fortified place with speed and with numbers sufficient to overwhelm all opposition.

2. As a verb, to make such an assault.

Stormberg, Battle of (10–11 December 1899), Second Anglo-Boer War. At Stormberg, a railroad junction 50 miles south of the Orange River in Cape Colony, South Africa, a British force of 3,000 men and supporting artillery under General William Forbes Gatacre [q.v.] was defeated by 2,300 Boers under Jan Hendrik Olivier [q.v.] and Esias Reinier Grobler (1861–1937). The unfortunate Gatacre had lost his way on the approach march and on his retreat forgot and left behind 696 of his soldiers. This was one of three British disasters in South Africa during Black Week [q.v.], the others being the battles of Colenso and Magersfontein [qq.v.]. Boer losses were minor; the British lost 135 killed and wounded and 696 captured.

Storming Party. See Forlorn Hope.

Stössel, Anatoli Mikhailovich (1848–1915). A Russian who entered the Russian army in 1864 and served in the Russo-Turkish War [q.v.] of 1877–78 and the Boxer Rebellion [q.v.] of 1900. At the beginning of the Russo-Japanese War of 1904 he was in command of Port Arthur, which he stoutly defended until forced to surrender on 2 January 1905. For this he was tried by court-martial and imprisoned. He was released in 1909. His subsequent life is unknown.

Stoughton, Edwin Henry (1838–1868). An American soldier who was graduated from West Point in 1859, the first five-year class. He resigned on 4 March 1861, on the eve of the American Civil War, and on 25 September was appointed colonel of the 4th Vermont. He took part in the Peninsular Campaign [q.v.], and in November 1862, scarcely three years out of West Point, he was made a brigadier general, at age twenty-four the youngest general officer in the Union army at that time. At Fairfax Court House in northern Virginia on the night of 9 March 1863 he was roused from his bed by guerrillas under John S. Mosby [q.v.] and taken prisoner along with 29 other Union soldiers. J. E. B. Stuart [q.v.] called Mosby's raid a "feat unparalleled in the war." His capture ended Stoughton's military career. Although exchanged, he was not given another command. After the war he practiced law in New York City.

Straggling. The failure of some troops to keep up with a marching column or the wandering from the route of a column of march in search of food, loot, or rest.

Stralsund, Siege of (30 January–19 April 1807), Napoleonic Wars. French forces under Marshal Édouard Adolphe Mortier [q.v.] moved to subjugate Pomerania and capture the fortress of Stralsund on the western shore of the Strait of Straelsund, 88 miles northwest of Stettin, defended by Swedish Generals Jean Henri Essen and Johan Toll [qq.v.]. Although there were about 13,000 men on each side, the Swedes were driven back into their defenses. On 19 April Essen agreed to an armistice proposed by Mortier in which the Swedes agreed not to move beyond the Peene River and both sides promised not to renew hostilities without one month's notice.

Strasbourg, Siege of (14 August–28 September 1870), Franco-Prussian War. This ancient city in northeastern France had extensive fortifications, but they had been little improved since the time of Sébastien Vauban [q.v.]. Germans under General August von Werder [q.v.] began a bombardment of the city on 14 August 1870. The art gallery, the famous city library, and the Palais de Justice all were destroyed, and the roof of the cathedral was badly damaged. On 26 August Werder began a formal siege. On 17 September a

Strasbourg *Bombardment of Strasbourg*

breach was made in the enceinte wall, and on 28 September French General Jean Jacques Alexis Uhrich (1802–1886) surrendered.

Stratagem. A ruse or trick to gain an advantage by deceiving or outwitting an enemy.

Strategic Flank. The flank that, if turned, drives a force away from its line of communication.

Strategos. A war game designed by American army Lieutenant Charles Adelle Lewis Totten (1850?–1908) for the purpose of teaching tactics and strategy [see Kriegsspiel].

Strategy. The planning, coordination, and employment of the armed forces of a belligerent or group of belligerents, using all military, political, economic, and psychological resources available to gain victory or lessen the chance of defeat. "Grand strategy" refers to the ways and means of attaining the political objectives of a war. The nineteenth-century German military theorist Hans Delbrück [q.v.] spoke of the strategy of annihilation, in which the complete destruction of an enemy's army is sought, and of the strategy of exhaustion, in which the enemy's capacity and will to persist in the fighting are undermined. Karl von Clausewitz [q.v.] more simply said: "Strategy is the theory of the use of battles for the object of war" (*On War* [1833]). Field Marshal August von Gneisenau [q.v.] wrote: "Strategy is the science of making use of space and time. I am more jealous of the latter than the former. We can always recover lost ground, but never lost time."

Strategy of Survival. See Fabian Strategy.

Strathnairn, Baron. See Rose, Hugh Henry.

Strawberry Plains, Battle of. See Deep Bottom Run, Battle of.

Straw Blower. A colloquial term during the American Civil War for a fifer.

Strelkovaia. A body of Russian sharpshooters. After the 1870 reforms of General D. A. Miliutin [q.v.] each infantry battalion held at least one company of *strelkovaia*.

Strength, Unit. The number of men in a unit. When one attempts to determine the size of an army or smaller unit, it is frequently impossible to tell how strength was counted, who was included, and who was not. During the American Civil War, for example, the "effective strength" of a unit was the number of enlisted men present for duty. The "total strength" included the effective strength plus the sick, those under arrest, and those away on temporary duty. The "aggregate strength" included all officers and other ranks present for duty, and the "combat strength" was the effective strength plus the officers present. In actual usage these terms were often loosely applied.

Stress, Combat. An emotional state caused by the tensions, fears, and physical exertions of battle. In the first half of the nineteenth century stress was not considered a genuine malady. During the American Civil War it was considered merely nostalgia [q.v.], an immature homesickness, or cowardice. During the Spanish-American War [q.v.] it was often called tropical asthenia, and some thought it to be caused by a tropical infection. The first published reference to combat stress occurred in 1871. The term "shell shock" was unknown before World War I. Today the phenomenon is called combat stress reaction, which, if not promptly and properly treated, becomes posttraumatic stress disorder, defined by the American Psychiatric Association as "the development of characteristic symptoms following a psychologically distressing event that is outside the range of usual human experience."

Stretcher. A litter for carrying the disabled or dead [see Cacolet; Doolie; Litter].

Strike a Flag, to. To lower a flag (sometimes used figuratively) as a sign of a willingness to surrender.

Striker. A soldier servant in the American army; an officer's orderly or, in British usage, a batman. Strikers were often scornfully called dog robbers in the American army and accused of taking the scraps from the officers' tables that ought to have gone to the dogs. Strikers received extra pay for their services from the officers they served and were excused from many onerous duties. In 1870 the U.S. Congress forbade the use of soldiers as servants, but officers protested, and the law was generally ignored.

In the British army, many senior noncommissioned officers, such as the regimental sergeant major, were also entitled to strikers.

Stripes. See Chevrons.

Strongpoint Defense. A battle position that affords all-round defense and is strongly defended. In German: *Schwerpunkt*.

Stuart, James Ewell Brown (1833–1864), from the initials of his first three names, known as Jeb Stuart. An American soldier who was graduated from West Point in 1854 and brevetted a second lieutenant in the Mounted Rifles. On 3 March 1855 he transferred to the 1st Cavalry on the Kansas frontier, where he took part in several engagements against Indians. On 29 July 1857 at Salmon's Fork on the Kansas River, while serving under Colonel E. V. Sumner [q.v.], he participated in a saber charge against an estimated 300 Cheyennes, perhaps the first and only one in Indian warfare. Several Indians were killed; Sumner suffered 2 killed and 10 wounded, one of whom was Stuart, who received a pistol ball in the chest. In 1857–58 he was a member of the Utah Expedition [q.v.] under General Albert Sidney Johnston [q.v.]. In 1859 he served as an aide to Robert E. Lee in the capture of John Brown [q.v.] at Harpers Ferry. He was promoted captain on 22 April 1861 but resigned on 14 May at the outbreak of the Civil War to join the Confederate army as colonel of the 1st Virginia Cavalry. He quickly established himself as a brilliant cavalry commander, distinguishing himself in the First Battle of Bull Run [q.v.]. He was promoted brigadier general in September 1861. In June 1862 he made a spectacular raid that took him completely around the army of General George B. McClellan [q.v.]. He took part in the Seven Days' Battles [q.v.], and in September 1862 he was promoted major general. In October he repeated his feat of encircling the Union army. In the Battle of Fredericksburg [q.v.] he commanded the extreme right of the Confederate line. After both Thomas ("Stonewall") Jackson and A. P. Hill [qq.v.] were wounded in the Battle of Chancellorsville [q.v.], he succeeded Jackson as corps commander. Stuart was defeated at Brandy Station [q.v.], one of his hardest-fought battles and the largest cavalry engagement of the war. On 2–4 July 1863 he commanded the cavalry in the Battle of Gettysburg [q.v.], but he did not arrive on the field until after the battle had begun. On 11 May 1864 he was mortally wounded while intercepting the raid of Philip Sheridan [q.v.] at Yellow Tavern [q.v.] in front of Richmond. He died the fol-

Stuart, Jeb *Stuart's raiders with new army clothing at Federal supply depot in Chambersburg, Pennsylvania*

lowing day. In an obituary the *Richmond Examiner* (17 May 1864) lauded him as "The Confederate lion, the shaking of whose mane and angry roar kept the Jackal North in a perpetual terror."

Stuart, John (1759–1815). A British soldier who fought against the Americans in the American Revolutionary War and was taken prisoner at Yorktown in 1781. In 1799 he fought in the capture of Minorca, and in 1801 he fought in Egypt. In 1806 he commanded an expedition to Calabria and defeated French General Jean Louis Reynier [q.v.] in the Battle of Maida [q.v.] on 6 July 1806 [see Naples, Anglo-Russian Expedition to; Calabrian War]. He had further successes in southern Italy and Sicily but resigned his command in 1810 because he received so little support.

Sturdza, Gregory / Grigorie (1821–1901). A Rumanian soldier educated in Germany and France. He became a general in the Turkish army and later held the same rank in the Moldavian army. In 1859 he was an unsuccessful candidate for the Rumanian throne.

Sturgis, Samuel Davis (1822–1889). An American soldier who was graduated from West Point in 1846 and was captured during the Mexican War [q.v.] and held at Buena Vista for eight days before being released. After the war he served with the 1st Dragoons in New Mexico, taking part in the operations against the Jicarilla Apaches in 1854 and against Mescalero Apaches the following year. He was a member of the Utah Expedition [q.v.] of 1857–58, and in 1860 he took part in a campaign against the Comanches and Kiowas. He was a captain in command at Fort Smith, Arkansas, on the right bank of the Poteau River near its junction with the Arkansas River, in April 1861, when, at the outbreak of the American Civil War, many of his officers resigned to join the Confederate army. Although the fort was surrounded by Confederate militia, Sturgis marched his troops out, carrying most of the government equipment with him, and reached Fort Leavenworth unscathed. He was promoted brigadier general of volunteers, to rank from 10 August 1861.

He saw action at the battles of Wilson Creek, Second Bull Run, South Mountain, Antietam, and Fredericksburg [qq.v.]. After his defeat in the Battle of Brice's Crossroads [q.v.] on 10 June 1864 a board of investigation was called to investigate the "disaster," and he spent the remainder of the war "awaiting orders." He ended the war a major general, but in the postwar reductions he was appointed lieutenant colonel of the 6th Cavalry and later of the 7th Cavalry. He retired in 1886.

Stutterheim, Carl Gustav Ludwig Wilhelm Julius von (1815–1871). A German soldier who entered the Prussian army in August 1830. He was given command of the German Legion [see Foreign Legion, British] raised by the British for the Crimean War [q.v.] but not used. He led those of the Legion who when discharged settled in South Africa in 1857. He returned to Germany to fight in the Schleswig-Holstein War in 1864 and in the Franco-Prussian War [qq.v.] of 1870–71. In 1871 he committed suicide in Wiesbaden. The town of Stutterheim on the Kubusie River at the foot of the Amatola Mountains in eastern Cape Province, South Africa, is named for him.

Subaltern. A commissioned officer below the rank of captain.

Subedar / Subadar. A rank in the Indian army [q.v.] native infantry equivalent to sergeant.

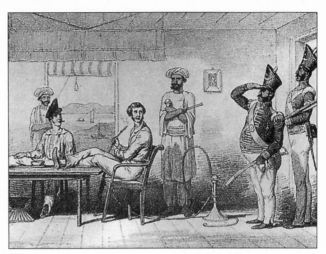

Subedar *A subaltern receives the subedar's morning report*

Sub-Lieutenant. The lowest commissioned rank in the British army, equivalent to second lieutenant in the American army, *sous-lieutenant* in the French army and *Leutnant* in the German army. The title replaced "ensign" and "cornet" in 1871.

Subordination. Submission to the orders of superiors. According to *Wilhelm's Military Dictionary* of 1881, "In effect, it is subordination that gives a soul and harmony to the service; it adds strength to authority, and merit to obedience; and while it secures efficacy of command, reflects honor upon its execution. It is subordination which prevents every disorder, and procures every advantage to an army."

Substantive Rank. The permanent rank of an officer, as opposed to temporary, local, or brevet rank. It is usually a rank below which an officer cannot be reduced without a court-martial. In the U.S. army the highest substantive rank was, and is, major general.

Substitute, Military. A man who takes the place, usually for a price, of one who has been conscripted. The practice was tolerated in many countries that conscripted soldiers.

Suchet, Louis Gabriel (1770–1826). A French soldier who began his military career in 1791 when he was commissioned in the Garde Nationale [q.v.]. He served in Italy, taking part in the battles of Loano, Dego, Lodi, and Castiglione. He was promoted general of brigade in 1798, and general of division the following year. In 1801 he was appointed inspector of infantry and governor of Padua. He fought at Ulm, Hollabrunn, Jena, Pultusk, and Austerlitz [qq.v.]. From 1808 to 1814 he played a prominent role in the Peninsular War [q.v.], in which he commanded the French III Corps, which he named the Army of Aragón. He became a kind of warlord in Catalonia and largely paid, fed, and clothed his troops from the taxes he levied. However, he increased the prosperity of the province by abolishing medieval laws restricting trade and he reduced corruption. In 1811 he was made a marshal and Duc d'Albufera. He continued to serve under the Bourbons but rallied to Napoleon in the Hundred Days [q.v.].

Sucre, Antonio José de (1795–1830). A soldier and revolutionary born in Venezuela. In 1811 he was a lieutenant in the Spanish colonial army. He became the chief lieutenant of Simón Bolívar [q.v.] in the 1821 campaign against Spain in Quito, Ecuador, and on 22 May 1822 won the Battle of Pichincha [q.v.]. He served under Bolívar in Peru in 1823–24 and with him won the Battle of Junín on 6 August 1824 and the Battle of Ayacucho [qq.v.] on 9 December that same year. In 1826 he became the first president of Bolivia. In 1828, forced to resign because of the opposition from native Bolivians, he took service with Colombia. On 4 June 1830 he was assassinated in the forest of Berueros, near Pasto, Colombia, on his way home from the Colombian Congress at Bogotá, at which he had been president. The town of Sucre, the legal capital of Bolivia, is named after him.

Sudan, British Reconquest of (1896–98). General Horatio Kitchener [q.v.], sirdar (commander-in-chief) of the Egyptian army, led an Anglo-Egyptian army in a methodical reconquest of the Sudan from the Mahdist Dervishes. Escorted by a flotilla of gunboats, he moved up the Nile, and to avoid a large bend in the river, he constructed a railroad across the desert. On 21 September 1896 he captured Dongola, on 7 August 1897 he defeated the Dervishes at Abu Hamed, and on 8 April 1898 he scored a major victory in the Battle of Atbara [qq.v.]. The final and decisive battle of the campaign took place on 2 September 1898 just north of Omdurman [q.v.], where Kitchener's superior weapons, including 20 machine guns, and disciplined troops soundly defeated the numerically superior but poorly armed Dervishes.

Sudan, British Reconquest of *Native woman gives water to Sudanese troops serving with Kitchener's army in the Sudan, 1898.*

Sudan, Egyptian Conquest of (1821–22). Most of the Sudan was conquered by the Egyptian armies of Muhammad Ali [q.v.], who administered it as his private estate and made Khartoum, at the juncture of the Blue and While Niles, its capital.

Suddasain, Battle of (1 July 1848), Second Sikh War. Lieutenant Herbert Edwardes [q.v.] collected a force of 18,000 Bhawlpuris and Pathans and at this town defeated 12,000 Sikhs, who withdrew into nearby Multan, on the Chenab River, 200 miles west-southwest of Lahore, in present-day Pakistan, where they were besieged for six months. [See Multan, Siege of.]

Suffolk, Siege of (11 April–4 May 1863), American Civil War. After an unsuccessful attempt to recapture New Bern [q.v.], North Carolina, Confederate General James Longstreet [q.v.] attacked Union General John James Peck (1821–1878) at Suffolk, Virginia. When forced to abandon his attempts to capture the town, he laid siege to it and foraged in the lush acres around it. Although he reported that the place could be taken in a few days, he added that he did not think "we can afford to spend the powder and ball." He abandoned the siege on being recalled to Lee's Army of Northern Virginia [q.v.]. Casualties were 260 Federals and 900 Confederates, 400 of whom were listed as missing.

Suicide. Army life separated men from families, friends, and sweethearts; depression, loneliness, and alcohol drove some to take their own lives. Especially the isolated, comfortless life on the American western frontier seemed to drive soldiers to suicide. A War Department report in 1891 revealed that the ratio of 76 suicides per 1,000 men in the American army from 1879 to 1888 was three times higher than that of the British and Belgian armies and twice as high as that of the disciplined Prussian army.

In fighting primitive peoples soldiers often preferred suicide to capture. This was true for American soldiers fighting Indians on the Great Plains and for British soldiers fighting Pathans on the Northwest Frontier. Rudyard Kipling [q.v.] advised in "The Young British Soldier":

> When you're wounded and left on Afghanistan's plains,
> An' the women come out to cut up what remains,
> Jest roll to your rifle an' blow out your brains.
> An' go to your Gawd like a soldier.

Sukhomlinov, Vladimir Aleksandrovich (1848–1926). A Russian soldier who won the Cross of St. George the Martyr [q.v.] as a cavalry officer in the Russo-Turkish War of 1877–78. Sergei Dmitrievich Sazonov (1866–1927), a Russian diplomat who became foreign minister in 1810, said of him: "It was very difficult to make him work, but to get him to tell the truth was impossible." He bragged of having never read a military manual and, an advocate of edged weapons, was never able to conceive that machine guns and breech-loading artillery had put an end to cavalry attacks. Nevertheless, he became a general, and he is generally credited with being responsible for Russian unpreparedness for World War I. In 1906 he married his fourth wife, a woman thirty-two years younger than he, and financed her extravagances by gambling and cheating his government. In 1917 he was convicted of treason and sentenced to life imprisonment, but he was released in 1918 by the Soviets and died in Berlin.

Sukoro, Battle of. See Tyrnau, Battle of.

Suleiman / Süleyman Pasha (1838–1892). A Turkish soldier who entered the army in 1854 and fought in

Montenegro, Crete, and Yemen. He taught at the military academy in Constantinople (Istanbul) and became its director. In 1876 he distinguished himself in the Turko-Serbian War, defeating the Serbs and Russian volunteers in the Battle of Alexinatz [q.v.]. He took an active part in the deposition of Sultan Abdul-Aziz (1830–1876). In the Russo-Turkish War of 1877–78 [q.v.] he held command in Bulgaria, but his army was nearly destroyed in fighting the Russians at the Shipka Pass [q.v.]. In October 1877 he was made commander-in-chief of the Army of the Danube. In January 1878 he was defeated and forced to retreat to Constantinople. For this he was charged with treason and court-martialed. He was sentenced to fifteen years in prison but was pardoned by the sultan.

Suliot Rebellions. Suliots were a people of mixed Greek and Albanian origin who in the seventeenth century fled from Turkish oppression to the Suli Mountains and the valley of the Acheron (Akheron) River, then in the pashalik of Jannina (today eastern Epirus). In 1800 they numbered about 560 families. Although they fought the encroachments of the egregious Ali Pasha of Jannina [q.v.], they were crushed in 1803, and many fled to Parga on the Ionian Sea, then ruled by the French. After the final fall of Napoleon, Parga came under British rule until 1819, when over the objections of the populace, it was ceded to Turkey. Many Suliots then fled to the Ionian Islands, particularly Cephalonia, at the time ruled by Britain. During the Greek War of Independence [q.v.] Suliots under Marcos Bozzaris [q.v.] took an active part in fighting the Turks, but their former homeland in Epirus was not included as part of independent Greece in the Treaty of 1829.

Sully, Alfred (1821–1879). An American soldier who was graduated from West Point in 1841 and commissioned in the infantry. He first saw action in the Second Seminole War [q.v.] of 1841–42. In the Mexican War [q.v.] he took part in the siege of Veracruz [q.v.] in March 1847. In 1853 he fought in the Rogue River War [q.v.], and in 1860–61 he cam-

paigned against the Cheyenne Indians. Soon after the outbreak of the American Civil War he was made colonel of the 1st Minnesota. He served through the Peninsular Campaign and distinguished himself at South Mountain and Antietam [qq.v.]. In September 1862 he was promoted brigadier general of volunteers. In that rank he fought at Fredericksburg on 13 December 1862 and at Chancellorsville [qq.v.] on 2–4 May 1863. He was then given command of the Department of the Dakotas and made his headquarters at Sioux City, Iowa. In cooperation with General Henry Sibley [q.v.] he undertook a campaign against the Sioux and defeated a band at Whitestone Hill, in what is now North Dakota, on 3 September 1863. In July 1864 he launched a second campaign and overcame the Sioux in the Battle of Killdeer Mountain [q.v.]. In March 1865 he was promoted major general of volunteers and a brigadier general in the regular army.

In the reorganization of the army after the war, Sully was made lieutenant colonel of the 10th Infantry and in December 1873 he was promoted colonel.

Sultana. Perhaps the most tragic accident ever to strike the American army was the sinking of the steamship *Sultana* in the Mississippi River near Memphis, Tennessee, on 27 April 1865. The ship was licensed to carry 376 passengers and a crew of 80, but on this date it was carrying perhaps as many as 2,400, including 1,300 recently released Union prisoners of war eager to return home, a few women and children, and 100 horses and mules plus 150 tons of sugar.

About 2:00 A.M. an enormous explosion created a massive hole, destroying the pilothouse and most of the deck beneath it. The wooden superstructure was soon engulfed in flames. Nicholas Karns, a soldier who survived, described the scene: "Everywhere steam was escaping, women were screaming, soldiers were swearing, horses neighing, mules braying, splinters flying—the once magnificent 'Sultana' was a wreck." About 1,800 people were drowned, scalded to death, or incinerated.

Thanks to a change in the course of the ever-unstable Mississippi River, the remains of the *Sultana* are now buried in a farmer's field near Mound City, Arkansas.

Sully, Alfred *General Sully's attack on Sioux at Whitestone Hill, Dakota Territory, 3 September, 1863*

Sumatra, Dutch Conquest of (1873–1908). In 1821 the British ceded Benkoelen, their last possession in Sumatra, to the Dutch, but even as late as 1873 the Dutch effectively controlled only coastal areas, and campaigns in the north against the sultan of Achin (Atjeh) carried over into the twentieth century [see Padri War].

Summer Palace, Destruction of the (24 October 1860), Second Opium War. Five miles outside Peking (Beijing) stood the large collection of buildings containing an immense treasure of books, cloths, jewels, vases, and other valuables known as the Summer Palace. General James Hope Grant [q.v.], commanding the British forces, was incensed when it was looted by the French, but when he learned of the torture of Sir Harry Smith Parkes (1828–1885) and his envoys [see Taku Forts], he ordered the palace burned. After the British in turn looted the place, the firing was overseen by British engineers [see Opium Wars, Second].

Summit Springs (11 July 1869), American Indian Wars. German-born Mrs. George (Maria) Weichel[l] had been in the United States only two months and had settled with her husband on the Solomon River in Kansas when on 30 May 1869 the Cheyenne dog soldiers of Tall Bull [q.v.] attacked. They killed her husband and took her captive. The wife of army scout Thomas Alderdice (1841–1925) was also taken, along with one of their four sons; the other three children were slain; the youngest, a baby, was strangled. This atrocity led to an expedition by the 5th Cavalry under Major Eugene Asa Carr [q.v.] that successfully attacked the eighty-four lodges of Cheyenne dog soldiers near present-day Sterling in northeast Colorado. All the lodges were demolished, and much other property was destroyed; 52 Indians were killed, and 17 were taken prisoner. Mrs. Alderdice was found dead, but Mrs. Weichel was released unharmed. The battle virtually ended the Cheyenne threat.

In the Cheyenne lodges thirteen hundred dollars were found, presumably stolen by the Indians. Nine hundred dollars were given to Mrs. Weichel, who was taken to Fort Sedgwick, Colorado, to recuperate. There she married the hospital steward who cared for her.

Sumner, Edwin Vose (1797–1863). An American soldier who received a direct commission in 1819 in the 2nd Infantry and, after serving in the Black Hawk War [q.v.], served on the western frontier. A major when the Mexican War [q.v.] began, he accompanied Philip Kearny [q.v.] to New Mexico and later served under General Winfield Scott [q.v.]. In the Battle of Cerro Gordo [q.v.] a musket ball bounced off his head, earning him the nickname of Bull Head.

He was not a popular officer. In 1847 Captain (later Confederate General) Richard Ewell called him "the greatest martinet in the service, who for our sins has got command of us. We are in perfect Purgatory here, and Major Sumner would be a perfect devil anywhere . . . we all put up daily petitions to get rid of him." In 1848 he was promoted lieutenant colonel of the 1st Dragoons and served in New Mexico against Apaches, Utes, and Navajos and established several new posts. In 1852 he was named acting governor of New Mexico. In 1855 he became colonel of the newly formed 1st Cavalry. The following year, when commander of Fort Leavenworth, Kansas, he worked against the free-soil and proslavery turmoil of Bloody Kansas. On 29 July 1857 he led a cavalry charge, rare in Indian fighting, and dispersed mounted Cheyennes at Soloman's Fork of the Kansas River.

On 16 March 1861 he was promoted brigadier general, one of only three in the American regular army at that time. At the beginning of the Civil War he commanded II Corps in the Army of the Potomac [q.v.], which he led in the Peninsular Campaign [q.v.] and in which he was twice wounded. He was the oldest active corps commander. General George B. McClellan [q.v.] praised his gallantry and his "judgement and energy." On 31 May 1862 he was promoted major general of volunteers. He fought in Antietam (Sharpsburg), and he commanded the Left Grand Division in the Battle of Fredericksburg [qq.v.]. He died of natural causes on 21 March 1863.

Sumner, Edwin Vose, Jr. (1835–1912). An American soldier, the eldest son of Civil War General Edwin Vose Sumner [q.v.]. He was commissioned in the 1st Cavalry of the Union Army on 5 August 1861 at the beginning of the Civil War. By the end of the war he was a captain with the brevet rank of brigadier general of volunteers. After the war he served nearly fourteen years on the Pacific coast. He took part in the Modoc War of 1872–73 and the Nez Percé War [qq.v.] of 1877. He became colonel of the 7th Cavalry in 1894 and retired a brigadier general in 1899.

Sumner, Samuel Storrow (1842–1937). A son of Civil War General Edwin Vose Sumner [q.v.] who served in the Union army in the American Civil War, emerging as a brevet major. After the war he remained in the army and saw much service fighting Indians. For his part in the defeat of the Cheyennes in the Battle of Summit Springs on 11 July 1869 and the Great Sioux War [qq.v.] of 1876 he won a brevet to lieutenant colonel. He fought in the Battle of Slim Buttes [q.v.] and commanded a battalion in the Wind River Expedition. During the Spanish-American War [q.v.] he became a brigadier general and a major general of volunteers. He retired in 1906.

Sumpitan. A blowpipe, usually five to eight feet long, used in Malaya and Borneo. The darts, made of wood from the sago palm, were usually about 10 inches long. Their tips were dipped in poison made from a mixture of ipoh tree juice and such other substances as scorpion venom, pepper, snake venom, etc. Raja James Brooke [q.v.], writing in 1841, described the manner in which the weapon was used: "In advancing the sumpitan is carried in the mouth and elevated, and they will discharge at least five arrows to one compared to the musket."

Sumurai. See Samurai.

Suomanlinna, Battles of. See Sveaborg, Battles of.

Superior Officer. Any officer of higher rank or one of the same rank who has priority by reason of earlier date of promotion or other reason.

Supernumeraries. Officers and men carried on the rolls of a unit in excess of the approved establishment. When there were not enough vacancies for second lieutenants in the U.S. army, graduates of the Military Academy were attached to units as brevet second lieutenants until vacancies occurred.

Supersede, to. To deprive an officer of his position for an offense or to place an officer over the head of another officer.

Support. 1. As a noun, the movement of a military force to aid, protect, supplement, or sustain another force.

2. As a verb, to be held back as a reserve.

Supporting Distance. The distance between units of an army that could be traveled quickly enough to give assistance if needed. When all of an army's units are so placed, it is said to be concentrated.

Surgeon. In the nineteenth century army doctors were called surgeons. Even when they held military rank, they were not entitled to command in line or staff positions.

Surgeon *Surgeon major of the medical service of the French army treats wounded on the field*

Surgeon's Mate. In the British army, a warrant officer (senior noncommissioned officer) who assisted regimental surgeons.

Surgery, Military. See Medicine and Surgery, Military.

Surinam, Capture of (5 May 1804), Napoleonic Wars. A British squadron under Commodore Sir Samuel Hood (1762–1814) with 2,000 troops under Sir Charles Green captured this West Indian stronghold held by about 1,000 Dutch plus some locally raised troops.

Surprise Attack. An attack against an enemy when or where he least expects attack or is least capable of effectively resisting. Surprise often leads to a victory out of proportion to the numbers engaged. The attack of Thomas ("Stonewall") Jackson [q.v.] on the Union flank at Chancellorsville is a classic example.

Surrender, to. To capitulate to an enemy [see Honors of War; Unconditional Surrender; Munfordville, Battle of].

Surveillance. The systematic observation of an area for intelligence purposes.

Suspension of Arms. Similar to an armistice [q.v.], but brief and restricted to a pressing local need, such as the burial of the dead or the collection of the wounded. It was sometimes agreed upon to allow opposing commanders to confer.

Surrender, to *Confederates surrender at Crampton's Gap, American Civil War.*

Suspensoir. A kind of athletic supporter that all mounted men in the French army were required to wear to guard their "organs of generation."

Sutler. A civilian who sold comestibles, necessities, and sometimes liquor to soldiers at army posts, to an army in the field, and in many prisoner of war camps. Found in all armies, sutlers sometimes had a quasi-official status. In Britain the position was first officially recognized in February 1717. During the Crimean War [q.v.] a small army of Greeks, Turks, and Armenians acted as sutlers. In India entire bazaars, often containing more civilians than the troops they served, grew up around cantonments and even accompanied armies on campaign.

In 1821 the U.S. War Department gave official recognition to sutlers and officially integrated them into the military establishment. Considered superior to enlisted men, they were without line authority. Their privileges and responsibilities were set forth in army regulations published in 1822, but there remained considerable confusion about their status. In 1829 regimental sutlers were banned, and sutlers were assigned only to army posts. In 1831 this was reversed. On 9 February 1832 it was decreed: "There will be one sutler per post known as the 'Post Sutler.' If more than one is allowed, he will be the 'extra' sutler." In 1835 it was determined that sutlers be appointed by the secretary of war for four-year periods. On 12 February 1839 troops in the field were allowed one sutler per unit. The army controlled prices and hours of trade. The business of the sutler was badly hurt when the sale of liquor on a post was forbidden, a regulation that flickered on and off for the next fifty years [see Nicks, Sally].

Much of the sutler's trade was on credit, and in the American army he sat at the pay table and received his due after the laundresses. If a soldier died, the sutler lost the money owed. Many established themselves as bankers and postmasters on military posts, but others traveled about in wagons and operated in unstable markets. Many were enterprising. When General Winfield Scott [q.v.] invaded Mexico at Veracruz [q.v.], some sutlers had landed ahead of the troops and had already set up shop on the beaches.

Not always popular, many were accused of overcharging and selling inferior goods or unfit food. Soldiers often stole from them, sometimes during the American Civil War organizing a rally, a mass attack upon a sutler's shop or wagon. Some were suspected of being spies. When baggage, women, and sutlers were ordered to the rear, it was a sure sign that an army was about to move.

As the century progressed, most armies placed their sutlers under increasing regulation. In the United States in the 1880s they were subject in all respects to the army's rules and regulation, and they were directly supervised on each post by a committee of three officers known as the Council of Administration. The sutler could not sublease, transfer, sell, or farm out his business, and he needed special permission to trade with Indians. A part of his profit went to the post or military command and was used for the benefit of the troops. The post commander set the rates and prices, which were required to be reasonable and fair.

In the United States in the late 1880s the sutlers (or post traders, as they had been officially named in 1870) began to be replaced by canteens, an idea copied from the British [see Canteen]. By General Order No. 11 on 8 February 1892 the name canteen was changed to post exchange [q.v.], and the licenses to post traders were revoked.

Sutler *A sutler's tent*

Suvorov, Aleksandr Vasilievich (1729–1800). A Russian soldier born in Finland. He served in the Seven Years' War (1756–63), the Russo-Turkish War of 1773–74, and commanded the Russian army against the Turks in 1787–92, winning the Battle of Kinburn with a bayonet charge. In 1794 he was created a field marshal, and in 1799 he defeated the French at Cassano d'Adda, Trebbia River, and Novi, but he was defeated by French General André Masséna in the Second Battle of Zurich on 25 September of that year. In 1800 he was commander-in-chief of the Russian army.

Sveaborg, Battles of. Also called the Battles of Soumenlinna. In the nineteenth century two attacks were launched upon this fortress, built by the Swedes in 1749 in the harbor of Helsinki, Finland.

Russo-Swedish War (February–3 May 1808). A garrison of 7,000 Swedes and Finns held off a Russian force for three months through winter weather so bitter that it prevented the Russians from bringing up siege guns and the fortress from receiving supplies. The garrison finally surrendered on 3 May. The Russians captured 200 guns and nineteen transports.

Crimean War (9–11 August 1855). A Russian fortress during the Crimean War [q.v.], it was bombarded by a British fleet under Admiral Richard Dundas (1802–1861), who commanded the Baltic Fleet, but it was not captured.

Svištov / Svishov, Battle of (26–27 June 1877), Russo-Turkish War of 1877–78. Following the Russian declaration of war on Turkey in support of Serbia on 24 April 1877, a Russian army advanced into Moldavia and Walachia (soon to be recognized as Rumania), and on 26 June an advance guard of 15,000 men under General Mikhail Dragomirov [q.v.] slipped across the Danube in boats during the night. The next day they attacked the Turkish fortress of Svištov, 14 miles east of Nikopol (Nicopolis), on the southern bank of the Danube. After reinforcements commanded by General Mikhail Skobolov [q.v.] arrived, the garrison surrendered. By achieving surprise, the Russians suffered fewer than 1,000 casualties in the assault, and they were then able to move on to Nikopol and later Plevna [see Plevna, Siege of].

Swayne, Wager (1834–1902). An American soldier and lawyer who was educated at Yale. On 31 August 1861 he entered the Union army as a major in the 43rd Ohio. He saw action under General John Pope [q.v.], took part in the advance upon Corinth, and won the Medal of Honor [q.v.] for his gallantry in the Battle of Corinth [q.v.] on 4 October 1862. He was promoted colonel and served in the Atlanta Campaign. On 2 February 1865 in the crossing of the Salkehatchi River he suffered a wound by a shell fragment that required amputation of his right leg above the knee. He was brevetted brigadier general, to rank from 5 February, and on 13 March he was given the full rank.

After the war he was promoted major general, the last such promotion in the Civil War period, and placed in charge of the Freedmen's Bureau [q.v.] in Alabama. He retired in 1870 and practiced law in Toledo, Ohio, and in 1881 in New York City.

Swearing. For some reason cursing has always been associated with soldiering. Shakespeare spoke of "a soldier, full of strange oaths" (*As You Like It*, II, vii), and General George Washington (1732–1799) in a general order to the army (1776) deplored "that unmeaning and abominable custom, swearing," although it was said that he himself could swear with the best.

Swedish Invasion of Norway (1814). Norway was given to Sweden by the Treaty of Kiel on 14 January 1814, but on 17 May the Norwegians declared their independence. On 16 July Swedish troops led by Count Hans von Essen [q.v.] entered the country. Charles Frederick, Duke of Holstein, who had been elected king of Norway, abdicated on 10 October, and on 4 November King Charles XIII of Sweden (1748–1818) was proclaimed king by the Storting, assembled at Christiania (Oslo). He accepted the constitution, which declared Norway a "free, independent, indivisible, and inalienable state united to Sweden," an arrangement perhaps understandable only to Scandinavians.

Swedish Mauser Rifle. A bolt-action rifle with a five-round fixed-box magazine introduced in 1896. It had an overall length of 49.6 inches, weighed 9.1 pounds, and had a muzzle velocity of 2,625 feet per second. A carbine version had been introduced two years earlier.

Swedish Military Coup d'État (13 March 1809). King Gustavus (Gustav) IV of Sweden (1778–1837), having become insane, was dethroned by a conspiracy of officers of the Western Army led by Count Karl Johan Adlercreutz [q.v.]. Thirteen officers broke into the king's apartments, seized him, and removed him to the Château of Gripsholm. He later wandered about Europe and died in poverty at St. Gallen, Switzerland. His childless uncle Karl (Charles), the Duke of Sudermania (1748–1818), succeeded him as Karl XIII under a new constitution. In 1810 Jean Baptiste Bernadotte [q.v.], a former marshal of Napoleon, was chosen to be crown prince, and upon the death of Karl he took the throne as King Charles XIV on 5 February 1818.

Sweeny, Thomas William (1820–1892). An Irish-born American soldier who emigrated to the United States when he was twelve. During the Mexican War [q.v.] he fought with a militia unit and lost his right arm in the Battle of Churubusco [q.v.]. On 3 March 1848 he was commissioned a second lieutenant in the 2nd Infantry. In January 1861 he was promoted captain and at the beginning of the Civil War was severely wounded in the Battle of Wilson's Creek [q.v.]. In January 1862 he was named colonel of the 52nd Illinois Infantry. In that rank he fought at Fort Donelson and at Shiloh [qq.v.], where he was again wounded. In the Battle of Corinth [q.v.] he commanded a brigade, and in March 1863 he was promoted brigadier general, to rank from 29 November 1862. He led a division in the Atlanta Campaign [q.v.], but after the Battle of Atlanta he was court-martialed on charges brought by his corps commander, General Grenville Mellen Dodge (1831–1916), whom he had assaulted and with whom he had frequently quarreled, calling him a "God-damned liar" and a "cowardly son of a bitch." Although acquitted, Sweeny was not restored to command. In December 1865 he was dismissed the service for being absent without leave. He soon involved himself in the Fenian Brotherhood and in a Fenian raid [qq.v.] on Canada [see O'Neil, John]. Although he was arrested with other Fenians, he was quickly released and in November 1866 was reinstated in the army. He was placed on the retired list as a brigadier general on 11 May 1870.

Sweet, Benjamin Jeffrey (1832–1874). An American politician and soldier who at age twenty-seven entered the Wisconsin legislature. At the beginning of the Civil War he was commissioned a major in the Union army. He took part in the Battle of Perryville [q.v.], quitting the ambulance in which he was confined with malaria to mount his horse and join the fight. He fell seriously wounded and, since his health was permanently impaired, was placed in the Veterans Reserve Corps [q.v.] and given command of Camp Douglas [q.v.], a prisoner of war camp at Chicago.

In June 1864 he uncovered a plot to liberate and arm the 10,000 Confederate prisoners held there on 4 July and then to sack and destroy the city. He moved quickly to strengthen his garrison, and the plot came to nothing. In November of the same year he learned of a plot planned for election night, when 5,000 armed men were to liberate the prisoners and supply them with 9,000 rifles. To oppose them, Sweet had only 796 men, few of whom were fit for active duty. Recruiting one of the prisoners, John T. Shanks (b. 1832), a former scout and Texas Ranger to lead police to the conspirators, Sweet arranged for him to escape. Closely followed, Shanks duly made contact with the ringleader, who was arrested.

As a reward Shanks was commissioned a captain, Company I, 6th United States Volunteers, a regiment composed of galvanized Yankees [q.v.], who fought Indians on the plains. He resigned on 11 October 1866. Sweet was brevetted brigadier general and in a mass meeting received the Thanks of the citizens of Chicago.

After the war Sweet resigned on 17 September 1866 and practiced law. He later served in the pension and internal revenue offices.

Swift, Joseph Gardener (1783–1865). An American soldier who was appointed a cadet in the Corps of Artillerists and Engineers in 1800. In 1801 he was assigned to West Point, New York, where the U.S. Military Academy was formally established on 16 March 1802. With one other cadet, he received his commission as an officer on 12 October of that year. His class of two is regarded as the first to be graduated from the new academy. Swift rose rapidly; in 1812, although not yet twenty-nine years old, he was promoted colonel and appointed chief of engineers. For his service in the War of 1812 [q.v.] he was promoted brigadier general in February 1814. In 1816 he became the superintendent of West Point. He resigned two years later. From 1829 to 1845 he worked as a civil engineer in charge of harbor improvements on the Great Lakes.

Swiss Army Knife. See Knife, Swiss Army.

Swiss Civil War. See Sunderbund War.

Switzerland, French Occupation of (1798–1802). French troops occupied Switzerland in 1798, and Napoleon formed the Helvetic Republic. When the troops were withdrawn in August 1801, there was at once an uprising in the canton of Schwyz, one of the forest cantons, the people seeking increased cantonal independence. Napoleon sent General Michel Ney [q.v.] with a force sufficient to quell the uprising, and the Swiss were forced to sign a fifty-year treaty of alliance, to provide 16,000 men to serve under French command, and to annex to France the canton of Valais. In 1815, after the final fall of Napoleon, Valais was restored, and Switzerland became a confederation of twenty-two cantons.

Sword. 1. Any hand-held edged weapon with a long blade for cutting or thrusting. Swords are manufactured in various sizes and shapes that bear specific names, such as saber, cutlass, tulwar, and épée. In all European and American armies in the nineteenth century a sword was carried as a symbol of an officer's authority. Swords of honor, beautifully engraved, were often presented to officers who had distinguished themselves.

2. War itself, as in the statement of Rear Admiral Alfred Thayer Mahan (1840–1914) that "Step by step in the past, man has ascended by means of the sword" (*The Peace Conference* [1899]).

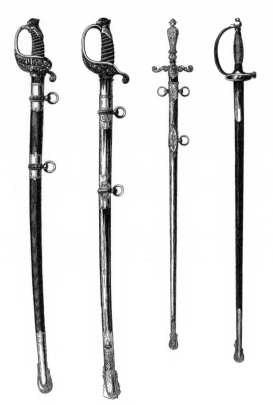

U.S. regulation swords

Sword Knot. An ornamental cord tied to the hilt of a sword. In the American army general officers wore gold cords with acorn ends; other officers wore gold lace straps with gold bullion tassels of the same material. Enlisted cavalrymen wore leather straps with bullion tassels of the same material. Black sword knots were worn as signs of mourning.

Sword Law. The will of the strongest.

Sword Master. See Master of the Sword.

Syce. A Hindi word for groom.

Sykes, George (1822–1880). An American soldier who was graduated from West Point in 1842 in a class that was to contribute twelve corps and army commanders to the northern and southern armies during the American Civil War. He served in the Second Seminole War, won a brevet in the Mexican War [qq.v.], and fought against Indians in Texas and New Mexico. In the American Civil War he commanded in the First Battle of Bull Run [q.v.] the battalion of U.S. regulars that did not join the flight of the panic-stricken volunteers after the Union defeat. On 28 September 1861 he was promoted brigadier general and led a brigade in the Peninsular Campaign [q.v.]. He fought at Second Bull Run, Antietam, and Fredericksburg [qq.v.] and on 29 November 1862 was promoted major general. He was at Chancellorsville [q.v.], but his troops were not involved in the rout of the Union troops there. In the Battle of Gettysburg [q.v.] on 2–4 July 1863 he commanded a corps and successfully defended Little Round Top [q.v.] and Big Round Top. Although a great defensive general, he was slow when alacrity was required and was often called Tardy George. In December 1863 he was relieved of his command by General George Meade, and he spent the remainder of the war in Kansas. After the war he reverted to the rank of lieutenant colonel and was later promoted colonel.

Sykes, Percy (1867–1945). A British soldier educated at Rugby and Sandhurst who in 1888 was commissioned in the 16th Lancers. During the Second Anglo-Boer War [q.v.] he served in the Intelligence Department and then commanded the Montgomery Imperial Yeomanry [see Yeomanry]. During World War I he was made a brigadier general and organized the Persian army to restore order in southern Persia (Iran).

Szczecin, Battle of. See Stettin, Battle of.

Széchenyi, Istávan (1791–1860). A Hungarian soldier who gained fame as a daring cavalryman when on 16–17 October 1813, on the eve of the Battle of Leipzig, he rode through the French lines [q.v.], carrying orders to Field Marshal Gebhard von Blücher and Marshal Jean Baptiste Bernadotte [qq.v.]. Two years later, in the Battle of Tolentino [q.v.], he added to his reputation for bravery and élan by leading a cavalry charge that scattered the bodyguard of Marshal Joachim Murat [q.v.].

He later became a successful statesman, initiating projects designed to open the Danube from Buda (Budapest) to the Black Sea, and he introduced steamboats on the Danube, Theis (Tisza), and Lake Balaton. He was appointed minister of war in 1848, and he opposed the radical politics of Lajos Kossuth (1802–1894] during the Hungarian Revolution [q.v.]. In 1860, under the strain of the times, he committed suicide.

Szeklers. Literally, frontier guards. A people, believed by some to be descended from Attila's Huns but probably descended from Magyars, who lived in the upper valleys of the Mures and the Olt rivers in eastern Transylvania. During the Hungarian Revolution of 1848–49 [q.v.] they fought voluntarily in the Army of Transylvania commanded by Jósef Bem [q.v.].

Sword knot

Tabar. An Indian or Persian battleax with a wide blade balanced by a hammerhead.

Table Money. An allowance granted to American general officers to fulfill the duties of hospitality within their command.

Tabor. A ring of baggage to deter cavalry attacks on infantry.

Tache d'Huile Strategy. A French colonial system for expanding control and pacification, successfully employed in Indochina, Madagascar, and Africa. When a small area had been seized and was securely held, control would be extended to surrounding areas, spreading like a spot of oil, first through foot and mounted patrols, then through the construction of roads and forts. The technique was developed by Colonel (later General) Joseph Gallieni [q.v.].

Tachi. A Japanese sword, single-edged and curved like a saber, not used in fighting in the nineteenth century but often worn as a ceremonial sword until 1877, when the wearing of swords was forbidden.

Tacna, Battle of (26 May 1880), War of the Pacific. Some 14,000 Chileans under General Manuel Baquedano defeated a slightly smaller allied force of Peruvians and Bolivians under Bolivian President Narciso Campero [q.v.] at Tacna, Peru, about 40 miles north of Arica in a mostly arid region enclosed on the east by foothills of the Andes Mountains. There were heavy casualties, the Allies losing about 3,000, including 197 officers, to the Chileans' 2,000. The Chileans then moved on Arica, which they took by assault on 7 June.

On 20 October 1883, by the Treaty of Ancón, the nitrate-rich province of Tarapacá was ceded to Chile along with the districts of Arica and Tacna, the two latter to be held for ten years, after which a plebiscite was to determine ownership. The plebiscite was never held, and the problem festered until in May 1929 both sides accepted an American compromise. The following year the region was divided between Peru and Chile.

Tacón, Miguel, Marqués de la Unión de Cuba (1777–1855). A Spanish soldier and sailor who in 1806 was military governor of Popayán, Colombia. From 1809 to 1814 he led Spanish forces against rebels in South America. Returning to Spain, he took part in the Spanish Civil War of 1820–23 [q.v.]. In 1834 he was appointed captain general of Cuba and in that office suppressed the newly written Cuban constitu-

tion. In 1837 he excluded Cuban deputies from the Spanish Cortes. He was recalled in 1838.

Tactical. Of or pertaining to tactics.

Tactical Formations. There were in the nineteenth century four basic tactical formations: soldiers in lines, shoulder to shoulder; soldiers in dense columns, a mobile formation that became offensive when deployed in lines; skirmishers, an open-order flexible formation usually used to harass an enemy; and the hollow square, a defensive formation much favored by the British.

Tactical Manuals. Handbooks designed to instruct and assist officers in the performance of military tasks to which they might be assigned.

Tactical Marches. Marches made in the immediate vicinity of the enemy, often observable by him.

Tactical Officers. Officers at American military academies responsible for instruction in military subjects and for instilling military discipline.

Tactical Unit. The largest body of men that could be controlled and deployed on a battlefield by the voice of one man. As the century progressed and shoulder weapons and artillery improved in performance, the use of massed units disappeared and the size of a tactical unit was reduced. When a unit's size was so large that couriers and "gallopers" and staff officers were used, it ceased to be a tactical unit and became a formation.

Tactics. The movements planned and used when an enemy is in close or near close contact or a battle is imminent or under way. The word is derived from the Greek *taktikē*, meaning ordered or arranged. Karl von Clausewitz [q.v.] defined tactics as "the use of military forces in combat." In the nineteenth century tactics was divided into grand tactics for large organizations and minor tactics when applied to a small organization or to organizations of only one arm (infantry, artillery, or cavalry). General Antoine Henri de Jomini [q.v.] wrote: "Grand Tactics is the art of forming good combinations preliminary to battles as well as during their progress. The guiding principle in tactical combinations, as in those of strategy, is to bring the masses of the force at hand against a part of the opposing army and upon that point the possession of which promises the most important results" (*Précis de l'art* *de la guerre* [1838]). British Colonel G. F. R. Henderson (1854–1903) referred to grand tactics as "those stratagems, manoeuvres, and devices by which victories are won, and concern only those officers who may find themselves in independent command" (*Science of War* [1906]).

In the early nineteenth century there was much discussion about the virtues of columns and lines in battle. The British were famous for their double lines of battle; the French for their heavy columns, which, when correctly used, had great shock value but were vulnerable to artillery. Although a column could rarely break unshaken infantry, it could shatter a formation that was seen to waver. The column was considered best for maintaining unit cohesion, particularly with inexperienced troops [see Tactical Formations]. Napoleon used both lines and columns and sometimes a mixture of the two. If not in column, his soldiers usually fought in three lines.

For most of the nineteenth century artillery was placed in front of or beside the infantry; cavalry was on the flanks or behind the infantry. These formations ended when the use of the percussion cap [q.v.] and the rifle ended the tactical utility of cavalry and the cylindroconoidal shell revolutionized artillery tactics. The percussion cap was invented in 1814, and the cylindroconical shell in 1824, but armies were slow to realize their advantages and to adjust tactics to conform to a changed battlefield. Not until 1839 was the percussion musket issued to British infantry, and not until 1851 were they equipped with Minié rifles [q.v.].

The value of percussion rifles and rifled artillery was never more dramatically demonstrated than in Bohemia during the Seven Weeks' War [q.v.]. Solid masses of Austrian troops, feebly protected by skirmishers, rushed at Prussian lines and were decimated by the Dreyse needle gun [q.v.] and the Prussian artillery.

Tacubaya, Battle of (11 April 1859), Mexican Revolution. At this town (now a suburb west of Mexico City) Mexican federal troops under General Leonardo Márquez decisively suppressed a Liberal uprising of 4,000 men under General Santos Degollado (1811–1861), who lost all his artillery and munitions. His wounded and captured survivors were massacred.

Tafalla / Tiebas, Battle of (9–11 February 1811), Peninsular War. Spanish General Francisco Espoz y Mina [q.v.] took receipt of two British siege guns that were landed at Deba and used them to besiege Tafalla, 20 miles south of Pamplona. The French governor of Navarre, marching with 3,000 men to relieve the town, was met by the Spanish at Tiebas, 10 miles from Tafalla, where Espoz y Mina had four battalions on the road. On 10 February, after a daylong attempt to break through, the French were repulsed and fell back upon Pamplona. The disheartened troops besieged at Tafalla surrendered the next day.

Tahiti, French Conquest of (1838–80). In 1838 a French frigate commanded by Captain Abel Aubert Dupetit-Thouars (1793–1864) landed at Tahiti, the largest of the Society Islands, and extorted from Queen Pomare (d. 1877) the right of Frenchmen, including the resident missionaries, who had proved disruptive and troublesome, to settle on her islands. In 1843 the queen was forced to place the islands under French protection. Under the terms of the treaty her authority and that of her chiefs were preserved, but soon after the treaty was signed, Dupetit-Thouars reappeared, deposed the queen, and took possession of the islands for France. Although not countenanced by the French government, the act was not corrected, and the islanders rose in a rebellion that lasted for two years. French troops were unable to conquer the western islands, which were left to their rightful owners, and unrest persisted until in 1880 Queen Pomare's son abdicated and the struggle was abandoned.

Taiping Rebellion (1850–1864). This Chinese civil war, waged mostly in the south, was the most bloody and most destructive of all the wars waged in the nineteenth century and perhaps the bloodiest civil war in the history of the world. Estimates of those killed, civilian and military, range from 20 million to 50 million. It was also the most sweeping revolution against an existing social order in the nineteenth century, for it was a rebellion not only against the Manchu Ching (Qing) dynasty (1644–1912) but also against Confucianism and a centuries-old way of life.

In 1837 Hung Hsiu-ch'üan (now spelled Hong Xiuquan) [q.v.], a young man who after four times failing the examinations that would have admitted him to the gentry, came under the spell of Protestant Christianity. He emerged from a trance one day to proclaim the Tai-Ping (*T'ai-p'ing T'ien-kuo*), or Great Peace, with himself the heavenly king. By 1844 he was preaching a kind of social utopia that appealed to the poor, and in 1847 in the mountains of Kwangtung (Guangdong) Province in southeast China he established a commune and attracted an army of "God Worshipers" that grew rapidly. Converts to the new religion gave up all their property, which was held in common; each was to be supplied according to his or her needs; all served in or in support of the Taiping army.

In 1850 the heavenly king proclaimed his temporal sovereignty over the world, thus coming into conflict with the Manchu Empire, and on 4 November of that year the Taipings clashed with imperial forces for the first time in the Battle of Chin T'ien [q.v.]. On 11 January 1851 Hung proclaimed an open rebellion.

On 15 August he issued a proclamation that established a system of command and control and divided the army among five generals who were proclaimed wangs (kings), each of whom was given an army of his own and the title of commander (*chu-chiang*). The army was thus divided into advance, right, left, central, and rear units.

The Taiping army was based upon the classical *chou-li* system, said to have been devised by the founder of the Chou dynasty (1122 B.C.–255 B.C.), but it probably had been conceived much more recently. Under this system civilian and military functions were not separated. The troops were militia, who took up arms as needed and served under officers who were also magistrates. The Taipings used the *chou-li* titles for their officers, followed its same division into units, and retained its size of units. The basic unit was the squad led by a sergeant (*liang-ssu-ma*) with 5 corporals and 20 privates. Five squads made a platoon under a lieutenant, five platoons made a company under a captain, five companies made a battalion, and five battalions an army corps, the largest unit, with 13,156 men. Most of the military organization and administration was under the command of the Wang Yang Hsiu-ch'ing [q.v.], commander of the central army and the Imperial Guard.

Taiping women were divided into identical units, and no contact was allowed between men and women until final victory (never reached) was achieved; even among married couples sex was forbidden, and those who disobeyed were beheaded. Only Hung and the wangs, all of whom developed large harems, were excepted, but anyone who gossiped about the heavenly king's own active sex life was beheaded, as were prostitutes. Homosexuals were tortured before their execution. Even having clothing laundered by someone of the opposite sex was a punishable offense.

In the autumn of 1851 the Taiping army moved east, capturing cities and defeating the forces of the Ching government. In the southern part of Kwangsi Province they fought a number of battles with government forces and with pirates, members of the Triad Society [q.v.], the largest and most powerful of the numerous Chinese secret societies. Many of the Triad leaders had been attracted to the Taipings, but most had deserted when they learned of the strict enforcement of the rules regarding private property and sex. When the army moved again, it marched through Kwangsi Province and besieged its capital, Kweilin, on the right bank of the Kwei River, but gave up the siege after a month and moved into Hunan Province. There it was defeated at Hsining (Siangtan) by a smaller force under well-trained provincial militia formed by a member of the local gentry, Chiang Chung-yüan (d. 1854), an imperialist general. Although Hung lost a number of his best-trained and most thoroughly indoctrinated followers, the march continued, and the ranks were expanded by increasing numbers of recruits, many of whom felt they had nothing to lose and something to gain by joining an organization that promised to feed them.

From 11 September until 30 November 1852 the Taipings besieged Changsha [q.v.], on the right bank of the Siang River, 45 miles south of Lake Tungting (Tunting Ho) but failed to capture it. In the attempt Hsiao Ch'ao-kuei [q.v.], became the second of the five wangs to be killed. In January 1853 the Taipings captured Wuchang (Wuhan), on the south bank of the Yangtze River, 425 miles west of Shanghai. On Lake Tungting they captured hundreds of boats, enabling them to move troops by water down the Yangtze. On 15 February the town of Wu-Hsüeh [q.v.] in Hupeh Province, on the left bank of the Yangtze, fell to the Taipings. On 18 February 1853, after a weeklong siege, the port city of Kiukiang [q.v.] was taken, and on 24 February, Anking (Hwaining), on the north bank of the Yangtze, the main stronghold guarding the approach to Nanking (Nanjing or Nanxiang), China's second-largest city, fell.

On 19 March 1853 the Taipings captured the great city of Nanking, which Hung entered like an emperor, borne on a sedan chair. He renamed the city T'ien-ching (heavenly capital) and established his headquarters there, dallying with his dozens of wives and concubines in an ornate palace while Yang steadily increased his authority. It was soon clear that Yang was the wang who was chief among equals, the executive head of the entire army. He tightened discipline and increased indoctrination. Now he himself had trances in which he claimed to speak for the Holy Ghost.

The Taipings at the time numbered more than a million people, and Yang established a new system of government based on a mixture of bureaucracy and etiquette requiring multiple staffs and bureaus. Because two of the original five wangs had been killed in battle, he reorganized the army into three corps, the largest, centered on Nanking, under his direct command.

To expand their territory, armies were sent north toward Peking (Beijing) and westward up the Yangtze. On 1 April 1853 the northern army captured Yangchow (Kiangtu), 15 miles north of Chinkiang, but wasted two months unsuccessfully besieging Hsuchang in Honan Province. The delay enabled the imperial forces to organize their resources, and the northern army, although it eventually managed to reach the outskirts of Tientsin, was virtually destroyed.

The western army marched out of Nanking on 19 May 1853, and 14 January 1854 it captured Hwaining, capital of Anhwei Province. Here Chiang Chun-yüan, who had been made governor of the province for his earlier victories, was defeated and wounded and drowned himself. Hsiang-t'an (Siangtan), on the Siang River 20 miles south-southwest of Changsha, was captured on 24 April 1854.

The greatest threat to the Taiping forces now arose under the leadership of the remarkably able Tsêng Kuo-fan [q.v.] governor of Hunan Province, whose provincial army raised units that were recruited, officered, disciplined, and paid for by local gentry. He had begun in 1853 with an army of 1,000, which was blooded by fighting local bandits, and when it swelled to 20,000 (eventually to reach 120,000), he began his battles with the Taipings. Tsêng's first triumph was the recapture of Hsiang-t'an on 1 May 1854. Two months later his forces scored a major victory at Yochow (Yoyang or Yueyang) in northeast Hunan Province, 85 miles northeast of Chungsha on Lake Tungting. The victory greatly increased his prestige and, in capturing half the Taipings' boats, cost them the control of the central Yangtze River.

The Taipings sent another expedition up the Yangtze, this time under Shih Ta-k'ai [q.v.], one of the ablest of the surviving wangs. Between 5 April and 9 August 1856 at Kiangnan Province in eastern China the Taipings under Yang defeated the largest imperial force ever fielded. It was said that each side numbered 2.5 million men. However, in December 1856 Wuchang was retaken by Tsêng's provincial forces.

The imperial government placed two blockading forces near Nanking: a Northern Camp (*chiang-nan ta-ying*) and a Southern Camp (*chiang-pei te-ying*). The city began to suffer from a lack of supplies, and Yang was forced to withdraw a part of the army fighting Tsêng to fight the blockading imperial armies. The Taipings first attacked the imperial army on the north bank of the Yangtze River and defeated it in the Battle of Yangchow (Kiangtu), 15 miles north of Chinkiang. In June 1856, reinforced by the army under Shih Ta-k'ai, they attacked the Southern Camp, and the imperial forces were routed. The blockade was broken.

With the immediate danger over, Taiping leaders began a vicious war among themselves. Hung Hsiu-ch'üan at this time laid claim to be the son of God and the younger brother of Jesus Christ while Yang Hsiu-ch'ing, who in trances had previously spoken through the Holy Ghost, now claimed to speak for God the Father. A growing threat to Hung, Yang even rebuked him for ill-treating his concubines and for his fits of temper that sometimes resulted in summary executions. Yang sealed his fate when he claimed precedence over the other wangs. On 2 September 1856 Wei Ch'ang-hui [q.v.], the *pei wang* (north king), killed him. In the following days all of his family and followers—an estimated 20,000 people—were slain. Historians differ on whether Wei was following Hung's orders or was acting on his own.

The slaying of Yang and his people did not end the infighting. Wei Ch'ang-hui then tried without success to kill Shih Ta-k'ai. Soon after, on orders from Hung, Wei was himself assassinated with all his family and some 200 followers. Of the original chief leaders, the founders and organizers, only Hung and Shih remained.

Shih left his army in the field and from November 1856 until the end of May 1857 attempted to take Yang's place and to control all of the Taipings' forces. However, he lacked Yang's administrative talents, and he felt threatened by Hung's two elder brothers, Hung Jen-ta and Hung Jen-fa, who appeared on the scene as power players and were created wangs. Leaving Nanking, Shih took with him large numbers, said to be 200,000, of the central army and began a campaign of his own. In 1858 his forces were said to be in the "hundreds of thousands," according to government sources, but eventually these were decimated in Hunan by the forces of Tsêng Kuo-fan in 1859.

The main Taiping forces remained in the lower Yangtze area, principally at Nanking and in Anhwei Province, but each commander acted independently, for there was no real commander-in-chief. In 1857 Li Hsiu-ch'eng (d. 1864) a leading commander, made common cause against imperial forces with the leaders of the Nien Rebellion [q.v.], notably Chang Lo-hsing [q.v.], who commanded the largest of the Nien armies. The Nien [q.v.] at this time controlled part of northern Anhwei along the borders of Shantung, Honan, and Kiangsu. Li Hsiu-ch'eng achieved such prestige through the

victories he achieved with the Nien in the upper Yangtze area that he was created *chung wang* (faithful king). On 24 February 1857 he scored a significant victory over government troops in the Northern Camp and pursued the fleeing forces northward.

Meanwhile, the forces of Tsêng Kuo-fan continued a slow advance, denying the Taipings the upper Yangtze area. Imperial forces again gathered around Nanking and rebuilt the Northern and Southern camps and prepared to advance upon Chen Chiang (Chenkiang) in east Yunan Province, 28 miles southeast of Kunming. To meet this threat, the Taiping commanders joined forces and on 15 November 1858 decisively defeated the Hunan army under Tsêng's brother, who was killed.

Numerous Europeans and Americans served on both sides in the war. Initially it was believed in Europe and the United States that the Taipings were indeed Christians. Their defeats were met with sympathy and their successes with applause while British and American newspapers reported the cruelties and tortures of the imperialists. But as the Taipings' destructions and butcheries were revealed and their twisted brand of Christianity became apparent, popular opinion in the Western world shifted toward the Manchu imperialists. In the United States an act of Congress of 22 June 1860 made it a capital offense to join the Taipings.

Although the various Taiping armies managed to hold their own, affairs became increasingly chaotic in Nanking. Hung Hsiu-ch'üan's brothers had no grasp of military or administrative problems and no influence at all over the military commanders. Then on 22 April 1859 Hung Jan-kan (d. 1864), a

Taiping Rebellion *Battle of Tianjin, the Qing Imperial Army surrounding the Taiping Expeditionary Force, February 1854. (The civil war lasted almost fifteen years and took an estimated 20 to 40 million lives.)*

young cousin of the heavenly king, arrived in Nanking. He had studied Christianity in Shanghai and worked in Hong Kong and thus knew more about the Western world than did the Taiping leaders. He was soon created a *wang* and assumed the position of chief of staff. Although he was a good administrator and strategist, he was unable to control the army commanders, who had grown vain, powerful, and self-willed. Their autonomy, combined with the confusion at the court, doomed the Taipings.

When a Taiping army approached Shanghai in May 1860, the British and French announced that they would defend the city itself from the rebels. The Chinese commercial community reacted by raising, with the assent of the imperial government, the 3,000-man Ever Victorious Army [q.v.], commanded by an American, Frederick Townsend Ward [q.v.], who was killed in 1862. In March 1863 British Major Charles Gordon [q.v.] took command. The French also raised a small Chinese army that was officered by Frenchmen. The initial objective of the two armies was to clear a 35-mile area around Shanghai.

The Ever Victorious Army under Gordon captured Quinsan in May and in September invested Soochow (Suzhou). Although Gordon was initially defeated, Soochow fell in December. On 19 July 1864 Nanking was captured after a siege, and its fall was the beginning of a great slaughter of Taipings [see Nanking, Sieges of]. Hung Hsiu-ch'üan was found to have killed himself. The remnants of the Taipings were driven out of Changchow (Wutsin), near Amoy, in April 1865.

The few leaders who managed to escape from Nanking were soon caught and executed. The Taiping armies disintegrated, and the great rebellion drew to an end. Shih Ta-k'ai was beheaded in Szechwan Province when he surrendered. The last major Taiping force was annihilated on 7 February 1866, when 10,000 were killed and 50,000 surrendered. This was officially proclaimed the end of the rebellion [see Li Hsu-pin; Li Hung-chang; Lin Feng-hsiang; Hunan Braves; Hung Chen-kan; Nien / Nienfei Rebellion].

Although British accounts give the impression that Gordon and his little army defeated the Taipings, their part in the fourteen-year-long rebellion was merely supportive of the imperial efforts. The Taipings were eventually defeated not by Gordon or the imperial regular forces but by dissension in the ranks of the wangs and by provincial armies that came into being throughout the country, particularly the forces raised by Tsêng Kuo-fan in Hunan.

Tait, Peter (fl. 1860s). An Irish clothier of Limerick who in the 1860s was the largest manufacturer of ready-made clothes in the world. He made uniforms for the British army and during the American Civil War for the Confederate army, delivering them in his own blockade-runners. His short Confederate jackets were made of cadet gray kersey with eight buttons in front, each stamped "P. Tait, Limerick."

Taiwan. See Formosa.

Take by Storm, to. To capture an enemy position by a violent assault.

Take the Queen's / King's Shilling, to. To enlist as a soldier in the British army. The shilling represented the bounty, which was sometimes more than a shilling.

Takouba. A sword carried by the Tuaregs [q.v.] of the Sahara. The blades were sometimes of European origin. The hilts were variations of a design called cross of Agades, named after a town in the Air massif of central Niger [see Telek].

Taku Forts, Attacks on the (1858–60 and 1900), Second Opium War. The Taku (Degu) forts were on the Hai River, 37 miles east of Tientsin (Tianjin), China. They were stoutly built and were improved in the 1850s by Seng-ko-Lin-Ch'in [q.v.].

Second Opium War (20 May 1858). An Anglo-French force under British Admiral Sir Michael Seymour (1802–1887) captured Canton (Guangzhou) on 28–29 December 1857. It then moved north and captured the Taku forts but held them only briefly.

Second Opium War (25 June 1859). When the Chinese refused to admit foreign diplomats in Peking (Beijing), British Admiral Sir James Hope (1808–1881) attempted to force passage of the Peiho (Han) River with eleven gunboats and a landing force of 1,100 men, but met severe resistance. He was himself twice wounded, and two ships were sunk beneath him. Of the eleven gunboats, six were sunk or disabled. The landing force became bogged down in mud and had to retreat. The British lost 89 killed and 345 wounded.

American Commodore Josiah Tattnall (1795–1871), commanding a squadron in Asian waters, violated American neutrality by coming to the aid of the British, an act he justified by saying, "Blood is thicker than water." Britain and France then agreed on joint action against the Chinese.

Second Opium War (21 August 1860). A joint Anglo-French force of 11,000 British and Indian troops and 7,000 French took by assault the Taku forts, manned by about 5,000 Chinese under Governor Hang Foo. British and Indian casualties were 21 killed and 184 wounded; there were fewer French casualties. The Chinese suffered 400 killed and wounded; 2,100 Chinese were captured, disarmed, and released. The Allied expedition then moved up the Peiho River, the British and Indians on the right bank and the French on the left. The Chinese asked for an armistice, and to arrange terms a small delegation, headed by Henry Brougham Loch [q.v.] and Sir Harry Smith Parkes (1828–1885), traveled to Canton. There on 18 September they were seized, imprisoned, and tortured. Half died as a result of their usage or succumbed to infections. The survivors were released after three weeks and a mere ten minutes before orders were received

Taku Forts *A captured Taku fort*

from the emperor to kill them. Parkes and Loch both survived, but Loch never completely recovered from his ordeal. In retaliation the British looted and burned the Summer Palace [q.v.].

The forts were again attacked in 1900, during the Boxer Rebellion [q.v.], and by terms of a treaty signed at the end of the conflict were destroyed in 1902.

Talana Hill, Battle of (20 October 1899), Second Anglo-Boer War. In Zulu *talana* means little shelf. The battle is sometimes called the Battle of Dundee. Boers under Lucas Johannes Meyer [q.v.], holding the Talana heights above Dundee, Natal, 120 miles northwest of Durban, were dislodged by the British at a cost of 20 officers and 142 men killed and wounded, including their commander, Sir William Penn Symons (1843–1899), who was mortally wounded, and 331 taken prisoner.

Talavera de la Reina, Battle of (27–28 July 1809), Peninsular War. Sir Arthur Wellesley (later Duke of Wellington), invading Spain from Portugal along the Tagus Valley with about 20,000 men, 60 guns, and a friendly Spanish force of 34,800 under General Gregorio García de la Cuesta [q.v.] reached Talavera, 70 miles southwest of Madrid, where he halted, for the Spanish authorities, who had promised to supply him with food, had failed to make good. While wrestling with his supply problems, he learned that two French armies were converging upon him: one from the north commanded by Marshal Nicolas Soult and another from the south commanded by Marshal Claude Victor [qq.v.]. Arriving in the area first, without waiting for Soult, Victor launched a night attack on 27–28 July 1809 with 30,000 men upon Wellesley's left. Wellesley's army was distributed along the Cerro de Medellín, a dominating height, and the French were repulsed. Four major attacks were beaten back on the 28th. The bulk of the fighting was done by 16,000 British troops. The Spaniards, having seen a few French horsemen in the distance, fired their muskets and fled. They were, said Wellesley, "frightened only by the noise of their own fire." French losses were 761 killed, 6,391 wounded, 206 missing, and 20 guns. The British suffered 801 killed, 3,915 wounded, and 645 missing. Many British and French died when a grass fire spread over the dry plain. The Spanish claimed a loss of 1,200 killed or wounded, but this seems unlikely; probably most should be numbered among the missing.

Wellesley withdrew into Portugal before Soult appeared on the scene. Late in life Wellington pronounced this battle the most bitter he had fought, but he also said this of several other battles. It was for this victory that Lieutenant General Wellesley was created Viscount Wellington.

Taliaferro, William Booth (1822–1898). An American soldier who was graduated from the College of William and Mary in Virginia in 1841 and for a time studied law at Harvard. On 23 February 1847, during the Mexican War [q.v.], he was commissioned a captain in the 11th Infantry. He was promoted major in August of the same year and was mustered out a year later. From 1850 to 1853 he served in the Virginia legislature. At the time of John Brown's raid [q.v.] on Harpers Ferry he commanded the Virginia militia and in that position was present at the hanging of John Brown [see Brown's Raid, John]. In May 1861, at the beginning of the American Civil War, he was commissioned a colonel in the Virginia provisional army and was for a time a major general of militia. He joined the Confederate army as colonel of the 23rd Virginia. After taking part in several small engagements, he was promoted brigadier general from 4 March 1862. He served under General Thomas ("Stonewall") Jackson [q.v.] in the Valley Campaign, and although Jackson despised him, he won the Battle of McDowell [q.v.] for him.

In August 1862 he was severely wounded in the Battle of Groveton [q.v.]. After fighting in the Battle of Fredericksburg [q.v.], he served under General Pierre Beauregard [q.v.] in Florida, Georgia, and South Carolina, where in July 1863, with fewer than 1,200 men, he successfully defended Fort Wagner [q.v.] against 5,000 Federals.

After the war he again served in the Virginia legislature (1874–79) and as a judge (1891–97). He was a member of the Board of Visitors of the Virginia Military Institute [q.v.] and of the College of William and Mary.

Talladega, Battle of (9 November 1813), Creek War. After the massacre of more than 500 whites by Creek Indians at Fort Mims [q.v.] on 30 August 1813, General Andrew Jackson collected a force of Tennessee militia and volunteers and defeated a band of Creeks near this town, 44 miles east of Birmingham, Alabama.

Tall Bull (1830?–1869). A Cheyenne dog soldier [q.v.] and head of one of the most militant of the Cheyenne warrior societies. He was active in the wars on the western plains in 1868–69 and took part in the Battle of Beecher's Island [q.v.], where he was one of those who persuaded Roman Nose [q.v.] to make his fatal charge. He was killed in the Battle of Summit Springs [q.v.], Colorado, on 11 July 1869. Tall Bull's death signaled the end of the dog soldiers' power.

No one knows who killed Tall Bull, but many, including numerous Pawnee Indians and Buffalo Bill Cody [q.v.], claimed the kill. Modern American historian James T. King has stated that "the circumstances of the death of Tall Bull have given rise to the longest continuing, one of the most involved, and perhaps one of the least important controversies in frontier history" (*War Eagle*).

Talleyrand, Élie Charles de, Duc de Périgord (1788–1879). A French soldier who fought at Wagram [q.v.] in 1809 and took part in Napoleon's Russian Campaign [q.v.] in 1812. In 1814 he participated in the battles for the defense of France, but after Waterloo he went over to the Bourbons. In 1816 he was created a field marshal.

Talma. A gutta-percha rain cloak extending to the knees with long sleeves worn by enlisted men in the U.S. cavalry from 1861.

Talneer, Affair at (17 February 1818), Third Maratha War. By the Treaty of 6 January 1818 the Marathas agreed to surrender certain border fortresses to the British, but when a division under the command of General Thomas Hislop (1764–1843) arrived before the fort at Talneer, its commander refused to surrender it. After successfully storming the fort, Hislop ordered the commander hanged and the 300 men of the garrison put to the sword. There was a furor over the harshness of this action when it became known in Britain, and although he was defended in the House of Lords by Wellington, Parliament specifically excluded Hislop from its Thanks to the Deccan army [see Deccan Prize].

Talus. The slope of the face of a work in a fortification.

Talwar. A saber used in India, Persia (Iran), Afghanistan, and elsewhere in Asia.

Tamai, Battle of (13 March 1884), campaign against Dervishes in the eastern Sudan. A British force of 4,000 with four guns and some Gatlings under General Gerald Graham [q.v.] defeated a force of an estimated 12,000 Hadenowas [see Fuzzy-Wuzzy] under Osman Digna [q.v.] about 20 miles west of Suakin. The British advanced in two squares. One of them was briefly broken by the Hadenowas, but the second square moved up to give support, and the Hadenowas were repulsed. British casualties were 10 officers and 204 other ranks killed or wounded; estimated Dervish casualties were 2,200.

Tamai *The British recapture a gatling gun from the Hadenowas, 13 March 1884*

Tamames, Battle of (18 October 1809), Peninsular War. Spanish General Don Lorenzo del Parque [q.v.] with 20,000 infantry, 1,500 cavalry, and 18 guns occupied a strong position in hills behind the village of Tamames in Salamanca Province in western Spain, 23 miles east-northeast of Ciudad Rodrigo. There he was unsuccessfully attacked by 14,000 infantry with 14 guns under French General Jean Gabriel Marchand [q.v.]. The French lost 1,400 killed and wounded; del Parque 700. This was the first victory of a Spanish field army since the Battle of Alcañiz [q.v.] on 23 May 1809.

Tamboekie War. See Kaffir Wars.

Tam-o-Shanter. A Scottish bonnet with a broad top and a tourie (toorie or bobble) on top. It was said to be named after the poem "Tam o'Shanter" by Robert Burns (1759–1796),

written about 1789, in which Tam, leaving his inn in wind and rain, riding his old mare

> Whiles holding fast his gude blue bonnet,
> Whiles crooning o'er some auld Scots sonnet,

encounters a witches revel.

Tampion. See Tompion.

Tananarive (Antananarivo), Capture of (30 September 1895), French occupation of Madagascar. After a short bombardment by the French, the capital of Madagascar surrendered to a 15,000-man French army under General Jacques Duchesnes (1837–1918). This triggered in the interior a violent revolution that was with some difficulty suppressed. On 6 August 1896 Madagascar was proclaimed a French colony, and General Joseph Gallieni [q.v.], who replaced Duchesnes, deposed the queen and established a military government [see Madagascar, Warfare in].

Tang. 1. The projecting part of the breech of a musket by which the barrel is secured to the stock.
   2. The part of a sword blade to which the hilt is attached.

Tang Ts'u, Battle of (16 June 1900), Boxer Rebellion. A 2,000-man international force of marines and sailors under British Admiral Edward Hobart Seymour (1840–1929), marching from Tientsin to relieve the besieged legations in Peking (Beijing) [see Boxer Rebellion], was defeated at this town about halfway to Peking and forced to turn back by a Chinese force under General Nieh Shih-cheng [q.v.].

Tani, Tateki (1837–1911). A Japanese soldier who fought in the Boshin Civil War in 1868, the Japanese invasion of Formosa (Taiwan) in 1874, and the Satsuma Rebellion of 1876–77 [qq.v.]. In 1876, leading an imperial army of 50,000, mostly conscripts, he successfully defeated the forces of Saigo Takamori [q.v.] in the Battle of Kamamoto.

Tanner, James (1844–1927). An American soldier and politician known as Corporal Tanner who enlisted in the Union army at the beginning of the American Civil War, rose to the rank of corporal, and lost both legs in the Second Battle of Bull Run. Appointed commissioner of pensions early in 1889, he determined to give the maximum benefit to "every old comrade that needs it." He greatly increased pension payments without investigation into claims and made a hash of administrative procedures and his budget. He was forced to resign in September of the same year, but there were no accusations of personal dishonesty. In 1905–06 he was commander-in-chief of the Grand Army of the Republic [q.v.].

Tantia Topi (1819?–1859). A Maratha Brahman originally named Ramchandra Panduroga who was a rebel leader in the Indian Mutiny [q.v.]. He was in the service of Nana Sahib [q.v.] and was responsible for the Cawnpore Massacre [q.v.] in July 1857. Although he defeated a British force at Bithur, he was beaten by British General Colin Campbell [q.v.] a few days later. He joined forces with the rani of Jhansi [q.v.], and on 1 April 1858 was defeated at the siege of Jhansi by General Hugh Henry Rose [q.v.]. On 18 June he fled into the jungles of Rajputana with a small force and carried on a hit-and-run campaign until betrayed by the raja of Narwar. He was captured by forces under General Robert Napier [q.v.] and hanged on 18 April 1859.

Taos Rebellion (1847). On 19 January 1847 Charles Bent (1799–1847), a fur trader who had been appointed the first civilian governor of New Mexico Territory, was attacked at his home in Taos by Mexicans and Pueblos who opposed American rule. He and 10 others were killed. Troops sent on a punitive expedition under Colonel Sterling Price [q.v.] found and killed 150 Pueblos and wounded another 300 on 19 August. American losses were 10 soldiers killed. New Mexico was thereafter ruled by a military governor.

Tapajo. A leather blinder used by packers while packing or adjusting a disarranged load on an animal.

Tapingchaun, Battle of (21–23 February 1895), Sino-Japanese War. In bitter cold weather Japanese General Michitsura Nozu [q.v.] advanced upon and defeated the Chinese under General Sung Ching at Tapingchaun, 50 miles west of Ussuriysk. This was one of the last battles of the Sino-Japanese War [q.v.].

Taps. An American bugle call composed by General Daniel Butterfield [q.v.] at Harrison's Landing, Virginia, in 1862. It was, and is sometimes still, sounded at night as a signal to extinguish lights. The derivation of the term is uncertain. Before this call Americans used the French *l'extinction des feux* (extinguish fires). Taps is also played at military funerals and memorial services. The British equivalent is last post [q.v.].

Taranaki Wars. See Maori Wars: Second Maori War.

Tarapacá, Battle of (27 November 1879), War of the Pacific. The Chileans landed an expeditionary force at Pisagua, a small town now in Chile, 40 miles north of Iquique, and pushed through heavy opposition from Peruvian and Bolivian forces on 16 November 1879. On 27 November the Chileans suffered a repulse in the province of Tarapacá, but the Allies failed to exploit their victory, and the entire seacoast was soon in Chilean hands.

Tarbes, Battle of (20 March 1814), Peninsular War. At this city on the Adour River in southwestern France, Wellington attempted to trap Marshal Jean Soult [q.v.], who had his back to the Pyrenees, but two French divisions fought a successful rearguard action, and Soult slipped away and marched toward Toulouse.

Target. A mark at which to shoot; a point at which a weapon is aimed.

Tarifa, Siege of (19 December 1811–5 January 1812), Peninsular War. French forces, part of the army under Marshal Jean Soult [q.v.] that was besieging Cádiz, attempted to capture this seaport town, 51 miles southeast of Cádiz, but the governor of Gibraltar had moved to strengthen the town's defenses and had garrisoned it with 2,500 men, including 600 Spanish infantry. On 29 December the French created a breach in the defenses, and on 31 December 1811 they launched an assault with French grenadiers that was repulsed by the British 87th Foot. On 5 January the French abandoned their efforts, which had cost them about 1,000 casualties. The British lost 150.

Tarleton Helmet. A crested metal or leather helmet with a peaked front and plume named after British Lieutenant Colonel (later General) Banastre Tarleton (1754–1833), the "Green Dragoon," who during the American Revolution was known as Butcher Tarleton by American patriots. The helmet was worn in the British army by regular light dragoons until 1812, by the Royal Horse Artillery until 1827, and still later by some Yeomanry regiments.

Tarleton's Quarter. Showing no mercy; killing prisoners. An early nineteenth-century American colloquialism derived from the ruthless practice of British Lieutenant Colonel (later General) Banastre Tarleton (1754–1833) in the American Revolutionary War.

Tarqui, Battle of (27 February 1829), Peruvian aggression, also known as the Battle of Jirón. In 1827 José Lamar, later president of Peru, launched an invasion of Bolivia and forced President Antonio Sucre [q.v.] to flee to Ecuador. Lamar then attacked Ecuador, and a Peruvian naval squadron captured Guayaquil in January 1829, but Sucre and Ecuadorian General Juan José Flores [q.v.] led an army that defeated the Peruvians at Tarqui, on 27 February and recaptured Guayaquil the following day.

Tarragona, Sieges of. During the Peninsular War there were two sieges of this town on the Mediterranean Sea, 54 miles west-southwest of Barcelona.

Siege by the French (3 May–28 June 1811). In May 1811, when French General Louis Suchet [q.v.] laid siege to Tarragona, the Spanish garrison put up a stout defense but was gradually pushed back, and by 21 June Suchet had obtained a lodgment in the lower town. A week later he took the upper town by storm, and 8,000 survivors surrendered. Total Spanish losses were 18,000. Suchet suffered 6,000 casualties but was able to advance upon Valencia. On 1 July Suchet was created a marshal of the empire by Napoleon.

Siege by the British (2–13 June 1812). On 2 June 1812 an Allied force of 24,000 men, half Spaniards, attempted to recapture Tarragona and laid siege to it. The French garrison consisted of only 1,600, but the British commander, Major General George Murray (1772–1846), needlessly fearing a French relieving force, abandoned the siege and left in a panic after spiking his guns. Wellington believed that he lacked "sound sense" and ordered him court-martialed. The court treated him leniently, sentencing him only to be admonished, and the prince regent dispensed with that. In 1825 he was promoted full general.

Tartan. 1. Woolen cloth of varying patterns and stripes worn by Scots Highland regiments.

2. In the last part of the nineteenth century, the plain blue or green trousers worn by infantry (tartan was the type of weave).

Taruhito, Arisugawa (1835–1895). A Japanese general and the adoptive uncle of the emperor who led imperial troops against the rebels at the time of the Meiji Restoration (1868–69). In 1877 he suppressed the Satsuma Rebellion [q.v.]. As a field marshal he took part in the Sino-Japanese War [q.v.]. He represented Japan at Queen Victoria's Diamond Jubilee.

His brother Arisugawa Takehito (1862–1913) served in the Royal Navy from 1879 to 1882.

Tarutino, Battle of (18 October 1812), Napoleon's invasion of Russia. Russian General Levin Bennigsen defeated French Marshal Joachim Murat [qq.v.] near this Ukrainian town, 60 miles west of Belgorod-Dnestrovski during the French retreat from Moscow.

Tashkent / Tashkend, Siege of. See Khokand, Russian Conquest of.

Tasmania, British Conquest of (1802–30). The British attempts to occupy and settle Tasmania, a large island and many small islands south of Australia, were resisted by the estimated 5,000 Tasmanians. Near-constant warfare in the form of skirmishes took place until in 1831 the remnants of the native population, by then reduced to only 202, were induced to emigrate first to South Brunei, a 149-square-mile island, 32 miles southwest of Tasmania, and subsequently to Flinders Island, 20 miles wide and 40 miles long, off the northeast coast of Tasmania. The last pure-blooded Tasmanian died at the age of seventy-six in 1876.

Tatsumi / Tachimi, Naobumi (1845–1907). A Japanese soldier who fought in the Boshin Civil War of 1868, the Satsuma Rebellion of 1877, and the Sino-Japanese War of 1894–95 [qq.v.], in which he distinguished himself in the Battle of Pyongyang [q.v.] in 1894. He also served as a general in the Russo-Japanese War of 1904–05.

Tattoo. 1. As a noun, a nighttime drum or bugle call for soldiers to return to their quarters. In the American army it is played about fifteen minutes before taps [q.v.]. As late as 1813 it was called tapto, probably from the Dutch *taptoe*. Originally a drumbeat sounded through a camp or garrison town to alert sutlers and tavernkeepers to turn their taps "to" (to close) and troops to return to their quarters for roll call.

2. In British usage, as a noun, a military exercise held outdoors or in a large indoor arena as an entertainment.

3. As a noun, an indelible mark or design on the skin, sometimes used to mark a deserter or other military criminal [see Branding].

4. As a verb, to mark the skin with a tattoo.

5. In India, as a noun, a locally bred pony.

Taunay, Visconde de, Alfredo d'Escragnolle (1843–1899). A Brazilian military engineer, politician, and writer who served in the War of the Triple Alliance [q.v.] in 1865–70. He was the author of many plays, novels, poems, and historical sketches.

Tayeizan, Battle of (4 July 1868), Boshin Civil War. Sometimes called the Battle of Tokyo. The followers of the Takugawa shogunate made their last stand at the Tayeizan Temple in the Park of Eyeno in Edo (Tokyo), where they were defeated and massacred.

Taylor, Richard (1826–1879). The son of Zachary Taylor and the brother of the first wife of Jefferson Davis [qq.v.]. He was educated in Europe and at Harvard (briefly) and Yale, from which he was graduated in 1845. During the Mexican War [q.v.] he served for a time as his father's military secretary. At the beginning of the American Civil War he joined the Confederate army and was appointed colonel of the 9th Louisiana and arrived at Manassas on the night of the First Battle of Bull Run. He was appointed brigadier general on 21 October 1861 and advanced to major general the following 28 July. He served for a time under Thomas ("Stonewall") Jackson in the Valley Campaign [q.v.] and in the Seven Days' Battles [qq.v.]. He successfully defeated the Red River Expedition [q.v.] of Nathaniel Banks [q.v.] and was promoted lieutenant general, to rank from 8 April 1865. The following month he surrendered the last Confederate force west of the Mississippi River. After the war he attempted with little success to obtain a diminution of the severity of the Reconstruction Acts.

Taylor's Bridge, Battle of. See North Anna River, Battle of.

Taylor, Zachary (1784–1850). An American soldier and politician (nicknamed Old Rough and Ready) who entered the army as a first lieutenant in 1808 and was promoted captain two years later. In the War of 1812 [q.v.] he won distinction for his defense of Fort Harrison on the Wabash River in Indiana Territory and was brevetted major. He was a colonel in the Black Hawk War [q.v.] and took part in the Battle of Bad Axe [q.v.]. In 1837, during the Second Seminole War [q.v.], he defeated Seminole and Mikisuki Indians on the north shore of Lake Okeechobee in south-central Florida [see

General Zachary Taylor

Okeechobee, Battle of] and was made a brevet brigadier general.

On 8 May 1846 at Palo Alto he fought and won the first pitched battle of the Mexican War [q.v.]. The following day he fought and won a battle at Resaca de la Palma [q.v.]. He occupied Matamoros on 18 May and soon after was promoted major general. On 21–24 September he captured Monterrey [q.v.]. On 21–23 February 1847 he defeated a vastly superior Mexican force under Santa Anna [q.v.] at Buena Vista [q.v.].

In June 1848 the Whig Party nominated Taylor, who had no discernible opinion on any of the major issues of the day, had no political experience, and had never voted in a presidential election and was thus an atttractive political figure, as its candidate for president of the United States. He won the nomination, but since he was notoriously stingy, he did not learn of his nomination for several weeks because he refused to pay the postage due on a letter from Whig party leaders. He was elected president but died after only a year and four months in office.

Tchapka. See Shapska.

Tchernaiev, Mikhail Gregorjovich. See Chernyaiev, Mikhail Grigorievich.

Tchernaya, Battle of. See Chernaya.

Teb, El, Battle of. See El Teb, Battles of.

Tebe, Marie (fl. 1860s). An American vivandière [q.v.] with the 114th Pennsylvania Volunteers during the American Civil War. The regiment, dressed as Zouaves, was composed of wealthy young men from Philadelphia who provided the young woman, probably in her twenties, with a uniform and paid her a salary. She joined on 17 August 1861 and served with the regiment through all its campaigns in the eastern theater. General David Birney [q.v.] awarded her a medal for her gallantry in the Battle of Chancellorsville [q.v.], in which she braved bullets to move among the thirsty troops with a canteen. She found fault with the medal, complaining that it was copper, not gold. She was said to have lost heavily in a gambling craze that swept through the Army of the Potomac. She was mustered out with her regiment on 29 May 1865. Her subsequent life is unknown.

Teck, Francis Paul Louis Alexander, Duke of (1830?–1900). The Duke of Teck was educated at the Austrian Academy of Engineers (1849–53) and served as a soldier in the Austrian and British armies. During the Austro-Piedmontese War he accompanied Field Marshal Emmanuel Wimpffen [q.v.] to Italy, and in 1859 he distinguished himself in the Battle of Solferino [q.v.]. In 1882, during Arabi's Revolt [q.v.], he served on the staff of Sir Garnet Wolseley [q.v.] and distinguished himself in the Battle of Tell el-Kebir [q.v.]. In 1892 he became a British major general.

Tecovac, Battle of (16 November 1876), Mexican Revolution. The death of Benito Pablo Juárez [q.v.] was followed by more than the usual turmoil in Mexico until General Porfirio Díaz [q.v.] defeated the forces of his principal rival, Sebastián

Lerdo de Tejada (1825–1889), in this battle. On 12 May 1877 Díaz was elected president. He remained Mexico's strong man until 1911. Lerdo de Tejada was exiled and died in New York.

Tecumseh (1768–1813). An American Indian leader who was born in a Shawnee village in the Ohio wilderness. In 1774 his father was brutally murdered by white men who had crossed onto Indian lands in violation of a recent treaty. Although he was a child at the time, Tecumseh resolved that when he was grown, he would become a warrior like his father and be "a fire spreading in the hill and valley, consuming the race of dark souls."

At the age of sixteen he joined a band of Shawnees who attempted to stop the white invasion of their lands by intercepting settlers' flatboats coming down the Ohio River from Pennsylvania. On one occasion a captured white man was burned alive, a practice that is said to have revolted Tecumseh. Eventually he became the leader of his own band, and for a time the Indians were so effective that river traffic was almost stopped.

In 1805 Tecumseh allied himself with his younger brother Elskwatawa or Tenskwatawa, known as the Shawnee Prophet, who preached a return to fundamental Shawnee values, an end to tribal wars and a rejection of all aspects of white civilization, an ardent appeal that spread quickly across the Northwest Territory. Gen. William Henry Harrison [q.v.], the governor of Indiana Territory, attempted without success to destroy his influence.

In August 1809 Tecumseh and his brother met with Harrison, and in a tense confrontation in front of the governor's mansion, Harrison demanded that they have faith in the protections provided by treaties. Tecumseh answered, "How can we have confidence in the white people? When Jesus Christ came upon the earth you killed Him and nailed Him to a cross." Harrison assessed Tecumseh as "one of those uncommon geniuses who spring up occasionally to produce revolutions and overturn the established order of things."

With the failure of the conference Harrison decided that Tecumseh would have to be crushed. When Tecumseh began to travel in the South, attempting to garner support for an Indian confederation that could oppose the white men, Harrison decided that the time had come. On 7 November 1811, during Tecumseh's absence, Harrison struck at the village Tecumseh and his brother had established to accommodate the numerous converts from other tribes who had joined them [see Tippecanoe, Battle of].

Undeterred, Tecumseh rallied support for the British during the War of 1812 [q.v.] and raised a force of about 3,000 that aided British General Isaac Brock [q.v.] in repelling the invasion of Canada and the capture of Detroit from Brigadier General William Hull [q.v.]. He fell mortally wounded in the Battle of the Thames [q.v.] in Ontario on 5 October 1813, and his dream of an Indian confederation died with him. He was said to have been killed by Colonel Richard Mentor Johnson (1780–1850), who fought in the battle as a cavalry commander and in 1836 became the only vice president of the United States ever to be elected by the Senate. Still, no one was certain that Tecumseh was killed, only that he was never seen again.

On the battlefield an impressive-looking dead Indian was thought to be Tecumseh by some soldiers, who cut strips of his flesh to tan and make razor strops or other leather souvenirs of the occasion.

Tecumseh *Popular rendition of reputed rescue by Tecumseh of tortured white captives.*

Tekke Campaign, Russian (1779–1881). In 1879 the Russians launched an attack upon the Dengeel Tepe fortifications of the Tekkes, a Muslim tribe of Turkomens who inhabited Transcaspia, the area between the Caspian Sea and Amu Darya (ancient Oxus) River. They were repulsed with heavy losses. The following year the Russians laid a single-track railroad across the desert from the Caspian Sea to Mulla Kari, where they built a water distillation plant. Then an army of 8,000 men with 52 guns and 12 Gatling-type machine guns under General Mikhail Skobelev, with Aleksei Kuropatkin [qq.v.] as chief of staff, was transported to the railhead, from which they marched 500 miles to attack Akkal Oasis. There on 4 January 1881 they laid siege to the sizable fortress of Geok Tepe. On 17 January a Russian mine breached the wall. The place was taken by storm, and the Tekkes fled, pursued by Cossacks [see Geok Tepe, Sieges of]. In spite of the campaign's success the pacification of Transcaspia remained a problem for years and gave rise to considerable bloodshed.

Telegraph. The invention of the electrical telegraph by Samuel Finley Breese Morse (1791–1872) in 1844 was one of the many inventions of the nineteenth century that eventually changed strategy and tactics. In 1853 Wilhelm Julius Gintl, an Austrian telegraphist, invented the duplex system, enabling two messages to be sent in opposite directions simultaneously.

The first military use of the telegraph occurred in 1854, during the Crimean War [q.v.], when a submarine cable 547 kilometers long was laid between Varna, Bulgaria, and the Crimean Peninsula. From Varna a regular telegraph linked Paris and London. Later the telegraph was used effectively by the British during the Indian Mutiny [q.v.]. The electrical telegraph soon replaced the Chappe visual telegraph [q.v.], and in the 1860s all major locations in Europe were linked, greatly expediting mobilization. However, it was 1870 before the British army formed its first telegraph troop, with Binden Blood [q.v.] as its first commander. In 1871 the Society of Telegraph Engineers (later the Institution of Electrical Engineers) was formed.

On 29 April 1861, during the American Civil War, the War Department seized the commercial telegraph systems around Washington, D.C., and gave control of them to Thomas Alexander Scott (1823–1881), vice-president of the Pennsylvania Railroad, who in August was appointed to the newly created post of assistant secretary of war. In October of the same year the U.S. army established the Military Telegraph Service as a civilian unit in the Quartermaster's Department under Anson Stagger (1825–1912), superintendent of Western Union, who was commissioned a colonel [see Beardslee Magneto-Electric Field Telegraph Machine]. By 1864 it had put into use more than 6,500 miles of wire, 76 miles of which were underwater cables. The corps was disbanded in 1866.

Telek. A dagger used by the Tuaregs [q.v.] in the Sahara. It had a straight double-edged blade 12 to 16 inches long, diamond-shaped in cross section, and tapered to a fine point. The pommel was in the form of a cross, and the sheath was often of decorated leather [see Takouba].

Telephone. In 1876 Alexander Graham Bell (1847–1922),

Telegraph *Union military telegraph construction corps, April 1864. Photograph by Alexander Gardner*

an American speech therapist, invented the telephone. Four years later it was in general use, but its employment in nineteenth-century warfare was limited, for the equipment was not sufficiently robust for field service, and it made no real contribution to the conduct of war. In 1878 George C. Maynard, an electrician, ran a telephone line from the office of the chief signal officer in Washington, D.C., across the Potomac River to Fort Myer. In 1885 the German army first used telephones for the direction of artillery fire by forward observers. That same year in the United States a field telephone was used between the firing line and target shelters on a rifle range. In 1895 two American Signal Corps officers, Captain Charles E. Kilbourne (1848?–1903) and Captain Richard E. Thompson (1846?–1903), designed a portable model. The British used the instrument to some extent in the Second Anglo-Boer War, and the Americans in the Spanish-American War [qq.v.].

Tell el-Kebir, Battle of (13 September 1882), Arabi's Revolt. After deceiving the Egyptains into thinking he would land at Alexandria, Sir Garnet Wolseley [q.v.] landed nearly 40,000 men at Ismailia, beginning on 20 August. General Gerald Graham [q.v.] was dispatched with 2,000 men to seize the Sweetwater Canal at Kassassin. Wolseley, with 17,400 men and 67 guns, made a rare night approach march across the Egyptian desert, using naval officers as navigators, and at first light he attacked 22,000 Egyptians with 60 guns entrenched along the railway and the sweet-water canal between Cairo and Zigazag. British surprise was complete, and the Egyptians, driven from their positions, fled toward Cairo. British losses were 58 killed, 379 wounded, and 22 missing; Egyptian losses were estimated at 2,500, and all their guns were taken.

Tell el-Kebir *Sir Garnet Wolseley at the Battle of Tell el-Kebir, Egypt, 13 September 1882*

Temesvár, Battle of. See Timişoara / Temesvár, Battle of.

Temperance / Abstinence Societies. Measures designed to keep soldiers from drink have been common but usually unsuccessful. In Britain, service temperance societies offered medals to men who were able to stay sober for a specified period. In 1862 an organization formed in India as the Soldiers' Total Abstinence Association grew to become the Royal Army Temperance Association, headed by generals of high rank,

most of whom would not themselves have considered giving up their wine.

Until 1830 whiskey was issued as a ration in the American army, and even after that date it was issued to the sick, to all on Christmas and other holidays, and to men on special duty. The French soldier was issued wine; the British soldier, rum; the German soldier, beer.

Temple, Richard Carnac (1850–1931). A British soldier and Orientalist who served in the Second Afghan War and the Third Anglo-Burmese War [qq.v.] in 1885. In 1894 he was chief commissioner of the Andaman and Nicobar Islands. He founded and edited *Punjab Notes and Queries*.

Tenaille. An outwork with two faces in fortifications located in the main ditch between two bastions.

Tenaillon. In fortifications, works constructed on each side of a ravelin to cover the shoulders of the bastions or to provide extra strength. It is similar to a lunette.

Tennessee, Confederate Army of. In the American Civil War, the principal Confederate army in the western theater, formed under General Braxton Bragg [q.v.] on 20 November 1862 by a merger of the Central Army of Kentucky under General Edmund Kirby Smith [q.v.] with Bragg's smaller Army of Mississippi. Its first engagement was at Stones River [q.v.], and at that time it numbered about 38,000 effectives. In September 1863 Bragg was reinforced to 47,500 infantry and 14,500 cavalry. After the Battle of Chickamauga [q.v.] the army was reorganized into three corps.

On 2 December 1863 Bragg was relieved of his command and replaced by General Joseph E. Johnston [q.v.], who in turn on 18 July 1864 was replaced by General John Hood [q.v.], who, after an unsuccessful tour, was relieved at his own request. On 23 January 1865 Hood was replaced by Richard Taylor [q.v.]. On 23 February Johnston again assumed command of a much-weakened army of about 20,000, which on 26 April he surrendered.

Tennessee, Hood's Invasion of (18 September 1864–10 January 1865), American Civil War. After abandoning Atlanta on 1 September 1864, Confederate General John Hood [q.v.] determined to strike the line of communications of Union General William Tecumseh Sherman [q.v.]. In October he destroyed some railroad facilities, but he was repulsed at Allattoona Pass [q.v.]. After suffering setbacks at Franklin and Nashville [qq.v.], Hood retreated, having accomplished little, and was relieved at his own request.

Tennessee, Union Army of the, American Civil War. The Union Department and Army of the Tennessee was formed on 16 October 1862 under the command of Major General U. S. Grant, but from 24 October 1863 to 26 March 1864 it was commanded by William Tecumseh Sherman [q.v.]. Major General James B. McPherson [q.v.] then commanded the army until he was killed at Atlanta on 22 July 1864. Subsequently the army was commanded by John A. Logan and Otis O. Howard [qq.v.].

Tennessee Quick Step. During the American Civil War

the grimly humorous soldier's term for diarrhea and dysentery.

Tents. Except for use as hospitals and unit headquarters, tents were seldom seen in nineteenth-century field armies. Napoleon disapproved of them, claiming they were "injurious to health" and that they "attract the attention of the enemy's staff." But the practice of soldiers' sleeping on the ground in all weathers led Elzéar Blaze, a French officer, to remark that "heroes have the gout and rheumatism." [See Pup Tent.]

Tents *Hospital tent (left) and Sibley tent*

Ten Years' War (1868–78), Cuban Revolutions. In the 1860s many Cubans opposed Spanish rule, which levied and increased taxes while it excluded them from the government. After Queen Isabella II (1830–1904) was deposed in the Spanish Revolution of 1868, many saw this as an opportunity to throw off the Spanish yoke. Hostilities began on 10 October 1868, when Carlos Manuel de Céspedes (1819–1874), a wealthy landowner at Yara, proclaimed a revolution and promised reforms, including the gradual emancipation of slaves with compensation to their owners. Most of the fighting took place in western Cuba, and as the war dragged on, it was marked by excesses on both sides. The government became increasingly repressive, and the rebels became more cruel and violent. Among the rebel leaders who emerged were Máximo Gómez y Báez, José Julián Martí, and Calixto García y Íñiguez [qq.v.], all of whom took part in later revolutions. The Spanish forces were led by General Valeriano Weyler y Nicolau [q.v.].

In January 1878 Spanish General Arsenio Martínez de Campos [q.v.] signed the Convention of Zanjón, by which the government agreed to an amnesty and the liberation of slaves. The insurgents laid down their arms, but the promised reforms were more superficial than substantive, and the level of discontent increased. There was a Little War in 1879–80, but it was soon ended. An estimated 200,000 Cubans and Spaniards were killed in the Ten Years' War, which was a prelude to the Cuban War of Independence [see Cuban Revolutions].

Terauchi, Makakata (1852–1919). A Japanese soldier who fought in the Choshu clan army during the Boshin Civil War [q.v.] of 1868 and entered the imperial army as a sergeant in

1870. He was commissioned a lieutenant in 1871 and was severely wounded during the Satsuma Rebellion [q.v.] in 1877, losing the use of one arm. In 1897 he became a major general. He was on the joint staff during the Sino-Japanese War [q.v.] of 1894–95. From 1902 to 1911 he was minister of war. He was promoted field marshal in 1916.

Terreplein. 1. The level space behind a parapet where guns are mounted or the level ground around the interior of any fortification. It is ground upon which men can stand protected and ready to fight.

2. The rear talus of a rampart.

Terry, Alfred Howe (1827–1890). A lawyer educated at Yale, he turned Union soldier during the American Civil War and fought as a colonel of the 2nd Connecticut at First Bull Run [q.v.]. He took part in the capture of Port Royal, South Carolina, in November 1861 and Fort Pulaski, Georgia [q.v.], in April 1862. In December 1864 and January 1865 he commanded the land forces in the assault and capture of Fort Fisher [q.v.], for which on 24 January he was tendered the Thanks of Congress. He rose to the rank of major general and commanded a corps. After the war he remained in the army and commanded the Department of the Dakotas from 1866 to 1868 and from 1873 to 1886. It was he who sent Lieutenant Colonel George Custer [q.v.] to reconnoiter toward the Bighorn River, and his arrival with the rest of his command on the battlefield of the Little Bighorn [q.v.] on 27 June 1876, two days after the main battle, rescued the battle's survivors. He became a major general on 3 March 1886, one of only three authorized at that time and the first Civil War volunteer to reach that grade in the regular army.

Terzo. The middle third of the blade of an edged weapon.

Tesak / Tessak. A short sword worn by Russian artillerymen in the Caucasian Corps [q.v.].

Tête-de-Pont. A fortified semicircle with its back to a river covering one or more crossings. A bridgehead.

Teton Sioux. A confederation of American Indian tribes—Oglala Sioux, Brûlé, Hunkpapa, Miniconjou, Sans Arc, Two Kettle, and Blackfoot—who lived in territory bounded by the Missouri, Yellowstone, Powder, and North Platte rivers and with whom the U.S. army often contended between 1850 and 1890 [see Great Sioux War].

Tetuán, Battle of (4 February 1860), Spanish-Moroccan War. Near this city on the Mediterranean coast, 25 miles south of Ceuta, a Spanish army of 30,000 under Marshal Leopoldo O'Donnell [q.v.] drove 40,000 Moors out of their entrenchments. Three days later the Spanish entered the town.

Texas Rangers. 1. A semimilitary police force organized in Texas in 1835–36 to protect settlers from Indians, rustlers, and desperadoes. In the 1840s General Sam Houston [q.v.]

A rare photograph of Texas Rangers

increased its strength to 1,600. Its members were picked men, equipped with revolvers and saddle guns; they never drilled and never wore uniforms. In the 1870s they reached their peak of usefulness.

2. During the American Civil War a volunteer regiment, the 8th Texas Cavalry, was generally called the Texas Rangers. It acquired a fine war record fighting in the West.

Texas War of Independence (1836). The migration of Americans into Texas began in 1821, when Moses Austin (1761–1821) received a charter and a grant of land from the government of New Spain to form a settlement of 200 families. Before the settlers arrived, Austin died, and the newly independent state of Mexico replaced the Spanish government. However, Austin's son Stephen Fuller Austin (1793–1836) had the charter confirmed, and in 1824, when the Republic of Mexico was established under a constitution, Texas became a Mexican state. In 1830 the Mexican government prohibited further settlements by Americans in one of several laws enacted that the settlers regarded as a violation of their rights. When Austin went to Mexico City to protest, he was imprisoned for eight months. Relations between Texan colonists and Mexico deteriorated steadily until on 12 October 1835 the first clash between rebel Texans and Mexican troops occurred just south of Gonzales. The Mexicans were defeated. On 28 October the Texans routed a larger Mexican force two miles south of San Antonio. Although the United States was neutral, a number of American volunteers, such as the Alabama Red Shirts [q.v.], came to help the "Texians," as they were sometimes called. On 7 December 1835 Texans briefly seized San Antonio [q.v.]. Mexican General Antonio López de Santa Anna [q.v.] led an army of 6,000 against them and entered the city on 23 February.

On 1 March 1836 a convention was convened in Washington, Texas. Within a few days it declared Texas independent and appointed Sam Houston [q.v.] to command a provisional army. On 6 March, while the convention was still in session, Santa Anna captured the Alamo [q.v.], where for twelve days 182 Texans had held out. Three weeks later he defeated a force of 300 Texans in the Battle of Goliad and killed all the prisoners [see Goliad Massacre].

On 21 April Houston led his quickly assembled army in an attack upon 1,200 Mexicans under Santa Anna camped on the western side of the San Jacinto River. Shouting, "Remember the Alamo!," in twenty minutes the Texans scored a decisive victory and captured Santa Anna [see San Jacinto, Battle of]. Santa Anna then ordered the remainder of his army to leave Texas and acceded to Texan independence. The Mexican Congress repudiated his agreement, but an independent Texas had become a reality.

Although in 1836 the citizens of Texas voted overwhelmingly to become part of the United States, the American government rejected the notion. Texas was not admitted as the twenty-eighth state until 29 December 1845.

Texas War of Independence *Texas volunteers capture San Antonio, 7 December 1835.*

Thaba Bosigo / Thaba Bosiu. A flat-topped mountain about four miles in circumference in Basutoland (Lesotho) where Moshesh [q.v.], a Basuto chief, established a stronghold in 1832. It is a natural fortress, rising 400 feet above the plain and surrounded by cliffs that are broken only by six easily defended passes to the summit. Its name means "mountain of the night." It was frequently but unsuccessfully attacked by Zulus and other South African tribes. In August 1865 Boers from the Orange Free State under Lourens Jacobus Wepener [q.v.] attempted to storm the place, but they were beaten off, and Wepener was killed. Neither white nor black antagonists ever succeeded in capturing it.

Thaba Bosigo *Boers unsuccessfully attack Moshesh's stronghold at Thaba Bosigo, August 1865*

Thackwell, Joseph (1781–1859). A British soldier who began his military career in 1798 as a cornet in the Worcester Fencible Cavalry and served with it in Ireland. When the unit was disbanded in 1800, he obtained a commission in the 15th Light Dragoons. In 1808, during the Peninsular War [q.v.], he went with his regiment to Spain, where he took part in the Battle of Vitoria [q.v.] and the final battles of the war. In 1815 he fought in the Battle of Waterloo [q.v.], in which he lost his left arm. He married at the age of forty-four and sired four sons and three daughters. In 1837 he was sent to India, where he commanded the cavalry of the Army of the Indus in the First Afghan War [q.v.]. He served in the Gwalior Campaign and both Sikh wars [qq.v.]. In 1854 he was appointed inspector of cavalry and promoted lieutenant general.

Thames, Battle of the (5 October 1813), War of 1812.

Against the advice of Tecumseh [q.v.], the Shawnee chief, the 800 British regulars and their 1,000 Indian allies, all under Brigadier General Henry A. Procter, evacuated Detroit and retreated into Canada. They were pursued by 4,500 American regulars and militia under Major General William Henry Harrison [q.v.], who overtook them in southeastern Ontario and decisively defeated them on the banks of the Thames River, near Moraviantown, just east of Thanesville, about 55 miles east of Detroit. The Indians held firm until Tecumseh was killed, perhaps by Richard Mentor Johnson [q.v.], later vice president of the United States.

Without Tecumseh's leadership the Indians fled the field, leaving 35 dead. The British lost 12 killed, 22 wounded, and 477 taken prisoner. The Americans lost 7 killed and 22 wounded. Harrison became a national hero. When he was ordered to disband his militia and send his regulars to the Niagara area, he resigned his commission in a fit of anger.

Thanks of Congress or Parliament. The expression of formal, official gratitude to a soldier, usually a victorious general, for war services. A public acknowledgment given by the American Congress or the British Parliament for distinguished services.

Thayer, Sylvanus (1785–1872). An American soldier and educator who was graduated from West Point in 1808 and commissioned in the Corps of Engineers. In 1815 he was sent to Europe to study European armies, fortifications, and military schools. On his return in 1817 he was appointed superintendent of the U.S. Military Academy at West Point, New York, a post he held until 1833, earning the accolade of the Father of the Military Academy. He organized the corps of cadets into tactical units; held cadets and professors to high academic standards; established the Academic Board [q.v.], composed of the permanent faculty members, to advise him on academic requirements; insisted on weekly reports on each cadet; and created the post of commandant of cadets to instill military discipline. The high standards of personal conduct to which he held the cadets more than once sparked rebellions [see Egg Nog Riot]. During his first year he court-martialed and dismissed 5 cadets who, speaking for 200 others, demanded a say in the management of the academy. The dismissed cadets appealed to Congress, demanding an investigation of the "monarchical ideas of its present ruler, whom they described as advanced in depravity." Francis H. Smith [q.v.], who was graduated in Thayer's last year and became superintendent of the Virginia Military Institute [q.v.], said of him: "It was useless to attempt to awaken tender emotions in him. He was not without feeling, but never displayed it in his *office*. That office . . . a judgement hall, which no cadet entered without a sentiment of awe, or left without a feeling of relief."

From 1833 to 1863 he served on harbor fortifications and improvements. In 1867 he established and endowed the Thayer School of Engineering at Dartmouth College.

Theater of War. Synonymous with "seat of war." Any extent of land upon which war is being waged or is expected to be waged.

Theodore of Abyssinia (1818?–1868), originally Kasa or Kassa Tewodorus. An Abyssinian (Ethiopian) whose father was a local chief and whose uncle was a governor of Kwara,

Thames *Death of Tecumseh at the Battle of the Thames*

three districts between Lake Tana and Abyssinia's ill-defined northwestern frontier. In 1855 Theodore overthrew the ras (chief) of Tigre, a northern province. He proceeded to lead revolts and military expeditions, warring against the Gallas and conquering the central Ethiopian province and former kingdom of Shoa, and he finally had himself crowned negus of Abyssinia. His tyrannical rule provoked rebellion, and in 1861–62 the Boghos in the Keren (Cheren) region, later part of Eritrea, successfully threw off his yoke [see Abyssinian Civil Wars].

In 1864, accusing Britain of aiding Egypt and Turkey in opposing him, he imprisoned among other Europeans, C. A. Cameron, the British consul, an act that provoked the British to launch the Abyssinian Expedition [q.v.] under General Robert Napier [q.v.]. When Napier successfully assaulted his stronghold at Magdala on 13 April 1868, Theodore killed himself.

Theron, Daniel (1870–1900). An Afrikaner hero of the Second Anglo-Boer War [q.v.]. Before the war he had been a law agent in Krugersdorp whose only claim to fame was the drubbing he once gave a newspaper editor who had published remarks he considered insulting to womanhood. At the beginning of the war he was made captain of the Transvaal Cyclist Corps, but after the Battle of Colenso [q.v.] he was put in charge of a band of scouts whose feats of daring became legendary. He was killed in action in 1900.

Thesiger, Frederic Augustus, Second Baron Chelmsford (1827–1905). A British soldier educated at Eton and commissioned into the Rifle Brigade on 31 December 1844. He served in the Crimean War and the Indian Mutiny [qq.v.]. On 15 March 1877 he was promoted major general, and in February 1878 he was sent to South Africa with the local rank of lieutenant general. In January 1879 he invaded Zululand in three columns, he himself accompanying the central column [see Zulu War]. While he led half the column on a reconnaissance, the remainder was destroyed by Zulus in the Battle of

Isandhlwana [q.v.] on 22 January, a disaster that brought the invasion to a halt. It was not resumed until June, when reinforcements arrived. Dismay over Isandhlwana caused the home government to replace Chelmsford with Lord Wolseley [q.v.], but before Wolseley could arrive, Chelmsford had captured the Zulu capital of Ulundi, routed the Zulus, and ended the war.

He was promoted lieutenant general in 1882 and was placed on the retired list in 1893. He died while playing billiards at the United Service Club [q.v.] in London.

Thesiger, Frederic *Return of King Cetewayo's ambassadors to Lord Chelmsford's camp, 27 June 1879*

Thielmann, Johann Adolf, Freiherr von (1765–1824). A German soldier, born a Saxon, who fought in the Prussian army in the Battle of Jena [q.v.] on 14 October 1806 and in the defense of Danzig (Gdansk) from 18 March until 27 May 1807 [see Danzig / Gdansk, Sieges of]. On 14 June he took part in the Battle of Friedland [q.v.]. As a colonel in a *Freikorps* in 1809 he opposed the invasion of Saxony by

Austria. In the same year he was promoted major general. The following year he became a lieutenant general, and in 1812 he commanded a brigade of Saxon cuirassiers in the Russian army and served with distinction in the Battle of Borodino [q.v.] on 7 September [see Russian Campaign, Napoleon's]. In 1813 he commanded the fortress of Torgau on the Elbe River. When ordered to join Napoleon, he refused and on 12 May deserted to the Allies. On 28 September he defeated General Charles Lefebvre-Desnouëttes [q.v.] in the Battle of Altenberg. In 1815 he commanded the Prussian III Corps under Field Marshal Gebhard von Blücher [q.v.] and was engaged at Ligny, where he commanded the left of the line, and at Wavre [qq.v.], where he fought a valiant rearguard action with only 25,000 men against two French army corps under General Emmanuel Grouchy [q.v.], an action that enabled Blücher and the rest of the Prussian army to assist Wellington in the Battle of Waterloo [q.v.].

Thin Red Line. This expression for a line of red-coated British infantry in battle was a corruption of the words of *The Times* (London) correspondent William Howard Russell [q.v.], who during the Crimean War [q.v.], reporting the charge of the Russian Kievski Hussar Regiment No. 11 against the 93rd Highlanders (later Argyll and Sutherland Highlanders) under General Colin Campbell [q.v.] on 25 October 1854 at Balaclava, wrote: "The Russians dashed on towards that thin red streak tipped with a line of steel." Rudyard Kipling helped immortalize the expression in the poem "Tommy" when he wrote: "But it's 'Thin red line of 'eroes' when the drums begin to roll. . . ."

Third Lieutenant. In the American army, a rank just below a second lieutenant established in January 1813. One such officer, called a coronet in the cavalry and an ensign [q.v.] in the infantry, was authorized for each company. The rank was abolished in the cavalry in 1814, in the infantry in 1815, and in the artillery in 1818. In the twentieth century it was revived for the lowest rank in the Philippine Scouts. [See Ensign.]

Thirty Days' War. See Graeco-Turkish War.

Thirty Years' Peace. A name for the period in American history between 1815, when the War of 1812 [q.v.] ended, and the beginning of the Mexican War [qq.v.], in 1846. In this period, however, the United States fought three major campaigns: the First Seminole War in 1817–19, the Black Hawk War in 1832, and the Second Seminole War [qq.v.] in 1835–43, as well as numerous lesser engagements with Indians east of the Mississippi River.

Thomas, Evan (1843–1873). An American soldier and a son of Lorenzo Thomas [q.v.]. He was commissioned a second lieutenant in the 4th Artillery on 9 April 1861 and as a Union officer won brevets to captain in the course of the American Civil War. In November 1865 he was charged with wounding a civilian in Georgetown, D.C. (annexed to Washington, D.C., in 1878), and, together with two fellow 4th Artillery officers who had tried to abet his escape from jail, was court-martialed and sentenced to suspension of rank and pay for a year.

In 1873, during the Modoc War [q.v.], he fought in the lava beds of northeastern California, and there on 26 April

with a reconnaissance party of 5 officers and 59 enlisted men he was ambushed by Scarface Charlie [q.v.], one of the more effective warrior leaders of Captain Jack [q.v.]. Many of the soldiers panicked. While their officers struggled to keep them from fleeing, Thomas rallied them with the cry "We must fight and die like men and soldiers." When he fell mortally wounded, he refused to allow himself to be moved to the rear, saying, "I will not retreat a step farther. This is as good a place to die as any." Only 1 officer survived the ambush; 5, including Thomas, were killed or mortally wounded. Of the 59 enlisted men, 18 were killed, and about as many more wounded.

Thomas, George (1756?–1802). An Irish adventurer and soldier of fortune who began his career as a sailor in the British navy but about 1781 deserted a man-of-war at Madras and joined the service of the Poligar chiefs of the Carnatic. In 1787 he served the begum Sumru of Sirdhana, who appointed him her commander-in-chief. In 1788 he distinguished himself in the siege of Gokalgarh, saving the life of the Mogul emperor. In 1792 he was degraded and left the begum's army for the service of the Scindia ruler of Meerut, in northern India, for whom he raised and drilled an army. Having been rewarded by gifts of lands, he built a fort which he called Georgegarh, established a military post at Hansi, and began a program of expansion, finally forming a separate state and becoming the most powerful ruler on the right bank of the Jumna River. He acquired enormous wealth and maintained a large army that made forays upon his Sikh neighbors. In 1802 Sikhs and Marathas united to defeat him with 32,000 men and 110 cannon, and he was forced to surrender Georgegarh [see Skinner, James]. He was captured at Hansi and, carrying a concealed fortune in rubies, was escorted over the border into British territory. He died that same year.

Thomas, George Henry (1816–1870). An American soldier who was graduated from West Point in 1840 and entered the artillery. He earned a brevet in the Second Seminole War, and in the Mexican War [qq.v.] he gained brevets to captain and major for gallantry in the battles of Monterrey and Buena Vista [qq.v.]. On 26 August 1860 he was wounded by arrows in a fight with Indians while on a scouting expedition at the headwaters of the Colorado and Concho rivers.

Thomas, George Henry *General Thomas's bivouac after the first day's battle at Chickamauga, 19–20 September 1863.*

Although born in Virginia, he remained loyal to the Union in the American Civil War in spite of the objections of his sisters, who never again spoke to him. In August 1861, after the First Battle of Bull Run [q.v.], he was appointed brigadier general of volunteers. Almost all his service was in the western theater, where he commanded the forces that dispersed the Confederates under F. K. Zollicoffer [q.v.] at Mill Springs [q.v.], Kentucky, on 19 January 1862. He took part in the Battle of Shiloh [q.v.] and was promoted major general of volunteers to rank from 25 April. He distinguished himself in the battles of Corinth, Perryville, Stones River, and Chickamauga [qq.v.]. For his heroic stand in the latter he was dubbed the Rock of Chickamauga. He fought at Chattanooga, and in the Atlanta Campaign he commanded the Army of the Cumberland [qq.v.]. In September 1864 he was sent to repel the attempt of General John Hood [q.v.] to destroy the line of communications of William T. Sherman [q.v.], and on 15–16 December 1864 he defeated Hood at the Battle of Nashville [q.v.]. After the war he was commander of the Division of the Pacific. He died of apoplexy in San Francisco on 28 March 1870.

Thomas, Lorenzo (1804–1875). An American soldier who was graduated from West Point in 1823. He served in the Mexican War [q.v.] and won a brevet to lieutenant colonel for gallantry in the Battle of Monterrey [q.v.]. From 1861 to 1863, during the American Civil War, he was adjutant general of the Union army. In 1863–65 he was in Mississippi organizing regiments of blacks. In March 1865 he was brevetted major general, and after the war he was again appointed adjutant general.

In 1868, at the height of the conflict between President Andrew Johnson (1808–1875) and Secretary of War Edwin Stanton [q.v.], Johnson dismissed Stanton and appointed Thomas interim secretary of war. Stanton, backed by Congress, resisted removal, and Thomas was arrested for violation of the Tenure of Office Act, over which Johnson was subsequently impeached. Thomas resumed his duties as adjutant general and retired in February 1869.

Thomas, Minor T. (1830–1897). An American engineer and soldier who on 29 April 1861, at the beginning of the American Civil War, joined the Union army as a second lieutenant in the 1st Minnesota. He was wounded at First Bull Run [q.v.] and on 18 October was named lieutenant colonel of the 4th Minnesota. During the Sioux uprising in Minnesota [q.v.] he took command of Fort Ripley and in the summer of 1864 assembled a brigade of 2,100 men of all arms that, under the command of General Alfred Sully [q.v.], defeated the Sioux in the Battle of Killdeer Mountain [q.v.] on 28 July. Because Sully was ill, Thomas actually commanded during the battle. Later he fought in the Battle of Murfreesboro [q.v.] and at the end of the war was brevetted brigadier general. After the war he practiced civil engineering in Minnesota.

Thomas Cook and Son. A British travel agency that became famous for its circular tours of Europe and the completeness of its travel arrangements and its provision of modern comforts to Europeans visiting Egypt and the Middle East. In 1870 John Mason Cook (1834–1899), the son of the founder, Thomas Cook (1808–1892), was appointed travel agent for passenger traffic on the Nile by both steamer and *dhahabiya,* the sturdy sailboats of the Nile. In 1884 the British government gave the company a contract to carry army stores and personnel from Asyut to Wadi Halfa for the Gordon Relief Expedition [q.v.]. In 1884 and 1885 it transported 17,000 British and Egyptian troops, 800 small boats, 40,000 tons of stores, and 40,000 tons of coal in 27 steamers and 650 sailboats of from 70 to 200 tons capacity. The company is still in existence.

Thompson, John Reuben (1823–1873). A journalist and poet who from 1846 to 1860 was editor of the *Southern Literary Messenger*. During the American Civil War he served as an assistant secretary to John Letcher (1813–1884), the governor of Virginia.

Many of his war poems became popular: "Ashby," "Lee to the Rear," and "The Burial of Latane" [see Latane, William]. He also assisted in the writing of Johann Heros von Borcke's [q.v.] *Memoirs of the Confederate War of Independence* (1866).

Thompson, Thomas Perronet (1783–1869). A British soldier, colonial administrator, and politician who at age fifteen was sent to Queen's College, Cambridge, where he took his degree at the age of nineteen. He then entered the Royal Navy as a midshipman. On the Newfoundland station, when several West Indiamen were recaptured from the French, he was given command of one and sailed it safely to port. In 1804 he was elected a fellow of Queen's College, "a sort of promotion," he said, "which has not often gone along with the rank and dignity of midshipman." After nearly four years in the navy, he was commissioned in 1806 in the 95th Rifles (later the Rifle Brigade) and in 1807 took part in the British expedition to Buenos Aires [q.v.], in the course of which he was captured by the Spanish. Released after a short imprisonment, he returned to England, where in July 1808, at the age of twenty-five, he was appointed governor of the newly acquired colony of Sierra Leone. He was recalled in his second year, and in 1811 he married the daughter of a clergyman and was sent to Spain, where he fought in the final battles of the Peninsular War [q.v.]. At the end of the war he transferred to the 17th Light Dragoons, then serving in India, and he arrived in Bombay in 1815. He fought the Pindaris [q.v.] and took part in an expedition against the Wahhabis in the Persian Gulf. When peace was made, he was left behind with a few hundred sepoys and some European artillerymen. In an attack upon Arab pirates, he was defeated. For his defeat he was court-martialed but acquitted.

He returned to England a captain in 1822 and saw no further action, but he advanced steadily, becoming a full general in 1868, the year before his death. His son C. W. Thompson fought in the Second Sikh War [q.v.] and also became a general.

From the time of his return Thompson devoted himself to politics and writing on political subjects. He was interested in the Greek struggles for independence and in 1825 published two pamphlets in modern Greek and French on outposts and on a system of telegraphing for armies in the field [see Telegraph]. In 1828 he was elected a fellow of the Royal Society, and the following year he became the proprietor of the *Westminster Review,* which he owned for seven years, and for which he wrote more than a hundred articles. In 1836 he was elected a member of Parliament for Hull.

Thousand Days, War of a. See Colombian Revolts.

Thouvenot, Pierre (1757–1817). A French soldier who was commissioned into the colonial artillery in 1780 and spent eight years in the West Indies. He served as chief of staff to General Charles Dumouriez [q.v.] in Holland and in April 1793 defected with him, living abroad until permitted to return to France in 1800. He was sent to Santo Domingo and in 1802 was promoted general of brigade. The following year he returned to Europe and served in the Peninsular War [q.v.] in Spain, where as governor of Bayonne he was wounded during the siege of the city [see Bayonne, Siege of]. On 5 May 1814 he signed a convention with the Allies, one of the last of the French generals to continue resistance in the Peninsular War.

Three Emperors, Battle of. See Austerlitz, Battle of.

Three-Inch Ordnance Gun. A rifled three-inch gun popular during the American Civil War. It was often called a Rodman, although gun designer Thomas J. Rodman [q.v.] had no connection with its design or manufacture. The barrel was of heavy wrought iron, needing no breech reinforcement, and weighed about 820 pounds. The powder charge was usually one pound, and a shell could be thrown accurately up to 2,000 yards at an elevation of only five degrees. The Union army acquired 925 of these guns.

Three-Month / Ninety-Day Regiments. At the beginning of the American Civil War it was not anticipated that the rebellion of the southern states would last more than ninety days. Consequently, in the North many regiments were raised in which enlistments were for only three months.

Three Years' War. See Peruvian-Bolivian Confederation, War of the.

Throat. 1. In fortifications, the narrow space between the flanks of a bastion and the place where they join the curtain.
2. The backs of the faces of a redan.

Thumb Stall. A leather thumb covering worn by a cannoneer when serving the vent of a gun. The protected thumb was held over the vent while the artillery piece was being sponged and loaded [see Serving the Vent].

Tientsin, Capture of (13 July 1900), Boxer Rebellion. An international force of 5,000 stormed the city walls and captured the citadel at Tientsin (Tianzin) in northeastern China at the junction of the Pei River and Grand Canal where they form the Hai River. The Japanese and Americans distinguished themselves, the U.S. 9th Infantry suffering heavy losses, including its commander, Colonel (brevet Brigadier General) Emerson Hamilton Liscum (1850?–1900). Total Allied losses were about 800; Chinese losses are unknown.

Tilsit, Treaties of (7 and 9 July 1807). On 25 June 1807 Napoleon and Tsar Alexander I [q.v.] met for private discussions on a specially constructed raft in the middle of the lower Niemen River. On 7 July a number of documents were signed: a peace treaty, an agreement upon alliances, and secret articles. Two days later a treaty with Prussia was added. Under the terms of the treaties Prussia lost all its lands west of the Elbe; a new kingdom of Westphalia was created with Jérôme Bonaparte (1784–1860) as king; the status of Danzig (Gdańsk) as a free city was restored; Russia accepted Napoleon as a mediator in its quarrel with Turkey and ceded the Ionian Islands and other Mediterranean possessions to France, among other concessions.

Tilton, Henry Remsen (1836–after 1900). An American surgeon educated at the medical department of the University of Pennsylvania, from which he was graduated in 1859. During the American Civil War he served as a first lieutenant and assistant surgeon in various federal hospitals. He remained in the army after the war and served in the West, taking part in several Indian campaigns. In 1876, during the Great Sioux War [q.v], he was promoted major. The following year he served in the Nez Percé War [q.v.], winning a Medal of Honor in the Battle of Bear Paw Mountain [q.v.], where on 30 September 1877 he "fearlessly exposed his life and displayed great gallantry in rescuing and protecting the wounded men. . . ." He retired from the army as a lieutenant colonel in 1900.

Tilton, James (1745–1822). An American army doctor who served in the American Revolution and when it ended returned to private practice. He wrote *Economical Observations on Military Hospitals and the Prevention and Cure of Diseases Incident to an Army* (1813). Probably as a consequence of this publication he was offered and accepted the position of physician and surgeon general of the army, a post created by an act of 8 March 1813. He served exactly two years until 1815 and, by improving hospitals, establishing new hospitals, and eliminating the incompetent, did much to improve the medical services of the army. In December 1814, at the end of the War of 1812 [q.v.], he issued *Regulations for the Medical Department,* which defined clearly for the first time the duties of medical officers and the sanitary staff.

Timişoara / Temesvár, Battle of (9 August 1849), Hungarian Revolution. On 13 April 1849 Hungarians rebelled against Austrian rule and proclaimed a Hungarian republic. Austria called upon Russia for help, and Russian troops invaded from the north while an Austrian army under General Julius von Haynau [q.v.] advanced into Hungary from the west. At Timişoara, a city on the Timiş River, 75 miles northeast of Belgrade, near the Serbian border, the rebels, commanded by Hungarian General Henryk Dembínski [q.v.], were utterly defeated. This was the last pitched battle of the war, and it broke Hungarian resistance. Four days later the remaining rebel forces surrendered to the Russians. After his victory Haynau hanged nine Hungarian generals and shot four others, conduct that led the British press to condemn him as General Hyena.

Timrod, Henry (1828–1867). A Confederate soldier and poet who was known as the poet laureate of the Confederacy. He dropped out of college and failed as a law student, but his verses had found an audience even before the war. In the winter of 1861–62 he served as a private in the 13th South Carolina before being discharged because of tuberculosis. His most famous poems were "The Cotton Boll," "Carolina," and "Ethnogenesis."

Tinah Khan, Battle of (3 January 1870), Afghan Civil War.

Deposed Afghan Amir Shere Ali [q.v.], having been defeated in the Battle of Sheikhabad [q.v.] on 10 May 1866, returned four years later to fight Abdur Rahman Khan [q.v.], his nephew, and Afzul Khan, his brother. In this battle he was more successful [see Afghan Civil Wars].

Tippecanoe, Battle of (7 November 1811). After the Battle of Fallen Timbers (20 August 1794) settlers pushed into Ohio Territory and beyond, into lands claimed by the Indians. To resist the encroachments onto tribal territory, Tecumseh [q.v.], a Shawnee chief, and his brother, Elskwatawa (Tenskwatawa), known as the Prophet, organized a confederacy of the affected tribes and demanded that the American government remove those settlers already on tribal lands and prohibit further settlement. William Harrison [q.v.], governor of Indiana Territory, rejected their demands and, with the approval of the secretary of war, who sent him 300 regular infantry, decided to confront the Indians before they descended upon the settlements.

At the end of September 1811 Harrison moved out of Vincennes with the regulars and 650 militia. He paused to build a fort on the edge of the tribal lands and then moved on. He halted his force about a mile west of Tecumseh's village, where Tippecanoe Creek joins the Wabash River at a place that is now the site of the small town of Battle Ground, Indiana, 7 miles north-northeast of Lafayette and about 50 miles from present-day Chicago. The expedition made its camp in the form of a trapezoid on some high ground with half the regulars and the 300 militia on the side facing the village. Harrison then invited the Indians to a conference. Tecumseh was absent, but the Prophet accepted, promising peace as long as the conference lasted. However, before dawn on 7 November the date of the conference, his warriors launched a surprise attack upon the camp, which Harrison repulsed with difficulty. In a counterattack his troops sent the Indians flying and burned the village. Harrison lost 39 killed and 151 wounded, 29 mortally; Indian losses are unknown, but 36 dead were left on the field.

Tirah Campaign (1897). Depredation by Afridis and Orakzais on India's Northwest Frontier [q.v.] led to a British punitive expedition against them. Two divisions, about 35,000 men under General Sir William Stephen Alexander Lockhart [q.v.], the largest such frontier expedition ever launched, penetrated the Tirah country, never before entered by Europeans. It was a fertile land, which the British laid waste, cutting fruit trees and burning crops and barns. Only one pitched battle was fought [see Dargai, Battle of], but the British columns were pursued by snipers, and there were small actions until the expedition left [see Findlater, George].

Tirah Campaign *British advance into the Tirah Valley after the Battle of Dargai, on Northwest Frontier, 9 November 1897.*

Tippecanoe *Battle of Tippecanoe River, Indiana, 7 November 1811*

Tirailleur. A French rifleman, sharpshooter, skirmisher, light infantryman. The word came into use during the Napoleonic Wars [q.v.]. In the French Armée d'Afrique [q.v.] the term was used to designate units of Africans organized as light infantry and commanded mostly by French officers.

The first locally raised African tirailleur unit was the Tirailleurs Algérien, one of three regiments formed in 1842. They were originally dressed in baggy *sarouel* trousers and turbans. During the Crimean War [q.v.] 2,500 served in the Crimea. From 1858 they were uniformed as Zouaves [q.v.]. In 1875 they were reorganized to make three regiments of four battalions each. Traditionally recruits came from Kabylia and the Tell areas of Algeria.

The largest tirailleur unit was the Tirailleur Sénégalais [see Senegalese Tirailleurs], a unit founded by Louis Faidherbe [q.v.] in 1857 with a mixture of 500 slaves, captives, and impressed men. A detachment of Senegalese Tirailleurs accompanied Captain Jean Marchand [q.v.] to Fashoda [see Fashoda Incident], and on 14 July 1899 the detachment marched in the Bastille Day parade in Paris. A decree of 1889 authorized Senegalese to be commissioned, but few were, and these were generally the illegitimate sons of French officers and black African women.

In 1884 the 4th Tirailleurs Algérien, composed of Tunisian conscripts, was formed: the name Tunisian was not added until 1921. The Tirailleurs Gabonais, a unit recruited in the French colony of Gabon existed only from 1887 to 1891.

In 1883 in Madagascar the French formed the Tirailleurs Sakalaves, intended originally simply to hold the area around Diego-Suarez. The Sakalavas were one of the mainly African peoples on the west coast of the island. In 1893 this unit was reduced to battalion strength, and in October 1896 it formed the nucleus of the Tirailleurs Malgaches, to which a second regiment was added in 1897 and a third in 1903. The primary purpose of these units was the pacification and suppression of rebellions.

TNT. See Trinitrotoluene.

Tobra Gup. Hindustani term for "nose bag gossip." Camp gossip and rumors.

Todd, George (d. 1864). In the American Civil War Todd was the principal lieutenant of Confederate guerrilla leader William Clarke Quantrill [q.v.] until the two men quarreled and Todd took command of most of the cutthroat band [see Quantrill's Raids]. He was part of most of the guerrilla actions in Missouri and led the band in the Centralia Massacre [q.v.]. He was killed in October 1864 just outside Independence, Missouri, while scouting for Confederate General Sterling Price [q.v.].

Todleben / Totleben, Franz Eduard Ivanovich (1818–1884). A Russian military engineer who was commissioned in the engineers in 1836. In 1848–50 he was a captain in a campaign against Shamyl [q.v.] in the Caucasus, and in 1853 he was part of the campaign in the Danubian principalities. During the Crimean War [q.v.] he distinguished himself by his design of the fortifications of Sevastopol, where he was severely wounded on 20 June 1855. Later in the war he completed the defenses of Nikolaev and Cronstadt (Kronshtadt or Kronstadt). In 1869 he was promoted general and chief of engineers. During the Russo-Turkish War of 1877–78 [q.v.] he made the plans for the successful siege of Plevna [q.v.], and he besieged and captured several Bulgarian forts. In 1878 he was briefly in command of the entire Russian army. In 1880 he was made a count and appointed governor of Vilna (Vilnius or Vilnyus or Vilno or Wilno or Wilna) in Lithuania.

Tofrek / Tofrik, Battle of (22 March 1885), British Sudan campaigns. Because of poor scouting by the British 5th Lancers, a British force of three battalions of Anglo-Indian troops and one and one-half battalions of British troops under Major General John Carstairs McNeill, VC (1831–1904), was taken by surprise by 4,000 Dervishes in the northeastern Sudan, about halfway between Suakim and Tamai. Although one of the sepoy battalions broke and the Dervishes penetrated the unfinished zeriba [q.v.], they were repulsed with about 2,000 killed. The British lost 294 combatants and 176 camp followers killed, wounded, or missing.

Tohopeka, Battle of. See Horseshoe Bend, Battle of.

Toise. A measurement frequently used in the construction of fortifications and military surveying. It was equal to 6.3946 feet or 2.1315 yards.

Tokuho. The Japanese soldier's code, promulgated in 1872, which listed seven virtues: loyalty, obedience, courage, controlled force, frugality, honor, and respect for superiors. It was similar to bushido [q.v.] but lacked its sensitivity and compassion. It was given a fuller expression in the Imperial Rescript [q.v.] to Soldiers and Sailors in 1882.

Tokyo, Battle of. See Tayeizan, Battle of.

Tolentino, Battle of (3 May 1815), Hundred Days. An Austrian army of 11,000 with 28 guns under General Vincenz von Bianchi [q.v.] defeated a Neapolitan force of 29,000 with 35 guns under Marshal Joachim Murat [q.v.] at this central Italian town, 100 miles north of Rome and 12 miles west-southwest of Macerata. In this battle Istáván Széchenyi [q.v.], a Hungarian soldier, led a memorable cavalry charge that scattered Murat's bodyguard. The Neapolitans sustained 4,000 casualties; the Austrians, 800. Murat fled to France.

Toll, Count Johan Kristoffer (1743–1817). A Swedish soldier and statesman who in 1783 headed a commission on national defense. In 1807, during the Russo-Swedish War [q.v.], he aided in the defense of Stralsund [q.v.] and persuaded the Russians to agree to a convention whereby the Swedish troops were allowed to return unmolested to Sweden. Soon after, he was created a marshal of Sweden. In 1814 he was created a count.

Tolosa, Battle of (26 June 1813), Peninsular War. Around Tolosa, a fortified town on an important road junction in northern Spain, 11 miles southwest of San Sebastián, French General Maximilien Foy [q.v.] occupied strong positions with 12,000 men. Here he was attacked in the flank by 30,000 Portuguese, Spanish, British, and the King's German Legion [q.v.] under Lieutenant General Sir Thomas Graham [q.v.]. After an indecisive battle the French withdrew. Casualties were about 600 on each side. Foy, after leaving a garrison at San Sebastián [q.v.], retreated into France.

Tolstoy, Count Lev or Lyov (English: Leo) Nikolaievich (1828–1910). A Russian soldier, novelist, social philosopher, and religious mystic. In 1844 he matriculated at Kazan University. In 1851, while visiting his elder brother, Nikolai, an army officer in the Caucasus, he enrolled as a gentleman volunteer in an artillery unit and took part in an attack upon Grozny in Chechnya. In 1854, at the beginning of the Crimean War [q.v.], he was commissioned and at his own request served in the army operating against the Turks, first on the Danube and then at Sevastopol [q.v.], where he commanded a battery throughout the siege. In 1857 he resigned from the army. Among his books are a number with military themes, including *The Cossacks* (1854, published in 1862), *Two Hussars* (1856), and *War and Peace* (1866).

Tombeau. A French punishment in which a soldier was made to crouch in a pit for a long period. Although officially forbidden, it was used in the Armée d'Afrique.

Tombs, Henry (1824–1874). A British soldier born in India who was educated at the military college of the Honourable East India Company at Addiscombe [q.v.] and was commissioned a lieutenant in the Bengal artillery in 1841. He fought in the Battle of Punniar in the Gwalior Campaign and in the battles of Mudki and Ferozeshah in the First Sikh War [qq.v.]. In the Battle of Aliwal [q.v.] he served as an aide-de-camp to Sir Harry Smith [q.v.]. During the Second Sikh War [q.v.] he served as deputy assistant quartermaster general of the artillery division and was present at the battles of Ramnagar, Chilianwala, and Gujerat [qq.v.].

During the Indian Mutiny [q.v.] he served through the siege of Delhi [q.v.] and won the Victoria Cross on 9 July 1857. He served under Sir Colin Campbell [q.v.] in the relief of Lucknow. In 1861 he was promoted lieutenant colonel. In 1864 he took part in the Bhutan Campaign [q.v.], and in 1867 he was promoted major general. He commanded the Allahabad Division of the army in 1871.

Tombs Memorial Prize. A medal commemorating Major General Sir Henry Tombs [q.v.], which was first awarded in 1877 at the Royal Military Academy, Woolwich, to the "Best Qualified Cadet entering the Royal Artillery."

Tommy Atkins. Nickname for a British soldier in the ranks. Its origin is obscure, but Thomas Atkins is said to have been used as a specimen name on forms. Its use as an affectionate term for a British soldier was little known before it was popularized in the 1890s by Rudyard Kipling [q.v.]. Sir George Younghusband, a British officer, wrote: "I myself had served for many years with soldiers, but had never heard the words or expressions that Rudyard Kipling's soldiers used. Many a time did I ask my brother officers whether they had heard them. No, never. But sure enough, a few years later the soldiers thought, and talked, and expressed themselves exactly like Rudyard Kipling's soldiers. . . . Rudyard Kipling made the modern soldier" (*A Soldier's Memories in Peace and War* [1917]).

Tompion. A plug or cover for the muzzle of a cannon to keep out dirt and water.

Tompkins, Charles Henry (b. 1830). An American soldier who in 1849 dropped out of West Point after two years and in 1856 enlisted as a private. He was a first lieutenant in the 2nd Cavalry at the beginning of the American Civil War. On 1 June 1861 he led a daring reconnaissance at Fairfax Court House in which in a brief engagement the first Confederate soldier was killed in an action. (Tompkins was later (1893) awarded the Medal of Honor [q.v.]). He ended the war as a captain and brevet brigadier general. After the war he remained in the army. He retired as a colonel and assistant quartermaster general in 1894.

Tompkins, Sally Louisa (1833–1916). A wealthy woman in Richmond, Virginia, who established a hospital for Confederate soldiers at her own expense after the First Battle of Bull Run. From 1 August 1861, the date it was established, to 2 April 1865 there were only 73 deaths of the 1,333 admissions, an astonishing record unsurpassed by any other military hospital. When all army hospitals were put under military control, President Jefferson Davis [q.v.] on 9 September 1861 commissioned her a captain of cavalry to retain her services. She thus became the only woman officially to hold a commission in the Confederate army. She was known as Captain Sally for the rest of her life.

Her charity and hospitality depleted her fortune, and in 1905 she moved into the Confederate Women's Home in Richmond, where she died. She was buried with military honors. Four chapters of the United Daughters of the Confederacy are named in her honor.

Tonga, Revolts in. The Tonga (or Friendly) Islands constitute an archipelago in the western South Pacific Ocean about midway between Samoa and Fiji. A revolt broke out among warring factions in 1799 and dragged on until checked by Taufa'ahua (1797–1893), a strong man who in 1845 became king under the name George Tubou (Tapou) I.

The successes of Methodist missionaries, who had arrived in 1822, created a division that erupted in a war between the new Christians and those who still worshiped the old gods. Although the king supported the missionaries, the war did not end until 1852, and its end brought no diminution of the religious discord. When a retired Wesleyan missionary, Shirley Baker, became Tonga's premier, he persuaded the king to break relations with the Wesleyans in Sydney, Australia, and establish a state religion. Persecution of members of the old church and much social turmoil followed until in 1890 Baker was removed. When King George Tubou died at the age of ninety-six, he was succeeded by his great-grandson, who in 1900 was persuaded to place his kingdom under British protection. It remains a monarchy but is now a constitutional one.

Tongue River, Battle of (8 January 1877), American Indian Wars. In the Wolf Mountains of Montana Territory the 5th Infantry and two companies of the 22 Infantry, all under Colonel (later General) Nelson A. Miles [q.v.], in a blizzard in sub-zero weather stormed a snow-covered ridge and successfully attacked an Indian force twice its size under Crazy Horse [q.v.]. The Indians surrendered soon after.

Tonkin Campaign, French. See French Indochina War, Third.

Toombs, Robert Augustus (1810–1885). An American who on the eve of the American Civil War was one of the wealthiest planters in Georgia. On 19 July 1861 he was appointed brigadier general in the Confederate army and ordered to take command of the Georgia brigade in Virginia. He was a fiery volunteer, contemptuous of professional soldiers, declaring that the epitaph of the Confederacy would be "Died by West Point." When West Pointer General A. P. Hill [q.v.] reprimanded him after the Battle of Malvern Hill [q.v.] for allowing his men to break ranks and failing to rally them, he challenged Hill to a duel, earning him another reprimand. He was severely wounded in the Battle of Antietam [q.v.], but it was men of his brigade who held the stone bridge (Burnside Bridge) on the right of the Confederate line.

Because he was not promoted, he resigned on 4 March 1863 and spent most of the rest of the war criticizing the government, although as William Tecumseh Sherman [q.v.] advanced upon Atlanta, he accepted an appointment as inspector general of the Georgia militia. At war's end he fled first to Cuba and then to England. He returned in 1867 to build a large law practice, but he never requested amnesty. His later years were tragic. Just as he began to recover his fortune, his wife became insane and died. He lost his sight and died an alcoholic.

Tope. In Hindustani, a cannon.

Tope Khana. In Hindustani, the artillery, an artillery park, an arsenal, or the ordnance department. Sometimes written Topikhannah.

Topographical Engineers. A separate branch of the service in the American army, authorized in May 1816, consisting of a small group of officers concerned primarily with exploration and mapping. It was amalgamated with the Corps of Engineers on 31 March 1863.

Toppibachi / Topgi-Bachi. Grand master of artillery in the Turkish army.

Torbert, Alfred Thomas Archimedes (1833–1880). An American soldier who was graduated from West Point in 1855 and served with the 5th Infantry on the western frontier, in the Third Seminole War [q.v.], and on the Utah Expedition [q.v.]. At the beginning of the American Civil War he became the only officer to hold commissions in both the Union and Confederate armies at the same time. On 25 February 1861 he was promoted lieutenant in the Union army, and in April, through some confusion, he was nominated and confirmed a first lieutenant in the Confederate army. He fought in the Union army in the Peninsular Campaign, Chancellorsville, Fredericksburg, South Mountain, Antietam, and Gettysburg [qq.v.], commanding both infantry and cavalry and winning brevets in both the volunteer service and the regular army through major general.

In the postbellum reorganization of the army in 1866 he found himself a mere captain in the 5th Infantry. He resigned his commission and served in several diplomatic posts. He resigned in 1878 as consul general in Paris and returned to the United States. In 1880 he shipped on the steamer *Vera Cruz* for Mexico and was drowned when the ship foundered off Cape Canaveral on 29 August.

Torpedo. Originally a moored sea mine invented by Robert Fulton (1765–1815) and named after an electric ray fish. The name was also applied to land mines [q.v.] [see Rains, Gabriel].

Torrens, Henry (1779–1828). A British soldier commissioned in 1793 who served under General Ralph Abercromby [q.v.] in the West Indies. He served in Portugal in 1798 and in the Netherlands in 1799, where he was wounded at Egmont-op-Zee. He fought in the Maratha Wars [q.v.] in India and took part in the disastrous expedition to Buenos Aires [q.v.] in 1807. In 1808, during the Peninsular War [q.v.], he was military secretary to Wellesley (later Duke of Wellington) in Portugal and fought at Roliça and Vimeiro [qq.v.]. In 1814 he was promoted major general, and in 1820 he was appointed adjutant general to the forces. In that post he did much to revise and improve the infantry regulations.

Torres Vedras, Lines of (10 October 1810–5 March 1811), Peninsular War. In October 1809 Wellington had given orders for the construction of a line of fortifications north of Lisbon to protect the city and the British embarkation point at São Julião da Barra, to the west. The works were built under the direction of Lieutenant Colonel Richard Fletcher (1768–1813), a British military engineer, with the aid of 17 other engineer officers and 10,000 local laborers. When they were completed, a series of enclosed works stretched in noncontiguous triple lines for 28 miles from the estuary of the Tagus River on the east to the sea on the west. They included 108 redoubts (42 more were added in 1810) and mounted 447 guns. Five signal stations were established on dominant peaks. The lines took their name from the commune of Torres Vedras, 26 miles north of Lisbon.

Incredible as it seems, these formidable works had been constructed in secrecy, and when on 11 October 1810 Marshal André Masséna [q.v.] arrived before the lines with 60,000 men, he was taken completely by surprise. Masséna soon realized that the position was impregnable, and after vainly hoping that Wellington would emerge from the safety of his lines and fight, he retreated toward the Mondego River.

Tortosa, Battle of (20 December 1810–2 January 1811), Peninsular War. On 15 December 1810 a French force of

Tortosa *The French seize Tortosa, January 1811*

7,000 under Marshal Louis Gabriel Suchet [q.v.] arrived in front of this town on the Ebro River in northeastern Spain, 40 miles southwest of Tarragona, garrisoned by 7,179 Spanish under the Conde de Alacha. Commanding the only land route between Catalonia and Valencia and a major bridge over the Ebro, it had to be taken before Tarragona [q.v.] could be besieged and the invasion of Valencia could begin.

On the night of 20–21 December 1810 the French began the siege at the bastion of San Pedro, one of the weakest points in the defenses. Siege guns were brought up, and a breach 15 yards across was blown in the defenses on 29 December. Just as Suchet was about to attack, Alacha surrendered. The French then sacked the town. The Spaniards suffered 1,400 killed and wounded; the remainder were taken prisoner.

Tosei-Guso Ku. See Gusoku.

Toski, Battle of (3 August 1889), War in the Sudan. On 22 June a Dervish force of 6,000 warriors and 8,000 followers under Abd al-Rahman wad al-Najumi [q.v.] tried for a second time to invade Egypt from the Sudan. Near the Sudanese village of Toski on the Nile, near Abu Simbel, an Anglo-Egyptian force of about 2,000 under General Francis Wallace Grenfell (1841–1925), the sirdar of the Egyptian army, defeated the Dervishes, and al-Najumi was killed. Dervish losses were about 1,200 killed and wounded. Anglo-Egyptian losses were 25 killed and 140 wounded. On 3 and 4 August some 3,000 prisoners were taken.

Total Strength. See Strength, Unit.

Totenköpfe Hussars. See Hussars.

Totten, Joseph Gilbert (1788–1864). An American soldier who was appointed a cadet at West Point in November 1802 and became the tenth graduate in July 1805. From 1808 to 1838 he was engaged in work on harbor defenses and in river and harbor improvements. During the Mexican War [q.v.] he served under General Winfield Scott [q.v.] and planned the operations against Veracruz. During the American Civil War he was promoted brigadier general in 1863 and brevetted major general in April 1864, but he died the following day. Fort Totten in New York Harbor is named in his honor.

Touchhole. The vent of a muzzle-loading artillery piece by which fire is sent to the powder of the charge.

Toug. A Mameluke standard that consisted of one or more horsehair tails mounted on a pole.

Toulouse, Battle of (10 April 1814), Peninsular War. When Spain and Portugal were freed from all French control, 50,000 British, Spanish, and Portuguese troops under Wellington advanced over the Pyrenees into southern France. Marshal Nicolas Soult [q.v.] fell back over the Garonne River into Toulouse, 133 miles southeast of Bordeaux, and took position on Calvinet Ridge, one-half mile north of the city, with some 42,000 French troops. Here he was attacked by the Allied army. Soult threw back a premature assault by Spanish troops against the northern defenses, but the British under General

William Carr Beresford [q.v.] advanced successfully in the center and took the heights. Abandoning Toulouse, Soult retreated eastward, having suffered some 3,200 casualties. The Allies lost 4,659, of whom some 2,000 were Spanish. This was the last battle of the war, for on 12 April Wellington learned of Napoleon's abdication.

Tourie / Toorie. The short ends (bobble) worn on top of Scottish bonnets: tam-o'-shanter, kilmarnock, or glengarry.

Tousard, Anna Louis de (1749–1817). An army officer born in Paris who came to the United States in 1777 and fought for the Americans in the Revolutionary War, losing his right arm in action on 28 August 1778. He was commissioned a major of artillery in the American army and promoted colonel in 1798. He planned and supervised construction of fortifications at Fort Mifflin, Pennsylvania; West Point, New York; and Newport, Rhode Island. In 1801–02 he reorganized the garrison at West Point as a military academy. In 1802 he returned to France and was given a pension by Napoleon. He then served as French agent and later vice-consul in several American cities.

Toussaint L'Ouverture / Louverture, Pierre Dominique (1743–1803). A Haitian black general born of slave parents who in 1791 took a prominent part in an abortive slave insurrection. In 1793, after the slaves were freed, he joined the French republicans and became their recognized leader, successfully forcing the British to evacuate the island in 1798. In 1799 he defeated André Rigaud [q.v.], the leader of the mulattoes in a civil war. By 1801 he was master of the entire island of Hispaniola. He resisted when Napoleon tried to reinstate slavery, but he was overcome by a French force under General Charles Victor Leclerc [q.v.] in 1802. He was captured, charged with conspiracy, and sent as a prisoner to France. He was imprisoned in the Château de Joux, where he starved to death.

Toussaint L'Ouverture

Towarczys. A corps of Polish lancers in the Prussian army who were recruited from the lesser Polish nobility in what were then New East Prussia and South Prussia.

Tower Bastion. A casemented tower in the form of a bastion.

Town Major. The officer who regulates the duties of a garrison or occupied town. He assigns quarters and guard details, maintains rosters, arranges for countersigns, etc.

Townsend, Edward Davis (1817–1893). An American soldier who was graduated from West Point in 1833. From 1862 to 1880 he was adjutant general of the army, and it was under his direction that the papers from the American Civil War were collected and later published between 1881 and 1901

as *War of the Rebellion: Official Records of the Union and Confederate Armies* [see Official Records].

Townsend, George Alfred (1841–1914). A successful American journalist who was one of the first syndicated columnists. During the American Civil War he covered the Union side for various newspapers under the name Gath. He also covered the Seven Weeks' War [q.v.] in Europe. He then became an equally successful writer of fiction. In 1896 on his estate, Gapland (today Gathland State Park), on South Mountain in western Maryland, he dedicated an ornate and incredibly ugly stone arch, 50 feet high and 40 feet wide, the only monument ever erected to American war correspondents and artists. Built at a cost of five thousand dollars, it bears the names of 157 American Civil War newsmen, 9 of whom were Southerners.

Townshend, Charles Vere Ferrers (1861–1924). A British soldier who in 1881 was commissioned in the Royal Marine Light Infantry. He took part in the Gordon Relief Expedition [q.v.] in 1884–85 and fought in the Battle of Abu Klea [q.v.] on 17 January 1885. He transferred to the Indian army in 1886 and as a captain in 1895 was in command at the fort in Chitral that withstood a siege of forty-six days [see Chitral Campaign]. During the reconquest of the Sudan [q.v.] by General Horatio Kitchener [q.v.] in 1898 he fought in the battles at the Atbara River on 8 April and at Omdurman [qq.v.] on 2 September. He served in the Second Anglo-Boer War [q.v.] and was promoted major general in 1911. In 1916, during the First World War, he was besieged at Kut-el-Amara, 100 miles southeast of Baghdad, by the Turks and after a month surrendered 10,000 men. At the time this was the largest surrender ever of a British army. While his men endured the most deplorable conditions and suffered an enormously high death rate, Townshend lived luxuriously and became an admirer of the Turks, who released him to plead their cause in England, to the outrage of most Britons.

Towse, Beachcroft (1864–1948). A British soldier and pioneer of assistance to the blind. He was commissioned in the Seaforth Highlanders in 1883 and three years later he transferred to the Gordon Highlanders. He served in the Chitral Relief Expedition and the Battle of Malakand [qq.v.]. In 1899 he went with his battalion to South Africa for the Second Anglo-Boer War [q.v.] and was present in the advance upon Kimberley [see Kimberley, Siege of]. In the Battle of Magersfontein [q.v.] he distinguished himself by carrying his mortally wounded commanding officer from the field. On 30 April 1900, while rallying his men on Thaba Mountain to attack a group of Boers, he was seriously wounded, losing his sight. For his gallantry on these occasions he was awarded the Victoria Cross. Renowned as the Blind VC, he threw himself into organizations and causes that aided the blind, particularly blinded soldiers, and was knighted for his efforts.

Traces. The ropes, straps, and chains connecting horses with limbers, caissons, or other carriages.

Tracing. Marking on the ground the outlines of a fortification to be constructed.

Trail. 1. That part of a gun carriage that extends back from the axle to rest on the ground and helps stabilize a piece when fired. It is also the part connected to a limber or caisson by resting on a pintle when traveling.

2. "To trail arms" is to carry a musket or rifle with the hand near the middle, the barrel facing forward.

Trail of Tears (1830s–1840s). In 1830 Congress passed the Indian Removal Acts, giving the government the power to move all Indians to lands west of the Mississippi River. The Cherokees and others refused to leave [see Cherokee Disturbances and Removal]. In 1838 American troops began their forcible removal from North Carolina, Tennessee, Alabama, and Georgia. The migration was badly organized, and on the long trail about a quarter of the tribe, men, women, and children, died of starvation, exposure, and diseases.

Trail of Tears *Cherokee forced march, the Trail of Tears. Painting by Richard Lindneux*

Trainer. In American usage a militiaman called out on training day for drill and instruction.

Trajectory. The path of a projectile through the air from the weapon to its point of impact. Air resistance and gravity contrive to make this a compound curve, steeper at the target end than at the end of a gun's barrel.

Traktir Ridge, Battle of. See Chernaya, Battle of.

Transfuge. A deserter.

Transport. 1. A troopship [q.v.].
2. The noncombat vehicles of a military unit.

Transvaal Civil War of 1862–64. After the Great Trek of the Boers north from Cape Colony in South Africa, four small republics were established in the Transvaal. Quarrels soon erupted over boundaries, religion, and political affairs. In 1856 the South African Republic was formed in the southwest of the Transvaal, and Marthinus Wessels Pretorius [q.v.] was elected its president. He tried without success to unify the entire area north of the Vaal River into a single republic. In 1859 he was also elected president of the Orange Free State in the south. He attempted to join the two republics, but negotiations fell apart, and war erupted. In 1863 Pretorius resigned from the presidency of the Orange Free State, and in 1864 he was able to put an end to the strife and unite the Transvaal. In that same year he was reelected president of the South African Republic, usually called the Transvaal and now Transvaal Province in the Republic of South Africa.

Transvaal War. See Anglo-Boer Wars: First Anglo-Boer War.

Tranter, William (1816–1890). A British gunmaker in Birmingham, England, who developed a double-trigger-action breech-loading revolver, which he patented in 1853. It was manufactured in caliber .433 and fired metallic cartridges. Called the Tranter, it was popular with army officers. It was adopted by the British army in 1878 and remained in service until 1887.

Trant, Nicholas (1769–1839). A British soldier who was educated at a military college in France and in 1794 was commissioned in the British 84th Foot. He served with that regiment on Walcheren Island in the Netherlands and in Cape Colony, South Africa. In 1798 he took part in the capture of Minorca. On 17 January 1799 he was appointed major in the Minorcan Regiment, a Portuguese unit he helped raise. After the Treaty of Amiens [q.v.] on 25 March 1802 he resigned from the army, but returned in 1803 and was promoted lieutenant in 1805. Posted to Portugal in 1808, during the Peninsular War [q.v.], with the local rank of lieutenant colonel, he commanded a Portuguese brigade of 1,500 infantry and 250 cavalry in the battles of Roliça and Vimeiro [qq.v.]. In 1809 he raised a regiment from among the students at the University of Coimbra, which grew to contain 3,000 men. He took part in the advance of Wellesley's army to the Douro (Duero) River and was made governor of Oporto when it was recaptured. On 1 June 1809 he was promoted captain in the British army while at the same time he held the rank of brigadier general in the Portuguese army. In 1810 he was ordered back to England but was saved by Wellington, who wrote: "There is no officer the loss of whose services in this country would be more sensibly felt."

On 7 October 1810 Trant launched a successful attack upon Coimbra [q.v.], where Marshal André Masséna [q.v.] had left 5,000 sick and wounded with a small guard. Most of the sick and wounded were slaughtered by the Portuguese; the remainder were made prisoner and shipped to Oporto. It was, according to William Napier [q.v.], "the most daring and hardy enterprise executed by any partisan during the whole war." In 1811 the Portuguese knighted Trant with the Order of the Tower and the Sword.

In 1813 he was recalled to England, where his only reward was a brevet majority. In 1816 he was placed on half pay, and in 1825 he resigned from the army. He died impoverished in the vicarage of his son-in-law.

Trapdoor Springfield. The 1866 Springfield carbine, .50 and .70 calibers to which there were many modifications.

Trautenau, Battle of (27 June 1866), Seven Weeks' War. At this town (Trutnow) in northeast Bohemia, 83 miles northeast of Prague, Prussian forces under Eduard von Bonin [q.v.] drove back the Austrians under Ludwig von Gablenz [q.v.], but Gablenz was reinforced, and the Prussians, near exhaustion after a long, hot march, retreated. Although the Prussians left the field, Austrians suffered 5,732 casualties to their 1,227.

Travancore Rebellion (1809). A disagreement between the British and the ruler of this Madrasi state on the Malabar coast of India led to a plot by the Travancoreans to kill the British Resident and attack the small British garrison there. The plot failed, and the British garrison held out until reinforcements arrived. At Palamcotta a British column drove off a second attack.

Traveling Forges. A blacksmith's establishment on wheels, usually one for each battery of field artillery. In the American army the forge was housed in a cart and a limber.

Traveling Kitchens. Wagons or carts fitted with stoves or ovens that enable food to be cooked on the march.

Traverse. 1. A bank of earth built at right angles to the line of defense to protect parapets or trenches from being enfiladed.
2. A compartment or recess formed by a protecting screen.
3. Any obstacle.
4. A communications gallery or trench in a defensive work.
5. The lateral movement of a gun on a pivot or carriage to change its direction of fire to the left or right.

Travis, William Barret (1809–1836). An American lawyer who in 1831, believing his wife unfaithful, left her and their son and daughter in Alabama and emigrated to Texas, where he rose to leadership among the aggressive Texans who were

Traverse *Three first traverses on land end, Fort Fisher, North Carolina, January 1865*

ready to resist Mexican authority. On 29 June 1835 he raised a company of 25 volunteers and took prisoner a Mexican captain at Anahuac, a military post 35 miles northeast of Galveston. In November he captured 200 Mexican horses within 40 miles of Bexar (San Antonio). On 24 December he was commissioned a cavalry lieutenant colonel in the Texas army. In January 1836 he was ordered to take 30 men to aid Jim Bowie [q.v.] at Bexar. There the two were to share the command at the Alamo [q.v.], a mission station converted into a fort. Because Bowie fell sick with typhoid and pneumonia, Travis was in sole command of the fort with its 188 men when it was besieged on 24 February by a Mexican army under General Antonio López de Santa Anna [q.v.]. On 6 March 1836 the Alamo was taken, and all survivors were shot.

Travois / Travée. A kind of primitive vehicle made of two shafts bearing a platform or net and trailed from a horse, mule, or other animal. Travois were common among Indians on

Travois

the American plains and were sometimes adopted by American army units, often serving as crude stretchers for the sick or wounded.

Accounts differ as to their comfort. In November 1876 they were used to transport the wounded after the Dull Knife fight [see Dull Knife Outbreak]. One hardy soul, strapped to a travois dragged by a runaway mule, sang out to the officer who stopped it, "Let 'er go, Lieutenant! If I had sleigh bells I'd think I was taken a sleigh ride." But Sergeant James B. Kincaid, wounded in the same fight, had a grim reaction: "Make this easier for me or kill me to get me out of my misery."

The wounded sometimes traveled for days before their wounds were properly dressed and treated by a doctor. American Indian War soldiers carried no first-aid kits.

Tread. The surface of a banquette on which a soldier stood to fire over the parapet.

Treason. 1. The betrayal of a trust.
2. Overt acts designed to overthrow a country's government or assassinate its ruler. This was usually defined as high treason and in the early days of the nineteenth century was widely interpreted. In Britain the last two executions for high treason occurred when two British soldiers were found in French uniforms after the British capture of the isle of Bourbon (Réunion) in the Indian Ocean. Their defense was that they had assumed the French uniform to facilitate their escape to England. On 16 March 1812 they were hanged and beheaded at Horsemonger Lane Gaol (Jail).

In the United States, according to the Constitution (Art. III, sec. 3) treason can consist only in making war against the United States or assisting its enemies, and no one can be convicted unless he or she confesses or unless two witnesses testify to the same act. Cases of treason against the United States have rarely been tried. The most notable of the nineteenth century was the trial of former Vice President Aaron Burr (1756–1836), who was acquitted in 1807. Although there were wholesale indictments after the American Civil War, all were dropped and amnesty was extended.

Tredegar Iron Works. This major Confederate arsenal on the Kanawha Canal in Richmond, Virginia, was the most

valuable manufactory in the Confederacy during the American Civil War. It contained the only major rolling mill in the South capable of producing cannon and railroad rails. Although the Confederate army relied mostly on artillery purchased in Europe and on captured Union guns, the facility manufactured 1,099 guns, nearly half of all the guns manufactured in the Confederacy. The works also rebored many obsolete guns from Virginia armories.

The private company had been owned by Joseph R. Anderson [q.v.], a West Pointer, since 1843. At the outbreak of the war it employed 900 workers. By 1863 it had increased its work force to 2,500. The company also operated nine canalboats, a tannery, shoemaking shops, and a firebrick factory.

Tredegar Iron Works *Most important gun manufactory in the Confederacy, Richmond, Virginia*

Trenches. Although usually used in siege operations [see Bayou; Sap; Parallels; Traverse], they were seldom used by infantry until the last half of the American Civil War.

Trenches *Shelter trenches*

Trepov, F. F. (1812–1889). A Russian general who in January 1878, while governor-general of St. Petersburg, was seriously wounded by a young woman revolutionary, Vera Ivanova Zasulich (1849–1919). The evidence against her was incontrovertible, but after a sensational trial a jury acquitted her.

Trevilian Raid (7–28 June 1864), American Civil War. When General U. S. Grant abandoned his operations around Cold Harbor, he ordered Philip Sheridan [q.v.] to make a diversion. On 7 June Sheridan crossed the Pamunkey River with two divisions and moved westward between the North Anna and Mattapony rivers. On the 10th he crossed the North Anna and encamped near Louisa Court House. Lee sent two divisions under Wade Hampton [q.v.] to block his path. In a daring move Brigadier General George Armstrong Custer [q.v.] rode between two Confederate brigades and captured most of Hampton's wagons as well as 800 horses. Hampton was forced to break off the action against Sheridan in his front to deal with Custer, who had taken a position at Trevilian Station. Although Hampton recaptured his horses and wagons and took several hundred of Custer's men prisoner, Custer managed to hold his position.

On 12 June Sheridan attacked Hampton's entrenched men and was repulsed with heavy losses. He abandoned his mission and on 28 June rejoined Grant. Union losses were 1,007 killed, wounded, and captured, of which the Michigan Brigade under General Custer suffered the most, 416 casualties.

Trews. Scottish for trousers [q.v.]. Trews were worn by Lowland Scottish regiments that did not wear kilts.

Triad Occupation of Shanghai (September 1853). The Shanghai branch of the secret Triad Society [q.v.], called the Small Sword Society, was led by Liu Li-ch'uan, a physician and sometime interpreter for Western merchants. On 7 September 1853 he seized control of the city, threw open the jails, and robbed the banks of some five million dollars, which he distributed to his followers. He then proceeded to capture other towns in the Yangtze Delta.

Triad Society. One of the largest of the many secret societies in imperial China that aimed to drive out the Manchu imperialists and restore the Ming dynasty (1368–1644), the last dynasty before the Manchu conquest. Many of its branches, each with its own name, were simply bands of bandits. During the Taiping Rebellion [q.v.] eight Triad chiefs petitioned to join the Taiping movement and were told that they would be accepted only if they were tutored in the new religion by Taiping teachers. When one of their tutors was discovered to have stolen their tuition money, he was executed. Such an extreme punishment for such a trivial offense so horrified the chiefs that they decamped. They were, however, active in other antigovernment rebellions [see Red Turban Revolt].

Triangle. A triangular framework of spontoons or poles to which a prisoner was tied to be flogged. "To go to the triangle" was to be flogged.

Tribal Regiments. In the British army, a term sometimes applied to regiments of Scots, Welsh, and Irish.

Tribulus. See Caltrop.

Trigger. A lever connected with a latch as a means of releasing it that on a hand-held or shoulder weapon fires the gun when it is pulled with the finger.

Trimble, Isaac Ridgeway (1802–1888). An American soldier who was graduated from West Point in 1822 and served for ten years in the artillery before resigning to work as a construction engineer for a series of eastern and southern railroads. At the beginning of the American Civil War he burned bridges north of Baltimore to prevent the passage of Federal troops. In May 1861 he accepted a commission in the Confederate army as colonel of engineers in Virginia, and in August he was promoted brigadier general. He commanded a brigade in the division of General Richard Ewell [q.v.] in the Shenandoah Valley Campaign of "Stonewall" Jackson [q.v.].

He fought in the Seven Days' Battles, Cedar Mountain, and the Second Battle of Bull Run [qq.v.], in which he was severely wounded. He returned to duty in time to fight at Gettysburg [q.v.], where he lost a leg and was captured. He was not exchanged until February 1865, but he was promoted major general to rank from 17 January 1863.

Trimble, Joel Graham (1832–1911). An American soldier who attended but did not graduate from Kenyon College. In 1851 as a civilian he accompanied the 1st Dragoons to California, where he took part in two of the initial engagements of the Rogue River War [q.v.], in one of which he was wounded in the head. On 5 February 1855 he enlisted in the 1st Dragoons and on 31 October fought in the Battle of Hungry Hill, between Grave and Cow creeks in Oregon. Later he was involved in small engagements in Washington Territory. When his enlistment expired in 1860, he rode for a time for the pony express before reenlisting in the 2nd Dragoons. He fought with this unit at the beginning of the American Civil War and was twice wounded. In 1863 he was commissioned a second lieutenant in the 1st Cavalry, and he ended the war as a first lieutenant with two brevets. With this regiment he served in Texas and Oregon, and on 26 December 1868 he was promoted captain. He fought in the Modoc War [q.v.] of 1873 and received the surrender of Captain Jack [q.v.]. On 17 June 1877 he took part in the Battle of White Bird Canyon [q.v.], and he fought in the subsequent Nez Percé War [q.v.]. Since he had lost the sight in his right eye and most of his left, he retired for disability in 1879. He lived for another twenty-two years, married, and sired three sons and two daughters.

Trinitrotoluene. A flammable toxic derivative $CH_3C_3H_2$ $[NO_2]$ of toluene used in high explosives when nitrated with toluene. Commonly called TNT.

Trinkitat, Battle of. See El Teb, Battles of.

Triple Alliance, War of the (1864–70). In 1864 Uruguay's Colorado (Red) Party revolted against the Blanco (White) Party, then in power. The Brazilian state of Rio Grande do Sol supported the rebels and rebuffed the offer to mediate held out by Francisco Solano López [q.v.], the dictator of Paraguay, who then warned that if Brazil invaded Uruguay (then called Banda Oriental), it would mean war. In October 1864 Brazilian troops crossed the frontier into Uruguay, and on 11 November 1864 López seized a Brazilian ship on the Río Paraguay. On 1 May 1865 Brazil, Uruguay, and Argentina signed a secret pact, the Triple Alliance, agreeing jointly to make war on Paraguay.

The war that followed is sometimes called the Paraguayan War. Some arms for the Paraguayan army and officers to train its men had been acquired in Europe, and by November 1864 Paraguay had an army of 30,000 well-trained soldiers, mostly Guarani-speaking Indians; a reserve of 34,000 boys aged fourteen to eighteen; and a third reserve of badly armed younger boys and old men. However, of the first line troops, only 250 were armed with breech-loading carbines, and most had only Brown Bess muskets [q.v.].

On 29 March 1865 Paraguayan forces invaded the Argentina province of Corrientes, and on 14 April Argentina declared war on Paraguay. In response López declared war on

Argentina and Uruguay and, with the intent of invading southern Brazil, marched an army of 12,400 from the Paraná River through northeast Argentine territory, capturing supplies and weapons as it went. However, on 18 September an Allied army of 30,000 under Venancio Flores [q.v.], chief of the Uruguayan army, defeated a Paraguayan army of 4,000 on the banks of the Uruguay River near the town of Uruguayana. In June 1865 in an unsuccessful attempt to gain control of the rivers the Paraguayans made a surprise attack upon nine Brazilian armored steamers in the Riachuelo (Matanzas) River.

As the Allies prepared to invade Paraguay, López concentrated 25,000 men at the great fortress of Humaitá, on a peninsula between the Paraná and Paraguay rivers. His force was defeated by the Allies on the Paraná River [see Paraná, Battle of] on 16–17 April 1866, and at Estero Velhaco on 2 May. On 24 May the bloodiest battle of the war was fought [see Tuyutí, Battles of]. López was defeated, but the Allies were too exhausted to pursue, and he was able to fall back and reorganize. On 14 June the camp of the Allies on the Paraná was bombarded. On 22 September Paraguay virtually knocked the Argentineans out of the war by defeating them in the Battle of Curupayty [q.v.], Paraguay's greatest victory, but also its last.

An attempted invasion of northwestern Paraguay through the Matto Grosso in 1867 was a fiasco. Cholera raged on both sides. On 17 February of the same year two Allied monitors steamed past Curupayty, and on 21 February six Allied ironclads forced the passage of the Humaitá River but found the capital, Asunción, abandoned, for López had drawn his army, now reduced to about 10,000, back to Ypacarai, just north of Angostura. There on 25 December 1867 López suffered a decisive defeat in the Battle of Ypacaraí [q.v.] and fled north with a handful of cavalry.

On 5 August 1868 Colonel Francisco Martínez (d. 1868), the besieged commander at Humaitá, was forced to surrender the extensive fortifications there, for the starving garrison was reduced to 3,000. Martínez was so weak he could neither stand nor speak. On López's orders the few who managed to struggle back to their own lines were executed as traitors. Among them was Colonel Martínez's wife, who was flogged and executed. Five days later the town of Angostura surrendered, and the next day Brazilian troops entered and sacked Asunción.

A paranoid López formed a police organization, *fiscoles de sangre* (blood prosecutors) to seek out traitors. Between June and December 1868 some 400 people were tortured and executed. They included the bishop of Paraguay, López's brothers and brothers-in-law, and numerous women. His own mother and sisters were condemned to death but were saved by the ending of the war.

On 24 March 1869 Prince Louis d'Eu [q.v.] of the Brazilian army was appointed commander-in-chief of the Allied army, and on 8 May he surprised and captured Rosario. In a running battle in August with fights on the 12th, 16th, 18th, and 21st López was defeated, but he refused to surrender. From 21 to 27 December 1868 he was besieged at Lomas Valentinas [q.v.], and in the fighting there his army was virtually annihilated. He made his escape with only about 2,000 men. From Chaco tribes and from children, old men, and some women he raised a fresh army of 10,000 and established a new capital at the village of Piribebuy in central Paraguay.

On 12 August the pursuing Allies outflanked his force and attacked, killing 2,000, some of whom were found to be mere boys wearing false beards. With the remnants of his ragtag army López retreated into the most remote corner of Paraguay. Hundreds died on the way. In February 1870, with his mistress, Eliza Lynch [q.v.], their sons, and about 500 troops, he sought refuge at Cerro Cora, a low depression in the foothills of the Serra (Cordillera) de Amambahy in the Matto Grosso along the Brazil-Paraguay border. In a fifteen-minute fight on the bank of the Aquidabán River [see Aquidabán River, Battle of] on 1 March 1870 he was killed by Brazilian lancers. Mrs. Lynch and her fifteen-year-old son, a colonel, tried to escape but were caught, and the boy was killed when he refused to surrender. His mother buried her lover and their son with her own hands. On 20 June a peace treaty was signed between the Allies and Paraguay. Four years later Mrs. Lynch was seen in London, where she was described as a distinguished-looking woman.

During this war every male Paraguayan capable of fighting, regardless of age, was conscripted. Entire regiments were formed of boys twelve to fifteen years old. Women were conscripted as well. Mrs. Lynch organized a regiment of amazons, and women were used to dig fortifications and as beasts of burden to carry food and ammunition. When no longer capable of working, they were left by the road to die or were killed to prevent them from revealing information to the enemy.

At the beginning of the war the population of Paraguay had been 1,337,439, mostly Guarani-speaking Indians. At war's end the population had shrunk to 28,746 men and 106,254 women above the age of fifteen and 86,079 children. Allied losses were estimated to be 1 million.

A Brazilian army of occupation remained in Paraguay until 1876. There were revolutions in 1881, 1894, and 1898 and spasmodic uprisings into the twentieth century, but none improved the welfare of the country. Not until May 1993 was there a free election of a civilian president.

Tripolitan War (1801–05). In 1801 Yusuf Kabamanli, ruler of the Barbary state of Tripoli, to whom the United States had paid ransom money and yearly blackmail, declared war upon the United States when the authorities refused to pay a two-hundred-thousand-dollar ransom for the return of captured American seamen. In response, the United States dispatched to the Mediterranean a four-vessel squadron under Captain Isaac Hull (1773–1843). The war was waged mostly in a series of naval engagements against the Barbary pirates. Land operations were conducted by William Eaton [q.v.], who in 1801 was U.S. consul in Tunis. Using forty thousand dollars supplied by the Secret Service Fund [q.v.], he planned to overthrow Yusuf Kabamanli and replace him with his brother Hamet Kabamanli, then in exile in Egypt.

In November 1804 Eaton, accompanied by seven marines and a midshipman under the command of First Lieutenant Presley N. O'Bannon, arrived in Egypt. He assembled a mercenary army of assorted nationalities; Hamet provided 80 mounted Bedouins and 150 infantry. Accompanied by Hamet, Eaton and his little army of about 400 with 107 camels began their march across the Libyan desert on 6 March 1805. In spite of the hardships of the journey, mutinies, and Hamet's timidity, Eaton rendezvoused with USS *Argus* at the Gulf of Bomba, 20 miles east of Derna, on 18 April. On 27

April, with the help of three warships, he successfully attacked Derna, and for the first time the American flag flew over captured foreign soil [see Derna, Battle of].

The capture of Derna inspired Yusuf Kabamanli to reduce the ransom he was asking for the return of the captured seamen to sixty thousand dollars on condition that Eaton yield the town. American negotiators cravenly agreed, and Eaton, enraged, returned to the United States. Hamet Kabamanli and his people were left to their fate.

Tripolitan War *William Eaton leaves Egypt to attack Tripoli, March 1805*

Tripolitsa Massacre (5 October 1851), Greek War of Independence. At the outset of the revolt of the Greeks in the Morea (Peloponnesus) some 10,000 Turks were massacred in this city in central Peloponnesus, 39 miles southwest of Corinth, an act that brought on savage Turkish reprisals. On 30 June 1825 the city was retaken and destroyed by Ibrahim Pasha [q.v.].

Trocadero, Battle of (31 August 1823), French intervention in Spain. French forces under General Louis Antoine de Bourbon, Duc de Angoulême (1775–1844), defeated the Spanish republican revolutionaries under Colonel Rafael del Riego y Núñez [q.v.], eight miles from Cádiz, capturing two forts, the principal of which was known as Trocadero [see Cádiz, Siege of]. In memory of its capture the hill on the right

Trocadero *French attack on the Trocadero, 1823*

bank of the Seine in Paris was named Trocadéro, and on this ground a palace so named was erected for the international exhibition of 1878.

Trochu, Louis Jules (1815–1896). A French soldier who served as a captain in Algeria, as a colonel in the Crimean War [q.v.], and as a division commander in Italy in 1859. In 1866 he was employed at the Ministry of War preparing army reorganization schemes. On 17 August 1870, during the Franco-Prussian War, he was governor of Paris [see Buzenval, Battle of]. Under the republic he became president of the Government of National Defense during the siege of Paris [q.v.] in 1870–71. He resigned in 1873.

Troop. 1. A unit in a cavalry regiment corresponding to an infantry company and usually commanded by a captain. The term was not officially used in the U.S. army until 1883.
2. A body of soldiers of indeterminate size.
3. A beat of drum as a signal to assemble, usually to march.

Troop Corporal Major. The chief British noncommissioned officer of a troop of the Household Cavalry, which had no sergeants.

Trooper. 1. A cavalryman.
2. A cavalry horse.

Troop Horse. A trooper's cavalry horse. An officer's horse, usually of better quality, was a charger.

Trooping the Colors / Colours. A British military ceremony in the public mounting of guards.

Troopship. Usually a merchant ship "taken up" to transport soldiers. Britain with its far-flung empire made the greatest use of troopships. These were seldom of the best, and the tales of misery and discomfort on board were legendary. The ships were always overcrowded, and when cholera or other infectious diseases broke out, the results were often catastrophic. Shipwrecks were common, and some gained renown through the bravery and fortitude of the troops, for there were never enough lifeboats. When the *Sarah Sands* sank in November 1847, the British commander-in-chief issued a general order on the splendid behavior of the soldiers of the 54th Regiment, who had not panicked, but he did nothing to improve the conditions or the safety of troopships.

At two-thirty on the morning of 27 October 1848 the 177-ton brig *Governor Phillips,* on a voyage from Sydney, Australia, to Hobart, Tasmania, struck a reef off Gull Island in high seas. There were 85 on board, including 5 young children, 40 convicts in chains, and a military guard of a lieutenant, a sergeant, and 13 privates of the 96th Regiment. Waves ripped up the decks, and 2 of the guards were killed by falling planks. The remainder worked feverishly to free the convicts and saved all but 4. Of the 85 passengers on board, 16 were lost, including the lieutenant and 6 privates.

In 1857 the *Transit* (soldiers called her Chance It) sailed from England for China. She encountered a heavy storm and sprang a leak in the Bay of Biscay. Later she broke her mainmast and foundered on a rock in the Strait of Banda off the coast of Malaya. Survivors waited two days on slim rations before being rescued and carried to Singapore.

Conditions aboard troopships were exposed by Charles Dickens (1812–1870) and others when the situation aboard the *Great Tasmania* [q.v.] was revealed.

The most celebrated sinking of a British troopship was the wreck of the *Birkenhead* on 26 February 1852 off Sanya Point, a headland near Cape Agulhas in South Africa. The ship carried 638, of whom 551, including women and children, were passengers. There were only three lifeboats. Of those on board, 184 were saved, a number that included all the women and children. As the ship sank, the troops, drafts for several regiments, were drawn up on deck, where the men and their officers stood fast, knowing that if they swam to the launched boats they would swamp them. In his poem "Soldier an' Sailor Too" Rudyard Kipling [q.v.] paid tribute to their heroism: "to stand and be still to the Birken'ead drill is a damn tough bullet to chew."

The worst troopship disaster for Americans occurred at the end of the Civil War, when the *Sultana* [q.v.], a side-wheel Mississippi steamboat, blew its boilers on 27 April 1865 near Memphis Tennessee.

Troops of the Line. See Arms of the Service.

Trotha, Lothar von (1848–1920). A German soldier who served in the Franco-Prussian War [q.v.]. He was commander of troops in German East Africa (mainland Tanzania) in 1894–97. In 1900 he commanded the First East Asian Brigade during the Boxer Rebellion [q.v.]. In 1904 he commanded in German South-West Africa (Namibia) and led the troops in the Herero War.

Trou-de-Loup. Literally, wolf's hole.

1. A sloping pit, usually pointed at the bottom like an inverted cone, with sharpened sticks in the middle.

2. In the manufacture of cannon, the hole in which the superfluous metal of a cast is run.

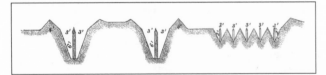

Drawings of Trou-de-Loup

Troupes de Marine. Units originally raised to defend French naval posts and colonial possessions. Two regiments of infantry with a corps of artillery were formed in 1822 and in 1828 came under the naval ministry. By 1840 there were 140 companies distributed in the French colonies. Officers rarely came from St. Cyr; most were promoted from the ranks. Conscripts were not allowed to serve unless they volunteered after six months' home service. Enlistees came mainly from Corsica and southern France. Serving more often on land than on sea, marines saw service in the Peninsular War and in the Russian Campaign [qq.v.]. After 1900 they were called La Coloniale.

Troupes de Marine   *A color party of French marines*

Trousers. Loose pants reaching the ankle were originally used in armies only by soldiers during drill or while doing fatigues. In the early nineteenth century they were introduced for campaign wear. They became common wear about 1830.

Trowel Bayonet. A bayonet designed to be used as an entrenching tool introduced into the American army as an experiment in 1879. It was soon discontinued, for when soldiers used it as a shovel, dirt clogged the barrel of the rifle.

Trunions / Trunnions. The two cylindrical arms attached to the sides of a cannon to support it in its carriage. They formed the horizontal axis on which the piece rotated when elevated or depressed. The outer face of the trunion was often used to record a gun's type, number, manufacturer, and date of manufacture.

It was a considerable advance in the design of artillery when trunions were introduced in the last half of the fifteenth century. They were placed not at the gun's center of gravity but forward so that most of the weight of guns and howitzers was toward the breech.

Ts'ao-chow, Battle of (18–19 May 1865), Nien Rebellion. Northwest of this town in Shantung (now Ho-tse), imperial forces under Manchu General Seng-ko-lin-ch'in [q.v.] were lured into a Nien ambush sprung by Chang Tsung-yü (d. 1868) and suffered a crushing defeat in one of the bloodiest battles of the war. Seng-ko-lin-ch'in finally managed to draw back into a village, but he was soon surrounded by the Nien army, which was supplemented by members of secret societies and local bandits. Late that night he attempted to cut his way out. Although he broke through the first line of besiegers, his troops became confused in the dark and ran into more Nien and a local force. Seng-ko-lin-ch'in was wounded eight times before he was killed.

Tsao-ho-ku / Tsaokohow, Battle of (30 November 1894), Sino-Japanese War. A small but hard-fought battle in which Japanese forces under Prince Aritimo Yamagata [q.v.] defeated Chinese forces near this Manchurian town about 60 miles south-southeast of Mukden (Shenyang). Soon after, cold weather and a shortage of supplies brought the Japanese advance into Manchuria to a temporary halt.

Tsêng Kuo-Fan (1811–1872). A Chinese soldier and statesman who was born in Hunan Province and took three degrees in Chinese scholarship, including the highest, *chin shih*. In 1852, during the Taiping Rebellion [q.v.], as governor of Hunan Province he raised an army of volunteers recruited mainly from the hardy peasants of the mountainous areas of the province and adjacent regions and trained them after the manner of famed Ming General Ch'i Chi-kuang (1528–1587). His troops were organized into battalions containing 500 soldiers and 180 camp followers. Even after the rebellion had been put down, his example was followed by the governors of other provinces that were threatened by rebels and bandits so that by the end of the nineteenth century China was a patchwork of regional armies over which the central government exercised little control.

The Hunan forces were blooded in fights with local bandits and secret societies. In their first encounter with the Taipings in 1854 they were defeated, but on 1 May of that year they won a victory at Hsiang-t'an [see Taiping Rebellion]. In July a victory at Yüeh-chou (Chihkiang) in western Hunan on the Yüan River, 210 miles south-southwest of Changsha, proved to be the turning point in Tsêng's campaign, giving him enormous prestige and proof of the soundness of his strategy.

With a fleet of 240 war junks he destroyed half of the Taipings' riverboats, wresting from them the control of the central portion of the Yangtze River. He captured Wuchang, the capital of Hupeh Province, and Hanyang, near Hankow. Although the rebels retook Wuchang, Tsêng cleared first the country around Lake Poyang Hu and then the province of Kiangsu in eastern China. In 1857 he took command of Cheh-kiang and cleared the province of Ngan-hui. In 1860 he had an army of 120,000 men. He was appointed viceroy of the two Kiang provinces and imperial war minister. Two years later he was appointed assistant grand secretary of state. He besieged Nanking (Nanjing or Nanxiang), the Taiping capital, and on 19 July 1864 it capitulated [see Nanking, Siege of]. In 1865, at the end of the Taiping Rebellion, he was sent, after the death of Seng-ko-lin-ch'in [q.v.], to quell the Nien Rebellion [q.v.] in Shantung (Shandong). Although he failed and in 1866 was relieved of his command, he continued to be effective. He built the Kiangnan arsenal at Shanghai.

Tshitsagov / Chichagov, Paul / Pavel Vasilievich (1767–1849). A Russian admiral and general who served in the fleet of Catherine the Great (1729–1796). In May 1812 he was in command of the Black Sea Fleet and governor of Moldavia and Walachia. In August 1812 he moved north with 35,000 troops to put pressure upon Napoleon's southern flank [see Russian Campaign, Napoleon's]. In mid-September he was reinforced by other Russian troops and formed one of the three armies threatening Napoleon's retreat. After capturing the French supply base at Minsk on 16 November, he turned east and took Borisov on Napoleon's line of retreat and destroyed the bridges across the Berezina River [q.v.]. Although he effectively harassed Napoleon in the crossing of the Berezina on 27–28 November, his army was roughly handled. Nevertheless, he pursued the French to the Niemen River. Nothing is known of Tshitsagov's subsequent career.

Tsingtao, German Occupation of (November 1897). Until 1891, when the Chinese built a naval base in this seaport on the southeast shore of Kiaochow Bay in northeast China, Tsingtao (today Qingdao) was a mere fishing village. Using the murder of two German missionaries in Shantung (Shandong) Province as an excuse, Germany occupied it in 1897 and in 1898 forced the Chinese to lease the area to Germany for ninety-nine years. Kaiser William boasted: "Hundreds of German traders will revel in the knowledge that the German Empire has at last secured a firm footing in Asia" and "hundreds of thousands of Chinese will quiver when they feel the iron fist of Germany heavy on their necks, while the whole German nation will be delighted that its government has done a manly act." Tsingtao was captured by the Japanese in 1914.

Tso Tsung-t'ang (1812–1885). A Chinese general and statesman who aided Tsêng Kuo-fan [q.v.] of Hunan in 1861–65 and was credited with reclaiming the province of Chekiang from the Taipings in 1862 [see Taiping Rebellion]. He was governor of Shensi (Shaanxi) and Kansu (Gansu) from 1866 until 1873. He suppressed the Muslim Rebellion, captured Suchow in Kansu, put down the Nien Rebellion [q.v.] with a provincial army in 1868, and in 1875 crushed the Tungan Revolt. In March 1876 he launched a campaign that ended in the defeat of Yakub Beg [q.v.] in May 1877, and in 1878 he extended Chinese control of Sinkiang (Xinjiang) as far as Ili [see Chinese Turkestan, Conquest of]. In 1881 he was made a member of the Tsung-li Yamen (a high honor), and in 1884 he took part in the war against the French in Foochow (Fuzhou) [see Indochina, French Invasion and Occupation of].

Tsuba. The plate guard on Japanese swords. It was almost always highly decorated. In the nineteenth century the number of styles multiplied greatly, and every variety of technique was used.

Tuareg. A Berber people of the central Sahara, who call themselves *Keh Tagelmoust* (people of the veil), for the men wear dark blue veils. They inhabit an area from Tuat [q.v.] in the north to northern Nigeria and from Lake Chad in the east to modern Mauritania. Fiercely independent, they were constantly at odds with the French, attacking caravans, columns, and detachments.

Tuat, French Invasions of (1899–1901). Tuat was a complex of oases around the Hammada of Tademaït in southwestern Algeria and southeastern Morocco. The chief settlement, Salah, was claimed by the sultan of Morocco. On 28 November 1899 French Captain Théodore Pein (1868–1930?) with 90 cameleers, 15 horsemen, and 40 goumiers (Chamba irregulars) escorted what was purportedly a scientific expedition under a geologist, M. Flamand, out of Ouargla, Algeria. On 27 December the party reached the edge of Tuat. After fighting a battle at Igosten in which about 50 Arabs were killed, Pein moved on Salah, which on 29 December surrendered without a fight.

In February–April, reinforced by two companies of tirailleurs, a company of Bats d'Af and a half company of spahis, a section of sappers [qq.v.], and some 80 mm guns, he completed the conquest of Tuat.

In 1900, after the bulk of the French had departed, leaving behind only garrisons, the inhabitants revolted. For the second expedition in 1901 the French requisitioned 35,000 camels, 25,000 of which perished. This campaign destroyed the fragile economy of the region. A report of 29 March 1901 spoke of "a country which is unhealthy, miserable, hardly able to nourish its inhabitants, producing only dates, uninhabitable for European troops. In a word: not worth the sacrifices made."

Tube. The barrel of an artillery piece.

Tuchune. A Chinese warlord.

Tucker, Henry H. (1841?–1908). An American soldier and scout who during the American Civil War served as a Union army enlisted man in the Ohio infantry. Although he was wounded and discharged for disability, he reenlisted in the 143rd Illinois. After the war he moved to Kansas.

One of the scouts of George Forsyth [q.v.], Tucker was present at the Battle of Beecher's Island [q.v.], in which he was posted as a sharpshooter. His arm was broken by a bullet the first day, 17 September 1868. John Haley, who came to his aid, was himself wounded, and while young Eli Ziegler (1852–1916) attempted to apply a tourniquet to Tucker's arm, Tucker was struck by an arrow. After the rescue on 25 September, he walked most of the nearly 100 miles to Fort Wallace because the jouncing of the army wagon was too painful. In 1869 he was a lieutenant in the Kansas militia but then disappeared from history.

Tucumán, Battle of (24 September 1812), Argentine revolt against Spain. Near this Argentinean town at the eastern end of the Andes, patriot forces under Manuel Belgrano [q.v.] defeated royalists. On 6 July 1816 the united provinces of Río de la Plata met here to declare their independence.

Tudela, Battle of (23 November 1808), Peninsular War. A French army of 30,000 under Marshal Jean Lannes [q.v.] defeated a Spanish army of 45,000 under General Francisco de Castaños [q.v.] near this commune on the Ebro River, 52 miles south of Pamplona. Castaños had failed to put out cavalry pickets, and the arrival of the French before he completed his line of battle caught him by surprise. The Spanish lost nearly 4,000 men and 26 guns; the French lost about 600. The French remained in occupation of Tudela until 1813.

Tu Duc (1829–1883). The emperor of Annam from 1847 to 1883 who fought unsuccessfully to keep European missionaries and French soldiers out of his empire in Indochina (Vietnam).

Tuğ. The war standard of the Turkish sultans.

Tugendbund. Literally, league of virtue. A Prussian patriotic society, formed in 1808 in Königsberg following the humiliations of the Treaties of Tilsit [q.v.], that gained wide support among intellectuals. Its aim was to revive Prussian morale and achieve independence through an anti-Napoleon propaganda campaign. When Napoleon ordered it suppressed, it pursued its work underground. Its influence is credited for the 1813 Prussian defection from the French alliance. In 1815 its

views were deemed too radical, and it was effectively suppressed.

Tuiuti, Battle of (3 November 1867), War of the Triple Alliance. Although the Paraguayans were defeated by the Allies near this village (no longer extant), Paraguayan dictator Francisco Solano López [q.v.] rewarded the survivors with a medal, a rare instance of a medal being awarded for a defeat.

Tukulor-French Wars. See Franco-Tukulor Wars.

Tula Arsenal. In 1595 Tsar Boris Fedorovich Godunov (1551?–1605) established the first Russian gun factory at Tula, an industrial city on the Oka River, 110 miles south of Moscow. In 1705 it was developed into a great arsenal by Pëtr Alekseevich I, known as Peter the Great (1672–1725). In the nineteenth century it employed many foreign craftsmen and pioneered in the manufacture and use of machine-made parts.

Tulwar. See Talwar.

Tumander. A Baluchi headman.

Tumbril. A covered cart used to carry ammunition, tools, and sometimes money or prisoners.

Tung Wang. See Yang Hsiu-ch'ing.

Tunisia, French Capture of (April–May 1881). In spite of numerous interventions by British, French, and Italians, Tunis (Tunisia) retained some measure of independence until France, using a raid by Kroumir tribesmen into Algeria as an excuse, launched a punitive expedition. In April 1861 French seaborne forces captured the port city of Bizerte while a second force from Algeria moved across the border. Tunis surrendered in May, and the Treaty of Bardo declared Tunisia a French protectorate.

Tupelo, Battle of (14–15 July 1864), American Civil War. Union General Andrew Jackson Smith [q.v.] with 14,200 troops moved from Memphis, Tennessee, to protect the railroad line used to send supplies to General William Tecumseh Sherman [q.v.], then advancing upon Atlanta, Georgia. On 11 July he reached Pontotoc, in northwest Mississippi, 17 miles west of the town of Tupelo, 57 miles north-northwest of Columbus. Confederate General Nathan Bedford Forrest [q.v.], who commanded 6,000 troops in Mississippi, concentrated his force at Okolona, 16 miles south of Tupelo. On 13 July, as Smith swerved toward the town, Lieutenant General Stephen D. Lee [q.v.] joined Forrest with 2,000 men, and the combined force took up a strong position in a line about two miles from Tupelo, from which they launched gallant but uncoordinated charges that were repulsed. Instead of counterattacking, Smith, having lost 674 men (77 killed, 559 wounded, and 38 missing), withdrew northward, a decision for which he was criticized by Sherman. The Confederates lost 210 killed and 1,116 wounded, including Forrest.

Tupiza, Battle of (7 November 1810), Argentine revolt against Spain. Argentine troops under Colonel Antonio González defeated a Spanish royalist force under General José

María de Córdoba y Rosas (1800?–1830) at this small mining town in Upper Peru (Bolivia) near the Argentine border. The government of Buenos Aires awarded an escudo [q.v.] to each of the victorious participants.

Turbans. See Pagri.

Turchin, John Basil (1822–1901), originally Ivan Vasilovich Turchinoff. A Russian soldier, educated at the Imperial Military Academy at St. Petersburg, who fought in the Hungarian Revolution and the Crimean War [qq.v.], rising to the rank of colonel. After marrying a Polish woman, he emigrated to the United States in 1856. He worked as an engineer for the Illinois Central Railroad until, at the beginning of the American Civil War, he was made colonel of the 19th Illinois. While with that unit he wrote a manual, *Brigade Drill*. When he was given command of a brigade under General Don Carlos Buell [q.v.], his troops predictably were well drilled, but with his tacit approval, they soon gained a reputation for pillaging and wreaking havoc. After one of his regiments had occupied Bowling Green, Kentucky, a correspondent for the *Cincinnati Gazette* reported that the town "presented a scene of desolation seldom witnessed," and in late April 1862, when he captured Huntsville, Alabama, he gave his men free rein. Twenty miles west of the town Confederate cavalry, helped by about 100 of the townsmen, had routed the 18th Ohio, killing more than 30 Union soldiers. Forming his men in the town square, Turchin reminded them of the townsmen's part in the battle, ending with the words "I shut mine eyes for one hour." In the melee that followed black servant girls were raped, houses ransacked, and an estimated fifty thousand dollars' worth of plate, clocks, jewelry, and other valuables were taken.

On 2 July Buell ordered a court-martial for Turchin and Lieutenant Colonel Joseph R. Scott, his second-in-command. Turchin was charged with neglect of duty, conduct unbecoming an officer, and disobedience of lawful orders; the latter charge referred to his taking his wife to war (on at least one occasion she was known to have assumed command when her husband was ill). On 5 July he tried to avoid the court-martial by writing a letter of resignation, but the court convened on 20 July with Brigadier James Garfield [q.v.], the future president of the United States, as president of the court. During the trial Turchin learned that he had been nominated for promotion to brigadier general and that the Senate had already given its approval. On 27 July he requested that his letter of resignation be canceled.

On 6 August 1862 both Turchin and Scott were found guilty and dishonorably discharged. Public opinion, rallied by the press in the North, roundly damned General Buell for prosecuting him. When Turchin arrived home in Chicago, he received a hero's welcome and was greeted by an army colonel with a letter from President Lincoln dated 19 July. Mrs. Turchin had appealed directly to the president. Turchin was confirmed as a brigadier general, and his court-martial conviction was vacated. Scott too was cleared and promoted colonel.

Turchin went on to distinguish himself in the Battle of Chickamauga, where his brilliant charges earned him the sobriquet of the Russian Thunderbolt, and later in the Atlanta Campaign [qq.v.]. Major General Absalom Baird (1824–1905), his division commander, spoke of him as "one of the most thoroughly educated and scientific soldiers in the country, and a more devoted patriot than most of those born upon our soil." On 15 July 1864 he went on sick leave, and on 4 October he resigned because of ill health.

After the war he became a solicitor of patents in Chicago, and in 1873 he founded a Polish colony at Radom (named after Radom, Poland), a small village, 16 miles south of Centralia, Illinois. Late in life he became mentally deranged. He died in 1901 in the Southern Hospital for the Insane in Anna, Illinois.

Turcos. Algerian riflemen, Tirailleurs Algérien [q.v.], in the French army (Armée d'Afrique). In 1875 there were three regiments organized as Zouaves [q.v.].

Turcos *A local turco lieutenant*

Turkestan. See Chinese Turkestan, Conquest of.

Turkey Bend, Battle of. See White Oak Swamp, Battle of.

Turkish Bells. See Jingling Johnny.

Turkish Cavalry, Mutiny of (1831). While Ibrahim Pasha [q.v.] was conquering Syria, Turkish cavalry at Jiddah mutinied because it had not been paid. The mutiny was led by Tarçe Bilmez, a Georgian Mameluke, who proclaimed himself ruler of the Hejaz and marched on Mecca (Makkah). The Porte recognized his claim and attempted unsuccessfully to persuade him to attack Ibrahim Pasha in Syria. Instead he turned south and plundered al-Qunfidha and Asir. At the seaport town of Mocha in southwest Arabia the Arabs put up a stout resistance, and Bilmez suffered heavy casualties. The survivors were transported by British ships to Bombay and then to Constantinople (Istanbul).

Turkish Civil War (1808). Mustafa Bairakdar (1775–1808), a former grand vizier, led an army in an unsuccessful attack upon Constantinople (Istanbul) in an effort to restore Selim III (1761–1808), who had been deposed as sultan by janissaries [q.v.], and replaced with Mustafa IV (1779–1808). In response, the janissaries strangled Selim. Mustafa too was soon assassinated, and Selim's twenty-three-year-old nephew assumed the throne as Mahmud II (1785–1839), beginning a thirty-one-year reign.

Turkish Mauser 7.65 mm Rifle, Model 1890. A rifle that was essentially the same as the Belgian Mauser 7.65 mm Model 1889. The Turkish Mauser 7.65 mm Model 1893 was a slightly modified version of the Spanish Mauser Model 1893.

Turko-Egyptian Wars. See Egyptian-Turkish Wars; Egyptian Revolt.

Turko-Greek War. See Graeco-Turkish War.

Turko-Montenegrin Wars. After the Battle of Kosovo in 1389 defeated Serbs took refuge in the Black Mountain (Monte Negro), where, ruled by bishop princes and known as Montenegrins, they defied Turkish authority. In the nineteenth century they sided with Russia in its wars with Turkey, in 1852–53 and 1861–62, and allied themselves with Serbia in the Turko-Serbian War [q.v.] in 1876–77.

First War (1852–53). In 1851 Prince-Bishop Danilo I (1826–1860) separated the offices of prince and bishop and proclaimed the first to be hereditary. The Turkish sultan, declaring that Danilo had exceeded his authority, sent troops under Omar Pasha [q.v.] into Montenegro. Austria moved troops to the border of Bosnia and Herzegovina and ordered Omar Pasha to withdraw. After Russia had applied pressure as well, he complied.

Second War (1861–62). When disorder and rebellion followed the death of Danilo I in 1860, the Turks sent a large expedition under Omar Pasha into Montenegro and overran the country. Peace was arranged at the Convention of Scutari (Shkoder). Montenegro agreed not to build forts on the frontier or to import arms.

Third War (1876). In 1875 Montenegro supported the insurrection of Bosnia-Herzegovina, and in 1876 it joined with Serbia in the Turko-Serbian War [q.v.], during which it scored a signal victory in the capture of Niksich [q.v.] (Nikšić). At the Congress of Berlin in 1878 it was declared an autonomous state.

Turko-Persian War (1821–23 and 1826). Following the severe Persian losses in the Russo-Persian War of 1804–12 [q.v.], Crown Prince Abbas Mirza [q.v.] began the modernization of the Persian army, sending officers to England and inviting British officers to come to Persia (Iran). In 1821 Turkish protection of rebellious Azerbaijani tribes prompted him to lead an expedition into eastern Anatolia. There was

fighting in the Lake Van region, and the Persians won a victory over numerically superior forces in the Battle of Erzurum [q.v.]. A peace treaty was signed two years later. The war achieved nothing. Both sides recognized the previous frontiers, and no territory was exchanged.

Turko-Russian Wars. See Russo-Turkish Wars.

Turko-Serbian War (June 1876–March 1877). Christian insurrections against Turkish rule in Bosnia and Herzegovina were brutally put down by the Turks, leading to declarations of war by Serbia on 30 June 1876 and by Montenegro on 2 July. The Turks sent an army into the Balkans and crushed the revolt with great ruthlessness [see Bulgarian Atrocities]. Turkish forces under Suleiman Pasha [q.v.] defeated Serbian forces that contained large numbers of Russian volunteers, in the Battle of Alexinatz on 1 September and in the Battle of Djunis on 29 October [qq.v.]. The Serbs were in danger of being completely overrun when Russia intervened. The war thus became the prelude to the Russo-Turkish War of 1877–78 [q.v.].

Turko-Serbian War *Turkish atrocities included the burning of three Serbians near Tesica. Drawing by Frederic Villiers 1875–6*

Turk's Head Brush. A brush on a staff used in cleaning the bores of guns in the artillery.

Turncoat. A person or unit that changes sides during a war or a battle.

Turner, Nat. See Nat Turner's Insurrection.

Turner, Thomas Elwyn (d. 1862). An American officer commissioned in 1857 who served under General George Crook [q.v.] in operations against hostile Indians in northern California. In 1858 he was with Crook in Washington Territory operating against Indians who had defeated troops at Steptoe's Butte on 17 May. After capturing an Indian village in which several hostiles believed to have killed whites were found, Crook, as commanded, ordered them to be executed. He later wrote that he found "this whole business exceedingly distasteful," but as "Lt. Turner rather enjoyed that kind of thing, I detailed him to execute them, which was done. . . ."

During the American Civil War Turner became a captain and was brevetted major for his gallantry in the Battle of Gaines's Mill [q.v.] on 27 June 1862. He died on 1 August.

Turner, Tomkyns Hilgrove (1766?–1843). A British soldier who saw considerable action in the low countries under Frederick, Duke of York [q.v.], in the 1790s. In 1801 he fought at Aboukir [q.v.], Egypt, and he was present at the surrender of the French at Alexandria. Article 6 of the surrender terms stipulated that all of the looted antiquities and scientific collections the French had accumulated were to be given up, but General Jacque François Menou [q.v.] tried to evade this by claiming that all loot was private property. To prevent wholesale destruction, the British sent Turner, who had a deep interest in antiquaries, to negotiate, and it was finally agreed that the French collections of insects and animals could be retained but that the remainder, including the Rosetta stone, had to be surrendered. With a large detail of artillerymen Turner entered Alexandria to claim Britain's due only to find that the French had already destroyed some of the packing materials. In the face of French abuse he saw the antiquities packed and loaded aboard ship. He accompanied them to England. In 1830 Turner was promoted to general.

Turner's Gap, Battle of. See South Mountain, Battle of.

Turning Movement. A movement aimed not directly at an enemy but at a point in his rear or on his flank, which compels him to abandon his position and become more vulnerable or causes him to divert major forces to meet the threat. [See Envelopment.]

Tuyen Quang, Siege of (16 January–3 March 1885), Sino-French War. At this town (now Tuyenquang) in North Vietnam on the Clear River, 70 miles northwest of Hanoi, on 16 January 1885 Chinese Black Flags [q.v.] and regulars under Liu Yung-fu [q.v.] attacked a French force of 390 Foreign Legionnaires and 200 Tirailleurs Tonkinois under Major Marc Edmond Dominé, who defended an almost indefensible position for more than six weeks. By the end of February the French had only 180 riflemen available to defend a perimeter 1,200 yards long. They were rescued by a relief force under General Louis Alexandre Brière de L'Isles on 3 March. Nearly half the defenders had been killed or wounded.

Tuyutí, Battles of. Two important battles of the War of the Triple Alliance [q.v.] were fought at Estancia Tuyutí, approximately 40 miles northeast of Encarnación, Paraguay.

First Battle of Tuyutí (24 May 1866), sometimes called the Battle of Paso de Patria. By whatever name, this was, for the numbers engaged, the bloodiest battle in Latin American history. An Allied army of 45,000 Brazilian and Uruguayans under General Venancio Flores [q.v.] crossed the Paraná River and advanced into southeastern Paraguay. On 2 May General Francesco Solano López [q.v.] with 25,000 Paraguayans moved into defensive positions to meet the advancing Allies, but López changed his mind at the last minute and launched an attack. He was repulsed, and the Allies surrounded him on three sides, but he refused to surrender. The result was a near massacre, the Paraguayans losing 6,000 killed and 7,000 wounded; the Allies losing 8,000 killed and wounded. Only 350 wounded Paraguayans were taken prisoner. The Allied forces failed to follow up their victory, and López was able to fall back and reorganize.

Second Battle of Tuyutí (3 November 1867). After two years of war the Allies had boxed the Paraguayans into defensive positions near Estancia Tuyutí. Paraguayan General Francisco Solano López with 6,000 men launched a surprise attack upon the right flank of the Allied positions holding 16,000. Paraguayan cavalry led the attack and broke through the lines. This was followed by infantry, who also succeeded but who broke up inside the lines to loot. The Allies counterattacked and drove the Paraguayans out. Each side lost about 2,400 in this inconclusive battle.

Twiggs, David Emmanuel (1790–1862). An American soldier who was educated at Franklin College in Athens, Georgia. He studied law before the War of 1812 [q.v.], when he was commissioned a captain in the 8th Infantry on 12 March 1812. He ended the war [q.v.] as a major in the 28th Infantry. In 1817–18 he served in the First Seminole War [q.v.] under General Edmund Gaines [q.v.]. In 1828 troops under his command built Fort Winnebago on the right bank of the Fox River at the portage between the Fox and Wisconsin rivers. He commanded there until he became a lieutenant colonel in 1831. During the Black Hawk War [q.v.] he was stricken by cholera and did not see action. In the Second Seminole War [q.v.] he was colonel of the 2nd Dragoons in Florida, and on 21 March 1838 he captured more than 500 Indians, 151 of whom were warriors. In the Mexican War [q.v.] he served first as a colonel under General Zachary Taylor [q.v.] and then as a brigadier general under General Winfield Scott [q.v.]. He fought at Veracruz and Cerro Gordo [qq.v.]. At the beginning of the Civil War he commanded the Department of Texas. In February 1861 he surrendered to Confederate Colonel Ben McCulloch, an act for which he was dismissed from the service. On 22 May he was appointed major general in the Provisional Army of the Confederacy, but he was too old and infirm for field service and was compelled to retire on 15 June 1862. He died on 15 July.

Twiggs was noted for his crude behavior. George Ballantine, who served with him in the Mexican War, claimed that he had a contempt for "even the common courtesies of civilized life."

Two Brothers, War of. See Miguelite Wars.

Tyler, Robert Charles (1833?–1865). An American soldier of fortune who in 1856 served under William Walker [q.v.] in Nicaragua. Nothing more is known of his life until the

American Civil War. On 18 April 1861 he enlisted in the Confederate 15th Tennessee Infantry and in December was elected lieutenant colonel. The following May he was colonel. He served as provost marshal under Braxton Bragg [q.v.] in Kentucky. He fought at Perryville, was wounded at Shiloh, and commanded a brigade at Chickamauga [qq.v.], where he lost a leg, after which he was promoted brigadier general. He was killed defending a small earthwork at West Point, Georgia.

Tyler Gabion. A gabion made from a single sheet of galvanized iron. Each weighed 28 pounds, and no pickets were needed. It could be rolled into a cylinder and tied with strong wire ties through four eyelets by two men in about ten minutes.

Typhoid Fever. One of the great scourges of the nineteenth century. It was responsible for the largest mortality of any disease affecting armies in the field. Even at the end of the century the death rate from typhoid during the Second Anglo-Boer War [q.v.] was 15 per 1,000 among the troops and still higher among the Boers in the concentration camps [q.v.]. Some 31,000 British troops who contracted the disease were invalided to England.

In 1896 hypodermic injection of the dead organism was developed by Sir Almroth Wright (1861–1947), but even after proof of its effectiveness was evident, many refused to believe in antityphoid inoculation. By 1909 it was used in major European armies. Only the British and Russian armies refused to make it mandatory.

Tyrnau / Trnava, Battle of (29 September 1848), Hungarian Revolution. Rebel forces under Richard Guyon [q.v.] defeated Josef Ječlaić od Bužima [q.v.], the ban of Croatia, at this Slovakian town (*Nagyszombat* in Hungarian) 23 miles northeast of Bratislava.

Tyrnavos, Battle of. See Graeco-Turkish War.

Tyrolean Revolt (April 1809–February 1810). After the French conquered the Tyrol in 1805, Napoleon, by the Treaty of Pressburg, united it with Bavaria. In 1809 a revolt against Bavarian rule was led by Andreas Hofer [q.v.], who received moral support from Austria. After Hofer's sturdy mountaineers defeated a Bavarian force sent to suppress them, a joint French-Bavarian army was mounted and crushed the revolt. Hofer was betrayed, captured, and shot at Mantua on 10 February 1810. In 1814 the Treaty of Paris reunited the Tyrol with Austria. In 1819 the Austrian emperor ennobled the Hofer family.

Tytler, John Adam (1835–1880). A British soldier who served under Colin Campbell [q.v.] in an expedition against Adam Khel Afridis on the Northwest Frontier [q.v.] in 1850. He won the Victoria Cross as a lieutenant on 10 February 1858, during the Indian Mutiny [q.v.], in the course of which he was shot in the arm and received a spear thrust into his chest in hand-to-hand fighting. He also served in the Umbeyla Campaign of 1863 and the Hazara Field Force on Black Mountain in 1868 [see Hazara Expeditions].

Tzú-chi / Tzeki, Battle of (20 August 1862). Frederick Townsend Ward [q.v.], after clearing a 30-mile cordon around Shanghai of Taiping rebels [see Taiping Rebellion] and winning, with some French and British help, eleven victories within four months, led his mercenary army in an attack upon the walled city of Tzú-chi, near Ningpo (Ningo). Although successful, Ward was mortally wounded in the battle.

U

Uchatius, Franz von (1811–1881). An Austro-Hungarian soldier, inventor, and artillerist who in 1856 introduced an improved process of manufacturing steel. Among his later improvements and inventions were a ballistic apparatus, ring grenades, and a steel bronze (called Uchatius bronze) used in the manufacture of cannon.

Uclés, Battle of (13 January 1809), Peninsular War. In east-central Spain, 40 miles west of Cuenca, at the fortified town of Uclés, which lies at the foot of a monastery once owned by the Military Order of Santiago, a French force of 16,300 men with 32 guns under Marshal Claude Victor [q.v.] defeated a Spanish force of 12,000 with 4 guns under General Francisco Xavier Venegas (d. 1838). The French lost barely 200; the Spanish lost 1,000 killed and wounded and 6,000 taken prisoner.

Ueno, Battle of (4 July 1868), Boshin Civil War. In this last battle of the Boshin Civil War [q.v.] fought near Edo (renamed Tokyo in November 1868) the forces of the shogun were defeated, ending the Tokugawa shogunate (1603–1868). The rebel troops were transported to Edo by ships provided by shipping magnate Yataro Iwasaki (1834–1885), who later founded Mitsubishi.

Ueno is now a district in northern Tokyo centered on Japan's first public park, zoo, and museum.

Uganda Mutiny (1897–1901). British Major James Macdonald [q.v.] with 300 Sudanese troops embarked from Mombasa in East Africa on an exploring expedition to Fashoda, on the Nile below Khartoum, Sudan. His troops had not been paid for six months, were in need of new clothing, and were unhappy about being sent on an expedition without their wives. In the Nandi district of what is today Kenya they mutinied and set off for Uganda, looting as they moved. Macdonald pursued them with a force of Zanzibaris and on 19 October 1897 found and defeated one group of mutineers. After being reinforced, he attacked and defeated others. Four years later, in 1901, the last of the mutineers were suppressed.

Uhlans. Originally these were Tatars from the 26,200-square-mile area at the bend of the Middle Volga who had settled in communities in Poland and Lithuania. Dressed in their traditional costumes, they formed regiments (*polks*) of lancers in the Polish army. In 1740 Uhlans were introduced into the Prussian army, which came to apply their name loosely to all its light cavalry. In addition to the lance, most were armed with sabers and later in the nineteenth century with pistols as well. The uhlans won renown for their dash and gallantry in the Franco-Prussian War of 1870–71.

Uhlans *Prussian uhlan in uniform worn at Sadowa*

Ulanka. A type of coat, sometimes called a spenser, first worn by German and Polish lancers. In the mid-nineteenth century it became popular and was adopted by other European armies.

Ulm, Battle of (17 October 1805), Napoleonic Wars. When Austria and Russia joined the Third Coalition against France in 1805, Napoleon moved to destroy the Austrians before a Russian army under General Mikhail Kutuzov [q.v.] could join them. Accordingly he left his positions around Boulogne on 27 August, abandoned plans to invade Britain, and marched southeast across the Rhine toward the Danube. Austrian General Karl Mack [q.v.], learning of the French advance, concentrated his army in the area of Ulm, on the upper Danube, 48 miles southeast of Stuttgart, anticipating that

Napoleon would penetrate the Black Forest. On 7 October he learned that Napoleon had moved farther east and, having crossed the Danube at Neuburg, threatened Austrian communications with Vienna. After attempting and failing to check Marshal Michel Ney's [q.v.] corps on the north bank, Mack fell back upon Ulm. On 17 October he was surrounded, and three days later he capitulated with 20,000 troops, said to have been the "flower of the Austrian army." In the several engagements fought after 7 October, the Austrians lost 50,000 men to France's 6,000. Mack was subsequently court-martialed for his failure and condemned to death, but his sentence was reduced to twenty years in prison, and he was pardoned in 1809.

An anonymous Prussian officer gave his opinion of Napoleon's style in war: "In my youth we used to march and countermarch all summer without gaining or losing a square league, and then we went into winter quarters, but now comes an ignorant, hot-headed young man who flies from Boulogne to Ulm, and from Ulm to the middle of Moravia, and fights battles in December. The whole system of his tactics is monstrously incorrect."

Ulundi, Battle of (4 July 1879), Zulu War. At the Zulu capital of Ulundi, 115 miles northeast of Durban, just south of the White Umfolozi River, some 20,000 Zulus under Cetewayo [q.v.] were routed by a British army of 5,317 infantry and 899 mounted men with 12 field guns and 2 Gatling guns under Frederick Augustus Thesiger, newly created Lord Chelmsford [q.v.]. The battle lasted for only thirty minutes and ended with the 17th Lancers and the 5th Dragoon Guards pursuing the fleeing Zulus. British losses were 1 officer, 9 other ranks, 5 "native horse" killed and 78 wounded; Zulu dead were estimated to be 1,500.

This was the final battle of the Zulu War. After the battle Cetewayo is reputed to have said: "There are not tears enough to grieve for all our dead." He managed to escape but was captured later by troops under Lord Wolseley.

Ulundi *The 17th Lancers charge the Zulus at Ulundi, 1879.*

Umara wad Nimr Muhammad (d. 1863). A Jali refugee chief in the Sudan; the son of Nimr Muhammad Nimr (1785?–1846), the last king of Shendi. He became the leader of an outlawed band of Jaliyins who harassed the Egyptians and Turks. In 1850, with a force of Abyssinians, he ranged in the eastern Sudan, attacking the Hadendowas (Kipling's "Fuzzy-Wuzzies"), raiding Egyptian posts, and bartering women for arms with Ilyas Bey Kiridli (d. 1862?), a Cretan in the Egyptian service. In 1863 the Egyptians burned his village. He escaped, but later in the year he was mortally wounded in a fight with an Egyptian patrol.

Umar bin Said Tall (1795?–1864). A Tukulor Muslim leader in West Africa. After making the haj to Mecca (Makkah) in 1826, he married into the ruling family of Bornu and spent several years in the Sokoto Empire, which he left in 1837. For reasons now obscure, he was imprisoned for a time by the Bambara king of Segu. In the 1840s he established a religious hostel at Diagouku in the Fouta Djallon (Futa Jallon) massif and attracted a wide following, gaining prestige and wealth. In 1849 he established a new headquarters at Dinguiraye, Guinea, 25 miles west of Dabola, and from here he successfully attacked a nearby small animist kingdom. In 1852 he declared a jihad against all animists in the western Sudan. In 1861 he defeated the Segu Bambaras and soon after Sultan Ahmadu of Masina. By 1862 he was in control of the western Sudan from Timbuktu to the frontier of French Senegal.

Umar considered himself primarily a religious reformer with a mission to purify Islam and to impose the Sharia (Islamic law). His followers, known as Talibés (students of religion), were mostly Tukulors from the Fouta Djallon area. These formed the elite of his forces; many were mounted [see Franco-Tukulor War]. In 1862 Ahmad al-Bakkai, his religious rival, who was supported by the Bambaras of Segu, rebelled. Umar was besieged at Hamdallahi, near Timbuktu, where in February 1864, in an attempt to break the siege, he was killed.

Umbeyla Campaign (1863). On the Northwest Frontier of India many tribesmen, filled with religious zeal, became a menace to Europeans and non-Muslims. One group, centered on the village of Sitana in a rugged mountain area on the west side of the Indus River about 75 miles northwest of Peshawar, became particularly troublesome. "Their principal occupation," according to Sir John Adye [q.v.], "consisted of incursions into the plains . . . and in robbing and murdering peaceful traders in our territories."

Known first as the Sitana Fanatics, and then, when driven from the village, as the Hindustani fanatics, they mounted a holy war against non-Muslims, making increasingly larger raids. In October 1863 the British, under General Neville Bowles Chamberlain [q.v.], led a force of 6,000, mostly Indian troops, in a campaign against them, and the fighting was particularly bitter. One outlying position, known as Crag Picket, was taken and retaken three times. After a three-month campaign the Hindustani fanatics were suppressed and their villages burned. British losses were 15 officers, 34 British other ranks, and 189 natives killed; 24 British officers, 118 British soldiers, and 541 native troops wounded.

Umm Dibaikarat / Diwaykarat, Battle of (23 November 1899). Reconquest of the Sudan. An Anglo-Egyptian force of 3,700 under Francis Wingate [q.v.] defeated 5,000 Dervishes under Khalifa Abdullahi [q.v.] in a half-hour battle near Kosti. Abdullahi was killed. This was the last battle between the British and the Mahdist Dervishes.

Umpande / Umpanda. See Panda.

Unao, Battle of (29 July 1857), Indian Mutiny. British General Sir Henry Havelock [q.v.], after relieving Cawnpore [q.v.], left a 300-man garrison there and with 1,500 men and 10 guns pressed on to relieve Lucknow [q.v.]. At Unao, a village 12 miles northeast of Cawnpore, he encountered a force of mutineers and rebels in strong positions with their flanks protected by swamps. The position and the village were taken by storm, but Havelock found himself attacked by a newly arrived force of mutineers. These were scattered by artillery and small-arms fire. Of the 6,000 mutineers and rebels, some 300 were killed. Fifteen guns were captured.

Unattached List. A term used in the British army for the list of officers who are no longer serving in their regiment. Officers on the list were usually serving on the staff of a brigade or higher unit.

Uncase, to. To uncover or display the colors of a unit.

Unconditional Surrender. A surrender of a military force or post without condition or stipulation. The term was made memorable in the United States during the American Civil War by the reply of Brigadier General U. S. Grant on 16 February 1862 to Confederate General Simon Bolivar Bruckner [q.v.], at Fort Donelson [q.v.], who had asked for terms to surrender: "Yours of this date proposing Armistice, and appointment of Commissioners, to settle terms of capitulation is just received. No terms except unconditional and immediate surrender can be accepted. I propose to move immediately upon your works."

Uncover, to. 1. To remove one's headgear.
2. To expose or leave unprotected a unit by a movement, maneuver, or positioning.

Under Arms, to be. To carry or bear weapons and to be ready to fight.

Under Fire, to be. To be exposed to the fire of artillery or musketry.

Undress Uniform. A British term for any uniform that was not dress uniform but was worn for work or on informal occasions.

Uniform. The distinctive clothing and insignia worn by the military or some professionals.

Union Army. The commonly used name for the U.S. Army during the American Civil War. In April 1861, at the beginning of the war, the regular army consisted of 16,000 officers and men, a number reduced by the 313 officers who resigned their commissions to fight for the Confederacy and the 28 enlisted men who deserted for the same reason. By 1 April governors of northern states had volunteered to supply 300,000 men. On 15 April Lincoln called for 75,000 militia committed to serve for three months. On 3 May he called for 42,000 three-year volunteers. On 22 July Congress voted its approval of Lincoln's action and authorized an army of 500,000 men. On 2 July 1862 there was a call for another 300,000 volunteers to serve ninety days.

Since by 4 August 1862 martial ardor had cooled somewhat, the volunteers Lincoln had called for had not materialized. A draft of 300,000 nine-month militia failed, but bounties [q.v.] from the federal, state, and local governments supplied the needed men. The states were responsible for recruiting, equipping, and outfitting the troops, and throughout the war the regiments and batteries of artillery were numbered by the states and carried the state designation—e.g., 14th Ohio Infantry or 3rd Ohio Cavalry.

When still more men were needed, Congress passed the Enrollment Act of 3 March 1863 [see Conscription]. However, payment of three hundred dollars or the hiring of a substitute excused a man from service, an inequity that inspired draft riots [q.v.]. The Union army, however, remained basically a volunteer force, and only 52,068 were forced to serve; 86,724 of those drafted received exemptions, and another 118,010, mostly foreign-born, enlisted as substitutes.

In the course of the war more than 250,000 men were honorably discharged as physically unfit because of wounds or diseases. There were about 200,000 deserters, 76,526 of whom were arrested and returned to duty. The highest deser-

SERGEANT MAJOR, ARTILLERY, U.S. ARMY.
FULL DRESS.

SERGEANT, INFANTRY, U.S. ARMY.
FULL DRESS.

PRIVATE, U.S. INFANTRY.
FATIGUE MARCHING ORDER.

CORPORAL, CAVALRY, U.S. ARMY.
FULL DRESS.

PRIVATE, LIGHT ARTILLERY, U.S. ARMY.
FULL DRESS.

GREAT COAT
FOR ALL MOUNTED MEN.

Union Army *Uniforms of the Union Army*

tion rate, more than 24 percent, was among the regulars, who in peace and war always had high rates [see Desertion]. Among the volunteers, only 6 percent deserted. On 1 May 1865 there were 1 million men in the Union army, and in the course of the war 2.3 million had served three-year enlistments.

Union League Clubs. One of the many "Loyal League" all-male clubs formed in the United States during the American Civil War. The Union League was formed in 1862 in the East and Mideast to rally state and local support for the Republican Party's policies, particularly those regarding the war. The all-male clubs grew rapidly; there were said to be 75,000 members in Illinois alone. They have survived in many cities as expensive social clubs.

Union Loyal League. An organization formed by eighteen representatives of three counties in Texas populated principally by German immigrants. In June 1861, during the Civil War, members vowed never to bear arms against the United States. On 4 July 1862 some 500 men met and formed three companies under Fritz Tegener (d. 1861). Confederate Brigadier General Hamilton Prioleau Bee (1822–1895), commander of the military district of the Rio Grande, sent a captain and four companies of the 2nd Texas Mounted Rifles to the area to "restore order."

Tegener's men were disbanded, but many decided to reassemble in Mexico. They were pursued, and most, including those taken prisoner, were killed [see Nueces, Affair at].

Union Repeating Gun. Official name for a primitive machine gun popularly called a coffee grinder whose inventor was unknown. It had a single barrel and was operated by means of a crank, as was the later Gatling gun [q.v.]. Two were carried into action in the American Civil War by the 28th Pennsylvania, then commanded by Colonel John White Geary [q.v.]. They were first fired in a skirmish with Confederate cavalry near Middleburg, Virginia, on 29 March 1862. Colonel Geary found the guns "inefficient and unsafe to the operators" and sent them to the Washington Arsenal. They were later sold for scrap at eight dollars each.

Unit Cohesion. Men working and fighting together each with reliance upon the others. The term was not used in the nineteenth century, but the principle was well understood. Ardant du Picq [q.v.] wrote: "Four brave men who do not know each other will not dare to attack a lion. Four less brave, but knowing each other well, sure of their reliability and consequently of mutual aid, will attack resolutely. There is the science of the organization of armies in a nutshell" (*Battle Studies* [1868]).

United Confederate Veterans. An organization established in New Orleans in 1889 for the protection of Confederate widows and orphans, the maintenance of camaraderie, and the collection of information on the American Civil War.

United Service Club. In 1815 a group of senior British officers, meeting at the Thatched House Tavern in St. James's Street formed the General Military Club, renamed the United Service Club when naval officers joined the following year. In 1817–19 a clubhouse was built in Charles Street, the first clubhouse to be erected in London. The present building in Pall Mall was built in 1827–28 by John Nash (1752–1835).

United Service Institution. A British service institution founded in 1831 and first known as the Naval and Military Library and Museum. It took its present name in 1839 and was incorporated in 1860. It was open to all officers of all services, including the Yeomanry and the officers of the Honourable East India Company. When it was founded, the hope was expressed that the institution would "detach many of our friends from the club house and billiard table." It has published a *Journal* since 1857.

United States Army. The Constitution of the United States gives the states the authority to raise militias and appoint their officers. It gives Congress the authority to raise armies and declare war, and it appoints the president commander-in-chief. The War Department was created in 1789, and in 1792 Congress created the Legion (army) of the United States. In 1802 a military academy to provide officers was established at West Point, New York. The regular army remained small and even in the last quarter of the century was less than half the size of Belgium's army. There was a general feeling among political leaders that in case of war soldiers could be supplied from the militias and volunteers.

In 1802, under the direction of Henry Dearborn [q.v.], then secretary of war, the army underwent a radical transformation. It became politicized and Federalist officers were pushed aside. Also, considerable changes were made in appearance: Short hair replaced wigs, trousers replaced knee breeches, and stylish shoe buckles were abolished. In 1808 noncommissioned rank was shown by yellow epaulets on the right shoulders of sergeants and left shoulders of corporals. Militia units generally wore gray; regulars wore red coats until 1821, when blue uniforms were introduced, and red coats were restricted to bandsmen. (The present United States Army Band is still uniformed in red coats.) In the same year officers' insignia of rank were introduced. They resembled those of the present day except that captains wore two gold bars, first lieutenants wore one gold bar, and second lieutenants none. (In current usage, captains and first lieutenants wear silver bars, and second lieutenants wear a gold bar.)

Because cavalry was more expensive than infantry, the army had no regular cavalry until 1833, when the 1st Dragoons was activated, followed three years later by the 2nd Dragoons. On 19 May 1846 a regiment of mounted rifles was formed. In 1853 two regiments named the 1st Cavalry and the 2nd Cavalry were formed. All were light cavalry, and all usually fought on foot. Each regiment was authorized 652 men, but usually contained only 300 to 400.

In peacetime, recruiting was difficult, and desertions were common [see Desertion]. Many of the enlisted men in the regular army in peacetime and many of the volunteers during the American Civil War were foreign-born. In 1821–23 about 25 percent had been born in Europe, most in Ireland or one of the German states. In 1825, when it was decreed that only native Americans could serve, enlistments plummeted. The restriction was removed on 13 August 1828. The first federal draft law was enacted on 3 March 1863 [see Conscription; Draft; Draft Riots].

Until the Civil War there were no units of blacks or Indians. Eventually two regiments of regular black cavalry and

Annual Strength of the American Regular Army in the Nineteenth Century

YEAR	AGGREGATE STRENGTH	YEAR	AGGREGATE STRENGTH
1800	No returns	1851	10,538
1801	4,051	1852	11,202
1802	No returns	1853	10,417
1803	2,576	1854	10,745
1804	2,730	1855	15,752
1805	No returns	1856	15,562
1806	" "	1857	15,764
1807	" "	1858	17,498
1808	" "	1859	16,435
1809	6,954	1860	16,367
1810	No returns	1861	16,422
1811	" "	1862	No returns
1812	6,686	1863	" "
1813	19,036	1864	" "
1814	38,186	1865	22,310
1815	33,424	1866	Not consolidated
1816	10,024	1867	56,815
1817	8,220	1868	50,916
1818	7,676	1869	36,774
1819	8,688	1870	37,075
1820	No returns	1871	28,953
1821	" "	1872	28,175
1822	5,211	1873	28,652
1823	5,949	1874	28,444
1824	5,779	1875	25,318
1825	5,719	1876	28,280
1826	5,809	1877	23,945
1827	5,722	1878	25,818
1828	5,529	1879	26,389
1829	6,169	1880	26,411
1830	5,951	1881	25,670
1831	5,869	1882	25,186
1832	6,102	1883	25,478
1833	6,412	1884	26,383
1834	6,824	1885	26,859
1835	7,151	1886	26,544
1837	7,834	1887	26,436
1838	8,653	1888	26,738
1839	9,704	1889	27,478
1840	10,570	1890	27,089
1841	11,169	1891	26,175
1842	10,628	1892	26,900
1843	8,935	1893	27,519
1844	8,573	1894	27,934
1845	8,349	1895	27,172
1846	10,690	1896	27,038
1847	21,686	1897	27,532
1848	10,035	1898	47,867
1849	10,585	1899	64,729
1850	10,763	1900	68,155

For the greater part of the century most of the army was deployed on the western frontier in a constabulary role. Army forts, camps, and stations were widely scattered and usually inadequately garrisoned. In 1818, of 64 posts, only 23 had more than 100 men. In 1855 there were 74 posts, only 44 of which had more than 100 men. By 1870 the army had 197 posts, 88 of which held fewer than 100 men. Although the country grew larger in the course of the century, in 1889 with the end of the Indian Wars the army posts were reduced to 77, only 7 of which had fewer than 100 men.

Because the president presides as the commander-in-chief of the armed forces, there was some question about the title of the army's senior uniformed officer. From December 1779 to 1 June 1821 the title was merely senior officer; thereafter it was commanding general. In 1885 U. S. Grant was designated general-in-chief but was stripped of all control over the administration and supply of the army, responsibilities that were undertaken by the secretary of war, to whom all the staff bureau chiefs reported. Not until August 1903 did the title change to chief of staff.

Except in wartime, promotion for officers was glacially slow. Promotion for regimental officers was by seniority within the regiment until October 1890, when it was changed to promotion by seniority within the branch of the service. At the same time Congress ordered physical and professional examinations before promotion. In 1899 there were 110 officers who had not received promotions in twenty years. Arthur MacArthur [q.v.] was a captain for twenty-three years. In 1900 there were 37 Civil War veterans serving as captains. Small as were the classes graduating from West Point, many graduates had to serve as brevet second lieutenants until an opening occurred.

In the nineteenth century there were three major components to the land forces: regulars; volunteers in time of war; and militia, serving only in wartime. Militia were organized by each state with officers appointed by the governor, and until 15 April 1861, when President Lincoln incorporated 75,000 militia into the army, they did not serve outside their own states. Most volunteers enlisted in state-raised units, which were numbered by the states, although during the American Civil War there were a few units of United States volunteers.

United States Military Academy. See West Point.

Unit Strength. The number of men, supplies, arms, and equipment of a unit.

Universal Military Service. See Conscription.

Unshot, to. To remove the projectile loaded in a piece of ordnance.

Unteroffizier. A German noncommissioned officer.

Uprising. An insurrection, émeute.

Upton, Emory (1839–1881). An American soldier who was graduated from West Point in 1861. While a cadet, Upton, an ardent abolitionist, fought a duel with swords over this issue with Cadet Wade Hampton Gibbes (1840?–1904) of South Carolina, later a major in the Confederate army. During the

two of infantry were raised, and the four regiments boasted the lowest desertion rates and the highest reenlistment rates in the army [see Black Troops in the U.S. Army]. Most Indians did not take well to army discipline, but for a time Troop L of the 1st Cavalry contained only Indians. Others were used as scouts. Their insignia was a badge of crossed arrows.

course of the American Civil War Upton rose from second lieutenant to brevet major general in both the regular army and the volunteers, commanding with distinction units of all three arms. He fought at First Bull Run, where he aimed and fired the first gun of the battle; Spotsylvania, where he was wounded; and Antietam, Fredericksburg, and Chancellorsville [qq.v.]. He won acclaim for his action on 7 November 1863 at Rappahannock Bridge, where he took a Confederate bridgehead, capturing 1,600 prisoners, 8 colors, 2,000 stand of arms, and a pontoon bridge. He commanded first a brigade and then a division in Sheridan's Valley Campaign [q.v.]. After the war he reverted to his permanent rank of captain, but in the reorganization of the army in 1866 he was promoted lieutenant colonel of the newly organized 25th Infantry, one of the two infantry regiments of black soldiers with white officers.In 1867 he published *A New System of Tactics, Double and Single Rank, Adopted to American Topography and Improved Firearms* (generally known as Upton's *Tactics*), which was soon adopted by the U.S. army. From 1870 to 1875 he was commandant of cadets at West Point. A tour of European and Asian armies convinced him that the expansible German army was the superior model, and in 1878 he published *Armies of Asia and Europe*. He was a prolific writer, many of whose works were published only after his death.

For many years Upton suffered what were apparently migraine headaches, for which there was then no remedy. His young wife died in 1870. On 14 March 1881 he wrote his resignation from the army, and on the 15th shot himself with his Colt .45.

Urquiza, Justo José (1800–1870). An Argentine general who was governor of Entre Ríos Province from 1842 to 1854. In 1845 he revolted and defeated General José Rivera [q.v.], leader of the Colorados (Reds), in the Battle of India Muerta. In 1852 he revolted and defeated General Juan de Rosas [qq.v.]. On 20 November 1853 he was elected the first constitutional president of Argentina. He served until 12 April 1860 and then became commander of the national forces and, after 1860, again governor of Entre Ríos. He was defeated in the 1861 revolution by Bartolomé Mitre [q.v.] and on 12 April 1870 was assassinated.

Urrea, José Cosme de (1797?–1849). A Mexican soldier who in 1809 became a cadet in the presidial company of San Rafael Buenavista and in 1811 fought insurgents in Sinaloa, western Mexico, Jalisco, and Michoacán. He was commissioned in 1816 and in 1829 became associated with Santa Anna [q.v.]. By 1835 he was a colonel and engaged in expeditions against Comanche Indians.

He was for a time governor and military commander in Durango before taking part in Santa Anna's expedition against insurgent Texans, in which he fought engagements at San Patricio, Bexar (San Antonio), the Alamo [q.v.], and Goliad [see Goliad Massacre]. Although he recommended clemency for the prisoners taken at Goliad, on orders from Santa Anna, who insisted that he honor the Mexican Parliament's decree of 30 December 1835 calling for the execution of all prisoners (a decree Santa Anna had sought), he was forced to execute 342. Somehow 48 escaped. In the Battle of San Jacinto [q.v.] only the men commanded by Urrea retreated in good order to Guadalupe Victoria. In 1837 he was named governor of Sonora, but he became tangled in Mexican politics and in 1845 was forced to flee the country.

Uruguayana, Captures of (1865), War of the Triple Alliance. This Brazilian town on the Uruguay River was captured by Paraguayans under General Estigarribia on 5 August 1865 and recaptured without a fight by General Bartolomé Mitre [q.v.] on 18 September.

Uruguayan Revolutions. The control of Uruguay, known as Banda Oriental, was frequently disputed by Spain and Portugal when Argentina was owned by Spain and Brazil by Portugal. In 1776 it was included in the Spanish viceroyalty of the Río de la Plata, a large area that included present-day Argentina, Bolivia, and Paraguay. In 1808, when Napoleon forced King Ferdinand VII (1784–1833) to abdicate and replaced him with his brother Joseph (1768–1844), Argentina attempted to seize control.

Civil War of 1811–16. When Francisco Javier de Elio (1767–1822), the Spanish viceroy in Buenos Aires, was ousted and replaced by a junta that established the United Provinces of the Río de la Plata, he fled to Montevideo, from which Uruguayans under José Gervasio Artigas [q.v.] tried forcibly to remove him. Elio sought aid from Carlota Joaquina (1775–1830), King Ferdinand's sister and the wife of the Brazilian regent. In 1811 a Portuguese army invaded the state to protect Elio from the Uruguayan revolutionaries and those in Buenos Aires who wanted independence from Spain, but Artigas successfully held the province, which he hoped to establish as a new state independent of both Spain and Portugal.

In 1814 Argentine troops attacked Montevideo but were repulsed. In 1816 a Brazilian army invaded and succeeded in driving out Artigas and in 1821 uniting Banda Oriental to Brazil. It remained a part of Brazil until the Argentine-Brazilian War of 1825–28 [q.v.], when it established its independence as Uruguay.

Civil War of 1842–51. What began as a local affair centered in Montevideo between political conservatives, called Blancos (Whites), and liberals, called Colorados (Reds), became an international war. The Argentine dictator Juan Manuel de Rosas [q.v.] joined forces with the Blancos and besieged Montevideo; the Colorados were aided by France, Britain, Brazil, and Paraguay [see Argentine Intervention in Uruguay]. On 23 February 1852 Allied forces decisively defeated the Blanco forces at the Battle of Monte Caseros [q.v.].

Urvina / Urbina, José María (1808–1891). A Ecuadorian soldier and political leader who from 1852 to 1856 was president of Ecuador. He was overthrown and for twenty years lived in exile in Peru. In 1876 he returned, and until 1878 he was commander-in-chief of the Ecuadorian army.

Usibepu (d. 1914). A Zulu chief who was at one time subordinate to Cetewayo [q.v.]. After the Zulu War [q.v.] of 1879, when the Zulu kingdom was broken up into thirteen separate states, the British granted him northeast Zululand. In 1883, after Cetewayo's return from captivity in England, he repelled an attack by Cetewayo's warriors and destroyed his kraal. In 1884 he was attacked and defeated by Dinizulu [q.v.], a son of Cetewayo, who was assisted by some 200 Boers. He spent his final years on a special reserve set aside by Sir Melmoth Osborn (1833–1899), the British Resident in Zululand.

Utah Expedition (October 1857–May 1858). On 24 July 1847 Mormon leader Brigham Young (1801–1877), looking out over the valley of Salt Lake in present-day Utah, announced, "This is the place." There his followers (Latter-day Saints) established almost a separate state, which they called Deseret. In 1850 it was declared a U.S. territory. Although Brigham Young was appointed its governor, federal authority was ignored, and emigration of non-Mormons was viewed as a serious threat. Local Indians were incited to attack them and even, on at least one occasion, to massacre a party passing through the territory [see Mountain Meadows Massacre].

In October 1857 an expedition of about 2,500 troops, including the 5th and 10th Infantry with two batteries of artillery, assembled at Fort Leavenworth, Kansas, and moved out toward Utah to restore U.S. authority. Brevet Brigadier General Albert Sidney Johnston [q.v.] took command in November. While the troops skirmished with Utes, Shoshonis, and Bannocks, Mormon militia (Danites) slowed their advance by stampeding horses, destroying wagon trains, and burning prairie grass. Johnston was compelled by his slow progress and bad weather to winter east of the Wasatch Mountains. When spring came, Young called on male followers to come to Salt Lake City to defend their capital, and Johnston, whose force had been increased to 5,500, moved forward. Hostilities were averted through the efforts of Thomas Kane [q.v.], a non-Mormon but a trusted friend of Young, who succeeded in bringing Johnston and Young together, enabling Johnston to establish federal authority peacefully.

Uthman abu Bakr Diqna. See Osman Digna.

Uthman Adam / Uthman Janu (1866?–1889). A Mahdist leader in the Sudan and a relative of Khalifa Abdullahi [q.v.]. He displayed exceptional military knowledge at an early age and about 1886 was made an amir and appointed governor of Kordofan. There he mobilized the Dervishes to fight the rebellious Kabbabish tribe. In May 1887 he routed the tribesmen in the Battle of Umm Badr in northern Kordofan and killed their leader at Jebel al-Ain. Later in 1887 he joined Amir Karam Allah Muhammad Kurkusawi [q.v.] in Darfur in a successful campaign against the rebellious Rizaiquats and killed Yusuf Ibrahim Muhammad (d. 1888), the puppet sultan of Darfur, in battle. He was raised to the elevated rank of Amir al-Umra and appointed governor of both Kordofan and Darfur. In 1889 he waged a bloody but successful war against Ahmad abu Jummaiza (d. 1889) and his Masalit tribe. He died shortly after.

Uxbridge, Lord Henry William Paget, First Marques of Anglesey and Second Earl of. See Paget, Henry William.

Vaal Krantz, Battle of (5–6 February 1900), Second Anglo-Boer War. In Natal General Sir Redvers Buller [q.v.] with 20,000 men tried for a third time to relieve besieged Ladysmith [q.v.]. On 5 February 1900 he forced a crossing of the Tugela River and seized Vaal Krantz, a height just southwest of the city. Boers under Louis Botha [q.v.] attempted without success to drive the British off, but on his own initiative Buller called off his offensive and again withdrew his forces behind the Tugela River. British casualties were 374; Boer casualties were less. This was, however, the last Boer victory in Natal.

Vaillant, Jean Baptiste Philibert (1790–1872). A French officer who first saw action in Napoleon's Russian Campaign [q.v.] in 1812 and later fought at Ligny and Waterloo [qq.v.]. He was an engineer officer at the siege of Antwerp in 1832 [q.v.] and at the siege and capture of Rome in 1849. In 1851 he was created a marshal of France, and he served as minister of war from 1854 to 1859. In the Austro-Piedmontese War [q.v.] of 1859 he commanded the French forces. For ten years, beginning in 1860, he was minister of the emperor's household.

Valdiva, Capture of (18 June 1820), Chilean War of Independence. Admiral Thomas Cochrane, Tenth Earl of Dundonald (1775–1860), who commanded the Chilean navy, sailed his flagship, *O'Higgins,* 50 guns, to Valdiva, in south-central Chile, about 16 miles from the mouth of the Valdiva River. After bombarding the forts, he landed a party that captured the place, the last Spanish stronghold on the Chilean coast.

Valencia, Battle of (27–28 June 1808), Peninsular War. On 27 June 1808 French Marshal Bon Adrien Jannot de Moncey [q.v.] attacked Valencia in eastern Spain on the Mediterranean. The city was defended by three regular Spanish battalions and by 7,000 Valencian levies, who took up positions outside the city. It took Moncey a day to push them back. The next day he launched three assaults upon the town. All failed. He then retreated to Madrid, 188 miles west-northwest, where he arrived on 15 July.

Valencia, Siege of (25 December 1811–9 January 1812), Peninsular War. On Christmas Day 1811 French Marshal Louis Suchet [q.v.] with 33,000 men advanced on Valencia, Spain, before which Joachim Blake [q.v.] with 20,000 Spaniards and Portuguese had thrown up an eight-mile line of earthworks. Suchet duped Blake into expecting that he would attack his center, then threw 25,000 men against his left. Blake retreated and was soon bottled up in the city. After an ineffectual attempt to break out, he surrendered on 9 January. Suchet captured 16,000 men, 370 guns, and a mountain of supplies and matériel and levied a heavy fine on the city.

Valise. 1. In British parlance, an infantryman's knapsack, originally worn on the hip but transferred to the center of the back in 1882.
2. A cloth or leather container, usually tubular, tied to the cantle of a saddle on a cavalry horse.
3. In the American artillery, a leather cylinder, 18 inches long, placed on the saddle of each horse of an artillery carriage. It carried the driver's small personal articles.

Vallejo, Mariano Guadalupe (1808–1890). A soldier and pioneer in California. In 1823 he joined the Mexican army, and in 1829 he helped suppress an Indian uprising at San José Mission near San Francisco. In 1836 he supported the rebellion of his nephew Juan Bautista Alvarado (1809–1882) that established California as practically a free state. Alvarado served as its governor until 1841, and Vallejo was appointed commander of the provincial military forces. He established himself in Sonoma, living as a semi-independent chief with Indian allies and Mexican troops devoted to his cause. He was active in securing the submission of California to U.S. authority, and when California was admitted to the Union in 1850, he served as a state senator in its first legislature.

Valley Campaign, Stonewall Jackson's. See Shenandoah Valley Campaign of Jackson.

Valls, Battle of (25 February 1809), Peninsular War. A French army of 13,350 under Marshal Laurent Gouvion St. Cyr [q.v.] defeated an Allied army of 11,240 under General Teodora Reding (1755–1809) at Valls, a town in northeast Spain, 11 miles north of Tarragona, and then sacked the town. French casualties were 900; Allied casualties were about 3,000, half of whom were prisoners. Reding suffered three wounds that proved fatal.

Valor. Bravery. The caustic Ambrose Bierce [q.v.], who fought in the American Civil War, defined valor as "A soldierly compound of vanity, duty, and the gambler's hope."

Valutino, Battle of. See Smolensk, Battle of.

Valverde, Battle of (21 February 1862), American Civil War.

Confederate General Henry Hopkins Sibley [q.v.], advancing up the Rio Grande with 2,600 men, defeated a Union force of 3,810 under Brigadier General Edward Canby [q.v.] outside Fort Craig, New Mexico, near the present town of San Marcial [see New Mexico, Confederate Army of]. The Federals lost 68 killed, 160 wounded, and 35 missing; the Confederates lost 36 killed and 160 wounded. Sibley was soon after defeated in the Battle of Glorieta [q.v.].

Vandamme, Dominique Joseph René (1770–1830). A French soldier who fought as an infantry officer in Belgium in 1793–94. He was promoted general of brigade in 1793 but was temporarily suspended from rank in June 1795 for looting and using bad language; he was restored in September. In 1799 he was promoted general of division. In 1800 he was accused of embezzlement but talked his way out of the scandal. At Austerlitz [q.v.] in 1805 he distinguished himself in command of a division of IV Corps that stormed the Pratzen Heights. In 1809 he fought at Abensberg, Landshut, and Eckmühl [qq.v.]. In 1813 he was defeated and captured at Kulm [q.v.]. He rallied to Napoleon during the Hundred Days [q.v.] and commanded III Corps. He distinguished himself, displaying both courage and initiative in the battles of Ligny and Wavre [qq.v.]. After the Battle of Waterloo [q.v.] in 1815, he fled to the United States, where he remained until he returned to France in 1819.

Van Dorn, Earl (1820–1863). An American soldier who was graduated from West Point in 1842 and served in Florida, Louisiana, and Alabama. During the Mexican War [q.v.] he won two brevets. He was then stationed at Pilatka, Florida, in 1849–50 and operated against the Seminoles. From 1856 to 1861 he served under Colonel Robert E. Lee in operations against the Comanches, establishing a reputation as a daring commander. On 1 October 1859 he was wounded in the abdomen and wrist by Comanche arrows. Although his abdominal wound was thought to be mortal, he reported back to duty only five weeks later. He was promoted major in June 1860, but he resigned in January 1861 at the beginning of the American Civil War, and on 5 June he was commissioned in the Confederate army as a colonel of cavalry. In June 1861 he was promoted brigadier general, and on 19 September he was named major general.

He was defeated in the battles of Pea Ridge (Elkhorn) and Corinth [qq.v.], but in December 1862 he disrupted General U. S. Grant's operations by destroying his supply depot at Holly Spring, Mississippi.

On 8 May 1863 a Dr. Peters requested a pass of Van Dorn and, after it was signed, shot him in the head. His killer then picked up the pass and with it made his way through the lines. He was never brought to justice.

Van Lew, Elizabeth (1818–1900). A Union sympathizer and spy in Richmond, Virginia, during the American Civil War. An ardent abolitionist even before the war, she had freed the family slaves when her father died and had helped blacks escape on the Underground Railroad. During the war she provided refuge and aid to fleeing prisoners of war. She is said to have worked with Samuel Ruth [q.v.], the pro-Union superintendent of the Richmond, Fredericksburg & Potomac Railroad. After the war President U. S. Grant appointed her postmaster in Richmond.

Vannovskii, Pëtr Semenovich (1822–1904). A Russian soldier who served as minister of war from 1881 to 1897.

Van Rensselaer, Stephen (1764–1839). An American soldier and politician, the eighth patroon of a vast estate of about 436,000 acres in New York, which he inherited in 1769. When not yet nineteen, he eloped with Margaret Schuyler, the daughter of Major General Philip Schuyler (1773–1804). In 1786 he joined the militia as a major of infantry. From 1795 to 1801 he was lieutenant governor of New York. In the War of 1812 [q.v.], as major general of the New York militia, he was given command of the American forces on the northeast frontier, although he had no active military experience. On 12 October 1812 he was defeated in the Battle of Queenston Heights [q.v.] in Canada. Later he took an active part in the construction of the Erie Canal, and in 1824 he founded the technical school that in 1826 became the Rensselaer Polytechnic Institute.

Van / Vanguard. The front or forward edge of an army on the march or troops operating in front of a military force.

Varese, Battle of (25 May 1859), Italian War of Independence. This battle, sometimes called the Battle of Malnate, was fought in Lombardy near the commune of Varese on the shore of Lake Varese, 30 miles northwest of Milan. Giuseppe Garibaldi [q.v.] with 3,000 men repulsed an Austrian army of 5,000.

Varna, Siege of (July–October 1828), Russo-Turkish War of 1828–29. In the summer of 1828 Russian armies crossed the Danube at several points and advanced toward Constantinople (Istanbul). Scattered Turkish strongpoints delayed their advance. One of these was Varna, a fortified port on the Black Sea in northeast Bulgaria, defended by 20,000 Turks. In July 1828 Prince Aleksandr Menshikov [q.v.] detached a Russian force under General Hans Diebitsch [q.v.] to take the town, but he encountered Turkish resistance so strong that he was forced to lay siege to it in July. Varna was not captured until 11 October, when its walls were stormed; the next day the garrison surrendered.

Vauban, Sébastien le Prestre de (1633–1707). A French military engineer who, although certainly not a nineteenth-century soldier, created fortifications that were still in use in that century and who conceived methods for both attacking and defending those fortifications. In his lifetime he took part in forty-eight sieges and repaired or constructed 160 fortifications.

At age eighteen he joined the army of Louis II de Bourbon, Prince de Condé (1621–1686), as a cadet. In 1653 he entered the French service, and two years later he was appointed a royal engineer. At the siege of Maestricht (Maastricht) in 5–30 July 1673 he introduced the system of advancing upon a fortification by means of several parallel trenches [see Parallels]. From 1678 to 1688 he surrounded the French kingdom with fortifications of his design [see Sieges]. He also planned the great aqueduct of Maintenon, and he is credited with inventing the socket bayonet in 1687. At the siege of Philippsburg in 1688 he introduced ricochet batteries of his own devising. From 15 March to 10 April 1691 he conducted the siege of Mons; from 25 May to 1 July 1692 the siege of

Namur; and from 15 May to 5 June 1697 the siege of Aith. On 14 January 1703 he became a marshal of France.

He wrote widely on a variety of subjects, including *Traité des mines* and *Traité de l'attaque des places*.

Vauchamps, Battle of (14 February 1814), Napoleonic Wars. Napoleon with 20,000 men defeated an army of 20,000 under Field Marshal Gebhard von Blücher [q.v.] in this battle fought near Château-Thierry and one mile west of Montmirail. The French lost 600; Blücher lost 7,000 men, 16 guns, and much transport.

Vaughan Road, Battle of. See Dabney's Mill, Battle of.

Vedel, Dominique Honoré Antoine Marie (1771–1848). A French soldier born in Monaco who enlisted in 1784 and was commissioned in 1787. He served mostly in Italy until he was posted to Switzerland in 1799. He fought at Austerlitz [q.v.] in 1805 and soon after was promoted general of brigade. In 1806 he fought at Saalfeld and Jena [qq.v.]. In December 1806 he was wounded in the knee in the Battle of Pultusk [q.v.], and in 1807 he was twice wounded, at Heilsberg and at Friedland [qq.v.]. In 1807 he was promoted general of division and sent to fight in Spain. In 1808 he had the misfortune to be present at the calamity of Bailén [q.v.] and was returned to France in disgrace and even imprisoned for a time. He was reappointed to command in 1813 and served in Italy and under Marshal Pierre Augereau [q.v.] at Lyons. He did not rally to Napoleon during the Hundred Days [q.v.] but served the Bourbons and was honored by them. He retired in 1831.

Vedette. A mounted outguard or sentinel.

Veintemilla, Ignacio de (1830–1909). An Ecuadorian general and dictator. He led a successful liberal revolution in 1876 and became provisional president. In 1878 he was elected president, but in 1883 he was deposed during a civil war and exiled.

Vekilchares. A quartermaster in the Turkish army.

Velestinos, Battle of. See Pharsalus, Battle of.

Velites. In Roman armies, velites were nimble young soldiers who acted as light skirmishers. Napoleon adopted the term, applying it to physically fit, educated young men who aspired to be officers and were willing to pay two hundred francs per year to serve in Guards infantry or three hundred francs to serve in Guards cavalry or artillery. Schooling was provided, and after three years a conscientious and able young man could become a *sous-lieutenant* in a line regiment.

Vellore, Mutiny at (July 1806). General Sir John Francis Cradoc (1762–1839), as he was known before he changed his name to Caradoc in 1820, was commander-in-chief of the Madras army when, with the blessing of Lord William Cavendish Bentinck (1774–1839), governor of Madras (1803–07), he foolishly issued in December 1805 an edict prohibiting the wearing of beards and turbans by sepoys. In 1797 a military board had discussed the matter of changing the pattern of Indian soldiers' turbans, giving the matter

"every consideration which a subject of that delicate and important nature required," and had decided it would be unwise to make changes. In the event the military board had proved to be wise. Sir John's order met with vehement opposition and in July 1806 occasioned a mutiny among the 1,500 sepoys stationed at Vellore, a city with a strong fortress on the banks of the Palar River, 80 miles west-southwest of the city of Madras. Spurred on by the sons of Tipu Sahib (1751–1799), princes confined to the city, the mutineers murdered a number of Europeans before the 69th Foot, stationed there, could spring into action. Many of its officers had been shot and the garrison was low on ammunition before they were rescued by Colonel Rollo Gillespie [q.v.], who marched from Arcot with the 19th Light Dragoons and some loyal Indian sowars. More than 800 mutineers and about 130 British soldiers were killed in the fighting. Other small outbreaks in the area were easily suppressed.

Vendée, Revolts in. In 1793–96 this maritime department in west-central France was the scene of a series of insurrections in support of the Bourbons. The revolts are sometimes called the Vendée Wars. During Napoleon's Hundred Days [q.v.] hostility to republicanism revived in the department, forcing Napoleon to divert a strong corps he could have used elsewhere to suppress an uprising. In 1832 it was the scene of still-another aborted uprising.

Venereal Disease. Except for epidemics of cholera, yellow fever, typhoid, and similar contagious diseases, most military hospitals were largely filled with patients suffering from sexually related diseases, seemingly the occupational disorders of soldiers. In war and peace they impaired the efficiency of armies.

In 1806–07 Napoleon's Grande Armée opened six hospitals for soldiers in and near Warsaw: two for sick, two for wounded, and two for venereal diseases. The British army at home and abroad had the highest incidence of venereal diseases of any of the armies of regulated countries. Dr. James McGrigor [q.v.], the British army's chief medical officer, reported that between December 1816 and December 1818 there were 4,767 venereal disease patients in British military hospitals, a rate of 26.5 per 1,000. In 1859 in Britain it was found that of every 1,000 hospital admissions, 422 were for venereal diseases. In comparison, from 1880 to 1890 the venereal disease rate for the entire American army was 80 out of every 1,000.

During the American Civil War the surgeon general reported that among Union troops there were 103,000 cases of gonorrhea and 73,000 cases of syphilis. Confederate figures were probably comparable. Memphis was reported to be a "beehive of women of ill fame." Authorities in Nashville, another such beehive, loaded 111 disruptive prostitutes aboard a river steamer and dispatched them to any river port that would accept them. None would, but soldiers swam out to the boat when it was anchored and climbed aboard. When the women were denied even these customers, they trashed the steamer. Two months later they were all back in Nashville.

American General Tasker Bliss [q.v.], speaking of the army in the 1870s, remarked that post surgeons "had nothing to do but confine laundresses and treat the clap [gonorrhea]." Even senior officers were not always untouched. Confederate General A. P. Hill [q.v.] suffered from bouts of a then-incurable strain of gonorrhea contracted while still a cadet at West Point.

Whenever an army sought to reduce the incidence of the disease by licensing prostitutes and requiring compulsory medical examinations, as did the French in North Africa, the British in Britain and India for a time, and the Union army in the United States, the incidence of venereal diseases dropped dramatically.

In Britain the Contagious Diseases Prevention Act of 1864 provided for the compulsory medical examination of prostitutes in eleven garrison towns and the detention in a hospital for those found infected. The act was amended later and applied to eighteen towns.

There was considerable objection to the acts from those who thought that sin should not be made safe or those who believed the compulsory examination of women was unjust. Josephine Elizabeth Butler (1828–1906), wife of the canon of Winchester, led a campaign against them and against licensed brothels. She was not alone. In 1869 Josephine Baker, wife of the principal of Liverpool College, founded the Ladies National Association for the Repeal of the Contagious Diseases Act. In 1875 she was instrumental in the formation in Geneva, Switzerland, of the International Federation for the Abolition of State Regulation of Vice. Florence Nightingale [q.v.] joined the campaign because she considered the scheme unworkable and ineffectual. "You cannot reclaim prostitutes. You must prevent prostitution," she said, and she advocated better recreational facilities in the army. Although a royal commission in 1871 and a select committee in 1879 approved of the acts, in 1883 the House of Commons condemned the compulsory examination of women, and in 1886 the acts were formally repealed.

As early as 1834 Thomas Carr, archbishop of Bombay, had protested any regulation of the lal bazaars [q.v.] in India, maintaining that "it has pleased Providence to order that sin and misery should be connected, and the arrangement of which I complain is an attempt to make sinning safe." Nevertheless, the examination of prostitutes was introduced at all cantonments in India in 1865, but as a result of a public outcry in Britain, it was partially suspended in 1884 and ceased in 1888. In 1889 a new cantonment act was passed. Amended in 1893, the act prohibited the periodic and compulsory examination of women. The syphilis rate at once jumped from 75.5 per 1,000 to 174.1 for primary and from 29.4 to 84.9 for secondary infections. Consequently, in 1897 a new order gave commanders the authority to require infected soldiers to attend a dispensary and to remove brothels and loitering prostitutes near cantonments.

Some countries instituted state-controlled brothels without arousing public outcries. In France there had been *maisons de tolérance* since 1778, and they were not closed until after World War II, when a female deputy pushed through a change in the law [see Bordel Militaire Controllé / Bordel Mobile de Campagne]. Sweden permitted state-registered brothels in 1847, and Denmark followed in 1874.

Venetian Revolution of 1848–49. See Venice, Siege of; Manin, Daniele.

Venezuela Revolutions. 1. 1810–21. With the exception of a few short intervals, war against Spanish rule was waged in Venezuela from 1810 to 1821. On 14 July 1811 the country declared itself free of Spain. A year later the first phase of the revolution ended with the defeat of the rebel army under Francisco de Miranda [q.v.], who had made himself dictator, and his surrender to the forces of Spanish General Domingo Monteverdi (1772–1823) at La Victoria on 12 July 1812. Miranda, who had been promised deportation to the United States, was put in chains and sent to Spain.

In 1813 Simón Bolívar [q.v.] returned from Curaçao and defeated Monteverdi's army in a series of battles. On 6 August he occupied Caracas. In September he unsuccessfully besieged Monteverdi at Puerto Cabello, a seaport 70 miles west of Caracas. Spanish reinforcements arrived and on 15 June 1814 defeated Bolívar at La Puerta [q.v.]; on 16 July Spanish forces reoccupied Caracas. On 18 August a Spanish army of 10,000 destroyed Bolívar's 3,000-man force in the Battle of Aragua in northern Venezuela, and once more Bolívar was forced to flee the country. In December 1816 he returned to Venezuela and again led an unsuccessful revolution that collapsed in 1818.

Venezuelan freedom from Spain was not accomplished until a rebel army under Antonio de Sucre [q.v.] defeated royalists near the village of Carabobo [q.v.], 20 miles southwest of Valencia, on 24 June 1821.

2. 1848–49. From 1830 to 1848 José Antonio Páez [q.v.], a Conservative, dominated Venezuela, serving either as president or power broker. In 1846 his friend General José Tadeo Monagas [q.v.] was elected president. Breaking with Páez, he appointed Liberals as ministers. In 1848–49 Páez led a revolt that failed and he was forced into exile. José Tadeo Monagas alternated with his brother, José Gregorio Monagas (1795–1858), as president.

3. 1858–64. In March 1858 the dictatorial Monagas brothers were overthrown in a revolution that both Liberals and

Venezuela Revolutions *Soldiers of the Venezuelan army, 1820*

Conservatives supported. Venezuela then dissolved into political disorder as various caudillos struggled for power. The presidency was an uncertain seat until José Antonio Páez [q.v.] was recalled in 1861. In 1863 he was overthrown and again went into exile.

4. 1868–70. Liberal General Juan Falcón (1820–1870), whose tenure provoked an increasing number of civil disorders, served as president from 1863 until overthrown by a revolution in 1868. In 1870 Antonio Guzmán Blanco (1829–1899) led a counterrevolution and was elected president. He ruled as a benevolent dictator until overthrown in a revolution in 1888–89. For the next two years no one effectively ruled.

5. 1891–92. General Joaquín Crespo [q.v.] led a revolution that brought him to power, and in 1894 he was elected president for four years.

6. 1898–1900. In 1898 Ignacio Andrade became the first civilian to be elected president. A revolt against his government a few months later was crushed, but Andrade was driven from office by another revolution in 1900.

Venice, Siege of (20 July-28 August 1849), Italian Wars of Independence. Venice ceased to be a republic in 1797, when it was ceded to Austria. By the Treaty of Pressburg in December 1805 it was annexed to Napoleon's kingdom of Italy. In 1814 it was restored to Austria. On 22 March 1848 Venice declared itself the Republic of St. Mark. On 20 July 1849, after the Austrian victory in the Battle of Novara on 23 March, Austrians under Field Marshal Josef Radetzky [q.v.] laid siege to the city. Venetians under Daniele Manin [q.v.] put up a stout resistance. When the Austrian artillery proved unable to destroy the city's defenses, an Austrian artillery officer, Oberleutnant Franz Uchatius, arrived with paper balloons, each designed to hold a $13\frac{1}{2}$-pound bomb that could be released over a target by a time fuze. The balloons were tried—the first aerial bombardment of a city under siege—but occasioned neither destruction nor panic. However, Venice was starved into submission and surrendered on 28 August. Manin fled to Paris.

Venice remained in Austrian hands for the next seventeen years.

Vent. On muzzle-loading cannon the vent is the aperture through which fire is passed to the charge.

Venta del Pozo, Battle of (23 October 1812), Peninsular War. After his failure to capture Burgos [q.v.], Wellington [q.v.] ordered a retreat west toward Portugal. The advance guard of the French Army of Portugal, commanded by General Joseph Souham [q.v.], came upon British vedettes of Wellington's army as they were trying to cross the Pisuerga River over a narrow bridge. There was a confused cavalry melee at the bridge, but Wellington was able to withdraw behind the river, thanks in large part to the steadiness of the King's German Legion. Wellington lost 230 men; Souham lost 300.

Vera, Battles for the Bridge of (1 September and 7 October 1813), Peninsular War.

1. On 1 September 1813 Marshal Nicolas Soult [q.v.], unaware that the besieged French garrison at San Sebastián had surrendered the day before, made a final effort to bring relief. With 10,000 men he approached the town but was halted at the bridge at Vera that arched over the swollen Bidassoa River. It was stoutly defended by 70 British riflemen under Captain

Daniel Cadoux of the 95th Regiment (later Rifle Brigade). Two sentries guarding the bridge were quickly killed, but Cadoux's riflemen shot all who attempted to cross. Cadoux sent word of the attack to the commander of his brigade, a mile away, who, instead of sending support, ordered him to retreat, a command he refused to follow. He held his position until the next day, when he ran out of ammunition. Trying then to retreat and being exposed to French fire, he and 15 of his men were killed; 45 were wounded. Soult crossed unopposed.

2. On 7 October 1813 four brigades of Allied troops launched a major attack northward over the bridge at Vera. The ridges north of the town held by 4,700 French were successfully attacked by troops under Colonel (later Field Marshal) John Colburn [q.v.]. The French lost 1,300 men and four guns; the Allies lost 850 out of 6,500 engaged. On 30 October, Pamplona, the last French garrison on Spanish soil, surrendered.

Veracruz / Vera Cruz, American Siege and Capture of (9–29 March 1847), Mexican War. At five-thirty on the afternoon of 9 March 1847 the armed forces of the United States launched their first full-scale amphibious operation, landing near Veracruz, Mexico, 13,000 soldiers and marines under General Winfield Scott [q.v.] in sixty-five specially constructed surf boats. The boats, designed by Colonel Joseph Gilbert Totten [q.v.], were from 35 feet 9 inches to 40 feet long, double-ended, flat-bottomed, and broad-beamed. Each carried 40 men plus a crew of 8. The landing was unopposed, and not a man was lost.

Veracruz, on the Atlantic Ocean, Mexico's largest port, was considered by many officers to be the most formidably defended city in North America. On the land side it was guarded by two large forts, Fort Santiago and Fort Concepción, which stood at each end of a line of nine small forts linked by a defendable wall. Manned by more than 3,300 Mexican troops, the eleven forts held 86 guns. Just 1,000 yards offshore was a massive fortress, San Juan de Ulúa, mounting 135 guns and manned by 1,030 men. Unknown to the Americans, much of the defensive structure had been allowed to deteriorate, the supply of powder was low, and only four days' provisions were kept in the city.

On 29 March, after American artillery and large naval guns had bombarded the city and forts for six days, the Mexicans surrendered. Mexican losses were 100 civilians and 80 soldiers; American losses were 19 killed and 63 wounded.

Verdi, Giuseppe (1813–1901). The Italian musician who became an invigorator of the "Risorgimento" [q.v.]. In 1842, when his opera *Nabucco* was first performed, a near riot erupted in the third act when the chorus of enslaved and exiled Israelites sang "*Va, pensiero* [Flee, thought]," a lament for their homeland. The audience, recognizing in the words their own political condition, forced the orchestra and cast to repeat the chorus, and although this was forbidden by law, it was done. "Viva Verdi!" became the shibboleth of the revolutionaries, and the letters of Verdi's name came to stand for "Vive Emmanuel, Re d'Italia," a reference to the future King Victor Emmanuel II (1820–1878).

Verdun, Siege of (October–November 1870), Franco-Prussian War. This fortified French town on the right bank of the Meuse River, 150 miles east-northeast of Paris, was besieged by the Germans. On 28 October 1870 the French made two unsuccessful sorties, and on 8 November they surrendered. The Germans took 4,000 men and 108 guns as well as much ammunition and matériel.

Beginning in 1874, the fortifications were modernized and strengthened by the French. They were to play a bloody role in World War I.

Vereshchagin, Vasili (1842–1904). A Russian war correspondent and painter of miliary scenes who entered the navy in 1859 and later studied art in Paris. He was known for the realism of his paintings depicting mutilated soldiers and military executions.

Vergier, Auguste, Comte de la Rochejacquelein (1784–1868). A French soldier involved in the Vendéan Uprising of 1815 [see Vendée, Revolts in]. In 1818, after the restoration, he was created a field marshal and took part in the French intervention in Spain [q.v.] in 1823. He also fought in the Russo-Turkish War of 1828–29.

Very / Verry / Verey Light. A colored signal flare fired from a special pistol, sometimes called a Very signal light. It was invented in 1877 by an American naval officer and ordnance expert, Edward Wilson Very (1847–1907), and originally was called Very's night signal.

Veteran. 1. A surviving soldier of a war.
2. A long-service, experienced soldier.

When nineteenth century wars were over, discharged soldiers were abandoned; many became beggars. Sir William Napier wrote after the Peninsular War, "Thus the war terminated, and with it all remembrance of the veteran's service" (*History of the War in the Peninsula* [1850]).

Veterans' Preference. In 1865 the U.S. Congress affirmed that "persons honorably discharged from the military or naval service by reason of disability resulting from wounds or sickness incurred in the line of duty, shall be preferred for appointment to civil offices, provided they are found to possess the business capacity necessary for the proper discharge of the duties of such offices." This was expanded in 1919 to include all "honorably discharged" veterans. It was further expanded by the Veterans' Preference Act of 1944.

Veterans Reserve Corps. See Invalid Corps.

Veterinary Surgeon. A profession new in the nineteenth century, for farriers were usually charged with the treatment of sick or disabled horses. The term "veterinary surgeon" was first noticed in print in 1802. In 1809 an article in the *European Magazine* spoke disparagingly of farriers who have "conferred on themselves a title highly pre-eminent, that of veterinary surgeon."

Vetterli, Friedrich (1822–1882). A Swiss inventor and gunsmith who in 1864 joined the Waffen-Department of Schweizerische Industrie-Gesellschaft. He designed the Vetterli rifle [q.v.], adopted by the Swiss army in 1868, and a machine gun that was adopted by the Swiss army in 1869 and by the Italian army two years later.

Vetterli Rifle. A rifle designed by the Swiss inventor Friedrich Vetterli [q.v.] and introduced into the Swiss army in 1868. The first model was a 10.4 mm caliber, magazine-load, bolt-action rifle weighing 9.75 pounds and using a rimfire metallic cartridge. It was the first magazine-fed rifle accepted for universal military service. Various improvements were added, and models, including the Vetterli-Vitall introduced in 1871, were in use until 1889.

Viceroy's Commissioned Officer. In the Indian army, a native soldier who had been commissioned not by the sovereign but by the viceroy of India. Before India passed from the Honourable East India Company to the crown and the governor-general became the viceroy, such officers were called native officers. Both under the company and under the crown they ranked below the most junior officer commissioned by the British sovereign. Three ranks were available to them, beginning with jemadar, the lowest, succeeded by risaldar in the cavalry or subedar (subadar) in the infantry, followed by the highest, risaldar major in the cavalry and subedar major in the infantry.

Vickers. In 1828 Edward Vickers (1804–1897) and his father-in-law, George Naylor, formed a British company to manufacture tools, files, and other steel products. In 1867 this became Vickers' Sons & Co., which in 1869 made steel forgings for guns and in 1888 began to manufacture entire guns. In 1884 it bought shares in the Maxim Gun Company, and in 1896 it became Vickers' Sons and Maxim (see Maxim, Hiram Stevens). In 1897 the company bought the Maxim-Nordenfelt Gun and Ammunition Company and added the manufactory of machine guns and ammunition.

Vicksburg, Campaign and Siege of, (29 March–4 July 1863), American Civil War. On 29 March 1863, General U. S. Grant boldly launched his Union Army of the Tennessee on a march south through Louisiana from its base camps at Milliken's Bend and Young's Point in a daring campaign to capture Vicksburg. Situated on the east bank of the Mississippi atop a line of bluffs that tower above the river, Vicksburg was known as the "Gibraltar of the Confederacy." Protected by eight miles of earthworks containing nine forts, Vicksburg was the most strategic site in the western theater for it prevented Union control of the Mississippi River.

On 16 April, as Grant's army pushed south through Louisiana, the vessels of the Mississippi Squadron, commanded by R. Adm. David Dixon Porter, battled their way past the batteries at Vicksburg and later rendezvoused with Grant at Hard Times. On 29 April, Porter's gunboats failed to silence Confederate shore batteries at Grand Gulf, 25 miles below Vicksburg, causing Grant to cross the river farther south at Bruinsburg on 30 April–May 1.

On 1 May, Grant's forces overcame Confederate resistance at Port Gibson. Union victory secured Grant's landing site and compelled the evacuation of Grand Gulf. Over the next seventeen days, Grant's army pushed deep into Mississippi, overcame Confederate forces at Raymond on 12 May and on 14 May captured Jackson, Mississippi's capital city, and scattered Confederate troops that were assembling there under General Joseph E. Johnston. Turning west, Grant drove on Vicksburg. On 16 May his army defeated the Vicksburg field army under Lt. Gen. John C. Pemberton at Champion Hill,

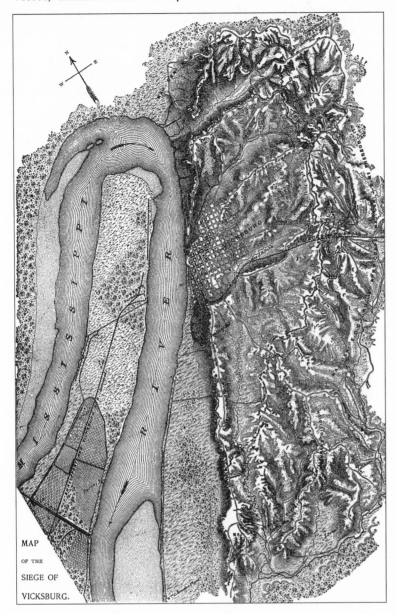

MAP
OF THE
SIEGE OF
VICKSBURG.

Victoria Cross

against Agustín de Iturbide [q.v.], and in 1824 he became the first president of the republic. He served until 1829.

Victoria Cross. The first British medal for valor open to all ranks in the army and navy was authorized by royal warrant, signed on 29 January 1856. It provided that those awarded the cross also receive an annual gratuity of £10, increased to £50 in 1898 and to £1,300 in 1995. The medal bears a Maltese cross ensigned with the royal crest and a scroll bearing the word "Valor," a design chosen by Queen Victoria. In the army it was and is worn suspended on a red ribbon; prior to 1920 the navy ribbon was blue. Nineteenth-century medals were made of bronze from melted-down Russian guns captured in the Crimean War [q.v.]; later the remaining metal became mixed with that of some melted-down Chinese guns. A bar is awarded for a second award of the medal; only three men have won the medal twice. Recipients of the award are authorized to use the postnominal letters VC.

A unique provision stipulated that if an entire company or troop had distinguished itself, its officers could select one officer to receive the award, its noncommissioned officers could select a noncommissioned officer, and two privates could be voted medals by their peers. This method was first used during the Indian Mutiny [q.v.], in the course of which 181 earned the award.

The medal's first awards were announced in the *London Gazette* of 24 February 1857, and in a ceremony in Hyde Park on 26 June Queen Victoria invested 62 Crimean veterans. Later an additional 49 Crimean veterans were awarded the medal.

A royal warrant of 10 August 1858 provided for "non-military persons" to receive the award, and four civilians won the medal for their gallantry in the Indian Mutiny [see Kavanagh, Thomas Henry]. On 23 April 1881 a royal warrant extended eligibility to the "Indian Ecclesiastical Establishments," allowing the Reverend James Adams (1839–1903) to be awarded the medal for his gallantry in the Second Afghan War [q.v.].

A royal warrant of 25 January 1867 extended eligibility to those serving in local forces. Major Charles Heaphy (1822–1881) of the Auckland Militia was given the award for an act of bravery in a Maori War [q.v.].

The first posthumous award of the medal was given to the son of Field Marshal Lord Roberts, VC, Frederick Hugh Sherston Roberts (1872–1899), who was mortally wounded in the Battle of Colenso [q.v.], during the Second Anglo-Boer War [q.v.]. No woman has as yet been awarded the cross.

Provision was made for the Victoria Cross to be forfeited in case of dishonorable behavior, and 8 recipients have been deprived of the honor, 7 in the nineteenth century. Gunner

the most decisive action of the campaign, and the following day routed Pemberton's army at Big Black River, hurling the southern army into the Vicksburg defenses.

Anxious for a quick victory, Grant stormed the city's defenses on both 19 and 22 May only to be driven back with heavy loss. His army then settled down to a tight seige. On 4 July, the day after the Union victory at Gettysburg [q.v.], Pemberton capitulated. The 20,000 Confederates who surrendered were for the most part too weak from hunger or disease to offer further resistance. Grant also captured 172 guns.

Victor, Claude Perrin. See Perrin, Claude Victor.

Victoria, Battle of. See La Victoria, Battle of.

Victoria, Guadalupe (1789–1843), real name: Manuel Félix Fernández. A Mexican soldier and political leader who in 1810 joined the unsuccessful revolution of Miguel Hidalgo y Costilla [q.v.]. In 1823 he joined Santa Anna [q.v.] in a successful revolt

John Collis (1856–1918), who won his cross in the Battle of Maiwand [q.v.] in 1880, lost it in 1895 for committing bigamy.

A curious statistic: Although in the late nineteenth century the homicide rate in Britain was about 8 per 100,000, among the 166 who received the Victoria Cross in the nineteenth century, 7 committed suicide.

Victorio (1825?–1880). An Apache warrior who became head of a Chihennes band that was incorporated into the Mimbres Apaches. From his territory in the Chiricahua Mountains in southeast Arizona, he led numerous raids into Mexico. During the summer of 1855 he and other Indians under Chief Juh [q.v.] won a victory over a Mexican force at Namiquipa, Chihuahua. In 1857, when the Mexicans accounted for many Apache deaths by distributing among a gathering whiskey laced with arsenic, Victorio, who appears to have been abstemious, went unscathed. During the American Civil War he undoubtedly participated in the numerous Apache raids and depredations in the Southwest.

In 1876 he was described by an Indian inspector as "short and stout, with a heavy, firm-set jaw, and an eye [of a] politician." In the spring of 1877 he and his people were settled on the reservation at San Carlos, Arizona, a place described by one of his followers as having "nothing but cactus, rattlesnakes, heat, rocks, insects. No game; no edible plants." Some died of starvation. On 2 September of that year Victorio and Loco (1823?–1905), another Mimbres leader, broke out with about 300 followers. Two days later Victorio and 60 warriors pounced upon a detachment of the 9th Cavalry, a black regiment, near Ojo Caliente, New Mexico, the first engagement of what came to be called the Victorio War. Not long afterward the two leaders and their followers surrendered themselves at Fort Wingate, New Mexico, near the headwaters of the Puerco River, but on learning that they were to be returned to San Carlos, Victorio and some of the band broke away. After a few depredations they finally drifted into Fort Stanton, New Mexico, the Mescalero reservation on the Rio Bonita, some 20 miles east of the Sierra Blanca range. There they were permitted to remain and to draw rations, but mistaking the visit of a government official as a plot to arrest and imprison him, Victorio again bolted with his band on 21 August 1879.

After successfully fighting several skirmishes with troops, he led the way to the Black-Mimbres Mountains west of the Rio Grande. There with his friend Juh [q.v.] he drove south into Mexico. Major Albert Payson Morrow (1842–1911), with detachments from the 3rd and 9th Cavalry and some Indian scouts, pursued the band across the border, suffering near-incredible hardships. Morrow confided to a friend: "I am heartily sick of this business. . . . I have had eight engagements with Victorio Indians . . . and in each I have driven and beaten them . . . but there is no appreciable advantage."

Victorio next moved east into the Candelaria Mountains in Chihuahua, where he twice ambushed Mexican militia, killing 30 with no loss to the band. In January 1880 he was back in New Mexico, playing cat and mouse with the columns sent against him, sometimes winning and sometimes fighting indecisive engagements. In April he was in the San Andrés Mountains, fighting small actions on the 5th, 6th, 7th, and 9th. One veteran army officer described him as "the greatest Indian who had ever appeared on the American con-

tinent." On 24 May 1880, however, 59 Apache scouts under Henry Kinney Parker (1854–pre-1929), chief of scouts, trapped him at the head of a canyon at the headwaters of the Palomas River. Caught off guard, he lost at least 30 of his people, some of whom were women. He himself was wounded in the leg. Parker lost none of his scouts and captured 160 horses but was forced to fall back when out of ammunition. Victorio survived his wound and retreated into Mexico. (Parker later killed one of Victorio's sons, who had become a famous raider in his own right.)

After a long, hard campaign Mexican Lieutenant Colonel Joaquín Terrazas, a cousin of the governor of Chihuahua, with the help of Tarahumara allies laid an ambush in Chihuahua in an area called Tres Castillos where three low peaks rise out of the desert plain. There on 15 October the main body of the band was trapped. In the battle, which began at dawn and lasted into the night, all the warriors fell. Terrazas lost only 3 killed. In all, 78 Apaches, including Victorio were killed; 68 women were taken prisoner, and 2 boys were captured but released.

Victorio had fathered one daughter and four sons, three of whom were killed in the war. The surviving and youngest son attended the Indian School at Carlisle, Pennsylvania, and returned to Fort Sill, where he married. His descendants are numerous today.

Victorio War. See Victorio.

Victory. The overcoming of an enemy in a battle, campaign, or war. There are degrees of victory. German Field Marshal Alfred von Schlieffen [q.v.] said: "A victory on the battlefield is of little account if it has not resulted in a breakthrough or encirclement. Though pushed back, the enemy will appear again on different ground to renew the resistance he momentarily gave up. The campaign will go on."

Vidette. See Vedette.

Viele, Egbert Ludovicus (1825–1902). An American soldier and engineer who upon graduation from West Point in 1847 was sent immediately to Mexico City. [See: Mexican War.] He then served on the western frontier, retiring as a first lieutenant in 1853 to work as an engineer in New Jersey. At the beginning of the American Civil War [q.v.] he served as a captain in the 7th New York Militia. On 17 August 1861 he was appointed brigadier general of volunteers. That same year he published *Handbook for Active Service,* a book that proved popular for young officers both North and South. He served in the South Carolina coastal operations and was for a time military governor of Norfolk. In 1863, when ordered to Ohio to assist in conscription, he resigned and began a distinguished career as an engineer. He served for a time as park commissioner for New York City.

Vifquain, Jean Baptiste Victor (1836?–1904). A Belgian-born American soldier who was graduated from the École Militaire Belge in 1856 and was commissioned in the cavalry. In 1857 he came to the United States. Although he was living in Nebraska when the American Civil War began, he returned to the East and in July 1861 enlisted in the 53rd New York, a regiment largely composed of French-born Americans who were uniformed as Zouaves. In October he was promoted first lieutenant and adjutant, but in March 1862 his unit, being a ninety-day regiment [q.v.], was disbanded. Vifquain and three French-Americans then hatched a plot to capture President Jefferson Davis. It was soon aborted. They arrived in Richmond but found that Davis was not there, and they were for a time jailed. Vifquain next joined the 97th Illinois as adjutant and rose rapidly. By war's end he had won a brevet to brigadier general and the Medal of Honor [q.v.].

After the war he returned to Nebraska and became the state's adjutant general. For a time he served in diplomatic posts in South America. At the outbreak of the Spanish-American War [q.v.] he was commissioned a lieutenant colonel of the 3rd Nebraska Regiment, commanded by William Jennings Bryan (1860–1925), recently defeated as a presidential candidate. When Bryan resigned, Vifquain became colonel. He served in Cuba and was mustered out in May 1899.

Világos. See Siria, Battle of.

Viljoen, Ben (1868–1917). A South African Boer soldier who helped capture Leander Starr Jameson [q.v.] in 1896 [see Jameson Raid]. During the Second Anglo-Boer War [q.v.] he repeatedly distinguished himself, particularly as a guerrilla leader. He was ultimately captured and sent to St. Helena as a prisoner of war. After the war he and a number of followers, diehards who refused to acknowledge defeat, established themselves in Mexico and in some cases the United States, where Viljoen died.

Villafranca, Action at (3 January 1809), Peninsular War. During Sir John Moore's retreat to Corunna [q.v.] his much-demoralized 25,000-man Allied army reached Villafranca, near Aragón, 15 miles north-northwest of Tudela. His troops found and looted the town's wine cellars. Moore himself was commanding the rear guard, holding the bridge over the Coa River at Cacabellos, three miles from Villafranca, until the French drew back and the Allies were able to blow it up. Wellington was horrified by the pandemonium when he reached Villafranca. The hanging of a trooper for breaking into a rum store failed to bring order. The retreat to Corunna proceeded.

Villard, Henry (1835–1900), originally Ferdinand Heinrich Gustav Hilgard. A Bavarian who studied in Germany before coming to the United States, where he changed his name, studied the law, and became a newspaper reporter. In 1859 he traveled to Colorado, and the following year he published a guidebook for emigrants, *The Past and Present of Pike's Peak Gold Regions*. In 1861 at the beginning of the American Civil War, in the employ of the *Cincinnati Commercial,* he filed the earliest story of the First Battle of Bull Run. He later achieved some notoriety with a story in which he affirmed that Secretary of War Simon Cameron (1799–1889) considered William Tecumseh Sherman [q.v.] insane. When the army-controlled telegraph refused to transmit his report of the Union disaster in the Battle of Fredericksburg [q.v.], he carried his story to Washington, where he personally informed President Lincoln of the defeat. Working chiefly for the *New York Tribune,* he covered the majority of the war's major battles and is generally considered one of the outstanding war

correspondents of his time. After the war he returned to Germany to report on the Seven Weeks' War [q.v.]. He then left journalism and amassed a fortune as a financier of railroads and newspapers in the United States.

Villiers, Battle of (30 November–3 December 1870), Franco-Prussian War. One of the large-scale unsuccessful sorties made by the French during the siege of Paris. It was led by General Auguste Ducrot [q.v.] against Württembergers. After an initial success the French were repulsed for a loss of 424 officers and 9,053 other ranks. German casualties were 156 officers and 3,373 other ranks.

Villiers, Frederic (1852–1927). A British war artist who covered campaigns in the Sudan for the *Graphic* and was present at the Battle of Abu Klea [q.v.]. In the Graeco-Turkish War [q.v.] of 1897 he operated the first cinematograph camera used in the history of warfare.

Vimeiro, Battle of (21 August 1808), Peninsular War. In July 1808, taking advantage of the unrest that followed the French occupation of Portugal, 17,000 British and Portuguese troops led by Arthur Wellesley (later Duke of Wellington) landed north of Lisbon. Unchecked at Roliça [q.v.], he continued south. French General Jean Junot [q.v.] then made a rapid march with 13,050 troops and 24 guns to meet him. When Junot's attempt to outflank the Allies was detected, Wellesley redeployed his forces so that his right center was anchored on a hill just above the village of Vimeiro, 32 miles northwest of Lisbon, near the mouth of the Maceira (Alcabrichel) River.

Junot launched two attacks upon the hill, led by Generals Jean Thomières (1771–1812) and François Étienne Kellerman (1770–1835). Both were repulsed by British infantry. Two further attacks were made by the French to the left of the British line, but these also failed, and Junot, having lost 2,000 men and 13 guns, retired toward Torres Vedras. When the French retreated, Wellesley launched the 20th Light Dragoons in pursuit, but the cavalry ventured too far, and out of 240 troopers, 45 were killed or wounded and 11 were taken prisoner. Wellesley suffered only 720 casualties. Wellesley was preparing to pursue with his entire force, but at this moment Lieutenant General Sir Harry Burrard (1755–1813), his superior, arrived on the scene, assumed command, and forbade a pursuit.

Vinkovo, Battle of (18 October 1812), Napoleon's Russian Campaign. On 18 October 1812 Napoleon decided to begin his retreat from Moscow. He was confirmed in his belief that this was the right move by two successful attacks launched by Russian General Mikhail Kutusov [q.v.], one against the cavalry of General Horace Sebastiani [q.v.] near the town of Vinkovo on the Motsha River, 30 miles southwest of Moscow, and one upon the center of Joachim Murat [q.v.], 2 miles from Vinkovo. Sebastiani lost six guns.

Vionville, Battle of. See Mars-la-Tour–Vionville, Battle of.

Virginia, Army of. The short-lived Union army of 47,000 men formed on 26 June 1862 under John Pope [q.v.] consisted of three smaller armies under John Frémont, Irvin McDowell, and Nathaniel Banks [qq.v.]. Frémont, who refused to serve under Pope, resigned his commission and was replaced by Franz Sigel [q.v.]. The army was soundly defeated by General Robert E. Lee in the Second Battle of Bull Run [q.v.], and its existence ended in September after the Battle of Chantilly [q.v.].

Virginia Military Institute. A state military academy founded in 1839 at Lexington, Virginia. It was modeled after the U.S. Military Academy at West Point, New York, and combined college-level studies with military instruction and strict discipline. From its beginning through the American Civil War the superintendent was Francis H. Smith [q.v.]. Of its 1,902 matriculates through 1865, 1,781 served in the Confederate army and 17 became generals. Many professors also served, notable among them Thomas Jackson [q.v.]. The institute functioned throughout the war although studies were briefly interrupted when Stonewall Jackson borrowed some cadets in May 1862. The only service they saw was to bury the dead after the Battle of McDowell. There was a more serious interruption when 229 cadets fought in the Battle of New Market [q.v.] on 15 May 1864. In June of that year Union General David Hunter [q.v.] burned the institute's buildings, but Smith was able to resume classes later in the year.

Virginia Military Institute, 1857

Virtues, Military. Those qualities in the character of men that are particularly valued in soldiers, such as courage, fortitude, loyalty, and obedience to authority.

Visor. The projecting front piece of a headgear. In Britain, it is called a peak.

Vitkevich, Yan (1810?–1839). A Lithuanian aristocrat who while a student in Poland became caught up in anti-Russian movements. At age seventeen he was stripped of his rank and sent as a conscript to Siberia. There he learned several Central Asian languages and was commissioned a lieutenant. He successfully carried out dangerous missions to Bokhara and Kabul. When for political reasons his work was unacknowledged, he destroyed his notes and shot himself.

Vitoria / Vittoria, Battle of (21 June 1813), Peninsular War. Taking advantage of the withdrawal of French forces from the Iberian Peninsula following Napoleon's setbacks in Russia and Central Europe, Wellington led nearly 80,000 British, Portuguese, and Spanish troops with 90 guns out of Portugal into northern Spain. Crossing the upper Ebro, he outflanked 57,000 French troops, including 7,000 cavalry, with 153 guns under Marshal Jean Baptiste Jourdan [q.v.], who had been joined by Joseph Bonaparte (1768–1844), nominally king of Spain. On 21 June 1813 at Vitoria, 50 miles west of Pamplona and 175 miles northeast of Madrid, Wellington, with 8,317 cavalry and 27,372 British, 17,569 Portuguese, and 6,800 Spanish infantry (75,152 total) with 153 guns, launched a three-column assault on the enemy and drove him back through the town in considerable confusion. The pursuit was hampered by undisciplined troops. Wellington missed an opportunity to destroy the French completely when his men turned to looting and drinking. As military writer John F. C. Fuller once pointed out, in every army there is a mob waiting to break out. It was on this occasion that the duke referred to his men as "the scum of the earth."

Wellington lost 22 officers and 479 men killed and 167 officers and 2,640 men wounded. Jourdan lost 756 killed, 4,414 wounded, 2,826 missing, and almost all his artillery and baggage trains: 151 guns, 451 wagons of ammunition, cattle provisions, and treasure. He also lost his marshal's baton, which the British found and sent to the prince regent, who replied by sending Wellington his own field marshal's baton. The battle of Vitoria ended French domination in Spain. Former King Joseph fled over the Pyrenees to France. Austria, encouraged by this victory, joined the Sixth Coalition [see Napoleonic Wars].

Vivandières. Women who accompanied troops and sold provisions, wine, and liquor. Their place in the French army was officially recognized in 1800, when each was issued a *patente de vivandière*. Four were allowed in each battalion of infantry, and two per squadron of cavalry. They were forbidden to sell to civilians or to soldiers in other units. All were wives of serving privates or noncommissioned officers. When they could, they established little canteens; some fortunate ones owned a tent and a pony cart. After 1804 they were given free treatment in military hospitals in time of war. French vivandières carried a small keg (*tonnelet*), usually painted red, white, and blue, on a broad leather belt [compare Sutlers].

French Napoleonic vivandière

During the American Civil War a few vivandières established themselves in the armies of both sides of the conflict, all serving in regiments of foreign-born soldiers, usually French, except for a unit composed mostly of Harvard boys, who thought it would be classy to have one.

One of the most famous of the American vivandières was Marie Tepe, called French Mary, a French immigrant who had married Bernardo Tepe, a Philadelphia tailor. When he enlisted in a Zouave regiment in 1861, she went along as a vivandière. She took part in thirteen battles and was wounded in the heel at the Battle of Fredericksburg [q.v.]. The wound pained her the remainder of her life. She committed suicide in 1900.

Vizetelly, Frank (1830–1883). A British war correspondent and artist who was the younger brother of Henry Vizetelly (1820–1894), the pioneer of the illustrated press. In 1857 he helped found *Monde Illustré* in Paris. As a war correspondent he covered the Battle of Solferino and the campaigns of Giuseppe Garibaldi in Italy, the American Civil War, and the Battle of Sadowa [qq.v.]. In 1883 he was in the Sudan, accompanying the ill-fated army of Hicks Pasha [see Hicks Pasha, William]. He was killed with Hicks Pasha in the Battle of Kashgil [q.v.] on 5 November.

Vladimirescu, Tudor (d. 1821). A Rumanian soldier and political leader who in 1812 raised a corps of Rumanian pandours [q.v.] to fight on the side of the Russians against the Turks. In return the Russians commissioned him a major and awarded him a decoration. In 1820 he was approached by an emissary of the Greek patriot Prince Alexander Ypsilanti [q.v.], who asked him to organize a rebellion in Rumania to assist the Greek rising. Vladimirescu raised a force of Rumanian irregulars and proclaimed a Rumanian national crusade directed against Greek Orthodox priests and boyars, a move that won him wide support from the Rumanian peasantry. By January 1821 he had captured Oltenita [q.v.] in eastern Rumania, at the confluence of the Arges and Danube rivers, as well as the country around it. He then marched on Bucharest. Ypsilanti, finding that Vladimirescu had his own agenda, had him arrested and allowed him to be assassinated at Targoviste.

Vogel von Falkenstein, Eduard (1797–1885). A Prussian soldier who was commissioned a second lieutenant on 8 December 1813 and served in the 1814 campaign in France. In 1843 he was a battalion commander. He was wounded during the rioting in Berlin in 1848 [see Revolutions of 1848]. In May 1850 he was appointed a colonel on the general staff. During the Schleswig-Holstein War [q.v.] of 1864 he served as general chief of staff to General Friedrich von Wrangel [q.v.] and was for a time governor of Jutland (August–October 1864). In the Seven Weeks' War [q.v.] of 1866, as commander of the Prussian army in southern Germany, he invaded Saxony and in June defeated the Hanoverians in the Battle of Langensalza [q.v.] and besieged Frankfurt-am-Main.

During the Franco-Prussian War he was governor-general of the German coast provinces. There, after reading a pamphlet advocating an end to German nobility, he arrested the leading Social Democrats. Upon their release they sued him. A Prussian court ruled in their favor and required him to pay compensation and court costs. He was placed on the reserve list in April 1871.

Voisko. A Cossack tribal regiment or host in the Russian army.

Voivode. A title among some Slavonic peoples, meaning leader of a host. The first holder of this title was Radimir Putnik [q.v.]. The title was used for a Serbian field marshal and at times for Russian, Polish, and Turkish governors, administrators, or military commanders.

Volcanic Arms Company. An American company formed in New Haven, Connecticut, in 1855 that collapsed in 1858. The Volcanic rifle it manufactured was not a success, but it was a stepping-stone to better weapons. After its bankruptcy the remains of the company were purchased by Oliver Winchester [q.v.], one of its shareholders, who then established the New Haven Arms Company and hired Benjamin Henry [q.v.] to redesign the gun. From the ashes of this company the famous Winchester repeating rifle [q.v.] eventually appeared.

Volkonski, Prince Pëtr Mikhailovich (1776–1852). A Russian officer who served in the fight against Napoleon [see Russian Campaign, Napoleon's] in 1812. In 1813 he was the first to advise the tsar to march on Paris.

Volley. 1. The simultaneous discharge of a number of missile-firing weapons on command.
2. A round of artillery fire with each gun in a battery firing a single shot as soon as it is ready.
3. A burst of firing; a salvo.

Volley Gun. See Ribauld / Ribalde / Ribauldequin.

Voltigeurs. Literally, leapers. Highly mobile light infantry composed of short, strong, nimble men first formed in the French Army in 1804. All line and tirailleur units had one such company. They were usually used as skirmishers.

During the Mexican War [q.v.] the United States formed a voltigeur unit. It was in existence only from 11 February 1847 to 25 August 1848.

Volturno, Battle of (1 October 1860), Italian Wars of Independence. Giuseppe Garibaldi [q.v.] with 20,000 of his Red Shirts [q.v.] was attacked by 40,000 Neapolitans attempting to prevent him from capturing Capua, 18 miles north of Naples, on the Volturno River. The Neapolitans were repulsed, and Garibaldi captured the town but suffered heavy losses: 2,023 killed or wounded. The Neapolitans lost 400 killed and 2,070 captured.

Volunteers. Soldiers who are not professionals, men who willingly, often eagerly offered their services to armies, almost always during a major war.

Vomito. See Yellow Fever / Yellow Jack.

Von Borcke, Heros (1836?–1895). A six-foot four-inch-tall blond Prussian who, after service in the Prussian army, sailed to the United States during the American Civil War and served as a major on the staff of Confederate General J. E. B. Stuart [q.v.]. In June 1863 he was severely wounded in a cavalry action near Middleburg, Virginia, and retired from active service. In 1866 he fought on the side of the Prussians in the Seven Weeks' War [q.v.], then retired to his country estate.

He was the author of *Memoirs of the Confederate War for Independence* (1866) and, in collaboration with Justus Scheibert, wrote *Die gross Reiterschlacht bei Brandy Station* (*The Great Cavalry Battle at Brandy Station*) (1893).

Von Bredow's Death Ride. See Death Ride.

Von Steinwehr, Adolph Wilhelm August Friedrich (1822–1877). A German-born soldier who served in the

Volunteers *Call for Irish volunteers for the Civil War*

American army. The son and grandson of high-ranking Prussian officers, he was educated at the Brunswick Military Academy and served as a lieutenant in the Duke of Brunswick's army. In 1847 he obtained a year's leave and sailed to the United States, where he tried without success to procure a regular army commission for the Mexican War [q.v.]. However, he succeeded in obtaining an appointment in the Coast Survey, and while surveying in Mobile Bay, he met and married a young Alabama woman. He took his bride back to Prussia, resigned his commission, and in 1849 returned to become an American citizen and a "Latin Farmer" near Wallingford, Connecticut, one of a number of highly educated Germans who, unable to find professional employment, turned to farming.

At the beginning of the American Civil War he was commissioned colonel of the 29th New York, an all-German regiment known as the Astor Rifles. On 12 October 1861 he was promoted brigadier general and commanded a brigade in the division of Ludwig (Louis) Blenker [q.v.]. He fought in the Shenandoah Valley [see Shenandoah Valley Campaign of Jackson) and was given command of a division that fought at Second Bull Run, Chancellorsville, Gettysburg, and

Chattanooga [qq.v.]. When he was reduced to the command of a brigade after having been briefly a corps commander, he felt he had been overslaughed. He resigned on 3 July 1865.

After the war he taught military science at Yale and built a reputation as a geographer and cartographer.

Von Trotha, Lothar (1848–1920). A German soldier who in 1894 was given command of the forces in German East Africa (roughly mainland Tanzania). Promoted to brigadier general, he commanded the German contingent sent to China during the Boxer Rebellion [q.v.]. He was later governor of South-West Africa (Namibia) and gained a reputation for ruthlessness during the Herero War of 1904. He retired in 1906.

Von Vegesack, Baron Ernest Mattais Peter (d. 1903). A Swedish officer who fought as a captain on the side of Denmark in the Schleswig-Holstein War [q.v.] and on the Union side in the American Civil War. After serving on the staff of General George B. McClellan [q.v.] in the Peninsular Campaign [q.v.], in which he earned the Medal of Honor (awarded in April 1863, for his gallantry in the Battle of Gaine's Mill [q.v.] on 27 June 1862), he became colonel of the 24th New York. In the Second Battle of Bull Run he commanded a corps and covered the retreat of General Fitz John Porter [q.v.]. He was mustered out on 1 June 1863, and in August he returned to Sweden, where the king permitted him to wear his foreign decoration. He retired a major general in the Swedish army.

Vorontsov / Voronzov, Mikhail Semënovich (1782–1856). A Russian soldier who fought against Napoleon in 1805–07. In 1809–11 he fought the Turks, and he again fought against Napoleon in 1812–14 [see Russian Campaign, Napoleon's]. He commanded the Corps of Occupation in France from 1815 to 1818. In 1828 he played a commanding role in the Siege of Varna [q.v.]. He was appointed governor-general of what was called New Russia (the southern provinces of the Russian Empire, today roughly Ukraine and Bessarabia), where he developed the city of Odessa and was the first to introduce steamboats on the Black Sea. He was responsible for constructing most of the defenses of Sevastopol [see Crimean War]. In 1844 he was named governor and commander-in-chief of the Caucasus with plenipotentiary powers, and by 1848 he had succeeded in conquering most of Dagestan [see Shamyl / Schamyl / Shamil]. In 1856 he was created prince and promoted field marshal.

Voyageurs. Canadian rivermen expert in handling canoes and riverboats. They were originally employed by the Hudson's Bay Company and by fur traders to transport men and goods to and from remote Canadian trading posts. Colonel Garnet Wolseley, who used them on his Red River Expedition [q.v.], brought a number of them to Egypt to work on the Nile during the Gordon Relief Expedition [q.v.].

W

Wachtmantel. See Watch Coat.

Wachtmeister. A sergeant major in German artillery and cavalry.

Wadsworth, Decius (1768–1821). An American soldier who matriculated at Yale College at age fourteen and obtained a master's degree in 1788. In 1794, when Congress created the Corps of Artillerists and Engineers, he applied for and received a commission as a captain in the corps but resigned two years later. In 1798 he was reappointed as a captain. By 1802, when the size of the army was reduced, he was a major and survived the cut. In that year the artillery and engineers were separated, and he became an engineer officer. In 1803 he was appointed chief of engineers and superintendent of West Point. In February 1805 he again resigned and went into business in Montreal, but when the War of 1812 [q.v.] began, he closed his business and accepted the appointment of commissary general of ordnance in command of the newly created Ordnance Department.

Wadsworth created a small, efficient staff in Washington and established arsenals at Albany, New York, and Pittsburgh, Pennsylvania. He attempted to standardize the artillery and to improve gun carriages. He served until Congress virtually abolished the Ordnance Department [q.v.] as a separate service in 1821, when he resigned.

Wadsworth, James Samuel (1807–1864). A wealthy New Yorker educated at Harvard who was a member of the Washington Peace Conference [q.v.] in 1861. Although he had no military experience, he served as a volunteer aide to Union General Irvin McDowell during the First Battle of Bull Run [q.v.] and was rewarded by being appointed brigadier general and given command of a brigade near Washington, D.C., a command he held until he was named to command the Military District of Washington. He took leave from that position to run an unsuccessful campaign for governor of New York. On his return to duty he was given command of a division that saw some action in the Battle of Chancellorsville [q.v.]. He fought at Gettysburg and at the Battle of the Wilderness [qq.v.], on the second day of which he was mortally wounded by a bullet in his brain.

Wagner, Arthur Lockwood (1853–1905). An American soldier and educator who was graduated from West Point in 1875 and took part in the Great Sioux War [q.v.] of 1876–77 and in campaigns against the Sioux in Montana and Dakota Territory. He also fought in the Nez Percé War [q.v.], and in

1880–81 he fought the Utes in Utah. In 1882 he was promoted first lieutenant and assigned as professor of military science and tactics to the East Florida Seminary (now the University of Florida), where he remained until 1885. In 1887 he was appointed instructor in the art of war at the Infantry and Cavalry School (known between 1881 and 1886 as the School of Application for Infantry and Cavalry). While there he published *The Campaign of Königgrätz* (1889), *The Service of Security and Information* (1893), *Organization and Tactics* (1895), and *A Catechism of Outpost Duty* (1896). In 1892 he was promoted captain, and in 1896 he left the school and was named major and assistant adjutant general. In May 1898 he was promoted lieutenant colonel and in that rank served on the staff of General Henry Lawton [q.v.] in Cuba and then on the staff of Nelson A. Miles [q.v.] in Puerto Rico. He was sent in December 1899 to the Philippines, where he served in several staff positions, becoming a colonel in 1901. He died on 17 June 1905, the day his commission as brigadier general was signed.

Wagon Box Fight (2 August 1867), American Indian Wars. Near Fort Phil Kearny, Wyoming, the principal army post on the Bozeman Trail [q.v.], a company of the 27th Infantry under Captain James Powell (1828–1893) was guarding a party of woodcutters when they were attacked by Sioux and Northern Cheyenne Indians, who at once swept up a herd of army mules and drove off both the woodcutters and their guards. Some reached the fort; others took refuge in the wagon box corral, where Captain Powell found himself with First Lieutenant John C. Jenness (1842?–1867), 26 soldiers, and 4 civilians.

The circumstances and the nature of the battle resembled the Hayfield Fight [q.v.], which had occurred the previous day near Fort C. F. Smith. The Indians launched several charges, but all were beaten back by the soldiers' newly issued breech-loading but single-shot Springfield rifles [q.v.]. When, after four and a half hours, a relief force with a howitzer arrived, the Indians were driven off. Powell suffered 6 killed, including Lieutenant Jenness, and 2 wounded. He estimated that the Indians lost at least 60 killed and twice as many wounded, although this seems unlikely.

Wagon Soldier. An American colloquial term for an artilleryman.

Wagram, Battle of (5–6 July 1809), Napoleonic Wars. Following his unsuccessful battle at Aspern-Essling [q.v.], Napoleon, reinforced by troops from Italy under his stepson

Eugène de Beauharnais [q.v.], passed the bulk of his 188,000 men and 554 guns onto Lobau Island in the Danube, four miles due east of Vienna, and converted it into an impregnable base. From there during the night of 4–5 July 1809 French troops crossed to the east bank, establishing a bridgehead in the face of weak Austrian opposition. That evening, with the Austrians retiring before him, Napoleon advanced toward the village of Wagram, 11 miles northeast of the Austrian capital, where Archduke Charles Louis [q.v.] waited with 181,000 men and 446 guns in defensive positions on heights above the village. Initial French attempts to storm the heights failed. Shortly after dawn on 6 July, Charles Louis launched an attack along the riverbank toward Lobau Island in an attempt to sever Napoleon's line of communications. It was repulsed by the French IV Corps under Marshal André Masséna [q.v.]. After another surprise Austrian advance early in the day had been checked by Marshal Louis Davout [q.v.] with III Corps, General Jacques Macdonald [q.v.] with 8,000 men attacked the Austrians' left, and when II Corps under General Nicolas Oudinot [q.v.], supported by reserve artillery, successfully pierced their center, the Austrians began to withdraw, their rear guard commanded by Field Marshal Ignatius Gyulas (1763–1831). Although Archduke John [q.v.] came up with 12,500 reserves, they were too late and too few to be effective. By nightfall the French were completely victorious. The price of success was high: 23,000 killed or wounded and 7,000 missing. Austrian losses were 19,110 killed or wounded and 6,740 missing. The French were too exhausted to mount a pursuit that night. Four days later Charles requested an armistice.

After the battle Napoleon stopped by a regiment of infantry and asked the colonel who was his bravest man. A bandsman was brought forward and introduced to the emperor, who said to him: "I am told that you are the bravest man in this regiment. I appoint you a knight of the Legion of Honor, Baron of the Empire, and award you a pension of 4,000 francs." Such gestures, which were soon known throughout the army, had a profound effect upon morale. Napoleon never believed that the peerage he created should be limited to gentlemen; he preferred bravery to manners.

Peace between Austria and France was made by the Treaty of Schönbrunn, signed on 14 October, and Austria joined Napoleon's Continental System [q.v.].

Wahoo Swamp, Battle of (17–21 November 1836), Second Seminole War. An American force of 1,835 under militia Brigadier General Richard Keith Call (1792–1836) was attacked in this swamp by Seminole Indians. American losses were 58; Seminole losses were about 95.

Waizan, Battle of (10 April 1849), Hungarian Revolution. Near this town (Hungarian: *Vác*) on the left bank of the Danube, about 20 miles north of Budapest, some 7,000 Hungarians under János Damjanich [q.v.] defeated two Austrian brigades.

Wakizashi. A short Japanese sword usually carried by samurai with the katana [q.v.], the longer fighting sword. Samurai sometimes referred to the *wakizashi* as the "guardian of their honor," for it was also used for seppuku, or hara-kiri [q.v.].

Walcheren Expedition (28 July–30 September 1809), Napoleonic Wars. On 28 July 1809, to open up a new front in Europe, 264 ships and transports carried nearly 40,000 troops under General Sir John Pitt, Second Earl of Chatham (1756–1835), from England up the Scheldt River to Walcheren Island, an 82-square-mile island in the North Sea on the southwest coast of the Netherlands. They landed on 30 July. A French brigade tried to interfere but was driven back by the ships' guns.

Henri Clarke, Napoleon's efficient war minister, was able to scrape up an army of nearly 40,000 for the defense of Holland. There were only minor actions until 13 August, when the British began a bombardment of Du Flushing (Vlissingen). The city surrendered on 16 August [see Flushing, Du, Siege of], but Chatham failed to take advantage of his initial success and, instead of marching directly upon Antwerp, wasted time handling supply problems, giving the Dutch and French time to counter the threat, and for Jean Baptiste Bernadotte [q.v.] to establish a defensive line that effectively sealed off Walcheren. Malaria, along with typhus and other gastrointestinal diseases, swept through the ranks of the British, and by the time Chatham reembarked his army on 30 September he had lost 3,960 dead, only 106 of whom were killed in action. In all, 11,296 sick were evacuated, most of whom were stricken by malaria.

Walcheren Fever. The name given to the malaria that struck down so many British soldiers in the ill-fated Walcheren Expedition [q.v.].

Walcutt, Charles Carroll (1838–1898). An American soldier educated at the Kentucky Military Institute, near Frankfort, Kentucky. In 1861, at the beginning of the American Civil War, he raised a company for the Union army, but it was not taken into service. On 1 October he was commissioned a major in the 46th Ohio, and in the spring of the following year he was wounded in his left shoulder in the Battle of Shiloh [q.v.]. He carried the bullet for the rest of his life. In March 1865 he was brevetted major general for "special gallantry." On the March to the Sea [q.v.] of General William Tecumseh Sherman [q.v.] he was again wounded. General Oliver O. Howard, commanding the Army of Tennessee [q.v.], said of him that "there is not a braver or better officer."

Walcutt took part in the siege of Vicksburg, the Battle of Chattanooga, and the principal battles of the Atlanta Campaign [qq.v.]. He ended the war as a divisional commander. He was mustered out in January 1866 and was appointed warden of the Ohio Penitentiary. In July he accepted appointment as lieutenant colonel of the 16th Infantry, but he resigned four months later and returned to his post at the prison, where he served until 1869, when President U. S. Grant [q.v.] appointed him collector of internal revenue. From 1883 to 1887 he was mayor of Columbus, Ohio. He was a prominent Mason and a member of the Loyal Order.

Waldersee, Alfred von (1832–1904). A German soldier who joined the Prussian general staff during the Seven Weeks' War [q.v.] of June–August 1866. During the Franco-Prussian War [q.v.] he was present at the siege of Metz [q.v.], and in 1871 he was chief of staff to Frederick Francis II, Grand Duke of Mecklenburg-Schwerin (1842–1883), and later to the governor of Paris. In 1882 he was quartermaster of the Prussian staff, and in 1888 he succeeded Helmuth von Moltke the Elder as chief of staff. He alienated the kaiser by his opposition to the expansive naval program proposed by Admiral Alfred von Tirpitz (1849–1930), and in 1891 he was replaced by Alfred von Schlieffen [q.v.]. In 1900 he was named field marshal general and placed in command of the German contingent sent to China during the Boxer Rebellion [q.v.]. Although he arrived too late for the major actions, he conducted nearly three dozen punitive expeditions between September 1900 and May 1901 around Peking (Beijing).

Walers. Horses sent to the British and Indian armies in India from New South Wales, Australia, from about 1830. They were usually 15 to 16 hands high, sired by English Thoroughbreds from mares that were part draft horse. A military veterinarian described walers as having "fine clean legs and bones, with a short back, large barreled, fine neck and broad head."

Walk About. An expression employed by British officers to waive the ceremony of a sentinel's salute.

Walker, James Alexander (1832–1901). In 1852, while a student at the Virginia Military Institute [q.v.], young Walker threatened to kill one of his professors, Major Thomas Jackson [q.v.]. General Stonewall Jackson later became his commanding officer in the American Civil War. At the beginning of the war Walker was colonel of the 13th Virginia, which he led in Jackson's Valley Campaign, in the Seven Days' Battles, and at Second Bull Run [qq.v.]. He commanded a brigade at Antietam, where he was wounded, at Fredericksburg, and at Chancellorsville [qq.v.]. He was promoted brigadier general at Jackson's request, to rank from 15 May 1863, and was given command of the Stonewall Brigade, which he led at Bristoe Station, Gettysburg, the Wilderness, and Spotsylvania [qq.v.], where he was severely wounded. At Petersburg and Appomattox [qq.v.] he commanded a division.

After the war he farmed near Pulaski and interested himself in politics. He became lieutenant governor of Virginia in 1876 and later served two terms (1895–99) in Congress.

Walker, James Thomas (1826–1896). A British army field engineer who served in India during the Indian Mutiny [q.v.]. From 1861 to 1863 he was superintendent of the great trigonometrical survey of India. He was named major general in 1884.

Walker, Mary (1832–1919). An American "doctor" whose medical education consisted of two terms at Syracuse Medical College, which specialized in herbs, in 1855 and graduation in 1862 from the New York Hygeio-Therapeutic College. Her application to be an army surgeon was refused, but in November 1862, during the American Civil War, she began work as a volunteer field surgeon. Clad in her own version of a uniform—officer's trousers, a surgeon's green sash, and a straw hat with an ostrich feather—she served the Union army for two years and treated wounded at Fredericksburg and Chickamauga [qq.v.]. General George H. Thomas [q.v.] appointed her assistant surgeon of the 52nd Ohio, but that regiment's historian, Nixon Steward, said: "She did little or nothing for the sick of the regiment. . . . Many of the boys believed she was a spy." General Thomas finally concluded: "She

is probably unqualified to administer aspirin." She was captured a month later but in four months was exchanged for a Confederate officer and ever after took pride in the "man for man" exchange.

The government hired her as a contract surgeon at a hundred dollars a month, and she spent the remainder of the war practicing in a Louisville, Kentucky, female prison and in a Tennessee orphanage. On 8 March 1864 a medical board examined her qualifications and determined that "Her practical acquaintance with disease and the use of medicine is not greater than most housewives."

In January 1866 she was awarded the Medal of Honor [q.v.], the only woman ever to receive it, and from the time of its presentation proudly wore it every day. Her medal was revoked in 1917, together with 910 others, but she refused to return it and continued to wear it; it was restored in 1977 by a split vote of the Army Board of Correction of Military Records, which had been asked by four members of Congress to reconsider her case. In 1982 she was honored on a postage stamp.

As the years passed, she grew increasingly eccentric, insisting on wearing only male clothing, including wing collars and top hats, although she was often arrested for masquerading as a man. In 1887 she exhibited herself in sideshows. She spent the remainder of her active life in constant and unreasonable scheming against friends and relations.

Walker, William (1824–1860). An American filibuster. At age twenty he was graduated from the University of Pennsylvania Medical College, and he then spent two years in Europe, studying at Paris, Edinburgh, and Heidelberg. On his return he studied law in New Orleans and practiced briefly before becoming editor of the *New Orleans Crescent*. He was described at this time as standing only five feet five inches tall, having blond hair, and weighing 120 pounds. In 1850 he joined the gold rush to California. On 12 January 1851 at the Mission Dolores in San Francisco, in the first of four duels in his career, he was wounded in the arm by William Hicks Graham (1829–1866), a gunman and later lawyer. In this, as in all subsequent duels, he failed to hit his opponent. While in California, he conceived a scheme for colonizing Mexico. By 1853 he had gathered a force of 45 volunteers and in that year led it in an invasion of Lower California. Initially successful, he proclaimed it a republic with himself as president, and in January 1854 he announced the annexation of the Mexican state of Sonora, but his supply ship on the Pacific Coast was seized on orders of American Colonel Ethan Allen Hitchcock [q.v.]. After he was attacked by Mexican troops and driven out of the country, Walker surrendered to American Brigadier General John Ellis Wool [q.v.] at the border. In May 1854 he was tried in San Francisco for violations of American neutrality laws and was acquitted.

He soon assembled another force of 58 adventurers, grandly named La Falange Americana (the American Phalanx), and on 4 May 1855 he slipped out of San Francisco's harbor to join a revolutionary faction in Nicaragua. On 26 June, after a voyage of 2,700 miles, he landed his force at Realejo. His first fight was an unsuccessful attempt to capture Rivas, a town on the west shore of Lake Nicaragua. On October 11, after acquiring two small cannon and being reinforced to a total strength of about 400 by fresh volunteers from California and by some 250 local recruits, he marched his little army on Granada, the oldest city in the country, with a population of about 10,000, on the southwest shore of Lake Nicaragua. On 13 October he took it by assault with the loss of only a drummer boy.

As a result of his success, the government agreed to terms, and a new regime was formed with Walker as commander-in-chief of an army of 1,200, mostly distributed in small garrisons around the country. Victory brought him fresh recruits; a recruiting office was opened in San Francisco.

On 28 February 1856 Costa Rica declared war on Nicaragua, its leaders promising to drive the foreign invaders from Central American soil. It was soon joined by other Central American states. Rallying his army, Walker announced a "war to the knife and the knife to the hilt" and dispatched a force of 200 men to invade the Costa Rican province of Guanacaste. The officer commanding the force was incompetent, and on 20 March in the first battle, at the Hacienda of Santa Rosa, 12 miles inside Costa Rica, he was surprised and quickly defeated. While the remnants of the army retreated across the border, their wounded, left on the ground, were killed by the Costa Ricans.

In spite of this setback and the invasion of Nicaragua by Costa Rica, Walker was elected president and was inaugurated on 12 July 1856. He was strongly supported in the American South, for his aim was to establish a strong confederacy of slave states in Central America. Although slavery had been outlawed in Nicaragua in 1824, he reinstated it on 22 September 1856.

His government was recognized by the United States, but in trying to recover money owed the country by the steamship company the Accessory Transit Company, he ran afoul of its famous owner, Cornelius Vanderbilt (1794–1877). When Vanderbilt refused to recognize the claim, Walker ordered all the property of the company seized, although in doing so, he cut off his line of communication with California. Determined to bring him down as well as his government, Vanderbilt sent money, men, and supplies to oppose him.

On 11 April 1857 Walker led a force of 500 men, mostly Americans, in a successful attack upon Rivas, which had been captured by Costa Rica. He was besieged there by a Central American army equipped by the British and led by Juan Rafael Mora, the president of Costa Rica, and in May 1857 he was forced to seek refuge on board an American man-of-war. In the United States Walker was given a hero's welcome, particularly in the South. Later that same year he led another filibustering force to Nicaragua, but on 8 December he was arrested at San Juan del Norte by American Commodore Hiram Paulding (1797–1878), who returned him to the United States. After a brief stay, determined to return, he sailed once again to Central America. In September 1860 he was arrested in Honduras by a British naval officer and turned over to Honduran authorities, who court-martialed him on 11 September and shot him the following morning.

Walker, William Henry Talbot (1816–1864). An American soldier who was graduated from West Point in 1837 and saw service in Florida during the Second Seminole War [q.v.]. He was severely wounded in the Battle of Okeechobee [q.v.] on 25 December 1837. During the Mexican War [q.v.] he won brevets to lieutenant colonel and was severely wounded in the Battle of Molino del Rey [q.v.] on 8 September 1857. After the war he was commandant of cadets at West Point.

In December 1860 he resigned his commission, and in 1861, at the beginning of the American Civil War, he was appointed major general of Georgia volunteers and fought at Chickamauga. He was killed on 22 July 1864 while leading a sortie out of Atlanta, Georgia, against Federal General James B. McPherson [q.v.] at Peachtree Creek [q.v.].

Walking Out Uniform. In British usage, an enlisted soldier's good uniform for off-duty wear.

Wallace, Lewis (Lew) (1827–1905). An American soldier, lawyer, and author. At age sixteen, when his father was governor of Indiana, he joined a state militia unit. He served as a first lieutenant in the 1st Indiana during the Mexican War [q.v.] but saw little action. At the beginning of the American Civil War he was appointed Indiana adjutant general and helped raise 150 Indiana companies. He was commissioned a colonel in the 11th Indiana, a three-month regiment. On 3 September 1861 he was promoted to brigadier general, and he took part in the capture of Fort Donelson [q.v.]; in March 1862 he was promoted major general, the youngest in the Union army at that time. He commanded a division in the Battle of Shiloh [q.v.], but Grant blamed him for arriving late on the battlefield, and he was relieved of his command. Assigned to Baltimore, out of the fighting, he was in place to scrape together a small force, and in the Battle of Monocacy [q.v.] in July 1864 he was able to delay the march of Jubal Early [q.v.] on Washington.

Fully cognizant of the horrors of war he was still enthralled by it. He wrote: "Battle has a fascination which draws men as birds are said to be drawn by serpents. . . . [They] thrill with fierce delight to find themselves within the heat and fury of its deadly circle."

After the war he was a member of the court-martial that tried those accused of taking part in the assassination of President Lincoln and was president of the court that tried and convicted Confederate Captain Henry Wirz [q.v.], commandant of the infamous prison at Andersonville [q.v.]. From 1878 to 1881 he was governor of New Mexico Territory, where, on the night of 17 March 1879, he met and accepted the surrender of the outlaw Billy the Kid (real name: Henry McCarty [1859–1881]). Wallace was subsequently minister to Turkey. He was the author of many novels, including *Ben Hur, A Tale of the Christ* (1880). Although seventy-one years old at the outbreak of the Spanish-American War [q.v.] he energetically tried, but in vain, to obtain a general's commission.

Wantie. A wagon rope.

War. A state of life in which an armed and organized political, religious, or ethnic entity directs great violence of some duration and magnitude against similar entities, now particularly nation against nation. War is the most enduring nonbiological function of mankind.

The object of war is to impose the will of one such entity upon another, and it is begun by a leader who believes his side can win. "No one starts a war—or rather, no one in his senses ought to do so—without first being clear in his mind what he intends to achieve by that war and how he intends to conduct it," wrote Karl von Clausewitz [q.v.] in *On War* (1833). However, a belligerent's intent frequently changes in the course of a war or at its end. The aim of war is its political purpose; the way in which a war is conducted is its operational objective.

The character or nature of any given war is determined by the available technology, the experience of past wars, the political milieu, the human and material resources available, the national wills, the terrain over which it is fought, and the education and character of the troops, particularly the officer corps. In the last quarter of the nineteenth century technology emerged as the dominant arbiter of change.

Clausewitz sagely observed: "War is no pastime; it is no mere joy in daring and winning, no place for irresponsible enthusiasts. It is a serious means to a serious end, and all its colorful resemblance to a game of chance, all the vicissitudes of passion, courage, imagination, and enthusiasm it includes are merely its special characteristics." The best-known and most often quoted or misquoted statement of Clausewitz is: "War is not merely a political act, but also a political instrument, a continuation of political relations, a carrying out of the same by other means" (*On War*).

While most people, even generals, deplore war, there have always been a few who speak of its virtues or at least its necessity. On 11 December 1880 General Helmuth von Moltke the Elder [q.v.], in a letter to the Swiss legal scholar and statesman Johann Kaspar Bluntschli (1808–1881) wrote: "War is part of God's world order. . . . Without war the world would sink into materialism." Even Ralph Waldo Emerson (1803–1882), who believed that "universal peace is as sure as is the prevalence of civilization over barbarism, of liberal governments over feudal forms," said: "War educates the senses, calls into action the will, perfects the physical condition, brings men into such swift and close collision in critical moments that man measures man." Future General Henry Wager Halleck [q.v.], writing just before the American Civil War, pointed out: "The Bible nowhere prohibits war. In the Old Testament we find war and even conquest positively commanded, and although war was raging in the time of Christ and his Apostles, still they said not a word of its unlawfulness and immorality" (*Elements of Military Art and Science* [1846]).

War, Causes of. See Casus Belli.

War between the States. A name for the American Civil War used by some southerners after the war. The term was not used during the war. Many southerners then spoke of the Second War of Independence. The official name, established after the war, was War of the Rebellion.

Warbonnet Creek, Skirmish at (17 July 1876), Great Sioux War. A large party of Cheyenne warriors decamping from the Red Cloud Agency in northwestern Nebraska to join other bands of hostile Indians in Montana encountered troops of the 5th Cavalry under Colonel Wesley Merritt [q.v.] with Buffalo Bill Cody [q.v.] as his chief of scouts. The fight was brief, and the Indians fled back to the safety of their reservation. It was in this skirmish that Buffalo Bill killed in personal combat the Northern Cheyenne chief Yellow Hair (1850?–1876).

Warburton, Robert (1842–1899). An Indian army soldier whose father was a British artillery officer taken prisoner at Kabul in 1842 during the First Afghan War [q.v.]. His mother was an Afghan princess. He was commissioned in the Royal Artillery in 1861 and took part in the Abyssinian Campaign [q.v.]. He transferred to the Bengal Staff Corps and in 1878 took part in an expedition against the Uthman Khel on the Northwest Frontier [q.v.]. In 1878–80 he took an active part in the Second Afghan War. Between 1879 and 1882, with intervals of other duties, and from 1882 continuously to 1890 he was a political officer in the Khyber Pass. There he formed the Khyber Rifles [q.v.], recruited from Afridi tribesmen, and made the road through the pass safe. In 1897, when the Afridis were on the verge of revolting, he was sent for but arrived too late to prevent the uprising. He died not long after in Kensington.

War Correspondents. Newspaper reporters with armies. This was a new phenomenon in the nineteenth century. General Garnet Wolseley [q.v.] in his *The Soldier's Pocket Book* (1869) described war correspondents as "Those newly invented curse to armies . . . that race of drones who are an encumbrance to an army; they eat the rations of the fighting man, they do no work at all."

Although the epitaph of war correspondent Sir William Howard Russell [q.v.] in St. Paul's Cathedral proclaims that he was "the first and the greatest," he certainly was not the first, for before his time there were at least two who covered the Peninsular War [q.v.] in Spain, notably Henry Crabb Robinson (1775–1867) of *The Times* (London).

In the nineteenth century many officers doubled as correspondents, as did Winston Churchill [q.v.]. Some of the civilian reporters carried arms and did not hesitate to join in a fight, as did Henry Morton Stanley (1841–1904) in the Ashanti War and artist Alfred R. Waud [q.v.] in the American Civil War. Nevertheless, few officers cared for newsmen.

During the American Civil War more than 150 newspapers, almost all from the North, sent "specials" to cover the action. General Irvin McDowell [q.v.] scornfully suggested that they wear white uniforms "to indicate the purity of their profession." General William Tecumseh Sherman [q.v.] called them "mischievous," among other names. In January 1862 he arrested a reporter for the *New York Herald* and demanded that he be court-martialed as a spy. Colonel (later Field Marshal) Douglas Haig [q.v.], writing from the Sudan to his sister in 1898, declared that "the best war correspondent is he who can tell the most thrilling lies" [see Censorship]. Although generally despised by the military, the war correspondents of the American Civil War are honored in a memorial arch erected by George Alfred Townsend [q.v.], one of their own, at Gaplands Park, not far from the battlefield of South Mountain in Maryland.

In the nineteenth century a few war correspondents became influential, stirring the hearts of their readers to the point of influencing political action. Among these were William Howard Russell whose reports of the needless hardships of British soldiers in the Crimean War [q.v.] brought down the government at home, and Januarius MacGahan [q.v.], whose graphic depiction of Turkish atrocities in Bulgaria led William Gladstone (1809–1898) to write his most fiery pamphlet (*Bulgarian Horrors* [1876–77]).

Ward, Frederick Townsend (1828–1862). An American soldier of fortune who was said to have begun his adventurous career as a sailor and to have taken part in the Crimean War and the Mexican War [qq.v.] and to have served under

William Walker [q.v.], the filibuster, in Central America. He emigrated to China in 1859 and married the twenty-one-year-old daughter of a rich Shanghai merchant. When Shanghai was threatened by Taiping rebels, he raised a small force of foreigners to oppose them [see Taiping Rebellion]. In June 1860 he raised and was the first commander of the Shanghai Foreign Arms Corps, a Chinese force with mostly European officers that became the Ever Victorious Army [q.v.]. He was wounded several times, but his victories earned him a mandarin rank, and he was made a general in the imperial army. On 21 September in an attack upon Tzú-chi [q.v.], near Ningpo, he was shot in the abdomen. He died the next day. British Major Charles Gordon [q.v.] succeeded him, earning the sobriquet of "Chinese Gordon."

Ward was buried in the Confucian cemetery at Sungkiang, 25 miles northwest of Shanghai. On the day of his funeral the merchants of Shanghai closed their shops. In 1877 a memorial hall with a shrine was erected in his honor. It was desecrated by the Japanese in World War II and destroyed by the Communists, who in 1955 paved over his grave.

Frederick Townsend Ward, 1862

Warde, Henry (1766–1834). A British soldier who took part in the capture of Mauritius in 1810 and acted as governor from 1811 to 1813. He was governor of Barbados from 1821 until 1827.

War Department. The U.S. Department of War was created by Congress in 1789 and in its first ten years included the administration of the navy as well as the army. The separate system of staff departments was not created until 1816, under Secretary of War John Caldwell Calhoun (1782–1850). It changed little until 1903, when a general staff was established.

War Establishment. The size of an army with its weapons and equipment in time of war when reserves and auxiliaries are added and peacetime units are augmented.

War Games. See Kriegsspiel.

Warning Order. A preliminary notice of a movement or action, alerting a subordinate that a more detailed order will follow.

War of 1812 (1812–15), called the Patriot's War in Canada. The American name of this war is somewhat of a misnomer, for although it began when the U.S. Congress declared war upon Great Britain on 18 June 1812, the fighting did not end until the Battle of New Orleans on 8 January 1815, fought after peace had been signed in Europe. At issue, said the Americans, were free trade and sailors' rights, both violated by Britain's impressment of American sailors.

The congressional mandate was less than overwhelming. The measure passed the Senate by only 19 to 13 and the House by 79 to 49. The war was certainly not popular with all Americans, some of whom were apathetic and some in open opposition. Many in New England continued to sell grain and supplies to the British and Canadians.

Although the American regular army consisted of only 414 officers and 5,149 enlisted men scattered about in twenty-three forts and posts, most with fewer than 200 men each, it was believed that the deficiency of numbers could be made up by state militia, although even before war was declared, the governors of Massachusetts, Connecticut, and Rhode Island announced that they would refuse to call up their militias. No real war plans existed, and the War Department was headed by an inefficient secretary, William Eustis (1753–1825). He was soon replaced by John Armstrong (1758–1843), who was forced to resign after the British expeditionary force led by Admiral Sir George Cockburn (1771–1853) and General Robert Ross [q.v.] burned Washington, D.C. [q.v.]. Major General Henry Dearborn [q.v.], the senior American general, who assumed command of the northwestern frontier, proved so inept that he was soon recalled. (Dearborn had been a militia captain in the Battle of Bunker Hill in the Revolutionary War. Fort Dearborn, built on the site of Chicago, was named after him in 1803.)

Except for the Battle of New Orleans, all the significant American victories were at sea. The center of the war on land was in the lower Great Lakes area. Although Britain, with a population of 18 million and an army of nearly 100,000, was militarily far superior to the United States, struggling to raise an army of 44,500 from a population of 7.7 million, its troops were still engaged in fighting Napoleon in the Iberian Peninsula [see Peninsular War]. Canada, with a population of only about 500,000, had a small reservoir from which to draw militia. Its defensive forces ultimately consisted of about 7,000 British and Canadian regulars and 10,000 militia under Major General Isaac Brock [q.v.], the governor and military commander in Upper Canada. Also, there were 3,500 Indian auxiliaries.

During the initial stage of the war Britain was too hard pressed in Europe to supply more men, ships, and war matériel to Canada, but the country possessed a fine general in Brock, and it was in this period the Americans made their biggest blunders.

American strategy called for a two-pronged invasion of Canada. Many Americans hoped that Lower Canada (Ontario) could be added to the United States. Although the plan was sound, the forces available were inadequate, and able generals were thin on the ground.

On 12 July fifty-nine-year-old American General William Hull [q.v.], a hero of the Revolutionary War and governor of Michigan Territory, was given command of the western theater of operations. He arrived at Fort Detroit with 300 regulars and 1,500 Ohio militiamen and a week later led them across the Detroit River into Canada. Instead of moving directly upon the nearest enemy strongpoint at Fort Malden, 20 miles south of Detroit, he lingered close to the river and contented himself with sending out reconnaissance and raiding parties. General Brock, more energetic, sent troops and Indians across the river and in doing so cut Hull's communications with Ohio. Fearing that Detroit was in danger, on 7 August Hull began to withdraw his forces to the fort. Brock followed him up with a force of half the size. On 16 August, after firing a few rounds of artillery, he was about to attack when Hull abruptly surrendered [see Detroit, Capture of]. Brock thus acquired an immense store of supplies. (In 1814 Hull was court-martialed and sentenced to be shot, a sentence never executed because of his record in the Revolutionary War.)

The quality of Hull's troops was not high; at least that was the opinion of British Major John Richardson, who described a batch of prisoners thusly: "Their appearance was miserable to the last degree. They had the air of men to whom cleanliness was a virtue unknown and their squalid bodies were covered by habiliments that had evidently undergone every change of season."

At Fort Dearborn Captain Nathan Heald (1778?–1832), acting on Hull's orders, abandoned the fort and marched toward Detroit. On 15 August he was nearly wiped out in an attack by Indians. Ninety-six men, women, and children were killed; only 43 survived, including Heald, who was wounded. Fort Michilimackinac, on the straits between Lake Huron and Lake Michigan, also fell.

Immediately after the capture of Detroit, Brock marched to the Niagara frontier, where American General Stephen Van Rensselaer [q.v.], a man of great social prestige and no military experience whatsoever, was assembling a force of New York militiamen. By the beginning of October Van Rensselaer had some 2,300 militia at the village of Lewiston, New York, on the Niagara River seven miles north of Niagara Falls. At nearby Buffalo, New York, there were 1,650 regulars and 400 militia under Brigadier General Alexander Smyth (d. 1830), a regular army general who refused to serve under or cooperate with a militia general such as Van Rensselaer. Another force of about 1,300 was assembled at Fort Niagara, built in 1796 on a point of land where the Niagara River flows into Lake Ontario.

Opposite Van Rensselaer's camp the Canadian side was protected by a battery deployed on top of a steep-sided height between the town and the Niagara River manned by about 300 men. During the early hours of 13 October 1812 Van Rensselaer crossed the river, stormed the heights, and drove

War of 1812 *Cartoon critical of British behavior during the war of 1812*

the British into the town. There the Canadians and British were reinforced, but Van Rensselaer was not, General Smyth having refused to come to his aid. The height was retaken. The Americans lost 90 killed and nearly 1,000 taken prisoner [see Queenston Heights, Battle of].

Van Rensselaer resigned, and General Smyth replaced him, but unable to control the militia, which melted away, he requested three months' leave, after which he disappeared from the rolls. Except for a few raids, there was no further action on this front.

Major General Dearborn at Albany, New York, with seven regiments of regular infantry, artillery, and some dragoons proposed to attack Montreal and in November marched his army first to Plattsburg and then to the frontier. There he changed his mind, turned about face, marched back to Plattsburg, and went into winter quarters.

At the end of October 1812 Brigadier General William Harrison [q.v.], the "Hero of Tippecanoe," started toward Lake Erie with the object of recapturing Detroit, but when a detachment of 1,000 he had pushed forward as far as Fort Malden was massacred by Indians and Canadians, he halted and built two forts: Fort Meigs, at the rapids of the Maumee River, and Fort Stephenson, both in Ohio on the Michigan border at the western end of Lake Erie.

On 26 April 1813 Americans under Dearborn and Brigadier General Zebulon Pike [qq.v.] were ferried across Lake Ontario and successfully attacked York [q.v.] (today Toronto, Ontario), but at a high cost, including Pike's death. American troops, out of hand, looted and burned the town; many provincial records were destroyed.

On the night of 26–27 May a British force under Major General Sir George Prevost [q.v.], governor-general of Lower Canada, moved from Kingston across the lake to attack Sackets Harbor [q.v.], which was defended by 1,150 men, mostly militia, under Brigadier General Jacob Brown [q.v.]. The British, repulsed with heavy losses, retreated to their ships, and returned to Canada.

On the same day that Prevost sailed to attack Sackets Harbor, General Dearborn at the western end of Lake Ontario invaded Canada with an army of 4,000 men. The amphibious assault was led by Colonel Winfield Scott [q.v.] and Commodore Oliver Hazard Perry (1785–1819). Badly outnumbered, the British retreated, abandoning Queenstown. Two days later Dearborn sent 2,000 men in pursuit. They were attacked and routed in a night attack by 700 British. A smaller contingent surrendered to a force of British and Indians half its size. Until the Battle of the Thames [q.v.] on 5 October there was no further action on land. Dearborn, in poor health, resigned on 15 June.

On 10 September Commodore Perry defeated the British naval forces on Lake Erie. As soon as Perry's fleet had been repaired, Harrison embarked a small army and moved to retake Fort Malden while a land force of 3,500 moved toward Detroit. The British, outnumbered, abandoned both Fort Malden and Detroit. On the banks of the Thames River, about 25 miles from Fort Malden and 55 miles east of Detroit, Harrison defeated the British and their Indian allies. Tecumseh [q.v.] was killed in the battle. There was no further fighting in this area for the remainder of the war.

Harrison moved the bulk of his army to Niagara, where the Americans were planning a two-pronged assault upon Montreal. An army of 4,000 men under Brigadier General Wade Hampton [q.v.] was assembled at Plattsburg, New York, and another of 6,000 under Major General James Wilkinson [q.v.] was gathered at Sackets Harbor. Although the operation depended upon close cooperation between the two forces, the personal relations between the two generals were so strained that they scarcely spoke to each other. Hampton, advanced a short way down the Chateaugay River, made contact with the British, and a part of his force suffered a repulse [see Christler's Farm, Battle of]. He immediately retreated back to Plattsburg and resigned his commission. Wilkinson, after some 2,000 of his men were severely defeated north of Ogdensburg, 55 miles west-northwest of Watertown, New York, also retreated into Plattsburg. So ended one of the biggest American fiascos of the war.

In December 1813 the British under Major General Phineas Riall [q.v.], taking advantage of the disarray of the American forces, seized Fort George and Fort Niagara, which remained in British hands until the end of the war. Before evacuating Fort George, the Americans had burned the town of Newark and part of Queenstown. In retaliation the British after taking Fort Niagara, loosed their Indian allies on the surrounding countryside and burned Buffalo and the village of Black Rock.

Just as many in the northern part of the United States had hoped in the beginning of the war that Canada would be conquered, so many in the South hoped that parts of Mississippi Territory and Florida, both Spanish possessions, could be added to the United States. Andrew Jackson [q.v.], then commander of the Tennessee militia, wrote the secretary of war that he would "rejoice at the opportunity of placing the American eagle on the ramparts of Mobile, Pensacola and Fort St. Augustine." After much debate Congress had approved an expedition into that portion known as West Florida, a strip of land running from the Mississippi River to the Apalachicola River, and this had been undertaken by General Hampton before he marched north to take part in the disastrous aborted Montreal Expedition. Mobile was occupied without opposition.

In the summer of 1813 the Creek Indians had engaged in a series of outrages that culminated in the attack upon Fort Mims [q.v.], near the junction of the Alabama and Tombigbee rivers, and the massacre that followed. This gave Jackson an excuse to assemble his army of Tennessee militia and move into Mississippi Territory, which then included all of Alabama and Mississippi. Many of his volunteers were quickly disillusioned, and some defected, but supported by 600 regulars, in March 1813 Jackson moved to the attack, defeating the Creeks in the Battle of Horseshoe Bend [q.v.] on the Tallapoosa River. This action had no bearing on the outcome of the war against Britain, but neither did most of the land battles that took place in the course of this war.

In March 1813 Congress authorized an increase in the staff of the army, adding an adjutant general, an inspector general, a surgeon general, and an apothecary general. Early in 1814 it authorized the increase of the army to forty-five regiments of infantry, four rifle regiments, two regiments of dragoons, and four artillery regiments. In March General Wilkinson again attempted to invade Canada. Leading 4,000 men, he advanced about eight miles into Canada before being halted by 200 British and Canadians supported by some gunboats on the Richelieu River. This second invasion proved an even greater disaster than the first.

On 3 July Major General Brown and Brigadier General Scott with 3,500 men crossed the Niagara River. Two days later they defeated a numerically inferior force of British regulars and Indians under General Riall on the banks of the Chippewa River [see Chippewa, Battle of; Indian Wars, American].

Brown followed up the retreating British as far as Queenstown, but after waiting two weeks and not receiving the naval support he needed, he withdrew to the Chippewa. He then intended to move on Burlington Heights at the head of Lake Ontario by way of a road known as Lundy's Lane. Meanwhile, following the Treaty of Amiens [q.v.], the British in Canada had received 16,000 reinforcements, mostly veterans of the Peninsular War [q.v.]. As Brown was advancing down Lundy's Lane, he unexpectedly encountered a British force under Riall, and there, on 25 July 1814, ensued the most stubbornly contested engagement of the war [see Lundy's Lane, Battle of]. Both sides claimed victory, but Brown's advance into Canada was halted.

At the beginning of August the reinforced British laid siege to Fort Erie [q.v.], but they withdrew on 21 September after sustaining heavy losses. On 5 November the Americans destroyed Fort Erie and retreated to American soil.

In September 1814 British General Prevost led 16,000 troops in an invasion of New York by way of Lake Champlain. He was defeated when he launched a badly coordinated attack upon Plattsburg on 13 September. The British lost a naval battle on the lake the same day.

The British navy maintained a blockade of American harbors and moved at will on the East Coast. An expeditionary force landed at Cape Cod, and in August 1814 Major General John Ross [q.v.], commanding a force of 4,500 men, was transported up the Chesapeake Bay and the Patuxent River. After defeating the Americans at Bladensburg [q.v.] on 24 August, he captured Washington, D.C., and burned its public buildings [see Washington, D.C., Burning of]. Ross was killed soon after in an abortive attack on Baltimore.

In December 1814–January 1815 British General Sir Edward Michael Pakenham (1778–1815) made an ill-conceived attack on New Orleans [q.v.], which was defended by Andrew Jackson with the help of a local pirate, Jean Laffite [q.v.]. Pakenham was killed in a failed assault on 8 January 1815, and his force was with difficulty extracted. Unknown to the belligerents, the war had ended more than two weeks before the battle.

In September 1812 Tsar Alexander I (1777–1825) of Russia had offered to mediate, and on 11 March 1813 his offer was accepted by the Americans. The British initially rejected mediation, but peace talks finally began in January 1814 and ended at the Charterhouse at Ghent, Belgium, where a peace treaty was signed on 24 December 1814. The United States achieved none of the objectives for which it had gone to war. However, the treaty did provide for the release of prisoners, the arbitration of Canadian and American boundary disputes, and the restoration of occupied territory. News of the Treaty of Ghent reached New York on 11 February, and relations between the United States and Britain returned to a status quo ante bellum.

Total American battle deaths among the regular forces were 65 officers and 1,235 other ranks killed and 227 officers and 2,758 other ranks wounded; among the militia and volunteers, 577 were killed and 1,015 were wounded. British losses are unknown.

War of 1866. See Seven Weeks' War.

War Office. A British government office responsible for army administration and operations. It was established in 1785 and headed by the secretary of state for war, who, from 1801 to 1854, was also the secretary for the colonies. In 1863 the office of secretary of state at war, which had emerged under the reign of Charles II (1630–1685), was abolished.

War of Resistance. See Peninsular War.

War of the Axe. See Axe War.

War of the Castes (1847–55). From about 1835 the Yucatán Peninsula was effectively independent from Mexico. A European-descended landowning elite controlled all political power and made a fortune raising henequen using Mayan labor. In 1847 the Mayans revolted. Plantations were destroyed, and landowners killed. When the United States refused a request for annexation, Mexican troops were called in to suppress the revolt in exchange for reincorporation into Mexico.

War of the Pacific. See Pacific, War of the.

War of the Rebellion. The official name of the American Civil War. Acts of Congress in 1874 and 1880 concerning the compilation of official records of the war so describe it [see Official Records].

War of the Reform (1857–60). The Mexican constitution of 1857 contained reforms that were supported by Liberals led by President Ignacio Comonfort (1812–1863). In the same year he was forced into exile by General Félix Zuloaga [q.v.], a Conservative who seized power in Mexico City until replaced by Miguel Miramón [q.v.], another Conservative, the following year. However, later in the year a rump congress, meeting at Querétaro, 160 miles northwest of Mexico City, proclaimed Benito Pablo Juárez [qq.v.], a Liberal, president.

Conservatives in Mexico City, who controlled the church and the army and were supported by the wealthy families, refused to accept Juárez and moved against him, forcing his government and his army to move to Guadalajara on the Pacific coast and even to Panama before they managed a defiant stand at the port city of Veracruz. Miramón made an attempt to attack them there, but his army was defeated by the diseases of the lowlands. The American government recognized Juárez and his Liberal government.

The ill-trained militia army of the Liberals, commanded by General Santos Degollado (d. 1861), lost every battle, including notable defeats in the Battle of Tacubaya on 11 April 1859 and the Battle of Celaya in November. To finance his revolution, Juárez seized church property, which he used to purchase better arms and equipment. Liberal General Jesús González Ortega (1824–1881) was then able to win a victory at Guadalajara and delivered the forces of Miramón a decisive defeat in the Battle of Calpulálpam [q.v.] on 20 December 1860. Juárez entered Mexico City in triumph on 1 January 1871. He then put into effect the reforms of the constitution.

War of the Two Brothers. See Miguelite Wars.

Warrant Officer. In the British army, a high-ranking non-commissioned officer. The rank did not exist in the American army until the twentieth century.

Warren, Charles (1840–1927). A British soldier and archaeologist who joined the Royal Engineers in 1857 and from 1867 to 1870 made a reconnaissance of the Jordan Valley, Philistia, and Gilead for the Palestine Exploration Fund and excavated extensively in Palestine. During the Kaffir War of 1877–78 in South Africa [see Kaffir Wars], he was in command of the Diamond Fields Horse. He took part in several actions and was severely wounded in a fight at Perie Bush, a large natural forest near King William's Town.

From 1880 to 1884 he was an instructor at the school of military engineering at Chatham. He was detached for a time to search for Professor Edward Henry Palmer (1840–1882), who, sent by the government to pacify Arabs following Arabi's Revolt [q.v.], had disappeared. After discovering that the professor had been robbed and murdered, Warren recovered his remains and arranged for the murderers to be punished. For these services he was knighted. In 1884 he was sent on a military expedition to Bechuanaland [q.v.] to restore order where clashes had occurred between Boer immigrants and natives. In 1886 he took the post of chief commissioner of the London Metropolitan Police; he resigned two years later. From 1889 to 1894 he was commander of troops in Singapore. In November 1899, at the beginning of the Second Anglo-Boer War [q.v.], he was promoted lieutenant general and sent to South Africa to command a division under General Sir Redvers Buller, VC [q.v.]. He proved a disaster as a division commander, suffering defeat by a handful of Boers in the Battle of Spion Kop [q.v.]. He returned to England in 1900 and became a full general in 1904. The rest of his life was devoted to the Boy Scout movement and to Masonic research.

Warren, Gouverneur Kemble (1830–1882). An American soldier who was graduated from West Point in 1850 and served in the Corps of Engineers. In August 1861, at the beginning of the Civil War he was named colonel of volunteers and commanded the newly raised 5th New York. He commanded a brigade in the battles of Gaines's Mill, Second Bull Run, and Antietam [qq.v.]. In September of the following year he was promoted brigadier general, and in February 1863 he was appointed chief topographical engineer of the Army of the Potomac [q.v.]. On 2 July 1863 at Gettysburg his prompt action in seizing Little Round Top saved the day for the Union army (his action is commemorated by a bronze statue there). On 4 March 1864 he was given a corps, with which he fought at the Wilderness, Spotsylvania, Cold Harbor, and Five Forks [qq.v.]. In the latter battle General Philip Sheridan [q.v.] thought him apathetic, late in reaching Dinwiddie Court House the day before and late in attacking at Five Forks. Grant supported Sheridan, and Warren was relieved of his command.

After the war, from 1865 to 1882, he was engaged in military engineering works. He repeatedly asked for a court of inquiry, but this was not granted until 1879. The court under Rutherford B. Hayes [q.v.], which sat irregularly for nearly two years, exonerated him of the most serious charges, but he died before the verdict was announced. Bitter at his treatment, he left instructions that he not be buried in his uniform and that no patriotic emblems be present at his funeral.

Warrior. Although often used as a synonym for "soldier," the term is more strictly used for a fighting man with fewer restraints upon the kinds of people attacked and the degree of violence employed than those imposed upon professional soldiers.

Warsaw, Battle of (6–7 September 1831), Polish Revolution of 1831. By the summer of 1831 the last center of Polish resistance to Russian rule was Warsaw, where Governor Count Jan Krukowiecki [q.v.] with 30,000 troops under General Henryk Dembiński and General Jósef Bem [qq.v.] still occupied strong defensive positions. On 6 September 1831 General Ivan Paskievich [q.v.] with 60,000 Russian troops attacked and took the first line of the Polish defenses, but the Poles stubbornly held out for another day before surrendering. Of the 3,000 defenders of the Wola Redoubt, only 10 men were left unscathed. The revolution was crushed at a cost of 10,500 Russian casualties, 3,000 of whom were killed; the Poles lost about 9,000.

Warsaw Massacre (2 February 1861). A mass demonstration in Warsaw of Poles against Russian rule was crushed when Russian regulars fired upon the mob, killing many [see Polish Revolutions].

Wartenberg, Battle of (1 October 1813), Napoleonic Wars. Near this East Prussian town (Polish: *Barczewo*), nine miles east-northeast of Allenstein (Polish: *Olsztyn*), 16,000 French under General Henri Bertrand [q.v.], occupying strong positions protected by a dike and swampland, were attacked by 60,000 Prussians under Field Marshal Gebhard von Blücher [q.v.]. The battle lasted for five hours until Blücher turned Bertrand's flank. Prussian casualties were about 5,000 to the French 500.

"War to the Knife." During the Peninsular War [q.v.], the defiant reply given by Spanish General José Palafox [q.v.] to the French demand for the surrender of Saragossa [q.v.] in 1808. This was echoed in 1856 by William Walker [q.v.] in his defiant "war to the knife and knife to the hilt" when Costa Rica declared war on Nicaragua.

Washington, D.C., Burning of (24–25 August 1814), War of 1812. On 19 August Major General Robert Ross [q.v.], leading a force of 4,500 British soldiers and marines with three light guns and some rockets, landed at Benedict, Maryland, a fishing village on the Patuxent River, 33 miles southeast of Washington, D.C. On 24 August he defeated 6,000 Americans, mostly militia, under General William Henry Winder [q.v.] in the Battle of Bladensburg [q.v.]. It took only three hours to rout the Americans, so Ross marched on and that night occupied the American capital. "So unexpected was our entry and capture of Washington," Ross wrote, "and so confident was [President] Madison of the defeat of our troops, that he had prepared a supper for the expected conquerors; and when our advance party entered the President's house, they found a table laid with forty covers." Beginning that night and continuing the next day, the British destroyed the bridge across the Potomac and burned the public buildings, including the halls of Congress, the Supreme Court building, the National Archives, and the Library. (The Constitution, the Declaration of Independence, and other important papers had been carried away and safely hidden across the Potomac River in Loudoun County, Virginia.) The only public building not burned was the Patent Office, saved by its superintendent, architect William Thornton (1759–1828), who prevailed upon the British to spare it. The Americans themselves had set fire to the arsenal and dockyard. The only private home destroyed was one from which shots had been fired. A heavy rain in the early hours of the 25th quenched some flames. At dawn high winds brought down a number of damaged buildings, killing 30 British soldiers. At Greenleaf's Point a dry well filled with gun-powder exploded and killed others. On 30 August the British reembarked.

General Henri de Jomini [q.v.] in *Des Expéditions d'outremer* (*Overseas Expeditions*) wrote: "To the great astonishment of the world, a handful of seven or eight thousand English were seen to land in the middle of a state of ten million inhabitants, and penetrate far enough to get possession of the capital, and destroy all the public buildings; results for a parallel to which we should search history in vain. One would be tempted to put it down to the republican and unmilitary spirit of those states, if we had not seen the militia of Greece, Rome, and Switzerland make a better defense of their homes against far more powerful attacks, and if in this same year another and more numerous English expedition had not been totally defeated by the militia of Louisiana under the orders of General Jackson." (The reference was to Andrew Jackson and the Battle of New Orleans [qq.v.].)

The American government had had ample warning that an attempt would be made to capture Washington, but General John Armstrong [q.v.], then secretary of war, had scoffed at the idea. His scoffing cost him his appointment, for the burning of Washington and other debacles of the war were laid at his door, and he was forced to resign.

Washington, D.C., Union Defenses of. During the American Civil War General George B. McClellan selected Major John G. Barnard [qq.v.] to build the defenses of the Union capital. By the end of 1861 Barnard had encircled Washington with 37 miles of lines. These were continually improved upon during the course of the war until the defenses consisted of 20 miles of rifle pits connected by 60 forts and 93 batteries of 762 guns and 74 mortars. However, the only threat to the capital came on 11 July 1864, when the army of Lieutenant General Jubal Early [q.v.] arrived at the city gates to find itself confronted and repulsed by the most powerful fortifications of any American city.

Washington, John Macrea. (1797–1853). An American soldier who was graduated from West Point in 1817, fought in the Second Seminole War [q.v.] and was present in the Battle of Lockahatchee [q.v.]. Serving under General Winfield Scott in 1838–39, he assisted in the removal of the Cherokees to present-day Oklahoma. He then helped to quell border disputes with Canada. During the Mexican War [q.v.] he commanded a battery under General John Wool [q.v.] and won a brevet for his conduct in the Battle of Buena Vista [q.v.]. In 1848–49 he was civil and military governor in New Mexico. In that capacity he called up the militia and led an expedition against the Navajos. During a skirmish on 31 August 1849 Chief Narbona (1776?–1849) was killed and was scalped by

one of the militiamen. Washington was soon after transferred to a post in New Hampshire. In December 1853 he was drowned, when his ship, the *San Francisco*, was lost in a storm near the mouth of the Delaware River.

Washington Horse Artillery. One of the most famous Confederate artillery units in the American Civil War. It was organized in New Orleans in 1838 as the Native American Artillery, a militia unit. During the Mexican War [q.v.] it served under General Zachary Taylor [q.v.]. It was renamed the Washington Artillery in 1852 and by this time contained some of New Orleans's most prominent and wealthy citizens. Just before the American Civil War it expanded to five batteries. On 11 April 1861, at the outbreak of the war, it seized the Baton Rouge Arsenal and equipped itself with guns and ammunition. The following month it entered the Confederate service and arrived in Richmond, Virginia, on 4 June with six 6-pounders, two 2-pounder howitzers, and one rifled gun. It first saw action on 18 June in the Battle of Blackburn's Ford [q.v.], in which it lost 1 officer and 5 enlisted men killed. As part of the Army of Northern Virginia [q.v.] it took part in the Peninsular Campaign, Second Bull Run, Antietam, Fredericksburg, Chancellorsville, and Gettysburg [qq.v.]. One company was at Chickamauga and Petersburg [qq.v.]. In the course of the war 719 men served in the Washington Horse Artillery; 62 were killed in action, 2 from accidents, and 20 died of diseases.

It later served in the Spanish-American War [q.v.] and both world wars. It is today part of the 256th Infantry Brigade of the Louisiana National Guard.

Washington Peace Conference (4–27 February 1861). An unofficial conference of prominent moderates from the North and the South that met at the Willard Hotel in Washington, D.C., to discuss how civil war could be averted. It was presided over by John Tyler (1790–1862), tenth president of the United States (1841–45). General Winfield Scott [q.v.] called it "a collection of visionaries and fanatics" and the *New York Herald* termed many of its conferees "political fossils." As Lincoln had predicted, nothing came of the debates, accusations, and lectures.

Washita, Battle of (27 November 1868). In retaliation for the depredations of several Indian braves, Lieutenant Colonel George Custer [q.v.] with his 7th Cavalry was ordered on a punitive expedition. On 27 November 1868 he led a three-pronged dawn attack upon the camp of Black Kettle (1803?–1868) on the Washita River in Indian Territory (Oklahoma), killing 103 peace-seeking Cheyenne Indians, including 16 Indian women and 9 children, and capturing 53 other women and children. Black Kettle was killed as he tried to flee. Custer lost 2 officers and 14 enlisted men killed. His soldiers slaughtered 900 of the Indians' ponies.

Custer violated a basic military precept by attacking an enemy of unknown strength on unreconnoitered terrain, a mistake he was to repeat at the Battle of the Little Bighorn [q.v.], where it proved fatal. This time, however, it brought him new renown as an Indian fighter.

General Philip Sheridan [q.v.], commanding the Department of Missouri, was elated by Custer's initial report and wrote General William Sherman [q.v.], his superior, "[I]f we can get one or two more good blows there will be no more Indian troubles in my Department."

There has been debate on whether Custer's attack was justified. Black Kettle and the majority of his band had been peaceful, and the chief had steadily pursued a policy of peace with the white men, but it seems certain that some of his young warriors had indeed killed Kansas settlers and then returned to his camp. The army never found a suitable way to discriminate between guilty and innocent Indians on the Great Plains, and Indian chiefs rarely achieved the authority over their people that the soldiers and politicians imagined or desired.

Watch Coat. An overcoat (greatcoat) so called because it was originally supplied only for sentries going on watch on cold nights. *Wachtmantel* in German.

Watchword. 1. A password given in response to a challenge. 2. A word or expression used as a signal or a rallying cry.

Waterloo, Battle of (18 June 1815), Napoleon's Hundred Days. Believing that Field Marshal Gebhard von Blücher [q.v.] and his Prussian troops, following their defeat at Ligny [q.v.] on 16 June, were too far east to take any effective part in the impending battle with Wellington, Napoleon dispatched Marshal Emmanuel Grouchy [q.v.] to protect his right flank [see Wavre, Battle of] and then gathered 72,000 men and 246 guns on a low ridge, making his headquarters at an inn called La Belle Alliance [q.v.] on the road south of Brussels. Before him, Wellington had deployed 68,000 British, Dutch, Flemish, and German troops with 156 guns behind a low ridge called Mont-St. Jean, 4 miles south of the village of Waterloo and 12 miles from Brussels. In front of the ridge Wellington's men also held the farm of La Haye Sainte and on the right the Château of Hougoumont [qq.v.], which were to be important features on the battlefield. The battle was fought on a 4-mile front between the villages of Mont-St. Jean and Plancenoit.

Waterloo *Wellington orders his troops to advance at Waterloo*

Waterloo *Charge of the Scot's Greys at Waterloo*

The French, under cover of their artillery, moved forward shortly before noon on 18 June 1815 but failed to make immediate progress against Hougoumont and did not take La Haye Sainte until six o'clock in the evening. Meanwhile, despite the pressure of French artillery and cavalry attacks, the squares of Allied infantry on the ridge held firm, while Blücher's Prussians were gradually closing on the French right flank from the east. Late in the afternoon 31,000 Prussians attacked and captured Plancenoit in the rear of La Belle Alliance, and although it was retaken by French reserves, Napoleon, realizing that he must win the main battle, made a last desperate attack. Stiffened by nine battalions of the Old Guard led by Marshal Michel Ney [q.v.], he launched an attack on the Allied center at seven o'clock. When this failed and the Prussians again took Plancenoit, the French began to retreat.

Wellington suffered 15,000 casualties, the Prussians 7,000, and the French a total of 44,000. Wellington's victory saved Brussels. Napoleon abdicated for a second and final time four days later.

In a letter to William Wellesley-Pole (1763–1845) after the battle Wellington wrote: "It was the most desperate business I ever was in; I never took so much trouble about any Battle; and never was so near being beat."

The first British government issue of a war medal was awarded to all ranks who fought at Waterloo. Prize money was also distributed: Wellington was awarded £61,000, other generals received £1,275, and privates received £2 11s 4d.

Watertown Arsenal. An American arsenal, established in 1816, seven miles west of Boston, Massachusetts, which manufactured field guns and artillery ammunition, made alterations in coast artillery, and tested experimental guns. It contained the U.S. Testing Machine, the most elaborate and accurate machine in the world for testing the strength of materials.

Watervliet Arsenal. An American arsenal on the Hudson River just north of Albany, New York. It was founded in 1812, and by 1889 it was the principal factory for cannon.

Watie, Stand (1806–1871). A three-quarters Cherokee Indian who, during the American Civil War, became a Confederate brigadier general, the highest-ranking Indian in the Confederate army. He had learned English at a Moravian mission school and become a planter and businessman. From 1845 to 1861 he was a member of the Cherokee Tribal Council and was its speaker from 1857 to 1859. In 1861 he raised and commanded a company that fought in the Battle of Wilson's Creek and at Peabody Ridge [qq.v.]. He was named colonel of the 2nd Cherokee Mounted Rifles and took part in the invasion of Missouri by Sterling Price [q.v.]. On 6 May 1865 he became a brigadier general and commanded a brigade. He did not surrender until 23 June 1865.

Wauchope, Andrew Gilbert (1846–1899). A Scottish soldier who was commissioned in the Black Watch [q.v.] in 1865, after serving for two years as a midshipman. After service in Cyprus, Egypt, and the Sudan, he was promoted major general and given command of the Highland brigade at the beginning of the Second Anglo-Boer War [q.v.]. He was killed leading his troops in the Battle of Magersfontein [q.v.] on 11 December 1899. He was buried on the battlefield, but through a curious misunderstanding a monument was erected to him at Matjesfontein, a small town several hundred miles distant in the Karroo.

Waud, Alfred R. (1828–1891). An English-born artist who was trained at the Royal Academy's School of Design and emigrated to the United States in 1850. In 1861, at the beginning of the American Civil War, he was working for the *New York Illustrated News,* in which his battlefield sketches appeared until February 1862, when he moved to *Harper's Weekly,* for which he worked the rest of his life. During the war he carried a gun and frequently put himself in danger to obtain a better view. His works, with those of his brother William, also an artist, make a collection of twenty-three hundred sketches, now in the Library of Congress in Washington, D.C. Waud died of a heart attack while sketching the battlefields of Georgia in 1891.

Alfred Waud sketches at Gettysburg.
Photograph by Matthew Brady

Wauhatchie, Attack on (28–29 October 1863), American Civil War. At the foot of the west side of Lookout Mountain on Wauhatchie Creek in Tennessee a division under Union Brigadier General John W. Geary [q.v.] defended the rear of the army of Major General Joseph Hooker [q.v.] and his line of communication. Night attacks were rare in nineteenth-century land warfare, but on the night of 28 October 1863 Confederate General James Longstreet launched four brigades against Geary. In spite of considerable confusion, the assault was made at midnight from the north and east and took Geary by surprise. Hooker, about three miles away, hearing the sounds of battle, dispatched two divisions to his aid. Repeated Confederate attacks were beaten back, and repeated counterattacks by the Federals were repulsed, all with heavy losses. The Confederates retreated at about 3:00 A.M. [see Night Attack].

Alfred Waud sketch of the charge of Humphrey's division, Battle of Fredericksburg, 13 December 1862

Because of the confused nature of the fighting, the after-action reports of the commanders make little sense, and the casualty figures are more unreliable than most. However, Federal losses were reported as 76 killed, 339 wounded, and 22 missing; Confederate losses were about 460.

Waving the Bloody Shirt. See Bloody Shirt.

Wavre, Battle of (18 June 1815), Napoleon's Hundred Days. After the reverse at Ligny [q.v.] on 16 June 1815, Field Marshal Gebhard von Blücher [q.v.] with his Prussian troops retired toward Wavre, 14 miles southeast of Brussels. To guard against a flank attack by Blücher, as he moved his main body toward Brussels, Napoleon detached Marshal Emmanuel Grouchy [q.v.] with 33,000 men to protect his right flank. Probing forward during the morning of 18 June, Grouchy encountered Prussian forces in the area of Wavre. Aware that a general action was imminent near Brussels, Blücher had left General Johann Thielmann [q.v.] with 25,000 men to defend the village, which Grouchy attacked fiercely throughout the day, oblivious of the fact that Blücher was marching 10 miles southwest with the bulk of the Prussians to intervene decisively on the battlefield of Waterloo. On the morning of 19 June Grouchy captured Wavre, but because the Battle of Waterloo [q.v.] had by then been won by Wellington and Blücher, his victory was irrelevant. Losses were about 2,500 on each side.

Wawz / Wawer, Battle of (30–31 March 1831), Polish Revolution of 1831. Polish forces under General Jan Skrzynecki [q.v.], after two days of hard fighting, defeated the Russians, who lost 12,000 in killed and wounded and 2,000 taken prisoner. The loss to the Poles was small, but this victory was soon followed by defeat and ruin.

Waynesborough, Battle of (2 March 1865), American Civil War. On 28 February 1865 Union General Philip Sheridan [q.v.] led two cavalry divisions—about 10,000 men—south of Winchester, Virginia, up the Shenandoah Valley to attack Staunton, a Confederate supply depot. Sheridan reached it on 1 March to find the town deserted and the supplies gone, removed by the troops of Lieutenant General Jubal Early [q.v.], who had retreated southward. The following day Sheridan directed General George Custer [q.v.] to pursue, and Custer encountered 1,700 Confederate troops, a portion of Early's army under General Gabriel Colvin Wharton (1824–1906), on a low ridge just west of Waynesborough. About three-thirty in the afternoon, having found a one-eighth-mile gap in the Confederate line, Custer pushed three regiments through it and followed with an attack by a brigade of cavalry. Early vainly tried to rally his men before making his own escape. Custer captured more than 1,600 Confederates, nearly 200 wagons, 11 guns, and 17 flags.

Weaponry. The science of designing and manufacturing weapons. Although first printed in 1844, the word was not used much in the nineteenth century and is absent from most pre-World War II dictionaries. Journalists have corrupted the meaning and now often use it as the plural of weapon.

Weapons. Instruments to fight with. The Bible states: "Wisdom is better than weapons of war" (Ecclesiastes 11:18), but men seem never to have believed this or never to have been sufficiently wise.

Although General Henri de Jomini [q.v.] in 1838 in his *Précis de l'art de la guerre* considered that the "means of destruction were approaching perfection with frightful rapidity," except for the development of shrapnel [q.v.] and improved rockets, there were few noteworthy improvements in weapons in the first half of the century. It was not until the last half and particularly the last third that a remarkable escalation in the destructive power and efficiency of weapons occurred. In a mere fifty years breech-loading rifles replaced muskets, breech-loading rifled cannon replaced muzzleloaders, and the machine gun was invented and improved; smokeless powder and rim-fired metallic cartridges changed tactics. The value of cavalry as an offensive tool ebbed with these developments, and the saber and lance became almost obsolete. The bayonet, for reasons that remain obscure, has never been abandoned in spite of its inutility. Hand grenades, for reasons equally obscure, were seldom used. Land mines came to be used extensively only toward the end of the American Civil War although explosives used for demolition purposes were in use throughout the century in sieges. Rockets were not new but were much improved as weapons by William Congreve [q.v.] and were particularly effective against primitive tribesmen.

Weatherford, William. See Red Eagle.

Webb, Alexander Stewart (1835–1911). An American soldier who was graduated from West Point in 1855 and fought in the Third Seminole War in 1856. In the American Civil War he was present at First Bull Run and fought in the Peninsular Campaign [qq.v.]. On 23 June 1863 he was promoted brigadier general and given command of a brigade consisting of four Pennsylvania regiments. On the third day of the Battle of Gettysburg his brigade was posted at the "little clump of trees" that was the focal point for Pickett's Charge [q.v.], and Webb and his brigade were in large part responsible for the repulse of the Confederate assault. Webb was awarded the Medal of Honor [q.v.] for his gallantry in the action. The brigade suffered 451 men killed and wounded; Webb was among the wounded. In the Battle of Spotsylvania on 10–12 May 1864 he was severely wounded, but he returned to duty in January 1865 as chief of staff to General George Meade [q.v.].

After the war, in the reorganized army of 1866, he was appointed lieutenant colonel of the 44th Infantry, and he taught for a time at West Point. He resigned in 1870 to become president of the College of the City of New York, a post he held for thirty-three years.

Weber, Max (1824–1901). A soldier who was born in the grand duchy of Baden and after graduation from the Karlsruhe Military Academy was commissioned a lieutenant in the army of the grand duke. He became involved in the revolutions that swept through Europe in 1848–49. After the German revolts were crushed, he fled to the United States and opened the Konstanz Hotel in New York City, a haven for German immigrants. At the beginning of the American Civil War he organized the rifle regiment, composed mostly of Germans, that became the 20th New York. On 28 April 1862 he was promoted brigadier general. He distinguished himself in the Battle of Antietam [q.v.], in which he was wounded, losing permanently the use of his right arm. In April 1864 at Harpers Ferry he was in charge of the troops from the Monocacy River to Sleepy Creek. He was driven out of his position by Jubal Early but reoccupied it soon after when the Confederates withdrew.

After the war he served as American consul at Nantes, France, and as collector of internal revenue for New York.

Webley Pistol. A revolver manufactured by P. Webley & Son in Britain and adopted by the British army in 1887. The first models were six-shot hinged-frame pistols in .442 caliber with a four-inch barrel. A model in .455 caliber was introduced in 1899.

Webster, Joseph Dana (1811–1876). An American soldier educated at Dartmouth College, from which he was graduated in 1832. In 1838 he was commissioned in the Topographical Engineers, and he served in the Mexican War [q.v.]. In 1854 he resigned as a captain and settled in Chicago, but on 1 July 1861, at the beginning of the Civil War, he returned to the army and was soon engaged in constructing defenses in Cairo, Illinois. On 1 February he was appointed a colonel and became General Grant's chief of staff. He served at Shiloh [q.v.] and was promoted brigadier general on 29 November 1862. During Grant's Vicksburg Campaign he was in charge of all the railroads serving Grant's forces and later Sherman's.

After the war he was appointed collector of internal revenue.

Wedge Block. A triangular block of wood inserted beneath the breech of a muzzle-loading gun and hammered toward the muzzle to depress the elevation of the tube.

Wei Ch'ang (d. 1856). A rebel Chinese general appointed north wang in the Taiping Rebellion [q.v.]. In 1853 he commanded the rear guard in the march on the Yangtze River and later that year took part in the capture of Nanking (Nanjing or Nanxiang), which became the Taiping capital [see Nanking, Siege of]. When Yang Hsiu Ch'ing [q.v.] appeared to threaten the leadership of Hung Hsiu-Ch'uan [q.v.], the Taiping founder and ruler, Wei was ordered to kill Yang, an order he followed with such zeal that an estimated 20,000 of Yang's family, friends, and followers were slaughtered as well. He then attempted to kill Shih Ta-k'ai [q.v.], another wang, and to supersede Hung himself, but in November 1856 he was arrested and executed.

Weihaiwei, Battle of (30 January–12 February 1895), Sino-Japanese War. On 19 January 1895 the Japanese Third Army under Iwao Oyama [q.v.] was landed unopposed at Jungcheng, on the eastern tip of the Shantung Peninsula, 20 miles east of the Chinese naval base at the port town of Weihaiwei. While the Japanese fleet under Yuko (or Sukenori) Ito (1843–1913) shelled the port's shore fortifications from the sea, Oyama marched west in bitter winter weather and captured the town on 12 February. The Chinese commander, Admiral Ting Ju-ch'ang, committed suicide. This battle ended the war.

Weissenburg, Battle of. See Wissembourg, Battle of.

Weissenfels, Battle of (1 May 1813), Napoleonic Wars. Napoleon, advancing upon Lützen, ordered Marshals Michel Ney and Jean Baptiste Bessières [qq.v.] with an army corps and the Imperial Guard cavalry to press forward and engage the Allied forces under General Ludwig Wittgenstein [q.v.] even though the French army was still incomplete, for he feared that Wittgenstein would take flight. They clashed at this town, 20 miles west-southwest of Leipzig. When the Russian cavalry of Marshal Ferdinand Winzingerode (1770–1818) tried to prevent the French from crossing the Rippach River, they were repulsed by French infantry, composed for the most part of young conscripts. The Allies drew back, and the French advanced on Lützen [q.v.]. Napoleon used the engagement with telling effect to inspire his army. In the course of the battle Bessières was struck by a round shot and killed instantly.

Weitzel, Godfrey (1835–1884). An American soldier who was graduated from West Point in 1855. The son of German immigrants, he had been educated only in local schools, but he was graduated second in his class and was commissioned in the engineers. In the two years before the outbreak of the American Civil War he taught engineering at West Point. In the spring of 1862, one year after the war had begun, he was chief engineer and second-in-command in the successful expedition led by Major General Benjamin Butler [q.v.] against New Orleans [q.v.], and he was appointed acting mayor of the captured city. On 29 August 1862 he was promoted brigadier general of volunteers and commanded a division at the siege of Fort Hudson. Two years later he was a major general, and in December 1864 he was again second-in-command under Butler in the attack upon Fort Fisher [q.v.]. In the final stage of the war in the East he commanded all troops north of the Appomattox River. On 3 April he telegraphed Washington: "We entered Richmond at eight o'clock this morning."

In March 1866 he was mustered out of the volunteer service and reverted to his substantive rank of captain. In August he was promoted major, a rank he held for sixteen years. In 1882 he was mustered out as a lieutenant colonel.

Weldon Railroad Operations (22–23 June 1864), American Civil War. During the Petersburg Campaign [q.v.] General U. S. Grant sent a cavalry division and two corps of infantry to extend his line westward and to cut Confederate lines of communication south of Petersburg, particularly to destroy the Weldon Railroad connecting Petersburg to North Carolina. Confederate Lieutenant General A. P. Hill [q.v.], exploiting a gap in the Union advance, sent three divisions to separate and attack the flanks of the divided Federal forces. The Federals retreated after losing 2,962 men.

Wellesley, Arthur. See Wellington, Arthur Wellesley, First Duke of.

Wellington, Arthur Wellesley, First Duke of (1769–1852). In 1787, at the age of eighteen, Arthur Wellesley entered the army. In 1797 he sailed to India with his regiment, the 33rd Foot. In 1799 he commanded a division in the Fourth Mysore War against Tipu (Tippoo) Tib (1751–1799) and was then appointed to the supreme military and civil command in the Deccan. His rapid rise was due in large part to his eldest brother, Richard Colley Wellesley, later Lord Mornington (1760–1842), governor general in India from 1797 to 1805, who bought him the command of his regiment. In 1803 he defeated the Maratha chiefs in the Second Maratha War [q.v.]. He returned to England in 1805, and in 1806 he married Lady Katherine ("Kitty") Pakenham, who was to bear him three sons and three daughters. In 1807 he took part in the siege of Copenhagen [q.v.], defeating the Danes at Köge (Kjöge) on the east-central coast of Sjaelland Island. In 1808 he was promoted lieutenant general and sent to the Iberian Peninsula to aid the Portuguese in driving out the French [see Peninsular War]. After his victories in the bat-

Wellington at San Trinidad breach cheered by his troops

tles of Roliça and Vimeiro [qq.v.] he was recalled to England [see Cintra, Convention of], but on the death of Sir John Moore [q.v.] he returned to the seat of war and was given the chief command. In that capacity he drove the French out of Spain and fought the final battle of the war at Toulouse [q.v.].

In the course of the war his victories were rewarded with advances in the peerage. On a single day he heard five successive patents of nobility, from baron to First Duke of Wellington, read in the House of Lords. In 1814 he was ambassador to France and Britain's representative at the Congress of Vienna in 1814–15. After Napoleon's return from Elba Wellington was given command of the Anglo-Dutch army in the Low Countries, and with Field Marshal Gerhard von Blücher [q.v.] he defeated Napoleon in the Battle of Waterloo [q.v.] on 18 June 1815. In 1818 Wellington was made master general of the ordnance, an office he held until 1827. From January 1828 to November 1830 he was prime minister. He was again appointed commander-in-chief, and in 1842 he was confirmed for life in that office. Appointed lord high constable, in 1848 he organized the military in London against the Chartists [see Chartist Riots].

On his death his body lay in state at Chelsea Hospital [q.v.]. So many came to view it that two people were killed in the crush.

Wepener, Lourens Jacobus (1812–1865). An Afrikaner soldier of Swedish descent who fought in South African wars against native tribes and was killed while leading a party of volunteers against the Basuto stronghold of Thaba Bosigo [q.v.] on 15 August 1865.

Wepener, Siege of (9–25 April 1900), Second Anglo-Boer War. About 1,000 Boers under Christiaan De Wet [q.v.] laid siege to some 1,700 British of the Colonial Division at this Orange Free State town on the Caledon River, 63 miles southeast of Bloemfontein. The Boers shelled the town and inflicted about 300 casualties, but the British held out until relieved. Boer losses were 5 killed and 13 wounded.

Werder, Johann Ludwig (1808–1885). A German gunmaker who began his career as an apprentice to a locksmith and became a mechanical engineer. After studying production methods in the United States, he returned to Europe to develop and manufacture machine tools, locomotives, and many types of mechanisms. In the late 1860s he operated an arms factory in Nuremberg, where he developed the Werder system [q.v.] for rifles.

Werder System. A breech-loading system for small arms invented by Johann Ludwig Werder [q.v.] of Nuremberg and adopted by the Bavarian army in 1869. It employed a falling breechblock similar to that of the Peabody rifle [q.v.] and a finger-operated lever inside the trigger guard that unlocked the falling block. It was closed and locked by a thumb-operated lever that also cocked the internal hammer.

Werndl, Josef (1831–1889). A gunmaker from a family of gunsmiths who honed his skills in gun factories in Europe and the United States, where he worked for Colt and Remington, until in 1853 he returned to Europe to take over the family business in Steyr. In 1863 he developed the successful Werndl military rifle, a single-shot weapon with a unique breech closure that inspired the Nordenfeldt breechblock [q.v.].

West, Army of the (1846), Mexican War. An American army of 1,660 men commanded by Brigadier General Stephen Watts Kearny [q.v.] that, in 1846 during the Mexican War [q.v.], marched west from Fort Leavenworth, Kansas, to wrest California from Mexico. On 15 August 1846 it reached Las Vegas, then a small village of adobe buildings in the Sangre de Cristo Mountains, which marked the northeast frontier of New Mexico. Standing on the roof of an adobe building overlooking the plaza, Kearny formally took possession of New Mexico. On 25 September he resumed his march westward with 300 dragoons, the rest he sent back when he learned that California had already surrendered to Captain John Frémont [q.v.] and a number of naval officers. On 25 November he forded the Colorado River; on 2 December he reached Warner's Ranch in the highlands beyond the Imperial Valley desert. On 7–8 December he suffered a defeat at the hands of Californios in the Battle of San Pasqual [q.v.], in which he was wounded by lances. There followed an unseemly dispute with Frémont over which of the two was in command. Since Kearny was clearly the superior, Frémont was later court-martialed for his presumption.

Kearny served briefly in Mexico and won a brevet to major general, but he contracted a disease in Veracruz that seriously impaired his health, and he died soon after in St. Louis.

West Point. The popular name for the United States Military Academy located adjacent to the small town of West Point, New York, where during the Revolutionary War a strong fort was built on the heights overlooking the Hudson River. During the first presidential administration (1789–97) of General George Washington (1732–1799) the rank of cadet was created in the Corps of Artillerists and Engineers, and two cadets were assigned to each company for instruction. On 16 March 1802 the artillery and engineers were separated. In April the Corps of Engineers, consisting of 7 officers and 10 cadets, was established at the fort as a military academy, with Jonathan Williams [q.v.] as post commander and superintendent and Anna Louis de Tousard [q.v.], a French officer, as head of instruction. By 1812 the academy had graduated 89, of whom 69 were still in the service. The academy remained under the Corps of Engineers with all its superintendents appointed from the corps until 1868.

On 28 July 1817 Captain Sylvanus Thayer [q.v.], an 1808 graduate, became superintendent. Generally considered the father of the academy, he served until July 1833. It was he who instituted the academic and training system still used, and he made the academy a school of scientific distinction. In 1818 he inaugurated the system of ranking cadets, a system that continued until 1977. Highest-ranking graduates were given first choice of arms and usually chose the Corps of Engineers. Those in lower ranks usually vied for commissions in the artillery, and the lowest were commissioned in the infantry or cavalry.

Although most of the fighting that was to be done by West Point cadets in the nineteenth century, aside from the Mexican War and the Civil War [qq.v.], was to be against Indians on the western frontier, there were no classes, not even a lecture, on Indian fighting or the construction or management of a western fort, nor were there classes on Indian languages or culture. The emphasis was entirely upon European-style warfare.

For most of the nineteenth century the academy's rate of attrition was high, from one-third to one-half of the enrolled cadets failing or dropping out, especially those from western states, who generally lacked the necessary academic background. There were also those dismissed for indiscipline [see Egg Nog Riot]. Most cadets were (and are) appointed by members of Congress, and for the greater part of the century there was little screening before their appointment. Some of the first appointees, it was discovered, could not read or write. Most of the graduates came from eastern states, where there were better schools.

The first black cadet was James Webster Smith of South Carolina, who was admitted in June 1870 but was not graduated. The first black to be graduated was Henry O. Flipper [q.v.] in 1877; the second was John Hanke Alexander (1865?–1894), who was graduated in 1887; the third, Charles Young (1867?–1922), was graduated at the bottom of his class in 1889 but rose to become a colonel. No other black was graduated until 1936.

Not until 1860 did an academy graduate, Joseph E. Johnston [q.v.], class of 1829, become a brigadier general. Except when acting as engineers and explorers, West Pointers were not considered exceptional soldiers until the Mexican War [q.v.], in which many distinguished themselves. In a speech at a dinner after the capture of Mexico City,

West Point *Military Academy at West Point, 1817*

8 December 1847, General Winfield Scott [q.v.] declared: "I give it as my fixed opinion that but for our graduated cadets the war between the United States and Mexico might, and probably would, have lasted some four or five years, with, in its first half, more defeats than victories falling to our share, whereas in two campaigns we conquered a great country . . . without the loss of a single battle or skirmish." An eloquent testimonial, even if not quite true.

The class of 1842, many of whose alumni fought in the Mexican War, went on to greater glory in the American Civil War, during which 22 of the 37 class members still alive when the war began became generals in either the Union or Confederate army.

In 1861, on the outbreak of the Civil War, there were 278 cadets in the academy, 86 of whom came from the South; 65 of these resigned or were discharged for refusing to take the oath of allegiance, and only 21 stayed on. Classes were accelerated so that two classes were graduated that year. In the course of the war the academy produced 159 officers and maintained a student body of just over 200.

"Duty Honor Country" is the motto of the academy. General Douglas MacArthur (1880–1964), a 1902 graduate, speaking to the Corps of Cadets on 12 May 1962, told them: "In my dreams I hear again the crash of guns, the rattle of musketry, the strange mournful mutter of the battlefield. But in the evening of my memory, always I come back to West Point. Always there echoes and re-echoes in my ears—Duty Honor Country."

West Point Electro-Ballistic Machine. A machine invented by James Gilcrest Benton (1818?–1881) to determine by electricity the initial velocity of a projectile.

West Pointer. A graduate of the U.S. Military Academy located at West Point, New York [see West Point].

West Point Iron and Cannon Foundry. Sometimes called the Cold Springs Foundry, it was established under government patronage in 1817 and located across the Hudson River from West Point, 20 miles south of Poughkeepsie, New York. From 1836 to 1867 its supervisor was Robert Parrott [q.v.]. During the American Civil War it produced more than seventeen hundred pieces of ordnance and three million projectiles. In 1861 Parrott invented, and patented, a method of strengthening cast-iron guns by shrinking wrought-iron hoops on the breech, and the same year he invented an expanding projectile for rifled cannon. Parrott 12-pounder guns were used by Union artillery throughout the Civil War.

On 24 June 1862 President Lincoln, always curious about ordnance, paid a visit to the foundry.

Westport, Battle of (23 October 1864), American Civil War. Confederate General Sterling Price [q.v.] with 12,000 cavalry and 14 guns tried to reclaim Missouri for the Confederacy by invading from Arkansas. At Westport, Missouri, now a suburb of Kansas City, he fought a four-hour battle with Union forces under Alfred Pleasanton and Samuel Curtis [qq.v.]. Each side lost about 1,500, and Price was forced to retreat. On 25 October he fought a costly battle at Mine Creek, Kansas. By the time he reached safety in Arkansas he had lost half of his men.

Weyler y Nicolau, Valeriano (1838–1930). A Spanish officer of German descent who was born in Palma de Majorca. He was graduated from the military college in Toledo and later the Spanish staff college. As a lieutenant colonel he distinguished himself in 1863–65 in Santo Domingo (Dominican Republic) and in 1868–72 in fighting against rebels in Cuba. In 1874–75 he took part in the Second Carlist War [q.v.] in Spain as a Cristino, and in 1876 he was promoted major general. From 1888 to 1892 he was in the Philippines, where he brutally suppressed the Caroline rebels on Mindanao and elsewhere in the islands. In 1892–93 he was back in Spain, suppressing émeutes among the Basques, and in Navarre. He was appointed captain general of Cuba and arrived in Havana on 10 February 1896. He believed that "Mercy has no place in war," and within six days announced his *reconcentrado* policy, beginning in sections of Oriente and Camagüey provinces [see Concentration Camps]. In October 1897 he was recalled. In the early twentieth century he served three times as minister of war, and in 1910 he was appointed to the Supreme War Council.

Weyrother, Franz von (1755–1806). An Austrian soldier who first saw action against the Turks in 1788–90. He was promoted general in 1804. On the eve of the Battle of Austerlitz [q.v.] he spent three hours convincing the Allied commanders of the value of his plan for the massive envelopment movement that failed. Prince Adam Jerzy Czartoryski (1770–1861), Russia's Polish-born acting foreign minister, who witnessed the battle, wrote: "The wretched Weyrother wandered from place to place, bravely risking his life to redeem the disaster of which he was the chief cause." He died ten weeks later.

Wheat, Chatham Roberdeau (1826–1862). An American soldier, born the son of an Episcopal minister, who was graduated from the University of Nashville in 1845. After a year studying law, he volunteered for the Mexican War [q.v.] and rose to the rank of captain. After the war he practiced law in New Orleans and was elected to the Louisiana legislature, but the war had given him a taste for combat and adventure that the law and politics failed to satisfy. He served in several filibustering expeditions to Central America and Cuba, and in 1860 he was serving with English volunteers in the revolutionary army of Giuseppe Garibaldi [q.v.] in Italy.

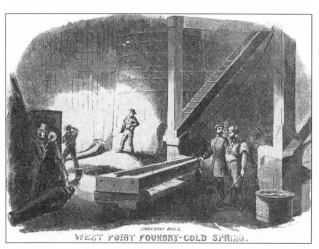

West Point foundry at Cold Spring, New York

At the beginning of the American Civil War he organized the 1st Louisiana Special Battalion, familiarly known as the Louisiana Tigers, taking in, among others, many who were the sweepings of the New Orleans docks, men unaccustomed to discipline. Wheat, standing six feet four inches, was able to control them, but he was the only man who could. When he was shot through both lungs at First Bull Run, the battalion's first battle, and told by a surgeon that the wound was fatal, he replied, "I don't feel like dying yet." He survived to fight with his battalion in the Shenandoah Valley and in the Seven Days' Battles [q.v.]. He was wounded again, this time mortally, in the Battle of Gaines's Mill [q.v.] on 27 June 1862. He died the same day. His battalion was disbanded.

Wheaton, Frank (1833–1903). An American army officer who spent one year at Brown University in 1849–50 before serving at age seventeen as a "chain bearer and station marker" for the Mexican Boundary Commission. In March 1855 he was commissioned a first lieutenant in the 1st Cavalry, and he spent six years on the frontier. In August 1855 he fought the Cheyenne Indians on the Wood River near Fort Kearney, Nebraska, and in July 1857 he took part in the expedition against the Cheyennes. In 1857–58 he served in the Utah Expedition [q.v.] under Albert S. Johnston [q.v.], and he was engaged in quelling the violence in Bloody Kansas.

In July 1861, at the beginning of the American Civil War, he was named lieutenant colonel of the 2nd Rhode Island Volunteers and distinguished himself at First Bull Run [q.v.]. Promoted to colonel, he served with the Army of the Potomac [q.v.] in the Peninsular Campaign [q.v.] and in Maryland, winning promotion to brigadier general of volunteers. He led a brigade in the Battle of Fredericksburg [q.v.] on 13 December 1862 and fought on the third day of the Battle of Gettysburg [q.v.], 3 July 1863. He fought at Spotsylvania on 8–12 May 1864 and later in June in the first assaults upon Petersburg [qq.v.]. He was promoted major general and repulsed the raid of Jubal Early [q.v.] upon Washington.

In April 1866 he was mustered out of the volunteer service and reverted to the rank of major but was soon promoted to lieutenant colonel of the 39th Infantry. During the Modoc War [q.v.] he led the first assaults on the lava beds [q.v.] on 16–17 January 1873. He oversaw the trial of Captain Jack [q.v.] and his fellow chiefs and the day before they were hanged informed them that President U. S. Grant would not commute their sentence. He retired in 1897, soon after being promoted major general.

Wheaton, Loyd (1838–1918). An American soldier who in April 1861, at the beginning of the American Civil War, enlisted in the Union army for three months as a sergeant in the 8th Illinois Infantry. At the end of his enlistment he was commissioned a first lieutenant in the same regiment. He served throughout the war and, as a colonel, was wounded in the Battle of Shiloh [q.v.] on 7 April 1862. On 9 April 1865 his gallantry in an assault upon Fort Blakely won him a Medal of Honor [q.v.], although it was not awarded until 1894. In May 1866 he was mustered out of the volunteer service a brevet colonel and in July was appointed a captain in the 34th Infantry. After serving on the frontier, he was named brigadier general of volunteers in May 1898 at the beginning of the Spanish-American War [q.v.]. In August 1899 he was ordered to the Philippines, where he earned a brevet to major general

for his gallantry in the Battle of Imus, seven miles southeast of Cavite, on 19 June 1899. With Generals Henry W. Lawton and Arthur MacArthur [qq.v.] he fragmented the insurrectionists under Emilio Aguinaldo [q.v.]. In March 1901 he became a major general in the regular army, and he retired in July 1902.

Wheeler, Joseph (1836–1906). An American soldier whose maternal grandfather was General William Hull [q.v.]. He was graduated from West Point in 1859. On 22 April 1861, at the beginning of the American Civil War, he resigned as a second lieutenant in the Mounted Rifles. And twenty-one months later, at the age of twenty-six, he was a major general in the Confederate army in command of all the cavalry in the Army of Tennessee [q.v.]. In 1863 he published *A Revised System of Cavalry Tactics for the Use of Cavalry and Mounted Infantry*, the first unequivocal advocacy for the use of mounted infantry rather than heavy cavalry. A small man, only five feet five inches tall, he weighed no more than 120 pounds throughout the war, in which he saw more action than most. He was three times wounded, 36 staff officers fell at his side, and sixteen horses were shot from under him. In May 1865 he was captured while trying to prevent the capture of President Jefferson Davis. He was paroled after spending two months in a federal prison, and he ended the war a lieutenant general.

After the war he entered the hardware business and in 1866 married a wealthy widow. He became a successful planter, studied the law, and was admitted to the bar. In 1883 he began serving the first of eight terms in the House of Representatives, where he was a member of the Military Affairs Committee.

During the Spanish-American War [q.v.] he served as a major general of volunteers and commanded the dismounted cavalry in Cuba, where his aggressive actions brought on the Battle of Las Guásimas [q.v.] on 24 June 1898. On 1 July he was present in the Battle of San Juan Hill [q.v.]. In 1898 he published *The Santiago Campaign*. In 1899 he commanded a brigade in the Philippines. He was retired on 10 September 1900 as a brigadier general in the regular army.

Wheeler and General William Fitzhugh Lee [q.v.] were the only Confederate officers to become generals in the U.S. army. Wheeler had no qualms about serving in the army against which he had fought, declaring that he would face General Robert E. Lee at the gate of heaven wearing his blue uniform. He is one of only a handful of Confederate officers buried in Arlington National Cemetery [q.v.].

"When Johnny Comes Marching Home Again." A popular song of the American Civil War written by Irish-born bandmaster Patrick Sarsfield Gilmore (1829–1892) under the pseudonym Louis Lambert. The best-known lines were "The men will cheer and the boys will shout and the ladies they will all turn out, and we'll all drink deep when Johnny comes marching home."

Whipple Hat. Also known as the excelsior hat, it had a brim around two-thirds of the crown and a leather visor. It was patented on 16 July 1861 by J. F. Whipple and manufactured by the Seamless Clothing Manufacturing Company. Whipple hats were worn during the American Civil War by Union troops in the United States Sharpshooters and by some units from New York and New Hampshire.

Whistling Dick. The most celebrated single gun of the American Civil War was a rifled and banded gun, originally a smoothbore 18-pounder manufactured at the Tredegar Iron Works [q.v.] in Richmond, Virginia. It was subsequently rifled in a manner that gave an erratic spin to projectiles and produced a distinctive whistling sound when they were in flight. It was installed to be part of the Confederate river defenses at Vicksburg [q.v.], Mississippi, where on 27 May 1863 it sank the Union gunboat *Cincinnati*.

Since shortly after the war until the present there has been displayed at West Point a 7.44-inch Blakely gun, its muzzle shortened by about two feet, that until 1957 was considered to be Whistling Dick. It has recently been established that although also at Vicksburg, it was known as Widow Blakely. The whereabouts or fate of the true Whistling Dick is unknown.

White, George Stuart (1835–1912). A British soldier who entered the army in 1855. In the Second Afghan War [q.v.] in 1878–79 he was second-in-command of the 2nd Battalion, 92nd Regiment (later the Gordon Highlanders), when he led a charge during the Battle of Charasiab [q.v.] on 6 October 1879 that won for him the Victoria Cross. In 1884–85 he commanded a battalion of the Gordons in the Gordon Relief Expedition [q.v.]. In 1885–86 he commanded a brigade in the Third Anglo-Burmese War [q.v.], after which he was promoted major general. In 1890 he saw action on the Northwest Frontier [q.v.] in the Zhob Expedition. From 1893 to 1898 he was commander-in-chief, India, and directed the conduct of the Chitral and Tirah campaigns [qq.v.]. During the Second Anglo-Boer War [q.v.] he was commander of the troops besieged in Ladysmith [q.v.] in 1899–1900 for 119 days until relieved by General Redvers Buller [q.v.]. From 1900 to 1904 he was governor of Gibraltar; while there, he was promoted field marshal. An equestrian statue of him adorns Portland Place in London.

White, Rollin (1817–1892). An American inventor and gun designer who worked for a time for Samuel Colt [q.v.]. He sold or licensed his patents to Smith & Wesson and others. He grew rich from his design for a sewing machine.

White Arm. A romantic name for an edged weapon, particularly a saber. The French term, *arme blanche*, is frequently used. Occasionally used as a synonym for cavalry.

White Bird (1807?–1882). An Indian leader and medicine man of the Nez Percés who fought in the Nez Percé War [q.v.] and refused to surrender, even at the close of the Battle of Bear Paw Mountain [q.v.], which ended the war. With some 200 followers he made his way to Canada, where he was well received by Sitting Bull [q.v.]. He remained there for five years. He was killed after his return by an Indian who accused him of making medicine that had killed his two sons.

Whitebird Canyon, Battle of (17 June 1877), Nez Percé War. On 13 June 1877, three young Nez Percé Indians raided several farms and killed four white settlers. Fearing retribution, they fled for protection to the band of White Bird [q.v.] in the gorge of Salmon River, about one mile northeast of present-day Whitebird, Idaho. Captain David Perry (1841–1908), commanding Company F, 1st Cavalry, set off with some volunteers, about 109 whites, to attack the band. He was soundly defeated in the battle that followed and suffered 34 dead; 3 Indians were wounded. This was the opening battle of the Nez Percé War [q.v.].

White Cockade. The badge of French royalists. French emigrant units serving in foreign armies wore the cockade as a sign of their allegiance to the Bourbons.

White Feather. Symbol of cowardice. "To show the white feather" was to be a coward.

White Flag. See Flag of Truce.

White Lotus Sect. A Chinese secret society begun by a Buddhist monk, Mao Tzu-yüan, of Suchow (Kiuchuan) in the fourteenth century. It was originally an ascetic religious organization, but government persecution and the rising of rival sects altered its doctrines and practices. Its members came to resist Manchu authority, and in the nineteenth century they led numerous revolts against the imperial government. The Boxer Rebellion [q.v.] at the end of the century was said to have been instigated by the sect.

Red was the favored color of the society, and its members wore red turbans.

White Mutiny (1858–59). In November 1858, at the end of the Indian Mutiny [q.v.], a British royal proclamation abolished the Honourable East India Company [q.v.]. The crown assumed the governing power of the company, and the European officers and men of the company's army were transferred into the British army, a move not universally popular. It was particularly resented by the enlisted men in the so-called European regiments of the company. Within two weeks the Madras Fusiliers staged a protest; the 1st Bengal European Cavalry followed suit, and then others. At Meerut men of the 4th Bengal European Cavalry refused to parade, and on 5 June 1859 the men of the 5th Bengal European Cavalry barricaded themselves in barracks and refused to obey their officers until they were starved into submission. Private William Johnson, judged to be the ringleader, was shot by firing squad.

Although government law officers ruled that it was legal for the crown to shanghai the company's soldiers, many army officers were uneasy about the move, and in the end the government capitulated; only 2,809 men had proved willing to enlist in the queen's army. The remainder, 10,116 strong, were shipped back to Britain, packed with their families into troopships [q.v.] often lacking sufficient food and water. Some arrived in England in such pitiable condition that a national scandal erupted.

White Oak Swamp, Battle of (30 June 1862), American Civil War. A battle in southern Virginia, one of the Seven Days' Battles [q.v.] of the Peninsular Campaign [q.v.], also known as the Battle of Glendale, New Market Roads, Charles City Crossroad, Nelson's or Frayser's Farm, Turkey Bridge, Turkey Bend, or Willis's Church. On the night of 29–30 June in a heavy rain Union General George B. McClellan [q.v.] drew his army behind White Oak Swamp. Lee ordered attacks that had little chance of success. In a stupor from lack of sleep, Confederate General Thomas ("Stonewall") Jackson, instead of crossing one of the several fords available, sat on a log and contented himself with shelling the enemy. Only the attacks of James Longstreet and A. P. Hill [qq.v.] made any progress. During the night McClellan was able to move his entire army to Malvern Hill [q.v.], where four Union corps took up strong defensive positions. Federal losses were 2,853; Confederate losses, 3,615.

White Sergeant. A British term of derision applied "to those ladies who, taking advantage of the weakness of their husbands, neglect their domestic concerns to interfere in military matters" (*Wilhelm's Military Dictionary and Gazetteer* [1881], and repeated exactly in *Farrow's Military Encyclopedia* [1884]).

Whiting. A chalk used like pipe clay to whiten leather equipment.

Whiting, William Henry Chase (1824–1865). An American soldier who, after being graduated from Georgetown College (now University) in 1840, went on to West Point, from which he was graduated first in his class with the highest grades ever obtained up to that time. The brilliant Whiting acted as mentor for and tutor to a slower fellow student named Thomas Jackson [q.v.], later known as Stonewall. Whiting resigned from the army in 1861 to join the Confederate service and distinguished himself at First Bull Run and in the Peninsular Campaign [qq.v.], where he commanded a division under Jackson. After the Battle of Malvern Hill [q.v.] he was ordered to North Carolina, where he developed Fort Fisher at the mouth of Cape Fear River into the strongest fortification in the Confederacy. He was promoted major general on 22 April 1863, and in the summer of 1864 he was at Petersburg. Here his failure to bring his troops into action on time at Port Walthall Junction gave rise to the accusation that he was drunk or on drugs. On 15 January 1865 at Fort Fisher [q.v.] he was severely wounded and captured. Imprisoned in Fort Columbus (Fort Jay) on Governor's Island in New York Harbor, he died of his wounds on 10 March.

Whitman, Walt(er) (1819–1892). An American journalist and poet who in late 1862, during the American Civil War, after tending to his wounded brother George in Virginia, returned to his home in Washington, D.C., and appointed himself an unofficial nurse to the sick and wounded soldiers in Washington hospitals. War, he concluded, was "about 999 parts diarrhea and one part glory."

He left a record of his experiences in *Memoranda during the War* (1875), in poems published in *Drum Taps* (1865) and *Sequel to Drum Taps* (1865–66), and in *The Wound-Dresser*, a volume of wartime letters to his mother. He was dismissed from his job as a clerk in the Indian Bureau of the Department of the Interior by order of the secretary, who pronounced his *Leaves of Grass* (1855, reprinted with Civil War poems in 1867) immoral.

Whitman Massacre (29 November 1847). In 1836 Dr. Marcus Whitman (1802–1847), an American physician and prominent Congregational missionary, and his wife, Narcissa Prentiss Whitman (1808–1847), founded an Indian mission near present-day Walla Walla, Washington, southeast of the Columbia River. In 1842 he began an arduous seven-month journey back east on horseback to collect emigrants. He re-

turned in 1843 with a sizable company, whose arrival alarmed the resident Cayuse Indians, who resented the ever-increasing number of settlers. Four years later, when measles devastated the tribe, they blamed its outbreak (probably correctly) on the whites. On 29 November 1847 Whitman, his wife, and 12 others were murdered. Taken captive were 53 women and children, who were not released until they were ransomed. The massacre began the Cayuse War [q.v.] and helped spur passage of the bill that made Oregon a state the following year.

Whitman Massacre *Dr. Marcus Whitman is massacred by a Cayuse Indian*

Whitney, Eli (1765–1825). An American inventor and manufacturer best known as the inventor of the cotton gin, which he patented in 1794. He was also a manufacturer of firearms and obtained a government contract to provide 10,000 stand of arms within two years. In filling the contract, he opened a factory at Whitneyville, Connecticut, near New Haven, where he introduced dies that produced interchangeable parts, probably the first use of such a system.

Whitworth, Joseph (1803–1887). A British mechanical engineer and inventor who secured an accepted standard for screws (Whitworth thread), discovered a new way to make ductile steel for guns, devised a hexagonal bore with a twist that improved the accuracy and aim of guns, and developed a unique breech closure, using a screw block outside the barrel. Guns manufactured to his design fired a long hexagonal projectile of lead and could be deadly up to 1,500–1,800 yards. Although the British army refused to adopt them, many, in various calibers, were sold in the United States during the American Civil War. If they were cleaned regularly and loaded properly, they performed well.

Whitworth Gun. See Whitworth, Joseph.

Wichita, Battle of (1 October 1858). On 15 September 1858 Captain and brevet Major Earl Van Dorn [q.v.] left Fort Belknap on the north bank of the Salt Fork of the Brazos River, near present-day Graham, Texas, leading a column of four companies of the 2nd Cavalry (225 men) and 135 Indian auxiliaries from the Brazos reservation. On 23 September they built a stockade on Otter Creek at the foot of the Wichita Mountains and named it Fort Radziminski in honor of a recently killed lieutenant of the 2nd Cavalry. On the 29th Van Dorn learned of a Comanche camp near Wichita Village, Choctaw Nation, Indian Territory. Assuming the Indians to be hostile, he attacked on 1 October. After a battle lasting an hour and a half the Indians fled, leaving 56 warriors and 2 women killed. Van Dorn lost 2 killed and 13 wounded, 1 mortally. He himself was wounded by arrows in his abdomen and wrist. The troops burned 120 lodges, destroyed food, ammunition, and camp furnishings, and captured 300 horses.

Unknown to Van Dorn, the camp he had attacked was that of Buffalo Hump (fl.1844–1865), a Comanche chief who, at the army's invitation, was on his way to Fort Atkinson to talk peace.

Wilcox, Cadmus Marcellus (1824–1891). An American soldier who was graduated from West Point in 1846 and fought in the Mexican War and the Third Seminole War [qq.v.]. He was a groomsman for U. S. Grant when he was married in 1848. He resigned in April 1861 as a captain to enter the Confederate service as colonel of the 9th Alabama. He fought in the Army of Northern Virginia from First Bull Run to Appomattox [qq.v.], becoming a brigadier general in October 1861 and a major general, to rank from August 1863.

After the war he refused commissions in the Egyptian and Korean armies to care for his widowed sister-in-law and her children, his only family.

Wild, Edward Augustus (1825–1891). An American medical doctor and soldier who became a partisan of Giuseppe Garibaldi [q.v.]. He served as a surgeon in the Turkish army during the Crimean War [q.v.]. During the American Civil War he served in the Union army as a captain in the 1st Massachusetts and fought at First Bull Run and in the Peninsular Campaign [qq.v.] until he was severely wounded in the hand in the Battle of Seven Pines [q.v.]. While recuperating at home, he raised another regiment and became its colonel. At South Mountain he was severely wounded in the left arm and, using his own medical judgment, ordered the surgeons to amputate.

Wild believed that black soldiers were equal to white soldiers, a notion inimical to the beliefs of most officers. While recovering, he began recruiting blacks and soon led a brigade, known as Wild's African Brigade, in operations against Charleston, South Carolina.

On a raid in northeastern North Carolina he captured Daniel Bright (d. 1863), who was, or had been, a member of the 62nd Georgia Cavalry; the issue is not clear. Wild claimed he was a guerrilla, convicted him in a drumhead court-martial, and on 18 December 1863 hanged him from a beam of his own house. The body, bearing a placard reading "This Guerrilla hanged by order of Brigadier General Wild," was left hanging for forty hours. The Confederates were outraged, claiming that Bright was on leave, and in retaliation, on 12 January 1864, they hanged Private Samuel Jones of the 5th United States Colored Troops.

Wild was transferred to the Norfolk area, where he was arrested on 19 June 1864 by General Edward Winslow Hinks (1830–1894), his division commander, for insubordination in his rough handling of southern sympathizers. Tried by court-martial, he was convicted but freed on a technicality: Because of the prejudice among many Union officers against officers commanding black troops, it had been ordered that they could be tried only by other officers serving with black troops, an order not followed in his case.

Unreformed, Wild engaged in a feud with O. C. Ord [q.v.], his army commander, and was transferred to the Freedmen's Bureau [q.v.] in Georgia. He was mustered out on 15 January 1866 and entered the mining business in the West, becoming the superintendent of a silver mine in Nevada. He died in Medellín, Colombia, on 28 August 1891.

Wild Cat (1810–1857), also called Coacoochee. A Seminole Indian leader in Florida who, refusing to leave for Indian Territory (Oklahoma), led attacks upon American soldiers. In the spring of 1837 General Thomas Sidney Jesup [q.v.], who considered him the ablest of the Seminole leaders, seized and imprisoned him when he came in to parlay under a white flag. On the night of 29 November he escaped, having fasted until he was thin enough to squeeze through the bars of his cell. He then collected a band and launched a series of attacks upon troops, including the Battle of Lake Okeechobee [q.v.] and the attack of 19 May 1840 upon Second Lieutenant James S. Sanderson near Micanopy, Florida, in which that officer was killed. Soon after, on the route from Picolata to St. Augustine, the band attacked a carriage and two wagons of a theatrical troupe and killed several of its members. Wild Cat was delighted with the costumes found in the baggage, and on 5 March 1841 he arrived at Fort Cummings to talk peace arrayed as Hamlet. At the parlay he agreed to bring in his men and to move to Indian Territory. Lieutenant William Tecumseh Sherman [q.v.] was in charge of his escort for part of the way.

The Seminoles found life in the inhospitable territory unendurable, and in 1844 Wild Cat made an unsuccessful journey to Washington, D.C., to seek assistance. In December 1849 he led a band of Seminoles, blacks, and a few Creeks into Texas to establish a free colony on Cow Bayou in the Brazos Valley. There they faced the hostility of the local whites, who wanted to enslave the blacks. When the Mexican government offered them land in Coahuila, they resettled. Wild Cat died from smallpox in 1857.

Wilderness, Battle of the (5–6 May 1864), American Civil War. A bloody, disjointed, and indecisive battle fought in the wilderness area west of Fredericksburg at the beginning of General U. S. Grant's Wilderness Campaign [q.v.]. On 4 May Grant crossed the Rapidan River with 108,000 men to engage 59,000 Confederates under General Robert E. Lee [see Wilderness Campaign]. In the two-day battle that began the next day Grant lost 17,600, and Lee 7,750.

Wilderness Campaign (May–June 1864), American Civil War. After the Battle of Gettysburg in July 1863 the next major engagement in the eastern theater was a campaign undertaken by General U. S. Grant west of Fredericksburg, Virginia, south of the Rapidan River, in the nearly impenetrable Wilderness, an area 14 miles long and 10 miles wide. On 5–6 May the indecisive and bloody Battle of the Wilderness [q.v.] was fought. This was followed on 8–12 May by the even more bloody Battle of Spotsylvania Court House [q.v.], in which Grant was repulsed. Fearing that Lee might withdraw into the defenses of Richmond, Grant attacked the Confederates on 1–3 June at Cold Harbor, a futile engagement costly in terms of lives. Grant then withdrew across the James River and in the summer initiated the Petersburg Campaign [q.v.].

Grant lost 50,000 men, about 41 percent of his original strength, in the Wilderness Campaign; Lee lost about 32,000, but this was 46 percent of his strength. Grant was able to replace his losses with fresh recruits, but the Confederates were near the end of their resources.

Wilkinson, James (1757–1825). An American soldier who served in the Revolutionary War and in clashes with hostile Indians. He became the ranking officer in the American army when General Anthony Wayne (1745–1796) died. In 1805–06 he was governor of Louisiana. His 2,000-man army was quartered at Terre aux Boeufs, a swamp where mosquitoes abounded, sanitation was nonexistent, and the water was brackish. Scurvy and dysentery swept through the camp, and 127 men died within three months. The camp was, however, near Baton Rouge and thus convenient for Wilkinson, who ignored orders to move his men to a more healthful location.

He was implicated in the conspiracy of Aaron Burr but was acquitted by a court-martial in 1811. Winfield Scott [q.v.], then a young officer, was court-martialed and suspended from the army for calling him a liar and a traitor, saying, among other things, that serving under Wilkinson was like living with a whore. Many agreed. Nevertheless, on 2 March 1813 he was commissioned a major general and placed in command of American forces on the Canadian frontier [see War of 1812]. He failed to distinguish himself but was honorably discharged in 1815 [see Canada, American Invasion of]. In 1821 he traveled to Mexico and secured a land grant in Texas. He died four years later in Mexico before he could establish possession.

He was in the pay of the Spanish in return for aligning himself with their interests in Mexican-American boundary disputes. He appears to have been a man for whom honesty was a mere abstraction and to have earned a reputation as "an unprincipled scoundrel and contemptible opportunist." David L. Bongard, a modern historian, has called him "one of the sleaziest characters ever to wear an American uniform." In his own time he was said to have been a general who never won a battle or lost a court-martial.

Wilkinson, John (1728–1808). An Englishman known as the Great Ironmaster. He developed a superior method for boring cylinders, designed an improved bellows, and developed a plant that supplied artillery, shells, and assorted equipment for the British and other armies. He grew to be enormously wealthy. By all accounts he was not an amiable man. He quarreled with his brother William (d. 1808), who left England to establish forges and foundries in France [see Schneider-Creusot Company], and his enormous fortune was largely lost through twelve years of legal disputes with his nephews and his three illegitimate sons. According to the *Dictionary of National Biography*, "Wilkinson's domestic arrangements were of a very peculiar character." When he died, he was appositely buried in an iron coffin.

Willcox, Orlando Bolivar (1823–1907). An American soldier who was graduated from West Point in 1847 and fought in the Mexican War and the Second Seminole War [qq.v.]. He resigned as a first lieutenant in 1857 and practiced law in Detroit. At the outbreak of the American Civil War he gave up his practice to join the Union army and was appointed colonel of the 1st Michigan. Two months later he was given command of a brigade, which he led at First Bull Run [q.v.], where he was wounded and captured. Imprisoned in Richmond, he was one of several officers held hostage at the county jail and destined to be hanged if, as threatened, the federal government executed as pirates several captured Confederate privateers. The federal authorities reconsidered, and Willcox was exchanged on 19 August 1862. He was promoted brigadier general, to rank from the date of his capture. In that rank he fought in the battles of Antietam and Fredericksburg, in the Wilderness, and at Spotsylvania [qq.v.].

On 15 January 1866 he was mustered out of the volunteers and named colonel of the 29th Infantry. In 1868 he transferred to the 12th Infantry, which he long commanded. He was appointed commander of the Department of Arizona in 1878, at a time of great unrest among the Apaches. He was superseded in 1882 by George Crook [q.v.]. In 1886 he was promoted brigadier general, but he retired the following year.

Willcox was the author of an artillery manual and under the name Walter March wrote two unnoteworthy novels. He was twice married and sired six children.

William I (1772–1843), full Dutch name: Willem Frederik. A Dutch soldier and king, son of the last stadtholder of Holland. From 1793 to 1795 he commanded the Dutch army against France. He later joined the Prussian army and was captured at Jena [q.v.] in 1806. He fought in the Austrian army in the Battle of Wagram [q.v.] in 1809. In 1815 the Congress of Vienna named him to rule the new Kingdom of the Netherlands, created out of Belgium and Holland. Belgian revolts, aided by the French [see Antwerp, Sieges of], forced him to ratify a treaty of separation in 1839. In 1840 he abdicated in favor of his son, William II [q.v.].

William I (1781–1864). A soldier and king of Württemberg. He commanded troops of his kingdom in Napoleon's army during the Russian Campaign [q.v.] in 1812 but in 1813–14 led an army corps of anti-Napoleonic allies. He favored a Germanic union and helped form the Zollverein (customs union) in 1828–30.

William I (1797–1888), full German name: Wilhelm Friedrich Ludwig. A German soldier and prince who became king of Prussia in 1861 and German emperor in 1871. During the Revolutions of 1848 his absolutist ideas and his brutal suppression of insurrection earned him such unpopularity that he had to flee to England. Nevertheless, in 1858, when his elder brother, King Frederick William IV (1795–1861), became insane, he was named regent. In 1861 he was crowned king, declaring that he "ruled by the favor of God, and of no one else." During the Seven Weeks' War [q.v.] he was in nominal command in the Battle of Sadowa [q.v.]. In 1867 he was head of the North German Confederation, and in 1870–71 he led the German armies in the Franco-Prussian War [q.v.], being personally on site at Gravelotte–St. Privat and at Sedan [qq.v.]. At Versailles on 18 January 1871 he was proclaimed emperor of Germany. In 1872 he broke off relations with the Vatican and pressed the enactment of severe laws against Catholics. In 1878 two attempts to assassinate him failed. He supported his generals in strengthening Prussian hegemony over Germany.

William II (1792–1849), full Dutch name: Willem Frederik George Lodewijk. A Dutch soldier and ruler. As Prince of Orange he fought under Wellington in Spain during the Peninsular War [q.v.] and commanded the Dutch forces in the Battle of Waterloo [q.v.] in 1815. In 1832 he commanded the Dutch army that was defeated by the French allies of the Belgians [see Antwerp, Sieges of]. In 1840 he succeeded his father, William I [q.v.], who abdicated in his favor.

Williams, Jonathan (1750–1815). An American public official and army officer educated in London under the eyes of his granduncle Benjamin Franklin (1706–1790). He accompanied Franklin to France and then back to Philadelphia, where in 1796 he was appointed a judge. In February 1801 he was commissioned a major in the Corps of Artillerists and Engineers, and in December he was appointed inspector of fortifications and commander of the post at West Point, New York. When the Military Academy was established there in 1802, Williams became its first superintendent [see West Point]. In a squabble over who had authority over cadets, he resigned in June 1803. In April 1805 he was persuaded to return as a lieutenant colonel. In July 1812 he again resigned when he failed to be given a position he craved. Shortly thereafter he was appointed brigadier general of New York militia, but he soon resigned and returned to Philadelphia. In 1814 he was elected to Congress, but he died before he could take his seat.

Williams, Thomas (1815–1862). An American soldier who served as a private under his father, a militia general, in the Black Hawk War [q.v.]. In 1837 he was graduated from West Point and was commissioned in the artillery. He served in the Second Seminole War [q.v.] and in the Mexican War [q.v.] won two brevets while serving as an aide to General Winfield Scott [q.v.]. On 14 May 1861, at the beginning of the American Civil War, he was promoted major, and on 28 September brigadier general of volunteers. In October he took part in the expedition to North Carolina commanded by General Ambrose Burnside [q.v.], and in 1862 he was in the army under General Nathaniel Banks [q.v.] that captured New Orleans. While conducting a defense of Baton Rouge [q.v.] against an attack by General John C. Breckinridge [q.v.], he was killed by a bullet in his chest.

Williams, William Fenwick (1800–1883). A British soldier born in Nova Scotia and educated as a military engineer at Woolwich [q.v.]. In 1841 he was sent to Constantinople (Istanbul), and he remained in Turkey for the next fourteen years. He was an engineer colonel engaged in defining the Turkish-Persian frontier when the Crimean War [q.v.] broke out. He was then appointed British military commissioner with the Turkish army in Asia. In September 1854 he reached Kars, and there he reformed and invigorated the Turkish forces. In January 1855 he was made *ferik* (lieutenant general) and pasha in the Turkish army. Besieged at Kars [q.v.] from June 1855 until 28 November, when lack of supplies forced him to surrender [see Crimean War]. Russian General Mikhail Nikolaevich Muraviëv [see Muraviëv Family], who captured the city, said to him: "You have made yourself a name in history, and posterity will stand amazed at the endurance, courage and discipline which this siege has called forth in the remains of an army." For his gallant defense he was made a baronet and knight commander of the Bath and granted an annuity of £1,000. The City of London presented him with a sword of honor, and Oxford conferred a degree upon him. France and Turkey also decorated him. From 1859 to 1865 he was commander of forces in Canada. In 1864 he was promoted major general, and in 1881 he was appointed constable of the Tower of London.

Williams Rapid-Fire Gun. A rapid-fire breech-loading gun that fired a one-pound shell and required a three-man crew. It was invented by R. S. Williams of Kentucky, and in 1862–63 forty-two of the guns with a caliber of 1.25 inches were manufactured. The Tredegar Iron Works [q.v.] in Richmond made twenty-four. The gun could fire at the rate of 20 rounds per minute and had a maximum range of 2,000 yards. Like the Gatling [q.v.], it was operated by a handcrank, but it was not, as sometimes claimed, the first true machine gun. It was first used in action on 31 May 1862 in the Battle of Seven Pines [q.v.] under the direction of the inventor. At Blue Ridge, Tennessee, in October 1863, Captain Theodore V. Allen, of the 7th Ohio Cavalry, against whom the guns were directed, said, "We had heard artillery before, but we had never heard anything that made such a horrible noise as the shot from these breech-loaders. . . ." However, the guns tended to jam when overheated, and they were not manufactured in quantity.

Willoughby, Digby (1845–1901). A British soldier and adventurer who went to seek his fortune in South Africa in 1871. He first saw action in command of a native mounted corps in the Zulu War [q.v.] of 1879. After working as an auctioneer and later as an actor, he raised a unit known as Willoughby's Horse, which saw service in the Gun War [q.v.] against the Basutos in 1880. In January 1884 he sailed to Madagascar and there on 18 May was appointed to command the native army that fought the invading French [see Madagascar, Warfare in]. In December 1885 he helped negotiate a peace. He was then sent to London as the Malagasy envoy but was rejected as such because he was still a British subject. In 1893 at the World's Columbian Exposition in Chicago, Illinois, he conducted a much-admired military spectacle dressed as a British field marshal. In October of that year he returned to South Africa and took part in the final days of the First Matabele War [see Matabele Wars]. The following year he was in London giving lectures on the war. In 1896, on the outbreak of the Second Matabele War, he formed and was a member of the council of defense at Bulawayo. At the beginning of the Second Anglo-Boer War [q.v.] he was in South Africa but took no part in the fighting and soon returned to England. He had lost an eye and was in poor health, but he had been made wealthy by a second marriage.

Willoughby, John Christopher (1859–1918). A British soldier and South African pioneer who was educated at Eton and Cambridge and was commissioned in 1879. After service in Egypt he resigned his commission and emigrated to South Africa, where he served in the Matabele War of 1893 [q.v.] and took part in the Jameson Raid [q.v.], for which he spent a few months in a British jail. During the Second Anglo-Boer War [q.v.] he was in charge of the transport for the Flying Column in the relief of the siege of Mafeking [q.v.].

Wilson, Allan (1856–1893). A Scottish-born Rhodesian soldier who as a young man joined the Cape Mounted Rifles [q.v.] and served in Basutoland (Lesotho) and Bechuanaland (Botswana). At the beginning of the Matabele War of 1893 [q.v.] he was a major. He was in command of the ill-fated Shangani Patrol [q.v.], in which he was killed with all his men on 4 December 1893.

Wilson, Jack. See Wovoka.

Wilson, James Harrison ("Harry") (1837–1925). An American soldier who was graduated from West Point in 1860, when the course was five years, and was commissioned in the engineers. During the American Civil War he served as an aide to General George B. McClellan in the Maryland Campaign of 1862 and fought at South Mountain and Antietam [qq.v.]. He took part in all the battles of the Vicksburg Campaign, and on 30 October 1863 he was promoted brigadier general of volunteers, the only officer on Grant's staff ever to receive unit command. He commanded a division under Philip Sheridan [q.v.] and was appointed chief of cavalry under William Tecumseh Sherman [q.v.]. Grant thought so highly of him that he told Sherman: "I believe Wilson will add 50 per cent to the effectiveness of your cavalry." In October 1864 he was named a brevet major general and appointed chief of cavalry in the Division of Mississippi. In a raid through Alabama and Georgia with 14,000 men, he cut a wide swath of destruction. He defeated Nathan Bedford Forrest [q.v.] in the Battle of Franklin on 30 November 1864 and again at Ebenezer Church [qq.v.] on 1 April 1865. He captured Selma and Montgomery, Alabama, and Columbus, Georgia, and had reached Macon when hostilities ended [see Wilson's Raid]. Wilson, never a modest man, later wrote: "I regard the capture of Selma as the most remarkable achievement in the history of modern cavalry." He is said to have been the most able of the "boy generals" in the war.

In the reorganization of the army in 1866 he was appointed lieutenant colonel of the newly organized 35th Infantry. He resigned on 31 December 1870 to work in railway engineering and management and to write. During the Spanish-American War [q.v.], being the only senior major general in civil life under retirement age, he volunteered and served as a major general of volunteers in Cuba and Puerto Rico. During the Boxer Rebellion [q.v.] in 1900 he served in China as second-in-command of the American contingent under General Adna R. Chaffee [q.v.]. He resigned in March 1901 and was granted the rank of major general on the retired list. He resumed his writing, producing biographies of Grant and other Civil War figures, numerous magazine articles, and in 1912 a flavorful two-volume autobiography, *Under the Old Flag*. He was the last survivor of his West Point class.

Wilson, Robert Thomas (1777–1849). A British soldier who had taken part in the disastrous Walcheren Expedition [q.v.] and fought against Irish rebels and in 1802 against the

French in Egypt before becoming a brigade commander in the Peninsular War [q.v.]. In 1811 he was British military commissioner with the Russian army, and he was the first eyewitness to report the burning of Moscow to Britain. In 1813 he commanded the Prussian reserve in the Battle of Lützen [q.v.]. Although he had been decorated by the tsar, he wrote *Sketch of the Military and Political Power of Russia* (1817), in which he recounted many of the barbarities he had seen committed by Cossacks and other Russian troops, and warned of Russia's growing power. He was promoted general in 1841 and from 1842 to 1849 was governor of Gibraltar.

Wilson's Creek (10 August 1861), American Civil War. Confederate Brigadier General Ben McCulloch [q.v.], moving to attack a newly formed Union force under Brigadier General Nathaniel Lyon [q.v.] at Springfield, Missouri, camped on Wilson's Creek, about 15 miles from Springfield, on 9 August. His force consisted of Missouri state guard and Arkansas militia. Instead of waiting to be attacked, Lyon attacked the Confederates at five o'clock on the morning of the 10th. In a fiercely contested but indecisive battle Lyon was killed, and the command fell upon Major Samuel D. Sturgis [q.v.], who withdrew his force to Springfield. The Confederates were too exhausted and had too little ammunition to pursue.

The Union army contained 5,400 effectives, 223 of whom were killed, 721 wounded, and 291 missing; Confederate losses were 257 killed, 900 wounded, and 27 missing out of 11,600 effectives.

Wilson's Raid (22 March–20 April 1865), American Civil War. An incursion of three cavalry divisions (13,500 men) moving in three columns under Union General James H. Wilson [q.v.] from the extreme northwest corner of Alabama to Selma, the Confederates' most important military center in the area, holding arsenals, factories, foundries, and stores of supplies. Wilson concentrated his force at Jasper, 38 miles northwest of Birmingham, on 27 March, and on 31 March he put to rout both a section of the cavalry of Nathan Bedford Forrest [q.v.] at Montevallo, 32 miles south of Birmingham, and another section near Plantersville, Mississippi, 4 miles southeast of Tupelo. Selma, Alabama, was protected by a strong line of earthworks, but they were manned by about 7,000 militia, who soon bolted. Wilson took the town on 2 April. He then marched on Montgomery, which he took on the 12th. On 20 April he captured Macon and learned that the war had ended.

In his 525-mile march Wilson captured 288 guns and nearly 100,000 small arms. He destroyed factories, mills, warehouses, depots, 35 locomotives, 500 railroad cars, and much track. Federal losses were 725; Wilson claimed a capture of 6,820 prisoners and an estimated 1,200 Confederates killed or wounded.

Wimpffen, Emmanuel Félix de (1811–1884). A French soldier who served in the Crimean War, in the Austro-Piedmontese War [qq.v.], and in Algeria [see Algeria, Conquest and Occupation of]. In the Franco-Prussian War [q.v.] he commanded an army corps. He succeeded General Marie MacMahon [q.v.] in the Battle of Sedan [q.v.] on 1 September 1870 and signed the capitulation the following day.

Winans, Thomas (1819–1878). An American mechanical engineer and inventor who was the son of Ross Winans (d. 1878), inventor of the camelback railroad locomotive. He amassed an enormous fortune working in Russia, where he married a Russian woman. He was a native of Baltimore whose sympathies were with the Confederates during the American Civil War. He invented a steam gun [q.v.], said to be "of a most destructive character," and attempted to ship it to Harpers Ferry by way of the Baltimore & Ohio Railroad, but at Rolay House, then about five miles from Baltimore, it was confiscated by Union General Benjamin Butler [q.v.]. Winans then sailed to Europe for the duration of the war.

Winchester, Battles of, American Civil War. Winchester, Virginia, at the lower end of the Shenandoah Valley, 70 miles west-northwest of Washington, D.C., changed hands dozens of times in the course of the American Civil War and was the site of three main battles:

First Battle (25 May 1862). Thomas ("Stonewall") Jackson with 17,000 men successfully attacked Federal forces under Major General Nathaniel Banks [q.v.] entrenched south of the town and drove them out of Virginia. Banks had about 25,000, but only about 8,500 were effectives. Federal losses were nearly 3,000; Confederate losses were about 400 [see Shenandoah Valley Campaign of Jackson].

Second Battle (14–15 June 1863). Just outside the town a Confederate corps under General Richard Ewell [q.v.] successfully attacked a Union division under General Robert Milroy [q.v.] and captured an enormous amount of guns, ammunition, and supplies. Union losses were about 1,000 killed and wounded and 3,358 captured. Ewell suffered 269 casualties. A court of inquiry cleared Milroy of responsibility for the disaster.

Third Battle (19 September 1864). Near Opequon, a village on Opequon Creek, just east of Winchester, some 38,000 Federals under Philip Sheridan [q.v.] defeated 13,000 Confederates under Jubal Early [q.v.]. It was a costly victory for the Union. Its losses were about 1,000 killed and missing, plus 3,983 wounded; Confederate losses were 276 killed, 1,827 wounded, and 1,818 missing. The battle is sometimes called the Battle of Opequon.

Winchester, James (1752–1826). An American soldier who served in the Revolutionary War and was twice captured by the British. After the war he moved to what is now central Tennessee and rose to become a brigadier general in the militia. In March 1812, in anticipation of the coming War of 1812 [q.v.], he was commissioned a brigadier general in the U.S. army. By August he had several regiments assembled in Cincinnati, and by early September he was confirmed as commander of the Army of the Northwest, a position he held for only a few days, being superseded by Major General William Henry Harrison [q.v.]. With a wing of this army he was sent to recapture Frenchtown (Monroe, Michigan), but not far from the town, on the Raisin River, on 22 January 1813 he was attacked and defeated by a force of Indians and British under Colonel Henry Procter. After the Americans had given up their arms, they were attacked by the Indians, and more than 100 were killed [see Raisin River Massacre]. Winchester, for a third time a prisoner of the British, spent more than a year in confinement in Canada. When exchanged, he was given command at Mobile. In March 1815 he resigned his commission.

Winchester, Oliver Fisher (1810–1880). An American industrialist who at age fourteen was apprenticed to a carpenter and at twenty was a master builder. In 1833 he began work as a clerk in a dry goods store and haberdashery. In 1847 he patented an improved method of making men's dress shirts and in their manufactory became rich. In 1855 he purchased stock in the Volcanic Arms Company [q.v.] in New Haven, Connecticut, and in 1857, when the company failed, he purchased its entire assets for $39,000. He then established the New Haven Arms Company and hired Benjamin Tyler Henry [q.v.], who developed a .44 caliber cartridge and modified a rifle to accept it. In 1860 he offered the Henry rifle [q.v.] to the government. The federal government, always ultraconservative when considering new weapons, refused to adopt the rifle, but it was purchased by many state militias and was popular with settlers in fear of raiders. In time Winchester acquired the rights to a variety of inventions, including those of John M. Browning, who between 1883 and 1900 sold almost all his patents to him. In 1866 he reorganized the New Haven Arms Company as the Winchester Repeating Arms Company, whose first new product was the Winchester Model 1866, a .44 caliber, rimfire lever-action rifle, that owed much to the Henry Rifle. Sometimes called a yellow belly, it became famous on the western frontier, and it proved valuable to the Turks, who, armed with it, inflicted heavy casualties on the Russians at Plevna [q.v.] in 1877. The company is still in existence.

Windage. 1. The difference between the size of the bore and the size of the shot. The greater the windage, the less accurate the rifle or musket.

2. An allowance made in aiming a weapon to compensate for the effect of wind upon the trajectory of the bullet.

Winder, Charles Sidney (1829–1862). An American soldier who was graduated from West Point in 1850. In 1854, while en route to Panama on a troopship, he behaved so heroically during a hurricane that he was promoted captain on 3 March 1855, supposedly the youngest in the American army. On 1 April 1861 he resigned and joined the Confederate army as a major. He took part in the reduction of Fort Sumter and in July was appointed colonel of the 6th South Carolina. On 1 March 1862 he was promoted brigadier general. He commanded the Stonewall Brigade in General Thomas Jackson's division, taking part in all of the battles of Jackson's Valley Campaign [q.v.] and the Seven Days' Battles [q.v.]. He was mortally wounded by a shell in the Battle of Cedar Mountain [q.v.] on 9 August 1862.

Winder, John Henry (1800–1865). An American soldier who was graduated from West Point in 1820 and commissioned in the artillery. During the Mexican War [q.v.] he held the rank of captain but won brevets to major and lieutenant colonel serving under General Winfield Scott [q.v.]. In April 1861 he resigned and joined the Confederate army. In July he was appointed provost marshal and commander of military prisons in Virginia. When the first large batch of prisoners arrived after First Bull Run, he commandeered several tobacco warehouses in Richmond and established Libby Prison [q.v.]. In May 1864 most prisoners were moved to Macon, Georgia, and Winder was put in charge of all prisons in Georgia and Alabama; in November 1864 he commanded all military prisons east of the Mississippi River.

Winder, William Henry (1775–1824). An American lawyer, politician, and soldier who was educated at the University of Pennsylvania. At the beginning of the War of 1812 [q.v.] he was commissioned a lieutenant colonel of the newly raised 14th Infantry and was soon promoted colonel of the regiment. He saw some action on the Niagara frontier, and on 12 March 1813 he was promoted brigadier general. On 5 June he was captured in the Battle of Stoney Creek [q.v.]. While in captivity, he successfully negotiated with the British for an exchange of prisoners.

He was freed in April 1814 and was given command of a military district that included Maryland, the District of Columbia, and part of Virginia. When the British under Robert Ross [q.v.] landed and threatened Washington, he met them with a force of 6,000, mostly militia, at Bladensburg, Maryland, seven miles east-northeast of the capital [see Bladensburg, Battle of]. His troops failed to stand, and he retreated through Washington to Montgomery Court House. The next day he learned of the burning of Washington and hurried to Baltimore to take part in its defense.

A congressional inquiry was made into the defeat at Bladensburg, and Winder demanded and received a military court of inquiry, which on 26 January 1815 exonerated him and commended his conduct. After the war he was again given command of a military district, but he soon resigned and returned to his law practice. He was twice elected to the Maryland senate.

Windisch-Graetz, Prince Alfred Candidus Ferdinand zu (1787–1862). An Austrian soldier who became a field marshal and commanded in Bohemia in 1840–48. In 1848 he suppressed the Czech uprising in Prague and defeated the Hungarians in the Battle of Schwechat [q.v.]. He occupied Budapest [q.v.] and defeated the Hungarian rebels at Kápolna [q.v.] on 26–27 February 1849, but he was defeated at Gödöllo. He was relieved of his command and made governor of the fortress at Mainz [see Hungarian Revolution of 1848]. In 1861 he served in Austria's upper house.

Wing. 1. A vague term that indicated a part of a command, usually a cavalry command. In the British army and in the Indian army it was often used in place of a squadron. After the Indian Mutiny [q.v.] all Indian cavalry regiments were divided into two wings, each commanded by a captain or a major. Although a wing was usually a unit larger than a company but smaller than a battalion, Confederate General Joseph Johnston at the beginning of the American Civil War organized wings in the Army of the Potomac [q.v.] that were actually divisions or corps.

2. A unit on a flank; that part of a force on the right or left of the main body.

3. A shell-like epaulet.

Wingate, Francis Reginald (1861–1953). A British soldier and colonial administrator who joined the army in 1880 and served in India and at Aden. He spoke perfect Arabic and served on the Egypt-Sudan frontier in 1889 and 1891. In 1898 he took part in the reconquest of the Sudan [q.v.] under H. H. Kitchener [q.v.], whom he succeeded as governor-general of the Sudan in 1899. He won the Battle of Umm Dibaikarat [q.v.] on 23 November 1899, the final battle of the war against the Mahdist Dervishes, in which the khalifa Abdullahi [q.v.] was killed. From 1916 to 1919 he was British high commissioner in Egypt. He was the author of *Madhiism and the Egyptian Sudan* (1891).

Wingate, George Wood (1840–1928). A New York City lawyer who was active in the New York militia regiments (called National Guards) and formulated rules for systematic rifle practice. He was instrumental in forming the National Rifle Association [q.v.] and served as its president for twenty-five years.

Wing Officer. An officer, usually a captain or major, commanding a wing of cavalry in the British or Indian service.

Wirz, Henry (1823–1865). A Swiss educated in Zurich, Paris, and Berlin who emmigrated to Kentucky in 1849 and was a practicing lawyer when the American Civil War began. He enlisted in the Confederate army in the 4th Louisiana Battalion on 16 June 1861, and by August 1862 he was a captain. He suffered a severe wound that paralyzed his right arm in the Battle of Seven Pines. In March 1864 he took command of the prisoner of war camp at Andersonville, in Sumter County in southwest Georgia [see Andersonville Prison]. After the war he was accused of ordering prisoners killed and was tried by a military court that convicted him and sentenced him to be hanged. He was executed in the courtyard of the District of Columbia's Old Capitol Prison (now the site of the Supreme Court) on 10 November 1865.

Henry S. White, the chaplain of the 5th Rhode Island, described Wirz as "lean, tall, rough, coarse . . . swears incessantly and curses most cruelly."

Wissembourg, Battle of (4 August 1870), Franco-Prussian War. At this town, 40 miles northeast of Strasbourg, 4,000 French troops under General Charles Abel Douay (1809–1870), a part of I Corps of Marshal Marie MacMahon [q.v.], were attacked by 25,000 troops of the Prussian Third Army commanded by Crown Prince Frederick William [q.v.], which was advancing into eastern France in four columns. The garrison resisted for six hours until the Prussians stormed the defenses and captured the town. This was the first major action of the war. Their victory cost the Germans 1,551 casualties and the French 1,600 in killed and wounded, including General Douay, who was killed, and 700 taken prisoner. MacMahon retreated and adopted a defensive position on a wooded plateau.

Witbooi, Hendrik (1838–1905). The *kaptein* (captain or head) from 1884 of the Witbois, part of a larger group, a mixture of Afrikaners, Hottentots, and Bantus who lived in South West Africa (Namibia) and proudly called themselves bastards until missionaries taught them the word was pejorative. Witbooi had a Christian education and was reputed to be "always neatly and cleanly dressed" and to be "very well grounded in the Bible."

He led his people in numerous cattle wars and raids on the Hereros. When the Hereros agreed to German protection, German Reichskommissar Dr. Heinrich Göring (father of Nazi Reichsmarschall Hermann Göring [1893–1946]) tried without success to coerce Witbooi to accept it as well. On 12 April 1891 a German force under Landeshauptmann Kurt von François [q.v.] moved against him, surprising him and his clan at Hoornkranz, near Rehoboth, 90 miles southwest of Windhoek. In the battle that followed the Germans fired 16,000 rounds from repeating rifles, killing 85, of whom 78 were women. The Germans lost one man. Hendrik Witbooi escaped.

On 1 January 1894 François was replaced by Major Theodor Leutwein [q.v.], a veteran of the Franco-Prussian War [q.v.], who built a series of forts in the interior. In late August of that year Leutwein won a pyrrhic victory, but he pursued Witbooi until on 15 September 1894 he surrendered.

Soon after, at the beginning of the German-Herero War, Witbooi revolted but was quickly subdued. In 1903 he revolted once more. He was brought to bay in 1905 at Keetmanshoop, where on 29 October he died of wounds. His diary was published in South Africa by the Van Riebeeck Society in 1929.

Withdrawal. The deliberate disengagement from the enemy in which a force moves to the rear or takes up a new or alternate position not in direct contact with the enemy, as did the Russian army after the Battle of Borodino [q.v.].

Withlacoochee, Battles on the. During the Second Seminole War there were two engagements on the shores of this river in west Florida, 65 miles from Tampa.

First Battle (28 December 1835). About 250 regulars and volunteers under Duncan Lamont Clinch [q.v.] fought about 300 Seminoles in an undecisive battle. The Americans lost 4 killed and 59 wounded; Indian losses were estimated at 40.

Second Battle (27 February 1836). General Edmund Pendleton Gaines [q.v.] with 1,100 troops was ambushed by more than 1,000 Seminoles and lost 26 killed and 111 wounded; Indian losses are unknown.

Wittgenstein, Ludwig Adolf Peter, Prince of Sayn-Wittgenstein-Ludwigsburg (1769–1843). The son of a Prussian general in the Russian service who followed his father into the Russian army. He fought at Austerlitz [q.v.] on 2 December 1805, against Napoleon in 1807, and against Nicolas Oudinot and Claude Victor [qq.v.] in 1812. In 1809 he commanded a corps in the Russo-Swedish War [q.v.]. In 1813 he was relieved of his command after his defeat in the Battle of Bautzen [q.v.] on 20–21 May. In 1825 he was made a field marshal, and in 1828 he was sent to fight the Turks [see Russo-Turkish Wars]. He retired because of ill health soon after.

Wives, Soldiers'. In the American, British, and numerous other armies soldiers needed permission to marry. In the British army the wives of those granted permission were said to be on the strength, and received certain privileges, such as the permission to take in washing or to work as maids for officers' wives. In the early years of the nineteenth century many lived in screened-off portions of the barracks. In Britain, Queen's Regulations allowed 6 wives per company of infantry and 12 per troop of cavalry.

In the American army, rations, medical care, and bedding straw were provided for laundresses, all wives of soldiers, and 1 laundress was provided for every 17 soldiers, but not more than 4 per company. In the 1870s there were 1,316 official laundresses. At the pay table, the money due them was deducted before that of the sutlers [q.v.].

When a British army unit was sent overseas, the few wives permitted to accompany it were chosen by lot, usually slips of paper marked "To go" or "Not to Go." Those fortunate enough to go washed clothes, cooked, nursed sick and wounded, and performed all the tasks "for which women accompany an army." Those left behind were usually reduced to begging or prostitution. Kipling's poem "The Absent-Minded Beggar" was written during the Second Anglo-Boer War to raise money for the families soldiers left behind:

> There are girls he married secret, asking no permission to,
>   For he knew he wouldn't get it if he did.
> There is gas and coals and vittles, and the house-rent falling due,
>   And it's more than rather likely there's a kid.

The Crimean War was the last in which wives of other ranks were allowed to accompany the troops. Officers' wives rarely accompanied their husbands on campaign, but Frances ("Fanny") Duberley [q.v.], wife of Captain Henry Duberley, paymaster of the 8th Light Dragoons, always did. She was present in the Crimea throughout the Crimean War [q.v.], and in India during the Indian Mutiny [q.v.] she took part in a cavalry charge against the troops of the rani of Jhansi [q.v.].

Wolf Mountains, Battle of the (8 January 1877), Great Sioux War. In the Wolf Mountains, near the Tongue River, in Montana in a raging snowstorm five companies and two half companies of the 5th Infantry and two companies of the 22nd Infantry (476 men) with one Napoleon howitzer and one Rodman gun, all under General Nelson A. Miles [q.v.], defeated more than 500 Sioux and Cheyenne Indians under Crazy Horse [q.v.]. The battle in the snow lasted five hours. Miles suffered 1 soldier killed and 8 wounded, 1 mortally; 50 men suffered from frostbite during the campaign. Crazy Horse lost 1 Cheyenne and 2 Sioux killed. Miles thought this small engagement "one of the most successful in [the] history of Indian warfare." On his return to his base he wrote in a letter to his wife that he had "taught the destroyers of Custer that there was one small command that could whip them as long as they dared face it."

Wolseley, Garnet Joseph (1833–1913). A British soldier who entered the army in March 1852 as an ensign in the 12th Foot. He soon transferred to the 80th Foot, with which he served in the Second Anglo-Burmese War [q.v.], in which he was severely wounded. He was again wounded in the Crimean War [q.v.] and lost an eye. In 1857, while on his way to China in the *Transit*, he was shipwrecked in the Strait of Banka [see Troopship]. When he was rescued, he was taken to Singapore, where because of the Indian Mutiny [q.v.], he was diverted to Calcutta. He saw much action in the mutiny, including the relief of Lucknow [q.v.], while serving under Sir Colin Campbell [q.v.]. In 1860 he finally reached China, where he fought in the Second Opium War [q.v.]. In 1869, while deputy quartermaster general in Canada, he published *Soldiers' Pocket Book for Field Service*, and in 1870 as a colonel he successfully conducted the Red River Expedition [q.v.] against the Canadian rebel Louis Riel [q.v.]. In 1871 he was in London as assistant adjutant general, assisting Edward Cardwell [q.v.] in initiating the army reforms that abolished the purchase of commissions and offered shorter terms of service for other ranks. On the outbreak of the Second Ashanti

War in 1873 [q.v.] he was appointed to command the expeditionary force sent to the Gold Coast (Ghana) and on his victorious return was given the Thanks of Parliament [q.v.] and £25,000. The expression "All Sir Garnet" came into use at the time to signify any action performed with efficiency and dispatch. In 1875 Wolseley held high command in Natal, and in 1878 he briefly held command in Cyprus. In 1879, after the defeat of the British in the Battle of Isandhlwana [q.v.] at the beginning of the Zulu War [q.v.], he was sent to Natal to relieve Lord Chelmsford [q.v.]. The war was almost over by the time he reached South Africa, and after defeating Sekukuni [q.v.], he returned in May 1880 to London. There he was appointed quartermaster general.

In 1882 he commanded the army that suppressed Arabi's Revolt [q.v.] in Egypt, winning a complete victory in the Battle of Tell el-Kebir [q.v.]. He was made a full general the same year. In 1884 he commanded the expedition sent to the Sudan to relieve General Charles ("Chinese") Gordon [q.v.] besieged in Khartoum [q.v.]. Although he moved with his usual expedition, his advance force arrived just two days after the death of Gordon and the fall of the city. From 1890 to 1895 he was commander-in-chief of the British army. He was made a field marshal in 1894.

Although Wolseley had little formal education, he was generally conceded to be the most intelligent British general of the Victorian era. His erudition was satirized by William Gilbert (1836–1911) in *The Pirates of Penzance* in the patter song: "I am the very model of a modern major general." Wolseley was amused by it and himself sometimes sang it.

Wolseley, Garnet *Wolseley as a young officer leading a forlorn hope against Myat-toon's stronghold at Burma, February 1853*

Wolseley Gang. The name often applied to the select group of officers in whom Garnet Wolseley [q.v.] reposed confidence and whenever possible included in his campaigns, either on his staff or as subordinate commanders. Among them were Evelyn Wood, Redvers Buller, William Francis Butler, George Pomeroy Colley, and Henry Brackenbury [qq.v.].

Wolves. Indians serving as scouts or auxiliaries with the U.S. army on the western frontier.

Woman Order. See General Orders No. 28.

Women Soldiers. Although no women were enlisted or conscripted in the nineteenth century in any American,

European, or Asian army, there have always been some women who have wished to become soldiers, and a few have managed to do so. During the American Civil War an estimated 400 avoided detection in the makeshift and casual physical examinations for the Union army.

In Napoleon's army the "Chaste Suzanne" began her career as a "drummer boy" at age fourteen and served until she was wounded in the Battle of Waterloo [q.v.]. In the British army Dr. "James" Barry [q.v.] passed her entire career as an army surgeon, her sex undetected until she died. [See: Vivandière; Amazons; Blanchisseuse; Troopship.]

Women's Union for Nursing Sick and Wounded in War. An organization founded during the Franco-Prussian War [q.v.] of 1870–71 by Princess Alice Maud Mary (1843–1878), Grand Duchess of Hesse-Darmstadt and the second daughter of Queen Victoria. The organization provided nurses for German army hospitals.

Wood, Henry Evelyn (1838–1919). A British soldier nicknamed Sailor Wood because he began his career as a teenaged midshipman and fought with the naval brigade in the Crimean War [q.v.], in which he was severely wounded. Perhaps no soldier in the British army ever suffered as many wounds, injuries, and illnesses as did Evelyn Wood [his first name was never used]. After the Crimean War, in which he was seriously wounded in the arm and suffered pneumonia and typhoid fever, he transferred to the cavalry, reporting in spite of a severe ingrown toenail. He served in the Indian Mutiny [q.v.], where he won a Victoria Cross in spite of an aching jaw, broke a collarbone when he galloped his pony into a tree, and had his face smashed by the hoof of a giraffe he was attempting to ride. As a lieutenant colonel he served with Sir Garnet Wolseley [q.v.] in the Second Ashanti War [q.v.], where he was shot by an Ashanti with a musket loaded with nails. He studied law and was called to the bar in 1874 but never practiced. In 1879 he commanded a column in the Zulu War [q.v.], and during the First Anglo-Boer War of 1881 [q.v.] he assumed the chief command on the death of Sir George Colley [q.v.]. In South Africa he was thrown from a buggy, and his spine was injured when he fell on the horse's head; soon after his feet swelled to an enormous size. In 1882 he took part in the suppression of Arabi's Revolt [q.v.] in spite of a bad case of diarrhea, and immediately after he was appointed the first British sirdar (commander-in-chief) of the British-controlled Egyptian army. In 1893 he was named quartermaster general. While in London he tried to learn to ride a bicycle and collided with a horse, which viciously bit him on the arm. Later he was forced to have several teeth removed. He served in the Gordon Relief Expedition [q.v.] although he had grown quite deaf, and in Egypt he crushed his thumb in the joints of a folding chair. In 1895 he was made a full general, and in 1898 he was appointed adjutant general of the British army. In 1900, while riding to hounds, he was thrown, and a crucifix he was wearing was driven into his ribs. In spite of his many accidents, wounds, and ailments, he lived to be eighty-one and died a field marshal.

Wood wrote several books, including an autobiography, *From Midshipman to Field Marshal* (1894) and a volume of reminiscences, *Winnowed Memories* (1917).

Wood, Leonard (1860–1927). An American soldier who began his military career as an army surgeon after being graduated from Harvard Medical School in 1884. As a first lieutenant and assistant surgeon he accompanied the expedition against the Apaches that led to the capture of Geronimo [q.v.]. He was awarded the Medal of Honor in 1898 for "distinguished conduct" on the expedition. He was promoted captain in 1891 and, while stationed in Washington, D.C., was appointed White House physician to President Grover Cleveland (1837–1908), a position he also held under President William McKinley (1843–1901), who took office in March 1897. During this time he developed a close friendship with Theodore Roosevelt [q.v.], then assistant secretary of the navy.

In 1898, at the beginning of the Spanish-American War [q.v.], he and Roosevelt organized the 1st Volunteer Cavalry, known as the Rough Riders [q.v.], and Wood gained appointment to command it as a colonel of volunteers. He commanded in the Battle of Las Guásimas [q.v.] on 24 June 1898 and then was given command of a cavalry brigade, which he led in the Battle of San Juan Hill [q.v.] on 1 July and in the subsequent operations that resulted in the capture of Santiago de Cuba on 17 July. In July he was promoted brigadier general and appointed governor of Santiago. In December he was promoted major general.

Following the postwar reductions, he reverted to brigadier general in April 1899, but in December he was again promoted major general of volunteers and made governor of Cuba, a post he held until he turned over executive authority to newly elected President Tomás Estrada Palma (1835–1908) on 20 May 1902. In February 1900 he had been made a brigadier general in the regular army. After service in the Philippines he became the army chief of staff in April 1910. When the United States entered World War I, he fully expected to command the American Expeditionary Force, a position given instead to General John Pershing. In January 1917 President Wilson, speaking to Secretary of War Newton Baker, said: "Personally, I have no confidence either in General Wood's discretion or in his loyalty to his superiors." Secretary Baker considered him "the most insubordinate general in the entire army." In 1920 he was an unsuccessful candidate for president, and in October 1921 he was appointed governor-general of the Philippines, where he died.

Wood, Thomas John (1823–1906). An American soldier who was graduated from West Point in 1845. He won a brevet during the Mexican War and took part in the Utah Expedition [qq.v.]. During the American Civil War he fought at Shiloh and Murfreesboro [qq.v.], where he was wounded. After the latter battle, although he was criticized for obeying an order from General William Rosecrans [q.v.] that left a hole in the Union lines, he was brevetted brigadier general in the regular army. (Rosecrans was relieved of his command.) In the Battle of Chattanooga [q.v.] Wood's men were among the first to reach the crest of Missionary Ridge. He distinguished himself in the Atlanta Campaign [q.v.], in which he was gravely wounded in the leg. He retired in 1868.

Wood Lake, Battle of (23 September 1862), Sioux uprising in Minnesota. Sioux Indians under Little Crow [q.v.] planned an attack upon volunteers under Colonel Henry Sibley [q.v.], but Sibley fortuitously discovered the plan and decisively defeated them near the village of Wood Lake, in southwest Minnesota, 10 miles south of Granite Falls [see Minnesota, Sioux Uprising in].

Woodville, Robert (1856–1927). A British painter of battle scenes of the Crimean War, Arabi's Revolt, and the Second Anglo-Boer War [qq.v.].

Wool, John Ellis (1784–1869). An American soldier who joined the militia in Troy, New York, in 1807 and, although he had little formal education, became its adjutant and quartermaster. In April 1812, at the beginning of the War of 1812 [q.v.], he was commissioned a captain in the 13th Infantry. In subsequent actions he was wounded in the Battle of Queenstown Heights [q.v.] and was promoted major. He won a brevet to lieutenant colonel. In 1816 he was named inspector general in the newly created Northern Division under General Jacob Jennings Brown [q.v.]. In 1821, when the army was reorganized, he remained as one of two inspector generals of the army. In 1826 he was brevetted brigadier general, and fifteen years later he was made a substantive brigadier general. He pressed for the creation of an ordnance department and the acquisition of more modern artillery, and in 1832 he sailed for Europe, where he observed French maneuvers, visited the British artillery school at Woolwich [q.v.], and witnessed the siege of Antwerp [q.v.].

Wool carried out a number of special assignments: He mediated a strike at the Springfield Arsenal [q.v.] in 1833, directed the operation that moved the Cherokees west of the Mississippi in 1836–37, and in 1837–38 blocked gunrunning to Canadian rebels over the New York-Vermont frontier. In 1841 he was promoted brigadier general in the regular army and succeeded Winfield Scott [q.v.] as commander of the Eastern Department.

In May 1846, when the United States declared war on Mexico [see Mexican War], he was sent to the Ohio Valley to raise 10,000 volunteers for the army of Zachary Taylor [q.v.]. In September he was in Texas, and in February 1847 he took an active role in the Battle of Buena Vista [q.v.], for which he was later given the Thanks of Congress and a sword of honor. In 1847–48 he commanded the occupation forces in northern Mexico. At war's end he was brevetted major general.

In 1854 he was sent to California, where he halted the recruiting efforts of William Walker [q.v.], the filibuster, and calmed settlers' efforts to fight local Indian tribes in Oregon and Washington. Although he was seventy-seven years old when the Civil War [q.v.] began, he was in command at Fort Monroe, Virginia, and subsequently commanded in Maryland, where he moved to stamp out secessionist sympathy. He was promoted major general in the regular service on 17 May 1862, the oldest officer on either side to hold an active command. His last act was the suppression of the draft riots [q.v.] in New York City in 1863. He retired on 1 August of that year.

Woolson, Albert (1848–1956). A drummer boy who served in Battery C, 1st Minnesota Heavy Artillery, during the American Civil War. He became the last veteran of that war, living until 2 August 1956.

Although there were many who claimed the title of last Confederate veteran, including three fraudulent claimants who attended the final reunion of the United Confederate Veterans, the last living Confederate veteran was Pleasant Crump, who served in the 10th Alabama and died on 31 December 1951.

Wools-Sampson, Aubrey (1856–1924). A South African soldier born and educated at Cape Town. He took part in the Sekukuni, Zulu, and Gun wars [qq.v.]. On the Witwatersrand he became involved in the aborted revolution that resulted in the unsuccessful Jameson Raid [q.v.]. During the Second Anglo-Boer War he raised the Imperial Light Horse [q.v.] and was recommended for, but failed to receive, the Victoria Cross [q.v.].

Woolwich. Short name for the Royal Military Academy, Woolwich [q.v.]. It was colloquially known as the shop.

Woolwich Arsenal. Popular name for the Royal Arsenal, Woolwich, the principal British gun factory from the seventeenth century until World War II, at Woolwich, England, now a southeastern suburb of London. It was composed of three parts: Royal Gun Factory, Royal Carriage Department, and Royal Laboratory. The laboratory, built in 1669 at the east end of town and used for the testing and development of guns and shot, was closed in the 1860s. The main government foundry moved to Woolwich from Moorfields in 1715–17. In 1805 the arsenal was named the Royal Arsenal by King George III (1738–1820).

Woordie Major. In the Indian army, the name of the native or viceroy commissioned officer who assisted the adjutant in cavalry regiments.

Work. As a noun in military usage, a work was any man-made defensive structure or earthwork.

Wörth, Battle of. See Fröschwiller / Froeschwiller / Wörth, Battle of.

Worth, William Jenkins (1794–1849). An American army officer who in March 1813, during the War of 1812 [q.v.], went from store clerk to first lieutenant in the 23rd Infantry. He distinguished himself as an aide to General Winfield Scott [q.v.] in the battles of Chippewa [q.v.] on 5 July 1814, and Lundy's Lane [q.v.] on 25 July, in which he was seriously wounded. He remained in the army after the war and for

eight years beginning in 1820 was commandant of cadets at West Point. In 1838 he was colonel of the 8th Infantry, and on 19 April 1842, during the Second Seminole War [q.v.], he defeated the Seminoles in the Battle of Pelikalkaha in Florida near Lake Ahapopka. In 1846, at the outbreak of the Mexican War [q.v.], he was appointed second-in-command to General Zachary Taylor [q.v.] in the Army of Texas and in that year took part in the battles of Palo Alto on 8 May, Resaca de la Palma the following day, and Monterrey [qq.v.], where he led the assault, on 23 September. Later, under General Winfield Scott, he fought at Cerro Gordo on 18 April 1847, received the capitulation of Puebla on 15 May, fought at Contreras and Churubusco on 19–20 August, and stormed Molino del Rey on 8 September [qq.v.]. In the assault on Mexico City he seized the San Cosme Gate. At the time of his death from cholera on 7 May 1849 he was in command of the Department of Texas.

Wounded Knee, Battle of (29 December 1890), American Indian Wars. On 15 December 1890 old Chief Sitting Bull [q.v.] was arrested by Indian police at the Standing Rock Reservation (North Dakota). Members of his band protested the arrest, and a brawl erupted in which Sitting Bull, a number of tribesmen, and several Indian police were killed. Many of the band then fled under the leadership of the Miniconjou Sioux leader Big Foot [q.v.]. On 28 December they were found in the Dakota Badlands by a patrol of the 7th Cavalry. Big Foot was suffering from pneumonia, and he and the band of about 350 were escorted to a campsite in the valley of Wounded Knee Creek, about 70 miles west of the Pine Ridge Agency.

Colonel James William Forsyth [q.v.], commanding the 7th Cavalry, had orders to disarm the Sioux, and he began the operation at dawn on 29 December. "We were not expecting any trouble," wrote Private Jesse Harris later. The camp was surrounded by seven troops of the 7th Cavalry, some Indian scouts, and a four-gun battery of the 1st Artillery. Tensions arose when the disarming began; a medicine man exhorted the young men to fight, assuring them that their ghost shirts would protect them. [see Ghost Dance Disturbances]; soldiers nervously kept their fingers on the triggers of their carbines. When one of Forsyth's men tried to take a gun from a deaf

Wounded Knee *Scouts returning from the Wounded Knee battlefield*

Indian, the gun discharged; the medicine man with a shout threw dust in the air, upon which several warriors dropped their blankets and raised their Winchester rifles. Indians and cavalrymen were at once engaged in a bloody conflict at close quarters unwanted by either side.

Captain Edward Godfrey (1843?–1932), who had won a Medal of Honor [q.v.] in the Battle of Bear Paw Mountain [q.v.] in the Nez Percé War [q.v.], shouted a command not to shoot the women and children, but a sergeant growled, "To hell with the women." As Private C. O. Norman later wrote, "Everyone was trying to look out for himself."

The two sides broke away from their close contact, giving the artillery targets for the guns. The battle lasted less than an hour, but at its end there were at least 146 dead and 50 wounded Sioux whose blood-stained Ghost Shirts destroyed the ghost dance myth. Among the soldiers, 25 were dead and 39 wounded.

The following day the remaining Sioux ambushed troops near a Catholic mission (Drexel Mission), near White Clay Creek in South Dakota. Forsyth's men were saved by the arrival of four troops of the 9th Cavalry. The fighting at Wounded Knee Creek and at the mission were the last major battles of the Indian Wars in the United States.

Wounds. Although in every nineteenth century war except the Maori Wars [q.v.] in New Zealand and the Franco-Prussian War there were far more sick than wounded and far greater death rates from disease than from enemy action, hospitals overflowed with the wounded after battles. The battle wounds of the Union army during the American Civil War might serve as prototypes for those suffered in other fighting armies of the century. Of these, 94 percent were caused by bullets, about 5½ percent by artillery, and less than 0.5 percent by edged weapons, some of which were the result of fights among soldiers of the same unit. Wounds to the arms or legs accounted for 71 percent of the bullet wounds treated in hospitals, explaining the high ratio of amputees. Abdominal bullet wounds were seldom treated by surgery; bed rest was recommended. Large wounds from artillery shell fragments were simply cleaned and sewn up. The mortality rate for wounds to the large intestine in those who reached hospitals was 41 percent.

Many bore the pain of their wounds stoically. American Captain Guy Vernor Henry (1834?–1899), probably spoke for many when, severely wounded by a bullet through the face, he said to commiseraters, "It is nothing. For this, we are soldiers."

Wovoka (1856?–1932). A Paiute Indian medicine man and mystic. He was orphaned at an early age and was taken in by a white rancher's family, who named him Jack Wilson.

About 1887 he claimed to have had a vision in which he had been lifted "up to the other world," where he met God, who told him to teach his people to love each other, to live in peace with the whites and with each other, and to work and not to steal so that they could pass to the other world, where there would be no death, no sickness, and no old age. He was then given a dance to be performed for five consecutive days [see Ghost Dance Disturbances]. The dance came to be known as the ghost dance, and his message spread among the tribes, but as it spread, it was frequently distorted, as it was at Wounded Knee [q.v.].

Wrangel, Baron Friedrich Heinrich Ernst von (1784–1877). A Prussian soldier who fought in the Napoleonic Wars and was known as Papa Wrangel. In 1848 he commanded the federal troops in the Schleswig-Holstein Revolt [q.v.], and in 1848–49 he crushed the insurrection in Berlin [see Revolutions of 1848]. In 1856 he was made field marshal. In the Schleswig-Holstein War [q.v.] in 1864 he held supreme command over Prussian and Austrian forces. In 1866 he fought in the Seven Weeks' War [q.v.] against Austria.

Wrede, Prince Karl Philipp (1767–1838). A Bavarian soldier who was a major general in the Battle of Hohenlinden in 1800 and commanded a Bavarian division against Austria in 1805, leading the invasion of the Tyrol. He was wounded in the Battle of Wagram [q.v.]. In Napoleon's invasion of Russia [q.v.] in 1812 he led the Bavarian contingent. In 1813 he negotiated an alliance with Austria and commanded the Austro-Bavarian army against the French in the Battle of Hanau [q.v.], in which he was defeated. In 1814 he took part in the battles of La Rothière [q.v.], Rosny, Bar-sur-Aube [q.v.] and Arlis-sur-Aube and was made a field marshal. He represented Bavaria in the Congress of Vienna in 1814–15 and led the Bavarian forces into France in 1815. In 1822 he became the generalissimo of the Bavarian army.

Wright, Horatio Gouverneur (1820–1899). An American soldier who was graduated from West Point in 1841 second in his class and then served ten years in Florida. In the American Civil War he fought in the Union army at First Bull Run [q.v.]. On 16 September 1861 he was named brigadier general of volunteers, and in February 1862 he led an expedition against the Florida coast. In 1862 he was promoted major general and commanded the Department of the Ohio, but the Senate refused to confirm his promotion until 12 May 1864. He commanded a division in the Battle of Gettysburg and in the Battle of the Wilderness [qq.v.]. When General John Sedgwick [q.v.] fell in the Battle of Chancellorsville [q.v.], Wright succeeded to the command of his corps. He repulsed the raid of Jubal Early [q.v.] on Washington in July 1864 and then served under Philip Sheridan [q.v.] in his Shenandoah Valley Campaign [q.v.], where he failed to rally his troops in the Battle of Cedar Creek [q.v.]. On 2 April 1865 he led the first troops into the Confederate works at Petersburg [q.v.]. After the war he reverted to the rank of lieutenant colonel and was promoted colonel and chief of engineers in 1879. He retired in 1884.

Wright, Marcus Joseph (1831–1922). An American lawyer and soldier who began his military career in the militia. For several years before the American Civil War he was lieutenant colonel of the 154th Tennessee Militia, and he was mustered into the Confederate service with that regiment, renamed the 154th Senior Tennessee Infantry. He served for a time as military governor of Columbus, Kentucky, and then fought at Belmont and at Shiloh [qq.v.], where he was wounded. On 13 December 1862 he was promoted major general. He commanded a brigade in the Battle of Chickamauga [q.v.].

After the war he returned to the practice of law in Memphis. In 1878 he was made agent for the collection of Confederate records for use in the *War of the Rebellion: Official Records of the Union and Confederate Armies* (see Official Records). He worked on this project until his retirement in 1917, making invaluable contributions to the history of the war.

Wu-Hsüeh, Capture of (15 February 1853), Taiping Rebellion. The Taiping army, advancing down the Yangtze River by boat and by land administered a crushing defeat to the imperial forces at this town (now Wusüeh) on the left bank of the Yangtze, 16 miles south of Kwangtsi.

Wuntho, Capture of (1891–92), Third Anglo-Burmese War. In 1885 the British annexed Upper Burma. In 1891 the sawbwa (ruler) was deposed in an open rebellion. In response, the British formed a force of 1,800 troops that occupied the capital, Wuntho, 135 miles north of Mandalay, and restored order.

Würst Wagon. A light two-wheeled ammunition wagon on which soldiers sat in two rows facing outward with ammunition stacked between them. It was used in some European armies during the Napoleonic Wars.

Württemberg, Frederick (1759–1830). A Württemberg duke who became elector in 1803 as Frederick II. After the Battle of Austerlitz [q.v.] on 2 December 1805 the country became a French satellite. When it was upgraded to a kingdom in 1806, Frederick was crowned King Frederick I.

Wyndham, Percy (fl. 1861–1863). An English soldier of fortune who served under Giuseppe Garibaldi [q.v.] in Italy. Claiming that an Italian decoration he had been awarded was the equivalent of a knighthood, he called himself Sir Percy. In the United States during the American Civil War he raised a cavalry regiment for the Union army and fought against Thomas ("Stonewall") Jackson [q.v.] in the Shenandoah Valley. He had boasted that he would capture Turner Ashby [q.v.], Jackson's cavalry commander, but he was himself captured by Ashby's men. He was exchanged on 21 September 1862 and commanded a brigade under General George Stoneman [q.v.] in his raid during the Chancellorsville Campaign. He was wounded in the Battle of Brandy Station [q.v.] but recovered to take part in other raids during the Chancellorsville Campaign, after which his whereabouts are unknown. His regiment was mustered out on 24 July 1865.

Wynkoop, Edward Wanshear (1836–1891). An American soldier who was sheriff of Arapahoe County, Kansas Territory (Colorado), and helped to found the community that became Denver. In 1860 two companies of militia were formed, and he became first lieutenant of the Denver Cavalry. In 1861 he married Louise Wakely, a professional actress and by her had eight children. On 31 March of that year he was commissioned a second lieutenant in the 1st Colorado Cavalry and with the outbreak of the American Civil War was elected captain of Company A. He remained in the West, fighting at Apache Pass and Glorieta [qq.v.]. On 28 March 1862, two days after the Battle of Glorieta, he fought again at Pigeon Ranch. On 8 May 1864 he was a major placed in command at Fort Lyon in eastern Colorado. There he made peace with a number of prominent Indian chiefs, including Black Kettle [q.v.], and secured the release of several white hostages. Although he made no promises, the Indians understood that they were under government protection. He was succeeded at Fort Lyon in November 1864 and ordered to Fort Riley, Kansas. Two days after his departure he was horrified to learn of the massacre of the Indians at Sand Creek [q.v.] by troops under Colonel John Chivington [q.v.].

Wynkoop was sent back to investigate, and it was said that "his fearless testimony won the respect of military officers and federal officials who repudiated Chivington's brutality." He was, however, excoriated by many in Colorado Territory who, like Chivington, believed the only good Indian was a dead one. On 17 June 1865 he was appointed chief of cavalry for the District of Upper Arkansas. In July 1866 he resigned his commission and was appointed agent to the Cheyennes, Arapahos, and Plains Apaches with headquarters at Larned, Kansas. He resigned in 1868 to look for gold in the Black Hills, where he organized and became captain of the Black Hills Rangers. His second-in-command and chief scout was John Wallace ("Jack") Crawford (1847–1917), the so-called poet scout. In the 1880s he served as special agent for the U.S. Land Office, first in Denver and then in Santa Fe. In 1889 he became adjutant general of the New Mexico Territorial Militia. He died of Bright's disease.

X Y

Xaintrailles, Charles Antoine Dominique (1763–1833). A French soldier who was trained in the artillery and commissioned in 1779. When his regiment was disbanded in 1783 he reenlisted as a simple gunner. He later regained his commission and by 1796 was a general of division. In 1801, charged with and acquitted of peculation, he retired. In 1813 he returned to the army and was placed in charge of the supply of the Bavarian Corps of Observation. He was captured in the Battle of Leipzig [q.v.], but in June 1814 he was allowed to return to France. He died in Paris in abject poverty.

Yager. See Jäger.

Yakiba. The tempered edge of a blade on a Japanese sword. It was about one-third to one-half inch wide along the cutting edge and appeared to have a "cloudy pearl luster."

Yakima War (1855–58). Many of the Yakima Indians living on the shores of the Columbia and Yakima rivers in Washington Territory struggled against the efforts of whites to move them elsewhere. Other Indians in the area rose to support them, and for nearly three years they fought off U.S. troops in numerous skirmishes, ambushes, and battles until they were defeated on 10 September 1858 by three companies of the 9th Infantry in the Battle of Four Lakes, fought at Four Lakes and Spokane Plains in Washington Territory. After the battle 24 chiefs were hanged or shot, and most of the Indians moved to an area south of the present-day city of Yakima.

Yakub Beg. See Chinese Turkestan, Conquest of.

Yakub Khan, Muhammad (1849–1923). An Afghan amir, son of Shere Ali [q.v.]. From 1863 to 1874 he was governor of Herat. In 1867–68 he aided his father in his successful struggle to regain Kabul, but in 1870 he rebelled against his father, who imprisoned him at Kabul for four years (1874–78). When Shere Ali was forced by the British to flee the country in 1878, Yakub became amir. Although he signed a peace treaty with the British at Gandamak, he was forced to abdicate after Pierre Cavagnari [q.v.], the British Resident, was massacred with his guards at Kabul by mutinous Afghan troops. In 1880 he surrendered to the British and lived the rest of his life on a pension in India.

Yalman. Incorrectly, Jelman. The pointed cutting part of a saber, a widened and cutting part that extends from the point to about a third or fourth of the length of a blade.

Yamagata, Prince Aritomo (1838–1922). A Japanese soldier and statesman. During the European naval attack on the

Yakima War *Depiction of a Cavalry charge against the Yakimas. Such charges were rare in Indian Wars, and this illustration may be highly exaggerated.*

three forts at Shimonoseki in September 1864, he was in command of one and was wounded in the forearm [see Japanese Army]. He served with distinction in the Boshin Civil War [q.v.] of 1868, and two years later he was sent to the United States and to Europe, where he saw something of the Franco-Prussian War [q.v.]. In 1873 he became war minister, and after the suppression of the Satsuma Rebellion [q.v.] in 1877 he was appointed the army's first chief of staff in the following year. In these capacities he did more than anyone else to shape the Japanese imperial army. He introduced conscription, founded and organized the general staff, and established the independence of the army from civilian control. In 1889–93 he was premier. In 1894, during the Sino-Japanese War [q.v.] of 1894–95, he commanded the Japanese First Army in Korea until he fell seriously ill and was relieved. On his recovery he served as war minister for the remainder of the war. He was promoted field marshal in 1898 and again served as premier in 1898–1900. At the beginning of the Russo-Japanese War in 1904 he was chief of staff and served throughout the war, then retired from active service. He has been called the father of the modern Japanese army.

Yamaji, Motoharu (1841–1897). A Japanese soldier known as *Dokuganryu* (one-eyed dragon). During the Boshin Civil War [q.v.] of 1868 he led clan troops against shogunate forces, and in 1871 he entered the new imperial army as a major. He served as a brigade staff officer during the Satsuma Rebellion [q.v.], and in 1881 he was promoted major general. He served with great distinction as a division commander in the Sino-Japanese War [q.v.] of 1894–95 and is considered by many to have been one of Japan's finest field commanders in the nineteenth century.

Yamato. A general term for things Japanese, encompassing the national spirit of Japan and the belief in the superiority of the Japanese people.

Yamazuki / Yamasakii, Battle of (May 1814). Near this town in southern Honshu, 15 miles northwest of Himeji, the samurai of the rebellious Yoshitsune family defeated the forces of the Taira family. Sometimes called the Taira War.

Yang Hsiu-tsin (1817?–1856), last name sometimes rendered Hsiu-ch'ing. A Chinese rebel in the Taiping Rebellion [q.v.] who joined the Taipings in 1848 and quickly rose to power, becoming *tung wang* (eastern king), one of the original five wangs, and one of the best Taiping generals. When the main Taiping force was surrounded at Yungan (Mengcheng), 50 miles east-northeast of Fowyang, on the Kwa River, he devised and led a brilliant breakout on 3 April 1852. He then marched north toward the valley of the Yangtze and attacked Kweilin (Guilin), but he lacked sufficient artillery and was repulsed. However, on 3 December he captured the huge arsenal at Yochow (Yueyang), giving him enough weapons and ammunition to capture in January 1853 the Wuhan city complex on the Yangtze. Marching eastward, he took on 19–21 March the great city of Nanking (Nanxiang or Nanjing), which became the Taiping capital. In August he repulsed efforts by imperial forces to recapture it [see Nanking, Siege of].

As he assumed ever more power, he aroused the jealousy of Hung Hsiu-ch'üan [q.v.], the founder and head of the Taipings, who ordered him murdered when Yang claimed to be the Holy Ghost and aspired to the supreme command. The order was carried out by Wei Ch'ang-hui [q.v.], the north wang, who killed not only Yang but all his relatives and, it is said, some 20,000 of his followers.

"Yankee Doodle." A popular song of uncertain origin sung during the American Revolution by the British in derision of American militia and provincial troops. It was soon adopted by the Americans and made their own. It was first published in the United States in 1794 and has been steadily used in many versions as a quasi-national American marching song and military air.

Yap, European Conquest of (1890–98). Yap (Uap) is an island group consisting of four large islands and ten small ones, close together and surrounded by a coral reef in the south Caroline Islands in the western Pacific Ocean, 225 miles northeast of Palau. Yap itself is the largest and one of the most beautiful and productive of the Carolines. In 1885 Germany seized these islands, which were claimed by both Britain and Spain. The three claimants referred the matter to the pope, who, not surprisingly, sided with Catholic Spain, which garrisoned the islands. In January 1891 dissension flared on Yap among the Spanish and American missionaries and the natives. About 300 people were killed. The Spanish attempted to pacify the natives, but in December the Yap garrison was massacred.

In June 1899 Spain ceded the islands to Germany, which lost them at the end of World War I. Ownership, then disputed between the United States and Japan in 1921–22, was settled by mandating the islands to Japan but with the United States retaining cable and radio rights. In World War II Yap was a large Japanese naval base. After the war it became part of a strategic trust territory administered by the United States.

Yashiki. Fortified mansions of Japanese daimyos. Most were destroyed after the Meiji Restoration in the 1870s and 1880s.

Yasukuni Shrine. The central shrine of state Shinto (*Kokka Shinto*), erected at the request of Emperor Meiji (1852–1912) in 1869 on Kudan Hill, on the north side of the Imperial Palace in Tokyo, in which were enshrined the spirits of Japanese soldiers and civilians who had died in wars since 1853, specifically the 6,971 who were killed in the Boshin Civil War [q.v.], which ended the Tokugawa shogunate. Originally named Shokonsha (shrine for inviting the spirits), it was renamed Shrine of National Peace in 1879.

In 1881 the *yushukan,* a memorial hall, was established to exhibit articles left behind by the war dead. It was destroyed by an earthquake in 1923 but rebuilt in 1931.

Since World War II the shrine has become controversial, particularly since 1979, when Prime Minister Ohira Masayoshi and several cabinet ministers visited it shortly after General Tojo Hideki (1884–1948) and six others who had been hanged as war criminals were enshrined there.

Yataghan. 1. A Turkish and Middle Eastern sword with a Damascus blade, double-edged and pointed, with a ridge in the middle of its entire length. The scabbard and handle were often highly ornamented, but it was without a cross guard.

2. A bayonet with a double curved blade developed in the early nineteenth century.

Yataghan *A janissary's 1½-foot yataghan*

Yellow Fever / Yellow Jack. A destructive infectious disease, often called *vomito negro,* which was more fatal to European armies in the West Indies and central America than bullets and blades. It was said to progress from constipation to headaches, high fever, and nausea, to cramps in the neck that spread to the entire body, and finally to the vomiting of dark red blood that was, according to a French Foreign Legion officer, "like coffee with the grounds suspended in it." Death usually followed within six to twelve hours. If the victim survived, he had a lifelong immunity.

It had a devastating effect upon the French forces under General Charles Leclerc [q.v.] in Haiti in 1801–04. Sixty percent of his staff succumbed, as on 2 November 1802, less than nine months after arriving, did Leclerc himself. In 1865 it killed a third of the French Foreign Legion in Mexico [see Mexico, French Invasion and Occupation of]. The disease ravaged the American army in Cuba during the Spanish-American War [q.v.].

John Crawford of Baltimore was the first to suggest that a mosquito might be responsible for the transmission of the disease, but he was ignored. In 1881 a Cuban physician of Scottish-French heritage, Dr. Carlos Juan Finlay (1833–1915), suggested in a paper that a mosquito might be the agent of transmission of the disease. In 1900 in Havana, Cuba, an American army medical officer, Walter Reed [q.v.], headed a board to study its cause and mode of transmission. By controlled experiments the commission proved that it was carried by a small dark mosquito (*Aëdes aegypti*), making possible the virtual elimination of yellow fever in that country and world-wide in any location in which effective mosquito control measures could be implemented.

Yellow Flag. Before the formation of the International Red Cross and the general recognition of the red cross symbol, a yellow flag was placed near hospital buildings, tents, and areas to signal their use.

Yellowstone Command. The troops under Colonel (later General) Nelson A. Miles [q.v.] who undertook the arduous winter campaign against the Teton Sioux and their Cheyenne compatriots in 1876–77 that ended the Great Sioux War [q.v.].

Yellow Tavern, Battle of (11 May 1864), American Civil War. While the Battle of Spotsylvania [q.v.] raged, General U. S. Grant sent Major General Philip Sheridan [qq.v.] with 10,000 cavalry to raid the line of communication of Confederate General Robert E. Lee. At Yellow Tavern, about 10 miles north of Richmond, Virginia, Sheridan engaged 4,500 cavalry under Lieutenant General J. E. B. Stuart [q.v.].

The Union troops drove the Confederates from the field, and Stuart was killed. Federal losses were 625 to the Confederates' 1,000. A number of recently captured Federal prisoners of war were released.

Yellow Wolf (1779?–1864). A Cheyenne chief who first distinguished himself in raids on other Indian tribes. About 1833 he led a successful war against the Kiowas, and in 1835 and 1838 he waged wars against other tribes. However, recognizing the hopelessness of trying to overcome the white men, he advised his people that their only hope of survival lay in adopting the white man's ways. In 1863 he was one of the chiefs from the plains who traveled to Washington and met President Lincoln and P. T. Barnum. On 29 December 1864 he was among the peaceful Indians killed when John Chivington [q.v.] attacked Black Kettle's [q.v.] camp on the Sand Creek [q.v.].

Yeomanry. British part-time volunteer cavalry. On 27 March 1794, at the beginning of the Napoleonic Wars, when Britain feared invasion, a bill was introduced in Parliament to take advantage of volunteers who did not wish to be part of either the regular service or the militia. It was swiftly passed, and thus was established the basis for "encouraging and disciplining such Corps and companies of men, as shall voluntarily enroll themselves for . . . the General defence of the Kingdom." Officially known as Gentlemen and Yeomanry Cavalry, it was to be called to duty for the defense of the country in case of invasion and for "the suppression of riots and tumults." Commissions were given to the nobility and gentry while the ranks were formed of yeomen, freeholders under the social class of gentlemen but men of respectable standing. Each man had to provide his own mount; saddlery and uniforms were provided by the officers or by county subscriptions. The government provided arms. The Yeomanry soon became an exclusive and prestigious organization.

By the time of the Treaty of Amiens [q.v.] most English, many Welsh, and some Scottish counties had from one to twenty troops. In 1803, when the war with France resumed, the Yeomanry was increased to 36,000 officers and other ranks. Until 1871 its control was the responsibility of the home secretary; it then passed to the secretary of state for war.

Although its size was much reduced after the departure of Napoleon for St. Helena, the corps was retained to suppress civil disorders [see British Civil Disorders; Peterloo Massacre; Chartist Riots]. The last such use was in 1867, when the Royal 1st Devon Yeomanry was mustered to overawe food rioters in Devon.

The Yeomanry was primarily rural, and its annual camps were usually timed to avoid the seasons for seeding, haymaking, and harvesting. It was never intended to be used abroad, but in 1888 units became liable for service anywhere in the kingdom in case of invasion. In December 1899, in response to Black Week [q.v.], during the Second Anglo-Boer War [q.v.], it was organized into regiments and known as the Imperial Yeomanry. It served well in South Africa as mounted infantry. Although the units had always been noted for their elaborate uniforms, they readily switched to khaki for the war.

The Wiltshire Yeomany takes precedence over all others. Ten troops were regimented in 1797 as the Regiment of Wiltshire Yeomanry Cavalry. In 1831 it became "Royal," and in 1863 the "Prince of Wales Own." In 1859 it included dismounted riflemen, but this deviation was discontinued in 1876.

The name was also for a time used to designate an Irish volunteer corps that consisted of both cavalry and infantry.

Yeomen of the Guard. Sometimes called Beefeaters [q.v.]. The oldest military unit in the world. It was formed by Henry VII (1457–1509) in 1485, the first year of his reign, as *Valecti garde [corporis] domini Regis* (Guard [of our Body] of Our Lord the King), a title it still retains. When a regular army was formed for the first time in the reign of Charles II (1630–1668; king: 1660–85), the Yeomen of the Guard consisted of 5 officers and 81 other ranks, a size that it has more or less retained. Since 1743 its duties have been almost entirely ceremonial. In the nineteenth century it consisted mostly of old soldiers, although for a time civilians were allowed to purchase positions. William IV (1765–1837) stopped the practice, and the last civilian retired in 1848.

The Yeomen are armed with swords and partisans (antique weapons with broad blades on long shafts). Their uniform consists of purple Tudor hats, voluminous red doublet tunics trimmed in velvet and gold lace, scarlet hose, knee breeches, and black shoes. There have been minor changes over the centuries, but the uniform has remained basically Tudor.

Yerevan, Battle and Siege of. See Erivan / Yerevan / Erevan, Battles of; Erivan / Yerevan / Erevan Siege of.

Yermalov, Aleksis (1772–1861). A Russian officer who became a general and fought in the Caucasus, becoming known as the Lion of the Caucasus.

Yngaut, Battle of. See Ingavi / Yngavi, Battle of.

Yohannes IV. See Johannes IV.

Yorck von Wartenburg, Johan David Ludwig (1759–1830). A Prussian soldier who entered the army in 1772 but was cashiered for insubordination in 1778. He then entered the service of the Dutch East India Company and served in South Africa and in 1783–85 in the Dutch East Indies. In 1785 he returned to Prussia and was reinstated in the Prussian army. He fought in the Polish Campaign of 1794 and in the Fourth Coalition against Napoleon in 1806 [see Coalition Wars]. He was severely wounded and captured in the Battle of Lübeck [q.v.] on 6–7 November 1806. In 1807 he became a major general and after a tour of commanding the West Prussian Brigade was appointed inspector general of light infantry. In 1811 he was appointed governor-general of East and West Prussia. He commanded the Prussian contingent of Napoleon's army in Napoleon's Russian Campaign [q.v.]. On 30 December 1812 he "neutralized" the Prussian army by defecting with his corps. It was a popular step among the Prussian people, but one that made him subject to court-martial. He was absolved when the Treaty of Kalisch ranged Prussia on the side of the Allies. In 1813–14 he was a corps commander and fought at Leipzig, Bautzen [qq.v.], and elsewhere. He fought against the French in Napoleon's final campaign of 1814 and was ennobled. In 1821 he was made a field marshal.

York, Duke of. See Frederick Augustus, Duke of York and Albany.

York (Toronto), Attack on (26 April 1813), War of 1812. Some 1,700 American troops, under General Henry Dearborn [q.v.], ferried across Lake Ontario by ships under Commodore Isaac Chauncey (1772–1840), landed without opposition four miles west of York (Toronto, Ontario, Canada). Because Dearborn was in poor health, the assault was commanded by Brigadier General Zebulon Pike [q.v.]. The British garrison of 600 in fortifications between the town and the lake was soon overwhelmed, but when the Americans were pushing through the fort into the town, a powder magazine exploded, killing a fifth of the force, including General Pike. The surviving American troops rampaged through the town, burning and looting; provincial records were destroyed. After occupying York for a week, the Americans recrossed the lake to the United States.

Yoruba-Fulani War (1817). In West Africa the Yoruba kingdom of Oyo collapsed when its northernmost province was captured by Fulani forces.

Young, Bennett H. See St. Albans, Raid on.

Young, Pierce Manning Butler (1836–1896). An American soldier who attended the Georgia Military Academy until in 1857 he won an appointment to West Point. At the beginning of the American Civil War on 16 March 1861, three months before graduation, he resigned his cadetship and soon after joined the Confederate service as a second lieutenant. On 30 December 1864 he was promoted major general. He fought in the Seven Days' Battles, was wounded at South Mountain, but survived to serve at Fredericksburg, Brandy Station, and Gettysburg [qq.v.]. He fought in the Wilderness and in the Petersburg Campaign [qq.v.]. After the war he was a planter, congressman, and diplomatic representative to Russia, Honduras, and Guatemala.

Young, Samuel Baldwin Marks (1840–1924). An American soldier who on 25 April 1861, at the beginning of the American Civil War, enlisted in the Union army as a private in the 12th Pennsylvania Infantry, a ninety-day regiment [q.v.]. When it was mustered out, he raised and was named captain of a company that became part of the 4th Pennsylvania Cavalry. He served in the Peninsular Campaign [q.v.] and distinguished himself at Antietam and Brandy Station [qq.v.]. He rose to be a colonel in June 1864 and ended the war in command of a brigade; he was later brevetted brigadier general. In the reorganized army of 1866 he was commissioned a second lieutenant of the 12th Infantry, and in July he was promoted captain. In service on the western frontier he took part in the Hualapais War [q.v.] and in numerous smaller affairs in Arizona and Texas. In 1881 he began a four-year tour as an instructor at the Infantry and Cavalry School, which opened in the same year at Fort Leavenworth. He commanded a squadron of cavalry at Sacramento, California, during a labor disturbance in 1894, and that year he was made acting superintendent of Yellowstone National Park. During the Spanish-American War [q.v.] he served as a brigadier general of volunteers in Cuba. Malaria sent him back to the United States after the Battle of Las Guásimas [q.v.], but he recovered to serve in the campaign against Emilio Aguinaldo [q.v.] in the Philippines.

Young was promoted brigadier general in the regular army in January 1900 and major general the following year. He was president of the War College Board, and on 9 August 1903 he was promoted lieutenant general and commanding general of the army. Six days later he became the army's first chief of staff. He retired in 1904 but continued to serve in various capacities, including ten years as president of the Soldiers' Home [q.v.] in Washington, D.C.

Younger, Thomas Coleman ("Cole") (1844–1916). An American desperado who during the American Civil War became a Confederate officer and guerrilla leader. After the war he joined the gang of Jesse James (1847–1882). On 7 September 1876 he took part in a bank robbery in which two citizens were killed. He was captured, tried, and imprisoned. He was pardoned in 1903 and was said to have led an exemplary life thereafter.

Young Guard. See Garde Impériale.

Ypacarai, Battle of. See Angostura, Paraguay, Fighting near.

Ypsilanti, Alexandros (1792–1828). A Greek soldier, brother of Demetrios Ypsilanti [q.v.]. His father, Constantine Ypsilanti (1760–1816), was the hospodar (governor) of Moldavia from 1799 to 1806 and of Walachia from 1802 to 1806 and again in 1807 until, having encouraged the Serbs to rebel against Turkey, he was forced to flee to Russia. His sons accompanied him, and in 1809 Alexandros was commissioned in the Russian Imperial Guard. He served with distinction in the Russian army in 1812–13, losing an arm in the Battle of Dresden [q.v.] on 27 August 1813. In 1820 he was chosen by the Greek Hetairia Philike (Greek nationalists) as their chief, and the following year he proclaimed the independence of Greece from Turkey.

Assuming that all the Balkans would support the Greek Revolution, he led an invasion of Moldavia in March 1821 and seized its capital, Jassy (Iasi, Rumania), then marched into Bucharest. Although he received some Balkan support, it was not enough. He had expected support as well from Russia, Turkey's traditional enemy, but Russia, pressured by Prince Klemens von Metternich (1773–1859), Austria's powerful foreign minister, repudiated him, and the Greek ecumenical patriarch excommunicated him. On 9 June 1821 his forces were decisively defeated by the Turks in the Battle of Dragasani, 90 miles west of Bucharest. He fled to Austria, seeking asylum, but was imprisoned there for more than six years. He died soon after gaining his freedom.

Ypsilanti, Demetrios (1793–1832). A brother of Alexandros Ypsilanti [q.v.], he fought in the Russian army against the French in 1814, and he helped his brother in his Greek revolt against Ottoman rule. After the Turkish victory in the Battle of Dragasani on 9 June 1821, he fled into the Morea (Peloponnesus), where he carried on the fight for Greek independence. In 1823 he successfully defended Argos, and in 1825 Naples. From 1828 to 1830 he was commander-in-chief of the Greek forces.

Ytororó, Battle of the (December 1868), War of the Triple Alliance. A Paraguayan force of 5,000 with 12 guns under General Bernardino Caballero [q.v.] attempted to hold a bridge over the Ytororó River against an attack by a numerically superior force of Brazilians under the Duque de Caxias [q.v.], who was pursuing the main Paraguayan army. In bitter hand-to-hand fighting the bridge changed hands three times, but the Paraguayans, having suffered a loss of 1,200, were at last forced to retreat. Brazilian losses were about 3,000. The Brazilians, although delayed, regrouped to overtake the Paraguayans and defeated them in the Battle of Avay [q.v.].

Yüan Shih-k'ai (1859–1916). A Chinese soldier and statesman who served in the army from 1882 to 1885. For nine years, beginning in 1885, he was resident in Seoul, Korea. In 1897 he commanded an army corps, and the following year he was adviser to the emperor. In 1900 he was governor of Shantung. He remained neutral during the Boxer Rebellion [q.v.]. After the overthrow of the Manchus in 1911 he became commander-in-chief of northern forces. From 1913 to 1916, as president of China, he tried unsuccessfully to assume dictatorial powers. The manner of his death is unknown.

Yü-chi-chan. Literally: roving attack warfare. A Chinese expression used to describe the tactics of the Nien in China in the 1850s [see Nien Rebellion].

Yungay, Battle of (20 January 1839), War of the Peruvian-Bolivian Confederation. Andrés de Santa Cruz [q.v.], who in 1820–23 had fought in the War for Peruvian Independence from Spain, became president of Bolivia in 1829. In 1837 he formed the Peruvian-Bolivian Confederation, a virtual reuniting of the two countries. Facing dominion by the confederation, Chile built up a strong army under Manuel Bulnes [q.v.] and defeated an invading force of Peruvians and Bolivians near the Chilean village of Yungay in Ñuble Province southeast of Concepción. Santa Cruz fled to Europe, and the confederation dissolved.

Yung-lung-ho / Yinlung-ho, Battle of (19 February 1867), Nien Rebellion. On the banks of this river near Anlu (until 1912 called Teian), in east-central Hupeh, China, about 60 miles northwest of Hankow, imperial forces under Liu Ming-ch'uan (fl. 1860s), a former salt smuggler who commanded the Anhwei army (*Huai-chün*) of about 10,000, and Pao Ch'ao (d. 1886), commanding about 16,000 of the Hunan army, launched a two-pronged attack upon the Nien [q.v.] under Jen Chu. The two generals were jealous of each other, and Liu personally led the attack across the Yung-lung River two hours before the agreed-upon hour. After a short skirmish the Nien feigned defeat and ran away, pursued by the government troops, upon which reserve Nien forces then came in behind the pursuers with the intention of capturing their ammunition and supplies left on the other side of the river. Liu hurriedly dispatched six battalions to protect his supply depot, but these troops were met by a strong counterattack. The government troops were forced to fall back defeated.

Yusuf Ibrahim Muhammad (d. 1888). A puppet sultan of Darfur who in 1887 rose in rebellion against Mahdist rule in the Sudan. In the following year his army was decisively defeated by Mahdist forces near El Fasher (Al Fashir), the capital of Darfur, and he fled into the Marra Mountains, where he was soon killed near Kabkabiya.

Yusuf Shuhdi Pasha (d. 1899). An Egyptian soldier educated in Cairo and Berlin who took part in the Abyssinian-Egyptian War [q.v.] of 1875–76. He assisted the Turks in suppressing the Serbian rebellion in 1876 [see Serbian Revolts] and fought in the Russo-Turkish War [q.v.] of 1877–78. After the collapse of Arabi's Revolt [q.v.] in 1882 he was appointed a member of the court that tried Ahmed Arabi. In the new Egyptian army formed by the British he commanded a brigade. In 1893–94 he was minister of war and marine.

Yuzbachi. A Turkish captain of 100 men. A captain.

Z

Zaatcha, Siege of (July–November 1849), French conquest of Algeria. On 16 July 1849 French Foreign Legion and Bat d'Af [qq.v.] forces first skirmished with hostile Arabs at this desert village, on the fringe of the Chott Melghir (Melrir) depression south of Biskra, and lost 5 killed and 12 wounded. Three days later they again clashed with Arabs in the area and, having lost a further 31 killed and 117 wounded, retreated to Biskra.

On 7 October 1849 a French force of 4,403, including 1,000 Foreign Legion and 11 guns advanced upon Zaatcha. On 12 October the French were reinforced to about 6,000. On 20 October the French began an ineffective bombardment of the place. On 8 November a column of 1,200 Zouaves under François Canrobert [q.v.] arrived with 3,000 goats he had captured in razzias [q.v.] on his way south. Canrobert stormed the Arab fortifications, and the place was taken. The Zouaves then massacred every Arab in sight, including Sheikh Bou Zian, the dissident chief. French total losses were 193 killed and 804 wounded.

Zaharoff, Basil (1850–1936), originally Basileios Zacharias. A Greek born in Turkey who became a French arms merchant and international financier. In the 1880s he entered the munitions industry as an agent for Vickers in Spain, and in the 1890s he was named chairman of Vickers-Maxim. He was said to be associated with Krupp, Schneider-Creusot, Skoda [qq.v.], and other arms manufacturers and became a shadowy but influential world figure, amassing an enormous fortune dealing in arms, oil, shipping, and banking. He became a French citizen in 1913 and was knighted by the British in 1918.

Zaki Tamal (d. 1892). A Mahdist amir in the Sudan who saw much active service in command of Dervish armies in Darfur. In the Abyssinian-Egyptian War [q.v.] he won a decisive victory in the Battle of Gallabat [q.v.]. In 1882, when he was governor of Kassala, he was accused by Ahmad wad Ali wad Ahmad [q.v.], a cousin of the khalifa Abdullahi [q.v.], then ruler of the Sudan, of conspiring to hand over Kassala to the Italians. He was summoned to Khartoum, where he was stoned to death. His place as governor of Kassala was taken by his accuser.

Zalinski, Edmund Louis Gray (1849–1909). A Polish-born American army officer and inventor who emigrated to the United States in 1852 and served in the Union army during part of the American Civil War. He was commissioned in the regular army in 1866 and served until 1894. He was the inventor of an entrenching tool and an improved telescopic sight and the developer of a pneumatic dynamite gun [q.v.].

Zaragoza, Ignacio (1829–1862). A Mexican soldier who as a general in command at La Puebla in 1862 successfully resisted the first French attacks [see Mexico, French Invasion and Occupation of; La Puebla, Battle of]. La Puebla, originally La Puebla de los Angeles, was renamed Puebla de Zaragoza in his honor.

Zariba. A camp in the Sudan protected by a wall of thornbushes.

Zeilin, Jacob (1806–1880). A Marine Corps officer who attended West Point but was not graduated. Commissioned a second lieutenant in the Marine Corps in 1831, he saw much sea duty. During the Mexican War [q.v.] he earned a brevet to major for his services in California, where he fought in the Battle of San Gabriel [q.v.]. During the American Civil War he commanded one of the four companies of marines that took part in the First Battle of Bull Run [q.v.], in which he was wounded. On 10 June 1864 he was promoted colonel and appointed commandant of the corps over the heads of more senior officers, all of whom were ordered to retire because of age. In 1867 he was promoted brigadier general, the Marine Corps's first general officer. He commanded the corps until he retired in 1876.

Zeim, Battle of (20 April 1877), Russo-Turkish War. A Russian army under General Mikhail Loris-Melikov [q.v.] attacked strongly entrenched Turks under Ahmed Mukhtar Pasha [q.v.] at this tiny village near Plevna (now Pleven in northern Bulgaria). It was repulsed with considerable loss.

Zell / Mariazell, Battle of (8 November 1805), Napoleonic Wars. Marshals Louis Davout and Auguste de Marmont [qq.v.] were sent by Napoleon to keep the Austrian forces in northern Italy from joining the forces opposing him as he advanced into Austria from Ulm [q.v.]. In Styria on 6 November 1805 Davout captured large quantities of Austrian stores and equipment, and two days later he fought a sharp battle at Zell (Mariazell), 29 miles north-northeast of Leoben. The Austrians lost 8,000 men killed or taken prisoner. Only 2,000 escaped into Hungary.

Zembourek. A camel corps in the Persian army in which light artillery pieces were mounted on the saddles. In 1853 it numbered 200 men.

Zemio / Zemoi Ikpiro (1842–1917). An Azande chief who began his rule about 1885 in Central Africa. By a series of victories over the Bandias and other Azande chiefs, he made himself the most powerful chief of the Anunaga group in the valley of the Mbommu (Bpomu) River, the 500-mile stream that unites with the Ulle River to form the Ubangi.

Zeppelin, Graf Ferdinand von (1838–1917). A German soldier and airship inventor who was commissioned at the age of twenty in the Württemberg army. In 1863, during the American Civil War, he took leave to observe and serve in the Union army. He wanted, he said, to discover if as a Christian he could take part in a war. The Prussian ambassador in Washington, D.C., arranged for him to meet with President Lincoln [q.v.], who authorized a pass allowing him to move freely in the Union army. Using his pass, he became acquainted with German-born General Carl Schurz [q.v.], of whose generalship he formed a poor opinion. As a member of the staff of General Alfred Pleasonton [q.v.] he took part in one of the cavalry engagements preceding the Battle of Gettysburg [q.v.]. On 17 August 1863 he first ascended in a balloon.

Returning to Württemberg, he served in the Seven Weeks' War and the Franco-Prussian War [qq.v.]. In 1891 he retired from the army with the rank of lieutenant general and devoted himself to the study of aeronautics. In 1900 in his factory at Friedrichshafen he constructed the zeppelin, the first rigid-frame airship; on 2 July 1900 it rose from the ground and remained aloft for twenty minutes but was wrecked in landing. In 1906 he made two successful flights, reaching a speed of 30 miles per hour; the following year he reached a speed of 36 miles per hour.

The zeppelin was first used in war by Germany on 19 January 1915 against Britain.

Zhob Valley Expeditions. The Zhob River, a tributary of the Gumal, flows through an extensive valley that is the most direct route between what was India's Northwest Frontier [q.v.] and Quetta in Baluchistan (Pakistan). It was almost unknown to Europeans until opened by the British Zhob River Expedition in 1884. Later that year the British, after launching a punitive expedition against the Pathans in the valley, occupied the area. A second punitive expedition was sent against the inhabitants in 1890 and a third in 1919.

Zichy, Wilhelm (d. 1875). A Hungarian officer who served in the Austrian cavalry in the Hungarian Revolution of 1848–49 and in the Seven Weeks' War of 1866 [qq.v.]. In 1875 he left the army and traveled to East Africa, where, after some exploring, he joined the Egyptian army there under General Søren Arendrup [q.v.] [see Abyssinian-Egyptian Wars]. He was mortally wounded in the Battle of Gundet [q.v.].

Ziethen, Hans Ernst Karl, Graf von (1770–1848). A German soldier who was commissioned in the Prussian Queen's Dragoons in 1806 and fought against Napoleon's armies in 1813 and 1814, particularly distinguishing himself in the Battle of Leipzig [q.v.] on 16–18 October 1813. In 1815 he was promoted lieutenant general and commanded the Prussian I Corps in the battles of Ligny and Waterloo [qq.v.]. He was appointed commander of the Prussian army of occupation in France after Waterloo. In 1835 he was promoted field marshal.

Zigzags. The approach trenches used by besiegers.

Zitácuaro, Battle of (1–2 January 1812), Mexican War of Independence. Some 20,000 Mexican revolutionaries led by Ignacio López Rayón were defeated by 5,000 Spanish and loyalists under Colonel Félix María Calleja del Rey [q.v.], who stormed this town, in southwest Mexico, 80 miles west of Mexico City. The rebels suffered 7,000 casualties; the Spanish and loyalists lost 2,000. Calleja del Rey burned every building except the churches and returned in triumph to Mexico City.

Znaim, Battle of (10–11 July 1809), Napoleonic Wars. Following the Battle of Wagram [q.v.] on 5–6 July 1809 French cavalry, about 8,000 sabers under Marshal André Masséna, pursued Archduke Charles [qq.v.], who mounted a strong rear guard of perhaps 30,000 Austrians. Contact was made late in the day on 9 July 1809 near Znaim (Znojmo), in southern Moravia, 35 miles southwest of Brno. There was bitter fighting in the next two days as each side received ever-greater reinforcements. The battle ended about seven o'clock on the evening of 11 July, when a general armistice was declared. Peace was not signed until the Treaty of Schönbrunn on 14 October.

Zollicoffer, Felix Kirk (1812–1862). An American journalist and politician of little education who in 1836 served for a year as a volunteer in the Second Seminole War [q.v.]. In 1845–49 he was adjutant general and comptroller of Tennessee, and from 1849 to 1852 he was a state senator. In 1861 he took part in the abortive Washington Peace Conference [q.v.], and soon after, at the beginning of the Civil War, he accepted a commission as a brigadier general in the Provisional Confederate States Army. He was killed in the Battle of Mill Springs [q.v.] on 19 January 1862.

Zouaves. A corps of the French Armée d'Afrique (African army) formed in 1830 or 1831 in Algeria of Berbers of the Zouaoua tribe, who lived in the Djurdjura country, in the Little Atlas Mountains northeast of Algiers. For reasons now obscure, the Zouaves soon became all French, but they continued to wear a colorful Moorish-style uniform: a short jacket decorated with rose madder braid; a blue vest, also decorated; baggy *sarouel* pantaloons, red in winter and for ceremonies, otherwise white; a blue cotton girdle; and a red fez with a turban. The Zouaves were the first unit in the French army to use *galons*—braiding on the sleeves—as rank badges.

The corps soon established a reputation for its élan. As its prestige increased, its uniform was much copied. Papal Zouaves and many volunteer units of the American Civil War were so uniformed, and the British West African regiments wore a simplified version.

In 1832, shortly after the corps was founded, it consisted of one battalion of 38 officers, 10 boy soldiers, and 1,085 enlisted men organized into ten companies. A second battalion was added in 1835–36, to form a regiment under the command of Colonel Louis Lamoricière [q.v.], and in 1852 the corps was expanded to three regiments. The French *Loi des Cadre* of 1874 provided for four regiments of four battalions, each with four fighting companies of 3 officers and 85 other ranks.

Between 1831 and 1851 the Zouaves fought in 330 engagements, including the Battle of Isly [q.v.] in 1844, operations in Kabylia in 1849, and the attack and bloody sack of Zaatcha [q.v.] in November 1849. During the Crimean War [q.v.], the first in which the Zouaves served outside North Africa, they fought at the Alma, before Sevastopol, and at Inkerman [qq.v.], where, it is said, the 3rd Zouaves charged with a pretty vivandière [q.v.] at their head. They fought in the Austro-Sardinian War [q.v.] of 1859, and when Victor Emmanuel II (1820–1894) gave them Sardinia's highest award, they responded by making the king an honorary corporal. They later served in Indochina and in China during the Boxer Rebellion.

Zubair / Zubayr / Zubeir / Zobeir, Rahma Mansur (1830–1913), often referred to as simply Zubair Pasha. An ivory and slave trader who, although technically an Egyptian, by 1865 had created his own army and carved out an independent empire for himself in the Bahr el Ghazal district of southwestern Sudan. In 1873, when he attacked the sultan of Darfur, Egyptian troops were sent to help him. After the sultan's defeat in 1874 Zubair was made a pasha and appointed governor of the provinces of Bahr el Ghazal and Darfur. Both British and Egyptian authorities quickly came to distrust his influence, and in 1876 he was lured to Cairo, where he was prevented from returning to the Sudan. In 1877 he served with the Egyptian contingent of the Turkish army in Rumelia during the Russo-Turkish War [q.v.] of 1877–78. In 1884 General Charles Gordon [q.v.], then governor-general of the Sudan, asked that he be sent to him to help suppress the Mahdist movement, a request that was denied. In 1899, after the Anglo-Egyptian reconquest, he was permitted to return to the Sudan.

Zulu-Boer Conflicts. When white settlers arrived in Natal, Shaka [q.v.], the Zulu chief, established and maintained good relations with them and even presented them with large tracts of land. However, in 1828 he was assassinated by his half brother Dingaan [q.v.], who succeeded him. Less friendly to the white settlers, Dingaan sought to stop the voortrekkers (Boers fleeing the British government in Cape Colony) from entering Natal. In 1837, when Pieter Retief [q.v.], a Boer leader, approached Dingaan for permission to establish a settlement, Dingaan promised land if the Boers would help him recover cattle that he claimed had been stolen. Retief agreed and retrieved the cattle, but in February 1838, while enjoying Dingaan's hospitality, Retief and his party were set upon and murdered.

The Boers declared war, and on 16 September 1838, at a site on the Blood River [q.v.], Boers under Andries Pretorius [q.v.] won a notable victory, the Zulus losing some 3,000, the Boers only a few. Most of the tribe then moved north of the Tugela River, which came to be accepted as a natural boundary.

In 1840 Umpande, a brother of Dingaan's, led a revolution and, with the help of Boer commandos, made himself king.

Zulu Civil Wars. After Dingiswayo [q.v.], paramount chief of the Abatetwa (Mtetwa) people, was killed by Chief Zwide of the Ndwandwes, the Abatetwas placed themselves under Shaka [q.v.], chief of the Zulus, who revolutionized warfare in South Africa by replacing the throwing spear with the stabbing assegai and by developing radical new tactics. Use of the short, stout assegai meant that warriors could no longer throw their spears and run but had to close with their foe. His army in fighting formation was likened to the head of an ox; from either side of the main body came "horns," troops that ran ahead to envelop the enemy. Regiments were organized by age-groups, and no man could marry until he had washed his assegai in the blood of an enemy. Footware was forbidden, and to make sure his warriors' feet were tough, he required them to dance on thorns; those whose dancing was not vigorous enough were clubbed to death.

In the Battle of Gqokoli Hill in 1819 Shaka's newly built army defeated a numerically superior Ndwandwe army; Zwide was killed, and most of his people fled. Then began the *mfecane* [see Mfecane and Mfengu], the great "crushing" that in the early 1820s devastated wide swaths of southern Africa. In his wars Shaka is estimated to have killed more than a million people. Captured enemy warriors were slaughtered; captured young women were spared to become wives of his warriors. In an ever-expanding empire he absorbed land and peoples.

A Zulu warrior

Zulu War *Chief Ntshingwayo kaMahole, the most senior Zulu general in the war of 1879*

In 1856 rivalry and competition between Cetewayo [q.v.] and Mbulazi (d. 1856), sons of the reigning Zulu chief Umpande [q.v.], led to civil war in Zululand. The two armies, each led by one of the brothers, fought in the Battle of the Tugela River in December 1856, and Cetewayo won a decisive victory. Mbulazi and his surviving followers were captured and killed. Although Umpande lived for another sixteen years, Cetewayo became the de facto Zulu ruler.

After the defeat of Cetewayo's army by the British in the Zulu War [q.v.] of 1879, Cetewayo went into hiding, but he was eventually captured and sent to England, where he met and impressed Queen Victoria. On 29 January 1883 he was allowed to return to Zululand. Civil war immediately erupted between his supporters and the forces under his brother Usibepu (d. 1884?). After a year of inconclusive fighting, Cetewayo was killed, but the fighting went on under his son Dinizulu [q.v.], who called for the help of Boers in the Transvaal, promising them in return a large slice of land in northern Natal. This turned the tide, and Dinizulu became undisputed chief. When the British annexed Zululand in 1887, he revolted, and in 1889 he was arrested and shipped to St. Helena for a time. In 1906 he became involved in the Bambata Revolution and was exiled to the Transvaal.

Zulu War (1879). In 1842 Natal became a British colony. From 1840 until the death of Zulu Chief Umpande [q.v.] in 1872 peace was maintained. Umpande's son Cetewayo [q.v.], who succeeded him on his death, aroused considerable apprehension among the white settlers [see Zulu Civil Wars]. As he attempted to extend his authority over those who had fled his tyranny into Natal, friction on the frontier mounted.

The British demanded that the Zulus dismantle their army. When this was refused, General Frederic Thesiger, Viscount Chelmsford [q.v.], on 10 January 1879 led an army of 5,000

British and 8,200 African troops into Zululand in three widely dispersed columns. Thus began the Zulu War [q.v.]. On 22 January, while he was absent with a portion of his force seeking out the Zulus, his central column of about 1,000 Africans and 1,800 British, most from the 2nd Battalion of the 24th Regiment (later South Wales Borderers) camped at the base of a tall craig called Isandhlwana. There it was attacked by some 10,000 Zulus. All but 55 British and 300 Africans were slaughtered. No prisoners were taken [see Isandhlwana, Battle of]. Among the acclaimed heroes were two young officers, Lieutenant Nevill Josiah Aylmer Coghill and Lieutenant Teignmouth Melvill, who were killed trying to cross the Buffalo River carrying the colors of the 24th Foot. In 1907 they were posthumously awarded Victoria Crosses.

At Rorke's Drift [q.v.], a ford on the Buffalo River near Isandhlwana, the British had established a small hospital in a mission station. On the night following the battle it was attacked by 4,000 Zulus led by a half brother of Cetewayo. The station was successfully defended for twelve hours by 139 British soldiers, 35 of whom were sick. When the Zulus left the field, they had lost about 400 warriors; the British lost 17 killed.

No fewer than 11 British soldiers were awarded the Victoria Cross [q.v.] for their part in this fight, the highest number ever awarded for a single action. Among those decorated were the two officers present: Lieutenant John Chard, an engineer officer, and Lieutenant Granville Bromhead [qq.v.] of the 24th Foot.

Chelmsford, heavily reinforced, again invaded Zululand in March, and this time the Zulus were defeated. In August Cetewayo was captured. The British then departed, leaving

Zulu War *Men of HMS Shah part of a naval brigade in Chelmsford's army.*

Zululand in turmoil as minor chiefs struggled for supremacy [see Zulu Civil Wars]. In 1897 Zululand was annexed to Natal; it remained quiet until 1906, when troops had to be called in to suppress an uprising against British rule.

An event that at the time seemed greatly significant and received more treatment in the press than any single victory or defeat in any of the Zulu Wars was the death of the French prince imperial, the twenty-three-year-old heir to the French throne, who on 1 June 1879 was killed while on a routine patrol [see Napoleon, Eugène Louis Jean Joseph].

Zumalacárreguy, Tomás (1788–1835). A Spanish soldier who was born in the Basque province of Guipúzcoa. On the reestablishment of absolutism, he was made governor of Ferrol, but in 1832 he was dismissed from the army as a Carlist. In 1833 he took command of Carlist forces in Biscay, where he waged successful campaigns and guerrilla wars against the Cristinos and in two years had control of all the area north of the Ebro River [see Carlist War, First]. On 14 June 1835 he was severely wounded by a musket ball in his leg at the siege of Bilbao [q.v.]. The wound was treated by incompetent surgeons, and he died ten days later.

Zündnadelgewehr. See Dreyse Needle Gun.

Selected Bibliography

Alger, John I. *Definitions and Doctrine of the Military Art, Past and Present.* Wayne, N.J.: Avery Publishing Group, 1985.

American Military History. Washington, D.C.: Center of Military History United States Army, 1969.

Ammer, Christine. *Fighting Words: From War, Rebellion, and Other Combative Capers.* New York: Paragon House, 1989.

Anon. *Dictionary of Military Terms: Joint Chief of Staff.* New York and Elstree, U.K.: Greenhill Books, 1987.

Boatner, Mark Mayo. *The Civil War Dictionary,* rev. ed. New York: David McKay Company, 1988.

Brassey's Encyclopedia of Military History and Biography, ed. Franklin D. Margiotta. Washington and London: Brassey's, 1994.

Calvert, Michael, and Peter Young. *A Dictionary of Battles 1715–1815.* New York: Mayflower Books, 1979.

Cambridge Biographical Dictionary, gen. ed. Magnus Magnusson. Cambridge, U.K.: Cambridge University Press, 1990.

Carman, W. Y. *Dictionary of Military Uniforms.* New York: Scribners, 1977.

Chandler, David. *Dictionary of the Napoleonic Wars.* New York: Macmillan Publishing Co., 1979.

Dictionary of American Biography, ed. Allen Johnson and Dumas Malone. 20 vols. New York: Published under the auspices of the American Council of Learned Societies, 1928–36.

Dictionary of National Biography, ed. Leslie Stephen and Sidney Lee. 22 vols. plus supplements. Oxford, U.K.: George Smith, 1882–1913; since 1917 Oxford University Press.

Dupuy, R. Ernest, and Trevor N. Dupuy. *The Encyclopedia of Military History from 3500 B.C. to the Present,* 2d rev. ed. New York: Harper & Row, 1986.

Dupuy, Trevor N. *The Harper Encyclopedia of Military Biography.* New York: Harper Collins, 1992.

Eggenberger, David. *A Dictionary of Battles.* London: George Allen & Unwin, 1967.

Elting, John R., Dan Cragg, and Ernest Deal. *A Dictionary of Soldier Talk.* New York: Charles Scribner's Sons, 1984.

Encyclopaedia Britannica, 14th ed. London and New York: 1929.

The Encyclopedia of Twentieth Century Warfare, ed. Dr. Noble Frankland. New York: Crown Publishers, 1989.

Farrow, Edward S. *Farrow's Military Encyclopedia, a Dictionary of Military Knowledge.* 3 vols. New York: Published for the author, 1885.

Frazer, Robert W. *Forts of the West.* Norman and London: University of Oklahoma Press, 1965.

German Military Dictionary. Washington, D.C.: War Department, 1944.

Harbottle's Dictionary of Battles, 3d ed, rev. George Bruce. New York: Van Nostrand Reinhold Co., 1981.

Haydn, Joseph. *Dictionary of Dates,* 25th ed. London and other cities: 1918.

Haythornthwaite, Philip J. *The Napoleonic Source Book.* New York; Oxford, U.K.; Sydney, Australia: Facts on File, 1990.

Heitman, Frances B. *Historical Register and Dictionary of the United States Army, from Its Organization September 1789, to March 2, 1903.* 2 vols. Washington, D.C.: Government Printing Office, 1903.

Hill, Richard. *A Biographical Dictionary of the Anglo-Egyptian Sudan.* Oxford, U.K.: Clarendon Press, 1951.

Historical Times Encyclopedia of the Civil War, ed. Patricia L. Faust. New York: Harper & Row, 1986.

Hobson-Jobson: A Glossary of Anglo-Indian Colloquial Words and Phrases and of Kindred Terms, by Col. Henry Yule and A. C. Burnell in 1886. New ed. by William Crooke in 1903. London: Routledge & Kegan Paul, 1968.

Hogg, Ian V. *The Illustrated Encyclopedia of Artillery.* Secaucus, N.J.: Chartwell Books, 1988.

———. *Fortress: A History of Military Defence.* New York: St. Martin's Press, 1975.

———. *Illustrated Encyclopedia of Firearms.* Secaucus, N.J.: Chartwell Books, 1978.

Johnson, Thomas H., in consultation with Harvey Wish. *The Oxford Companion to American History.* New York: Oxford University Press, 1966.

International Military and Defense Encyclopedia. 6 vols. New York: Macmillan Publishing Co., 1993.

Kenyon, J. P. *A Dictionary of British History.* Ware, U.K.: Wordsworth, 1992.

Kohn, George C. *Dictionary of Wars.* New York and Oxford, U.K.: Facts on File, 1986.

Laffin, John. *Brassey's Battles.* London: Brassey's Defence Publishers, 1985.

Livermore, Thomas L. *Numbers and Losses in the Civil War in America, 1861–1865.* Boston: Houghton Mifflin Co., 1901.

Macksey, Kenneth. *The Penguin Encyclopedia of Weapons and Military Technology from Prehistory until the Present Day.* London: Viking, 1994.

———, and William Woodhouse. *The Penguin Encyclopedia of Modern Warfare, 1850 to the Present Day.* London: Viking, 1991.

Magnusson, Magnus, ed. *Cambridge Biographical Dictionary.* Cambridge U.K.: Cambridge University Press, 1990.

Oxford English Dictionary, ed. Herbert Coleridge, F. J. Furnivall, J. A. H. Murray, H. Bradley, William Alexander Cragie, and Charles Talbut Onions. Oxford, U.K.: Clarendon Press, 1884–1928.

Palmer, Alan. *An Encyclopedia of Napoleon's Europe.* New York: St. Martin's Press, 1984.

Palmer, Dave Richard, and James W. Stryker. *Early American Wars and Military Institutions.* West Point, N.Y.: Department of History, United States Military Academy (Avery Publishing Group, Wayne, N.J.), 1986.

Perkins, Dorothy. *Encyclopedia of Japan: Japanese History and Culture, from Abacus to Zori.* New York: Facts on File, 1991.

Perrett, Bryan. *The Battle Book: Crucial Conflicts in History from 1469 BC to the Present.* London: Arms and Armour Press, 1992.

Phister, Frederick. *Statistical Record of the Armies of the United States.* New York: New York: Charles Scribner's Sons, 1889.

Prucha, Francis Paul. *Guide to the Military Posts of the United States.* Milwaukee: State Historical Society of Wisconsin, 1966.

Quick, John. *Dictionary of Weapons and Military Terms.* New York: McGraw-Hill, 1973.

Quotations. Annapolis, Md.: United States Naval Institute, 1966.

Reference Guide to United States Military History, 1815–1865, ed. Charles Reginald Schrader. New York: Facts on File, 1993.

Rosenthal, Eric. *Encyclopedia of Southern Africa.* London and New York: Frederick Warne, 1961.

———. *Southern African Dictionary of National Biography.* London and New York: Frederick Warne, 1966.

Royle, Trevor. *A Dictionary of Military Quotations.* London: Routledge, 1990.

Scott, Colonel H. L. *Military Dictionary.* Reprint of 1861 edition by D. Van Nostrand. New York: Greenwood Press, 1968.

Seltzer, Leon E., ed. *The Columbia Lippincott Gazetteer of the World, with 1961 Supplement.* New York: Columbia University Press by arrangement with J. B. Lippincott Company, 1962.

Shafritz, Jay M. *Words on War: Military Quotations from Ancient Times to the Present.* New York, London, et al.: Prentice Hall, 1990.

———, J. A. Todd, and David B. Robertson. *The Facts on File Dictionary of Military Science.* New York and Oxford, U.K.: Facts on File, 1989.

Spiller, Roger A., ed. *Dictionary of American Military Biography.* 3 vols. Westport, Conn., and London: Greenwood Press, 1984.

Spring, Christopher. *African Arms and Armor.* Washington, D.C.: Smithsonian Institution Press, 1993.

Steinberg, S. H. *A New Dictionary of British History,* reprinted with corrections. London: Edward Arnold, 1964.

Stocqueler, J. H. *The Military Encyclopedia; a Technical, Biographical and Historical Dicionary, referring Exclusively to the Military Sciences, the Memoirs of Distinquished Soldiers, and the Narratives of Remarkable Battles.* London: Wm. H. Allen & Co., 1853.

Sweetman, John. *A Dictionary of European Land Battles from the Earliest Times to 1945.* London: Robert Hale, 1984.

Tarassuk, Leonid, and Claude Blair, eds. *The Complete Encyclopedia of Arms and Weapons.* Verona, Italy: Bonanza, 1982.

Thrapp, Dan L. *Encyclopedia of Frontier Biography.* 3 vols. Lincoln and London: University of Nebraska Press, 1988.

Tsouras, Peter G. *Warriors Words: A Quotation Book.* London: Cassell Arms and Armour, 1992.

Upton, Emory. *Armies of Asia and Europe.* New York: Reprint of original 1877 edition by Greenwood Press, 1968.

U.S. Department of Defense. *Dictionary of Military Terms.* New York: Greenhill Books, 1987.

Vincent, Benjamin. *Haydn's Dictionary of Dates and Universal Information,* 25th ed. Graz, Austria: Akademische Druck-u. Verlagsanstalt, 1910.

Warner, Ezra J. *Generals in Blue: Lives of the Union Commanders.* Baton Rouge and London: Louisiana State University Press, 1964.

———. *Generals in Gray: Lives of the Confederate Commanders.* Baton Rouge and London: Louisiana State University Press, 1986.

Watts, Peter. *A Dictionary of the Old West.* New York: Promontory Press, 1977.

Webster's American Military Biographies. Springfield, Mass.: G. & C. Merriam, 1978.

Webster's Biographical Dictionary. Springfield, Mass.: G. & C. Merriam, 1957.

Webster's Geographical Dictionary, 10th ed. Springfield, Mass.: Merriam-Webster, 1998.

Wilhelm, Thomas. *A Military Dictionary and Gazetteer.* Philadelphia: L. R. Hamersly, 1881.

Willcox, Cornélis de Witt. *A French-English Military Technical Dictionary with a Supplement Containing Recent Military and Technical Terms.* War Department Document No. 95. Washington, D.C.: Government Printing Office, 1917.

Young, Brigadier Peter. *A Dictionary of Battles* (1816–1976). London: New English Library, 1977.

———, gen. ed. *The Dictionary of Battles.* New York: Henry Holt and Company, 1988.

Illustration Credits

Image research by Linda Sykes Picture Research, Hilton Head, South Carolina

Africana Museum, Johannesburg: 713; Analectic Magazine: 873; Anne S. K. Brown Military Collection, Brown University Library: 3, 4(right), 7(right), 10, 27, 46(top),48, 54(top right), 69, 77(bottom) 81(left), 89, 103, 128(left), 138(bottom), 141, 145(bottom), 150 (left), 162, 173, 179(right), 253(right), 266(left), 281, 304, 306, 312, 338(left), 379, 432(top), 465, 491 (both),506 (bottom right), 529, 530, 544(left), 557, 613, 654, 657(left), 727, 736, 745, 748, 764, 776(right), 830, 847, 898; Atlas to Accompany the Official Records of the Union and Confederate Armies, 1891–1895: 170, 186(bottom), 190, 198, 315, 319, 325(right), 328(top), 354(bottom), 506(left), 548, 582, 595, 668, 680(left), 690, 697, 701, 840; Basel Museum: 56(top); Battles and Leaders of the Civil War, 1888: 37(both), 79, 87(top), 88, 106, 113, 176, 128,130, 145(top), 156(bottom), 220, 236(right), 253(bottom left), 254, 257, 264(bottom), 284(top), 308, 311(both), 316, 327, 345, 368, 394, 405, 408, 410(left), 435(right), 455, 457, 488(top), 498, 499, 502, 506(top right), 514, 522(top left), 527, 539, 544(right), 578, 620, 632, 639, 645, 652, 668, 675(right), 683, 693, 696, 797, 816, 829(right), 850; Bernard, George, War Talks of Confederate Veterans, 1892: 796(right); Bibliotheque Nationale, Paris: 212, 528; Bibliotheque Publique et Universitaire Cabinet des Estampes, Geneva: 269; Billings, John: Hard Tack and Coffee, 1888: 389; Black and White magazine: 46(bottom), 205, 617, 662, 819(top); British Museum: 174, 299(right); Cailliaud, Voyage a Meroe, Paris, 1826: 430; Cape Archives, Capetown: 210; Carnavalet Museum, Paris: 829(bottom left); Casa Pardos, Buenos Aires: 44; Century magazine: 1, 30(bottom), 32, 38, 94, 142(bottom), 161(right), 175(right), 214, 267, 367, 642, 651(right), 680(top right), 758(left), 768; Chicago Historical Society: 110(left), 321, 353, 651(left), 720(top), 754, 854; Civic Print Collection 'Achille Bertarelli' Milan: 101, 164(left), 263, 325(left), 422(top), 438, 439, 496(left), 837, 853(right); Colorado Historical Society: 195; Congreve, William, Details of the Rocket System, 1814: 215, 276, 406(top), 705; Cooke, John Esten: A Life of General Robert E. Lee, New York: Appleton, 1871: 488(bottom); Cooper Hewitt, Smithsonian Institution: 423; Corbis-Bettmann: 64, 65, 74(top), 81(top right), 82, 99(both), 120, 150(right), 246, 249(right), 264(top), 272, 294, 298, 306(bottom), 313, 352(top left), 359, 382, 387(right), 427, 436, 450(right), 522(right), 639, 731, 749; Cosmopolitan magazine, February, 1897: 262; Culver Pictures: 583(right), 601, 679; Daily Graphic: 13, 61(bottom), 132, 147, 399, 365, 597(bottom), 673(left), 834; Das Illustrierte Mississippithal, 1857: 109; Daughters of the Republic of Texas Library, Alamo: 123; Di Carpeno, The Fight for Freedom, Palermo, 1860: 343; Du Boulay, Japanese Official Reports: 673; Dunn, J. P. Jr., Massacres of the Mountains, 1886: 890; Eastern Montana College Library Special Collections: 235(top): Essex Institute, Salem, MA: 861; Farrow, Edward S., Farrow's Military Encyclopedia, Volumes 1–3, 1884 /Anne S. K. Brown Military Collection, Brown University Library: 4(left), 7(left), 16, 30(top), 42, 55(top), 74(bottom), 75, 84, 87(bottom right), 111(both), 129, 151, 153, 163, 169, 171, 183, 185, 202, 258, 274(right), 283, 285, 287, 288(both), 297, 309, 311(top), 321, 322, 333, 336, 338, 340, 342, 345, 363, 375, 376, 379, 395, 403, 405, 428, 458, 471, 500 (both), 516, 522(bottom left), 531, 536, 539, 542, 561, 572, 577, 579, 608, 632, 635 (both), 638, 644, 656, 652, 655, 658, 706, 719, 753, 770, 773 (both), 762, 785, 826 (both), 850; Frank Leslie's Illustrated Newspaper: 98, 135, 234, 244; Franklin Delano Roosevelt Library, Hyde Park, New York: 478(top); Frederick Todd Collection, Croton-on Hudson, NY: 73; Lt. Col. Alessandro Gasparinetti Collection, Rome: 41, 124, 481, 833; Gilcrease Institute: 108; Giraudon: 2, 22; Halstead, The Story of Cuba, 1896: 61(top), 235(bottom), 274(bottom left), 360, 387(left), 625; Halstead, The Story of the Philippines, 1898: 15, 61, 650; C. Hamilton Smith, Costume of the British Army: 373; Harper's Weekly: 29, 51(top), 320, 355(top right), 378, 421, 583(left), 648, 675(right), 730(right), 754, 742, 763, 787, 791, 794, 873; Histoire de la Guerre de la Peninsula sous Napoleon, 1827: 549(top); Historisches Museum St. Gallen: 776(left); Horace Nicholls: 156(top); Hulton/Getty: 437, 468; Huntington Library,